PARIMAL SANSKRIT SERIES N0. 73

112 UPANIṢADS

(AN EXHAUSTIVE INTRODUCTION, SANSKRIT TEXT, ENGLISH TRANSLATION & INDEX OF VERSES)

Thoroughly Revised New Edition

Vol. 1

Translated by
Board of Scholars

Editors
K. L. Joshi
O. N. Bimali
Bindiya Trivedi

PARIMAL PUBLICATIONS
DELHI

Published by
PARIMAL PUBLICATIONS
27/28, Shakti Nagar, Delhi-110007 (INDIA)
ph. : +91-11-23845456
e-mail : order@parimalpublication.com
url : http://www.parimalpublication.com

Sixth Reprint Edition : Year 2022

ISBN : 978-81-7110-243-3 (Set)
978-81-7110-244-0 (Vol. I)

Price : ₹ 2000.00 (Set of 2 Vols.)

Printed at
Vishal Kaushik Printers
Near GTB Hospital, Delhi

INTRODUCTION

The Upaniṣads are philosophical and theological mystical treatises forming the third division of the Veda; the preceding portions being the Mantras or Hymns, which are largely prayers, and the Brāhmaṇas or sacrificial rituals– the utterance, successively, of poet, priest and philosopher.

There are two great departments of the Veda. The first is called Karma-kāṇḍa, the department of works, which embraces both Mantras and Brāhmaṇas; and is followed by the vast majority of persons whose action of religion is laying up of merit by means of ceremonial prayers and sacrificial rites. The second is called Jñāna-kāṇḍa, the department of knowledges—the theosophic portion of the Vedic revelation; and this is embraced by the Upaniṣads, and is intended for the select few who are capable of attaining the true doctrine.

The most important of the Upaniṣads belong to what are called Āraṇyakas or forest-books, which form an appendix to the Brāhmaṇas; and, treating as they do of the release of the soul from metaphsychosis, by means of a recognition of the oneness of its real nature with the great impersonal Self and are so profound that they were required to be read in the solitude of forests, by persons, who, having performed all the duties of a student and a house-holder, retired from the world and their days passed in the contemplation of the Deity.

The Upaniṣads are as far removed from the ancient poetry of the Veda as the Talmud is from the Old Testament and Sufism is from the Quran. They represent the results of the first plunge of the human mind into the depths of metaphysical speculation; and investigate such abstruse problems as the origin of the universe, the nature of the Deity, the nature of the human soul, and the relation of spirit and matter.

The etymology of the word is doubtful. It probably signifies sitting down near somebody, in order to listen or meditate and worship (Upa-ni-ṣad); so that it would express the idea of a session or assembly of pupils sitting down at a respectful distance secret doctrine—a digest of the principles and mysteries contained in the Vedas; and some Indian philosophers derive the word from the root sad, in the sense of destruction; meaning thereby that the secret doctrine, fully apprehended, would destroy all passion and ignorance, and all knowledge derived from the senses merely—all knowledge save that of the Self.

Now about the number and divisions of the Upaniṣads, with the disappearance of many of the recessions of the Vedas, many Brāhmaṇas, Āraṇyakas and Upaniṣads also disappeared. The fact that the sacred books were not committed to writing in ancient times is partly responsible for this loss. Further more, among the works surviving, it is difficult to ascertain the exact number that should be regarded as authentic Upaniṣads. A religious system is considered valid in India only when it is supported by Śruti (the Vedas); hence the founders of religious sects have sometimes written books and called them Upaniṣads in order to give their views scriptural authority. The Allāḥ Upaniṣad, for instance, was composed in the sixteenth century, at the time of the Muslim emperor Akbar.

One hundred and eight Upaniṣads are enumerated in the Muktikopaniṣad, which is a work belonging to the tradition of the Yajurveda. Among these, the Aitaerya Upaniṣad and Kauṣītaki Upaniṣad belong to the Ṛgveda; the Chāndogya and Kena, to the Sāmaveda; the Taittirīya, Mahānārayaṇa, Kaṭha, Śvetāśvatara and Maitrāyaṇī, to the Kṛṣṇa Yajurveda; the Īśa and Bṛhadāraṇyaka, to the Śukla Yajurveda; and the Muṇḍaka, Praśna and Māṇḍukya, to the Atharvaveda. It may be stated, also, that these Upaniṣads belong to differing recensions of their respective Vedas. Thus, for instance, the Muṇḍaka Upaniṣad belongs to the Śaunaka recension of the Atharvaveda, while the Praśna Upaniṣad belongs to the Pippalāda recension. The Brahma Sūtras, which is the most authoritative work on the Vedānta philosophy, has been based upon the Aitareya, Taittirīya, Chāndogya, Bṛhadāraṇyaka, Kauṣītaki, Kaṭha, Śvetāśvatara, Muṇḍaka, Praśna and possibly also the Jāhāla Upaniṣad. Śaṅkarācārya wrote his celebrated commentaries on the Īśa, Kena, Kaṭha, Praśna, Muṇḍaka, Māṇḍukya, Aitareya, Taittirīya, Chāndogya, Bṛhadāraṇyaka and possibly also the Śvetāśvatara Upaniṣad. These latter are regarded as the major works.

These are probably as old as the sixth century B.C. or anterior to the rise of Buddhism and the fundamental Upaniṣads of the Vedānta philosophy.

The teachings of the Upaniṣads, Bahmasūtras and the Bhagavad Gītā form the basis of the Vedānta philosophy.

But the Vedānta has different schools of interpretation, represented by the three great Ācāryas—Śaṅkara, Rāmānuja and Mādhava; that Śaṅkara being the oldest and most orthodox and in closest harmony with the ancient patheistic thoughts of India. The Upaniṣads undoubtedly admit of different interpretations. Their authors belonged to different sections of society, some of the most important being Kṣatriyas or Rajput kings; and these generations of Vedic theologians had their own favourite sacred texts which they studied and speculated upon; these speculations coming in course of time to be locked upon as sacred too. There is unquestionably a certain uniformity of leading conceptions running throughout the Upaniṣads, though with considerable divergence in detail. They were, however, never meant to form a philosophical system coherent in all its parts, and free from contradictions. Their authors belonged to different periods of time and do not claim any Divine inspiration that would preserve a continuous revelation of truth. The views of one sage do not seem to agree in several important points with another, as to the nature of the Supreme Being, whether He possesses qualities (saguṇa) or is destitute of qualities (nirguṇa), though the latter represents, as we shall see, the prevailing thought. They differ also as to the reality or unreality of the external world; and as to the nature of that soul, whether it is of minute size and an agent, and therefore finite, or whether it is identical with the Supreme and therefore infinite. All this invests these ancient treatises with not a little difficulty to those who study them; though their interest and value are not thereby diminished.

The Upaniṣads undoubtedly represent the highest product of the Indian mind; and one of the most imposing and subtle of the systems of ontology yet known in the history of philosophy; and the Vedānta, styled by Śaṅkarācārya 'the string upon which the gems of the Upaniṣads are strung,' is regarded as the finest flower and the ripest fruit of Indian spirituality. They contain the highest authority on which the various systems of Indian philosophy rest; and are practically the only portion of Vedic literature which is extensively studied by orthodox educated Hindus in the present day.

The Vedānta philosophy has also its appreciators in Europe. Not to speak of its similarity in some respects to Berkeley's Idealism, though essentially different, Professor Max Muller has represented it in an attractive light; and some German philosophers such as Schopenhauer and his ardent disciple, Professor Deussen of Kiel, confess to much enthusiasm for this particular wisdom of the East. These two speak of the study of the Upaniṣads as elevating and consoling. It is urged by modern Hindu Vedāntists, that the school of German thought first expressed by Kant, completed by Schopenhauer and further elaborated by Deussen, brings the western world nearer and nearer to the Advaita or monistic position; and the Vedānta is claimed to be the key to all religions, the lamp by which all can be studied. Professor Deussen says of this system that it is "equal in rank to Plato and Kant", and is one of the most valuable products of the genius of mankind in its search for the eternal truth.

This is precisely what one can feel in studying the Upaniṣads. Though a persual of the literature is a great intellectual treat, there is a strange medley of the sublime and the common place, of profundities and trivialities, of philosophy and superstition. One can find there the nature worship of the Vedas, especially of the sun and mention made of 33 gods. One can find sexual relations even in the Supreme; that the Self divided himself into two and so produced husband and wife; and from these were "created everything that exists in pairs, down to the ants." One can find details of Vedic sacrifices, of oblations of curds and honey and many puerile rites and superstitious ceremonies. One can find human greatness associated with children and cattle and fame and long life. One can find astrology and strange astronomy, such as the soul leaving the body and passing through the air, coming first to the sun, and then at a greater distance, ascending to the moon; and the Hindu belief about eclipses—the moon escaping from the mouth of Rāhu. One can find interesting evidence of the knowledge and practice of certain arts and sciences, such as melting of iron, pottery, wheel-making and the chemistry of metals; also that a Divine origin is claimed for caste; and such bewildering morality as this, that a man who knows a certain thing, even if he commits what seems much evils, consumes it all and becomes pure and clean. One can find a full blown and elaborated doctrine of transmigration; and that those whose conduct has been evil, are born again as dog or hog, worm, insect, fish, bird, lion, boar and serpent, rice and corn, herbs and trees, sesamum and beans.

One can find also much importance attached to protracted bodily stillness and fixity of lock, to certain modes of breathing and to suppression of breath, to the mental repetition of strange sets of formulae, and to meditations on the unfathomable mysteries contained in certain monosyllables, such as the famous Oṁ— the symbol of the Absolute under its three-fold personalisation. One can find great subtleties of thought, expressed in such pregnant brevity that in very sentence we seem to read a page; a labyrinth of mystic language, tedious repetitions and puerile conceits; the use of fanciful metaphors and unconnected images, of defective analogies in place of proof, such as arguing from a rope being mistaken for a serpent to the unreality of the visible universe; or from the man with diseased eye who sees two moons where there in reality only one, to show that it is only ignorance (avidyā) that takes the world as real; or from the fact that all earthen pots are in truth only earth, that the whole world is nothing but Brahman. One can find a want of system and of common sense; a tendency to speculate rather than investigate; and, therefore, controversies always beginning afresh, the solving of insoluble enigmas, the attaining unattainable frames of mind.

But all these one passes over, unaccounted for and unexplained, and desire to notice rather the best features of the Upaniṣads, those that lift the human heart from the earthly to a higher level; the elevated thoughts and noble conceptions; the deep spirituality; the pathetic guesses at truth and relation to the highest questions that the human mind can propose to itself. For in the groping after something felt to be needed, in the yearning of hearts dissatisfied and empty, lies the value of the Upaniṣads. In their seeking and searching after the Infinite, these "Songs before Sunrise," as they have been styled, must always have a profound interest for every devout mind. They do not claim as does the Bible to have a divine message for the world; neither do they contain as do the Vedas any fervid and beautiful prayers to God; they are rather psychological excursions about God. The Bible shows God in quest of man, rather than man in quest of God; and when thoughtfully studied and experienced, will be found to meet the questions raised by this ancient philosophy and to supply its only true solution.

What now is the fundamental idea and the highest object of the Upaniṣads, as interpreted by the first great commentator Śaṅkarācārya, and in part also by Rāmānujācārya? It is this : that behind all the phenomena and mythology of Nature, behind the Vedic deities, there is the Supreme Soul of the Universe, the Highest Self, the Paramātman—the Absolute; offering certain parallels to the Idealism of Plato, or to the Infinite Being of Spinoza, or to Hegel's Rationality of the Universe, though more psychological or spiritual than either of them. And, further, that behind the veil of the body and the senses, behind one reason and all psychological, manifestation, beyond the Ego with all its accidents and limitations, there is another Ātman or subjective Self. This Self can only by discovered by a severe moral and intellectual discipline, such as is practised by the sannyāsin or mendicant, ascetic or yogī; a person having his senses and passions under complete control; and those who wish to know not themselves but their Self have to penetrate behind the mind and the personality before they can find "the Self of Selves, the Old Man, the Looker-on." The highest knowledge possible to man begins to dawn when the individual Self being a mere transitory reflection of the Eternal Self; and the highest aim of all thought and study is, through this knowledge, to return to the Highest Self and regain identity with it. "The jar is broken, and the ether that was in it is one with the one and undivided ether, from which the jar once seemed to severe it." "Here to know is to be; to know the Ātman is to be the Ātman; and the reward of this highest knowledge after death is freedom from new births, or immortality."

Such was the dream of ancient India, and the loftiest peak of its philosophic thought; the first attempt at the philosophy of the Absolute instinct with the spirit of speculative daring; and it undoubtedly shows us the very best that the human mind is capable of reaching. The Highest Self, the Ātman—than which perhaps no happier philosophical expression has been found for the Universal Principle—was the goal of the endeavour. It was also the starting point of all phenomenal existence, "the root of the world"—the Sat or Satya—the only true and real Existence. Whatever else exists—the universe and gods and men—has but an emanative existence or an illusory existence under the influence of Māyā; the whole creation, visible and invisible, being due to the one Sat or Self; is upheld by it and will ultimately return to it. As one of the Upaniṣads profoundly and beautifully says :—

"There is one Eternal Thinker, thinking non-eternal thoughts, He, though one, fulfils the desires of many. The wise who perceive Him within their Self, to them belongs eternal life, eternal peace." The highest wisdom of Greece, it has been observed, was "to know ourselves;" the highest wisdom of India is "to know our Self."

Thus we see the transcendental character of Indian thought; the yearning after the Beyond, the Unseen, the Infinite; the necessity to transcend the limits of all mere empirical knowledge; to penetrate the mere shell, and grasp the innermost kernel—the last of the several enclosing envelopes or sheaths, beyond which we cannot pierce. To such a mind, the finite is meaningless without the Infinite. This material earth has no abiding. Life is a dream and death a birth and an awakening. India is the land of the Infinite. Its skies are so deep and blue; its mountains are lofty and inaccessible; its forests are so dense and boundless; its rivers are so broad and long, that it is natural for the Indian to conceive the Infinite.

And herein lies the peculiar strength of the Vedāntist position, which all opponents of a materialistic or naturalistic philosophy must admire. When attacked, Hinduism has always kept open a line of retreat upon transcendental fortifications and has not attempted to make compromise with scientific research. In harmony with what is best in the present philosophical thought of the West, the Vedāntist affirms that the empirical school as expounded in recent years by Spencer, Mill, Huxley and others, leads logically to agnosticism, since its sphere of knowledge is limited to the world of sense perception. It is thorough going in its grasp of the physical half of the phenomenal world, but cannot comprehend the psychical— the region of man's religious convictions and beliefs. It is here where philosophy steps into emancipate the scientific reason. It contrasts phenomenal with noumenal realities; it deals primarily with consciousness, or the mental world, maintaining that it is only of the Ego that a direct knowledge is possible; and the element of permanency in the material world of perception and in the mental world of self-consciousness, of which western philosophy has not obtained the clearest vision, is set up as an ultimate fact of philosophic analysis by the Vedāntist, who always inquires into the ultimate bases of phenomena and declares that the Eternal cannot be known through the transient.

The Supreme Being is believed, by the non-dualistic, Vedāntist, to be associated with a certain power called Māyā or Avidyā, to which the appearance of the universe is due; and it is urged by some that it is called Māyā or nescience, ignorance or illusion, because the world and its belongings stand in the way of our reaching to a knowledge of the ultimate truth—the eternal substratum of the world, the underlying principle of existence. The first step to the knowledge of the Supreme is the recognition of this permanent element.

And if we would get at the truths which lie beyond and behind this world of action and the play of the senses, we must, according to the Vedānta, cultivate self-restraint and tranquillity, suppress our actions and senses, or at any rate, renounce the desire for the fruit of one's actions; since it is this fruit or karma that chains one to this world by repeated births and deaths. The various systems of Yoga philosophy current among Hindus—as these self restraining exercises are termed—have for their foundation the national belief in the necessity for human souls to seek liberation from the bondage of the flesh by realising, as the Advaitin or non-dualist does, that the eternal principle of all being the power that creates, supports and again withdraws into itself, all worlds, is identical with the Ātman, the self or soul in us. These systems of Yoga teach each its own method of attaining the desired end; but all enjoin the performance of works in a spirit that renounces all attachment to results.

The latent capacity of men of transcending the finite and his affinity to what is universal and infinite, is the key to the evolution of religion; and ancient India supplies us with its earliest form.

At first sight, the personification of the objects and forces of Nature—the sun, the dawn, the firmament, the winds and storms—such as we find in the Vedic hymns, seems to present a polytheistic nature-worship. A closer study, however, shows us that the various divinities have not that distinct individuality which marks the mythologies of Greece and Rome; but that beyond and beneath them all there is an invisible Reality, a Unity, in which they blend, and for which they are only varied expressions : as a passage of the Ṛgveda states :—"That which exists is One; sages call it variously."

Now what was it that led the mind first of all to deify certain natural objects, and then to find beneath them all an enduring substance, passing from the worship of the elements personified to the worship of the power that rules over the elements? It was the sense of the vanity and unreality and fleeting character of all finite things; "the inadequacy of their satisfactions, the insecurity of their possessions, the lack of any fixed stay." This feeling undoubtedly represents the earliest dawn of the religious consciousness, the elementary form of religious faith, such as we find in ancient India. It is a later stage of thought that argues from the existence of the world to the notion of a First Cause—all-wise and omnipotent Creator. To the Indian, the all-embracing sky, the majestic sun, the silent stars, the everlasting hills, the noble rivers, become to the mind types of permanence and power, in the midst of a feeble and fleeting life; and these are forthwith deified. There we have the earliest and rudest form of religious worship.

Gradually, however, as the mind became more reflective and philosophical, these separate nature-divinities fade away and Nature is regarded as a whole; till, in the Upaniṣads, the religious consciousness attempts to pass beyond Nature, beyond everything, beyond 'where words cannot go, nor mind,' and to grasp an invisible Essence, which is neither the heavens nor the earth, but something infinitely greater and more abiding than all—pure Being the innermost Being both of nature and man.

This philosophical synthesis, this pantheistic idea of God, implicit in the Vedas, explicit in the Upaniṣads, thus early rooted itself in Hindu thought; and out of it has grown all the moral and social life of the people. Pantheism in some form or another has pervaded the intellectual history of mankind, and fascinated some of the greatest thinkers of the world. For there is pantheism and pantheism. European pantheism has commonly made God to be co-extensive with all material things it has identified the world with God—all things being parts of the Divine nature, i.e. the finite is the Infinite. Indian mystic pantheism, however, is very different, and is far more spiritual. It affirms not the deification of the finite world, but its nothingness : the formula that expresses it is not, the world is God, but the world is nothing and God is all in all—the One only Infinite Reality.

It was thus, primarily, a true consciousness—the consciousness of the world's nothingness—that gave rise to this conception, of a Substance beneath the shadows; that beyond the finite is the Infinite, summed up in the Indian dictum—"There is but one Being—on Second—" ekam ava advitiyam. It is the answer that the human mind at an early stage gives to the problem of the One in many; an attempt to give unity to its ideas by the aid of the logical category of Substance. For, just as behind the various qualities and changes of a flower there is something we regard as constant and permanent, so beneath all the surface appearances of things there is one and only one Reality that never changes—one Being, Brahman. And he who would know Him or It, must turn away from all sense perception and contemplate Pure Existence.

At such a stage, when the mind was groping and guessing after truth, metaphors rather than formal reasoning governed thought; and the deepest reflections of philosophy were embodied in sensuous images. The Supreme Being is represented as saying, I am the light in the sun, the brilliancy in flame, the fragrance in the earth, the goodness of the good, the beginning, middle and end of all;" but what was meant was that God is the only Being that really is.

The writers of the Upaniṣads seem to have clearly seen the distinction between dogmatic and rational Theism, the Theism that is based on mere traditional or instinctive belief, and the higher faith that comes out of insight and deep reflection on the nature of the world and of the soul. Having seen this distinction, they could not but further see that the passage from the one of the other was not an easy one. Every one that professed to be a believer and worshipper of God and felt a curiosity to know God, could not be admitted into the privileges of a theological student. Notwithstanding his belief and inquisitiveness, he might not possess the moral and spiritual attainments necessary for a successful student, His mind might be too restless and too much taken up with things external to be able to fix itself upon supersensuous realities and if, by mere dint of intellectual concentration, he succeeded in understanding the nature of the Deity, his heart unless purified and warmed by devotional exercises, would fail to establish itself in God, and would not thus truly find him. Our Theologians, therefore, insisted upon their pupils going through a long course of moral and spiritual exercise before they were admitted as regular students of the science of God. In the Praśnopaniṣad, we find the Ṛṣi Pippalāda sending away six inquirers after God, ...inquirers who are described as worshippers of God, . . .sending away even such men, for another year of disciplinary exercises before undertaking their regular instruction. In the Chāndogya Upaniṣad, Satyakāma Jābāla is turned out to tend his teacher's cattle which not only tests his theological ardour and teaches him to be dutiful and obedient under the most trying circumstances, but further brings him into direct contact with Nature and gives him special opportunities for cultivating habits of solitary reflection so essential to the knowledge of things divine, so that after his long and rigorous course of apprenticeship, he is enabled to know God with only a little help from his master. In the Kaṭhopaniṣad, Mṛtyu consents to instruct Naciketā in the mysteries of the soul only when, after offering him all the attractions of his divine palace, including all that men value most, he saw that the young man was insensible to them, and would not be satisfied by anything else than the knowledge he sought. The same Upaniṣad says :-

"He who has not given up bad habits, whose mind is not tranquil and used the spiritual concentration cannot find him (i.e. God) even by knowledge."

Showing that knowledge, which is so essential to the finding of God is not in itself sufficient to lead to him. We need not multiply instances. The following quotation indicates briefly how very difficult the Ṛṣis considered the passage from the religion of mere belief to that of philosophical or spiritual insight to be : "Arise, awake, seek competent instructors and try to know God. The wise say that way is as difficult to be passed as the sharp edge of a razor."

Once admitted into the privileged circle of Theistic inquirers the pupil must have been made to go through prescribed courses of meditation and reasoning. What the lines of thought were which he followed in his attempt to reach rational or philosophical Theism, it is scarcely possible for us to discover with any amount of certainty. The instruction imparted must have been largely, if not exclusively, oral. The art of writing, even if introduced at all, must have been in its infancy, so that no records, properly so called, remain of the teachings of those who founded the philosophy of the Upaniṣads. The Upaniṣads, however, are not systematic treatises on Philosophy. They contain, like the Bible and other ancient scriptures, exhortations on ethical and spiritual life, anecdotes, stories, poetry, psychology and devout utterances that are as often poetical as philosophical. But notwithstanding their unsystematic character, they contain the elements of system, a profound and magnificent system of Philosophy. Being the product of various authors and even of different ages, they are not free from contradictions even on important matters, though the philosophical reader, accustomed to tentative expressions of apparently conflicting but really complementary aspects of the same truth in philosophical literature, will find fewer contradictions in them than the ordinary reader. Though, however, a strictly self-consistent system can no more be gathered from the Upaniṣads than from any body of "sacred books" a general current of thought towards certain Philosophical doctrines may clearly be traced in them. This general current of thought in the writers of the Upaniṣads is all that we mean by the "philosophy of the Upaniṣads". However, though as we have already observed, we have no proper record of the lines of thought which our old Theistic thinkers followed in reaching their conclusions, the conclusions themselves, and often the language in which they are clothed, indicate with sufficient clearness, the method adopted by them. There are, besides, here and there, passages containing more or less luminous philosophical analysis which throw much light on the logical processes through which the minds of the Ṛṣis moved. Gathering these scattered fragments of light, we shall give a rough idea of the theistic philosophy of the Upaniṣads.

On the subject of the relation of mind and matter, all indications lead us to conclude that the writers of the Upaniṣads were Idealists. To them, as much as to Berkeley and Hegel and their followers the world is through and through a mental construction. Whether manifested or unmanifested, it rests in mind. Objects to them, as to the European Idealist, are essentially related to knowledge and can therefore exist only in knowledge. The Aitareya enumerates the various classes of objects, animate and inanimate including even the highest gods, and says. . . . . "All is produced by Reason and rests in reasonm the World is produced by Reason and rests in Reason and Reason is Brahman. The Kaṭha says, . . . "In him rest all worlds and none are apart from him." The Praśna says, ... "As my dear birds rest on trees, so all rests in the Supreme-Self." These and innumerable other passages of similar import can be explained only in the light of Idealism. That can the resting of all things in the Supreme Mind mean but the correlation of subject and object. The Ṛṣis must have seen that objects, with all other qualities, appear to mind, to knowledge, and that they can be believed in and thought of only in relation to mind. As the Muṇḍaka says, ...“In whom, the luminous one, all things rest and shine,” and elsewhere, ...“His, the shining one, all things shine after, all shine through His light.”

Such utterances may seem to some to indicate a Being whose existence is inferred from the indications of law and order in the world, a Being whose relation to Nature cannot be explained by the familiar relation of subject and object, and who, if he is directly cognisable at all, is so only in supreme moments of mystical insight. But the authors of the Upaniṣads' unlike the natural Theologians of Europe, made little use of the Design Argument. The Reason in which they saw the world shine is not one of which they had any need to go in search of by the aid of ingeniously constructed arguments. They found it in themselves. It is identical with what every one calls his own Reason his own Self. It is that which is the subjects appear and exist for us. Let us hear how the Kenopaniṣad distinguishes subject and object and identifies God with the former (1-4-8).

But by identifying Brahman with the subject or self in each person, do not the Upaniṣads make him limited and plural? They would indeed do so if by the ‘Self’ they meant anything that is, in its every nature, individual, particular. But by ‘Self’ the Upaniṣads do not meant any such thing. They mean by it, something that is, in its very nature, universal, that is common to all thinking individuals, the common basis of all subjects, animate and inanimate. At each step of analysis, the Ṛṣis names a category which comprehends the lower categories, till he comes to the highest category the Supreme Self, which transcends not only the sensorium and the intellect, where time and space end, but also that centre of spiritual activity to which, as a substance, intellect itself is referred as a mode or attribute. By the Supreme person or Self therefore, the Upaniṣads mean something that transcends time, space and quantity, which belongs not only to me, a particular centre of spiritual activity, but to all such centres. As the same Upaniṣad says :—What is here is there; what is there is here. He who sees plurality in this goes from death to death. This is made much more clear in the dialogue between Nārada and Sanatkumāra in the Chāndogya Upaniṣad. Sanatkumāra enumerates a number of categories, coming to a higher one at each step as Nārada feels dissatisfied with each last, and at last he comes to Prāṇa, Nārada seems satisfied, as he cannot think of a higher category than life, with the departure of which every activity in us ceases. But Sanatkumāra leads him to the highest category, where alone final satisfaction can be obtained, and that is the Infinite (Bhūmā). But Nārada like all minds in which the highest enlightenment has not dawned, asks, “Where does the Infinite abide, O Lord”? Just as we ask, “Where is the Self”? or say, “The Self is here,” thus making space a higher category than Self. Sanatkumāra at first says, “The Infinite abides in its own glory,” but as if in anticipation of Nārada's question “Where is that glory”? Sanatkumāra withdraws even this seeming limitation of Infinite and says, “It does not abide in its glory.” This Infinite, which comprehends all space and so cannot be anywhere in particular, is then identified with the Self, and the infinitude of the Self described in the words—"Verily I extend from below, I extend from above, I extend from behind, I extend from before, I extend from the South, I extend from the North. Of a truth I am all this". It is then said that all the categories or objects enumerated above are products of the Self.

No demonstration, in the ordinary sense of the term, is offered of this apparently starting position that the Self in us—that which makes us knowing, thinking beings, is infinite and one in all. This may be partly due to the Ṛṣis not being perfect masters of the art of exposition, but it seems also in part, due to the fact that the truth appeared to them too plain to require any formal demonstration. To us it seems that when one has brought to a focus all the scattered rays of light, the Ṛṣis have thrown on the problem, it strikes one as a real demonstration, if 'demonstration' is the word for the revelation of a truth which forms the background of all knowledge, all thinking, all demonstration. In thinking of objects, we necessarily think of a subject. In knowing and thinking of the limitations of objects, even of mutually exclusive thinking objects or minds, we necessarily do so from the standpoint of subject which transcends all limitations, we do so only by identifying ourselves with a Universal which, since it is the condition of knowing and thinking limits, cannot itself be limited. In other words, it is not any individual, any particular centre of spiritual activity as distinguished from other centres, that knows and thinks limits as such, by the Infinite itself that does so; and in as much as the Infinite thinks my thoughts for me, I am one with it. There are also passages which seem to teach the utter annihilation of all that is finite and objective. Much depends upon how these passages are interpreted. We think, however, that spiritual experience confirms the interpretation which construes such 'annihilation' into the real subsumption of the finite into the infinite, the full consciousness on the part of the finite that in itself it is nothing, the Infinite is all-in-all.

The Search for the Cause of the Universe

The earliest philosophic view with regard to the supreme Being appears to have arisen out of an attempt to answer the question, whence this universe? Consequently the Upaniṣads abound in numerous creation theories, each seeking to trace the universe to some First Cause and describing how and why this First Cause created the universe. A very early creation theory is to be found in Bṛhadāraṇyaka, which says that "In the beginning this world was Soul alone in the form of a Puruṣa. Looking around, he saw nothing else than himself. . . . He desired a second."[1]

We rise to a distinctly higher level of Philosophical thought when we pass from attempts to explain the universe in terms of a magnified person to explanations in terms of natural phenomena, such as Water, or Food (earth) and again from such obviously visible

1. Bṛ. Upaniṣad, V.5.1.

and particular elements to elements less visible and more universal, such as air, space, non-being, being and the Imperishable. Thus with regard to Water as the First Principle, it said in the Bṛ. Up. "In the beginning this world was just Water. That Water emitted the Real. . . . and in the Chānd. Up., "It is just Water solidified that is this earth. . . .atmosphere. . . .sky... Gods and men, beas and birds, grass and trees. . .Reverence Water."[1] The reason why Water was regarded as the source of all things seems to be that life is impossible without water. As the Chāndogya tells us, living beings perish if there is no rain.[2] In a similar manner, it is argued that Food (earth) is the source of all things, for without Food, creatures Perish.[3] Crude as these theories are, they make a tremendous advance in philosophical thought, for here the thinker turns away from the anthropomorphism of an earlier day and all explanations in terms of gods and goddesses, and seeks to interpret the universe, not in terms of some creation of his imagination, but in terms of a Principle known to him in everyday experience.

With Water and Food as the Ultimate Principle, however, we still move in the realm of the particular and the sensible. Wind or Breath, being invisible and less sharply defined, tend to lead the mind away from attachment to the sensible—which again could not have been easy for these pioneer thinkers. The reason for regarding this as Ultimate seems to have been derived chiefly from the observation that an individual dies when breath ceases, and also from the fact that it is breath alone which functions untiringly in the individual while other organs soon become exhausted and require rest. This is true of Air or Wind, the counterpart in the inorganic world of Breath in the living body, for Air never seems to require rest, unlike Fire, which soon exhausts itself, and the Sun and Moon, which daily set and thus take their rest.[4] Moreover, just as all the other functions of the body disappear in sleep into breath, and Breath alone remains. The elemental forces of nature such as fire, water, sun and moon are seen to disappear into Air or Wind, "The Wind verily, is a snatcher unto itself. Verily, when a fire blows out, it just goes to the wind. When the sun sets, it just goes to the Wind. When the moon sets, it just goes to the Wind. When Water dries, it goes up, it just goes to the Wind. For the Wind, truly snatches all here to itself. Now with reference to oneself Prāṇa, verily, is a snatcher unto itself. When one sleeps, speech just goes to breath, the eye to breath, the ear to breath; the mind to breath; for the breath, truly, snatches all here to himself. Verily, there are two snatcher unto themselves.[5] And with regard to the supremacy of Breath among all the vital elements in the body. We have the dramatic portrayal of rivalry among the five organs of the body, speech, sight,

1. Tait. Up. II.6.
2. Tait. Up. II.6.
3. Taitt. Up. 11.1.
4. Bṛ. Up. 1.5.21, 22.
5. Chānd. Up. IV.3.1-4.

hearing, mind and breath, and the victory gained by Breath by its showing that without it none of the others can function, while without the other organs, it can still function.[1] It is primarily on the basis of the indispensability of Breath for living beings that it is acclaimed as Supreme. If so, it is obvious that while the philosopher who regarded breath or Wind as the ultimate Principle made an advance over those who put forward a sensible element like water or Food as ultimate, still he did not, any more than they, succeed in rising above anthropomorphism, if by anthropomorphism we mean the way of thinking which argues purely on the analogy of what is true in human experience. Whether the ultimately soul is conceived of as Water, Food, or Breath, it is precisely because these are absolutely essential to human life.

When, however, we pass to a comparatively universal and omnipresent such as space as the First Principle, we seem for the first time to pass to the level of abstract thought which has succeeded in dissociating itself from the sensible and the anthropomorphic. Thus we have the question asked, "To what does this world go back?" and the answer is, "To space. .. verily all things here arise out of space. They disappear back into space, for space alone is greater than these; space is the final goal.[2] From this, the transition to such highly abstract conceptions such as that of Non-being, Being, or the Imperishable as ultimate was not very difficult, and we have these three principles put forward as the source of all things. Non-being was not mean mere nothingness, but some form of characterless existence.[3] "To be sure, some people say : "In the beginning this world was just non-being (asat). One only without a second; from that non-being, Being, (sat) was produced. But verily, my dear whence could this be? How from non-being could being be produced? On the contrary my dear, in the beginning this world was just being, one only, without a second. It bethought itself : Would that I were many? Let me procreate myself; It emitted heat . . . that heat be thought itself. . .'would that I were many? Let me procreate myself. It emitted water. . .that water be thought itself. . .Would that I were many? Let me procreate myself. It emitted food."[4] Thus we are told that the whole universe, including man is nothing but a product of these three elements, heat, water and food which have for their animating principle the primal being. It does not seem likely that this being was conceived as characterised by consciousness. The thought that is ascribed to this being in the passage above cited must not, it would seem, be taken literally, for the same word here translated 'thought' is also used in the case of heat and water as each of these differentiates itself. Further the very materialistic account that is given of men and his conscious faculties, as the product of heat, water and food, the thrice repeated maxim that "The mind consists of food," and the

1. Tait. Up. II.6.
2. Chānd. Up. I.9.1.
3. Chānd. Up. III.19.1.
4. Tait. Up. II.6.

striking illustration of this truth in the fact that without food for 15 days Śvetaketu is unable to employ his mind, all seem to point to the view that consciousness was regarded by this philosopher as the result of non-conscious processes, and as therefore not ultimate. Then also the view that in sleep, where there is a total lack of consciousness or in death, where we are told that mind has passed into breath, and breath into heat one reaches being, seem to indicate that being was conceived as some primeval unconscious substance which underlies all things and which is best represented by the three elements of heat, water, and food. This being is also described some primeval stuff out of which everything in the universe, whether conscious soul or unconscious object, is ultimately constituted, Like the Greek philosopher, Thales, it seems the philosophers of the Upaniṣads, tried to discover the material cause of the universe. And later on one see that they identified the efficient cause of the universe with this material cause. This ultimate essence which form the stuff of all that exists is just the primeval substance out of which everything has come, whether as non-being or being. Ultimate reality is some abstract potency or essence from which the universe has sprung and into which it will finally return. In Taitt. Up., Varuṇa, the father of Bhṛgu teaches his son about the cause of the universe. He said : "That from that into which (at the time of dissolution) they enter, they merge seek to know that– That is Brahman."[1] Bhṛgu, the son of Varuṇa realised that food is Brahman; far from food, verily, are these beings born, by food, when form, do they live; into food (at the time of dissolution) do they enter, do they merge. Again he realised Prāṇa, mind and intellect (Vijñāna) as Brahman, for the same reason. And lastly he realised that bliss (ānanda) in Brahman; far from bliss, verily, are these beings, by bliss, when born, do they live into bliss (at the time of dissolution) do they enter, merge.[2] Ṛṣis, discoursing on Brahman as the cause of the universe ask; "Is Brahman the cause? Whence are we born? By what do we live? Where do we dwell at the end (after death)? Should time, or nature, or necessity, or chance or the elements be regarded as the cause? Or he who is called the Puruṣa, the living self?[3] To answer above questions the sages say that it is not possible to discover the final cause of the universe by means of reason based upon sense experience. Therefore, the seers pursued the path of Yoga, and came to the conclusion that the Supreme lord evolved the world with the help of His own Māyā.[4] Here, it seems, the cause of the universe is consciousness one. He is māyin. With the help of his own māyā the Lord creates the universe. He can desire, so He, the Supreme Soul desired, May I be many, may I be born.[5] In Aitareya Upaniṣads also we find the similar version : "He bethought Himself; 'Let me now create the world. Then

1. Tait. Up. II.6.
2. Tait. Up. II.6.
3. Chānd. Up. IV.4.15.
4. Chānd. Up. IV.4.15.
5. Chānd. Up. IV.4.15.

He created these worlds. . . .[1] Taitt. Up. again describes that "From that (Brahman) was born ākāśa; from air, fire; from fire, water; from water, earth; from earth, herbs; from herbs, food; from food, man.[2] So, we can say the worlds are created from Brahman and by Brahman. It is said that only Brahman is the cause of the universe, the universe comes out from Brahman and returns back into Brahman again. Now that distinguishes the concept of Brahman from concepts such as water, Breath, or Space, is that, unlike these concepts, Brahman as cosmic power came to be thought of primarily as a conscious principle. It thus implied that what underlies the external universe is one with what exists within one's own self; may; more, that as conscious principle it is more akin to self than to not self. The seeds of monistic idealism, which characterises the teaching of the Upaniṣads, as well as much of the later development of Indian thought, were sown, it would appear, by men like Yājñavalkya with their philosophic insight that Brahman the ultimate ground of all things, is a conscious principle.

The development which we have so far traced in the view of Supreme Reality as some impersonal sensible element such as water and food to more and more abstract and universal elements such as breath or air, space, non-being, being, the Imperishable, till finally we reach the view of Brahman as a conscious principle, represents only one among numerous lines of thought that came to development of this time.

This Brahman is essence of all. All the gods and all the powers hitherto recognised are subordinate to Him. The gods Agni and Vāyu are unable respectively to burn or to blow away so much as a piece of straw without the power given to them by Brahman.[3] The Upaniṣads make it perfectly clear that nothing does or can exist outside of Brahman. Within the all-comprehensive self or Brahman, everything will be found to exist; therefore it is said: "Just as, my dear, by one clod of clay all that is made of clay is known, the modification being only a name, arising from speech, while the truth is that all is clay; just as, my dear by one nagget of gold all that is made of gold is known, the modification being only a name, arising from speech, while the truth is that all is gold."[4] Existence apart from Brahman is difficult to conceive, according to the Upaniṣads. Brahman as the cause of the universe, is all pervading. Therefore "All this is Brahman."[5] It is pointed out that Brahman is shining one in the East, West, South and North, as the Endless or the infinite in the earth, air, sky, and ocean, as the luminous in the fire, sun, moon and lightning and as possessing a support in breath, eye, ear and mind. This discourse also ends by adding that above all Brahman is to be known as the conscious Principle in oneself.[6]

---

1. Chānd. Up. IV.4.15.
2. Chānd. Up. IV.4.15.
3. Chānd. Up. IV.4.15.
4. Chānd. Up. IV.4.15.
5. Chānd. Up. IV.4.15.
6. Chānd. Up. IV.4.15.

The Ātman

From the subjective stand point we can say the reality is the Ātman. In the Chānd. Upaniṣad[1] the another narrates a story to arrive at the conception of the self-conscious being from the subjective stand point. He brings out how the ultimate reality must not be mistaken with the bodily consciousness; how it must not be confused with the dream consciousness; how it transcends even the deep sleep consciousness; how finally it is the Pure self consciousness, which is beyond all bodily or mental limitations. We are told in the Chāndogya Upaniṣad that Indra, among the gods and Virocana among the demons, went to Prajāpati to know the real nature of Ātman. They wanted to know the self which is free from sin, free from old age, free from death, free from grief, free from hunger, free from thirst, whose desires come true and whose thoughts come true that it is which should be searched out, that it is which one should desire to understand. Prajāpati would not immediately tell them the final truth. He tried to delude them by saying first that the self was nothing more than the image that we see in the eye, in water, or in a mirror. Indra and Virocana want back, Virocana was satisfied with the teaching in Prajāpati; and thought that the self was nothing more than the mere consciousness of body. But Indra was not satisfied with the first teaching of Prajāpati. He went back again to Prajāpati to request him once more to tell him what ultimate reality was. Prajāpati tried to confuse him again to examine his worthiness by saying that dream consciousness was the true self. Third time Indra went back to Prajāpati. Again he confused him (Indra) by saying that deep sleep conscious was the true self. Finally when Indra went back to Prajāpati to learn the real nature of Ātman, Prajāpati said : "Verily O Indra, this body is subject to death, but it is at the same time the vesture of an immortal soul. It is only when the Soul is encased in the body, that it is cognisant of pleasure and pain. There is neither pleasure nor pain for the soul once relieved of its body. Just as the wind and the cloud, the lightning and the thunder, are without body and arise from heavenly space and appear in their own form, so does this serene being, namely, the Self, arise from this mortal body, reach the highest light, and then appear in his own form. This Serene being who appear in his own form is the highest person.[2] The pure self is immortal and incorporeal. The embodied self is the victim of pleasure and pain. So long as one is identified with the body, there is no cessation of pleasure and pain. But neither pleasure nor pain touches one who is not identified with the body. [3]

When the self comes to inhabit the body, it must be recognised as passing through certain psychical states. The Māṇḍukya Upaniṣad makes the analysis of the four states of consciousness. The quarter (pāda) of the self is called Vaiśvānara, whose sphere of activity is the waking state, who is conscious of external objects. The second pāda is Taijas, sphere of activity is dream state, who is conscious of internal objects. The third is Prājña, whose

1. Chānd. Up. IV.4.15.
2. Tait. Up. II.6.
3. Chānd. Up. IV.4.15.

sphere is deep sleep in whom all experiences become unified. The Turīya is not that which is conscious of the outer (objective) world, nor that which is conscious of both, nor that which that which is a mass of consciousness. It is not simple consciousness nor is it unconsciousness. It is unperceived, unrelated, incomprehensible, uninferable, and indescribable. It is the cessation of all phenomena : it is all peace, all bliss, and non-dual. This is Ātman, and this has to be realised.[1]

In Praśna Upaniṣad, Pippalāda describes the self as Puruṣa with sixteen parts. 'He said to Sukeśa : That person He from whom these sixteen parts arise is verily here within the body.' He created Prāṇa; from Prāṇa faith, space, air, fire, water, earth, the organs, mind, food, from food virility, austerity, the Vedic hymns, sacrifice, the worlds; and in the worlds. He created names.[2]

Like Brahman, the Ātman was also postulated as the world ground by the Upaniṣadic philosophers. Finally these two world grounds, Brahman and Ātman, are not different and separate.[3] We find it directly stated : 'verily, that great unborn Soul, undecaying, undying, immortal, fearless, is Brahman.[4] As oil (exists) in sesame seeds, butter in milk, water in river-beds and fire in wood, so the self is realised (as existing) within the self, when a man looks for it by means of truthfulness and austerity that is the Brahman. . . [5] The Upaniṣadic Philosophers regard the Ātman as identical with Brahman the world ground which is the Absolute. The Ātman is Self-conscious and Brahman is identical with the Ātman the Self consciousness. Professor R.D. Ranade says 'Here we have unmistakably the ontological argument, namely, that ultimate existence must be identified with Self consciousness. Thus by a survey of the different approaches to the problem of Reality, namely, the cosmological, the theological, and the psychological, we see that the Upaniṣadic philosophers try to establish Reality on the firm footing of Self-consciousness to them is eternal verily. God to them is not God, unless He is identical with Self-consciousness. Existence is not existence if it does not mean Self-consciousness. Reality is not reality, if it does not express throughout its structure the marks of pure Self consciousness. Self consciousness thus constitutes the ultimate category of existence to the Upaniṣadic philosophers. [6]

This ultimate reality or Ātman is described as Puruṣa. We are told that Ātman shaped a Puruṣa and drew him forth from the water, and brooded upon him. From the mouth of this Puruṣa came Fire; from his nostrils, Air, from his eyes, the Sun; from his ears, the quarters, of heaven; from his skin, plants and trees; from his heart, the moon; from his navel, death;

1. Chānd. Up. IV.4.15.
2. Chānd. Up. IV.4.15.
3. Chānd. Up. IV.4.15.
4. Tait. Up. II.6.
5. Chānd. Up. IV.4.15.
6. Chānd. Up. IV.4.15.

and from his virile member, water. And in creating man, we are told that the Deity ordered those various elements in the external world to enter into man, and 'fire became speech and entered the mouth. Wind became breath and entered the nostrils. The sun became sight and entered the eyes. The quarters of heaven became hearing and entered the ears. Plants and trees became hairs, and entered the skin. The moon became mind, and entered the heart. Death became the out breath (apāna) and entered the navel. Water became semen and entered the virile member.[1] What is not worthy is that both the self and the not-self, which seem so entirely different from each other, are here regarded as having a mutual correspondence, since both of them are permeated by the same forces which emanated from the primeval Puruṣa. Further, the old Ṛgvedic idea[2] of cosmic Puruṣa, from the parts of whose body various elements in the universe are regarded as emanating an idea which occurs frequently in he Upaniṣads, as well as later Indian writings—is here assimilated by the Ātman theory. The view that ultimate Reality was Puruṣa or presiding genius of the universe appears thus to have developed side by side with the view that it was Ātman. May more, as evidenced by these early Ātman theories, it would appear that the distinction between Puruṣa and Ātman was not maintained, the two being freely identified with each other. Thus the Upaniṣadic philosophers describe cosmic Puruṣa as identical with Ātman and already said that Ātman is not different from Brahman.

Kaikeya's instruction of the six Brahmans who come to him each with a different nation as to what Brahman is, viz., that he is heaven, sun, wind, space, water and earth, is not only to show that Brahman is all these, but also to deduce from each of these partial definitions of Brahman, a corresponding attribute in Him. Thus, as heaven, He is the brightly shining One; as sun, the manifold one; as wind, one who possesses various paths; as space, one who is expanded; as water, one who is all wealth; as earth, one who is a support. Here again obviously the philosopher attempts to describe Brahman in terms of what is most striking and significant in each of these various elements with which He is identified, and concludes by pointing out that Brahman is the Soul which is within one self.[3]

The progressive instruction of Nārada by Sanatkumāra,[4] where by Nārada is led from lower to higher conceptions of Brahman—from Brahman as name, speech, mind, conception, thought, meditation, understanding, etc. to Soul (Ātman) as the highest—has for its characteristic the fact, the each category, which is mentioned as descriptive of Brahman, is mentioned on the ground that it is important and indispensable and if it is transcended it is only because there is a still higher category, which is also important and indispensable, and which has the added merit of subsuming under itself the previous

1. Chānd. Up. IV.4.15.
2. Chānd. Up. IV.4.15.
3. Chānd. Up. IV.4.15.
4. Chānd. Up. IV.4.15.

categories. Thus an effort is made to describe Brahman in terms of qualities, the most significant and all-inclusive. In this way, it would seem, philosophers sought to go beyond the view that Brahman, the ultimate ground of all things, is a conscious principle, and to describe it in terms suggestive of value and pre-eminence. It is true that they do not tell us very much about the attributes of Brahman beyond what has been mentioned above. Nevertheless it is significant that Brahman the all-pervading conscious principle, tended to be regarded as possessed of value. Brahman is the unity which explains all this diversity, straightway identified everything in the universe with Brahman. To the Upaniṣadic philosophers nothing can exist without Brahman. They therefore, proclaim, "Lo, here all is Brahman," verily, this whole world is Brahman. Tranquil, let one worship it as that in which he come forth, as that into which he will be dissolved, as that in which he breathes.[1] Verily, what is called Brahman—that is the same as what the space outside of a person is verily, what the space outside of a person is—that is the same as what the space within a person is verily, what the space within a person is—that is the same as what the space here within the heart is.[2] Verily, this whole world containing all desires, containing all odours, containing all tastes, encompassing this whole world, the unspeaking, the unconcerned—this is the Soul of mine within the heart, this is Brahman.[3]

The Upaniṣadic doctrine of the self and some systems of Indian Philosophy

The Vedāntic school of Śaṅkara is completely based on the Upaniṣadic Doctrine of the Self. Śaṅkara has successfully interpreted the Upaniṣadic texts in favour of Advaitism. Rāmānuja also has claimed himself to be the real follower of the Upaniṣadic Doctrine. One can find the germs of other philosophies too such as Nyāya and Sāṁkhya in the Upaniṣads.

(i) Dualism of Nyāya

Nyāya is a system of atomistic and spiritualistic pluralism. It recognises the dualism of matter and spirit. Though Nyāya refers to God as the creator, preserver and destroyer of this world, but He, as an eternal external reality, is always, limited by the co-eternal atoms and souls and has to be guided by the law of Karma.[4] Nyāya recognises God to be as the efficient cause of this universe. According to Nyāya philosophy the eternal atoms are the material cause of this universe. So Nyāya has diverted its philosophical theories from the original teachings of the Upaniṣads. The Upaniṣads do not teach such extreme dualism as one finds in Nyāya system of philosophy. Nyāya accepts the plurality of souls. The finite souls are completely separated from the Supreme Self, the God. Apart from identity of the finite souls with the infinite Supreme One, Nyāya does not accept even any kind of unity of

1. Chānd. Up. IV.4.15.
2. Chānd. Up. IV.4.15.
3. Chānd. Up. IV.4.15.
4. Tait. Up. II.6.

them with the Supreme. One cannot find this type of extreme dualism and pluralism in the Upaniṣads. The Upaniṣads teach us that there is only one reality that is Brahman. Apart from Brahman there cannot be any separate entity. Everything is dependent on Brahman for its existence.

It has already stated that according to Nyāya, God is the creator, preserver and destroyer of the universe. We can find germs of this creation theory of Nyāya in the Upaniṣads. Even some difference will remain there between the creation theory of the Upaniṣad and that of Nyāya. Because Nyāya has accepted eternal atoms to be as material cause of the universe. According to the Upaniṣads, Brahman the Supreme Self is the efficient as well as the material cause of the universe. "Having performed austerities, He created all this whatever there is. . . .The Satya became all this."[1]

(ii) Sāṁkhya System

The root ideas of Sāṁkhya are to be found in the Chāndogya, Kaṭha and Praśna Upaniṣads. But the Śvetāśvatara gives us a fuller and more detailed account of Sāṁkhya philosophy. The Sāṁkhya philosophy of the Upaniṣads, specially that of the Śvetāśvatara Upaniṣad was the theistic one. It recognises the god head as the creating principle of the universe.[2] But the later system of Sāṁkhya philosophy does not recognise the God head for the same purpose. We find the germs of the Sāṁkhya philosophy in the Kaṭhopaniṣad too. When we are told in that Upaniṣad that beyond the mind is Buddhi, beyond the Buddhi is the Mahat Ātman, beyond the Mahat Ātman is the Avyakta, beyond the Avyakta is the Puruṣa, and beyond the Puruṣa there is nothing else. Again we are told in the Śvetāśvatara that there is one unborn Prakṛti– red, white and black, which gives birth to many creatures like itself.[3] These are root ideas of the Sāṁkhya philosophy which are clearly found in the Upaniṣads. But even these Upaniṣads too do not support the atheistic Sāṁkhya and the plurality of the souls. The learned Professor Dr. Radhakrishnan says– "The Upaniṣads do not support the theory of a plurality of Puruṣas. . .[4] It is already stated that central teaching of the Upaniṣads is the doctrine of one self, the Supreme Self. It is transcendent and as well as immanent. It is the cause of the universe. But the latter Sāṁkhya philosophers have modified this doctrine of one reality and developed their conception of the plurality of Puruṣas. The causality of the world is transferred from Brahman to Prakṛti. According to the Sāṁkhya philosophy, Puruṣa is beginningless and eternaly unchanging. It is timeless and spaceless, mere sentient and entirely passive. Puruṣa is devoid of the three guṇas.[5] It is

1. Tait. Up. II.6.
2. Tait. Up. II.6.
3. Tait. Up. II.6.
4. Tait. Up. II.6.
5. Tait. Up. II.6.

the eternal seer behind the phenomena of Prakṛti and its changes. It is without parts and attributes, all-pervasive and subtle. Puruṣa is pure consciousness.

Sāṁkhya adheres uncompromisingly to the doctrine of the plurality of Puruṣas. The monistic philosophers assert that the individual souls are illusory and that only the world-soul is real. Sāṁkhya does not accept this monistic theory of the soul. Sāṁkhya gives some arguments for proving the plurality of the Puruṣas.[1]

The crucial point, that marks the difference between the doctrine of Ātman of the Upaniṣads and Sāṁkhya Puruṣa, is the doctrine of the plurality of souls. According to the Upaniṣadic doctrine of the Self, individual souls are only temporal and apparent forms of the cosmic Soul. In the final analysis, individuals are only appearance.[2] The nature of Puruṣa is the same like that of Brahman of the Upaniṣads because Puruṣa is also pure consciousness the ultimate knower which is the source of all knowledge. It is self luminous and self-proved, uncaused, eternal and all pervading. Only transfer of the causality to Prakṛti and the plurality of the souls separate the Sāṁkhya system from the Ātman doctrine of the Upaniṣads. The three arguments which are given for proving the plurality of the Puruṣas, actually do not touch the transcendent and pure conscious Puruṣas, and so they do not prove the plurality of the Puruṣas. The three arguments prove only the plurality of Jīvas who suffer from Janma-maraṇa and karaṇa. Therefore Iśvarakṛṣṇa says– Puruṣa, therefore is really neither found nor is it liberated nor does it transmigrate. Bondage, liberation and transmigration belong to Prakṛti in its manifold forms.[3] Jīva is not Guṇātīta. It is related with the three guṇās of Prakṛti. So one can say that Jīvatva is a product of Prakṛti with the three guṇas. Therefore Jīvas or in other words Prakṛti is suffering from Janana and maraṇa and not pure conscious puruṣa. Now it is clear that the Sāṁkhya philosophers have created a confusion between the puruṣa, the transcendental pure one and the Jīva; the empirical ego with the three arguments which are given to prove the plurality of the puruṣa. Actually the three arguments should be given to prove the plurality of Jīvas. Dr. C.D. Sharma correctly points out in his book "Sāṁkhya throughout makes a confusion between the puruṣa, the transcendental subject and the Jīva, the empirical ego, the product of the reflection of puruṣa in Buddhi or Mahat."[4] Ācārya Śaṅkara has pointed out that unintelligent Prakṛti cannot be the creator of this universe. Without being conscious Prakṛti of Sāṁkhya cannot be the efficient cause of the world. If the Sāṁkhya philosophers hold that the universe can come from unintelligent Prakṛti without help of any conscious principle which is called the efficient cause, then the acceptance of puruṣa as pure consciousness will be useless and if so the Sāṁkhya philosophers should shakes hand with those western thinkers who give the mechanistic explanations of evolution without accepting any conscious agent for creation.

---

1. Tait. Up. II.6.
2. Tait. Up. II.6.
3. Tait. Up. II.6.
4. Tait. Up. II.6.

(iii) Viśiṣṭādvaitavāda

Ācārya Rāmānuja's philosophy is called qualitative monism. He also claims himself to be the real interpreter of the Self-doctrine of the Upaniṣads. According to Rāmānuja, the Absolute is an organic unity which is qualified by diversity. Rāmānuja recognises three tattvas as ultimately real. These are matter, souls and god. The matter and souls are absolutely dependent on God. There are substances in themselves, but for their dependence on God, they become His attributes. God is qualified by matter and souls. [1]

Rāmānuja finds justification for his Viśiṣṭādvaitavāda in the Śvetāsvatara Upaniṣad which tells us that there are three ultimate existences—The Supreme Lord, the eternal omniscient and imperishable and all-knowing God, the eternal Jīva of limited knowledge and power and the unborn Prakṛti. There are three tattvas : The enjoyer (Jīva), the objects of enjoyment, and the Ruler (Īśvara). The triad is described by the knowers of Brahman.[2]

According to Rāmānuja, God is the Soul of souls. God is also the Soul of nature. The Bṛhadāraṇyaka tells us that God is the Antaryāmin of the universe : He who inhabits water, yet is within water, whom water does not know. . . . .Who controls water from within. He is yourself, the Inner controller, the Immortal. Who controls fire from within. .. .who controls sky from within. . . . . who controls the air from within . .. . . who controls heaven from within. . . . .who controls the sun from within . . . .who controls all beings from within . . . . the Inner controller, the Immortal. . . . [3]

This doctrine of Antaryāmin constitutes the fundamental position in the philosophy of Rāmānuja when he calls God the Soul of nature.[4] God is identified with the Absolute in Rāmānuja's philosophy. God is Brahman and Brahman is a qualified unity. God may be viewed through to stages—as Kāraṇa Brahma and a Kārya Brahma. Brahman is the Supreme cause of this universe. Therefore, the world is fully dependent on Brahman. Though the finite self is real, yet it is not independent. It is dependent on God. The matter and the soul-both are the attributes of God.

Rāmānuja criticises carefully the Advaitic view of the nature of Ultimate Reality. He examines the Advaitin's view that Brahman or Ultimate Reality in Advaita or one without a second, that is, a pure one which excludes all differences. His contention is that such a pure non differenced being cannot be established by an appeal to experience. According to Rāmānuja, Brahman is Saviśeṣa. Brahman cannot be regarded as pure non-differenced consciousness. Brahman must be regarded as Self or person with excellent attributes.[5] The Advaitin interprets the text, one only without a second, to mean that Brahman is a pure

---

1. Tait. Up. II.6.
2. Tait. Up. II.6.
3. Tait. Up. II.6.
4. Tait. Up. II.6.
5. Tait. Up. II.6.

unity devoid of all differences. But Rāmānuja asks, if this be true, what about other passages which predicate "eternity and other attributes of Brahman?" When these passages are also taken into consideration, the text that Brahman is 'one only without a second' will have to be viewed as teaching, not that Brahman is devoid of qualities, but that He is one, like whom there is none other. "What the phrase 'Without a second' really aims at intimating is that Brahman possesses manifold powers, and this it does by denying the existence of another ruling principle different from Brahman. The clause 'Being only this was in the beginning, one only'; teaches that Brahman when about to create constitutes the substantial cause of the world. Here the idea of some further operative cause capable of giving rise to the effect naturally presents itself to the mind and hence we understand that the added clause, without a second, is meant to negative such an additional cause.[1] Rāmānuja says that the passages which declare that Brahman is without qualities are meant to negative the evil qualities depending on Prakṛti, and not all qualities as such.[2] Rāmānuja says that the Scripture means to teach such way is that Brahman has many excellent qualities, but is devoid of all evil qualities. Moreover, he adds, the bliss of Brahman may be said to indicate His excellent qualities, for in the scriptural section, which speaks of the relative bliss enjoyed by souls in different worlds, the highest bliss is said to be the bliss of Brahman.

According to Rāmānuja's view it would seem that the teaching of Scripture is not that Brahman is a substance void of qualities, nor thought void of attributes, but that he is highest Self, whose essential attribute is knowledge characterised by bliss, who is possessed of an unlimited number of auspicious qualities but excludes all evil qualities, and similar to, or higher than, whom there is no other.

Regarding the relationship of Brahman to the world, Rāmānuja seeks for such scriptural texts as relate Brahman to the world without sacrificing either the distinctive nature of Brahman or the reality of the world. In other words, Rāmānuja's teaching, as derived from authoritative works, in regard to the relation of Brahman to the world, is this; The world, consisting of matter and souls is the body of Brahman. He is distinct from it and from its Soul.

Rāmānuja believes in Brahma-pariṇāmavāda. According to this theory the entire universe is a real modification of Brahman. Rāmānuja states that the essential nature of the soul is to be a knowing subject. Sometimes he states that the soul is a part of Brahman. Rāmānuja makes it clear that he means nothing more than that. Souls are attributes or modes of Brahman. The relation between Brahman and the soul is apṛthaksiddhi. This means that the relation between God and the soul is inseparable once. In any case Rāmānuja does not accept identity of the soul with God. Even in the state of release the souls are not identified with God.

1. Tait. Up. II.6.
2. Tait. Up. II.6.

Now it may be asked—When did Rāmānuja obtain this doctrine of qualified monism? He claims that Scripture teaches it. But our account of the Upaniṣads shows that no such clearly formulated doctrine is to be found in them. Rāmānuja himself is aware of this fact. Further the Upaniṣadic passages which he cites as teaching his view of the nature of Brahman are so few and uncertain in meaning that we may sure that he did not derive his doctrine from them. Besides his very eagerness to claim support for his view from scripture seems to reveal the fact that he obtained his doctrine from other sources. Regarding his view of the nature of Brahman, Rāmānuja himself proceeds to show that it is also taught by the Viṣṇu Purāṇa and the passages which he cites so fully reflect the view which he advocates throughout the Śrī Bhāṣya. The passages of the Bṛhadāraṇyaka and the Śvetāsvatara do not support directly his view of three tattvas and Viśiṣṭādvaitavāda.

(iv) Advaita vedānta

Ācārya Śaṅkara has developed Advaitavāda from the Upaniṣadic doctrine of Ātman. Numerous passages of the Upaniṣads can be cited to claim support of Śaṅkara's view of Advaita. We have already cited passages from Upaniṣads to support the doctrine of one Supreme Self in previous chapters. 'From death to death does he go say the Upaniṣads, who sees difference in this world. Just as by the knowledge of a bump of earth, everything that is made of earth comes to be known, all this being merely a world, a modification and a name, the Ultimate substratum of it all being the earth; that just as by the knowledge of a piece of iron everything made of iron becomes known. . .. similarly by the knowledge of Brahman everything is known, because Brahman is the Ultimate substratum of all.'[1] Āruṇi says ' In the beginning my dear, this universe was being alone, one only without a second. . . .being alone that existed in the beginning one only without a second.[2] Yājñavalkya says 'It is only when there seems to be aduality that one. . . . thinks about the other, but where the Ātman alone is, what and where by may one. . . .think?'

According to Advaita Vedānta, Brahman is the Ultimate Reality. In ultimate sense Brahman is devoid of all qualities. It is indeterminate and non-dual. It is Nirviśeṣa and transcendent. Brahman is pure consciousness. Brahman associated with māyā appears as qualified or Saguṇa or Īśvara who is the creator, preserver and destroyer of this universe. Brahman is the ground of the world which appears through Māyā. According to Śaṅkara, Brahman is the efficient and as well as the material cause of the universe through Māyā. There is no causality in Brahman without Māyā. The world is an appearance. But from the phenomenal point of view, the world is quite real. It is practical reality so long as true knowledge does not dawn.

According to Advaita view, the self is pure consciousness and pure being. Jīvatva is an appearance. It is phenomenal reality from the phenomenal point of view. Jīvas are many but

1. Tait. Up. II.6.
2. Tait. Up. II.6.

actually the plurality of the soul is an imposition. Pure self is only one. Therefore the Upaniṣad says : tattvamasi, the self is identified with Brahman. In true sense Brahman is an Absolute. Therefore it is said that Brahman is everything and everything is Brahman. Śaṅkara criticises Brahmapariṇāmavāda. The world is vivarta of Brahman. Appearance is Vivarta, Śaṅkara does not declare the world to be an illusion. According to him, the world is not an illusion. It is Mithyā. Mithyā means the world is neither real nor unreal, but Mithyā.[1] It appears to be real. The passages of the Upaniṣads mostly support Advaita view of Śaṅkara, Śaṅkara does not say that the world and Jīvatva are mere dream. He says that there is a great difference between Svapna and Jāgrat.[2]

To explain the worldly creation according to Advaita view, the Advaitavādins introduce the concept of Vivarta. In all the creations we find in the world, the effect is produced through a transformation of the cause into something else. The cause dies in order to give birth to the effect. In any case in order to account for the emergence of the effect, some form of alteration in the cause has some how to be admitted. The vivartavāda makes a bold attempt in this line. It tries to show that even in this there are illustrations of an effect being produce without any change or modification whatsoever is the cause. The rope snake etc. are the classic examples. The examples have been taken in the wrong way every where and their true significance has been missed. It is assumed that by these examples the Vedānta has sought to explain away the world as mere illusion, where as the examples have quite another bearing. They only seek to show the unsullied nature of the cause, which is not touched in any away by the effect imposed upon it. As Śaṅkara says : Not by the fact that a water snake is taken to be a snake does it become full of poison nor a snake being taken for a water-snake becomes poisonless. Similarly all the imperfections and limitations in creation do not touch Brahman at all. The Vivartavāda keeps the whole cause unmodified and yet explains the modification. The Vedānta cites the classic examples of illusion because on the intellectual plan there is no other analogy through which the unmodified nature of the cause along with the production of the effect can be illustrated. So Śaṅkara preserves the real spirit of the self doctrine of the Upaniṣads when he develops his non-dualistic philosophy from them.

(v) Controversy between Advaita and Viśiṣṭādvaita

The question at issue between the advocates of Advaita on the one hand and Viśiṣṭādvaita on the other, resolves itself into the problem whether Nature is apparent or real, whether finite objects, objects in time and space, do really exist or only seem to exist. The controversy is not to be found in the Upaniṣads in an explicit form. It has grown in times much later than those when these treatises were composed, and out of attempts to expound certain utterances contained in them one way or the other. After devoting a good

1. Tait. Up. II.6.
2. Tait. Up. II.6.

deal of attention to the study of the question, we have come to the conclusion that the controversy is little more than war or worlds. There is, it seems to us, an unsectarian Vedantism which neither the one nor the other school truly represents, and the truth of which both, in there different ways, testify to the fact is, there is not a single truth which one of them accepts and the other rejects and not a single false doctrine which the one does not abjure equally with the other. But in doing the one of the other in their acceptances and rejections, they use quite different terms and phrases, so that what the one seems to assert, the other seems to deny, and vice versa. What we have said will become clear as we proceed.

The controversy arises out of the relativity of subject and object, both in its individual and universal aspects. We have seen how the phenomena of the mind are related to it. They are relative to it, dependent on it; they are many, while it is one; they are ever-changing impermanent, while it is unchangeable and permanent. In times of dreamless sleep they are all but not existent. . .they exist only in a potential form, unified with the causal power of the mind. The question we have now to ask is, are the phenomena apparent or real? That they have some sort of existence, they are not absolutely unreal, admits of no question. The question is as to the nature of their existence. That they are relative to the mind, dependent on the mind, is also clear to reflection if not to ordinary common sense. That colour has no existence independent of a seeing mind and that sound can exist only in relation to the power of hearing, may be unintelligible to unreflective people, but cannot admit of moment's doubt to a philosopher. Independent and absolute existence, therefore, can, in no case, be attributed to phenomena. You may choose to call them real, but you must remember that, in this case, you use the word "reality" not in the sense of absolute existence, but in a different sense, in the sense of "relative or dependent existence." But the mind is real in the former sense; it is absolutely real, its existence not depending upon anything else. So, phenomena are not real in the same sense in which the mind is real, and we may even say that they are not real in the same degree in which the mind is real. If then, by "reality" one understood only absolute reality, one might say that if the mind is real, phenomena are unreal, that as they are nothing but the mind, all that needs to be said about them is already said in the proposition, "the mind is real" and they do not deserve to be affirmed in a co-ordinate proposition. Looked at in this way therefore, phenomena are not real, but only apparent. Even when they seem to be most real, in our waking hours, their existence is only relative, dependent, not for themselves but for another, apparent, therefore and not real.

Looked at, again, from another stand-point, from the standpoint of their changefulness, their transitoryness, phenomena will appear to lose a large part of the reality ascribed to them by common sense. What is red now, becomes white the next moment; what is hard, may be made soft with no great difficulty; what is human body now with every beauty of form, colour and proportion, will be reduced to ashes in the course of few hours. Do such fitful, evanescent things deserve to be called real? Are they not appearances rather than realities?

Again, in the hours of dreamless sleep, phenomena seem to lose even that relative, apparent existence that they possess in our waking hours. It cannot indeed, be said that they become absolutely non-existent in those hours. Were it so, they would not re-start into their relative existence and be recognised in their identity in waking hours. But it is evident that their mode of existence in the former condition is very different from their existence in the latter. In the former their existence is only potential, causal and not actual and their differences only implicit, not explicit. Now, how can things that can thus cease to exist for all practical purposes be said to be real? They are only apparent. Phenomenal or apparent existence—seeming to exist—is the only sort of existence that can be attributed to them.

Now, it will be seen that, the facts remaining exactly the same, a very different description may be given of them and a very different phraseology used with reference to them, if one chooses to do so. It may be said, for instance, that though the phenomena of the mind are not independent of it, they are, in a sense, distinguished from it—distinguished as modes or modifications from the thing modified. The thing modified and its modifications are indeed related, but they are not absolutely the same. Phenomena are many and different, whereas the mind is one. As modifications then, phenomena, with their plurality and difference, are as real as the mind, the thing modified. Hence their existence is not merely apparent, it is real. Secondly, as to their transitoriness, their changefulness, it must be observed that though they change in form, their substance remains unexhausted. This substance is indeed, nothing but the power of the mind to produce phenomena, to assume various forms, but this power itself is something real and not apparent. It is also, as the power of modifying itself in various ways, something distinguishable from the permanent, unchangeable aspect of the mind, that aspect in which it is the seat of eternal ideas. Both these expects of them, as distinct from each other, are equally real and non-apparent. In the third place, the state of dreamless sleep, though a state in which phenomena and their differences remain unmanifested, is, by no means, a state of indifference or perfect homogeneity. Though unmanifested the objects are there, with all their differences in fact; otherwise they could not be reproduced in waking life in all their variety and fullness. In this case also, then, there is no room for saying that identity only is real and difference only apparent. Reality has to be affirmed of both identity and difference.

We have only to universalise our case and we are face to face with the problem in hand. Put God in the place of the mind and the objects of Nature, in that of the phenomena of the mind and we understand the point at issue between the Vivartavāda and the Pariṇāmavāda. Nature is relative to God, dependent on Him; it is only a mode assumed by Him. It is constantly changing, it is in a perpetual flux. And then, a time comes, at the end of every cycle, when it loses all its wonderful complexity and is reduced to a causal form in which the germs of variety are only potential. And even in this casual form it is nothing but the power of God to project a variety of appearances in time and space and not an independent reality. What should we say of such a thing? Is its existence apparent or real? We may choose one or the other form of expression according as we look at the facts from one or another stand-point. The facts themselves will remain all the same. Emphasising the relative and dependent character of Nature, we may say that as it has no absolute existence, it does not deserve to be called real, it is only apparent. Again, directing our attention particularly to the fact that Nature, as relative and dependent, as phenomenal, is, by these very characteristics, distinct from God, the Supreme Reality. We may say that as thus distinguished, it has a reality as much as the Supreme Reality. Again, as to the homogeneity to which Nature is reduced at the end of one and the beginning of another period of creation, we may bring into prominence the fact that the homogeneity is more apparent than real. To the Supreme Intellect, to which the past and the future are as real as the present, the infinite complexity of Nature is present even in its potential condition. To Him, therefore, if not to finite intelligence, Nature is as real in its potentiality as in its actuality.

The repugnance of the Advaitin to admitting the reality of Nature is due to his firm faith in the absolute attributes of God, in his infinitude, eternality, unchangeableness, absolute intelligence and indivisibility. He thinks that the admission of the reality of Nature amounts to a denial of these attributes. If finite things really exist, do not they form so many limitations of the Infinite, which, in that ceases to be infinite? Secondly, as the Eternal is neither born, nor dies, and as He is Infinite. One only without a second, where is the room for other things coming into and going out of real existence? Again to say that change is real, is to say that the Absolute Reality changes, that it becomes what it was not before, which means that it is subject to the law of causation and is therefore no Absolute at all. Further if, to the Supreme Intellect, everything is equally present, what possible meaning can be attached to thinks past and future? Then, as to finite intelligence subject to error and ignorance, where is the room for such a thing in the midst of Infinite Knowledge? To say, as the Pariṇāmavādin says, that God assumes the form of the world, that he Himself becomes the various objects of the world, animate and inanimate, is to say that the Infinite One divests Himself of His infinitude, cases to be infinite—a doctrine which is absurd on the face of it, and which makes all spiritual exercises, all efforts to attain unity with the Infinite utterly unmeaning. The Vivartavādin therefore concludes that objects in time and space, including finite intelligence, or to speak more correctly, all things that make intelligence appear limited, are only appearances and not realities and the power by which God projects these appearances is like that by which a magician performs his wonderful feats. It is a most mysterious power, its nature transcending human comprehension. It is, on the one hand, one with God; it is His power and nothing apart from Him. On the other hand, as something manifesting itself in innumerable finite objects, in a series of innumerable changes without beginning and end, it is something distinguishable from the Divine essence, into which no notion of finitude, mutability and divisibility enters. The mysteriousness of this power further consists in its apparently making things come to pass which are contradictory and therefore impossible. By this power, He who is one and infinite seems to make Himself many and finite; He who is unchangeable seems to change himself perpetually he who is absolute knowledge and holiness seems to make himself ignorant and unholy. Hence our philosophers call this power Māyā. It is most expressive term, indicating the incrustableness of a power whose nature can no more be understood than its existence denied. The Advaitin do not claim that the postulation of this incomprehensible power affords any real explanation of the enigmas of the world; they candidly admit the final incomprehensibility of things, the mysteriousness of creation and gives this mystery a name, Māyā or Avidyā. This term, Avidyā when spoken of as the cause of the world, does not exactly mean ignorance, but rather 'knot-knowledge' i.e., something seemingly different from knowledge, which constitutes the essence of Divinity. Now God, as contemplated in Himself in His infinite and immutable essence, apart from Māyā, is the Nirguṇa Brahman, of whom or which nothing more can be said than that it is Truth, Intelligence and Bliss, Sat, Cit, Ānandam. As contemplated with reference of Māyā, as producing the world of finite objects by this mysterious power, God is Īśvara, the Ruler, the Lord, what western theologians call the Personal God, the omniscient and omnipotent Creator, Preserver and destroyer of the world, the Father, Guide, Instructor and Saviour of finite souls. The Advaitin do not say that these attributes of God, attributes which are called 'personal; are not true. What they say is that they are relatively true, true, that is, with reference to that mysterious power by which God seems to produce things different from him. These attributes imply a certain difference, a duality between God and the world; and duality is the result of Māyā. As Māyā is without beginning and without end, being the power of the Eternal Being, the Saguṇa character of God is also eternal; he is eternally Īśvara Lord, as well as Brahman.

As we said the controversy is little more than a war of words. Nothing is contended for on one side which is not admitted in some shape or other by the opposite side. An Infinite Being which is the final explanation and Ultimate Reality of all existence, a creative power out of which all things come, a start of potential existence in which all differences are unmanifested, the causal and mundane aspects of the Deity, finite souls distinct from Infinite and seeking union with the latter, all these appear in both the contending systems. The difference is not so much of doctrine, if a difference of phraseology is not taken as such, as of emphasis. Though the same things are recognised in both the systems, they do not put the same emphasis on all things. The Advaita emphasise the relativity and evanescence of finite things; the Pariṇāmavādin ask us not to forget the relative and changeful, these things are manifestations of a real Divine Power. The Advaitin draws attention to the unity and identity of God amid the apparent difference of natural objects. The Pariṇāmavādin points out that difference is not opposed to identity, and is as real as the latter. The one gives prominence to the truth that the Divine essence is untouched by the imperfections of the world; the other adds that things, with all their imperfections are nevertheless full of the Divine presence. The former insists upon our constantly keeping in view the ultimate unity of God and man, a unity which alone makes salvation attainable the latter tells us not to lose sight of out difference with the Infinite, a difference which alone gives a meaning to our search after salvation. We need not dwell upon the point. This difference of emphasis pervades the two systems and constitutes their main distinction.

We have confide ourselves to the exposition of the philosophical aspect of the question and have not touched its scriptural aspect. A good deal of energy is spent on either side in interpreting scriptural texts, in trying to find out, for instance, whether the admission of duality or difference in a passage is final or only tentative, made merely for the purpose of enjoining a preliminary spiritual discipline, or as an expression of final truth; whether, again, an ascertain of unity does or does not exclude a real diversity of modes; and thirdly, to what extent and in what respects an illustration drawn from natural objects or from the practical life of man to explain the relation of God to the world is to be accepted as a representation of ultimate truth; and so on. However important, from one point of view, such discussions may be, we have purposely refrained from entering into them, and have tried only to set forth, in brief, the appeals that the two theories make to reason as distinct from faith in the scriptures. An elaborate discussion of the question in its scriptural aspects, with occasional resorts to independent reasoning will be found in Śaṅkara's commentary on the 14th aphorism, pāda I, chapter II of the Śāriraka Mīmāṁsā. Important statements on the points at issue between the two schools will be found in the commentary on some of the other aphorisms of the same pāda.

Central Teaching of the Upaniṣads

Still a question may arise : what is the real and central teaching of the Upaniṣads? The Iśopaniṣad answers : "Īśa Vāsyamidam Sarvam."[1] Everything is inhabited by Īśa or Brahman. "Nehānānāsti Kincan :" there is no plurality at all. Paul Deuseen desribes; 'In the conception of unity as it is expressed in the words of Ṛg. 1.164. 'Ekam Sad viprā bahudhā vadanti' the poets give many names to that which is one only, the fundamental thought of the whole teaching of the Upaniṣads lay already hidden gem. For this verse, strictly understood, really asserts that all plurality, consequently all proximity in space, all succession in time, all relation of cause and effect, all interdependence of subject and object, rests only upon words (*Vadanti*) or, as was said later, is "a mere matter of words (*Vācāranbhaṇa*), and that only unity is in the full sense real.[2] The central teaching of the Upaniṣads is that the Ātman is the soul reality, that there can be nothing beside it, and therefore, with the knowledge of the Ātman all is known. From this point of view there is no universe outside of the Ātman. But the loftiness of this metaphysical conception forbade its maintenance in the presence of the empirical consciousness which teaches the existence

1. Tait. Up. II.6.
2. Tait. Up. II.6.

of a real universe. It was necessary to concede the reality of the universe, and to reconcile with this the idealistic dogma of the sole reality of the Ātman by asserting that the universe exists, but is in truth nothing but the Ātman.[1] The Upaniṣadic view that Brahman is the sole reality, does not mean that there are things outside Brahman, which, are illusory. There is no such thing as unreal; everything is real, since all are moments in the all-comprehensive reality of Brahman.[2] Nothing can exist outside of Brahman. Everything is within the all-comprehensive Self or Brahman. The neti-neti of Yājñavalkya also simply signifies the distinction of the Ātman from all this that is here and does not convey any sense of the excluding everything from it, as is ordinarily supposed. The Brahman of the Upaniṣads has no opposition whatsoever to anything and as such need to exclude anything in order to maintain its reality or purity. Thus 'neti-neti' does not deny the reality of existence, it denies all the empirical characterisation of reality. It just signifies that Reality is something unique and distinct from the empirical.[3] According to R.E. Hume, the Ātman theory and the Brahman theory became merged together in an absolute pantheism in the Upaniṣads.[4] He calls it intelligent monism; "intelligent monism it may, in general, be called; for, although very different types of philosophy have been shown to be represented in the Upaniṣads, monism is their most prevalent type and the one which has continued their chief heritage. Still, even as monism, it is hardly the monism of the west, nor is it the monism that is based upon science."[5]

The fundamental thought that runs through the whole body of the Upaniṣads is the sole reality of Brahman, or Ātman. Even when the reality of the universe is conceded, the purpose is to maintain that the manifold world is not different from Brahman. Though Brahman is immanent. It is at the same time remained transcendent. "It is inside all this and outside all this." The Ṛgveda states that Brahman covers the whole universe and yet transcends it by the measure of ten figures. The Upaniṣads declare 'other than the known, and more than the unknown is that.'

* * *

1. Tait. Up. II.6.
2. Tait. Up. II.6.
3. Tait. Up. II.6.
4. Tait. Up. II.6.
5. Tait. Up. II.6.

CONTENTS

1. ĪŚĀVĀSYOPANIṢAD

ईशावास्योपनिषद्

Recognition of the unity underlying the diversity of the world

The fortieth chapter of Yajurveda is called Īśāvāsyopaniṣad. It has been given first place in the series of Upaniṣads. The visible world and life within this gigantic creation presuming as abode of God and thus, developing conscious to realise omnipresent and almighty features of God, this Upaniṣad has advised living discipline, with peace and satisfaction and further establishing integrity with no distinction. Its 18 hymns are said of same significance as that of eighteen chapters in Gītā.

Instruction given in the first hymn is that the life and world both are God's above, hence, use the treasure of life abiding the rules. The sage has given a predominate formulae for keeping oneself scot-free from the proud of achievements and wealth by simply raising a question "whose money is this?" In second hymn there are formulae of living long life and performing activity without least bondage or ties. In third hymn, dire consequence arising due to infringement of discipline are indicated. The fourth, fifth and eighth hymns explain the feature of perfect knowledge (Parabrahman) and hymn six and seventh highlight the characteristics of the people who realise it. From nineth to fourteenth, the secret of establishing a balance between learning and ignorance and the creation as also destruction has been disclosed. Hymn 15 and 16 describes the pray to God for enabling to understand his feature and the aptitude for realisation of the same. In hymn 17 and 18 the lord of fire have been solicited for enabling to know the mortal body and leading to aim of life through the best route.

The perfect knowledge (Parabrahman) expressed as Oṁ is absolute in itself with all respects and this universe is also absolute in itself like Oṁ. The perfect world has arisen from that absolute element. The balance resulted on an extraction of perfect from the perfect also remains perfect in itself. May the pains and pricks either super divine, super material or spiritual be turn in peace.

The opinion of the Ṛṣi is excellent when he says the balance or result of extracting perfect from the perfect is also perfect.

ॐ पूर्णमदः पूर्णमिदं पूर्णात्पूर्णमुदच्यते।

पूर्णस्य पूर्णमादाय पूर्णमेवावशिष्यते।।

ॐ शान्तिः शान्तिः शान्तिः।।

Oṁ! The yon is fulness; fulness, this. From fulness, fulness doth proceed. Withdrawing fulness's fulness off, even fulness then itself remains.

[Parbrahman expressed as "Oṁ" is absolute from all angles and this creation is also perfect in itself. This whole (complete) universe has been originated from that perfect element. In case this perfection is extracted out from that perfect element, the resultant or the residual part also remains perfect. May the fevers and fatigues of material, metaphysical and celestial be cooled-down.]

ईशा वास्यमिदꣳ सर्वं यत्किञ्च जगत्यां जगत्। तेन त्यक्तेन भुञ्जीथा मा गृधः कस्य स्विद्धनम्॥१॥

By the Lord (*īśā*) enveloped must this all be—

Whatever moving thing there is in the moving world.

With this renounced, you may enjoy. Covet not the wealth of anyone at all.

[Whatever either inert or alive is seen in this world, that all is covered embedded within God viz., under jurisdiction of God. Use only the part abandoned (entrusted) by him for you.]

कुर्वन्नेवेह कर्माणि जिजीविषेच्छतꣳ समाः। एवं त्वयि नान्यथेतोऽस्ति न कर्म लिप्यते नरे॥२॥

Even while doing deeds here, one may desire to live a hundred years. Thus on you— not otherwise than this is it— The deed (*karman*) adheres not on the man.

[The sages have told such disciplines following which a man can avail long life as also live free from ties usually created due to Karma.]

असुर्या नाम ते लोका अन्धेन तमसावृताः। ताꣳस्ते प्रेत्याभिगच्छन्ति ये के चात्महनो जनाः॥३॥

Devilish (*asurya*) are called those worlds, which are covered over with blind darkness (*tamas*). Unto them, on deceasing, go whatever folk are slayers of the Self.

[The people violating the discipline are known as Asurya (Dependent to the physical and sensual power but not following the true discretion). They are surrounded with the immeasuring darkness *i.e.* ignorance through out their life.]

अनेजदेकं मनसो जवीयो नैनद्देवा आप्नुवन्पूर्वमर्षत्।

तद्धावतोऽन्यानत्येति तिष्ठत्तस्मिन्नपो मातरिश्वा दधाति॥४॥

Unmoving, the One (*ekam*) is swifter than the mind.

The sense-powers (*devas*) reached not It, speeding on before.

Past others running, This goes standing.

In It Mātariśvān places action.

[The unvariated God is one who is more dynamic than the mind itself. He cannot be chased *i.e.* known to deities viz., the senses irrespective of stable, he goes ahead running to the dynamic bodies.]

तदेजति तन्नैजति तद्दूरे तद्वन्तिके। तदन्तरस्य सर्वस्य तदु सर्वस्यास्य बाह्यतः॥५॥

It moves. It moves not. It is far and It is near. It is within all this. It is outside of all this.

[He is at immeasuring distant and at the same time, nearest to all. He too is present within these all.]

यस्तु सर्वाणि भूतान्यात्मन्येवानुपश्यति। सर्वभूतेषु चात्मानं ततो न विजुगुप्सते॥६॥

Now, he who on all beings looks as just (*eva*) in the Self (Ātman). And on the Self as in all beings— He does not shrink away from Him.

[The knowledge acquired by virtue of reading cannot remove the illusion and the knowledge well experienced is sine-qua-non for this.]

यस्मिन्सर्वाणि भूतान्यात्मैवाभूद्विजानतः। तत्र को मोहः कः शोक एकत्वमनुपश्यतः॥७॥

In whom all beings have become just (*eva*) the Self of the discerner— Then what delusion (*moha*), what sorrow (*śoka*) is there of him who perceives the unity!

[At which stage, the man is known to the fact that this Ātma tattva is appeared in the nature of all beings, where the attachment or grief may stand or arise in this stage of knowing all in one.]

स पर्यगाच्छुक्रमकायमव्रणमस्नाविरꣳ शुद्धमपापविद्धम्।
कविर्मनीषी परिभूः स्वयंभूर्याथातथ्यतोऽर्थान्व्यदधाच्छाश्वतीभ्यः समाभ्यः॥८॥

He has environed, The bright, the bodiless, the scatheless,
The sinewless, the pure (*śuddha*), unpierced by evil (*a-pāpa-viddha*)!
Wise (*kavi*), intelligent (*manīṣī*), encompassing (*paribhū*), self-existent (*svayambhū*),
Appropriately he distributed objects (*arthas*) through the eternal years.

अन्धं तमः प्रविशन्ति येऽविद्यामुपासते। ततो भूय इव ते तमो य उ विद्यायाꣳ रताः॥९॥

They enter into blind darkness, who worship ignorance; and They also enter into darkness greater than that, as it were, who delight in knowledge.

[The persons who are mere devotee to the evil-learning (Avidyā), surround in the gross ignorance (darkness) and they also same way surround (trapped) with ignorance who are only devoted to learning (conscience).]

अन्यदेवाहुर्विद्ययान्यदाहुरविद्यया॥ इति शुश्रुम धीराणां ये नस्तद्विचचक्षिरे॥१०॥

Other, indeed, they say, than knowledge! Other, they say, than non-knowledge! Thus we have heard from the wise (*dhīra*) who have explained it to us.

[Knowledge leads to a different path, while Ignorance (Avidyā) leads to another different path, this teaching has been transmitted to us by the ancient sages.]

विद्यां चाविद्यां च यस्तद्वेदोभयꣳ सह। अविद्यया मृत्युं तीर्त्वा विद्ययामृतमश्नुते॥११॥

One who knows the knowledge and non-knowledge— this pair conjointly (*saha*), he transcends with non-knowledge passing over death and with knowledge wins the immortal.

अन्धं तमः प्रविशन्ति येऽसंभूतिमुपासते। ततो भूय इव ते तमो य उ संभूत्याꣳरताः॥१२॥

They enter into blind darkness, who worship non-becoming (*a-sambhūti*);

They enter into darkness greater than that, as it were, who delight in becoming (*sambhūti*).

[*sambhūti* is the origination and *asambhūti* is non-becoming, perishing.]

अन्यदेवाहुः संभवादन्यदाहुरसंभवात्। इति शुश्रुम धीराणां ये नस्तद्विचचक्षिरे॥१३॥

Other, indeed—they say—than origin (*sambhava*)! Other—they say—than non-origin (*a-sambhava*)! —Thus we have heard from the wise, who have explained it to us.

सम्भूतिं च विनाशं च यस्तद्वेदोभयꣳ सह। विनाशेन मृत्युं तीर्त्वा सम्भूत्याऽमृतमश्नुते।।१४।।

Becoming (*sambhūti*) and destruction (*vināśa*)—He who knows this pair conjointly (*saha*) with destruction passing over death and with becoming wins the immortal.

हिरण्मयेन पात्रेण सत्यस्यापिहितं मुखम्। तत्त्वं पूषन्नपावृणु सत्यधर्माय दृष्टये।।१५।।

With a vessel wholly of gold the mouth of truth is covered over. O Pūṣan, do you uncover or open that for one whose law is the Real to see.

पूषन्नेकर्षे यम सूर्य प्राजापत्य व्यूह रश्मीन्समूह।

तेजो यत्ते रूपं कल्याणं तत्ते पश्यामि योऽसावसौ पुरुषः सोऽहमस्मि।।१६।।

O Pūṣan, the sole Seer (*ekarṣi*), O Controller (*yama*), O Sun (*sūrya*), O son of Prajāpati, spread forth your rays! Gather your splendour (*tejas*)! What is your lovable form—that of you I see. He who is yonder, yonder Person (*puruṣa*)—I myself am he!

वायुरनिलममृतमथेदं भस्मान्तꣳ शरीरम्। ॐ क्रतो स्मर कृतꣳ स्मर क्रतो स्मर कृतꣳ स्मर।।१७।।

[My] breath (*vāyu*) to the immortal wind (*anila*)! This body then ends in ashes! *Oṁ*!

O Purpose (*kratu*), remember! The deed (*kṛta*) remember!

O Purpose, remember! The deed remember!

अग्ने नय सुपथा राये अस्मान्विश्वानि देव वयुनानि विद्वान्।

युयोध्यस्मज्जुहुराणमेनो भूयिष्ठां ते नम उक्तिं विधेम।।१८।।

General prayer of petition and adoration

O Agni! lead us on an even (a good) way to prosperity (*rai*), O God, you know all the ways! Keep far away from us crooked-going sin (*enas*)! we render most ample expression of adoration to you.

ॐ पूर्णमदः पूर्णमिदं...... इति शान्तिः।।

।।इति ईशावास्योपनिषत्समाप्ता।।

***

2. KENOPANIṢAD

केनोपनिषद्

This Upaniṣad is within ninth chapter of "Tavalkāra Brāhmaṇa" (Sāmvediya). This is also called Tavalkāra Upaniṣad and Brahmaṇopaniṣad. It starts with a question "Keneṣitaṁ......(By whom this life is motivated?). The starting word being "Ken" (By whom), this Upaniṣad is said Kenopaniṣad. The Ṛṣi has made it clear while explaining the nature and glory of all motivator perfect knowledge (Parabrahman) that the Brahmatattva (Absolute element) is very easy to talk and listen about but it is most difficult to understand and digest. In the first and second part the peculiarities of that motivating entity, his realisation and the unavoidable necessities to know him have been described vividly through colloquy arranged between the teacher and pupil. In the third and fourth part, illustration has been given from the vanity arising in Gods and the appearance of Brāhmī Cetanā (conscience) to suppress that super ego in the form of Yakṣa. Subsequently the Brahmatattva (element of knowledge) has been described for the Gods by Goddess Umā. At the ending shore, the importance of knowing the secret of Brahmavidyā (conscience) alongwith the resources has been elaborated and the manner of Parabrahman worship and the fruits (result) inherent therein have been explained.

॥ शान्तिपाठः ॥

ॐ आप्यायन्तु ममाङ्गानि वाक् प्राणश्चक्षुः श्रोत्रमथो बलमिन्द्रियाणि च सर्वाणि सर्वं ब्रह्मौपनिषदं माहं ब्रह्म निराकुर्यां मा मा ब्रह्म निराकरोदनिराकरणमस्त्वनिराकरणं मेऽस्तु तदात्मनि निरते य उपनिषत्सु धर्मास्ते मयि सन्तु ते मयि सन्तु॥

ॐ शान्तिः शान्तिः शान्तिः॥

O the Supreme Soul! may our all organs healthy and our voice, breathing, eyes, ears, force and all sensory organs be strong. The Upaniṣad (proposed knowledge) is Brahma, we don't refuse it. This do not abandon us. May our inseparable relation with one another maintained. Whatever (religion, knowledge etc.) described in Upaniṣad, be insert in us, be incorporate in us. May the three pains be cool.

॥प्रथमः खण्डः॥

ॐ केनेषितं पतति प्रेषितं मनः केन प्राणः प्रथमः प्रैति युक्तः। केनेषितां वाचमिमां वदन्ति चक्षुः श्रोत्रं क उ देवो युनक्ति॥१॥

Query : The real agent in the individual?

By whose motivation, do this mind assess to its subjects? By whose engaged this breathe does function proper? By whose activation the voice does exercise in people? Who is that intangible God that engages our eyes and ears in their functions?

श्रोत्रस्य श्रोत्रं मनसो मनो यद्वाचो ह वाचꣳ स उ प्राणस्य प्राणः। चक्षुषश्चक्षुरतिमुच्य धीराः प्रेत्यास्माल्लोकादमृता भवन्ति॥२॥

[Answer :]

That which is the hearing of the ear, the thought of the mind,

The voice of speech, as also the breathing of the breath,

And the sight of the eye! Past these escaping, the wise,

On departing from this world, become immortal.

न तत्र चक्षुर्गच्छति न वाग्गच्छति नो मनः। न विद्मो न विजानीमो यथैतदनुशिष्यादन्यदेव तद्विदितादथो अविदितादधि। इति शुश्रुम पूर्वेषां ये नस्तद्व्याचचक्षिरे॥३॥

There the eye goes not, speech goes not, nor the mind.

We know not, we understand not; How one would teach It.

Other, indeed, is It than the known, And moreover above the unknown.

—Thus have we heard of the ancients (*pūrva*) who have explained it to us.

यद्वाचानभ्युदितं येन वागभ्युद्यते। तदेव ब्रह्म त्वं विद्धि नेदं यदिदमुपासते॥४॥

That which is unexpressed with speech (*vāc*, voice),

That with which speech is expressed—

That indeed know as Brahma,

Not this that people worship as this.

यन्मनसा न मनुते येनाहुर्मनो मतम्। तदेव ब्रह्म त्वं विद्धि नेदं यदिदमुपासते॥५॥

That which one thinks not with thought (*manas*, mind),

[or, That which thinks not with a mind,]

That with which they say thought (*manas*, mind) is thought—

That indeed know as Brahma,

Not this that people worship as this.

यच्चक्षुषा न पश्यति येन चक्षूꣳसि पश्यति। तदेव ब्रह्म त्वं विद्धि नेदं यदिदमुपासते॥६॥

That which one sees not with sight (*cakṣus*, eye),

[or, That which sees not with an eye]

That with which one sees sights (*cakṣūṁsi*)—

That indeed known as Brahma,

Not this that people worship as this.

यच्छ्रोत्रेण न शृणोति येन श्रोत्रमिदꣳ श्रुतम्। तदेव ब्रह्म त्वं विद्धि नेदं यदिदमुपासते॥७॥

That which one hears not with hearing (*śrotra*, ear),

[or, That which hears not with an ear,]

That with which hearing here is heard—
That indeed know as Brahma,
Not this that people worship as this.

यत्प्राणेन न प्राणिति येन प्राणः प्रणीयते। तदेव ब्रह्म त्वं विद्धि नेदं यदिदमुपासते।।८।।

That which one breathes (*prāṇiti*) not with breathing (*prāṇa*, breath),
[or, That which breathes not with breath,]
That with which breathing (*prāṇa*) is conducted (*praṇīyate*)—
That indeed known as Brahma,
Not this that people worship as this.

।।द्वितीयः खण्डः।।

The paradox of Its inscrutability

यदि मन्यसे सुवेदेति दभ्रमेवापि नूनं त्वं वेत्थ ब्रह्मणो रूपम्।
यदस्य त्वं यदस्य देवेष्वथ नु मीमांस्यमेव ते मन्ये विदितम्।।१।।

[Ācārya say] If you think 'I know well,' only very slightly now do you know!— a form of Brahma!—what thereof is yourself, and what thereof is among the gods! So then it is to be pondered upon (*mīmāṁsyam*) indeed by you.

[Pupil:] I think it is known.

नाहं मन्ये सुवेदेति नो न वेदेति वेद च। यो नस्तद्वेद तद्वेद नो न वेदेति वेद च।।२।।

I think not 'I know well'; Yet I know not 'I know not'!
He of us who knows It, knows It; Yet he knows not ' I know not'.

यस्यामतं तस्य मतं मतं यस्य न वेद सः। अविज्ञातं विजानतां विज्ञातमविजानताम्।।३।।

[Ācārya]
It is conceived of by him, by whom It is not conceived of.
He by whom It is conceived of, knows It not.
It is not understood by those who [say they] understand It.
It is understood by those who [say they] understand It not.

प्रतिबोधविदितं मतममृतत्वं हि विन्दते। आत्मना विन्दते वीर्यं विद्यया विन्दतेऽमृतम्।।४।।

When known by an awakening, It is conceived of;
Truly it is immortality one finds.
With the Soul (Ātman) one finds power;
With knowledge one finds the immortal.

इह चेदवेदीदथ सत्यमस्ति न चेदिहावेदीन्महती विनष्टिः।

भूतेषु भूतेषु विचित्य धीराः प्रेत्यास्माल्लोकादमृता भवन्ति॥५॥

If one have known [It] here, then there is truth.

If one have known [It] not here, great is the destruction (*vinaṣṭi*).

Discerning [It] in every single being, the wise,

On departing from this world, become immortal.

[He who has attained that perfect knowledge (Parabrahma), has attained the reality, but who could not realise him in existing life, has sustained considerable loss (loss of precious time). The wise man therefore realise that supreme entity present in every being and every element and thus, moving from the route of this world ultimately attains the immortality.]

॥तृतीयः खण्डः॥

Allegory of the Vedic gods' ignorance of Brahma

ब्रह्म ह देवेभ्यो विजिग्ये तस्य ह ब्रह्मणो विजये देवा अमहीयन्त। त ऐक्षन्तास्माकमेवायं विजयोऽस्माकमेवायं महिमेति॥१॥

Now, Brahma won a victory for the gods. Now, in the victory of this Brahma the gods were exulting. They bethought themselves : 'Ours indeed is this victory! Ours indeed is this greatness!'

तद्धैषां विजज्ञौ तेभ्यो ह प्रादुर्बभूव तन्न व्यजानत किमिदं यक्षमिति॥२॥

Now, It understood this of them. It appeared to them. They did not understand It. 'What wonderful being (*yakṣa*) is this?' they said.

तेऽग्निमब्रुवञ्जातवेद एतद्विजानीहि किमेतद्यक्षमिति तथेति॥३॥

They said to Agni (Fire) : 'Jātavedas, find out this—what this wonderful being it.'

'So be it.'

तदभ्यद्रवत्तमभ्यवदत्कोऽसीत्यग्निर्वा अहमस्मीत्यब्रवीज्ञातवेदा वा अहमस्मीति॥४॥

He ran unto It.

Unto him It spoke : 'Who are you?' 'Verily, I am Agni,' he said. 'Verily, I am Jātavedas.'

तस्मिंस्त्वयि किं वीर्यमित्यपीदꣳ सर्वं दहेयं यदिदं पृथिव्यामिति॥५॥

Yakṣa asked the fire-god– 'In such as you what power is there?'

'Indeed, I might burn everything here, whatever there is here in the earth!'

तस्मै तृणं निदधावेतद्दहेति। तदुपप्रेयाय सर्वजवेन तन्न शशाक दग्धुं स तत एव निववृते नैतदशकं विज्ञातुं यदेतद्यक्षमिति॥६॥

It put down a straw before him. 'Burn that!' He went forth at it with all speed. He was not able to burn it. Thereupon indeed he returned, saying : 'I have not been able to find out this—what this wonderful being is.'

अथ वायुमब्रुवन्वायवेतद्विजानीहि किमेतद्यक्षमिति तथेति।।७।।

Then they said to Vāyu (Wind) : 'O Vāyu, find out this—what this wonderful being is.'

'So be it.'

तदभ्यद्रवत्तमभ्यवदत्कोऽसीति वायुर्वा अहमस्मीत्यब्रवीन्मातरिश्वा वा अहमस्मीति।।८।।

He ran unto It.

Unto him It spoke : 'Who are you?'

'Verily, I am Vāyu,' he said. 'Verily, I am Mātariśvan.'

तस्मिंस्त्वयि किं वीर्यमित्यपीदं सर्वमाददीयम् यदिदं पृथिव्यामिति।।९।।

'In such as you what power is there?'

'Indeed, I might carry off everything here, whatever there is here in the earth.'

तस्मै तृणं निदधावेतदादत्स्वेति। तदुपप्रेयाय सर्वजवेन तन्न शशाकादातुं स तत एव निववृते नैतदशकं विज्ञातुं यदेतद्यक्षमिति।।१०।।

It put down a straw before him. 'Carry that off!'

He went at it with all speed. He was not able to carry it off. Thereupon indeed he returned, saying : 'I have not been able to find out this—what this wonderful being is.'

अथेन्द्रमब्रुवन्मघवन्नेतद्विजानीहि किमेतद्यक्षमिति। तथेति तदभ्यद्रवत्तस्मात्तिरोदधे।।११।।

Then they said to Indra : 'Maghavan ('Liberal'), find out this—what this wonderful being is.'

'So be it.' He ran unto It. It disappeared from him.

स तस्मिन्नेवाकाशे स्त्रियमाजगाम बहुशोभमानामुमां हैमवतीं तां होवाच किमेतद्यक्षमिति।।१२।।

In that very space he came upon a woman exceedingly beautiful, Umā, daughter of the Snowy Mountain (*Haimavat*) or Brahmavidyā in the form of Umā.

To her he said : 'what is this wonderful being?'

।।चतुर्थः खण्डः।।

Knowledge of Brahman, the ground of superiority

सा ब्रह्मेति होवाच ब्रह्मणो वा एतद्विजये महीयध्वमिति ततो हैव विदांचकार ब्रह्मेति।।१।।

She said- 'It is Brahman.' 'In that victory of Brahman, verily, exult you.'

Thereupon he knew it was Brahman.

तस्माद्वा एते देवा अतितरामिवान्यान्देवान्यदग्निर्वायुरिन्द्रस्तेन ह्येनन्नेदिष्ठं पस्पृशुस्ते ह्येनत्प्रथमो विदांचकार ब्रह्मेति।।२।।

Therefore, verily, these gods, namely Agni, Vāyu and Indra, are above the other gods, as it were; for these touched It nearest, for these and [especially] he [i.e. Indra] first knew It was Brahman.

तस्माद्वा इन्द्रोऽतितरामिवान्यान्देवान्स ह्येनन्नेदिष्ठं पस्पर्श स ह्येनत्प्रथमो विदांचकार ब्रह्मेति।।३।।

Therefore, verily, Indra is above the other gods, as it were; for he touched It nearest, for he first knew It was Brahman.

Brahman in cosmic and in individual phenomena

तस्यैष आदेशो यदेतद्विद्युतो व्यद्युतदा इतीन्न्यमीमिषदा इत्यधिदैवतम्।।४।।

Of It there is this teaching.

That in the lightning which flashes forth, which makes one blink, and say 'Ah!'—that 'Ah!' refers to divinity.

अथाध्यात्मं यदेतद्गच्छतीव च मनोऽनेन चैतदुपस्मरत्यभीक्ष्णꣳ संकल्पः।।५।।

Now with regard to oneself.

That which comes, as it were, to the mind, by which one repeatedly remembers—that conception (*saṁkalpa*) [is It]!

तद्ध तद्वनं नाम तद्वनमित्युपासितव्यं स य एतदेवं वेदाऽभि हैनꣳ सर्वाणि भूतानि संवाञ्छन्ति।।६।।

Brahma, the great object of desire

It is called *Tad-vana* ('It-is-the-desire'). As 'It-is-the-desire' (*Tad-vana*) It should be worshipped. For him who knows it thus, all beings together yearn.

[The Brahman as *"Tadvana"*. Ācārya Saṅkara has given its meaning as Tad-Bhajanīyam *i.e.* worth to meditate *"Vana"* is used in purportion to *"Ras"* (juice) also. On this premise, it transpires that the Brahma in radical form is "juicy". The devotee whose motion merges in Ātma-tattva, his intimacy extends so large as all beings are impressed by him.]

उपनिषदं भो ब्रूहीत्युक्ता य उपनिषद्ब्राह्मीं वाव त उपनिषदमब्रूमेति।।७।।

'Sir, tell me the mystic doctrine (*upaniṣad*)!'

'The mystic doctrine has been declared to you. Verily, we have told you the mystic doctrine of Brahma (*brāhmī upaniṣad*).'

तस्यै तपो दमः कर्मेति प्रतिष्ठा वेदाः सर्वाङ्गानि सत्यमायतनम्।।८।।

Austerity (*tapas*), restraint (*dama*), and work (*karman*) are the foundation of it [i.e. the mystic doctrine]. The Vedas are all its limbs. Truth is its abode.

यो वा एतामेवं वेदापहत्य पाप्मानमनन्ते स्वर्गे लोके ज्येये प्रतितिष्ठति प्रतितिष्ठति।।९।।

He, verily, who knows it [i.e. the mystic doctrine] thus, striking off evil (*pāpmān*), becomes established in the most excellent, endless, heavenly world— yea, he becomes established!

।। इति केनोपनिषत्समाप्ता।।

****

3. KAṬHOPANIṢAD

कठोपनिषद्

This upaniṣad is under the school of Kaṭha in Kṛṣṇa Yajurveda. Herein are two chapters and each chapter contains 3 cantos (Vallīs). The famous episode (tale) of the dialogue between Yama and Naciketā, the son of Vājaśrava is described in this upaniṣad. Vājaśrava was intended to worship merely the symbolic (not actual) demonstration of the gift by providing the donees' the trivial things. His son Naciketā, who was well learned to the meaning of gift, intended to motivate his father performing the custom in true sense, asked him that to whom will be give his son? On retention of his question, Vājaśrava annoyed and he fanatically said that he will be gored to yama, the god of death.

Naciketā as a result of his special efforts, met finally with lord Yama. Yama pleased and asked him to have three boons. He asks for his father's satisfaction as the very first boon, heavenly pleasure rendering Agnividyā (fire learning) as the second and Ātmavidyā (self-realisation) as the third boon. Yama happily sanctioned the first two boons but he wants to allow him not to stress on the third boon having it impossible. Naciketā stood unvariated. This subject-matter is elaborated in the first chapter under first vallī. In second and third vallī, lord Yama makes him to understand several aspects relating to the soul and the supreme soul. In second chapter, the hurdles befalling in way to seek God, their solution and god's existence in the heart has been described. Further, omnipresence of god, Aśvattha (mortality) in garb of the world, yoga-penance, faith on god and emancipation etc. has been described. Finally, the attainment of Brahma (perfect knowledge) by the grace of Brahma vidyā has been enunciated.

।।शान्तिपाठ:।।

ॐ सह नाववतु। सह नौ भुनक्तु। सह वीर्यं करवावहै। तेजस्विनावधीतमस्तु मा विद्विषावहै।।
ॐ शान्ति: शान्ति: शान्ति:।।

The supreme soul! Wish you please protect both of us (the teacher and disciple) simultaneously. Nourish us simultaneously. May both of us be powerful simultaneously. The learning acquired by us be full of splendour and intelligence should there be no place for inimity and rivalry between us. O mighty! may the trio fevers (material, metaphysical and celestial) be cooled down and undepleting peace attained.

First Vallī

prologue : Naciketas devoted to Death

Part -I

ॐ उशन् ह वै वाजश्रवस: सर्ववेदसं ददौ। तस्य ह नचिकेता नाम पुत्र आस।।१।।

Now verily, with zeal did Vājaśravasa (in the Viśvajit sacrifice) give his whole possession [as a religious gift]. He had a son, Naciketā by name.

तꣳह कुमारꣳ सन्तं दक्षिणासु नीयमासु श्रद्धाविवेश सोऽमन्यत॥२॥

Into him, boy as he was, while the sacrificial gifts were being led up, faith (*śraddhā*) entered. He thought to himself :

पीतोदका जग्धतृणा दुग्धदोहा निरिन्द्रियाः। अनन्दा नाम ते लोकास्तान्स गच्छति ता ददत्॥३॥

'Their water drunk, their grass eaten,

Their milk milked, barren!

Joyless (*a-nanda*) certainly are those worlds

He goes to, who gives such [cows]!'

स होवाच पितरं तत कस्मै मां दास्यसीति। द्वितीयं तृतीयं तꣳहोवाच मृत्यवे त्वा ददामीति॥४॥

Then he said to his father : 'Papa, to whom will you give me?'— a second time– a third time.

To him then he said : 'To Death I give you!'

बहूनामेमि प्रथमो बहूनामेमि मध्यमः। किꣳस्विद्यमस्य कर्त्तव्य यन्मयाद्य करिष्यति॥५॥

Naciketā in the house of Death

[Naciketā reflects :]

Of many I go as the first. Of many I go as an intermediate. What pray, has Yama (Death) to be done? That he will do with me today?

अनुपश्य यथा पूर्वे प्रतिपश्य तथापरे। सस्यमिव मर्त्यः पच्यते सस्यमिवाजायते पुनः॥६॥

Look forward, how [fared] the former ones. Look backward; so [will] the after ones.

Like grain a mortal ripens! Like grain he is born hither (*ā-jāyate*) again!

[Aggrieved of the word expressed in a state of temper his father, was again asked by Naciketā– "O Dear father! ponder on the behaviour as your father and fore-fathers had made and further look at the behaviour as being made by other highest enlightened presently. The mortal man becomes mature (attains death having too old) like the harvest in a certain point of time and further regains birth comensurating with the certain time frame.]

वैश्वानरः प्रविशत्यतिथिर्ब्राह्मणो गृहान्। तस्यैताꣳ शान्तिं हर वैवस्वतोदकम्॥७॥

As fire (Vaiśvānara Agni) enters,

A Brahma (*brāhmaṇa*) guest into houses.

They make this the quieting thereof :—

Fetch water, Vaivasvata!

[The Vaiśvānara Agni in garb of Brāhmaṇa may only enter the houses. The affluent people entertain them by providing Arghya-pādya etc. You should therefore however offer the water for arghya.]

आशाप्रतीक्षे सङ्गतं सूनृतां चेष्टापूर्ते पुत्रपशूंश्च सर्वान्।

एतद्वृङ्क्ते पुरुषस्याल्पमेधसो यस्यानश्नन्वसति ब्राह्मणो गृहे॥८॥

Hope and expectation, intercourse and pleasantness,

Sacrifices and meritorious deeds, sons and cattle, all—

This he snatches away from the man of little understanding

In whose home a Brahman remains without eating.

तिस्रो रात्रीर्यदवात्सीर्गृहे मेऽनश्नन्ब्रह्मन्नतिथिर्नमस्यः।

नमस्तेऽस्तु ब्रह्मन्स्वस्ति मेऽस्तु तस्मात्प्रति त्रीन्वरान्वृणीष्व॥९॥

[Death (Yama), returning from a three days' absence and finding that Naciketā has not received the hospitality which is due to a Brāhmaṇa, says :]

Since for three nights you has abode in my house

Without eating, O Brāhmaṇa a guest to be reverenced,

Reverence be to you, O Brāhmaṇa! Well-being (*svasti*) be to me!

Therefore in return choose three boons!

शान्तसंकल्पः सुमना यथा स्याद्वीतमन्युर्गतमो माभि मृत्यो।

त्वत्प्रसृष्टं माभिवदेत्प्रतीत एतत्त्रयाणां प्रथमं वरं वृणे॥१०॥

Naciketā's first wish : return to an appeased father on earth.

(Naciketā said) O Yamarāja! With intent appeased, well-minded, with passion departed, let Gautama my father be again toward me, Death;

That cheerfully he may greet me, when from you dismissed—This of the three as boon the first I choose!

[My father may love me as before when I am allowed by you to return my home. This is the first boon out of the three you already have committed to sanction.]

यथा पुरस्ताद्भविता प्रतीत औद्दालकिरारुणिर्मत्प्रसृष्टः।

सुखंरात्रीः शयिता वीतमन्युस्त्वां ददृशिवान्मृत्युमुखात्प्रमुक्तम्॥११॥

(O Naciketā) Cheerful as formerly will he be—Auddālaki Āruṇi, from me dismissed.

Happily will he sleep during nights, with passion departed, when he has seen you from the mouth of Death released.

स्वर्गे लोके न भयं किंचनास्ति न तत्र त्वं न जरया बिभेति।

उभे तीर्त्वाशनायापिपासे शोकातिगो मोदते स्वर्गलोके॥१२॥

[Naciketā's second wish : an understanding of the Naciketā's sacrificial fire that leads to heaven]

In the world of heaven, is no fear any more. There you are not. Not from old age does one fear. Over both having crossed—the hunger and the thirst gone beyond sorrow, one rejoices in the heaven-world.

स त्वमग्निः स्वर्ग्यमध्येषि मृत्यो प्रब्रूहि त्वःश्रद्दधानाय मह्यम्।
स्वर्गलोका अमृतत्वं भजन्त एतद्द्वितीयेन वृणे वरेण।।१३।।

Yourself, O Death, understand the heavenly fire. Declare it to me who have faith (*śraddhadhāna*).

Heaven-world people partake of immortality. This I choose with boon the second.

[O Yamarāja! you are well known to the sole source of heaven, the agnividyā (learning of fire). Please, let me know that learning (Agnividyā), known to which the people access to heaven and enjoy the immortality there. I am curious enough to know and please, explain that learning supposing that I am asking your grace as the second boon, you already have given the privilege to ask for.]

प्र ते ब्रवीमि तदु मे निबोध स्वर्ग्यमग्निं नचिकेतः प्रजानन्।
अनन्तलोकाप्तिमथो प्रतिष्ठां विद्धि त्वमेतन्निहितं गुहायाम्।।१४।।

On request (supra) made by Naciketā, the god of death said– O' Naciketā!

I do declare to you, and to you learn it of me—

Understanding about the heavenly fire, O Naciketā!

The attainment of the infinite world, likewise too its establishment—

Know you that as set down in the secret place [of the heart].

[The thing kept within cavity is rare to find about and it needs Herculean endeavour to attain because of most cryptic nature in itself. The heart (bosom) too is called the cavity. Yama has given hint that Agnividyā dwells in the heart. As the wood inherited with the material fire, the heaven providing energy vested with the heart.]

लोकादमग्निं तमुवाच तस्मै या इष्टका यावतीर्वा यथा वा।
स चापि तत्प्रत्यवदद्यथोक्तमथास्य मृत्युः पुनरेवाह तुष्टः।।१५।।

He told him of that fire as the beginning of the world, what bricks, and how many, and how [built].

And he too repeated that, as it was told. Then, pleased with him, Death said again—

[The Yamarāja then explained before Naciketā, the Bhūta Agnividyā, a learning which is the sole cause of the worlds (Lokas). The complete procedure of choosing what kind of and by what method the bricks or the units was explained. Naciketā repeated the same before Yama whatever was told to him without any pause. Having satisfied of the understanding power of Naciketā, Yama then proceeded.]

तमब्रवीत्प्रीयमाणो महात्मा वरं तवेहाद्य ददामि भूयः।
तवैव नाम्ना भवितायमग्निः सृंकां चेमामनेकरूपां गृहाण।।१६।।

Delighting, the great soul (*mahātman*) said to him :—

[Death resumes :]

A further boon I give you here today.

By your name indeed shall this fire be [known].

This multifold garland (*sṛṅkā*), too, accept.

[Naciketā means a person who is not attached with the prapañca (worldly mortal thinking). Only the person so unattached may hold the discipline. The person involved in passions (worldly affairs) indulge his influence or the powers for the worldly hunger and cannot safe them to amply with the divine discipline. Naciketā had not involved him within the worldly ambitions or devices of his father and devoted himself for attaining the higher ideals. This was the sole reason for his access to Yama and thereby benefited with the divine boons. Yama is the god preferring and maintaining the divine discipline. He has raised a question in Ṛgveda 10.135 that on which carrier Naciketā has arrived here? Keeping himself unattached to the *prapañca* (worldly affairs) and all surrendering trend for the divine discipline is the only basis on which Naciketā could acquire the divine Agnividyā. It is therefore, cogent to say such vidyā as Naciketāgni (learning that keeps unattached.]

त्रिणाचिकेतस्त्रिभिरेत्य सन्धिं त्रिकर्मकृत्तरति जन्ममृत्यू।
ब्रह्मजज्ञं देवमीड्यं विदित्वा निचाय्येमाः शान्तिमत्यन्तमेति॥१७॥

Having kindled a triple Naciketā-fire, having attained union with the three, performing the triple work, one crosses over birth and death.

By knowing the knower of what is born from Brahman, the god to be praised,

[And] by revering [him], one goes forever to this peace (*śānti*).

[Naciketas vidyā (learning) is called the thrice manner learning. The scholars have accepted it consisting of three manners *i.e.* access, study and ceremony. The devotee has to establish a combination of soul sense with these three or the inert, micro and the reason bodies has to be motivated with this learning. This process can be said the trio-combined. Some school say the trio-combination consisting of mother, father and the teacher. Three deeds are considered as creation, nutrition and destruction or worship to god, co-ordination therewith and the donation in context to the offering.]

त्रिणाचिकेतस्त्रयमेतद्विदित्वा य एवं विद्वाःश्चिनुते नाचिकेतम्।
स मृत्युपाशान्पुरतः प्रणोद्य शोकातिगो मोदते स्वर्गलोके॥१८॥

Having kindled a triple Naciketas-fire, having known this triad,
he who knowing thus, builds up the Naciketas-fire.
He, having cast off in advance the bonds of death,
With sorrow overpassed, rejoices in the heaven-world.

एष तेऽग्निर्नचिकेतः स्वर्ग्यो यमवृणीथा द्वितीयेन वरेण।
एतमग्निं तवैव प्रवक्ष्यन्ति जनासस्तृतीयं वरं नचिकेतो वृणीष्व॥१९॥

This, O Naciketas, is your heavenly fire,

Which you did choose with the second boon.

As you, indeed, will folks proclaim this fire,

The third boon, Naciketas, choose!

येयं प्रेते विचिकित्सा मनुष्येऽस्तीत्येके नायमस्तीति चैके।

एतद्विद्यामनुशिष्यस्त्वयाहं वराणामेष वरस्तृतीयः॥२०॥

Naciketas's third wish : knowledge concerning the effect of dying.

(Naciketā said) - This doubt that there is in regard to a man deceased :

'He exists,' say some' 'He exists not,' say others—This would I know, instructed by you!

Of the boons this is boon the third.

देवैरत्रापि विचिकित्सितं पुरा न हि सुविज्ञेयमणुरेष धर्मः।

अन्यं वरं नचिकेतो वृणीष्व मा मोपरोत्सीरति मा सृजैनम्॥२१॥

(Yama said) O' Naciketā!

Even the gods had doubt as to this of yore.

For truly, it is not easily to be understood. Subtile is this matter (*dharma*).

Another boon, O Naciketas, choose!

Press me not! Give up this one for me!

देवैरत्रापि विचिकित्सितं किल त्वं च मृत्यो यन्न सुविज्ञेयमात्थ।

वक्ता चास्य त्वादृगन्यो न लभ्यो नान्यो वरस्तुल्य एतस्य कश्चित्॥२२॥

This knowledge preferable to the greatest earthly pleasures.

(Naciketā said) O' god of death!

Even the gods had doubt, indeed, as to this,

And you, O Death, say that it is not easily to be understood

And another declarer of it the like of you is not to be obtained.

No other boon the equal of it is there at all.

शतायुषः पुत्रपौत्रान्वृणीष्व बहून्पशून्हस्तिहिरण्यमश्वान्।

भूमेर्महदायतनं वृणीष्व स्वयं च जीव शरदो यावदिच्छसि॥२३॥

Yama told– Choose centenarian sons and grandsons,

Many cattle, elephants, gold and horses.

Choose a great abode of earth.

And yourself live as many autumns as you desire.

एतत्तुल्यं यदि मन्यसे वरं वृणीष्व वित्तं चिरजीविकां च।
महाभूमौ नचिकेतस्त्वमेधि कामानां त्वा कामभाजं करोमि॥२४॥

This, if you think an equal boon, choose—wealth and long life!
A great one on earth, O Naciketas, be you.
The enjoyer of your desires I make you.

ये ये कामा दुर्लभा मर्त्यलोके सर्वान्कामाꣳ श्छन्दतः प्रार्थयस्व।
इमा रामाः सरथाः सतूर्या न हीदृशा लम्भनीया मनुष्यैः।
आभिर्मत्प्रत्ताभिः प्ररिचारयस्व नचिकेतो मरणं मानुप्राक्षीः॥२५॥

Whatever desires are hard to get in the mortal world—
For all desires at pleasure make request.
These lovely maidens with chariots, with lyres—
Such [maidens], indeed, are not obtainable by men—
By these, from me bestowed, be waited on!
O Naciketas, question me not regarding dying (*maraṇa*)!

श्वोभावा मर्त्यस्य यदन्तकैतत्सर्वेन्द्रियाणां जरयन्ति तेजः।
अपि सर्वं जीवितमल्पमेव तवैव वाहास्तव नृत्यगीते॥२६॥

(Naciketā said) Ephemeral things! That which is a mortal's, O End-maker,
Even the vigour (*tejas*) of all the powers, they wear away.
Even a whole life is slight indeed.
You be the vehicles (*vāha*! You be the dance and song!

न वित्तेन तर्पणीयो मनुष्यो लप्स्यामहे वित्तमद्राक्ष्म चेत्त्वा।
जीविष्यामो यावदीशिष्यसि त्वं वरस्तु मे वरणीयः स एव॥२७॥

Not with wealth is a man to be satisfied.
Shall we take wealth, if we have seen you?
Shall we live so long as you shall rule?
—This, in truth, is the boon to be chosen by me.

अजीर्यताममृतानामुपेत्य जीर्यन्मर्त्यःस्थः प्रजानन्।
अभिध्यायन्वर्णरतिप्रमोदानतिदीर्घे जीविते को रमेत॥२८॥

When one has come into the presence of undecaying immortals.
What decaying mortal, here below, that understands,
That mediates upon the pleasures of beauty and delight,
Would delight in a life over-long?

यस्मिन्निदं विचिकित्सन्ति मृत्यो यत्साम्पराये महति ब्रूहि नस्तत्।
योऽयं वरो गूढमनुप्रविष्टो नान्यं तस्मान्नचिकेता वृणीते॥२९॥

This thing whereon they doubt, O Death :
What there is in the great passing on—tell us that !
This boon, that has entered into the hidden—
No other than that does Naciketas choose.

[Only the person like Naciketā, full detached to the material pleasure, can reject such allurements. On the premise of this very self-loyalty, he becomes entitle to attain the essence of soul.]

Second Vallī

The failure of pleasure and of ignorance; the wisdom of the better knowledge

अन्यच्छ्रेयोऽन्यदुतैव प्रेयस्ते उभे नानार्थे पुरुषꣳसिनीतः।
तयोः श्रेय आददानस्य साधु भवति हीयतेऽर्थाद्य उ प्रेयो वृणीते॥१॥

Yamarāja said Naciketā -
The better (*śreyas*) is one thing, and the pleasanter (*preyas*) quite another.
Both these, of different aim, bind a person.
Of these two, well is it for him who takes the better;
He fails of his aim who chooses the pleasanter.

श्रेयश्च प्रेयश्च मनुष्यमेतस्तौ संपरीत्य विविनक्ति धीरः।
श्रेयो हि धीरोऽभि प्रेयसो वृणीते प्रेयो मन्दो योगक्षेमाद्वृणीते॥२॥

Both the better an the pleasanter come to a man.
Going all around the two, the wise man discriminates.
The wise man chooses the better, indeed, rather than the pleasanter.
The stupid man, from getting and keeping (*yoga-kṣema*), chooses the pleasanter.

स त्वं प्रियान्प्रियरूपाꣳश्च कामानभिध्यायन्नचिकेतोऽत्यस्राक्षीः।
नैतां सृङ्कां वित्तमयीमवाप्तो यस्यां मज्जन्ति बहवो मनुष्याः॥३॥

You indeed, upon the pleasant and pleasantly appearing desires
Meditating, has let them go, O Naciketas.
You are not one who has taken that garland of wealth
In which many men sink down.

दूरमेते विपरीते विषूची अविद्या या च विद्येति ज्ञाता।
विद्याभीप्सिनं नचिकेतसं मन्ये न त्वा कामा बहवो लोलुपन्त॥४॥

Widely opposite and asunder are these two :
Ignorance (*avidyā*) and what is known as 'knowledge' (*vidyā*).
I think Naciketas desirous of obtaining knowledge!
Many desires rend you not.

अविद्यायामन्तरे वर्तमानाः स्वयं धीराः पण्डितं मन्यमानाः।
दन्द्रम्यमाणाः परियन्ति मूढा अन्धेनैव नीयमाना यथान्धाः॥५॥

Those abiding in the midst of ignorance,
Self-wise, thinking themselves learned,
Running hither and thither, go around deluded,
Like blind men led by one who is himself blind.

न सांपरायः प्रतिभाति बालं प्रमाद्यन्तं वित्तमोहेन मूढम्।
अयं लोको नास्ति पर इति मानी पुनः पुनर्वशमापद्यते मे॥६॥

[Heedlessness the cause of rebirth]
The passing-on is not clear to him who is childish,
Heedless, deluded with the delusion of wealth.
Thinking 'This is the world! There is no other!'
Again and again he comes under my control.

श्रवणायापि बहुभिर्यो न लभ्यः शृण्वन्तोऽपि बहवो यं न विद्युः।
आश्चर्यो वक्ता कुशलोऽस्य लब्धाश्चर्यो ज्ञाता कुशलानुशिष्टः॥७॥

[The need for a competent teacher of the soul]
He who by many is not obtainable even to hear of,
He whom many, even when hearing, know not—
Wonderful is the declarer, proficient the obtainer of Him!
Wonderful the knower, proficiently taught!

न नरेणावरेण प्रोक्त एष सुविज्ञेयो बहुधा चिन्त्यमानः।
अनन्यप्रोक्ते गतिरत्र नास्त्यणीयान्ह्यतर्क्यमणुप्रमाणात्॥८॥

Not, when proclaimed by an inferior man, is He
To be well understood, [thought] being manifoldly considered.
Unless declared by another, there is no going thither;
For He is inconceivably more subtile than what is of subtile measure.

नैषा तर्केण मतिरापनेया प्रोक्तान्येनैव सुज्ञानाय प्रेष्ठ।
यां त्वमापः सत्यधृतिर्बतासि त्वादृङ्नो भूयान्नचिकेतः प्रष्टा॥९॥

Not by reasoning (*tarka*) is this thought (*mati*) to be attained.

Proclaimed by another, indeed, it is for easy understanding, dearest friend (*preṣṭha*)!

This which you has attained! Ah, you are of true steadfastness!

May there be for us a questioner (*praṣṭā*) the like of you, O Naciketas!

जानाम्यहꣳ शेवधिरित्यनित्यं न ह्यध्रुवैः प्राप्यते हि ध्रुवं तत्।
ततो मया नाचिकेतश्चितोऽग्निरनित्यैर्द्रव्यैः प्राप्तवानस्मि नित्यम्॥१०॥

I know that what is known as treasure is something inconstant.

For truly, that which is steadfast is not obtained by those who are unsteadfast.

Therefore the Naciketas-fire has been built up by me,

And with means which are inconstant I have obtained that which is constant.

कामस्याप्तिं जगतः प्रतिष्ठां क्रतोरनन्त्यमभयस्य पारम्।
स्तोममहदुरुगायं प्रतिष्ठां दृष्ट्वा धृत्या धीरो नचिकेतोऽत्यस्राक्षीः॥११॥

O dear Naciketā! The obtainment of desire, the foundation of the world (*jagat*),

The endlessness of will, the safe shore of fearlessness,

The greatness of praise, the wide extent, the foundation (having seen),

You, O Naciketas, a wise one, has with steadfastness let [these] go!

तं दुर्दर्शं गूढमनुप्रविष्टं गुहाहितं गह्वरेष्ठं पुराणम्।
अध्यात्मयोगाधिगमेन देवं मत्वा धीरो हर्षशोकौ जहाति॥१२॥

Him who is hard to see, entered into the hidden,

Set in the secret place [of the heart], dwelling in the depth, primeval—

By considering him as God, through the Yoga-study of what pertains to self,

The wise man leaves joy and sorrow behind.

एतच्छ्रुत्वा संपरिगृह्य मर्त्यः प्रवृह्य धर्म्यमणुमेतमाप्य।
स मोदते मोदनीयꣳ ह लब्ध्वा विवृतꣳसद्म नचिकेतसं मन्ये॥१३॥

When a mortal has heard this and fully comprehended, has torn off what is concerned with the right (*dharmya*), and has taken Him as the subtile,

Then he rejoices, for indeed he has obtained what is to be rejoiced in.

I regard Naciketas a dwelling open [for Ātman].

अन्यत्र धर्मादन्यत्राधर्मादन्यत्रास्मात्कृताकृतात्। अन्यत्र भूताच्च भव्याच्च यत्तत्पश्यसि तद्वद॥१४॥

(Naciketā said) Apart from the right (*dharma*) and apart from the unright (*a-dharma*),

Apart from both what has been done and what has not been done here,

Apart from what has been and what is to be—What you see as that, speak that!

सर्वे वेदा यत्पदमामनन्ति तपाꣳसि सर्वाणि च यद्वदन्ति।

यदिच्छन्तो ब्रह्मचर्यं चरन्ति तत्ते पदꣳ संग्रहेण ब्रवीम्योमित्येतत्॥१५॥

[The mystic syllable 'Oṁ' as an aid] (Yama said)

The word which all the Vedas proclaim, and which is expressed in all austerities.

Desiring which men live the life of religious studentship (*brahmacarya*)—

That word to you I briefly explain. That is *Oṁ*!

एतद्ध्येवाक्षरं ब्रह्म एतद्ध्येवाक्षरं परम्। एतद्ध्येवाक्षरं ज्ञात्वा यो यदिच्छति तस्य तत्॥१६॥

That syllable, truly, indeed, is Brahman! That syllable indeed is the supreme!

Knowing that syllable, truly, indeed, Whatever one desires is his!

एतदालम्बनꣳ श्रेष्ठमेतदालम्बनं परम्। एतदालम्बनं ज्ञात्वा ब्रह्मलोके महीयते॥१७॥

That is the best support. That is the supreme support. Knowing that support, one becomes happy in the Brahma-world.

न जायते म्रियते वा विपश्चिन्नायं कुतश्चिन्न बभूव कश्चित्।

अजो नित्यःशाश्वतोऽयं पुराणो न हन्यते हन्यमाने शरीरे॥१८॥

The wise one [i.e. the soul, the *ātman*, the self] is not born, nor dies.

This one has not come from anywhere, has not become anyone.

Unborn, constant, eternal, primeval, this one is not slain when the body is slain.

हन्ता चेन्मन्यते हन्तुꣳ हतश्चेन्मन्यते हतम्। उभौ तौ न विजानीतो नायꣳ हन्ति न हन्यते॥१९॥

If the slayer think to slay, If the slain think himself slain,

Both these understand not. This one slays not, nor is slain.

अणोरणीयान्महतो महीयानात्मास्य जन्तोर्निहितो गुहायाम्।

तमक्रतुः पश्यति वीतशोको धातुप्रसादान्महिमानमात्मनः॥२०॥

More minute than the minute, greater than the great, is the Soul (Ātman) that is set in the heart of a creature here.

One who is without the active will (*a-kratu*) beholds Him, and becomes freed from sorrow—When through the grace (*prasāda*) of the Creator (*dhātṛ*) he beholds the greatness of the Soul (Ātman).

आसीनो दूरं व्रजति शयानो याति सर्वतः। कस्तं मदामदं देव मदन्यो ज्ञातुमर्हति॥२१॥

Sitting, he proceeds a far; Lying, he goes everywhere.

Who else than I (*mad*) is able to know; The god (*deva*) who rejoices and rejoices not (*madāmada*)?

अशरीरꣳशरीरेष्वनवस्थेष्ववस्थितम्। महान्तं विभुमात्मानं मत्वा धीरो न शोचति॥२२॥

Him who is the bodiless among bodies, stable among the unstable, the great, all-pervading Soul (Ātman)—

On recognising Him, the wise man sorrows not.

नायमात्मा प्रवचनेन लभ्यो न मेधया न बहुना श्रुतेन।

यमेवैष वृणुते तेन लभ्यस्तस्यैष आत्मा विवृणुते तनूंस्वाम्।।२३।।

This Soul (Ātman) is not to be obtained by instruction,

Nor by intellect, nor by much learning.

He is to be obtained only by the one whom he chooses;

To such a one that Soul (Ātman) reveals his own person (*tanūm svām*).

नाविरतो दुश्चरितान्नाशान्तो नासमाहितः। नाशान्तमानसो वापि प्रज्ञानेनैनमाप्नुयात्।।२४।।

Not he who has not ceased from bad conduct,

Not he who is not tranquil, not he who is not composed,

Not he who is not of peaceful mind

Can obtain Him by intelligence (*prajñā*).

The all-comprehending incomprehensible

यस्य ब्रह्म च क्षत्रं चोभे भवत ओदनः। मृत्युर्यस्योपसेचनं क इत्था वेद यत्र सः।।२५।।

He for whom the priesthood (*brahman*) and the nobility (*kṣatra*)

Both are as food, And death is as a sauce—

Who really knows where He is?

[The symbolic use of "Brahma" and "Kṣatra" in this hymn appear as the sub-characteristic of the supreme soul. Brahma indicates easy discipline of religion or the power of discretion while "Kṣatra" indicates the power of endeavour of industry. Thus, these expressions prove as the symbol of the characteristic of the living organism. That element of supreme soul, rolls up all beings at the material tone through the instrument of death within it.]

Third Vallī

The universal and the individual soul

ऋतं पिबन्तौ सुकृतस्य लोके गुहां प्रविष्टौ परमे परार्धे।

छायातपौ ब्रह्मविदो वदन्ति पञ्चाग्नयो ये च त्रिणाचिकेताः।।१।।

(Yama said) There are two that drink of righteousness (*ṛta*) in the world of good deeds;

Both are entered into the secret place [of the heart], and in the highest upper sphere.

Brahma-knowers speak of them as 'light' and 'shade',

And so do householders who maintain the five sacrificial fires,

and those too who perform the triple Naciketas-fire.

यः सेतुरीजानानामक्षरं ब्रह्म यत्परम्। अभयं तितीर्षतां पारं नाचिकेतꣳ शकेमहि।।२।।

This which is the bridge for those who sacrifice,

And which is the highest imperishable Brahma

For those who seek to cross over to the fearless farther shore—

The Naciketas-fire may we master!

आत्मानꣳ रथिनं विद्धि शरीरꣳ रथमेव तु। बुद्धिं तु सारथिं विद्धि मनः प्रग्रहमेव च।।३।।

[Parable of the individual soul in a chariot]

O' Naciketā! Know you the soul (*ātman*, self) as riding in a chariot,

The body as the chariot.

Know you the intellect (*buddhi*) as the chariot-driver,

And the mind (*manas*) as the reins.

इन्द्रियाणि हयानाहुर्विषयाँस्तेषु गोचरान्। आत्मेन्द्रियमनोयुक्तं भोक्तेत्याहुर्मनीषिणः।।४।।

The senses (*indriya*), they say, are the horses;

The objects of sense, what they range over.

The self combined with senses and mind

Wise men call 'the enjoyer' (*bhoktṛ*).

यस्त्वविज्ञानवान्भवत्ययुक्तेन मनसा सदा। तस्येन्द्रियाण्यवश्यानि दुष्टाश्व इव सारथेः।।५।।

He who has not understanding (*a-vijñāna*),

Whose mind is not constantly held firm—

His senses are uncontrolled,

Like the vicious horses of a chariot-driver.

यस्तु विज्ञानवान्भवति युक्तेन मनसा सदा। तस्येन्द्रियाणि वश्यानि सदश्वा इव सारथेः।।६।।

He, however, who has understanding,

Whose mind is constantly held firm—

His senses are under control,

Like the good horses of a chariot-driver.

यस्त्वविज्ञानवान्भवत्यमनस्कः सदाऽशुचिः। न स तत्पदमाप्नोति सꣳसारं चाधिगच्छति।।७।।

He, however, who has not understanding, who is unmindful and ever impure, reaches not the goal, But goes on to reincarnation (*saṁsāra*).

यस्तु विज्ञानवान्भवति समनस्कः सदा शुचिः। स तु तत्पदमाप्नोति यस्माद्भूयो न जायते।।८।।

He, however, who has understanding, Who is mindful and ever pure, reaches the goal from which he is born no more.

विज्ञानसारथिर्यस्तु मन:प्रग्रहवान्नर:। सोऽध्वन: पारमाप्नोति तद्विष्णो: परमं पदम्॥९॥

He, however, who has the understanding of a chariot-driver, A man who reins in his mind— He reaches the end of his journey. That is the highest place of Viṣṇu.

इन्द्रियेभ्य: परा ह्यर्था अर्थेभ्यश्च परं मन:। मनसस्तु परा बुद्धिर्बुद्धेरात्मा महान्पर:॥१०॥

Higher than the senses are the objects of sense.

Higher than the objects of sense is the mind (*manas*);

and higher than the mind is the intellect (*buddhi*).

Higher than the intellect is the Great Self (Ātman).

महत: परमव्यक्तमव्यक्तात्पुरुष: पर:। पुरुषान्न परं किंचित्सा काष्ठा सा परा गति:॥११॥

Higher than the Great is the Unmanifest (*avyakta*).

Higher than the Unmanifest is the Person.

Higher than the Person there is nothing at all.

That is the goal. That is the highest course.

एष सर्वेषु भूतेषु गूढोत्मा न प्रकाशते। दृश्यते त्वग्र्यया बुद्ध्या सूक्ष्मया सूक्ष्मदर्शिभि:॥१२॥

Though He is hidden in all things,

That Soul (Ātman, Self) shines not forth,

But he is seen by subtle seers

With superior, subtle intellect.

यच्छेद्वाङ्मनसी प्राज्ञस्तद्यच्छेज्ज्ञानं आत्मनि। ज्ञानमात्मनि महति नियच्छेत्तद्यच्छेच्छान्त आत्मनि॥१३॥

[The Yoga method—of suppression]

An intelligent man should suppress his speech and his mind.

The latter he should suppress in the Understanding-Self (*jñāna ātman*).

The understanding he should suppress in the Great Self [= *buddhi*, intellect].

That he should suppress in the Tranquil Self (*śānta ātman*).

उत्तिष्ठत जाग्रत प्राप्य वरान्निबोधत। क्षुरस्य धारा निशिता दुरत्यया दुर्गं पथस्तत्कवयो वदन्ति॥१४॥

[Exhortation to the way of liberation from death]

Arise ye! Awake ye! Obtain your boons and understand them!

A sharpened edge of a razor, hard to traverse,

A difficult path is this—poets (*kavi*) declare!

अशब्दमस्पर्शमरूपमव्ययं तथाऽरसं नित्यमगन्धवच्च यत्।

अनाद्यन्तं महत: परं ध्रुवं निचाय्य तन्मृत्युमुखात्प्रमुच्यते॥१५॥

What is soundless, touchless, formless, imperishable, likewise tasteless, constant, odourless, without beginning, without end, higher than the great, stable—

By discerning That, one is liberated from the mouth of death.

नाचिकेतमुपाख्यानं मृत्युप्रोक्तꣳ सनातनम्। उक्त्वा श्रुत्वा च मेधावी ब्रह्मलोके महीयते॥१६॥

[The immortal value of this teaching]

The Naciketas tale, which is narrated by Death, A wise man by teaching and hearing this, becomes magnified in the Brahma-world.

य इमं परमं गुह्यं श्रावयेद् ब्रह्मसंसदि। प्रयत: श्राद्धकाले वा तदानन्त्याय कल्पते तदानन्त्याय कल्पत इति॥१७॥

If one recites this supreme secret, in an assembly of Brahmans, or at a time of the ceremony for the dead, devoutly—

That makes for immortality! —That makes for immortality!

[The couplet "Brahma sansad" refers to the group of persons or professions that meditate for attainment of knowledge. Similarly "Śrāddhakāla" refers to the point of time when difference emerges among such group of persons. The persons knowledge oriented and obeisanct should be clearly made known of this fact because this will fructify manifold. In case, the circumstances as described are not available, this learning confines only to enhance the self-knowledge.]

Fourth Vallī

The immortal Soul not to be sought through outward senses

Part -1

पराञ्चि खानि व्यतृणत्स्वयंभूस्तस्मात्पराङ् पश्यति नान्तरात्मन्।
कश्चिद्धीर: प्रत्यगात्मानमैक्षदावृत्तचक्षुरमृतत्वमिच्छन्॥१॥

The Self-existent (*svayambhū*) pierced the openings [of the senses] outward;

Therefore one looks outward, not within himself (*antarātman*).

A certain wise man, while seeking immortality,

Introspectively beheld the Soul (Ātman) face to face.

पराच: कामाननुयन्ति बालास्ते मृत्योर्यन्ति विततस्य पाशम्।
अथ धीरा अमृतत्वं विदित्वा ध्रुवमध्रुवेष्विह न प्रार्थयन्ते॥२॥

The childish go after outward pleasures ;

They walk into the net of widespread death.

But the wise, knowing immortality,

Seek not the stable among things which are unstable here.

[From hymn 3 to 13, lord Yama has said "This is only". It appears that simultaneous to explanation, Yama is going to demonstrate that element and while making this fact apparent, he says

"That secret, learning, element of soul or supreme soul, to which you want to understand, is only this."]

येन रूपं रसं गन्धं शब्दान्स्पर्शांश्च मैथुनान्। एतेनैव विजानाति किमत्र परिशिष्यते एतद्वै तत्॥३॥

That by which [one discerns] form, taste, smell, sound, and mutual touches —

It is with That indeed that one discerns.

What is there left over here! This, verily, is That!

स्वप्नान्तं जागरितान्तं चोभौ येनानुपश्यति। महान्तं विभुमात्मानं मत्वा धीरो न शोचति॥४॥

By recognizing as the great and all-pervading Soul (Ātman)

That whereby one perceives both the states of sleeping and the waking,

The wise man does not sorrows.

[By the knowledge or sense the man sees the apparent or tangible things while he is awaken and even slept, the prudent man knowing that omnipresent and great universal soul, do not fall in gloom at any of the situation.]

य इमं मध्वदं वेद आत्मानं जीवमन्तिकात्। ईशानं भूतभव्यस्य न ततो विजुगुप्सते एतद्वै तत्॥५॥

[The universal Soul (Ātman), identical with the individual and with all creation]

He who knows him, to whom everything is honey,

As the living Soul (Ātman) near at hand,

Lord of what has been and of what is to be—

He does not shrink away from Him. This, verily, is That!

यः पूर्वं तपसो जातमद्भ्यः पूर्वमजायत। गुहां प्रविश्य तिष्ठन्तं यो भूतेभिर्व्यपश्यते, एतद्वै तत्॥६॥

He who was born of old from austerity (*tapas*), was born of old from the waters,

Who stands entered into the secret place [of the heart],

Who looked forth through beings— This, verily, is That!

[One who by virtue of his penance sees the brahma (knowledge) brought in before the pañcabhūtas (five elements) like water, ether etc. and residing in the cavity of heart in all, knows the truth. This only is that brahma (knowledge).]

या प्राणेन संभवत्यदितिदेवतामयी। गुहां प्रविश्य तिष्ठन्तं यो भूतेभिर्व्यपश्यते, एतद्वै तत्॥७॥

She who arises with life (*prāṇa*), Aditi (Infinity), maker of divinity,

Who stands entered into the secret place [of the heart],

Who was born forth through beings— This, verily, is That!

अरण्योर्निहितो जातवेदा गर्भ इव सुभृतो गर्भिणीभिः।

दिवे दिव ईड्यो जागृवद्भिर्हविष्मद्भिर्मनुष्येभिरग्निः, एतद्वै तत्॥८॥

Fire (Agni), the all-knower (*jātavedas*), hidden away in the two fire-sticks, like the embryo well borne by pregnant women, worthy to be worshipped day by day, by watchful men with oblations— This, verily, is That!

यतश्चोदेति सूर्योऽस्तं यत्र च गच्छति। तं देवाः सर्वेर्पितास्तदु नात्येति कश्चन, एतद्वै तत्।।९।।

Whence the sun rises, And where it goes to rest—

On Him all the gods are founded; And no one ever goes beyond it.

This, verily, is That!

[The place to the extent the sun rises and sets is enshrined by the divine powers. Nobody may cross that place. This is that absolute god.]

यदेवेह तदमुत्र यदमुत्र तदन्विह। मृत्योः स मृत्युमाप्नोति य इह नानेव पश्यति।।१०।।

Whatever is here, that is there. What is there, that again is here.

He obtains death after death. Who seems to see a difference here.

मनसैवेदमाप्तव्यं नेह नानास्ति किंचन। मृत्योः स मृत्युं गच्छति य इह नानेव पश्यति।।११।।

By the mind, indeed, is this [realization] to be attained :—

There is no difference here at all!

He goes from death to death who seems to see a difference here.

[The element of supreme soul may be known only when the mind is true or holy. Nothing in this world is besides god. But the man who sees difference in this, attains the death from death.]

अङ्गुष्ठमात्रः पुरुषो मध्य आत्मनि तिष्ठति। ईशानो भूतभव्यस्य न ततो विजुगुप्सते, एतद्वै तत्।।१२।।

A Person of the measure of a thumb stands in the midst of one's self (*ātman*),

Lord of what has been and of what is to be.

One does not shrink away from Him. This, verily, is That!

अङ्गुष्ठमात्रः पुरुषो ज्योतिरिवाधूमकः। ईशानो भूतभव्यस्य स एवाद्य स उ श्वः, एतद्वै तत्।।१३।।

A Person of the measure of a thumb, like a light without smoke,

Lord of what has been and what is to be.

He alone is today, and tomorrow too.

[The supreme soul as little as a thumb is a severe light like without any smoke. It governs all. It remains unvariated *i.e.* unchangeable all through. This is perfect knowledge (Parabrahman).]

यथोदकं दुर्गे वृष्टं पर्वतेषु विधावति। एवं धर्मान्पृथक् पश्यंस्तानेवानुविधावति।।१४।।

[The result of seeing multiplicity or else pure unity]

As water rained upon rough ground runs to waste among the hills,

So he who sees qualities (*dharma*) separately, runs to waste after them.

[As the rain water flows various places coming down from the high mountains where it first rained, the same way who considers different from the absolute god the different religions and the communities (or distinct nature as of man, demon and gods), follows then. It means he wanders through the several worlds of gods and demons and the several species of beings like the scattered water of the rain down from the mountains.]

यथोदकं शुद्धे शुद्धमासिक्तं तादृगेव भवति। एवं मुनेर्विजानत आत्मा भवति गौतम।।१५।।

As pure water poured forth into pure becomes the very same,

So becomes the soul (*ātman*), O Gautama, of the seer (*muni*) who has understanding.

[Yama is taking the example of the pure water while explaining, the essence of the soul. The pure water changes its features according to the pot in which it is kept. In plants, it becomes their fluid and in beings it turns into the blood. There is no defects in it. The learned person keeps his senses detached from the luxuries (material). He therefore, may be integrated with everybody. Naciketā the term is used for a devotee who possess the power of keeping himself detached from the material luxuries. Starting from several subjects (material) to the divine powers and the supreme element of soul, such a man may establish the harmony. Assuming Naciketā, an eligible devotee, Yama makes him to know this learning.]

Fifth Vallī

The real soul of the individual and of the world

पुरमेकादशद्वारमजस्यावक्रचेतसः। अनुष्ठाय न शोचति विमुक्तश्च विमुच्यते, एतद्वै तत्।।१।।

By ruling over the eleven-gated citadel Of the Unborn, the Un-crooked-minded one, One sorrows not.

But when liberated [from the body], he is liberated indeed. This, verily, is That!

हꣳसः शुचिषद्वसुरन्तरिक्षसद्धोता वेदिषदतिथिर्दुरोणसत्।

नृषद्वरसदृतसद्व्योमसदब्जा गोजा ऋतजा अद्रिजा ऋतं बृहत्।।२।।

The swan [i.e. the sun] in the clear, the Vasu in the atmosphere,

The priest by the altar, the guest in the house,

In man, in broad space, in the right (*ṛta*), in the sky,

Born in water, born in cattle, born in the right, born in rock, is the Right, the Great!

ऊर्ध्वं प्राणमुन्नयत्यपानं प्रत्यगस्यति। मध्ये वामनमासीनं विश्वेदेवा उपासते।।३।।

Upwards the out-breath (*prāṇa*) he leadeth.

The in-breath (*apāna*) inward he casts.

The dwarf who is seated in the middle all the gods (*deva*) reverence!

अस्य विस्रꣳसमानस्य शरीरस्थस्य देहिनः। देहाद्विमुच्यमानस्य किमत्र परिशिष्यते, एतद्वै तत्।।४।।

When this incorporate one that stands in the body is dissolved, and is released from the body, what is there left over here? This, verily, is That!

[What remain when this soul of being exited in body moves from a body to another as its usual dynamic nature after the death? The same that remains thereafter is brahma (the knowledge).]

न प्राणेन नापानेन मर्त्यो जीवति कश्चन। इतरेण तु जीवन्ति यस्मिन्नेतावुपाश्रितौ।।५।।

Not by the out-breath (*prāṇa*) and the in-breath (*apāna*) do any mortal whatsoever live.

But by another do men live—even that whereon both these depend.

हन्त त इदं प्रवक्ष्यामि गुह्यं ब्रह्म सनातनम्। यथा च मरणं प्राप्य आत्मा भवति गौतम॥६॥

Come! I will proclaim this to you , the hidden, eternal Brahman;

And how, after it reaches death, The soul (*ātman*) fares, O Gautama!

योनिमन्ये प्रपद्यन्ते शरीरत्वाय देहिनः। स्थाणुमन्येऽनुसंयन्ति यथाकर्म यथाश्रुतम्॥७॥

Some go into a womb for the embodiment of a corporeal being. Others go into a stationary thing according to their deeds (*karman*) and according to their knowledge.

[The motive as adopted by the soul of the beings as a result of their deeds and the study of literature (Branch of learning) some obtain several species (yoni) of creatures for holding with the body and others receive inertia like trees, creeper, mountain etc. immovable species.]

य एष सुप्तेषु जागर्ति कामं कामं पुरुषो निर्मिमाणः। तदेव शुक्रं तद्ब्रह्म तदेवामृतमुच्यते। तस्मिँल्लोकाः श्रिताः सर्वे तदु नान्येति कश्चन, एतद्वै तत्॥८॥

He who is awake in those that sleep, The Person who fashions desire after desire—

That indeed is the Pure. That is Brahma.

That indeed is called the Immortal.

On it all the worlds do rest; And no one soever goes beyond it. This, verily, is That!

[The super man (absolute soul) provides for the consumption of all creatures according to their deeds and remains awaken when all retires on their beds. That pure element is called non-perishing perfect knowledge (Parabrahma) to which nobody may cross or go further than him. All worlds (lokas) depend on him. This is that brahma (knowledge).]

अग्निर्यथैको भुवनं प्रविष्टो रूपं रूपं प्रतिरूपो बभूव।

एकस्तथा सर्वभूतान्तरात्मा रूप रूपं प्रतिरूपो बहिश्च॥९॥

[The Yama now explains that like absolute soul (Paramātman) the fire etc. elements also get universal form through detachment.]

As the one fire has entered the world and becomes corresponding in form to every form, so the one Inner Soul (*antarātman*) of all things is corresponding in form to every form, and yet is outside.

वायुर्यथैको भुवनं प्रविष्टो रूपं रूपं प्रतिरूपो बभूव।

एकस्तथा सर्वभूतान्तरात्मा रूपं रूपं प्रतिरूपो बहिश्च॥१०॥

As the one wind has entered the world and becomes corresponding in form to every form, so the one Inner Soul of all things is corresponding in form to every form, and yet is outside.

[Though wind enters in various things of this world in one'form, it still appears to us in different forms (because of various shapes of different things). In the same way, Paramātman appears in various forms in the beings even then it is one and alone. This is also existed in the outer atmosphere.]

सूर्यो यथा सर्वलोकस्य चक्षुर्न लिप्यते चाक्षुषैर्बाह्यदोषैः।
एकस्तथा सर्वभूतान्तरात्मा न लिप्यते लोकदुःखेन बाह्यः॥११॥

As the sun, the eye of the whole world, is not sullied by the external faults of the eyes. So the one Inner Soul of all things is not sullied by the evil in the world, being external to it.

[The indescribable bliss of recognizing the world-soul in one's own soul]

एको वशी सर्वभूतान्तरात्मा एकं रूपं बहुधा यः करोति।
तमात्मस्थं येऽनुपश्यन्ति धीरास्तेषां सुखं शाश्वतं नेतरेषाम्॥१२॥

The Inner Soul (*antarātman*) of all things, the One Controller, who makes his one form manifold—The wise who perceive Him as standing in oneself, they, and no others, have eternal happiness!

नित्यो नित्यानां चेतनश्चेतनानामेको बहूनां यो विदधाति कामान्।
तमात्मस्तं येऽनुपश्यन्ति धीरास्तेषां शान्तिः शाश्वती नेतरेषाम्॥१३॥

Him who is the Constant among the inconstant, the Intelligent among intelligences, the One among many, who grants desires—

The wise who perceive Him as standing in oneself, they, and no other, have eternal peace!

तदेतदिति मन्यन्तेऽनिर्देश्यं परमं सुखम्। कथं नु तद्विजानीयां किमु भाति विभाति वा॥१४॥

'This is it!'—thus they recognize The highest, indescribable happiness. How, now, shall I understand 'this'?

Does it shine [of itself] or does it shine in reflection?

[The self-luminous light of the world]

न तत्र सूर्यो भाति न चन्द्रतारकं नेमा विद्युतो भान्ति कुतोऽयमग्निः।
तमेव भान्तमनुभाति सर्वं तस्य भासा सर्वमिदं विभाति॥१५॥

The sun shines not there, nor the moon and stars,
These lightnings shine not, much less this (earthly) fire!
After Him, as He shines, do everything shine,
This whole world is illumined with His light.

Sixth Vallī

The world-tree rooted in Brahman

ऊर्ध्वमूलोऽवाक्शाख एषोऽश्वत्थः सनातनः। तदेव शुक्रं तद्ब्रह्म तदेवामृतमुच्यते। तस्मिँल्लोकाः श्रिताः सर्वे तदु नात्येति कश्चन, एतद्वै तत्॥१॥

Its root is above, its branches below—This eternal fig-tree!

That (root) indeed is the Pure. That is Brahman. That indeed is called the immortal one.

On it all the worlds rest and no one soever goes beyond it. This, verily, is That!

[Same liquid circulates from the roots of the tree, in leaves of the tree. The roots of immortal tree in garb of the creation (Śṛṣṭi) are above the infinite sky. The liquid circulated therefrom, appears in varied forms when it reaches to the components of the creation.]

यदिदं किं च जगत्सर्वं प्राण एजति निःसृतम्। महद्भयं वज्रमुद्यतं य एतद्विदुरमृतास्ते भवन्ति।।२।।

Whatever there is, this whole world, was created from and moves in Life (*prāṇa*).

The great fear, the upraised thunderbolt— they who know That, become immortal.

भयादस्याग्निस्तपति भयात्तपति सूर्यः। भयादिन्द्रश्च वायुश्च मृत्युर्धावति पञ्चमः।।३।।

From fear of Him fire (Agni) do burn.

From fear the sun (Sūrya) gives forth heat.

From fear both Indra and Wind (Vāyu),

And Death (Mṛtyu) as fifth, do speed along.

इह चेदशकद्बोद्धुं प्राक् शरीरस्य विस्रसः। ततः सर्गेषु लोकेषु शरीरत्वाय कल्पते।।४।।

[Degrees of perception of the Soul (Ātman)]

If one has been able to perceive [Him] here on earth before the dissolution of the body, according to that [knowledge] he becomes fitted for embodiment in the world-creations.

यथादर्शे तथात्मनि यथा स्वप्ने पितृलोके। यथाप्सु परीव ददृशे तथा गन्धर्वलोके छायातपयोरिव ब्रह्मलोके।।५।।

As in a mirror, so is it seen in the body (*ātman*);
As in a dream, so in the world of the fathers;
As if in water, so in the world of the Gandharvas (genii);
As if in light and shade, so in the world of Brahma.

[The pure heart is like a mirror viz. as the clear image of the article exposed to mirror is seen, the image of Brahma (knowledge) looks clear in the pure heart. The image of Brahma does not look clear in Pitṛloka (parental world). Its reason is that the memory factor relating to pre-birth keeps their relation with the relatives of pre-birth. In gandharvaloka too the image of Brahma looks indistinct like the wares of the water because having involvement in material luxuries, the Brahma does not appear apparent. But in brahmaloka (abode of knowledge) the image of soul and the supreme soul is seen all apparent like the shadow and the sun.]

[The gradation up to the supersensible Person]

इन्द्रियाणां पृथग्भावमुदयास्तमयौ च यत्। पृथगुत्पद्यमानानां मत्वा धीरो न शोचति।।६।।

The separate nature of the senses, And that their arising and setting,

Is of things that come into being apart [from himself],

The wise man recognizes these, and does not sorrows.

इन्द्रियेभ्यः परं मनो मनसः सत्त्वमुत्तमम्। सत्त्वादधि महानात्मा महतोऽव्यक्तमुत्तमम्।।७।।

Higher than the senses (*indriya*) is the mind (*manas*);

Above the mind is the true being (*sattva*).

Over the true being is the Great Self [i.e. *buddhi*, intellect];

Above the Great is the Unmanifest (*avyakta*).

[Mind is superior than the sensory organs, wisdom is than the mind, the soul of the beings is than the wisdom and the undescribable power is superior than the soul of the beings.]

अव्यक्तात्तु परः पुरुषो व्यापकोऽलिङ्ग एव च। यं ज्ञात्वा मुच्यते जन्तुरमृतत्वं च गच्छति।।८।।

Higher than the Unmanifest, however, is the Person (Puruṣa).

All-pervading and without any mark (*a-liṅga*) whatever.

Knowing which, a man is liberated and goes to immortality.

न संदृशे तिष्ठति रूपमस्य न चक्षुषा पश्यति कश्चनैनम्।

हृदा मनीषी मनसाऽभिक्लृप्तो य एतद्विदुरमृतास्ते भवन्ति।।९।।

His form (*rūpa*) is not to be beheld. No one soever sees Him with the eye.

He is framed by the heart, by the thought, by the mind.

They who know That become immoratl.

[The method of Yoga, suppressive of the lower activity]

यदा पञ्चावतिष्ठन्ते ज्ञानानि मनसा सह। बुद्धिश्च न विचेष्टति तामाहुः परमां गतिम्।।१०।।

When cease the five [Sense-] knowledge, together with the mind (*manas*),

And the intellect (*buddhi*) stirs not—that, they say, is the highest course.

[When the five sensory organs including mind are concentrated in the element of soul and the wisdom too becomes inactive, the stage is called the supreme position of the soul of the beings.]

तां योगमिति मन्यन्ते स्थिरामिन्द्रियधारणाम्। अप्रमत्तस्तदा भवति योगो हि प्रभवाप्ययौ।।११।।

This they consider as Yoga —The firm holding back of the senses.

Then one becomes undistracted. Yoga, truly, is the origin and the end.

[The Soul incomprehensible except as existent]

नैव वाचा न मनसा प्राप्तुं शक्यो न चक्षुषा। अस्तीति ब्रुवतोऽन्यत्र कथं तदुपलभ्यते।।१२।।

Not by speech, not by mind, not by sight can He be apprehended.

How can He be comprehended otherwise than by one's saying 'He is'?

अस्तीत्येवोपलब्धव्यस्तत्त्वभावेन चोभयोः। अस्तीत्येवोपलब्धस्य तत्त्वभावः प्रसीदति।।१३।।

He can indeed be comprehended by the thought 'He is' (*asti*) and by [admitting] the real nature of both [his comprehensibility and his incomprehensibility].

When he has been comprehended by the thought 'He is' His real nature manifests itself.

[A renunciation of all desires and attachments the condition of immortality]

यदा सर्वे प्रमुच्यन्ते कामा येऽस्य हृदि श्रिताः। अथ मर्त्योऽमृतो भवत्यत्र ब्रह्म समश्नुते।

When are liberated all the desires that lodge in one's heart,

Then a mortal becomes immortal! Therein he reaches Brahman!

[The assumption of element (tattva bhāva) is scattered unless the other passion are removed. An integration of such assumption only leads to realise the god.]

यदा सर्वे प्रभिद्यन्ते हृदयस्येह ग्रन्थयः। अथ मर्त्योऽमृतो भवत्येतावद्ध्यनुशासनम्॥१५॥

When are cut all, the knots of the heart here on earth, then a mortal becomes immortal!

— Thus far is the instruction.

शतं चैका च हृदयस्य नाड्यस्तासां मूर्धानमभिनिःसृतैका।

तयोर्ध्वमायन्नमृतत्वमेति विष्वङ्ङन्या उत्क्रमणे भवन्ति॥१६॥

There are a hundred and one channels of the heart.

One of these passes up to the crown of the head.

Going up by it, one goes to immortality.

The others are for departing in various directions.

अङ्गुष्ठमात्रः पुरुषोऽन्तरात्मा सदा जनानां हृदये संनिविष्टः। तं स्वाच्छरीरात् प्रवृहेन्मुञ्जादिवेषीकां धैर्येण। तं विद्याच्छुक्रममृतं तं विद्याच्छुक्रममृतमिति॥१७॥

A Person of the measure of a thumb is the inner soul (*antarātman*), ever seated in the heart of creatures. Him one should draw out from one's own body like an arrow-shaft out from a reed, with firmness.

Him one should know as the Pure, the Immortal—Yea, Him one should know as the Pure, the Immortal.

This teaching, the means of attaining Brahma and immortality

मृत्युप्रोक्तां नचिकेतोऽथ लब्ध्वा विद्यामेतां योगविधिं च कृत्स्नम्।

ब्रह्मप्राप्तो विरजोऽभूद्विमृत्युरन्योऽप्येवं यो विदध्यात्ममेव॥१८॥

Then Naciketas, having received this knowledge declared by Death, and the entire rule of Yoga, attained Brahman and became free from passion, free from death.

And so may any other who knows this in regard to the Soul (Ātman).

[Thus Naciketā became free from all perplexions and thus, by virtue of purity exonerated from the cycle of the life and death thereby attained the knowledge (brahmatva). This became through the learning predicted by the Yama.]

ॐ सह नाववतु........ इति शान्तिः॥

॥ इति कठोपनिषत्समाप्ता॥

4. PRAŚNOPANIṢAD

प्रश्नोपनिषद्

This upaniṣad is brāhmaṇa part of the branch of Pippalāda to the Atharvaveda. The six questions asked by the eager disciples from Maharṣi Pippalāda and the answers given by him have been made subject-matter of this upaniṣad. In the first question, Kabandhi wished to know about "Prāṇa" (the breathing) and "Rayi". In second question, Bhārgava has raised three questions about the basis of subject (the public). Under the third question, Āśvalāyana has asked six questions regarding the origin of Prāṇa (breathing). In the fourth question, Gāgrya has raised five quests regarding the soul of the beings (Jīvātmā) and the supreme soul (Paramātman). Under the fifth question, Satyakāma has wished to know the worship of Oṁkara. Sixth question was raised by Sukeśa in which curiosity about the person equipped of sixteen arts has been made. At last, the questions have expressed gratitude for providing with the appropriate solutions to Maharṣi Pippalāda and prayed him.

।।शान्तिपाठः।।

ॐ भद्रं कर्णेभिः श्रृणुयाम देवा भद्रं पश्येमाभिर्यजत्राः। स्थिरैरङ्गैस्तुष्टुवाꣳसस्तनूभिर्व्यशेम देवहितं यदायुः।। स्वस्ति न इन्द्रो वृद्धश्रवाः स्वस्ति नः पूषा विश्ववेदाः। स्वस्ति नस्तार्क्ष्यो अरिष्टनेमिः स्वस्ति नो बृहस्पतिर्दधातु।। ॐ शान्तिः शान्तिः शान्तिः।।

O gods! may we listen benevolent averments through our ears. May we see charming scenes and having body with sturdy limbs, engage in the interests of god throughout life. Indradeva (king of gods) be pleased with us, the sun-god do welfare, the Ganiradeva, competent to remove the hurdles be at our support and lord Jupiter enhance our knowledge (asti bhāva). Let three kind of fevers be cool-down.

First Praśna

Six questioners seek the highest Brahma from a teacher

ॐ सुकेशा च भारद्वाजः शैब्यश्च सत्यकामः सौर्यायणी च गार्ग्यः कौसल्यश्चाश्वलायनो भार्गवो वैदर्भिः कबन्धी कात्यायनस्ते हैते ब्रह्मपरा ब्रह्मनिष्ठाः परं ब्रह्मान्वेषमाणा एष ह वै तत्सर्वं वक्ष्यतीति ते ह समित्पाणयो भगवन्तं पिप्पलादमुपसन्नाः।।१।।

Sukeśan Bhāradvāja and Śaibya Satyakāma and Sauryāyaṇin Gārgya and Kauśalya, Āśvalāyana and Bhārgava Vaidarbhi and Kabandhin Kātyāyana— these, indeed, were devoted to Brahma, intent upon Brahma, in search of the highest Brahma. Thinking 'He, verily, will tell it all,' with fuel in hand they approached the honourable Pippalāda.

तान्हं स ऋषिरुवाच भूय एव तपसा ब्रह्मचर्येण श्रद्धया संवत्सरं संवत्स्यथ यथाकामं प्रश्नान्पृच्छत यदि विज्ञास्यामः सर्वं ह वो वक्ष्याम इति।।२।।

To them then that seer (*ṛṣi*) said : 'Dwell with me (*samvatsyatha*) a year (*samvatsara*) more, with austerity (*tapas*), chastity (*brahmacarya*), and faith (*śraddhā*). Then ask what questions you will. If we know, we will tell you all.'

अथ कबन्धी कात्यायन उपेत्य पप्रच्छ। भगवन्कुतो ह वा इमाः प्रजाः प्रजायन्त इति।।३।।

(After living a year in the cottage of Pippalāda) Katyāyana Kabandhi asked the sage Pippalāda– 'Sir, whence, verily, are creatures here born?'

तस्मै स होवाच प्रजाकामो वै प्रजापतिः स तपोऽतप्यत स तपस्तप्त्वा स मिथुनमुत्पादयते। रयिं च प्राणं चेत्येतौ मे बहुधा प्रजाः करिष्यत इति।।४।।

Then Pippalāda said to him– 'The Lord of Creation (Prajāpati), verily, was desirous of creatures (offspring, *prajā*). He performed austerity. Having performed austerity, he produced a pair, matter (*rayi*, fem.) and life (*prāṇa*, masc.), thinking "These two will make creatures for me in manifold ways."

[Prāṇa is an element of sense or the power that gives motion, the Rayi is nature that is able to hold and provide several forms. In the most modern language, these can be known as life energy and the matter. A combination or harmony of these two, originates the creation (Sṛṣṭi).]

आदित्यो ह वै प्राणो रयिरेव चन्द्रमा रयिर्वा एतत्सर्वं यन्मूर्तं चामूर्तं च तस्मान्मूर्तिरेव रयिः।।५।।

The sun, verily, is life; matter, indeed, is the moon.

Matter, verily, is everything here, both what is formed and what is formless. Therefore material form (*mūrti*) indeed is matter.

The sun, identified with the life of creatures.

[The tangible source of breathing circulation is the sun on this earth. Being light giver and motivator, the sun is in garb of Prāṇa. The moon having lighted and motivated of the light from the sun is the symbol of Rayi. All components of micro and macro nature are called Rayi.]

अथादित्य उदयन्यत्प्राचीं दिशं प्रतिशति ते प्राच्यान्प्राणान् रश्मिषु संनिधत्ते। यद्दक्षिणां यत्प्रतीचीं यदुदीचीं यदधो यदूर्ध्वं यदन्तरा दिशो यत्सर्वं प्रकाशयति तेन सर्वान्प्राणान् रश्मिषु संनिधत्ते।।६।।

Now the sun, when it rises, enters the eastern quarter. Thereby it collects the living beings (*prāṇa*) of the east in its rays. When it illumines the southern, the western, the northern, the lower, the upper, the intervening quarters, when it illumines everything– thereby it collects all living beings in its rays.

स एष वैश्वानरो विश्वरूपः प्राणोऽग्निरुदयते तदेतदृचाभ्युक्तम्।।७।।

That fire rises as the universal, all-formed life. This very [doctrine] has been declared in the verse :–

विश्वरूपं हरिणं जातवेदसं परायणं ज्योतिरेकं तपन्तम्।

सहस्त्ररश्मिः शतधा वर्तमानः प्राणः प्रजानामुदयत्येष सूर्यः॥८॥

That sun is in all forms, basis of all, full of beams, omniscient, loyal to penance and unique. That sun with its thousands rays, existing in hundreds of forms rises as the Prāṇa form to all living beings.

संवत्सरो वै प्रजापतिस्तस्यायने दक्षिणं चोत्तरं च। तद्ये ह वै तदिष्टापूर्ते कृतमित्युपासते ते चान्द्रमसमेव लोकमभिजयन्ते। त एव पुनरावर्तन्ते तस्मादेतऽऋषयः प्रजाकामा दक्षिणं प्रतिपद्यन्ते। एष ह वै रयिर्यः पितृयाणः॥९॥

[The year identified with the Lord of Creation; the two paths; of reincarnation and of non-reincarnation]

The year, verily, is Lord of Creation (Prajāpati). This has two paths, the Southern and the Northern.

Now, those, verily, indeed, who worship, thinking "Sacrifice and merit are our work (*kṛta*)!" They win only the lunar world. They, indeed, return hither again. Therefore those seers (*ṛṣis*) who are desirous of offspring go the Southern course. This matter (*rayi*) verily it is, that leads to the fathers (*pitṛyāṇa*).

[The term candra is formed of the speech "Cadi" which means "pleasure". Appropriating, energy with an objective of material pleasure, the men reproducing children are helpful in conducting the cycle of life and death.]

अथोत्तेरण तपसा ब्रह्मचर्येण श्रद्धया विद्यमात्मानमन्विष्यादित्यमभिजयन्ते। एतद्वै प्राणानामायतनमेतदमृतमभयमेतत्परायणमेतस्मान्न पुनरावर्तन्त इत्येष निरोधस्तदेष श्लोकः॥१०॥

But they who seek the Soul (Ātman) by austerity, chastity, faith and knoweldge—they by the Northern course win the sun. That, verily, is the support of life-breaths. That is the immortal, the fearless. That is the final goal. From that they do not return—as they say (*iti*). That is the stopping [of rebirth]. As to that there is this verse (*śloka*) : —

[The devotees establish solidarity with the supreme soul by appropriating their energy through persuasion of the sun, the source of motivating energy, celibacy and obeisance etc. are to be exercised in this process.]

पञ्चपादं पितरं द्वादशाकृतिं दिव आहुः परे अर्धे पुरीषिणम्। अथेमे अन्य उ परे विचक्षणं सप्तचक्रे षळर आहुरर्पितमिति॥११॥

They speak of a father, five-footed, twelve-formed,

Rich in moisture, as in the higher half of heaven.

But others here speak of a sage in the lower half,

Set in a seven-wheeled, six-spoked [chariot].

मासो वै प्रजापतिस्तस्य कृष्णपक्ष एव रयिः शुक्लः प्राणस्तस्मादेतऽऋषयः शुक्ल इष्टिं कुर्वन्तीतर इतरस्मिन्॥१२॥

The month, verily, is the Lord of Creation (Prajāpati). Its dark half, indeed, is matter; its bright half, life. Therefore these seers (*ṛṣi*) perform sacrifice in the bright half; other people, in the other half.

[The light enhances in light fortnight. The desirous activity's motive in light fortnight is the activity of producing the energy. The motive for performance in dark fortnight is the activity of energy appropriation.]

अहोरात्रो वै प्रजापतिस्तस्याहरेव प्राणो रात्रिरेव रयिः प्राणं वा एते प्रस्कन्दन्ति। ये दिवा रत्या संयुज्यन्ते ब्रह्मचर्यमेव तद्यद्रात्रौ रत्या संयुज्यन्ते॥१३॥

Day and night, verily, are the Lord of Creation (Prajāpati). Of this, day indeed is life; the night, matter. Verily, they waste their life who join in sexual enjoyment by day; it is chastity that they join in sexual enjoyment by night.

अन्नं वै प्रजापतिस्ततो ह वै तद्रेतस्तस्मादिमाः प्रजाः प्रजायन्त इति॥१४॥

Food, verily, is the Lord of Creation (Prajāpati). From this, verily, is semen. From this creatures here are born. (Food is the direct source of creatures.)

तद्ये ह वै तत्प्रजापतिव्रतं चरन्ति ते मिथुनमुत्पादयन्ते। तेषामेवैष ब्रह्मलोको येषां तपो ब्रह्मचर्यं येषु सत्यं प्रतिष्ठितम्॥१५॥

Now, they who practise this rule of Prajāpati produce a pair.

They indeed possess that Brahma-world,

Who possess austerity (*tapas*) and chastity (*brahmacarya*),

In whom the truth is established.

तेषामसौ विरजो ब्रह्मलोको न येषु जिह्ममनृतं न माया चेति॥१६॥

To them belongs you stainless Brahma-world,

In whom there is no crookedness and falsehood, nor trickery (*māyā*).'

Second Praśna

Concerning the several personal powers and their chiefest

अथ हैनं भार्गवो वैदर्भिः पप्रच्छ। भगवन्कत्येव देवाः प्रजां विधारयन्ते? कतर एतत्प्रकाशयन्ते? कः पुनरेषां वरिष्ठः? इति॥१॥

Then the native of Vidarbha country Bhārgava asked Pippalāda -

'Sir, how many powers (*deva*) support a creature?

How many illumine this [body]?

Which one again is the chiefest of them?'

तस्मै स होवाचाकाशो ह वा एष देवो वायुरग्निरापः पृथिवी वाङ्मनश्चक्षुः श्रोत्रं च। ते प्रकाश्याभिवन्दन्ति वयमेतद्बाणमवष्टभ्य विधारयामः॥२॥

Pippalāda said to Bhārgava– 'Space (*ākāśa*), verily, is such a power (*devu*)—wind, fire, water, earth, speech, mind, sight, and hearing, too. These, having illumined it, declare : "We uphold and support this trunk (*bāṇa*)!"

तान्वरिष्ठः प्राण उवाच मा मोहमापद्यथा। अहमेवैतत्पञ्चधात्मानं प्रविभज्यैतद्बाणमवष्टभ्य विधारयामीति।।३।।

To them Life (*prāṇa*, the life-breath), the chiefest, said : "Fall not into delusion! I indeed, dividing myself (*ātmānam*) fivefold, support and sustain this body!"

तेऽश्रद्दधाना बभूवुः सोऽभिमानादूर्ध्वमुत्क्रमत इव तस्मिन्नुत्क्रामत्यथेतरे सर्व एवोत्क्रामन्ते तस्मिंश्च प्रतिष्ठमाने सर्व एव प्रातिष्ठन्ते तद्यथा मक्षिका मधुकरराजानमुत्क्रामन्तं सर्वा एवोत्क्रामन्ते एवमस्मिंश्च प्रतिष्ठमाने सर्वा एव प्रातिष्ठन्त एवं वाङ्मनश्चक्षुः श्रोत्रं च ते प्रीताः प्राणं स्तुन्वन्ति।।४।।

They were incredulous. He, from pride, as it were, rises up aloft. Now when he rises up, then all the others also rise up; and when he settles down, they all settle down with him.

Now, as all the bees rise up after the king been when he rises up, and all settle down when he settles down, even so speech, mind, sight and hearing. They, being satisfied, praise Life (*prāṇa*, the life-breath).

The Universal Life

एषोऽग्निस्तपत्येष सूर्य एष पर्जन्यो मघवानेष वायुः। एष पृथिवी रयिर्देवः सदसच्चामृतं च यत्।।५।।

As fire (Agni), he warms. He is the sun (Sūrya).

He is the bountiful rain (Parjanya). He is the wind (Vāyu).

He is the earth, matter (*rayi*), God (*deva*),

Being (*sat*) and Non-being (*asat*), and what is immortal.

अरा इव रथनाभौ प्राणे सर्वं प्रतिष्ठितम्। ऋचो यजूंषि सामानि यज्ञः क्षत्रं ब्रह्म च।।६।।

Like the spokes on the hub of a wheel, Everything is established on Life (*prāṇa*) :—

The Ṛg verses, the Yajus formulas, the Sāman chants,

The sacrifice, the nobility (*kṣatra*), and the priesthood (*brahman*)!

प्रजापतिश्चरसि गर्भे त्वमेव प्रतिजायसे। तुभ्यं प्राण! प्रजास्त्विमा बलिं हरन्ति यः प्राणैः प्रतितिष्ठसि।।७।।

As the Lord of Creation (Prajāpati), you move in the womb.

It is you yourself that are born again.

To you, O life, creatures here bring tribute—You, who dwell with living beings!

देवानामसि वह्नितमः पितॄणां प्रथमा स्वधा। ऋषीणां चरितं सत्यमथर्वाङ्गिरसामसि।।८।।

You are the chief bearer [of oblations] to the gods!

You are the first offering to the fathers!

You are the true practice of the seers, descendants of Atharvan and Aṅgiras.

इन्द्रस्त्वं प्राण! तेजसा रुद्रोऽसि परिरक्षिता। त्वमन्तरिक्षे चरसि सूर्यस्त्वं ज्योतिषां पतिः॥९॥

Indra are you, O Life, with your brilliance! Rudra are you as a protector!

You move in the atmosphere as the sun (Sūrya), you Lord of lights!

यदा त्वमभिवर्षस्यथेमाः प्राण ते प्रजाः। आनन्दरूपास्तिष्ठन्ति कामायान्नं भविष्यतीति॥१०॥

When you rain upon them, then these creatures of you, O Life,

Are blissful, thinking : "There will be food for all desire!"

व्रात्यस्त्वं प्राणैकर्षिरत्ता विश्वस्य सत्पतिः। वयमाद्यस्य दातारः पिता त्वं मातरिश्व नः॥११॥

A Vrātya are you, O Life, the only seer, an eater, the real lord of all!

We are the givers of your food! You are the father of the wind (Mātariśvan).

या ते तनूर्वाचि प्रतिष्ठिता या श्रोत्रे या च चक्षुषि। या च मनसि संतता शिवां तां कुरु मोत्क्रमीः॥१२॥

That form of you which abides in speech, which abides in hearing, which abides in sight, and which is extended in the mind, make propitious! Go not away!

प्राणस्येदं वशे सर्वं त्रिदिवे यत्प्रतिष्ठितम्। मातेव पुत्रान् रक्षत्व श्रीश्च प्रज्ञां च विधेहि न इति॥१३॥

This whole world is in the control of Life, even what is established in the third heaven!

As a mother her son, do you protect [us]! Grant to us prosperity (*śrī*) and wisdom (*prajñā*)!'

[The earth is called the first, the space the second and the heaven or tridiva as the third.]

Third Praśna

Six questions concerning a peron's life

अथ हैनं कौसल्यश्चाश्वलायनः पप्रच्छ। भगवन्कुत एष प्राणो जायते? कथमायात्यस्मिञ्छरीरे? आत्मानं वा प्रविभज्य कथं प्रातिष्ठते? केनोत्क्रमते? कथं बाह्यमभिधत्ते? कथमध्यात्ममिति॥१॥

Then Kausalya Āśvalāyana asked the sage Pippalāda -

[i] 'Whence, sir, is this life (*prāṇa*) born?

[ii] How does it come into this body?

[iii] And how does it distribute itself (*ātmānam*), and establish itself?

[iv] Through what does it depart?

[v] How does it relate itself to the external?

[vi] How with reference to the self?'

तस्मै स होवाचातिप्रश्नान्पृच्छसि ब्रह्मिष्ठोऽसीति तस्मात्तेऽहं ब्रवीमि॥२॥

The sage Pippalāda said him– 'You are asking questions excessively. But you are pre-eminently a Brahman— methinks (*iti*). Therefore I tell you.

[Generally, it is difficult to feel the element of Prāṇa. Its origin and appropriation is more difficult but only curious may understand it and the Ṛṣi therefore, make clear that subject.]

आत्मन एष प्राणो जायते। यथैषा पुरुषे छायैतस्मिन्नेतदाततं मनोकृतेनायात्यस्मिञ्छरीरे।।३।।

[i] The source of a person's life

This life (*prāṇa*) is born from the Spirit (Ātman, Self).

[ii] Its embodiment

As in the case of a person there is this shadow extended, so it is in this case. By the action of the mind [in one's previous existence] it comes into this body.

यथा सम्राडेवाधिकृतान्विनियुङ्क्ते एतान्ग्रामानेतान्ग्रामानधितिष्ठस्वेत्येवमेवैष प्राण इतरान्प्राणान्पृथक्पृथगेव संनिधत्ते।।४।।

[iii] Its establisment and distribution in the body as an overlord commands his overseers, saying : "Superintend such and such villages," even so this life (*prāṇa*) controls the other life-breaths one by one.

पायूपस्थेऽपानं चक्षुःश्रोत्रे मुखनासिकाभ्यां प्राणः स्वयं प्रातिष्ठते मध्ये तु समानः। एष ह्येतद्धुतमन्नं समं नयति तस्मादेताः सप्तार्चिषो भवन्ति।।५।।

The out-breath (*apāna*) is in the organs of excretion and generation. The life-breath (*prāṇa*) as such (*svayam*) establishes itself in the eye and ear together with the mouth and nose. While in the middle is the equalizing breath (*samāna*), for it is this [breath] that equalizes [in distribution] whatever has been offered as food. From this arise the seven flames.

हृदि ह्येष आत्मा। अत्रैतदेकशतं नाडीनां तासां शतं शतमेकैकस्या द्वासप्ततिर्द्वासप्ततिः प्रतिशाखानाडीसहस्राणि भवन्त्यासु व्यानश्चरति।।६।।

In the hearth, truly, is the self (*ātman*). Here there are those hundred and one channels. To each one of these belong a hundred smaller channels. To each of these belong seventy-two thousand branching channels (*kitā*). Within them moves the diffused breath (*vyāna*).

अथैकयोर्ध्व उदानः पुण्येन पुण्यं लोकं नयति पापेन पापमुभाभ्यामेव मनुष्यलोकम्।।७।।

[iv] Its departure

Now, rising upward through one of these [channels], the up-breath (*udāna*) leads in consequence of good [work] (*puṇya*) to the good world; in consequence of evil (*pāpa*), to the evil world; in consequence of both, to the world of men.

आदित्यो ह वै बाह्यः प्राण उदयत्येष ह्येनं चाक्षुषं प्राणमनुगृह्णानः। पृथिव्यां या देवता सैषा पुरुषस्यापानमवष्टभ्यान्तरा यदाकाशः स समानो वायुर्व्यानः।।८।।

[v and vi] Its cosmic and personal relations :

The sun, verily, rises externally as life; for it is that which helps the life-breath in the eye. The divinity which is in the earth supports a person's out-breath (*apāna*). What is between [the sun and the earth], namely space (*ākāśa*), is the equalizing breath (*samāna*). The wind (Vāyu) is the diffused breath (*vyāna*).

तेजो ह वा उदानस्तस्मादुपशान्ततेजाः। पुनर्भवमिन्द्रियैर्मनसि संपद्यमानैः॥९॥

Heat (*tejas*), verily, is the up-breath (*udāna*). Therefore one whose heat has ceased goes to rebirth, with his senses (*indriya*) sunk in mind (*manas*).

यच्चित्तस्तेनैष प्राणमायाति प्राणस्तेजसा युक्तः। सहात्मना यथासंकल्पितं लोकं नयति॥१०॥

Whatever is one's thinking (*citta*), therewith he enters into life (*prāṇa*). His life joined with his heat, together with the self (*ātman*), leads to whatever, world has been fashioned [in thought].

य एवं विद्वान्प्राणं वेद न हास्य प्रजा हीयतेऽमृतो भवति तदेष श्लोकः॥११॥

The knower who knows life (*prāṇa*) thus—his offspring truly is not lost; he becomes immortal. As to this there is this verse (*śloka*) :—

उत्पत्तिमायतिं स्थानं विभुत्वं चैव पञ्चधा। अध्यात्मं चैव प्राणस्य विज्ञायामृतमश्नुते विज्ञायामृतमश्नुत इति॥१२॥

The source, the entrance, the location,
The fivefold extension,
And the relation to self (*adhyātma*) of the life (*prāṇa*)—
By knowing these one attains immortality! By knowing these one attains immortality!

Fourth Praśna

Concerning sleep and the ultimate basis of things

अथ हैनं सौर्यायणी गार्ग्यः पप्रच्छ। भगवन्नेतस्मिन्पुरुषे कानि स्वपन्ति? कान्यस्मिन् जाग्रति? कतर एष देवः स्वप्नान्पश्यति? कस्यैतत्सुखं भवति? कस्मिन्नु सर्वे संप्रतिष्ठिता भवन्तीति॥१॥

Then Gārgya, the grandson of sun raised a question before the sage Pippalāda -

[i] 'Sir, what are they that sleep in a person here?

[ii] What are they that remain awake in him?

[iii] Which is the god (*deva*) that sees the dreams?

[iv] Whose is the happiness?

[v] In whom, pray, are all things established?

तस्मै स होवाच। यथा गार्ग्य। मरीचयोऽर्कस्यास्तं गच्छतः सर्वा एतस्मिंस्तेजोमण्डल एकीभवन्ति। ताः पुनःपुनरुदयतः ह वै तत्सर्वं परे देवे मनस्येकीभवति। तेन तर्ह्येष पुरुषो न श्रृणोति न पश्यति न जिघ्रति न रसयते न स्पृशते नाभिवदते नादत्ते नानन्दयते न विसृजते नेयायते स्वपितीत्याचक्षते॥२॥

[i] All sense-functions unified in the mind during sleep

To him then he said : 'O Gārgya, as the rays of the setting sun all become one in an orb of brilliance and go forth, again and again when it rises, even so, verily, everything here becomes one in mind (*manas*), the highest god.'

Therefore in that condition (*tarhi*) the person hears not, sees not, smells not, tastes not, touches not, speaks not, takes not, enjoys not, emits not, moves not about. "He sleeps!" they say.

प्राणाग्नय एवैतस्मिन्पुरे जाग्रति गार्हपत्यो ह वा एषोऽ पानो व्यानोऽ न्वाहार्यपचनो यद्गार्हपत्यात्प्रणीयते प्रणयनादाहवनीय: प्राण:।।३।।

[ii] The five life-functions, like sacrificial fires, slumber not

Life's fires, in truth, remain awake in this city.

The out-breath (*apāna*) is the Gārhapatya (Householder's) fire. The diffused breath (*vyāna*) is the Anvāhāryapacana (Southern Sacrificial) fire. The in-breath (*prāṇa*) is the Āhavanīya (Oblation) fire, from "being taken" (*praṇayana*), since it is taken (*praṇīyate*) from the Gārhapatya fire.

[Herein is expressing the process of offering in garb of the life that perpetuates in body.]

यदुच्छ्वासनि: श्वासावेतावाहुती समं नयतीति स समान:। मनो ह वाव यजमान इष्टफलमेवेदान: स एनं यजमानमहरहर्ब्रह्म गमयति।।४।।

The equalizing breath (*samāna*) is so called because it "equalizes" (*samaṁ nayati*) the two oblations : the in-breathing and the out-breathing (*ucchvāsa-niḥśvāsa*). The mind, verily, indeed, is the sacrificer. The fruit of the sacrifice is the up-breath (*udāna*). It leads the sacrificer to Brahma day by day.

अत्रैष देव: स्वप्ने महिमानमनुभवति यद्दृष्टं दृष्टमनुपश्यति श्रुतं श्रुतमेवार्थमनुशृणोति देशदिगन्तरैश्च प्रत्यनुभूतं पुन: पुन: प्रत्यनुभवति दृष्टं चादृष्टं च श्रुतं चानुभूतं चाननुभूतं च सच्चासच्च सर्वं पश्यति सर्व: पश्यति।।५।।

[iii] The universal mind, the beholder of dreams

There, in sleep, that god experiences greatness. Whatever object has been seen, he sees again; whatever has been heard, he hears again. That which has been severally experienced in different places and regions, he severally experiences again and again. Both what has been seen and what has not been seen, both what has been heard and what has not been heard, both what has been experienced and what has not been experienced, both the real (*sat*) and the unreal (*a-sat*)— he sees all. He sees it, himself being all.

स यदा तेजसाभिभूतो भवत्यत्रैष देव: स्वप्नान्न पश्यत्यथ तदैतस्मिञ्छरीरे एतत्सुखं भवति।।६।।

[iv] The brilliant happiness of dreamless sleep, in the mind's non-action

When he is overcome with brilliance (*tejas*), then that god sees no dreams; then here in this body arises this happiness (*sukha*).

स यथा सोम्य! वयांसि वासोवृक्षं संप्रतिष्ठन्ते एवं ह वै तत्सर्वं पर आत्मनि संप्रतिष्ठते॥७॥

[v] The supreme Soul the ultimate basis of the manifold world and of the individual

As birds resort to a tree for a resting-place, even so, O friend, it is to the supreme Soul (Ātman) that everything here resorts :—

पृथिवी च पृथिवीमात्रा चापश्चापोमात्रा च तेजश्च तेजोमात्रा च वायुश्च वायुमात्रा चाकाशश्चाकाशमात्रा च चक्षुश्च द्रष्टव्यं च श्रोत्रं च श्रोतव्यं च घ्राणं च घ्रातव्यं च रसश्च रसयितव्यं च त्वक् च स्पर्शयितव्यं च वाक् च वक्तव्यं च हस्तौ चादातव्यं चोपस्थश्चानन्दयितव्यं च पायुश्च विसर्जयितव्यं च पादौ च गन्तव्यं च मनश्च च बुद्धिश्च बोद्धव्यं चाहङ्कारश्चाहङ्कर्तव्यं च चित्तं च चेतयितव्यं विद्योतयितव्यं च प्राणश्च विधारयितव्यं च॥८॥

Earth and the elements (*mātra*) of earth, water and the elements of water, heat (*tejas*) and the elements of heat, wind and the elements of wind, space and the elements of space, sight and what can be seen, hearing and what can be heard, smell and what can be smelled, taste and what can be tasted, the skin and what can be touched, speech and what can be spoken, the hand and what can be taken, the organ of generation and what can be enjoyed, the anus and what can be excreted, the feet and what can be walked, mind (*manas*) and what can be perceived, intellect (*buddhi*) and what can be conceived, egoism (*ahaṁkāra*) and what can be connected with "me", thought (*citta*) and what can be thought, brilliance (*tejas*) and what can be illumined, life-breath (*prāṇa*) and what can be supported.

एष हि द्रष्टा स्प्रष्टा श्रोता घ्राता रसयिता मन्ता बोद्धाकर्ता विज्ञानात्मा पुरुषः स परेऽक्षर आत्मनि संप्रतिष्ठते॥९॥

Truly, this seer, toucher, hearer, smeller, taster, thinker (*mantṛ*), conceiver (*boddhṛ*), doer, the conscious self (*vijñānātman*), the person— his resort is in the supreme imperishable Soul (Ātman, Self).

परमेवाक्षरं प्रतिपद्यते स यो ह वै तदच्छयमशरीरमलोहितं शुभ्रमक्षरं वेदयते यस्तु सोम्य! स सर्वज्ञः सर्वो भवति॥ तदेष श्लोकः॥१०॥

Verily, O friend! He who recognizes that shadowless, bodiless, bloodless, pure Imperishable, arrives at the Imperishable itself.

He, knowing all, becomes the All. On this there is the verse (*śloka*) :—

विज्ञानात्मा सह देवैश्च सर्वैः प्राणा भूतानि संप्रतिष्ठन्ति यत्र। तदक्षरं वेदयते यस्तु सोम्य! स सर्वज्ञः सर्वमेवाविवेशेति॥११॥

O friend! He who recognizes as the Imperishable

That whereon the conscious self, with all its powers (*deva*),

And the life-breaths (*prāṇa*) and the elements (*bhūta*) do rest—

He, knowing all, into the All has entered.

Fifth Praśna

Concerning the value of meditation on 'Oṁ'

अथ हैनं शैब्यः सत्यकामः पप्रच्छ। स यो ह वै तद्भगवन्मनुष्येषु प्रायणान्तमोङ्कारमभिध्यायीत। कतमं वाव स तेन लोकं जयतीति॥१॥

Later on Satyakāma, son of Śibi asked Pippalāda– 'Verily, sir, if some one among men here should meditate on the syllable *Oṁ* until the end of his life, which world, verily, does he win thereby?

तस्मै स होवाच। एतद्वै सत्यकाम। परं चापरं च ब्रह्म यदोंकारस्तस्माद्विद्वानेतेनैवायतनेनैकतरमन्वेति॥२॥

Then Pippalāda said to him– 'Verily, O Satyakāma, that which is the syllable *Oṁ* is both the higher and the lower Brahma. Therefore with this support, in truth, a knower reaches one or the other.

स यद्येकमात्रमभिध्यायीत स तेनैव संवेदितस्तूर्णमेव जगत्यामभिसंपद्यत। तमृचो मनुष्यलोकमुपनयन्ते स तत्र तपसा ब्रह्मचर्येण श्रद्धया संपन्नो महिमानमनुभवति॥३॥

If he meditates on one element [namely *a*], having been instructed by that alone he quickly comes into the earth [after death]. The Ṛg verses lead him to the world of men. There, united with austerity, chastity and faith, he experiences greatness.

अथ यदि द्विमात्रेण मनसि संपद्यते सोऽन्तरिक्षं यजुर्भिरुन्नीये सोमलोकं स सोमलोके विभूतिमनुभूय पुनरावर्तते॥४॥

Now, if he is united in mind with two elements [namely *a* + *u*], he is led by the Yajus formulas to the intermediate space, to the world of the moon. Having experienced greatness in the world of the moon, he returns hither again.

यः पुनरेतन्त्रिमात्रेणोमित्येतेनैवाक्षरेण परं पुरुषमभिध्यायीत स तेजसि सूर्ये संपन्नः। यथा पादोदरस्त्वचा विनिर्मुच्यत एवं ह वै स पाप्मना विनिर्मुक्तः स सामभिरुन्नीयते ब्रह्मलोकं स एतस्माज्जीवघनात्परात्परं पुरिशयं पुरुषमीक्षते तदेतौ श्लोकौ भवतः॥५॥

Again, he who meditates on the highest Person (Puruṣa) with the three elements of the syllable *Oṁ* [namely *a* + *u* +*m*] is united with brilliance (*tejas*) in the sun. As a snake is freed from its skin, even so, verily, is he freed from sin (*pāpman*). He is led by the Sāman chants to the world of Brahma. He beholds the Person that dwells in the body and that is higher than the highest living complex. As to this there are these two verses (*śloka*) :-

तिस्रो मात्रा मृत्युमत्यः प्रयुक्ता अन्योन्यसक्ता अनविप्रयुक्ताः।

क्रियासु बाह्याभ्यन्तरमध्यमासु सम्यक्प्रयुक्तासु न कम्पते ज्ञः॥६॥

The three elements are deadly when employed (mutually intertwined and comprising the death) ; One after the other, separately.

In actions external, internal, or intermediate when they are properly employed, the knower trembles not.

ऋग्भिरेतं यजुर्भिरन्तरिक्षं सामभिर्यत्तत्कवयो वेदयन्ते।

तमोंकारेणैवायतनेनान्वेति विद्वान्यत्तच्छान्तमजरममृतमभयं परं चेति॥७॥

With the Ṛg verses, to this world; with the Sāman chants, to the intermediate space;

With the Yajus formulas, to that which sages (*kavi*) recognize;

With the syllable *Oṁ* in truth as a support, the knower reaches That

Which is peaceful, unaging, immortal, fearless and supreme!'

Sixth Praśna

Concerning the Person with sixteen parts

अथ हैनं सुकेशा भारद्वाजः पप्रच्छ। भगवन्हिरण्यनाभः कौसल्यो राजपुत्रो मामुपेत्यैतं प्रश्नमपृच्छत। षोडशकलं भारद्वाज! पुरुषं वेत्थ? तमहं कुमारमब्रुवं नाहमिमं वेद यद्यहमिममवेदिषं कथं ते नावक्ष्यमिति। समूलो वा एष परिशुष्यति योऽ नृतमभिवदति तस्मान्नार्हाम्यनृतं वक्तुम्। स तूष्णीं रथमारुह्य प्रवव्राज। तं त्वा पृच्छामि क्वासौ पुरुषः? इति॥१॥

Then Sukeśan Bhāradvāja asked him [i.e. Pippalāda] : 'Sir, Hiraṇyanābha, a prince of the Kośalas, came to me and asked this question : "Bhāradvāja, do you know the Person with the sixteen parts?" I said to the youth : "I know him not. If I had known him, would I not have told you? Verily, he dries up even to the roots, who speaks untruth. Therefore it is not proper that I should speak untruth." In silence he mounted his chariot and departed. I ask it of you : "Where is that Person?"

तस्मै स होवाच। इहैवान्तः शरीरे सोम्य स पुरुषो यस्मिन्नेताः षोडशकलाः प्रभवन्तीति॥२॥

To him he then said : 'Even here within the body, O friend, is that Person in whom they say the sixteen parts arise.

स ईक्षांचक्रे। कस्मिन्नहमुत्क्रान्त उत्क्रान्त भविष्यामि कस्मिन्वा प्रतिष्ठिते प्रतिष्ठास्यामीति॥३॥

He [i.e. the Person] thought to himself : "In whose departure shall I be departing? In whose resting firm, verily, shall I be resting firm?"

स प्राणमसृजत प्राणाच्छ्रद्धां खं वायुर्ज्योतिरापः पृथिवीन्द्रियं मनोऽन्नमन्नाद्वीर्यं तपो मंत्राः कर्मलोका लोकेषु च नाम च॥४॥

He created life (*prāṇa*); from life, faith (*śraddhā*), space (*kha*), wind light, water earth, sense-faculty (*indriya*), mind, food; from food, virility, austerity, sacred sayings (*mantra*), sacrifice, the worlds; and in the worlds, name [i.e. the individual].

स यथेमा नद्यः स्यन्दमानाः समुद्रायणाः समुद्रं प्राप्यास्तं गच्छन्ति भिद्येते तासां नामरूपे समुद्र इत्येव प्रोच्यते। एवमेवास्य परिद्रष्टुरिमाः षोडशकलाः पुरुषायणाः पुरुषं प्राप्यास्तं गच्छन्ति भिद्येते चासां नामरूपे

पुरुष इत्येवं प्रोच्यते स एषोऽकलोऽमृतो भवति। तदेष श्लोकः॥५॥

As these flowing rivers that tend towards the ocean, on reaching the ocean, disappear, their name and form (*nāma-rūpa*) are destroyed, and it is called simply "the ocean"—even so of this spectator these sixteen parts that tend toward the Person, on reaching the Person, disappear, their name and form are destroyed, and it is called simply "the Person". That one continued without parts, immortal! As to that there is this verse :—

अरा इव रथनाभौ कला यस्मिन्प्रतिष्ठिताः। तं वेद्यं पुरुषं वेद यथा मा वो मृत्युः परिव्यथा इति॥६॥

Whereon the parts rest firm; Like the spokes on the hub of a wheel—

Him I know as the Person to the known! So let death disturb you not!'

तान्होवाचैतावदेवाहमेतत्परं ब्रह्मं वेद नातः परमस्तीति॥७॥

Pippalāda said to them– 'Thus far, in truth, I know that supreme Brahman. There is naught higher than It.'

ते तमर्चयन्तस्त्वं हि नः पिता योऽस्माकमविद्यायाः परं पारं तारयसीति। नमः परमऋषिभ्यो नमः परमऋषिभ्यः॥८॥

They praised him and said : 'You truly are our father— you who lead us across to the shore beyond ignorance.'

॥शान्तिपाठः॥

ॐ भद्रं कर्णेभिः श्रृणुयाम.....॥

स्वस्ति इन्द्रो वृद्धश्रवा...... इति शान्ति॥

॥ इति प्रश्नोपनिषत्समाप्ता॥

***

5. MUṆḌAKOPANIṢAD

मुण्डकोपनिषद्

This Upaniṣad is related with Śaunkīya branch of the Atharvaveda. There are three Muṇḍaka's in it and every Muṇḍaka contains two parts. The connotation of the term 'Muṇḍaka' is the knowledge that rectifies the mind conceiving of thoughts thereby releasing from ignorance. The Ṛṣi Aṅgirā has made Śaunaka to understand the Parā and Aparā learning (vidyā). In the first part of the first Muṇḍaka, the parā and aparā learning has been described as the colloquy of Ṛṣi just after the tradition of the Brahmavidyā. Herein the realisation of Brahman through Parāvidyā and the origin of world by the supreme god has been described. In the second part the Aparā vidyā, the offering and its fruits, detachment from the luxuries and the teacher loyal to the Brahma and the eligible disciple has been told as sine-qua-non for conjointly for the realisation of knowledge. In second Muṇḍaka, the origin of world through the knowledge in garb of the splinter of the fire and its drowning has been described. The significance of the feature of Brahma and the attainment of Brahma has been described as the bow in garb of Oṁkāra and an arrow of the soul can hit the target of the supreme soul. In the third Muṇḍaka, realisation of knowledge by the purification of heart and the position of expert in knowledge or realisation as also significance has been described by giving example that the body in garb of tree and two birds in garb of the supreme soul.

।। शान्तिपाठः।।

ॐ भद्रं कर्णेभिः शृणुयाम देवा भद्रं पश्येमाक्षभिर्यजत्राः।
स्थिरैरङ्गैस्तुष्टुवाꣳसस्तनूभिर्व्यशेम देवहितं यदायुः।।
स्वस्ति न इन्द्रो वृद्धश्रवाः स्वस्ति नः पूषा विश्ववेदाः। स्वस्ति नस्तार्क्ष्यो अरिष्टनेमिः स्वस्ति नो
बृहस्पतिर्दधातु ।। ॐ शान्तिः शान्तिः शान्तिः।।

First Muṇḍaka

Preparation for the knowledge of Brahman

Part - 1

The line of tradition of this knowledge from Brahmā himself

ॐ ब्रह्मा देवानां प्रथमः संबभूव विश्वस्य कर्ता भुवनस्य गोप्ता।
स ब्रह्मविद्यां सर्वविद्याप्रतिष्ठामथर्वाय ज्येष्ठपुत्राय प्राह।।१।।

Brahmā arose as the first of the gods—The maker of all, the protector of the world.

He told the knowledge of Brahma (*brahma-vidyā*), the foundation of all knowledge, to Atharva[n], his eldest son.

अथर्वणे यां प्रवदेत ब्रह्माथर्वा तां पुरोवाचाङ्गिरे ब्रह्मविद्याम्।

स भारद्वाजाय सत्यवाहाय प्राह भारद्वाजोऽङ्गिरसे परावराम्।।२।।

What Brahmā taught to Atharvan, even that knowledge of Brahman, Atharvan told in ancient time to Aṅgira.

He told it to Bhāradvāja Satyavāha; Bhāradvāja to Aṅgiras—both the higher and the lower [knowledge].

शौनको ह वै महाशालोऽङ्गिरसं विधिवदुपसन्नः पप्रच्छ।

कस्मिन्नु भगवो विज्ञाते सर्वमिदं विज्ञातं भवतीति।।३।।

Śaunaka, verily, indeed, a great householder, approached Aṅgiras according to rule, and asked : 'Through understanding of what, pray, does all this world become understood, sir?'

[This is Śaunaka's quest for the clue to an understanding of the world]

तस्मै स होवाच। द्वे विद्ये वेदितव्ये इति ह स्म यद्ब्रह्मविदो वदन्ति पर चैवापरा च।।४।।

[Two kinds of knowledge ! the traditions of religion and the knoweldge of the eternal]

To him then he said ! 'There are two knowledges to be known—as indeed the knowers of Brahma are wont to say : a higher (*para*) and also a lower (*apara*).

तत्रापरा ऋग्वेदो यजुर्वेदः सामवेदोऽथर्ववेदः शिक्षा कल्पो व्याकरणं निरुक्तं छन्दो ज्योतिषमिति। अथ परा यया तदक्षरमधिगम्यते।।५।।

Of these, the lower is the Ṛgveda, the Yajurveda, the Sāmaveda, the Atharvaveda,

Pronunciation (*śikṣā*), Ritual (*kalpa*), Grammar (*vyākaraṇa*), Definition (*nirukta*), Metrics (*chandas*), and Astrology (*jyotiṣa*).

Now, the higher is that whereby that Imperishable (*akṣara*) is apprehended.

यत्तदद्रेश्यमग्राह्यमगोत्रमवर्णमचक्षुःश्रोत्रं तदपाणिपादं नित्यं विभुं सर्वगतं सुसूक्ष्मं तदव्ययं यद्भूतयोनिं परिपश्यन्ति धीराः।।६।।

That which is invisible, ungraspable, without family, without caste (*a-varṇa*)—

Without sight or hearing is It, without hand or foot,

Eternal, all-pervading, omnipresent, exceedingly subtile;

That is the imperishable, which the wise perceive as the source of beings.

यथोर्णनाभिः सृजते गृह्णते च यथा पृथिव्यामोषधयः संभवन्ति।

यथा सतः पुरुषात्केशलोमानि तथाक्षरात्संभवतीह विश्वम्।।७।।

As a spider emits and draws in [its thread],

As herbs arise on the earth,

As the hairs of the head and body from a living person,

So from the Imperishable arises everything here.

तपसा चीयते ब्रह्म ततोऽन्नमभिजायते।

अन्नात्प्राणो मनः सत्यं लोकाः कर्मसु चामृतम्॥८॥

By austerity (*tapas*) Brahma becomes built up.

From that, food is produced; From food— life-breath, mind, truth, the worlds, immortality too in works.

यः सर्वज्ञः सर्वविद्यस्य ज्ञानमयं तपः। तस्मादेतद्ब्रह्म नाम रूपमन्नं च जायते॥९॥

He who is all-knowing, all-wise, Whose austerity consists of knowledge—

From Him are produced the Brahma here, [Namely] name and form, and food.

[The perfect knowledge has nobody. The penance made through it therefore, cannot be understood on the basis of material trends in vogue. Whatever motion he does in the position of ceaseless peace and inaccessible stage by virtue of resolution is his penance.]

Part - 2

All the ceremonies of religion scrupulously to be practised

तदेतत्सत्यं मन्त्रेषु कर्माणि कवयो यान्यपश्यंस्तानि त्रेतायां बहुधा संततानि। तान्याचरथ नियतं सत्यकामा एष वः पन्थाः सुकृतस्य लोके॥१॥

This is the truth :— The works which the sages (*kavi*) saw in the sacred sayings (*mantra*, i.e. Vedic hymns).

Are manifoldly spread forth in the triad [of the Vedas].

Follow them (*ācaratha*) constantly, ye lovers of truth (*satyakāma*)!

This is your path to the world of good deeds.

यदा लेलायते ह्यर्चिः समिद्धे हव्यवाहने।

तदाज्यभागावन्तरेणाहुतीः प्रतिपादयेच्छ्रद्धया हुतम्॥२॥

When the flame flickers, after the oblation fire has been kindled,

Then, between the two portions of melted butter, his oblations

One should throw—an offering made with faith (*śraddhā*).

यस्याग्निहोत्रमदर्शमपौर्णमासमचातुर्मास्यमनाग्रयणमतिथिवर्जितं च।

अहुतमवैश्वदेवमविधिना हुतमासप्तमांस्तस्य लोकान्हिनस्ति॥३॥

If one's Agnihotra sacrifice is not followed by the sacrifice of the new moon and of the full moon, by the four-months sacrifice, by the harvest sacrifice, if it is unattended by guests, or not offered at all, or without the ceremony to all the gods, or not according to rule, it destroys his seven worlds.

काली कराली च मनोजवा च सुलोहिता या च सुधूम्रवर्णा।

स्फुलिङ्गिनी विश्वरुची च देवी लेलायमाना इति सप्त जिह्वाः॥४॥

The Black (*kālī*), and the Terrible, and the Swift-as-Thought, The Very-red, and the Very-smoky-coloured,

The Scintillating, and the All-formed, divine one,

Are the seven so-called flickering tongues [of flame].

एतेषु यश्चरते भ्राजमानेषु यथाकालं चाहुतयो ह्याददायन्।

तन्नयन्त्येताः सूर्यस्य रश्मयो यत्र देवानां पतिरेकोऽधिवासः॥५॥

If one performs sacrifices when these are shining,

Offering the oblations at the proper time, too,

These (flames) as rays of the sun lead him

To where is resident the one lord (*pati*) of the gods.

एह्येहीति तमाहुतयः सुवर्चसः सूर्यस्य रश्मिभिर्यजमानं वहन्ति।

प्रियां वाचमभिवदन्त्योऽर्चयन्त्य एष वः पुण्यः सुकृतो ब्रह्मलोकः॥६॥

Saying to him "Come! Come!" the splendid offerings

Carry the sacrificer with the rays of the sun,

Addressing pleasant speech, praising, and saying :

"This is your meritorious (*puṇya*) Brahma-world, gained by good works."

प्लवा ह्येते अदृढा यज्ञरूपा अष्टादशोक्तमवरं येषु कर्म।

एतच्छ्रेयो येऽभिनन्दन्ति मूढा जरामृत्युं ते पुनरेवापि यन्ति॥७॥

Unsafe boats, however, are these sacrificial forms,

The eighteen, (16 Ṛtvija, Yajamāna and wife of Yajamāna) in which is expressed the lower work.

The fools who approve that as the better,

Go again to old age and death. (It means the sacrificial forms are ineffective against rebirth).

अविद्यायामन्तरे वर्तमानाः स्वयं धीराः पण्डितम्मन्यमानाः।

जङ्घन्यमानाः परियन्ति मूढा अन्धेनैव नीयमाना यथान्धाः॥८॥

Those abiding in the midst of ignorance,

Self-wise, thinking themselves learned,

Hard smitten, go around deluded,

Like blind men led by one who is himself blind.

अविद्यायां बहुधा वर्तमाना वयं कृतार्था इत्यभिमन्यन्ति बालाः।
यत्कर्मिणो न प्रवेदयन्ति रागात्तेनातुराः क्षीणलोकाश्च्यवन्ते॥ ९॥

Manifoldly living in ignorance, they think to themselves, childishly : "We have accomplished our aim!"

Since doers of deeds (*karmin*) do not understand, because of passion (*rāga*),

Therefore, when their worlds are exhausted, they sink down wretched.

इष्टापूर्तं मन्यमाना वरिष्ठं नान्यच्छ्रेयो वेदयन्ते प्रमूढाः।
नाकस्य पृष्ठे ते सुकृतेऽनुभूत्वेमं लोकं हीनतरं वा विशन्ति॥ १०॥

Thinking sacrifice and merit is the chiefest thing,

Naught better do they know—deluded!

Having had enjoyment on the top of the heaven won by good works,

They re-enter this world, or a lower.

तपः श्रद्धे ये ह्युपवसन्त्यरण्ये शान्ता विद्वांसो भैक्षचर्यां चरन्तः।
सूर्यद्वारेण ते विरजाः प्रयान्ति यत्रामृतः स पुरुषो ह्यव्ययात्मा॥ ११॥

They who practise austerity (*tapas*) and faith (*śraddhā*) in the forest.

The peaceful (*śānta*) knowers who live on alms,

Depart passionless (*virajā*) through the door of the sun,

To where is that immortal Person (Puruṣa), even the imperishable Spirit (Ātman).

परीक्ष्य लोकान्कर्मचितान्ब्राह्मणो निर्वेदमायान्नास्त्यकृतः कृतेन।
तद्विज्ञानार्थं स गुरुमेवाभिगच्छेत्समित्पाणिः श्रोत्रियं ब्रह्मनिष्ठम्॥ १२॥

[This knowledge of Brahman to be sought properly from a qualified teacher]

Having scrutinized the worlds that are built up by work, a Brahman

Should arrive at indifference. The [word] that was not made is not [won] by what is done.

For the sake of this knowledge let him go, fuel in hand,

To a spiritual teacher (*guru*) who is learned in the scriptures and established on Brahman.

तस्मै स विद्वानुपसन्नाय सम्यक् प्रशान्तचित्ताय शमान्विताय।
येनाक्षरं पुरुषं वेद सत्यं प्रोवाच तां तत्त्वतो ब्रह्मविद्याम्॥ १३॥

Such a knowing [teacher] unto one who has approached properly,

Whose thought is tranquilized, who has reached peace,

Teaches in its very truth that knowledge of Brahma

Whereby one knows the Imperishable, the Person, the True.

Second Muṇḍaka

The Doctrine of Brahma-Ātman

Part - 1

The Imperishable, the source and the goal of all beings

तदेतत्सत्यं यथा सुदीप्तात्पावकाद्विस्फुलिङ्गाः सहस्रशः प्रभवन्ते सरूपाः तथाक्षराद्विविधाः सोम्य भावाः प्रजायन्ते तत्र चैवापि यन्ति॥ १॥

This is the truth :—

As, from a well-blazing fire, sparks by the thousand issue forth of like form, so from the Imperishable, my friend, beings manifold are produced, and thither also go.

दिव्यो ह्यमूर्तः पुरुषः सबाह्याभ्यन्तरो ह्यजः। अप्राणो ह्यमनाः शुभ्रो ह्यक्षरात्परतः परः॥ २॥

Heavenly (*divya*), formless (*a-mūrtta*) is the Person (Puruṣa).

He is without and within, unborn, breathless (*a-prāṇa*), mindless (*a-manas*), pure (*śubhra*), higher than the high Imperishable.

एतस्माज्जायते प्राणो मनः सर्वेन्द्रियाणि च। खं वायुर्ज्योतिरापः पृथिवी विश्वस्य धारिणी॥ ३॥

From Him is produced breath (*prāṇa*), mind (*manas*), and all the senses (*indriya*), space (*kha*), wind, light, water and earth, the supporter of all.

[Prāṇa, mind and all sensory organs arise from this eternal Brahman. This is the source of the human person and of the cosmic elements.]

अग्निर्मूर्धा चक्षुषी चन्द्रसूर्यौ दिशः श्रोत्रे वाग्विवृताश्च वेदाः।

वायुः प्राणो हृदयं विश्वमस्य पद्भ्यां पृथिवी ह्येष सर्वभूतान्तरात्मा॥ ४॥

The macrocosmic Person–

Fire is His head; His eyes, the moon and sun;

The regions of space, His voice, the revealed Vedas;

Wind, His breath (*prāṇa*), His heart, the whole world. Out of His feet,

The earth. Truly, He is the Inner Soul (Ātman) of all.

तस्मादग्निः समिधो यस्य सूर्यः सोमात्पर्जन्य ओषधयः पृथिव्याम्।

पुमान् रेतः सिञ्चति योषितायां बह्वीः प्रजाः पुरुषात्संप्रसूताः॥ ५॥

From Him [proceeds] fire, whose fuel is the sun; From the moon (Soma), rain; herbs, on the earth.

The male pours seed in the female. Many creatures are produced from the Person (Puruṣa).

तस्मादृचः साम यजूꣳषि दीक्षा यज्ञाश्च सर्वे क्रतवो दक्षिणाश्च।

संवत्सरश्च यजमानश्च लोकाः सोमो यत्र पवते यत्र सूर्यः॥ ६॥

From him the Ṛg verses, the Sāman Chant, the sacrificial formulas (*yajus*), the initiation rite (*dīkṣā*).

And all the sacrifices, ceremonies and sacrificial gifts (*dakṣiṇā*),

The year too, and the sarcificer (Yajamāna), the worlds (Lokas)

Where the moon (Soma) shines brightly, and were the sun. (Thus he is the source of all religious rites)

तस्माच्च देवा बहुधा संप्रसूता: साध्या मनुष्या: पशवो वयांसि।

प्राणापानौ व्रीहियवौ तपश्च श्रद्धा सत्यं ब्रह्मचर्यं विधिश्च॥७॥

From Him, too, gods are manifoldly produced.

The celestials (Sādhyas), men, cattle, birds,

The in-breath and the out-breath (*prāṇāpanau*), rice and barley, austerity (*tapas*),

Faith (*śraddhā*), truth, chastity, and the law (*vidhi*).

सप्त प्राणा: प्रभवन्ति तस्मात्सप्तार्चिष: समिध: सप्त होमा:।

सप्त इमे लोका येषु चरन्ति प्राणा गुहाशया निहिता: सप्त सप्त॥८॥

From Him come forth the seven life-breaths (*prāṇa*),

The seven flames, their fuel, the seven oblations,

These seven worlds, wherein do move

The life-breaths that dwell in the secret place [of the heart] placed seven and seven.

[According to Ācārya Śaṅkara the even Prāṇa (two eyes, two ears, two nostrils, a tongue.]

अत: समुद्रा गिरयश्च सर्वेऽस्मात्स्यदन्ते सिन्धव: सर्वरूपा:।

अतश्च सर्वा ओषधयो रसाश्च येनैष भूतैस्तिष्ठते ह्यन्तरात्मा॥९॥

From Him, the seas and the mountains all.

From Him roll rivers of every kind.

And from Him all herbs, the essence, too,

Whereby that Inner Soul (*antarātman*) dwells in beings.

पुरुष एवेदं विश्वं कर्म तपो ब्रह्म परामृतम्।

एतद्यो वेद निहितं गुहायां सोऽविद्याग्रन्थिं विकिरतीह सोम्य॥१०॥

The Person (Puruṣa) himself is everything here :

Work (*karman*) and austerity (*tapas*) and Brahman, beyond death.

He who knows That, set in the secret place [of the heart]—

He here on earth, my friend, rends asunder the knot of ignorance.

Part - 2

The all-inclusive Brahman

आवि:संनिहितं गुहाचरन्नाम महत्पदमत्रैतत्समर्पितम्। एजत्प्राणन्निमिषच्च
यदेतज्ञानथ सदसद्वरेण्यं परं विज्ञानाद्यद्वरिष्ठं प्रजानाम्॥ १॥

Manifest, [yet] hidden; called 'Moving-in-secret';

The great abode! Therein is placed that which moves and breaths and winks.

What that is, know as Being (*sad*) and Non-being (*a-sad*),

As the object of desire, higher than understanding,

As what is the best of creatures!

यदर्चिमद्यदणुभ्योऽ णु च यस्मिँल्लोका निहिता लोकिनश्च।
तदेतदक्षरं ब्रह्म स प्राणस्तदु वाङ् मनः तदेतत्सत्यं तदमृतं सोम्य विद्धि॥ २॥

That which is flaming, which is subtler than the subtle,

On which the worlds are set, and their inhabitants—

That is the imperishable Brahma. It is life (*prāṇa*), and It is speech and mind. That is the real. It is immortal.

It is [a mark] to be penetrated. Penetrate It, my friend!

[A target to be penetrated by meditation on 'Oṁ']

धनुर्गृहीत्वौपनिषदं महास्त्रं शरं ह्युपासानिशितं संधयीत।
आयम्य तद्भावगतेन चेतसा लक्ष्यं तदेवाक्षरं सोम्य विद्धि॥ ३॥

Taking as a bow the great weapon of the Upaniṣad,

One should put upon it an arrow sharpened by meditation.

Stretching it with a thought directed to the essence of That,

Penetrate that Imperishable as the mark, my friend.

प्रणवो धनुः शरो ह्यात्मा ब्रह्म तल्लक्ष्यमुच्यते। अप्रमत्तेन वेद्धव्यं शरवत्तन्मयो भवेत्॥ ४॥

The mystic syllable *Oṁ (praṇava)* is the bow. The arrow is the soul (*ātman*). Brahma is said to be the mark (*lakṣya*). By the undistracted man is It to be penetrated. One should come to be in It, as the arrow [in the mark]. The immortal Soul, the one warp of the world and of the individual.

यस्मिन्द्यौः पृथिवी चान्तरिक्षमोतं मनः सह प्राणैश्च सर्वैः।
तमेवैकं जानथ आत्मानमन्या वाचो विमुञ्चथामृतस्यैष सेतुः॥ ५॥

He on whom the sky, the earth, and the atmosphere are woven, and the mind, together with all the life-breaths (*prāṇa*),

Him alone know as the one Soul (Ātman). Other words dismiss. He is the bridge to immortality.

अरा इव रथनाभौ संहता यत्र नाड्यः स एषोऽन्तश्चरते बहुधा जायमानः।

ओमित्येवं ध्यायथ आत्मानं स्वस्ति वः पाराय तमसः परस्तात्॥ ६॥

Where the channels are brought together

Like the spokes in the hub of a wheel—

Therein he moves about, Becoming manifold.

Oṁ! thus speaking meditate upon the Soul (Ātman).

Hail to you! go to the bank beyond darkness.

यः सर्वज्ञः सर्वविद्यस्यैष महिमा भुवि दिव्ये ब्रह्मपुरे ह्येष व्योम्न्यात्मा प्रतिष्ठितः।

मनोमयः प्राणशरीरनेता प्रतिष्ठितोऽन्ने हृदयं संनिधाय।

तद्विज्ञानेन परिपश्यन्ति धीरा आनन्दरूपममृतं यद्विभाति॥ ७॥

He who is all-knowing, all-wise, whose is this greatness on the earth— He is in the divine Brahma city and in the heaven established! The Soul (Ātman)!

Consisting of mind, leader of the life-breaths and of the body,

He is established on food, controlling the heart.

By this knowledge the wise perceive; The blissful Immortal that gleams forth.

भिद्यते हृदयग्रन्थिश्छिद्यन्ते सर्वसंशयाः। क्षीयन्ते चास्य कर्माणि तस्मिन्दृष्टे परावरे॥ ८॥

When He is seen— both the higher and the lower, the knot of the heart is loosened, all doubts are cut off, and one's deeds (*karman*) cease.

हिरण्मये परे कोशे विरजं ब्रह्म निष्कलम्। तच्छुभ्रं ज्योतिषां ज्योतिस्तद्यदात्मविदो विदुः॥ ९॥

In the highest golden sheath is Brahma, without stain, without parts. Brilliant is It, the light of lights— That which knowers of the Soul (Ātman) do know!

न तत्र सूर्यो भाति न चंद्रतारकं नेमा विद्युतो भान्ति कुतोऽयमग्निः।

तमेव भान्तमनुभाति सर्वं तस्य भासा सर्वमिदं विभाति॥ १०॥

The sun shines not there, nor the moon and stars;

These lightnings shine not, much less this [earthly] fire!

After Him, as He shines, do everything shine.

This whole world is illumined with His light.

ब्रह्मैवेदममृतं पुरस्ताद्ब्रह्म दक्षिणतश्चोत्तरेण। अधश्चोर्ध्वं च प्रसृतं ब्रह्मैवेदं विश्वमिदं वरिष्ठम्॥ ११॥

Brahman, indeed, is this immortal. Brahma before, Brahma behind, to right and to left. Stretched forth below and above,

Brahma, indeed, is this whole world, this widest extent.

Third Muṇḍaka

(The Way to Brahman)

Part - 1

Recognition of the Great Companion, the supreme salvation

द्वा सुपर्णा सयुजा सखाया समानं वृक्षं परिषस्वजाते।

तयोरन्यः पिप्पलं स्वाद्वत्त्यनश्नन्नन्यो अभिचाकशीति॥ १॥

Two birds, fast bound companions,

Clasp close the self-same tree.

Of these two, the one eats sweet fruit;

The other looks on without eating.

समाने वृक्षे पुरुषो निमग्नोऽनीशया शोचति मुह्यमानः।

जुष्टं यदा पश्यत्यन्यमीशमस्य महिमानमिति वीतशोकः॥ २॥

On the self-same tree a person, sunken, Grieves for his impotence, deluded; When he sees the other, the Lord (*iśa*), contented,

And his greatness, he becomes freed from sorrow.

यदा पश्यः पश्यते रुक्मवर्णं कर्तारमीशं पुरुषं ब्रह्मयोनिम्।

तदा विद्वान्पुण्यपापे विधूय निरञ्जनः परमं साम्यमुपैति॥ ३॥

When a seer sees the brilliant Maker, Lord, Person, the Brahma-source, Then, being a knower, shaking off good an evil,

Stainless, he attains supreme identity (*sāmya*) [with Him].

प्राणो ह्येष यः सर्वभूतैर्विभाति विजानन्विद्वान्भवते नातिवादी।

आत्मक्रीड आत्मरतिः क्रियावानेष ब्रह्मविदां वरिष्ठः॥ ४॥

Truly, it is Life (*prāṇa*) that shines forth in all things!

Understanding this, one becomes a knower There is no superior speaker.

Having delight in the Soul (Ātman), having pleasure in the Soul, doing the rites,

सत्येन लभ्यस्तपसा ह्येष आत्मा सम्यग्ज्ञानेन ब्रह्मचर्येण नित्यम्।

अन्तःशरीरे ज्योतिर्मयो हि शुभ्रो यं पश्यन्ति यतयः क्षीणदोषा॥ ५॥

This Soul (Ātman) is obtainable by truth, by austerity (*tapas*),

By proper knowledge (*jñāna*), by the student's life of chastity (*brahmacarya*) constantly [practised].

Within the body, consisting of light, pure is He

Whom the ascetics (*yati*), with imperfections done away, behold.

सत्यमेव जयते नानृतं सत्येन पन्था विततो देवयानः।
येनाक्रमन्त्यृषयो ह्याप्तकामा यत्र तत्सत्यस्य परमं निधानम्॥ ६॥

Truth alone conquers, not untruth.
By truth is laid out the path leading to the gods (*devayāna*)
By which the sages whose desire is satisfied ascend
To where is the highest repository of truth.

बृहच्च तद्दिव्यमचिन्त्यरूपं सूक्ष्माच्च तत्सूक्ष्मतरं विभाति।
दूरात्सुदूरे तदिहान्तिके च पश्यत्स्विहैव निहितं गुहायाम्॥ ७॥

Vast, heavenly, of unthinkable form, And more minute than the minute, it shines forth.
It is farther than the far, yet here near at hand,
Set down in the secret place [of the heart], even here among those who behold [It].

न चक्षुषा गृह्यते नापि वाचा नान्यैर्देवैस्तपसा कर्मणा वा।
ज्ञानप्रसादेन विशुद्धसत्त्वस्ततस्तु तं पश्यते निष्कलं ध्यायमानः॥ ८॥

Not by sight is It grasped, not even by speech,
Not by any other sense-organs (*deva*), austerity, or work.
By the peace of knowledge (*jñāna-prasāda*), one's nature purified—
In that way, however, by meditating, one does behold Him who is without parts.

एषोऽणुरात्मा चेतसा वेदितव्यो यस्मिन्प्राणः पञ्चधा संविवेश।
प्राणैश्चित्तं सर्वमोतं प्रजानां यस्मिन्विशुद्धे विभवत्येष आत्मा॥ ९॥

That subtile Soul (Ātman) is to be known by thought (*cetas*)
Wherein the senses (*prāṇa*) fivefoldly have entered.
The whole of men's thinking is interwoven with the senses.
When that is purified, the Soul (Ātman) shines forth.

यं यं लोकं मनसा संविभाति विशुद्धसत्त्वः कामयते यांश्च कामान्।
तं तं लोकं जयते तांश्च कामांस्तस्मादात्मज्ञं ह्यर्चयेद्भूतिकामः॥ १०॥

Whatever world a man of purified nature makes clear in mind, And whatever desires he desires for himself— That world he wins, those desires too.

Therefore he who is desirous of welfare should praise the knower of the Soul (Ātman).

[An important mystery herein is revealed. The man who wishes for the worldly pleasures and exerts all possible in the direction, feels pleasure of collecting them considering it an achievement. The man of sacrosanct heart receives that pleasure merely when he resolute. The former persons who seek their pleasure in collection of material luxuries therefore, should follow the metaphysician considering him the supreme soul.]

Part - 2

Desires as the cause of rebirth

स वेदैतत्परमं ब्रह्म धाम यत्र विश्वं निहितं भाति शुभ्रम्।
उपासते पुरुषं ह्यकामास्ते शुक्रमेतदतिवर्तन्ति धीराः॥ १॥

He knows that Supreme Brahma-abode,
Founded on which the whole world shines radiantly.
They who, being without desire, worship the Person (Puruṣa)
And are wise, pass beyond the seed (*śukra*) [of rebirth] here.

कामान्यः कामयते मन्यमानः स कामभिर्जायते तत्र तत्र।
पर्याप्तकामस्य कृतात्मनस्तु इहैव सर्वे प्रविलीयन्ति कामाः॥ २॥

He who in fancy forms desires,
Because of his desires is born [again] here and there.
But of him whose desire is satisfied, who is a perfected soul (*kṛtātman*),
For him all desires here on earth vanish away.

The Soul (Ātman) known only by revelation to His own elect

नायमात्मा प्रवचनेन लभ्यो न मेधया न बहुना श्रुतेन।
यमेवैष वृणुते तेन लभ्यस्तस्यैष आत्मा विवृणुते तनुं स्वाम्॥ ३॥

This Soul (Ātman) is not to be obtained by instruction,
Nor by intellect, nor by much learning.
He is to be obtained only by the one whom He chooses;
To such a one that Soul (Ātman) reveals His own person (*tanūm svām*).

[The methods attaining material knowledge are not the methods for attaining the metaphysics. The material knowledge is like the matter, attainable through the manual or metal labour. Metaphysics is sensitive (related to super-conscious) and it reveals its nature ipso-facto when the devotee is found eligible].

नायमात्मा बलहीनेन लभ्यो न च प्रमादात्तपसो वाप्यलिङ्गात्।
एतैरुपायैर्यतते यस्तु विद्वांस्तस्यैष आत्मा विशते ब्रह्मधाम॥ ४॥

This Soul (Ātman) is not to be obtained by one destitute of fortitude,
Nor through heedlessness, nor through a false notion of austerity (*tapas*).
But he who strives by these means, provided he knows—
Into his Brahma-abode this Soul (Ātman) enters.

संप्राप्यैनमृषयो ज्ञानतृप्ताः कृतात्मानो वीतरागाः प्रशान्ताः।
ते सर्वगं सर्वतः प्राप्य धीरा युक्तात्मानः सर्वमेवाविशन्ति॥ ५॥

Attaining Him, the seers (*ṛṣi*) who are satisfied with knowledge,

Who are perfected souls (*kṛtātman*), from passion free (*vīta-rāga*), tranquil—

Attaining Him who is the universally omnipresent, those wise,

Devout souls (*yuktātman*) into the All itself do enter.

वेदान्तविज्ञानसुनिश्चितार्थाः संन्यासयोगाद्यतयः शुद्धसत्त्वाः।

ते ब्रह्मलोकेषु परान्तकाले परामृताः परिमुच्यन्ति सर्वे॥ ६॥

They who have ascertained the meaning of the Vedānta-knowledge.

Ascetics (*yati*) with natures purified through the application of renunciation (*saṁnyāsa-yoga*)—

They in the Brahma-worlds at the end of time are all liberated beyond death.

गताः कलाः पञ्चदश प्रतिष्ठा देवाश्च सर्वे प्रतिदेवतासु।

कर्माणि विज्ञानमयश्च आत्मा परेऽव्यये सर्व एकीभवन्ति॥ ७॥

Gone are the fifteen parts according to their station,

Even all the sense-organs (*deva*) in their corresponding divinities!

One's deeds (*karman*), and the self that consist of understanding (*vijñāna-maya ātman*)— All become unified in the supreme Imperishable.

[In Praśnopaniṣad 6.4, the fifteen arts have been described as five elements including ether etc., cereal, semen, sensory organs, mind, obeisance, penance, hymns, deeds, loka and the name. If someone wants to dedicate himself in knowledge, he should firstly abandon the ego relating to his arts achievements (expertise) and let them surrender to the God. Only then the soul of living organism can be dedicated to that supreme soul.]

यथा नद्यः स्यन्दमानाः समुद्रेऽस्तं गच्छन्ति नामरूपे विहाय।

तथा विद्वान्नामरूपाद्विमुक्तः परात्परं पुरुषमुपैति दिव्यम्॥ ८॥

As the flowing rivers in the ocean, disappear, quitting name and form,

So the knower, being liberated from name and form, Goes unto the Heavenly Person, higher than the high.

स यो ह वै तत्परमं ब्रह्म वेद ब्रह्मैव भवति नास्याब्रह्मवित्कुले भवति।

तरति शोकं तरति पाप्मानं गुहाग्रन्थिभ्यो विमुक्तोऽमृतो भवति॥ ९॥

He, verily, who knows that supreme Brahman, becomes very Brahman. In his family no one ignorant of Brahman arises.

He crosses over sorrow. He crosses over sin (*pāpman*). Liberated from the knots of the heart, he becomes immortal.

तदेतदृचाऽभ्युक्तम्–

क्रियावन्तः श्रोत्रिया ब्रह्मनिष्ठाः स्वयं जुह्वत एकर्षिं श्रद्धयन्तः।

तेषामेवैतां ब्रह्मविद्यां वदेत शिरोव्रतं विधिवद्यैस्तु चीर्णम्॥ १०॥

[The rewards and the requisite conditions of this knowledge of Brahma]

This very [doctrine] has been declared in the verse :—

They who do the rites, who are learned in the Vedas, who are intent on Brahma,

They who, possessing faith (*śraddhayan*), make oblation of themselves, even of the one seer —

To them indeed one may declare this knowledge of Brahma,

When, however, the Muṇḍaka-vow has been performed by them according to rule.'

तदेतत्सत्यमृषिरङ्गिराः पुरोवाच नैतदचीर्णव्रतोऽधीते। नमः परमऋषिभ्यो नमः परमऋषिभ्यः॥ ११॥

This is the truth. The seer (*ṛṣi*) Aṅgiras declared it in ancient time. One who has not performed the vow does not read this.

Adoration to the highest seers!

Adoration to the highest seers!

॥ शान्तिपाठः॥

॥ॐ भद्रं कर्णेभिः .... इति शान्तिः॥

॥इति मुण्डकोपनिषत्समाप्ता॥

***

6. MĀṆḌŪKYOPANIṢAD

माण्डूक्योपनिषद्

॥शान्तिपाठः॥

ॐ भद्रं कर्णेभिः शृणुयाम देवा........।

स्वस्ति न इन्द्रो वृद्धश्रवाः..... इति शान्तिः॥

This upaniṣad is a part of the subject-matter in Atharvaveda. In this upaniṣad, it has been presumed that the whole universe is addressed under the syllable Oṁ. It has been considered as best symbol to the absolute soul and a knowledge pertaining to this very syllable. The syllable Oṁ has been described with all the application it bears within and the echos it governs. This upaniṣad is distinct as compared with the verbosity of the older upaniṣad. As opposed to the most of the upaniṣad of the Atharvaveda, the Māṇḍūkyopniṣad makes a more enthusiastic impression because it distinguishes only 3 and not 3 and a half moras in the word Oṁ. This upaniṣad furnishes the proof for this thesis of providing with the supremacy to the syllable Oṁ.

It says the word is Brahma, Brahma is Ātman, the Ātman is the sound Oṁ because its moras correspond the four quarters or feet *i.e.* the four stages of Ātman. These four stages are– the waking, Vaiśvānara in which the Ātman perceives outward? The dream state, Taijas in which the Ātman perceives inward, 3-the deep sleep, Prājña *i.e.* the Brāhmaṇa for the time being, 4-this fourth is the extinction of the word expanse not affected unconsciously as in the third state but with consensus. At the first state, the A corresponds of Oṁ; the 2nd, the U; the 3rd the M and the 4th, without an element.

The mystic symbolism of the word 'Oṁ'

ओमित्येतदक्षरमिदꣳसर्वं तस्योपव्याख्यानभूतं भवद्भविष्यदिति सर्वमोङ्कार एव। यच्चान्यत्त्रिकालातीतं तदप्योङ्कार एव॥१॥

Oṁ! This syllable is this whole world.

Its further explanation is :—

The past, the present, the future—everything is just the word *Oṁ*.

And whatever else that transcends threefold time— that, too, is just the word *Oṁ*.

[What has been described by the above hymn is a scope of syllable Oṁ that embeds within it all the visible as also invisible objects of this universe. It envisages that this universe as also the knowledge that identity with it as also the cycle of time classified in present, past and future are also the part and parcel of the syllable Oṁ. All elements as found in this universe are also the form of this significant syllable.]

सर्वंऽह्येतद्ब्रह्मायमात्मा ब्रह्म सोऽयमात्मा चतुष्पात्॥२॥

For truly, everything here is Brahma; this self (*ātman*) is Brahma. This same self has four fourths.

[It has been conveyed that knowledge is supreme because all kinds of presumptions, assumptions, as also the perceptions get their worth when the knowledge get in touch with the soul and the soul govern the body. The location, the property as also the effects of all the four feet of the knowledge and the soul have been described in the successive hymns.]

जागरितस्थानो बहि:प्रज्ञ: सप्ताङ्ग एकोनविंशतिमुख: स्थूलभुग्वैश्वानर: प्रथम: पाद:॥३॥

The waking state (*jāgarita-sthāna*), outwardly cognitive, having seven limbs, having nineteen mouths, enjoying the gross (*sthūla-bhuj*), the Common-to-all-men (*vaiśvānara*), is the first fourth.

[The first feet of the knowledge and the soul in consonance with its effects has been described in the above hymn. Assuming the first feet as conducting all the affairs of this universe, it has been told that as the director should always keep himself alert and well aware of his affairs, conversant with the outer knowledge and well intelligent with all the 7 premier issues (These have been described as 7 lokas or the 7 rays), he should have 19 kinds of styles to give way to the expressions regarding the affairs and should take the cognizance of the consequential effects or the results in the other words show that these consequences may be leaden with the contextual fruits which may be distributed among all units engaged and assigned with the specific part of the issues as a whole. The Vaiśvānara or the director of this universe has been presumed ever awaken *i.e.* intelligent with exterior objects of this universe and a shining personality bearing 7 kinds of intelligence or the crystallized knowledge of all pros and cons conducted in this universe. Vaiśvānara or the director of this universe has 19 mouths *i.e.* manner of expressions consisting of 10 sensory organs, 5 prāṇas (breathing) and the 4 kinds of the feelings in the heart. He is responsible for the results obtained under his direction from the universe and the objects dwelling in it.]

स्वप्नस्थानोऽन्त:प्रज्ञ: सप्ताङ्ग एकोनविंशतिमुख: प्रविविक्तभुक् तैजसो द्वितीय: पाद:॥४॥

The dreaming state (*svapna-sthāna*), inwardly cognitive, having seven limbs, having nineteen mouths, enjoying the exquisite (*pravivikta-bhuj*), the Brilliant (*taijasa*), is the second fourth.

[The base to stand for this 2nd foot has been told this mortal world yet it has inner eyes or intuition by virtue of which this foot is competent enough to know everything regarding the word which has no visible shape and form. The objects of luxuries that it enjoys with are also in micro form which cannot be seen by the mortal living organisms. It has been told that always illuminating this hymn conveys that the knowledge has the 2nd foot which has no bearing with the mortal world. However, it has been presumed that its base also stands the earth or this ever-perishing world.]

यत्र सुप्तो न कंचन कामं कामयते न कंचन स्वप्नं पश्यति तत्सुषुप्तम्। सुषुप्तस्थान एकीभूत: प्रज्ञानघन एवानन्दमयो ह्यानन्दभुक् चेतोमुख: प्राज्ञस्तृतीय: पाद:॥५॥

If one asleep desires no desire whatsoever, sees no dream whatsoever, that is deep sleep (*suṣupta*).

The deep-sleep state (*suṣupta-sthāna*), unified (*ekī-bhūta*), just (*eva*) a cognition-mass (*prajñāna-ghana*), consisting of bliss (*ānanda-maya*), enjoying bliss (*ānanda-bhuj*), whose mouth is thought (*cetas-*), the Cognitional (*prājña*), is the third fourth.

[The knowledge as it is equipped with excellent powers, its holder or the possessor could however be intelligent extraordinarily. However, he could have no choice of interest to think about or enjoy the worldly luxuries. As everyone knows that the dreams are merely representative of the thoughts as well as passions never fulfilled in the daylight, it is but natural that the learned person as he accepts the objects by their facts and not by imagination. When the power to analyse the facts is with an intelligent man, his mind will never be so looming in the trench of imagination and there would be no place for dreams at night. Again the learned person however sleepy, never losses his power of concentration because of well checked on his senses. As the men lives under the illuminating sun, it is natural that he will always be happy least caring for the worldly feelings or the calculations of the events and incidence. Such illuminating face fellow is the 3rd foot of knowledge or in other words, an ascetic who has passed the 3 standards of the knowledge or the fact.]

एष सर्वेश्वर एष सर्वज्ञ एषोऽन्तर्याम्येष योनिः सर्वस्य प्रभवाप्ययौ हि भूतानाम्॥६॥

This is the lord of all (*sarveśvara*). This is the all-knowing (*sarva-jña*). This is the inner controller (*antar-yāmin*). This is the source (*yoni*) of all, for this is the origin and the end (*prabhavāpyayau*) of beings.

[The knowledge herein has been described above all. It has been told that it is the cause of creation, nutrition as also the disruption. The movable as well as the immovable objects, visible or invisible whatever their form, all get their origination from the knowledge. It is the beginning the extension as also the conclusion of everything that comprises of or compounded this world as a whole. The cause and effect theory widely accepted by the scientists embedded in the ever extended scope of knowledge.]

नान्तःप्रज्ञं न बहिष्प्रज्ञं नोभयतःप्रज्ञं न प्रज्ञानघनं न प्रज्ञं नाप्रज्ञम्। अदृष्टमव्यवहार्यमग्राह्यमलक्षण-मचिन्त्यमव्यपदेश्यमेकात्मप्रत्ययसारं प्रपञ्चोपशमं शान्तं शिवमद्वैतं चतुर्थं मन्यन्ते स आत्मा स विज्ञेयः॥७॥

Not inwardly cognitive (*antaḥ-prajña*), not outwardly cognitive (*bahiṣ-prajña*), not both-wise cognitive (*ubhayataḥ-prajña*), not a cognition-mass (*prajñāna-ghana*), not cognitive (*prajña*), not non-cognitive (*a-prajña*), unseen (*a-dṛṣṭa*), with which there can be no dealing (*a-vyavahārya*), ungraspable (*a-grāhya*), having no distinctive mark (*a-lakṣaṇa*), non-thinkable (*a-cintya*), that cannot be designated (*a-vyapadeśya*), the essence of the assurance of which is the state of being one with the Self (*ekātmya-pratyaya-sāra*), the cessation of development (*prapañcośama*), tranquil (*śānta*), benign (*śiva*), without a second (*a-dvaita*)—[such] they think is the fourth. He is the Self (Ātman). He should be discerned.

[The fourth foot of the knowledge or Brahma has been explained here in its entirity. As the hymn itself convey the idea, the fourth step if it is accessed by the ascetic, the characteristics as appear in his personalia are that he becomes scot-free from knowing about anything. This is the reason why this fourth foot of knowledge has been explained as unaware of internal or external happening. It is, indeed, appeared in the ascetic that he has no meaning for having any option because his mental powers at that stage merge into one and there is no scope for the other. At this stage, the senses by which intelligence and ignorance are defined, loss their identity in toto. He becomes such an idol to which neither fine sensory organs *i.e.* eyes, ears, mouth, nose and skin nor the five functionary organs *i.e.* mouth, belly, anus, hands and feet can motivate or divide anyway or in any form whatsoever. At this stage of penance, activities of any kinds have no meaning, the criterion cannot measure this stage as also it is the stage where no limit for thinking can be prescribed and nothing can be said in appreciation to this stage. There are only experiences that this subject (ascetic) only feels but cannot describe as to what has been felt by him. Naturally, with so many characteristics this subject could have no cognizance whatsoever taken by the common mass of this material world and such a subject enjoying the fourth foot of the knowledge will attain the peace, welfare and at this stage, there will be no chaos or the common circumstances. As we see, this upaniṣad *i.e.* Māṇḍūkyopaniṣad has described this systematic and ascendant stages for the ascetics and the knowledge in itself has been described as the supreme lord, supreme soul as also bearer of the recognition of the power itself. The worldly feelings and pains are only for those who reside here but the knowledge having its peculiar essence makes the subject scot-free from the mortal senses. Lastly, the hymn expects that this fourth foot of knowledge is only worth-knowing because the rest are otherwise than knowledge is ever perishing.]

सोऽयमात्माध्यक्षरमोङ्कारोऽधिमात्रं पादा मात्रा मात्राश्च पादा अकार उकारो मकार इति॥८॥

This is the Self with regard to the word *Oṁ*, with regard to its elements. The elements (*mātra*) are the fourths; the fourths, the elements : the letter *a*, the letter *u*, the letter *m*.

[In this hymn, the moras of the knowledge or the soul appeared in their multi-meanings. Three moras *i.e.* a, u, m are rested with the syllable Oṁ. This word in itself is three-dimensional. According to the theory of relativity, there are three dimensions– 1. The Time, 2. The Voiume and 3. The Mars respectively. The first dimension *i.e.* Time also bears three moras *i.e.* the past, the present and the future. The 2nd dimension *i.e.* Volume also bears 3 other dimensions like the length, the width and the height in itself. In internal property of a man, we also see that there are mainly three kinds of priorities *i.e.* Sat (cool-temperament), Raja (ambitious temperament) and Tama (aggressive temperament). What this description envisages is that this knowledge or in other words, the Brahma has been revealed in three moras. There are a number of other facts found in 3 species, some of them are– The study is also consisting of reading, writing and learning, the age of human being has also 3 dimensions– childhood, the youth and the old, the necessity as per the well-settled theorem by Economics is also comprised of 3 dimensions *i.e.* passion for anything, Assessment of the material requirements and the third promptness in use of the material to satisfy the passion.]

जागरितस्थानो वैश्वानरोऽकारः प्रथमा मात्राप्तेरादिमत्त्वाद्वा आप्नोति ह वै सर्वान्कामानादिश्च भवति य एवं वेद॥९॥

The waking state, the Common-to-all-men, is the letter *a*, the first element, from *āpti* ('obtaining') or from *ādimatvā* ('being first').

He obtains, verily, indeed, all desires, he becomes first— he who knows this.

[As this first foot of knowledge *i.e.* Vaiśvānara has been described in the opening lines of this upaniṣad, this hymn again highlights the reasons for having it the first foot of the knowledge. It clarifies that the Vaiśvānara stage of the ascetic is well-aware of the material senses and thus it is just beginning therefore, described as the first stage or the first foot of the anus. The ascetic who arrives at Vaiśvānara actually possesses the skills and expertise in the field or what he does his efforts. In material achievements, this part of knowledge makes a man to get on the outstanding success in his life and guarantees a topmost place wherever are to which he wants to achieve. Thus, this stage have been full of material sciences is benevolent and most advantageous for the material achievement. However, the scope is only confined to the particular ambition and the goal as well.]

स्वप्नस्थानस्तैजस उकारो द्वितीया मात्रोत्कर्षादुभयत्वाद्वोत्कर्षति ह वै ज्ञानसंततिं समानश्च भवति नास्याऽब्रह्मवित्कुले भवति य एवं वेद॥१०॥

The sleeping state, the Brilliant, is the letter *u*, the second element, from *utkarṣa* ('exaltation') or from *ubhayatvā* ('intermediateness').

He exalts, verily, indeed, the continuity of knowledge; and he becomes equal (*samāna*); no one ignorant of Brahma is born in the family of him who knows this.

[This upaniṣad herein describes the position of a man who makes himself able to stand on the 2nd steer of the knowledge. It explains that it is the middle stage of a man where the two words (The material and the metaphysical) are well-known to and the acquirer of the 2nd foot have excellent power of imagination. When this is the position, it is but certain that the man could have balanced ideas and he could establish an equal parameters for the both senses *i.e.* material senses and the metaphysical senses. In other words, we may say that he will be the best known person to how one should pass his worldly life. Thus, his life will act like a balance where one side is the wait of dignity and the other side, the worldly affairs and achievements as well. This is the reason for telling this stage as Tejas. All kinds of school of thoughts assemble to such a mind and the accumulated stream like Brahmaputra of Assam ultimately merges into the ocean of knowledge. What it conveys nothing than telling that such a man reaps the highest achievements in his worldly life and again destines to higher position in heavenly abode also.]

सुषुप्तस्थानः प्राज्ञो मकारस्तृतीया मात्रा मितेरपीतेर्वा मिनोति ह वा इदं सर्वमपीतिश्च भवति य एवं वेद॥११॥

The deep-sleep state, the Cognitional, is the letter *m*, the third element, from *miti* ('erecting') or from *apīti* ('immerging').

He, verily, indeed, erects (*minoti*) this whole world, and he becomes its immerging—he who knows this.

[The 3rd foot of knowledge is hereby explained and it has been told that his foot is not less than the extreme power of the eliminator to which Lord Śiva possesses. The man learned to Prājña is well-aware of the causative entity of the consciousness. At this stage, only an exclusively consciousness is seen activated everywhere. The man arriving at this stage becomes so able as to feel this whole universe within him, however, in its micro-form *i.e.* in seed form. His consciousness assumes that the senses of the word comprising all movable, immovable, tangible, intangible, visible as also invisible entities of this world are not at all different than him and these all are vested within him, however, in their minuscule form.]

अमात्रश्चतुर्थोऽव्यवहार्यः प्रपञ्चोपशमः शिवोऽद्वैत एवमोङ्कार आत्मैव संविशत्यात्मनात्मानं य एवं वेद य एवं वेद॥१२॥

The fourth is without an element, with which there can be no dealing, the cessation of development, benign, without a second.

Thus *Oṁ* is the Self (Ātman) indeed.

He who knows this, with his self enters the Self— yea, he who knows this!

[This hymn makes it crystal clear that this is the last and the fourth stage of the knowledge. The worldly attachments and temptations have nothing to do when a man is assessed to such highest position. Hence, it is natural that he could be free from all kinds of activities because activities also have their tangible form and they are much or less related to the worldly achievements. For an instance, someone reads the book. The verb 'reading' is an activity till the reader has not digested the ideas inherent to the concerned book. As and when he arise at the stage when everything is digested therefrom and the nut-shell is entered into the conscious, nobody may see him further doing that activity. So the activity as we have told here is tangible *i.e.* the book is also framed on the material object *i.e.* paper, the machines used for printing are also objects, therefore, activity is always tangible, however, at the ultimate stage, when there is no material objects are required, it will be said the inactive stage, however, most active at that stage. The same is with the 4th foot of the knowledge. The ascetic who have crossed the 3 precedent stages, will certainly be so extra-ordinary or exceptional in regard to knowledge that he need not any base that may be purported to the worldly objects thereby revealing him that he is performing any kind of activity. Such a man, indeed, will be learned by soul (Ātma-Jñāni) it is, therefore, most easy for him to insert his soul into the perfect knowledge (Brahma). Further, having arrived at this stage there would remain no illusions in his mind thereby no dual thoughts or two sorts of assumptions for a single thing will be seen in his personality. What this mean is that everything will be apparent before him and there will remain no illusions for conjecture and surmise.]

ॐ भद्रं कर्णेभिः शृणुयाम देवा........।

स्वस्ति न इन्द्रो वृद्धश्रवाः..... इति शान्तिः।।

।।इति माण्डूक्योपनिषत्समाप्ता।।

***

7. TAITTIRĪYOPANIṢAD

तैत्तिरीयोपनिषद्

This very upaniṣad is a part of the subject-matter of the Taittirīyāraṇyaka to the branch of Taittirīya in Kṛṣṇayajurveda. Out of the total 10 chapters in Āraṇyaka, only 7th, 8th and 9th chapters have been recognised as upaniṣad. In these 3 chapters of Āraṇyaka, there are 3 *vallīs i.e.,* Śikṣā vallī, Brahmānand-vallī and Bhṛgu vallī respectively. Just at the outset of Śikṣā vallī, the 5 broad codes namely Adhiloka, Adhijyotiṣ, Adhivijña and Adhyātma (metaphysics) have been described and the consequences of listening to and following them have also been elaborately given. So far as penance (साधना) is concerned, the syllable Oṁ and Bhuḥ, Svaḥ, Mahaḥ etc. recitals are described as most significant. Finally in this upaniṣad some formulae regarding study and teaching with modesty and the culture have been described and an importance of practical behaviour concomitant to ideal thoughts has also been highlighted.

In the 2nd vallī *i.e.* Brahmānanda vallī an importance to realise the supreme lord in the cavity of heart has been thoroughly explained and various complexions of the supreme lord like pertaining to the food, breathing (Prāṇa), mind, conscious and the pleasure have been broadly described. While discussing the scope of pleasure it has been taken from the material pleasure with sequel developments and the gradual superior forms of it have been described comprising the pleasure of knowledge (Brahmānanda) in toto. The stages of a person who are having to realise the divine pleasure have been also being the subject-matter of this upaniṣad.

Now on the 3rd vallī *i.e.* Bhṛgu vallī taking place in the heart of Bhṛgu for realising the knowledge has been satisfied by his father Varuṇa. He made him to know the element of knowledge and instructed him to realise himself by the way of penance and perpetual exercises. In pursuance with the instructions given by the father Bhṛgu had realised in the thought of knowledge in a sequel before the breathing, the mind, the conscious as well as the pleasure. It means that while pondering over the exercises– physical, mental as well as spiritual, he could make him having to realise the scope of knowledge gradually from the material objects to the inner and material feelings. When Bhṛgu was well equipped with the realisation to the extent of his father's instructions, Lord Varuṇa then made him to understand the appropriate use of the food-stuffs including cereals and educated him to the manner of due appropriation of all kinds of food-stuffs. This upaniṣad finally describes the stage of devotee, well realised to the supreme lord thereby duly reformed in behaviour and their feelings as well as expressions completely based on the theorem of equality.

।।शान्तिपाठः।।

ॐ शं नो मित्रः शं वरुणः। शं नो भवत्वर्यमा। शं न इन्द्रो बृहस्पतिः। शं नो विष्णुरुरुक्रमः। नमो ब्रह्मणे। नमस्ते वायो। त्वमेव प्रत्यक्षं ब्रह्मासि। त्वामेव प्रत्यक्षं ब्रह्म वदिष्यामि। ऋतं वदिष्यामि। सत्यं वदिष्यामि। तन्मामवतु। तद्वक्तारमवतु। अवतु माम्। अवतु वक्तारम्।। ॐ शान्तिः शान्तिः शान्तिः।।

शीक्षावल्ली

।। प्रथमोऽनुवाकः।।

ॐ शं नो मित्रः शं वरुणः। शं नो भवत्वर्यमा। शं न इन्द्रो बृहस्पतिः। शं नो विष्णुरुरुक्रमः। नमो ब्रह्मणे। नमस्ते वायो। त्वमेव प्रत्यक्षं ब्रह्मासि। त्वामेव प्रत्यक्षं ब्रह्म वदिष्यामि। ऋतं वदिष्यामि। सत्यं वदिष्यामि। तद्वक्तारमवतु। अवतु माम्। अवतु वक्तारम्।। ॐ शान्तिः शान्तिः शान्तिः।।

First Vallī– Śikṣā Vallī

(Chapter concerning Instruction)

First Anuvāka

Propitious unto us, Mitra! Propitious, Varuṇa! Propitious unto us let Aryaman be! Propitious unto us, Indra! Bṛhaspati! Propitious unto us, Viṣṇu, the Wide-strider! Adoration to Brahmā! Adoration to you, Vāyu!

You, indeed, are the perceptible Brahma. Of you, indeed, the perceptible Brahma, will I speak. I will speak of the right (*rta*). I will speak of the true. Let that favour me! Let that Favour the speaker! Let it favour me! Let is favour the speaker!

Oṁ! Peace! Peace! Peace!

[The air had been told as an apparent knowledge because the flow of the breathing air circulates with the wind only. The knowledge is so degenetic that it covers all in itself and this knowledge is circulating in the form of life with all the living organism. According to this fact, an element of the supreme soul is always felt as the breathing air and the wind that blows throughout the universe. Perhaps, this was the reason why the scent has degenerated the air as apparent knowledge or the Brahman.]

।। द्वितीयोऽनुवाकः।।

ॐ शीक्षां व्याख्यास्यामः। वर्णः। स्वरः। मात्रा बलम्। साम संतानः। इत्युक्तः शीक्षाध्यायः।।१।।

Second Anuvāka

Lesson Pronunciation

Oṁ! We will expound Pronunciation; the sound (*varṇa*); the accent (*svara*); the quantity (*mātrā*); the force (*bala*); the articulation (*sāma*); the combination (*santāna*). Thus has been declared the lesson on Pronunciation.

[The sound or letters *i.e.* a, i etc. the vowels *i.e.* a, e, i, o, u or Udatya, Anudatya and Svarik etc. in Veda, the matrā small and big etc., the breathing power consumed while pronunciation of the letters is made (Bala), the method of pronunciation in balanced sound (Sāma) and the process of joining the words (Santāna). The above experiment pertains a Vedic experiment on education. The hymn envisages that without knowledge of letter or sound, expression, the accentuation, the balancing and the adding, one cannot be educated. What it means is that the education is consist of all these components within it.]

॥ तृतीयोऽनुवाकः॥

सह नौ यशः। सह नौ ब्रह्मवर्चसम्। अथातः संहिताया उपनिषदं व्याख्यास्यामः॥ पञ्चस्वधिकरणेषु। अधिलोकमधिज्यौतिषमधिविद्यमधिप्रजमध्यात्मम्। ता महासंहिता इत्याचक्षते। अथाधिलोकम्। पृथिवी पूर्वरूपम्। द्यौरुत्तररूपम्। आकाशः संधिः। वायुःसंधानम्। इत्यधिलोकम्॥१॥

अथाधिज्यौतिषम्। अग्निः पूर्वरूपम्। आदित्य उत्तररूपम्। आपः संधिः। वैद्युतः संधानम्। इत्यधिज्यौतिषम् ॥२॥

अथाधिविद्यम्। आचार्यः पूर्वरूपम्। अन्तेवास्युत्तररूपम्। विद्या संधिः। प्रवचनं संधानम्। इत्यधिविद्यम्। अथाधिप्रजम्। माता पूर्वरूपम्। पितोत्तररूपम्। प्रजा संधिः। प्रजननं संधानम्। इत्यधिप्रजम्॥३॥

Third Anuvāka

The mystic significance of combinations

Glory (*yaśas*) be with us two!

Pre-eminence in sacred knowledge (*brahma-varcasa*) be with us two.

Now next, we will expound the mystic meaning (*upaniṣad*) of combination (*saṁhitā*) in five heads :

with regard to the world; with regard to the luminaries; with regard to knowledge; with regard to progeny; with regard to oneself.

Now, with regard to the world.

The earth is the prior form; the heaven, the latter form. Space is their conjunction;

wind, the connection. Thus with regard to the world.

Now, with regard to the luminaries.

Fire is the prior form; the sun, the latter form. Water is their conjunction; lightning, the connection. Thus with regard to the luminaries.

Now, with regard to knowledge.

The teacher is the prior form; the pupil, the latter form. Knowledge is their conjunction; instruction, the connection. Thus with regard to knowledge.

Now, with regard to progeny.

The mother is the prior form; the father, the latter form. Progeny is their conjunction; procreation, the connection. Thus with regard to progeny.

अथाध्यात्मम्। अधरा हनुः पूर्वरूपम्। उत्तरा हनुरुत्तररूपम्। वाक् संधिः। जिह्वा संधानम्। इत्यध्यात्मम्। इतीमा महासंहिताः। य एवमेता महासंहिता व्याख्याता वेद। संधीयते प्रजया पशुभिः ब्रह्मवर्चसेनान्नाद्येन सुवर्ग्येण लोकेन॥४॥

Now, with regard to oneself.

The lower jaw is the prior form; the upper jaw, the latter form. Speech is their conjunction; the tongue, the connection. Thus with regard to oneself.

These are the great combinations. He who knows these combinations, thus expounded, becomes conjoined with offspring, with cattle, with pre-eminence in sacred knowledge, with food, with the heavenly world.

।। चतुर्थोऽनुवाकः।।

यश्छन्दसामृषभो विश्वरूपः। छन्दोभ्योऽध्यमृतात्संबभूव। स मेन्द्रो मेधया स्पृणोतु। अमृतस्य देव धारणो भूयासम्। शरीरं मे विचर्षणम्। जिह्वा मे मधुमत्तमा। कर्णाभ्यां भूरि विश्रुवम्। ब्रह्मणः कोशोऽसि मेधया पिहितः। श्रुतं मे गोपाय।।१।।

Fourth Anuvāka

A teacher's prayer

He who is pre-eminent among the Vedic hymns (*chandas*), who is the all-formed (*viśva-rūpa*).

Who has sprung into being from immortality above the Vedic hymns—

Let this Indra deliver (√*spṛ*) me with intelligence!

O God (*deva*), I would become possessor of immortality!

May my body be very vigorous!

May my tongue be exceeding sweet!

May I hear abundantly with my ears!

You are the sheath of Brahma,

With intelligence covered over!

Guard for me what I have heard!

[it is Prosperity] who brings, extends

आवहन्ती वितन्वाना कुर्वाणाचीरमात्मनः। वासाꣳसि मम गावश्च। अन्नपाने च सर्वदा। ततो मे श्रियमावह। लोमशां पशुभिः सह स्वाहा। आ मायन्तु ब्रह्मचारिणः स्वाहा। विमायन्तु ब्रह्मचारिणः स्वाहा। प्रमायन्तु ब्रह्मचारिणः स्वाहा। दमायन्तु ब्रह्मचारिणः स्वाहा। शमायन्तु ब्रह्मचारिणः स्वाहा।।२।।

And long makes her own—

My garments and cows,

And food and drink always.

Therefore bring me prosperity (*śrī*)

In wool, along with cattle!

Hail!

May students of sacred knowledge (*brahmacārin*) come unto me! Hail!

May students of sacred knowledge come apart unto me! Hail!

May students of sacred knowledge come forth unto me! Hail!

May students of sacred knowledge subdue themselves! Hail!

May students of sacred knowledge tranquillise themselves! Hail!

यशो जनेऽसानि स्वाहा। श्रेयान् वस्यसोऽसानि स्वाहा। तं त्वा भग प्रविशानि स्वाहा। स मा भग प्रविश स्वाहा। तस्मिन् सहस्रशाखे। निभगाहं त्वयि मृजे स्वाहा यथापः प्रवता यन्ति। यथा मासा अहर्जरम्। एवं मां ब्रह्मचारिणः। धातरायन्तु सर्वतः स्वाहा। प्रतिवेशोऽसि प्र मा भाहि प्र मा पद्यस्व।।३।।

May I become glorious among men! Hail!

May I be better than the very rich! Hail!

Into you yourself, O Gracious Lord (*bhaga*), may I enter! Hail!

Do you yourself, O Gracious Lord, enter into me! Hail!

In such a one, a thousand-fold ramified—O Gracious Lord, in you I am cleansed! Hail!

As waters run downward, as months into the year, so, O Establisher (*dhātṛ*), may students of sacred knowledge run unto me from all sides! Hail!

You are a refuge! Shine upon me! Come unto me!

।। पञ्चमोऽनुवाकः।।

भूर्भुवः सुवरिति वा एतास्तिस्रो व्याहृतयः। तासामु ह स्मैतां चतुर्थीं माहाचमस्यः प्रवेदयते। मह इति। तद्ब्रह्म। स आत्मा। अङ्गान्यन्या देवताः। भूरिति वा अयं लोकः। भुव इत्यन्तरिक्षम्। सुवरित्यसौ लोकः।।१।।

मह इत्यादित्यः। आदित्येन वाव सर्वे लोका महीयन्ते। भूरिति वा अग्निः। भुव इति वायुः। सुवरित्यादित्यः। मह इति चन्द्रमाः। चन्द्रमसा वाव सर्वाणि ज्योतींषि महीयन्ते। भूरिति वा ऋचः। भुव इति सामानि। सुवरिति यजूंषि।।२।।

Fifth Anuvāka

The fourfold mystic Utterances

Bhūr! *Bhuvas*! *Suvar*! Verily, these are the three Utterances (*vyāhṛti*). And beside these, too, Māhācamasya made known as fourth, namely *Mahas* (Greatness)! That is Brahma. That is the body (*ātman*); other divinities are the limbs.

Bhūr, verily, is this world; *Bhuvas*, the atmosphere; *Suvar*, yonder world;

Mahas, the sun. Verily, all worlds are made greater (*mahīyante*) by the sun.

Bhūr, verily, is Agni (Fire); *Bhuvas*, Vāyu (Wind); *Suvar*, Āditya (Sun); *Mahas*, the moon. Verily, all lights are made greater by the moon.

Bhūr, verily, is the Ṛg verses; *Bhuvas*, the Sāman chants; *Suvar*, the Yajus formulas;

मह इति ब्रह्म। ब्रह्मणा वाव सर्वे वेदा महीयन्ते भूरिति वै प्राणः। भुव इत्यपानः। सुवरिति व्यानः। मह इत्यन्नम्। अन्नेन वाव सर्वे प्राणा महीयन्ते। ता वा एताश्चतस्रश्चतुर्धा। चतस्रश्चतस्रो व्याहृतयः। ता यो वेद। स वेद ब्रह्म। सर्वेऽस्मै देवा बलिमावहन्ति॥३॥

Mahas, sacred knowledge (*brahman*). Verily, all the Vedas are made greater by sacred knowledge.

Bhūr, verily, is the in-breath (*prāṇa*); *Bhuvas*, the out-breath (*apāna*); *Suvar*, the diffused breath (*vyāna*); *Mahas*, food (*anna*). Verily, all the vital breaths (*prāṇa*) are made greater by food.

Verily, these four are fourfold. The Utterances are four ạnd four. He who knows these, knows Brahma; to him all the gods bring strength.

॥ षष्ठोऽनुवाकः॥

स य एषोऽन्तर्हृदय आकाशः। तस्मिन्नयं पुरुषो मनोमयः। अमृतो हिरण्मयः। अन्तरेण तालुके। य एष स्तन इवालम्बते सेन्द्रयोनिः। यत्रासौ केशान्तो विवर्तते। व्यपोह्य शीर्षकपाले भूरित्यग्नौ प्रतितिष्ठति। भुव इति वायौ॥१॥

सुवरित्यादित्ये मह इति ब्रह्मणि। आप्नोति स्वाराज्यम्। आप्नोति मनसस्पतिम्। वाक्पतिश्चक्षुष्पतिः। श्रोत्रपतिर्विज्ञानपतिः। एतत्ततो भवति। आकाशशरीरं ब्रह्म। सत्यात्म प्राणारामं मन आनन्दम्। शान्तिसमृद्धममृतम्। इति प्राचीनयोग्योपास्स्व॥२॥

Sixth Anuvāka

A departing person's attainment with the four Utterances

This space that is within the heart— therein is the person, consisting of mind "(*mano-maya*), immortal, resplendent. That which hangs down between the palates like a nipple— that is Indra's place of exist.

Piercing the head at the point where is the edge of the hair, with the word *Bhūr* he stands upon Agni (Fire); with the word *Bhuvas*, upon Vāyu (Wind);

With the word *Suvar*, upon Āditya (the Sun); with the word *Mahas*, upon Brahma. He obtains self-rule (*svā-rājya*). He obtains the lord of the mind, lord of the voice, lord of the eye, lord of the ear, lord of the understanding—this and more he becomes, even Brahma, whose body is space (*ākāśa-śarīra*), whose soul is the real (*satyātman*), whose pleasure-ground is the breathing spirit, whose mind is bliss (*mana-ānanda*), abounding in tranquillity (*śānti-samṛddha*), immortal. Thus, O Prācīnayogya (Man of the Ancient Yoga), worship.

॥ सप्तमोऽनुवाकः॥

Seventh Anuvāka

The fivefoldness of the world and of the individual

पृथिव्यन्तरिक्षं द्यौर्दिशोऽवान्तरदिशाः। अग्निर्वायुरादित्यश्चन्द्रमा नक्षत्राणि। आप ओषधयो वनस्पतय आकाश आत्मा। इत्यधिभूतम्। अथाध्यात्मम्। प्राणो व्यानोऽपान उदानः समानः। चक्षुः श्रोत्रं मनो वाक् त्वक्। चर्म माꣳसꣳ स्नावस्थिमज्जा। एतदधि विधाय ऋषिरवोचत्। पाङ्क्तं वा इदं सर्वम्। पाङ्क्तेनैव पाङ्क्तꣳ स्पृणोतीति॥१॥

Earth,	atmosphere,	heaven,	quarters of heaven,	intermediate quarters;
fire,	wind,	sun,	moon,	stars;
water,	plants,	trees,	space,	one's body.

Thus with regard to material existence (*adhi-bhūta*).

Now with regard to oneself (*adhy-ātma*).

Prāṇa breath,	Vyāna breath,	Apāna breath,	Udāna breath,	Samāna breath;
sight,	hearing,	mind,	speech,	touch;
skin,	flesh,	muscle,	bone,	marrow.

Having analyzed in this manner, a seer has said : 'Fivefold, verily, is this whole world. With the fivefold, indeed, one wins the fivefold.'

॥ अष्टमोऽनुवाकः॥

ओमिति ब्रह्म। ओमतीदꣳसर्वम्। ओमित्येदनुकृतिर्हस्म वा अप्यो श्रावयेत्याश्रावयन्ति। ओमिति सामानि गायन्ति। ओꣳशोमिति। शस्त्राणि शꣳसन्ति। ओमित्यध्वर्युः प्रतिगरं प्रतिगृणाति। ओमिति ब्रह्मा प्रसौति। ओमित्यग्निहोत्रमनुजानाति। ओमिति ब्राह्मणः प्रवक्ष्यन्नाह ब्रह्मोपाप्नवानीति ब्रह्मैवोपाप्नोति॥१॥

Eighth Anuvāka

Glorification of the sacred word 'Oṁ'

Oṁ is *brahman*. *Oṁ* is the whole world. *Oṁ*—that is compliance. As also, verily, it is well known—upon the words 'O! Call forth!' they call forth.

With '*Oṁ*' they sing the Sāman chants.

With '*Oṁ! Śom!*' they recite the Invocations of Praise (*śastra*).

With '*Oṁ*' the Adhvaryu priest utters the Response.

With '*Oṁ*' the Brahman priest (Brahmā) utters the Introductory Eulogy (*pra*+$\sqrt{}$*stu*).

With '*Oṁ*' one assents to the Agni-oblation (*agnihotra*).

'*Oṁ*', says a Brahman (*Brāhmaṇa*) about to recite, 'may I get the sacred word (*brahma*)!' He does get the sacred word.

।। नवमोऽनुवाकः।।

ऋतं च स्वाध्यायप्रवचने च। सत्यं च स्वाध्यायप्रवचने च। तपश्च स्वाध्यायप्रवचने च। दमश्च स्वाध्यायप्रवचने च। शमश्च स्वाध्यायप्रवचने च। अग्नयश्च स्वाधायप्रवचने च। अग्निहोत्रं च स्वाध्यायप्रवचने च। अतिथयश्च स्वाध्यायप्रवचने च। मानुषं च स्वाध्यायप्रवचने च। प्रजा च स्वाध्यायप्रवचने च। प्रजनश्च स्वाध्यायप्रवचने च। प्रजातिश्च स्वाध्यायप्रवचने च। सत्यमिति सत्यवचा राथीतरः। तप इति तपोनित्यः पौरुशिष्टिः। स्वाध्यायप्रवचने एवेति नाको मौद्गल्यः। तद्धि तपस्तद्धि तपः।।१।।

Ninth Anuvāka

Study of the sacred word the most important of all duties

The right (*ṛta*), and also study and teaching.

The true (*satya*), and also study and teaching.

Austerity (*tapas*), and also study and teaching.

Self-control (*dama*), and also study and teaching.

Tranquility (*śama*), and also study and teaching.

The [sacrificial] fires, and also study and teaching.

The Agnihotra sacrifice, and also study and teaching.

Guests, and also study and teaching.

Humanity (*mānuṣa*), and also study and teaching.

Offspring, and also study and teaching.

Begetting, and also study and teaching.

Procreation, and also study and teaching.

'The true!'—says Satyavacas ('Truthful') Rathītara.

'Austerity!'—says Taponitya ('Devoted-to-austerity') Pauruśiṣṭi.

'Just study and teaching!'— says Nāka ('Painless') Maudgalya, 'for that is austerity—for that is austerity.'

।। दशमोऽनुवाकः।।

अहं वृक्षस्य रेरिवा कीर्तिः पृष्ठं गिरेरिव। ऊर्ध्वपवित्रो वाजिनीव स्वमृतमस्मि। द्रविणꣳ सवर्चसम्। सुमेधा अमृतोक्षितः। इति त्रिशङ्कोर्वेदानुवचनम्।।१।।

Tenth Anuvāka

The excellence of Veda-knowledge– a meditation

I am the mover of the tree! My fame is like a mountain's peak!

Exaltedly pure, like the excellent nectar in the sun,
I am a shining treasure, wise, immortal, indestructible!
This is Triśaṅku's recitation on Veda-knowledge.

॥ एकादशोऽनुवाकः॥

वेदमनूच्याचार्योऽन्तेवासिनमनुशास्ति। सत्यं वद। धर्मं चर। स्वाध्यायान्मा प्रमदः। आचार्याय प्रियं धनमाहृत्य प्रजातन्तुं मा व्यवच्छेत्सीः। सत्यान्न प्रमदितव्यम्। धर्मान्न प्रमदितव्यम्। कुशलान्न प्रमदितव्यम्। भूत्यै न प्रमदितव्यम्। स्वाध्यायप्रवचनाभ्यां न प्रमदितव्यम्। देवपितृकार्याभ्यां न प्रमदितव्यम्॥१॥

मातृदेवो भव। पितृदेवो भव। आचार्यदेवो भव। अतिथिदेवो भव। यान्यनवद्यानि कर्माणि तानि सेवितव्यानि नो इतराणि। यान्यस्माकꣳ सुचरितानि तानि त्वयोपास्यानि॥२॥

नो इतराणि ये के चास्मच्छ्रेयाꣳसो ब्राह्मणः तेषां त्वयाऽऽसने न प्रश्वसितव्यम् श्रद्धया देयम्। अश्रद्धयाऽ देयम्। श्रिया देयम्। ह्रिया देयम्। भिया देयम्। संविदा देयम्। अथ यदि ते कर्मविचिकित्सा वा वृत्तविचिकित्सा वा स्यात्॥३॥

ये यत्र ब्राह्मणाः संमर्शिनः। युक्ता आयुक्ताः अलूक्षा धर्मकामाः स्युः। यथा ते तत्र वर्तेरन्। तथा वर्तेथाः। अथाभ्याख्यातेषु। ये तत्र ब्राह्मणाः संमर्शिनः। युक्ता आयुक्ताः। अलूक्षा धर्मकामाः स्युः। यथा ते तेषु वर्तेरन्। तथा तेषु वर्तेथाः। एष आदेशः। एष उपदेशः। एषा वेदोपनिषत्। एतदनुशासनम्। एवमुपासितव्यम्। एवमु चैतदुपास्यम्॥४॥

Eleventh Anuvāka

Practical precepts to a student

Having taught the Veda, a teacher further instructs a pupil :-

Speak the truth. Practise virtue (*dharma*). Neglect not study [of the Vedas].

Having brought an acceptable gift to the teacher, cut not off the line of progeny.

One should not be negligent of truth. One should not be negligent of virtue.

One should not be negligent of welfare. One should not be negligent of prosperity.

One should not be negligent of study and teaching.

2. One should not be negligent of duties to the gods and to the fathers.

Be one to whom a mother is as a god.

Be one to whom a father is as a god.

Be one to whom a teacher is as a god.

Be one to whom a guest is as a god.

Those acts which are irreproachable should be practised, and no others.

Those things which among us are god deeds should be revered by you,

3. and no others.

Whatever Brahmans (*Brāhmaṇa*) are superior to us, for them refreshment should be procured by you with a seat.

One should give with faith (*śraddhā*).

One should not give without faith.

One should not give with plenty (*śrī*).

One should give with modesty.

One should give with fear.

One should give with sympathy (*sam-vid*).

Now, if you should have doubt concerning an act, or doubt concerning conduct,

4. if there should be there Brahmans competent to judge, apt, devoted, not harsh, lovers of virtue (*dharma*)—as they may behave themselves in such a case, so should you behave yourself in such a case.

Now, with regard to [people] spoken against, if there should be there Brāhmaṇas competent to judge, apt, devoted, not harsh, lovers of virtue—as they may behave themselves with regard to such, so should you behave yourself with regard to such.

[This is the teaching. This is the admonition. This is the mystic doctrine of the Veda (*veda-upaniṣad*). This is the instruction. Thus should one worship. Thus, indeed, should one worship. In this hymn, we see that the teacher is making an enquiry of the knowledge acquired by his pupil on successful completion of their studies unto Vedas and preaching them the modas-operandi as also modas-bevandi according to which they have to transmit their knowledge in their behavioural world. In fact, the knowledge only shines when it is brought out while one is activating in his respective fields. The study or the knowledge that remains confined to the books is worthless if it cannot bring any specific change in the personality of the concerned man. This is the reason why the respective teacher preaching his pupil herein some salient features which they have to follow on their return to material world. He is teaching the salient part of character popularly known as discipline but he doesn't draw any limit that the knowledge is only but he had taught them. He inspires them getting their concerneds with most learned person if they deem any confusion or doubt on the aspect they could study while in acquaintance with their teacher. The noun "Brahmin" is only used for that person who is well-illuminating by virtue of knowledge and has no attachment, ego etc. as the other persons of the society are expected. The man who have converted all the aspects of knowledge in his practical life is only eligible to provide with the right advice unbiased and free from attachment as also of fear.]

।। द्वादशोऽनुवाकः।।

शं नो मित्रः शं वरुणः। शं नो भवत्वर्यमा। शं नो इन्द्रो बृहस्पतिः। शं नो विष्णुरुरुक्रमः। नमो ब्रह्मणे। नमस्ते वायो। त्वमेव प्रत्यक्षं ब्रह्मासि। त्वामेव प्रत्यक्षं ब्रह्मावादिषम्। ऋतमवादिषम्। सत्यमवादिषम्। तन्मामावीत्। तद्वक्तारमावीत्। आवीन्माम्। आवीद्वक्तारम्।। ॐ शान्तिः शान्तिः शान्तिः।।१।।

Twelfth Anuvāka

Invocation, adoration and acknowledgement

Propitious unto us, Propitious, Varuṇa! Propitious unto us, let Aryaman be! Propitious unto us, Indra! Bṛhaspati! Propitious unto us, Viṣṇu, the Wide-strider!

Adoration to Brahmā! Adoration to you, Vāyu!

You, indeed, are the perceptible Brahma. Of you, indeed, the perceptible Brahma, have I spoken. I have spoken of the right. I have spoken of the true. That has favoured me. That has favoured the speaker. It has favoured me. It has favoured the speaker.

Oṁ! Peace! Peace! Peace!

ब्रह्मानन्दवल्ली

॥शान्तिपाठः॥

ॐ सह नाववतु। सह नौ भुनक्तु। सह वीर्यं करवावहै। तेजस्वि नावधीतमस्तु मा विद्विषावहै॥
ॐ शान्तिः शान्तिः शान्तिः॥१॥

2. Brahmānandavallī

Pray for the peace :

May the supreme soul protect both of us (the teacher and the pupil). May it provide us nutrition altogether. May both of us do exertion together. Be our study blessed with splendour. May we get rid of the mutual envy and malaphides with one another. May the peace remove all the trio suffering *i.e.* physical, mental and spiritual.

॥ प्रथमोऽनुवाकः॥

ॐ ब्रह्मविदाप्नोति परम्। तदेषाऽभ्युक्ता। सत्यं ज्ञानमनन्तं ब्रह्म। यो वेद निहितं गुहायां परमे व्योमन्। सोऽश्नुते सर्वान् कामान् सह ब्रह्मणा विपश्चितेति। तस्माद्वा एतस्मादात्मन आकाशः संभूतः। आकाशाद्वायुः। वायोरग्निः। अग्नेरापः। अद्भ्यः पृथिवी। पृथिव्या ओषधयः। ओषधीभ्योऽन्नम्। अन्नात्पुरुषः। स वा एषा पुरुषोऽन्नरसमयः। तस्येदमेव शिरः। अयं दक्षिणः पक्षः। अयमुत्तरः पक्षः। अयमात्मा इदं पुच्छं प्रतिष्ठा। तदप्येष श्लोको भवति॥१॥

First Anuvāka

The all-comprehensive Brahma of the world and of the individual; knowledge thereof the supreme success

Oṁ! He who knows Brahma, attains the highest! For which this [verse] has been declared :-

He who knows Brahma as the real (*satya*), as knowledge (*jñāna*), as the infinite (*ananta*),

Set down in the secret lace [of the heart] and in the highest heaven (*parame vyoman*),

He obtains all desires, along with the intelligent (*vipaścit*) Brahma.

From this Soul (Ātman), verily, space (*ākāśa*) arose; from space, wind (*vāyu*); from wind, fire; from fire, water; from water, the earth; from the earth, herbs; from herbs, food; from food, semen; from semen, the person (*puruṣa*).

[The person consisting of food]

This, verily, is the person that consists of the essence of food. This, indeed, is his head; this, the right side; this, the left side; this, the body (*ātman*); this, the lower part, the foundation.

As to that there is also this verse :-

[The above hymn classifies the systematic consumption process of the perfect knowledge when it gets the touch of a body. A scientific process in respect of creation of the living organism indeed has been described here fantastically. The modern sciences also accept that in the origin of this nature ether was the first element and the air, the fire, the water and the earth has got their birth systematically as a chain reaction.]

।। द्वितीयोऽनुवाकः।।

In succeeding hymns the origin of 5 elements from the god as also the 5 kinds of elements incorporated in the human body have been described. It has been made crystal clear that the size of all these 5 elements inserted into the human body is proportionate to the body. These 5 elements have been described by taking a bird suitable for the comparison while discussing on division of a human body as the head, the trunk and the tail. The head of mankind has been compared with the head of a bird, the two arms with his right and left wing and the feet with the tail of the bird.

अन्नाद्वै प्रजाः प्रजायन्ते यः काश्च पृथिवीᳫश्रिताः। अथो अन्नेनैव जीवन्ति। अथैनदपि यन्त्यन्ततः। अन्नᳫहि भूतानां ज्येष्ठम्। तस्मात्सर्वौषधमुच्यते। सर्वं वै तेऽन्नमाप्नुवन्ति। येऽन्नं ब्रह्मोपासते। अन्नᳫहि भूतानां ज्येष्ठम्। तस्मात्सर्वौषधमुच्यते। अन्नाद्भूतानि जायन्ते। जातान्यन्नेन वर्धन्ते। अद्यतेऽत्ति च भूतानि तस्मादन्नं तदुच्यत इति। तस्माद्वा एतस्मादन्नरसमयात्। अन्योऽन्तर आत्मा प्राणमयः। तेनैष पूर्णः। स एव पुरुषविध एव। तस्य पुरुषविधताम्। अन्वयं पुरुषविधः। तस्या प्राण एव शिरः। व्यानो दक्षिणः पक्षः। अपान उत्तरः पक्षः। आकाश आत्मा। पृथिवी पुच्छं प्रतिष्ठा। तदप्येष श्लोको भवति।।१।।

Second Anuvāka

Food the supporting, yet consuming, substance of all life; a phase of Brahman

From food, verily, creatures are produced, Whatsoever [creatures] dwell on the earth.

Moreover by food, in truth, they live. Moreover into it also they finally pass.

For truly, food is the chief of beings; Therefore it is called a panacea. Verily, they obtain all food who worship Brahma as food.

For truly, food is the chief of beings; Therefore it is called a panacea.

From food created things are born. By food, when born, do they grow up.

It both is eaten and eats things. Because of that it is called food.

The person consisting of breath Verily, other than and within that one that consists of the essence of food is the self that consists of breath. By that this is filled. This, verily, has the form of a person. According to that one's personal form is this one with the form of a person. The in-breath (*prāṇa*) is its head; the diffused breath (*vyāna*), the right wing; the out-breath (*apāna*), the left wing; space, the body (*ātman*); the earth, the lower part, the foundation.

As to that there is also this verse :—

[In these hymns, the supremacy of cereals in human life has been described. These emphasize on the vitality of the cereals and say that cereals are only cause of the origin of body. Cereals provide nutrition and ultimately these also become the cause of death. It has been expected herein that the mankind should pay the special care to the cereals and may never spoil it because it is the supreme among all elements. Further, it has been made clear that the soul not withstanding live in body, it never be affected either by the positive or the negative virtues of the body. In other words, there is a sheer distinction between the soul and the body. The form of the Prāṇa has been assumed as a person.]

।। तृतीयोऽनुवाकः।।

प्राणं देवा अनु प्राणन्ति। मनुष्याः पशवश्च ये। प्राणो हि भूतानामायुः। तस्मा त्सर्वायुषमुच्यते। सर्वमेव च आयुर्यन्ति। ये प्राणं ब्रह्मोपासते। प्राणो हि भूतानामायुः। तस्मात्सर्वायुषमुच्यत इति। तस्यैष एव शारीर आत्मा। यः पूर्वस्य तस्माद्वा एतस्मात्प्राणमयात्। अन्योऽन्तर आत्मा मनोमयः। तेनैष पूर्णः। स वा एष पुरुषविध एव। तस्य पुरुषविधताम्। अन्वयं पुरुषविधः। तस्य यजुरेव शिरः। ऋग् दक्षिणः पक्षः। सामोत्तरः पक्षः। आदेश आत्मा। अथर्वाङ्गिरसः पुच्छं प्रतिष्ठा। तदप्येष श्लोको भवति।।

Third Anuvāka

Breath, the life of all living beings; a phase of Brahma

The gods do breathe along with breath (*prāṇa*), as also men and beasts.

For truly, breath is the life (*āyus*) of beings therefore, it is called the Life-of-all (*sarvāyuṣa*).

To a full life (*sarvam āyus*) go they who worship Brahma as breath.

For truly, breath is the life of beings;

Therefore it is called the Life-of-all.

This, indeed, is its bodily self (*śarīra-ātman*), as of the former.

The person consisting of mind

Verily, other than and within that one that consists of breath is a self that consists of mind (*mano-maya*). By that this is filled. This, verily, has the form of a person. According to that one's personal form is this one with the form of a person. The Yajurveda is its head; the Ṛgveda, the right side; the Sāmaveda, the left side; teaching, the body (*ātman*); the Hymns of the Atharvans and Aṅgirasas, the lower part, the foundation.

As to that there is also this verse :—

[In these hymns, the breathing (Prāṇa) has been appreciated describing that it is the life of all beings and the inner soul of the body made of cereals. Another body within the same living body has been assumed and named as the body of the mind. This another body *i.e.* the body of mind has features of a man and all the 4 Vedas have been told the different organs of this body. We see here that how beautifully these hymns have drawn a distinction between two kinds of bodies - 1. the body made of cereal and 2. the body of mind.

The pupil unguided by the brain and particularly those who don't apply their mind while performing any activity are devoid of the body of mind. They have only a single body which is made of cereals and their activities are only confined to earning money and their food without applying their discretion, they perform their activities which have merely nexus with their pitty interests while the body of mind is acquired only through a prolong penance on devoting oneself in the study of Vedas or the knowledge in itself.]

।। चतुर्थोऽनुवाकः।।

यतो वाचो निवर्तन्ते अप्राप्य मनसा सह। आनन्दं ब्रह्मणो विद्वान्। न बिभेति कदाचनेति। तस्यैष एव शारीर आत्मा। यः पूर्वस्य तस्माद्वा एतस्मान्मनोमयात्। अन्योऽन्तर आत्मा विज्ञानमयः। तेनैषः पूर्णः। स वा एष पुरुषविध एव। तस्य पुरुषविधताम्। अन्वयं पुरुषविधः। तस्य श्रद्धैव शिरः। ऋतं दक्षिणः पक्षः। सत्यमुत्तरः पक्षः। योग आत्मा। महः पुच्छं प्रतिष्ठा। तदप्येष श्लोको भवति।।१।।

Fourth Anuvāka

Inexpressible, fearless bliss; a phase of Brahman

Wherefrom words turn back, together with the mind, not having attained—

The bliss of Brahma he who knows; Fears not at any time at all.

This, indeed, is its bodily self (*śarīra-ātman*), as of the former.

The person consisting of understanding

Verily, other than and within that one that consists of mind is a self that consists of understanding (*vijñāna-maya*). By that this is filled. This, verily, has the form of a person. According to that one's personal form is this one with the form of a person. Faith (*śraddhā*) is its head; the right (*ṛta*), the right side; the true (*satya*), the left side; contemplation (*yoga*), the body (*ātman*); might (*mahas*), the lower part, the foundation.

As to that there is also this verse :—

[A third body has been also assumed alongwith the first two already described in the precedent hymn. It has been told that this body of conscious dwells in the body of mind, its feature has been also told the same as the body of mind and the parts of body have been described distinctly. Thus we see that gradually the structurization of the body is availing varied shapes. The body of conscious as implies from its name is the purified soul carefully cleaned and with regular practice made able to bear some specific properties like obeisance, the sense of right and wrong, the truth while speaking, the art of meditation and the etiquette and its entirity. Thus, the macro or apparent feature of the body is going to see its micro features.]

।। पञ्चमोऽनुवाकः।।

विज्ञानं यज्ञं तनुते। कर्माणि तनुतेऽपि च। विज्ञानं देवाः सर्वे। ब्रह्म ज्येष्ठमुपासते। विज्ञानं ब्रह्म चेद्वेद। तस्माच्चेन्न प्रमाद्यति शरीरे पाप्मनो हित्वा। सर्वान्कामान्समश्नुत इति। तस्यैष एव शारीर आत्मा। यः पूर्वस्य। तस्माद्वा एतस्माद्विज्ञानमयात्। अन्योऽन्तर आत्मानन्दमयः। तेनैष पूर्णः। स वा एष पुरुषविध एव। तस्य

पुरुषविधताम्। अन्वयं पुरुषविधः। तस्य प्रियमेव शिरः। मोदो दक्षिणः पक्षः। प्रमोद उत्तरः पक्षः। आनन्द आत्मा। ब्रह्म पुच्छं प्रतिष्ठा। तदप्येष श्लोको भवति॥१॥

Fifth Anuvāka

Understanding, all-directing; a saving and satisfying phase of Brahma

Understanding directs the sacrifice;

And deeds also it directs.

This understanding that all the gods do worship as Brahman, as chief.

If one knows Brahman as understanding, and if he is not heedless thereto, He leaves his sins (*pāpman*) in the body and attains all desires.

This, indeed, is its bodily self, as of the former.

Verily, other than and within that one that consists of understanding is a self that consists of bliss (*ānanda-maya*). By that this is filled. That one, verily, has the form of a person. According to that one's personal form is this one with the form of a person. Pleasure (*priya*) is its head; delight (*moda*), the right side; great delight (*pra-moda*), the left side; bliss (*ānanda*), the body (*ātman*); Brahma, the lower part, the foundation.

As to that there is also this verse :—

[Again in this fifth lesson another body has been also invented. This body is assumed as the body providing with pleasure. It has been told that this body of pleasure is inserted within the body of conscious. Having its direct nexus with the pleasure the deity, the enjoyment, the meriments etc. has been described as the parts of this body. It has now become clear that there are 4 kinds of micro bodies within the common body fed on the cereals. The body described herein is the last because human life or even life of all beings long for the pleasure. They indeed enjoy the real pleasure *i.e.* eternal.]

॥ षष्ठोऽनुवाकः॥

असन्नेव स भवति असद्ब्रह्मेति वेद चेत्। ब्रह्मेति चेद्वेद। सन्तमेनं ततो विदुरिति। तस्यैष एव शारीर आत्मा यः पूर्वस्य। अथातोऽनुप्रश्नाः। उताविद्वानमुं लोकं प्रेत्य कश्चन गच्छती३। आहो विद्वानमुं लोकं प्रेत्य। कश्चित्समश्नुता३ उ। सोऽकामयत। बहुभ्यां प्रजायेयेति। स तपोऽतप्यत। स तपस्तप्त्वा इदꣳ सर्वमसृजत। यदिदं किंच। तत्सृष्ट्वा तदेवानुप्राविशत्। तदनु प्रविश्य सच्च त्यच्चाभवत्। निरुक्तं चानिरुक्तं च। निलयनं चानिलयनं च। विज्ञानं चाविज्ञानं च। सत्यं चानृतं च सत्यमभवत्। यदिदं किं च। तत्सत्यमित्याचक्षते। तदप्येष श्लोको भवति॥१॥

Sixth Anuvāka

Assimilation either to the original or to the derivative Brahma which one knows

Non-existent (*a-sat*) himself does one become, If he knows that Brahma is non-existent.

If one knows that Brahma exists, Such a one people thereby know as existent.

This, indeed, is its bodily self, as of the former.

Query : Who reaches the Brahma-word of bliss?

Now next, the appurtenant questions (*anu-praśna*) :—

Does any one who knows not,

On deceasing, go to yonder world?

Or is it that any one who knows,

On deceasing attains yonder world?

All plurality and antitheses of existence developed from an original and still immanent unity

He desired : 'Would that I were many! Let me procreate myself!' He performed austerity. Having performed austerity he created this whole world, whatever there is here. Having created it into it, indeed, he entered. Having entered it, he became both the actual (*sat*) and the yon (*tya*), both the defined (*nirukta*) and the undefined, both the based and the non-based, both the conscious (*vijñāna*) and the unconscious, both the real (*satya*) and the false (*anṛta*). As the real, he became whatever there is here. That is what they call the real.

As to that there is also this verse :—

[It is beautifully explained here that whatever be learned persons observed unbiased is certainly true. The question raises here is that to whom we can say the learned person? Whether the invader, the torcherer, the terrorist and evil doers can be said learned person? Certainly not because here is always found a sheer difference between activities, the routine, the behaviour etc. of a learned person and the shrewd one. Whose mind is involved in performing great deeds will certainly ponder upon the philanthropy and his acts will definitely benevolent however much or less in proportion to his caliber and capacity both. When this is the position, the statements or the advises given by them will certainly be for the welfare of mankind. How a learned person develops his career to realize the truth has been compared here with the systematic efforts of the God itself. As the God wished to appear in countless features and with a view to fill this necessity, the almighty did penance, the learned person also involved themselves in sheer exertion. However, as the God has many features and the pupil have different faiths on him, a learned person has also different identities in the public. Everyone observes him in the light of his activities *i.e.* a thief will certainly imagine him as thief while a businessman as businessman, while the man about whom are different identities is the Ṛṣi person always unavariated in his nature and the deeds performed by him.]

।। सप्तमोऽनुवाकः।।

असद्वा इदमग्र आसीत्। ततो वै सदजायत। तदात्मानꣳ स्वयमकुरुत। तस्मात्तत्सुकृतमुच्यत इति। यद्वै तत्सुकृतम्। रसो वै सः। रसꣳ ह्येवायं लब्ध्वानन्दी भवति। को ह्येवान्यात्कः प्राण्यात्। यदेष आकाश आनन्दो न स्यात्। एष ह्येवानन्दयाति यदा ह्येवैष एतस्मिन्नदृश्येऽनात्म्येऽनिरुक्तेऽनिलयनेऽभयं प्रतिष्ठां विन्दते। अथ सोऽभयं गतो भवति यदा ह्येवैष एतस्मिन्नुदरमन्तरं कुरुते। अथ तस्य भयं भवति। तत्त्वेव भयं विदुषोऽमन्वानस्य। तदप्येष श्लोको भवति।।१।।

Seventh Anuvāka

The original self-developing non-existence, the essence of existence and the sole basis of fearless bliss

In the beginning, verily, this [world] was non-existent.

Therefrom, verily, Being (*sat*) was produced.

That made itself (*svayam akuruta*) a Soul (Ātman).

Therefore it is called the well-done (*su-kṛta*).

Verily, what that well done is—that, verily, is the essence (*rasa*) [of existence]. For truly, on getting the essence, one becomes blissful. For who indeed would breathe, who would live, if there were not this bliss in space! For truly, this (essence) cause bliss. For truly, when one finds fearlessness as a foundation in that which is invisible, bodiless (*an-ātmya*), undefined, non-based, then he has reached fearlessness. When, however, one makes a cavity, an interval therein, then he comes to have fear. But that indeed is the fear of one who thinks of himself as a knower.

As to that there is also this verse :—

[It has been told in these hymns that prior to become an apparent deed the human mind gets the information and merge it with his perceptions and only thereafter the concerned activity is performed. The nature or Prakṛti in its micro sense reveals the mental world of mankind. The Indian Jurisprudence also accepts the fact that prior to determining the gravity of crime, it is essential to measure or investigate the proportionate guilty of the concerned accuse. What is intangible is the premier thing that gives birth to the tangible objects, however, while intangible form the process goes on and the thought is organized which result is the deed which can be observed later. By virtue of the preaching, through these hymns it has been told that however, intangible but one should reform to it so that its result, the tangible one is appreciated by the concerned society that observes it.]

॥ अष्टमोऽनुवाकः॥

भीषाऽस्माद्वातः पवते। भीषोदेति सूर्यः। भीषाऽस्मादग्निश्चेन्द्रश्च मृत्युर्धावति पञ्चम इति। सैषाऽऽनन्दस्य मीमाꣳसा भवति। युवा स्यात्साधुयुवाध्यायक आशिष्ठो द्रढिष्ठो बलिष्ठः। तस्येयं पृथिवी सर्वा वित्तस्य पूर्णा स्यात्। स एको मानुष आनन्दः। ते ये शतं मानुषा आनन्दाः। स एको मनुष्यगन्धर्वाणामानन्दः। क्षोत्रियस्य चाकामहतस्य। ते ते शतं मनुष्यगन्धर्वाणामानन्दः। स एको देवगन्धर्वाणामानन्दः। क्षोत्रियस्य चाकामहतस्य। ते ते शतं देवगन्धर्वाणामानन्दः। स एकः पितॄणां चिरलोकलोकानामानन्दः। श्रोत्रियस्य चाकामहतस्य। ते ये शतं पितॄणां चिरलोकलोकानामानन्दाः। स एक आजानजानां देवानामानन्दः। श्रोत्रियस्य चाकामहतस्य। ते ये शतमाजानजानां देवानामानन्दाः। स एकः कर्मदेवानां देवानामानन्दः। ये कर्मणा देवानपि यन्ति श्रोत्रियस्य चाकामहतस्य। ते ये शतं कर्मदेवानां देवानामानन्दाः। स एको देवानामानन्दः। श्रोत्रियस्य चाकामहतस्य। ते ये शतं देवानामानन्दाः। स एक इन्द्रस्यानन्दः। श्रोत्रियस्य चाकामहतस्य। ते ये शतमिन्द्रस्यानन्दाः। स एको बृहस्पतेरानन्दः। श्रोत्रियस्य चाकामहतस्य। ते ये शतं बृहस्पतेरानन्दाः। स एकः प्रजापतेरानन्दः। श्रोत्रियस्य

चाकामहतस्य। ते ये शतं प्रजापतेरानन्दाः। स एको ब्रह्मण आनन्दः। श्रोत्रियस्य चाकामहतस्य। स यश्चायं पुरुषे। यश्चासावादित्ये। स एकः। स य एवंवित्। अस्माल्लोकात्प्रेत्य। एतमन्नमयमात्मानमुपसंक्रामति। एतं प्राणमयमात्मानमुपसंक्रामति। एतं मनोमयमात्मानमुपसंक्रामति। एतं विज्ञानमयमात्मानमुपसंक्रामति। एतमानन्दमयमात्मानमुपसंक्रामति। तदप्येष श्लोको भवति।।१।।

Eighth Anuvāka

All cosmic activity through fear of the Supreme

Through fear of Him the Wind (Vāyu) doth blow.

Through fear of Him the Sun (Sūrya) doth rise.

Through fear of Him both Agni (Fire) and Indra

And Death (Mṛtyu) as fifth do speed along.

The gradation of blisses up to the bliss of Brahma

This is a consideration (*mīmāṁsā*) of bliss.

Let there be a youth, a good (*sādhu*) youth, well read, very quick, very firm, very strong. Let this whole earth be full of wealth for him. That is one human bliss.

A hundred human blisses are one bliss of the human Gandharvas (genii)—also of a man who is versed in the scriptures (*śrotriya*) and who is not smitten with desire.

A hundred blisses of the human Gandharvas are one bliss of the divine Gandharvas—also of a man who is versed in the scriptures and who is not smitten with desire.

A hundred blisses of the divine Gandharvas are one bliss of the fathers in their long enduring world—also fo a man who is versed in the scriptures and who is not smitten with desire.

A hundred blisses of the fathers in their long enduring world are one bliss of the gods who are born so by birth (*ājāna-ja*)—also of a man who is versed in the scriptures and who is not smitten with desire.

A hundred blisses of the gods who are born so by birth are one bliss of the gods who are gods by work (*karma-deva*), who go to the gods by work—also of a man who is versed in the scriptures and who is not smitten with desire.

A hundred blisses of the gods who are gods by work are one bliss of the gods—also of a man who is versed in the scriptures and who is not smitten with desire.

A hundred blisses of the gods are one bliss of Indra—also of a man who is versed in the scriptures and who is not smitten with desire.

A hundred blisses of Indra are one bliss of Bṛhaspati—also of a man who is versed in the scriptures and who is not smitten with desire.

A hundred blisses of Bṛhaspati are one bliss of Prajāpati—also of a man who is versed in the scriptures and who is not smitten with desire.

A hundred blisses of Prajāpati are one bliss of Brahma—also of a man who is versed in the scriptures and who is not smitten with desire.

The knower of the unity of the human person with the personality in the world reaches the self consisting of bliss

Both he who is here in a person and he who is yonder in the sun—he is one.

He who knows this, on departing from this world, proceeds on to that self which consists of food, proceeds on to that self which consists of breath, proceeds on to that self which consists of mind, proceeds on to that self which consists of understanding, proceeds on to that self which consists of bliss.

As to that there is also this verse :—

[It is worth mentioned here that the attainment of pleasure is not merely possible when one has suffice estate and the property. He needs a supreme personality by all the four corners. In succeeding hymns, this pleasure is classified in degrees or duly categorized. The Ṛṣi has envisaged repeatedly that this pleasure can only availed to a person who is enriched of knowledge and get rid of the passions or any kind of temptations. He says that the ignorant, wanders hither and thither by fascinating in the minor feelings of pleasure, therefore, he can't access to the supreme pleasure throughout his life. As the ailing tongue can't feel the taste in the respective fusion, the mind hung on the passions in the same way can't feel the taste of supreme pleasure. What is intended through these hymns is a message to human beings that they shouldn't be indulged with the material pleasures because all such kinds of gaieties are momentary and only stand in the way to search for the supreme pleasure. One should therefore protect him from indulging in the material pleasure which have no longer existence than the bubble of the water.]

।। नवमोऽनुवाकः।।

यतो वाचो निवर्तन्ते अप्राप्य मनसा सह। आनन्दं ब्रह्मणो विद्वान्। न बिभेति कुतश्चनेति। एतꣳह वाव न तपति किमहꣳ साधु नाकरवम्। किमहं पापमकरवमिति। स य एवं विद्वानेति आत्मानꣳ स्पृणुते उभे ह्येवैष एते आत्मानꣳ स्पृणुते य एवं वेद। इत्युपनिषत्।।१।।

Ninth Anuvāka

The knower of the bliss of Brahma is saved from all fear and from all moral self-reproach

Wherefrom words turn back,

Together with the mind, not having attained—

The bliss of Brahman he who knows,

Fears not from anything at all.

Such a one, verily, the thought dose not torment : 'Why have I not done the good (*sādhu*)? Why have I done the evil (*pāpa*)?' He who knows this, delivers (*spṛṇute*) himself (*ātmānam*) from these two [thoughts]. For truly, from both of these he delivers himself—he who knows this!

Such is the mystic doctrine (*upaniṣad*)!

[The supremacy of knowledge is again stretched upon and it has been said very clearly that the knowledge is like a beam of light that makes the man to know where are the dark places or the loopholes in his personality. Thus having reckoned with the nature of deeds either good or evil, he brooms out the great deeds instead of the evils. When the deeds are performed so benevolent why world he lament later on when the consequences are turned upon or the crop of deeds will be ripen. Again a learned person have no attachment with the great deeds because he knows that if a slight attachment takes place, it could expect praise from the person or the class of pupil for whom he had done well. In case, this expectation is not fulfilled, either anger or disgust will take place in his heart. On the other hand, if he receives warm appreciation from the public, an ego will certainly insert into his personality thereby making him egoistic. This is the reason a learned person is never attached with the great deeds performed by him and acts on the principle that to do and forget.]

• • • • •

भृगुवल्ली

।। प्रथमोऽनुवाकः।।

भृगुर्वै वारुणिः। वरुणं पितरमुपससार। अधीहि भगवो ब्रह्मेति। तस्मा। एतत्प्रोवाच। अन्नं प्राणं चक्षुः श्रोत्रं वाचमिति। तꣳ होवाच। यतो वा इमानि भूतानि जायन्ते। येन जातानि जीवन्ति। यत्प्रयन्त्यभिसंविशन्ति। तद्विजिज्ञासस्व। तद्ब्रह्मेति। स तपोऽतप्यत। स तपस्तप्त्वा।।१।।

Bhṛguvallī

Bhṛgu's progressive learning through austerity of five phases of Brahma

First Anuvāka

Bhṛgu Vāruṇi, verily, approached his father Varuṇa and said : 'Declare Brahma, sir!'

To him he taught that as food, as breath, as sight, as hearing, as mind, as speech.

Then he said to him : 'That, verily, whence beings here are born, that by which when born they live, that into which on deceasing they enter—that be desirous of understanding. That is Brahma.'

He performed austerity. Having performed austerity,

।। द्वितीयोऽनुवाकः।।

अन्नं ब्रह्मेति व्यजानात्। अन्नाद्ध्येव खल्विमानि भूतानि जायन्ते। अन्नेन जातानि जीवन्ति। अन्नं प्रयन्त्यभिसंविशन्तीति। तद्विज्ञाय। पुनरेव वरुणं पितरमुपससार। अधीहि भगवो ब्रह्मेति। तꣳहोवाच। तपसा ब्रह्म विजिज्ञासस्व। तपो ब्रह्मेति स तपोऽतप्यत। स तपस्तप्त्वा।।१।।

Lesson - 2

He understood that Brahma is food. For truly, indeed, beings here are born from food, when born they live by food, on deceasing they enter into food.

Having understood that, he again approached his father Varuṇa and said : 'Declare Brahma, sir!'

Then he said to him : 'Desire to understand Brahma by austerity. Brahma is austerity (*tapas*).'

He performed austerity. Having performed austerity.

।। तृतीयोऽनुवाकः।।

प्राणो ब्रह्मेति व्यजानात्। प्राणाद्ध्येव खल्विमानि भूतानि जायन्ते। प्राणेन जातानि जीवन्ति। प्राणं प्रयन्त्यभिसंविशन्तीति। तद्विज्ञाय पुनरेव वरुणं पितरमुपससार। अधीहि भगवो ब्रह्मेति। तꣳहोवाच। तपसा ब्रह्म विजिज्ञासस्व। तपो ब्रह्मेति। स तपोऽतप्य। स तपस्तप्त्वा।।१।।

Lesson - 3

He understood that Brahma is breath (*prāṇa*). For truly, indeed, beings here are born from breath, when born they live by breath, on deceasing they enter into breath.

Having understood that, he again approached his father Varuṇa, and said : 'Declare Brahma, sir!'

Then he said to him : 'Desire to understand Brahma by austerity Brahma is austerity!'

He performed austerity. Having performed austerity.

।। चतुर्थोऽनुवाकः।।

मनो ब्रह्मेति व्यजानात्‌ मनसो ह्येव खल्विमानि भूतानि जायन्ते। मनसा जातानि जीवन्ति। मनः प्रयन्त्यभिसंविशन्तीति। तद्विज्ञाय पुनरेव वरुणं पितरमुपससार। अधीहि भगवो ब्रह्मेति। तꣳहोवाच। तपसा ब्रह्म विजिज्ञासस्व। तपो ब्रह्मेति। स तपोऽतप्यत। स तपस्तप्त्वा।।१।।

Lesson - 4

He understood that Brahma is mind (*manas*). For truly, indeed, beings here are born from mind, when born they live by mind, on deceasing they enter into mind.

Having understood that, he again approached his father Varuṇa, and said : 'Pronounce Brahman, sir!'

Then he said to him : 'Desire to understand Brahman by austerity. Brahman is austerity.'

He performed austerity. Having performed austerity,

।। पञ्चमोऽनुवाकः।।

विज्ञानं ब्रह्मेति व्यजानात्‌ विज्ञानाद्ध्येव खल्विमानि भूतानि जायन्ते। विज्ञानेन जातानि जीवन्ति। विज्ञानं प्रयन्त्यभिसंविशन्तीति। तद्विज्ञाय पुनरेव वरुणं पितरमुपससार। अधीहि भगवो ब्रह्मेति। तꣳहोवाच। तपसा ब्रह्म विजिज्ञासस्व। तपो ब्रह्मेति। स तपोऽतप्यत। स तपस्तप्त्वा।।१।।

Lesson - 5

He understood that Brahma is understanding (*vijñāna*). For truly, indeed, beings here are born from understanding, when born they live by understanding, on deceasing they enter into understanding.

Having understood that, he again approached his father Varuṇa and said : 'Declare Brahma, sir!'

Then he said to him : 'Desire to understand Brahma by austerity. Brahma is austerity.'

He performed austerity. Having performed austerity,

।। षष्ठोऽनुवाकः।।

आनन्दो ब्रह्मेति व्यजानात् आनन्दाद्ध्येव खल्विमानि भूतानि जायन्ते। आनन्देन जातानि जीवन्ति। आनन्दं प्रयन्त्यभिसंविशन्तीति। सैषा भार्गवी वारुणी विद्या। परमे व्योमन् प्रतिष्ठिता। स य एवं वेद प्रतिष्ठति। अन्नवानन्नदो भवति। महान् भवति प्रजया पशुभिर्ब्रह्मवर्चसेन महान् कीर्त्या।।

Lesson - 6

He understood that Brahma is bliss (*ānanda*). For truly, indeed, beings here are born from bliss, when born they live by bliss, on deceasing they enter into bliss.

This is the knowledge of Bhṛgu Vārurṇi, established in the highest heaven. He who knows this, becomes established. He becomes an eater of food, possessing food. He becomes great in offspring, in cattle, in the splendour of sacred knowledge, great in fame.

[The Ṛsi has expressed here very clearly that the art of learning knowledge or Brahmavidyā is not subordinate to any man in particular but it resides at the unending sky. The curious devotee like Ṛsi Bhṛgu may accessed it by virtue of enhancing his experience through the penance and thus as a result of bringing gradual reforms until the ultimate mystery of knowledge is disclosed before him.]

।। सप्तमोऽनुवाकः।।

अन्नं न निन्द्यात्। तद्व्रतम्। प्राणो वा अन्नम्। शरीरमन्नादम्। प्राणे शरीरं प्रतिष्ठितम्। शरीरे प्राणः प्रतिष्ठितः। तदेतदन्नमन्ने प्रतिष्ठितम्। स य एतदन्नमन्ने प्रतिष्ठितं वेद प्रतितिष्ठति। अन्नवानन्नादो भवति। महान् भवति प्रजया पशुभिर्ब्रह्मवर्चसेन महान् कीर्त्या।।

Lesson - 7

One should not blame food. That is the rule.

Breath (*prāṇa*), verily, is food. The body is an eater of food. The body is established on breath; breath is established on the body. So food is established on food.

He who knows that food which is established on food, becomes established. He becomes an eater of food, possessing food. He becomes great in offspring, in cattle, in the splendour of sacred knowledge, great in fame.

।। अष्टमोऽनुवाकः।।

अन्नं न परिचक्षीत। तद्व्रतम्। आपो वा अन्नम्। ज्योतिरन्नादम्। अप्सु ज्योतिः प्रतिष्ठितम्। ज्योतिष्यापः प्रतिष्ठिताः। तदेतदन्नमन्ने प्रतिष्ठितम्। स य एतदन्नमन्ने प्रतिष्ठितं वेद प्रतितिष्ठति। अन्नवानन्नादो भवति। महान् भवति प्रजया पशुभिर्ब्रह्मवर्चसेन महान् कीर्त्या।।

Lesson - 8

One should not despise food. That is the rule.

Water, verily, is food. Light is an eater of food. Light is established on water; water is established on light. So food is established on food.

He who knows that food which is founded on food, becomes established. He becomes an eater of food, possessing food. He becomes great in offspring, in cattle, in the splendour of sacred knowledge, great in fame.

[The splendour or the brilliance can be felt easily in water when the lustre of the pearl or any radiant thing precedes, it is said that its water has receded or its shining has faded.]

।। नवमोऽनुवाकः।।

अन्नं बहु कुर्वीत। तद्व्रतम्। पृथिवी वा अन्नम्। आकाशोऽ न्नादः। पृथिव्यामाकाशः प्रतिष्ठितम्। आकाशे पृथिवी प्रतिष्ठितः। तदेतदन्नमन्ने प्रतिष्ठितम्। स य एतदन्नमन्ने प्रतिष्ठितं वेद प्रतितिष्ठति। अन्नवानन्नादो भवति। महान् भवति प्रजया पशुभिर्ब्रह्मवर्चसेन महान् कीर्त्या।।

Lesson - 9

One should make for himself much food. That is the rule.

The earth, verily, is food. Space is an eater of food. Space is established on the earth; the earth is established on space. So food is established on food.

He who knows that food which is established on food, becomes established. He becomes an eater of food, possessing food. He becomes great in offspring, in cattle, in the splendour of sacred knowledge, great in fame.

A giver of food is prospered accordingly.

[The earth in the sky can be seen apparently but to know the location of sky in the earth it is necessary to reckon with the atomic structure. We see that as per science, the centre part of an atom is nucleus and the electrons revolve around it. The space emit the revolving electrons and the nucleus is equal to the space between the earth and the sun. This space between the two particles of the atom is sky. Thus, in every solid matter there is suffice sky in it.]

।। दशमोऽनुवाकः।।

न कचनं वसतौ प्रत्याचक्षीत। तद्व्रतम्। तस्माद्यया कया च विधया बह्वन्नं प्राप्नुयात्। आराध्यस्मा अन्नमित्याचक्षते। एतद्वै मुखतोऽन्नꣳराद्धम्। मुखतोऽस्मा अन्नꣳ राध्यते। एतद्वै मध्यतोऽन्नꣳराद्धम्। मध्यतोऽस्मा अन्नꣳराध्यते। एतद्वा अन्ततोऽन्नꣳराद्धम्। अन्ततोऽस्मा अन्नꣳराध्यते।।१।। य एवं वेद। क्षेम इति वाचि योगक्षेम इति प्राणापानयोः। कर्मेति हस्तयोः। गतिरिति पादयोः। विमुक्तिरिति पायौ इति मानुषीः समाज्ञाः। अथ दैवीः। तृप्तिरिति वृष्टो बलमिति विद्युति।।२।।

Lesson - 10

(1) One should not refuse anyone at one's dwelling. That is the rule.

Therefore in any way whatsoever one should obtain much food. Of such a one people say : 'Food has succeeded (*arādhi*) for him!'

This food, verily, being prepared (*rāddha*) [for the suppliant] at the beginning, for him food is prepared at the beginning.

This food, verily, being prepared in the middle, for him food is prepared in the middle. This food, verily, being prepared at the end, for him food is prepared at the end— (2) for him who knows this.

Manifestations of Brahma as food

As preservation (*kṣema*) in speech, acquisition and preservation (*yoga-kṣema*) in the in-breath and the off-breath (*prāṇa-apāna*), work in the hands, motion in the feet, evacuation in the anus; these are the human recognitions [of Brahma as food].

Now the divine : satisfaction in rain, strength in lightning,

यश इति पशुषु। ज्योतिरिति नक्षत्रेषु। प्रजापतिरमृतमानन्द इत्युपस्थे। सर्वमित्याकाशे। तत्प्रतिष्ठेत्युपासीत।
प्रतिष्ठावान् भवति। तन्मह इत्युपासीत। महान् भवति। तन्मन इत्युपासीत। महान् भवति। तन्मन इत्युपासीत।
मानवान् भवति॥३॥

Splendour in cattle, light in the stars, procreation, immortality, and bliss in the generative organ, the all in space.

The worshiper thereof appropriates the object of his worship

One should worship It as a foundation; one [then] becomes possessed of a foundation.

One should worship It as greatness; one becomes great.

One should worship It as mind (*manas*); one becomes possessed of mindfulness.

तन्नम इत्युपासीत। नम्यन्तेऽस्मै कामा:। तद्ब्रह्मेत्युपासीत। ब्रह्मवान् भवति। तद्ब्रह्मण: परिमर इत्युपासीत
पर्येणं म्रियन्ते द्विषन्त: सपत्ना:। परि येऽप्रिया भ्रातृव्या:। स यश्चायं पुरुषे। यश्चासावादित्ये। स एक:॥४॥

One should worship It as adoration; desires make adoration to one.

One should worship It as magic formula (*brahma*); one becomes possessed of magic formula.

One should worship It as 'the dying around the magic formula' (*brahmaṇaḥ parimara*); around one die his hateful rivals, and those who are his unfriendly foes.

The knower of the unity of the human person with the universal Being attains unhampered desire

Both he who is here in a person and he who is yonder in the sun—he is one.

स य एवंवित्। अस्माल्लोकाप्रेत्य। एतमन्नमयमात्मानमुपसंक्र म्य। एतं प्राणमयमात्माममुपसंक्रम्य। एत
मनोमयमात्माममुपसंक्रम्य।   एतं   विज्ञानमयमात्माममुपसंक्रम्य।   एत   मानंमयमात्माममुपसंक्रम्य।
इमाँल्लोकान्कामान्नी कामरूप्यनुसंचरन्। एतत्साम गायन्नास्ते। हा ३ वु हा ३ वु हा ३ वु॥५॥

He who knows this, on departing from this world, proceeding on to that self which consists of food, proceeding on to that self which consists of breath, proceeding on to that self which consists of mind, proceeding on to that self which consists of understanding, proceeding on to that self which consists of bliss, goes up and down these worlds, eating what he desires, assuming what form he desires. He sits singing this chant (*sāman*) :—

A mystical rapture of the knower of the universal unity
Oh, wonderful! Oh, wonderful! Oh, wonderful!

अहमन्नमहमन्नमहमन्नम्। अहमन्नादो ३ ऽहमन्नादो ३ ऽहमन्नादः। अहꣳश्लोककृदहꣳश्लोककृद-हꣳश्लोककृत्। अहमस्मि प्रथमजा ऋता३स्य। पूर्वं देवेभ्योऽमृतस्य ना ३ भायि। यो मा ददाति स इदेव मा३वाः। अहमन्नमन्नमदन्तमा ३द्मि। अहं विश्वं भुवनमभ्यभवा३म्। सुवर्णज्योतीः य एवं वे। इत्युपनिषत्॥६॥

I am food! I am food! I am food!
I am a food-eater! I am a food-eater! I am a food-eater!
I am a fame-maker (*śloka-kṛt*)! I am a fame-maker! I am a fame-maker!
I am the first-born of the world-order (*ṛta*),
Earlier than the gods, in the navel of immortality!
Who gives me away, he indeed has aided me!
I, who am food, eat the eater of food!
I have overcome the whole world!
He who knows this, has a brilliantly shining light.
Such is the mystic doctrine (*upaniṣad*)!

ॐ शं नो मित्रः शं वरुणः..... इति शान्तिः॥

॥ इति तैत्तिरीयोपनिषत्समाप्ता॥

***

8. AITAREYOPANIṢAD

ऐतरेयोपनिषद्

The 4th, 5th and 6th chapter in 2nd Āraṇyaka of the Vedic Aitareya Āraṇyaka, since contain the art of learning knowledge or Brahma Vidyā; these chapters have been recognised as Aitareyopaniṣad. There are 3 parts in the 1st chapter while one each in the 2nd and the 3rd chapter. In 1st part of the 1st chapter, the subject-matter covers the resolution of the supreme soul or Paramātman as regards to create the world as Śṛṣṭi, and the structurisation of the Lokapālas or the protector of the creation have been described. The degenetic man from Hiraṇyagarbha and reproduction of all gods has been elaborately explained from his genetic organs. In its 2nd part, the subject-matter covers the creation of human body as a dwelling place for the gods and the food for satisfying his hunger. In the 3rd part, an illustration regarding the food taking by the breathing (Prāṇa) and an entrance of the supreme soul from the Mūrdha (palate) have been given. The curiosity taking birth in the man so reproduced and his achievement by virtue of realising the element of supreme soul has also been described. In 2nd chapter, a process of learning life cycle by the Ṛṣi Vāmadeva has been explained. The entrance of the breathing (Jīva) in mother's boom, his first birth there in the process of coming out and the 2nd birth as also taking birth in various bodies after death has been called his 3rd birth. In the 3rd chapter, a question has been raised about the god worth adoration and thus the supreme soul has been proved as the only adorable god. It has been explained that the salvation is only possible after death and when the supreme soul is attained.

॥शान्तिपाठः॥

वाङ्मे मनसि प्रतिष्ठिता मनो मे वाचि प्रतिष्ठितमाविरावीर्म एधि। वेदस्य म आणीस्थः श्रुतं मे मा प्रहासीरनेनाधीतेनाहोरात्रान्संदधाम्यृतं वदिष्यामि सत्यं वदिष्यामि।

तन्मामवतु तद्वक्तारमवतु अवतु मामवतु वक्तारमवतु वक्तारम्॥

ॐ शान्तिः शान्तिः शान्तिः॥

Pray for Peace

O Supreme soul! Establish yourself in my tongue and the mind. Please come and lead my expressions. O supreme soul! Be appear before me. Make me to realise the Vedas. Don't make me so deviated that I could forget the knowledge which has been acquired before and by listening to. Make me able to keep myself busy throughout the day and night in my existing tendency of perseverance (my industry on study may continue). I shall always speak the truth and what is right may the knowledge (Brahma) protect me. He also protect the speaker (the teacher). Let all the 3 fevers be cool down.

Chapter - 1

Part - 1

[In this Upaniṣad, The creation of the four worlds, of the cosmic person, and of cosmic powers by the primeval Self and the degenetic life cycle inter-alia to the emancipation have been elaborated.]

आत्मा वा इदमेव एवाग्र आसीन्नान्यत्किञ्चनमिषत्। स ईक्षत लोकान्नु सृजा इति॥१॥

Verily, this world in the beginning was Ātman (Self, Soul), one only,—no other winking thing whatever. Then the supreme soul had made up his mind that I should create the world (Lokas).

[In this hymn, The term "Miṣat" is used in the sense of eye-winking which is the visible attitude taking place with the least effort. The sense of this phrase, therefore, appropriate to be taken that there was nothing in existence and if anyone, that was inert. The first effort has been made in the garb of resolution by the knowledge (Brahma).]

स इमाँल्लोकानसृजत अम्भो मरीचीर्मरमापोऽदोऽम्भः परेण दिवं द्यौः प्रतिष्ठाऽन्तरिक्षं मरीचयः। पृथिवी मरो या अधस्तात्ता आपः॥२॥

He created these (four) worlds : water (*ambhas*), light-rays (*marīci*), death (*mara*), and the waters (*ap*). Yon is the water, above the heaven; the heaven is its support. The light-rays are the atmosphere; death, the earth; what is underneath, the waters.

[The name and location of the worlds are herein worth-considering. The earth is called Mara or the mortal world. The space is Marīci which the world fully lighted by the beams of light. The meaning of Marīci is purported to the Kalpa-tree (a tree fulfilling all desires). According to it, this world is the killer of evils, the micro-organism or the dark. The modern science also confirms such an acute killing flow existed in the space. The term *Ambha* is consisting of *Am*, the breathing and "Bhaḥ" *i.e.* nutriatar. Beyond the world of the sun, it provides maintenance to the micro-breathings invisibly and the world of the sun is established as its apparent feature. A number of learned persons have accepted that the world of *Āpaḥ* is existed below the earth but such an opinion doesn't likely to be true.

The Āpaḥ in reality has been envisaged by Ṛgveda as the fundamental activating flow of the creation. Āpaḥ is the fundamental matter of the creation. This too is Hiraṇyagarbha to which Veda has told that it is the base of the earth and the world of the sun. The water is also called Āpaḥ but in case, such meaning is adopted the real connotation of the hymn cannot be arrived at. The *Āpaḥ*, therefore, to be accepted commensurate with the assumption as made by Veda because it will only be appropriate to understand the hymn. It has been addressed in the plural form of feminine gender as *Taḥ*. In the womb of this element *i.e.* Āpaḥ the resolution of Brahma turns into universal form while matured in this seed like formation of the resolution. This properly have been eating of the mother, it is appropriate to say the Āpaḥ as Devi-Āpaḥ or Taḥ-Āpaḥ. In this upaniṣad too, the productive use of Āpaḥ in succeeding hymns can be seen repeatedly.]

स ईक्षतेमे नु लोका लोकपालान्नु सृजा इति। सोऽद्भ्य एव पुरुषं समुद्धृत्यामूर्च्छयत्॥३॥

He bethought himself : 'Here now are worlds. Let me now create world-guardians (Loka-pālās).' Right (*eva*) from the waters he drew forth and shaped (√*mūrcch*) a person (in the form of Hiraṇyagarbha).

[The term "Man" (Puruṣa) is applied for a person competent to do creative industry. The knowledge (Brahma) had given a stature to the degenetic man from that fundamental flow *i.e.* Āpaḥ, it means the power of degenetic structurization was awaken. The Ṛṣi has said it extraction as the water. The meaning of the term *Adbhyaḥ* is the water but its application here in is *Āpaḥ i.e.* a flow competent to create the universe.]

तमभ्यतपत्तस्याभितप्तस्य मुखं निरभिद्यत यथाण्डं मुखाद्वाग्वाचोऽग्निर्नासिके निरभिद्येतां नासिकाभ्यां प्राणः। प्राणाद्वायुरक्षिणी निरभिद्येतामक्षिभ्यां चक्षुश्चक्षुष आदित्यः कर्णौ निरभिद्येतां कर्णाभ्यां श्रोत्रं श्रोत्राद्दिशस्त्वङ् निरभिद्यत त्वचो लोमानि लोमभ्य ओषधिवनस्पतयो हृदयं निरभिद्यत हृदयान्मनो मनसश्चन्द्रमा नाभिर्निरभिद्यत नाभ्या अपानोऽपानान्मृत्युः शिश्नं निरभिद्यत शिश्नाद्रेतो रेतसः आपः॥४॥

Upon him (puruṣa) he (Ātman) brooded (*abhi* +√*tap*). When he had been brooded upon, his mouth was separated out, egg-like; from the mouth, speech (*vāc*); from speech, Agni (Fire).

Nostrils were separated out; from the nostrils, breath (*prāṇa*); from breath, Vāyu (Wind).

Eyes were separated out; from the eyes, sight (*cakṣus*); from sight, Āditya (the Sun).

Ears were separated out; from the ears, hearing (*śrotra*); from hearing, the quarters of heaven.

Skin was separated out; from the skin, hairs; from the hairs, plants an trees.

A heart was separated out; from the heart, mind (*manas*); from mind, the moon.

A navel was separated out; from the navel, the out-breath (*apāna*); from the out-breath, death (*mṛtyu*).

A virile member was separated out; from the virile member, semen; from the semen, water (*ap*).

[It has been said herein that the *Āpaḥ* was originated again from the semen while at a place, it was told the first and foremost element which had originated the degenetic man itself. It is really a very scientific as also a vivid statement. Āpaḥ is the fundamental flow and the main causative in the function of creating the world. In the semen too there inherits the seed for reproducing this world or it is the 2nd power of Āpaḥ that maintains the function subsequent to the creation made by it. The semen is, therefore, the micro-form of the Āpaḥ and competent enough to carry on the creation as was firstly made by the Āpaḥ. The Ṛṣi has after a long course of observation found it true in the same element of Āpaḥ the sensitivity again used to accept the new form or the complexion.]

Part -2

The ingredience of the cosmic powers in the human person

ता एता देवता सृष्टा अस्मिन्महत्यर्णवे प्रापतंस्तमशनायापिपासाभ्यामन्ववार्जत्। ता एनमब्रुवन्नायतनं नः प्रजानीहि यस्मिन्प्रतिष्ठिता अन्नमदामेति॥१॥

These divinities, having been created, fell headlong in this great restless sea. He visited it with hunger and thirst.

They [i.e. the divinities] said to him : 'Find out for us an abode wherein we may be established and may eat food.'

ताभ्यो गामानायत्ता अब्रुवन्न वै नोऽयमलमिति। ताभ्योऽश्वमानयत्ता अब्रुवन्न वै नोऽयमलमिति।।२।।

He led up a bull to them. They said : 'Verily, this is not sufficient for us.'

He led up a horse to them. They said : 'Verily, this is not sufficient for us.'

ताभ्यः पुरुषमानयत्ता अब्रुवन् सुकृतं बतेति। पुरुषो वाव सुकृतम्। ता अब्रवीद्यथाऽऽयतनं प्रविशतेति।।३।।

He led up a person to them. They said : 'Oh! Well done!'— Verily, a person is a thing well done.

He said to them : 'Enter into your respective abodes.'

अग्निर्वाग्भूत्वा मुखं प्राविशद्वायुः प्राणो भूत्वा नासिके प्राविशदादित्यश्चक्षुर्भूत्वाक्षिणी प्राविशद्दिशः श्रोत्रं भूत्वा कर्णौ प्राविशन्नोषधिवनस्पतयो लोमानि भूत्वा त्वचं प्राविशंश्चन्द्रमा मनो भूत्वा हृदयं प्राविशन्मृत्युरपानो भूत्वा नाभिं प्राविशदापो रेतो भूत्वा शिश्नं प्राविशन्।।४।।

Fire became breath and entered the nostrils. The sun became sight, and entered the eyes. The quarters of heaven became hearing, and entered the ears. Plants and trees became hairs and entered the skin. The moon became mind, and entered the heart. Death became the out-breath (*apāna*), and entered the navel. Waters became semen, and entered the virile member.

[It is worth to keep in mind that the gods as they got their birth from the organs of degenetic man, established themselves in the same, regions (organs) of the man.]

तमशनायापिपासे अब्रूतामावाभ्यामभिप्रजानीहीति। ते अब्रवीदेतास्वेव वां देवतास्वाभजाम्येतासु भागिन्यौ करोमीति। तस्माद्यस्यै कस्यै च देवतायै हविर्गृह्यते भागिन्यावेवास्यामशनायापिपासे भवतः।।५।।

Hunger and thirst said to him [i.e. Ātman] : 'For us two also find out [an abode].'

Unto the two he said : 'I assign you two a part among these divinities. I make you two partakers among them.' Therefore to whatever divinity an oblation is made, hunger and thirst become partakers in it.

[The Ṛṣi makes it clear that there is no independent place for the hunger and the thirst. They are aided with the divine powers spreaded in distinct organs and parts of the human body. The conclusions arrived at through the research made by the physiologists also accepts this truth. The hunger and thirst is existed within the every cell of body unless the stock of food and water depleted in the belly, the thirst and hunger is not felt at all. When the man is suffering from ailment, this hunger and thirst is satiated by the food and water issued through the drops. This makes it clear that the hunger and food is added with every living cell of the body.]

Part - 3

The creation of food of fleeting material form and the inability of various personal functions to obtain it

स ईक्षतेमे तु लोकाश्च लोकपालाश्चान्नमेभ्य: सृजा इति।।१।।

He bethought himself : 'Here now are worlds and world-guardians. Let me create food for them.'

सोऽपोऽभ्यतपत् ताभ्योऽभितप्ताभ्यो मूर्तिरजायत। या वै सा मूर्तिरजायतान्नं वै तत्।।२।।

He brooded upon the waters. From them, when they had been brooded upon, a material form (*mūrti*) was produced. Verily, that material form which was produced—verily, that is food.

[It is worth taking into consideration that the flow of *Ap* too in this new creation was boiled or matured by this supreme soul.]

तदेनत्सृष्टं पराङत्यजिघांसत् तद्वाचा जिघृक्षत्तन्नाशक्नोद्वाचा ग्रहीतुम्। स यद्धैनद्वाचाऽग्रहैष्यदभिव्याहृत्य हैवान्नमत्रप्स्यत्।।४।।

Having been created, it sought to flee away.

He sought to seize it with speech. He was not able to grasp it with speech. If indeed he had grasped it with speech, merely with uttering food one would have been satisfied.

तत्प्राणेनाजिघृक्षत् तन्नाशक्नोत्प्राणेन ग्रहीतुम्। स यद्धैनत्प्राणेनाग्रहैष्यदभिप्राण्य हैवान्नमत्रप्स्यत्।।४।।

He sought to grasp it with breath. He was not able to grasp it with breath. If indeed he had grasped it with breath, merely with breathing toward food one would have been satisfied.

तच्चक्षुषाजिघृक्षत् तन्नाशक्नोच्चक्षुषा ग्रहीतुम्। स यद्धैनच्चक्षुषाग्रहैष्यद् दृष्ट्वा हैवान्नमत्रप्स्यत्।।५।।

He sought to grasp it with sight. He was not able to grasp it with sight. If indeed he had grasped it with sight, merely with seeing food one would have been satisfied.

तच्छ्रोत्रेणाजिघृक्षत् तन्नाशक्नोच्छ्रोत्रेण ग्रहीतुम्। स यद्धैनच्छ्रोत्रेणाग्रहैष्यच्छ्रुत्वा हैवान्नमत्रप्स्यत्।।६।।

He sought to grasp it with hearing. He was not able to grasp it with hearing. If indeed he had grasped it with hearing, merely with hearing food one would have been satisfied.

तत्त्वचाजिघृक्षत् तन्नाशक्नोत्त्वचा ग्रहीतुम्। स यद्धैनत्त्वचाग्रहैष्यत्स्पृष्ट्वा हैवान्नमत्रप्स्यत्।।७।।

He sought to grasp it with the skin. He was not able to grasp it with the skin. If indeed he had grasped it with the skin, merely with touching food one would have been satisfied.

तन्मनसाजिघृक्षत् तन्नाशक्नोन्मनसा ग्रहीतुम्। स यद्धैनत्त्वचाग्रहैष्यत्स्पृष्ट्वा हैवान्नमत्रप्स्यत्।।८।।

He sought to grasp it with the mind. He was not able to grasp it with the mind. If indeed he had grasped it with the mind, merely with thinking on food one would been satisfied.

तच्छिश्नेनाजिघृक्षत्तन्नाशक्नोच्छिश्नेन ग्रहीतुम्। स यद्धैनच्छिश्नेनाग्रहैष्यद्विसृज्य हैवान्नमत्रप्स्यत्।।९।।

He sought to grasp it with the virile member. He was not able to grasp it with the virile member. If indeed he had grasped it with the virile member, merely with emitting food one would have been satisfied.

तदपानेनाजिघृक्षत् तदावयत्। सैषोऽन्नस्य ग्रहो यद्वायुरन्नायुर्वा एष यद्वायुः॥१०॥

He sought to grasp it with the out-breath (*apāna*– the digestive breath). He consumed it. This grasper of food is what wind (*vāyu*) is. This one living on food (*annāyu*), verily, is what wind is.

[According to Ācārya Śaṅkara the meaning of breathing is as the cavity of mouth. In Vācastatyan too, the breathing in, has been told the holder of breathing. In Ayurveda, the digestion, discharge of excreta etc., activities are accepted possible only by the breathing in or by Apāna. This wind, therefore, is the holder of the food. Enhancing the age through this food, this wind is called as the food year (Annāyu).]

The entrance of the Self into the body

स ईक्षत कथं न्विदं मदृते स्यादिति स ईक्षत कतरेण प्रपद्या इति। स ईक्षत यदि वाचाभिव्याहृतं यदि प्राणेनाभिप्राणितं यदि चक्षुषा दृष्टं यदि श्रोत्रेण श्रुतं यदि त्वचा स्पृष्टं यदि मनसा ध्यातं यद्यपानेनाभ्यपानितं यदि शिश्ने विसृष्टमथ कोऽहमिति॥११॥

He [i.e. Ātman] bethought himself : 'How now could this thing exist without me?'

He bethought himself : 'With which should I enter?'

He bethought himself : 'If with speech there is uttered, if with breath (*prāṇa*) there is breathed, if with sight there is seen, if with hearing there is heard, if with the skin there is touched, if with the mind there is thought, if with the out-breath (*apāna*) there is breathed out, if with the virile member there is emitted, then who am I?'

स एतमव सीमानं विदार्यैतया द्वारा प्रापद्यत। सैषा विदृतिर्नाम द्वास्तदेतन्नान्दनम्। तस्य त्रय आवसथास्त्रयः स्वप्ना अयमावसथोऽयमावसथोऽयमावसथ इति॥१२॥

So, cleaving asunder this very hair-part (*sīmān*), by that door he entered. This is the door named 'the cleft' (*vidṛti*). That is the delighting (*nāndana*).

He has three dwelling-places, three conditions of sleep. This is a dwelling-place. This is a dwelling-place. This is a dwelling-place.

[The phrase "This very place is" has been repeated 3 times. It is a well-settled therein of space that to make anything most confirmed, it is repeated 3 times. This is the reason for reiterating the place in the above hymn. What the statement wants to confirm is that this body is the abode of that supreme soul. Another proportion may also be in existence, there are 3 automatic systems in the body that are under control of the supreme soul. These blends found in human body are- 1. raticular activating system in the mind, pacemaker in the heart and the digestion as also the cycle of reproduction *i.e.* the naval blend. The body, the mind and the supreme ether in the 3 places are residing and the apparent, micro and the causative forms or the creation, nutrition and the changes may be called 3 dreams of that supreme soul.]

स जातो भूतान्यभिव्यैख्यत् किमिहान्यं वावदिषदिति।

स एतमेव पुरुषं ब्रह्म ततममपश्यदिदमदर्शमिती३।।१३।।

Having been born, he looked around on beings (*bhūta*), [thinking] : 'Of what here would one desire to speak as another?' He saw this very person as veriest (*tatama*) Brahma. 'I have seen It (*idaṁ adarśa*), said he (*iti*).

तस्मादिदन्द्रो नामेदन्द्रो ह वै नाम तमिदन्द्रं सन्तमिन्द्र।

इत्याचक्षते परोक्षेण परोक्षप्रिया इव हि देवा: परोक्षप्रिया इव हि देवा:।।१४।।

Therefore his name is Idaṁ-dra ('It-seeing'). Idaṁ-dra, verily, is his name. Him who is Idaṁ-dra they call 'Indra' cryptically, for the gods are fond of the cryptic (*parokṣa-priya*) as it were—for the gods are fond of the cryptic, as it were.

Chapter - 2

Part - 1

A self's three successive births

This Jīva (the living body) very first enshrines in the human body like an womb. The semen as found in the body of a man is the splendour arising from all the organs of this body. The man provides maintenance to the splendour inherent in him and then discharging it into ovary or the female male it creates the womb. This is the first birth of this Jiva (living body).

पुरुषे ह वा अयमादितो गर्भो भवति। यदेतद्रेतस्तदेतत्सर्वेभ्योऽङ्गेभ्यस्तेज: संभूतमात्मन्येवात्मानं बिभर्ति तद्यदा स्त्रियां सिञ्चत्यथैनज्जनयति तदस्य प्रथमं जन्म।।१।।

In a person (*puruṣa*), verily, this one becomes at first an embryo (*garbha*). That which is semen (*retas*), is the vigour (*tejas*) come together from all the limbs. In the self, indeed, one bears a self. When he pours this in a woman, then he begets it. This is one's first birth.

तत् स्त्रिया आत्मभूयं गच्छति यथा स्वमङ्गं तथा तस्मादेनां न हिनस्ति।

सास्यैतमात्मानमत्र गतं भावयति।।२।।

It comes into self-becoming (*ātma-bhūya*) with the woman, just as a limb of her own. Therefore it injures her not. She nourishes this self of his that has come to her.

[This combination or the eventuality is the same as between the degenetic man and the nature itself at the time of first creation of the earth.]

सा भावयित्री भावयितव्या भवति तं स्त्री गर्भं बिभर्ति सोऽग्र एव कुमारं जन्मनोऽग्रेऽधिभावयति। स यत्कुमारं जन्मनोऽग्रेऽधिभावयत्यात्मानमेव तद्भावयत्येषां लोकानां सन्तत्या एवं सन्तता हीमे लोकास्तदस्य द्वितीयं जन्म।।३।।

She, being a nourisher, should be nourished. The woman bears him as an embryo. In the beginning, indeed, he nourishes the child [and] from birth onward. While he nourishes the child from birth onward, he thus nourishes his own self, for the continuation of these worlds; for thus are these worlds continued. This is one's second birth.

सोऽस्यायमात्मा पुण्येभ्यः कर्मभ्यः प्रतिधीयते। अथास्यायमितर आत्मा कृतकृत्यो वयोगतः प्रैतिः स इतः प्रयन्नेव पुनर्जायते तदस्य तृतीयं जन्म॥४॥

This self of one is put in one's place for pious deeds (*puṇya karman*). Then this other self of one, having done his work (*kṛta-kṛtya*), having reached his age, deceases. So, deceasing hence indeed, he is born again. This is one's third birth.

तदुक्तमृषिणा– गर्भे नु सन्नन्वेषामवेदमहं देवानां जनिमानि विश्वा। शतं मा पुर आयसीररक्षन्नधः श्येनो जवसा निरदीयमिति गर्भ एवैतच्छयानो वामदेव एवमुवाच॥५॥

As to this it has been said by a seer (Vāmadeva)- Being yet in embryo, I knew well All the births of these gods! A hundred iron citadels confined me,

And yet, a hawk (*śyena*) with swiftness, forth I flew!

In embryo indeed thus lying (*śayāna*), Vāmadeva spoke in this wise.

This very issue has been described by the Ṛṣi as under - "I have duly understood the mystery of gods in the stage of womb. I was tight and thrown in the iron made cases. These cases were in 100 numbers. I have now realised the knowledge of element and now I have came out like an eagle and I have penetrated all those cases." Thus sleeping in the womb the Ṛṣi Vāmadeva have revealed this fact.

स एवं विद्वानंस्माच्छरीरभेदादूर्ध्व उत्क्रम्यामुष्मिन् स्वर्गे।

लोके सर्वान् कामानाप्त्वामृतः समभवत् समभवत्॥६॥

So he, knowing this, having ascended aloft from this separation from the body (*śarīra-bheda*), obtained all desires in the heavenly world (*svarga-loka*), and became immortal—yea, became [immortal]!

Chapter - 3

Part -1

The pantheistic Self

कोऽयमात्मेति वयमुपास्महे कतरः स आत्मा येन वा पश्यति येन वा शृणोति येन वा गन्धानाजिघ्रति येन वा वाचं व्याकरोति येन वा स्वादु चास्वादु च विजानाति॥१॥

[Question :] Who is this one?

[Answer :] We worship him as the Self (Ātman).

[Question :] Which one is the Self?

[Answer :] [He] whereby one sees, or whereby one hears, or whereby one smells odours, or whereby one articulates speech, or whereby one discriminates the sweet and the unsweet;

यदेतत् हृदय मनश्चैतत्। संज्ञानमाज्ञानं विज्ञानं प्रज्ञानं मेधा दृष्टिर्धृतिर्मतिर्मनीषा जूतिः स्मृतिः संकल्पः क्रतुरसुः कामो वश इति सर्वाण्येवैतानि नामधेयानि भवन्ति॥२॥

That which is heart (*hṛdaya*) and mind (*manas*)—that is, consciousness (*saṁjñāna*), perception (*ājñāna*), discrimination (*vijñāna*), intelligence (*prajñāna*), wisdom (*medhas*), insight (*dṛṣṭi*), steadfastness (*dhṛti*), thought (*mati*), thoughtfulness (*manīṣā*), impulse (*jūti*), memory (*smṛti*), conception (*saṁkalpa*), purpose (*kratu*), life (*asu*), desire (*kāma*), will (*vaśa*).

All these, indeed are appellations of intelligence (*prajñāna*).

एष ब्रह्मैष इन्द्र एष प्रजापतिरेते सर्वे देवा इमानि च पञ्च महाभूतानि पृथिवी वायुराकाश आपो ज्योतींषीत्येतानीमानि च क्षुद्रमिश्राणीव। बीजानीतराणि चेतराणि चाण्डजानि च जारूजानि च स्वेदजानि चोद्भिज्ञानि चाश्वा गावः पुरुषा हस्तिनो यत्किंचेदं प्राणि जङ्गमं च पतत्रि च यच्च स्थावरं सर्वं तत्प्रज्ञानेत्रं प्रज्ञाने प्रतिष्ठितं प्रज्ञानेत्रो लोकः प्रज्ञा प्रतिष्ठा प्रज्ञानं ब्रह्म।।३।।

He is Brahman; he is Indra; he is Prajāpati; [he is] all these gods : and these five gross elements (*mahā-bhūtāni*), namely earth (*pṛthivī*), wind (*vāyu*), space (*ākāśa*), water (*āpas*), light (*jyotīṁṣi*); these things and those which are mingled of the fine (*kṣudra*), as it were; origins (*bīja*) of one sort and another : those born from an egg (*aṇḍa-ja*), and those born from a womb (*jāru-ja*), and those born from sweat (*sveda-ja*), and those born from a sprout (*udbhij-ja*); horses, cows, persons, elephants; whatever breathing thing there is here—whether moving or flying and what is stationary.

All this is guided by intelligence, is based on intelligence. The world is guided by intelligence. The basis is intelligence. Brahma is intelligence.

स एतेन प्रज्ञेनात्मनास्माल्लोकादुत्क्रम्यामुष्मिन् स्वर्गे लोके सर्वान्कामानाप्त्वामृतः समभवत् समभवत्।। इत्योम्।।४।।

So he [i.e. Vāmadeva], having ascended aloft from this world with that intelligent Self (Ātman), obtained all desires in heavenly world and became immortal—yea, became [immortal]!

Thus (*iti*)! *Oṁ*!

वाङ्मे मनसि प्रतिष्ठिता ......मामवतु वक्तारमवतु वक्तारम्।।

ॐ शान्तिः शान्तिः शान्तिः

।। इति ऐतरेयोपनिषत्समाप्ता।।

***

9. CHĀNDOGYA-UPANIṢAD

छान्दोग्योपनिषद्

The part of Chāndogya Brāhmaṇa under the Talavkāra branch of Sāmaveda has been accepted as upaniṣad with this very name Chāndogyopaniṣad. There are 10 chapters in the above Chāndogya-Brāhmaṇa out of which only 8 chapters have been incorporated in this upaniṣad. This is one of the Upaniṣad which has the prolix subject-matter.

As its name indicates, Chandaḥ is the basis of this upaniṣad. The connotation of Chandaḥ is not confined only to a sort of literary composition of the verse but it impose a meaning also. The meaning of the term Chandaḥ is a thing that covers other things. The poet uses the literary rhyme for breasting with the spirit of the path with whom he has come in such with the letters, sentences, the vowels covering that path or the spirit are the part and parcel of that hymns used therein. Similarly, the Ṛṣi sees emanation as revelation of the ultimate reading of this creation through different sources and covered by various factors of the nature. Hence he has depicted them all as the rhyming as same as Udgītha.

In the 1st chapter, the Oṁkāra and an essence of Ṛk, Sāma etc. has been explained by inserting an illustration of a battle fought between the gods and the demons. The rhyme of Oṁkāra has not been confined to only the breathing and the letters but the secrets of joining it with the vibrations of main breathing has been explained very clearly. Thereafter the metaphysical and celestial ways of worship for Oṁkāra have been made to understand and its various forms have been defined. In 2nd chapter, a number of ways of adoration have been described by joining the Sāma with the etiquette and the modesty. In the 3rd chapter, the Sun is addressed as the honey to the gods and various sorts of nectars from its different directions has been described for attainment thereof. An inventory of the eligible person for this Madhuvidyā (art of honey) has been made and the universal forms of Gāyatrī has been proved as also an inspection to worship the Sun knowing it as Brahma has been given. In the 4th chapter, a story of educating Satyakāma Jābāla by an ox, the fire, the flamingo and the donkey has been elaborated in a sequence and the reference of education by the various fires has been illustrated. The 5th chapter relates to the art of breathing (Prāṇa vidyā). In a colloquy between Śvetaketu and Pravāhaṇa the process of turning the 5th offering into person related by Apatattva and a colloquy between Aśvapati and the saints on various natures of the breathing has been discussed. In the 6th chapter, various forms of the god and the soul have been made clear by referring to a number of instances and referenced. In the 7th chapter, the adoration of Brahma in its various forms has been explained. In the 8th chapter by inserting the plot of Indra and Virocana an importance of acquiring eligibility by the way of penance for interviewing with as realizing to the element of soul as element of knowledge have been depicted. Lastly the tradition of self-knowledge and its results have been discussed.

।।शान्तिपाठः।।

ॐ आप्यायन्तु ममाङ्गानि वाक् प्राणश्चक्षुः श्रोत्रमथो बलमिन्द्रियाणि च सर्वाणि सर्वं ब्रह्मौपनिषदं माहं ब्रह्म निराकुर्यां मा मा ब्रह्म निराकरोदनिराकरणमस्त्वनिराकरणं मेऽस्तु तदात्मनि निरते य उपनिषत्सु धर्मास्तु मयि सन्तु ते मयि सन्तु।।

ॐ शान्तिः शान्तिः शान्तिः।।

First Chapter

Part-1

ओमित्येतदक्षरमुद्गीथमुपासीत, ओमिति ह्युद्गायति तस्योपव्याख्यानम्।।१।।

Oṁ! One should reverence the Udgītha (Loud Chant) as this syllable, for one sings the loud chant (*ud* + √ *gī*) [beginning] with 'Oṁ'. He performs Sāmagāna by receiving this very syllable of Oṁ. Such a worship is explained herein.

एषा भूतानां पृथिवी रसः पृथिव्या आपो रसोऽपामोषधयो रस ओषधीनां पुरुषो रसः पुरुषस्य वाग्रसो वाच ऋग्रसः ऋचः साम रस साम्न उद्गीथो रसः।।२।।

The essence of all living organisms is the earth. The essence of the earth is water. The essence of water is plants. The essence of plants is a person (*puruṣa*). The essence of a person is speech. The essence of speech is the Ṛg ('hymn'). The essence of the Ṛg is the Sāman ('chant'). The essence of the Sāman is the Udgītha ('loud singing').

स एष रसानाँ रसतमः परमः पराध्योंऽष्टमो य उद्गीथः।।३।।

This is the quintessence of the essences, the highest, the supreme, the eighth– namely the Udgītha.

[This takes the VIIIth place among the earth etc. essences. A particular significance is of getting 8th place by echo of Oṁ. This whole creation is distributed in 7 of each class, like 7 lokas, 7 Ragas, 7 colours, 7 expressions etc. The VIIIth place comes after 7 and thus the beginning of next seven. All essences are embedded in the echo of Oṁ and all appear out from them. In a cryptic meaning, the VIIIth place seems depicting the same perceptions within it.]

कतमा कतमर्क्कतमत्कतमत्साम कतमः कतम उद्गीथ इति विमृष्टं भवति।।४।।

'Which one is the Ṛg? Which one is the Sāman? Which one is the Udgītha?' Thus has there been considered.

वागेवर्क् प्राणः सामोमित्येतदक्षरमुद्गीथस्तद्वा एतन्मिथुनं यद्वाक् च प्राणश्चर्क् च साम च।५।।

The Ṛg is speech. The Sāman is breath (*prāṇa*). The Udgītha is this syllable '*Oṁ*'.

Verily, this is a pair– namely speech and breath, and also the Ṛg and Sāman.

[The breathing too is Sāma. Sāmagāna is not only an art of the speech by the vibration of the breathing and should not be adhered to. If no attentive waves get their motion in the breathing, it cannot be tantamounted as Sāma of the Sāma. In the common singing too this fact functions for making it influencive as otherwise.]

तदेतन्मिथुनमोमित्येतस्मिन्नक्षरे सꣳसृज्यते यदा वै मिथुनौ समागच्छत आपयतो वै तावन्योन्यस्य कामम्॥६॥

This pair is joined together in this syllable '*Oṁ*'. Verily, when a pair come together, verily, the two procure each the other's desire.

आपयिता ह वै कामानां भवति य एतदेवं विद्वानक्षरमुद्गीथमुपास्ते॥७॥

A procurer of desires, verily, indeed, becomes he who, knowing this thus, reverences the Udgītha as this syllable.

तद्वाएतदनुज्ञाक्षरं यद्धि किंचानुजानात्योमित्येव तदाह एषा एव समृद्धिर्यदनुज्ञा समर्धयिता ह वै कामानां भवति य एतदेवं विद्वानक्षरमुद्गीथमुपास्ते॥८॥

Verily, this syllable is assent; for whenever one assents to anything he says simply '*Oṁ*'. This, indeed, is fulfilment– that is, assent is. A fulfiller of desires, verily, indeed, becomes he who, knowing this thus, reverences the Udgītha as this syllable.

[This universe is created by virtue of the resolution made by the Brahma. His permission for the creation of this universe is the cardinal cause behind the universe as created. Whatever the source or the purpose for which permission is given by the Brahma, that element certainly comes into existence, therefore the permission of Brahma too is prosperity. This statement of the Ṛṣi is very vital and vivid.]

तेनेयं त्रयी विद्या वर्तत ओमित्याश्रावयत्योमितिशꣳसत्योमित्युद्गायत्येतस्यैवाक्षरस्यापचित्यै महिम्ना रसेन॥९॥

This threefold knowledge proceeds with it : saying '*Oṁ*' one called forth; saying '*Oṁ*' one recites; saying '*Oṁ*', one sings aloud, to the honour of that syllable, with its greatness, with its essence.

तेनोभौ कुरुतो यश्चैतदेवं वेद यश्च न वेद। नाना तु विद्या चाविद्या च यदेव विद्यया करोति श्रद्धयोपनिषदा तदेव वीर्यवत्तरं भवतीति खल्वेतस्यैवाक्षरस्योपव्याख्यानं भवति॥१०॥

He who knows this thus and he who knows not, both perform with it. Diverse, however, are knowledge and ignorance. What, indeed, one performs with knowledge, with faith (*śraddhā*) with mystic doctrine (*upaniṣad*)– that, indeed, becomes the more effective.

Such is the further explanation of this syllable.

॥इति प्रथमः खण्डः॥

Part-2

The Udgītha identified with breath

देवासुरा ह वै यत्र संयेतिर उभये प्राजापत्यास्तद्ध देवा उद्गीथमाजह्रुरनेनैनानभिभविष्याम इति॥१॥

Verily, when the gods (Devas) and the demons (Asuras) both descendants of Prajāpati, contended with each other, the gods took unto themselves the Udgītha, thinking : 'With this we shall overcome them!'

[The supreme soul has been said the father of creation or the master or even the ruler. The god and demon, the matter and anti-matter, the creative and destructive flow, the genuine motivation and the cunning motivation all have been originated from him therefore he is the matter of them all.

In case, all these merge into one, the retrospective stage of the inactive creation may again come into existence. These both aspects therefore are engaged in their prescribed functions. A man can fructify any of the flow through his resolution. The worship of syllable Oṁ is provided for keeping one save from the germinating effect.]

ते ह नासिक्यं प्राणमुद्गीथमुपासांचक्रिरे। तꣳहासुराः पाप्मना विविधुस्तस्मात्तेनोभयं जिघ्रति सुरभि च दुर्गन्धि च पाप्मना ह्येष विद्धः॥२॥

Then they worshipped the Udgītha (the syllable Oṁ) as the breath in the nose. The devils afflicted that with evil. Therefore with it one smells both the sweet-smelling and the ill-smelling, for it is afflicted with evil.

अथ ह वाचमुद्गीथमुपासांचक्रिरे। ताꣳहासुराः पाप्मना विविधुस्तस्मात्तयोभयं वदति सत्यं चानृतं च पाप्मना ह्येषा विद्धा॥३॥

Then the gods worshipped the Udgītha (the echo of Oṁ) as speech. The devils afflicted that with evil. Therefore with it one speaks both the true and the false, for it is afflicted with evil.

अथ ह चक्षुरुद्गीथमुपासांचक्रिरे। तद्धासुराः पाप्मना विविधुस्तस्मात्तेनोभयꣳ पश्यति दर्शनीयं चादर्शनीयं च पाप्मना ह्येतद्विद्धम्॥४॥

The gods then worshipped the Udgītha as the eye. The devils afflicted that with evil. Therefore with it one sees both the slightly and the unsightly, for it is afflicted with evil.

अथ ह श्रोत्रमुद्गीथमुपासांचक्रिरे। तद्धासुराः पाप्मना विविधुस्तस्मात्तेनोभयꣳ शृणोति श्रवणीयं चाश्रवणीयं च पाप्मना ह्येतद्विद्धम्॥५॥

Then they reverenced the Udgītha as the ear, but the demons vitiated it too. Therefore with it one hears both what should be listened to and what should not be listened to, for it is afflicted with evil.

अथ ह मन उद्गीथमुपासांचक्रिरे। तद्धासुराः। पाप्मना विविधुस्तस्मात्तेनोभयꣳ संकल्पयते संकल्पनीयं चासंकल्पनीयं च पाप्मना ह्येतद्विद्धम्॥६॥

The gods then worshipped the Udgītha as the mind. The demons afflicted that with evil.

Therefore with it one imagines both what should be imagined and what should not be imagined, for it is afflicted with evil.

[The sage has here explained that the echo of Oṁ may be worshipped by the breathings coherent to the sensory organs but even a little omission may viciates it owing to a slight lift even to the flow given to the evils.

It has been explained in successive hymns that the complexes created by the demons become known as rescinded when the syllable Oṁ is worshipped through the cardinal breathing.]

अथ ह य एवायं मुख्यः प्राणस्तमुद्गीथमुपासांचक्रिरे। तꣳहासुरा ऋत्वा विदध्वꣳसुर्यथाश्मानमाखणमृत्वा विध्वꣳसेत॥७॥

Then they reverenced the Udgītha as that which is the breath in the mouth. When the devils struck that, they fell to pieces, as one would fall to pieces in striking against a solid stone.

एवं यथाश्मानमाखणमृत्वा विध्वꣳसत एवꣳहैव स विध्वꣳसते य एवंविदि पापं कामयते यश्चैनमभिसादसि स एषोऽश्माखणः॥८॥

As a lump of clay would fall to pieces in striking against a solid stone, so falls to pieces he who wishes evil to one who knows this, and he, too, who injures him. Such a one is a solid stone.

नैवैतेन सुरभि न दुर्गन्धि विजानात्यपहतपाप्मा ह्येष तेन यदश्नाति यत्पिबति तेनेतरान् प्राणानवति। एतमु एवान्ततोऽवित्त्वोत्क्रामति व्याददात्येवान्तत इति॥९॥

With this [breath] one discerns neither the sweet-smelling nor the ill-smelling, for it is free from evil. Whatever one eats with this, whatever one drinks with this, he protects the other vital breaths. And not finding this [breath in the mouth], one finally deceases; one finally leaves his mouth open.

[When the cardinal breathing of the body engages in worship the Udgītha (the echo of Oṁ), it awakes his high qualities while digesting the food. The maintenance of the breathings as located in bodily organs through the food, the arising qualities save him from the attacks made by the deficiencies. The succeeding hymn explains the cardinal breathing.]

तꣳहाङ्गिरा उद्गीथमुपासाचक्र एतमु एवाङ्गिरसं मन्यन्तेऽङ्गानां यद्रसः॥१०॥

Aṅgirā too had worshipped the syllable Oṁ as the Udgītha. People think that it is indeed Aṅgiras, because it is the essence (*rasa*) of the limbs (*aṅga*)– for that reason.

तेन तꣳह बृहस्पतिरुद्गीथमुपासांचक्र एतमु एव बृहस्पतिं मन्यन्ते वाग्धि बृहती तस्या एष पतिः॥११॥

Bṛhaspati reverenced this as the Udgītha. People think that it is indeed Bṛhaspati, because speech is great (*bṛhatī*) and it is the lord (*pati*) thereof– for that reason.

तेन तꣳहायास्य उद्गीथमुपासांचक्र एतमु एवायास्यं मन्यन्त आस्याद्यदयते॥१२॥

Ayāsya reverenced this as the Udgītha. People think that it is indeed Ayāsya, because it goes (*ayate*) from the mouth (*āsya*)– for that reason.

तेन तꣳ ह बको दाल्भ्यो विदांचकार। स ह नैमिशीयानामुद्गाता बभूव सह स्मैभ्यः कामानागायति॥१३॥

Baka, the son of Dālbhya knew it. He became Udgātri priest of the people of Naimiṣa. He used to sing to them their desires.

[The devotee of Udgītha (the syllable Oṁ) who has acquired expertise may fill his breathing with the waves in accordance with the resolution while engaged in the offering etc. functions and thus competent enough to spread the same spirits in the whole atmosphere.]

आगाता ह वै कामानां भवति य एतदेवं विद्वानक्षरमुद्गीथमुपास्त इत्यध्यात्मम्॥१४॥

An effective singer of desires, verily, indeed, becomes he who, knowing this thus, reverences the syllable as the Udgītha.

Thus with reference to the self.

॥इति द्वितीयः खण्ड॥

Part-3

Various identifications of the Udgītha and of its syllables

अथाधिदैवतं य एवासौ तपति तमुद्गीथमुपासीतोद्यन्वा एष प्रजाभ्य उद्गायति उद्यꣳस्तमो भयमपहन्त्यपहन्ता ह वै भयस्य तमसो भवति य एवं वेद॥१॥

Now we will discuss on the worship of the celestial glory. Him who glows yonder [i.e. the sun] one should reverence as an Udgītha. Verily, on rising (*ud-yan*), he sings aloud (*ud-gāyati*) for creatures. On rising, he dispels darkness and fear. He, verily, who knows this becomes a dispeller of fear and darkness.

समान उ एवायं चासौ चोष्णोऽयमनुष्णोऽसौ स्वर इतीममाचक्षते स्वर इति प्रत्यास्वर इत्यमुं तस्माद्वा एतमिममुं चोद्गीथमुपासीत॥२॥

This [breath in the mouth] and that [sun] are alike. This is warm. That is warm. People designate this as sound (*svara*) that as sound (*svara*) and as the reflecting (*pratyāsvara*). Therefore, verily, one should reverence this and that as an Udgītha.

अथ खलु व्यानमेवोद्गीथमुपासीत यद्वै प्राणिति स प्राणो यदपानिति सोऽपानोऽथ यः प्राणापानयोः सन्धिः स व्यानो यो व्यानः सा वाक् तस्मादप्राणन्ननपानन्वाचमभिव्याहरति॥३॥

The Udgītha (the syllable Oṁ) should be worshipped in garb of the breathing known as the Vyāna. When one breathes in– that is the in-breath (*prāṇa*). When one breathes out– that is the out-breath (*apāna*). The junction of the in-breath and the out-breath is the diffused breath. Speech is the diffused breath. Therefore one utters speech without in breathing, without out-breathing.

[The activities of breathing in and breathing out in the element of breathing are automatic. In Vyāna, the employment of the breathing by resolution takes place in the particular direction. Motivating the breathing to the higher ideals by resolution while worshipping is called Udgītha (the syllable Oṁ). This activity is performed by restricting the functions of breathing in and breathing out. This issue has been further made clear in the successive hymns.]

या वाक्स ऋक् तस्मादप्राणन्ननपानन्नृचमभिव्याहरति यत् ऋक् तत्साम तस्मादप्राणन्ननपानन्साम गायति यत्साम स उद्गीथस्तस्मादप्राणन्ननपानन्नुद्गायति॥४॥

The Ṛk is speech. Therefore one utters the Ṛk without in-breathing, without out-breathing. The Sāman is the Ṛk. Therefore one sings the Sāman without in-breathing, without out-breathing. The Udgītha is the Sāman. Therefore one chants the Udgītha without in-breathing, without out-breathing.

अतो यान्यन्यानि वीर्यवन्ति कर्माणि यथोग्नेर्मन्थनमाजे: सरणं दृढस्य धनुष आयमनप्राणन्ननपानꣳस्तानि करोत्येतस्य हेतोर्व्यानमेवोद्गीथमुपासीत॥५॥

Apart from it, the otherwise function require strength, like the kindling of fire by friction, the running of a race, the bending of a stiff bow– one performs them without in-breathing, without out-breathing. For this reason one should reverence the diffused breath as an Udgītha.

अथ खलूद्गीथाक्षराण्युपासीतोद्गीथ इति प्राण एवोत्प्राणेन ह्युत्तिष्ठति वाग्गीर्वाचो ह गिर इत्याचक्षतेऽन्नं थमन्ने हीदꣳ सर्वꣳ स्थितम्॥६॥

But one should also reverence the syllables of the Udgītha– *ud, gī, tha. Ud* is breath, for through breath one arises (*ut-tiṣṭhati*); *gī* is speech, for people designate speeches as words (*giras*); *tha* is food, for upon food this whole world is established (*sthita*).

[While worshipping Udgītha, the breathing in the bodily organs in garb of the food, the breathing (Vyāna) in actions and cardinal breathing providing with the upward motion are worth-worshipping. The worship of Udgītha harmonizing the close of holder, exhibitor and the promoter breathings in various forms in the nature has been explained in the successive hymns.]

द्यौरेवोदन्तरिक्षं गी: पृथिवी थमादित्य एवोद्वायुर्गीरग्निस्थꣳसामवेद एवोद्यजुर्वेदो गीर्ऋग्वेदस्थं दुग्धेऽस्मै वाग्दोहं यो वाचो दोहोऽन्नवानन्नादो भवति य एतान्येवं विद्वानुद्गीथा क्षराण्युपास्त उद्गीथ इति॥७॥

Ud is heaven; *gī* is atmosphere; *tha* is the earth. *ud* is the sun; *gī* is wind; *tha* is fire. *Ud* is Sāmaveda; *gī* is Yajurveda; *tha* is Ṛgveda. Speech yields milk– that is, the milk of speech itself– for him, he becomes rich in food, an eater of food, who knows and reverences these syllables of the Udgītha thus : *ud, gī, tha*.

[In the successive hymns, it has been made clear that the devotee to Udgītha must keep his devotion in an absolute form for the desired success. The penance of spirit or devotion for the person who resides Sāma or the pray requires self-meditation which has been clearly discussed in the successive hymns.]

अथ खल्वाशी: समृद्धिरुपसरणानीत्युपासीत येन साम्नास्तोष्यन्स्यात्तत्सामोपधावेत्॥८॥

Now then, the fulfilment of wishes— One would reverence the following as places of refuge. One should take refuge in the Sāman with which he may be about to sing a Stotra.

यस्यामृति तामृचं यदार्षेयं तमृषिं यां देवतामभिष्टोष्यन्स्यात्तां देवतामुपधावेत्॥९॥

One should take refuge in the Ṛk in which it was contained, in the Ṛṣi, who was the poet, in the divinity unto whom he may be about to sing a Stotra.

येन च्छन्दसा स्तोष्यन्स्यात्तच्छन्द उपधावेद्येन स्तोमेन स्तोष्यमाणः स्यात्तꣳस्तोममुपधावेत्॥१०॥

One should take refuge in the meter with which he may be about to sing a Stotra. One should take refuge in the hymn-form with which he may be about to sing a Stotra for himself.

यां दिशमभिष्टोष्यन्स्यात्तां दिशमुपधावेत्॥११॥

One should take refuge in the quarter of heaven toward which he may be about to sing a Stotra.

आत्मानमन्तत उपसृत्य स्तुवीत कामं ध्यायन्नप्रमत्तोऽभ्याशो ह यदस्मै स कामः समृद्ध्येत यत्कामः स्तुवीतेति यत्कामः स्तुवीतेति॥१२॥

Finally, one should go unto himself and sing a Stotra, meditating carefully upon his desire. Truly the prospect is that the desire will be fulfilled for him, desiring which he may sing a Stotra—yea, desiring which he may sing a Stotra!

॥इति तृतीयः खण्डः॥

Part-4

'*Oṁ*', superior to the three Vedas, the immortal refuge

ओमित्येतदक्षरमुद्गीथमुपासीतोमिति ह्युद्गायति तस्योपव्याख्यानम्॥१॥

'*Oṁ*'! One should reverence the Udgītha as this syllable for one sings the loud chant [beginning] with '*Oṁ*'.

This very Udgītha is hereby explained.

देवा वै मृत्योर्बिभ्यतस्त्रयीं विद्यां प्राविशꣳस्ते छन्दोभिरच्छादयन्यदेभिरच्छादयꣳस्तच्छन्दसां छन्दस्त्वम्॥२॥

Verily, the gods, when they were afraid of death, took refuge in the threefold knowledge [i.e. the three Vedas]. They covered (*acchādayan*) themselves with meters. Because they covered themselves with these, therefore the meters are called *chandas*.

[The gods have been told immortal then how they frightened of death? The gods as referred herein are purported to the divine powers enshrined into body.

In Śvetāśvatara upaniṣad, it has been described that the gods arising from the various organs of the degenetic man entered into the parts and the organs of the human body. As the man is mortal, the gods entered into his limbs and organs and therefore feel the fear of death.]

तानु तत्र मृत्युर्यथा मत्स्यमुदके परिपश्येदेवं पर्यपश्यदृचि साम्नि यजुषि। ते नु वित्त्वोर्ध्वा ऋचः साम्नो यजुषः स्वरमेव प्राविशन्॥३॥

Death saw them there, in the Ṛk, in the Sāman, in the Yajus, just as one might see a fish in water. When they found this out, they arose out of the Ṛk, out of the Sāman, out of the Yajus, and took refuge in sound.

यदा वा ऋचमाप्नोत्योमित्येवातिस्वरत्येवꣳ सामैवं यजुरेष उ स्वरो यदेतदक्षरमेतदमृतमभयं तत्प्रविश्य देवा अमृता अभया अभवन्॥४॥

While reciting Ṛca, he sounds out '*Oṁ*'; similarly a Sāman; similarly a Yajus. This sound is that syllable. It is immortal fearless. By taking refuge in it the god became immortal, fearless.

[The gods unless give up observing, their entity in the essences of the ever mortal sensory organs etc. could not free from the fear of death even if they comply with the discipline prescribed by the Veda as and when they get entrance into the pleasure of supreme essence in garb of the Brahma as Oṁ, they attain immortality.]

स य एतदेवं विद्वानक्षरं प्रणौत्येतदेवाक्षरꣳ स्वममृतमभयं प्रविशति तत्प्रविश्य यदमृता देवास्तदमृतो भवति॥५॥

He who pronounces the syllable, knowing it thus, takes refuge in that syllable, in the immortal, fearless sound. Since the gods became immortal by taking refuge in it, therefore he becomes immortal.

॥इति चतुर्थः खण्डः॥

Part-5

The Udgītha identified with the sun and with breath

अथ खलु य उद्गीथः स प्रणवो यः प्रणवः स उद्गीथ इत्यसौ वा आदित्य उद्गीथ एष प्रणव ओमिति ह्येष स्वरन्नेति॥१॥

In fact, what is Udgītha is the Praṇava (Oṁ) too and what is Praṇava if Udgītha too, And so, verily, the Udgītha is yonder sun, and it is *Oṁ*, for it is continually sounding '*Oṁ*'.

[The modern science accepts that the Sun with its solar family is also dynamic. The revival of the breathing by the Sun has already been called Udgītha in recedent hymns of this very upaniṣad at 1.31.]

एतमु एवाहमभ्यगासिषं तस्मान्मम त्वमेकोऽसीति ह कौषीतकिः पुत्रमुवाच रश्मीꣳस्त्वं पर्यावर्तयाद्बहवो वै ते भविष्यन्तीत्यधिदैवतम्॥२॥

'I sang praise unto it alone; therefore you are my only [son],' said Kauṣītaki to his son. 'Reflect upon its [various] rays. Verily, you will have many [sons]'.

This is a description on the divinities.

[In proportionate to the resolution made by the devotee, the power of breathing is appropriated. As per this fact, the above hymn envisages that one or a number of Suns can be obtained by way of focussing the brain at Sun.]

अथाध्यात्मं य एवायं मुख्यः प्राणस्तमुद्गीथमुपासीतोमिति ह्येष स्वरन्नेति॥३॥

Now with reference to the self. One should reverence the Udgītha as that which is the breath in the mouth, for it is continually sound '*Oṁ*'.

एतमु एवाहमभ्यगासिषं तस्मान्मम त्वमेकोऽसीति ह कौषीतकिः पुत्रमुवाच प्राणाꣳस्त्वं भूमानमभिगायताद्बहवो वै मे भविष्यन्तीति॥४॥

'I sang praise unto it alone; therefore you are my only [son],' spoke Kauṣītaki unto his son. 'Sing praise unto the breaths as a multitude. Verily, you will have many [sons].'

अथ खलु य उद्गीथः स प्रणवो यः प्रणवः स उद्गीथ इति होतृषदनाद्धैवापि दुरुद्गीतमनुसमाहरतीत्यनु समाहरतीति॥५॥

Now then, the Udgītha is *Oṁ*; *Oṁ* is the Udgītha. With this thought, verily, from the seat of a Hotṛ priest one puts in order again the Udgītha which has been falsely chanted—yea, puts it in order again.

[In case, the person engaged for performing the offering is not competent to use the hymns accurately and thereby if the vibration is not thrilling right, the learned person by virtue of reciting the Oṁ energises the cardinal breathing and the deficiency thereby sat aright.]

॥इति पञ्चमः खण्डः॥

Part-6

The cosmic and personal interrelations of the Udgītha

इयमेवर्गग्निः साम तदेतदेतस्यामृच्यध्यूढꣳ साम तस्मादृच्यध्यूढꣳ साम गीयत इयमेव साग्निरमस्तत्साम॥१॥

The Ṛk is this [earth]; the Sāman is fire. This Sāman rests upon that Ṛk. Therefore, the Sāman is sung as resting upon the Ṛk. *sā* is this [earth]; *ama* is fire. That makes *sāma.*

[The Sāma, viz., Udgītha has been said the circulation of breathing when the breathing is circulated the element of earth (wood etc.) jointly make the fire. Similarly, the circulation of breathing in the space forms the wind and the circulation of breathing by ether forms the Sun.]

अन्तरिक्षमेवर्ग्वायुः साम तदेतदेतस्यमृच्यध्यूढꣳ साम। तस्मादृच्यध्यूढꣳ साम गीयतेऽन्तरिक्षमेव सा वायुरमस्तत्साम॥२॥

The atmosphere is Ṛk and the wind is Sāma. This Sāman rests upon that Ṛk. Therefore the Sāman is sung as resting upon the Ṛk. *sā* is the atmosphere; *ama* is the wind. That make *sāma*.

द्यौरेवर्गादित्यः साम तदेतदेतस्यामृच्यध्यूढꣳ साम। तस्मादृच्यध्यूढꣳ साम गीयते द्यौरेव सादित्योऽमस्तत्साम॥३॥

The Ṛk is heaven; the Sāman is the sun. This Sāman rests upon that Ṛk. Therefore the Sāman is sung as resting upon the Ṛk. *sā* is heaven; *ama* is the sun. That makes *sāma.*

नक्षत्राण्येवर्क् चन्द्रमा: साम तदेतदेतस्यामृच्यध्यूढꣳ साम। तस्मादृच्यध्यूढꣳ साम गीयते नक्षत्राण्येव सा चन्द्रमा अमस्तत्साम॥४॥

The Ṛk is the lunar mansions; the Sāman is the moon. This Sāman rests upon that Ṛk. Therefore the Sāman is sung as resting upon the Ṛk. *sā* is the lunar mansions; *ama* is the moon. That makes *sāma*.

अथ यदेतदादित्यस्य शुक्लं भा: सैवर्गथ: यन्नीलं पर: कृष्णं तत्साम तदेतदेतस्यामृच्यध्यूढꣳ साम तस्मादृच्यध्यूढꣳ साम गीयते॥५॥

Now, the Ṛk is the white shining of the sun; the Sāman is the dark, the ultra-black. This Sāman rests upon that Ṛk. Therefore the Sāman is sung as resting upon the Ṛk.

अथ यदेतदादित्यस्य शुक्लं भा: सैव साथ यन्नीलं पर: कृष्णं तदमस्तत्सामाथ एषोऽन्तरादित्ये हिरण्य: पुरुषो दृश्यते हिरण्यश्मश्रुर्हिरण्यकेश आप्रणखात्सर्व एव सुवर्ण:॥६॥

Now, *sā* is the white shining of the sun; *ama* is the dark, the ultra-black. That makes *sāma*.

Now, that golden person who is seen within the sun has a golden beard and golden hair. He is exceedingly brilliant all, even to the fingernail tip.

तस्य यथा कप्यासं पुण्डरीकमेवमक्षिणी तस्योदिति नाम स एष सर्वेभ्य: पाप्मभ्य उदित उदेति ह वै सर्वेभ्य: पाप्मभ्यो य एवं वेद॥७॥

His eyes are even as a Kapyāsa (the buttocks of an ape) lotus-flower. His name is High (*ud*). He is raised high above all evils. Verily, he who knows this rises high above all evils.

तस्यर्क् च साम च गेष्णौ तस्मादुद्गीथस्तस्मात्त्वेवोद्गातैतस्य हि गाता स एष ये चामुष्मात्पराञ्चो लोकास्तेषां चेष्टे देवकामानां चेत्यधिदैवतम्॥८॥

His songs (*geṣṇau*) are the Ṛk and the Sāman. Therefore [they are called] the Udgītha. Therefore also the Udgātṛ priest [is so called], for he is the singer (*gātṛ*) of this [High (*ud*)]. He is the lord of the worlds which are beyond yonder sun, and also of the gods' desires.— Thus with reference to the divinities.

॥इति षष्ठ: खण्ड:॥

Part-7

अथाध्यात्मं वागेवर्क् प्राण: साम तदेतदेतस्यामृच्यध्यूढꣳ साम तस्मादृच्यध्यूढꣳ साम गीयते वागेव सा प्राणोऽमस्तत्साम॥१॥

Now with reference to the self.—

The Ṛk is speech; the Sāman is breath. This Sāman rests upon that Ṛk. Therefore the Sāman is sung as resting upon the Ṛk. *sā* is speech; *ama* is breath. That makes *sāma*.

चक्षुरेवर्गात्मा साम तदेतदेतस्यामृच्यध्यूढꣳ साम तस्मादृच्यध्यूढꣳ साम गीयते चक्षुरेव सात्माऽमस्तत्साम॥२॥

The Ṛk is the eye; the Sāman is the soul (*ātman*). This Sāman rests upon that Ṛk. Therefore the Sāman is sung as resting upon the Ṛk. *sā* is the eyes; *ama* is the soul. That makes *sāma*.

श्रोत्रमेवर्ङ्मनः साम तदेतदेतस्यामृच्यध्यूढꣳ साम तस्मादृच्यध्यूढꣳ साम गीयते श्रोत्रमेव सा मनोऽमस्तत्साम॥३॥

The Ṛk is the ear; the Sāman is the mind. This Sāman rests upon that Ṛk. Therefore the Sāman is sung as resting upon the Ṛk. *sā* is the ear; *ama* is the mind. That makes *sāma.*

अथ यदेतदक्ष्णः शुक्लं भाः सैवर्गथ यन्नीलं परः कृष्णं तत्साम तदेतदेतस्यामृच्यध्यूढꣳ तस्मादृच्यध्यूढꣳ साम गीलयते। अथ यदेतदक्ष्णः शुक्लं भाः सैव साथ यन्नीलं परः कृष्णं तदमस्तत्साम॥४॥

Now, the Ṛk is the bright shining of the eye; the Sāman is the dark, the ultra-black. This Sāman rests upon that Ṛk. Therefore the Sāman is sung as resting upon the Ṛk. *sā* is the bright shining of the eye; *ama* is the dark, the ultra-black. That makes *sāma.*

अथ य एषोऽन्तरक्षिणि पुरुषो दृश्यते सैव ऋक् तत्साम तदुक्थं तद्यजुस्तद्ब्रह्म तस्यैतस्य तदेव रूपं यदमुष्य रूपं यावमुष्य गेष्णौ तौ गेष्णौ यन्नाम तन्नाम॥५॥

Now, this person who is seen within the eye is the hymn (*ṛk*), is the chant *sāman*), is the recitation (*uktha*), is the sacrificial formula (*yajus*), is the prayer (*brahman*).

The form of this one is the same as the form of that [Person seen in the sun]. The songs of the former are the songs of this. The name of the one is the name of the other.

स एष ये चैतस्मादर्वाञ्चो लोकास्तेषां चेष्टे मनुष्यकामानां चेति तद्य इमे वीणायां गायन्त्येतं ते गायन्ति तस्मात्ते धनसनयः॥६॥

He is lord of the worlds which are under this one, and also of men's desires. So those who sing on the lute sing of him. Therefore they are winners of wealth.

अथ य एतदेवं विद्वान्साम गायत्युभौ स गायति सोऽमुनैव स एष ये चामुष्मात्पराञ्चो लोकास्ताꣳश्चाप्नोति देवकामास्ताꣳश्च॥७॥

Now, he who sings the Sāman, knowing it thus, sings of both; through the former he wins the worlds which are beyond the former, and also the gods' desires.

अथानेनैव ये चैतस्मादर्वाञ्चो लोकास्ताꣳश्चाप्नोति मनुष्यकामाꣳश्च तस्मादु हैवंविदुद्गाता ब्रूयात्॥८॥

Through the latter he wins the worlds which are under the latter, and also men's desires. Therefore an Udgītṛ priest who knows this may say :

कं ते काममागायानीत्येष ह्येव कामगानस्येष्टे य एवं विद्वान्साम गायति साम गायति॥९॥

'What desire may I win for you by singing?' For truly he is lord of the winning of desires by singing, who, knowing this, sings the Sāman—yea, sings the Sāman!

॥इति सप्तमः खण्डः॥

Part-8

The Udgītha identified with the ultimate, i.e. space

त्रयो होद्गीथे कुशला बभूवुः शिलकः शालावत्यश्चैकितायनो दाल्भ्यः प्रवाहणो जैवलिरिति ते होचुरुद्गीथे वै कुशलाः स्मो हन्तोद्गीथे कथां वदाम इति॥१॥

There were three men proficient in the Udgītha : Śilaka Śālāvatya, Caikitāyana, Dālbhya and Pravāhaṇa, Jaivali. These said : 'We are proficient in the Udgītha. Come! Let us have a discussion on the Udgītha!'.

तथेति ह समुपविविशुः स ह प्रवाहणो जैवलिरुवाच भगवन्तावग्रे वदतां ब्राह्मणयोर्वदतोर्वाचꣳ श्रोष्यामीति॥२॥

'So be it,' said they, and sat down together on appropriate place. Then Pravāhaṇa Jaivali said : 'Do you two, sirs, speak first. While there are two Brāhmaṇas speaking, I will listen to their word.'

स ह शिलकः शालावत्यश्चैकितायनं दाल्भ्यमुवाच हन्त त्वा पृच्छानीति पृच्छेति होवाच॥३॥

Then Śilaka Śālāvatya said to Caikitāyana Dālbhya : 'Come! Let me question you.'

'Question', said he.

का साम्नो गतिरिति स्वर इति होवाच स्वरस्य का गतिरिति प्राण इति होवाच प्राणस्य का गतिरित्यन्नमिति होवाचान्नस्य का गतिरित्याप इति होवाच॥४॥

'To what does the Sāman go back?' 'To sound,' said he.

'To what does sound go back?' 'To breath,' said he.

'To what does breath go back?' 'To food,' said he.

'To what does food go back?' 'To water,' said he.

अपां का गतिरित्यसौ लोक इति होवाचामुष्य लोकस्य का गतिरिति न स्वर्गं लोकमतिनयेदिति होवाच स्वर्गं वयं लोकꣳ सामाभिसंस्थापयामः स्वर्गसꣳस्तावꣳहि सामेति॥५॥

"What is the essence of this water?" 'Yonder world,' he said.

"What is the essence of yonder world?"

He said– 'One should not lead beyond the heavenly world,' 'We establish the Sāman upon the heavenly world, for the Sāman is praised as heaven'.

तꣳह शिलकः शालावत्यश्चैकितायनं दाल्भ्यमुवाचाप्रतिष्ठितं वै किल ते दाल्भ्य साम यस्त्वेतर्हि ब्रूयान्मूर्धा ते विपतिष्यतीति मूर्धा ते विपतिष्यतीति मूर्धा ते विपतेदिति॥६॥

Then Śilaka Śālāvatya said to Caikitāyana Dālbhya; 'Verily, indeed, your Sāman, O Dālbhya, is unsupported. If some one now were to say "Your head will fall off," your head would fall off.'

हन्ताहमेतद्भगवतो वेदानीति विद्धीति होवाचामुष्य लोकस्य का गतिरित्ययं लोक इति होवाचास्य लोकस्य का गतिरिति न प्रतिष्ठां लोकमतिनयेदिति होवाच प्रतिष्ठां वयं लोकꣳ सामाभिसꣳस्थापयामः प्रतिष्ठासꣳस्तावꣳहि सामेति॥७॥

'Come! Let learn this from you, sir.' 'Learn,' said he (Dālbhya).

'To what does yonder world go back?' 'To this world,' said he.

'To what does this world go back?' 'One should not lead beyond the world-support,' said he.

'We establish the Sāman upon the world as a support, for the Sāman is praised as a support.'

तꣳ ह प्रवाहणो जैवलिरुवाचान्तवद्वै किल ते शालावत्य साम यस्त्वेतर्हि ब्रूयान्मूर्धा ते विपतिष्यतीति मूर्धा ते विपतेदिति हन्ताहमेतद्भगवतो वेदानीति विद्धीति होवाच॥८॥

Then Pravāhaṇa Jaivali said to him : 'Verily, indeed, your Sāman, O Śālāvatya, comes to an end. If some one now were to say "Your head will fall off," your head would fall off.'

'Come! Let me learn this from you, sir.'

'Learn,' said he.

॥ इति अष्टमः खण्डः॥

Part-9

अस्य लोकस्य का गतिरित्याकाश इति होवाच सर्वाणि ह वा इमानि भूतान्याकाशादेव समुत्पद्यन्त आकाशं प्रत्यस्तं यन्त्याकाशो ह्येवैभ्यो ज्यायानाकाशः परायणम्॥१॥

Śilaka said– 'What is the essence of this world?' He said– "space," 'Verily, all things here arise out of space. They disappear back into space, for space alone is greater than these; space is the final goal.

स एष परोवरीयानुद्गीथः स एषोऽनन्तः परोवरीयो हास्य भवति परोवरीयसो ह लोकाञ्जयति य एतदेवं विद्वान्परोवरीयाꣳ समुद्गीथमुपास्ते॥२॥

This is the most highest and excellent Udgītha. This is endless. The most excellent is his, the most excellent worlds does he win, who, knowing it thus, reverences the most excellent Udgītha.

तꣳ हैतमतिधन्वा शौनक उदरशाण्डिल्यायोक्त्वोवाच यावत्त एनं प्रजायामुद्गीथं वेदिष्यन्ते परोवरीयो हैभ्यस्तावदस्मिँल्लोके जीवनं भविष्यति॥३॥

तथामुष्मिँल्लोके लोक इति स य एतमेवं विद्वानुपास्ते परोवरीय एव हास्यास्मिँल्लोके जीवनं भवति तथामुष्मिँल्लोके लोक इति लोके लोक इति॥४॥

When Atidhanvān Śaunaka told this Udgītha to Udara-śāṇḍilya, he also said : "As far as they shall know this Udgītha among your offspring, so far will they have the most excellent life in this world, and likewise a world in yonder world." He who knows and reverence sit thus has the most excellent life in this world, and likewise a world in yonder world—yea, a world in yonder world.'

॥ इति नवमः खण्डः॥

Part-10

The divinities connected with the three parts of the Chant

मटचीहतेषु कुरुष्वाटिक्या सह जाययोषस्तिर्ह चाक्रायण इभ्यग्रामे प्रद्राणक उवास॥१॥

The land of the state of Kuru spoiled owing to sudden fall of the hailstorms, there lived in the Ibhya village of a Elephant-man a very poor man, Uṣasti Cākrāyaṇa, with his wife Āṭikī.

स हेभ्यं कुल्माषान्खादन्तं बिभिक्षे तꣳहोवाच। नेतोऽन्ये विद्यन्ते यच्च ये म इम उपनिहिता इति॥२॥

He begged of the Elephant-man, while he was eating Kulmāṣa grains. The latter said to him : 'I have no others than these which are set before me'.

एतेषां मे देहीति होवाच तानस्मै प्रददौ हन्तानुपानमित्युच्छिष्टं वै मे पीतꣳ स्यादिति होवाच॥३॥

Uṣasti said– "Give me some of them". He gave them to him and said : 'Well, here is water'.

'Verily, that would be for me to drink leavings!' said he.

Uṣasti replied– "I could be accused of drinking stole water if I have it."

न स्विदेतेऽप्युच्छिष्टा इति न वा अजीविष्यामिमा न खादन्निति होवाच कामो म उदपानमिति॥४॥

'Are not these [beans] also leavings?'

'Verily, I could not live, if I did not eat those,' said he. 'The drinking of water is at my will.'

स ह खादित्वातिशेषाञ्जायाया आजहार साग्र एव सुभिक्षा बभूव तान्प्रतिगृह्य निदधौ॥५॥

Having eaten, Uṣasti gave the remainder to his wife. She had already begged enough to eat. She took these and put them away.

स ह प्रातः संजिहान उवाच यद् बतान्नस्य लभेमहि लभेमहि धनमात्राꣳराजासौ यक्ष्यते स मा सर्वैरार्त्विज्यैर्वृणीतेति॥६॥

On the next morning, having got up from the bed, Uṣasti said to his wife- 'Oh, if we could get some food, we might get a little money! The king over there is going to have a sacrifice performed for himself. He might, choose me to perform all the priestly offices.'

तं जायोवाच हन्त पत इम एव कुल्माषा इति तान्खादित्वामुं यज्ञं विततमेयाय॥७॥

His wife said to him : 'Here, my lord, are the beans.' He ate them and went off to that sacrifice, which had already been begun.

तत्रोद्गातृनास्तावे स्तोष्यमाणानुपोपविवेश स ह प्रस्तोतारमुवाच॥८॥

There he approached the Udgātṛ priests as they were about to chant the hymns of praise in the place of the singing. Then he said to the Prastotā priest :

प्रस्तोतर्या देवता प्रस्तावमन्वायत्ता तां चेदविद्वान्प्रस्तोष्यसि मूर्धा ते विपतिष्यतीति॥९॥

'Prastotā priest, if you shall sing the Prastāva (Introductory Praise) without knowing the divinity which is connected with the Prastāva, your head will fall off.'

एवमेवोद्गातारमुवाचोद्गातर्या देवतोद्गीथमन्वायत्ता तां चेदविद्वानुद्गास्यसि मूर्धा ते विपतिष्यतीति॥१०॥

Similarly also he said to the Udgātṛi priest : 'UdgātṛI priest, if you shall chant the Udgītha (Loud Chant) without knowing the divinity which is connected with the Udgītha, your head will fall off.'

एवमेव प्रतिहर्तारमुवाच प्रतिहर्तर्या देवता प्रतिहारमन्वायत्ता तां चेदविद्वान्प्रति हरिष्यसि मूर्धा ते विपतिष्यतीति ते ह समारतास्तूष्णीमासांचक्रिरे॥११॥

Similarly also he said to the Pratihartā priest : 'O Pratihartā priest, if you shall take up the Pratihāra (Response) without knowing the divinity which is connected with the Pratihāra, your head will fall off.' Then they ceased and quietly seated themselves.

[Such precautions were given by the saints who were expert in the functions like offerings to the half-learned persons with a view to by the depth of their knowledge. Having, this a terrifying ultimatum, the half-learned Brāhmaṇa, the clients etc. used to refrain from the work handled that time by them.]

Part-11

अथ हैनं यजमान उवाच भगवन्तं वा अहं विविदिषाणीत्युषस्तिरस्मि चाक्रायण इति होवाच॥१॥

Then the institutor of the sacrifice said to him : 'Verily, I want to know about you, sir. "I am Uṣasti Cākrāyaṇa," said he.

स होवाच भगवन्तं वा अहमेभिः सर्वैरार्त्विज्यैः पर्यैषिषं भगवतो वा अहमवित्त्वान्यानवृषि॥२॥

Then he [i.e. the institutor) said : 'Verily, I have been searching around for you, sir, for all these priestly offices. Verily, not finding you, sir, I have chosen others.

भगवाꣳस्त्वे मे सर्वैरार्त्विज्यैरिति तथेत्यथ तर्ह्येत एव समतिसृष्टाः स्तुवतां यावत्त्वेभ्यो धनं दद्यास्तावन्मम दद्या इति तथेति ह यजमान उवाच॥३॥

But do you, sir, perform all the priestly offices for me.'

'So be it,' said he (*iti*). 'But in this matter (*tarhi*) let these indeed, being permitted, sing the Stotra; but you should give me as much money as you would give them.'

Yajamāna said– 'So be it,'

अथ हैनं प्रस्तोतोपससाद प्रस्तोतर्या देवता प्रस्तावमन्वायत्ता तां चेदविद्वान्प्रस्तोष्यसि मूर्धा ते विपतिष्यतीति मा भगवानवोचत्कतमा सा देवतेति॥४॥

Then the Prastotṛi priest approached him and said : 'You sir, said unto me : "Prastotṛi priest, if you shall sing the Prastāva without knowing the divinity which is connected with the Prastāva, your head will fall off." Which is that divinity?

प्राण इति होवाच सर्वाणि ह वा इमानि भूतानि प्राणमेवाभिसंविशन्ति प्राणमभ्युज्जिहते सैषा देवता प्रस्तावमन्वायत्ता तां चेदविद्वान्प्रास्तोष्यो मूर्धा ते व्यपतिष्यत्तथोक्तस्य मयेति॥५॥

'Breath *(prāṇa)*,' said he. 'Verily, indeed, all being here enter [into life] with breath and depart [from life] with breath. This is the divinity connected with the Prastāva. If you had sung the Prastāva without knowing it, your head would have fallen off, after your had been told so by me.'

अथ हैनमुद्गातोपससादोद्गातर्या देवतोद्गीथमन्वायत्ता तां चेदविद्वानुद्गास्यसि मूर्धा ते विपतिष्यतीति मा भगवानवोचत्कतमा सा देवतेति॥६॥

Then the Udgātṛi priest approached him and said; 'You sir, said unto me : "Udgātṛi priest, if you shall chant the Udgītha without knowing the divinity which is connected with the Udgītha, your head will fall off." Which is that divinity?'

आदित्य इति होवाच सर्वाणि ह वा इमानि भूतान्यादित्यमुच्चैः सन्तं गायन्ति सैषा देवतोद्गीथमन्वायत्ता तां चेदविद्वानुदगास्यो मूर्धा ते व्यपतिष्यत्तथोक्तस्य मयेति॥७॥

'The Sun,' said he. 'Verily, indeed, all beings here sing (*gāyanti*) of the sun when he is up (*uccais*). This is the divinity connected with the Udgītha. If you had chanted the Udgītha without knowing it, your head would have fallen off, after you had been told so by me.'

अथ हैनं प्रतिहर्तोपससाद प्रतिहर्तर्यो देवता प्रतिहारमन्वायत्ता तां चेदविद्वान्प्रतिहरिष्यसि मूर्धा ते विपतिष्यतीति मा भगवानवोचत्कतमा सा देवतेति॥८॥

Then the Pratihartṛ priest approached him and said : 'You, sir, said unto me : "Pratihartṛ priest, if you shall take up the Pratihāra without knowing the divinity which is connected with the Pratihāra, your head will fall off." Which is that divinity?'

अन्नमिति होवाच सर्वाणि ह वा इमानि भूतान्यन्नमेव प्रतिहरमाणानि जीवन्ति सैषा देवता प्रतिहारमन्वायत्ता तां चेदविद्वान्प्रत्यहरिष्यो मूर्धा ते व्यपतिष्यत्तथोक्तस्य मयेति तथोक्तस्य मयेति॥९॥

He said 'Food,' 'Verily, indeed, all beings here live by taking up to themselves (*pratiharamāṇa*) food. This is the divinity connected with the Pratihāra. If you had taken up the Pratihāra without knowing it, your head would have fallen off, after you had been told so by me.'

॥इति एकादशः खण्डः॥

Part-12

In this part, the 'Śauva' Udgītha is described. According to the reference books, the term 'Śauva' is the abbreviated form of the 'Śauvana'. 'Śauvana' is meant for anything related to the motion (Śvāna). This is a trimming illustration. The term 'Śvāna' is formed of the 'Śuṅ root'. According to 'Śuṅ' to go, the term Śvāna is meant for dynamically. The proportion to this illustration seems clear by assuming the meaning of 'Śauva' as relating to the breathing. According to the story, the sons of the Ṛṣi have gone to the far natural place for perseverance. They introduced their with the purified breathing or the wind full of oxygen. Other 'Śvānas' (the breathing defected of the sensory organs) refer to their hunger and submit to them singing Udgītha for attainment of food. In the precedent parts of this upaniṣad, it has been already said that the penance of Udgītha performed by the purified breathing is only fructified. The group of breathings spreaded all through in the nature sing Udgītha under the leading of the purified breathing. The illustration or the context described herein obtains clarity.

अथात: शौव उद्गीथस्तद्ध बको दाल्भ्यो ग्लावो वा मैत्रेय: स्वाध्यायमुद्वाव्राज॥१॥

Now next, the 'Śauva' Udgītha, connected with Dogs is described —

So Bāka Dālbhya or Glāva Maitreya—went forth for Veda-study.

तस्मै श्वा श्वेता: प्रादुर्बभूव तमन्ये श्वान उपसमेत्योचुरन्नं नो भगवानागायत्वशनायाम वा इति॥२॥

A white dog appeared before him. Around this one other dogs gathered and said : 'Do you sir, obtain food for us by singing. Verily, we are hungry.'

तान्होवाचेहैव मा प्रातरुपसमीयातेति तद्ध बाको दाल्भ्यो ग्वालो वा मैत्रेय: प्रतिपालयांचकार॥३॥

Then he said to them : 'In the morning you may assemble unto me here at this spot'. So Bāka Dālbhya—or Glāva Maitreya—awaited.

ते ह यथैवेदं बहिष्पवमानेन स्तोष्यमाणा: सꣳरब्धा: सर्पन्तीत्येव माससृपुस्ते ह समुपविश्य हिंचक्रु:॥४॥

Then, even as [priests] here, when they are about to chant with the Bahiṣpavamāna hymn, glide hand in hand, so did they glide on. Then they sat down together and performed the preliminary vocalizing (*hiṅkāra*).

[The hymn of 'Bahiṣpavamāna' is recited in the morning not at the later but by moving in a batch around the altar. The aim of such movement is for attaining the best cereal for the offering on fire. Here to the tendencies coherent with the breathing *i.e.* the hunger and the thirst etc. do pray for the food so that they may survive. In the succeeding hymn this very psalms has been described. It has been called 'Trita'. It has been made to the three gods.]

ओ३मदा३मों३पिबा३मों३देवो वरुण: प्रजापति: सविता३न्नमिहा२हर-दन्नपते२ऽन्नमिहा हरा२हरो३मिति॥५॥

'*Oṁ*! Let us eat. *Oṁ*! Let us drink. *Oṁ*! May the god Varuṇa, Prajāpati and Savitā bring food here! O Lord of food, bring food here! yea, bring it here! *Oṁ*!'

॥इति द्वादश: खण्ड:॥

Part-13

The mystical meaning of certain sounds in the Chant

The penance known as 'Stobha' which relates to the 'Sāma' is described in this part. The vowels are recited like the classical music but the words depicting particular meanings are not used herein.

The spirit attached with the vowels in that very process has been elaborated here.

अयं वाव लोको हाउकारो वायुर्हाइकारश्चन्द्रमा अथकार आत्मेहकारोऽग्निरीकारः॥१॥

Verily, the sound *hā-u* is the world, [for this interjectional trill occurs in the Rathantara Sāman, which is identified with the earth'.

The sound *hā-ī* is wind, [for this interjectional trill occurs in the Vāmadevya Sāman, which has for its subject the origin of wind and water].

The sound *atha* is the moon, [for on food (*anna*) everything is established (*sthita*), and the moon consists of food].

The sound *iha* is oneself, [for oneself is here (*iha*)].

The sound *ī* is Agni, [for all Sāmans sacred to Agni end with the sound *ī*].

आदित्य ऊकारो निहव एकारो विश्वदेवा औहोयिकारः प्रजापतिर्हिंकारः प्राणः स्वरोऽन्नं या वाग्विराट्॥२॥

The sound *ū* is the sun, [for people sing of the sun when it is up (*ū-rdhvam*)].

The sound *e* is the Invocation, [for people call with 'Come! (*e-hi*)'].

The sound *au-ho-i* is the Viśvaveda gods, [for this interjectional trill occurs in the Sāman to the Viśvaeva gods].

The sound *hiṅ* is Prajāpati, [for Prajāpati is undefined, an the sound *hiṅ* also is indistinct].

svara (sound) is breath, [for that is the source of sound].

yā is food, [for everything here moves (*yati*) through the help of food].

vāc is Virāj, [for this interjectional trill occurs in the Sāman to Virāj].

अनिरुक्तस्त्रयोदशः स्तोभः संचरो हुंकारः॥३॥

The sound *hum*, the variable thirteenth interjectional till, is the Undefined.

दुग्धेऽस्मै वाग्दोहं यो वाचो दोहोऽन्नवानन्नदो भवति य एतामेवꣳ साम्नामुपनिषदं वेदोपनिषदं वेद इति॥४॥

Speech yields milk—that is, the milk of speech itself—for him, he becomes rich in food, an eater of food, who knows thus this mystic meaning (*upaniṣad*) of the Sāmans—yea, who knows the mystic meaning!

Second Chapter

Part-1

The Meditation of the Whole Sāman

ॐ समस्तस्य खलु साम्न उपासनꣳ साधु यत्खलु साधु तत्सामेत्याचक्षते तदसाधु तदसामेति॥१॥

Oṁ! Assuredly, the reverence of the Sāman entire (*samasta*) is good (*sādhu*). Assuredly, anything that is good, people call *sāman* (abundance); anything that is not good, *a-sāman* (deficiency).

[The root cause of the recital of Sāma is clarified here. Recital of Sāma is purported to the best recital performed for the benevolent purpose. The recital of Sāma on the basis of elocution of singing but with the selfish interest as also with greed cannot be tantamounted to the recital of Sāma. The benevolent spirits full of appearing only are desired for the recital Sāma. The Ṛṣi has made it clear in the 4th and the last hymn under this part.]

तदुताप्याहुः साम्नैनमुपागादिति साधुनैनमुपागादित्येव तदाहुरसाम्नैनमुपागादित्यसाधुनैनमुपागादित्येव तदाहुः॥२॥

So also people say : 'He approached him with *sāman* (kindliness)'; that is, they say : 'He approached him with good manner (*sādhu*).'— 'He approached him with no *sāman*'; that is, they say : 'He approached him with no good manner.'

अथोताप्याहुः साम नो बतेति यत्साधु भवति साधु बतेत्येव तदाहुरसाम न बतेति यदासाधु भवत्यसाधु बतेत्येव तदाहुः॥३॥

So also, further, people say : 'Oh! We have *sāman* (goods)!' if it is something good (*sādhu*); that is, they say : 'Oh! Good!' 'Oh! We have no *saman*!' if it is not good; that is, they say : 'Oh! No good!'

स य एतदेवं विद्वान्साधु सामेत्युपास्तेऽभ्याशो ह यदेनꣳ साधवो धर्मा आ च गच्छेयुरुप च नमेयुः॥४॥

He who, knowing this, reverence the Sāman the best among all,— truly the prospect is that good qualities will come unto him and attend him.

Part-2

Some analogies to the fivefold Chant

In this very upaniṣad, it has been made clear in the precedent hymns that Udgītha too is the 'Sāman', and the spirit of 'Sāman' is purported to the gentle and bonafied spirits. The breathings are motivated and inclined to perform the particular purpose in Udgītha. The ceretum are the orders of motivating the breathings for the greatest deeds is continued in various forms throughout the tangible as also intangible nature. In recital of the hymns pertaining to the offerings, five divisions or the devotion of 'Sāma', have been told. The Ṛṣi has highlighted various forms of 'Sāma' in the degenetic offering of nature as also its divisions from 1st to 7th part. It has been said that the devotee able to accustom himself with the application of Sāma by the breathings in course of a number of natural activities can obtain a power to control that cycle in toto.

लोकेषु पञ्चविधꣳसामोपासीत पृथिवी हिंकारोऽग्निः प्रस्तावोऽन्तरिक्षमुद्गीथ आदित्यः प्रतिहारो द्यौर्निधनमित्यूर्ध्वेषु॥१॥

In the worlds one should reverence a fivefold Sāman (Chant). The earth is a Hiṅkāra (Preliminary Vocalizing). Fire is a Prastāva (Introductory Praise). The atmosphere is an Udgītha (Loud Chant). The sun is a Pratihāra (Response). The sky is a Nidhana (Conclusion).

Thus in their ascending order.

अथावृत्तेषु द्यौर्हिंकार आदित्यः प्रस्तावोऽन्तरिक्षमुद्गीथोऽग्निः प्रतिहारः पृथिवी निधनम्॥२॥

Now in their reverse order.

The sky is a Hiṅkāra. The sun is a Prastāva. The atmosphere is an Udgītha. Fire is a Pratihāra. The earth is a Nidhana.

[The 'Hiṁkāra' and 'Nidhana' is recital of Sāman are an indicator of the beginning and the end respectively. When the breathing is motivated targeting the upper worlds from the earth, the situation availed is as described in hymn number one. However, when the 'Sāma' is recited from the upper worlds by targeting the earth, the situating becomes as described in the hymn number 2.]

कल्पन्ते हास्मै लोका ऊर्ध्वाश्चावृत्ताश्च य एतदेवं विद्वाँल्लोकेषु पञ्चविधꣳसामोपास्ते॥३॥

The worlds, both in their ascending order and in their reverse order, serve him who, knowing this thus, reverences a fivefold Sāman in the worlds.

Part-3

वृष्टौ पञ्चविधꣳ सामोपासीत पुरो वातो हिंकारो मेघो जायते स प्रस्तावो वर्षति स उद्गीथो विद्योतते स्तनयति स प्रतिहारः॥१॥

In a rain-storm one should reverence a fivefold Sāman.

The preceding wind is a Hiṅkāra. A cloud is formed—that is a Prastāva. It rains—that is an Udgītha. It lightens, it thunders—that is a Pratihāra.

उद्गृह्णाति तन्निधनं वर्षति हास्मै वर्षयति ह य एतदेवं विद्वान्वृष्टौ पञ्चविधꣳसामोपास्ते॥२॥

It lifts—that is a Nidhana. It rains for him, indeed, he causes it to rain, who, knowing this thus, reverences a fivefold Sāman in a rainstorm.

Part-4

सर्वास्वप्सु पञ्चविधꣳसामोपासीत मेघो यत्संप्लवते स हिंकारो यद्वर्षति स प्रस्तावो याः प्राच्यः स्यन्दन्ते स उद्गीथो याः प्रतीच्यः स प्रतिहारः समुद्रो निधनम्॥१॥

In all waters one should reverence a fivefold Sāman.

When a cloud gathers—that is a Hiṅkāra. When it rains—that is a Prastāva. Those [waters] which flows to the east—they are an Udgītha. Those which flow to the west—they are a Pratihāra. The ocean is a Nidhana.

न हाप्सु प्रैत्यप्सुमान्भवति य एतदेवं विद्वान्सर्वास्वप्सु पञ्चविधꣳसामोपास्ते॥२॥

He perishes not in water, he becomes rich in water, who, knowing this thus, reverence a fivefold Sāman in all waters.

Part-5

ऋतुषु पञ्चविधꣳ सामोपासीत वसन्तो हिंकारो ग्रीष्मः प्रस्तावो वर्षा उद्गीथः शरत्प्रतिहारो हेमन्तो निधनम्॥१॥

In the seasons one should reverence a fivefold Sāman.

The spring is a Hiṅkāra. The summer is a Prastāva. The rainy season is an Udgītha. The autumn is a Pratihāra. The winter is a Nidhana.

कल्पन्ते हास्मा ऋतव ऋतुमान्भवति य एतदेवं विद्वानृतुषु पञ्चविधꣳसामोपास्ते॥२॥

The seasons serve him, he becomes rich in seasons, who, knowing this thus, reverences a fivefold Sāman in the seasons.

Part-6

पशुषु पञ्चविधꣳसामोपासीताजा हिंकारोऽवयः प्रस्तावो गाव उद्गीथोऽश्वाः प्रतिहारः पुरुषो निधनम्॥१॥

In animals one should reverence a fivefold Sāman.

Goats are a Hiṅkāra. Sheep are a Prastāva. Cows are an Udgītha. Horses are a Pratihāra.

भवन्ति हास्य पशवः पशुमान्भवति य एतदेवं विद्वान्पशुषु पञ्चविधꣳ सामोपास्ते॥२॥

Animals come into his possession, he becomes rich in animals, who, knowing this thus, reverences a fivefold Sāman in animals.

Part-7

प्राणेषु पञ्चविधं परोवरीयः सामोपासीत प्राणो हिंकारो वाक्प्रस्तावश्चक्षुरुद्गीथः श्रोत्रं प्रतिहारो मनो निधनं परोवरीयाꣳसि वैतानि॥१॥

In the vital breaths (*prāṇa*) one should reverence the most excellent fivefold Sāman.

Breath is a Hiṅkāra. Speech is a Prastāva. The eye is an Udgītha. The ear is a Pratihāra. The mind is a Nidhana. Verily, these are the most excellent.

परोवरीयो हास्य भवति परोवरीयसो ह लोकाञ्जयति य एतदेवं विद्वान्प्राणेषु पञ्चविधं परोवरीयः सामोपास्त इति तु पञ्चविधस्य॥२॥

The most excellent becomes his, he wins the most excellent worlds, who, knowing this thus, reverences the most excellent fivefold Sāman in the vital breaths.—So much for the fivefold.

Part-8

Some analogies to the sevenfold Chant

अथ सप्तविधस्य वाचि सप्तविधꣳसामोपासीत यत्किंच वाचो हुमिति स हिंकारो यत्प्रेति स प्रस्तावो यदेति स आदिः॥१॥

Now for the sevenfold. In speech one should reverence a sevenfold Sāman. Whatsoever of speech is *huṁ*—that is a Hiṅkāra (Preliminary Vocalizing). Whatsoever is *pra*—that is a Prastāva (Introductory Praise). Whatsoever is *ā*—that is an Ādi (Beginning).

यदुदिति स उद्गीथो यत्प्रतीति स प्रतिहारो यदुपेति स उपद्रवो यन्नीति तन्निधनम्॥२॥

Whatsoever is *ud*—that is an Udgītha (Loud Chant).

Whatsoever is *prati*—that is a Pratihāra (Response).

Whatsoever is *upa*—that is an Upadrava (Approach to the End).

Whatsoever is *ni*—that is a Nidhana (Conclusion).

दुग्धेऽस्मै वाग्दोहं यो वाचो दोहोऽन्नवानन्नादो भवति य एतदेवं विद्वान्वाचि सप्तविधꣳसामोपास्ते।।३।।

Speech yields milk—that is, the milk of speech itself—for him, be becomes rich in food, an eater of food, who knowing this thus, reverences a sevenfold Sāman in speech.

Part-9

अथ खल्वमुमादित्यꣳ सप्तविधꣳ सामोपासीत सर्वदा समस्तेन साम मां प्रति मां प्रतीति सर्वेण समस्तेन साम।।१।।

Now, verily, one should reverence yonder sun as a sevenfold Sāman. It is always the same (*sama*); therefore it is a Sāman. It is the same with everyone, since people think: 'It faces me! It faces me!' Therefore it is a Sāman.

तस्मिन्निमानि सर्वाणि भूतान्यन्वायत्तानीति विद्यात्तस्य यत्पुरोदयात्स हिंकारस्तदस्य पशवोऽन्वायत्तास्तस्मात्ते हिंकुर्वन्ति हिंकारभाजिनो ह्येतस्य साम्नः।।२।।

One should know that all beings here are connected with it.

When it is before sunrise—that is a Hiṅkāra (Preliminary Vocalizing). Animals are connected with this [part] of it. Therefore they perform preliminary vocalizing. Truly, they are partakers in the Hiṅkāra of that Sāman.

अथ यत्प्रथमोदिते स प्रस्तावस्तदस्य मनुष्या३ अन्वायत्तास्तस्मात्ते प्रस्तुतिकामाः प्रशꣳसाकामाः प्रस्तावभाजिनो ह्येतस्य साम्नः।।३।।

Now, when it is just after sunrise—that is a Prastāva (Introductory Praise). Men are connected with this [part] of it. Therefore they are desirous of praise (*prastuti*), desirous of laudation. Truly, they are partakers in the Prastāva of that Sāman.

अथ यत्सङ्गववेलायाꣳ स आदिस्तदस्य वयाꣳस्यन्वायत्तानि तस्मात्तान्यन्तरिक्षेऽनारम्भणान्यादायात्मानं परिपतन्त्यादिभाजीनि ह्येतस्य साम्नः।।४।।

Now, when it is the cow gathering-time— that is an Ādi (Beginning). The birds are connected with this [part] of it. Therefore they support (*ādāya*) themselves without support (*an-ārambaṇa*) in the atmosphere and fly around. Truly, they are partakers in the Ādi of that Sāman.

अथ यत्संप्रति मध्यन्दिने स उद्गीथस्तदस्य देवा अन्वायत्तास्तस्मात्ते सत्तमाः प्राजापत्यानामुद्गीथभाजिनो ह्येतस्य साम्नः।।५।।

Now, when it is just at midday— that is an Udgītha (Loud Chant). The gods are connected with this [part] of it. Therefore they are the best of Prajāpati's offspring. Truly, they are partakers in the Udgītha of that Sāman.

अथ यदूर्ध्वं मध्यन्दिनात्प्रागपराह्णात्स प्रतिहारस्तदस्य गर्भा अन्वायत्तास्तस्मात्ते प्रतिहृता नावपद्यन्ते प्रतिहारभाजिनो ह्येतस्य साम्नः॥६॥

Now, when it is past midday and before [the latter part of] the afternoon—that is a Pratihāra (Response). Fetuses are connected with this [part] of it. Therefore they are taken [or, held] up (*pratihṛta*) and do not drop down. Truly, they are partakers in the Pratihāra of that Sāman.

अथ यदूर्ध्वमपराह्णात्प्रागस्तमयात्स उपद्रवस्तदस्यारण्या अन्वायत्तास्तस्मात्ते पुरुषं दृष्ट्वा कक्षꣳ श्वभ्रमित्युपद्रवन्त्युपद्रवभाजिनो ह्येतस्य साम्नः॥७॥

Now, when it is past afternoon and before sunet—that is an Upadrava (Approach to the end). Wild beasts are connected with this [part] of it. Therefore when they see a man, they approach (*upadravanti*) a hiding place as their hold. Truly, they are partakers in the Upadrava of that Sāman.

अथ यत्प्रथमास्तमिते तन्निधनं तदस्य पितरोऽन्वायत्तास्तस्मात्तान्निदधति निधनभाजिनो ह्येतस्य साम्न एवं खल्वमुमादित्यꣳ सप्तविधꣳ सामोपास्ते॥८॥

Now, when it is just after sunset—that is the Nidhana (Conclusion). The Pitṛs are connected with this [part] of it. Therefore people lay aside (*ni* + √*dhā*) the manes. Truly, they are partakers in the Nidhana of that Sāman.

Part-10

अथ खल्वात्मसंमितमतिमृत्यु सप्तविधꣳसामोपासीत हिंकार इति त्र्यक्षरं प्रस्ताव इति त्र्यक्षरं तत्समम्॥१॥

Thereafter, one should meditate upon the seven-fold Sāman. Now then, one should reverence the Sāman, measured (*sammita*) in itself, as leading beyond death. *Hiṅkāra* has three syllables. *Prastāva* has three syllables. That is the same (*sama*).

आदिरिति द्व्यक्षरं प्रतिहार इति चतुरक्षरं तत इहैकं तत्समम्॥२॥

The term 'Ādi' is formed with 2 letters and 'Pratihāra' is formed with 4 letters. A single letter if removed from 'Pratihāra' and added with the 'Ādi', both words become equal.

उद्गीथ इति त्र्यक्षरमुपद्रव इति चतुरक्षरं त्रिभिस्त्रिभिः समं भवत्यक्षरमतिशिष्यते त्र्यक्षरं तत्समम्॥३॥

The word Udgītha consists of three letters and 'Updrava' consists of four letters. To the extent of 3 letters these are equal and a single letter remains. This residual letter is called 'Akṣara'. It also consists of 3 letters, therefore, it also is equal.

निधनमिति त्र्यक्षरं तत्सममेव भवति तानि ह वा एतानि द्वाविꣳशतिरक्षराणि॥४॥

Nidhana has three syllables. That is the same, too. These are twenty-two syllables.

एकविꣳशत्यादित्यमाप्नोत्येकविꣳशो वा इतोऽसावादित्यो द्वाविꣳशेन परमादित्याज्जयति तन्नाकं तद्विशोकम्॥५॥

With the twenty-one one obtains the sun. Verily, the sun is the twenty-first from here.

With the twenty-two one wins what is beyond the sun. That is heaven (*nākam*). That is the sorrowless.

आप्नोति हादित्यस्य जयं परो हास्यादित्यजयाज्जयो भवति य एतदेवं विद्वानात्मसंमितमतिमृत्यु सप्तविधः सामोपास्ते सामोपास्ते॥६॥

He obtains the victory of the sun, indeed, a victory higher than the victory of the sun in his, who, knowing this thus, reverences the sevenfold Sāman, measured in itself, as leading beyond death—yea, who reverences the Sāman!

Part-11

मनो हिंकारो वाक्प्रस्तावश्चक्षुरुद्गीथः श्रोत्रं प्रतिहारः प्राणो निधनमेतद्गायत्रं प्राणेषु प्रोतम्॥१॥

Now the peculiar worship relating to Gāyatra is described. The mind is 'Hiṁkāra', Speech is a Prastāva. The eye is an Udgītha. The ear is a Pratihāra. The breath is a Nidhana. This is the Gāyatra Sāman as woven upon the vital breaths (*prāṇa*).

स य एवमेतद्गायत्रं प्राणेषु प्रोतं वेद प्राणी भवति सर्वमायुरेति ज्योग्जीवति महान्प्रजया पशुभिर्भवति महान्कीर्त्या महामनाः स्यात्तद्व्रतम्॥२॥

He who knows thus this Gāyatra Sāman as woven upon the vital breaths becomes possessor of vital breaths, reaches a full length of life, lives long, becomes great in offspring and in cattle, great in fame. One should be great-minded. That is his rule.

Part-12

अभिमन्थति स हिंकारो धूमो जायते स प्रस्तावो ज्वलति स उद्गीथोऽङ्गारा भवन्ति स प्रतिहार उपशाम्यति तन्निधनः सः शाम्यति तन्निधनमेतद्रथन्तरमग्नौ प्रोतम्॥१॥

The fire emerging out as a result of rubbing is 'Hiṁkāra', Smoke is produced—that is a Prastāva. It blazes—that is an Udgītha. Coals are formed—that is a Pratihāra. It become extinct—that is a Nidhana. It becomes completely extinct—that is a Nidhana. This is the Rathantara Sāman as woven upon fire.

स य एवमेतद्रथन्तरमग्नौ प्रोतं वेद ब्रह्मवर्चस्यन्नादो भवति सर्वमायुरेति ज्योग्जीवति महान्प्रजया पशुभिर्भवति महान्कीर्त्या न प्रत्यङ्ङग्निमाचामेन्न निष्ठीवेत्तद्व्रतम्॥२॥

One who knows thus this Rathantara Sāman as woven upon fire becomes an eater of food, eminent in sacred knowledge, reaches a full length of life, lives long, becomes great in offspring and in cattle, great in fame. One should not take a sip and spit toward fire. That is his rule.

Part-13

उपमन्त्रयते स हिंकारो ज्ञपयते स प्रस्तावः स्त्रिया सह शेते स उद्गीथः प्रति स्त्रीं सह शेते स प्रतिहारः कालं गच्छति तन्निधनं पारं गच्छति तन्निधनमेतद्वामदेव्यं मिथुने प्रोतम्॥१॥

Now the worship of Vāmadevya Sāma in the form of couple is described. One summons—that is a Hiṅkāra. He makes request—that is a Prastāva. Together with the woman he lies down—that is an Udgītha. He lies upon the woman—that is a Pratihāra. He comes to the end—that is a Nidhana. He comes to the finish—that is a Nidhana.

[The sage has said the couple life and the cycle of reproduction by way of it as under the Vāmadevya Sāma. A few pupil alleged to this context as being trivial but it is worth consideration that he is explaining a number of ways for the worship of Sāman in the cycle of Sāma, the flow of breathing according to the flow of nature. When this is the position, how the genetic signs conducted by the couples can be abandoned. The sage observed here a particular Sāma (a Supreme penance of the development through the breathing). Thus there is no scope for futility in this context of discussion on the knowledge as also the scientific matter.]

स य एवमेतद्वामदेव्यं मिथुने प्रोतं वेद मिथुनीभवति मिथुनान्मिथुनात्प्रजायते सर्वमायुरेति ज्योग्जीवति महान्प्रजया पशुभिर्भवति महान्कीर्त्या न कां च न परिहेत्तद्व्रतम्॥२॥

He who knows thus this Vāmadevya Sāman as woven upon copulation comes to copulation, procreates himself from every copulation, reaches a full length of life, lives long, becomes great in offspring and in cattle, great in fame. One should never abstain from any woman. That is his rule.

Part-14

उद्यन्हिंकार उदितः प्रस्तावो मध्यन्दिन उद्गीथोऽपराह्णः प्रतिहारोऽस्तं यन्निधनमेतद्बृहदादित्ये प्रोतम्॥१॥

The rising sun is a Hiṅkāra. The risen sun is a Prastāva. Mid-day is an Udgītha. Afternoon is a Pratihāra. When it is set—that is a Nidhana.

This degentic Sāma is established in the Sun.

स य एवमेतद्बृहदादित्ये प्रोतं वेद तेजस्व्यन्नादो भवति सर्वमायुरेति ज्योग्जीवति महान्प्रजया पशुभिर्भवति महान्कीर्त्या तपन्तं न निन्देत्तद्व्रतम्॥२॥

He who knows thus this Bṛhad Sāman as woven upon the sun becomes a brilliant eater of food, reaches a full length of life, lives long, becomes great in offspring and in cattle, great in fame. One should not find fault with it when it is hot. That is his rule.

Part-15

अभ्राणि संप्लवन्ते स हिंकारो मेघो जायते स प्रस्तावो वर्षति स उद्गीथो विद्योतते स्तनयति स प्रतिहार उद्गृह्णाति तन्निधनमेतद्वैरूपं पर्जन्ये प्रोतम्॥१॥

Mists come together—that is a Hiṅkāra. A cloud is formed—that is a Prastāva. It rains—that is an Udgītha. It lightens and thunders—that is a Pratihāra. It holds up—that is a Nidhana. This is the Virūpa Sāman as woven upon cloud (*pārjanya*).

स य एवमेतद्वैरूपं पर्जन्ये प्रोतं वेद विरूपाꣳश्च सुरूपाꣳश्च पशूनवरुन्धे सर्वमायुरेति ज्योग्जीवति महान्प्रजया पशुभिर्भवति महान्कीर्त्या वर्षन्तं न निन्देत्तद्व्रतम्॥२॥

He who knows thus this Vairūpa Sāman as woven upon rain acquires cattle both of various form (*vi-rūpa*) and of beautiful form (*su-rūpa*), reaches a full length of life, lives long, becomes great in children and in cattle, great in fame. One should not find fault with it when it rains. That is his rule.

Part-16

वसन्तो हिंकारो ग्रीष्मः प्रस्तावो वर्षा उद्गीथः शरत्प्रतिहारो हेमन्तो निधनमेतद्वैराजमृतुषु प्रोतम्।।१।।

Spring is a Hiṅkāra. Summer is a Prastāva. The rainy season is an Udgītha. Autumn is a Pratihāra. Winter is a Nidhana. This is the Vairāja Sāman as woven upon the seasons.

स य एवमेतद्वैराजमृतुषु प्रोतं वेद विराजति प्रजया पशुभिर्ब्रह्मवर्चसेन सर्वमायुरेति ज्योग्जीवति महान्प्रजया पशुभिर्भवति महान्कीर्त्यर्तूंन्न निन्देत्तद्व्रतम्।।२।।

He who knows thus this Vairāja Sāman as woven upon the seasons shines like a king (*virājati*) with offspring, cattle and eminence in sacred knowledge, reaches a full length of life, lives long, becomes great in offspring and cattle, great in fame. One should not find fault with the seasons. That is his rule.

Part-17

पृथिवी हिंकारोऽन्तरिक्षं प्रस्तावो द्यौरुद्गीथो दिशः प्रतिहारः समुद्रो निधनमेताः शक्वर्यो लोकेषु प्रोताः।।१।।

The earth is a Hiṅkāra. The atmosphere is a Prastāva. The sky is an Udgītha. The regions of the compass are a Pratihāra. The ocean is a Nidhana. These are the verses of the Śakvarī Sāman as woven upon the worlds.

स य एवमेताः शक्वर्यो लोकेषु प्रोता वेद लोकी भवति सर्वमायुरेति ज्योग्जीवति महान्प्रजया पशुभिर्भवति महान्कीर्त्या लोकान्न निन्देत्तद्व्रतम्।।२।।

He who knows thus these verses of the Śakvarī Sāman as woven upon the worlds becomes possessor of a world, reaches a full length of life, lives long, becomes great in offspring and in cattle, great in fame. One should not find fault with the worlds. That is his rule.

Part-18

अजा हिंकारोऽवयः प्रस्तावो गाव उद्गीथोऽश्वाः प्रतिहारः पुरुषो निधनमेता रेवत्यः पशुषु प्रोताः।।१।।

The goat is Hiṁkāra, Sheep are a Prastāva, the cows are Udgītha, the horses are Pratihāra and the man is Nidhana. These are the verses of the Revatī Sāman as woven upon animals.

स य एवमेताः रेवत्यः पशुषु प्रोता वेद पशुमान्भवति सर्वमायुरेति ज्योग्जीवति महान्प्रजया पशुभिर्भवति महान्कीर्त्या पशून्न निन्देत्तद्व्रतम्।।२।।

He who knows thus these verses of the Revatī Sāman as woven upon animals becomes possessor of animals, reaches a full length of life, lives long, becomes great in offspring and in cattle, great in fame. One should not find fault with animals. That is his rule.

Part-19

लोम हिंकारस्त्वक्प्रस्तावो माꣳ समुद्गीथोस्थि प्रतिहारो मज्जा निधनमेतद्यज्ञायज्ञीयमङ्गेषु प्रोतम्।।१।।

Hair is a Hiṅkāra. Skin is a Prastāva. Flesh is an Udgītha. Bone is a Pratihāra. Marrow is a Nidhana. This is the Yajñāyajñīya Sāman as woven upon the members of the body.

स य एवमेतद्यज्ञायज्ञीयमङ्गेषु प्रोता वेदङ्गी भवति नाङ्गेन विहूर्च्छति सर्वमायुरेति ज्योग्जीवति महान्प्रजया पशुभिर्भवति महान्कीर्त्या संवत्सरं मज्ज्ञो नाश्नीयात्तद्व्रतम् मज्ज्ञो नाश्नीयादिति वा।।२।।

He who knows thus this Yajñāyajñīya Sāman as woven upon the members of the body becomes possessor of the members of his body, does not become defective in any member of the body, reaches a full length of life, live long, becomes great in offspring and in cattle, great in fame. One should not eat of marrow for a year. That is his rule. Rather, one should not eat of marrow at all.

Part-20

अग्निर्हिंकारो वायुः प्रस्ताव आदित्य उद्गीथो नक्षत्राणि प्रतिहारश्चन्द्रमा निधनमेतद्राजनं देवतासु प्रोतम्।।१।।

The fire is hiṁkāra, the wind is Prastāva, the sun is Udgītha, the planet is Pratihāra and the moon is Nidhana. This is the Rājana Sāman as woven upon the divinities.

स य एवमेतद्राजनं देवतासु प्रोतं वेदैतासामेव देवतानाꣳ सलोकताꣳ सार्ष्टिताꣳ सायुज्यं गच्छति सर्वमायुरेति ज्योग्जीवति महान्प्रजया पशुभिर्भवति महान्कीर्त्या ब्राह्मणान्न निन्देत्तद्व्रतम्।।२।।

He who knows thus this Rājana Sāman as woven upon the divinities goes to the same world, to equality and to complete union (*sāyujya*) with those very divinities, reaches a full length of life, lives long, becomes great in offspring and in cattle, great in fame. One should not find fault with the Brāhmaṇas. That is his rule.

Part-21

The Sāman itself based on the world-all

त्रयी विद्या हिंकारस्त्रय इमे लोकाः स प्रस्तावोऽग्निर्वायुरादित्यः स उद्गीथो नक्षत्राणि वयाꣳसि मरीचयः स प्रतिहारः सर्पा गन्धर्वाः पितरस्तन्निधनमेतत्साम सर्वस्मिन्प्रोतम्।।१।।

The Three-fold science is a Hiṅkāra. The three worlds here are a Prastāva. Agni, Vāyu and Āditya are an Udgītha. Stars, birds and light-rays are a Pratihāra. Serpents, Gandharvas and the Fathers are a Nidhana. This is the Sāman as woven upon the world-all.

स य एवमेतत्साम सर्वस्मिन्प्रोतं वेद सर्वꣳ ह भवति।।२।।

He who knows thus this Sāman as woven upon the world-all become the world-all itself.

तदेष श्लोकः। यानि पञ्चधा त्रीणि त्रीणि तेभ्यो न ज्यायः परमन्यदस्ति।।३।।

On this line there is this verse :- Whatever triple things are fivefold— Than these things there is nothing better, higher.

यस्तद्वेद स वेद सर्वं सर्वा दिशो बलिमस्मै हरन्ति। सर्वमस्मीत्युपासीत तद्व्रतं तद्व्रतम्।।४।।

Who knows this fact, he knows the world-all; All regions of the compass bring him tribute. One should reverence the thought 'I am the world-all!' That is his rule. That is his rule!

Part - 22

Seven different modes of singing the chant, characteristic of different gods

विनर्दि साम्नो वृणे पशव्यमित्यग्नेरुद्गीथोऽनिरुक्तः प्रजापतेर्निरुक्तः सोमस्य मृदु श्लक्ष्णं वायोः श्लक्ष्णं बलवदिन्द्रस्य क्रौञ्चं बृहस्पतेरपध्वान्तं वरुणस्य तान्सर्वानेवोपसेवेत वारुणं त्वेव वर्जयेत्।।१।।

'I prefer the high-sounding animal-like form of the Sāman'—such is the Udgītha belonging to Agni. The indistinct form belongs to Prajāpati; the distinct, to Soma; the soft and smooth, to Vāyu; the smooth and strong, to Indra; the heron-like, to Bṛhaspati; the ill-sounding to Varuṇa. One may practise all these, but one should avoid that belonging to Varuṇa.

अमृतत्वं देवेभ्य आगायानीत्यागायेत्स्वधां पितृभ्य आशां मनुष्येभ्यस्तृणोदकं पशुभ्यः स्वर्गं लोकं यजमानायान्नमात्मन आगायानीत्येतानि मनसा ध्यायन्नप्रमत्तः स्तुवीत।।२।।

'Let me obtain immortality for the gods by singing'—thus should one obtain with his singing. 'Let me obtain oblation for the fathers by singing, hope for men, grass and water for cattle, a heavenly world for the sacrificer, food for myself (*ātman*)'—one should sing the Stotra carefully, meditating these things in mind.

सर्वे स्वरा इन्द्रस्यात्मानः सर्व ऊष्माणः प्रजापतेरात्मानः सर्वे स्पर्शा मृत्योरात्मानस्तं यदि स्वरेषूपालभेतेन्द्रꣳशरणं प्रपन्नोऽभूवं स त्वा प्रति वक्ष्यतीत्येनं ब्रूयात्।।३।।

All vowels are embodiments (*ātman*) of Indra. all spirants are embodiments of Prajāpati. All [other] consonants are embodiments of Mṛtyu (Death).

If one should reproach a person on his vowels, let him say to that one : 'I have been a suppliant to Indra for protection. He will answer you.'

अथ यद्येनमूष्मसूपालभेत प्रजापतिꣳशरणं प्रपन्नोऽभूवं स त्वा प्रतिपेक्ष्यतीत्येनं ब्रूयादथ यद्येनꣳ स्पर्शेषूपालभेत मृत्युꣳशरणं प्रपन्नोऽभूवं स त्वा प्रतिधक्ष्यतीत्येनं ब्रयात्।।४।।

So, if one should reproach him on his spirants, let him say to that one : 'I have been a suppliant to Prajāpati for protection. He will thrash you.'

So, if one should reproach him on his [other] consonants, let him say to that one : 'I have been a suppliant to Mṛtyu (Death) for protection. He will burn you up.'

सर्वे स्वरा घोषवन्तो बलवन्तो वक्तव्या इन्द्रे बलं ददानीति सर्व ऊष्माणोऽग्रस्ता अनिरस्ता विवृता वक्तव्याः प्रजापतेरात्मानं परिददानीति सर्वे स्पर्शा लेशेनानभिनिहिता वक्तव्या मृत्योरात्मानं परिहराणीति॥५॥

All the vowels should be pronounced strong and sonant, with the thought : 'To Indra let me give strength.' All the spirants should be pronounced well open, without being slurred over, without being elided, with the thought : 'To Prajāpati let me entrust myself.' All the [other] consonants should be pronounced slowly, without being merged together, with the thought : 'From Mṛtyu (Death) let me withdraw myself (*ātman*).'

Part - 23

Different modes of religious life

त्रयो धर्मस्कन्धा यज्ञोऽध्ययनं दानमिति प्रथमस्तप एव द्वितीयो ब्रह्मचार्याचार्यकुलवासी तृतीयोऽत्यन्तमात्मानमाचार्यकुलेऽवसादयन्सर्व एते पुण्यलोका भवन्ति ब्रह्मसꣳस्थोऽमृतत्वमेति॥१॥

There are three branches of duty. Sacrifice, study of the Vedas, alms-giving—that is the first. Austerity, indeed, is the second. A student of sacred knowledge (*brahmacārin*) dwelling in the house of a teacher, settling himself permanently in the house of a teacher, is the third. All these become possessors of meritorious worlds. He who stands firm in Brahma attains immortality.

The syllable 'Oṁ', the acme of the cosmogony

प्रजापतिर्लोकानभ्यतपत्तेभ्योऽभितप्तेभ्यस्त्रयी विद्या संप्रास्रवत्तामभ्यतपत्तस्या अभितप्ताया एतान्यक्षराणि संप्रास्रवन्त भूर्भुवः स्वरिति॥२॥

Prajāpati brooded upon the worlds. From them, when they had been brooded upon, issued forth the threefold knowledge. He brooded upon this. From it, when it had been brooded upon, issued forth these syllables : *bhūr, bhuvaḥ, svar*.

तान्यभ्यतपत्तेभ्योऽभितप्तेभ्य ॐकारः संप्रास्रवत्तद्यथा शङ्कुना सर्वाणि पर्णानि संतृण्णान्येवमोंकारेण सर्वा वाक् संतृण्णोंकार एवेदꣳ सर्वमोंकार एवेदꣳसर्वम्॥३॥

He brooded upon them. From them, when they had been brooded upon, issued forth the syllable *Oṁ*. As all leaves are held together by a spike, so all speech is held together by *Oṁ*. Verily, *Oṁ* is the world-all. Verily, *Oṁ* is this world-all.

Part - 24

Earth, atmosphere, and sky the reward for performers of the morning, noon and evening oblations.

ब्रह्मवादिनो वदन्ति यद्वसूनां प्रातः सवनꣳ रुद्राणां माध्यन्दिनꣳ सवनमादित्यानां च विश्वेषां च देवानां तृतीयसवनम्॥१॥

The expounders of sacred knowledge (*brahmavādin*) say : 'Since to the Vasus belongs the morning Soma-libation, to the Rudras the mid-day Soma-libation, to the Ādityas and the Viśvadevas the third Soma-libation.

क्व तर्हि यजमानस्य लोक इति स यस्तं न विद्यात्कथं कुर्यादथ विद्वान्कुर्यात्॥२॥

Where, then (*tarhi*), is the sacrificer's world?'

If one knows not, how can he perform [the sacrifice with success]? So let him who knows perform.

पुरा प्रातरनुवाकस्योपाकरणाज्जघनेन गार्हपत्यस्योदङ्मुख उपविश्य स वासवꣳसामाभिगायति॥३॥

Before the commencement of the morning litany he sits down behind the Gārhapatya fire, facing the north and sings forth the Sāman to the Vasus :-

लो३कद्वारमपावा३र्णू३३पश्येम त्वा वयꣳरा ३३३३३ हुं ३ आ ३३ ज्या ३ यो ३ आ ३२१११ इति॥४॥

O the god of fire! 'Open the door to Your world, And let us see You, For the obtaining of Your sovereignty!'

अथ जुहोति नमोऽग्नये पृथिवीक्षिते लोकक्षिते लोकं मे यजमानाय विन्दैष वै यजमानस्य लोक एतास्मि॥५॥

So he offers the oblation and says : 'Adoration to Agni, earth-inhabiting, world-inhabiting! Find a world for me, the sacrificer! Verily, that is the sacrificer's world! I will go.

अत्र यजमानः परस्तादायुषः स्वाहाऽपजहि परिघमित्युक्त्वोत्तिष्ठति तस्मै वसवः प्रातः सवनꣳ संप्रयच्छन्ति॥६॥

Thither, I, the sacrificer, after life. Hail! Thrust back the bar!' Thus having spoken, he rises. At the same time the Vasus bestow upon him the morning Soma-libation.

[The Vasus are the gods providing the accommodation (residence). For the sake of attaining prosperous and happy life under the blessing of god in this world Vasus are prayed.]

पुरा माध्यन्दिनस्य सवनस्योपाकरणाज्जघनेनाग्नीध्रीयस्योदङ्मुख उपविश्य स रौद्रꣳसामाभिगायति॥७॥

Before the commencement of the mid-day Soma-libation he sits down behind the Āgnīdhrīya fire, facing the north, and sings forth the Sāman to the Rudras :-

लो३कद्वारमापावा३र्णू३३ पश्येम त्वा वयं वैरा ३३३३३ हुं ३ आ ३३ ज्या ३ यो ३ आ ३२१११ इति॥८॥

O wind! 'Open the door to Your world, And let us see You, For the obtaining of Wide sovereignty!'

अथ जुहोति नमो वायवेऽन्तरिक्षक्षिते लोकक्षिते लोकं मे यजमानाय विन्दैष वै यजमानस्य लोक एतास्मि॥९॥

So he offers the libation and says : 'Adoration to Vāyu, atmosphere-inhabiting, world-inhabiting! Find a world for me, the sacrificer! Verily, that is the sacrificer's world! I will go.

[At the IInd Stage of life when the liability of couple life has been completed, the devotee should pass his life in Vānaprastha (Half seclusion from the domestic liabilities). The Rudras are the gods who destroy the deficiencies. By worshipping Rudra, the devotee should endeavour for rectifying the deficiencies from his individual as also the social life.]

अत्र यजमानः परस्तादायुषः स्वाहाऽपजहि परिघमित्युक्त्वोत्तिष्ठति तस्मै रुद्रा माध्यन्दिनꣳ सवनꣳ संप्रयच्छन्ति॥१०॥

Thither, I, the sacrificer, after life. Hail! Thrust back the bar!' Thus having spoken he rises. At the same time the Rudras bestow upon him the mid-day Soma-libation.

पुरा तृतीयसवनस्योपाकरणाज्जघनेनाहवनीयस्योदङ्मुख उपविश्य स आदित्यꣳ स वैश्वदेवꣳ सामाभिगायति॥११॥

Before the commencement of the third Soma-libation he sits down behind the Āhavanīya fire, facing the north and sings forth the Sāman to the Ādityas and the Viśvadevas :-

लो३कद्वारमपावा३र्णू ३३ पश्येम त्वा वयꣳस्वारा ३३३३३ हुं ३ आ ३३ ज्या ३ यो ३ आ ३२१११ इति॥१२॥

O sun god! 'Open the door to Your world, And let us see You, For the obtaining of Chief sovereignty!'

आदित्यमथ वैश्वदेवं लो३कद्वारमपावा३र्णू ३३ पश्येम त्वा वयꣳ साम्ना ३३३३३ हुं ३ आ ३३ ज्या ३ यो ३ आ ३२१११ इति॥१३॥

Thus the [Sāman] to the Ādityas. Now the [Sāman] to the Viśvadevas :-

'Open the door to Your world, And let us see You, For the obtaining of Full sovereignty!'

अथ जुहोति नम आदित्येभ्यश्च विश्वेभ्यश्च देवेभ्यो दिविक्षिद्भ्यो लोकक्षिद्भ्यो लोकं मे यजमानाय विन्दत॥१४॥

So he offers the oblations and says : 'Adoration to the Ādityas and to the Viśvadevas, sky-inhabiting, world-inhabiting! Find a world for me, the sacrificer!

एष वै यजमानस्य लोक एतास्म्यत्र यजमानः परस्तादायुषः स्वाहाऽपहतपरिघमित्युक्त्वोत्तिष्ठति॥१५॥

Verily, that is the sacrificer's world! I will go thither, I, the sacrificer, after life. Hair! Thrust back the bar!' Thus having spoken, he rises.

तस्मा आदित्याश्च विश्वे च देवास्तृतीयꣳसवनꣳ संप्रयच्छन्त्येष ह वै यज्ञस्य मात्रां वेद य एवं वेद य एवं वेद॥१६॥

At the same time the Ādityas and the Viśvadevas bestow upon him the third Soma-libation. Verily, he knows the fullness of the sacrifice who knows this— yea, who knows this!

[At the last stage of life, the devotee should bring into practice the knowledge and the inspiration in accordance with the dictum of "this whole world is like our family" by virtue of the penance offered to the Sun-god and the Viśvadevas.]

Third Chapter

Part - 1

The sun as the honey extracted from all the Vedas

असौ वा आदित्यो देवमधु तस्य द्यौरेव तिरश्चीनवꣳशोऽन्तरिक्षमपूपो मरीचयः पुत्राः॥१॥

Verily, yonder sun is the honey of the gods. The cross-beam for it is the sky. The honey comb is the atmosphere. The brood are the particles of light. Verily, these Ṛg verses.

तस्य ये प्राञ्चो रश्मयस्ता एवास्य प्राच्यो मधुनाड्यः। ऋच एव मधुकृत ऋग्वेद एव पुष्पं ता अमृता आपस्ता वा एता ऋचः॥२॥

The eastern rays of that sun are its eastern honey-cells. The bees are the Ṛg verses. The flower is the Ṛg-veda. The drops of nectar fluid [arose as follows].

एतमृग्वेदमभ्यतपꣳस्तस्याभितप्तस्य यशस्तेज इन्द्रियं वीर्यमन्नाद्यꣳरसोऽजायत॥३॥

Brooded upon that Ṛgveda; from it, when it had been brooded upon, there was produced as its essence splendour, brightness, power, vigor, and food.

तद्व्यक्षरत्तदादित्यमभितोऽश्रयत्तद्वा एतद्यतेददादित्यस्य रोहितꣳरूपम्॥४॥

It flowed forth. It repaired to the sun. Verily, that is what that red appearance of the sun is.

Part - 2

अथ येऽस्य दक्षिणा रश्मयस्ता एवास्य दक्षिणा मधुनाड्यो यजूꣳष्येव मधुकृतो यजुर्वेद एव पुष्पं ता अमृता आपः॥१॥

So its southern rays are its southern honey-cells. The bees are the Yajus formulas. The flower is the Yajurveda. The drops of nectar fluid [arose as follows].

तानि वा एतानि यजूꣳष्येतं यजुर्वेदमभ्यतपꣳस्तस्याभितप्तस्य यशस्तेज इन्द्रियं वीर्यमन्नाद्यꣳरसोऽजायत॥२॥

Certainly, these Yajus formulas brooded upon that Yajurveda; from it, when it had been brooded upon, there was produced as its essence splendour, brightness, power, vigor and food.

तद्व्यक्षरत्तदादित्यमभितोऽश्रयत्तद्वा एतद्यदेतदादित्यस्य शुक्लꣳ रूपम्॥३॥

It flowed forth. It repaired to the sun. Certainly, that is what that white appearance of the sun is.

Part - 3

अथ येऽस्य प्रत्यञ्चो रश्मयस्ता एवास्य प्रतीच्यो मधुनाड्यः सामान्येव मधुकृतः सामवेद एव पुष्पं ता अमृता आपः॥१॥

The western rays of the Sun are now its western honey-cells. The bees are the Sāman chants. The flower is the Sāmaveda. The drops of nectar fluid [arose as follows].

तानि वा एतानि सामान्येतः सामवेदमभ्यतपःस्तस्याभितप्तस्य यशस्तेज इन्द्रियं वीर्यमन्नाद्यः रसोऽजायत।।२।।

Indeed, those Sāman chants brooded upon that Sāmaveda; from it, when it had been brooded upon, there was produced as its essence splendour, brightness, power, vigor and food.

तद्व्यक्षरत्तदादित्यमभितोऽश्रयत्तद्वा एतद्यदेतदादित्यस्य परं कृष्णःरूपम्।।३।।

It flowed forth. It repaired to the sun. Certainly, that is what that dark appearance of the sun is.

Part - 4

अथ येऽस्योदञ्चो रश्मयस्ता एवास्योदीच्यो मधुनाड्योऽथर्वाङ्गिरस एव मधुकृत इतिहासपुराणं पुष्पं ता अमृता आपः।।१।।

So its northern rays are its northern honey-cells. The bees are the [Hymns] of the Atharvans and Aṅgirasas. The flower is Legend and Ancient Lore (*itihāsa-purāṇa*). The drops of nectar fluid [arose as follows].

ते वा एतेऽथर्वाङ्गिरस एतदितिहासपुराणमभ्यतपःस्तस्याभितप्तस्य यशस्तेज इन्द्रियं वीर्यमान्नाद्यःरसोऽजायत।।२।।

Verily, those [Hymns] of the Atharvans and Aṅgirasas brooded upon that Legend and Ancient Lore; from it, when it had been brooded upon, there was produced as its essence splendour, brightness, power, vigor and food.

तद्व्यक्षरत्तदादित्यमभितोऽश्रयत्तद्वा एतद्यदेतदादित्यस्य परं कृष्णः रूपम्।।३।।

It flowed forth. It repaired to the sun. Verily, that is what that exceedingly dark appearance of the sun is.

Part - 5

अथ येऽस्योर्ध्वा रश्मयस्ता एवास्योर्ध्वा मधुनाड्यो गुह्या एवादेशा मधुकृतो ब्रह्मैव पुष्पं ता अमृता आप।।१।।

Then, its upward rays are the upper honey-cells. The bees are the Hidden Teachings [i.e. the Upaniṣads]. The flower is Brahma. The drops of nectar fluid [arose as follows].

ते वा एते गुह्या आदेशा एतद्ब्रह्माभ्यतपःस्तस्याभितप्तस्य यशस्तेज इन्द्रियं वीर्यमान्नाद्यःरसोऽजायत।।२।।

Verily, those Hidden Teachings brooded upon that Brahma; from it, when it had been brooded upon, there was produced as its essence splendour, brightness, power, vigour and food.

[The material science assumes the activation of the particles in the matter as the cause for the activation of the Sun etc. The Ṛṣi opines that the apparent process of the Sun etc. is because a resolution of the senses or an order is acting behind it. The computer is seen doing all the functions but the computer scientist only knows that the cause for activation of the computer is absolutely the command given to it. Similarly, the Ṛṣi assumes that any secret command is in existence behind all the functions of this world.]

तद्व्यक्षरत्तदादित्यमभितोऽश्रयत्तद्वा एतद्यदेतदादित्यस्य मध्ये क्षोभत इव॥३॥

It flowed forth. It repaired to the sun. Verily, that is what seems to tremble in the middle of the sun.

ते वा एते रसानाः रसा वेदा हि रसास्तेषामेते रसास्तानि वा एतान्यमृतानाममृतानि वेदा ह्यमृतास्तेषामेतान्यमृतानि॥४॥

Verily, these are the essences of the essences, for the Vedas are essences and these are their essences. Verily, these are the nectars of the nectars, for the Vedas are nectars and these are their nectars.

[From the first to the 5th part, the essences located at the east, south, west and north parts as also at the upper portion of the Sun have been described. According to the saint, the visible colours of the Sun are also coherent with certain micro flow of the senses. The red and white divisions of the Sun are easy to understand. What are the dark and gross dark? These may be that division of the Sun to which the material scientists say eclipse of the Sun. The establishment of particular flows in the eastern etc. divisions of the Sun have been described in above 5 parts. In the successive 5 parts *i.e.* from 6 to 10 the similar arising of the nectar flows from those very parts of the sun and its impact has been described.]

Part - 6

The knower of the cosmic significance of the sacred scriptures advances to the world-sun, Brahma

तद्यत्प्रथममममृतं तद्वसव उपजीवन्त्यग्निना मुखेन न वै देवा अश्नन्ति न पिबन्त्येतदेवामृतं दृष्ट्वा तृप्यन्ति॥१॥

The Vasus live upon that which is the first nectar [i.e. the Ṛgveda] through Agni as their mouth. Verily, the gods neither eat nor drink. They are satisfied merely with seeing that nectar.

त एतदेव रूपमभिसंविशन्त्येतस्माद्रूपादुद्यन्ति॥२॥

These enter that [red] form of the sun and come forth from that form.

स य एतदेवममृतं वेद वसूनामेवैको भूत्वाग्निनैव मुखेनैतदेवामृतं दृष्ट्वा तृप्यति स य एतदेव रूपमभिसंविशत्येतस्माद्रूपादुदेति॥३॥

One who knows thus that nectar becomes one of the Vasus themselves and through Agni as his mouth is satisfied merely with seeing that nectar. He enters that very form and comes forth from that form.

[As per the opinion of the ṚṣI, only the Vasu established among the devotees can only know the essence of nectar flown by the Vasus. In the successive parts a discussion has been made about the Rudras. As per Upaniṣad, the parts of gods as establish in degenetic are also within the man. Hence, they establish their contact with the homologous flows. As the various apparatus fixed on the space crafts at the far distance in the sky are either activated or made inert by issuing special frequency signals suited to them, the special circuits within a man becomes active or dormant by the divine flows coming from the space.]

स यावदादित्यः पुरस्तादुदेता पश्चादस्तमेता वसूनामेव तावदाधिपत्यꣳस्वाराज्यं पर्येता॥४॥

Till the Sun arises from the east and sets in the west, so long will he compass the overlordship and the chief sovereignty (*svārājya*) of the Vasus.

[From the 6th to the 10th part of this Upaniṣad various directions have been described in the process of sun-rising and its setting. A majority of scholars have endeavour to explain them by assuming as the direction of the sun for these directions but such endeavour do not satisfy the discretion. These directions indeed are not the directions of the earth. As it has been clearly mentioned in the precedent part that the establishment of the special divine flows has been made in the particular parts (the east etc.) of the Sun. What has been discussed herein pertains to the special nectar flows from those parts of the Sun. It should be purported to the rising of the Sun in the east that till the east part of the Sun is visible and the west part is invisible (because of setting), the impact of Vasus and the nectar flow coherent to them remains on the atmosphere as also on the devotee. In the successive parts, the rising and setting of the other south, west etc. parts of the sun should be taken with the same proportion.]

Part - 7

अथ यद्द्वितीयममृतं तद्रुद्रा उपजीवन्तीन्द्रेण मुखेन न वै देवा अश्नन्ति न पिबन्त्येतदेवामृतं दृष्ट्वा तृप्यन्ति॥१॥

Now, the Rudras live upon what is the second nectar [i.e. the Yajurveda] through Indra as their mouth. Verily, the gods neither eat nor drink. They are satisfied merely with seeing that nectar.

त एतदेव रूपमभिसंविशन्त्येतस्माद्रूपादुद्यन्ति॥२॥

By seeing this (nectar) they mediate (inert) and encourage also.

स य एतदेवममृतं वेद वसूनामेवैको भूत्वाग्निनैव मुखेनैतदेवामृतं दृष्ट्वा तृप्यति स य एतदेव रूपमभिसंविशत्येतस्माद्रूपादुदेति॥३॥

He who knows thus that nectar becomes one of the Rudras themselves and through Indra as his mouth is satisfied merely with seeing that nectar. He enters that very form and comes forth from that form.

स यावदादित्यः पुरस्तादुदेता पश्चादस्तमेता द्विस्तावद्दक्षिणत उदेतोत्तरतोऽस्तमेता रुद्राणामेव तावदाधिपत्यꣳस्वाराज्यं पर्येता॥४॥

As long as the sun shall rise in the east and set in the west, twice so long will it rise in the south and set in the north, and just that long will he compass the overlordship and the chief sovereignty of the Rudras.

Part - 8

अथ यत्तृतीयममृतं तदादित्या उपजीवन्ति वरुणेन मुखेन न वै देवा अश्नन्ति न पिबन्त्येतदेवामृतं दृष्ट्वा तृप्यन्ति॥१॥

That which is the third nectar, upon that the Ādityas live [i.e. the Sāmaveda] through Varuṇa as their mouth. Verily, the gods neither eat nor drink. They are satisfied merely with seeing that nectar.

त एतदेव रूपमभिसंविशन्त्येतस्माद्रूपादुद्यन्ति॥२॥

They feel comfort in this form and get encouragement too.

स य एतदेवममृतं वेदादित्यानामेवैको भूत्वा वरुणेनैव मुखेनैतदेवामृतं दृष्ट्वा तृप्यति स य एतदेव रूपमभिसंविशत्येतस्माद्रूपादुदेति॥३॥

He who knows thus that nectar becomes one of the Ādityas themselves and through Varuṇa as his mouth is satisfied merely with seeing that nectar. He enters that very form and comes forth from that form.

स यावदादित्यः दक्षिणत उदेतोत्तरतोऽस्तमेता द्विस्तावत्पश्चादुदेता पुरस्तादस्तमेताऽऽदित्यानामेव तावदाधिपत्यꣳस्वाराज्यं पर्येता॥४॥

So long as the sun shall rise in the south and set in the north, twice so long will it rise in the west and set in the east, and just that long will he compass the overlordship and the chief sovereignty of the Ādityas.

Part - 9

अथ यच्चतुर्थममृतं तन्मरुत उपजीवन्ति सोमेन मुखेन न वै देवा अश्नन्ति न पिबन्त्येतदेवामृतं दृष्ट्वा तृप्यन्ति॥१॥

Now, the Maruts live upon what is the fourth nectar [i.e. the Athravaveda] through Soma as their mouth. Verily, the gods neither eat nor drink. They are satisfied merely with seeing that nectar.

त एतदेव रूपमभिसंविशन्त्येतस्माद्रूपादुद्यन्ति॥२॥

These enter that [exceedingly dark] form and come forth from that form.

स य एतदेवममृतं वेद मरुतामेवैको भूत्वा सोमेनैव मुखेनैतदेवामृतं दृष्ट्वा तृप्यति स य एतदेव रूपमभिसंविशत्येतस्माद्रूपादुदेति॥३॥

He who knows thus that nectar becomes one of the Maruts themselves and through Soma as his mouth is satisfied merely with seeing that nectar. He enters that very form and comes forth from that form.

स यावदादित्यः पुरस्तादुदेता पुरस्तादस्तमेता द्विस्तावदुत्तरत उदेता दक्षिणतोऽस्तमेता मरुतामेव तावदाधिपत्यꣳस्वाराज्यं पर्येता॥४॥

As long as the sun shall rise in the west and set in the cast, twice so long will it rise in the north and set in the south, and just that long will he compass the overlordship and the chief sovereignty of the Maruts.

Part - 10

अथ यत्पञ्चमममृतं तत्साध्या उपजीवन्ति ब्रह्मणा मुखेन न वै देवा अश्नन्ति न पिबन्त्येतदेवामृतं दृष्ट्वा तृप्यन्ति।।१।।

The fifth nectar circulating and vibrating at the middle of the sun becomes the cause of birth for the 'Sādhya' gods under the lead of Brahmā. These gods satiates only by seeing this nectar because they neither eat it nor drink it.

त एतदेव रूपमभिसंविशन्त्येतस्माद्रूपादुद्यन्ति।।२।।

These enter that form [which seems to tremble in the middle of the sun] and come forth from that form.

स य एतदेवममृतं वेद साध्यानामेवैको भूत्वा ब्रह्मणैव मुखेनैतदेवामृतं दृष्ट्वा तृप्यति स एतदेव रूपमभिसंविशत्येतस्माद्रूपादुदेति।।३।।

He who knows thus that nectar becomes one of the Sādhyas themselves and through Brahma as his mouth is satisfied merely with seeing that nectar. He enters that very form and comes forth from that form.

स यावदादित्यः उत्तरत उदेता दक्षिणतोऽस्तमेता द्विस्तावदूर्ध्वमुदेतार्वागस्तमेता साध्यानामेव तावदाधिपत्यꣳस्वाराज्यं पर्येता।।४।।

As long as the sun shall rise in the north and set in the south, twice so long will it rise in the zenith and set in the nadir, and just that long will he compass the overlordship and the chief sovereignty of the Sādhyas.

Part -11

अथ तत ऊर्ध्व उदेत्य नैवोदेता नास्तमेतैकल एव मध्ये स्थाता तदेष श्लोकः।।१।।

Henceforth, after having risen in the zenith, it will no more rise nor set. It will stand alone in the middle. On this point there is this verse :-

न वै तत्र न निम्लोच नोदियाय कदाचन। देवास्तेनाहꣳ सत्येन मा विराधिषि ब्रह्मणेति।।२।।

In yonder sphere it has not set, Nor even has it risen up; and by the truth of this, ye gods, of Brahma let me not be robbed.

[The sun as described herein is absolutely different than the apparent sun *i.e.* it is self-illuminating and omnipresent element. This has been broadly explained at 8.6.1-2 of this very Upaniṣad.]

न ह वा अस्मा उदेति न निम्लोचति सकृद्दिवा हैवास्मै भवति य एतामेवं ब्रह्मोपनिषदं वेद।।३।।

Verily, it neither rises nor sets for him, it is ever more day for him, who knows thus this mystic doctrine (*upaniṣad*) of Brahma.

तद्धैतद्ब्रह्मा प्रजापतय उवाच प्रजापतिर्मनवे मनुः प्रजाभ्यस्तद्धैतदुद्दालकायारुणये ज्येष्ठाय पुत्राय पिता ब्रह्म प्रोवाच॥४॥

Brahmā expounded this to Prajāpati; Prajāpati, to Manu; Manu, to his descendants. To Uddālaka Āruṇi, as being the eldest son, his father decalred this Brahman.

इदं वाव तज्जेष्ठाय पुत्राय पिता ब्रह्म प्रब्रूयात्प्रणाय्याय वान्तेवासिने॥५॥

नान्यस्मै कस्मैचन यद्यप्यस्मा इमामद्भिः परिगृहीतां धनस्य पूर्णां दद्यादेतदेव ततो भूय इत्येतदेव ततो भूय इति॥६॥

Verily, a father may teach this Brahma to his eldest son or to a worthy pupil,

[but] to no one else at all. Even if one should offer him this [earth] that is encompassed by water and filled with treasure, [he should say] : 'This, truly, is more than that! This, truly, is more than that!'

Part - 12

The Gāyatrī meter as a symbol of all

गायत्री वा इदꣳ सर्वं भूतं यदिदं किंच वाग्वै गायत्री वाग्वा इदꣳ सर्वं भूतं गायति च त्रायते च॥१॥

Verily, the Gāyatrī meter is everything here that has come to be, whatsoever there is here. Verily, the Gāyatrī is speech. Verily, speech both sings of (*gāyati*) and protects (*trāyate*) everything here that has come to be.

या वै सा गायत्रीयं वाव सा येयं पृथिव्यस्याꣳ हीदꣳ सर्वं भूतं प्रतिष्ठितमेतामेव नातिशीयते॥२॥

Verily, what this Gāyatrī is—that is the same as what this earth is; for on it everything here that has come to be is established. It does not extend beyond it.

या वै सा पृथिवीयं वाव सा यदिदमस्मिन्पुरुषे शरीरमस्मिन्हीमे प्राणाः प्रतिष्ठिता एतदेव नातिशीयन्ते॥३॥

Verily, what this earth is—that is the same as what the body in man here is; for in it these vital breaths are established. They do not extend beyond it.

तद्वै तत्पुरुषे शरीरमिदं वाव तद्यदिदमस्मिन्नतः पुरुषे हृदयमस्मिन्हीमे प्राणाः प्रतिष्ठिता एतदेव नातिशीयन्ते॥४॥

Verily, what the body in man is—that is the same as what the heart within man here is; for on it these vital breaths are established. They do not extend beyond it.

सैषा चतुष्पदा षड्विधा गायत्री तदेतदृचाभ्यनूक्तम्॥५॥

This Gāyatrī is the four-footed and sixfold. With reference to it a Ṛg verse states :

[A majority of scholars have attempted to match the meaning of this hymn with the great hymn of Gāyatrī.]

[It is worth taking into notice that in this hymn , Gāyatrī form is not confined only in a hymn but in the number of hymns. Hence, instead of matching it with the Gāyatrī hymn, it should be matched with the Prāṇavidyā of Gāyatrī. The same is revealed in the Vedic hymns. Four Vedas are its 4 feet. This Gāyatrī is enriched of 6 properties of 6 kinds at flowing from 6 directions *i.e.* the east, the west, the south, the north, up and down]

तावानस्य महिमा ततो ज्यायाꣳश्च पूरुषः। पादोऽस्य सर्वा भूतानि त्रिपादस्यामृतं दिवीति॥६॥

His greatness is of such extent, Yet Puruṣa is greater still. All beings are one-fourth of him; Three-fourths the immortal in the sky.

यद्वै तद्ब्रह्मेतीदं वाव तद्योऽयं बहिर्धा पुरुषादाकाशो यो वै स बहिर्धा पुरुषादाकाशः॥७॥

अयं वाव स योऽयमन्तः पुरुष आकाशो यो वै सोऽन्तपुरुष आकाशः॥८॥

अयं वाव स योऽयमन्तर्हृदय आकाशस्तदेतत्पूर्णमप्रवर्ति पूर्णामप्रवर्तिनीꣳ श्रिय लभते य एवं वेद॥९॥

Indeed, which is that Brahman—that is the same as what the space outside of a person is. Verily, what the space outside of a person is that is the same as what the space within a person is. Verily, what the space within a person is that is the same as what the space here within the heart is. That is the Full, the Non-active. Full non-active prosperity he obtains who knows this.

Part - 13

The five doorkeepers of the heavenly world

तस्य ह वा एतस्य हृदयस्य पञ्च देवसुषयः स योऽस्य प्राङ्सुषिः स प्राणस्तच्चक्षुः स आदित्यस्तदेतत्तेजोऽन्नाद्यमित्युपासीत तेजस्व्यन्नादो भवति य एवं वेद॥१॥

Verily, indeed, this heart here has five openings for the gods. As for its eastern opening—that is the Prāṇa breath, that is the eye, that is the sun. One should reverence that as glow and as food. He becomes glowing and an eater of food who knows this.

अथ योऽस्य दक्षिणः सुषिः स व्यानस्तच्छ्रोत्रꣳ स चन्द्रमास्तदेतच्छ्रीश्च यशश्चेत्युपासीत श्रीमान्यशस्वी भवति य एवं वेद॥२॥

Now, as for its southern opening—that is the Vyāna breath, that is the ear, that is the moon. One should reverence that as prosperity and splendour. He becomes prosperous and splendid who knows this.

अथ योऽस्य प्रत्यङ् सुषिः सोऽपानः सा वाक् सोऽग्निस्तदेतद्ब्रह्मवर्चसमन्नाद्यमित्युपासीत ब्रह्मवर्चस्यन्नादो भवति य एवं वेद॥३॥

Now, as for its western opening—that is the Apāna breath, that is speech, that is fire. One should reverence that as eminence in sacred knowledge and as food. He becomes eminent in sacred knowledge and an eater of food who knows this.

अथ योऽस्योदङ् सुषिः स समानस्तन्मनः स पर्जन्यस्तदेतत्कीर्तिश्च व्युष्टिश्चेत्युपासीत कीर्तिमान्व्युष्टिमान्भवति य एवं वेद॥४॥

Now, as for its northern opening—that is the Samāna breath, that is mind, that is the rain-god (Parjanya). One should reverence that as fame and beauty. He becomes famous and beauteous who knows this.

अथ योऽस्योर्ध्वः सुषिः स उदानः स वायुः स आकाशस्तदेतदोजश्च महश्चेत्युपासीतौजस्वी महस्वान्भवति य एवं वेद॥५॥

Now as for its upper opening—that is the Udāna breath, that is wind, that is space. One should reverence that as vigour and greatness. He becomes vigorous and great who knows this.

ते वा एते पञ्च ब्रह्मपुरुषाः स्वर्गस्य लोकस्य द्वारपाः स य एतानेवं पञ्च ब्रह्मपुरुषान्स्वर्गस्य लोकस्य द्वारपान्वेदास्य कुले वीरो जाये प्रतिपद्यते स्वर्गं लोकं य एतानेव पञ्च ब्रह्मपुरुषान्स्वर्गस्य लोकस्य द्वारपान्वेद॥६॥

Verily, these same are five Brahman-men, doorkeepers of the heavenly world. Who knows these thus as five Brahman-men, as doorkeepers of the heavenly world, in his family a hero is born. He reaches the heavenly world who knows these thus as five Brahman-men, doorkeepers of the heavenly world.

The ultimate exists within oneself.

अथ यदतः परो दिवो ज्योतिर्दीप्यते विश्वतः पृष्ठेषु सर्वतः पृष्ठेष्वनुत्तमेषूत्तमेषु लोकेष्विदं वाव तद्यदिदमस्मिन्नन्तः पुरुषो ज्योतिस्तस्यैषा दृष्टिः॥७॥

Now, the light which shines higher than this heaven, on the backs of all, on the backs of everything, in the highest worlds, than which there are no higher—verily, that is the same as this light which is here within a person.

There is this seeing of it—

यत्रैतदस्मिञ्छरीरे सꣳस्पर्शेनोष्णिमानं विजानाति तस्यैषा श्रुतिर्यत्रैतत्कर्णावपिगृह्य निनदमिव नदथुरिवाग्नेरिव ज्वलत उपशृणोति तदेतद्दृष्टं च श्रुतं चेत्युपासीत चक्षुष्यः श्रुतो भवति य एवं वेद य एवं वेद॥८॥

When one perceives by touch this heart here in the body. There is this hearing of it—when one closes his ears and hears as it were a sound, as it were a noise, as of a fire blazing. One should reverence that flight as something that has been seen and heard. He becomes one beautiful to see, one heard of in renown, who knows this—yea, who knows this!

Part - 14

The individual soul identical with the infinite Brahman

सर्वं खल्विदं ब्रह्म तज्जलानिति शान्त उपासीत। अथ खलु क्रतुमयः पुरुषो यथा क्रतुरस्मिँल्लोके पुरुषो भवति तथेतः प्रेत्य भवति स क्रतुं कुर्वीत॥१॥

'Verily, this whole world is Brahma. Tranquil let one worship. It as that from which he came forth, as that into which he will be dissolved, as that in which he breathes.

Now, verily, a person consists of purpose (*kratu-maya*). According to the purpose which a person has in this world, thus does he become on departing hence. So let him form for himself a purpose.

मनोमय प्राणशरीरो भारूपः सत्यसंकल्प आकाशात्मा सर्वकर्मा सर्वकामः सर्वगन्धः सर्वरसः सर्वमिदमभ्यात्तोऽवाक्यनादरः॥२॥

He who consists of mind, whose body is life (*prāṇa*) whose form is light, whose conception is truth, whose soul (*ātman*) is space, containing all works, containing all desires, containing all odours, containing all tastes, encompassing this whole world, the unspeaking, the unconcerned—

एष म आत्मान्तर्हृदयेऽणीयान्व्रीहेर्वा यवाद्वा सर्षपाद्वा श्यामाकाद्वा श्यामाकतण्डुलाद्वा एष म आत्मान्तहृदये ज्यायान्पृथिव्या ज्यायानन्तरिक्षाज्जायान्दिवो ज्यायानेभ्यो लोकेभ्यः॥३॥

This Soul of mine within the heart is smaller than a grain of rice, or a barley-corn, or a mustard-seed, or a grain of millet, or the kernel of a grain of millet; this Soul of mine within the heart is greater than the earth, greater than the atmosphere, greater than the sky, greater than these worlds.

सर्वकर्मा सर्वकामः सर्वगन्धः सर्वरसः सर्वमिदमभ्यात्तोऽवाक्यनादर एष म आत्मान्तर्हृदय एतद् ब्रह्मैतमितः प्रेत्याभिसंभवितास्मीति यस्य स्यादद्धा न विचिकित्सास्तीति ह स्माह शाण्डिल्यः शाण्डिल्यः॥४॥

Containing all works, containing all desires, containing all odours, containing all tastes, encompassing this whole world, the unspeaking, the unconcerned—this is the Soul of mine within the heart, this is Brahma. Into him I shall enter on departing hence.

If one would believe this, he would have no more doubt. Thus used Śāṇḍilya to say—yea, Śāṇḍilya!

Part - 15

The universe as a treasure-chest and refuge

अन्तरिक्षोदरः कोशो भूमिर्बुध्नो न जीर्यति दिशो ह्यस्य स्त्रक्तयो द्यौरस्योत्तरं बिलꣳ स एष कोशो वसुधानस्तस्मिन्विश्वमिदꣳ श्रितम्॥१॥

The chest whose space is atmosphere, With earth for bottom, never decays. Its corners are the poles of heaven. Its upper opening is the sky. This chest is one containing wealth. Within it everything here rests.

तस्य प्राची दिक् जुहूर्नाम सहमाना नाम दक्षिणा राज्ञी नाम प्रतीची सुभूता नामोदीची तासां वायुर्वत्सः स य एतमेवं वायुं दिशां वत्सं वेद न पुत्ररोदꣳरोदिति सोऽहमेतमेवं वायुं दिशां वत्सं वेद मा पुत्ररोदꣳ रुदम्॥२॥

Its eastern quarter is named Sacrificial Ladle (*juhū*). Its southern quarter is named Overpowering. Its western quarter is named Queen (*rājñī*). Its northern quarter is named Wealthy. The wind is the child of these quarters of heaven. He who knows this wind thus as the child of the quarters of heaven mourns not for a son.

'I here know this wind thus as the child of the quarters of heaven. Let me not mourn for a son.'

अरिष्टं कोश प्रपद्येऽमुनाऽमुनाऽमुना प्राणं प्रपद्येऽमुनाऽमुनाऽमुना भूः प्रपद्येऽमुनाऽमुनाऽमुना भुवः प्रपद्येऽमुनाऽमुनाऽमुना स्वः प्रपद्येऽमुनाऽमुनाऽमुना॥३॥

'I take refuge in the imperishable chest with this one, with this one, with this one.'

'I take refuge in breath (*prāṇa*) with this one, with this one, with this one.'

'I take refuge in *bhūr* with this one, with this one, with this one.'

'I take refuge in *bhuvas* with this one, with this one, with this one.'

'I take refuge in *svar* with this one, with this one, with this one.'

स यदवोचं प्राणं प्रपद्य इति प्राणो वा इदꣳ सर्वं भूतं यदिदं किंच तमेव तत्प्रापत्सि॥४॥

When I said, 'I take refuge in breath'—breath, verily, is everything here that has come to be, whatsoever there is. So it was in this I took refuge.

अथ यदवोचं भूवः प्रपद्य इति पृथिवीं प्रपद्येऽन्तरिक्ष प्रपद्ये दिव प्रपद्ये इत्येव तदवोचम्॥५॥

So when I said, 'I take refuge in *bhūr*', what I said was : 'I take refuge in earth; I take refuge in atmosphere; I take refuge in sky.'

अथ यदवोचं भूवः प्रपद्य इत्यग्निं प्रपद्ये वायु प्रपद्ये आदित्य प्रपद्य इत्येव तदवोचम्॥६॥

So when I said, 'I take refuge in *bhuvas*', what I said was : 'I take refuge in Agni (Fire); I take refuge in Vāyu (Wind); I take refuge in Āditya (Sun).'

अथ यदवोचꣳ स्व प्रपद्य इत्यृग्वेदं प्रपद्ये यजुर्वेदं प्रपद्ये सामवेदं प्रपद्य इत्येव तदवोचं तदवोचम्॥७॥

Lastly, when I said, 'I take refuge in *svar*,' what I said was : 'I take refuge in the Ṛgveda; I take refuge in the Yajurveda; I take refuge in the Sāmaveda'. That was what I said.

Part - 16

A person's entire life symbolically a Soma-sacrifice

पुरुषो वाव यज्ञस्तस्य यानि चतुर्विꣳशतिवर्षाणि तत्प्रातःसवनं चतुर्विꣳशत्यक्षरा गायत्री गायत्रं प्रातःसवनं तदस्य वसवोऽन्वायत्ताः प्राणा वाव वसव एते हीदꣳ सर्वं वायसन्ति॥१॥

Verily, a person is a sacrifice. His [first] twenty-four years are the morning Soma-libation, for the Gāyatrī meter has twenty-four syllables and the morning Soma-libation is offered with a Gāyatrī hymn. The Vasus are connected with this part of the sacrifice. Verily, the vital breaths (*prāṇa*) are the Vasus, for they cause everything here to continue (√*vas*).

तं चेदेतस्मिन्वयसि किंचिदुपतपेत्स ब्रूयात्प्राणा वसव इदं मे प्रातः सवनं माध्यन्दिनꣳ सवनमनुसन्तनुतेति माहं प्राणानां वसूनां मध्ये यज्ञो विलोप्सीयेत्युद्धैव तत एत्यगदो ह भवति॥२॥

If any sickness should overtake him in this period of life, let him say : 'Ye vital breaths, ye Vasus, let this morning libation of mine continue over to the mid-day libation. Let not me, the sacrifice, be broken off in the midst of the vital breaths, of the Vasus.' He arises from it; he becomes free from sickness.

अथ यानि चतुश्चत्वारिंशद्वर्षाणि तन्माध्यन्दिनꣳ सवनं चतुश्चत्वारिꣳशदक्षरा त्रिष्टुप् त्रैष्टुभं माध्यन्दिनꣳ सवनं तदस्य रुद्रा अन्वायत्ताः प्राणा वाव रुद्रा एते हीदꣳ सर्वꣳ रोदयन्ति॥३॥

Now the [next] forty-four years are the mid-day libation, for the Triṣṭubh meter has forty-four syllables and the mid-day libation is offered with a Triṣṭubh hymn. The Rudras are connected with this part of the sacrifice. Verily, the vital breaths are the Rudras, for [on departing] they cause everything here to lament (√*rud*).

तं चेदेतस्मिन्वयसि किंचिदुपतपेत्स ब्रूयात्प्राणा रुद्रा इदं मे माध्यन्दिनꣳ सवनं तृतीयसवनमनुसन्तनुतेति माहं प्राणानाꣳ रुद्राणां मध्ये यज्ञो विलोप्सीयेत्युद्धैव तत एत्यगदो ह भवति॥४॥

If any sickness should overtake him in this period of life, let him say : 'Ye vital breaths, ye Rudras, let this mid-day libation of mine continue over to the third libation. Let not me, the sacrifice, be broken off in the midst of the vital breaths, of the Rudras.' He arises from it; he becomes free from sickness.

अथ यान्यष्टाचत्वारिꣳशद्वर्षाणि तृतीयसवनमष्टाचत्वारिꣳशदक्षरा जगती जागतं तृतीयसवनं तदस्यादित्या अन्वायत्ताः प्राणा वावादित्या एते हीदꣳ सर्वमाददते॥५॥

Now, the [next] forty-eight years are the third libation, for the Jagatī meter has forty-eight syllables and the third libation is offered with a Jagatī hymn. The Ādityas are connected with this part of the sacrifice. Verily, the vital breaths are the Ādityas, for [on departing] they take everything to themselves (*ādadate*).

तं चेदेतस्मिन्वयसि किंचिदुपतपेत्स ब्रूयात्प्राणा आदित्य इदं मे तृतीयसवनमायरनुसन्तनुतेति माहं प्राणानामादित्यानां मध्ये यज्ञो विलोप्सीयेत्युद्धैव तत एत्यगदो हैव भवति॥६॥

If any sickness should overtake him in this period of life, let him say : 'Ye vital breaths, ye Ādityas, let this third libation of mine continue to a full length of life. Let not me, the sacrifice, be broken off in the midst of the vital breaths, of the Ādityas'. He arises from it; he becomes free from sickness.

एतद्ध स्म वै तद्विद्वानाह महिदास ऐतरेयः स किं म एतदुपतपसि योऽहमनेन न प्रेष्यामीति स ह षोडशं वर्षशतमजीवत्प्रह षोडशं वर्षशतं जीवति य एवं वेद॥७॥

Verily, it was this that Mahidāsa Aitareya knew when he used to say : 'Here, why do you afflict me with this sickness—me, who am not going to die with it?' He lived a hundred and sixteen years. He lives to a hundred and sixteen years who knows this.

Part - 17

स यदशिशिषति यत्पिपासति यन्न रमते ता अस्य दीक्षा:॥१॥

When one hungers and thirsts and does not enjoy himself—that is a Preparatory Consecration Ceremony (*dīkṣā*).

अथ यदश्नाति यत्पिबति यद्रमते तदुपसदैरेति॥२॥

When one eats and drinks and enjoys himself—then he joins the Upasada ceremonies.

अथ यद्धसति यज्ञक्षति यन्मैथुनं चरति स्तुतशस्त्रैरेव तदेति॥३॥

When one laughs and eats and practises sexual intercourse —then he joins in the chant and Recitation (*stuta-śāstra*).

अथ यत्तपो दानमार्जवमहिꣳसा सत्यवचनमिति ता अस्य दक्षिणा:॥४॥

Austerity, alms-giving, uprightness, harmlessness, truthfulness— these are one's gifts for the priests.

तस्मादाहु: सोष्यत्यसोष्टेति पुनरुत्पादनमेवास्य तन्मरणमेवास्यावभृथ:॥५॥

Therefore they say : 'He will procreate (*sosyati*)! He has procreated (*asoṣṭa*)!'— that is his rebirth (*punar-utpādana*). Death is an ablution after the ceremony.

तद्धैतद्घोर आङ्गिरस: कृष्णाय देवकीपुत्रायोक्त्वोवाचापिपास एव स बभूव सोऽन्तवेलायामेतत्त्रयं प्रतिपद्येताक्षितमस्यच्युतमसि प्राणसꣳशितमसीति तत्रैते द्वे ऋचौ भवत:॥६॥

When Ghora Āṅgirasa explained this to Kṛṣṇa, the son of Devakī, he also explained—that he had become free from desire—'In the final hour one should take refuge in these three thoughts : "You are the Indestructible; you are the Unshaken; you are the very essence of life (*prāṇa*)." On this point there are these two Ṛg verses :—

आदित्प्रत्नस्य रेतस:। उद्वयन्तमसस्परि ज्योति: पश्यन्त: उत्तरꣳस्व: पश्यन्त उत्तरं देवं देवत्रा सूर्यमगन्म ज्योतिरुत्तममिति ज्योतिरुत्तममिति॥७॥

Proceeding from primeaval seed, [The early morning light they see, That gleameth higher than the heaven], From out of darkens all around, We, gazing on the higher light—Yea, gazing on the higher light—To Sūrya, god among the gods, We have attained—the highest light! —Yea, the highest light!

Part - 18

The fourfold Brahman in the individual and in the world

मनो ब्रह्मेत्युपासीतेत्यध्यात्ममथाधिदैवतमाकाशो ब्रह्मेत्युभयमादिष्टं भवत्यध्यात्मं चाधिदैवतं च॥१॥

One should reverence the mind as Brahman.— Thus with reference to the self.

Now with reference to the divinities. One should reverence space as Brahman.

This is the twofold instruction with reference to the self and with reference to the divinities.

तदेतच्चतुष्पाद्ब्रह्म। वाक् पादः प्राणः पादश्चक्षुः पादः श्रोत्रं पाद इत्यध्यात्ममथाधिदैवतमग्निः पादो वायुः पाद आदित्यः पादो दिशः पाद इत्युभयमेवादिष्टं भवत्यध्यात्मं चैवाधिदैवतं च।।२।।

That Brahma has four quarters. One quarter is speech, One quarter is breath. One quarter is the eye. One quarter is the ear. Thus with reference to the self.

Now with reference to the divinities. One quarter is Agni (Fire). One quarter is Vāyu (Wind). One quarter is Āditya (the Sun). One quarter is the quarters of heaven.

This is the twofold instruction with reference to the self and with reference to the divinities.

वागेव ब्रह्मणश्चतुर्थः पादः। सोऽग्निना ज्योतिषा भाति च तपति च भाति च तपति च कीर्त्या यशसा ब्रह्मवर्चसेन य एवं वेद।।३।।

Speech, truly, is a fourth part of Brahma. It shines and glows with Agni as its light. He shines and glows with fame, with splendour and with eminence in sacred knowledge who knows this.

प्राण एव ब्रह्मणश्चतुर्थः पादः। स वायुना ज्योतिषा भाति च तपति च भाति च तपति च कीर्त्या यशसा ब्रह्मवर्चसेन य एवं वेद।।४।।

Breath, truly, is a fourth part of Brahma. It shines and glows with Vāyu a sits light. He shines and glows with fame, with splendour and with eminence in sacred knowledge who knows this.

चक्षुरेव ब्रह्मणश्चतुर्थः पादः। स आदित्येन ज्योतिषा भाति च तपति च भाति च तपति च कीर्त्या यशसा ब्रह्मवर्चसेन य एवं वेद।।५।।

The eye, truly, is a fourth part of Brahma. It shines and glows with Āditya as its light. He shines and glows with fame, with splendour and with eminence in sacred knowledge who knows this.

श्रोत्रमेव ब्रह्मणश्चतुर्थः पादः। स दिग्भिज्योतिषा भाति च तपति च भाति च तपति च कीर्त्या यशसा ब्रह्मवर्चसेन य एवं वेद य एवं वेद।।६।।

The ear, truly, is a fourth part of Brahma. It shines and glows with the quarters of heaven as its light. He shines and glows with fame, with splendour and with eminence in sacred knowledge who knows this—yea, who knows this!

Part - 19

The cosmic egg

आदित्यो ब्रह्मेत्यादेशस्तस्योपव्याख्यानमसदेवेदमग्र आसीत्तत्सदासीत्तत्समभवत्तदाण्डं निरवर्तत तत्संवत्सरस्य मात्रामशयत तन्निरभिद्यत ते आण्डकपाले रजतं च सुवर्णं चाभवताम्।।१।।

A description is found that the Sun is Brahman. A number of explanations are given on it. In the beginning this world was merely non-being. It was existent. It developed. It turned into an egg. It lay for the period of a year. It was split asunder. One of the two eggshell-parts became silver, one gold.

तद्यद्रजतꣳ सेयं पृथिवी यत्सुवर्णꣳ सा द्यौर्यज्जरायु ते पर्वता यदुल्बꣳ समेघो नीहारो या धमनयस्ता नद्यो यद्वास्तेयमुदकꣳ स समुद्रः॥२॥

That which was of silver is this earth. That which was of gold is the sky. What was the outer membrane is the mountains. What was the inner membrane is cloud and mist. What were the veins are the rivers. What was the fluid within is the ocean.

अथ यत्तदजायत सोऽसावादित्यस्तं जायमानं घोषा उलूलवोऽनूदतिष्ठन् सर्वाणि च भूतानि च सर्वे च कामास्तस्मात्तस्योदयं प्रति प्रत्यायनं प्रति घोषा उलूलवोऽनूत्तिष्ठन्ति सर्वाणि च भूतानि सर्वे चैव कामाः॥३॥

Now, what was born therefrom is yonder sun. When it was born, shouts and hurrahs, all beings and all desires rose up toward it. Therefore at its rising and at its every return shouts and hurrahs, all beings and all desires rise up toward it.

स य एतमेवं विद्वानादित्यं ब्रह्मेत्युपास्तेऽभ्याशो ह यदेनꣳ साधवो घोषा आ च गच्छेयुरुप च निम्रेडेरन्निम्रेडेरन्॥४॥

He who, knowing it thus, reverences the sun as Brahma—the prospect is that pleasant shouts will come unto him and delight him—yea, delight him!

Fourth Chapter

Part - 1

Conversational instructions; The story of Jānaśruti and Raikva : wind and breath as snatchers-unto themselves.

जानश्रुतिर्ह पौत्रायणः श्रद्धादेयो बहुदायी बहुपाक्य आस स ह सर्वत आवसथान्मापयांचक्रे सर्वत एव मेऽत्स्यन्तीति॥१॥

Oṁ! Now there was Jānaśruti, the great-grandson [of Janaśruta], a pious dispenser, a liberal giver, a preparer of much food. He had rest-houses built everywhere with the thought, 'Everywhere people will be eating of my food.'

अथ ह हꣳसा निशायामतिपेतुस्तद्धैवꣳ हꣳसो हꣳसमभ्युवाद हो होऽयि भल्लाक्ष भल्लाक्ष जानश्रुतेः पौत्रायणस्य समं दिवा ज्योतिराततं तन्मा प्रसाङ्क्षीस्तत्त्वा मा प्रधाक्षीरिति॥२॥

Now then, one time swans flew past in the night, and one swan spoke to another thus: 'Hey! Ho! Short-sight! Short-sight! The light of Jānaśruti, the great-grandson [of Janaśruta], has spread like the sky. Do not touch it, lest it burn you up!'

तमु ह परः प्रत्युवाच कम्बर एनमेतत्सन्तꣳ सयुग्वानमिव रैक्वमात्थेति यो नु कथꣳ सयुग्वा रैक्व इति॥३॥

To it the other one then replied : 'Come! Who is that man of whom you speak as if he were Raikva, the man with the cart?' 'Pray, how is it with Raikva, the man with the cart?'

यथा कृतायविजितायाधरेयाः संयन्त्येवमेनः सर्वं तदभिसमेति यत्किंच प्रजाः साधु कुर्वन्ति यस्तद्वेद यत्स वेद स मयैतदुक्त इति॥४॥

'As the lower throws of dice all go to the highest throw to the winner, so whatever good thing creatures do, all goes to him. I say the same thing of whoever knows what he knows.'

तदु ह जानश्रुतिः पौत्रायण उपशुश्राव स ह संजिहान एव क्षत्तारमुवाचाङ्गारे ह सयुग्वानमिव रैक्वमात्थेति यो नु कथः सयुग्वा रैक्व इति॥५॥

Now Jānaśruti, the great-grandson [of Janaśruta], overheard this. Then when he rose he said to the attendant : 'Lo! You speak [of me] as if I were Raikva, the man with the cart!' 'Pray, how is it with Raikva, the man with the cart?'

यथा कृतायविजितायाधरेयाः संयन्त्येवमेनः सर्वं तदभिसमेति यत्किंच प्रजाः साधु कुर्वन्ति यस्तद्वेद यत्स वेद स मयैतदुक्त इति॥६॥

'As the lower throws of dice all go to the highest throw, to the winner, so to this man, whatever good thing creatures do, all goes to him. I say the same thing of whoever knows what he knows.'

स ह क्षत्तान्विष्य नाविदमिति प्रत्येयाय तः होवाच यत्रारे ब्राह्मणस्यान्वेषणा तदेनमर्च्छेति॥७॥

Then the attendant, having sought, came back, saying, 'I did not find him.'

Then he said to him : 'Oh! Where one searches for a Brāhmaṇa, there seek for him.'

सोऽधस्ताच्छकटस्य पामानं कषमाणमुपोपविवेश तः हाभ्युवाद त्वं नु भगवः सयुग्वा रैक्व इत्यहः ह्यरा ३ इति प्रतिजज्ञे स ह क्षत्ताऽविदमिति प्रत्येयाय॥८॥

He approached a man who was scratching the itch underneath a cart and said to him : 'Pray, sir, are you Raikva, the man with the cart?' 'Oh! I am , indeed,' he acknowledged.

Then the attendant went back, and said : 'I have found him.'

Part -2

तदुह जानश्रुतिः पौत्रायणः षट् शतानि गवां निष्कमश्वतरीरथं तदादाय प्रतिचक्रमे तः हाभ्युवाद॥१॥

Then Jānaśruti, the great-grandson [of Janaśruta], took six hundred cows and a gold necklace and a chariot drawn by a she-mule, and went back to him. He said to him :

रैक्वेमानि षट् शतानि गवामयं निष्कोऽयमश्वतरीरथो नु म एतां भगवो देवताः शाधि यां देवतामुपास्स इति॥२॥

'Raikva, here are six hundred cows and here is a gold necklace, and here is a chariot drawn by a she-mule. Now, sir, teach me that divinity—the divinity which you reverence.'

तमु ह परः प्रत्युवाचाह हारेत्वा शूद्र तवैव सह गोभिरस्त्विति तदुह पुनरेव जानश्रुतिः पौत्रायणः सहस्रं गवां निष्कमश्वतरीरथं दुहितरं तदादाय प्रतिचक्रमे॥३॥

And to him then the other replied : 'Oh! Necklace and carriage along with the cows be yours, O Śūdra!'

And then again Jānaśruti, the great-grandson [of Janaśruta'], taking a thousand cows and a gold necklace and a chariot drawn by a she-mule, and his daughter too, went unto him.

तꣳ हाभ्युवाद रैक्वेदꣳ सहस्रं गवामयं निष्कोऽयमश्वतरीरथ इयं जायाऽयं ग्रामो यस्मिन्नास्सेऽन्वेव मा भगवः शाधीति॥४॥

Then he spoke unto him : 'Raikva, here are a thousand cows and here is a gold necklace, and here is a chariot drawn by a she-mule, and here is a wife, and here is the village in which you dwell. Pray, sir, do you teach me.'

तस्या ह मुखमुपोद्गृह्णन्नुवाचाजहारेमाः शूद्रानेनैव मुखेनालापयिष्यथा इति ते हैते रैक्वपर्णा नाम महावृषेषु यत्रास्मा उवास तस्मै होवाच॥५॥

Then, lifting up her face towards himself, he [i.e. Raikva] said : 'He has brought these [cows] along!– Śūdra, merely with this face you would cause me to speak.'

So those are called the Raikvaparṇa [villages], among the people of the Mahāvṛṣas, where at his offer he lived.

Then he said to him :-

Part - 3

वायुर्वाव संवर्गो यदा वा अग्निरुद्वायति वायुमेवाप्येति यदा सूर्योऽस्तमेति वायुमेवाप्येति यदा चन्द्रोऽस्तमेति वायुमेवाप्येति॥१॥

'The Wind (Vāyu), verily, is a snatcher-unto itself. Verily, when a fire blows out, it just goes to the Wind. When the sun sets, it just goes to the Wind. When the moon sets, it just goes to the Wind.

यदाप उच्छुष्यन्ति वायुमेवापियन्ति वायुर्ह्येवैतान्सर्वान्संवृङ्क्त इत्यधिदैवतम्॥२॥

When water dries, goes up, it just goes to the Wind. For the Wind, truly, snatches all here to itself. Thus with reference to the divinities.

अथाध्यात्मं प्राणो वाव संवर्गः स यदा स्वपिति प्राणमेव वागप्येति प्राणं चक्षुः प्राणꣳश्रोत्रं प्राणं मनः प्राणो ह्येवैतान्सर्वान्संवृङ्क्त इति॥३॥

Now with reference to oneself. Breath (*prāṇa*), verily, is a snatcher-unto itself. When one sleeps, speech just goes to breath; the eye, to breath; the ear, to breath; the mind, to breath; for the breath, truly, snatches all here to itself.

तौ वा एतौ द्वौ संवर्गौ वायुरेव देवेषु प्राणः प्राणेषु॥४॥

Verily, these are two snatchers-unto themselves : the Wind among the gods, breath among the vital breaths.

अथ ह शौनकं च कापेयमभिप्रतारिणं च काक्षसेनिं परिविष्यमाणौ ब्रह्मचारी बिभिक्षे तस्मा उ ह न ददतुः॥५॥

Now, once upon a time when Śaunaka Kāpeya and Abhipratāriṇ Kākṣaseni were being served with food, a student of sacred knowledge begged of them. They did not give to him.

स होवाच महात्मनश्चतुरो देव एकः कः स जगार भुवनस्य गोपास्तं कापेय नाभिपश्यन्ति मर्त्या अभिप्रतारिन्बहुधा वसन्तं यस्मै वा एतदन्नं दत्तमिति॥६॥

Then he said : "One God (*deva*) has swallowed up four mighty beings (*mahātman*). Who is that world's protector, O Kāpeya? Him mortal men perceive not, though abiding. In manifolded forms, Abhipratāriṇ. Verily, this food has not been offered to whom it belongs."

तदु ह शौनकः कापेयः प्रतिमन्वानः प्रत्येयायात्मा देवानां जनिता प्रजानाꣳहिरण्यदꣳष्ट्रो बभसोऽनसूरिर्महान्तमस्य महिमानमाहुरनद्यमानो यदनन्नमत्तीति वै वयं ब्रह्मचारिन्नेदमुपास्महे दत्तास्मै भिक्षामिति॥७॥

Then Śaunaka Kāpeya, considering this, replied- "The Self (*ātman*) of gods, of creatures, Procreator, with golden teeth Devourer, truly Wise One—His mightiness they say is truly mighty; He eats what is not food and is not eaten. Thus, verily, O student of sacred knowledge, do we reverence it. Give ye him alms."

तस्मा उ ह ददुस्ते वा एते पञ्चान्ये पञ्चान्ये दश संतस्तत्कृतं तस्मात्सर्वासु दिक्ष्वन्नमेव दशकृतꣳ सैषा विराडन्नादी तयेदꣳ सर्वं दृष्टꣳ सर्वमस्येदं दृष्टं भवत्यन्नादो भवति य एवं वेद य एवं वेद॥८॥

Then they gave to him.

These five and the other five make ten and that is the highest throw in dice. Therefore in all regions ten, the highest throw, is food. That is Virāj and an eater of food. Through it this whole world came to light. The whole world comes to light for him, he becomes an eater of food, who knows this —yea, who knows this.'

Part - 4

Satyakāma instructed concerning four quarters of Brahma

सत्यकामो ह जाबालो जबालां मातरमामन्त्रयांचक्रे ब्रह्मचर्यं भवति विवत्स्यामि किं गोत्रोन्वहमस्मीति॥१॥

Once upon a time Satyakāma Jābāla addressed his mother Jabālā : 'O Mother! I desire to live the life of a student of sacred knowledge. Of what family, pray, am I?'

सा हैनमुवाच नाहमेतद्वेद तात यद्गोत्रस्त्वमसि बह्वहं चरन्ती परिचारिणी यौवने त्वामलभे साहमेतन्न वेद यद्गोत्रस्त्वमसि जबाला तु नामाहमस्मि सत्यकामो नाम त्वमसि स सत्यकाम एव जाबालो ब्रुवीथा इति॥२॥

Then she said to him : 'I do not know this, my dear—of what family you are. In my youth, when I went about a great deal serving as a maid, I got you. So I do not know of what family you are. However, I am Jabālā by name; you are Satyakāma by name. So you may speak of yourself as Satyakāma Jābāla.'

स ह हारिद्रुमतं गौतममेत्योवाच ब्रह्मचर्यं भगवति वत्स्याम्युपेयां भगवन्तमिति॥३॥

Then he went to Hāridrumata Gautama and said : 'I will live the life of a student of sacred knowledge. I will become a pupil of yours, sir.'

तꣳ होवाच किंगोत्रो नु सोम्यासीति स होवाच नाहमेतद्वेद भो यद्गोत्रोऽहमस्म्यपृच्छं मातरꣳ सा मा प्रत्यब्रवीद्बह्वहं चरन्ती परिचारिणी यौवने त्वामलभे साहमेतन्न वेद यद्गोत्रस्त्वमसि जबाला तु नामाहमस्मि सत्यकामो नाम त्वमसीति सोऽहꣳ सत्यकामो जाबालोऽस्मि भो इति।।४।।

To him he then said : 'Of what family, pray, are you, my dear?'

Then he said : 'I do not know this, sir, of what family I am. I asked my mother. She answered me : "In my youth, when I went about a great deal serving as a maid, I got you. So I do not know this, of what family you are. However, I am Jabālā by name; you are Satyakāma by name." So I am Satyakāma Jābāla, sir.'

तꣳ होवाच नैतदब्राह्मणो विवक्तुमर्हति समिधꣳ सोम्याहरोप त्वा नेष्ये न सत्यादगा इति तमुपनीय कृशानामबलानां चतुःशता गा निराकृत्योवाचेमाः सोम्यानुसंव्रजेति ता अभिप्रस्थापयन्नुवाच नासहस्रेणावर्तयेति स ह वर्षगणं प्रोवास ता यदा सहस्रꣳ संपेदुः।।५।।

The Gautama said– A non-Brāhmaṇa (*a-Brāhmaṇa*) would not be able to explain thus. Bring the fuel, my dear. I will receive you as a pupil. You have not deviated from the truth.'

After having received him as a pupil, he separated out four hundred lean, weak cows and said : 'Follow these, my dear.'

As he was driving them on, he said : 'I may not return without a thousand.' So he lived away a number of years. When they came to be a thousand,

Part - 5

अथ हैनमृषभोऽभ्युवाद सत्यकाम ३ इति भगव इति ह प्रतिशुश्राव प्राप्ताः सोम्य सहस्रꣳ स्मः प्रापय न आचार्यकुलम्।।१।।

The bull spoke to him, saying : 'Satyakāma!' 'Sir!' he replied.

'We have reached a thousand, my dear. Bring us to the teacher's house.

ब्रह्मणश्च ते पादं ब्रवाणीति ब्रवीतु मे भगवानिस्ति तस्मै होवाच प्राची दिक्कला प्रतीची दिक्कला दक्षिणा दिक्कलोदीची दिक्कलैष वै सोम्य चतुष्कलः पादो ब्रह्मणः प्रकाशवान्नाम।।२।।

And let me tell you a quarter of Brahma.' 'Tell me, sir.' To him it then said : 'One sixteenth is the east. One sixteenth is the west. One sixteenth is the south. One sixteenth is the north. This, verily, my dear, is the quarter of Brahma, consisting of four sixteenths, named the Shining.

स य एतमेवं विद्वाꣳश्चतुष्कलं पादं ब्रह्मणः प्रकाशवानित्युपास्ते प्रकाशवानस्मिँल्लोके भवति प्रकाशवत ह लोकाञ्जयति य एतमेवं विद्वाꣳश्चतुष्कलं पादं ब्रह्मणः प्रकाशवानित्युपास्ते।।३।।

He who, knowing it thus, reverences a quarter of Brahma, consisting of four sixteenths, as the Shining, becomes shining in this world. Then he wins shining worlds who, knowing it thus, reverences a quarter of Brahma, consisting of four sixteenths, as the Shining.

Part - 6

अग्निष्टे पादं वक्तेति स ह श्वोभूते गा अभिप्रस्थापयांचकार ता यत्राभिसायं बभूवुस्तत्राग्निमुपसमाधाय गा उपरुध्य समिधमाधाय पश्चादग्नेः प्राङुपोपविवेश॥१॥

Fire will tell you a quarter.' He then, when it was the marrow, drove the cows on. Where they came at evening, there he built a fire, penned in the cows, laid on fuel, and sat down to the west of the fire, facing the east.

तमग्निरभ्युवाद सत्यकाम ३ इति भगव इति ह प्रतिशुश्राव॥२॥

The fire god addressed Satyakāma, he replied - "Yes Lord!"

ब्रह्मणः सोम्य ते पादं ब्रवाणीति ब्रवीतु मे भगवानिति तस्मै होवाच पृथिवी कलान्तरिक्षं कला द्यौः कला समुद्रः कलैष वै सोम्य चतुष्कलः पादो ब्रह्मणोऽनन्तवान्नाम॥३॥

The fire god said to him– "O gentle young chap! Should I tell you the 2nd foot of Brahman?" He replied– "O Lord! Tell me immediately." Then the fire god said– 'One sixteenth is the earth. One sixteenth is the atmosphere. One sixteenth is the sky. One sixteenth is the ocean. This, verily, my dear, is the quarter of Brahma, consisting of four sixteenths, named the Endless.

स य एतमेवं विद्वाꣳश्चतुष्कलं पादं ब्रह्मणोऽनन्तवानित्युपास्तेऽनन्तवानस्मिँल्लोके भवत्यनन्ततो ह लोकाञ्जयति य एतमेवं विद्वाꣳश्चतुष्कलं पादं ब्रह्मणोऽनन्तवानित्युपास्ते॥४॥

He who, knowing it thus, reverences a quarter of Brahma, consisting of four sixteenths, as the Endless, becomes endless in this world. Then he wins endless worlds who, knowing it thus, reverences a quarter of Brahma, consisting of four sixteenths, as the Endless.

Part - 7

हꣳसस्ते पादं वक्तेति स ह श्वोभूते गा अभिप्रस्थापयांचकार ता यत्राभिसायं बभूवुस्तत्राग्निमुपसमाधाय गा उपरुध्य समिधमाधाय पश्चादग्नेः प्राङुपोपविवेश॥१॥

A swan will tell you a quarter.' He then, when it was the marrow, drove the cows on. Where they came at evening, there he built a fire, penned in the cows, laid on the fuel, and sat down to the west of the fire, facing the east.

तꣳ हꣳस उप निपत्याभ्युवाद सत्यकाम ३ इति भगव इति ह प्रतिशुश्राव॥२॥

A swan flew down to him, and spoke to him, saying : 'Satyakāma!' 'Sir!' he replied.

ब्रह्मणः सोम्य ते पादं ब्रवाणीति ब्रवीतु मे भगवानिति तस्मै होवाचाग्निः कला सूर्यः कला चन्द्रः कला विद्युत्कलैष वै सोम्य चतुष्कलः पादो ब्रह्मणो ज्योतिष्मान्नाम॥३॥

'Let me tell you, my dear, a quarter of Brahma'. 'Tell me, sir.' To him it then said : 'One sixteenth is fire. One sixteenth is the sun. One sixteenth is the moon. One sixteenth is lightning. This, verily, my dear, is the quarter of Brahma, consisting of four sixteenths, named the Luminous.

स य एतमेवं विद्वाꣳश्चतुष्कलं पादं ब्रह्मणो ज्योतिष्मानित्युपास्ते ज्योतिष्मानस्मिँल्लोके भवति ज्योतिष्मतो ह लोकाञ्जयति य एतमेवं विद्वाꣳश्चतुष्कलं पादं ब्रह्मणो ज्योतिष्मानित्युपास्ते॥४॥

He who, knowing it thus, reverences a quarter of Brahma, consisting of four sixteenths, as the Luminous, becomes luminous in this world. Then he wins luminous worlds who, knowing it thus, reverences a quarter of Brahma, consisting of four sixteenths, as the Luminous.

Part - 8

मद्गुष्टे पादं वक्तेति स ह श्वोभूते गा अभिप्रस्थापयांचकार ता यत्राभि सायं बभूवुस्तत्राग्निमुपसमाधाय गा उपरुध्य समिधमाधाय पश्चादग्नेः प्राङुपोपविवेश॥१॥

A diver-bird will tell you a quarter.' He then, when it was the morrow, drove the cows on. Where they came at evening, there he built a fire, penned in the cows, laid on fuel, and sat down to the west of the fire, facing the east.

तं मद्गुरुपनिपत्याभ्युवाद सत्यकाम ३ इति भगव इति ह प्रतिशुश्राव॥२॥

A diver-bird flew down to him, and spoke to him, saying : 'Satyakāma! He replied - "Yes Lord!"

ब्रह्मणः सोम्य ते पादं ब्रवाणीति ब्रवीतु मे भगवानिति तस्मै होवाच प्राणः कला चक्षुः कला श्रोत्रं कला मनः कलैष वै सोम्य चतुष्कलः पादो ब्रह्मण आयतनवान्नाम॥३॥

Madgu then said to him– "O dear! I will tell you the 4th foot of Brahman?" Satyakāma replied– "O Lord! Tell me immediately." Then he said to him : 'One sixteenth is breath. One sixteenth is the eye. One sixteenth is the ear. One sixteenth is mind. This, verily, my dear, is the quarter of Brahma, consisting of four sixteenths, named Possessing-a-support.

स य एतमेवं विद्वाꣳश्चतुष्कलं पादं ब्रह्मण आयतनवानित्युपास्त आयतनवानस्मिँल्लोके भवत्यायतनवतो ह लोकाञ्जयति य एतमेवं विद्वाꣳश्चतुष्कलं पादं ब्रह्मण आयतनवानित्युपास्ते॥४॥

He who, knowing it thus, reverences a quarter of Brahma, consisting of four sixteenths, as Possessing-a-support, comes to possess a support in this world. Then he wins worlds possessing a support who, knowing it thus, reverence a quarter of Brahma, consisting of four sixteenths, as Possessing-a-support.'

Part - 9

प्राप हाचार्यकुलं तमाचार्योऽभ्युवाद सत्यकाम ३ इति भगव इति ह प्रतिशुश्राव॥१॥

Then he reached the teacher's house. The teacher spoke to him, saying : 'Satyakāma!' 'Sir!' he replied.

ब्रह्मविदिव वै सोम्य भासि को नु त्वानुशशासेत्यन्ये मनुष्येभ्य इति ह प्रतिजज्ञे भगवाꣳस्त्वेव मे कामे ब्रूयात्॥२॥

श्रुतꣳ ह्येव मे भगवद्दृशेभ्य आचार्याद्धैव विद्या विदिता साधिष्ठं प्रापतीति तस्मै हैतदेवोवाचात्र ह न किंचन वीयायेति वीयायेति॥३॥

'Verily, my dear, you shine like a Brahma-knower. Who, pray, has instructed you?'

'Others than men,' he acknowledge. 'But do you yourself please speak to me; for I have heard from those who are like you, sir, that the knowledge which has been learned from a teacher best helps one to attain his end.'

To him he then declared it. In it then nothing whatsoever was omitted—yea, nothing was omitted.

Part - 10

Brahma as life, joy and the void

उपकोसलो ह वै कामलायनः सत्यकामे जाबाले ब्रह्मचर्यमुवास तस्य ह द्वादशवर्षाण्यग्नीन्परिचचार स ह स्मान्यानन्तेवासिनः समावर्तयꣳस्तꣳ ह स्मैव न समावर्तयति॥१॥

Now, verily, Upakosala Kāmalāyana dwelt with Satyakāma Jābāla as a student of sacred knowledge. For twelve years he tended his fires. Then, although accustomed to allow other pupils to return home, him he did not allow to return.

तं जायोवाच तप्तो ब्रह्मचारी कुशलमग्नीन्परिचचारीन्मा त्वाग्नयः परिप्रवोचन्प्रब्रूह्यस्मा इति तस्मै हाप्रोच्यैव प्रवासांचक्रे॥२॥

His wife said to him : 'The student of sacred knowledge has performed his penance. He has tended the fires well. Let not the fires anticipate you in teaching him. Teach him yourself.' But he went off on a journey without having told him.

स ह व्याधिनानशितुं दध्रे तमाचार्यजायोवाच ब्रह्मचारिन्नशान किंनु नाश्नासीति स होवाच बहव इमेऽस्मिन्पुरुषे कामा नानात्यया व्याधिभिः प्रतिपूर्णोऽस्मि नाशिष्यामीति॥३॥

Then, on account of sickness, he [i.e. Upakosala] took to not eating. The teacher's wife said to him : 'Student of sacred knowledge, eat. Why, pray, do you not eat?'

Then he said : 'Many and various are the desires here in this man. I am filled up with sickness. I will not eat.'

अथ हाग्नयः समूदिरे तप्तो ब्रह्मचारी कुशलं नः पर्यचारीद्धन्तास्मै प्रब्रवामेत तस्मै होचुः॥४॥

So then the fires said among themselves : 'The student of sacred knowledge has performed his penance. He has tended us well. Come! Let us teach him.' Then they said to him :

प्राणो ब्रह्म कं ब्रह्म खं ब्रह्मेति स होवाच विजानाम्यहं यत्प्राणो ब्रह्म कं च तु खं च न विजानामीति ते होचुर्यद्वाव कं तदेव खं तदेव खं कमिति प्राणं च हास्मै तदाकाशं चोचुः॥५॥

'Brahma is life (*prāṇa*). Brahma is joy. Brahma is the void.'

Then he said : 'I understand that Brahma is life. But joy and void I do not understand.'

They said : 'Joy (*ka*)—verily, that is the same as the Void (*kha*). The Void—verily, that is the same as Joy.' And then they explained to him life and space.

Part - 11

अथ हैनं गार्हपत्योऽनुशशास पृथिव्यग्निरन्नमादित्य इति य एष आदित्ये पुरुषो दृश्यते सोऽहमस्मि स एवाहमस्मीति॥१॥

So then the householder's (Gārhapatya) fire instructed him : 'Earth, fire, food, sun [are forms of me. But] the Person who is seen in the sun—I am he; I am he indeed!'

स य एतमेवं विद्वानुपास्तेऽपहते पापकृत्यां लोकीभवति सर्वमायुरेति ज्योग्जीवति नास्यावरपुरुषाः क्षीयन्त उप वयं तं भुञ्जामोऽस्मिंश्च लोकेऽमुष्मिंश्च य एतमेवं विद्वानुपास्ते॥२॥

[Chorus of the fires:] 'He who knows and reverences this fire thus, repels evil-doing from himself, becomes possessor of a world, reaches a full length of life, lives long. His descendants do not become destroyed. Both in this world and in the yonder we serve him who knows and reverences this fire thus.'

Part - 12

अथ हैनमन्वाहार्यपचनोऽनुशशासापो दिशो नक्षत्राणि चन्द्रमा इति य एष चन्द्रमसि पुरुषो दृश्यते सोऽहमस्मि स एवाहमस्मीति॥१॥

So then the southern sacrificial (Anvāhāryapacana) fire instructed him : 'Water, the quarters of heaven, the stars, the moon [are forms of me. But] the Person who is seen in the moon—I am he; I am he indeed!'

स य एतमेवं विद्वानुपास्तेऽपहते पापकृत्यां लोकीभवति सर्वमायुरेति ज्योग्जीवति नास्यावरपुरुषाः क्षीयन्त उप वयं तं भुञ्जामोऽस्मिंश्च लोकेऽमुष्मिंश्च य एतमेवं विद्वानुपास्ते॥२॥

[Chorus of the fires:] 'He who knows and reverences this fire thus, repels evil-doing from himself, becomes possessor of a world, reaches a full length of life, lives long. His descendants do not become destroyed. Both in this world and in the yonder we serve him who knows and reverences this fire thus.'

Part -13

अथ हैनमाहवनीयोऽनुशशास प्राण आकाशो द्यौर्विद्युदिति य एष विद्युति पुरुषो दृश्यते सोऽहमस्मि स एवाहमस्मीति॥१॥

So then the eastern (Āhavanīya) fire instructed him : 'Breath, space, sky, lightning [are forms of me. But] the Person who is seen in the lightning—I am he; I am he indeed!'

स ह एतमेव विद्वानुपास्तेऽपहते पापकृत्यां लोकीभवति सर्वमायुरेति ज्योग्जीवति नास्यावरपुरुषाः क्षीयन्त उप वयं तं भुञ्जामोऽस्मिंश्च लोकेऽमुष्मिंश्च य एतमेवं विद्वानुपास्ते॥२॥

[Chorus of the fires:] 'He who knows and reverences this fire thus, repels evil-doing from himself, becomes possessor of a world, reaches a full length of life, lives long. His descendants do not become destroyed. Both in this world and in the yonder we serve him who knows and reverences this fire thus.'

Part - 14

The soul and its way to Brahman

ते होचुरुपकोसलैषा सोम्य तेऽस्मद्विद्यात्मविद्या चाचार्यस्तु ते गतिं वक्तेत्याजगाम हास्याचार्यस्तमाचार्योऽभ्युवादोपकोसल ३ इति।।१।।

Those fires said to Upakosala– "O Upakosala! Dear one! you have this knowledge of ourselves and the knowledge of the Soul (Ātman). But the teacher will tell you the way." Then the teacher returned. The teacher spoke to him, saying : 'Upakosala!'

भगव इति ह प्रतिशुश्राव ब्रह्मविद इव सोम्य ते मुखं भाति को नु त्वानुशशासेति को नु मानुशिष्याद्भो इतीहापेव निह्नुत इमे नूनमीदृशा अन्यादृशा इतीहाग्नीनभ्यूदे किं नु सोम्य किल तेऽवोचन्निति।।२।।

'Sir!' he then replied.' 'Your face, my dear, shines like a Brahma-knower's. Who, pray, has instructed you?'

'Who, pray, would instruct me, sir?'—Here he denied it, as it were. 'These! They are of this appearance now, but they were of a different appearance!' Here he alluded to the fires.

'What, pray, my dear, did they indeed tell you?'

इदमिति ह प्रतिजज्ञे लोकान्वाव किल सोम्य तेऽवोचन्नहं तु ते तद्वक्ष्यामि यथा पुष्करपलाश? आपो न श्लिष्यन्त एवमेवंविदि पापं कर्म न श्लिष्यत इति ब्रवीतु मे भगवानिति तस्मै होवाच।।३।।

'This,' he acknowledged. 'Verily, my dear, they did indeed tell you the worlds. But I will tell you something. As water adheres not to the leaf of a lotus-flower, so evil action adheres not to him who knows this.'

'Tell me, sir'. To him he then said :

Part - 15

य एषोऽक्षिणि पुरुषो दृश्यत एष आत्मेति होवाचैतदमृतमभयमेतद्ब्रह्मेति तद्यद्यप्यस्मिन्सर्पिर्वोदकं वा सिञ्चन्ति वर्त्मनी एव गच्छति।।१।।

'That Person who is seen in the eye—He is the Self (Ātman),' said he. 'That is the immortal, the fearless. That is Brahma. So even if they pour clarified butter or water on that, it goes away to the edges.

एतꣳ संयद्वाम इत्याचक्षत एतꣳ हि सर्वाणि वामान्यभिसंयन्ति सर्वाण्येनं वामान्यभिसंयन्ति य एवं वेद।।२।।

They call this "Loveliness-uniter" (*saṁyadvāma*), for all lovely things (*vāma*) come together (*saṁyanti*) unto it. All lovely things come together unto him who knows this.

एष उ एव वामनीरेष हि सर्वाणि वामानि नयति सर्वाणि वामानि नयति य एवं वेद।।३।।

And this is also "Goods-bringer" (*vāmanī*), for it brings (√*nī*) all gods (*vāma*). He brings all goods who knows this.

एष उ एव भामनीरेष हि सर्वेषु लोकेषु भाति सर्वेषु लोकेषु भाति य एवं वेद॥४॥

And this one is also "Light-bringer" (*bhāmanī*), for it shines (√*bhā*) in all worlds. He shines in all worlds who knows this.

अथ यदु चैवास्मिञ्छव्यं कुर्वन्ति यदि च नार्चिषमेवाभिसंभवन्त्यर्चिषोऽहरह्न आपूर्यमाणपक्षमापूर्यमाणपक्षाद्यान्षडुदङ्ङेति मासाꣳस्तान्मासेभ्यः संवत्सरꣳ संवत्सरादादित्यमादित्याच्चन्द्रमसं चन्द्रमसो विद्युतं तत्पुरुषोऽमानवः॥५॥

Now, whether they perform the cremation obsequies in the case of such a person or not, they [i.e. the dead] pass over into a flame; from a flame, into the day; from the day, into the half-month of the waxing moon; from the half-month of the waxing moon, into the six months during which the sun moves northwards; from the months, into the year; from the year, into the sun; from the sun, into the moon; from the moon, into lightning. Then there is a Person (*puruṣa*) who is non-human (*a-mānava*).

स एनान्ब्रह्म गमयत्येष देवपथो ब्रह्मपथ एतेन प्रतिपद्यमाना इमं मानवमावर्तं नावर्तन्ते नावर्तन्ते॥६॥

He leads them on to Brahman. This is the way to the gods, the way to Brahman. They who proceed by it return not to the human condition here—yea, they return not!'

Part - 16

The Brāhmaṇa priest properly silent at the sacrifice

एष ह वै यज्ञो योऽयं पवत एष ह यन्निदꣳ सर्वं पुनाति। यदेष यन्निदꣳसर्वं पुनाति तस्मादेष एव यज्ञस्तस्य मनश्च वाक् च वर्तनी॥१॥

Verily, he who purifies here is a sacrifice. Truly, when he moves, he purifies this whole world. Since when he moves (*yan*) he purifies this whole world, therefore indeed he is a sacrifice (*yajña*).

His two paths are mind and speech.

तयोरन्यतरां मनसा सꣳस्करोति ब्रह्मा वाचा होताध्वर्युरुद्गातान्यतराꣳ स यत्रोपाकृते प्रातरनुवाके पुरा परिधानीयाया ब्रह्मा व्यववदति॥२॥

अन्यतरामेव वर्तनीꣳ सꣳस्करोति हीयतेऽन्यतरा स यथैकपाद्व्रजन्रथो वैकेन चक्रेण वर्तमानो रिष्यत्येवमस्य यज्ञो रिष्यति यज्ञꣳ रिष्यन्तं यजमानोऽनुरिष्यति स इष्ट्वा पापीयान्भवति॥३॥

Of these the Brāhmaṇa priest (*brahmā*) forms one with his mind; the Hotṛi, the Adhvaryu and the Udāgtṛi priests, the other with speech.

In case, after the morning litany has commenced, the Brāhmaṇa priest interrupts before the concluding verse, he forms only one path. The other becomes discontinued.

As a one-legged man walking or a chariot proceeding with one wheel, suffers injury, so his sacrifice suffers injury. The institutor of the sacrifice suffers injury after the sacrifice which suffers injury. He becomes worse off by having sacrificed.

अथ यत्रोपाकृते प्रातरनुवाके न पुरा परिधानीयाया ब्रह्मा व्यववदत्युभे एव वर्तनी सꣳस्कुर्वन्ति न हीयतेऽन्यतरा॥४॥

But in case, after the morning litany has commenced, the Brāhmaṇa priest does not interrupt before the concluding verse, they form both paths; the other does not become discontinued.

स यथोभयपाद्व्रजन्रथो वोभाभ्यां चक्राभ्यां वर्तमानः प्रतितिष्ठत्येवमस्य यज्ञः प्रतितिष्ठति यज्ञं प्रतितिष्ठन्तं यजमानोऽनुप्रतितिष्ठति स इष्ट्वा श्रेयान्भवति॥५॥

As a two-legged man walking, or a chariot proceeding with both wheels, is well supported, so his sacrifice is well supported. The institute of the sacrifice is well supported after the sacrifice which is well supported. He becomes better off by having sacrificed.

Part -17

How the Brāhmaṇa priest rectifies mistakes in the sacrificial ritual

प्रजापतिर्लोकान्यतपत्तेषां तप्यमानानाꣳ रसान्प्रावृहदग्निं पृथिव्या वायुमन्तरिक्षादादित्यं दिवः॥१॥

Prajāpati brooded upon the worlds. As they were being brooded upon, he extracted their essences : fire from the earth, wind from the atmosphere, the sun from the sky.

स एतास्तिस्रो देवता अभ्यतपत्तासां तप्यमानानाꣳ रसान्प्रावृहदग्नेर्ऋचो वायोर्यजूꣳषि सामान्यादित्यात्॥२॥

Upon these three deities he brooded. As they were being brooded upon, he extracted their essences : from the fire, the Ṛg verses; from the wind, the Yajus formulas; the Sāman chants, from the sun.

स एतां त्रयीं विद्यामभ्यतपत्तस्यास्तप्यमानाय रसान्प्रावृहद्भूरित्यृग्भ्यो भुवरिति यजुर्भ्यः स्वरितिः सामभ्यः॥३॥

Upon this threefold knowledge he brooded. As it was being brooded upon, he extracted its essences : *bhūr* from the Ṛg verses, *bhuvas* from the Yajus formulas, *svar* from the Sāman chants.

तद्यद्ध्यृक्तो रिष्येद्भूः स्वाहेति गार्हपत्ये जुहुयादृचामेव तद्रसेनर्चां वीर्येणर्चां यज्ञस्य विरिष्टꣳ संदधाति॥४॥

So if there should come an injury in connection with the Ṛg verses, one should make an oblation in the householder's (Gārhapatya) fire with the words '*bhūr*! Hail!' So by the essence of the Ṛg verses themselves, by the power of the Ṛg verses, he mends the injury to the Ṛg verses of the sacrifice.

अथ यदि यजुष्टो रिष्येद्भुवः स्वाहेति दक्षिणाग्नौ जुहुयाद्यजुषामेव तद्रसेन यदुषां वीर्येण यजुषां यज्ञस्य विरिष्टꣳ संदधाति॥५॥

Moreover, if there should come an injury in connection with the Yajus formulas, one should make an oblation in the southern (Dakṣiṇa) fire with the words '*bhuvas*! Hail!' So by the essence of the Yajus formulas themselves, by the power of the Yajus formulas, he mends the injury to the Yajus formulas of the sacrifice.

अथ यदि सामतो रिष्येत्स्वः स्वाहेत्याहवनीये जुहुयात्साम्नामेव तद्रसेन साम्नां वीर्येण साम्नां यज्ञस्य विरिष्टꣳ संदधाति॥६॥

Moreover, if there should come an injury in connection with the Sāman chants, one should make an oblation in the eastern (Āhavanīya) fire with the words '*svar*! Hail!' So by the essence of the Sāman chants themselves, by the power of the Sāman chants, he mends the injury to the Sāman chants of the sacrifice.

तद्यथा लवणेन सुवर्णꣳ संदध्यात्सुवर्णेन रजतꣳ रजतेन त्रपु त्रपुणा सीसꣳ सीसेन लोहं लोहेन दारु दारु चर्मणा॥७॥

एवमेषां लोकानामासां देवतानामस्यास्त्रय्या विद्याया वीर्येण यज्ञस्य विरिष्टꣳ संदधाति भेषजकृतो ह वा एष यज्ञो यत्रैवंविद्ब्रह्मा भवति॥८॥

So, as one would mend gold with borax-salt, silver with gold, tin with silver, lead with tin, brass with lead, wood with brass or with leather, even so with the power of those worlds, of those divinities, of that triple knowledge one mends the injury to the sacrifice. Verily, that sacrifice is healed in which there is a Brāhmaṇa priest who knows this.

एष ह वा उदक्प्रवणो यज्ञो यत्रैवंविद्ब्रह्मा भवत्येवंविदꣳ ह वा एषा ब्रह्माणमनु गाथा यतो यत आवर्तते तत्तद्गच्छति॥९॥

Verily, that sacrifice is inclined to the north in which there is a Brāhmaṇa priest who knows this. Verily, there is this song on the Brāhmaṇa priest who knows this :—

Whichever way he turns himself,
In that same way goes.

मानवो ब्रह्मैवैक ऋत्विक्कुरूनश्वाभिरक्षत्येवंविद्ध वै ब्रह्मा यज्ञं यजमानꣳ सर्वांश्चर्त्विजोऽभिरक्षति तस्मादेवंविदमेव ब्रह्माणं कुर्वीत नानेवंविदं नानेवंविदम्॥१०॥

The silent Brāhmaṇa (because he has taken vow of silent, called 'Mānava') priest alone protects the sacrificers like a dog.

Verily, the Brāhmaṇa priest who knows this guards the sacrifice, the institutor of the sacrifice and all the priests. Therefore one should make as his Brahman priest one who knows this, not one who does not know this— yea, not one who does not know this.

Fifth Chapter

On breath, the soul and the Universal Soul

Part - 1

यो ह वै ज्येष्ठं च श्रेष्ठं च वेद ज्येष्ठ ह वै श्रेष्ठश्च भवति प्राणो वाव ज्येष्ठ श्रेष्ठश्च॥१॥

Oṁ! Verily, he who knows the chiefest and best, becomes the chiefest and best. Breath, indeed, is the chiefest and best.

यो ह वै वसिष्ठं वेद वसिष्ठो ह स्वानां भवति वाग्वाव वसिष्ठः।।२।।

यो ह वै प्रतिष्ठां वेद प्रति ह तिष्ठत्यस्मिꣳश्च लोकेऽमुष्मिꣳश्च चक्षुर्वाव प्रतिष्ठा।।३।।

यो ह वै संपदं वेद सꣳहास्मै कामाः पद्यन्ते दैवाश्च मानुषाश्च श्रोत्रं वाव संपत्।।४।।

Verily, he who knows the most excellent, becomes the most excellent of his own [people]. Speech, verily, is the most excellent.

Verily, he who knows the firm basis, has a firm basis both in this world and in the yonder. The eye, verily, is a firm basis.

Verily, he who knows attainment— for him wishes are attained both human and divine. The ear verily, is attainment.

यो ह वा आयतनं वेदायतनꣳ ह स्वानां भवति मनो ह वा आयतनम्।।५।।

Verily, he who knows the abode, becomes an abode of his own [people]. The mind, verily, is the abode.

अथ ह प्राणा अहꣳ श्रेयसि व्यूदिरेऽहꣳ श्रेयानस्म्यहꣳ श्रेयानस्मीति।।६।।

Now, the Vital Breaths (*prāṇa*) disputed among themselves on self-superiority, saying [in turn] : 'I am superior!' 'I am superior!'

ते ह प्राणाः प्रजापतिं पितरमेत्योचुर्भगवन्को नः श्रेष्ठ उति तान्होवाच यस्मिन्व उत्क्रान्ते शरीरं पापिष्ठतरमिव दृश्येत स वः श्रेष्ठ इति।।७।।

Those Vital Breaths went to Father Prajāpati, and said : 'Sir! Which of us is the most superior?'

He said to them : 'That one of you after whose going off the body appears as if it were the very worst off— he is the most superior of you.'

सा ह वागुच्चक्राम सा संवत्सरं प्रोष्य पर्येत्योवाच कथमशकतर्ते मज्जीवितुमिति यथा कला अवदन्तः प्राणन्तः प्राणेन पश्यन्तश्चक्षुषा शृण्वन्तः श्रोत्रेण ध्यायन्तो मनसैवमिति प्रविवेश ह वाक्।।८।।

Speech went off. Having remained away a year, it came around again and said : 'How have you been able to live without me?' Hearing this the speech again entered into body.

चक्षुर्होच्चक्राम तत्संवत्सरं प्रोष्य पर्येत्योवाच कथमशकतर्ते मज्जीवितुमिति यथान्धा अपश्यन्तः प्राणन्तः प्राणेन वदन्तो वाचा शृण्वन्तः श्रोत्रेण ध्यायन्तो मनसैवमिति प्रविवेश ह चक्षुः।।९।।

The Eye went off. Having remained away a year, it came around again and said : 'How have you been able to live without me?'

'As the blind, not seeing, but breathing with the breath, speaking with speech, hearing with the ear, thinking with the mind. Thus,' Hearing this the Eye entered in.

श्रोत्रꣳ होच्चक्राम तत्संवत्सरं प्रोष्य पर्येत्योवाच कथमशकतर्ते मज्जीवितुमिति यथा बधिरा अशृण्वन्तः प्राणन्तः प्राणेन वदन्तो वाचा पश्यन्तश्चक्षुषा ध्यायन्तो मनसैवमिति प्रविवेश ह श्रोत्रम्॥१०॥

The Ear went off. Having remained away a year, it came around again, and said : 'How have you been able to live without me?'

'As the deaf, not hearing, but breathing with the breath, speaking with speech, seeing with the eye, thinking with the mind. Thus.' The Ear entered in.

मनो होच्चक्राम तत्संवत्सरं प्रोष्य पर्येत्योवाच कथमशकतर्ते मज्जीवितुमिति यथा बाला अमनसः प्राणन्तः प्राणेन वदन्तो वाचा पश्यन्तश्चक्षुषा शृण्वन्तः श्रोत्रेणैवमिति प्रविवेश ह मनः॥११॥

The Mind went off. Having remained away a year, it came around again, and said : 'How have you been able to live without me?'

'As simpletons, mindless, but breathing with the breath, speaking with speech, seeing with the eye, hearing with the ear. Thus.' The Mind entered in.

अथ ह प्राण उच्चिक्रमिषन्स यथासुहयः पड्वीशशङ्कून् संखिदेदेवमितरान् प्राणान् समखिदत्तꣳ हाभिसमेत्योचुर्भगवन्नेधि त्वं नः श्रेष्ठोऽसि मोत्क्रमीरिति॥१२॥

Now when the Breath was about to go off— as a fine horse might tear out the pegs of his foot-tethers all together, thus did it tear out the other Breaths all together. They all came to it and said : 'Sir! Remain. You are the most superior of us. Do not go off.'

अथ हैनं वागुवाचं यदहं वसिष्ठोऽस्मि त्वं तद्वसिष्ठोऽसीत्यथ हैनं चक्षुरुवाच यदहं प्रतिष्ठास्मि त्वं तत्प्रतिष्ठासीति॥१३॥

Then Speech said unto that one : 'If I am the most excellent, so are you the most excellent.' Then the Eye said unto that one : 'If I am a firm basis, so are you a firm basis.'

अथ हैनꣳ श्रोत्रमुवाच यदहꣳ संपदस्मि त्वं तत्संपदसीत्यथ हैनं मन उवाच यदहमायतनमस्मि त्वं तदायतनमसीति॥१४॥

Then the Ear said unto the one : 'If I am attainment, so are you attainment.' Then the Mind said unto that one ; 'If I am an abode, so are you an abode.'

न वै वाचो न चक्षूꣳषि न श्रोत्राणि न मनाꣳसीत्याचक्षते प्राणा इत्येवाचक्षते प्राणो ह्येवैतानि सर्वाणि भवति॥१५॥

Verily, they do not call them 'Speeches', nor 'Eyes', nor 'Ears', nor 'Minds'. They call them 'Breaths' (*prāṇa*), for the vital breath is all these.

Part -2

स होवाच किं मेऽन्नं भविष्यतीति यत्किंचिदिदमा श्वभ्य आ शकुनिभ्य इति होचुस्तद्वा एतदनस्यान्नमो ह वै नाम प्रत्यक्षं न ह वा एवंविदि किंचनानन्नं भवतीति॥१॥

It said. 'What will be my food?'

'Whatever there is here, even to dogs and birds,' they said. So this, verily, is the food (*anna*) of breath (*ana*). Verily, breath is its evident name. Verily, in the case of one who knows this, there is nothing whatever that is not food.

[The food is required for the living organism only till the breathing is in them. This requirement is ceased when the breathing leaves the body, therefore, all kinds of foods are only for the breathing]

स होवाच किं मे वासो भविष्यतीत्याप इति होचुस्तस्माद्वा एतदशिष्यन्तः पुरस्ताच्चोपरिष्टाच्चाद्भिः परिदधति लम्भुको ह वासो भवत्यनग्नो ह भवति॥२॥

It said : 'What will be my garment?' 'Water', they said.

Therefore, verily, when people are about to eat, they enswathe it [i.e. the breath] with water both before and after. It is accustomed to receive a garment; it becomes not naked.

तद्धैतत्सत्यकामो जाबालो गोश्रुतये वैयाघ्रपद्यायोक्त्वोवाच यद्यप्येतच्छुष्काय स्थाणवे ब्रूयाज्जायेरन्नेवास्मिञ्छाखाः प्ररोहेयुः पलाशानीति॥३॥

When Satyakāma Jābāla told this to Gośruti Vaiyāgrapadya, he also said : 'Even if one should tell this to a dried-up stump, branches would be produced on it and leaves would spring forth.'

The 'mixed potion' incantation for the attainment of greatness

[In the hymn number 1 and 3 extra-ordinary advantage to the person knowing the process of breathing and that of listening has been described. During that period to know meant capacity to conduct the process of that breathing and to hear meant to digest that process of breathing perhaps was prevailed. In the same circumstance getting nutrition from the food and revival of the dry stump can be possible.]

अथ यदि महज्जिगमिषेदमावास्यायां दीक्षित्वा पौर्णमास्याᳫं रात्रौ सर्वौषधस्य मन्थं दधिमधुनोरुपमथ्य ज्येष्ठाय श्रेष्ठाय स्वाहेत्यग्नावाज्यस्य हुत्वा मन्थे संपातमवनयेत्॥४॥

Now, if one should wish to come to something great, let him on the night of a new moon perform the Preparatory Consecration Ceremony (Dīkṣā) and on the night of the full moon mix a mixed potion of all sorts of herbs with sour, milk and honey.

'Hail to the chiefest and best!' with these words he should offer a libation of melted butter in the fire and pour the residue into the potion.

वसिष्ठाय स्वाहेत्यग्नावाज्यस्य हुत्वा मन्थे संपातमवनयेत्प्रतिष्ठायै स्वाहेत्यग्नावाज्यस्य हुत्वा मन्थे संपातमवनयेत्संपदे स्वाहेत्यग्नावाज्यस्य हुत्वा मन्थे संपातमवनयेदायतनाय स्वाहेत्यग्नावाज्यस्य हुत्वा मन्थे संपातमवनयेत्॥५॥

'Hail to the most excellent!' with these words he should offer a libation of melted butter in the fire and pour the residue into the potion.

'Hail to the firm basis!' with these words he should offer a libation of melted butter in the fire and pour the residue into the potion.

'Hail to the abode!' with these words he should offer a libation of melted butter in the fire and pour the residue into the potion.

अथ प्रतिसृप्याञ्जलौ मन्थमाधाय जपत्यमो नामास्यमा हि ते सर्वमिदꣳ स हि ज्येष्ठः श्रेष्ठो राजाधिपतिः स मा ज्यैष्ठ्यꣳ श्रेष्ठ्यꣳ राज्यमाधिपत्यं गमयत्वहमेवेदꣳ सर्वमसानीति॥६॥

Then, creeping back [from the fire], and taking the potion in his hollowed hands, he mutters : 'You are He (*ama*) by name, for this whole world is at home (*amā*) in you, for you are pre-eminent and supreme (*śreṣtha*), king and overlord. Let him bring me to pre-eminence and supremacy (*śraiṣthya*), kingship and overlordship! Let me be all this!'

अथ खल्वेतयर्चा पच्छ आचामति तत्सवितुर्वृणीमह इत्याचामति वयं देवस्य भोजनमित्याचामति श्रेष्ठꣳ सर्वधातममित्याचामति तुरं भगस्य धीमहीति सर्वं पिबति॥७॥

Verily, then with this Ṛg verse he takes a sip at each hemstitch : 'The food which is god Savitṛ's,' (Tatsaviturvṛṇīmahe)—here he take a sip— 'That for ourselves do we prefer,' (Vayam devasya Bhojanam)—here he takes a sip—'The best, the all-refreshing food;' (Śreṣṭham Sarvadhātamam)—here he takes a sip—'The Giver's strength may we attain!' (Turam Bhagasya Dhīmahi)—here he takes a sip.

निर्णिज्य कꣳसं चमसं वा पश्चादग्ने संविशति चर्मणि वा स्थण्डिले वा वाचंयमोऽप्रसाहः स यदि स्त्रियं पश्येत्समृद्धं कर्मेति विद्यात्॥८॥

After having cleansed the drinking-vessel or goblet, he lies down to the west of the fire either on a skin or on the bare ground with voice restrained and self-possessed. If he should see a woman, he may know that the rite is successful.

तदेष श्लोकः। यदा कर्मसु काम्येषु स्त्रियꣳ स्वप्नेषु पश्यति। समृद्धिं तत्र जानीयात्तस्मिन्स्वप्ननिदर्शने तस्मिन्स्वप्ननिदर्शन इति॥९॥

As to this there is the following verse :-

If during rites done for a wish; One sees a woman in his dream, Success he there may recognize; In this appearance of his dream,

— In this appearance of his dream.

Part - 3

The course of the soul in its reincarnations

श्वेतकेतुर्हारुणेयः पञ्चालानाꣳसमितिमेयाय तꣳह प्रवाहणो जैवलिरुवाच कुमारानु त्वाशिषत्पितेत्यनु हि भगव इति॥१॥

Once upon a time 'Śvetaketu', the son of Āruṇi visited in the court of the king of Pañcāla. Pravāhaṇa, the son of Jaivala asked him in the assembly– 'Young man, has your father instructed you?' He replied– "Yes Lord!"

वेत्थ यदितोऽधि प्रजाः प्रयन्तीति न भगव इति वेत्थ यथा पुनरावर्तन्त ३ इति न भगव इति वेत्थ पथोर्देवयानस्य पितृयाणस्य च व्यावर्तना ३ इति न भगव इति॥२॥

'Do you know unto what creatures go' Śvetaketu replied– 'No, sir.'

'Do you know how they return again?' He replied– 'No, sir.'

'Do you know the parting of the two ways, one leading to the gods and one leading to the fathers?' He replied– 'No, sir.'

वेत्थ यथासौ लोको न संपूर्यत ३ इति न भगव इति वेत्थ यथा पञ्चम्यामाहुतावापः पुरुषवचसो भवन्तीति नैव भगव इति॥३॥

Pravāhaṇa again asked– 'Do you know how [it is that] yonder world is not filled up?'

Śvetaketu replied– 'No, sir.'

'Do you know how in the fifth oblation water comes to have a human voice?'

He replied– 'No, indeed, sir.'

अथानु किमनुशिष्टोऽवोचथा यो हीमानि न विद्यात्कथꣳसोऽनुशिष्टो ब्रुवीतेति स हायस्तः पितुरर्धमेयाय तꣳहोवाचाऽननुशिष्य वाव किल मा भगवानब्रवीदनु त्वाशिषमिति॥४॥

'Now, pray, how did you say of yourself that you had been instructed? Indeed, how could one who would not know these things speak of himself as having been instructed?'

Distressed, he then went to his father's place. Then he said to him : 'Verily, indeed, without having instructed me, your, sir, said : "I have instructed you."'

पञ्च मा राजन्यबन्धुः प्रश्नानप्राक्षीत्तेषां नैकञ्चनाशकं विवक्तुमिति स होवाच यथा मा त्वं तदैतानवदो यथाहमेषां नैकंचन वेद यद्यहमिमानवेदिष्यं कथं ते नावक्ष्यमिति॥५॥

Śvetaketu said to his father– Five questions a fellow of the princely class (*rājanya-bandhu*) has asked me. I was not able to explain even one of them.'

Then he [i.e. the father] said : 'As you have told them to me here, I do not know even one of them. If I had known them, how would I not have told them to you?'

स ह गौतमो राज्ञोऽर्धमेयाय तस्मै ह प्राप्तायार्हाञ्चकार स ह प्रातः सभाग उदेयाय तꣳहोवाच मानुषस्य भगवन्गौतम वित्तस्य वरं वृणीथा इति होवाच तवैव राजन्मानुषं वित्तं यामेव कुमारस्यान्ते वाचमभाषथास्तामेव मे ब्रूहीति स ह कृच्छ्रीबभूव॥६॥

Then Gautama went to the king's place. To him, when he arrived, he [i.e. the king' had proper attention shown. Then on the morrow he went up to the audience-hall. Then he [i.e. the king] said to him : 'Honoured Gautama, you may choose for yourself a boon of human wealth.'

Then he said : 'Human wealth be yours, O king! The word which you said in the presence of the young man, even that do you speak to me.'

Then he became troubled.

तꣳह चिरं वसेत्याज्ञापयांचकार तꣳ होवाच यथा मा त्वं गौतमावदो यथेयं न प्राक् त्वत्तः पुरा विद्या ब्राह्मणान्गच्छति तस्मादु सर्वेषु लोकेषु क्षत्रस्यैव प्रशासनमभूदिति तस्मै होवाच॥७॥

'Wait a while,' he commanded him. Then he said : 'As to what you have told me, O Gautama, this knowledge has never yet come to Brāhmaṇas before you; and therefore in all the worlds has the rule belonged to the Kṣatriya only.' Then he said to him :—

Part - 4

The 1st question asked by Pravāhaṇa to Śvetaketu was that– "How the Apaḥ becomes personal in the 5th Āhuti?" The answer of this question has been given in this part. Along with the solution of this question, a way of solution of other questions is automatically disclosed. The Veda has said this creation as full of offering. The Ṛṣi explains various stages of the cycle of creation by appreciating the physical offering. The Soma by virtue of 1st Āhuti in the world of Sun, the raining by virtue of IInd Āhuti in the space, the food by virtue of IIIrd Āhuti on the earth, the semen by the 4th Āhuti in the man and the personal living organisms originates when 5th Āhuti in the female is given. The question was how the Apaḥ becomes indicating to a man. The 1st Āhuti has been said being of the obeisance.

The obeisance and the Apaḥ are the synonyms. The Veda considers Apaḥ as the radical active matter of the creation brought in by virtue of the penance of Brahma. By the connotation this cycle discloses all the secret stages from the Brāhmaṇa consent to its appearance as the senses of the living organism.

असौ वाव लोको गौतमाग्निस्तस्यादित्य एव समिद्रश्मयो धूमोऽहरर्चिश्चन्द्रमा अङ्गारा नक्षत्राणि विस्फुलिङ्गाः॥१॥

'Yonder world, verily, O Gautama, is a sacrificial fire. In this case the sun is the fuel; the light-rays, the smoke; the day, the flame; the moon, the coals, the stars, the sparks.

तस्मिन्नेतस्मिन्नग्नौ देवाः श्रद्धां जुह्वति तस्या आहुतेः सोमो राजा संभवति॥२॥

In this fire the gods offer faith (*śraddhā*). From this oblation arises King Soma.

[In the 1st stage of the offering of creation by offering the obeisance or the element of Apaḥ, the Soma, viz., the fundamental flow of nutrition is originated.]

Part - 5

पर्जन्यो वाव गौतमाग्निस्तस्य वायुरेव समिदभ्रं धूमो विद्युदर्चिरशनिरङ्गारा ह्रादुनयो विस्फुलिङ्गाः॥१॥

The rain-cloud, verily, O Gautama, is a sacrificial fire. In this case wind is the fuel; mist, the smoke; lightning, the flame; the thunderbolt, the coals; hailstones, the sparks.

तस्मिन्नेतस्मिन्नग्नौ देवाः सोमꣳ राजानं जुह्वति तस्या आहुतेर्वर्षꣳ संभवति॥२॥

In this divine fire, the gods jointly perform the offering for the king Soma and this particular offering makes the rain to appear.

[The clouds are the production capacity of that world, at the 2nd stage of offering the rain is originated by Soma.]

Part - 6

पृथिवी वाव गौतमाग्निस्तस्याः संवत्सर एव समिदाकाशो धूमो रात्रिरर्चिर्दिशोऽङ्गारा अवान्तरदिशो विस्फुलिङ्गाः॥१॥

The earth, verily, O Gautama, is a sacrificial fire. In this case the year is the fuel; space, the smoke; night, the flame; the quarters of heaven, the coals; the intermediate quarters of heaven, the sparks.

तस्मिन्नेतस्मिन्नग्नौ देवा वर्षं जुह्वति तस्या आहुतेरन्नꣳ संभवति॥२॥

In this fire the gods offer rain. From this oblation arises food.

[In the 3rd stage of the offering, the life element is converted into the food.]

Part - 7

पुरुषो वाव गौतमाग्निस्तस्य वागेव समित्प्राणो धूमो जिह्वार्चिश्चक्षुरङ्गाराः श्रोत्रं विस्फुलिङ्गाः॥१॥

Man, verily, O Gautama, is a sacrificial fire. In this case speech is the fuel; breath, the smoke; the tongue, the flame; the eyes, the coals; the ear, the sparks.

तस्मिन्नेतस्मिन्नग्नौ देवा अन्नं जुह्वति तस्या आहुते रेतः संभवति॥२॥

In this fire the gods offer food. From this oblation arises semen.

[After the offering of this 4th stage, the intangible life element is appeared in the form of semen, an element (Apaḥ) in the semen.]

Part -8

योषा वाव गौतमाग्निस्तस्य उपस्थ एव समिद्यदुपमन्त्रयते स धूमो योनिरर्चिर्यदन्तः करोति तेऽङ्गारा अभिनन्दा विस्फुलिङ्गाः॥१॥

Woman, verily, O Gautama, is a sacrificial fire. In this case the sexual organ is the fuel; when one invites, the smoke; the vulva, the flame; when one inserts, the coals; the sexual pleasure, the sparks.

तस्मिन्नेतस्मिन्नग्नौ देवा रेतो जुह्वति तस्या आहुतेर्गर्भः संभवति॥२॥

In this fire the gods offer semen. From this oblation arises the foetus.

[On maturing this 5th offering the Apaḥ (the radical life) element as offered in the 1st time develops in the form of the living organism and a person established in the body.]

Part - 9

इति तु पञ्चम्यामाहुतावापः पुरुषवचसो भवन्तीति स उल्बावृतो गर्भो दश वा नव वा मासानन्तः शयित्वा यावद्वाथ जायते॥१॥

Thus indeed in the fifth oblation water comes to have a human voice.

After he has lain within for ten months, or for however long it is, as a foetus covered with membrane, then he is born.

(Āpaḥ herein is purported to the basic and active flow of the creation offered with obeisance in the 1st offering. It remains in the womb till the period of 9 or 10 months or until the whole feature is not developed and having relaxed within womb upto such period, this man gets birth.)

[The 5th question asked on disclosure of the secret regarding the fire-learning (Agnividyā) avails herein the clear answer. Subsequently, the other questions relating to the motion of the children born in the manly form are answered.]

स जातो यावदायुषं जीवति तं प्रेतं दिष्टमितोऽग्नय एव हरन्ति यत एवेतो यतः संभूतो भवति॥२॥

When born, he lives for as long as is his length of life. When deceased, they carry him hence to the appointed place for the fire from whence indeed he came, from whence he arose.

Part - 10

In this part, 5 questions asked about the fire-learning (Agni vidyā) have been answered -

तद्य इत्थं विदुर्ये चेमेऽरण्ये श्रद्धा तप इत्युपासते तेऽर्चिषमभिसंभवन्त्यर्चिषोऽहरह्न आपूर्यमाणपक्षमापूर्यमाणपक्षाद्यान्षडुदङ्ङेति मासाꣳस्तान्॥१॥

So those who know this, and those too who worship in a forest with the thought that "Faith is austerity," pass into the flame; from the flame, into the day; from the day, into the Pakṣa (half-circle of the month) of the waxing moon; from the half-month of the waxing moon, into the six months during which the sun moves northward (Uttarāyaṇa);

मासेभ्यः संवत्सरꣳ संवत्सरादादित्यमादित्याच्चन्द्रमसं चन्द्रमसो विद्युतं तत्पुरुषोऽमानवः स एनान्ब्रह्म गमयत्येष देवयानः पन्था इति॥२॥

From those months, into the year; from the year, into the sun; from the sun, into the moon; from the moon, into the lightning. There is a Person (*puruṣa*) who is non-human *(a-mānava)*. He leads them on to Brahman. This is the way leading to the gods (Devayāna).

अथ य इमे ग्राम इष्टापूर्ते दत्तमित्युपासते ते धूममभिसंभवन्ति धूमाद्रात्रिꣳ रात्रेरपरपक्षमपरपक्षाद्यान्षड्दक्षिणैति मासाꣳस्तान्नैते संवत्सरमभिप्राप्नुवन्ति॥३॥

मासेभ्यः पितृलोकं पितृलोकादाकाशमाकाशाच्चन्द्रमसमेष सोमो राजा तद्देवानामन्नं तं देवा भक्षयन्ति॥४॥

But those who in the village reverence a belief in sacrifice, merit, and alms giving—they pass into the smoke; from the smoke, into the night; from the night, into the latter half of the month; from the latter half of the month, into the six months during which the sun moves southward—these do not reach the year; from those months, into the world of the fathers; from the world of the fathers, into space; from space, into the moon. That is king Soma. That is the food of the gods. The gods eat that.

तस्मिन्यावत्संपातमुषित्वाथैतमेवाध्वानं पुनर्निवर्तन्ते यथेतमाकाशमाकाशाद्वायुं वायुर्भूत्वा धूमो भवति धूमो भूत्वाभ्रं भवति॥५॥

After having remained in it as long as there is a residue [of their good works], then by that course by which they came they return again, just as they came, into space; from space, into wind. After having become wind, one becomes smoke. After having become smoke, he becomes mist.

अभ्रं भूत्वा मेघो भवति मेघो भूत्वा प्रवर्षति त इह व्रीहियवा ओषधिवनस्पतयस्तिलमाषा इति जायन्तेऽतो वै खलु दुर्निष्प्रपतरं यो यो ह्यन्नमत्ति यो रेतः सिञ्चति तद्भूय एव भवति॥६॥

After having become mist, he becomes cloud. After having become cloud, he rains down. They are born here as rice and barley, as herbs and trees, as sesame plants and beans. Thence, verily, indeed, it is difficult to emerge; for only if some one or other eats him as food and emits him as semen, does he develop further.

तद्य इह रमणीयचरणा अभ्याशो ह यत्ते रमणीयां योनिमापद्येरन्ब्राह्मणयोनिं वा क्षत्रिययोनिं वा वैश्ययोनिं वाथ य इह कपूयचरणा अभ्याशो ह यत्ते कपूयां योनिमापद्येरन् श्वयोनिं वा सूकरयोनिं वा चण्डालयोनिं वा॥७॥

Accordingly, those who are of pleasant conduct here— the prospect is, indeed, that they will enter a pleasant womb, either the womb of a Brāhmaṇa, or the womb of stinking conduct here—the prospect is, indeed, that they will enter a stinking womb, either the womb of a dog, or the womb of a swine, or the womb of an outcast (*caṇḍāla*).

अथैतयोः पथोर्न कतरेण च न तानीमानि क्षुद्राण्यसकृदावर्तीनि भूतानि भवन्ति जायस्व म्रियस्वेत्येतत्तृतीयꣳ स्थानं तेनासौ लोको न संपूर्यते तस्माज्जुगुप्सेत तदेष श्लोकः॥८॥

But on neither of these ways are the small, continually returning creatures, [those of whom it is said:] "Be born and die"– theirs is a third state.

Thereby [it comes about that] yonder world is not filled up. Therefore one should seek to guard himself. As to this there is the following verse:-

स्तेनो हिरण्यस्य सुरां पिबꣳश्च गुरोस्तल्पमावसन्ब्रह्महा च। एते पतन्ति चत्वारः पञ्चमश्चाचरꣳस्तैरिति॥९॥

The plunderer of gold, the liquor-drinker,

The invader of a teacher's bed, the Brahman-killer

These four sink downward in the scale,

And, fifth, he who consorts with them.

अथ ह य एतानेवं पञ्चाग्नीन्वेद न स ह तैरप्याचरन्पाप्मना लिप्यते शुद्धः पूतः पुण्यलोको भवति य एवं वेद य एवं वेद॥१०॥

But he who knows these five fires thus, is not stained with evil, even though consorting with those people. He becomes pure, clean, possessor of a pure world, who knows this—yea, he who knows this!'

Part -11
The Universal Soul

प्राचीनशाल औपमन्यवः सत्ययज्ञः पौलुषिरिन्द्रद्युम्नो भाल्लवेयो जनः शार्कराक्ष्यो बुडिल आश्वतराश्विस्ते हैते महाशाला महाश्रोत्रियाः समेत्य मीमाꣳसां चक्रुः को नु आत्मा किं ब्रह्मेति॥१॥

Prācīnaśāla Aupamanyava (the son of Upamanyu), Satyayajña Pauluṣi (the son of Puluṣa), Indradyumna Bhālaveya (the son of Bhallavi), Jana Śārkarākṣya, and Buḍila Āśvatarāśvi—these great householders, greatly learned in sacred lore (*śrotriya*), having come together, pondered : 'Who is our Ātman (Soul)? What is Brahman?'

ते ह संपादयांचक्रुरुद्दालको वै भगवन्तोऽयमारुणिः संप्रतीममात्मानं वैश्वानरमध्येति तꣳहन्ताभ्यागच्छामेति तꣳ हाभ्याजग्मुः॥२॥

Then they agreed among themselves : 'Verily, sirs, Uddālaka Āruṇi here studies exactly this Universal (*vaiśvānara*) Ātman (Soul). Come, let us go unto him.'

Then unto him they went.

स ह संपादयांचकार प्रक्ष्यन्ति मामिमे महाशाला महाश्रोत्रियास्तेभ्यो न सर्वमिव प्रतिपत्स्ये हन्ताहमन्यमभ्यनुशासानीति॥३॥

Then he agreed with himself : 'These great householders, greatly learned in sacred lore, will question me. I may not be able to answer them everything. Come! Let me direct them to another.'

तान्होवाचाश्वपतिर्वै भगवन्तोऽयं कैकेयः संप्रतीममात्मानं वैश्वानरमध्येति तꣳहन्ताभ्यागच्छामेति तꣳहाभ्याजग्मुः॥४॥

Āruṇi, then told them– 'Verily, sirs, Aśvapati Kaikeya studies just this Universal Ātman (Soul). Come! Let us go unto him.'

Then unto him they went.

तेभ्यो ह प्राप्तेभ्यः पृथगर्हाणि कारयांचकार स ह प्रातः संजिहान उवाच न मे स्तेनो जनपदे न कदर्यो न मद्यपो नानाहिताग्निर्नाविद्वान्न स्वैरी स्वैरिणी कुतो यक्ष्यमाणो वै भगवन्तोऽहमस्मि यावदेकैकस्मा ऋत्विजे धनं दास्यामि तावद्भगवद्भ्यो दास्यामि वसन्तु भगवन्त इति॥५॥

Then to them severally, when they arrived, he had proper attentions shown. He was indeed a man who, on rising, could say :

'Within my realm there is no thief, no miser, nor a drinking man,

None altarless, none ignorant,

No man unchaste, no wife unchaste.'

'Verily, sirs, I am about to have a sacrifice performed. As large a gift as I shall give to each priest, so large a gift will I give to you, sirs. Remain, my sirs.'

ते होचुर्येन हैवार्थेन पुरुषश्चरेत्तꣳहैव वदेदात्मानमेवेमं वैश्वानरꣳ संप्रत्यध्येषि तमेव नो ब्रूहीति॥६॥

Then they said : With whatever subject a person is concerned, of that indeed he should speak. You know just this Universal Ātman (Soul). Him indeed do you tell to us.'

तान्होवाच प्रातर्वः प्रतिवक्तास्मीति ते ह समित्पाणयः पूर्वाह्णे प्रतिचक्रमिरे तान्हानुपनीयै वैतदुवाच॥७॥

Then he said to them : 'On the morrow will I make reply.' Then with fuel in their hands in the morning they returned. Then, without having first received them as pupils, he spoke to them as follows :

Part - 12

औपमन्यव कं त्वमात्मानमुपास्स इति दिवमेव भगवो राजन्निति होवाचैष वै सुतेजा आत्मा वैश्वानरो यं त्वमात्मानमुपास्से तस्मात्तव सुतं प्रसुतमासुतं कुले दृश्यते॥१॥

The king Aśvapati asked Aupamanyava, the son of Upamanyu– "O Aupamanyava, whom do you reverence as the Ātman (Soul)?' Prācīnaśāla answered– 'The heaven indeed, sir, O King,' 'The Universal Ātman (Soul) is, verily, that brightly shining one (*sutejas*) which you reverence as the Ātman (Soul). Therefore Soma is seen pressed out (*suta*) and continually pressed out in your family.

अत्स्यन्नं पश्यसि प्रियमत्त्यन्नं पश्यति प्रियं भवत्यस्य ब्रह्मवर्चसं कुले य एतमेवमात्मानं वैश्वानरमुपास्ते मूर्धा त्वेष आत्मन इति होवाच मूर्धा ते व्यपतिष्यद्यन्मां नागमिष्य इति॥२॥

King Aśvapati again said– You eat food; you see what is pleasing. He eats food; he sees what is pleasing. There is eminence in sacred knowledge in the family of him who reverences the Universal Ātman (Soul) thus. That, however, is only the head of the Ātman (Soul),' said he. 'Your head would have fallen off, if you had not come unto me.'

Part - 13

अथ होवाच सत्ययज्ञं पौलूषिं प्राचीनयोग्यं कं त्वमात्मानमुपास्स इत्यादित्यमेव भगवो राजन्निति होवाचैष वै विश्वरूप आत्मा वैश्वानरो यं त्वमात्मानुपास्से तस्मात्तव बहु विश्वरूपं कुले दृश्यते॥१॥

Then he said to Śatyayajña Paulūṣi : 'Prācīnayogya! Whom do you reverence as the Ātman (Soul)?' He said– 'The sun indeed, sir, O King!

'The Universal Ātman (Soul) is, verily, that manifold one which you reverence as the Ātman (Soul). Therefore much of all sorts is seen in your family.

प्रवृत्तोऽश्वतरीरथो दासीनिष्कोऽत्स्यन्नं पश्यसि प्रियमत्त्यन्नं पश्यति प्रियं भवत्यस्य ब्रह्मवर्चसं कुले य एतमेवमात्मानं वैश्वानरमुपास्ते चक्षुष्ट्वे तदात्मन इति होवाचान्धोऽभविष्यो यन्मां नागमिष्य इति॥२॥

A chariot drawn by a she-mule rolled up [before your door], a female slave, a gold necklace. You eat food; you see what is pleasing. He eats food; he sees what is pleasing. There is eminence in sacred knowledge in the family of him who reverences that Universal Ātman (Soul) thus. That, however, is only the eye of the Ātman (Soul),' said he. King Aśvapati again said– 'You would have become blind, if you had not come unto me.'

Part - 14

अथ होवाचेन्द्रद्युम्नं भाल्लवेयं वैयाघ्रपद्य कं त्वमात्मानमुपास्स इति वायुमेव भगवो राजन्निति होवाचैष वै पृथग्वर्त्मात्मा वैश्वानरो यं त्वमात्मानमुपास्से तस्मात्त्वां पृथग्बलय आयन्ति पृथग्रथश्रेणयोऽनुयन्ति॥१॥

Then said to Indradyumna Bhāllaveya : 'Vaiyāghrapadya! Whom do you reverence as the Ātman (Soul)?'

'The wind indeed, sir, O King,' said he.

'The Universal Ātman (Soul) is, verily, that which possesses various paths, which you reverence as the Ātman (Soul). Therefore offerings come unto you in various ways; rows of chariots follow you in various ways.

अत्स्यन्नं पश्यसि प्रियमत्त्यन्नं पश्यति प्रियं भवत्यस्य ब्रह्मवर्चसं कुले च एतमेवमात्मानं वैश्वानरमुपास्ते प्राणस्त्वेष आत्मन इति होवाच प्राणस्त उदक्रमिष्यद्यन्मां नागमिष्य इति॥२॥

The king told that "You eat food; you see what is pleasing. He eats food; he sees what is pleasing". There is eminence in sacred knowledge in the family of him who reverences that Universal Ātman (Soul) thus.

That, however, is only the breath of the Ātman (Soul),' said he. 'Your breath would have departed, if you had not come unto me.'

Part - 15

अथ होवाच जनः शार्कराक्ष्य कं त्वमात्मानमुपास्स इत्याकाशमेव भगवो राजन्निति होवाचैष वै बहुल आत्मा वैश्वानरो यं त्वमात्मानमुपास्से तस्मात्त्वं बहुलोऽसि प्रजया च धनेन च॥१॥

Then he said to Jana : 'Śārkarākṣya! Whom do you reverence as the Ātman (Soul)?'

'Space indeed, sir, O King,' said he.

'The Universal (Vaiśvānara) Ātman (Soul) is, verily, that expanded one, which you reverence as the Ātman (Soul). Therefore, you are expanded with offspring and wealth.

अत्स्यन्नं पश्यसि प्रियमत्त्यन्नं पश्यति प्रियं भवत्यस्य ब्रह्मवर्चसं कुले य एतमेवमात्मानं वैश्वानरमुपास्ते संदेहस्त्वेष आत्मन इति होवाच संदेहस्ते व्यशीर्यद्यन्मां नागमिष्य इति॥२॥

You eat food; you see what is pleasing. He eats food; he sees what is pleasing. There is eminence in sacred knowledge in the family of him who reverences that Universal Ātman (Soul) thus.

That, however, is only the body (*saṁdeha*) of the Ātman (Soul),' said he. 'Your body would have fallen to pieces, if you had not come unto me.'

Part - 16

अथ होवाच बुडिलमाश्वतराश्विं वैयाघ्रपदा कं त्वमात्मानमुपास्स इत्यप एव भगवो राजन्निति होवाचैष वै रयिरात्मा वैश्वानरो यं त्वमात्मानमुपास्से तस्मात्त्वः रयिमान्पुष्टिमानसि॥१॥

The king Aśvapati again asked Buḍila Āśvatarāśvi : 'Vaiyāghrapadya! Whom do you reverence as the Ātman (Soul)?'

Water indeed, sir, O King,' said he.

'The Universal Ātman (Soul) is, verily, that wealth, which you reverence as the Ātman (Soul). Therefore you are wealthy and thriving.

अत्स्यन्नं पश्यसि प्रियमत्त्यन्नं पश्यति प्रियं भवत्यस्य ब्रह्मवर्चसं कुले य एतमेवमात्मानं वैश्वानरमुपास्ते बस्तिस्त्वेष आत्मन इति होवाच बस्तिस्ते व्यभेत्स्यद्यन्मां नागमिष्य इति॥२॥

You eat food; you see what is pleasing. He eats food; he sees what is pleasing. There is eminence in sacred knowledge in the family of him who reverences that Universal Ātman (Soul) thus.

That, however, in only the bladder of the Ātman (Soul),' said he. 'Your bladder would have burst, if you had not come unto me.'

Part - 17

अथ होवाचोद्दालकमारुणिं गौतम कं त्वमात्मानमुपास्स इति पृथिवीमेव भगवो राजन्निति होवाचैष वै प्रतिष्ठात्मा वैश्वानरो यं त्वमात्मानमुपास्से तस्मात्त्वं प्रतिष्ठितोऽसि प्रजया च पशुभिश्च॥१॥

Then the king Aśvapati asked Uddālaka, the son of Aruṇa - 'O Gautama! Whom do you reverence as the Ātman (Soul)?' He said– 'The earth indeed, sir, O King!'

'The Universal Ātman (Soul) is, verily, that support, which you reverence as the Ātman (Soul). Therefore you are supported with offspring and cattle.

अत्स्यन्नं पश्यसि प्रियमत्त्यन्नं पश्यति प्रियं भवत्यस्य ब्रह्मवर्चसं कुले य एतमेवमात्मानं वैश्वानरमुपास्ते पादौ त्वेतावात्मन इति होवाच पादौ ते व्यम्लास्येतां यन्मां नागमिष्य इति॥२॥

You eat food; you see what is pleasing. He eats food; he sees what is pleasing. There is eminence in sacred knowledge in the family of him who reverences that Universal Ātman (Soul) thus.

That, however, is only the feet of the Ātman (Soul),' said he. 'Your feet would have withered away, if you had not come unto me.'

Part -18

तान्होवाचैते वै खलु यूयं पृथगिवेममात्मानं वैश्वानरं विद्वांसोऽन्नमत्थ यस्त्वेतमेवं प्रादेशमात्रमभिविमानमात्मानं वैश्वानरमुपास्ते स सर्वेषु लोकेषु सर्वेषु भूतेषु सर्वेष्वात्मस्वन्नमत्ति॥१॥

Then he said to them : 'Verily, indeed, you here eat food, knowing this Universal Ātman (Soul) as if something separate. He, however, who reverences this Universal Ātman (Soul) that is of the measure of the span—thus, [yet] is to be measured by thinking of oneself—he eats food in all worlds, in all beings, in all selves.

तस्य ह वा एतस्यात्मनो वैश्वानरस्य मूर्धैव सुतेजाश्चक्षुर्विश्वरूपः प्राणः पृथग्वर्त्मात्मा संदेहो बहुलो बस्तिरेव रयिः पृथिव्येव पादावुर एव वेदिर्लोमानि बर्हिर्हृदयं गार्हपत्यो मनोऽन्वाहार्यपचन आस्यमाहवनीयः॥२॥

The brightly shining [heaven] is indeed the head of that Universal Ātman (Soul). The manifold [sun] is his eye. That which possesses various paths [i.e. the wind] is his breath. The extended [space] is his body. Wealth [i.e. water] is indeed his bladder. The support [i.e. the earth] is indeed his feet. The sacrificial area is indeed his breast. The sacrificial grass is his hair. The Gārhapatya fire is his heart. The Anvāhāryapacana fire is his mind. The Āhavanīya fire is his mouth.

[Virāṭ, the son of a sage was worshipped every limb of the Vaiśvānara, the element of the soul may be realised by the worship of the soul located in a particular limb but it cannot be confined to that stage only. In case, an omission is committed as to confine that gigantic soul in any particular limb, it may damage that particular limb in order to maintain its incessant flow. This was the reason why king Aśvapati expressed the possibility of the damage to the particular organs of the sons of the saints.]

Part - 19

The mystical Agnihotra sacrifice to the Universal Soul in one's own self

तद्यद्भक्तं प्रथममागच्छेत्तद्धोमीयꣳस यां प्रथमामाहुतिं जुहियात्तां जुहुयात्प्राणाय स्वाहेति प्राणस्तृप्यति॥१॥

Therefore the first food which one may come to, should be offered. The first oblation which he would offer he should offer with "Hail to the Prāṇa breath!" The Prāṇa breath is satisfied.

प्राणे तृप्यति चक्षुस्तृप्यति चक्षुषि तृप्यत्यादित्यस्तृप्यत्यादित्ये तृप्यति द्यौस्तृप्यति दिवि तृप्यन्त्यां यत्किंच द्यौश्चादित्यश्चाधितिष्ठतस्तत्तृप्यति तस्यानृतृप्तिं प्रजया पशुभिरन्नाद्येन तेजसा ब्रह्मवर्चसेनेति॥२॥

The Prāṇa breath being satisfied, the eye is satisfied. The eye being satisfied, the sun is satisfied. The sun being satisfied, the heaven is satisfied. The heaven being satisfied, whatever the heaven and the sun rule over is satisfied. Along with the satisfaction thereof, he is satisfied with offspring, with cattle, with food, with the glow of health, and with eminence in sacred knowledge.

Part - 20

अथ यां द्वितीयां जुहुयात्तां जुहुयाद्व्यानाय स्वाहेति व्यानस्तृप्यति॥१॥

Then the second oblation which he would offer he should offer with "Hail to the Vyāna breath!" The Vyāna breath is satisfied.

व्याने तृप्यति श्रोत्रं तृप्यति श्रोत्रे तृप्यति चन्द्रमास्तृप्यति चन्द्रमसि तृप्यति दिशस्तृप्यन्ति दिक्षु तृप्यन्तीषु यत्किंच दिशश्च चन्द्रमाश्चाधितिष्ठन्ति तत्तृप्यति तस्यानुतृप्तिं तृप्यति प्रजया पशुभिरन्नाद्येन तेजसा ब्रह्मवर्चसेनेति॥२॥

The Vyāna breath being satisfied, the ear is satisfied. The ear being satisfied, the moon is satisfied. The moon being satisfied, the quarters of heaven are satisfied. The quarters of heaven being satisfied, whatever the moon and the quarters of heaven rule over is satisfied. Along with the satisfaction thereof, he is satisfied with offspring, with cattle, with food, with the glow of health, and with eminence in sacred knowledge.

Part - 21

अथ यां तृतीयां जुहुयात्तां जुहुयाद्व्यानाय स्वाहेत्यपानस्तृप्यति।।१।।

Then the third offering which he would offer he should offer with "Hail to the Apāna breath!" The Apāna breath is satisfied.

अपाने तृप्यति वाक्तृप्यति वाचि तृप्यन्त्यामग्निस्तृप्यत्यग्नौ तृप्यति पृथिव्यां तृप्यन्त्यां यत्किंच पृथिवी चाग्निश्चाधितिष्ठतस्तत्तृप्यति तस्यानुतृप्तिं तृप्यति प्रजया पशुभिरन्नाद्येन तेजसा ब्रह्मवर्चसेनेति।।२।।

The Apāna breath being satisfied, speech is satisfied. Speech being satisfied, fire is satisfied. Fire being satisfied, the earth is satisfied. The earth being satisfied, whatever the earth and fire rule over is satisfied. Along with the satisfaction thereof, he is satisfied with offspring, with cattle, with food, with the glow of health, and with eminence in sacred knowledge.

Part - 22

अथ यां चतुर्थीं जुहुयात्तां जुहुयाद्व्यानाय स्वाहेति समानस्तृप्यति।।१।।

Then the fourth offering which he would offer he should offer with "Hail to the Samāna breath!" The Samāna breath is satisfied.

समाने तृप्यति मनस्तृप्यति मनसि तृप्यति विद्युत्तृप्यति विद्युति तृप्यन्त्यां यत्किंच विद्युच्च पर्जन्यश्चाधितिष्ठतस्तत्तृप्यति तस्यानुतृप्तिं तृप्यति प्रजया पशुभिरन्नाद्येन तेजसा ब्रह्मवर्चसेनेति।।२।।

The Samāna breath being satisfied, the mind is satisfied. The mind being satisfied, the rain-god (Parjanya) is satisfied. The rain-god being satisfied, lightning is satisfied. Lightning being satisfied, whatever the rain-god and lightning rule over is satisfied. Along with the satisfaction thereof, he is satisfied with offspring with cattle, with food, with the glow of health, and with eminence in sacred knowledge.

Part - 23

अथ यां पञ्चमीं जुहुयात्तां जुहुयाद्व्यानाय स्वाहेत्युदानस्तृप्यति।।१।।

Then the fifth offering which he would offer he should offer with "Hail to the Udāna breath!" The Udāna breath is satisfied.

उदाने तृप्यति त्वक् तृप्यति त्वचि तृप्यन्त्यां वायुस्तृप्यति वायौ तृप्यत्याकाशस्तृप्यत्याकाशे तृप्यति यत्किंच वायुश्चाकाशश्चाधितिष्ठतस्तत्तृप्यति तस्यानुतृप्तिं तृप्यति प्रजया पशुभिरन्नाद्येन तेजसा ब्रह्मवर्चसेनेति।।२।।

On satiation of Udāna, the skin satiates, after the skin the wind satiates, Wind being satisfied, space is satisfied. Space being satisfied, whatever wind and space rule over is satisfied. Along with the satisfaction thereof, he is satisfied with offspring, with cattle, with food, with the glow of health, and with eminence in sacred knowledge.

Part - 24

स य इदमविद्वानग्निहोत्रं जुहोति यथाङ्गारानपोह्य भस्मनि जुहुयात्तादृक्तत्स्यात्।।१।।

If one offers the Agnihotra (fire) sacrifice without knowing this—that would be just as if he were to remove the live coals and pour the offering on ashes.

अथ य एतदेवं विद्वानग्निहोत्रं जुहोति तस्य सर्वेषु लोकेषु सर्वेषु भूतेषु सर्वेष्वात्मसु हुतं भवति।।२।।

But if one offers the Agnihotra sacrifice knowing it thus, his offering is made in all worlds, in all beings, in all selves.

तद्यथेषीकातूलमग्नौ प्रोतं प्रदूयेतैवꣳहास्य सर्वे पाप्मानः प्रदूयन्ते य एतदेवं विद्वानग्निहोत्रं जुहोति।।३।।

So, as the top of a reed laid on a fire would be burned up, even so are burned up all the evils of him who offers the Agnihotra sacrifice knowing it thus.

तस्मादु हैवंविद्यद्यपि चण्डालायोच्छिष्टं प्रयच्छेदात्मनि हैवास्य तद्वैश्वानरे हुतꣳस्यादिति तदेष श्लोकः।।४।।

यथेह क्षुधिता बाला मातरं पर्युपासते। एवꣳसर्वाणि भूतान्यग्निहोत्रमुपासत इत्यग्निहोत्रमुपासत इति।।५।।

And therefore, if one who knows this should offer the leavings even to an outcast (*caṇḍāla*), it would be offered in his Universal Ātman (Soul). As to this there is the following verse :—

'As hungry children sit around; About their mother here in life,

Even so all beings sit around; The Agnihotra sacrifice.'

Sixth Chapter

Part -1

The instruction of Śvetaketu by Uddālaka concerning the key to all knowledge

श्वेतकेतुर्हारुणेय आस तꣳह पितोवाच श्वेतकतो वस ब्रह्मचर्यम्। न वै सोम्यास्मत्कुलीनोऽननूच्य ब्रह्मबन्धुरिव भवतीति।।१।।

Oṁ! Now, there was Śvetaketu, the grandson of Aruṇa, To him his father said : 'Live the life of a student of sacred knowledge (Brahmacarya Āśrama). Verily, my dear, from our family there is no one unlearned (in the Vedas (*an-ucya*), a Brāhmaṇa by connection (*brahma-bandhu*), as it were.'

[Brahmabandhu is the man who doesn't behave like Brahmins but associated to them. By using this term the Ṛsi wants to convey that all persons in his clan are well-known to the Brahma.]

स ह द्वादशवर्ष उपेत्य चतुर्विंशतिवर्षः सर्वान्वेदानधीत्य महामना अनूचानमानी स्तब्ध एयाय तꣳह पितोवाच श्वेतकेतो यन्नु सोम्येदं महामना अनूचानमानी स्तब्धोऽस्युत तमादेशमप्राक्ष्यः॥२॥

येनाश्रुतꣳश्रुतं भवत्यमतं मतमविज्ञातं विज्ञातमिति। कथं नु भगवः स आदेशो भवतीति॥३॥

He then, having become a pupil at the age of twelve, having studied all the Vedas, returned at the age of twenty-four, conceited, thinking himself a great scholar and arrogent.

Then his father said to him : 'O Śvetaketu, my dear, since now you are conceited, think yourself learned, and are proud, did you also ask for that teaching whereby what has not been heard of becomes heard of, what has not been thought of becomes thought of, what has not been understood becomes understood?'

'What is that teaching, Sir?'

यथा सोम्यैकेन मृत्पिण्डेन सर्वं मृन्मयं विज्ञातꣳस्याद्वाचारम्भणं विकारो नामधेयं मृत्तिकेत्येव सत्यम्॥४॥

"Just as, my dear, through a clod of clay everything made of clay may be known—the modification is merely a verbal distinction, a name; the reality is just "clay"—

यथा सोम्यैकेन लोहमणिना सर्वं लोहमयं विज्ञातꣳस्याद्वाचारम्भणं विकारो नामधेयं लोहमित्येव सत्यम्॥५॥

Just as, my dear, through a single ingot of gold all that is made of gold may be known— the modification is merely a verbal distinction, a name; the reality is just "gold"—

यथा सोम्यैकेन नखनिकृन्तनेन सर्वं कार्ष्णायसं विज्ञातꣳस्याद्वाचारम्भणं विकारो नामधेयं कृष्णायसमित्येव सत्यमेवꣳ सोम्य स आदेशो भवतीति॥६॥

My dear, Just as by one nail-scissors everything made of iron may be known— the modification is merely a verbal distinction, a name; the reality is just "iron"—so, my dear, is that teaching.'

न वै नूनं भगवन्तस्त एतदवेदिषुर्यद्ध्येतदवेदिष्यन् कथं मे नावक्ष्यन्निति भगवाꣳस्त्वेवमेतद्ब्रवीत्विति तथा सोम्येति होवाच॥७॥

'Verily, those honoured men did not know this; for, if they had known it, why would they not have told me? But do you, sir, tell me it.'

'So be it, my dear,' said he.

Part - 2

सदेव सोम्येदमग्र आसीदेकमेवाद्वितीयं तद्धैक आहुरसदेवेदमग्र आसीदेकमेवाद्वितीयं तस्मादसतः सज्जायत॥१॥

Uddālaka told Śvetaketu– 'In the beginning, my dear, this world was just Being (*sat*), one only, without a second. To be sure, some people say– "In the beginning this world was just Non-being (*a-sat*), one only, without a second; from that Non-being Being was produced."

कुतस्तु खलु सोम्यैवं स्यादिति होवाच कथमसतः सज्जायेतेति। सत्त्वेव सोम्येदमग्र आसीदेकमेवाद्वितीयम्।।२।।

But verily, my dear, whence could this be?' said he. 'How from Non-being could Being be produced? On the contrary, my dear, in the beginning this world was just Being, one only, without a second.

तदैक्षत बहु स्यां प्रजायेयेति तत्तेजोऽसृजत। तत्तेज ऐक्षत बहुस्यां प्रजायेयेति तदपोऽसृजत। तस्माद्यत्र क्वच शोचति स्वेदते वा पुरुषस्तेजस एव तदध्यापो जायन्ते।।३।।

It bethought itself : "Would that I were many! Let me procreate myself!" It emitted heat. That heat bethought itself : "Would that I were many! Let me procreate myself." It emitted water. Therefore whenever a person grieves or perspires from the heat, then water [i.e. either tears or perspiration] is produced.

ता आप ऐक्षन्त बह्वयः स्याम प्रजायेमहीति ता अन्नमसृजन्त। तस्माद्यत्र क्वच वर्षति तदेव भूयिष्ठमन्नं भवत्यद्भ्य एव तदध्यन्नाद्यं जायते।।४।।

That water bethought itself : "Would that I were many! Let me procreate myself." It emitted food. Therefore whenever it rains, then there is abundant food. So food for eating is produced just from water.

[The Ṛṣi already have explained in the precedent Chapter 5 that the 1st offering was made in the world of Sun in course of the creation of earth. The truth gave birth to splendour as the world of earth is known as the world of Sun. This very splendour as a result of resolution for the creation is called as the Hiraṇyagarbha by the Veda. As a result of dividing that splendour, the element of Ap (water) was originated. The Veda has assumed it as the radically activated flow of the creation. This can be said as the water from the world of sun. By resolution of this flow of water (Ap) sub-atomic particles were formed which can he said as the earth element of the world of sun. In the next stage, the splendour is called as the sun etc. By virtue of the conflict in the element of water the splendour originated the atomic particles and the water in the space. By virtue of the water and the micro particles the element of earth was formed by the crystallised and stable particles. The Ṛṣi observes the process of the both stages. In his statement, both the forms *i.e.* micro and macro, visible and invisible of the splendour, water and the earth are blended. The meaning of his statement can be understood when this very assumption is made.]

Part -3

तेषां खल्वेषां भूतानां त्रीण्येव बीजानि भवन्त्याण्डजं जीवजमुद्भिज्जमिति।।१।।

(Thereafter Uddālaka clarified his statement further while making Śvetaketu to understand the course of creation) Now, of these beings here there are just three origins : [there are beings] born from an egg *i.e.* Aṇḍaja, born from a living thing *i.e.* Jarāyuja, born from a sprout *i.e.* Udbhijja.

सेयं देवतैक्षत हन्ताहमिमास्तिस्रो देवता अनेन जीवेनात्मनानुप्रविश्य नामरूपे व्याकरवाणीति।।२।।

That divinity [i.e. Being] bethought itself : "Come! Let me enter these three divinities [i.e. heat, water, and food] with this living Soul (*ātman*), and separate out name and form.

तासां त्रिवृतं त्रिवृतमेकैकां करवाणीति सेयं देवतेमास्तिस्रो देवता अनेनैव जीवेनात्मनानुप्रविश्य नामरूपे व्याकरोत्॥३॥

Let me make each one of them threefold." That divinity entered into these three divinities with this living Soul and separated out name and form.

तासां त्रिवृतं त्रिवृतमेकैकामकरोद्यथा तु खलु सोम्येमास्तिस्रो देवतास्त्रिवृत्त्रिवृदेकैका भवति तन्मे विजानीहीति॥४॥

It made each of them threefold. Now, verily, my dear, understand from me how each of these three divinities becomes threefold.

Part - 4

यदग्ने रोहितꣳरूपं तेजसस्तद्रूपं यच्छुक्लं तदपां यत्कृष्णं तदन्नस्यापागादग्नेरग्नित्वं वाचारम्भणं विकारो नामधेयं त्रीणि रूपाणीत्येव सत्यम्॥१॥

Whatever red form fire has, is the form of heat; whatever white, the form of water; whatever dark, the form of food. The fire-hood has gone from fire : the modification is merely a verbal distinction, a name. The reality is just "the three forms."

यदादित्यस्य रोहितꣳरूपं तेजसस्तद्रूपं यच्छुक्लं तदपां यत्कृष्णं तदन्नस्यापागादग्नेरग्नित्वं वाचारम्भणं विकारो नामधेयं त्रीणि रूपाणीत्येव सत्यम्॥२॥

Whatever red form the sun has, is the form of heat; whatever white, the form of water; whatever dark, the form of food. The sunhood has gone from the sun : the modification is merely a verbal distinction, a name. The reality is just "the three forms."

यच्चन्द्रमसो रोहितꣳरूपं तेजसस्तद्रूपं यच्छुक्लं तदपां यत्कृष्णं तदन्नस्यापागादग्नेरग्नित्वं वाचारम्भणं विकारो नामधेयं त्रीणि रूपाणीत्येव सत्यम्॥३॥

Whatever red form the moon has, is the form of heat; whatever white, the form of water; whatever dark, the form of food. The moonhood has gone from the moon : the modification is merely a verbal distinction, a name. The reality is just "the three forms."

यद्विद्युतो रोहितꣳ रूपं तेजसस्तद्रूपं यच्छुक्लं तदपां यत्कृष्णं तदन्नस्यापागादग्नेरग्नित्वं वाचारम्भणं विकारो नामधेयं त्रीणि रूपाणीत्येव सत्यम्॥४॥

Whatever red form the lightning has, is the form of heat; whatever white, the form of water; whatever dark, the form of food. The lightninghood has gone from the lightning : the modification is merely a verbal distinction, a name. The reality is just "the three forms."

एतद्ध स्म वै तद्विद्वांꣳस आहुः पूर्वे महाशाला महाश्रोत्रिया न नोऽद्य कश्चनाश्रुतममतमविज्ञात-मुदाहरिष्यतीति ह्येभ्यो विदांचक्रुः॥५॥

Verily, it was just this that the great householders, greatly learned in sacred lore, knew when they said of old : "No one now will bring up to us what has not been heard of, what has not been thought of, what has not been understood." For from these [three forms] they knew [everything].

यदु रोहितमिवाभूदिति तेजसस्तद्रूपमिति तद्विदाञ्चक्रुर्यदु शुक्लमिवाभूदित्यपाꣳरूपमिति तद्विदाञ्चक्रुर्यदु कृष्णमिवाभूदित्यन्नस्य रूपमिति तद्विदांचक्रुः॥६॥

They knew that whatever appeared red was the form of heat. They knew that whatever appeared white was the form of water. They knew that whatever appeared dark was the form of food.

यद्विज्ञातमिवाभूदित्येतासामेव देवतानाꣳ समास इति तद्विदांचक्रुर्यथा नु खलु सोम्येमास्तिस्रो देवताः पुरुषं प्राप्य त्रिवृत्त्रिवृदेकैका भवति तन्मे विजानीहीति॥७॥

They knew that whatever appeared un-understood is a combination of just these divinities.

Verily, my dear, understand from me how each of these three divinities, upon reaching man, becomes threefold.

Part - 5

अन्नमशितं त्रेधा विधीयते तस्य यः स्थविष्ठो धातुस्तत्पुरीषं भवति यो मध्यमस्तन्माꣳसं योऽणिष्ठस्तन्मनः॥१॥

Food, when eaten, becomes divided into three parts. That which is its coarsest constituent becomes the feces; that which is medium, the flesh; that which is finest, the mind.

आपः पीतास्त्रेधा विधीयन्ते तासां यः स्थविष्ठो धातुस्तन्मूत्रं भवति यो मध्यमस्तल्लोहितं योऽणिष्ठः स प्राणः॥२॥

Water, when drunk, become divided into three parts. That which is its coarsest constituent, becomes the urine; that which is medium, the blood; that which is finest, the breath (*prāṇa*).

तेजोऽशितं त्रेधा विधीयते तस्य यः स्थविष्ठो धातुस्तदस्थि भवति यो मध्यमः स मज्जा योऽणिष्ठः सा वाक्॥३॥

Heat, when eaten, becomes divided into three parts. That which is its coarsest constituent, becomes bone; that which is medium, the marrow; that which is finest, the voice.

अन्नमयꣳ हि सोम्य मन आपोमयः प्राणस्तेजोमयी वागिति भूय एव मा भगवान्विज्ञापयत्विति तथा सोम्येति होवाच॥४॥

Uddālaka again said– For, my dear, the mind consists of food; the breath consists of water; the voice consists of heat.'

'Do you, sir, cause me to understand even more.' He said– 'So be it, my dear.'

Part - 6

दध्न: सोम्य मथ्यमानस्य योऽणिमा स ऊर्ध्व: समुदीषति तत्सर्पिर्भवति।।१।।

Uddālaka, the father of Śvetaketu again said– 'Of coagulated milk, my dear, when churned, that which is the finest essence all moves upward; it becomes butter.

एवमेव खलु सोम्यान्नस्याश्यमानस्य योऽणिमा स ऊर्ध्व: समुदीषति तन्मनो भवति।।२।।

Even so, verily, my dear, of food, when eaten, that which is the finest essence all moves upward; it becomes the mind.

अपाः सोम्य पीयमानानां योऽणिमा स ऊर्ध्व: समुदीषति स प्राणो भवति।।३।।

Of water, my dear, when drunk, that which is the finest essence all moves upward; it becomes the breath.

तेजस: सोम्याश्यमानस्य योऽणिमा स ऊर्ध्व: समुदीषति स वाग्भवति।।३।।

Of heat, my dear, when eaten, that which is the finest essence all moves upward; it becomes the voice.

अन्नमयःहि सोम्य मन आपोमय: प्राणस्तेजोमयी वागिति भूय एव मा भगवान्विज्ञापयत्विति तथा सोम्येति होवाच।।५।।

For, my dear, the mind consists of food; the breath consists of water; the voice consists of heat.'

'Do you, sir, cause me to understand even more.' He said– 'So be it, my dear.'

Part - 7

षोडशकल: सोम्य पुरुष: पञ्चदशाहानि माशी: काममप: पिबापोमय: प्राणो न पिबतो विच्छेत्स्यत इति।।१।।

'A person, my dear, consists of sixteen parts. For fifteen days do not eat; drink water at will. Breath, which consists of water, will not be cut off from one who drinks water.'

स ह पञ्चदशाहानि नाशाथ हैनमुपससाद किं ब्रवीमि भो इत्यृच: सोम्य यजूःषि सामानीति स होवाच न वै मा प्रतिभान्ति भो इति।।२।।

Then for fifteen days he did not eat. So then he approached him, saying, 'What shall I say, sir?'

'The Ṛg verses, my dear, the Yajus formulas, the Sāman chants.'

Then he said : 'Verily, they do not come to me, sir.'

तः होवाच यथा सोम्य महतोऽभ्याहितस्यैकोऽङ्गार: खद्योतमात्र: परिशिष्ट: स्यात्तेन ततोऽपि न बहु दहेदेवःसोम्य ते षोडशानां कलानामेका कलातिशिष्टा स्यात्तयैतर्हि वेदान्नानुभवस्यशानाथ मे विज्ञास्यसीति।।३।।

To him he then said : 'Just as, my dear, a single coal of the size of a fire-fly may be left over from a great kindled fire, but with it the fire would not thereafter burn much—so, my dear, of your sixteen parts a single sixteenth part may be left over, but with it you do not now apprehend the Vedas. Now eat, then you will understand from me.

स हाशाथ हैनमुपससाद तꣳह यत्किञ्च पप्रच्छ सर्वꣳह प्रतिपेदे॥४॥

Then he ate. So then he approached him. Then whatsoever he asked him, he answered everything.

तꣳहोवाच यथा सोम्य महतोऽभ्याहितस्यैकमङ्गारं खद्योतमात्रं परिशिष्टं तं तृणैरुपसमाधाय प्राज्वलयेत्तेन ततोऽपि बहु दहेत्॥५॥

Āruṇi said to him– 'Just as, my dear, one may, be covering it with straw, make a single coal of the size of a fire-fly that has been left over from a great kindled fire blaze up, and with it the fire would thereafter burn much—

एवꣳसोम्य ते षोडशानां कलानामेका कलातिशिष्टाभूत्सान्नेनोपसमाहिता प्राज्वालीत्तयैतर्हि वेदाननुभवस्यन्नमयꣳहि सोम्य मन आपोमयः प्राणस्तेजोमयी वागिति तद्धास्य विजज्ञाविति विजज्ञाविति॥६॥

So, my dear, of your sixteen parts a single sixteenth part has been left over. After having been covered with food it has blazed up. With it you now apprehend the Vedas; for, my dear, the mind consists of food, the breath consists of water, the voice consists of heat.'

Then he understood from him—yea, he understood.

Part - 8

Concerning sleep, hunger and thirst, and dying

उद्दालको हारुणिः श्वेतकेतुं पुत्रमुवाच स्वप्नान्तं मे सोम्य विजानीहीति यत्रैतत्पुरुषः स्वपिति नाम सता सोम्य तदा संपन्नो भवति स्वमपीतो भवति तस्मादेनꣳस्वपितीत्याचक्षते स्वꣳह्यपीतो भवति॥१॥

Then Uddālaka Āruṇi, said to his son Śvetaketu– Understand from me, my dear, the condition of sleep. When a person here sleeps (*svapiti*), as it is called, then, my dear, he has reached Being, he has gone to his own (*svamapīta*). Therefore they say of him "he sleeps"; for he has gone to his own.

स यथा शकुनिः सूत्रेण प्रबद्धो दिशं दिशं पतित्वान्यत्रायतनमलब्ध्वा बन्धनमेवोपश्रयत एवमेव खलु सोम्य तन्मनो दिशं दिशं पतित्वान्यत्रायतनमलब्ध्वा प्राणमेवोपश्रयते प्राणबन्धनꣳ हि सोम्य मन इति॥२॥

As a bird fastened with a string, after flying in this direction and in that without finding an abode elsewhere, rests down just upon its fastening—even so, my dear, the mind, after flying in this direction and I that without finding an abode elsewhere, rests down just upon breath; for the mind, my dear, has breath as its fastening.

अशनापिपासे मे सोम्य विजानीहीति तत्रैतत्पुरुषोऽशिशिषति नामाप एव तदशितं नयन्ते तद्यथा गोनायोऽश्वनायः पुरु षनाय इत्येव तदप आचक्षतेऽशनायेति तत्रैतच्छुङ्गमुत्पतितꣳ सोम्य विजानीहि नेदममूलं भविष्यतीति॥३॥

Āruṇi said– "O dear! Understand from me, my dear, hunger (*aśanā*) and thirst. When a person here is hungry (*aśiśiṣati*), as it is called, just water is leading off (*nayanti*) that which has been eaten (√*aś*). So, as they speak of "a leader-of-cows"(*go-nāya*), "a leader-of-horses" (*aśva-nāya*), "a leader-of-men" (*puruṣa-nāya*), so they speak of water as "a leader-of-food" (*aśa-nāya,* hunger).

On this point, my dear, understand that this [body] is a sprout which has sprung up. It will not be without a root.

तस्य क्व मूलꣲ स्यादन्यत्रान्नादेवमेव खलु सोम्यान्नेन शुङ्गेनापो मूलमन्विच्छाद्भिः सोम्य शुङ्गेन तेजोमूलमन्विच्छ तेजसा सोम्य शुङ्गेन सन्मूलमन्विच्छ सन्मूलाः सोम्येमाः सर्वाः प्रजाः सदायतनाः सत्प्रतिष्ठाः॥४॥

What else could its root be than food? Even so, my dear, with food for a sprout, look for water as the root. With water, my dear, as a sprout, look for heat as the root. With heat, my dear, as a sprout, look for Being as the root. All creatures here, my dear, have Being as their root, have Being as their home, have Being as their support.

अथ यत्रैतत्पुरुषः पिपासति नाम तेज एव तत्पीतं नयते तद्यथा गोनायोऽश्वनायः पुरुषनाय इत्येव तत्तेज आचष्ट उदन्येति तत्रैतदेव शुङ्गमुत्पतितꣲ सोम्य विजानीहि नेदममूलं भविष्यतीति॥५॥

Now, when a person here is thirsty, as it is called, just heat is leading off that which has been drunk. So, as they speak of "a leader-of-cows" (*go-nāya*), "a leader-of-horses" (*aśva-nāya*), "a leader-of-men" (*puruṣa-nāya*), so one speaks of heat as "a leader-of-water" (*uda-nāya*, thirst).

On this point, my dear, understand that this [body] is a sprout which has sprung up. It will not be without a root.

[The physiology of the modern age has already accepted the fact that the water carries the food to the every cell of the body and the water is carried by the bio-electricity in course of the process of metabolism. The Ṛṣi is explaining the same process by his own way.]

तस्य क्व मूलꣲ स्यादन्यत्राद्भ्योऽद्भिः सोम्य शुङ्गेन तेजो मूलमन्विच्छ तेजसा सोम्य शुङ्गेन सन्मूलमन्विच्छ सन्मूलाः सोम्येमाः सर्वाः प्रजाः सदायतनाः सत्प्रतिष्ठा यथा नु खलु सोम्येमास्तिस्रो देवताः पुरुषं प्राप्य त्रिवृत्त्रिवृदेकैका भवति तदुक्तं पुरस्तादेव भवत्यस्य सोम्य पुरुषस्य प्रयतो वाङ्मनसि संपद्यते मनः प्राणे प्राणस्तेजसि तेजः परस्यां देवतायाम्॥६॥

Where else could its root be than in water? With water, my dear, as a sprout, look for heat as the root. With heat, my dear, as a sprout, look for being as the root. All creatures here, my dear, have Being as their root, have being as their abode, have Being as their support.

But how, verily, my dear, each of these three divinities, upon reaching man, becomes threefold, has previously been said.

When a person here is deceasing, my dear, his voice goes into his mind; his mind, into his breath; his breath, into heat; the heat, into the highest divinity.

स य एषोऽणिमैतदात्म्यमिदꣳ सर्वं तत्सत्यꣳ स आत्मा तत्त्वमसि श्वेतकेतो इति भूय एव मा भगवान् विज्ञापयत्विति तथा सोम्येति होवाच॥७॥

That which is the finest essence— this whole world has that as its soul. That is Reality (*satya*). That is Ātman (Soul). That are you, Śvetaketu.'

'Do you, sir, cause me to understand even more.' He said– 'So be it, my dear.'

Part - 9

The unitary World-Soul, the immanent reality of all things and of man

यथा सोम्य मधु मधुकृतो निस्तिष्ठन्ति नानात्ययानां वृक्षाणाꣳरसान्समवहारमेकताꣳ रसं गमयन्ति॥१॥

ते यथा तत्र न विवेकं लभन्तेऽमुष्याहं वृक्षस्य रसोऽस्म्यमनुष्याहं वृक्षस्य रसोऽस्मीत्येवमेव खलु सोम्येमाः सर्वाः प्रजाः सति संपद्य न विदुः सति संपद्यामह इति॥२॥

Uddālaka again said to Śvetaketu– 'As the bees, my dear, prepare honey by collecting the essences of different trees and reducing the essence to a unity, as they are not able to discriminate "I am the essence of this tree," "I am the essence of that tree"—even so, indeed, my dear, all creatures here, though they reach Being, know not "We have reached Being."

त इह व्याघ्रो वा सिꣳहो वा वृको वा वराहो वा कीटो वा पतङ्गो वा दꣳशो वा मशको वा यद्यद्भवन्ति तदाभवन्ति॥३॥

Whatever they are in this world, whether tiger, the lion, the owl, the pig, the insects and the flies, wiper or the mosquitoes etc. get their birth as a chain reaction frequently in this world as a whole.

स य एषोऽणिमैतदात्म्यमिदꣳ सर्वं तत्सत्यꣳ स आत्मा तत्त्वमसि श्वेतकेतो इति भूय एव मा भगवान् विज्ञापयत्विति तथा सोम्येति होवाच॥४॥

That which is the finest essence—this whole world has that as its soul. That is Reality. That is Ātman (Soul). That are you, Śvetaketu."

'Do you, sir, cause me to understand even more.' He said– 'So be it, my dear.'

Part - 10

इमाः सोम्य नद्यः पुरस्तात्प्राच्यः स्यन्दन्ते पश्चात्प्रतच्यस्ताः समुद्रात्समुद्रमेवापियन्ति स समुद्र एव भवति ता यथा तत्र न विदुरियमहमस्मीति॥१॥

Uddālaka again explained– "O dear! 'These rivers flow, the eastern toward the east, the western toward the west (always move through their appropriate route). They go just from the ocean to the ocean. They become the ocean itself. As there they know not "I am this one," "I am that one"—

एवमेव खलु सोम्येमाः सर्वाः प्रजाः सत आगत्य न विदुः सत आगच्छामह इति त इह व्याघ्रो वा सिꣳहो वा वृको वा वराहो वा कीटो वा पतङ्गो वा दꣳशो वा मशको वा यद्यद्भवन्ति तदाभवन्ति॥२॥

Even so, indeed, my dear, all creatures here, though they have come forth from Being, know not "We have come forth from Being." Whatever they are in this world, tier, or lion, or wolf, or boar, or worm, or fly, or gnat, or mosquito, that they become.

स य एषोऽणिमैतदात्म्यमिदꣳ सर्वं तत्सत्यꣳ स आत्मा तत्त्वमसि श्वेतकेतो इति भूय एव मा भगवान् विज्ञापयत्विति तथा सोम्येति होवाच॥३॥

Āruṇi said– "O Śvetaketu! That which is the finest essence—this whole world has that as its soul. That is Reality. That is Ātman (Soul). That are you, Śvetaketu.'

'Do you, sir, cause me to understand even more.' 'So be it, my dear,' said he.

Part - 11

अस्य सोम्य महतो वृक्षस्य यो मूलेऽभ्याहन्याज्जीवन् स्रवेद्यो मध्येऽभ्याहन्याज्जीवन्स्रवेद्योऽग्रेऽभ्याहन्याज्जीवन्स्रवेत्स एष जीवेनात्मानुप्रभूतः पेपीयमानो मोदमानस्तिष्ठति॥१॥

O my dear! 'Of this great tree, if some one should strike at the root, it would bleed, but still live. If some one should strike at its middle, it would bleed, but still live. If some one should strike at its top, it would bleed, but still live. Being pervaded by Ātman (Soul), it continues to stand, eagerly drinking in moisture and rejoicing.

अस्य यदेकाꣳ शाखां जीवो जहात्यथ सा शुष्यति द्वितीयां जहात्यथ सा शुष्यति तृतीयां जहात्यथ सा शुष्यति सर्वं जहति सर्वः शुष्यत्येवमेव खलु सोम्य विद्धीति होवाच॥२॥

If the life leaves one branch of it, then it dries up. It leaves a second; then that dries up. It leaves a third; then that dries up. It leaves the whole; the whole dries up. Even so, indeed, my dear, understand,' said he.

जीवापेतं वाव किलेदं म्रियते न जीवो म्रियत इति स य एषोऽणिमैतदात्म्यमिदꣳ सर्वं तत्सत्यꣳ स आत्मा तत्त्वमसि श्वेतकेतो इति भूय एव मा भगवान् विज्ञापयत्विति तथा सोम्येति होवाच॥३॥

'Verily, indeed, when life has left it, this body dies. The life does not die.

That which is the finest essence—this whole world has that as its soul. That is Reality. That is Ātman (Soul). That are you, Śvetaketu.'

'Do you, sir, cause me to understand even more.' 'So be it, my dear', said he.

Part - 12

न्यग्रोधफलमत आहरेतीदं भगव इति भिन्द्धीति भिन्नं भगव इति किमत्र पश्यसीत्यण्व्य इवेमा धाना भगव इत्यासामङ्गैकां भिन्द्धीति भिन्ना भगव इति किमत्र पश्यसीति न किंचन भगव इति॥१॥

'Bring hither a fig from there.' 'Here it is, sir'.

'Divide it.' 'It is divided, sir.'

'What do you see there?' 'These rather (*iva*) fine seeds, sir.'

'Of these, please (*aṅga*), divide one.' 'It is divided, sir.'

'What do you see there?' 'Nothing at all, sir'.

तꣳ होवाच यं वै सोम्यैतमणिमानं न निभालयस एतस्य वै सोम्यैषोऽणिम्न एवं महान्यग्रोधस्तिष्ठति श्रद्धस्त्व सोम्येति।।२।।

Then Uddālaka said– "O dear! 'Verily, that finest essence which you do not perceive—verily, my dear, from that finest essence this great Nyagrodha (sacred fig) tree thus arises.

स य एषोऽणिमैतदात्म्यमिदꣳ सर्वं तत्सत्यꣳ स आत्मा तत्त्वमसि श्वेतकेतो इति भूय एव मा भगवान् विज्ञापयत्विति तथा सोम्येति होवाच।।३।।

He said– O Śvetaketu! Believe me, my dear,' 'that which is the finest essence—this whole world has that as its soul. That is Reality. That is Ātman (Soul). That are you, Śvetaketu.'

'Do you, sir, cause me to understand even more.' Uddālaka said– 'So be it, my dear.'

Part - 13

लवणमेतदुदकेऽवधायाथ मा प्रातरुपसीदथा इति स ह तथा चकार तꣳ होवाच यद्दोषा लवणमुदकेऽवाधा अङ्ग तदाहरेति तद्धावमृश्य न विवेद।।१।।

Uddālaka again explained to his son Śvetaketu– "O dear! 'Place this salt in the water. In the morning come unto me.' Then he did so.

Then he said to him : 'That salt you placed in the water last evening—please bring it hither.'

Then he grasped for it, but did not find it, as it was completely dissolved.

यथा विलीनमेवाङ्गास्यान्तादाचामेति कथमिति लवणमिति मध्यादाचामेति कथमिति लवणमित्यन्तादाचामेति कथमिति लवणमित्यभिप्रास्यैनदथ मोपसीदथा इति तद्ध तथा चकार तच्छश्वत्संवर्तते तꣳहोवाचात्र वाव किल सत्सोम्य न निभालयसेऽत्रैव किलेति।।२।।

'Please take a sip of it from this end,' said he. 'How is it?'– 'Salt'.

'Take a sip from the middle,' said he. 'How is it?'– 'Salt'.

'Take a sip from that end,' said he. 'How is it?'– 'Salt'.

'Set it aside. Then come unto me.'

He did so, saying, 'It is always the same.'

Then he said to him : 'Verily, indeed, my dear, you do not perceive Being here. Verily, indeed, it is here.

स य एषोऽणिमैतदात्म्यमिदꣳ सर्वं तत्सत्यꣳ स आत्मा तत्त्वमसि श्वेतकेतो इति भूय एव मा भगवान् विज्ञापयत्विति तथा सोम्येति होवाच।।३।।

Āruṇi told– "O dear! That which is the finest essence—this whole world has that as its soul. That is Reality. That is Ātman (Soul). That are you, Śvetaketu.'

'Do you sir, cause me to understand even more.'

'So be it, my dear,' said he.

Part - 14

यथा सोम्य पुरुषं गन्धारेभ्योऽभिनद्धाक्षमानीय तं ततोऽतिजने विसृजेत्स यथा तत्र प्राङ्वोदङ् वाधराङ्वा प्रत्यङ्वा प्रध्मायीताभिनद्धाक्ष आनीतोऽभिनद्धाक्षो विसृष्टः॥१॥

Uddālaka again explained– 'O dear! just as, one might lead away from the Gandhāras a person with his eyes bandaged, and then abandon him in an uninhabited place; as there he might be blown forth either to the east, to the north, or to the south, since he had been led off with his eyes bandaged and deserted with his eyes bandaged;

तस्य यथाभिनहनं प्रमुच्य प्रब्रूयादेतां दिशं गन्धारा एतां दिशं व्रजेति स ग्रामाद्ग्रामं पृच्छन् पण्डितो मेधावी गन्धारानेवोपसंपद्येतैवमेवेहाचार्यवान् पुरुषो वेद तस्य तावदेव चिरं यावन्न विमोक्ष्येऽथ संपत्स्य इति॥२॥

As, if one released his bandage and told him, "In that direction are the Gandhāras; go in that direction!" he would, if he were a sensible man, by asking [his way] from village to village, and being informed, arrive home at the Gandhāras—even so here on earth one who has a teacher knows : "I shall remain here only so long as I shall not be released [from the bonds of ignorance]. Then I shall arrive home."

स य एषोऽणिमैतदात्म्यमिदꣳ सर्वं तत्सत्यꣳ स आत्मा तत्त्वमसि श्वेतकेतो इति भूय एव मा भगवान् विज्ञापयत्विति तथा सोम्येति होवाच॥३॥

"O dear! That which is the finest essence—this whole world has that as its soul. That is Reality. That is Ātman (Soul). That are you, Śvetaketu.'

'Do you, sir, cause me to understand even more!' 'So be it, my dear,' said he.

Part - 15

पुरुषꣳ सोम्योतोपतापिनं ज्ञातव्यः पर्युपासते जानासि मां जानासि मामिति। तस्य यावन्न वाङ्मनसि संपद्यते मनः प्राणो प्राणस्तेजसि तेजः परस्यां देवतायं तावज्जानाति॥१॥

"O dear! 'Also, around a [deathly] sick person his kinsmen gather, and ask, "Do you know me?" "Do you know me?" So long as his voice does not go into his mind, his mind into his breath, his breath into heat, the heat into the highest divinity—so long he knows.

अथ यदास्य वाङ्मनसि संपद्यते मनः प्राणे प्राणस्तेजसि तेजः परस्यां देवतायामथ न जानाति॥२॥

Then when his voice goes into his mind, his mind into his breath, his breath into heat, the heat into the highest divinity —then he knows not.

स य एषोऽणिमैतदात्म्यमिदꣳ सर्वं तत्सत्यꣳ स आत्मा तत्त्वमसि श्वेतकेतो इति भूय एव मा भगवान् विज्ञापयत्विति तथा सोम्येति होवाच॥३॥

"O dear! That which is the finest essence—this whole world has that as its soul. That is Reality. That is Ātman (Soul). That are you, Śvetaketu.

'Do you, sir, cause me to understand even more.'

'So be it, my dear,' said he.

Part - 16

पुरुषꣳ सोम्योत हस्तगृहीतमानयन्त्यपहार्षीत्स्तेयमकार्षीत्परशुमस्मै तपतेति स यदि तस्य कर्ता भवति तत एवानृतमात्मानं कुरुते सोऽनृताभिसन्धोऽनृतेनात्मानमन्तर्धाय परशुं तप्तं प्रतिगृह्णाति स दह्यतेऽथ हन्यते॥१॥

'And also, my dear, they lead up a man seized by the hand, and call : "He has stolen! He has committed a theft! Heat the axe for him!" If he is the doer thereof, thereupon he makes himself (*ātmānam*) untrue. Speaking untruth, covering himself with untruth, he seizes hold of the heated ax and is burned. Then he is slain.

अथ यदि तस्याकर्ता भवति तत एव सत्यमात्मानं कुरुते स सत्याभिसन्धः सत्येनात्मानमन्तर्धाय परशुं तप्तं प्रतिगृह्णाति स न दह्यतेऽथ मुच्यते॥२॥

But if he is not the doer thereof, thereupon he makes himself true. Speaking truth, covering himself with truth, he seizes hold of the heated ax and is not burned. Then he is released.

स यथा तत्र नादाह्येतैतदात्म्यमिदꣳ सर्वं तत्सत्यꣳ स आत्मा तत्त्वमसि श्वेतकेतो इति तद्धास्य विजज्ञाविति विजज्ञाविति॥३॥

As in this case he would not be burned [because of the truth], so this whole world has that [truth] as its soul. That is Reality. That is Ātman (Soul). That are you, Śvetaketu.'

Then he understood it from him—yea, he understood.

Seventh Chapter

Part - 1

The instruction of Nārada by Sanatkumāra

Progressive worship of Brahman up to the Universal Soul

अधीहि भगव इति होपससाद सनत्कुमारं नारदस्तꣳ होवाच यद्वेत्थ तेन मोपसद ततस्त ऊर्ध्वं वक्ष्यामीति॥१॥

Oṁ! 'Teach me, sir,!'— with these words Nārada came to Sanatkumāra.

To him he then said : 'Come to me with what you know. Then I will tell you still further.'

स होवाचर्ग्वेदं भगवोऽध्येमि यजुर्वेदः सामवेदमाथर्वणं चतुर्थमितिहासपुराणं पञ्चमं वेदानां वेदं पित्र्यः राशिं दैवं निधिं वाकोवाक्यमेकायनं देवविद्यां ब्रह्मविद्यां भूतविद्यां क्षत्रविद्यां नक्षत्रविद्याः सर्पदेवजनविद्यामेतद्भगवोऽध्येमि॥२॥

Then he (Nārada) said to him– 'O Lord!, I know the Ṛgveda, the Yajurveda, the Sāmaveda, the Atharvaveda as the fourth, Legend and Ancient Lore (*itihāsa-purāṇa*) as the fifth, the Veda of the Vedas [i.e. Grammar], Propitiation of the Manes, mathematics, Augury (*daiva*), Chronology, Logic, Polity, the Science of the Gods (*deva-vidyā*), the Science of Sacred Knowledge (*brahma-vidyā*), Demonology (*bhūta-vidyā*), the Science of Rulership (*kṣatra-vidyā*), Astrology (*nakṣatra-vidyā*), the Science of Snake-charming, and the Fine Arts (*sarpa-devajana-vidyā*). This, sir, I know.

सोऽहं भगवो मन्त्रविदेवास्मि नात्मविच्छुतः ह्येव मे भगवद्दृशेभ्यस्तरति शोकमात्मविदिति सोऽहं भगवः शोचामि तं मा भगवाञ्छोकस्य पारं तारयत्विति तःहोवाच यद्वै किंचैतदध्यगीष्ठा नामैवैतत्॥३॥

"O Lord! Such a one am I, sir, knowing the sacred sayings (*mantra-vid*), but not knowing the Soul (Ātman). It has been heard by me from those who are like you, sir, that he who knows the Soul (Ātman) crosses over sorrow. Such a sorrowing one am I, sir, Do you sir, cause me, who am such a one, to cross over to the other side of sorrow.'

To him he then said : 'Verily, whatever you have here learned, verily, that is mere name (*nāman*).

नाम वा ऋग्वेदो यजुर्वेदः सामवेद आथर्वणश्चतुर्थ इतिहासपुराणः पञ्चमो वेदानां वेदः पित्र्यो राशिर्दैवो निधिर्वाकोवाक्यमेकायनं देवविद्या ब्रह्मविद्या भूतविद्या क्षत्रविद्या नक्षत्रविद्या सर्पदेवजनविद्या नामैवेतन्नामोपास्स्वेति॥४॥

Verily, a Name are the Ṛgveda, the Yajurveda, the Sāmaveda, the Atharvaveda as the fourth, Legend and Ancient Lore (*itihāsa-purāṇa*) as the fifth, the Veda of the Vedas [i.e. Grammar], Propitiation of the Manes, Mathematics, Augury (*daiva*), Chronology, Logic, Polity, the Science of the Gods (*deva-vidyā*), the Science of Sacred Knowledge (*brahma-vidyā*), Demonology (*bhūta-vidyā*), the Science of Rulership (*kṣatra-vidyā*), Astrology (*nakṣatra-vidyā*), the Science of Snake-charming, and the Fine Arts (*sarpa-devajana-vidyā*). This is mere Name. Reverence Name.

स यो नाम ब्रह्मेत्युपास्ते यावन्नाम्नो गतं तत्रास्य यथाकामचारो भवति यो नाम ब्रह्मेत्युपास्तेऽस्ति भगवो नाम्नो भूय इति नाम्नो वाव भूयोऽस्तीति तन्मे भगवान्ब्रवीत्विति॥५॥

He who reverences Name as Brahma—as far as Name goes, so far he has unlimited freedom, he who reverences Name as Brahma.'

'Is there, sir, more than Name?'

'There is, assuredly, more than Name.'

'Do you, sir, tell me it.'

Part - 2

वाग्वाव नाम्नो भूयसी वाग्वा ऋग्वेदं विज्ञापयति यजुर्वेदꣳ सामवेदमाथर्वणं चतुर्थमितिहापुराणं पञ्चमं वेदानां वेद पित्र्यं राशिं दैवं निधिं वाकोवाक्यमेकायनं देवविद्यां ब्रह्मविद्यां भूतविद्यां क्षत्रविद्यां नक्षत्रविद्याꣳ सर्पदेवजनविद्यां दिवं च पृथिवीं च वायुं चाकाशं चापश्च तेजश्च देवाꣳश्च मनुष्याꣳश्च पशूꣳश्च वयाꣳसि च तृणवनस्पतीञ्छ्वापदान्याकीटपतङ्गपिपीलिकं धर्मं चाधर्मं च सत्यं चानृतं च साधु चासाधु च हृदयज्ञं चाहृदयज्ञं च यद्वै वाङ्नाभविष्यन्न धर्मो नाधर्मो व्यज्ञापयिष्यन्न सत्यं नानृतं न साधु नासाधु न हृदयज्ञो नाहृदयज्ञो वागेवैतत्सर्वं विज्ञापयति वाचमुपास्स्वेति॥१॥

(Sanatkumāra said) 'Speech (*vāc*), assuredly, is more than Name. Speech, verily, makes knows the Ṛgveda, the Yajurveda, the Sāmaveda, the Atharva-vedas the fourth, Legend and Ancient Lore as the fifth, the Veda of the Vedas [i.e. Grammar], Propitiation of the Manes, Mathematics, Augury, Chronology, Logic, Polity, the Science of the Gods, the Science of Sacred Knowledge, Demonology, the Science of Rulership, Astrology, the Science of Snake-charming, and the Fine Arts, as well as heaven and earth, wind and space, water and heat, gods and men, beasts and birds, grass and trees, animals together with worms, flies, and ants, right and wrong, true and false, good and bad, pleasant and unpleasant. Verily, if there were no speech, neither right nor wrong would be known, neither true nor false, neither good nor bad, neither pleasant nor unpleasant. Speech, indeed, makes all this known. Reverence Speech.

स यो वाचं ब्रह्मेत्युपास्ते यावद्वाचो गतं तत्रास्य यथाकामचारो भवति यो वाचं ब्रह्मेत्युपास्तेऽस्ति भगवो वाचो भूय इति वाचो वाव भूयोऽस्तीति तन्मे भगवान्ब्रवीत्विति॥२॥

He who reverences Speech as Brahman—as far as Speech goes, so far he has unlimited freedom, he who reverences Speech as Brahman.'

'Is there, sir, more than Speech?'

'There is, assuredly, more than Speech.'

'Do you, sir, tell me it.'

Part - 3

मनो वाव वाचो भूयो यथा वै द्वे वामलके द्वे वा कोले द्वौ वाक्षौ मुष्टिरनुभवत्येवं वाचं च नाम च मनोऽनुभवति स यदा मनसा मनस्यति मन्त्रानधीयीयेत्यथाधीते कर्माणि कुर्वीयेत्यथ कुरुते पुत्राꣳश्च पशूꣳश्चेच्छेयेत्यथेच्छत इमं च लोकममुं चेच्छेयेत्यतेच्छते मनो ह्यात्मा मनो हि लोको मनो हि ब्रह्म मन उपास्स्वेत॥१॥

Sanatkumāra says–

'Mind (*manas*), assuredly, is more than Speech. Verily, as the closed hand compasses two acorns, or two kola-berries, or two dice-nuts (belleric myrobalam), so Mind compasses both Speech and Name. When through Mind one has in mind "I wish to learn the sacred sayings (*mantra*)," then he learns them; "I wish to perform sacred works (*karma*)," then he performs them; "I would desire sons and cattle," then he desired them; "I would desire this world and the yonder," then he desires them. Truly the self (*ātman*) is Mind. Truly, the world (*loka*) is Mind. Truly, Brahman is Mind.

स यो मनो ब्रह्मेत्युपास्ते यावन्मनसो गतं तत्रास्य यथाकामचारो भवति यो मनो ब्रह्मेत्युपास्तेऽस्ति भगवो मनसो भूय इति मनसो वाव भूयोऽस्तीति तन्मे भगवान्ब्रवीत्विति।।२।।

He who reverences Mind as Brahma—as far as Mind goes, so far he has unlimited freedom, he who reverences Mind as Brahma.'

'Is there, sir, more than Mind?'

'There is, assuredly, more than Mind'.

'Do you, sir, tell me it.'

Part - 4

संकल्पो वाव मनसो भूयान्यदा वै संकल्पयतेऽथ मनस्यत्यथ वाचमीरयति तामु नाम्नीरयति नाम्नि मन्त्रा एकं भवन्ति मन्त्रेषु कर्माणि।।१।।

(Sanatkumāra said) 'Conception (*saṁkalpa*), assuredly, is more than Mind. Verily, when one forms a Conception, then he has in Mind, then he utters Speech, and he utters it in Name. The sacred sayings (*mantra*) are included in Name and sacred works in the sacred sayings.

तानि ह वा एतानि संकल्पैकायनानि संकल्पात्मकानि संकल्पे प्रतिष्ठितानि समक्लृपतां द्यावापृथिवी समकल्पेतां वायुश्चाकाशं च समकल्पन्तापश्च तेजश्च तेषाᳬ संक्लृप्त्यै वर्षᳬ संकल्पते वर्षस्य संक्लृप्त्या अन्नᳬसंकल्पतेऽन्नस्य संक्लृप्त्यै प्राणा: संकल्पन्ते प्राणानाᳬ संक्लृप्त्यै मन्त्रा: संकल्पन्ते मन्त्राणाᳬ संक्लृप्त्यै कर्माणि संकल्पन्ते कर्मणाᳬ संक्लृप्त्यै लोक: संकल्पते लोकस्य संक्लृप्त्यै सर्वᳬ संकल्पते स एष संकल्प: संकल्पमुपास्स्वेति।।२।।

(O Nārada!) Verily, these have Conception as their union-point, have Conception as their soul, are established on Conception. Heaven and earth were formed through Conception. Wind and space were formed through Conception. Water and heat were formed through Conception. Through their having been formed, rain becomes formed. Through rain having been formed, food becomes formed. Through food having been formed, living creatures (*prāṇa*) become formed. Through living creatures having been formed, sacred sayings (*mantra*) become formed. Through sacred sayings having been formed, sacred works (*karma*) become [per]formed. Through sacred works having been [per]formed, the world becomes formed. Through the world having been formed, everything becomes formed. Such is Conception. Reverence Conception.

स य: संकल्पं ब्रह्मेत्युपास्ते क्लृप्तान्वै स लोकान् ध्रुवान् ध्रुव: प्रतिष्ठितान् प्रतिष्ठितोऽव्यथमानानव्यथमानोऽभिसिध्यति यावत्संकल्पस्य गतं तत्रास्य यथाकामचारो भवति य: संकल्पं ब्रह्मेत्युपास्तेऽस्ति भगव: संकल्पाद्भूय इति संकल्पाद्वाव भूयोऽस्तीति तन्मे भगवान्ब्रवीत्विति।।३।।

(O Nārada!) He who reverences Conception as Brahma—he, verily, attains the Conception-worlds; himself being enduring, the enduring worlds; himself established, the established worlds; himself unwavering, the unwavering worlds As far as Conception goes, so far he has unlimited freedom, he who reverences Conception as Brahma.'

'Is there, sir, more than Conception?'

'There is, assuredly, more than Conception.'

'Do you sir, tell me it.'

Part - 5

चित्तं वाव संकल्पाद्भूयो यदा वै चेतयतेऽथ मनस्यत्यथ वाचमीरयति तामु नाम्नीरयति नाम्नि मन्त्रा एकं भवन्ति मन्त्रेषु कर्माणि॥१॥

(O Nārada!) 'Thought (*citta*), assuredly, is more than Conception. Verily, when one thinks, then he forms a conception, then he has in Mind, then he utters Speech, and he utters it in Name. The sacred sayings (*mantra*) are included in Name and sacred works in the sacred sayings.

तानि ह वा एतानि चित्तैकायनानि चित्तात्मानि चित्ते प्रतिष्ठितानि तस्माद्यद्यपि बहुविदचित्तो भवति नायमस्तीत्येवैनमाहुर्यदयं वेद यद्वा अयं विद्वान्नेत्थमचित्तः स्यादित्यथ यद्यल्पविच्चित्तवान्भवति तस्मा एवोत शुश्रूषन्ते चित्तꣳह्येवैषामेकायनं चित्तमात्मा चित्तं प्रतिष्ठा चित्तमुपास्स्वेति॥२॥

(O Nārada!) Verily, these things have Thought as their union-point, have Thought as their soul, are established on Thought. Therefore, even if one who knows much is without Thought, people say of him : "He is not anybody, whatever he knows! Verily, if he did know, he would not be so without Thought!" On the other hand, if one who knows little possesses Thought, people are desirous of listening to him. Truly, indeed, Thought is the union-point, Thought is the soul (*ātman*), Thought is the support of these things. Reverence Thought.

स यश्चित्तं ब्रह्मेत्युपास्ते चित्तान्वै स लोकान् ध्रुवान् ध्रुवः प्रतिष्ठितान् प्रतिष्ठितोऽव्यथमानानव्यथमानोऽभिसिद्ध्यति यावच्चित्तस्य गतं तत्रास्य यथाकामचारो भवति यश्चित्तं ब्रह्मेत्युपास्तेऽस्ति भगवश्चित्ताद्भूय इति चित्ताद्वाव भूयोऽस्तीति तन्मे भगवान्ब्रवीत्विति॥३॥

O Nārada! He who reverences Thought as Brahma—he, verily, attains the Thought-worlds; himself being enduring, the enduring worlds; himself being established, the established worlds; himself being unwavering, the unwavering worlds. As far as Thought goes, so far he has unlimited freedom, he who reverences Thought as Brahma.'

'Is there, sir, more than Thought?'

'There is, assuredly, more than Thought.'

'Do you, sir, tell me it.'

Part - 6

ध्यानं वाव चित्ताद्भूयो ध्यायतीव पृथिवी ध्यायतीवान्तरिक्षं ध्यायतीव द्यौर्ध्यायन्तीवापो ध्यायन्तीव पर्वता ध्यायन्तीव देवमनुष्यास्तस्माद्य इह मनुष्याणां महत्तां प्राप्नुवन्ति ध्यानापादाꣳशा इवैव ते भवन्त्यथ येऽल्पाः कलहिनः पिशुना उपवादिनस्तेऽथ ये प्रभवो ध्यानापादाꣳशा इवैव ते भवन्ति ध्यानमुपास्स्वेति॥१॥

(O Nārada!) 'Meditation (*dhyāna*), assuredly, is more than Thought. The earth meditates, as it were (*iva*). The atmosphere meditates, as it were. The heaven meditates, as it were. Water meditates, as it were. Mountains meditate, as it were. Gods and men meditate, as it were. Therefore whoever among men here attain greatness—they have, as it were, a part of the reward of meditation. Now, those who are small are quarrellers, tale-bearers, slanderers. But those who are superior—they have, as it were, a part of the reward of Meditation. Reverence Meditation.

स यो ध्यानं ब्रह्मेत्युपास्ते यावद्ध्यानस्य गतं तत्रास्य यथाकामचारो भवति यो ध्यानं ब्रह्मेत्युपास्तेऽस्ति भगवो ध्यानाद्भूय इति ध्यानाद्वाव भूयोऽस्तीति तन्मे भगवान्ब्रवीत्विति॥२॥

(O Nārada!) He who reverences Meditation as Brahma—as far as Meditation goes, so far he has unlimited freedom, he who reverences Meditation as Brahma.'

'Is there, sir, more than Meditation?'

'There is, assuredly, more than Meditation'.

'Do you, sir, tell me it.'

Part - 7

विज्ञानं वाव ध्यानाद्भूयो विज्ञानेन वा ऋग्वेदं विजानाति यजुर्वेदꣳसामवेदमाथर्वणं चतुर्थमितिहासपुराणं पञ्चमं वेदानां वेदं पित्र्यꣳ राशिं दैवं निधिं वाकोवाक्यमेकायनं देवविद्यां ब्रह्मविद्यां भूतविद्यां क्षत्रविद्यां नक्षत्रविद्याꣳ सर्पदेवजनविद्यां दिवं च पृथिवीं च वायुं चाकाशं चापश्च तेजश्च देवाꣳश्च मनुष्याꣳश्च पशूꣳश्च वयाꣳसि च तृणवनस्पतीञ्छ्वापदान्याकीटपतङ्गपिपीलिकं धर्मं चाधर्मं च सत्यं चानृतं च साधु चासाधु च हृदयज्ञं चाहृदयज्ञं चान्नं च रसं चेमं च लोकममुं च विज्ञानेनैव विजानाति विज्ञानमुपास्स्वेति॥१॥

(O Nārada!) 'Understanding (*vijñāna*), assuredly, is more than Meditation. Verily, by Understanding one understands the Ṛgveda, the Yajurveda, the Sāmaveda, the Atharvaveda as the fourth, Legend and Ancient Lore (*itihāsa-purāṇa*) as the fifth, the Veda of the Vedas [i.e. Grammar], Propitiation of the Manes, Mathematics, Augury (*daiva*), Chronology, Logic, Polity, the Science of the Gods (*deva-vidyā*), the Science of Sacred Knowledge (*brahma-vidyā*), Demonology (*bhūta-vidyā*), the Science of Rulership (*kṣetra-vidyā*), Astrology (*nakṣatra-vidyā*), the Science of Snake-charming, and the Fine Arts (*sarpa-devajana-vidyā*), as well as heaven and earth, wind and space, water and heat, gods and men, beasts and birds, grass and trees, animals together with worms, flies, and ants, right and wrong, true and false, good and bad, pleasant and unpleasant, food and drink, this world and the yonder—all this one understands just with Understanding. Reverence Understanding.

स यो विज्ञानं ब्रह्मेत्युपास्ते विज्ञानवतो वै स लोकाञ्ज्ञानवतोऽभिसिद्ध्यति यावद्विज्ञानस्य गतं तत्रास्य यथाकामचारो भवति यो विज्ञानं ब्रह्मेत्युपास्तेऽस्ति भगवो विज्ञानाद्भूय इति विज्ञानाद्वाव भूयोऽस्तीति तन्मे भगवान्ब्रवीत्विति॥२॥

He who reverences Understanding as Brahma—he, verily, attains the worlds of Understanding (*vijñāna*) and of Knowledge (*jñāna*). As far as Understanding goes, so far he has unlimited freedom, he who reverences Understanding as Brahma.'

'Is there, sir, more than Understanding?'

'There is, assuredly, more than Understanding.'

'Do you, sir, tell me it.'

Part - 8

बलं वाव विज्ञानाद्भूयोऽपि ह शतं विज्ञानवतामेको बलवानाकम्पयते। स यदा बली भवत्यथोत्थाता भवत्युत्तिष्ठन्परिचरिता भवति परिचरन्नुपसत्ता भवत्युपसीदन्द्रष्टा भवति श्रोता भवति मन्ता भवति बोद्धा भवति कर्ता भवति विज्ञाता भवति। बलेन वै पृथिवी तिष्ठति बलेनान्तरिक्षं बलेन द्यौर्बलेन पर्वता बलेन देवमनुष्या बलेन पशवश्च वयाꣳसि च तृणवनस्पतयः श्वापदान्याकीटपतङ्गपिपीलकं बलेन लोकस्तिष्ठति बलमुपास्स्वेति॥१॥

(O Nārada!) 'Strength (*bala*), assuredly, is more than Understanding. Indeed, one man of Strength causes a hundred men of Understanding to tremble. When one is becoming strong, he becomes a rising man. Rising, he becomes an attendant. Attending, he becomes attached as a pupil. Attached as a pupil, he becomes a seer, he becomes a hearer, he becomes a thinker, he becomes a perceiver, he becomes a doer, he becomes an understander. By Strength, verily, the earth stands; by Strength, the atmosphere; by Strength, the sky; by Strength, the mountains; by Strength, gods and men; by Strength, beasts and birds, grass and trees, animals together with worms, flies, and ants. By Strength the world stands. Reverence Strength.

स यो बलं ब्रह्मेत्युपास्ते यावद्बलस्य गतं तत्रास्य यथाकामचारो भवति यो बलं ब्रह्मेत्युपास्तेऽस्ति भगवो बलाद्भूय इति बलाद्वाव भूयोऽस्तीति तन्मे भगवान्ब्रवीत्विति॥२॥

He who reverences Strength as Brahma—as far as Strength goes, so far he has unlimited freedom, he who reverences Strength as Brahma.'

'Is there, sir, more than Strength?'

'There is, assuredly, more than Strength.'

'Do you, sir, tell me it.'

Part - 9

अन्नं वाव बलाद्भूयस्तस्माद्यद्यपि दशरात्रीर्नाश्नीयाद्यद्युह जीवेदथवाद्रष्टाश्रोतामन्ताबोद्धाकर्ताविज्ञाता भवत्यथान्नस्यायै द्रष्टा भवति बोद्धा भवति कर्ता भवति विज्ञाता भवत्यन्नमुपास्स्वेति॥१॥

'Food (*anna*), assuredly, is more than Strength. Therefore, if one should not eat for ten days, even though he might live, yet verily he becomes a non-seer, a non-hearer, a non-thinker, a non-perceiver, a non-doer, a non-understander. But on the entrance of food he becomes a seer, he becomes a hearer, he becomes a thinker, he becomes a perceiver, he becomes a doer, he becomes an understander. Reverence Food.

स योऽन्नं ब्रह्मेत्युपास्तेऽन्नवतो वै स लोकान्पानवतोऽभिसिद्ध्यति यावदन्नस्य गतं तत्रास्य यथाकामचारो भवति योऽन्नं ब्रह्मेत्युपास्तेऽस्ति भगवोऽन्नाद्भूय इत्यन्नाद्वाव भूयोऽस्तीति तन्मे भगवान्ब्रवीत्विति॥२॥

He who reverences Food as Brahma—he, verily, attains the worlds of Food and Drink. As far as food goes, so far he has unlimited freedom, he who reverences Food as Brahma.'

'Is there, sir, more than Food?' 'There is, assuredly, more than Food.'

'Do you, sir, tell me it.'

Part - 10

आपो वावान्नाद्भूयस्यस्तस्माद्यदा सुवृष्टिर्न भवति व्याधीयन्ते प्राणा अन्नं कनीयो भविष्यतीत्यथ यदा सुवृष्टिर्भवत्यानन्दिनः प्राण भवन्त्यन्नं बहु भविष्यतीत्याप एवेमा मूर्ता येयं पृथिवी यदन्तरिक्षं यद् द्यौर्यत्पर्वता यद्देवमनुष्या यत्पशवश्च वयाꣳसि च तृणवनस्पतयः श्वापदान्याकीटपतङ्गपिपीलकमाप एवेमा मूर्ता अप उपास्स्वेति॥१॥

(O Nārada!) 'Water (*āpas*), verily, is more than Food. Therefore, when there is not a good rain, living creatures (*prāṇa*) sicken with the thought, "Food will become scarce." But when there is a good rain, living creatures become happy with the thought, "Food will become abundant." It is just Water solidified that is this earth, that is the atmosphere, that is the sky, that is gods and men, beasts and birds, grass and trees, animals together with worms, flies and ants; all these are just Water solidified. Reverence Water.

स योऽपो ब्रह्मेत्युपास्त आप्नोति सर्वान्कामाꣳस्तृप्तिमान्भवति यावदपां गतं तत्रास्य यथाकामचारो भवति। योऽपो ब्रह्मेत्युपास्तेऽस्ति भगवोऽद्भ्यो भूय इत्यद्भ्यो वाव भूयोऽस्तीति तन्मे भगवान्ब्रवीत्विति॥२॥

He who reverences Water (*āpas*) as Brahma obtains (*āpnoti*) all his desires and becomes satisfied. As far as Water goes, so far he has unlimited freedom, he who reverences Water as Brahma.'

'Is there, sir, more than Water?' 'There is, assuredly, more than Water.'

'Do you sir, tell me it.'

Part - 11

तेजो वावाद्भ्यो भूयस्तद्वा एतद्वायुमागृह्याकाशमभितपति तदाहुर्निशोचति नितपति वर्षिष्यति वा इति तेज एव तत्पूर्वं दर्शयित्वाथापः सृजते तदेतदूर्ध्वाभिश्च तिरश्चीभिश्च विद्युद्भिराह्रादाश्चरन्ति तस्मादाहुर्विद्योतते स्तनयति वर्षिष्यति वा इति तेज एव तत्पूर्वं दर्शयित्वाथापः सृजते तेज उपास्स्वेति॥१॥

'Heat (*tejas*), verily, is more than Water. That, verily, seizes hold of the wind, and heats the ether (*ākāśa*). Then people say : "It is hot! It is burning hot! Surely it will rain!" Heat indeed first indicates this, and then lets out water. So, with lightnings darting up and across the sky, thunders roll. Therefore people say : "It lightens! It thunders! Surely it will rain!" Heat indeed first indicates this, and then lets out water. Reverence Heat.

स यस्तेजो ब्रह्मेत्युपास्ते तेजस्वी वै स तेजस्वतो लोकान्भास्वतोऽपहततमस्कानभिसिद्ध्यति यावत्तेजसो गतं तत्रास्य तथाकामचारो भवति यस्तेजो ब्रह्मेत्युपास्तेऽस्ति भगवस्तेजसो भूय इति तेजसो वाव भूयोऽस्तीति तन्मे भगवान्ब्रवीत्विति॥२॥

He who reverences Heat as Brahma—he, verily, being glowing, attains glowing, shining worlds freed from darkness. As far as Heat goes, so far he has unlimited Freedom, he who reverences Heat as Brahma.'

'Is there, sir, more than Heat?' 'There is, assuredly, more than Heat.'

'Do you, sir, tell me it.'

Part - 12

आकाशो वाव तेजसो भूयानाकाशे वै सूर्याचन्द्रमसावुभौ विद्युन्नक्षत्राण्यग्निराकाशेनाह्वयत्याकाशेन श्रणोत्याकाशेन प्रतिश्रृणोत्याकाशे रमत आकाशे न रमत आकाशे जायत आकाशमभिजायत आकाशमुपास्स्वेति॥१॥

'Space (*ākāśa*), assuredly, is more than Heat. In Space, verily, are both sun and moon lightning stars and fire. Through Space one calls out; through Space one hears; through Space one answers. In Space one enjoys himself; in Space one does not enjoy himself. In Space one is born; unto Space one is born. Reverence Space.

स य आकाशं ब्रह्मेत्युपास्त आकाशवतो वै स लोकान्प्रकाशवतोऽसंबाधानुरुगायवतोऽभिसिद्ध्यति यावदाकाशस्य गतं तत्रास्य यथाकामचारो भवति य आकाशं ब्रह्मेत्युपास्तेऽस्ति भगव आकाशाद्भूय इत्याकाशाद्वाव भूयोऽस्तीति तन्मे भगवान्ब्रवीत्विति॥२॥

(O Nārada!) He who reverences Space as Brahma—he, verily, attains spacious, gleaming, unconfined, wide-extending worlds. As far as Space goes, so far he has unlimited freedom, he who reverences Space as Brahma.'

'Is there, sir, more than Space?' 'There is, assuredly, more than Space.'

'Do you, sir, tell me it.'

Part -13

स्मरो वावाकाशाद्भूयस्तस्माद्यद्यपि बहव आसीरन्न स्मरन्तो नैव ते कंचन श्रृणुयुर्न मन्वीरन्न विजानीरन् यदा वाव ते स्मरेयुरथ श्रृणुयुरथ मन्वीरन्नथ विजानीरन् स्मरेण वै पुत्रान्विजानाति स्मरेण पशून् स्मरमुपास्स्वेति॥१॥

O Nārada! 'Memory (*smara*), verily, is more than Space. Therefore, even if many not possessing Memory should be assembled, indeed they would not hear any one at all, they would not think, they would not understand. But assuredly, if they should remember, then they would hear, then they would think, then they would understand. Through Memory, assuredly, one discerns his children; through Memory, his cattle. Reverence Memory.

स यः स्मरं ब्रह्मेत्युपास्ते यावत्स्मरस्य गतं तत्रास्य यथाकामचारो भवति यः स्मरं ब्रह्मेत्युपास्तेऽस्ति भगवः स्मराद्भूय इति स्मराद्वाव भूयोऽस्तीति तन्मे भगवान्ब्रवीत्विति।।२।।

He who reverence Memory as Brahma—as far as Memory goes, so far he has unlimited freedom, he who reverence memory as Brahma.'

'Is there, sir, more than Memory?' 'There is, assuredly, more than Memory.'

'Do you, sir, tell me it.'

Part - 14

आशा वाव स्मराद्भूयस्याशेद्धो वै स्मरो मन्त्रानधीते कर्माणि कुरुते पुत्रांश्च पशूंश्चेच्छत इमं च लोकममुं चेच्छत आशामुपास्स्वेति।।१।।

O Nārada! 'Hope (*āśā*), assuredly, is more than Memory. When kindled by Hope, verily, Memory learns the sacred sayings (*mantra*); [kindled by Hope] one performs sacred works (*karma*), longs for sons and cattle, for this world and the yonder. Reverence Hope.

स य आशां ब्रह्मेत्युपास्त आशयास्य सर्वे कामाः समृद्ध्यन्त्यमोघा हास्याशिषो भवन्ति यावदाशाया गतं तत्रास्य यथाकामचारो भवति य आशां ब्रह्मेत्युपास्तेऽस्ति भगव आशाया भूय इत्याशाया वाव भूयोऽस्तीति तन्मे भगवान् ब्रवीत्विति।।२।।

He who reverences Hope as Brahma—through Hope all his desires prosper, his wishes are not unavailing. As far as Hope goes, so far he has unlimited freedom, he who reverences Hope as Brahma.'

'Is there, sir, more than Hope?'

'There is, assuredly, more than Hope.'

'Do you, sir, tell me it.'

Part - 15

प्राणो वा आशाया भूयान्यथा वा अरा नाभौ समर्पिता एवमस्मिन् प्राणो सर्वꣳ समर्पितं प्राणः प्राणेन याति प्राणः प्राणं ददाति प्राणाय ददाति। प्राणो ह पिता प्राणो माता प्राणो भ्राता प्राणः स्वसा प्राण आचार्यः प्राणो ब्राह्मणः।।१।।

(O Nārada!) 'Life ((*prāṇa*, breath), verily, is more than Hope. Just as, verily, the spokes are fastened in the hub, so on this vital breath everything is fastened. Life (*prāṇa*) goes on with vital breath (*prāṇa*). Vital breath (*prāṇa*) gives life (*prāṇa*); it gives [life] to a living creature (*prāṇa*). One's father is vital breath; one's mother, vital breath; one's brother, vital breath; one's sister, vital breath; one's teacher (*ācārya*), vital breath; a Brahman is vital breath.

स यदि पितरं वा मातरं वा भ्रातरं वा स्वसारं वाचार्यं वा ब्राह्मणं वा किंचिद् भृशमिव प्रत्याह धिक्त्वाऽस्त्वित्येवैनमाहुः पितृहा वै त्वमसि मातृहा वै त्वमसि भ्रातृहा वै त्वमसि स्वसृहा वै त्वमस्याचार्यहा वै त्वमसि ब्राह्मणहा वै त्वमसीति॥२॥

If one answers harshly, as it were (*iva*), a father, or a mother, or a brother, or a sister, or a teacher, or a Brahman, people say to him : "Shame on you! Verily, you are a slayer of your father! Verily, you are a slayer of your mother! Verily, you are a slayer of your brother! Verily, you are a slayer of your sister! Verily, you are a slayer of your teacher! Verily, you are a slayer of a Brahman!"

अथ यद्यप्येनानुत्क्रान्तप्राणाञ्छूलेन समासं व्यतिषं दहेन्नैवैनं ब्रूयुः पितृहासीति न मातृमासीति न भ्रातृहासीति न स्वसृहासीति नाचार्यहासीति न ब्राह्मणहासीति॥३॥

But if, when the vital breath has departed from them, one should even shove them with a poker and burn up every bit of them, people would not say to him : "You are a slayer of your father," nor "You are a slayer of your mother," nor "You are a slayer of your brother," nor "You are a slayer of your sister," nor "You are a slayer of your teacher," nor "You are a slayer of a Brahman."

प्राणो ह्येवैतानि सर्वाणि भवति स वा एषा एवं पश्यन्नेवं मन्वान एवं विजानन्नतिवादी भवति तं चेद्ब्रूयुरतिवाद्यसीत्यतिवाद्यस्मीति ब्रूयान्नापह्नुवीत॥४॥

For indeed, vital breath (*prāṇa*) is all these things. Verily, he who sees this, thinks this, understands this, becomes a superior speaker. Even if people should say to him "You are a superior speaker," he should say "I am a superior speaker." He should not deny it.

Part - 16

एष तु वा अतिवदति यः सत्येनातिवदति सोऽहं भगवः सत्येनातिवदानीति सत्यं त्वेव विजिज्ञासितव्यमिति सत्यं भगवो विजिज्ञास इति॥१॥

(O Nārada!) But he, verily, speaks superiorly who speaks superiorly with Truth (*satya*).'

'Then I, sir, would speak superiorly with Truth.'

'But one must desire to understand the Truth.'

'Sir, I desire to understand the Truth.'

Part - 17

यदा वै विजानात्यथ सत्यं वदति नाविजानन् सत्यं वदति विजानन्नेव सत्यं वदति विज्ञानं त्वेव विजिज्ञासितव्यमिति विज्ञानं भगवो विजिज्ञास इति॥१॥

(Sanatkumāra said "O Nārada!") 'Verily, when one understands, then he speaks the Truth. One who does not understand, does not speak the Truth. Only he who understands speaks the Truth. But one must desire to understand Understanding (*vjñāna*).'

'Sir, I desire to understand Understanding.'

Part - 18

यदा वै मनुतेऽथ विजानाति नामत्वा विजानाति मत्वैव विजानाति मतिस्त्वेव विजिज्ञासितव्येति। मतिं भगवो विजिज्ञास इति॥१॥

'Verily, when one thinks, then he understands. Without thinking one does not understand. Only after having thought does one understand. But one must desire to understand Thought (*mati*).'

'Sir, I desire to understand Thought.'

Part -19

यदा वै श्रद्दधात्यथ मनुते नाश्रद्दधन्मनुते श्रद्दधदेव मनुते श्रद्धा त्वेव विजिज्ञासितव्येति श्रद्धां भगवो विजिज्ञास इति॥१॥

'Verily, when one has Faith, then he thinks. One who has not Faith does not think. Only he who has Faith thinks. But one must desire to understand Faith (*śraddhā*).'

Sir, I desire to understand Faith.'

Part - 20

यदा वै निस्तिष्ठत्यथ श्रद्दधाति नानिस्तिष्ठञ्छ्रद्दधाति निस्तिष्ठन्नेव श्रद्दधाति निष्ठा त्वेव विजिज्ञासितव्येति निष्ठां भगवो विजिज्ञास इति॥१॥

'Verily, when one grows forth, then he has faith. One who does not grow forth does not have Faith. Only he who grows forth (*niḥ* +√*sthā*) has Faith. But one must desire to understand the Growing Forth (*niḥ* +√*ṣṭhā*).'

'Sir, I desire to understand the Growing Forth.'

Part - 21

यदा वै करोत्यथ निस्तिष्ठति नाकृत्वा निस्तिष्ठति कृत्वैव निस्तिष्ठति कृतिस्त्वेव विजिज्ञासितव्येति। कृतिं भगवो विजिज्ञास इति॥१॥

'Verily, when one is active, then he grows forth. Without being active one does not grow forth. Only by activity does one grow forth. But one must desire to understand Activity (*kṛti*).'

'Sir, I desire to understand Activity.'

Part - 22

यदा वै सुखं लभतेऽथ करोति नासुखं लब्ध्वा करोति सुखमेव लब्ध्वा करोति सुखं त्वेव विजिज्ञासितव्यमिति। सुखं भगवो विजिज्ञास इति॥१॥

'Verily, when one gets Pleasure for himself, then he is active. Without getting Pleasure one is not active. Only by getting Pleasure is one active. But one must desire to understand Pleasure (*sukha*).'

'Sir, I desire to understand Pleasure.'

Part - 23

यो वै भूमा तत्सुखं नाल्पे सुखमस्ति भूमैव सुखं भूमा त्वेव विजिज्ञासितव्य इति भूमानं भगवो विजिज्ञास इति॥१॥

'Verily, a Plenum is the same as Pleasure. There is no Pleasure in the small. Only a Plenum is Pleasure. But one must desire to understand the Plenum (*bhūman*).'

'Sir, I desire to understand the Plenum'.

Part - 24

यत्र नान्यत्पश्यति नान्यच्छृणोति नान्यद्विजानाति स भूमाऽथ यत्रान्यत्पश्यत्यन्यच्छृणोत्यन्यद्विजानाति तदल्पं यो वै भूमा तदमृतमथ यदल्पं तन्मर्त्यꣳ स भगवः कस्मिन्प्रतिष्ठित इति। स्वे महिम्नि यदि वा न महिम्नीति॥१॥

'Where one sees nothing else, hears nothing else, understands nothing else—that is a Plenum. But where one sees something else— that is the small. Verily, the Plenum is the same as the immortal; but the small is the same as the mortal.'

'That Plenum, sir—on what is it established?'

'On its own greatness—unless, not on greatness at all.

गोअश्वमिह महिमेत्याचक्षते हस्तिहिरण्यं दासभार्यं क्षेत्राण्यायतनानीति नाहमेवं ब्रवीमि ब्रवीमीति होवाचान्यो ह्यन्यस्मिन्प्रतिष्ठित इति॥२॥

Here on earth people call cows and horses, elephants and gold, slaves and wives, fields and abodes "greatness". I do not speak thus; I do not speak thus, said he; 'for [in that case] one thing is established upon another.

Part - 25

स एवाधस्तात्स उपरिष्टात्स पश्चात्स पुरस्तात्स दक्षिणतः स उत्तरतः स एवेदꣳसर्वमित्यथातोऽहङ्कारादेश एवाहमेवाधस्तादहमुपरिष्टादहं पश्चादहं पुरस्तादहं दक्षिणतोऽहमुत्तरतोऽहमेवेदꣳ सर्वमिति॥१॥

(O Nārada!) That [Plenum], indeed, is below. It is above. It is to the west. It is to the east. It is to the south. It is to the north. It, indeed, is this whole world.

Now next, the instruction with regard to the Ego (*ahaṁkārā-deśa*).

I, indeed, am below. I am above. Am to the west. I am to the east. I am to the south. I am to the north. I, indeed, am this whole world.

अथात आत्मादेश एवात्मैवाधस्तादात्मोपरिष्टादात्मा पश्चादात्मा पुरस्तादात्मा दक्षिणत आत्मोत्तरत आत्मैवेदꣳ सर्वमिति। स वा एष पश्यन्नेवं मन्वान एवं विजानन्नात्मरतिरात्मक्रीड आत्ममिथुन आत्मानन्दः स स्वराड् भवति तस्य सर्वेषु लोकेषु कामचारो भवति। अथ येऽन्यथातो विदुरन्यराजानस्ते क्षय्यलोका भवन्ति तेषाꣳ सर्वेषु लोकेष्वकामचारो भवति॥२॥

Now next, the instruction with regard to the soul (*ātmādeśa*).

The Soul (Ātman), indeed, is below. The Soul is above. The Soul is to the west. The Soul is to the east. The Soul is to the south. The Soul is to the north. The Soul, indeed, is this whole world.

Verily, he who sees this, who thinks this, who understands this, who has pleasure in the Soul, who has delight in the Soul, who has intercourse with the Soul, who has bliss in the Soul—he is autonomous (*sva-rāj*); he has unlimited freedom in all worlds. But they who know otherwise than this are heteronomous (*anya-rājan*); they have perishable worlds; in all worlds they have no freedom.

Part - 26

तस्य ह वा एतस्यैवं पश्यत एवं मन्वानस्यैवं विजानत आत्मत: प्राण आत्मत आशात्मत: स्मर आत्मत आकाश आत्मतस्तेज आत्मत आप आत्मत आविर्भावतिरोभावावात्मतोऽन्नमात्मतोबलामात्मतोविज्ञानमात्मतो ध्यानमात्मतश्चित्तमात्मत: संकल्प आत्मतो मन आत्मतो वागात्मतो नामात्मतो मन्त्रा आत्मत: कर्माण्यात्मत एवेदꣳ सर्वमिति।।१।।

Sanatkumāra said– Verily, for him who sees this, who thinks this, who understands this, Vital Breath (*prāṇa*) arises from the Soul (Ātman); Hope, from the Soul; Memory, from the Soul; Space (*ākāśa*), from the Soul; Heat, from the Soul; Water, from the Soul; Appearance and Disappearance, from the Soul; Food, from the Soul; Strength, from the Soul; Understanding, from the Soul; Meditation, from the Soul; Thought, from the Soul; Conception, from the Soul; Mind, from the Soul; Speech, from the Soul; Name, from the Soul; sacred sayings (*mantra*), from the Soul; sacred works (*karman*), from the Soul; indeed this whole world, from the Soul.

तदेष श्लोको न पश्यो मृत्यु पश्यति न रोगं नोत दु:खताꣳ सर्वꣳ ह पश्य: पश्यति सर्वमाप्नोति सर्वश इति। स एकधा भवति त्रिधा भवति पञ्चधा सप्तधा नवधा चैव पुनश्चैकादश: स्मृत: शतं च दश चैकश्च सहस्राणि च विꣳशतिराहारशुद्धौ सत्त्वशुद्धि: सत्त्वशुद्धौ ध्रुवा स्मृति: स्मृतिलम्भे सर्वग्रन्थीनां विप्रमोक्षस्तस्मै मृदितकषायाय तमसस्पारं दर्शयति भगवान् सनत्कुमारस्तꣳ स्कन्द इत्याचक्षते तꣳ स्कन्द इत्याचक्षते।।२।।

As to this there is the following verse :—

The seer sees not death, nor sickness, nor any distress.

The seer sees only the All, obtains the All entirely.

That [Soul] is onefold, is threefold, fivefold, sevenfold, and also ninefold;

Again, declared elevenfold, hundred-and-eleven-fold, And also twenty-thousand-fold.

In pure nourishment (*āhāra-śuddhi*) there is a pure nature (*sattva-śuddhi*). In a pure nature the traditional doctrine (*smṛti*) becomes firmly fixed. In acquiring the traditional doctrine there is release from all knots [of the heart]. To such a one who has his stains wiped away the blessed Sanatkumāra shows the further shore of darkness. People call him Skanda —yea, they call him Skanda.'

Eigth Chapter

Concerning the nature of the soul

Part - 1

The universal real Soul, within the heart and in the world

अथ यदिदमस्मिन्ब्रह्मपुरे दहरं पुण्डरीकं वेश्म दहरोऽस्मिन्नन्तराकाशस्तस्मिन्यदन्तस्तदन्वेष्टव्यं तद्वाव विजिज्ञासितव्यमिति॥१॥

Oṁ! [The teacher should say:] 'Now, what is here in this city of Brahma, is an abode, a small lotus-flower. Within that is a small space. What is within that, should be searched out; that, assuredly, is what one should desire to understand.'

तं चेद्ब्रूयुर्यदिदमस्मिन्ब्रह्मपुरे दहरं पुण्डरीकं वेश्म दहरोऽस्मिन्नन्तराकाशः किं तदत्र विद्यते यदन्वेष्टव्यं यद्वाव विजिज्ञासितव्यमिति स ब्रुयात्॥२॥

If they [i.e. the pupils] should say to him : 'This abode, the small lotus-flower that is here in this city of Brahma, and the small space within that—what is there which should be searched out, which assuredly one should desire to understand?'

यावान्वा अयमाकाशस्तावानेषोऽन्तर्हृदय आकाश उभे अस्मिन् द्यावापृथिवी अन्तरेव समाहित उभावग्निश्च वायुश्च सूर्याचन्द्रमसावुभौ विद्युन्नक्षत्राणि यच्चास्येहास्ति यच्च नास्ति सर्वं तदस्मिन्समाहितमिति॥३॥

He should say : 'As far, verily, as this world-space (*ayam ākāśa*) extends, so far extends the space within the heart. Within it, indeed, are contained both heaven and earth, both fire and wind, both sun and moon, lightning and the stars, both what one possesses here and what one does not possess; everything here is contained within it.'

तं चेद्ब्रूयुरस्मिँश्चेदिदं ब्रह्मपुरे सर्वꣳ समाहितꣳ सर्वाणि च भूतानि सर्वे च कामा यदैतज्जरामाप्नोति प्रध्वꣳसते वा किं ततोऽतिशिष्यत इति॥४॥

If they should say to him : 'If within this city of Brahma is contained everything here, all beings as well as all desires, when old age overtakes it or it perishes, what is left over therefrom?'

स ब्रूयान्नास्य जरयैतज्जीर्यति न वधेनास्य हन्यत एतत्सत्यं ब्रह्मपुरमस्मिन्कामाः समाहिता एष आत्मापहतपाप्मा विजरो विमृत्युर्विशोको विजिघत्सोऽपिपासः सत्यकामः सत्यसंकल्पो यथा ह्येवेह प्रजा अन्वाविशन्ति यथानुशासनं यं यमन्तमभिकामा भवन्ति यं जनपदं यं क्षेत्रभागं तं तमेवोपजीवन्ति॥५॥

He should say : 'That does not grow old with one's old age; it is not slain with one's murder. That is the real city of Brahma. In it desires are contained. That is the Soul (Ātman), free from evil, ageless, deathless, sorrowless, hungerless, thirstless, whose desire is the Real, whose conception is the Real.

For, just as here on earth human beings follow along in subjection to command; of whatever object they are desirous, whether a realm or a part of a field, upon that they live dependent—

तद्यथेह कर्मजितो लोकः क्षीयत एवमेवामुत्र पुण्यजितो लोकः क्षीयते तद्य इहात्मानमननुविद्य व्रजन्त्येतांश्च सत्यान् कामांस्तेषां सर्वेषु लोकेष्वकामचारो भवत्यथ य इहात्मानमनुविद्य व्रजन्त्येतांश्च सत्यान् कामांस्तेषां सर्वेषु लोकेषु कामचारो भवति॥६॥

As hereon earth the world which is won by work (*karma-jita loka*) becomes destroyed, even so there the world which is won by merit (*puṇya-jit loka*) becomes destroyed.

Those who go hence without here having found the Soul (Ātman) and those real desires (*satya kāma*)—for them in all the worlds there is no freedom. But those who go hence having found here the Soul and those real desires—for them in all worlds there is freedom.

Part - 2

स यदि पितृलोककामो भवति संकल्पादेवास्य पितरः समुत्तिष्ठन्ति तेन पितृलोकेन संपन्नो महीयते॥१॥

If he becomes desirous of the world of fathers, merely out of his conception (*saṁkalpa*) fathers arise. Possessed of that world of fathers, he is happy.

अथ यदि मातृलोककामो भवति संकल्पादेवास्य मातरः समुत्तिष्ठन्ति तेन मातृलोकेन संपन्नो महीयते॥२॥

So, if he becomes desirous of the world of mothers, merely out of his conception mothers arise. Possessed of that world of mothers, he is happy.

अथ यदि भ्रातृलोककामो भवति संकल्पादेवास्य भ्रातरः समुत्तिष्ठन्ति तेन भ्रातृलोकेन संपन्नो महीयते॥३॥

So, if he becomes desirous of the world of brothers, merely out of his conception brothers arise. Possessed of that world of brothers, he is happy.

अथ यदि स्वसृलोककामो भवति संकल्पादेवास्य स्वसारः समुत्तिष्ठन्ति तेन स्वसृलोकेन सम्पन्नो महीयते॥४॥

So, if he becomes desirous of the world of sisters, merely out of his conception sisters arise. Possessed of that world of sisters, he is happy.

अथ यदि सखिलोककामो भवति संकल्पादेवास्य सखायः समुत्तिष्ठन्ति तेन सखिलोकेन संपन्नो महीयते॥५॥

So, if he becomes desirous of the world of friends, merely out of his conception friends arise. Possessed of that world of friends, he is happy.

अथ यदि गन्धमाल्यलोककामो भवति संकल्पादेवास्य गन्धमाल्ये समुत्तिष्ठन्ति गन्धमाल्यलोकेन संपन्नो महीयते॥६॥

So, if he becomes desirous of the world of perfume and garlands, merely out of his conception perfume and garlands arise. Possessed of that world of perfume and garlands, he is happy.

अथ यद्यन्नपानलोककामो भवति संकल्पादेवास्य समुत्तिष्ठतस्तेनान्नपानलोकेन संपन्नो महीयते।।७।।

So, if he becomes desirous of the world of food and drink, merely out of his conception food and drink arise. Possessed of that world of food and drink, he is happy.

अथ यदि गीतवादित्रलोककामो भवति संकल्पादेवास्य गीतवादित्रे समुत्तिष्ठन्ति गीतवादित्रलोकेन संपन्नो महीयते।।८।।

So, if he becomes desirous of the world of song and music, merely out of his conception song and music arise. Possessed of that world of song and music, he is happy.

अथ यदि स्त्रीलोककामो भवति संकल्पादेवास्य स्त्रियः समुत्तिष्ठन्ति तेन स्त्रीलोकेन संपन्नो महीयते।।९।।

So, if he becomes desirous of the world of women, merely out of his conception women arise. Possessed of that world of women, he is happy.

यं यमन्तमभिकामो भवति यं कामं कामयते सोऽस्य संकल्पादेव समुत्तिष्ठन्ति तेन संपन्नो महीयते।।६।।

Of whatever object he becomes desirous, whatever desire he desire, merely out of his conception it arises. Possessed of it, he is happy.

Part - 3

त इमे सत्याः कामा अनृतापिधानास्तेषाः सत्यानाः सतामनृतमपिधानं यो यो ह्यस्येतः प्रैति न तमिह दर्शनाय लभते।।१।।

These same are real desires (*satya kāma*) with a covering of what is false. Although they are real, there is a covering that is false.

For truly, whoever of one's [fellows] departs hence, one does not get him [back] to look at here.

अथ ये चास्येह जीवा ये च प्रेता यच्चान्यदिच्छन्न लभते सर्वं तदत्र गत्वा विदन्तेऽत्र ह्यस्यैते सत्याः कामा अनृतापिधानास्तद्यथापि हिरण्यनिधिं निहितमक्षेत्रज्ञा उपर्युपरि संचरन्तो न विन्देयुरेवमेवेमाः सर्वाः प्रजा अहरहर्गच्छन्त्य एतं ब्रह्मलोकं न विन्दन्त्यनृतेन हि प्रत्यूढाः।।२।।

But those of one's [fellows] who are alive there, and those who have departed, and whatever else one desires but does not get—all this one finds by going in there [i.e. in the Soul]; for there, truly, are those real desires of his which have a covering of what is false.

So, just as those who do not know the spot might go over a hid treasure of gold again and again, but not find it, even so all creatures here go day by day to that Brahma-world (*brahma-loka*) [in deep sleep], but do not find it; for truly they are carried astray by what is false.

स वा एष आत्मा हृदि तस्यैतदेव निरुक्तः हृद्ययमिति तस्माद्धृदयमहरहर्वा एवंवित्स्वर्गं लोकमेति॥३॥

Verily, this Soul (Ātman) is in the heart. The etymological explanation (*nirukta*) thereof is this : This one is in the heart (*hṛdy ayam*); therefore it is the heart (*hṛdayam*). Day by day, verily, he who knows this goes to the heavenly world (*svarga loka*).

अथ य एष संप्रसादोऽस्माच्छरीरात्समुत्थाय परं ज्योतिरुपसंपद्य स्वेन रूपेणाभिनिष्पद्यत एष आत्मेत होवाचैतदमृतमभयमेतद्ब्रह्मेति तस्य ह वा एतस्य ब्रह्मणो नाम सत्यमिति॥४॥

Now, that serene one who, rising up out of this body, reaches the highest light and appears with his own form—he is the Soul (Ātman),' said he [i.e. the teacher']. 'That is the immortal, the fearless. That is Brahma.'

Verily, the name of that Brahma is the Real (*satyam*).

तानि ह वा एतानि त्रीण्यक्षराणि सतीयमिति तद्यत्सत्तदमृतमथ यत्ति तन्मर्त्यमथ यद्यं तेनोभे यच्छति यदनेनोभे यच्छति तस्माद्यमहरहर्वा एवंवित्स्वर्गं लोकमेति॥५॥

Verily, these are the three syllables : *sat-ti-yam*. The *sat* (Being)—that is the immortal. The *ti*—that is the mortal. Now the *yam*—with that one holds the two together. Because with it one holds (√*yam*) the two together, therefore it is *yam*. Day by day, verily, he who knows this goes to the heavenly world.

Part - 4

अथ य आत्मा स सेतुर्विधृतिरेषां लोकानामसंभेदाय नैतः सेतुमहोरात्रे तरतो न जरा न मृत्युर्न शोको न सुकृतं न दुष्कृतः सर्वे पाप्मानोऽतो निवर्तन्तेऽपहतपाप्मा ह्येष ब्रह्मलोकः॥१॥

Now, the Soul (Ātman) is the bridge [or dam], the separation for keeping these worlds apart. Over that bridge [or dam] there cross neither day, nor night, nor old age, nor death, nor sorrow, nor well-doing, nor evil-doing.

तस्माद्वा एतः सेतुं तीर्त्वान्धः सन्ननन्धो भवति विद्धः सन्नविद्धो भवत्युपतापी सन्ननुपतापी भवति तस्माद्वा एतः सेतुं तीर्त्वापि नक्तमहरेवाभिनिष्पद्यते सकृद्विभातो ह्येवैष ब्रह्मलोकः॥२॥

All evils turn back therefrom, for that Brahma-world is freed from evil. Therefore, verily, upon crossing that bridge, if one is blind, he becomes no longer blind; if he is sick, he becomes no longer sick. Therefore, verily, upon crossing that bridge, the night appears even as the day, for that Brahma-world is ever illumined.

तद्य एवैतं ब्रह्मलोकं ब्रह्मचर्येणानुविन्दन्ति तेषामेवैष ब्रह्मलोकस्तेषाः सर्वेषु लोकेषु कामचारो भवति॥३॥

But only they who find that Brahma-world through the chaste life of a student of sacred knowledge (*brahmacarya*)—only they possess that Brahma-world. In all worlds they possess unlimited freedom.

Part - 5

The true way to the Brahma-loka

अथ यद्यज्ञ इत्याचक्षते ब्रह्मचर्यमेव तद्ब्रह्मचर्येण ह्येव यो ज्ञाता तं विन्दतेऽथ यदिष्टमित्याचक्षते ब्रह्मचर्यमेव तद्ब्रह्मचर्येण ह्येवेष्ट्वात्मानमनुविन्दते॥१॥

Now, what people call 'sacrifice' (*vajña*) is really the chaste life of a student of sacred knowledge (*brahmacarya*), for only through the chaste life of a student of sacred knowledge does he who is a knower (*yajñātṛ*) find that [world].

Now, what people call 'what has been sacrificed' (*iṣta*) is really the chaste life of a student of sacred knowledge, for only after having searched (*iṣṭvā*) with the chaste life of a student of sacred knowledge does one find the Soul (Ātman).

अथ यत्सत्त्रायणमित्याचक्षते ब्रह्मचर्यमेव तद्ब्रह्मचर्येण ह्येव सत आत्मनस्त्राणं विन्दतेऽथ यन्मौनमित्याचक्षते ब्रह्मचर्यमेव तद्ब्रह्मचर्येण ह्येवात्मानमनुविद्य मनुते॥२॥

Now, what people call 'the protracted sacrifice' (*satrāyaṇa*) is really the chaste life of a student of sacred knowledge, for only through the chaste life of a student of sacred knowledge does one find the protection (*trāṇa*) of the real (*sat*) Soul (Ātman).

Now, what people call 'silent asceticism' (*mauna*) is really the chaste life of a student of sacred knowledge, for only in finding the Soul through the chaste life of a student of sacred knowledge does one [really] think (*manute*).

अथ यदनाशकायनमित्याचक्षते ब्रह्मचर्यमेव तदेष ह्यात्मा न नश्यति यं ब्रह्मचर्येणानुविन्दतेऽथ यदरण्यायनमित्याचक्षते ब्रह्मचर्यमेव तत्तदरश्च ह वै ण्यश्चार्णवौ ब्रह्मलोके तृतीयस्यामितो दिवि तदैरंमदीयꣳ सरस्तदश्वत्थः सोमसवनस्तदपराजिता पूर्ब्रह्मणः प्रभुविमितꣳ हिरण्मयम्॥३॥

Now, what people call 'a course of fasting' (*an-āśakāyana*) is really the chaste life of a student of sacred knowledge, for the Soul (Ātman) which one finds through the chaste life of a student of sacred knowledge perishes not (*na-naśyati*).

Now, what people call 'betaking oneself to hermit life in the forest' (*araṇyāyana*) is really the chaste life of a student of sacred knowledge. Verily, the two seas in the Brahma-world, in the third heaven from here, are *Ara* and *Ṇya*. There is the lake Airaṁmadīya ('Affording Refreshment and Ecstasy'); there, the fig-tree Somasavana ('the Soma-yielding')' there, Brahma's citadel, Aparājitā ('the Unconquered'), the golden hall of the Lord (*prabhu*).

तद्य एवैतावरं च ण्यं चार्णवौ ब्रह्मलोके ब्रह्मचर्येणानुविन्दन्ति तेषामेवैष ब्रह्मलोकस्तेषाꣳ सर्वेषु लोकेषु कामचारो भवति॥४॥

But only they who find those two seas, Ara and Ṇya, in the Brahma-world through the chaste life of a student of sacred knowledge—only they possess that Brahma-world. In all the worlds they possess unlimited freedom.

Part - 6

Passing out from the heart through the sun to immortality

अथ या एता हृदयस्य नाड्यस्ताः पिङ्गलस्याणिम्नस्तिष्ठन्ति शुक्लस्य नीलस्य पीतस्य लोहितस्येत्यसौ वा आदित्यः पिङ्गल एष शुक्ल एष नील एष पीत एष लोहितः॥१॥

Now, as for these channels of the heart—they arise from the finest essence, which is reddish brown, white, blue, yellow, and red : so it is said. Verily, yonder sun is reddish brown; it is white; it is blue; it is yellow; it is red.

[In this very Upaniṣad in the first to fifth part of the chapter three, different colours, aspects as also the nectar flows associated there to have been described. That description is relevant here. It is clear that this 'Āditya' is different than the sun and something analogous to omnipresent self-luminating element of soul.]

तद्यथा महापथ आतत उभौ ग्रामौ गच्छतीमं चामुं चैवमेवैता आदित्यस्य रश्मय उभौ लोकौ गच्छन्तीमं चामुं चामुष्मादादित्यात्प्रतायन्ते ता आसु नाडीषु सृप्ता आभ्यो नाडीभ्यः प्रतायन्ते तेऽमुष्मिन्नादित्ये सृप्ताः॥२॥

Now, as a great extending highway goes to two villages, this one and the yonder, even so these rays of the sun go to two worlds, this one and the yonder. They extend from yonder sun, and creep into these channels. They extend from these channels, and creep into yonder sun.

तद्यत्रैतत्सुप्तः समस्तः संप्रसन्नः स्वप्नं न विजानात्यासु तदा नाडीषु सृप्तो भवति तन्न कश्चन पाप्मा स्पृशति तेजसा हि तदा संपन्नो भवति॥३॥

Now, when one is thus sound asleep, composed, serene, he knows no dream; then he has crept into these channels; so no evil touches him, for then he has reached the Bright Power (*tejas*).

अथ यत्रैतदबलिमानं नीतो भवति तमभित आसीना आहुर्जानासि मां जानासि मामिति स यावदस्माच्छरीरादनुत्क्रान्तो भवति तावज्जानाति॥४॥

Now, when one thus becomes reduced to weakness, those sitting around say : 'Do you know me?' 'Do you know me?' As long as he has not departed from this body, he knows them.

अथ यत्रैतदस्माच्छरीरादुत्क्रामत्यथैतैरेव रश्मिभिरूर्ध्वमाक्रमते स ओमिति वा होद्वा मीयते स यावत्क्षिप्येन्मनस्तावदादित्यं गच्छत्येतद्वै खलु लोकद्वारं विदुषां प्रपदनं निरोधोऽविदुषाम्॥५॥

But when he thus departs from this body, then he ascends upward with these very rays of the sun. With the thought of *Oṁ*, verily, he passes up. As quickly as one could direct his mind to it, he comes to the sun. That, verily, indeed, is the world-door, an entrance for knowers, a stopping for non-knowers.

तदेष श्लोकः। शतं चैका च हृदयस्य नाड्यस्तासां मूर्धानमभिनिःसृतैका। तयोर्ध्वमायन्नमृतत्वमेति विष्वङ्ङन्या उत्क्रमणे भवन्त्युत्क्रमणे भवन्ति॥६॥

An hymn is quoted in this context. There are a hundred and one channels of the heart.

One of these passes up to the crown of the head.

Going up by it, one goes to immortality.

The others are for departing in various directions.

Part - 7

The progressive instruction of Indra by Prajāpati concerning the real self

य आत्मापहतपाप्मा विजरो विमृत्युर्विशोको विजिघत्सोऽपिपासः सत्यकामः सत्यसंकल्पः सोऽन्वेष्टव्यः स विजिज्ञासितव्यः स सर्वाꣳश्च लोकानाप्नोति सर्वाꣳश्च कामान्यस्तमात्मानमनुविद्य विजानातीति ह प्रजापतिरुवाच॥१॥

(Now, we describe the illustrations pertaining to Indra and Virocana while making clarity on the nature of soul.) Prajāpati Brahma said– 'The Self (Ātman), which is free from evil, ageless, deathless, sorrowless, hungerless, thirstless, whose desire is the Real, whose conception is the Real—He should be searched out, Him one should desire to understand. He obtains all worlds and all desires who has found out and who understands that Self.'

तद्धोभये देवासुरा अनुबुबुधिरे ते होचुर्हन्त तमात्मानमन्विच्छामो यमात्मानमन्विष्य सर्वाꣳश्च लोकानाप्नोति सर्वाꣳश्च कामानितीन्द्रो हैव देवानामभिप्रवव्राज विरोचनोऽसुराणां तौ हासंविदानावेव समित्पाणी प्रजापतिसकाशमाजग्मतुः॥२॥

Then both the gods and the devils (*deva-asura*) heard it. Then they said : 'Come! Let us search out that Self, the Self by searching out whom one obtains all worlds and all desires!'

Then Indra from among the gods went forth unto him, and Virocana from among the devils. Then, without communicating with each other, the two came into the presence of Prajāpati, fuel in hand.

तौ ह द्वात्रिꣳशतं वर्षाणि ब्रह्मचर्यमूषतुस्तौ ह प्रजापतिरुवाच किमिच्छन्तावववास्तमिति। तौ होचतुर्य आत्मापहतपाप्मा विजरो विमृत्युर्विशोको विजिघत्सोऽपिपासः सत्यकामः सत्यसंकल्पः सोऽन्वेष्टव्यः स विजिज्ञासितव्यः स सर्वाꣳश्च लोकानाप्नोति सर्वाꣳश्च कामान्यस्तमात्मानमनुविद्य विजानातीति भगवतो वचो वेदयन्ते तमिच्छन्तावववास्तमिति॥३॥

Then for thirty-two years the two lived the chaste life of a student of sacred knowledge (*brahmacarya*).

Then Prajāpati said to the two : 'Desiring what have you been living?'

Then the two said : "The Self (Ātman), which is free from evil, ageless, deathless, sorrowless, hungerless, thirstless, whose desire is the Real, whose conception is the Real—He should be searched out, Him one should desire to understand. He obtains all worlds and all desires who has found out and who understands that Self." Such do people declare to be your words, sir. We have been living desiring Him.'

तौ ह प्रजापतिरुवाच य एषोऽक्षिणि पुरुषो दृश्यत एष आत्मेति होवाचैतदमृतमभयमेतद्ब्रह्मेत्यथ योऽयं भगवोऽप्सु परिख्यायते यश्चायमादर्शे कतम एष इत्येष उ एवैषु सर्वेष्वन्तेषु परिख्यायत इति होवाच॥४॥

Then Prajāpati said to the two : 'That Person who is seen in the eye—He is the Self (Ātman) of whom I spoke. That is the immortal, the fearless. That is Brahma.'

'But this one, sir, who is observed in water and in a mirror—which one is he?'

'The same one, indeed, is observed in all these,' said he.

Part - 8

उदशराव आत्मानमवेक्ष्य यदात्मनो न विजानीथस्तन्मे प्रब्रूतमिति तौ होदशरावेऽवेक्षांचक्राते तौ ह प्रजापतिरुवाच किं पश्यथेति तौ होचतुः सर्वमेवेदमावां भगव आत्मानं पश्याव आलोमभ्य आनखेभ्यः प्रतिरूपमिति॥१॥

Prajāpati told to them– 'Look at yourself in a pan of water. Anything that you do not understand of the Self, tell me.'

Then the two looked in a pan of water.

Then Prajāpati said to the two : 'What do you see?'

Then the two said : 'We see everything here, sir, a Self corresponding exactly, even to the hair and fingernails!'

तौ ह प्रजापतिरुवाच साध्वलंकृतौ सुवसनौ परिष्कृतौ भूत्वोदशरावेऽवेक्षेथामिति तौ ह साध्वलङ्कृतौ सुवसनौ परिष्कृतौ भूत्वोदशरावेऽवेक्षांचक्राते तौ ह प्रजापतिरुवाच किं पश्यथ इति॥२॥

Prajāpati again said to them– 'Make yourselves well-ornamented, well-dressed, adorned, and look in a pan of water.'

Then the two made themselves well-ornamented, well-dressed, adorned, and looked in a pan of water.

Then Prajāpati said to the two : 'What do you see?'

तौ होचतुर्यथैवेदमावां भगवः साध्वलंकृतौ सुवसनौ परिष्कृतौ स्व एवमेवेमौ भगवः साध्वलंकृतौ सुवसनौ परिष्कृतावित्येष आत्मेति होवाचैतदमृतमभयमेतद्ब्रह्मेति तौ ह शान्तहृदयौ प्रवव्रजतुः॥३॥

Then the two said : 'Just as we ourselves are here, sir, well-ornamented, well-dressed, adorned—so there, sir, well-ornamented, well-dressed, adorned.'

'That is the Self,' said he. 'That is the immortal, the fearless. That is Brahma.'

Then with tranquil heart (*śānta-hṛdaya*) the two went forth.

[They could not understand the secret behind the statement of Prajāpati and returned back.]

तौ हान्वीक्ष्य प्रजापतिरुवाचानुपलभ्यात्मानमनुविद्य व्रजतो यतर एतदुपनिषदो भविष्यन्ति देवा वासुरा वा ते पराभविष्यन्तीति स ह शान्तहृदय एव विरोचनोऽसुराञ्जगाम तेभ्यो हैतामुपनिषदं प्रोवाचात्मैवेह महय्य आत्मा परिचर्य आत्मानमेवेह महयन्नात्मानं परिचरन्नुभौ लोकाववाप्नोतीमं चामुं चेति॥४॥

Then Prajāpati glanced after them, and said : 'They go without having comprehended, without having found the Self (Ātman). Whosoever shall have such a doctrine (*upaniṣad*), be they gods or be they devils, they shall perish.'

Then with tranquil heart Virocana came to the devils. To them he then declared this doctrine (*upaniṣad*) : 'Oneself (*ātman*) is to be made happy here on earth. Oneself is to be waited upon. He who makes his own self (*ātman*) happy here on earth, who waits upon himself—he obtains both worlds, both this world and the yonder.'

तस्मादप्यद्येहाददानमश्रद्दधानमयजमानमाहुरासुरो बतेत्यसुराणाꣳ ह्येषोपनिषत्प्रेतस्य शरीरं भिक्षया वसनेनालंकारेणेति सꣳस्कुर्वन्त्येतेन ह्यमुं लोकं जेष्यन्तो मन्यते॥५॥

Therefore even now here on earth they say of one who is not a giver, who is not a believer (*a-śraddadhāna*), who is not a sacrificer, 'Oh! Devilish (*āsura*)!' for such is the doctrine (*upaniṣad*) of the devils. They adorn the body (*śarīra*) of one deceased with what they have begged, with dress, with ornament, as they call it, for they think that thereby they will win yonder world.

Part - 9

अथ हेन्द्रोऽप्राप्यैव देवानेतद्भयं ददर्श यथैव खल्वयमस्मिञ्छरीरे साध्वंकृते साध्वलंकृतो भवति सुवसने सुवसनः परिष्कृते एवमेवायमस्मिन्नन्धेऽन्धो भवति स्रामे स्रामः परिवृक्णे परिवृक्णोऽस्यैव शरीरस्य नाशमन्वेष नश्यति नाहमत्र भोग्यं पश्यामीति॥१॥

But then Indra, even before reaching the gods, saw this danger : 'Just as, indeed, that one [i.e. the bodily self] is well-ornamented when this body (*śarīra*) is well-ornamented, well-dressed when this is well-dressed, adorned with this is adorned, even so that one is blind when this is blind, lame when this is lame, maimed when this is maimed. It perishes immediately upon the perishing of this body. I see nothing enjoyable in this.'

स समित्पाणिः पुनरेयाय तꣳ ह प्रजापतिरुवाच मघवन्यच्छान्तहृदयः प्राव्राजीः सार्धं विरोचनेन किमिच्छन् पुनरागम इति स होवाच यथैव खल्वयं भगवोऽस्मिञ्छरीरे साध्वलंकृते साध्वलंकृतो भवति सुवसने सुवसनः परिष्कृते परिष्कृत एवमेवायमस्मिन्नन्धेऽन्धो भवति स्रामे स्रामः परिवृक्णे परिवृक्णोऽस्यैव शरीरस्य नाशमन्वेष नश्यति नाहमत्र भोग्यं पश्यामीति॥२॥

He came back again with fuel in hand. Then Prajāpati said to him : 'Desiring what, O Maghavan ('Munificent One'), have you come back again, since you along with Virocana went forth with tranquil heart?'

Then he said : 'Just as, indeed, that one [i.e. the bodily self] is well-ornamented when this body is well-ornamented, well-dressed when this is well-dressed, adorned when this is adorned even so it is blind when this is blind, lame when this is lame, maimed when this is maimed. It perishes immediately upon the perishing of this body. I see nothing enjoyable in this.'

एवमेवैष मघवन्निति होवाचैतं त्वेव ते भूयोऽनुव्याख्यास्यामि वसापराणि द्वात्रिंशतं वर्षाणीति स हापराणि द्वात्रिंशतं वर्षाण्युवास तस्मै होवाच॥३॥

'He is even so, O Maghavan,' said he. 'However, I will explain this further to you. Live with me thirty-two years more.'

Then he lived with him thirty-two years more.

To him [i.e. to Indra] he [i.e. Prajāpati] then said :—

Part - 10

य एष स्वप्ने महीयमानश्चरत्येष आत्मेति होवाचैतदमृतमभयमेतद्ब्रह्मेति स ह शान्तहृदयः प्रवव्राज स हाप्राप्यैव देवानेतद्भयं ददर्श तद्यद्यपीदꣳ शरीरमन्धं भवत्यन्धः स भवति यदि स्राममस्रामो नैवैषोऽस्य दोषेण दुष्यति॥१॥

'He who moves about happy in a dream—he is the Self (Ātman),' said he. 'That is the immortal, the fearless. That is Brahman.'

Then with tranquil heart he [i.e. Indra] went forth.

Then, even before reaching the gods, he saw this danger : 'Now, even if this body is blind, that one [i.e. the Self, Ātman] is not blind. If this is lame, he is not lame. Indeed, he does not suffer defect through defect of his.

न वधेनास्य हन्यते नास्य स्राम्येण स्रामो घ्नन्ति त्वेवैनं विच्छादयन्तीवाप्रियवेत्तेव भवत्यपि रोदितीव नाहमत्र भोग्यं पश्यामीति॥२॥

He is not slain with one's murder. He is not lame with one's lameness. Nevertheless, as it were (*iva*), they kill him; as it were, they unclothe him; as it were, he comes to experience what is unpleasant; as it were, he even weeps. I see nothing enjoyable in this.'

स समित्पाणिः पुनरेयाय तꣳ ह प्रजापतिरुवाच मघवन्यच्छान्तहृदयः प्राव्राजीः किमिच्छन् पुनरागम इति स होवाच तद्यद्यपीदं भगवः शरीरमन्धं भवत्यनन्धः स भवति यदि स्राममस्रामो नैवेषोऽस्य दोषेण दुष्यति॥३॥

Indra again returned to Prajāpati with the offering fuel in his hands. Then Prajāpati said to him : 'Desiring what, O Maghavan, have you come back again, since you went forth with tranquil heart?'

Then he said : 'Now, sir, even if this body is blind, that one [i.e. the Self] is not blind. If this is lame, he is not lame. Indeed, he does not suffer defect through defect of this.

न वधेनास्य हन्यते नास्य स्राम्येण स्रामो घ्नन्ति त्वेवैन्नं विच्छादयन्तीवाप्रियवेत्तेव भवत्यपि रोदितीव नाहमत्र भोग्यं पश्यामीत्येवमेवैष मघवन्निति होवाचैतं त्वेव ते भूयोऽनुव्याख्यास्यामि वसापराणि द्वात्रिंशतं वर्षाणीति स हापराणि द्वात्रिंशतं वर्षाण्युवास तस्मै होवाच॥४॥

He is not slain with one's murder. He is not lame with one's lameness. Nevertheless, as it were, they kill him; as it were, they unclothe him; as it were, he comes to experience what is unpleasant; as it were, he even weeps. I see nothing enjoyable in this.'

'He is even so, O Maghavan,' said he. 'However, I will explain this further to you. Live with me thirty-two years more.'

Then he lived with him thirty-two years more.

To him [i.e. to Indra] he [i.e. Prajāpati] then said :—

Part - 11

तद्यत्रैतत् सुप्तः समस्तः संप्रसन्नः स्वप्नं न विजानात्येष आत्मेति होवाचैतदमृतमभयमेतद्ब्रह्मेति स ह शान्तहृदयः प्रवव्राज स हाप्राप्यैव देवानेतद्भयं ददर्श नाह खल्वयमेवꣳ संप्रत्यात्मानं जानात्ययमहमस्मीति नो एवेमानि भूतानि विनाशमेवापीतो भवति नाहमत्र भोग्यं पश्यामीति॥१॥

'Now, when one is sound asleep, composed, serene, and knows no dream—that is the Self (Ātman),' said he. 'That is the immortal, the fearless. That is Brahma.'

Then with tranquil heart he went forth.

Then, even before reaching the gods, he saw this danger: 'Assuredly, indeed, this one does not exactly know himself (*ātmānam*) with the thought "I am he," nor indeed the things here. He becomes one who has gone to destruction. I see nothing enjoyable in this.'

स समित्पाणिः पुनरेयाय तꣳ ह प्रजापतिरुवाच मघवन्यच्छान्तहृदयः प्राव्राजीः किमिच्छन्पुनरागम इति स होवाच नाह खल्वयं भगव एवꣳ संप्रत्यात्मानं जानात्ययमहमस्मीति नो एवेमानि भूतानि विनाशमेवापीतो भवति नाहमत्र भोग्यं पश्यामीति॥२॥

Fuel in hand, back again he came. Then Prajāpati said to him : 'Desiring what, O Maghavan, have you come back again, since you went forth with tranquil heart?'

Then he [i.e. Indra] said : 'Assuredly, this [self] does not exactly know himself with the thought "I am he," nor indeed the things here. He becomes one who has gone to destruction. I see nothing enjoyable in this.'

एवमेवैष मघवन्निति होवाचैतं त्वेव ते भूयोऽनुव्याख्यास्यामि नो एवान्यत्रैतस्माद्वसापराणि पञ्च वर्षाणीति स हापराणि पञ्च वर्षाण्युवास तान्येकशतꣳ संपेदुरेतत्तद्यदाहुरेकशतꣳ ह वै वर्षाणि मघवान्प्रजापतौ ब्रह्मचर्यमुवास तस्मै होवाच॥३॥

'He is even so, O Maghavan,' said he. 'However, I will explain this further to you, and there is nothing else besides this. Live with me five years more.'

Then he lives with him five years more. That makes one hundred and one years. Thus it is that people say, 'Verily, for one hundred and one years Maghavan lived the chaste life of a student of sacred knowledge (*brahmacarya*) with Prajāpati.'

To him [i.e. to Indra] he [i.e. Prajāpati] then said :—

Part - 12

मघवन्मर्त्यं वा इदꣳशरीरमात्तं मृत्युना तदस्यामृतस्याशरीरस्यात्मनोऽधिष्ठानमात्तो वै सशरीरः प्रियाप्रियाभ्यां न वै सशरीरस्य सतः प्रियाप्रिययोरपहतिरस्त्यशरीरं वाव सन्तं न प्रियाप्रिये स्पृशतः॥१॥

'O Maghavan, verily, this body (*śarīra*) is mortal. It has been appropriated by Death (Mṛtyu). [But] it is the standing ground of that deathless, bodiless Self (Ātman). Verily, he who is incorporate has been appropriated by pleasure and pain. Verily, there is no freedom from pleasure and pain for one while he is incorporate. Verily, while one is bodiless, pleasure and pain do not touch him.

अशरीरो वायुरभ्रं विद्युत्स्तनयित्नुरशरीराण्येतानि तद्यथैतान्यमुष्मादाकाशात्समुत्थाय परं ज्योतिरुपसंपद्य स्वेन रूपेणाभिनिष्पद्यन्ते॥२॥

एवमेवैष सम्प्रसादोऽस्माच्छरीरात्समुत्थाय परं ज्योतिरुपसम्पद्य स्वेन रूपेणाभिनिष्पद्यते स उत्तमः पुरुषः स तत्र पर्येति जक्षत्क्रीडन्रममाणः स्त्रीभिर्वा यानैर्वाज्ञातिभिर्वा नोपजनꣳ स्मरन्निदꣳ शरीरꣳ स यथा प्रयोग्य आचरणे युक्त एवमेवायमस्मिञ्छरीरे प्राणो युक्तः॥३॥

The wind is bodiless. Clouds, lightning, thunder—these are bodiless. Now as these, when they arise from yonder space and reach the highest light, appear each with its own form.

Even so that serene one (*samprasāda*), when he rises up from this body (*śarīra*) and reaches the highest light, appears with his own form. Such a one is the supreme person (*uttama puruṣa*). There such a one goes around laughing, sporting, having enjoyment with women or chariots or friends, not remembering the appendage of this body. As a draft-animal is yoked in a wagon, even so this spirit (*prāṇa*) is yoked in this body.

अथ यत्रैताकाशमनुविषण्णं चक्षुः स चाक्षुषः पुरुषो दर्शनाय चक्षुरथ यो वेदेदं जिघ्राणीति स आत्मा गन्धाय घ्राणमथ यो वेदेदमभिव्याहराणीति स आत्माभिव्याहाराय वागथ यो वेदेदꣳ शृणवानीति स आत्मा श्रवणाय श्रोत्रम्॥४॥

Now, when the eye is directed thus toward space, that is the seeing person (*cākṣuṣa puruṣa*); the eye is [the instrument] for seeing. Now, he who knows "Let me smell this"—that is the Self (Ātman); the nose is [the instrument] for smelling. Now, he who knows "Let me utter this"—that is the Self; the voice is [the instrument] for utterance. Now, he who knows "Let me hear this"—that is the Self; the ear is [the instrument] for hearing.

अथ यो वेदेदं मन्वानीति स आत्मा मनोऽस्य दैवं चक्षुः स वा एष एतेन दैवेन चक्षुषा मनसैतान् कामान् पश्यन् रमते॥५॥

Now, he who knows "Let me think this"—that is the Self; the mind (*manas*) is his divine eye (*daiva cakṣu*). He, verily, with that divine eye the mind, sees, desires here, and experiences enjoyment.

य एते ब्रह्मलोके तं वा एतं देवा आत्मानमुपासते तस्मात्तेषाꣳ सर्वे च लोका आत्ताः सर्वे च कामाः स सर्वाꣳश्च लोकानाप्नोति सर्वाꣳश्च कामान्यस्तमात्मानमनुविद्य विजानातीति ह प्रजापतिरुवाच प्रजापतिरुवाच॥६॥

Verily, those gods who are in the Brahma-world reverence that Self. Therefore all worlds and all desires have been appropriated by them. He obtains all worlds and all desires who has found out and who understands that Self (Ātman).'

Thus spoke Prajāpati—yea, thus spoke Prajāpati!

Part - 13

A paean of the perfected soul

श्यामाच्छबलं प्रपद्ये शबलाच्छ्यामं प्रपद्येऽश्व इव रोमाणि विधूय पापं चन्द्र इव राहोर्मुखात्प्रमुच्य धूत्वा शरीरमकृतं कृतात्मा ब्रह्मलोकमभिसंभवामीत्यभिसंभवामीति॥१॥

From the dark I go to the varicoloured. From the varicoloured I go to the dark. Shaking off evil, as a horse his hairs; shaking off the body (*śarīra*), as the moon release itself from the mouth of Rāhu; I, a perfected soul (*kṛtātman*), pass into the uncreated Brahma-world—yea, into it I pass!

Part -14

The exultation and prayer of a glorious learner

आकाशो वै नाम नामरूपयोर्निर्वहिता ते यदन्तरा तद्ब्रहम तदमृतꣳ स आत्मा प्रजापतेः सभां वेश्म प्रपद्ये यशोऽहं भवामि ब्राह्मणानां यशो राज्ञां यशो विशां यशोऽहमनुप्रापत्सि स हाहं यशसां यशः श्येतमदत्कमदत्कꣳ श्येतं लिन्दु माभिगां लिन्दु माभिगाम्॥१॥

Indeed, what is called space (*ākāśa*) is the accomplisher of name and form. That within which they are, is Brahma. That is the immortal. That is the Self (Ātman, Soul).

I go to Prajāpati's abode and assembly-hall.

I am the glory of the Brahmans (*brāhmaṇas*), the glory of the princes (*rājan*), the glory of the people (*viś*).

I have attained unto glory.

May I, who am the glory of the glories, not go to hoary and toothless, year to toothless and hoary and drivelling [old age]!

Yea, may I not go to drivelling [old age]!

Part - 15

Final words to the departing pupil

तद्धैतद्ब्रह्मा प्रजापतय उवाच प्रजापतिर्मनवे मनुः प्रजाभ्य आचार्यकुलाद्वेदमधीत्य यथाविधानं गुरोः कर्मातिशेषेणाभिसमावृत्य कुटुम्बे शुचौ देशे स्वाध्यायमधीयानो धार्मिकान्विदधदात्मनि सर्वेन्द्रियाणि

संप्रतिष्ठाप्याहिꣳसन्सर्वभूतान्यन्यत्र तीर्थेभ्यः स खल्वेवं वर्तयन्यावदायुषं ब्रह्मलोकमभिसंपद्यते न च पुनरावर्तते न च पुनरावर्तते॥१॥

Lord Brahmā describe this knowledge of soul before Prajāpati. Prajāpati to Manu and Manu preached this supreme knowledge to human beings (*prajā*). He who according to rule has learned the Veda from the family of a teacher, in time left over from doing work for the teacher; he who, after having come back again, in a home of his own continues Veda-study in a clean place and produces [sons and pupils]; he who has concentrated all his senses upon the Soul (Ātman); he who is harmless (*ahiṁsant*) towards all things elsewhere than at holy places (*tīrtha*)—he, indeed, who lives thus throughout his length of life, reaches the Brahma-world and does not return hither again—yea, he does not return hither again!

ॐ आप्यायन्तु ममाङ्गानि ... सन्तु ते मयि सन्तु॥

ॐ शान्तिः शान्तिः शान्तिः॥

इति छान्दोग्योपनिषत्समाप्ता॥

***

10. BṚHADĀRAṆYAKOPANIṢAD

बृहदारण्यकोपनिषद्

।। शान्तिपाठः।।

ॐ पूर्णमदः पूर्णमिदं...... इति शान्ति।।

This upaniṣad is the subject-matter of 'Śatapatha Brāhmaṇa' of 'Vājasaneyī Brāhmaṇa' to the Kāṇva branch of the Śukla Yajurveda. The term 'Bṛhat' is meant by the large and 'Āraṇyaka' is meant by the forest therefore this upaniṣad having been written in the forest is called 'Bṛhadāraṇyaka'. There are six chapters and several Brahmins in every chapter of it.

In the first chapter, there are six Brahmins. In the first Brāhmaṇa (relating to horse-offering), the creative offering has been revealed by giving sheer importance to a gigantic horse and in the second Brāhmaṇa, the origin of Sṛṣṭi (creation) after the great devastation is described. In the third Brāhmaṇa, the significance of breathings and its kinds have been made clear by referring to the context of the gods and demons. In the fourth Brāhmaṇa, the Brahma is considered as of universal form and the evolution of four Varṇas (the Brāhmaṇa, Kṣatriya, the Vaiśya and the Śūdra) by him are described. In the sixth Brāhmaṇa, origin of various cereals and an importance of the mind, the speech and the breathing has been described. Simultaneously, the significance of the name, the complexions and the act has also been described. In the first Brāhmaṇa of the second chapter the Brahma and the element of soul has been clearly described by the colloquy between the boosting Gāgrya Bālāki and the learned king Ajātaśatru. In the second and the third Brahmins of the second chapter, the worship of breathing and two forms of Brahma (tangible and intangible) have been described. In the fourth Brāhmaṇa a colloquy between Yājñavalkya and Maitreyī is given. This colloquy is about the same in the fifth Brāhmaṇa under the fourth chapter of this upaniṣad. In the fifth and sixth Brāhmaṇa the Madhuvidya and its tradition has been described. Under the nineth Brāhmaṇa of the third chapter, a questionaire submitted before the renowned Ṛṣi Yājñavalkya by a section of the experts in metaphysics in an offering performed by the king Janaka. The Ṛṣi Gārgī has raised questions twice. At the outset the Ṛṣi Yājñavalkya restricted him by warning that he will lost his head if more questions are before raised him. Secondly, he raised two questions by the permission of the council and having received the answers pronounce before the audience that nobody may conquer him but the Ṛṣi Śākalya, Vidagdha did not put his ears on the warning therefore he lost his head owing to more questions raised. In the fourth chapter, two colloquies have been referred. Out of them one is between the saint Yājñavalkya and Janaka while the other is between Yājñavalkya and Maitreyī. Finally, the tradition of the conclusion has been followed. In the fifth chapter, the varied forms of worship to the Brahma as also the worship of the intellectual man (Manomaya Puruṣa) and the speech has been elaborated. The manner of worship in its varied form to be offered for the food and breathing coincides to the upward motion after the death has been made ex-faci clear to understand. In the worship of Gāyatrī the fourth foot namely, 'Darśata' is mentioned alongwith the three feet worth reciting. In the sixth chapter, the supremacy of breathing, the learning of five kinds fire (Pañcāgni Vidyā), Manth Vidyā and the genetic science have been thoroughly described. Lastly, a succinct note covering all the topics in this upaniṣad has been given.

॥ प्रथमोऽध्याय:॥

प्रथमं ब्राह्मणम्

उषा वा अश्वस्य मेध्यस्य शिर:। सूर्यश्चक्षुर्वात: प्राणो व्यात्तमग्निर्वैश्वानर: संवत्सर आत्माश्वस्य मेध्यस्य द्यौ: पृष्ठमन्तरिक्षमुदरं पृथिवी पाजस्यम्। दिश: पार्श्वे अवान्तरदिश: पर्शव ऋतवोऽङ्गानि मासाश्चार्धमासाश्च पर्वण्यहोरात्राणि प्रतिष्ठा नक्षत्राण्यस्थीनि नभो मा◌ंसानि। ऊवध्य◌ं सिकता: सिन्धवो गुदा यकृच्च क्लोमानश्च पर्वता ओषधयश्च वनस्पतयश्च लोमानि उद्यन् पूर्वोर्धो निम्लोचञ्जघनार्थो यद्विजृम्भते यद्विद्योतते यद्विधूनुते तत्स्नयति यन्मेहति तद्वर्षति वागेवास्य वाक्॥१॥

[In the first Brāhmaṇa, a gigantic horse for the offering has been described. It has been said that the limbs and the organs of such a horse are spreaded all over the three worlds. This is an explanation by using the figure of speech. The term 'horse' is the indicator of power and the motion. This world is always dynamic. This power making it dynamic has been called the horse. The term 'horse' denotes anything that moves very fast. This horse (described herein) is for the purpose of offering. This word is synonymous to the offering (Yajña). Therefore, the circulation of power that conducts this world as a whole is definitely worth-offering. This word should be applied strictly while describing the matter regarding the divine offering. The root Medha has three meanings– the wisdom, the infringement or violation and the harmony or co-ordination. The gigantic process of offering cannot be said violative or infringing process, therefore, this meaning is not worth to accept here. Instead of it, it can be said undoubtedly worth entertaining by the wit or worth influencing by the wisdom. Such a meaning is really worth to accept. It is necessary to keep this flow of power adhered to or add with it.]

This horse for the purpose of offering or the flow of world-wide power has its head the dawn, the sun is its eyes, the wind is its breathing, the fire of Vaiśvānara is its opened mouth and the Saṁvatsara (period of one year) is its soul. The world of sun is the back portion of that horse, the space is his belly, the earth is the place under his hoofs, the directions are his collateral parts of the body, the directions in the angles are the ribs, the seasons are his other limbs, the month and the Pakṣa (period of 15 days) are his joints, the day and night are his two feet, the group of planets are his bones and the ether is his flesh. The little objects of this universe are his undigested grains of food, the rivers are the group of his nerves, the group of mountains are his liver and the flesh forming the heart. The flora world is his hair, the sun at the moon is his upper part of body from the navel, the setting sun is the lower part of his body. Similarly, When he yawns, then it lightens. When he shakes himself, then it thunders. When he urinates, then it rains. Voice, indeed, is his voice.

[The figure of speech, however, are not real in themselves but they are able to explain thoroughly the reality. Hence, the use of figure of speech for providing with the description or part of the body including the head of that horse are most appropriate. The space has been said the belly of the horse, therefore the undigested grains of food should not be deemed the common grain of food but the sub-particles existing in the space particularly which are immature and in the process of converting in the matter.]

अहर्वा अश्वं पुरस्तान्महिमान्वजायत तस्य पूर्वे समुद्रे रात्रिरेनं पश्चान्महिमान्वजायत तस्यापरे समुद्रे योनिरेतौ वा अश्वं महिमानावभितः संबभूवतुः। हयो भूत्वा देवानवहद्वाजी गन्धर्वानर्वाऽसुरानश्वो मनुष्यान् समुद्र एवास्य बन्धुः समुद्रो योनिः॥२॥

Verily, the day arose for the horse as the sacrificial vessel which stands before. Its place is the eastern sea. Verily, the night arose for him as the sacrificial vessel which stands behind. Its place is the western sea. Verily, these two arose on both sides of the horse as the two sacrificial vessels. Becoming a steed (haya), he carries the gods; a stallion, the Gandharvas; a courser, the demons; a horse, men. The sea, indeed, is his relative. The sea is his place.

[The Haya, Vāji, Arva, Aśva all these words are synonyms and refers to the meaning speedy but in view of the connotation there is lying some distinction among them. Haya is the word meant by one who goes ahead by abandoning. As the medicines known as Vājīkaraṇa increase the power of cohesion, therefore, the term Vāji is linked with Yoga. Similarly, Arva means caprice and aggressive as also the horse has been said vociferous (Mahāśano). The origin place and intimate friend of horse is the sea. This is not an ordinary sea but a sea in which the causative nature (the element of Apaḥ) swings on it, by the impact of the waves of this sea the world is created and destroyed. This sea is the gigantic and activated Vyoma. Veda too has said it 'Samudro Arṇavaḥ' etc.]

द्वितीयं ब्राह्मणम्

नैवेह किंचनाग्र आसीन्मृत्युनैवेदमावृतमासीत्। अशनाययाशनाया हि मृत्युस्तन्मनोऽकुरुतात्मन्वी स्यामिति। सोऽर्चन्नचरत्तस्यार्चत आपोऽजायन्तार्चते वै मे कमभूदिति तदेवार्कस्यार्कत्वम् कः ह वा अस्मै भवति य एवमेतदर्कस्यार्कत्वं वेद॥१॥

Initially, nothing was existed in this world, everything was covered under the claw of death. This world was covered by the hunger and the hunger is the death (As the god merges the world with it, it too is called the death). Then he made up his mind (*manas*) : 'Would that I had a self!' So he went on (*acarat*) praising (*arcan*). From him, while he was praising water was produced. 'Verily, while I was praising, I had pleasure (*ka*)!' thought he. This, indeed, is the *arka*-nature of what pertains to brightness (*arkya*). Verily, there is pleasure for him who knows thus that *arka*-nature of what pertains to brightness.

[The sentence that everything was covered in the claw of death and hunger is a trimmed dictum. The death is the stage of inactiveness and the stage of great devastation. The desire of god as to merging this whole world within him can be said the hunger. As a result of this desire of merging the world or a hunger, the stage of great devastation arises. When that Brahma again wished to create this world, the cycle of creation again started revolving. The word 'Arka' is derived from the root 'Arca'.

It is considered as saying something regarding god. Hence, it is all appropriate to have leisure or the grace of divine with the man who knows the mystery pertaining to the god.]

आपो वा अर्कस्तद्यदपाः शर आसीत्समहन्यत सा पृथिव्यभवत्तस्यामश्राम्यत्तस्य श्रान्तस्य तप्तस्य तेजोरसो निरवर्ततााग्निः॥ २॥

The water, verily, was brightness. That which was the froth of the water became solidified. That became the earth.

On it he [i.e. death] tortured himself (√*śram*). When he had tortured himself and practised austerity, his heat (*tejas*) and essence (*rasa*) turned into fire.

स त्रेधात्मानं व्यकुरुतादित्यं तृतीयं वायुं तृतीयः स एष प्राणस्त्रेधा विहितः। तस्य प्राची दिक्शिरोऽसौ चासौ चेमौ। अथास्य प्रतीची दिक् पुच्छमसौ चासौ च सक्थ्यौ दक्षिणा चोदीची च पार्श्वे द्यौः पृष्ठमन्तरिक्षमुदरमियमुरः स एषोप्सु प्रतिष्ठितो यत्र क्व चैति तदेव प्रतितिष्ठत्येवं विद्वान्॥ ३॥

He divided himself (*ātmānam*) threefold : [fire (*agni*) one third], the sun (*āditya*) one third, wind (*vāyu*) one third. He also is Life (*prāṇa*) divided threefold.

The eastern direction is his head. Yonder one and yonder one are the fore quarters. Likewise the western direction is his tail. Yonder one and yonder one are the hind quarters. South and north are the flanks. The sky is the back. The atmosphere is the belly. This [earth] is the chest. He stands firm in the waters. He who knows this, stands firm wherever he goes.

सोऽकामयत द्वितीयो म आत्मा जायेतेति स मनसा वाचं मिथुनः समभवदशनाया मृत्युस्तद्यद्रेत आसीत्स संवत्सरोऽभवत्। न ह पुरा ततः संवत्सर आस तमेतावन्तं कालमबिभः। यावान्संवत्सरस्तमेतावतः कालस्य परस्तादसृजत। तं जातमभिव्याददात्स भाणकरोत्सैव वागभवत्॥ ४॥

He desired : 'Would that a second self of me were produced!' He—death, hunger—by mind copulated with speech (*vāc*). That which was the semen (*retas*), became the year (Saṁvatsara). Previous to that there was no year. He bore him for a time as long as a year. After that long time he brought him forth. When he was born, Death opened his mouth on him. He cried '*bhāṇ*!' That, indeed, became speech.

[The events referred to above is personified. It has been referred that as a result of combination between the mind that the speech, the dynamic splendour *i.e.* knowledge appeared. As a result of condensation or crystallization that was become the Saṁvatsara *i.e.* a reservoir of the knowledge formed as a result of the combination between the mind and the speech. Should that knowledge not elapsed by the flux of time, he used the term 'Bhāṇ' which means an experiment with the decent breathing viz., extension of the sensitive and learned living-organism. This fact has been proved in the successive hymns.]

स ऐक्षत यदि वा इममभिमःस्ये कनीयोऽन्नं करिष्य इति स तया वाचा तेनात्मनेदः सर्वमसृजत यदिदं किंचर्चो यजूःषि सामानि छन्दाःसि यज्ञान् प्रजाः पशून्। स यद्यदेवासृजत तत्तदत्तुमध्रियत सर्वं वा अत्तीति तददितेरदितित्वः सर्वस्यैतस्यात्ता भवति सर्वमस्यान्नं भवति य एवमेतददितेरदितित्वं वेद॥ ५॥

He bethought himself : 'Verily, if I shall intend against him, I shall make the less food for myself.' With that speech, with that self he brought forth this whole world, whatsoever exists here : the Hymns (*ṛk*) [i.e. the Ṛgveda], the Formulas (*yajus*) [i.e. the Yajurveda], the chants (*sāman*) [i.e. the Sāmaveda], meters, sacrifices, men, cattle.

Whatever he brought forth, that he began to eat. Verily, he eats (√*ad*) everything : that is the *aditi*-nature of Aditi (the Infinite). He who knows thus the *aditi*-nature of Aditi, becomes an eater of everything here; everything becomes food for him.

सोऽकामयत भूयसा यज्ञेन भूयो यजेयेति। सोऽश्राम्यत्स तपोऽतप्यत तस् श्रान्तस्य तप्तस्य यशो वीर्यमुदक्रामत्। प्राणा वै यशो वीर्यं तत्प्राणेषूत्क्रान्तेषु शरीरꣳ श्वयितुमध्रियत तस्य शरीर एव मन आसीत्॥ ६॥

He desired : 'Let me sacrifice further with a greater sacrifice (*yajña*)!' He tortured himself. He practised austerity. When he had tortured himself and practised austerity, glory and vigour went forth. The glory and vigour, verily, are the vital breaths. So when the vital breaths departed, his body began to swell. His mind, indeed, was in his body (*śarīra*).

[On the premises of the scientific research as made in the modern era, they accept the fact that the breathing process was extended with the big bang theory (a grand explosion and this apparent world was spreaded as a reason of that grand explosion). The matter at the earlier stage was excessively densed. Since it was extended, the world worth considering as the genesis of offering was evolved.]

सोऽकामयत मेध्यं म इदꣳ स्यादात्मन्व्यनेन स्यामिति ततोऽश्वः समभवद्यदश्वत्तन्मेध्यमभूदिति तदेवाश्वमेधस्याश्वमेधत्वम्। एष ह वा अश्वमेधं वेद य एनमेवं वेद तमनवरुद्ध्यैवामन्यत तꣳ संवत्सरस्य परस्तादात्मन आलभत पशून्देवताभ्यः प्रत्यौहत्। तस्मात्सर्वदेवत्यं प्रोक्षितं प्राजापत्यमालभन्ते। एष ह वा अश्वमेधो य एष तपति तस्य संवत्सर आत्मायमग्निरर्कस्तस्येमे लोका आत्मानस्तावेतावर्काश्वमेधौ सोपुनरेकैव देवता भवति मृत्युरेवाप पुनर्मृत्युं जयति नैनं मृत्युराप्नोति मृत्युरस्यात्मा भवत्येतासां देवतानामेको भवति॥ ७॥

He desired : 'Would that this [body] of mine were fit for sacrifice! Would that by it I had a self (*ātmanvin*)!' Thereupon it became a horse (*aśva*), because it swelled (*aśvat*). 'It has become fit for sacrifice (*medhya*)!' thought he. Therefore the horse-sacrifice is called Aśva-medha. He, verily, knows the Aśva-medha, who knows it thus.

He kept him [i.e. the horse] in mind without confining him. After a year he sacrificed him for himself. [Other] animals he delivered over to the divinities. Therefore men sacrifice the victim which is consecrated to Prajāpati as though offered unto all the gods.

Verily, that [sun] which gives forth heat is the Aśva-medha. The year is its embodiment (*ātman*).

This [earthly] fire is the *arka*. The worlds are its embodiments These are two, the *arka* sacrificial fire and the Aśva-medha sacrifice. Yet again they are one divinity, even Death. He [who knows this] wards off repeated death (*punarmṛtyu*), death obtains him not, death becomes his body (*ātman*), he becomes one of these deities.

तृतीयं ब्राह्मणम्

This part of Udgītha Vidyā (learning of the syllable Oṁ) has been elaborated in the second part of the first chapter in Chāndogya upaniṣad also. Thus, only slight changes can be seen in this subject-matter in Bṛhadāraṇyakopaniṣad.

द्वया ह प्राजापत्या देवाश्चासुराश्च ततः कानीयसा एव देवा ज्यायसा असुरास्त एषु लोकेष्वस्पर्धन्त ते ह देवा ऊचुर्हन्तासुरान्यज्ञ उद्गीथेनात्ययामेति॥ १॥

The superiority of breath among the bodily functions

The gods (*deva*) and the devils (*asura*) were the twofold offspring of Prajāpati. Of these the gods were the younger, the devils the older. They were struggling with each other for these worlds.

The gods said : 'Come, let us overcome the devils at the sacrifice with the Udgītha. were of the sons of Prajāpati.

ते ह वाचमूचुस्त्वं न उद्गायेति तथेति तेभ्यो वागुदगायत्। यो वाचि भोगस्तं देवेभ्य आगायद्यत् कल्याणं वदति तदात्मने। ते विदुरनेन वै न उद्गात्रात्येष्यन्तीति तमभिद्रुत्य पाप्मनाविध्यन्त्स यः स पाप्मा यदेवेदमप्रतिरूपं वदति स एव स पाप्मा॥ २॥

Having decided this, the gods urged the god of the speech (proudly of style) for reciting Udgītha. The god of speech accepted their request and recited the syllable Oṁ on behalf of them. Whatever pleasure there is in speech, that it sang for the gods, whatever good one speaks, that for itself.

Owing to this the demons were known to the fact that the gods may attack on them by means of recital of Oṁ. Hence, they approached to the god of speech and vitiated him. The vicious application or use of speech indeed is the evil.

अथ ह प्राणमूचुस्त्वं न उद्गायेति। तथेति तेभ्यः प्राण उदगायद्यः प्राणे भोगस्तदेवेभ्य आगायद्यत् कल्याणं जिघ्रति तदात्मने ते विदुरनेन वै न उद्गात्रात्येष्यन्तीति तमभिद्रुत्य पाप्मनाविध्यन्त्स यः स पाप्मा यदेवेदमप्रतिरूपं जिघ्रति स एव स पाप्मा॥ ३॥

Then they [i.e. the gods] said to the In-breath (*prāṇa*) 'Sing for us the Udgītha.'

'So be it,' said the In-breath, and sang for them. Whatever pleasure there is in the in-breath, that it sang for the gods; whatever god one breathes in, that for itself.

They [i.e. the devils] knew : 'Verily, by this singer they will overcome us.' They rushed upon it and pierced it with evil. That evil was the improper thing that one breathes in. This, truly, was that evil.

अथ ह चक्षुरूचुस्त्वं न उद्गायेति। तथेति तेभ्यश्चक्षुरुदगायद् यश्चक्षुषि भोगस्तं देवेभ्य आगायद्यत्कल्याणं पश्यति तदात्मने ते विदुरनेन वै न उद्गात्रात्येष्यन्तीति तमभिद्रुत्य पाप्मनाविध्यन्त्स यः स पाप्मा यदेवेदमप्रतिरूपं पश्यति स एव स पाप्मा॥ ४॥

Then they [i.e. the gods] said to the Eye : 'Sing for us the Udgītha.'

'So be it,' said the Eye, and sang for them. Whatever pleasure there is in the eye, that it sang for the gods; whatever good one sees, that for itself.

They [i.e. the devils] knew : 'Verily, by this singer they will overcome us.' They rushed upon it and pierced it with evil. That evil was the improper thing that one sees. This, truly, was that evil.

अथ ह श्रोत्रमूचुस्त्वं न उद्गायेति। तथेति तेभ्यः श्रोत्रे भोगस्तं देवेभ्य आगायद्यत्कल्याणꣳशृणोति तदात्मने ते विदुरनेन वै न उद्गात्रात्येष्यन्तीति तमभिद्रुत्य पाप्मनाऽविध्यन्त्स यः स पाप्मा यदेवेदमप्रतिरूपꣳ शृणोति स एव स पाप्मा॥ ५॥

Then they [i.e. the gods] said to the Ear : 'Sing for us the Udgītha.'

'So be it,' said the Ear, and sang for them. Whatever pleasure there is in the ear, that it sang for the gods; whatever good one hears, that for itself.

They [i.e. the devils] knew : 'Verily, by this singer they will overcome us.' They rushed upon it and pierced it with evil. That evil was the improper thing that one hears. This, truly, was that evil.

अथ ह मन ऊचुस्त्वं न उद्गायेति तथेति तेभ्यो मन उद्गायद्यो मनसि भोगस्तं देवेभ्य आगायद्यत् कल्याणꣳ संकल्पयति तदात्मने ते विदुरनेन वै न उद्गात्रात्येष्यन्तीति तमभिद्रुत्य पाप्मनाऽविध्यन्त्स यः स पाप्मा यदेवेदमप्रतिरूपꣳ संकल्पयति स एव स पाप्मैवमु खल्वेता देवतः पाप्मभिरुपासृजन्नेवमेनाः पाप्मेनाविध्यन्॥ ६॥

Subsequently, the gods prayed for reciting Udgītha through the mind. The mind has accepted this offer and started the recital of Udgītha. Whatever pleasure there is in the mind, that it sang for the gods; whatever good one imagines, that for itself.

They [i.e. the devils] knew : 'Verily, by this singer they will overcome us.' They rushed upon him and pierced him with evil. That evil was the improper thing that one imagines. This, truly, was that evil. Hence, the gods when indulged into the evils penetrated by the evil which was inflicted by the demons on them.

अथ हेममासन्यं प्राणमूचुस्त्वं न उद्गायेति। तथेति तेभ्य एष प्राण उदगायत्ते विदुरनेन वै न उद्गात्रात्येष्यन्तीति तमभिद्रुत्य पाप्मनाविव्यत्स्यन्स यथाश्मानमृत्वा लोष्टो विध्वꣳसेतैवꣳ हैव विध्वꣳसमाना विष्वञ्चो विनेशुस्ततो देवा अभवन् परासुराः। भवत्यात्मना परास्य द्विषन्भ्रातृव्यो भवति य एवं वेद॥ ७॥

Then they [i.e. the gods] said to this Breath in the mouth : 'Sing for us the Udgītha'.

'So be it,' said this Breath, and sang for them.

They [i.e. the devils] knew : 'Verily, by this singer they will overcome us.' They rushed upon him and desired to pierce him with evil. As a clod of earth would be scattered by striking on a stone, even so they were scattered in all directions and perished. Therefore the gods increased, the demons became inferior. He increases with himself, a hateful enemy becomes inferior for him who knows this.

ते होचुः क्व नु सोऽभूद्यो न इत्थमसक्तेत्ययमास्येऽन्तरितिसोऽयास्य आङ्गिरसोऽङ्गानाꣳ हि रसः॥ ८॥

Then they said, 'What, pray, has become of him who stuck to us thus?' 'This one here (*ayam*) is within the mouth (*asya*)!' He is called Ayāsya Āṅgirasa, for he is the essence (*rasa*) of the limbs (*aṅga*).

सा वा एषा देवता दूर्नाम दूरꣳ ह्यस्या मृत्युर्दूरꣳ ह वा अस्मान्मृत्युर्भवति य एवं वेद॥ ९॥

This breathing god is also known as Dūra (distant) by name because the death stands far away from him. The man who knows this mystery (the death stands far away), always is protected from the death.

सा वा एषा देवतैतासां देवतानां पाप्मानं मृत्युमपहत्य यत्रासां दिशामन्तस्तद्गमयांचकार तदासां पाप्मनो विन्यदधात्तस्मान्न जनमियान्नातन्तमियान्नेत्पाप्मानं मृत्युमन्ववायानीति॥ १०॥

Verily, that divinity having struck off the evil of these divinities, even death, made this go to where is the end of the quarters of heaven. There is set down their evils. Therefore one should not go to [foreign] people, one should not go to the end [of the earth], lest he fall in with evil, with death.

सा वा एषा देवतैतासां देवतानां पाप्मानं मृत्युमपहत्याथैनां मृत्युमत्यवहत्॥ ११॥

Verily, that divinity by striking off the evil, the death, of those divinities carried them beyond death. (It conveys that the man obtains the nectar like emancipation by abandoning the evils).

स वै वाचमेव प्रथमामत्यवहत्सा यदा मृत्युमत्यमुच्यत सोऽग्निरभवत्सोऽयमग्निः परेण मृत्युमतिक्रान्तो दीप्यते॥ १२॥

Verily, it carried Speech over as the first. When that was freed from death, it became fire. This fire, when it has crossed beyond death, shines forth.

अथ ह प्राणमत्यवहत्स यदा मृत्युमत्यमुच्यत स वायुरभवत्सोऽयं वायुः परेण मृत्युमतिक्रान्तः पवते॥ १३॥

The god of breathing then provided the smelling power with the immortality. That smelling power turned into the wind form as soon as it crossed the death (evils). That very wind is blowing ceaselessly after being and free from the clutches of the death.

अथ चक्षुरत्यवहत्तद्यदा मृत्युमत्यमुच्यत स आदित्योऽभवत् सोऽसावादित्यः परेण मृत्युमतिक्रान्तास्तपति॥ १४॥

Subsequently, he took the eyes beyond the death. Absolving from the ties of the death, the eyes turned into form of the Sun. That very eyes now luminates as the Sun having free from the clutches of the death.

अथ श्रोत्रमत्यवहत्तद्यदा मृत्युमत्यमुच्यत ता दिशोऽभवꣳस्ता इमा दिशः परेण मृत्युमतिक्रान्ताः॥ १५॥

The breathing then enabled the ears to cross the death. They turned in the form of directions after liberty. Thus, the ears were acquitted from the ties of death and became the directions.

अथ मनोऽत्यवहत्तद्यदा मृत्युमत्यमुच्यत स चन्द्रमा अभवत्सोऽसौ परेण मृत्युमतिक्रान्तो भात्येवꣳ ह वा एनमेषा देवता मृत्युमतिवहति य एवं वेद॥ १६॥

Likewise it carried the Mind across. When that was freed from death, it became the moon. That moon, when it has crossed beyond death, shines.

Thus, verily, that divinity carries beyond death him who knows this.

अथात्मनेऽन्नाद्यमागायद्यद्धि किंचान्नमद्यतेऽनेनैव तदद्यत इह प्रतितिष्ठति॥ १७॥

Then it [i.e. breath] sang out food for itself, for whatever food is eaten is eaten by it. Hereon one is established.

ते देवा अब्रुवन्नेतावद्वा इदꣳ सर्वं यदन्नं तदात्मन आगासीरनु नोऽस्मिन्नन्न आभजस्वेति ते वै माभिसंविशतेति तथेति तꣳ समन्तं परिण्यविशन्त तस्माद्यदनेनान्नमत्ति तेनैतास्तृप्यन्त्येवꣳ ह वा एनꣳ स्वा अभिसंविशन्ति भर्ता स्वानाꣳ श्रेष्ठः पुर एता भवत्यन्नादोऽधिपतिर्य एवं वेद य उ हैवंविदꣳ स्वेषु प्रति प्रतिबुभूषति न हैवालं भार्येभ्यो भवत्यथ य एवैतमनुभवति यो वै तमनु भार्यान् बुभूर्षति स हैवालं भार्येभ्यो भवति॥ १८॥

Those gods said : 'Of such extent, verily, is this universe as food. You have sung it into your own possession. Give us an after-share in this food.'

'As such, verily, do you enter into me.'

'So be it.' They entered into him from all sides. Therefore whatever food one eats by this breath, these are satisfied by it. Thus, verily, his people come to him, he becomes the supporter of his people, their chief, foremost leader, an eater of food, an overlord—he who knows this. And whoever among his people desires to be the equal of him who has this knowledge suffices not for his dependents. But whoever follows after him and whoever, following after him, desire to support his dependents, he truly suffices for his dependents.

सोऽयास्य आङ्गिरसोऽङ्गानाꣳ हि रसः प्राणो वा अङ्गानाꣳ रसः प्राणो हि वा अङ्गानाꣳ रसस्तस्माद्यस्मात्कस्माच्चाङ्गात्प्राण उत्क्रामति तदेव तच्छुष्यत्येष हि वा अङ्गानाꣳ रसः॥ १९॥

He is Ayāsya Āṅgirasa, for he is the essence (*rasa*) of the limbs (*aṅga*). Verily, breath is the essence of the limbs, for verily breath is the essence of the limbs. Therefore from whatever limb the breath departs, that indeed dries up, for it is verily the essence of the limbs.

एष उ एव बृहस्पतिर्वाग् वै बृहती तस्या एष पतिस्तस्मादु बृहस्पतिः॥ २०॥

And it is also Bṛhaspati. The Bṛhatī is speech. He is her lord (*pati*) and is therefore Bṛhaspati.

एष उ एव ब्रह्मणस्पतिर्वाग् वै ब्रह्म तस्या एष पतिस्तस्मादु ब्रह्मणस्पतिः॥ २१॥

And it is also Brahmaṇaspati. Prayer (*brahman*), verily, is speech. He is her lord (*pati*) and is therefore Brahmaṇaspati.

एष उ एव साम वाग् वै सामैष सा चामश्चेति तत्साम्नः सामत्वं यद्वेव समः प्लुषिणा समो मशकेन समो नागेन सम एभिस्त्रिभिर्लोकैः समोऽनेन सर्वेण तस्माद्वेव सामाश्नुते साम्नः सायुज्यꣳ सलोकतां जयति य एवमेतत्साम वेद॥ २२॥

[A glorification of the Chant as breath]

This breathing too is Sāma because this speech is 'Sa' and the breathing is 'Āma' and a combination of 'Sa' and 'Āma' makes the word *sāman*.

Or because it is equal (*sama*) to a gnat, equal to a fly, equal to an elephant, equal to these three worlds, equal to this universe, therefore, indeed, it is the Sāmaveda. He obtains intimate union with the Sāman, he wins its world who knows thus that Sāman.

एष उ वा उद्गीथः प्राणो वा उत्प्राणेन हीदꣳ सर्वमुत्तब्धं वागेव गीथोच्चगीथा चेति स उद्गीथः॥ २३॥

His breathing too is called Udgītha. The breath verily is up (*ut*), for by breath this whole world is upheld (*ut-tabdha*). Song (*gītha*), verily, is speech; *ut* and *gītha*—that is Udgītha.

तद्धापि ब्रह्मदत्तश्चैकितानेयो राजानं भक्षयन्नुवाचायं त्यस्य राजा मूर्धानं विपातयताद्यदितोऽवास्य आङ्गिरसोऽन्येनोदगायदिति वाचा च ह्येव स प्राणेन चोदगायदिति॥ २४॥

As also Brahmadatta Caikitāneya, while partaking of King [Soma], said : 'Let this king cause this man's head to fall off, if Ayāsya Āṅgirasa sang the Udgītha with any other means than that, for,' said he, 'only with speech and with breath did he sing the Udgītha.'

[If the revelation made by mouth and the speech is without vibration of the breathing, it is redundant and only pomp and show. By reason of not being the ever felt conduction of the breathing in the worlds parrotly pronunciated, they become worth nothing. The combination of breathing as also of the speech is sina-cua-non in the lifelong meditation or penance.]

तस्य हैतस्य साम्नो यः स्वं वेद भवति हास्य स्वं तस्य वै स्वर एव स्वं तस्मादार्त्विज्यं करिष्यन्वाचि स्वरमिच्छेत तया वाचा स्वरसंपन्नयार्त्विज्यं कुर्यात्तस्माद्यज्ञे स्वरवन्तं दिदृक्षन्त एवाथो यस्य स्वं भवति भवति हास्य स्वं य एवमेतत्साम्नः स्वं वेद॥ २५॥

He who knows the property of that Sāman has that property. Its property, truly, is tone. Therefore let him who is about to perform the duties of a Ṛtvij priest desire a good tone in his voice. Being possessed of such a voice, let him perform the duties of the Ṛtvij priest. Therefore people desire to see at the sacrifice one who has a good tone, as being one who has a possession. He has a possession who knows thus the property of the Sāman.

तस्य हैतस्य साम्नो यः सुवर्णं वेद भवति हास्य सुवर्णं तस्य वै स्वर एव सुवर्णं भवति हास्य सुवर्णं य एवमेतत्साम्नः सुवर्णं वेद॥ २६॥

He who knows the gold of that Sāman comes to have gold. The tone (*svara*), verily, is its gold. He comes to have gold who knows thus that gold of the Sāman.

तस्य हैतस्य साम्नो यः प्रतिष्ठां वेद प्रति ह तिष्ठति तस्य वै वागेव प्रतिष्ठा वाचि हि खल्वेष एतत्प्राणः प्रतिष्ठितो गीयतेऽन्न इत्यु हैक आहुः॥ २७॥

He who knows the support of that Sāman is indeed supported. Voice, verily, is its support, for when supported on voice the breath sings. But some say it is supported on food.

अथातः पवमानानामेवाभ्यारोहः स वै खलु प्रस्तोता साम प्रस्तौति स यत्र प्रस्तुयात्तदेतानि जपेदसतो मा सद्गमय तमसो मा ज्योतिर्गमय मृत्योर्मामृतं गमयेति स यदाहासतो मा सद्गमयेति मृत्युर्वा असत्सदमृतं मृत्योर्मामृतं गमयामृतं मा कुर्वित्येवैतदाह तमसो मा ज्योतिर्गमयेति मृत्युर्वै तमो ज्योतिरमृतं मृत्योर्मामृतं गमयामृतं मा कुर्वित्येवैतदाह मृत्योर्मामृतं गमयेति नात्र तिरोहितमिवास्ति। अथ यानीतराणि स्तोत्राणि तेष्वात्मनेऽन्नाद्यमागायेत्तस्मादु तेषु वरं वृणीत यं कामं कामयेत तꣳस एष एवंविदुद्गातात्मने वा यजमानाय वा यं कामं कामयते तमागायति तद्धैतल्लोकजिदेव न हैवालोक्यताया आशास्ति य एवमेतत्साम वेद॥ २८॥

[Prayers to accompany an intelligent performance of the Chant]

Now next, the praying of the purificatory formulas (*pavamāna*).

The Prastotā priest (Praiser), verily begins to praise with the Chant (*sāman*). When he begins to praise, then let [the sacrificer] mutter the following :—

'From the unreal (*asat*) lead me to the real (*sat*)! From darkness lead me to light! From death lead me to immortality!'

When he says 'From the unreal lead me to the real,' the unreal, verily, is death, the real is immortality. 'From death lead me to immortality. Make me immortal' that is what he says.

'From darkness lead me to light' the darkness, verily, is death, the light is immortality. 'From death lead me to immortality. Make me immortal' that is what he says.

'From death lead me to immortality' there is nothing there that seems obscure.

Now whatever other verses there are of a hymn of praise (*stotra*), in them one may win food for himself by singing. And, therefore, in them he should choose a boon, whatever desire he may desire. That Udgātṛi priest who knows this— whatever desire he desires, either for himself or for the sacrificer, that he obtains by singing. This, indeed, is world-conquering. There is no prospect of his being without a world who knows thus this Sāman.

चतुर्थं ब्राह्मणम्

आत्मैवेदमग्र आसीत् पुरुषविधः सोऽनुवीक्ष्य नान्यदात्मनोऽपश्यत् सोऽहमस्मीत्यग्रे व्याहरत्ततोऽहंनामाभवत्तस्मादप्येतर्ह्यामन्त्रितोऽहमयमित्येवाग्र उक्त्वाथान्यन्नाम प्रब्रूते यदस्य भवति स यत्पूर्वोऽस्मात्सर्वस्मात्सर्वान्पाप्मन औषत्तस्मात्पुरुष ओषति ह वै स तं योऽस्मात्पूर्वो बुभूषति य एवं वेद॥ १॥

[The creation of the manifold world from the unitary Soul]

In the beginning this world was Soul (*Ātman*) along in the form of a Person. Looking around, he saw nothing else than himself. He said first : 'I am.' Then arose the name 'I'.

Therefore even today, when one is addressed, he says first just 'It is I' and then speaks whatever name he has. Since before (*pūrva*) all this world he burned up (√*uṣ*) all evils, therefore he is a person (*pur-uṣ-a*). He who knows this, verily, burns up him who desires to be ahead of him.

[In the above hymns, Pur is meant very first and 'uṣa' means competent to burn. Therefore, Puruṣa is meant for burning the deficiencies as also the evils very first and when these are sprouting. What is conveyed as a lesson to the people is that one is only able to be addressed as Puruṣa, who burns the evils sprouting in his mind.]

सोऽबिभेत्तस्मादेकाकी बिभेति स हायमीक्षांचक्रे यन्मदन्यन्नास्ति कस्मान्नु बिभेमीति तत एवास्य भयं वीयाय कस्माद्ध्यभेष्यद् द्वितीयाद्वै भयं भवति॥ २॥

He was afraid. Therefore one who is alone is afraid. This one then thought to himself : 'Since there is nothing else than myself, of what am I afraid?' Thereupon, verily, his fear departed, for of what should he have been afraid? Assuredly it is from a second that fear arises.

स वै नैव रेमे तस्मादेकाकी न रमते स द्वितीयमैच्छत् स हैतावानास यथा स्त्रीपुमाꣳसौ संपरिष्वक्तौ स इममेवात्मानं द्वेधापातयत्ततः पतिश्च पत्नी चाभवतां तस्मादिदमर्धबृगलमिव स्व इति ह स्माह याज्ञवल्क्यस्तस्मादयमाकाशः स्त्रिया पूर्यत एव ताꣳ समभवत्ततो मनुष्या अजायन्त॥ ३॥

Verily, he had no delight. Therefore one alone has no delight. He desired a second. He was, indeed, as large as a woman and a man closely embraced. He caused that self to fall (√*pat*) into two pieces. Therefrom arose a husband (*pati*) and a wife (*patni*). Therefore this [is true] : 'Oneself (*sva*) is like a half-fragment,' as Yājñavalkya used to say. Therefore this space is filled by a wife. He copulated with her. Therefrom human beings were produced.

[The presumption of lord Śiva's being Naṭeśvara (half male and half female) has been made very clear in the above hymns. At the first is the genesis of man and the nature was not taken place like the birth of a baby from the womb. Contrary to it, this process of genesis started like the opening of two parts by the purse or oyster on being nature. By the same process the man and the nature from the Brahmā, Śiva and Śakti from Mahādeva, Brahmā and Sāvitrī from Prajāpati were originated.]

सो हेयमीक्षांचक्रे कथं नु मात्मन एव जनयित्वा संभवति हन्त तिरोऽसानीति सा गौरभवदृषभ इतरस्ताꣳ समेवाभवत्ततो गावोऽजायन्त वडवेतराभवदश्ववृष इतरो गर्दभीतरा गर्दभ इतरस्ताꣳ समेवाभवत्तत एकशफमजायताजेतराभवद्बस्त इतरोऽविरितरा मेष इतरस्ताꣳसमेवाभवत्ततोऽजायन्तैवमेव यदिदं किंच मिथुनमापिपीलिकाभ्यस्तत्सर्वमसृजत॥ ४॥

And she then bethought herself : 'How now does he copulate with me after he has produced me just from himself? Come, let me hide myself.' She became a cow. He became a bull. With her he did indeed copulate. Then cattle were born. She became a mare, he a stallion. She became a female ass, he a male ass; with her he copulated, of a truth. Then were born solid-hoofed animals. She became a she-goat, he a he-goat; she a ewe, he a ram. With her he did verily copulate. Therefrom were born goats and sheep. Thus, indeed, he created all, whatever pairs there are, even down to the ants.

[The Ṛṣi reveals here very clearly that the presumption according to the evolution theory is not correct. It is worth to mention that according to this theory, it has been presumed that all the creatures got their birth gradually from amoeba to the various species of living-organisms. At the first stage and by its resolution, the nature casted into different forms according to the necessity, the man also forms accordingly by the power of resolution. The second stage of the reproduction process in the world was then commenced.]

सोऽवेदहं वाव सृष्टिरस्म्यहꣳ हीदꣳसर्वमसृक्षीति ततः सृष्टिरभवत्सृष्ट्याꣳ हास्यैतस्यां भवति य एवं वेद॥५॥

After originating all these, that man came to know that 'I, indeed, am this creation. Verily, he who has this knowledge comes to be in that creation of his.

अथेत्यभ्यमन्थस्त मुखाच्च योनेर्हस्ताभ्यां चाग्निमसृजत तस्मादेतदुभयमलोमकमन्तरतोऽलोमका हि योनिरन्तरतस्तद्यदिदमाहुरमुं यजामुं देवमेतस्यैव सा विसृष्टिरेव उ ह्येव सर्वे देवा अथ यत्किंचेदमार्द्रं तद्रेतसोऽसृजत तदु सोम एतावद्वा इदꣳसर्वमन्नं चैवान्नादश्च सोम एवान्नमग्निरन्नादः सैषा ब्रह्मणोऽतिसृष्टिच्छ्रेयसो देवानसृजताथ यन्मर्त्यः सन्नमृतानसृजत तस्मादतिसृष्टिरतिसृष्ट्याꣳ हास्यैतस्यां भवति य एवं वेद॥६॥

Then he rubbed thus. From his mouth as the fire-hole (*yoni*) and from his hands he created fire (*agni*). Both these [i.e. the hands and the mouth] are hairless on the inside, for the fire-hole (*yoni*) is hairless on the inside.

This that people say, 'Worship this god! Worship that god!' one god after another—this is his creation indeed! And he himself is all the gods.

Now, whatever is moist, that he created from semen, and that is Soma. This whole world, verily, is just food and the eater of food.

That was Brahma's super-creation : namely, that he created the gods, his superiors; likewise that, being mortal, he created the immortals. Therefore was it a super-creation. Verily, he who knows this comes to be in that super-creation of his.

तद्धेदं तर्ह्यव्याकृतमासीत्तन्नामरूपाभ्यामेव व्याक्रियतेऽसौनामायमिदꣳरूप इति तदिदमप्येतर्हि नामरूपाभ्यामेव व्याक्रियतेऽसौनामायमिदꣳरूप इति, स एष इह प्रविष्ट आ नखाग्रेभ्यो यथा क्षुरः क्षुरधानेऽवहितः स्याद्विश्वंभरो वा विश्वंभरकुला ये तं न पश्यन्ति। अकृत्स्नो हि स प्राणन्नेव प्राणो नाम भवति वदन् वाक्पश्यꣳश्चक्षुः शृण्वन् श्रोत्रं मन्वानो मनस्तान्यस्यैतानि कर्मनामान्येव, स योऽत एकैकमुपास्ते न स वेदाकृत्स्नो ह्येषोऽत एकैकेन भवत्यात्मेत्येवोपासीतात्र ह्येते सर्व एकं भवन्ति तदेतत्पदनीयमस्य सर्वस्य यदयमात्मानेन ह्येतत्सर्वं वेद। यथा ह वै पदेनानुविन्देदेवं कीर्तिꣳ श्लोकं विन्दते य एवं वेद॥७॥

Verily, at that time the world was undifferentiated. It became differentiated just by name and form, as the saying is : 'He has such a name, such a form.' Even today this world is differentiated just by name and form, as the saying is : 'He has such a name, such a form.'

He entered in here, even to the fingernail-tips, as a razor would be hidden in a razor-case, or fire in a fire-holder. Him they see not, for [as seen] he is incomplete. When breathing, he becomes breath (*prāṇa*) by name; when speaking, voice; when seeing, the eye; when hearing, the ear; when thinking, the mind : these are merely the names of his acts. Whoever worships one or another of these—he knows not; for he is incomplete with one or another of these. One should worship with the thought that he is just one's self (*ātman*), for therein all these become one. That same thing, namely, this self, is the trace (*padanīya*) of this All, for by it one knows this All. Just as, verily, one might find by a footprint (*pada*), thus. He finds fame and praise who knows this.

तदेतत्प्रेयः पुत्रात्प्रेयो वित्तात्प्रेयोऽन्यस्मात्सर्वस्मादन्तरतरं यदयमात्मा स योऽन्यमात्मनः प्रियं ब्रुवाणं ब्रूयात् प्रियꣳ रोत्स्यतीतीश्वरो ह तथैव स्यादात्मानमेव प्रियमुपासीत स य आत्मानमेव प्रियमुपास्ते न हास्य प्रियं प्रमायुकं भवति॥८॥

That self is dearer than a son, is dearer than wealth, is dearer than all else, since this self is nearer.

If of one who speaks of anything else than the self as dear, one should say, ' He will lose what he holds dear,' he would indeed be likely to do so. One should reverence the self alone as dear. He who reverences the self alone as dear—what he hold dear, verily, is not perishable.

तदाहुर्यद्ब्रह्मविद्या सर्वं भविष्यन्तो मनुष्या मन्यन्ते किमु तद्ब्रह्मावेद्यस्मात्तत्सर्वमभवदिति॥९॥

Some curious Brāhmaṇas have raised a question: 'Since men think that by the knowledge of Brahma they become the All, what, pray, was it that Brahma knew whereby he became the All?'

ब्रह्म वा इदमग्र आसीत् तदात्मानमेवावेदहं ब्रह्मास्मीति, तस्मात्तत् सर्वमभवत् तद्यो यो देवानां प्रत्यबुध्यत स एव तदभवत्तथर्षीणां तथा मनुष्याणां तद्धैतत्पश्यन्नृषिर्वामदेवः प्रतिपेदेऽहं मनुरभवꣳ सूर्यश्चेति तदिदमप्येतर्हि य एवं वेदाऽहं ब्रह्मास्मीति स इदꣳसर्वं भवति तस्य ह न देवाश्च नाभूत्या ईशते, आत्मा ह्येषाꣳस भवत्यथ योऽन्यां देवतामुपास्तेऽन्योऽसावन्योऽहमस्मीति न स वेद यथा पशुरेवꣳ स देवानां यथा ह वै बहवः पशवो मनुष्यं भुञ्ज्युरेवमेकैकः पुरुषो देवान् भुनक्त्येकस्मिन्नेव पशावादीयमानेऽप्रियं भवति किमु बहुषु तस्मादेषां तन्न प्रियं यदेतन्मनुष्या विद्युः॥१०॥

Verily, in the beginning this world was Brahma.

It knew only itself (*ātmānam*); 'I am Brahma!' Therefore it became the All. Whoever of the gods became awakened to this, he indeed became it; likewise in the case of seers (*ṛṣi*), likewise in the case of men. Seeing this, indeed, the seer Vāmadeva began :—

I was Manu and the sun (*Sūrya*)!

This is so now also. Whoever thus knows 'I am Brahma!' becomes this All; even the gods have not power to prevent his becoming thus, for he becomes their self (*ātman*).

So whoever worships another divinity [than his Self], thinking 'He is one and I another', he knows not. He is like a sacrificial animal for the gods. Verily, indeed, as many animals would be of service to a man, even so each single person is of service to the gods. If even one animal is taken away, it is not pleasant. What, then, if many? Therefore it is not pleasing to those [gods] that men should know this.

ब्रह्म वा इदमग्र आसीदेकमेव तदेकꣳ सन्न व्यभवत्तच्छ्रेयोरूपमत्यसृजत क्षत्रं यान्येतानि देवत्रा क्षत्राणीन्द्रो वरुणः सोमो रुद्रः पर्यन्यो यमो मृत्युरीशान इति तस्मात् क्षत्रात्परं नास्ति तस्माद्ब्राह्मणः क्षत्रियमधस्तादुपास्ते राजसूये क्षत्र एव तद्यशो दधाति सैषा क्षत्रस्य योनिर्यद्ब्रह्म तस्माद्यद्यपि राजा परमतां गच्छति ब्रह्मैवान्तत उपनिश्रयति स्वां योनिं य उ एनꣳ हिनस्ति स्वाꣳ स योनिमृच्छति स पापीयान् भवति यथा श्रेयाꣳसꣳ हिꣳसित्वा॥ ११॥

Verily, in the beginning this world was Brahma, one only. Being one, he was not developed. He created still further a superior form, the Kṣatrahood, even those who are Kṣatras (rulers) among the gods : Indra, Varuṇa, Soma, Rudra, Parjanya, Yama, Mṛtyu, Īśāna. Therefore there is nothing higher than Kṣatra. Therefore at the Rājasūya ceremony the Brahman sits below the Kṣatriya. Upon Kṣatrahood alone does he confer this honour. This same thing, namely Brahmanhood (*brahma*), is the source of Kṣatrahood. Therefore, even if the king attains supremacy, he rests finally upon Brahmanhood as his own source. So whoever injures him [i.e. a Brahman] attacks his own source. He fares worse in proportion as he injures one who is better.

[Initially, all persons knowing Brahma were like the life of Brāhmaṇa with the enhancement of society, men were required for providing the defence. The persons providing defence (Kṣatriya) were selected and appointed out from those Brahma knowing persons. In context to the word providing defence those only were given the most importance.]

स नैव व्यभवत् स विशमसृजत यान्येतानि देवजातानि गणश आख्यायन्ते वसवो रुद्रा आदित्या विश्वेदेवा मरुत इति॥ १२॥

He was not yet developed. He created the Viś (the commonalty), those kinds of gods that are mentioned in numbers : the Vasus, the Rudras, the Ādityas, the Viśvedevas, the Maruts.

[The society was developed with more paces and to satisfy the emerging needs the Vaiśya Varṁa was developed from that very society particularly to tackle with the issues like production, exchange, distribution etc.]

स नैव व्यभवत्सशौद्रंवर्णमसृजत पूषणमियं वैपूषेयꣳ हीदꣳ सर्वं पुष्यति यदिदं किंच॥ १३॥

He was not yet developed. He created the Śūdra caste (*varṇa*), Pūṣan. Verily, this [earth] is Pūṣan, for she nourishes (√*puṣ*) everything that is.

स नैव व्यभवत्तच्छ्रेयोरूपमत्यसृजत धर्मं तदेतत् क्षत्रस्य क्षत्रं यद्धर्मस्तस्माद्धर्मात्परं नास्त्यथो अबलीयान् बलीयाꣳ समाशꣳसते धर्मेण यथा राज्ञैवं यो वै स धर्मः सत्यं वै तत्तस्मात् सत्यं वदन्तमाहुर्धर्मं वदतीति धर्मं वा वदन्तꣳ सत्यं वदतीत्येतद्ध्येवैतदुभयं भवति॥ १४॥

He was not yet developed. He created still further a better form, Law (*dharma*). This is the power (*kṣatra*) of the Kṣatriya class (*kṣatra*), viz. Law. Therefore there is nothing higher than Law. So a weak man controls a strong man by Law, just as if by a king. Verily, that which is Law is truth. Therefore they say of a man who speaks the truth, 'he speaks the Law', or of a man who speaks the Law, 'He speaks the truth.' Verily, both these are the same thing.

तदेतद्ब्रह्म क्षत्रं विट् शूद्रस्तदग्निनैव देवेषु ब्रह्माभवद्ब्राह्मणो मनुष्येषु क्षत्रियेण क्षत्रियो वैश्येन वैश्यः शूद्रेण शूद्रस्तस्मादग्नावेव देवेषु लोकमिच्छन्ते ब्राह्मणे मनुष्येष्वेताभ्याꣳहि रूपाभ्यां ब्रह्माभवत्। अथ यो ह वा अस्माल्लोकात्स्वं लोकमदृष्ट्वा प्रैति स एनमविदितो न भुनक्ति यथा वेदो वाननूक्तोऽन्यद्वा कर्माकृतं यदिह वा अप्यनेवंविद् महत्पुण्यं कर्म करोति तद्धास्यान्ततः क्षीयत एवात्मानमेव लोकमुपासीत स य आत्मानमेव लोकमुपास्ते न हास्य कर्म क्षीयते अस्माद्ध्येवात्मनो यद्यत्कामयते तत्तत्सृजते।। १५।।

So that Brahma [appeared as] Kṣatra, Viś and Śūdra. So among the gods Brahma appeared by means of Agni, among men as a Brahman, as a Kṣatriya by means of the [divine] Kṣatriya, as a Vaiśya by means of the [divine] Vaiśya, as a Śūdra by means of the [divine] Śūdra. Therefore people desire a place among the gods in Agni, among men in a Brahman, for by these two forms [pre-eminently] Brahma appeared.

Now whoever departs from this world [i.e. the world of the Ātman] without having recognized it as his own, to him it is of no service, because it is unknown, as the unrecited Vedas or any other undone deed [do not help a man].

Verily, even if one performs a great and holy work, but without knowing this, that work of his merely perishes in the end. One should worship the Self alone as this world does not perish, for out of that very Self he creates whatsoever he desires.

अथो अयं वा आत्मा सर्वेषां भूतानां लोकः स यज्जुहोति यद्यजते तेन देवानां लोकोऽथ यदनुब्रूते तेन ऋषीणामथ यत्पितृभ्यो निपृणाति यत्प्रजामिच्छते तेन पितृणामथ यन्मनुष्यान्वासयते यदेभ्योऽशनं ददाति तेन मनुष्याणामथ यत्पशुभ्यस्तृणोदकं विन्दति तेन पशूनां यदस्य गृहेषु श्वापदा वयाꣳस्यापिपीलिकाभ्य उपजीवन्ति तेन तेषां लोको यथा ह वै स्वाय लोकायारिष्टिमिच्छेदेवꣳ हैवंविदे सर्वाणि भूतान्यरिष्टिमिच्छन्ति तद्वा एतद्विदितं मीमाꣳसितम्।। १६।।

Now this Self, verily, is a world of all created things. Insofar as a man makes offerings and sacrifices, he becomes the world of the gods. Insofar as he learns [the Vedas], he becomes the world of the seers (*ṛṣi*). Insofar as he offers libations to the fathers and desires offspring, he becomes the world of the fathers. Insofar as he gives lodging and food to men, he becomes the world of men. Insofar as he finds grass and water for animals, he becomes the world of animals. Insofar as beasts and birds, even to the ants, find a living in his houses, he becomes their world. Verily, as one would desire security for his own world, so all creatures wish security for him who has this knowledge. This fact, verily, is known when it is thought one.

आत्मैवेदमग्र आसीदेक एव सोऽकामयत जाया मे स्यादथ प्रजायेयाथ वित्तं मे स्यादथ कर्म कुर्वीयेत्येतावान् वै कामो नेच्छꣳश्चनातो भूयो विन्देत्तस्मादप्येतर्ह्येकाकी कामयते जाया मे स्यादथ प्रजायेयाथ वित्तं मे स्यादथ कर्म कुर्वीयेति स यावदप्येतेषामेकैकं न प्राप्नोत्यकृत्स्न एव तावन्मन्यते तस्यो कृत्स्नता मन एवास्यात्मा वाग्जाया प्राणः प्रजा चक्षुर्मानुषं वित्तं चक्षुषा हि तद्विन्दते श्रोत्रं दैवꣳ श्रोत्रेण हि तच्छृणोत्यात्मैवास्य कर्मात्मना हि कर्म करोति स एष पाङ्क्तो यज्ञः पाङ्क्तः पशुः पाङ्क्तः पुरुषः पाङ्क्तमिदꣳ सर्वं यदिदं किंच तदिदꣳ सर्वमाप्नोति य एवं वेद॥ १७॥

In the beginning this world was just the Self (*Ātman*), one only. He wished : 'Would that I had a wife; then I would procreate. Would that I had wealth; then I would offer sacrifice.' So great, indeed, is desire. Not even if one desired, would he get more than that. Therefore even today when one is lonely one wishes : 'Would that I had a wife, then I would procreate. Would that I had wealth, then I would offer sacrifice.' So far as he does not obtain any one of these, he thinks that he is, assuredly, incomplete. Now his completeness is as follows : his mind truly is his self (*ātman*); his voice is his wife; his breath is his offspring; his eye is his worldly wealth, for with his eye he finds; his ear is his heavenly [wealth], for with his ear he hears it; his body (*ātman*), indeed, is his work, for with his body he performs work.

The sacrifice is fivefold. The sacrificial animal is fivefold. A person is fivefold. This whole world, whatever there is, is fivefold. He obtains this whole world who knows this.

पञ्चमं ब्राह्मणम्

यत्सप्तान्नानि मेधया तपसाजनयत्पिता। एकमस्य साधारणं द्वे देवानभाजयत्। त्रीण्यात्मनेऽकुरुत पशुभ्य एकं प्रायच्छत्तस्मिन्सर्वं प्रतिष्ठितं यच्च प्राणिति यच्च न कस्मात्तानि न क्षीयन्तेऽद्यमानानि सर्वदा। यो वैतामक्षितिं वेद सोऽन्नमत्ति प्रतीकेन स देवानपि यच्छति स ऊर्जमुपजीवतीति श्लोकाः॥ १॥

[The threefold production of the world by Prajāpati as food for himself]

When the Father produced by intellect and austerity seven kinds of food, one of his [foods] was common to all, of two he let the gods partake, three he made for himself, one he bestowed upon the animals.

On this [food] everything depends, both what breaths and what does not. How is it that these do not perish? When they are being eaten all the time?

He who knows this imperishableness— he eats food with his mouth (*pratīka*), he goes to the gods, he lives on strength. Thus the verses.

यत्सप्तान्नानि मेधया तपसाजनयत्पितेति मेधया हि तपसाऽजनयत्पितैकमस्य साधारणमितीदमेवास्य तत्साधारणमन्नं यदिदमद्यते स य एतदुपास्ते न स पाप्मनो व्यावर्तते मिश्रꣳ ह्येतत् द्वे देवानभाजयदिति हुतं च प्रहुतं च तस्माद्देवेभ्यो जुह्वति च प्र च जुह्वत्यथो आहुर्दर्शपूर्णमासाविति। तस्मान्नेष्टियाजुकः स्यात्पशुभ्य एकं प्रायच्छदिति तत्पयः पयो ह्येवाग्रे मनुष्याश्च पशवश्चोपजीवन्ति तस्मात् कुमारं जातं घृतं वै वाग्रे प्रतिलेहयन्ति

स्तनं वानुधापयन्त्यथ वत्सं जातमाहुरतृणाद इति। तस्मिन् सर्वं प्रतिष्ठितं यच्च प्राणिति यच्च नेति पयसि हीदꣳ सर्वं प्रतिष्ठितं यच्च प्राणिति यच्च न। तद्यदिदमाहुः संवत्सरं पयसा जुह्वदप पुनर्मृत्युं जयतीति न तथा विद्याद्यदहरेव जुहोति तदहः पुनर्मृत्युमपजयत्येवं विद्वान्सर्वꣳ हि देवेभ्योऽन्नाद्यं प्रयच्छति। कस्मात्तानि न क्षीयन्तेऽद्यमानानि सर्वदेति पुरुषो वा अक्षितिः स हीदमन्नं पुनः पुनर्जनयते यो वै तामक्षितिं वेदेति पुरुषो वा अक्षितिः स हीदमन्नं धिया धिया जनयते। कर्मभिर्यद्धैतन्न कुर्यात्क्षीयेत ह सोऽन्नमत्ति प्रतीकेनेति मुखं प्रतीकं मुखेनेत्येतत्स देवानपि गच्छति स ऊर्जमुपजीवतीति प्रशꣳसा॥ २॥

'When the Father produced by intellect and austerity seven kinds of food' truly by intellect and austerity the Father did produce them.

'One of his [foods] was common to all.' That of his which is common to all is the food that is eaten here. He who worships that, is not turned from evil, for it is mixed [i.e. common, not selected]. 'Of two he let the gods partake.' They are the *huta* [fire-sacrifice) and the *prahuta* (offering). For this reason one sacrifices and offers to the gods. People also say that these two are the new-moon and the full-moon sacrifices. Therefore one should not offer sacrifice [merely] to secure a wish.

'One he bestowed upon the animals' that is milk, for at first both men and animals live upon milk. Therefore they either make a new-born babe lick butter or put it to the breast. Likewise they call a new-born calf 'one that does not eat grass.'

'On this [food] everything depends, both what breathes and what does not' for upon milk everything depends, both what breathes and what does not. This that people say, 'By offering milk for a year one escapes repeated death (*punarmṛtyu*)' one should know that this is not so, since on the very day that he makes the offering he who knows escapes repeated death, for he offers all his food to the gods.

'How is it that these do not perish when they are being eaten all the time?' Verily, the Person is imperishableness, for he produces this food again and again.

'He who knows this imperishableness' verily, a person is imperishableness, for by continuous meditation he produces this food as his work. Should he not do this, all the food would perish.

'He eats food with his mouth (pratīka).' The *pratīka* is the mouth. So he eats food with his mouth.

'He goes to the gods, he lives on strength' this is praise.

[One should not take the apparent meaning of the milk from the above said statement revealing that a respiring and non-respiring all living-organisms are depended on the milk. It should be purported as the nourishing flow. Similarly, the sensitivity tied with the worldly bondage may be purported as animal fastened with a rope.]

त्रीण्यात्मनेऽकुरुतेति मनो वाचं प्राणं तान्यात्मनेऽकुरुतान्यत्रमना अभूवं नादर्शमन्यत्रमना अभूवं नाश्रौषमिति मनसा ह्येव पश्यति मनसा शृणोति। कामः संकल्पो विचिकित्सा श्रद्धाश्रद्धा

धृतिरधृतिर्ह्रीर्धीर्भीरित्येतत्सर्वं मन एव तस्मादपि पृष्ठत उपस्पृष्टो मनसा विजानाति यः कश्च शब्दो वागेव सैषा ह्यन्तमायत्तैषा हि न प्राणोऽपानो व्यान उदानः समानोऽन इत्येतत्सर्वं प्राण एवैतन्मयो वा अयमात्मा वाङ्मयो मनोमयः प्राणमयः॥ ३॥

'Three he made for himself.' Mind, speech, breath — these he made for himself.

People say : 'My mind was elsewhere; I did not see. My mind was elsewhere; I did not hear. It is with the mind, truly, that one sees. It is with the mind that one hears. Desire, imagination, doubt, faith, lack of faith, steadfastness, lack of steadfastness, shame, meditation, fear—all this is truly mind. Therefore even if one is touched on his back, he discerns it with the mind.

Whatever sound there is, it is just speech. Verily, it comes to an end [as human speech]; verily, it does not [as the heavenly voice].

The in-breath, the out-breath, the diffused breath, the up-breath, the middle-breath– all this is just breath. Indeed, the self (*ātman*) consists of speech, mind and breath.

[As the gods existed in the body and the nature are satiated and provided with power by the 'Huta' and 'Prahuta', the Brahma as existed in the body and the sensitivity of the Brahma prevailing in the nature can be made powerful and satiated by the mind, speech and the breathing. The use of these three elements should be made for knowledge and no way for the enjoyments of any kinds. The man who does this can only be said a Brāhmaṇa loyal to the knowledge or a celibate man.]

त्रयो लोका एत एव वागेवायं लोको मनोऽन्तरिक्षलोकः प्राणोऽसौ लोकः॥ ४॥

These same (mind, speech and the breathing as described herein) are the three worlds. this [terrestrial] world is Speech. The middle [atmospheric] world is Mind. That [celestial] world is Breath.

त्रयो वेदा एत एव वागेवर्ग्वेदो मनो यजुर्वेदः प्राणः सामवेदः॥ ५॥

These same are the three Vedas. The Ṛgveda is Speech. The Yajurveda is Mind. The Sāmaveda is Breath.

देवाः पितरो मनुष्या एत एव वागेव देवा मनः पितरः प्राणो मनुष्याः॥ ६॥

The same are the gods, Manes and men. The gods are Speech. The Manes are Mind. Men are Breath.

पिता माता प्रजैत एव मन एव पिता वाङ्माता प्राणः प्रजा॥ ७॥

These same are father, mother and offspring. The father is Mind. The mother is Speech. The offspring is Breath.

विज्ञातं विजिज्ञास्यमविज्ञातमेत एव यत् किंच विज्ञातं वाचस्तद्रूपं वाग्घि विज्ञाता वागेनं तद्भूत्वावति॥ ८॥

These are Vijñāta (duly known), Vijijñāsya (what is to be known) and Avijñāta (what is unknown). The known (knowledge) is speech, the power of speech too is known. This speech too protects the concerned living-organism by virtue of knowledge.

यत्किञ्च विजिज्ञास्यं मनसस्तद्रूपं मनो हि विजिज्ञास्यं मन एनं तद्भूत्वावति॥ ९॥

Whatever is to be known is a form of Mind, for mind is to be known. Mind, having become this, helps him.

यत्किञ्चाविज्ञातं प्राणस्त तद्रूपं प्राणो ह्यविज्ञातः प्राण एनं तद्भूत्वावति॥ १०॥

What is unknown is a form of Breath, for Breath is unknown. Breath, having become this, helps him.

तस्यै वाचः पृथिवी शरीरं ज्योतीरूपमयमग्निस्तद्यावत्येव वाक्तावती पृथिवी तावानयमग्निः॥ ११॥

Of this Speech the earth is the body. Its light-form is this [terrestrial] fire. As far as Speech extends, so far extends the earth, so far this fire.

अथैतस्य मनसो द्यौः शरीरं ज्योतीरूपमसावादित्यस्तद्यावदेव मनस्तावती द्यौस्तावानसावादित्यस्तौ मिथुनꣳ समैतां ततः प्राणोऽजायत स इन्द्रः स एषोऽसपत्नो द्वितीयो वै सपत्नो नास्य सपत्नो भवतो य एवं वेद॥ १२॥

The world of sun is the body of mind and the sun is its (of mind) luminating form. As far as Mind extends, so far extends the sky, so far you sun. These two [the fire and the sun] entered sexual union. Therefrom was born Breath. He is Indra. He is without a rival. Verily, a second person is a rival. He who knows this has no rival.

अथैतस्य प्राणस्यापः शरीरं ज्योतीरूपमसौ चन्द्रस्तद्यावानेव प्राणस्तावत्य आपस्तावानसौ चन्द्रस्त एते सर्व एव समाः सर्वेऽनन्ताः स यो हैतानन्तवत उपास्तेऽन्तवन्तꣳ स लोकं जयत्यथ यो हैताननन्तानुपास्तेऽनन्तꣳ स लोकं जयति॥ १३॥

The water is the body of that breathing, the moon is its luminating form, the quantum of water and the moon is equal to the quantum of breathing. All these are equal and endless. Verily he who worships them as finite wins a finite world. Likewise he who worships them as infinite wins an infinite world.

स एष संवत्सरः प्रजापतिः षोडशकलस्तस्य रात्रय एव पञ्चदशकला ध्रुवैवास्य षोडशी कला स रात्रिभिरेवा च पूर्यतेऽप च क्षीयते सोऽमावास्याꣳ रात्रिमेतया षोडश्या कलया सर्वमिदं प्राणभृदनुप्रविश्य ततः प्रातर्जायते तस्मादेताꣳ रात्रि प्राणभृतः प्राणं न विच्छिन्द्यादपि कृकलासस्यैतस्या एव देवताया अपचित्यै॥ १४॥

That above described Saṁvatsara too is Prajāpati. He is composed of sixteen parts. The nights are his fifteen parts and the sixteenth part is Dhruva (steadfast). He is increased and diminished by his nights alone. Having, on the new-moon night, entered with that sixteenth part into everything here that has breath, he is born thence on the following morning [as the new moon]. Therefore on that night one should not cut off the breath of any breathing thing, not even of a lizard, in honour of that divinity.

यो वै स संवत्सरः प्रजापतिः षोडशकलोऽयमेव स योऽयमेवंवित्पुरुषस्तस्य वित्तमेव पञ्चदशकला

आत्मैवास्य षोडशी कला स वित्तेनैवा च पूर्यतेऽप च क्षीयते तदेतन्नभ्यं यदयमात्मा प्रधिर्वित्तं तस्माद्यद्यपि सर्वज्यानिं जीर्यत आत्मना चेज्जीवति प्रधिनागादित्येवाहुः॥ १५॥

Verily, the person here who knows this, is himself that Prajāpati with the sixteen parts who is the year (Saṁvatsara). The fifteen parts are his wealth. The sixteenth part is his self (*ātman*). In wealth alone [not in self] is one increased and diminished.

That which is the self (*ātman*) is a hub; wealth, a felly. Therefore even if one is overcome by the loss of everything, provided he himself lives, people say merely : 'He has come off with the loss of a felly!'

अथ त्रयो वाव लोका मनुष्यलोकः पितृलोको देवलोक इति सोऽयं मनुष्यलोकः पुत्रेणैव जय्यो नान्येन कर्मणा कर्मणा पितृलोको विद्यया देवलोको देवलोको वै लोकानाꣳ श्रेष्ठस्तस्माद्विद्यां प्रशꣳसन्ति॥ १६॥

Now, there are of a truth three worlds—the world of men, the world of the fathers, and the world of the gods. This world of men is to be obtained by a son only, by no other means; the world of the fathers, by sacrifice; the world of the gods, by knowledge. The world of the gods is verily the best of worlds. Therefore they praise knowledge.

अथातः संप्रत्तिर्यदा प्रैष्यन्मन्यतेऽथ पुत्रमाहु त्वं ब्रह्म त्वं यज्ञस्त्वं लोक इति स पुत्रः प्रत्याहाहं ब्रह्माहं यज्ञोऽहं लोक इति यद्वै किंचानूक्तं तस्य सर्वस्य ब्रह्मेत्येकता। ये वै के च यज्ञास्तेषाꣳ सर्वेषां यज्ञ इत्येकता ये वै के च लोकास्तेषाꣳ सर्वेषां लोक इत्येकतैतावद्वा इदꣳ सर्वमेतन्मा सर्वꣳ सन्नयमितोऽभुनजदिति तस्मात् पुत्रमनुशिष्टं लोक्यमाहुस्तस्मादेनमनुशासति स यदैवंविदस्माल्लोकात्प्रैत्यथैभिरेव प्राणैः सह पुत्रमाविशति, स यद्यनेन किंचिदक्ष्णयाकृतं भवति तस्मादेनꣳ सर्वस्मात्पुत्रो नाम स पुत्रेणैवास्मिँल्लोके प्रतितिष्ठत्यथैनमेते देवाः प्राणा अमृता आविशन्ति॥ १७॥

Now, the process known by this name is described. When the father is about to move out from this world or considers himself a guide to his son, he says to him -

'You are Brahman (holy knowledge). You are sacrifice. You are the world.' The son replies : 'I am holy knowledge. I am sacrifice. I am the world'. Verily, whatever has been learned [from the Vedas], the sum of all this is expressed by the word 'knowledge' (*brahman*). Verily, whatever sacrifices have been made, the sum of them all is expressed by the word 'sacrifice'. Whatever worlds there are, they are all comprehended under the word 'world'. So great, verily, is this all.

'Being thus the all, let him assist me from this world,' thus [the father considers]. Therefore they call 'world-procuring' a son who has been instructed. Therefore they instruct him. When one who has this knowledge departs from this world, he enters into his son with these vital breaths [i.e. faculties : Speech, Mind and Breath]. Whatever wrong has been done by him, his son frees him from it all. Therefore he is called a son (*putra*). By his son a father stands firm in this world. Then into him [who has made over to his son his mortal breaths] enter those divine immortal breaths.

पृथिव्यै चैनमग्नेश्च दैवी वागाविशति सा वै दैवी वाग्यया यद्यदेव वदति तत्तद्भवति॥ १८॥

From the earth and from the fire the divine Speech enters him. Verily, that is the divine Speech whereby whatever one says comes to be.

दिवश्चैनमादित्याच्च दैवं मन आविशति तद्वै दैवं मनो येनानन्द्येव भवत्यथो न शोचति॥ १९॥

Out of the sky and out of the sun the divine Mind enters him. Verily, that is the divine Mind whereby one becomes blissful and sorrows not.

Out of the water and out of the moon the divine Breath enters him. Verily, that is the divine Breath which, whether moving or not moving, is not perturbed, nor injured.

He who knows this becomes the Self of all beings. As is that divinity [i.e. Prajāpati], so is he. As all beings favour that divinity, so to him who knows this all beings show favour. Whatever sufferings creatures endure, these remain with them. Only good goes to him. Evil, verily, does not go to the gods.

अथातो व्रतमीमाꣳसा प्रजापतिर्ह कर्माणि ससृजे तानि सृष्टान्यन्योन्येनास्पर्धन्त वदिष्याम्येवाहमिति वाग्दध्रे द्रक्ष्याम्यहमिति चक्षुः श्रोष्याम्यहमिति श्रोत्रमेवमन्यानि कर्माणि यथाकर्म तानि मृत्युः श्रमो भूत्वोपयेमे तान्याप्नोत्तान्याप्त्वा मृत्युरवारुन्ध तस्माच्छ्राम्यत्येव वाक् श्राम्यति चक्षुः श्राम्यति श्रोत्रमथेममेव नाप्नोद्योऽयं मध्यमः प्राणस्तानि ज्ञातुं दध्रिर अयं वै नः श्रेष्ठो यः संचरꣳश्चासंचरꣳश्च न व्यथतेऽथो न रिष्यति हन्तास्यैव सर्वे रूपमसामेति त एतस्यैव सर्वे रूपमभवꣳस्तस्मादेत एतेनाख्यायन्ते प्राणा इति तेन ह वाव तत्कुलमाचक्षते यस्मिन्कुले भवति य एवं वेद य उ हैवंविदा स्पर्धतेऽनुशुष्यत्यनुशुष्य हैवान्ततो म्रियत इत्यध्यात्मम्॥ २१॥

Prajāpati created the active functions (*karma*). They, when they had been created, strove with one another. 'I am going to speak,' the voice began. 'I am going to see,' said to eye. 'I am going to hear,' said the ear. So spake the other functions, each according to his function. Death, appearing as weariness, laid hold and took possession of them; and, taking possession of them, Death checked them. Therefore the voice become weary, the eye becomes weary, the ear becomes weary. But Death did not take possession of him who was the middle breath. They sought to know him. They said : 'Verily, he is the best of us, since whether moving or not moving, he is not perturbed, nor perishes. Come, let us all become a form of him.' Of him, indeed, they became a form. Therefore they are named 'vital breaths' after him. In whatever family there is a man who has this knowledge, they call that family after him. Whoever strives with one who knows this, dries up and finally dies. So much with reference to the self.

अथाधिदैवतं ज्वलिष्याम्येवाहमित्यग्निर्दध्रे तप्स्याम्यहमित्यादित्यो भास्याम्यहमिति चन्द्रमा एवमन्या देवता यथादैवतꣳ स यथैषां प्राणानां मध्यमः प्राण एवमेतासां देवतानां वायुर्म्लोचन्ति ह्यन्या देवता न वायुः सैषानस्तमिता देवता यद्वायुः॥ २२॥

Now with reference to the divinities.

'Verily, I am going to blaze,' began the Fire. 'I am going to give forth heat,' said the Sun. 'I am going to shine,' said the Moon. So said the other divinities, each according to his divine nature. As Breath holds the central position among the vital breaths [or functions], so Wind among these divinities; for the other divinities have their decline, but not Wind. The

Wind is that divinity which never goes to rest.

अथैष श्लोको भवति यतश्चोदेति सूर्योऽस्तं यत्र च गच्छतीति प्राणाद्वा एष उदेति प्राणेऽस्तमेति तं देवाश्चक्रिरे धर्मꣳ स एवाद्य स उ श्व इति यद्वा एतेऽमुर्ह्यध्रियन्त तदेवाप्यद्य कुर्वन्ति। तस्मादेकमेव व्रतं चरेत्प्राण्याच्चैवापान्याच्च नेन्मा पाप्मा मृत्युराप्नुवदिति यद्यु चरेत्समापिपयिषेत्तेनो देवतायै सायुज्यꣳ सलोकतां जयति॥ २३॥

There is this verse on the subject :—

From whom the sun rises and in whom it sets- in truth, from Breath it rises, and in Breath it sets—him the gods made law (*dharma*); He only today and tomorrow will be.

Verily, what those [functions] undertook of old, even that they accomplish today. Therefore one should practise but one activity. He should breathe in and breathe out, wishing, 'May not the evil one, Death, get me.' And the observance which he practises he should desire to fulfil to the end. Thereby he wins complete union with that divinity [i.e. Breath] and residence in the same world.

षष्ठं ब्राह्मणम्

त्रयं वा इदं नामरूपं कर्म तेषां नाम्नां वागित्येतदेषामुक्थमतो हि सर्वाणि नामान्युत्तिष्ठन्त्येतदेषाꣳ सामैतद्धि सर्वैर्नामभिः सममेतदेषा ब्रह्मैतद्धि सर्वाणि नामानि बिभर्ति॥ १॥

Whatever is existing in this universe is a commune of the three things *i.e.* the name, form, and work.

Of these, as regards names, that which is called Speech is their hymn of praise (*uktha*), for from it arise (*ut-thā*) all names. It is their Sāman (chant), for it is the same (*sama*) as all names. It is their prayer (*brahman*), for it supports (√*bhar*) all names.

अथ रूपाणां चक्षुरित्येतदेषामुक्थमतो हि सर्वाणि रूपाण्युत्तिष्ठन्त्येतदेषाꣳ सामैतद्धि सर्वै रूपैः सममेतदेषा ब्रह्मैतद्धि सर्वाणि रूपाणि बिभर्ति॥ २॥

Now of forms. That which is called the Eye is their hymn of praise (*uktha*), for from it arise (*ut-thā*) all forms. It is their Sāman (chant), for it is the same (*sama*) as all forms. It is their prayer (*brahman*), for it supports (√*bhar*) all forms.

अथ कर्मणामात्मेत्येतदेषामुक्थमतो हि सर्वाणि कर्माण्युत्तिष्ठन्त्येतदेषाꣳ सामैतद्धि सर्वैः कर्मभिः सममेतदेषां ब्रह्मैतद्धि सर्वाणि कर्माणि बिभर्ति तदेतत्त्रयꣳ सदेकमयमात्मात्मो एकः सन्नेतत्त्रयं तदेतदमृतꣳ सत्येन छन्नं प्राणो वा अमृतं नामरूपे सत्यं ताभ्यामयं प्राणश्छन्नः॥ ३॥

Now of works. That which is called the Body (*ātman*) is their hymn of praise (*uktha*), for from it arise (*ut-thā*) all actions. It is their Sāman (chant), for it is the same (*sama*) as all works. It is their prayer (*brahman*), for it supports (√*bhar*) all works.

Although it is that triad, this Soul (*Ātman*) is one. Although it is one, it is that triad. That is the Immortal veiled by the real (*satya*). Life (*prāṇa*, 'breath') [a designation of the Ātman], verily, is the Immortal. Name and form are the real. By them this Life is veiled.

।।द्वितीयोऽध्याय:।।

प्रथमं ब्राह्मणम्

Gārgya and Ajātaśatru's progressive definition of Brahma as the world-source, entered in sleep

दृप्तबालाकिर्हानूचानो गार्ग्य आस स होवाचाजातशत्रुं काश्यं ब्रह्म ते ब्रवाणीति स होवाचाजातशत्रुः सहस्रमेतस्यां वाचि दद्मो जनको जनक इति वै जना धावन्तीति।। १।।

Dṛptabālāki was a learned Gārgya. He said to Ajātaśatru, [king] of Benares : 'I will tell you about Brahma.' Ajātaśatru said : 'We will give a thousand [cows] for such a speech. Verily, people will run hither, crying, "A Janaka! A Janaka!"'

स होवाच गार्ग्यो य एवासावादित्ये पुरुष एतमेवाहं ब्रह्मोपास इति स होवाचाजातशत्रुर्मा मैतस्मिन्संवदिष्ठा अतिष्ठाः सर्वेषां भूतानां मूर्धा राजेति वा अहमेतमुपास इति स य एतमेवमुपास्तेऽतिष्ठाः सर्वेषां भूतानां मूर्धा राजा भवति।। २।।

Bālāki Gārgya then said : 'The Person who is yonder in the sun—him indeed, I worship as Brahma!'

Ajātaśatru said : 'Talk not to me about him! I worship him as the pre-eminent, the head and king of all beings. He who worships him as such becomes per-eminent, the head and king of all beings.'

स होवाच गार्ग्यो य एवासौ चन्द्रे पुरुष एतमेवाहं ब्रह्मोपास इति स होवाचाजातशत्रुर्मा मैतस्मिन्संवदिष्ठा बृहत्पाण्डरवासाः सोमो राजेति वा अहमेतमुपास इति स य एतमेवमुपास्तेऽहरहर्ह सुतः प्रसुतो भवति नास्यान्नं क्षीयते।। ३।।

Gārgya said : 'The Person who is yonder in the moon—him, indeed, I worship as Brahma!'

Ajātaśatru said : 'Talk not to me about him! I worship him as the great, white-robed king Soma. He who worships him as such, for him soma is pressed out and continually pressed out day by day. His food does not fail.'

स होवाच गार्ग्यो य एवासौ विद्युति पुरुष एतमेवाहं ब्रह्मोपास इति स होवाचाजातशत्रुर्मा मैतस्मिन्संवदिष्ठास्तेजस्वीति वा अहमेतमुपास इति स य एतमेवमुपास्ते तेजस्वी ह भवति तेजस्विनी हास्य प्रजा भवति।। ४।।

Gārgya said : 'The Person who is yonder in lightning —him, indeed, I worship as Brahma!'

Ajātaśatru said : 'Talk not to me about him! I worship him, verily, as the Brilliant. He who worships him as such becomes brilliant indeed. His offspring becomes brilliant.'

स होवाच गार्ग्यो य एवायमाकाशे पुरुष एतमेवाहं ब्रह्मोपास इति स होवाचाजातशत्रुर्मा मैतस्मिन्संवदिष्ठाः पूर्णमप्रवर्तीति वा अहमेतमुपास इति स य एतमेवमुपास्ते पूर्यते प्रजया पशुभिर्नास्यास्माल्लोकात्प्रजोद्वर्तते॥ ५॥

Gārgya said : 'The Person who is here in space—him indeed, I worship as Brahma!'

Ajātaśatru said : 'Talk not to me about him! I worship him, verily, as the Full, the non-active. He who worships him as such is filled with offspring and cattle. His offspring goes not forth from this earth.'

स होवाच गार्ग्यो य एवायं वायौ पुरुष एतमेवाहं ब्रह्मोपास इति स होवाचाजातशत्रुर्मा मैतस्मिन्संवदिष्ठा इन्द्रो वैकुण्ठोऽपराजिता सेनेति वा अहमेतमुपास इति स य एतमेवमुपास्ते जिष्णुर्हापराजिष्णुर्भवत्यन्यतस्त्यजायी॥ ६॥

Gārgya said : 'The Person who is here in wind—him, indeed, I worship as Brahma!'

Ajātaśatru said : 'Talk not to me about him! Verily, I worship him as Indra, the terrible (*vaikuṇṭha*), and the unconquered army. He who worships him as such becomes indeed triumphant, unconquerable, and a conqueror of adversaries.'

स होवाच गार्ग्यो य एवायमग्नौ पुरुष एतमेवाहं ब्रह्मोपास इति स होवाचाजातशत्रुर्मा मैतस्मिन्संवदिष्ठा विषासहिरिति वा अहमेतमुपास इति स य एतमेवमुपास्ते विषासहिर्ह भवति विषासहिर्हास्य प्रजा भवति॥ ७॥

Gārgya said : 'The Person who is here in fire—him, indeed, I worship as Brahma!'

Ajātaśatru said : 'Talk not to me about him! I worship him, verily, as the Vanquisher. He who worships him as such becomes a vanquisher indeed. His offspring become vanquishers.'

स होवाच गार्ग्यो य एवायमप्सु पुरुष एतमेवाहं ब्रह्मोपास इति स होवाचाजातशत्रुर्मा मैतस्मिन्संवदिष्ठाः प्रतिरूप इति वा अहमेतमुपास इति स य एतमेवमुपास्ते प्रतिरूपꣳ हैवैनमुपगच्छति नाप्रतिरूपमथो प्रतिरूपोऽस्माज्जायते॥ ८॥

Gārgya said : 'The Person who is here in water — him, indeed, I worship as Brahma!'

Ajātaśatru said : 'Talk not to me about him! I worship him, verily, as the Counterpart [of phenomenal objects]. His counterpart comes to him [in his children], not that which is not his counterpart. His counterpart is born from him.'

स होवाच गार्ग्यो य एवायमादर्शे पुरुष एतमेवाहं ब्रह्मोपास इति स होवाचाजातशत्रुर्मा मैतस्मिन्संवदिष्ठा रोचिष्णुरिति वा अहमेतमुपास इति स य एतमेवमुपास्ते रोचिष्णुर्ह भवति रोचिष्णुर्हास्य प्रजा भवत्यथो यैः सन्निगच्छति सर्वाꣳस्तानतिरोचते॥ ९॥

Gārgya said : 'The Person who is here in a mirror—him, indeed, I worship as Brahma!'

Ajātaśatru said : 'Talk not to me about him! I worship him, verily, as the Shining One. He who worships him as such becomes shining indeed. His offspring shine. He outshines all those with whom he goes.'

स होवाच गार्ग्यो य एवायं यन्तं पश्चाच्छब्दोऽनूदेत्येतमेवाहं ब्रह्मोपास इति स होवाचाजातशत्रुर्मा मैतस्मिन्संवदिष्ठा असुरिति वा अहमेतमुपास इति स य एतमेवमुपास्ते सर्वꣳ हैवास्मिँल्लोक आयुरेति नैनं पुरा कालात्प्राणो जहाति॥ १०॥

Gārgya said : 'The sound here which follows after one as he goes—him, indeed, I worship as Brahma!'

Ajātaśatru said : 'Talk not to me about him! I worship him, verily, as Life (*asu*). To him who worships him as such there comes a full length of life (*āyu*) in this world. Breath (*prāṇa*) leaves him not before the time.'

स होवाच गार्ग्यो य एवायं दिक्षु पुरुष एतमेवाहं ब्रह्मोपास इति होवाचाजातशत्रुर्मा मैतस्मिन्संवदिष्ठा द्वितीयोऽनपग इति वा अहमेतमुपास इति स य एतमेवमुपास्ते द्वितीयवान् ह भवति नास्माद्गणश्छिद्यते॥ ११॥

Gārgya said : 'The Person who is here in the quarters of heaven—him, indeed, I worship as Brahma!'

Ajātaśatru said : 'Talk not to me about him! I worship him, verily, as the Inseparable Companion. He who worships him as such has a companion. His company is not separated from him.'

स होवाच गार्ग्यो य एवायं छायामयः पुरुष एतमेवाहं ब्रह्मोपास इति स होवाचाजातशत्रुर्मा मैतस्मिन्संवदिष्ठा मृत्युरिति वा अहमेतमुपास इति स य एतमेवमुपास्ते सर्वꣳ हैवास्मिँल्लोक आयुरेति नैनं पुरा कालान्मृत्युरागच्छति॥ १२॥

Gārgya said : 'The Person here who consists of shadow —him, indeed, I worship as Brahma!'

Ajātaśatru said : 'Talk not to me about him! I worship him, verily, as Death. To him who worships him as such there comes a full length of life in this world. Death does not come to him before the time.'

स होवाच गार्ग्यो य एवायमात्मनि पुरुष एतमेवाहं ब्रह्मोपास इति स होवाचाजातशत्रुर्मा मैतस्मिन्संवदिष्ठा आत्मन्वीति वा अहमेतमुपास इति स य एतमेवमुपास्त आत्मन्वीह भवत्यात्मन्विनी हास्य प्रजा भवति स ह तूष्णीमास गार्ग्यः॥ १३॥

Gārgya said : 'The Person here who is in the body (*ātman*)—him, indeed, I worship as Brahma!'

Ajātaśatru said : 'Talk not to me about him! I worship him, verily, as the Embodied One (*ātmanvin*). He who worships him as such becomes embodied indeed. His offspring becomes embodied.' Gārgya became silent.

स होवाचाजातशत्रुरेतावन्नू३ इत्येतावद्धीति नैतावता विदितं भवतीति स होवाच गार्ग्य उप त्वा यानीति॥ १४॥

Ajātaśatru said : 'Is that all?' Gārgya said : 'That is all.' Ajātaśatru said : 'With that much [only] it is not known.' Gārgya said : 'Let me come to you as a pupil.'

स होवाचाजातशत्रुः प्रतिलोमं चैतद्यद्ब्राह्मणः क्षत्रियमुपेयाद्ब्रह्म मे वक्ष्यतीति व्येव त्वा ज्ञपयिष्यामीति तं पाणावादायोत्तस्थौ तौ ह पुरुषꣳ सुप्तमाजग्मतुस्तमेतैर्नामभिरामन्त्रयांचक्रे बृहन् पाण्डरवासः सोमराजन्निति स नोत्तस्थौ तं पाणिना पेषं बोधयांचकार स होत्तस्थौ॥ १५॥

Ajātaśatru said : 'Verily, it is contrary to the course of things that a Brahman should come to a Kṣatriya, thinking "He will tell me Brahma." However, I shall cause you to know him clearly.'

He took him by the hand and rose. The two went up to a man who was asleep. They addressed him with these words : 'You great, white-robed king Soma!' He did not rise. He [i.e. Ajātaśatru] woke him by rubbing him with his hand. That one arose.

स होवाचाजातशत्रुर्यत्रैष एतत्सुप्तोऽभूद्य एष विज्ञानमयः पुरुषः क्वैष तदाभूत्कुत एतदागादिति तदु ह न मेने गार्ग्यः॥ १६॥

Ajātaśatru said : 'When this man fell asleep thus, where then was the person who consists of intelligence (*vijñāna*)? When did he thus come back?' And this also Gārgya did not know.

स होवाचाजातशत्रुर्यत्रैष एतत्सुप्तोऽभूद्य एष विज्ञानमयः पुरुषस्तदेषां प्राणानां विज्ञानेन विज्ञानमादाय य एषोऽन्तर्हृदय आकाशस्तस्मिञ्छेते तानि यदा गृह्णात्यथ हैतत्पुरुषः स्वपिति नाम तद्गृहीत एव प्राणो भवति गृहीता वाग् गृहीत चक्षुर्गृहीतꣳ गृहीतं मनः॥ १७॥

Ajātaśatru said : 'When this man has fallen asleep thus, then the person who consists of intelligence, having by his intelligence taken to himself the intelligence of these senses (*prāṇa*), rests in that place which is the space within the heart. When that person restrains the senses, that person is said to be asleep. Then the breath is restrained. The voice is restrained. The eye is restrained. The ear is restrained. The mind is restrained.

स यत्रैतत्स्वप्न्ययाचरति ते हास्य लोकास्तदुतेव महाराजो भवत्युतेव महाब्राह्मण उतेवोच्चावचं निगच्छति स यथा महाराजो जानपदान् गृहीत्वा स्वे जनपदे यथाकामं परिवर्तेतैवमेवैष एतत्प्राणान् गृहीत्वा स्वे शरीरे यथाकामं परिवर्तते॥ १८॥

When he goes to sleep, these worlds are his. Then he becomes a great king, as it were. Then he becomes a great Brahman, as it were. He enters the high and the low, as it were. As a great king, taking with him his people, moves around in his own country as he please, even so here this one, taking with him his senses, moves around in his own body (*śarīra*) as he pleases.

अथ यदा सुषुप्तो भवति यदा न कस्यचन वेद हिता नाम नाड्यो द्वासप्ततिसहस्राणि हृदयात्पुरीततमभिप्रतिष्ठन्ते ताभिः प्रत्यवसृप्य पुरीतति शेते स यथा कुमारो वा महाराजो वा महाब्राह्मणो वातिघ्नीमानन्दस्य गत्वा शयीतैवमेवैष एतच्छेते॥ १९॥

Now when one falls sound asleep (*suṣupta*), when one knows nothing whatsoever, having crept out through the seventy-two thousand channels called *hitā*, which lead from the heart to the pericardium, one rests in the pericardium, Verily, as a youth or a great king or a great Brahman might rest when he has reached the summit of bliss, so this one now rests.'

स यथोर्णनाभिस्तन्तुनोच्चरेद्यथाग्नेः क्षुद्रा विस्फुलिङ्गा व्युच्चरन्त्येवमेवास्मादात्मनः सर्वे प्राणाः सर्वे लोकाः सर्वे देवाः सर्वाणि भूतानि व्युच्चरन्ति तस्योपनिषत्सत्यस्य सत्यमिति प्राणा वै सत्यं तेषामेष सत्यम्॥ २०॥

As a spider might come out with his thread, as small sparks come forth from the fire, even so from this Soul come forth all vital energies (*prāṇa*), all worlds, all gods, all beings. The mystic meaning (*upaniṣad*) thereof is 'the Real of the real (*satyasya satya*). Vital energies, verily, are the real. He is their Real.'

द्वितीयं ब्राह्मणम्

The embodiment of Breath in a person

यो ह वै शिशुꣳ साधानꣳ सप्रत्याधानꣳ सस्थूणꣳ सदामं वेद सप्त ह द्विषतो भ्रातृव्यानवरुणद्ध्ययं वाव शिशुर्योऽयं मध्यमः प्राणस्तस्येदमेवाधानमिदं प्रत्याधानं प्राणः स्थूणान्नं दाम॥ १॥

Verily, he who knows the new-born infant with his housing, his covering, his post, and his rope, keeps off seven hostile relatives.

Verily, this infant is Breath (*prāṇa*) in the middle. Its housing is this [body]. Its covering is this [head]. Its post is breath (*prāṇa*). Its rope is food.

तमेताः सप्ताक्षितय उपतिष्ठन्ते तद्या इमा अक्षन् लोहिन्यो राजयस्ताभिरेनꣳ रुद्रोऽन्वायत्तोऽथ या अक्षन्नापस्ताभिः पर्जन्यो या कनीनिका तयादित्यो यत्कृष्णं तेनाग्निर्यच्छुक्लं तेनेन्द्रोऽधरयैनं वर्तन्या पृथिव्यन्वायत्ता द्यौरुत्तरया नास्यान्नं क्षीयते य एवं वेद॥ २॥

Seven imperishable beings stand near to serve him. Thus there are these red streaks in the eye. By them Rudra is united with him. Then there is the water in the eye. By it Parjanya is united with him. There is the pupil of the eye. By it the sun is united with him. By the black of the eye, Agni; by the white of the eye, Indra; by the lower eyelash, Earth is united with him; by the upper eyelash, Heaven. He who knows this—his food does not fail.

तदेष श्लोको भवति। अर्वाग्बिलश्चमस ऊर्ध्वबुध्नस्तस्मिन्यशो निहितं विश्वरूपम्। तस्यासत ऋषयः सप्त तीरे वागष्टमी ब्रह्मणा संविदानेत्यर्वाग्बिलश्चमस ऊर्ध्वबुध्न इतीदं तच्छिर एष ह्यर्वाग्बिलश्चमस ऊर्ध्वबुध्नस्तस्मिन्यशो निहितं विश्वरूपमिति प्राणा वै यशो विश्वरूपं प्राणनेतदाह तस्यासत ऋषयः सप्त तीर इति प्राणा वा ऋषयः प्राणानेतदाह वागष्टमी ब्रह्मणा संविदानेति वाग्ध्यष्टमी ब्रह्मणा संवित्ते॥ ३॥

In connection herewith there is this verse :—

There is a cup with its mouth below and its bottom up. In it is placed every form of glory. On its rim sit seven seers. Voice as an eight is united with prayer (*brahman*).

'There is a cup having its mouth below and its bottom up' this is the head, for that is a cup having its mouth below and its bottom up. 'In it is placed every form of glory' breaths, verily, are the 'every form of glory' placed in it; thus he says breaths (*prāṇa*). 'On its rim sit seven seers'— verily, the breaths are the seers. Thus he says breaths. 'Voice as an eight is united with prayer' for voice as an eight is united with prayer.

इमावेव गोतमभरद्वाजावयमेव गोतमोऽयं भरद्वाज इमावेव विश्वामित्रजमदग्नी अयमेव विश्वामित्रोऽयं जमदग्निरिमावेव वसिष्ठकश्यपावयमेव वसिष्ठोऽयं कश्यपो वागेवात्रिर्वाचा ह्यन्नमद्यतेऽत्तिर्ह वै नामैतद्यदत्रिरिति सर्वस्यात्ता भवति सर्वमस्यान्नं भवति य एवं वेद॥ ४॥

These two [sense-organs] here [i.e. the ears] are Gotama and Bharadvāja. This is Gotama and this is Bharadvāja. These two here [i.e. the eyes] are Viśvāmitra and Jamadagni. This is Viśvāmitra. This is Jamadagni. These two here [i.e. the nostrils] are Vasiṣṭha and Kaśyapa. This is Vasiṣṭha. This is Kaśyapa. The voice is Atri, for by the voice food is eaten (√*ad*). Verily, eating (*at-ti*) is the same as the name Atri. He who knows this becomes the eater of everything; everything becomes his food.

तृतीयं ब्राह्मणम्

The two forms of Brahman

द्वे वाव ब्रह्मणो रूपे मूर्तं चैवामूर्तं च मर्त्यं चामृतं च स्थितं च यच्च सच्च त्यच्च॥ १॥

There are, assuredly, two forms of Brahma : the formed (*mūrta*) and the formless, the mortal and the immortal, the stationary and the moving, the actual (*sat*) and the yon (*tya*).

तदेतन्मूर्तं यदन्यद्वायोश्चान्तरिक्षाच्च तन्मर्त्यमेतत्स्थितमेतत्सत्तस्यैतस्य मूर्तस्यैतस्य मर्त्यस्यैतस्य स्थितस्यैतस्य सत एष रसो य एष तपति सतो ह्येष रसः॥ २॥

This is the formed [Brahma]– whatever is different from the wind and the atmosphere. This is mortal; this is stationary; this is actual. The essence of this formed, mortal, stationary, actual [Brahma] is yonder [sun] which gives forth heat, for that is the essence of the actual.

अथामूर्तं वायुश्चान्तरिक्षं चैतदमृतमेतद्यदेतत्त्यत्तस्यैतस्यामूर्तस्यैतस्यामृतस्यैतस्य यत एतस्य त्यस्यैष रसो य एष एतस्मिन्मण्डले पुरुषस्तस्य ह्येष रस इत्यधिदैवतम्॥ ३॥

Now the formless [Brahman] is the wind and the atmosphere. This is immortal, this is moving, this is the yon. The essence of this unformed, immortal, moving, yonder [Brahma] is the Person in that sun-disk, for he is the essence of the yon. Thus with reference to the divinities.

अथाध्यात्ममिदमेव मूर्तं यदन्यत्प्राणाच्च यश्चायमन्तरात्मन्नाकाश एतन्मर्त्यमेतत्स्थितमेतत्सत्तस्यैतस्य मूर्तस्यैतस्य मर्त्यस्यैतस्य स्थितस्यैतस्य सत एष रसो यच्चक्षुः ह्येष रसः॥ ४॥

Now, with reference to the self.

Just that is the formed [Brahma] which is different from breath (*prāṇa*) and from the space which is within the self (*ātman*). This is mortal, this is stationary, this is actual. The essence of this formed, mortal, stationary, actual [Brahma] is the eye, for it is the essence of the actual.

अथामूर्तं प्राणश्च यश्चायमन्तरात्मन्नाकाश एतदमृतमेतद्यदेतत्त्यं तस्यैतस्यामूर्तस्यैतस्यामृतस्यैतस्य यत एतस्य त्यस्यैष रसो योऽयं दक्षिणेऽक्षन्पुरुषस्त्यस्य ह्येष रसः॥५॥

Now the formless [Brahma] is the breath and the space which is within the self. This is immortal, this is moving, this is the yon. The essence of this unformed, immortal, moving, yonder [Brahma] is this Person who is in the right eye, for he is the essence of the yonder.

तस्य हैतस्य पुरुषस्य रूपं यथा माहारजनं वासो यथा पाण्ड्वाविकं यथेन्द्रगोपो यथाग्न्यर्चिर्यथा पुण्डरीकं यथा सकृद्विद्युत्तः सकृद्विद्युत्तेव ह वा अस्य श्रीर्भवति य एवं वेदाथात आदेशो नेति नेति न ह्येतस्मादिति नेत्यन्यत्परमस्त्यथ नामधेयः सत्यस्य सत्यमिति प्राणा वै सत्यं तेषामेष सत्यम्॥६॥

The form of this Person is like a saffron-coloured robe, like white wool, like the [red] Indragopa beetle, like a flame of fire, like the [white] lotus-flower, like a sudden flash of lightning. Verily, like a sudden lightning-flash is the glory of him who knows this.

Hence, now, there is the teaching 'Not thus! not so!' (*neti, neti*), for there is nothing higher than this, that he is thus. Now the designation for him is 'the Real of the real.' Verily, breathing creatures are the real. He is their Real.

चतुर्थं ब्राह्मणम्

The conversation of Yājñavalkya and Maitreyī concerning the pantheistic Soul

मैत्रेयीति होवाच याज्ञवल्क्य उद्यास्यन्वा अरेऽहमस्मात्स्थानादस्मि हन्त तेऽनया कात्यायन्यान्तं करवाणीति॥१॥

Yājñavalkya said to his wife Maitreyī– 'lo, verily, I am about to go forth from this state. Behold! let me make a final settlement for you and that Kātyāyanī.'

सा होवाच मैत्रेयी यन्नु म इयं भगोः सर्वा पृथिवी वित्तेन पूर्णा स्यात्कथं तेनामृता स्यामिति नेति होवाच याज्ञवल्क्यो यथैवोपकरणवतां जीवितं तथैव ते जीवितः स्यादमृतत्वस्य तु नाशास्ति वित्तेनेति॥२॥

Maitreyī replied– "O Lord! Whether I will access to the immortal position if the whole earth with the prosperity would be under my ownership?" Yājñavalkya said– 'No, As the life of the rich, even so would your life be. Of immortality, however, there is no hope through wealth.'

सा होवाच मैत्रेयी येनाहं नामृता स्यां किमहं तेन कुर्यां? यदेव भगवान्वेद तदेव मे ब्रूहीति॥३॥

Then said Maitreyī : 'What should I do with that through which I may not be immortal? What you know, sir— that, indeed, tell me!'

स होवाच याज्ञवल्क्यः प्रिया बतारे नः सती प्रियं भाषस एह्यास्स्व व्याख्यास्यामि ते व्याचक्षाणस्य तु मे निदिध्यासस्वेति॥ ४॥

Then Yājñavalkya said– "O Maitreyī! : 'Ah (*bata*)! Lo (*are*), dear (*priyā*) as you are to us, dear is what you say! Come, sit down. I will explain to you. But while I am expounding, do you seek to ponder thereon.'

स होवाच न वा अरे पत्युः कामाय पतिः प्रियो भवत्यात्मनस्तु कामाय पतिः प्रियो भवति न वा अरे जायायै कामाय जाया प्रिया भवत्यात्मनस्तु कामाय जाया प्रिया भवति न वा अरे पुत्राणां कामाय पुत्राः प्रिया भवन्त्यात्मनस्तु कामाय पुत्राः प्रिया भवन्ति न वा अरे वितस्य कामाय वित्तं प्रियं भवत्यात्मनस्तु कामाय वित्तं प्रियं भवति न वा अरे ब्रह्मणः कामाय ब्रह्म प्रियं भवति न वा अरे लोकानां कामाय लोकाः प्रिया भवन्त्यात्मनस्तु कामाय लोकाः प्रिया भवन्ति न वा अरे देवानां कामाय देवाः प्रिया भवन्त्यात्मनस्तु कामाय देवाः प्रिया भवन्ति न वा अरे भूतानां कामाय भूतानि प्रियाणि भवन्त्यात्मनस्तु कामाय भूतानि प्रियाणि भवन्ति न वा अरे सर्वस्य कामाय सर्वं प्रियं भवत्यात्मनस्तु कामाय सर्वं प्रियं भवत्यात्मा वा अरे द्रष्टव्यः श्रोत्रव्यो मन्तव्यो निदिध्यासितव्यो मैत्रेय्यात्मनो वा अरे दर्शनेन श्रवणेन मत्या विज्ञानेनेदꣳ सर्वं विदितम्॥ ५॥

The Ṛṣi Yajñavalkya said– 'Lo, verily, not for love of the husband is a husband dear, but for love of the Soul (*Ātman*) a husband is dear.

Lo, verily, not for love of the wife is a wife dear, but for love of the Soul a wife is dear.

Lo, verily, not for love of the sons are sons dear, but for love of the Soul sons are dear.

Lo, verily, not for love of the wealth is wealth dear, but for love of the Soul wealth is dear.

Lo, verily, not for love of Brahmanhood (*brahma*) is Brahmanhood dear, but for love of the Soul Brahmanhood is dear.

Lo, verily, not for love of Kṣatrahood (*kṣatra*) is Kṣatrahood dear, but for love of the Soul Kṣatrahood is dear.

Lo, verily, not for love of the worlds are the worlds dear, but for love of the Soul the worlds are dear.

Lo, verily, not for love of the gods are the gods dear, but for love of the Soul the gods are dear.

Lo, verily, not for love of the beings (*bhūta*) are beings dear, but for love of the Soul beings are dear.

Lo, verily, not for love of all is all dear, but for love of the Soul all is dear.

Lo, verily, it is the Soul (*Ātman*) that should be seen, that should be hearkened to, that should be thought on, that should be pondered on, O Maitreyī. Lo, verily, with the seeing of, with the hearkening to, with the thinking of, and with the understanding of the Soul, this world-all is known.

ब्रह्म तं परादाद्योऽन्यत्रात्मनो ब्रह्म वेद क्षत्रं तं परादाद्योऽन्यत्रात्मनः क्षत्रं वेद लोकास्तं परादुर्योऽन्यत्रात्मनो लोकान्वेद देवास्तं परादुर्योऽन्यत्रात्मनो देवान्वेद भूतानि तं परादुर्योऽन्यत्रात्मनो भूतानि वेद सर्वं तं परादाद्योऽन्यत्रात्मनः सर्वं वेदेदं ब्रह्मेदं क्षत्रमिमे लोका इमे देवा इमानि भूतानीदꣳ सर्वं यदयमात्मा॥ ६॥

The man who considers that the Brāhmaṇa or the knowledge exists not in soul but in another thing, is abandoned by the Brāhmaṇa or the knowledge. Similarly, the power or the Kṣatriya abandons the man who observes it otherwise than the soul. The world abandons the man who looks it otherwise than the soul. The gods abandon such a man who looks them otherwise than the soul and all living-beings abandon such a man who looks them otherwise than in the soul. Thus, the knowledge, the power, the world, the gods and all living-organism are the soul and nothing else than the soul itself.

स यथा दुन्दुभेर्हन्यमानस्य न बाह्याञ्छब्दाञ्छक्नुयाद्ग्रहणाय दुन्दुभेस्तु ग्रहणेन दुन्दुभ्याघातस्य वा शब्दो गृहीतः॥ ७॥

It is as, when a drum is being beaten, one would not be able to grasp the external sounds, but by grasping the drum or the beater of the drum the sound is grasped.

स यथा शङ्खस्य ध्मायमानस्य न बाह्याञ्छब्दाञ्छक्नुयाद्ग्रहणाय शङ्खस्य तु ग्रहणेन शङ्खध्मस्य वा शब्दो गृहीतः॥ ८॥

It is—as, when a conch-shell is being blown, one would not be able to grasp the external sounds, but by grasping the conch-shell or the blower of the conch-shell the sound is grasped.

स यथा वीणायै वाद्यमानायै न बाह्यान् शब्दान् शक्नुयात् ग्रहणाय वीणायै तु ग्रहणेन वीणावादस्य वा शब्दो गहीतः॥ ९॥

It is—as, when a lute is being played, one would not be able to grasp the external sounds, but by grasping the lute or the player of the lute the sound is grasped.

स यथार्द्रैधाग्नेरभ्याहितात्पृथग्धूमा विनिश्चरन्त्येवं वा अरेऽस्य महतो भूतस्य निःश्वसितमेतद्यदृग्वेदो यजुर्वेदः सामवेदोऽथर्वाङ्गिरस इतिहासः पुराणं विद्या उपनिषदः श्लोकाः सूत्राण्यनुव्याख्यानानि व्याख्यानान्यस्यैवैतानि सर्वाणि निःश्वसितानि॥ १०॥

It is—as, from a fire laid with damp fuel, clouds of smoke separately issue forth, so, lo, verily, from this great Being (*bhūta*) has been breathed forth that which is Ṛgveda, Yajurveda, Sāmaveda, [Hymns] of the Atharvans and Aṅgirases, Legend (*itihāsa*), Ancient Lore (*purāṇa*), Sciences (*vidyā*), Mystic Doctrines (*upaniṣad*), Verses (*śloka*), Aphorisms (*sūtra*), Explanations (*anuvyākhyāna*) and Commentaries (*vyākhyāna*). From it, indeed, are all these breathed forth.

स यथा सर्वासामपाꣳ समुद्र एकायनमेवꣳ सर्वेषाꣳ स्पर्शानां त्वगेकायनमेवꣳ सर्वेषा गन्धानां नासिके एकायनमेवꣳ सर्वेषाꣳ रसानां जिह्वैकायनमेवꣳ सर्वेषाꣳ रूपाणां चक्षुरेकायनमेवꣳ सर्वेषाꣳ श्रोत्रमेकायनमेवꣳ

सर्वेषाः संकल्पानां मन एकायनमेवः सर्वासां विद्यानाः हृदयमेकायनमेवः सर्वेषां कर्मणाः हस्तावेकायनमेवः सर्वेषामानन्दानामुपस्थ एकायनमेवः सर्वेषां विसर्गाणां पायुरेकायनमेवः सर्वेषामध्वनां पादावेकायनमेवः सर्वेषा वेदानां वागेकायनम्॥ ११॥

It is—as of all waters the uniting-point is the sea, so of all touches the uniting-point is the skin, so of all tastes the uniting-point is the tongue, so of all smells the uniting-point is the nostrils, so of all forms the uniting-point is the eye, so of all sounds the uniting-point is the ear, so of all intentions (*saṁkalpa*) the uniting-point is the mind (*manas*), so of all knowledges the uniting-point is the mind (*manas*), so of all knowledges the uniting-point is the heart, so of all acts (*karma*) the uniting-point is the hands, so of all pleasures (*ānanda*) the uniting-point is the generative organ, so of all evacuations the uniting-point is the anus, so of all journeys the uniting-point is the feet, so of all the Vedas the uniting-point is speech.

स यथा सैन्धवखिल्य उदके प्रास्त उदकमेवानुविलीयेत न हास्योद्ग्रहणायेव स्याद्यतो यतस्त्वाददीत लवणमेवैवं वा अर इदं महद्भूतमनन्तमपारं विज्ञानघन एवैतेभ्यो भूतेभ्यः समुत्थाय तान्येवानुविनश्यति न प्रेत्य संज्ञास्तीत्यरे ब्रवीमीति होवाच याज्ञवल्क्यः॥ १२॥

It is—as a lump of salt cast in water would dissolve right into the water; there would not be [any] of it to seize forth, as it were (*iva*), but wherever one may take, it is salty indeed—so, lo, verily, this great Being (*bhūta*), infinite, limitless, is just a mass of knowledge (*vijñāna-ghana*).

Arising out of these elements (*bhūta*), into them also one vanishes away. After death there is no consciousness (*na pretya saṁjñā 'sti*). Thus, lo, say I.' Thus spake Yājñavalkya.

सा होवाच मैत्रेय्यत्रैव मा भगवानमूमुहन्न प्रेत्य संज्ञास्तीति स होवाच याज्ञवल्क्यो न वा अरेऽहं मोहं ब्रवीम्यलं वा अर इदं विज्ञानाय॥ १३॥

Then spake Maitreyī : 'Herein, indeed, you have bewildered me, sir — in saying (*iti*) : "After death there is no consciousness"!'

Then spake Yājñavalkya : Lo, verily, I speak not bewilderement (*moha*). Sufficient, lo, verily, is this for understanding.

यत्र हि द्वैतमिव भवति तदितर इतरं जिघ्रति तदितर इतरं पश्यति तदितर इतरः शृणोति तदितर इतरमभिवदति तदितर इतरं मनुते तदितर इतरं विजानाति यत्र वा अस्य सर्वमात्मैवाभूत्तत्केन कं जिघ्रेत्तत्केन कं पश्येत्तत्केन कः शृणुयात्तत्केन कमभिवदेत्तत् केन कं मन्वीत तत्केन कं विजानीयाद्येनेदः सर्वं विजानाति तं केन विजानीयाद्विज्ञातारमरे केन विजानीयादिति॥ १४॥

For where there is a duality (*dvaita*), as it were (*iva*), there one sees another; there one smells another; there one hears another; there one speaks to another; there one thinks of another; there one understands another. Where, verily, everything has become just one's own self, then whereby and whom would one smell? then whereby and whom would one see? then whereby and whom would one hear? then whereby and to whom would one speak? then whereby and on whom would one think? then whereby and whom would one understand? Whereby would one understand him by whom one understands this All? Lo, whereby would one understand the understander?'

पञ्चमं ब्राह्मणम्

The co-relativity of all things cosmic and personal, and the absoluteness of the immanent Soul

इयं पृथिवी सर्वेषा भूतानां मध्वस्यै पृथिव्यै सर्वाणि भूतानि मधु यश्चायमस्यां पृथिव्यां तेजोमयोऽमृतमयः पुरुषो यश्चायमध्यात्मᳬ शारीरस्तेजोमयोऽमृतमयः पुरुषोऽयमेव स योऽयमात्मेदममृतमिदं ब्रह्मेदᳬ सर्वम्॥ १॥

This earth is honey for all creatures, and all creatures are honey for this earth. This shining, immortal Person who is in this earth, and with reference to oneself, this shining, immortal Person who is in the body—he, indeed, is just this Soul (*Ātman*), this Immortal, this Brahma, this All.

[Honey is tasty and an excellent nutrient. The earth is interesting and nourishing all the living-organisms and the living-organisms are interesting and nutrients for the earth itself, therefore both of them are called honey to each other. This consortium or the consistency is a skill and phenomenon of the creator. Similarly, the other factors of the nature has been also described with such a harmony established between them.]

इमा आपः सर्वेषा भूतानां मध्वासामपाᳬ सर्वाणि भूतानि मधु यश्चायमास्वप्सु तेजोमयोऽमृतमयः पुरुषो यश्चायमध्यात्मᳬ रैतसस्तेजोमयोऽमृतमयः पुरुषोऽयमेव स योऽयमात्मेदममृतमिदं ब्रह्मेदᳬ सर्वम्॥ २॥

These waters are honey for all things, and all things are honey for these waters. This shining, immortal Person who is in these waters and with reference to oneself, this shining, Immortal Person who is made of semen—he is just this Soul, this immortal, this Brahma, this All.

अयमग्निः सर्वेषां भूतानां मध्वस्याग्नेः सर्वाणि भूतानि मधु यश्चायमस्मिन्नग्नौ तेजोमयोऽमृतमयः पुरुषो यश्चायमध्यात्मं वाङ्मयस्तेजोमयोऽमृतमयः पुरुषोऽयमेव स योऽयमात्मेदममृतमिदं ब्रह्मेदᳬ सर्वम्॥ ३॥

This fire is honey for all things, and all things are honey for this fire. This shining, Immortal Person who is in this fire, and with reference to oneself, this shining, immortal Person who is made of speech—he is just this Soul, this Immortal, this Brahma, this All.

अयं वायुः सर्वेषा भूतानां मध्वस्य वायोः सर्वाणि भूतानि मधु यश्चायमस्मिन्वायौ तेजोमयोऽमृतमयः पुरुषो यश्चायमध्यात्मं प्राणस्तेजोमयोऽमृतमयः पुरुषोऽयमेव स योऽयमात्मेदममृतमिदं ब्रह्मेदᳬ सर्वम्॥ ४॥

This wind is honey for all things, and all things are honey for this wind. This shining, immortal Person who is in this wind, and with reference to oneself, this shining, immortal Person who is breath—he is just this Soul, this Immortal, this Brahma, this All.

अयमादित्यः सर्वेषां भूतानां मध्वस्यादित्यस्य सर्वाणि भूतानि मधु यश्चायमस्मिन्नादित्ये

तेजोमयोऽमृतमयः पुरुषो यश्चायमध्यात्मं चाक्षुषस्तेजोमयोऽमृतमयः पुरुषोऽयमेव स योऽयमात्मेदममृतमिदं ब्रह्मेदꣳ सर्वम्॥५॥

This sun is honey for all things, and all things are honey for this sun. This shining, immortal Person who is in this sun, and, with reference to oneself, this shining, immortal Person who is in the eye—he is just this Soul, this Immortal, this Brahma, this All.

इमा दिशः सर्वेषा भूतानां मध्वासां दिशाꣳ सर्वाणि भूतानि मधु यश्चायमासु दिक्षु तेजोमयोऽमृतमयः पुरुषो यश्चायमध्यात्मꣳ श्रौत्रः प्रातिश्रुत्कस्तेजोमयोऽमृतमयः पुरुषोऽयमेव स योऽयमात्मेदममृतमिदं ब्रह्मेदꣳ सर्वम्॥६॥

These quarters of heaven are honey for all things, and all things are honey for these quarters of heaven. This shining, immortal Person who is in these quarters of heaven, and with reference to oneself, this shining, immortal Person who is in the ear and in the echo—he is just this Soul, this Immortal, this Brahma, this All.

अयं चन्द्रः सर्वेषां भूतानां मध्वस्य चन्द्रस्य सर्वाणि भूतानि मधु यश्चायमस्मिꣳश्चन्द्रे तेजोमयोऽमृतमयः पुरुषो यश्चायमध्यात्मं मानसस्तेजोमयोऽमृतमयः पुरुषोऽयमेव स योऽयमात्मेदममृतमिदं ब्रह्मेदꣳ सर्वम्॥७॥

This moon is honey for all things, and all things are honey for this moon. This shining, immortal Person who is in this moon, and with reference to oneself, this shining, immortal person consisting of mind—he is just this Soul, this Immortal, this Brahma, this All.

इयं विद्युत्सर्वेषां भूतानां मध्वस्यै विद्युतः सर्वाणि भूतानि मधु यश्चायमस्यां विद्युति तेजोमयोऽमृतमयः पुरुषो यश्चायमध्यात्मं तैजसस्तेजोमयोऽमृतमयः पुरुषोऽयमेव स योऽयमात्मेदममृतमिदं ब्रह्मेदꣳ सर्वम्॥८॥

This lightning is honey for all things, and all things are honey tor this lightning. This shining, immortal Person who is in this lightning, and with reference to oneself, this shining, immortal Person who exists as heat—he is just this Soul, this Immortal, this Brahma, this All.

अयꣳ स्तनयित्नुः सर्वेषां भूतानां मध्वस्य स्तनयित्नोः सर्वाणि भूतानि मधु यश्चायमस्मिन्स्तनयित्नौ तेजोमयोऽमृतमयः पुरुषो यश्चायमध्यात्मꣳ शाब्दः सौवरस्तेजोमयोऽमृतमयः पुरुषोऽयमेव स योऽयमात्मेदममृतमिदं ब्रह्मेदꣳ सर्वम्॥९॥

This thunder is honey for all things, and all things are honey for this thunder. This shining, immortal Person who is in thunder and with reference to oneself, this shining, immortal Person who is in sound and in tone—he is just this Soul, this Immortal, this Brahman, this All.

अयमाकाशः सर्वेषां भूतानां मध्वस्याकाशस्य सर्वाणि भूतानि मधु यश्चायमस्मिन्नाकाशे तेजोमयोऽमृतमयः पुरुषो यश्चायमध्यात्मꣳ हृद्याकाशस्तेजो मेयोऽमृतमयः पुरुषोऽयमेव स योऽयमात्मेदममृतमिदं ब्रह्मेदꣳ सर्वम्॥१०॥

This space is honey for all things, and all things are honey for this space. This shining, immortal Person who is in this space, and with reference to oneself, this shining, immortal

Person who is in the space in the heart—he is just this Soul, this Immortal, this Brahma, this All.

अयं धर्मः सर्वेषां भूतानां मध्वस्य सर्वाणि भूतानि मधु यश्चायमस्मिन्धर्मे तेजोमयोऽमृतमयः पुरुषो यश्चायमध्यात्मं धार्मस्तेजोमयोऽमृतमयः पुरुषोऽयमेव स योऽयमात्मेदममृतमिदं ब्रह्मेदꣳ सर्वम्॥ ११॥

This Law (*dharma*) is honey for all things, and all things are honey for this Law. This shining, immortal Person who is in this Law, and with reference to oneself, this shining, immortal Person who exists as virtuousness—he is just this Soul, this Immortal, this Brahma, this All.

इदꣳ सत्यꣳ सर्वेषां भूतानां मध्वस्य सत्यस्य सर्वाणि भूतानि मधु यश्चायमस्मिन्सत्ये तेजोमयोऽमृतमयः पुरुषो यश्चायमध्यात्मꣳ सात्यस्तेजोमयोऽमृतमयः पुरुषोऽयमेव स योऽयमात्मेदममृतमिदं ब्रह्मेदꣳ सर्वम्॥ १२॥

This Truth is honey for all things, and all things are honey for this Truth. This shining, immortal Person who is in this Truth, and with reference to oneself, this shining, immortal Person who exists as truthfulness—he is just this Soul, this Immortal, this Brahma, this All.

इदं मानुषꣳ सर्वेषां भूतानां मध्वस्व मानुषस्य सर्वाणि भूतानि मधु यश्चायमस्मिन्मानुषे तेजोमयोऽमृतमयः पुरुषः यश्चायमध्यात्मं मानुषः तेजोमयोऽमृतमयः पुरुषोऽयमेव स योऽयमात्मेदममृतमिदं ब्रह्मेदꣳ सर्वम्॥ १३॥

This mankind (*mānuṣa*) is honey for all things and all things are honey for this mankind. This shining, immortal Person who is in this mankind, and with reference to oneself, this shining, immortal Person who exists as a human being—he is just this Soul, this Immortal, this Brahma, this All.

अयमात्मा सर्वेषां भूतानां मध्वस्यात्मनः सर्वाणि भूतानि मधु यश्चायमस्मिन्नात्मनि तेजोमयोऽमृतमयः पुरुषो यश्चायमात्मा तेजोमयोऽमृतमयः पुरुषोऽयमेव स योऽयमात्मेदममृतमिदं ब्रह्मेदꣳ सर्वम्॥ १४॥

This Soul (*Ātman*) is honey for all things, and all things are honey for this Soul. This shining, immortal Person who is in this Soul, and with reference to oneself, this shining, immortal Person who exists as Soul—he is just this Soul, this Immortal, this Brahma, this All.

स वा अयमात्मा सर्वेषा भूतानामदिपतिः सर्वेषां भूतानाꣳ राजा तद्यथा रथनाभौ च रथनेमौ चाराः सर्वे समर्पिता एवमेवास्मिन्नात्मनि सर्वाणि भूतानि सर्वे देवाः सर्वे लोकाः सर्वे प्राणाः सर्व एत आत्मानः समर्पिताः॥ १५॥

Verily, this Soul is the overlord of all things, the king of all things. As all the spokes are held together in the hub and felly of a wheel, just so in this Soul all things, all gods, all worlds, all breathing things, all these selves are held together.

इदं वै तन्मधु दध्यङ्ङाथर्वणोऽश्विभ्यामुवाच तदेतदृषिः पश्यन्नवोचत्। तद्वां नरा सनये दꣳस उग्रमाविष्कृणोमि तन्यतुर्न वृष्टिम्। दध्यङ् ह यन्मध्वाथर्वणो वामश्वस्य शीर्ष्णा प्रयदीमुवाचेति॥ १६॥

This, verily, is the honey which Dadhyañc Ātharvaṇa declared unto the two Aśvins. Seeing this, the seer spoke :—

'That mighty deed of yours, O you two heroes, [which you did] for gain,

I make known, as thunder [makes known the coming] rain,

Even the honey which Dadhyañc Ātharvaṇa to you did declare by the head of a horse.'

इदं वै तन्मधु दध्यङ्ङाथर्वणोऽश्विभ्यामुवाच तदेतदृषिः पश्यन्नवोचदाथर्वणायाश्विना दधीचेऽश्व्यꣳशिरः प्रत्यैरयतम्। स वां मधु प्रवोचदृतायन्त्वाष्ट्रं यद्दस्रावपि कक्ष्यं वामिति॥ १७॥

This Madhu Vidyā was provided by Ātharvaṇa Dadhyañc to Aśvinī Kumāras.

Seeing this, the seer spoke :—

'Upon Dadhyañc Ātharvaṇa you Aśvins did substitute a horse's head. He, keeping true, declared to you the honey of Tvaṣṭā, which is your secret, O you mighty ones.'

इदं वै तन्मधु दध्यङ्ङाथर्वणोऽश्विभ्यामुवाच तदेतदृषिः पश्यन्नवोचत्। पुरश्चक्रे द्विपदः पुरश्चक्रे चतुष्पदः पुरः स पक्षी भूत्वा पुरः पुरुष आविशदिति। स वा अयं पुरुषः सर्वासु पूर्षु पुरिशयो नैनेन किंचनानावृतम्॥ १८॥

This, verily, is the honey which Dadhyañc Ātharvaṇa declared unto the two Aśvins. Seeing this, the seer spoke :—

'Citadels with two feet he did make. Citadels with four feet he did make.

Into the citadels he, having become a bird—

Into the citadels (*puras*) the Person (*puruṣa*) entered.'

This, verily, is the person (*puruṣa*) dwelling in all cities (*puriśaya*). There is nothing by which he is not covered, nothing by which he is not hide.

इदं वै तन्मधु दध्यङ्ङाथर्वणोऽश्विभ्यामुवाच तदेतदृषिः पश्यन्नवोचद्रूपꣳरूपं प्रतिरूपो बभूव तदस्य रूपं प्रतिचक्षणाय। इन्द्रो मायाभिः पुरुरूप ईयते युक्ता ह्यस्य हरयः शता दशेत्ययं वै हरयोऽयं वै दश च सहस्राणि बहूनि चानन्तानि च तदेतद्ब्रह्मापूर्वमनपरमनन्तरमबाह्यमयमात्मा ब्रह्म सर्वानुभूरित्यनुशासनम्॥ १९॥

This, verily, is the honey which Dadhyañc Ātharvaṇa declared unto the two Aśvins. Seeing this, the seer spoke:— He became corresponding in form to every form.

This is to be looked upon as a form of him. Indra by his magic powers (*māyā*) goes about in many forms yoked are his ten-hundred steeds.'

He [i.e. the Soul, *Ātman*], verily, is the steeds. He, verily, is tens and thousands, many and endless. This Brahma is without an earlier and without a later, without an inside and without an outside. This Soul is Brahma, the all-perceiving. Such is the instruction.

षष्ठं ब्राह्मणम्

The teachers of this doctrine

अथ वꣳश पौतिमाष्यो गौपवनाद्गौपवनः पौतिमाष्यात्पौतिमाष्यो गौपवनाद्गौपवनः कौशिकात्कौशिकः कौण्डिन्यात्कौण्डिन्यः शाण्डिल्याच्छाण्डिल्यः कौशिकाच्च गौतमाच्च गौतमः॥ १॥

आग्निवेश्यादाग्निवेश्यः शाण्डिल्याच्चानभिम्लाताच्चानभिम्लात आनभिम्लातादानभिम्लातआनभिम्लाता-दान भिम्लातो गौतमाद्गौतमः सैतवप्राचीनयोग्याभ्याꣳ सैतवप्राचीनयोग्यौ पाराशर्यात्पाराशर्यो भारद्वाजाद्भारद्वाजो भारद्वाजाच्च गौतमाच्च गौतमो भारद्वाजाद्भारद्वाजः पाराशर्यात् पाराशर्यो बैजवापायनाद्बैजवापायनः कौशिकायनेः कौशिकायनिः॥ २॥

घृतकौशिकाद्घृतकौशिकः पाराशर्यायणात्पाराशर्यायणः पाराशर्यात् पाराशर्यो जातूकर्ण्याज्जातूकर्ण्य आसुरायणाच्च यास्काच्चासुरायणस्त्रैवणेस्त्रैवणिरौपजन्धनेरौपजन्धनिरासुरेरासुरिर्भारद्वाजाद्भारद्वाज आत्रेयादत्रेयो माण्टेर्माण्टिर्गौतमाद्गौतमो गौतमाद्गौतमो वात्स्याद्वात्स्यः शाण्डिल्याच्छांण्डिल्यः कैशोर्यात्काप्यात्कैशोर्यः काप्यः कुमारहारितात्कुमारहारितो गालवाद्गालवो विदर्भीकौण्डिन्याद्विदर्भीकौण्डिन्यो वत्सनपातो बाभ्र-वाद्वत्सनपाद्बाभ्रवः पथः सौभरात्पन्थाः सौभरोऽयास्यादाङ्गिरसादयास्य आङ्गिरस आभूतेस्त्वाष्ट्रादाभूतिस्त्वाष्ट्रो विश्वरूपात्त्वाष्ट्राद्विश्वरूपस्त्वाष्ट्रोऽश्विभ्यामश्विनौ दधीच आथर्वणाद्दध्यङ्ङाथर्वणोऽथर्वणो दैवादथर्वा दैवो मृत्योः प्राध्वꣳसनान्मृत्युः प्राध्वꣳसनः प्रध्वꣳसनात्प्रध्वꣳसन एकर्षेरेकर्षिर्विप्रचित्तेर्विप्रचित्तिर्व्यष्टेर्व्यष्टिः सनारोः सनारुः सनातनात्सनातनः सनगात्सनगः परमेष्ठिनः परमेष्ठी ब्रह्मणो ब्रह्म स्वयंभु ब्रह्मणे नमः॥ ३॥

Now the clan-tree of this Madhu Khaṇḍa is described. Pauti Māṣya received this teaching from Gaupavana. Similarly, Gaupavana from Pauti Māṣya and Pauti Māṣya from Gaupavana obtained the learning. This trend ran on as Gaupavana from Kauśika, Kauśika from Kauṇḍinya, Kauṇḍinya from Śāṇḍilya, Śāṇḍilya from Kauśika, Kauśika from Gautama, Gautama from Agniveśya, Agniveśya from Śāṇḍilya and Ānabhimlāta from Gautama, Gautama from Saitava and from Prācīnayogya, Saitava and Prācīnayogya from Pārāśarya, Pārāśarya from Bhāradvāja, Bhāradvāja from Bhāradvāja and Gautama, Gautama from Bhāradvāja, Bhāradvāja from Pārāśarya, Pārāśarya from Baijavapāyana, Baijavapāyana from Kauṣīkāyani, Kauṣīkāyanī from Ghṛtakauśika, Ghṛtakauśika from Pārāśaryāyaṇa, Pārāśaryāyaṇa from Pārāśarya, Pārāśarya from Jātūkarṇya, Jātūkarṇya from Āsurāyaṇa and Yāskamuni, Āsurāyaṇa from Trivaṇi, Trivaṇi from Aupajandhani, Aupajandhani from Āsuri, Āsuri from Bhāradvāja, Bhāradvāja from Ātreya, Ātreya from Māṇṭi, Māṇṭi from Gautama, Gautama from Vātsya, Vātsya from Śāṇḍilya, Śāṇḍilya from Kaiśorya kāpya, Kaiśorya kāpya from Kumāra Hārita, Kumāra Hārita from Gālava, Gālava from Vidarbhī Kauṇḍinya, Vidarbhī Kauṇḍinya from Vatsanapāt Bābhrava, Vatsanapāt Bābhrava from Panthāsaubhara, Panthāsaubhara from Ayāsya Āṅgirasa, Ayāsya Āṅgirasa from Ābhūti Tvāṣṭra, Ābhūti Tvāṣṭra from Viśvarūpa Tvāṣṭra, Viśvarūpa Tvāṣṭra from Aśvinīkumāras, Aśvinīkumāras from Dadhyañ Ātharvaṇa, Dadhyañ Ātharvaṇa from Atharvadaiva, Atharvadaiva from Mṛtyu Prādhvaṅsana, Mṛtyu Prādhvaṅsana from Pradhvaṅsana, Pradhvaṅsana from Ekarṣi, Ekarṣi from Vipracitti, Vipracitti from Vyaṣṭi, Vyaṣṭi from Sanāru, Sanāru from Sanātana, Sanātana from Sanaga, Sanaga from Parameṣṭhi and Parameṣṭhi received this divine knowledge from Lord Brahmā. Lord Brahmā was the first man who self acquired this knowledge. Lord Brahmā is therefore saluted.

[In this Brāhmaṇa, a tradition of the sages who had obtained the knowledge are described. Some Ṛṣi have mutually acquired the knowledge and some have mutually obtained the knowledge more than once. It appears that the saints have mutually disclosed their feelings they obtained regarding the supreme almighty and thus both were benefited. It is also possible that they would have felt the metaphysical senses more than one time.]

॥तृतीयोऽध्यायः॥

प्रथमं ब्राह्मणम्

जनको ह वैदेहो बहुदक्षिणेन यज्ञेनेजे तत्र ह कुरुपञ्चालानां ब्राह्मणा अभिसमेता बभूवुस्तस्य ह जनकस्य वैदेहस्य विजिज्ञासा बभूव कःस्विदेषां ब्राह्मणानामनूचानतम इति स ह गवाᳬ सहस्रमवरुरोध दश दश पादा एकैकस्याः शृङ्गयोराबद्धा बभूवुः॥ १॥

Janaka, the king of Vaideha, sacrificed with a sacrifice at which many presents were distributed. Brāhmaṇas of the Kurupañcālas were gathered together there. In this Janaka of Vaideha there arose a desire to know which of these Brāhmaṇas was the most learned in scripture. He enclosed a thousand cows. To the horns of each ten *pādas* [of gold] were bound.

तान्होवाच ब्राह्मणा भगवन्तो यो वो ब्रह्मिष्ठः स एता गा उदजतामिति ते ह ब्राह्मणा न दधृषुरथ ह याज्ञवल्क्यः स्वमेव ब्रह्मचारिणमुवाचैताः सोम्योदज सामश्रवा ३ इति ता होदाचकार ते ह ब्राह्मणाश्चुक्रुधुः कथं नो ब्रह्मिष्ठो ब्रुवीतेत्यथ ह जनकस्य वैदेहस्य होताश्वलो बभूव स हैनं पप्रच्छ त्वं नु खलु नो याज्ञवल्क्य ब्रह्मिष्ठोऽसी३ति स होवाच नमो वयं ब्रह्मिष्ठाय कुर्मो गोकामा एव वयᳬ स्म इति तᳬ ह तत एव प्रष्टुं दध्रे होताश्वलः॥ २॥

He said to them : 'Venerable Brāhmaṇas, let him of you who is the best Brāhmaṇa drive away these cows.'

Those Brāhmaṇas burst not.

Then Yājñavalkya said to his pupil : 'Sāmaśravas, my dear, drive them away.' He drove them away. The Brāhmaṇas were angry. 'How can he declare himself to be the best Brāhmaṇa among us?'

He replied : 'We give honour to the best Brāhmaṇa. But we are really desirous of having those cows.'

Thereupon Aśvala, the Hotā-priest, began to question him.

याज्ञवल्क्येति होवाच यदिदᳬ सर्वं मृत्युनाप्तᳬ सर्वं मृत्युनाभिपन्नं केन यजमानो मृत्योराप्तिमतिमुच्यत इति होत्रर्त्विजाग्निना वाचा वाग्वै यज्ञस्य होता तद्येयं वाक् सोऽयमग्निः स होता स मुक्तिः सातिमुक्तिः॥ ३॥

'Yājñavalkya', said he, 'since everything here is overtaken by death, since everything is overcome by death, whereby is a sacrificer liberated beyond the reach of death?'

'By the Hotā-priest, by fire, by speech. Verily, speech is the Hotṛi of sacrifice. That which is this speech is this fire, is the Hotṛi. This is release (*mukti*), this is complete release.'

याज्ञवल्क्येति होवाच यदिद॰ सर्वमहोरात्राभ्यामाप्त॰ सर्वमहोरात्राभ्याममभिपन्नं केन यजमानोऽहोरात्रयोराप्तिमतिमुच्यत इत्यध्वर्युणर्त्विजा चक्षुपादित्येन चक्षुर्वै यज्ञस्याध्वर्युस्तद्यदिदं चक्षु: सोऽसावादित्य: सोऽध्वर्यु: स मुक्ति: सातिमुक्ति:॥४॥

'Yājñavalkya,' said he, 'since everything here is overtaken by day and night, since everything is overcome by day and night, whereby is a sacrificer liberated beyond day and night?'

'By the Adhvaryu-priest, by the eye, by the sun. Verily, the eye is the Adhvaryu of sacrifice. That which is this eye is yonder sun, is the Adhvaryu. This is release, this is complete release.'

याज्ञवल्क्येति होवाच यदिद॰ सर्वं पूर्वपक्षापरपक्षाभ्यामाप्त॰ सर्वं पूर्वपक्षापरपक्षाभ्याममभिपन्नं केन यजमान: पूर्वपक्षापरपक्षयोराप्तिमतिमुच्यत इत्युद्गात्रर्त्विजा वायुना प्राणेन प्राणो वै यज्ञस्योद्गाता तद्योऽयं प्राणं स वायु: स उद्गाता स मुक्ति: सातिमुक्ति:॥५॥

Aśvala again asked - "O Yājñavalkya! 'since everything here is overtaken by the waxing and waning moon, by what means does a sacrificer obtain release from the waxing and waning moon?"

'By the Udgātā-priest, by the wind, by breath. Verily, breath is the Udgātṛ of the sacrifice. That which is this breath is wind, is the Udgātṛ. This is release, this is complete release.'

याज्ञवल्क्येति होवाच यदिदमन्तरिक्षमनारम्बणमिव केनाक्रमेण यजमान: स्वर्गं लोकमाक्रमत इति ब्रह्मणर्त्विजा मनसा चन्द्रेण मनो वै यज्ञस्य ब्रह्मा तद्यदिदं मन: सोऽसौ चन्द्र: स ब्रह्मा स मुक्ति: सातिमुक्तिरित्यतिमोक्षा अथ संपद:॥६॥

Aśvala asked - "O Yājñavalkya! 'since this atmosphere does not afford a [foot] hold, as it were, by what means of ascent does a sacrificer ascend to the heavenly world?

'By the Brahman-priest, by the mind, by the moon. Verily, the mind is the Brahman of the sacrifice. That which is this mind is yonder moon, is the Brahman. This is release, this is complete release.' Thus [concerning] liberation.

याज्ञवल्क्येति होवाच कतिभिरयमद्यर्ग्भिर्होतत्समिन्यज्ञे करिष्यतीति तिसृभिरिति कतमास्तास्तिस्त्र इति पुरोऽनुवाक्या च याज्या च शस्यैव तृतीय किं ताभिर्जयतीति यत्किंचेदं प्राणभृदिति॥७॥

Aśvala asked - 'O Yājñavalkya! how many Ṛg verses will the Hotṛi make use of today in this sacrifice?' 'Three.' 'Which are those three?'

'The introductory verse, the accompanying verse, and the benediction as the third.'

'What does one win by these?' 'Whatever there is here that has breath.'

याज्ञवल्क्येति होवाच कत्ययमद्याध्वर्युरस्मिन्यज्ञ आहुतीर्होष्यतीति तिस्र इति कतमास्तास्तिस्र इति या हुता उज्ज्वलन्ति या हुता अतिनेदन्ते या हुता अधिशेरते किं ताभिर्जयतीति या हुता उज्ज्वलन्ति देवलोकमेव ताभिर्जयति दीप्यत इव हि देवलोको या हुता अतिनेदन्ते पितृलोकमेव ताभिर्जयत्यतीव हि पितृलोको या हुता अधिशेरते मनुष्यलोकमेव ताभिर्जयत्यध इव हि मनुष्यलोकः॥८॥

'Yājñavalkya,' said he, 'how many oblations will the Adhvaryu pour out today in this sacrifice?' 'Three'. 'Which are those three?'

'Those which when offered flame up, those which when offered flow over, those which when offered sink down.'

'What does one win by these?'

'By those which when offered flame up, one wins the world of the gods, for the world of the gods gleams, as it were. By those which when offered flow over (*ati-nedante*), one wins the world of the fathers, for the world of the fathers is over (*ati*), as it were. By those which when offered sink down (*adhiśerate*) one wins the world of men, for the world of men as below (*adhas*), as it were.'

याज्ञवल्क्येति होवाच कतिभिरयमद्य ब्रह्मा यज्ञं दक्षिणतो देवताभिर्गोपायतीत्येकयेति कतमा सैकेति मन एवेत्यनन्तं वै मनोऽनन्ता विश्वेदेवा अनन्तमेव स तेन लोकं जयति॥९॥

Aśvala asked– 'with how many divinities does the Brahman protect the sacrifice on the right today?'

'With one.'

'Which is that one?'

'The mind. Verily, endless is the mind. Endless are the All-gods. An endless world he wins thereby.'

याज्ञवल्क्येति होवाच कत्ययमद्योद्गातास्मिन्यज्ञे स्तोत्रियाः स्तोष्यतीति तिस्र इति कतमास्तास्तिस्र इति पुरोनुवाक्या च याज्या च शस्यैव तृतीया कतमास्ता या अध्यात्ममिति प्राण एव पुरोनुवाक्याऽपानो याज्या व्यानः शस्या किं ताभिर्जयतीति पृथिवीलोकमेव पुरोनुवाक्यया यजत्यन्तरिक्षलोकं याज्यया द्युलोकः शस्यया ततो ह होताश्वल उपरराम॥१०॥

Aśvala asked– "O Yājñavalkya! 'how many hymns of praise will the Udgātṛi chant today in this sacrifice?' 'Three'.

'Which are those three?'

'The introductory hymn, the accompanying hymn, and the benediction hymn as the third.'

'Which are those three with reference to the self?'

'The introductory hymn is the in-breath (*prāṇa*). The accompanying hymn is the out-breath (*apāna*). The benediction hymn is the diffused breath (*vyāna*).'

'What does one win by these?'

'One wins the earth-world by the introductory hymn, the atmosphere-world by the accompanying hymn, the sky-world by the benediction hymn.'

Thereupon the Hotṛi-priest Aśvala held his peace.

द्वितीयं ब्राह्मणम्

The fettered soul, and its fate at death

अथ हैनं जारत्कारव आर्तभागः पप्रच्छ याज्ञवल्क्येति होवाच ग्रहाः कत्यतिग्रहा इत्यष्टौ ग्रहा अष्टावतिग्रहा इति ये ते तेऽष्टौ ग्रहा अष्टावतिग्रहाः कतमे त इति॥ १॥

Then Jāratkārava Ārtabhāga questioned him. 'Yājñavalkya,' said he, 'how many apprehenders are there? How many over-apprehenders (*atigrāha*– one who takes or seizes to an extraordinary extent or organ of apprehension which are eight in number)?

'Eight apprehenders. Eight over-apprehenders.'

'Those eight apprehenders and eight over- apprehenders—which are they?'

प्राणो वै ग्रहः सोऽपानेनातिग्राहेण गृहीतोऽपानेन हि गन्धाञ्जिघ्रति॥ २॥

'Breath (*prāṇa*), veirly, is an apprehender. It is seized by the out-breath (*apāna*) as an over-apprehender, for by the out-breath one smells an odour.

वाग्वै ग्रहः स नाम्नातिग्राहेण गृहीतो वाचा हि नामान्यभिवदति॥ ३॥

Speech, verily, is an apprehender. It is seized by name as an over-apprehender, for by speech one speaks names.

जिह्वा वै ग्रहः स रसेनातिग्राहेण गृहीतो जिह्वया हि रसान्विजानाति॥ ४॥

The tongue, verily, is an apprehender. It is seized by taste as an over-apprehender, for by the tongue one knows tastes.

चक्षुर्वै ग्रहः स रूपेणातिग्राहेण गृहीतश्चक्षुषा हि रूपाणि पश्यति॥ ५॥

The eye, verily, is an apprehender. It is seized by appearance as an over-apprehender, for by the eye one sees.

श्रोत्रं वै ग्रहः स शब्देनातिग्राहेण गृहीतः श्रोत्रेण हि शब्दाञ्छृणोति॥ ६॥

The ear, verily, is an apprehender. It is seized by sound as an over-apprehender, for by the ear one hears sounds.

मनो वै ग्रहः स कामेनातिग्राहेण गृहीतो मनसा हि कामान्कामयते॥ ७॥

The mind, verily, is an apprehender. It is seized by desire as an over-apprehender, for by the mind one desires.

हस्तौ वै ग्रहः स कर्मणातिग्राहेण गृहीतो हस्ताभ्याꣳ हि कर्म करोति॥ ८॥

The hands, verily, are an apprehender. It is seized by action as an over-apprehender, for by the hands one performs action.

त्वग्वै ग्रहः स स्पर्शेनातिग्राहेण गृहीतस्त्वचा हि स्पर्शान्वेदयत इत्येतेऽष्टौ ग्रहाअष्टावतिग्रहाः॥ ९॥

The skin, verily, is an apprehender. It is seized by touch as an over-apprehender, for by the skin one is made to know touches.'

याज्ञवल्क्येति होवाच यदिदꣳ सर्वं मृत्योरन्नं का स्वित्सा देवता यस्या मृत्युरन्नमित्यग्निर्वै मृत्युः सोऽपामन्नमप पुनर्मृत्युं जयति॥ १०॥

Ārtabhāga Jāratkārava asked - "O Yājñavalkya! 'since everything here is food for death, who, pray, is that divinity for whom death is food?'

'Death, verily, is a fire. It is the food of water (*āpas*). He wards off (*apa-jayati*) repeated death [who knows this].'

याज्ञवल्क्येति होवाच यत्रायं पुरुषो म्रियत यदस्मात्प्राणाः क्रामनत्याहो ३ नेति नेति होवाच याज्ञवल्क्योऽत्रैव समवनीयन्ते स उच्छ्वयत्याध्मायत्याध्मातो मृतः शेते॥ ११॥

Ārtabhāga again asked - "O Yājñavalkya! 'when a man dies, do the breaths go out of him, or no?'

'No,' said Yājñavalkya. 'They are gathered together right there. He swells up. He is inflated. The dead man lies inflated.'

याज्ञवल्क्येति होवाच यत्रायं पुरुषो म्रियते किमेनं न जहातीति नामेत्यनन्तं वै नामानन्ता विश्वेदेवा अनन्तमेव स तेन लोकं जयति॥ १२॥

'Yājñavalkya,' said he, 'when a man dies, what does not leave him?'

'The name. Endless, verily, is the name. Endless are the All-gods. An endless world he wins thereby.'

याज्ञवल्क्येति होवाच यत्रास्य पुरुषस्य मृतस्याग्निं वागप्येति वातं प्राणश्चक्षुरादित्यं मनश्चन्द्रं दिशः श्रोत्रं पृथिवीꣳ शरीरमाकाशमात्मौषधीर्लोमानि वनस्पतीन्केशा अप्सु लोहितं च रेतश्च निधीयते क्वायं तदा पुरुषो भवतीत्याहर सोम्य हस्तमार्तभागावामेवैतस्य वेदिष्यावो न नावेतत् सजन इति तौ होत्क्रम्य मन्त्रयांचक्राते तौ ह यदूचतुः कर्म हैव तदूचतुरथ यत्प्रशशꣳसतुः कर्म हैव तत्प्रशशꣳसतुः पुण्यो वै पुण्येन कर्मणा भवति पापः पापेनेति ततो ह जारत्कारव आर्तभाग उपरराम॥ १३॥

Ārtabhāga asked again - "O Yājñavalkya! 'Yājñavalkya,' said he, 'when the voice of a dead man goes into fire, his breath into wind, his eye into the sun, his mind into the moon, his hearing into the quartes of heaven, his body into the earth, his soul (*ātman*) into space, the hairs of his head into plants, the hairs of his body into trees, and his blood and semen are placed in water, what then becomes of this person (*puruṣa*)?'

'Ārtabhāga, my dear, take my hand. We two only will know of this. This is not for us two [to speak of] in public.'

The two went away and deliberated. What they said was *karma* (action). What they praised was *karma*. Verily, one becomes good by good action, bad by bad action.

Thereupon Jāratkārava Ārtabhāga held his peace.

[It becomes clear now that the conversations among the saints were arranged to seek out proper solutions of the curiosity as also with a view to approach to the truth. In course of the discussions, they only use to pronounce the facts definitely known and the facts requiring consultation amid the scholars were used to be discussed among them with more clarity and without concealing anything.]

तृतीयं ब्राह्मणम्

Where the offerers of the horse-sacrifice go

अथ हैनं भुज्युर्लाह्यायनिः पप्रच्छ याज्ञवल्क्येति होवाच मद्रेषु चरकाः पर्यव्रजाम ते पतञ्चलस्य काप्यस्य गृहानैम तस्यासीद्दुहिता गन्धर्वगृहीता तमपृच्छाम कोऽसीति सोऽब्रवीत्सुधन्वाऽऽङ्गिरस इति तं यदा लोकानामन्तानपृच्छामाथैनमब्रूम क्व पारिक्षिता अभवन्निति क्व पारिक्षिता अभवन् स त्वा पृच्छामि याज्ञवल्क्य क्व पारिक्षिता अभवन्निति॥ १॥

Then Bhujyu Lāhyāyani questioned him. 'Yājñavalkya,' said he, 'we were travelling around as wanderers among the Madras. As such we came to the house of Patañcala Kāpya. He had a daughter who was possessed by a Gandharva. We asked him : "Who are you?" He said : "I am Sudhanvan, a descendant of Aṅgiras." When we were asking him about the ends of the earth, we said to him : "What has become of the Pārikṣitas? What has become of the Pārikṣitas?" I now ask you, Yājñavalkya. What has become of the Pārikṣitas?'

स होवाचोवाच वै सोगच्छन्वै ते तद्यत्राश्वमेधयाजिनो गच्छन्तीति क्वन्वश्वमेधयाजिनो गच्छन्तीति द्वात्रिꣳशतं वै देवरथाह्न्यान्ययं लोकस्तꣳ समन्तं पृथिवी द्विस्तावत्पर्येति ताꣳ समन्तं पृथिवीं द्विस्तावत्समुद्रः पर्येति तद्यावती क्षुरस्य धारा यावद्वा मक्षिकायः पत्रं तावानन्तरेणाकाशस्तानिन्द्रः सुपर्णो भूत्वा वायवे प्रायच्छत्तान्वायुरात्मनि धित्वा तत्रागमयद्यत्राश्वमेधयाजिनोऽभवन्नित्येवमेव वै स वायुमेव प्रशशꣳस तस्माद्वायुरेव व्यष्टिर्वायुः समष्टिरप पुनर्मृत्युं जयति य एवं वेद ततो ह भुज्युर्लाह्यायनिरुपरराम॥ २॥

He said : 'That one doubtless said, "They have, in truth, gone whither the offerers of the horse-sacrifice go." '

'Where, pray, do the offerers of the horse-sacrifice go?'

'This inhabited world, of a truth, is as broad as thirty-two days [i.e. days' journeys] of the sun-god's chariot. The earth, which is twice as wide, surrounds it on all sides. The ocean, which is twice as wide, surrounds the earth on all sides. Then there is an interspace as broad as the edge of a razor or the wing of a mosquito. Indra, taking the form of a bird, delivered them [i.e. the Pārikṣitas] to wind. Wind, placing them in himself, led them where the offerers of the horse-sacrifice were. Somewhat thus he [i.e. Sudhanvan] praised Wind. Therefore Wind alone is individuality (*vyaṣṭi*). Wind is totality (*samaṣṭi*). He who knows this wards off repeated death.'

चतुर्थ ब्राह्मणम्

The theoretical unknowability of the immanent Brahma

अथ हैनमुषस्तश्चाक्रायणः पप्रच्छ याज्ञवल्क्येति होवाच यत्साक्षादपरोक्षाद्ब्रह्म य आत्मा सर्वान्तरस्तं मे व्याचक्ष्व इत्येष त आत्मा सर्वान्तरः कतमो याज्ञवल्क्य सर्वान्तरो यः प्राणेन प्राणिति स त आत्मा सर्वान्तरो योऽपानेनापानीति स त आत्मा सर्वान्तरो यो व्यानेन व्यानिति स त आत्मा सर्वान्तरो य उदानेनोदानिति स त आत्मा सर्वान्तर एष त आत्मा सर्वान्तरः॥ १॥

Then Uṣasta Cākrāyaṇa questioned him. 'Yājñavalkya said he, 'explain to me him, who is the Brahma present and not beyond our ken, him who is the Soul in all things.'

'He is your soul (*ātman*), which is in all things.'

'Which one, O Yājñavalkya, is in all things?'

'He who breathes in with your breathing in (*prāṇa*) is the Soul of yours, which is in all things. He who breathes out with your breathing out (*apāna*) is the Soul of yours, which is in all things. He who breathes about with your breathing about (*vyāna*) is the Soul of yours, which is in all things. He who breathes up with your breathing up (*udāna*) is the Soul of yours, which is in all things. He is your soul, which is in all things.'

स होवाचोषस्तश्चाक्रायणो यथा विब्रूयादमौ गौरसावश्व इत्येवमेवैतद्व्यपदिष्टं भवति यदेव साक्षादपरोक्षाद्ब्रह्म य आत्मा सर्वान्तरस्तं मे व्याचक्ष्वेत्येष त आत्मा सर्वान्तरः कतमो याज्ञावल्क्य सर्वान्तरो न दृष्टेर्द्रष्टारं पश्येर्न श्रुतेः शृणुयात्र मतेर्मन्तारं मन्वीथा न विज्ञातेर्विज्ञातारं विजीनीया एष त आत्मा सर्वान्तरोऽतोऽन्यदार्तं ततो होषस्तश्चाक्रायण उपरराम॥ २॥

Uṣasta Cākrāyaṇa said : 'This has been explained to me just as one might say, "This is a cow. This is a horse." Explain to me him who is just the Brahma present and not beyond our ken, him who is the Soul in all things.'

'He is your soul, which is in all things.'

'Which one, O Yājñavalkya, is in all things?'

'You could not see the seer of seeing. You could not hear the hearer of hearing. You could not think the thinker of thinking. You could not understand the understander of understanding. He is your soul, which is in all things. Ought else than Him [or, than this] is wretched.'

Uṣasta kept a silence because he was then satisfied by the answers.

पञ्चमं ब्राह्मणम्

The practical way of knowing Brahma—by renunciation

अथ हैनं कहोलः कौषीतकेयः पप्रच्छ याज्ञावल्क्येति होवाच यदेव साक्षादपरोक्षाद्ब्रह्म य आत्मा सर्वान्तरस्तं मे व्याचक्ष्वेत्येष त आत्मा सर्वान्तरः कतमो याज्ञवल्क्य सर्वान्तरो योऽशनायापिपासे शोकं मोहं जरां मृत्युमत्येति। एतं वै तमात्मानं विदित्वा ब्राह्मणाः पुत्रैषणायाश्च वित्तैषणायाश्च लोकैषणायाश्च व्युत्थायाथ भिक्षाचर्यं चरन्ति या ह्येव पुत्रैषणा सा वित्तैषणा या वित्तैषणा सा लोकैषणोभे ह्येते एषणे एव भवतस्तस्माद् ब्राह्मणः पाण्डित्यं निर्विद्य बाल्येन तिष्ठासेद्बाल्यं च पाण्डित्यं च न निर्विद्याथ मुनिरमौनं च मौनं च निर्विद्याऽथ ब्राह्मणः स ब्राह्मणः केन स्याद्येन स्यात्तेनेदृश एवातोऽन्यदार्तं ततो ह कहोलः कौषीतकेय उपरराम॥ १॥

Now Kahola Kauśītakeya questioned him. 'Yājñavalkya,' said he, 'explain to me him who is just the Brahma present and not beyond our ken, him who is the Soul in all things.'

'He is your soul, which is in all things.'

'Which one, O Yājñavalkya, is in all things?'

'He who passed beyond hunger and thirst, beyond sorrow and delusion, beyond old age and death—Brāhmaṇas who know such a Soul overcome desire for sons, desire for wealth, desire for worlds, and live the life of mendicants. For desire for sons is desire for wealth, and desire for wealth is desire for worlds, for both these are merely desires. Therefore let a Brāhmaṇa become disgusted with learning and desire to live as a child. When he has become disgusted both with the state of childhood and with learning, then he becomes an ascetic (*muni*). When he has become disgusted both with the non-ascetic state and with the ascetic state, then he becomes a Brahman.

'By what means would he become a Brahman?'

'By that means by which he does become such a one. Aught else than this Soul (*Ātman*) is wretched.'

Satisfied with the answers Kauṣītakeya Kahola kept silence.

षष्ठं ब्राह्मणम्

The regresses to Brahma, the ultimate world-ground

अथ हैनं गार्गी वाचक्नवी पप्रच्छ याज्ञवल्क्येति होवाच यदिदꣳ सर्वमप्स्वोतं च प्रोतं च कस्मिन्नु खल्वाप ओताश्च प्रोताश्चेति वायौ गार्गीति कस्मिन्नु खलु वायुरोतश्च प्रोतश्चेत्यन्तरिक्षलोकेषु गार्गीति कस्मिन्नु खल्वन्तरिक्षलोका ओताश्च प्रोताश्चेति गन्धर्वलोकेषु गार्गीति कस्मिन्नु खलु गन्धर्वलोका ओताश्च प्रोताश्चेत्यादित्यलोकेषु गार्गीति कस्मिन्नु खल्वादित्यलोका ओताश्च प्रोताश्चेति चन्द्रलोकेषु गार्गीति कस्मिन्नु खलु चन्द्रलोका ओताश्च प्रोताश्चेति नक्षत्रलोकेषु गार्गीति कस्मिन्नु खलु नक्षत्रलोका ओताश्च प्रोताश्चेति देवलोकेषु गार्गीति कस्मिन्नु खलु देवलोका ओताश्च प्रोताश्चेतीन्द्रलोकेषु गार्गीति कस्मिन्नु खल्विचन्द्रलोका

ओताश्च प्रोताश्चेति प्रजापतिलोकेषु गार्गीति कस्मिन्नु खलु प्रजापतिलोका ओताश्च प्रोताश्चेति ब्रह्मलोकेषु गार्गीति कस्मिन्नु खलु ब्रह्मलोका ओताश्च प्रोताश्चेति स होवाच गार्गि मातिप्राक्षीर्मा ते मूर्धा व्यपप्तदनतिप्रश्नयां वै देवातामतिपृच्छसि गार्गि मातिप्राक्षीरिति ततो ह गार्गी वाचक्रव्युपरराम॥ १॥

Then Gārgī Vācaknavī questioned him. 'Yājñavalkya,' said she, 'since all this world is woven, warp and woof, on water, on what, pray, is the water woven, warp and woof?'

'On wind, O Gārgī.'

'On what then, pray, is the wind woven, warp and woof?'

'On the atmosphere-worlds, O Gārgī.'

'On what then, pray, are the atmosphere-worlds woven, warp and woof?'

'On the worlds of the Gandharvas, O Gārgī?'

'On what then, pray, are the worlds of the Gandharvas woven, warp and woof?'

'On the worlds of the Gandharvas, O Gārgī.'

'On what then, pray, are the world of the Gandharvas woven, warp and woof?'

'On the worlds of the sun, O Gārgī.'

'On what then, pray, are the worlds of the sun woven, warp and woof?'

'On the worlds of the moon, O Gārgī.'

'On what then, pray, are the worlds of the moon woven, warp and woof?'

'On the world of the stars, O Gārgī.'

'On what then, pray, are the worlds of the stars woven, warp and woof?'

'On the worlds of the gods, O Gārgī.'

'On what then, pray, are the worlds of the gods woven, warp and woof?'

'On the worlds of Indra, O Gārgī.'

'On what then, pray, are the worlds of Indra woven, warp and woof?'

'On the worlds of Prajāpati, O Gārgī.'

'On what then, pray, are the worlds of Prajāpati woven, warp and woof?'

'On the worlds of Brahma, O Gārgī.'

'On what then, pray, are the worlds of Brahma woven, warp and woof?'

Yājñavalkya said : 'Gārgī, do not question too much, lest your head fall off. In truth, you are questioning too much about a divinity about which further questions cannot be asked. Gārgī, do not over-question.'

Thereupon Gārgī Vācaknavī held her peace.

[The matter which is undescribably if attempted to prove by the mere logic, it is called the excess enquiry. The learned person who deliberately and to satisfy his ego abuses his mind in such futile context, the metaphysics (the eternal nature) may punish him.]

सप्तमं ब्राह्मणम्

Wind, the string holding the world together; the immortal immanent Soul, the Inner Controller

अथ हैनमुद्दालक आरुणिः पप्रच्छ याज्ञवल्क्येति होवाच मद्रेष्ववसाम पतञ्चलस्य काप्यस्य गृहेषु यज्ञमधीयानास्तस्यासीद्भार्या गन्धर्वगृहीता तमपृच्छाम कोऽसीति सोऽब्रवीत् कबन्ध आथर्वण इति सोऽब्रवीत्पतञ्चलं काप्यं याज्ञिकाꣳश्च वेत्थ नु त्वं काप्य तत्सूत्रं येनायं च लोकः परश्च लोकः सर्वाणि च भूतानि संदृब्धानि भवन्तीति सोऽब्रवीत्पतञ्चलः काप्यो नाहं तद्भगवन्वेदेति सोऽब्रवीत्पतञ्चलं काप्यं याज्ञिकाꣳश्च वेत्थ नु त्वं काप्य तमन्तर्यामिणं य इमं च लोकं परं च लोकꣳ सर्वाणि च भूतानि योऽन्तरो यमयतीति सोऽब्रवीत्पतञ्चलः काप्यो नाहं त भगवन्वेदेति सोऽब्रवीत्पतञ्चलं काप्यं याज्ञिकाꣳश्च यो वै तत्काप्यसूत्रं विद्यात्तं चान्तर्यामिणमिति स ब्रह्मवित्स लोकवित्स देववित्स वेदवित्स भूतवित्स आत्मवित्स सर्वविदिति तेभ्योऽब्रवीत्तदहं वेद तच्चेत्त्वं याज्ञवल्क्य सूत्रमविद्वाꣳस्तं चान्तर्यामिणं ब्रह्मगवीरुदजसे मूर्धा ते विपतिष्यतीति वेद वा अहं गौतम तत्सूत्रं तं चान्तर्यामिणमिति यो वा इदं कश्चिद्ब्रूयाद्वेद वेदेति यथा वेत्थ तथा ब्रूहीति॥ १॥

Then Uddālaka Āruṇi questioned him. 'Yājñavalkya,' said he, 'we were dwelling among the Madras in the house of Patañcala Kāpya, studying the sacrifice. He had a wife possessed by a spirit (*gandharva*). We asked him : "Who are you?" He said : "I am Kabandha Ātharvaṇa." He said to Patañcala Kāpya and to us students of the sacrifice : "Do you know, O Kāpya, that thread by which this world and the other world and all things are tied together?" Patañcala Kāpya said : "I do not know it, sir." He said to Patañcala Kāpya and to us students of the sacrifice : "Pray do you know, O Kāpya that Inner Controller who from within controls this world and the other world and all things?" Patañcala Kāpya said : "I do not know him, sir." He said to Patañcala Kāpya and to us students of the sacrifice : "Verily, Kāpya, he who knows that thread and the so-called Inner Controller knows Brahma, he knows the worlds, he knows the gods, he knows the Vedas, he knows created things, he knows the Soul, he knows everything." Thus he [i.e. the spirit] explained it to them. And I know it. If you, O Yājñavalkya, drive away the Brahma-cows without knowing that thread and the Inner Controller, your head will fall off.'

'Verily, I know that thread and the Inner Controller, O Gautama.'

'Any one might say "I know, I know." Do you tell what you know.'

स होवाच वायुर्वै गौतम तत्सूत्रं वायुना वै गौतम सूत्रेणायं च चलोकः परश्च लोकः सर्वाणि च भूतानि संदृब्धानि भवन्ति तस्माद्वै गौतम पुरुषं प्रेतमाहुर्व्यस्रꣳसिषतास्याङ्गानीति वायुना हि गौतम सूत्रेण संदृब्धानि भवन्तीत्येवमेवैतद्याज्ञवल्क्यान्तर्यामिणं ब्रूहीति॥ २॥

He [i.e. Yājñavalkya] said : 'Wind, verily, O Gautama, is that thread. By wind, verily, O Gautama, as by a thread, this world and the other world and all things are tied together.

Therefore, verily, O Gautama, they say of a deceased person, "His limbs become unstrung," for by wind, O Gautama, as by a thread, they are strung together.'

'Quite so, O Yājñavalkya. Declare the Inner Controller.'

यः पृथिव्यां तिष्ठन् पृथिव्या अन्तरो यं पृथिवी न वेद यस्य पृथिवी शरीरं यः पृथिवीमन्तरो यमयत्येष त आत्मान्तर्याम्यमृतः॥ ३॥

'He who, dwelling in the earth, yet is other than the earth, whom the earth does not know, whose body the earth is, who controls the earth from within—He is your Soul, the Inner Controller, the Immortal.

योऽप्सु तिष्ठन्नद्भ्योऽन्तरो यमापो न विदुर्यस्यापः शरीरं योऽपोऽन्तरो यमयत्येष त आत्मान्तर्याम्यमृतः॥ ४॥

He who, dwelling in the waters, yet is other than the waters, whom the waters do not know, whose body the waters are, who controls the waters from within—He is your Soul, the Inner Controller, the Immortal.

योऽग्नौ तिष्ठन्नग्नेरन्तरो यमग्निर्न वेद यस्याग्निः शरीरं योऽग्निमन्तरो यमयत्येष त आत्मान्तर्याम्यमृतः॥ ५॥

He who, dwelling in the fire, yet is other than the fire, whom the fire does not know, whose body the fire is, who controls the fire from within—He is your Soul, the Inner Controller, the Immortal.

योऽन्तरिक्षे तिष्ठन्नन्तरिक्षादन्तरो यमन्तरिक्षं न वेद यस्यान्तरिक्षꣳ शरीरं योऽन्तरिक्षमन्तरो यमयत्येष त आत्मान्तर्याम्यमृतः॥ ६॥

He who, dwelling in the atmosphere, yet is other than the atmosphere, whom the atmosphere does not know, whose body the atmosphere is, who controls the atmosphere from within—He is your Soul, the Inner Controller, the Immortal.

यो वायौ तिष्ठन्वायोरन्तरो यं वायुर्न वेद यस्य वायुः शरीरं यो वायुमन्तरो यमयत्येष त आत्मान्तर्याम्यमृतः॥ ७॥

He who, dwelling in the wind, yet is other than the wind, whom the wind does not know, whose body the wind is, who controls the wind from within—He is your Soul, the Inner Controller, the Immortal.

यो दिवि तिष्ठन्दिवोऽन्तरो यं द्यौर्न वेद यस्य द्यौः शरीरं यो दिवमन्तरो यमयत्येष त आत्मान्तर्याम्यमृतः॥ ८॥

He who, dwelling in the sky, yet is other than the sky, whom the sky does not know, whose body the sky is, who controls the sky from within—He is your Soul, the Inner Controller, the Immortal.

य आदित्ये तिष्ठन्नादित्यादन्तरो यमादित्यो न वेद यस्यादित्यः शरीरं य आदित्यन्तरो यमयत्येष त आत्मान्तर्याम्यमृतः॥ ९॥

He who, dwelling in the sun, yet is other than the sun, whom the sun does not know, whose body the sun is, who controls the sun from within—He is your Soul, the Inner Controller, the Immortal.

यो दिक्षु तिष्ठन्दिग्भ्योऽन्तरो यं दिशो न विदुर्यस्य दिशः शरीरं यो दिशोऽन्तरो यमयत्येष त आत्मान्तर्याम्यमृतः॥ १०॥

He who, dwelling in the quarters of heaven, yet is other than the quarters of heaven, whom the quarters of heaven do not know, whose body the quarters of heaven are, who controls the quarters of heaven from within—He is your Soul, the Inner Controller, the Immortal.

यश्चन्द्रतारके तिष्ठꣳश्चन्द्रतारकादन्तरो यं चन्द्रतारकं न वेद यस्य चन्द्रतारकꣳ शरीरं यश्चन्द्रतारकमन्तरो यमयत्येष त आत्मान्तर्याम्यमृतः॥ ११॥

He who, dwelling in the moon and stars, yet is other than the moon and the stars, whom the moon and stars do not know, whose body the moon and stars are, who controls the moon and stars from within—He is your Soul, the Inner Controller, the Immortal.

य आकाशे तिष्ठन्नाकाशादन्तरो यमाकाशो न वेद यस्याकाशः शरीरं य आकाशमन्तरो यमयत्येष त आत्मान्तर्याम्यमृतः॥ १२॥

He who, dwelling in space, yet is other than space, whom space does not know, whose body space is, who controls space from within—He is your Soul, the Inner Controller, the Immortal.

यस्तमसि तिष्ठꣳस्तमसोऽन्तरो यं तमो न वेद यस्य तमः शरीरं यस्तमोऽन्तरो यमयत्येष त आत्मान्तर्याम्यमृतः॥ १३॥

He who, dwelling in the darkness, yet is other than the darkness, whom the darkness does not know, whose body the darkness is, who controls the darkness from within—He is your Soul, the Inner Controller, the Immortal.

यस्तेजसि तिष्ठꣳस्तेजसोऽन्तरो यं तेजो न वेद यस्य तेजः शरीरं यस्तेजोऽन्तरो यमयत्येष त आत्मान्तर्याम्यमृत इत्यधिदैवतमथाधिभूतम्॥ १४॥

He who, dwelling the light, yet is other than the light, whom the light does not know, whose body the light is, who controls the light from within—He is your Soul, the Inner Controller, the Immortal.

Thus far with reference to the divinities. Now with reference to material existence (*adhi-bhūta*).

यः सर्वेषु भूतेषु तिष्ठन्सर्वेभ्यो भूतेभ्योऽन्तरो यꣳ सर्वाणि भूतानि न विदुर्यस्य सर्वाणि भूतानि शरीरं यः सर्वाणि भूतान्यन्तरो यमयत्येष त आत्मान्तर्याम्यमृत इत्यधिभूतमथाध्यात्मम्॥ १५॥

He who, dwelling in all things, yet is other than all things, whom all things do not know, whose body all things are, who controls all things from within—He is your Soul, the

Inner Controller, the Immortal.

यः प्राणे तिष्ठन्प्राणादन्तरो यं प्राणो न वेद यस्य प्राणः शरीरं यः प्राणन्तरो यमयत्येष त आत्मान्तर्याम्यमृतः॥ १६॥

He who, dwelling in breath, yet is other than breath, whom the breath does not know, whose body the breath is, who controls the breath from within—He is your Soul, the Inner Controller, the Immortal.

यो वाचि तिष्ठन्वाचोऽन्तरो यं वाङ् न वेद यस्य वाक् शरीरं यो वाचमन्तरो यमयत्येष त आत्मान्तर्याम्यमृतः॥ १७॥

He who, dwelling in speech, yet is other than speech, whom the speech does not know, whose body the speech is, who controls the speech from within—He is your Soul the Inner Controller, the Immortal.

यश्चक्षुषि तिष्ठꣳश्चक्षुषोऽन्तरो यं चक्षुर्न वेद यस्य चक्षुः शरीरं यश्चक्षुरन्तरो यमयत्येष त आत्मान्तर्याम्यमृतः॥ १८॥

He who, dwelling in the eye, yet is other than the eye, whom the eye does not know, whose body the eye is, who controls the eye from within—He is your Soul, the Inner Controller, the Immortal.

यः श्रोत्रे तिष्ठञ्छ्रोत्रादन्तरो यꣳ श्रोत्रं न वेद यस्य श्रोत्रꣳ शरीरं यः श्रोत्रमन्तरो यमयत्येष त आत्मान्तर्याम्यमृतः॥ १९॥

He who, dwelling in the ear, yet is other than the ear, whom the ear does not know, whose body the ear is, who controls the ear from within—He is your Soul, the Inner Controller, the Immortal.

यो म नसि तिष्ठन्मनसोऽन्तरो यं मनो न वेद यस्य मनः शरीरं यो मनोऽन्तरो यमयत्येष त आत्मान्तर्याम्यमृतः॥ २०॥

He who, dwelling in the mind, yet is other than the mind, whom the mind does not know, whose body the mind is, who controls the mind from within—He is your Soul, the Inner Controller, the Immortal.

यस्त्वचि तिष्ठꣳस्त्वचोऽन्तरो यं त्वङ् न वेद यस्य त्वक् शरीरं यस्त्वचमन्तरो यमयत्येष त आत्मान्तर्याम्यमृतः॥ २१॥

He who, dwelling in the skin, yet is other than the skin, whom the skin does not know, whose body the skin is, who controls the skin from within —He is your Soul, the Inner Controller, the Immortal.

यो विज्ञाने तिष्ठन्विज्ञानादन्तरो यं विज्ञानं न वेद य्य विज्ञानꣳ शरीरं यो विज्ञानमन्तरो मयत्येष त आत्मान्तर्याम्यमृतः॥ २२॥

He who, dwelling in the understanding, yet is other than the understanding, whom the understanding does not know, whose body the understanding is, who controls the understanding from within—He is your Soul, the Inner Controller, the Immortal.

यो रेति तिष्ठन् रेतसोऽन्तरो यः रेतो न वेद यस्य रेतः शरीरं यो रेतोऽन्तरो यमयत्येष त आत्मान्तर्याम्यमृतोऽदृष्टो द्रष्टाश्रुतः श्रोतामतो मन्ताविज्ञातो विज्ञाता नान्योऽतोऽस्ति द्रष्टा नान्योऽतोऽस्ति श्रोता नान्योऽतोऽस्ति मन्ता नान्योऽतोऽस्ति विज्ञातैष त आत्मान्तर्याम्यमृतोऽतोऽन्यदार्तं ततो होद्दालक आरुणिरुपरराम॥ २३॥

He who, dwelling in the semen, yet is other than the semen, whom the semen does not know, whose body the semen is, who controls the semen from within—He is your Soul, the Inner Controller, the Immortal.

He is unseen Seer, the unheard Hearer, the unthought Thinker, the understood Understander. Other than He there is no seer. Other than He there is no hearer. Other than He there is no thinker. Other than He there is no understander. He is your Soul, the Inner Controller, the Immortal.

Thereupon Uddālaka Āruṇi held his peace.

अष्टमं ब्राह्मणम्

The ultimate warp of the world—the unqualified Imperishable

अथ ह वाचक्नव्युवाच ब्राह्मणा भगवन्तो हन्ताहमिमं द्वौ प्रश्नौ प्रक्ष्यामि तौ चेन्मे वक्ष्यति न वै जातु युष्माकमिमं कश्चिद्ब्रह्मोद्यं जेतेति पृच्छ गार्गीति॥ १॥

Then [Gārgī] Vācaknavī said : 'Venerable Brāhmaṇas, lo, I will ask him [i.e. Yājñavalkya] two questions. If he will answer me these, not one of you will surpass him in discussions about Brahma.'

Ask, Gārgī.

सा होवाचाहं वै त्वा याज्ञवल्क्य यथा काश्यो वा वैदेहो वोग्रपुत्र उज्ज्यं धनुरधिज्यं कृत्वा द्वौ बाणवन्तौ सपत्नातिव्याधिनौ हस्ते कृत्वोपोत्तिष्ठेदेवमेवाहं त्वा द्वाभ्यां प्रश्नाभ्यामुपोदस्थां तौ मे ब्रूहीति पृच्छ गार्गीति॥ २॥

She said : 'As a noble youth of the Kāśīs or of the Vaidehas might rise up against you, having strung his unstrung bow and taken two foe-piercing arrows in his hand, even so, O Yājñavalkya, have I risen up against you with two questions. Answer me these.'

Yājñavalkya said : 'Ask, Gārgī.'

सा होवाच यदूर्ध्वं याज्ञवल्क्य दिवो यदवाक् पृथिव्या यदन्तरा द्यावापृथिवी इमे यद्भूतं च भवच्च भविष्यच्चेत्याचक्षते कस्मिंस्तदोतं च प्रोतं चेति॥ ३॥

She said : 'That, O Yājñavalkya, which is above the sky, that which is beneath the earth, that which is between these two, sky and earth, that which people call the past and the present and the future—across what is that woven, warp and woof?'

स होवाच यदूर्ध्वं गार्गि दिवो यदवाक् पृथिव्या यदन्तरा द्यावापृथिवी इमे यद्भूतं च भवच्च भविष्यच्चेत्याचक्षत आकाशे तदोतं च प्रोतं चेति॥ ४॥

Yājñavalkya replied– 'That, O Gārgī, which is above the sky, that which is beneath the earth, that which is between these two, sky and earth, that which people call the past and the present and the future—across space is that woven, warp and woof.'

सा होवाच नमस्तेऽस्तु याज्ञवल्क्य यो म एतं व्यवोचोऽपरस्मै धारयस्वेति पृच्छ गार्गीति॥ ५॥

She said : 'Adoration to you, Yājñavalkya, in that you have solved this question for me. Prepare yourself for the other.'

'Ask, Gārgī.'

सा होवाच यदूर्ध्वं याज्ञवल्क्य दिवो यदवाक् पृथिव्या यदन्तरा द्यावापृथिवी इमे यद्भूतं च भवच्च भविष्यच्चेत्याचक्षते कस्मिँस्तदोतं च प्रोतं चेति॥ ६॥

She said : 'That, O Yājñavalkya, which is above the sky, that which is beneath the earth, that which is between these two, sky and earth, that which people call the past and the present and the future—across what is that woven, warp and woof?'

स होवाच यदूर्ध्वं गार्गि दिवो यदवाक् पृथिव्या यदन्तरा द्यावापृथिवी इमे यद्भूतं च भवच्च भविष्यच्चेत्याचक्षत आकाश एव तदोतं च प्रोतं चेति कस्मिन्नु खल्वाकाश ओतश्च प्रोतश्चेति॥ ७॥

The Ṛṣi Yājñavalkya replied– "O Gārgī, which is above the sky, that which is beneath the earth, that which is between these two, sky and earth, that which people call the past and the present and the future—across space alone is that woven, warp and woof ?"

'Across what then, pray, is space woven, warp and woof.'

स होवाचैतद्वै तदक्षरं गार्गि ब्राह्मणा अभिवदन्त्यस्थूलमनण्वह्रस्वमदीर्घमलोहित-मस्नेहमच्छायमतमोऽवाय्वनाकाशमसङ्गमरसमगन्धमचक्षुष्कमश्रोत्रमवागमनोऽतेजस्कमप्राणममुखममात्र-मनन्तरमबाह्यं न तदश्नाति किंचन न तदश्नाति कश्चन॥ ८॥

He said : 'That, O Gārgī, Brāhmaṇas call the Imperishable (*akṣara*). It is not coarse, not fine, not short, not long, not glowing [like fire], not adhesive [like water], without shadow and without darkness, without air and without space, without stickiness, (intangible), odourless, tasteless, without eye, without ear, without voice, without wind, without energy, without breath, without mouth, (without personal or family name, unaging, undying, without fear, immortal, stainless, not uncovered, not covered), without measure, without inside and without outside.

It consumes nothing soever. No one soever consumes it.

एतस्य वा अक्षरस्य प्रशासने गार्गि सूर्याचन्द्रमसौ विधृतौ तिष्ठत एतस्य वा अक्षरस्य प्रशासने गार्गि द्यावापृथिव्यौ विधृते तिष्ठत एतस्य वा अक्षरस्य प्रशासने गार्गि निमेषा मुहूर्ता अहोरात्रकण्यर्धमासा मासा ऋतवः संवत्सरा इति विधृतास्तिष्ठन्त्येतस्य वा अक्षरस्य प्रशासने गार्गि प्राच्योऽन्या नद्यः स्यन्दन्ते श्वेतेभ्यः पर्वतेभ्यः प्रतीच्योऽन्या यां यां च दिशमन्वेतस्य वा अक्षरस्य यप्रशासने गार्गि ददतो मनुष्याः प्रशꣳसन्ति यजमानं देवा दर्वीं पितरोऽन्वायत्ताः॥ ९॥

Verily, O Gārgī, at the command of that Imperishable the sun and the moon stand apart.

Verily, O Gārgī, at the command of that imperishable the earth and the sky stand apart. Verily, O Gārgī, at the command of that Imperishable the moments, the hours, the days, the nights, the fortnights, the months, the seasons, and the years stand apart. Verily, O Gārgī, at the command of that Imperishable some rivers flow from the snowy mountains to the east, others to the west, in whatever direction each flows. Verily, O Gārgī, at the command of that Imperishable men praise those who give, the gods are desirous of a sacrificer, and the fathers [are desirous] of the Manes-sacrifice.

यो वा एतदक्षरं गार्ग्यविदित्वाऽस्मिँल्लोके जुहोति यजते तपस्तप्यते बहूनि वर्षसहस्राण्यन्तवदेवास्य तद्भवति यो वा एतक्षरं गार्ग्यविदित्वास्माल्लोकात्प्रैति स कृपणोऽथ य एतदक्षरं गार्गि विदित्वास्माल्लोकात्प्रैति स ब्राह्मणः॥ १०॥

The Ṛṣi Yājñavalkya said– "Verily, O Gārgī, if one performs sacrifices and worship and undergoes austerity in this world for many thousands of years, but without knowing that imperishable, limited indeed is that [work] of his. Verily, O Gārgī, he who departs from this world without knowing that Imperishable is pitiable. But, O Gārgī, he who departs from this world knowing that Imperishable is a Brahman."

तद्वा एतदक्षरं गार्ग्यदृष्टं द्रष्ट्रश्रुतः श्रोत्रमतं मन्त्रविज्ञातं विज्ञातृ नान्यदतोऽस्ति द्रष्ट नान्यदतोऽस्ति श्रोतृ नान्यदतोऽस्ति मन्तृ नान्यदतोऽस्ति विज्ञात्रेतस्मिन्नु खल्वक्षरे गार्ग्याकाश ओतश्च प्रोतश्चेति॥ ११॥

Yājñavalkya said– "Verily, O Gārgī, that Imperishable is the unseen Seer, the unheard Hearer, the unthought Thinker, the ununderstood Understander. Other than It there is naught that sees. Other than It there is naught that hears. Other than It there is naught that thinks. Other than It there is naught that understands. Across this Imperishable, O Gārgī, is space woven, warp and woof."

सा होवाच ब्राह्मणा भगवन्तस्तदेव बहु मन्येध्वं यदस्मान्नमस्कारेण मुच्येध्वं न वै जातु युष्माकमिमं कश्चिकमिमं कश्चिद्ब्रह्मोद्यं जेतेति ततो ह वाचक्नव्युपरराम॥ १२॥

She said : 'Venerable Brāhmaṇas, you may think it a great thing if you escape from this man with [merely] making a bow. Not one of you will surpass him in discussions about Brahma.'

Thereupon [Gārgī] Vācaknavī held her peace.

[Gārgī was most learned lady in respect of Brahma. Hence, all saints gathered there were agreed to her statement but only 'Śākalya Vidagdha' did not accede to it, owing to his egoistic nature. It has been elaborated in the successive Brāhmaṇas. It is sufficient to indicate here that he had to suffer from his obnoxious behaviour.]

नवमं ब्राह्मणम्

Regresses of the numerous gods to the unitary Brahma

अथ हैनं विदग्धः शाकल्यः पप्रच्छ कति देवा याज्ञवल्क्येति स हैतयैव निविदा प्रतिपेदे यावन्तो वैश्वदेवस्य निविद्युच्यन्ते त्रयश्च त्री च शता त्रयश्च त्री च सहस्रेत्योमिति होवाच कत्येव देवा याज्ञवल्क्येति

त्रयस्त्रिंशदित्योमिति होवाच कत्येव देवा याज्ञवल्क्येति षडित्योमिति होवाच कत्येव देवा याज्ञवल्क्येति त्रय इत्योमिति होवाच कत्येव देवा याज्ञवल्क्येति द्वावित्योमिति होवाच कत्येव देवा याज्ञवल्क्येत्यध्यर्ध इत्योमिति होवाच कत्येव देवा याज्ञवल्क्येत्येक इत्योमिति होवा कतमे ते त्रयश्च त्री शता त्रयश्च त्री च सहस्रेति॥ १॥

Then Vidagdha Śākalya questioned him. 'How many gods are there, Yājñavalkya?'

He answered in accord with the following *Nivid* (invocationary formula) : 'As many as are mentioned in the *Nivid* of the Hymn to All the Gods, namely, three hundred and three and three thousand and three 3+300+3+3000 (=3306).'

'Yes,' said he, 'but just how many gods are there, Yājñavalkya?' 'Thirty-three.'

'Yes,' said he, 'but just how many gods are there, Yājñavalkya?' 'Six'.

'Yes,' said he, 'but just how many gods are there, Yājñavalkya?' 'Three'.

'Yes,' said he, 'but just how many gods are there, Yājñavalkya?' 'Two'.

'Yes,' said he, 'but just how many gods are there, Yājñavalkya?' 'One and a half.'

'Yes,' said he, 'but just how many gods are there, Yājñavalkya?' 'One'.

'Yes,' said he, 'which are those three hundred and three, and those three thousand and three?'

स होवाच महिमान एवैषामेते त्रयस्त्रिंशत्त्वेव देवा इति कतमे ते त्रयस्त्रिंशदित्यष्टौ वसव एकादश रुद्रा द्वादशादित्यास्त एकत्रिंशदिन्द्रश्चैव प्रजापतिश्च त्रयस्त्रिंशाविति॥ २॥

He [i.e. Yājñavalkya] said : 'Those are only their powers (*mahiman*). There are just thirty-three gods.'

'Which are those thirty-three?'

'Eight Vasus, eleven Rudras, twelve Ādityas. Those are thirty-one. Indra and Prajāpati make thirty-three.'

कतमे वसव इत्यग्निश्च पृथिवी च वायुश्चान्तरिक्षं चादित्यश्च द्यौश्च चन्द्रमाश्च नक्षत्राणि चैते वसव एतेषु हीदं सर्वंहितमिति तस्माद्वसव इति॥ ३॥

Śākalya asked– 'Which are the Vasus?'

'Fire, earth, wind, atmosphere, sun, sky, moon and stars. These are Vasus, for upon them this excellent (*vasu*) world is set, (for they give a dwelling (*vāsayante*) to the world). Therefore, they are called Vasus.'

कतमे रुद्रा इति दशेमे पुरुषे प्राणा आत्मैकादशस्ते यदास्माच्छरीरान्मर्त्यादुत्क्रामन्त्यथ रोदयन्ति तद्यद्रोदयन्ति तस्माद्रुद्रा इति॥ ४॥

Śākalya asked again– "Who are these 'Rudras'?" Yājñavalkya said– 'These ten breaths in a person, and the self as the eleventh. When they go out from this mortal body, they make us lament. So, because they make us lament (√*rud*), therefore they are Rudras.'

कतय आदित्या इति द्वादश वै मासाः संवत्सरस्यैत आदित्या एते हीदं सर्वमाददाना यन्ति ते यदिदं सर्वमाददाना यन्ति तस्मादादित्या इति॥ ५॥

'Which are the Ādityas?'

'Verily, the twelve months of the year. These are Ādityas, for they go carrying along this whole world. Since they go (*yanti*) carrying along (*ā-dā*) this whole world, therefore they are called Ādityas.'

कतम इन्द्रः कतमः प्रजापतिरिति स्तनयित्नुरेवेन्द्रो यज्ञः प्रजापतिरिति कतमः स्तनयित्नुरित्यशनिरिति कतमो यज्ञ इति पशव इति॥ ६॥

'Which is Indra? Which is Prajāpati?'

'The thunder, verily, is Indra. The sacrifice is Prajāpati.'

'Which is the thunder?' 'The thunderbolt.'

'Which is the sacrifice?' 'The sacrificial animals.'

कतमे षडित्यग्निश्च पृथिवी च वायुश्चान्तरिक्षं चादित्यश्च द्यौश्चैते षडेते हीदꣳ सर्वं षडिति॥ ७॥

Śākalya again asked -"Which are six gods?" Yājñavalkya replied - "These are the earth, the fire, the air, the space, the world of sun (Dan) and the Sun. These are everything.

कतमे ते त्रयो देवा इतीम एव त्रयो लोका एषु हीमे सर्वे देवा इति कतमौ तौ द्वौ देवावित्यन्नं चैव प्राणश्चेति कतमोऽध्यर्ध इति योऽय पवत इति॥ ८॥

Śākalya asked again - "Who are those three gods?" Yājñavalkya replied - "Three worlds are the three gods and all gods reside in them" Śākalya again asked - "Who are those two gods?" The Ṛṣi replied - "The food and the breathing are those two gods." Śākalya again asked - "Who are the one and half god?" Yājñavalkya replied - "This ever-blowing wind is one and half god?"

तदाहुर्यदयमेक इवैव पवतेऽथ कथमध्यर्ध इति यदस्मिन्निदꣳ सर्वमध्यार्ध्नोत्तेनाध्यर्ध इति कतम एको देव इति प्राण इति स ब्रह्म तदित्याचक्षते॥ ९॥

Then Śākalya asked : 'Since he who purifies is just like one, how then is he one and a half?'

'Because in him this whole world did prosper (*adhyārdhnot*). Therefore he is one and a half (*adhyardha*).'

'Which is the one god?' 'Breath,' said he. 'They call him Brahma, the Yon (*tya*).'

Eight different Persons and their corresponding divinities

पृथिव्येव यस्यायतनमग्निर्लोको मनोज्योतिर्यो वै तं पुरुषं विद्यात्सर्वस्यात्मनः परायणꣳ स वै वेदिता स्याद्याज्ञवल्क्य वेद वा अहं तं पुरुषꣳ सर्वस्यात्मनः परायणं यमात्थ य एवायꣳ शारीरः पुरुषः स एष वदैव शाकल्य तस्य का देवतेत्यमृतमिति होवाच॥ १०॥

Śākalya said : 'Verily, he who knows that Person whose abode is the earth, whose world is fire, whose light is mind, who is the last source of every soul—he, verily, would be a knower, O Yājñavalkya.'

(Yājñavalkya said) 'Verily, I know that Person, the last source of every soul, of whom you speak. This very person who is in the body is He. Tell me, Śākalya, who is his god?'

'The Immortal,' said he.

काम एव यस्यायतनꣳ हृदयं लोको मनोज्योतिर्यो वै तं पुरुषं विद्यात्सर्वस्यात्मनः परायणꣳ स वै वेदिता स्याद्याज्ञवल्क्य वेद वा अहं तं पुरुषꣳ सर्वस्यात्मनः परायणं यमात्थ य एवायं काममयः पुरुषः स एष वदैव शाकल्य तस्य का देवतेति स्त्रिय इति होवाच॥ ११॥

[Śākalya said:] 'Verily, he who knows that Person whose abode is desire, whose world is the heart, whose light is mind, who is the last source of every soul—he, verily, would be a knower, O Yājñavalkya.'

[Yājñavalkya said:] 'Verily, I know that Person, the last source of every soul, of whom you speak. This very person who is made of desire is He. Tell me, Śākalya, who is his god?'

'Women,' said he.

रूपाण्येव यस्यायतनं चक्षुर्लोको मनोज्योतिर्यो वै तं पुरुषं विद्यात्सर्वस्यात्मनः परायणꣳ स वै वेदिता स्याद्याज्ञवल्क्य वेद वा अहं तं पुरुषꣳ सर्वस्यात्मनः परायणं यमात्थ य एवासावादित्ये पुरुषः स एष वदैव शाकल्य तस्य का देवतेति सत्यमिति होवाच॥ १२॥

[Śākalya said:] 'Verily, he who knows that Person whose abode is forms (*rūpa*), whose world is the eye, whose light is mind, who is the last source of every soul—he, verily, would be a knower, O Yājñavalkya.'

'Verily, I know that Person, the last source of every soul, of whom you speak. That very person who is in the sun is He. Tell me, Śākalya, who is his god?'

'Truth,' said he.

आकाश एव यस्यायतनꣳ श्रोत्र लोको मनोज्योतिर्यो वै तं पुरुषं विद्यात्सर्वस्यात्मनः परायणꣳ स वै वेदिता स्याद्याज्ञवल्क्य वेद वा अहं तं पुरुषꣳ सर्वस्यात्मनः परायणं यमात्थ य एवायꣳ श्रौत्रः प्रातिश्रुत्कः पुरुषः स एष वदैव शाकल्य तस्य का देवतेति दिश इति होवाच॥ १३॥

[Śākalya said:] 'Verily, he who knows that Person whose abode is space (*ākāśa*), whose world is the ear, whose light is mind, who is the last source of every soul—he, verily, would be a knower, O Yājñavalkya.'

'Verily, I know that Person, the last source of every soul, of whom you speak. This person who is in hearing and who is in the echo is He. Tell me, Śākalya, who is his god?'

'The quarters of heaven,' said he.

तम एव यम्यायतनꣳ हृदयं लोको मनोज्योतिर्यो वै तं पुरुषं विद्यात्सर्वस्यात्मनः परायणꣳ स वै वेदिता स्याद्याज्ञवल्क्य वेद वा अहं तं पुरुषꣳ सर्वस्यात्मनः परायणं यमात्थ य एवायं छायामयः पुरुषः स एष वदैव शाकल्य तस्य का देवतेति मृत्युरिति होवाच॥ १४॥

[Śākalya said:] 'Verily, he who knows that Person whose abode is darkness (*tamas*), whose world is the heart, whose light is mind, who is the last source of every soul—he, verily, would be a knower, O Yājñavalkya.'

'Verily, I know that Person, the last source of every soul, of whom you speak. This very person who is made of shadow is He. Tell me, Śākalya, who is his god?'

'Death,' said he.

रूपाण्येव यस्यायतनं चक्षुर्लोको मनोज्योतिर्यो वै तं पुरुषं विद्यात्सर्वस्यात्मनः परायणꣳ स वै वेदिता स्याद्याज्ञवल्क्य वेद वा अहं तं पुरुषꣳ सर्वस्यात्मनः परायणं यमात्थ य एवायमादर्शे पुरुषः स एष वदैव शाकल्य तस्य का देवतेत्यसुरिति होवाच॥ १५॥

[Śākalya said:] 'Verily, he who knows that Person whose abode is forms (*rūpa*), whose world is the eye, whose light is mind, who is the last source of every soul—he, verily, would be a knower, O Yājñavalkya.'

Verily, I know that Person, the last source of every soul, of whom you speak. This very person who is in the mirror is He. Tell me, Śākalya, who is his god? He said- 'Life (*asu*),'

आप एव यस्यायतनꣳ हृदयं लोको मनोज्योतिर्यो वै तं पुरुषं विद्यात्सर्वस्यात्मनः परायणꣳ स वै वेदिता स्याद्याज्ञवल्क्य वेद वा अहं तं पुरुषꣳ सर्वस्यात्मनः परायणं यमात्थ य एवायमप्सु पुरुषः स एव वदैव शाकल्य तस्य का देवतेति वरुण इति होवाच॥ १६॥

[Śākalya said:] 'Verily, he who knows that Person whose abode is water, whose world is the heart, whose light is mind, who is the last source of every soul—he, verily, would be a knower, O Yājñavalkya.'

'Verily, I know that Person, the last source of every soul, of whom you speak. This very person who is in the waters is He. Tell me, Śākalya, who is his god?'

Yājñavalkya replied - "His god is Varuṇa."

रेत एव यस्यायतनꣳ हृदयं लोको मनोज्योतिर्यो वै तं पुरुषं विद्यात्सर्वस्यात्मनः परायणꣳ स वै वेदिता स्याद्याज्ञवल्क्य वेद वा अहं तं पुरुषꣳ सर्वस्यात्मनः परायणं यमात्थ स एवायं पुत्रमयः पुरुषः स एष वदैव शाकल्य तस्य का देवतेति प्रजापतिरिति होवाच॥ १७॥

Śākalya said - "One who knows the person who is shelterer to all living-organisms becomes omniscient. His body is the semen, heart is the world and the mind is the flame." Yājñavalkya said - "I am well-introduced with that man to whom you say shelterer of all living-organisms. He is the man in the garb of sun. O Śākalya! Ask some more questions." Śākalya asked again - "Who is the god of him?" Yājñavalkya answered - "He is Prajāpati."

शाकल्येति होवाच याज्ञवल्क्यस्त्वाꣳ स्विदिमे ब्राह्मणा अङ्गारावक्षयणमक्रता ३ इति॥ १८॥

Yājñavalkya said to Śākalya - "O Śākalya! These Brāhmaṇas definitely have made you a long used for lifting the conflaggerated piece of fuel up."

याज्ञवल्क्येति होवाच शाकल्यो यदिदं कुरुपञ्चालानां ब्राह्मणानत्यवादीः किं ब्रह्म विद्वानिति दिशो वेद सदेवाः सप्रतिष्ठा इति यद्दिशो वेत्थ सदेवाः सप्रतिष्ठाः॥ १९॥

Śākalya said - "O Yājñavalkya! Whether you presume yourself as identified with the Brahma while condemning the Brāhmaṇas from Kurū and Pāñcāla states by alleging to them." Yājñavalkya replied - "I know about gods and the directions inclu.ling their abode." Śākalya told- "If you know about the gods and the directions where these are existing.

किंदेवतोऽस्य प्राच्यां दिश्यसीत्यादित्यदेवत इति स आदित्यः कस्मिन्प्रतिष्ठित इति चक्षुषीति कस्मिन्नु चक्षुः प्रतिष्ठितमिति रूपेष्विति चक्षुषा हि रूपाणि पश्यति कस्मिन्नु रूपाणि प्रतिष्ठितानीति हृदय इति होवाच हृदयेन हि रूपाणि जानाति हृदये ह्येव रूपाणि प्रतिष्ठितानि भवन्तीत्येवमेवैतद्याज्ञवल्क्य॥ २०॥

Please, tell that at the east directions who is the god existed with you?" Yājñavalkya replied - "I am with the sun there." Śākalya again asked - "In whom that sun is existed?" Yājñavalkya replied - "In the eye." Śākalya asked - "Where the eyes are existed?" The Ṛṣi replied -"It is in the complexion because the man looks at the complexion only by the eyes." Śākalya asked - "Where the complexion is existed?" Yājñavalkya replied - "It is in the heart because the man recognises the complexions only by his heart." Śākalya accepted this truth.

किं देवतोऽस्यां दक्षिणायां दिश्यसीति यमदेवत इति स यमः कस्मिन्प्रतिष्ठित इति यज्ञ इति कस्मिन्नु यज्ञः प्रतिष्ठित इति दक्षिणायामिति कस्मिन्नु दक्षिणा प्रतिष्ठितेति श्रद्धायामिति यदा ह्येव श्रद्धत्तेऽथ दक्षिणां ददाति श्रद्धायाः ह्येव दक्षिणा प्रतिष्ठितेति कस्मिन्नु श्रद्धा प्रतिष्ठितेति हृदय इति होवाच हृदयेन हि श्रद्धां जानाति हृदये ह्येव श्रद्धा प्रतिष्ठिता भवतीत्येवमेवैतद्याज्ञवल्क्य॥ २१॥

Śākalya asked - "Who is the god with you in the south?" Yājñavalkya replied - "I am with the god of death." Śākalya again asked - "Where the god of death is existed?" The Ṛṣi replied - "It is existed in the obeisance." He again ask the location of obeisance on which the Ṛṣi replied - "It is in the heart because a man is known to the obeisance by the heart." Śākalya said - "O Yājñavalkya! It is true."

किंदेवतोऽस्यां प्रतीच्यां दिश्यसीति वरुणदेवत इति स वरुणः कस्मिन्प्रतिष्ठित इत्यप्स्विति कस्मिन्न्वापः प्रतिष्ठिता इति रेतसीति कस्मिन्नु रेतः प्रतिष्ठितमिति हृदय इति तस्मादपि प्रतिरूपं जातमाहुर्हृदयादिव सृप्तो हृदयादिव निर्मित इति हृदये ह्येव रेतः प्रतिष्ठित भवतीत्येवमेवैतद्याज्ञवल्क्य॥ २२॥

Śākalya further asked - "Who is the god with you in the west?" Yājñavalkya replied - "It is Varuṇa." Śākalya asked - "Where the Varuṇa is existed?" The Ṛṣi replied - "It is in the water." Again when asked the location of the water, the Ṛṣi replied that it is in the semen. Śākalya then asked - "Where the semen is existed?" Yājñavalkya replied - "It is in the heart and this is the reason the pupil address the sun analogous to the nature of his father that it is as if born from the heart of his father or framed by the father's heart." Śākalya said - "This too is true."

किंदेवतोऽस्यामुदीच्यां दिश्यसीति सोमदेवत इति स सोमः कस्मिन्प्रतिष्ठित इति दीक्षायामिति कस्मिन्नु दीक्षा प्रतिष्ठितेति सत्य इति तस्मादपि दीक्षितमाहुः सत्यं वदेति सत्ये ह्येव दीक्षा प्रतिष्ठितेति कस्मिन्नु सत्यं

प्रतिष्ठितमिति हृदय इति होवाच हृदयेन हि सत्यं जानाति हृदये ह्येव सत्यं प्रतिष्ठितं भवतीत्येवमेवैतद्याज्ञवल्क्य॥ २ ३॥

Śākalya asked Yājñavalkya - "Who is the god with you in the North?" Yājñavalkya replied - "It is Soma." Śākalya asked - "Where it is existed?" The Ṛṣi replied it is in the consecration. Then Śākalya asked - "Where the consecration is existed?" The Ṛṣi replied - "It is in the heart because a man can only become familiar to the truth by heart therefore the truth is existed in the heart." Then Śākalya said - "O Yājñavalkya said! It is also true."

किंदेवतोऽस्या ध्रुवायां दिश्यसीत्यग्निदेवत इति सोऽग्निः कस्मिन्प्रतिष्ठित इति वाचीति कस्मिन्नु वाक् प्रतिष्ठितेति हृदय इति कस्मिन्नु हृदयं प्रतिष्ठितमिति॥ २ ४॥

Śākalya asked Yājñavalkya - "Who is the god with you in the Dhruva direction?" Yājñavalkya replied - "It is fire." A question again raised - "Where the fire is existed?" Yājñavalkya replied - "It is in the power of speech." It was again asked that where the power of speech is existed. Yājñavalkya replied - "It is in the heart." Śākalya again asked - "Then tell me where heart is located?"

अहल्लिकेति होवाच याज्ञवल्क्यो यत्रैतदन्यत्रास्मन्मन्यासै यद्ध्येतदन्यत्रास्मत्स्याच्छ्वानो वैनदद्युर्वयाꣳसि वैनद्विमथ्नीरन्निति॥ २ ५॥

Yājñavalkya replied - "O Preta! When you take the heart separate then the body, it would have certainly eaten by the dogs or pierced into pieces by the attack of the birds. (As the birds use their beak to make a hole in the dead bodies and for extracting out the soft flesh therefrom. These birds are including vulture, the crow, the eagle etc.?

कस्मिन्नु त्वं चात्मा च प्रतिष्ठितौ स्थ इति प्राण इति कस्मिन्नु प्राणः प्रतिष्ठित इत्यपान इति कस्मिन्न्वपानः प्रतिष्ठित इति व्यान इति कस्मिन्नु व्यानः प्रतिष्ठित इत्युदान इति कस्मिन्नूदानः प्रतिष्ठित इति समान इति स एष नेति नेत्यात्माऽगृह्यो न हि गृह्यतेऽशीर्यो न हि शीर्यतेऽसङ्गो न हि सज्यतेऽसितो न व्यथते न रिष्यत्येतान्यष्टावायतनान्यष्टौ लोका अष्टौ देवा अष्टौ पुरुषाः स यस्तान्पुरुषान्निरुह्य प्रत्युह्यात्यक्रामत्तं त्वौपनिषदं पुरुषं पृच्छामि तं चेन्मे न विवक्ष्यसि मूर्धा ते विपतिष्यतीति तꣳ ह न मेने शाकल्यस्तस्य ह मूर्धा विपपातापि हास्य परिमोषिणोऽस्थीन्यपजह्रुरन्यन्मन्यमानाः॥ २ ६॥

Śākalya again asked - "Where the body and the soul are existed?" Yājñavalkya replied - "It is in the body." Śākalya again asked - "Where the breathings are existed?" The Ṛṣi replied - "It is in the Apāna (breathing in)." He again asked - "Where the Apāna is existed?" the Ṛṣi replied - "It is in Vyāna." He again asked - "Where the Vyāna is existed?" The Ṛṣi replied - "It is in Udāna." He again inquired - "Where Udāna is existed?" Yājñavalkya replied - "It is in Samāna." Yājñavalkya further said - "This soul is called Neti-Neti (endless). It is meant something not entertainable and immortal. It is without company, unmanaged and unpenetrated. There are eight bodies, eight gods and eight men. He has contravened the designated deeds by joining together these persons in his heart by turning into individual form. The knowable person by Upaniṣad is the topic of my curiosity. In case, you could not provide me with clear description, your head will be fell down. As Śākalya was unknown to that man therefore he was beheaded and his skeleton too was picked up considering something, valuable by the thieves.

अथ होवाच ब्राह्मण भगवन्तो यो वः कामयते स मा पृच्छतु सर्वे वा मा पृच्छत यो वः कामयते तं वः पृच्छामि सर्वान्वा वः पृच्छामीति ते ह ब्राह्मणा न दधृषुः॥२७॥

Yājñavalkya said - "O revered Brāhmanas! Anyone among you or conjointly you all may ask questions to me. In case, you are not willing to raise any question, I myself should ask questions from the curious persons either in a sequence or common questions from all. However, nobody could dare to ask any of the questions from Yājñavalkya.

तान् हैतैः लोकैः प्रपच्छ। यथा वृक्षो वनस्पतिस्तथैव पुरुषोऽमृषा। तस्य लोमानि पर्णानि त्वगस्योत्पाटिका बहिः॥१॥ त्वच एवास्य रुधिरं प्रस्यन्दि त्वच उत्पटः। तस्मात्तदा तृण्णात्प्रैति रसो वृक्षादिवाहतात्॥२॥ मा:ऽसान्यस्य शकराणि किनाटःस्नाव तत्स्थिरम्। अस्थीन्यन्तरतो दारूणि मज्जा मज्जोपमा कृता॥३॥ यद्वृक्षो वृक्णो रोहति मूलान्नवतरः पुनः। मर्त्यः स्विन्मृत्युना वृक्णः कस्मान्मूलात्प्ररोहति॥४॥ रेतस इति मा वोचतजीवतस्तत्प्रजायते। धानारुह इव वै वृक्षोऽञ्जसा प्रेत्स संभवः॥५॥ यत्समूलमावृहेयुर्वृक्षं न पुनराभवेत्। मर्त्यः स्विन्मृत्युना वृक्णः कस्मान्मूलात्प्ररोहति॥६॥ जात एव न जायते को न्वेनं जनयेत्पुनः। विज्ञानमानन्दं ब्रह्म रातिर्दातुः परायणं तिष्ठमानस्य तद्विद इति॥७॥॥८॥

Yājñavalkya asked the successive questions through these hymns from the Brāhmaṇas - "The man and the vegetables including trees possess the same properties. As the trees have green leaves, the man has hair in the body and the bark of the tree is analogous to the skin in the human body. The blood is the essence as the blood oozes from the skin of man, the essence (gum) emanates from the bark of the tree. The tree emanates the essence when any of its parts are injured and the blood oozes from the human body when it is injured. The flesh of human body is pari-meteria to the endodermis of the tree, the nerve system of human body is analogous to the hard fibre of the tree. The tree fibre is stable like the nerves of man. Analogous to the bones existed within the human nerves, the tree also have Kinata inside the fibre. The marrow existing in the human body is like the seed of the tree. Notwithstanding so uniformity the tree is competent to sprout from the root in case its trunk is cut down but the man cannot be renewed in the same body after death. Don't say that the man is originated by the semen because it also arises in the living man and not in the dead person. Again the tree gets rebirth through its seed and sprouts again if it is fell down. In case, the tree is uprooted, its revival is impossible. Similarly, the man cannot revive if he is cut down by the death. A man cannot revive because he already have taken birth. Who will give birth him after the death? (The Brāhmaṇas did not answer this question therefore the Veda say about it that) The Brahma is in garb of science and the pleasure. He too is the supreme position of the donor. That Brahma also is the perfect shelter of a man loyal to Brahma and introduced with the Brahma.

।।चतुर्थोऽध्याय:।।

प्रथमं ब्राह्मणम्

King Janaka instructed by Yājñavalkya : six partial definitions of Brahma

जनको ह वैदेह आसांचक्रेऽथ ह याज्ञवल्क्य आवव्राज तं होवाच याज्ञवल्क्य किमर्थमचारी: पशूनिच्छन्नण्वन्तानीत्युभयमेव सम्राडिति होवाच।। १।।

Janaka, [king] of Vaideha, was seated. Yājñavalkya came up. To him he said : 'Yājñavalkya, for what purpose have you come? Because you desire cattle or subtle disputatons?' He said– 'Indeed, for both, your Majesty,'

यत्ते कश्चिदब्रवीत्तच्छृणवामेत्यब्रवीन्मे जित्वा शैलिनिर्वाग्वै ब्रह्मेति यथा मातृमान्पितृमानाचार्यवान्ब्रूयात्तथा तच्छैलिनिरब्रवीद्वाग्वै ब्रह्मेत्यवदतो हि किं स्यादित्यब्रवीत्तु ते तस्यायतनं प्रतिष्ठां न मेऽब्रवीदित्येकपाद्वा एतत्सम्राडिति स वै नो ब्रूहि याज्ञवल्क्य वागेवायतनमाकाश: प्रतिष्ठा प्रज्ञेत्येनदुपासीत का प्रज्ञता याज्ञवल्क्य वागेव सम्राडिति होवाच वाचा वै सम्राड् बन्धु: प्रज्ञायत ऋग्वेदो यजुर्वेद: सामवेदोऽथर्वाङ्गिरस इतिहास: पुराणं विद्या उपनिषद: श्लोका: सूत्राण्यनुव्याख्यानानि व्याख्यानानीष्टं हुतमासितं पायितमयं च लोक: परश्च लोक: सर्वाणि च भूतानि वाचैव सम्राट् प्रज्ञायन्ते वाग्वै सम्राट् परमं ब्रह्म नैनं वाग्जहाति सर्वाण्येनं भूतान्यभिक्षरन्ति देवो भूत्वा देवानप्येति एवं विद्वानेतदुपास्ते हस्त्यृषभं सहस्रं ददामीति होवाच जनको वैदेह: स होवाच याज्ञवल्क्य: पिता मेऽमन्यत ना ननुशिष्य हरेतेति।। २।।

Yājñavalkya said - "O king! I have come here to listen everything whatever has been told by anybody regarding Brahman." Janaka replied - "Śailini Jitvan has presumed Brahman as the power of speech.

Yājñavalkya replied- 'As a man might say that he had a mother, that he had a father, that he had a teacher, so did that Śailini say "Brahma, verily, is speech." For he might have thought (*iti*), "What can one have who cannot speak?" But did he tell you Its seat and support?'

Janaka told– 'He did not tell me.'

Yājñavalkya further said - 'Forsooth, your Majesty, that is a one-legged [Brahma].'

'Verily, Yājñavalkya, do you here tell us.'

'Its seat is just speech; Its support, space (*ākāśa*). One should worship It as intelligence (*prajñā*).'

'What is Its quality of intelligence, Yājñavalkya?'

'Just speech, your Majesty,' said he. 'Verily, by speech, your Majesty, a friend is recognized. By speech alone, your Majesty, the Ṛgveda, the Yajurveda, the Sāmaveda, the [Hymns] of the Atharvans and Aṅgirases, Legends (*itihāsa*), Ancient Lore (*purāṇa*), Sciences (*vidyā*), Mystic Doctrines (*upaniṣad*), Verses (*śloka*), Aphorisms (*sūtra*), Explanations (*anuvyākhyāna*), Commentaries (*vyākhyāna*), what is offered in sacrifice and as oblation, food and drink, this world and the other, and all beings are known. The highest Brahma, your Majesty, is in truth speech. Speech does not desert him who, knowing this, worships it as such. All things run unto him. He, having become a god, goes even to the gods.'

'I will give you a thousand cows with a bull as large as an elephant,' said Janaka, [king] of Vaideha.

Yājñavalkya replied : 'My father thought that without having instructed one should not accept.'

यदेव ते कश्चिदब्रवीत्तच्छृणवामेत्यब्रवीन्म उदङ्कः शौल्बायनः प्राणो वै ब्रह्मेति यथा मातृमान्पितृमानाचार्यवान्ब्रूयात्तथा तच्छौल्बायनोऽब्रवीत्प्राणो वै ब्रह्मेत्यप्राणतो हि किꣳ स्यादित्यब्रवीत्तु ते तस्यायतनं प्रतिष्ठां न मेऽब्रवीदित्येकपाद्वा एतत्सम्राडिति स वै नो ब्रूहि याज्ञवल्क्य प्राण एवायतनमाकाशः प्रतिष्ठा प्रियमित्येनदुपासीत का प्रियता याज्ञवल्क्य प्राण एव सम्राडिति होवाच प्राणस्य वै सम्राट् कामायायाज्य याजयत्यप्रतिगृह्यस्य प्रतिगृह्णात्यपि तत्र वधाशङ्कं भवति यां दिशमेति प्राणस्यैव सम्राट् कामाय प्राणो वै सम्राट् परमं ब्रह्म नैनं प्राणो जहाति सर्वाण्येनं भूतान्यभिक्षरन्ति देवो भूत्वा देवानप्येति य एवं विद्वानेतदुपास्ते हस्त्यृषभꣳ सहस्रं ददामीति होवाच जनको वैदेहः स होवाच याज्ञवल्क्यः पिता मेऽमन्यत नाननुशिष्य हरेतेति॥ ३॥

'Let us hear what anybody may have told you,' [continued Yājñavalkya].

Udaṅka Śaulbāyana told me : "Brahma, verily, is the breath of life (*prāṇa*)."

'As a man might say that he had a mother, that he had a father, that he had a teacher, so did that Śaulbāyana say, "Brahma is the breath of life." For he might have thought, "What can one have who is without the breath of life?" But did he tell you Its seat and support?'

'He did not tell me.'

'Forsooth, your Majesty, that is a one-legged [Brahma].'

'Verily, Yājñavalkya, do you here tell us.'

'Its seat is just the breath of life; Its support, space. One should worship It as the dear (*priya*).'

'What is Its dearness, Yājñavalkya?'

'The breath of life itself, your Majesty,' said he. 'Verily, out of love for the breath of life, your Majesty, one has sacrifice offered for him for whom one should not offer sacrifice, one accepts from him from whom one should not accept. Out of love of just the breath of life, your Majesty, there arises fear of being killed wherever one goes. The highest Brahma, your Majesty, is in truth the breath of life. The breath of life leaves not him who, knowing this, worships it as such. All things run unto him. He, having become a god, goes even to the gods.

'I will give you a thousand cows with a bull as large as an elephant,' said Janaka, [king] of Vaideha.

Yājñavalkya replied : 'My father thought that without having instructed one should not accept.'

यदेव ते कश्चिदब्रवीत्तच्छृणवामेत्यब्रवीन्मे बर्कुर्वार्ष्णश्चक्षुर्वै ब्रह्मेति यथा मातृमान्पितृमानाचार्यवान्ब्रूयात्तथा तद्वार्ष्णोऽब्रवीच्चक्षुर्वै ब्रह्मेत्यपश्यतो हि किꣳ स्यादित्यब्रवीत्तु ते तस्यायतनं प्रतिष्ठां न मेऽब्रवीदित्येकपाद्वा एतत्सम्राडिति स वै नो ब्रूहि याज्ञवल्क्य चक्षुरेवायतनमाकाशः प्रतिष्ठा सत्यमित्येनदुपासीत का सत्यता याज्ञावल्क्य चक्षुरेव सम्राडिति होवाच चक्षुषा वै सम्राट् पश्यन्तमाहुरद्राक्षीरिति स आहाद्राक्षमिति तत्सत्यं भवति चक्षुर्वै सम्राट् परमं ब्रह्म नैनं चक्षुर्जहाति सर्वाण्येनं भूतान्यभिक्षरन्ति देवो भूत्वा देवानप्येति य एवं विद्वानेतदुपास्ते हस्त्यृषभꣳ सरस्त्रं ददामीति होवाच जनको वैदेहः स होवा याज्ञवल्क्यः पिता मेऽमन्यत नाननुशिष्य हरेतेति॥४॥

Then Yājñavalkya again said to king Janaka– 'Let us hear what anybody may have told you,'

'Barku Vārṣṇa told me : "Brahma, verily, is sight."

'As a man might say that he had a mother, that he had a father, that he had a teacher, so did that Vārṣṇa say, "Brahma is sight (*cakṣu*)." For he mighty have thought, "what can one have who cannot see?" But did he tell you Its seat and support?'

'He did not tell me.' (Janaka said)

'Forsooth, your Majesty, that is a one-legged [Brahma].'

'Verily, Yājñavalkya, do you here tell us.'

'Its seat is just sight; Its support, space. One should worship It as the true (*satya*).'

'What is Its truthfulness, Yājñavalkya?'

'Sight alone, your Majesty,' said he. 'Verily, your Majesty, when they say to a man who sees with his eyes, "Have you seen?" and he says, "I have seen," that is the truth. Verily, your Majesty, the highest Brahma is sight. Sight leaves not him who, knowing this worships it as such. All things run unto him. He, becoming a god, goes to the gods.'

'I will give you a thousand cows with a bull as large as an elephant,' said Janaka, [king] of Vaideha.

Yājñavalkya replied : 'My father thought that without having instructed one should not accept.'

यदेव ते कश्चिदब्रवीत्तच्छृणवामेत्यब्रवीन्मे गर्दबीविपीतो भारद्वाजः श्रोत्रं वै ब्रह्मेति यथा मातृमान्पितृमानाचार्यवान्ब्रूयात्तथा तद्भारद्वाजोऽब्रवीच्छ्रोत्रं वै ब्रह्मेत्यश्रृण्वतो हि किꣳ स्यादित्यब्रवीत्तु ते तस्यायतनं प्रतिष्ठां न मेऽब्रवीदित्येकपाद्वा एतत्सम्राडिति स वै नो ब्रूहि याज्ञवल्क्य श्रोत्रमेवायतनमाकाशः प्रतिष्ठानन्त इत्येनदुपासीत कानन्तता याज्ञवल्क्य दिश एव सम्राडिति होवाच तस्माद्वै सम्राडिति यां कां च दिशं गच्छति नैवास्या अन्तं गच्छत्यनन्ता हि दिशो दिशो वै सम्राट् श्रोत्रꣳ श्रोत्रं वै सम्राट् परमं ब्रह्म नैनꣳ श्रोत्रं जहाति सर्वाण्येनं भूतान्यभिक्षरन्ति देवो भूत्वा देवानप्येति य एवं विद्वानेतदुपास्ते हस्त्यृषभꣳ सहस्त्रं ददामीति होवाच जनको वैदेहः स होवाच याज्ञवल्क्यः पिता मेऽमन्यत नाननुशिष्य हरेतेति॥५॥

Yājñavalkya told king Janaka– 'Let us hear what anybody may have told you,'

Janaka said– 'Gardabhīvipīta Bhāradvāja told me : "Brahma, verily, is hearing."

Yājñavalkya said– 'As a man might say that he had a mother, that he had a father, that he had a teacher, so did that Bhāradvāja say, "Brahma is hearing." For he might have thought, "What can one have who cannot hear?" But did he tell you Its seat and support?

King Janaka replied– "No Sir! He did not tell anything about it."

'Forsooth, your Majesty, that is a one-legged [Brahma].'

'Verily, Yājñavalkya, do you here tell us.'

'Its seat is just hearing; Its support, space. One should worship It as the endless (*ananta*).'

'What is Its endlessness, Yājñavalkya?'

'Just the quarters of heaven, your Majesty,' said he. 'Therefore, verily, your Majesty, to whatever quarter one goes, he does not come to the end of it, for the quarters of heaven are endless. Verily, your Majesty, the quarters of heaven are hearing. Verily, your Majesty, the highest Brahma is hearing. Hearing does not desert him who, knowing this, worships it as such. All things run unto him. He, becoming a god, goes to the gods.'

'I will give you a thousand cows with a bull as large as an elephant,' said Janaka, [king] of Vaideha.

Yājñavalkya replied : 'My father thought that without having instructed one should not accept.'

यदेव ते कश्चिदब्रवीत्तच्छृणवामेत्यब्रवीन्मे सत्यकामो जाबालो मनो वै ब्रह्मेति यथा मातृमान्पितृमानाचार्यवान्ब्रूयात्तथा तज्जाबालोऽवीन्मनो वै ब्रह्मेत्यमनसो हि किꣳ स्यादित्यब्रवीत्तु ते तस्यायतनं प्रतिष्ठां न मेऽब्रवीदित्येकपाद्वा एतत्सम्राडिति स वै नो ब्रूहि याज्ञवल्क्य मन एवायतनमाकाशः प्रतिष्ठाऽऽनन्द इत्येनदुपासीत का आनन्दता याज्ञवल्क्य मन एव सम्राडिति होवाच मनसा वै सम्राट् स्त्रियमभिहार्यते तस्यां प्रतिरूपः पुत्रो जायते स आनन्दो मनो वै सम्राट् परमं ब्रह्म नैनं मनो जहाति सर्वाण्येनं भूतान्यभिक्षरन्ति देवो भूत्वा देवानप्येति य एवं विद्वानेतदुपास्ते हस्त्यृषभꣳ सहस्रं ददामीति होवाच जनको वैदेहः स होवाच याज्ञवल्क्यः पिता मेऽमन्यत नाननुशिष्य हरेतेति॥ ६॥

'Let us hear what anybody may have told you,' [continued Yājñavalkya].

'Satyakāma Jābāla told me : "Brahma, verily, is mind." '

'As a man might say that he had a mother, that he had a father, that he had a teacher, so did that Jābāla say, "Brahma is mind." For he might have thought, "What can one have who is without a mind?" But did he tell you Its seat and support?'

'He did not tell me.'

'Forsooth, your Majesty, that is a one-legged [Brahma].'

'Verily, Yājñavalkya, do you here tell us.'

'Its seat is just the mind; Its support, space. One should worship It as the blissful (*ānanda*).'

'What is Its blissfulness, Yājñavalkya?'

'Just the mind, your Majesty,' said he. 'Verily, your Majesty, by the mind one betakes himself to a woman. A son like himself is born of her. He is bliss. Verily, your majesty, the highest Brahma is mind. Mind does not desert him who, knowing this, worships it as such. All things run unto him. He, becoming a god, goes to the gods.'

'I will give you a thousand cows with a bull as large as an elephant,' said Janaka, [king] of Vaideha.

Yājñavalkya replied : 'My father thought that without having instructed one should not accept.'

यदेव ते कश्चिदब्रवीत्तच्छृणवामेत्यब्रवीन्मे विदग्धः शाकल्यो हृदयं वै ब्रह्मेति यथा मातृमान्पितृमानाचार्यवान्ब्रूयात्तथा तच्छाकल्योऽब्रवीद्धृदयं वै ब्रह्मेत्यहृदयस्य हि किꣳ स्यादित्यब्रवीत्तु ते तस्यायतनं प्रतिष्ठां न मेऽब्रवीदित्येकपाद्वा एतत्सम्राडिति स वै नो ब्रूहि याज्ञवल्क्य हृदयमेवायतनमाकाशः प्रतिष्ठा स्थितिरित्येनदुपासीत का स्थितता याज्ञवल्क्य हृदयमेव सम्राडिति होवाच हृदयं वै सम्राट् सर्वेषां भूतानामायतनꣳ हृदयं वै सम्राट् सर्वेषा भूतानां प्रतिष्ठा हृदये ह्येव सम्राट् सर्वाणि भूतानि प्रतिष्ठितानि भवन्ति हृदयं वै सम्राट् परमं ब्रह्म नैनꣳ हृदयं जहाति सर्वाण्येनं भूतान्यभिक्षरन्ति देवा भूत्वा देवानप्येति य एवं विद्वानेतदुपास्ते हस्त्यृषभꣳ सहस्रं ददामीति होवाच जनको वैदेहः स होवाच याज्ञवल्क्यः पिता मेऽमन्यत नाननुशिष्य हरेतेति॥७॥

'Let us hear what anybody may have told you,'[continued Yājñavalkya].

'Vidagdha Śākalya told me : "Brahma, verily, is the heart." '

'As a man mighty say that he had a mother, that he had a father, that he had a teacher, so did that Śākalya say, "Brahma is the heart." For he might have thought, "What can one have who is without a heart?" But did he not tell you Its seat and support?'

'He did not tell me.'

'Forsooth, your Majesty, that is a one-legged [Brahma].'

'Verily, Yājñavalkya, do you here tell us.'

'Its seat is just the heart; Its support, space. One should worship It as the steadfast (*sthiti*).'

'What is Its steadfastness, Yājñavalkya?'

'Just the heart, your Majesty,' said he. 'Verily, your Majesty, the heart is the seat of all things. Verily, your Majesty, the heart is the support (*pratiṣṭhā*) of all things, for on the heart alone, your Majesty, all things are established (*pratiṣṭhita*). Verily, your Majesty, the highest Brahma is the heart. The heart does not leave him who, knowing this, worships it as such. All things run unto him. He, becoming a god, goes to the gods.'

'I will give you a thousand cows with a bull as large as an elephant,' said Janaka, [king] of Vaideha.

Yājñavalkya replied : 'My father thought that without having instructed one should not accept.'

द्वितीयं ब्राह्मणम्

Concerning the soul, its bodily and universal relations

जनको ह वैदेहः कूर्चादुपावसर्पन्नुवाच नमस्तेऽस्तु याज्ञवल्क्यानु मा शाधीति स होवाच यथा वै सम्राण्महान्तमध्वानमेष्यन् रथं वा नावं वा समाददीतैवमेवैताभिरुपनिषद्भिः समाहितात्मास्येवं वृन्दारक आढ्यः सन्नधीतवेद उक्तोपनिषत्क इतो विमुच्यमानः क्व गमिष्यसीति नाहं तद्भगवन्वेद यत्र गमिष्यामीत्यथ वै तेऽहं तद्वक्ष्यामि यत्र गमिष्यसीति ब्रवीतु भगवानिति॥ १॥

Janaka [king] of Vaideha, descending from his cushion and approaching, said : 'Adoration to you, Yājñavalkya. Do you instruct me.'

He [i.e. Yājñavalkya], said : 'Verily, as a king about to go on a great journey would prepare a chariot or a ship, even so you have a soul (*ātman*) prepared with these mystic doctrines (*upaniṣad*). So, being at the head of a troop, and wealthy, learned in the Vedas, and instructed in mystic doctrines, where, when released hence, will you go?'

'That I know not, noble sir—where I shall go.'

'Then truly I shall tell you that—where you will go.'

'Tell me, noble sir.'

इन्धो ह वै नामैष योऽयं दक्षिणेऽक्षन्पुरुषस्तं वा एतमिन्धꣳ सन्तमिन्द्र इत्याचक्षते परोक्षेणैव परोक्षप्रिया इव हि देवाः प्रत्यक्षद्विषः॥ २॥

Yājñavalkya said - 'Indha (i.e. the Kindler) by name is this person here in the right eye. Him, verily, who is that Indha people call "Indra" cryptically, for the gods are fond of the cryptic, as it were, and dislike the evident.

[The divine powers are the micro flow of the breathings and this can be felt directly. The eyes or the ears directly seen as bearer of the power to see and listen but the power inherent to see and listen are divine and these are in their indirect form. To clear this statement, it is plausible to mention that the deaf and the blind also have the exterior eyes and the ears both but due to lack of the divine power these are unable to see and hear. This is reason the gods prefer not exterior but the interior or the indirect.]

अथैतद्वामेऽक्षणि पुरुषरूपमेषास्य पत्नी विराट् तयोरेष सꣳस्तावो य एषोऽन्तर्हृदय आकाशोऽथैनयोरेतदन्नं य एषोऽन्तर्हृदये लोहितपिण्डोऽथैनयोरेतत्प्रावरणं यदेतदन्तर्हृदये जालकमिवाथैनयोरेषा सृतिः संचरणी यैषा हृदयादूर्ध्वा नाड्युच्चरति यथा केशः सहस्रधा भिन्न एवमस्यैता हिता नाम नाड्योऽन्तर्हृदये प्रतिष्ठिता भवन्त्येताभिर्वा एतदास्रवदास्रवति तस्मादेष प्रविविक्ताहारतर इवैव भवत्यस्माच्छारीरादात्मनः॥ ३॥

Now that which has the form of a person in the left eye is his wife, Virāj. Their meeting-place [literally, their common praise, or concord] is the space in the heart. Their food is the red lump in the heart. Their covering is the net-like work in the heart. The path that they go is that channel which goes upward from the heart. Like a hair divided a thousandfold, so are the channels called *hitā*, which are established within the heart. Through these flows that which flows on [i.e. the food]. Therefore that [soul which is composed of Indha and Virāj] is, as it were, an eater of finer food than is this bodily self.

[This statement of the sage referring to the right and left eye as the husband and wife is really a cryptic statement. The modern science could only receive a captive knowledge or minuscule knowledge in this context. The powers inherent to both eyes are addressed as the man but they are compliment to one another like a husband and the wife. By the same reason, one can be said as the half part of the other.]

तस्य प्राची दिक् प्राञ्चः प्राणा दक्षिणा दिग्दक्षिणे प्राणाः प्रतीची दिक् प्रत्यञ्चः प्राणा उदीची दिगुदञ्चः प्राणा ऊर्ध्वा दिगूर्ध्वाः प्राणा अवाची दिगवाञ्चः प्राणाः सर्वा दिशः सर्वे प्राणाः स एष नेति नेत्यात्माऽगृह्यो नहि गृह्यतेऽशीर्यो नहि शीर्यतेऽसङ्गो नहि सज्यतेऽसितो न व्यथते न रिष्यत्यभयं वै जनक प्राप्तोऽसीति होवाच याज्ञवल्क्यः स होवाच जनको वैदेहोऽभयं त्वा गच्छताद्याज्ञवल्क्य यो नो भगवन्नभयं वेदयसे नमस्तेऽस्त्विमे विदेहा अयमहमस्मि॥ ४॥

The eastern breaths are his eastern quarter. The southern breaths are his southern quarter. The western breaths are his western quarter. The northern breaths are his northern quarter. The upper breaths are his upper quarter [i.e. the zenith]. The lower breaths are his lower quarter [i.e. the nadir]. All the breaths are all his quarters.

But the soul (*Ātman*) is not this, it is not that (*neti, neti*). It is unseizable, for it cannot be seized. It is indestructible, for it cannot be destroyed. It is unattached, for it does not attach itself. It is unbound. It does not tremble. It is not injured.

'Verily, Janaka, you have reached fearlessness.' Thus spoke Yājñavalkya.

Janaka [king] of Vaideha, said : 'May fearlessness come unto you, noble Sir, you who make us to know fearlessness.' Adoration to you! Here are the Vaidehas, here am I [as your servants].

तृतीयं ब्राह्मणम्

The light of man is the soul

जनकꣳ ह वैदहं याज्ञवल्क्यो जगाम स मेने न वदिष्य इत्यथ ह यज्जनकश्च वैदेहो याज्ञवल्क्यश्चाग्निहोत्रे समूदाते तस्मै ह याज्ञवल्क्यो वरं ददौ स ह कामप्रश्नमेव वव्रे तꣳ हास्मै ददौ तꣳ सम्राडेव पूर्वं पप्रच्छ॥ १॥

Yājñavalkya came to Janaka [king] of Vaideha. He thought to himself : 'I will not talk.'

But [once] when Janaka, [king] of Vaideha, and Yājñavalkya were discussing together at an Agnihotra, Yājñavalkya granted the former a boon. He chose asking whatever question he wished. He granted it to him. So [now] the king, [speaking] first, asked him :

याज्ञवल्क्य किंज्योतिरयं पुरुष इति आदित्यज्योतिः सम्राडिति होवाचादित्येनैवायं ज्योतिषास्ते पल्ययते कर्म कुरुते विपल्येतीत्येवमेवैतद्याज्ञवल्क्य॥ २॥

'Yājñavalkya, what light does a person here have?'

'He has the light of the sun, O king,' he said, 'for with the sun, indeed, as his light one sits, moves around, does his work, and returns.'

Janaka said– "Yes, it is quite right."

अस्तमित आदित्य याज्ञवल्क्य किंज्योतिरेवायं पुरुष इति चन्द्रमा एवास्य ज्योतिर्भवतीति चन्द्रमसैवायं ज्योतिषास्ते पल्ययते कर्म कुरुते विपल्येतीत्येवमेवातद्याज्ञवल्क्य॥ ३॥

But when the sun has set, Yājñavalkya, 'what light does a person here have?'

'The moon, indeed, is his light,' said he, 'for with the moon indeed, as his light one sits, moves around, does his work, and returns.'

'Quite so, Yājñavalkya.

अस्तमित आदित्ये याज्ञवल्क्य चन्द्रमस्यस्तमिते किंज्योतिरेवायं पुरुष इत्यग्निरेवास्य ज्योतिर्भवतीत्यग्निनैवायं ज्योतिषास्ते पल्ययते कर्म कुरुते विपल्येतीत्येवमेवैतद्याज्ञवल्क्य॥ ४॥

But when the sun has set, and the moon has set, what light does a person here have?'

'Fire, indeed, is his light,' said he, 'for with fire, indeed, as his light one sits, moves around, does his work, and returns.'

'Quite so, Yājñavalkya.

अस्तमित आदित्ये याज्ञवल्क्य चन्द्रमस्यस्तमिते शान्तेऽग्नौ किंज्योतिरेवायं पुरुष इति वागेवास्य ज्योतिर्भवतीति वाचैवायं ज्योतिषास्ते पल्ययते कर्म कुरुते विपल्येतीति तस्माद्वै सम्राडिति यत्र स्वः पाणिर्न विनिर्ज्ञायतेऽथ यत्र वागुच्चरत्युपैव तत्र न्येतीत्येवमेवैतद्याज्ञवल्क्य॥ ५॥

But when the sun has set, Yājñavalkya, and the moon has set, and the fire has gone out, what light does a person here have?'

'Speech, indeed, is his light,' said he, 'for with speech, indeed, as his light one sits, moves around, does his work, and returns. Therefore, verily, O king, where one does not discern even his own hands, when a voice is raised, then one goes straight towards it.'

'Quite so, Yājñavalkya.

अस्तमित आदित्ये याज्ञवल्क्य चन्द्रमस्यस्तमिते शान्तेऽग्नौ शान्तायां वाचि किंज्योतिरेवायं पुरुष इत्यात्मैवास्य ज्योतिर्भवतीत्यात्मनैवायं ज्योतिषास्ते पल्ययते कर्म कुरुते विपल्येतीति॥ ६॥

Janaka again asked– But when the sun has set, Yājñavalkya, and the moon has set, and the fire has gone out, and speech is hushed, what light does a person here have?'

'The soul (*ātman*), indeed, is his light,' said he, 'for with the soul, indeed, as his light one sits, moves around, does his work, and returns.'

कतम आत्मेति योऽयं विज्ञानमयः प्राणेषु हृद्यन्तर्ज्योतिः पुरुषः स समानः सन्नुभौ लोकावनुसंचरति ध्यायतीव लेलायतीव स हि स्वप्नो भूत्वेमं लोकमतिक्रामति मृत्यो रूपाणि॥ ७॥

King Janaka again asked– 'Which (*katama*) is the soul?'

'The person here who among the senses is made of knowledge, who is the light in the heart. He, remaining the same, goes along both worlds, appearing to think, appearing to move about, for upon becoming asleep he transcends this world and the forms of death.'

स वा अयं पुरुषो जायमानः शरीरमभिसंपद्यमानः पाप्मभिः सꣳसृज्यते स उत्क्रामन् म्रियमाणः पाप्मनो विजहाति॥ ८॥

Verily, this person, by being born and obtaining a body, is joined with evils. When he departs, on dying, he leaves evils behind.

तस्य वा एतस्य पुरुषस्य द्वे एव स्थाने भवत इदं च परलोकस्थानं च सन्ध्यं तृतीयꣳ स्वप्नस्थानं तस्मिन्सन्ध्ये स्थाने तिष्ठन्नेते उभे स्थाने पश्यतीदं च परलोकस्थानं च। अथ यथाक्रमोऽयं परलोकस्थाने भवति तमाक्रममाक्रम्योभयान् पाप्मन आनन्दाꣳश्च पश्यति स यत्र प्रस्वपित्यस्य लोकस्य सर्वावतो मात्रामुपादाय स्वयं विहत्य स्वयं निर्माय स्वेन भासा स्वेन ज्योतिषा प्रस्वपित्यत्रायं पुरुषः स्वयं ज्योतिर्भवति॥ ९॥

Verily, there are just two conditions of this person : the condition of being in this world and the condition of being in the other world. There is an intermediate third condition, namely, that of being in sleep. By standing in this intermediate condition one sees both those conditions, namely being in this world and being in the other world. Now whatever the approach is to the condition of being in the other world, by making that approach one sees the evils [of this world] and the joys [of yonder world].

When one goes to sleep, he takes along the material (*mātra*) of this all-containing world, himself tears it apart, himself builds it up, and dreams by his own brightness, by his own light. Then this person becomes self-illuminated.

न तत्र रथा न रथयोगा न पन्थानो भवन्त्यथ रथान् रथयोगान्पथः सृजते न तत्रानन्दा मुदः प्रमुदो भवन्त्यथानन्दान् मुदः प्रमुदः सृजते न तत्र वेशान्ताः पुष्करिण्यः स्रवन्त्यो भवन्त्यथ वेशान्तान् पुष्करिणीः स्रवन्तीः सृजते स हि कर्ता॥ १०॥

There are no chariots there, no spans, no roads. But he projects from himself chariots, spans, roads. There are no blisses there, no pleasures, no delights. But he projects from himself blisses, pleasures, delights. There are no tanks there, no lotus-pools, no streams. But he projects from himself tanks, lotus-pools, streams. For he is a creator.

तदेते श्लोका भवन्ति। स्वप्नेन शारीरमभिप्रहत्याऽसुप्तः सुप्तानभिचाकशीति। शुक्रमादाय पुनरेति स्थानꣳ हिरण्मयः पुरुष एकहꣳसः॥ ११॥

On this point there are the following verses :—

Striking down in sleep what is bodily, sleepless he looks down upon the sleeping [senses].

Having taken to himself light, there returns to his place the golden person, the one spirit (*haṁsa*).

प्राणेन रक्षन्नवरं कुलायं बहिष्कुलायादमृतश्चरित्वा। स ईयतेऽमृतो यत्र कामꣳ हिरणमयः पुरुष एकहꣳसः॥ १२॥

Guarding his low nest with the breath, the Immortal goes forth out of the nest.

He goes wherever he pleases—the immortal, the golden person, the one spirit (*haṁsa*).

स्वप्नान्त उच्चावचमीयमानो रुपाणि देवः कुरुते बहूनि। उतेव स्त्रीभीः सह मोदमानो जक्षदुतेवापि भयानि पश्यन्॥ १३॥

In the state of sleep going aloft and alow, a god, he makes many forms for himself—

Now, as it were, enjoying pleasure with women,

Now, as it were, laughing, and even beholding fearful sights.

आराममस्य पश्यन्ति न तं पश्यति कश्चनेति तं नायतं बोधयेदित्याहुः। दुर्भिषज्यꣳहास्मै भवति यमेष न प्रतिपद्यतेऽथो खल्वाहुर्जागरितदेश एवास्यैष इति यानि ह्येव जाग्रत्पश्यति तानि सुप्त इत्यत्रायं पुरुषः स्वयंज्योतिर्भवति सोऽहं भगवते सहस्त्रं ददाम्यत ऊर्ध्वं विमोक्षाय ब्रूहीति॥ १४॥

People see his pleasure-ground; Him no one sees at all.

"Therefore one should not wake him suddenly," they say. Hard is the curing for a man to whom He does not return.

Now some people say : "That is just his waking state, for whatever things he sees when awake, those too he sees when asleep." [This is not so, for] there [i.e. in sleep] the person is self-illuminated.

[Janaka said:] 'I will give you, noble sir, a thousand [cows]. Declare what is higher than this, for my release [from reincarnation].'

[According to a certain group of people, this stage of dreaming too is the stage of awakening because whatever the man observes in dreams, the same he too observes in the stage of awakening and at this stage, this man becomes self-illuminating. King Janaka said– "I provide you with one thousand currencies (Mudrā). O Lord! Let me know what is emancipation."]

स वा एष एतस्मिन्संप्रसादे रत्वा चरित्वा दृष्ट्वैव पुण्यं च पापं च पुनः प्रतिन्यायं प्रतियोन्याद्रवति स्वप्नायैव स यत्तत्र किंचित्पश्यत्यनन्वागतस्तेन भवत्यसङ्गो ह्ययं पुरुष इत्येवमेवैतद्याज्ञवल्क्य सोऽहं भगवते सहस्त्रं ददाम्यत ऊर्ध्वं विमोक्षायैव ब्रूहीति॥ १५॥

'Having had enjoyment in this state of deep sleep, having travelled around and seen good and bad, he hastens again, according to the entrance and place of origin, back to sleep. Whatever he sees there [i.e. in the state of deep sleep], he is not followed by it, for this person is without attachments.'

[Janaka said:] 'Quite so, Yājñavalkya. I will give you, noble sir, a thousand [cows]. Declare what is higher than this, for my release.'

स वा एष एतस्मिन्स्वप्ने रत्वा चरित्वा दृष्ट्वैव पुण्यं च पापं च पुनः प्रतिन्यायं प्रतियोन्याद्रवति बुद्धान्तायैव स यत्तत्र किंचित्पश्यत्यनन्वागतस्तेन भवत्यसङ्गो ह्ययं पुरुष इत्येवमेवैतद्याज्ञवल्क्य सोऽहं भगवते

सहस्त्रं ददाम्यत ऊर्ध्वं विमोक्षायैव ब्रूहीति॥ १६॥

Having had enjoyment in this state of sleep, having travelled around and seen good and bad, he hastens again, according to the entrance and place of origin, back to the state of waking. Whatever he sees there [i.e. in dreaming sleep], he is not followed by it, for this person is without attachments.'

[Janaka said:] 'Quite so. Yājñavalkya. I will give you, noble sir, a thousand [cows]. Declare what is higher than this, for my release.'

स वा एष एतस्मिन्बुद्धान्ते रत्वा चरित्वा दृष्ट्वैव पुण्यं च पापं च पुनः प्रतिन्यायं प्रतियोन्याद्रवति स्वप्नान्तायैव॥ १७॥

'Having had enjoyment in this state of waking, having travelled around and seen good and evil, he hastens again, according to the entrance and place of origin, back to dreaming sleep.

तद्यथा महामत्स्य उभे कूलेऽनुसंचरति पूर्वं चापरं चैवमेवायं पुरुष एतावुभावन्तावनुसंचरति स्वप्नान्तं च बुद्धान्तं च॥ १८॥

As a great fish goes along both banks of a river, both the hither and the further, just so this person goes along both these conditions, the condition of sleeping and the condition of waking.

तद्यथास्मिन्नाकाशे श्येनो वा सुपर्णो वा विपरिपत्य श्रान्तः सꣳहत्य पक्षौ संलयायैव ध्रियत एवमेवायं पुरुष एतस्मा अन्ताय धावति यत्र सुप्तो न कंचन कामं कामयते न कंचन स्वप्नं पश्यति॥ १९॥

As a falcon, or an eagle, having flown around here in space, becomes weary, folds its wings, and is borne down to its nest, just so this person hastens to that state where, asleep, he desires no desire and sees no dream.

ता वा अस्यैता हिता नाम नाड्यो यथा केशः सहस्रधा भिन्नस्तावताणिम्ना तिष्ठन्ति शुक्लस्य नीलस्य पिङ्गलस्य हरितस्य लोहितस्य पूर्णा अथ यत्रैनं घ्नन्तीव जिनन्तीव हस्तीव विच्छाययति गर्तमिव पतति यदेव जाग्रद्भयं पश्यति तदत्राविद्यया मन्यतेऽथ यत्र देव इव राजेवाहमेवेदꣳ सर्वोऽस्मीति मन्यते सोऽस्य परमो लोकः॥ २०॥

Verily, a person has those channels called *hitā*; as a hair subdivided a thousandfold, so minute are they, full of white, blue, yellow, green, and red. Now when people seem to be killing him, when they seem to be overpowering him, when an elephant seems to be tearing him to pieces, when he seems to be falling into a hole—in these circumstances he is imagining through ignorance the very fear which he sees when awake. When, imagining that he is a god, that he is a king, he thinks "I am this world-all", that is his highest world.

तद्वा अस्यैतदतिच्छन्दा अपहतपाप्माऽभयꣳ रूपं तद्यथा प्रियया स्त्रिया संपरिष्वक्तो न बाह्यं किंचन वेद नान्तरमेवमेवायं पुरुषः प्राज्ञेनात्मना संपरिष्वक्तो न बाह्यं किंचन वेद नान्तरं तद्वा अस्यैतदाप्तकाममात्मकाममकामꣳ रूपꣳ शोकान्तरम्॥ २१॥

This, verily, is that form of his which is beyond desires, free from evil, without fear. As a man, when in the embrace of a beloved wife, knows nothing within or without, so this person, when in the embrace of the intelligent Soul, knows nothing within or without. Verily, that is his [true] form in which his desire is satisfied, in which the Soul is his desire, in which he is without desire and without sorrow.

अत्र पिताऽपिता भवति माताऽमाता लोका अलोका देवा अदेवा वेदा अवेदा अत्र स्तेनोऽस्तेनो भवति भ्रूणहाऽभ्रूणहा चाण्डालोऽचाण्डालः पौल्कसोऽपल्कसः श्रमणोऽश्रमणस्तापसोऽतापसोऽनन्वागतं पुण्येनानन्वागतं पापेन तीर्णो हि तदा सर्वाञ्छोकान्हृदयस्य भवति॥ २२॥

There a father becomes not a father; a mother, not a mother; the worlds, not the worlds; the gods, not the gods; the Vedas, not the Vedas; a thief, not a thief. There the destroyer of an embryo become not the destroyer of an embryo; a Cāṇḍāla [the son of a Śūdra father and a Brahman mother] is not a Cāṇḍāla; a Paulkasa [the son of a Śūdra father and a Kṣatriya mother] is not a Paulkasa; a mendicant is not a mendicant; an ascetic is not an ascetic. He is not followed by good, he is not followed by evil, for then he has passed beyond all sorrows of the heart.

यद्वै तत्र पश्यति पश्न्वै तत्र पश्यति न हि द्रष्टुर्द्वष्टेर्विपरिलोपो विद्यलेऽविनाशित्वान्न तु तद्द्वितीयमस्ति ततोऽन्यद्विभक्तं यत् पश्येत्॥ २३॥

Verily, while he does not there see [with the eyes], he is verily seeing, though he does not see (what is [usually] to be seen); for there is no cessation of the seeing of a seer, because of his imperishability [as a seer]. It is not, however, a second thing, other than himself and separate, that he may see.

यद्वै तत्र जिघ्नति जिघ्नन् वै तत्र जिघ्नति न हि घ्नातुर्घ्नातेर्विपरिलोपो विद्यतेऽविनाशित्वान्न तु तद्द्वितीयमस्ति ततोऽन्यद्विभक्तं यज्जिघ्नेत्॥ २४॥

Verily, while he does not there smell, he is verily smelling, though he does not smell (what is [usually] to be smelled); for there is no cessation of the smelling of a smeller, because of his imperishability [as a smeller]. It is not, however, a second thing, other than himself and separate, that he may smell.

यद्वै तत्र रसयते रसयन्वै तत्र रसयते नहि रसयितू रसयतेर्विपरिलोपो विद्यतेऽविनाशित्वान्न तु तद्द्वितीयमस्ति ततोऽन्यद्विभक्तं यद्रसयेत्॥ २५॥

Verily, while he does not there taste, he is verily tasting, though he does not taste (what is [usually] to be tasted); for there is no cessation of the tasting of a taster, because of his imperishability [as a taster]. It is not, however, a second thing, other than himself and separate, that he may taste.

यद्वै तत्र वदति वदन्वै तत्र वदति न हि वक्तुर्वक्तेर्विपरिलोपो विद्यतेऽविनाशित्वान्न तु तद्द्वितीयमस्ति ततोऽन्यद्विभक्तं यद्वदेत्॥ २६॥

Verily, while he does not there speak, he is verily speaking, though he does not speak (what is [usually) to be spoken); for there is no cessation of the speaking of a speaker, because of his imperishability [as a speaker]. It is not, however, a second thing, other than himself and separate, to which he may speak.

यद्वै तन्न शृणोति शृण्वन्वै तन्न शृणोति न हि श्रोतुः श्रुतेर्विपरिलोपो विद्यतेविनाशित्वान्न तु तद्द्वितीयमस्ति ततोऽन्यद्विभक्तं यच्छृणुयात्॥ २७॥

Verily, while he does not there hear, he is verily hearing, though he does not hear (what is [usually] to be heard); for there is no cessation of the hearing of a hearer, because of his imperishability [as a hearer]. It is not, however, a second thing, other than himself and separate, which he may hear.

यद्वै तन्न मनुते मन्वानो वै तन्न मनुते न हि मन्तुर्मतेर्विपरिलोपो विद्यतेऽविनाशित्वान्न तु तद्द्वितीयमस्ति ततोऽन्यद्विभक्तं यन्मन्वीत॥ २८॥

Verily, while he does not there think, he is verily thinking, though he does not think (what is [usually] to be thought); for there is no cessation of the thinking of a thinker, because of his imperishability [as a thinker]. It is not, however, a second thing, other than himself and separate, of which he may think.

यद्वै तन्न स्पृशति स्पृशन् वै तन्न स्पृशति न हि स्प्रष्टुः स्पृष्टेर्विपरिलोपो विद्यतेऽविनाशत्वान्न तु तद्द्वितीयमस्ति ततोऽन्यद्विभक्तं यत्स्पृशेत्॥ २९॥

Verily, while he does not there touch, he is verily touching, though he does not touch (what is [usually] to be touched); for there is no cessation of the touching of a toucher, because of his imperishability [as a toucher]. It is not, however, a second thing, other than himself and separate, which he may touch.

यद्वै तन्न विजानाति विजानन्वै तन्न विजानाति न हि विज्ञातुर्विज्ञातेर्विपरिलोपो विद्यतेऽविनाशित्वान्न तु तद्द्वितीयमस्ति ततोऽन्यद्विभक्तं यद्विजानीयात्॥ ३०॥

Verily, while he does not there know, he is verily knowing, though he does not know (what is [usually] to be known); for there is no cessation of the knowing of a knower, because of his imperishability [as a knower]. It is not, however, a second thing, other than himself and separate, which he may know.

(The above are the dormant stages and we will now describe the stages of awaken.)

यत्र वान्यदिव स्यात्तत्रान्योऽन्यत्पश्येदन्योऽन्यज्जिघ्रेदन्योऽन्यद्रसयेदन्योऽन्यद्वदेदन्योऽन्यच्छृणुयादन्योऽन्यन्मन्वीतान्योऽन्यत्स्पृशेदन्योऽन्यद्विजानीयात्॥ ३१॥

Verily, where there seems to be another, there the one might see the other; the one might smell the other; the one might taste the other; the one might speak to the other; the one might hear the other; the one might think of the other; the one might touch the other; the one might know the other.

सलिल एको द्रष्टाऽद्वैतो भवत्येष ब्रह्मलोकः सम्राडिति हैनमनुशशास याज्ञवल्क्य एषास्य परमा

गतिरेषास्य परमा संपदेषोऽस्य परमो लोक एषोऽस्य परम आनन्द एतस्यैवानन्दस्यान्यानि भूतानि मात्रामुपजीवन्ति॥ ३२॥

An ocean, a seer alone without duality, becomes he whose world is Brahma, O King!—thus Yājñavalkya instructed him. 'This is a man's highest path. This is his highest achievement. This is his highest world. This is his highest bliss. On a part of just this bliss other creatures have their living.'

स यो मनुष्याणाꣳ राद्धः समृद्धो भवत्यन्येषामधिपतिः सर्वैर्मानुष्यकैर्भोगैः संपन्नतमः स मनुष्याणां परम आनन्दोऽथ ये शतं मनुष्याणामानन्दाः स एकः पितृणां जितलोकानामानन्दोऽथ ये शतं पितृणां जितलोकानामानन्दाः स एको गन्धर्वलोक आनन्दोऽथ ये शतं गन्धर्वलोक आनन्दा:स एकः कर्मदेवानामानन्दो ये कर्मणा देवत्वमभिसंपद्यन्तेऽथ ये शतं कर्मदेवानामानन्दाः स एक आजानदेवानामानन्दो यश्च श्रोत्रियोऽवृजिनोऽकामहतोऽथ ये शतमाजानदेवानामानन्नदाः स एकः प्रजापतिलोक आनन्दो यश्च श्रोत्रियोऽवृजिनोऽकामहतोऽथ ये शतं प्रजापतिलोक आनन्दाः स एको ब्रह्मलोक आनन्दो यश्च श्रोत्रियोऽवृजिनोऽकामहतोऽथैष एव परम आनन्द एष ब्रह्मलोकः सम्राडिति होवाच याज्ञवल्क्यः सोऽहं भगवते सहस्रं ददाम्यत ऊर्ध्वं विमोक्षायैव ब्रूहीत्यत्र ह याज्ञवल्क्यो बिभयांचकार मेधावी राजा सर्वेभ्यो मान्तेभ्य उदरौत्सीदिति॥ ३३॥

If one is fortunate among men and wealthy, lord over others, best provided with all human enjoyments—that is the highest bliss of men. Now a hundredfold the bliss of men is one bliss of those who have won the fathers' world. Now a hundredfold the bliss of those who have won the fathers' world is one bliss in the Gandharva-world. A hundredfold the bliss in the Gandharva-world is one bliss of the gods who gain their divinity by meritorious works. A hundredfold the bliss of the gods by works is one bliss of the gods by birth and of him who is learned in the Vedas, who is without crookedness, and who is free from desire. A hundredfold the bliss of the gods by birth is one bliss in the Prajāpati-world and of him who is learned in the Vedas, who is without crookedness, and who is free from desire. A hundredfold the bliss in the Prajāpati-world is one bliss in the Brahına-world and of him who is learned in the Vedas, who is without crookedness, and who is free from desire. This truly is the highest world. This is the Brahma-world, O king. Thus spoke Yājñavalkya.

[Janaka said:] 'I will give you, noble sir, a thousand [cows]. Speak further than this, for my release.'

Then Yājñavalkya feared, thinking : 'This intelligent king has driven me out of every corner.'

स वा एष एतस्मिन्स्वप्नान्ते रत्वा चारित्वा दृष्ट्वैव पुण्यं च पापं च पुनः प्रतिन्यायं प्रतियोन्याद्रवति बुद्धान्तायैव॥ ३४॥

[He said:] 'Having had enjoyment in this state of sleep, having travelled around and seen good and bad, he hastens again, according to the entrance and place of origin, back to the state of waking.

तद्यथाऽनः सुसमाहितमुत्सर्जद्यायादेवमेवायꣳ शारीर आत्मा प्राज्ञेनात्मनान्वारूढ उत्सर्जन्याति यत्रैतदूर्ध्वोच्छ्वासी भवति॥ ३५॥

[The soul at death]

As a heavily loaded cart goes creaking, just so this bodily self, mounted by the intelligent Self, goes groaning when one is breathing one's last.

स यत्रायमणिमानं न्येति जरया वोपतपतावाणिमानं निगच्छति तद्यथाम्रं वौदुम्बर वा पिप्पलं वा बन्धनात्प्रमुच्यत एवमेवायं पुरुष एभ्योऽङ्गेभ्यः संप्रमुच्य पुनः प्रतिन्यायं प्रतियोन्याद्रवति प्राणायैव॥ ३६॥

When he comes to weakness—whether he come to weakness through old age or through disease—this person frees himself from these limbs just as a mango, or a fig, or a berry releases itself from its bond; and he hastens again, according to the entrance and place of origin, back to life.

तद्यथा राजानमायान्तमुग्राःप्रत्येनसःसूतग्रामण्योऽन्नैःपानैरावसथैः प्रतिकल्पन्तेऽयमायात्ययमागच्छतीत्येवꣳ हैवंविदꣳ सर्वाणि भूतानि प्रतिकल्पन्त इदं ब्रह्मायातीदमागच्छतीति॥ ३७॥

As noblemen, policemen, chariot-drivers, village-heads wait with food, drink, and lodgings for a king who is coming, and cry : "Here he comes! Here he comes!" so indeed do all things wait for him who has this knowledge and cry : "Here is Brahma coming! Here is Brahma coming!"

तद्यथा राजानं प्रयियासन्तमुग्राः प्रत्येनसः सूतग्रामण्योऽभिसमायन्त्येवमेवेममात्मानमन्तकाले सर्वे प्राणा अभिसमायन्ति यत्रैतदूर्ध्वोच्छ्वासी भवति॥ ३८॥

As noblemen, policemen, chariot-drivers, village-heads gather around a king who is about to depart, just so do all the breaths gather around the soul at the end, when one is breathing one's last.

चतुर्थं ब्राह्मणम्

स यत्रायमात्माऽबल्यं न्येत्य संमोहमिव न्येत्यथैनमेते प्राणा अभिसमायन्ति स एतास्तेजोमात्राः समभ्याददानो हृदयमेवान्ववक्रामति स यत्रैष चाक्षुषः पराङ् पर्यावर्ततेऽथारूपज्ञो भवति॥ १॥

When this self comes to weakness and to confusedness of mind, as it were, then the breaths gather around him. He takes to himself those particles of energy and descends into the heart. When the person in the eye turns away, back [to the sun], then one becomes non-knowing of forms.

एकीभवति न पश्यतीत्याहुरेकीभवति न जिघ्रतीत्याहुरेकीभवति न रसयत इत्याहुरेकीभवति न वदतीत्याहुरेकीभवति न शृणोतीत्याहुरेकीभवति न मनुत इत्याहुरेकीभवति न स्पृशतीत्याहुरेकीभवति न विज्ञानातीत्याहुस्तस्य हैतस्य हृदयस्याग्रं प्रद्योतते तेन प्रद्योतेनैष आत्मा निष्क्रामति चक्षुष्टो वा मूर्ध्नो वाऽन्येभ्यो वा शरीरदेशेभ्यस्तमुत्क्रामन्तं प्राणोऽनूत्क्रामति प्राणमनूत्क्रामन्तꣳ सर्वे प्राणा अनुत्क्रामन्ति सविज्ञानो भवति सविज्ञानमेवान्ववक्रामतिं तं विद्याकर्मणी समन्वारभेते पूर्वप्रज्ञा च॥ २॥

"He is becoming one," they say; "he does not see." "He is becoming one," they say; "he does not smell." "He is becoming one," they say; "he does not taste." "He is becoming one," they say; "he does not speak." "He is becoming one," they say; "he does not hear." "He is becoming one," they say; "he does not think." "He is becoming one," they say; "he does not touch." "He is becoming one," they say; "he does not know." The point of his heart becomes lighted up. By that light the self departs, either by the eye, or by the head, or by other bodily parts. After him, as he goes out, the life (*prāṇa*) goes out. After the life, as it goes out, all the breaths (*prāṇa*) go out. He becomes one with intelligence. What has intelligence departs with him. His knowledge and his works and his former intelligence [i.e. instinct] lay hold of him.

तद्यथा तृणजलायुका तृणस्यान्तं गत्वाऽन्यमाक्रममाक्रम्यात्मानमुपसꣳहरत्येवमेवायमात्मेदꣳशरीरं निहत्याऽविद्यां गमयित्वा॥ न्यमाक्रममाक्रम्यात्मानमुपसꣳ हरति॥ ३॥

[The soul of the unreleased after death]

Now as a caterpillar, when it has come to the end of a blade of grass, in taking the next step draws itself together towards it, just so this soul in taking the next step strikes down this body, dispels its ignorance, and draws itself together [for making the transition].

तद्यथा पेशस्कारी पेशसो मात्रामुपादायान्यन्नवतरं कल्याणतरꣳ रूपं तनुत एवमेवायमात्मेदꣳ शरीरं निहत्याऽविद्यां गमयित्वाऽन्यन्नवतरं कल्याणतरꣳ रूपं कुरुते पित्र्यं वा गान्धर्वं वा दैवं प्राजापत्यं वा ब्राह्मं वाऽन्येषा वा भूतानाम्॥ ४॥

As a goldsmith, taking a piece of gold, reduces it to another newer and more beautiful form, just so this soul, striking down this body and dispelling its ignorance, makes for itself another newer and more beautiful form like that either of the fathers, or of the Gandharvas, or of the gods, or of Prajāpati, or of Brahma, or of other beings.

स वा अयमात्मा ब्रह्म विज्ञानमयो मनोमयः प्राणयश्चक्षुर्मयः श्रोत्रमयः पृथिवीमय आपोमयो वायुमय आकाशमयस्तेजोमयोऽतेजोमयः काममयोऽकाममयः क्रोधमयोऽक्रोधमयो धर्ममयोऽधर्ममयः सर्वमयस्तद्यदेतदिदंमयोऽदोमय इति यथाकारी यथाकारी तथा भवति साधुकारी साधुर्भवति पापकारी पापो भवति पुण्यः पुण्येन कर्मणा भवति पापः पापेन। अथो खल्वाहुः काममय एवायं पुरुष इति स यथाकामो भवति तत्क्रतुर्भवति यत्क्रतुर्भवति तत्कर्म कुरुते यत्कर्म् कुरुते तदभिसंपद्यते॥ ५॥

Verily, this soul is Brahma, made of knowledge, of mind, of breath, of seeing, of hearing, of earth, of water, of wind, of space, of energy and of non-energy, of desire and of non-desire, of anger and of non-anger, of virtuousness and of non-virtuousness. It is made of everything. This is what is meant by the saying "made of this, made of that."

According as one acts, according as one conducts himself, so does he become. The doer of good becomes good. The doer of evil becomes evil. One becomes virtuous by virtuous action, bad by bad action.

But people say : "A person is made [not of acts, but] of desires only." [In reply to this I say:] As is his desire, such is his resolve; as is his resolve, such the action he performs;

what action (*karma*) he performs, that he procures for himself.

तदेष श्लोको भवति। तदेव सक्तः सह कर्मणैति लिङ्गं मनो यत्र निषक्तमस्य। प्राप्यान्तं कर्मणस्तस्य यत्किंचेह करोत्ययम्। तस्माल्लोकात्पुनरैत्यस्मै लोकाय कर्मण इति नु कामयमानोऽथाकामयमानो योऽकामो निष्काम आत्मकामो न तस्य प्राणा उत्क्रामन्ति ब्रह्मैव सन्ब्रह्माप्येति॥६॥

On this point there is this verse :—

Where one's mind is attached—the inner self goes thereto with action, being attached to it alone. Obtaining the end of his action, whatever he does in this world, he comes again from that world to this world of action.

—So the man who desires.

Now the man who does not desire. He who is without desire, who is freed from desire, whose desire is satisfied, whose desire is the Soul—his breaths do not depart. Being very Brahma, he goes to Brahma.

तदेष श्लोको भवति। यदा सर्वे प्रमुच्यन्ते कामा येऽस्य हृदि श्रिताः।

अथ मर्त्योऽमृतो भवत्यत्र ब्रह्म समश्नुत इति।

तद्यथाऽहिनिर्ल्वयनी वल्मीके मृता प्रत्यस्ता शयीतैवमेवेदꣳ शरीरꣳ शेतेऽथायमशरीरोऽमृतः प्राणो ब्रह्मैव तेज एव सोऽहं भगवते सहस्रं ददामीति होवाच जनको वैदेहः॥७॥

On this point there is this verse :—

When are liberated all the desires that lodge in one's heart, then a mortal becomes immortal! Therein he reaches Brahma!

As the slough of a snake lies on an ant-hill, dead, cast off, even so lies this body. But this incorporeal, immortal Life (*prāṇa*) is Brahma indeed, is light indeed.

'I will give you, noble sir, a thousand [cows],' said Janaka, [king] of Vaideha.

तदेते श्लोको भवन्ति। अणुः पन्था विततः पुराणो माꣳस्पृष्टोऽनुवित्तो मयैव।

तेन धीरा अपियन्ति ब्रह्मविदः स्वर्गं लोकमित ऊर्ध्वं विमुक्ताः॥८॥

[Yājñavalkya continued :] 'On this point there are these verses :—

The ancient narrow path that stretches far away has been touched by me, has been found by me. By it the wise, the knowers of Brahma, go up hence to the heavenly world, released.

तस्मिञ्छुक्लमुत नीलमाहुः पिङ्गलꣳ हरितं लोहितं च।

एष पन्था ब्रह्मणा हानुवित्तस्तेनैति ब्रह्मवित्पुण्यकृत्तैजसश्च॥९॥

On it, they say, is white and blue and yellow and green and red. That was the path by Brahma found by it goes the knower of Brahma, the doer of right (*puṇya kṛt*), and every shining one.

अन्धं तमः प्रविशन्ति येऽविद्यामुपासते। ततो भूय इव ते तमो य उ विद्यायाꣳरताः॥१०॥

They enter into blind darkness who worship ignorance;

Into darkness greater than that, as it were, they that delight in knowledge.

अनन्दा नाम ते लोका अन्धेन तमसाऽवृताः। ताꣳस्ते प्रेत्याभिगच्छन्त्यविद्वाꣳसोऽबुधो जनाः॥ ११॥

Joyless are those worlds called, covered with blind darkness.

To them after death go those people that have not knowledge, that are not awakened.

आत्मानं चेद्विजानीयादयमस्मीति पूरुषः। किमिच्छन्कस्य कामाय शरीरमनुसंज्वरेत्॥ १२॥

If a person knew the Soul (*Ātman*), with the thought "I am he!"

With what desire, for love of what would he cling unto the body?

यस्यानुवित्तः प्रतिबुद्ध आत्माऽस्मिन्संदेह्ये गहने प्रविष्टः।

स विश्वकृत्स हि सर्वस्य कर्ता तस्य लोकः स उ लोक एव॥ १३॥

He who has found and has awakened to the Soul that has entered this conglomerate abode— He is the maker of everything, for he is the creator of all the world is his : indeed, he is the world itself.

इहैव सन्तोऽथ विद्मस्तद्वयं न चेदवेदीर्महती विनष्टिः।

ये तद्विदुरमृतास्ते भवन्त्यथेतरे दुःखमेवापियन्ति॥ १४॥

Verily, while we are here we may know this. If you have known it not, great is the destruction. Those who know this become immortal, but others go only to sorrow.

यदैतमनुपश्यत्यात्मानं देवमञ्जसा। ईशानं भूतभव्यस्य न ततो विजुगुप्सते॥ १५॥

If one perceives Him as the Soul, as God (*deva*), clearly, as the Lord of what has been and of what is to be—one does not shrink away from Him.

यस्मादर्वाक्संवत्सरोऽहोभिः परिवर्तते। तद्देवा ज्योतिषां ज्योतिरायुर्होपासतेऽमृतम्॥ १६॥

That before which the year revolves with its days—that the gods revere as the light of lights, as life immortal.

यस्मिन्पञ्च पञ्चजना आकाशश्च प्रतिष्ठितः। तमेव मन्य आत्मानं विद्वान्ब्रह्मामृतोऽमृतम्॥ १७॥

On whom the five peoples and space are established—Him alone I, the knowing, I, the immortal, believe to be the Soul, the immortal Brahman.

प्राणस्य प्राणमुत चक्षुषश्चक्षुरुत श्रोत्रस्य श्रोत्रं मनसो ये मनो विदुः। ते निचिक्युर्ब्रह्म पुराणमग्र्यम्॥ १८॥

They who know the breathing of the breath, the seeing of the eye, the hearing of the ear, (the food of food), the thinking of the mind—They have recognized the ancient, primeval Brahma.

मनसैवानुद्रष्टव्यं नेह नानास्ति किंचन। मृत्योः स मृत्युमाप्नोति य इह नानेव पश्यति॥ १९॥

By the mind alone is It to be perceived. There is no earth no diversity.

He gets death after death, who perceives here seeming diversity.

एकधैवानुद्रष्टव्यमेतदप्रमेयं ध्रुवम्। विरजः पर आकाशादज आत्मा महान्ध्रुवः॥ २०॥

As a unity only is It to be looked upon this indemonstrable, enduring Being, spotless, beyond space, the unborn Soul, great, enduring.

तमेव धीरो विज्ञाय प्रज्ञां कुर्वीत ब्राह्मणः। नानुध्यायाद्बहूञ्छब्दान्वाचो विग्लापनꣳहि तदिति॥ २१॥

By knowing Him only, a wise Brāhmaṇa should get for himself intelligence.

He should not meditate upon many words, for that is a weariness of speech.

[Words are merely an indicative and this Brahma is felt only by the direct experience, therefore it is advised that one should try to avoid from the redundant jungle of please and submissions.]

स वा एष महानज आत्मा योऽयं विज्ञानमयः प्राणेषु य एषोऽन्तर्हृदय आकाशस्तस्मिञ्छेते सर्वस्य वशी सर्वस्येशानः सर्वस्याधिपतिः स न साधुना कर्मणा भूयान्नो एवासाधुना कनीयानेष सर्वेश्वर एष भूताधिपतिरेष भूतपाल एष सेतुर्विधरण एषां लोकानामसंभेदाय तमेतं वेदानुवचनेन ब्राह्मणा विविदिषन्ति यज्ञेन दानेन तपसाऽनाशकेनैतमेव विदित्वा मुनिर्भवति एतमेव प्रव्राजिनो लोकमिच्छन्तः प्रव्रजन्ति एतद्ध स्म वैतत्पूर्वे विद्वाꣳसः प्रजां न कामयन्ते किं प्रजया करिष्यामो येषां नोऽयमात्माऽयं लोक इति ते ह स्म पुत्रैषणायाश्च वित्तैषणायाश्च लोकैषणायाश्च व्युत्थायाथ भिक्षाचर्यं चरन्ति या ह्येव पुत्रैषणा सा वित्तैषणा या वित्तैषणा सा लोकैषणोभे ह्येते एषणे एव भवतः। स एष नेति नेत्यात्माऽगृह्यो नहि गृह्यतेऽशीर्यो नहि शीर्यतेऽसङ्गो नहि सज्यतेऽसितो न व्यथते न रिष्यत्येतमु हैवैते न तरत इत्यतः पापमकरवमित्यतः कल्याणमकरवमित्युभे उ हैवैष एते तरति नैनं कृताकृते तपतः॥ २२॥

Verily, he is the great, unborn Soul, who is this [person] consisting of knowledge among the senses. In the space within the heart lies the ruler of all, the lord of all, the king of all. He does not become greater by good action nor inferior by bad action. He is the lord of all, the overlord of beings, the protector of beings. he is the separating dam for keeping these worlds apart.

Such a one the Brāhmaṇas desire to know by repetition of the Vedas, by sacrifices, by offerings, by penance, by fasting. On knowing him, in truth, one becomes an ascetic (*muni*). Desiring him only as their home, mendicants wander forth.

Verily, because they know this, the ancients desires not offspring, saying : "What shall we do with offspring, we whose is this Soul, this world?" They, verily, rising above the desire for sons and the desire for wealth and the desire for worlds, lived the life of a mendicant. For the desire for sons is the desire for wealth, and the desire for wealth is the desire for worlds; for both these are desires.

That Soul (*Ātman*) is not this, it is not that (*neti, neti*). It is unseizable, for it cannot be seized. It is indestructible, for it cannot be destroyed. It is unattached, for it does not attach itself. It is unbound. It does not tremble. It is not injured.

Him [who knows this] these two do not overcome—neither the thought "Hence I did wrong," nor the thought "Hence I did right." Verily, he overcomes them both. What he has done and what he has not done do not affect him.

तदेतदृचाभ्युक्तम्। एष नित्यो महिमा ब्राह्मणस्य न वर्धते कर्मणा नो कनीयान्। तस्यैव स्यात्पदवित्तं विदित्वा न लिप्यते कर्मणा पापकेनेति। तस्मादेवंविच्छान्तो दान्त उपरतस्तितिक्षुः समाहितो भूत्वाऽत्मन्येवात्मानं पश्यति सर्वमात्मानं पश्यति नैनं पाप्मा तरति सर्वं पाप्मानं तरति नैनं पाप्मा तपति सर्वं पाप्मानं तपति विपापो विरजोऽविचिकित्सो ब्राह्मणो भवत्येष ब्रह्मलोकः सम्राडेनं प्रापितोऽसीति होवाच याज्ञवल्क्यः सोऽहं भगवते विदेहान् ददामि मां चापि सह दास्यायेति॥ २३॥

This very [doctrine] has been declared in the verse :—

This eternal greatness of a Brahman is not increased by deeds (*karman*), nor diminished.

One should be familiar with it. By knowing it, one is not stained by evil action.

Therefore, having this knowledge, having become calm, subdued, quiet, patiently enduring and collected one sees the Soul just in the soul. One sees everything as the Soul. Evil does not overcome him; he overcomes all evil. Evil does not burn him; he burns all evil. Free from evil, free from impurity, free from doubt, he becomes a Brāhmaṇa.

This is the Brahma-world, O king, said Yājñavalkya.

[Janaka said:]– I will give you, noble sir, the Vaidehas and myself also to be your slave.

स वा एष महानज आत्माऽन्नादो वसुदानो विन्दते वसु य एवं वेद॥ २४॥

[Yājñavalkya continued:] ‘This is that great, unborn Soul, who eats the food [which people eat], the giver of good. He finds good who knows this.

स वा एष महानज आत्माजरोऽमरोऽमृतोऽभयो ब्रह्माभयं वै ब्रह्माभयꣳ हि वै ब्रह्म भवति य एवं वेद॥ २५॥

Verily, that great, unborn Soul, undecaying, undying, immortal, fearless, is Brahma. Verily, Brahma is fearless. He who knows this becomes the fearless Brahma.’

पञ्चमं ब्राह्मणम्

The conversation of Yājñavalkya and Maitreyī concerning the pantheistic Soul

अथ ह याज्ञवल्क्यस्य द्वे भार्ये बभूवतुः मैत्रेयी च कात्यायनी च तयोर्ह मैत्रेयी ब्रह्मवादिनी बभूव स्त्रीप्रज्ञैव तर्हि कात्यायन्यथ ह याज्ञवल्क्योऽन्यद्वृत्तमुपाकरिष्यन्॥ १॥

It is renowned that the sage Yājñavalkya had two wives. The name of one was Maitreyī and other was Kātyāyanī. Out of them Maitreyī was a dicourser on sacred knowledge (*brahma-vādinī*); Kātyāyanī had just (*eva*) a woman’s knowledge in that matter (*tarhi*).

Now they, Yājñavalkya was about to commence another mode of life.

मैत्रेयीति होवाच याज्ञवल्क्यः प्रव्रजिष्यन्वा अरेऽयमस्मात्स्थानादस्मि हन्त तेऽनया कात्यायन्यान्तं करवाणीति॥ २॥

‘Maitreyī!’ said Yājñavalkya, ‘lo, verily, I am about to wander forth from this state. Behold! Let me make a final settlement for you and that Kātyāyanī.

सा होवाच मैत्रेयी यन्नु म इयं भगोः सर्वा पृथिवी वित्तेन पूर्णा स्यात्स्यां न्वहं तेनामृताऽऽहो ३ नेति नेति होवाच याज्ञवल्क्यो यथैवोपकरणवतां जीवितं तथैव ते जीवितꣳ स्यादमृतत्वस्य तु नाशास्ति वित्तेनेति॥ ३॥

Maitreyī replied– 'If now, sir, this whole earth filled with wealth were mine, would I now thereby be immortal.'

'No, no!' said Yājñavalkya. 'As the life of the rich, even so would your life be. Of immortality, however, there is no hope through wealth.'

सा होवाच मैत्रेयी येनाहं नामृता स्यां किमहं तेन कुर्यां यदेव भगवान्वेद तदेव मे विब्रूहीति॥ ४॥

Then Maitreyī said : 'What should I do with that through which I may not be immortal? What you know, sir—that, indeed, explain to me.'

स होवाच याज्ञवल्क्यः प्रिया वै खलु नो भवती सती प्रियमवृधद्धन्त तर्हि भवत्येतद्व्याख्यास्यामि ते व्याचक्षाणस्य तु मे निदिध्यासस्वेति॥ ५॥

Yājñavalkya replied - "O Maitreyī! You always are darling of my heart and your instant statement too is enhancing my joy. Behold, then, lady, I will explain it to you. But, while I am expounding, do you seek to ponder thereon."

स होवाच न वा अरे पत्युः कामाय पतिः प्रियो भवत्यात्मनस्तु कामाय पतिः प्रियो भवति न वा अरे जायायै कामाय जाया प्रिया भवत्यात्मनस्तु कामाय जाया प्रिया भवति न वा अरे पुत्राणां कामाय पुत्राः प्रिया भवन्त्यात्मनस्तु कामाय पुत्राः प्रिया भवन्ति न वा अरे वित्तस्य कामाय वित्तं प्रियं भवत्यात्मनस्तु कामाय वित्तं प्रियं भवति न वा अरे ब्रह्मणः कामाय ब्रह्म प्रियं भवत्यात्मनस्तु कामाय ब्रह्म प्रियं भवति न वा अरे क्षत्रस्य कामाय क्षत्रं प्रियं भवत्यात्मनस्तु कामाय क्षत्रं प्रियं भवति न वा अरे लोकानां कामाय लोकाः प्रिया भवन्त्यामनस्तु कामाय लोकाः प्रिया भवन्ति न वा अरे देवानां कामाय देवाः प्रिया भवन्ति न वा अरे वेदानां कामाय वेदाः प्रिया भवन्त्यात्मनस्तु कामाय वेदाः प्रिया भवन्ति न वा अरे भूतानां कामाय भूतानि प्रियाणि भवन्त्यात्मनस्तु कामाय भूतानि प्रियाणि भवन्ति न वा अरे सर्वस्य कामाय सर्वं प्रियं भवत्यात्मनस्तु कामाय सर्वं प्रियं भवति आत्मा वा अरे द्रष्टव्यः श्रोतव्यो मन्तव्यो न र्दिध्यासितव्यो मैत्रेय्यात्मनि खल्वरे दृष्टे श्रुते मते विज्ञात इदꣳ सर्वं विदितम्॥ ६॥

'Lo, verily, not for love of the husband is a husband dear, but for love of the Soul (*Ātman*) a husband is dear.

Lo, verily, not for love of the wife is a wife dear, but for love of the Soul a wife is dear.

Lo, verily, not for love of the sons are sons dear, but for love of the Soul sons are dear.

Lo, verily, not for love of the sons are sons dear, but for love of the Soul sons are dear.

Lo, verily, not for love of the wealth is wealth dear, but for love of the Soul wealth is dear.

Lo, verily, not for love of the cattle are cattle dear, but for love of the Soul cattle are dear.

Lo, verily, not for love of Brahmanhood is Brahmanhood dear, but for love of the Soul Brahmanhood is dear.

Lo, verily, not for love of Kṣatrahood is Kṣatrahood dear, but for love of the Soul Kṣatrahood is dear.

Lo, verily, not for love of the worlds are the worlds dear, but for love of the Soul the worlds are dear.

Lo, verily, not for love of the gods are the gods dear, but for love of the Soul the gods are dear.

Lo, verily, not for love of the Vedas are the Vedas dear, but for love of the Soul the Vedas are dear.

Lo, verily, not for love of the beings (*bhūta*) are beings dear, but for love of the Soul beings are dear.

Lo, verily, not for love of all is all dear, but for love of the Soul all is dear.

Lo, verily, it is the Soul (*Ātman*) that should be seen, that should be hearkened to, that should be thought on, that should be pondered on, O Maitreyī.

Lo, verily, in the Soul's being seen, hearkened to, thought on, understood, this world-all is known.

ब्रह्म तं परादाद्योऽन्यत्रात्मनो ब्रह्म वेद क्षत्रं त परादाद्योऽन्यत्रात्मनः क्षत्रं वेद लोकास्तं परादुर्योऽन्यात्रात्मनो लोकान्वेद देवास्तं परादुर्योऽन्यत्रात्मनो देवान्वेद वेदास्तं परादुर्योऽन्यत्रात्मनो वेदान्वेद भूतानि तं परादुर्योऽन्यात्रात्मनो भूतानि वेद सर्वं तं परादाद्योऽन्यत्रात्मनः सर्वं वेदेहं ब्रह्मेदं क्षत्रमिमे लोका इमे देवा इमे वेदा इमानि भूतानीदꣳ सर्वं यदयमात्मा॥७॥

Brahmanhood deserts him who knows Brahmanhood in aught else than the Soul. Kṣatrahood deserts him who knows Kṣatrahood in aught else than the Soul. The gods desert him who knows the gods in aught else than the Soul. The Vedas desert him who knows the Vedas in aught else than the Soul. Beings desert him who knows beings in aught else than the Soul. Everything deserts him who knows everything in aught else than the Soul. This Brahmanhood, this Kṣatrahood, these worlds, these gods, these Vedas, all these beings, everything here is what this Soul is.

[The actual advantage of the knowledge, power, world, gods and Vedas etc. ceases when these are not considered as the soul. In case, their exterior complexion remains, there will be no advantages at all.]

स यथा दुन्दुभेर्हन्यमानस्य न बाह्याञ्छब्दाञ्छक्नुयद्ग्रहणाय दुन्दुभेर्ग्रहणेन दुन्दुभ्याघातस्य वा शब्दो गृहीतः॥८॥

It is—as, when a drum is being beaten, one would not be able to grasp the external sounds, but by grasping the drum or the beater of the drum the sound is grasped.

स यथा शङ्खस्य ध्मायमानस्य न बाह्याञ्छब्दान्छक्नुयाद्ग्रहणाय शङ्खस्य तु ग्रहणेन शङ्खध्मस्य वा शब्दो गृहीतः॥९॥

It is—as, when a conch-shell is being blown, one would not be able to grasp the external sounds, but by grasping the conch-shell or the blower of the conch-shell the sound is grasped.

स यथा वीणायै वाद्यमानायै न बाह्याञ्छब्दाञ्छक्नुयाद्ग्रहणाय वीणायै तु ग्रहणेन वीणावादस्य वा शब्दो गृहीतः॥ १०॥

It is—as, when a lute is being played, one would not be able to grasp the external sounds, but by grasping the lute or the player of the lute the sound is grasped.

स यथार्द्रैधाग्नेरभ्याहितस्य पृथग्धूमा विनिश्चरन्त्येवं वा अरेऽस्य महतो भूतस्य निःश्वसितमेतद्यदृग्वेदो यजुर्वेदः सामवेदोऽथर्वाङ्गिरस इतिहासः पुराणं विद्या उपनिषदः श्लोकाः सूत्राण्यनुव्याख्यानानि व्याख्यानानीष्टꣳ हुतमाशितं पायितमयं च लोकः परश्च लोकः सर्वाणि च भूतान्यस्यैवैतानि सर्वाणि निःश्वसितानि॥ ११॥

It is—as, from a fire laid with damp fuel, clouds of smoke separately issue forth, so, lo, verily, from this great being (*bhūta*) has been breathed forth that which is Ṛgveda, Yajurveda, Sāmaveda [Hymns] of the Atharvans and Aṅgirases, Legend (*itihāṣa*), Ancient Lore (*purāṇa*), Sciences (*vidyā*), Mystic Doctrines (*upaniṣad*), Verses (*śloka*), Aphorisms (*sūtra*), Explanations (*anuvyākhyāna*), Commentaries (*vyākhyāna*), sacrifice, oblation, food, drink, this world and the other, and all beings. From it, indeed, have all these been breathed forth.

स यथा सर्वासामपाꣳ समुद्र एकायनमेवꣳ सर्वेषाꣳ स्पर्शानां त्वगेकायनमेवꣳ सर्वेषा गन्धानां नासिके एकायनमेवꣳ सर्वेषाꣳ रसानां जिह्वैकायनमेवꣳ सर्वेषाꣳ रूपाणां चक्षुरेकायनमेवꣳ सर्वेषाꣳ शब्दानाꣳ श्रोत्रमेकायनमेवꣳ सर्वेषाꣳ संकल्पानां मन एकायनमेवꣳ सर्वासां विद्यानाꣳ हृदयमेकायनमेवꣳ सर्वेषां कर्मणाꣳ हस्तावेकायनमेवꣳ सर्वेषामानन्दानामुपस्थ एकायनमेवꣳ सर्वेषां विसर्गाणां पायुरेकायनमेवꣳ सर्वेषामध्वनां पादावेकायनमेवꣳ सर्वेषां वेदानां वागेकायनम्॥ १२॥

It is—as the uniting place of all waters is the sea, likewise the uniting-place of all touches is the skin, likewise the uniting-place of all tastes is the tongue; likewise the uniting place of all odours is the nose; likewise the uniting-place of all forms is the eye; likewise the uniting-place of all sounds is the ear; likewise the uniting-place of all intentions is the mind; likewise the uniting-place of all knowledges is the heart; likewise the uniting-place of all actions is the hands; likewise the uniting-place of all pleasures is the generative organ; likewise the uniting-place of all evacuations is the anus; likewise the uniting-place of all journeys is the feet; likewise the uniting-place of all Vedas is speech.

स यथा सैन्धवघनोऽनन्तरोऽबाह्यः कृत्स्नो रसघन एवैवं वा अरेऽयमात्माऽनन्तरोऽबाह्यः कृत्स्नः प्रज्ञानघन एवैतेभ्यो भूतेभ्यः समुत्थाय तान्येवानुविनश्यति न प्रेत्य संज्ञास्तीत्यरे ब्रवीमीति होवाच याज्ञवल्क्यः॥ १३॥

It is—as is a mass of salt, without inside, without outside, entirely a mass of taste, even so, verily, is this Soul, without inside, without outside, entriely a mass of knowledge.

Arising out of these elements, into them also one vanishes away. After death there is no consciousness (*saṁjñā*). Thus, lo, say I.' Thus spoke Yājñavalkya.

सा होवाच मैत्रेय्यत्रैव मा भगवान्मोहान्तमापीपिपन्न वा अहमिमं विजानामीति स होवाच न वा अरेऽहं मोहं ब्रवीम्यविनाशी वा अरेऽयमात्माऽनुच्छित्तिधर्मा॥ १४॥

Then said Maitreyī : 'Herein, indeed, you have caused me, sir, to arrive at the extreme of bewilderment. Verily, I understand It [i.e. this *Ātman*] not.'

Then said he : 'Lo, verily, I speak not bewilderment. Imperishable, lo, verily, is this Soul, and of indestructible quality.

यत्र हि द्वैतमिव भवति तदितर इतरं पश्यति तदितरं इतरं जिघ्नति तदितर इतरꣳ रसयते तदितर इतरमभिवदति तदितर इतरꣳ शृणोति तदितर इतरं मनुते तदितर इतरꣳ स्पृशति तदितर इतरं विजानाति यत्र त्वस्य सर्वमात्मैवाभूत्तत्केन कं पश्येत्तत्केन कं जिघ्रत्तत्केन कꣳ रसयेत्तत्केन कमभिवदेत्तत्केन कꣳ शृणुयानत्केन कं मन्वीत तत्केन कꣳस्पृशेत्तत्केन कं विजानीयाद्येनेदꣳ सर्वं विजानाति तं केन विजानीयात्स एषं नेति नेत्यात्माऽगृह्यो न हि गृह्यतेऽशीर्यो नहि शीर्यतेऽसङ्गो न हि सज्यतेऽसितो न व्यथते न रिष्यति विज्ञातारमरे केन विजानीयादित्युक्तानुशासनासि मैत्रेय्येतावदरे खल्वमृतत्वमिति होक्त्वा याज्ञवल्क्यो विजहार॥ १५॥

For where there is a duality, as it were, there one sees another; there one smells another; there one tastes another; there one speaks another; there one hears another; there one thinks of another; there one touches another; there one understands another. But where everything has become just one's own self, then whereby and whom would one see? then whereby and whom would one smell? then whereby and whom would one taste? then whereby and to whom would one speak? then whereby and whom would one hear? then whereby and of whom would one think? then whereby and whom would one touch? then whereby and whom would one understand? whereby would one understand him by means of whom one understands this All?

That Soul (*Ātman*) is not this, it is not that (*neti, neti*). It is unseizable, for it cannot be seized; indestructible, for it cannot be destroyed; unattached, for it does not attach itself; is unbound, does not tremble, is not injured.

Lo, whereby would one understand the understander? Thus you have the instruction told to you, Maitreyī. Such, lo, indeed, is immortality.' After speaking thus, Yājñavalkya departed.

षष्ठं ब्राह्मणम्

The teachers of this doctrine

अथ वꣳशः (पौतिमाष्यात्) पौतिमाष्यो गौपवनाद्गौपवनः पौतिमाष्यात्पौतिमाष्यो गौपवनाद्गौपवनः कौशिकात्कौशिकः कौण्डिन्यात्कौण्डिन्यः शाण्डिल्याच्छाण्डिल्यः कौशिकाच्च गौतमाच्च गौतमः॥ १॥

आग्निवेश्यादाग्निवेश्यो गार्ग्याद्गार्ग्यो गार्ग्याद्गार्ग्यो गौतमाद्गौतमः सैतवात्सैतवः पाराशर्यायणात्पाराशर्यायणो गार्ग्यायणाद्गार्ग्यायण उद्दालकायनादुद्दालकायनो जाबालायनाज्जाबालायनो माध्यन्दिनायनान्माध्यन्दिनायनः सौकरायणात्सौकरायणः काषायणात्काषायणः सायकायनात्सायकायनः कौशिकायनेः कौशिकायनिः॥ २॥

घृतकौशिकाद्घृतकौशिक:पाराशर्यायणात्पाराशर्यायण:पाराशर्यात्पाराशर्यो जातूकर्ण्याज्ञातूकर्ण्य आसुरायणाद्य यास्काद्यासुरायणस्त्रैवणेस्त्रैवणिरौपजङ्घनेरौपजङ्घनिरासुरेरासुरिर्भारद्वाजाद्भारद्वाज आत्रेयादात्रेयो माण्टेर्माण्टिर्गौतमाद्गौतमो गौतमाद्गौतमो वात्स्याद्वात्स्य: शाण्डिल्याच्छाण्डिल्य: कैशोर्यात्काप्यात्कैशोर्य: काप्य: कुमारहारितात्कुमारहारितो कालवाद्गालवो विदर्भकौण्डिन्याद्विदर्भीकौण्डिन्यो वत्सनपातो बाभ्रवाद्वत्सनपाद्बाभ्रव: पथ: सौभरात्पन्था: सौभरोऽयास्यादाङ्गिरसादयास्यआङ्गिरसआभूतेस्त्वाष्ट्रादाभूतिस्त्वाष्ट्रो विश्वरूपात्त्वाष्ट्राद्विश्वरूपस्त्वाष्ट्रोऽश्विभ्यामश्विनौ दधीच आथर्वणाद्दध्यङ्ङाथर्वणो दैवादथर्वादैवो मृत्यो: प्राध्वंसनान्मृत्यु:प्राध्वंसन:प्रध्वंसनात्प्रध्वंसन एकऋषेरेकर्षिर्विप्रचित्तेर्विप्रचित्तिर्व्यष्टेर्व्यष्टि: सनारो: सनारु: सनातनात्सनातन: सनगात्सनग: परमेष्ठिन: परमेष्ठी ब्रह्मणो ब्रह्म स्वयंभु ब्रह्मणे नम:॥ ३॥

Now the lineage (of the chapter dedicated to Yājñavalkya) is described. Pautimāṣya had acquired this knowledge from Gaupavana, Gaupavana from Pautimāṣya, Pautimāṣya from Gaupavana, Gaupavana from Kauśika, Kauśika from Kauṇḍinya, Kauṇḍinya from Śāṇḍilya, Śāṇḍilya from Kauśika and Gautama, Gautama from Āgniveśya, Āgniveśya from Gāgrya, Gargavaṅśī from Gargavaṅśī, Gārgāyaṇa from Gautama, Gautama from Saitava, Saitava from Pārāśaryāyaṇa, Pārāśaryāyaṇa from son of Gāgrya, son of Gāgrya from Uddālakāyana, Uddālakāyana from Jābālayana, Jābālayana from Mādhyandināyana, Mādhyandināyana from Śaukarāyaṇa, Śaukarāyaṇa from Kāṣāyaṇa, Kāṣāyaṇa from Sāyakāyana, Sāyakāyana from Kauśikāyani, Kauśikāyani from Gṛtakauśika, Gṛtakauśika from Pārāśaryāyaṇa, Pārāśaryāyaṇa from Pārāśarya, Pārāśarya from Jātūkarṇya, Jātūkarṇya from Āsurāyaṇa and Yāska, Āsurāyaṇa from Traivaṇi, Traivaṇi from Aupajanghani, Aupajanghani from Āsuri, Āsuri from Bhāradvāja, Bhāradvāja from Ātreya, Ātreya from Māṇṭi, Māṇṭi from Gautama, Gautama from Gautama, Gautama from Vātsya, Vātsya from Śāṇḍilya, Śāṇḍilya from Kaiśorya Kāpya, Kaiśorya Kāpya from Kumārahārita, Kumārahārita from Gālava, Gālava from Vidarbhī Kauṇḍinya, Vidarbhī Kauṇḍinya from Vatsanapāta Vābhrata, Vātsanapāta Vābhrata from Panthāsaubhara, Panthāsaubhara from Ayāsya Aṅgirā, Ayāsya Aṅgirā from Ābhūti Tvāstra, Ābhūti Tvāstra from Viśvarūpa Tvāstra, Viśvarūpa Tvāstra from Aśvinī Kumāras, Aśvidvaya from Dadhyaṅātharvaṇa, Dadhyaṅāthrvaṇa from Ātharvadaiva, Ātharvadaiva from Mṛtyu Pradhvaṅsana, Mṛtyu Prādhvaṅsana from Prādhvaṅsana, Pradhvaṅsana from Ekarṣi, Ekarṣi from Vipracitti, Vipracitti from Vyaṣṭi, Vyaṣṭi from Sanāru, Sanāru from Sanātana, Sanātana from Sanaga, Sanaga from Parameṣṭhi and Parameṣṭhi from the Brahma. Brahma is the Self-existent (*svayam-bhū*). Adoration to Brahma!

॥पञ्चमोऽध्यायः॥

प्रथमं ब्राह्मणम्

The inexhaustible Brahman

ॐ पूर्णमदः पूर्णमिदं पूर्णात्पूर्णमुदच्यते। पूर्णस्य पूर्णमादाय पूर्णमेवावशिष्यते॥ ॐ ३ खं ब्रह्म खं पुराणं वायुरं खमिति ह स्माह कौरव्यायणीपुत्रो वेदो यं ब्राह्मणा विदुर्वेदैनेन यद्वेदितव्यम्॥ १॥

Oṁ! The yon is fulness; fulness, this. From fulness, fulness does proceed. Withdrawing fulness's fulness off, even fulness then itself remains.

Oṁ! 'Brahma is the ether (*kha*)—the ether primeval, the ether that blows.' Thus, verily, was the son of Kauravyāyanī wont to say.

This is the knowledge (*veda*) the Brāhmaṇas know. Thereby I know (*veda*) what is to be known.

द्वितीयं ब्राह्मणम्

The three cardinal virtues

त्रयः प्राजापत्याः प्रजापतौ पितरि ब्रह्मचर्यमूषुर्देवा मनुष्या असुरा उषित्वा ब्रह्मचर्यं देवा ऊचुर्ब्रवीतु नो भवानिति तेभ्यो हैतदक्षरमुवाच द इति व्यज्ञासिष्टा ३ इति व्यज्ञासिष्मेति होचुर्दाम्यतेति न आत्थेत्योमिति होवाच व्यज्ञासिष्टेति॥ १॥

The threefold offspring of Prajāpati—gods, men, and devils (*asura*)—dwelt with their father Prajāpati as students of sacred knowledge (*brahmacarya*).

Having lived the life of a student of sacred knowledge, the gods said : 'Speak to us, sir.' To them then he spoke this syllable, '*Da*'. Did you understand?' 'We did understand', said they. 'You said to us, "Restrain yourselves (*damyata*)." 'Yes (*Oṁ*)!' said he. 'You did understand.'

अथ हैनं मनुष्य ऊर्ब्रवीतु नो भवानिति तेभ्यो हैतदेवाक्षरमुवाच द इति व्यज्ञासिष्टा ३ इति व्यज्ञासिष्मेति होचुर्दत्तेति न आत्थेत्योमिति होवाच व्यज्ञासिष्टेति॥ २॥

So then the men said to him : 'Speak to us, sir.' To them then he spoke this syllable, '*Da*'. 'Did you understand?' 'We did understand,' said they. 'You said to us, "give (*datta*)." 'Yes (*Oṁ*)!' said he. 'You did understand.'

अथ हैनमसुरा ऊचुर्ब्रवीतु नो भवानिति तेभ्यो हैतदेवाक्षरमुवाच द इति व्यज्ञासिष्टा ३ इति व्यज्ञासिष्मेति होचुर्दयध्वमिति न आत्थेत्योमिति होवाच व्यज्ञासिष्टेति तदेतदेवैषा दैवी वागनुवदति स्तनयित्नुर्द द द इति दाम्यत दत्त दयध्वमिति तदेतत्त्रयꣳ शिक्षेद्दमं दानं दयामिति॥ ३॥

So then the devils said to him : 'Speak to us, sir.' To them then he spoke this syllable, '*Da*'. 'did you understand?' 'We did understand,' said they. 'You said to us, "Be compassionate (*dayadhvam*)." 'Yes (*Oṁ*)!' said he. 'You did understand.'

This same thing does the divine voice here, thunder, repeat : *Da! Da! Da!* that is, restrain yourselves, give, be compassionate. One should practise this same triad : self-restraint, giving, compassion.

[All the three sons of Prajāpati have adopted the self-suitable meaning of the single letter 'Da'. Prajāpati satisfied by it. How it became possible? Its answer is that it could be possible on the basis of the pure heart as a result of following celibacy. Otherwise the audience cannot entertain the vibration of truth owing to the defects in their physique inspite of a complete sentence is told. The sage inspires that we should follow these three instructions of Prajāpati even today. The second question arising now is that we are man so why should we follow all the three instructions given to the gods, men and the demons? Its answer is that by virtue of celibacy (they behave with knowledge), it becomes apparent that when the divine element arises in the heart, one should resort to the oppression of the ego that motivates a man to suffer from superiority complex. Similarly, when the manly desires arise, one should give donation to avoid from selfishness and finally when the demon's desire arise, one should resort to the kindness to avoid from the cruelty.]

तृतीयं ब्राह्मणम्

Brahma as the heart

एष प्रजापतिर्यद्धृदयमेतद्ब्रह्मैतत्सर्वं तदेतत्त्र्यक्षरꣳहृदयमिति हृ इत्येकमक्षरमभिहरन्त्यस्मै स्वाश्चान्ये च य एवं वेद द इत्येकमक्षरं ददत्यस्मै स्वाश्चान्ये च य एवं वेद यमित्येकमक्षरमेति स्वर्गं लोकं य एवं वेद॥ १॥

This heart is Prajāpati, Brahma and everything. This heart consist of three letters *i.e.* the Varṇas or non-perishing properties.

hṛ is one syllable. Both his own people and others bring ($\sqrt{}$*hṛ*) offerings unto him who knows this.

da is one syllable. Both his own people and others give ($\sqrt{}$*dā*) unto him who knows this.

yam is one syllable. To the heavenly world goes (*eti* [Pl. *yanti*]) he who knows this.

[A heart possesses three kinds of attitudes. It motivates to gain what is not with it but necessary, to give the thing far better uses already available and always ready to go ahead to achieve the aim. These three attitudes of a heart conjointly provides the pleasure and the better contribution to this world and that world as also these provide him with the high position of the truth.]

चतुर्थं ब्राह्मणम्

तद्वैतदेव तदास सत्यमेव स यो हैतं महद्यक्षं प्रथमजं वेद सत्यं ब्रह्मेति जयतीमाँल्लोकान् जित इन्न्वसावसद्य एवमेतं महद्यक्षं प्रथमजं वेद सत्यं ब्रह्मेति सत्यꣳ ह्येव ब्रह्म॥ १॥

This, verily, is That. This, indeed, was That, even the Real. He who knows that wonderful being (*yakṣa*) as the first born—namely, that Brahma is the Real—conquers these worlds. Would he be conquered who knows thus that great spirit as the first-born—namely, that Brahma is the Real? [No!] for indeed, Brahma is the Real.

पञ्चमं ब्राह्मणम्

The Real, etymologically and cosmologically explained

आप एवेदमग्र आसुस्ता आपः सत्यमसृजन्त सत्यं ब्रह्म ब्रह्म प्रजापतिं प्रजापतिर्देवाꣳस्ते देवाः सत्यमेवोपासते तदेतत्त्र्यक्षरꣳ सत्यमिति स इत्येकमक्षरं तीत्येकमक्षरं यमित्येकमक्षरं प्रथमोत्तमे अक्षरे सत्य मध्यतोऽनृतं तदेतदमृतमुभयतः सत्येन परिगृहीतꣳ सत्यभूयमेव भवति नैवं विद्वाꣳसमनृतꣳ हिनस्ति॥ १॥

In the beginning this world was just Water. That Water emitted the Real—Brahma [being] the Real; Brahma, Prajāpati; Prajāpati, the gods. Those gods reverenced the Real (*satyam*). That is trisyllabic : *sa-ti-yam—sa* is one syllable, *ti* is one syllable, *yam* is one syllable. The first and last syllables are truth (*satyam*). In the middle is falsehood (*anṛtam*). This falsehood is embraced on both sides by truth; it partakes of the nature of truth itself. Falsehood dose not injure him who knows this.

[This perishing matter or the world is originated by the truth and finally it merges with the truth also. The man known to this fact inspite of making contemporary use of perishing matter, doesn't destroy by involving the same and the sage wants to convey the same.]

तद्यत्तत्सत्यमसौ स आदित्यो य एष एतस्मिन्मण्डले पुरुषो यश्चायं दक्षिणोऽक्षन्पुरुषस्तावेतावन्योन्यस्मिन्प्रतिष्ठितौ रश्मिभिरेषोऽस्मिन्प्रतिष्ठितः प्राणैरयममुष्मिन् स यदोत्क्रमिष्यन्भवति शुद्धमेवैतन्मण्डलं पश्यति नैनमेते रश्मयः प्रत्यायन्ति॥ २॥

Yonder sun is the same as that Real. The Person who is there in that orb and the Person who is here in the right eye—these two depend the one upon the other. Through his rays that one depends upon this one; through his vital breaths this one upon that. When one is about to decease, he sees that orb quite clear [i.e. free from rays]; those rays come to him no more.

य एष एतस्मिन्मण्डले पुरुषस्तस्य भूरिति शिर एकꣳ शिर एकमेतदक्षरं भुव इति बाहू द्वौ बाहू द्वे एते अक्षरे स्वरिति प्रतिष्ठा द्वे प्रतिष्ठे द्वे एते अक्षरे तस्योपनिषदहरिति हन्ति पाप्मानं जहाति च य एवं वेद॥ ३॥

The head of the person who is there in that orb is *Bhūr*—there is one head, this is one syllable. *Bhuvar* is the arms—there are two arms, these are two syllables. *Svar* is the feet—there are two feet, these are two syllables (*su-ar*). The mystic name (*upaniṣad*) thereof is 'Day' (*ahan*). He slays (√*han*) evil, he leaves it behind (√*hā*), who knows this.

योऽयं दक्षिणेऽक्षन्पुरुषस्तस्य बूरिति शिर एकꣳ शिर एकमेतदक्षरं भुव इति बाहू द्वौ बाहू द्वे एते अक्षरे स्वरिति प्रतिष्ठा द्वे प्रतिष्ठे द्वे एते अक्षरे तस्योपनिषदहमिति हन्ति पाप्मानं जहाति च य एवं वेद॥ ४॥

The head of the person who is here in the right eye is *Bhūr*—there is one head, this is one syllable. *Bhuvar* is the arms—there are two arms, these are two syllables. *Svar* is the feet—there are two feet, these are two syllables (*su-ar*). The mystic name (*upaniṣad*) thereof is 'I' (*aham*). He slays (√*han*) evil, he leaves it behind (√*hā*), who knows this.

षष्ठं ब्राह्मणम्

मनोमयोऽयं पुरुषो भाः सत्यस्तस्मिन्नन्तर्हृदये यथा व्रीहिर्वा यवो वा स एष सर्वस्येशानः सर्वस्याधिपतिः सर्वमिदं प्रशास्ति यदिदं किंच॥ १॥

[The individual person, monastically explained]

This person (*puruṣa*) here in the heart is made of mind, is of the nature of light, is like a little grain of rice, is a grain of barley. This very one is ruler of everything, is lord of everything, governs this whole universe, whatsoever there is.

सप्तमं ब्राह्मणम्

[Brahma as lightning, etymologically explained]

विद्युद्ब्रह्मेत्याहुर्विदानाद्विद्युद्विद्यत्येनं पाप्मनो य एवं वेद विद्युद्ब्रह्मेति विद्युद्ध्येव ब्रह्म॥ १॥

Brahman is lightning (*vidyut*), they say, because of unloosing (*vidāna*). Lightning unlooses (*vidyati*) him from evil who knows this, that Brahma is lightning—for Brahma is indeed lightning.

अष्टमं ब्राह्मणम्

वाचं धेनुमुपासीत तस्याश्चत्वारः स्तनाः स्वाहाकारो वषट्कारो हन्तकारः स्वधाकारस्तस्या द्वौ स्तनौ देवा उपजीवन्ति स्वाहाकारं च वषट्कारं च हन्तकारं मनुष्याः स्वधाकारं पितरस्तस्याः प्राण ऋषभो मनो वत्सः॥ १॥

One should reverence Speech as a milch-cow (Kāmadhenu). She has four udders : the *Svāhā* (Invocation), the *Vaṣaṭ* (Presentation), the *Hanta* (Salutation), the *Svadhā* (Benediction). The gods subsist upon her two udders, the *Svāhā* and the *Vaṣaṭ*; men, upon the *Hanta;* the fathers, upon the *Svadhā*. The breath is her bull; the mind, her calf.

नवमं ब्राह्मणम्

अयमग्निर्वैश्वानरो योऽयमन्तः पुरुषो येनेदमन्नं पच्यते यदिदमद्यते तस्यैष घोषो भवति यमेत्कर्णावपिधाय शृणोति स यदोत्क्रमिष्यन्भवति नैनं घोषꣳ शृणोति॥ १॥

This is the universal fire (Vaiśvānara) which is here within a person, by means of which the food that is eaten is cooked. It is the noise thereof that one hears on covering the ears thus. When one is about to depart, one hears not this sound.

दशमं ब्राह्मणम्

The course of Brahma after death

यदा वै पुरुषोऽस्माल्लोकात्प्रैति स वायुमागच्छति तस्मै स तत्र विजिहीते यथा रथचक्रस्य खं तेन स ऊर्ध्व आक्रमते स आदित्यमागच्छति तस्मै स तत्र विजिहीते यथा लम्बरस्य खं तेन स ऊर्ध्व आक्रमते स

चन्द्रमसमागच्छति तस्मै स तत्र विजिहीते यथा दुन्दुभेः खं तेन स ऊर्ध्व आक्रमते स लोकमागच्छत्यशोकमहिमं तस्मिन्वसति शाश्वतीः समाः॥ १॥

Verily, when a person (*puruṣa*) departs from this world he goes to the wind. It opens out there for him like the hole of a chariot-wheel. Through it he mounts higher.

He goes to the sun. It opens out there for him like the hole of a drum. Through it he mounts higher. He goes to the moon. It opens out for him there like the hole of a kettle-drum. Through it he mounts higher. He goes to the world that is without heat, without cold. Therein he dwells eternal years.

एकादशं ब्राह्मणम्

एतद्वै परमं तपो यद्व्याहितस्तप्यते परमꣳ हैव लोकं जयति य एवं वेदैतद्वै परमं तपो यं प्रेतमरण्यꣳ हरन्ति परमꣳ हैव लोकं जयति य एवं वेदैतद्वै परमं तपो यं प्रेतमग्नावभ्यादधति परमꣳ हैव लोकं जयति य एवं वेद॥ १॥

Verily, that is the supreme austerity which a sick man suffers. The supreme world, assuredly, he wins who knows this.

Verily, that is the supreme austerity when they carry a dead man into the wilderness. The supreme world, assuredly, he wins who knows this.

Verily, that is the supreme austerity when they lay a dead man on the fire. The supreme world, assuredly, he wins who knows this.

द्वादशं ब्राह्मणम्

अन्नं ब्रह्मेत्येक आहुस्तन्न तथा पूयति वा अन्नमृते प्राणात्प्राणो ब्रह्मेत्येक आहुस्तन्न तथा शुष्यति वै प्राण ऋतेऽन्नादेते ह त्वेव देवते एकधाभूयं भूत्वा परमतां गच्छतस्तद्ध स्माह प्रातृदः पितरं किꣳस्विदेवैवं विदुषे साधु कुर्यां किमेवास्मा असाधु कुर्यामिति स ह स्माह पाणिना मा प्रातृद कस्त्वेनयोरेकधाभूयं भूत्वा परमतां गच्छतीति तस्मा उ हैतदुवाच वीत्यन्नं वै वि अन्ने हीमानि सर्वाणि भूतानि विष्टानि रमिति प्राणो वै रं प्राणे हीमानि सर्वाणि भूतानि रमन्ते सर्वाणि ह वा अस्मिन्भूतानि विशन्ति सर्वाणि भूतानि रमन्ते य एवं वेद॥ १॥

[Brahma as food, life and renunciation]

'Brahma is food' Thus some say. This is not so. Verily, food becomes putrid without life (*prāṇa*).

'Brahma is life'—thus some say. This is not so. Verily, life dries up without food. Rather, only by entering into a unity do these deities reach the highest state.

Now it was in this connection that Prātṛda said to his father :

'What good, pray, could I do to one who knows this? What evil could I do to him?'

He then said, with [a wave of] his hand : 'No, Prātṛda. Who reaches the highest state [merely] by entering into a unity with these two?'

And he also spoke to him thus : '*vi*'—verily, *vi* is food, for all beings here enter (√*viś*) into food; and '*ram*'—verily, *ram* is life, for all beings here delight (√*ram*) in life. Verily, indeed, all beings enter into him, all beings delight in him who knows this.

त्रयोदशं ब्राह्मणम्

उक्थं प्राणो वा उक्थं प्राणो हीदꣳ सर्वमुत्थापयत्युद्धास्मादुक्थविद्वीरस्तिष्ठत्युक्थस्य सायुज्यꣳ सलोकतां जयति य एवं वेद॥ १॥

The *Uktha* : Verily, the Uktha is life (*prāṇa*), for it is life that causes everything here to rise up (*ut-thā*). From him there rises up an Uktha-knowing son, he wins co-union and co-status with the Uktha, who knows this.

यजुः प्राणो वै यजुः प्राणे हीमानि सर्वाणि भूतानि युज्यन्ते युज्यन्ते हास्मै सर्वाणि भूतानि श्रैष्ठ्याय यजुषः सायुज्यꣳ सलोकतां जयति य एवं वेद॥ २॥

The *Yajus* : Verily, the Yajus is life (*prāṇa*), for in life are all beings here united (√*yuj*). United, indeed, are all beings for his supremacy, he wins co-union and co-status with the Yajus, who knows this.

साम प्राणो वै साम प्राणे हीमानि सर्वाणि भूतानि सम्यञ्चि सम्यञ्चि हास्मै सर्वाणि भूतानि श्रैष्ठ्याय कल्पन्ते साम्नः सायुज्यꣳ सलोकतां जयति य एवं वेद॥ ३॥

The *Sāman* : Verily, the Sāman is life (*prāṇa*), for in life are all beings here combined (*samyañci*). Combined, indeed, are all beings here serving him for his supremacy, he wins co-union and co-status with the Sāman, who knows this.

क्षत्रं प्राणो वै क्षत्रं हि वै क्षत्रं त्रायते हैनं प्राणः क्षणितोः प्र क्षत्रमत्रमाप्नोति क्षत्रस्य सायुज्यꣳ सलोकतां जयति य एवं वेद॥ ४॥

The *Kṣatra* : Verily, rule is life (*prāṇa*), for verily, rule is life. Life protects (√*trā*) one from hurting (*kṣaṇitos*). He attains a rule that needs no protection (*a-tra*), he wins co-union and co-status with the Kṣatra, who knows this.

चतुर्दशं ब्राह्मणम्

[In this Brāhmaṇa, the essence of Gāyatrī and its significance has been described]

भूमिरन्तरिक्षं द्यौरित्यष्टावक्षराण्यष्टाक्षरꣳ ह वा एकं गायत्र्यै पदमेतदु हैवास्या एतत्स यावदेषु त्रिषु लोकेषु तावद्ध जयति योऽस्या एतदेवं पदं वेद॥ १॥

The sage while explaining the importance of the first food of Gāyatrī, says– *bhū-mir* (earth), *an-ta-ri-kṣa* (interspace), *dy-aur* (sky)—eight syllables. Of eight syllables, verily, is one line of the Gāyatrī. And that [series], indeed, is that [line] of it. As much as there is in the three worlds, so much indeed does he win who knows thus that line of it.

ऋचो यजूꣳषि सामानीत्यष्टावक्षराण्यष्टाक्षरꣳ ह वा एकं गायत्र्यै पदमेतदु हैवास्या एतत्स यावतीयं त्रयी विद्या तावद्ध जयति योऽस्या एतदेवं पदं वेद॥ २॥

Ṛcaḥ (verses), *ya-jūṁṭi* (sacrificial formulas), *sā-mā-ni* (chants)—eight syllables. Of eight syllables, verily, is one line of the Gāyatrī. And that [series], indeed, is that [line] of it. As much as is this threefold knowledge, so much indeed does he win who knows thus that line of it.

प्राणोऽपानो व्यान इत्यष्टावक्षराण्यष्टाक्षरः ह वा एकं गायत्र्यै पदमेतदु हैवास्या एतत्स यावदिदं प्राणि तावद्ध जयति योऽस्या एतदेवं पदं वेदाथास्या एतदेव तुरीयं दर्शतं पदं परोरजा य एष तपति यद्वै चतुर्थं तत्तुरीयं दर्शतं पदमिति ददृश इव ह्येष परोरजा इति सर्वमु ह्येवैष रज उपर्युपरि तपत्येवः हैव श्रिया यशसा तपति योऽस्या एतदेवं पदं वेद॥ ३॥

Prā-ṇa (in-breath), *ap-ā-na* (out-breath), *vy-ā-na* (diffused breath)—eight syllables. Of eight syllables, verily, is one line of the Gāyatrī. And that [series], indeed, is that [line] of it. As much breathing as there is here, so much indeed does he win who knows thus that line of it.

That is its fourth, the slightly, foot, namely the one above-the-darksome who glows yonder. This fourth is the same as the Turīya. It is called the 'slightly (*darśatam*) foot,' because it has come into sight (*dadṛśe*), as it were. And he is called 'above-the-darksome' (*paro-rajas*), because he glows yonder far above everything darksome. Thus he glows with luster and glory who knows thus that foot of it.

[The fourth foot of Gāyatrī too consist of eight letters. Its reference can be seen in 'Viśvāmitra Kalpa' and the appreciating of ancient 'Sāndhya' (sacrificial pray). It has been said in 'Upaniṣad' that only three feet of Gāyatrī are worth reciting while the fourth foot *i.e.* the 'Darśata' is worth feeling. It is classified as *Prorajasi-Asau-Adahom i.e.* beyond the worldly matter or light everything here is the Brahma in garb of the syllable Oṁ. When the vibration of the breathing establish integrity with the three feet, the devotee automatically starts feeling the fourth foot. This is the reason it is called 'Darśata'.]

सैषा गायत्र्येतस्मिंःस्तुरीये दर्शते पदे परोरजसि प्रतिष्ठिता तद्वैतत्सत्ये प्रतिष्ठितं चक्षुर्वै सत्यं चक्षुर्हि वै सत्यं तस्माद्यदिदानीं द्वौ विवदमानावेयातामहमदर्शमहमश्रौषमिति य एवं ब्रूयादहमदर्शमिति तस्मा एवं श्रद्धध्याम तद्वै तत्सत्यं बले प्रतिष्ठितं प्राणो वै बलं तत्प्राणे प्रतिष्ठितं तस्मादाहुर्बलः सत्यादोजीय इत्येवं वैषा गायत्र्यध्यात्मं प्रतिष्ठिता सा हैषा गयाःस्तत्रे प्राणा वै गयास्तत्प्राणाःस्तत्रे तद्यद्गयाःस्तत्रे तस्माद्गायत्री नाम स यामेवामूः सावित्रीमन्वाहैषैव स यस्मा अन्वाह तस्य प्राणाःस्त्रायते॥ ४॥

This Gāyatrī is based upon that fourth, slightly foot, the one above-the-darksome. That is based upon truth (*satya*). Verily, truth is sight, for verily, truth is sight. Therefore if now two should come disputing, saying 'I have seen!' 'I have heard!' we should trust the one who would say 'I have seen'.

Verily, that truth is based on strength (*bala*). Verily, strength is life (*prāṇa*). It is based on life. Therefore they say, 'Strength is more powerful than truth.'

Thus is that Gāyatrī based with regard to the Self (*adhyātmam*). It protects the house-servants. Verily, the house-servants are the vital breaths (*prāṇa*). So it protects the vital breaths. Because it protects (√*trā*) the house-servants (*gaya*), therefore it is called Gāyatrī. That Sāvitrī stanza which one repeats is just this. For whomever one repeats it, it protects his vital breaths.

ताꣳहैतामेके सावित्रीमनुष्टुभमन्वाहुर्वागनुष्टुबेतद्वाचमनुब्रूम इति न तथा कुर्यादगायत्रीमेव सावित्रीमनुब्रूयाद्यदिह वा अप्येवंविद्बह्विव प्रतिगृह्णाति न हैव तद्गायत्र्या एकंचन पदं प्रति।।५।।

Some recite this Sāvitrī stanza as Anuṣṭubha meter, saying : 'The speech is Anuṣṭubha meter. We recite the speech accordingly.' One should not do so. One should recite the Sāvitrī stanza as Gāyatrī meter. Verily, even if one who knows thus receives very much, that is not at all in comparison with one single line of the Gāyatrī.

[The Upaniṣad accepts as 'Guru Mantra' (hymns taught by the teacher) to the Gāyatrī hymn with its three feet consisting of 'Gāyatrī Chaṇḍavala' eight alphabets. It, therefore, makes clear that it is not appropriate to provide as 'Guru Mantra' or applied the same way the Gāyatrī hymn with its fourth foot or with other rhymes.]

स य इमाꣳस्त्रींल्लोकान्पूर्णान्प्रतिगृह्णीयात्सोऽस्या एतत्प्रथमं पदमाप्नुयादथ यावतीयं त्रयी विद्या यस्तावत्प्रतिगृह्णीयात्सोऽस्या एतद्द्वितीयं पदमाप्नुयादथ यावदिदं प्राणि यस्तावत्प्रतिगृह्णीयात्सोऽस्या एतत्तृतीय पदमाप्नुयादथास्या एतदेव तुरीयं दर्शतं पदं परोरजा य एष तपति नैव केनचनाप्यं कुत उ एतावत्प्रतिगृह्णीयात्।।६।।

If one should receive these three worlds full, he would receive that first line of it [i.e. the Gāyatrī]. If one should receive as much as is this three fold knowledge, he would receive that second line of it. If one should receive as much as there is breathing here, he would receive that third line of it. But that fourth (*turīya*), slightly foot, the one above-the-darksome, who glows yonder, is not obtainable by anyone whatsoever. When, pray, would one receive so much!

[The sub-place of Gāyatrī has been given here. Sub-place is meant by psalms recited by going near. Commonly, this hymn is recited by the proximate feeling with the great power of Gāyatrī. At the higher position, when the breathing of devotee are cleaned to the extent, they attain the direct touch of this power, the stage of sub-place then automatically is formed.]

तस्या उपस्थनं गायत्र्यस्येकपदी द्विपदी त्रिपदी चतुष्पद्यपदसि नहि पद्यसे नमस्ते तुरीयाय दर्शताय पदाय परोरजसेऽसावदो मा प्रापदिति यं द्विष्यादसावस्मै कामो मा समृद्धीति वा न हैवास्मै स कामः समृद्ध्यते यस्मा एवमुपतिष्ठतेऽहमदः प्रापमिति वा।।७।।

The veneration of it : 'O Gāyatrī, you are one-footed, two-footed, three-footed, four-footed. You are without a foot, because you do not go afoot. You are without a foot, because you do not go afoot. Adoration to your fourth, slightly foot, the one above-the-darksome! Let not so-and-so obtain such-and-such!' namely, the one whom one hates. Or, 'So-and-so— let not his wish propser!' Indeed, that wish is not prospered for him in regard to whom one venerates thus. Or, 'Let me obtain such-and-such!'

एतद्ध वै तज्जनक वैदेहो बुडिलमाश्वतराश्विमुवाच यन्नु हो तद्गायत्रीविदब्रूथा अथ कथꣳहस्तीभूतो वहसीति मुखꣳ ह्यस्याः सम्राण्न विदांचकारेति होवाच तस्या अग्निरेव मुखं यदिह वा अपि बह्विवाग्नावभ्यादधति सर्वमेव तत्संदहत्येवꣳ हैवेवंविद्यद्यपि बह्विव पापं कुरुते सर्वमेव तत्संप्साय शुद्धः पूतोऽजरोऽमृतः संभवति॥८॥

On this point, verily, Janaka, [king] of Vaideha, spoke as follows to Buḍila Āśvatarāśvi: 'Ho! Now if you spoke of yourself thus as a knower of the Gāyatrī, how then have you come to be an elephant and are carrying?'

'Because, great king, I did not know its mouth,' said he.

Its mouth is fire. Verily, indeed, even if they lay very much on a fire, it burns it all. Even so one who knows this, although he commits very much evil, consumes it all and becomes clean and pure, ageless and immortal.

पञ्चदशं ब्राह्मणम्

A dying person's prayer

हिरण्मयेन पात्रेण सत्यस्यापिहितं मुखम्। तत्त्वं पूषन्नपावृणु सत्यधर्माय दृष्टये। पूषन्नेकर्षे यम सूर्य प्राजापत्य व्यूह रश्मीन्समूह तेजो यत्ते रूपं कल्याणतमं तत्ते पश्यामि योऽसावसौ पुरुषः सोऽहमस्मि। वायुरनिलममृतमथेदं भस्मान्तꣳ शरीरम्। ॐ ३ क्रतो स्मर कृतꣳस्मर क्रतो स्मर कृतꣳ स्मर। अग्ने नय सुपथा राये अस्मान्विश्वानि देव वयुनानि विद्वान्। युयोध्यस्मज्जुहुराणमेनो भूयिष्ठां ते नम उक्तिं विधेम॥१॥

With a golden vessel the Real's face is covered over. That do you, O Pūṣan, uncover for one whose law is the Real (*satya-dharma*) to see.

O Nourisher (*Pūṣan*), the sole Seer, O Controller (*Yama*), O Sun, offspring of Prajāpati, spread forth your rays! Gather your brilliance! What is your fairest form—that of you I see. He who is yonder, yonder Person (*puruṣa*)—I myself am he!

[My] breath (*vāyu*) to the immortal wind (*anilam amṛtam*)! This body then ends in ashes! *Oṁ!*

O Purpose (*kratu*), remember! The deed (*kṛta*) remember! O Purpose, remember! The deed remember!

O Agni, by a goodly path to prosperity (*rai*) lead us, You god who knows all the ways!

Keep far from us crooked-going sin (*enas*)! most ample expression of adoration to you would be render.

।।षष्ठोऽध्याय:।।

प्रथमं ब्राह्मणम्

The characteristic excellence of six bodily functions, and the value of the knowledge thereof

योो ह वै ज्येष्ठं च श्रेष्ठं च वेद ज्येष्ठ श्रेष्ठश्च स्वानां भवति प्राणो वै ज्येष्ठश्च श्रेष्ठश्च ज्येष्ठश्च श्रेष्ठश्च स्वानां भवत्यपि च येषां बुभूषति य एवं वेद।।१।।

Om! Verily, he who knows the chiefest and best, becomes the chiefest and best of his own [people].

Breath (*prāṇa*), verily, is chiefest and best. He who knows this becomes the chiefest and best of his own [people] and even of those of whom he wishes so to become.

यो ह वै वसिष्ठां वेद वसिष्ठ: स्वानां भवति वाग्वै वसिष्ठा वसिष्ठ: स्वानां भवत्यपि च येषां बुभूषति य एवं वेद।।२।।

Verily, he who knows the most excellent becomes the most excellent of his own [people].

Speech, verily, is the most excellent. He who knows this becomes the most excellent of his own [people] and even of those of whom he wishes so to become.

यो ह वै प्रतिष्ठां वेद प्रतितिष्ठति समे प्रतितिष्ठति दुर्गे चक्षुर्वै प्रतिष्ठा चक्षुषा हि समे च दुर्गे च प्रतितिष्ठति प्रतितिष्ठति समे प्रतितिष्ठति दुर्गे च एवं वेद।।३।।

Verily, he who knows the firm basis (*prati-ṣṭhā*) has a firm basis (verb *prati-ṣṭhā*) on even ground, has a firm basis on rough ground.

The Eye, verily, is a firm basis, for with the eye both on even ground and on rough ground one has a firm basis. He has a firm basis on even ground, he has a firm basis on rough ground, who knows this.

यो ह वै सम्पदं वेद सꣳहास्मै पद्यते यं कामं कामयते श्रोत्रं वै सम्पच्छ्रोत्रे हीमे सर्वे वेदा अभिसम्पन्ना: सꣳहास्मै पद्यते यं कामं कायमते य एवं वेद।।४।।

Verily, he who knows attainment—for him, indeed, is attained what wish he wishes.

The Ear, verily, is attainment, for in the ear all these Vedas are attained. The wish that he wishes is attained for him who knows this.

यो ह वा आयतनं वेदायतनꣳस्वानां भवत्यायतनं जनानां मनो वा आयतनमायतनꣳ स्वानां भवत्यायतनं जनानां य एवं वेद।।५।।

Verily, he who knows the abode becomes the abode of his own [people], an abode of folk.

The Mind, verily, is an abode. He becomes an abode of his own [people], an abode of folk, who knows this.

यो ह वै प्रजापतिं वेद प्रजापते ह प्रजया पशुभी रेतो वै प्रजापतिः प्रजायते ह प्रजया पशुभिर्य एवं वेद॥५॥

Verily, he who knows procreation (*prajāti*) procreates himself with progeny and cattle.

Semen, verily, is procreation. He procreates himself with progeny and cattle, who knows this.

ते हेमे प्राणा अहꣳश्रेयसे विवदमाना ब्रह्म जग्मुस्तद्धोचुः को नो वसिष्ठ इति तद्धोवाच यस्मिन्व उत्क्रान्त इदꣳ शरीरं पापीयो मन्यते स वो वसिष्ठ इति॥७॥

These vital Breaths (*prāṇa*), disputing among themselves on self-superiority, went to Brahma. Then they said : 'Which of us is the most excellent?'

Then he said : 'The one of you after whose going off this body is thought to be worse off, he is the most excellent of you.'

वाग्घोच्चक्राम सा संवत्सरं प्रोष्यागत्योवाच कथमशकत मदृते जीवितुमिति ते होचुर्यथाकला अवदन्तो वाचा प्राणन्तः प्राणेन पश्यन्तश्चक्षुषा शृण्वन्तः श्रोत्रेण विद्वाꣳसो मनसा प्रजायमाना रेतसैवमजीविष्मेति प्रविवेश ह वाक्॥८॥

Speech went off. Having remained away a year, it came back and said : 'How have you been able to live without me?'

They said : 'As the dumb, not speaking with speech, but breathing with breath, seeing with the eye, hearing with the ear, knowing with the mind, procreating with semen. Thus have we lived.' Speech entered in.

चक्षुर्होच्चक्रामं तत्संवत्सरं प्रोष्यागत्योवाच कथमशकत मदृते जीवितुमिति ते होचुर्यथा अन्धा अपशन्तश्चक्षुषा प्राणन्तः प्राणेन वदन्तो वाचा शृण्वन्तः श्रोत्रेण विद्वाꣳसो मनसा प्रजायमाना रेतसैवमजीविष्मेति प्रविवेश ह चक्षु॥९॥

Then the eyes departed for a year out from the body. On its return, it said– "How did you live without me." They said : 'As the blind, not seeing with the eye, but breathing with breath, speaking with speech, hearing with the ear, knowing with the mind, procreating with semen. Thus have we lived.' The eye entered in.

श्रोत्रꣳ होच्चक्राम तत्संवत्सरं प्रोष्यागत्योवाच कथमशकत मदृते जीवितुमिति ते होचुर्यथा बधिरा अश्रृण्वन्तः श्रोत्रेण प्राणन्तः प्राणेन वदन्तो वाचा पश्यन्तश्चक्षुषा विद्वाꣳसो मनसा प्रजायमाना रेतसैवमजीविष्मेति प्रविवेश ह श्रोत्रम्॥१॥

Then the ears departed after the eyes. They also lived out from the body for a year asked on their return to other sensory organs– "How all of you did live without me?" The sensory organs replied– 'As the deaf, not hearing with the ear, but breathing with breath, speaking with speech, seeing with the eye, knowing with the mind, procreating with semen. Thus have we lived.' The ear entered in.

मनो होच्चक्राम तत्संवत्सरं प्रोष्यागत्योवाच कथमशकत मदृते जीवितुमिति ते होचुर्यथा मुग्धा अविद्वांसो मनसा प्राणन्तः प्राणेन वदन्तो वाचा पश्यन्तश्चक्षुषा शृण्वन्तः श्रोत्रेण प्रजायमाना रेतसैवमजीविष्मेति प्रविवेश ह मनः॥११॥

The Mind went off. Having remained away a year, it came back and said : 'How have you been able to live without me?'

They said : 'As the stupid, not knowing with the mind, but breathing with breath, speaking with speech, seeing with the eye, hearing with the ear, procreating with semen. Thus have we lived.' The mind entered in.

रेतो होच्चक्राम तत्संवत्सरं प्रोष्यागत्योवाच कथमशकत मदृते जीवितुमिति ते होचुर्यथा क्लीबा अप्रजायमाना रेतसा प्राणन्तः प्राणेन वदन्तो वाचा पश्यन्तश्चक्षुषा शृण्वन्तः श्रोत्रेण प्रजायमाना विद्वांसो मनसैवमजीविष्मेति प्रविवेश ह रेतः॥१२॥

After the mind, the semen also departed out from the body. It also did returned after a year and asked the others on return– "How did you live in my absence?" The sensory organs replied– "As the impotent person inspite of crippled in reproducing the children lives on breathing, speech, eyes, ears and the mind, we also lived the same." Hearing this the semen again took its place in the body.

अथ ह प्राण उत्क्रमिष्यन्यथा महासुहयः सैन्धवः पड्वीशशंकून्संवृहेदेवं हैवेमान्प्राणान्त्संववर्ह ते होचुर्मा भगव उत्क्रमीर्न वै शक्ष्यामस्त्वदृते जीवितुमिति तस्यो मे बलिं कुरुतेति तथेति॥१३॥

Then Breath was about to go off. As a large fine horse of the Indus-land might pull up the pegs of his foot-tethers together, thus indeed did it pull up those vital breaths together. They said : 'Sir, go no off! Verily, we shall not be able to live without you!'

'If such I am, make me an offering'. 'So be it.'

सा ह वागुवाच यद्वा अहं वसिष्ठास्मि त्वं तद्वसिष्ठोऽसीति यद्वा अहं प्रतिष्ठास्मि त्वं तत्प्रतिष्ठोऽसीति चक्षुर्यद्वा अहं संपदस्मि त्वं तत्संपदसीति श्रोत्रं यद्वा अहमायतनमस्मि त्वं तदायतनमसीति मनो यद्वा अहं प्रजातिरस्मि त्वं तत्प्रजातिरसीति रेतस्तस्यो मे किमन्नं किं वास इति यदिदं किंचाश्वभ्य आकृमिभ्य आ कीटपतङ्गेभ्यस्तत्तेऽन्नमापो वास इति न ह वा अस्यानन्नं जग्धं भवति नानन्नं परिगृहीतं य एवमेतदनस्यान्नं वेद तद्विद्वांसः श्रोत्रिया अशिष्यन्त आचामन्त्यशित्वाचामन्त्येतमेव तदनमनग्नं कुर्वन्तो मन्यन्ते॥१४॥

Speech said : 'Verily, wherein I am the most excellent, therein are you the most excellent.'

The eye said- 'Verily, wherein I am a firm basis, therein are you a firm basis,'

The ear said- 'Verily, wherein I am attainment, therein are you attainment,'

The mind said- 'Verily, wherein I am an abode, therein are you an abode,'

The semen said- 'Verily, wherein I am procreation, therein are you procreation,'

'If such I am, what is my food? what is my dwelling?'

'Whatever there is here, even to gods, worms, crawling and flying insects—that is your food. Water is your dwelling.'

Verily, what is not food is not eaten; what is not food is not taken by him who thus knows that [i.e. water] as the food (*anna*) of breath (*ana*). Those who know this, who are versed in sacred learning (*śrotriya*), when they are about to eat, take a sip; after they have eaten, they take a sip. So, indeed, they think they make that breath (*ana*) not naked (*anagna*).

द्वितीयं ब्राह्मणम्

The course of the soul in its incarnations

श्वेतकेतुर्ह वा आरुणेयः पञ्चालानां परिषदमाजगाम स आजगाम जैवलिं प्रवाहणं परिचारयमाणं तमुदीक्ष्याभ्युवाद कुमार३ इति स भो३ इति प्रतिशुश्रावानुशिष्टोऽन्वसि पित्रेत्योमिति होवाच॥१॥

Śvetaketu, son of Āruṇi visited at the conference of Pañcālas and appeared before 'Pravāhaṇa', the son of Jaivala who was enjoying the services of his servants. Looking at 'Pravāhaṇa', Śvetaketu addressed him with the words– "O young man! He replied– "What do you want (Bho)?" Pravāhaṇa raised a question– 'Have you been instructed by your father?' Śvetaketu replied– "Yes!".

वेत्थ यथेमाः प्रजाः प्रयत्यो विप्रतिपद्यन्ता ३ इति नेति होवाच वेत्थो यथेमं लोकं पुनरापद्यन्ता३ इति नेति हैवोवाच वेत्थो यथासौ लोक एवं बहुभिः पुनः पुनः प्रयद्भिर्न संपूर्यता३ इति नेति हैवोवाच वेत्थो यतिथ्यामाहुत्यां हुतायामापः पुरुषवाचो भूत्वा समुत्थाय वदन्ती३ इति नेति हैवोवाच वेत्थो देवयानस्य वा पथः प्रतिपदं पितृयाणस्य वा यत्कृत्वा देवयानं वा पन्थानं प्रतिपद्यन्ते पितृयाणं वापि हि ऋषेर्वचः श्रुतम् द्वे सृती अशृणवं पितृणामहं देवानामुत मर्त्यानाम्। ताभ्यामिदं विश्वमेजत्समेति यदन्तरा पितरं मातरं चेति नाहमत एकंचन वेदेति होवाच॥२॥

'Know you how people here, on deceasing, separate in different directions?'

'No,' said he.

'Know you how they come back again to this world?' 'No,' said he.

'Know you why yonder world is not filled up with the many who continually thus go hence?' 'No,' said he.

'Know you in which oblation that is offered the water becomes the voice of a person, rises up, and speaks?' 'No', said he.

'Know you the access of the path leading to the gods, or of the one leading to the fathers? By doing what, people go to the path of the gods or of the fathers? For we have heard the word of the seer :—

Two paths, I've heard—the one that leads to fathers, and one that leads to gods—belong to mortals.

By these two, every moving thing here travels, that is between the Father and the Mother.'

'Not a single one of them do I know,' said he.

अथैनं वसत्योपमन्त्रयांचक्रेऽनादृत्य वसतिं कुमारः प्रदुद्राव स आजगाम पितरं तꣳहोवाचेति वाव किल नो भवान्पुरानुशिष्टानवोचदिति कथꣳ सुमेध इति पञ्च मा प्रश्नान् राजन्यबन्धुरप्राक्षीत्ततो नैकंचन वेदेति कतमे त इतीम ह प्रतिकान्युदाजहार॥३॥

Then he addressed him with an invitation to remain. Not respecting the invitation to remain, the boy ran off. He went to his father. He said to him : 'Verily, aforetime you have spoken of me, sir, as having been instructed!'

'How now, wise one?'

'Five questions a fellow of the princely class (*rājanya-bandhu*) has asked me. Not a single one of them do I know.'

'What are they?'

'These'—and he repeated the topics.

स होवाच तथा नस्त्वं तात जानीथा यथा यदहं किंचन वेद सर्वमहं तत्तुभ्यमवोचं प्रेहि तु तत्र प्रतीत्य ब्रह्मचर्यं वत्स्याव इति भवानेव गच्छत्विति स आजगाम गौतमो यत्र प्रवाहणस्य जैवलेराम तस्मा आसनमाहृत्योदकमाहारयांचकाराथ हास्मा अर्घ्यं चकार तꣳ होवाच वरं भगवते गौतमाय दद्म इति॥४॥

He said : 'You should know me, my dear, as such, that whatsoever I myself know, I have told all to you. But, come! Let us go there and take up studentship.'

'Go yourself, sir.'

So Gautama went forth to where [the place] of Pravāhaṇa Jaibāli was.

He brought him a seat, and had water brought; so he made him a respectful welcome. Then he said to him : 'A boon we offer to the honourable Gautama!'

स होवाच प्रतिज्ञातो म एष वरो यां तु कुमारस्यान्ते वाचमभाषथास्तां मे ब्रूहीति॥५॥

The father of Śvetaketu replied– 'The boon acceptable to me is this :—Pray tell me the word which you spoke in the presence of the young man.'

स होवाच दैवेषु वै गौतम तद्वरेषु मानुषाणां ब्रूहीति॥६॥

King Pravāhaṇa said– "O Gautama! that is among divine boons. Mention [one] of human boons.'

स होवाच विज्ञायते हास्ति हिरण्यस्यापात्तं गोअश्वानां दासीनां प्रवाराणां परिधानस्य मा नो भवान्बहोरनन्तस्यापर्यन्तस्याभ्यवदान्योऽभूदिति स वै गौतम तीर्थेनिच्छासा इत्युपैम्यहं भवन्तमिति वाचा ह स्मैव पूर्व उपयन्ति स होपायनकीर्त्योवास॥७॥

Then he said : 'It is well known that I have a full share of gold, of cows and horses, of females slaves, of rugs, of apparel. Be not ungenerous toward me, Sir, in regard to that which is the abundant, the infinite, the unlimited.'

'Then, verily, O Gautama, you should seek in the usual manner.'

'I come to you, sir, as a pupil!' With [this] word, verily, indeed, men aforetime came as pupils. So with the acknowledgement of coming as a pupil he remained.

स होवाच यथा नस्त्वं गौतम मापराधास्तव च पितामहा यथेयं विद्येतः पूर्वं न कस्मिꣳश्चन ब्राह्मण उवास तां त्वहं तुभ्यं वक्ष्यामि को हि त्वैवं ब्रुवन्तमर्हति प्रत्याख्यातुमिति॥८॥

The king said– "O Gautama! 'As truly as this knowledge has never heretofore dwelt with any Brahman (*brāhmaṇa*) whatsoever, so truly may not you and your grandfathers injure us. But I will tell it to you, for who is able to refuse you when you speak thus!' He continued (*iti*).

असौ वै लोकोऽग्निर्गौतम तस्यादित्य एव समिद्रश्मयो धूमोऽहरर्चिर्दिशोऽङ्गारा अवान्तरदिशो विस्फुलिङ्गास्तस्मिन्नेतस्मिन्नग्नौ देवाः श्रद्धां जुह्वति तस्या आहुत्यै सोमो राजा संभवति॥९॥

'Yonder world, verily, is a sacrificial fire, O Gautama. The sun, in truth, is its fuel; the light-rays, the smoke; the day, the flame; the quarters of heaven, the coals; the intermediate quarters, the sparks. In this fire the gods offer faith (*śraddhā*). From this oblation King Soma arises.

पर्जन्यो वाग्निर्गौतम तस्य संवत्सर एव समिदभ्राणि धूमो विद्युदर्चिरशनिरङ्गारा ह्रादुनयो विस्फुलिङ्गास्तस्मिन्नेतस्मिन्नग्नौ देवाः सोमꣳ राजानं जुह्वति तस्या आहुत्यै वृष्टिः संभवति॥१०॥

A rain-cloud, verily, is a sacrificial fire, O Gautama. The year, in truth, is its fuel; the thunder-clouds, the smoke; the lightning, the flame; the thunder-bolts, the coals; the hail-stones, the sparks. In this fire the gods offer King Soma. From this oblation rain arises.

अयं वै लोकोऽग्निर्गौतम तस्य पृथिव्येव समिदग्निर्धूमो रात्रिरर्चिश्चन्द्रमाङ्गारा नक्षत्राणि विस्फुलिङ्गास्तस्मिन्नेतस्मिन्नग्नौ देवाः वृष्टिं जुह्वति तस्या आहुत्या अन्नꣳ संभवति॥११॥

This world, verily, is a sacrificial fire, O Gautama. The earth, in truth, is its fuel; fire, the smoke; night, the flame; the moon, the coals; the stars, the sparks. In this fire the gods offer rain. From this oblation food arises.

पुरुषो वाऽग्निर्गौतम तस्य व्यात्तमेव समित्प्राणो धूमो वागर्चिश्चक्षुरङ्गारा श्रोत्रं विस्फुलिङ्गास्तस्मिन्नेतस्मिन्नग्नौ देवाः अन्नं जुह्वति तस्या आहुत्यै रेतः संभवति॥१२॥

Man (*puruṣa*), verily, is a sacrificial fire, O Gautama. The open mouth, verily, is its fuel; breath (*prāṇa*), the smoke; speech, the flame; the eye, the coals; the ear, the sparks. In this fire the gods offer food. From this oblation semen arises.

योषा वा अग्निर्गौतम तस्या उपस्थ एव समिल्लोमानि धूमो योनिरर्चिर्यदन्तः करोति तेऽङ्गारा अभिनन्दा विस्फुलिङ्गास्तस्मिन्नेतस्मिन्नग्नौ देवाः रेतो जुह्वति तस्या आहुत्यै पुरुषः संभवति स जीवति यावज्जीवत्यथ यदा म्रियते॥१३॥

अथैनमग्नये हरन्ति तस्याग्निरेवाग्निर्भवति समित्समिद्धूमो धूमोऽर्चिरर्चिरङ्गारा अङ्गारा विस्फुलिङ्गा विस्फुलिङ्गास्तस्मिन्नेतस्मिन्नग्नौ देवाः पुरुषं जुह्वति तस्या आहुत्यै पुरुषो भास्वरवर्णः संभवति॥१४॥

Woman, verily, is a sacrificial fire, O Gautama. The sexual organ, in truth, is its fuel; the hairs, the smoke; the vulva, the flame; when on inserts, the coals; the feelings of pleasure, the sparks. In this oblation the gods offer semen. From this oblation a person (*puruṣa*) arises. He lives as long as he lives. Then when he dies, they carry him to the fire. His fire, in truth, becomes the fire, fuel, the fuel; smoke, the smoke; flame, the flame; coals, the coals; sparks, the sparks. In this fire the gods offer a person (*puruṣa*). From this obaltion the man arises, having the colour of light.

ते य एवमेतद्विदुर्ये चामी अरण्ये श्रद्धाꣳ सत्यमुपासते तेऽर्चिरभिसंभवन्त्यर्चिषोऽहरह्न आपूर्यमाणपक्षमापूर्यमाणपक्षा-द्यान्षण्मासानुदङ्ङादित्य एति मासेभ्यो देवलोकं देवलोकादादित्यमादित्याद्वैद्युतं तान्वैद्युतान्पुरुषो मानस एत्य ब्रह्मलोकान् गमयति ते तेषु ब्रह्मलोकेषु पराः परावतो वसन्ति तेषां न पुनरावृत्तिः॥१५॥

Those who know this, and those too who in the forest truly worship (*upāsate*) faith (*śraddhā*), pass into the flame [of the cremation-fire]; from, the flame, into the day; from the day, into the half month of the waxing moon; from the half month of the waxing moon, into the six months during which the sun moves northward; from these months, into the world of the gods (*deva-loka*); from the world of the gods, into the sun; from the sun, into the lightning-fire. A Person (*puruṣa*) consisting of mind (*mānasa*) goes to those regions of lightning and conducts them to the Brahma-worlds. In those Brahma-worlds they dwell for long extents. Of these there is no return.

अथ ये यज्ञेन दानेन तपसा लोकाञ्जयन्ति ते धूममभिसंभवन्ति धूमाद्रात्रिꣳ रात्रेरपक्षीयमाणपक्षमक्षीयमाणपक्षा-द्यान्षण्मासान्दक्षिणादित्य एति मासेभ्यः पितृलोकं पितृलोकाच्चन्द्रं ते चन्द्रं प्राप्यान्नं भवन्ति ताꣳस्तत्र देवा यथा सोमꣳ राजनमाप्यायस्वापक्षीयस्वेत्येवमेनाꣳस्तत्र भक्षयन्ति तेषां यदा तत्पर्यवैत्यथैममेवाकाशमभनिष्पद्यन्त आकाशाद्वायुं वायोर्वृष्टिं वृष्टेः पृथिवीं ते पृथिवीं प्राप्यान्नं भवन्ति ते पुनः पुरुषाग्नौ हूयन्ते ततो योषाग्नौ जायन्ते लोकान्प्रत्युत्थायिनस्त एवमेवानुपरिवर्तन्तेऽथ य एतौ पन्थानौ न विदुस्ते कीटाः पतङ्गा यदिदं दन्दशूकम्॥१६॥

But they who by sacrificial offering, charity, and austerity conquer the worlds, pass into the smoke [of the cremation-fire]; from the smoke, into the night; from the night, into the half month of the waning moon; from the half month of the waning moon, into the six months during which the sun moves southward; from those months, into the world of the fathers; from the world of the fathers, into the moon. Reaching the moon, they become food. There the gods—as they say to King Soma, "Increase! Decrease!"— even so feed upon them there. When that passes away from them, then they pass forth into this space; from space, into air; from air, into rain; from rain, into the earth. On reaching the earth they become food. Again they are offered in the fire of man. Then they are born in the fire of woman. Rising up into the world, they cycle round again thus.

But those who know not these two ways, become crawling and flying insects and whatever there is here that bites.'

तृतीयं ब्राह्मणम्

Incantation and ceremony for the attainment of a great wish

स यः कामयेत महत्प्राप्नुयामित्युदगयन आपूर्यमाणपक्षस्य पुण्याहे द्वादशाहमुपसद्व्रती भूत्वौदुम्बरे कꣳसे चमसे वा सर्वौषधं संभृत्य परिसमुह्य परिलिप्याग्निमुपसमाधाय परिस्तीर्यावृताज्यꣳ सꣳस्कृत्य पुꣳसा नक्षत्रेण मन्थꣳ संनीय जुहोतियावन्तो देवास्त्वयि जातवेदस्तिर्यञ्चो घ्नन्ति पुरुषस्य कामान्। तेभ्योऽहं भागधेयं जुहोमि ते मा तृप्ताः सर्वैः कामैस्तर्पयन्तु स्वाहा। या तिरश्ची निपद्यतेऽहं विधरणी इति।। तां त्वा घृतस्य धारया यजे सꣳराधनीमहꣳ स्वाहा।।१।।

Whoever may wish, 'I would attain something great!' in the northern course of the sun, on an auspicious day of the half month of the waxing moon, having performed the Upasad ceremony for twelve days, having collected in a dish of the wood of the sacred fig-tree (*udumbara*), or in a cup, all sorts of herbs including fruits, having swept around, having smeared around, having built up a fire, having strewn it around, having prepared the melted butter according to rule, having compounded the mixed potion under a male star, he makes an oblation, saying :—

'However many gods in you, All-knower, adversely slay desires of a person,

To them participation I here offer! Let them, pleased, please me with all desires! Hail!

Whoever lays herself adverse, and says, "I the deposer am!"

To you, O such appeasing one, with stream of ghee I sacrifice. Hail!'

ज्येष्ठाय स्वाहा श्रेष्ठाय स्वाहेत्यग्नौ हुत्वा मन्थे सꣳस्रवमवनयति प्राणाय स्वाहा वसिष्ठायै स्वाहेत्यग्नौ हुत्वा मन्थे सꣳस्रवमवनयति वाचे प्रतिष्ठायै स्वाहेत्यग्नौ हुत्वा मन्थे सꣳस्रवमवनयति चक्षुषे स्वाहा संपदे स्वाहेत्यग्नौ हुत्वा मन्थे सꣳस्रवमवनयति श्रोत्राय स्वाहाऽयतनाय स्वाहेत्यग्नौ हुत्वा मन्थे सꣳस्रवमवनयति मनसे स्वाहा प्रजात्यै स्वाहेत्यग्नौ हुत्वा मन्थे सꣳस्रवमवनयति रेतसे स्वाहेत्यग्नौ हुत्वा मन्थे सꣳस्रवमवनयति।।२।।

'To the chiefest, hail! To the best, hail!' he makes an oblation in the fire, and pours off the remainder in the mixed potion. A Hail to breath (*prāṇa*).

'To the most excellent, hail!' he makes an oblation in the fire and pours off the remainder in the mixed potion. A Hail to speech!

'To the firm basis, hail!'— he makes an oblation in the fire and pours off the remainder in the mixed potion. A Hail to the eye!

'To attainment, hail!' he makes an oblation in the fire and pours off the remainder in the mixed potion. A Hail to the ear!

'To the abode, hail!'—he makes an oblation in the fire and pours off the remainder in the mixed potion. A Hail to the mind!

'To procreation, hail!'—he makes an oblation in the fire and pours off the remainder in the mixed potion. A Hail to the semen!

Thus he makes an oblation in the fire and pours off the remainder in the mixed potion.

अग्नये स्वाहेत्यग्नौ हुत्वा मन्थे सꣳस्रवमवनयति सोमाय स्वाहेत्यग्नौ हुत्वा मन्थे सꣳस्रवमवनयति भूः स्वाहेत्यग्नौ हुत्वा मन्थे सꣳस्रवमवनयति भुवः स्वाहेत्यग्नौ हुत्वा मन्थे सꣳस्रवमवनयति स्वः स्वाहेत्यग्नौ हुत्वा मन्थे सꣳस्रवमवनयति भूर्भुवः स्वः स्वाहेत्यग्नौ हुत्वा मन्थे सꣳस्रवमवनयति ब्रह्मणे स्वाहेत्यग्नौ हुत्वा मन्थे सꣳस्रवमवनयति क्षत्राय स्वाहेत्यग्नौ हुत्वा मन्थे सꣳस्रवमवनयति भूताय स्वाहेत्यग्नौ हुत्वा मन्थे सꣳस्रवमवनयति भविष्यते स्वाहेत्यग्नौ हुत्वा मन्थे सꣳस्रवमवनयति विश्वाय स्वाहेत्यग्नौ हुत्वा मन्थे सꣳस्रवमवनयति सर्वाय स्वाहेत्यग्नौ हुत्वा मन्थे सꣳस्रवमवनयति प्रजापते स्वाहेत्यग्नौ हुत्वा मन्थे सꣳस्रवमवनयति।।३।।

'To Agni (fire), hail!'—he makes an oblation in the fire and pours off the remainder in the mixed potion.

'To Soma, hail!' —he make an oblation in the fire and pours off the remainder in the mixed potion.

'O Earth (*bhūr*), hail!' —he makes an oblation in the fire and pours off the remainder in the mixed potion.

'O Atmosphere (*bhuvas*), hail!' —he makes an oblation in the fire and pours off the remainder in the mixed potion.

'O Sky (*svar*), hail!' —he makes an oblation in the fire and pours off the remainder in the mixed potion.

'O Earth, Atmosphere, and Sky, hail!' —he makes an oblation in the fire and pours off the remainder in the mixed potion.

'To the Brahmanhood, hail!' —he makes an oblation in the fire and pours off the remainder in the mixed potion.

'To the Kṣatrahood, hail!' —he makes an oblation in the fire and pours off the remainder in the mixed potion.

'To the past, hail!' —he makes an oblation in the fire and pours off the remainder in the mixed potion.

'To the future, hail!' —he makes an oblation in the fire and pours off the remainder in the mixed potion.

'To everything, hail!' —he makes an oblation in the fire and pours off the remainder in the mixed potion.

'To the All, hail!' —he makes an oblation in the fire and pours off the remainder in the mixed potion.

'To Prajāpati, hail!' —he makes an oblation in the fire and pours off the remainder in the mixed potion.

अथैनमभिमृशति भ्रमदसि ज्वलदसि पूर्णमसि प्रस्तब्धमस्येकसभमसि हिंकृतमसि हिङ्क्रियमाणमस्युद्गीथमस्युद्गीयमानमसि श्रावितमसि प्रत्याश्रावितमस्यार्द्रे संदीप्तमसि विभूरसि प्रभूरस्यन्नमसि ज्योतिरसि निधनमसि संवर्गोऽसीति।।४।।

Then he touches it, saying : 'You are the moving. You are the glowing. You are the full. You are the steadfast. You are the sole resort. You are the sound *hiṅ*. You are the Loud Chant (*udgītha*). You are the chanting. You are that which is proclaimed. You are that which is proclaimed in the antiphon. You are the flaming in the moist. You are the pervading. You are surpassing. You are food. You are light. You are destruction. You are the despoiler.'

अथैनमुद्यच्छत्यामꣳस्यामꣳहि ते महि हि राजेशानोऽधिपतिः स माꣳराजेशानोऽधिपतिं करोत्विति॥५॥

Then he raises it, saying : 'You think. Think of your greatness! He is, indeed, king and ruler and overlord. Let the king and ruler make me overlord.'

अथैनमाचामति तत्सवितुर्वरेण्यं मधु वाता ऋतायते मधु क्षरन्ति सिन्धवः माध्वीर्नः सन्त्वोषधीर्भूः स्वाहा, भर्गो देवस्य धीमहि मधु नक्तमुतोषसो मधुमत्पार्थिवꣳरजः मधु द्यौरस्तु नः पिता भुवः स्वाहा, धियो यो नः प्रयोदयान्मधुमान्नो वनस्पतिर्मधुमाँ ३ अस्तु सूर्यः माधवीर्गावो भवन्तु नः स्वः स्वाहेति सर्वां च सावित्रीमन्वाह सर्वाश्च मधुमतीरहमेवेदꣳ सर्वं भूयासं भूर्भुवः स्वः स्वाहेत्यन्तत आचम्य पाणी प्रक्षाल्य जघनेनाग्निं प्राक्शिराः संविशति प्रातरादित्यमुपतिष्ठते दिशामेकपुण्डरीकमस्यहं मनुष्याणामेकापुण्डरीकं भूयासमिति यथेतमेत्य जघनेनाग्निमासानो वꣳशं जपति॥६॥

Then he takes a sip, saying :—

'On this choice [glory] of Savitā—this sweetness, winds for pious man—

This sweetness, too, the streams pour forth. Sweet-filled for us let be the herbs!

To Earth (*bhūr*), hail!

[On this choice] glory of the god let us meditate.' Sweet be the night and morning glows! Sweet be the atmosphere of earth!

And sweet the Heaven-father (*dyaus pitā*) be to us! To Atmosphere (*bhuvas*), hail!

And may he himself inspire our thoughts! The tree be full of sweet for us! And let the sun be full of sweet! Sweet-filled the cows become for us! To the Sky (*svar*), hail!'

He repeats all the Sāvitrī Hymn and all the 'Sweet-verses,' and says : 'May I indeed become this world-all! O Earth (*bhūr*) and Atmosphere (*bhuvas*) and Sky (*svar*)! Hail!'

Finally, having taken a sip, having washed his hands, he lies down behind the fire, head eastward. In the morning he worships the sun, and says : 'Of the quarters of heaven you are the one lotus-flower! May I of men become the one lotus-flower!'

Then he goes back the same way that he came, and seated behind the fire, mutters the Line of Tradition (*vaṁśa*).

तꣳहैतमुद्दालक आरुणिर्वाजसनेनाय याज्ञवल्क्यायान्तेवासिन उक्त्वोवाचापि य एनꣳशुष्के स्थाणौ निषिञ्चेज्जायेरञ्छाखाः प्ररोहेयुः पलाशानीति॥७॥

This, indeed, did Uddālaka Āruṇi tell to his pupil Vājasaneya Yājñavalkya, and say : 'Even if one should pour this on a dry stump, branches would be produced and leaves would spring forth.'

एतमु हैव वाजसनेयो याज्ञवल्क्यो मधुकाय पैङ्ग्यायान्तेवासिन उक्त्वोवाचापि य एनं शुष्के स्थाणौ निषिञ्चेज्जायेरञ्छाखाः प्ररोहेयुः पलाशानीति॥८॥

This, indeed, did Vājasaneya Yājñavalkya tell to his pupil Madhuka Paiṅgya, and say : 'Even if one should pour this on a dry stump, branches would be produced and leaves would spring forth.

एतमु हैव मधुकः पैङ्ग्यश्चूलाय भागवित्तयेऽन्तेवासिन उक्त्वोवाचापि य एनं शुष्के स्थाणौ निषिञ्चेज्जायेरञ्छाखाः प्ररोहेयुः पलाशानीति॥९॥

This, indeed, did Madhuka Paiṅgya tell to his pupil Cūla Bhāgavitti, and say : 'Even if one should pour this on a dry stump, branches would be produced and leaves would spring forth.'

एतमु हैव चलो भागवित्तिर्जानकय आयस्थूणायान्तेवासिन उक्त्वोवाचापि य एनं शुष्के स्थाणौ निषिञ्चेज्जायेरञ्छाखाः प्ररोहेयुः पलाशानीति॥१०॥

This, indeed, did Cūla Bhāgavitti tell to his pupil Jānaki Āyasthūṇa, and say : 'Even if one should pour this on a dry stump, branches would be produced and leaves would spring forth.'

एतमु हैव जानकिरायस्थूणः सत्यकामाय जाबालायान्तेवासिन उक्त्वोवाचापि य एनं शुष्के स्थाणौ निषिञ्चेज्जायेरञ्छाखाः प्ररोहेयुः पलाशानीति॥११॥

This, indeed, did Jānaki Āyasthūṇa tell to his pupil Satyakāma Jābāla, and say : 'Even if one should pour this on a dry stump, branches would be produced and leaves would spring forth.'

एतमु हैव सत्यकामो जाबालोऽन्तेवासिभ्य उक्त्वोवाचापि य एनं शुष्के स्थाणौ निषिञ्चेज्जायेरञ्छाखाः प्ररोहेयुः पलाशानीति तमेतन्नापुत्राय वानन्तेवासिने वा ब्रूयात्॥१२॥

This, indeed, did Satyakāma Jābāla tell to his pupils, and say : 'Even if one should pour this on a dry stump, branches would be produced and leaves would spring forth.'

One should not tell this to one who is not a son or to one who is not a pupil.

चतुरौदुम्बरो भवत्यौदुम्बरः स्रुव औदुम्बरश्चमस औदुम्बर इध्म औदुम्बर्या उपमन्थन्यौ दश ग्राम्याणि धान्यानि भवन्ति व्रीहियवास्तिलमाषा अणुप्रियङ्गवो गोधूमाश्च मसूराश्च खल्वाश्च खलकुलाश्च तान् पिष्टान्दधनि मधुनि घृत उपसिञ्चत्याज्यस्य जुहोति॥१३॥

Fourfold is the wood of the sacred fig-tree [in the ceremony] : the spoon (*sruva*) is of the wood of the sacred fig-tree; the cup is of the wood of the sacred fig-tree; the fuel is of the wood of the sacred fig-tree; the two mixing-sticks are of the wood of the sacred fig-tree. There are ten cultivated grains [used] : rice and barley, sesamum and beans, millet and panic, and wheat, and lentils, and pulse, and vetches. These, when they have been ground, one sprinkles with curdled milk, honey, and ghee; and one makes an oblation of melted butter.

चतुर्थं ब्राह्मणम्

In this Brāhmaṇa, the reproduction process, the basis of the world of living-organisms, is highlighted. According to the Ṛṣi, this whole universe is like offering or full of offerings, therefore the reproduction process that always maintains the dynamicity of the cycle of this universe is also a part and parcel of the offerings which should be properly administered. This part therefore is worth understanding and practising by taking in consideration the reproduction process also a kind of offering.

एषां वै भूतानां पृथिवी रसः पृथिव्या आपोऽपामोषधय ओषधीनां पुष्पाणि पुष्पाणां फलानि फलानां पुरुषः पुरुषस्य रेतः॥१॥

[Incantations and ceremonies for procreation]

Verily, of created things here earth is the essence; of earth, water; of water, plants; of plants, flowers; of flowers, fruits; of fruits, man (*puruṣa*); of man, semen.

स ह प्रजापतिरीक्षांचक्रे हन्तास्मै प्रतिष्ठां कल्पयानीति स स्त्रियꣳ ससृजे ताꣳसृष्ट्वाऽध उपासत तस्मात्स्त्रियमध उपासीत स एतं प्राञ्चं ग्रावणमात्मन एव समुदपारयत्तेनैनामभ्यसृजत्॥२॥

Prajāpati ('Lord of creatures') bethought himself : 'Come, let me provide him a firm basis!' So he created woman. When he had created her, he revered her below. Therefore one should revere woman below. He stretched out for himself that stone which projects. With that he impregnated her.

The Ṛṣi while describing the components of the reproduction offering giving birth to the divine man says–

तस्या वेदिरुपस्थो लोमानि बर्हिश्चर्माधिषवणे समिद्धो मध्यतस्तौ मुष्कौ स यावान् ह वै वाजपेयेन यजमानस्य लोको भवति तावानस्य लोको भवति य एवं विद्वानधोपहासं चरत्यासाꣳ स्त्रीणाꣳसुकृतं वृङ्क्तेऽथ य इदमविद्वानधोपहासं चरत्यस्य स्त्रियः सुकृतं वृञ्जते॥३॥

Her lap is a sacrificial altar; her hairs, the sacrificial grass; her skin, the soma-press. The two labia of the vulva are the fire in the middle. Verily, indeed, as great as in the world of him who sacrifices with the Vājapeya ('Strength-libation') sacrifice, so great is the world of him who practises sexual intercourse, knowing this; he turns the good deeds of women to himself. But he who practises sexual intercourse without knowing this—women turn his good deeds unto themselves.

[The person who engages him in cohesion abiding by the prescribed rules in order to fulfill the necessity of reproduction after having a knowledge of this reproduction offering, usually attains the fruit of such offering but the man not able to control his lust if engages him in the cohesion, the rules are infringed and he thus losses the fruit of his deed.]

एतद्ध स्म वै तद्विद्वानुद्दालक आरुणिराहैतद्ध स्म वै तद्विद्वान्नाको मौद्गल्य आहैतद्ध स्म वै तद्विद्वान्कुमारहारित आह बहवो मर्या ब्राह्मणायना निरिन्द्रिया विसुकृतोऽस्माल्लोकात्प्रयन्ति य इदमविद्वाꣳसोऽधोपहासं चरन्तीति बहु वा इदꣳ सुप्तस्य वा जाग्रतो वा रेतः स्कन्दति॥४॥

तदभिमृशेदनु वा मन्त्रयेत यन्मेऽद्य रेतः पृथिवीमस्कान्त्सीद्यदोषधीरप्यसरद्यदप इदमहं तद्रेत आददे पुनर्मामैत्विन्द्रियं पुनस्तेजः पुनर्भगः पुनरग्निर्धिष्ण्या यथास्थानं कल्पन्तामित्यनामिकाङ्गुष्ठाभ्यामादायन्तरेण स्तनौ वा भ्रुवौ वा निमृज्यात्॥५॥

This, verily, indeed, it was that Uddālaka Āruṇi knew when he said :—

This, verily, indeed, it was that Kumārahārita knew when he said : 'Many mortal men, Brāhmaṇas by descent, go forth from this world, impotent and devoid of merit, namely those who practise sexual intercourse without knowing this.'

[If] even this much semen is spilled, whether of one asleep or of one awake,

then he should touch it, or [without touching] repeat :—

'What semen has of mine to earth been spit now,

Whatever to herb has flowed, whatever to water—

This very semen I reclaim! Again to me let vigor come! Again, my strength; again, my glow! Again the altars and the fire be found in their accustomed place!'

Having spoken thus, he should take it with ring-finger and thumb, and rub it on between his breasts or his eye-brows.

अथ यद्युतक आत्मानं पश्येत्तदभिमन्त्रयेत मयि ते इन्द्रियं यशो द्रविणꣳ सुकृतमिति श्रीर्ह वा एषां स्त्रीणां यन्मलोद्वासास्तस्मान्मलोद्वाससं यशस्विनीमभिक्रम्योपमन्त्रयेत॥६॥

Now, if one should see himself in water, he should recite over it the formula : 'In me be vigor, power, beauty, wealth, merit!'

This, verily, indeed, is loveliness among women : when she has removed the clothes of her impurity. Therefore when she has removed the clothes of her impurity and is beautiful, one should approach and invite her.

सा चेदस्मै न दद्यात्काममेनामवक्रीणीयात् सा चेदस्मै नैव दद्यात्काममगेनां यष्ट्या वा पाणिना वोपहत्यतिक्रामेदिन्द्रियेण ते यशसा यश आदद इत्ययशा एव भवति॥७॥

If she should not grant him his desire, he should bribe her. If she still does not grant him his desire, he should hit her with a stick or with his hand, and overcome her, saying : 'With power, with glory I take away your glory!' Thus she becomes inglorious.

सा चेदस्मै दद्यादिन्द्रियेण ते यशसा यश आदधामीति यशस्विनावेव भवतः॥८॥

If she should yield to him, he says : 'With power, with glory I give you glory!' Thus they two become glorious.

स यामिच्छेत्कामयेत मेति तस्यामर्थं निष्ठाय मुखेन मुखꣳ सधायोपस्थमस्या अभिमृश्य जपेदङ्गादात्संभवसि हृदयादधि जायसे। स त्वमङ्गकषायोऽसि दिग्धाविद्धामिव मादयेमाममूं मयीति॥९॥

The woman whom one may desire with the thought, 'May she enjoy love with me!' after inserting the member in her, joining mouth with mouth, and stoking her lap, he should mutter :—

'You that from every limb are come, that from the heart are generate,

You are the essence of the limbs! Distract this woman here in me, as if by poisoned arrow pierced!'

अथ यामिच्छेन्न गर्भं दधीतेति तस्यामर्थं निष्ठाय मुखेन मुखꣳ संधायाभिप्राण्यापान्यादिन्द्रियेण ते रेतसा रेत आदद इत्यरेता एव भवति॥१०॥

Now, the woman whom one may desire with the thought, 'may she not conceive offspring!' —after inserting the member in her and joining mouth with mouth, he should first inhale, then exhale, and say : 'With power, with semen, I reclaim the semen from you!' Thus she comes to be without seed.

अथ यामिच्छेद्दधीतेति तस्यामर्थं निष्ठायं मुखेन मुखꣳ संधायाभिप्राण्यापान्यादिन्द्रियेण ते रेतसा रेत आदधामीति गर्भिण्येव भवति॥११॥

Now, the woman whom one may desire with the thought, 'May she conceive!' —after inserting the member in her and joining mouth with mouth, he should first exhale, then inhale, and say : 'With power, with semen, I deposit semen in you!' Thus she becomes pregnant.

[In the above hymns, first breathing and then breathing-in is suggested for non-conceiving and first breathing-in and then breathing is suggested for conceiving. It seems that the teachers perhaps would have made their pupils to exercise the same during ancient period.]

अथ यस्य जायायै जारः स्यात्तं चेद् द्विष्यादामपात्रेऽग्निमुपसमाधाय प्रतिलोमꣳ शरबर्हिस्तीर्त्वा तस्मिन्नेताः शरभृष्टीः प्रतिलोमाः सर्पिषाक्ता जुहुयान्मम समिद्धेऽहौषीः प्राणापानौ त आददेऽसाविति मम समिद्धेऽहौषीः पुत्रपशूꣳस्त आददेऽसावीति मम समिद्धेहौषीरिष्टासुकृते त आददेऽसाविति मम समिद्धेऽहौषीराशापराकाशौ त आददेऽसाविति। स एव एष निरिन्द्रियो विसकृतोऽस्माल्लोकात्प्रैति यमेवंविद्ब्राह्मणः शपति तस्मादेवंविच्छ्रोत्रियस्य दारेण नोपहासमिच्छेदुत ह्येवंवित्परो भवति॥१२॥

Now, if one's wife have a paramour, and she hates him, let him put fire in an unannealed vessel, spread out a row of reed arrows in inverse order, and therein sacrifice in inverse order those reed arrows, their heads smeared with ghee, saying :—

'You have made a libation in my fire! I take away your in-breath and out-breath (*prāṇāpānau*)—you, so-and-so!

You have made a libation in my fire! I take away your sons and cattle—you, so-and-so!

You have made a libation in my fire! I take away your sacrifices and meritorious deeds—you, so-and-so!

You have made a libation in my fire! I take away your hope and expectation—you, so-and-so!'

Verily, he whom a Brāhmaṇa who knows this curses—he departs from this world impotent and devoid of merit. Therefore one should not desire dalliance with the spouse of a person learned in sacred lore (*śrotriya*) who knows this, for indeed he who knows this becomes superior.

अथ यस्य जायामार्तवं विन्देत्त्र्यहं कंसेन पिबेदहतवासा नैनां वृषलो न वृषल्युपहन्यात्त्रिरात्रान्त आप्लुत्य व्रीहीनवघोतयेत्।।१३।।

Now, when the monthly sickness comes upon anyone's wife, for three days she should not drink from a metal cup, nor put on fresh clothes. Neither a low-caste man nor a low-caste woman should touch her. At the end of the three nights she should bathe and should have rice threshed.

[The woman should avoid from excess heat and cold as also labour in course of menstruation so that the physical energy could properly clear the menstrual flow. Balanced diet and movements should also be followed. On expiry of three days, she may start her common routine.]

स य इच्छेत्पुत्रो मे शुक्लो जायेत वेदमनुब्रुवीत सर्वमायुरियादिति क्षीरौदनं पाचयित्वा सर्पिष्मन्तमश्नीयातामीश्वरौ जनयितवै।।१४।।

In case one wishes, 'that a white son be born to me! that he be able to repeat a Veda! that he attain the full length of life!' —they two should have rice cooked with milk and should eat it prepared with ghee. They two are likely to beget [him].

अथ य इच्छेत्पुत्रो मे कपिलः पिङ्गलो जायेत द्वौ वेदावनुब्रुवीत सर्वमायुरियादिति दध्योदनं पाचयित्वा सर्पिष्मन्तमश्नीयातामीश्वरौ जनयितवै।।१५।।

Now, in case one wishes, 'That a tawny son with reddish-brown eyes be born to me! that he be able to recite two Vedas! that he attain the full length of life!' they two should have rice cooked with sour milk and should eat it prepared with ghee. They two are likely to beget [him].

अथ य इच्छेत्पुत्रो मे श्यामो लोहिताक्षो जायेत त्रीन्वेदाननुब्रुवीत सर्वमायुरियादित्युदौदनं पाचयित्वा सर्पिष्मन्तमश्नीयातामीश्वरौ जनयितवै।।१६।।

Now, in case one wishes, 'That a swarthy son with red eyes be born to me! that he be able to repeat three Vedas! that hc attain the full length of life!' —they two should have rice boiled with water and should eat it prepared with ghee. They two are likely to beget [him].

अथ य इच्छेद्दुहिता मे पण्डिता जायेत सर्वमायुरियादिति तिलौदनं पाचयित्वा सर्पिष्मन्तमश्नीयातामीश्वरौ जनयितवै।।१७।।

Now, in case one wishes, 'That a learned (*paṇḍita*) daughter be born to me! that she attain the full length of life!' —they two should have rice boiled with sesame and should eat it prepared with ghee. They two are likely to beget [her].

अथ य इच्छेत्पुत्रो मे पण्डितो विगीतः समितिंगमः शुश्रूषितां वाचं भाषिता जायेत सर्वान्वेदाननुब्रुवीत सर्वमायुरियादिति मांसौदनं पाचयित्वा सर्पिष्मन्तमश्नीयातामीश्वरौ जनयितवै औक्षेण वार्षभेण वा।।१८।।

Now, in case one wishes, 'That a son, learned, famed, a frequenter of council-assemblies, a speaker of discourse desired to be heard, be born to me! that he be able to repeat all the Vedas! that he attain the full length of life!' —they two should have rice boiled with meat and should eat it prepared with ghee. They two are likely to beget [him], with meat, either veal or beef.

अथाभिप्रातरेव स्थालीपाकावृताज्यं चेष्टित्वा स्थालीपाकस्योपघातं जुहोत्यग्नये स्वाहानुमतये स्वाहा देवाय सवित्रे सत्यप्रसवाय स्वाहेति हुत्वोद्धृत्य प्राश्नाति प्राश्येतरस्याः प्रयच्छति प्रक्षाल्य पाणी उदपात्रं पूरयित्वा तेनैनां त्रिरभ्युक्षत्युत्तिष्ठातो विश्वावसोऽन्यामिच्छ प्रपूर्व्यां सं जायां पत्या सहेति॥१९॥

Now, toward morning, having prepared melted butter in the manner of the Sthālīpāka, he takes of the Sthālīpāka and makes a libation, saying : 'To Agni, hail! To Anumati, hail! To the god Savitri ('Enlivener,' the Sun), whose is true procreation (*satya-prasava*), hail!' Having made the libation, he takes and eats. Having eaten, he offers to the other [i.e. to her]. Having washed his hands, he fills a vessel with water and therewith sprinkles her thrice, saying :—

'Arise from hence, Viśvavasu!

Some other choicer maiden seek!

This wife together with her lord—'

अथैनामभिपद्यतेऽमोहमस्मि सा त्वꣳ सा त्वमस्यमोऽहं सामाहमस्मि ऋक्त्वं द्यौरहं पृथिवी त्वं तावेहि सꣳरभावहै सह रेतो दधावहै पुꣳसे पुत्राय वित्तय इति॥२०॥

Then he comes to her and says :—

'This man (*ama*) am I; that woman (*sā*), you! That woman, you; this man am I! I am the Sāman; you, the Ṛg! I am the heaven; you, the earth!

Come, let us two together clasp! together let us semen mix, a male, a son for to procure!'

अथास्या ऊरु विहापयति विजिहीथां द्यावापृथिवी इति तस्यामर्थं निष्ठाय मुखेन मुखꣳ संधाय त्रिरेनामुलोमामनुमार्ष्टि विष्णुर्योनिं कल्पयतु त्वष्टा रूपाणि पिꣳशतु। आसिञ्चतु प्रजापतिर्धाता गर्भं दधातु ते। गर्भं धेहि सिनीवालि गर्भं धेहि पृथुष्टुके। गर्भं ते अश्विनौ देवावाधत्तां पुष्करस्रजौ॥२१॥

Then he spreads apart her thighs, saying : 'Spread yourselves apart, heaven and earth!' Inserting the member in her and joining mouth with mouth, he strokes her three times as the hair lies, saying :—

'Let Viṣṇu make the womb prepared!

Let Tvaṣṭri shape the various forms!

Prajāpati—let him pour in!

Let Dhātṛi place the germ for you!

O Sinīvālī, give the germ;

O give the germ, you broad-tressed dame!

Let the Twin Gods implace you germ—

The Aśvins, crowned with lotus-wreaths!

हिरण्मयी अरणी याभ्यां निर्मन्थतामश्विनौ तं ते गर्भं हवामहे दशमे मासि सूतये यथाऽग्निगर्भा पृथिवी यथा द्यौरिन्द्रेण गर्भिणी। वायुर्दिशां यथा गर्भं एवं गर्भं दधामि तेऽसाविति॥२२॥

With twain attrition-sticks of gold the Aśvin Twins twirl forth a flame;

This such a germ we beg for you, in the tenth month to be brought forth.

As earth contains the germ of Fire (*agni*), as heaven is pregnant with the Storm (*indra*),

As of the points of Wind (*vāyu*) is germ, even so a germ I place in you, So-and-so!'

सोष्यन्तीमद्भिरभ्युक्षति यथा वायुः पुष्करिणीꣳसमिङ्गयति सर्वतः। एवा ते गर्भ एजतु सहावैतु जरायुणा। इन्द्रस्यायं व्रजः कृतः सार्गलः सपरिश्रयः। तमिन्द्र निर्जहि गर्भेण सावराꣳसहेति॥२३॥

When she is about to bring forth, he sprinkles her with water, saying :—

'Like as the wind does agitate a lotus-pond on every side, so also let your fetus stir.

Let it come with its chorion.

This fold of Indra's has been made with barricade enclosed around.

O Indra, cause him to come forth—the after-birth along with babe!'

जातेऽग्निमुपसमाधायाङ्क आधाय कꣳसे पृषदाज्यꣳ सनीय पृषदाज्यस्योपघातं जुहोत्यस्मिन्सहस्रं पुष्यासमेधमानः स्वे गृहे। अस्योपसंद्यां मा च्छैत्सीत् प्रजया च पशुभिश्च स्वाहा। मयि प्राणꣳस्त्वयि मनसा जुहोमि स्वाहा। यत्कर्मणात्यरीरिचं यद्वा न्यूनमिहाकरम्। अग्निष्टत्स्विष्टकृद्विद्वान्स्विष्टꣳ सुहुतं करोतु नः स्वाहेति॥२४॥

When [the son] is born, he [i.e. the father] builds up a fire, places him on his lap, mingles ghee and coagulated milk in a metal dish, and makes an oblation, ladling out of the mingled ghee and coagulated milk, and saying :—

'In this son may I be increased, and have a thousand in mine house!

May nothing rob his retinue of offspring or of animals! Hail!

This vital powers (*prāṇa*) which are in me, my mind, I offer in you. Hail!

What in this rite I overdid, or what I have here scanty made—

Let Agni, wise, the Prosperer, make fit and good our sacrifice! Hail!'

अथास्य दक्षिणं कर्णमभिनिधाय वाग्वागिति त्रिरथ दधिमधुघृतꣳ संनीयानन्तर्हितेन जातरूपेण प्राशयति। भूस्ते दधामि भुवस्ते दधामि स्वस्ते दधामि भूर्भुवः स्वः सर्वं त्वयि दधामीति॥२५॥

Then he draws down to the child's right ear and says 'Speech! Speech!' three times. Then he mingles coagulated milk, honey, and ghee and feeds [his son] out of a gold [spoon] which is not placed within [with mouth], saying : 'I place in you *Bhūr*! I place in you *Bhuvas*! I place in your *Svar*! *Bhūr, Bhuvas, Svar* — everything I place in you!'

अथास्य नाम करोति वेदोऽसीति तदस्य तद्गुह्यमेव नाम भवति॥२६॥

Then he gives him a name, saying : 'You are Veda.' So this becomes his secret name.

अथौनं मात्रे प्रदाय स्तनं प्रयच्छति यस्ते स्तनः शशयो यो मयोभूर्यो रत्नधा वसुविद्यः सुदत्रः।
येन विश्वा पुष्यसि वार्याणि सरस्वति तमिह धातवे करिति॥२७॥

Then he presents him to the mother and offers the breast, saying :—

'Your breast which is unfailing and refreshing,
Wealth-bearer, treasure-finder, rich bestower,
With which you nourish all things esteemed—
Give it here, O Sarasvatī, to suck from.'

अथास्य मातरमभिमन्त्रयते इलासि मैत्रावरुणी वीरे वीरमजीजनत्। सा त्वां वीरवती भव यास्मान् वीरवतोऽकरदिति। तं वा एतमाहुरतिपिता बताभूरतिपितामहो बताभूः परमां बत काष्ठां प्रापच्छ्रिया यशसा ब्रह्मवर्चसेन य एवंविदो ब्राह्मणस्य पुत्रो जायत इति॥२८॥

Then he addresses the child's mother :—

'You are Ilā, of the lineage of Mitra and Varuṇa!
O heroine! She has borne a hero!
Continue to be such a woman abounding in heroes—
She who has made us abound in a hero!'

Of such a son, verily, they say : 'Ah, you have gone beyond your father! Ah, you have gone beyond your grandfather!'

Ah, he reaches the highest pinnacle of splendour, glory and sacred knowledge who is born as the son of a Brahman who knows this!

पञ्चमं ब्राह्मणम्

The tradition of teachers in the Vājasaneyi school

अथ वꣳशः पौतिमाषीपुत्रः कात्यायनीपुत्रात् कात्यायनीपुत्रो गौतमीपुत्राद्गौतमीपुत्रो भारद्वाजीपुत्राद्भारद्वाजीपुत्रः पाराशरीपुत्रत्पाराशरीपुत्र औपस्वस्तीपुत्रादौपस्वस्तीपुत्रः पाराशरीपुत्रात् पाराशरीपुत्रः कात्यायनीपुत्रात्कात्यायनीपुत्रः कौशिकीपुत्रात्कौशिकीपुत्र आलम्बीपुत्राच्च वैयाघ्रपदीपुत्राच्च वैयाघ्रपदीपुत्रः काण्वीपुत्राच्च कापीपुत्राच्च कापीपुत्रः॥१॥

आत्रेयीपुत्रादात्रेयीपुत्रो गौतमीपुत्राद्गौतमीपुत्रो भारद्वाजीपुत्राद्भारद्वाजीपुत्रः पाराशरीपुत्रात्पाराशरीपुत्रो वात्सीपुत्राद्वात्सीपुत्रः पाराशरीपुत्रात्पाराशरीपुत्रो वार्कारुणीपुत्राद्वार्कारुणीपुत्रो वार्कारुणीपुत्राद्वार्कारुणीपुत्र आर्तभागीपुत्रादार्तभागीपुत्रः शौङ्गीपुत्राच्छौङ्गीपुत्रः सांकृतीपुत्रात्सांकृतीपुत्र आलम्बायनीपुत्रादालम्बायनीपुत्र आलम्बीपुत्रादालम्बीपुत्रो जायन्तीपुत्राज्जायन्तीपुत्रो माण्डूकायनीपुत्रान्माण्डूकायनीपुत्रो माण्डूकीपुत्राद्भालुकीपुत्रः शाण्डिलीपुत्राच्छाण्डिलीपुत्रो राथीतरीपुत्राद्राथीतरीपुत्रो भालुकीपुत्राद्भालुकीपुत्रः क्रौञ्चिकीपुत्राभ्यां

क्रौञ्चिकीपुत्रौ वैदभृतोपुत्राद्वैदभृतीपुत्रः कार्शकेयीपुत्रात्कार्शकेयीपुत्रः प्राचीनयोगीपुत्रात्प्राचीनयोगीपुत्रः सांजीवीपुत्रात्सांजीवीपुत्रः प्राश्नीपुत्रादसुरिवासिनः प्राश्नीपुत्र आसुरायणादासुरायण आसुरेरासुरिः॥२॥

याज्ञवल्क्याद्याज्ञवल्क्य उद्दालकादुद्दालकोऽरुणादरुण उपवेशेरुपवेशिः कुश्रेः कुश्रिर्वाजश्रवसो वाजश्रवा जिह्वावतो बाध्योगाज्जिह्वावान्बाध्योगोऽसिताद्वार्षगणादसितो वार्षगणो हरितात्कश्यपाद्धरितः कश्यपः शिल्पात्कश्यपाच्छिल्पः कश्यपः कश्यपान्नैध्रुवेः कश्यपो नैध्रुविर्वाचो वागम्भिण्या अम्भिण्यादित्यादादित्यानीमानि शुल्कानि यजुंषि वाजसनेयेन याज्ञवल्क्येनाख्यायन्ते॥३॥

Now the progeny of the saints well-known to Brahma is described. The son of Pautimāṣi obtained education from the son of Katyāyanī, the son of Katyāyanī from the son of Gautamī, the son of Gautamī from the son of Bhāradvāji, the son of Bhāradvāji from the son of Pārāśarī, the son of Pārāśarī from Aupasvasti, the son of Aupasvasti from the son of Pārāśarī, the son of Pārāśarī from the son of Kātyāyanī, the son of Kātyāyanī from the son of Kauśiki, the son of Kauśiki from the son of Ālambi and the son of Vaiyāghrapadi, the son of Vaiyāghrapadi from the son of Kānvī and the son of Kāpī. The son of Kāpī from the son of Ātreyī, the son of Ātreyī from the son of Gautamī, the son of Gautamī from the son of Bhāradvājī, the son of Bhāradvājī from the son of Pārāśarī, the son of Pārāśarī from the son of Vātsī, the son of Vātsī from the son of Pārāśarī, the son of Pārāśarī from the son of Vārkāruṇī, the son of Vārkāruṇī from the son of Ārtabhāgī, the son of Ārtabhāgī from the son of Sauṅgi, the son of Sauṅgi from the son of Sānkṛti, the son of Sānkṛti from the son of Ālambayānī, the son of Ālambayānī from the son of Ālambī, the son of Ālambī from the son of Jāyantī, the son of Jāyantī from the son of Māṇḍūkāyanī, the son of Māṇḍūkāyanī from the son of Māṇḍūkī, the son of Māṇḍūkī from the son of Śāṇḍilī, the son of Śāṇḍilī from the son of Rāthītarī, the son of Rāthītarī from the son of Bhāluki, the son of Bhāluki from the two sons of the Krauñciki, the two sons of Krauñciki from the son of Vaidabhṛtī, the son of Vaidabhṛtī from the son of Kārśakeyī, the son of Kārśakeyī from Prācīnayogī, Prācīnayogī from the son of Sāñjivī, the son of Sāñjivī from the son of Āsurivāsī Prāṣṇī, the son of Prāṣṇī from Āsurāyaṇa and the Āsurāyaṇa obtained the education from the Āsuri. Thereafter Āsuri obtained education from Yājñavalkya, Yājñavalkya from Uddālaka, Uddālaka from Āruṇa, Āruṇa from Upaveśi, Upaveśi from Kusri, Kusri from Vājaśravas, Vājaśravas from Jihvāvān Bādhyoga, Jihvāvān Bādhyoga from Asita Vārṣagaṇa, Asita Vārṣagaṇa from Hārita Kaśyapa, Hārita Kaśyapa from Śilpa Kaśyapa, Śilpa Kaśyapa from Naidhruvi Kaśyapa, Naidhruvi Kaśyapa from Vāk, Vāk from Ambhiṇī and Ambhiṇī obtained education from Āditya. The hymns of Śukla Yajurveda conferred by Āditya too are propagated by Vājasaneya Yājñavalkya.

समानसा सांजीवीपुत्रात्सांजीवीपुत्रो माण्डूकायनेर्माण्डूकायनिर्माण्डव्यान्माण्डव्यः कौत्सात्कौत्सो माहित्थेर्माहित्थिर्वामकक्षा-यणाद्वामकक्षायणः शाण्डिल्याच्छण्डिल्यो वात्स्याद्वात्स्यः कुश्रेः कुश्रिर्यज्ञवचसो राजस्तम्बायनाद्यज्ञवचा राजस्तम्बायनस्तुरात्कावषेयात्तुरः कावषेयः प्रजापतेः प्रजापतिर्ब्रह्मणो ब्रह्म स्वयंभु ब्रह्मणे नमः॥४॥

Only a clan is existed till Sānjīvi. Thereafter the son of Sānjīvi obtained knowledge from Māṇḍūkāyani, Māṇḍūkāyani from Māṇḍavya, Māṇḍavya from Kautsa, Kautsa from Mahitthi, Mahitthi from Vāmakakṣāyaṇa, Vāmakakṣāyaṇa from Śāṇḍilya, Śāṇḍilya from Vātsya, Vātsya from Kusri, Kusri from Yajñavacas Rājastambāyana, Yajñavacas Rājastambāyana from Turakāvaṣeya, Turakāvaṣeya from Prajāpati and Prajāpati obtained knowledge from the Brahma. Brahma is the Self-existent (*svayam-bhū*). Adoration to Brahma!

॥शान्तिपाठः॥

ॐ पूर्णमदः पूणमिदं......इति शान्तिः॥

॥ इति बृहदारण्यकोपनिषत्समाप्ता॥

***

11. ŚVETĀŚVATARA-UPANIṢAD

श्वेताश्वतरोपनिषद्

This Upaniṣad falls under the branch of Kṛṣṇa Yajurveda. There are six chapters in it. The ground reason for the genesis of this world has been asked in its first chapter. It has been described here that in case, the position looms in dark even if a long discussion made, the creation on the basis of perception through meditation is a cycle and a particular flow respectively. The root element, the necessity to know the element of supreme soul, its significance and the nature of living-organism, the nature and the god as also the supreme soul, the enjoyer and the enjoyable etc. divisions has been clearly discussed. Finally a penance by reciting Oṁ has been suggested. It has been said that the Oṁ like the oil makes apparent the element of supreme soul residing in the region of heart. The second chapter pertains to the 'Dhyāna Yoga' (meditation) and the 'Sādhanā' (penance). The significance of meditation has been made properly worth understanding. Its method and procedure, Praṇāyāma (breathing control), the place, etc., rules and the symptoms of progress also made visible in this chapter. Salutation is conveyed to the supreme element by explaining command on the five elements through penance under 'Yoga' and the measures making apparent the element of Brahma from the element of soul. In the third and fourth chapter, the topics like the genesis of the world, the omnipresence of this supreme entity of soul competent to generate, to maintain and to destroy and the significance of reckoning with this has been described. He has been told the greatest, beyond comparison and the minutest, competent to do everything, without the sensory organs still residing in the castle holding the nine doors. To explain easily the position of living soul and the supreme soul, an example of the two words on the same branch has been referred. An impetus is given to know the illusions and their creator and the significance of his knowledge has been elaborated. Finally the creator of illusion has been prayed for emancipation.

In the chapter fifth and the sixth, the eccentricity of the learning, ignorance and the administrator of them *i.e.* the supreme soul has been told and suggestions have been forwarded to follow the knowledge embedded in upaniṣad whose contemplation's lead to this supreme soul. Again the various movements of the living soul according to the deeds performed, uncountable species (Yoni), they obtain has been described alongwith the measures for exonerating from them. The cause for universe has been described the supreme element of soul instead of the inert nature (Prakṛti). The omnipresence and omnipotence of the supreme soul has been proved clearly by suggesting to resort the meditation, worship and the yoga related to knowledge. Finally, an instruction has been given with effect that this learning (Vidyā) should be given only to its eligible person who can follow with letter and spirit.

॥शान्तिपाठः॥

ॐ सह नाववतु। सह नौ भुनक्तु। सह वीर्यं करवावहै।

तेजस्विनावधीतमस्तु ममा विद्विषावहै॥

ॐ शान्तिः शान्तिः शान्तिः॥

Chapter - 1
Conjectures concerning the First Cause

ॐ ब्रह्मवादिनो वदन्ति।

किं कारणं ब्रह्म कुतः स्म जाता जीवाम केन क्व च संप्रतिष्ठाः।

अधिष्ठिताः केन सुखेतरेषु वर्तामहे ब्रह्मविदो व्यवस्थाम्।।१।।

Discourses or Brahman (*brahma-vādin*) say :—

What is the cause? Brahman? Whence are we born?

Whereby do we live? And on what are we established?

Overruled by whom; in pains and pleasures,

Do we live our various conditions, O you theologians (*brahmavid*)?

कालः स्वभावो नियतिर्यदृच्छा भूतानि योनिः पुरुष इति चिन्त्यम्।

संयोग एषां न त्वात्मभावादात्माप्यनीशः सुखदुःखहेतोः।।२।।

Time (*kāla*), or inherent nature (*sva-bhāva*), or necessity (*niyati*), or chance (*yadṛcchā*),

Or the elements (*bhūta*), or a [female] womb (*yoni*), or a [male] person (*puruṣa*) are to be considered [as the cause];

Not a combination of these, because of the existence of the soul (*ātman*).

The soul certainly is impotent over the cause of pleasure and pain.

ते ध्यानयोगानुगता अपश्यन्देवात्मशक्तिं स्वगुणैर्निगूढाम्।

यः कारणानि निखिलानि तानि कालात्मयुक्तान्यधितिष्ठत्येकः।।३।।

Those who followed after meditation (*dhyāna*) and abstraction (*yoga*)

Saw the self-power (*ātma-śakti*) of God (*deva*) hidden in his own qualities (*guṇa*).

He is the One who rules over all these causes, from 'time' to 'the soul'.

[The recognition of Brahman cannot be possible on mere discussion but it is the sensitivity of the soul under the meditation that penetrates the cover of properties and it only enables to realise the supreme element.]

तमेकनेमिं त्रिवृतं षोडशान्तं शतार्धारं विंशतिप्रत्यराभिः।

अष्टकैः षड्भिर्विश्वरूपैकपाशं त्रिमार्गभेदं द्विनिमित्तैकमोहम्।।४।।

We understand him [as a wheel] with one felly, with a triple tire,

With sixteen end-parts, fifty spokes, twenty counter-spokes,

With six sets of eights, whose one rope is manifold,

Which has three different paths, whose one illusion (*moha*) has two conditioning causes.

[The complete pattern of arrangement to this universe has been described in the from of a wheel, the nemi is meant for the periphery (the Prakṛti) that fastens the wheel and three circles are meant for the three properties *i.e.* Satva, Rajas and Tamas. Sixteen arts are the joint of the periphery from the beginning to the end. These have been described in the fourth and fifth hymn under the sixth question as contemplated in the 'Praśnopaniṣad'. The fifty columns (Arc) are the contradiction, powerlessness, satiation etc. fifty prefixes. Similarly, the attitudes of heart (feeling) has been classified into fifty forms and the twenty other auxiliary columns are the ten sensory organs, five subjects and five breathings. It is not clear that which has been said 'Aṣṭaka' in the wheel. Further, each out of these six have eight kinds which are the nature, the marrow (Dhātu) in the body, axioms, spirits, divine species and the specific merits. The three routes are performing great deeds, committing crimes and acquiring knowledge while two objectives are the good deeds and the evils respectively. All these are revolving around the nucleus of attachment.]

पञ्चस्रोतोम्बुं पञ्चयोन्युग्रवक्त्रां पञ्चप्राणोर्मिं पञ्चबुद्ध्यादिमूलाम्।
पञ्चावर्तां पञ्चदु:खौघवेगां पञ्चाशद्भेदां पञ्चपर्वामधीम:।।५।।

We understand him as a river of five streams from five sources, impetuous and crooked, whose waves are the five vital breaths, whose original source is fivefold perception (*buddhi*),

With five whirlpools, an impetuous flood of fivefold misery, divided into five distresses, with five branches.

सर्वाजीवे सर्वसंस्थे बृहन्ते तस्मिन्हंसो भ्राम्यते ब्रह्मचक्रे।
पृथगात्मानं प्रेरितारं च मत्वा जुष्टस्ततस्तेनामृतत्वमेति।।६।।

In this which vital all things, which appears in all things, the Great—

In this Brahma-wheel the soul (*haṁsa*) flutters about,

Thinking that itself (*ātmānam*) and the Actuator are different.

When favoured by Him, it attains immortality.

उद्गीतमेतत्परमं तु ब्रह्म तस्मिंस्त्रयं सुप्रतिष्ठाक्षरं च।
अत्रान्तरं ब्रह्मविदो विदित्वा लीना ब्रह्मणि तत्परा योनिमुक्ता:।।७।।

This has been sung as the supreme Brahma.

In it there is a triad. It is the firm support, the Imperishable.

By knowing what is therein, Brahma-knowers become merged in Brahma, intent thereon, liberated from the womb [i.e. from rebirth].

संयुक्तमेतत्क्षरमक्षरं च व्यक्ताव्यक्तं भरते विश्वमीश:।
अनीशश्चात्मा बुध्यते भोक्तृभावाज्ज्ञात्वा देवं मुच्यते सर्वपाशै:।।८।।

That which is joined together as perishable and imperishable,

As manifest and unmanifest— the Lord (*īśa*, Potentate) supports it all.

Now, without the Lord the soul (*ātman*) is bound, because of being an enjoyer;

By known God (*deva*) one is released from all fetters.

ज्ञाज्ञौ द्वावजावीशनीशावजा ह्येका भोक्तृभोगार्थयुक्ता।

अनन्तश्चात्मा विश्वरूपो ह्यकर्ता त्रयं यदा विन्दते ब्रह्ममेतत्॥९॥

There are two unborn ones : the knowing [Lord] and the unknowing [individual soul], the Omnipotent and the impotent.

She [i.e. nature, Prakṛti], too, is unborn, who is connected with the enjoyer and objects of enjoyment.

Now, the soul (*ātman*) is infinite, universal, inactive.

When one finds out this triad, that is Brahman.

क्षरं प्रधानममृताक्षरं हरः क्षरात्मानावीशते देव एकः।

तस्याभिध्यानाद्योजनात्तत्त्वभावाद्भूयश्चान्ते विश्वमायानिवृत्तिः॥१०॥

What is perishable, is Primary Matter (*pradhāna*). What is immortal and imperishable, is Hara (the 'Bearer,' the soul).

Over both the perishable and the soul the One God (*deva*) rules.

By meditation upon Him, by union with Him, and by entering into His being.

More and more, there is finally cessation from every illusion (*māyā-nivṛtti*).

ज्ञात्वा देवं सर्वपाशापहानिः क्षीणैः क्लेशैर्जन्ममृत्युप्रहाणिः।

तस्याभिध्यानात्तृतीयं देहभेदे विश्वैश्वर्यं केवल आप्तकामः॥११॥

By knowing God (*deva*), one becomes free from all bonds, with distresses destroyed, there is cessation of birth and death.

By meditating upon Him there is a third stage at the dissolution of the body, even universal lordship; being absolute (*kevala*), his desire is satisfied.

एतज्ज्ञेयं नित्यमेवात्मसंस्थं नातः परं वेदितव्यं हि किंचित्।

भोक्ता भोग्यं प्रेरितारं च मत्वा सर्वं प्रोक्तं त्रिविधं ब्रह्ममेतत्॥१२॥

That Eternal should be known as present in the self (*ātmasaṁstha*). Truly there is nothing higher than that to be known.

When one recognizes the enjoyer, the object of enjoyment and the universal Actuator, all has been said. This is the three fold Brahman.

वह्नेर्यथा योनिगतस्य मूर्तिर्न दृश्यते नैव च लिङ्गनाशः।

स भूय एवेन्धनयोनिगृह्यस्तद्वोभयं वै प्रणवेन देहे॥१३॥

[Made manifest like latent fire, by the exercise of meditation]

As the material form (*mūrti*) of fire when latent in its source [i.e. the fire-wood]

Is not perceived—and yet there is no envanishment of its subtile form (*liṅga*)—

But may be caught again by means of the drill in its source,

So, verily, both [the universal and the individual Brahma] are [to be found] in the body by the use of *Oṁ*.

स्वदेहमरणिं कृत्वा प्रणवं चोत्तरारणिम्। ध्याननिर्मथनाभ्यासाद्देवं पश्येन्निगूढवत्।।१४।।

By making one's own body the lower friction-stick and the syllable *Oṁ* the upper friction-stick,

By practising the friction of meditation (*dhyāna*), one may see the God (*deva*) who is hidden, as it were.

तिलेषु तैलं दधनीव सर्पिरापः स्रोतस्स्वरणीषु चाग्निः।

एवमात्मात्मनि गृह्यतेऽसौ सत्येनैनं तपसा योऽनुपश्यति।।१५।।

As oil in sesame seeds, as butter in cream, as water in river-beds, and as fire in the friction-sticks, so is the Soul (Ātman) apprehended in one's own soul, if one looks for Him with true austerity (*tapas*).

सर्वव्यापिनमात्मानं क्षीरे सर्पिरिवार्पितम्। आत्मविद्यातपोमूलं तद्ब्रह्मोपनिषत्परं तद्ब्रह्मोपनिषत्परमिति।।१६।।

The Soul (Ātman), which pervades all things as butter is contained in cream,

which is rooted in self-knowledge and austerity—This is Brahman, the highest mystic doctrine (*upaniṣad*)!

This is Brahman, the highest mystic doctrine!

Chapter - 2

Invocation to the god of inspiration for inspiration and self-control

युञ्जानः प्रथमं मनस्तत्त्वाय सविता धियः। अग्नेर्ज्योतिर्निचाय्य पृथिव्या अध्याभरत्।।१।।

God Savitṛ (the Inspirer), first controlling mind and thought for truth,

discerned the light of Agni (Fire) and brought it out of the earth.

युक्तेन मनसा वयं देवस्य सवितुः सवे। सुवर्गेयाय शक्त्या।।२।।

With mind controlled, we are in the inspiration of the god Savitṛ, for heaven and strength.

युक्त्वाय मनसा देवान्सुवर्यतो धिया दिवम्।

बृहज्ज्योतिः करिष्यतः सविता प्रसुवाति तान्।।३।।

With mind having controlled the powers that unto bright heaven through thought do go,

May Savitṛ inspire them, that they may make a mighty light!

युञ्जते मन उत युञ्जते धियो विप्रा विप्रस्य बृहतो विपश्चितः।

विहोत्रा दधे वयुनाविदेक इन्मही देवस्य सवितुः परिष्टुतिः।।४।।

They are the sages among the great wise sages who control their mind and control their thoughts.

The One who knows the rules has arranged the priestly functions.

Mighty is the chorus-praise of the god Savitṛ.

युजे वां ब्रह्म पूर्व्यं नमोभिर्विश्लोक एतु पथ्येव सूराः।

शृण्वन्तु विश्वे अमृतस्य पुत्रा आ ये धामानि दिव्यानि तस्थुः॥५॥

I join your ancient prayer (*brahma-pūrvyam*) with adorations! My verses go forth like suns upon their course.

All the sons of the immortal listen, even those who ascended to heavenly stations!

[Owing to excessive attachment with the defects of the mind and the wit, the persons of this universe move on beggary of the mind and in ego. This procedure of salutation is an exercise of support for the desired aim. When the mind and the wit of the devotee are sacred and enjoined with the great aim, his dynamicity and the power both are extended. How can the mind be cooled down and make sacred, this process has been made clear in the successive hymns.]

अग्निर्यत्राभिमथ्यते वायुर्यत्राभियुज्यते। सोमो यत्रातिरिच्यते तत्र संजायते मनः॥६॥

[Spiritual significance of the sacrificial worship]

Where the fire is being kindled, where the wind is applied thereto, where the Soma overflows, there is inspiration (*manas*) born.

सवित्रा प्रसवेन जुषेत ब्रह्म पूर्व्यम्। तत्र योनिं कृ णवसे नहि ते पूर्वमक्षिपत्॥७॥

With Savitṛ as the inspirer one should delight in the ancient prayer (*brahma-pūrvyam*).

If there you make your source, the former [work] besmears you not.

त्रिरुन्नतं स्थाप्य समं शरीरं हृदीन्द्रियाणि मनसा संनिरुध्य।

ब्रह्मोडुपेन प्रतरेत विद्वान्स्रोतांसि सर्वाणि भयावहानि॥८॥

[Rules and results of Yoga]

Holding his body steady with the three [upper parts] erect, and causing the sense with the mind to enter into the heart,

A wise man with the Brahma-boat should cross over all the fear-bringing streams.

[All kinds of passions are originated from the heart. In case, these ambitions are inserted in the heart, the pleasure of all senses can be perceived within heart and a man needn't to wander to and fro.]

प्राणान्प्रपीड्येह स युक्तचेष्टः क्षीणे प्राणे नासिकयोच्छ्वसीत।

दुष्टाश्वयुक्तमिव वाहमेनं विद्वान्मनो धारयेताप्रमत्तः॥९॥

Having repressed his breathings here in the body, and having his movements checked, one should breathe through his nostrils with diminished breath.

Like that chariot yoked with vicious horses, his mind the wise man should restrain undistractedly.

समे शुचौ शर्करावह्निवालुकाविवर्जिते शब्दजलाश्रयादिभिः।

मनोनुकूले न तु चक्षुपीडने गुहानिवातश्रयणे प्रयोजयेत्॥१०॥

In a clean level spot, free from pebbles, fire and gravel, by the sound of water and other propinquities favourable to thought, not offensive to the eye in a hidden retreat protected from the wind, one should practise Yoga.

नीहारधूमार्कानलानिलानां खद्योतविद्युत्स्फटिकशशीनाम्।

एतानि रूपाणि पुरः सराणि ब्रह्मण्यभिव्यक्तिकराणि योगे॥११॥

Fog, smoke, sun, fire, wind, fire-flies, lightning, a crystal, a moon—These are the preliminary appearances, which produce the mainfestation of Brahma in Yoga.

पृथ्व्याप्यतेजोऽनिलखे समुत्थिते पञ्चात्मके योगगुणे प्रवृत्ते।

न तस्य रोगो न जरा न मृत्युः प्राप्तस्य योगाग्निमयं शरीरम्॥१२॥

When the fivefold quality of Yoga has been produced, arising from earth, water, fire, air and space,

No sickness, no old age, no death has he who has obtained a body made out of the fire of Yoga.

[On attaining this stage, he neither suffers from ailment nor the old age as also he seldom meet to the premature death. The word 'Pṛthvyāpyatejo' as used in this hymn is the application of Sanskrit elocution, otherwise the word 'Pṛthvyāptejo' more suitable in place of it.]

लघुत्वमारोग्यमलोलुपत्वं वर्णप्रसादं स्वरसौष्ठवं च।

गन्धः शुभो मूत्रपुरीषमल्पं योगप्रवृत्तिं प्रथमां वदन्ति॥१३॥

Lightness, healthiness, steadiness, clearness of countenance and pleasantness of voice, sweetness of odour, and scanty excretions—

These, they say, are the first stage in the progress of Yoga.

यथैव बिम्बं मृदयोपलिप्तं तेजोमयं भ्राजते तत्सुधान्तम्।

तद्वात्मतत्त्वं प्रसमीक्ष्य देही एकः कृतार्थो भवति वीतशोकः॥१४॥

Even as a mirror stained by dust shines brilliantly when it has been cleansed, so the embodied one, on seeing the nature of the Soul (Ātman), becomes unitary, his end attained, from sorrow freed.

यदात्मतत्त्वेन तु ब्रह्मतत्त्वं दीपोपमेनेह युक्तः प्रपश्येत्।

अजं ध्रुवं सर्वतत्त्वैर्विशुद्धं ज्ञात्वा देवं मुच्यते सर्वपाशैः॥१५॥

When with the nature of the self, as with a lamp, a practiser of Yoga beholds here the nature of Brahman, unborn, steadfast, from every nature free— by knowing God (*deva*) one is released from all fetters!

एषो ह देवः प्रदिशोऽनु सर्वाः पूर्वो ह जातः स उ गर्भे अन्तः।

एषो ह देवः प्रदिशोऽनु सर्वा पूर्वो ह जातः स उ गर्भे अन्तः।

स एव जातः स जनिष्यमाणः प्रत्यङ्जनास्तिष्ठति सर्वतोमुखः॥१६॥

That God faces all the quarters of heaven.

Aforetime was he born, and he it is within the womb.

He has been born forth. He will be born.

He stands opposite creatures, having his face in all directions.

यो देवोऽग्नौ योऽप्सु यो विश्वं भुवनमाविवेश।

य ओषधीषु यो वनस्पतिषु तस्मै देवाय नमो नमः॥१७॥

The God who is in fire, who is in water, who has entered into the whole world, who is in plants, who is in trees—to that God be adoration!— yea, be adoration!

Chapter - 3

The One God identified with Rudra

य एको जालवानीशत ईशनीभिः सर्वांल्लोकानीशत ईशनीभिः।

य एवैक उद्भवे संभवे च य एतद्विदुरमृतास्ते भवन्ति॥१॥

The One spreader of the net, who rules with his ruling powers, who rules all the worlds with his ruling powers,

The one who alone stands in their arising and in their continued existence—they who know That, become immortal.

एको हि रुद्रो न द्वितीयाय तस्थुर्य इमाँल्लोकानीशत ईशनीभिः।

प्रत्यङ्जनास्तिष्ठति संचुकोपान्तकाले संसृज्य विश्वा भुवनानि गोपाः॥२॥

For truly, Rudra (the Terrible) is the One—they stand not for a second—who rules all the worlds with his ruling powers.

He stands opposite creatures. He, the Protector, after creating all being, merges them together at the end of time.

विश्वतश्चक्षुरुत विश्वतोमुखो विश्वतोबाहुरुत विश्वतस्पात्।

संबाहुभ्यां धमति सं पतत्रैर्द्यावाभूमी जनयन्देव एकः॥३॥

Having an eye on every side and a face on every side, having an arm on every side and a foot on every side,

The One God forges together with hands, with wings, creating the heaven and the earth.

यो देवानां प्रभवश्चोद्भवश्च विश्वाधिपो रुद्रो महर्षिः।

हिरण्यगर्भं जनयामास पूर्वं स नो बुद्ध्या शुभया संयुनक्तु॥४॥

He who is the source and origin of the gods, the rulers of all, Rudra, the great seer,

Who of old created the Golden Germ (Hiraṇyagarbha)— may he endow us with clear intellect!

या ते रुद्रा शिवा तनूरघोराऽपापकाशिनी।

तया नस्तनुवा शंतमया गिरिशन्ताभिचाकशीहि॥५॥

[Prayers from the Scriptures unto Rudra for favour]

The form of your, O Rudra, which is kindly (*śiva*), unterrifying, revealing no evil—

With that most benign form to us appear, O dweller among the mountains!

यामिषुं गिरिशन्त हस्ते बिभर्ष्यस्तवे।

शिवां गिरित्र तां कुरु मा हिंसी: पुरुषं जगत्॥६॥

O dweller among the mountains, the arrow which you hold in your hand to throw make kindly (*śiva*), O mountain-protector! do not injure man or beast!

ततः परं ब्रह्म परं बृहन्तं यथा निकायं सर्वभूतेषु गूढम्।

विश्वस्यैकं परिवेष्टितारमीशं तं ज्ञात्वाऽमृता भवन्ति॥७॥

Higher than this is Brahma. The Supreme, the Great, Hidden in all things, body by body,

The One embracer of the universe— by knowing Him as Lord (*īśa*) men become immortal.

वेदाहमेतं पुरुषं महान्तमादित्यवर्णं तमसः परस्तात्।

तमेव विदित्वातिमृत्युमेति नान्यः पन्था विद्यतेऽयनाय॥८॥

I know this mighty Person (Puruṣa) of the colour of the sun, beyond darkness.

Only by knowing Him does one pass over death. There is no other path for going there.

यस्मात्परं नापरमस्ति किंचिद्यस्मान्नाणीयो न ज्यायोऽस्ति कश्चित्।

वृक्ष इव स्तब्धो दिवि तिष्ठत्येकस्तेनेदं पूर्णं पुरुषेण सर्वम्॥९॥

Than whom there is naught else higher, than whom there is naught smaller, naught greater,

The One stands like a tree established in heaven. By Him, the Person, this whole world is filled.

ततो यदुत्तरतरं तदरूपमनामयम्।

य एतद्विदुरमृतास्ते भवन्त्यथेतरे दुःखमेवापियन्ति॥१०॥

That which is beyond this world, is without form and without ill.

They who know That, become immortal; But others go only to sorrow.

सर्वाननशिरोग्रीवः सर्वभूतगुहाशयः। सर्वव्यापी स भगवान् तस्मात्सर्वगतः शिवः॥११॥

Who is the face, the head, the neck of all. Who dwells in the heart of all things, He is All-pervading and bountiful (*maghavan*); Therefore omnipresent, and kindly (*śiva*).

महान्प्रभूर्वै पुरुषः सत्त्वस्यैष प्रवर्तकः। सुनिर्मलामिमां प्राप्तिमीशानो ज्योतिरव्ययः।।१२।।

A mighty lord (*prabhu*) is the Person (Puruṣa), the instigator of the highest being (*sattva*) unto the purest attainment. He is the ruler, a light and imperishable.

अङ्गुष्ठमात्रः पुरुषोऽन्तरात्मा सदा जनानां हृदये संनिविष्टः।

हृदा मनीषी मनसाभिक्लृप्तो य एतद्विदुरमृतास्ते भवन्ति।।१३।।

A Person of the measure of a thumb is the inner soul (*antarātman*), Ever seated in the heart of creatures. He is framed by the heart, by the thought, by the mind. They who know That, become immortal.

[In 'Bhagavadgītā', the size of living soul has also contemplated as small as the thumb in the heart of all living-organisms. According to physiology, it is the same as the pacemaker is existed in the heart. The scientists also accept this fact that the root vibrations of the heart are arisen from that space maker.]

सहस्रशीर्षा पुरुषः सहस्राक्षः सहस्रपात्। स भूमिं विश्वतो वृत्वाऽत्यतिष्ठद्दशाङ्गुलम्।।१४।।

That *Puruṣa* has a thousand heads, a thousand eyes, a thousand feet;

He surrounds the earth on all sides, and stands ten fingers breadth beyond.

पुरुष एवेदं सर्वं यद्भूतं यच्च भव्यम्। उतामृतत्वस्येशानो यदन्नेनातिरोहति।।१५।।

Puruṣa is in truth this All, what has been and what yet shall be;

Lord too, of immortality which waxes greater still by food.

[The second line is variously explained. The meaning of the words seems to be: he is lord of immortality or the immortal world of the Gods, which grows greater by food, that is, by the sacrifical offerings of men. According to Sāyaṇa: he is the lord or distributer of immortality because he becomes the visible world in order that living beings may obtain the fruits of their actions and gain *mokṣa* or final liberation from their bonds; 'he is also the lord of immortality; for he mounts beyond (his own condition) for the food (of living beings).']

सर्वतः पाणिपादं तत्सर्वतोऽक्षिशिरोमुखम्। सर्वतः श्रुतिमल्लोके सर्वमावृत्य तिष्ठति।।१६।।

It has a hand and foot on every side, on every side an eye and head and face,

It has an ear everywhere in the world. It stands encompassing all.

सर्वेन्द्रियगुणाभासं सर्वेन्द्रियविवर्जितम्। सर्वस्य प्रभुमीशानं सर्वस्य शरणं बृहत्।।१७।।

Seeming to possess the quality (*guṇa*) of all the senses, it is devoid of all the senses!

The lord (*prabhu*), the ruler of all, the great shelter of all—

नवद्वारे पुरे देही हंसो लेलायते बहिः। वशी सर्वस्य लोकस्य स्थावरस्य चरस्य च।।१८।।

Though in the nine-gated city embodied, back and forth to the external hovers the soul (*haṁsa*),

The Controller of the whole world, both the stationary and the moving.

अपाणिपादो जवनो ग्रहीता पश्यत्यचक्षुः स शृणोत्यकर्णः।

स वेत्ति वेद्यं न च तस्यास्ति वेत्ता तमाहुरग्र्यं पुरुषं महान्तम्॥१९॥

Without foot or hand, he is swift and a seizer!

He sees without eye; he hears without ear!

He knows whatever is to be known; him there is none who knows!

Men call him the Great primeval Person.

अणोरणीयान्महतो महीयानात्मा गुहायां निहितोऽस्य जन्तोः।

तमक्रतुं पश्यति वीतशोको धातुः प्रसादान्महिमानमीशम्॥२०॥

More minute than the minute, greater than the great,

Is the Soul (Ātman) that is set in the heart of a creature here.

One beholds Him as being without the active will, and becomes freed from sorrow—

When through the grace (*prasāda*) of the Creator, he sees the Lord (*īśa*) and his greatness.

वेदाहमेतमजरं पुराणं सर्वात्मानं सर्वगतं विभुत्वात्।

जन्मविरोधं प्रवदन्ति यस्य ब्रह्मवादिनो हि प्रवदन्ति नित्यम्॥२१॥

I know this undecaying, primeval

Soul of all, present in everything through immanence,

Of whose exemption from birth they speak—

For the expounders of Brahma (*brahma-vādin*) speak of Him as eternal.

Chapter -4

The One God of the manifold world

य एकोऽवर्णो बहुधा शक्तियोगाद्वर्णाननेकान्निहितार्थो दधाति।

वि चैति चान्ते विश्वमादौ स देवः स नो बुद्ध्या शुभया संयुनक्तु॥१॥

The One who, himself without colour, by the manifold application of his power (*śakti-yoga*) distributes many colours in his hidden purpose,

And into whom, its end and its beginning, the whole world dissolves—He is God (*deva*)! May He endow us with clear intellect!

तदेवाग्निस्तदादित्यस्तद्वायुस्तदु चन्द्रमाः। तदेव शुक्रं तद्ब्रह्म तदापस्तत्प्रजापतिः॥२॥

That surely is Agni (fire). That is Āditya (the sun). That is Vāyu (the wind), and That is the moon. That surely is the pure. That is Brahma. That is the waters. That is Prajāpati (Lord of Creation).

त्वं स्त्री त्वं पुमानसि त्वं कुमार उत वा कुमारी।
त्वं जीर्णो दण्डेन वंचसि त्वं जातो भवसि विश्वतोमुखः।।३।।

You are the female, you are the male. You are the youth and the maiden too.

You totter as an old man with a staff. Being born, you become facing in every direction.

नीलः पतङ्गो हरितो लोहिताक्षस्तडिद्गर्भ ऋतवः समुद्राः।
अनादिमत्त्वं विभुत्वेन वर्तसे यतो जातानि भुवनानि विश्वा।।४।।

You are the dark-blue bird and the green [parrot] with red eyes,

You are pregnant with lightning as cloud. You are the seasons and the seas.

Having no beginning, you do abide with immanence, wherefrom all beings are born.

[Some scholars had derivated the meaning for the terms 'Nīlaḥ Pataṅgaḥ' and 'Haritaḥ Lohitākṣaḥ' as the blue colour bee and the parrot which have green complexion and red eyes but the wide factors of nature has been described in this hymn as also in the successive hymns and the meaning as an insect and the words are not consistent herein. As the sun has a meaning as Pataṅga and the sky is blue, therefore the meaning as sun, the green colour as vegetation and the red-eyed as the planet or fire is more appropriate.]

[The universal and the individual soul]

अजामेकां लोहितशुक्लकृष्णां बह्वीः प्रजाः सृजमानां सरूपाः।
अजो ह्येको जुषमाणोऽनुशेते जहात्येनां भुक्तभोगामजोऽन्यः।।५।।

With the one unborn female, red, white and black, who produces many creatures which are alike in form.

There lies the one unborn male taking his delight. Another unborn male leaves her with whom he has had his delight.

द्वा सुपर्णा सयुजा सखाया समानं वृक्षं परिषस्वजाते।
तयोरन्यः पिप्पलं स्वाद्वत्त्यनश्नन्नन्योऽभिचाकशीति।।६।।

Two birds, of pretty wings, closely-knit friends, clasp close the self-same tree.

Of these two, the one eats sweet fruit; The other looks on without eating.

[Here, two birds indicate the living soul and the supreme soul, they resort to a single tree (body) and always live jointly and amicably. The one bird (the living soul) consumes the fruits of that tree (fruit of deed) but the other bird (the supreme soul) does not consumes the fruit and only observes them.]

समाने वृक्षे पुरुषो निमग्नोऽनीशया शोचति मुह्यमानः।
जुष्टं यदा पश्यत्यन्यमीशमस्य महिमानमिति वीतशोकः।।७।।

On the self-same tree a person, sunken, grieves for his impotence, deluded;

When he sees the other, the lord (*īśa*), contented, and his greatness, he becomes freed from sorrow.

[The ignorant soul in the illusion of a manifold universe]

ऋचो अक्षरे परमे व्योमन्यस्मिन्देवा अधि विश्वे निषेदुः।
यस्तन्न वेद किमृता करिष्यति य इत्तद्विदुस्त इमे समासते॥८॥

That syllable of the sacred hymn (*ṛc,* Ṛgveda) whereon, in highest heaven,
All the gods are seated—
Of what avail is the sacred hymn (*ṛc*, Ṛgveda) to him who knows not That?
They, indeed, who know That, are here assembled.

[One who have no realisation of that knowledge can do nothing as a result of their study on Vedas while the persons who have realised that supreme soul always are existed blissfully in him.]

छन्दांसि यज्ञाः क्रतवो व्रतानि भूतं भव्यं यच्च वेदा वदन्ति।
अस्मान्मायी सृजते विश्वमेतत्तस्मिंश्चान्यो मायया संनिरुद्धः॥९॥

Sacred poetry (*chandas*), the sacrifices, the ceremonies, the ordinances,
The past, the future, and what the Vedas declare—
This whole world the illusion-maker (*māyin*) projects out of this [Brahma].
And in it by illusion (*māyā*) the other is confined.

मायां तु प्रकृतिं विद्यान्मायिनं तं महेश्वरम्। तस्यावयवभूतैस्तु व्याप्तं सर्वमिदं जगत्॥१०॥

Now, one should know that Nature (Prakṛti) is illusion (*māyā*),
And that the Mighty Lord (*maheśvara*) is the illusion-maker (*māyin*).
This whole world is pervaded.
With beings that are parts of Him.

यो योनिं योनिमधितिष्ठत्येको यस्मिन्निदं सं च वि चैति सर्वम्।
तमीशानं वरदं देवमीड्यं निचाय्येमां शान्तिमत्यन्तमेति॥११॥

The One who rules over every single source,
In whom this whole world comes together and dissolves,
The Lord (*īśana*), the blessing-giver, God (*deva*) adorable—
By revering Him one goes for ever to this peace (*śānti*).

[This whole universe merges in him at the time of great devastation (Pralaya) and again originated in multiform at the time of creation.]

यो देवानां प्रभवश्चोद्भवश्च विश्वाधिपो रुद्रो महर्षिः।
हिरण्यगर्भं पश्यत जायमानं स नो बुद्ध्या शुभया संयुनक्तु॥१२॥

He who is the source and origin of the gods,

The ruler of all, Rudra (the Terrible), the great seer,

Who beheld the Golden Germ (Hiraṇyagarbha) when he was born—

May He endow us with clear intellect!

यो देवानामधिपो यस्मिँल्लोका अधिश्रिताः।

य ईशेऽस्य द्विपदश्चतुष्पदः कस्मै देवाय हविषा विधेम॥१३॥

Who is the overlord of the gods, on whom the worlds do rest,

Who is lord of biped and quadruped here—

To what god will we give reverence with oblations?

सूक्ष्मातिसूक्ष्मं कलिलस्य मध्ये विश्वस्य स्रष्टारमनेकरूपम्।

विश्वस्यैकं परिवेष्टितारं ज्ञात्वा शिवं शान्तिमत्यन्तमेति॥१४॥

More minute than the minute, in the midst of confusion the Creator of all, of manifold forms,

The One embracer of the universe—by knowing Him as kindly (*śiva*) one attains peace forever.

स एव काले भुवनस्य गोप्ता विश्वाधिपः सर्वभूतेषु गूढः।

यस्मिन्युक्ता ब्रह्मर्षयो देवताश्च तमेवं ज्ञात्वा मृत्युपाशांश्छिनत्ति॥१५॥

He indeed is the protector of the world in time,

The overlord of all, hidden in all things,

With whom the seers of Brahma and the divinities are joined in union.

By knowing Him thus, one cuts the cords of death.

घृतात्परं मण्डमिवातिसूक्ष्मं ज्ञात्वा शिवं सर्वभूतेषु गूढम्।

विश्वस्यैकं परिवेष्टितारं ज्ञात्वा देवं मुच्यते सर्वपाशैः॥१६॥

By knowing as kindly (*śiva*) Him who is hidden in all things,

Exceedingly fine, like the cream that is finer than butter,

The One embracer of the universe—

By knowing God (*deva*) one is released from all fetters.

एष देवो विश्वकर्मा महात्मा सदा जनानां हृदये संनिविष्टः।

हृदा मनीषा मनसाऽभिक्लृप्तो य एतद्विदुरमृतास्ते भवन्ति॥१७॥

That God, the All-worker, the Great Soul (*mahātman*),

Ever seated in the heart of creatures,

Is framed by the heart, by the thought, by the mind—

They who know That, become immortal.

[This creator of universe and ever-luminating supreme soul is duly existed in the heart of all people. The devotee who realises it by establishing meditation through their heart, wit and mind, always attain immortality.]

यदाऽतमस्तन्न दिवा न रात्रिर्न सन्न चासच्छिव एव केवलः।

तदक्षरं तत्सवितुर्वरेण्यं प्रज्ञा च तस्मात्प्रसृता पुराणी॥१८॥

When there is no darkness, then there is no day or night,

Nor being, nor non-being, only the Kindly One (*śiva*) alone.

That is the Imperishable. 'That [is the] choice [splendour] of Savitṛ (the Sun).'

And from that was primeval Intelligence (*prajñā*) created.

[Only a single benevolent god Śiva is remained when the darkness of ignorance is decayed. There is no distinction remain between a day and a night and neither truth nor fallacy is existed. He is always immortal, worshipped by the sun-god and the perception has been emanated from him.]

नैनमूर्ध्वं न तिर्यञ्चं न मध्ये परिजग्रभत्।

न तस्य प्रतिमा अस्ति यस्य नाम महद्यशः॥१९॥

Not above, not across, nor in the middle has one grasped Him.

There is no likeness of Him whose name is Great Glory (*mahad yaśas*).

न संदृशे तिष्ठति रूपमस्य न चक्षुषा पश्यति कश्चनैनम्।

हृदा हृदिस्थं मनसा य एनमेवं विदुरमृतास्ते भवन्ति॥२०॥

His form is not to be beheld. No one soever sees Him with the eye.

They who thus know Him with heart and mind as abiding in the heart, become immortal.

[Nobody in this universe can see that supreme soul with his material eyes and no complexion of this supreme soul stays before the eyesight. The devotee who realises this supreme soul existing in their heart by virtue of an innocent mind and spiritual feeling, attains the immortality.]

अजात इत्येवं कश्चिद्भीरु प्रतिपद्यते।

रुद्र यत्ते दक्षिणं मुखं तेन मां पाहि नित्यम्॥२१॥

With the thought 'He is eternal!' A certain one in fear approaches.

O Rudra, that face of your which is propitious—with that do you protect me ever!

[You are liberated from the cycle of the birth and the death. If someone who fears of death like me, shelters to you and request for protection through your benevolent complexion (the right mouth), you should honour his request.]

मा नस्तोके तनये मा न आयुषि मा नो गोषु मा नो अश्वेषु रीरिषः।

वीरान्मा नो रुद्र भामितोऽवधीर्हविष्मन्तः सदमित्त्वा हवामहे॥२२॥

Injure us not in child or grandchild, nor in life!

Injure us not in cattle! Injure us not in horses!

Slay not our strong men in anger, O Rudra!

With oblations ever we call upon you.

Chapter - 5

Brahma, the One God of the manifold world

द्वे अक्षरे ब्रह्मपरे त्वनन्ते विद्याविद्ये निहिते यत्र गूढे।

क्षरं त्वविद्यां ह्यमृतं तु विद्या विद्याविद्ये ईशते यस्तु सोऽन्यः॥१॥

In the imperishable, infinite, supreme Brahma are two things;

For therein are knowledge and ignorance placed hidden.

Now ignorance is a thing perishable, but knowledge is a thing immortal.

And He who rules the ignorance and the knowledge is another,

यो योनिं योनिमधितिष्ठत्येको विश्वानि रूपाणि योनीश्च सर्वाः।

ऋषिं प्रसूतं कपिलं यस्तमग्रे ज्ञानैर्बिभर्ति जायमानं च पश्येत्॥२॥

[Even] the One who rules over every single source, all forms and all sources;

Who bears in his thoughts, and beholds when born, that red (*kapila*) seer who was engendered in the beginning.

एकैकं जालं बहुधा विकुर्वन्नस्मिन्क्षेत्रे संहरत्येष देवः।

भूयः सृष्ट्वा पतयस्तथेशः सर्वाधिपत्यं कुरुते महात्मा॥३॥

That God spreads out each single net [of illusion] manifoldy, and draws it together here in the world.

Thus again, having created his Yatis, the Lord (*īśa*), the Great Soul (*mahātman*), exercises universal overlordship.

सर्वा दिश ऊर्ध्वमधश्च तिर्यक्प्रकाशयन्भ्राजते यद्वनड्वान्।

एवं स देवो भगवान्वरेण्यो योनिस्वभावानधितिष्ठत्येकः॥४॥

As the illumining sun shines upon All regions, above, below, and across, So that One God, glorious, adorable,

Rules over whatever creatures are born from a womb.

यच्च स्वभावं पचति विश्वयोनिः पाच्यांश्च सर्वान्परिणामयेद्यः।

सर्वमेतद्विश्वमधितिष्ठत्येको गुणांश्च सर्वान्विनियोजयेद्यः॥५॥

The source of all, who develops his own nature,

Who brings to maturity whatever can be ripened, and who distributes all qualities (*guṇa*)— over this whole world rules the One.

तद्वेदगुह्योपनिषत्सु गूढं तद्ब्रह्मा वेदयते ब्रह्मयोनिम्।
ये पूर्वं देवा ऋषयश्च तद्विदुस्ते तन्मया अमृता वै बभूवु:॥६॥

That which is hidden in the secret of the Vedas, even the Mystic Doctrines (*upaniṣad*)— Brahmā knows That as the source of the sacred word (*brahman*).

The gods and seers of old who knew That, they, [coming to be] of Is nature, verily, have become immortal.

गुणान्वयो य: फलकर्मकर्ता कृतस्य तस्यैव न चोपभोक्ता।
स विश्वरूपस्त्रिगुणस्त्रिवर्त्मा प्राणाधिप: संचरति स्वकर्मभि:॥७॥

Whoever has qualities (*guṇa*, distinctions) is the doer of deeds that bring recompense; and of such action surely he experiences the consequence.

Undergoing all forms, characterized by the three Qualities, treading the three paths, the individual self roams about according to its deeds (*karman*).

अङ्गुष्ठमात्रो रवितुल्यरूप: संकल्पाहंकारसमन्वितो य:।
बुद्धेर्गुणेनात्मगुणेन चैव आराग्रमात्रोऽप्यपरोऽपि दृष्ट:॥८॥

He is of the measure of a thumb, of sun-like appearance, when coupled with conception (*saṁkalpa*) and egoism (*ahaṁkāra*).

But with only the qualities of intellect and of self, the lower [self] appears of the size of the point of an awl.

वालाग्रशतभागस्य शतधा कल्पितस्य च। भागो जीव: स विज्ञेय: स चानन्त्याय कल्पते॥९॥

This living [self] is to be known as a part of the hundredth part of the point of a hair

Subdivided a hundredfold; and yet it partakes of infinity.

[The form of living-organism should be deemed so micro as a hair firstly divided in hundred parts and the resultant part again divided into hundred parts and thus one fraction or the part is equal to the form of that living-organism. However, such a minutest part extended in multiform which cannot be counted.]

नैव स्त्री न पुमानेष न चैवायं नपुंसक:। यद्यच्छरीरमादत्ते तेन तेन स युज्यते॥१०॥

Not female, nor yet male is it; nor yet is this neuter.

Whatever body he take to himself, with that he becomes connected.

संकल्पनस्पर्शनदृष्टिमोहैर्ग्रासांबुवृष्ट्यात्मविवृद्धिजन्म।
कर्मानुगान्यनुक्रमेण देही स्थानेषु रूपाण्यभिसंप्रपद्यते॥११॥

By the delusions (*moha*) of imagination, touch and sight, and by eating, drinking, and impregnation there is a birth and development of the self (*ātman*).

According to his deeds (*karman*) the embodied one successively assumes forms in various conditions.

स्थूलानि सूक्ष्मानि बहूनि चैव रूपाणि देही स्वगुणैर्वृणोति।
क्रियागुणैरात्मगुणैश्च तेषां संयोगहेतुरपरोऽपि दृष्टः॥१२॥

Coarse and fine, many in number, the embodied one chooses forms according to his own qualities.

[Each] subsequent cause of his union with them is seen to be because of the quality of his acts and of himself.

अनाद्यन्तं कलिलस्य मध्ये विश्वस्य स्रष्टारमनेकरूपम्।
विश्वस्यैकं परिवेष्टितारं ज्ञात्वा देवं मुच्यते सर्वपाशैः॥१३॥

[Liberation through knowledge of the One God]

Him who is without beginning and without end, in the midst of confusion, the Creator of all, of manifold form,

The One embracer of the universe—by knowing God (*deva*) one is released from all fetters.

भावग्राह्यमनीडाख्यं भावाभावकरं शिवम्। कलासर्गकरं देवं ये विदुस्ते जहुस्तनुम्॥१४॥

Him who is to be apprehended in existence, who is called 'incorporeal,' the maker of existence (*bhāva*) and non-existence, the kindly one (*śiva*),

God (*deva*), the maker of the creation and its parts— they who know Him, have left the body behind.

Chapter - 6

The One God, Creator and Lord, in and over the world

स्वभावमेके कवयो वदन्ति कालं तथान्ये परिमुह्यमानाः।
देवस्यैष महिमा नु लोके येनेदं भ्राम्यते ब्रह्मचक्रम्॥१॥

Some sages discourse of inherent nature (*sva-bhāva*); others likewise, of time. Deluded men!

It is the greatness of God in the world by which this Brahma-wheel is caused to revolve.

[Some say the nature of mankind a cause of the cycle of birth, Others say the time its cause but all these very far from the reality. Actually, it is the magnificence of that supreme soul by which this cycle of creation is rotated in this world.]

येनावृतं नित्यमिदं हि सर्वं ज्ञः कालकालो गुणी सर्वविद्यः।
तेनेशितं कर्म विवर्तते ह पृथ्व्याप्यतेजोऽनिलखानि चिन्त्यम्॥२॥

He by whom this whole world is constantly enveloped is intelligent, the author of time, possessor of qualities (*guṇin*), omniscient.

Rules over by Him, [his] work (*karman*) revolves—this which is regarded as earth, water, fire, air and space!

तत्कर्म कृत्वा विनिवर्त्य भूयस्तत्त्वस्य तत्त्वेन समेत्य योगम्।

एकेन द्वाभ्यां त्रिभिरष्टभिर्वा कालेन चैवात्मगुणैश्च सूक्ष्मैः॥३॥

He creates this work, and rests again. Having entered intō union (*yoga*) with principle (*tattva*) after principle, with one, with two, with three, or with eight, with time, too, and the subtile qualities of a self—

आरभ्य कर्माणि गुणान्वितानि भावांश्च सर्वान्विनियोजयेद्यः।

तेषामभावे कृतकर्मनाशः कमक्षये याति स तत्त्वतोऽन्यः॥४॥

He begins with works which are connected with qualities (*guṇa*), and distributes all existences (*bhāva*).

In the absence of these [qualities] there is a disappearance of the work that has been done. [Yet] in the destruction of the work he continues essentially other [than it].

[The devotee who initiates the actions covered by the three properties (Guṇa) and dedicates the motivations as also the resultant deeds to the supreme soul, becomes unaffected to those deeds and thus the deeds performed in the previous life also are decayed.]

आदिः स संयोगनिमित्तहेतुः परस्त्रिकालादकलोऽपि दृष्टः।

तं विश्वरूपं भवभूतमीड्यं देवं स्वचित्तस्थमुपास्य पूर्वम्॥५॥

The beginning, the efficient cause of combinations, He is to be seen as beyond the three times (*kāla*), without parts (*a-kala*) too!

Worship Him as the manifold, the origin of all being, the adorable God who abides in one's own thoughts, the primeval.

[That primitive person, the supreme soul have been observed as a cause for combination of the nature with the living-organisms. He is beyond the three times (past, present and future) and sixteen kalās.]

स वृक्षकालाकृतिभिः परोऽन्यो यस्मात्प्रपञ्चः परिवर्ततेऽयम्।

धर्मावहं पापनुदं भगेशं ज्ञात्वात्मस्थममृतं विश्वधाम॥६॥

Higher and other than the world-tree, time, and all forms out of him, from whom this expanse proceeds.

The bringer of right (*dharma*), the remover of evil (*pāpa*), the lord of prosperity—know Him as in one's own self (*ātma-stha*), as the immortal abode of all.

[That supreme soul is beyond and different than the elements motivating to live in illusion, in worldly cycle, under time (Kāla) and in a specific feature.]

तमीश्वराणां परमं महेश्वरं तं देवतानां परमं च दैवतम्।

पतिं पतीनां परमं परस्ताद्विदाम देवं भुवनेशमीड्यम्॥७॥

Him who is the supreme Mighty Lord (*maheśvara*) of lords, the supreme Divinity of divinities,

The supreme Ruler of rulers, paramount, Him let us know as the adorable God, the Lord (*īśa*) of the world.

न तस्य कार्यं करणं च विद्यते न तत्समश्चाभ्यधिकश्च दृश्यते।

परास्य शक्तिर्विविधैव श्रूयते स्वाभाविकी ज्ञानबलक्रिया च॥८॥

No action or organ of his is found; there is not seen his equal, nor a superior.

His high power (*śakti*) is revealed to be various indeed; and innate is the working of his intelligence and strength.

न तस्य कश्चित्पतिरस्ति लोके न चेशिता नैव च तस्य लिङ्गम्।

स कारणं करणाधिपाधिपो न चास्य कश्चिज्जनिता न चाधिपः॥९॥

Of Him there is no ruler in the world, nor lord; nor is there any mark (*liṅga*) of Him.

He is the Cause (*kāraṇa*), lord of the lords of sense-organs. Of Him there is no progenitor, nor lord.

यस्तूर्णपनाभ इव तन्तुभिः प्रधानजैः स्वभावतः।

देव एकः स्वमावृणोति स नो दधातु ब्रह्माव्ययम्॥१०॥

The one God who covers himself, like a spider, with threads produced from Primary Matter (*pradhāna*), according to his own nature (*svabhāvatas*)—may He grant us entrance in Brahman!

एको देवः सर्वभूतेषु गूढः सर्वव्यापी सर्वभूतान्तरात्मा।

कर्माध्यक्षः सर्वभूताधिवासः साक्षी चेता केवलो निर्गुणश्च॥११॥

The one god, hidden in all things, all-pervading, the Inner Soul of all things,

The overseer of deeds (*karman*), in all things abiding, the witness, the sole thinker, devoid of qualities (*nir-guṇa*),

[That alone god resides within all, he is witness to all and further he is sensitive, sacred and beyond the physical properties *i.e.* Sattva, Rajas and Tamas.]

एको वशी निष्क्रियाणां बहूनामेकं बीजं बहुधा यः करोति।

तमात्मस्थं येऽनुपश्यन्ति धीरास्तेषां सुखं शाश्वतं नेतरेषाम्॥१२॥

The one controller of the inactive many, who makes the one seed manifold—

The wise who perceive Him as standing in one's self—they, and no others, have eternal happiness.

[The unique supreme soul, administrator of all who converts a single seat of all inactive living-organisms into varied forms, is seen only by the bold persons by virtue of their perception in the cavity of heart. They only attains ever-lasting pleasure, no body else.]

नित्यो नित्यानां चेतनश्चेतनानामेको बहूनां यो विदधाति कामान्।
तत्कारणं सांख्ययोगाधिगम्यं ज्ञात्वा देवं मुच्यते सर्वपाशैः॥१३॥

Him who is the constant among the inconstant, the intelligent among intelligences,
The One among many, who grants desires,
That Cause, attainable by discrimination and abstraction (*sāṁkhya-yoga*)—
By knowing God, one is released from all fetters!

[The devotee who knows that causative supreme soul by virtue of the perception through 'Sāṁkhya' and 'Yoga' (Jñāna Yoga and Karma Yoga), he is liberated from all ties.]

न तत्र सूर्यो भाति न चन्द्रतारकं नेमा विद्युतो भान्ति कुतोऽयमग्निः।
तमेव भान्तमनुभाति सर्वं तस्य भासा सर्वमिदं विभाति॥१४॥

The sun shines not there, nor the moon and stars; these lightnings shine not, much less this [earthly] fire!

After Him, as He shines, do everything shine. This whole world is illumined with his light.

एको हꣳसो भुवनस्यास्य मध्ये स एवाग्निः सलिले संनिविष्टः।
तमेव विदित्वातिमृत्युमेति नान्यः पन्था विद्यतेऽयनाय॥१५॥

The one soul (*haṁsa*) in the midst of this world—this indeed is the fire which has entered into the ocean.

Only by knowing Him does one pass over death. There is no other path for going there.

[The scientists also accept the fact that the water is originated by the fire and the fire is embedded with the water in the form of 'Vaḍavānala' (sea-fire). For example -

$H_2 + O_2 + \text{Heat} = \text{Water}$

is the formula as per science.]

स विश्वकृद्विश्वविदात्मयोनिर्ज्ञः कालकालो गुणी सर्वविद्यः।
प्रधानक्षेत्रज्ञपतिर्गुणेशः संसारमोक्षस्थितिबन्धहेतुः॥१६॥

He who is the maker of all, the all-knower, self-sourced, intelligent, the author of time, possessor of qualities, omniscient, is the ruler of Primary Matter (*pradhāna*) and of the spirit (*kṣetra-jña*), the lord of qualities (*guṇa*), the cause of reincarnation (*saṁsāra*) and of liberation (*mokṣa*), of continuance and of bondage.

स तन्मयो ह्यमृत ईशसंस्थो ज्ञः सर्वगो भुवनस्यास्य गोप्ता।
य ईशेऽस्य जगतो नित्यमेव नान्यो हेतुर्विद्यत ईशनाय॥१७॥

Consisting of That, immortal, existing as the Lord, intelligent, omnipresent, the guardian of this world, is He who constantly rule this world. There is no other cause found for the ruling.

[He is the supreme soul in the universal form or illuminator of all. He is the standing regulator to this whole universe because no body else is competent to take over the affairs of this universe.]

यो ब्रह्माणं विदधाति पूर्वं यो वै वेदांश्च प्रहिणोति तस्मै।

तꣳ ह देवमात्मबुद्धिप्रकाशं मुमुक्षुर्वै शरणमहं प्रपद्ये॥१८॥

To Him who of old creates Brahmā, and who, verily, delivers to him the Vedas—

To that God, who is lighted by his own intellect, do I, being desirous of liberation, resort as a shelter—

निष्कलं निष्क्रियꣳ शान्त निरवद्यं निरञ्जनम्। अमृतस्य परꣳ सेतुं दग्धेन्धनमिवानलम्॥१९॥

To Him who is without parts, without activity, tranquil (*śānta*), irreproachable, spotless,

The highest bridge of immortality, like a fire with fuel burned.

यदा चर्मवदाकाशं वेष्टयिष्यन्ति मानवा:। तदा देवमविज्ञाय दु:खस्यान्तो भविष्यति॥२०॥

When men shall roll up space as it were a piece of leather,

Then will there be an end of evil apart from knowing God!

[The above hymn conveys the sense that the miseries will absolutely destroy when realisation with the supreme element is made.]

तप: प्रभावाद्देवप्रसादाच्च ब्रह्म ह श्वेताश्वतरोऽथ विद्वान्।

अत्याश्रमिभ्य: परमं पवित्रं प्रोवाच सम्यगृषिसङ्घजुष्टम्॥२१॥

By the efficacy of his austerity and by the grace of God (*deva-prasāda*) the wise Śvetāśvatara in proper manner declared Brahman to the ascetics of the most advanced stage as the supreme means of purification—this which is well-pleasing to the company of seers.

वेदान्ते परमं गुह्यं पुराकल्पे प्रचोदितम्। नाप्रशान्ताय दातव्यं नापुत्रायाशिष्याय वा पुन:॥२२॥

The supreme mystery in the Veda's end (Vedānta), which has been declared in former time,

Should not be given to one not tranquil, nor again to one who is not a son or a pupil.

यस्य देवे परा भक्तिर्यथा देवे तथा गुरौ।

तस्यैते कथिता ह्यर्था: प्रकाशन्ते महात्मन: प्रकाशन्ते महात्मन इति॥२३॥

To one who has the highest devotion (*bhakti*) for God, and for his spiritual teacher (*guru*) even as for God,

To him these matters which have been declared become manifest [if he be] a great soul (*mahātman*)—

Yea, become manifest [if he be] a great soul!

ॐ सह नाववतु...........इति शान्ति:॥

॥इति श्वेताश्वतरोपनिषत्समाप्ता॥

***

12. BRAHMABINDŪPANIṢAD

ब्रह्मबिन्दूपनिषत्

मनो हि द्विविधं प्रोक्तं शुद्धं चाशुद्धमेव च। अशुद्धं कामसंकल्पं शुद्धं कामविवर्जितम्॥ १॥

The Manas (mind) is twofold, one is pure and the other is impure. The mind in which the desires come frequently is an impure and which is free from all desires is called pure.

मन एव मनुष्याणां कारणं बन्धमोक्षयोः। बन्धाय विषयासक्तं मुक्त्यै निर्विषयं स्मृतम्॥ २॥

The mind is the main cause of bondage and emancipation to us. When this engrossed in the worldly issues is the cause for bondage and when devoid of all passions and desires it is cause of emancipation.

यतो निर्विषयस्यास्य मनसो मुक्तिरिष्यते। अतो निर्विषयं नित्यं मनः कार्यं मुमुक्षुणा॥ ३॥

निरस्तविषयासङ्गं संनिरुद्धं मनो हृदि। यदा यात्युन्मनीभावं तदा तत्परमं पदम्॥ ४॥

Indeed, by the objectless Manas (mind) one can attain final emancipation. Hence, it is suggested to the ascetic desirous of emancipation should keep him mind away from all worldly affairs. It is the ultimate state where there is no place for worldly attachments. One locks up his mind in the heart and thus turns into state of deep attention, then he attains the highest position.

तावदेव निरोद्धव्यं यावद्धृदि गतं क्षयम्। एतज्ज्ञानं च मोक्षं च अतोऽन्यो ग्रन्थविस्तरः॥ ५॥

Therefore, one should restrain his mind until it emerges in the heart. This state of the mind is the knowledge and emancipation. Nothing else it whatever may be, that all is only adding a prolix to a volume.

नैव चिन्त्यं न चाचिन्त्यमचिन्त्यं चिन्त्यमेव च। पक्षपातविनिर्मुक्तं ब्रह्म संपद्यते तदा॥ ६॥

It is not thinkable and not unthinkable. It is thinkable and unthinkable together. One attains Brahman when there remains no difference regarding what to think and what is not worthy to think. Free from partisanship, one can attain Brahman.

स्वरेण संधयेद्योगमस्वरं भावयेत्परम्। अस्वरेण हि भावेन भावो नाभाव इष्यते॥ ७॥

One should perceive Yoga with Praṇava (Oṁ) and as a subsequent step, he should meditate wordlessly on highest Brahman. Through meditation without word, the attainment of that great one is not mere and non-being.

तदेव निष्कलं ब्रह्म निर्विकल्पं निरञ्जनम्। तद्ब्रह्माहमिति ज्ञात्वा ब्रह्म संपद्यते ध्रुवम्॥ ८॥

That Brahman is devoid of part, changeless and spotless (pure). When a man considers that "I am Brahman" he definitely becomes Brahman himself.

निर्विकल्पमनन्तं च हेतुदृष्टान्तवर्जितम्। अप्रमेयमनादिं च यत् ज्ञात्वा मुच्यते बुधः॥ ९॥

That Brahman is changeless, unending, devoid of cause, incomparable, limitless and without beginning. Realising thus a wise attains the liberation.

न निरोधो न चोत्पत्तिर्न बद्धो न च साधकः। न मुमुक्षा न मुक्तिश्च इत्येषा परमार्थता॥ १०॥

There is no devastation, no origin, no bondage and none aspirant. There is no desire for emancipation and no liberation. That is the highest reality.

एक एवात्मा मन्तव्यो जाग्रत्स्वप्नसुषुप्तिषु। स्थानत्रयव्यतीतस्य पुनर्जन्म न विद्यते॥ ११॥

One should consider Ātman as one, in the three stages *i.e.*, awaking, dream and deep sleep. The person who has jumped beyond these three stages does not born again.

एक एव हि भूतात्मा भूते भूते व्यवस्थितः। एकधा बहुधा चैव दृश्यते जलचन्द्रवत्॥ १२॥

There is only one being-soul which dwells in (the heart of) every creature. It appears in oneform and yet multiform as the reflection of the moon looks differently in pond.

घटसंवृतमाकाशं लीयमाने घटे यथा। घटो लीयेत नाकाशं तद्वज्जीवो नभोपमः॥ १३॥

The space is filled in a pitcher but when the pitcher is destroyed in pieces, truly the jar alone breaks, not the space. Thus Jīva is like the pitcher. [A man can die but the soul seldom dies as it is immortal].

घटवद्विविधाकारं भिद्यमानं पुनः पुनः। तद्भग्नं न च जानाति स जानाति च नित्यशः॥ १४॥

The distinct forms of living-organisms are like a pitcher and it ceaselessly cracks and destroy. They all are unaware when this departs, but still he is aware eternally.

[This inert body doesn't know the Brahman residing within heart but that supreme soul a witness to all, knows always the pros and cons of the bodies. It is an everlasting fact that the soul doesn't destroy while the body is all mortal.]

शब्दमायावृतो यावत्तावत्तिष्ठति पुष्करे। भिन्ने तमसि चैकत्वमेकमेवानुपश्यति॥ १५॥

Upto the time this living-soul is covered by the illusion having existence in the form of name and complexion, then the soul resides in the heart-lotus duly tied therewith. But when the darkness grows clear, he sees oneness all alone.

शब्दाक्षरं परं ब्रह्म तस्मिन्क्षीणे यदक्षरम्। तद्विद्वानक्षरं ध्यायेद्यदीच्छेच्छान्तिमात्मनः॥ १६॥

The words 'Brahman' is the syllable of the Oṁ sound. When this fades off, what remains, the learned person desirous of peace should meditate upon eternal one.

द्वे विद्ये वेदितव्ये तु शब्दब्रह्म परं च यत्। शब्दब्रह्मणि निष्णातः परं ब्रह्माधिगच्छति॥ १७॥

Two sciences are to be considered, one is Śabdabrahman and another is Parabrahman. One who is expert in the knowledge of Śabdabrahman (*i.e.* the knowledge of Vedas) attains to the highest Brahman.

ग्रन्थमभ्यस्य मेधावी ज्ञानविज्ञानतत्त्वतः। पलालमिव धान्यार्थी त्यजेद्ग्रन्थमशेषतः॥ १८॥

An intelligent for searching true knowledge through the study of scriptures and after attaining the real knowledge, throws off the mass of bookish stuff, like a man who is wishing corn strives away all husk.

गवामनेकवर्णानां क्षीरस्याप्येकवर्णता। क्षीरवत्पश्यते ज्ञानं लिङ्गिनस्तु गवां यथा॥ १९॥

The cows may be of different colours but the colour of their milk is the same. In the same way, the Self-knowledge is like the milk and its characteristic like cows.

[The learned person observes like the milk of cows of the discretion of people who bears a number of communal marks of symbols. No difference in the knowledge arises merely by the discrepancy of the symbols.]

घृतमिव पयसि निगूढं भूते भूते च वसति विज्ञानम्। सततं मन्थयितव्यं मनसा मन्थानभूतेन॥ २०॥

As the clarified butter is hidden in the milk, the conscious always exists in all beings. As the milk is churned out to obtain the ghṛt, everyone should churn it out in himself with mind as the churning rod with a motto to obtain the conscious Brahman. One should live in perfect meditation.

ज्ञाननेत्रं समादाय चोद्धरेद्वह्निवत् परम्। निष्कलं निश्चलं शान्तं तद्ब्रह्माहमिति स्मृतम्॥ २१॥

Subsequently, one should perceive fire by friction using the eyes of knowledge, which is partless, stainless, most peaceful and it is realized by himself "I am that Brahman".

सर्वभूताधिवासं च यद्भूतेषु वसत्यपि। सर्वानुग्राहकत्वेन तदस्म्यहं वासुदेवः तदस्म्यहं वासुदेव इति॥ २२॥

That which is abode of all creatures and to which all creatures are abode, which holds in it all mercily, I am that Vāsudeva, that Vāsudeva (supreme and universal soul).

ॐ सह नाववतु............ इति शान्तिः॥

॥इति ब्रह्मबिन्दूपनिषत्समाप्ता॥

****

13. KAIVALYOPANIṢAD

कैवल्योपनिषद्

॥शान्तिपाठः॥

ॐ सह नाववतु ....इति शान्तिः॥

अथाश्वलायनो भगवन्तं परमेष्ठिनमुपसमेत्योवाच।
अधीहि भगवन्ब्रह्मविद्यां वरिष्ठां सदा सद्भिः सेव्यमानां निगूढाम्।
यथाऽचिरात्सर्वपापं व्यपोह्य परात्परं पुरुषं याति विद्वान्॥ १॥

Once upon a time, Āśvalāyana went to Lord Parameṣṭī (Brahmā) and addressed Him thus : "O illustrious one! instruct me into *Brahmavidyā* (Divine wisdom), which is the most excellent, which is ever enjoyed by the wise, which is mystic, and by which the learned, after having soon freed themselves from all sins, reach *Puruṣa*, the Supreme of the supreme."

तस्मै स होवाच पितामहश्च श्रद्धाभक्तिध्यानयोगादवैहि॥ २॥
न कर्मणा न प्रजया धनेन त्यागेनैके अमृतत्वमानशुः।
परेण नाकं निहितं गुहायां विभ्राजते यद्यतयो विशन्ति॥ ३॥
वेदान्तविज्ञानसुनिश्चितार्थाः संन्यासयोगाद्यतयः शुद्धसत्त्वाः।
ते ब्रह्मलोकेषु परान्तकाले परामृताः परिमुच्यन्ति सर्वे॥ ४॥

To him the Grandfather (thus) replied: "Know (It) through Śraddhā (faith), Bhakti (devotion), Dhyāna (meditation), and Yoga. Persons attain salvation not through Karma, progeny or wealth but through renunciation alone. Ascetics of pure mind through (the realisation of) the meaning well-ascertained by Vedānta-Vijñāna and through Saṁnyāsa-Yoga enter into That which is above Svarga (heaven) and is in the cave (of the heart). They all attain Paramātman in the Brahman's-world and are (finally) emancipated.

विविक्तदेशे च सुखासनस्थः शुचिः समग्रीवशिरः शरीरः।
अन्त्याश्रमस्थः सकलेन्द्रियाणि निरुध्य भक्त्या स्वगुरुं प्रणम्य॥ ५॥
हृत्पुण्डरीकं विरजं विशुद्धं विचिन्त्य मध्ये विशदं विशोकम्।
अचिन्त्यमव्यक्तमनन्तरूपं शिवं प्रशान्तममृतं ब्रह्मयोनिम्॥ ६॥
तमादिमध्यान्तविहीनमेकं विभुं चिदानन्दमरूपमद्भुतम्।
उमासहायं परमेश्वरं प्रभुं त्रिलोचनं नीलकण्ठं प्रशान्तम्।
ध्यात्वा मुनिर्गच्छति भूतयोनिं समस्तसाक्षिं तमसः परस्तात्॥ ७॥
स ब्रह्मा स शिवः सेन्द्रः सोऽक्षरः परमः स्वराट्।

स एव विष्णुः स प्राणः स कालोऽग्निः स चन्द्रमाः॥८॥

स एव सर्वं यद्भूतं यच्च भव्यं सनातनम्। ज्ञात्वा तं मृत्युमत्येति नान्यः पन्था विमुक्तये॥९॥

सर्वभूतस्थमात्मानं सर्वभूतानि चात्मनि। संपश्यन्ब्रह्म परमं याति नान्येन हेतुना॥१०॥

आत्मानमरणिं कृत्वा प्रणवं चोत्तरारणिम्। ज्ञाननिर्मथनाभ्यासात्पापं दहति पण्डितः॥११॥

"Being seated in a pleasant posture in an unfrequented place with a pure mind, and with his neck, head, and body erect, having given up the duties of the (four) orders of life, having subjugated all the organs, having saluted his preceptor with devotion, Meditating the pure, dustless or without Rajas heart-lotus and having contemplated in its (heart's) centre Parameśvara who is always with His consort Umā, who is pure and free from sorrow, who is unthinkable and invisible, who is of endless forms, who is of the nature of happiness, who is very quiescent, who is of the form of emancipation, who is the source of Māyā, who has no beginning, middle or end, who is One, who is All-Pervading, who is Cidānanda (Consciousness-Bliss), who is formless, who is wonderful, who is the Lord (of all), who has three eyes, who has a blue neck, (Nīlakaṇṭha), and who is serenity (itself)— the Muni attains Paramātmā, the womb of all elements, the All Witness, and above Tamas.

He only is Brahmā. He only is Śiva. He only is Indra. He only is the indestructible. He only is the Supreme. He only is the Self-Shining. He only is Viṣṇu. He only is Prāṇa. He only is Time. He only is Agni (fire). He only is the moon. He only is all things that exist or will hereafter exist. He only is eternal. Having known Him, one crosses death. There is no other path to salvation. He only attains Parabrahman who sees in himself all elements and himself in all elements. There is no other means. Having constituted his body an Araṇi (the lower attritional piece of wood) and praṇava (Oṁ), the upper Araṇi, a wise man burns Ajñāna by the churning of meditation.

स एव मायापरिमोहितात्मा शरीरमास्थाय करोति सर्वम्।
स्त्रियन्नपानादिविचित्रभोगैः स एव जाग्रत्परितृप्तिमेति॥१२॥

स्वप्ने स जीवः सुखदुःखभोक्ता स्वमायया कल्पितजीवलोके।
सुषुप्तिकाले सकले विलीने तमोऽभिभूतः सुखरूपमेति॥१३॥

पुनश्च जन्मान्तरकर्मयोगात्स एव जीवः स्वपिति प्रबुद्धः।
पुरत्रये क्रीडति यश्च जीवस्ततस्तु जातं सकलं विचित्रम्।
आधारमानन्दमखण्डबोधं यस्मिँल्लयं याति पुरत्रयं च॥१४॥

एतस्माज्जायते प्राणो मनः सर्वेन्द्रियाणि च। खं वायुर्ज्योतिरापश्च पृथ्वी विश्वस्य धारिणी॥१५॥

यत्परं ब्रह्म सर्वात्मा विश्वस्यायतनं महत्। सूक्ष्मात्सूक्ष्मतरं नित्यं तत्त्वमेव त्वमेव तत्॥१६॥

जाग्रत्स्वप्नसुषुप्त्यादिप्रपञ्चं यत्प्रकाशते। तद्ब्रह्माहमिति ज्ञात्वा सर्वबन्धैः प्रमुच्यते॥१७॥

त्रिषु धामसु यद्भोग्यं भोक्ता भोगश्च यद्भवेत्। तेभ्यो विलक्षणः साक्षी चिन्मात्रोऽहं सदाशिवः॥

मय्येव सकलं जातं मयि सर्वं प्रतिष्ठितम्। मयि सर्वं लयं याति तद्ब्रह्माद्वयमस्म्यहम्॥१९॥

अणोरणीयानहमेव तद्वन्महानहं विश्वमहं विचित्रम्।
पुरातनोऽहं पुरुषोऽहमीशो हिरणमयोऽहं शिवरूपमस्मि॥ २०॥
अपाणिपादोऽहमचिन्त्यशक्तिः पश्याम्यचक्षुः स शृणोम्यकर्णः।
अहं विजानामि विविक्तरूपो न चास्ति वेत्ता मम चित्सदाहम्॥ २१॥
वेदैरनेकैरहमेव वेद्यो वेदान्तकृद्वेदविदेव चाहम्॥ २२॥
न पुण्यपापे मम नास्ति नाशो न जन्म देहेन्द्रियबुद्धिरस्ति।
न भूमिरापो न च वह्निरस्ति न चानिलो मेऽस्ति न चाम्बरं च॥ २३॥
एवं विदित्वा परमात्मरूपं गुहाशयं निष्कलमद्वितीयम्।
समस्तसाक्षिं सदसद्विहीनं प्रयाति शुद्धं परमात्मरूपम्॥ २४॥

It is only He (Paramātmā) who, deluded by Māyā, assumes a body with the internal organs and does everything. It is only He who in the waking state is gratified with women, food, drink, and other diverse enjoyments. In the dream too, the Jīva enjoys pleasures and sorrow in the several worlds which are created by His Māyā. In the deep sleep when all illusion vanished, He, replace with darkness (Tamas), attains the state of happiness. Then through the force of the Karmas of previous births, the Jīva again wakes up and goes to sleep. All the diversified objects (of the universe) emanate from the Jīva, who sports in the three bodies (gross, subtle and casual). The three bodies are finally absorbed in Him who is the source of all, who is Bliss, and who is Absolute Wisdom. From Him, arise Prāṇa. Manas, all the organs of sense and action Ākāśa, Vāyu, Agni, water and earth supporting all. Parabrahman, which is of all forms, which is the Supreme Abode of this universe, which is the most subtle of the subtle and which is eternal, is only yourself. You are only That. One who knows himself to be that Parabrahman that shines as the universe in the waking, dreaming, dreamless and other states, will be relieved from all bondage. I am that Sadāśiva, (or the eternal happiness) who is other than the enjoyer, the enjoyed, and the enjoyment in the three seats (or bodies), and who is witness and cinmātra. All emanate from me alone. All exist in Me alone. All merge into Me alone. I am that non-dual Brahman. I am the atom of atoms; so am I the biggest (of all). I am this diversified universe. I am the oldest of all. I am Puruṣa. I am Īśa (the Lord). I am of the form of Jyotis (light) and of the form of happiness. I have neither hands nor feet. I have power unthinkable. I see without eyes, I hear without ears. I am omniscient. I have one kind of form only. None is able to know Me fully. I am always of the form of Cit. I am the One that should be known through all the Vedas. I am the Guru who revealed the Vedānta. I am only He who knows the true meaning of Vedānta. I have no sins or virtues. I have no destruction. I have no birth, body, organs of sense or action, or Buddhi. To me there is no earth water or fire. There is no Vāyu; there is no Ākāśa. He who thinks Paramātman as being in the cave (of the heart), as having no form, as being secondless, as being the witness of all and as being neither Sat nor Asat, attains the pure form of supreme Ātman.

य: शतरुद्रियमधीते सोऽग्निपूतो भवति स वायुपूतो भवति स आत्मपूतो भवति स सुरापानात्पूतो भवति स ब्रह्महत्याया: पूतो भवति स सुवर्णस्तेयात्पूतो भवति स कृत्याकृत्यात्पूतो भवति तस्मादविमुक्तमाश्रितो भवत्यत्याश्रमी सर्वदा सकृद्वा जपेत्॥ २५॥

अनेन ज्ञानमाप्नोति संसारार्णवनाशनम्।
तस्मादेवं विदित्वैनं कैवल्यं पदमश्नुते कैवल्यं पदमश्नुत इति॥ २६॥

One who recites this Śatarudriya, becomes as pure as Agni (fire). He becomes purified by wind, purified by Ātman. He becomes purified from the sins of drinking alcohol. He becomes purified from the sins of murder of a Brāhmaṇa. He becomes purified from the sins of theft of gold. He becomes purified from the sins of commission (of those that ought not to be done) and the sins of omission (of those that ought to be done). Therefore he goes into the Avimukta. Rising above the Āśramas, one should recite (this Upaniṣad) always or even once (in a day).

By the virtues of this, he acquires the knowledge that destroys the ocean of Saṁsāra. Therefore having known Him, he attains the Kaivalya State (reward of final emancipation)— yea, he attains the Kaivalya State.

ॐ सह नाववतु........................इति शान्ति:॥

॥इति कैवल्योपनिषत्समाप्ता॥

***

14. JĀBĀLOPANIṢAD

जाबालोपनिषद्

This Upaniṣad is related to the tradition of Śukla Yajurveda. There are six parts in it. In the first part, a colloquy between Lord Bṛhaspati and Yājñavalkya regarding Prāṇa-vidyā (learning) has been given. The Ṛṣi Yājñavalkya has explained the place of breathing, abode of Brahman and the only place for offering *i.e.*, Avimukta (Brahmarandhra-Kāśī). Lord Rudra provides with emancipation to the living soul by preaching Tāraka Brahma to the man at his hermit Atri and Yājñavalkya has been introduced in the second part in which the region of Avimukta has been told at the middle of the eyebrows on the basis of the knowledge acquired as a result of its worship. A man can preach the knowledge of soul to other. A way to attain the element of an immortality has been described in the third part by the Ṛṣi Yājñavalkya. The measure so described is a Jāpa of Śatarudra. The devotee can conquer his death by virtue of this Jāpa. The Ṛṣi Yājñavalkya in reply to the question raised regarding seclusion by the king Janaka has told its system, the procedure and the activities to be performed in the fourth part. In the fifth part, the hermit, Atri has obtained a guideline regarding the sacrificial thread (Yajñopavīta), the garments, the Muṇḍana, the alms etc. of a recluse. A conclusion has been arrived to the effect that a recluse should keep himself away from the distortions of worldly issues by his mind and speech both. In the sixth part, a commentory on the activities performed by the renowned recluse like Saṁvartaka, Āruṇī, Śvetaketu, Durvāsā, Ribhu etc. has been made and finally the characteristics of a naked Paramahaṁsa (great scholar) has been explained.

॥शान्तिपाठः॥

ॐ पूर्णमदः.............इति शान्तिः॥

बृहस्पतिरुवाच याज्ञवल्क्यं यदनु कुरुक्षेत्रं देवानां देवयजनं सर्वेषां भूतानां ब्रह्मसदनम्। अविमुक्तं वै कुरुक्षेत्रं देवानां देवयजनं सर्वेषां भूतानां ब्रह्मसदनम्। तस्माद्यत्र क्वचन गच्छति तदेव मन्येत तदविमुक्तमेव। इदं वै कुरुक्षेत्रं देवानां देवयजनं सर्वेषां भूतानां ब्रह्मसदनम्। अत्र हि जन्तोः प्राणेषूत्क्रममाणेषु रुद्रस्तारकं ब्रह्म व्याचष्टे येनासावमृतीभूत्वा मोक्षीभवति। तस्मादविमुक्तमेव निषेवेत अविमुक्तं न विमुञ्चेदेवमेवैतद्याज्ञवल्क्यः॥ १॥

Bṛhaspati said to Yājñavalkya– "After Kurukṣetra, what is the region of sacrifice of gods and the abode of Brahman for all beings? Yājñavalkya replied– "Avimukta (Kāśī) is the true Kurukṣetra (the region of breathing). This very region has been called the sacrificial place of gods and it too is the abode of Brahman for all beings. Hence, the person moving at any place should consider it. This is Kurukṣetra, the sacrificial place of gods and Brahman-seat of all creatures. For here, when the vital breaths depart out of a person, Rudra preach regarding formula of Tāraka Brahma, to the living soul by virtue of which he attains the immortality and becomes liberated. One should not leave Avimukta [which is not left]!"— "It is so, O Yājñavalkya."

॥द्वितीयः खण्डः॥

अथ हैनमत्रिः पप्रच्छ याज्ञवल्क्यं य एषोऽनन्तोऽव्यक्त आत्मा तं कथमहं विजानीयामिति। स होवाच याज्ञवल्क्यः सोऽविमुक्त उपास्यो य एषोऽनन्तोऽव्यक्त आत्मा सोऽविमुक्ते प्रतिष्ठित इति॥ १॥

Then Atri asked Yājñavalkya : "This infinite, not manifest Ātman, how can I know him?" Yājñavalkya replied– "He is to be worshipped in Avimukta. That endless and unmanifested soul resides in Avimukta."

सोऽविमुक्तः कस्मिन्प्रतिष्ठित इति वरणायां नास्यां च मध्ये प्रतिष्ठित इति। का वै वरणा का च नासीति सर्वानिन्द्रियकृतान्दोषान्वारयतीति तेन वरणा भवति। सर्वानिन्द्रियकृतान्पापान्नाशयतीति तेन नासी भवतीति। कतमच्चास्य स्थानं भवतीति। भ्रुवोर्घ्राणस्य च यः संधिः स एष द्यौर्लोकस्य परस्य च संधिर्भवतीति। एतद्वै संधिं संध्यां ब्रह्मविद उपासत इति सोऽविमुक्त उपास्य इति। सोऽविमुक्तं ज्ञानमाचष्टे यो वै तदेतदेवं वेदेति॥ २॥

Where is situated that Avimukta place? In reply to this Ṛṣi Yājñavalkya said– "It is enshrined in the middle of the Varaṇā and Nāśī" (Atri asked further) "what is Varaṇā and what the Nāśī?" Yājñavalkya replied– "The thing that eliminates (*vārayati*) the defect or evils committed by the organs of body is called Varaṇā and which that dispels the sins committed by all senses is called Nāśī". (Atri further asked) Where is its location? Then Yājñavalkya replied "Its location is at the adjunction of the eyebrow and nose. For that is the meeting place of heaven (*dyuloka*) and the highest region. Therefore, one who knows Brahman, adores this connecting place as the union-time (Sandhyā). Hence, that Avimukta is only adorable. The person who has duly acquired knowledge of a result of his worship to Avimukta is only competent to preach regarding soul to others.

॥तृतीयः खण्डः॥

अथ हैनं ब्रह्मचारिण ऊचुः किं जप्येनामृतत्वं ब्रूहीति। स होवाच याज्ञवल्क्यः। शतरुद्रियेणेत्येतानि ह वा अमृतनामधेयान्येतैर्ह वा अमृतो भवतीति॥ १॥

The celibate disciples then asked to Yājñavalkya– "By what recitation one can attain the immortality, tell us?" Then Yājñavalkya replied– "Immortality is attained only by recitation of Śatarudriya (Vāj. Saṁhitā xvi)." One who occurs there, is conceived as many epithes of immortal. He becomes immortal.

॥चतुर्थः खण्डः॥

अथ ह जनको ह वैदेहो याज्ञवल्क्यमुपसमेत्योवाच भगवन् संन्यासमनुब्रूहीति। स होवाच याज्ञवल्क्यो ब्रह्मचर्यं समाप्य गृही भवेत्, गृही भूत्वा वनी भवेत्, वनी भूत्वा प्रव्रजेत्। यदि वेतरथा ब्रह्मचर्यादेव प्रव्रजेद्गृहाद्वा वनाद्वा। अथ पुनरव्रती वा व्रती वा स्नातको वाऽस्नातको वा उत्सन्नाग्निरनग्निको वा यदहरेव विरजेत्तदहरेव प्रव्रजेत्॥ १॥

Then Janaka, the king of Vaideha, approached Yājñavalkya and said : "Explain to me, O exalted sir, the renunciation (*Saṁnyāsa*)!" Ṛṣi Yājñavalkya replied– "One should first observe the rules of celibacy. On its successful completion, he should become a householder, then he should become a Vānaprasthin (forest-resident). After that, he should finally accept the life of reclusion. However, a direct entry into reclusion may be made after Brahmacarya, Gṛhastha or Vānaprastha.

And even otherwise, whether he may have observed a vow or not, whether he has taken the final ablution or not, whether he has caused the household fires to extinguish or whether he is (already) without fire, from that day on, on which he renounces, he should wander as a pilgrim.

तद्धैके प्राजापत्यामेवेष्टिं कुर्वन्ति। तदु तथा न कुर्यादाग्नेयीमेव कुर्यात्। अग्निर्ह वै प्राणः। प्राणमेवैतया करोति पश्चात्त्रैधातवीयामेव कुर्यात्। एतयैव त्रयो धातवो यदुत सत्त्वं रजस्तम इति। अयं ते योनिर्ऋत्वियो यतो जातो अरोचथाः। तं जानन्नग्न आरोहाथा नो वर्धयरयिम् इत्यनेन मन्त्रेणाग्निमाजिघ्रेत्। एष ह वा अग्नेर्योनिर्यः प्राणः। प्राणं गच्छ स्वाहेत्येव मेवैतदाह॥

On occasion of entrance into reclusion, a few people perform a *Prājāpatya* sacrifice; if one does not do that, he should offer a sacrifice to Agni alone, for Agni is the Prāṇa; so thereby one offers to the Prāṇa. As a next step, he should offer the *Traidhātavīya* sacrifice; thereby the three Dhātus (elements), namely Sattva, Rajas and Tamas are worshipped.

By reciting the hymn– *Ayam te yoni...* etc. (Atharva. 3.20,1) one should inhale the fire. O fire! This breathing is a common cause because you are originated through this breathing. O fire! You burn the breathing and you attain to the light and growth. Please ensure our growth. Indeed, this Prāṇa is the vagina of fire (producer of fire). "Go to that Prāṇa, Svāhā" thus he says. (He offers oblation by reciting these hymns).

ग्रामादग्निमाहृत्य पूर्ववदग्निमाघ्रापयेत्। यद्यग्निं न विन्देदप्सु जुहुयात्। आपो वै सर्वा देवताः। सर्वाभ्यो देवताभ्यो जुहोमि स्वाहेति हुत्वा समुद्धृत्य प्राश्नीयात्साज्यं हविरनामयं मोक्षमन्त्रस्त्रय्येवं विन्देत्। तद्ब्रह्मैतदुपासितव्यम्। एवमेवैतद्भगवन्निति वै याज्ञवल्क्यः॥ ३॥

One [the priest] may also bring the fire from a village and make him [the Saṁnyāsin] inhale the fire as described. If he cannot get fire, he should make an offering in water, for water is all godheads. And after performing the sacrifice with the words "Oṁ, I offer to all godheads, svāhā." After performing thus, he should take out of it and the wholesome sacrificial food should be eaten along with clarified butter. One should make a conception that the hymn for emancipation is Oṁ consisting of three letters *i.e.*, (अ उ म्) Lord Yājñavalkya pronounced that this very is Brahma and it is only adorable.

॥पञ्चमः खण्डः॥

अथ हैनमत्रिः पप्रच्छ याज्ञवल्क्यम्। पृच्छामि त्वा याज्ञवल्क्य अयज्ञोपवीती कथं ब्राह्मण इति। स होवाच याज्ञवल्क्य इदमेवास्य तद्यज्ञोपवीतं य आत्मा अपः प्राश्याचम्यायं विधिः परिव्राजकानाम्॥ १॥

Then Atri asked Yājñavalkya– "I am curious to know the type of Brāhmaṇa which has not put on the sacrificial thread (Yajñopavīta)." Yājñavalkya replied– "This Ātman is only sacrificial thread to him, that he feeds himself and that he rinses the mouth (Prāśana and Ācamana) with water. That is the sacrificial precept of the Parivrājakas.

वीराध्वाने वाऽनाशके वाऽपां प्रवेशे वाऽग्निप्रवेशे वा महाप्रस्थाने वाऽथ परिव्राड्- विवर्णवासा मुण्डोऽपरिग्रहः शुचिरद्रोही भैक्षाणो ब्रह्मभूयाय भवति। यद्यातुरः स्यान्मनसा वाचा संन्यसेत्। एष पन्था ब्रह्मणा हानुवित्तस्तेनैति संन्यासी ब्रह्मविदित्येवमेवैष भगवन्निति वै याज्ञवल्क्यः॥ २॥

The recluse at the time when he is on the way of a warrior, in the stage of hunger, while entering into the water of a river like Gaṅgā etc., while entering into the fire and at the time of Mahāprasthāna should put one colourless garments, with shaven head, without belongings, pure, free from deceipt, living on begging, becomes fit for Brahmanhood. In case, he is too ill, and wish to observe reclusion, then the subjects of worldly enjoyments should be abandoned by mind and the speech. This path is propounded by Brahman (Vedas). The recluse being well-known to Brahman, it is necessary for him to observe these rules. Thus Yājñavalkya said.

॥षष्ठः खण्डः॥

तत्र परमहंसा नाम संवर्तकारुणिश्वेतकेतुदुर्वासऋभुनिदाघजडभरतदत्तात्रेयरैवतकप्रभृतयोऽव्यक्तलिङ्गा अव्यक्ताचारा अनुन्मत्ता उन्मत्तवदाचरन्तः॥ १॥

The great recluse like Saṁvartaka, Āruṇi, Śvetaketu, Durvāsas, Ṛbhu, Nidāgha, Jaḍabharata, Dattātreya and Raivataka etc. were without any visible sign or the symbol of reclusion. Their behaviour was invisible. They were behaving like mad, but were not mad.

त्रिदण्डं कमण्डलुं शिक्यं पात्रं जलपवित्रं शिखां यज्ञोपवीतं चेत्येतत्सर्वं भूः स्वाहेत्यप्सु परित्यज्यात्मानमन्विच्छेत्॥ २॥

The recluse of the above stage should immerse the three staves, Kamaṇḍalu, drinking bowl, water-flasks, water-filter, a braid of hair and sacrificial thread etc. into water by reciting the hymn "Bhūḥ Svāhā" and seek the Ātman.

यथाजातरूपधरो निर्द्वन्द्वो निष्परिग्रहस्तत्तत्त्वब्रह्ममार्गे सम्यक्संपन्नः शुद्धमानसः प्राणसंधारणार्थं यथोक्तकाले विमुक्तो भैक्षमाचरन्नुदरपात्रेण लाभालाभौ समौ भूत्वा शून्यागारदेवगृहतृणकूटवल्मीकवृक्षमूल कुलालशालाग्निहोत्रशालानदीपुलिन गिरिकुहरकन्दरकोटरनिर्झरस्थण्डिलेष्वनिकेतवास्यप्रयत्नो निर्ममः शुक्लध्यानपरायणोऽध्यात्मनिष्ठः शुभाशुभकर्मनिर्मूलनपरः संन्यासेन देहत्यागं करोति स परमहंसो नाम स परमहंसो नामेति॥ ३॥

The recluse always remains naked as he was born, free from pairs of opposites (*dvandva*), without belonging, firmly devoted to the way of true knowledge, the Brahman, and pure-minded. He is a liberated, but in order to survive, he is begging alms at prescribed hours, with the belly as his utensil. He don't fall in the trap of worry whether he gets anything or not. He lives without taking care for an appropriate residence in the deserted place, temples, huts, in the hold of the snakes, under a tree, in the residence of pot-maker, at the place of offering, at the bank of river, in mountains, trenches or in caves and near the streams. He always engrosses himself in concentration to the great deeds and uplifts his soul from the state where discrimination of good and bad deeds reside. Who becomes free from body by means of renunciation, he is called Paramahaṁsa when be breathes his last.

ॐ पूर्णमदः .... इति शान्तिः॥

॥इति जाबालोपनिषत्समाप्ता॥

***

15. HAṀSOPANIṢAD

हंसोपनिषद्

॥शान्तिपाठः॥

ॐ पूर्णमदः .... इति शान्तिः।

गौतम उवाच– भगवन्सर्वधर्मज्ञ सर्वशास्त्रविशारद। ब्रह्मविद्याप्रबोधो हि केनोपायेन जायते॥

सनत्कुमार उवाच- विचार्य सर्वधर्मेषु मतं ज्ञात्वा पिनाकिनः। पार्वत्या कथितं तत्त्वं शृणु गौतम तन्मम॥ २॥ अनाख्येयमिदं गुह्यं योगिने कोशसंनिभम्। हंसस्याकृतिविस्तारं भुक्तिमुक्तिफलप्रदम्॥ ३॥

Gautama addressed Sanatkumāra thus : "O Lord, You are the knower of all dharmas and are well versed in all Śāstras, please tell me the means by which I may obtain a knowledge of Brahma-vidyā. Sanatkumāra replied thus :

"Hear, O Gautama, that Tattva as expounded by Pārvatī after inquiring into all dharmas and ascertaining Śiva's opinion. This treatise on the nature of Haṁsa which gives the fruit of bliss and salvation and which is like a treasure to the yogin, is (a) very mystic (science) and should not be revealed (to the public).

अथ हंसपरमहंसनिर्णयं व्याख्यास्यामः। ब्रह्मचारिणे शान्ताय दान्ताय गुरुभक्ताय। हंसहंसेति सदा ध्यायन्॥ ४॥ सर्वेषु देहेषु व्याप्तो वर्तते। यथा ह्यग्निः काष्ठेषु तिलेषु तैलमिव तं विदित्वा मृत्युमत्येति॥ ५॥

"Now we shall explain the true nature of Haṁsa and Paramahaṁsa for the benefit of a brahmacārin (a seeker after Brahman or celibate), who has his desires under control, is devoted to his Guru and always contemplates (as) Haṁsa, and realises thus : It (Haṁsa) is permeating all bodies like fire (or heat) in all kinds of wood or oil in all kinds of gingelly seeds. Having known (It) thus, one does not meet with death.

गुदमवष्टभ्याधाराद्वायुमुत्थाप्य स्वाधिष्ठानं त्रिः प्रदक्षिणीकृत्य मणिपूरकं गत्वा अनाहतमतिक्रम्य विशुद्धौ प्राणान्निरुध्याज्ञामनुध्यायन्ब्रह्मरन्ध्रं ध्यायन् त्रिमात्रोऽहमित्येव सर्वदा पश्यत्यनाकारश्च भवति॥ ६॥

एषोऽसौ परमहंसो भानुकोटिप्रतीकाशो येनेदं सर्वं व्याप्तम्॥ ७॥

"Having contracted the anus (with the heels pressed against it), having raised the vāyu (breath) from (Mūlādhāra cakra), having made circuit thrice round Svādhiṣṭhāna, having gone to Maṇipūraka, having crossed Anāhata, having controlled Prāṇa in Viśuddhi and then having reached Ājñyā, one contemplates in Brahmarandhra (in the head), and having meditated there always 'I am of three mātrās', cognises (his Self) and becomes formless. The Śiṣṇa (penis) has two sides (left and right from head to foot). This is that Paramahaṁsa (Supreme Haṁsa or Higher Self) having the resplendence of crores of suns and by whom all this world is pervaded.

तस्याष्टधा वृत्तिर्भवति। पूर्वदले पुण्ये मतिः। आग्नेये निद्रालस्यादयो भवन्ति। याम्ये क्रौर्ये मतिः। नैर्ऋते पापे मनीषा। वारुण्यां क्रीडा। वायव्यां गमनादौ बुद्धिः। सौम्ये रतिप्रीतिः। ईशान्ये द्रव्यादानम्। मध्ये वैराग्यम्। केसरे जाग्रदवस्था। कर्णिकायां स्वप्नम्। लिङ्गे सुषुप्तिः। पद्मत्यागे तुरीयम्। यदा हंसे नादो विलीनो भवति तत् तुरीयातीतम्॥ ८॥

अथो नाद आधाराद्ब्रह्मरन्ध्रपर्यन्तं शुद्धस्फटिकसंकाशः। स वै ब्रह्म परमात्मेत्युच्यते॥ ९॥

"It (this Haṁsa which has buddhi as vehicle) has eight-fold vṛtti. (When it is) in the eastern petal, there is the inclination (in a person) to virtuous actions; in the south-eastern petal, there arise sleep, laziness, etc.; in the southern, there is the inclination to cruelty; in the south-western, there is the inclination to sins; in the western, there is the inclination to sensual sport; in the north-western, there arises the desire of walking, and others; in the northern, there arises the desire of lust; in the north-eastern, there arises the desire of amassing money; in the middle (or the interpaces between the petals), there is the indifference to material pleasures. In the filament (of the lotus), there arises the waking state; in the pericarp, there arises the svapna (dreaming state); in the bīja (seed of pericarp), there arises the suṣupti (dreamless sleeping state); when leaving the lotus, there is the turīya (fourth state). When Haṁsa is absorbed in Nāda (spiritual sound), the state beyond the fourth is reached. Nāda (which is at the end of sound and beyond speech and mind) is like a pure crystal extending from (Mūla) Ādhāra to Brahmarandhra. It is that which is spoken of as Brahma Paramātmā.

अथ हंस ऋषिः। अव्यक्तगायत्री छन्दः। परमहंसो देवता। हमिति बीजम्। स इति शक्तिः। सोऽहमिति कीलकम्॥ १०॥

षट्संख्यया अहोरात्रयोरेकविंशतिसहस्राणि षट्शतान्यधिकानि भवन्ति। सूर्याय सोमाय निरञ्जनाय निराभासायातनुसूक्ष्म प्रचोदयादिति॥ ११॥

अग्नीषोमाभ्यां वौषट् हृदयाद्यङ्गन्यासकरन्यासौ भवतः॥ १२॥

एवं कृत्वा हृदयेऽष्टदले हंसात्मानं ध्यायेत्॥ १३॥

अग्नीषोमौ पक्षावोंकारः शिर उकारो बिन्दु स्त्रिणेत्रं मुखं रुद्रो रुद्राणी चरणौ।

द्विविधं कण्ठतः कुर्यादित्युन्मनाः अजपोपसंहार इत्यभिधीयते॥ १४॥

[Here the performance of Ajapā Gāyatrī is given.]

"Now Haṁsa is the Ṛṣi; the metre is Avyakta Gāyatrī; Paramahaṁsa is the devatā (or presiding deity) 'Ham' is the bīja; 'Sa' is the śaktī' So'ham is the kīlaka. Thus these are six. There are 21,600 Haṁsas (or breaths) in a day and night. (Salutation to) Surya, Soma, Nirañjana (the stainless) and Nirābhāsa (the universeless), Ajapā-mantra. (May) the bodiless and subtle one guide (or illuminate my understanding). Vauṣaṭ to Agni-Soma. Then Aṅganyāsas and Kara-nyāsas occur (or should be performed after the mantras as they are performed before the mantras) in the heart and other (seats). Having done so, one should contemplate upon Haṁsa as the Ātman in his heart. Agni and Soma are its wings (right and left sides); Oṁkāra is its head; Ukāra and bindu are the three eyes and face rspectively; Rudra and Rudrāṇī (or Rudra's wife) are the feet kaṇṭhata (or the realisation of the oneness of jīvātmā or Haṁsa, the lower self with Paramātmā or Paramahaṁsa, the Higher Self) is done in two ways, (samprajñāta and asamprajñāta). After that, Unmanī is the end of the Ajapā (Mantra).

एवं हंसवशात्तस्मान्मनो विचार्यते॥ १५॥

अस्यैव जपकोट्यां नादमनुभवति एवं सर्वं हंसवशान्नादो दशविधो जायते। चिणीति प्रथमः। चिञ्चिणीति द्वितीयः। घण्टानादस्तृतीयः। शङ्खनादश्चतुर्थम्। पञ्चमस्तन्त्रीनादः। षष्ठस्तालनादः। सप्तमो वेणुनादः। अष्टमो मृदङ्गनादः। नवमो भेरीनादः। दशमो मेघनादः॥ १६॥

नवमं परित्यज्य दशममेवाभ्यसेत्॥ १७॥

प्रथमे चिञ्चिणीगात्रं द्वितीये गात्रभञ्जनम्। तृतीये खेदनं याति चतुर्थे कम्पते शिरः॥ १८॥

पञ्चमे स्रवते तालु षष्ठेऽमृतनिषेवणम्। सप्तमे गूढविज्ञानं परा वाचा तथाऽष्टमे॥ १९॥

अदृश्यं नवमे देहं दिव्यं चक्षुस्तथाऽमलम्। दशमं परमं ब्रह्म भवेद्ब्रह्मात्मसंनिधौ॥ २०॥

तस्मिन्मनो विलीयते मनसि संकल्पविकल्पे दग्धं पुण्यपापे सदाशिवः शक्त्यात्मा सर्वत्रावस्थितः स्वयंज्योतिः शुद्धो बुद्धो नित्यो निरञ्जनः शान्तः प्रकाशत इति वेदानुवचनं भवतीत्युपनिषत्॥ २१॥

Having thus reflected upon manas by means of this (Haṁsa), one hears Nāda after the uttering of this japa (mantra) a crore of times. It (Nāda) is (begun to heard as) of ten kinds. The first is ciṇī (like the sound of that word); the second is ciṇī-ciṇī; the third is the sound of bell; the fourth is that of conch; the fifth is that of tantri (lute); the sixth is that sound of tāla (cymbals); the seventh is that of flute; the eighth is that of bheri (drum); the ninth is that of mṛdaṅga (double drum); and the tenth is that of clouds (viz., thunder). He may experience the tenth without the first nine sounds (through the initiation of a Guru). In the first stage, his body becomes ciṇī- ciṇī; in the second, there is the (bhañjana) breaking (or affecting) in the body; in the third, there is the (bhedana) piercing; in the fourth, the head shakes; in the fifth, the palate produces saliva; in the sixth, nectar is attained; in the seventh, the knowledge of the hidden (things in the world) arises; in the eighth, Parāvāk is heard; in the ninth, the body becomes invisible and the pure divine eye is developed; in the tenth, he attains Parabrahman in the presence of (or with) Ātman which is Brahman. After that, when manas is destroyed, when it which is the source of saṅkalpa and vikalpa disappears, owing to the destruction of these two, and when virtues and sins are burnt away, then he shines as Sadāśiva of the nature of Śakti pervading everywhere, being effulgence in its very essence, the immaculate, the eternal, the stainless and the most quiescent Oṁ. Thus is the teaching of the Vedas."

ॐ पूर्णमदः .... इति शान्तिः॥

॥इति हंसोपनिषत्समाप्ता॥

16. ĀRUṆYUPANIṢAD

आरुण्युपनिषद्

This Upaniṣad is related to the tradition of Sāmaveda. It is also called as Āruṇikopaniṣad. Lord Brahmā had explained some aphorism for acquiring perfection in recluse and thus satisfy the curiosity of the sage Āruṇi regarding renounce. The celibate, couple and the successive Āśram (Vānaprastha) are authorised or held entitle to enter into reclusion. The vital framework of renunciation to the symbol of offering, sacrificial thread etc. rituals of the recluse. The recluse doesn't abandon the offering and becomes himself the offering itself. He doesn't abandon the sacrificial thread but his life itself becomes the sacrificial thread. He doesn't abandon the hymns but his speech itself kept the form of hymn. Owing to hold these important aphorism, he is called as Sannyāsī i.e, the person or rituals in course of entering in life of recluse, has been also enumerated.

॥ शान्तिपाठः॥

ॐ आप्यायन्तु ममाङ्गानि वाक् प्राणश्चक्षुः श्रोत्रमथो बलमिन्द्रियाणि च सर्वाणि सर्वं ब्रह्मौपनिषदं माहं ब्रह्म निराकुर्यां मा मा ब्रह्म निराकरोदनिराकरणमस्त्वनिराकरणं मेऽस्तु तदात्मनि निरते य उपनिषत्सु धर्मास्ते मयि सन्तु ते मयि सन्तु॥ ॐ शान्तिः शान्तिः शान्तिः॥

May my all organs and parts of the body avail growth. May the speech, the breathing, the eyes, the ears, the power and all sensory organs obtain due growth. All Upaniṣads are Brahman. May the Brahma is not abandoned by me and the Brahma on its part should not abandon me. I further repeat that the Brahman shouldn't abandon me. Thus, the religion as propounded by Upaniṣad should be obtained to us viz., who are engrossed with Brahma. May the trio-fevers cooled down and may we attain peace.

ॐ आरुणिः प्रजापतेर्लोकं जगाम। तं गत्वोवाच। केन भगवन्कर्माण्यशेषतो विसृजानीति। तं होवाच प्रजापतिस्तव पुत्रान्भ्रातृन्बन्ध्वादिञ्छिखां यज्ञोपवीतं यागं सूत्रं स्वाध्यायं च भूर्लोकभुवर्लोकस्वर्लोक-महर्लोकजनोलोकतपोलोकसत्यलोकं चातलतलातलवितलसुतलरसातलमहातलपातालं ब्रह्माण्डं च विसृजेत्। दण्डमाच्छादनं चैव कौपीनं च परिग्रहेत्। शेषं विसृजेदिति॥१॥

Āruṇi, the son of Aruṇa appeared before Lord Brahmā in the abode of Brahma. He pray to Prajāpati that he should suggest some versatile ways to him. He asked "O Lord! How can I abandon all activities?" Lord Brahmā said to him "O Saint! One should abandon to put sacrificial thread, organise the offering, keeping the braid, the perseverance, ones son, near and dears, sanguine, relatives and the whole Brahmāṇḍa comprising the abode of Bhū, Bhuvaḥ, Svaḥ, Mahaḥ, Janaḥ, Tapaḥ, Satyaḥ and Atala; Talātal, Vitala, Sutala, Rasātala, Mahātala and Pātāla. He should only keep with him a stick, a single cloth to cover the body and once nicker (Kaupīna). All other things besides these should be abandoned.

गृहस्थो ब्रह्मचारी वा वानप्रस्थो वा उपवीतं भूमावप्सु वा विसृजेत्। अलौकिकाग्नीनुदराग्नौ समारोपयेत्। गायत्रीं च स्ववाच्यग्नौ समारोपयेत्। कुटीचरो ब्रह्मचारी कुटुम्बं विसृजेत्। पात्रं विसृजेत्। पवित्रं विसृजेत्। दण्डाँल्लोकाग्नीन् विसृजेदिति होवाच। अत ऊर्ध्वममन्त्रवदाचरेत्। ऊर्ध्वगमनं विसृजेत्। औषधवदशनमाचरेत्। त्रिसंध्यादौ स्नानमाचरेत्। संधिं समाधावात्मन्याचरेत् सर्वेषु वेदेष्वारण्यकमावर्तयेदुपनिषदमावर्तयेदुपनिषदमावर्तयेदिति॥२॥

Either he is celibate, couple or in the stage after couple life should impose all divine fires on his digestive power (Jaṭharāgnī). He should enshrine Gāyatrī in the fire of his speech, the sacrificial thread on the earth or it should be flown with the water. The celibate residing in a hermittage should wreck all attachments with his family members. He should abandon the vessels (pots) and the seat (Kuśa) as also the stick and the material fire too. It was suggested by Lord Brahmā to Āruṇi. He added further that he should behave as a man without hymn. He shouldn't desire to reside in the heavens. He should take the food like a medicine and take bath daily thrice in a day. At the time of his pray, he should do research on the supreme soul, a perfect knowledge in the state of meditation, concomittantly, he should go over the Āraṇyaka and churn the topic in his mind. He should read Upaniṣads again and again.

खल्वहं ब्रह्मसूत्रं सूचनात्सूत्रं ब्रह्मसूत्रमहमेव विद्वांस्त्रिवृत्सूत्रं त्यजेद्विद्वान्य एवं वेद संन्यस्तं मया संन्यस्तं मया संन्यस्तं मयेति त्रिरुक्त्वाऽभयं सर्वभूतेभ्यो मत्तः सर्वं प्रवर्तते। सखा मा गोपायोजःसखायोऽसीन्द्रस्य वज्रोऽसि वार्त्रघ्नः शर्म मे भव यत्पापं तन्निवारयेति। अनेन मन्त्रेण कृतं वैणवं दण्डं कौपीनं परिग्रहेदौषधवदशनमाचरेदौषधवदशनं प्राश्नीयाद्यथालाभमश्नीयात्। ब्रह्मचर्यमहिंसां चापरिग्रहं च सत्यं च यत्नेन हे रक्षते३ हे रक्षतो३ हे रक्षत इति॥३॥

The desirous of reclusion should give up putting sacrificial thread with the presumption that he himself is the sacrificial thread that enables the Brahma to know. The scholar known to this should then repeat three times "Mayā Saṅnyastam" viz., I have adopted the life of a recluse, I have left everything, I have left everything. He should then put on the nicker and a bamboo stick duly spelled with hymns with the letter and the spirit that this whole world is residing within him. Let the creatures violent and non-violent enjoy fearlessness. Further, addressing to the bamboo stick, he should say that the stick is his friend and it will protect his splendour. He should further say that the stick is his friend and it is the thunderbolt of Lord Indra enabling him to kill the demon Vṛtra. O thunderbolt! Make us to enjoy pleasure and destroy the evil that may stand as hurdle in the way of reclusion. He should take the food considering it as medicine *i.e.* be cautious at the time of eating and take a lesser diet. O Āruṇi! one should rigidly maintain celibacy, non-violence, check on desires and the truth after attaining to the life of a recluse.

O Son! Protect very carefully and with the best attempts, the discipline prescribed for the life of a recluse.

अथातः परमहंसपरिव्राजकानामासनशयनादिकं भूमौ ब्रह्मचारिणां मृत्पात्रं वाऽलाबुपात्रं दारुपात्रं वा। कामक्रोधहर्षरोषलोभमोहदम्भदर्पेच्छासूयाममत्वाहंकारादीनपि परित्यजेत्। वर्षासु ध्रुवशीलोऽष्टौ मासानेकाकी यतिश्चरेद् द्वावे वा चरेद् द्वावे वा चरेदिति॥४॥

Lord Brahmā further added that the sacrosanct recluse, known to Brahma; should only take seat on the earth and should never use cot etc. for sleeping. He should keep a wooden jug or an earthern pot with him. The recluse should abandon entirely the vices like sensuality, anger, happiness, gloom, fury, greed, attachment, ego, envy, desire, critical approach for others, excess affliction and the proud etc. He should live at a single place upto four month of the rainy season. Besides it, the rest of eight months should be passed by moving alone or atleast he should stay at a place for two months.

स खल्वेवं यो विद्वान्सोपनयनादूर्ध्वमेतानि प्रागवा त्यजेत्। पितरं पुत्रमग्निमुपवीतं कर्म कलत्रं चान्यदपीह। यतयो भिक्षार्थं ग्रामं प्रविशन्ति पाणिपात्रमुदरपात्रं वा। ॐ हि ॐ हि ॐ हीत्येतदुपनिषद् विन्यसेत्। खल्वेतदुपिषदं विद्वान्यं एवं वेद पालाशं बैल्वमाश्वत्थमौदुम्बरं दण्डं मौञ्जीं मेखलां यज्ञोपवीतं च त्यक्त्वा शूरो य एवं वेद। तद्विष्णोः परमं पदं सदा पश्यन्ति सूरयः। दिवीव चक्षुराततम्। तद्विप्रासो विपन्यवो जागृवांसः समिन्धते। विष्णोर्यत्परमं पदमिति। एवं निर्वाणानुशासनं वेदानुशासनं वेदानुशासनम्। इत्युपनिषद्॥५॥

If a scholar known to all rules and by laws of the life in renounce should abandon his parents, sun, fire, sacrificial thread, activities, wife and all that which is existed in the form of material objects or articles either prior or after the ceremony of Upanayana. The person entering into life of a recluse should use his hands at the pot or his stomach as the vessel while visiting at the villages for alms. He should first recite the syllable 'Oṁ' thrice and then enter in the village. It has been contemplated by this Upaniṣad and the person known to it is truly a scholar. The person is a gallant and the great who abandons the sacrificial thread and accepts a stick of Palāśa, Bela, Pīpal (holy fig tree) and Gulara (sycamore) etc. Such ascetics always watch the supreme abode of Lord Viṣṇu, existed everywhere with its gigantic splendour like the Sun in the sky. The devotees free from attachment and engrossed with ceaseless meditation give more light to that supreme abode when he accesses there. This position is called the supreme abode of Lord Viṣṇu. Thus, it is a discipline to be followed for emancipation, a discipline prescribed by the Veda and this is the Upaniṣad.

ॐ आप्यायन्तु ममाङ्गानि...... इति शान्तिः॥

॥ इति आरुण्युपनिषत्समाप्ता॥

***

17. GARBHOPANIṢAD

गर्भोपनिषद्

यद्गर्भोपनिषद्वेद्यं गर्भस्य स्वात्मबोधकम्।

शरीरापह्नवात्सिद्धं स्वमात्रं कलये हरिम्।।

ॐ सह नाववत्विति शान्तिः।।

ॐ पञ्चात्मकं पञ्चसु वर्तमानं षडाश्रयं षड्गुणयोगयुक्तम्। तं सप्तधातुं त्रिमलं द्वियोनिं चतुर्विधाहारमयं शरीरं भवति। पञ्चात्मकमिति कस्मात् पृथिव्यापस्तेजो वायुराकाशमित्यस्मिन्पञ्चात्मके शरीरे का पृथिवी का आपः किं तेजः को वायुः किमाकाशमित्यस्मिन्पञ्चात्मके शरीरे तत्र यत्कठिनं सा पृथिवी यद्द्रवं ता आपः यदुष्णं तत्तेजः यत्संचरति स वायुः यत्सुषिरं तदाकाशमित्यच्युते। तत्र पृथिवी धारणे आपः पिण्डीकरणे तेजः प्रकाशने वायुर्व्यूहने आकाशमवकाशप्रदाने। पृथक्श्रोत्रे शब्दोपलब्धौ त्वक् स्पर्शे चक्षुषी रूपे जिह्वा रसने नासिका घ्राणे वदति।

षडाश्रयमिति कस्मात्। मधुराम्ललवणतिक्तकटुकषायरसान्विन्दतीति। षड्जऋषभगान्धारमध्यमपञ्चम-धैवतनिषादाश्चेतीष्टानिष्टशब्दसंज्ञा प्रणिधानाद्दशविधा भवन्ति।।१।।

शुक्लो रक्तः कृष्णो धूम्रः पीतः कपिलः पाण्डर इति।।

Oṁ. The body is composed of the five (elements); it exists in the five (objects of sense, etc.); it has six supports : it is associated with the six guṇas; it has seven dhātus (essential ingredients) and three malas (impurities); it has three yonis (wombs) and is formed of four kinds of food.

Why is the body said to be composed of five? Because there are five elements in this body (viz.,), pṛthivī, āpas, agni, vāyu and ākāśa? In this body of five elements, What is the pṛthivī elements? What āpas ? What agni? What vāyu? and What ākāśa? Pṛthivī is said to be that which is hard; āpas is said to be that which is liquid; agni is said to be that which is hot; vāyu is that which moves; ākāśa is that which is full of holes (or tubes). Of these, pṛthivī is seen in supporting (objects), āpas in cohesion, tejas (or agni) is making forms visible, vāyu in moving, ākāśa chiefly in avakāṣa (viz., giving space). (Then what are the five objects of sense, etc.?) The ear exists in sound, the skin in touch, the eye iṇ forms, the tongue in taste, and the nose in odour. (Then) the mouth (exists) in speech, the hand in lifting, the feet in walking, the anus in excreting, and the genitals in enjoying. (Then through buddhi, one knows and determines; through manas, he thinks and fancies; through citta, he recollects; through ahaṁkāra, he feels the idea of 'I'. Thus these perform their respective functions.

Which are the six supports? There are six kinds of rasas (essence or tastes)— sweet, sour, saltish, bitter, astringent, and pungent. The body depends upon them while they depend upon the body.

There are six changes of state (viz.,), the body exists, is born, grows, matures, decay, and dies. And there are also six cakras (wheels) depending on the dhamani (nerves), (viz.,), mūlādhāra, svādhiṣṭhāna, maṇipūrraka, anāhata, viśuddhi, and ājñā. Also the guṇas are six— kāma (passion) and others and śama (mental restraint) and others; there being properly— association (with the former) and devotion (to the latter). Then there are seven kinds of sounds, (viz.,). ṣadja (sa), ṛṣabha (ri), gāndhāra (ga), madhyama (ma) pañcama (pa), daivata (da), and niṣāda (ni), which are stated to be seven agreeable and disagreeable ones; and there are seven kinds of dhātus having seven colours, (viz.,) śukla (white), rakta (red), kṛṣṇa (dark-blue or indigo), dhūmara (blue), pīta (yellow), kapila (orange-red), and pāndara (yellowish white).

सप्तधातुकमिति कस्मात् यदा देवदत्तस्य द्रव्यादिविषया जायन्ते। परस्परं सौम्यगुणत्वात् षड्विधो रसो रसाच्छोणितं शोणितान्मांसं मांसान्मेदो मेदसः स्नायवः स्नायुभ्योऽस्थीति अस्थिभ्यो मज्जा मज्जातः शुक्रं शुक्रशोणितसंयोगादावर्तते गर्भो हृदि व्यवस्थां नयति हृदयेन्तराग्निः अग्निस्थाने पित्तं पित्तस्थाने वायुः वायुतो हृदयं प्राजापत्यात्क्रमात्॥२॥

In whomsoever these substances arise and increase, the rasa (essence) is the cause of the one following and so on (as stated below). (These rasas are six in number; from the rasas (probably chyme) arises blood : from blood, flesh; from flesh, fat; from fat, bones; from bones, marrow; and from marrow, śukla (the male seminal fluid). From the union of śukla and śoṇita (the female vital energy), occurs garbha (conception in the womb). Being stationed in the heart, it is led. In the heart of persons, (there is) an internal agni; in the seat of agni, there is bile; in the seat of bile, there is vāyu; in the seat of vāyu, is hṛdaya (heart or Ātmā).

ऋतुकाले संप्रयोगादेकरात्रोषितं कललं भवति सप्तरात्रोषितं बुद्बुदं भवति अर्धमासाभ्यन्तरे पिण्डो भवति। मासाभ्यन्तरे कठिनो भवति मासद्वयेन शिरः संपद्यते। मासत्रयेण पादप्रदेशो भवति। अथ चतुर्थे मासे गुल्फजठरकटिप्रदेशा भवन्ति।

पञ्चमे मासे पृष्ठवंशो भवति। षष्ठे मासे मुखनासिकाक्षिश्रोत्राणि भवन्ति। सप्तमे मासे जीवेन संयुक्तो भवति। अष्टमे मासे सर्वलक्षणसंपूर्णो भवति। पितू रेतोऽतिरेकात्पुरुषो मातू रेतोऽतिरेकात्स्त्री उभयोर्बीजतुल्यत्वान्नपुंसको भवति। व्याकुलितमनसोऽन्धाः खञ्जाः कुब्जा वामना भवन्ति। अन्योन्यवायुपरिपीडितशुक्रद्वैविध्यात्तनु स्यात्ततो युग्माः प्रजायन्ते। पञ्चात्मकः समर्थः पञ्चात्मिका चेतसा बुद्धिर्गन्धरसादिज्ञानाक्षराक्षरमोंकारं चिन्तयतीति तदेतदेकाक्षरं ज्ञात्वाष्टौ प्रकृतयः षोडश विकाराः शरीरे तस्यैव देहिनः अथ मात्राशितपीतनाडीसूत्रगतेन प्राण आप्यायते। अथ नवमे मासि सर्वलक्षणज्ञानकरणसंपूर्णो भवति। पूर्वजातिं स्मरति। शुभाशुभं च कर्म विन्दति॥३॥

Through having connection at the ṛtu (seasons) fit for raising issues, it (the embryo formed in the womb) is like water in the first night; in seven nights, it is like a bubble; at the end of half a months, it becomes a ball. At the end of a month, it is hardened; in two months, the head is formed; in three months, the region about the feet; and in fourth month, the region about the stomach and the loin and also ankle is formed, in the fifth month, the back (or spinal) bone; in the sixth, the face, the nose, eyes, and ears; in the seventh, it becomes united with Jīva (Ātmā); in the eighth month, it becomes full (of all organs); in the ninth, it becomes fatty. Śukla belongs to men and śoṇita to women. Each (by itself) is neutral (of is powerless). (But in their combination) a son is born when the father's seed preponderates. A daughter is born when the mother's seed preponderates. Should both be equal, a eunuch is born. Since females have more of passion, on account of their deriving more pleasure (than male from sexual union), a greater number of females are born. Action corresponds to mental state (of the actor). Hence the child (born) takes after (the thought of) the parents. From parents with minds full of anxieties (at the time of union) are born the blind, the lame, the hunchback, the dwarf, and the limbless. (From impregnation) during the eclipses of the sun and the moon, children are born with defective limbs. Increase or decrease, similarities or dissimilarities of bodies arise (in children) through the influence of time, place, action, dravya (substance), and enjoyment. From a well-conducted intercourse (or union), the child being born with the form of the father possesses, his qualities, just as the image in a glass reflects truly the original. When śukla bursts into two through the interaction (or blowing against one another) of the vāyu of both śukla and śoṇita, then twins (of the same sex) are born. In the same manner when the retas (the seminal fluids), viz., (śukla and śoṇita) of both the parents burst into two, then mixed progeny (male and female) is the result. Among mankind, five embryos (only can be formed at a pregnancy in the womb), A womb with one embryo is common. There are some with two. Those with three are only to be found (as rarely) as one in a thousand. Where there is a frequent pouring (of seminal fluid into the womb), a greater number of limbs is produced (in the child). When the pouring (within the womb) is only once, then the child becomes dried up (or contracted). By pouring (within) more than once, couples are (sometimes) born.

पूर्वयोनिसहस्राणि दृष्ट्वा चैव ततो मया। आहारा विविधा भुक्ताः पीता नानाविधाः स्तनाः।। जातश्चैव मृतश्चैव जन्म चैव पुनः पुनः। यन्मया परिजनस्यार्थे कृतं कर्म शुभाशुभम्। एकाकी तेन दह्येऽहं गतास्ते फलभोगिनः। अहो दुःखोदधौ मग्नो न पश्यामि प्रतिक्रियाम्। यदि योन्याः प्रमुच्येऽहं तत्प्रपद्ये महेश्वरम्। अशुभक्षयकर्तारं फलमुक्तिप्रदायकम्। यदि योन्याः प्रमुच्येऽहं तत्प्रपद्ये नारायणम्। अशुभक्षयकर्तारं फलमुक्तिप्रदायकम्। यदि योन्याः प्रमुच्येऽहं तत्सांख्यं योगमभ्यसे। अशुभक्षयकर्तारं फलमुक्तिप्रदायकम्। यदि योन्याः प्रमुच्येऽहं ध्याये ब्रह्म सनातनम्। अथ योनिद्वारं संप्राप्तो यन्त्रेणपीड्यमानो महता दुःखेन जातमात्रस्तु वैष्णवेन वायुना संस्पृष्टस्तदा न स्मरति जन्ममरणानि न च कर्म शुभाशुभं विन्दति।।४।।

Then (viz., in the ninth month), this (in the body) made of five elements and able to sense odour, taste, etc., through tejas (spiritual fire), etc., which is also made up of the five elements— this cognizes the indestructible oṁkāra through its deep wisdom and contemplation. It cognizes as the one letter (Oṁ).

Then there arise in the body the eight prakṛtis and the sixteen vikāras (changes). Through the food and drink of the mother transmitted through her nādis, the chid obtains prāṇa. In the ninth month, it is full of all attributes.

It then remembers its previous births, finds out what has been done and what has not been done, and discriminates between actions, right and wrong. (Then it thinks thus:) "Many thousands of wombs have been seen by me, many kinds of food have been tasted (by me), and many breasts have been sucked (by me). All parts of the world have been my place of birth, as also my burning-ground in the past. In eighty-four lakhs of wombs, have I been born. I have often born and have often died. I have been subject to the cycle of re-births very often. I have had birth and death, again birth and death, and again birth (and so on). There is much suffering while living in the womb. Delusion and sorrow attended every birth. In youth are sorrow, grief, dependence on others, ignorance, the non-performance of what is beneficial laziness, and the performance of what is unfavourable. In adult age, (the sources of sorrow are) attachment to sensual objects and groaning under the three kinds of pain. In old age anxiety, disease, fear of death, desires, love of self, passion, anger, and non-independence— all these produce very great suffering. This birth is a sea of sorrow and is unbearable. I have not attained the dharma of nivṛtti, (viz., the means of overcoming the cycle of re-birth) nor have I acquired the means of yoga and jñāna. Alas ! I am sunk in the ocean of sorrow and find no remedy for it. Fie on ajñāna ! fie on ajñāna ! fie on the troubles caused by passion and anger; fie on the fetters of saṁsāra (the mundane existence) ! I shall attain wisdom from a Guru. If I get myself freed from the womb, then I shall practise sāṁkyha yoga which is the cause of the extinction of all evil and the bestower of the fruit of emancipation. If I get myself freed from the womb, I shall seek refuge of Maheśvara (the great Lord) who is cause of the extinction of all evil and bestower of the (four) ends of life. If I get myself freed from the womb, then I shall seek refuge in that Lord of the world who is the cidātmā of all śakti and the cause of all causes. If I get myself freed from the womb, then I shall seek refuge in that supreme Lord Bhargaḥ (Śiva or light) who is paśupati (the lord of paśus or souls), Rudra, Mahādeva (the great Deva) and the Guru of the world. If I get myself freed from the bondage of the womb, I shall perform great penances. If I get myself freed from the passage of the womb, I shall worship Viṣṇu in my heart who is the bestower of nectar, who is bliss, who is Nārāyaṇa, and who never decays. I am now confined in my mother's womb; and were I freed from its bonds, I shall please the divine Vāsudeva without diverting my mind. I am burnt through actions, good and bad, committed by me alone before for the sake of others, while those who enjoyed the fruits thereof have disappeared. Through non-belief (unspirituality), I formely gave up all fears (of sin) and committed sins. I now reap their fruits. I shall becme a believer hereafter."

Thus does the Jīva (Ātmā) within the (mother's womb) contemplate again and again the many kinds of miseries (it had undergone), and remembering always the miseries of the cycle or re-births, becomes disgusted (with the material enjoyments of the world), often fainting in the innermost centre (viz., heart) of all creatures of (the idea of) his avidyā, desire, the karma. Then this being, who had entered many hundreds of female wombs of beings (in the previous births), comes to the mouth of the womb wishing to obtain release. Here being pressed by the yantra (neck of the uterus), it suffers much trouble. Moreover it is much affected by parsūti (delivery) vāyu and ceases to remember anything of the past; it also ceases to see far and to be the cognizer of the real. Coming into contact with the earth, it becomes fiercy-eyed and debased. The evail of the eye after it, if rubbed with (or cleaned by) water vanishes; and with it, vanishes memory of birth and death, good and bad actions and their affinities. Then how does he understand vāyu, bile, and śleṣma (phlegm)? When they are in their proper state, they produce health : with their disturbance, diseases are generated. It should be known that one becomes capable of knowing through a proper quantity of bile; through having a little more or a little less of it, he cornes of know more. When the bile is changed (otherwise), he becomes changed and acts lik a mad man. And that bile is agni. Agni influenced by karma is kindled by vāyu, the source (or seat) of virtue and vice, fuel is kindled within (by fire) from without (by the wind).

And of how many kinds is *agni*? It has three bodies, three (seeds or progeny), three puras (cities), three *dhātus*, and three kinds of *agni* threefold. Of these three, *Vaiśvānara* is bodiless. And that *agni* becomes (or is subdivided into) *Jñānāgni* (wisdom-fire), *Darśanāgni* (eye-fire), and *Koṣṭhāgni* (digestive fire). Of these *Jñānāgni* pertains to the mind; *Darśanāgni* pertains of the senses; and *Koṣṭhāgni* pertains to daily cooks (of disgests) equally whatever is eaten, drunk, licked, or sucked through *prāṇa* and *apāna*. *Darśanāgni* is (in) the eye itself and is the cause of the *vijñāna* and enables one to see all objects of form. It has three seats, The (spiritual) eye itself being the (primary) seat, and the eyeballs being the accessory seats. *Dakśināgni* is in the heart, *Gārhapatya* is in the belly, and in the face is *Āhavanīya*. (In these sacrifices with the three *agnis*), the *Puruṣa* is himself the sacrificer; *buddhi* becomes his wife; santoṣa (contentment) becomes the *dīkṣā* (vow) taken; the mind and the organs of the senses become the sacrificial vessels; the *karmendriyas* (organs of action) are the sacrificial instruments. In this sacrifice of the body, the several devas who become the *ṛtvijas* (sacrificial priests) perform their parts following the master of the sacrifice, (*viz.*, the true individuality), wherever he goes. In this (sacrifice), the body is the sacrificial place, the skull of the head is the fire-pit, the hairs are the *kuśa* grass; the mouth is the antarvedi (raised platform in sacrifice); *kāma* (or passion) is the clarified butter; the period of life is the period of sacrifice; *nāda* (sound) produced in (heart) is the *sāmaveda* (recited during the sacrifice; *vaikharī* in the *yajus* (or *yajurveda* hymns); *parā*, *paśyanti*, and *madhyamā* are the ṛks (or ṛgveda hymns); cruel worlds are the atharvas (*atharvaveda* hymns) and *khilas* (supplementary texts of each veda); true; words are the *vyāhṛtis*. Life, strength, and bile are the *paśus* (sacrificial creatures) and death is *avabhṛta* (the bath which concludes the sacrifice). In this sacrifice, the (three) fires blaze up and then according to (the desires of) the worldly, the devas bless him. All who are living (in this world) are the sacrificers. There is none living who does not perform *yajña* (sacrifice). This body is (created) for *yajña*, and arises out of *yajña* and changes according to *yajña*. If this *yajña* is continued in a direction changed (from the right course, or is abused), then it leads to an ocean of misery.

शरीरमिति कस्मात्। अग्नयो ह्यत्र श्रियन्ते ज्ञानाग्निदर्शनाग्निः कोष्ठाग्निरिति। तत्र कोष्ठाग्निर्नामाशितपीतलेह्यचोष्यं पचति। दर्शनाग्नी रूपाणां दर्शनं करोति। ज्ञानाग्निः शुभाशुभं च कर्म विन्दति। त्रीणि स्थानानि भवन्ति मुखे आहवनीय उदरे गार्हपत्यो हृदि दक्षिणाग्निः आत्मा यजमानो मनो ब्रह्म लोभादयः पशवो धृतिर्दीक्षा संतोषश्च बुद्धीन्द्रियाणि यज्ञपात्राणि हवींषि कर्मेन्द्रियाणि शिरः कपालं केशा दर्भा मुखमन्तर्वेदिः चतुष्कपालं शिरः षोडश पार्श्वदन्तपटलानि सप्तोत्तरं मर्मशतं साशीतिकं संधिशतं सनवकं स्नायुशतं सप्त शिराशतानि पञ्च मज्जाशतानि अस्थीनि च ह वै त्रीणि शतानि षष्टीः सार्धचतस्रो रोमाणि कोट्यो हृदयं पलान्यष्टौ द्वादश पला जिह्वा पित्तप्रस्थं कफस्याढकं शुक्रकुडवं मेदः प्रस्थौ द्वावनियत मूत्रपुरीषमाहारपरिमाणात्। पैप्पलादं मोक्षशास्त्रं पैप्पलादं मोक्षशास्त्रमिति।।

In this body, there are sixteen side-teeth, having each a membrane (as its root) and fifteen openings. It (the body) is measured by ninety-six digits, there are in it fourteen nādis seats and 108 joints. There are seventy-two tubes seats with seventy-two nādis between them, of which three are important, viz., iḍā, piṅgalā, and suṣumnā, the fourth is purītati, and jīvata the fifth. Above Jīvata is bile and near bile is purītati. Above the navel, two digits to the left of it, is seated the source of bile.

The food taken in is divided into three parts— urine, fæces, and sāra (the essence of chyme). The urine dividing itself into two, spreads to the left below the navel. The fæces is in the right side and is of seven kinds. The sāra is of five kinds and spread itself over the body. Hence the semen and blood are produced from food and drink. In this body, vāyu which is moving as prāṇa is the Sūtrātmā. Through it, one inspires and expires and moves (his limbs). Without it, no limb of the body will be animated. Through vāyu, the current of blood is driven into the nādis from the cakra (plexus) of the heart, and those which can be touched (on the body) are easily discernible. The juicy essences (of food) which arise out of digestion enter the womb which is suspended in the stomach of the mother and coming near the child's head nourishes the child's prāṇa through the suṣumnā (on the head or pineal gland). Suṣumnā is the Brahma-nāḍī. Prāṇa and others are found there. It (prāṇa) descends lower and lower as the time of birth approaches and settles in the heart when the child is born. Through yoga, it should be brought from the midle of the eyebrows to the end of suṣumnā (viz., the pineal gland), when he becomes the cognizer of the Real like the child in the womb. In the body of this nature, Ātman is latent and deathless, and is the witness and Puruṣa. It lives in this body, being enveloped (by māyā). Prāṇī (or the jīva having prāṇa) has abhimāna (identification with the body) on account of avidyā. Ajñāna which surrounds it is seed; the antaḥkaraṇa (internal organ) is the sprout and the body is the tree. In this tree (of body), there are eight crores of hairs, eighty hundreds of joints, nine hundreds of tendons, eight palams of heart, twelve palams of tongue, one prastha (or two palams) of bile; one ādhaka of phlegm, one kudupa (or 1/4 prastha) of śukla and two prasthas of marrow. One should consider everything as evanescent, like the child in the womb (with its prāṇa. etc.,) stationed in the suṣumnā (of the head). Then he becomes freed and gets on more body. If not, an ignorant man becomes subject to the cycle of re-births, etc., is exposed like a worm to the drink of urine and fæces, and undergoes in this body the sufferings of hell. Therefore knowing all this, one should be averse to worldly objects. Thus ends the mokṣa-śāstra of Pippalāda— thus ends the mokṣa-śāstra of Pippalāda.

ॐ सहनाववत्विति शान्तिः॥

॥इति गर्भोपनिषत्समाप्ता॥

***

18. NĀRĀYAṆOPANIṢAD

नारायणोपनिषद्

॥शान्तिपाठः॥

ॐ सह नाववतु .... इति शान्तिः॥

अथ पुरुषो ह वै नारायणोऽकामयत प्रजाः सृजेयेति। नारायणात्प्राणो जायते। मनः सर्वेन्द्रियाणि च। खं वायुर्ज्योतिरापः पृथिवी विश्वस्य धारिणी। नारायणादब्रह्मा जायते। नारायणा-द्रुद्रो जायते। नारायणादिन्द्रो जायते। नारायणात्प्रजापतिः प्रजायते। नारायणाद्द्वादशादित्या रुद्रा वसवः सर्वाणि छन्दांसि नारायणादेव समुत्पद्यन्ते। नारायणात्प्रवर्तन्ते। नारायणे प्रलीयन्ते। एतदृग्वेदशिरोऽधीते॥ १॥

Oṁ. Then Nārāyaṇa, the supreme Puruṣa desired– "I shall create offspring." From Nārāyaṇa emanates prāṇa, manas, the several organs of sense and action, ākāśa, vāyu, agni, āpas and pṛthivī that supports all. From Nārāyaṇa emanates Brahmā. From Nārāyaṇa emanates Rudra. From Nārāyaṇa emanates Indra. From Nārāyaṇa emanates Prajāpati (the divine progenitor). From Nārāyaṇa emanates the twelve ādityas, rudras, vasus, and all the chanḍas (Vedas). From Nārāyaṇa only do (all these) proceed. Through Nārāyaṇa do (they) prosper. In Nārāyaṇa (they) are absorbed. The Ṛgveda teaches this.

अथ नित्यो नारायणः। ब्रह्मा नारायणः। शिवश्च नारायणः। शक्रश्च नारायणः। कालश्च नारायणः। दिशश्च नारायणः। विदिशश्च नारायणः। ऊर्ध्वं च नारायणः। अधश्च नारायणः। अन्तर्बहिश्च नारायणः। नारायण एवेदं सर्वं यद्भूतं यच्च भव्यम्। निष्कलंको निरञ्जनो निर्विकल्पो निराख्यातः शुद्धो देव एको नारायणो न द्वितीयोऽस्ति कश्चित्। य एवं वेद स विष्णुरेव भवति स विष्णुरेव भवति। एतद्यजुर्वेदशिरोऽधीते॥ २॥

Then Nārāyaṇa is eternal. Brahmā is Nārāyaṇa, Śiva is Nārāyaṇa. Indra is Nārāyaṇa, Kāla (Time) is Nārāyaṇa, Dik (space) is Nārāyaṇa, the intermediate quarters also are Nārāyaṇa; that which is above is Nārāyaṇa, that which is below is Nārāyaṇa, that which is in and out is Nārāyaṇa, that whole universe which that existed and will exist is Nārāyaṇa. Nārāyaṇa is the only one that is stainless, sinless, changeless, and unnameable, and that is pure and divine. There is no second. Whoever knows Him thus, becomes Viṣṇu Himself. The Yajurveda teaches this.

ॐ इत्यग्रे व्याहरेत्। नम इति पश्चात्। नारायणायेत्युपरिष्टात्। ॐ इत्येकाक्षरम्। नम इति द्वे अक्षरे। नारायणायेति पञ्चाक्षराणि। एतद्वै नारायणस्याष्टाक्षरं पदम्। यो ह वै नारायणस्याष्टाक्षरं पदमध्येति। अनपब्रुवः सर्वमायुरेति। विन्दते प्राजापत्यं रायस्पोषं गौपत्यं ततोऽमृतत्वमश्नुते ततोऽमृतत्वमश्नुत इति। एतत्सामवेदशिरोऽधीते॥ ३॥

One should utter "Oṁ" first, then "namaḥ" and then "Nārāyaṇa." "Oṁ" (is) a single syllable; "Namaḥ" contains two syllables : Nārāyaṇāye contains five syllables. this is the sentence known as the Aṣṭākṣara of Nārāyaṇa. Whoever studies this Aṣṭākṣara of Nārāyaṇa and recites it constantly, attains full life and supremacy over men, enjoys the pleasures of royalty and becomes the master of all souls. He attains Mokṣa; yea, he attains mokṣa. The Sāmaveda teaches this.

प्रत्यगानन्दं ब्रह्मपुरुषं प्रणवस्वरूपम्। अकार उकारो मकार इति। ता अनेकधा समभवत्तदेतदोमिति। यमुक्त्वा मुच्यते योगी जन्मसंसारबन्धनात्। ॐ नमो नारायणायेति मन्त्रोपासको वैकुण्ठभुवनं गमिष्यति। तदिदं पुण्डरीकं विज्ञानघनं तस्मात्तडिदाभमात्रम्। ब्रह्मण्यो देवकीपुत्रो ब्रह्मण्यो मधुसूदनः। ब्रह्मण्यः पुण्डरीकाक्षो ब्रह्मण्यो विष्णुरच्युत इति। सर्वभूतस्थमेकं वै नारायणं कारणपुरुषमकारणं परं ब्रह्मोम्। एतदथर्वशिरोऽधीते।। ४।।

The Yogin having pronounced (the name of) Him who is complete bliss, who is Brahma-puruṣa and who is of the nature of Praṇava (Oṁ)— combination of A, U, and M— is released from the bondage of birth and mundane existence. He who practises the mantra "Oṁ-Namo-Nārāyaṇāye" reaches Vaikuṇṭha (the abode of Viṣṇu). It is this lotus (heart). It is replete with vijñāna : It has the brilliancy of lightning. The son of Devakī is Brahmaṇya Madhusūdana is Brahmaṇya. Nārāyaṇa who pervades all elements, who is one only, who is the cause Puruṣa and who is causeless, is known as Parabrahman. The Atharvaṇa Upaniṣaḍ teaches this.

प्रातरधीयानो रात्रिकृतं पापं नाशयति। सायमधीयानो दिवसकृतं पापं नाशयति। तत्सायं-प्रातरधीयानः पापोऽपापो भवति। माध्यंदिनमादित्याभिमुखोऽधीयानः पञ्चमहापातकोपपातकात्प्रमुच्यते। सर्ववेदपारायणपुण्यं लभते। नारायणसायुज्यमवाप्नोति श्रीमन्नारायणसायुज्यमवाप्नोति य एवं वेद।। ५।।

Whoever recites (this Upaniṣad) in the morning destroys the sins committed the night (before). Whoever recites it in the evening destroys the sins committed during the day. Whoever recites morning and evening becomes free from sins, however sinful he may be. Whoever recites (it) in the noon facing the sun is freed from all the five great sins as well as from the minor ones. He derives the good effects of the recitation of all the Vedas. Whoever knows thus attains Sāyujya of Nārāyaṇa (viz., is absorbed in the essence of Nārāyaṇa). He attains Sāyujya of Nārāyaṇa.

।।इति नारायणोपनिषत्समाप्ता।।

***

19. PARAMAHAṀSOPANIṢAD

परमहंसोपनिषद्

This Upaniṣad is related to Śukla Yajurveda. There are only four hymns in it. The great hermit Nārada has asked Lord Brahmā regarding the position of Paramahaṁsa and the guidelines of this route. In reply to which Lord Brahmā has enumerated broadly the nature of Paramahaṁsa, his outwards perceiving, the cardinal consecration, his behaviour etc. The man doing reverse to it has been stated as an enigma to the name of recluse and suffering from the dire consequences of the grass hell of Raurava. The Paramahaṁsa should not retain the gold etc. wealth with him and if he does; it leads him to a position analogous to self-suicide, murder of Brahma and Caṇḍāla. Paramahaṁsa is an ascetic free from desires, vicissitudes, affection and envies and he is much above than the mean feelings of good and bad. He is celibate, engrossed in the soul and in the form of perfect pleasure and knowledge. He has a well-check on the temptations and senses. Their very is the supreme position of life.

॥शान्तिपाठः॥

ॐ पूर्णमदः .... इति शान्तिः॥ (द्रष्टव्य-अध्यात्मोपनिषद्)

अथ योगिनां परमहंसानां कोऽयं मार्गस्तेषां का स्थितिरिति नारदो भगवन्तमुपगत्योवाच। तं भगवानाह। योऽयं परमहंसमार्गो लोके दुर्लभतरो न तु बाहुल्यो यद्येको भवति स एव नित्यपूतस्थः स एव वेदपुरुष इति विदुषो मन्यन्ते महापुरुषो यच्चित्तं तत्सर्वदा मय्येवावतिष्ठते तस्मादहं च तस्मिन्नेवावस्थीयते। असौ स्वपुत्रमित्रकलत्रबन्ध्वादीञ्छिखायज्ञोपवीतं स्वाध्यायं च सर्वकर्माणि संन्यस्यायं ब्रह्माण्डं च हित्वा कौपीनं दण्डमाच्छादनं च स्वशरीरोपभोगार्थाय च लोकस्योपकारार्थाय च परिग्रहेत्। तच्च न मुख्योऽस्ति कोऽयं मुख्य इति चेदयं मुख्यः॥ १॥

Once the hermit Nārada went to Lord Brahmā and asked— "The Paramahaṁsa among the yogis live at what position and what is their modus operandi and doctrines?" Lord Brahmā replied– "The modus operandi of Paramahaṁsa is most scarce in this world and hardly a few persons are Paramahaṁsa. Only one or two recluse are found Paramahaṁsa and they live with all sacrosanct spirit. According to the scholars. Paramahaṁsa of this nature are the man of Vedas. The mind of such great person always enshrines with me and I myself abandons his sons, wife, relatives, near and dears, braid sacrificial thread, the perseverance etc. all activities and holds mere copying, a stick and few garments mere sufficient to protect the body for the interest of entire world. However,, merely doing this is not the prime consecration of Paramahaṁsa." Nārada asked again— "Then tell me. What is the main consecration?"

न दण्डं न शिखां न यज्ञोपवीतं न चाच्छादनं चरति परमहंसो न शीतं न चोष्णं न सुखं न दुःखं न मानावमाने च षडूर्मिवर्जं निन्दागर्वमत्सरदम्भदर्पेच्छाद्वेषसुखदुःखकामक्रोधलोभमो-हहर्षासूयाहंकारादींश्च हित्वा

स्ववपुः कुणपमिव दृश्यते यतस्तद्वपुरपध्वस्तं संशयविपरीत-मिथ्याज्ञानानां यो हेतुस्तेन नित्यनिवृत्तस्तन्नित्यबोधस्तत्स्वयमेवावस्थितिस्तं शान्तमचलमद्वयानन्दचिद्घन एवास्मि। तदेव मम परमधाम तदेव शिखा च तदेवोपवीतं च। परमात्मात्मनोरेकत्वज्ञानेन तयोर्भेद एव विभग्नः सा संध्या॥ २॥

Main consecration of a Paramahaṁsa is that he should not hold stick, braid, sacrificial thread and the garments. Apart from it he should be without the feeling of hot and cold, insult and respect as also the vicissitudes of worldly life *i.e.* six kinds of brain vagaries. He observes his body as a corpse and abandons the criticism, proud, malice, ego, vanity, desire, envy, gaiety, sorrow, sensuality, anger, greed, affection, pleasure, impurity etc. He is always in the form of conscious and never expects or tempts for any worldly things. He deems that he is exclusively undeviated pleasure and of sound mind. He treats it as his supreme abode and the braid as also sacrificial thread. He observes the soul and supreme soul equally. It is his Sandhyā or worship that he goes beyond the discrimination which is observed by common people between the soul and supreme soul.

सर्वान्कामान्परित्यज्य अद्वैते परमे स्थितिः। ज्ञानदण्डो धृतो येन एकदण्डी स उच्यते। काष्ठदण्डो धृतो येन सर्वाशी ज्ञानवर्जितः। तितिक्षाज्ञानवैराग्यशमादिगुणवर्जितः। भिक्षामात्रेण यो जीवेत्स पापी यतिवृत्तिहा। स याति नरकान्घोरान्महारौरवसंज्ञकान्। इदमन्तरं ज्ञात्वा स परमहंसः॥ ३॥

That Paramahaṁsa exists in its unduel Parabrahma form often giving up all desires. He bears a stick of knowledge, therefore, called Ekadaṇḍī svāmī, but the person who is fulfilled with hopes holding a wooden stick, ignorant, void of the spirit for renunciation, knowledge, detachment, control etc. properties and who has destroyed the profession of yogī by living on the alms, certainly is plucked down in a gross hellish stage. Paramahaṁsa is the person who understands the difference between an evil, does recluse and is the supreme saint.

आशाम्बरो न नमस्कारो न स्वाहाकारो न स्वधाकारो न निन्दा न स्तुतिर्यादृच्छिको भवेद्भिक्षुः। नावाहनं न विसर्जनं न मन्त्रं न ध्यानं नोपासनं च। न लक्ष्यं नालक्ष्यं न पृथङ् नापृथगहं न न त्वं न सर्वं चानिकेतस्थिरमतिरेव स भिक्षुः सौवर्णादीनां नैव परिग्रहेन्न लोक नं नावलोक नं च न च बाधकः क इति चेद्बाधकोऽस्त्येव। यस्माद्भिक्षुर्हिरण्यं रसेन दृष्टं चेत्स ब्रह्महा भवेद्यस्माद्भिक्षुर्हिरण्यं रसेन स्पृष्टं चेत्स पौल्कसो भवेद्यस्माद्भिक्षु हिरण्यं रसेन ग्राह्यं चेत्स आत्महा भवेत्तस्माद्भिक्षुर्हिरण्यं रसेन न दृष्टं च न स्पृष्टं च न ग्राह्यं च। सर्वे कामा मनोगता व्यावर्तन्ते। दुःखे नोद्विग्नः सुखे न स्पृहा त्यागो रागे सर्वत्र शुभाशुभयोरनभिस्नेहो न द्वेष्टि न मोदं च। सर्वेषामिन्द्रियाणां गतिरुपरमते य आत्मन्येवावस्थीयते। तत्पूर्णानन्दैकबोधस्त-द्ब्रह्मैवाहमस्मीति कृतकृत्यो भवति कृतकृत्यो भवति॥ ४॥

He becomes a beggar voluntarily without putting ears on condemnation or praise, the reverence, respect, the spirit to offer has nothing the remain as summation surrendering, hymn the concentration, worship and the visible or invisible. He has no spirit to discriminate between the narrow thinking of– "it is mine and that is yours" and devoid of the universal spirit. He is a man without home but a most strong, mind. He doesn't involve himself in the collection of the gold etc. as also the money, viz., he never runs after money. He doesn't think any discrimination between an attractive and unattractive thing. Nothing is a hindrance for him viz., he can attain whatever he desire. In case, on attainment of supreme soul and detached form the worldly issues, his lure for the gold or money throws him to commit heinous crime like to murder a Brahma, such a beggar does self suicide. Such person living on alms should not either see, touch, becomes anxious in the state of sorrow and remains uncaused for the feeling of pleasure. He becomes unattached even to the good or bad leaving all kinds of attachments to the extent that he neither has any exhilaration and his all sense organs are perfectly cooled down. He carries himself in the orbit where he only engrosses himself in thinking on the element of soul. He always thinks himself the perfect pleasure, the full conscious Brahma and by the power of summoning such a pleasure, he feels himself always in gaiety.

ॐ पूर्णमदः .... इति शान्तिः॥

॥इति परमहंसोपनिषत्समाप्ता॥

***

20. BRAHMOPANIṢAD

ब्रह्मोपनिषद्

॥शान्तिपाठः॥

ॐ सह नाववतु ....इति शान्तिः॥

अथास्य पुरुषस्य चत्वारि स्थानानि भवन्ति। नाभिर्हृदयं कण्ठं मूर्धेति। तत्र चतुष्पादं ब्रह्म विभाति। जागरितं स्वप्नं सुषुप्तं तुरीयमिति। जागरिते ब्रह्मा स्वप्ने विष्णुः सुषुप्तौ रुद्रस्तुरीय-मक्षरम्। स आदित्यो विष्णुश्चेश्वरश्च स्वयममनस्कमश्रोत्रमपाणिपादं ज्योतिर्विदितम्॥ १॥

The Puruṣa has four seats— navel, heart, neck, and head. There Brahman with the four feet specially shines. Those feet are jāgrata, svapna, suṣupti, and turya. In Jégrata, he is Brahmā, in svapna Viṣṇu, in suṣupti Rudra, and in turya the supreme Akṣara. He is Āditya, Viṣṇu, Īśvara, Puruṣa, Jīva, Agani, the resplendent. The Para-brahman shines in the midst of these. He is without manas, ear, hands, feet, and light.

यत्र लोका न लोका देवा न देवा वेदा न वेदा यज्ञा न यज्ञा माता न माता पिता न पिता स्नुषा न स्नुषा चाण्डालो न चाण्डालः पौल्कसो न पौल्कसः श्रमणो न श्रमणः तापसो न तापस इत्येकमेव परं ब्रह्म विभाति निर्वाणम्॥ २॥

न तत्र देवा ऋषयः पितर ईशते प्रतिबुद्धः सर्वविद्येति॥ ३॥

There the worlds are no worlds, Devas no Devas, Vedas no Vedas, sacrifices no sacrifices, mother no mother, father no father, daughter-in-law no daughter-in-law, caṇḍāla no caṇḍala, paulkasa no paulkasa, śramaṇa no śramaṇa, hermits no hermits; so one only Brahman shines as different. In the Hṛḍayākāśa (ākāśa in the heart) in the Cidākāś, that is Brahman. It is extermely subtle. The Hṛḍayākāśa can be known. This moves in it. In Brahman, everthing is strung. Those who thus know the Lord, know everything. In him the Devas, the worlds, the Pitṛs and the Ṛṣis do not rule. He who has awakened knows everything.

हृदिस्था देवताः सर्वा हृदि प्राणाः प्रतिष्ठिताः।
हृदि प्राणश्च ज्योतिश्च त्रिवृत्सूत्रं च तद्विदुः। हृदि चैतन्ये तिष्ठति॥ ४॥
यज्ञोपवीतं परमं पवित्रं प्रजापतेर्यत्सहजं पुरस्तात्।
आयुष्यमग्र्यं प्रतिमुञ्च शुभ्रं यज्ञोपवीतं बलमस्तु तेजः॥ ५॥
सशिखं वपनं कृत्वा बहिःसूत्रं त्यजेद्बुधः। यदक्षरं परं ब्रह्म तत्सूत्रमिति धारयेत्॥ ६॥
सूचनात्सूत्रमित्याहुः सूत्रं नाम परं पदम्। तत्सूत्रं विदितं येन स विप्रो वेदपारगः॥ ७॥
येन सर्वमिदं प्रोतं सूत्रे मणिगणा इव। तत्सूत्रं धारयेद्योगी योगवित्तत्त्वदर्शिवान्॥ ८॥

All the Devas are in the heart; in the heart are all the prāṇa : in the heart are prāṇa, jyoti and that three-plied holy thread. In the heart in caitanya, it (prāṇa) is. Put on the yajñopavīta (holy thread), the supreme, the holy, which came into existence along with the Prajāpati, which gives long life and which is very excellent; let this give you strength and tejas. The wise man having shaved his head completely, should throw away the external thread. He should wear, as the holy thread, the supreme and indestructible Brahman. It is called sūtra, because sūcanāt (indicating) (that the Ātman is in the heart). Sūtra means the supreme abode. He who knows that sūtra is a vipra (Brāhmaṇa), he has crossed the ocean of the Vedas. On that sūtra (thread), everything is strung, like the beads on the thread.

बहि:सूत्रं त्यजेद्विद्वान्योगमुत्तममास्थित:।

ब्रह्मभावमिदं सूत्रं धारयेद्य: स चेतन:। धारणात्तस्य सूत्रस्य नोच्छिष्टो नाशुचिर्भवेत्॥ ९॥

सूत्रमन्तर्गतं येषां ज्ञानयज्ञोपवीतिनाम्। ते वै सूत्रविदो लोके ते च यज्ञोपवीतिन:॥ १०॥

ज्ञानशिखिनो ज्ञाननिष्ठा ज्ञानयज्ञोपवीतिन:। ज्ञानमेव परं तेषां पवित्रं ज्ञानमुच्यते॥ ११॥

अग्नेरिव शिखा नान्या यस्य ज्ञानमयी शिखा। स शिखीत्युच्यते विद्वान्नेतरे केशधारिण:॥ १२

The yogin, well versed in yoga and having a clear perception of Truth, should wear the thread. Practising the noble yoga, the wise man should abandon the external thread. He who wears the sūtra, as Brahman, he is an intelligent being. By wearing the sūtra, he is not polluted. They whose sūtra, is within, whose yajñopavīta is jñāna— they only know the sūtra, and, they only wear the yajñopavīta in this world. Those whose tuft of hair is jñāna, who are firmly grounded in jñāna and whose yajñopavīta is jñāna, consider jñāna only as supreme. Jñāna is holy and excellent. He whose śikhā (tuft of hair) is jñāna like the śikhī (flame of agni)— he, the wise one; only wears a true śikhā; others wear a mere tuft of hair.

कर्मण्यधिकृता ये तु वैदिके ब्राह्मणादय:। तै: संधार्यमिदं सूत्रं क्रियाङ्गं तद्धि वै स्मृतम्॥ १३॥

शिखा ज्ञानमयी यस्य उपवीतं च तन्मयम्। ब्राह्मण्यं सकलं तस्य इति ब्रह्मविदो विदु:॥ १४॥

इदं यज्ञोपवीतं तु पवित्रं यत्परायणम्। स विद्वान्यज्ञोपवीती स्यात्स यज्ञ: तं यज्वानं विदु:॥ १५॥

Those brāhmaṇas and others who perform the ceremonies prescribed in the Vedas— they wear this thread only as a symbol of their ceremonies. Those who know the Vedas say that he only is a true brāhmaṇa who wears the śikhā of jñāna and whose yajñopavīta is the same (jñāna). This yajñopavīta (Yajña means Viṣṇu or sacrifice and Upavīta is that which surrounds; hence that which surrounds Viṣṇu) is supreme and is the supreme refuge. He who wears that really knows— he only wears the sūtra, he is Yajña (Viṣṇu) and he only knows Yajña (Viṣṇu).

एको देव: सर्वभूतेषु गूढ: सर्वव्यापी सर्वभूतान्तरात्मा।

कर्माध्यक्ष: सर्वभूताधिवास: साक्षी चेता केवलो निर्गुणश्च॥ १६॥

एको वशी सर्वभूतान्तरात्मा एकं रूपं बहुधा य: करोति।

तमात्मस्थं येऽनुपश्यन्ति धीरास्तेषां शांति: शाश्वती नेतरेषाम्॥ १७॥

आत्मानमरणिं कृत्वा प्रणवं चोत्तरारणिम्।

ध्याननिर्मथनाभ्यासद्देवं पश्येन्निगूढवत्॥ १८॥

तिलेषु तैलं दधनीव सर्पिराप: स्रोत: स्वरणीषु चाग्नि:।
एवमात्मात्मनि गृह्यतेऽसौ सत्येनैनं तपसा योऽनुपश्यति॥ १९॥
ऊर्णनाभिर्यथा तन्तून्सृजते संहरत्यपि।
जाग्रत्स्वप्ने तथा जीवो गच्छत्यागच्छते पुन:॥ २०॥
नेत्रस्थं जागरितं विद्यात्कण्ठे स्वप्नं समाविशेत्।
सुषुप्तं हृदयस्थं तु तुरीयं मूर्ध्नि संस्थितम्॥ २१॥
यतो वाचो निवर्तन्ते अप्राप्य मनसा सह।
आनन्दमेतज्जीवस्य यं ज्ञात्वा मुच्यते बुध:॥ २२॥
सर्वव्यापिनमात्मानं क्षीरे सर्पिरिवान्वितम्।
आत्मविद्यातपोमूलं तद्ब्रह्मोपनिषत्पदं तद्ब्रह्मोपनिषत्पदमिति॥ २३॥

One God hidden in all things, pervades all things and the Inner Life of all things. He awards the fruits of karma, he lives in all things, he sees all things without any extraneous help, he is the soul of all. There is nothing like him and he is without any guṇas (being secondless). He is the great wise one. He is the one doer among the many actionless objects. He is always making one thing appear as several (by māyā). Those wise men who see him in buddhi, they only obtain eternal peace. Having made Ātman, as the upper araṇi (attritional piece of wood) and Praṇava, the lower araṇi, by constant practice of dhyāna, one should see the concealed deity. As the oil in the sesamum seed, as the ghee in the curds, as the water in the rivers, and as the fire in the araṇi, so they who practise turth and austerities see Him in the buddhi. As the spider throws out and draws into itself the threads, so the Jīva goes and returns during the jāgrata and the svapna states. The heart is in the form of a closed lotus-flower, with its head-hanging down; it has a hole in the top. Know it to be the great abode of all. Know that during jāgrata it (Jīva) dwells in the eye, and during svapna in the throat; during suṣupti, it is in the heart and during turya in the head. (Because buddhi unites) the Paratyagātma with the Paramātmā, the worship of sandhyā (union) arose. So we should perform sandhyāvandana (rites). The sandhyāvandana performed by dhyāna requires no water. It gives no trouble to the body or the speech. Knowing That which unites all things in the sandhyā of the one-staffed sannyāsins, knowing That from which speech and mind turn back without being able to obtain it and That which is the bliss of Jīva, the wise one is freed. The secret of Brahmavidyā is to reveal the real nature of the Ātmā, that is all-pervading, that is like ghee in the milk, that is the source of ātmavidyā and tapas and to show that everything is in essence one.

सह नाववतु ....इति शान्ति:॥

॥इति ब्रह्मोपनिषत्समाप्ता॥

21. AMṚTANĀDOPANIṢAD

अमृतनादोपनिषद्

।।शान्तिपाठः।।

ॐ सह नाववतु। सह नौ भुनक्तु। सह वीर्यं करवावहै।

तेजस्विनावधीतमस्तु मा विद्विषावहै।।

ॐ शान्तिः शान्तिः शान्तिः।।

शास्त्राण्यधीत्य मेधावी अभ्यस्य च पुनः पुनः। परमं ब्रह्म विज्ञाय उल्कावत्तान्यथोत्सृजेत्।। १।।

ओंकाररथमारुह्य विष्णुं कृत्वाथ सारथिम्। ब्रह्मलोकपदान्वेषी रुद्राराधनतत्परः।। २।।

तावद्रथेन गन्तव्यं यावद्रथपथि स्थितः। स्थात्वा रथपतिस्थानं रथमुत्सृज्य गच्छति।। ३।।

मात्रालिङ्गपदं त्यक्त्वा शब्दव्यञ्जनवर्जितम्। अस्वरेण मकारेण पदं सूक्ष्मं हि गच्छति।। ४।।

शब्दादि विषयान्पञ्च मनश्चैवातिचञ्चलम्। चिन्तयेदात्मनो रश्मीन्प्रत्याहारः स उच्यते।। ५।।

प्रत्याहारस्तथा ध्यानं प्राणायामोऽथ धारणा। तर्कश्चैव समाधिश्च षडङ्गो योग उच्यते।। ६।।

यथा पर्वतधातूनां दह्यन्ते धमनान्मलाः। तथेन्द्रियकृता दोषा दह्यन्ते प्राणधारणात्।। ७।।

प्राणायामैर्दहेद्दोषान्धारणाभिश्च किल्बिषम्। प्रत्याहारेण संसर्गान् ध्यानेनानीश्वरान्गुणान्।। ८।।

किल्बिषं हि क्षयं नीत्वा रुचिरं चैव चिन्तयेत्।। ९।।

रुचिरं रेचकं चैव वायोराकर्षणं तथा। प्राणायामास्त्रयः प्रोक्ता रेचपूरककुम्भकाः।। १०।।

सव्याहर्ति सप्रणवां गायत्रीं शिरसा सह। त्रिः पठेदायतप्राणः प्राणायामः स उच्यते।। ११।।

उत्क्षिप्य वायुमाकाशे शून्ये कृत्वा निरात्मकम्। शून्यभावे नियुञ्जीयाद्रेचकस्येति लक्षणम्।। १२।।

वक्त्रेणोत्पलनालेन तोयमाकर्षयेन्नरः। एवं वायुर्ग्रहीतव्यः पूरकस्येति लक्षणम्।। १३।।

नोच्छ्वसेन्न च निश्वसेन्नैव गात्राणि चालयेत्। एवं भावं नियुञ्जीयात्कुम्भकस्येति लक्षणम्।। १४।।

अन्धवत्पश्य रूपाणि शब्दं बधिरवच्छृणु। काष्ठवत्पश्य वै देहं प्रशान्तस्येति लक्षणम्।। १५।।

मनःसंकल्पकं ध्यात्वा संक्षिप्यात्मनि बुद्धिमान्। धारयित्वा तथात्मानं धारणा परिकीर्तिता।। १६।।

आगमस्याविरोधेन ऊहनं तर्क उच्यते। समं मन्येत यल्लब्ध्वा स समाधिः प्रकीर्तितः।। १७।।

The wise having studied the Śāstras and reflected on them again and again and having come to know Brahman, should abandon them all like a firebrand. Having ascended the car of Oṁ with Viṣṇu (the Higher Self) as the charioteer, one wishing to go to the seat of Brahmaloka intent on the worship of Rudra, should go in the chariot so long as he can go. Then abandoning the car, he reaches the place of the Lord of the car. Having given up mātrās, liṅga, and pada, he attains the subtle pada (seat or word) without vowels or consonants by means of the letter M without the svara (accent). That is called pratyāhāra when one merely thinks of the five objects of sense, such as sound, etc., as also the very unsteady mind as the reins of Ātman. Pratyāhāra (subjugation of the senses), dhyāna (contemplation), prāṇāyāma (control of breath), dhāraṇā (concentration), tārka and samādhī are said to be the six parts of yoga. Just as the impurities of mountain-minerals are burnt by the blower, so the stains committed by the organs are burned by checking prāṇa. Through prāṇāyāma should be burnt the stains; through dhāraṇā, the sins; through pratyāhāra, the (bad) association; and through dhyāna, the godless qualities. Having destroyed the sins, one should think of Rucira (the shining). Rucira (cessation), expiration and inspiration— these three are prāṇāyāma of (recaka, pūraka and kumbhaka) expiration, inspiration and cessation of breath. That is called (one) prāṇāyāma when one repeats with a prolonged (or elongated) breath three times the Gāyatrī with its vyāhrutis and Praṇava (before it) along with the śiras (the head) joining after it. Raising up the vāyu from the ākāśa (region, viz., the heart) and making the body void (of vāyu) and empty and uniting (the soul) to the state of void, is called recaka (expiration). That is called pūraka (inspiration) when one takes in vāyu, as a man would take water into his mouth through the lotus-stalk. That is called kumbhaka (cessation of breath) when there is no expiration or inspiration and the body is motionless, remaining still in one state. Then he sees forms like the blind, hears sounds like the deaf and sees the body like wood. This is the characteristic of one that has attained much quiescence. That is called dhāraṇā when the wise man regards the mind as saṅkalpa and merging saṅkalpa into Ātmā, contemplates upon his Ātman (alone). That is called tāraka when one makes inference which does not conflict with the Vedas. That is called samādhi in which one, on attaining it, thinks (all) equal.

भूमौ दर्भासने रम्ये सर्वदोषविवर्जिते। कृत्वा मनोमयीं रक्षां जप्त्वा वै रथमण्डले॥ १८॥
पद्मकं स्वस्तिकं वापि भद्रासनमथापि वा। बद्ध्वा योगासनं सम्यगुत्तराभिमुखः स्थितः॥ १९॥
नासिकापुटमङ्गुल्या पिधायैकेन मारुतम्। आकृष्य धारयेदग्निं शब्दमेव विचिन्तयेत्॥ २०॥
ओमित्येकाक्षरं ब्रह्म ओमित्येतन्न रेचयेत्। दिव्यमन्त्रेण बहुधा कुर्यादामलमुक्तये॥ २१॥
पश्चाद्ध्यायीत पूर्वोक्तक्रमशो मन्त्रविद्बुधः। स्थूलादिस्थूलसूक्ष्मं च नाभेरूर्ध्वमुपक्रमः॥ २२॥
तिर्यगूर्ध्वमधोदृष्टि विहाय च महामतिः। स्थिरस्थायी विनिष्कम्पः सदा योगं समभ्यसेत्॥ २३॥
तालमात्राविनिष्कम्पो धारणायोजनं तथा। द्वादशमात्रो योगस्तु कालतो नियमः स्मृतः॥ २४॥
अघोषमव्यञ्जनमस्वरं च अतालुकण्ठोष्ठमनासिकं च यत्।
अरेफजातमुभयोष्मवर्जितं यदक्षरं न क्षरते कथंचित्॥ २५॥
येनासौ गच्छते मार्गं प्राणस्तेनाभिगच्छति। अतस्तमभ्यसेन्नित्यं यन्मार्गगमनाय वै॥ २६॥
हृद्द्वारं वायुद्वारं च मूर्धद्वारमथापरम्। मोक्षद्वारं बिलं चैव सुषिरं मण्डलं विदुः॥ २७॥

Seating himself on the ground on a seat of kuśa grass which is pleasant and devoid of all evils, having protected himself mentally (from all evil influences), uttering ratha-maṇḍala, assuming either padma, svastika, or bhadra posture or any other which can be practised easily, facing the north and closing the nostril with the thumb, one should inspire through the other nostril and retain breath inside and preserve the Agni (fire). Then he should think of the sound (Oṁ) alone. Oṁ, the one letter is Brahman; Oṁ should not be breathed out. Through this divine mantra (Oṁ), it should be done many times to get rid himself of impurity. Then as said before, the mantra-knowing wise should regularly meditate, beginning with the navel upwards in the gross, the primary (or less) gross and subtle (states). The greatly wise should give up all (sight) seeing across, up or down, and should practise yoga always being motionless and without tremor. The union as stated (done) by remaining without tremor in the hollow stalk (viz., Suṣumnā) alone is dhāraṇā. The yoga with the ordained duration of twelve mātrās is called (dhāraṇā). That which never decays is Akṣara (Oṁ) which is without ghoṣa (third, fourth, and fifth letters from K), consonant, vowel, palatal, guttural, nasal, letter R and sibilants. Prāṇa travels through (or goes by) that path through which this Akṣara (Oṁ) goes. Therefore it should be practised daily, in order to pass along that (course). It is through the opening (or hole) of the heart, through the opening of vāyu (probably navel), through the opening of the head and through the opening of mokṣa. They call it bila (cave), suṣira (hole), or maṇḍala (wheel).

भयं क्रोधमथालस्यमतिस्वप्नातिजागरम्। अत्याहारमनाहारं नित्यं योगी विवर्जयेत्॥ २८॥
अनेन विधिना सम्यङ् नित्यमभ्यस्यते क्रमात्। स्वयमुत्पद्यते ज्ञानं त्रिभिर्मासैर्न संशयः॥ २९॥
चतुर्भिः पश्यते देवान्पञ्चभिर्विततःक्रमः। इच्छयाप्नोति कैवल्यं षष्ठे मासि न संशयः॥ ३०॥

A yogin should always avoid fear, anger, laziness, too much sleep or waking and too much food or fasting. If the above rule be well and strictly practised each day, spiritual wisdom will arise of itself in three months without doubt. In four months, he sees the devas; in five months, he knows (or becomes) Brahmaniṣṭha; and truely in six months he attains kaivalya at will. There is no doubt.

पार्थिवः पञ्चमात्रस्तु चतुर्मात्रस्तु वारुणः। आग्नेयस्तु त्रिमात्रोऽसौ वायव्यस्तु द्विमात्रकः॥ ३१॥
एकमात्रस्तथाकाशो ह्यर्धमात्रं तु चिन्तयेत्। संधिं कृत्वा तु मनसा चिन्तयेदात्मनात्मनि॥ ३२॥
त्रिंशत्सार्धाङ्गुलः प्राणो यत्र प्राणैः प्रतिष्ठितः। एष प्राण इति ख्यातो बाह्यप्राणस्य गोचरः॥ ३३॥
अशीतिश्च शतं चैव सहस्राणि त्रयोदश। लक्षश्चैको विनिश्वास अहोरात्रप्रमाणतः॥ ३४॥
प्राण आद्यो हृदि स्थाने अपानस्तु पुनर्गुदे। समानो नाभिदेशे तु उदानः कण्ठमाश्रितः॥ ३५॥
व्यानः सर्वेषु चाङ्गेषु व्याप्य तिष्ठति सर्वदा। अथ वर्णास्तु पञ्चानां प्राणादीनामनुक्रमात्॥ ३६॥
रक्तवर्णो मणिप्रख्यः प्राणवायुः प्रकीर्तितः। अपनास्तस्य मध्ये तु इन्द्रगोपसमप्रभः॥ ३७॥
समानस्तु द्वयोर्मध्ये गोक्षीरधवलप्रभः। आपाण्डुर उदानश्च व्यानो ह्यर्चिःसमप्रभः॥ ३८॥
यस्येदं मण्डलं भित्त्वा मारुतो याति मूर्धनि।
यत्र कुत्र म्रियेद्वापि न स भूयोऽभिजायते न स भूयोऽभिजायत इत्युपनिषत्॥ ३९॥

That which is of the earth is of five mātrās (or it takes five mātrās to pronounce

Pārthiva-Praṇava) That which is of water of four mātrās; of agni, three mātrās; of vāyu, two; and of ākāśa, one. But he should think of that which is with no mātrās. Having united Ātman with manas, one should contemplate upon Ātman by means of ātmā. Prāṇa is thirty digits long. Such is the position (or range) of prāṇas. This is called Prāṇa which is the seat of the external prāṇas. The breaths by day and night are numbered as 1, 13, 180. (Of the prāṇas) the first (viz.,) Prāṇa is pervading the heart; Apāna, the anus; samāna, the navel; Udāna, the throat; and Vyāna, all parts of the body. Then come the colours of the five prāṇas in order. Prāṇa is said to be of the colour of a blood-red gem or coral); Apāna which is in the middle is of the colour of Indra-gopa (in insect of white or red colour); Samāna is between the colour of pure milk and crystal (or oily and shining), between both (Prāṇa and Apāna: Udāna is apāṇdura (pale white); and Vyāna resembles the colour of light. That man is never reborn wherever he may die, whose breath goes out of the head after piercing through this maṇḍala (of the pineal gland). That man is never reborn.

ॐ सह नाववतु.... इति शान्तिः॥

॥अमृतनादोपनिषद् समाप्ता॥

***

22. ATHARVAŚIRA UPANIṢAD

अथर्वशिर उपनिषद्

This Upaniṣad is related to the tradition of Atharvaveda. In the first three Kaṇḍikās, a description of the realisation to the entity of supreme Soul in the form of Rudra by the gods as also the hymns recited for, his pleasure; are given. He has been stated as the primitive cause, the past future and the present, the male and female, the perishable, the immortal, the confident, the secret; he too is the power that adorns the inert and sensitive world with peculiarities. He has been stated beyond Oṁ, the letter 'A' 'U' and 'M'. Describing Lord Rudra as Praṇava his peculiarities, the power and importance of his worship has been described in fourth Kaṇḍikā. In the Sixth Kaṇḍikā the Origin of Sattva, Rajas, Tamas etc. properties and the basic activated element 'Apaḥ' and the evolvement of it has been described. The importance of reciting this Upaniṣad has been described in the Seventh Kaṇḍikā.

॥शान्तिपाठः॥

ॐ भद्रं कर्णेभिः शृणुयाम देवा भद्रं पश्येमाक्षभिर्यत्राः।
स्थिरैरङ्गैस्तुष्टुवाꣳ सस्तनूभिर्व्यशेम देवहितं यदायुः॥
स्वस्ति न ऽ इन्द्रो वृद्धश्रवाः स्वस्ति नः पूषा विश्ववेदाः।
स्वस्ति नस्ताक्ष्र्यो अरिष्टनेमिः स्वस्ति नो बृहस्पतिर्दधातु॥
ॐ शान्तिः शान्तिः शान्तिः॥

O God! May we listen to the benevolent speech (words) from our ear and see the benevolent scenes always. O god! May we live full life praying you ceaselessly with healthy body. So that we can perform the great deeds. May Lord Indra, the king of gods and great illustrious; do our welfare. May the omniscient god Pūṣā do our welfare.

देवा ह वै स्वर्गं लोकमायँस्ते देवा रुद्रमपृच्छन्को भवानिति। सोऽब्रवीदहमेकः प्रथममासं वर्तामि च भविष्यामि च नान्यः कश्चिन्मत्तो व्यतिरिक्त इति। सोऽन्तरादन्तरं प्राविशत् दिशश्चान्तरं प्राविशत् सोऽहं नित्यानित्योऽहं व्यक्ताव्यक्तो ब्रह्माहमब्रह्माहं प्राञ्चः प्रत्यञ्चोऽहं दक्षिणाञ्च उदञ्चोऽहं अधश्चोर्ध्वं चाहं दिशश्च प्रतिदिशश्चाहं पुमानपुमान् स्त्रियश्चाहं गायत्र्यहं सावित्र्यहं सरस्वत्यहं त्रिष्टुब्जगत्यनुष्टुप् चाहं छन्दोऽहं गार्हपत्यो दक्षिणाग्निराहवनीयोऽहं सत्योऽहं गौरहं गौर्यहमृगहं यजुरहं सामाहमथर्वाङ्गिरसोऽहं ज्येष्ठोऽहं श्रेष्ठोऽहं वरिष्ठोऽहमापोऽहं तेजोऽहं गुह्योऽहमरण्योऽहमक्षरमहं क्षरमहं पुष्करमहं पवित्रमहमग्रं च मध्यं च बहिश्च पुरस्ताज्ज्यो-तिरित्यहमेव सर्वे मामेव स सर्वे स मां यो मां वेद स देवान्वेद स सर्वांश्च वेदान्साङ्गानपि ब्रह्म ब्राह्मणैश्च गां गोभिर्ब्राह्मणान्ब्राह्मण्येन हविर्हविषा आयुरायुषा सत्येन सत्यं धर्मेण धर्मं तर्पयामि स्वेन तेजसा। ततो ह वै ते देवा रुद्रमपृच्छन् ते देवा रुद्रमपश्यन्। ते देवा रुद्रमध्यायंस्ततो देवा ऊर्ध्वबाहवो रुद्रं स्तुन्वन्ति॥ १॥

The god once visited at the heavenly abode and asked Lord Rudra "Who are you?" Lord Rudra answered– I am one. I am past, present and future also. There is nothing except me. The god residing in the heart of all living organisms and inserted in all directions too is I myself. I am eternal and non-eternal, visible and invisible, Brāhmaṇa and non-Brāhmaṇa. I am eastern and western, southern and northern, I am below and above (Chānd. 7,25,1), I am the quarters and the sub-quarters. I am masculine and neuter and feminine. I am Gāyatrī, Sāvitrī and Sarasvatī. Triṣṭubh, the Jagatī and the Anuṣṭubh. I am the fire in all forms viz., Gārhapatya, Daksiṇāgni and Āhavanīya. I am the cow and the she-buffalo. I am Ṛc, Yajus and Sāman and I am the Atharvāṅgiras.' I am the eldest, the noblest and the best. I am the water and the fire, I am hidden in the fire-sticks. I am the imperishable and the perishable. I am the lotus flower and I am the Soma-filter. I am the powerful, I am within and without, I am 'the light [born] in the East'. I am all, I am the unending. He who knows me, becomes all at the same time. He knows the gods and all the Vedas and the Vedāṅgas. And I am also that, I who with my power satisfy the Brāhmaṇa by the Brāhmaṇas, the cow with the cows, the Brāhmaṇas with the Brāhmaṇahood, the sacrificial food with the sacrificial food, the life with the life, the truth with the truth, the law with the law." Then the gods asked Rudra, the gods looked at Rudra, the gods thought over Rudra, the gods started praying him with their arms lifted up.

ॐ यो वै रुद्रः स भगवान्यश्च ब्रह्मा तस्मै वै नमो नमः॥१॥ यो वै रुद्रः स भगवान्यश्च विष्णुस्तस्मै वै नमो नमः॥२॥ यो वै रुद्रः स भगवान्यश्च स्कन्दस्तस्मै वै नमो नमः॥३॥ यो वै रुद्रः स भगवान्यश्चेन्द्रस्तस्मै वै नमो नमः॥४॥ यो वै रुद्रः स भगवान्यश्चाग्निस्तस्मै वै नमो नमः॥५॥ यो वै रुद्रः स भगवान्यश्च वायुस्तस्मै वै नमो नमः॥६॥ यो वै रुद्रः स भगवान्यश्च सूर्यस्तस्मै वै नमो नमः॥७॥ यो वै रुद्रः स भगवान्यश्च सोमस्तस्मै वै नमो नमः॥८॥ यो वै रुद्रः स भगवान्ये चाष्टौ ग्रहास्तस्मै वै नमो नमः॥९॥ यो वै रुद्रः स भगवान्ये चाष्टौ प्रतिग्रहास्तस्मै वै नमो नमः॥१०॥ यो वै रुद्रः स भगवान्यच्च भूस्तस्मै वै नमो नमः॥११॥ यो वै रुद्रः स भगवान्यच्च भुवस्तस्मै वै नमो नमः॥१२॥ यो वै रुद्रः स भगवान्यच्च स्वस्तस्मै वै नमो नमः॥१३॥ यो वै रुद्रः स भगवान्यच्च महस्तस्मै वै नमो नमः॥१४॥ यो वै रुद्रः स भगवान्या च पृथिवी तस्मै वै नमो नमः॥१५॥ यो वै रुद्रः स भगवान्यच्चान्तरिक्षं तस्मै वै नमो नमः॥१६॥ यो वै रुद्रः स भगवान्या च द्यौस्तस्मै वै नमो नमः॥१७॥ यो वै रुद्रः स भगवान्याश्चापस्तस्मै वै नमो नमः॥१८॥ यो वै रुद्रः स भगवान्यच्च तेजस्तस्मै वै नमो नमः॥१९॥ यो वै रुद्रः स भगवान्यच्चाकाशं तस्मै वै नमो नमः॥२०॥ यो वै रुद्रः स भगवान्यश्च कालस्तस्मै वै नमो नमः॥२१॥ यो वै रुद्रः स भगवान्यश्च यमस्तस्मै वै नमो नमः॥२२॥ यो वै रुद्रः स भगवान्यश्च मृत्युस्तस्मै वै नमो नमः॥२३॥ यो वै रुद्रः स भगवान्यच्चामृतं तस्मै वै नमो नमः॥२४॥ यो वै रुद्रः स भगवान्यच्च विश्वं तस्मै वै नमो नमः॥२५॥ यो वै रुद्रः स भगवान्यच्च स्थूलं तस्मै वै नमो नमः॥२६॥ यो वै रुद्रः स भगवान्यच्च सूक्ष्मं तस्मै वै नमो नमः॥२७॥ यो वै रुद्रः स भगवान्यच्च शुक्लं तस्मै वै नमो नमः॥२८॥ यो वै रुद्रः स भगवान्यच्च कृष्णं तस्मै वै नमो नमः॥२९॥ यो वै रुद्रः स भगवान्यच्च कृत्स्नं तस्मै वै नमो नमः॥३०॥ यो वै रुद्रः स भगवान्यच्च सत्यं तस्मै वै नमो नमः॥३१॥ यो वै रुद्रः स भगवान्यच्च सर्वं तस्मै वै नमो नमः॥३२॥॥२॥

O Lord Rudra! You are in the form of Brahmā, we salute you O Lord Rudra! You are in the form of Lord Viṣṇu and we salute you. O Lord Rudra! You are saluted in the form of Skanda. You are saluted in the form of Indra, the fire, the wind and the sun. O Lord Rudra! You are in the form of eight stars and sub-stars, you are saluted in these forms too. You are further saluted in the form of Bhūḥ, Bhuvaḥ, Svaḥ, Mahaḥ. Rudra is this exalted one and the earth, to him the salutation, Rudra is this exalted one and the mid-region, to him the salutation, Rudra is this exalted one and the heaven, to him the salutation, Rudra is this exalted one and the water, to him the salutation, Rudra is this exalted one and the fire, to him the salutation, Rudra is this exalted one and the Kāla, to him the salutation, Rudra is this exalted one and the Yama, to him the salutation, the salutation!

Rudra is this exalted one and the Mṛtyu, to him the salutation, the salutation! Rudra is this exalted one and the immortal, to him the salutation, the salutation! Rudra is this exalted one and the ether, to him the salutation, the salutation! Rudra is this exalted one and the all, to him the salutation, the salutation! Rudra is this exalted one and the gross, to him the salutation, the salutation! Rudra is this exalted one and the fine, to him the salutation, the salutation! Rudra is this exalted one and the white, to him the salutation, the salutation! Rudra is this exalted one and the black, to him the salutation, the salutation! Rudra is this exalted one and the whole, to him the salutation, the salutation! Rudra is this exalted one and-the true, to him the salutation, the salutation! Rudra is this exalted one and the universe, to him the salutation, the salutation!

भूस्ते आदिर्मध्यं भुवस्ते स्वस्ते शीर्षं विश्वरूपोऽसि ब्रह्मैकस्त्वं द्विधा त्रिधा बद्धस्त्वं शान्तिस्त्वं पुष्टिस्त्वं हुतमहुतं दत्तमदत्तं सर्वमसर्वं विश्वमविश्वं कृतमकृतं परमपरं परायणं च त्वम्। अपाम सोमममृता अभूमागन्म ज्योतिरविदाम देवान्। किं नूनमस्मान्कृणवदरातिः किमु धूर्तिरमृतं मर्त्यस्य च।

Lord Rudra! *Bhūr* is your beginning, *bhuvar* your middle, *svar* your head. You are in universal form and an exclusive Brāhmaṇa. You are one, twofold, threefold. You are growth, you are peace, you are prosperity. What is offered in sacrifice and what not offered in sacrifice, given and not given, all and non-all, whole and non-whole, done and undone, the highest of the highest (*parama-param*, that is how it is to be split), the highest goal, you are it. We have drunk Soma, have become immortal. We have entered into the light, found out the gods! What could the hostility harm us now, What, O immortal, the malice of man! (See Ṛg. 8, 48, 3).

सोमसूर्य पुरस्तात् सूक्ष्मः पुरुषः। सर्वं जगद्धितं वा एतदक्षरं प्राजापत्यं सौम्यं सूक्ष्मं पुरुषमग्राह्यमग्राह्येण भावं भावेन सौम्यं सौम्येन सूक्ष्मं सूक्ष्मेण वायव्यं वायव्येंन ग्रसति स्वेन तेजसा तस्मा उपसंहर्त्रे महाग्रासाय वै नमो नमः। हृदिस्था देवताः सर्वा हृदि प्राणाः प्रतिष्ठिताः। हृदि त्वमसि यो नित्यं तिस्रो मात्राः परस्तु सः। तस्योत्तरतः शिरो दक्षिणतः पादौ य उत्तरतः स ओङ्कारः य ओङ्कारः स प्रणवो यः प्रणवः स सर्वव्यापी यः सर्वव्यापी सोऽनन्तो योऽनन्तस्तत्तारं यत्तारं तत्सूक्ष्मं यत्सूक्ष्मं तच्छुक्लं यच्छुक्लं तद्वैद्युतं यद्वैद्युतं तत्परं ब्रह्म यत्परं ब्रह्म स एकः य एकः स रुद्रो यो रुद्रः स ईशानो य ईशानः स भगवान् महेश्वरः॥ ३॥

O God! You are subtle soul (Puruṣa) appeared earlier than the Sun and moon. You are modest man (Puruṣa). The whole world is that syllable [Oṁ], which swallows what is Prajāpati-like, what is soma-like, the subtle soul, the seizable by its unseizable, the existence by its existence, the Soma-like by its Soma-like, the subtle by its subtle, the wind-like by its wind-like. To it as the greatest swallower, the salutation, the salutation!

All deities are in the heart and the vital breaths. You are beyond the three moras *i.e.* A. U and M and resides in the heart of all living organisms. Its head is in the North, feet are in the South. He who is to the North, is the sound Oṁ, as the sound Oṁ he is the holy call, as the holy call, he is all-pervading, as all-pervading he is infinite, as infinite he is the protecting (*tāram*), as the protecting he is the pure, as the pure he is the subtle, as the subtle he is the lightning-like, as the lightning-like he is the highest Brāhmaṇa, as the highest Brāhmaṇa he is the one, as the one he is Rudra, as Rudra he is the ruler, as the ruler he is the exalted Maheśvara.

अथ कस्मादुच्यत ओङ्कारो यस्मादुच्चार्यमाण एव प्राणानूर्ध्वमुत्क्रामयति तस्मादुच्यते ओङ्कारः। अथ कस्मादुच्यते प्रणवः यस्मादुच्चार्यमाण एव ऋग्यजुःसामाथर्वाङ्गिरसो ब्रह्म ब्राह्मणेभ्यः प्रणामयति नामयति च तस्मादुच्यते प्रणवः।

अथ कस्मादुच्यते सर्वव्यापी यस्मादुच्चार्यमाण एव सर्वान् लोकान् व्याप्नोति स्नेहो यथा पललपिण्डमिव शान्तरूपमोतप्रोतमनुप्राप्तो व्यतिषिक्तश्च तस्मादुच्यते सर्वव्यापी। अथ कस्मादुच्यतेऽनन्तो यस्मादुच्चार्यमाण एव तिर्यगूर्ध्वमधस्ताच्चास्यान्तो नोपलभ्यते तस्मादुच्यतेऽनन्तः।

अथ कस्मादुच्यते तारं यस्मादुच्चार्यमाण एव गर्भजन्मव्याधिजरामरणसंसारमहाभयात्तारयति त्रायते च तस्मादुच्यते तारम्। अथ कस्मादुच्यते शुक्लं यस्मादुच्चार्यमाण एव क्लन्दते क्लामयते च तस्मादुच्यते शुक्लम्।

अथ कस्मादुच्यते सूक्ष्मं यस्मादुच्चार्यमाण एव सूक्ष्मो भूत्वा शरीराण्यधितिष्ठति सर्वाणि चाङ्गान्यभिमृशति तस्मादुच्यते सूक्ष्मम्। अथ कस्मादुच्यते वैद्युतं यस्मादुच्चार्यमाण एवाव्यक्ते महति तमसि द्योतयते तस्मादुच्यते वैद्युतम्।

अथ कस्मादुच्यते परं ब्रह्म यस्मात्परमपरं परायणं च बृहद्बृहत्या बृंहयति तस्मादुच्यते परं ब्रह्म। अथ कस्मादुच्यते एको यः सर्वान्प्राणान्संभक्ष्य संभक्षणेनाजः संसृजति विसृजति च। तीर्थमेके व्रजन्ति तीर्थमेके दक्षिणाः प्रत्यञ्च उदञ्चः प्राञ्चोऽभिव्रजन्त्येके तेषां सर्वेषामिह संगतिः। साकं स एको भूतश्चरति प्रजानां तस्मादुच्यत एकः।

अथ कस्मादुच्यते रुद्रः यस्मादृषिभिर्नान्यैर्भक्तैर्द्रुतमस्य रूपमुपलभ्यते तस्मादुच्यते रुद्रः। अथ कस्मादुच्यते ईशानः यःसर्वान्देवानीशते ईशनीभिर्जननीभिश्च परम शक्तिभिः। अभि त्वा शूर नोनुमो दुग्धा इव धेनवः। ईशानमस्य जगतः स्वर्दृशमीशानमिन्द्र तस्थुष इति तस्मादुच्यत ईशानः।

अथ कस्मादुच्यते भगवान्महेश्वरः यस्माद्भक्ताज्ञानेन भजन्त्यनुगृह्णाति च वाचं संसृजति विसृजति च सर्वान्भावान्परित्यज्यात्मज्ञानेन योगैश्वर्येण महति महीयते तस्मादुच्यते भगवान्महेश्वरः। तदेतद्रुद्रचरितम्॥ ४॥

But why is he called the sound Oṁ? Because, being uttered he makes the vital breaths go upwards on high, therefore he is called the sound Oṁ. It is recited for conveying salute to Ṛg, Yajuḥ, Sāma, Atharva and the Brāhmaṇas, hence, it is called Praṇava. Why is it said omnipresent? Because, being uttered, he pervades and permeates that quiet one (Kāṭh.3,13), sewn lengthwise and crosswise (Bṛh.3,6), as a lump of sesame-dough with oil, therefore he is called all-pervading. It is called unending (Ananta) because ending is not perceived irrespective of the recital made upward, downward and slantly.

But why is he called the Tāram (protecting)? Because, being uttered, he rescues from the dire fear of conception, birth, illness, old age, death and from the transmigration of the soul and protects, therefore, it is called the protecting.

But why is he called the pure (*śu-klam*)? Because, being uttered, he makes noise (*klandate*) and makes one tired (*klāmayati*), therefore he is called the pure.

But why is he called the subtle? Because, being uttered, he takes possession of the body in a subtle form and tinges all the limbs, therefore he is called the subtle.

But why is he called lightning-like? Because, being uttered, he illumines it in the great unmanifest darkness, therefore he is called lightning-like.

But why is he called the highest Brahman? Because he is the highest of the highest, the highest goal, the strong and strengthens by the strong [magic power] (*bṛhatyā bṛṁhayati*), therefore he is called the highest Brahman. But why is he called the one? He who, the devourer of all vital powers (*prāṇāḥ*), by the act of devouring them, as being more eternal unites them and again spreads them apart, so that some hasten to their master and some others hasten to their master and some others hasten to their master and yet others [as the natural powers corresponding to the Prāṇas] hasten to the South, the West, the North and the East, who is the meeting place of all here, and has become one by uniting, moves along [as the vital breath] of the creatures, therefore he is called that one.

But why is he called Rudra? Because his essence (*rū-pam*) is grasped instantly (*dru-tam*) only by the seers (*ṛ-ṣi*), not by other devotees, therefore he is called *Ru-dra*.

But why is he called the ruler? Because it is he,

Who rules over all the gods,

With his regal and procreative powers (cf. Śvet. 3,1),

To you, O here, we cry out,

Like cows, which go for milking,

To the lord of what moves, to the heaven-seer,

To the lord, O Indra, of what stays (Ṛg. 7,32,22),

therefore he is called the ruler.

But why is he called the exalted Maheśvara? Because he permits the devotees (*bhakta*) in the participation of perception and is gracious towards them; because he withdraws the speech [of the Veda] in himself and again allows it to flow out (Bṛh. 2,4,10); because, giving up all forms, he raises himself and is elevated through the perception of the Ātman and the mastery of the Yoga, therefore he is called the exalted Maheśvara.

This is the knowledge of Rudra.

एषो ह देवः प्रदिशो नु सर्वाः पूर्वो ह जातः स उ गर्भे अन्तः। स एव जातः स जनिष्यमाणः प्रत्यङ्जनास्तिष्ठति सर्वतोमुखः। एको रुद्रो न द्वितीयाय तस्मै य इमाँल्लोकानीशत ईशनीभिः। प्रत्यङ्जनास्तिष्ठति संचुकोचान्तकाले संसृज्य विश्वा भुवनानि गोप्ता। यो योनिं योनिमधितिष्ठत्येको येनेदं संचरति विचरति सर्वम्। तमीशानं वरदं देवमीड्यं निचाय्येमां शान्तिमत्यन्तमेति। क्षमां हित्वा हेतुजालस्य मूलं बुद्ध्या संचितं स्थापयित्वा तु रुद्रे रुद्रमेकत्वमाहुः। शाश्वतं वै पुराणमिषमूर्जेन पशवोऽनुनामयन्तं मृत्युपाशान्। तदेतेनात्मन्नेतेनार्धचतुर्थमात्रेण शान्तिं संसृजति पाशविमोक्षणम्। या सा प्रथमा मात्रा ब्रह्मदेवत्या रक्ता वर्णेन यस्तां ध्यायते नित्यं स गच्छेद्ब्राह्मं पदम्। या सा द्वितीया मात्रा विष्णुदेवत्या कृष्णा वर्णेन यस्तां ध्यायते नित्यं स गच्छेद्वैष्णवं पदम्। या सा तृतीया मात्रा ईशानदेवत्या कपिला वर्णेन यस्तां ध्यायते नित्यं स गच्छेदैशानं पदम्। या साऽर्धचतुर्थी मात्रा सर्वदेवत्याऽव्यक्तीभूता खं विचरति शुद्धस्फटिकसन्निभा वर्णेन यस्तां ध्यायते नित्यं स गच्छेत्पदमनामयम् तदेतमुपासीत मुनयोऽर्वाग्वदन्ति न तस्य ग्रहणमयं पन्था विहित उत्तरेण येन देवा यान्ति येन पितरो येन ऋषयः परमपरं परायणं चेति। बालाग्रमात्रं हृदयस्य मध्ये विश्वं देवं जातरूपं वरेण्यम्। तमात्मस्थं ये नु पश्यन्ति धीरास्तेषां शान्तिर्भवति नेतरेषाम्। यस्मिन्क्रोधं यां च तृष्णां क्षमां च तृष्णां हित्वा हेतुजालस्य मूलम्। बुद्ध्या संचितं स्थापयित्वा तु रुद्रे रुद्रमेकत्वमाहुः। रुद्रो हि शाश्वतेन वै पुराणेनेषमूर्जेण तपसा नियन्ता। अग्निरिति भस्म वायुरिति भस्म जलमिति भस्म स्थलमिति भस्म व्योमेति भस्म सर्वंꣳह वा इदं भस्म मन एतानि चक्षूंषि भस्मानि यस्माद्व्रतमिदं पाशुपतं यद्भस्मनाङ्गानि संस्पृशेत्तस्माद्ब्रह्म तदेतत्पाशुपतं पशुपाशविमोक्षणाय॥ ५॥

The one god in all the world-spaces, born of old and in mother's womb. He was born, he will be born, He is in men and omnipresent. One Rudra there is, [don't worship] him as second! Who with his regal powers rule over the world; He dwells in the creatures and gathers them in him at the end, when he, the guardian, devours all creatures.

Who, as one, presides over every womb, through whom the whole universe spreads out;

Who knows him as ruler, as God, liberal giver, praise-worthy. He enters into that peace forever.

Shunning the world, the root of the casual net, wisely surrendering to Rudra all acquisition, [they] acknowledged Rudra as the unity, as the eternal, the senior in refreshment and energy, the creature, as the one who cuts their bonds of death.

Thus it happens that, by means of that [sacred sound], when he penetrates into the soul, [the Īśvara] grants peace, the release of creatures (*paśu*) from their bonds (*pāśa*) by the three-and-half mora [of Oṁ].

The first mora [of Oṁ = *a* + *u* + *m*] has Brāhmaṇa as its deity and is red in colour; he who meditates on it continuously, goes to the abode of Brāhmaṇa.

The second mora has Viṣṇu as its deity and is black in colour; he who meditates on it continuously, goes to the abode of Viṣṇu.

The third mora has Īśāna as its deity and is brown in colour; he who meditates on it continuously, goes to the abode of Īśāna as its deity and is brown in colour; he who meditates on it continuously, goes to the abode of Īśāna.

But the three-and-half moras has all these as its deities, is unmanifest, goes out into the wide, is pure and resembles a mountain-crystal in colour; he who meditates on it continuously, goes to the abode of the bliss.

Therefore one should revere this! The silent ones (ascetics) proclaim it worldlessly, because there is no grasping of it.

That is the prescribed way to the North, by which the gods go (Chānd. 5,10,1), and the fathers and the Ṛṣis to the highest of the highest, to the supreme goal.

Minute like hair's tip, in the midst of heart, omnipresent, the God, golden dear,

The wise who sees him as dwelling in himself, he alone attains peace, and none else.

[Leaving] anger to him, greed and worldly desires, shunning the world, the root of the casual net wisely surrendering to Rudra all acquisition, they acknowledged Rudra as the unity; for Rudra is the controller through eternal, old refreshment-and-energy and austerities. What is called fire is ashes, and what wind, is ashes; and what water, is ashes; and what earth, is ashes; and what ether, is ashes; and the whole universe is ashes, and the mind and these eyes! Because this is the vow of the Pāśupata, viz. that he covers his limbs with ashes, therefore this is the Pāśupata form of prayer, so that the creation be freed from his bonds.

योऽग्नौ रुद्रो योऽप्स्वन्तर्य ओषधीर्वीरुध आविवेश। य इमा विश्वा भुवनानि चक्लृपे तस्मै रुद्राय नमोऽस्त्वग्नये। यो रुद्रोऽग्नौ यो रुद्रोप्स्वन्तर्यो रुद्र ओषधीर्वीरुध आविवेश। यो रुद्र इमा विश्वा भुवनानि चक्लृपे तस्मै रुद्राय वै नमो नमः।

यो रुद्रोऽप्सु यो रुद्र ओषधीषु यो रुद्रो वनस्पतिषु। येन रुद्रेण जगदूर्ध्वं धारितं पृथिवी द्विधा त्रिधाधर्ता धारिता नागा येऽन्तरिक्षे तस्मै रुद्राय वै नमो नमः।

मूर्धानमस्य संसीव्याथर्वा हृदयं च यत्। मस्तिष्कादूर्ध्वं प्रेरयन् पवमानोऽधि शीर्षतः। तद्वा अथर्वणः शिरो देवकोशः समुज्झितः। तत्प्राणोऽभिरक्षति शिरोऽन्तमथो मनः। न च दिवो देवजनेन गुप्ता नचान्तरिक्षाणि न च भूम इमाः। यस्मिन्निदं सर्वमोतप्रोतं यस्मादन्यन्न परं किंचनास्ति। न तस्मात्पूर्वं न परं तदस्ति न भूतं नोत भव्यं यदासीत्। सहस्रपादेकमूर्ध्ना व्याप्तं स एवेदमावरीवर्ति भूतम्। अक्षरात्संजायते कालः कालाद्व्यापक उच्यते। व्यापको हि भगवान्रुद्रो भोगायमानो यदा शेते रुद्रस्तदा संहार्यते प्रजाः। उच्छ्वसिते तमो भवति तमस आपोऽप्स्वङ्गुल्या मथिते मथितं शिशिरे शिशिरं मथ्यमानं फेनो भवति, फेनादण्डं भवत्यण्डाद्ब्रह्मा भवति, ब्रह्मणो वायुः वायोरोंकार ॐकारात्सावित्री सावित्र्या गायत्री गायत्र्या लोका भवन्ति। अर्चयन्ति तपः सत्यं मधु क्षरन्ति यद्ध्रुवम्। एतद्धि परमं तप आपो ज्योतीरसोऽमृतं ब्रह्म भूर्भुवः स्वरों नम इति॥ ६॥

Salutation to that Rudra, who is in fire, in water, who has entered plants and creepers, who has become all these creatures. To this Rudra, salutation, as Agni! To Rudra, who is in fire, in water, who has entered plants and creepers, who has become all these creatures, to this Rudra, salutation, salutation!

Rudra who is in water, Rudra in plants, Rudra in trees, Rudra by whom the world is held on high, by whom is supported the earth in a two-fold or three-fold as supporter, and the snakes who dwell in the atmosphere, to this Rudra, salutation, salutation!

[Rudra as Prāṇa in the human head :]

When Atharvan sewed together his head and the heart in him, he stimulated him over the brain, as purifier, from the head down. This head belongs to Atharvan,

A cask stuffed with gods. This head is guarded by Prāṇa, Food and Manas in union. There are nine heavens, guarded by divine community, Nine atmospheres, and nine of these earths; He who is seen lengthwise and crosswise in all; From him nothing exists apart.

Nothing is earlier than him, nothing later, Nothing what had been or was going to be;

With a thousand feet and only one head. He pervades the world and makes it roll.

From the Eternal, time is born, From time he is called the pervader, from the pervader is the exalted Rudra. When Rudra lies down in the manner of a serpent's coil, then the creatures are withdrawn within. When he breathes out, there originates darkness, from darkness the water; when he stirs in the water with a finger, what is stirred becomes cold in the cold and, when it is stirred, it becomes foam; out of the foam originates the (universe-) egg, out of the egg Brāhmaṇa, out of Brāhmaṇa the wind, out of the wind the sound Oṁ, out of the sound Oṁ Sāvitrī, out of Sāvitrī Gāyatrī, out of Gāyatrī the worlds.

They praise Tapas and truth when they pour out the sweet drink, who does not forget (liberation). Indeed, this is the highest Tapas, is water, light, essence, the Immortal, Brāhmaṇa.

Bhūr, bhuvaḥ, svar! Oṁ! Salutation!

य इदमथर्वशिरो ब्राह्मणोऽधीते अश्रोत्रियः श्रोत्रियो भवति अनुपनीत उपनीतो भवति सोऽग्निपूतो भवति स वायुपूतो भवति स सूर्यपूतो भवति स सोमपूतो भवति स सत्यपूतो भवति स सर्वपूतो भवति स सर्वैर्देवैर्ज्ञातो भवति स सर्वैर्वेदैरनुध्यातो भवति स सर्वेषु तीर्थेषु स्नातो भवति तेन सर्वैः क्रतुभिरिष्टं भवति गायत्र्याः षष्टिसहस्राणि जप्तानि भवन्ति इतिहासपुराणानां रुद्राणां शतसहस्राणि जप्तानि भवन्ति। प्रणवानामयुतं जप्तं भवति। आ चक्षुषः पङ्क्तिं पुनाति। आ सप्तमात्पुरुषयुगान्पुनातीत्याह भगवानथर्वशिरः सकृज्जप्त्वैव शुचिः स पूतः कर्मण्यो भवति। द्वितीयं जप्त्वा गणाधिपत्यमवाप्नोति। तृतीयं जप्त्वैवमेवानुप्रविशत्यों सत्यमों सत्यम्॥७॥

The Brāhmaṇa who studies this Atharvaśiras, one who is not an authority on scriptures becomes an authority on scriptures, an uninitiated becomes initiated; he is purified by fire, purified by wind, purified by Soma, purified by truth; he is known by all the gods, is meditated upon by all the Vedas, becomes one who has bathed in all the holy bathing places, and all sacrifices are performed by him. Sixty thousand Gāyatrī stanzas are muttered by him, a hundred thousand [stanzas] of the Itihāsa-Purāṇas and of the Rudra hymns are muttered by him, ten thousand Praṇavas are muttered by him. He purifies the assembly as far as his sight reaches (*ācakṣuṣaḥ*) he purifies up to the seventh generation (ancestors and descendants) : thus has the exalted one promised.

He who mutters the Atharvaśiras once, becomes pure, purified, fit for activity?—he who mutters it a second time, attains supremacy over the host of the supreme god; he who mutters it a third time, enters into a similar existence.

Oṁ! The truth! Oṁ! The truth! Oṁ! The truth!

ॐ भद्रं कर्णेभिः............इति शान्तिः।।

।।इति अथर्वशिर उपनिषत्समाप्ता।।

***

23. KAUṢĪTAKI BRĀHMAṆOPANIṢAD

कौषीतकि ब्राह्मणोपनिषद्

It is well known, that such actions as rubbing, etc., produce purity in substances like mirrors, etc., capable of reflecting light; and similarly the sound, of actions, commencing with the Agnihotra and ending with the Aśvamedha, produces purity in the understanding, capable as it is of reflecting the divine light; it is also understood from a passage of the Śruti that sacrifice, charity and penance are the means of the desire to know. And again, since heaven, etc., which are the fruits of actions, are a kind of happiness, and this is a synonym for the serenity of the understanding, therefore even those persons who are devoted to ceremonial actions, allow that actions to produce purity in the understanding. Hence the Śruti, having declared the system of works at great length, now takes the occasion to declare the knowledge of Brahma. Here follows the Kauṣītaki Brāhmaṇa Upaniṣad in four chapters, commencing with the words "Once on a time Citrā, the son of Gārgya," and ending with "who knows thus." In the first chapter, it declares the knowledge of Brahmā's couch, with the northern and southern paths; in the second the knowledge of prāṇa, and certain external and internal actions of him who knows it for the attainment of various blessings; and in the third and fourth the knowledge of soul. Although this latter portion, commencing "Pratardana" verily, ought properly to be read first, yet even the purified understanding, not knowing the true nature of Brahma, would feel fear before the unconditioned Brahma even though it really causes no fear, just as even a virtuous lad, whose father had left his home on a distant journey while he was yet unborn, might well be afraid at the first sight of him. Hence to remove his fear and to lead him to the northern path, the Śruti first describes the conditioned Brahma sitting in the world of Brahma like a king in this world. In the first chapter, therefore, by the passage, "he comes to the couch of unmeasured splendour; this is Prāṇa," it is declared that Prāṇa is the couch of Brahma. At the mention thereof there arises in the hearers a desire to know, is this Prāṇa only breath, or is it endowed with various supernatural powers? To satisfy this desire, the worship of prāṇa is commenced in the second chapter; and afterwards, having thus made a good opportunity, the Śruti proceeds to declare the knowledge of Brahma. And since here, too, even the conditioned knowledge of Brahma was only attained from the mouth of the teacher by such great saints, endued with humility, as (Gautama, Śvetaketu and others, hence the conditioned or the unconditioned knowledge of Brahma can be alone attained by modern students who are likewise endued with humility. With this object in view, the following narrative opens the Upaniṣad.

॥शान्तिपाठः॥

ॐ वाङ् मे मनसि......................इति शान्तिः॥

॥प्रथमोऽध्यायः॥

चित्रो ह वै गार्ग्यायणिर्यक्ष्यमाण आरुणिं वव्रे। स ह पुत्रं श्वेतकेतुं प्रजिघाय याजयेति। तं हासीनं पप्रच्छ गौतमस्य पुत्रास्ते संवृतं लोके यस्मिन्माधास्यस्यन्यमुताहो बोद्धवा तस्य मा लोके धास्यसीति। स होवाच

नाहमेतद्वेद हन्ताचार्यं पृच्छानीति। स ह पितरमासाद्य पप्रच्छेतीति मा प्राक्षीत्कथं प्रतिब्रवाणीति। स होवाचाहमप्येतन्न वेद सदस्येव वयं स्वाध्यायमधीत्य हरामहे यन्नः परे ददत्येह्युभौ गमिष्याव इति। स ह समित्पाणिश्चित्रं गार्ग्यायणिं प्रतिचक्राम उपायानीति। तं होवाच ब्रह्मार्घोऽसि गौतम यो मानमुपागा एहि त्वा ज्ञपयिष्यामीति॥ १॥

Once on a time Citrā, the son of Gārgya, being about to offer a sacrifice, chose Āruṇi as his priest. He sent his son Śvetaketu instead, "Go you and offer the sacrifice." When he came, Citrā asked him, "You are the son of Gautama, is there any secret place in the world where you can set me or is there one of two roads, which leads to a world where you can set me?" He answered, "I know it not; well, let me ask my father." He went to his father and asked him, "thus and thus did he ask me, how should I make reply?" He answered, "I also know it not. We will go to his house and read the Veda there and gain this knowledge from him; since others give to us (he too will not deny us). Come, we will both set out." So he went, as a pupil, with fuel in his hand, to Citrā, the son of Gārgya, saying, "Let me come into your presence." He answered, 'Oh Gautama, you are worthy to receive divine wisdom, in that you has not been too proud, come, I will make you to know all.'

स होवाच ये वै के चास्माल्लोकात्प्रयन्ति चन्द्रमसमेव ते सर्वे गच्छन्ति। तेषां प्राणैः पूर्वपक्ष आप्यायते। अथापरपक्षे न प्रजनयति। एतद्वै स्वर्गस्य लोकस्य द्वारं यश्चन्द्रमास्तं यत्प्रत्याह तमतिसृजतेऽथ य एनं प्रत्याहतमिह वृष्टिर्भूत्वा वर्षति स इह कीटो वा पतङ्गो वा शकुनिर्वा शार्दूलो वा सिंहो वा मत्स्यो वा परश्वा वा पुरुषो वान्यो वैतेषु स्थानेषु प्रत्याजायते यथाकर्म यथाविद्यम्। तमागतं पृच्छति कोऽसीति तं प्रतिब्रूयाद्विचक्षणादृतवो रेत आभृतं पञ्चदशात्प्रसूतात्पित्र्यावतस्तन्मा पुंसि कर्तर्येरयध्वं पुंसा कर्त्रा मातरि मा निषिक्तः स जायमान उपजायमानो द्वादश त्रयोदश उपमासो द्वादशत्रयोदशेन पित्रा संतद्विदेहं तन्म ऋतवो मर्त्यव आरभध्वम्। तेन सत्येन तपसर्तुरस्म्यार्तवोऽस्मि कोऽसि त्वमस्मीति तमतिसृजते॥ २॥

He said "All who depart from this world, go to the moon. In the bright fortnight the moon is gladdened by their spirits; but in the dark fortnight it sends them forth into new births. Verily the moon is the door of Svarga. Him who rejects it, it sends on beyond; but whoso rejects it not, him it rains down upon this world; and here is he born either as a worm or a grasshopper or a fish or a bird or a lion or a boar or a serpent or a tiger or a man or some other creature, according to his deeds and his knowledge. Him, when he comes, the Guru asks, "Who are you?" Let him thus make answer; "Seed was collected from the wise season-ordaining moon, the ruler of the bright and dark fortnights, the home of the ancestors, itself produced from the daily oblations, that seed, even me, the deities placed in a man, by that man they placed it in a woman, from her I was born, in mortal birth, of twelve months, of thirteen months, identical with the year, I was united to a father of twelve and thirteen months, to know the knowledge that is truth and to know the knowledge that is against the truth; uphold, then, O gods, the due times of my life that I may win immortality. By my words of truth, by my toils and sufferings, I am time, I am dependent on time." "Who are you?" "I am yourself." Then he lets him proceed beyond.

स एतं देवयानं पन्थानमासाद्याग्निलोकमागच्छति स वायुलोकं स वरुणलोकं स आदित्यलोकं स इन्द्रलोकं स प्रजापतिलोकं स ब्रह्मलोकं तस्य ह वा एतस्य ब्रह्मलोकस्य आरो ह्रदो मुहूर्तोऽन्वेष्टिहा विरजा नदील्यो वृक्षः सालज्यं संस्थानमपराजितमायतनमिन्द्रप्रजापती द्वारगोपौ। विभुप्रमितं विचक्षणाऽऽसन्द्यमितौजाः पर्यङ्कः प्रिया च मानसी प्रतिरूपा च चाक्षुषी पुष्पाण्यावयतौ वै च जगान्यम्बाश्चाम्बावयवीश्चाप्सरसः। अम्बया नद्यस्तमित्थंविदा गच्छति तं ब्रह्मा हाभिधावत मम यशसा विरजां वा अयं नदीं प्रापन्न वा अयं जरयिष्यतीति॥ ३॥

He having reached the divine road, goes to the world of Agni, then to the world of Vāyu, then to the world of Varuṇa, then to the world of Indra, then to the world of Prajāpati, then to the world of Brahmā. Verily in that world of Brahmā are the Lake of enemies; the sacrifice-destroying moments; the Age-less river; the Ilya tree; the Sālajya city; the impregnable Palace; Indra and Prajāpati the door keepers; Brahmā's hall Vibhu; his throne Vicakṣaṇā; his couch of unmeasured splendour; and his wife (nature), the cause of the mind and her reflection, the cause of the eye, who weave the worlds like flowers and the Apsarasas, the mothers of all, the undecaying and the streams that roll on to the knowledge of Brahmā. Onward the knower advances, Brahmā cries to his attendants, "Run and meet him with the glory due to me; he has gained the age-less river, he shall never grow old."

तं पञ्चशतान्यप्सरसां प्रतियन्ति शतं चूर्णहस्ताः शतं वासोहस्ताः शतं फलहस्ताः शतमाञ्जनहस्ताः शतं माल्यहस्तास्तं ब्रह्मालंकारेणालंकुर्वन्ति स ब्रह्मालंकारेणालंकृतो ब्रह्म विद्वान्ब्रह्माभिप्रैति स आगच्छत्यारं ह्रदं तं मनसाऽत्येति। तमित्वा संप्रतिविदो मज्जन्ति स आगच्छति मुहूर्तान्विहेष्टिहास्तेऽस्मादपद्रवन्ति स आगच्छति विरजां नदीं तां मनसैवात्येति। तत्सुकृतदुष्कृते धुनुते। तस्य प्रिया ज्ञातयः सुकृतमुपयन्त्यप्रिया दुष्कृतं तद्यथा रथेन धावयन्रथचक्रे पर्यवेक्षत, एवमहोरात्रे पर्यवेक्षत एवं सुकृतदुष्कृते सर्वाणि च द्वंद्वानि स एष विसुकृतो विदुष्कृतो ब्रह्म विद्वान्ब्रह्मैवाभिप्रैति॥ ४॥

Five hundred Apsarasas go to meet him, one hundred with fruits in their hands, one hundred with perfumes in their hands, one hundred with garlands in their hands, one hundred with garments in their hands, one hundred with pounded aromatics in their hands; they adorn him with the adornment of Brahmā. He, adorned with the adornment of Brahmā, knowing Brahmā, advances toward Brahmā everywhere. He comes to the lake of enemies, he crosses it by his mind. When they who know only the present, come thereto, they are drowned. He comes to the sacrifice-destroying moments, they fly from him : He comes to the age-less river, he crosses it by his mind, then he shakes off his good and bad deeds [as a horse shakes his mane.] His dear kindred obtain his good deeds, his enemies obtain his bad deeds. Just as one driving swiftly in a chariot looks down on the two wheels revolving, so too he looks down on day and night, on good deeds and bad deeds and on all the pairs; he, free from good deeds, free from bad deeds, knowing Brahmā, advances toward Brahmā.

स आगच्छतील्यं वृक्षं तं ब्रह्मगन्धः प्रविशति, स आगच्छति सालज्यं संस्थानं तं ब्रह्मरसः प्रविशति, स आगच्छत्यपराजितमायतनं तं ब्रह्मतेजः प्रविशति स आगच्छति। इन्द्रप्रजापती द्वारगोपौ तावस्मादपद्रवतः स

आगच्छति विभुप्रमितं तं ब्रह्मतेजः प्रविशति स आगच्छति विचक्षणामासन्दीं बृहद्रथन्तरे सामनी पूर्वौ पादौ श्यैतनौधसे चापरौ वैरूपवैराजे अनूच्येते शाक्वररैवते तिरश्ची सा प्रज्ञा प्रज्ञया हि विपश्यति स आगच्छत्यमितौजसं पर्यङ्कं स प्राणस्तस्य भूतं च भविष्यच्च पूर्वौ पादौ श्रीश्चेरा चापरौ बृहद्रथंतरे अनूच्ये भद्रयज्ञायज्ञीये शीर्षण्ये ऋचश्च सामानि च प्राचीनातानानि यजूंषि तिरश्चीनानि सोमांशव उपस्तरणमुद्गीथ उपश्रीः श्रीरुपबर्हणं तस्मिन्ब्रह्मास्ते तमित्थंवित्पादेनैवाग्र आरोहति। तं ब्रह्मा पृच्छति कोऽसीति तं प्रतिब्रूयात्॥ ५॥

He comes to the Ilya tree, the odour of Brahmā reaches him; he comes to the Sālajya city, the flavour of Brahmā reaches him; he comes to the impregnable Palace, the splendour of Brahmā reaches him; he comes to the door-keepers Indra and Prajāpati; they fly from him; he comes to the hall Vibhu, the glory of Brahmā reaches him; he comes to his throne Vicakṣaṇā, the Sāmas Bṛhad and Rathantara are its eastern feet, the Sāmas Śyaita and Naudhasa its western feet, the Sāmas Vairūpa and Vairāja its edges north and south, the Sāmas Śākvara and Raivata its edges east and west; his throne is knowledge; by knowledge he sees it all. He comes to the couch of unmeasured splendour; this is Prāṇa. Past and future are its two eastern feet, prosperity and earth its two western; the Sāmas Bhadra and Yajñāyajñīya are the short bars east and west, at the head and foot; the Sāmas Bṛhad and Rathantara the long bars north and south at the sides; the Ṛcs and Sāmas are the cornices east and west, the Yajuṣ verses the cornices south and north; the moon-beams the cushion, the Udgītha the coverlet, prosperity the pillow. Thereon sits Brahmā. He, knowing the truth, first mounts thereon with one foot. Brahmā asks him, "Who are you?" Let him then thus answer:

ऋतुरस्म्यार्तवोऽस्म्याकाशाद्योनेः संभूतो भार्या एतत्संवत्सरस्य तेजोभूतस्य भूतस्य भूतस्य भूतस्यात्मा त्वमात्मासि यस्त्वमसि सोऽहमस्मीति तमाह कोऽहमस्मीति सत्यमिति ब्रूयात्किं तद्यत्सत्यमिति यदन्यद्देवेभ्यश्च प्राणेभ्यश्च तत्सदथ यद्देवाश्च प्राणाश्च तत्त्यं तदेतया वाचाऽभिव्या ह्रियते सत्यमित्येतावदिदं सर्वमिदं सर्वमसि। इत्येवैनं तदाह। तदेतदृक्श्लोकेनाभ्युक्तम् यजूदरः सामशिरा आसावृङ्मूर्तिरव्ययः। स ब्रह्मेति स विज्ञेय ऋषिर्ब्रह्ममयो महानिति। तमाह केन मे पौंस्यानि नामान्याप्नोतीति प्राणेनेति ब्रूयात्। केन स्त्रीनामानीति वाचेति केन नपुंसकानीति मनसेति केन गन्धानिति प्राणेनेत्येव ब्रूयात्। केन रूपाणीति चक्षुषेति केन शब्दानिति श्रोत्रेणेति केनान्नरसानिति जिह्वयेति केन कर्माणीति हस्ताभ्यामिति केन सुखदुःखे इति शरीरेणेति केनानन्दं रतिं प्रजातिमित्युपस्थेनेति। केनेत्या इति पादाभ्यामिति केन धियो विज्ञातव्यं कामानिति प्रज्ञयेति ब्रूयात्तमाह। आपो वै खलु मे ह्यसावयं ते लोक इति सा या ब्रह्मणो जितिर्या व्यष्टिस्तां जितिं जयति तां व्यष्टिं व्यश्नुते य एवं वेद य एवं वेद॥ ६॥

"I am time, I am what is in time; I am born from the womb of space, from the (self-manifesting) light of Brahma; the seed of the year, the splendour of the past and the cause, the soul of all that is sensible and insensible and of the five elements. You are soul. What you are, that am I." Brahmā says to him, "Who am I?" Let him answer, "You are the Truth." "What is the truth?" "What is other than the gods (who preside over the senses) and the vital airs, that is *being (sat);* what is the gods and the vital airs, that is *that (tya);* all this is called by the word *sattya,* the Truth; such is all this (universe); all this are you." Thus he speaks to him. This is also said by a verse of the Veda.

"The Yajur his belly, the Sāma his head, the Ṛk his form, this is to be recognised as the indestructible Brahmā, the great Ṛṣi identified with Brahmā."

Brahmā says to him, "How did you obtain my male names?" "By the breath." "How neuter names?" "By the mind." "How female names?" "By the voice." "How smells?" "By the breath." "How forms?" "By the eye." "How sounds?" "By the ear." "How the flavours of food?" "By the tongue." "How actions?" "By the hands." "How joy and sorrow?" "By the body." "How pleasure, dalliance, offspring?" "By the organ of generation." "How journeyings?" "By the feet." "How thoughts, that which is to be known, and desired?" "By intuition alone." Then Brahmā says to him, 'The waters (and the other elements) are mine, therefore this world is yours.' Whatever victory belongs to Brahmā, whatever extended power, that victory *he* wins, that extended power *he* obtains, who knows thus, who knows thus. (7.)

।।द्वितीयोऽध्याय:।।

प्राणो ब्रह्मेति ह स्माह कौषीतकिस्तस्य ह वा एतस्य प्राणस्य ब्रह्मणो मनो दूतं वाक्परिवेष्ट्री चक्षुर्गोप्तृ श्रोत्रं संश्रावयितृ तस्मै वा एतस्मै प्राणाय ब्रह्मण एता: सर्वा देवता अयाचमानाय बलिं हरन्ति तथो एवास्मै सर्वाणि भूतान्ययाचमानायैव बलिं हरन्ति य एवं वेद तस्योपनिषन्न याचेदिति। तद्यथा ग्रामं भिक्षित्वाऽलब्ध्वोपविशेन्नाहमतो दत्तमश्नीयामिति। य एवैनं पुरस्तात्प्रत्याचक्षीरंस्त एवैनमुपमन्त्रयन्ते ददाम त इति। एष धर्मो याचितो भवति। अन्यतस्त्वेवैनमुपमन्त्रयन्ते ददाम त इति।। १।।

'Prāṇa is Brahma,' thus said Kauṣītaki. Of this prāṇa identical with Brahma, the mind is the messenger, the eye the guard, the ear the door-keeper, the speech the tire-woman. He who knows mind as the messenger of prāṇa which is Brahma, becomes himself possessed of the messenger; he who knows the eye as the guard becomes himself possessed of the guard; he who knows the ear as the door-keeper becomes himself possessed of the door-keeper; he who knows the speech as the tire-woman becomes himself possessed of the tire-woman. To him, this prāṇa, identical with Brahma, all these deities bring offerings, though he asks not; thus to him (the worshipper), though he asks not, all creatures bring offerings. Whoso thus knows, his is the secret vow, 'he will never beg.' Just as when one, having begged in a village and received nothing, sits down (saying), 'I will not eat hence even if they give it,' then the others forthwith invite him who had before rejected him. This is the character of him who asks not, but the alms-givers invite him (saying) 'Let us give to you.'

प्राणो ब्रह्मेति ह स्माह पैङ्ग्यस्तस्य ह वा एतस्य प्राणस्य ब्रह्मणो वाक्परस्ताच्चक्षुरारुन्धे चक्षु: परस्ताच्छ्रोत्रमारुन्धे श्रोत्रं परस्तान्मन आरुन्धे मन: परस्तात्प्राण आरुन्धे तस्मै वा एतस्मै प्राणाय ब्रह्मण एता: सर्वा देवता अयाचमानाय बलिं हरन्ति तथो एवास्मै सर्वाणि भूतान्ययाचमानायैव बलिं हरन्ति य एवं वेद

तस्योपनिषन्न याचेदिति तद्यथा ग्रामं भिक्षित्वाऽलब्ध्वोपविशेन्नाहमतो दत्तमश्नीयामिति य एवैनं पुरस्तात्प्रत्याचक्षीरंस्त एवैनमुपमन्त्रयन्ते ददाम त इत्येष धर्मो याचितो भवत्यन्यतस्त्वेवैनमुपमन्त्रयन्ते ददाम त इति॥ २॥

'Prāṇa is Brahma,' thus said Paiṅgya. In this prāṇa, identical with Brahma, after the speech, the eye envelopes; after the eye, the ear envelopes; after the ear, the mind envelopes; after the mind, prāṇa envelopes. To this prāṇa, identical with Brahma, all these deities bring offerings, though he asks not; thus to him (the worshipper), though he asks not, all creatures bring offerings. Whoso thus knows, his is the secret vow 'he will never beg.' Just as when one, having begged in a village and received nothing, sits down, (saying) 'I will not eat hence, even if they give it;' then the others invite him who had before rejected him. This is the character of him who asks not, but the alms-givers invite him (saying) 'Let us give to you.'

अथात एकधनावरोधनं यदेकधनमभिध्यायात्पौर्णमास्यां वाऽमावास्यायां वा शुद्धपक्षे वा पुण्ये नक्षत्रेऽग्निमुपसमाधाय परिसमूह्य परिस्तीर्य पर्युक्ष्योत्पूय दक्षिणं जान्वाच्य स्रुवेण वा चमसेन वा कंसेन वैता आज्याहुतीर्जुहोति वाङ्नाम देवताऽवरोधिनी सा मेऽमुष्मादिदमवरुन्धां तस्यै स्वाहा। प्राणो नाम देवताऽवरोधिनी सा मेऽमुष्मादिदमवरुन्धां तस्यै स्वाहा। चक्षुर्नाम देवताऽवरोधिनी सा मेऽमुष्मादिदमवरुन्धां तस्यै स्वाहा। श्रोत्रं नाम देवताऽवरोधिनी सा मेऽमुष्मादिदमवरुन्धां तस्यै स्वाहा। मनो नाम देवताऽवरोधिनी सा मेऽमुष्मादिदमवरुन्धां तस्यै स्वाहा। प्रज्ञा नाम देवताऽवरोधिनी सा मेऽमुष्मादिदमवरुन्धां तस्यै स्वाहेत्यथ धूमगन्धं प्रजिघ्रायाज्यलेपेनाङ्गान्यनु विमृज्य वाचंयमोऽभिप्रव्रज्यार्थं ब्रुवीत दूतं वा प्रहिणुयाल्लभते हैव॥ ३॥

Next follows the attainment of some special wealth. If a man meditates on some special wealth; then, on a full moon or a new moon or a pure fortnight or an auspicious constellation on one of these holy seasons, having placed the fire, swept the sacrificial floor, strewn the sacred grass, sprinkled the holy water, kneeling on the right knee, let him offer the oblations of ghee with the sruva, (saying) 'The deity named speech is the obtainer, may it obtain this for me from that man; svāhā unto it, the deity named prāṇa is the obtainer, may it obtain this for me from that man; svāhā unto it; the deity named the eye is the obtainer, may it obtain this for me from that man; svāhā unto it; the deity named the ear is the obtainer, may it obtain this for me from that man; svāhā unto it, the deity named mind is the obtainer, may it obtain this for me from that man; svāhā unto it; the deity named knowledge (prajñā) is the obtainer, may it obtain this for me from that man; svāhā unto it.' Then, having inhaled the smell of the smoke and having anointed his limbs with the ghee, let him go forth, restraining his speech and declare his request to that man or send to him a messenger. Of a truth he obtains it.

अथातो दैवः स्मरो यस्य प्रियो बुभूषेद्यस्यै वा एषां वै तेषामेवैकस्मिन्पर्वण्यग्निमुपसमाधायैतयैवावृतैता आज्याहुतीर्जुहोति वाचं ते मयि जुहोम्यसौ स्वाहा। प्राणं ते मयि जुहोम्यसौ स्वाहा। चक्षुस्ते मयि जुहोम्यसौ स्वाहा। श्रोत्रं ते मयि जुहोम्यसौ स्वाहा। मनस्ते मयि जुहोम्यसौ स्वाहा। प्रज्ञां ते मयि जुहोम्यसौ स्वाहेत्यथ

धूमगन्धं प्रजिघ्रायाज्यलेपेनाङ्गान्यनु विमृज्य वाचंयमोऽभिप्रव्रज्य संस्पर्शं जिगमिषेदपि वाताद्वा संभाषमाणस्तिष्ठेत्प्रियो हैव भवति स्मरन्ति हैवास्य॥ ४॥

Next comes the divine desire (Daivah Smaraḥ). If (the worshipper) desires to be beloved by any man or woman or by any men or women, then in the name of these same deities, on a sacred day, let him offer the oblations of ghee in this (aforementioned) manner, (saying) 'I here offer your speech in myself, svāhā; I here offer your prāṇa in myself, svāhā; I here offer your eye in myself, svāhā; I here offer your ear in myself, svāhā; I here offer your mind in myself, svāhā; I here offer your knowledge in myself, svāhā.' Then having inhaled the smell of the smoke and anointed his limbs with the ghee, let him go forth (towards that person), restraining his speech; let him seek to touch him or else let him stand addressing him by his breath. Of a truth he becomes beloved, they remember him even in absence.

अथात: सांयमनं प्रातर्दनमान्तरमग्निहोत्रमिति चाचक्षते यावद्वै पुरुषो भाषते न तावत्प्राणितुं शक्नोति प्राणं तदा वाचि जुहोति। यावद्वै पुरुष: प्राणिति न तावद्भाषितुं शक्नोति वाचं तदा प्राणे जुहोति। एते अनन्ते अमृताहुती जाग्रच्च स्वपंश्च संततमव्यवच्छिन्नं जुहोत्यथ या अन्या आहुतयोऽन्तवत्यस्ता: कर्ममय्यो हि भवन्त्येतद्ध वै पूर्वे विद्वांसोऽग्निहोत्रं न जुहवांचक्रु:॥ ५॥

Next comes the self-subjection of Prātardana; they call it 'the inner Agnihotra.' As long as a man speaks, so long he cannot breathe, then he offers the breath in the speech; as long as a man breathes, so long he cannot speak, then he offers the speech in the breath. These are the two never-ending immortal oblations; waking and sleeping, he continually offers them. All other oblations have an end and possess the nature of works. The ancients, knowing this true sacrifice, did not use to offer the Agnihotra.

उक्थं ब्रह्मेति ह स्माह शुष्कभृङ्गारस्तदृगित्युपासीत सर्वाणि हास्मै भूतानि श्रैष्ठ्यायाभ्यर्चन्ते तद्यजुरित्युपासीत सर्वाणि हास्मै भूतानि श्रैष्ठ्याय युज्यन्ते तत्सामेत्युपासीत सर्वाणि हास्मै भूतानि श्रैष्ठ्याय संनमन्ते तच्छ्रीरित्युपासीत तद्यश इत्युपासीत तत्तेज इत्युपासीत तद्यथैतच्छास्त्राणां श्रीमत्तमं यशस्वितमं तेजस्वितमं भवति। तथैवैवं विद्वान् सर्वेषां भूतानां श्रीमत्तमो यशस्वितमस्तेजस्वितमो भवति। तमेतमैष्टकं कर्ममयमात्मानमध्वर्यु: संस्करोति तस्मिन्यजुर्मयं प्रवयति यजुर्मय ऋङ्मयं होता ऋङ्मये साममयमुद्गाता स एष सर्वस्यै त्रयीविद्याया आत्मैष उ एवास्यात्मा एतदात्मा भवति य एवं वेद॥ ६॥

'Uktha is Brahma,' thus said Śuṣkabhṛṅgāra. Let him worship it as the Ṛk; all beings adore him for his excellence. Let him worship it as the Yajur; all beings are joined (yuj) to him for his excellence. Let him worship it as the Sāma; all beings bow (sannam) to him for his excellence. Let him worship it as beauty, let him worship it as glory, let him worship it as splendour. Just as this (bow) is among weapons, the most beautiful, the most glorious, the most splendid, so he who knows thus is, among all beings, the most beautiful, the most glorious, the most splendid. This same prāṇa, connected with the sacrificial bricks, endued with the character of works and of a truth himself, does the adhvaryu purify. In it he weaves what has the character of the Yajur, in the Yajur the hotṛi weaves what has the character of the Ṛk, in the Ṛk the udgātṛi weaves what has the character of the Sāma. He this adhvaryu (prāṇa) is the soul of the three Vedas, he of a truth is the soul of Indra who knows thus.

अथातः सर्वजितः कौषीतकेस्त्रीण्युपासनानि भवन्ति यज्ञोपवीतं कृत्वाऽप आचम्य त्रिरुदपात्रं प्रसिच्योद्यन्तमादित्यमुपतिष्ठेत वर्गोऽसि पाप्मानं मे वृङ्धीत्येतयैवावृता मध्ये सन्तमुद्वर्गोऽसि पाप्मानं मे वृङ्धीत्येतयैवावृताऽस्तं यन्तं संवर्गोऽसि पाप्मानं मे संवृङ्धीति। यदहोरात्राभ्यां पापं करोति सं तद्वृङ्क्ते॥७॥

Next come the three forms of worship of the all-conquering Kauṣītaki. The all-conquering Kauṣītaki adores the rising sun, having put on the sacrificial thread and brought water and thrice sprinkled the sacred cup (saying) "You are the scatterer, scatter away my sin." In this way he adores the sun at high noon, 'You are the utter scatterer, utterly scatter away my sin.' In this way he adores the setting sun, 'You are the complete scatterer, completely scatter away my sin.' Whatever sin he has committed by day or by night, he completely scatters it away. So he who knows thus, in this way adores the sun, and whatever sin he commits by day or by night he completely scatters away.

अथ मासि मास्यमावास्यायां पश्चाच्चन्द्रमसं दृश्यमानमुपतिष्ठेतैतयैवावृता हरिततृणाभ्यां वाक्प्रत्यस्यति यत्ते सुसीमं हृदयमधि चन्द्रमसि श्रितं तेनामृतत्वस्येशाने माऽहं पौत्रमघं रुदमिति न हास्मात्पूर्वाः प्रजाः प्रैतीति नु जातपुत्रस्याथाजातपुत्रस्याप्यायस्व समेतु ते सं ते पयांसि समु यन्तु वाजा यमादित्या अंशुमाप्याययन्तीत्येतास्तिस्त्र ऋचो जपित्वा माऽस्माकं प्राणेन प्रजया पशुभिराप्याययिष्ठा योऽस्मान्द्वेष्टि यं च वयं द्विष्मस्तस्य प्राणेन प्रजया पशुभिराप्याययस्वेति दैवीमावृतमावर्त आदित्यस्यावृतमन्वावर्त इति दक्षिणं बाहुमन्वावर्तते॥८॥

Next, month by month, on the day after the new moon, let him in this same way adore the moon when seen to the west of the sun or let him throw towards it two young blades of grass (saying,) 'That fair-proportioned heart of mine placed on the moon in the sky, I hold myself as the knower thereof; may I never weep for evil concerning my children.' His children die not before him. Such is the worship for one who has children born to him. Next is the worship for him who has no children. (Let him say) 'Increase, O Soma, may vigour come to you; 'May the milky juices flow round you, may the sacrificial offerings;' 'That beam (named Suṣumnā) which the ādityas gladden.' Having muttered these three ṛks, let him turn his right arm round (saying), 'Gladden not by our breath or children or cattle, him who hates us and whom we hate; gladden us by his breath, his children and his cattle. Thus I turn the turning of Indra, I turn the turning of the sun.'

अथ पौर्णमास्यां पुरस्ताच्चन्द्रमसं दृश्यमानमुपतिष्ठेतैतयैवावृता सोमो राजाऽसि विचक्षणः पञ्चमुखोऽसि प्रजापतिर्ब्राह्मणस्त एकं मुखं तेन मुखेन राज्ञोऽत्सि तेन मुखेन मामन्नादं कुरु राजा त एकं मुखं तेन मुखेन विशोऽत्सि तेन मुखेन मामन्नादं कुरु श्येनस्त एकं मुखं तेन मुखेन पक्षिणोऽत्सि तेन मुखेन मामन्नादं कुर्वग्निष्ट एकं मुखं तेन मुखेनेमं लोकमत्सि तेन मुखेन मामन्नादं कुरु त्वयि पञ्चमं मुखं तेन मुखेन सर्वाणि भूतान्यत्सि तेन मुखेन मामन्नादं कुरु माऽस्माकं प्राणेन प्रजया पशुभिरवक्षेष्ठा योऽस्मान्द्वेष्टि यं च वयं

द्विष्मस्तस्य प्राणेन प्रजया पशुभिरवक्षीयस्वेति दैवीमावृतमावर्त आदित्यस्यावृतमन्वावर्तन्त इति दक्षिणं बाहुमन्वावर्तते॥ ९॥

Next on the day of the full moon let him in this same way adore the moon when it is seen in front of him, (saying), 'You are Soma, the brilliant, the wise, the five-mouthed, the lord of creatures. The Brahman is one mouth of your, with that mouth you eat kings, with that mouth make me to eat food. The king is one mouth of your, with that mouth you eat common men, with that mouth make me to eat food. The hawk is one mouth of your, with that mouth you eat birds, with that mouth make me to eat food. The fire is one mouth of your, with that mouth you eat this world, with that mouth make me to eat food. The fifth mouth is in you yourself, with that mouth you eat all beings, with that mouth, make me to eat food. Destroy not our life or children or cattle; whoso hate us and whoso we hate, destroy his life, his children, his cattle. Thus do I turn the turning of the deities, I turn the turning of the sun.' He, thus saying, turns his right arm round.

अथ संवेश्यञ्जायायै हृदयमभिमृशेद्यत्ते सुसीमे हृदये हितमन्तः प्रजापतौ मन्येऽहं मां तद्विद्वांसं तेन माऽहं पौत्रमघं रुदमिति न हास्मात्पूर्वाः प्रजाः प्रैतीति॥ १०॥

Next wishing to lie with his wife, let him touch her heart (saying) "As joy is placed in your heart, the lord of progeny, O fair one, so, O mistress of immortality, may you never have sorrow concerning your children." Her children die not before her.

अथ प्रोष्यायन्पुत्रस्य मूर्धानमभिमृशेत्। अङ्गादङ्गात्संभवसि हृदयादधिजायसे। आत्मा त्वं पुत्र माविथ स जीव शरदः शतमसाविति नामास्य गृह्णाति। अश्मा भव परशुर्भव हिरण्यमस्तृतं भव तेजो वै पुत्रनामासि स जीव शरदः शतमसाविति नामास्य गृह्णाति येन प्रजापतिः प्रजाः पर्यगृह्णादरिष्ट्यै तेन त्वा परिगृह्णाम्यसाविति नामास्य गृह्णात्यथास्य दक्षिणे कर्णे जपत्यस्मै प्रयन्धि मघवन्नृजीषिन्नितीन्द्र श्रेष्ठानि द्रविणानि धेहीति सव्ये मा च्छित्था मा व्यथिष्ठाः शतं शरद आयुषो जीव पुत्र ते नाम्ना मूर्धानमवजिघ्राम्यसाविति त्रिर्मूर्धानमवजिघ्रेद्गवां त्वा हिंकारेणाभि हिं करोमीति त्रिर्मूर्धानमभि हिंकुर्यात्॥ ११॥

Next, when returning after an absence from home, let a man smell his son's head (saying), 'You arise from me, limb by limb, above all are you born from my heart; you are verily my soul, my son; live you a hundred years;' he then gives his name. 'Be you a stone, be you an axe, be you as widely scattered gold; you are verily called splendour, my son; live you a hundred years;' thus (saying) he calls him by his name. Then he embraces him, (saying), 'As Prajāpati embraced his creatures for their weal, so I here embrace you.' Then he whispers in his right ear, 'O Maghavan, O on-rusher, give to this one.' 'O Indra, bestow the best riches,' thus (saying), he whispers in his left ear. 'Cut not off my line (of posterity), vex not yourself, live you the hundred years of life; I smell your head calling you by your name,' thus (saying) let him thrice smell his head. 'I greet you with the lowing sound of the cows,' thus (saying) let him thrice make a lowing sound *(hing)* over his head.

अथातो दैवः परिमर एतद्वै ब्रह्म दीप्यते यदग्निर्ज्वलत्यथैतन्म्रियते यन्न ज्वलति तस्यादित्यमेव तेजो गच्छति वायुं प्राण एतद्वै ब्रह्म दीप्यते यदादित्यो दृश्यतेऽथैतन्म्रियते यन्न दृश्यते तस्य चन्द्रमसमेव तेजो गच्छति वायुं प्राण एतद्वै ब्रह्म दीप्यते यच्चन्द्रमा दृश्यते। अथैतन्म्रियते यन्न दृश्यते तस्य विद्युतमेव तेजो गच्छति वायुं प्राण एतद्वै ब्रह्म दीप्यते यद्विद्युद्विद्योततेऽथैतन्म्रियते यन्न विद्योतते तस्य वायुमेव तेजो गच्छति वायुं प्राणः। ता वा एताः सर्वा देवता वायुमेव प्रविश्य वायौ मृता न मृच्छन्ते तस्मादेव उ पुनरुदीरत इत्यधिदैवत-मथाध्यात्मम्॥ १२॥

Next prāṇa is called the death of the deities, (*Daivaḥ parimaraḥ*). This Brahma shines forth when the fire blazes, it dies when it blazes not; the splendour of the fire goes to the sun, the prāṇa goes to the wind. This Brahma shines forth when the sun is seen, it dies when it is not seen; the sun's splendour goes to the moon, the prāṇa to the wind. This Brahma shines forth when the moon is seen, it dies when it is not seen; its splendour goes to the lightning, the prāṇa to the wind. This Brahma shines forth when the lightning flashes, it dies when it flashes not forth; its splendour goes to the quarters of space, the prāṇa to the wind. All these deities having entered into the wind only and having died in the wind, die not, therefore they rise again. Such is the topic of the deities, now follows that of the soul.

एतद्वै ब्रह्म दीप्यते यद्वाचा वदत्यथैतन्म्रियते यन्न वदति तस्य चक्षुरेव तेजो गच्छति प्राणं प्राण एतद्वै ब्रह्म दीप्यते यच्चक्षुषा पश्यत्यथैतन्म्रियते यन्न पश्यति तस्य श्रोत्रमेव तेजो गच्छति प्राणं प्राण एतद्वै ब्रह्म दीप्यते यच्छ्रोत्रेण शृणोत्यथैतन्म्रियते यन्न शृणोति तस्य मन एव तेजो गच्छति प्राणं प्राण एतद्वै ब्रह्म दीप्यते यन्मनसा ध्यायत्यथैतन्म्रियते यन्न ध्यायति तस्य प्राणमेव तेजो गच्छति प्राणं प्राणस्ता वा एताः सर्वा देवताः प्राणमेव प्रविश्य प्राणे मृता न मृच्छन्ते तस्मा देव उ पुनरुदीरते तद्यदिह वा एवं विद्वांस उभौ पर्वतावभिप्रवर्तेयातां तुस्तूर्षमाणौ दक्षिणश्चोत्तरश्च न हैवैनं स्तृण्वीयाताम्। अथ य एनं द्विषन्ति यांश्च स्वयं द्वेष्टि त एनं सर्वे परिम्रियन्ते॥ १३॥

This Brahma shines forth when it speaks by the speech, it dies when it speaks not; its splendour goes to the eye, the prāṇa to prāṇa. This Brahma shines forth when it sees by the eye, it dies when it sees not; its splendour goes to the ear, the prāṇa to prāṇa. This Brahma shines forth when it hears by the ear, it dies when it hears not; its splendour goes to the mind, the prāṇa to prāṇa. This Brahma shines forth when it thinks by the mind, it dies when it thinks not; its splendour goes to prāṇa, the prāṇa to prāṇa. All these deities, having, thus entered into prāṇa only and having died in prāṇa, die not; therefore they rise again. Therefore if both mountain ranges, the Southern and the Northern, should close in on him who knows thus, threatening to destroy him, they would harm him not. Then those who hate him and those whom he himself hates, die round him on every side.

अथातो निःश्रेयसादानं सर्वा ह वै देवता अहंश्रेयसे विवदमानाः। अस्माच्छरीरादुच्चक्रमुस्तद्दारुभूतं शिश्येऽथैनद्वाक्प्रविवेश तद्वाचा वदच्छिश्य एव। अथैनच्चक्षुः प्रविवेश तद्वाचा वदच्चक्षुषा पश्यच्छिश्य एवाथैनच्छ्रोत्रं प्रविवेश तद्वाचा वदच्चक्षुषा पश्यच्छ्रोत्रेण शृण्वच्छिश्य एवाथैनन्मनः प्रविवेश तद्वाचा वदच्चक्षुषा पश्यच्छ्रोत्रेण शृण्वन्मनसा ध्यायच्छिश्य एवाथैनत्प्राणः प्रविवेश तत्तत एव समुत्तस्थौ ते देवाः

प्राणे निःश्रेयसं विदित्वा प्राणमेव प्रज्ञात्मानमभिसंभूय सहैतैः सर्वैरस्माल्लोकादुच्चक्रमुः। ते वायुप्रतिष्ठा आकाशात्मानः स्वरीयुस्तथो एवैवं विद्वान्सर्वेषां भूतानां प्राणमेव प्रज्ञात्मानमभिसंभूय सहैतैः सर्वैरस्माच्छरीरादुत्क्रामति स वायुप्रतिष्ठ आकाशात्मा स्वरेति स तद्भवति यत्रैते देवास्तत्प्राप्य तदमृतो भवति यदमृता देवाः॥ १४॥

Next comes the accepting the pre-eminence (of prāṇa). These deities, contending each for his own pre-eminence, went out from this body. It lay breathing not, dry, a very log of wood. Then speech entered into it; it spoke by speech, still it lay. Then the sight entered into it, it spoke by speech, it saw by sight, still it lay. Then the hearing entered into it; it spoke by speech, it saw by sight, it heard by hearing, still it lay. Then the mind entered into it; it spoke by speech, it saw by sight, it heard by hearing, it thought by mind, still it lay. Then prāṇa entered into it, it rose up from its place. All these deities, having recognised the pre-eminence to be in prāṇa, having honoured prāṇa as alone the soul of knowledge, went out from this body with all these. Then they went to heaven lost in the wind, identified with the ether. So too he who knows thus, having recognised the pre-eminence to be in prāṇa, haying honoured prāṇa as alone the soul of knowledge, goes out from this body with all these (five vital airs). He goes to heaven, lost in the wind, identified with ether; he goes to that, wherein those deities abide. With the immortality of the deities, did he become immortal who knows thus.

अथातः पितापुत्रीयं संप्रदानमिति चाचक्षते। पिता पुत्रं प्रेष्यन्नाह्वयति नवैस्तृणैरगारं संस्तीर्याग्निमुपसमाधायोदकुम्भं सपात्रमुपनिधायाहतेन वाससा संप्रच्छन्नः स्वयं श्येत एत्य पुत्र उपरिष्टादभिनिपद्यते, इन्द्रियैरस्येन्द्रियाणि संस्पृश्यापि वाऽस्याभिमुखत एवासीताथास्मै संप्रयच्छति वाचं मे त्वयि दधानीति पिता वाचं ते मयि दध इति पुत्रः प्राणं मे त्वयि दधानीति पिता प्राणं ते मयि दध इति पुत्रः। चक्षुर्मे त्वयि दधानीति पिता चक्षुस्ते मयि दध इति पुत्रः। श्रोत्रं मे त्वयि दधानीति पिता श्रोत्रं ते मयि दध इति पुत्रः। मनो मे त्वयि दधानीति पिता मनस्ते मयि दध इति पुत्रः। अन्नरसान्मे त्वयि दधानीति पिता अन्नरसांस्ते मयि दध इति पुत्रः। कर्माणि मे त्वयि दधानीति पिता कर्माणि ते मयि दध इति पुत्रः। सुखदुःखे मे त्वयि दधानीति पिता सुखदुःखे ते मयि दध इति पुत्रः। आनन्दं रतिं प्रजातिं मे त्वयि दधानीति पिता, आनन्दं रतिं प्रजातिं ते मयि दध इति पुत्रः। इत्या मे त्वयि दधानीति पिता, इत्यास्ते मयि दध इति पुत्रः। धियो विज्ञातव्यं कामान्मे त्वयि दधानीति पिता धियो विज्ञातव्यं कामांस्ते मयि दध इति पुत्रः। अथ दक्षिणावृत्प्राङुपनिष्क्रामति तं पिताऽनुमन्त्रयते यशो ब्रह्मवर्चसमन्नाद्यं कीर्तिस्त्वा जुषतामित्यथेतरः सव्यमंसमन्ववेक्षते पाणिनाऽन्तर्धाय वसनान्तेन वा प्रच्छाद्य स्वर्गान्‌ लोकान्‌ कामानाप्नुहीति स यद्यगदः स्यात्पुत्रस्यैश्वर्ये पिता वसेत्परि वा व्रजेद्यद्यु वै प्रेयाद्यदेवैनं समापयति तथा समापयितव्यो भवति तथा समापयितव्यो भवति॥ १५॥

Next follows the father's tradition to the son. Thus do they in truth relate it. The father, when about to die, calls his son. Having spread the house with new grass and duly laid the fire and placed a vessel of water with a pot of rice, clothed with an unworn garment, the father lies (awaiting him). The son having come approaches him from above, having touched all his organs with his own organs; or else let the father perform the tradition with his son seated in front of him. Then he delivers the organs over. "Let me place my speech in you," said the father; "I take your speech in me," said the son. "Let me place my breath in you," said the father, "I take your breath in me," said the son. "Let me place my sight in you," said the father; "I take your sight in me," said the son. "Let me place my hearing in you," said the father; "I take your hearing in me," said the son. "Let me place my flavours of food in you," said the father; "I take your flavours of food in me," said the son. "Let me place my actions in you," said the father; "I take your actions in me," said the son. "Let me place my pleasure and pain in you," said the father; "I take your pleasure and pain in me," said the son. "Let me place my enjoyment, dalliance and offspring in you," said the father; "I take your enjoyment, dalliance and offspring in me," said the son. "Let me place my walking in you," said the father; "I take your walking in me," said the son. "Let me place my mind in you," said the father; "I take your mind in me," said the son. "Let me place my knowledge in you," said the father; "I take your knowledge in me," said the son. Or if the father be unable to speak much, let him say at once, "Let me place my vital airs in you," and let the son say, "I take your vital airs in me." Then the son goes out, having walked round his father, keeping his right side towards him and the father cries after him. "May glory, holiness and honour attend you." Then the son looks back over his left shoulder, holding his hand or the end of his garment before his face, (saying) "Obtain you the svarga worlds and your desires." Should the father afterwards recover let him dwell in the authority of his son (as a guest) or let him become a wandering ascetic. If he dies, thus let them cause the son duly to receive the tradition, as the tradition is to be given.

।।तृतीयोऽध्याय:।।

प्रतर्दनो ह दैवोदासिरिन्द्रस्य प्रियं धामोपजगाम। युद्धेन च पौरुषेण च तं हेन्द्र उवाच। प्रतर्दन वरं ते ददानीति स होवाच प्रतर्दन:। त्वमेव मे वृणीष्व यं त्वं मनुष्याय हिततमं मन्यस इति तं हेन्द्र उवाच। न वै वरोऽवरस्मै वृणीते त्वमेव वृणीष्वेत्येवमवरो वै किल म इति होवाच प्रतर्दनोऽथो खल्विन्द्र: सत्यादेव नेयाय। सत्यं हीन्द्र: स होवाच। मामेव विजानीह्येतदेवाहं मनुष्याय हिततमं मन्ये। यन्मां विजानीयात्। त्रिशीर्षाणं त्वाष्ट्रमहनमरुन्मुखान्यतीन्सालावृकेभ्य: प्रायच्छं बह्वी: सन्धा अतिक्रम्य दिवि प्रह्लादीयानतृणमहमन्तरिक्षे पौलोमान्पृथिव्यां कालखाञ्जान्। तस्य मे तत्र न लोम च मा मीयते। स यो मां विजानीयान्नास्य केन च कर्मणा लोको मीयते। न मातृवधेन न पितृवधेन न स्तेयेन न भ्रूणहत्यया नास्य पापं च न चकृषो मुखान्नीलं वेत्तीति।। १।।

Pratardana verily, the ṣon of Daivodāsa, went to the loved mansion of Indra, by (the sacrifice of) battle and by manly valour; Indra said to him, "Oh Pratardana, choose a boon." Pratardana answered, "Choose you for me what you think best for man." Indra said to him, "The superior chooses not for the inferior; choose you for yourself." Pratardana said, "Let not the inferior (choose)." Indra swerved not from the truth, for Indra is truth; Indra said to him, "Verily know me; this I think the best for man, that he should know me. I slew the three-headed son of Tvaṣṭṛ; I gave to the wolves the devotees the Arunmukhas; violating many a treaty I slew the hosts of Prahlāda, (I slew) the sons of Puloman in the sky and the Kālakhāñjas on the earth and not one hair of my head was harmed. Whoso knows me, by no deed so ever is his future bliss harmed, not by theft, not by a Brāhmaṇa's murder, nor by a mother's murder, nor by a father's murder; nor, if he wishes to commit sin, departs the bloom from his face."

स होवाच प्राणोऽस्मि प्रज्ञात्मा तं मामायुरमृतमित्युपास्स्व। आयुः प्राणः प्राणो वा आयुः प्राण एवामृतम्। यावद्ध्यस्मिञ्छरीरे प्राणो वसति तावदायुः। प्राणेन ह्येवामुष्मिँल्लोकेऽमृतत्वमाप्नोति। प्रज्ञया सत्यं संकल्पम्। स यो ममायुरमृतमित्युपास्ते सर्वमायुरस्मिँल्लोक एति। आप्नोत्यमृतत्वमक्षितिं स्वर्गे लोके। तद्धैक आहुरेकभूयं वै प्राणा गच्छन्तीति। न हि कश्चन शक्नुयात्सकृद्वाचा नाम प्रज्ञापयितुं चक्षुषा रूपं श्रोत्रेण शब्दं मनसा ध्यातुमित्येकभूयं वै प्राणाः। एकैकमेतानि सर्वाण्येव प्रज्ञापयन्ति। वाचं वदन्तीं सर्वे प्राणा अनुवदन्ति। चक्षुः पश्यत्सर्वे प्राणा अनुपश्यन्ति श्रोत्रं शृण्वत्सर्वे प्राणा अनुशृण्वन्ति मनो ध्यायत्सर्वे प्राणा अनुध्यायन्ति प्राणं प्राणन्तं सर्वे प्राणा अनुप्राणन्तीति। एवमु हैवैतदिति हेन्द्र उवाच। अस्ति त्वेव प्राणानां निःश्रेयसमिति॥ २॥

Indra said, "I am prāṇa. Worship me as identical with knowledge, as life, as immortal; life is prāṇa, prāṇa is life. While prāṇa abides in this body, so long does life abide. By prāṇa a man obtains in this world immortality; by knowledge he obtains true resolve. He who worships me as life and immortal, reaches his full life in this world and in heaven obtains immortality and becomes indestructible." (Pratardana said) "Therefore say some, the prāṇas become one, for none at the same time can make known a name by the speech, a form by the eye, a sound by the ear, a thought by the mind; the prāṇas, having become one, make known all these one by one. Thus when speech speaks, all the prāṇas speak after it; when the eye sees, all the prāṇas see after it; when the ear hears, all the prāṇas hear after it; when the mind thinks, all the prāṇas think after it; when the breath breathes, all the prāṇas breathe after it," Indra answered, "Thus indeed it is, but the highest weal belongs only to the prāṇas."

जीवति वागपेतो मूकान्हि पश्यामो जीवति चक्षुरपेतोऽन्धान्हि पश्यामो जीवति श्रोत्रापेतो बधिरान्हि पश्यामो जीवति मनोपेतो बालान्हि पश्यामो जीवति बाहुच्छिन्नो जीवत्यूरुच्छिन्न इति। एवं हि पश्याम इति। अथ खलु प्राण एव प्रज्ञात्मेदं शरीरं परिगृह्योत्थापयति। तस्मादेतदेवोऽथमुपासीत। यो वै प्राणः सा प्रज्ञा या वा प्रज्ञा स प्राणः। सह ह्येतावस्मिञ्शरीरे वसतः सहोत्क्रामतस्तस्यैषैव दृष्टिः। एतद्विज्ञानम्। यत्रैतत्पुरुषः सुप्तः स्वप्नं न कंचन पश्यत्यथास्मिन्प्राण एवैकधा भवति। तदैनं वाक्सर्वैर्नामभिः सहाप्येति चक्षुः सर्वै रूपैः सहाप्येति श्रोत्रं सर्वैः शब्दैः सहाप्येति मनः सर्वैर्ध्यानैः सहाप्येति। स यदा प्रतिबुध्यते। यथाग्नेर्ज्वलतः सर्वा दिशो विस्फुलिङ्गा विप्रतिष्ठेरन्नेवमेवैतस्मादात्मनः प्राणा यथायतनं विप्रतिष्ठन्ते प्राणेभ्यो देवा देवेभ्यो लोकाः। तस्यैषैव सिद्धिः एतद्विज्ञानम्। यत्रैतत्पुरुष आर्तो मरिष्यन्नाबल्यं न्येत्य संमोहं न्येति तदाहुः। उदक्रमीच्चित्तम्। न शृणोति न पश्यति न वाचा वदति न ध्यायत्यथास्मिन्प्राण एवैकधा भवति तदैनं वाक्सर्वैर्नामभिः सहाप्येति

चक्षुः सर्वै रूपैः सहाप्येति श्रोत्रं सर्वैः शब्दैः सहाप्येति मनः सर्वैर्ध्यानैः सहाप्येति यदा प्रतिबुध्यते यथाग्नेर्ज्वलतो विस्फुलिङ्गा विप्रतिष्ठेरन्नेवमेवैतस्मादात्मनः प्राणा याथायतनं विप्रतिष्ठन्ते प्राणेभ्यो देवा देवेभ्यो लोकाः॥ ३॥

One lives bereft of speech, for we see the dumb; one lives bereft of sight, for we see the blind; one lives bereft of hearing, for we see the deaf; one lives bereft of mind, for we see infants; one lives bereft of arms and bereft of legs, for we see it thus. Hence verily prāṇa is identical with knowledge (prajñā). Having assumed this body it raises it up, therefore let men worship this as Uktha; it is thus that we find everything in prāṇa. What prāṇa is, that is knowledge; what knowledge is, that is prāṇa. This is the only true vision of prāṇa, this its true knowledge. When a man is so asleep that he sees no dream so ever, then he becomes absorbed in this prāṇa. Then the speech enters into it with all names, the eye enters into it with all forms, the hearing enters into it with all sounds, the mind enters into it with all thoughts. When the man awakes, as from blazing fire sparks go forth in all directions, so from this soul all the prāṇas go forth to their several stations; from the prāṇas go forth the devas, from the devas the worlds. This Prāṇa is alone identical with knowledge, having assumed this body it raises it up, therefore let him worship this as the true Uktha. Thus do we find all in Prāṇa. What Prāṇa is, that is knowledge, (Prajñā) what knowledge is, that is Prāṇa. This is the final proof thereof, this its true understanding. When yonder man, sick, about to die and very feeble, falls into fainting, his friends (standing around) say, 'His mind has departed, he hears not, he sees not, he speaks not with his speech, he thinks not;' then he becomes absorbed in this prāṇa, then the speech enters it with all names, the eye enters it with all forms, the hearing enters it with all sounds, the mind enters it with all thoughts. When he departs from this body, he departs with all these.

स यदाऽस्माच्छरीरादुत्क्रामति सहैवैतैः सर्वैरुत्क्रामति वागस्मात्सर्वाणि नामान्यभिवि सृजते। वाचा सर्वाणि नामान्याप्नोति प्राणोऽस्मात्सर्वान्गन्धानभिविसृजते प्राणेन सर्वान्गन्धाना-प्नोति चक्षुरस्मात्सर्वाणि रूपाण्यभिविसृजते चक्षुषा सर्वाणि रूपाण्याप्नोति श्रोत्रमस्मात्सर्वाञ्श-ब्दानभिविसृजते श्रोत्रेण सर्वाञ्शब्दानाप्नोति मनोऽस्मात्सर्वाणि ध्यानान्यभिविसृजते मनसा सर्वाणि ध्यानान्याप्नोति सैषा प्राणे सर्वाप्तिः। यो वै प्राणः सा प्रज्ञा या वा प्रज्ञा स प्राणः सह ह्येतावस्मिञ्शरीरे वसतः सहोत्क्रामतः। अथ खलु यथाऽस्यै प्रज्ञायै सर्वाणि भूतान्येकं भवन्ति तद्व्याख्यास्यामः॥ ४॥

All names, which are verily speech, are left in him, by speech he obtains all names; all odours, which are verily prāṇa, are left in him, by prāṇa he obtains all odours; all forms, which are verily the eye, are left in him, by the eye he obtains all forms; all sounds, which are verily the ear, are left in him, by the ear he obtains all sounds; all thoughts, which are verily the mind, are left in him, by the mind he obtains all thoughts. Together they two dwell in this body, together they two depart from it. Now will we explain how in this same knowledge (Prajñā) all beings are also absorbed.

वागेवास्या एकमङ्गमदूहळं तस्यै नाम परस्तात्प्रतिविहिता भूतमात्रा। घ्राणमेवास्या एकमङ्गमदूहळं तस्य गन्धः परस्तात्प्रतिविहिता भूतमात्रा चक्षुरेवास्या एकमङ्गमदूहळं तस्य रूपं परस्तात्प्रतिविहिता भूतमात्रा श्रोत्रमेवास्या एकमङ्गमदूहळं तस्य शब्दः परस्तात्प्रतिविहिता भूतमात्रा जिह्वैवास्या एकमङ्गमदूहळं तस्या अन्नरसः परस्तात्प्रतिविहिता भूतमात्रा हस्तावेवास्या एकमङ्गमदूहळं तयोः कर्म परस्तात्प्रतिविहिता भूतमात्रा शरीरमेवास्या एकमङ्गमदूहळं तस्य सुखदुःखे परस्तात्प्रतिविहिता भूतमात्रोपस्थ एवास्या एकमङ्गमदूहळं तस्यानन्दो रतिः प्रजातिः परस्तात्प्रतिविहिता भूतमात्रा पादावेवास्या एकमङ्गमदूहळं तयोरित्या परस्तात्प्रतिविहिता भूतमात्रा प्रज्ञैवास्या एकमङ्गमदूहळं तस्यै धियो विज्ञातव्यं कामाः परस्तात्प्रतिविहिता भूतमात्रा॥ ५॥

Speech verily milked one portion thereof; its object, the name, was placed outside as a rudimentary element; the vital air verily milked a portion thereof; its object, the smell, was placed outside as a rudimentary element; the eye verily milked a portion thereof; its object, the form, was placed outside as a rudimentary element; the ear verily milked a portion thereof; its object, the sound, was placed outside as a rudimentary element; the tongue verily milked a portion thereof; its object, the taste of food, was placed outside as a rudimentary element; the two hands verily milked a portion thereof; their object, action, was placed outside as a rudimentary element; the body verily milked a portion thereof; its objects, pleasure and pain, were placed outside as a rudimentary element; the organ of generation verily milked a portion thereof; its objects, enjoyment, dalliance and offspring were placed outside as a rudimentary element; the feet verily milked a portion thereof; their objects, walkings, were placed outside as a rudimentary element; the mind verily milked a portion thereof; its objects, thought and desires, were placed outside as a rudimentary element.

प्रज्ञया वाचं समारुह्य वाचा सर्वाणि नामान्याप्नोति। प्रज्ञया प्राणं समारुह्य प्राणेन सर्वान्गन्धानाप्नोति प्रज्ञया चक्षुः समारुह्य चक्षुषा सर्वाणि रूपाण्याप्नोति प्रज्ञया श्रोत्रं समारुह्य श्रोत्रेण सर्वाञ्शब्दानाप्नोति प्रज्ञया जिह्वां समारुह्य जिह्वया सर्वानन्नरसानाप्नोति प्रज्ञया हस्तौ समारुह्य हस्ताभ्यां सर्वाणि कर्माण्याप्नोति प्रज्ञया शरीरं समारुह्य शरीरेण सुखदुःखे आप्नोति प्रज्ञयोपस्थं समारुह्योपस्थेनानन्दं रतिं प्रजातिमाप्नोति प्रज्ञया पादौ समारुह्य पादाभ्यां सर्वा इत्या आप्नोति प्रज्ञयैव धियं समारुह्य प्रज्ञयैव धियो विज्ञातव्यं कामानाप्नोति॥ ६॥

Having mounted by Prajñā on speech, he finds by speech all names; having mounted by Prajñā on the vital air, he finds by the vital air all odours; having mounted by Prajñā on the eye, he finds by the eye all forms; having mounted by Prajñā on the ear, he finds by the ear all sounds; having mounted by Prajñā on the tongue, he finds by the tongue all flavours of food; having mounted by Prajñā on the hands, he finds by the hands, all actions; having mounted by Prajñā on the body, he finds by the body pleasure and pain; having mounted by Prajñā on the organ of generation, he finds by the organ of generation enjoyment, dalliance and offspring; having mounted by Prajñā on the feet, he finds by the feet all walkings; having mounted by Prajñā on the mind, he finds by the mind all thoughts.

न हि प्रज्ञापेता वाङ् नाम किंचन प्रज्ञापयेत्। अन्यत्र मे मनोऽभूदित्याह। नाहमेतन्नाम प्राज्ञासिषमिति। न हि प्रज्ञापेतः प्राणो गन्धं कंचन प्रज्ञापयेदन्यत्र मे मनोऽभूदित्याह नाहमेतं गन्धं प्राज्ञासिषमिति। न हि प्रज्ञापेतं चक्षू रूपं किंचन प्रज्ञापयेदन्यत्र मे मनोऽभूदित्याह। नाहमेतद्रूपं प्राज्ञासिषमिति न प्रज्ञापेतं श्रोत्रं शब्दं कंचन प्रज्ञापयेदन्यत्र मे मनोऽभूदित्याह। नाहमेतं शब्दं प्राज्ञासिषमिति न हि प्रज्ञापेता जिह्वाऽन्नरसं कंचन प्रज्ञापयेदन्यत्र मे मनोऽभूदित्याह। नाहमेतमन्नरसं प्राज्ञासिषमिति न प्रज्ञापेतौ हस्तौ कर्म किंचन प्रज्ञापयेतामन्यत्र मे मनोऽभूदित्याह नाहमेतत्कर्म प्राज्ञाससिषमिति न हि प्रज्ञापेतं शरीरं सुखं दुःखं किंचन प्रज्ञापयेदन्यत्र मे मनोऽभूदित्याह नाहमेतत्सुखं दुःखं प्राज्ञासिषमिति न हि प्रज्ञापेत उपस्थ आनन्दं रतिं प्रजातिं कांचन प्रज्ञापयेदन्यत्र मे मनोऽभूदित्याह। नाहमेतमानन्दं न रतिं न प्रजातिं प्राज्ञासिषमिति न हि प्रज्ञापेतौ पादावित्यां कांचन प्रज्ञापयेतामन्यत्र मे मनोऽभूदित्याह। नाहमेतामित्यां प्राज्ञासिषमिति। न हि प्रज्ञापेता धीः काचन सिध्येन्न प्रज्ञातव्यं प्रज्ञायेत॥ ७॥

Verily, bereft of prajñā, the speech can make known no name so ever, 'My mind,' it says, 'was elsewhere, I perceived not that name.' Verily, bereft of prajñā, the vital air can make known no odour so ever, 'My mind,' it says, 'was elsewhere, I perceived not that odour.' Verily, bereft of prajñā, the eye can make known no form so ever, 'My mind,' it says, 'was elsewhere, I perceived not that form.' Verily, bereft of prajñā, the ear can make known no sound so ever, 'My mind,' it says, 'was elsewhere, I perceived not that sound.' Verily, bereft of prajñā, the tongue can make known no flavour of food so ever, 'My mind,' it says, 'was elsewhere, I perceived not that flavour.' Verily, bereft of prajñā, the hands can make known no action so ever, 'Our mind,' they say, 'was elsewhere, we perceived not that action.' Verily, bereft of prajña, the body can make known no pleasure, no pain so ever, 'My mind,' it says, 'was elsewhere, I perceived not that pleasure nor that pain.' Verily bereft of prajñā, the organ of generation can make known no enjoyment nor dalliance nor offspring so ever, 'My mind,' it says, 'was elsewhere, I perceived not that enjoyment nor dalliance nor offspring.' Verily, bereft of prajñā, the feet can make known no walking so ever, 'Our mind,' they say, 'was elsewhere, we perceived not that walking.' Verily, bereft of prajñā, no thought can be completed, nor any thing known which should be known.

न वाचं विजिज्ञासीत वक्तारं विद्यान्न गन्धं विजिज्ञासीत घ्रातारं विद्यान्न रूपं विजिज्ञासीत रूपविद्यं विद्यान्न शब्दं विजिज्ञासीत श्रोतारं विद्यान्नान्नरसं विजिज्ञासीतान्नरसस्य विज्ञातारं विद्यान्न कर्म विजिज्ञासीत कर्तारं विद्यान्न सुखदुःखे विजिज्ञासीत सुखदुःखयोर्विज्ञातारं विद्यान्नानन्दं न रतिं न प्रजातिं विजिज्ञासीतानन्दस्य रतेः प्रजातेर्विज्ञातारं विद्यान्नेत्यां विजिज्ञासीतैतारं विद्यात्। न मनो विजिज्ञासीत मन्तारं विद्यात्। ता वा एता दशैव भूतमात्रा अधिप्रज्ञं दश प्रज्ञामात्रा अधिभूतं यद्धि भूतमात्रा न स्युर्न प्रज्ञामात्राः स्युर्यद्वा प्रज्ञामात्रा न स्युर्न भूतमात्राः स्युः॥ ८॥

न ह्यन्यतरतो रूपं किंचन सिध्येत्। नो एतन्नाना, तद्यथा रथस्यारेषु नेमिरर्पितो नाभावरा अर्पिता एवमेवैता भूतमात्राः प्रज्ञामात्रास्वर्पिताः प्रज्ञामात्राः प्राणेऽर्पिताः स एष प्राण एव प्रज्ञात्मानन्दोऽजरोऽमृतः। न साधुना कर्मणा भूयान्नो एवासाधुना कनीयान्। एष ह्येवैनं साधु कर्म कारयति तं यमेभ्यो लोकेभ्य उन्निनीषत एष उ एवैनमसाधु कर्म कारयति तं यमधो निनीषते। एष लोकपाल एष लोकाधिपतिरेष सर्वेशः स म आत्मेति विद्यात्स म आत्मेति विद्यात्॥ ९॥

Let not a man wish to know the speech, let him know the speaker; let not a man wish to know the smell, let him know the smeller; let not a man wish to know the form, let him know the seer; let not a man wish to know the sound, let him know the hearer; let not a man wish to know the flavour of food, let him know the, knower; let not a man wish to know the action, let him know the agent; let not a man wish to know the pleasure and pain, let him know the knower of the pleasure and pain; let not a man wish to know enjoyment, dalliance nor offspring, let him know the knower of the enjoyment, dalliance and offspring; let not a man wish to know the walking, let him know the walker; let not a man wish to know the mind, let him know the thinker. Verily these ten rudimentary elements depend on prajñā and the ten rudiments of prajñā depend on the elements. Were there no rudimentary elements, there would be no rudiments of prajñā; were there no rudiments of prajñā, there would be no rudimentary elements; from either alone no form would be accomplished. There is no division of this union; just as the circumference of a wheel is placed upon the spokes and the spokes upon the nave, so the rudimentary elements are placed upon the rudiments of prajñā and the rudiments of prajñā are placed upon prāṇa. This Prāṇa is verily prajñā, it is joy, it is eternally young and immortal; it is not increased by good deeds, it is not decreased by bad deeds. Verily him it causes to do good deeds, whom it desires to uplift from these worlds; while him it causes to do bad deeds whom it desires to sink down. This is the guardian of the world, this the king of the world, this the lord of the world, this is my soul. Thus let a man know, thus let a man know.

॥चतुर्थोऽध्यायः॥

अथ गार्ग्यो ह वै बालाकिरनूचानः संस्पृष्ट आस सोऽवददुशीनरेषु स वसन्मत्स्येषु कुरुपञ्चालेषु काशिविदेहेष्विति स हाजातशत्रुं काश्यमेत्योवाच। ब्रह्म ते ब्रवाणीति तं होवाचाजातशत्रुः। सहस्रं दद्मस्त इत्येतस्यां वाचि जनको जनक इति वा उ जना धावन्तीति॥ १॥

Now Gārgya, the son of Balāka Ṛṣi, was renowned as a reader of the Veda. He wandered about and so journeyed among the Uśīnaras, the Matsyas, the Kurus, the Pañcālas, the Kāśis and the Videhas. He came to Ajātśatru, the king of the Kāśī and said, "Let me tell you Brahma." Ajātaśatru said to him, "I give you one thousand cows for these words of your. Many are the persons who run hither (foolishly) crying, 'Janaka, Janaka.'"

स होवाच बालाकिर्य एवैष आदित्ये पुरुषस्तमेवाहमुपास इति तं होवाचाजातशत्रुर्मा मैतस्मिन्संवादयिष्ठाः। बृहन्पाण्डरवासा अतिष्ठाः सर्वेषां भूतानां मूर्धेति वा अहमेतमुपास इति स यो

हैतमेवमुपास्तेऽतिष्ठाः सर्वेषां भूतानां मूर्धा भवति॥ २॥

The son of Balāka said, "I adore him who is the spirit in the sun." Ajātaśatru said, "Speak not proudly, speak not proudly of this; I adore him as the vast one, clothed in white raiment, all-excelling, the head of all beings; whoso thus adores him, excels all and becomes the head of all beings."

स होवाच बालाकिर्य एवैष चन्द्रमसि पुरुषस्तमेवाहमुपास इति तं होवाचाजातशत्रुर्मा मैतस्मिन्संवादयिष्ठाः सोमो राजाऽन्नस्यात्मेति वा अहमेतमुपास इति स यो मेवमुपास्तेऽन्नस्यात्मा भवति॥ ३॥

The son of Balāka said, "I adore him who is the spirit in the moon." Ajātaśatru said, "Speak not proudly, speak not proudly of this; I adore him as the soul of food; whoso thus adores him, becomes the soul of food."

स होवाच बालाकिर्य एवैष विद्युति पुरुषस्तमेवाहमुपास इति तं होवाचाजातशत्रुर्मा मैतस्मिन्संवादयिष्ठाः सत्यस्यात्मेति वा अहमेतमुपास इति स यो हैतमेवमुपास्ते सत्यस्यात्मा भवति॥ ४॥

The son of Balāka said, "I adore him who is the spirit in the lightning." Ajātaśatru said, "Speak not proudly, speak not proudly of this; I adore him as the soul of truth; whoso thus adores him, becomes the soul of truth."

स होवाच बालाकिर्य एवैष स्तनयित्नौ पुरुषस्तमेवाहमुपास इति तं होवाचाजातशत्रुर्मा मैतस्मिन्संवादयिष्ठाः शब्दस्यात्मेति वा अहमेतमुपास इति स यो हैतमेवमुपास्ते शब्दस्यात्मा भवति॥ ५॥

The son of Balāka said, "I adore him who is the spirit in the thunder-cloud." Ajātaśatru said, "Speak not proudly, Speak not proudly of this; I adore him as the soul of sound; whoso thus adores him, becomes the soul of sound."

स होवाच बालाकिर्य एवैष वायौ पुरुषस्तमेवाहमुपास इति तं होवाचाजातशत्रुर्मा मैतस्मिन्संवादयिष्ठाः इन्द्रो वैकुण्ठोऽपराजिता सेनेति वा अहमेतमुपास इति स यो हैतमेवमुपास्ते पूर्यते जिष्णुर्ह वा अपराजयिष्णुरन्यतस्त्यजायी भवति॥ ६॥

The son of Balāka said, "I adore him who is the spirit in the wind." Ajātaśatru said, "Speak not proudly, speak not proudly of this; I adore him as Indra, whom none can stay, whose hosts are unconquerable; whoso thus adores him, becomes a conqueror, unconquerable by others and himself conquering others."

स होवाच बालाकिर्य एवैष आकाशे पुरुषस्तमेवाहमुपास इति तं होवाचाजातशत्रुर्मा मैतस्मिन्संवादयिष्ठाः पूर्णमप्रवर्ति ब्रह्मेति वा अहमेतमुपास इति स यो हैतमेवमुपास्ते पूर्यते प्रजया पशुभिर्यशसा ब्रह्मवर्चसेन स्वर्गेण लोकेन सर्वमायुरेति॥ ७॥

The son of Balāka said, "I adore him who is the spirit in the ether." Ajātaśatru said, "Speak not proudly, speak not proudly of this; I adore him as the full and actionless Brahma; who so thus adores him, is filled with progeny, cattle, fame, holiness and svarga, and accomplishes his full life in this world."

स होवाच बालाकिर्य एवैषोऽग्नौ पुरुषस्तमेवाहमुपास इति तं होवाचाजातशत्रुर्मा मैतस्मिन्संवादयिष्ठा विषासहिरिति वा अहमेतमुपास इति स यो हैतमेवमुपास्ते विषासहिर्हैवान्वेष भवति॥ ८॥

The son of Balāka said, "I adore him who is the spirit in the fire." Ajātaśatru said, "Speak not proudly, speak not proudly of this; I adore him as the irresistible; whoso thus adores him, becomes irresistible among others."

स होवाच बालाकिर्य एवैषोऽप्सु पुरुषस्तमेवाहमुपास इति तं होवाचाजातशत्रुर्मा मैतस्मिन्संवादयिष्ठा स्तेजस आत्मेति वा अहमेतमुपास इति स यो हैतमेवमुपास्ते तेजस आत्मा भवतीत्यधिदैवतमथाध्यात्मम्॥ ९॥

The son of Balāka said, "I adore him who is the spirit in the waters." Ajātaśatru said, "Speak not proudly, speak not proudly of this; I adore him as the soul of light; whoso thus adores him, becomes the soul of light." Thus far the adoration depending on the deities, now that which depends on the soul.

स होवाच बालाकिर्य एवैष आदर्शे पुरुषस्तमेवाहमुपास इति तं होवाचाजातशत्रुर्मा मैतस्मिन्संवादयिष्ठाः प्रतिरूप इति वा अहमेतमुपास इति स यो हैतमेवमुपास्ते प्रतिरूपो हैवास्य प्रजायामाजायते नाप्रतिरूपः॥ १०॥

The son of Balāka said, "I adore him who is the spirit in the mirror." Ajātaśatru said, "Speak not proudly, speak not proudly of this; I adore him as the reflection; whoso thus adores him, is born truly reflected in his children, not falsely reflected."

स होवाच बालाकिर्य एवैष छायायां पुरुषस्तमेवाहमुपास इति तं होवाचाजातशत्रुर्मा मैतस्मिन्संवादयिष्ठा द्वितीयोऽनपग इति वा अहमेतमुपास इति स यो हैतमेवमुपास्ते विन्दते द्वितीयाद्द्वितीयवान् हि भवति॥ ११॥

The son of Balāka said, "I adore him who is the spirit in the shadow." Ajātaśatru said, "Speak not proudly, speak not proudly of this; I adore him as the double and inseparable; whoso thus adores him, obtains (offspring) from the double and himself becomes doubled."

स होवाच बालाकिर्य एवैष प्रतिश्रुत्कायां पुरुषस्तमेवाहमुपास इति तं होवाचाजातशत्रुर्मा मैतस्मिन्संवादयिष्ठा असुरिति वा अहमेतमुपास इति स यो हैतमेवमुपास्ते न पुरा कालात् सम्मोहमेति॥ १२॥

The son of Balāka said, "I adore him who is the spirit in the echo." Ajātaśatru said, "Speak not proudly, speak not proudly of this; I adore him as the life; whoso thus adores him, faints not before his time."

स होवाच बालाकिर्य एवैष शब्दे पुरुषस्तमेवाहमुपास इति तं होवाचाजातशत्रुर्मा मैतस्मिन्संवादयिष्ठा मृत्युरिति वा अहमेतमुपास इति स यो हैतमेवमुपास्ते न पुरा कालात्प्रैतीति॥ १३॥

The son of Balāka said, "I adore him who is the spirit in sound." Ajātaśatru said, "Speak not proudly, speak not proudly of this; I adore him as death; whoso thus adores him, dies not before his time."

स होवाच बालाकिर्य एवैतत्पुरुषः सुप्तः स्वप्नया चरति तमेवाहमुपास इति तं होवाचाजातशत्रुर्मा मैतस्मिन्संवादयिष्ठा यमो राजेति वा अहमेतमुपास इति स यो हैतमेवमुपास्ते सर्वं हास्मा इदं श्रैयाय यम्यते॥ १४॥

The son of Balāka said, "I adore him who as that sleeping spirit, goes forth by sleep." Ajātaśatru said, "Speak not proudly, speak not proudly of this; I adore him as king Yama; whoso thus adores him, to him all this (world) is subdued for his weal."

स होवाच बालाकिर्य एवैष शारीरः पुरुषस्तमेवाहमुपास इति तं होवाचाजातशत्रुर्मा मैतस्मिन्संवादयिष्ठाः प्रजापतिरिति वा अहमेतमुपास इति स यो हैतमेवमुपास्ते प्रजायते प्रजया पशुभिर्यशसा ब्रह्मवर्चसेन स्वर्गेण लोकेन सर्वमायुरेति॥ १५॥

The son of Balāka said, "I adore him who is the spirit in the body." Ajātaśatru said, "Speak not proudly, speak not proudly of this; I adore him as Prajāpati; whoso thus adores him, is multiplied in children, cattle, glory, holiness, heaven; and accomplishes his full life."

स होवाच बालाकिर्य एवैष दक्षिणेऽक्षिणि पुरुषस्तमेवाहमुपास इति तं होवाचाजातशत्रुर्मा मैतस्मिन्संवादयिष्ठा वाच आत्माऽग्नेरात्मा ज्योतिष आत्मेति वा अहमेतमुपास इति स यो हैतमेवमुपास्त एतेषां सर्वेषामात्मा भवति॥ १६॥

The son of Balāka said, "I adore him who is the spirit in the right eye." Ajātaśatru said, "Speak not proudly, speak not proudly of this; I adore him as the soul of speech, the soul of fire, the soul of splendour; whoso thus adores him, becomes the soul of all these."

स होवाच बालाकिर्य एवैष सव्येऽक्षिणि पुरुषस्तमेवाहमुपास इति तं होवाचाजातशत्रुर्मा मैतस्मिन्संवादयिष्ठाः सत्यस्यात्मा विद्युत आत्मा तेजस आत्मेति वा अहमेतमुपास इति स यो हैतमेवमुपास्त एतेषां सर्वेषामात्मा भवतीति॥ १७॥

The son of Balāka said, "I adore him who is the spirit in the left eye." Ajātaśatru said, "Speak not proudly, speak not proudly of this; I adore him as the soul of truth, the soul of the lightning, the soul of light; whoso thus adores him, becomes the soul of all these."

तत उ ह बालाकिस्तूष्णीमास तं होवाचाजातशत्रुः। एतावन्नु बालाका३इ इत्येतावद्धीति होवाच बालाकिस्तं होवाचाजातशत्रुर्मृषा वै किल मा समवादयिष्ठा ब्रह्म ते ब्रवाणीति। स होवाच। यो वै बालाक एतेषां पुरुषाणां कर्ता यस्य वैतत्कर्म स वै वेदितव्य इति तत उ ह बालाकिः समित्पाणिः प्रतिचक्रम उपायानीति तं होवाचाजातशत्रुः प्रतिलोमरूपमेव तत्स्याद्यत्क्षत्रियो ब्राह्मणमुपनयेत्। एहि व्येव त्वा ज्ञपयिष्यामीति तं ह पाणावभिपद्य प्रवव्राज तौ ह सुप्तं पुरुषमाजग्मतुस्तं हाजातशत्रुरामन्त्रयांचक्रे। बृहन्पाण्डरवासः सोमराजन्निति। स उ ह तूष्णीमेव शिश्ये। तत उ हैनं यष्ट्याविचिक्षेप स तत एव समुत्तस्थौ तं होवाचाजातशत्रुः। क्वैष एतद्बालाके पुरुषोऽशयिष्ट क्वैतदभूत्कुत एतदागा३दिति। तत उ ह बालाकिर्न विजज्ञौ॥ १८॥

Then verily the son of Balāka became silent. Ajātaśatru said to him, "Thus far only (reaches your knowledge,) O son of Balāka?" "Thus far only," he replied. Ajātaśatru said, "Speak not proudly without cause, (saying) 'Let me tell you Brahma.' O son of Balāka, He who is the maker of these spirits, whose work is all this. *He* verily is the Being to be known." Then truly the son of Balāka came up to him with fuel in his hand, saying, "Let me attend you (as my guru)." Ajātaśatru said to him, "This I consider contrary to nature that a Kṣatriya should instruct a Brāhmaṇa. Come, I will tell you all I know."

Then having taken him by the hand, he set forth. They came to a man asleep. Ajātaśatru called him, (saying) "Oh you vast one, clothed in white raiment, king Soma." The man still lay asleep. Then he pushed him with his staff and he at once rose up. Ajātaśatru said to the son of Balāka, "Where, O son of Balāka, lay this spirit asleep, where was all this done, whence came he thus back?" Then the son of Balāka knew not what to reply.

तं होवाचाजातशत्रुर्यत्रैष एतद्बालाके पुरुषोऽशयिष्ट यत्रैतदभूद्यत एतदागादिति। हिता नाम हृदयस्य नाड्यो हृदयात्पुरीततमभिप्रतन्वन्ति तद्यथा सहस्रधा केशो विपाटितस्तावदण्व्यः पिङ्गलस्याणिम्ना तिष्ठन्ति। शुक्लस्य कृष्णास्य पीतस्य लोहितस्येति तासु तदा भवति। यदा सुप्तः स्वप्नं न कंचन पश्यत्यस्मिन्प्राण एवैकधा भवति तदैनं वाक्सर्वैर्नामभिः सहाप्येति चक्षुः सर्वै रूपैः सहाप्येति श्रोत्रं सर्वैः शब्दैः सहाप्येति मनः सर्वैर्ध्यानैः सहाप्येति स यदा प्रतिबुध्यते यथाऽग्नेर्ज्वलतः सर्वा दिशो विस्फुलिङ्गा विप्रतिष्ठेरन्नेवमेवैतस्मादात्मनः प्राणा यथायतनं विप्रतिष्ठन्ते प्राणेभ्यो देवा देवेभ्यो लोकाः तद्यथा क्षुरः क्षुरधानेऽवहितः स्यात्। विश्वंभरो वा विश्वंभरकुलाय एवमेवैष प्रज्ञ आत्मेदं शरीरमात्मानमनुप्रविष्ट आलोमभ्य आनखेभ्यः॥ १९॥

Ajātaśatru said to him, "This is where, O son of Balāka, this spirit lay asleep, where all this was done and whence he thus came back. The vessels of the heart named *Hitā,* proceeding from the heart, surround the great membrane (round the heart); thin as a hair divided into a thousand parts and filled with the minute essence of various colours, of white, of black, of yellow and of red. When the sleeping man sees no dreams so ever, he abides in these."

Then is he absorbed in that Prāṇa. Then the speech enters into it with all names, the sight enters with all forms, the hearing enters with all sounds, the mind enters with all thoughts. When he awakes, as from blazing fire sparks go forth in all directions, so from this Soul all the prāṇas go forth to their several stations, from the prāṇas go forth the devas, from the devas the worlds. This is the true Prāṇa, identical with Prajñā; entering this body and soul, it penetrates to the nails and hairs of the skin.

तमेतमात्मानमेत आत्मानोऽन्ववस्यन्ते यथा श्रेष्ठिनं स्वाः। तद्यथा श्रेष्ठी स्वर्भुङ्क्ते यथा वा स्वाः श्रेष्ठिनं भुञ्जन्त्येवमेवैष प्रज्ञात्मैतैरात्मभिर्भुङ्क्ते। एवं वै तमात्मानमेत आत्मानो भुञ्जन्ति। स यावद्ध वा इन्द्र एतमात्मानं न विजज्ञे तावदेनमसुरा अभिबभूवुः। स यदा विजज्ञेऽथ हत्वाऽसुरान्विजित्य सर्वेषां देवानां श्रैष्ठ्यं स्वाराज्यमाधिपत्यं परीयाय तथो एवैवं विद्वान्सर्वान्पाप्मनोऽपहत्य सर्वेषां भूतानां श्रैष्ठ्यं स्वाराज्यमाधिपत्यं पर्येति य एवं वेद य एवं वेद॥ २०॥

Just as a razor placed in a razor case or fire in the home of fire, thus this Soul, itself Prajñā, enters this body and soul to the hairs and nails. The inferior souls follow this Soul as the household the householder. As the householder feeds with his household and as the household feed on the householder, so this Soul, itself Prajñā, feeds with those souls and thus those souls feed on this Soul. As long as Indra knew not this Soul, so long the Asuras overcame him. When he knew it, then having conquered and slain the Asuras, he attained the pre-eminence of all gods and all beings, he attained sovereignty and empire. Thus too is it with him who have this knowledge, having destroyed all sins and he attain the pre-eminence of all beings and sovereignty and empire, who knows thus, who knows thus.

वाङ्मे मनसि ....इति शान्तिः।।

।।इति कौषीतकिब्राह्मणोपनिषत्समाप्ता।।

***

24. NṚSIṀHAPŪRVATĀPINYUPANIṢAD

नृसिंहपूर्वतापिन्युपनिषद्

॥शान्तिपाठ:॥

ॐ भद्रं कर्णेभि: .... इति शान्ति:॥

This upaniṣad is related to the tradition of Atharvaveda. The tangible (Sanśeṣa) and intangible (Nirākāra) Brahma has been enunciated by the means of questionnaire between the gods and Prajāpati in this upaniṣad. The subject-matter of this upaniṣad has been divided in five sub-parts. These five sub-parts are also renowned with the name of upaniṣad too. The supreme soul (Paramātman) has been revealed as supreme industrious person (Nṛsiṁha). It has been said that this creation (Sṛṣṭi) has been developed as a result of the penance made by the supreme person. The involvement of creation can be said as the penance made by him previously. The upaniṣad explaining the series of the development of creation (Sṛṣṭi) has been stated 'Pūrvatāpinī'. The contents of first upaniṣad is– The desire of Prajāpati just at the root of creation, observance of the Anuṣṭubha hymn, this whole creation embedded within Anuṣṭubha hymn, four feet (Pāda) of the king hymn (Mantrarāja), the questions relating to saints, god, rhyme etc., the fruits of reciting Anuṣṭubha hymn, meditation on Sāma in the form of Loka (people), Veda, Brahma etc., the magnificence of the king hymn and the significance of this learning. The contents embedded with the second upaniṣad are crossing the world by observance to Nārsiṁha Mantrarāja, the merger of the Sāma's feet with the feet of Praṇava , Anuṣṭupatā of Sāma, Pancañgatā of Sāma, the Nyāsa (summoning process of gods on several organs of body) procedure of 'Oṁ, Nyāsa by every foot of Mantrarāja, the importance and use of the violent, gallant etc. 'pādas. In the third upaniṣad, the curiosity for the power seed of mantrarāja and power as also seed (key) has been described.

The contents in the fourth upaniṣad are preaching of Aṅga mantra, the Brahma in the form of Praṇava (Oṁ), the description of four feet of Praṇava, the form of Sāvitrī, Gāyatrī hymn, hymn of Yajurlakṣmī, Nṛsiṁha Gāyatrī hymn etc. The subject matter of the fifth upaniṣad is the curiosity gods for Mahācakra, description of six, eighth, twelfth, thirty second splints bearing discus, observance of organs, observance of Mahācakra, magnificence of penetrating Mahācakra, fruit of reading Mantrarāja, the supremacy of reciting the king hymn and the description of attainment of Brahma (knowledge) by the devotee reciting the king-hymn. Thus, the intangible Brahma has been related with the tangible Brahma *i.e.* lord Nṛsiṁha.

॥प्रथमोपनिषद्॥

आपो वा इदमासन् सलिलमेव। स प्रजापतिरेक: पुष्करपर्णे समभवत्। तस्यान्तर्मनसि काम: समवर्तत इदं सृजेयमिति। तस्माद्यत्पुरुषो मनसाभिगच्छति तद्वाचा वदति तत्कर्मणा करोति। तदेषाभ्यनूक्ता- कामस्तदग्रे समवर्तताधि मनसो रेत: प्रथमं यदासीत्। सतो बन्धुमसति निरविन्दन्हृदि प्रतीष्या कवयो मनीषेति उपैनं तदुपनमति यत्कामो भवति य एवं वेद॥ १॥

The Ist Upaniṣad

It has been said that Prajāpati Brahmā was appeared on the lotus petals standing amid the immeasurable quantum of the water when only water was spreaded everywhere and there was nothing like creation (Sṛṣṭi). The Prajāpati lord Brahmā then resolved for creating the world. It is a dictum popularly known and used that "the speech and activities are lead by the resolutions made by a man." The saints have said in this prospect– In course of creating this universe what originated in the mind of the primitive man was the sensuality. The scholars doing self-analysis in a regular manner consider the sensuality or lust as bondage of the inner-soul or conscience. The scholars consider that the sensuality arises in the mind engrossed in causative or functional nature (Prakṛti). This basic active element (Āpaḥ) had become the root cause for the creation of this universe. The people known to this mystery, receive everything to which they desire.

स तपोऽतप्यत स तपस्तप्त्वा स एतं मन्त्रराजं नारसिंहमानुष्टुभमपश्यत्। तेन वै सर्वमिदमसृजत यदिदं किंच। तस्मात्सर्वमानुष्टुभमित्याचक्षते यदिदं किंच। अनुष्टुभो वा इमानि भूतानि जायन्ते। अनुष्टुभा जातानि जीवन्ति। अनुष्टुभं प्रयन्त्यभिसंविशन्ति तस्यैषा भवत्यनुष्टुप्प्रथमा भवत्यनुष्टुबुत्तमा भवति वाग्वा अनुष्टुब्वाचैव प्रयन्ति वाचोद्यन्ति परमा वा एषा छन्दसां यदनुष्टुबिति॥ २॥

Lord Brahmā sat on penance for the objective of the creation of the world. As a result of that penance, this Nārasiṁha king-hymn appended with the Anuṣṭup rhyme has been introduced in the conscience. He created this tangible world of virtue of the king hymn. This tangible or apparent world is by this very reason called embedded in the king-hymn *i.e.* Anuṣṭubha. All living-organisms have been originated by this hymn of Anuṣṭup. They receive the power of existence of reason of Anuṣṭup and they entered into Anuṣṭup after their death also. This profession or concept of Anuṣṭup is the speech too. The people attain to their birth and death by this speech (hymn). Anuṣṭup definitely is the best among all other rhymes.

[Anuṣṭup has been stated as the cause for origin, development and the destruction. There are four feet in the rhyme of Anuṣṭup. One meaning of the rhyme is specific structurisation of the poetry but the second meaning is too wide *i.e.* ·hat covers. As the Anuṣṭup is revealed in the four feet, the different streams of creation (Sṛṣṭi) are further revealed in four feet each as– four Vedas, four kinds of living-organism (perspiratory, ovarian, wombic and aquatic), four kind of conscience, four Varṇas and four Aśramas etc. In the successive hymns several species of creation in the four numbers has been stated. This is the reason the creation has been stated as embedding with the rhyme Anuṣṭup.]

ससागरां सपर्वतां सप्तद्वीपां वसुन्धरां तत्साम्नः प्रथमं पादं जानीयात्। यक्षगन्धर्वाप्सरोगणसेवितमन्तरिक्षं तत्साम्नो द्वितीयं पादं जानीयाद्वसुरुद्रादित्यैः सर्वैर्देवैः सेवितं दिवं तत्साम्नस्तृतीयं पादं जानीयात्। ब्रह्मस्वरूपं निरञ्जनं परमं व्योमकं तत्साम्नश्चतुर्थं पादं जानीयाद्यो जानीते सोऽमृतत्वं च गच्छति॥ ३॥

It should be considered that the earth consisting of the seven islands, the mountain and the ocean have been originated from the first foot of this king-hymn in garb of Sāma. This space enjoyed by the Yakṣa, Gandharva and the fairies (dancing damsel in heaven), has been originated from the second foot of that Sāma. Further, it should be deemed that the world of sun surrounded by Vasu, Rudra and the Sun has been originated from the third foot of that Sāma. Similarly, the intangible, free from the pollution of illusion (Māyā), sacrosanct and supreme ether in garb of Brahma should be considered as origin from the fourth foot. By knowing this fact, the creatures attain to immortality.

ऋग्यजुःसामाथर्वाणश्चत्वारो वेदाः साङ्गाः सशाखाश्चत्वारः पादा भवन्ति॥४॥

किं ध्यानं किं दैवतं कान्यङ्गानि कानि दैवतानि किं छन्दः क ऋषिरिति॥५॥

The four feet of this king-hymn are– Ṛk, Yajuḥ, Sāma and Atharva *i.e.* four Vedas including all sub-parts (Aṅgas) and branches.

How meditation on king hymn should be made? Who is the god of it? What are the organs? What is the Gaṇa and rhyme of gods and who are the sage to this king-hymn?

स होवाच प्रजापतिः स यो ह वै सावित्रस्याष्टाक्षरं पदं श्रियाऽभिषिक्तं तत्साम्नोऽङ्गं वेद श्रिया हैवाभिषिच्यते। सर्वे वेदाः प्रणवादिकास्तं प्रणवं तत्साम्नोऽङ्गं वेद स त्रींल्लोकाञ्जयति चतुर्विंशत्यक्षरा महालक्ष्मीर्यजुस्तत्साम्नोऽङ्गं वेद स आयुर्यशःकीर्तिज्ञानैश्वर्यवान्भवति। तस्मादिदं साङ्गं साम जानीयाद्यो जानीते सोऽमृतत्वं च गच्छति॥६॥

The renowned Prajāpati Brahma said– "The person who knows the feature of this king-hymn as eight letters Gāyatrī hymn processed (enthroned) by Śrī seed (key), definitely becomes prosperous with knowledge and the wealth both. The Praṇava (Oṁ) is recited at the beginning of Vedic hymns. The person considering Praṇava as a part to this very Sāma becomes victorious in all the three worlds. The scholar who knows the Mahālakṣmi hymn consisting of twenty four letters in the form of Yajuḥ, attains to fame, knowledge, long-life and prosperity. This Sāma should be known with its all parts because the person known to three parts attains to immortality.

सावित्रीं प्रणवं यजुर्लक्ष्मीं स्त्रीशूद्राय नेच्छन्ति। द्वात्रिंशदक्षरं साम जानीयाद्यो जानीते सोऽमृतत्वं च गच्छति। सावित्रीं लक्ष्मीं यजुः प्रणवं यदि जानीयात् स्त्रीशूद्रः स मृतोऽधो गच्छति तस्मात्सर्वदा नाचष्टे यद्याचष्टे स आचार्यस्तेनैव स मृतोऽधो गच्छति॥७॥

The scholars do not want preaching Praṇava Gāyatrī and Mahālakṣmi hymn in the form of Yajuḥ to the female and śūdras because those are not entitle to have knowledge of this most sacrosanct hymn. They should know the Sāma containing the thirty two letters as the person known to it, attains to immortality. In case the hymns of Gāyatrī Praṇava and Mahālakṣmi hymn in the form of Yajurveda is learnt by the females and śūdras even having unauthorised or forbidden, they do not receive any fruit for such perseverance and suffer from adversities after their death. The Ācāryas should also take precautions because those will also suffer from doer consequences if they preach these hymns to above said unauthorised persons.

[A specific purpose intervenes herein behind considering the females and śūdras as unauthorised. The world female is used for a woman who is engaged every time in taking foolishly and futile, frequently conceived and busy with providing maintenance and protection to the babies. How does the most holy procedure can be followed by such female? Similarly, the word śūdra is used for a man who suffers from agony every moment. As the recital of hymns etc. requires cool and tender temperament, the person suffering from such melancholia will not concentrate his mind. Hence, the purpose cannot be achieved. These are the reasons, the female and śūdra are barred from learning and doing attempts of perseverance of the same. The persons not falling under this definition are however fully entitled to this purpose.]

स होवाच प्रजापतिः–अग्निर्वै देवा इदं सर्वं विश्वा भूतानि प्राणा वा इन्द्रियाणि पशवोऽन्नममृतं सम्राट् स्वराड्विराट् तत्साम्नः प्रथमं पादं जानीयात्। ऋग्यजुःसामाथर्वरूपः सूर्योऽन्तरादित्ये हिरण्मयः पुरुषस्तत्साम्नो द्वितीयं पादं जानीयात्। य ओषधीनां प्रभुर्भवति ताराधिपतिः सोमस्तत्साम्नस्तृतीयं पादं जानीयात्। स ब्रह्मा स शिवः स हरिः सेन्द्रः सोऽक्षरः परमः स्वराट् तत्साम्नश्चतुर्थं पादं जानीयाद्यो जानीते सोऽमृतत्वं च गच्छति॥ ८॥

Prajāpati Brahma again started saying– One should know all gods, fires, creatures, breathings, sensory organs, animals, food (cereals), nectar, Samrāṭ, Svarāṭ and Virāt. Ṛk, Yajuḥ, Sāma and Atharvaveda, the sun and the Hiraṇyamaya person existed in the orbit of sun should be known as the second foot. All medicines and the moon, kind of stars are to be considered as the third foot and lord Viṣṇu, Brahmā, Śiva, Indra and immortal supreme soul should be considered as the fourth foot. The person knowing four feet this way, attains to the immortality.

उग्रं प्रथमस्याद्यं ज्वलं द्वितीयस्याद्यं नृसिं तृतीयस्याद्यं मृत्युं चतुर्थस्याद्यं साम जानीयाद्यो जानीते सोऽमृतत्वं च गच्छति। तस्मादिदं साम यत्र कुत्रचिन्नाचष्टे यदि दातुमपेक्षते पुत्राय शुश्रूषवे दास्यत्यन्यस्मै शिष्याय वा चेति॥ ९॥

The foot *"ugram"* in king-hymn Anuṣṭubha is the beginning part of the first foot. The foot *"jvalam"* is the initial part of the second foot. The starting part of third food is *"Nṛsiṅ"* and the initial part to fourth foot is *"Mṛtyu"*. These four feets are the forms of Sāma. The person known to this fact attains immortality. This Sāma is desired to give someone other, it can be given only to the obedient son or the disciple whose conduct is duly proved. To preach this to un-entitled is strictly prohibited.

क्षीरोदार्णवशायिनं नृकेसरिं योगिध्येयं परमं पदं साम जानीयाद्यो जानीते सोऽमृतत्वं च गच्छति॥ १०॥

Prajāpati continued further that the Nṛsiṁha form of lord that rests in Kṣīrasāgara is the form worth doing meditation for yogis. The person known to Sāma this way, attains to the immortality.

[The fact as to attainment of nectar (Amṛta) as a result of meditation on Nṛsiṁha god retiring on Kṣīrasāgara (ocean of milk) is fully reasonable. Kṣīrasāgara is meant by an eatable (entertainable) matter that gives immortality. It can also be said as the flow of the element of creation (Sṛṣṭi) earlier than the time when the matter was created. Herein Nṛsiṁha (the inbuer of splendour in the living soul of the men) is in sleeping posture *i.e.* the most mighty divine power within him is in dormance.

Meditation on such divine element and imbibing the same, definitely make the devotee to attain immortality.]

वीरं प्रथमस्याद्यार्धान्त्यं तं स द्वितीयस्याद्यार्धान्त्यं हंभी तृतीयस्याद्यार्धान्त्यं मृत्युं चतुर्थस्याद्यार्धान्त्यं साम जानीयाद्यो जानीते सोऽमृतत्वं च गच्छति। तस्मादिदं साम येन केनचिदाचार्यमुखेन यो जानीते स तेनैव शरीरेण संसारान्मुच्यते मोचयति मुमुक्षुर्भवति। जपात्तेनैव शरीरेण देवतादर्शनं करोति तस्मादिदमेव मुख्यद्वारं कलौ नान्येषां भवति तस्मादिदं साङ्गं साम जानीयाद्यो जानीते सोऽमृतत्वं च गच्छति॥ ११॥

The foot "Vīra" should be deemed the last part to the first holy of the first foot in the king hymn Anuṣṭubha. The foot "Taṅ Sa" should be considered as the last part of the first half of the second foot to this Sāma. The foot "Haṁbhī" should be considered the last part to the first half of the fourth foot to this Sāma. The person who knows that all this is Sāma, attains to the immortality. The person who develops his knowledge to this fact by duly receiving it from Ācārya, attains emancipation in this very body and further becomes a cause for providing others with emancipation. Irrespective of the devotee knowing it involved in the worldly attachments, starts thinking to have emancipation's. The person reciting this hymn of Sāma gets direct perception of lord Nṛsiṁha in his existing life. No other way so easy particularly in this Kaliyuga is available. The person who knows this Sāma with all its organs (Aṅgas), attains to the emancipation.

ऋतं सत्यं परं ब्रह्म पुरुषं नरकेसरिविग्रहं कृष्णपिङ्गलम्। ऊर्ध्वरेतं विरूपाक्षं शंकरं नीललोहितम्। उमापतिः पशुपतिः पिनाकी ह्यमितद्युतिः। ईशानः सर्वविद्यानामीश्वरः सर्वभूतानां ब्रह्माधिपतिर्ब्रह्मणोऽधिपतिर्यो वै यजुर्वेदवाच्यस्तं हि साम जानीयाद्यो जानीते सोऽमृतत्वं च गच्छति॥ १२॥

Lord Nṛsiṁha in garb of Ṛta and the truth are omni-initutive and omnipresent god. He is of black and grey complexion. His stature is a fine blend of the man and the lion. The eyes of lord Nṛsiṁha are most dreadful and fierce. He gazes on the objects straightly (ūrdhvaretā). He is benevolent to all. Having blue throat and reddish complexion upside, the devotees worship him by reciting his name as Nīlalohita. Lord Nṛsiṁha too is Umāpati, Paśupati, Pinākadhārin (holder of the bow named Pināka) and most luminating (holder of light) lord Maheśvara. Lord Nṛsiṁha too is the ruler of all learning's and the living organisms. Lord Nṛsiṁha too is the master of lord Brahmā, the supreme god of Brahma (knowledge) and the connotation (embodiment) of Yajurveda. He should be considered Sāma. The person who knows this fact, attains to immortality.

[The form of Nṛsiṁha and his power has been revealed herein. It is full of mystery. Lord Nṛsiṁha has been stated as Ṛta and the truth, which are the primitive factors of the creation (world). Ṛtaṁ ca satyaṁ.......Sūryācandramasau dhātā yathā pūrvamakalpayai..... (Ṛg.10.190.1-3) etc. hymns describe that these factors hand made the creature possible. Three names of Nṛsiṁha as– Kṛṣṇapiṅgala, Nīlalohita and Dyutimān has been described herein. These all reveal the seriatim form for the revelation of the matter. The first form is of Kṛṣṇapiṅgala– Blackish brown. It reveals unclarity, the second form is of Nīlalohita (Bluish red) which reveals some lesser unclarity and the third form is of luminating (full of light) which is of full clarity. The hint as having creation of the matter in the same order has been given here.]

महा प्रथमान्तार्धस्याद्यं र्वतो द्वितीयान्तार्धस्याद्यं षणं तृतीयान्तार्धस्याद्यं नमा चतुर्थान्तार्धस्याद्यं साम जानीयाद्यो जानीते सोऽमृतत्वं च गच्छति। तस्मादिदं साम सच्चिदानन्दमयं परं ब्रह्म तमेवं विद्वानमृत इह भवति। तस्मादिदं साङ्गं साम जानीयाद्यो जानीते सोऽमृतत्वं च गच्छति॥ १३॥

The foot "Mahā" is the beginning part of the last half to the first foot of king hymn Anuṣṭubha. The foot "Rvato" is the starting part of the last half of second foot to the king hymn Anuṣṭubha and the foot "Namā" is the initial part to the last half of the fourth foot. The person who knows that this all is Sāma, attains to immortality. Sāma too is the supreme Brahma in garb of Saccidānanda. Knowing this fact properly, we attains to immortality in this very life. The person who knows this Sāma with all its parts, attains to the emancipation.

विश्वसृज एतेन वै विश्वमिदमसृजन्त यद्विश्वमसृजन्त तस्माद्विश्वसृजो विश्वमेनाननु प्रजायते ब्रह्मण: सलोकतां सार्ष्टितां सायुज्यं यन्ति तस्मादिदं साङ्गं साम जानीयाद्यो जानीते सोऽमृतत्वं च गच्छति॥ १४॥

The Prajāpati is creator to this earth, has created this whole universe by reciting the hymns of Sāma. This is the reason, he has been said as creator of universe. This world has been created by him. The persons known to this very mystery attain to the abode of Brahma and merge with the same. This Sāma, therefore, should be understood with all its auxiliaries. The person so known, attains to the immortality.

विष्णुं प्रथमान्त्यं मुखं द्वितीयान्त्यं भद्रं तृतीयान्त्यं म्यहं चतुर्थान्त्यं साम जानीयाद्यो जानीते सोऽमृतत्वं च गच्छति। योऽसौ वेद यदिदं किंचात्मनि ब्रह्मण्येवानुष्टुभं जानीयाद्यो जानीते सोऽमृतत्वं च गच्छति स्त्रीपुंसयोर्वा। य इहैव स्थातुमपेक्षते तस्मै सर्वैश्वर्यं ददाति। यत्र कुत्रापि म्रियते देहान्ते देव: परमं ब्रह्म तारकं व्याचष्टे येनासावमृतीभूत्वा सोऽमृतत्वं च गच्छति॥ १५॥

The last foot to the first foot of king hymn Anuṣṭubha is Viṣṇu. The last word of second foot is 'Mukham', the last word to third foot is 'Bhadram' and the last word to fourth foot is 'Myaham'. The person known to Sāma this way attains to salvation. The above said elements of worship etc. are only known to lord Brahmā. The king hymn Anuṣṭubha is in the form of the souls of living organisms and its sinus is in Brahma. The person knowing this, attains to the immortality. Lord Nṛsiṁha provides the persons of good conduct with all kinds of pleasure and prosperity as desired by him. Lord Nṛsiṁha preaches his devotee Tāraka hymn, the embodiment of perfect knowledge irrespective of the place of his death. Having known to the hymn, he attains to the emancipation after having obtained the immortal complexion.

तस्मादिदं साममध्यगं जपति तस्मादिदं सामाङ्गं प्रजापतिस्तस्मादिदं सामाङ्गं प्रजापतिर्य एवं वेदेति महोपनिषत्। य एतां महोपनिषदं वेद स कृतपुरश्चरणो महाविष्णुर्भवति महाविष्णुर्भवति॥ १६॥

The Japa (silent recital) of Sāma in garb of Tāraka hymn should therefore, made always because the power of Prajāpati Brahma is inherited to the hymn of Sāma. The person known to this, is the real devotee. As this hymn reckons with the element of supreme god (Parameśvara), it is called Mahopaniṣad. The person sitting on the penance known as Puraścaraṇa duly observing the procedure told herein, obtains the fruit definitely and becomes Mahāviṣṇu.

॥द्वितीयोपनिषद्॥

देवा ह वै मृत्योः पाप्मभ्यः संसाराच्च बिभीयुस्ते प्रजापतिमुपाधावंस्तेभ्य एतं मन्त्रराजं नारसिंहमानुष्टुभं प्रायच्छत्तेन वै ते मृत्युमजयन् पाप्मानं चातरन्संसारं चातरंस्तस्माद्यो मृत्योः पाप्मभ्यः संसाराच्च बिभीयात्स एतं मन्त्रराजं नारसिंहमानुष्टुभं प्रतिगृह्णीयात्स मृत्युं जयति स पाप्मानं तरति स संसारं तरति॥ १॥

Second Upaniṣad

Once in ancient time, all gods went to Prajāpati Brahma having afraid of the world, vices and the death. Prajāpati Brahma preached them the king hymn Anuṣṭubha of lord Nṛsiṁha. They conquered the death and crossed the ocean of world by making them to avoid from all vices. The person threatened of the death, vices and the ocean of this material world, should therefore; shelter to the king-hymn Anuṣṭubha. The person resorting to king-hymn conquers death, compounds the vices and thus, easily crosses this worldly ocean.

तस्य ह वै प्रणवस्य या पूर्वा मात्रा पृथिव्यकारः स ऋग्भिर्ऋग्वेदो ब्रह्मा वसवो गायत्री गार्हपत्यः स साम्नः प्रथमः पादो भवति। द्वितीयाऽन्तरिक्षं स उकारः स यजुर्भिर्यजुर्वेदो विष्णुरुद्रास्त्रिष्टुब्दक्षिणाग्निः स साम्नो द्वितीयः पादो भवति। तृतीया द्यौः स मकारः स सामभिः सामवेदो रुद्रा आदित्या जगत्याहवनीयः स साम्नस्तृतीयः पादो भवति। याऽवसानेऽस्य चतुर्थ्यर्धमात्रा सा सोमलोक ओंकारः सोऽथर्वणैर्मन्त्रैरथर्ववेदः संवर्तकोऽग्निर्मरुतो विराडेकर्षिर्भास्वती स्मृता सा साम्नश्चतुर्थः पादो भवति॥ २॥

The inseparable part to king-hymn is Praṇava (Oṁ). Its first mora is 'A'. Its abode is the earth, gaṇa are Aṣṭavasu, the Veda is Ṛgveda, god is Brahma, rhyme is Gāyatrī and fire is Gārhapatya. All these are embedded with the first mora of Praṇava (Oṁ). This first mora too is the first foot of Sāma, 'U' is the second mora. The abode of this second mora is space, the god is Viṣṇu, Guṇa is the eleven Rudras, its Veda is Yajurveda consisting of all Yajuḥ hymns, rhyme is Triṣṭup and the fire is Dakṣiṇāgni. This is the second foot of the king hymn Sāma. The inseparable part of king hymn Sāma is the 'M'. Its abode is 'the abode of sun', Veda is Sāmaveda, God is Rudra, Guṇa are the twelve suns, rhyme is Jagatī and the fire is Āhavanīya. This all is within the third mora. The third foot of Sāma is this third mora. The sound creating half-mora which is heard last while reciting Praṇava has the abode of Soma, the perfect knowledge (Parabrahman) expressed as 'Oṁ' is its god, its Veda is Atharvaveda, its fire is Saṁpravartaka, Gaṇa are forty nine Maruts and rhyme is

Virāt and its Ṛsi is Brahmā. This most luminating mora is in garb of Brahma (knowledge). This fourth mora to Praṇava too is the fourth foot.

अष्टाक्षर: प्रथम: पादो भवत्यष्टाक्षरास्त्रय: पादा भवन्त्येवं द्वात्रिंशदक्षराणि संपद्यन्ते द्वात्रिंशदक्षरा वा अनुष्टुब्भवत्यनुष्टुभा सर्वमिदं सृष्टमनुष्टुभा सर्वमुपसंहृतम्॥ ३॥

This Anuṣṭup hymn contains thirty two letters in aggregate. Its first foot contains eight letters and the rest of feet *i.e.* three feet also contain eight letters each. This Anuṣṭup hymn is the nucleus of the whole world. It is the cause of creation and destruction too.

तस्य हैतस्य पञ्चाङ्गानि भवन्ति चत्वार: पादाश्चत्वार्यङ्गानि भवन्ति सप्रणवं सर्वं पञ्चमं भवति हृदयाय नम: शिरसे स्वाहा शिखायै वषट् कवचाय हुं अस्त्राय फडिति प्रथमं प्रथमेन संयुज्यते द्वितीयं द्वितीयेन तृतीयं तृतीयेन चतुर्थं चतुर्थेन पञ्चमं पञ्चमेन व्यतिषजति व्यतिषिक्ता वा इमे लोकास्तस्माद्व्यतिषिक्तान्यङ्गानि भवन्ति॥ ४॥

This Anuṣṭup hymn contains five organs (Aṅga). The fifth Praṇava alongwith four feet too is its one of organs. This hymn is concluded wish Praṇava (Oṁ). Five parts in human body have also been stated. These are the heart, head, braid, arms and the skull. All parts (organs) of Praṇava should therefore, be added with recital of Hṛdayāya Namaḥ, Śirase Svahā, Śikhāya Vaṣat, Kavacāya Huṁ, Astrāya phat. The first part of the body should be touched while reciting the first part of the hymn, second with the second, third with third and thus, systematically fifth part of the body should be touched while reciting the fifth part of the hymn. As all worlds are related mutually, the above parts too are mutually related.

ओमित्येतदक्षरमिदं सर्वं तस्मात्प्रत्यक्षरमुभयत ओंकारो भवति। अक्षराणां न्यासमुपदिशन्ति ब्रह्मवादिन:॥ ५॥

This 'Oṁ' is the whole world. One should therefore, does Nyāsa by adding 'Oṁ' syllable before and after each letter of this Anuṣṭup hymn. The scholars known to Brahma, suggest for doing Aṅganyāsa with each other.

तस्य ह वा उग्रं प्रथमं स्थानं जानीयाद्यो जानीते सोऽमृतत्वं च गच्छति वीरं द्वितीयं स्थानं महाविष्णुं तृतीयं स्थानं ज्वलन्तं चतुर्थं स्थानं सर्वतोमुखं पञ्चमं स्थानं नृसिंहं षष्ठं स्थानं भीषणं सप्तमं स्थानं भद्रमष्टमं स्थानं मृत्युमृत्युं नवमं स्थानं नमामि दशमं स्थानमहमेकादशं स्थानं जानीयाद्यो जानीते सोऽमृतत्वं च गच्छति॥ ६॥

The first foot to this Anuṣṭup is 'Ugram' and it is the first place of hymn. The person known to this fact attains to immortality. 'Vīrama' is at the second place in the hymn, 'Mahāviṣṇu is the third, 'Jvalaṅtam is fourth, Sarvatomukham is fifth, Nṛsiṁham is sixth, Bhīṣaṇam is seventh, Bhadram is the eighth, Mṛtyumṛtyum is ninth, Namāmi is the tenth and Aham is eleventh. The person known to these places, attains to the immortality.

[According to the hints given here, the Anuṣṭubha hymn will be as- 'Oṁ ugraṁ vīraṁ mahāviṣṇuṁ jvalantaṁ sarvatomukham, Nṛsiṁhaṁ bhīṣaṇaṁ bhadraṁ mṛtyumṛtyuṁ namāmyaham]

एकादशपदा वा अनुष्टुब्भवत्यनुष्टुभा सर्वमिदं सृष्टमनुष्टुभा सर्वमिदमुपसंहृतं तस्मात्सर्वानुष्टुभं जानीयाद्यो जानीते सोऽमृतत्वं च गच्छति॥७॥

This is Anuṣṭup Vṛtti consisting of eleven feet. Creation of this whole world has been made by it and it to becomes the cause for destruction. One should consider it as the magnificence of Anuṣṭup. The person knowing this, attains to immortality.

देवा ह वै प्रजापतिमब्रुवन्नथ कस्मादुच्यत उग्रमिति। स होवाच प्रजापतिर्यस्मात्स्व-महिम्ना सर्वांल्लोकान्सर्वान्देवान्सर्वानात्मन: सर्वाणि भूतान्युद्गृह्णात्यजस्रं सृजति विसृजति वासयत्युद्ग्राह्यत उद्गृह्यते। स्तुहि श्रुतं गर्तसदं युवानं मृगं न भीममुपहत्नुमुग्रम्। मृडा जरित्रे रुद्र स्तवानो अन्यं ते अस्मन्निवपन्तु सेना: तस्मादुच्यत उग्रमिति॥८॥

Prajāpati lord Brahmā was once asked by the gods– Why the adjective 'violent' has been used for lord Nṛsiṁha? Prajāpati replied– Lord Nṛsiṁha does upliftment of all world, gods, all living organisms and all souls incessantly and in a regular manner by virtue of his magnificence. He creates, provides maintenance and he too does the destruction's. He merges this whole universe with him. He does grace on the world and persue others to do the same. Hence, he is called violent (ugra). It has been stated in Ṛgveda that one should pray the god which is prayed by the Vedas (Śrutis). The supreme soul is enshrined as a young chap in the cavity of heart. That lord is not fierce for his devotees even in the form of a lion. He does grace on all by accessing to them. He is called violent because he does welfare of devotees and kills the shrewd. O lord Nṛsiṁha! We pray you. Please, do our welfare. May your grand army not attack on us and go somewhere other place. Owing to these reasons, lord Nṛsiṁha has been called as violent.

अथ कस्मादुच्यते वीरमिति। यस्मात्स्वमहिम्ना सर्वांल्लोकान्सर्वान्देवान्सर्वानात्मन: सर्वाणि भूतानि विरमति विरामयत्यजस्रं सृजति विसृजति वासयति। यतो वीर: कर्मण्य: सुदक्षो युक्तग्रावा जायते देवकामस्तस्मादुच्यते वीरमिति॥९॥

The gods had again asked– O lord! Why has the adjective 'Vīram' been given to Nṛsiṁha? Brahma told– He plays various ways with all worlds, souls, gods and the living beings by virtue of his magnificence, enjoys the plays so played, create all continuously, destroy them and provides them stability.

(It has been said in Ṛcās of Ṛgveda that) lord Nṛsiṁha does immediate grace on his devotees. He is warrior and dutious. He becomes Adhvaryu in stone form and thus, co-operate in processing the Soma. He too wish summoning to gods. This is the reason, he is addressed as 'Vīram'.

अथ कस्मादुच्यते महाविष्णुमिति। यस्मात्स्वमहिम्ना सर्वांल्लोकान्सर्वान्देवान्सर्वानात्मन: सर्वाणि भूतानि व्याप्नोति व्यापयति स्नेहो यथा पललपिण्डं शान्तमूलमोतं प्रोतमनुव्याप्तं व्यतिषिक्तो व्याप्यते व्यापयते। यस्मान्न जात: परो अन्यो अस्ति य आविवेश भुवनानि विश्वा। प्रजापति: प्रजया संविदान: त्रीणि ज्योतींषि सचते स षोडशीं तस्मादुच्यते महाविष्णुमिति॥१०॥

(The gods asked– Lord! Please tell us that why lord Nṛsiṁha) is addressed with the name of Mahāviṣṇum. (Prajāpati replied)– Lord Nṛsiṁha is uniformly present everywhere with his magnificence. As the fat is found in the piece of flesh, he is present in entire body will all organs. This world having embedded within him, merges with him at the time of great devastation (Mahāpralaya). (His magnificence has been described in Ṛgveda). Lord Nṛsiṁha exists with sixteen arts (learning or kalās) in several flames. He is surviving the subject, adorable for them, equally present everywhere and provides maintenance to the subject. Nobody can be compared with lord Nṛsiṁha *i.e.* he is unique.

अथ कस्मादुच्यते ज्वलन्तमिति यस्मात्स्वमहिम्ना सर्वांल्लोकान्सर्वान्देवान्सर्वानात्मनः सर्वाणि भूतानि स्वतेजसा ज्वलति ज्वालयति ज्वाल्यते ज्वालयते। सविता प्रसविता दीप्तो दीपयन्दीप्यमानः ज्वलञ्ज्वलिता तपन्वितपन्त्संतपन्रोचनो रोचमानः शोभनः शोभमानः कल्याणस्तस्मादुच्यते ज्वलन्तमिति॥ ११॥

(The gods again asked) Why the adjective 'Jvalantam' is used for lord Nṛsiṁha? (Brahma told)– Lord Nṛsiṁha is self-luminating and enlightens to all living-organisms, all gods and the souls with his magnificence. (It has been contemplated in Ṛgveda while describing the magnificence of lord Nṛsiṁha that) he spreads light like lord Sun (Savitā) and always present as renowned for production in garb of fertility (Prasavitā). He is self luminated and gives light to others too. He does penance and make others to do penance. He is illustrious himself and provides other the opportunity to become illustrious. He does welfare for all and make others to perform all benevolent deeds.

अथ कस्मादुच्यते सर्वतोमुखमिति। यस्मात्स्वमहिम्ना सर्वांल्लोकान्सर्वान्देवान्सर्वानात्मनः सर्वाणि भूतानि स्वयमनिन्द्रियोऽपि सर्वतः पश्यति सर्वतः शृणोति सर्वतो गच्छति सर्वत आदत्ते सर्वगः सर्वगतस्तिष्ठति। एकः पुरस्ताद्य इदं बभूव यतो बभूव भुवनस्य गोपाः। यमप्येति भुवनं सांपराये नमामि तमहं सर्वतोमुखमिति तस्मादुच्यते सर्वतोमुखमिति॥ १२॥

(Gods again asked– O Prajāpati!) Why the adjective 'Sarvatomukham' has been used for lord Nṛsiṁha? (Lord Brahmā said)– he exists everywhere equally in all places, moves to all places, observes all from all directions, hears to and entertains to all souls, living-organisms, all gods and all worlds with his magnificence inspite of having beyond to the sensory organs. (It has also been stated in Ṛgveda that) the god who was one in himself at the beginning of world, appeared in garb of this world. That god is the creator, nourisher and destroyer of this world. Such 'Sarvatomukha' (present and observe everywhere) god is saluted. This is the reason for saying him 'Sarvatomukha'.

अथ कस्मादुच्यते नृसिंहमिति। यस्मात्सर्वेषां भूतानां ना वीर्यतमः श्रेष्ठतमश्च सिंहो वीर्यतमः श्रेष्ठतमश्च। तस्मान्नृसिंह आसीत्परमेश्वरो जगद्धितं वा एतद्रूपं यदक्षरं भवति। प्रतद्विष्णुःस्तवते वीर्याय मृगो न भीमः कुचरो गिरिष्ठाः। यस्योरुषु त्रिषु विक्रमणेष्वधिक्षियन्ति भुवनानि विश्वा। तस्मादुच्यते नृसिंहमिति॥ १३॥

(The gods again asked) 'Why the adjective 'Nṛsiṁhaṁ' has been given?" (Lord Brahmā said)– The man is the most chivalrous and the best among all living-organisms. The lord by this reason has been stated holding the characteristic of a man and lion both.

This form of lord is immortal, benevolent and unending for the world. The devotees pray for acquiring several kind of power. He is not dreadful to his devotees even in the form of a lion. Lord Nṛsiṁha moves everywhere on earth and mountains. He is present in multiforms. He is inherent to the speech of priests too. The three worlds are measured in his three steps. These are the reasons for calling him 'Nṛsiṁham'.

अथ कस्मादुच्यते भीषणमिति। यस्माद्भीषणं यस्य रूपं दृष्ट्वा सर्वे लोकाः सर्वे देवाः सर्वाणि भूतानि भीत्या पलायन्ते स्वयं यतः कुतश्च न बिभेति। भीषाऽस्माद्वातः पवते भीषोदेति सूर्यः। भीषाऽस्मादग्निश्चेन्द्रश्च मृत्युर्धावति पञ्चम इति तस्मादुच्यते भीषणमिति॥ १४॥

(The gods asked) O god! Please tell us that why the word 'horrible' has been used for the god in this hymn. (Prajāpati replied that) all worlds, gods and living-organisms start fleeing to and fro in a tense of fear merely by a single sight at this horrible form of lord. However, lord himself seldom afraid of anybody. (Vedas say) owing to fear of this lord, the wind god blows and lord sun gives light to the earth. Lord fire and Indra too perform their respective duties owing to fear of him and the fifth god, the god of death too does his duty actively. This is the reason for calling lord as 'horrible'.

अथ कस्मादुच्यते भद्रमिति। यस्मात्स्वयं भद्रो भूत्वा सर्वदा भद्रं ददाति। रोचनो रोचमानः शोभनः शोभमानः कल्याणः। भद्रं कर्णेभिः शृणुयाम देवा भद्रं पश्येमाक्षभिर्यजत्राः। स्थिरैरङ्गैस्तुष्टुवाꣳसस्तनूभिर्व्यशेम देवहितं यदायुः। तस्मादुच्यते भद्रमिति॥ १५॥

(The gods asked– O lord! Please tell us that) why lord Nṛsiṁha has been addressed as 'Bhadram'? (Prajāpati said that) Lord is *Bhadra i.e.* benevolent to all. He himself acquires fame and makes others also to acquire the fame. He establishes his high image and inspire others too for the same. (It has been said in Veda) O gods! You support the clients. May we listen to the benevolent speech (words) from our ear and see the benevolent scenes always. O god! May we live full life praying you ceaselessly with healthy body so that we can perform the great deeds. This is the reason for calling lord as benevolent (Bhadram).

अथ कस्मादुच्यते मृत्युमृत्युमिति। यस्मात्स्वमहिम्ना स्वभक्तानां स्मृत एव मृत्युमपमृत्युं च मारयति। य आत्मदा बलदा यस्य विश्व उपासते प्रशिषं यस्य देवाः। यस्य छायामृतं यो मृत्युमृत्युः कस्मै देवाय हविषा विधेम। तस्मादुच्यते मृत्युमृत्युमिति॥ १६॥

(The gods raised a question further that O god!) why the foot 'Mṛtyumṛtyum' has been come in this king-hymn? (Prajāpati said) the gods on being prayed by devotees, drives their death and premature death too with his magnificence. (It has been said in Veda) we offer morsels (Āhutis) to that supreme soul, full of truth, mind and pleasure (Saccidānanda) that gives us physical and metaphysical power, immortal pleasure. When living in shelter and physical or material pains, when not prayed is attained as return and all gods performing great deeds follows to whose best preaching. On this very basis he is said Mṛtyu-Mṛtyum.

अथ कस्मादुच्यते नमामीति। यस्माद्यं सर्वे देवा नमन्ति मुमुक्षवो ब्रह्मवादिनश्च। प्र नूनं ब्रह्मणस्पतिर्मन्त्रं वदत्युक्थ्यम्। यस्मिन्निन्द्रो वरुणो मित्रो अर्यमा देवा ओकांसि चक्रिरे। तस्मादुच्यते नमामीति॥ १७॥

(The gods asked that) why the foot 'Namāmi' has come in this Anuṣṭubha? (Prajāpati said) all gods, the persons known to Brahma and desirous of emancipation do worship of lord Nṛsiṁha. He therefore, is adorable. (Lord reva says) salute is conveyed to the lord prayed by Brahma, shelter to Brahma and Vedas and who is made Iṣṭa (aim or destination) by the gods like Indra, Varuṇa, Mitra and Aryamā etc. This is the reason for appearance of the word 'Namāmi' in this king-hymn.

अथ कस्मादुच्यतेऽहमिति। अहमस्मि प्रथमजा ऋतस्य पूर्वं देवेभ्यो अमृतस्य नाभिः। यो मा ददाति स इ देवमावाः अहमन्नमन्नमदन्तमद्मि। अहं विश्वं भुवनमभ्यभवां सुवर्णज्योतीः। य एवं वेदेति महोपनिषत्॥ १८॥

(The gods again asked) O god! Why the foot 'Aham' inserted in this hymn? (Brahma said) The Veda says– "I have born even prior to the everlasting (Sanātana) Yajña of Sṛṣṭi (creation). I am also the place of nectar's origin. I also am the cereals. I give all flames and powers. The eligible things offered to me ensures welfare of all. The persons who alone consume the cereals are gobbled by me." The people known to this fact are the true devotees. This is the preaching of this great upaniṣad (the great knowledge acquired through experience or perception).

॥तृतीयोपनिषद्॥

देवा ह वै प्रजापतिमब्रुवन्नानुष्टुभस्य मन्त्रराजस्य नारसिंहस्य शक्तिं बीजं नो ब्रूहि भगव इति॥ १

The Third Upaniṣad

Once the gods asked lord Brahmā– O God! Please, have a grace for telling the power and the seed (key) to the Anuṣṭubha hymn of lord Nṛsiṁha.

स होवाच प्रजापतिर्माया वा एषा नारसिंही सर्वमिदं सृजति सर्वमिदं रक्षति सर्वमिदं संहरति। तस्मान्मायामेतां शक्तिं विद्याद्य एतां मायां शक्तिं वेद स पाप्मानं तरति स मृत्युं तरति स संसारं तरति सोऽमृतत्वं च गच्छति महतीं श्रियमश्नुते॥ २॥

Prajāpati said– This world has been created by the illusion (Māyā), the everlasting power of lord Nṛsiṁha. This illusion of lord therefore, is the power of the king-hymn. The man get rid of the evils on having known to this illusion, conquers the death and attains to immortality. He crosses the ocean of world and obtains all kinds of prosperity.

मीमांसन्ते ब्रह्मवादिनो ह्रस्वा दीर्घा प्लुता चेति। यदि ह्रस्वा भवति सर्वं पाप्मानं दहत्यमृतत्वं च गच्छति यदि दीर्घा भवति महतीं श्रियमाप्नोत्यमृतत्वं च गच्छति यदि प्लुता भवति ज्ञानवान्भवत्यमृतत्वं च गच्छति॥ ३॥

The Brahma knowing persons consider that if the illusory power of lord of Nṛsiṁha is slight, prolong or under current (plut)? If it is momentary or slight, the evils of the devotee are effaced as soon as he is known of illusion and he attains to immortality. If the devotee is known in depth, he attains to the immortality after having great prosperity with him. If he knows as under current (plut), the devotee so known to illusion attains to immortality.

तदेतदृषिणोक्तं निदर्शनं-स ईं पाहि य ऋजीषी तरुत्रः श्रियं लक्ष्मीमौपलामम्बिकां गां षष्ठीं च यामिन्द्रसेनेत्युदाहुः तां विद्यां ब्रह्मयोनिं सरूपामिहायुषे शरणं प्रपद्ये॥ ४॥

The Ṛṣi says– O the novel with the point (bindu) in garb of illusion power! I am shelter to the power of learning (vidyā śakti) that enables knowing the Brahma, Indrasena, Ṣaṣṭhī Śakti (Skanda Śakti), Brahmaśakti (Sarasvatī), Śivaśakti (Ambikā), Śrīśakti (goddess Lakṣmī) of lord for attaining to long life with useful means as the fruit for simple and attentive endeavour made in order to cross the ocean of world. Please, protect me with all powers.

सर्वेषां वा एतद्भूतानामाकाशः परायणं सर्वाणि ह वा इमानि भूतान्याकाशादेव जायन्त आकाशादेव जातानि जीवन्त्याकाशं प्रयन्त्यभिसंविशन्ति तस्मादाकाशं बीजं विद्यात्॥ ५॥

The ether is the shelter to all living-beings. All commune of creatures is originated by the ether. The creatures live after taking birth from ether and merge with the ether too. Hence, the key to creation of the living-organisms is the ether.

तदेतदृषिणोक्तं निदर्शनं- हंसः शुचिषद्वसुरन्तरिक्षसद्धोता वेदिषदतिथिर्दुरोणसत्। नृषद्वरसदृत-सद्व्योमसदब्जा गोजा ऋतजा अद्रिजा ऋतं बृहत्। य एवं वेदेति महोपनिषत्॥ ६॥

The saints have stated in this prospect that the self-luminating lord exists in the supreme abode. He too is Vasu residing in the space. He comes to homes as Atithi (unexpected and alien persons visit at home). He also is the honoured fire at the alter for offering and the clients giving morsel Āhuti) too. The ether is his residence. He appears on earth, the heaven and the best abode of the truth also. He appears on earth, water, mountain and great deeds in garb of the greatest and supreme truth. The aforesaid fruit is availed by such knowledge. This and this is said in this very Mahopaniṣad.

॥चतुर्थोपनिषद्॥

देवा ह वै प्रजापतिमब्रुवन्नानुष्टुभस्य मन्त्रराजस्य नारसिंहस्याङ्गमन्त्रान्नो ब्रूहि भगव इति॥ १

Fourth Upaniṣad

The gods again asked the Prajāpati Brahma– "O God! Please, tell the imbibed hymns (inseparable) of the king-hymn Anuṣṭubha."

स होवाच प्रजापतिः प्रणवं सावित्रीं यजुर्लक्ष्मीं नृसिंहगायत्रीमित्यङ्गानि जानीयाद्यो जानीते सोऽमृतत्वं च गच्छति॥ २॥

Lord Brahmā then said– The syllable Oṁ (Praṇava) Sāvitrī (Gāyatrī), Yajurlakṣmī and Nṛsiṁha Gāyatrī should be known imbibed to the king-hymn. The person attains to immortality including the physical prosperity who knows them.

ओमित्येतदक्षरमिदं सर्वं तस्योपव्याख्यानं भूतं भवद्भविष्यदिति सर्वमोंकार एव यच्चान्यत्त्रिकालातीतं तदप्योंकार एव। सर्वं ह्येतद्ब्रह्मायमात्मा ब्रह्म सोऽयमात्मा चतुष्पात्॥ ३॥

Oṁ is everlasting. This apparent world is conducted under the magnificence of Oṁ. The past, future and present is related to this syllable. Whatever is beyond the three times (Kalās) that too is 'Oṁ'. Lord Nṛsiṁha in the form of supreme soul too is Brahma. Lord Nṛsiṁha in the form of all souls has four feet.

जागरितस्थानो बहि:प्रज्ञः सप्ताङ्ग एकोनविंशतिमुखः स्थूलभुग्वैश्वानरः प्रथमः पादः॥ ४॥

The lord Vaiśvānara whose abode is the awaking state and this whole apparent world embedded within that state, who makes the subject of knowledge in exterior world, the seven worlds including Bhūḥ, Bhuvaḥ etc. are whose parts of body, who have nineteen mouths comprising five sensory organs, five functionary organs, five breathings and four consciences, who is the enjoyer (Bhoktā) of this physical world, whose body is this whole universe and having intuitive person existing within it who is addressed as Vaiśvānara; is the first foot of supreme and perfect soul lord Nṛsiṁha.

[The seven organs are purported to the abode of sun, the sun, the wind, ether, water, earth and the summoning (Āhavanīya) fire respectively. The nineteen mouths are purported to five sensory organs, five functionary of executive organs, five breathings and the four consciences.]

स्वप्नस्थानोऽन्त:प्रज्ञः सप्ताङ्ग एकोनविंशतिमुखः प्रविविक्तभुक्तैजसो द्वितीय:पादः॥ ५॥

The person luminating Hiraṇyagarbha whose residence is the state of dreaming and the micro world embedded within it, whose knowledge is spreaded in internal and micro-world with its entirity, who has seven parts of body, nineteen mouths, who exists in micro world, enjoy and provides maintenance to it is the second foot of lord Nṛsiṁha.

यत्र सुप्तो न कंचन कामं कामयते न कंचन स्वप्नं पश्यति तत्सुषुप्तम्। सुषुप्तस्थान एकी-भूतः प्रज्ञानघन एवानन्दमयो ह्यानन्दभुक् चेतोमुखः प्राज्ञस्तृतीयः पादः। एष सर्वेश्वर एष सर्वज्ञ एषोऽन्तर्याम्येष योनिः सर्वस्य प्रभवाप्ययौ हि भूतानाम्॥ ६॥

The state of dormance is said when the sleeping man neither wish anything nor seen any dream. Whose abode is state of dormance and the state of devastation (Pralaya) of the world so seemed, who exists in a single form, whose complexion is the perfect science, who is in humour and whose face shine with divine glory, who enjoys the pleasure arisen to his complexion, such conscious person is the third foot of Nṛsiṁha. He is the supreme soul, omniscient, omni-intuitive, cause for the world, origin, nutrition and the destruction (Pralaya) of all.

नान्त:प्रज्ञं न बहि:प्रज्ञं नोभयत:प्रज्ञं न प्रज्ञं नाप्रज्ञं न प्रज्ञानघनमदृष्टमव्यवहार्यमग्राह्यमलक्षणम-चिन्त्यमव्यपदेश्यमैकात्म्यप्रत्ययसारं प्रपञ्चोपशमं शान्तं शिवमद्वैतं चतुर्थं मन्यन्ते स आत्मा स विज्ञेयः॥ ७॥

The element unique, always silent, unknown, either formidable or micro, who is unknown to both formations, to whom nothing either as learned or stupid can be said, who is not the concentrated form of even perceiving, who is not seen, cannot be gripped, cannot be brought in practical application and who is intangible, beyond conceiving or judging and undescribable, who can be felt only in the form of soul entity and who is benevolent as also free from the worldly ties of malice is the fourth foot of lord Nṛsiṁha. It has been stated by the scholars. He is soul (supreme soul) and worth knowing.

अथ सावित्री गायत्र्या यजुषा प्रोक्ता तया सर्वमिदं व्याप्तं घृणिरिति द्वे अक्षरे सूर्य इति त्रीणि आदित्य इति त्रीणि। एतद्वै सावित्रस्याष्टाक्षरं पदं श्रियाभिषिक्तं य एवं वेद श्रिया हैवाभिषिच्यते॥ ८॥

Now, the Sāvitrī hymn is told– This hymn has been stated as added to the Gāyatrī rhyme in the form of Yajur mantra. This world is covered by it. The hymn Ghṛṇiḥ Sūryaḥ ādityaḥ, two letters are in Ghṛṇiḥ, three are in Sūryaḥ (Sūryaḥ having functions of surrounding) and three are in Ādityaḥ. Thus, this Sāvitrī hymn containing eight letters is adorned with Śrī (prosperity). The person known to hymn this way always adorned with Lakṣmī (the wealth).

तदेतदृचाभ्युक्तं- ऋचो अक्षरे परमे व्योमन्यस्मिन्देवा अधि विश्वे निषेदुः। यस्तन्न वेद किमृचा करिष्यति य इत्तद्विदुस्त इमे समासत इति॥ ९॥

It has been stated in Ṛcas that the Ṛcas of Ṛgveda are enshrined in the everlasting Brahma in the form of self-luminating ether. The devotees known to this fact reside where all gods reside. The devotees not known to the self-luminating supreme soul, cannot achieve any fruit for reciting the Veda. The worshippers who knows that Brahma accordingly, reside in the supreme abode with all pleasure.

न ह वा एतस्यर्चा न यजुषा न साम्नाऽर्थोऽस्ति यः सावित्रं वेदेति॥ १०॥

The devotee known to the Sāvitrī hymn does not require to recite the hymns of Ṛg, Yajuḥ and Sāmaveda.

ॐ भूर्लक्ष्मीर्भुवर्लक्ष्मीः स्वर्लक्ष्मीः कालकर्णी तन्नो महालक्ष्मीः प्रचोदयात् इत्येषा वै महालक्ष्मीर्यजुर्गायत्री चतुर्विंशत्यक्षरा भवति॥ ११॥

May the goddess Mahālakṣmī inspire us for performing the great deeds who is the goddess full of the prosperity, wealth to the world of earth, wealth of Bhuvaḥ and the Svaḥ worlds as well and whose name is Kālakarṇī, the Gāyatrī of Mahālakṣmī. It contains twenty four letters.

गायत्री वा इदं सर्वं यदिदं किंच तस्माद्य एतां महालक्ष्मीं याजुषीं वेद महतीं श्रियमश्नुते॥ १२

This apparent or visible world definitely is in the form of Gāyatrī. The devotee who is known to this Mahālakṣmī in the form of Yajurveda and in gigantic form also he attains to the great prosperity.

ॐ नृसिंहाय विद्महे वज्रनखाय धीमहि। तन्नः सिंहः प्रचोदयात् इत्येषा वै नृसिंहगायत्री देवानां वेदानां निदानं भवति य एवं वेद निदानवान्भवति॥ १३॥

We know god Nṛsiṁha by virtue of kind guidance and grace of our teacher and the scripture. We hold that supreme soul having nails like thunderbolt in our heart. May that lord Nṛsiṁha inspire us processing on the path of welfare. This Nṛsiṁha Gāyatrī too is the cause for the gods and the Vedas. The person known to this fact, attains to the god.

देवा ह वै प्रजापतिमब्रुवन्नथ कैर्मन्त्रैः स्तुतो देवः प्रीतो भवति स्वात्मानं दर्शयति तन्नो ब्रूहि भगवन्निति॥ १४॥

Prajāpati Brahmā asked the gods– O Prajāpati! Please, tell us the hymns that please lord Nṛsiṁha.

स होवाच प्रजापतिः ॐ यो ह वै नृसिंहो देवो भगवान्यश्च ब्रह्मा भूर्भुवः स्वस्तस्मै वै नमो नमः॥ १॥ (यथा प्रथममन्त्रोक्तावाद्यन्तौ तथा सर्वमन्त्रेषु द्रष्टव्यौ) ...यश्च विष्णुः ...॥ २॥......... यश्च महेश्वरः ...॥ ३॥......... यश्च पुरुषः .....॥ ४॥............ यश्चेश्वरः॥ ५॥.......या सरस्वती .....॥ ६॥..... या श्रीः .....॥ ७॥..... या गौरी.....॥ ८॥..... या प्रकृतिः.....॥ ९॥..... या विद्या....॥ १०॥.....यश्चोंकारः ......॥ ११॥.... याश्चतस्रोऽर्धमात्राः ....॥ १२॥....... ये वेदाः साङ्गाः सशाखाः सेतिहासाः ....॥ १३॥....... ये पञ्चाग्नयः ....॥ १४॥........ याः सप्त महाव्याहृतयः......॥ १५॥........ये चाष्टौ लोकपालाः.......॥ १६॥......ये चाष्टौ वसवः ....॥ १७॥..... ये चैकादश रुद्राः.......॥ १८॥........ये च द्वादशादित्याः ......॥ १९॥...... ये चाष्टौ ग्रहाः......॥ २०॥.......यानि च पञ्च महाभूतानि.....॥ २१॥.....यश्च कालः.......॥ २२॥.......यश्च मनुः.......॥ २३॥....... यश्च मृत्युः.......॥ २४॥......यश्च यमः .....॥ २५॥.....यश्चान्तकः......॥ २६॥.......यश्च प्राणः ......॥ २७॥..... यश्च सूर्यः .....॥ २८॥.....यश्च सोमः .....॥ २९॥..... यश्च विराट् पुरुषः.....॥ ३०॥.....यश्च जीवः .....॥ ३१॥....यश्च सर्वम्.........॥ ३२॥इति द्वात्रिंशत् इति तान्प्रजापतिरब्रवीदेतैर्मन्त्रैर्नित्यं देवं स्तुवध्वम्॥ १५॥

Prajāpati replied (having heard this)– Out of thirty two letters in king-hymn Anuṣṭubha, every letter originate a hymn and one should do worship with these hymns.

[Prajāpati herein has revealed (discussed) thirty two hymns in the form of praying lord Nṛsiṁha. Lord Nṛsiṁha has been stated introduced with Anuṣṭup. He has been accepted as the fundamental element of the origin and development of the creation (Sṛṣṭi). Pray to the lord Nṛsiṁha has been made by assuming the thirty two factors as the base thereto. It is all pertinent to pray lord Nṛsiṁha by reciting thirty two hymns of Anuṣṭup rhyme containing thirty two letters and to attain the fruit of imbibing his thirty two streams of power.]

ततो देवः प्रीतो भवति स्वात्मानं दर्शयति तस्माद्य एतैर्मन्त्रैर्नित्यं देवं स्तौति स देवं पश्यति सोऽमृतत्वं च गच्छति य एवं वेदेति महोपनिषत्॥ १६॥

Lord is pleased by following this procedure for worship and makes himself apparent for the devotees. The person who prays by reciting these hymns daily, observes his gigantic form as a result of seeing him through his divine sight graced by lord. He thus attains to the immortality. The person known to this fact definitely attains to the fruit (supra). It has been pronounced by this Mahopaniṣad.

॥पञ्चमोपनिषद्॥

देवा ह वै प्रजापतिमब्रुवन्नानुष्टुभस्य मन्त्रराजस्य नारसिंहस्य महाचक्रं नाम चक्रं नो ब्रूहि भगव इति सार्वकामिकं मोक्षद्वारं यद्योगिन उपदिशन्ति॥ १॥

Fifth Upaniṣad

Once the gods most humbly asked lord Brahmā– "O lord! Please tell us about the discus (cakra) namely, gigantic discus (Mahācakra) of the king hymn Anuṣṭubha. This Mahācakra fulfils all desires and ensures emancipation– it has been stated by Yogīs.

[It is all appropriate to say Mahācakra of the supreme person (Parama Puruṣa), which has been made in garb of the cycle of management for conducting the tangible and intangible creation (Sṛṣṭi) in a disciplined manner. Several forms of discus (cakras) has been described in Nṛsiṁha Ṣaṭcakropaniṣad.]

स होवाच प्रजापतिः षडक्षरं वा एतत्सुदर्शनं महाचक्रं तस्मात्षडरं भवति षट्पत्रं चक्रं भवति षड्वा ऋतव ऋतुभिः संमितं भवति मध्ये नाभिर्भवति नाभ्यां वा एतेऽराः प्रतिष्ठिता मायया एतत्सर्वं वेष्टितं भवति नात्मानं माया स्पृशति तस्मान्मायया बहिर्वेष्टितं भवति॥ २॥

Brahma replied (having heard the question raised)– The Mahācakra is named Sudarśana and it contains six letters. The six seasons are like six sticks in it. These sticks are fixed in its navel (Nucleus). The whole discus is surrounded by the Nemi of illusion (Māyā).

अथाष्टारमष्टपत्रं चक्रं भवत्यष्टाक्षरा वै गायत्री गायत्र्या संमितं भवति बहिर्मायया वेष्टितं भवति क्षेत्रं क्षेत्रं वै मायैषा संपद्यते॥ ३॥

Subsequently, a discus containing eight Aras (sticks) known as Eight petal cakra (Aṣṭadala cakra) is formed. It contains eight letters. There are eight letters in a foot of Gāyatrī. Hence, the Aras of this discus establish an uniform relation with the eight letters of Gāyatrī. This too has been covered by illusion (Māyā) from outside. This illusion is pervaded in each and every field.

अथ द्वादशारं द्वादशपत्रं चक्रं भवति द्वादशाक्षरा वै जगती जगत्या संमितं भवति बहिर्मायया वेष्टितं भवति॥ ४॥

Then the discus containing twelve letters (Dvādaśākṣarī cakra) is formed and it is compared with the rhyme Jagatī. Its one foot contains twelve letters. This cakra too is extraneously covered by illusion (Māyā).

अथ षोडशारं षोडशपत्रं चक्रं भवति षोडशकलो वै पुरुषः पुरुष एवेदं सर्वं पुरुषेण संमितं भवति मायया बहिर्वेष्टितं भवति॥ ५॥

Then sixteen petal discus (Ṣoḍaśāra cakra) is formed. These sixteen petals (kalās) are in the form of sixteen kalās of lord Nṛsiṁha. The lord is enriched with sixteen kalās, hence, this discus should be considered as an apparent god. This discus too is extraneously covered by illusion (Māyā).

अथ द्वात्रिंशदरं द्वात्रिंशत्पत्रं चक्रं भवति द्वात्रिंशदक्षरा वा अनुष्टुब्भवत्यनुष्टुभा सर्वमिदं भवति बहिर्मायया वेष्टितं भवति॥ ६॥

Then the discus containing thirty two petals is formed same way as thirty two aras (sticks). This rhyme Anuṣṭup contains thirty two letters. An Ara (stick or pallet) should be presumed in each letter. It too is extraneously covered by illusion (Māyā).

अरैर्वा एतत्सुबद्धं भवति वेदा वा एतेऽराः पत्रैर्वा एतत्सर्वतः परिक्रामति छन्दांसि वै पत्राणि॥ ७॥

It (discus) is duly fastened with Aras (pallets). The Aras (pallets) of this discus are Vedas, its leaves are rhymes and this discus revolves all around by the leaves in garb of rhymes.

एतत्सुदर्शनं महाचक्रं तस्य मध्ये नाभ्यां तारकं यदक्षरं नारसिंहमेकाक्षरं तद्भवति षट्सु पत्रेषु षडक्षरं सुदर्शनं भवत्यष्टसु पत्रेष्वष्टाक्षरं नारायणं भवति द्वादशसु पत्रेषु द्वादशाक्षरं वासुदेवं भवति। षोडशसु पत्रेषु मातृकाद्याः सबिन्दुकाः षोडश स्वरा भवन्ति। द्वात्रिंशत्सु पत्रेषु द्वात्रिंशदक्षरं मन्त्रराजं नारसिंहमानुष्टुभं भवति। तद्वा एतत्सुदर्शनं नाम चक्रं महाचक्रं सार्वकामिकं मोक्षद्वारमृङ्मयं यजुर्मयं साममयं ब्रह्ममयममृतमयं भवति। तस्य पुरस्ताद्वसव आसते रुद्रा दक्षिणत आदित्याः पश्चाद्विश्वेदेवा उत्तरतो ब्रह्मविष्णुमहेश्वरा नाभ्यां सूर्याचन्द्रमसौ पार्श्वयोः॥ ८॥

This Sudarśana named 'Mahācakra' is renowned owing to its thirty two petals. One should do Nyāsa (summoning god on several parts of body) of single letter Tāraka hymn 'Oṁ' relating to lord Nṛsinha at the navel place amids it. This Tāraka hymn contains single letter. Nyāsa of Sudarśana hymn containing six letters *i.e.* 'Sahastrāra huṁ phaṭ' in six petals of discus should be made. In the eight petals of discus, the eight letter Nārāyaṇa hymn (*i.e.* Oṁ Namo Nārāyaṇa) resides. Hence, one should do Nyāsa presuming the same. Vāsudeva hymn containing twelve letters (Oṁ Namo Bhagavate Vāsudevaya) should be enshrined in the twelve petals of the discus. Nyāsa of sixteen letters including the vowel at beginning and point (Bindu) of the label of letters (Varṇa mālā) should be made in sixteen petals. The king-hymn Anuṣṭubha containing thirty two letters in thirty two petals should be duly summoned through Nyāsa. This Sudarśana named Mahācakra fulfils the projections proposed, it is the gateway to emancipation, it is in the form of Ṛk, Yajuḥ, Sāmaveda and it is apparent perfect knowledge (Parabrahma) and full of immortality. Aṣtavasu is in its east, eleven Rudra in the south, twelve suns in the west and similarly Viśvedevā is in the north. Lord Brahmā, Viṣṇu and Maheśvara in navel and the sun and moon are in the collateral parts.

[The procedure to construct the Sudarśana Mahācakra as described herein also has a sketch form (Yantra) duly make. Under the ceremony (ritual), the hymn, Tantra and Yantra is also described, special use or importance has been explained for holding these yantras.]

तदेतदृचाभ्युक्तं– ऋचो अक्षरे परमे व्योमन्यस्मिन्देवा अधिविश्वे निषेदुः। यस्तन्न वेद किमृचा करिष्यति य इत्तद्विदुस्त इमे समासत इति॥ ९॥

The Ṛcā of Veda says– All Vedas are situated in everlasting (Lord Nṛsiṁha) who is in the form of supreme ether. All gods too are located in them. The person who does not know the supreme god (lord Nṛsiṁha and his Mahācakra Sudarśana) cannot gain anything even if he is well learnt to Ṛgveda etc. The devotee known to lord Nṛsiṁha and his discus, attains to the supreme position.

तदेतत्सुदर्शनं महाचक्रं बालो वा युवा वा वेद स महान्भवति स गुरु:सर्वेषां मन्त्राणामुपदेष्टा भवत्यनुष्टुभा होमं कुर्यादनुष्टुभार्चनं कुर्यात्तदेतद्रक्षोघ्नं मृत्युतारकं गुरुणा लब्धं कण्ठे बाहौ शिखायां वा बध्नीत सप्तद्वीपवती भूमिर्दक्षिणार्थं नावकल्पते तस्माच्छ्रद्धया यां कांचिद्गां दद्यात्सा दक्षिणा भवति॥ १०॥

If any child or young-chap is known to the Mahācakra Sudarśana, he becomes teacher to all by attaining greatness. He becomes preacher to all hymns. The worship and offering of this yantra is made by the king-hymn Anuṣṭubha. This yantra named Sudarśana has been stated as relieving from the fear of monsters and crossing the mortality (death). One should hold this yantra preached by teacher (Guru) on the throat, arm or braid. If the earth containing seven islands is given to teacher in the form of fees (dakṣiṇa), it too falls short. One should therefore, donate the land to the extent his capacity allows.

देवा ह वै प्रजापतिमब्रुवन्नानुष्टुभस्य मन्त्रराजस्य नारसिंहस्य फलं नो ब्रूहि भगव इति॥ ११॥

The gods asked Prajāpati– O lord! What is the fruit of king-hymn Anuṣṭubha? Kindly, tell us the same.

स होवाच प्रजापतिर्य एतं मन्त्रराजं नारसिंहमानुष्टुभं नित्यमधीते सोऽग्निपूतो भवति स वायुपूतो भवति स आदित्यपूतो भवति स सोमपूतो भवति स सत्यपूतो भवति स ब्रह्मपूतो भवति स विष्णुपूतो भवति स रुद्रपूतो भवति स देवपूतो भवति स सर्वपूतो भवति स सर्वपूतो भवति॥ १२॥

Prajāpati said– The person reciting and making Japa of this hymn becomes like the gold heated on the fire. He is made pure by the sun, moon and wind too. Becoming holy made by the observance of truth, he is made holy by the world, Brahmā, Viṣṇu and Rudra including all gods. He is made holy by all of them.

य एतं मन्त्रराजं नारसिंहमानुष्टुभं नित्यमधीते स मृत्युं तरति स पाप्मानं तरति स ब्रह्महत्यां तरति स भ्रूणहत्यां तरति स वीरहत्यां तरति स सर्वहत्यां तरति स संसारं तरति स सर्वं तरति स सर्वं तरति॥ १३॥

The person doing Japa in a regular manner, this king-hymn Anuṣṭubha for lord Nṛsiṁha, attains victory in the death. He get rid of evils. He avoids from killing Brahma, womb (Bhrūṇa) and Vīra (Brother). He is liberated from all kind of slaughtering or murder. He crosses the ocean of world. He makes others too to cross the same.

य एतं मन्त्रराजं नारसिंहमानुष्टुभं नित्यमधीते सोऽग्निं स्तम्भयति स वायुं स्तम्भयति स आदित्यं स्तम्भयति स सोमं स्तम्भयति स उदकं स्तम्भयति स सर्वान्देवांस्तम्भयति स सर्वान्ग्रहांस्तम्भयति स विषं स्तम्भयति स विषं स्तम्भयति॥ १४॥

The person doing regular Japa of this king hymn Anuṣṭubha in order to please lord Nṛsiṁha, can resist the motion of the fire, wind, sun, moon and the flow of the water too.

He can fascinate or shine the gods. He can resist the motion of all planets and can fascinate even the poison too.

य एतं मन्त्रराजं नारसिंहमानुष्टुभं नित्यमधीते स देवानाकर्षयति स यक्षानाकर्षयति स नागानाकर्षयति स ग्रहानाकर्षयति स मनुष्यानाकर्षयति स सर्वानाकर्षयति स सर्वानाकर्षयति॥ १५॥

The person doing regular Japa (silent recital) of this king-hymn Anuṣṭubha can summon Gods, Yakṣas, Nagas, stars and all people easily by virtue of creating an attractions. He can attract all.

य एतं मन्त्रराजं नारसिंहमानुष्टुभं नित्यमधीते स भूर्लोकं जयति स भुवर्लोकं जयति स स्वर्लोकं जयति स महर्लोकं जयति स जनोलोकं जयति स तपोलोकं जयति स सत्यलोकं जयति स सर्वांल्लोकाञ्जयति स सर्वांल्लोकाञ्जयति॥ १६॥

The person doing regular Japa on this king-hymn Anuṣṭubha conquers the earth, Bhuvaḥ, Svaḥ, Mahaḥ, Janaḥ, Tapaḥ and the world (abode) of truth. He establishes his victory on all worlds.

य एतं मन्त्रराजमानुष्टुभं नित्यमधीते सोऽग्निष्टोमेन यजते स उक्थ्येन यजते स षोडशिना यजते स वाजपेयेन यजते सोऽतिरात्रेण यजते सोऽप्तोर्यामेण यजते सोऽश्वमेधेन यजते स सर्वैः क्रतुभिर्यजते स सर्वैः क्रतुभिर्यजते॥ १७॥

The person doing regular Japa of this king-hymn for the pleasure of lord Nṛsiṁha, attains to the fruit of all offerings like Agniṣṭoma Yajña, Ukthya Yajña, Ṣoḍaśī Yajña, Vājapeya Yajña, Atirātra Yajña, Aptoryāma Yajña and Aśvamedha Yajña automatically and without arranging them. He naturally do Yajña from all Kratus.

य एतं मन्त्रराजं नारसिंहमानुष्टुभं नित्यमधीते स ऋचोऽधीते स यजूंष्यधीते स सामान्यधीते सोऽथर्वणमधीते सोऽङ्गिरसमधीते स शाखा अधीते स पुराणान्यधीते स कल्पानधीते स गाथामधीते स नाराशंसीरधीते स प्रणवमधीते यः प्रणवमधीते स सर्वमधीते स सर्वमधीते॥ १८॥

The person doing regular Japa of Anuṣṭubha hymn, attains to the fruit of perseverance to Ṛg, Yajuḥ, Sāma and Atharvaveda. He attains the fruit of perseverance made on the Aṅgirasa part of Veda. He attains the fruit of perseverance on Puraṇa, tales, Nārāśaṅsī and Praṇava. The person doing Japa automatically does the perseverance of all.

अनुपनीतशतमेकमेकेनोपनीतेन तत्समममुपनीतशतमेकमेकेन गृहस्थेन तत्समं गृहस्थश-तमेकमेकेन वानप्रस्थेन तत्समं वानप्रस्थशतमेकमेकेन यतिना तत्समं यतीनां तु शतं पूर्णमेकमे-केन रुद्रजापकेन तत्समं रुद्रजापकशतमेकमेकेनाथर्वशिरः शिखाध्यापकेन तत्सममथर्वशिरः शिखाध्यापकशतमेकमेकेन तापनीयोपनिषदध्यापकेन तत्समं तापनीयोपनिषदध्यापकशतमेकमेकेन मन्त्रराजाध्यापकेन तत्समम्॥ १९॥

A single person holding sacrificial thread (yajñopavīta) is equal to the one hundred boys without that thread. One Vānaprastha (Āśrama after Gṛhastha) is equal to one hundred persons living couple life (Gṛhastha). One recluse (Saṁyasī) is equal to such one hundred persons living with Vānaprastha Āśrama. One person doing Japa of doing perseverance on one Atharvaśiras and Atharvaśikhās of Rudra, such one hundred persons doing perseverance of Atharvaśiras are equal to the person doing Japa of one Nṛsiṁha hymn.

तद्वा एतत्परमं धाम मन्त्रराजाध्यापकस्य यत्र न सूर्यस्तपति यत्र न वायुर्वाति यत्र न चन्द्रमा भाति यत्र न नक्षत्राणि भान्ति यत्र नाग्निर्दहति यत्र न मृत्युः प्रविशति यत्र न दुःखं सदानन्दं परमानन्दं शान्तं शाश्वतं सदाशिवं ब्रह्मादिवन्दितं योगिध्येयं परमं पदं यत्र गत्वा न निवर्तन्ते योगिनः॥२०॥

The devotees (ascetic) to this king-hymn pertaining to lord Nārasiṁha attains to that supreme abode where the wind does not access, the sun rays cannot go, moon cannot light, stars do not twinkle, fire does not blaze, the death does not enter, a place without any sorrow, always pleasing, supreme pleasure giver, full of peace, everlasting, supreme benevolent, prayed by Brahmā etc. gods, supreme aim of yogis and supreme position accessing to where, they are liberated from all worldly ties.

तदेतदृचाभ्युक्तम्- तद्विष्णोः परमं पदं सदा पश्यन्ति सूरयः। दिवीव चक्षुराततम्। तद्विप्रासो विपन्यवो जागृवांसः समिन्धते। विष्णोर्यत्परमं पदम्। तदेतन्निष्कामस्य भवति तदेतन्निष्कामस्य भवति य एवं वेदेति महोपनिषत्॥२१॥

The Ṛcā of Ṛgveda has also stated– as lord Sun located in the ether can be easily seen by naked eyes, the scholars in the similar fashion, see and acquire, the supreme place (supreme position of divinity) of lord Viṣṇu through their eyes of knowledge. Ever curious learned priests, illumine that supreme position of lord Viṣṇu (viz. reveal it for the public in common). The person known to this fact, attains to that divine position (destination). It has been pronounced by this Mahopaniṣad.

ॐ भद्रं कर्णेभिः .... इति शान्तिः॥

॥इति नृसिंहपूर्वतापिन्युपनिषत्समाप्ता॥

***

25. KĀLĀGNIRUDROPANIṢAD

कालाग्निरुद्रोपनिषद्

This upaniṣad falls under the tradition of Kṛṣṇa Yajurveda. A special method of holding ash (Bhasma Dhāraṇa) as a mean of knowledge of Brahma has been described in it. The questions and answers as taken place between Sanatkumāra and Kālāgnirudra has been described in this upaniṣad. The Ṛṣi of this upaniṣad hymn Kālāgnirudra etc. has been elaborated very first in it. Subsequently, the method of holding Tripuṇḍa has been asked. Thus, method of Tripuṇḍa called as Śāmbhara vrata, the measurement (length etc.) of the Tripuṇḍa line and the power god of three lines has been propounded. Hastily, it has been said while propounding the magnificent fruits of upaniṣad, learning and the study of this scripture that the person going over attentively turns in to the form of Śiva.

॥शान्तिपाठः॥

ॐ सह नाववतु......... इति शान्तिः॥

अथ कालाग्निरुद्रोपनिषदः संवर्तकोऽग्निर्ऋषिरनुष्टुप्छन्दः श्रीकालाग्निरुद्रो देवता श्री कालाग्निरुद्रप्रीत्यर्थे विनियोगः॥१॥

The Ṛṣi of this Kālāgnirudropaniṣad is Saṁvartaka fire (Agni), Chanda is anuṣṭup and Devatā is Śrīkālāgni Rudra. It is offering for the pleasure of Kālāgnirudra.

अथ कालाग्निरुद्रं भगवन्तं सनत्कुमारं पप्रच्छ अधीहि भगवंस्त्रिपुण्ड्रविधिं सतत्त्वं किं द्रव्यं कियत्स्थानं कति प्रमाणं का रेखाः के मंत्राः का शक्तिः किं दैवतं कः कर्ता किं फलमिति च॥२॥

Once upon a time god Kālāgnirudra was asked by Sanatkumāra– "Teach me, O exalted sir, the truth in respect to the rule of the Tripuṇḍram (a sect-mark consisting of three streaks) and what material, which place? What is the measurement (size) of it? How many lines are erected? What is the hymn pertaining to it? What power does it hold? Which divinity, which formula, which powers and which reward there are."

तं होवाच भगवान्कालाग्निरुद्रः यद्द्रव्यं तदोग्नेयं भस्म सद्योजातादिपञ्चब्रह्ममन्त्रैः परिगृह्याग्निरिति भस्म वायुरिति भस्म जलमिति भस्म स्थलमिति भस्म व्योमेति भस्मेत्यनेनाभिमन्त्र्य मानस्तोक इति समुद्धृत्य मा नो महान्तमिति जलेन संसृज्य त्रियायुषमिति शिरोललाटवक्षःस्कन्धेषु त्रियायुषैस्त्र्यम्बकैस्त्रिशक्तिभिस्तिर्यक्तिस्रो रेखाः प्रकुर्वीत व्रतमेच्छाम्भवं सर्वेषु वेदेषु वेदवादिभिरुक्तं भवति तस्मात्तत्समाचरेन्मुमुक्षुर्न पुनर्भवाय॥३॥

Hearing this, god Kālāgnirudra said to Sanatkumāra describing in detail that the matter of tripuṇḍa is the ash of Agnihotra (the offering). This ash should be held with recital of "sadyojāta" etc. five hymns of Brāhmaṇa. It should be dually worshipped by the hymns pertaining to *Agniriti bhasma, Vāyuriti bhasma, Khamiti bhasma, Jalamiti bhasma, Sthalamiti bhasma* (five element etc. Atharvaśiras 5). That ash should be picked up on tip of a finger, take out with the formula *mā nas toke* (Ṛg. 1, 114, 8) and [after consecrating] with the formula *tryambakaṁ yajāmahe* (Ṛg. 7,59,12) should apply it as three lines across on the head, forehead, breast and shoulders under the three *tryāyuṣa*-formulas, *tryambaka*-formulas and *triśakti*-formulas.

The persons learnt to Vedas has described this "Śambhu-vow". The desirous people for emancipation should hold it specially who do not want to move through the cycle of rebirth.

अथ सनत्कुमारः पप्रच्छ प्रमाणमस्य त्रिपुण्ड्रधारणस्य॥४॥

Having heard this, Sanatkumāra further asked the measurement (length etc.) of the three lines to be drawn in the "tripuṇḍra.

त्रिधा रेखा भवत्याललाटादाचक्षुषोरामूर्ध्नोराभ्रुवोर्मध्यतश्च॥५॥

[Lord Kālāgnirudra replied] three lines should be drawn from the middle point of both brows to the next end of forehead from where the head starts.

यास्य प्रथमा रेखा सा गार्हपत्यश्चाकारो रजो भूर्लोकः स्वात्मा क्रियाशक्तिर्ऋग्वेदः प्रातःसवनं महेश्वरो देवतेति॥६॥

The first line is in the forms of gārhapatya Agni, the *a*-sound, the Rajas, the terrestrial world, the external Ātman, the acting power, the Ṛgveda, the morning pressing [of the Soma], and Maheśvara is its divinity.

यास्य द्वितीया देखा सा दक्षिणाग्निरुकारः सत्त्वमन्तरिक्षमन्तरात्मा चेच्छाशक्तिर्यजुर्वेदो माध्यंदिनं सवनं सदाशिवो देवतेति॥७॥

Its second line is in the forms of Dakṣiṇagni, the '*u*-sound' the Sattvam, the atmosphere, the inner Ātman, the willing power, the Yajurveda, the midday pressing [of the Soma] and *Sadāśiva* is its divinity.

यास्य तृतीया रेखा साहवनीयो मकारस्तमो द्यौर्लोकः परमात्मा ज्ञानशक्तिः सामवेदस्तृतीयसवनं महादेवो देवतेति॥८।

The third line is in the forms of Āhavanīya fire, the *m*-sound, the Tamas, the heaven, the highest Ātman, the perceiving power, the Sāmaveda, the evening pressing [of the Soma] and Mahādeva is its divinity.

एवं त्रिपुण्ड्रविधिं भस्मना करोति यो विद्वान्ब्रह्मचारी गृही वानप्रस्थो यतिर्वा स महापातकोपपातकेभ्यः पूतो भवति स सर्वेषु तीर्थेषु स्नातो भवति स सर्वान्वेदानधीतो भवति स सर्वान्देवाञ्ज्ञातो भवति स सततं सकलरुद्रमन्त्रजापी भवति स सकलभोगान्भुङ्क्ते देहं त्यक्त्वा शिवसायुज्यमेति न स पुनरावर्तते न स पुनरावर्तत इत्याह भगवान्कालाग्निरुद्रः॥९॥

Therefore, he makes the Tripuṇḍram from the ashes. He who knows this, whether he be a Brāhmaṇa-student, a house-holder, a forest-resident or an ascetic, he is thereby purified of all the great sins and minor sins. Thereby all the gods are meditated upon by him, he is known by all the gods, becomes one who has bathed in all the holy bathing places, one who has all the time muttered the Rudra-prayer. And after enjoying all the pleasures he enters, giving up the body, into union with Śiva and does not return—and does not return."

यस्त्वेद्वाधीते सोऽप्येवमेव भवतीत्योम् सत्यमित्युपनिषत्॥१०॥

The person who recites it here, he also attains to a similar position. "Oṁ" is only the truth. This upaniṣad describes the same.

ॐ सह नाववतु......... इति शान्तिः॥

॥इति कालाग्निरुद्रोपनिषत्समाप्ता॥

***

26. MAITREYYUPANIṢAD

मैत्रेय्युपनिषद्

॥शान्तिपाठः॥

ॐ आप्यायन्तु .... इति शान्तिः॥

First Prapāṭhaka

The ascetic king Bṛhadratha, being offered a boon, choose knowledge of the Soul (Ātman)

ॐ बृहद्रथो वै नाम राजा राज्ये ज्येष्ठं पुत्रं निधापयित्वेदमशाश्वतं मन्यमानः शरीरं वैराग्यमुपेतोऽरण्यं निर्जगाम। स तत्र परमं तप आस्थायादित्यमीक्षमाण ऊर्ध्वबाहुस्तिष्ठत्यन्ते सहस्रस्य मुनेरन्तिकमाजगामाग्निरिवाधूमकस्तेजसा निर्दहन्निवात्मविद्भगवाञ्छाकायन्य उत्तिष्ठोत्तिष्ठ वरं वृणीष्वेति राजानमब्रवीत्स तस्मै नमस्कृत्योवाच भगवन्नाहमात्मवित्त्वं तत्त्वविच्छृणुमो वयं स त्वं नो ब्रूहीत्येतद्वृत्तं पुरस्तादशक्यं मा पृच्छ प्रश्नमैक्ष्वाकान्यान्कामान्वृणीष्वेति शाकायन्यस्य चरणावभिमृश्यमानो राजेमां गाथां जगाद॥ १॥

A King named Bṛhadratha, after having established his son in the kingdom, thinking that this body is non-eternal, reached the state of indifference towards the world (*vairāgya*), and went forth into the forest. There he stood, performing extreme austerity, keeping his arms erect, looking up at the sun.

At the end of a thousand [days] there came into the presence of the ascetic, the honourable knower of the Soul (Ātman), Śākāyanya, like a smokeless fire, burning as it were with glow. 'Arise! Arise! Choose a boon!' said he to the king.

He did obeisance to him and said : 'Sir, I am no knower of the Soul (Ātman). You are one who knows its true nature, we have heard. So, do you tell us.'

'Such things used to occur! Very difficult [to answer] is this question! Aikṣvāka, choose other desires!' said Śākāyanya.

With his head touching that one's feet, the king uttered this speech :—

अथ किमेतैर्वान्यानां शोषणं महार्णवानां शिखरिणां प्रपतनं ध्रुवस्य प्रचलनं स्थानं वा तरूणां निमज्जनं पृथिव्याः स्थानादपसरणं सुराणां सोऽहमित्येतद्विधेऽस्मिन्संसारे किं कामोपभोगैर्यैरेवाश्रितस्यासकृदुपावर्तनं दृश्यत इत्युद्धर्तुमर्हसीत्यन्धोदपानस्थो भेक इवाहमस्मिन्संसारे भगवंस्त्वं नो गतिरिति॥ २॥

"What is the use of these to me or any other? Oceans dry up, Mountains sink down. The positions of Dhruva (the Polar Star) and of trees change. Earth is drowned. The Suras (angels) run away, leaving their (respective) places. (While such is the case), I am He in reality. Therefore of what avail to me is the gratification of desires since one who clings to the gratification of desires is found to return again and again to this Saṁsāra (mundane existence). You are able to extricate me (out of this Saṁsāra). I am drowned like a frog in a dry well. You are my refuge.

भगवच्छरीरमिदं मैथुनादेवोद्भूतं संविदपेतं निरय एव मूत्रद्वारेण निष्क्रान्तमस्थिभिश्चितं मांसेनानुलिप्तं चर्मणावबद्धं विण्मूत्रवातपित्तकफमज्जामेदोवसाभिरन्यैश्च मलैर्बहुभिः परिपूर्णमेतादृशे शरीरे वर्तमानस्य भगवंस्त्वं नो गतिरिति॥ ३॥

"O Lord! this body was the result of sexual intercourse. It is without wisdom; it is hell (itself). It came out through the urinary orifice. It is linked together by bones. It is coated over with flesh. It is bound by skin. It is replete with faeces, urine, *Vāyu* (air), bile, phlegm, marrow, fat, serum and many other impurities. O Lord ! to me in such a foul body (as this), You are my refuge."

अथ भगवाञ्छाकायन्यः सुप्रीतोऽब्रवीद्राजानं महाराज बृहद्रथेक्ष्वाकुवंशध्वजशीर्षात्मज्ञः कृतकृत्यस्त्वं मरुन्नाम्नो विश्रुतोऽसीत्ययं खल्वात्मा ते कतमो भगवन्वर्ण्य इति तं होवाच॥ ४॥

शब्दस्पर्शादयो येऽर्था अनर्था इव ते स्थिताः। येषां सक्तस्तु भूतात्मा न स्मरेच्च परं पदम्॥ ५॥

तपसा प्राप्यते सत्त्वं सत्त्वात्संप्राप्यते मनः। मनसा प्राप्यते ह्यात्मा ह्यात्मापत्त्या निवर्तते॥ ६॥

यथा निरिन्धनो वह्निः स्वयोनावुपशाम्यति। तथा वृत्तिक्षयाच्चित्तं स्वयोनावुपशाम्यति॥ ७॥

स्वयोनावुपशान्तस्य मनसः सत्यगामिनः। इन्द्रियार्थविमूढस्यानृताः कर्मवशानुगाः॥ ८॥

चित्तमेव हि संसारस्तत्प्रयत्नेन शोधयेत्। यच्चित्तस्तन्मयो भवति गुह्यमेतत्सनातनम्॥ ९॥

चित्तस्य हि प्रसादेन हन्ति कर्म शुभाशुभम्। प्रसन्नात्मात्मनि स्थित्वा सुखमक्षयमश्नुते॥ १०॥

समासक्तं यदा चित्तं जन्तोर्विषयगोचरम्। यद्येवं ब्रह्मणि स्यात्तत्को न मुच्येत बन्धनात्॥ ११॥

हृत्पुण्डरीकमध्ये तु भावयेत्परमेश्वरम्। साक्षिणं बुद्धिवृत्तस्य परमप्रेमगोचरम्॥ १२॥

अगोचरं मनोवाचामवधूताधिसंप्लवम्। सत्तामात्रप्रकाशैकप्रकाशं भावनातिगम्॥ १३॥

अहेयमनुपादेयमसामान्यविशेषणम्। ध्रुवं स्तिमितगम्भीरं न तेजो न तमस्ततम्। निर्विकल्पं निराभासं निर्वाणमयसंविदम्॥ १४॥

नित्यः शुद्धो बुद्धमुक्तस्वभावः सत्यः सूक्ष्मः संविभुश्चाद्वितीयः।
आनन्दाब्धिर्यः परः सोऽहमस्मि प्रत्यग्धातुर्नात्र संशीतिरस्ति॥ १५॥

आनन्दमन्तर्निजमाश्रयं तमाशापिशाचीमवमानयन्तम्।
आलोकयन्तं जगदिन्द्रजालमापत्कथं मां प्रविशेदसङ्गम्॥ १६॥

वर्णाश्रमाचारयुता विमूढाः कर्मानुसारेण फलं लभन्ते।
वर्णादिधर्मं हि परित्यजन्तः स्वानन्दतृप्ताः पुरुषा भवन्ति॥ १७॥

वर्णाश्रमं सावयवं स्वरूपमाद्यन्तयुक्तं ह्यतिकृच्छ्रमात्रम्।
पुत्रादिदेहेष्वभिमानशून्यं भूत्वा वसेत्सौख्यतमे ह्यनन्त इति॥ १८॥

Thereupon Lord Śākāyanya was pleased and addressed the King thus: "O Mahārāja, Bṛhadratha, the flag of the Ikṣvāku race, you are an Ātmajñānī. You are one that has done his duty. You are famous by the name of Marut." At which the King asked: "O Lord ! in what way, can you describe Ātmā?" To which he replied thus: "Sound, touch, and others which seem to be Artha (wealth) are in fact Anartha (evil). The Bhūtātmā (the lower Self) clinging to these never remembers the Supreme Seat. Through Tapas, Sattva (quality) is acquired; through Sattva, a (pure) mind is acquired; and through mind, (Parama) Ātmā, (the higher Self) is reached. Through attaining Ātmā, one gets liberation. Just as fire without fuel is absorbed into its own womb, so Citta (thought) through the destruction of its modifications is absorbed into its own womb (source). To a mind that has attained quiescence and truth, and which is not affected by sense-objects, the events that occur to it through the bondage of Karma are merely unreal. It is Citta alone that is Saṁsāra. It should be cleansed with effort. Whatever his Citta (Thinks), of that nature he becomes. This is an archaic mystery. With the purifying of Citta, one makes both good and bad Karmas to perish. One whose mind is thus cleansed attains the indestructible Bliss (through his own Self). Just as Citta becomes united with an object that comes across it, so why should not one (be released) from bondage, when one is united with Brahman. One should meditate in the middle of the lotus of the heart, Parameśvara (the highest Lord) who is the witness to the play of Buddhi, who is the object of supreme love, who is beyond the reach of mind and speech, who has no beginning or end, who is Sat alone being of the nature of light only, who is beyond meditation, who can neither be given up nor grasped (by the mind), who is without equal or superior, who is the permanent, who is of unshaken depth, who is without light or darkness, who is all-pervading, changeless and vehicleless, and who is wisdom of the nature of Mokṣa (salvation). I am He— that Paramātmā who is the eternal, the pure, the liberated, of the nature of wisdom, the true, the subtle, the all-pervading, the secondless, the ocean of bliss, and one that is superior to Pratyagātmā (the lower Self). There is no doubt about it. How will calamity (or bondage) approach me who am depending upon my own bliss in my heart, who have put to shame the ghost of desires, who look upon this universe as (but) a jugglery and who am not associated with anything. The ignorant with their observance of the castes and orders of life obtain their fruits according to their Karmas. Men who have given up all duties of castes, etc., rest content in the bliss on their own Self. The distinctions of caste and orders of life have divisions among them, have beginning and end, and are very painful. Therefore having given up all identification with sons and as well as body, one should dwell in that endless and most supreme Bliss."

Second Prapāṭhaka

Śākāyanya's instruction concerning the Soul (Ātman)

अथ भगवान्मैत्रेयः कैलासं जगाम तं गत्वोवाच भो भगवन्परमतत्त्वरहस्यमनुब्रूहीति। स होवाच महादेवः। देहो देवालयः प्रोक्तः स जीवः केवलः शिवः। त्यजेदज्ञाननिर्माल्यं सोऽहंभावेन पूजयेत्॥ १॥

अभेददर्शनं ज्ञानं ध्यानं निर्विषयं मनः। स्नानं मनोमलत्यागः शौचमिन्द्रियनिग्रहः॥ २॥

ब्रह्मामृतं पिबेद्भैक्षमाचरेद्देहरक्षणे। वसेदेकान्तिको भूत्वा चैकान्ते द्वैतवर्जिते। इत्येवमाचरेद्धीमान्स एवं मुक्तिमाप्नुयात्॥ ३॥

Then Lord Maitreya went to Kailāśa and having reached it asked Him thus: "O Lord ! Please initiate me into the mysteries of the highest Tattva." To which Mahādeva replied: "The body is said to be a temple. The Jīva in it is Śiva alone. Having given up all the cost-off offerings of Ajñāna, one should worship Him with So'ham (I am He). The cognition of everything as non-different from oneself of Jñāna (wisdom). Abstracting the mind from sensual objects is Dhyāna (meditation). Purifying the mind of its impurities is Snāna (bathing). The subjugation of the Indriyas (sensual organs) is Śauca (purification). One should drink the nectar of Brahman and beg food for maintaining the body. Having one (though) alone, he should live at a solitary place without a second. The wise man should observe thus: then he obtains Absolution.

जातं मृतमिदं देहं मातापितृमलात्मकम्। सुखदुःखालयामेध्यं स्पृष्ट्वा स्नानं विधीयते॥ ४॥

धातुबद्धं महारोगं पापमन्दिरमध्रुवम्। विकाराकारविस्तीर्णं स्पृष्ट्वा स्नानं विधीयते॥ ५॥

नवद्वारमलस्रावं सदा काले स्वभावजम्। दुर्गन्धं दुर्मलोपेतं स्पृष्ट्वा स्नानं विधीयते॥ ६॥

मातृसूतकसंबन्धं सूतके सह जायते। मृतसूतकजं देहं स्पृष्ट्वा स्नानं विधीयते॥ ७॥

अहंममेति विण्मूत्रलेपगन्धादिमोचनम्। शुद्धशौचमिति प्रोक्तं मृज्जलाभ्यां तु लौकिकम्॥ ८॥

चित्तशुद्धिकरं शौचं वासनात्रयनाशनम्। ज्ञानवैराग्यमृत्तोयैः क्षालनाच्छौचमुच्यते॥ ९॥

"This body is subject to birth and death. It is of the nature of the secretion of the father and mother. It is impure, being the seat of happiness and misery. (Therefore) bathing is prescribed for touching it. It is bound by the *Dhātus* (skin, blood, etc.), is liable to severe diseases, is a house of sins, is impermanent and is of changing appearance and size. (Therefore) bathing is prescribed for touching it. Foul matter is naturally oozing out always from the nine holes. It (body) contains bad odour and foul excrement. (Therefore) bathing is prescribed for touching it. It is connected (or tainted) with the child-birth impurity of the mother and is born with it. It is also tainted with death impurity. (Therefore) bathing is prescribed for touching it. (The conception of) "I and mine" is the odour arising from the besmeared dung and urine. The release from it is spoken of as the perfect purification. The (external) purification by means of water and earth is on account of the worldly concerns. The destruction of the threefold affinities (of *Śāstras*, world and body) generates the purity for cleansing *Citta*. That is called the (real) purification which is done by means of the earth and water of *Jñāna* (wisdom) and *Vairāgya* (indifference to objects).

अद्वैतभावना भैक्षमभक्ष्यं द्वैतभावनम्। गुरुशास्त्रोक्तभावेन भिक्षोर्भैक्षं विधीयते॥ १०॥

विद्वान्स्वदेशमुत्सृज्य संन्यासानन्तरं स्वतः। कारागारविनिर्मुक्तचोरवद्दूरतो वसेत्॥ ११॥

अहंकारसुतं वित्तभ्रातरं मोहमन्दिरम्। आशापत्नीं त्यजेद्यावत्तावन्मुक्तो न संशयः॥ १२॥

मृता मोहमयी माता जातो बोधमयः सुतः। सूतकद्वयसंप्राप्तौ कथं संध्यामुपास्महे॥ १३॥

हृदाकाशे चिदादित्यः सदा भासति भासति। नास्तमेति न चोदेति कथं संध्यामुपास्महे॥ १४॥
एकमेवाद्वितीयं यद्गुरोर्वाक्येन निश्चितम्। एतदेकान्तमित्युक्तं न मठो न वनान्तरम्॥ १५॥
असंशयवतां मुक्तिः संशयाविष्टचेतसाम्। न मुक्तिर्जन्मजन्मान्ते तस्माद्विश्वासमाप्नुयात्॥। १६॥
कर्मत्यागान्न संन्यासो न प्रैषोच्चारणेन तु। संधौ जीवात्मनोरैक्यं संन्यासः परिकीर्तितः॥ १७॥
वमनाहारवद्यस्य भाति सर्वेषणादिषु। तस्याधिकारः संन्यासे त्यक्तदेहाभिमानिनः॥ १८॥
यदा मनसि वैराग्यं जातं सर्वेषु वस्तुषु। तदैव संन्यसेद्विद्वानन्यथा पतितो भवेत्॥ १९॥
द्रव्यार्थमन्नवस्त्रार्थं यः प्रतिष्ठार्थमेव वा। संन्यसेदुभयभ्रष्टः स मुक्तिं नाप्तुमर्हति॥ २०॥

"The conception of Advaita (non-dualism) should be taken in as the Bhikṣā (alms-food); (but) the conception of Dvaita (dualism) should not be taken in. To a Sannyāsī (ascetic), Bhikṣā is ordained as dictated by the Śāstra and the Guru. After becoming a Sannyāsī, a learned man should himself abandon his native place and live at a distance, like a thief released from prison. When a person gives up Ahaṁkāra (I-am-ness) the son, wealth, the brother, delusion, the house, and desire, the wife, there is no doubt that he is an emancipated person. Delusion, the mother is dead. Wisdom, the son is born. In this manner while two kinds of pollution have occurred, how shall we (the ascetics) observe the Sandhyās (conjunction periods)? The Cit (consciousness) of the sun is ever shining in the resplendent Ākāśa of the heart. He neither sets nor rises; while so, how shall we perform the Sandhyās? Ekānta (solitude) is that state of one without second as determined by the words of a Guru. Monasteries or forests are not solitudes. Emancipation is only for those who do not doubt. To those who doubt, there is no salvation even after many births. Therefore one should attain faith. (Mere) abandoning of the Karmas or of the Mantras uttered at the initiation of a Sannyāsī (ascetic) will not constitute Sannyāsa. The union of Jīva (-Ātmā) (the lower self) and Parama (-Ātmā) (the higher Self) at the two Sandhis (morning and evening) is termed Sannyāsa. Whoever has a nausea for all Īśaṇā (desires) and the rest as for vomited food, and is devoid of all affection for the body, is qualified for Sannyāsa. At the moment when indifference towards all objects arises in the mind, a learned person may take up Sannyāsa. Otherwise, he is fallen person. Whoever becomes a Sannyāsī on account of wealth, food, clothes and fame, becomes fallen in both (as a Sannyāsī and as a householder); (then) he is not worthy of salvation.

उत्तमा तत्त्वचिन्तैव मध्यमं शास्त्रचिन्तनम्। अधमा मन्त्रचिन्ता च तीर्थभ्रान्त्यधमाधमा॥ २१॥
अनुभूतिं विना मूढो वृथा ब्रह्मणि मोदते। प्रतिबिम्बितशाखाग्रफलास्वादनमोदवत्॥ २२॥
न त्यजेच्चेद्यतिर्मुक्तो यो माधूकरमान्तरम्। वैराग्यजनकं श्रद्धाकलत्रं ज्ञाननन्दनम्॥ २३॥
धनवृद्धा वयोवृद्धा विद्यावृद्धास्तथैव च। ते सर्वे ज्ञानवृद्धस्य किंकराः शिष्यकिंकराः॥ २४॥
यन्मायया मोहितचेतसो मामात्मानमापूर्णमलब्धवन्तः।
परं विदग्धोदरपूरणाय भ्रमन्ति काका इव सूरयोऽपि॥ २५॥
पाषाणलोहमणिमृण्मयविग्रहेषु पूजा पुनर्जननभोगकरी मुमुक्षोः।

तस्माद्यतिः स्वहृदयार्चनमेव कुर्याद्बाह्यार्चनं परिहरेदपुनर्भवाय॥ २६॥

अन्तःपूर्णो बहिःपूर्णः पूर्णकुम्भ इवार्णवे। अन्तःशून्यो बहिःशून्यः शून्यकुम्भ इवाम्बरे॥ २७॥

मा भव ग्राह्यभावात्मा ग्राहकात्मा च मा भव। भावनामखिलां त्यक्त्वा यच्छिष्टं तन्मयो भव॥ २८॥

द्रष्टृदर्शनदृश्यानि त्यक्त्वा वासनया सह। दर्शनप्रथमाभासमात्मानं केवलं भज॥ २९॥

संशान्तसर्वसंकल्पा या शिलावदवस्थितिः। जाग्रन्निद्राविनिर्मुक्ता सा स्वरूपस्थितिः परा॥ ३०॥

"The thought of (contemplation upon) Tattvas is the transcendental one; that of the Śāstras, the middling, and that of Mantras, the lowest. The delusion of pilgrimages is the lowest of the lowest. Like one, who, having seen in water the reflection of fruits in the branches of trees, tastes and enjoys them, the ignorant without self-congnition are in vain overjoyed with (as if they reached) Brahman. That ascetic is an emancipated person who does not abandon the internal alms-taking (viz., the meditation upon the non-dual), generating Vairāgya as well as faith the wife, and wisdom the son. Those men (termed) great through wealth, age, and knowledge, are only servants to those that are great through their wisdom as also to their disciples. Those whose minds are deluded by Māyā, however learned they may be, do not attain Me, the all-full Ātmā, and roam about like crows, simply for the purpose of filling up their belly, well burnt up (by hunger, etc.). For one that longs after salvation, the worship of images made of stone, metals, gem, or earth, is productive of rebirth and enjoyment. Therefore the ascetic should perform his own heart-worship alone, and relinquish external worship in order that he may not be born again. Then like a vessel full to its brim in an ocean, he is full within and full without. Like a vessel void in the ether, he is void within and void without. Do not become (or differentiate between) the Ātman that knows or the Ātman that is known. Do become of the form of that which remains, after having given up all thoughts. Relinquishing with their Vāsanās the seer, the seen and the visual, worship Ātman alone, the resplendent supreme presence. That is the real supreme State wherein all Saṅkalpas (thoughts) are at rest, which resembles the state of a stone, and which is neither waking nor sleeping."

॥तृतीयोऽध्यायः॥

अहमस्मि परश्चास्मि ब्रह्मास्मि प्रभवोऽस्म्यहम्। सर्वलोकगुरुश्चास्मि सर्वलोकेऽस्मि सोऽस्म्यहम्॥ १॥

अहमेवास्मि सिद्धोऽस्मि शुद्धोऽस्मि परमोऽस्म्यहम्। अहमस्मि सदासोऽस्मि नित्योऽस्मि विमलोऽस्म्यहम्॥ २॥

विज्ञानोऽस्मि विशेषोऽस्मि सोमोऽस्मि सकलोऽस्म्यहम्। शुभोऽस्मि शोकहीनोऽस्मि चैतन्योऽस्मि समोऽस्म्यहम्॥ ३॥

मानावमानहीनोऽस्मि निर्गुणोऽस्मि शिवोऽस्म्यहम्। द्वैताद्वैतविहीनोऽस्मि द्वन्द्वहीनोऽस्मि सोऽस्म्यहम्॥ ४॥

भावाभावविहीनोऽस्मि भासाहीनोऽस्मि भास्म्यहम्। शून्याशून्यप्रभावोऽस्मि शोभनाशोभनोऽस्म्यहम्॥ ५॥

तुल्यातुल्यविहीनोऽस्मि नित्यः शुद्धः सदाशिवः। सर्वासर्वविहीनोऽस्मि सात्त्विकोऽस्मि सदास्म्यहम्॥ ६॥

एकसंख्याविहीनोऽस्मि द्विसंख्यावानहं न च। सदसद्भेदहीनोऽस्मि संकल्परहितोऽस्म्यहम्॥ ७॥

नानात्मभेदहीनोऽस्मि ह्यखण्डानन्दविग्रहः। नाहमस्मि न चान्योऽस्मि देहादिरहितोऽस्म्यहम्॥ ८
आश्रयाश्रयहीनोऽस्मि आधाररहितोऽस्म्यहम्। बन्धमोक्षादिहीनोऽस्मि शुद्धब्रह्मास्मि सोऽस्म्यहम्॥ ९॥
चित्तादिसर्वहीनोऽस्मि परमोऽस्मि परात्परः। सदा विचाररूपोऽस्मि निर्विचारोऽस्मि सोऽस्म्यहम्॥ १०॥
अकारोकाररूपोऽस्मि मकारोऽस्मि सनातनः। ध्यातृध्यानविहीनोऽस्मि ध्येयहीनोऽस्मि सोऽस्म्यहम्॥ ११॥

"I am "I" (the Self). I am also another (the not-Self). I am Brahman. I am the Source (of all things). I am also the Guru of all worlds. I am of all the worlds. I am He. I am Myself alone. I am Siddha. I am the Pure. I am the Supreme. I am. I am always He. I am the Eternal. I am stainless, I am Vijñāna. I am the Excellent. I am Soma. I am the All. I am without honour or dishonour. I am without Guṇas (qualities). I am Śiva (the auspicious). I am neither dual or non-dual. I am without the dualities (of heat or cold, etc.) I am He. I am neither existence nor non-existence. I am without language. I am the Shining. I am the Glory of void and non-void. I am the good and the bad. I am Happiness. I am without grief. I am Caitanya. I am equal (in all). I am the like and the non-like. I am the eternal, the pure, and the ever felicitous. I am without all and without not all. I am Sāttvika. I am always existing. I am without the number one. I am without the number two. I am without the difference of Sat and Asat. I am without Saṅkalpa. I am without the difference of manyness. I am the form of immeasurable Bliss. I am one that exist not. I am the one that is not another. I am without body, etc. I am with asylum. I am without asylum. I am without support. I am without bondage or emancipation. I am pure Brahma. I am He. I am without Citta, etc. I am the supreme and the Supreme of the supreme. I am ever of the form of deliberation and yet am I without deliberation. I am He. I am of the nature of the Akāra and Ukāra as also of Makāra. I am the earliest. The contemplator and contemplator I am without. I am One that cannot be contemplated upon.

सर्वत्रपूर्णरूपोऽस्मि सच्चिदानन्दलक्षणः। सर्वतीर्थस्वरूपोऽस्मि परमात्मास्म्यहं शिवः॥ १२॥
लक्ष्यालक्ष्यविहीनोऽस्मि लयहीनरसोऽस्म्यहम्। मातृमानविहीनोऽस्मि मेयहीनः शिवोऽस्म्यहम्॥
न जगत्सर्वद्रष्टास्मि नेत्रादिरहितोऽस्म्यहम्। प्रवृद्धोऽस्मि प्रबुद्धोस्मि प्रसन्नोऽस्मि हरोऽस्म्यहम्॥ १४॥
सर्वेन्द्रियविहीनोऽस्मि सर्वकर्मकृदप्यहम्। सर्ववेदान्ततृप्तोऽस्मि सर्वदा सुलभोऽस्म्यहम्॥ १५॥
मुदितामुदिताख्योऽस्मि सर्वमौनफलोऽस्म्यहम्। नित्यचिन्मात्ररूपोऽस्मि सदा सच्चिन्मयोऽस्म्यहम्॥ १६॥
यत्किंचिदपि हीनोऽस्मि स्वल्पमप्यति नास्म्यहम्। हृदयग्रन्थिहीनोऽस्मि हृदयाम्बुजमध्यगः॥ १७॥
षड्विकारविहीनोऽस्मि षट्कोशरहितोऽस्म्यहम्। अरिषड्वर्गमुक्तोऽस्मि अन्तरादन्तरोऽस्म्यहम्॥ १८॥
देशकालविमुक्तोऽस्मि दिगम्बरसुखोऽस्म्यहम्। नास्ति नास्ति विमुक्तोऽस्मि नकाररहितोऽस्म्यहम्॥ १९॥
अखण्डाकाशरूपोऽस्मि ह्यखण्डाकारमस्म्यहम्। प्रपञ्चमुक्तचित्तोस्मि प्रपञ्चरहितोऽस्म्यहम्॥ २०॥
सर्वप्रकाशरूपोऽस्मि चिन्मात्रज्योतिरस्म्यहम्। कालत्रयविमुक्तोऽस्मि कामादिरहितोऽस्म्यहम्॥ २१॥
कायिकादिविमुक्तोऽस्मि निर्गुणः केवलोऽस्म्यहम्। मुक्तिहीनोऽस्मि मुक्तोऽस्मि मोक्षहीनोऽस्म्यहं सदा॥
सत्यासत्यादिहीनोऽस्मि सन्मात्रान्नास्म्यहं सदा। गन्तव्यदेशहीनोऽस्मि गमनादिविवर्जितः॥ २३॥
सर्वदा समरूपोऽस्मि शान्तोऽस्मि पुरुषोत्तमः। एवं स्वानुभवो यस्य सोऽहमस्मि न संशयः॥ २४॥

यः शृणोति सकृद्वापि ब्रह्मैव भवति स्वयमित्युपनिषत्॥ २५॥

Am He. I have full form in all. I have the characteristics of Saccidānanda. I am of the form of places of pilgrimages. I am the higher Self and Śiva. I am neither the thing defined nor non-defined. I am the non-absorbed Essence. I am not the measurer, the measure or the measured. I am Śiva. I am not the universe. I am the Seer of all. I am without the eyes, etc. I am the full grown. I am the Wise. I am the quiescent. I am the Destroyer. I am without any sensual organs. I am the doer of all actions. I am One that is content with all Vedāntas (either books or Ātmik Wisdom). I am the easily attainable. I have the name of one that is pleased as well as one that is not. I am the fruits of all silence. I am always of the form of Cinmātra (Absolute consciousness). I am always Sat (Be-ness) and Cit (Consciousness). I am one that has not anything in the least. I am not one that has not anything in the least. I am without the heart-knot (Granthi). I am the Being in the middle of the lotus. I am without the six changes. I am without the six sheaths and without the six enemies. I am within the within. I am without place and time. I am of the form of happiness having the quarters as My garment. I am the emancipated One. Without bondage. I am without the "no". I am of the form of the partless. I am the partless. I have Citta, though released from the universe. I am without the universe. I am of the form of all light. I am the Light (Jyotis) in Cinmātra (Absolute Consciousness). I am free from the three periods (of time past, present, and future). I am without desires. I am without body. I am One that has no body. I am Guṇaless. I am alone. I am without emancipation. I am the emancipated One. I am ever without emancipation. I am without truth or untruth. I am always One that is not different from Sat (Be-ness). I have no place to travel. I have no going, etc. I am always of the same form. I am the Quiescent. I am Puruṣottama (the Lord of Souls). There is no doubt that he who has realised himself thus is Myself. Whoever hears (this) once becomes himself Brahman, yea, he becomes himself Brahman. Thus is the Upaniṣaḍ."

ॐ आप्यायन्तु ....इति शान्तिः॥

॥इति मैत्रेय्युपनिषत्समाप्ता॥

***

27. SUBĀLOPANIṢAD

सुबालोपनिषद्

॥शान्तिपाठः॥

ॐ पूर्णमदः .... इति शान्तिः॥

॥प्रथमः खण्डः॥

तदाहुः किं तदासीत्तस्मै स होवाच न सन्नासन्न सदसदिति॥ १॥

तस्मात्तमः संजायते तमसो भूतादिर्भूतादेराकाशमाकाशाद्वायुर्वायोरग्निरग्नेरापोऽद्भ्यः पृथिवी॥ २॥

तदण्डं समभवत्तत्संवत्सरमात्रमुषित्वा द्विधाऽकरोदधस्ताद्भूमिमुपरिष्टादाकाशं मध्ये पुरुषो दिव्यः सहस्रशीर्षा पुरुषः सहस्राक्षः सहस्रपात्। सहस्रबाहुरिति॥ ३॥

सोऽग्रे भूतानां मृत्युमसृजत्त्र्यक्षं त्रिशिरस्कं त्रिपादं खण्डपरशुम्॥ ४॥

तस्य ब्रह्मा बिभेति स ब्रह्माणमेव विवेश स मानसान्सप्त पुत्रानसृजत्ते ह विराजः सप्त मानसानसृजन्ते ह प्रजापतयः॥ ५॥

ब्राह्मणोऽस्य मुखमासीद्बाहू राजन्यः कृतः। ऊरू तदस्य यद्वैश्यः पद्भ्यां शूद्रो अजायत। चन्द्रमा मनसो जातश्चक्षोः सूर्यो अजायत। श्रोत्राद्वायुश्च प्राणश्च हृदयात्सर्वमिदं जायते॥ ६॥

Then he (Raikva) asked : "What was at first" to which (He the Lord) replied :

"There was neither Sat nor asat nor sat-asat. From it, tamas (darkness) was evolved. From tamas came bhūtādi; from bhūtādi came ākāśa, from ākāśa, vāyu; from vāyu, agni (fire); from agni āpas (water); and from āpas, pṛthivī (earth). Then it became an egg. After remaining so for one divine year, it split into two and became earth below, the ākāśa above and in the midst, the infinite Puruṣa of a divine form of myriads of heads, eyes, feet and hands. Prior to the bhūtas (elements), he had evolved Mṛtyu (time or death) of three letters, three heads, and three feet, and having a Khaṇḍa-paraśu (broken axe). To him, Brahmā (the Puruṣa) spoke. He entered Brahmā himself and evolved mentally the seven sons and these sons as well as the seven Prajāpatis (progenitors). Brāhmaṇas were born from His mouth, Kṣatriyas from His hands, Vaiśyas from His thighs, and from the feet were born the Śūdras. The moon was born from His manas (mind), the sun from His eyes, vāyu from (His) ears and prāṇas from (His) heart. Thus all things were born."

॥द्वितीयः खण्डः॥

अपानान्निषादा यक्षराक्षसगन्धर्वाश्चास्थिभ्यः पर्वता लोमभ्य ओषधिवनस्पतयो ललाटात्क्रोधजो रुद्रो जायते॥ १॥

तस्यैतस्य महतो भूतस्य निःश्वसितमेतद्यदृग्वेदो यजुर्वेदः सामवेदोऽथर्ववेदः शिक्षा कल्पो व्याकरणं निरुक्तं छन्दो ज्योतिषामयनं न्यायो मीमांसा धर्मशास्त्राणि व्याख्यानान्युप-व्याख्यानानि च सर्वाणि च

भूतानि॥ २॥

हिरण्यज्योतिर्यस्मिन्नयमात्माधिक्षियन्ति भुवनानि विश्वा। आत्मानं द्विधाऽकरोदर्धेन स्त्री अर्धेन पुरुषो देवो भूत्वा देवानसृजदृषिर्भूत्वा ऋषीन्यक्षराक्षसगन्धर्वान्ग्राम्यानारण्यांश्च पशूनसृज-दितरा गौरितरोऽनड्वानितरा वडवेतरोऽश्व इतरा गर्दभीतरो गर्दभ इतरा विश्वंभरीतरो विश्वंभरः॥ ३॥

सोऽन्ते वैश्वानरो भूत्वा संदग्ध्वा सर्वाणि भूतानि पृथिव्यप्सु प्रलीयत आपस्तेजसि प्रलीयन्ते तेजो वायौ विलीयते वायुराकाशे विलीयत आकाशमिन्द्रियेष्विन्द्रियाणि तन्मात्रेषु तन्मात्राणि भूतादौ विलीयन्ते भूतादिर्महति विलीयते महानव्यक्ते विलीयतेऽव्यक्तमक्षरे विलीयते अक्षरं तमसि विलीयते तमः परे देव एकीभवति परस्तान्न सन्नासन्न सदसदित्येतन्निर्वाणा-नुशासनमिति वेदानुशासनमिति वेदानुशासनम्॥ ४॥

"From apāna came Niṣādas, Yakṣas, Rākṣasas and Gandharvas. From (His) bones, arose the mountains. From His hairs arose the herbs and the trees. From His forehead, Rudra was born through His anger, the breath of this great Being became the Ṛgveda, Yajurveda, Sāmveda, Atharvaveda, Śīkṣā (the science of the proper pronunciation and articulation of sounds), Kalpa (the science of methodology), Vyākaraṇa (grammar), Nirukta (glossarial explanation of absolute and other terms in Vedas), Chandas (prosody or vedic metre), Jyotiṣa (astrology), Nyāya (logic), Mīmāṁsā (including rituals and vedānta), Dharmaśāstras, commentaries, glosses and all beings. This Ātman (or the Self of Puruṣa) is Hiraṇyajyotis (or golden or effulgent Light) into which all the universe is absorbed. He divided Ātman (his Self) into two moieties; out of one moiety, the woman was created; and out of the other man. Having become a Deva, he created the Devas. Having become a Ṛṣi, He created the Ṛṣis; also He created Yakṣas, Rākṣasas, Gandharvas, wild and domestic beasts and others such as cows, bulls, mares and horses, she-asses and asses and Viśvambhara (the Supporter) and Viśvambharā (the earth). Becoming Vaiśvānara (fire) at the end (of creation), He burnt up all objects, then (in dissolution). Pṛthivī was absorbed in āpas, āpas in agni, agni in vāyu, vāyu in ākāśa, ākāśa in indriyas (organs), indriyas into tanmātras (rudimentary properties), tanmātras into bhūtādi, bhūtādi into mahat, mahat into avyakta, avyakta into akṣara (the indestructible), akṣara into tamas (darkness) and tamas becomes one with the supreme Lord. And then there is neither Sat nor asat, nor Sat-asat. This is the teaching of Nirvāṇa and this is the teaching of the Vedas. Yea, this is the teaching of the Vedas."

॥तृतीयः खण्डः॥

असद्वा इदमग्र आसीदजातमभूतमप्रतिष्ठितमशब्दमस्पर्शमरूपमरसमगन्धमव्ययममहान्तमबृहन्त-मजमात्मानं मत्वा धीरो न शोचति॥ १॥

अप्राणममुखमश्रोत्रमवागमनोऽतेजस्कमचक्षुष्कमनामगोत्रमशिरस्कमपाणिपादमस्निग्धमलोहितमप्रमेय-मह्रस्वमदीर्घमस्थूलमनणवनल्पमपारमनिर्देश्यमनपावृतम-प्रतर्क्यमप्रकाश्यमसंवृतमनन्तरमबाह्यं न तदश्नाति किंचन न तदश्नाति कश्चन॥ २॥ एतद्वै सत्येन दानेन तपसाऽनाशकेन ब्रह्मचर्येण निर्वेदनेनानाशकेन षडङ्गेनैव साधयेदेतत्त्रयं वीक्षेत दमं दानं दयामिति न तस्य प्राणा उत्क्रामन्त्यत्रैव समवलीयन्ते ब्रह्मैव सन्ब्रह्माप्येति य एवं वेद॥ ३॥

"As first, there was Asat, unborn, non-existent, unsupported, soundless, touchless, formless, tasteless, odourless and decayless. The undaunted man never grieves, as he knows Ātman to be great, all-pervading and unborn. It (Ātmā) is prāṇaless, mouthless, earless, tongueless, manas-less, tejas-less, eyeless, nameless, gotraless (or clanless), headless, handless, feetless, non-unctuous, bloodless, non-measurable, neither long nor short, neither gross nor atomic, neither great nor small, endless, indescribable, non-returnable, non-luminious, not hidden, having neither inside nor outside, neither eating anything nor being eaten by others. Some one (out of many) attains to this (Ātmā) by the six means of satya (truth), dāna (charity), tapas (religious austerities), non-injury to any creature, celibacy and complete indifference to worldy objects; and there are no other means. Whoever feels happy with the thought 'I know that', that learned person, prāṇa will never get out of his body at the moment of death, but will become absorbed in Brahman; and being absorbed in Brahman, he attains the state of Brahman Itself as he who knows this."

॥चतुर्थः खण्डः॥

हृदयस्य मध्ये लोहितं मांसपिण्डं यस्मिंस्तद्दहरं पुण्डरीकं कुमुदमिवानेकधा विकसितं हृदयस्य दश छिद्राणि भवन्ति येषु प्राणाः प्रतिष्ठिताः॥ १॥

स यदा प्राणेन सह संयुज्यते तदा पश्यति नद्यो नगराणि बहूनि विविधानि च यदा व्यानेन सह संयुज्यते तदा पश्यति देवांश्च ऋषींश्च यदाऽपानेन सह संयुज्यते तदा पश्यति यक्षराक्षसगन्धर्वान्यदोदानेन सह संयुज्यते तदा पश्यति देवलोकान्देवान्स्कन्दं जयन्तं चेति यदा समानेन सह संयुज्यते तदा पश्यति देवलोकान्धनानि च यदा वैरम्भेण सह संयुज्यते तदा पश्यति दृष्टं च श्रुतं च भुक्तं चाभुक्तं च सच्चासच्च सर्वं पश्यति॥ २॥

अथेमा दश दश नाड्यो भवन्ति। तासामेकैकस्या द्वासप्ततिर्द्वासप्ततिः शाखा नाडीसहस्राणि भवन्ति यस्मिन्नयमात्मा स्वपिति शब्दानां च करोत्यथ यद्द्वितीये स कोशे स्वपिति तदेमं च लोकं परं च लोकं पश्यति सर्वाञ्छब्दान्विजानाति स संप्रसाद इत्याचक्षते प्राणः शरीरं परिरक्षति हरितस्य नीलस्य पीतस्य लोहितस्य श्वेतस्य नाड्यो रुधिरस्य पूर्णाः॥ ३॥

अथात्रैतद्दहरं पुण्डरीकं कुमुदमिवानेकधा विकसितं यथा केशः सहस्रधा भिन्नस्तथा हिता नाम नाड्यो भवन्ति हृद्याकाशे परे कोशे दिव्योऽयमात्मा स्वपिति यत्र सुप्तो न कंचन कामं कामयते न कंचन स्वप्नं पश्यति न तत्र देवा न देवलोका यज्ञा न यज्ञा वा न माता न पिता न बन्धुर्न बान्धवो न स्तेनो न ब्रह्महा तेजस्कायममृतं सलिल एवेदं सलिलं वनं भूयस्तेनैव मार्गेण जाग्राय धावति सम्राडिति होवाच॥ ४॥

"In the middle of the heart is a red fleshy mass in which is the dahara-lotus. Like the lotus, it opens into many (petals). There are ten openings in the heart. The (different kinds of) prāṇas are located there. Whenever the (Ātmā) is united with prāṇa, he sees cities with rivers and other variegated things; when united with vyāna, he sees Devas and Ṛṣis; when united with apāna, he sees Yakṣas, Rākṣasas and Gandharvas; when united with Udāna, he perceives the celestial world, Devas, Skanda (Kārtikeya or the six-faced Mars), and Jayanta (Indra's son); when united with Samāna, he sees the celestial world and the treasures (of

Kubera); when united with Rambhā (a nādi hereafter given out), he sees whatever is seen or not seen, heard or not heard, eaten or not eaten, asat or sat and all else.

"There are ten nāḍis; in each of these are seventy-one. And these become 72,000 branch nāḍis. When Ātman sleeps therein, it produces sound; but when Ātman sleeps in the second kośa (or sheath) then it sees this world and the higher as also knows all the sounds. This is spoken of as samprasāda (deep sleep rest). Then prāṇa protects the body. The nāḍis are full of blood, of the colours green, blue, yellow, red, and white. Now this dahara-lotus has many petals like a lilly. Like a hair divided into 1,000 parts, the nāḍis called hita are. The divine Ātman sleeps in the ākāśa of the heart, in the supreme kośa (or ānandamaya sheath); sleeping there, it has no desires, no dreams, no deva-worlds, no yajñas or sacrificer, no mother or father, no relative, no kinsman, no thief, or no Brāhman-slayer. Its body is tejas (resplendent effulgence) and of the nature of nectar (or the immortal). It is as if in sport, a water-lotus. When he returns again to the waking state by the same way (he quitted or went in before to the heart), he is Samrāt. Thus says he."

॥पञ्चमः खण्डः॥

स्थानानि स्थानिभ्यो यच्छति नाडी तेषां निबन्धनं चक्षुरध्यात्मं द्रष्टव्यमधिभूतमादित्य-स्तत्राधिदैवतं नाडी तेषां निबन्धनं यश्चक्षुषि यो द्रष्टव्ये य आदित्ये यो नाड्यां यः प्राणे यो विज्ञाने य आनन्दे यो हृद्याकाशे य एतस्मिन्सर्वस्मिन्नन्तरे संचरति सोऽयमात्मा तमात्मा-नमुपासीताजरममृतमभयमशोकमनन्तम्॥ १॥

श्रोत्रमध्यात्मं श्रोतव्यमधिभूतं दिशस्तत्राधिदैवतं नाडी तेषां निबन्धनं यः श्रोत्रे यः श्रोतव्ये यो दिक्षु यो नाड्यां यः प्राणे यो विज्ञाने य आनन्दे यो हृद्याकाशे य एतस्मिन्सर्वस्मि-न्नन्तरे संचरति सोऽयमात्मा तमात्मानमुपासीताजरममृतमभयमशोकमनन्तम्॥ २॥

नासाध्यात्मं घ्रातव्यमधिभूतं पृथिवी तत्राधिदैवतं नाडी तेषां निबन्धनं यो नासायां यो घ्रातव्ये यः पृथिव्यां यो नाड्यां ....नन्तम्॥ ३॥

जिह्वाध्यात्मं यो रसयितव्यमधिभूतं वरुणस्तत्राधिदैवतं नाडी तेषां निबन्धनं यो जिह्वायां यो रसयितव्ये यो वरुणे यो नाड्यां ....नन्तम्॥ ४॥

त्वगध्यात्मं स्पर्शयितव्यमधिभूतं वायुस्तत्राधिदैवतं नाडी तेषां निबन्धनं यस्त्वचि यः स्पर्शयितव्ये यो वायौ यो नाड्यां...........नन्तम्॥ ५॥

मनोऽध्यात्मं मन्तव्यमधिभूतं चन्द्रस्तत्राधिदैवतं नाडी तेषां निबन्धनं यो मनसि यो मन्तव्ये यश्चन्द्रे यो नाड्यां ....नन्तम्॥ ६॥

बुद्धिरध्यात्मं बोद्धव्यमधिभूतं ब्रह्मा तत्राधिदैवतं नाडी तेषां निबन्धनं यो बुद्धौ यो बोद्धव्ये यो ब्रह्मणि यो नाड्यां............. नन्तम्॥ ७॥

अहंकारोऽध्यात्ममहंकर्तव्यमधिभूतं रुद्रस्तत्राधिदैवतं नाडी तेषां निबन्धनं योऽहंकारे योऽहंकर्तव्ये यो रुद्रे यो नाड्यां.......... नन्तम्॥ ८॥

चित्तमध्यात्मं चेतयितव्यमधिभूतं क्षेत्रज्ञस्तत्राधिदैवतं नाडी तेषां निबन्धनं यश्चित्ते यश्चेतयितव्ये यः क्षेत्रज्ञे यो नाड्यां........... नन्तम्॥ ९॥

वागध्यात्मं वक्तव्यमधिभूतमग्निस्तत्राधिदैवतं नाडी तेषां निबन्धनं यो वाचि यो वक्तव्ये योऽग्नौ यो नाड्यां............नन्तम्॥ १०॥

हस्तावध्यात्ममादातव्यमधिभूतमिन्द्रस्तत्राधिदैवतं नाडी तेषां निबन्धनं यो हस्ते य आदातव्ये य इन्द्रे यो नाड्यां............ नन्तम्॥ ११॥

पादावध्यात्मं गन्तव्यमधिभूतं विष्णुस्तत्राधिदैवतं नाडी तेषां निबन्धनं यः पादे यो गन्तव्ये यो विष्णौ यो नाड्यां............... नन्तम्॥ १२॥

पायुरध्यात्मं विसर्जयितव्यमधिभूतं मृत्युस्तत्राधिदैवतं नाडी तेषां निबन्धनं यः पायौ यो विर्जयितव्ये यो मृत्यौ यो नाड्यां ....नन्तम्॥ १३॥

उपस्थोऽध्यात्ममानन्दयितव्यमधिभूतं प्रजापतिस्तत्राधिदैवतं नाडी तेषां निबन्धनं य उपस्थे य आनन्दयितव्ये यः प्रजापतौ यो नाड्यां यः प्राणे यो विज्ञाने य आनन्दे यो हृद्याकाशे य एतस्मिन्सर्वस्मिन्नन्तरे संचरति सोऽयमात्मा तमात्मानमुपासीताजरममृतमभयमशोकमनन्तम्॥ १४

एष सर्वज्ञ एष सर्वेश्वर एष सर्वाधिपतिरेषोऽन्तर्याम्येष योनिः सर्वस्य सर्वसौख्यैरुपा-स्यमानो न च सर्वसौख्यान्युपास्यति वेदशास्त्रैरुपास्यमानो न च वेदशास्त्राण्युपास्यति यस्यान्नमिदं सर्वे न च योऽन्नं भवत्यतः परं सर्वनयनः प्रशास्तान्नमयो भूतात्मा प्राणमय इन्द्रियात्मा मनोमयः संकल्पात्मा विज्ञानमयः कालात्मानन्दमयो लयात्मैकत्वं नास्ति द्वैतं कुतो मर्त्यं नास्त्यमृतं कुतो नान्तःप्रज्ञो न बहिःप्रज्ञो नोभयतःप्रज्ञो न प्रज्ञानघनो न प्रज्ञो नाप्रज्ञोऽपि नो विदितं वेद्यं नास्तीत्येतन्निर्वाणानुशासनमिति वेदानुशासनमिति वेदानुशासनम्॥ १५॥

"That which joins one place (or centre) with another is the nāḍis which bind them. The eye is adhyātma (pertaining to the body); the visible objects are adhibhūta (pertaining to the elements and the sun is adhidaivata (spiritual). The nāḍis form their bond (or connect them). He who moves in the eye, in the visible, in the sun, in the nāḍis, in prāṇa, in vijñāna, in ānanda, in the ākāśa of the heart, and within all else— That is Ātman. It is that which should be worshipped. It is without old age, death, fear, sorrow, or end.

"The ear is adhyātma, the audible adhibhūta, and dik (the quarters) is adhidaivata. The nāḍis bind them. He who moves in the ear, in the audible, in the quarters, in the nāḍis, in prāṇa, in vijñāna, in ānanda, in the ākāśa of the heart, and within all else— That is Ātman. It is that which should be worshipped. It is without old age, death, fear, sorrow, or end.

"The nose is adhyātma, the odoriferous adhibhūta, and the earth is adhidaivata. The nāḍīs bind them. He who moves in the nose, the odoriferous, the earth, the nāḍīs, prāṇa, vijñāna, ānanda, the ākāśa of the heart, and within all else— That is Ātman. It is that which should be worshipped. It is without old age, death, fear, sorrow, or end.

"The tongue is adhyātma : the tastable adhibhūta, and Varuṇa is adhidaivata. The nāḍīs bind them. He who moves in the tongue, the tastable, Varuṇa, the nāḍīs, prāṇa, vijñāna, ānanda, tha ākāśa of the heart, and within all else— That is Ātman. It is that which should be worshipped. It is without old age, death, fear, sorrow, or end.

"The skin is adhyātma, the tangiferous adhibhūta, and the vāyu is adhidaivata. The nāḍis bind them. He who moves in the skin, the tangiferous, the vāyu, the nāḍis, prāṇa, vijñāna, ānanda, the ākāśa of the heart, and within all else— That is Ātman. It is that which should be worshipped. It is without old age, death, fear, sorrow, or end.

"Vāk (speech) is adhyātma, that which is acted upon by vāk is adhibhūta, and Agni is Adhidaivata. The nāḍis bind them. He who moves in vāk, that which is acted upon by vāk, Agni, the nāḍis, prāṇa, vijñāna, the ākāśa of the heart, and within all else— That is Ātman. It is that which should be worshipped. It is without old age, death, fear, sorrow, or end.

"The hand is adhyātma, that which can be handled is adhibhūta, and Indra is adhidaivata. The nāḍis bind them. He who moves in the hand, that which can be handled by it, Indra, the nāḍīs, prāṇa, vijñāna, ānanda, the ākāśa of the heart, and within all else— That is Ātman. It is that which should be worshipped. It is without old age, death, fear, sorrow, or end.

"The feet is adhyātma, that which is walked upon is adhibhūta, and Viṣṇu (or Upendra) is adhidaivata. The nāḍis bind them. He who moves in the feet, that which is walked upon, Viṣṇu, the nāḍis, prāṇa, vijñāna, ānanda, the ākāśa of the heart, and within all else— That is Ātman. It is that which should be worshipped. It is without old age, death, fear, sorrow, or end.

"The anus is adhyātma, the excreta is adhibhūta, and Mṛtyu is adhidaivata. The nāḍīs bind them. He who moves the anus, the excreta, Mṛtyu, the nāḍīs, prāṇa, vijñāna, ānanda, the ākāśa of the heart, and within all else— That is Ātman. It is that which should be worshipped. It is without old age, death, fear, sorrow, or end.

"The genitals is adhyātma, the secretion is adhibhūta, and Prajāpati is adhidaivata. The nāḍīs bind them. He who moves in the genitals, secretion Prajāpati, the nāḍis, prāṇa, vijñāna, ānanda, the ākāśa of the heart, and within all else— That is Ātman. It is that which should be worshipped. It is without old age, death, fear, sorrow, or end.

"Manas is adhyātma, the thinkable is adhibhūta, and the moon is adhidaivata. The nāḍis bind them. He who moves in the manas, the thinkable, the moon, the nāḍis, prāṇa, vijñāna, ānanda, the ākāśa of the heart, and within all else— That is Ātman. It is that which should be worshipped. It is without old age, death, fear, sorrow, or end.

"Buddhi is adhyātma, the certainly knowable is adhibhūta, and Brahmā is adhidaivata. The nāḍis bind them. He who moves in buddhi, the certainly knowable, Brahmā, the nāḍis, prāṇa, vijñāna, ānanda, the ākāśa of the heart, and within all else— That is Ātman. It is that which should be worshipped. It is without old age, death, fear, sorrow, or end.

"Ahaṁkāra is adhyātma, that which is acted upon by ahaṁkāra is adhibhūta, and Rudra is adidaivata. The nāḍis bind them. He who moves in ahaṁkāra, that which is acted upon by ahaṁkāra, Rudra, the nāḍīs, prāṇa, vijñāna, ānanda, the ākāśa of the heart, and within all else— That is Ātman. It is that which should be worshipped. It is without old age, death, fear, sorrow, or end.

"Citta is adhyātma, that which is acted upon by citta (producing fluctuation of thought) is adhibhūta, and Kṣetrajña is adhidaivata. The nadis bind them. He who moves in citta, that which is acted upon by citta, Kṣetrajña, naḍīs, prāṇa, vijñāna, ānanda, the ākāśa of the heart, and within all else— That is Ātman. It is that which should be worshipped. It is without old age, death, fear, sorrow, or end.

"He is the knower of all, the Lord of all, the ruler of all, the one latent in all, the one worshipped for the happiness of all, but Himself not worshipping (or seeking) any happiness, the one worshipped by all, the Vedas and other books and to which all this is food, but who does not become the food of another; moreover, the one who, as the eye, is the ordainer of all, the one who as annamaya is Bhūtātmā; the one who is prāṇamaya is Indriyātmā, the one as manomaya is Saṅkalpātmā, the one who as vijñānamaya is Kālātmā, the one who as ānandamaya is Layātmā, is one and not dual. How can it be said to be mortal? How can it be said that there is not immortality in It? It is neither internal prajñā nor external prajñā nor both, nor Prajñāghana; It is neither prajñā nor not-prajñā, it is neither known nor is it to know anything. Thus is the exposition of Nirvāṇa; and thus is the exposition of the Vedas; yea, thus is the exposition of the Vedas."

॥षष्ठ:खण्ड:॥

नैवेह किंचनाग्र आसीदमूलमनाधारा इमा: प्रजा: प्रजायन्ते॥ १॥

चक्षुश्च द्रष्टव्यं च नारायण: श्रोत्रं च श्रोतव्यं च नारायणो घ्राणं च घ्रातव्यं च नारायणो जिह्वा च रसयितव्यं च नारायणस्त्वक् च स्पर्शयितव्यं च नारायणो मनश्च मन्तव्यं च नारायणो बुद्धिश्च बोद्धव्यं च नारायणोऽहंकारश्चाहंकर्तव्यं च नारायणश्चित्तं च चेतयितव्यं च नारायणो वाक् च वक्तव्यं च नारायणो हस्तौ चादातव्यं च नारायण:पादौ च गन्तव्यं च नारायण: पायुश्च विसर्जयितव्यं च नारायण उपस्थश्चानन्दयितव्यं च नारायणो धाता विधाता कर्ता विकर्ता दिव्यो देव एको नारायण:॥ २॥

आदित्या रुद्रा मरुतो वसवोऽश्विनावृचो यजूंषि सामानि मन्त्रोऽग्निराज्याहुतिर्नारायण उद्भव: संभवो दिव्यो देव एको नारायण:॥ ३॥

माता पिता भ्राता निवास: शरणं सुहृद्गतिर्नारायण:॥ ४॥

विराजा सुदर्शनाजितासोम्यामोघाकुमारामृतासत्यामध्यमानासीराशिशुरासुरासूर्या-भास्वतीविज्ञेयानि नाडीनामानि दिव्यानि॥ ५॥

गर्जति गायति वाति वर्षति वरुणोऽर्यमा चन्द्रमा: काल: कविर्धाता ब्रह्मा प्रजापतिर्मघवा दिवसाश्चार्धदिवसाश्च कला: कल्पाश्चोर्ध्वं य दिशश्च सर्वं नारायण:॥ ६॥

पुरुष एवेदं सर्वं यद्भूतं यच्च भव्यम्। उतामृतत्वस्येशानो यदन्नेनातिरोहति। तद्विष्णो: परमं पदं सदा पश्यन्ति सूरय:। दिवीव चक्षुराततम्। तद्विप्रासो विपन्यवो जागृवांस: समिन्धते। विष्णोर्यत्परमं पदम्। तदेतन्निर्वाणानुशासनमिति वेदानुशासनमिति वेदानुशासनम्॥ ७॥

"At first there was not anything in the least. These creatures were born through no root, no support but the Divine Deva, the one Nārāyaṇa. The eye and the visible are Nārāyaṇa; the ear and the audible are Nārāyaṇa; the tongue and the 'tastable' are Nārāyaṇa; the nose and the 'smellable' are Nārāyaṇa; the skin and the tangible are Nārāyaṇa; manas and that which is acted upon by it are Nārāyaṇa; buddhi and that which is acted upon by it are Nārāyaṇa; ahaṁkāra and that which is acted upon by it are Nārāyaṇa; citta and that which is acted upon by it are Nārāyaṇa; vāk and that which is spoken are Nārāyaṇa; the hand and that which is lifted are Nārāyaṇa; the leg and that which is walked upon are Nārāyaṇa; the anus and the excreted are Nārāyaṇa; the genitals and the enjoyment of pleasure are Nārāyaṇa. The originator and the ordainer as also the agent and the causer of changes, are the Divine Deva Nārāyaṇa only. Ādityas, Rudras, Maruts, Vasus, Aśvins, the Ṛk, Yajuṣ, and Sāma, Mantras, Agni, clarified butter and oblation— all these are Nārāyaṇa. The origin and the combination are the Divine Deva Nārāyaṇa only. Mother, father, brother, residence, asylum, friends and dependents are Nārāyaṇa only. The divine nāḍis known as Virājā, Sudarśanā, Jitā, Saumyā, Moghā, Kumārā, Amṛtā, Satyā, Samadhyamā, Nāsīrā, Śiśirā, Surā, Sūryā, and Bhāsvatī (fourteen nāḍis in all), that which thunders, sings and rains, viz., Varuṇa, Aryamā (sun), Candramas (moon) Kalā (part), Kavi (Śukra), the creator Brahmā and Prajāpati, Indra, Kāla (or time) of days, half-days, Kalpa, the upper, and the directions— all these are Nārāyaṇa. That which was and will be is this Puruṣa only. Like the eye (which sees without any obstacle) the thing spread in the ākāśa, the wise ever see this supreme seat of Viṣṇu. Brāhmaṇas who are ever spiritually awake, praise in diverse ways and illuminate the suprme abode of Viṣṇu, thus is the exposition to the attaining of Nirvāṇa; thus is the teaching of the Vedas; yea, this is the teaching of the Vedas.

॥सप्तम: खण्ड:॥

अन्त:शरीरे निहितो गुहायामज एको नित्यो यस्य पृथिवी शरीरं य: पृथिवीमन्तरे संचरन् यं पृथिवी न वेद। यस्याप: शरीरं योऽपोऽन्तरे संचरन्यमापो न विदु:। यस्य तेज: शरीरं यस्तेजोन्तरे संचरन् यं तेजो न वेद। यस्य वायु: शरीरं यो वायुमन्तरे संचरन् यं वायुर्न वेद। यस्याकाश: शरीरं य आकाशमन्तरे संचरन् यमाकाशो न वेद। यस्य मन: शरीरं यो मनोन्तरे संचरन् यं मनो न वेद। यस्य बुद्धि: शरीरं यो बुद्धिमन्तरे संचरन् यं बुद्धिर्न वेद। यस्याहंकार: शरीरं योऽहंकारमन्तरे संचरन् यमहंकारो न वेद। यस्य चित्तं शरीरं यश्चित्तमन्तरे संचरन् यं चित्तं न वेद। यस्याव्यक्तं शरीरं योऽव्यक्तमन्तरे संचरन् यमव्यक्तं न वेद। यस्याक्षरं शरीरं योऽक्षरमन्तरे संचरन् यमक्षरं न वेद। यस्य मृत्यु: शरीरं यो मृत्युमन्तरे संचरन् यं मृत्युर्न वेद। स एष सर्वभूतान्तरात्माऽपहतपाप्मा दिव्यो देव एको नारायण:॥ १॥

एतां विद्यामपान्तरतमाय ददावपान्तरतमो ब्रह्मणे ददौ ब्रह्मा घोराङ्गिरसे ददौ घोराङ्गिरा रैत्वाय ददौ रैत्वो रामाय ददौ राम: सर्वेभ्यो भूतेभ्यो ददावित्येवं निर्वाणानुशासनमिति वेदानुशासनमिति वेदानुशासनम्॥ २॥

"Within the body, is the one eternal Aja (unborn), located in the cave (of the heart). Earth is His body. Though He moves in the earth, earth does not know Him. Waters are His body. Though He moves in the waters, waters do not know Him. Tejas is His body. Though He moves in tejas, tejas does not know Him. Vāyu is His body. Though He moves in vāyu, vāyu does not know Him. Ākāśa is His body. Though He moves in ākāśa, ākāśa does not know Him. Manas is His body. Though He moves in manas, manas does not know Him.

Buddhi is his body. Though He moves in buddhi, buddhi does not know Him. Ahaṁkāra is His body. Though He moves in ahaṁkāra, ahaṁkāra does not know Him. Citta is His body. Though He moves in citta, citta does not know Him. Avyakta is His body. Though He moves in Avyakta, Avyakta does not know Him. Akṣara is His body. Though He moves in Akṣara, akṣara does not know Him. Mṛtyu (death) is His body. Though He moves in Mṛtyu, Mṛtyu does not know Him. Such an one is the Ātman within all creatures, the remover of all sins and the Divine Deva, the one Nārāyaṇa.

"This knowledge was imparted (by Nārāyaṇa) to Apāntaratama who in turn imparted it to Brahmā. Brahmā imparted it to Ghora-Aṅgiras. He imparted it to Raikva, who in turn imparted it to Rāma. Rāma imparted it to all creatures. This is the teaching of Nirvāṇa; this is the teaching of the Vedas; yea, this is the teaching of the Vedas."

॥अष्टम: खण्ड:॥

अन्त:शरीरे निहितो गुहायां शुद्ध: सोऽयमात्मा सर्वस्य मेदोमांसक्लेदावकीर्णे शरीर-मध्येऽत्यन्तोपहते चित्रभित्तिप्रतीकाशे गान्धर्वनगरोपमे कदलीगर्भवन्नि:सारे जलबुद्बुदव-च्चञ्चले नि:सृतमात्मानमचिन्त्यरूपं दिव्यं देवमसङ्गं शुद्धं तेजस्कायमरूपं सर्वेश्वरमचि-न्त्यमशरीरं निहितं गुहायाममृतं विभ्राजमानमानन्दं तं पश्यन्ति विद्वांसस्तेन लये न पश्यन्ति॥ १

"The Ātman of all which is immaculate, is located within the cave in the body. Ātman which lives in the midst of the body filled with fat, flesh and phlegm in a seat very closely shut up with shining many-coloured walls resembling a Gandharva city and with the (subtle) essence going out of it (to other parts of the body), which seat may be likened to a plantain flower and is ever agitated like a water-bubble— this Ātman is of an unthinkable form, the Divine Deva, associateless and pure, has tejas as its body, is of all forms, the Lord of all, the unthinkable and the bodiless, placed within the cave, immortal, shining, and bliss itself. He is a wise person who cognizes Ātman thus, and not one who does not do so."

॥नवम: खण्ड:॥

अथ हैनं रैक्व: पप्रच्छ भगवन्कस्मिन्सर्वेऽस्तं गच्छन्तीति। तस्मै स होवाच चक्षुरेवाप्येति यच्चक्षुरेवास्तमेति द्रष्टव्यमेवाप्येति यो द्रष्टव्यमेवास्तमेत्यादित्यमेवाप्येति य आदित्यमेवास्त-मेति विराजामेवाप्येति यो विराजामेवास्तमेति प्राणमेवाप्येति य: प्राणमेवास्तमेति विज्ञानमेवाप्येति यो विज्ञानमेवास्तमेत्यानन्दमेवाप्येति य आनन्दमेवास्तमेति तुरीयमेवाप्येति यस्तुरीयमेवास्तमेति तदमृतमभयमशोकमनन्तनिर्बीजमेवाप्येतीति होवाच॥ १॥

Once Raikva questioned Him (Lord) thus : "O Lord, in whom does everything disappear (or merge)?" He replied thus : "That which (or he who) disappears in the eye becomes the eye only; that which disappears in the visible becomes the visible only; that which disappears in the sun becomes sun only; that which disappears in Virāṭ becomes Virāṭ only; that which disappears in prāṇa becomes prāṇa only; that which disappears in vijñāna becomes vijñāna only; that which disappears in ānanda becomes ānanda only; that which disappears in turya becomes turya only— (all these) attain that which is deathless, fearless, sorrowless, endless, and seedless."

श्रोत्रमेवाप्येति यः श्रोत्रमेवास्तमेति श्रोतव्यमेवाप्येति यः श्रोतव्यमेवास्तमेति दिशमेवाप्येति यो दिशमेवास्तमेति सुदर्शनामेवाप्येति यः सुदर्शनामेवास्तमेत्यपानमेवाप्येति योऽपानमेवास्तमेति विज्ञानमेवाप्येति यो विज्ञानमेवास्तमेति तदमृतमभयमशोकमनन्त-निर्बीजमेवाप्येतीति होवाच॥ २॥

Then He continued : "That which disappears in the ear becomes ear itself; that which disappears in the audible becomes the audible only; that which disappears in dik (space) becomes dik only; that which disappears in sudarśana (discus) becomes sudarśana only : that which disappears in apāna becomes apāna only; that which disappears in vijñāna becomes vijñāna only; that which disappears in ānanda becomes ānanda only; that which disappears in turya becomes turya only— (all these) attain that which is deathless, fearless, sorrowless, endless, and seedless."

नासामेवाप्येति यो नासामेवास्तमेति घ्रातव्यमेवाप्येति यो घ्रातव्यमेवास्तमेति पृथिवीमेवाप्येति यः पृथिवीमेवास्तमेति जितामेवाप्येति यो जितामेवास्तमेति व्यानमेवाप्येति यो व्यानमेवास्तमेति विज्ञानमेवाप्येति तदमृत................ होवाच॥ ३॥

Then He continued : "That which disappears in the nose becomes nose only; that which disappears in the odoriferous becomes odoriferous only; that which disappears in pṛthivī becomes pṛthivī only; that which disappears in jitam (victory) becomes victory only; that which disappears in vyāna becomes vyāna only; that which disappears in vijñāna becomes vijñāna only; that which disappears in bliss becomes bliss only; that which disappears in turya becomes turya only— (all these) attain that which is deathless, fearless, sorrowless, endless, and seedless."

जिह्वामेवाप्येति यो जिह्वामेवास्तमेति रसयितव्यमेवाप्येति यो रसयितव्यमेवास्तमेति वरुणमेवाप्येति यो वरुणमेवास्तमेति सौम्यामेवाप्येति यः सौम्यामेवास्तमेत्युदानमेवाप्येति य उदानमेवास्तमेति विज्ञानमेवाप्येति तदमृत.................. होवाच॥ ४॥

Then He continued : "That which disappears in the mouth becomes the mouth only; that which disappears in the taste becomes the taste only; that which disappears in Varuṇa becomes Varuṇa only; that which disappears in Saumya (moon or Mercury) becomes saumya only; that which disappears in udāna becomes udāna only; that which disappears in vijñāna becomes vijñāna only; that which disappears in bliss becomes bliss only; that which disappears in turya becomes turya only— (all these) attain that which is deathless, fearless, sorrowless, endless, and seedless."

त्वचमेवाप्येति यस्त्वचमेवास्तमेति स्पर्शयितव्यमेवाप्येति यः स्पर्शयितव्यमेवास्तमेति वायुमेवाप्येति यो वायुमेवास्तमेति मोघामेवाप्येति यो मोघामेवास्तमेति समानमेवाप्येति यः समानमेवास्तमेति विज्ञानमेवाप्येति तदमृत.............. होवाच॥ ५॥

Then He continued : "That which disappears in the skin becomes the skin only; that which disappears in touch becomes touch only; that which disappears in vāyu becomes vāyu only; that which disappears in cloud becomes cloud only; that which disappears in samāna becomes samāna only; that which disappears in vijñāna becomes vijñāna only; that which disappears in bliss becomes bliss only; that which disappears in turya becomes turya only— (all these) attain that which is deathless, fearless, sorrowless, endless, and seedless."

वाचमेवाप्येति यो वाचमेवास्तमेति वक्तव्यमेवाप्येति यो वक्तव्यमेवास्तमेत्य-ग्निमेवाप्येति योऽग्निमेवास्तमेति कुमारामेवाप्येति यः कुमारामेवास्तमेति वैरम्भमेवाप्येति यो वैरम्भमेवास्तमेति विज्ञानमेवाप्येति तदमृत............... होवाच॥ ६॥

Then He continued : "That which disappears in vāk becomes vāk only; that which disappears in speech becomes speech only; that which disappears in *Agni* becomes *agni* only; that which disappears in Kumārā becomes kumārā only; that which disappears in hostility becomes hostility itself; that which disappears in *vijñāna* become *vijñāna* only; that which disappears in bliss becomes bliss only; that which disappears in turya becomes turya only— (all these) attain that which is deathless, fearless, sorrowless, endless, and seedless."

हस्तमेवाप्येति यो हस्तमेवास्तमेत्यादातव्यमेवाप्येति य आदातव्यमेवास्तमे-तीन्द्रमेवाप्येति य इन्द्रमेवास्तमेत्यमृतामेवाप्येति योऽमृतामेवास्तमेति मुख्यमेवाप्येति यो मुख्यमेवास्तमेति विज्ञानमेवाप्येति तदमृत....................... होवाच॥ ७॥

Then He continued : "That which disappears in the hand becomes the hand only; that which disappears in that which is lifted by the hand becomes that which is lifted by the hand; that which disappears in Indra becomes Indra only; that which disappears in the nectar becomes nectar only; that which disappears in mukhya becomes mukhya only; that which disappears in *vijñāna* becomes *vijñāna* only; that which disappears in bliss becomes bliss only; that which disappears in turya becomes turya only— (all these) attain, that which is deathless, fearless, sorrowless, endless and seedless."

पादमेवाप्येति यः पादमेवास्तमेति गन्तव्यमेवाप्येति यो गन्तव्यमेवास्तमेति विष्णुमेवाप्येति यो विष्णुमेवास्तमेति सत्यामेवाप्येति यः सत्यामेवास्तमेत्यन्तर्याममेवाप्येति योऽन्तर्याममेवास्तमेति विज्ञानमेवाप्येति तद.............. होवाच॥ ८॥

Then He continued : "That which disappears in the leg becomes the leg only; that which disappears in that which is walked upon becomes that which is walked upon; that which disappears in Viṣṇu becomes Viṣṇu only; that which disappears in satya becomes satya only; that which disappears in the suppression of the breath and voice becomes the suppression of the breath and voice; that which disappears in vijñāna becomes vijñāna only; that which disappears in bliss becomes bliss only; that which disappears in turya becomes turya only— (all these) attain that which is deathless, fearless, sorrowless, endless, and seedless."

पायुमेवाप्येति यः पायुमेवास्तमेति विसर्जयितव्यमेवाप्येति यो विसर्जयितव्य-मेवास्तमेति मृत्युमेवाप्येति यो मृत्युमेवास्तमेति मध्यमामेवाप्येति यो मध्यमामेवास्तमेति प्रभञ्जनमेवाप्येति यः प्रभञ्जनमेवास्तमेति विज्ञानमेवाप्येति तद......... होवाच॥ ९॥

Then He continued : "That which disappears in the anus becomes the anus only; that which disappears in that which is excreted becomes that which is excreted; that which disappears in Mṛtyu becomes Mṛtyu only; that which disappears in spirituous liquor becomes spiritous liquor only; that which disappears in hurricane becomes hurricane only; that which disappears in vijñāna becomes vijñāna only; that wich disappears in bliss becomes bliss only; that which disappears in turya becomes turya only— (all these) attain that which is deathless, fearless, sorrowless, endless, and seedless."

उपस्थमेवाप्येति य उपस्थमेवास्तमेत्यानन्दयितव्यमेवाप्येति य आनन्दयितव्यमे-वास्तमेति प्रजापतिमेवाप्येति यः प्रजापतिमेवास्तमेति नासीराममेवाप्येति यो नासीराममेवास्तमेति कुर्मिरमेवाप्येति यः कुर्मिरमेवास्तमेति विज्ञानमेवाप्येति तदमृत .... होवाच॥ १०॥

Then He continued : "That which disappears in the genitals becomes the genitals only; that which disappears in that which is enjoyed becomes that which is enjoyed; that which disappears in that which is Prajāpati becomes Prajāpati only; that which disappears in nāsīrām becomes nāsīrām only; that which disappears in kurmira becomes kurmira only; that which disappears in vijñāna becomes vijñāna only; that which disappears in bliss becomes bliss only; that which disappears in turya becomes turya only— (all these) attain that which is deathless, fearless, sorrowless, endless, and seedless."

मन एवाप्येति यो मन एवास्तमेति मन्तव्यमेवाप्येति यो मन्तव्यमेवास्तमेति चन्द्रमेवाप्येति यश्चन्द्रमेवास्तमेति शिशुमेवाप्येति यः शिशुमेवास्तमेति श्येनमेवाप्येति यः श्येनमेवास्तमेति विज्ञानमेवाप्येति तदमृत............ होवाच॥ ११॥

Then He continued : "That which disappears in *manas* becomes *manas* itself; that which disappears in the thinkable becomes thinkable itself; that which disappears in the moon becomes the moon itself; that which disappears in śiśu becomes śiśu itself; that which disappears in śyena becomes śyena itself; that which disappears in *vijñāna* becomes *vijñāna* only; that which disappears in *ānanda* becomes *ānanda* itself; that which disappears in turya becomes turya itself— (all these) attain that which is deathless, fearless, sorrowless, endless, and seedless."

बुद्धिमेवाप्येति यो बुद्धिमेवास्तमेति बोद्धव्यमेवाप्येति यो बोद्धव्यमेवास्तमेति ब्रह्माणमेवाप्येति यो ब्रह्माणमेवास्तमेति सूर्यामेवाप्येति यः सूर्यामेवास्तमेति कृष्णमेवाप्येति यः कृष्णमेवास्तमेति विज्ञानमेवाप्येति तदमृत............ होवाच॥ १२॥

Then He continued : "That which disappears in buddhi becomes buddhi itself; that which disappears in the certainly knowable becomes the certainly knowable itself; that which disappears in Brahmā becomes Brahmā himself; that which disappears in Kṛṣṇa becomes Kṛṣṇa himself; that which disappears in Sūrya becomes Sūrya itself; that which disappears in vijñāna becomes vijñāna itself; that which disappears in ānanda becomes ānanda itself; that which disappears in turya becomes turya itself— (all these) attain that which is deathless, fearless, sorrowless, endless, and seedless."

अहंकारमेवाप्येति योऽहंकारमेवास्तमेत्यहंकर्तव्यमेवाप्येति योऽहंकर्तव्यमेवास्तमेति रुद्रमेवाप्येति यो रुद्रमेवास्तमेत्यसुरामेवाप्येति योऽसुरामेवास्तमेति श्वेतमेवाप्येति यः श्वेतमेवास्तमेति विज्ञानमेवाप्येति तदमृत............ होवाच॥ १३॥

Then He continued : "That which disappears in ahaṁkāra becomes ahaṁkāra itself; that which disappears in that which is acted upon by ahaṁkāra becomes that itself; that which disappears in Rudra becomes Rudra himself; that which disappears in asura becomes asura itself; that which disappears in śveta becomes śveta itself; that which disappears in vijñāna becomes vijñāna itself; that which disappears in ānanda becomes ānanda itself; that which disappears in turya becomes turya itself— (all these) attain that which is deathless, fearless, sorrowless, endless, and seedless."

चित्तमेवाप्येति यश्चित्तमेवास्तमेति चेतयितव्यमेवाप्येति यश्चेतयितव्यमेवास्तमेति क्षेत्रज्ञमेवाप्येति यः क्षेत्रज्ञमेवास्तमेति भास्वतीमेवाप्येति यो भास्वतीमेवास्तमेति नागमेवाप्येति यो नागमेवास्तमेति विज्ञानमेवाप्येति यो विज्ञानमेवास्तमेत्यानन्दमेवाप्येति य आनन्दमेवास्तमेति तुरीयमेवाप्येति यस्तुरीयमेवास्तमेति तदमृतमभयमशोकमनन्तं निर्बीजमेवाप्येति तदमृत............... होवाच॥ १४॥

Then He continued : "That which disappears in citta becomes citta itself; that which disappears in that which is acted upon by citta becoming that itself; that which disappears in Kṣetrajña becomes Kṣetrajña itself; that which disappears in bhāsvatī becomes bhāsvatī itself; that which disappears in nāga becomes nāga itself; that which disappears in vijñāna becomes vijñāna itself; that which disappears in ānanda becomes ānanda itself; that which disappears in turya becomes turya itself— (all these) attain that which is deathless, fearless, sorrowless, endless, and seedless."

य एवं निर्बीजं वेद निर्बीज एव स भवति न जायते न म्रियते न मुह्यते न भिद्यते न दह्यते न छिद्यते न कम्पते न कुप्यते सर्वदहनोऽयमात्मेत्याचक्षते॥ १५॥

नैवमात्मा प्रवचनशतेनापि लभ्यते न बहुश्रुतेन न बुद्धिज्ञानाश्रितेन न मेधया न वेदैर्न यज्ञैर्न तपोभिरुग्रैर्न सांख्यैर्न योगैर्नाश्रमैर्नान्यैरात्मानमुपलभन्ते प्रवचनेन प्रशंसया व्युत्थानेन तमेतं ब्राह्मणाः शुश्रुवांसोऽनूचाना उपलभन्ते शान्तो दान्त उपरतस्तितिक्षुः समाहितो भूत्वात्मन्येवात्मानं पश्यति सर्वस्यात्मा भवति य एवं वेद॥ १६॥

"He who knows this as seedless in this manner becomes himself seedless. He is neither born, nor dies, nor is deluded nor split, nor burnt, nor cut— yea, he does not feel angry, and hence he is said to be Ātmā, capable of burning all. Such an Ātman is neither attained by a hundred sayings, nor by (the reading of) many scriptures, nor by mere intelligence, nor by hearing from others, nor by understanding, nor by Vedas, nor by scriptures, nor by severe tapas, nor sāṁkhya, nor yoga, nor observances of the orders of the life, nor by any other means (than the following). Devoted Brāhmaṇas who repeat the Vedas according to rules and who worship Him with praise attain Him. He who is quiescent, self-controlled, indifferent to worldly objects and resigned, having centred his mind on Ātman sees Ātman and becomes one with the Ātman of all, as also he who knows this."

॥दशमः खण्डः॥

अथ हैनं रैक्वः पप्रच्छ भगवन्कस्मिन्सर्वे संप्रतिष्ठिता भवन्तीति रसातललोकेष्विति होवाच कस्मिन्रसातललोका ओताश्च प्रोताश्चेति भूर्लोकेष्विति होवाच। कस्मिन्भूर्लोका ओताश्च प्रोताश्चेति भुवर्लोकेष्विति होवाच। कस्मिन्भुवर्लोका ओताश्च प्रोताश्चेति सुवर्लोकेष्विति होवाच। कस्मिन्सुवर्लोका ओताश्च प्रोताश्चेति महर्लोकेष्विति होवाच। कस्मिन्महर्लोका ओताश्च प्रोताश्चेति जनोलोकेष्विति होवाच। कस्मिन् जनोलोका ओताश्च प्रोताश्चेति तपोलोकेष्विति होवाच। कस्मिँस्तपोलोका ओताश्च प्रोताश्चेति सत्यलोकेष्विति होवाच। कस्मिन्सत्यलोका ओताश्च प्रोताश्चेति प्रजापतिलोकेष्विति होवाच। कस्मिन्प्रजापतिलोका ओताश्च प्रोताश्चेति ब्रह्मलोकेष्विति होवाच। कस्मिन्ब्रह्मलोका ओताश्च प्रोताश्चेति सर्वलोका आत्मनि ब्रह्मणि मणय इवौताश्च प्रोताश्चेति स होवाच॥ १॥

एवमेतान् लोकानात्मनि प्रतिष्ठितान्वेदात्मैव स भवतीत्येतन्निर्वाणानुशासनमिति वेदानुशासनमिति वेदानुशासनम्॥ २॥

Then Raikva asked Him : "O Lord, where do all things rest? He replied : "In the worlds of Rasātala (or nether worlds)."

"In what are these (Rasātala world) woven warp and woof?" He replied : "In the worlds of Bhūḥ."

"In what are these (worlds of Bhūḥ) woven warp and woof?" he replied : "In the worlds of Bhuvaḥ."

"In what are these (Bhuvaḥ worlds) woven warp and woof?" "In the worlds of Suvaḥ."

"In what are these (Suvaḥ worlds) woven warp and woof?" In the worlds of Mahaḥ."

"In what are these (Mahaḥ worlds) woven warp and woof.?" "In the Janaloka."

"In what are these (Jana worlds) woven warp and woof?" "In the Tapoloka."

"In what are these (Tapolokas) woven warp and woof?" "In the Satya Loka."

"In what are these (Satya worlds) woven warp and woof." "In the Prajāpati lok."

"In what are these (Prajāpati worlds) woven warp and woof?" In the Brahmaloka."

"In what are these (Brahma worlds) woven warp and woof." "In the Sarvaloka."

"In what are these (Sarva lokas) woven warp and woof." "In Ātmā— which is Brahman, like beads (in a rosary) warp-wise and woof-wise."

Then he said : "All these rest in Ātmā, and he who knows this, becomes Ātman itself. Thus is the exposition of Nirvāṇa. Thus is the exposition of the Vedas; yea, thus is the exposition of the Vedas."

॥एकादशः खण्डः॥

अथ हैनं रैक्वः पप्रच्छ भगवन्योऽयं विज्ञानघन उत्क्रामन्स केन कतरद्वाव स्थानमुत्सृ-ज्यापक्रामतीति तस्मै स होवाच। हृदयस्य मध्ये लोहितं मांसपिण्डं यस्मिंस्तद्दहरं पुण्डरीकं कुमुदमिवानेकधा विकसितं तस्य मध्ये समुद्रः समुद्रस्य मध्ये कोशस्तस्मिन्नाड्यश्चतस्रो भवन्ति रमारमेच्छाऽपुनर्भवेति तत्र रमा पुण्येन पुण्यं

लोकं नयत्यरमा पापेन पापमिच्छया यत्स्मरति तदभिसंपद्यते अपुनर्भवया कोशं भिनत्ति कोशं भित्त्वा शीर्षकपालं भिनत्ति शीर्षकपालं भित्त्वा पृथिवीं भिनत्ति पृथिवीं भित्त्वाऽपो भिनत्त्यपो भित्त्वा तेजो भिनत्ति तेजो भित्त्वा वायुं भिनत्ति वायुं भित्त्वाकाशं भिनत्त्याकाशं भित्त्वा मनो भिनत्ति मनो भित्त्वा भूतादिं भिनत्ति भूतादिं भित्त्वा महान्तं भिनत्ति महान्तं भित्त्वाव्यक्तं भिनत्त्यव्यक्तं भित्त्वाक्षरं भिनत्त्यक्षरं भित्त्वा मृत्युं भिनत्ति मृत्युर्वै परे देव एकीभवतीति परस्तान्न सन्नासन्न सदसदित्येतन्निर्वाणा-नुशासनमिति वेदानुशासनमिति वेदानुशासनम्॥ १॥

Again Raikva asked Him : "O Lord ! what is the seat of Ātman which is replete with vijñāna? and how does it leave the body and pervade the universe?" To this He replied : "There is a mass of red flesh in the middle of the heart. In it, there is a lotus called dahara. It buds forth in many petals like a water-lilly. In the middle of it is an ocean (samudra). In its midst a koka (bird). In it there are four nāḍis. They are ramā, aramā, Icchā and punarbhava. Of these, ramā leads a man of virtue to a happy world. Aramā leads one of sins into the world of sins. (Passing) through Icchā (Nāḍi), one gets whatever he remembers. Through Punarbhava, he splits opon the sheaths after splitting open the sheaths, he splits open the skull of the head; then he splits open pṛthvī; then āpas; then tejas; then vāyu; then ākāśa. Then he splits open manas; then bhūtādi; then mahat; then avyakta; then akṣara; then he splits open mrtyu and mrtyu becomes one with the supreme God. Beyond this, there is neither Sat nor asat, nor Sat-asat. Thus is the exposition of Nirvāṇa; and thus is the exposition of the Vedas; yea, thus is the exposition of Vedas."

॥द्वादशः खण्डः॥

ॐ नारायणाद्वा अन्नमागतं पक्वं ब्रह्मलोके महासंवर्तके पुनः पक्वमादित्ये पुनः पक्वं क्रव्यादि पुनः पक्वं जालकिलक्लिन्नं पर्युषितं पूतमन्नमयाचितमसंक्लृप्तमश्नीयान्न कंचन याचेत॥ १॥

"Anna (food) came from Nārāyaṇa. It was first cooked in Brahmaloka in the Mahā-samvartaka fire. Again it was cooked in the sun; again it was cooked in kravyādi (lit., the fire that burns raw flesh, etc.); again it was cooked in jālakila (the flaming kila); then it became pure and not stale (or fresh). One should eat whatever has fallen to his share and without begging; one should never beg any (food)."

॥त्रयोदशः खण्डः॥

बाल्येन तिष्ठासेद्बालस्वभावोऽसङ्गो निरवद्यो मौनेन पाण्डित्येन निरवधिकारतयोपलभ्येत कैवल्यमुक्तं निगमनं प्रजापतिरुवाच महत्पदं ज्ञात्वा वृक्षमूले वसेत कुचेलोऽसहाय एकाकी समाधिस्थ आत्मकाम आप्तकामो निष्कामो जीर्णकामो हस्तिनि सिंहे दंशे मशके नकुले सर्पराक्षसगन्धर्वे मृत्यो रूपाणि विदित्वा न बिभेति कुतश्चनेति वृक्षमिव तिष्ठासेच्छिद्यमानोऽपि न कुप्येत न कम्पेतोत्पलमिव तिष्ठासेच्छिद्यमानोऽपि न कुप्येत न कम्पेताकाशमिव तिष्ठासेच्छिद्यमानोऽपि न कुप्येत न कम्पेत सत्येन तिष्ठासेत्सत्योऽ यमात्मा॥ १॥

"The wise man should conduct himself like a lad, with the nature of a child, without company, blameless, silent and wise and without exercising any authority. This description of Kaivalya is stated by Prajāpati. Having found with certitude the supreme seat, one should dwell under a tree with torn cloths, unaccompanied, single and engaged in samādhi. He should be longing after the attaining of Ātman having attained this object, he is desireless, his desires have decayed. He fears none, though he finds the cause of death in such as elephants, lions, gadflies, mosquitoes, ichneuma, serpents, Yakṣas, Rākṣasas and Gandharvas. He will stand like a tree. Though cut down, he will neither get angry nor tremble. He will stand (or remain) like a lotus. Though pierced, he will neither get angry nor tremble. He will stand like ākāśa; though struck, he will neither get angry nor tremble. He will stand by Satya (truth), since Ātman is Satya.

सर्वेषामेव गन्धानां पृथिवी हृदयं सर्वेषामेव रसानामापो हृदयं सर्वेषामेव रूपाणां तेजो हृदयं सर्वेषामेव स्पर्शानां वायुर्हृदयं सर्वेषामेव शब्दानामाकाशं हृदयं सर्वेषामेव गतीनामव्यक्तं हृदयं सर्वेषामेव सत्त्वानां मृत्युर्हृदयं मृत्युर्वै परे देव एकीभवतीति परस्तान्न सन्नासन्न सदसदित्येतन्निर्वाणानुशासनमिति वेदानुशासनमिति वेदानुशासनम्॥ २॥

"Pṛthivī is the heart (or centre) of all odours; āpas is the heart of all tastes; tejas is the heart of all forms; vāyu is the heart of all touch; ākāśa is the heart of all sounds; avyakta is the heart of gītās (or sounds); mṛtyu is the heart of all Sattvas; and mṛtyu becomes one with the Supreme. And beyond Him, there is neither Sat nor asat, nor Sat-asat. Thus is the exposition of Nirvāṇa; thus is the exposition of the Vedas; yea, thus is the exposition of the Vedas."

॥चतुर्दश: खण्ड:॥

पृथिवी वान्नमापोऽन्नादा आपो वान्नं ज्योतिरन्नादं ज्योतिर्वान्नं वायुरन्नादो वायुर्वान्नमाकाशोऽन्नाद आकाशो वान्नमिन्द्रियाण्यन्नादानीन्द्रियाणि वान्नं मनोऽन्नादं मनो वान्नं बुद्धिरन्नादा बुद्धिर्वान्नमव्यक्तमन्नादमव्यक्तं वान्नमक्षरमन्नादमक्षरं वान्नं मृत्युरन्नादो मृत्युर्वै परे देव एकीभवतीति परस्तान्न सन्नासन्न सदसदित्येतन्निर्वाणानुशासनमिति वेदानुशासनमिति वेदानुशासनम्॥ १॥

"Pṛthivī is the food, and āpas is the eater; āpas is the food and jyotis (or fire) is the eater; jyotis is the food, and vāyu is the eater; vāyu is the food, and ākāśa is the eater; and ākāśa is the food and the indriyas (organs) are the eaters; indriyas are the food and manas is the eater; manas is the food, and buddhi is the eater; buddhi is the food, and avyakta is the eater; avyakta is the food, and akṣara is the eater; akṣara is the food, and mṛtyu is the eater; and mṛtyu becomes one with the Supreme. Beyond Him, there is neither Sat and asat, nor Sat-asat. Thus is the exposition of Nirvāṇa, and thus is the exposition of the Vedas; yea, thus is the exposition of the Vedas."

॥पञ्चदश: खण्ड:॥

अथ हैनं रैक्व: पप्रच्छ भगवन्योऽयं विज्ञानघन उत्क्रामन्स केन कतरद्वाव स्थानं दहतीति तस्मै स होवाच योऽयं विज्ञानघन उत्क्रामन्प्राणं दहत्यपानं व्यानमुदानं समानं वैरम्भं मुख्यमन्तर्यामं प्रभञ्जनं कुमारं श्येनं श्वेतं कृष्णं नागं दहति पृथिव्यापस्तेजोवाय्वाकाशं दहति जागरितं स्वप्नं सुषुप्तं तुरीयं च महतां च लोकं परं च लोकं दहति लोकालोकं दहति धर्माधम दहत्यभास्करममर्यादं निरालोकमत: परं दहति महान्तं

दहत्यव्यक्तं दहत्यक्षरं दहति मृत्युं दहति मृत्युर्वै परे देव एकीभवतीति परस्तान्न सन्नासन्न सदसदित्येतन्निर्वाणानुशासन मिति वेदानुशासनमिति वेदानुशासनम्॥ १॥

Again Raikva aksed : "O Lord, when this Vijñāna-ghana goes out (of the body or the universe), what does it burn and how?" To which He replied : When it goes away, it burns prāṇa, apāna, vyāna, udāna, samāna, vairambha, mukhya, antaryāma, prabhañjana, kumāra, śyena, kṛṣṇa, śveta and nāga. Then it burns pṛthivī, āpas, tejas, vāyu, and ākāśa; then it burns the waking, the dreaming, the dreamless sleeping and the fourth states as well as the mahariokas and worlds higher; then it burns the lokāloka (the highest world forming a limit to the other worlds). Then it burns dharma and adharama. Then it burns that which is beyond, is sunless, limitless, and worldless. Then it burns mahat; it burns avyakta; it burns akṣara; it burns mṛtyu; and mṛtyu becomes one with the great Lord. Beyond Him, there is neither Sat and asat, nor Sat-asat. Thus is the exposition of Nirvāṇa, and thus is the exposition of the Vedas; yea, thus is the exposition of the Vedas."

॥षोडशः खण्डः॥

सौबालबीजब्रह्मोपनिषन्नाप्रशान्ताय दातव्या नापुत्राय नाशिष्याय नासंवत्सररात्रोषिताय नापरिज्ञातकुलशीलाय दातव्या नैव च प्रवक्तव्या। यस्य देवे परा भक्तिर्यथा देवे तथा गुरौ। तस्यैते कथिता ह्यर्थाः प्रकाशन्ते महात्मन इत्येतन्निर्वाणानुशासनमिति वेदानुशासनमिति वेदानुशासनम्॥ १॥

"This Saubāla-Bīja, Brahma-Upaniṣad should neither be given out nor taught to one who has not controlled his passions, who has no sons, who has not gone to a Guru, and having become his disciple has not resided with him for a year, and whose family and conduct are not known. These doctrines should be taught to him who has supreme devotion to the Lord and as much to his Guru. Then these truths shine in his great soul. Thus is the exposition of Nirvāṇa; thus is the exposition of the Vedas; yea, thus is the exposition of the Vadas."

ॐ पूर्णमदः .... इति शान्तिः॥

॥इति सुबालोपनिषत्समाप्ता॥

----

28. KṢURIKOPANIṢAD

क्षुरिकोपनिषद्

This Upaniṣad is related to Kṛṣṇa Yajurveda. There are twenty-five hymns in it. This Upaniṣad is competent like a knife or the cutter to cut the factor imposing hurdles for, or bounds in the way of the knowledge of element. The eight parts of Yoga *i.e.*, Yama, Niyama, Āsana, Prāṇāyāma, Pratyāhāra, Dhāraṇā, Dhyāna and Samādhi and their nexus with accomplishment with the purpose or the aim or its result is also specifically discussed herein. It has been stated in this Upaniṣad that as the spider creates network or a nest for him by knitting the saliva extracted from its mouth, the breathing should enter in the same way into all sensitive zones in the body by exercising a number of Yogāsanās including control on breathing. Subsequently, by developing upward the element of breathing is circulated out from the spinal nerve existed in the heart lotus. Thus adding other seventy two thousand nerves; the perfect knowledge can be accessed to through the process of penetration of all these nerves. On arrival of that supreme place, the living-organism becomes competent to cut all kinds of ties. At that stage, it merges with the supreme element by burning all ties of deeds, the same way of a lamp that merges with it the entire quantum of oil and cotton lace in the supreme flame. Thus, the living-organisms so liberated, no mere ties with the worldly chords. This all as stated above is an essence of this Upaniṣad.

॥शान्तिपाठः॥

ॐ सह नाववतु.................इति शान्तिः॥

क्षुरिकां संप्रवक्ष्यामि धारणां योगसिद्धये। यां प्राप्य न पुनर्जन्म योगयुक्तस्य जायते॥ १॥

I will describe here cutting concentration for attaining to the accomplishment on Yoga. One who attains it as a Yogin, is liberated from the cycle of rebirth.

[The man enjoys the pleasure of liberty if the presumption suggested above is duly made. This is the reason it is called as a knife that cut the ties. The worldly people are tied to the worldly relations particularly owing to compulsions of the worldly passions. When the Yogis arrive at the state of knitting assumption through adopting perpetual exercise of Yama, Niyama, Āsana, Prāṇāyāma and Pratyāhara, the man is engrossed in the activity to exercise the entity of soul and entity of the supreme soul and also the affairs transacted between them. As a result of their assumption, all the worldly ties are shattered.

The Prāṇāyāma, a preparatory exercise to be able for framing assumption has been described in the hymn number 2 to 5.]

वेदतत्त्वार्थविहितं यथोक्तं हि स्वयंभुवा। निःशब्दं देशमास्थाय तत्रासनमवस्थितः॥ २॥

कूर्मोऽङ्गानीव संहृत्य मनो हृदि निरुध्य च। मात्राद्वादशयोगेन प्रणवेन शनैः शनैः॥ ३॥

पूरयेत्सर्वमात्मानं सर्वद्वारं निरुध्य च। उरोमुखकटिग्रीवं किंचिद्धृदयमुन्नतम्॥ ४॥

प्राणान्संधारयेत्तस्मिन्नासाभ्यन्तरचारिणः। भूत्वा तत्र गतप्राणः शनैरथ समुत्सृजेत्॥ ५॥

The main contents of the Veda, as pronounced by the self-born Brahmā and the spirit embedded within the meaning of element, one should take an appropriate posture in a silent place, the same way as the tortoise shrinks his all organs within him. The devotee in the same way put a check on desolution or the disorganisation of the spirits arising in the mind and heart enploying the twelve moras under reciting Oṁkāra gradually. The whole body one fills with breath (exercising the *Pūraka*). At this stage, all the routes, of the breathing are to be restricted and the chest, mouth, the waist and the neck duly in erect position and the heart region should also be advanced.

The breathing circulated through the body should be established in all the cells of cardinal organs through *kumbhaka.* At the time when the breathing is duly circulated, it should be exhaled very steadily by adopting the process of recaka.

[There are three moras in the syllable of Oṁ. The twelve moras are purported that the time consumed while easily pronunciating the syllable Oṁ four times, should also be fixed for the exercise of Kumbhaka and recaka.]

स्थिरमात्रादृढं कृत्वा अङ्गुष्ठेन समाहितः। द्वे तु गुल्फे प्रकुर्वीत जङ्घे चैव त्रयस्त्रयः॥ ६॥
द्वे जानुनी तथोरुभ्यां गुदे शिश्ने त्रयस्त्रयः। वायोरायतनं चात्र नाभिदेशे समाश्रयेत्॥ ७॥

Having a formidable exercise on Prāṇāyama, by adopting the above procedure, the devotee should most cautiously make an assumption notion that the breathing has duly entered as a result of thrice time each frequency of Prāṇāyāma adopted, twice time each in the ankles including the thumb, two calves, three to the right and three to the left. Then in the knees and thighs two times each and thrice time each in anus and penis. He should thereafter assume the breathing in the navel region.

[The lower portion of the waist region, connected with the discus like Mūlādhāra and Svādhiṣṭhāna are very first zones where one has to establish his assumption. Then gradually, the flow of breathing is imagined in the zone of navel, heart, throat and the mind and wisdom on upside it, respectively. How this assumption or notion is to be made formidable and strong, its description has been made in the successive hymns.]

तत्र नाडी सुषुम्ना तु नाडीभिर्बहुभिर्वृता। अणुरक्ताश्च पीताश्च कृष्णास्ताम्रविलोहिताः॥ ८॥

The nerve of Brahma namely Suṣumnā artery is covered by many arteries including Iḍā, Piṅgalā etc. These are in most micro form and found in red, yellow, black, and copper colour.

अतिसूक्ष्मां च तन्वीं च शुक्लां नाडीं समाश्रयेत्। ततः संचारयेत्प्राणानूर्णनाभीव तन्तुना॥ ९॥

The nerve most subtle, thin and white should be resorted to. Then, like the spider moves through the fibres created by its saliva, the yogī should circulate the breathing within that cluster of nerves.

[It is pertinent to state here that the spider creates most micro fibre through its mouth and it moves to the desired direction, hanging on this fibre. The fibre so created by nerve get their origination from the breathing. The power of breathing is made dynamic in the physical system by these means too.]

ततो रक्तोत्पलाभासं हृदयायतनं महत्। दहरं पुण्डरीकं तद् वेदान्तेषु निगद्यते॥ १०॥

तद्भित्त्वा कण्ठमायाति तां नाडीं पूरयन्यत:। मनसस्तु परं गुह्यं सुतीक्ष्णं बुद्धिनिर्मलम्॥ ११॥

It is the region of heart most spacious called as the Dahara or Puṇḍarīka in Vedānta adjacent to that navel. That region is always laminated like a reddish lotus. Then in the seriation there comes the breathing in the throat carrying sensitivity to all the nerves. Then, there comes the place of mind and the secret beyond it, the pious and the place of acute wisdom.

पादस्योपरि यन्मर्म तद्रूपं नाम चिन्तयेत्। मनोद्वारेण तीक्ष्णेन योगमाश्रित्य नित्यश:॥ १२॥

इन्द्रवज्र इति प्रोक्तं मर्मजङ्घानुकृन्तनम्। तद्ध्यानबलयोगेन धारणाभिर्निकृन्तयेत्॥ १३॥

ऊर्वोर्मध्ये तु संस्थाप्य मर्मप्राणविमोचनम्। चतुरभ्यासयोगेन छिन्देदनभिशङ्कित:॥ १४॥

Thus the sensitive regions existing upside the feet are worth concentration with their names and shape. The region known as Indravajra (Indra's thunderbolt) adjacent to the legs should be penetrated by developing an acute mind through the perpetual practise on yoga. Untill through power of meditation, through Yoga and concentration he cuts them off. Shifting himself, he cuts off the breath and joints through Yoga repeated four times without hesitation.

तत: कण्ठान्तरे योगी समूहं नाडिसंचयम्। एकोत्तरं नाडिशतं तासां मध्ये परा स्थिरा॥ १५॥

सुषुम्ना तु परे लीना विरजा ब्रह्मरूपिणी। इडा तिष्ठति वामेन पिङ्गला दक्षिणेन च॥ १६॥

The yogi should subsequently circulate the breathing in the cluster of nerves existing within the throat of yogi. There are one hundred one nerves which are regarded as best in that cluster. The Parāśakti or the metaphysical power is existed in the middle of them. The Suṣumnā engrosses in the supreme element and the Virajā nerve is in the form of Brahman. The Iḍā nerve is located at the right while the Piṅgalā is at the south direction.

तयोर्मध्ये वरं स्थानं यस्तं वेद स वेदवित्। द्वासप्ततिसहस्राणि प्रति नाडीषु तैतिलम्॥ १७॥

The person who knows the best-place existed in middle of the both nerves *i.e.* Iḍā and Piṅgalā becomes competent to know the vedas *i.e.*, the eternal knowledge. The strength of micro nerves has been stated seventy two thousand in total. These have been stated Taitila.

छिन्द्यते ध्यानयोगेन सुषुम्नैका न छिद्यते। योगनिर्मलधारेण क्षुरेणानलवर्चसा॥ १८॥

छिन्देन्नाडीशतं धीर: प्रभावादिह जन्मनि। जातीपुष्पसमायोगैर्यथा वास्यति वै तिलम्॥ १९॥

All nerves can be split by the concetration through Yoga. However, Suṣumnā is the only nerve which cannot be penetrated. With the lightning-sharp razor of Yogic power, shining like the fire, the wise one, here on earth itself should split the hundred nerves, like a pillow is perfumed with jasmine flowers.

एवं शुभाशुभैर्भावैः सा नाडी तां विभावयेत्। तद्भाविताः प्रपद्यन्ते पुनर्जन्मविवर्जिताः॥ २०॥

Thus, the yogi ought to know the different nerves holding the respective spirits either good or evil. The yogi obtains the everlasting supreme Brahman (knowledge) by liberating himself from the cycle of rebirth.

तपोविजितचित्तस्तु निःशब्दं देशमास्थितः। निःसङ्गस्तत्त्वयोगज्ञो निरपेक्षः शनैः शनैः॥ २१॥

The person who has conquered his heart by virtue of the strong penance should do an exercise on Yoga that educates the advantage of living in solitude freed from all worldly inclination and expectation.

पाशं छित्त्वा यथा हंसो निर्विशङ्कः खमुत्क्रमेत्। छिन्नपाशस्तथा जीवः संसारं तरते सदा॥ २२॥

As the Svāna (bird) independently flies in the sky after piercing into pieces the nets within which it is captured; the knower of yoga similarly crosses the worldly ocean by liberating himself from all worldly ties under the grace of perceptual practise of yoga.

यथा निर्वाणकाले तु दीपो दग्ध्वा लयं व्रजेत्। तथा सर्वाणि कर्माणि योगी दग्ध्वा लयं व्रजेत्॥ २३॥

As the cotton lace used in the lamp merges in the supreme light at the time of extinction, the master in yoga merges with the supreme element of soul and thus burns into ashes all his deeds in the blazing fire of yoga.

प्राणायामसुतीक्ष्णेन मात्राधारेण योगवित्। वैराग्योपलघृष्टेन छित्त्वा तं तु न बध्यते॥ २४॥

The razor made sharp by friction perpetually made through the exercise of Prāṇāyāma reciting Oṁ on the stone of detachment, the yogi cuts off all the worldly ties and thus he is never trapped in the worldly network.

अमृतत्वं समाप्नोति यदा कामात्प्रमुच्यते। सर्वैषणाविनिर्मुक्तश्छित्त्वा तन्तुं न बध्यते छित्त्वा तन्तुं न बध्यते। इत्युपनिषत्॥ २५॥

Having liberated from the desires, the yogi becomes blank of the passions and only then he attain to the immortality and further ties are cut away with by such yogi. This is the mystery of this Kṣurikopaniṣad.

ॐ सह नाववतु ....इति शान्तिः॥

॥इति क्षुरिकोपनिषत्समाप्ता॥

***

29. SARVASĀROPANIṢAD

सर्वसारोपनिषद्

।।शान्तिपाठः।।

ॐ सह नाववतु........ इति शान्तिः।।

[In the text, all the questions are given first and then the answers follow. But the following arrangement is adopted to facilitate reference.]

कथं बन्धः कथं मोक्षः का विद्या काऽविद्येति। जाग्रत्स्वप्नसुषुप्तितुरीयं च कथम्। अन्नमयप्राणमयमनोमयविज्ञानमयानन्दमयकोशाः कथम्। कर्ता जीवः पञ्चवर्गः क्षेत्रज्ञः साक्षी कूटस्थोऽन्तर्यामी कथम्। प्रत्यगात्मा माया चेति कथम्।।१।।

What is *Bandha* (bondage)?

Ātman [the Self] falsely superimposing the body and others which are non-Self upon Himself, and identifying Himself with them— this identification forms the bondage of the Self.

आत्मेश्वरजीवोऽनात्मनां देहादीनामात्मत्वेनाभिमन्यतेसोऽभिमान आत्मनो बन्धः तन्निवृत्तिर्मोक्षः।।२।।

What is *Mokṣa* [emancipation]?

The freedom from the [identification] is *Mokṣa.*

या तदभिमानं कारयति सा अविद्या। सोऽभिमानो यया निवर्तते सा विद्या।।३।।

What is *Avidyā* (Nescience)?

That which cause this identification— that indeed is *Avidyā.*

मन आदिचतुर्दशकरणैः पुष्कलैरादित्याद्यनुगृहीतैः शब्दादीन्विषयान्स्थूलान्यदोपलभते तदात्मनो जागरणम्। तद्वासनासहितैश्चतुर्दशकरणैः शब्दाद्याभावेऽपि वासनामयाञ्छब्दादीन्यदोपलभते तदात्मनःस्वप्नम्। चतुर्दशकरणोपरमाद्विशेषविज्ञानाभावाद्यदा शब्दादीन्नोपलभते तदात्मनः सुषुप्तम्। अवस्थात्रयभावाभावसाक्षी स्वयंभावरहितं नैरन्तर्यं चैतन्यं यदा तदा तुरीयं चैतन्यमित्युच्यते।।४।।

What is Vidyā (knowledge)?

That which removes this identification is Vidyā.

What are (meant by) the states of Jāgrata [the waking], Svapna [the dreaming], Suṣupti [the dreamless sleeping] and Turīya [the fourth]?

Jāgrata is that [state] during which Ātman enjoys the gross objects of senses as sound, etc., through the 14 organs as Manas, etc., having the sun and the rest as their presiding deities.

Svapna is that [state] during which Ātman experiences, through the 14 organs associated with the Vāsanās (affinities], of the waking condition, sound and other objects which are of the form of the Vāsanās created for the time being, even in the absence of [the gross] sound and the others. Ātman experiences Suṣupti when it does not experience sound and other objects of sense from the cessation of the functions of the 14 organs, there being no special enjoying consciousness on account of the absence of these organs.

Turīya is that state during which Ātman is a witness to the existence of the above-mentioned three states, though it is in itself without (their) existence and non-existence and during which it is one uninterrupted Caitanya (consciousness) alone. And that Caitanya is that which is connected with the three states, which is without the three states, and which is pure.

अन्नकार्याणां कोशानां समूहोऽन्नमयः कोश इत्युच्यते। प्राणादिचतुर्दशवायुभेदा अन्नमयकोशे यदा वर्तन्ते तदा प्राणमयः कोश इत्युच्यते। एतत्कोशद्वयसंसक्तं मनआदिचतुर्दशकरणैरात्मा शब्दादिविषयसंकल्पादीन्धर्मान्यदा करोति तदा मनोमयः कोश इत्युच्ये। एतत्कोशत्रयसंसक्तं तद्गतविशेषज्ञो यदा भासते तदा विज्ञानमयः कोश इत्युच्यते। एतत्कोशचतुष्टयं संसक्तं स्वकारणाज्ञाने वटकणिकायामिव वृक्षो यदा वर्तते तदानन्दमयः कोश इत्युच्यते॥५॥

What are the Annamaya, Prāṇamaya, Manomaya, Vijñānamaya and Ānandamaya Kośas (sheaths)?

Annamaya sheath is the aggregate of the materials formed by food. When the ten Vāyus (vital airs), Prāṇas and others, flow through the Annamaya sheath, then it is called the Prāṇamaya sheath. When Ātman connected with the above two sheaths performs the functions of hearing, etc., through the 14 organs of Manas and others, then it is called Manomaya Sheath.

When in the (Antaḥ-Karaṇa) internal organs connected with the above three sheaths, there arise the modifications of contemplation, meditation, etc., about the peculiarities of the sheaths, then it is called Vijñānamaya sheath.

When the self-cause Jñāna is in its self-bliss like the banyan tree in its seed, though associated with these four sheaths caused by Ajñāna, then it is called Ānandamaya sheath. Ātman which is associated with the upādhi [vehicle] of these sheaths is figuratively called Kośa.

सुखदुःखबुद्ध्या श्रेयोऽन्तः कर्ता यदा तदा इष्टविषये बुद्धिः सुखबुद्धिरनिष्टविषये बुद्धिर्दुःखबुद्धिः। शब्दस्पर्शरूपरसगन्धाः सुखदुःखहेतवः। पुण्यपापकर्मानुसारी भूत्वा प्राप्तशरीरसंयोगमप्राप्तशरीरसंयोगमिव कुर्वाणो यदा दृश्यते तदोपहितजीव इत्युच्यते॥६॥

मन आदिश्च प्राणादिश्चेच्छादिश्च सत्त्वादिश्च पुण्यादिश्चैते पञ्चवर्गाणां धर्मीभूतात्मज्ञानादृते न विनश्यत्यात्मसन्निधौ नित्यत्वेन प्रतीयमान आत्मोपाधिर्यस्तल्लिङ्गशरीरं हृद्ग्रन्थिरित्युच्यते॥७॥

What is meant by Kartā (actor), Jīva, Pañcavarga (the five groups], Kṣetrajña (the lord of the place), Sākṣi [the witness], Kūtastha and antaryāmin (the latent guide)?

Kartā (the actor) is the one who possesses the body and the internal organs through their respective desires proceeding from the idea of pleasure and pain. The idea of pleasure is that modification of the mind known as love. The idea of pain is that modification of the mind know as hate. The cause of pleasure and pain are sound, touch, form, taste and odour.

Jīva is that Adhyāsi [deluded one] that thinks that this body, which is obtained through the effects of good and bad Karmas, is one not so obtained.

Pañcavarga (the five groups) are (1) Manas, viz., Manas, Buddhi, Citta and Ahaṁkāra (creating uncertainly, certitude, flitting thought and egoism), (2) Prāṇa, i.e., Prāṇa. Apāna, Vyāna, Samāna and Udāna, (3) Sattva, i.e., Sattva, Rajas, and Tamas. (4) the [five] elements: earth, water, fire, Vāyu and Ākāśa and (5) Dharma and its opposite Adharma.

The original Avidyā which has the characteristics of the above 5 groups, which does not perish without Ātma-Jñāna, which appears eternal through the presence of Ātman and which is the vehicle for [the manifestation of] Ātmā, is the seed of the liṅga [subtle] body. It is also called Hṛdaya-granthi [the heart-knot].

तत्र यत्प्रकाशते चैतन्य स क्षेत्रज्ञ इत्युच्यते॥ ८॥

The Caitanya [consciousness] which is reflected and shines in it is Kṣetrajña.

ज्ञातृज्ञानज्ञेनयानामाविर्भावतिरोभावज्ञाता स्वयमाविर्भावतिरोभावरहित: स्वयंज्योति: साक्षीत्युच्यते॥ ९॥

Sākṣi [the witness] is that conscious one that is aware of the appearance and disappearance [of the three states] of the knower, the knowledge and the known, who is himself without [or not affected by] this appearance and disappearance, and who is self-radiant.

ब्रह्मादिपिपीलिकापर्यन्त सर्वप्राणिबुद्धिष्ववशिष्टतयोपलभ्यमान: सर्वप्राणिबुद्धिस्थो यदा तदा कूटस्थ इत्युच्यते॥ १०॥

Kūṭastha is he who is found without exception in the Buddhi of all creatures from Brahmā down to ants, and who is shining as Ātman and dwells as witness to the Buddhi of all creatures.

कूटस्थोपहितभेदानां स्वरूपलाभहेतुर्भूत्वा मणिगणे सूत्रमिव सर्वक्षेत्रेष्वनुस्यूतत्वेन यदा काश्यते आत्मा तदान्तर्यामीत्युच्यते॥ ११॥

Antaryāmin is the Ātman that shines as the Ordainer, being within all bodies like the thread [on which] beads [are strung] and serving to know the cause of the several differences of Kūṭastha and others associated with him.

सत्यं ज्ञानमनन्तमान्दं सर्वोपाधिविनिर्मुक्तं कटकमुकुटाद्युपाधिरहितसुवर्णघनवद्विज्ञानचिन्मात्रस्वभावात्मा यदा भासते तदा त्वंपदार्थ:प्रत्यगात्मेत्युच्यते।

Who is Pratyagātmā?

He is of the nature of truth, wisdom, eternity and bliss. He has no vehicles of body. He is abstract wisdom itself, like a mass of pure gold that is devoid of the changes of bracelet, crown, etc. He is of the nature of mere consciousness. He is that which shines as Caitanya and Brahman. When He is subject to the vehicle of Avidyā and is the meaning of the word "Tvam" ('Thou' in "Tattvamasi"), then He is Pratyagātmā.

सत्यं ज्ञानमनन्तं ब्रह्म। सत्यमविनाशि। अविनाशि नाम देशकालवस्तुनिमित्तेषु विनश्यत्सु यन्न विनश्यति तदविनाशि। ज्ञानं नामोत्पत्तिविनाशरहित नैरन्तर्य चैतन्यं ज्ञानमित्युच्यते।

अनन्तं नाम मृद्विकारेषु मृदिव स्वर्णविकारेषु स्वर्णमिव तन्तुविकारेषु तन्तुरिवाव्यक्तादिसृष्टिप्रपञ्चेषु पूर्ण व्यापकं चैतन्यमनन्तमित्युच्यते। आनन्दं नाम सुखचैतन्यस्वरूपोऽपरिमितानन्दसमुद्रोऽवशिष्टसुखस्वरूपश्चानन्द इत्युच्यते॥ १२॥

And what is Satya (the true)?

It is the Sat (Be-ness) which is the aim pointed out by the Vedas. It is that which cannot be said to be Asat (non-Be-ness). It is that which is not affected by the three periods of time. It is that which continues to exist during the three periods of time. It is one without a second. It has not the differences of similarity or dissimilarity; or it is that which is the source of all ideas. It is that which does not perish even though space, time, matter, cause, etc., perish.

And what is Jñāna (wisdom) ?

It is self-light. It is that which illuminates all. It is that Absolute Consciousness which is without any obscuration. It is that Consciousness which has no beginning or end, which is perpetual and which is the witness to all modifications and their opposites.

And what is Ananta (the eternal)?

It is that which is without origin and destruction. It is that which is not subject to the six changes (viz., birth, growth, manhood, decay, old age and death). It is free from all Upādhis. It is that Consciousness which, being all full and without destruction, permeates the created universe composed of Avyakta and others, like the earth in the modifications of clay, the gold in the modifications of gold and thread in the modifications of thread.

And what is Ānanda (bliss)?

It is the seat of all sentient beings, like the ocean of the water, is eternal, pure, partless and non-dual, and is the sole essence of Cidānanda (consciousness-bliss).

एतद्वस्तुचतुष्टयं यस्य लक्षणं देशकालवस्तुनिमित्तेष्वव्यभिचारी तत्पदार्थः परमात्मेत्युच्यते॥ १३॥

Who is Paramātmā?

It is He who is associated with truth, wisdom, eternity, bliss, omniscience, etc., who is subject to the vehicle of Māyā and who is the meaning of the word "Tat" (or 'That' in "Tattvamasi").

त्वंपदार्थादौपाधिकात्तत्पदार्थादौपाधिकभेदाद्विलक्षणमाकाशवत्सूक्ष्मं केवलं सत्तामात्रस्वभावं परं ब्रह्मेत्युच्यते॥ १४॥

What is *Brahman*?

Brahman is that which is free from all vehicles, which is the Absolute Consciousness devoid of particularities, which is Sat (Be-ness), which is without a second, which is bliss and which is Māyā-less. It is different from characteristics of that expressed by the word

"Tvam" (Thou) subject to Upādhis (vehicles), or the characteristics of 'That' expressed by the word "Tat" subject to Upādhis. It is itself differenceless and is seen as the Seat of everything. It is the pure, the numeral, the true and the indestructible.

माया नाम अनादिरन्तवती प्रमाणाऽप्रमाणसाधारणा न सती नासती न सदसती स्वयमधिका विकाररहिता निरूप्यमाणा सतीतरलक्षणशून्या सा मायेत्युच्यते। अज्ञानं तुच्छाप्यसती कालत्रयेऽपि पामराणां वास्तवी च सत्त्वबुद्धिर्लौकिकानामिदमित्यनिर्वचनीया वक्तुं न शक्यते॥ १५॥

नाहं भवाम्यहं देवो नेन्द्रियाणि दशैव तु। न बुद्धिर्न मनः शश्वन्नाहंकारस्तथैव च।

अप्राणो ह्यमनाः शुभ्रो बुद्ध्यादीनां हि सर्वदा। साक्ष्यहं सर्वदा नित्यश्चिन्मात्रोऽहं न संशयः।

नाहं कर्ता नैव भोक्ता प्रकृतेः साक्षिरूपकः। मत्सान्निध्यात्प्रवर्तन्ते देहाद्या अजडा अव।

स्थाणुर्नित्यः सदानन्दः शुद्धो ज्ञानमयोऽमलः। आत्माहं सर्वभूतानां विभुः साक्षी न संशयः॥ १६-१९॥

ब्रह्मैवाहं सर्ववेदान्तवेद्यं नाहं वेद्यं व्योमवातादिरूपम्।

रूपं नाहं नाम नाहं न कर्म ब्रह्मैवाहं सच्चिदानन्दरूपम्॥ २०॥

नाहं देहो जन्ममृत्यु कुतो मे नाहं प्राणः क्षुत्पिपासे कुतो मे।

नाहं चेतः शोकमोहौ कुतो मे नाहं कर्ता बन्धमोक्षौ कुतो मे इत्युपनिषत्॥ २१॥

What is Māyā ?

The root of this not-Ātman is Māyā. She appears in Brahman like clouds, etc., in the sky. She has no beginning but has an end. She is subject to proof and not-proof. She neither is; nor is not; nor is she a combination of both (Sat and Asat). Her seat is indescribable. She has the varieties of differences as extolled by the wise. It is she that truly is not. Her nature is Ajñāna. She appears as Mūlaprakṛti, Guṇa-Sāmya (a state where the three Guṇas are found in equilibrium), Avidyā (Nescience) and other forms, transforming herself into the form of the universe. Thus does a knower of Brahman cognize her.

Of how many kinds are substances?

There are three kinds, Sat (Bee-ness), Asat (not-Be-ness) and Mithyā (Illusion).

Sat alone is Brahman. Asat is that which is not. Mithyā is the illusory ascription to Brahman of the universe that is not.

What is fit to be known is Brahman, the Ātman alone.

Brahma-Jñāna is the rooting out of all— bodies and such like— that are not Self, and the merging in Brahman, the Sat. The universe of Ākāśa and others including Jīva is not-Ātman.

ॐ सह नाववतु.... इति शान्तिः॥

॥इति सर्वसारोपनिषत्समाप्ता॥

***

30. NIRĀLAMBA-UPANIṢAD

निरालम्बोपनिषद्

॥शान्तिपाठः॥

ॐ पूर्णमदः पूर्णमिदं....... इति शान्तिः॥

ॐ नमः शिवाय गुरवे सच्चिदानन्दमूर्तये। निष्प्रपञ्चाय शान्ताय निरालम्बाय तेजसे। निरालम्बं समाश्रित्य सालम्बं विजहाति यः। स संन्यासी च योगी च कैवल्यं पदमश्नुते॥१॥

एषामज्ञानजन्तूनां समस्तारिष्टशान्तये। यद्यद्बोद्धव्यमखिलं तदाशङ्क्य ब्रवीम्यम्॥२॥

किं ब्रह्म। क ईश्वरः। को जीवः। का प्रकृतिः। कः परमात्मा। को ब्रह्मा। को विष्णुः। को रुद्रः। क इन्द्रः। सः शमनः। कः सूर्य। कश्चन्द्र। के सुराः। के असुराः। के पिशाचाः। के मनुष्याः। काः स्त्रियः। के पश्वादयः। किं स्थावरम्। के ब्राह्मणादयः। का जातिः। किं कर्म। किमकर्म। किं ज्ञानम। किमज्ञानम्। किं सुखम्। किं दुखम्। कः स्वर्गः। को नरकः। को बन्धः को मोक्षः। क उपास्यः। कः शिष्यः। को विद्वान्। को मूढः। किमासुरम्। किं तपः। किं पदमं पदम्। किं ग्राह्यम्। किमग्राह्यम्। कः संन्यासीत्याशङ्क्याह ब्रह्मेति॥३॥

Oṁ. I shall relate in the form of a catechism whatever should be known for the removal of all miseries that befall on these ignorant creatures (men).

What is Brahman? Who is Īśvara? Who is Jīva? What is Prakṛti? Who is Paramātmā? Who is Brahmā? Who is Viṣṇu? Who is Rudra? Who is Indra? Who is Yama? Who is Sūrya? Who is Candra? Who are Devas? Who are Rākṣasas ? Who are Piśācas? Who are Manuṣyas? Who are Women? Who are Paśus, etc.? What is Sthāvara? Who are Brāhmaṇas and others? What is Jāti (caste)? What is Karma? What is Akarma? What is Jñāna? What is Ajñāna? What is Sukha? What is Duḥkha? What is Svarga? What is Naraka? What is Bandha? What is Mokṣa? Who is Upāsya? Who is Vidvān? Who is Mūḍha? What is Āsura? What is Tapas? What is Paramapada? What is Grāhya? What is Agrāhya? Who is Sannyāsi? Thus are the questions.

स होवाच महदहंकारपृथिव्यप्तेजोवाय्वाकाशत्वेन बृहद्रूपेणाण्डकोशेन कर्मज्ञानार्थरूपतया भासमानमद्वितीयमखिलोपादिविनिर्मुक्तं तत्सकलशक्त्युपबृंहितमनाद्यनन्तं शुद्धं शिवं शान्तं निर्गुणमित्यादिवाच्यमनिर्वाच्यं चैतन्यं ब्रह्म। ईश्वर इति च। ब्रह्मैव स्वशक्तिं प्रकृत्यभिधेयामाश्रित्य लोकान्सृष्ट्वा प्रविश्यान्तर्यामित्वेन ब्रह्मादीनां बुद्धीन्द्रियनियन्तृत्वादीश्वरः॥४॥

What is Brahman?

It is the Caitanya that appears, through the aspects of Karma and Jñāna, as this vast mundane egg composed of Mahat' Ahaṁkāra and the five elements, earth, water, fire, Vāyu and Ākāśa— that is secondless— that is devoid of all Upādhis [vehicles], that is full of all Śaktis [potencies], that is without beginning and end, that is described as pure, beneficial, peaceful, and Guṇa-less and that is indescribable.

Who is Īśvara? and what are His characteristics? Brahman itself, having through His Śakti called Prakṛti (matter) created the worlds and being latent in them, becomes the ruler of Buddhi and Indriyas (organs of sense and action) as well as Brahmā (the creator) and others, Hence he is named Īśvara.

जीव इति च ब्रह्मविष्णवीशानेन्द्रादीनां नामरूपद्वारा स्थूलोऽहमिति मिथ्याध्यासवशाज्जीवः। सोऽहमेकोऽपि देहारम्भकभेदवशाद्बहुजीवः॥५॥

Who is Jīva?

Īśvara Himself, subject to the false superimposition upon Himself [or the idea] "I am the gross" through the [assumption of the] names and forms of Brahmā, Viṣṇu, Rudra, Indra, and others is Jīvas. Though one, he appears as many Jīvas, through the force of the different Karmans originating in the bodies.

प्रकृतिरिति च ब्रह्मणः सकाशान्नानाविचित्रजगन्निर्माणसामर्थ्यबुद्धिरूपा ब्रह्मशक्तिरेव प्रकृतिः॥६॥

What is Prakṛti (matter)?

It is nothing else but the Śakti [potency] of Brahman which is of the nature of Buddhi that is able to produce the many motley worlds by virtue of the mere presence of Brahman.

परमात्मेति च देहादेः परतरत्वाद् ब्रह्मैव परमात्मा॥७॥

What is Paramātmā? The supreme Ātman or soul.

It is Brahman alone that is Paramātmā as it (the former) is far superior to bodies and others.

स ब्रह्मा स विष्णुः स इन्द्रः स शमनः स सूर्यः स चन्द्रस्ते असुरास्ते पिशाचास्ते मनुष्यास्ताः स्त्रियते पश्वादयस्तत्स्थावरं ते ब्राह्मणादयः॥८॥

That *Brahman* is Brahmā, Viṣṇu, Rudra and Indra, Yama, Sun and Moon, Devas, Asuras, Piśācas, men, women, beasts, etc., the fixed ones, Brāhmaṇas and others. Here there is no manyness in the least degree: all this is verily *Brahman.*

सर्वं खल्विदं ब्रह्म नेह नानास्ति किंचन॥९॥

जातिरिति च। न चर्मणो न रक्तस्य न मांसस्य न चास्थिनः।

न जातिरात्मनो जातिर्व्यवहारप्रकल्पिता॥१०॥

कर्मेति च क्रियमाणेन्द्रियैः कर्माण्यहं करोमीत्यध्यात्मनिष्ठतया कृतं कर्मैव कर्म। अकर्मेति च कर्तुव्यभोक्तृत्वाद्यंकारतया बन्धरूपं जन्मादिकारणं नित्यनैमित्तिकयागव्रततपोदानादिषु फलाभिसंधानं यत्तदकर्म॥११-१२॥

It cannot refer to the skin, the blood, the flesh or the bone. There is no caste for Ātmā; caste is only conventional.

What is Karma?

Karma is that action alone which is performed by the organs and ascribed to Ātmā; as "I do" (viz., agency being attributed to Ātmā).

What is Akarma [or non-Karma]?

Akarma is the performance, without any desire for the fruits, of the daily and occasional rites, sacrifices, vows, austerities, gifts and other actions that are associated with the egoism of the actor and the enjoyer, and that are productive of bondage, rebirth, etc.

ज्ञानमिति देहेन्द्रिनिग्रहसद्‌गुरूपासनश्रवणमनननिदिध्यासनैर्यद्यद्‌दृग्दृश्यस्वरूपं सर्वान्तरस्थं सर्वसमं घटपचादिपदार्थमिवाविकारं विकारेषु चैतन्यं विना किंचिन्नास्तीति साक्षात्कारानुभवो ज्ञानम्।।१३।।

What is Jñāna?

It is the realisation by direct cognition of the fact that in this changing universe there is nothing but Caitanya [the one life] that is Consciousness, that is of the form of the seer and the seen, pervading all things, that is the same in all, and that is not subject to changes like pot, cloth, etc. This realisation is brought about by means of the subjugation of the body and the senses, the serving of a good Guru (teacher), the hearing of the exposition of Vedānta doctrines and constant meditation thereon.

अज्ञानमिति च रज्जौ सर्पभ्रान्तिरिवाद्वितीये सर्वानुस्यूते सर्वमये ब्रह्मणि देवतिर्यङ्नस्थावरस्त्रीपुरुषवर्णाश्रम- बन्धमोक्षोपाधिनानात्मभेदकल्पितं ज्ञानमज्ञानम्।।१४।।

What is Ajñāna?

It is the illusory attribution, like the snake in the rope, of many Ātmās (souls) through the diverse Upādhis [or vehicles] of the angels, beasts, men, the fixed ones, females, males, castes and orders of life, bondage and emancipation, etc., to Brahman that is secondless, all-permeating and of the nature of all.

सुखमिति च सच्चिदानन्दस्वरूपं ज्ञात्वानन्दरूपा या स्थितिः सैव सुखम्।।१५।।

दुःखमिति अनात्मरूपो विषयसंकल्प एव दुःखम्।।१६।।

स्वर्ग इति च सत्संसर्गः स्वर्गः। नरक इति च असत्संसारविषयजनसंसर्ग एव नरकः।।१७।।

बन्ध इति च अनाद्यविद्यावासनया जातोऽहमित्यादिसंकल्पो बन्धः।।१८।।

पितृमातृसहोदरदारापत्यगृहरामक्षेत्रममतासंसारावरणसङ्कल्पो बन्धः।।१९।।

What is Sukha (happiness)?

It is a state of being of the nature of bliss, having cognized through experience the Reality of Saccidānanda [or that which is be-ness, consciousness and bliss].

What is Duḥkha (pains)?

It is the mere Saṅkalpa [or the thinking] of the objects of mundane existence [or of not-Self].

What is Svarga (heaven)?

It is the association with Sat [either good men or Brahman which is Sat, the true].

What is Naraka (hell)?

It is association with that which brings about this mundane existence which is Asat [the false].

कर्तृत्वाद्यहंकारसंकल्पो बन्धः॥२०॥

अणिमाद्यष्टैश्वर्याशासिद्धसंकल्पो बन्धः॥२१॥

देवमनुष्याद्युपासनाकामसंकल्पो बन्धः॥२२॥

यमाद्यष्टाङ्गयोगसंकल्पो बन्धः॥२३॥

वर्णाश्रमधर्मकर्मसंकल्पो बन्धः॥२४॥

आज्ञाभयसंशयात्मगुणसंकल्पो बन्धः॥२५॥

यागव्रततपोदानविधिविधानज्ञानसंकल्पो बन्ध॥२६॥

केवलमोक्षापेक्षासंकल्पो बन्धः॥२७॥

संकल्पमात्रसंभवो बन्धः॥२८॥

What is Bandha [bondage]?

Such Saṅkalpas [thoughts] as "I was born," etc., arising from the affinities of beginningless ajñāna form bondage.

The thought obscuration [or mental ignorance] of the mundane existence of "mine" in such as father, mother, brother, wife, child, house, gardens, lands, etc., are bondages.

The thought of I-ness as actor, etc., are bondage.

The thought of the development in oneself of the eight siddhis (higher psychical powers) as Aṇimā and others is bondage.

The thought of propitiating the angels, men, etc., is bondage.

The thought of going through the eight means of Yoga practice, Yama, etc., is bondage.

The thought of performing the duties of one's own caste and orders of life is bondage.

The thought that command, fear and doubt are the attributes of [or pertain to] Ātman is bondage.

The thought of knowing the rules of performing sacrifices, vows, austerity and gift is bondage. Even the mere thought of desire for Mokṣa (emancipation) is bondage. By the very act of thought, bondage is caused.

मोक्ष इति च नित्यानित्यवस्तुविचारादनित्यसंसारसुखदुःखविषयसमस्तक्षेत्र ममताबन्धक्षयो मोक्षः॥२९॥

What is Mokṣa [emancipation]?

Mokṣa is the (state of) the annihilation, through the discrimination of the eternal from the non-eternal, of all thoughts of bondage, like those of "mine" in objects of pleasure and pain, lands, etc., in this transitory mundane existence.

उपास्य इति च सर्वशरीरस्थचैतन्यब्रह्मप्रापको गुरुरुपास्य॥३०॥

Who is Upāsya [or fit to be worshipped]?

That Guru (or spiritual instructor) who enables (the disciple) to attain to Brahman, the Consciousness that is in all bodies.

शिष्य इति च विद्याध्वस्तप्रपञ्चावगाहितज्ञानावशिष्टं ब्रह्मैव शिष्यः॥३१॥

Who is Śiṣya (the disciple)?

The disciple is that brahman alone that remains after the consciousness of the universe has been lost (in him) through Brāhmic wisdom.

विद्वानिति च सर्वान्तरस्थस्वसंविद्रूपविद्विद्वान्॥३२॥

Who is Vidvān (the learned)?

It is he who has cognized the true form (or reality) of his own consciousness that is latent in all.

मूढ इति च कर्तृत्वाद्यहंकारभावारूढो मूढः॥३३॥

Who is Mūḍha [the ignorant]?

He who has the egoistic conception of the body, caste, orders of life, actor, enjoyer and others.

आसुरमिति च ब्रह्मविष्णवीशानेन्द्रादीनामैश्वर्यकामनया निरशनजपाग्निहोत्रादिष्वन्तरात्मानं संतापयति चात्युग्ररागद्वेष-विहिंसादम्भाद्यपेक्षितं तप आसुरम्॥३४॥

What is Āsura [the demoniacal]?

It is the Tapas [austerity] practised by one inflicting trouble on the Ātman within through Japa (or inaudible muttering of Mantras], abstinence from food, Agnihotra [the performance of the worship of fire], etc., attended with cruel desire, hatred, pain, hypocrisy and the rest for the purpose of acquiring the powers of Viṣṇu, Brahmā, Rudra, Indra and others.

तप इति च ब्रह्म सत्यं जगन्मिथ्येत्यपरोक्षज्ञानाग्निना। ब्रह्माद्यैश्वर्याशासिद्धसङ्कल्पबीजसन्तापं तपः॥३५॥

What is Tapas?

Tapas is the act of burning— through the fire of direct cognition of the knowledge that Brahman is the truth and the universe, a myth— the seed of the deep-rooted desire to attain the powers of Brahmā, etc.

परमं पदमिति च प्राणेन्द्रियाद्यन्तः करुणगुणादेः। परतरं सच्चिदानन्दमयं नित्युमुक्तब्रह्मस्थानं परमं पदम्॥३६॥

What is Paramapada [the supreme abode]?

It is the seat of the eternal and emancipated brahman which is far superior to Prāṇas (the vital airs), the organs of sense and actions, the internal organs (of thought), the Guṇas and others, which is of the nature of Saccidānanda and which is the witness to all.

ग्राह्यमिति च देशकालवस्तुपरिच्छेदराहित्यचिन्मात्रस्वरूपं ग्राह्यम्॥३७॥

What is *Grāhya* [or fit to be taken in]?

Only that Reality of Absolute Consciousness which is not conditioned by space, time or substance.

अग्राह्यमिति च स्वस्वरूपव्यतिरिक्तमायामयबुद्धीन्द्रियगोचरजगत्सत्यत्वचिन्तनमग्राह्यम्॥३८॥

What is Agrāhya?

The thought that this universe is truth— this universe which is different from one's Self and which being subject to Māyā (or illusion) forms the object of (cognition of) Buddhi and the organs.

संन्यासीति च सर्वधर्मान्परित्यज्य निर्ममो निरहंकारो भूत्वा ब्रह्मेष्टं शरणमुपगम्य तत्त्वमसि अहं ब्रह्मास्मि सर्वं खल्विदं ब्रह्म नेह नानास्ति किंचनेत्यादिमहावाक्यार्थानुभवज्ञानाद् ब्रह्मैवाहमस्मीति निश्चित्य निर्विकल्पसमाधिना स्वतन्त्रो यतिश्चरति स संन्यासी स मुक्तः स पूज्यः स योगी स परमहंसः सोऽवधूतः स ब्राह्मण इति॥३९॥

Who is the Sannyāsī [ascetic]?

A Sannyāsī is an ascetic who having given up all the duties of caste and orders of life, good and bad actions, etc., being freed from [the conception of] "I" and "mine" and having taken his refuge in Brahman alone, roams at large practising Nirvikalpa Samādhi and being firmly convinced of "I am Brahman" through the realisation of the meaning of such sacred (Vedic) sentences as "Thou are That" "All this is verily Brahman" and "Here there is no manyness in the least". He only is an emancipated person. He only is fit to be adored. He only is a Yogin. He only a Paramahaṁsa. He only is an Avadhūta. He only is a Brahman.

इदं निरालम्बोपनिषदं योऽधीते गुर्वनुग्रहतः सोऽग्निपूतो भवति स वायुपूतो भवति न स पुनरावर्तते न स पुनरावर्तते पुनर्नाभिजायते पुनर्नाभिजायत इत्युपनिषत्॥४०॥

Whoever studies the Nirālamba-Upaniṣad becomes, through the grace of Guru, pure like fire. He becomes pure like Vāyu (air). He does not return. He is not born again: may he is not born again.

ॐ पूर्णमदः पूर्णमिदं... इति शान्तिः॥

॥निरालम्बोपनिषद् समाप्त॥

***

31. ŚUKARAHASYOPANIṢAD

शुकरहस्योपनिषद्

ॐ सह नाववतु.... इति शान्तिः।।

This Upaniṣad is under the Kṛṣṇa Yajurveda. Lord Śiva has preached the Ṛṣi Śukadeva in pursuance with the request made by the great hermit Vyāsa in this Upaniṣad. The Ṛṣi Śukadeva brought forward his curiosity to know with classification of the Brahma in six parts before Lord Śiva in which four gigantic sentences– (i) 'Oṁ Prajñanam Brahma', (ii) Oṁ Aham Brahmāsmi, (iii) Oṁ Tattvamasi and (iv) Oṁ Ayamātmā Brahma were asked. In its third part, these four sentences have been explained broadly and with splitting up the feet joined to make a sentence. In the last part of it, it has been described that the Ṛṣi Śukadeva was known to integration of his sensitivity with all living and dead matters of this universe by virtue of attaining this knowledge.

अथातो रहस्योपनिषदं व्याख्यास्यामः।।१।।

Now, the Rahasyopaniṣad is described.

देवर्षयो ब्रह्माणं संपूज्य प्रणिपत्य पप्रच्छुर्भगवन्नस्माकं रहस्योपनिषद् ब्रूहीति।।२।।

Once the great hermits in heaven worshipped lord Brahmā and after formal salutation, they requested him to preach on Rahasyopaniṣad.

सोऽब्रवीत्–पुरा व्यासो महातेजाः सर्ववेदः तपोनिधिः। प्रणिपत्य शिवं साम्बं कृताञ्जलिरुवाच।।३।।

Lord Brahmā replied that in ancient times, the great Ṛṣi Vedavyāsa had classified all Vedas. He once went to lord Śiva and offered his keen obeisance to him with the following requests.

श्रीवेदव्यास उवाच– देवदेव महाप्राज्ञ पाशच्छेददृढव्रत। शुकस्य मम पुत्रस्य वेदसंस्कारकर्मणि।।४।।

ब्रह्मोपदेशकालोऽयमिदानीं समुपस्थितः। ब्रह्मोपदेशः कर्त्तव्यो भवताद्य जगद्गुरो।।५।।

Saint Vedavyāsa requested that "O the king of gods! Supreme Lord! Remover of all hurdles occurring due to worldly bounds! O a great resolution maker! Now the time has come to preach my son Śukadeva, the hymns of Gāyatrī and the syllable Oṁ in the ceremony of study on Veda. O the teacher of this universe! Please accept my invitation to preach him all these hymns.

ईश्वर उवाच-मयोपदिष्टे कैवल्ये साक्षाद्ब्रह्मणि शाश्वते। विहाय पुत्रो निर्वेदात्प्रकाशं यास्यति स्वयम्।।६।।

Lord Śiva said– "O great saint! Your son will renounce everything and will attain the light within him which will detach him from the pleasure of this material world if I preach him the knowledge of everlasting Brahma."

श्री वेदव्यास उवाच यथा तथा वा भवतु ह्युपनयनकर्मणि। उपदिष्टे मम सुते ब्रह्मणि त्वत्प्रसादतः।।७।।

Śrī Vedavyāsa requested– "Whatever be its result but I humbly request you to preach him the knowledge of Brahma in this opportuned time when a ceremony is hasted."

सर्वज्ञो भवतु क्षिप्रं मम पुत्रो महेश्वर। तव प्रसादसंपन्नो लभेन्मुक्तिं चतुर्विधाम्॥८॥

"O lord of this universe! I wish my son be learnt to all knowledge and could be able to obtain the emancipation through the four ways *i.e.* co-ordination, proximation, integration and absolute merge under your kind grace."

तच्छुत्वा व्यासवचनं सर्वदेवर्षिसंसदि। उपदेष्टुं स्थितः शम्भुः साम्बो दिव्यासने मुदा॥९॥

Lord Śiva accepted to the pray of Saint Vedavyāsa and visited to the assembly of the saints with goddess Umā with an intention to preach his son. Thus, he merrily enshrined on a divine seat.

कृतकृत्यः शुकस्तत्र समागत्य सुभक्तिमान्। तस्मात् स प्रणवं लब्ध्वा पुनरित्यब्रवीच्छिवम्॥१०॥

The Ṛṣi Śukadeva was thus fructified in company of lord Śiva while attending his preaching with keen devotion. Having obtained the consecration of Praṇava (Oṁ), he further prayed to lord Śiva.

श्रीशुक उवाच–

देवादिदेव सर्वज्ञ सच्चिदानन्दलक्षण। उमारमण भूतेश प्रसीद करुणानिधे॥११॥

The Ṛṣi Śukadeva requested– "O the prime adorable god! O omnipresent! O endower with real pleasure! O the husband of goddess Umā! Have mercy on me because you are the treasure of kindness for all living-organisms.

उपदिष्टं परंब्रह्म प्रणवान्तर्गतं परम्। तत्त्वमस्यादिवाक्यानां प्रज्ञादीनां विशेषतः॥१२॥

श्रोतुमिच्छामि तत्त्वेन षडङ्गानि यथाक्रमम्। वक्तव्यानि रहस्यानि कृपयाद्य सदाशिव॥१३॥

"You have preached me all about the syllable Oṁ and the perfect Brahma beyond it but I am curious to listen systematically about the element of gigantic sentences like 'Tattvamasi', 'Prajñānam Brahma' etc. duly classified in six parts. O God of welfare! Kindly disclose the secret hidden within these gigantic sentences.

श्रीसदाशिव उवाच–

साधु साधु महाप्राज्ञ शुक ज्ञाननिधे मुने। प्रष्टव्यं तु त्वया पृष्टं रहस्यं वेदगर्भितम्॥१४॥

Lord Śiva replied– "O most learned Śukadeva! You definitely are possessor of outstanding knowledge. You have asked about the practical form of the cryptic mysteries."

रहस्योपनिषन्नाम्ना सषडङ्गमिहोच्यते। यस्य विज्ञानमात्रेण मोक्षः साक्षान्न संशयः॥१५॥

"I, therefore, describe this cryptic subject of Rahasyopaniṣad duly classifying it in six parts. On attaining this specific knowledge, no scope for the doubt is left for availing salvation."

अङ्गहीनानि वाक्यानि गुरुर्नोपदिशेत्पुनः। सषडङ्गान्युपदिशेन्महावाक्यानि कृत्स्नशः॥१६॥

It is an appropriate fact to say that a teacher should not teach the sentences without classifying them in parts and all gigantic sentences should be explained with their six parts.

चतुर्णामपि वेदानां यथोपनिषद: शिर:। इयं रहस्योपनिषदत्तथोपनिषदां शिर:॥१७॥

As Upaniṣads are the supreme among the four Vedas, Rahasyopaniṣad is the supreme among all the upaniṣads.

रहस्योपनिषद्ब्रह्म ध्यातं येन विपश्चिता। तीर्थैर्मन्त्रै: श्रुतैर्जप्यैस्तस्य किं पुण्यहेतुभि:॥१८॥

The metaphysician who have gone in depth on the Brahma as described in this Rahasyopaniṣad, he needn't to go on pilgrimage to recite mantras, to study on Vedas and even to do Japa (silent recital) etc. causes.

वाक्यार्थस्य विचारेण यदाप्नोति शरच्छतम्। एकवारजपेनैव ऋष्यादिध्यानतश्च यत्॥१९॥

The fruit which is obtained as a result of deliberating on the meanings to gigantic sentences last upto hundred pleasant seasons *i.e.* years, the same can be obtained only with a silent recital including recollection of the saints etc. of these sentences.

ॐ अस्य श्रीमहावाक्यमहामन्त्रस्य हंस ऋषि:। अव्यक्तगायत्री छन्द:। परमहंसो देवता। हं बीजम्। स: शक्ति:। सोऽहं कीलकम्। मम परमहंसप्रीत्यर्थे महावाक्यजपे विनियोग:। सत्यं ज्ञानमनन्तं ब्रह्म अङ्गुष्ठाभ्यां नम:। नित्यानन्दो ब्रह्म तर्जनीभ्यां स्वाहा। नित्यानन्दमयं ब्रह्म मध्यमाभ्यां वषट्। यो वै भूमा अनामिकाभ्यां हुम्। यो वै भूमाधिपति: कनिष्ठिकाभ्यां वौषट्। एकमेवाद्वितीयं ब्रह्म करतलकरपृष्ठाभ्यां फट्। सत्यं ज्ञानमनन्तं ब्रह्म हृदयाय नम:। नित्यानन्दो ब्रह्म शिरसे स्वाहा। नित्यानन्दमयं ब्रह्म शिखायै वषट्। यो वै भूमा कवचाय हुम्। यो वै भूमाधिपति: नेत्रत्रयाय वौषट्। एकमेवाद्वितीयं ब्रह्म अस्त्राय फट्। भूर्भुव:सुवरोमिति दिग्बन्ध:॥२०॥

The Ṛṣi to the great hymn of Oṁ gigantic sentence is Haṁsa, indescribable is the rhyme of 'Gāyatrī', Paramahaṁsa is the god, 'Haṁ' is the root hymn, 'Saḥ' is the power and 'So'haṁ Kīlaka. 'Viniyoga' (keep attention) is made by me for recital of the gigantic sentence with a view to please the god 'Paramahaṁsa'. For 'Kara-nyāsa' (summation of hymn power to the hands) the Brahma is truth, full of knowledge and limitless. Salutation is made to him. The touch of thumb endows with the everlasting pleasure, it is saluted and a touch should be made to the index finger. The Brahma is always source of pleasure it is saluted (touch to the little finger). Brahma is one and unique it is saluted (touch the palm and the back part of the palm). The Brahma is truth, full of knowledge and infinite– it is saluted (touch the heart (chest)). The Brahma is the source of everlasting pleasure it is saluted (touch the head). Brahma is always pleasing it is saluted (touch the braid). The Brahma is all extended it is saluted (touch left and the right shoulders). The administrator of the wide-extended is Brahma it is saluted (touch both eyes). The Brahma is one and unique it is saluted (move the right hand over the head and then clap on the left hand). Oṁ (the perfect Brahma) is embedded within Bhūḥ (the earth), Bhuvaḥ (the space) and Svaḥ (the world of sun) it is saluted (a provision of safety from all directions).

ध्यानम्–

नित्यानन्दं परमसुखदं केवलं ज्ञानमूर्तिं द्वन्द्वातीतं गगनसदृशं तत्त्वमस्यादिलक्ष्यम्।

एकं नित्यं विमलमचलं सर्वधीसाक्षिभूतं भावातीतं त्रिगुणरहितं सद्गुरुं तं नमामि॥२१॥

Meditation– We salute to the great teacher who always is the source of pleasure, endower of the supreme gaiety, the image of the knowledge himself, who is beyond the material vicissitudes, un-biased like the wide ether and whose aim always is to attain the element of supreme soul. Further, who is one, immortal, always sacrosanct, undivided, enshrining on the wit of all, witness to all living-organisms free from the attachments and untouched by the greed, affection, ego etc. common properties.

अथ महावाक्यानि चत्वारि। यथा ॐ प्रज्ञानं ब्रह्म॥१॥ ॐ अहं ब्रह्मास्मि॥ ॐ तत्त्वमसि॥३॥ ॐ अयमात्मा ब्रह्म॥४॥ तत्त्वमसीत्यभेदवाचकमिदं ये जपन्ति ते शिवसायुज्यमुक्तिभाजो भवन्ति॥२२॥

Now four gigantic sentences are given. The first sentence is 'Oṁ Prajñānam Brahma' (outstanding knowledge is Brahma). The second sentence is 'Oṁ Aham Brahmāsmi' (I am the Brahma). The third is 'Oṁ Tattvamasi' (you are that Brahma) and the fourth sentence is 'Oṁ Ayamātmā Brahma' (this soul is Brahma). Out of these sentences, the 'Tattvamasi' lays down the integration or inspiration from the Brahma. The devotee thinking and considering upon this sentence, receive the fruit of salvation (physical) of lord Śiva.

[In the successive hymns, the foot 'Tat' as used with 'Oṁ Tattvamasi' is given with its meditation through six parts alongwith meditation including 'Digbandḥ' (safety from all directions) has been described.]

तत्पदमहामन्त्रस्य। हंस ऋषिः। अव्यक्तगायत्री छन्दः। परमहंसो देवता। हं बीजम्। सः शक्तिः। सोऽहं कीलकम्। मम सायुज्यमुक्त्यर्थे जपे विनियोगः तत्पुरुषाय अङ्गुष्ठाभ्यां नमः। ईशानाय तर्जनीभ्यां स्वाहा। अघोराय मध्यमाभ्यां वषट्। सद्योजाताय अनामिकाभ्यां हुम्। वामदेवाय कनिष्ठिकाभ्यां वौषट्। तत्पुरुषेशानाघोरसद्योजातवामदेवेभ्यो नमः करतलकरपृष्ठाभ्यां फट्। एवं हृदयादिन्यासः। भूर्भुवः सुवरोमिति दिग्बन्धः॥२३॥

(The Nyāsa should be made as) By touching the thumb, it is recited that we salute to 'Tat Puruṣa', by touching the index finger– salute to 'Īśāna', by touching the middle finger salute to 'Aghora', by touching the ring finger– salute to 'Sadyojāta' (that automatically takes birth), by touching the little finger– salute to Vāmadeva should be recited. Thereafter both palms should touch one another, face and back both sides with a recital that salute to Īśāna, Aghora, Sadyojāta and Vāmadeva. Similarly, the Nyāsa (common to gods to enshrine on limbs of the body) for the heart etc. limbs should be made with a recital we salute to Oṁ (the supreme soul), 'Bhūḥ' (the earth), 'Bhuvaḥ' (the space) and 'Svaḥ' (the world of sun). Similarly, a defensive provision from all directions should be made.

ध्यानम्–

ज्ञानं ज्ञेयं ज्ञानगम्यादतीतं शुद्धं बुद्धं मुक्तमप्यव्ययं च।
सत्यं ज्ञानं सच्चिदानन्दरूपं ध्यायेदेवं तन्महो भ्राजमानम्॥२४॥

(Now one should meditate with the recital of) We should bring in our attention that god of a great splendour who is knowledge in himself, worth to know and who is beyond access of the knowledge itself. He is in the form of wit, most sacred, liberate and immortal. He only is worth meditation in the form of truth, knowledge and the real pleasure.

[In the successive hymns, the detail regarding meditation on the gigantic sentence 'Oṁ Tattvamasi' including its spell in six organs of the body particularly of the foot 'Tvam' and defensive provision for all directions has been described.]

त्वंपदमहामन्त्रस्य विष्णुर्ऋषिः। गायत्रीछन्दः। परमात्मा देवता। ऐं बीजम्। क्लीं शक्ति। सौः कीलकम्। मम मुक्त्यर्थे जपे विनियोगः। वासुदेवाय अङ्गुष्ठाभ्यां नमः। संकर्षणाय तर्जनीभ्यां स्वाहा। प्रद्युम्नाय मध्यमाभ्यां वषट्। अनिरुद्धाय अनामिकाभ्यां हुम्। वासुदेवाय कनिष्ठिकाभ्यां वौषट्। वासुदेवसंकर्षणप्रद्युम्नानिरुद्धेभ्यः करतलकरपृष्ठाभ्यां फट्। एवं हृदयादिन्यासः। भूर्भुवः सुवरोमिति दिग्बन्धः॥२५॥

Herein the Ṛṣi to the foot 'Tvam' of the great hymn is lord Viṣṇu, the rhyme is 'Gāyatrī', the god is the supreme soul, the seed (nuclei) is 'Aeṁ', the power is 'Klīṁ', 'Kīlaka' is 'Sauḥ'. The 'Viniyoga' (meditation of 'Japa' (silent recital) is for the salvation. The hands are spelled as salutation to Vāsudeva (touch the thumb), salutation to 'Saṅkarṣaṇa' (touch the index finger), salutation to 'Pradyumna' (touch the middle finger), salutation to 'Anirudha' (touch the ring finger), salutation to Vāsudeva (touch the little finger) and salutation to 'Vāsudeva', 'Saṅkarṣaṇa', 'Pradyumna' and 'Anirudha' (touch the palm up and down side). Similarly, spell to heart etc. organs is made. The recital for defence of all directions is 'Bhūr Bhuvaḥ Svaḥ Oṁ'.

ध्यानम्–

जीवत्वं सर्वभूतानां सर्वत्राखण्डविग्रहम्। चित्ताहंकारयन्तारं जीवाख्यं त्वं पदं भजे॥२६॥

We meditate on the foot 'Tvam' (under 'Tattvamasi') in the form of all living-organisms, spiritually considering you as the breathing essence in all living-organisms and you are integral part in the form of diversity and you control our impulses as our ego both.

[In the successive hymn, the foot 'Asi' in the great hymn of 'Oṁ Tattvamasi' has been described with the six way meditation and defensive provision for all directions.]

असिपदमहामन्त्रस्य मन ऋषिः। गायत्री छन्दः। अर्धनारीश्वरो देवता। अव्यक्तादिर्बीजम्। नृसिंहः शक्तिः। परमात्मा कीलकम्। जीवब्रह्मैक्यार्थे जपे विनियोगः। पृथ्वीद्व्यणुकाय अङ्गुष्ठाभ्यां नमः। अब्द्व्यणुकाय तर्जनीभ्यां स्वाहा। तेजोद्व्यणुकाय मध्यमाभ्यां वषट्। वायुद्व्यणुकाय अनामिकाभ्यां हुम्। आकाशद्व्यणुकाय कनिष्ठिकाभ्यां वौषट्। पृथिव्यप्तेजोवाय्वाकाशद्व्यणुकेभ्यः करतलकरपृष्ठाभ्यां फट्। एवं हृदयादि न्यासः भूर्भुवः सुवरोमिति दिग्बन्धः॥२७॥

The Ṛṣi to 'Asi' word of the great hymn is the mind, the rhyme is 'Gāyatrī', the god is 'Ardhanārīśvara', the seed (nuclei) is the undescribable etc. the power is 'Nṛsiṁha' and Kīlaka is the supreme soul. For the unity of 'Jīva Brahma', the following meditation in

'Japa' is prescribed– salutation to the double molecular earth (touch the thumb), salutation to the double molecular water (touch the index finger), salutation to the double molecular fire (touch the middle finger), salutation to the double molecular wind (touch the ring finger), salutation to the double molecular ether (touch the little finger), and salutation to the double molecular of earth, water, fire, wind and ether (touch the palm up and down side). Similarly, the manner to spell the heart etc. organs is prescribed. For defence of all directions, the recitals is 'Bhūr Bhuvaḥ Svaḥ . . . .Oṁ'.

ध्यानम्–

जीवो ब्रह्मेति वाक्यार्थं यावदस्ति मनःस्थितिः। ऐक्यं तत्त्वं लये कुर्वन्ध्यायेदसिपदं सदा॥२८॥

The person becomes able to integrate the element (the five elements merge in an integral Brahma on death) who gets concentration on this gigantic sentence which is meant by the living-organisms too is Brahma and ponders over its word 'Asi' always.

एवं महावाक्यषडङ्गान्युक्तानि॥२९॥

Thus the six way classification of gigantic sentences has been made.

अथ रहस्योपनिषद्विभागशो वाक्यार्थश्लोकाः प्रोच्यन्ते॥३०॥

Now the hymns enabling to understand the meaning of these sentences in 'Rahasyopaniṣad' is explained.

येनेक्षते शृणोतीदं जिघ्रति व्याकरोति च। स्वाद्वस्वादु विजानाति तत्प्रज्ञानमुदीरितम्॥३१॥

The sensitivity enabling the living-organisms to see, to hear, to smell, to express and to taste is called perception.

चतुर्मुखेन्द्रदेवेषु मनुष्याश्वगवादिषु चैतन्यमेकं ब्रह्मातः प्रज्ञानं ब्रह्म मय्यपि॥३२॥

The Brahma of perception vested with the four headed Brahma, lord Indra, all gods, the man, the horse, the cow etc. animals and all other living-organisms is also vested with me.

परिपूर्णः परात्मास्मिन्देहे विद्याधिकारिणि। बुद्धेः साक्षितया स्थित्वा स्फुरन्नहमितीर्यते॥३३॥

Ours body is entitled to acquire the perfect learning of Brahma. The wit of supreme soul as existed in the form of witness, is called ego when it is our burst.

स्वतः पूर्णः परात्मात्र ब्रह्मशब्देन वर्णितः। अस्मीत्यैक्यपरामर्शस्तेन ब्रह्म भवाम्यहम्॥३४॥

The supreme soul as perfectly and automatically established has been described herein with the application of the word 'Brahma'. The word 'Asmī' indicates the unity established between the Brahma and the living-organisms. Thus the meaning purported to is 'I myself is the Brahma.'

एकमेवाद्वितीयं सन्नामरूपविवर्जितम्। सृष्टेः पुराधुनाप्यस्य तादृक्त्वं तदितीर्यते॥३५॥
श्रोतुर्देहेन्द्रियातीतं वस्त्वत्र त्वंपदेरितम्। एकता ग्राह्यतेऽसीते तदैक्यमनुभूयताम्॥३६॥

The Brahma is the same existed even today as it was before the creation, an absolute, without any name and the complexion, single and real and unique. That Brahma is described in the foot of 'Tattvamasi' *i.e.* 'Tat'. The element of soul, beyond the body and the senses as existed within the disciple listening to the preachings from his teacher has been described here by the foot 'Tvam'. The connotation of the feet 'Tat' and 'Tvam' of the foot 'Asi' should be perceived as an integration of the Brahma and the element of soul.

स्वप्रकाशापरोक्षत्वमयमित्युक्तितो मतम्। अहंकारादिदेहान्तं प्रत्यगात्मेति गीयते॥३७॥

The element auto-luminated beyond the apparent body under 'Ayamātmā Brahma' (the Brahma within this soul) has been led down by the foot 'Ayam'. From ego to the body has been considered as 'Pratyagātmā' (the physical soul).

दृश्यमानस्य सर्वस्य जगतस्तत्त्वमीर्यते। ब्रह्मशब्देन तद्ब्रह्म स्वप्रकाशात्मरूपकम्॥३८॥

The element embedded with this whole apparent world is described with the word 'Brahma'. That Brahma is dwelling in the heart of all living-beings in the garb of their soul.

अनात्मदृष्टेरविवेकनिद्रामहं मम स्वप्नगतिं गतोऽहम्।
स्वरूपसूर्येऽभ्युदिते स्फुटोक्तेर्गुरोर्महावाक्यपदैः प्रबुद्धः॥३९॥

I was wandering in a condition analogous as in dreaming because of dormant power of discretion in the ego revealing world of 'My', 'mine' where self-satisfaction was the main cause in the material objects. My son of the soul has now been arisen by the blissful preaching of my teacher on the feet of great sentences and I am now able to know what is reality (these are the feelings of Ṛṣi Śukadeva).

वाच्यं लक्ष्यमिति द्विधार्थसरणीवाच्यस्य हि त्वंपदे वाच्यं भौतिकमिन्द्रियादिरपि यल्लक्ष्यं त्वमर्थश्च सः। वाच्यं तत्पदमीशताकृतमतिर्लक्ष्यं तु सच्चित्सुखानन्दब्रह्म तदर्थ एष च तयोरैक्यं त्वसीदं पदम्॥४०॥

In order to know the meaning of great sentences, one should follow the expression and the aim both. As per the expression, the material senses too are the subject of the foot 'Tvam' but the all sensitive supreme soul is its intended meaning who is beyond these physical senses. Similarly, the expression of foot 'Tat' is the supreme soul who is sovereign and cause for all actions. Its intended meaning is the Brahma in garb of true pleasure. By the intended meaning of both above feet, the foot 'Asi' herein lays down the integrity of the living soul and the Brahma. (It is necessary to understand the expressive meaning and the intended meaning of each hymn and the gigantic sentence).

त्वमिति तदिति कार्ये कारणे सत्युपाधौ द्वितयमितरथैकं सच्चिदानन्दरूपम्। उभयवचनहेतू देशकालौ च हित्वा जगति भवति सोऽयं देवदत्तो यथैकः॥४१॥

By the two designations *i.e.* cause and effect, the distinction between 'Tvam' and 'Tat' feet has been made. These both are an absolute real pleasure if the designation is not added with them. In the material world, this and that words are frequently used in every place and the time. If these words are deleted, an absolute Brahma remains. For example, if we say this is Devadatta and again that is Devadatta. We see in both these sentences that Devadatta is a person who is addressed by this and that.

कार्योपाधिरयं जीवः कारणोपाधिरीश्वरः। कार्यकारणतां हित्वा पूर्णबोधोऽवशिष्यते॥४२॥

This living soul bears the designation of the effect and the god, the designation of cause. The Brahma is purified form of knowledge and only remains if these cause and effect designations are deleted.

श्रवणं तु गुरोः पूर्वं मननं तदनन्तरम्। निदिध्यासनमित्येतत् पूर्वबोधस्य कारणम्॥४३॥

A disciple can acquire the perfect knowledge only when he listens to from his teacher, ponders over the same in depth and then brings into action whatever he has perceived.

अन्यविद्यापरिज्ञानमवश्यं नश्वरं भवेत्। ब्रह्मविद्यापरिज्ञानं ब्रह्मप्राप्तिकरं स्थितम्॥४४॥

The knowledge acquired if pertains to other learning's is definitely perishable but the knowledge of Brahma learning (Vidyā) makes a person able to attain Brahma if it is duly acquired.

महावाक्यान्युपदिशेत्सषडङ्गानि देशिकः। केवलं नहि वाक्यानि ब्रह्मणो वचनं यथा॥४५॥

The lord Brahmā has pronounced that a teacher should not merely explain the gigantic sentences to his disciples but their feet, the six forms of summoning various gods etc. should also be taught.

ईश्वर उवाच–

एवमुक्त्वा मुनिश्रेष्ठ रहस्योपनिषच्छुक। मया पित्रानुनीतेन व्यासेन ब्रह्मवादिना॥४६॥

Lord Śiva said to the Ṛṣi Śukadeva– "O Śukadeva! Your father Vedavyāsa is well-learnt to Brahma. I have explained this 'Rahasyopaniṣad' to you only when he requested for the same."

ततो ब्रह्मोपदिष्टं वै सच्चिदानन्दलक्षणम्। जीवन्मुक्तः सदा ध्यायन्नित्यस्त्वं विहरिष्यसि॥४७॥

"The preaching of the real pleasure 'Brahma' is existed in it and it can be obtained only by virtue of a deep penance. You will obtain emancipation from the cycle of birth and death as a result of your perseverance on that Brahma."

यो वेदादौ स्वरः प्रोक्तो वेदान्ते च प्रतिष्ठितः। तस्य प्रकृतिलीनस्य यः परः स महेश्वरः॥४८॥

The syllable Oṁ as pronounciated just at the beginning of Vedas and as enshrined in the Vedānta as also who is beyond the nature even while it is absolutely merged with it. This is Maheśvara.

उपदिष्टः शिवेनेति जगत्तन्मयतां गतः। उत्थाय प्रणिपत्येशं त्यक्ताशेषपरिग्रहः॥४९॥

Having heard the preaching from lord Śiva, the Ṛṣi Śukadeva was engrossed in the universal god. Then he stood from his seat, saluted to lord Śiva and moved to the forest for penance by renouncing everything which he had.

परब्रह्मपयोराशौ प्लवन्निव ययौ तदा। प्रव्रजन्तं तमालोक्य कृष्णद्वैपायनो मुनिः॥५०॥

The Ṛṣi Vedavyāsa was aggrieved and start lamenting when Śukadeva had left for the forest but Ṛṣi Śukadeva was unknown to the feelings of his father because he was engrossed in the pleasure of swimming in the ocean of perfect knowledge (Brahma).

अनुव्रजन्नाजुहाव पुत्रविश्लेषकातरः। प्रतिनेदुस्तदा सर्वे जगत्स्थावरजङ्गमाः॥५१॥

The Ṛṣi Vedavyāsa started calling him and bean to follow him with the sheer sorrow of bereavement. All the living and dead objects of the whole universe responded his call full of sorrow.

तच्छ्रुत्वा सकलाकारं व्यासः सत्यवतीसुतः। पुत्रेण सहितः प्रीत्या परानन्दमुपेयिवान्॥५२॥

यो रहस्योपनिषदमधीते गुर्वनुग्रहात्। सर्वपापविनिर्मुक्तः साक्षात्कैवल्यमश्नुते साक्षात्कैवल्यमश्नुत इत्युपनिषत्॥५३॥

Having heard the response from all worldly objects and having confirmed with the fact that his son was merged within the whole world, the Ṛṣi Vedavyāsa (the son of Satyavatī) attained the perfect knowledge (Brahma) with his son. The devotee who attains to this philosophy of element attached with this 'Rahasyopaniṣad' by the grace of his teacher, attains high position of emancipation and exonerated from all evils committed. This is the mysterious knowledge of this Upaniṣad.

॥शान्तिपाठः॥

ॐ सहनाववतु...... इति शान्तिः॥

॥शुकरहस्योपनिषत्समाप्ता॥

***

32. VAJRASŪCIKOPANIṢAD

वज्रसूचिकोपनिषद्

॥शान्तिपाठः॥

ॐ आप्यायन्तु .... इति शान्तिः॥

वज्रसूचीं प्रवक्ष्यामि शास्त्रमज्ञानभेदनम्। दूषणं ज्ञानहीनानां भूषणं ज्ञानचक्षुषाम्॥ १॥

I now proceed to declare the Vajrasūcī— the weapon that is the destroyer of ignorance— which condemns the ignorant and praises the man of divine vision.

ब्रह्मक्षत्रियवैश्यशूद्रा इति चत्वारो वर्णास्तेषां वर्णानां ब्राह्मण एव प्रधान इति वेदवचनानुरूपं स्मृतिभिरप्युक्तम्। तत्र चोद्यमस्ति को वा ब्राह्मणो नाम किं जीवः किं देहः किं जातिः किं ज्ञानं किं कर्म किं धार्मिक इति॥ २॥

There are four castes— the brāhmaṇa, the kṣatriya, the vaiśya, and the śūdra. Even the smṛtis declare in accordance with the words of the vedas that the brāhmaṇa alone is the most important of them.

[Then this remains to be examined– what is meant by the *brāhmaṇa*? Is it a *jīva*? Is it a body? Is it a class? Is it *Jñāna*? Is it *karma*? Or is it a doer of dharma.]

तत्र प्रथमो जीवो ब्राह्मण इति चेत्तन्न। अतीतानागतानेकदेहानां जीवस्यैकरूपत्वात् एकस्यापि कर्मवशादनेकदेहसंभवात् सर्वशरीराणां जीवस्यैकरूपत्वाच्च। तस्मान्न जीवो ब्राह्मण इति॥ ३॥

To begin with : is Jīva is the brāhmaṇa? No. since the jīva is the same in the many past and future bodies (of all persons), and since the jīva is the same in all of the many bodies obtained through the force of karma, therefore jīva is not the brāhmaṇa.

तर्हि देहो ब्राह्मण इति चेत्तन्न। आचाण्डालादिपर्यन्तानां मनुष्याणां पाञ्चभौतिकत्वेन देहस्यैकरूपत्वाज्जरामरणधर्माधर्मादिसाम्यदर्शनाद् ब्राह्मणः श्वेतवर्णः क्षत्रियो रक्तवर्णो वैश्यः पीतवर्णः शूद्रः कृष्णवर्ण इति नियमाभावात्। पित्रादिशरीरदहने पुत्रादीनां ब्रह्महत्यादिदोष-संभवाच्च। तस्मान्न देहो ब्राह्मण इति॥ ४॥

Then is the body the brāhmaṇa? No. Since the body, as it is made up of the five elements, is the same for all people down to caṇḍālas, etc., since old age and death, dhrama and adharma are found to be common to them all, since there is no absolute distinction that the brāhmaṇas are white-coloured, the kṣatriyas red, the vaiśyas yellow, and the śūdras dark, and since in burning the corpse of his father, etc., the stain of the murder of a brāhmaṇa, etc., will accrue to the son, etc., therefore the body is not the brāhmaṇa.

तर्हि जातिर्ब्राह्मण इति चेत्तन्न। तत्र जात्यन्तरजन्तुष्वनेकजातिसंभवा महर्षयो बहवः सन्ति। ऋष्यशृङ्गो मृग्याः कौशिकः कुशात् जाम्बूको जम्बूकात्। वाल्मीको वल्मीकात् व्यासः कैवर्तकन्यकायाम् शशपृष्ठात्

गौतमः वसिष्ठ उर्वश्याम् अगस्त्यः कलशे जात इति श्रुतत्वात्। एतेषां जात्या विनाप्यग्रे ज्ञानप्रतिपादिता ऋषयो बहवः सन्ति। तस्मान्न जातिर्ब्राह्मण इति॥ ५

Then is a class the brāhmaṇa? No. Since many great Ṛṣis have sprung from other castes and orders of creation— Ṛṣyaśṛṅga was born of deer; Kauśika, of Kuśa grass; Jāmbuka of a jackal; Vālmīki of valmīka (an ant-hill); Vyāsa of a fisherman's daughter; Gautama, of the posteriors of a hare; Vasiṣṭha of Ūrvaśi; and Agastya of a water-pot; thus have we heard. Of these, many Ṛṣis outside the caste even have stood first among the teachers of divine Wisdom; therefore a class is not the brāhmaṇa.

तर्हि ज्ञानं ब्राह्मण इति चेत्तन्न। क्षत्रियादयोऽपि परमार्थदर्शिनोऽभिज्ञा बहवः सन्ति। तस्मान्न ज्ञानं ब्राह्मण इति॥ ६॥

Is jñāna the brāhmaṇa? No. Since there were many kṣatriyas and others well versed in the cognition of divine Truth, therefore jñāna is not the brāhmaṇa.

तर्हि कर्म ब्राह्मण इति चेत्तन्न। सर्वेषां प्राणिनां प्रारब्धसंचितागामिकर्मसा-धर्म्यदर्शनात्कर्माभिप्रेरिताः सन्तो जनाः क्रियाः कुर्वन्तीति। तस्मान्न कर्म ब्राह्मण इति॥ ७॥

Then is karma the brāhmaṇa? No. Since the prārabdha, sañcita, and āgāmi karmas are the same for all beings, and since all people perform their actions as impelled by karma, therefore karma is not the brāhmaṇa.

तर्हि धार्मिको ब्राह्मण इति चेत्तन्न। क्षत्रियादयो हिरण्यदातारो बहवः सन्ति। तस्मान्न धार्मिको ब्राह्मण इति॥ ८॥

Then is a doer of dharma (virtuous actions) the brāhmaṇa? No. Since there are many kṣatriyas, etc., who are givers of gold, therefore a doer of virtuous actions is not the brāhmaṇa.

तर्हि को वा ब्राह्मणो नाम। यः कश्चिदात्मानमद्वितीयं जातिगुणक्रियाहीनं षडूर्मिषड्भावे-त्यादिसर्वदोषरहितं सत्यज्ञानानन्दानन्तस्वरूपं स्वयं निर्विकल्पमशेषकल्पाधारमशेषभूतान्तर्यामित्वेन वर्तमानमन्तर्बहिश्चाकाशवदनुस्यूतमखण्डानन्द स्वभावमप्रमेयमनुभवैकवेद्यमापरोक्षतया भासमानं करतलामलकवत्साक्षादपरोक्षीकृत्य कृतार्थतया कामरागादिदोषरहितः शमदमादिसंपन्नो भावमात्सर्यतृष्णाशामोहादिरहितो दम्भाहंकारादिभिरसंस्पृष्टचेता वर्तत एवमुक्तलक्षणो यः स एव ब्राह्मण इति श्रुतिस्मृतिपुराणेतिहासानामभिप्रायः। अन्यथा हि ब्राह्मणत्वसिद्धिर्नास्त्येव। सच्चिदानन्दमात्मानमद्वितीयं ब्रह्म भावयेदात्मानं सच्चिदानन्दं ब्रह्म भावयेदित्युपनिषत्॥ ९॥

Who indeed then is brāhmaṇa? Whoever he may be, he who had directly realised his Ātman and who is directly cognizant, like the myrobalan in his palm, of his Ātman that is without a second, that is devoid of class and actions, that is free from the faults of the six stains and the six changes, that is of the nature of truth, knowledge, bliss, and eternity, that is without any change in itself, that is the substratum of all the kalpas, that exists penetrating all things, that pervades everything within and without as ākāśa, that is of natue of undivided bliss, that cannot be reasoned about and that is known only by direct cognition. He who by the reason of having obtained his wishes is devoid of the faults of thirst after worldly objects and passions, who is the possessor of the qualifications beginning with śama, who is free from emotion, malice, thirst after worldly objects, desire, delusion, etc., whose mind is untouched by pride, egoism, etc., who possesses all these qualities and means— he only is the brāhmaṇa.

Such is the opinion of the vedas, the smṛtis, the itihāsa and the purāṇas. Otherwise one cannot obtain the status of a brāhmaṇa. One should meditate of his Ātman as Saccidānanda, and the non-dual Brahman, Yea, one should meditate on his Ātman as the Saccidānanda Brahman.

ॐ आप्यायन्तु .... इति शान्तिः॥

॥इति वज्रसूच्युपनिषत्समाप्ता॥

***

33. TEJO-BINDU UPANIṢAD

तेजोबिन्दूपनिषद्

।।शान्तिपाठः।।

ॐ यत्र चिन्मात्रकलना यात्यपह्नवमञ्जसा।

तच्चिन्मात्रमखण्डैकरसं ब्रह्म भवाम्यहम्।।

ॐ सह नाववत्विति शान्तिः।।

ॐ तेजोबिन्दूः परं ध्यानं विश्वात्महृदि संस्थितम्।

।।प्रथमोऽध्यायः।।

ॐ तेजोबिन्दुः परं ध्यानं विश्वात्महृदि संस्थितम्। आणवं शांभवं शान्त स्थूलं सूक्ष्म पर च यत्।।१।।
दुःखाढ्यं च दुराराध्यं दुष्प्रेक्ष्यं मुक्तमव्ययम्। दुर्लभं तत्स्वयं ध्यानं मुनीनां च मनीषिणाम्।।२।।
यताहारो जितक्रोधो जितसङ्गो जितेन्द्रियः। निर्द्वन्द्वो निरहंकारो निराशीरप्रिग्रहः।।३।।
अगम्यागमकर्ता यो गम्याऽगमनमानसः। मुखे त्रीणि च विन्दन्ति त्रिधामा हंस उच्यते।।४।।

Param-Dhyāna (the supreme meditation) should be upon tejobindu, which is the Ātman of the universe, which is seated in the heart, which is of the size of an atom, which pertains to Śiva, which is quiescent and which is gross and subtle, as also above these qualities. That alone should be the dhyāna of the Munis as well as the men, which is full of pains, which is difficult to meditate on, which is difficult to perceive, which is the emancipated one, which is decayless and which is difficult to attain. One whose food is moderate, whose anger has been controlled, who has given up all love for society, who has subdued his passions, who has overcome all pairs (heat and cold etc.), who has given up his egoism, who does not bless anyone nor take anything from others, and also who goes where they naturally ought not to go, and naturally would not go where they like to go— such persons also obtain three in the face. Haṁsa is said to have three seats.

परं गुह्यतमं विद्धि ह्यस्ततन्द्रो निराश्रयः। सोमरूपकला सूक्ष्मा विष्णोस्तत्परमं पदम्।।५।।
त्रिवक्त्रं त्रिगुणं स्थानं त्रिधातुं रूपवर्जितम्। निश्चलं निर्विकल्पं च निराकारं निराश्रयम्।।६।।
उपाधिरहितं स्थानं वाङ्मनोऽतीतगोचरम्। स्वभावं भावसंग्राह्यमसंघातं पदाच्युतम्।।७।।
अनानानन्दनातीतं तुष्प्रेक्ष्य मुक्तमव्ययम्। चिन्त्यमेवं विनिर्मुक्तं शाश्वतं ध्रुवमच्युतम्।।८।।
तद्ब्रह्मणस्तदध्यात्मं तद्विष्णोस्तत्परायणम्। अचिन्त्यं चिन्मयात्मानं यद्व्योमं परमं स्थितम्।।९।।
अशून्यं शून्यभावं तु शून्यातीतं हृदि स्थितम्। न ध्यानं च न च ध्याता न ध्येयो ध्येय एव च।।१०।।
सर्वं च न परं शून्यं न परं नापरात्परम्। अचिन्त्यमप्रबुद्धं च न सत्यं न परं विदुः।।११।।

मुनीनां संप्रयुक्तं च न देवा न परं विदुः। लोभं मोहं भयं दर्पं कामं क्रोधं च किल्बिषम्॥१२॥
शीतोष्णे क्षुत्पिपासे च संकल्पकविकल्पकम्। न ब्रह्मकुलदर्पं च न मुक्तिग्रन्थिसंचयम्॥१३॥
न भयं न सुखं दुःखं तथा मानावमानयोः। एतद्भावविनिर्मुक्तं तद्ग्राह्यं ब्रह्म तत्परम्॥१४॥

Therefore know it is the greatest of mysteries, without sleep and without support. It is very subtle, of the form of Sōma, and is the supreme seat of Viṣṇu. That seat has three faces, three guṇas and three dhātus, and is formless, motionless, changeless, sizeless, and supportless. That seat is without upādhi, and is above the reach of speech and mind. It is Svabhāva (self or nature) reachable only by bhāva (being). The indestructible seat is associateless, without bliss, beyond mind, difficult to perceive, emancipated and changeless. It should be meditated upon as the liberated, the eternal, the permanent and the indestructible. It is Brahman, is adhyātma (or the deity presiding as Ātmā) and is the highest seat of Viṣṇu. It is inconceivable, of the nature of Cidātmā and above the ākāśa, is void and non-void, and beyond the void, and is abiding in the heart. There is (in It) neither meditation nor meditator, nor the meditated, nor the non-meditated. It is not the universe. It is the highest. It is neither supreme nor above the supreme. It is inconceivable, unknowable, non-truth and not the highest. It is realised by the Munis, but the Devas do not know the supreme One. Avarice, delusion, fear, pride, passion, anger, sin, heat, cold, hunger, thirst, thought and fancy— (all these do not exist in It). (In It) there is no pride of (belonging to) the Brāhmaṇa caste, nor is there the collection of the knot of salvation. (In It) there is no fear, no happiness, no pains, neither fame nor disgrace. That which is without these states is the supreme Brahman.

यमो हि नियमस्त्यागो मौनं देशश्च कालतः। आसनं मूलबन्धश्च देहसाम्यं च दृक्स्थितिः॥१५॥
प्राणसंयमनं चैव प्रत्याहारश्च धारणा। आत्मध्यानं समाधिश्च प्रोक्तान्यङ्गानि वै क्रमात्॥१६॥
सर्वं ब्रह्मेति वै ज्ञानादिन्द्रियग्रामसंयमः। यमोऽयमिति संप्रोक्तोऽभ्यसनीयो मुहुर्मुहुः॥१७॥
सजातीयप्रवाहश्च विजातीयतिरस्कृतिः। नियमो हि परानन्दो नियमात्क्रियते बुधैः॥१८॥
त्यागो हि महता पूज्यः सद्यो मोक्षप्रदायकः॥१९॥

Yama (forbearance), niyama (religious observance), tyāga (renunciation), mauna (silence) according to time and place, āsana (posture), mūlabandha, seeing all bodies as equal, the position of the eye, prāṇa-saṁyamana (control of breath), pratyāhāra (subjugation of the senses), dhāraṇā, ātma-dhyāna and samādhi— these are spoken of as the parts (of yoga) in order. That is called yama in which one controls all his organs (of sense and actions) through the vijñāna that all is Brahman; this should be practised often and often. Niyama, in which there is the supreme bliss enjoyed through the flowing (or inclination) of the mind towards things of the same (spiritual) kind, (viz., Brahman) and the abandoning of things differing from one another is practised by the sages as a rule. In tyāga (renunciation), one abandons the manifestations (or objects) of the universe through the cognition of Ātman that is Sat and Cit. This is practised by the great and is the giver of immediate salvation.

यस्माद्वाचो निवर्तन्ते अप्राप्य मनसा सह। यन्मौनं योगिभिर्गम्यं तद्भजेत्सर्वदा बुधः॥२०॥

वाचो यस्मान्निवर्तन्ते तद्वक्तुं केन शक्यते। प्रपञ्चो यदि वक्तव्यः सोऽपि शब्दविवर्जितः॥२१॥

इति वा तद्भवेन्मौनं सर्वं सहजसंज्ञितम्। गिरां मौनं तु बालानामयुक्तं ब्रह्मवादिनाम्॥२२॥

आदावन्ते च मध्ये च जनो यस्मिन्न विद्यते। येनेदं सततं व्याप्तं स देशो विजनः स्मृतः॥२३॥

कल्पना सर्वभूतानां ब्रह्मादीनां निमेषतः। कालशब्देन निर्दिष्टः ह्यखण्डानन्दमद्वयम्॥२४॥

सुखेनैव भवेद्यस्मिन्नजस्रं ब्रह्मचिन्तनम्। आसनं तद्विजानीयादन्यत्सुखविनाशनम्॥२५॥

सिद्धये सर्वभूतादि विश्वाधिष्ठानमद्वयम्। यस्मिन्सिद्धिं गताः सिद्धास्तत्सिद्धासनमुच्यते॥२६॥

यन्मूलं सर्वलोकानां यन्मूलं चित्तबन्धनम्। मूलबन्धः सदा सेव्यो समानत्वमृजुत्वं शुष्कवृक्षवत्॥२७॥

Mauna (the silence), in which, without reaching That, speech returns along with mind, is fit to be attained by the Yogins and should be ever worshipped by the ignorant even.

How is it possible to speak of "That", from which speech returns? How should it be described as the universe as there is no word to describe it? It is "That" which is (really) called silence, and which is naturally understood (as such). There is silence in children, but with words (latent); whereas the knowers of Brahman have it (silence) but without words. That should be known as "the lonely seat" in which there is no man in the beginning, middle, or end, and through which all this (universe) is fully pervaded. The illusion of Brahmā and all other beings takes place within one twinkling (of His eye). That should be known as āsana (posture), in which one has with ease and without fatigue (uninterrupted) meditation of Brahman; that is described by the word kāla (time), that is endless bliss and that is secondless. Everything else is the destroyer of happiness. That is called siddhāsana (siddha-posture) in which the siddhas (psychical personages) have succeeded in realising the endless One as the support of the universe containing all the elements, etc. That is called the mūlabandha, which is the Mūla (root) of all words, and through which the root Citta is (bandha) bound. It should be always practised by the Rājayogins.

अङ्गानां समतां विद्यात्समे ब्रह्मणि लीयते। नो चेन्नैव समानत्वमृजुत्वं शुष्कवृक्षवत्॥२८॥

दृष्टिं ज्ञानमयीं कृत्वा पश्येद्ब्रह्ममयं जगत्। सा दृष्टिः परमोदारा न नासाग्रावलोकिनी॥२९॥

द्रष्टृदर्शनदृश्यानां विरामो यत्र वा भवेत्। दृष्टिस्तत्रैव कर्तव्या न नासाग्रावलोकिनी॥३०॥

चित्तासिर्वभावेषु ब्रह्मत्वेनैव भावनात्। निरोधः सर्ववृत्तीनां प्राणायामः स उच्यते॥३१॥

निषेधनं प्रपञ्चस्य रेचकाख्यः समीरितः। ब्रह्मैवास्मीति या वृत्तिः पूरको वायुरुच्यते॥३२॥

निषेधनं प्रपञ्चस्य रेचकाख्यः समीरितः। ब्रह्मैवास्मीति या वृत्तिः पूरको वायुरुच्यते॥३२॥

One after having known the equality of the aṅgas (or parts of yoga) point to one and the same Brahman, should be absorbed in that equal (or uniform) Brahman; if not, there is not that equality (attained). Then like a dry tree, there is straightness (or uniformity throughout). Making one's vision full of spiritual wisdom, one should look upon the world as full of Brahman. That vision is very noble. It is (generally) aimed at the tip of the nose; but it should be directed towards that seat (of Brahman) wherein the cessation of seer, the seen, and sight will take place, and not towards the tip of the nose. That is called prāṇāyāma (the control of breath), in which there is the control of the modifications (of mind) through the cognition of Brahman in all the states of citta, and others. The checking of (the conception of the reality of) the universe, is said to be expiration. The conception of "I am Brahman" is inspiration.

ततस्तद्वृत्तिनैश्चल्यं कुम्भकः प्राणसंयमः। अयं चापि प्रबुद्धानामज्ञानां घ्राणपीडनम्॥३३॥
विषयेष्वात्मतां दृष्ट्वा मनसश्चित्तरञ्जकम्। प्रत्याहारः स विज्ञेयोऽभ्यसनीयो मुहुर्मुहुः॥३४॥
यत्र यत्र मनो याति ब्रह्मणस्तत्र दर्शनात्। मनसा धारणं चैव धारणा सा परा मता॥३५॥
ब्रह्मैवास्मीति सद्वृत्त्या निरालम्बतया स्थितिः। ध्यानशब्देन विख्यातः परमानन्ददायकः॥३६॥
निर्विकारतया वृत्त्या ब्रह्माकारतया पुनः। वृत्तिविस्मरणं सम्यक्समाधिरभिधीयते॥३७॥

The holding on (long) to this conception without agitation is cessation of breath. Such is the practice of the enlightened. The ignorant close their nose. That should be known as pratyāhāra, through which one sees Ātman (even) in the objects of sense, and pleases citta through manas. It should be practised often and often. Through seeing Brahman wherever the mind goes, the dhāraṇā of mind is obtained. Dhāraṇā is thought of highly by wise. By dhāraṇā is meant that state where one indulges in the good thought, "I am Brahman alone," and is without any support. This dhyāna is the giver of supreme bliss. Being first in a state of changelessness, and then forgetting (even) that state owing to the cognition of the (true) nature of Brahman— this is called samādhi.

इमं चाकृत्रिमानन्दं तावत्साधुं समभ्यसेत्। लक्ष्यो यावत्क्षणात्पुंसः प्रत्यक्त्वं संभवेत्स्वयम्॥३८॥
ततः साधननिर्मुक्तः सिद्धो भवति योगिराट्। तत्स्वं रूपं भवेत्तस्य विषयो मनसो गिराम्॥३९॥

This kind of bliss should be practised (or enjoyed) by a wise person till his cognition itself united in a moment with the state of *pratyak* (Ātman). Then this King of Yogins becomes a Siddha, and is without any aid (outside himself). Then he will attain a state, inexpressible and unthinkable.

समाधौ क्रियमाणे तु विघ्नान्यायान्ति वै बलात्। अनुसंधानराहित्यमालस्यं भोगलालसम्॥४०॥
लयस्तमश्च विक्षेपस्तेजः स्वेदश्च शून्यता। एवं हि विघ्नबाहुल्यं त्याज्यं ब्रह्मविशारदैः॥४१॥
भाववृत्त्या हि भावत्वं शून्यवृत्त्या हि शून्यता। ब्रह्मवृत्त्या हि पूर्णत्वं तया पूर्णत्वमभ्यसेत्॥४२॥

When samādhi is practised, the following obstacles arise with great force— absence of right inquiry, laziness, inclination to enjoyment, absorption (in material object), tamas, distraction, impatience, sweat, and absent-mindedness. All these obstacles should be overcome by curiosity into Brahman. Through bhāvavṛttis (worldly thoughts) one gets into them. Through Śūnya-vṛttis (void or empty thoughts), one gets into them. But through the vṛttis of Brahman, one gets fullness. Therefore one should develop fullness through this means (of Brahman).

ये हि वृत्तिं विहायैनां ब्रह्माख्यां पावनीं पराम्। वृथैव ते तु जीवन्ति पशुभिश्च समा नराः॥४३॥

ये तु वृत्तिं विजानन्ति ज्ञात्वा वै वर्धयन्ति ये। ते वै सत्पुरुषा धन्यां वन्द्यास्ते भुवनत्रये।।४४।।

येषां वृत्तिः समा वृद्धा परिपक्वा च सा पुनः। ते वै सद्ब्रह्मतां प्राप्ता नेतरे शब्दवादिनः।।४५।।

कुशला ब्रह्मवार्तायां वृत्तिहीनाः सुरागिणः। तेऽप्यज्ञानतया नूनं पुनरायान्ति यान्ति च।।४६।।

निमिषार्धं न तिष्ठन्ति वृत्तिं ब्रह्ममयीं विना। यथा तिष्ठन्ति ब्रह्माद्याः सनकाद्याः शुकादयः।।४७।।

He who abandons this vṛtti of Brahman, which is very purifying and supreme— that man lives in vain like a beast. But he who understands this vṛtti (of Brahman), and having understood it makes advances in its, becomes a good and blessed person, deserving to be worshipped by the three worlds. Those who are greatly developed through the ripening (of their past karmas) attain the state of Brahman : others are simply reciters of words. Those who are clever in arguments about Brahman, but are without the action pertaining to Brahman, and who are greatly attached to the world— those certainly are born again and again (in this world) through their ajñāna; (the former) never remain, even for half a moment— without the vṛtti of Brahman, like Brahmā and others, Sanaka, Śuka and others.

कारणं यस्य वै कार्यं कारणं तस्य जायते। कारणं तत्त्वतो नश्येत्कार्याभावे विचारतः।।४८।।

अथ शुद्धं भवेद्वस्तु यद्वै वाचामगोचरम्। उदेति शुद्धचित्तानां वृत्तिज्ञानं ततः परम्।।४९।।

भावितं तीव्रवेगेन यद्वस्तु निश्चयात्मकम्। दृश्यह्यदृश्यतां नीत्वा ब्रह्माकारेण चिन्तयेत्।।५०।।

विद्वान्नित्यं सुखे तिष्ठेद्धिया चिद्रसपूर्णया।।

When a cause is subject to changes, it (as an effect) must also have its cause. When the cause ceases to exist in truth, the effect perishes through right discrimination. Then that substance (or principle) which is beyond the scope of words, remains pure. After that, vṛtti jñāna arises in their purfied mind; through meditation with transcendental energy, there arises a firm certitude. After reducing the visible into the invisible state, one should see everything as Brahman. The wise should every stay in bliss with their understanding full of essence of cit. Thus ends the first chapter of Tejobindu.

।।अथ द्वितीयोऽध्यायः।।

अथ ह कुमारः शिवं पप्रच्छाऽखण्डैकरसचिन्मात्रस्वरूपमनुब्रूहीति। स होवाच परमः शिवः।

अखण्डैकरसं दृश्यमखण्डैकरसं जगत्। अखण्डैकरसं भावमखण्डैकरसं स्वयम्।।१।।

अखण्डैकरसो मन्त्र अखण्डैकरसा क्रिया। अखण्डैकरसं ज्ञानखण्डैकरसं जलम्।।२।।

अखण्डैकरसा भूमिरखण्डैकरसं वियत्। अखण्डैकरसं शास्त्रमखण्डैकरसात्रयी।।३।।

अखण्डैकरसं ब्रह्म चाखण्डैकरसं व्रतम्। अखण्डैकरसो जीव अखण्डैकरसो ह्यजः।।४।।

अखण्डैकरसो ब्रह्म अखण्डैकरसो हरिः। अखण्डैकरसो रुद्र अखण्डैकरसोऽस्म्यहम्।।५।।

अखण्डैकरसो ह्यात्मा ह्यखण्डैकरसो गुरुः। अखण्डैकरसं लक्ष्यमखण्डैकरसं महः।।६।।

अखण्डैकरसो देह अखण्डैकरसं मनः। अखण्डैकरसं चित्तमखण्डैकरसं सुखम्।।७।।

अखण्डैकरसा विद्या अखण्डैकरसोऽव्ययः। अखण्डैकरसं नित्यमखण्डैकरसं परम्।।८।।

अखण्डैकरसं किंचिदखण्डैकरसं परम्। अखण्डैकरसादन्यन्नास्ति अखण्डैकरसान्न हि।
अखण्डैकरसात्किंचिदखण्डैकरसादरम्।।१०।।
अखण्डैकरसं स्थूलं सूक्ष्मं चाखण्डरूपकम्। अखण्डैकरसं वेद्यमखण्डैकरसो भवान्।।११।।
अखण्डैकरसं गुह्यमखण्डैकरसादिकम्। अखण्डैकरसो ज्ञाता ह्यखण्डैकरसा स्थितिः।।१२।।
अखण्डैकरसा माता अखण्डैकरसः पिता। अखण्डैकरसो भ्राता अखण्डैकरसः पतिः।।१३।।
अखण्डैकरसं सूत्रमखण्डैकरसो विराट्। अखण्डैकरसं गात्रमखण्डैकरसं शिरः।।१४।।
अखण्डैकरसं चान्तरखण्डैकरसं वहिः। अखण्डैकरसं पूर्णमखण्डैकरसं शिरः।।१४।।
अखण्डैकरसं चान्तरखण्डैकरसं गृहम्। अखण्डैकरसं गोप्यमखण्डैकरसामृतम्।।१५।।
अखण्डैकरसं गोत्रमखण्डैकरसं गृहम्। अखण्डैकरसं गोप्यमखण्डैकरसशशशी।।१६।।
अखण्डैकरसास्तारा अखण्डैकरसो रविः। अखण्डैकरसं क्षेत्रमखण्डैकरसा क्षमा।।१७।।
अखण्डैकरसः शान्त अखण्डैकरसोऽगुणः। अखण्डैकरसः साक्षी अखण्डैकरसः सुहृत।।१८।।
अखण्डकरसो बन्धुरखण्डैकरसः सखा। अखण्डैकरसो राजा अखण्डैकरसं पुरम्।।१९।।
अखण्डैकरसं राज्यमखण्डैकरसाः प्रजाः। अखण्डैकरसं तारमखण्डैकरसो जपः।।२०।।
अखण्डैकरसं ध्यानमखण्डैकरसं पदम्। अखण्डैकरसं ग्राह्यमखण्डैकरसं महत्।।२१।।
अखण्डैकरसो होम अखण्डैकरसोः जपः। अखण्डैकरसं स्वर्गमखण्डैकरसः स्वयम्।।२३।।

Then the Kumāra asked Śiva : "Please explain to me the nature of Cinmātra, that is the partless non-dual essence." The great Śiva replied : "The partless non-dual essence is the visible. It is the world, it is the existence, it is the Self, it is mantra, it is action, it is spiritual wisdom, it is water. It is the earth, it is ākāśa, it is the books, it is the three Vedas, it is the Brahman, it is the religious vow, it is Jīva, it is Aja (the unborn), it is Brahmā, it is Viṣṇu, it is Rudra; it is I, it Ātmā, it is the Guru. It is the aim, it is sacrifice, it is the body, it is manas, it is citta, it is happiness, it is vidyā; it is the undifferentiated, it is the eternal, it is the supreme, it is everything. O six-faced one, different form It there is nothing. None, none but It; It is I. It is gross, it is subtle, it is knowable, it is thou; it is the mysterious; it is the knower; it is existence, it is mother, it is father, it is brother, it is husband, it is Sūtra (Ātmā), it is Virāṭ. It is the body, it is the head, it is the internal, it is the external, it is full, it is nectar, it is gotra (clan), it is gṛha (the house), it is the preservable, it is the moon, it is the stars, it is the sun, it is the holy seat. It is forgiveness, it is patience, it is the guṇas, it is the witness. It is a friend, it is a relative, it is an ally, it is the king, town, kingdom and subjects. It is Oṁ, japa, meditation, the seat, the one worthy to be taken (in), the heart, the Jyotis, Svarga (heaven) and Self."

अखण्डैकरसं सर्वं चिन्मात्रमिति भावयेत्। चिन्मात्रमेव चिन्मात्रमखण्डैकरसं परम्।।२४।।
भववर्जितचिन्मात्रं सर्वं चिन्मात्रमेव हि। किं च सर्वं चिन्मात्रमयं चिन्मयमेव हि।।२५।।
आत्मभावं च चिन्मात्रमखण्डैकरसं विदुः। सर्वलोकं चं चिन्मात्रं वत्ता मत्ता च चिन्मयम्।।२६।।
आकाशो भूर्जलं वायुरग्निर्ब्रह्मा: हरिः शिवः। यत्किंचिद्यन्नं किंचिच्च सर्वं चिन्मात्रमेव हि।।२७।।

अखण्डैकरसं सर्वं यद्यच्चिन्मात्रमेव हि। भूतं भव्यं भविष्यच्च सर्वं चिन्मात्रमेव हि॥२८॥
द्रव्यं कालं च चिन्मात्रं ज्ञानं ज्ञेयं चिदेव हि। ज्ञाता चिन्मात्ररूपश्च सर्वं चिन्मयमेव हि॥२९॥
संभाषणं च चिन्मात्रं यद्यच्चिन्मात्रमेव हि। असच्च सच्च चिन्मात्रमाद्यन्तं चिन्मयं सदा॥३०॥
आदिरन्तश्च चिन्मात्रं गुरुशिष्यादि चिन्मयम्। दृगदृश्यं यदि चिन्मात्रमस्ति चेच्चिन्मयं सदा॥३१॥
सर्वाश्चर्यं हि चिन्मात्रं देहं चिन्मात्रमेव हि। लिङ्गं च कारणं चैव चिन्मात्रान्न हि विद्यते॥३२॥
अहं त्वं चैव चिन्मात्रं मूर्तामूर्तादिचिन्मयम्। पुण्यं पापं च चिन्मात्रं जीवश्चिन्मात्रविग्रहः॥३३॥
चिन्मात्रान्नास्ति संकल्पश्चिन्मात्रान्नास्ति वेदनम्। चिन्मात्रान्नास्ति मन्त्रादि चिन्मात्रान्नास्ति देवता॥३४॥
चिन्मात्रान्नास्ति दिक्पालश्चिन्मात्राद्व्यवहारिकम्। चिन्मात्रात्परमं ब्रह्म चिन्मात्रान्नास्ति कोऽपि हि॥३५॥
चिन्मात्रान्नास्ति माया च चिन्मात्रान्नास्ति पूजनम्। चिन्मात्रान्नास्ति मन्तव्य चिन्मात्रान्नास्ति सत्यकम्॥३६॥
चिन्मात्रान्नास्ति कोशादि चिन्मात्रान्नास्ति वै वसु। चिन्मात्रान्नास्ति मौनं च चिन्मात्रान्नास्त्यमौनकम्॥३७॥
चिन्मात्रान्नास्ति वैराग्यं सर्वं चिन्मात्रमेव हि। यच्च यावच्च चिन्मात्रं यच्च यावच्च दृश्यते॥३८॥
यच्च यावच्च दूरस्थं सर्वं चिन्मात्रमेव हि। यच्च यावच्च भूतादि यच्च यावच्च लक्ष्यते॥३९॥
यच्च यावच्च वेदान्ताः सर्वं चिन्मात्रमेव हि। चिन्मात्रान्नास्ति गमनं चिन्मात्रान्नास्ति मोक्षकम्॥४०॥
चिन्मात्रान्नास्ति लक्ष्यं च सर्वं चिन्मात्रेव हि। अखण्डैकरसं ब्रह्म चिन्मात्रान्न हि विद्यते॥४१॥
शास्त्रे मयि त्वयीशे च ह्यखण्डैकरसो भवान्। इत्येकरूपकतया यो वा जानात्यहं त्विति॥४२॥
सकृज्ज्ञानेन मुक्तिः स्यात्सम्यग्ज्ञाने स्वयं गुरुः॥४३॥

"All the partless and non-dual essence should be regarded as Cinmātra. Cinmātra alone is the Absolute Consciousness; and this partless non-dual essence alone is the (real) essence. All having consciousness alone except those having changes, are cinmātra. All this is Cinmātra. He is Cinmātra; the state of Ātman is known as Cinmātra and the partless non-dual essence. The whole world is cinmātra. Our state and my state are cinmātra. Ākāśa, earth, water, vāyu, agni, Brahmā, Viṣṇu, Śiva and all else that exist or do not, are Cinmātra. That which is the partless non-dual essence is Cinmātra. All the past, present, and future are Cinmātra. Substance and time are Cinmātra. Knowledge and the knowable are Cinmātra, the knower is Cinmātra. Everything is Cinmātra. Every speech is Cinmātra. Whatever else is Cinmātra. Asat and Sat are Cinmātra. The beginning and end are Cinmātra; that which is in the beginning and end is Cinmātra ever. The Guru and the disciple are Cinmātra. If the seer and the seen are Cinmātra, then they are always Cinmaya. All things wondrous are Cinmātra. The (gross) body is Cinmātra. The (gross) body is Cinmātra, as also the subtle and causal bodies. There is nothing beyond Cinmātra. I and thou are Cinmātra. Form and non-form are Cinmātra. Virtue and vice are Cinmātra. The body is a symbol of Cinmātra. Saṅkalpa, knowing, mantra, and others, the gods invoked in mantras, the gods presiding over the eight quarters, the phenomenal and the supreme Brahman are nothing but Cinmātra. There is nothing without Cinmātra. Māyā is nothing without Cinmātra. Pūjā (worship) is nothing without Cinmātra, Mediation, truth, sheaths and others, the (eight) vasus, silence, non-silence, and indifference to objects— are nothing without Cinmātra.

Everything is from Cinmātra. Whatever is seen and however seen— it is Cinmātra so far. Whatever exists and however distant, is Cinmātra. Whatever elements exist, whatever is perceived, and whatever is Vedānta— all these are Cinmātra. Without Cinmātra, there is no motion, no mokṣa and no goal aimed at. Everything is cinmātra. Brahman that is the partless non-dual essence is known to be nothing but Cinmātra. You, O Lord, are the partless non-dual essence (stated) in the books, in me, in You, and in the ruler. He who thus perceives 'I' as of one homogeneity (pervading everywhere) will at once be emancipated through this spiritual wisdom. He is his own Guru with this profound spiritual wisdom. Thus ends the second chapter of Tejobindu.

।।अथ तृतीयोऽध्याय:।।

कुमार: पितरमात्मानुभवमनुब्रूहीति पप्रच्छ।
स होवाच पर: शिव:।
परब्रह्मस्वरूपोऽहं परमानन्दमस्म्यहम्। केवलं ज्ञानरूपोऽहं केवलं परमोऽस्म्यहम्।।१।।
केवलं शान्तरूपोऽहं केवलं चिन्मयोऽस्म्यहम्। केवलं नित्यरूपोऽहं केवलं शाश्वतोऽस्म्यहम्।।२।।
केवलं सत्त्वरूपोऽहमहं त्यक्त्वाहमस्म्यहम्। सर्वहीननस्वरूपोऽहं चिदाकाशमयोऽस्म्यहम्।।३।।
केवलं तुर्यरूपोऽस्मि तुर्यातीतोऽस्मि केवल:। सदा चैतन्यरूपोऽस्मि चिदानन्दमयोऽस्म्यहम्।।४।।
केवलाकाररूपोऽस्मि शुद्धरूपोऽस्म्यहं सदा। केवलं ज्ञानरूपोऽस्मि केवलं प्रियमस्म्यहम्।।५।।
निर्विकल्पस्वरूपोऽस्मि निरीहोऽस्मि निरामय:। सदाऽसङ्गस्वरूपोऽस्मि निर्विकारोऽहमव्यय:।।६।।
सदैकरसरूपोऽस्मि सदा चिन्मात्रविग्रह:। अपरिच्छिन्नरूपोऽस्मि ह्यखण्डानन्दरूपवान्।।७।।
सत्परानन्दरूपोऽस्मि चित्परानन्दमस्म्यहम्। अन्तरान्तररूपोऽहमवाङ्मनसगोचर:।।८।।
आत्मानन्दस्वरूपोऽहं सत्यानन्दोऽस्म्यहं सदा। आत्मारामस्वरूपोऽस्मि ह्यहमात्मा सदाशिव:।।९।।
आत्मप्रकाशरूपोऽस्मि ह्यात्मज्योती रसोऽस्म्यहम्। आदिमध्यान्तहीनोऽस्मि ह्याकाशसदृशोऽस्म्यहम्।।१०।।
नित्यशुद्धचिदानन्दसत्तामात्रोऽहमव्यय:। नित्यबुद्धविशुद्धैकसच्चिदानन्दमस्म्यहम्।।११।।

Then Kumāra addressed his father (again) : "Please explain to me the realisation of Ātman. "To which the great Śiva said : "I am of the nature of the Parabrahman. I am the supreme bliss. I am solely of the nature of divine wisdom. I am the sole supreme, the sole quiescence, the sole Cinmaya, the sole unconditioned, the sole permanent and the sole Sattva. I am the 'I' that has given up 'I'. I am one that is without anything. I am full of Cidākāśa. I am the sole fourth one. I am the sole one above the fourth (state of turya). I am the nature of (pure) consciousness. I am ever of the nature of bliss-consciousness. I am of the nature of the non-dual. I am ever of a pure nature, solely of the nature of divine wisdom, of the nature of happiness, without fancies, desires or diseases, of the nature of bliss, without changes or differentiations, and of the nature of the eternal one essence and Cinmātra. My real nature is indescribable, of endless bliss, the bliss above Sat and Cit and the interior of the interior. I am beyond reach of manas and speech. I am of the nature of

Ātmic bliss, true bliss and one who plays with (my) Ātman. I am Ātman and Sadāśiva. My nature is Ātmic spiritual effulgence. I am the essence of the jyotis of Ātman. I am without beginning, middle or end. I am like the sky. I am solely Sat, Ānanda, and Cit which is unconditioned and pure. I am the Saccidānanda that is eternal, enlightened and pure. I am ever of the nature of the eternal Śeṣa (serpent-time). I am ever beyond all. My nature is beyond form. My form is supreme ākāśa. My nature is of the bliss of earth. I am ever without speech. My nature is the all-seat (foundation of all). I am ever replete with consciousness, without the attachment of body, without thought, without the modifications of citta, the sole essence of Cidātman, beyond the visibility of all and of the form of vision. My nature is ever full. I am ever fully contented, the all, and Brahman, and the very consciousness; I am 'I'. My nature is of the earth. I am the great Ātman and the supreme of the supreme; I appear sometimes as different from myself; sometimes as possessing a body, sometimes as a pupil and sometimes as the basis of the words. I am beyond the three periods of time, am worshipped by the Vedas, am determined by the sciences and am fixed in the citta. There is nothing left out by me, neither the earth nor any other objects here. Know that there is nothing which is out of myself. I am Brahmā, a Siddha, the eternally pure, non-dual one, Brahman, without old age or death. I shine by myself; I am my own Ātmā, my own goal, enjoy myself, play in myself, have my own spiritual effulgence, am my own greatness, and am used to play in my own Ātmā, look on my own Ātman and am in myself happily seated. I have my own Ātman as the residue, stay in my own consciousness, and play happily in the kingdom of my own Ātmā, Sitting on the real throne of my own Ātman. I think of nothing else but my own Ātmā, I am Cid-rūpa alone, Brahman alone, Saccidānanda, the secondless, the one replete with bliss and the sole brahman and ever without anything, have the bliss of my own Ātmā, the unconditioned bliss, and am always Ātma-Ākāśa. I alone am in the heart like Cidāditya (the consciousness-sun). I am content in my own Ātmā, have no form, or no decay, am without the number one, have the nature of an unconditioned and emancipated one and I am subtler than ākāśa; I am without the existence of beginning or end, of the nature of the all-illuminating, the bliss greater than the great, of the sole nature of Sat, of the nature of pure mokṣa, of the nature of truth and bliss, full of spiritual wisdom and bliss, of the nature of wisdom alone, and of the nature of Saccidānanda. All this is Brahman alone. There is none other than Brahman and that is 'I'.

नित्यशेषस्वरूपोऽस्मि सर्वातीतोऽस्म्यहं सदा। रूपातीतस्वरूपोऽस्मि परमाकाशविग्रहः।।१२।।
भूमानन्दस्वरूपोऽस्मि भाषाहीनोऽस्म्यहं सदा। सर्वाधिष्ठानरूपोऽस्मि सर्वदा चिद्घनोऽस्म्यहम्।।१३।।
देहभावविहीनोऽस्मि चिन्ताहीनोऽस्मि सर्वदा। चित्तवृत्तिविहीनोऽहं चिदात्मैकरसोऽस्म्यहम्।।१४।।
सर्वदृश्यविहीनोऽहं दृग्रूपोऽस्म्यहमेव हि। सर्वदा पूर्णरूपोऽस्मि नित्यतृप्तोऽस्म्यहं सदा।।१५।।
अहं ब्रह्मैव सर्वं स्यादहं चैतन्यमेव हि। अहमेवाहमेवास्मि भूमाकाशस्वरूपवा्।।१६।।
अहमेव महानात्मा ह्यहमेव परात्परः। अहमन्यवदाभामि ह्यहमेव शरीरवत्।।१७।।
अहं शिष्यवदाभामि ह्ययं लोकत्रयाश्रयः। अहं कालत्रयातीत अहं वेदैरुपासितः।।१८।।

अहं शास्त्रेण निर्णीत अहं चित्ते व्यवस्थित:। मत्त्यक्तं नास्ति किंचिद्वा मत्त्यक्तं पृथिवी च वा॥१९॥
मयातिरिक्तं यद्यद्वा तत्तन्नास्तीति निश्चिनु। अहं ब्रह्मास्मि सिद्धोऽस्मि नित्यशुद्धोऽस्म्यहं सदा॥२०॥
निर्गुण: केवलात्मास्मि निराकारोऽस्म्यहं सदा। केवलं ब्रह्ममात्रोऽस्मि ह्यजरोऽस्म्यमरोऽस्म्यहम्॥२१॥
स्वयमेव स्वयं भामि स्वयमेव सदात्मक:। स्वयमेवात्मनि स्वस्थ: स्वयमेव परा गति:॥२२॥
स्वयमेव स्वयं भञ्जे स्वयमेव स्वयं रमे। स्वयमेव स्वयं ज्योति: स्वयमेव स्वयं मह:॥२३॥
स्वस्यात्मनि स्वयं स्वात्मन्येव विलोक्ये। स्वात्मन्येव सुखासीन: स्वात्ममात्रावशेषक:॥२४॥
स्वचैतन्ये स्वयं स्थास्ये स्वात्मराज्ये सुखे रमे। स्वात्मसिंहासने स्थित्वा स्वात्मनोऽन्यन्न चिन्तये॥२५॥
चिद्रूपमात्रं ब्रह्मैव सच्चिदान्दमद्वयम्। आन्दनघन एवाहमहं ब्रह्मास्मि केवलम्॥२६॥
सर्वदा सर्वसून्योऽहं सर्वात्मानन्दवाहनम्। नित्यानन्दस्वरूपोऽहमात्माकाशोऽस्मि नित्यदा॥२७॥
अहमेव हृदाकाशश्चिदादित्यस्वरूपवान्। आत्मनात्मनि तृप्तोऽस्मि ह्यरूपोऽस्म्यहमव्यय:॥२८॥
एकसंख्याविहीनोऽस्मि नित्यमुक्तस्वरूपवान्। आकाशादपि सूक्ष्मोऽहमाद्यन्ताभाववानहम्॥२९॥
सर्वप्रकाशरूपोऽहं परवरसुखोऽस्म्यहम्। सत्तामात्रस्वरूपोऽहं शुद्धमोक्षस्वरूपवान्॥३०॥
सत्यानन्दस्वरूपोऽहं ज्ञानानन्दघनोऽस्म्यहम्। विज्ञानमात्ररूपोऽहं सच्चिदानन्दलक्षण:॥३१॥
ब्रह्ममात्रमिदं सर्वं ब्रह्मणोऽन्यत्र किंचन। तदेवाहं सदानन्दं ब्रह्मैवाहं सनातनम्॥३२॥
त्वमित्येतत्तदित्येन्मत्तोऽन्यन्नास्ति किंचन। चिच्चैतन्यस्वरूपोऽहमहमेव पर शिव:॥३३॥
अतिभावस्वरूपोऽहमहमेव सखात्मक:। साक्षिवस्तुविहीनत्वात्साक्षित्वं नास्ति मे सदा॥३४॥
केवलं ब्रह्ममात्रत्वादहमात्मा सनातन:। अहमेवादिशेषोऽहमहं शेषोऽहमेव हि॥३५॥
नामरूपविमुक्तोऽहमहमानन्दविग्रह:। इन्द्रियाभावरूपोऽहं सर्वभावस्वरूपक:॥३६॥
बन्धमुक्तिविहीनोऽहं शाश्वतानन्दविग्रह:। आदिचैत्तन्यमात्रोऽहमखण्डैकरसोऽस्म्यहम्॥३७॥
वाङ्मनोऽगोचरश्चाहं सर्वत्र सखवानहम्। सर्वत्र पूर्णरूपोऽहं भूमानन्दमयोऽस्म्यहम्॥३८॥
सर्वत्र तृप्तिरूपोऽहं परामृतरसोऽस्म्यहम्। एकमेवाद्वितीयं सद्ब्रह्मैवाहं न संशय:॥३९॥
सर्वशून्यस्वरूपोऽहं सकलागमगोचर:। मुक्तोऽहं मोक्षरूपोऽहं निर्वाणसुखरूपवान्॥४०॥
सत्यविज्ञानमात्रोऽहं सन्मात्रानन्दवाहनम्। तुरीयातीतरूपोऽहं निर्विकल्पस्वरूपवान्॥४१॥

"I am Brahman that is Sat, and bliss, and the ancient. The word 'thou' and the word 'that' are not different from me. I am of the nature of consciousness. I am alone the great Śiva. I am beyond the nature of existence. I am of the nature of happiness. As there is nothing that can witness me, I am without the state of witness. Being purely of the nature of Brahman, I am the eternal Ātman. I alone am the Ādiśeṣa (the primeval Śeṣa). I alone am the Śeṣa. I am without name and form, of the nature of bliss, of the nature of being unperceivable by the senses, and of the nature of all beings; I have neither bondage nor salvation. I am of the form of eternal bliss. I am the primeval consciousness alone, the partless and non-dual essence, beyond reach of speech and mind, of the nature of bliss everywhere, of the nature of fullness everywhere, of the nature of earthly bliss, of the nature of contentment everywhere, the supreme nectary essence, and the one and secondless Sat (viz.,), Brahman. There is no doubt of it. I am of the nature of all-void. I am the one that is given out by the Vedas. I am of the nature of the emancipated and emancipation, of Nirvāṇic bliss, of truth and wisdom, of Sat alone and bliss, of the one beyond the fourth, of one without fancy.

सर्वदा ह्यजरूपोऽहं नीरागोऽस्मि निरञ्जनः। अहं शुद्धोऽस्मि बुद्धोऽस्मि नित्योऽस्मि प्रभुरस्म्यहम्॥४२॥
ओङ्कारार्थस्वरूपोऽस्मि निष्कलङ्कमयोऽस्म्यहम्। चिदाकारस्वरूपोऽस्मि नाहमस्मि न सोऽस्म्यहम्॥४३॥
न हि किंचित्स्वरूपोऽस्मि निर्व्यापारस्वरूपवान्। निरंशोऽस्मि निराभासो न मनोनेन्द्रियोऽस्म्यहम्॥४४॥
न बुद्धिर्नविकल्पोऽहं न देहादित्रयोऽस्म्यहम्। न जाग्रत्स्वप्नरूपोऽहं सुषुप्तिस्वरूपवान्॥४५॥
न तापत्रयरूपोऽहं नेषणात्रयवानहम्। श्रवणं नास्ति मे सिद्धेर्मननं च चिदात्मनि॥४६॥
सजातीयं न मे किंचिद्विजातीयं न मे क्वचित्। स्वगतं च न मे किंचिन्न मे भेदत्रयं क्वचित्॥४७॥

I am always with the nature of Aja (the unborn). I am without passion or faults. I am the pure, the enlightened, the eternal, the all-pervading and of the nature of the significance of Oṁ, of the spotless, and of Cit. I am neither existing nor non-existing. I am not of the nature of anything. I am of the nature of the actionless. I am without parts. I have no semblance, no manas, no sense, no buddhi, no change, none of the three bodies, neither the waking, dreaming, or dreamless sleeping states. I am neither of the nature of the three pains nor of the three desires. I have neither *śravaṇa* nor *manana* in cidātmā in order to attain salvation. There is nothing like me or unlike me. There is nothing within me. I have none of the three bodies.

असत्यं हि मनोरूपमसत्यं बुद्धिरूपकम्। अहंकारमसद्धीति नित्योऽहं शाश्वत ह्यजः॥४८॥
देहत्रयमसद्विद्धि कालत्रयमसत्सदा। गुणत्रयमसद्विद्धि ह्यहं सत्यात्मकः शुचिः॥४९॥
श्रुतं सर्वमसद्विद्धि वेदं सर्वमसत्सदा। शास्त्रं सर्वमसद्विद्धि ह्यहं सत्यचिदात्मकः॥५०॥
मूर्तित्रयमसद्विद्धि सर्वभूतमसत्सदा। सर्वतत्त्वमसद्विद्धि ह्याहं भूमा सदाशिवः॥५१॥
गुरुशिष्यमसद्विद्धि गुरोर्मन्त्रमसत्ततः। यदृश्यं तदसद्विद्धि न मां विद्धि तथाविधम्॥५२॥
यच्चिन्त्यं तदसद्विद्धि यन्नयाय्य तदसत्सदा। यद्धितं तदसद्विद्धि न मां विद्धितथाविधम्॥५३॥
सर्वान्प्राणानसद्विद्धि सर्वान्भोगानसत्त्विति। दृष्टिं श्रुतमसद्विद्धि ओतं प्रोतसमन्मयम्॥५४॥
कार्याकार्यमसद्विद्धि नष्टं प्राप्तमसन्मयम्। दुःखादुःखमसद्विद्धि सर्वासर्वमसन्मयम्॥५५॥
पूर्णापूर्णमसद्विद्धि धर्माधर्ममसन्मयम्। लाभालाभावसद्विद्धि जयाजयमसन्मयम्॥५६॥
शब्दं सर्वमसद्विद्धि स्पर्शं सर्वमसत्सदा। रूपं सर्वमसद्विद्धि रसं सर्वमसन्मयम्॥५७॥
गन्धं सर्वमसद्विद्धि सर्वात्रानमसन्मयम्! असदेव सदा सर्वमसदेव भवोद्भवम्॥५८॥
असदेव गुणं सर्वं सन्मात्रमहमेव हि।

"The nature of manas is unreal, the nature of buddhi is unreal, the nature of *aham* (the 'I') is unreal; but I am the unconditioned, the permanent and the unborn. The three bodies are unreal, the three periods of time are unreal, the three guṇas are unreal, but I am of the nature of the real and the pure. That which is heard is unreal, all the Vedas are unreal, the

Śāstras are unreal, but I am the Real and of the nature of cit. The Mūrtis (Brahmā, Viṣṇu and Rudra having limitation) are unreal, all the creation is unreal, all the *tattvas* are unreal, but know that I am the great Sadāśiva. The master and the disciple are unreal, the mantra of the Guru is unreal, that which is seen is unreal, but know me to be Real. Whatever is thought of is unreal, whatever is lawful is unreal, whatever is beneficial is unreal, but know me to be the Real. Know the Puruṣa (ego) to be unreal, know the enjoyments to be unreal, know things seen and heard are unreal as also the one woven warp-wise and woof-wise, viz., this universe; cause and non-cause are unreal, things lost or obtained are unreal. Pains and happiness are unreal, all and non-all are unreal, gain and loss are unreal, victory and defeat are unreal. All the sound, all the touch, all the forms, all the taste, all the smell, and all ajñāna are unreal. Everthing is always unreal— the mundane existence is unreal— all the guṇas are unreal. I am of the nature of Sat.

स्वात्ममन्त्रं सदा पश्येत्स्वात्ममन्त्रं सदाभ्यसेत्।।५९।।

अहं ब्रह्मास्मिमन्त्रोऽयं दृश्यपापं विनाशयेत्। अहं ब्रह्मास्मि मन्त्रोऽयमन्यमन्त्रं विनाशयेत्।।६०।।

अहं ब्रह्मास्मि मन्त्रोऽयं देहदोषं विनाशयेत्। अहं ब्रह्मास्मि मन्त्रोऽयं जन्मपापं विनाशयेत्।।६१।।

अहं ब्रह्मास्मि मन्त्रोऽयं मृत्युपाशं विनाशयेत्। अहं ब्रह्मास्मि मन्त्रोऽयं द्वैतदु:खं विनाशयेत्।।६२।।

अहं ब्रह्मास्मि मन्त्रोऽयं भेदबुद्धिं विनाशयेत्। अहं ब्रह्मास्मि मन्त्रोऽयं चिन्तादु:ख विनाशयेत्।।६३।।

अहं ब्रह्मास्मि मन्त्रोऽयं बुद्धिव्याधि विनाशयेत्। अहं ब्रह्मास्मि मन्त्रोऽयं चित्तबन्धं विनाशयेत्।।६४।।

अहं ब्रह्मास्मि मन्त्रोऽयं सर्वव्याधीन्विनाशयेत्। अहं ब्रह्मास्मि मन्त्रोऽयं सर्वशोकं विनाशयेत्।।६५।।

अहं ब्रह्मास्मि मन्त्रोऽयं कामादिन्नाशयेत्क्षणात्। अहं ब्रह्मास्मि मन्त्रोऽयं क्रोधशक्तिं विनाशयेत्।।६६।।

अहं ब्रह्मास्मि मन्त्रोऽयं चित्तवृत्तिं विनाशयेत्। अहं ब्रह्मास्मि मन्त्रोऽयं संकल्पादीन्विनाशयेत्।।६७।।

अहं ब्रह्मास्मि मन्त्रोऽयं कोटिदोषं विनाशयेत्। अहं ब्रह्मास्मि मन्त्रोऽयं सर्वतन्त्रं विनाशयेत्।।६८।।

अहं ब्रह्मास्मि मन्त्रोऽयं मन्त्रोऽयमात्माज्ञानं विनाशयेत्। अहं ब्रह्मास्मि मन्त्रोऽयमात्मलोकजयप्रद:।।६९।।

अहं ब्रह्मास्मि मन्त्रोऽयमप्रतर्क्यसुखप्रद:।। अहं ब्रह्मास्मि मन्त्रोऽयमजढत्वं प्रयच्छति।।७०।।

अहं ब्रह्मास्मि मन्त्रोऽयमनात्मासुरमर्दन:। अहं ब्रह्मास्मि वज्रोऽयमानत्माखग्रिन्हेत्।।७१।।

अहं ब्रह्मास्मि मन्त्रोऽयमनात्माख्यासुरान्हरेत्। अहं ब्रह्मास्मि मन्त्रोऽयं सर्वांस्तान्मोक्षयिष्यति।।७२।।

अहं ब्रह्मास्मि मन्त्रोऽयं ज्ञानान्दं प्रयच्छति। सप्तकोटिमहामन्त्रं जन्मकोटिशतप्रदम्।।७३।।

सर्वमन्त्रान्समुत्सृज्य एतं मन्त्र समभ्यसेत्। सद्यो मोक्षमवाप्नोति नात्र संदेहमण्वपि।।७४।।

"One should cognize his own Ātman alone. One should always practise the mantra of his Ātman alone the mantra (Aham-brahmāsmi) 'I am brahman' removes all the sins of sight, destroys all other mantras, destroys all the sins of body and birth, the noose of Yama, the pains of duality, the thought of difference, the pains of thought, the disease of buddhi, the bondage of Citta, all diseases, all griefs and passions instantaneously, the power of anger, the modifications of citta, saṅkalpa, crores of sins, all actions and the ajñāna of Ātman. The mantra 'I am brahman' gives indescribable bliss, gives the state of ajada (the non-inertness or the undecaying) and kills the demon of non-Ātman. The thunderbolt 'I am Brahman' clears all the hill of not-Ātman. The wheel 'I am Brahman' destroys the asuras of not-Ātman. The mantras 'I am Brahman' will relieve all (persons). The mantra 'I am Brahman' gives spiritual wisdom and bliss. There are seven crores of great mantras and there are viratas (vows) of (or yielding) hundred crores of births. Having given up all other mantras, one should ever practise this mantra. He obtains at once salvation, and there is not even a particle of doubt about it. Thus ends the third chapter of the Tejobindu Upaniṣad."

।।अथ चतुर्थोऽध्याय:।।

कुमार: परमेश्वरं पप्रच्छ जीवन्मुक्तविदेहमुक्तयो: स्थितिमनुब्रूहीति:। स होवाच पर शिव:।
चिदात्माहं परात्माहं निर्गुणोऽहं परात्पर:। आत्ममात्रेण यस्तिष्ठेत्स जीवन्मुक्त उच्यते।।१।।
देहत्रयातिरिक्तोऽहं शुद्धचैतन्यमस्म्यहम्। ब्रह्माहमिति यस्यान्त: स जीवन्मुक्त उच्यते।।२।।
आनन्दघनरूपोऽस्मि परानन्दघनोऽस्म्यहम्। यस्य देहादिकं नास्ति यस्य ब्रह्मेति निश्चय:।
परमानन्दपूर्णो य: स जीवन्मुक्त उच्यते।।३।।
यस्य देहादिकं नास्ति यस्य ब्रह्मेति निश्चय:। परमानन्दपूर्णो य: स जीवन्मुक्त उच्यते।।४।।
सर्वत्र पूर्णरूपात्मा सर्वत्रात्मावशेषक:। आनन्दरतिरव्यक्त: परिपूर्णश्चिदात्मक:।।५।।
शुद्धचैतन्यरूपात्मा सर्वसङ्गविवर्जित:। नित्यानन्द: प्रसन्नात्मा ह्यन्यचिन्ताविवर्जित:।।६।।
किं चिदस्तित्वहीनो य: स जीवन्मुक्त उच्यते। न मे चित्तं न मे बुद्धिर्नाहंकारो न चेन्द्रियम्।।७।।
न मे देह: कदाचिद्वा न मे प्राणादय: क्वचित्। न मे माया न मे कामो न मे क्रोध: परोऽस्म्यहम्।।८।।
न मे किंचिदिदं वापि न मे किंचित्क्वचिज्जगत्। न मे दोषो न मे लिङ्गं न मे चक्षुर्न मे मन:।।९।।
न मे श्रोत्रं न मे नासा न मे जिह्वा न मे कर:। न मे जाग्रन्न मे स्वप्नं न मे कारणमण्वपि।।१०।।
न मे तुरीयमिति य: स जीवन्मुक्त उच्यते। इदं सर्वं न में किंचिदयं सर्वं न मे क्वचित्।।११।।
न मे कालो न मे देशो न मे वस्तु न मे मति:। न मे स्नानं न मे संध्या न मे दैवं न मे स्थलम्।।१२।।
न मे तीर्थं न मे सेवा न मे ज्ञानं न मे पदम्। न मे बन्धो न मे जन्म न मे वाक्यं न मे रवि:।।१३।।
न मे पुण्यं न मे पापं न मे कार्यं न मे शुभम्। न मे जीव इति स्वात्मा न मे किंचिज्जगन्त्रयम्।।१४।।
न मे मोक्षो न मे द्वैतं न मे वेदो न मे विधि:। न मेऽन्तिकं न मे दूरं न मे बोधो न मे रह:।।१५।।
न मे म गुरुर्न मे शिष्यो न म हीनो न चाधिक:। न मे ब्रह्म न मे विष्णुर्न मे रुद्रो न चन्द्रमा:।।१६।।
न मे पृथ्वी न मे तोयं न मे वायुर्न मे वियत्। न मे वह्निर्न मे गोत्रं न मे लक्ष्यं न मे भव:।।१७।।
न मे ध्याता न मे ध्येयं न मे ध्यानं न मे मनु:। न मे शीतं न मे चोष्णं न मे तृष्णा न मे क्षुधा:।।१८।।
न मे मित्रं न मे शुत्रुर्न मे मोहो न मे जय:। न मे पूर्वं न मे पश्चान्न मे चोर्ध्वं न मे दिश:।।१९।।
न मे वक्तव्यमल्पं वा न मे श्रोतव्यमण्वपि। न मे गन्तव्यमीषद्वा न मे ध्यातव्यमण्वपि।।२०।।
न मे भोक्तव्यमीषद्वा न मे स्मर्तव्यमण्वपि। न मे भोगो न मे रागो न मे यागो न मे लय:।
न मे मौर्ख्यं न मे शान्तं न मे बन्धो न मे प्रियम्।

न मे मोदः प्रमोदो वा न मे स्थूलं न मे कृशम्।।२२।।

न मे दीर्घं न मे ह्रस्वं न मे वृद्धिर्न मे क्षयः। अध्यारोपोऽपवादो वा न मे चैकं न मे बहु।।२३।।

न मे आन्ध्यं न मे मान्द्यं न मे पट्विदमण्वपि। न मे मांसं न मे रक्तं न मे मेदो न मे ह्यसृक्।।२४।।

न मे मज्जा न मेऽस्थिर्वा न मे त्वग्धातुसप्तकम्। न मे शुक्लं न मे रक्तं न मे नीलं न मे पृथक्।।२५।।

न मे तापो न मे लाभो मुख्यं गौणं न मे क्वचित्। न मे भ्रान्तिर्न मे स्थैर्यं न मे गुह्यं न मे कुलम्।।२६।।

न मे त्याज्यं न मे ग्राह्यं न मे हास्यं न मे नयः। न मे वृत्तं न मे ग्लानिर्न मे शोष्यं न मे सुखम्।।२७।।

न मे ज्ञाता न मे ज्ञानं न मे ज्ञेयं न मे स्वयम्। न मे तुभ्यं न मे मह्यं न मे त्वं च न मे त्वहम्।।२८।।

न मे जरा न मे बाल्यं न मे यौवनमण्वपि। अहं ब्रह्मास्म्यहं ब्रह्मास्म्यहं ब्रह्मेति निश्चयः।।२९।।

चिदहं चिदहं चेति स जीवन्मुक्त उच्यते। ब्रह्मैवाहं चिदेवाहं परो वाहं न संशयः।।३०।।

स्वयमेव स्वयं हंसः स्वयमेव स्वयं स्थितः। स्वयमेव स्वयं पश्येत्स्वात्मराज्ये सुखं वसेत्।।३१।।

स्वात्मानन्दं स्वयं भोक्ष्येत्स जीवन्मुक्त उच्यते। स्वयमेवैकवीरोऽग्रे स्वयमेव प्रभुः स्मृतः।

स्वस्वरूपे स्वयं स्वप्स्ये स जीवन्मुक्त उच्यते।।३२।।

The Kumāra asked the great Lord : "Please explain to me the nature of Jīvanmukti (embodied salvation) and videhamukti (disembodied salvation)." To which the great Śiva replied : "I am cidātmā. I am Para-Ātman. I am the Nirguṇa, greater than the great. One who will simply stay in Ātman is called a Jīvanmukta. He who realises : 'I am beyond the three bodies, I am the pure consciousness and I am Brahman', is said to be a Jīvanmukta. He is said to be a Jīvanmukta, who realises : "I am of the nature of the blissful and of the supreme bliss and I have neither body nor any other thing except the certitude "I am Brahman" Only. He is said to be a Jīvanmukta who has not at all got the 'I' in myself, but who stays in cinmātra (absolute consciousness) alone, whose interior is consciousness alone, who is only of the nature of Cinmātra, whose Ātman is of the nature of the all-full, who has Ātman left over in all, who is devoted to bliss, who is undifferentiated, who is all-full of the nature of consciousness, whose Ātman is of the nature of pure consciousness, who has given up all affinities (for objects), who has unconditioned bliss, whose Ātman is tranquil, who has got no other thought (then Itself), and who is devoid of the thought of the existence of anything. He is said to be a Jīvanmukta who realises : 'I have no citta, no buddhi, no ahaṁkāra, no sense, no body at any time, no prāṇas, no Māyā, no passion and no anger, I am the great, I have nothing of these objects or of the world, and I have no sin, no characteristics, no eye, no manas, no ear, no nose, no tongue, no hand, no waking, no dreaming, or causal state in the least or the fourth state.' He is said to be a Jīvanmukta, who realises : 'All this is not mine, I have no time, no space, no object. no thought, no snāna (bathing), no sandhyās (junction-period ceremonies), no deity, no place, no sacred places, no worship, no spiritual wisdom, no seat, no relative, no birth, no speech, no wealth, no virtue, no vice, no duty, no auspiciousness, no Jīva, not even the three worlds, no salvation, no duality, no Vedas, no mandatory rules, no proximity, no distance, no knowledge, no secrecy, no Guru, no disciple, no diminution, no excess, no Brahmā, no Viṣṇu, no Rudra, no moon, no earth, no water, no vāyu, no ākāśa, no agni, no clan, no lakṣya (object aimed at), no mundane existence, no meditator, no object of meditation, no manas, no cold, no heat, no thirst, no hunger, no friend, no foe, no illusion, no victory, no past, present, or future, no quarters, nothing to be said or heard in the least, nothing to be gone (or attained) to, nothing to be contemplated enjoyed or remembered, no enjoyment, no desire, no yoga, no absorption, no garrulity, no quietude, no bondage, no love, no joy, no instant joy, no hugeness, no smallness, neither length nor shortness, neither increase nor decrease, neither adhyāropa (illusory attribution) nor apavāda (withdrawl of the conception) no oneness, no manyness, no blindness, no dullness, no skull, no flesh, no blood, no lymph, no skin, no marrow, no bone, no skin, none of the seven dhātus, no whiteness, no redness, no blueness, no heat, no gain, neither importance nor non-importance, no delusion, no perseverance, no mystery, no race, nothing to be abandoned or received, nothing to be laughed at, no policy, no religious vow, no fault, no bewailments, no happiness, neither knower nor knowledge nor the knowable, no Self, nothing belonging to you or to me, neither you nor I, and neither old age nor youth nor manhood; but I am certainly Brahman. "I am certainly Brahman. I am Cit, I am Cit." He is said to be a Jīvanmukta who cognizes : 'I am Brahman alone, I am Cit alone, I am the supreme'. No doubt need be entertained about this : 'I am Haṁsa itself, I remain of my own will, I can see myself through myself, I reign happy in the kingdom of Ātman and enjoy in myself the bliss of my own Ātmā'. He is a Jīvanmukta who is himself, the foremost and the one undaunted person who is himself the lord and rests in his own Self.

ब्रह्मभूत: प्रशान्तात्मा ब्रह्मानन्दमय: सुखी। स्वच्छरूपो महामौनी वैदेही मुक्त एव स:।।३३।।
सर्वात्मा समरूपात्मा शुद्धात्मा त्वहमुत्थित:। एकवर्जित एकात्मा सर्वात्मा स्वात्ममात्रक:।।३४।।
अजात्मा चामृतात्माहं स्वयमात्माहमव्यय:। लक्ष्यात्मा ललितात्माहं तूष्णीमात्मस्वभाववान्।।३५।।
आनन्दात्मा प्रियो ह्यात्मा मोक्षात्मा बन्धवर्जित:। ब्रह्मैवाहं चिदेवाहमेवं वापि न चिन्त्यते।।३६।।
चिन्मात्रेणैव यस्तिष्ठैद्वैदेही मुक्त एव: स:।।३७।।

"He is a *Videhamukta* who has become *Brahman*, whose *Ātman* has attained quiescence, who is of the nature of Brāhmic bliss, who is happy, who is of a pure nature, and who is a great mauni (observer of silence). He is *videhamukta* who remains in *Cinmātra* alone without (even) thinking thus : 'I am all *Ātmā*, the Atmā that is equal (or the same) in all, the pure, without one, the non-dual, the all, the self only, the birthless and the deathless— I am myself the undecaying *Ātman* that is the object aimed at, the sporting, the silent, the blissful, the beloved and the bondless salvation— I am *Brahman* alone— I am *Cit* alone'. He is a *Videhamukta* who having abandoned the thought : 'I alone am the *Brahman*' is filled with bliss.

निश्चयं च परित्यज्य अहं ब्रह्मेति निश्चयम्। आनन्दभरितस्वान्तो वैदेही मुक्त एव स:।।३७।।
सर्वमस्तीति नास्तीति निश्चयं त्यज्य तिष्ठति। अहं ब्रह्मास्मि नास्मीति सच्चिदान्दमात्रक:।।३९।।

किंचित्क्वचित्कदाचिच्च आत्मानं न स्पृशत्यसौ। तूष्णीमेव स्थिरस्तूष्णीं तूष्णीं सत्यं न किंचन।।४०।।
परमात्मा गुणातीतः सर्वात्मा भूतभावनः। कालभेदं वस्तुभेदं देशभेदं स्वभेदकम्।।४१।।
किंचिद्भेदं न तस्यास्ति किंचिद्वापि न विद्यते। अहं त्वं तदिदं सोऽयं कालात्मा कालहीनकः।।४२।।
शून्यात्मा सूक्ष्मरूपात्मा विश्वात्मा विश्वहीनकः। देवात्मा देवहीनात्मा मेयात्मा मेयवर्जितः।।४३।।
सर्वत्र जडहीनात्मा सर्वेषामन्तरात्मकः। सर्वसंकल्पहीनात्मा चिन्मात्रोऽस्मीति सर्वदा।।४४।।
केवलः परमात्माहं केवलो ज्ञानविग्रहः। सत्तामात्रस्वरूपात्मा नान्यत्किंचिज्जगद्भयम्।।४५।।
जीवेश्वरेति वाक् क्वेति वेदशास्त्राद्यहं त्विति। इदं चैतन्यमात्रसंसिद्धः अहं चैतन्यमित्यपि।।४६।।

He is a Videhamukta who having given up the certainty of the existence of non-existence of all objects, is pure Cidānanda (the consciousness bliss), who having abandoned (the thought): 'I am Brahman' (or) 'I am not Brahman' does not mingle his Ātman with anything, anywere or at any time, who is ever silent with the silence of Satya, who does nothing, who has gone beyond guṇas, whose Ātman has become the All, the great, and the purifier of the elements, who does not cognize the change of time, matter, place, himself or other differences, who does not see (the difference of) 'I', 'thou', 'this' or 'that', who being of the nature of time is yet without it, whose Ātmā is void, subtle and universal, but yet without (them), whose Ātman is divine and yet without Devas, whose Ātman is measurable and yet without measure, whose Ātman is without inertness and within every one, whose Ātman devoid of any saṅkalpa, who thinks always : 'I am Cinmātra, I am simply Paramātman, I am only of the nature of spiritual wisdom, I am only of the nature of Sat, I am afraid of nothing in this world,' and who is without the conception of Devas, Vedas and sciences, 'All this is consciousness, etc.,' and regards all as void.

इति निश्चयशून्यो यो वैदेही मुक्त एव सः। चैतन्यमात्र संसिद्धः स्वात्मारामः सुखासनः।।४७।।
अपरिच्छिन्नरूपात्मा अणुस्थूलादिवर्जितः। तुर्यतुर्यः परानन्दो वैदेही मुक्त एव सः।।४८।।
नामरूपविनीनात्मा परसंवित्सुखात्मकः। तुरीयातीरूपात्मा शुभाशुभविवर्जितः।।४९।।
योगात्मा योगयुक्तात्मा बन्धमोक्षविवर्जितः। गुणागुणविहीनात्मा देशकालविवर्जितः।।५०।।
साक्ष्यसाक्षित्वहीनात्मा किंचित्किंचिन्न किंचन। यस्य प्रपञ्चमानं न ब्रह्माकारमपीह न।।५१।।
स्वस्वरूपे स्वयंज्योतिः स्वस्वरूपे स्वयंरतिः। वाचामगोचरानन्दो वाङ्मनोगोचरः स्वयम्।।५२।।
अतीतातीतभावो यो वैदेही मुक्त एव सः।

He is a Videhamukta who has realised himself to be Caitanya alone, who is remaining at ease in the pleasure-garden of own Ātmā, whose Ātman is of an illimitable nature, who is without the conception of the small and the great, and who is the fourth of the fourth state and the supreme bliss. He is a Videhamukta whose Ātman is nameless and formless, who is the great spiritual wisdom of the nature of bliss, and of the nature of the state beyond turya, who is neither auspicious not inauspicious, who has yoga as his Ātmā, whose Ātman is associated with yoga, who is free from bondage or freedom, without guṇa or non-guṇa, without space, time, etc., without the witnessable and the witness, without the small or the great, and without the cognition of the universe or even the cognition of the nature of Brahman, but who finds his spiritual efflugence in his own nature, who finds bliss in himself, whose bliss is beyond the scope of words and mind, and whose thought is beyond and beyond.

चित्तवृत्तेरतीतो यश्चित्तवृत्त्यवभासकः॥५३॥
सर्ववृत्तिविहीनात्मा वैदेही मुक्त एव सः।
तस्मिन्काले विदेहीति देहस्मरणवर्जितः॥५४॥
ईषन्मात्रं स्मृतं चेद्यस्तदा सर्वसमन्वितः।

He is said to be Videhamukta who has gone beyond (or mastered quite) the modifications of citta, who illumines such modifications, and whose Ātman is without any modifications at all. In that case, he is neither embodied nor disembodied. If such a thought in entertained (even), for a moment, then he is surrounded (in thought) by all.

परैरदृष्टबाह्यात्मा परमानन्दचिद्घनः॥५५॥
परैदृष्टबाह्यात्मा सर्ववेदान्तगोचरः। ब्रह्मामृतरसास्वादो ब्रह्मामृतरसायनः॥५६॥
ब्रह्मामृतरसासक्तो ब्रह्मामृतरसः स्वयम्। ब्रह्मामृतरसे मग्नो ब्रह्मानन्दशिवार्चनः॥५७॥
ब्रह्मामृतरसे तृप्तो ब्रह्मानन्दानुभावकः। ब्रह्मानन्दशिवानन्दो ब्रह्मानन्दरसप्रभः॥५८॥
ब्रह्मानन्दपरं ज्योतिर्ब्रह्मानन्दनिरन्तरः। ब्रह्मानन्दरसान्नादो ब्रह्मानन्दकुटुम्बकः॥५९॥
ब्रह्मानन्दरसारूढो ब्रह्मानन्दैकचिद्घनः। ब्रह्मानन्दरसोद्वाहो ब्रह्मानन्दरसंभरः॥६०॥
ब्रह्मानन्दजनैर्युक्तो ब्रह्मानन्दात्मनि स्थितः। आत्मरूपमिदं सर्वमात्मनोऽन्यत्र किंचन॥६१॥
सर्वमात्माहमात्मास्मि परमात्मा परात्मकः।

He is a Videhamukta whose external Ātman invisible to others is the supreme bliss aiming at the highest vedānta, who drinks the juice of the nectar of Brahman, who has the nectar of Brahman as medicine, who is devoted to the juice of the nectar of Brahman, who is immersed in that juice, who has the beneficent worship of the Brāhmic bliss, who is not satiated with the juice of the nectar or Brahman, who realises Brāhmic bliss, who cognized the Śiva bliss in Brāhmic bliss, who has the effulgence of the essence of Brāhmic bliss, who has become one with it, who lives in the household of Brāhmic bliss, has mounted the car of Brāhmic bliss, who has an imponderable Cit being one with it, who is supporting (all), being full of it, who associated with me having it, who says in Ātman having that bliss and who thinks : 'All this is of the nature of Ātmā, there is nothing else beside Ātmā, all is Ātmā, I am Ātmā, the great Ātmā, the supreme Ātmā, and Ātman of the form of bliss.'

नित्यानन्दस्वरूपात्मा वैदेही मुक्त एव सः॥६२॥
पूर्णरूपो महानात्मा प्रीतात्मा शाश्वतात्मकः। सर्वान्तर्यामिरूपात्मा निर्मलात्मा निरात्मकः॥६३॥
निर्विकारस्वरूपात्मा शुद्धात्मा शान्तरूपकः। शान्ताशान्तस्वरूपात्मा नैकात्मत्वविवर्जितः॥६४॥
जीवात्मपरमात्मेति चिन्तासर्वस्ववर्जितः। मुक्तामुक्तस्वरूपात्मा मुक्तामुक्तविवर्जितः॥६५॥

बन्धमोक्षस्वरूपात्मा बन्धमोक्षविवर्जितः। द्वैताद्वैतस्वरूपात्मा द्वैताद्वैतविवर्जितः॥६६॥
सर्वासर्वस्वरूपात्मा सर्वासर्वविवर्जितः। मोदप्रमोदरूपात्मा मोदादिविनिवर्जितः॥६७॥
सर्वसंकल्पहीनात्मा वैदेही मुक्त एव सः। निष्कलात्मा निर्मलात्मा बुद्धात्म पुरुषात्मकः॥६८॥
आनन्दादिविहीनात्मा अमृतात्मामृतात्मकः। कालत्रयस्वरूपात्मा कालत्रयविवर्जितः॥६९॥
अखिलात्मा ह्यमेयात्मा मानात्मा मानवर्जितः। नित्यप्रत्यक्षरूपात्मा नित्यप्रत्यक्षनिर्णयः॥७०॥
अन्यहीनस्वभावात्मा अन्यहीनस्वयंप्रभः। विद्याविद्यादिमेयात्मा विद्याविद्यादिवर्जितः॥७१॥
नित्यानित्यविहीनात्मा इहामुत्रविवर्जितः। शमादिषट्कशून्यात्मा मुमुक्षत्वादिवर्जितः॥७२॥
स्थूलदेहविहीनात्मा सूक्ष्मदेहविवर्जितः। कारणादिविहीनात्मा तुरीयादिविवर्जितः॥७३॥
अन्नकोशविहीनात्मा प्राणकोशविवर्जितः। मनःकोशविहीनात्मा विज्ञानादिविवर्जितः॥७४॥
आनन्दकोशहीन्त्मा पञ्चकोशविवर्जितः। निर्विकल्पस्वरूपात्मा सविकल्पविवर्जितः॥७५॥
दृश्यानुविद्धहीनात्मा शब्दविद्धविवर्जितः। सदा समाधिशून्यात्मा आदिमध्यान्तवर्जितः॥७६॥
प्रज्ञानवाक्यहीनात्मा अहंब्रह्मास्मिवर्जितः। तत्त्वमस्यादिहीनात्मा अयमात्मेत्यभावकः॥७७॥
ओंकारवाच्यहीनात्मा सर्ववाच्यविवर्जितः। अवस्थात्रयहीनात्मा अक्षरात्मा चिदात्मकः॥७८॥
आत्मज्ञेयादिहीनात्मा यत्किंचिदिदमात्मकः। भानाभानविहीनात्मा वैदेही मुक्त एव सः॥७९॥
आत्मानमेव वीक्षस्व आत्मानं बोधय स्वकम्। स्वमात्मानं स्वयं भुङ्क्ष्व स्वस्थो भव षडानन॥८०॥
स्वमात्मनि स्वयं तृप्तः स्वमात्मनि स्वयं चर। आत्मानमेव मोदस्व वैदेही मुक्तिको भवेत्युपनिषद्॥

He who thinks : 'My nature is full, I am the great Ātmā, I am the all-contented ana the permanent Ātman. I am the Ātman pervading the heart of all, which is stained by anything, but which has no Ātmā; I am the Ātman whose nature is changeless, I am the quiescent Ātmā; and I am the many Ātmā' He who does not think this is Jīvātmā and that is Paramātmā, whose Ātman is of the nature of the emancipated and the non-emancipated, but without emancipation or bondage, whose Ātman is of the nature of the dual and the non-dual one, but without duality and non-duality; whose Ātman is of the nature of All and the non-All, but without them; whose Ātman is of the nature of the happiness arising from objects obtained and enjoyed, but without it; and who is devoid of any saṅkalpa— such a man is a videhamukta. He whose Ātman is partless, stainless, enlightened, Puruṣa, without bliss, etc., of the nature of nectar, of the nature of the three periods of time, but without them; whose Ātman is entire and non-measurable, being subject to proof though without proof; whose Ātman is the eternal and the witness, but without eternality and witness; whose Ātman is nature of the secondless, who is the self-shining one without a second, whose Ātman cannot be measured by vidyā and avidyā but without them; whose Ātman is without conditionedness or unconditionedness, who is without this or the higher worlds, whose Ātman is without the six things beginning with śama, who is without the qualifications of the aspirant after salvation, whose Ātman is without gross, subtle, causal, and the fourth bodies, and without the anna, prāṇa, manas, and vijñāna sheaths; whose Ātman is of the nature of ānanda (bliss) sheath, but without five sheaths; whose Ātman is the nature of nirvikalpa, is devoid of saṅkalpa, without the characteristics of the visible or the audible, and of the nature of void, owing to unceasing samādhi, who is without beginning, samādhi, who is without beginning, middle, or end; whose Ātman is devoid of the word Prajñāna, who is without the idea 'I am Brahman,' whose Ātman is devoid (of the thought) of 'thou art', who is without the thought of 'this is Ātmā', whose Ātman is devoid of that which is described by Oṁ, who is above the reach of any speech or the three states, and is the indestructible and the cidātmā, whose Ātman is not the one which can be known by Ātman and whose Ātman has neither light nor darkness. Such a personage is a Videhamukta. Look only upon Ātmā; know It as your own. Enjoy your Ātman yourself, and stay in peace. O six-faced one, be content in your own Ātmā, be wandering in your own Ātmā, and be enjoying your own Ātman. Then you will attain Videhamukti."

।।अथ पञ्चमोऽध्यायः।।

निदाघो नाम वै मुनिः पप्रच्छ ऋभुं भगवन्तमात्मानात्मविवेकमनुब्रूहीति। स होवाच ऋभुः।

The Sage named Nīdāgha addressed the venerable Ṛbhu : "O Lord please explain to me the discrimination of *Ātman* from non-*Ātman.*" The Sage replied thus :

सर्ववाचोऽवधिर्ब्रह्म सर्वचिन्तावधिर्गुरुः। सर्वकारणकार्यात्मा कार्यकारणवर्जितः।।१।।
सर्वसंकल्परहितः सर्वनादमयः शिवः। सर्ववर्जितचिन्मात्रः सर्वानन्दमयः परः।।२।।
सर्वतेजः प्रकाशात्मा नादानन्दमयात्मकः। सर्वानुभवनिर्मुक्तः सर्वध्यानविवर्जितः।।३।।
सर्वनादकलातीत एष आत्माहमव्ययः। आत्मानात्मविवेकादिभेदाभेदविवर्जितः।।४।।
शान्ताशान्तादिहीनात्मा नादान्तर्ज्योतिरूपकः। महावाक्यार्थतोदूरो ब्रह्मास्मीत्यतिदूरतः।।५।।
तच्छब्दवर्ज्यस्त्वंशब्दहीनो वाक्यार्थवर्जितः। क्षराक्षरविहीनो यो नादान्तर्ज्योतिरेव सः।।६।।
अखण्डैकरसो वाहमानन्दोऽस्मीतिवर्जितः। सर्वातीतस्वभावात्मा नादान्तर्ज्योतिरेव सः।।७।।
आत्मेति शब्दहीनो य आत्मशब्दार्थवर्जितः। सच्चिदानन्दहीनो य एषैवात्मा सनानतः।।८।।
स निर्देष्टुमशक्यो यो वेदवाक्यैरगम्यतः। यस्य किंचिद्बहिर्नास्ति किंचिदन्तः कियन्न स।।९।।
यस्य लिङ्गं प्रपञ्चं वा ब्रह्मैवात्मा न संशयः। नास्ति यस्य शरीरं वा जीवो वा भूतभौतिकः।।१०।।
नामरूपादिकं नास्ति भोज्यं वा भोगभुक्व वा। सद्वाऽसद्वा स्थितिर्वापि यस्य नास्ति क्षराक्षरम्।।११।।
गुणं वा विगुणं वापि सम आत्मा न संशयः। यस्य वाच्यं वाचकं वा श्रवणं मननं च वा।।१२।।
गुरुशिष्यादिभेदं वा देवलोकाः सुरासुराः। यत्र धर्ममधर्मं वा शुद्धं वाशुद्धमण्वपि।।१३।।
यक्ष कालमकालं वा निश्चयः संशयो न हि। यत्र मन्त्रममन्त्रं वा विद्याविद्ये न विद्यते।।१४।।
द्रष्टृदर्शनदृश्यं वा ईषन्मात्रं कलात्मकम्। अनात्मेति प्रसङ्गो वा ह्यनात्मेति मनोऽपि वा।।१५।।
अनात्मेति जगद्वापि नास्ति नास्तीति निश्चिनु। सर्वसंकल्पशून्यत्वात्सर्वकार्यविवर्जनात्।।१६।।
केवलं ब्रह्ममात्रत्वान्नास्त्यनात्मेति निश्चिनु। देहत्रयविहीनत्वात्कालत्रयविवर्जनात्।।१७।।
जीवत्रयगुणाभावात्तापत्रयविवर्जनात्। लोकत्रयविहीनत्वात्सर्वमात्मेति शासनात्।।१८।।

चित्ताभावाच्चिन्तनीयं देहाभावाज्जरा न च। पादाभावाद्गतिर्नास्ति हस्ताभावात्क्रिया न च॥१९॥
मृत्युर्नास्ति जनाभावद्बुद्ध्यभावात्सुखादिकम्। धर्मो नास्ति शुचिर्नास्ति सत्यं नास्ति भयं न च॥२०॥
अक्षरोच्चारणं नास्ति गुरुशिष्यादि नास्त्यपि। एकाभावे द्वितीयं न न द्वितीये न चैकता॥२१॥
सत्यत्वमस्ति चेत्किंचिदसत्यं न च संभवेत्। असत्यत्वं यदि भवेत्सत्यत्वं न घटिष्यति॥२२॥
शुभं यद्यशुभं विद्धि अशुभाच्छुभमिष्यते। भयं यद्यभयं विद्धि अभयाद्भयमापतेत्॥२३॥
बन्धत्वमपि चेन्मोक्षो बन्धाभावे क्व मोक्षता। मरणं यदि चेज्जन्म जन्माभावे मृतिर्न च॥२४॥
त्वमित्यपि भवेच्चाहं त्वं नो चेदहमेव न। इदं यदि तदेवास्ति तदभावादिदं न च॥२५॥
अस्तीति चेन्नास्ति तदा नास्ति चेदस्ति किंचन। कार्यं चेत्कारणं किंचित्कार्याभावे न कारणम्॥२६॥
द्वैतं यदि तदाऽद्वैतं द्वैताभावे द्वयं न च। दृश्यं यदि दृगप्यस्ति दृश्याभावे दृगेव न॥२७॥
अन्तर्यदि बहिः सत्यमन्ताभावे बहिर्न च। पूर्णत्वमस्ति चेत्किंचिदपूर्णत्वं प्रसज्यते।२८॥
तस्मादेतत्क्वचिन्नास्ति त्वं चाहं वा इमे इदम्। नास्ति दृष्टान्तिकं सत्ये नास्ति दार्ष्टान्तिकं ह्यजे॥२९॥
परंब्रह्माहमस्मीति स्मरणस्य मनो न हि। ब्रह्ममात्रं जगदिदं ब्रह्ममात्रं त्वमप्यहम्॥३०॥
चिन्मात्रं केवलं चाहं नास्त्यनात्म्येति निश्चिनु। इदं प्रपञ्चं नास्त्येव नोत्पन्नं नो स्थितं क्वचित्॥३१॥
चित्तं प्रपञ्चमित्याहुर्नास्ति नास्त्येव सर्वदा। न प्रपञ्चं न चित्तादि नाहंकारो न जीवकः॥३२॥
मायाकार्यादिकं नास्ति माया नास्ति भयं नहि। कर्ता नास्ति क्रिया नास्ति श्रवणं मननं नहि॥३३॥
समाधिद्वितयं नास्ति मातृमानादि नास्ति हि। अज्ञानं चापि नास्त्येव ह्यविवेकं कदाचन॥३४॥
अनुबन्धचतुष्कं न संबन्धक्षयमेव न। न गङ्गा न गया सेतुर्न भूतं नान्यदस्ति हि॥३५॥
न भूमिर्न जलं नाग्निर्न वायुर्नं च ख क्वचित्। न देवा न च दिक्पाला न वेद न गुरुः क्वचित्॥३६॥
न दूरं नान्तिकं नालं न मध्यं न क्वचित्थितम्। नाद्वैतं द्वैतसत्यं वा ह्यसत्यं वा इदं न च॥३७॥
बन्धमोक्षादिकं नास्ति सद्वाऽसद्वा सुखादि वा। जातिर्नास्ति गतिर्नास्ति वर्णो नास्ति न लौकिकम्॥३८॥

"The furthest limit of all vāk (speech) is Brahman; the furthest limit to all the thoughts is the Guru. That which is of the nature of all causes and effects but yet without them, that which is without saṅkalpa, of the nature of all bliss, that which illuminates all luminaries and that which is full of the bliss of nāda (spiritual sound), without any enjoyment and contemplation and beyond nādas and kalās (parts)— that is Ātmā, that is the 'I', the indestructible. Being devoid of all the difference of Ātman and non-Ātmā, of heterogeneity and homogeneity and of quiescence and non-quiescence— that is the one Jyotis at the end of nāda. Being remote from the conception of Mahā-vākyārtha (i.e., the meaning of Mahā-vākyas) as well 'I am Brahman', being devoid of or without the conception of the world and the meaning, and being devoid of the conception of the destructible and indestructible— that is the one Jyotis at the end of nāda. Being without the conception 'I am the partless non-dual essence' or 'I am the blissful', and being of the nature of the one beyond all-that is one Jyotis at the end of nāda. He who is devoid of the significance of Ātman (viz., motion) and devoid of Saccidānanda— he is alone Ātmā, the eternal. He who is undefinable and unreachable by the words of the vedas, who has neither externals nor internals, and whose symbol is either the universe or Brahman— he is undoubtedly Ātman. He who has no body, nor is a Jīva made up of the elements their compounds, who has neither form nor name, neither the enjoyable nor the enjoyer, neither Sat nor asat, neither preservation nor regeneration, neither guṇa nor non-guṇa— that is undoubtedly my Ātman. He who has neither the described nor description, neither śravaṇa nor manana, neither Guru nor disciple, neither the world of the Devas nor Devas nor Asuras, neither duty nor non-duty, neither the immaculate nor non-immaculate, neither time nor non-time, neither certainty nor doubt, neither mantra nor non-mantra, neither science nor non-science, neither the seer nor the sight which is subtle, nor the nectar of time— that is Ātman. Rest assured that not-Ātman is a misnomer. There is no manas as not-Ātman. There is no world as not-Ātman. Owing to the absence of all saṅkalpas and to the giving up of all actions, brahman alone remains, and there is no not-Ātman. Being devoid of the three bodies, the three periods of time, the three guṇas of Jīva, the three pains and the three worlds, and following the saying 'All is Brahman', know that there is nothing to be known through the absence of citta; there is no old age through the absence of body; no motion through the absence of legs; no action through the absence of hands; no death through the absence of creatures; no happiness through the absence of buddhi; no virtue, no purity, no fear, no repetition of mantras, no Guru nor disciple, There is no second in the absence of one. Where there is not the second, there is not the first. Where there is truth alone, there is no non-truth possible; where there is non-truth alone, there is no truth possible. You regard a thing auspicious as inauspicious, then auspiciousness is desired (as separate) from inauspiciousness. If you regard fear as non-fear, then fear will arise out of non-fear. If bondage should become emancipation, then in the absence of bondage will be no emancipation. If birth should imply death, then in the absence of birth, there is no death. If 'thou' should imply 'I', then in the absence of 'thou' there is no 'I', if 'this' should be 'that', 'this' does not exist in the absence of 'that'. If being should imply nor being, then non-being will imply being. If an effect implies a cause, then in the absence of effect, there is no cause. If duality implies non-duality, then in the absence of duality, there is no non-deality. If there should be the seen, then there is the eye (or sight); in the absence of the seen, there is no eye. In the absence of the interior, there is no exterior. If there should be fullness, then non-fullness is possible. Therefore (all) this exists nowhere. Neither you nor I, nor this nor these exist. There exists no (object of) comparison in the true one. There is no simile in the unborn. There is (in it) no mind to think. I am the supreme Brahman. This world is Brahman only. Thou and I are Brahman only. I am cinmātra simply, and there is no not-Ātman. Rest assured of it. This universe is not (really at all). It was nowhere produced and stays nowhere. Some say that citta is the universe. Not at all. It exist not. Neither the universe nor citta nor ahaṁkara nor Jīva exists (really). Neither the creation of Māyā nor Māyā itself exists (really). Fear does not (really) exit. Actor, action, hearing, thinking, the two samādhis, the measurer, the measure, ajñāna and aviveka— none of these exists (truly) anywhere. Therefore the four more moving considerations and the three kinds of relationship exist not. There is no Gaṅgā, no Gayā, no Setu (bridge), no elements or anything else, no earth, water, fire, vāyu, and ākāśa anywhere, no Devas, no guardians of the four quarters, no Vedas, no Guru, no distance, no proximity, no time, no middle, no non-duality, no turth, no untruth, no bondage, no emancipation, no Sat, no asat, no happiness, etc., no class, no motion, no caste, and no worldly business.

सर्वं ब्रह्मेति नास्त्येव ब्रह्म इत्यपि नास्ति हि। चिदित्येवेति नास्त्येव चिदहंभाषणं नहि॥३९॥
अहं ब्रह्मास्मि नास्त्येव नित्यशुद्धोऽस्मि न क्वचित्। वाचा यदुच्यते किंचिन्मनसा मनुते क्वचित्॥४०॥
बुद्ध्या निश्चिनुते नास्ति चित्तेन ज्ञायते नहि। योगी योगादिकं नास्ति सदा सर्वं सदा न च॥४१॥
अहोरात्रादिकं नास्ति स्नानध्यानादिकं नहि। भ्रान्तिरभ्रान्तिर्नास्त्येव नास्त्यनात्मेति न निश्चिनु॥४२॥

All is Brahman only and nothing else— all is Brahman only and nothing else. There exists then nothing (or statement) as that 'consciousness alone is'; there is (then) no saying such as 'Cit is I'. The statement 'I am Brahman' does not exist (then); nor does exist (then) the statement : 'I am the eternally pure'. Whatever is uttered by the mouth, whatever is thought by manas, whatever is determined by buddhi, whatever is cognized by citta— all these do not exist. There is no Yogin or yoga then. All are and are not. Neither day nor night, neither bathing nor contemplating, neither delusion nor not-delusion— all these do not exist then. Know that is no not-Ātman.

वेदशास्त्रं पुराणं च कार्यं कारणमीश्वरः। लोको भूतं जनस्त्वैक्यं सर्वं मिथ्या न संशयः॥४३॥
बन्धो मोक्षः सुखः दुःखं ध्यानं चित्तं सुरासुराः। गौणं मुख्यं परं चान्यत्सर्वं मिथ्या न संशयः॥४४॥
वाचा वदति यत्किंचित्संकल्पै कल्प्यते च यत्। मनसा चिन्त्यते यद्यत्सर्वं मिथ्या न संशयः॥४५॥
बुद्ध्या निश्चीयते किंचिच्चिते निश्चीयते क्वचित्। शास्त्रैः प्रपञ्चयते यद्यन्नेत्रेणैव निरीक्ष्यते॥४६॥
श्रोत्राभ्यां श्रूयते यद्यदन्यत्सद्भावमेव च। नेत्रं श्रोत्रं गात्रमेव मिथ्येति च सुनिश्चितम्॥४७॥
इदमित्येव निर्दिष्टमयमित्येव कल्प्यते। त्वमहं तदिदं सोऽहमन्यत्सद्भावमेव च॥४८॥
यद्यत्संभाव्यते लोके सर्वसंकल्पसंभ्रमः। सर्वाध्यासं सर्वगोप्यं सर्वभोगप्रभेदकम्॥४९॥
सर्वदोषप्रभेदाद्य नास्त्यनात्मेति निश्चिनु। मदीयं च त्वदीयं च ममेति च तवेति च॥५०॥
मह्यं तुभ्यं मयेत्यादि तत्सर्वं वितथं भवेत्। रक्षको विष्णुरित्यादि ब्रह्मा सृष्टेस्तु कारणम्॥५१॥
संहारे रुद्र इत्येव सर्वं मिथ्येति निश्चिनु। स्नानं जपस्तपो होमः स्वाध्यायो देवपूजनम्॥५२॥
मन्त्रं तन्त्रं च सत्सङ्गो गुणदोषविजृम्भणम्। अन्तःकरणसद्भाव अविद्यायाश्च संभवः॥५३॥
अनेककोटिब्रह्माण्डं सर्वं मिथ्येति निश्चिनु। सर्वदेशिकवाक्योक्तिर्येन केनापि निश्चितम्॥५४॥
दृश्यते जगति यद्यद्यज्जगति वीक्ष्यते। वर्तते जगति यद्यत्सर्वं मिथ्येति निश्चिनु॥५५॥
येन केनाक्षरेणोक्तं येन केन विनिश्चितम्। येन केनापि गदितं येन केनापि मोदितम्॥५६॥
येन कनापि यद्दत्तं येन केनापि यत्कृतम्। यत्र यत्र शुभं कर्म यत्र यत्र च दुष्कृतम्॥५७॥
यद्यत्करोषि सत्येन सर्वं मिथ्येति निश्चिनु। त्वमेव परमात्मासि त्वमेव परमो गुरुः॥५८॥

त्वमेवाकाशरूपोऽसि साक्षिहीनोऽसि सर्वदा। त्वमेव सर्वभावोऽसि त्वं ब्रह्मासि न संशयः।।५९।।
कालहीनोऽसि कालोऽसि सदा ब्रह्मासि चिद्धनः। सर्वतः स्वस्वरूपोसि चैतन्यघनवानसि।।६०।।
सत्योऽसि सिद्धोऽसि सनातनोऽसि मुक्तोऽसि मोक्षोऽसि मुदामृतोऽसि।
देवोऽसि शान्तोऽसि नारामयोऽसि ब्रह्मासि पूर्णोऽसि परात्परोऽसि।।६१।।
समोऽसि सच्चापि सनातनोऽपि सत्यादिवाक्यैः प्रतिबोधितोऽसि।
सर्वाङ्गहीनोऽसि सदा स्थितोऽसि ब्रह्मेन्द्ररुद्रादिविभावितोऽसि।।६२।।
सर्वप्रपञ्चभ्रमवर्जितोऽसि सर्वेषु भूतेषु च भासितोऽसि।
सर्वत्र संकल्पविवर्जितोऽसि सर्वागमान्तार्थविभावितोऽसि।।६३।।
सर्वत्र संतोषसुखासनोऽसि सर्वत्र गत्यादिविवर्जितोऽसि।
सर्वत्र लक्ष्यादिविवर्जितोऽसि ध्यातोऽसि विष्णवादिसुरैरजस्रम्।।६४।।
चिदाकारस्वरूपोऽसि चिन्मात्रोऽसि निरङ्कुशः। आत्मन्येव स्थितोऽसि त्वं सर्वशून्योऽसि निर्गुणः।।६५।।
आनन्दोऽसि परोऽसि त्वमेक एवाद्वितीयकः। चिद्धनानन्दरूपोऽसि परिपूर्णस्वरूपकः।।६६।।
सदसि त्वमसे ज्ञोऽसि सोऽसि जानासि वीक्षसि। सच्चिदानन्दरूपोऽसि वासुदेवोऽसि वै प्रभुः।।६७।।
अमृतोऽसि विभुश्चासि चञ्चलो ह्यचलो ह्यसि। सर्वेऽसि सर्वहीनोऽसि शान्ताशान्तविवर्जितः।।६८।।
सत्तामात्रप्रकाशोऽसि सत्तासामान्यको ह्यसि। नित्यसिद्धिस्वरूपोऽसि सर्वसिद्धिविवर्जितः।।६९।।
ईषन्मात्रविशून्योऽसि अणुमात्राविवर्जितः। अस्तित्ववर्जितोऽसि त्वं नास्तित्वादिविवर्जितः।।७०।।
लक्ष्यलक्षणहीनोऽसि निर्विकारो निरामयः। सर्वनादान्तरोऽसि त्वं कलाकाष्ठाविवर्जितः।।७१।।
ब्रह्मविष्णवीशहीनोऽसि स्वस्वरूपं प्रपश्यसि। स्वस्वरूपावशेषोऽसि स्वानन्दाब्धौ निमज्जसि।।७२।।
स्वात्मराज्ये स्वमेवासि स्वयंभावविवर्जितः। शिष्टपूर्णस्वरूपोऽसि स्वस्मात्किंचिन्न पश्यसि।।७३।।
स्वस्वरूपान्न चलसि स्वस्वरूपेण जृम्भसि। स्वस्वरूपादन्योऽसि ह्यहमेवासि निश्चिनु।।७४।।
इदं प्रपञ्चं यत्किंचिद्यद्यज्जगति विद्यते। दृश्यरूपं च दृग्रुपं सर्वं शशविषाणवत्।।७५।।
भूमिरापोऽजलो वायुः खं मनो बुद्धिरेव च। अहंकारश्च तेजश्च लोकं भुवनमण्डलम्।।७६।।
नाशो जन्म च सत्यं च पुण्यपापजयादिकम्। रागः कामः क्रोधलोभौ ध्यानं ध्येयं गुणं परम्।।७७।।
गुरुशिष्योपदेशादिरादिरन्तं शमं शुभम्। भूतं भव्यं वर्तमानं लक्ष्यं लक्षणमद्वयम्।।७८।।
शमो विचारः संतोषो भोक्तृभोज्यादिरूपकम्। यमाद्यष्टाङ्गयोगं च गमनागमनात्मकम्।।७९।।
आदिमध्यान्तरङ्गं च ग्राह्यं त्याज्यं हरिः शिवः। इन्द्रियाणि मनश्चैव अवस्थात्रितयं तथा।।८०।।
चतुर्विंशतितत्त्वं च साधनानां चतुष्टयम्। सजातीयं विजातीयं लोका भूरादयः क्रमात्।।८१।।
सर्ववर्णाश्रमचारं मन्त्रतन्त्रादिसंग्रहम्। विद्याविद्यादिरूपं च सर्ववेदं जडाजडम्।।८२।।
बन्धमोक्षविभागं च ज्ञानविज्ञानरूपकम्। बोधाबोधस्वरूपं वा द्वैताद्वैतादिभाषणम्।।८३।।
सर्ववेदान्तसिद्धान्त सर्वशास्त्रार्थनिर्णयम्। अनेक जीवसद्भावमेकजीवादिनिर्णयम्।।८४।।

यद्यद्ध्यायति चित्तेन यद्यत्संकल्पते क्वचित्। बुद्ध्या निश्चीयते यद्यद्गुरुणा संश्लृणोति यत्॥ ८५॥
यद्यद्वाचा व्याकरोति यद्यदाचार्यभाषणम्। यद्यत्स्वरेन्द्रियैर्भाव्यं यद्यन्मीमांस्यते पृथक्॥ ८६॥
यद्यन्यायेन निर्णीतं महद्भिर्वेदपारगैः। शिवः क्षरति लोकान्वै विष्णुः पाति जगत्त्रयम्॥ ८७॥
ब्रह्म सृजति लोकान्वै एकमादिक्रियादिकम्। यद्यदस्ति पुराणेषु यद्यद्वेदेषु निर्णयम्॥ ८८॥
सर्वोपनिषदां भावं सर्वं शशविषाणवत्। देहोऽहमिति संकल्पं तदन्तःकरणं स्मृतम्॥ ८९॥
देहोऽमहिति संकल्पो महत्संसार उच्यते। देहोऽहमिति संकल्पस्तद्बन्धमिति चोच्यते॥ ९०॥
देहोऽहमिति संकल्पस्तद्दुःखमिति चोच्यते। देहोऽहमिति यद्भानं तदेव नरकं स्मृतम्॥ ९१॥
देहोऽहमिति संकल्पो जगत्सर्वमितीर्यते। देहोऽहमिति संकल्पो हृदयग्रन्थिरीरितिः॥ ९२॥
देहोऽहमिति यज्ज्ञानं तदेवाज्ञानमुच्यते। देहोऽहमिति यज्ज्ञानं तदसद्भावमेव च॥ ९३॥
देहोऽहमिति या बुद्धिः सा चाविद्येति भण्यते। देहोऽहमिति यज्ज्ञानं तदेव द्वैतमुच्यते॥ ९४॥
देहोऽहमिति संकल्पः सत्यजीवः स एव हि। देहोऽहमिति यज्ज्ञानं परिच्छिन्नमितीरितम्॥ ९५॥
देहोऽहमिति संकल्पो महापापमिति स्फुटम्। देहोऽहमिति या बुद्धिस्तृष्णा दोषामयः किल॥ ९६॥
यत्किंचिदपि संकल्पस्तापत्रमितीरित्। कामं क्रोधं बन्धनं सर्वदुःखं विश्वं दोषं कालनानास्वरूपम्।
यत्किंचेदं सर्वसंकल्पजालं तत्किंचेदं मानसं सोम्य विद्धि॥ ९७॥

॥अथ षष्ठोऽध्यायः॥

"The Vedas, Science, Purāṇas, effect and cause, Īśvara and the world and the elements and mankind— all these are unreal. There is no doubt about it. Bondage, salvation, happiness, relatives, meditation, citta, the Devas, the demons, the secondary and the primary, the high and the low— all these are unreal. There is no doubt of it. Whatever is uttered by the mouth, whatever is wished by saṅkalpa, whatever is thought by manas— all these unreal. Whatever is determined by the buddhi, whatever is cognized by citta, whatever is discussed by the religious books, whatever is seen by the eye and heard by the ears, and whatever exists as Sat, as also the ear, the eye, and the limbs— all these are unreal. Whatever is described as such and such, whatever is thought as so-and-so, all the existing thoughts such as 'thou are I', 'that is this', and 'He is I', and whatever happens in mokṣa, as also all saṅkalpas, delusion, illusory attribution, mysteries and all the diversities of enjoyment and sin— all these do not exist. So is also not— all these do not exist. So is also not-Ātman. Mine and thine, my and thy, for me and for thee, by me and by thee— all these are unreal. (The statement) that Viṣṇu is the preserver, Brahmā is the creator, Rudra is the destroyer— know that these undoubtedly are false. Bathing, uttering of mantras, japas (religious austerities), homa (sacrifice), study of Vedas, worship of the Devas, mantra, tantra, association with the good, the unfolding of the faults of guṇas, the working of the internal organ, the result of avidyā, and the many crores of mundane eggs— all these are unreal. Whatever is spoken of as true according to the verdict of all teachers, whatever is seen in this world and whatever exists— all these are unreal. Whatever is uttered by words, whatever is ascertained, spoken, enjoyed, given or done by any one, whatever action is done, good or bad, whatever is done as truth— Know all these to be unreal. Thou alone are the transcendental Ātman and the supreme Guru of the form of ākāśa, which is devoid of fitness (for it) and of the nature of all creatures. Thou are Brahman; thou time; and thou are Brahman, that is ever and imponderable. Thou are of everywhere, of all forms, and full of consciousness. Thou are the truth. Thou are one that has mastered the siddhis, and thou are the ancient, the emancipated, emancipation, the nectar of bliss, the God, the quiescent, the diseaseless, Brahman, the full, and greater than the great. Thou are impartial, Sat and the ancient knowledge, recognised by the words 'Truth, etc'. Thou are devoid of all parts. Thou are the ever-existing— thou appeares as Brahmā, Rudra, Indra, etc.— thou are above the illusion of the universe— thou shines in all element— thou are without saṅkalpa in all— thou are known by means of the underlying meaning of all scriptures; thou are ever content and ever happily seated (in thyself): thou are without motion, etc. In all things, thou are without any characteristics; in all things thou are contemplated by Viṣṇu and other Devas at all times; thou have the nature of Cit, thou are Cinmātra unchecked, thou stayes in Ātman itself, thou are void of everything and without guṇas, thou are bliss, the great, the one secondless, the state of Sat and asat, the knower, the known, the seer, the nature of Saccidānanda, the lord of Devas, the all-prevading, the deathless, the moving, the motionless, the all and the non-all with quiescence and non-quiescence, sat alone, Sat commonly (found in all), of the form of Nitya-Siddha (the unconditioned developed one), and yet devoid of all siddhis. There is not an atom which thou does not penetrate; but yet thou are without it. Thou are devoid of existence and non-existence as also the aim and object aims at. Thou are changelss, decayless, beyond all nādas, without kāla or kartā (divisions of time) and without Brahmā, Viṣṇu and Śiva. Thou looks into the nature of each and are above the nature of each. Thou are immersed in the bliss of Self. Thou are the monarch of the kingdom of Self, and yet without the conception of Self. Thou are of the nature of fullness and incompleteness. There is nothing that thou see which is not in thyself. Thou does not stir out of thy nature. Thou acts accoding to the nature of each. Thou are nothing but the nature of each. Have no doubt 'thou are I'.

"This universe and everything in it, whether the seer or the seen, resembles the horns of a hare (or are illusory). Earth, water, agni, vāyu, ākāśa, manas, buddhi, ahaṁkāra, tejas, the worlds and the sphere of the universe, destruction, birth, truth, virtue, vice, gain, desires, passion, anger, greed, the object of meditation, wisdom, Guru, disciple, limitation, the beginning and end, auspiciousness, the past, present, and future, the aim and the object of aim, mental restraint, inquiry, contentment, enjoyer, enjoyment, etc., the eight parts of yoga, yama, etc., the going and coming (of life), the beginning, middle and end, that which can be taken and rejected, Hari, Śiva, the organs, manas, the three states, the twenty-four tattvas, the four means, one of the same class or different classes, Bhūh and other worlds, all the castes and orders of life with the rules laid down for each, mantras and tantras, science and nonscience, all the vedas, the inert and the non-inert, bondage and salvation, spiritual wisdom and non-wisdom, the enlightened and the non-enlightened, duality and non-duality, the conclusion of all Vedāntas and Śāstras, the theory of the existence of all souls and that one soul only, whatever is thought by citta, whatever is willed by saṅkalpa, whatever is determined by buddhi, whatever one hears and sees, whatever the Guru instruct, whatever is sensed by all the organs, whatever is discussed in mīmāṁsā, whatever is ascertained by nyāya (philosophy) and by the great ones who have reached the other side of the Vedas, the saying 'Śiva destroys the world, Viṣṇu protects it, and Brahmā creates it', whatever is found in the purāṇas, whatever is ascertained by the Vedas, and is the signification of all the Vedas— all these resemble the horns of a hare. The conception 'I am the body' is spoken of as the internal organ; the conception 'I am the body' is spoken of as the great mundane existence; the conception 'I am the body' constitutes the whole universe. The conception 'I am the body' is spoken of as the knot of the heart, as non-wisdom, as the state of asat, as nonscience, as the dual, as the true Jīva and with parts, is certainly the great sin, and is the disease generated by the fault of thirst after desires. That which is saṅkalpa, the three pains, passion, anger, bondage, all the miseries, all the faults and the various forms of time— know these to be the result of manas.

मन एव जगत्सर्वं मन एव महारिपुः। मन एव हि संसारो मन एव जगत्त्रयम्॥ ९८॥

मन एव महद्दुःखं मन एव जरादिकम्। मन एव हि कालश्च मन एव मलं तथा॥ ९९॥

मन एव हि संकल्पो मन एव हि जीवकः। मन एव हि चित्तं च मनोऽहंकार एव च॥ १००॥

मन एव महद्बन्धं मनोऽन्तःकरणं च तत्। मन एव हि भूमिश्च मन एव हि तोयकम्॥ १०१॥

मन एव हि तेजश्च मन एव मरुन्महान्। मन एव हि चाकाशं मन एव हि शब्दकम्॥ १०२॥

स्पर्शं रूपं रसं गन्धं कोशाः पञ्च मनोभवाः। जाग्रत्स्वप्नसुषुप्त्यादि मनोमयमितीरितम्॥ १०३॥

दिक्पाला वसवो रुद्रा आदित्याश्च मनोमयाः। दृश्यं जडं द्वन्द्वजातमज्ञानं मानसं स्मृतम्॥ १०४॥

संकल्पमेव यत्किंचित्तत्तन्नास्तीति निश्चिनु। नास्ति नास्ति जगत्सर्वं गुरुशिष्यादिकं नहीत्युपनिषत्॥ १०५॥

Manas alone is the whole world, ever-deluding, the mundane existence, the three worlds, the great pains, the old age and others, death and the great sin, the saṅkalpa, the Jīva, the citta, the ahaṁkāra, the bondage, the internal organ and earth, water, agni, vāyū, and ākāśa. Sound, touch, form, taste, and odour, the five sheaths, the waking, the dreaming, and dreamless sleeping states, the guradians of the eight quarters, Vasus, Rudras, Ādityas, the seen, the inert, the pairs and non-wisdom— all these are the products of manas. Rest assured that there is no reality in all that is saṅkalpa. The whole world, the Guru, disciple, etc., do not exist, yea, do not exist.

Thus ends the sixth chapter of this Upaniṣad."

॥अथ सप्तमोऽध्यायः॥

ऋभुः॥

सर्वं सच्चिन्मयं विद्धि सर्वं सच्चिन्मयं ततम्। सच्चिदानन्दमद्वैतं सच्चिदानन्दमद्वयम्॥१॥

सच्चिदानन्दमात्रं हि सच्चिदानन्दमन्यकम्। सच्चिदानन्दरूपोऽहं सच्चिदानन्दमेव खम्॥ २॥

सच्चिदानन्दमेव त्वं सच्चिदानन्दकोऽस्म्यहम्। मनोबुद्धिरहंकारचित्तसंघातका अमी॥ ३॥

न त्वं नाहं च चान्यद्वा सर्वं ब्रह्मैव केवलम्। न वाक्यं न पदं वेदं नाक्षरं न जडं क्वचित्॥ ४॥

न मध्यं नादि नान्तं वा न सत्यं न निबन्धनम्। न दुखं न सुःखं भावं न माया प्रकृतिस्तथा॥ ५॥

न देहं न मुखं घ्राणं न जिह्वा न च तालुनी। न दन्तोष्ठौ ललाटं च निश्वासोच्छ्वास एव च॥ ६॥

न स्वेदमस्थि मांसं च न रक्तं न च मूत्रकम्। न दूरं नान्तिकं नाङ्गं नोदरं न किरीटकम्॥७॥

न हस्तपादचलनं न शास्त्रं न च शासनम्। न वेत्ता वेदनं वेद्यं न जाग्रत्स्वप्नसुप्तयः॥ ८॥

Ṛbhu continues again : "Know everything as Saccinmaya (full of Sat and consciousness). It pervades everything. Saccidānanda is non-dual, decayless, alone and other than all. It is 'I'. It alone is ākāśa and 'thou'. It is I. There is (in it) no manas, no buddhi, no ahaṁkāra, no citta, or the collection of these— neither 'thou' no I, nor anything else nor everything. Brahman alone is sentence, words, Vedas, letters, beginning, middle, or end, truth, law, pleasure, pain, existence, māyā, prakṛti, body, face, nose, tongue, plate, teeth, lip, forehead, expiration and inspiration, sweat, bone, blood, urine, distance, proximity, limb, belly, crown, the movement of hands and feet, Śāstras, command, the knower, the known, and the knowledge, the waking, dreaming and dreamless sleeping and the fourth state— all these do not belong to me.

तुर्यातीतं न मे किंचित्सर्वं सच्चिन्मयं ततम्। नाध्यात्मिकं नाधिभूतं नाधिदैवं न मायिकम्॥ ९॥

न विश्वस्तैजसः प्राज्ञो विराट्सूत्रात्मकेश्वराः। न गमागमचेष्टा च न नष्टं न प्रयोजनम्॥ १०॥

त्याज्यं ग्राह्यं न दूष्यं वा ह्यमेध्यामेध्यकं तथा। न पीनं न कृशं क्लेदं न कालं देशभाषणम्॥ ११॥

न सर्वं न भयं द्वैतं न वृक्षतृणपर्वताः। न ध्यानं योगसंसिद्धिर्न ब्रह्मक्षत्रवैश्यकम्॥ १२॥

न पक्षी न मृगो नाङ्गी न लोभो मोह एव च। न मदो न च मात्सर्यं कामक्रोधादयस्तथा॥ १३॥

न स्त्रीशूद्रबिडालादि भक्ष्यभोज्यादिकं च यत्। न प्रौढहीनो नास्तिक्यं न वार्तावसरोऽस्ति हि॥ १४॥

न लौकिको न लोको वा न व्यापारो न मूढता। न भोक्ता भोजनं भोज्यं न पात्रं पानपेयकम्॥ १५॥

न शत्रुमित्रपुत्रादिर्न माता न पिता स्वसा। न जन्म न मृतिर्वृद्धिर्न देहोऽहमिति भ्रमः॥ १६॥

न शून्यं नापि चाशून्यं नान्तःकरणसंसृति। न रात्रिर्न दिवा नक्तं न ब्रह्मा न हरिः शिवः॥ १७॥

न वारपक्षमासादि वत्सरं न च चञ्चलम्। न ब्रह्मलोको वैकुण्ठो न कैलासो न चान्यकः॥ १८॥

न स्वर्गो न च देवेन्द्रो नाग्निलोको न चाग्निकः। न यमो यमलोको वा न लोका लोकपालकाः॥ १९॥

न भूर्भुवःस्वस्त्रैलोक्यं न पातालं न भूतलम्। नाविद्या न च विद्या च न माया प्रकृतिर्जडा॥ २०॥

न स्थिरं क्षणिकं नाशं न गतिर्न च धावनम्। न ध्यातव्यं न मे ध्यानं न मन्त्रो न जपः क्वचित्॥ २१॥
न पदार्था न पूजार्हं नाभिषेको न चार्चनम्। न पुष्पं न फलं पत्रं गन्धपुष्पादिधूपकम्॥ २२॥
न स्तोत्रं न नमस्कारो न प्रदक्षिणमण्वपि। न प्रार्थना पृथग्भावो न हविर्नाग्निवन्दनम्॥ २३॥
न होमो न च कर्माणि न दुर्वाक्यं सुभाषणम्। न गायत्री न वा संधिर्न मनस्यं न दुःस्थितिः॥ २४॥
न दुराशा न दुष्टात्मा न चाण्डालो न पौल्कसः। न दुःसहं दुरालां न किरातो न कैतवम्॥ २५॥
न पक्षपातं पत्रं वा न विभूषणतस्करौ। न च दम्भो दाम्भिको वा न हीनो नाधिको नरः॥ २६॥
नैकं द्वयं त्रयं तुर्यं न महत्वं न चाल्पता। न पूर्णं न परिच्छिन्नं न काशी न व्रतं तपः॥ २७॥
न गोत्रं न कुलं सूत्रं न विभूत्वं न शून्यता। न स्त्री न योषिन्नो वृद्धा न कन्या न वितन्तुता॥ २८॥
न सूतकं न जातं वा नान्तर्मुखसुविभ्रमः। न महावाक्यमैक्यं वा नाणिमादिविभूतयः॥ २९॥

Everything is Saccinmaya interwoven. No attributes pertaining to body, elements and spirit, no root, no vision, no Taijasa, no Prāṇa, no Virāṭ, no Sūtrātmā, no Īśvara, and no going or coming, neither gain nor loss, neither the acceptable nor the rejectable, nor the censurable, neither the pure nor the impure, neither the stout nor the lean, no sorrow, time, space, speech, fear, duality, tree, grass or mountain, no meditation, no siddhi of yoga, no Brāhmaṇa, Kṣatriya or Vaiśya, no bird or beast, or limb, no greed, delusion, pride, malice, passion, anger or others, no woman, Śūdra, castes or others, nothing that is eatable or enjoyable, no increase or decrease, no belief in the Vedas, no speech, no worldliness or unworldliness, no transaction, no folly, no measure or measured, no enjoyment or enjoyed, no friends, son, etc., father, mother, or sister, no birth or death, no growth, body of 'I', no emptiness or fullness, no internal organs or mundane existence, no night, no day, no Brahmā, Viṣṇu or Śiva, no week, fortnight, month, or year, no unsteadiness, no brahmaloka, Vaikunṭha, Kailāśa and others, no Svarga, Indra, Agniloka, Agni, Yamaloka, Yama, Vāyuloka, guardians of the world, three worlds— Bhūḥ, Bhuvaḥ, Svaḥ, Pātāla or surface of earth, no science, nescience, māyā, prakṛti, inertness, permanency, transcience, destruction, movement, running, object of meditation, bathing, mantra or object, no adorable object, anoinment or siping with water, no flower, fruit, sandal, light waved before god, praise, prostrations, or circumambulation, no entreaty, conception of separateness even obliation of food, offered food, sacrifice, actions, abuse, praise, Gāyatrī and sandhi (period of junction, such as twilight, etc.), no mental state, calamity, evil desire, bad soul, caṇḍāla (low caste person), pulkasa, unbearableness, unspeakableness, kirāta (hunter), kaitava (demon), partiality, partisanship, ornament, chief, or pride, no manyness, no oneness, durability, triad, tetrad, greatness, smallness, fullness, or delusion, no kaitava, Benares, tapas, clan, family, sūtra, greatness, poverty, girl, old woman or widow, no pollution, birth, introvision or illusion, no sacred sentences, identity, or the siddhis, aṇimā, etc.

सर्वचैतन्यमात्रत्वात्सर्वदोषः सदा न हि। सर्वं सन्मात्ररूपत्वात्सच्चिदानन्दमात्रकम्॥ ३०॥
ब्रह्मैव सर्वं नान्योऽस्ति तदहं तदहं तथा। तदेवाहं तदेवाहं ब्रह्मैवाहं सनातनम्॥ ३१॥

ब्रह्मैवाहं न संसारी ब्रह्मैवाहं न मे मनः। ब्रह्मैवाहं न मे बुद्धिर्ब्रह्मैवाहं न चेन्द्रियः॥ ३२॥

ब्रह्मैवाहं न देहोऽहं ब्रह्मैवाहं न गोचरः। ब्रह्मैवाहं न जीवोऽहं ब्रह्मैवाहं न भेदभूः॥ ३३॥

ब्रह्मैवाहं जडो नाहमहं ब्रह्म न मे मृतिः। ब्रह्मैवाहं न च प्राणे ब्रह्मैवाहं परात्परः॥ ३४॥

इदं ब्रह्म परं ब्रह्म सत्यं ब्रह्म प्रभुर्हि सः। कालो ब्रह्म कला ब्रह्म सुखं ब्रह्म स्वयंप्रभम्॥ ३५॥

"Everything being consciousness alone, there is no fault in anything. Everything being of the nature of Sat alone, is saccidānanda only. Brahman alone is everything and there is nothing else. So 'That' is 'I' 'That' is 'I'. 'That' alone is 'I'. 'That' alone is 'I'. 'That' alone is 'I'. The eternal Brahman alone is 'I'. I am Brahman alone without being subject to mundane existence. I am Brahman alone without manas, any buddhi, organs or body. I am Brahman alone not perceivable. I am Brahman alone and not Jīva. I am Brahman alone and not liable to change. I am Brahman alone and not inert. I am Brahman alone and have no death. I am Brahman alone and have no prāṇas. I am Brahman alone and greater than the great. This is Brahman. Great is Brahman. Truth is Brahman. It is all-pervading. Time is Brahman. Kalā is Brahman. Happiness is Brahman. It is self-shining.

एकं ब्रह्म द्वयं ब्रह्म मोहो ब्रह्म शमादिकम्। दोषो ब्रह्म गुणो ब्रह्म दमः शान्तं विभुः प्रभुः॥ ३६॥

लोको ब्रह्म गुरुर्ब्रह्म शिष्यो ब्रह्म सदाशिवः। पूर्वं ब्रह्म परं ब्रह्म शुद्धं ब्रह्म शुभाशुभम्॥ ३७॥

जीव एव सदा ब्रह्म सच्चिदानन्दमस्म्यहम्। सर्वं ब्रह्ममयं प्रोक्तं सर्वं ब्रह्ममयं जगत्॥ ३८॥

One is Brahman. Two is Brahman. Delusion is Brahman. Śama and others are Brahman. Badness is Brahman. Goodness is Brahman. It is of the form of restraint, quiesence, the all-pervading and the all-powerful. The Loka (world) is Brahman. Guru is Brahman. Disciple is Brahman. It is Sadāśiva (That which) is Brahman. (That which will be) hereafter is Brahman. Purity is Brahman. Auspiciousness and inauspiciousness are Brahman. Jīva always is Brahman. I am Saccidānanda. All are of the nature of brahman. The universe is said to be of the nature of Brahman.

स्वयं ब्रह्म न संदेहः स्वस्मादन्यन्न किंचन। सर्वमात्मैरशुद्धात्मा सर्वं चिन्मात्रमद्वयम्॥ ३९॥

नित्यनिर्मलरूपात्मा ह्यात्मनोऽन्यन्न किंचन। अणुमात्रलसद्रूपमणुमात्रमिदं जगत्॥ ४०॥

अणुमात्रं शरीरं वा ह्यणुमात्रमसत्यकम्। अणुमात्रमचिन्त्यं वा चिन्त्यं वा ह्यणुमात्रकम्॥ ४१॥

ब्रह्मैव सर्वं चिन्मात्रं ब्रह्ममात्रं जगत्त्रयम्। आनन्दं रमानन्दमन्यत्किंचिन्नकिंचन॥ ४२॥

चैतन्यमात्रमोंकारं ब्रह्मैव सकलं स्वयम्। अहमेव जगत्सर्वमहमेव परं पदम्॥ ४३॥

अहमेव गुणातीत अहमेव परात्परः। अहमेव परं ब्रह्म अहमेव गुरोर्गुरुः॥ ४४॥

अहमेवाखिलाधार अहमेव सुखात्सुखम्। आत्मनोऽन्यज्जगन्नास्ति आत्मनोऽन्यत्सुखं न च॥ ४५॥

आत्मनोऽन्या गतिर्नास्ति सर्वमात्ममयं जगत्। आत्मनोऽन्यन्नहि क्वापि आत्मनोऽन्यत्तृणं नहि॥ ४६॥

आत्मनोऽन्यत्तुषं नास्ति सर्वमात्ममयं जगत्। ब्रह्ममात्रमिदं सर्वं ब्रह्ममात्रमसन्न हि॥ ४७॥

ब्रह्ममात्रं श्रुतं सर्वं स्वयं ब्रह्मैव केवलम्। ब्रह्ममात्रं वृतं सर्वं ब्रह्ममात्रं रसं सुखम्॥ ४८॥

ब्रह्ममात्रं चिदाकाशं सच्चिदानन्दमव्ययम्। ब्रह्मणोऽन्यतरन्नास्ति ब्रह्मणोऽन्यज्जगन्न च॥४९॥

ब्रह्मणोऽन्यदह नास्ति ब्रह्मणोऽन्यत्फलं नहि। ब्रह्मणोऽन्यत्तृणं नास्ति ब्रह्मणोऽन्यत्पदं नहि॥५०॥

ब्रह्मणोऽन्यद्गुरुर्नास्ति ब्रह्मणोऽन्यमसद्वपुः। ब्रह्मणोऽन्यन्न चाहंता त्वत्तेदन्ते नहि क्वचित्॥५१॥

स्वयं ब्रह्मात्मकं विद्धि स्वस्मादन्यन्न किंचन। यत्किंचिदृश्यते लोके यत्किंचिद्भाष्यते जनैः॥५२॥

यत्किंचिद्भुज्यते क्वापि तत्सर्वमसदेव हि। कर्तृभेदं क्रियाभेदं गुणभेदं रसादिकम्॥५३॥

लिङ्गभेदमिदं सर्वमसदेव सदा सुखम्। कालभेद देशभेदं वस्तुभेदं जयाजयम्॥५४॥

यद्यद्भेदं च तत्सर्वमसदेव हि केवलम्। असदन्तःकरणकमसदेवेन्द्रियादिकम्॥५५॥

असत्प्राणादिकं सर्वं संघातमसदात्मकम्। असत्यं पञ्चकोशाख्यमसत्यं पञ्च देवताः॥५६॥

असत्यं षड्विकारादि असत्यमरिवर्गकम्। असत्यं षड्तुश्चैव असत्यं षड्रसस्तथा॥५७॥

Brahman is itself. There is no doubt of it. There is nothing out of itself. The letter Oṁ of the form of consciousness is Brahman alone. Everything is itself. I alone am the whole universe and the highest seat, have crossed the guṇas and am greater than the great, the supreme Brahman, Guru of Gurus, the support of all and the bliss of bliss. There is no universe besides Ātman. The universe is of the nature of Ātman. There is nowhere (or no place) without Ātman. There is not even grass different from Ātman. There is not husk different from Brahman. The whole universe is of the nature of Ātman. All this is of the nature of Brahman. Asat is not of the nature of brahman. There is not a grass different from Brahman. There is not a seat different from Brahman; there is not a Guru different from Brahman. There is not a body different from Brahman. There is nothing different from Brahman like I-ness or you-ness. Whatever is seen in this world, whatever is spoken of by the people, whatever is enjoyed everywhere— all these are asat (unreal) only. The differences arising from the actor, action, qualities, likes, taste and gender— all these arise from asat and are (but) pleasurable. The differences arising from time, objects, actions, success or defeat and whatever else— all these are simply asat. The internal organ is asat. The organs are asat. All the prāṇas, the collections of all these, the five sheaths, the five deities, the six changes, the six enemies, the six seasons, and the six tastes, are asat.

सच्चिदानन्दमात्रोऽहमनुत्पन्नमिदं जगत्। आत्मैवाहं परं सत्यं नान्यासंसारदृष्टयः॥५८॥

सत्यमानन्दरूपऽहं चिद्घनानन्दविग्रहः। अहमेव परानन्द अहमेव परात्परः॥५९॥

ज्ञानाकारमिदं सर्वं ज्ञानानन्दोऽहमद्वयः। सर्वप्रकाशरूपोऽहं सर्वाभारस्वरूपकम्॥६०॥

I am Saccidānanda. The universe is rootless. I am Ātman alone, Cit and Ānanda. The scenes of mundane existence are not different. I am the Truth of the nature of Ānanda and of the nature of the imponderable Cit. All this is of the nature of jñāna. I am the secondless, having jñāna and bliss. I am of the nature of an illuminator of all things. I am of the nature of all non-being.

अहमेव सदा भामीत्येवं रूपं कुतोऽप्यसत्। त्वमित्येवं परं ब्रह्म चिन्मयानन्दरूपवान्॥६१॥

चिदाकारं चिदाकाशं चिदेव परमं सुखम्। आत्मैवाहमसन्नाहं कूटस्थोऽहं गुरुः परः॥६२॥

सच्चिदानन्दमात्रोऽहमनुत्पन्नमिदं जगत्। कालो नास्ति जगन्नास्ति मायाप्रकृतिरेव न॥६३॥

I alone shines always. Therefore how can I with such a nature become asat? That which is called 'thou' is the great brahman of the nature of the bliss of consciousness and of the nature of Cit having cidākāśa and cit alone as the great bliss. Ātman alone is 'I'. Asat is not 'I'. I am Kūṭastha, the great Guru and Saccidānanda alone. I am this born universe. No time, no universe, no māyā, no prakṛti (in me).

अहमेव हरिः साक्षादहमेव सदाशिवः। शुद्धचैतन्यभावोऽहं शुद्धसत्त्वानुभावनः॥६४॥

अद्वयानन्दमात्रोऽहं चिद्घनैकरसोऽस्म्यहम्। सर्वं ब्रह्मैव सततं सर्वं ब्रह्मैव केवलम्॥६५॥

सर्वं ब्रह्मैव सततं सर्वं ब्रह्मैव चेतनम्। सर्वान्तर्यामिरूपोऽहं सर्वसाक्षित्वलक्षणः॥६६॥

परमात्मा परं ज्योतिः परं धाम परा गतिः। सर्ववेदान्तसारोऽहं सर्वशास्त्रसुनिश्चितः॥६७॥

योगानन्दस्वरूपोऽहं मुख्यानन्दमहोदयः। सर्वज्ञानप्रकाशोऽस्मि मुख्यविज्ञानविग्रहः॥६८॥

तुर्यातुर्यप्रकाशोऽस्मि तुर्यातुर्यादिवर्जितः। चिदक्षरोऽहं सत्योऽहं वासुदेवोऽजरोऽमरः॥६९॥

अहं ब्रह्म चिदाकाशं नित्यं ब्रह्म निरञ्जनम्। शुद्धं बुद्धं सदामुक्तमनामकमरूपकम्॥७०॥

सच्चिदानन्दरूपोऽहमनुत्पन्नमिदं जगत्।

I alone am the Hari Personally, I alone am the Sadāśiva. I am of the nature of pure consciousness. I am the enjoyer of pure sattva. I am the only essence full of cit. Everything is Brahman and Brahman alone. Everything Brahman and is cit alone. I am of the nature of all-latent and the all-witness. I am the supreme Ātmā, the supreme jyotis, the supreme wealth, the supreme goal, the essence of all vedāntas, the subject discussed in all the Śāstras the nature of yogic bliss, the ocean of the chief wisdom, the brightness of the fourth state and the non-fourth but devoid of them, the indestructible cit, truth, Vāsudeva, the birthless, and the deathless Brahman, Cidākāśa, the unconditioned, the stainless, the immaculate, the emancipated, the utterly emancipated, the soulless, the formless and of the nature of the non-created universe.

सत्यासत्यं जगन्नास्ति संकल्पकलनादिकम्॥७१॥

नित्यानन्दमयं ब्रह्म केवलं सर्वदा स्वयम्। अनन्तमव्ययं शान्तमेकरूपमनामयम्॥७२॥

मत्तोऽन्यदस्ति चेन्मिथ्या यथा मरुमरीचिका। वन्ध्याकुमारवचने भीतिश्चेदस्ति किंचन॥७३॥

शशशृङ्गेण नागेन्द्रो मृतश्चेज्जगदस्ति तत्। मृगतृष्णाजलं पीत्वा तृप्तश्चेदस्त्विदं जगत्॥७४॥

नरशृङ्गेण नष्टश्चेत्कश्चिदस्त्विदमेव हि। गन्धर्वनगरे सत्ये जगद्भवति सर्वदा॥७५॥

"The universe which is assumed as truth and non-truth does not really exist. Brahman is of the nature of eternal bliss and is even by itself. It is endless, decayless, quiescent and of one nature only. If anything is other than myself, then it is as unreal as the mirage in an oasis. If one should be afraid of the son of a barren woman, of if a powerful elephant be killed by means of the horns of a hare, then the world (really is). If one (person) can quench his thirst by drinking the waters of the mirage, or if one should be killed by the horns of a man, then the universe really is. The universe exists always in the true Gandharva city (merely unreal).

गगने नीलिमासत्ये जगत्सत्यं भविष्यति। शुक्तिकारजतं सत्यं भूषणं चेज्जगद्भवेत्॥७६॥
रज्जुसर्पेण दष्टश्चेन्नरो भवतु संसृतिः। जातरूपेण बाणेन ज्वालाग्नौ नाशिते जगत्॥७७॥
विन्ध्याटव्यां पायसान्नमस्ति चेज्जगदुद्भवः। रम्भास्तम्भेन काष्ठेन पाकसिद्धौ जगद्भवेत्॥७८॥
सद्यः कुमारिकारूपैः पाके सिद्धे जगद्भवेत्। चित्रस्थदीपैस्तमसो नाशश्चेदस्त्विदं जगत्॥७९॥
मासात्पूर्वं मृतो मर्त्यो ह्यागतश्चेज्जगद्भवेत्। तक्रं क्षीरस्वरूपं चेतक्वचिन्नित्यं जगद्भवेत्॥८०॥
गोस्तनादुद्भवं क्षीरं पुनरारोपणे जगत्। भूरजोऽब्धौ समुत्पन्ने जगदभवतु सर्वदा॥८१॥
कूर्मरोम्णा गजे बद्धे जगदस्तु मदोत्कटे। नालस्थतन्तुना मेरुश्चालितश्चेज्जगद्भवेत्॥८२॥
तरङ्गमालया सिन्धुर्बद्धश्चेदस्त्विदं जगत्। अग्नेरधश्चेज्जवलनं जगद्भवतु सर्वदा॥८३॥
ज्वालावह्निः शीतलश्चेदस्तिरूपमिदं जगत्। ज्वालाग्निमण्डले पद्मवृद्धिश्चेज्जगदस्त्विदम्॥८४॥
महच्छैलेन्द्रनीलं वा संभवच्चेदिदं जगत्। मेरुरागत्य पद्माक्षे स्थितश्चेदस्त्विदं जगत्॥८५॥
निगिरेच्चेद्भृङ्गसूनुर्मेरुं चलवदस्त्विदम्। मशकेन हते सिंहे जगत्सत्यं तदास्तु ते॥८६॥
अणुकोटरविस्तीर्णे त्रैलोक्यं चेज्जगद्भवेत्। तृणानलश्च नित्यश्चेत् क्षणिकं तज्जगद्भवेत्॥८७॥
स्वप्नदृष्टं च यद्वस्तु जागरे चेज्जगद्भवः। नदीवेगो निश्चलश्चेत्केनापीदं भवेज्जगत्॥८८॥
क्षुधितस्याग्निर्भोज्यश्चेन्निमिषं कल्पितं भवेत्। जात्यन्धै रत्नविषयः सुज्ञातश्चेज्जगत्सदा॥८९॥
नपुंसककुमारस्य स्त्रीसुखं चेद्भवेज्जगत्। निर्मितः शशशृङ्गेण रथश्चेज्जगदस्ति तत्॥९०॥
सद्योजाता तु या कन्या भोगयोग्या भवेज्जगत्। वन्ध्या गर्भाप्ततत्सौख्यं ज्ञाता चेदस्त्विदं जगत्॥९१॥
काको वा हंसवद्गच्छेज्जगद्भवतु निश्चलम्। महाखरो वा सिंहेन युध्यते चेज्जगत्स्थितिः॥९२॥
महाखरो गजगतिं गतश्चेज्जगदस्तु तत्। संपूर्णचन्द्रसूर्यश्चेज्जगद्भातु स्वयं जडम्॥९३॥
चन्द्रसूर्यादिको त्यक्त्वा राहुश्चेद्दृश्यते जगत्। भृष्टबीजसमुत्पन्नवृद्धिश्चेज्जगदस्तु सत्॥९४॥
दरिद्रो धनिकानां च सुखं भुङ्क्ते तदा जगत्। शुना वीर्येण सिंहस्तु जितो यदि जगत्तदा॥९५॥
ज्ञानिनो हृदयं मूढैर्ज्ञातं चेत्कल्पनं तदा। श्वानेन सागरे पीते निःशेषेण मनो भवेत्॥९६॥
शुद्धाकाशो मनुष्येषु पतितश्चेत्तदा जगत्। भूमौ वा पतितं व्योम व्योमपुष्पं सुगन्धकम्॥९७॥
शुद्धाकाशे वने जाते चलिते तु तदा जगत्। केवले दर्पणे नास्ति प्रतिबिम्बं तदा जगत्॥९८॥

When the blueness of the sky really exists in it, then the universe really is. When the silver in mother-of-pearl can be used in making an ornament, when a man is bitten by (the conception of) a snake in a rope, when the flaming fire is quenched by means of a golden arrow, when milky food is obtained in the (barren) forest of Vindhya (mountains), when cooking can take place by means of the fuel of (wet) plantain trees, when a female (baby) just born begins to cook, when curds resume the state of milk, or when the milk (milked) goes back through the teats of a cow, then will the universe really be. When the dust of the earth shall be produced in the ocean, when the maddened elephant is tied by means of the hair of a tortoise, when (mountain) Meru is shaken by the thread in the stalk of a lotus, when the ocean is bound by its rows of tides, when the fire flames downwards, when flame shall become (really) cold, when the lotus shall grow out of flaming fire, when Indranīla (sapphire) arises in the great mountains, when Meru comes and sits in the lotus-eye, when a mountain can become the offspring of a black bee, when Meru shall shake, when a lion is killed by a gnat, when the three worlds can be found in the space of the hollow of an atom, when the fire which burns a straw shall last for a long time, when the objects seen a dream shall come in the waking state, when the current of a river shall stand still (of itself), when the delivery of a barren woman shall be fruitful, when the crow shall walk like a swan, when the mule shall fight with a lion, when a great ass shall walk like an elephant, when the full moon shall become a sun, when Rāhu shall abandon the sun and the moon, when a good crop shall arise out of the waste (burnt) seeds, when the poor shall enjoy the happiness of the rich, when the lions shall be conquered by the bravery of dogs, when the heart of Jñānīs is known by fools, when the ocean is drunk by the dogs without any remainder, when the pure ākāśa shall fall upon men, when heaven shall fall on the earth, when the flower in the sky shall emit fragrance, when a forest appearing in pure ākāśa shall move, and when reflection shall arise in a glass simply (without mercury or anything else in its back), then the world really is.

अजकुक्षौ जगन्नास्ति ह्यात्मकुक्षौ जगन्नहि। सर्वथा भेदकलनं द्वैताद्वैतं न विद्यते॥ ९९॥

मायाकार्यमिदं भेदमस्ति चेद्ब्रह्मभावनम्। देहोऽहमिति दुःखं चेद्ब्रह्माहमिति निश्चयः॥ १००॥

हृदयग्रन्थिरस्तित्वे छिद्यते ब्रह्मचक्रकम्। संशये समनुप्राप्ते ब्रह्मनिश्चयमाश्रयेत्॥ १०१॥

अनात्मरूपचोरश्चेदात्मरत्नस्य रक्षणम्। नित्यानन्दमयं ब्रह्म केवलं सर्वदा स्वयम्॥ १०२॥

There is no universe in the womb of Aja (the unborn Brahman)— there is no universe is the womb of Ātman. Duality and non-duality, which are but the results of differentiation, are really not. All this is the result of māyā. Therefore, there should be Brahma-Bhāvanā. If misery should arise from the conception of 'I am the body', then it is certain 'I am Brahman'. The knot of the heart is the wheel of Brahman, which cuts asunder the knot of existence. When doubt arises in one, he should have faith of Brahman. The non-dual brahman, which is eternal and of the form of unconditioned bliss, is the guard of Ātman against the chief of the form of non-Ātman.

एवमादिसुदृष्टान्तैः साधितं ब्रह्ममात्रकम्। ब्रह्मैव सर्वभवनं भुवनं नाम संत्यज॥ १०३॥

अहं ब्रह्मेति निश्चित्य अहंभावं परित्यज। सर्वमेव लयं याति सुप्तहस्तस्थपुष्पवत्॥ १०४॥

न देहो न च कर्माणि सर्वं ब्रह्मैव केवलम्। न भूतं न च कार्यं च न चावस्थाचतुष्टयम्॥ १०५॥

लक्षणात्रयविज्ञानं सर्वं ब्रह्मैव केवलम्। सर्वव्यापारमुत्सृज्य ह्यहं ब्रह्मेति भावय॥ १०६॥

अहं ब्रह्म न संदेहो ह्यहं ब्रह्म चिदात्मकम्। सच्चिदानन्दमात्रोऽहमिति निश्चित्य तत्त्यज॥ १०७॥

Through instance like the above is established the nature of Brahman. Brahman alone is the all-abode. Abandon the name even of the universe. Knowing for certain 'I am Brahman', give up the 'I'. Everything disappears as the flower from the hands of sleeping person. There is neither body nor karma. Everything is Brahman alone. There are neither objects, nor actions, nor the four states. Everything which has the three characteristics of vijñāna is Brahman alone. Abondoning all actions, contemplate 'I am Brahman', 'I am Brahman'. There is no doubt of this. I am Brahman of the nature of cit— I am of the nature of saccidānanda.

शांकरीयं महाशास्त्रं न देयं यस्य कस्यचित्। नास्तिकाय कृतघ्नाय दुर्वृत्ताय दुरात्मने॥ १०८॥

गुरुभक्तिविशुद्धान्तःकरणाय महात्मने। सम्यक् परीक्ष्य दातव्यं मासं षाणमासवत्सरम्॥ १०९॥

सर्वोपनिषदभ्यासं दूरतस्त्यज्य सादरम्। तेजोबिन्दूपनिषदमभ्यसेत्सर्वदा मुदा॥ ११०॥

सकृदभ्यासमात्रेण ब्रह्मैव भवति स्वयं ब्रह्मैव भवति स्वयमित्युपनिषत्॥

"This great science of Śaṅkara should never be explained to any ordinary person, to an atheist or to a faithless, ill-behaved or evil-minded person. It should be, after due examination, given to the high-soul ones whose minds are purified with devotion to their Gurus. It should be taught for a year and a half. Leaving off thoroughly and entirely the practice recommended by the (other) Upaniṣad one should study the Tejobindu-Upaniṣad always with delight. By once studying it, he becomes one with Brahman. Thus ends the sixth chapter.

ॐ सह नाववत्विति शान्तिः॥

॥इति तेजोबिन्दूपनिषत्समाप्ता॥

***

34. NĀDA-BINDU-UPANIṢAD

नादबिन्दूपनिषद्

॥शांतिपाठः॥

ॐ वाङ्मे मनसि ....इति शान्तिः॥

ॐ अकारो दक्षिणः पक्ष उकारस्तूत्तरः स्मृतः। मकारं पुच्छमित्याहुरर्धमात्रा तु मस्तकम्॥ १॥
पादादिकं गुणास्तस्य शरीरं तत्त्वमुच्यते। धर्मोऽस्य दक्षिणं चक्षुरधर्मोऽथो परः स्मृतः॥ २॥

Oṁ! This Ātman is as bird. Syllable A is considered to be its right wing, U, its left : M, its tail-feathers; and the half mora (ardhamātrā) is its head.

The Rajas and Tamas are its feet, the Sattva is called its body, dharma (righteousness) is considered to be its right eye, and adharma (wrong) its left.

भूर्लोकः पादयोस्तस्य भुवर्लोकस्तु जानुनि। सुवर्लोकः कटीदेशे नाभिदेशे महर्जगत्॥ ३॥
जनोलोकस्तु हृद्देशे कण्ठे लोकस्तपस्ततः। भ्रुवोर्ललाटमध्ये तु सत्यलोको व्यवस्थितः॥ ४॥
सहस्त्रार्णमतीवात्र मन्त्र एष प्रदर्शितः। एवमेतां समारूढो हंसयोगविचक्षणः॥ ५॥
न भिद्यते कर्मचारैः पापकोटिशतैरपि।

The Bhūrloka is situtated in its feet; the Bhuvarloka, in its knees; the Svarloka, in its loins; and the Maharloka, in its navel.

In its heart is situated the jana-loka; the tapoloka in its neck, and the satyaloka is located in the centre of the forehead between the eyebrows.

"He speaks to a thousand days' width." In this hymn he is meant, one who is skilled in the Yoga, he ascends on that Haṁsa (bird). Thus he is not affected by the influences of Karman and is not bound by many a thouand sins.

आग्नेयी प्रथमा मात्रा वायव्येषा तथापरा॥ ६॥
भानुमण्डलसंकाशा भवेन्मात्रा तथोत्तरा। परमा चार्धमात्रा या वारुणीं तां विदुर्बुधा॥ ७॥

The first mātrā (mora) has Agni, (presiding deity); the second, Vāyu as its deity; then next third mora has the lustre of the solar orb, and the last (three and half), the wises know as belonging to Varuṇa (the presiding deity of water).

कालत्रयेऽपि यस्येमा मात्रा नूनं प्रतिष्ठिताः। एष ओंकार आख्यातो धारणाभिर्निबोधत॥ ८॥
घोषिणी प्रथमा मात्रा विद्युन्मात्रा तथापरा। पतङ्गिनी तृतीया स्याच्चतुर्थी वायुवेगिनी॥ ९॥
पञ्चमी नामधेया तु षष्ठी चैन्द्र्यभिधीयते। सप्तमी वैष्णवी नाम अष्टमी शांकरीति च॥ १०॥
नवमी महती नाम धृतिस्तु दशमी मता। एकादशी भवेन्नारी ब्राह्मी तु द्वादशी परा॥ ११॥

Each of these mātrās has indeed three kalās (parts). This is called Oṁkāra (Oṁ-sound). Know it by means of the dhāraṇās, (viz., concentration on each of the twelve kalās, or the variations of the mātras produced by the difference of svaras or intonation). The first mātrā is called ghoṣiṇī (rich in sound); the second is vidyunmāli (wreathed with lightning); the third is Pataṅginī (flight-enjoyer); the fourth Vāyuveginī (swift as wind); the fifth is called Nāmadheya (namable); the sixth is Aindrī (belonging to Indra); the seventh is Vaiṣṇavī (belong to Viṣṇu); the eighth, Śaṅkarī (after Śaṅkara); the ninth is Mahatī (great); the tenth, Dhṛti (regarding to firmness); the eleventh is Nārī (women, another reading is maunī-silent); and the twelfth is called Brāhmī (the Brāhmic).

प्रथमायां तु मात्रायां यदि प्राणैर्वियुज्यते। भरते वर्षराजासौ सार्वभौमः प्रजायते॥ १२॥

द्वितीयायां समुत्क्रान्तो भवेद्यक्षो महात्मवान्। विद्याधरस्तृतीयायां गान्धर्वस्तु चतुर्थिका॥ १३॥

पञ्चम्यामथ मात्रायां यदि प्राणैर्वियुज्यते। उषितः सह देवत्वं सोमलोके महीयते॥ १४॥

[Reward for the meditation at the time of death]

If a person happens to die in the first mātrā (while contemplating on it), he is born as a sovereign king in Bhāratavarṣa.

One gives up life in the second mātrā, he becomes an illustrious Yakṣa; if one departs in the third mora becomes a Vidyādhara; and in the fourth he becomes a Gandharva (these three beings the celestial hosts). If happens to die in the fifth, viz., ardhamātrā, He lives among gods and roams in the Somaloka (region of moon) magnificently.

षष्ठ्यामिन्द्रस्य सायुज्यं सप्तम्यां वैष्णवं पदम्। अष्टम्यां व्रजते रुद्रं पशूनां च पतिं तथा॥ १५॥

नवम्यां तु महर्लोकं दशम्यां तु जनं व्रजेत्। एकादश्यां तपोलोकं द्वादश्यां ब्रह्म शाश्वतम्॥ १६॥

ततः परतरं शुद्धं व्यापकं निर्मलं शिवम्। सदोदितं परं ब्रह्म ज्योतिषामुदयो यतः॥ १७॥

At the time of meditation one gives up his life in the sixth mora, he merges into Indra; if in the seventh, he reaches the seat of Viṣṇu; and if in the eighth, attains Rudra, the Lord of all creatures. If in the ninth, in Maharloka; if in the tenth, in Jana-loka (Another reading-Dhruvaloka); if in the eleventh, Tapoloka, and if in the twelfth, he attains the eternal state of Brahma.

That which is beyond these (viz.,) Parabrahman which is beyond (the above mātrās), the pure, the all-pervading, partless, holy, benevolent, the very resplendent and the origin of all jyotis (luminaries) should be known.

अतीन्द्रियं गुणातीतं मनो लीनं यदा भवेत्। अनूपमं शिवं शान्तं योगयुक्तं सदाविशेत्॥ १८॥

तद्युक्तस्तन्मयो जन्तुः शनैर्मुञ्चेत्कलेवरम्। संस्थितो योगचारेण सर्वसङ्गविवर्जितः॥ १९॥

ततो विलीनपाशोऽसौ विमलः कमलाप्रभुः। तेनैव ब्रह्मभावेन परमानन्दमश्नुते॥ २०॥

आत्मानं सततं ज्ञात्वा कालं नय महामते। प्रारब्धमखिलं भुञ्जन्नोद्वेगं कर्तुमर्हसि॥ २१॥

The Yoga and its reward

When the mind goes beyond the senses and the guṇas, it is dissolved in itself. Uncomparable, not imagining, auspicious and peaceful— That is called the correct art of Yoga. That person always engaged in its contemplation and always absorbed in it should gradually leave off his body following the course of Yoga and avoiding all worldly attachment.

Then he, being freed from the bonds of karma and the existence as a jīva and being pure, enjoys the supreme bliss by his attaining of the state of Brahman.

O intelligent man, spend your life always in the knowing of the supreme bliss, enjoying the whole of your prārabdha (that portion of past karmas now being enjoyed) without making any complaint (of it).

उत्पन्ने तत्त्वविज्ञाने प्रारब्धं नैव मुञ्चति। तत्त्वज्ञानोदयादूर्ध्वं प्रारब्धं नैव विद्यते॥ २२॥

देहादीनामसत्त्वात्तु यथा स्वप्ने विबोधतः। कर्म जन्मान्तरीयं यत्प्रारब्धमिति कीर्तितम्॥ २३॥

यत्तु जन्मान्तराभावात्पुंसो नैवास्ति कर्हिचित्। स्वप्नदेहो यथाध्यस्तस्तथैवायं हि देहकः॥ २४॥

Even after ātmajñāna (knowledge of Self) has awakened (in one), prārabdha does not leave (him); but he is liberated from prārabdha after the attainment of knowledge of Brahman because the body and other things are asat (unreal) like the things seen in a dream to one on awaking from it. That (portion of the) karmas which is done in former births are called prārabdha.

As the body that exists in the dreaming state is untrue, so is this body. Where then is rebirth to a thing that is illusory? How can a thing have any existence, when there is no birth (to it)?

अध्यस्तस्य कुतो जन्म जन्माभावे कुतः स्थितिः। उपादानं प्रपञ्चस्य मृद्भाण्डस्येव पश्यति॥ २५॥

अज्ञानं चेति वेदान्तैस्तस्मिन्नष्टे क्व विश्वता। यथा रज्जुं परित्यज्य सर्पं गृह्णाति वै भ्रमात्॥ २६॥

तद्वत्सत्यमविज्ञाय जगत्पश्यति मूढधीः। रज्जुखण्डे परिज्ञाते सर्परूपं न तिष्ठति॥ २७॥

अधिष्ठाने तथा ज्ञाते प्रपञ्चे शून्यतां गते। देहस्यापि प्पपञ्चत्वात्प्रारब्धावस्थितिः कुतः॥ २८॥

अज्ञानजनबोधार्थं प्रारब्धमिति चोच्यते। ततः कालवशादेव प्रारब्धे तु क्षयं गते॥ २९॥

ब्रह्मप्रणवसंधानं नादो ज्योतिर्मयः शिवः। स्वयमाविर्भवेदात्मा मेघापायेंऽशुमानिव॥ ३०॥

As the clay is the material cause of the pot, so one learns from Vedānta that ajñāna is the material cause of the universe : and when ajñāna ceases to exist, where then is the cosmos?

As a person through illusion mistakes a rope for a serpent, so the fool not knowing the truth sees the world (to be true).

When he knows it to be a piece of rope, the illusory idea of a serpent vanishes.

So when he knows the eternal substratum of everything and all the universe bcomes (therefore) void (to him), where then is prārabdha to him, the body being a part of the world? Therefore, the word prārabdha is accepted to enlighten the ignorant (only).

Then as prārabdha has, in course of time, worn out he who is the sound resulting from the union of Praṇava (Oṁ) with brahman who is the absolute effulgence itself, and who is the bestower of all good, shines himself like the sun at the dispersion of the clouds.

सिद्धासने स्थितो योगी मुद्रां संधाय वैष्णवीम्। शृणुयाद्दक्षिणे कर्णे नादमन्तर्गतं सदा।। ३१।।

अभ्यस्यमानो नादोऽयं बाह्यमावृणुते ध्वनिः। पक्षाद्विपक्षमखिलं जित्वा तुर्यपदं व्रजेत्।। ३२।।

The yogin being in the siddhāsana (posture) and practising the Vaiṣṇavī-mudrā, should always hear the internal sound through the right ear.

The sound which he thus practises makes him deaf to all external sounds. Having overcome all obstacles, he enters the turīya state within fifteen days.

श्रूयते प्रथमाभ्यासे नादो नानाविधो महान्। वर्धमाने तथाभ्यासे श्रूयते सूक्ष्मसूक्ष्मतः।। ३३।।

आदौ जलधिजीमूतभेरीनिर्झरसंभवः। मध्ये मर्दलशब्दाभो घण्टाकाहलजस्तथा।। ३४।।

अन्ते तु किंकिणीवंशवीणाभ्रमरनिःस्वनः। इति नानाविधा नादाः श्रूयन्ते सूक्ष्मसूक्ष्मतः।। ३५।।

In the beginning of his practice, he hears many loud sounds. They gradually increase in pitch and are heard more and more minute.

At first, the sounds are like those proceeding from the ocean, clouds, kettle-drum, and cataracts : in the middle (stage) those proceeding from mardala (a musical instrument), bell, and horn.

At the last stage, those proceeding from tinkling bless, flute, vīṇā (a musical instrument), and bells. Thus he hears many such sounds more and more minute.

महति श्रूयमाणे तु महाभेर्यादिकध्वनौ। तत्र सूक्ष्म सूक्ष्मतरं नादमेव परामृशेत्।। ३६।।

घनमुत्सृज्य वा सूक्ष्मे सूक्ष्ममुत्सृज्य वा घने। रममाणमपि क्षिप्तं मनो नान्यत्र चालयेत्।। ३७।।

यत्र कुत्रापि वा नादे लगति प्रथमं मनः। तत्र तत्र स्थिरीभूत्वा तेन सार्धं विलीयते।। ३८।।

विस्मृत्य सकलं बाह्यं नादे दुग्धाम्बुवन्मनः। एकीभूयाथ सहसा चिदाकाशे विलीयते।। ३९।।

When he comes to that stage when the sound of the great kettle-drum is being heard, he should try to distinguish only sounds more and more minute.

He may change his concentration from the gross sound to the subtle, of from the subtle to the gross, but he should not allow his mind to be diverted from them towards others.

The mind having at first concentrated itself on any one sound fixes firmly to that and is absorbed in it.

It (the mind) becoming insensible to the external impressions, becomes one with the sound as milk water, and then becomes rapidly absorbed in cidākāśa (the ākāśa where Cit prevails).

उदासीनस्ततो भूत्वा सदाभ्यासेन संयमी। उन्मनीकारकं सद्यो नादमेवावधारयेत्॥ ४०॥
सर्वचिन्तां समुत्सृज्य सर्वचेष्टाविवर्जितः। नादमेवानुसंदध्यान्नादे चित्तं विलीयते॥ ४१॥
मकरन्दं पिबन्भृङ्गो गन्धान्नापेक्षते यथा। नादासक्तं सदा चित्तं विषयं न हि काङ्क्षति॥ ४२॥
बद्धः सुनादगन्धेन सद्यः संत्यक्तचापलः।

Being indifferent towards all objects, the yogin having controlled his passions, should by continual practice concentrate his attention upon the sound which destroys the mind.

Having abandoned all thoughts and being freed from all actions, he should always concentrate his attention on the sound, and (then) his citta becomes absorbed in it.

Just as the bee drinking the honey (alone) does not care for the odour, so the citta which is always absorbed in sound, does not long for sensual objects as it is bound by the sweet smell of nāda and has abandoned its fitting nature.

नादग्रहणतश्चित्तमन्तरङ्गभुजङ्गमः॥ ४३॥
विस्मृत्य विश्वमेकाग्रः कुत्रचिन्न हि धावति। मनोमत्तगजेन्द्रस्य विषयोद्यानचारिणः॥ ४४॥
नियामनसमर्थोऽयं निनादो निशिताङ्कुशः। नादोऽन्तरङ्गसारङ्गबन्धने वागुरायते॥ ४५॥
अन्तरङ्गसमुद्रस्य रोधे वेलायतेऽपि वा। ब्रह्मप्रणवसंलग्ननादो ज्योतिर्मयात्मकः॥ ४६॥
मनस्तत्र लयं याति तद्विष्णोः परमं पदम्।

The serpent citta through listening to the nāda is entirely absorbed in it, and becoming unconscious of everything concentrates itself on the sound.

The sound serves the purpose of a sharp good to control the maddened elephant— citta which roves in the pleasure-garden of the sensual objects.

It serves the purpose of a snare for binding the deer— citta. It also serves the purpose of a shore to the ocean waves of citta.

The sound proceeding from Praṇava which is Brahman is of the nature of effulgence; the mind becomes absorbed in it; that is the supreme seat of Viṣṇu.

तावदाकाशसंकल्पो यावच्छब्दः प्रवर्तते॥ ४७॥
निःशब्दं तत्परं ब्रह्म परमात्मा समीयते। नादो यावन्मनस्तावन्नादान्तेऽपि मनोन्मनी॥ ४८॥
सशब्दश्चाक्षरे क्षीणे निःशब्दं परमं पदम्। सदा नादानुसंधानात्संक्षीणा वासना तु या॥ ४९॥
निरञ्जने विलीयेते मनोवायू न संशयः। नादकोटिसहस्राणि बिन्दुकोटिशतानि च॥ ५०॥
सर्वे तत्र लयं यान्ति ब्रह्मप्रणवनादके। सर्वावस्थाविनिर्मुक्तः सर्वचिन्ताविवर्जितः॥ ५१॥
मृतवत्तिष्ठते योगी स मुक्तो नात्र संशयः।

The sound exists till there is the ākāśic conception (ākāśa-saṅkalpa). Beyond this, is the (aśabda) soundless Parabrahman which is Pramātmā.

The mind exists so long as there is sound, but with its (sound's) cessation, there is the state called unmanī manas (viz., the state of being above the mind).

This sound is absorbed in the Akṣara (indestructible) and the soundless state is the supreme seat.

The mind which along with Prāṇa (Vāyu) has (its) kārmic affinities destroyed by the constant concetration upon nāda is absorbed in the unstained One. There is no doubt of it.

Many myriads of nādas and many more of bindus-(all) become absorbed in the Brahma-Praṇava sound.

Being freed from all states and all thoughts whatever, the yogin remains like one dead. He is a mukta. There is no doubt about this.

शङ्खदुन्दुभिनादं च न श्रृणोति कदाचन॥५२॥
काष्ठवज्ज्ञायते देह उन्मन्यावस्थया ध्रुवम्। न जानाति स शीतोष्णं न दुःखं न सुखं तथा॥५३॥
न मानं नावमानं च संत्यक्त्वा तु समाधिना। अवस्थात्रयमन्वेति न चित्तं योगिनः सदा॥५४॥
जाग्रन्निद्राविनिर्मुक्तः स्वरूपावस्थतामियात्॥५५॥
दृष्टिः स्थिरा यस्य विनासदृश्यं वायुः स्थिरो यस्य विना प्रयत्नम्।
चित्तं स्थिरं यस्य विनावलम्बं स ब्रह्मतारान्तरनादरूप इत्युपनिषत्॥५६॥

After that, he does not any time hear the sounds of conch or dundubhi (large kettle-drum).

The body in the state of unmanī is certainly like a log and does not feel heat or cold, joy or sorrow.

The yogin's citta having given up fame or disgrace is in samādhi above the three states.

Being freed from the waking and the sleeping states, he attains to his true state.

When the (spiritual) sight becomes fixed without any object to be seen, when the vāyu (prāṇa) becomes still without any effort, and when the citta becomes firm without any support, he becomes of the form of the internal sound of Brahma-Praṇava.

ॐ वाङ्मे मनसि ..... इति शान्तिः॥

॥ इति नादबिन्दूपनिषत्समाप्ता॥

----

35. DVAYOPANIṢAD

द्वयोपनिषद्

It is still unknown as to what tradition of and to what Veda this Upaniṣad is related. There are only seven hymns in it whereas origin and the nature of dual has been laid down in a most cryptic way.

ॐ अथातः श्रीमद्द्वयोत्पत्तिः। वाक्यो द्वितीयः। षट्पदान्यष्टादश। पञ्चविंशत्यक्षराणि। पञ्चदशाक्षरं पूर्वम्। दशाक्षरं परम्। पूर्वो नारायणः प्रोक्तोऽनादिसिद्धो मन्त्ररत्नः सदाचार्यमूलः। आचार्यो वेदसंपन्नो विष्णुभक्तो विमत्सरः। मन्त्रज्ञो मन्त्रभक्तश्च सदामन्त्राश्रयः शुचिः॥१॥ गुरुभक्तिसमायुक्तः पुराणज्ञो विशेषवित्। एवं लक्षणसंपन्नो गुरुरित्यभिधीयते॥२॥

Now, the origin of Śrīmaddvaya is described. The second is the sentence. The six foot are consisting of eighteen numbers. There are twenty-five letters. Fifteen letters are preceding and the ten letters are succeeding. Initially Nārāyaṇa has been stated as Anādisiddha who is rationale to etiquette and Jam-like in hymns.

[This Upaniṣad *i.e.* Dvaya starts with a resolution to the origin of the dual. It becomes clear that letter is considered first when the sentence is stated as second. The letter is immortal and inexpressive too therefore it is first while the sentence carrying its expression falls in second place. The Ṛṣi has stated that first or the presiding as Anādisiddha, Jam-hymn Nārāyaṇa on this very basis that first letter is considered Oṁ. The first expression of Brahma is letter or Nārāyaṇa and it is the base of the teacher or the sentence. This second teacher has been described in the successive hymns.]

The person having characteristics of well-known to Veda, the hymns, the devotee, resorting to hymns, known to Purāṇa, expert, pure heart, free from envy, devotee to Lord Viṣṇu and teacher is called Guru.

आचिनोति हि शास्त्रार्थानाचारस्थापनादपि।
स्वयमाचरते यस्तु तस्मादाचार्य उच्यते॥३॥

The person who chooses the meaning of holy books duly, understands properly the same and who not only establishes well-behaviour but himself observe the rules to behave is called Ācārya.

गुशब्दस्त्वन्धकारः स्यात् रुशब्दस्तन्निरोधकः।
अन्धकारनिरोधित्वाद्गुरुरित्यभिधीयते॥४॥

The letter 'Gu' is meant darkness and 'Ru' means its resistance in the word 'Guru'. The person who resists the ignorance is therefore called Guru.

गुरुरेव परं ब्रह्म गुरुरेव परा गतिः।
गुरुरेव परं विद्या गुरुरेव परं धनम्॥५॥

Guru is the supreme Brahma, the supreme position, supreme learning and the supreme wealth.

गुरुरेव परः कामः गुरुरेव परायणः।
यस्मात्तदुपदेष्टासौ तस्माद्गुरुतरो गुरुः॥६॥

Guru is the desired thing, the Supreme resort and having a preacher of supreme knowledge, the Guru is great.

यस्सकृदुच्चारणः संसारविमोचनो भवति।
सर्वपुरुषार्थसिद्धिर्भवति। न च पुनरावर्तते न च पुनरावर्तत इति। य एवं वेदेत्युपनिषत्॥७॥

A man in liberated from worldly ties even if he once pronunciate the word Guru. All industry avail accomplishment when the word Guru is pronunciated. In fact, the man remembering and pronunciating the word Guru seldom rotates round the cycle of birth and death and seldom takes rebirth. The person attains to everything who is understood duly to it.

॥इति द्वयोपनिषत् समाप्ता॥

----

36. YĀJÑAVALKYOPANIṢAD

याज्ञवल्क्योपनिषद्

This Upaniṣad is related to Śukla Yajurveda, colloquy between king Janaka and Yājñavalkya has been described herein. A prolis detail on holding recession has also been given under this Upaniṣad. King Janaka was pleased by Yājñavalkya couple life after the celibacy, Vānaprastha (renunciation of worldly attachments) after the couple and the reclusion after Vānaprastha is the order by manner prescribed for the walks of the life. However due to excessive emotions, an abundant position of the detachment, reclusion can be accepted anytime whenever that state is occupied. The person accepting reclusion should give up the raising braid put on sacrificial thread etc. How the Brāhmaṇa name will be given without the sacrificial threat? Yājñavalkya responded that the Oṁ is the sacrificial thread of a recluse. The properties, behaviours and intentions have been further described. Simultaneously, the defect of woman that divide a recluse from him sacred way has been highlighted with hatred picturesque. It has been suggested to a recluse that he should avoid from greed, affection, sensuality and that anger presuming that the children too are cause for pain. Finally a suggestion has been given to recluse that he should only engross his mind pondering over the perfect Brahma (knowledge) because only then emancipation can be obtained by him.

।।शान्तिपाठः।।

ॐ पूर्णमदः .... इति शान्तिः।।

अथ जनको ह वैदेहो याज्ञवल्क्यमुपसमेत्योवाच भगवन्संन्यासमनुब्रूहीति। स होवाच याज्ञवल्क्यो ब्रह्मचर्यं समाप्य गृही भवेत्। गृही भूत्वा वनी भवेत् वनी भूत्वा प्रव्रजेत्। यदि वेतरथा ब्रह्मचर्यादेव प्रव्रजेद्गृहाद्वा वनाद्वा। अथ पुनर्व्रती वाऽव्रती वा स्नातको वाऽस्नातको वा उत्सन्नाग्निरनग्निको वा यदहरेव विरजेत्तदहरेव प्रव्रजेत्।।। १।।

Once the king Janaka went to hermit Yājñavalkya and requested "O Lord! kindly make me to understood the life of recluse." Yājñavalkya responded " O king! One should enter into the couple life after completing the period of celibacy with a due observance of the procedure. After enjoyment in glut with ones children, wife, etc. he should then give up his residence and stay in the forest. On completion of this Vānaprastha stage; the stage of renunciation should be entertained. In case, the process of crystallizing knowledge takes lesser period, a man erstwhile in the stage of celibacy can directly jump up to reculsion. It is a criteria founded on the presumption that the extent of attachment leads a man from one stage to another. A detachment to worldly affair is the common cause for a reclusion. The moment when a main fully detached to the worldly issues, should immediately accept the reclusion inspite of his not being the celibate, the coupler, have completed the ceremonies of fire or not.

तदेके प्राजापत्यामेवेष्टिं कुर्वन्ति। अथवा न कुर्यादाग्नेय्यामेव कुर्यात्। अग्निर्हि प्राणः। प्राणमेवैतया करोति। त्रैधातवीयामेव कुर्यात्। एतयैव त्रयो धातवो यदुत सत्त्वं रजस्तम इति। अयं ते योनिर्ऋत्विजो यतो जातो अरोचथाः। तं जानन्नग्न आरोहाथा नो वर्धया रयिमित्यनेन मन्त्रेणाग्निमाजिघ्रेत्। एष वा अग्नेर्योनिर्यः प्राणं गच्छ स्वां योनिं गच्छ स्वाहेत्येवमेवैतदाह॥ २॥

Some people do Prājāpatya offering thereafter. The Āgneya Yājña is the substitution of this offering because the fire is the breathing. The breathing is nourished as a result of this offering. One can do as an option an offering relating to the three properties *i.e.* Sattva, Rajas and Tamas. He should then smell the fire by reciting this hymn "O Lord fire! We wise should be progressed owing to knowledge of the reason for which you are born, blaze with extreme light and increase our prosperity." This is the root cause of fire and this is breathing. O Lord fire! Please enshrine in the breathing the form of Yoni.

ग्रामादग्निमाहृत्य पूर्ववदग्निमाजिघ्रेत्। यदग्निं न विन्देदप्सु जुहुयादापो वै सर्वा देवताः सर्वाभ्यो देवताभ्यो जुहोमि स्वाहेति हुत्वोद्धृत्य प्राश्नीयात् साज्यं हविरनामयम्। मोक्षमन्त्रैस्त्रय्येवं वेद तद्ब्रह्म तदुपासितव्यम्। शिखां यज्ञोपवीतं छित्त्वा संन्यस्तं मयेति त्रिवारमुच्चरेत्। एवमेवैतद्भगवन्निति वै याज्ञवल्क्यः॥ ३॥

One should bring fire from a village and smell it. In case, the fire is not available, one should do this offering in the water because the water embeds within it, all gods. The assumption should be– I offer for all gods them Svāhā viz., May this morsel (Āhuti) be accepted by them. The residual should be then eaten. This morsel mixed with ghee removes all ailments. Thus, the trio-Veda position should be acquired be reciting the hymns relating to the emancipation. He is Brahma and he should be worshipped. I have accepted the life of a recluse by giving up the sacrificial thread and the braid. "Thrice time recital should be made of it. Saint Yājñavalkya thus described the method of accepting reclusion before the scholar king Janaka.

अथ हैनमत्रिः पप्रच्छ याज्ञवल्क्यं अयज्ञोपवीती कथं ब्राह्मण इति। स होवाच याज्ञवल्क्य इदं प्रणवमेवास्य तद्यज्ञोपवीतं य आत्मा। प्राश्याचम्यायं विधिः॥ ४॥

Subsequently, hermit Atri asked to Yājñavalkya– "O hermit! How can a Brahmaṇa survive without putting on a sacrificial thread." The hermit Yājñavalkya replied– "This Oṁ only is the sacrificial thread of that recluse." This Oṁ is the soul. The person who abides by the methods for offering aforesaid, eats the residual and then does Ācaman, it is the only and exclusive method for him.

अथ वा परिव्राड्विवर्णवासा मुण्डोऽपरिग्रहः शुचिरद्रोही भैक्षमाणो ब्रह्मभूयाय भवति। एष पन्थाः परिव्राजकानां वीराध्वाने वाऽनाशके वापां प्रवेशे वाग्निप्रवेशे वा महाप्रस्थाने वा। एष पन्था ब्रह्मणा हानुवित्तस्तेनेति स संन्यासी ब्रह्मविदिति। एवमेवैष भगवन्निति वै याज्ञवल्क्य॥ ५॥

The recluse putting on brown clothes this way, all pure in heart, not greedy and tidy, attains to the position of Brahma by living on alms. He is the form of Brahma viz., competent enough to attain Brahma. This is the only way for recluse. This route is suggested for the recluse to enter into water, fire, the great, departure etc. Abiding by them only makes the recluse competent to know the Brahma. Yājñavalkya thus described this method before the great king Janaka.

तत्र परमहंसा नाम संवर्तकारुणिश्वेतकेतुदुर्वासऋभुनिदाघदत्तात्रेयशुकवामदेवहारी-तक प्रभृतयोऽव्यक्तलिङ्गाऽव्यक्ताचारा अनुन्मत्ता उन्मत्तवदाचरन्त:॥ ६॥

Here among these recluse some are the best Paramahaṁsa who holds invisible marks of symbols, seems introvert, they do like dipsomaniac, however, without any taste of intoxication. Some of these yogis are Saṁvartaka, Āruṇi, Śvetaketu, Durvāsā, Ṛbhu, Nidāgha, Dattātreya, Śuka, Vāmadeva and Hārītaka etc.

परस्त्रीपुरपराङ्मुखास्त्रिदण्डं कमण्डलुं भुक्तपात्रं जलपवित्रं शिखां यज्ञोपवीतं बहिरन्तश्चेत्येतत्सर्वं भू: स्वाहेत्यप्सु परित्यज्यात्मानमन्विच्छेत्॥ ७॥

It is sine-qua-non for a recluse that refraining to see the face of other's wife, resort to forest and by immersing the in and out symbols like trident, kamaṇḍala, the bowl, the water, purifying Kuśa, the braid and the sacrificial thread etc. in the water by reciting Bhūḥ Svāhā. He then starts investigation deep into the soul.

यथा जातरूपधरा निर्द्वन्द्वा निष्परिग्रहास्तत्त्वब्रह्ममार्गे सम्यक्संपन्ना: शुद्धमानसा: प्राणसंधारणार्थं यथोक्तकाले विमुक्तो भैक्षमाचरन्नुदरपात्रेण लाभालाभौ समौ भूत्वा करपात्रेण वा कमण्डलूदकपो भैक्षमाचरन्नुदरमात्रसंग्रह: पात्रान्तरशून्यो जलस्थलक मण्डलुरबाधकरह: स्थलनिकेतनो लाभालाभौ समौ भूत्वा शून्यागार देवगृहतृणकूट वल्मीकवृक्षमूलकुलाल-शालाग्निहोत्र शालानदीपुलिनगिरि कुहरकोटर कन्दरनिर्झर स्थण्डि लेष्वनिकेतनिवास्यप्रयत्न: शुभाशुभकर्मनिर्मूलनपर: संन्यासेन देहत्यागं करोति स परमहंसो नामेति॥ ८॥

The recluse should arrive at the stage where no effects are felt of worldly vicissitudes, the heat and cold, void of duality, without greed, duly engrossed in the investigation of the element of Brahma with a sacrosanct heart, only sustaining food to the body and that too by the source of alms, free from the worry of profit and loss, live with full contentment on a water to the extent in Kamaṇḍala and to the food to the extent only in a bowl. He should only take his food to keep non-stop the physical function. He should have no desire to have any stock of food. He should choose a clandestine place to live on hundred life. The vacated and depleted building, the temples, a cottage of thatch, the valmīka (the cave constructed by ants) near the root of a tree, the cottage of potter, place of offering, the bank of a river, the cavity or the heavy boulders thrown by the functions should be issued as his residence. One who abandons his body after reclusion and squaring up all the accounts of his good or evil activities, is only known as Paramahaṁsa (the most genius person).

आशाम्बरो न नमस्कारो न दारपुत्राभिलाषी लक्ष्यालक्ष्यनिर्वर्तक: परिव्राट् परमेश्वरो भवति। अत्रैते श्लोका भवन्ति॥ ९॥

The recluse himself is the supreme god who lives in a life where no garments are required, who thinks no person worth saluting except the Brahma, who has no attachment with his life and children, who is known by his modus-operandi and who has abundant the inherent and non-inherent intentions. The following hymns have been contemplated regarding this.

यो भवेत्पूर्वसंन्यासी तुल्यो वै धर्मतो यदि।
तस्मै प्रणामः कर्तव्यो नेतराय कदाचन॥ १०॥

The person who has accepted the life of recluse very early or who is superior in conduct and thoughts as also in the community is only worth to salute and no body otherwise.

प्रमादिनो बहिश्चित्ताः पिशुनाः कलहोत्सुकाः।
संन्यासिनोऽपि दृश्यन्ते वेदसंदूषिताशयाः॥ ११॥

The recluse drawn in laxity, who are extrovert, who have excess attachment to the worldly issues, quarrelsome, shrewd and propounding the intentions of Vedas of defective are also seen in abundance.

नामादिभ्यः परे भूम्नि स्वाराज्ये चेत्स्थितोऽद्वये।
प्रणमेत्कं तदात्मज्ञो न कार्यं कर्मणा तदा॥ १२॥

How, a recluse master in the element of soul, undeviated, resident in the regime of non-duality, enshrined at the top place and beyond the qualification as name, residence, sensuality and the stage, can salute to another because he observes his own complexion in all (viz., one can't salute oneself and thus the recluse treating all equal never accepts the formality of Salutation). There is no work impossible for him in this world.

ईश्वरो जीवकलया प्रविष्टो भगवानिति।
प्रणमेद्दण्डवद्भूमावाश्वचण्डालगोखरम्॥ १३॥

The master in Metaphysics doesn't salute to any person or He even salutes by duly going down on the earth even to a horse, Cāṇḍāla (shrewd person), a cow and a donkey etc. because be observes all them gods.

मांसपाञ्चालिकायास्तु यन्त्रलोकेऽङ्गपञ्जरे।
स्नाय्वस्थिग्रन्थिशालिन्याः स्त्रियाः किमिव शोभनम्॥ १४॥

What is good and worth appreciation is the body of a female constituted by adding the flesh and marrow a pitcher like moving here and there and in which only veins, bones and glands are existing.

त्वङ्मांसरक्तवाष्पाम्बु पृथक् कृत्वा विलोचने। समालोकय रम्यं चेत्किं मुधा परिमुह्यसि॥ १५॥

By separating this body into skin, flesh, tear, blood and eyes etc., there will remain no more attraction. If this is the position why the place redundantly are so attached to the body of fair sex.

मेरुशृङ्गतटोल्लासिगङ्गाजलरयोपमा।
दृष्टा यस्मिन्मुने मुक्ताहारस्योल्लासशालिता॥ १६॥

The breast of a female and a garland on it has been appreciated as the stream of Gaṅgā water that flows down from the middle of two ridges in the vast mountain Meru. Actually that garland looks the same way.

श्मशानेषु दिगन्तेषु स एव ललनास्तनः।
श्वभिरास्वाद्यते काले लघुपिण्ड इवान्धसः॥ १७॥

When this same breast falls on cremation ground, cut out from the rest of body and badly splitted up, can be seen eaten by the dogs. The imagination that time for the dogs is nothing else but a piece of meat only.

केशकज्जलधारिण्यो दुःस्पर्शा लोचनप्रियाः।
दुष्कृताग्निशिखा नार्यो दहन्ति तृणवन्नरम्॥ १८॥

The females who maintain their hair raven tress, who smears Kajjala on the eyes, scare to touch, enchanting eyes and ignited like the fire flames; burn down the man like a straw.

ज्वलिता अतिदूरेऽपि सरसा अपि नीरसाः।
स्त्रियो हि नरकाग्नीनामिन्धनं चारु दारुणम्॥ १९॥

These females burn the man even from a distance, these seem a store of essence but actually are void of affection, these are like fuel to the hellish fire, their beauty leads to pain everybody.

कामनाम्ना किरातेन विकीर्णा मुग्धचेतसः।
नार्यो नरविहङ्गानामङ्गबन्धनवागुराः॥ २०॥

The god of sex as a hunter has spreaded this network of females that enchants the heart in order to capture the men-birds.

जन्मपल्वलमत्स्यानां चित्तकर्दमचारिणाम्।
पुंसां दुर्वासनारज्जुर्नारी बडिशपिण्डिका॥ २१॥

These females are like the pin duly jointed with the Lord of evil passion for the man who is fish like and moves in the mud like dirty heart and resides in the pond of the birth.

सर्वेषां दोषरत्नानां सुसमुद्गिकयानया।
दुःखशृङ्खलया नित्यमलमस्तु मम स्त्रिया॥ २२॥

May god save from the chain like females or miserable position who is like the box of all defective gems.

यस्य स्त्री तस्य भोगेच्छा निःस्त्रीकस्य क्व भोगभूः।
स्त्रियं त्यक्त्वा जगत्त्यक्तं जगत्त्यक्त्वा सुखी भवेत्॥ २३॥

The wise to copulate only lies with a man who has a wife but it has no place in the heart of a man who has no wife. In case, any person gives up the wife, it should be deemed that he has left the world.

अलभ्यमानस्तनयः पितरौ क्लेशयेच्चिरम्।
लब्धो हि गर्भपातेन प्रसवेन च बाधते॥ २४॥

The son too is a cause of pain because the parents long for bitterly if those have no son. In case, it any how obtained, it further gives the pain of abortion or the pain at the time of delivery.

जातस्य ग्रहरोगादि कुमारस्य च धूर्तता।
उपनीतेऽप्यविद्यत्वमनुद्वाहश्च पण्डिते॥ २५॥

In case, the son is obtained, he suffers from the ailments and miseries or sometimes, the sun become the cause of enigma. He remains stupid even after. Ceremony for sacrificial thread is performed if anyhow he is educated, his marriage becomes the cause for puzzle.

यूनश्च परदारादि दारिद्र्यं च कुटुम्बिनः।
पुत्रदुःखस्य नास्त्यन्तो धनी चेन्म्रियते तदा॥ २६॥

Besides, if the parents fear of his possible involvement, the number of children comes into earth to the extent that their proper maintenance becomes the cause for miseries. Thus, the pains caused by sons are numerous. Beside it, it is also seen that the rich people mostly remain without children or if there are some, those die in their premature ages (one should therefore abandon the wife or remain bachelor throughout life because the female is the ground cause for pains.

न पाणिपादचपलो न नेत्रचपलो यतिः।
न च वाक्चपलश्चैव ब्रह्मभूतो जितेन्द्रियः॥ २७॥

The yogi should not be caprice of hands, feel, eyes and the speech viz., he should be a well-controlled personality. He can observe celibacy only when he is of grave temperament.

रिपौ बद्धे स्वदेहे च समैकात्म्यं प्रपश्यतः।
विवेकिनः कुतः कोपः स्वदेहावयवेष्विव॥ २८॥

The person who observes with equal eye to the enemies and worldly ties is the yogi scholar. He never express his fury on any person. The man doesn't become loose temperament about his hand and feet etc.

अपकारिणि कोपश्चेत्कोपे कोपः कथं न ते।
धर्मार्थकाममोक्षाणां प्रसह्य परिपन्थिनि॥ २९॥

A man of angry mood should be asked why does he not express his anger that disturbs him. It is the basic reason for all happenings. It is the mighty enemy to conception, wealth, sensuality and the emancipation.

नमोऽस्तु मम कोपाय स्वाश्रयज्वालिने भृशम्।
कोपस्य मम वैराग्यदायिने दोषबोधिने॥

I salute frequently to the anger that itself burns down its own base. I frequently salute to the anger that provides me with reclusion and makes me aware of my faults.

यत्र सुप्ता जना नित्यं प्रबुद्धस्तत्र संयमी।
प्रबुद्धा यत्र ते विद्वान्सुषुप्तिं याति योगिराट्॥ ३१॥

The ascetic awakes when the common people retires and the yogi resorts to the dormance when other common people are awake.

चिदिहास्तीति चिन्मात्रमिदं चिन्मयमेव च।
चित्त्वं चिदहमेते च लोकाश्चिदिति भावय॥ ३२॥

The yogi should presume that I am in the form of mind in this world. The integrated world is the state of cinmaya and everything here is in the form of Cid. I am also Cid and this entire reaction is also in the form of Cid.

यतीनां तदुपादेयं पारहंस्यं परं पदम्।
नातः परतरं किंचिद्विद्यते मुनिपुङ्गव इत्युपनिषत्॥ ३३॥

O Great hermit! The emancipation viz., the supreme position of a Paramahaṁsa is worth use for yogis. Nothing so great is here. It is best. Thus this Upaniṣad has been concluded.

ॐ पूर्णमदः............ इति शान्तिः॥

॥इति याज्ञवल्क्योपनिषत्समाप्ता॥

***

37. JĀBĀLADARŚANOPANIṢAD

जाबालदर्शनोपनिषद्

This Upaniṣad is related to Sāmaveda. It is also called as Darśanopaniṣad. There are ten sections in it. A questionaire like description has been made herein containing the questions and answers transacted between Dattātreya, an incarnation to Lord Visnu and his disciple on Aṣṭāṅga Yoga.

In the first division of this Upaniṣad, the eight parts of Yoga and ten kinds of Yamas has been enumerated. In the second division, there is a description of ten rules. In the third division, the nine kinds of Āsanas in Yoga has been described. The fourth division contains an introduction to the nerves and magnificience of the pilgrim place of soul as also the self-realization. In the fifth division, the procedure of refining the nerves and the method of refining soul has been described. The sixth division, contains the method of Prāṇāyāma, its kinds and applications of the same. The different kinds of Pratyāhāra and its fruits has been detailed in the seventh division. The perception (Dhāraṇā) and the concentration is the subject-matter of the tenth division. Its fruit simultaneously have been described. Thus, this Upaniṣad can be entirely said relating to Yoga.

ॐ आप्यायन्तु..................इति शान्तिः॥

॥प्रथमः खण्डः॥

दत्तात्रेयो महायोगी भगवान्भूतभावनः। चतुर्भुजो महाविष्णुर्योगसाम्राज्यदीक्षितः॥ १॥
तस्य शिष्यो मुनिकरः सांकृतिर्नाम भक्तिमान्। पप्रच्छ गुरुमेकान्ते प्राञ्जलिर्विनयान्वितः॥ २॥
भगवन्ब्रूहि मे योगं साष्टाङ्गं सप्रपञ्चकम्। येन विज्ञातमात्रेण जीवन्मुक्तो भवाम्यहम्॥ ३॥

Lord Viṣṇu, the nourisher of all creatures appeared in the form of the Yogarāja Lord Dattātreya. Lord Dattātreya has gained expertise to tackle the realm of yoga. His disciple, the best hermit is popularly known as Sāṅkṛti. He became an extreme devotee of his teacher. He asked one day to his teacher most humbly and in a solitary place and in a solitude– "O Lord! kindly explain with detail of Aṣṭāṅga yoga so that I can make myself free from all the worldly ties.

सांकृते शृणु वक्ष्यामि योगं साष्टाङ्गदर्शनम्। यमश्च नियमश्चैव तथैवासनमेव च॥ ४॥
प्राणायामस्तथा ब्रह्मन्प्रत्याहारस्ततः परम्। धारणा च तथा ध्यानं समाधिश्चाष्टमं मुने॥ ५॥
अहिंसा सत्यमस्तेयं ब्रह्मचर्यं दयार्जवम्। क्षमा धृतिर्मिताहारः शौचं चैव यमा दश॥ ६॥

The yogī Lord Dattātreya said to his disciple– "O Sāṅkṛti! I tell you the philosophy of Aṣṭāṅga yoga. Please listen to it. The eight parts of yoga are– Yama, Niyama, Āsana, Prāṇāyāma, Pratyāhāra, Dhāraṇā, concentration and the meditation respectively. The kinds of Yama has been described as– (i) non-violence, (ii) truth, (iii) utilitarian, (iv) celibacy, (v) generosity, (vi) forgiveness, (vii) the simplicity (viii) patience (ix) control on diet and the (x) purity in and out.

वेदोक्तेन प्रकारेण विना सत्यं तपोधन। कायेन मनसा वाचा हिंसा हिंसा न चान्यथा॥७॥

आत्मा सर्वगतोऽच्छेद्यो न ग्राह्य इति या मतिः। सा चाहिंसा वरा प्रोक्ता मुने वेदान्तवेदिभिः॥

O the rich in penance! An action committing murder or causing any pain to anybody either by application of mind, speech or body separately or severely not permitted in Vedas is actually called the violence. Nothing distinct and separate to it is the violence. O Saint! The devotee should develop a spirit that the element of soul is omnipresent and it can't be destroyed through application of any arm or weapon. Entertainment of the soul is even impossible either through application of hands or other sensory organs. Hence, the justified wisdom is only stated the best non-violence by the scholars who have duly examined the words of Vedas.

चक्षुरादीन्द्रियैर्दृष्टं श्रुतं घ्रातं मुनीश्वर। तस्यैवोक्तिर्भवेत्सत्यं विप्र तन्नान्यथा भवेत्॥९॥

सर्वं सत्यं परं ब्रह्म न चान्यदिति या मतिः। तच्च सत्यं वरं प्रोक्तं वेदान्तज्ञानपारगैः॥१०॥

अन्यदीये तृणे रत्ने काञ्चने मौक्तिकेऽपि च। मनसा विनिवृत्तिर्या तदस्तेयं विदुर्बुधाः॥११॥

आत्मन्यनात्मभावेन व्यवहारविवर्जितम्। यत्तदस्तेयमित्युक्तमात्मविद्भिर्महामुने॥१२॥

O Sāṅkṛti! It is the truth referred to expressively or impliedly which is seen, heard, smelled and understood by the means of the sensory organs including the eyes, ears, etc. No other complexion is worn by the truth incoherent to it. Everything is the supreme soul in the form of perfect knowledge and the truth and there is nothing errs and otherwise then this supreme soul. The firm determination so made has been stated by the scholars of Vedas as the best truth. Developing a rel ctance for the objects like ornaments and the gems, the gold or the pearls etc. not his own, imposing a stern check on the mind not to entice or enchant for other things either smaller or bigger is called the spirit of renunciation (Asteya). The scholars has stated it as Asteya. O hermit! The person who can keep all worldly dealings distinct and separate from the soul and seldom thinking their any bearing with the soul, is called Asteya by the learned persons.

कायेन वाचा मनसा स्त्रीणां परिविवर्जनम्। ऋतौ भार्यां तदा स्वस्य ब्रह्मचर्यं तदुच्यते॥१३॥

ब्रह्मभावे मनश्चारं ब्रह्मचर्यं परन्तप॥१४॥

स्वात्मवत्सर्वभूतेषु कायेन मनसा गिरा। अनुज्ञा या दया सैव प्रोक्ता वेदान्तवेदिभिः॥१५॥

It is celibacy to abandon the couplation with women by application of mind, speech and body, jointly or separately and enjoying intercourse with his only wife and that too confined to the prescribed period prior and after the menstruation. In other words, the mind expelling the enemies like sensuality and disgust and leading it to the concentration on the element of supreme soul in garb of everlasting perfect knowledge is the best celibacy. It is kindness duly confirmed by the scholars of Vedas inspiring by which the man thinks and behaves with all living-organisms by application of his mind, speech and the body, the same was as he would have behave with himself and a surplus spirit to serve the humanity to the extent capacity allows.

पुत्रे मित्रे कलत्रे च रिपौ स्वात्मनि संततम्।
एकरूपं मुने यत्तदार्जवं प्रोच्यते मया॥ १६॥

To keep the spirit of equity in mind among the son, friends, wife, enemy and his self soul is called the simplicity.

कायेन मनसा वाचा शत्रुभिः परिपीडिते।
बुद्धिक्षोभनिवृत्तिर्या क्षमा सा मुनिपुङ्गव॥ १७॥

O great hermit! It is forgiveness that enables the man not being feel insulted or injured even after pains to mind, speech and body are inflicted by the enemies.

वेदादेव विनिर्मोक्षः संसारस्य न चान्यथा। इति विज्ञाननिष्पत्तिर्धृतिः प्रोक्ता हि वैदिकैः। अहमात्मा न चान्योऽस्मीत्येवमप्रच्युता मतिः॥ १८॥

This entire world attains to emancipation only when the knowledge of Vedas is acquired. There are no other reasons or the factors leading towards it. Such a resolution made so firmly has been called as patience by the Vedic scholars. In other words, it is a state when the man thinks "I am the soul and nothing distinct than it." The wisdom undeviated in all circumstances is called the best patience.

अल्पमृष्टाशनाभ्यां च चतुर्थांशावशेषकम्।
तस्माद्योगानुगुण्येन भोजनं मितभोजनम्॥ १९॥

To entertain the food embedding the stuffs enhancing the peace of mind and purity and that too in the balanced preparation, viz., to eat in the ratio of two part food and one third part water and thus leaving blank the one-fourth part for the circulation of wind is the suitable food duly confirmed for the best yogi. The food so balanced is called Mitāhāra.

स्वदेहमलनिर्मोक्षो मृज्जलाभ्यां महामुने। यत्तच्छौचं भवेद्बाह्यं मानसं मननं विदुः।
अहं शुद्ध इति ज्ञानं शौचमाहुर्मनीषिणः॥ २०॥

O great hermit! The action by which the body is cleaned and the dirt is removed by water and the clay is called the exterior cleaning (Śauca) while the meditation made on the bonafide and benevolent spirit by means of mind is called the cleaning of mind. Apart from it, the learned persons called cleaning the best knowledge that assumes as "I am the sacrosanct soul."

अत्यन्तमलिनो देहो देही चात्यन्तनिर्मलः।
उभयोरन्तरं ज्ञात्वा कस्य शौचं विधीयते॥ २१॥

This body is most impure in and out and the soul holding body is most pure and free from the dirt particles. Thus, to whom should we made the purest when the innermost knowledge of the soul and the body is acquired.

ज्ञानशौचं परित्यज्य बाह्ये यो रमते नरः। स मूढः काञ्चनं त्यक्त्वा लोष्टं गृह्णाति सुव्रत॥ २२॥

ज्ञानामृतेन तृप्तस्य कृतकृत्यस्य योगिनः। न चास्ति किंचित्कर्तव्यमस्ति चेन्न स तत्त्ववित्॥ २३॥

O the great resolute hermit ! The person who neglects the purity of knowledge and only cleans his body is not better than a stupid who collects the lump of clay instead of the gold. The yogi who is satiated and whose desires are duly met to the contentment at the state when he acquires the nectar-like knowledge, nothing as the undoing or impossible is left for him in this world. It still remains anything that it is clear that he is not learnt to the element.

लोकत्रयेऽपि कर्तव्यं किंचिन्नास्त्यात्मवेदिनाम्॥ २४॥

तस्मात्सर्वप्रयत्नेन मुनेऽहिंसादि साधनैः। आत्मानमक्षरं ब्रह्म विद्धि ज्ञानात्तु वेदनात्॥ २५॥

No liability and the duty is lying for the great souls known to the soul, is left throughout the three worlds. O the king of Saint! You should know as the everlasting Brahma to your soul when it is equipped with the means of non-violence etc.

॥द्वितीयः खण्डः॥

तपः संतोषमास्तिक्यं दानमीश्वरपूजनम्।

सिद्धान्तश्रवणं चैव ह्रीर्मतिश्च जपो व्रतम्॥ १॥

एते च नियमाः प्रोक्तास्तान्वक्ष्यामि क्रमाच्छृणु॥ २॥

There are ten rules, i.e., penance, contentment, theism, generosity, devotion, modesty, Japa, wisdom, resolution and listening to the doctrine have been staed. These are described as under.

वेदोक्तेन प्रकारेण कृच्छ्रचान्द्रायणादिभिः।

शरीरशोषणं यत्तत्तप इत्युच्यते बुधैः॥ ३॥

According to the scholars, decaying the overflowing power of the body by holding the fast like Kṛcchracāndrāyaṇa as prescribed in Veda's is called penance.

को वा मोक्षः कथं तेन संसारं प्रतिपन्नवान्।

इत्यालोकनमर्थज्ञास्तपः शंसन्ति पण्डिताः॥ ४॥

The metaphysician accepts as penance when the concentration is made on the question like what is emancipation and how and by what reason this world is badly tied?

यदृच्छालाभतो नित्यं प्रीतिर्या जायते नृणाम्। तत्संतोषं विदुः प्राज्ञाः परिज्ञानैकतत्पराः॥ ५॥

ब्रह्मादिलोकपर्यन्ताद्विरक्त्या यल्लभेत्प्रियम्। सर्वत्र विगतस्नेहः संतोषं परमं विदुः।

श्रौते स्मार्ते च विश्वासो यत्तदास्तिक्यमुच्यते॥ ६॥

The scholars consider as contentment the state of pleasure in heart felt on having everything as per the god proposes. In other words, the pleasure in mind felt due to detachment for the pleasure of divine abode including the abode of Brahma too is called the contentment by the learned persons. It is theism as perceived in a man in garb of his firm self confidence on the modus-operandi (religion) as prescribed or contemplated in Vedas and other memoirs.

न्यायार्जितधनं श्रान्ते श्रद्धया वैदिके जने।
अन्यद्वा यत्प्रदीयन्ते तद्दानं प्रोच्यते मया॥७॥

I only deem the wealth in the category of donation which is given to the needy persons, the learned persons suffering from pains or given as to reveal respect for the great man of characters subject to such wealth is earned by using the legal means.

रागाद्यपेतं हृदयं वागदुष्टानृतादिना।
हिंसादिरहितं कर्म यत्तदीश्वरपूजनम्॥८॥

It is the worship of god if the activities are free from the defects prognosticated to arise in garb of violence and representing the false statements or speeches as also the work which is free from any kind of attachment.

सत्यं ज्ञानमनन्तं च परानन्दं परं ध्रुवम्।
प्रत्यगित्यवगन्तव्यं वेदान्तश्रवणं बुधाः॥९॥

This soul is the truth, the knowledge, unending, the best and everlasting. It too is undeviated and in the form of supreme pleasure. It is listening to or pursuance with the doctrine when one has strong faith on the doctrines in course of performing his activities.

वेदलौकिकमार्गेषु कुत्सितं कर्म यद्भवेत्।
तस्मिन्भवति या लज्जा ह्रीः सैवेति प्रकीर्तिता।
वैदिकेषु च सर्वेषु श्रद्धा या सा मतिर्भवेत्॥१०॥

It is the shyness or the modesty that makes a man to hesitate usually to involve in the deeds condemned by the Vedas and the rules and laws prevalent in the world. An obeisance on the preachings made in Vedas is called wisdom.

गुरुणा चोपदिष्टोऽपि तत्र संबन्धवर्जितः।
वेदोक्तेनैव मार्गेण मन्त्राभ्यासो जपः स्मृतः॥११॥

It is Japa duly allowed by the teachers in pursuance with the channel suggested by Vedas at the reciting manner as noted therein.

कल्पसूत्रे तथा वेदे धर्मशास्त्रे पुराणके। इतिहासे च वृत्तिर्या स जपः प्रोच्यते मया॥१२॥
जपस्तु द्विविधः प्रोक्तो वाचिको मानसस्तथा॥१३॥

In my opinion, the Japa is to engage the propensities of mind in Veda, Kalpasūtra, the holy books, Purāṇa and the history. The Japas are of two kinds. The first is made by reciting and the second is made mutely or merely in the mind.

वाचिकोपांशुरुच्चैश्च द्विविधः परिकीर्तितः।
मानसो मननध्यानभेदाद्द्वैविध्यमाश्रितः।। १४।।

The Japa made by reciting also are of two kinds. The first in which a man loudly recites the hymns and the second in which the man merely whispers. Similarly, the Japa made in the mind too is classified in the concentration and thinking.

उच्चैर्जपादुपांशुश्च सहस्रगुणमुच्यते।
मानसश्च तथोपांशोः सहस्रगुणमुच्यते।। १५।।
उच्चैर्जपश्च सर्वेषां यथोक्तफलदो भवेत्।
नीचैः श्रोत्रेण चेन्मन्त्रः श्रुतश्चेन्निष्फलं भवेत्।। १६।।

It has been stated that the Japa made by whispering is one thousand times better than the Japa made under loud recital. Further the Japa made in mind is better as much as thousand times then which is made by murmuring. The Japa made with a loud voice provides all persons the due consequences but it is unfructified in case the men of lower śrotra have heard to the hymns so recited.

।।तृतीयः खण्डः।।

स्वस्तिकं गोमुखं पद्मं वीरसिंहासने तथा। भद्रं मुक्तासनं चैव मयूरासनमेव च।। १।।
सुखासनसमाख्यं च नवमं मुनिपुङ्गव। जानूर्वोरन्तरे कृत्वा सम्यक् पादतले उभे।। २।।
समग्रीवशिरःकायः स्वस्तिकं नित्यमभ्यसेत्। सव्ये दक्षिणगुल्फं तु पृष्ठपार्श्वे नियोजयेत्।। ३।।
दक्षिणेऽपि तथा सव्यं गोमुखं तत्प्रचक्षते। अङ्गुष्ठावधि गृह्णीयाद्धस्ताभ्यां व्युत्क्रमेण तु।। ४।।
ऊर्वोरुपरि विप्रेन्द्र कृत्वा पादतलद्वयम्। पद्मासनं भवेत्प्राज्ञ सर्वरोगभयापहम्।। ५।।

O the great hermit! The Āsanas or postures have been stated as nine in numbers. These are Svastika, Gomukha, Padmāsana, Vīrāsana, Simhāsana, Muktāsana, Bhadrāsana, Mayurāsana and Sukhāsana. To maintain the neck, the head and the body duly erect by trapping both feet in the middle of knees and pubic is called Svastika Āsana. One should do a regular practise on this Āsana. To pull and put the ankle of right foot at the rear part of the left and the ankle of the left foot to the rear portion of the right is called Gomukhāsana. O Brahmaṇa! To keep both feet on the pubic and gripping their thumbs by moving both hands towards feet is called Padmāsana. This Āsana removes all kinds of ailments.

दक्षिणेतरपादं तु दक्षिणोरुणि विन्यसेत्। ऋजुकायः समासीनो वीरासनमुदाहृतम्।। ६।।

To sit at a place keeping the body erect and placing the left foot on the right thigh is called Vīrāsana.

गुल्फौ च वृषणस्याधः सीवन्याः पार्श्वयोः क्षिपेत्। दक्षिणं सव्यगुल्फेन दक्षिणेन तथेतरत्।।

हस्तौ जानौ समास्थाप्यं स्वाङ्गुलीश्च प्रसार्य च। व्यक्तवक्त्रो निरीक्षेत नासाग्रं सुसमाहित:॥

सिंहासनं भवेदेतत् पूजितं योगिभि: सदा॥ ६.१-३॥

In Siṁhāsana, both ankles are taken at the colateral part below the testis in a position that the left ankle should fix on the right colateral and by right ankle the left colateral part of the testis. Both hands are kept on the knees and fingers are stretched, the mouth is opened, concentration is made at the forepoint of the nose through eyes.

गुल्फौ तु वृषणस्याध: सीवन्या: पार्श्वयो: क्षिपेत्।

पार्श्वपादौ च पाणिभ्यां दृढं बद्ध्वा सुनिश्चलम्। भद्रासनं भवेदेतद्विषरोगविनाशनम्॥ ७॥

In Bhadrāsana, both ankles are placed in the colateral regions of the testis, the colateral parts and feet both are firmly tied by the hands and mind concentration is made. This posture compounds all ailments arising due to consumption of toxic substances.

निपीड्य सीवनीं सूक्ष्मं दक्षिणेतरगुल्फत:।

वामं याम्येन गुल्फेन मुक्तासनमिदं भवेत्॥ ८॥

In Muktāsana, the micro line drawn in the region of testis is pushed by the left ankle and the left line is pushed by the right ankle.

मेढ्रादुपरि निक्षिप्य सव्यं गुल्फं तथोपरि।

गुल्फान्तरं च संक्षिप्य मुक्तासनमिदं मुने॥ ९॥

O hermit! In Muktāsana, one should place the left ankle on the genital organ and the right ankle on the left ankle.

कूर्पराग्रे मुनिश्रेष्ठ निक्षिपेन्नाभिपार्श्वयो:। भूम्यां पाणितलद्वन्द्वं निक्षिप्यैकाग्रमानस:॥ १०॥

समुन्नतशिर:पादो दण्डवद्व्योम्नि संस्थित:। मयूरासनमेतत्स्यात्सर्वपापप्रणाशनम्॥ ११॥

O great hermit! One should place his both palms on the ground, the elbows in this posture should touch the both colateral parts of the navel. Then, he should be erect like stick by lifting up his head and the feet both. The posture so made effaces all kinds of evils.

येन केन प्रकारेण सुखं धैर्यं च जायते।

तत्सुखासनमित्युक्तमशक्तस्तत्समाश्रयेत्॥ १२॥

The posture that renders extreme comfort and the patience while sitting is called Sukhāsana. The devotees weak in body should resort to this very posture.

आसनं विजितं येन जितं तेन जगत्त्रयम्।

अनेन विधिना युक्त: प्राणायामं सदा कुरु॥ १३॥

The person conquers the trio-worlds in its entirety who have conquered or established a good control on these postures. Hence, O Sāṅkṛti! Do Prāṇāyāma always by practising the yoga in this manner.

।।चतुर्थः खण्डः।।

The contents of this part are introduction of the nerves, the pilgrim of the soul and the magnificence of the knowledge of the soul.

शरीरं तावदेव स्यात्षण्णवत्यङ्गुलात्मकम्। देहमध्ये शिखिस्थानं तप्तजाम्बूनदप्रभम्।। १।।

त्रिकोणं मनुजानां तु सत्यमुक्तं हि सांकृते। गुदात्तु द्व्यङ्गुलादूर्ध्वं मेढ्रात्तु द्व्यङ्गुलादधः।। २।।

देहमध्यं मुनिप्रोक्तमनुजानीहि सांकृते। कन्दस्थानं मुनिश्रेष्ठ मूलाधारान्नवाङ्गुलम्।। ३।।

O Sāṅkṛti! This human body is merely ninety six fingers in measurement made by the hand of the concerned person. The place for fire is existed in the centre of this body. Its colour has been stated analogous to the melting gold. It is of triangular shape. We have explained this utmost fact to you. The region to do finger up from the region of anus and two fingers below from the genital should be deemed as the middle part of the human body. It is the Mūlādhāra. However, nine fingers upside from this region is the place for the cluster of nerves (Kanda).

चतुरङ्गुलमायामविस्तारं मुनिपुङ्गव। कुक्कुटाण्डसमाकारं भूषितं तु त्वगादिभिः।। ४।।

तन्मध्ये नाभिरित्युक्तं योगज्ञैर्मुनिपुङ्गव। कन्दमध्यस्थिता नाडी सुषुम्नेति प्रकीर्तिता।। ५।।

The length and width of that cluster is four fingers each and it is just in oval shape of the hen. It is adorned or duly covered by the membranes at the upper side.

O the hermit laurette! The scientists also have stated that the nucleus of the navel is existed at the middle of the cluster. The nerve existing just at the middle has been described as Suṣumnā by the scientists.

तिष्ठन्ति परितस्तस्या नाडयो हि मुनिपुङ्गव। द्विसप्ततिसहस्राणि तासां मुख्याश्चतुर्दश।। ६।।

सुषुम्ना पिङ्गला तद्वदिडा चैव सरस्वती। पूषा च वरुणा चैव हस्तिजिह्वा यशस्विनी।। ७।।

अलम्बुसा कुहूश्चैव विश्वोदरी पयस्विनी। शङ्खिनी चैव गान्धारा इति मुख्याश्चतुर्दश।। ८।।

As much as 72,000 nerves exists around that cluster. The cardinal nerves among them are– Suṣumnā, Piṅgalā, Iḍā, Sarasvatī, Varuṇā, Pūṣā, Yaśasvinī, Hastijihvā, Alambusā, Kuhū, Viśvodarī, Payasvinī, Śaṅkhinī and Gāndhārī. These are fourteen in number.

आसां मुख्यतमास्तिस्रस्तिसृष्वेकोत्तमोत्तमा।
ब्रह्मनाडीति सा प्रोक्ता मुने वेदान्तवेदिभिः।। ९।।

Out of these fourteen nerves, the first three are most inportant and major. Further, Suṣumnā nerve is the greatest among these three. The metaphysicians have addressed it as Brahmanāḍī.

पृष्ठमध्यस्थितेनास्थ्ना वीणादण्डेन सुव्रत।
सह मस्तकपर्यन्तं सुषुम्ना सुप्रतिष्ठिता।। १०।।

The stick like formation is renowned as the spinal chord. It is a junction of bones. The Suṣumnā nerve accesses to the brain by making its way between the hole made in these bones.

नाभिकन्दादधः स्थानं कुण्डल्या द्व्यङ्गुलं मुने। अष्टप्रकृतिरूपा सा कुण्डली मुनिसत्तम॥ ११॥

यथावद्वायुचेष्टां च जलान्नादीनि नित्यशः। परितः कन्दपार्श्वेषु निरुध्यैव सदा स्थिता॥ १२॥

O the hermit Laurette! The kuṇḍalinī is existed just below two fingers from the cluster of navel. It has been stated in the form of the eight nature *i.e.* the earth, the water, the splendour, the wind, the ether, the mind, the wisdom and the ego. That wind exists by covering from all sides the colateral part of that cluster and restricts the attempts, the water and the food.

स्वमुखेन समावेष्ट्य ब्रह्मरन्ध्रमुखं मुने। सुषुम्नाया इडा सव्ये दक्षिणे पिङ्गला स्थिता॥ १३॥

सरस्वती कुहूश्चैव सुषुम्नापार्श्वयोः स्थिते। गान्धारा हस्तिजिह्वा च इडायाः पृष्ठपूर्वयोः॥ १४॥

पूषा यशस्विनी चैव पिङ्गला पृष्ठपूर्वयोः। कुहोश्च हस्तिजिह्वाया मध्ये विश्वोदरी स्थिता॥ १५॥

यशस्विन्याः कुहोर्मध्ये वरुणा सुप्रतिष्ठिता। पूषायाश्च सरस्वत्या मध्ये प्रोक्ता यशस्विनी॥ १६॥

O hermit! It keeps covered the mouth of Brahmarandhra through its extension. The nerves Iḍā and Piṅgalā are existed at the left and right to the spinal respectively. The nerves Sarasvatī and Kuhū are existed at both colateral parts of the spinal. The nerves Gāndhārī and Hastijihvā at the back and front to the Iḍā nerve respectively. The nerves Pūṣā and Yaśasvinī are respectively existed at the front and the rear of the Piṅgalā. The Viśvodarī nerve is existed in the middle of the kuhū and Hastijihvā. The Varuṇā nerve is existed in the middle of the Yaśasvinī and kuhū. The location of Payasvinī has been stated in the middle of the Pūṣā and Sarasvatī.

गान्धारायाःसरस्वत्या मध्ये प्रोक्ता च शङ्खिनी। अलम्बुसा स्थिता पायुपर्यन्तं कन्दमध्यगा॥ १७॥

पूर्वभागे सुषुम्नाया राकायाः संस्थिता कुहूः। अधश्चोर्ध्वं स्थिता नाडी याम्यनासान्तमिष्यते॥ १८॥

इडा तु सव्यनासान्तं संस्थिता मुनिपुङ्गव। यशस्विनी च वामस्य पादाङ्गुष्ठान्तमिष्यते॥ १९॥

पूषा वामाक्षिपर्यन्ता पिङ्गलायास्तु पृष्ठतः। पयस्विनी च याम्यस्य कर्णान्तं प्रोच्यते बुधैः॥ २०॥

The location of Śaṅkhinī is in the middle of Gāndhārī and Sarasvatī nerve. The alambusā nerve is extended from the middle portion of the cluster to the anus. The second nerve of Suṣumṇā is Rākā and the Kuhū nerve is existed at the east to it. This nerve is enshrined both sides *i.e.* up and down. Its location has been stated as extended upto the right nose. The Iḍā nerve is extended upto the left nose. The Yaśasvinī nerve is extended upto the thumb of foot. The Pūṣā nerve is extended upto the left eye by moving from the back side of Piṅgalā. As per the scholars, Payasvinī nerve has been stated that it extends upto the right ear.

सरस्वती तथा चोर्ध्वगता जिह्वा तथा मुने। हस्तिजिह्वा तथा सव्यपादाङ्गुष्ठान्तमिष्यते॥ २१॥

शङ्खिनी नाम या नाडी सव्यकर्णान्तमिष्यते। गान्धारा सव्यनेत्रान्ता प्रोक्ता वेदान्तवेदिभिः॥ २२॥

The Sarasvatī nerve is extended upto the tongue and the Hastijivhā nerve upto the left thumb of the foot. The Śaṅkhinī nerve is extended upto the left ear. The persons known to Veda have been stated that the Gāndhārī nerve is extended upto the left eye.

विश्वोदराभिधा नाडी कन्दमध्ये व्यवस्थिता। प्राणोऽपानस्तथा व्यानः समानोदान एव च॥ २३॥

नागः कूर्मश्च कृकरो देवदत्तो धनंजयः। एते नाडीषु सर्वासु चरन्ति दश वायवः॥ २४॥

तेषु प्राणादयः पञ्च मुख्याः पञ्चसु सुव्रत। प्राणसंज्ञस्तथापानः पूज्यः प्राणस्तयोर्मुने॥ २५॥

The position of Viśvodara nerve has been stated in the middle of the cluster. The ten breathings have been stated. These are Prāṇa, Apāna, Vyāna, Udāna, Samāna, Nāga, Kūrma, Kṛkara, Devadatta and Dhanañjaya. These beathings are circulated all over the nervous system. The fine winds are cardinal among these ten breathings. Further, the Prāṇa and Apāna have been given the utmost importance out of these cardinal breathings.

आस्यनासिकयोर्मध्ये नाभिमध्ये तथा हृदि। प्राणसंज्ञोऽनिलो नित्यं वर्तते मुनिसत्तम॥ २६॥

अपानो वर्तते नित्यं गुदमध्योरुजानुषु। उदरे सकले कट्यां नाभौ जङ्घे च सुव्रत॥ २७॥

व्यानः श्रोताक्षिमध्ये च ककुद्भ्यां गुल्फयोरपि। प्राणस्थाने गले चैव वर्तते मुनिपुङ्गव॥ २८॥

उदानसंज्ञो विज्ञेयः पादयोर्हस्तयोरपि। समानः सर्वदेहेषु व्याप्य तिष्ठत्यसंशयः॥ २९॥

The wind known as Prāṇa always exists in the middle of nose and the mouth, in the middle of navel and the heart. The Apāna wind always exists in anus, genital pubic, knees, the entire belly, waist, navel and the thighs. The Vyāna wind is circulated in both ears, both eyes, both shoulders, both ankles, the region of Prāṇa and the throat too. The Udāna wind circulates in both hands and the feet. The Samāna wind circulates with equal pace all over the body.

नागादिवायवः पञ्च त्वगस्थ्यादिषु संस्थिताः। निःश्वासोच्छ्वासकासाश्च प्राणकर्म हि सांकृते॥ ३०॥

अपानाख्यस्य वायोस्तु विण्मूत्रादिविसर्जनम्। समानः सर्वसामीप्यं करोति मुनिपुङ्गव॥ ३१॥

The five winds including Nāga, circulate in the skin and the bone. O Sānkṛti! The exhale, inhale as also coughing are the functions of the Prāṇa wind. The Apāna wind does the function of discharging the excreta and the urine. O the laurette of hermit! The Samāna wind accommodates adjustment all over the body.

उदान ऊर्ध्वगमनं करोत्येव न संशयः। व्यानो विवादकृत्प्रोक्तो मुने वेदान्तवेदिभिः॥ ३२॥

उद्गारादिगुणः प्रोक्तो नागाख्यस्य महामुने। धनंजयस्य शोभादि कर्म प्रोक्तं हि सांकृते॥ ३३॥

निमीलनादि कूर्मस्य क्षुधा तु कृकरस्य च। देवदत्तस्य विप्रेन्द्र तन्द्रीकर्म प्रकीर्तितम्॥ ३४॥

The Udāna wind circulates upward. The scholars expert in Vedas considered that the Udāna wind is only the originator of sound. O great hermit! The Nāga wind does the function of vomiting and eructation etc. The Dhanañjaya wind renders the beauty to all organs of the body. The kūrma wind does the function of opening and closing the eyes. The

Kṛkala wind makes to feel the hunger and thirst and the Devadatta wind does the function of creation, laxity and dormance to the body.

सुषुम्नायाः शिवो देव इडाया देवता हरिः। पिङ्गलाया विरञ्चिः स्यात्सरस्वत्या विराण्मुने॥ ३५॥

पूषाधिदेवता प्रोक्तो वरुणा वायुदेवता। हस्तिजिह्वाभिधायास्तु वरुणो देवता भवेत्॥ ३६॥

O the hermit laurette! The god to the spinal nerve is Lord Śiva, Lord to Iḍā nerve is Lord Viṣṇu and Lord to Piṅgalā nerve is Brahmā. The god to Sarasvatī nerve is Virāṭ (gigantic). The god to Pūṣā nerve is Sun konwn as Pūṣā, the god to Varuṇa nerve is the wind and god to Hastijihvā nerve is Varuṇa.

यशस्विन्या मुनिश्रेष्ठ भगवान्भास्करस्तथा। अलम्बुसाया अम्ब्वात्मा वरुणः परिकीर्तितः॥ ३७॥

कुहोः क्षुद्देवता प्रोक्ता गान्धारी चन्द्रदेवता। शङ्खिन्याश्चन्द्रमास्तद्वत्पयस्विन्याः प्रजापतिः॥ ३८॥

O great hermit! Lord Sun is the god of Yaśasvinī nerve. The god to Alambusā nerve is Varuṇa, the god of water. The goddess to Kuhū nerve is Kṣudda (hunger). The god to Gāndhārī nerve is moon, the god to Śaṅkhinī nerve is also the moon and the god to Payasvinī nerve is Prajāpati.

विश्वोदराभिधायास्तु भगवान्पावकः पतिः। इडायां चन्द्रमा नित्यं चरत्येव महामुने॥ ३९॥

पिङ्गलायां रविस्तद्वन्मुने वेदविदां वर। पिङ्गलायामिडायां तु वायोः संक्रमणं तु यत्॥ ४०॥

तदुत्तरायणं प्रोक्तं मुने वेदान्तवेदिभिः। इडायां पिङ्गलायां तु प्राणसंक्रमणं मुने॥ ४१॥

दक्षिणायनमित्युक्तं पिङ्गलायामिति श्रुतिः। इडापिङ्गलयोः संधिं यदा प्राणः समागतः॥ ४२॥

The god to Viśvodarā nerve is god of fire. O the great hermit and expert in Veda! The moon and Sun are circulated always in Iḍā nerve and Piṅgalā nerves respectively. The transition of the Sun from the Piṅgalā nerve to Iḍā is called Uttarāyaṇa by the learned hermits. In the similar fashion, a transition of Sun from Iḍā to Piṅgalā is called Dakṣiṇāyana. O hermit! When the breathing moves at the joining of Iḍā and Piṅgalā, the intervening time in called Amāvāsyā within that body.

अमावास्या तदा प्रोक्ता देहे देहभृतां वर। मूलाधारं यदा प्राणः प्रविष्टः पण्डितोत्तम॥ ४३॥

तदाद्यं विषुवं प्रोक्तं तापसैस्तापसोत्तम। प्राणसंज्ञो मुनिश्रेष्ठ मूर्धानं प्राविशद्यदा॥ ४४॥

तदन्त्यं विषुवं प्रोक्तं तापसैस्तत्त्वचिन्तकैः। निःश्वासोच्छ्वासनं सर्वं मासानां संक्रमो भवेत्॥ ४५॥

इडायाः कुण्डलीस्थानं यदा प्राणः समागतः। सोमग्रहणमित्युक्तं तदा तत्त्वविदां वर॥ ४६॥

यदा पिङ्गलया प्राणः कुण्डलीस्थानमागतः। तदा तदा भवेत्सूर्यग्रहणं मुनिपुङ्गव॥ ४७॥

The ascetics has stated the time as a yoga namely, Ādyaviṣuva, when the breathing inserts in Mūlādhāra. O great hermit! When the breathing wind enters into Sahasrāra Cakra, this time has been described by our great hermits as the climax state of the Viṣuva yoga. The exhale and inhale of breathing have been considered as the Saṅkrānti of respective then month. O master among metaphysician! The time when the breathing comes near to Kuṇḍalinī by means of Iḍā nerve is called the lunar eclipse. When the breathing enters in the region of Kuṇḍalinī through the Piṅgalā nerve, it has been accepted as the time of solar eclipse.

श्रीपर्वतं शिर:स्थाने केदारं तु ललाटके। वाराणसीं महाप्राज्ञ भ्रुवोर्घ्राणस्य मध्यमे॥ ४८॥

In this body too, there is existed the pilgrim place namely Śrī Śaila instead of the head. The popular pilgrim place *i.e.* Kedāra is enshrined on the forehead. O the hermit of great conscience! Kāśī is existed in the middle of the nose and both eyebrows.

कुरुक्षेत्रं कुचस्थाने प्रयागं हृत्सरोरुहे। चिदम्बरं तु हृन्मध्ये आधारे कमलालयम्॥ ४९॥

Kurukṣetra is existed in the region of both nipples. The king place of pilgrim *i.e* Prayāga is existed in the heart lotus. The pilgrim place *i.e.* Cidambara is existed in the central region of heart. Kamalālaya, the place of pilgrim is existed in the region of Mūlādhāra Cakra.

आत्मतीर्थं समुत्सृज्य बहिस्तीर्थानि यो व्रजेत्।
करस्थं स महारत्नं त्यक्त्वा काचं विमार्गते॥ ५०॥

The person who moves to and fro to visit in the exterior place of pilgrim by giving up his visit to such pilgrim place of soul; is a man who searches out the glass by giving up the precious gems already existed in his hands.

भावतीर्थं परं तीर्थं प्रमाणं सर्वकर्मसु। अन्यथालिङ्ग्यते कान्ता अन्यथालिङ्ग्यते सुता॥ ५१॥

तीर्थानि तोयपूर्णानि देवान्काष्ठादिनिर्मितान्। योगिनो न प्रपूज्यन्ते स्वात्मप्रत्ययकारणात्॥ ५२॥

The place of pilgrim known as spiritual place is the best among all. A man kisses and embraces his wife as also his daughter but spirit lying behind is thoroughly distinct and separate. The man perfect in yoga keeps extreme faith and obeisance on the place of his soul's pilgrim and seldom resorted to the hurdles made of wood and stone and the places where the rivers are flown.

बहिस्तीर्थात्परं तीर्थमन्तस्तीर्थं महामुने। आत्मतीर्थं महातीर्थमन्यत्तीर्थं निरर्थकम्॥ ५३॥

These places of pilgrim innermost are the best among the worldly places of pilgrim. These are the great pilgrim places and the places otherwise then are redundant in toto.

चित्तमन्तर्गतं दुष्टं तीर्थस्नानैर्न शुध्यति। शतशोऽपि जलैर्धौतं सुराभाण्डमिवाशुचि॥ ५४॥

विषुवायनकालेषु ग्रहणे चान्तरे सदा। वाराणस्यादिके स्थाने स्नात्वा शुद्धो भवेन्नरः॥ ५५॥

As a vessel full of liquor cannot attain purity even if it is watched outside many times; the impure mind or the propensity dwelling in the heart cannot be made pure by mere taking a dive in the worldly pilgrim places. The man can only make him holy when he takes a bath in Vārāṇasi etc. pilgrim places as these are existed in the middle of the nose and eyebrows in the intervening time of Viṣuva yoga, Uttarāyaṇa, Daksiṇāyana and the time when the sun and moon are eclipsed.

ज्ञानयोगपराणां तु पादप्रक्षालितं जलम्। भावशुद्ध्यर्थमज्ञानां तत्तीर्थं मुनिपुङ्गव॥५६॥

The water used for washing the feet of scholars stands as the best pilgrim place for cleaning the bosom of the persons looming large in the ignorance.

तीर्थे दाने जपे यज्ञे काष्ठे पाषाणके सदा।
शिवं पश्यति मूढात्मा शिवे देहे प्रतिष्ठिते॥५७॥

An entity of the supreme soul is residing in the form of Lord Śiva in this very body. The foolish and ignorant person continuously searches the god in the place of pilgrim, donation, Japa (silent recital), offering, wood and in the stone because of not realising Lord Śiva in his own body.

अन्तःस्थं मां परित्यज्य बहिष्ठं यस्तु सेवते।
हस्तस्थं पिण्डमुत्सृज्य लिहेत्कूर्परमात्मनः॥५८॥

O Sāṅkṛti! The person who only worship the icons and neglects the elements of supreme soul that remains ever-lasting in his heart is like a man who licks his elbow and throws the morsel in the hand.

शिवमात्मनि पश्यन्ति प्रतिमासु न योगिनः।
अज्ञानां भावनार्थाय प्रतिमाः परिकल्पिताः॥५९॥

The yogis perceive Lord Śiva in their own soul. They never resort to worship the pieces of stones and the wood. The icons are notional and only to inspire the men to have a spiritual faith on Lord Śiva who already is residing in the hearts of all living organisms.

अपूर्वमपरं ब्रह्म स्वात्मानं सत्यमद्वयम्।
प्रज्ञानघनमानन्दं यः पश्यति स पश्यति॥६०॥
नाडीपुञ्जं सदाऽसारं नरभावं महामुने।
समुत्सृज्यात्मनाऽऽत्मानमहमित्येव धारय॥६१॥

The person competent to peep into his soul and perceive the Brahma in garb of pleasure only observes in the true sense that Brahma is unborn, all causative, always true, excellent and in the form of conscience in depth. O great hermit! This human body is only a cluster of nerves and always void of essence. Give up all attachments with this trivial body and resolve by your wit that you yourself are in the form of supreme soul.

अशरीरं शरीरेषु महान्तं विभुमीश्वरम्। आनन्दमक्षरं साक्षान्मत्वा धीरो न शोचति॥६२॥
विभेदजनके ज्ञाने नष्टे ज्ञानबलान्मुने। आत्मनो ब्रह्मणो भेदमसन्तं किं करिष्यति॥६३॥

A scholar and the patient man seldom suffers agony when he duly realizes the everlasting element of supreme soul who is distinct from the body even after residing within it, a noble, omnipresent and god to all. O great hermit! who will discuss on the topic of establishing the false discrimination between the soul and Brahma at a state when the ignorance is entirely eliminated by virtue of the true knowledge.

।।पञ्चमः खण्डः।।

The method of purifying the soul has been described here under–

सम्यक्कथय मे ब्रह्मन्नाडीशुद्धिं समासतः।

यथा शुद्ध्या सदा ध्यायञ्जीवन्मुक्तो भवाम्यहम्।। १।।

Sāṅkṛti again asked Lord Dattātreya– "O Brahmaṇa! kindly tell me in brief and lucid the process of purifying the nerves so that I could be able to attain emancipation as a result of due concentration on the element of supreme soul after the nerves duly purified."

सांकृते शृणु वक्ष्यामि नाडीशुद्धिं समासतः।

विध्युक्तकर्मसंयुक्तः कामसंकल्पवर्जितः।। २।।

Lord Dattātreya replied– "O Sāṅkṛti! I am going to describe the method of purifying the nerve in a succinct way. One should very first do all activities prescribed by the holy books and the prevalent law of the country considering his pious duty to perform then. He should give up the desire as also the resolution to have to yield of favourable results. (The Ṛṣi herein wants to refer that a man has sometimes decide some reverse way unmatching with the worldly outlook in which nothing is expected as a favourable result. In case, if he hankers for the fruit, the activity of much importance will not be made by him thereby causing direct or indirect detriment to the interest of the society as a whole.)

यमाद्यष्टाङ्गसंयुक्तः शान्तः सत्यपरायणः।

स्वात्मन्यवस्थितः सम्यग्ज्ञानिभिश्च सुशिक्षितः।। ३।।

He should be in patience and truthful and follow spiritually, all the eight parts of Yoga including Yama, Niyama, etc. He should concentrate on his soul and obtain the education duly from the learned person and offer the possible services to them.

पर्वताग्रे नदीतीरे बिल्वमूले वनेऽथवा।

मनोरमे शुचौ देशे मठं कृत्वा समाहितः।। ४।।

आरभ्य चासनं पश्चात्प्राङ् मुखोदङ् मुखोऽपि वा।

समग्रीवशिरः कायः संवृतास्यः सुनिश्चलः।।

नासाग्रे शशभृद्बिम्बे बिन्दुमध्ये तुरीयकम्।

स्रवन्तममृतं पश्येन्नेत्राभ्यां सुसमाहितः।। ६।।

He should then reside in the state of a mind in concentration at a place with natural landscapes and by constructing a hermitage or at the peak of a mountain, at the back of the river, under the shade of a Bilba tree or a place in solitude anywhere in the forest. He should sit on any of the posture facing the east or the north direction. The neck, the head and the entire body should be kept erect and the mouth should be closed. The orbit of moon should be considered or concentrated at the foreportion of nose and an element of supreme soul in the form of Turīya flowing a spring of nectar at the iota of Oṁ; should be seen directly through his eyes. The mind should be kept fully concentrated in course of such presumption.

इडया प्राणमाकृष्य पूरयित्वोदरे स्थितम्। ततोऽग्निं देहमध्यस्थं ध्यायज्ज्वालावलीयुतम्॥ ७॥
बिन्दुनादसमायुक्तमग्निबीजं विचिन्तयेत्। पश्चाद्विरेचयेत्सम्यक्प्राणं पिङ्गलया बुधः॥ ८॥
पुनः पिङ्गलयापूर्य वह्निबीजमनुस्मरेत्। पुनर्विरेचयेद्धीमानिडयैव शनैः शनैः॥ ९॥
त्रिचतुर्वासरं वाथ त्रिचतुर्वारमेव च। षट्कृत्वा विचरेन्नित्यं रहस्येवं त्रिसंधिषु॥ १०॥

The breathing air should be inhaled through the Iḍā nerve viz. the left nostril and the same should be stored in the belly. As a second step, he should concentrate on the element of fire enshrined in the middle of the body and a notion should be made that the fire lord is blazed with flames as a result of getting the touch of that wind. In the third step, he should concentrate on the fire seed after joining the sound and the iota of Oṁ. After doing this all, the yogi should gradually exhale the stored wind of breathing through Piṅgalā nerve viz. the right nostril. This exercise should be made continuously upto three or four days or three to four times or six times daily.

नाडीशुद्धिमवाप्नोति पृथक्चिह्नोपलक्षितः। शरीरलघुता दीप्तिर्वह्नेर्जाठरवर्तिनः॥ ११॥
नादाभिव्यक्तिरित्येतच्चिह्नं तत्सिद्धिसूचकम्। यावदेतानि संपश्येत्तावदेवं समाचरेत्॥ १२॥

As a blessing to the exercise so made, the nerves of yogi are duly purified and its symptoms starts revealing. The symptoms mainly are– the body becomes light, the power of digestion awakend and the sound of Anāhata is felt. These symptoms express the mastery on the exercise. One should involve himself in regular practise unless these symptoms are apparently felt.

अथवैतत्परित्यज्य स्वात्मशुद्धिं समाचरेत्। आत्मा शुद्धः सदा नित्यः सुखरूपः स्वयम्प्रभः॥
अज्ञानान्मलिनो भाति ज्ञानाच्छुद्धो विभात्ययम्। अज्ञानमलपङ्कं यः क्षालयेज्ज्ञानतोयतः।
स एव सर्वदा शुद्धो नान्यः कर्मरतो हि सः॥ १४॥

In case, the yogi doesn't prefers the abovesaid exercise, he may do the exercise of purifying the soul. This soul is always pure, immortal, pleasure giving and luminated automatically. However, the ignorance perceives the impurity in it. This soul starts luminating with full radiance when true knowledge is acquired. The man is only pure and innocent who ways out the mud and dirt in the form of ignorance by application of the knowledge soap. Contrary to it, the person attached to the worldly activities is not of a pure soul.

॥षष्ठः खण्डः॥

The method of Prāṇāyāma, its kinds, the outcome and the application has been described hereunder-

प्राणायामक्रमं वक्ष्ये सांकृते शृणु सादरम्। प्राणायाम इति प्रोक्तो रेचपूरककुम्भकैः॥ १॥

वर्णत्रयात्मकाः प्रोक्ता रेचपूरककुम्भकाः। स एष प्रणवः प्रोक्तः प्राणायामस्तु तन्मयः॥ २॥

Lord Ḍattātreya said– "O Sāṅkṛti! Now I am going to tell you about Prāṇāyāma. Listen to it with perfect obeisance. Prāṇāyāma is a process of controlling the breathing by systematic adoption of Pūraka, Kumbhaka and Recaka viz., Inhale, retain and exhale. The three letters in Praṇava *i.e* A, U, and M are equated with Pūraka, Recaka and Kumbhaka. As the combination of these three letters is called Oṁ, the Prāṇāyāma too is equated with Praṇava.

इडया वायुमाकृष्य पूरयित्वोदरे स्थितम्। शनैः षोडशभिर्मात्रैरकारं तत्र संस्मरेत्॥ ३॥

पूरितं धारयेत्पश्चाच्चतुःषष्ट्या तु मात्रया। उकारमूर्तिमत्रापि संस्मरन्प्रणवं जपेत्॥ ४॥

यावद्वा शक्यते तावद्धारयेज्जपतत्परः। पूरितं रेचयेत्पश्चान्मकारेणानिलं बुधः॥ ५॥

शनैः पिङ्गलया तत्र द्वात्रिंशन्मात्रया पुनः। प्राणायामो भवेदेवं ततश्चैवं समभ्यसेत्॥ ६॥

One should gradually inhale the wind through the Iḍā nerve viz. the left nostril and restore it in the belly. In between the process, one should use the sixteen moras and concentrate on the first letter of Oṁ *i.e.,* As a next step, the wind so inhaled should be withheld in the belly. This time too a Japa on Oṁ should be made upto the counting of six moras. The wind should be withheld in a state of such concentration till it is possible. The wind so withheld is then exhaled gradually through the Piṅgalā nerve in the right nostril and the last letter of Oṁ *i.e.* M should be used for Japa upto the time required for reciting thirty-two moras. Thus, a single cycle of Prāṇāyāma gets completed. A regular exercise should be made by adopting this method.

पुनः पिङ्गलयापूर्य मात्रैः षोडशभिस्तथा। अकारमूर्तिमत्रापि स्मरेदेकाग्रमानसः॥ ७॥

धारयेत्पूरितं विद्वान्प्रणवं संजपन्वशी। उकारमूर्तिं स ध्यायंश्चतुःषष्ट्या तु मात्रया॥ ८॥

Having a mastery obtained on the process aforesaid; the yogi should inhale the wind through Piṅgalā nerve *i.e* right nostril and the mind should be concentrated on the first letter of Oṁ *i.e* 'A' upto the frequency of sixteen moras. The wind so inhaled and filled in the belly should be withheld by imposing a control and with concentration on second letter of Oṁ *i.e* 'U' upto the frequency of sixty-four moras.

मकारं तु स्मरन्पश्चाद्रेचयेदिडयाऽनिलम्। एवमेव पुनः कुर्यादिडयापूर्य बुद्धिमान्॥ ९॥

एवं समभ्यसेन्नित्यं प्राणायामं मुनीश्वर। एवमभ्यासतो नित्यं षण्मासाद् ज्ञानवान्भवेत्॥ १०॥

Then as a final effort, the wind so withheld should be exhaled gradually and with concentration on the third letter of Oṁ *i.e* 'M' upto the thirty-two frequencies. O great hermit! The exercise of Prāṇāyāma should be made as a routine affair. The man so practising, attains to the knowledge within the short span of six months.

वत्सराद्ब्रह्मविद्वान्स्यात्तस्मान्नित्यं समभ्यसेत्। योगाभ्यासरतो नित्यं स्वधर्मनिरतश्च यः॥ ११॥

प्राणसंयमनेनैव ज्ञानान्मुक्तो भविष्यति। बाह्यादापूरणं वायोरुदरे पूरको हि सः॥ १२॥
संपूर्णकुम्भवद्वायोर्धारणं कुम्भको भवेत्। बहिर्विरेचनं वायोरुदराद्रेचकः स्मृतः॥ १३॥

The person realizes the Brahma as a result of exercising Prāṇāyāma regularly upto the period of a year. Hence, Prāṇāyāma should be made regularly. The person performing his liabilities by engrossing himself in the great deeds, definitely attains the sacred knowledge through Prāṇāyāma and avails emancipation or liberty from the worldly ties. The process of pulling the wind and storing it in the belly is called inhale (Pūraka). The process of withholding the air in the belly by which it is formed like a pitcher is called retention (kumbhaka) and the process of exhaling the wind out from the belly is called exhale (Recaka).

प्रस्वेदजनको यस्तु प्राणायामेषु सोऽधमः। कम्पनं मध्यमं विद्यादुत्थानं चोत्तमंविदुः॥ १४॥
पूर्वं पूर्वं प्रकुर्वीत यावदुत्थानसंभवः। संभवत्युत्तमे प्राज्ञः प्राणायामे सुखी भवेत्॥ १५॥

It has been considered a Prāṇāyāma is mean category if the body is perspirated after excercise. In case, the body shivers, it is called the Prāṇāyāma of medium category and if the body is felt lifting upward, it is called the best category of Prāṇāyāma. A man therefore should involve in regular practise on Prāṇāyāma with aforesaid method unless its best category is accomplished. On completion of the best category Prāṇāyāma, the person enjoys the pleasure.

प्राणायामेन चित्तं तु शुद्धं भवति सुव्रत। चित्ते शुद्धे शुचिः साक्षात्प्रत्यग्ज्योति र्व्यवस्थितः॥ १६॥
प्राणश्चित्तेन संयुक्तः परमात्मनि तिष्ठति। प्राणायामपरस्यास्य पुरुषस्य महात्मनः॥ १७॥
देहश्चोत्तिष्ठते तेन किंचिज्ज्ञानाद्विमुक्तता। रेचकं पूरकं मुक्त्वा कुम्भकं नित्यमभ्यसेत्॥ १८॥

O great resolute! The Prāṇāyāma purifies the mind and the mind so purified starts realizing the all sacrosanct element of soul. The breathing of the great men practising Prāṇāyāma on regular basis joins with the mind and thus both of them are concentrated on the supreme soul. On arriving at that state, his body gradually starts uplifting. He attains to emancipation as a result of acquiring knowledge through Prāṇāyāma so exercised. Having mastery obtained on the process of inhale and exhale one should pay emphasis particularly on the process of withholding the inhaled air (kumbhaka).

सर्वपापविनिर्मुक्तः सम्यग्ज्ञानमवाप्नुयात्। मनोजवत्वमाप्नोति पलितादि च नश्यति॥ १९॥
प्राणायामैकनिष्ठस्य न किंचिदपि दुर्लभम्। तस्मात्सर्वप्रयत्नेन प्राणायामान्समभ्यसेत्॥ २०॥

The yogi so exercising, Prāṇāyāma daily, undoubtedly acquires the best knowledge and exonerates from all kinds of ills. That person becomes as dynamic as the mind and puts the mind under subjugation. The ailments pertaining to the hairs including their turning in grey and other defects are also effaced. The person with perfect loyalty in Prāṇāyāma can obtain everything whatever he desires. Hence, the man should exercise Prāṇāyāma with full concentration.

विनियोगान्प्रवक्ष्यामि प्राणायामस्य सुव्रत। संध्ययोर्ब्राह्मकालेऽपि मध्याह्ने वाऽथवासदा॥ २१॥
बाह्यं प्राणं समाकृष्य पूरयित्वोदरेण च। नासाग्रे नाभिमध्ये च पादाङ्गुष्ठे च धारयेत्॥ २२॥

O great hermit! I am now going to tell you the peculiar application of Prāṇāyāma. In the morning and evening or in the dawn or in the noon, the exterior wind should be inhaled and established or stored in the belly, in the foreportion of nose, in the middle of navel and on the thumb of foot.

सर्वरोगविनिर्मुक्तो जीवेद्वर्षशतं नरः। नासाग्रधारणाद्वापि जितो भवति सुव्रत॥ २३॥
सर्वरोगनिवृत्तिः स्यान्नाभिमध्ये तु धारणात्। शरीरलघुता विप्र पादाङ्गुष्ठनिरोधनात्॥ २४॥

The man known to such application is liberated from all kinds of ailments and enjoys longavity not less than hundred years. O the great hermit! As a result of retaining the breathing air on the foreportion of nose, an extreme control on wind is obtained. All kinds of ailments are removed when this wind is held in the middle portion of the navel and the body enjoyes refreshing when the wind is held on the thumb of the foot.

जिह्वया वायुमाकृष्य यः पिबेत्सततं नरः। श्रमदाहविनिर्मुक्तो योगी नीरोगतामियात्॥ २५॥
जिह्वया वायुमाकृष्य जिह्वामूले निरोधयेत्। पिबेदमृतमव्यग्रं सकलं सुखमाप्नुयात्॥ २६॥

The person exercising Yoga and competent to pull the air through the tongue; always remains free from ailments and seldom suffers from tiredness and the fever. The process of entertaining the wind through tongue is that so pulled air through tongue should be withheld at the route of tongue and it should be then duly sipped. The person attains to all pleasures by doing this.

इडया वायुमाकृष्य भ्रुवोर्मध्ये निरोधयेत्। यः पिबेदमृतं शुद्धं व्याधिभिर्मुच्यते हि सः॥ २७॥

O metaphysician Sāṅkṛti! The person who establishes the wind in the middle of the brows by pulling it through the Iḍā nerve and thus entertains the purified nectar, becomes free from all kinds of ailments.

इडया वेदतत्त्वज्ञस्तथा पिङ्गलयैव च। नाभौ निरोधयेत्तेन व्याधिभिर्मुच्यते नरः॥ २८॥

O great hermit! Sāṅkṛti! The wind retained in the region of the navel after inhaling it through Iḍā and Piṅgalā nerves, also makes the man concerned free from all kinds of ailments.

मासमात्रं त्रिसन्ध्यायां जिह्वयारोप्य मारुतम्। अमृतं च पिबेन्नाभौ मन्दं मन्दं निरोधयेत्॥ २९॥
वातजाः पित्तजा दोषा नश्यन्त्येव न संशयः। नासाभ्यां वायुमाकृष्य नेत्रद्वन्द्वे निरोधयेत्॥ ३०॥
नेत्ररोगा विनश्यन्ति तथा श्रोत्रनिरोधनात्। तथा वायुं समारोप्य धारयेच्छिरसि स्थितम्॥ ३१॥

If the wind is exhaled through the tongue with a spirit as if the nectar is being sipped in morning, at noon and in the beginning regularly upto the period of one month and process of its retention in navel zone is maintained; the defects or ills arising due to the distortions of Vāta and Pitta are undoubtedly eliminated. The aliments pertaining to the eyes are destroyed if the wind is entialed simultaneously and retained in both eyes. The ailments pertaining to the ears are eliminated if that wind is retained in the ears. Similarly, the head ailments are eliminated if the wind is retained on the head. O Sāṅkṛti! I have told you all these solemnly.

शिरोरोगा विनश्यन्ति सत्यमुक्तं हि सांकृते। स्वस्तिकासनमास्थाय समाहितमनास्तथा॥ ३२॥

अपानमूर्ध्वमुत्थाप्य प्रणवेन शनैः शनैः। हस्ताभ्यां धारयेत्सम्यक्कर्णादिकरणानि च॥ ३३॥

अङ्गुष्ठाभ्यां मुने श्रोत्रे तर्जनीभ्यां तु चक्षुषी। नासापुटावधानाभ्यां प्रच्छाद्य करणानि वै॥ ३४॥

One should concentrate the mind, establish the posture of Svastika, do the Japa of Praṇava, uplift Apāna wind gradually and the ears etc. sensory organs should be duly pressed by both hands. The ears should be closed by both thumbs, the eyes by both index fingers and both nostrils by using two fingers and the wind should be retained within the head until and unless the nectar in garb of pleasure is appeared. O great hermit! the breathing wind enters into Brahmarandhra by doing this process.

आनन्दाविर्भवो यावत्तावन्मूर्धनि धारणात्। प्राणः प्रयात्यनेनैव ब्रह्मरन्ध्रं महामुने॥ ३५॥

ब्रह्मरन्ध्रं गते वायौ नादश्चोत्पद्यतेऽनघ। शङ्खध्वनिनिभश्चादौ मध्येमेघध्वनिर्यथा॥ ३६॥

शिरोमध्यगते वायौ गिरिप्रस्रवणं यथा। पश्चात्प्रीतो महाप्राज्ञ साक्षादात्मोन्मुखो भवेत्॥ ३७॥

O innocent Sāṅkṛti! A sound starts coming out like the conch cell when the breathing wind enters into the Brahmarandhra. In between the exercise, that sound turns into thundering of clouds. A sound as emerges when a fountain flows down from a mountain arises when the breathing is duly established in the middle of the head. O great hermit! The yogi subsequently attains soul-orientation and feels extreme pleasure.

पुनस्तज्ज्ञाननिष्पत्तिर्योगात्संसारनिह्नुतिः। दक्षिणोत्तरगुल्फेन सीवनीं पीडयेत्स्थिरम्॥ ३८॥

सव्येतरेण गुल्फेन पीडयेद्बुद्धिमान्नरः। जान्वोरधःस्थितां सन्धिं स्मृत्वा देवं त्रियम्बकम्॥ ३९॥

Subsequently, the perfect knowledge of the element of soul is attained and the worldly ties are entirely eliminated by virtue of that yoga (an another way to control the breathing wind is herein described). The nerve existed in the middle of the anus and the genital is called Sīvanī. It joins the half-parts of the body. The scholar should press that Sīvanī by using his left and right ankle and presume the Jyotirliṅga namely Tryambaka at the joint below the knees.

विनायकं च संस्मृत्य तथा वागीश्वरीं पुनः। लिङ्गनालात्समाकृष्य वायुमप्यग्रतो मुने॥ ४०॥

प्रणवेन नियुक्तेन बिन्दुयुक्तेन बुद्धिमान्। मूलाधारस्य विप्रेन्द्र मध्ये तं तु निरोधयेत्॥ ४१॥

निरुध्य वायुना दीप्तो वह्निरूहति कुण्डलीम्। पुनः सुषुम्नया वायुर्वह्निना सह गच्छति॥ ४२॥

The yogi should concomittantly concentrate on mother Vāgiśvarī and Gaṇeśa also. Subsequently, Japa of Oṁ with iota is to be made and the breathing should be established in the middle of Mūlādhāra by pulling it towards forepart of genital through its hole.

Retention of breathing therein results in establishment of the fire duly blazed at Kuṇḍalinī. The breathing by carrying with it this fire starts uplifting through the route of spinal nerve.

एवमभ्यसतस्तस्य जितो वायुर्भवेद्धशम्। प्रस्वेदः प्रथमः पश्चात्कम्पनं मुनिपुङ्गव॥४३॥

उत्थानं च शरीरस्य चिह्नमेतज्जितेऽनिले। एवमभ्यसतस्तस्य मूलरोगो विनश्यति॥४४॥

O great hermit! A good control on breathing is made as a result of such exercises. The symptoms or indications revealing this control is felt initially through perspiration in the body, shivering and finally uplifting of the body. All ailments pertaining to body and mind are eliminated as a result of such exercises.

भगन्दरं च नष्टं स्यात्सर्वरोगाश्च सांकृते। पातकानि विनश्यन्ति क्षुद्राणि च महान्ति च॥४५॥

नष्टे पापे विशुद्धं स्याच्चित्तदर्पणमद्भुतम्। पुनर्ब्रह्मादिभोगेभ्यो वैराग्यं जायते हृदि॥४६॥

O Sāṅkṛti! The ailments like Bhagandara (fistula) and others are eliminated by virtue of exercising this Prāṇāyāma. All kinds of evils either greater or smaller are also eliminated. The heart and mind both become sacrosanct as a mirror when the malafides and likewise other ills are eliminated. On arriving at this stage, detachment towards all worldly pleasures even which are available in the abode of Brahma etc. is emerged.

विरक्तस्य तु संसाराज्ज्ञानं कैवल्यसाधनम्। तेन पाशापहानिः स्याज्ज्ञात्वा देवं सदाशिवम्॥४७॥

ज्ञानामृतरसो येन सकृदास्वादितो भवेत्। स सर्वकार्यमुत्सृज्य तत्रैव परिधावति॥४८॥

ज्ञानस्वरूपमेवाहुर्जगदेतद्विचक्षणाः। अर्थस्वरूपमज्ञानात्पश्यन्त्यन्ये कुदृष्टयः॥४९॥

आत्मस्वरूपविज्ञानादज्ञानस्य परिक्षयः। क्षीणेऽज्ञाने महाप्राज्ञ रागादीनां परिक्षयः॥५०॥

रागाद्यसंभवे प्राज्ञ पुण्यपापविमर्दनम्। तयोर्नाशे शरीरेण न पुनः संप्रयुज्यते॥५१॥

The person so detached from the pleasure of this worldly ocean attains to the knowledge that leads him to the emancipation. All kinds of worldly ties are eliminated as a result of attaining to the element of supreme soul through that knowledge. The person starts to engross in the pleasure of knowledge by giving up all activities if he had once enjoyed that pleasure. The people of high understanding, consider this world as the sole source of knowledge but the others not sacred in their approach observe this world in the form of enjoyments. The ignorance is eliminated when the knowledge of soul is duly acquired. The attachment as also affections etc. too are eliminated when the ignorance is fully decayed. Owing to the lack of good and bad feelings and the attachment towards worldly pleasures, the scholar is not compelled to revolve round the cycle of birth and death.

॥सप्तमः खण्डः॥

Different kinds of Pratyāhāra and its results are described herein.

अथातः संप्रवक्ष्यामि प्रत्याहारं महामुने। इन्द्रियाणां विचरतां विषयेषु स्वभावतः॥१॥

बलादाहरणं तेषां प्रत्याहारः स उच्यते। यत्पश्यति तु तत्सर्वं ब्रह्म पश्यन्समाहितः॥२॥

प्रत्याहारो भवेदेष ब्रह्मविद्भिः पुरोदितः। यद्यच्छुद्धमशुद्धं वा करोत्यामरणान्तिकम्॥ ३॥
तत्सर्वं ब्रह्मणे कुर्यात्प्रत्याहारः स उच्यते। अथवा नित्यकर्माणि ब्रह्माराधनबुद्धितः॥ ४॥

O great hermit! I am going to describe about Pratyāhāra. Pratyāhāra is a process by which all sensory organs usually enjoying and attracted towards the worldly pleasures are to call back forcibly. Whatever is observed by a man, that all is Brahma and this presumption or understanding when attained, the concentration of mind thereupon is called Pratyāhāra as it is defined by the person known to Brahma. A surrender of all activities either good or bad performed by a man throughout his life to the god or the supreme soul is also called Pratyāhāra. In other words, Pratyāhāra is a concept that enables a man to perform all desired activities, presuming that these are in the form of service to the god.

काम्यानि च तथा कुर्यात्प्रत्याहारः स उच्यते। अथवा वायुमाकृष्य स्थानात्स्थानं निरोधयेत्॥ ५॥
दन्तमूलात्तथा कण्ठे कण्ठादुरसि मारुतम्। उरोदेशात्समाकृष्य नाभिदेशे निरोधयेत्॥ ६॥
नाभिदेशात्समाकृष्य कुण्डल्यां तु निरोधयेत्। कुण्डलीदेशतो विद्वान्मूलाधारे निरोधयेत्॥ ७॥
अथापानात्कटिद्वन्द्वे तथोरौ च सुमध्यमे। तस्माज्जानुद्वये जङ्घे पादाङ्गुष्ठे निरोधयेत्॥ ८॥
प्रत्याहारोऽयमुक्तस्तु प्रत्याहारस्मरैः पुरा। एवमभ्यासयुक्तस्य पुरुषस्य महात्मनः॥ ९॥

To worship the lord by performing all desired activities too is called Pratyāhāra. So far as Pratyāhāra as an exercise is concerned, the man should establish the wind from one place to another like from the route of teeth to the throat, from throat to the heart, from heart to the navel region, from navel region to the Kuṇḍalinī, from Kuṇḍalinī to Mūlādhāra, from Mūlādhāra to the region of waist and from there to the middle of the pubic region. Then it should be transferred to the knees, from the knees to the thighs and from thighs to the thumb of feet. The scholars expert in Pratyāhāra since ancient period has named the above said exercise as Pratyāhāra.

सर्वपापानि नश्यन्ति भवरोगश्च सुव्रत। नासाभ्यां वायुमाकृष्य निश्चलः स्वस्तिकासनः॥ १०॥
पूरयेदनिलं विद्वानापादतलमस्तकम्। पश्चात्पादद्वये तद्वन्मूलाधारे तथैव च॥ ११॥
नाभिकन्दे च हृन्मध्ये कण्ठमूले च तालुके। भ्रुवोर्मध्ये ललाटे च तथा मूर्धनि धारयेत्॥ १२॥

All evils as also all ailments in the form of birth and death are automatically eliminated if the Pratyāhāra is made by aforesaid manner. The scholar should sit in Svastika posture, keep his mind free from tensions, inhale the breathing air through both nostrils and carry it over all regions starting from the foot to the head. He should retain the breathing air on both feet, Mūlādhāra, navel region, middle region of heart, at the root of throat, palate, in the middle of brows, forehead and in the head. The retention of the breathing air gradually on these all parts of the body is called Pratyāhāra.

देहे स्वात्ममतिं विद्वान्समाकृष्य समाहितः। आत्मनाऽऽत्मनि निर्द्वन्द्वे निर्विकल्पे निरोधयेत्॥ १३॥
प्रत्याहारः समाख्यातः साक्षाद्वेदान्तवेदिभिः। एवमभ्यसतस्तस्य न किंचिदपि दुर्लभम्॥ १४॥

The learned person should do concentration in mind, separate the feeling of soul from the body and making himself free from fatigues, do concentration on his inner soul exclusively. The scholars of the Vedānta element has told this the real Pratyāhāra. Nothing is scarce to gain for the man who does exercises on Pratyāhāra by the aforesaid manner.

।।अष्टम: खण्ड:।।

The kinds and sub-kinds of conception is herein described.

अथात: संप्रवक्ष्यामि धारणा: पञ्च सुव्रत। देहमध्यगते व्योम्नि बाह्याऽऽकाशं तु धारयेत्।। १।।

प्राणे बाह्यानिलं तद्वज्ज्वलने चाग्निमौदरे। तोयं तोयांशके भूमिं भूमिभागे महामुने।। २।।

हयरावलकाराख्यं मंत्रमुच्चारयेत्क्रमात्। धारणैषा परा प्रोक्ता सर्वपापविशोधिनी।। ३।।

O great hermit! I am now going to tell you about the five kinds of conceptions (Dhāraṇa). One should presume the extraneous ether within the ether element existed within the body. Similarly, a conception (Dhāraṇā) should be made of exterior element of the wind in breathing, exterior element of fire in the digestive fire (Jaṭharānala), the exterior element of water in the water existing in the body, and this whole earth should be presumed in the immortal part of the body. While making such conceptions (Dhāraṇā) for each and every element, one should recite the seed hymns– Haṁ Yaṁ, Raṁ, Vaṁ, Laṁ respectively. This conception has been told the best for eliminating all evils.

जान्वन्तं पृथिवी ह्यंशो ह्यपां पाय्वन्तमुच्यते। हृदयांशस्तथाग्न्यंशो भ्रूमध्यान्तोऽ निलांशक:।। ४।।

आकाशांशस्तथा प्राज्ञ मूर्धांश: परिकीर्तित:। ब्रह्माणं पृथिवीभागे विष्णुं तोयांशके तथा।। ५।।

अग्न्यंशे च महेशानमीश्वरं चानिलांशके। आकाशांशे महाप्राज्ञ धारयेत्तु सदाशिवम्।। ६।।

The portion starting from the foot to the knee has been called the part of the earth. The portion from knee to anus is the water, from anus to the heart region is considered the part of the fire. Similarly, the portion of the wind has been considered from heart to the middle of the brows and the region of forehead has been called the part of ether element. O great scholar! One should consider Lord Brahmā in the element of earth, Lord Viṣṇu in element of water, Lord Śiva in element of fire, Īśvara in element of wind and Sadāśiva in the element of ether.

अथवा तव वक्ष्यामि धारणां मुनिपुङ्गव। पुरुषे सर्वशास्तारं बोधानन्दमयं शिवम्।। ७।।

धारयेद्बुद्धिमान्नित्यं सर्वपापविशुद्धये। ब्रह्मादिकार्यरूपाणि स्वे स्वे संहृत्य कारणे।। ८।।

सर्वकारणमव्यक्तमनिरूप्यमचेतनम्। साक्षादात्मनि संपूर्णे धारयेत्प्रणवे मन:।

इन्द्रियाणि समाहृत्य मनसात्मनि योजयेत्।। ९।।

O great hermit! I further describe one more conception (Dhāraṇā) for you. The learned person should develop a conception of this element of supreme soul which is everlasting, benevolent, pleasure giver, full of conscience and intuitive person in a routine manner. All kinds of evils are eliminated by doing this. He should hold the best supreme soul within his inner soul with a presumption that it is undescribable element of supreme soul beyond from the wisdom, does welfare to all by merging in the respective cause of Brahmā etc. in the form of activity. In other words, he should firmly determine that the supreme soul too is existed in the form of intuitive souls. While engrossing with such conception, he should establish his mind in the supreme soul known as Praṇava. He should concomittantly pull forcely all his sensory organs from their usual subjects and employ them in the soul itself.

।।नवम: खण्ड:।।

Two kinds of concentration and its fruits or the outcome is being explained herein.

अथात: संप्रवक्ष्यामि ध्यानं संसारनाशनम्। ऋतं सत्यं परं ब्रह्म सर्वसंसारभेषजम्।। १।।

ऊर्ध्वरेतं विरूपाक्षं विश्वरूपं महेश्वरम्। सोऽहमित्यादरेणैव ध्यायेद्योगीश्वरेश्वरम्।। २।।

I am now going to describe the concentration that eliminates the worldly ties. It functions as a penacea to all worldly ills. One should therefore concentrate on the supreme soul, all immortal, in the form of truth presuming it in the form of his soul. The supreme soul is the god of yogis, it holds odd eyes, Urdhvaretā, universal form and Maheśvara. One should presume with full loyalty in his wisdom that he himself is Para Brahma, an everlasting element of supreme soul.

अथवा सत्यमीशानं ज्ञानमानन्दमद्वयम्। अत्यर्थममलं नित्यमादिमध्यान्तवर्जितम्।। ३।।

तथाऽस्थूलमनाकाशमसंस्पृश्यमचाक्षुषम्। न रसं न च गन्धाख्यमप्रमेयमनूपमम्।। ४।।

आत्मानं सच्चिदानन्दमनन्तं ब्रह्म सुव्रत। अहमस्मीत्यभिध्यायेद्ध्येयातीतं विमुक्तये।। ५।।

The second kind of concentration is that I myself is the supreme soul and it is in the form of truth, god to all, full of knowledge, pleasure, sacrosanct, excellent, immortal, beyond the beginning, middle and the end, beyond from the formidable ignorance, distinct from the ether, distinguished from the wind as felt distinct always from the element of fire as seen by the eyes, in the form of essence, water and distinct from the earth in the form of smell. There are no apparent proofs to know it, it is excellent beyond the physique and it is the truth, the mind, the pleasure and unending Para Brahma. The element of supreme soul having such peculiarities should be concentrated in the form of soul and establish direct relation with it. The concentration so made always ensures emancipation.

एवमभ्यासयुक्तस्य पुरुषस्य महात्मन:। क्रमाद्वेदान्तविज्ञानं विजायेत न संशय:।। ६।।

The man of wit who engrosses himself in the exercise of the concentration described aforesaid, undoubtedly attains to the specific knowledge of the element of Brahma as described in Vedas.

॥दशमः खण्डः॥

The meditation and its outcome has been described herein.

अथातः संप्रवक्ष्यामि समाधिं भवनाशनम्।
समाधिः संविदुत्पत्तिः परजीवैकतां प्रति॥ १॥

I am now going to describe the meditation that eliminates all kinds of worldly ties. The meditation is nothing else than the appearance of determined wisdom regarding the supreme soul and the living soul considering it one and all.

नित्यः सर्वगतो ह्यात्मा कूटस्थो दोषवर्जितः।
एकः संभिद्यते भ्रान्त्या मायया न स्वरूपतः॥ २॥

This soul is everlasting, immortal, omnipresent and free from all kinds of defects. It is one but due to the confusion created by illusion, it appears distinctive. There is no discrimination in it in real sense.

तस्मादद्वैतमेवास्ति न प्रपञ्चो न संसृतिः। यथाकाशो घटाकाशो मठाकाश इतीरितः॥ ३॥
तथा भ्रान्तैर्द्विधा प्रोक्तो ह्यात्मा जीवेश्वरात्मना। नाहं देहो न च प्राणो नेन्द्रियाणि मनो नहि॥ ४॥
सदा साक्षिस्वरूपत्वाच्छिव एवास्मि केवलः। इति धीर्या मुनिश्रेष्ठ सा समाधिरिहोच्यते॥ ५॥

Owing to this reason, only Advaita is the truth. There is nothing like the illusion or world. As the ether is called with two names *i.e.* Ghaṭākāśa and Maṭhākāśa, the people in ignorance consider the supreme soul in two forms *i.e* the living-soul and the Īśvara. I am neither body nor breathing, neither sensory organs nor mind but only the element of supreme soul in the form of Śiva because of my always existence as a witness. O great hermit! The determined wisdom presuming this only is the meditation.

सोऽहं ब्रह्म न संसारी न मत्तोऽन्यः कदाचन। यथा फेनतरङ्गादि समुद्रादुत्थितं पुनः॥ ६॥
समुद्रे लीयते तद्वज्जगन्मय्यनुलीयते। तस्मान्मनः पृथङ् नास्ति जगन्माया च नास्ति हि॥ ७॥

I am that supreme Īśvara and not the living-soul fastened in the world. Hence, no existence of anything different than me has been remained in any time. As the froth and waves ultimately merge with the ocean, this world is originated from me and ultimately it is merged with me. Hence, the causative mind for creation too is not distinct from me. No separate existence of this world and illusion than me is here.

यस्यैवं परमात्माऽयं प्रत्यग्भूतः प्रकाशितः। स तु याति च पुंभावं स्वयं साक्षात्परा मृतम्॥ ८॥

Thus, perceiving of this supreme soul as ones own soul enables the man concerned to attain the sense of supreme soul always immortal and the supreme industrious.

यदा मनसि चैतन्यं भाति सर्वत्रगं सदा। योगिनोऽव्यवधानेन तदा संपद्यते स्वयम्॥ ९॥
यदा सर्वाणि भूतानि स्वात्मन्येव हि पश्यति। सर्वभूतेषु चात्मानं ब्रह्म संपद्यते तदा॥ १०॥

The direct perceiving of the sensitive and omnipresent soul in the mind of yogi enable him to establish himself in the form of supreme soul. The scholar so emerged looks all creatures within him and himself among all creatures and thus he apparently gets the form of Brahma himself.

यदा सर्वाणि भूतानि समाधिस्थो न पश्यति। एकीभूत: परेणाऽसौ तदा भवतिकेवल:॥ ११॥

यदा पश्यति चात्मानं केवलं परमार्थत:। मायामात्रं जगत्कृत्स्नं तदा भवति निर्वृति:॥ १२॥

When the person establishes integrity with the supreme soul by virtue of his meditation to the extent that he does not observe distinctively all living-organisms, he at that state is established in the form of the supreme soul. The person with such accomplishment observes his soul in the form of all benevolent truth and treats the entire world as a game of illusion played; thus, he attains to the supreme pleasure.

एवमुक्त्वा स भगवान्दत्तात्रेयो महामुनि:। सांकृति: स्वस्वरूपेण सुखमास्तेऽतिनिर्भय:॥ १३॥

Thus, the great scholar called Dattātreya concluded and turned back to silence. The great hermit! Sāṅkṛti duly grasped the essence of the preaching and starts living fearlessly and with pleasure in his real form of the soul.

ॐ आप्यायन्तु............................ इति शान्ति:॥

॥इति जाबालदर्शनोपनिषत्समाप्ता॥

***

Thus ends the first volume of the present edition of 112 Upaniṣads (Sanskrit Text and English Translation)

PARIMAL SANSKRIT SERIES N0. 73

112 UPANIṢADS

(AN EXHAUSTIVE INTRODUCTION, SANSKRIT TEXT, ENGLISH TRANSLATION & INDEX OF VERSES)

Thoroughly Revised New Edition

Vol. 2

Translated by

Board of Scholars

Editors

K. L. Joshi
O. N. Bimali
Bindiya Trivedi

PARIMAL PUBLICATIONS

DELHI

Published by

PARIMAL PUBLICATIONS

27/28, Shakti Nagar, Delhi-110007 (INDIA)

ph. : +91-11-23845456

e-mail : order@parimalpublication.com

url : http://www.parimalpublication.com

Sixth Reprint Edition : Year 2022

ISBN : 978-81-7110-243-3 (Set)
978-81-7110-245-7 (Vol. II)

Price : ₹ 2000.00 (Set of 2 Vols.)

Printed at

Vishal Kaushik Printers

Near GTB Hospital, Delhi

CONTENTS

38. DHYĀNABINDU-UPANIṢAD

ध्यानबिन्दूपनिषद्

॥शान्तिपाठ:॥

ॐ सह नाववतु .... इति शान्ति:॥

यदि शैलसमं पापं विस्तीर्णं बहुयोजनम्। भिद्यते ध्यानयोगेन नान्यो भेद: कदाचन॥ १॥

बीजाक्षरं परं बिन्दुं नादं तस्योपरि स्थितम्। सशब्दं चाक्षरे क्षीणे नि:शब्दं परमं पदम्॥ २॥

अनाहतं तु यच्छब्दं तस्य शब्दस्य यत्परम्। तत्परं विन्दते यस्तु स योगी छिन्नसंशय:॥ ३॥

वालाग्रशतसाहस्रं तस्य भागस्य भागिन:। तस्य भागस्य भागार्धं तत्क्षये तु निरञ्जनम्॥ ४॥

पुष्पमध्ये यथा गन्ध: पयोमध्ये यथा घृतम्। तिलमध्ये यथा तैलं पाषाणेष्विव काञ्चनम्॥ ५॥

एवं सर्वाणि भूतानि मणौ सूत्र इवात्मनि। स्थिरबुद्धिरसंमूढो ब्रह्मविद्ब्रह्मणि स्थित:॥ ६॥

तिलानां तु यथा तैलं पुष्पे गन्ध इवाश्रित:। पुरुषस्य शरीरे तु स बाह्याभ्यन्तरे स्थित:॥ ७॥

वृक्षं तु सकलं विद्याच्छाया तस्यैव निष्कला। सकले निष्कले भावे सर्वत्रात्मा व्यवस्थित:॥ ८॥

Even if sin should accumulate to a mountain extending over many yojanas (distance), it is destroyed by dhyānayoga. At no time has been found a destroyer of sins like this. Bījākṣara (seed-letter) is the supreme bindu. Nāda (spiritual sound) is above it. When the nāda ceases along with letter, than the nāda-less is supreme state. That yogins who considers as the highest that which is above nāda, which is anāhata, has all his doubts destroyed. If the point of a hair be divided into one-hundred thousand parts, this (nāda) is one-half of that still further divided; and when (even) this is absorbed, the yogin attains to the stainless Brahman. One who is of a firm mind and without the delusion (of sensual pleasures) and ever resting in Brahman, should see like the string (in a rosary of beads) all creatures (as existing) in Ātmā like odour in flowers, ghee in milk, oil in gingelly seeds and gold in quartz. Again just as the oil depends for its manifestation upon gingelly seeds and odour upon flowers, so does the Puruṣa depends for its existence upon the body, both external and internal. The tree is with parts and its shadow is without parts but with and without parts, Ātmā exists everywhere.

ओमित्येकाक्षरं ब्रह्म ध्येयं सर्वमुमुक्षुभि:। पृथिव्यग्निश्च ऋग्वेदो भूरित्येव पितामह:॥ ९॥

अकारे तु लयं प्राप्ते प्रथमे प्रणवांशके। अन्तरिक्षं यजुर्वायुर्भुवो विष्णुर्जनार्दन:॥ १०॥

उकारे तु लयं प्राप्ते द्वितीये प्रणवांशके। द्यौ: सूर्य: सामवेदश्च स्वरित्येव महेश्वर:॥ ११॥

मकारे तु लयं प्राप्ते तृतीये प्रणवांशके। अकार: पीतवर्ण: स्याद्रजोगुण उदीरित:॥ १२॥

उकार: सात्त्विक: शुक्लो मकार: कृष्णतामस:। अष्टाङ्गं च चतुष्पादं त्रिस्थानं पञ्चदैवतम्॥ १३॥

The one akṣara (letter Oṁ) should be contemplated upon as Brahman by all who aspire for emancipation. Pṛthivī, agni, ṛgveda, bhūḥ and Brahmā— all these (are absorbed) when Akāra (A), the first aṁśa (part) of Praṇava (Oṁ) becomes absorbed. Antarikṣa, yajurveda, vāyu, bhuvaḥ and Viṣṇu, the Janārdana— all these (are absorbed) when Ukāra (U), the second aṁśa of praṇava becomes absorbed. Dyur, sun, sāmaveda, suvāhu and Maheśvara— all these (are absorbed) when Makāra (M), the third aṁśa of praṇava becomes absorbed. Akāra is of (pīta) yellow colour and is said to be of rajoguṇa; Ukāra is of white colour and of sattvaguṇa; Makāra is of dark colour and of tamoguṇa.

ओंकारं यो न जानाति ब्राह्मणो न भवेत्तु सः। प्रणवो धनुः शरो ह्यात्मा ब्रह्मतल्लक्ष्यमुच्यते॥ १४॥

अप्रमत्तेन वेद्धव्यं शरवत्तन्मयो भवेत्। निवर्तन्ते क्रियाः सर्वास्तस्मिन्दृष्टे परावरे॥ १५॥

ओंकारप्रभवा देवा ओंकारप्रभवाः स्वराः। ओंकारप्रभवं सर्वं त्रैलोक्यं सचराचरम्॥ १६॥

ह्रस्वो दहति पापानि दीर्घः संपत्प्रदोऽव्ययः। अर्धमात्रासमायुक्तः प्रणवो मोक्षदायकः॥ १७॥

तैलधारामिवाच्छिन्नं दीर्घघण्टानिनादवत्। अवाच्यं प्रणवस्याग्रं यस्तं वेद स वेदवित्॥ १८॥

He who does not know Oṁkāra as having eight aṅgas (parts), four pādas (feet), three sthānas (seats) and five devatās (presiding deities) is not a Brāhmaṇa. Praṇava is the bow. Ātmā is the arrow and Brahman is said to be aim. One should aim at it with great care and then he, like the arrow, becomes one with It. When that Highest is cognised, all karmas return (from him, viz., do not affect him). The Vedas have Oṁkāra as their cause. The svaras (sounds) have Oṁkāra as their cause. The three worlds with (all) the locomotive and the fixed (ones in them) have Oṁkāra as their cause. The short (accent of Oṁ) burns all sins, the long one is decayless and the bestower of prosperity. United with ardhamātrā (half-metre of Oṁ), the praṇava becomes the bestower of salvation. That man is the knower of the Vedas who knows that the end (viz., ardhamātrā) of praṇava should be worshipped (or recited) as uninterrupted as the flow of oil and (resounding) as long as the sound of a bell.

हृत्पद्मकर्णिकामध्ये स्थिरदीपनिभाकृतिम्। अङ्गुष्ठमात्रमचलं ध्यायेदोंकारमीश्वरम्॥ १९॥

इडया वायुमापूर्य पूरयित्वोदरस्थितम्। ओंकारं देहमध्यस्थं ध्यायेज्ज्वालावलीवृतम्॥ २०॥

ब्रह्मा पूरक इत्युक्तो विष्णुः कुम्भक उच्यते। रेचो रुद्र इति प्रोक्तः प्राणायामस्य देवताः॥ २१॥

आत्मानमरणिं कृत्वा प्रणवं चोत्तरारणिम्। ध्याननिर्मथनाभ्यासाद्देवं पश्येन्निगूढवत्॥ २२॥

ओंकारध्वनिनादेन वायोः संहरणान्तिकम्। यावद्बलं समादध्यात्सम्यङ्नादलयावधि॥ २३॥

One should contemplate upon Oṁkāra as Īśvara resembling an unshaken light, as of the size of a thumb and as motionless in the middle of the pericarp of the lotus of the heart. Taking in vāyu through the left nostril and filling the stomach with it, one should contemplate upon Oṁkāra as being in the middle of the body and as surrounded by circling flames. Brahmā is said to be inspiration; Viṣṇu is said to be cessation (of breath), and Rudra is said to be expiration. These are the devatās of Prāṇāyāma. Having made Ātmā as the (lower) araṇi (sacrificial wood) and praṇava as the upper araṇi, one should see the God in secret through the practice of churning which is dhyāna. One should practise restraint of breath as much as it lies in his power along with (the uttering of) Oṁkāra sound, until it ceases completely.

गमागमस्थं गमनादिशून्यमोंकारमेकं रविकोटिदीप्तम्।
पश्यन्ति ये सर्वजनान्तरस्थं हंसात्मकं ते विरजा भवन्ति॥ २४॥
यन्मनस्त्रिजगत्सृष्टिस्थितिव्यसनकर्मकृत्। तन्मनो विलयं याति तद्विष्णोः परमं पदम्॥ २५॥

Those who look upon Oṁ as of the form of Haṁsa staying in all, shining like crores of suns, being alone, staying in gamāgama (ever going and coming) and being devoid of motion— at last such persons are freed from sin. That manas which is the author of the actions (viz.,), creation, preservation and destruction of the three worlds, is (then) absorbed (in the supreme One). That is the highest state of Viṣṇu.

अष्टपत्रं तु हृत्पद्मं द्वात्रिंशत्केसरान्वितम्। तस्य मध्ये स्थितो भानुर्भानुमध्यगतः शशी॥ २६॥
शशिमध्यगतो वह्निर्वह्निमध्यगता प्रभा। प्रभामध्यगतं पीठं नानारत्नप्रवेष्टितम्॥ २७॥
तस्य मध्यगतं देवं वासुदेवं निरञ्जनम्। श्रीवत्सकौस्तुभोरस्कं मुक्तामणिविभूषितम्॥ २८॥
शुद्धस्फटिकसंकाशं चन्द्रकोटिसमप्रभम्। एवं ध्यायेन्महाविष्णुमेवं वा विनयान्वितः॥ २९॥

The lotus of the heart has eight petals and thirty-two filaments. The sun is in its midst : the moon is in the middle of the sun. Agni is in the middle of the moon : the prabhā (spiritual light) is in the middle of agni. Pīṭha (seat or centre) is in the midst of prabhā, being set in diverse gems. One should meditate upon the stainless Lord Vāsudeva as being (seated) upon the centre of Pīṭha, as having Śrīvatsa (black mark) and Kaustubha (garland of gems) on his chest and as adorned with gems and pearls resembling pure crystal in lustre and as resembling crores of moons in brightness.

अतसीपुष्पसंकाशं नाभिस्थाने प्रतिष्ठितम्। चतुर्भुजं महाविष्णुं पूरकेण विचिन्तयेत्॥ ३०॥
कुम्भकेन हृदि स्थाने चिन्तयेत्कमलासनम्। ब्रह्माणं रक्तगौराभं चतुर्वक्त्रं पितामहम्॥ ३१॥
रेचकेन तु विद्यात्मा ललाटस्थं त्रिलोचनम्। शुद्धस्फटिकसंकाशं निष्कलं पापनाशनम्॥ ३२॥
अब्जपत्रमधः पुष्पमूर्ध्वनालमधोमुखम्। कदलीपुष्पसंकाशं सर्ववेदमयं शिवम्॥ ३३॥
शतारं शतपत्राढ्यं विकीर्णाम्बुजकर्णिकम्। तत्रार्कचन्द्रवह्नीनामुपर्युपरि चिन्तयेत्॥ ३४॥
पद्मस्योद्घाटनं कृत्वा बोधचन्द्राग्निसूर्यकम्। तस्य हृद्बीजमाहृत्य आत्मानं चरते ध्रुवम्॥ ३५॥

He should meditate upon Mahā-Viṣṇu as above or in the following manner. (That is) he should meditate with inspiration (of breath) upon Mahā-Viṣṇu as resembling the atasī flower and as staying in the seat of navel with four hands; then with restraint of breath, he should meditate in the heart upon Brahmā, the Grandfather as being on the lotus with the gaura (pale-red) colour of gems and having four faces : then through expiration, he should meditate upon the three-eyed Śiva between the two eyebrows shining like the pure crystal, being stainless, destroying all sins, being in that which is like the lotus facing down with its flower (or face) below and the stalk above or like the flower of a plantain tree, being of the form of all Vedas, containing one hundred petals and one hundred leaves and having the pericarp full-expanded. There he should meditate upon the sun, the moon and the agni, one above another. Passing above through the lotus which has the brightness of the sun, moon and agni, and taking its Hrīm bīja (letter), one leads his Ātmā firmly.

त्रिस्थानं च त्रिमार्गं च त्रिब्रह्म च त्रयाक्षरम्। त्रिमात्रमर्धमात्रं वा यस्तं वेद स वेदवित्॥ ३६॥

तैलधारामिवाच्छिन्नदीर्घघण्टानिनादवत्। बिन्दुनादकलातीतं यस्तं वेद स वेदवित्॥ ३७॥

यथैवोत्पलनालेन तोयमाकर्षयेन्नरः। तथैवोत्कर्षयेद्वायुं योगी योगपथे स्थितः॥ ३८॥

अर्धमात्रात्मकं कृत्वा कोशभूतं तु पङ्कजम्। कर्षयेन्नालमात्रेण भ्रुवोर्मध्ये लयं नयेत्॥ ३९॥

भ्रुवोर्मध्ये ललाटे तु नासिकायास्तु मूलतः। जानीयादमृतं स्थानं तद्ब्रह्मायतनं महत्॥ ४०॥

He is the knower of Vedas who knows the three seats, the three mātrās, the three Brahmas, the three akṣaras (letters) and the three mātrās associated with the ardhamātrā. He who knows that which is above bindu, nāda and kalā as uninterrupted as the flow of oil and (resounding) as long as the sound of a bell— that man is a knower of the Vedas. Just as a man would draw up (with his mouth) the water through the (pores of the) lotus-stalk, so the yogin treading the path of yoga should draw up the breath. Having made the lotus-sheath of the form of ardhamātrā, one should draw up the breath through the stalk (of the nādis–Suṣumnā, Iḍā and Piṅgalā) and absorb it in the middle of the eyebrows. He should know that the middle of the eyebrows in the forehead which is also the root of the nose is the seat of nectar. That is the great place of Brahman.

आसनं प्राणसंरोधः प्रत्याहारश्च धारणा। ध्यानं समाधिरेतानि योगाङ्गानि भवन्ति षट्॥ ४१॥

आसनानि च तावन्ति यावन्त्यो जीवजातयः। एतेषामतुलान्भेदान्विजानाति महेश्वरः॥ ४२॥

सिद्धं भद्रं तथा सिंहं पद्मं चेति चतुष्टयम्। आधारं प्रथमं चक्रं स्वाधिष्ठानं द्वितीयकम्॥ ४३॥

योनिस्थानं तयोर्मध्ये कामरूपं निगद्यते। आधाराख्ये गुदस्थाने पङ्कजं यच्चतुर्दलम्॥ ४४॥

तन्मध्ये प्रोच्यते योनिः कामाख्या सिद्धवन्दिता।

Postures, restraint of breath, subjugation of the senses, dhāraṇā, dhyāna and samādhi are the six parts of yoga. There are as many postures as there are living creatures; and Maheśvara (the great Lord) knows their distinguishing features. Siddha, bhadra, siṁha and padma are the four chief postures. Mūlādhāra is the first cakra. Śvādhiṣṭhāna is the second. Between these two is said to be the seat of yoni (perineum), having the form of Kāma (God of love). In tha Ādhāra of the anus, there is the lotus of four petals. In its midst is said to be the yoni called Kāma and worshipped by the siddhas.

योनिमध्ये स्थितं लिङ्गं पश्चिमाभिमुखं तथा॥ ४५॥

मस्तके मणिवद्भिन्नं यो जानाति स योगवित्। तप्तचामीकराकारं तडिल्लेखेव विस्फुरत्॥ ४६॥

चतुरस्रमुपर्यग्नेरधो मेढ्रात्प्रतिष्ठितम्। स्वशब्देन भवेत्प्राणः स्वाधिष्ठानं तदाश्रयम्॥ ४७॥

स्वाधिष्ठानं ततश्चक्रं मेढ्रमेव निगद्यते। मणिवत्तन्तुना यत्र वायुना पूरितं वपुः॥ ४८॥

तन्नाभिमण्डलं चक्रं प्रोच्यते मणिपूरकम्।

In the midst of the yoni is the Liṅga facing the west and split at its head like the gem. He who knows this, is a knower of the Vedas. A four-sided figure is situated above agni and below the genital organ, of the form of molten gold and shining like streaks of lightning. Prāṇa is with its sva (own) sound, having Svādhiṣṭhāna (seat), (or since sva of prāṇa arise from it). The cakra Svādhiṣṭhāna is spoken of as the genital organ itself. The cakra in the sphere of the navel is called Maṇipūraka, since the body is pierced through by vāyu like (gems) by string.

द्वादशारमहाचक्रे पुण्यपापनियन्त्रितः॥४९॥

तावज्जीवो भ्रमत्येवं यावत्तत्त्वं न विन्दति। ऊर्ध्वं मेढ्रादधो नाभेः कन्दो योऽस्ति खगाण्डवत्॥५०

तत्र नाड्यः समुत्पन्नाः सहस्राणि द्विसप्ततिः। तेषु नाडीसहस्रेषु द्विसप्ततिरुदाहृताः॥५१॥

प्रधानाः प्राणवाहिन्यो भूयस्तत्र दश स्मृताः। इडा च पिङ्गला चैव सुषुम्ना च तृतीयका॥५२॥

गान्धारी हस्तिजिह्वा च पूषा चैव यशस्विनी। अलम्बुसा कुहूरत्र शङ्खिनी दशमी स्मृता॥५३॥

एवं नाडीमयं चक्रं विज्ञेयं योगिना सदा। सततं प्राणवाहिन्यः सोमसूर्याग्निदेवताः॥५४॥

इडापिङ्गलासुषुम्नास्तिस्रो नाड्यः प्रकीर्तिताः। इडा वामे स्थिता भागे पिङ्गला दक्षिणे स्थिता॥५५

सुषुम्ना मध्यदेशे तु प्राणमार्गास्त्रयः स्मृताः। प्राणोऽपानः समानश्चोदानो व्यानस्तथैव च॥५६

नागः कूर्मः कृकरको देवदत्तो धनंजयः। प्राणाद्याः पञ्च विख्याता नागाद्याः पञ्च वायवः॥५७॥

The jīva (ego) urged to actions by its past virtuous and sinful karmas whirls about in this great cakra of twelve spokes, so long as it does not grasp the truth. Above the genital organ and below the navel is kanda of the shape of a bird's egg. There arise (from it) nādis seventy-two thousand in number. Of these seventy-two are generally known. Of these, the chief ones are ten and carry the prāṇas. Iḍā, Piṅgalā, Suṣumnā, Gāndhārī, Hastijihvā, Pūṣā, Yaśasvinī, Alambusā, Kuhū and Śaṅkhinī are said to be the ten. This cakra of the nādis should ever be known by the yogins. The three nādis– Iḍā, Piṅgalā and Suṣumnā are said to carry prāṇa always and have as their devatās, moon, sun, and agni. Iḍā is on the left side and Piṅgalā on the right side, while the Suṣumnā is in the middle. These three are known to be the paths of prāṇa. Prāṇa, Apāna, Samāna, Udāna, and Vyāna; Nāga, Kūrma, Kṛkara, Devadatta and Dhanañjaya; of these, the first five are called prāṇas, etc., and last five Nāga, etc. are called vāyus (or sub-prāṇas).

एते नाडीसहस्रेषु वर्तन्ते जीवरूपिणः। प्राणापानवशो जीवो ह्यधश्चोर्ध्वं प्रधावति॥५८॥

वामदक्षिणमार्गेण चञ्चलत्वान्न दृश्यते। आक्षिप्तो भुजदण्डेन यथोच्चलति कन्दुकः॥५९॥

प्राणापानसमाक्षिप्तस्तद्वज्जीवो न विश्रमेत्। अपानात्कर्षति प्राणोऽपानः प्राणाच्च कर्षति॥६०॥

खगरज्जुवदित्येतद्यो जानाति स योगवित्। हकारेण बहिर्याति सकारेण विशेत्पुनः॥६१॥

All these are situated (or run along) the one thousand nādis, (being) in the form of (or producing) life. Jīva which is under the influence of prāṇa and apāna goes up and down.

Jīva on account of its ever moving by the left and right paths is not visible. Just as a ball struck down (on the earth) with the bat of the hand springs up, so jīva ever tossed by prāṇa and apāna is never at rest. He is knower of yoga who knows that prāṇa always draws itself from apāna and apāna draws itself from prāṇa, like a bird (drawing itself from and yet not freeing itself) from the string (to which it is tied).

हंसहंसेत्यमुं मन्त्रं जीवो जपति सर्वदा। शतानि षड् दिवारात्रं सहस्राण्येकविंशति:॥ ६२॥

एतत्संख्यान्वितं मन्त्रं जीवो जपति सर्वदा। अजपा नाम गायत्री योगिनां मोक्षदा सदा॥ ६३॥

The jīva comes out with the letter Ha and gets in again with the letter Sa. Thus jīva always utters the mantra 'Haṁsa', 'Haṁsa'. The jīva always utters the mantra twenty-one thousand and six hundred times in one day and night. This is called Ajapā Gāyatrī and is ever the bestower of nirvāṇa to the yogins.

अस्या: संकल्पमात्रेण नर: पापै: प्रमुच्यते। अनया सदृशी विद्या अनया सदृशो जप:॥ ६४॥

अनया सदृशं पुण्यं न भूतं न भविष्यति। येन मार्गेण गन्तव्यं ब्रह्मस्थानं निरामयम्॥ ६५॥

मुखेनाच्छाद्य तद्द्वारं प्रसुप्ता परमेश्वरी। प्रबुद्धा वह्नियोगेन मनसा मरुता सह॥ ६६॥

सूचिवद्गुणमादाय व्रजत्यूर्ध्वं सुषुम्नया। उद्घाटयेत्कपाटं तु यथा कुञ्चिकया हठात्॥ ६७॥

कुण्डलिन्या तया योगी मोक्षद्वारं विभेदयेत्॥ ६८॥

Through its very thought, man is freed from sins. Neither in the past nor in the future is there a science equal to this, a japa equal to this or a meritorious action equal to this. Parameśvarī (viz., kuṇḍalinī śakti) sleeps shutting with her mouth that door which leads to the decayless Brahma-hole. Being aroused by the contact of agni with manas and prāṇa, she takes the form of a needle and pierces up through Suṣumnā. The yogin should open with great effort this door which is shut. Then he will pierce the door to salvation by means of kuṇḍalinī.

कृत्वा संपुटितौ करौ दृढतरं बध्वाथ पद्मासनं गाढं वक्षसि सन्निधाय चुबुकं ध्यानं च तच्चेतसि।

वारंवारमपानमूर्ध्वमनिलं प्रोच्चारयन्पूरितं मुञ्चन्प्राणमुपैति बोधमतुलं शक्तिप्रभावान्नर:॥ ६९॥

पद्मासनस्थितो योगी नाडीद्वारेषु पूरयन्। मारुतं कुम्भयन्यस्तु स मुक्तो नात्र संशय:॥ ७०॥

अङ्गानां मर्दनं कृत्वा श्रमजातेन वारिणा। कट्वम्ललवणत्यागी क्षीरपानरत: सुखी॥ ७१॥

ब्रह्मचारी मिताहारी योगी योगपरायण:। अब्दादूर्ध्वं भवेत्सिद्धो नात्र कार्या विचारणा॥ ७२॥

कन्दोर्ध्वकुण्डली शक्ति: स योगी सिद्धिभाजनम्। अपानप्राणयोरैक्यं क्षयान्मूत्रपुरीषयो:॥ ७३॥

Folding firmly the fingers of the hands, assuming firmly the Padma posture, placing the chin firmly on the breast and fixing the mind in dhyāna, one should frequently raise up the apāna, fill up with air and then leave the prāṇa. Then the wise man gets matchless wisdom through (this) śakti. That yogins who assuming Padma posture worships (i.e., conrols) vāyu at the door of the nādis and then performs restraint of breath is released without doubt. Rubbing off the limbs, the sweat arising from fatigue, abandoning all acid, bitter and saltish (food), taking delight in the drinking of milk and rasa, practising celibacy, being moderate in eating and ever bent on yoga, the yogin becomes a siddha in little more than a year. No inquiry need be made concerning the result. Kuṇḍalinī śakti, when it is up in the throat, makes the yogi get siddhi. The union of prāṇa and apāna has the extinction of urine and fæces.

युवा भवति वृद्धोऽपि सततं मूलबन्धनात्। पार्ष्णिभागेन संपीड्य योनिमाकुञ्चयेद्गुदम्॥७४॥
अपानमूर्ध्वमुत्कृष्य मूलबन्धोऽयमुच्यते। उड्याणं कुरुते यस्मादविश्रान्तमहाखगः॥७५॥
उड्डियाणं तदेव स्यात्तत्र बन्धो विधीयते। उदरे पश्चिमं ताणं नाभेरूर्ध्वं तु कारयेत्॥७६॥
उड्डियाणोऽप्ययं बन्धो मृत्युमातङ्गकेसरी। बध्नाति हि शिरोजातमधोगामिनभोजलम्॥७७॥
ततो जालन्धरो बन्धः कर्मदुःखौघनाशनः। जालन्धरे कृते बन्धे कण्ठसंकोचलक्षणे॥७८॥
न पीयूषं पतत्यग्नौ न च वायुः प्रधावति।

One becomes young even when old through performing mūlabandha always. Pressing the yoni by means of the heels and contracting the anus and drawing up the apāna— this is called mūlabandha. Uḍḍiyāṇa bandha is so called because it is (like) a great bird that flies up always without rest. One should bring the western part of the stomach above the navel. This Uḍḍiyāṇa bandha is a lion to the elephant of death, since it binds the water (or nectar) of the ākāśa which arises in the head and flows down. The Jālandhara bandha is the destroyer of all the pains of the throat. When this Jālandhara bandha which is destroyer of the pains of the throat is performed, then nectar does not fall on agni nor does the vāyu move.

कपालकुहरे जिह्वा प्रविष्टा विपरीतगा॥७९॥
भ्रुवोरन्तर्गता दृष्टिर्मुद्रा भवति खेचरी। न रोगो मरणं तस्य न निद्रा न क्षुधा तृषा॥८०॥
न च मूर्च्छा भवेत्तस्य यो मुद्रां वेत्ति खेचरीम्। पीड्यते न च रोगेण लिप्यते न च कर्मणा॥८१॥
बध्यते न च कालेन यस्य मुद्रास्ति खेचरी। चित्तं चरति खे यस्माज्जिह्वा भवति खे गता॥८२॥
तेनैषा खेचरी नाम मुद्रा सिद्धनमस्कृता।

When the tongue enters backwards into the hole of the skull, then there is the mudrā of vision latent in the eyebrow called khecarī. He who knows the mudrā, khecarī has no disease, death, sleep, hunger, thirst, or swoon. He who practises this mudrā is not affected by illness or karma; nor is he bound by the limitations of time. Since citta moves in the kha (ākāśa) and since the tongue has entered (in the mudrā) kha (viz., the hole in the mouth), therefore this mudrā is called khecarī and worshipped by the siddhas.

खेचर्या मुद्रया यस्य विवरं लम्बिकोर्ध्वतः॥८३॥
बिन्दुः क्षरति नो यस्य कामिन्यालिङ्गितस्य च। यावद्बिन्दुः स्थितो देहे तावन्मृत्युभयं कुतः॥८४॥
यावद्बद्धा नभोमुद्रा तावद्बिन्दुर्न गच्छति। गलितोऽपि यदा बिन्दुः संप्राप्तो योनिमण्डले॥८५॥

व्रजत्यूर्ध्वं हठाच्छक्त्या निबद्धो योनिमुद्रया। स एव द्विविधो बिन्दुः पाण्डरो लोहितस्तथा॥८६॥
पाण्डरं शुक्रमित्याहुर्लोहिताख्यं महारजः। विद्रुमद्रुमसंकाशं योनिस्थाने स्थितं रजः॥८७॥

He whose hole (or passage) above the uvula is closed (with the tongue backwards) be means of khecarīmudrā never loses his virility, even when embraced by a lovely woman. Where is the fear of death, so long as the bindu (virility) stays in the body. Bindu does not go out of the body, so long as the khecarīmudrā is practised. (Even) when bindu comes down to the sphere of the perineum, it goes up, being prevented and forced up by violent effort through yonimudrā. This bindu is twofold, white and red. The white one is called śukla and red one is said to contain much rajas. The rajas which stays in yoni is like the colour of a coral.

शशिस्थाने वसेद्बिन्दुस्तयोरैक्यं सुदुर्लभम्। बिन्दुः शिवो रजः शक्तिर्बिन्दुरिन्दू रजो रविः॥८८॥
उभयोः संगमादेव प्राप्यते परमं वपुः। वायुना शक्तिचालेन प्रेरितं खे यथा रजः॥८९॥
रविणैकत्वमायाति भवेद्दिव्यं वपुस्तदा। शुक्लं चन्द्रेण संयुक्तं रजः सूर्यसमन्वितम्॥९०॥
द्वयोः समरसीभावं यो जानाति स योगवित्। शोधनं मलजालानां घटनं चन्द्रसूर्ययोः॥९१॥
रसानां शोषणं सम्यङ् महामुद्राभिधीयते॥९२॥
वक्षोन्यस्तहनुर्निपीड्य सुषिरं योनेश्च वामाङ्घ्रिणा हस्ताभ्यामनुधारयन्प्रविततं पादं तथा दक्षिणम्।
आपूर्य श्वसनेन कुक्षियुगलं बध्वा शनै रेचयेदेषा पातकनाशिनी ननु महामुद्रा नृणां प्रोच्यते॥९३॥

The bindu stays in the seat of the genital organs. The union of these two moon and rajas is the sun. Through the union of these two is attained the highest body; when rajas is roused up by agitating the śakti through vāyu which unites with the sun, then is produced the divine form. Śukla being united with the moon and rajas with the sun, he is a knower of yoga who knows the proper mixture of these two. The cleansing of the accumulated refuse, the unification of the sun and the moon and the complete drying of the rasas (essences), this is called mahāmudrā. Placing the chin of the breast, pressing the anus by means of the left heel, and seizing (the toe) of the extended right leg by the two hands, one should fill his belly (with air) and should slowly exhale. This is called mahāmudrā, the destroyer of the sins of men.

अथात्मनिर्णयं व्याख्यास्ये- हृदि स्थाने अष्टदलपद्मं वर्तते। तन्मध्ये रेखावलयं कृत्वा जीवात्मरूपं ज्योतीरूपमणुमात्रं वर्तते। तस्मिन्सर्वं प्रतिष्ठितं भवति सर्वं जानाति सर्वं करोति सर्वमेतच्चरितमहं कर्ताऽहं भोक्ता सुखी दुःखी काणः खञ्जो बधिरो मूकः कृशः स्थूलोऽनेन प्रकारेण स्वतन्त्रवादेन वर्तते॥९३-१॥

Now I shall give a description of Ātman. In the seat of the heart is a lotus of eight petals. In its centre is jīvātmā of the form of jyotis and atomic in size, moving in a circular line. In it is located everything. It knows everything. It does everything. It does all these actions attributing everything to its own power, (thinking) I do, I enjoy, I am happy, I am miserable, I am blind, I am lame, I am deaf, I am mute, I am lean, I am stout, etc.

पूर्वदले विश्रमते पूर्वं दलं श्वेतवर्णं तदा भक्तिपुर:सरं धर्मे मतिर्भवति॥ ९३-२॥

यदाऽऽग्नेयदले विश्रमते तदाग्नेयदलं रक्तवर्णं तदा निद्रालस्यमतिर्भवति॥ ९३-३॥

यदा दक्षिणदले विश्रमते तद्दक्षिणदलं कृष्णवर्णं तदा द्वेषकोपमतिर्भवति॥ ९३-४॥

यदा नैर्ऋतदले विश्रमते तन्नैर्ऋतदलं नीलवर्णं तदा पापकर्महिंसामतिर्भवति॥ ९३-५॥

यदा पश्चिमदले विश्रमते तत्पश्चिमदलं स्फटिकवर्णं तदा क्रीडाविनोदे मतिर्भवति॥ ९३-६॥

यदा वायव्यदले विश्रमते वायव्यदलं माणिक्यवर्णं तदा गमनचलनवैराग्यमतिर्भवति॥ ९३-७॥

When it rests on the eastern petal which is of śveta (white) colour, then it has a mind (or is inclined) to dharma with bhakti (devotion). When it rests on the south-eastern petal, which is of rakta (blood colour), then it is inclined to sleep and laziness. When it rests on the southern petal, which is of kṛṣṇa (black) colour, then it is inclined to hate and anger. When it rests on the south-western petal which is of nīla (blue) colour, then it gets desire for sinful or harmful actions. When it rests on the western petal which is of crystal colour, then it is inclined to flirt and amuse, when it rests on the north-western petal which is of ruby colour, then it has a mind to walk, rove and have vairāgya (or be indifferent).

यदोत्तरदले विश्रमते तदुत्तरदलं पीतवर्णं तदा सुखशृंगारमतिर्भवति॥ ९३-८॥

यदेशानदले विश्रमते तदीशानदलं वैडूर्यवर्णं तदा दानादिकृपामतिर्भवति॥ ९३-९॥

यदा संधिसंधिषु मतिर्भवति तदा वातपित्तश्लेष्ममहाव्याधिप्रकोपो भवति॥ ९३-१०॥

When it rests on the northern petal which is pīta (yellow) colour, then it is inclined to be happy and to be loving. When it rests on the north-eastern petal which is of vaidūrya (lapis lazuli) colour, then it is inclined to amassing money, charity and passion. When it stays in the interspace between any two petals, then it gets the wrath arising from diesases generated through (the disturbance) of the equilibrium of) vāyu, bile and phlegm (in the body).

यदा मध्ये तिष्ठति तदा सर्वं जानाति गायति नृत्यति पठत्यानन्दं करोति॥ ९३-११॥

यदा नेत्रश्रमो भवति श्रमनिर्भरणार्थं प्रथमरेखावलयं कृत्वा मध्ये निमज्जनं कुरुते प्रथमरेखा बन्धूकपुष्पवर्णं तदा निद्रावस्था भवति। निद्रावस्थामध्ये स्वप्नावस्था भवति। स्वप्नावस्थामध्ये दृष्टं श्रुतमनुमानसंभववार्ता इत्यादिकल्पनां करोति तदादिश्रमो भवति॥ ९३-१२॥

श्रमनिर्हरणार्थं द्वितीयरेखावलयं कृत्वा मध्ये निमज्जनं कुरुते द्वितीयरेखा इन्द्रगोपवर्णं तदा सुषुप्त्यवस्था भवति सुषुप्तौ केवलपरमेश्वरसंबन्धिनी बुद्धिर्भवति नित्यबोधस्वरूपा भवति पश्चात्परमेश्वरस्वरूपेण प्राप्तिर्भवति॥ ९३-१३॥

When it stays in the middle, then it knows everything, sings, dances, speaks and is blissful. When the eye is pained (after a day's work), then in order to remove (its) pain, it makes first a circular line and sinks in the middle. The first line is of the colour of bandhūka flower (Bassia). Then is the state of sleep. In the mddle of the state of sleep is the state of dream. In the middle of the state of dream, it experiences the ideas of perception, Vedas, inference, possibility, (sacred) words, etc. Then there arises much fatigue. In order to remove this fatigue, it circles the second line and sinks in the middle. the second is of the colour of (the insect) Indragopa (of red or white colour). Then comes the state of dreamless sleep. During the dreamless sleep, it has only the thought connected with Parameśvara (the highest Lord) aione. This state is of the nature of eternal wisdom. Afterwards it attains the nature of the highest Lord (Parameśvara).

तृतीयरेखावलयं कृत्वा मध्ये निमज्जनं कुरुते तृतीयरेखा पद्मरागवर्णं तदा तुरीयावस्था भवति तुरीये केवलपरमात्मसंबन्धिनी मतिर्भवति नित्यबोधस्वरूपा भवति तदा शनैः शनैरुपरमेद्बुद्ध्या धृतिगृहीतयात्मसंस्थं मनः कृत्वा न किंचिदपि चिन्तयेत्॥ १३-१४॥

तदा प्राणापानयोरैक्यं कृत्वा सर्वं विश्वमात्मस्वरूपेण लक्ष्यं धारयति। यदा तुरीयातीतावस्था तदा सर्वेषामानन्दस्वरूपो भवति द्वन्द्वातीतो भवति यावद्देहधारणा वर्तते– तावत्तिष्ठति पश्चात्परमात्मस्वरूपेण प्राप्तिर्भवति इत्यनेन प्रकारेण मोक्षो भवतीदमेवात्मदर्शनोपाया भवन्ति॥ १३-१५॥

Then it makes a round of the third circle and sinks in the middle. The third circle is of the colour of padmarāga (ruby). Then comes the state of turya (the fourth). In turya, there is only the connection of Paramātmā. It attains the nature of eternal wisdom. Then one should gradually attain the quiescence of buddhi with self-control. Placing the manas in Ātmā, one should think of nothing else. Then causing the union of prāṇa and apāna, he concentrates his aim upon the whole universe being of the nature of Ātmā. Then comes the state of turyātīta (viz., that state beyond the fourth). Then everythig appears as bliss. He is beyond the pairs (of happiness and pains, etc.). He stays here as long as he should wear his body. Then he attains the nature of Paramātmā and attains emancipation through this means. This alone is the means of knowing Ātmā.

चतुष्पथसमायुक्तमहाद्वारगवायुना। सहस्थितत्रिकोणार्धगमने दृश्यतेऽच्युतः॥ १४॥

पूर्वोक्तत्रिकोणस्थानादुपरि पृथिव्यादिपञ्चवर्णकं ध्येयम्। प्राणादिपञ्चवायुश्च बीजं वर्णं च स्थानकम्।

यकारं प्राणबीजं च नीलजीमूतसन्निभम्। रकारमग्निबीजं च अपानादित्यसंनिभम्॥ १५॥

लकारं पृथिवीरूपं व्यानं बन्धूकसंनिभम्। वकारं जीवबीजं च उदानं शङ्खवर्णकम्॥ १६॥

हकारं वियत्स्वरूपं च समानं स्फटिकप्रभम्। हन्नाभिनासाकर्णं च पादाङ्गुष्ठादिसंस्थितम्॥ १७॥

द्विसप्ततिसहस्राणि नाडीमार्गेषु वर्तते। अष्टाविंशतिकोटीषु रोमकूपेषु संस्थिताः॥ १८॥

समानप्राण एकस्तु जीवः स एक एव हि।

When vāyu (breath) which enters the great hole associated with a hall where four roads meet gets into the halp of the well-placed triangle, then is Acyuta (the indestructible) seen. Above the aforesaid triangle, one should meditate on the five bīja (seed) letters of (the elements) pṛthivī, etc., as also on the five prāṇas, the colour of the bījas and their position. The letter is the bīja of prāṇa and resembles the blue cloud. The letter j is the bīja of agni, is of apāna and resembles the sun. The letter y is the bīja of pṛthivī, is of vyāna and rsembless bandhūka flower. The letter o is the bīja of jīva (vāyu), is of udāna and is of the colour of the conch. The letter g is the bīja of ākāśa, is of samāna, and is of the colour of crystal. Prāṇa stays in the heart, navel, nose, ear, foot, finger, and other places, travels through the seventy-two thousand nādis, stays in the twenty-eight crores of hair-pores and is yet the same everywhere. It is that which is called jīva.

रेचकादित्रयं कुर्याद्दृढचित्तः समाहितः॥९९॥

शनैः समस्तमाकृष्य हृत्सरोरुहकोटरे। प्राणापानौ च बध्वा तु प्रणवेन समुच्चरेत्॥१००॥

कण्ठसंकोचनं कृत्वा लिङ्गसंकोचनं तथा। मूलाधारात्सुषुम्ना च पद्मतन्तुनिभा शुभा॥१०१॥

अमूर्तो वर्तते नादो वीणादण्डसमुत्थितः। शङ्खनादादिभिश्चैव मध्यमेव ध्वनिर्यथा॥१०२॥

व्योमरन्ध्रगतो नादो मायूरं नादमेव च। कपालकुहरे मध्ये चतुर्द्वारस्य मध्यमे॥१०३॥

तदात्मा राजते तत्र यथा व्योम्नि दिवाकरः। कोदण्डद्वयमध्ये तु ब्रह्मरन्ध्रेषु शक्ति च॥१०४॥

स्वात्मानं पुरुषं पश्येन्मनस्तत्र लयं गतम्। रत्नानि ज्योत्स्निनादं तु बिन्दुमाहेश्वरं पदम्॥१०५॥

य एवं वेद पुरुषः स कैवल्यं समश्नुत इत्युपनिषत्॥१०६॥

One should perform the three, expiration, etc., with a firm will and great control : and drawing in everything (with the breath) in slow degress, he should bind prāṇa and apāna in the cave of the lotus of the heart and utter praṇava, having contracted his throat and the genital organ. From the Mūlādhāra (to the head) is the Suṣumnā resembling the shining thread of the lotus. The nāda is located in the Vīṇādaṇḍa (spinal column); that sound from its middle resembles (that of) the conch, etc. When it goes to the hole, the ākāśa, it resembles that of the peacock. In the middle of cave of the skull between the four doors shines Ātmā, like the sun in the sky. Between the two bows in the Brahma-hole, one should see Puruṣa with śakti as his own Ātmā. Then his manas is absorbed there. That man attains kaivalya who understands the gems, moonlight, nāda, bindu, and the seat of Maheśvara (the great Lord).

ॐ सह नाववतु .... इति शान्तिः॥

॥इति ध्यानबिन्दूपनिषत्समाप्ता॥

***

39. BRAHMAVIDYĀ-UPANIṢAD

ब्रह्मविद्योपनिषद्

This Upaniṣad is related to Kṛṣṇa Yajurveda. A descriptive discussion has been made on the measures to attain Brahma and its form. The four mātrās of Praṇava has been enumerated while on describing Praṇava Brahma, a mystery of Brahmavidyā. The other contents of this Upaniṣad are the nature of a living-organisms, the cause for emancipation and bondage and attainment of supreme god through Haṁsavidyā, feature of Sakala and Niṣkala Brahma, attainment of good and bad only by the knowledge of holy books and performing the practical deeds accordingly, research on Praṇavahaṁsa as an apparent offering, attainment of meditation as a result of exercise on Haṁsa hymn, the procedure and practise on Haṁsa yoga and engrassment of the soul topics by such Haṁsayogis. All these issues make apparent the element form of Brahma. This is the reason this Upaniṣad is called Brahmavidyā.

ॐ सह नाववतु......... इति शान्तिः।।

अथ ब्रह्मविद्योपनिषदुच्यते।

प्रसादाद्ब्रह्मणस्तस्य विष्णोरद्भुतकर्मणः। रहस्यं ब्रह्मविद्याया ध्रुवाग्निं संप्रचक्षते।।१।।

Now, the Brahmavidyopaniṣad is described. The mystery of Brahmavidyā which has complexion of undeviated knowledge or fire with the grace of the supreme Brahma in the form of Viṣṇu who performs the great and excellent deeds.

ओमित्येकाक्षरं ब्रह्म यदुक्तं ब्रह्मवादिभिः। शरीरं तस्य वक्ष्यामि स्थानं कालत्रयं तथा।।२।।

As the scholars on Brahma state, Oṁ is a letter of Praṇava and it is Brahma, similarly, I describe the body, the place and the three times (kāla) of that Brahmavidyā.

The saint is explaining here the expression of Brahma with buttering Oṁ.

तत्र देवास्त्रयः प्रोक्ता लोका वेदास्त्रयोऽग्नयः। तिस्रो मात्रार्धमात्रा च त्र्यक्षरस्य शिवस्य तु।।३।।

There are three gods, three worlds, three Vedas (Ṛg, Yajuh, Sāma), and three fires in Oṁkara. This trio-letter Śiva has three and a half-mātrās i.e. A, V, M and Anusvāra (moon).

ऋग्वेदो गार्हपत्यं च पृथिवी ब्रह्म एव च। अकारस्य शरीरं तु व्याख्यातं ब्रह्मवादिभिः।।४।।

The scholar of Brahma have described the body of 'A' extended upto Ṛgveda, Gārhapatya fire, element of earth and Brahma.

यजर्वेदोऽन्तरिक्षं च दक्षिणाग्निस्तथैव च। विष्णुश्च भगवान्देव उकारः परिकीर्तितः।।५।।

The body of 'U' is extended upto Yajurveda, Daksiṇāgni, the element of ether and Lord Viṣnu.

सामवेदस्तथा द्यौश्चाहवनीयस्तथैव च। ईश्वरः परमो देवो मकारः परिकीर्तितः।।६।।

The body of 'M' has been 'Sāmaveda, Āhavaniya fire, the world of sun, Iśvara and the supreme god.

सूर्यमण्डलमध्येऽथ ह्यकारः शङ्खमध्यगः। उकारश्चन्द्रसंकाशस्तस्य मध्ये व्यवस्थितः॥७॥

मकारस्त्वग्निसंकाशो विधूमो विद्युतोपमः। तिस्रो मात्रास्तथा ज्ञेयाः सोमसूर्याग्निरूपिणः॥८॥

The 'A' is existed in the middle of the Sun-orbit like the middle part of a conch, the U is existed within that very moon orbit, the blazing fire and the fire inherent with the lightning enshrines with 'M' thus, these three mātrās should be known as the sun, moon and the fire.

शिखा तु दीपसंकाशा तस्मिन्नुपरि वर्तते। अर्धमात्रा तथा ज्ञेया प्रणवस्योपरि स्थिता॥९॥

As the flame of a lamp always ascends, the half-mora of a Praṇava should be considered in the same location.

[The flame of a lamp is always ascendant. The Anusvāra echoes in the upper part of the mind (sense) as remains with the route of nose. Due to this mora, a conjoint sound of A, U, M lifts upward so it has been stated as a flame.]

पद्मसूत्रनिभा सूक्ष्मा शिखा सा दृश्यते परा। सा नाडी सूर्यसंकाशा सूर्यं भित्त्वा तथा परा॥१०॥

द्विसप्ततिसहस्राणि नाडीं भित्त्वा च मूर्धनि। वरदः सर्वभूतानां सर्वं व्याप्येव तिष्ठति॥११॥

That flame is perceived analogous to the fibre of a lotus. That nerve alike sun penetrates the sun as also the seventy-two thousand nerves enshrines in the mind, blesses all creatures and resides embedding all within it.

कांस्यघण्टानिनादस्यु यथा लीयति शान्तये। ओङ्कारस्तु तथा योज्यः शान्तये सर्वमिच्छता॥१२॥

All kinds of desires are cooled down by virtue of worship to Om as the sound from a gong made of bronze (a mixture of copper and tin) arises peace-giving and then merge therewith.

यस्मिन्विलीयते शब्दस्तत्परं ब्रह्म गीयते। धियं हि लीयते ब्रह्म सोऽमृतत्वाय कल्पते॥१३॥

The element in which the word immerses, has been called as Parabrahman and the Brahma in which the intellect immerses, has been called as nectar form Brahma.

वायुस्तेजस्तथाकाशस्त्रिविधो जीवसंज्ञकः। स जीवः प्राण इत्युक्तो बालाग्रशतकल्पितः॥१२॥

The living-organism is compared with the wind, splendour and the ether. The magnitude of this living-organism has been taken on surmise as one by hundredth part of the point of a hair.

नाभिस्थाने स्थितं विश्वं शुद्धतत्त्वं सुनिर्मलम्। आदित्यमिव दीप्यन्तं रश्मिभिश्चाखिलं शिवम्॥१५॥

That living-organism is enshrined within the navel-region (nucleus), a pure element, sacrosanct, known with the universal name. It illuminates like the sun and its consequences are all benevolent.

सकारं च हकारं च जीवो जपति सर्वदा। नाभिरन्ध्राद्विनिष्क्रान्तं विषयव्याप्तिवर्जितम॥१६॥

Every living-organism usually do Japa of 'Sa' and 'Ha' while breathing i.e. inhaling and exhaling. Thus, he does the Japa of So'haṁ. He thus discharges through the hole of navel and the worldly issues do not put any hindrance on his way.

तेनेदं निष्कलं विद्यात्क्षीरात्सर्पिर्यथा तथा। कारणेनात्मना युक्तः प्राणायामैश्च पञ्चभिः॥१७॥

The element of soul, all causative, extracted as a result of long churning like the ghee from milk, this element is known by the five functions of breathing, the element of breathing are flown within the five elements of the body. Hence, these are considered the five functions of the breathing in these five elements.

चतुष्कलासमायुक्तो भ्राम्यते च हृदि स्थितः। गोलकस्तु यदा देहे क्षीरदण्डेन वाऽहतः॥१८॥

As the milk is churned by using a log, the element of breathing existing in the heart with four arts is given circulation to all the parts of the body.

एतस्मिन्वसते शीघ्रमविश्रान्तं महाखगः। यावन्निःश्वसितो जीवस्तावन्निष्कलता गतः॥१९॥

The great bird, the best racer living in this body doesn't take rest. The living-soul losses its art when the breathing is ceased.

[The saint has stated the heart containing four arts and divisions. The modern physiologist consider it distributed in the left and right oracle and the left and right ventric.]

नभस्थं निष्कलं ध्यात्वा मुच्यते भवबन्धनात्। अनाहतध्वनियुतं हंसं यो वेद हृद्गतम्॥२०॥

स्वप्रकाशचिदानन्दं स हंस गीयते। रेचकं पूरकं मुक्त्वा कुम्भकेन स्थितः सुधीः॥२१॥

नाभिकन्दे समौ कृत्वा प्राणापानौ समाहितः। मस्तकस्थामृतास्वादं पीत्वा ध्यानेन सादरम्॥२२॥

दीपाकारं महादेवं ज्वलन्तं नाभिमध्यमे। अभिषिच्यामृतेनैव हंसहंसेति यो जपेत्॥२३॥

जरामरणरोगादि न तस्य भुवि विद्यते। एवं दिने दिने कुर्यादणिमादिविभूतये॥२४॥

He becomes free from the worldly ties as a result of lighting his lamp-mind on the element residing in the ether. The person introduced with the bird (Haṁsa), all pleasure in mind, duly illuminated and with the sound of Anāhata in the heart. The scholar who sips with extreme honour, the nectar enshrined in the mind by using Prāṅa and Apāna for practising on Prāṇāyāma with its three steps i.e. exhale, inhale and retention. The person who does Japa repeatedly on Haṁsa, while pouring nectar on all-illuminating Mahādeva like a lamp in the middle of his navel doesn't suffer from the ailments, premature death and the effect of old age. He becomes entitled to all outstanding and accomplishments like Aṇimā etc.

[Haṁsa is formed when So'haṁ is reverted. The living-organism with breathing has been addressed as Haṁsa. The Haṁsa assuming himself the Brahma by indicating this element of supreme soul, is not affected by the material distortions.]

ईश्वरत्वमवाप्नोति सदाभ्यासरतः पुमान्। बहवौ नैकमार्गेण प्राप्ता नित्यत्वमागताः॥२५॥

The learned person always engrossed in the practise of this Brahmavidyā attains to the element of Iśvara. A number of people have been accessed to the everlasting position by virtue of this single route.

हंसविद्यामृते लोके नास्ति नित्यत्वसाधनम्। यो ददाति महाविद्यां हंसाख्यां पारमेश्वरीम्।।२६।।
तस्य दास्यं सदा कुर्यात्प्रज्ञया परया सह। शुभं वाऽशुभमन्यद्वा यदुक्तं गुरुणा भुवि।।२७।।
तत्कुर्यादविचारेण शिष्यः संतोषसंयुतः। हंसविद्यामिमां लब्ध्वा गुरुशुश्रूषया नरः।।२८।।

There is no other means for the element of immortality like the nectar of the Haṁsa-formed learning. The learned person who provides with this great learning, all holy and supreme divine known as the Haṁsa learning is always worth adoration with all subject. The disciple should follow the order either good or bad given by the teacher without raising any question unfavourable and with full contentment. After attaining to this Haṁsa learning from the teacher, the man should always surrender himself for the service of that teacher.

आत्मानमात्मना साक्षाद्ब्रह्म बुद्ध्वा सुनिश्चलम्। देहजात्यादिसंबन्धान्वर्णाश्रमसमन्वितान्।।२९।।
वेदशास्त्राणि चान्यानि पदपांसुमिव त्यजेत्। गुरुभक्तिं सदा कुर्याच्छ्रेयसे भूयसे नरः।।३०।।

A cognisance of soul by soul and knowledge of Brahma with determined wisdom as a result of resistance given by the teacher, one should abandon the discrimination based on cast and commune etc. and the topics of Vedas and holy books unhesitatingly and to serve the teacher, should be the motto of the disciple. Only then the disciple may access to the true welfare.

गुरुरेव हरिः साक्षान्नान्य इत्यब्रवीच्छ्रुतिः।।३१।।

The teacher himself is apparent Hari. Nobody other than him is the god as it is confirmed by Vedas.

श्रुत्या यदुक्तं परमार्थमेव तत्संशयो नात्र ततः समस्तम्।
श्रुत्या विरोधे न भवेत्प्रमाणं भवेदनर्थाय विना प्रमाणम्।।३२।।

The statement disclosing Veda undoubtedly is the supreme aim. There are no other proofs if proof of Veda is contradictory or opposed. Everything would be harmful if it is without any proof.

देहस्थः सकलो ज्ञेयो निष्कलो देहवर्जितः। आप्तोपदेशगम्योऽसौ सर्वतः समवस्थितः।।३३।।

One should treat the physical sensitivity as sensitivity of division and this supreme sensitivity as an exclusive art or beyond art. This element made known by the learned teacher is enshrined everywhere with equity.

हंसहंसेति यो ब्रूयाद्धंसो ब्रह्मा हरिः शिवः। गुरुवक्त्रात्तु लभ्येत प्रत्यक्षं सर्वतोमुखम्।।३४।।

The scholar reciting Haṁsa-haṁsa is the benevolent form of Lord Brahmā, Viṣṇu and Śivā. He can know the Brahma which is omnipresent.

तिलेषु च यथा तैलं पुष्पे गन्ध इवाश्रितः। पुरुषस्य शरीरेऽस्मिन्स बाह्याभ्यन्तरे तथा।।३५।।

As the oil in seasame and the odour in flower is always existed, the Brahma exists in and out of this body.

उल्काहस्तो यथालोके द्रव्यमालोक्य तां त्यजेत्। ज्ञानेन ज्ञेयमालोक्य पश्चाज्ज्ञानं परित्यजेत्।।३६।।

As the torch is abandoned, when the desired thing is searched out with its help, the knowledge is abandoned when knowledge of the subject worth knowing is obtained.

पुषुपवत्सकलं विद्याद्गन्धस्तस्य तु निष्कलः। वृक्षस्तु सकल विद्याच्छाया तस्य तु निष्कला।।३७।।

One should treat as flower to the artful and the odour as artless or the tree as artful and its shadow as artless.

निष्कलः सकलो भावः सर्वत्रैव व्यवस्थितः। उपायः सकलस्तद्वदुपेयश्चैव निष्कलः।।३८।।

This artful and artless assumption is perceived everywhere. The thing of art is the means or measure while the Brahma is artless.

सकलो सकलो भावो निष्कले निष्कलस्तथा। एकमात्रो द्विमात्रश्च त्रिमात्रश्चैव भेदतः।।३९।।

अर्धमात्रा परा ज्ञेया तत ऊर्ध्वं परत्परम्। पञ्चधा पञ्चदैवत्यं सकलं परिपठ्यते।।४०।।

The spirit of art resides in Sakala and the spirit of artlessness resides in Niṣkala. The half-mātrā consists of the discrimination as 1, 2, and 3 mātrās as per on Parātpara is above it. The Sakala should be considered of five gods and five kinds i.e. five breathings five elements.

ब्रह्मणो हृदयस्थानं कण्ठे विष्णुः समाश्रितः। तालुमध्ये स्थितो रुद्रो ललाटस्थो महेश्वरः।।४१।।

The place of Brahmā is in the heart, Viṣṇu in the kaṇṭha, Rudra in the palate and Lord Śivā in the forehead.

नासाग्रे अच्युतं विद्यात्तस्यान्ते तु परं पदम्। परत्वात्तु परं नास्तीत्येवं शास्त्रस्य निर्णयः।।४२।।

Acyuta (Sadāśiva) in the forepart of nose and the supreme position in the middle of brows should be considered. The holy books have pronounced that nothing is greater than it.

देहातीतं तु तं विद्यान्नासाग्रे द्वादशाङ्गुलम्। तदन्तं तं विजानीयात्तत्रस्थो व्यापयेत्प्रभुः।।४३।।

The sense of physiquelessness should be imagined twelve-finger up from the forepart of the nose and the sovereign God should be considered at the extreme part (Sahasrāra Cakra) of it.

मनोऽप्यन्यत्र निक्षिप्तं चक्षुरन्यत्र पातितम्। तथापि योगिनां योगो ह्यविच्छिन्नः प्रवर्तते।।४४।।

Irrespective of the dynamicity of mind as also of the yogis, the yoga of yogis moves with inseparated spirit.

एतत्तु परमं गुह्यमेतत्तु परमं शुभम्। नातः परतरं किंचिन्नातः परतरं शुभम्।।४५।।

It is the most cryptic mystery. It is the best among all and nothing greater and larger than it.

शुद्धज्ञानामृतं प्राप्य परमाक्षरनिर्णयम्। गुह्याद्गुह्यतमं गोप्यं ग्रहणीयं प्रयत्नतः।।४६।।

One should decide the element of supreme letter on having the pure nectar of knowledge acquired. It is worth conceal and confidential as also worth entertain with extreme endeavour.

नापुत्राय प्रदातव्यं नाशिष्याय कदाचन। गुरुदेवाय भक्ताय नित्यं भक्तिपराय च॥४७॥

प्रदातव्यमिदं शास्त्रं नेतरेभ्यः प्रदापयेत्। दाताऽस्य नरकं याति सिध्यते न कदाचन॥४८॥

This Brahmavidyā shouldn't be shared either with an issueless person or non-disciple. It should be given only to a true devotee to the teacher. He should always be spiritual but this learning should not be given any other than described above. In case, someone is, will make his place to hell and his learning will prove fruitless.

गृहस्थो ब्रह्मचारी वा वानप्रस्थोऽथ भिक्षुकः। यत्र तत्र स्थितो ज्ञानी परमाक्षरवित्सदा॥४९॥

The celibate, couple, ascetic and the recluse whatever he is and wherever he resides; only knower to the element of supreme letter is real scholar.

विषयी विषयासक्तो याति देहान्तर शुभम्। ज्ञानादेवास्य शास्त्रस्य सर्वावस्थोऽपि मानवः॥५०॥

In case, the person is attached with the worldly enjoyments and issues, he too acquires the higher position after death as a blessing of his knowledge to this learning.

ब्रह्महत्याश्वमेधाद्यैः पुण्यपापैर्न लिप्यते। चोदको बोधकश्चैव मोक्षदश्च परः स्मृतः॥५१॥

इत्येषा त्रिविधो ज्ञेय आचार्यस्तु महीतले। चोदको दर्शयेन्मार्गं बोधकः स्थानमाचरेत्॥५२॥

मोक्षदस्तु परं तत्त्वं यज्ज्ञावा परमश्नुते। प्रत्यक्षयजनं देहे संक्षेपाच्छृणु गौतम॥५३॥

The scholars not involved with the offence as murder of Brahma and the great deeds like arranging Aśvamedha become inspirer, monitor and giver of emancipation. All Āharyas in this world are classified in these three categories. The inspirer guides, makes the ideal introduction with the knowledge pragmatically and thus provides with this supreme element competent to provide with emancipation. This supreme soul can be obtained as a result of due introduction with it. O Gautama! listen to in reference with the homage in this body.

तेनेष्ट्वा स नरो याति शाश्वतं पदमव्ययम्। स्वयमेव तु संपश्येद्देहे बिन्दुं च निष्कलम्॥५४॥

The man attains to the everlasting and immortal position by performing this deed. He himself becomes so competent as to perceive the artful and artless iota within his body.

अयने द्वे च विषुवे सदा पश्यति मार्गवित्। कृत्वा यामं पुरा वत्स रेचकपूरककुम्भकान्॥५५॥

One should do Prāṇāyāma consisting of Recaka, Pūraka and Kumbhaka at each quarter of the day and night like both fortnight (viz. light and dark).

पूर्वं चोभयमुच्चार्य अर्चयेत्तु यथाक्रमम्। नमस्कारेण योगेन मुद्रयारभ्य चार्चयेत्॥५६॥

He should very first worship Oṁ and Haṁsa with procedure for reciting. He should then do worship through the postures like Sāmbhari, Khecari etc. and with yoga of salutation i.e. Haṁsah so'haṁ etc.

सूर्यस्य ग्रहणं वत्स प्रत्यक्षयजनं स्मृतम्। ज्ञानात्सायुज्यमेवोक्तं तोये तोयं यथा तथा॥५७॥

O son! the means for apparent worship of Lord sun has been stated the day of eclipse. As the water is within water, the supreme position can be obtained only by virtue of the bonafide knowledge.

एते गुणाः प्रवर्तन्ते योगाभ्यासकृतश्रमैः। तस्माद्योगं समादाय सर्वदुःखबहिष्कृतः॥५८॥

The industry made for the exercise of yoga is of so virtuous that one should apply it ceaselessly and with industry to remove all physical pains.

योगध्यानं सदा कृत्वा ज्ञानं तन्मयतां व्रजेत्। ज्ञानात्स्वरूपं परमं हंसमन्त्रं समुच्चरेत्॥५९॥

One should obtain the state of meditation gradually through conception on yoga and reciting the hymns of this Brahmavidyā. The knowledge is the single means to obtain the supreme form of Brahmā (the hymn of Haṁsa).

प्राणिनां देहमध्ये तु स्थितो हंसः सदाऽच्युतः। हंस एव परं सत्यं हंस एव तु शक्तिकम्॥६०॥

The Haṁsa (sensitive soul) in the form of Acyuta always enshrines with the body of living-organisms. The Haṁsa is the absolute reality and it is the form of power.

हंस एव परं वाक्यं हंस एव तु वैदिकम्। हंस एव परो रुद्रो हंस एव परात्परम्॥६१॥

The Haṁsa is the supreme sentence and it is the essence of Vedas. Further, it is supreme Rudra and the supreme soul.

सर्वदेवस्य मध्यस्थो हंस एव महेश्वरः। पृथिव्यादिशिवान्तं तु अकाराद्याश्च वर्णकाः॥६२॥

कूटान्ता हंस एव स्यान्मातृकेति व्यवस्थिताः। मातृकारहितं मन्त्रमादिशन्ते न कुत्रचित्॥६३॥

The Haṁsa only is the supreme god amidst all gods. From the earth to Lord Śiva and from 'A' to 'kṣa', this Haṁsa is existed like the alphabets. The preaching of hymn without letter is seldom given.

हंसज्योतिरनूपम्यं देव मध्ये व्यवस्थितम्। दक्षिणामुखमाश्रित्य ज्ञानमुद्रां प्रकल्पयेत्॥६४॥

सदा समाधिं कुर्वीत हंसमन्त्रमनुस्मरन्। निर्मलस्फटिकाकारं दिव्यरूपमनुत्तमम्॥६५॥

The supreme flame of Haṁsa is existed among the gods, one should do the knowledge posture by resorting to Lord Śiva and do concentration on Haṁsa in the state of meditation and should concentrate on the divine form of soul like the sphaṭika.

मध्यदेशे परं हंसं ज्ञानमुद्रात्मरूपकम्। प्राणोऽपानः समानश्चोदानव्यानौ च वायवः॥६६॥

पञ्चकर्मेन्द्रियैर्युक्ताः क्रियाशक्तिबलोद्यताः। नागः कूर्मश्च कृकरो देवदत्तो धनंजयः॥६७॥

पञ्चज्ञानेन्द्रियैर्युक्ता ज्ञानशक्तिबलोद्यताः। पावकः शक्तिमध्ये तु नाभिचक्रे रविः स्थितः॥६८॥

One should always concentrate on the supreme Haṁsa in the form of knowledge lustre in the middle region. The five winds (Prāṇa) i.e. Prāṇa, Apāna, Samāna, Udāna and Vyāna as also the action power of five executive organs is mighty. A knowledge of power enriches with the winds i.e. Nāga, Kūrma, Kṛkala, Devadatta, Dhanañjaya and the five sensory organs. The fire between kuṇḍalinī and the sun in the navel resides.

बन्धमुद्रा कृता येन नासग्रे तु स्वलोचने। अकारे वह्निरित्याहुरुकारे हृदि संस्थितः॥६९॥

मकारो च भ्रुवोर्मध्यो प्राणशक्त्या प्रबोधयेत्। ब्रह्मग्रन्थिरकारे च विष्णुग्रन्थिर्हृदि स्थितः॥७०॥

One should do exercise very first on Bandha and posture. The fire 'A' in both eyes as also in the forepoint of nose, 'U' fire in the heart and 'M' fire in the middle of brows has been stated as existing. The power of breathing should be added therewith. The knot of Brahmā is in Oṁ forepoint of nose and eyes and the knot of Lord Viṣṇu exist in the heart.

रुद्रग्रन्थिर्भ्रुवोर्मध्ये भिद्यतेऽक्षरवायुना। अकारे संस्थितो ब्रह्मा उकारे विष्णुरास्थित:।।७१।।

मकारे संस्थितो रुद्रस्ततोऽस्यान्त: परात्पर:। कण्ठं संकुच्य नाड्यादौ स्तम्भिते येन शक्तित:।।७२।।

रसना पीड्यमानेयं षोडशी वोर्ध्वगामिनी। त्रिकूटं त्रिविधा चैव गोलाखं निखरं तथा।।७३।।

त्रिशङ्खवज्रमोंकारमूर्ध्वनालं भ्रुवोर्मुखम्। कुण्डलीं चालयन्प्राणन्भेदयन्शशिमण्डलम्।।७४।।

The knot of Rudra exists in the middle of eyebrows. These trio-knots are penetrated by the wind of letter (knowledge of Haṁsa). The place of Brahmā in 'A', place of Viṣṇu in 'U' and place of Rudra in 'M' has been stated. Then there is the place for parātpara Brahma. One should shrink the throat (do the Jālandhara Bandha) and stun the power of kuṇḍalinī. Subsequently, the orbit of moon should be penetrated by giving dynamicity to the breathing and the power of kuṇḍalinī that moves towards brows as also by pressing the tongue and carrying the power of Kuṇḍalinī to push the wind through to Trikuṭa (the adjunction of Iḍā, Piṅgalā and Suṣumnā nerves). The Suṣumnā nerve is most micro and it enters into Brahmarandhra. Then the air should be pushed through Triśaṅkha (that gobbles up the pleasure sorrow and the pleasure as also the sorrow jointly, Vajra non-penetrable by the person who is not yogi, and the power of Kuṇḍalinī that bears the sound of Oṁ.

साधयन्वज्रकुम्भानि नव द्वाराणि बन्धयेत्। सुमन: पवनारूढ: सरागो निर्गुणस्तथा।।७५।।

One should do exercise on Vajra Kumbhaka (the Ujjāyī, Śitalī etc. Prāṇāyāma) after closing the nine doors of the senses. He should keep his mind happy and try to gain expertise on Prāṇāyāma even in a simple state of mind.

ब्रह्मस्थाने तु नाद: स्याच्छंकिन्यमृतवर्षिणी। षट्चक्रमण्डलोद्धारं ज्ञानदीपं प्रकाशयेत्।।७६।।

As a result of this concentration, a sound is heard in the place of Brahma and the Śaṅkhinī nerve start pouring nectar as also the lamp of knowledge by penetration of the orbit of six discus, the knowledge lamp starts lighted.

सर्वभूतस्थितं देवं सर्वेशं नित्यमर्चयेत्। आत्मरूपं तमालोक्य ज्ञानरूपं निरामयम्।।७७।।

One should always do the worship of the supreme god who is enshrining within all creatures. He is in the form of soul and knowledge as also he is free from ailments.

दृश्यन्तं दिव्यरूपेण सर्वव्यापी निरञ्जन:। हंस हंस वदेद्वाक्यं प्राणिनां देहमाश्रित:। स प्राणापानयोर्ग्रन्थिरजपेत्यभिधीयते।।७८।।

सहस्रमेकं द्व्ययतं षट्शतं चैव सर्वदा। उच्चरन्पठितो हंस: सोऽहमित्यभिधीयते।।७९।।

One should do constant Japa of Haṁsa by perceiving the divine form of that omnipresent god within it. The gland of Prāṇa and Apāna as existed in the body of living-organisms is stated as Ajapa Japa. It converts into So'haṁ by reciting it twenty-one thousand six hundred times daily.

पर्वभागे ह्यधोलिङ्गं शिखिन्यां चैव पश्चिमम्। ज्योतिर्लिङ्गं भ्रुवोर्मध्ये नित्यं ध्यायेत्सदा यतिः॥८०॥

The ascetic should do concentration on Jyotirliṅga existed of braid, Adholiṅga in front of Kuṇḍalinī.

अच्युतोऽहमचिन्त्योऽहमतर्क्योऽहमजोऽस्म्यहम्। अव्रणोऽहमकायोऽहमनङ्गोऽस्म्यभयोऽस्म्यहम्॥८१॥

I am Acyuta. I am beyond imagination. I am beyond the extent of logic, I am unborn, I am hale and hearty, I am without body, I am without parts of the body and in a fearless state.

अशब्दोऽहमरूपोऽहमस्पर्शोऽस्म्यहमद्वयः। अरसोऽहमगन्धोऽहमनादिरमृतोऽस्म्यहम्॥८२॥

I am without words, without complexion, beyond touch and duality. I am without essence, odour and I am the form of nectar beyond birth.

अक्षयोऽहमलिङ्गोऽहमजरोऽस्म्यकलोऽस्म्यहम्। अप्राणोऽहममूकोऽहमचिन्त्योऽस्म्यकृतोऽस्म्यहम्॥८३॥

I am non-decaying, without genital, free from the impact of old age and artless. I am in the form of speech and without creating, beyond imagination and I am without action.

अन्तर्याम्यहमग्राह्योऽनिर्देश्योऽहमलक्षणः। अगोत्रोऽहमगात्रोऽहमचक्षुष्कोऽस्म्यवागहम्॥८४॥

I am intuitive, untouched, without direction and the characteristic. I am without the clan, gotra and the body. I am without eyes and the speech.

अदृश्योऽहमवर्णोऽहमखण्डोऽस्म्यहमद्भुतः। अश्रुतोऽहमदृष्टोऽहमन्वेष्टव्योऽमरोऽस्म्यहम्॥८५॥

I am invisible, colourless, integrated and excellent, I am unheard, unseen, untraced and immortal.

अवायुरप्यनाकाशोऽतेजस्कोऽव्यभिचार्यहम्। अमतोऽहमजातोऽहमतिसक्ष्मोऽविकार्यहम्॥८६॥

I am without wind, without the element of ether, without splendour, without infringement of law, untraceable, unborn, most micro and without defects.

अरजस्कोऽतमस्कोऽहमसत्त्वोऽस्म्यगुणोऽस्म्यहम्। अमायोऽनुभवात्माहमनन्योऽविषयोऽस्म्यहम्॥८७॥

I am without the property either of Sattva, Rajas and Tamas, I am beyond the virtues, illusion and I am in the form of perceiving and an exclusive and without the subject.

अद्वैतोऽहमपूर्णोऽहमबाह्योऽहमनन्तरः। अश्रोत्रोऽहमलेपोऽहमकर्तास्म्यहमद्वयः॥८८॥

I am non dual, I am perfect, I am neither in nor out. I am nor without ears, I am tiny, I am inexpressible and without ailments.

अद्वयानन्दविज्ञानघनोऽस्म्यहमविक्रियः। अनिच्छोऽहमलेपोऽहमकर्तास्म्यहमद्वयः॥८९॥

I am non-dual, pleasure, supreme conscience and without defects. I am without desires, non-involved, inactive and non-dual.

अविद्याकार्यहीनोऽहमवाङ्मनसगोचरः। अनल्पोऽहमशोकोऽहमविकल्पोऽस्म्यविज्वलन्॥९०॥

I am without the work performed in illusion, I am beyond the approach of mind and the speech. I am extreme without agony, option and without any peculiar fire.

आदिमध्यान्तहीनोऽहमाकाशसदृशोऽस्म्यहम्। आत्मचैतन्यरूपोऽहममहमानन्दचिद्धन:॥९१॥

I am without beginning, middle and the last. I am alike the ether. I am in the form of sensitive soul and like the supreme sensitivity of pleasure.

आनन्दामृतरूपोऽहमात्मसंस्थोऽहमन्तर:। आत्मकामोऽहमकाशात्परमात्मेश्वरोऽस्म्यहम्॥९२॥

I am in the form of pleasure, nectar and I reside in the soul. I myself is within the inner soul of all living-organisms. I am desirous of soul and I myself is the supreme Iśvara in the form of supreme soul mare extended than ether.

ईशानोऽस्म्यहमीड्योऽहमहमुत्तमपूरुष:। उत्कृष्टोऽहमुपद्रष्टाऽहमुत्तरतरोऽस्म्यहम्॥९३॥

I am Iśāna, I am adorable, I am the best person. I am the supreme, the witness and much more than the extent of the term 'beyond'.

केवलोऽहंकवि: कर्माध्यक्षोऽहं करणाधिप:। गुहाशयोऽहं गोप्ताहं चक्षुषश्चक्षुरस्म्यहम्॥९४॥

I am exclusive, a poet and the administrator of the activities. I am the cause for the causes viz. the supreme Lord. I am the confidential intention, the confident and I am an eye to the eyes.

चिदानन्दोऽस्म्यहं चेता चिद्धनश्चिन्मयोऽरस्म्यहम्। ज्योतिर्मयोऽस्म्यहं ज्यायाज्ज्योतिषां ज्योतिरस्म्यहम्॥९५॥

I am in extreme pleasure. I give inspiration. I am in the form of supreme soul and the best state of mind. I am illuminated with the light and I am the best flame among the flames.

तमस: साक्ष्यहं तुर्यतुर्योऽहं तमस: पर:। दिव्यो देवोस्मि दुर्दर्शो दृष्टाध्यायो ध्रुवोऽस्म्यहम्॥९६॥

I am in the form of witness to the darkness. I am Turya of Turya and beyond the darkness. I am in the form of divine god as also the pole star (everlasting to the eyes and I am able to see most specific).

नित्योऽहं निरवद्योऽहं निष्क्रियोऽस्मि निरञ्जन:। निर्मलो निर्विकल्पोऽहं निराख्यातोऽस्मि निश्चल:॥९७॥

I am immortal, without defects, inactive and omniscient. I am pure, exclusive, beyond the speech and undeviated.

निर्विकारो नित्यपूतो निर्गुणो निस्पृहोऽस्म्यहम्। निरिन्द्रियो नियन्ताऽहं निरपेक्षोऽस्मि निष्कल:॥९८॥

I am without defect, always in purity, free from the clutches of property and free from envy. I am without the senses, I am regulator. I am extreme and artless.

पुरुष: परमात्माहं पुराण: परमोऽस्म्यहम्। परावरोऽस्म्यहं प्राज्ञ: प्रपञ्चोपशमोऽस्म्यहम्॥९९॥

I am the man of supreme soul, the supreme ocean of knowledge and able to compound the illusion mixed conscious.

परामृतोऽस्म्यहं पूर्णः प्रभुरस्मि पुरातनः। पूर्णानन्दैकबोधोऽहं प्रत्यगेकरसोऽस्म्यहम्॥१००॥

I am beyond the nectar and sovereign god. I am the perfect pleasure, a symbol of knowledge, the soul and always alone.

प्रज्ञातोऽहं प्रशान्तोऽहं प्रकाशः परमेश्वरः। एकधा चिन्त्यमानोऽहं द्वैताद्वैतविलक्षणः॥१०१॥

I am of master conscious, I am patient and I myself the supreme Lord in garb of light. I am only worth to concentrate and meditate absolutely different from the characteristics of duality and non-duality.

बुद्धोऽहं भूतपालोऽहं भारूपो भगवानहम्। महादेवो महानस्मि महाज्ञेयो महेश्वरः॥१०२॥

I am wisdom and I am nourisher of all living-organisms. I too am the god in the form of lights. I am Mahādeva, the great conscious and the great Maheśvara too.

विमुक्तोऽहं विभुरहं वरेण्यो व्यापकोऽस्म्यहम्। वैश्वानरो वासुदेवो विश्वतश्चक्षुरस्म्यहम्॥१०३॥

I am sovereign, literate, adorable and omnipresent. I am the best Vaiśvānara and Vāsudeva. I am in the form of an eye to this entire universe.

विश्वाधिकोऽहं विशदो विष्णुर्विश्वकृदस्म्यहम्।
शुद्धोऽस्मि शुक्रः शान्तोऽस्मि शाश्वतोऽस्मि शिवोऽस्म्यहम्॥१०४॥

I am more than the universe. I am the ever-extended Lord Viṣṇu who creates this universe. I am pure, patient, peace-loving, prosperous, everlasting and Śiva too.

सर्वभूतान्तरात्माहमहमस्मि सनातनः। अहं सकृद्विभातोऽस्मि स्वे महिम्नि सदा स्थितः॥१०५॥

I am the innermost soul of all living-organisms. I am everlasting and evergreen. I am always illuminated by establishing myself in the magnificience.

सर्वान्तरः स्वयंज्योतिः सर्वाधिपतिरस्म्यहम्। सर्वभूताधिवासोऽहं सर्वव्यापी स्वराडहम्॥१०६॥

I am in the form of flame to the heart of all living-organisms and thus master to them. All creatures reside within me and I am omnipresent as also the king to all.

समस्तसाक्षी सर्वात्मा सर्वभूतगुहाशयः। सर्वेन्द्रियगुणाभासः सर्वेन्द्रियविवर्जितः॥१०७॥

I am witness to all, universal soul, the confidential intention of the living-organism, the illuminator qualities of sensory organs and without all sensory organs.

स्थानत्रयव्यतीतोऽहं सर्वानुग्राहकोऽस्म्यहम्। सच्चिदानन्दपूर्णात्मा सर्वप्रेमास्पदोऽस्म्यहम्॥१०८॥

I am beyond the three stages i.e. awaking, dreaming and odbmance. I do mercy on all. I am perfect soul and a truth, mind and the pleasure. I love to all and all love to me.

सच्चिदानन्दमात्रोऽहं स्वप्रकाशोऽस्मि चिद्घनः। सत्त्वस्वरूपसन्मात्रसिद्धसर्वात्मकोऽस्म्यहम्॥१०९॥

I am only the true pleasure and in the form of dense sensitivity luminating automatically. I am in the form of truth. The Siddha (all perfect) and a soul to all.

सर्वाधिष्ठानसन्मात्रः सर्वबन्धहरोऽस्म्यहम्। सर्वग्रासोऽस्म्यहं सर्वद्रष्टा सर्वानुभूरहम्।।११०।।

एव यो वेद तत्त्वेन स वै पुरुष उच्यते इत्युपनिषत्।।

I am in the form of perceiving (observing), destroying, literating and true from base for all living-organisms. The knower of this element only is called Puruṣa. Thus Upaniṣad has been concluded.

ॐ सह नाववतु.......... इति शान्तिः।।

।।इति ब्रह्मविद्योपनिषत्समाप्ता।।

***

40. YOGATATTVA-UPANIṢAD

योगतत्त्वोपनिषद्

॥शान्तिपाठः॥

ॐ सह नाववतु.......... इति शान्तिः॥

योगतत्त्वं प्रवक्ष्यामि योगिनां हितकाम्यया। यच्छ्रुत्वा च पठित्वा च सर्वपापैः प्रमुच्यते॥ १॥
विष्णुर्नाम महायोगी महाभूतो महातपाः। तत्त्वमार्गे यथा दीपो दृश्यते पुरुषोत्तमः॥ २॥
तमाराध्य जगन्नाथं प्रणिपत्य पितामहः। पप्रच्छ योगतत्त्वं मे ब्रूहि चाष्टाङ्गसंयुतम्॥ ३॥
तमुवाच हृषीकेशो वक्ष्यामि श‍ृणु तत्त्वतः। सर्वे जीवाः सुखैर्दुःखैर्मायाजालेन वेष्टिताः॥ ४॥
तेषां मुक्तिकरं मार्गं मायाजालनिकृन्तनम्। जन्ममृत्युजरा व्याधिनाशनं मृत्युतारकम्॥ ५॥
नानामार्गैस्तु दुष्प्रापं कैवल्यं परमं पदम्। पतिताः शास्त्रजालेषु प्रज्ञया तेन मोहिताः॥ ६॥
अनिर्वाच्यं पदं वक्तुं न शक्यं तैः सुरैरपि। स्वात्मप्रकाशरूपं तत्किं शास्त्रेण प्रकाश्यते॥ ७॥
निष्कलं निर्मलं शान्तं सर्वातीतं निरामयम्। तदेव जीवरूपेण पुण्यपापफलैर्वृतम्॥ ८॥
परमात्मपदं नित्यं तत्कथं जीवतां गतम्। सर्वभावपदातीतं ज्ञानरूपं निरञ्जनम्॥ ९॥
वारिवत्स्फुरितं तस्मिंस्तत्राहंकृतिरुत्थिता। पञ्चात्मकमभूत्पिण्डं धातुबद्धं गुणात्मकम्॥ १०॥
सुखदुःखैः समायुक्तं जीवभावनया कुरु। तेन जीवाभिधा प्रोक्ता विशुद्धैः परमात्मनि॥ ११॥
कामक्रोधभयं चापि मोहलोभमदो रजः। जन्म मृत्युश्च कार्पण्यं शोकस्तन्द्रा क्षुधा तृषा॥ १२॥
तृष्णा लज्जा भयं दुःखं विषादो हर्ष एव च। एभिर्दोषैर्विनिर्मुक्तः स जीवः केवलो मतः॥ १३॥

I shall now describe yoga-tattva (yoga-truth) for the benefit of yogins who are freed from all sins through the hearing and the studying of it. The supreme Puruṣa called Viṣṇu, who is the great yogin, the great being the great tapasvin, is seen as a lamp in the path of the truth. The Grandfather (Brahmā) having saluted the Lord of the universe (Viṣṇu) and having paid Him due respects, askẹd Him (thus) : "Please, explain to us the truth of yoga which includes in it the eight subservients." To which Hṛṣīkeśa (the Lord Viṣṇu) replied thus : "Listen. I shall explain its truth. All souls are immersed in happiness and sorrow through the snare of māyā. Kaivalya, the supreme seat, is the path which gives them emancipation, which rends asunder the snare of māyā, which is the destroyer of birth, old age disease and which enables one to overcome death. There are no other paths to salvation. Those who go round the net of Śāstras are deluded by that knowledge. It is impossible even for the Devas to describe that indescribable state. How can that which is self-shining be illuminated by the Śāstras ? That only which is without parts and stains and which is quiescent beyond all the free from decay becomes the jīva (self) on account of the results of past virtues and sins. How did that which is the seat of paramātmā, is eternal, and above the state of all existing things and is of the form of wisdom and without stains attain the state of jīva? A bubble arose in it as in water and in this (bubble) arose ahaṁkāra. To it arose a ball (of body) made of the five (elements) and bound by dhātus. Know that to be jīva which is associated with happiness and misery and hence is the term jīva applied to Paramātmā which is pure. That jīva is considered to be the kevala (alone) which is freed from the stains of passion, anger, fear, delusion, greed, pride, lust, birth, death, miserliness, swoon, giddiness, hunger, thirst, ambition, shame, fright, heart-burning, grief and gladness.

तस्माद्दोषविनाशार्थमुपायं कथयामि ते। योगहीनं कथं ज्ञानं मोक्षदं भवति ध्रुवम्॥ १४॥
योगो हि ज्ञानहीनस्तु न क्षमो मोक्षकर्मणि। तस्माज्ज्ञानं च योगं च मुमुक्षुर्दृढमभ्यसेत्॥ १५॥
अज्ञानादेव संसारो ज्ञानादेव विमुच्यते। ज्ञानस्वरूपमेवादौ ज्ञानं ज्ञेयैकसाधनम्॥ १६॥
ज्ञातं येन निजं रूपं कैवल्यं परमं पदम्। निष्कलं निर्मलं साक्षात्सच्चिदानन्दरूपकम्॥ १७॥
उत्पत्तिस्थितिसंहारस्फूर्तिज्ञानविवर्जितम्। एतज्ज्ञानमिति प्रोक्तमथ योगं ब्रवीमि ते॥ १८॥
योगो हि बहुधा ब्रह्मन्भिद्यते व्यवहारतः। मन्त्रयोगो लयश्चैव हठोऽसौ राजयोगतः॥ १९॥
आरम्भश्च घटश्चैव तथा परिचयः स्मृतः। निष्पत्तिश्चेत्यवस्था च सर्वत्र परिकीर्तिता॥ २०॥

So I shall tell you the means of destroying (these) sins. How could jñāna capable of giving mokṣa arise certainly without yoga? And even yoga becomes powerless in (securing) mokṣa when it is devoid of jñāna. So the aspirant after emancipation should practise (firmly) both yoga and jñāna. The cycle of births and deaths come only through ajñāna and perishes only through jñāna. Jñāna along was originally. It should be known as the only means (of salvation). That is jñāna through which one cognises (in himself) the real nature of kaivalya as the supreme seat, the stainless, the partless, and of the nature of Saccidānanda without birth, existence and death and without motion and jñāna.

Now I shall proceed to describe yoga to you. Yoga is divided into many kinds on account of its actions : (viz.,) Mantrayoga, Layayoga, Haṭhayoga, and Rājayoga. There are four states common to all these : (viz.,) Ārambha, Ghaṭa, Paricaya, and Niṣpatti.

एतेषां लक्षणं ब्रह्मन्वक्ष्ये शृणु समासतः। मातृकादियुतं मन्त्रं द्वादशाब्दं तु यो जपेत्॥ २१॥
क्रमेण लभते ज्ञानमणिमादिगुणान्वितम्। अल्पबुद्धिरिमं योगं सेवते साधकाधमः॥ २२॥
लययोगश्चित्तलयः कोटिशः परिकीर्तितः। गच्छंस्तिष्ठन्स्वपन्भुञ्जन्ध्यायेन्निष्कलमीश्वरम्॥ २३॥
स एव लययोगः स्याद्धठयोगमतः शृणु। यमश्च नियमश्चैव आसनं प्राणसंयमः॥ २४॥
प्रत्याहारो धारणा च ध्यानं भ्रूमध्यमे हरिम्। समाधिः समतावस्था साष्टाङ्गो योग उच्यते॥ २५॥
महामुद्रा महाबन्धो महावेधश्च खेचरी। जालंधरोड्डियाणश्च मूलबन्धस्तथैव च॥ २६॥

दीर्घप्रणवसंधानं सिद्धान्तश्रवणं परम्। वज्रोली चामरोली च सहजोली त्रिधा मता॥ २७॥
एतेषां लक्षणं ब्रह्मन्प्रत्येकं शृणु तत्त्वत:। लघ्वाहारो यमेष्वेको मुख्यो भवति नेतर:॥ २८॥
अहिंसा नियमेष्वेका मुख्या वै चतुरानन। सिद्धं पद्मं तथा सिंहं भद्रं चेति चतुष्टयम्॥ २९॥
प्रथमाभ्यासकाले तु विघ्ना: स्युश्चतुरानन। आलस्यं कत्थनं धूर्तगोष्ठी मन्त्रादिसाधनम्॥ ३०॥
धातुस्त्रीलौल्यकादीनि मृगतृष्णामयानि वै। ज्ञात्वा सुधीस्त्यजेत्सर्वान् विघ्नान्पुण्यप्रभावत:॥ ३१॥

O Brahman, I shall describe these to you. Listen attentively. One should practise the Mantra along with its mātrikās (proper intonations of the sounds) and others for a period of twelve years; then he gradually obtains wisdom along with the siddhis, (such as) aṇimā etc. Persons of weak intellect who are the least qualified for yoga practise this. The (second) Laya-yoga tends towards the absorption of the citta and is described in myriads of ways; (one of which is)— one should contemplate upon the Lord who is without parts (even) while walking, sitting, sleeping, or eating. This is called Laya-yoga. Now hear (the description of) Haṭha-yoga. This yoga is said to possess (the following) eight subservients, yama (forbearance), niyama (religious observance), āsana (posture), prāṇāyāma (suppression of breath), pratyāhāra (sub-jugation of the senses), dhāraṇā (concentration), dhyāna, the contemplation on Hari in the middle of the eyebrows and samādhi that is the state of equality. Mahāmudrā, Mahābandha and Khecarī, Jālandhara, Uddiyāṇa, and Mūla-bandha, uttering without intermission Praṇava (Oṁ) for a long time, and hearing the exposition of the supreme truths, Vajrolī, Amarolī and Sahajolī, which from a triad— all these separately I shall give a true description of. O four-faced one (Brahmā), among (the duties of) yama moderate eating— and not others— forms the principal factor; and non-injury is most important in niyama. (The chief postures are) four (viz.,) Siddha, Padma, Siṁha, and Bhadra. During the early stages of practice, the following obstacles take place, O four-faced one, (viz.,) laziness, idle talk, association with bad characters, acquisition of mantras, etc., playing with metals (alchemy) and woman, etc., the mirage. A wise man having found out these should abandon them by the force of his virtues.

प्राणायामं तत: कुर्यात्पद्मासनगत: स्वयम्। सुशोभनं मठं कुर्यात्सूक्ष्मद्वारं तु निर्व्रणम्॥ ३२॥
सुष्ठु लिप्तं गोमयेन सुधया वा प्रयत्नत:। मत्कुणैर्मशकैर्लूतैर्वर्जितं च प्रयत्नत:॥ ३३॥
दिने दिने च संमृष्टं संमार्जन्या विशेषत:। वासितं च सुगन्धेन धूपितं गुग्गुलादिभि:॥ ३४॥
नात्युच्छ्रितं नातिनीचं चैलाजिनकुशोत्तरम्। तत्रोपविश्य मेधावी पद्मासनसमन्वित:॥ ३५॥
ऋजुकाय: प्राञ्जलिश्च प्रणमेदिष्टदेवताम्। ततो दक्षिणहस्तस्य अङ्गुष्ठेनैव पिङ्गलाम्॥ ३६॥
निरुध्य पूरयेद्वायुमिडया तु शनै: शनै:। यथाशक्त्यविरोधेन तत: कुर्याच्च कुम्भकम्॥ ३७॥
पुनस्त्यजेत्पिङ्गलया शनैरेव न वेगत:। पुन: पिङ्गलयापूर्य पूरयेदुदरं शनै:॥ ३८॥
धारयित्वा यथाशक्ति रेचयेदिडया शनै:। यया त्यजेत्तयापूर्य धारयेदविरोधत:॥ ३९॥

जानु प्रदक्षिणीकृत्य न द्रुतं न विलम्बितम्। अङ्गुलिस्फोटनं कुर्यात्सा मात्रा परिगीयते॥४०॥
इडया वायुमारोप्य शनैः षोडशमात्रया। कुम्भयेत्पूरितं पश्चाच्चतुःषष्ट्या तु मात्रया॥४१॥
रेचयेत्पिङ्गलानाड्या द्वात्रिंशन्मात्रया पुनः। पुनः पिङ्गलयापूर्य पूर्ववत्सुसमाहितः॥४२॥
प्रातर्मध्यंदिने सायमर्धरात्रे च कुम्भकान्। शनैरशीतिपर्यन्तं चतुर्वारं समभ्यसेत्॥४३॥

Then assuming Padma posture, he should practise prāṇāyāma. He should erect a beautiful monastery with a very small opening and with no crevices. It should be well pasted with cow-dung or with white coment. It should be carefully freed from dugs, mosquitoes and lice. It should be swept well every day with a broom. It should be perfumed with good odours; and fragrant resins should burn in it. Having taken his seat neither too high nor too low on a cloth, deerskin and kuśa grass spread, one over the other, the wise man should assume the Padma posture and keeping his body erect and his hands folded in respect, should salute his deity. Then closing the right nostril with his right thumb, he should gradually draw in the air through the left nostril. Having restrained it as long as possible, he should again expel it through the right nostril, he should retain it as long as he can and then expel it through the left nostril drawing the air through the nostril by which he expels, he should continue this in uninterrupted succession. The time taken in making a round of the knee with the palm of the hand, neither very slowly nor very rapidly, and snapping the fingers once is called a mātrā. Drawing the air through the left nostril for about sixteen mātrās and having retained it (within) for about sixty-four mātrās one should expel it again through the right nostril for about thirty-two mātrās. Again fill the right nostril as before (and continue the rest). Practise cessation of breath four times daily (viz.,) at sunrise, noon, sunset and midnight, till eighty (times are reached).

एवं मासत्रयाभ्यासान्नाडीशुद्धिस्ततो भवेत्। यदा तु नाडीशुद्धिः स्यात्तदा चिह्नानि बाह्यतः॥४४॥
जायन्ते योगिनो देहे तानि वक्ष्याम्यशेषतः। शरीरलघुता दीप्तिर्जाठराग्निविवर्धनम्॥४५॥
कृशत्वं च शरीरस्य तदा जायेत निश्चितम्। योगविघ्नकराहारं वर्जयेद्योगवित्तमः॥४६॥
लवणं सर्षपं चाम्लमुष्णं रूक्षं च तीक्ष्णकम्। शाकजातं रामठादि वह्निस्त्रीपथसेवनम्॥४७॥
प्रातः स्नानोपवासादिकायक्लेशांश्च वर्जयेत्। अभ्यासकाले प्रथमं शस्तं क्षीराज्यभोजनम्॥४८॥
गोधूममुद्गशाल्यन्नं योगवृद्धिकरं विदुः। ततः परं यथेष्टं तु शक्तः स्याद्वायुधारणे॥४९॥
यथेष्टधारणाद्वायोः सिध्येत्केवलकुम्भकः। केवले कुम्भके सिद्धे रेचपूरविवर्जिते॥५०॥

By a continual practice for about three months, the purification of the nādis takes place. When the nādis have become purified, certain external signs appear on the body of the yogin. I shall proceed to describe them. (They are) lightness of the body, brilliancy of complexion, increase of the gastric fire, leanness of the body, and along with these, absence of restlessness in the body. The proficient in yoga should abandon the food detriental to the practice of yoga. He should give up salt, mustard, things sour, hot, pungent, or bitter, vegetables, asafoetida, etc., worship of fire, woman, walking, bathing at sunrise, emaciation of the body by fasts, etc. During the early stages of practice, food of milk and ghee is ordained; also food consisting of wheat, green pulse and red rice are said to favour the progress. Then he will be able to retain his breath as long as he like. By thus retaining the breath as long as he likes, kevala kumbhaka (cessation of breath without inspiration and expiration) is attained. When kevala kumbhaka is attained by one, and thus expiration and inspiration are dispensed with, there is nothing unattainable in the three worlds to him. In the commencement (of his practice), sweat is given out; he should wipe it off.

न तस्य दुर्लभं किंचित्त्रिषु लोकेषु विद्यते। प्रस्वेदो जायते पूर्वं मर्दनं तेन कारयेत्॥५१॥
ततोऽपि धारणाद्वायोः क्रमेणैव शनैः शनैः। कम्पो भवति देहस्य आसनस्थस्य देहिनः॥५२॥
ततोऽधिकतराभ्यासाद्दार्दुरी स्वेन जायते। यथा च दर्दुरो भाव उत्प्लुत्योत्प्लुत्य गच्छति॥५३॥
पद्मासनस्थितो योगी तथा गच्छति भूतले। ततोऽधिक तराभ्यासाद्भूमित्यागश्च जायते॥५४॥
पद्मासनस्थ एवासौ भूमिमुत्सृज्य वर्तते। अतिमानुषचेष्टादि तथा सामर्थ्यमुद्भवेत्॥५५॥
न दर्शयेच्च सामर्थ्यं दर्शनं वीर्यवत्तरम्। स्वल्पं वा बहुधा दुःखं योगी न व्यथते तदा॥५६॥
अल्पमूत्रपुरीषश्च स्वल्पनिद्रश्च जायते। कीलवो दूषिका लाला स्वेददुर्गन्धताननेे॥५७॥
एतानि सर्वथा तस्य न जायन्ते ततः परम्। ततोऽधिकतराभ्यासाद्बलमुत्पद्यते बहु॥५८॥
येन भूचरसिद्धिः स्याद्भूचराणां जये क्षमः। व्याघ्रो वा शरभो वापि गजो गवय एव वा॥५९॥
सिंहो वा योगिना तेन म्रियन्ते हस्तताडिताः। कन्दर्पस्य यथा रूपं तथा स्यादपि योगिनः॥६०॥

Even after that, owing to the retaining of the breath, the person practising it gets phlegm. Then by increased practice of dhāraṇā, sweat arises. As a frog moves by leaps, so the yogin sitting in the Padma posture moves on the earth. With a (further) increased practice, he is able to rise from the ground. He, while seated in Padma posture, levitates. There arises to him the power to perform extraordinary feats. He does (or should) not disclose to others his feats of great powers (in the path). Any pain, small or great, does not affect the yogin. Then excretions and sleep are diminished, tears, dirty water in the eye, salivary flow, sweat and bad smell in the mouth do not arise in him. With a still further practisce, he acquires great strength by which he attains Bhūcara siddhi, which enables him to bring under his control all the creatures that tread this earth; tigers, śarabhas, elephants, wild bulls or lions, die on being struck by the palm of the yogin. He becomes as beautiful as the god of love himself.

तद्रूपवशगा नार्यः काङ्क्षन्ते तस्य सङ्गमम्। यदि सङ्गं करोत्येष तस्य बिन्दुक्षयो भवेत्॥६१॥
वर्जयित्वा स्त्रियाः सङ्गं कुर्यादभ्यासमादरात्। योगिनोऽङ्गे सुगन्धश्च जायते बिन्दुधारणात्॥६२॥
ततो रहस्युपाविष्टः प्रणवं प्लुतमात्रया। जपेत्पूर्वार्जितानां तु पापानां नाशहेतवे॥६३॥
सर्वविघ्नहरो मन्त्रः प्रणवः सर्वदोषहा। एवमभ्यासयोगेन सिद्धिरारम्भसंभवा॥६४॥

All female beings taken up with the beauty of his person will desire of have intercourse with him. If he so keeps connection, his virility will be lost; so abandoning all copulation with women, he should continue his practice with no lust. By the preservation of the semen, a good odour pervades the body of the yogin. Then sitting in a secluded place, he should repeat Praṇava (Oṁ) with there pluta-mātrās (or prolonged intonation) for the destruction of his former sins. The mantra, Praṇava (Oṁ) destroys all obstacles and all sins. By practising thus he attains the ārambha (beginning or first) state.

ततो भवेद्धटावस्था पवनाभ्यासतत्परा। प्राणोऽपानो मनो बुद्धिर्जीवात्मपरमात्मनोः॥६५॥

अन्योन्यस्याविरोधेन एकता घटते यदा। घटावस्थेति सा प्रोक्ता तच्चिह्नानि ब्रवीम्यहम्॥६६॥

पूर्वं यः कथितोऽभ्यासश्चतुर्थांशं परिग्रहेत्। दिवा वा यदि वा सायं याममात्रं समभ्यसेत्॥६७॥

एकवारं प्रतिदिनं कुर्यात्केवलकुम्भकम्। इन्द्रियाणीन्द्रियार्थेभ्यो यत्प्रत्याहरणं स्फुटम्॥६८॥

योगी कुम्भकमास्थाय प्रत्याहारः स उच्यते। यद्यत्पश्यति चक्षुर्भ्यां तत्तदात्मेति भावयेत्।६९॥

यद्यच्छृणोति कर्णाभ्यां तत्तदात्मेति भावयेत्। लभते नासया यद्यत्तत्तदात्मेति भावयेत्॥७०॥

जिह्वया यद्रसं ह्यत्ति तत्तदात्मेति भावयेत्। त्वचा यद्यत्स्पृशेद्योगी तत्तदात्मेति भावयेत्॥७१॥

Then follows the ghaṭa (second state)— one which is acquired by constantly practising suppresion of breath. When a perfect union takes place between prāṇa and apāna, manas and buddhi, or jīvātmā and Paramātmā without opposition, it is called the ghaṭa state. I shall describe its signs. He may now practice only for about one-fourth of the period prescribed for practice before. By day and evening let him practise only of a yāma (3 hours). Let him practise kevala kumbhaka once a day. Drawing away completely the organs from the objects of sense during cessation of breath is called pratyāhāra. Whatever he sees with his eyes, let him consider as Ātmā. Whatever he hears with his ears, let him consider as Ātmā. Whatever he smells with his nose let him consider as Ātmā. Whatever he tastes with his tongue let him consider as Ātmā. Whatever the yogin touches with his skin let him consider as Ātmā.

एवं ज्ञानेन्द्रियाणां तु तत्तदात्मनि धारयेत्। याममात्रं प्रतिदिनं योगी यत्नादतन्द्रितः॥७२॥

यथा वा चित्तसामर्थ्यं जायते योगिनो ध्रुवम्। दूरश्रुतिर्दूरदृष्टिः क्षणाद्दूरागमस्तथा॥७३॥

वाक्सिद्धिः कामरूपत्वमदृश्यकरणी तथा। मलमूत्रप्रलेपेन लोहादेः स्वर्णता भवेत्॥७४॥

The yogin should thus gratify his organs of sense for a period of one yāma every day with great effort. Then various wonderful powers are attained by the yogin, such as clairveyance, clairvoyance, clairaudience, ability to transport himself to great distances within a moment, great power of speech, ability to take any form, ability to become invisible and the transmutation of iron into gold when the former is smearted over with his excretion.

खे गतिस्तस्य जायेत संतताभ्यासयोगतः। सदा बुद्धिमता भाव्यं योगिना योगसिद्धये॥७५॥

एते विघ्ना महासिद्धेर्न रमेत्तेषु बुद्धिमान्। न दर्शयेत्स्वसामर्थ्यं यस्य कस्यापि योगिराट्॥ ७६॥
यथा मूढो यथा मूर्खो यथा बधिर एव वा। तथा वर्तेत लोकस्य स्वसामर्थ्यस्य गुप्तये॥ ७७॥
शिष्याश्च स्वस्वकार्येषु प्रार्थयन्ति न संशयः। तत्तत्कर्मकरव्यग्रः स्वाभ्यासेऽविस्मृतो भवेत्॥ ७८॥
सर्वव्यापारमुत्सृज्य योगनिष्ठो भवेद्यतिः। अविस्मृत्य गुरोर्वाक्यमभ्यसेत्तदहर्निशम्॥ ७९॥
एवं भवेद्धटावस्था संतताभ्यासयोगतः। अनभ्यासवतश्चैव वृथागोष्ठ्या न सिद्ध्यति॥ ८०॥
तस्मात्सर्वप्रयत्नेन योगमेव सदाभ्यसेत्। ततः परिचयावस्था जायतेऽभ्यासयोगतः॥ ८१॥

That yogin who is constantly practising yoga attains the power to levitate. Then should the wise yogin think that these powers are great obstacles to the attainment of yoga, and so he should never take delight in them. The king of yogins should not exercise his powers before any person whatsoever. He should live in the world as a fool, an idiot, or a deaf man, in order to keep his powers concealed. His disciples would, without doubt, request him to show his powers for the gratification of their own desires. One who is actively engaged in one's duties forgets to practise (yoga); so he should practise day and night yoga without forgetting the words of the Guru. Thus passes the ghaṭa state to one who is constantly engaged in yoga practice. To one nothing is gained by useless company, since thereby he does not practise yoga. So one should with great effort practise yoga. Then by this constant practice is gained the paricaya state (the third state).

वायुः परिचितो यत्नादग्निना सह कुण्डलीम्। भावयित्वा सुषुम्नायां प्रविशेदनिरोधतः॥ ८२॥
वायुना सह चित्तं च प्रविशेच्च महापथम्। यस्य चित्तं स्वपवनं सुषुम्नां प्रविशेदिह॥ ८३॥

Vāyu (or breath) through arduous practice pierces along with agni the Kuṇḍalinī thought and enters the Suṣumnā uninterrupted. When one's citta enters Suṣumnā along with prāṇa, it reaches the high seat (of the head) along with prāṇa.

भूमिरापोऽनलो वायुराकाशश्चेति पञ्चकः। येषु पञ्चसु देवानां धारणा पञ्चधोच्यते॥ ८४॥
पादादिजानुपर्यन्तं पृथिवीस्थानमुच्यते। पृथिवी चतुरस्रं च पीतवर्णं लवर्णकम्॥ ८५॥
पार्थिवे वायुमारोप्य लकारेण समन्वितम्। ध्यायंश्चतुर्भुजाकारं चतुर्वक्त्रं हिरण्मयम्॥ ८६॥
धारयेत्पञ्च घटिकाः पृथिवीजयमाप्नुयात्। पृथिवीयोगतो मृत्युर्न भवेदस्य योगिनः॥ ८७॥
आजानोः पायुपर्यन्तमपां स्थानं प्रकीर्तितम्। आपोऽर्धचन्द्रं शुक्लं च वंबीजं परिकीर्तितम्॥ ८८॥
वारुणे वायुमारोप्य वकारेण समन्वितम्। स्मरन्नारायणं देवं चतुर्बाहुं किरीटिनम्॥ ८९॥
शुद्धस्फटिकसंकाशं पीतवाससमच्युतम्। धारयेत्पञ्च घटिकाः सर्वपापैः प्रमुच्यते॥ ९०॥

"There are the five elements (viz.,) Pṛthivī, āpas, agni, vāyu and ākāśa. To the body of the five elements, there is the fivefold dhāraṇā. From the feet to the knees is said to be the region of pṛthivī, is four-sided in shape, is yellow in colour and has the varṇa (or letter) La. Carrying the breath with the letter La along the region of earth (viz., from the foot to the knees) and contemplating upon Brahmā with four faces and four mouths and of golden colour, one should perform dhāraṇā there for a period of two hours. He then attains mastery over the earth. Death does not trouble him, since he has obtained mastery over the earth element. The region of āpas is said to extend from the knees to the anus. Āpas is semi-lunar in shape and white in colour and has Va for its bīja (seed) letter. Carrying up the breath, with the letter Va along the region of āpas, he should contemplate on the God Nārāyaṇa having four arms and a crowned head, as being of the colour of pure crystal, as dressed in orange clothes and as decayless; and practising dhāraṇā there for a period of two hours, he is freed from all sins.

ततो जलाद्भयं नास्ति जले मृत्युर्न विद्यते। आपायोर्हृदयान्तं च वह्निस्थानं प्रकीर्तितम्॥ ९१॥
वह्निस्त्रिकोणं रक्तं च रेफाक्षरसमुद्भवम्। वह्नौ चानिलमारोप्य रेफाक्षरसमुज्ज्वलम्॥ ९२॥
त्रियक्षं वरदं रुद्रं तरुणादित्यसंनिभम्। भस्मोद्धूलितसर्वाङ्गं सुप्रसन्नमनुस्मरन्॥ ९३॥
धारयेत्पञ्च घटिका वह्निनासौ न दाह्यते। न दह्यते शरीरं च प्रविष्टस्याग्निमण्डले॥ ९४॥
आहृदयाद्भ्रुवोर्मध्यं वायुस्थानं प्रकीर्तितम्। वायुःषट्कोणकं कृष्णं यकाराक्षरभासुरम्॥ ९५॥
मारुतं मरुतां स्थाने यकाराक्षरभासुरम्। धारयेत्तत्र सर्वज्ञमीश्वरं विश्वतोमुखम्॥ ९६॥
धारयेत्पञ्च घटिका वायुवद्व्योमगो भवेत्। मरणं न तु वायोश्च भयं भवति योगिनः॥ ९७॥

Then there is no fear for him from water, and he does not meet his death in water. From the anus to the heart is said to be the region of agni. Agni is triangular in shape, of red colour, and has the letter Ra for its (bīja) seed. Raising the breath made resplendent through the letter Ra along the region of fire, he should contemplate on Rudra, who has three eyes, who grants all wishes, who is of the colour of the midday sun, who is smeared all over with holy ashes and who is of a pleased contenance. Practising dhāraṇā there for a period of two hours, he is not burnt by fire even though his body enters the fire-pit. From the heart to the middle of the eyebrows is said to be the region of vāyu. Vāyu is hexangular in shape, black in colour and shines with the letter Ya. Carrying the breath along the region of vāyu, he should contemplate on Īśvara, the Omniscient, as possessing faces on all sides; and practising dhāraṇā there for two hours, he enters vāyu and then ākāśa. The yogin does not meet his death through the fear of vāyu.

आभ्रूमध्यात्तु मूर्धान्तमाकाशस्थानमुच्यते। व्योम वृत्तं च धूम्रं च हकाराक्षरभासुरम्॥ ९८॥
आकाशे वायुमारोप्य हकारोपरि शंकरम्। बिन्दुरूपं महादेवं व्योमाकारं सदाशिवम्॥ ९९॥
शुद्धस्फटिकसंकाशं धृतबालेन्दुमौलिनम्। पञ्चवक्त्रयुतं सौम्यं दशबाहुं त्रिलोचनम्॥ १००॥
सर्वायुधैर्धृताकारं सर्वभूषणभूषितम्। उमार्धदेहं वरदं सर्वकारणकारणम्॥ १०१॥
आकाशधारणात्तस्य खेचरत्वं भवेद्ध्रुवम्। यत्र कुत्र स्थितो वापि सुखमत्यन्तमश्नुते॥ १०२॥
एवं च धारणाः पञ्च कुर्याद्योगी विचक्षणः। ततो दृढशरीरः स्यान्मृत्युस्तस्य न विद्यते॥ १०३॥
ब्रह्मणः प्रलयेनापि न सीदति महामतिः।

From the centre of the eyebrows to the top of the head is said to be the region of ākāśa, is circular in shape, smoky in colour and shining with the letter Ha. Rising the breath along the region of ākāśa, he should contemplate on Sadāśiva in the following manner, as producing happiness, as of the shape of bindu, as the great deva, as have the shape of ākāśa, as shining like pure crystal, as wearing the rising crescent of moon on his head, as having five faces, ten heads and three eyes, as being of a pleased countenance, as armed with all weapons, as adorned with all ornaments, as having Umā (the goddess) in one-half of his body, as ready to grant favours, and as the cause of all the causes. By practising dhāraṇā in the region of ākāśa, he obtains certainly the power of levitating in the ākāśa (ether). Wherever he stays, he enjoys supreme bliss. The proficient in yoga should practise these five dhāraṇās. Then his body becomes strong and he does not know death. That great-minded man does not die even during the deluge of Brahma.

समभ्यसेत्तथा ध्यानं घटिकाषष्टिमेव च। वायुं निरुध्य चाकाशे देवतामिष्टदामिति॥ १०४॥

सगुणं ध्यानमेतत्स्यादणिमादिगुणप्रदम्। निर्गुणध्यानयुक्तस्य समाधिश्च ततो भवेत्॥ १०५॥

दिनद्वादशकेनैव समाधिं समवाप्नुयात्। वायुं निरुध्य मेधावी जीवन्मुक्तो भवत्ययम्॥ १०६॥

समाधिः समतावस्था जीवात्मपरमात्मनोः। यदि स्वदेहमुत्स्रष्टुमिच्छा चेदुत्सृजेत्स्वयम्॥ १०७॥

परब्रह्मणि लीयेत न तस्योत्क्रान्तिरिष्यते। अथ नो चेत्समुत्स्रष्टुं स्वशरीरं प्रियं यदि॥ १०८॥

सर्वलोकेषु विहरन्नणिमादिगुणान्वितः। कदाचित्स्वेच्छया देवो भूत्वा स्वर्गे महीयते॥ १०९॥

मनुष्यो वापि यक्षो वा स्वेच्छयापि क्षणाद्भवेत्।

सिंहो व्याघ्रो गजो वाश्वः स्वेच्छया बहुतामियात्॥ ११०॥

यथेष्टमेव वर्तेत यद्वा योगी महेश्वरः। अभ्यासभेदतो भेदः फलं तु सममेव हि॥ १११॥

Then he should practise dhāraṇā for a period of six ghaṭakās (two hours, 24 minutes). Restraining the breath in (the region of) ākāśa and contemplating on the deity who grants his wishes— this is said to be saguṇa dhyāna capable of giving (the siddhis), aṇimā, etc. One who is engaged in nirguṇa dhyāna attains the stage of samādhi. Within twelve days at least, he attains the stage of samādhi. Restraining his breath, the wise one becomes an emancipated person. Samādhi is that state in which the jīvātmā (lower self) and the Paramātmā (higher self) are differenceless (or of equal state). If he desires to lay aside his body, he can do so. He will become absorbed in Parabrahman and does not require utkrānti (going out or up). But if he does not so desire, and if his body is dear to him, he lives in all the worlds possessing the siddhis of aṇimā, etc. Sometimes he becomes a deva and lives honoured in svarga; or he becomes a man or an yakṣa through his will. He can also take the form of a lion, tiger, elephant, or horse through his own will. The yogin becoming the great Lord can live as long as he likes. There is difference only in the modes of procedure but the result is the same.

पार्ष्णिं वामस्य पादस्य योनिस्थाने नियोजयेत्। प्रसार्य दक्षिणं पादं हस्ताभ्यां धारयेद्दृढम्॥ ११२॥
चुबुकं हृदि विन्यस्य पूरयेद्वायुना पुनः। कुम्भकेन यथाशक्ति धारयित्वा तु रेचयेत्॥ ११३॥
वामाङ्गेन समभ्यस्य दक्षाङ्गेन ततोऽभ्यसेत्। प्रसारितस्तु यः पादस्तमूरूपरि नामयेत्॥ ११४॥
अयमेव महाबन्ध उभयत्रैवमभ्यसेत्। महाबन्धस्थितो योगी कृत्वा पूरकमेकधीः॥ ११५॥
वायुना गतिमावृत्य निभृतं कण्ठमुद्रया। पुटद्वयं समाक्रम्य वायुः स्फुरति सत्वरम्॥ ११६॥
अयमेव महावेधः सिद्धैरभ्यस्यतेऽनिशम्। अन्तःकपालकुहरे जिह्वां व्यावृत्य धारयेत्॥ ११७॥
भ्रूमध्यदृष्टिरप्येषा मुद्रा भवति खेचरी। कण्ठमाकु ञ्च्य हृदये स्थापयेद्दृढया धिया॥ ११८॥
बन्धो जालंधराख्योऽयं मृत्युमातङ्गकेसरी। बन्धो येन सुषुम्नायां प्राणस्तूड्डीयते यतः॥ ११९॥
उड्यानाख्यो हि बन्धोऽयं योगिभिः समुदाहृतः।

Place the left heel pressed on the anus, stretch the right leg and hold it firmly with both hands, Place the head on the breast and inhale the air slowly. Restrain the breath as long as you can and then slowly breathe out. After practising it with the left foot, practise it with the right. Place the foot that was stretched before on the thigh. This is mahābandha and should be practised on both sides. The yogin sitting in mahābandha and having inhaled the air with intent mind, should stop the course of vāyu (inside) by means of the throat-mudrā, and occupying the two sides (of the throat) with speed. This is called mahāvedha and is frequently practised by the siddhas. With the tongue thrust into the interior cavity of the head (or throat) and with the eyes intent on the spot between the eyebrows, this is called khecarīmudrā. Contracting the muscles of the neck and placing the head with a firm on the breast, this is called the jālandhara (bandha) and is a lion to the elephant of death. That bandha by which prāṇa flies through Suṣumnā is called uddiyāṇabandha by the yogins.

पार्ष्णिभागेन संपीड्य योनिमाकुञ्चयेद्दृढम्॥ १२०॥
अपानमूर्ध्वमुत्थाप्य योनिबन्धोऽयमुच्यते। प्राणापानौ नादबिन्दू मूलबन्धेन चैकताम्॥ १२१॥
गत्वा योगस्य संसिद्धिं यच्छतो नात्र संशयः। करणी विपरीताख्या सर्वव्याधिविनाशिनी॥ १२२॥
नित्यमभ्यासयुक्तस्य जाठराग्निविवर्धनी। आहारो बहुलस्तस्य संपाद्यः साधकस्य च॥ १२३॥
अल्पाहारो यदि भवेदग्निर्देहं हरेत्क्षणात्।

Pressing the heel firmly against the anus, contracting the anus and drawing up the apāna, this is said to be yonibandha. Through mūlabandha, prāṇa and apāna as well as nāda and bindu are united and gives success in yoga : there is no doubt about this. To one practising in a reversed manner (or on both sides) which destroyes all diseases, the gastric fire is increased. Therefore a practitioner should collect a large quantity of provisions, (for) if he takes a small quantity of food, the fire (within) will consume his body in a moment.

अधः शिरश्चोर्ध्वपादः क्षणं स्यात्प्रथमे दिने॥ १२४॥
क्षणाच्च किंचिदधिकमभ्यसेत्तु दिनेदिने। वली च पलितं चैव षण्मासार्धान्न दृश्यते॥ १२५॥

याममात्रं तु यो नित्यमभ्यसेत्स तु कालजित्। वज्रोलीमभ्यसेद्यस्तु स योगी सिद्धिभाजनम्॥ १२६॥
लभ्यते यदि तस्यैव योगसिद्धिः करे स्थिता। अतीतानागतं वेत्ति खेचरी च भवेद्ध्रुवम्॥ १२७॥
अमरीं यः पिबेन्नित्यं नस्यं कुर्वन्दिने दिने। वज्रोलीमभ्यसेन्नित्यममरोलीति कथ्यते॥ १२८॥
ततो भवेद्राजयोगो नान्तरा भवति ध्रुवम्। यदा तु राजयोगेन निष्पन्ना योगिभिः क्रियाः॥ १२९॥
तदा विवेकवैराग्यं जायते योगिनो ध्रुवम्। विष्णुर्नाम महायोगी महाभूतो महातपाः॥ १३०॥
तत्त्वमार्गे यथा दीपो दृश्यते पुरुषोत्तमः।

On the first day, he should stand on his head with the feet raised up for a moment. He should increase this period gradually every day. Wrinkles and greyness of hair will disappear within three months. He who practises only for a period of a yama (twenty-four minutes) every day conquers time. He who practises vajrolī becomes a yogin and the respository of all siddhis. If the yoga siddhis are ever to be attained, he only has them within his reach. He knows the past and the future and certainly moves in the air. He who drinks of the nectar thus is rendered immortal day by day. He should daily practise vajrolī. Then it is called amarolī. Then he obtains the rājayoga and certainly he does not meet with obstacles. When a yogin fulfils his action by rājayoga, then he certainly obtain discrimination and indifference to objects. Viṣṇu, the great yogin, the grand one of great austerities and the most excellent Puruṣa is seen as a lamp in the path of truth.

यः स्तनः पूर्वपीतस्तं निष्पीड्य मुदमश्नुते॥ १३१॥
यस्माज्जातो भगात्पूर्वं तस्मिन्नेव भगे रमन्। या माता सा पुनर्भार्या या भार्या मातरेव हि॥ १३२॥
यः पिता स पुनः पुत्रो यः पुत्रः स पुनः पिता। एवं संसारचक्रेण कूपचक्रे घटा इव॥ १३३॥
भ्रमन्तो योनिजन्मानि श्रुत्वा लोकान्समश्नुते। त्रयो लोकास्त्रयो वेदास्तिस्रः संध्यास्त्रयः स्वराः॥ १३४॥
त्रयोऽग्नयश्च त्रिगुणाः स्थिताः सर्वे त्रयाक्षरे। त्रयाणामक्षराणां च योऽधीतेऽप्यर्धमक्षरम्॥ १३५॥
तेन सर्वमिदं प्रोतं तत्सत्यं तत्परं पदम्। पुष्पमध्ये यथा गन्धः पयोमध्ये यथा घृतम्॥ १३६॥
तिलमध्ये यथा तैलं पाषाणेष्विव काञ्चनम्। हृदि स्थाने स्थितं पद्मं तस्य वक्त्रमधोमुखम्॥ १३७॥
ऊर्ध्वनालमधोबिन्दुस्तस्य मध्ये स्थितं मनः। अकारे रेचितं पद्ममुकारेणैव भिद्यते॥ १३८॥
मकारे लभते नादमर्धमात्रा तु निश्चला। शुद्धस्फटिकसंकाशं निष्कलं पापनाशनम्॥ १३९॥
लभते योगयुक्तात्मा पुरुषस्तत्परं पदम्।

That breast from which one sucked before (in his previous birth) he now presses (in love) and obtains pleasure. He enjoys the same genital organ from which he was born before. She who was once his mother will now be wife and she who is now wife is (or will be) verily mother. He who is now father will be again son, and he who is now son will be again father. Thus are the egos of this world wandering in the womb of birth and death like a bucket in the wheel of a well and enjoying the worlds. There are the three worlds, three vadas, three sandhyās, (morning, noon and evening), three svaras (sounds), three agnis, and guṇas, and all these are placed in the three letters (Oṁ). He who understands that which is indestructible and is the meaning of the three (Oṁ)— by him are all these worlds strung. This is the Turth, the supreme seat. As the smell in the flower, as the ghee in the milk, as the oil in the gingelly seed and as the gold in the quartz, so is the lotus situated in the heart. Its face is downwards and its stem upwards. Its bindu is downwards and in its centre is situated manas. By the letter A, the lotus becomes expanded; by the letter U, it becomes split (or opened), by the latter M, it obtains nāda; and the ardhamātrā (half-metre) is silence. The person engaged in yoga obtains the supreme seat, which is like a pure crystal, which is without parts and which destroys all sins.

कूर्मः स्वपाणिपादादिशिरश्चात्मनि धारयेत्।। १४०।।
एवं द्वारेषु सर्वेषु वायुपूरितरेचितः। निषिद्धं तु नवद्वारे ऊर्ध्वं प्राङ्निःश्वसस्तथा।। १४१।।
घटमध्ये यथा दीपो निवातं कुम्भकं विदुः। निषिद्धैर्नवभिद्वारैर्निर्जने निरुपद्रवे।।
निश्चितं त्वात्ममात्रेणावशिष्टं योगसेवयेत्युपनिषत्।। १४२।।

As a tortoise draws its hand and head within itself, so drawing in air thus and expelling it through the nine holes of the body, he breathes upwards and forwards, like a lamp in an air-tight jar which is motionless, so that which is seen motionless through the process of yoga in the heart and which is free from turmoil, after having been drawn from the nine holes, is said to be Ātmā alone.

ॐ सह नाववतु............ इति शान्तिः।।

।।इति योगतत्त्वोपनिषत्समाप्ता।।

***

41. ĀTMABODHA- UPANIṢAD

आत्मबोधोपनिषद्

॥शान्तिपाठः॥

ॐ वाङ्मे मनसि प्रतिष्ठिता मनो मे वाचि प्रतिष्ठितमाविरावीर्य एधि। वेदस्य म आणीस्थः श्रुतं मे मा प्रहासीरनेनाधीते नाहोरात्रान्संदधाम्यृतं वदिष्यामि सत्यं वदिष्यामि। तन्मामवतु तद्वक्तारमवतु अवतु मामवतु वक्तारमवतु वक्तारम्॥

ॐ शान्तिः शान्तिः शान्तिः॥

॥प्रथमोऽध्यायः॥

ॐ प्रत्यगानन्दं ब्रह्मपुरुषं प्रणवस्वरूपं अकार उकारो मकार इति त्र्यक्षरं प्रणवं तदेतदोमिति। यमुक्त्वा मुच्यते योगी जन्मसंसारबन्धनात्। ॐ नमो नारायणाय शङ्खचक्रगदाधराय तस्मात् ॐ नमो नारायणायेति मंत्रोपासको वैकुण्ठभुवनं गमिष्यति॥ १॥

Oṁ. Prostrations of Nārāyaṇa wearing conch, discus, and mace, by whom the Yogī is released from the bondage of the cycle of rebirth through the utterance of Him who is of the form of Praṇava, the Oṁ, composed of the three letters A, U, and M, who is the uniform bliss and who is the Brahmapuruṣa (all-pervading Puruṣa). Oṁ. Therefore the reciter of the Mantra "Oṁ-namo-Nārāyaṇāya" reaches the Vaikuṇṭha world.

अथ यदिदं ब्रह्मपुरं पुण्डरीकं तस्मात्तडिदाभमात्रं दीपवत्प्रकाशम्॥ २॥

ब्रह्मण्यो देवकीपुत्रो ब्रह्मण्यो मधुसूदनः। ब्रह्मण्यः पुण्डरीकाक्षो ब्रह्मण्यो विष्णुरच्युतः॥ ३॥

सर्वभूतस्थमेकं नारायणं कारणपुरुषमकारणं परं ब्रह्मोम्॥ ४॥

शोकमोहविनिर्मुक्तो विष्णुं ध्यायन्न सीदति। द्वैताद्वैतमभयं भवति मृत्योः स मृत्युमाप्नोति य इह नानेव पश्यति॥ ५॥

It is the heart-Kamala (lotus), viz., the city of Brahman. It is effulgent like lightning, shining like a lamp. It is Brahmaṇya (the presider over the city of Brahman) that is the son of Devakī. It is Brahmaṇya that is Madhusūdana (the killer of Madhu). It is Brahmaṇya that is Puṇḍarīkākṣa (lotus-eyed). It is Brahmaṇya, Viṣṇu that is acyuta (the indestructible). He who meditates upon that sole Nārāyaṇa, who is latent in all beings, who is the causal Puruṣa, who is causeless, who is Parabrahman, the Oṁ, who is without pains and delusion and who is all-pervading— that person is never subject to pains. From the dual, he becomes the fearless non-dual. Whoever sees this (world) as manifold (with the difference of I, you, he, etc.), passes from death to death.

हृत्पद्ममध्ये सर्वं यत्तत्प्रज्ञाने प्रतिष्ठितम्। प्रज्ञानेत्रो लोकः प्रज्ञा प्रतिष्ठा प्रज्ञानं ब्रह्म॥ ६॥

स एतेन प्रज्ञेनात्मनास्माल्लोकादुत्क्रम्यामुष्मिन्स्वर्गे लोके सर्वान्कामानाप्त्वाऽमृतः समभवदमृतः समभवत्॥ ७॥

यत्र ज्योतिरजस्रं यस्मिंल्लोकेऽभ्यर्हितं तस्मिन्मां देहि स्वमानमृते लोके अक्षते अच्युते लोके अक्षते अमृतत्वं च गच्छत्यों नमः॥ ८॥

In the centre of the heart-lotus is Brahman, which is the All, which has Prājña as Its eye and which is established in Prajñāna alone. To creatures, Pranjñāna is the eye and Prājña is the seat. It is Prajñāna alone that is Brahman. A person who meditates (thus), leaves this world through Prajñāna, the Ātmā and ascending attains all his desires in the Supreme Svarga deathless. Oh! I pray You, place me in that nectar-everflowing unfailing world where Jyotis (the light) always shines and where one is revered. (There is no doubt) he attains nectar also. Oṁ-namaḥ.

॥द्वितीयोऽध्यायः॥

प्रगलितनिजमायोऽहं निस्तुलदृशिरूपवस्तुमात्रोऽहम्।
अस्तमिताहंतोऽहं प्रगलितजगदीशजीवभेदोऽहम्॥ १॥
प्रत्यगभिन्नपरोऽहं विध्वस्ताशेषविधिनिषेधोऽहम्।
समुदस्ताश्रमितोऽहं प्रविततसुखपूर्णसंविदेवाहम्॥ २॥
साक्ष्यनपेक्षोऽहं निजमहिम्नि संस्थोऽहमचलोऽहम्। अजरोऽहमव्ययोऽहं पक्षविपक्षादिभेदविधुरोऽहम्॥ ३॥
अवबोधैकरसोऽहं मोक्षानन्दैकसिन्धुरेवाहम्। सूक्ष्मोऽहमक्षरोऽहं विगलितगुणजालकेवलात्माहम्॥ ४॥
निस्त्रैगुण्यपदोऽहं कुक्षिस्थानेकलोककलनोऽहम्। कूटस्थचेतनोऽहं निष्क्रियधामाहमप्रतर्क्योऽहम्॥ ५॥
एकोऽहमविकलोऽहं निर्मलनिर्वाणमूर्तिरेवाहम्। निरवयवोऽहमजोऽहं केवलसन्मात्रसारभूतोऽहम्॥ ६॥
निरवधिनिजबोधोऽहं शुभतरभावोऽहमप्रभेद्योऽहम्।
विभुरहमनवद्योऽहं निरवधिनिःसीमतत्त्वमात्रोऽहम्॥ ७॥
वेद्योऽहमागमान्तैराराध्यः सकलभुवनहृद्योऽहम्। परमानन्दघनोऽहं परमानन्दैकभूमरूपोऽहम्॥ ८॥
शुद्धोऽहमद्वयोऽहं संततभावोऽहमादिशून्योऽहम्। शमितान्तत्रितयोऽहं बद्धो मुक्तोऽहमद्भुतात्माहम्॥ ९॥
शुद्धोऽहमान्तरोऽहं शाश्वतविज्ञानसमरसात्माहम्। शोधितपरतत्त्वोऽहं बोधानन्दैकमूर्तिरेवाहम्॥ १०॥
विवेकयुक्तिबुद्ध्याहं जानाम्यात्मानमद्वयम्। तथापि बन्धमोक्षादिव्यवहारः प्रतीयते॥ ११॥

I am without Māyā. I am without compare. I am solely the thing that is of the nature of wisdom. I am without Ahaṁkāra (I-am-ness). I am without the difference of the universe, Jīva and Īśvara. I am the Supreme that is not different from Pratyagātmā (individual (Ātmā). I am with ordinances and prohibitions destroyed without remainder. I am with Āśramas (observances of life) well given up. I am of the nature of the vast and all-full wisdom. I am one that is witness and without desire. I reside in My glory alone. I am without motion. I am without old age— without destruction— without the differences of My party or another. I have wisdom as chief essence. I am the mere ocean of bliss called salvation. I am the subtle. I am without change. I am Ātmā merely, without the illusion of qualities. I am the Seat devoid of the three Guṇas. I am the cause of the many worlds in (My) stomach. I am the Kūṭastha-Caitanya (supreme Cosmic mind). I am of the form of the Jyotis (light) free from motion. I am not one that can be known by inference. I alone am full. I am of the form of the stainless salvation. I am without limbs or birth. I am the essence which is Sat itself. I am of the nature of the true wisdom without limit. I am the state of excellent happiness. I am One that cannot be differentiated. I am the all-pervading and without stain. I am the limitless and endless Sattva alone. I am fit to be known through Vedānta. I am the one fit to be worshipped. I am the heart of all the worlds. I am replete with Supreme Bliss. I am of the nature of happiness, which is Supreme Bliss. I am pure, secondless, and eternal. I am devoid of beginning. I am free from the three bodies (gross, subtle, and causal). I am of the nature of wisdom. I am the emancipated One. I have a wondrous form. I am free from impurity. I am the One latent (in all). I am the equal Ātmā of eternal Vijñāna. I am the refined Supreme Truth. I am of the nature of Wisdom-Bliss alone. Through I cognize as the secondless Ātmā by means of discriminative wisdom and reason, yet is found the relation between bondage and salvation.

निवृत्तोऽपि प्रपञ्चो मे सत्यवद्भाति सर्वदा। सर्पादौ रज्जुसत्तेव ब्रह्मसत्तैव केवलम्।। १२।।
प्रपञ्चाधाररूपेण वर्ततेऽतो जगन्न हि। यथेक्षुरससंव्याप्ता शर्करा वर्तते तथा।। १३।।
अद्वयब्रह्मरूपेण व्याप्तोऽहं वै जगत्त्रयम्। ब्रह्मादिकीटपर्यन्ताः प्राणिनो मयि कल्पिताः।। १४।।
बुद्बुदादिविकारान्तस्तरङ्गः सागरे यथा। तरङ्गस्थं द्रवं सिन्धुर्न वाञ्छति यथा तथा।। १५।।
विषयानन्दवाञ्छा मे मा भूदानन्दरूपतः। दारिद्र्याशा यथा नास्ति संपन्नस्य तथा मम।। १६।।
ब्रह्मानन्दे निमग्नस्य विषयाशा न तद्भवेत्। विषं दृष्ट्वाऽमृतं दृष्ट्वा विषं त्यजति बुद्धिमान्।। १७।।
आत्मानमपि दृष्ट्वाहमनात्मानं त्यजाम्यहम्! घटावभासको भानुर्घटनाशे न नश्यति।। १८।।
देहावभासकः साक्षी देहनाशे न नश्यति।

Though to Me the universe is gone, yet it shines as true always. Like the truth in the (illusory conception of a) snake, etc., in the rope, so the truth of Brahman alone is, and is the substratum on which this universe is playing. Therefore the universe is not. Just as sugar is found permeating all the sugar-juice (from which the sugar is extracted), so I am full in the three worlds in the form of the non-dual Brahman. Like the bubbles waves, etc., in the ocean, so all beings, from Brahmā down to worm, are fashioned in Me; just as the ocean does not long after the motion of the waves, so to Me, there is no longing after sensual happiness, being Myself of the form of (spiritual) Bliss. Just as in a wealthy person the desire for poverty does not arise, so in Me who am immersed in Brāhmic Bliss, the desire for sensual happiness cannot arise. An intelligent person who sees both nectar and poison rejects poison; so having cognized Ātmā, I reject those that are not Ātmā. The sun that illuminates the pot (both within and without) is not destroyed with the destruction of the pot; so the Sākṣī (witness) that illuminates the body is not destroyed with the destruction of the body.

न मे बन्धो न मे मुक्तिर्न मे शास्त्रं न मे गुरुः॥ १९॥

मायामात्रविकासत्वान्मायातीतोऽहमद्वयः। प्राणाश्चलन्तु तद्धर्मैः कामैर्वा हन्यतां मनः॥ २०॥

आनन्दबुद्धिपूर्णस्य मम दुःखं कथं भवेत्। आत्मानमञ्जसा वेद्मि क्वाप्यज्ञानं पलायितम्॥ २१॥

कर्तृत्वमद्य मे नष्टं कर्तव्यं वापि न क्वचित्। ब्राह्मण्यं कुलगोत्रे च नामसौन्दर्यजातयः॥ २२॥

स्थूलदेहगता एते स्थूलाद्भिन्नस्य मे नहि। क्षुत्पिपासान्ध्यबाधिर्यकामक्रोधादयोऽखिलाः॥ २३॥

लिङ्गदेहगता एते ह्यलिङ्गस्य न सन्ति हि। जडत्वप्रियमोदत्वधर्माः कारणदेहगाः॥ २४॥

न सन्ति मम नित्यस्य निर्विकारस्वरूपिणः। उलूकस्य यथा भानुरन्धकारः प्रतीयते॥ २५॥

स्वप्रकाशे परानन्दे तमो मूढस्य जायते। चतुर्दृष्टिनिरोधेऽभ्रैः सूर्यो नास्तीति मन्यते॥ २६॥

तथाऽज्ञानावृतो देही ब्रह्म नास्तीति मन्यते। यथामृतं विषाद्भिन्नं विषदोषैर्न लिप्यते॥ २७॥

न स्पृशामि जडाद्भिन्नो जडदोषान् प्रकाशतः। स्वल्पापि दीपकणिका बहुलं नाशयेत्तमः॥ २८॥

स्वल्पोऽपि बोधो निबिडं बहुलं नाशयेत्तथा। कालत्रये यथा सर्पो रज्जौ नास्ति तथा मयि॥ २९॥

अहंकारादिदेहान्तं जगन्नास्त्यहमद्वयः। चिद्रूपत्वान्न मे जाड्यं सत्यत्वान्नानृतं मम॥ ३०॥

आनन्दत्वान्न मे दुःखमज्ञानाद्भाति सत्यवत्।

आत्मप्रबोधोपनिषन्मुहूर्तमुपासित्वा न स पुनरावर्तते। न स पुनरावर्तत इत्युपनिषत्॥ ३१॥

To Me there is no bondage; there is no salvation, there are no Śāstra, there is no Guru; for these shine through Māyā and I have crossed them and am secondless. Let Prāṇas (vital airs) according to their laws be fluctuating. Let Manas (mind) be blown about by desire. How can pains affect me who am by nature full of Bliss? I have truly known Ātmā. My Ajñāna has fled away. The egoism of actorship has left Me. There is nothing I should yet do. Brahman's duties, family, Gotra (clan), name, beauty, and class— all these belong to the gross body and not to Me who am without any mark (of body). Inertness, love, and joy— these attributes appertain to causal body and not to Me, who am eternal and of changeless nature. Just as an owl sees darkness only in the sun, so a fool sees only darkness in the self-shining Supreme Bliss. Should the clouds screen the eyesight a fool thinks there is no sun; so an embodied person full of Ajñāna thinks there is no Brahman. Just as nectar which is other than poison does not commingle with it, so I, who am different from inert matter, do not mix with its stains. As the light of a lamp, however small, dispels immense darkness, so wisdom, however slight makes Ajñāna, however immense, to perish. Just as (the delusion) of the serpent does not exist in the rope in all the three periods of time (past, present, and future), so the universe from Ahaṁkāra (down) to body does not exist in Me who am the non-dual One. Being of the nature of consciousness alone, there is not inertness in Me. Being of the nature of Truth, there is not non-truth to me. Being of the nature of Bliss, there is not sorrow in Me. It is through Ajñāna that the universe shines as truth.

Whoever recites this Ātmabodha-Upaniṣad for Muhūrta (48 minutes) is not born again— Yea, is not born again.

ॐ वाङ्मे मनसि.................. इति शान्तिः॥

॥इत्यात्मबोधोपनिषत्समाप्ता॥

***

42. NĀRADA-PARIVRĀJAKA-UPANIṢAD

नारदपरिव्राजकोपनिषद्

॥शान्तिपाठः॥

ॐ भद्रं कर्णेभिः ....इति शान्तिः॥

॥प्रथमोपदेशः॥

अथ कदाचित्परिव्राजकाभरणो नारदः सर्वलोकसंचारं कुर्वन्नपूर्वपुण्यस्थलानि पुण्यतीर्थानि तीर्थीकुर्वन्नवलोक्य चित्तशुद्धिं प्राप्य निर्वैरः शान्तो दान्तः सर्वतो निर्वेदमासाद्य स्वरूपानुसंधानमनुसंधाय नियमानन्दविशेषगण्यं मुनिजनैरुपसंकीर्णं नैमिषारण्यं पुण्यस्थलमवलोक्य सरिगमपधनिससंज्ञैर्वैराग्यबोधकरैः स्वरविशेषैःप्रापञ्चिकपराङ्मुखैर्हरिकथालापैःस्थावरजङ्गमनामकैर्भगवद्भक्तिविशेषैर्नरमृगकिंपुरुषामरकिंनराप्सरोगणान्संमोहयन्नागतं ब्रह्मात्मजं भगवद्भक्तं नारदमवलोक्य द्वादशवर्षसत्रयागोपस्थिताः श्रुताध्ययनसंपन्नाः सर्वज्ञास्तपोनिष्ठापराश्च ज्ञानवैराग्यसंपन्नाः शौनकादिमहर्षयः प्रत्युत्थानं कृत्वा नत्वा यथोचितातिथ्यपूर्वकमुपवेशयित्वा स्वयं सर्वेऽप्युपविष्टा भो भगवन् ब्रह्मपुत्र कथं मुक्त्युपायोऽस्माकं वक्तव्यम्॥ १॥

Oṁ. Once upon a time, Nārada, the greatest of Parivrājakas (roaming ascetics), after roaming over all worlds and cleansing, through merely by looking at the places of pilgrimage able to impart rare religious merits, observed with a mind that had attained purity, without hate, quiescent and patient, and indifferent towards all (objects), the forest of Naimiṣa (the modern Nimsār), filled with beings that were engaged in the contemplation of Reality and had attained the greatness of the ordained bliss; (there) through the recitation of stories about Hari (Viṣṇu), associated with the musical notes of Sa, Ri, Ga, Ma, Pa, Dha, and Ni (of the gamut), able to impart indifference to objects and to make one look down upon the universe, and instilling divine devotion, fixed and movable (or mental and bodily), he entered (the forest, fascinating the crowds of beings, human, animal, Kimpuruṣas, celestials, Kinnaras, Apsaras and Uragas (collected there). (Thereupon the) great Ṛṣis Śāunaka and others who had been engaged for twelve years in Sattra sacrifice well-skilled in the recitation of Vedas, the knowers of all, and the good practisers of tapas, observed Nārada, the son of Brahmā and the devotee of the Lord, and having risen up, paid due respect to him. Then having with due respect requested him to sit down, they also seated themselves and addressed him thus : "O Lord, son of Brahmā, what is the means of salvation for us? It is desired that it should be communicated (to us)."

इत्युक्तस्तान् स होवाच नारदः सत्कुलभवोपनीतः सम्यगुपनयनपूर्वकं चतुश्चत्वारिंशत्संस्कारसंपन्नः स्वाभिमतैकगुरुसमीपे स्वशाखाध्ययनपूर्वकं सर्वविद्याभ्यासं कृत्वा द्वादशवर्षशुश्रूषापूर्वकं ब्रह्मचर्यं पञ्चविंशतिवत्सरं गार्हस्थ्यं पञ्चविंशतिवत्सरं वानप्रस्थाश्रमं तद्विधिवत्क्रमान्निर्वर्त्य चतुर्विधब्रह्मचर्यं षड्विधं गार्हस्थ्यं चतुर्विधं वानप्रस्थधर्मं सम्यगभ्यस्य तदुचितं कर्म सर्वं निर्वर्त्य साधनचतुष्टयसंपन्नः सर्वसंसारोपरि मनोवाक्कायकर्मभिर्यथाशानिवृत्तस्तथा वासनैषणोपर्यपि निर्वैरः शान्तो दान्तः संन्यासी परमहंसाश्रमेणास्खलितस्वस्वरूपध्यानेन देहत्यागं करोति स मुक्तो भवति स मुक्तो भवतीत्युपनिषत्॥ २॥

Thus addressed, Nārada replied to them thus : "One born in a good family and fit to go through the forty-four saṁskāras, upanayana and others, should, under a teacher to whom he is devoted, study, after the recitation of the Veda of his own śākhā (division), all the different branches of knowledge; then should fulfil, according to the rules ordained, for twelve years the observance of Brahmacarya (celibacy), such as the service of the Guru, etc.; then for twenty-five years the āśrama (order of life) of a gṛhastha (house-holder), and for twenty-five years the āśrama of a vānaprastha (forester). After thus practising well the fourfold celibacy, the sixfold householder's life, and the fourfold forester's life, and having performed all the duties thereof, he should acquire the fourfold means of salvation; thus the sannyāsin who gives up the desires along with the karmas of mind, speech, and body in this saṁsāra as well as the vāsanā (attachment) towards the threefold desire (of son, wife, and wealth), being without malice and endowed with quiescence and patience, undisturbed in the order of life of Paramahaṁsa, quits the body in the contemplation of Reality, is an emancipated person. Such is the Upaniṣad.

॥द्वितीयोपदेशः॥

अथ हैनं भगवन्तं नारदं सर्वे शौनकादयः पप्रच्छुर्भो भगवन् संन्यासविधिं नो ब्रूहीति तानवलोक्य नारदस्तत्स्वरूपं सर्वं पितामहमुखेनैव ज्ञातुमुचितमित्युक्त्वा सत्रयागपूर्त्यनन्तरं तैः सह सत्यलोकं गत्वा विधिवद्ब्रह्मनिष्ठावरं परमेष्ठिनं नत्वा स्तुत्वा यथोचितं तदाज्ञया तैः सहोपविश्य नारदः पितामहमुवाच गुरुस्त्वं जनकस्त्वं सर्वविद्यारहस्यज्ञः सर्वज्ञस्त्वमतो मत्तो मदिष्टं रहस्यमेकं वक्तव्यं त्वद्विना मदभिमतरहस्यं वक्तुं कः समर्थः। किमिति चेत् पारिव्राज्यस्वरूपक्रमं नो ब्रूहीति नारदेन प्रार्थितः परमेष्ठी सर्वतः सर्वानवलोक्य मुहूर्तमात्रं समाधिनिष्ठो भूत्वा संसारार्तिनिवृत्त्यन्वेषण इति निश्चित्य नारदमवलोक्य तमाह पितामहः। पुरा मत्पुत्र पुरुषसूक्तोपनिषद्रहस्यप्रकारं निरतिशयाकारावलम्बिना विराट्पुरुषेणोपदिष्टं रहस्यं ते विविच्योच्यते तत्क्रममतिरहस्यं बाढमवहितो भूत्वा श्रूयताम्।

Upadeśa II

All the Ṛṣis, Śaunaka and others addressing Lord Nārada said thus : "O Lord, please tell us the rules of sannyāsa." At which, seeing them, Nārada replied : "It is but must that we should know the whole truth from the mouth of Brahmā Himself." After the sattra sacrifice was completed, he took the ṛṣis along with him to satyaloka; and after duly making prostrations to and eulogising Brahmā engaged in meditation upon Brahman, he along with others was duly seated under the orders of Brahmā. Then Nārada addressed Brahmā thus : "You are Guru; You are father; You are the knower of the secret of all learning; You are the knower of all; You shall therefore tell me one secret. Who else but You are fit to tell the secret dear unto me. It is this. Please tell us the rules of the real sannyāsa (asceticism).

Thus prayed to by Nārada, Brahmā surveyed all in the four quarters; and after meditating for one muhūrta (48 minutes), and assuring himself that the inquiry was truly for the purpose of escaping from the pain of saṁsāra, Brahmā eyeing Nārada, said thus : "The mystery that was imparted before by Virāṭ-Puruṣa of illimitable form according to the Puruṣa-Sūkta-Upaniṣad is now being divulged to you. It is very mysterious. It is fit to be hearkened to with great attention.

भो नारद विधिवदादावनुपनीतोपनयनानंतरं तत्सत्कुलप्रसूत: पितृमातृविधेय: पितृसमीपादन्यत्र सत्संप्रदायस्थं श्रद्धावन्तं सत्कुलभवं श्रोत्रियं शास्त्रवात्सल्यं गुणवंतमकुटिलं सद्गुरुमासाद्य नत्वा यथोपयोगशुश्रूषापूर्वकं स्वाभिमतं विज्ञाप्य द्वादशवर्षसेवापुर:सरं सर्वविद्याभ्यासं कृत्वा तदनुज्ञया स्वकुलानुरूपामभिमतकन्यां विवाह्य पञ्चविंशतिवत्सरं गुरुकुलवासं कृत्वाथ गुर्वनुज्ञया गृहस्थोचितकर्म कुर्वन्दौर्ब्राह्मण्यनिवृत्तिमेत्य स्ववंशवृद्धिकाम: पुत्रमेकमासाद्य गार्हस्थ्योचितपञ्चविंशतिवत्सरं तीर्त्वा तत: पञ्चविंशतिवत्सरपर्यन्तं त्रिषवणमुदकस्पर्शनपूर्वकं चतुर्थकालमेकवारमाहारमाहरन्नयमेक एव वनस्थो भूत्वा पुरग्रामप्राक्तनसंचारं विहाय निकिर विरहिततदाश्रितकर्मोचितकृत्यं दृष्टश्रवणविषयवैतृष्ण्यमेत्य चत्वारिंशत्संस्कारसंपन्न: सर्वतो विरक्तश्चित्तशुद्धिमेत्याशासूयेर्ष्याहंकारं दग्ध्वा साधनचतुष्टयसंपन्न: संन्यस्तुमर्हतीत्युपनिषत्॥ १॥

O Nārada, one born in a good family and obedient to his parents, should, after the performance of upanayana according to the rules, find a virtuous Guru that is other than his father, is of good custom and habits, of faith, born of good family, a knower of Vedas, a lover of Śāstras, of (good) qualities and free from duplicity. Having made prostrations and rendered useful service to him, he should respectfully acquaint him with his intention. Having studied all departments of knowledge and rendered service for twelve years, he should, under his (the Guru's) orders, marry a girl fit for his family and dear unto him. Then having performed for twenty-five years the karmas incidental to a householder and attained the status of a Brāhmaṇa that has performed sacrifices and the rest, he should beget a son with the only desire of perpetuating the family. After thus spending twenty-five years in the performance of household dharma, he should bathe thrice daily for twenty-five years and take only one meal in the fourth period; he should live alone in the forest, after giving up his previous wanderings in city and village; and without desire for fruit, should perform the karmas incidental to that (forester's) order of life, and be without desire for objects seen and heard. Being skilled in the forty saṁskāras, he should be devoid of desire for all, have a purified mind, have burnt up desire, jealousy, envy and egoism, and have developed the four means of salvation. Then he becomes fit for sannyāsa. Such is the Upaniṣad."

॥तृतीयोपदेश:॥

अथ हैनं नारद: पितामहं पप्रच्छ भगवन् केन संन्यासाधिकारी वेत्येवमादौ संन्यासाधिकारिणं निरूप्य पश्चात्संन्यासविधिरुच्यते अवहित: शृणु। अथ षण्ढ: पतितोऽङ्गविकल: स्त्रैणो बधिरोऽर्भको मूक: पाषण्डश्चक्री लिङ्गी वैखानसहरद्विजौ भृतकाध्यापक: शिपिविष्टोऽनग्निको वैराग्यवन्तोऽप्येते न संन्यासार्हा: संन्यस्ता यद्यपि महावाक्योपदेशेनाधिकारिण: पूर्वसंन्यासी परमहंसाधिकारी॥ १॥

परेणैवात्मनश्चापि परस्यैवात्मना तथा। अभयं समवाप्नोति स परिव्राडिति स्मृति:॥ २॥

Upadeśa III

Then Nārada addressed the grandfather thus :

"O Lord, by whom, after attaining the qualifications of sannyāsa, is it fit to be taken ?" To which Brahmā replied : "After first expounding the qualifications of sannyāsa, the rules of sannyāsa will then be stated. Hearken carefully. A eunuch, the outcaste, the maimed, the lewd, the deaf, the youth, the dumb, the heretic, the discus-bearer, the Liṅga-wearer, the vaikhānasa (forester), the Haradvija (carrier of Śiva's flag), the reciter of Vedas for hire, the bald-headed, one without (sacrificial) fire— all these, even though they have attained vairāgya are unfit for sannyāsa. Even though they have become sannyāsins, they are unfit to be initiated into the mahāvākyas (sacred vedic sentences). The Paramahaṁsa sannyāsin stated before (as fit to take sannyāsa) is the one qualified. It is stated in the smṛtis that he is a parivrāt who is not afraid of others, as others are not afraid of him.

षण्ढोऽथ विकलोऽप्यन्धो बालकश्चापि पातकी। पतितश्च परद्वारी वैखानसहरद्विजौ॥ ३॥

चक्री लिङ्गी च पाषण्डी शिपिविष्टोऽप्यनग्निक:। द्वित्रिवारेण संन्यस्तो भृतकाध्यापकोऽपि च।

एते नार्हन्ति संन्यासमातुरेण विना क्रमम्॥ ४॥

आतुरकाल: कथमार्यसम्मत:। प्राणस्योत्क्रमणासन्नकालस्त्वातुरसंज्ञक:।

नेतरस्त्वातुर: कालो मुक्तिमार्गप्रवर्तक:॥ ५॥

आतुरेऽपि च संन्यासे तत्तन्मन्त्रपुर:सरम्। मन्त्रावृत्तिं च कृत्वैव संन्यसेद्विधिवद्बुध:॥ ६॥

The eunuch, the limbless, the blind, the youth, the sinful, the outcaste, the door-keeper, the vaikhānasa, the Haradvija, the Cakrī (discus-bearer), the Liṅgī (Liṅga-wearer), the heretic, the bald-headed, one without fire (sacrifice), one that had undergone sannyāsa twice or thrice, the reciter of Vedas for hire— all these are not fit for regular sannyāsa but only for ātura-sannyāsa (viz., sannyāsa taken while a person is afflicted, etc.). What is the opinion of āryas (Hindus) on the (fit) time for ātura-sannyāsa (being taken)? The time when prāṇa (life) is about to rise (out of the body) is called ātura. The time other than it is incapable of conferring (upon one) the path of salvation and is not ātura. Even in ātura-sannyāsa, the wise should according to rules, initiate himself into sannyāsa after reciting the mantras again and again in the course of respective mantras.

आतुरेऽपि क्रमे वापि प्रैषभेदो न कुत्रचित्। न मन्त्रं कर्मरहितं कर्म मन्त्रमपेक्षते॥७॥

अकर्म मन्त्ररहितं नातो मन्त्रं परित्यजेत्। मन्त्रं विना कर्म कुर्याद्भस्मन्याहुतिवद्भवेत्॥८॥

विध्युक्तकर्म संक्षेपात्संन्यासस्त्वातुरः स्मृतः।

There is no difference between regular and ātura-sannyāsa in the mantras to be uttered at the time of taking sannyāsa. There is no karma without mantras; (hence) karma needs mantras. Anything done without mantra cannot be termed karma. Hence mantras should not be given up. Any karma done without mantra is like an offering made in ashes. Through the consciseness (of the performance) of the karmas, it is stated to be ātura-sannyāsa.

तस्मादातुरसंन्यासे मन्त्रावृत्तिविधिर्मुने॥९॥

आहिताग्निर्विरक्तश्चेद्देशान्तरगतो यदि। प्राजापत्येष्टिमप्स्वेव निर्वृत्यैवाथ संन्यसेत्॥१०॥

मनसा वाथ विध्युक्तमन्त्रावृत्त्याथ वा जले। श्रुत्यनुष्ठानमार्गेण कर्मानुष्ठानमेव वा।

समाप्य संन्यसेद्विद्वान्नो चेत्पातित्यमाप्नुयात्॥११॥

यदा मनसि संजातं वैतृष्ण्यं सर्ववस्तुषु। तदा संन्यासमिच्छेत पतितः स्याद्विपर्यये॥१२॥

विरक्तः प्रव्रजेद्धीमान्सरक्तस्तु गृहे वसेत्। सरागो नरकं याति प्रव्रजन्हि द्विजाधमः॥१३॥

यस्यैतानि सुगुप्तानि जिह्वोपस्थोदरं करः। संन्यसेदकृतोद्वाहो ब्राह्मणो ब्रह्मचर्यवान्॥१४॥

"Therefore, O Muni, the recitation of mantras is stated to be in ātura-sannyāsa. One who is always duly doing agni-hotra (fire-sacrifice) should, when he quits (the house) for foreign places through indifference, perform the prājāpatya sacrifice in water and then take up sannyāsa. After completing in water the observances of karma through the mind, or the recitation of mantras, the wise man should attain sannyāsa. Else he becomes a fallen man. When, in the mind, indifference to all objects arises, then men should long after sannyāsa, (that being the best time for it); otherwise they are fallen. One who attains vairāgya should take sannyāsa. One who does not, should remain at home. That vile twice-born with desire, should he take sannyāsa, reaches hell. That Brāhmaṇa who is a celibate, who has under control his tongue, sexual organ, stomach, and hand may become a sannyāsin without undergoing the ceremony of marriage.

संसारमेव निःसारं दृष्ट्वा सारदिदृक्षया। प्रव्रजन्त्यकृतोद्वाहः परं वैराग्यमाश्रितः॥१५॥

प्रवृत्तिलक्षणं कर्म ज्ञानं संन्यासलक्षणम्। तस्माज्ज्ञानं पुरस्कृत्य संन्यसेदिह बुद्धिमान्॥१६॥

यदा तु विदितं तत्त्वं परं ब्रह्म सनातनम्। तदैकदण्डं संगृह्य सोपवीतां शिखां त्यजेत्॥१७॥

परमात्मनि यो रक्तो विरक्तोऽपरमात्मनि। सर्वैषणाविनिर्मुक्तः स भैक्षं भोक्तुमर्हति॥१८॥

पूजितो वन्दितश्चैव सुप्रसन्नो यथा भवेत्। तथा चेत्ताड्यमानस्तु तदा भवति भैक्षभुक्॥१९॥

अहमेवाक्षरं ब्रह्म वासुदेवाख्यमद्वयम्। इति भावो ध्रुवो यस्य तदा भवति भैक्षभुक्॥२०॥

यस्मिन्शान्तिः शमः शौचं सत्यं संतोष आर्जवम्। अकिंचनमदम्भश्च स कैवल्याश्रमे वसेत्॥२१॥

यदा न कुरुते भावं सर्वभूतेषु पापकम्। कर्मणा मनसा वाचा तदा भवति भैक्षभुक्॥२२॥

Having known saṁsāra (world) as one without sāra (or essence) and not having undergone any marriage on account of the desire to know the sāra (or essence of God), they become sannyāsins on account of the practice of the supreme vairāgya. The characteristic of Pravṛtti (path) is the performance of karma; that of nivṛtti of jñāna. Therefore placing jñāna in the forefront, the wise man should take up sannyāsa. When the reality of the eternal Parabrahman is understood, then he should take up one daṇḍa (staff) and abandon the holy thread and tuft of hair. Then he becomes fit to eat the alms-food (of sannyāsa), having become devoted to Paramātmā, indifferent to those that are non-Paramātmā and freed from all desires. He becomes fit to be the eater of alms food who peserves the same countenance when he is beaten, as when he is worshipped or prostrated to. He becomes fit to be the eater of alms-food who is of the firm certitude that he is no other than the non-dual and indestructible Brahman, otherwise named Vāsudeva. He in whom are existent śānti (control of the organs), śama (control of mind), purity (of mind and body), satya (truth), santoṣa (contentment), ārjava (straight for wardness), poverty, and non-ostentatiousness should be in the order of life of kaivalya (sannyāsa). When one does not, through actions, mind, or speech, commit any sinful action to any being, then he becomes fit for eating alms-food.

दशलक्षणकं धर्ममनुतिष्ठन्समाहितः। वेदान्तान्विधिवच्छ्रुत्वा संन्यसेदनृणो द्विजः॥ २३॥

धृतिः क्षमा दमोऽस्तेयं शौचमिन्द्रियनिग्रहः। धीर्विद्या सत्यमक्रोधो दशकं धर्मलक्षणम्॥ २४॥

अतीतान्न स्मरेद्भोगान्न तथानागतानपि। प्राप्तांश्च नाभिनन्देद्यः स कैवल्याश्रमे वसेत्॥ २५॥

अन्तःस्थानीन्द्रियाण्यन्तर्बहिष्ठान्विषयान्बहिः। शक्नोति यः सदा कर्तुं स कैवल्याश्रमे वसेत्॥ २६॥

प्राणे गते यथा देहः सुखं दुःखं न विन्दति। तथा चेत्प्राणयुक्तोऽपि स कैवल्याश्रमे वसेत्॥ २७॥

Having become quiescent (through the control of the mind), having practised the ten kinds of dharmas, having, according to rules, studied vedānta, and having paid the three debts (to devas, ṛṣis, and pitṛs), one should take up sannyāsa. Courage, fortitude, the control of the body, honesty, purity of (mind and body), control of the (inner) organs, shame, knowledge, truth, and absence of anger— these ten are the characteristics of dharma. One who does not look back (with pleasure) upon past enjoyments, nor forward into the future, and one who does not rejoice in the present, is fit to become a sannyāsin. One who is able to control within, the inner organs and without, the external organs, may be in the order of life of Kaivalya. One who while in life is not affected by pleasures and pains, as the body is unaffected by them after death, may be in the order of life of Kaivalya.

कौपीनयुगलं कन्था दण्ड एकः परिग्रहः। यतेः परमहंसस्य नाधिकं तु विधीयते॥ २८॥

यदि वा कुरुते रागादधिकस्य परिग्रहम्। रौरवं नरकं गत्वा तिर्यग्योनिषु जायते॥ २९॥

विशीर्णान्यमलान्येव चेलानि ग्रथितानि तु। कृत्वा कन्थां बहिर्वासो धारयेद्धातुरञ्जितम्॥ ३०॥

एकवासा अवासा वा एकदृष्टिरलोलुपः। एक एव चरेन्नित्यं वर्षास्वेकत्र संवसेत्॥ ३१॥

कुटुम्बं पुत्रदारांश्च वेदाङ्गानि च सर्वशः। यज्ञं यज्ञोपवीतं च त्यक्त्वा गूढश्चरेद्यतिः॥ ३२॥
कामः क्रोधस्तथा दर्पो लोभमोहादयश्च ये। तांस्तु दोषान्परित्यज्य परिव्राण्निर्ममो भवेत्॥ ३३॥

"An ascetic of the Paramahaṁsa (order) shall wear two loin-cloths, one ragged cloth, and one staff. Nothing more is ordained (in his case). Should he through desire wear more than these, he will fall into the hell or raurava and be born into the womb of an animal. Having stitched together old and clean cloths into one and having coloured it with red (ochre), he should wear it as his upper cloth. He may be with one cloth or even without it. He should roam about alone with the sole vision (of Brahman), devoid of desires; but he may be in one place alone in the rainy season. Having quite abandoned his family, including son and wife, vedānta, sacrifice, and the sacred thread, the ascetic should wander incognition. Having given up all faults, such as passion, anger, pride, desire, and delusion, he parivrāt (ascetic) should become one that owns nothing.

रागद्वेषवियुक्तात्मा समलोष्टाश्मकाञ्चनः। प्राणिहिंसानिवृत्तश्च मुनिः स्यात्सर्वनिस्पृहः॥ ३४॥
दम्भाहंकारनिर्मुक्तो हिंसापैशुन्यवर्जितः। आत्मज्ञानगुणोपेतो यतिर्मोक्षमवाप्नुयात्॥ ३५॥
इन्द्रियाणां प्रसङ्गेन दोषमृच्छत्यसंशयः। संनियम्य तु तान्येव ततः सिद्धिं निगच्छति॥ ३६॥
न जातु कामः कामानामुपभोगेन शाम्यति। हविषा कृष्णवर्त्मेव भूय एवाभिवर्धते॥ ३७॥
श्रुत्वा स्पृष्ट्वा च भुक्त्वा च दृष्ट्वा घ्रात्वा च यो नरः। न हृष्यति ग्लायति वा स विज्ञेयो जितेन्द्रियः॥
यस्य वाङ्मनसी शुद्धे सम्यग्गुप्ते च सर्वदा। स वै सर्वमवाप्नोति वेदान्तोपगतं फलम्॥ ३९॥

He is a muni who is devoid of love and hate, who regards equally a clod of earth, stone, or gold, who does no injury to any living creature, and is freed from all. That ascetic reaches salvation who is associated with Ātmajñāna, who is freed from ostentation and egoism, from doing injury and tale-bearing. Through attraction to the senses, he becomes subject to fault, there is no doubt : through their control, he gains perfection. Lust when enjoyed is never gratified. Just as fire increases with the oblation (of ghee, etc., poured into it) so also lust waxes strong (with enjoyment). It should be known that that man who does not rejoice or grieve through hearing, touching, eating, seeing, or smelling is a jitendriya (conqueror of the organs). He whose speech and mind are well brought under control attains, completely and always, all the fruits of vedānta.

संमानाद्ब्राह्मणो नित्यमुद्विजेत विषादिव। अमृतस्येव चाकाङ्क्षेदवमानस्य सर्वदा॥ ४०॥
सुखं ह्यवमतः शेते सुखं च प्रतिबुध्यते। सुखं चरति लोकेऽस्मिन्नवमन्ता विनश्यति॥ ४१॥
अतिवादांस्तितिक्षेत नावमन्येत कंचन। न चेमं देहमाश्रित्य वैरं कुर्वीत केनचित्॥ ४२॥
क्रुध्यन्तं न प्रतिक्रुध्येदाक्रुष्टः कुशलं वदेत्। सप्तद्वारावकीर्णां च न वाचमनृतां वदेत्॥ ४३॥
अध्यात्मरतिरासीनो निरपेक्षो निराशिषः। आत्मनैव सहायेन सुखार्थी विचरेदिह॥ ४४॥
इन्द्रियाणां निरोधेन रागद्वेषक्षयेण च। अहिंसया च भूतानाममृतत्वाय कल्पते॥ ४५॥

अस्थिस्थूणं स्नायुबद्धं मांसशोणितलेपितम्। चर्मावबद्धं दुर्गन्धि पूर्णं मूत्रपुरीषयोः॥४६॥

जराशोकसमाविष्टं रोगायतनमातुरम्। रजस्वलमनित्यं च भूतावासमिमं त्यजेत्॥४७॥

मांसासृक्पूयविण्मूत्रस्नायुमज्जास्थिसंहतौ। देहे चेत्प्रीतिमान्मूढो भविता नरकेऽपि सः॥४८॥

सा कालपुत्रपदवी सा महावीचिवागुरा। सासिपत्रवनश्रेणी या देहेऽहमिति स्थितिः॥४९॥

सा त्याज्या सर्वयत्नेन सर्वनाशेऽप्युपस्थिते। स्प्रष्टव्या सा न भव्येन सश्वमांसेव पुल्कसी॥५०॥

"That Brāhmaṇa who is always afraid of respect as poison and always longs after disrespect as nectar, sleeps soundly and rises happily even though he is treated with disrespect. He moves about happily in this world. The one who treats him with disrespect perishes. All cruel words should be endured. None should be treated with disrespect. On account of bodily relationship, none should be made inimical. No anger should be directed in turn towards one who is angry. Soft words (only) shold be spoken, even when (violently) pulled by another. No untrue words should be uttered, even should afflictions arise to the seven gates (of the body). One desirous of bliss should dwell in this universe through the aid of Ātmā alone, intent upon Ātmā, free from desires, and without the desire of blessing (others). He becomes fit for salvation through the control of the organs, the destruction of love and hate and non-injury to beings. He should abandon (all identification with) this feeble, perishable, and impure body of five elements whereof the bones are the pillars, which is strung by the nerves, coated over with flesh and blood, covered up by the skin, is of bad odour, full of urine and faeces is ever haunted by dotage and miseries and is the seat of all ills. If an ignorant man be fond of this body firmly knit together with flesh, blood, pus, faeces, and urine, nerves, fat, and bones, he would, a fortiori, be fond of hell. That (identification of the body with the Self) is alone the seat of the Kālasūtra hell. That is alone the Mahā-Vīci-Vāgura (hell). That is alone the Asipatravanaśreṇi (hell). Such an idea of the body being the Self should be strenuously abandoned, though all should perish. That love of the body is not fit to be felt by one intent upon his welfare; just as a low-caste woman eating dog's flesh is unfit to be touched.

प्रियेषु स्वेषु सुकृतमप्रियेषु च दुष्कृतम्। विसृज्य ध्यानयोगेन ब्रह्माप्येति सनातनम्॥५१॥

अनेन विधिना सर्वांस्त्यक्त्वा सङ्गान्शनैः शनैः। सर्वद्वन्द्वैर्विनिर्मुक्तो ब्रह्मण्येवावतिष्ठते॥५२॥

एक एव चरेन्नित्यं सिद्ध्यर्थमसहायकः। सिद्धिमेकस्य पश्यन्हि न जहाति न हीयते॥५३॥

कपालं वृक्षमूलानि कुचेलान्यसहायता। समता चैव सर्वस्मिन्नेतन्मुक्तस्य लक्षणम्॥५४॥

सर्वभूतहितः शान्तस्त्रिदण्डी सकमण्डलुः। एकारामः परिव्रज्य भिक्षार्थं ग्राममाविशेत्॥५५॥

एको भिक्षुर्यथोक्तः स्याद्द्वावेव मिथुनं स्मृतम्। त्रयो ग्रामः समाख्यात ऊर्ध्वं तु नगरायते॥५६॥

नगरं नहि कर्त्तव्यं ग्रामो वा मिथुनं तथा। एतत्त्रयं प्रकुर्वाणः स्वधर्माच्च्यवते यतिः॥५७॥

"One (fit to reach salvation), after leaving all meritorious actions to those dear to him and all sins to those not dear, attains the eternal Brahman through dhyāna-yoga. Such a man, through the ordinances, gives up little by little all associations, and being freed from all pairs of opposites, remains in Brahman alone. On account of the accomplishment (of salvation), he should be moving about alone and without any help. He who having understood the effect of being alone never derogates from it, is never left in want. The bowl, the foot of the tree, the tattered robe, the state of being without help, the equality of vision in all, these are the characteristics of the emancipated one. One intent upon the welfare of all beings, with a quiescent mind, having the three-knotted staff and bowl, and ever devoted to the One (Brahman), after taking up sannyāsa, may enter a village. Such one is a bhikṣu (alms-taker). Should two unite, it is called mithuna (a pair or union); with three, it becomes a grāma (or village); with more it is a nagara (or city). No city or village, or mithuna should be made, and an ascetic who commits these three (offences) falls from his duty. Through such intercourse (or ascetics), all kinds of talks connected with the king and alms, friendship, tale-bearing, and malice occur between them. There is no doubt of it.

राजवार्तादि तेषां स्याद्भिक्षावार्ता परस्परम्। स्नेहपैशुन्यमात्सर्यं संनिकर्षान्न संशयः॥५८॥

एकाकी निःस्पृहस्तिष्ठेन्न हि केन सहालपेत्। दद्यान्नारायणेत्येव प्रतिवाक्यं सदा यतिः॥५९॥

एकाकी चिन्तयेद्ब्रह्म मनोवाक्कायकर्मभिः। मृत्युं च नाभिनन्देत जीवितं वा कथंचन॥६०॥

कालमेव प्रतीक्षेत यावदायुः समाप्यते। नाभिनन्देत मरणं नाभिनन्देत जीवितम्।

कालमेव प्रतीक्षेत निर्देशं भृतको यथा॥६१॥

अजिह्वः षण्डकः पङ्गुरन्धो बधिर एव च। मुग्धश्च मुच्यते भिक्षुः षड्भिरेतैर्न संशयः॥६२॥

इदमिष्टमिदं नेति योऽश्नन्नपि न सज्जति। हितं सत्यं मितं वक्ति तमजिह्वं प्रचक्षते॥६३॥

अद्यजातां यथा नारीं तथा षोडशवार्षिकीम्। शतवर्षां च यो दृष्ट्वा निर्विकारः स षण्डकः॥६४॥

"He (the ascetic) should be alone and desireless. He should not converse with anybody. The ascetic should ever be uttering the word Nārāyaṇa in each sentence. Being alone, he should be meditating upon Brahman in all mental, spoken, and bodily actions. He should neither rejoice at dying or living. He should be anticipating the time when life will close. He should not be glad of dying; nor should he be glad of living. He should be biding his time like a hireling (for his pay). An ascetic who plays the part of the dumb, the eunuch, the lame, the blind, the deaf, and the idiot is emancipated through the (above six) means. There is no doubt of this. He who has not fondness for eating, saying that this is good and that is bad, who speaks only words that are beneficial, true, and moderate is said to be the dumb. He is a eunuch who is no more affected by the sight of a sixteen years old girl than of a new-born female baby or a hundred-years old woman.

भिक्षार्थमटनं यस्य विण्मूत्रकरणाय च। योजनान्न परं याति सर्वथा पङ्गुरेव सः॥६५॥

तिष्ठतो व्रजतो वापि यस्य चक्षुर्न दूरगम्। चतुर्युगां भुवं मुक्त्वा परिव्राट् सोऽन्ध उच्यते॥६६॥

हिताहितं मनोरामं वचः शोकावहं तु यत्। श्रुत्वापि न शृणोतीव बधिरः स प्रकीर्तितः॥६७॥

सान्निध्ये विषयाणां यः समर्थो विकलेन्द्रियः। सुप्तवद्वर्तते नित्यं स भिक्षुर्मुग्ध उच्यते॥६८॥

नटादिप्रेक्षणं द्यूतं प्रमदासुहृदं तथा। भक्ष्यं भोज्यमुदक्यां च षण्न पश्येत्कदाचन॥६९॥

He who does not move about for more than the distance of yojana for alms or for the calls of nature is a lame man. That parivrāt (ascetic) is said to be a blind man, who whether sitting or walking, has his vision extended to no more than four yokes distance on the ground. He is said to be deaf who, though hearing words, beneficial or non-beneficial, pleasant or painful to the mind, is as if he does not hear them. That clever ascetic is said to be an idiot who is ever in a state of sleep, as it were, having his organs non-agitated by objects, even though near. He should never observe the following six— the scenes of dancing, etc., gambling, lovely women, eatables, enjoyables, and women in their monthly course.

रागं द्वेषं मदं मायां द्रोहं मोहं परात्मसु। षडेतानि यतिर्नित्यं मनसापि न चिन्तयेत्॥७०॥

मञ्चकं शुक्लवस्त्रं च स्त्रीकथालौल्यमेव च। दिवा स्वापं च यानं च यतीनां पातनानि षट्॥७१॥

दूरयात्रां प्रयत्नेन वर्जयेदात्मचिन्तकः। सदोपनिषदं विद्यामभ्यसेन्मुक्तिहैतुकीम्॥७२॥

न तीर्थसेवी नित्यं स्यान्नोपवासपरो यतिः। न चाध्ययनशीलः स्यान्न व्याख्यानपरो भवेत्॥७३॥

अपापमशठं वृत्तमजिह्मं नित्यमाचरेत्। इन्द्रियाणि समाहृत्य कूर्मोऽङ्गानीव सर्वशः॥७४॥

क्षीणेन्द्रियमनोवृत्तिर्निराशीर्निष्परिग्रहः। निर्द्वन्द्वो निर्नमस्कारो निःस्वधाकार एव च॥७५॥

निर्ममो निरहंकारो निरपेक्षो निराशिषः। विविक्तदेशसंसक्तो मुच्यते नात्र संशय इति॥७६॥

"The ascetic should never in thought even think of others with the six (viz.,) love, hate, pride, deceit, treachery, and the illusion (of confounding them). To the ascetics, the following six are sinful : cot, white cloth, the stories of women, love towards women, sleep during the day, and vehicles. He who is engaged in Ātmic contemplation should carefully avoid a long journey. He should ever practise the upaniṣadic vidyā-tending to salvation. The ascetic need not bathe daily. He need not observe upavāsa (fast). He need not be one that had studied Vedas. He need not be one that is able to produce a commentary (lecture). He should daily observe acts without sin, deceit, or falsehood. He who, having withdrawn the organs within, like a turtle its limbs (within its shell), is with the actions of the organs and the mind annihilated, without desires, without possessing any object as his own, without dualities, without prostrations, without the oblations to pitṛ devatās (they being with desires), without mine or I, without awaiting anything, without the desire to be happy, and living in places where men do not live— he alone is emancipated. There is no doubt of this.

अप्रमत्तः कर्मभक्तिज्ञानसंपन्नः स्वतन्त्रो वैराग्यमेत्य ब्रह्मचारी गृही वानप्रस्थो वा मुख्यवृत्तिका चेद्ब्रह्मचर्यं समाप्य गृही भवेद्गृहाद्वनी भूत्वा प्रव्रजेद्यदि वेतरथा ब्रह्मचर्यादेव प्रव्रजेद्गृहाद्वा वनाद्वाऽथ पुनरव्रती वा व्रती वा स्नातको वाऽस्नातको वोत्सन्नाग्निरनग्निको वा यदहरेव विरजेत्तदहरेव प्रव्रजेत्तद्धैके प्राजापत्यामेवेष्टिं कुर्वन्त्यथवा न कुर्यादाग्नेय्यामेव कुर्यादग्निर्हि प्राणः प्राणमेवैतया करोति तस्मात्त्रैधातवीयामेव कुर्यादेतयैव त्रयो धातवो यदुत सत्त्वं रजस्तम इति॥७७॥

अयं ते योनिर्ऋत्वियो यतो जातो अरोचथाः। तं जानन्नग्न आरोहाथानो वर्धया रयिम्॥७८॥

A celibate, or householder, or forester, who is (ever) vigilant, has karma, devotion, and knowledge and is independent, after understanding his peculiar tendency and having become indifferent (to his order of life), may become an householder after ending the celibate life, or may from the householder's life enter the life of a forester, and then the life of an ascetic; or from the life of a celibate, or householder, or forester may (directly) enter that of an ascetic. The moment vairāgya arises in him, he may become an ascetic that moment, whether he is with vrata (religious observance) or not, is snātaka or not, or with discontinued fire-sacrifice or not. On account of that, some perform Prājāpatya-sacrifice alone; or Āgneya-sacrifice may be performed. Is not agni, prāṇa? Through this alone, one should perform that sacrifice only which is connected with the three dhātus. The three dhātus are sattva, rajas, and tamas alone. With the mantra, अयं ते योनि)त्विजो यतो जातो अरोचथाः। तं जानन्नग्ना आरोह था नो वर्धाया रयिं॥, *agni* (fire) should be taken in. Thus it is said (in the Śrutis): एष वा अग्नेर्योनिर्यः प्राणः, प्राणं गच्छ स्वां योनिं गच्छ स्वाहा॥

इत्यनेन मन्त्रेणाग्निमाजिघ्रेदेष वा अग्नेर्योनिर्यः प्राणः प्राणं गच्छ स्वां योनिं गच्छ स्वाहेत्येवमेवैतदाहवनीयादग्निमाहृत्य पूर्ववदग्निमाजिघ्रेद्यदग्निं न विन्देदप्सु जुहुयादापो वै सर्वा देवताः सर्वाभ्यो देवताभ्यो जुहोमि स्वाहेति हुत्वोद्धृत्य तदुदकं प्राश्नीयात्साज्यं हविरनामयं मोदमिति शिखां यज्ञोपवीतं पितरं पुत्रं कलत्रं कर्म चाध्ययनं मन्त्रान्तरं विसृज्यैव परिव्रजत्यात्मविन्मोक्षमन्त्रैस्त्रैधातवीयैर्विधेस्तद्ब्रह्म तदुपासितव्यमेवैतदिति॥७९॥

The agni from āhavanīya should be brought and taken in as before (with the mantras above mentioned). Should such an agni be not obtainable, the homa (oblation) should be done in water with the mantras, आपो वै सर्वा देवतास्सर्वाभ्यो देवताभ्यो जुहोमि स्वाहा। After performing homa, the water should be taken in and sipped. After uttering the mantra, `साज्यं हविरनामयं मोक्षदं' he abandons the tuft of hair in the head, the holy thread, father, son, wife, karma, vedic study and mantra and becomes an ascetic. The Śrutis say that a knower of Ātmā should be engaged in meditation upon Brahman, through the three mantras tending to salvation.

पितामहं पुनः पप्रच्छ नारदः कथमयज्ञोपवीती ब्राह्मण इति। तमाह पितामहः॥८०॥

सशिखं वपनं कृत्वा बहिःसूत्रं त्यजेद्बुधः। यदक्षरं परं ब्रह्म तत्सूत्रमिति धारयेत्॥८१॥

सूचनात्सूत्रमित्याहुः सूत्रं नाम परं पदम्। तत्सूत्रं विदितं येन स विप्रो वेदपारगः॥८२॥

येन सर्वमिदं प्रोतं सूत्रे मणिगणा इव। तत्सूत्रं धारयेद्योगी योगवित्तत्त्वदर्शनः॥८३॥

Then Nārada asked Brahmā thus : "How can one, without the holy thread, be a Brāhmaṇa?" To which Brahmā replied : "The wise should, after shaving (the head) together with the tuft of hair, cast off the holy thread. He should wear, as his sūtra (thread), the indestructible and supreme Brahman. On account of (sācanāt) its being an indication, it (thread) is called sūtra. Sūtra is the Paramapada (supreme seat). He by whom that sūtra is known is Brahman. That sūtra (thread of Brahman) in which is strung the whole universe like beads on a sūtra (string), should be worn by the yogin that has known yoga and tattva.

बहिः सूत्रं त्यजेद्विद्वान्योगमुत्तममास्थितः। ब्रह्मभावमिदं सूत्रं धारयेद्यः सचेतनः।

धारणात्तस्य सूत्रस्य नोच्छिष्टो नाशुचिर्भवेत्॥ ८४॥

सूत्रमन्तर्गतं येषां ज्ञानयज्ञोपवीतिनाम्। ते वै सूत्रविदो लोके ते च यज्ञोपवीतिनः॥ ८५॥

ज्ञानशिखा ज्ञाननिष्ठा ज्ञानयज्ञोपवीतिनः। ज्ञानमेव परं तेषां पवित्रं ज्ञानमुच्यते॥ ८६॥

अग्नेरिव शिखा नान्या यस्य ज्ञानमयी शिखा। स शिखीत्युच्यते विद्वान्नेतरे केशधारिणः॥ ८७॥

कर्मण्यधिकृता ये तु वैदिके ब्राह्मणादयः। तैर्विधार्यमिदं सूत्रं क्रियाङ्गं तद्धि वै स्मृतम्॥ ८८॥

शिखा ज्ञानमयी यस्य उपवीतं च तन्मयम्। ब्राह्मण्यं सकलं तस्य इति ब्रह्मविदो विदुरिति॥ ८९॥

The wise man that is in supreme yoga should abandon the outer sūtra (thread). He who wears (in his heart) this sūtra of Brāhmic Reality is alone Brāhmaṇa. Through wearing this higher sūtra, it becomes not a rejected one, not an impure one. Those only whose sūtra is internal, having the holy thread as jñāna are the real knowers of the sūtra, they are said to possess the yajñopavīta (holy thread). To those whose śikhā (tuft of hair) is jñāna, whose holy thread is jñāna, and whose meditation is upon jñāna, jñāna alone is supreme. It is said that jñāna alone is able to purify. That wise man alone who possesses the jñāna-śikhā like the śikhā (flame) of agni (fire) is said to possess śikhā (tuft of hair). Those that have mere śikhā are no śikhās. The Brāhmaṇas and other that are entitled to perform the vedic karmas are allowed to wear the (external) thread, only as an auxiliary to the karmas. It is only vedic. The knowers of Brahman know that all Brāhmaṇya (the state of Brahman) accrues to him only that has the jñānamaya śikhā (knowledge-tuft of hair) and the tanmaya (that or Brahmanful) upavīta (holy thread).

तदेतद्विज्ञाय ब्राह्मणः परिव्रज्य परिव्राडेकशाटी मुण्डोऽपरिग्रहः शरीरक्लेशासहिष्णुश्चेदथवा यथाविधिश्चेज्जातरूपधरो भूत्वा सपुत्रमित्रकलत्राप्तबन्ध्वादीनि स्वाध्यायं सर्वकर्मणि संन्यस्यायं ब्रह्माण्डं च सर्वं कौपीनं दण्डमाच्छादनं च त्यक्त्वा द्वन्द्वसहिष्णुर्न शीतं न चोष्णं न सुखं न दुःखं न निद्रा न मानावमाने च षडूर्मिवर्जितो निन्दाहंकारमत्सरगर्वदम्भेर्ष्यासूयेच्छाद्वेषसुखदुःखकामक्रोधलोभमोहादीन्विसृज्य स्ववपुः शवाकारमिव स्मृत्वा स्वव्यतिरिक्तं सर्वमन्तर्बहिरमन्यमानः कस्यापि वन्दनमकृत्वा न नमस्कारो न स्वाहाकारो न स्वधाकारो न निन्दास्तुतिर्यादृच्छिको भवेद्यदृच्छालाभसंतुष्टः सुवर्णादीन्न परिग्रहेन्नावाहनं न विसर्जनं न मन्त्रं नामन्त्रं न ध्यानं नोपासनं न लक्ष्यं नालक्ष्यं न पृथक् नापृथक् न त्वन्यत्र सर्वत्रानिकेतः स्थिरमतिः शून्यागारवृक्षमूलदेवगृह तृणकूटकुलालशालाग्निहोत्रशालाग्निदिगन्तरनदीतटपुलिनभूगृहकन्दरनिर्झरस्थण्डिलेषु वने वा श्वेतकेतुऋभुनिदाघऋषभदुर्वासःसंवर्तकदत्तात्रेयरैवतकवदव्यक्तलिङ्गोऽव्यक्ताचारो बालोन्मत्तपिशाचवदनुन्मत्तोन्मत्तवदाचरंस्त्रिदण्डं शिक्यं पात्रं कमण्डलुं कटिसूत्रं कौपीनं च तत्सर्वं भूःस्वाहेत्यप्सु परित्यज्य॥ ९०॥

कटिसूत्रं च कौपीनं दण्डं वस्त्रं कमण्डलुं। सर्वमप्सु विसृज्याथ जातरूपधरश्चरेत्॥ ९१॥

आत्मानमन्विच्छेद्यथा जातरूपधरो निर्द्वन्द्वो निष्परिग्रहस्तत्त्वब्रह्ममार्गे सग्यक्सम्पन्नः शुद्धमानसः प्राणसंधारणार्थं यथोक्तकाले करपात्रेणान्येन वा याचिताहारमाहरन् लाभालाभे समो भूत्वा निर्ममः शुक्लध्यानपरायणोऽध्यात्मनिष्ठः शुभाशुभकर्मनिर्मूलनपरः संन्यस्य पूर्णानन्दैकबोधस्त द्ब्रह्माहमस्मीति ब्रह्मप्रणवमनुस्मरन्भ्रमरकीटन्यायेन शरीरत्रयमुत्सृज्य संन्यासेनैव देहत्यागं करोति स कृतकृत्यो भवतीत्युपनिषत्॥ ९ २॥

"Having known it, a Brāhmaṇa should take up sannyāsa. Such a sannyāsin, should be, in order to bear the bodily afflictions, with one cloth, bald-headed and without having anything as being required (for his use); or according to rules, he may be (naked) as nature made his body, and should abandon his son, friend, wife, trustworthy relatives, etc., as well as all karmas and love for the universe, the loin-cloth, staff, and covering. Enduring all pairs of opposites without cold or heat, happiness or grief, fame or disgrace, without the six changes, I-ness, malice, pride, ostentation, jealousy, slander of others, love and hate, pleasure and pain, passion, anger, greed and delusion and regarding his body as a mere carcase, without thinking of all the things, internal and external; that are other than Self. Without Prostrations, without the worship of devas and pitṛs and without praise or condemnation, he should wander about of his own accord. He should not receive gold and others. For him, these is no invocation or dismissal (of deities), mantra or non-mantra, meditation or worship, aim or non-aim, others or not-others without having another's or (his own) settled place of residence, and having a firm conviction, he should be in a desolate house or at the foot of trees, or in a temple, a plenteous turfed spot, a potter's place or that of agnihotra or sacrifice, river, tank, sand-heap, subterranean vault, cave, mountain-hill, the place prepared for sacrifice or forest; or like the asked personages, Śveta-ketu, Ṛbhu, Nidāgha, Jaḍabharata, Ṛṣabha, Durvāsās, Saṁvartaka, Sanatsujāta, Vaideha (Janaka), Vatasiddha, Śuka, Vāmadeva, Dattātreya, Raivataka, and Gorakṣa, he should roam about as nature made him, without being recognised and without any means of discovery of his course of life, like a lad, or an insane man, or a ghost, with the action of a madman though not mad, after discarding in water the three-knotted staff, the stringed sling (bag), vessel, bowl, waist-strint, loin-cloth, stick and cloth. He should ever be engaged in Ātmic deliberation. Being in his natural state without being affected by the pairs, without receiving anything, being ever settled firmly in the Brāhmic path, having a pure mind, eating the food that is obtained without asking, in the palm as vessel, or in another's vessel in order to merely protect the body at the time-required, being of equal mind whether the object is gained or not, without having aught of his own, always meditating upon Brahman, being with Ātma-niṣṭhā, having eradicated all actions, virtuous and sinful, and having given up all— that one who ever utters Brahma-Praṇava, that "I am Brahman" alone, with the blissful and non-dual jñāna, and after rising above the three bodies (to Brahman), like the analogy of the wasp and the worm, gives up the body as a sannyāsin, is said to have done all his work (in this world). Such is the Upaniṣad."

॥चतुर्थोपदेशः॥

त्यक्त्वा लोकांश्च वेदांश्च विषयानिन्द्रियाणि च। आत्मन्येव स्थितो यस्तु स याति परमां गतिम्॥ १॥

नामगोत्रादिवरणं देशं कालं श्रुतं कुलम्। वयो वृत्तं शीलं ख्यापयेन्नैव सद्यतिः॥ २॥

न संभाषेत्स्त्रियं कांचित्पूर्वदृष्टां च न स्मरेत्। कथां च वर्जयेत्तासां न पश्येल्लिखितामपि॥ ३॥

एतच्चतुष्टयं मोहात्स्त्रीणामाचरतो यतेः। चित्तं विक्रियतेऽवश्यं तद्विकारात्प्रणश्यति॥ ४॥

तृष्णा क्रोधोऽनृतं माया लोभमोहौ प्रियाप्रिये। शिल्पं व्याख्यानयोगश्च कामो रागपरिग्रहः॥ ५॥

अहंकारो ममत्वं च चिकित्सा धर्मसाहसम्। प्रायश्चित्तं प्रवासश्च मन्त्रौषधपराशिषः।

प्रतिषिद्धानि चैतानि सेवमानो व्रजेदधः॥ ६॥

Upadeśa IV

"One who after giving up the world, the Vedas, the objects and the organs is in Ātmā alone, attains the supreme abode. A good ascetic should not make known his caste, name, gotra (clan), etc., his place and time, the Vedas, etc. studied by him, his family, age, history, observance and conduct. He should neither converse with women nor remember the women he had seen. He should give up all stories conected with women. He should not even see the figure of a woman in a picture. The mind of an ascetic who through delusion adopts the above four things connected with women is necessarily affected and thereby perishes. The following are prohibited (in his case) : Thirst, malice, falsehood, deceit, greed, delusion, the pleasant and the unpleasant, manual work, lecture, yoga, kāma (passion), desire, begging, I-ness, mine-ness, the obstinacy of curing diseases, penance, pilgrimage and the accomplishment of fruits of mantras, and medicines. He who performs these interdicted things, goes into a debased state. A muni who has mokṣa as his supreme seat should address such respectful words as "Please come, please go, please stay, and welcome" to one, even though he be his intimate friend. He should neither receive presents, etc., nor ask for them to be given to others. Even in dream, an ascetic should never direct a person (to do work for him). Even should he witness or hear of the happiness or grief of his wife, brother, son, and other relatives, he should not be affected thereby. He should abandon all joy and sorrow.

आगच्छ गच्छ तिष्ठेति स्वागतं सुहृदोऽपि वा। सम्माननं च न ब्रूयान्मुनिर्मोक्षपरायणः॥ ७॥

प्रतिग्रहं न गृह्णीयान्नैव चान्यं प्रदापयेत्। प्रेरयेद्वा तया भिक्षुः स्वप्नेऽपि न कदाचन॥ ८॥

जायाभ्रातृसुतादीनां बन्धूनां च शुभाशुभम्। श्रुत्वा दृष्ट्वा न कम्पेत शोकहर्षौ त्यजेद्यतिः॥ ९॥

अहिंसा सत्यमस्तेयब्रह्मचर्यापरिग्रहाः। अनौद्धत्यमदीनत्वं प्रसादः स्थैर्यमार्जवम्॥ १०॥

अस्नेहो गुरुशुश्रूषा श्रद्धा क्षान्तिर्दमः शमः। उपेक्षा धैर्यमाधुर्ये तितिक्षा करुणा तथा॥ ११॥

ह्रीस्तथा ज्ञानविज्ञाने योगो लघ्वशनं धृतिः। एष स्वधर्मो विख्यातो यतीनां नियतात्मनाम्॥ १२॥

निर्द्वन्द्वो नित्यसत्त्वस्थः सर्वत्र समदर्शनः। तुरीयः परमो हंसः साक्षान्नारायणो यतिः॥ १३॥

एकरात्रं वसेद्ग्रामे नगरे पञ्चरात्रकम्। वर्षाभ्योऽन्यत्र वर्षासु मासांश्च चतुरो वसेत्॥ १४॥

द्विरात्रं न वसेद्ग्रामे भिक्षुर्यदि वसेत्तदा। रागादयः प्रसज्येरंस्तेनासौ नारकी भवेत्॥ १५॥

"To the ascetics controlling their mind, the following are their svadharmas (own duties): Harmlessness, truth, honesty, celibacy, non-coveting, humility, high-spiritedness, clearness of mind, steadiness of mind, straightforwardness, non-attachments (to any), service to the Guru, faith, patience, bodily restraint, mental restraint, indifference, firm and sweet words, endurance, compassion, shame, jñāna, vijñāna, yoga, moderate food, and courage. That paramahaṁsa of an ascetic in the order of life of a sannyāsin who is without dualities, always follows the pure sattvaguṇa and sees all equally, is no other than the actual Nārāyaṇa Himself. He may live one day in a village and five days in a city, but five months in the wintry season. At other times he should live in other places (such as forest, etc.). He should not live in a village for two days (even); should he do so, desires and the rest will arise in him and thereby he becomes fit for hell.

ग्रामान्ते निर्जने देशे नियतात्माऽनिकेतनः। पर्यटेत्कीटवद्भूमौ वर्षास्वेकत्र संवसेत्॥ १६॥

एकवासा अवासा वा एकदृष्टिरलोलुपः। अदूषयन्सतां मार्गं ध्यानयुक्तो महीं चरेत्॥ १७॥

शुचौ देशे सदा भिक्षुः स्वधर्ममनुपालयन्। पर्यटेत सदा योगी वीक्षयन्वसुधातलम्॥ १८॥

न रात्रौ न च मध्याह्ने संध्ययोर्नैव पर्यटन्। न शून्ये न च दुर्गे वा प्राणिबाधाकरे न च॥ १९॥

एकरात्रं वसेद्ग्रामे पत्तने तु दिनत्रयम्। पुरे दिनद्वयं भिक्षुर्नगरे पञ्चरात्रकम्।

वर्षास्वेकत्र तिष्ठेत स्थाने पुण्यजलावृते॥ २०॥

He should live like a (harmless) worm on the earth with his mind under control and with no settled place of residence, at the end of the village where there are no persons. He may live in the same place in the wintry season. He should roam about on the earth with one or no cloth, with the one vision (of Brahman) alone, with no desires (of objects), with no condemnation of the actions of the wise and with meditation. That yogin or an ascetic should go about, observing the duties of his order of life, and with the eyes cast on the earth, in pure places. He should not roam about in night, midday or the two twilight periods in which are places void or difficult to be waded through or likely to injure living creatures. He may live for one day in a village, for three days in a town, for two days in a hamlet and for five days in a city. He may live in the wintry season (longer) in one place surrounded fully by water.

आत्मवत्सर्वभूतानि पश्यन्भिक्षुश्चरेन्महीम्। अन्धवत्कुब्जवच्चैव बधिरोन्मत्तमूकवत्॥ २१॥

स्नानं त्रिषवणं प्रोक्तं बहूदकवनस्थयोः। हंसे तु सकृदेव स्यात्परहंसे न विद्यते॥ २२॥

मौनं योगासनं योगस्तितिक्षैकान्तशीलता। निःस्पृहत्वं समत्वं च सप्तैतान्येकदण्डिनाम्॥ २३॥

परहंसाश्रमस्थो हि स्नानादेरविधानतः। अशेषचित्तवृत्तीनां त्यागं केवलमाचरेत्॥ २४॥

त्वङ् मांसरुधिरस्नायुमज्जामेदोस्थिसंहतौ। विण्मूत्रपूये रमतां क्रिमीणां कियदन्तरम्॥ २५॥

क्व शरीरमशेषाणां श्लेष्मादीनां महाचयः। क्व चाङ्गशोभा सौभाग्यकमनीयादयो गुणाः॥ २६॥

The ascetic should regard all creatures as Self and dwell upon earth like the blind, the hunch-back, the deaf, the insane, and the dumb. The bahūdaka and the forester should bathe thrice a day. In the case of haṁsa, one bath only is ordained; but none in the case of paramahaṁsa. In the case of the one having one staff, seven things are ordained, viz., silence, yoga-posture, yoga, endurance, solitariness, desirelessness, and equal vision over all. Bathing being not prescribed for a paramahaṁsa, he should abandon all the modifications of the mind only; what is the difference between the worms and the men that rejoice over this ill-smelling body which is but a collection of skin, flesh, blood, nerves, fat, marrow, bone, offal and urine? What is the body but a collection of all, phlegm, etc.? And what are the qualities, the vāsanā of the body, effulgence, beauty, etc.? (They are opposed to one another.)

मांसासृक्पूयविण्मूत्रस्नायुमज्जास्थिसंहतौ। देहे चेत्प्रीतिमान्मूढो भविता नरकेऽपि सः॥ २७॥

स्त्रीणामवाच्यदेशस्य क्लिन्ननाडीव्रणस्य च। अभेदेऽपि मनोभेदाज्जनः प्रायेण वञ्च्यते॥ २८॥

चर्मखण्डं द्विधा भिन्नमपानोद्गारधूपितम्। ये रमन्ति नमस्तेभ्यः साहसं किमतः परम्॥ २९॥

The ignorant man that is fond of this body, which is but a compound of flesh, blood, the ill-smelling urine and offal, nerve, fat and bone, will be fond of hell too. Though there is not difference between the women's secret parts that cannot be described by words and an (ever) oozing tubular wound, yet through the difference of the mind, (men are deluded). Such men are said to be without prāṇa, (viz., dead) though alive. Prostrations to those that sport in that piece of flesh which is rent in twain and tainted with the breaking of the wind, etc. What more revolting thing is there than this?

न तस्य विद्यते कार्यं न लिङ्गं वा विपश्चितः। निर्ममो निर्भयः शान्तो निर्द्वन्द्वोऽवर्णभोजनः॥ ३०॥ मुनिः कौपीनवासाः स्यान्नग्नो वा ध्यानतत्परः। एवं ज्ञानपरो योगी ब्रह्मभूयाय कल्पते॥ ३१॥ लिङ्गे सत्यपि खल्वस्मिञ्ज्ञानमेव हि कारणम्। निर्मोक्षायेह भूतानां लिङ्गग्रामो निरर्थकः॥ ३२॥ यन्न सन्तं न चासन्तं नाश्रुतं न बहुश्रुतम्। न सुवृत्तं न दुर्वृत्तं वेद कश्चित्स ब्राह्मणः॥ ३३॥ तस्मादलिङ्गो धर्मज्ञो ब्रह्मवृत्तमनुव्रतम्। गूढधर्माश्रितो विद्वानज्ञातचरितं चरेत्॥ ३४॥

संदिग्धः सर्वभूतानां वर्णाश्रमविवर्जितः। अन्धवज्जडवच्चापि मूकवच्च महीं चरेत्॥ ३५॥

तं दृष्ट्वा शान्तमनसं स्पृहयन्ति दिवौकसः। लिङ्गाभावात्तु कैवल्यमिति ब्रह्मानुशासनमिति॥ ३६॥

To the wise, there is nothing to do, no sign (of identification). The muni who is without 'mine' and fear, with quiescence, without duality and eating leaf (alone), should ever be in meditation with either loin-cloth or no cloth. A yogin who is thus in meditation becomes fit to be Brahman. Though he may have some signs (of identification to pass under this order of life or that), such signs are useless for gaining mokṣa. The cause of salvation is jñāna alone. He is a (true) brāhmaṇa who cannot be identified as sat (good person) or asat, knower of religious books or not, follower of good conduct or bad conduct. Therefore that learned man who is without signs, a knower of dharma, engaged in the actions of Brahman and a knower of the secret mysteries, should roam about, incognito. He should go about on this earth without any caste or order of life and without being (even) doubted (regarding his identity) by any beings, like the blind, the idiot, or the mute. Then (even) the angels become fond of him who has a quiescent mind. It is the dictate of the Vedas that the sign (of non-identification) itself is Kaivalya."

अथ नारदः पितामहं संन्यासविधिं नो ब्रूहीति पप्रच्छ। पितामहस्तथेत्यङ्गीकृत्यातुरे वा क्रमे वापि तुरीयाश्रमस्वीकारार्थं कृच्छ्रप्रायश्चित्तपूर्वकमष्टश्राद्धं कुर्याद्देवर्षिदिव्यमनुष्यभूत पितृमात्रात्मेत्यष्टश्राद्धानि कुर्यात्। प्रथमं सत्यवसुसंज्ञकान्विश्वान्देवान्देवश्राद्धे ब्रह्मविष्णुमहेश्वरानृषिश्राद्धे देवर्षिक्षत्रियर्षिमनुष्यर्षीन् दिव्यश्राद्धे वसुरुद्रादित्यरूपान्मनुष्यश्राद्धे सनकसनन्दनसनत्कुमारसनत्सुजातान्भूतश्राद्धे पृथिव्यादिपञ्चमहाभूतानि चक्षुरादिकरणानि चतुर्विधभूतग्रामान्पितृश्राद्धे पितृपितामहप्रपितामहान्मातृश्राद्धे मातृपितामहीप्रपितामहीरात्मश्राद्धे आत्मपितृपितामहाञ्जीवत्पितृकश्चेत्पितरं त्यक्त्वा आत्मपितामहप्रपितामहानिति सर्वत्र युग्मक्लृप्त्या ब्राह्मणानर्चयेदेकाध्वरपक्षेऽष्टाध्वरपक्षे वा स्वशाखानुगतमन्त्रैरष्टश्राद्धान्यष्टदिनेषु वा एकदिने वा पितृयागोक्तविधानेन ब्राह्मणानभ्यर्च्य भुक्त्यन्तं यथाविधि निर्वर्त्य पिण्डप्रदानानि निर्वर्त्य दक्षिणाताम्बूलैस्तोषयित्वा ब्राह्मणान्प्रेषयित्वा शेषकर्मसिद्ध्यर्थं सप्तकेशान्विसृज्य-'शेषकर्मप्रसिद्ध्यर्थं केशान्सप्ताष्ट वा द्विजः। संक्षिप्य वापयेत्पूर्वं केशश्मश्रुनखानि च' इति सप्तकेशान्संरक्ष्य कक्षोपस्थवर्जं क्षौरपूर्वकं स्नात्वा सायंसंध्यावन्दनं निर्वर्त्य सहस्रगायत्रीं जप्त्वा ब्रह्मयज्ञं निर्वर्त्य स्वाधीनाग्निमुपस्थाप्य स्वशाखोपसंहरणं कृत्वा तदुक्तप्रकारेणाज्याहुतिमाज्यभागान्तं हुत्वाहुतिविधिं समाप्यात्मादिभिस्त्रिवारं सक्तुप्राशनं कृत्वाचमनपूर्वकमग्निं संरक्ष्य स्वयमग्नेरुत्तरतः कृष्णाजिनोपरि स्थित्वा पुराणश्रवणपूर्वकं जागरणं कृत्वा चतुर्थयामान्ते स्नात्वा तदग्नौ चरुं श्रपयित्वा पुरुषसूक्तेनान्नस्य षोडशाहुतीर्हुत्वा विरजाहोमं कृत्वा अथाचम्य सदक्षिणं वस्त्रं सुवर्णपात्रं धेनुं दत्त्वा समाप्य ब्रह्मोद्वासनं कृत्वा। सं मा सिञ्चन्तु मरुतः समिन्द्रः सं बृहस्पतिः। सं मायमग्निः सिञ्चत्वायुषा च धनेन च बलेन चायुष्मन्तं करोतु मा इति। या ते अग्ने यज्ञिया तनूस्तयेह्यारोहात्मात्मानम्। अच्छा वसूनि कृण्वन्नस्मे नर्या पुरूणि। यज्ञो भूत्वा यज्ञमासीद स्वां योनिं जातवेदो भुव आजायमानः स क्षय एधीत्यनेनाग्निमात्मन्यारोप्य ध्यात्वाग्निं प्रदक्षिणनमस्कारपूर्वकमुद्वास्य प्रातःसंध्यामुपास्य सहस्रगायत्रीपूर्वकं सूर्योपस्थानं कृत्वा नाभिदघ्नोदकमुपविश्याष्टदिक्पालकार्घ्यपूर्वकं गायत्र्युद्वासनं कृत्वा सावित्रीं व्याहृतिषु प्रवेशयित्वा। अहं वृक्षस्य रेरिव। कीर्तिः पृष्ठं गिरेरिव। ऊर्ध्वपवित्रो वाजिनीवस्वमृतमस्मि। द्रविणं मे सवर्चसं सुमेधा अमृतोक्षितः। इति त्रिशङ्कोर्वेदानुवचनम्। यश्छन्दसामृषभो विश्वरूपः। छन्दोभ्योऽध्यमृतात्संबभूव। स मे इन्द्रो मेधया स्पृणोतु। अमृतस्य देवधारणो भूयासम्। शरीरं मे विचर्षणम्। जिह्वा मे मधुमत्तमा। कर्णाभ्यां भूरि विश्रवम्। ब्रह्मणः कोशोऽसि मेधयापिहितः। श्रुतं मे गोपाय। दारेषणायाश्च वित्तेषणायाश्च लोकेषणायाश्च व्युत्थितोऽहं ॐ भूः संन्यस्तं मया ॐभुवः संन्यस्तं मया ॐ सुवः संन्यस्तं मया ॐ भूर्भुवः सुवः संन्यस्तं मयेति मन्द्रमध्यमतालजध्वनिभिर्मनसा वाचोच्चार्याभयं सर्वभूतेभ्यो मत्तः सर्वं प्रवर्तते स्वाहेत्यनेन जलं प्राश्य प्राच्यां दिशि पूर्णाञ्जलिं प्रक्षिप्यों स्वाहेति शिखामुत्पाट्य। यज्ञोपवीतं परमं पवित्रं प्रजापतेर्यत्सहजं पुरस्तात्। आयुष्यमग्र्यं प्रतिमुञ्च शुभ्रं यज्ञोपवीतं बलमस्तु तेजः। यज्ञोपवीत बहिर्न निवसेस्त्वमन्तः प्रविश्य मध्ये ह्यजस्रं परमं पवित्रं यशो बलं ज्ञानवैराग्यं

मेधां प्रयच्छेति यज्ञोपवीतं छित्त्वा उदकाञ्जलिना सह। ॐ भूः समुद्रं गच्छ स्वाहेत्यप्सु जुहुयात्। ॐ भूः संन्यस्तं मया। ॐ भुवः संन्यस्तं मया। ॐ सुवःसंन्यस्तं मयेति त्रिरुक्त्वा त्रिवारमभिमन्त्र्य तज्जलं प्राश्याचम्य ॐ भूः स्वाहेत्यप्सु वस्त्रं कटिसूत्रमपि विसृज्य सर्वकर्मनिवर्तकोऽहमिति स्मृत्वा जातरूपधरो भूत्वा स्वरूपानुसंधानपूर्वकमूर्ध्वबाहुरुदीचीं गच्छेत्।। ३७।।

Then Nārada asked the Grandfather about the rules of sannyāsa. To which Brahmā assented and said : "Before either the ātura or regular sannyāsa is taken, kṛcchra penance should be done and then the eight śrāddhas. In each of the (eight) śrāddhas, two brāhmaṇas should be fed, in lieu of Viśvedevas called Satyavasu and the (Trimūrtis called) Brahmā, Viṣṇu, and Maheśvara, in Devaśrāddha first; then in Ṛṣiśrāddha in lieu of Devarṣī, Rājarṣi, and Manuṣyarṣi; then in Divyaśrāddha, in lieu of Vasu, Rudra, and Ādityas; then in manuṣyaśrāddha in lieu of Sanaka, Sanandana, Sanatkumāra, and Sanatsujāta; then in bhūtaśraddha, in lieu of the five great elements, pṛthivī, etc., eye and other organs and the four kinds of collection of bhūtas; then in Piṭṛśrāddha, in lieu of father, grandfather and great-grandfather; then in māṭṛśrāddha, in lieu of mother, mother's father and mother's grandfather; and then in Ātmaśrāddha, in lieu of himself, his father and grandfather or of himself, grandfather and great-grandfather, should his father be alive. He should perform the eight śrāddhas in one day, or eight days, with the mantras of his śākhā in one yājñapakṣa or eight yājñapakṣas. Then he should worship and feed the brāhmaṇas according to the rules contained in piṭṛyajña. Then offering the piṇḍas (balls of rice to the piṭṛs), he should gladden the brāhmaṇas with the tāmbūla (nut and betel, etc.,) presents and dismiss them. Then for the accomplishment of the remaining karmas, he should pluck off seven hairs; then again for finishing the rest of the karmas, he should hold seven or eight hairs and have the head shaved. Except his arm-pit and secret parts, he should have the hairs of his head, whiskers and mustache and nails shaved. Afer shaving, he should bathe and perform the evening sandhyā, uttering Gāyatrī a thousand times. Then performing brahmayajña, he should establish his own fire and acting up to his śākhā, should perform the oblation of ghee according to what is said therein till the ājya portion with those (mantras beginning with) Ātmā, etc.; should eat thrice the fried rice-powder, and then sipping the water, he should maintain the fire; then seated north of the fire on a deer-skin, he should be engaged in the study of Purāṇas; without sleeping, he should bathe at the end of the four yāmas and after cooking the oblation of (rice) in the fire, he should offer it to the fire in sixteen oblations according to (the mantras of) Puruṣa-Sūkta. Then having done virajā-homa and sipped water, he should close it with the gift (to brāhmaṇas) of cloth, golden vessel, and cows along with presents of money are then dismiss Brāhma (who had been invoked). With the prescribed mantra, he should attract Agni (fire) unto himself. After meditating upon and coming round and prostrating before the fire, he should dismiss it. Then in the morning performing sandhyā and uttering Gāyatrī a thousand times, he should make upasthāna (worship) to the sun. Then descending into water up to the navel, he should make arghya (water-offering) to the guardians of the eight quarters; then he should give leave to Gāyatrī, making Sāvitrī enter into vyāhṛti.

The *mantra* prescribed for this should be uttered through the mind and voice in high, middling, and low tones. With the *mantra*, अभयं सर्वभूतेभ्यो मत्तः सर्वे प्रवतते। the water should be sipped and having taken the water with the two hands, it should be dropped on east. Having uttered स्वाहा he should pluck his hair (yet left) and uttering the prescribed *mantra* and having torn off the sacred thread and taken it in the hand with water, should utter ओ भूः 'go to the ocean' and cast them down as oblation in water— ओं भूः संन्यस्तं मया। ओं भुवः संन्यस्तं मया। ओं स्वाः संन्यस्तं मया॥ Having uttered thrice and saturated thrice (the water) with (the influence of) the *mantras*, he should sip the water; and then uttering the *mantras* ओं भूः, etc., he should cast aside in water the cloth and waist-cord. Having thought himself to be the abdicator of all *karmas*, he, being in the meditation of his own Reality as nature made him, should go as before northwards with hands upraised.

पूर्ववद्विद्वत्संन्यासी चेद्गुरोः सकाशात्प्रणवमहावाक्योपदेशं प्राप्य यथासुखं विहरन्मत्तः कश्चिन्नान्यो व्यतिरिक्त इति फलपत्रोदकाहारः पर्वतवनदेवतालयेषु संचरेत्संन्यस्याथ दिगम्बरः सकलसञ्चारकः सर्वदानन्दस्वानुभवैकपूर्णहृदयः कर्मातिदूरलाभः प्राणायामपरायणः फलरसत्वक्पत्रमूलोदकैर्मोक्षार्थी गिरिकन्दरेषु विसृजेद्देहं स्मरंस्तारकम्॥ ३८॥

विविदिषासंन्यासी चेच्छतपथं गत्वाचार्यादिभिर्विप्रैस्तिष्ठ तिष्ठ महाभाग दण्डं वस्त्रं कमण्डलुं गृहाण प्रणवमहावाक्यग्रहणार्थं गुरुनिकटमागच्छेत्याचार्यैर्दण्डकटिसूत्रकौपीनं शाटीमेकां कमण्डलुं पादादिमस्तकप्रमाणमव्रणं समं सौम्यमकालपृष्ठं सलक्षणं वैणवं दण्डमेकमाचमनपूर्वकं सखा मा गोपायौजः सखायोऽसीन्द्रस्य वज्रोऽसि वार्त्रघ्नः शर्म मे भव यत्पापं तन्निवारयेति दण्डं परिग्रहेज्जगज्जीवनं जीवनाधारभूतं माते मा मन्त्रयस्व सर्वदा सर्वसौम्येति प्रणवपूर्वकं कमण्डलुं परिगृह्य कौपीनाधारं कटिसूत्रमोमिति गुह्याच्छादकं कौपीनमोमिति शीतवातोष्णत्राणकरं देहैकरक्षणमोमिति कटिसूत्रकौपीनवस्त्रमाचमनपूर्वकं योगपट्टाभिषिक्तो भूत्वा कृतार्थोऽहमिति मत्वा स्वाश्रमाचारपरो भवेदित्युपनिषत्॥ ३९॥

Should he be a *sannyāsin* learned (in the Vedas, etc.), he should get himself initiated into *Praṇava* from his teacher and go about at his own free will with the thought of there being none other but his self, and feeding his body with fruits, leaves and water, live in mountains, forest and temples. That lover of salvation who after *sannyāsa* roams about nacked in all places with his heart full of the enjoyment of *Ātmic* bliss, with the fruit of avoidance of *karmas* and maintaining his life with fruits, juice, barks, leaves, roots and water should abandon his body on mountain caves, uttering the *Praṇava*. But an aspirant after wisdom, should be become a *sannyāsin*, should, after walking a hundred steps, be addressed by the teacher and other *Brāhmaṇas* thus : "O *Mahābhāga* (very fortunate person), stay, stay, wear the staff, cloth and blow, come to the teacher in order to learn the meaning of *Praṇava mantra vākya*". He should then take up the waist-cord, loin-cloth, red-coloured cloth and bowl. A bamboo staff which is not injured from top to bottom, equal, beautiful, and not spotted with black, should be worn by him, after sipping the water and uttering *mantra* prescribed for the purpose. Then the bowl should be taken up, after uttering the *mantra* with the *Praṇava* preceding it : ओं जगज्जीवनं जीवनाधारभूतं मातेव मा मन्त्रयस्व सर्वदा सर्व

सौम्य।। Then after first uttering (the *mantra*) गुह्याच्छादनं कौपीनं ओं। शीतवातोष्णत्राणकरं देहैकरक्षणं वस्त्रं ओं।। he should take up the waist cord, loin-cloth and cloth with the *ācamana* (sipping of water) preceding it.

"Thus consecreated with yoga and thinking that he had done all that should be done, he should be firm in the observances of his order of life. Thus is the Upaniṣad.

।।पञ्चमोपदेश:।।

अथ हैनं पितामहं नारद: पप्रच्छ भगवन्सर्वकर्मनिवर्तक: संन्यास इति त्वयैवोक्त: पुन: स्वाश्रमाचारपरो भवेदित्युच्यते। तत: पितामह उवाच। शरीरस्य देहिनो जाग्रत्स्वप्नसुषुप्तितुरीयावस्था: सन्ति। तदधीना: कर्मज्ञानवैराग्यप्रवर्तका: पुरुषा जन्तवस्तदनुकूलाचारा: सन्ति। तथैव चेद्भगवन्संन्यासा: कतिभेदास्तदनुष्ठानभेदा: कीदृशास्तत्त्वतोऽस्माकं वक्तुमर्हसीति। तथेत्यङ्गीकृत्य तं पितामहेन।। १।।

संन्यासभेदैराचारभेद: कथमिति चेत्तत्त्वतस्त्वेक एव संन्यास: अज्ञानेनाशक्तिवशात्कर्मलोपतश्च त्रैविध्यमेत्य वैराग्यसंन्यासो ज्ञानसंन्यासो ज्ञानवैराग्यसंन्यास: कर्मसंन्यासश्चेति चातुर्विध्यमुपागत:।। २।।

तद्यथेति दुष्टमदनाभावाच्चेति विषयवैतृष्ण्यमेत्य प्राक्पुण्यकर्मवशात्संन्यस्त: स वैराग्यसंन्यासी।। ३।।

शास्त्रज्ञानात्पाप पुण्यलोकानुभवश्रवणात्प्रपञ्चोपरत: क्रोधेर्ष्यासूयाहङ्काराभिमानात्मकसर्वसंसारं निर्वृत्य दारेषणाधनेषणालोकेषणात्मकदेहवासनां शास्त्रवासनां लोकवासनां त्यक्त्वा वमनान्नमिव प्रकृतीयं सर्वमिदं हेयं मत्वा साधनचतुष्टयसंपन्नो य: संन्यस्यति स एव ज्ञानसंन्यासी।। ४।।

क्रमेण सर्वमभ्यस्य सर्वमनुभूय ज्ञानवैराग्याभ्यां स्वरूपानुसंधानेन देहमात्रावशिष्ट: संन्यस्य जातरूपधरो भवति स ज्ञानवैराग्यसंन्यासी।। ५।।

ब्रह्मचर्यं समाप्य गृही भूत्वा वानप्रस्थाश्रममेत्य वैराग्यभावेऽप्याश्रमक्रमानुसारेण य: संन्यस्यति स कर्मसंन्यासी।। ६।।

Upadeśa V

Then Nārada said to the Grandfather thus :

"You said that sannyāsa was the liberator of all karmas. Now you say again that the sannyāsin is one that should be in the observance of his āśrama (order of life). (How to reconcile the two?)" To which the Grandfather replied thus : "To the jīva possessing the body, there are three avasthās— the waking, the dreaming, and the dreamless sleeping with turya (the fourth). Those beings of Puruṣas that are subject to these avasthās follow the observances, incidental to them, of karma, jñāna and vairāgya." Nārada said: "O Lord, if so, what are the differences of different orders of sannyāsa? And what are the differences of their observances? Please tell us truly."

Therefore the differences of sannyāsas, and the differences of observances were related for the sake of Nārada by Brahmā, after assenting to his (Nārada's) question thus :

"Truly sannyāsa is of one kind only. On account of ajñāna, inability and non-performance of karmas of persons, it is divided into three and then into four, thus :

vairāgya-sannyāsa, jñāna-sannyāsa, jñānavairāgya-sannyāsa and karma-sannyāsa. The vairāgya-sannyāsin is one who becomes an ascetic after being in a condition of lust, etc., and then, becomes disgusted with the objects through his former good karmas. A jñāna-sannyāsin is one who becomes an ascetic with the four means of salvation, after controlling the organs through book-wisdom, and becoming familiar with the experiences of the world of virtue and vice, after abandoning anger, jealousy, envy, ahaṁkāra and all sannyāsa productive of indentification, after giving up the three vāsanās of the body, books and world, which are of the form of desires for women, wealth and earth, and after thinking that the whole of the universe should be given up, like vomited food. A jñānavairāgya-sannyāsin is one who becomes an ascetic as nature made him, after practising and enjoying all, and having the body alone remaining, through jñāna and vairāgya, in the realisation of the Reality. A karma-sannyāsin is one who, though he has no vairāgya, becomes an ascetic by regularly passing from one āśrama to another, from the celibate, to the householder and then to the forester.

ब्रह्मचर्येण संन्यस्य संन्यासाज्जातरूपधरो वैराग्यसंन्यासी। विद्वत्संन्यासी ज्ञानसंन्यासी विविदिषासंन्यासी कर्मसंन्यासी॥७॥

कर्मसंन्यासोऽपि द्विविधः निमित्तसंन्यासोऽनिमित्तसंन्यासश्चेति। निमित्तस्त्वातुरः। अनिमित्तः क्रमसंन्यासः। आतुरः सर्वकर्मलोपः प्राणस्योत्क्रमणकालसंन्यासः सनिमित्तसंन्यासः। दृढाङ्गो भूत्वा सर्वं कृतकं नश्वरमिति देहादिकं सर्वं हेयं प्राप्य॥८-९॥

हंसः शुचिषद्वसुरन्तरिक्षसद्धोता वेदिषदतिथिर्दुरोणसत्। नृषद्वरसदृतसद्व्योमसदब्जा गोजा ऋतजा अद्रिजा ऋतं बृहत्॥१०॥

ब्रह्मव्यतिरिक्तं सर्वं नश्वरमिति निश्चित्याथो क्रमेण यः संन्यस्यति स संन्यासोऽनिमित्तसंन्यासः॥११॥

A vairāgya-sannyāsin is one who becomes an ascetic from the celibate order (directly), being as nature made him.

(There is another fourfold classification) The four kinds are : vidvat-sannyāsa, vividiṣa-sannyāsa and karma-sannyāsa.

In karma-sannyāsa, there are two (sub-) divisions, nimitta (causal) and animitta (non-causal). Ātura-sannyāsa (on account of the cause of approaching death, disease, etc.), is nimitta-sannyāsa. The karma (regular) sannyāsa is animitta. Ātura-sannyāsa is on account of defective karmas. When sannyāsa is taken at the time of death, it is called nimitta, Animitta is that when one becomes duly a sannyāsin when the body is strong, (after being convinced) that all created things are subject to destruction, that body and others should be given up, that all Ātmā (souls)— each one shining in the pure Ākāśa, dwelling in all, moving in the antarikṣa (middle world) as of the form of vāyu, in the sacrificial pit as of the form of fire, in the moon, in all men, in the supreme angels, in the form of truth, in ākāśa, in the form of the conch, pearl, fish, etc., in water, in the form of grain, etc., in the form of the limbs of Vedas, in the form of the rivers from the mountains, in the form of truth and the great one— are no other than brahman and that others are but perishable.

संन्यासः षड्विधो भवति। कुटीचको बहूदको हंसः परमहंसः तुरीयातीतोऽवधूतश्चेति॥ १२॥

कुटीचकः शिखायज्ञोपवीती दण्डकमण्डलुधरः कौपीनकन्थाधरः पितृमातृगुर्वाराधनपरः पिठरखनित्रशिक्यादिमन्त्रसाधनपर एकत्रान्नादनपरः श्वेतोर्ध्वपुण्ड्रधारी त्रिदण्डः। बहूदकः शिखादिकन्थाधरस्त्रिपुण्ड्रधारी कुटीचकवत्सर्वसमो मधुकरवृत्त्याष्टकवलाशी॥ १३॥

हंसो जटाधारी त्रिपुण्ड्रोर्ध्वपुण्ड्रधारी असंक्लृप्तमाधूकरान्नाशी कौपीनखण्डतुण्डधारी॥ १४॥

परमहंसः शिखायज्ञोपवीतरहितः पञ्चगृहेष्वेकरात्रान्नादनपरः करपात्री एककौपीनधारी शाटीमेकामेकं वैणवं दण्डमेकशाटीधरो वा भस्मोद्धूलनपरः सर्वत्यागी॥ १५॥

There are six classes of sannyāsins— Kuṭīcaka, bahūdaka, haṁsa, paramahaṁsa, turīyātīta and avadhūta. Kuṭīcaka is one who wears the tuft of hair, holy thread, staff, bowl, loin-cloth and tattered cloth, who worships mother, father, and teacher, who has potsherd and sling, who is uttering mantras, who takes food in one and the same place, who ears, varitically, the white earth (on the forehead as sect-mark) and who has a staff. Buhūdaka is one who, like kutīcaka, wears the tuft of hair, tattered cloth, etc., as well as the three (sect-) marks, but who eats eight morsels of food through getting alms. The haṁsa is one who wears matted hair and the three vertical sect-marks and eats the alms-food without any limit (as to the morsel) and wears the bare loin-cloth only. The Paramahaṁsa is he who is without tuft of hair and holy thread, begs food in one day from five houses, has one loin-cloth, wears one red cloth alone and sacred ashes and has given up all.

तुरीयातीतो गोमुखः फलाहारी। अन्नाहारी चेद्गृहत्रये देहमात्रावशिष्टो दिगम्बरः कुणपवच्छरीरवृत्तिकः॥ १६॥

अवधूतस्त्वनियमोऽभिशस्तपतितवर्जनपूर्वकं सर्ववर्णेष्वजगरवृत्त्याहारपरः स्वरूपानुसंधानपरः॥ १७॥

आतुरो जीवति चेत्क्रमसंन्यासः कर्तव्यः॥ १८॥

कुटीचकबहूदकहंसानां ब्रह्मचर्याश्रमादितुरीयाश्रमवत् कुटीचकादीनां संन्यासविधिः॥ १९॥

परमहंसादित्रयाणां न कटिसूत्रं न कौपीनं न वस्त्रं न कमण्डलुर्न दण्डः। सार्ववर्णैकभैक्षाटनपरत्वं जातरूपधरत्वं विधिः। संन्यासकालेऽप्यलंबुद्धिपर्यन्तमधीत्य तदनन्तरं कटिसूत्रं कौपीनं दण्डं वस्त्रं कमण्डलुं सर्वमप्सु विसृज्याथ जातरूपधरश्चरेन्न कन्थावेशो नाध्येतव्यो न वक्तव्यो न श्रोतव्यमन्यत्किंचित्प्रणवादन्यं न तर्कं पठेन्न शब्दमपि बृहच्छब्दान्नाध्यापयेन्न महद्वाचो विग्लापनं गिरा पाण्यादिना संभाषणं नान्यस्माद्वा विशेषेण न शूद्रस्त्रीपतितोदक्या संभाषणं न यतेर्देवपूजा नोत्सवदर्शनं तीर्थयात्रावृत्तिः॥ २०॥

The turīyātīta is one who either may take fruits, eating them with his mouth like cows, or if he is an eater of food, may beg food from three houses. The naked man having the body alone has the bodily actions (quiescent), like the dead body. Such an one is the turīyātīta. The avadhūta is he who is without any rules, gets his food (in his mouth), following the course of the boa constrictor, from all persons except persons of ill-repute and outcastes, and is ever engaged in the realisation of the Real. Should the Ātura-sannyāsin be alive (after taking sannyāsa), he should take up regular sannyāsa. The rules to be observed in the case of the (three), Kuṭīcaka, bahūdaka and haṁsa are the same as for the orders of life from the celibate to the sannyāsin. For the three, paramahaṁsa upwards, they have no waist-cord, loin-cloth, cloth, bowl, and staff. they may get food from all castes and should be as nature made them. Such are the rules.

"At the time of the sannyāsa, the recitation of the Vedas should be made till the mind is cleared; and after casting aside in water the waist-cord, loin-cloth, staff, cloth, bowl, etc., he should roam about. He should be without even the slightest tattered cloth. He should neither utter anythig other than Praṇava, nor talk nor hear. he should not study logic or grammar. He should not talk many words; they will but pain his vocal organ. He should not converse with people through the vocal organ. He should not talk in other language (than Sanskrit). He has no worship of God and no witnessing of festivals; he should be free from pilgrimage.

पुनर्यतिविशेषः। कुटीचकस्यैकत्र भिक्षा बहूदकस्यासंक्लृप्तं माधूकरं हंसस्याष्टगृहेष्वष्टकवलं परमहंसस्य पञ्चगृहेषु करपात्रं फलाहारो गोमुखं तुरीयातीतस्यावधूतस्याजगरवृत्तिः सार्ववर्णिकेषु यतिर्नैकरात्रं वसेन्न कस्यापि नमेत्तुरीयातीतावधूतयोर्न ज्येष्ठो यो न स्वरूपज्ञः। स ज्येष्ठोऽपि कनिष्ठो हस्ताभ्यां नद्युत्तरणं न कुर्यान्न वृक्षमारोहेन्न यानादिरूढो न क्र यविक्रयपरो न किंचिद्विनिमयपरो न दाम्भिको नानृतवादी न यतेः किंचित्कर्तव्यमस्त्यस्ति चेत्सांकर्यम्। तस्मान्मननादौ संन्यासिनामधिकारः॥ २१॥

The other rules of ascetics are : The kutīcaka should beg alms in one house only; for the bahūdaka, eight morsels in eight houses; for the haṁsa, there is no limit; for paramahaṁsa, he should beg with his hand as the vessel in five houses; for the turīyātīta, he should eat fruits with his mouth like cows; (for avadhūta), he should take food like a boa constrictor in all castes. The ascetic should not dwell in one place for many days. He should not make prostrations to any one. Among the truīyātīta, and avadhūta (ascetics), even though one in junior, he should not make prostrations to another, a senior who has known the Reality. He should not swim with his hands and cross the river. He should not climb up a tree, nor get into a carriage. Nothing should be purchased or sold (by him). No exchange should be made, no ostentation for him. There is nothing for the ascetic to do. If there is anything for him to do, he will perish. Therefore the only thing he is qualified to do is reflection, etc.

आतुरकुटीचकयोर्भूर्लोकभुवर्लोकौ बहूदकस्य स्वर्गलोको हंसस्य तपोलोकः परमहंसस्य सत्यलोकस्तुरीयातीतावधूतयोः स्वात्मन्येव कैवल्यं स्वरूपानुसन्धानेन भ्रमरकीटन्यायवत्॥ २२॥

यं यं वापि स्मरन्भावं त्यजत्यन्ते कलेवरम्। तं तमेव समाप्नोति नान्यथा श्रुतिशासनम्॥ २३॥

तदेवं ज्ञात्वा स्वरूपानुसंधानं विनान्यथाचारपरो न भवेत्तदाचारवशात्तत्तल्लोकप्राप्तिर्ज्ञानवैराग्यसंपन्नस्य स्वस्मिन्नेव मुक्तिरिति न सर्वत्राचारप्रसक्तिस्तदाचारः। जाग्रत्स्वप्नसुषुप्तिष्वेकशरीरस्य जाग्रत्काले विश्वः स्वप्नकाले तैजसः सुषुप्तिकाले प्राज्ञः अवस्थाभेदादवस्थेश्वरभेदः कार्यभेदात्कारणभेदस्तासु चतुर्दशकरणानां

बाह्यवृत्तयोऽन्तर्वृत्तयस्तेषामुपादानकारणम्। वृत्तयश्चत्वारः मनोबुद्धिरहंकारश्चित्तं चेति। तत्तद्वृत्तिव्यापारभेदेन पृथगाचारभेदः॥ २४॥

नेत्रस्थं जागरितं विद्यात्कण्ठे स्वप्नं समाविशेत्। सुषुप्तं हृदयस्थं तु तुरीयं मूर्ध्नि संस्थितम्॥ २५॥

तुरीयमक्षरमिति ज्ञात्वा जागरिते सुषुप्त्यवस्थापन्न इव यद्यच्छुतं यद्यद्दृष्टं तत्तत्सर्वमविज्ञातमिव यो वसेत्तस्य स्वप्नावस्थायामपि तादृगवस्था भवति। स जीवन्मुक्त इति वदन्ति। सर्वश्रुत्यर्थप्रतिपादनमपि तस्यैव मुक्तिरिति। भिक्षुर्नैहिकामुष्मिकापेक्षः। यद्यपेक्षास्ति तदनुरूपो भवति। स्वरूपानुसन्धानव्यतिरिक्तान्यशास्त्राभ्यासै- रुष्ट्रकुङ्कुमभारवद्व्यर्थो न योगशास्त्रप्रवृत्तिर्न सांख्यशास्त्राभ्यासो न मन्त्रतन्त्रव्यापारः। इतरशास्त्रप्रवृत्तिर्यतेरस्ति चेच्छवालंकारवच्चर्मकारवदतिविदूरकर्माचारविद्यादूरो न प्रणवकीर्तनपरो यद्यत्कर्म करोति तत्तत्फलमनुभवति। एरण्डतैलफेनवदतः सर्वं परित्यज्य तत्प्रसक्तं मनोदण्डं करपात्रं दिगम्बरं दृष्ट्वा परिव्रजेद्भिक्षुः। बालोन्मत्तपिशाचवन्मरणं जीवितं वा न काङ् क्षेत कालमेव प्रतीक्षेत निर्देशभृतकन्यायेन परिव्राडिति॥ २६॥

"To the āturas and Kuṭīcakas, the world they attain is bhūrloka and bhuvarloka; to the bāhūdakas, svargaloka; to the haṁsas, tapoloka; to the paramahaṁsas, satyaloka. To the turīyātīta and avadhūta, Kaivalya in Ātmā according to the analogy of wasp and the worm through the realisation of Reality. It is the command of the Vedas that whatever from one thinks of all the last (death) moment and before leaving the body is attained by him and no other. Knowing it thus, he should not be a practiser of anything but the realisation of Reality. Through the observance of any other, he goes to the world of that other. To one has attained jñāna-vairāgya, his salvation is in the Self, as there is no other observance for him. The same one (Ātmā) alone is styled Viśva in the walking state, Taijasa in the dreaming state and Prājña in the dreamless sleeping state. Through the difference of states, there is the difference of the agent presiding over them. To the fourteen organs (the ten organs of sense and fictions and the four organs of the mind in these states), the outer and inner vṛttis, (modifications) are the material cause. There are four vṛttis– viz., manas, buddhi, ahaṁkāra and Citta. Through the differences of actions of the vṛttis, there arise the differences of separate functions.

When (the presiding agent is) in the eyes, there is the waking state; in the throat, the dreaming state; in the heart, the dreamless sleeping state; and in the head, the turya (of fourth) state. Knowing these and that the turya is the indestructible, one should not hear or see anything in the waking state, as if he were in dreamless sleeping state. To such a one who does not apparently know them, even the dreaming state forms the same (dreamless sleeping) state. Such a one is termed Jīvanmukta. All the Vedas say that there is salvation to such a one.

"To the ascetic, there should be no desire of this world or the higher. Then he will be one that will practise accordingly. Through the practices of (the study of) books foreign to the realisation of Reality, he becomes a useless person like a camel bearing saffron paint. To him, there is no entry into yoga books, no study of sāṁkhya books, no practice of mantra or tantra. Should there be any entry into other books (than the one treating of

Reality), then it will be like an ornament to a dead body. Like a cobbler, he should be beyond karma and knowledge and unfit for salutation and repeating the names of the Lord. He will duly get the benefit of the karmas (of his order of life). Having given up all like the foam (separating itself) from the castor oil, having the mental staff which controls the mind clinging to objects, having the hand as the vessel (for eating) and having the quarters alone as the cloth, the ascetic should go about like a lad, idiot, or ghost. He should neither desire to live nor die. Like a coolie abiding his appointed time (of pay), the ascetic should bide his time (of death).

तितिक्षाज्ञानवैराग्यशमादिगुणवर्जितः। भिक्षामात्रेण जीवी स्यात्स यतिर्यतिवृत्तिहा॥ २७॥
न दण्डधारणेन न मुण्डनेन न वेषेण न दम्भाचारेण मुक्तिः॥॥ २८॥
ज्ञानदण्डो धृतो येन एकदण्डी स उच्यते। काष्ठदण्डो धृतो येन सर्वाशी ज्ञानवर्जितः।
स याति नरकान्घोरान्महारौरवसंज्ञितान्॥ २९॥
प्रतिष्ठा सूकरीविष्ठासमा गीता महर्षिभिः। तस्मादेनां परित्यज्य कीटवत्पर्यटेद्यतिः॥ ३०॥
अयाचितं यथालाभं भोजनाच्छादनं भवेत्। परेच्छया च दिग्वासाः स्नानं कुर्यात्परेच्छया॥ ३१॥
स्वप्नेऽपि यो हि युक्तः स्याज्जाग्रतीव विशेषतः। ईदृक्चेष्टः स्मृतः श्रेष्ठो वरिष्ठो ब्रह्मवादिनाम्॥ ३२॥
अलाभे न विषादी स्याल्लाभे चैव न हर्षयेत्। प्राणयात्रिकमात्रः स्यान्मात्रासङ्गविवर्जितः॥ ३३॥
अभिपूजितलाभांश्च जुगुप्सेतैव सर्वशः। अभिपूजितलाभैस्तु यतिर्मुक्तोऽपि बध्यते॥ ३४॥
प्राणयात्रानिमित्तं च व्यङ्गारे भुक्तवज्जने। काले प्रशस्ते वर्णानां भिक्षार्थं पर्यटेद्गृहान्॥ ३५॥
पाणिपात्रश्चरन्योगी नासकृद्भैक्षमाचरेत्। तिष्ठन्भुञ्ज्याच्चरन्भुञ्ज्यान्मध्येनाचमनं तथा॥ ३६॥
अब्धिवद्धृतमर्यादा भवन्ति विशदाशयाः। नियतिं न विमुञ्चन्ति महान्तो भास्करा इव॥ ३७॥
आस्येन तु यदाहारं गोवन्मृगयते मुनिः। तदा समः स्यात्सर्वेषु सोऽमृतत्वाय कल्पते॥ ३८॥
अनिन्द्यं वै व्रजेद्गेहं निन्द्यं गेहं तु वर्जयेत्। अनावृते विशेद्द्वारि गेहे नैवावृते व्रजेत्॥ ३९॥
पांसुना च प्रतिच्छन्नशून्यागारप्रतिश्रयः। वृक्षमूलनिकेतो वा त्यक्तसर्वप्रियाप्रियः॥ ४०॥
यत्रास्तमितशायी स्यान्निरग्निरनिकेतनः। यथालब्धोपजीवी स्यान्मुनिर्दान्तो जितेन्द्रियः॥ ४१॥

One who lives by taking alms without (the qualifications of) patience, wisdom, vairāgya and the qualifications beginning with śama (control of mind) is the spoiler of the order of life of an ascetic. There is no salvation obtained through the mere assumption of the staff or making the head bald or other disguise or through ostentatious observances. That man who has jñāna as his staff is said to be the ekadaṇḍī (one having Brahman alone as the staff). An ascetic who, having merely a wooden staff without jñāna, eats all (indiscriminately) in all places, goes to the terrible hells called Mahāraurava. (The sense of) greatness in his case is likened by the ṛṣis to the pig's dung. Having given it up, he should move about like a worm. Food and cloth without being begged for by him should be obtained involuntarily through the will of others. A naked (ascetic) may bathe at the wish of another. A man who practises the meditation upon Self in the dreaming state as in the waking is said to be the foremost and first of Brahmavādins. He should neither grieve for things not obtained, nor rejoice at things obtained. With the organs not attached to objects, he should be engaged in the sole protection of life. He should always look down upon the gains obtained with much respect (shown to him). Through the gains obtained with much respect, the ascetic though released becomes bound. What is meant by the protection of life, is this : When the fire (of the hearth in a house) had been extinguished and all have taken food, he may go to the houses of caste people that are fit for taking alms from : The yogin who has his hand only as his alms-bowl should not often take alms. He may take (food) standing or sitting; so in the middle (of taking food), he may sip water. Those who have pure mind should not over-step the limits like the ocean. The great ones do not give up their self-restraint like the sun. When the muni takes, like a cow, the food with the mouth only (without the use of the hand), he becomes of equal vision to all beings. Then he becomes fit for salvation. He may, for alms, go from a forbidden house to a non-forbidden one. He should go (for alms) to a house where the door is opened, but not to a house where it is closed. The muni who has dusty body, an uninhabited house or the foot of a tree as his abode, without anything dear or not dear to him, sleeping where the sun sets, without any fire-worship, without any settled place and with patience and the organs under control, should live without any desire in any place obtained.

निष्क्रम्य वनमास्थाय ज्ञानयज्ञो जितेन्द्रियः। कालकाङ्क्षी चरन्नेव ब्रह्मभूयाय कल्पते॥ ४२॥

अभयं सर्वभूतेभ्यो दत्त्वा चरति यो मुनिः। न तस्य सर्वभूतेभ्यो भयमुत्पद्यते क्वचित्॥ ४३॥

निर्मानश्चानहंकारो निर्द्वन्द्वश्छिन्नसंशयः। नैव क्रुध्यति न द्वेष्टि नानृतं भाषते गिरा॥ ४४॥

पुण्यायतनचारी च भूतानामविहिंसकः। काले प्राप्ते भवेद्भैक्षं कल्पते ब्रह्मभूयसे॥ ४५॥

वानप्रस्थगृहस्थाभ्यां न संसृज्येत कर्हिचित्। अज्ञातचर्यां लिप्सेत न चैनं हर्ष आविशेत्।

अध्वा सूर्येण निर्दिष्टः कीटवद्विचरेन्महीम्॥ ४६॥

आशीर्युक्तानि कर्माणि हिंसायुक्तानि यानि च। लोकसंग्रहयुक्तानि नैव कुर्यान्न कारयेत्॥ ४७॥

नासच्छास्त्रेषु सज्जेत नोपजीवेत जीविकाम्। अतिवादांस्त्यजेत्तर्कान्पक्षं कंचन नाश्रयेत्॥ ४८॥

न शिष्याननुबध्नीत ग्रन्थान्नैवाभ्यसेद्बहून्। न व्याख्यामुपयुञ्जीत नारम्भानारभेत्क्वचित्॥ ४९॥

अव्यक्तलिङ्गोऽव्यक्तार्थो मुनिरुन्मत्तबालवत्। कविर्मूकवदात्मानं तद्दृष्ट्या दर्शयेन्नृणाम्॥ ५०॥

न कुर्यान्न वदेत्किंचिन्न ध्यायेत्साध्वसाधु वा। आत्मारामोऽनया वृत्त्या विचरेज्जडवन्मुनिः॥ ५१॥

एकश्चरेन्महीमेतां निःसङ्गः संयतेन्द्रियः। आत्मक्रीड आत्मरतिरात्मवान्समदर्शनः॥ ५२॥

बुधो बालकवत्क्रीडेत्कुशलो जडवच्चरेत्। वदेदुन्मत्तवद्विद्वान् गोचर्यां नैगमश्चरेत्॥ ५३॥

He who after going to the forest dwells with jñāna as the sacrifice and the organs under his mastery and awaits his time (of death), is fit to be of the nature of Brahman. A muni who goes about with no cause for instilling fear into all beings need never have any fear from them. One without any abhimāna (identification with body) or egoism or dualities or doubt, never is angry, never hates, never lies through the vocal organ. That person who, having visited all sacred places does not do any injury to any living creature and gets alms at the proper time, is fit to be of the nature of Brahman. He should not associate with a forester or householder. He should conduct himself in such manner as not to be known to others. He should not be glad of anything. He should roam about on earth like a worm, according to the direction pointed out by the sun. He should not do or cause to do works tending to (his) fame or pains or people's benefit. He should not be inclined towards vicious books. He should not live dependent upon any. He should give up all over-disputatious reasoning. He should not join any party (fighting with another). He should not take any disciples. He should not study many books. He should not discourse. Neither should he commence any works. Without any distinguishing characteristics and without letting others know his opinions, that wise man, or muni, ever intent upon the Brāhmic vision, should exhibit himself to people like an idiot, or a lad, or a mute person. He should neither do nor talk anything. He should not think of a good or bad thing. Rejoicing in That within himself, the muni should go about like an idiot. He should roam about alone without associating with any, and with the senses under control. The clever jñānī sporting in Ātmā, ever delighting in Ātmā, looking upon all with equal vision like an Ātmā-jñānī, and playing like a child, should wander about like an idiot. That learned man versed in Brahmavidyā should talk like a madman. He should follow the observances of cows (by eating with the mouth, causing no trouble to anybody).

क्षिप्तोऽवमानितोऽसद्भिः प्रलब्धोऽसूयितोऽपि वा। ताडितः संनिरुद्धो वा वृत्त्या वा परितापितः॥५४॥
विष्ठितो मूत्रितो वाज्ञैर्बहुधैवं प्रकल्पितः। श्रेयस्कामः कृच्छ्रगत आत्मनात्मानमुद्धरेत्॥५५॥
संमाननं परां हानिं योगर्द्धेः कुरुते यतः। जनेनावमतो योगी योगसिद्धिं च विन्दति॥५६॥
तथा चरेत वै योगी सतां धर्ममदूषयन्। जना यथावमन्येरन्गच्छेयुर्नैव सङ्गतिम्॥५७॥
जरायुजाण्डजादीनां वाङ्मनःकायकर्मभिः। युक्तः कुर्वीत न द्रोहं सर्वसङ्गांश्च वर्जयेत्॥५८॥
कामक्रोधौ तथा दर्पलोभमोहादयश्च ये। तांस्तु दोषान्परित्यज्य परिव्राड् भयवर्जितः॥५९॥
भैक्षाशनं च मौनित्वं तपो ध्यानं विशेषतः। सम्यग्ज्ञानं च वैराग्यं धर्मोऽयं भिक्षुके मतः॥६०॥
काषायवासाः सततं ध्यानयोगपरायणः। ग्रामान्ते वृक्षमूले वा वसेद्देवालयेऽपि वा।
भैक्षेण वर्तयेन्नित्यं नैकान्नाशी भवेत्क्वचित्॥६१॥

A good jñānī whether pushed, disregarded, slighted, beaten, or hindered by the vicious, or burnt by their acts, or having urine and fæces thrown upon him by them, or afflicted in various other ways, should always think well of them, though pained, and thus make them lift themselves through their own Selves. A yogin whether praised or afflicted by others, never thinks of it in order to reach a superior state in yoga. A yogin who is slighted by people, attains a higher state in yoga. A yogin never goes against the actions of the virtuous. He is the same whether people sight him or do not desire his association. He should do all that is right through the actions of mind, speech and body to all beings born out of the embryo or the egg, etc. He should harbour no malice against any and give up all clinging to things. The ascetic after giving up passion, anger, pride, desire, delusion and other faults should be without fear. Eating alms-food, preserving silence, tapas, special meditation, a good jñāna, and vairāgya— these are said, in the opinion (of the great), to be the dharma of the ascetic. Wearing the red cloth, and being ever in dhyāna-yoga, he should live either at the foot of a tree, outside the village, or in the temple. Daily he should live upon begging. He should not eat one food alone (from one only).

चित्तशुद्धिर्भवेद्यावत्तावन्नित्यं चरेत्सुधीः। ततः प्रव्रज्य शुद्धात्मा संचरेद्यत्र कुत्रचित्॥ ६२॥

बहिरन्तश्च सर्वत्र संपश्यन्हि जनार्दनम्। सर्वत्र विचरेन्मौनी वायुवद्वीतकल्मषः॥ ६३॥

समदुःखसुखः क्षान्तो हस्तप्राप्तं च भक्षयेत्। निर्वैरेण समं पश्यन्द्विजगोऽश्वमृगादिषु॥ ६४॥

भावयन्मनसा विष्णुं परमात्मानमीश्वरम्। चिन्मयं परमानन्दं ब्रह्मैवाहमिति स्मरन्॥ ६५॥

ज्ञात्वैवं मनोदण्डं धृत्वा आशानिवृत्तो भूत्वा आशाम्बरधरो भूत्वा सर्वदा मनोवाक्कायकर्मभिः सर्वसंसारमुत्सृज्य प्रपञ्चावाङ्मुखः स्वरूपानुसन्धानेन भ्रमरकीटन्यायेन मुक्तो भवतीत्युपनिषत्॥ ६६॥

Till the mind becomes pure, the learned man should thus be moving about. Then when the mind is purified, he may be anywhere, as a parivrājaka. Seeing Janārdana in and out everywhere, preserving silence, being without stain like vāyu, roaming everywhere, being equal in happiness and pains, and with patience, eating whatever comes to hand, equally regarding without any hate, brāhmaṇa, cow, horse, beasts and others, meditating through the mind upon Viṣṇu that is Paramātmā and Īśvara, thinking ever of Brāhmic bliss and thinking himself to be Brahman alone— such a one having known thus, regarding the staff to be no other than the certitude of the mind as above, having no desire, being naked and having abandoned all saṁsāra through the actions ever done through the mind, speech, and body, attains salvation, according to the analogy of the wasp and the worm, through the practice of the realisation of Reality without ever seeing the universe. Such is the Upaniṣad."

॥षष्ठोपदेशः॥

अथ नारदः पितामहमुवाच। भगवन् तदभ्यासवशात् भ्रमरकीटन्यायवत्तदभ्यासः कथमिति। तमाह पितामहः। सत्यवाग्ज्ञानवैराग्याभ्यां विशिष्टदेहावशिष्टो वसेत्॥ १॥

ज्ञानं शरीरं वैराग्यं जीवनं विद्धि शान्तिदान्ती नेत्रे मनो मुखं बुद्धिः कला पञ्चविंशतितत्त्वान्यवयवा अवस्था पञ्चमहाभूतानि कर्म भक्तिज्ञानवैराग्यं शाखा जाग्रत्स्वप्नसुषुप्तितुरीयाश्चतुर्दशकरणानि पङ्कस्तम्भाकाराणीति। एवमपि नावमतिपङ्कं कर्णधार इव यन्तेव गजं स्वबुद्ध्या वशीकृत्य स्वव्यतिरिक्तं सर्वं कृतकं नश्वरमिति मत्वा विरक्तः पुरुषः सर्वदा ब्रह्माहमिति व्यवहरेन्नान्यत्किंचिद्वेदितव्यं स्वव्यतिरेकेण। जीवन्मुक्तो वसेत्कृतकृत्यो भवति। न नाहं ब्रह्मेति व्यवहरेत्किंतु ब्रह्माहमस्मीत्यजस्रं जाग्रत्स्वप्नसुषुप्तिषु। तुरीयावस्थां प्राप्य तुरीयातीतत्वं व्रजेत्॥ २॥

Upadeśa VI

Nārada addressing Brahmā asked : "O Lord ! You said of abhyāsa (practice) according to the analogy of wasp and the worm. What is that practice ?"

To which the Grandfather replied thus :

"One (viz., an ascetic) should live with true speech and jñāna-vairāgya and with the body alone as the remaining (possession). Know jñāna alone as the body, vairāgya alone as prāṇa, śānti (mental control) and dānti (bodily control) as the eyes, manas alone as the face, buddhi alone as kalā (parts of effulgence), the twenty-five tattvas as the limbs, the avasthās as the five great elements, karma, bhakti, jñāna, and vairāgya as the branches (of parts) and that the waking, dreaming, dreamless sleeping, and turya avasthās and the fourteen organs as being of the nature of a pillar planted in the mud. Through such is the case, the man who masters these through his buddhi like a boatman regarding the boat immersed in the mire, or the elephant-driver regarding the elephant (under his control), and has known that all else besides Self is illusory and destructible and become indifferent, should ever utter : 'I am Brahman alone.' He should not know anything as other than Self. A Jīvanmukta who lives thus is a doer of that which should be done. He should not discourse that he is other than Brahman. But he should ever be discoursing : 'I am Brahman'. From the waking, dreaming and dreamless sleeping states, he should reach the turīya state and then turīyātīta (the state beyond turya).

दिवा जाग्रन्नक्तं स्वप्नं सुषुप्तमर्धरात्रं गतमित्येकावस्थायां चतस्रोऽवस्थास्त्वेकैककरणाधीनानां चतुर्दशकरणानां व्यापारश्चक्षुरादीनाम्। चक्षुषो रूपग्रहणं श्रोत्रयोः शब्दग्रहणं जिह्वाया रसास्वादनं घ्राणस्य गन्धग्रहणं वचसो वाग्व्यापारः पाणेरादानं पादयोः संचारः पायोरुत्सर्ग उपस्थस्यानन्दग्रहणं त्वचः स्पर्शग्रहणम्। तदधीना च विषयग्रहणबुद्धिः बुद्ध्या बुद्ध्यति चित्तेन चेतयत्यहंकारेणाहंकरोति। विसृज्य जीव एतान्देहाभिमानेन जीवो भवति। गृहाभिमानेन गृहस्थ इव शरीरे जीवः संचरति। प्राग्दले पुण्यावृत्तिराग्नेय्यां निद्रालस्यौ दक्षिणायां क्रौर्यबुद्धिर्नैर्ऋत्यां पापबुद्धिः पश्चिमे क्रीडारतिर्वायव्यां गमने बुद्धिरुत्तरे शान्तिरीशान्ये ज्ञानं कर्णिकायां वैराग्यं केसरेष्वात्मचिन्ता इत्येवं वक्त्रं ज्ञात्वा॥ ३॥

The waking state is in the day; the dreaming in the night and the dreamless sleeping in the midnight. Each avasthā (or state) has its sub-states. The functions of the fourteen organs, eye and others mutually dependent are the following : The eyes perceive forms; the ears, sounds; the tongue perceives tastes; the nose, odours; the vocal organ speaks; the hand lifts; the leg walks; the anus excretes; the sexual organ enjoys; the skin feels; the buddhi perceives objects, being under the control of the organs; through buddhi, he understands; through citta, he thinks; through ahaṁkāra, be says 'I'. All these should be abandoned. Through the identification with the house (the body), he, like a householder, becomes a jīva thinking that the body is itself.

The jīva is dwelling in his body. When he is in the eastern petal (of the heart), he is inclined to virtuous actions; in the south-eastern petal, to sleep and laziness; in the southern petal, to cruel actions; in the south-western petal, to sinful actions; in the western petal, to love of sport (or to flirt); in the north-western petal, to travelling; in the northern petal, to peace of mind; in the north-eastern petal, to jñāna; in (the middle of) the pericarp, to vairāgya; in the filament, to Ātmā-deliberation. Such are the different aspects to be understood (in the heart).

जीवदवस्थां प्रथमं जाग्रद्द्वितीयं स्वप्नं तृतीयं सुषुप्तं चतुर्थं तुरीयं चतुर्भिर्विरहितं तुरीयातीतम्। विश्वतैजसप्राज्ञतटस्थभेदैरेक एव एको देवः साक्षी निर्गुणश्च तद्ब्रह्माहमिति व्याहरेत्। नो चेज्जाग्रदवस्थायां जाग्रदादिचतस्रोऽवस्थाः स्वप्ने स्वप्नादिचतस्रोऽवस्थाः सुषुप्ते सुषुप्त्यादिचतस्रोऽवस्थाः तुरीये तुरीयादिचतस्रोऽवस्थाः न त्वेवं तुरीयातीतस्य निर्गुणस्य। स्थूलसूक्ष्मकारणरूपैर्विश्वतैजसप्राज्ञेश्वरैः सर्वावस्थासु साक्षी त्वेक एवावतिष्ठते। उत तटस्थो द्रष्टा तटस्थो न द्रष्टा द्रष्टृत्वान्न द्रष्टैव कर्तृत्वभोक्तृत्वाहंकारादिभिः स्पृष्टो जीवः जीवेतरो न स्पृष्टः। जीवोऽपि न स्पृष्ट इति चेन्न। जीवाभिमानेन क्षेत्राभिमानःशरीराभिमानेन जीवत्वम्। जीवत्वं घटाकाशमहाकाशवद्व्यवधानोऽस्ति। व्यवधानवशादेव हंसः सोऽहमिति मन्त्रेणोच्छ्वासनिः - श्वासव्यपदेशेनानुसन्धानं करोति। एवं विज्ञाय शरीराभिमानं त्यजेन्न शरीराभिमानी भवति। स एव ब्रह्मेत्युच्यते॥४॥

The first living avasthā (of jīva) is the waking; the second is the dreaming; the third is the dreamless sleeping; the fourth turīya; that which is not these four turyātīta. The one Lord alone that is witness and without qualities appears (as many) through the differences of Viśva. Taijasa, Prājña, the Taṭastha (the neutral). One should (always) utter : 'I am brahman alone.' Else in the waking state, (he is) in the four states of the waking state and others: in the dreaming state (he is) in the four states of the dreaming state and others; in the dreamless sleeping state, (he is) in the four states of the dreamless sleeping and others; in the turya, (he is) in the four states of turya and others; to the turīyātīta that is nirguṇa, such states are not. There is only one witness in all the states of Viśva. Taijasa and Prājña, who is presiding over the gross, the subtle and the causal (bodies). Is Taṭastha the seer? or is he not? As (to Taṭastha), there is the property of seeing; the jīva that is affected by the egoism, etc., of agency and enjoyment is not the seer. The one other than jīva (viz., Taṭastha) is not concerned (with egoism, etc.). If it is said that the jīva is not so (concerned with egoism), then it is not a fact. Through the abhimāna of the jīva, there is the abhimāna of the body. And (conversely) through the abhimāna of the the body, there is the abhimāna of the jīva. The state of the jīva is as a screen (to screen Brahman) like (the pot and house in) the pot-ākāśa and the house-ākāśa. Through such a screen, he reaches self-realisation through the mantra— "Haṁsa-So'aham' having the characteristics of inspiration and expiration. Having known thus, if he should give up the identification with the body, then he does not attain the state of jīva. Such a one is stated to be Brahman.

त्यक्तसङ्गो जितक्रोधो लघ्वाहारो जितेन्द्रियः। पिधाय बुद्ध्या द्वाराणि मनो ध्याने निवेशयेत्॥५॥

शून्येष्वेवावकाशेषु गुहासु च वनेषु च। नित्ययुक्तः सदा योगी ध्यानं सम्यगुपक्रमेत्॥६॥

आतिथ्यश्राद्धयज्ञेषु देवयात्रोत्सवेषु च। महाजनेषु सिद्ध्यर्थी न गच्छेद्योगवित्क्वचित्॥ ७॥

यथैनमवमन्यन्ते जनाः परिभवन्ति च। तथा युक्तश्चरेद्योगी सतां वर्त्म न दूषयेत्॥ ८॥

वाग्दण्डः कर्मदण्डश्च मनोदण्डश्च ते त्रयः। यस्यैते नियता दण्डाः स त्रिदण्डी महायतिः॥ ९॥

विधूमे च प्रशान्ताग्नौ यस्तु माधूकरीं चरेत्। गृहे च विप्रमुख्यानां यतिः सर्वोत्तमः स्मृतः॥ १०॥

दण्डभिक्षां च यः कुर्यात्स्वधर्मे व्यसनं विना। यस्तिष्ठति न वैराग्यं याति नीचयतिर्हि सः॥ ११॥

यस्मिन्गृहे विशेषेण लभेद्भिक्षां च वासनात्। तत्र नो याति यो भूयः स यतिर्नेतरः स्मृतः॥ १२॥

यः शरीरेन्द्रियादिभ्यो विहीनं सर्वसाक्षिणम्। पारमार्थिकविज्ञानं सुखात्मानं स्वयंप्रभम्॥ १३॥

परतत्त्वं विजानाति सोऽतिवर्णाश्रमी भवेत्। वर्णाश्रमादयो देहे मायया परिकल्पिताः॥ १४॥

नात्मनो बोधरूपस्य मम ते सन्ति सर्वदा। इति यो वेद वेदान्तैः सोऽतिवर्णाश्रमी भवेत्॥ १५॥

यस्य वर्णाश्रमाचारो गलितः स्वात्मदर्शनात्। स वर्णानाश्रमान्सर्वानतीत्य स्वात्मनि स्थितः॥ १६

योऽतीत्य स्वाश्रमान्वर्णानात्मन्येव स्थितः पुमान्। सोऽतिवर्णाश्रमी प्रोक्तः सर्ववेदार्थवेदिभिः॥ १७

Having given up abhimāna and anger, being content with moderate food, having conquered the organs and having controlled the organs, one should make the mind enter into meditation. The yogin who has always controlled (his mind and organs) should ever deligently commence his meditation in empty places, caves and forests. The knower of yoga who is bent upon accomplishing the end should never be engaged in giving feasts to Brāhmaṇas, in śrāddha sacrifices, etc., or in going to places of pilgrimages, festivals or crowds. The well-controlled yogin should go about as if people had treated him with disrespect. He should not go against the actions of the wise. That great ascetic is said to be a tridaṇḍin (or having a three-knotted staff) who holds firmly the three-daṇḍa (control) of mind, speech, and body. That ascetic is said to be supreme person who begs alms-food of worthy brāhmaṇas, when smoke has ceased and fire has been extinguished (in their houses). is he not a degraded ascetic who, though holding the staff and begging food, is without vairāgya and is not intent upon the observances of his order? He is an ascetic— not any other, who does not go to the house where he expects to find special alms or which he already visited. He is said to transcend all castes and orders of life who realises the self-shinning supreme Tattva that is without body and organs, the all-witness, the real vijñāna that is of the form of bliss. To the Ātmā that is of the nature of jñāna, such an idea as : 'the order of life, etc., is mine', being generated out of māyā in this body, can never exist. He who knows thus through vedānta is beyond all castes and orders of life. He from whom all castes and orders of life slip away through Ātmic vision, transcends them all the remains in Ātmā alone. That person is said by knower of the meaning of the Vedas to be ativarṇāśramī (beyond caste and order of life) who after crossing all castes and orders of life abides in Ātmā alone.

तस्मादन्यगता वर्णा आश्रमा अपि नारद। आत्मन्यारोपिताः सर्वे भ्रान्त्या तेनात्मवेदिना॥ १८॥

न विधिर्न निषेधश्च न वर्ज्यावर्ज्यकल्पना। ब्रह्मविज्ञानिनामस्ति तथा नान्यच्च नारद॥ १९॥
विरज्य सर्वभूतेभ्य आ विरिञ्चिपदादपि। घृणां विपाट्य सर्वस्मिन्पुत्रवित्तादिकेष्वपि॥ २०॥
श्रद्धालुर्मुक्तिमार्गेषु वेदान्तज्ञानलिप्सया। उपायनकरो भूत्वा गुरुं ब्रह्मविदं व्रजेत्॥ २१॥
सेवाभिः परितोष्यैनं चिरकालं समाहितः। सदा वेदान्तवाक्यार्थं शृणुयात्सुसमाहितः॥ २२॥
निर्ममो निरहंकारः सर्वसङ्गविवर्जितः। सदा शान्त्यादियुक्तः सन्नात्मन्यात्मानमीक्षते॥ २३॥
संसारदोषदृष्ट्यैव विरक्तिर्जायते सदा। विरक्तस्य तु संसारात्संन्यासः स्यान्न संशयः॥ २४॥
मुमुक्षुः परहंसाख्यः साक्षान्मोक्षैकसाधनम्। अभ्यसेद्ब्रह्मविज्ञानं वेदान्तश्रवणादिना॥ २५॥
ब्रह्मविज्ञानलाभाय परहंससमाह्वयः। शान्तिदान्त्यादिभिः सर्वैः साधनैः सहितो भवेत्॥ २६॥
वेदान्ताभ्यासनिरतः शान्तो दान्तो जितेन्द्रियः। निर्भयो निर्ममो नित्यो निर्द्वन्द्वो निष्परिग्रहः॥ २७॥
जीर्णकौपीनवासाः स्यान्मुण्डी नग्नोऽथ वा भवेत्। प्राज्ञो वेदान्तविद्योगी निर्ममो निरहंकृतिः॥ २८
मित्रादिषु समो मैत्रः समस्तेष्वेव जन्तुषु। एको ज्ञानी प्रशान्तात्मा स संतरति नेतरः॥ २९॥
गुरूणां च हिते युक्तस्तत्र संवत्सरं वसेत्। नियमेष्वप्रमत्तस्तु यमेषु च सदा भवेत्॥ ३०॥
प्राप्य चान्ते ततश्चैव ज्ञानयोगमनुत्तमम्। अविरोधेन धर्मस्य संचरेत्पृथिवीमिमाम्॥ ३१॥
ततः संवत्सरस्यान्ते ज्ञानयोगमनुत्तमम्। आश्रमत्रयमुत्सृज्य प्राप्तश्च परमाश्रमम्॥ ३२॥
अनुज्ञाप्य गुरूंश्चैव चरेद्धि पृथिवीमिमाम्। त्यक्तसङ्गो जितक्रोधो लघ्वाहारो जितेन्द्रियः॥ ३३॥
द्वाविमौ न विरज्येते विपरीतेन कर्मणा। निरारम्भो गृहस्थश्च कार्यवांश्चैव भिक्षुकः॥ ३४॥
माद्यति प्रमदां दृष्ट्वा सुरां पीत्वा च माद्यति। तस्माद्दृष्टिविषां नारीं दूरतः परिवर्जयेत्॥ ३५॥
संभाषणं सह स्त्रीभिरालापः प्रेक्षणं तथा। नृत्तं गानं सहासं च परिवादांश्च वर्जयेत्॥ ३६॥
न स्नानं न जपः पूजा न होमो नैव साधनम्। नाग्निकार्यादिकार्यं च नैतस्यास्तीह नारद॥ ३७॥
नार्चनं पितृकार्यं च तीर्थयात्रा व्रतानि च। धर्माधर्मादिकं नास्ति न विधिर्लौकिकी क्रिया॥ ३८॥
संत्यजेत्सर्वकर्माणि लोकाचारं च सर्वशः। कृमिकीटपतङ्गांश्च तथा योगी वनस्पतीन्॥ ३९॥
न नाशयेद्बुधो जीवान्परमार्थमतिर्यतिः। नित्यमन्तर्मुखः स्वच्छः प्रशान्तात्मा स्वपूर्णधीः॥ ४०॥
अन्तःसङ्गपरित्यागी लोके विहर नारद। नाराजके जनपदे चरत्येकचरो मुनिः॥ ४१॥
निःस्तुतिर्निर्नमस्कारो निःस्वधाकार एव च। चलाचलनिकेतश्च यतिर्यादृच्छिको भवेत्॥ ४२॥
इत्युपनिषत्।

Therefore, O Nārada, the castes and orders of life which are foreign (to Ātmā) are attributed falsely, by the ignorant, to Ātmā. O Nārada, for those that are brahma-jñānīs, there are no rules ordained nor prohibited; there is nothing to be given up or not; similarly nothing else (for them). Having attained indifference to all objects even up to Brahmā's seat, having destroyed (or done away with) all fondness for everything, as for son, relatives, wife, etc., and having faith in the path of salvation, and through love of vedānta-jñāna, he should approach a Guru who is a knower of Brahman with gift (in his hand). Having an equilibrated mind, he should satisfy the Guru for a long time through service, etc., and learn with a steady firm mind the meaning of the sentences of Vedas. Then being devoid of 'I' and 'mine' and of all attractions, and having attained peace of mind, etc., he sees Ātmā in himself. Through observing the faults of saṁsāra, there arises indifference. There is no doubt that sannyāsa arises in one who becomes disgusted with saṁsāra. The aspirant after salvation who is called paramahaṁsa should, through the hearing, etc., of vedānta, practise Brahma-jñāna which is the direct and chief means of salvation. In order to attain Brahma-jñāna, the one named paramahaṁsa should possess the qualities of the control of mind and body, etc. He should always be a practiser of vedānta, being master of the mind, the body and the organs, being without fear and egoism, with a firm mind, without the pairs (of opposites), without attaching himself to any, having a worn-out loin-cloth, and being bald-headed or naked. He should have the great intelligence of the knower of vedānta, a yogin without 'I' and 'mine' and being equal and friendly to friends and other beings. That jñānī alone and none else is able to cross saṁsāra who has his mind at peace. With the grace of the Guru towards him, he should live with him for year. He should be careful to observe yama (restraint) and niyama (religious observance). At the end of that (year), he should attain the supreme jñāna-yoga, and roam about on this earth without going against dharma; (or) at the end of one year, he should give up the three orders of life and attain the chief āśrama (of sannyāsa), as well as the supreme jñāna-yoga. Then, taking leave of the Guru, he should wander over the earth, having given up association (with wife, etc.), as well as anger, and being content with moderate food and having controlled the senses. The householder who does not perform karma, and the ascetic who performs karma— both become fallen through their perverse doings. Each becomes intoxicated through seeing women. Each becomes intoxicated through drinking alcohol. Therefore, women, mere sight of whom is poison, should be shunned at a distance. Such things as conversation and proximity with, the sight of, women, dancing, singing, using violence against persons, and disputatious arguments should be given up. Therefore, O Nārada, to such a one, there is neither bath, nor muttering of mantras, nor worship, nor homa, nor means of accomplishment, nor any karma of fire-sacrifice, etc., nor worshipping with flowers, etc., nor karmas to the pitṛs, nor pilgrimages, nor religious observances, nor dharmas, nor adharmas, nor any rules of observance, nor any other worldly karmas. He should give up karmas and worldly observances. That yogin of an ascetic who is learned person, having his intelligence directed towards Reality, should never injure any worm or insect, birds or tree. O Nārada, roam through the world with vision ever directed inwards, with purity, with mind under control, with a mind that is full of Brahman and all attraction given up within. The muni that goes about alone, does (or should) not dwell in countries where there is no king. (In this case), there is neither praise nor prostration, nor the propitiation of devas or pitṛs. Thus the ascetic who has his abode changeful (in body), or changeless (in Ātmā), should be content with whatever he gets. Thus is the Upaniṣad.

॥ सप्तमोपदेश:॥

अथ यतेर्नियम: कथमिति पृष्टं नारदं पितामह: पुरस्कृत्य विरक्त: सन्यो वर्षासु ध्रुवशीलोऽष्टौ मास्येकाकी चरन्नैकत्र निवसेद्भिक्षुर्भयात्सारङ्गवदेकत्र न तिष्ठेत्स्वगमननिरोधग्रहणं न कुर्याद्धस्ताभ्यां नद्युत्तरणं न कुर्यान्न वृक्षारोहणमपि न देवोत्सवदर्शनं कुर्यान्नैकत्राशी न बाह्यदेवार्चनं कुर्यात्स्वव्यतिरिक्तं सर्वं त्यक्त्वा मधुकरवृत्त्याहारमाहरन्कृशो भूत्वा मेदोवृद्धिमकुर्वन्नाज्यं रुधिरमिव त्यजेदेकत्रान्नं पललमिव गन्धलेपनमशुद्धिलेपनमिव क्षारमन्त्यजमिव वस्त्रमुच्छिष्टपात्रमिवाभ्यङ्गं स्त्रीसङ्गमिव मित्राह्लादकं मूत्रमिव स्पृहां गोमांसमिव ज्ञातचरदेशं चण्डालवाटिकामिव स्त्रियमहिमिव सुवर्णं कालकूटमिव सभास्थलं श्मशानस्थलमिव राजधानीं कुम्भीपाकमिव शवपिण्डवदेकत्रान्नं न देहान्तरदर्शनं प्रपञ्चवृत्तिं परित्यज्य स्वदेशमुत्सृज्य ज्ञातचरदेशं विहाय विस्मृतपदार्थं पुन: प्राप्तहर्ष इव स्वमानन्दमनुस्मरन्स्वशरीराभिमानदेशविस्मरणं मत्वा स्वशरीरं शवमिव हेयमुपगम्य कारागृहविनिर्मुक्तचोरवत्पुत्राप्तबन्धुभवस्थलं विहाय दूरतो वसेत्॥ अयत्नेन प्राप्तमाहरन्ब्रह्मप्रणवध्यानानुसन्धानपरो भूत्वा सर्वकर्मनिर्मुक्त: कामक्रोधलोभमोहमदमात्सर्यादिकं दग्ध्वा त्रिगुणातीत: षडूर्मिरहित: षड्भावविकारशून्य: सत्यवाक् शुचिरद्रोही ग्रामैकरात्रं पत्तने पञ्चरात्रं क्षेत्रे पञ्चरात्रं तीर्थे पञ्चरात्रमनिकेत: स्थिरमतिर्नानृतवादी गिरिकन्दरेषु वसेदेक एव द्वौ वा चरेत् ग्रामं त्रिभिर्नगरं चतुर्भिर्ग्राममित्येकश्चरेत्। भिक्षुश्चतुर्दशकरणानां न तत्रावकाशं दद्यादविच्छिन्नज्ञानाद्वैराग्यसंपत्तिमनुभूय मत्तो न कश्चिन्नान्यो व्यतिरिक्त इत्यात्मन्यालोच्य सर्वत: स्वरूपमेव पश्यञ्जीवन्मुक्तिमवाप्य प्रारब्धप्रतिभासनाशपर्यन्तं चतुर्विधं स्वरूपं ज्ञात्वा देहपतनपर्यन्तं स्वरूपानुसंधानेन वसेत्॥ १॥

Upadeśa VII

The Grandfather, after eulogizing Nārada who asked about the observance of ascetics, replied thus :—

"The ascetic that has attained indifference (to objects), should stay in one and the same place in the rainy season (for four months), and then for (the remaining) eight months should wander alone. Then also the ascetic should not stay in one and the same place for more than a day. Like a deer that does not stay in one place on account of fear, he should not stay in one place. He should not create an attraction (in his mind) that may serve as an obstacle to his going about. He should not cross a stream (by swimming) with his hand, nor ascend a tree, nor witness the festival of a God, nor partake or regal food, nor do the external worship of God. Having discarded all things other than the Self, he should be with his body emanciated by taking food (from each house) like the bees (from each flower). He should not increase that fat (in the body): he should discard ghee like blood. Regarding such royal food as flesh, sandal-coating, etc., as offal, the different tastes as the degraded caste, the cloth as a defiled vessel, the oil-bath as sexual union, the gladdening of a friend as urine, desires as cow's flesh, the country known to him as the outcastes place, gold and women as cobra or deadly poison, the place of assembly as the burning ground, the capital of the town as the hell called Kumbhīpāka, and royal food as balls of rice offered to the dead, he should be without any worship of God other than the Self; and having given up all the actions of the world and his own country, and ever thinking of the bliss of his Self like the bliss arising from the discovery of a lost object, forgetting his country and the fondness for his body, and knowing that his body should be slighted like a carcase, he should dwell away from son, relations and native place, like a thief released from prison. Taking whatever comes to him without effort, ever intent upon the realisation, through meditation, of Brahma-Praṇava, being freed from all karmas, having burnt up all passion, anger, greed, delusion, pride, malice, etc., having transcended the three guṇas, being without the six human infirmities, without the six changes, speaking the truth and being opposed to all savoury things, he should live for one day in a village, five days in a town, five days in a sacred place, and five days in sacred waters. With no settled place of residence and with a firm mind, he should dwell alone in mountain caves without uttering falsehood. Two persons should not join together. Should three join, there is created a village thereby; with four, is formed a city. Therefore he should live alone in a village. In it, the ascetic should not give scope to his fourteen organs. Having attained wealth or vairāgya through the non-dissipated jñāna, and having deliberated within himself that there is none other than the Self, he should attain Jīvanmukti, having seen the Reality everywhere. Till prārabdha karma is over, he should understand the four kinds of svarūpa (in Tattvamasi) and should live in the realisation of Reality, till his body falls (a prey to death).

त्रिषवणस्नानं कुटीचकस्य बहूदकस्य द्विवारं हंसस्यैकवारं परमहंसस्य मानसस्नानं तुरीयातीतस्य भस्मस्नानमवधूतस्य वायव्यस्नानम्॥ २॥

ऊर्ध्वपुण्ड्रं कुटीचकस्य त्रिपुण्ड्रं बहूदकस्य ऊर्ध्वपुण्ड्रं त्रिपुण्ड्रं हंसस्य भस्मोद्धूलनं परमहंसस्य तुरीयातीतस्य तिलकपुण्ड्रमवधूतस्य न किंचित्। तुरीयातीतावधूतयो:॥ ३॥

ऋतुक्षौरं कुटीचकस्य ऋतुद्वयक्षौरं बहूदकस्य न क्षौरं हंसस्य परमहंसस्य च न क्षौरम्। अस्ति चेदयनक्षौरं तुरीयातीतावधूतयोर्न क्षौरम्॥ ४॥

कुटीचकस्यैकान्नं माधूकरं बहूदकस्य हंसपरमहंसयो: करपात्रं तुरीयातीतस्य गोमुखं अवधूतस्याजगरवृत्ति:॥ ५॥

शाटीद्वयं कुटीचकस्य बहूदकस्यैकशाटी हंसस्य खण्डं दिगम्बरं परमहंसस्य एककौपीनं वा तुरीयातीतावधूतयोर्जातरूपधरत्वं हंसपरमहंसयोरजिनं न त्वन्येषाम्॥ ६॥

कुटीचकबहूदकयोर्देवार्चनं हंसपरमहंसयोर्मानसार्चनं तुरीयातीतावधूतयो: सोहंभावना॥ ७॥

कुटीचकबहूदकयोर्मन्त्रजपाधिकारो हंसपरमहंसयोर्ध्यानाधिकारस्तुरीयातीतावधूतयोर्न त्वन्याधिकार-स्तुरीयातीतावधूतयोर्महावाक्योपदेशाधिकार: परमहंसस्यापि। कुटीचकबहूदकहंसानां नान्यस्योपदेशाधिकार:॥ ८॥

कुटीचकबहूदकयोर्मानुषप्रणव: हंसपरमहंसयोरान्तरप्रणव:। तुरीयातीतावधूतयोर्ब्रह्म प्रणव:॥ ९॥

कुटीचकबहूदकयोः श्रवणं हंसपरमहंसयोर्मननं तुरीयातीतावधूतयोर्निदिध्यासः। सर्वेषामात्मानुसन्धानं विधिरिति॥ १०॥

एवं मुमुक्षुः सर्वदा संसारतारकं तारकमनुस्मरञ्जीवन्मुक्तो वसेदधिकारविशेषेण कैवल्य-प्राप्त्युपायमन्विष्येद्यतिरित्युपनिषत्॥ ११॥

"To the kuṭīcaka there is (prescribed) a bath three times daily; to the bahūdaka, twice; to the haṁsa, once; to the paramahaṁsa there is the mental bath; to the turyātīta, there is the holy-ashes bath; to the avadhūta, there is the wind as the bath. For the kuṭīcaka, there is the vertical sect-mark; for the bahūdaka, there is the three-lined (horizontal) sect-mark; for the haṁsa, both; for the paramahaṁsa, there is the holy-ashes sect-mark; for the turyātīta, there is the spot-sect-mark; for the avadhūta or for the turyātīta and avadhūta, there is none. For the kuṭīcaka, shaving takes place once in two months; for the bahūdaka, once in four months; for the haṁsa and paramahaṁsa, none, or if wanted, once in a year; for the turyātīta and avadhūta, none at all. The kuṭīcaka should take the food in one (place only); the bahūdaka should take alms (in many places); for the haṁsa and paramahaṁsa, the hand is the vessel; the turyātīta, should take food with the mouth as the cow; for the avadhūta, it is like the action of the boa constrictor (opening the mouth and taking whatever comes into it). For the kuṭīcaka, there are two cloths; for the bahūdaka, there is one cloth; for the haṁsa there is a piece of cloth; and the paramahaṁsa should be naked or have only a loin-cloth; in the case of the turyātīta and avadhūta, they should be as nature made them. For the haṁsa and paramahaṁsa, there (prescribed) a deer-skin, and for no others. For the kuṭīcaka and bahūdaka, there is the worship of the divine (image); for the haṁsa and paramahaṁsa, there is mental worship; for the turyātīta and avadhūta, there is the idea that they alone are Brahman. The Kuṭīcaka and bahūdaka are entitled to mantras and japas; the haṁsa and paramahaṁsa, to dhyāna (meditation); the turyātīta and avadhūta are entitled to none; but they are entitled to the initiation of the sacred sentences of the Vedas; so also the paramahaṁsa. The kuṭīcaka and bahūdaka are not entitled to initiate others; for them, there is (the uttering of) the mental praṇava; for the haṁsa and paramahaṁsa, there is the internal praṇava; (in the heart); for the turyātīta and avadhūta, there is the Brahma-praṇava (always). For the kuṭīcaka and bahūdaka, there is śravaṇa (hearing and study): for the haṁsa and paramahaṁsa, there is manana (thinking and remembering); for the turyātīta and avadhūta there is nididhyāsana (profound meditation ever). For all these, there is necessarily the meditation upon Ātmā. Thus the aspirant after salvation should ever be uttering the Praṇava which enables one to cross saṁsāra, and be living as a Jīvanmukta. Thus the ascetic, according to each one's capacity, should ever be seeking the means to attain Kaivala. Such the Upaniṣad."

॥अष्टमोपदेशः॥

अथ हैनं भगवन्तं परमेष्ठिनं नारदः पप्रच्छ संसारतारकं प्रसन्नो ब्रूहीति। तथेति परमेष्ठी वक्तुमुपचक्रमे ओमिति ब्रह्मेति व्यष्टिसमष्टिप्रकारेण। का व्यष्टिः का समष्टिः संहारप्रणवः

सृष्टिप्रणवश्चान्तर्बहिश्चोभयात्मकत्वात्त्रिविधो ब्रह्मप्रणवः। अन्तःप्रणवो व्यावहारिकप्रणवः। बाह्यप्रणव आर्षप्रणवः। उभयात्मको विराट्प्रणवः। संहारप्रणवो ब्रह्मप्रणवोऽर्धमात्राप्रणवः॥ १॥

ओमिति ब्रह्म। ओमित्येकाक्षरमन्तःप्रणवं विद्धि। स चाष्टधा भिद्यते। अकारोकारमकारार्धमात्रानादबिन्दुकलाशक्तिश्चेति। तत्र चत्वार अकारश्चायुतावयवान्वित उकारः सहस्रावयवान्वितो मकारः शतावयवोपेतोऽर्धमात्राप्रणवोऽनन्तावयवाकारः। सगुणो विराट्प्रणवः संहारो निर्गुणप्रणव उभयात्मकोत्पत्तिप्रणवो यथाप्लुतो विराट्प्लुत प्लुतःसंहारः॥ २॥

विराट्प्रणवः षोडशमात्रात्मकः षट्त्रिंशत्तत्त्वातीतः। षोडशमात्रात्मकत्वं कथमित्युच्यते। अकारः प्रथमोकारो द्वितीया मकारस्तृतीयार्धमात्रा चतुर्थी नादः पञ्चमी बिन्दुः षष्ठी कला सप्तमी कलातीताष्टमी शान्तिर्नवमी शान्त्यतीता दशमी उन्मन्येकादशी मनोन्मनी द्वादशी पुरी त्रयोदशी मध्यमा चतुर्दशी पश्यन्ती पञ्चदशी परा षोडशी पुनश्चतुःषष्टिमात्रा प्रकृतिपुरुषद्वैविध्यमासाद्याष्टाविंशत्युत्तरभेदमात्रास्वरूपमासाद्य सगुणनिर्गुणत्वमुपेत्यैकोऽपि ब्रह्मप्रणवः॥ ३॥

सर्वाधारः परंज्योतिरेष सर्वेश्वरो विभुः। सर्वदेवमयः सर्वप्रपञ्चाधारगर्भितः॥ ४॥
सर्वाक्षरमयः कालः सर्वागममयः शिवः। सर्वश्रुत्युत्तमो मृग्यः सकलोपनिषन्मयः॥ ५॥
भूतं भव्यं भविष्यद्यत्त्रिकालोदितमव्ययम्। तदप्योंकारमेवायं विद्धि मोक्षप्रदायकम्॥ ६॥
तमेवात्मानमित्येतद्ब्रह्मशब्देन वर्णितम्। तदेकममृतमजरमनुभूय तथोमिति॥ ७॥
सशरीरं समारोप्य तन्मयत्वं तथोमिति। त्रिशरीरं तमात्मानं परं ब्रह्म विनिश्चिनु॥ ८॥
परं ब्रह्मानुसंदध्याद्विश्वादीनां क्रमः क्रमात्। स्थूलत्वात्स्थूलभुक्त्वाच्च सूक्ष्मत्वात्सूक्ष्म भुक् परम्॥ ९॥
ऐक्यत्वानन्दभोगाच्च सोऽयमात्मा चतुर्विधः। चतुष्पाज्जागरितः स्थूलः स्थूलप्रज्ञो हि विश्वभुक्॥ १०॥
एकोनविंशतिमुखः साष्टाङ्गः सर्वगः प्रभुः। स्थूलभुक् चतुरात्माथ विश्वो वैश्वानरः पुमान्॥ ११॥

Upadeśa VIII

Then Nārada asked Parameṣṭhī (Brahmā) to enlighten him, who had surrendered himself to Him, about saṁsāra-tāraka (or that tāraka or Praṇava which lifts one out of saṁsāra).

Assenting to which, Brahmā began thus : "Oṁkāra that is Brahman is the vyaṣṭi (individual) and the samaṣṭi (cosmic). What is the individual? What is the cosmic? Brahma-praṇava is of three kinds, saṁhāra (destructive) praṇava, sṛṣṭi (creative) praṇava, and ubhayātmaka (belonging to both) praṇava, as being of two forms, internal and external. (It is also eight:) Antaḥpraṇava, Vyāvahārika-praṇava, bāhya-praṇava, ārṣa-praṇava, ubhayātmaka or virāṭ-praṇava, saṁhāra-praṇava, brahma-praṇava, and ardhamātrā praṇava. Oṁ is Brahman, know that the mantra of the one-syllabled Oṁ is Praṇava. It has the eight difference of akāra, ukāra, makāra, ardhamātrā, nāda, bindu, kalā, and śakti. Know it is not four (alone). Akāra is associated with ten thousand limbs; ukāra with one thousand limbs, makāra with one hundred limbs; ardhamātrā is of the nature of endless limbs. That which is saguṇa (associated with guṇas) is virāṭ-(preservation) praṇava; that which is nirguṇa (not associated with guṇas) is saṁhāra (or destruction) praṇava; that which is associated with guṇas and is not so associated, is utpatti (or origination) praṇava. Pluta (the elongated accent) is virāṭ : plutapluta is samhāra. The virāṭ-praṇava is of the form of sixteen mātrās and is above the thirty-six tattvas. The sixteen mātrās are thus : Akāra is the first mātrā; ukāra is the second; makāra is the third; ardhamātrā is the fourth; nāda is the fifth; bindu is the sixth; kalā is the seventh; kalātīta is the eighth; śānti is the ninth; śāntyatīta is the tenth; unmanī is the eleventh; manonmanī is the twelfth; purītati is the thirteenth; tanumadhyamā is the fourteenth; pati is the fifteenth; parā is the sixteenth. Then (again) having sixty-four mātrās and their division into the two, Prakṛti and Puruṣa and resolving themselves into the one hundred and twenty-eight differences of mātrās, it becomes saguṇa and nirguṇa. Though Brahma-praṇava is one only, it is the substratum of all, the support of the whole universe, of the form of all akṣaras (letters), time, Vedas, and Śiva. This Oṁkāra should be sought after, that is mentioned in the Vedas of the nature of the Upaniṣads. Know that this Oṁkāra is the Ātmā that is indestructible during the three periods of time, past, present, and future, able to confer salvation and eulogized Brahma-sound (Vedas). Having experienced this one Oṁ as immortal and ageless, and having brought about the Brahma-nature in this body, become convinced that your Ātmā, associated with the three bodies, is Parabrahman. Through Viśva and others (viz., Taijasa, Prājña, the Turya) in order, the realisation of parabrahman should be attained since Ātmā is of four kinds through his identification with, and the enjoying of the gross as well as the enjoyer of the gross, the subtle as well as the enjoyer of the subtle, and through his identification (with the third body) enjoying bliss in the fourth. He has four feet. The one presiding over the waking state is gross; and since he is the enjoyer of Viśva (the universe), he becomes the sthūla-prājña (gross consciousness). He has nineteen facets and eight parts. He is pervading everywhere and Lord. He is the enjoyer of the gross and is the caturātmā called Viśva. He alone is the Puruṣa called Vaiśvānara.

विश्वजित्प्रथमः पादः स्वप्नस्थानगतः प्रभुः। सूक्ष्मप्रज्ञः स्वतोऽष्टाङ्ग एको नान्यः परंतपः॥ १२॥

सूक्ष्मभुक् चतुरात्माथ तैजसो भूतराडयम्। हिरण्यगर्भः स्थूलोऽन्तर्द्वितीयः पाद उच्यते॥ १३॥

कामं कामयते यावद्यत्र सुप्तो न कंचन। स्वप्नं पश्यति नैवात्र तत्सुषुप्तमपि स्फुटम्॥ १४॥

एकीभूतः सुषुप्तस्थः प्रज्ञानघनवान्सुखी। नित्यानन्दमयोऽप्यात्मा सर्वजीवान्तरस्थितः॥ १५॥

तथाप्यानन्दभुक् चेतोमुखः सर्वगतोऽव्ययः। चतुरात्मेश्वरः प्राज्ञस्तृतीयः पादसंज्ञितः॥ १६॥

एष सर्वेश्वरश्चैष सर्वज्ञः सूक्ष्मभावनः। एषोऽन्तर्याम्येष योनिः सर्वस्य प्रभवाप्ययौ॥ १७॥

भूतानां त्रयमप्येतत्सर्वोपरमबाधकम्। तत्सुषुप्तं हि यत्स्वप्नं मायामात्रं प्रकीर्तितम्॥ १८॥

चतुर्थश्चतुरात्मापि सच्चिदेकरसो ह्ययम्। तुरीयावसितत्वाच्च एकैकत्वानुसारतः॥ १९॥

ओतानुज्ञात्रनुज्ञातृविकल्पज्ञानसाधनम्। विकल्पत्रयमत्रापि सुषुप्तं स्वप्नमान्तरम्।

मायामात्रं विदित्वैवं सच्चिदेकरसो ह्यथ॥ २०॥

विभक्तो ह्ययमादेशो न स्थूलप्रज्ञमन्वहम्। न सूक्ष्मप्रज्ञमत्यन्तं न प्रज्ञं न क्वचिन्मुने॥ २१॥

नैवाप्रज्ञं नोभयत:प्रज्ञं न प्रज्ञमान्तरम्। नाप्रज्ञमपि न प्रज्ञाघनं चादृष्टमेव च॥ २२॥

तदलक्षणमग्राह्यं यदव्यवहार्यमचिन्त्यमव्यपदेश्यमेकात्मप्रत्ययसारं प्रपञ्चोपशमं शिवं शान्तमद्वैतं चतुर्थं मन्यन्ते। स ब्रह्मप्रणव: स विज्ञेयो नापरस्तुरीय: सर्वत्र भानुवन्मुमुक्षूणामाधार: स्वयंज्योतिर्ब्रह्माकाश: सर्वदा विराजते परंब्रह्मत्वादित्युपनिषत्॥ २३॥

He alone is Viśvajit (the conqueror of the universe). This is the first foot. When this Lord attains the dreaming condition, he is the sūkṣma-prājña (subtle consciousness). O conqueror of all, he is the one having eight limbs, and there is none else. He is the enjoyer of the subtle and is caturātmā, named Taijasa and the protector of elements. He alone is the Hiraṇyagarbha presiding over the gross (or subtle matter rather). He is said to form the second foot. Suṣupti (or the dreamless sleep) is that state where one sleeps without any desire and where one sees not any dreams. The one identified with this dreamless sleep is Prajñāna-ghana, is blissful, of the nature of eternal bliss and the Ātmā in all creatures; yet he is enjoyer of bliss, has cetas (consciousness) as his (one) foot, as all-pervading, indestructible caturātmā and the Lord, and is named Prājña, the third foot. He alone is the Lord of all, the knower of all, the subtle-thoughted, the latent one, and the cause of all creation. He alone is the origin and the destruction. These three (states) are obstacles to all creatures obtaining (the final) peace. As is svapna, so is suṣupti, it (also) being said to be illusory. The caturātmā, the fourth, as he is Sat, Cit and Ekarasa (the one essence), ends as the fourth the follows (upon the heels of each of the above states), is the knower of the means of vikalpa-jñāna and is the anujñātā (the one following knower). Having known them, and known as māyā the three vikalpas of suṣupti, svapna and āntara (the inner), even in this state, is he not (to be known as) Sat-Cit-Ekarasa? This shall be expressed as differentiated thus : It is not even the gross prajña; nor is it the very subtle prajña; nor is it prajña itself (of the causal body) : O muni neither is it the trifling prajña; nor is it the non-prajña; nor is it the dual prajña; nor is it internal prajña, though it is without prajña; it is Prajñāna-ghana. It can never be known by the organs; nor it can be known by the reason; it cannot be grasped by the organs of action. It cannot be proved. It cannot be reached by thought. It cannot be proved by analogy. It can be realised by Self-realisation alone. It is with the waking state. etc. It is the auspicious, with changes, without a second. Such a one is thought to be Turya. This alone is Brahman, Brahma-praṇava. This should be known. There is no other turya. To the aspirants after salvation, it is the support, like the sun everywhere; it is the Self-light. As it alone is Brahman, this Brahma-Ākāśa is shining always. Thus is the Upaniṣad."

॥नवमोपदेशः॥

अथ ब्रह्मस्वरूपं कथमिति नारदः पप्रच्छ। तं होवाच पितामहः किं ब्रह्मस्वरूपमिति। अन्योऽसावन्योऽहमस्मीति ये विदुस्ते पशवो न स्वभावपशवस्तमेवं ज्ञात्वा विद्वान्मृत्युमुखात्प्रमुच्यते नान्यः पन्था विद्यतेऽयनाय॥ १॥

Upadeśa IX

Nārada asked : "Who is Brahma-svarūpa?" To which Brahmā replied thus: "Brahma-svarūpa is thus : Those who know that 'he (Brahman) is one and I am another' are only paśus (animals). The real paśus (animals) are no animals. The wise man who knows Brahman thus (as himself, and himself as Brahman) escapes out of the mouth of death. There is no other path to salvation.

कालः स्वभावो नियतिर्यदृच्छा भूतानि योनिः पुरुष इति चिन्त्यम्।
संयोग एषां न त्वात्मभावादात्मा ह्यनीशः सुखदुःखहेतोः॥ २॥
ते ध्यानयोगानुगता अपश्यन्देवात्मशक्तिं स्वगुणैर्निगूढाम्।
यः कारणानि निखिलानि तानि कालात्मयुक्तान्यधितिष्ठत्येकः॥ ३॥
तमेकस्मिंस्त्रिवृतं षोडशान्तं शतार्धारं विंशतिप्रत्यराभिः।
अष्टकैः षड्भिर्विश्वरूपैकपाशं त्रिमार्गभेदं द्विनिमित्तैकमोहम्॥ ४॥
पञ्चस्रोतोम्बुं पञ्चयोन्युग्रवक्त्रां पञ्चप्राणोर्मिं पञ्चबुद्ध्यादिमूलाम्।
पञ्चावर्तां पञ्चदुःखौघवेगां पञ्चाशद्भेदां पञ्चपर्वामधीमः॥ ५॥
सर्वाजीवे सर्वसंस्थे बृहन्ते तस्मिन्हंसो भ्राम्यते ब्रह्मचक्रे।
पृथगात्मानं प्रेरितारं च मत्वा जुष्टस्ततस्तेनामृतत्वमेति॥ ६॥
उद्गीथमेतत्परमं तु ब्रह्म तस्मिंस्त्रियं स्वप्रतिष्ठाक्षरं च।
अत्रान्तरं वेदविदो विदित्वा लीनाः परे ब्रह्मणि तत्परायणाः॥ ७॥
संयुक्तमेतत्क्षरमक्षरं च व्यक्ताव्यक्तं भरते विश्वमीशः।
अनीशश्चात्मा बध्यते भोक्तृभावाज्ज्ञात्वा देवं मुच्यते सर्वपाशैः॥ ८॥
ज्ञाज्ञौ द्वावजावीशानीशावजा ह्येका भोक्तृभोगार्थयुक्ता।
अनन्तश्चात्मा विश्वरूपो ह्यकर्ता त्रयं यदा विन्दते ब्रह्म ह्येतत्॥ ९॥
क्षरं प्रधानममृताक्षरं हरः क्षरात्मानावीशते देव एकः।
तस्याभिध्यानाद्योजनात्तत्त्वभावाद्भूयश्चान्ते विश्वमायानिवृत्तिः॥ १०॥

"Is time the cause (of origination of universes)? or nature? or karma? or accident? or the (great) elements? or Puruṣ ? This should be considered. It is not the union of them. (Then) there is the Ātmā, but (jīva) Ātmā is not the Lord, as it is subject to pleasures and pains. Those (Ṛṣis) following dhyāna-yoga have beheld, as the cause, the devātma-śakti concealed by its own qualities of that One that presides over all the causes associated with time and Ātmā. Him (the Universal Soul), we consider as the wheel which has one circumference, which is covered by three (layers), which has sixteen end-parts, which has fifty spokes and twenty counter-spokes, which has six times eight (nails), which has one rope of various forms, which has the threefold path, and which has delusion arising from the twofold cause. Him (we worship as a river) which has (water) oozing out of the five currents (of organs), which is terrible and crooked through the five causes (of elements), whose praṇas are the five waves, which has buddhi, etc., as the root cause, which has five whirlpools, which is impelled by the velocity of the five pains, which has fifty different miseries and which has the five obstacles. In this wheel of Brahman, which is the support of life and the last abiding place of all beings, and which is infinite, is whirling deluded the jīva, thinking that it is different from the one (Lord) Ordainer. Being blessed by Him, he gains salvation through such (a blessing). This is declared as brahman, as the supreme and the indestructible. In it, are the three (the enjoyer, the enjoyed and enjoyment). Hence it is the firm abode (of all). The knowers of Brahman having known Brahman within (the universe, etc.,) attain samādhi in Brahman and are absorbed in Brahma. Īśvara upholds this universe, closely associated with the destructible and indestructible, which are manifest and unmanifest; but the not-ruler of (jīva) Ātmā is bound through the thought of its being the enjoyer; and having known the Lod is freed from all fetters. Both Īśvara and jīva are birthless; one (the former) is jñānī and the other (latter) is ajñānī. (The goddess of) Brahmātma-śakti, is birthless, is alone engaged (in this world), on account of the enjoyment of the enjoyers. Ātmā is endless. The universe is Him from. He is not the agent. Whoever knows the Brahman that is threefold (as jīva, Īśvara and the universe) is released from bondage. It is pradhāna alone that is destructible. It is Īśvara that is immortal and indestructible. The one Lord (Īśvara) ordains Pradhāna and Puruṣa. The illusion of the universe disappears through meditation on union (of absorption) and sattva-bhāva of Parameśvara always.

ज्ञात्वा देवं मुच्यते सर्वपाशैः क्षीणैः क्लेशैर्जन्ममृत्युप्रहाणिः।
तस्याभिध्यानात्त्रितयं देहभेदे विश्वैश्वर्यं केवल आप्तकामः॥ ११॥
एतज्ज्ञेयं नित्यमेवात्मसंस्थं नातः परं वेदितव्यं हि किंचित्।
भोक्ता भोग्यं प्रेरितारं च मत्वा सर्वं प्रोक्तं त्रिविधं ब्रह्म ह्येतत्॥ १२॥
आत्मविद्यातपोमूलं तद्ब्रह्मोपनिषत्परम्॥ १३॥

Through knowing the Lord, avidyā and the rest are destroyed. Through the removal of such pains, there is freedom from birth and death. Through the meditation of the Parameśvara, the third body is acquired after this (physical) body, all wealth is enjoyed, and he attains whatever should be attained. He should know with certitude that all the three things (viz.,) the enjoyer, the enjoyed, and enjoyment are nothing but Brahman, and are of the nature of his own Self. All Ātmic knowledge is through tapas (only). That, Brahman contains in itself all excellence.

य एवं विदित्वा स्वरूपमेवानुचिन्तयंस्तत्र को मोहः कः शोक एकत्वमनुपश्यतः। तस्माद्विराड्भूतं भव्यं भविष्यद्भवत्यनश्वरस्वरूपम्॥ १४॥

Having known thus, whoever meditates upon the Ātmasvarūpa, to him were where then is grief? Where then is delusion? Therefore the Virāṭ is the past, present, and future time, and is of indestructible nature.

अणोरणीयान्महतो महीयानात्मास्य जन्तोर्निहितो गुहायाम्।
तमक्रतुं पश्यति वीतशोको धातुः प्रसादान्महिमानमीशम्॥ १५॥
अपाणिपादो जवनो ग्रहीता पश्यत्यचक्षुः स शृणोत्यकर्णः।
स वेत्ति वेद्यं न च तस्यास्ति वेत्ता तमाहुरग्र्यं पुरुषं महान्तम्॥ १६॥
अशरीरं शरीरेष्वनवस्थेष्ववस्थितम्। महान्तं विभुमात्मानं मत्वा धीरो न शोचति॥ १७॥
सर्वस्य धातारमचिन्त्यशक्तिं सर्वागमान्तार्थविशेषवेद्यम्।
परात्परं परमं वेदितव्यं सर्वावसानेऽन्तकृद्वेदितव्यम्॥ १८॥
कविं पुराणं पुरुषोत्तमोत्तमं सर्वेश्वरं सर्वदेवैरुपास्यम्।
अनादिमध्यान्तमनन्तमव्ययं शिवाच्युताम्भोरुहगर्भभूधरम्॥ १९॥
स्वेनावृतं सर्वमिदं प्रपञ्चं पञ्चात्मकं पञ्चसु वर्तमानम्। पञ्चीकृतानन्तभवप्रपञ्चं पञ्चीकृतस्वावयवैरसंवृतम्।
परात्परं यन्महतो महान्तं स्वरूपतेजोमयशाश्वतं शिवम्॥ २०॥
नाविरतो दुश्चरितान्नाशान्तो नासमाहितः। नाशान्तमानसो वापि प्रज्ञानेनैनमाप्नुयात्॥ २१॥

"Ātmā, that is the atom of atoms and the greatest of the greatest, is in the cave of the heart of all creatures. One without the thought of objects and without grief, knows the Ātmā capable of neither increase nor decrease through the grace of Īśvara or through the non-attraction to the objects of the senses. He (Ātmā) walks speedily without legs, lifts objects without hands, sees without eyes and hears without ears. He knows all, but none knows Him. He is said to be the foremost Mahā-Puruṣa. Having known Ātmā that is bodiless in this fleeting body, the great, the all-pervading, the support of all, with incomprehensible power, fit to be known through the meaning, etc., of all the Upaniṣads, the supreme of the supreme, the supreme object fit to be known, the one remaining after all, the all-knowing, the eternal, the foremost of all foremost beings, the ordainer of all, the one fit to be worshipped by all angels, the one without beginning, end, and middle, without limit or destruction, the cause of Brahmā, Viṣṇu, and Rudra, the one that has all the universe latent in himself, of the nature of the five elements with the expansion of all the quintuplicated creation, without being enveloped by his own limbs of quintuplicated objects, superior to the supreme, greater than the greatest, of the nature of effulgence, the eternal and the auspicious, the undaunted personage never grieves. One who has neither given up vicious actions, nor controlled his organs, nor mastered his mind, nor given up longing after fruits of actions though the mind is undisturbed, nor brought his mind to one state (or point), will not attain this Ātmā.

नान्तःप्रज्ञं न बहिःप्रज्ञं न स्थूलं नास्थूलं न ज्ञानं नाज्ञानं नोभयतः प्रज्ञमग्राह्यमव्यवहार्यं स्वान्तःस्थितः स्वयमेवेति य एवं वेद स मुक्तो भवति स मुक्तो भवतीत्याह भगवान्पितामहः॥ २२॥

"This (Brahman) is neither internal nor external consciousness; is neither gross, nor jñāna, nor ajñāna; nor is it the state between the waking and the dreaming states. It cannot be cognised by the organs; is not subject to proof; is within. He who knows that wich is by itself alone is emancipated person."

स्वस्वरूपज्ञः परिव्राट् परिव्राडेकाकी चरति भयत्रस्तसारङ्गवत्तिष्ठति। गमनविरोधं न करोति। स्वशरीरव्यतिरिक्तं सर्वं त्यक्त्वा षट्पदवृत्त्या स्थित्वा स्वरूपानुसन्धानं कुर्वन्सर्वमनन्यबुद्ध्या स्वस्मिन्नेव मुक्तो भवति। स परिव्राट् सर्वक्रियाकारकनिवर्तको गुरुशिष्यशास्त्रादिविनिर्मुक्तः सर्वसंसारं विसृज्य चामोहितः परिव्राट् कथं निर्धनिकः सुखी धनवाज्ज्ञानाज्ञानोभयातीतः सुखदुःखातीतः स्वयंज्योतिः प्रकाशः सर्ववेद्यः सर्वज्ञः सर्वसिद्धिदः सर्वेश्वरः सोऽहमिति। तद्विष्णोः परमं पदं यत्र गत्वा न निवर्तन्ते योगिनः। सूर्यो न तत्र भाति न शशाङ्कोऽपि न स पुनरावर्तते न स पुनरावर्तते तत्कैवल्यमित्युपनिषत्॥ २३॥

The Lord Brahmā said that he becomes an emancipated person. He who knows Reality is a Parivrāṭ. Such a Parivrāṭ roams about alone. Through fear, he is like a terrified deer. He will not be opposed to going anywhere. Having given up all but his body, he will live like a bee, and without considering others as foreign to himself; ever meditating upon Reality, he attains liberation in himself. Such a Parivrāt will be without delusion, without action or causing other to act, being absolved from teacher, disciple, books, etc., and having abandoned all saṁsāra. Such a Parivrāt roams about thus— without wealth, being happy, able to get wealth (if wanted), having crossed jñāna and ajñāna as well as happiness and grief, being Self-effulgence, being fit to be known by the Vedas, having known all, able to confer siddhis and remaining himself as Brahman, the Lord. Such Parivrāt attains the supreme abode of Viṣṇu, from which a yogin that has gone to it does not return, and where the sun and moon do not shine. He does not return. Such is Kaivalya.

Thus ends the Upaniṣad.

ॐ भद्रं कर्णेभिः .... इति शान्तिः॥

॥इति नारदपरिव्राजकोपनिषत्समाप्ता॥

***

43. TRIŚIKHĪ-BRĀHMAṆOPANIṢAD

त्रिशिखीब्राह्मणोपनिषद्

This upaniṣad is related to the tradition of white (Śukla) Yajurveda. The Yoga consisting of eight parts as a mean to attain Brahma (knowledge) has been propounded in this upaniṣad. It commences with the questions and answers which take place between a Brāhmaṇa Triśikhī and lord sun regarding the soul and Brahma. It continuance, the existence of Śiva element everywhere, origin of this whole world from Brahma, multi-division of a single crystal (Piṇḍa), the proportional discrimination of ether etc., micro creation (sṛṣṭi) from lord Brahmā to the conglomeration of the five elements, creation of the inert and sensitive world, four stages, motions of the sun towards the south and the north, description of knowledge providing with emancipation, the means of attaining knowledge through Yoga, the Yoga consisting eight parts as a mean for attaining the common knowledge of Brahma including Karma Yoga and Jñāna Yoga, ten kinds of Yama and Niyama, Āsanas of Haṭha Yoga, rejuvenation of nerves and various methods of Prāṇāyāma, the nature of fire orbit, movement of living-organism in the cycle of nerves, the place of Kuṇḍalinī and its functions, location of Nāḍikanda (cluster of nerves) near navel region, the breathing airs blowing in the nerves, suitable place of Yoga exercise and the method of practise of six mouths, controlling measures for mind (manojaya), accession to of breathing (Pratyāhāra) in the sensitive organs, kinds and sub-kinds of Dhāraṇā (power of retain), presumption of five elements in the limbs and organs of body, meditation and its outcome and finally attainment of specific knowledge, thereby attainment of emancipation has been described in detail.

॥शान्तिपाठः॥

ॐ पूर्णमदः .... इति शान्तिः॥

॥ब्राह्मणम् - १॥

त्रिशिखी ब्राह्मण आदित्यलोकं जगाम तं गत्वोवाच। भगवन् किं देहः किं प्राणः किं कारणं किमात्मा॥ १॥

First Brāhmaṇa

A Brāhmaṇa namely Triśikhī once visited to the world of sun and asked lord– "O God! What is this body? What is breathing? What is the cause and what is the soul?"

स होवाच सर्वमिदं शिव एव विजानीहि। किंतु नित्यः शुद्धो निरञ्जनो विभुरद्वयानन्दः शिव एकः स्वेन भासेदं सर्वं दृष्ट्वा तप्तायः पिण्डवदेकं भिन्नवदवभासते। तद्भासकं किमिति चेदुच्यते। सच्छब्दवाच्यमविद्याशबलं ब्रह्म॥ २॥

Lord sun replied– "O Brāhmaṇa! Be known that everything here is nothing else but the form of Śiva. That Śiva which is known as everlasting, pure, free from attachment, sovereign, exclusive and the pleasure itself originates one in multiform like a hot iron-bar after observation of everything from the divine abode which is only one, if a question is raised regarding identity of the god who is providing the light then the answer will be that.

ब्रह्मणोऽव्यक्तम्। अव्यक्तान्महत्। महतोऽहंकारः। अहंकारात्पञ्चतन्मात्राणि। पञ्चतन्मात्रेभ्यः पञ्चमहाभूतानि। पञ्चमहाभूतेभ्योऽखिलं जगत्॥ ३॥

The strong illusion as a shadow to the word 'Sat' *i.e.* the additional Brahma comprised of acute illusion and spreaded in this material world. This Brahma originates intangible, the intangible to 'Mahat', the 'Mahat' to ego, the ego generates five Tanmātras, the five Tanmātras to the five elements and from these five elements this whole world has been originated.

तदखिलं किमिति। भूतविकारविभागादिरिति। एकस्मिन्पिण्डे कथं भूतविकारविभाग इति। तत्तत्कार्यकारणभेदरूपेणांशतत्त्ववाचकवाच्यस्थानभेदविषयदेवताकोशभेदविभागा भवन्ति॥

What is that world? It is a division created by the defects or the distortions arisen in the element. How the divisions are created by splitting-up a single 'piṇḍa' due to distortions taking place in the element? The divisions has been stated on the basis of the part of element, the discrimination between the speaker (Vācaka) and the speech (Vācya), the subjects, gods and the discrimination according to the cells which are made according to different actions and causes of those different elements. (The kinds of five elements has been clearly explained in the successive hymns.)

अथाकाशोऽन्तःकरणमनोबुद्धिचित्ताहंकाराः। वायुः समानोदानव्यानापानप्राणाः। वह्निः श्रोत्रत्वक्चक्षुर्जिह्वाघ्राणानि। आपः शब्दस्पर्शरूपरसगन्धाः। पृथिवी वाक्पाणिपादपायूपस्थाः॥ ५॥

The five kinds of ether are– conscience, mind, wit, water (citta) and the ego. The winds are also of five kinds. These are– Samāna, Udāna, Vyāna, Apāna and Prāṇa. The sensory organs *i.e.* ears, skin, eyes, tongue and the nose are originated from the fire. The five Tanmātras *i.e.* speech, touch, complexion, essence and smell are originated from the element of water. The executive organs *i.e.* the speech, hands, feet, anus and genetic organs are originated by the earth.

ज्ञानसंकल्पनिश्चयानुसंधानाभिमाना आकाशकार्यान्तःकरणविषयाः। समीकरणोन्नयनग्रहणश्रवणोच्छ्वासा वायुकार्यप्राणादिविषयाः। शब्दस्पर्शरूपरसगन्धा अग्निकार्यज्ञानेन्द्रियविषया अबाश्रिताः। वचनादानगमनविसर्गानन्दाः पृथिवीकार्यकर्मेन्द्रियविषयाः। कर्मज्ञानेन्द्रियविषयेषु प्राणतन्मात्रविषया अन्तर्भूताः। मनोबुद्ध्योश्चित्ताहंकारौ चान्तर्भूतौ॥ ६॥

The knowledge, resolution, strong-determination, research and ego, these are the functions of ether element and subjects of conscience. The adjustment (nature creating balance), accession to (to lift upward, to entertain, to hear, to flow or expel out the sound, inhale and exhale, these are the functions of air elements and are subjects of breathings etc. The sound, touch, complexion, essence and smell etc. are the functions of fire element and subjects of the sensory organs. These all are dependent to the element of water. The speech, donation (to give), to come and to go, to discharge and the pleasure are the functions of earth element and subjects of executive organs. The subjects of breathing and Tanmātras are embedded with the subjects of educative as also sensory organs. The water (citta) and the ego are inherent to the mind and the wit.

अवकाशविधूतदर्शनपिण्डीकरणधारणाः सूक्ष्मतमा जैवतन्मात्रविषयाः॥७॥

The vacation (void), deplete (the dynamicity to come and go), the sight, the crystallisation (Piṇḍikaraṇa), Dhāraṇā (conceive) etc. are the subjects of minutest Tanmātras *i.e.* related to the elements of ether, wind, fire, water and the earth.

एवं द्वादशाङ्गानि आध्यात्मिकान्याधिभौतिकान्याधिदैविकानि। अत्र निशाकरचतुर्मुखदिग्वातार्कवरुणाश्व्यग्नीन्द्रोपेन्द्रप्रजापतियमा इत्यक्षाधिदेवतारूपैर्द्वादशनाड्यन्तःप्रवृत्ताः प्राणा एवाङ्गानि अंगज्ञानं तदेव ज्ञातेति॥८॥

Thus, the twelve parts as mentioned have been described in three major parts which are known as celestial, material and metaphysical. The moon, Brahma, the directions, the wind, the sun, the Varuṇa, Aśvini kumāra, the fire, the Indra, Upendra, Prajāpati and Yama are situated within the twelve nerves as the ruling god of twelve senses. These have been told as the parts of breathing (Prāṇa). The person known to these parts has been stated a scholar.

अथ व्योमानिलानलजलान्नानां पञ्चीकरणमिति। ज्ञातृत्वं समानयोगेन श्रोत्रद्वारा शब्दगुणो वागधिष्ठित आकाशे तिष्ठति आकाशस्तिष्ठति। मनो व्यानयोगेन त्वग्द्वारा स्पर्शगुणः पाण्यधिष्ठितो वायौ तिष्ठति वायुस्तिष्ठति। बुद्धिरुदानयोगेन चक्षुर्द्वारा रूपगुणः पादाधिष्ठितोऽग्नौ तिष्ठत्यग्निस्तिष्ठति। चित्तमपानयोगेन जिह्वाद्वारा रसगुण उपस्थाधिष्ठितोऽप्सु तिष्ठत्यापस्तिष्ठन्ति। अहंकारः प्राणयोगेन घ्राणद्वारा गन्धगुणो गुदाधिष्ठितः पृथिव्यां तिष्ठति पृथिवी तिष्ठति य एवं वेद॥९॥

Now, the crystallisation of five elements (the process of involvement of the pragmatic five elements by the combination of five basic elements) of the ether, the wind, the fire, the water and the earth (cereal) is described. The Jñātṛtva (ether) is located in the ether as a result of adding with the Samāna Vāyu (wind) and by the support of the merit, speech is in garb of the word through ears and the ether too is also enshrined within the same. As a result of adding with the Vyāna Vāyu and through the hands enriched of touching sense through the skin, the mind is located in the wind and the wind too is also existing within the same. As a result of adding with the Udāna Vāyu and with the support of feet and powers to see the complexion through eyes, the wit is enshrined in the fire and the fire too is enshrined within the same. As a result of adding with the Apāna Vāyu and taste through the tongue as also with the support of genital organs, the citta (water) is located in the water. The water too is located within the same. As a result of adding with the Prāṇa Vāyu and through the smelling property of nose and by the means of anus is located on the earth and the earth too is located within the same. One should take the connotation accordingly.

॥मन्त्रः-२॥

अत्रैते श्लोका भवन्ति। पृथग्भूते षोडश कलाः स्वार्धभागान्परान्क्रमात्।
अन्तःकरणव्यानाक्षिरसपायुनभः क्रमात्॥ १॥

The following hymns has been stated in this context. The ether etc. with sixteen arts (apparent) has been originated as a result of joining with the half part of every micro element and the other elements *i.e.* conscience, ether, Vyāna (wind), eyes, fire, essence (water) and anus (earth) etc.

मुख्यात्पूर्वोत्तरैर्भागैर्भूतेभूते चतुश्चतुः। पूर्वमाकाशमाश्रित्य पृथिव्यादिषु संस्थिताः॥ २॥

The cardinal and foremost part of every element commencing from the ether element to the earth element and the successive and residual part of other elements each by one and fourth part resides in the five elements.

[In the element which is apparent half-part of the basic micro-element and the remaining half part is comprised of four elements. It is to be considered that every element has sixteen parts (Kalās). By presuming this a new apparent element is constructed consisting sixteen parts (Kalās) as a result of one by half of the cardinal element *i.e.* sixteen parts plus half parts of the other four (viz. fourth part of eight parts *i.e.* two parts each of the four which means eight parts aggregate.]

मुख्यादूर्ध्वे परा ज्ञेया न परानुत्तरान्विदुः। एवमंशो ह्यभूत्तस्मात्तेभ्यश्चांशो ह्यभूत्तथा॥ ३॥

The main part of the upper side should be deemed as a micro element and the successive part is to be considered as an apparent element (Sthūla). Thus, both of them are joined with the parts of one anther.

तस्मादन्योन्यमाश्रित्य ह्योतं प्रोतमनुक्रमात्। पञ्चभूतमयी भूमिः सा चेतनसमन्विता॥ ४॥

All these elements are added with one another by attaining the mutual support in the similar fashion. This earth also is sensitive because of consisting five elements.

तत ओषधयोऽन्नं च ततः पिण्डाश्चतुर्विधाः। रसासृङ्मांसमेदोऽस्थिमज्जाशुक्राणि धातवः॥ ५॥

Having this, the earth generates the medicines, cereals, piṇdas of four kinds (which gets birth from perspiration, eggs, water and vagina) the essence, blood, flesh, marrow, bones, semen etc. seven Dhātus (sub-elements).

केचित्तद्योगतः पिण्डा भूतेभ्यः संभवाः क्वचित्। तस्मिन्नन्नमयः पिण्डो नाभिमण्डलसंस्थितः॥ ६

As a result of the combination of those Dhātus, the origin of a number of crystals made of elements becomes possible. That crystal enriched of food resides in the middle of the navel region.

अस्य मध्येऽस्ति हृदयं सनालं पद्मकोशवत्। सत्त्वान्तर्वर्तिनो देवाः कर्त्रहंकारचेतनाः॥ ७॥

The heart analogous to the lotus-ovary with the tube is existed in the middle of it and all gods (living souls) bearing the element of ego presuming themselves the cause (Kartā) of action; reside within that heart.

अस्य बीजं तमःपिण्डं मोहरूपं जडं घनम्। वर्तते कण्ठमाश्रित्य मिश्रीभूतमिदं जगत्॥ ८॥

Its seed which is called the crystal of the Tamas property in garb of attachment spreads all over the world with its existence in the thread of ignorance.

प्रत्यगानन्दरूपात्मा मूर्ध्नि स्थाने परे पदे। अनन्तशक्तिसंयुक्तो जगद्रूपेण भासते॥ ९॥

The supreme position of every pleasing soul is luminating everywhere in the form of universe as a result of combination with the infinite powers within mind.

सर्वत्र वर्तते जाग्रत्स्वप्नं जाग्रति वर्तते। सुषुप्तं च तुरीयं च नान्यावस्थासु कुत्रचित्॥ १०॥

The stage of awaking is omnipresent while the stage of dreaming resides in the awaken. This dormance and awaken stage (Turīyāvasthā) does not find anywhere in other stages.

सर्वदेशेष्वनुस्यूतश्चतूरूपः शिवात्मकः। यथा महाफले सर्वे रसाः सर्वप्रवर्तकाः॥ ११॥

As the essence is spreaded everywhere in the fruit of delicious taste, the soul in garb of Śiva is existed in the four forms throughout the places and the bodies etc.

तथैवान्नमये कोशे कोशास्तिष्ठन्ति चान्तरे। यथा कोशस्तथा जीवो यथा जीवस्तथा शिवः॥ १२॥

In that body, four treasures (Kośa) are existed within the treasure of food. As per the nature of these treasures, the living-soul gets birth and according to the living-soul, Lord Śiva (the supreme soul) has been stated.

सविकारस्तथा जीवो निर्विकारस्तथा शिवः। कोशास्तस्य विकारास्ते ह्यवस्थासु प्रवर्तकाः॥ १३॥

The mere difference between both is that the living soul is with defects in it while Śiva is beyond the defects. These treasures too are the defects of living-soul which are stated the promoter of all stages.

यथा रसाशये फेनं मथनादेव जायते। मनोनिर्मथनादेव विकल्पा बहवस्तथा॥ १४॥

As the froth arises, as a result of churning of milk, a number of options arise when the mind is churned.

कर्मणा वर्तते कर्मी तत्त्यागाच्छान्तिमाप्नुयात्। अयने दक्षिणे प्राप्ते प्रपञ्चाभिमुखं गतः॥ १५॥

The existence of living-soul is determined by his activities. Peace is attained when the activities are abandoned. He is compelled to involve in the dragnet of illusion owing to his entrance in Dakṣiṇāyana (the southern motion of sun from equator to south direction).

अहंकाराभिमानेन जीवः स्याद्धि सदाशिवः। स चाविवेकप्रकृतिसङ्गत्या तत्र मुह्यते॥ १६॥

When Sadāśiva (perfect knowledge) is fell in the trap of ego, he has to move in the category of living soul only at that stage. He is involved in the attachment due to combination of ignorance and the nature.

नानायोनिशतं गत्वा शेतेऽसौ वासनावशात्। विमोक्षात्संचरत्येव मत्स्यः कूलद्वयं यथा॥ १७॥

Owing to enslaved of the passions, he sleeps in ignorance and moves through many hundreds species (Yonis) and strolls in the middle of both banks of a river like a fish when these passions are abandoned.

ततः कालवशादेव ह्यात्मज्ञानविवेकतः। उत्तराभिमुखो भूत्वा स्थानात्स्थानान्तरं क्रमात्॥ १८॥

He then attains one place (class) to another place (class) in a seriatim towards the north as a consequence of attaining the discretion and conscience under the administration of the impact of time.

मूर्ध्न्याधायात्मनः प्राणान्योगाभ्यासं स्थितश्चरन्। योगात्संजायते ज्ञानं ज्ञानाद्योगः प्रवर्तते॥ १९॥

He thereafter engages him in practise of Yoga by enthroning the element of breathing in the mind. A trend of knowledge through Yoga and Yoga through knowledge is generated.

योगज्ञानपरो नित्यं स योगी न प्रणश्यति। विकारस्थं शिवं पश्येद्विकारश्च शिवे न तु॥ २०॥

The supreme devotee (Yogī) who engages himself attentively in the practise of the Yoga of knowledge (Jñāna Yoga), seldom meets to destruction. He ceaselessly observes Śiva (perfect knowledge) existed in the defects but not observes the defects in the Śiva.

योगप्रकाशकं योगैर्ध्यायेच्चानन्यभावनः। योगज्ञाने न विद्येते तस्य भावो न सिध्यति॥ २१॥

Such a supreme yogi, free from all kinds of defects, should exclusively plunge himself in the thinking of Brahma. One who has not attain such yoga of knowledge, seldom attains success.

तस्मादभ्यासयोगेन मनः प्राणान्निरोधयेत्। योगी निशितधारेण क्षुरेणैव निकृन्तयेत्॥ २२॥

Thus, the mind should be injected (controlled) through the breathings while doing the regular practise of yoga. The yogi should be so firm-determined as analogous to the sharp edge of knife to cut the ties of attachment.

शिखा ज्ञानमयी वृत्तिर्यमाद्यष्टाङ्गसाधनैः। ज्ञानयोगः कर्मयोग इति योगो द्विधा मतः॥ २३॥

As a result of practise on yoga consisting eight parts including Yama, Niyama etc. a flame of knowledge is generated. Two ways of yoga has been stated in which the first is the yoga of knowledge and the second is the yoga of action.

क्रियायोगमथेदानीं शृणु ब्राह्मणसत्तम। अव्याकुलस्य चित्तस्य बन्धनं विषये क्वचित्॥ २४॥

O great Brāhmaṇa! The yoga of action is now described. The mind of yogi if not impatient, he does not fall in the trap of the worldly enjoyments.

यत्संयोगो द्विजश्रेष्ठ स च द्वैविध्यमश्नुते। कर्म कर्तव्यमित्येव विहितेष्वेव कर्मसु॥ २५॥

बन्धनं मनसो नित्यं कर्मयोगः स उच्यते। यत्तु चित्तस्य सततमर्थे श्रेयसि बन्धनम्॥ २६॥

ज्ञानयोगः स विज्ञेयः सर्वसिद्धिकरः शिवः। यस्योक्तलक्षणे योगे द्विविधेऽप्यव्ययं मनः॥ २७॥

स याति परमं श्रेयो मोक्षलक्षणमञ्जसा। देहेन्द्रियेषु वैराग्यं यम इत्युच्यते बुधैः॥ २८॥

O supreme Brāhmaṇa! Combinations also are of two kinds to engage one's mind ceaselessly and through the action and duty prescribed by the holy books is called the yoga of action. Employment of mind always in the upliftment of soul is called the yoga of soul.

All kinds of achievements pertaining to the welfare of the soul are attained by virtue of practise on yoga of knowledge. The person who engages himself in the practice innocently and without any distortion on both the yogas, definitely attains to the emancipation. The scholars have stated that Yama is spirit of detachment from body and the sensory organs in its entirety.

अनुरक्तिः परे तत्त्वे सततं नियमः स्मृतः। सर्ववस्तुन्युदासीनभावमासनमुत्तमम्॥ २९॥

जगत्सर्वमिदं मिथ्याप्रतीतिः प्राणसंयमः। चित्तस्यान्तर्मुखीभावः प्रत्याहारस्तु सत्तम॥ ३०॥

Niyama is nothing else but a perpetual love for the element of supreme soul. The spirit of reluctance or indifference regarding all subjects is the supreme Āsana. Similarly, Prāṇāyāma too is nothing else but a process to understand duly the fallacious form of this universe. The introvert sense of the mind is called Pratyāhāra.

चित्तस्य निश्चलीभावो धारणा धारणं विदुः। सोऽहं चिन्मात्रमेवेति चिन्तनं ध्यानमुच्यते॥ ३१॥

To hold an undivided stage of mind is called Dhāraṇā. The meditation too is a developed conscience that I am in the form of Cinmātra.

ध्यानस्य विस्मृतिः सम्यक्समाधिरभिधीयते। अहिंसा सत्यमस्तेयं ब्रह्मचर्यं दयार्जवम्॥ ३२॥

क्षमा धृतिर्मिताहारः शौचं चेति यमा दश। तपः सन्तुष्टिरास्तिक्यं दानमाराधनं हरेः॥ ३३॥

वेदान्तश्रवणं चैव ह्रीर्मतिश्च जपो व्रतम्॥ इति॥ आसनानि तदङ्गानि स्वस्तिकादीनि वै द्विज॥ ३४

वर्ण्यन्ते स्वस्तिकं पादतलयोरुभयोरपि। पूर्वोत्तरे जानुनी द्वे कृत्वासनमुदीरितम्॥ ३५॥

A thorough deletion of the memory of the attention (meditation) is called a Samādhi. There are ten Yamas stated by the scholars. These are non-violence, truthfulness, celibacy, kindness, simplicity, forgiveness, patience, diet-control, purity and greedlessness. The ten Niyamas are the penance, satisfaction, theism, generosity, meditation on God, hearing to Vedas, modesty, wit, Japa and resolution. Now, Svastika etc. Āsanas and the procedure for exercising them in the topic of Āsanas is described. A posture of sitting by trapping the toes of both feet in the middle of knees is called Svastika Āsana.

सव्ये दक्षिणगुल्फं तु पृष्ठपार्श्वे नियोजयेत्। दक्षिणेऽपि तथा सव्यं गोमुखं गोमुखं यथा॥ ३६॥

The posture (Āsana) of Gomukha is called when the right ankle is employed at the left portion of the back and the left ankle is set at the right portion of the back. Thus, it is seen like the mouth of a cow.

एकं चरणमन्यस्मिन्नूरावारोप्य निश्चलः। आस्ते यदिदमेनोघ्नं वीरासनमुदीरितम्॥ ३७॥

गुदं नियम्य गुल्फाभ्यां व्युत्क्रमेण समाहितः। योगासनं भवेदेतदिति योगविदो विदुः॥ ३८॥

Imposing right foot on the left pubic and the left foot on the right pubic undivided is called Vīrāsana. According to Yogīs, fixing the right heel at the left side of the anus region and the left heel at the right region is called Yogāsana.

ऊर्वोरुपरि वै धत्ते यदा पादतले उभे। पद्मासनं भवेदेतत्सर्वव्याधिविषापहम्॥ ३९॥

Setting the toes of both feet on both pubic is called Padmāsana. It is stated that this Āsana is killer of the impact of poisons as also the diseases.

पद्मासनं सुसंस्थाप्य तदङ्गुष्ठद्वयं पुनः। व्युत्क्रमेणैव हस्ताभ्यां बद्धपद्मासनं भवेत्॥ ४०॥

While sitting on Padmāsana, when the thumb of left foot is caught by the right hand and the thumb of right foot is caught by the left hand, the posture so made is called Baddhapadmāsana.

पद्मासनं सुसंस्थाप्य जानूर्वोरन्तरे करौ। निवेश्य भूमावातिष्ठेद्व्योमस्थः कुक्कुटासनः॥ ४१॥

Having seated on Padmāsana when both hands are taken out from the middle of the legs and pubics and fixed on land and thus when body weight is uplifted by the hands so fixed on the ground is called Kukkuṭāsana.

कुक्कुटासनबन्धस्थो दोर्भ्यां संबध्य कन्धरम्। शेते कूर्मवदुत्तान एतदुत्तानकूर्मकम्॥ ४२॥

Having seated on Kukkuṭāsana, when both shoulders are fastened by both arms and thus erecting the body lineal like a tortoise is called Uttānakūrmāsana.

पादाङ्गुष्ठौ तु पाणिभ्यां गृहीत्वा श्रवणावधि। धनुराकर्णकाकृष्टं धनुरासनमीरितम्॥ ४३॥

Pulling of arms upto the ears in the form of a bow by holding the thumbs of both feet by the hands is called Dhanurāsana.

सीवनीं गुल्फदेशाभ्यां निपीड्य व्युत्क्रमेण तु। प्रसार्य जानुनोर्हस्तावासनं सिंहरूपकम्॥ ४४॥

Providing stability to the body in a posture when both knees and hands are extended by pushing the stomach region from opposite sides through both heels is called Siṁhāsana.

गुल्फौ च वृषणस्याधः सीविन्युभयपार्श्वयोः। निवेश्य पादौ हस्ताभ्यां बध्वा भद्रासनं भवेत्॥ ४५॥

By stabilising both ankles at both sides of the anus below the testis and sitting by holding both feet by hands is called Bhadrāsana.

सीवनीपार्श्वमुभयं गुल्फाभ्यां व्युत्क्रमेण तु। निपीड्यासनमेतच्च मुक्तासनमुदीरितम्॥ ४६॥

Both the collateral parts of the bullock when pressed from opposite sides by both ankles and thus sitting posture is called Muktāsana.

अवष्टभ्य धरां सम्यक्तलाभ्यां हस्तयोर्द्वयोः। कूर्परौ नाभिपार्श्वे तु स्थापयित्वा मयूरवत्॥ ४७॥

समुन्नतशिरः पादं मयूरासनमिष्यते। वामोरूमूले दक्षाङ्घ्रिं जान्वोर्वेष्टितपाणिना॥ ४८॥

वामेन वामाङ्गुष्ठं तु गृहीतं मत्स्यपीठकम्। योनिं वामेन संपीड्य मेढ्रादुपरि दक्षिणम्॥ ४९॥

ऋजुकायः समासीनः सिद्धासनमुदीरितम्। प्रसार्य भुवि पादौ तु दोर्भ्यामङ्गुष्ठमादरात्॥ ५०॥

जानूपरि ललाटं तु पश्चिमं तानमुच्यते। येन केन प्रकारेण सुखं धार्यं च जायते॥ ५१॥

तत्सुखासनमित्युक्तमशक्तस्तत्समाचरेत्। आसनं विजितं येन जितं तेन जगत्त्रयम्॥ ५२॥

At this root of the left pubic when the thumb of right foot is held by the hand in the same posture, it is called Matsyendrāsana. When the ankle of the left foot is fixed on the bullock and right foot is kept in the upper portion of the genital organ thereby making the body is called Siddhāsana. When both feet are extended on the ground, the thumbs of both feet are held by both hands and placing the head on knee, the posture is called Paścimottānāsana. A sitting posture ensuring comfort and stability is called Sukhāsana. The person unable to exercise other Āsanas due to one or other reasons, should be seated in this very Āsana. The person who has established command on Āsanas has enslaved all the three worlds viz. it will be deemed that he has won all these worlds.

यमैश्च नियमैश्चैव आसनैश्च सुसंयतः। नाडीशुद्धिं च कृत्वादौ प्राणायामं समाचरेत्॥५३॥

Prāṇāyāma should be exercised only when a man has developed well-balance through Yama, Niyana and Āsana etc. and nerves of the body are made ready for.

देहमानं स्वाङ्गुलिभिः षण्णवत्यङ्गुलायतम्। प्राणः शरीरादधिको द्वादशाङ्गुलमानतः॥५४॥

The measurement of the woman body is ninety-six fingers by the fingers of that concerned man. The breathing (Prāṇa) is more than twelve fingers as compared to the body.

देहस्थमनिलं देहसमुद्भूतेन वह्निना। न्यूनं समं वा योगेन कुर्वन्ब्रह्मविदिष्यते॥५५॥

Knowledge of Brahma can be obtained by regulating the wind existing in the body through Prāṇāyāma either by receding or establishing the equilibrium by virtue of Yoga through the energy (fire) arisen in the body.

देहमध्ये शिखिस्थानं तप्तजाम्बूनदप्रभम्। त्रिकोणं द्विपदामन्यच्चतुरस्रं चतुष्पदम्॥५६॥

वृत्तं विहङ्गमानां तु षडस्रं सर्पजन्मनाम्। अष्टास्रं स्वेदजानां तु तस्मिन्दीपवदुज्ज्वलम्॥५७॥

कन्दस्थानं मनुष्याणां देहमध्यं नवाङ्गुलम्। चतुरङ्गुलमुत्सेधं चतुरङ्गुलमायतम्॥५८॥

The trainable shining with the radiance of heated gold in the middle of the human body is called the place of fire. In cattle's, this place of fire is square-shaped, it is circular in birds, hexagonal in the species of snake like serpents and octagonal in the living-organism originating from perspiration. A tuber-shaped fire place of the measurement of nine fingers is found in the human body. It luminates like a lamp. It is four-fingers in height and four-fingers in width.

अण्डाकृति तिरश्चां च द्विजानां च चतुष्पदाम्। तुन्दमध्यं तदिष्टं वै तन्मध्यं नाभिरिष्यते॥५९॥

तत्र चक्रं द्वादशारं तेषु विष्ण्वादिमूर्तयः। अहं तत्र स्थितश्चक्रं भ्रामयामि स्वमायया॥६०॥

अरेषु भ्रमते जीवः क्रमेण द्विजसत्तम। तन्तुपञ्जरमध्यस्था यथा भ्रमति लूतिका॥६१॥

This tuber (fire place) is oval-shaped in serpents, birds and the cattle's. Its nucleus is called navel. A discuss bearing twelve blades is existed within it. The idols of lord Viṣṇu etc. gods are existed within it. I (Brahma) rotate this discus through my own illusion. The living-soul revolves in these twelve blades in the same way as the spider moves hither and thither in her cobweb.

प्राणाविरूढश्चरति जीवस्तेन विना न हि। तस्योर्ध्वे कुण्डलीस्थानं नाभेस्तिर्यगथोर्ध्वतः॥६२॥

The living-soul moves by riding on the element of breathing as it cannot move without it. A slanting and the higher place for the great power of Kuṇḍalinī is existed on upper part of the same.

अष्टप्रकृतिरूपा सा चाष्टधा कुण्डलीकृता। यथावद्वायुसारं च ज्वलनादि च नित्यशः॥६३॥

परितः कन्दपार्श्वे तु निरुध्यैव सदा स्थिता। मुखेनैव समावेष्ट्य ब्रह्मरन्ध्रमुखं तथा॥६४॥

By virtue of its eight forms, the Kuṇḍalinī regulates the circulation of food and water as also the air by gripping it in eight ways. It is located collaterally by covering the tuber (fire place) all around. It has covered the mouth of Brahmarandhra by its own mouth.

योगकालेन मरुता साग्निना बोधिता सती। स्फुरिता हृदयाकाशे नागरूपा महोज्ज्वला॥६५॥

By virtue of the practise on yoga, this great power of Kuṇḍalinī in the form of serpent within the ether of heart blazes with the clean-light like the fire erupted by the wind.

अपानाद्द्व्यङ्गुलादूर्ध्वमधो मेढ्रस्य तावता। देहमध्यं मनुष्याणां हृन्मध्यं तु चतुष्पदाम्॥६६॥

The middle part of the human body has been considered two fingers measurement upward from the Apāna and below the urinating organ. The middle part of the cattle's body has been told existed in the region of their heart.

इतरेषां तुन्दमध्ये नानानाडीसमावृतम्। चतुष्प्रकारद्व्ययुते देहमध्ये सुषुम्नया॥६७॥

In other living-organisms, the middle part of the body is the middle region of the navel wherein a number of nerves are connected. The spinal (Suṣumnā) nerve with Prāṇa and Apāna is existing four ways in the body.

कन्दमध्ये स्थिता नाडी सुषुम्ना सुप्रतिष्ठिता। पद्मसूत्रप्रतीकाशा ऋजुरूर्ध्वप्रवर्तिनी॥६८॥

The spinal nerve enshrined in the middle of the (Kanda) is most micro and analogous to the thread of Padma and it has become dynamic straightly upward.

ब्रह्मणो विवरं यावद्विद्युदाभासनालकम्। वैष्णवी ब्रह्मनाडी च निर्वाणप्राप्तिपद्धतिः॥६९॥

This Brahma nerve namely Vaiṣṇavī which goes up to the Brahmrandhra is as bright as the lightening and competent enough to provide with emancipation.

इडा च पिङ्गला चैव तस्याः सव्येतरे स्थिते। इडा समुत्थिता कन्दाद्वामनासापुटावधिः॥७०॥

पिङ्गला चोत्थिता तस्माद्दक्षनासापुटावधिः। गान्धारी हस्तिजिह्वा च द्वे चान्ये नाडिके स्थिते॥७१

पुरतः पृष्ठतस्तस्य वामेतरदृशौ प्रति। पूषायशस्विनीनाड्यौ तस्मादेव समुत्थिते॥७२॥

सव्येतरश्रुत्यवधि पायुमूलादलम्बुसा। अधोगता शुभा नाडी मेढ्रान्तावधिरायता॥७३॥

Two nerves namely Iḍā and Piṅgalā are enshrined on both collateral sides of the Suṣumnā. The Iḍā nerve has extended upto the left nostril after its outlet from the tuber and the Piṅgalā has reached upto right nostril. Both other nerves namely Gāndhārī and Hastijihvā too are existed at the same place. These two nerves *i.e.* Gāndhārī and Hastijihvā have been extended front and rear side of Iḍā and Piṅgalā and upto the right eye. The Pūṣā and Yaśasvinī both nerves have been extended upto the right and left ear from their origin place *i.e.* the anus. The nerve namely Alambusā has been descended upto the last point of the backbone.

पादाङ्गुष्ठावधिः कन्दादधोयाता च कौशिकी। दशप्रकारभूतास्ताः कथिताः कन्दसंभवाः॥७४॥

The nerve Kauśikī has been extended from the tuber (cluster of the nerves) down to the thumb of the foot. These ten nerves have been stated coming from the cluster of the nerves.

तन्मूला बहवो नाड्यः स्थूलसूक्ष्माश्च नाडिकाः। द्वासप्ततिसहस्राणि स्थूलाः सूक्ष्माश्च नाडयः॥७५॥

There are a number of apparent as also the micro nerves in seventy-two thousand numbers commencing from the Kauśikī nerves.

संख्यातुं नैव शक्यन्ते स्थूलमूलाः पृथग्विधाः। यथाश्वत्थदले सूक्ष्माः स्थूलाश्च विततास्तथा॥७६॥

It is a very tough work to count separately these apparent and micro nerves. These are so extended as the nerves are seen on the leaf of a pipal tree.

प्राणापानौ समानश्च उदानो व्यान एव च। नागः कूर्मश्च कृकरो देवदत्तो धनंजयः॥७७॥ चरन्ति दशनाडीषु दश प्राणादिवायवः। प्राणादिपञ्चकं तेषु प्रधानं तत्र च द्वयम्॥७८॥

The ten breathings *i.e.* the Prāṇa, Apāna, Samāna, Udāna, Vyāna, Nāga, Kūrma, Kṛkara, Devadatta and Dhanañjaya too also are circulated within these nerves. The first five breathings are the main breathings that circulate within these nerves. Further, the two breathings *i.e.* Prāṇa and Apāna are the supreme among them.

प्राण एवाथवा ज्येष्ठो जीवात्मानं बिभर्ति यः। आस्यनासिकयोर्मध्यं हृदयं नाभिमण्डलम्॥७९॥

पादाङ्गुष्ठमिति प्राणस्थानानि द्विजसत्तम। अपानश्चरति ब्रह्मन्गुदमेढ्रोरुजानुषु॥८०॥

The breathing is the supreme among all as it holds the living soul. O the eminent Brāhmaṇa, five places has been stated as the abode of the prime breathing. These are the middle portion of the mouth and nose, the heart, the navel region and the thumb of the foot. O Brāhmaṇa! The Apāna wind is circulated in the anus, last point of the spinal cord, the pubic region and within the knee.

समानः सर्वगात्रेषु सर्वव्यापी व्यवस्थितः। उदानः सर्वसन्धिस्थः पादयोर्हस्तयोरपि॥८१॥

The Samāna wind is spreaded in all the organs of the human body and the Udāna wind is existed in hands as also feet and in all the joints of the organs.

व्यानः श्रोत्रोरुकट्यां च गुल्फस्कन्धगलेषु च। नागादिवायवः पञ्च त्वगस्थ्यादिषु संस्थिताः॥८२॥

The wind namely Vyāna resides in the ears, pubic, waist, heel, shoulder and the neck. The Nāga etc. five sub-winds are existed in the skin, bones etc.

तुन्दस्थजलमन्नं च रसादीनि समीकृतम्। तुन्दमध्यगतः प्राणस्तानि कुर्यात्पृथक्पृथक्॥८३॥

The breathing air very first collects the water, the foot, the essence as existed in the elementary canal. Subsequently, it establishes these things separately from one another.

इत्यादिचेष्टनं प्राणः करोति च पृथक् स्थितम्। अपानवायुर्मूत्रादेः करोति च विसर्जनम्॥ ८४॥

The breathing wind does all these functions by keeping itself detached from these. The Apāna wind does the function of discharging the urine etc.

प्राणापानादिचेष्टादि क्रियते व्यानवायुना। उज्जीर्यते शरीरस्थमुदानेन नभस्वता॥ ८५॥

The functions made by the Prāṇa and Apāna etc. wind are performed only when the Vyāna wind is added with them and by virtue of the Udāna wind, these all winds avail ascendancy in the body.

पोषणादिशरीरस्य समानः कुरुते सदा। उद्गारादिक्रियो नागः कूर्मोऽक्षादिनिमीलनः॥ ८६॥

The nutrition and maintenance of the body is always performed by the Samāna wind. The Nāga wind makes possible the functions of eructation etc. The Kūrma wind performs the functions of opening and closing of the eyes.

कृकरः क्षुतयोः कर्ता दत्तो निद्रादिकर्मकृत्। मृतगात्रस्य शोभादेर्धनंजय उदाहृतः॥ ८७॥

The functions of Kṛkara wind is to create appetite for food. The Devadatta wind handles the sleep etc. and the Dhanañjaya wind saves the corpse from rotting upto a certain time.

नाडीभेदं मरुद्भेदं मरुतां स्थानमेव च। चेष्टाश्च विविधास्तेषां ज्ञात्वैव द्विजसत्तम॥ ८८॥

O great Brāhmaṇa! The premises and the functions of the wind are in multiform. One should made endeavour to have identity with all of them.

शुद्धौ यतेत नाडीनां पूर्वोक्तज्ञानसंयुतः। विविक्तदेशमासाद्य सर्वसंबन्धवर्जितः॥ ८९॥

योगाङ्गद्रव्यसंपूर्णं तत्र दारुमये शुभे। आसने कल्पिते दर्भकुशकृष्णाजिनादिभिः॥ ९०॥

तावदासनमुत्सेधे तावद्द्वयसमायते। उपविश्यासनं सम्यक्स्वस्तिकादि यथारुचि॥ ९१॥

The nerves should be rectified by following the procedure in the precedent hymns. Subsequently, one should get rid of all attachments, choose a solitary place, collect all material required for exercise of yoga, make the seat of Darbha Kuśa or black deer etc. and should try to meditate till a good balance among all the organs is not established. To avail good results one should regularly practise on Svastika etc. Āsanas.

बद्ध्वा प्रागासनं विप्र ऋजुकायः समाहितः। नासाग्रन्यस्तनयनो दन्तैर्दन्तानसंस्पृशन्॥ ९२॥

रसनां तालुनि न्यस्य स्वस्थचित्तो निरामयः। आकुञ्चितशिरः किंचिन्निबध्नन्योगमुद्रया॥ ९३॥

हस्तौ यथोक्तविधिना प्राणायामं समाचरेत्। रेचनं पूरणं वायोः शोधनं रेचनं तथा॥ ९४॥

One should be seated in the Āsana with the body duly erected. The sight should be at the fore-portion of the nose, the teeth should not touch each other. The tongue should be touched with the palatine, the mind should be free from thoughts, the body slightly leaned and the posture of Yogāsana should be followed while exercising the Prāṇāyāma. The process of inhale, exhale and retention should be followed and then the process of 'recana' should be followed.

चतुर्भिः क्लेशनं वायोः प्राणायाम उदीर्यते। हस्तेन दक्षिणेनैव पीडयेन्नासिकापुटम्॥ ९५॥
शनैः शनैरथ बहिः प्रत्रिपेत्पिङ्गलानिलम्। इडया वायुमापूर्य ब्रह्मन्षोडशमात्रया॥ ९६॥
पूरितं कुम्भयेत्पश्चाच्चतुःषष्ट्या तु मात्रया। द्वात्रिंशन्मात्रया सम्यग्रेचयेत्पिङ्गलानिलम्॥ ९७॥

The process of making the wind dynamic with these four processes is called Prāṇāyāma. One should firstly push the left nostril by right hand and the wind existing in the lungs should be exhaled through the right nostril. The wind then to be inhaled through left nostril by sixteen counts and the retention (Kumbhaka) should be made by sixty four counts. Finally, that wind so retained, should be exhaled through the right nostril.

एवं पुनः पुनः कार्यं व्युत्क्रमानुक्रमेण तु। संपूर्णकुम्भवद्देहं कुम्भयेन्मातरिश्वना॥ ९८॥

This practise should be followed regularly in a seriatim and in the reverse order. The wind should be retained like a pitcher in the body.

पूरणान्नाडयः सर्वाः पूर्यन्ते मातरिश्वना। एवं कृते सति ब्रह्मंश्चरन्ति दश वायवः॥ ९९॥

O Brāhmaṇa! All nerves are filled with the wind by the exercises so made. The ten winds duly start circulating in all nerves of the body.

हृदयाम्भोरुहं चापि व्याकोचं भवति स्फुटम्। तत्र पश्येत्परात्मानं वासुदेवमकल्मषम्॥ १००॥

As a result of this practise, the lotus-form heart is extended and becomes pure and clean with all respects and the concerned person then perceives the innocent Vāsudeva in the form of supreme soul.

प्रातर्माध्यन्दिने सायमर्धरात्रे च कुम्भकान्। शनैरशीतिपर्यन्तं चतुर्वारं समभ्यसेत्॥ १०१॥

The process of retention (Kumbhaka) should be followed four times in a day *i.e.*, morning, afternoon, evening and the mid-night. This process should be increased gradually upto the eighty counts.

एकाहमात्रं कुर्वाणः सर्वपापैः प्रमुच्यते। संवत्सरत्रयादूर्ध्वं प्राणायामपरो नरः॥ १०२॥
योगसिद्धो भवेद्योगी वायुजिद्विजितेन्द्रियः। अल्पाशी स्वल्पनिद्रश्च तेजस्वी बलवान्भवेत्॥ १०३॥

All kinds of evils get compounded merely by the one day practise if the same is done as the procedure described above. The person who does Prāṇāyāma daily upto the three years, gets mastery in Yoga. Such a Yogī (devotee) can establish control over the wind, controls his sensory organs, eats less, sleeps for little hours, attain splendour and becomes mighty.

अपमृत्युमतिक्रम्य दीर्घमायुरवाप्नुयात्। प्रस्वेदजननं यस्य प्राणायामस्तु सोऽधमः॥ १०४॥
कम्पनं वपुषो यस्य प्राणायामेषु मध्यमः। उत्थानं वपुषो यस्य स उत्तम उदाहृतः॥ १०५॥

He enjoys long life by destroying the fear of premature death. Prāṇāyāma with perspiration is its meanest feature, Prāṇāyāma with shivering body is the medium and Prāṇāyāma that ascends the body upward is stated its best feature.

अधमे व्याधिपापानां नाशः स्यान्मध्यमे पुनः। पापरोगमहाव्याधिनाशः स्यादुत्तमे पुनः॥ १०६॥

अल्पमूत्रोऽल्पविष्ठश्च लघुदेहो मिताशनः। पट्विन्द्रियः पटुमतिः कालत्रयविदात्मवान्॥ १०७॥

All kinds of ailments and the evils are decayed even if the Prāṇāyāma is of meanest category. Similarly, the incurable diseases, evils and all kinds of ailments physical and mental both can be removed even if the Prāṇāyāma is of medium category while Prāṇāyāma of the best category makes the person concerned sleeping for few hours, excreting lesser (night soil and the urine etc.), small body and lesser diet. His senses as well as the wit both are sharpened and he becomes competent to know what had taken place, what will be in future and what is going at present *i.e.* the knowledge of three tenses.

रेचकं पूरकं मुक्त्वा कुम्भीकरणमेव यः। करोति त्रिषु कालेषु नैव तस्यास्ति दुर्लभम्॥ १०८॥

The Yogī who does only the retention (Kumbhaka) process of the Prāṇāyāma and seldom does the exhale and inhale, can attain everything easily in course of the trio-cycle of the time (Three Kālas).

नाभिकन्दे च नासाग्रे पादाङ्गुष्ठे च यत्नवान्। धारयेन्मनसा प्राणान्सन्ध्याकालेषु वा सदा॥ १०९॥

The devotee continuously cautious to his Yoga should presume the element of breathing by means of the mind and while praying to God in his navel region (cluster of all nerves), at the fore-portion of the nose and on both thumbs of the feet.

सर्वरोगैर्विनिर्मुक्तो जीवेद्योगी गतक्लमः। कुक्षिरोगविनाशः स्यान्नाभिकन्देषु धारणात्॥ ११०॥

The Yogī passes his life most pleasing way by keeping himself get rid of all elements as a result of following this process. By holding the breathing in the navel region, all kinds of ailments, pertaining to stomach as also the arm-pit are duly cured.

नासाग्रे धारणाद्दीर्घमायुः स्याद्देहलाघवम्। ब्राह्मे मुहूर्ते संप्राप्ते वायुमाकृष्य जिह्वया॥ १११॥

पिबतस्त्रिषु मासेषु वाक्सिद्धिर्महती भवेत्। अभ्यासतश्च षण्मासान्महारोगविनाशनम्॥ ११२॥

By holding the breathing air in fore-point of nose a man attains long-life and enjoys the body refreshing always. Power of speech can be obtained within three months if the wind is sucked by pulling through the tongue just in Brahmamuhūrta (four to six 'o' clock in the morning). The Yogī enjoys convalescence from the incurable disease if this practise is followed upto the six months.

यत्र यत्र धृतो वायुरङ्गे रोगादिदूषिते। धारणादेव मरुतस्तत्तदारोग्यमश्नुते॥ ११३॥

The Yogī becomes free from ailments by storing that breathing air in the concerned organs inflicted or affected by the incurable diseases due to fastening of wind everywhere in the entire body.

मनसो धारणादेव पवनो धारितो भवेत्। मनसः स्थापने हेतुरुच्यते द्विजपुङ्गव॥ ११४॥

The storing process of wind starts increasing with the same pace as the mind is concentrated. O Brāhmaṇa! The Prāṇāyāma has been pronunciated sine-quo-non in order to get concentration in the mind.

करणानि समाहृत्य विषयेभ्य: समाहित:। अपानमूर्ध्वमाकृष्येदुदरोपरि धारयेत्॥ ११५॥

बध्नन्कराभ्यां श्रोत्रादिकरणानि यथातथम्। युञ्जानस्य यथोक्तेन वर्त्मना स्ववशं मन:॥ ११६॥

The Apāna wind should be hold upside by separating it from the subjects pertaining to the sensory organs. Both ears should be closed by keeping fingers into their holes. By virtue of following the six-form posture *i.e.* closer of eyes, ears, mouth, nose etc. with the fingers of both hands, the mind is enslaved.

मनोवशात्प्राणवायु: स्ववशे स्थाप्यते सदा। नासिकापुटयो: प्राण: पर्यायेण प्रवर्तते॥ ११७॥

With the conquest on mind by this process, the breathing wind becomes well-regulated and its movements starts in a routine manner through the nose.

तिस्रश्च नाडिकास्तासु स यावन्तं चरत्ययम्। शङ्खिनीविवरे याम्ये प्राण: प्राणभृतां सताम्॥ ११८॥

तावन्तं च पुन: कालं सौम्ये चरति संततम्। इत्थं क्रमेण चरता वायुना वायुजिन्नर:॥ ११९॥

अहश्च रात्रिं पक्षं च मासमृत्वयनादिकम्। अन्तर्मुखो विजानीयात्कालभेदं समाहित:॥ १२०॥

There are three main nerves. Three persons (Yogīs) who do Prāṇāyāma enjoys the balanced circulation of the wind through their right and left nostrils. By virtue of such balanced flow of the breathing wind, the devotee gets triumph on the wind. That Yogī becomes so competent as to take cognisance of the discrimination in the day, night, fortnight, month, season and the movement of sun towards North as also the South (Uttarāyaṇa and Dakṣiṇāyaṇa) by virtue of his introvert powers. Thus he becomes able to accustom his body as also mind with the changing atmosphere.

अङ्गुष्ठादिस्वावयवस्फुरणादर्शनैरपि। अरिष्टैर्जीवितस्यापि जानीयात्क्षयमात्मन:॥ १२१॥

One should understand the end of life nearer when the vibration in the thumbs etc. organs *i.e.,* vibration due to circulation of blood in the nervous system is ceased.

ज्ञात्वा यतेत कैवल्यप्राप्तये योगवित्तम:। पादाङ्गुष्ठे कराङ्गुष्ठे स्फुरणं यस्य न श्रुति:॥ १२२॥

तस्य संवत्सरादूर्ध्वं जीवितस्य क्षयो भवेत्। मणिबन्धे तथा गुल्फे स्फुरणं यस्य नश्यति॥ १२३॥

षण्मासावधिरेतस्य जीवितस्य स्थितिर्भवेत्। कूर्परे स्फुरणं यस्य तस्य त्रैमासिकी स्थिति:॥ १२४॥

When the symptoms of proxy death are known, the Yogī should concentrate his mental powers on penance in order to attain emancipation. In case, vibration due to circulation of the blood in the nerves found absent in both hands and feet, it is indicative of only a year's period is now left for death. The man can only survive upto six months when the vibrations are found absent in the wrist and the ankles. Similarly, absence of vibration in elbow indicates that the concerned person has only three months to survive.

कुक्षिमेहनपार्श्वे च स्फुरणानुपलम्भने। मासावधिर्जीवितस्य तदर्धस्य तु दर्शने॥ १२५॥

A man meets to death only with in a month if there is no vibration seen in the collateral parts of the stomach as also in the genital organs.

आश्रिते जठरद्वारे दिनानि दश जीवितम्। ज्योति: खद्योतवद्यस्य तदर्धं तस्य जीवितम्॥ १२६॥

Only ten days remains for survival when the vibration in the inner stomach is found absent. Similarly, five days time for survival may be predicted when the light of sun and moon is seen by the concerned man not much extended than the light of a fire-fly.

जिह्वाग्रादर्शने त्रीणि दिनानि स्थितिरात्मनः। ज्वालाया दर्शने मृत्युर्द्विदिने भवति ध्रुवम्॥ १२७॥

Three days time for survival should be deemed when the front portion of the tongue is not seen by the concerned man and again two days time to survival is to be deemed when the man is enable to see the flame.

एवमादीन्यरिष्टानि दृष्टायुः क्षयकारणम्। निःश्रेयसाय युञ्जीत जपध्यानपरायणः॥ १२८॥

These all symptoms are the cause of decaying the age. It is therefore advisable to involve oneself in penance as also meditation for the ultimate welfare of the soul *i.e.* emancipation.

मनसा परमात्मानं ध्यात्वा तद्रूपतामियात्। यद्यष्टादशभेदेषु मर्मस्थानेषु धारणम्॥ १२९॥

The supreme soul should be summoned through the mind and one should try to be analogous to the supreme soul. The sensitivity of that supreme soul should be enshrined in the eighteen sensitive places of the body.

स्थानात्स्थानं समाकृष्य प्रत्याहारः स उच्यते। पादाङ्गुष्ठं तथा गुल्फं जङ्घामध्यं तथैव च॥ १३०॥

मध्यमूर्वोश्च मूलं च पायुर्हृदयमेव च। मेहनं देहमध्यं च नाभिं च गलकूर्परम्॥ १३१॥

तालुमूलं च मूलं च घ्राणस्याक्ष्णोश्च मण्डलम्। भ्रुवोर्मध्यं ललाटं च मूलमूर्ध्वं च जानुनी॥ १३२॥

मूलं च करयोर्मूलं महान्त्येतानि वै द्विज। पञ्चभूतमये देहे भूतेष्वेतेषु पञ्चसु॥ १३३॥

Pratyāhāra is called the process from pulling one place to another. O Brāhmaṇa! The thumb of foot, ankle, middle part of the pubic region, middle part of the genital organ, the root portion of anus, the heart, the genital organ, the navel region, the throat, the elbow, the root of palate, the root portion of the nose, eye-balls, the middle portion of the brows, the forehead, the root portion of the brain, the root portion of the knee and the root portion of the hands are called the eighteen sensitive places of this body consisting of five elements.

मनसो धारणं यत्तद्युक्तस्य च यमादिभिः। धारणा सा च संसारसागरोत्तारकारणम्॥ १३४॥

The meditation is nothing else but concentration of the mind obtained by virtue of practising the Yamas etc. The man becomes competent to cross this worldly sea when full concentration is originated.

आजानुपादपर्यन्तं पृथिवीस्थानमिष्यते। पित्तला चतुरस्रा च वसुधा वज्रलाञ्छिता॥ १३५॥

It is stated that the contribution of the element of the earth commences from the feet upto the knees. This earth with four-yellowish angles has been stated Vajralāñchata (studded with these angles).

स्मर्तव्या पञ्चघटिकास्तत्रारोप्य प्रभञ्जनम्। आजानुकटिपर्यन्तमपां स्थानं प्रकीर्तितम्॥ १३६॥

The Yogī should concentrate on the element of earth by inhaling the wind upto two hours (five Ghaṭis). The portion starting from the knees upto the waist has been stated the region of water.

अर्धचन्द्रसमाकारं श्वेतमर्जुनलाञ्छितम्। स्मर्तव्यमम्भ:श्वसनमारोप्य दश नाडिका:॥ १३७॥

The shape of this water is analogous to the half circle. Its colour is white and it is studded with silver. By retention of the ear upto four hours one should concentrate on the element of water.

आदेहमध्यकट्यन्तमग्निस्थानमुदाहृतम्। तत्र सिन्दूरवर्णोऽग्निर्ज्वलनं दश पञ्च च॥ १३८॥

स्मर्तव्या नाडिका: प्राणं कृत्वा कुम्भे तथेरितम्। नाभेरुपरि नासान्तं वायुस्थानं तु तत्र वै॥ १३९॥

वेदिकाकारवद्धूम्रो बलवान्भूतमारुत:। स्मर्तव्य: कुम्भकेनैव प्राणमारोप्य मारुतम्॥ १४०॥

घटिकाविंशतिस्तस्माद् घ्राणाद्ब्रह्मबिलावधि। व्योमस्थानं नभस्तत्र भिन्नाञ्जनसमप्रभम्॥ १४१॥

The place of fire has been stated in the middle of the waist in the body. Its shape is analogous to the flames of fire and its colour is like Sindūra (a reddish powdered article used while worshipping lord Hanumān). One should, therefore, concentrate on the element of breathing by the process of retention (Kumbhaka) upto six hours. The portion from navel to the nose has been stated the place of wind. Its shape is like the alṭar. The wind as mighty as the smoke should be taken under retention process upto eight hours. The element of ether has been stated starting from the nose upto the Brahmarandhra. It has the blue colour.

व्योम्नि मारुतमारोप्य कुम्भकेनैव यत्नवान्। पृथिव्यंशे तु देहस्य चतुर्बाहुं किरीटिनम्॥ १४२॥

अनिरुद्धं हरिं योगी यतेत भवमुक्तये। अबंशे पूरयेद्योगी नारायणमुदग्रधी:॥ १४३॥

प्रद्युम्नमग्नौ वाय्वंशे संकर्षणमत: परम्। व्योमांशे परमात्मानं वासुदेवं सदा स्मरेत्॥ १४४॥

The Yogī, engaged in his perpetual practise should establish the breathing air in the region of ether by practising the process of retention (Kumbhaka). Aniruddha Hari with four arms and a crown should be enshrined in the mind in the portion as stated the earth. The Yogī becomes able to attain emancipation by virtue of following this process. He should meditate on Śrī Nārāyaṇa in the portion of the water, Pradyumna in the region of the fire, Sankarṣaṇa in the region of the wind and the supreme soul Vāsudeva in the region of ether in a continuous manner.

अचिरादेव तत्प्राप्तिर्युञ्जानस्य न संशय:। बद्ध्वा योगासनं पूर्वं हृद्देशे हृदयाञ्जलि:॥ १४५॥

नासाग्रन्यस्तनयनो जिह्वां कृत्वा च तालुनि। दन्तैर्दन्तानसंस्पृश्य ऊर्ध्वकाय: समाहित:॥ १४६॥

संयमेच्चेन्द्रियग्राममात्मबुद्ध्या विशुद्धया। चिन्तनं वासुदेवस्य परस्य परमात्मन:॥ १४७॥

The devotee engaged continuously in this practise attains this supreme soul at the earliest. He should very first be seated on Yogāsana, call the particular shape (as described above) in the region of the heart and concentrate the sight on the fore-portion of the nose. He should stretch the tongue to touch palate, slight touch between teeth and erect his body white sitting on Yogāsana. He should meditate on the supreme soul Vāsudeva with proper control on the sensory organs through the sacrosanct metaphysical learning.

स्वरूपव्याप्तरूपस्य ध्यानं कैवल्यसिद्धिदम्। याममात्रं वासुदेवं चिन्तयेत्कुम्भकेन यः॥ १४८॥
सप्तजन्मार्जितं पापं तस्य नश्यति योगिनः। नाभिकन्दात्समारभ्य यावद्धृदयगोचरम्॥ १४९॥
जाग्रद्वृत्तिं विजानीयात्कण्ठस्थं स्वप्नवर्तनम्। सुषुप्तं तालुमध्यस्थं तुर्यं भ्रूमध्यसंस्थितम्॥ १५०॥

The Yogī avails the emancipation only by having meditation on the element of soul within his heart. Thus, the Yogī who meditates on the perfect knowledge Vāsudeva by virtue of establishing retention upto a quarter day, the evils committed by him upto seven previous years get destroyed. The place from the nuclei of the navel upto the region of the heart is indicative of the awakened stage. The stage of dreaming is in the throat, the dormance in the middle of the palate and the reverie (Turyavasthā) is existed in the middle of the brows.

तुर्यातीतं परं ब्रह्म ब्रह्मरन्ध्रे तु लक्षयेत्। जाग्रद्वृत्तिं समारभ्य यावद्ब्रह्मबिलान्तरम्॥ १५१॥
तत्रात्मायं तुरीयस्य तुर्यान्ते विष्णुरुच्यते। ध्यानेनैव समायुक्तो व्योम्नि चात्यन्तनिर्मले॥ १५२॥
सूर्यकोटिद्युतिधरं नित्योदितमधोक्षजम्। हृदयाम्बुरुहासीनं ध्यायेद्वा विश्वरूपिणम्॥ १५३॥

The region of Turyavasthā is existed in the Brahmarandhra and towards the perfect knowledge (Para Brahma). The element of soul pertaining to this stage existed starting from the awaken stage to the Brahmarandhra. At the last, it has been addressed as Viṣṇu. The Yogī should be seated on meditation for universal Viṣṇu luminating with the radiance of a crore suns by enshrining in the lotus heart grown in ever-clean and pure ether.

अनेकाकार खचितमनेकवदनान्वितम्। अनेकभुजसंयुक्तमनेकायुधमण्डितम्॥ १५४॥
नानावर्णधरं देवं शान्तमुग्रमुदायुधम्। अनेकनयनाकीर्णं सूर्यकोटिसमप्रभम्॥ १५५॥
ध्यायतो योगिनः सर्वमनोवृत्तिर्विनश्यति। हृत्पुण्डरीकमध्यस्थं चैतन्यज्योतिरव्ययम्॥ १५६॥
कदम्बगोलकाकारं तुर्यातीतं परात्परम्। अनन्तमानन्दमयं चिन्मयं भास्करं विभुम्॥ १५७॥
निवातदीपसदृशमकृत्रिममणिप्रभम्। ध्यायतो योगिनस्तस्य मुक्तिः करतले स्थिता॥ १५८॥

All tendencies of Yogī gets abolished by meditating on lord Śrī Viṣṇu who is in multiform and having varied features, who has multi-mouth, multi-arms, multi-weapons, multi-complexions, divine form, loose-tempered, enshrining peace, holder of a number of weapons, multi-eyes and universal form shining with the radiance of a crore suns. The emancipation is easily accessed to the Yogī by virtue of meditating on Para Brahma (perfect knowledge) shining with the original shine of gem enlighted in the void place, sensitive power residing in the middle of the lotus heart, a form of flame, perfect circular as the tree of Kadamba, beyond imagination, inaccessible, infinite, pleasing, omnipresent, illustrated and sovereign power.

विश्वरूपस्य देवस्य रूपं यत्किंचिदेव हि। स्थवीयः सूक्ष्ममन्यद्वा पश्यन्हृदयपङ्कजे॥ १५९॥

ध्यायतो योगिनो यस्तु साक्षादेव प्रकाशते। अणिमादिफलं चैव सुखेनैवोपजायते॥ १६०॥

The Yogī who meditates within his lotus heart either the apparent, micro or any other form of the universal god, becomes in the same form of the Para Brahma (perfect knowledge) to which he is meditated. Without the least efforts, he attains the fruits of all axioms (Siddhis) like Aṇimā, Laghimā etc.

जीवात्मनः परस्यापि यद्येवमुभयोरपि। अहमेव परंब्रह्म ब्रह्माहमिति संस्थितिः॥ १६१॥

समाधिः स तु विज्ञेयः सर्ववृत्तिविवर्जितः। ब्रह्म संपद्यते योगी न भूयः संसृतिं व्रजेत्॥ १६२॥

Samādhi or the soul meditation is nothing else but the indication of these things when the concerned Yogī becomes able to pronounce– 'I am the Brahma (knowledge)' after duly acquiring the knowledge of living soul as also the supreme soul. His all tendencies and passions gets retirement prior to availing this stage. Hence, he feels no attachment for the worldly things and the relations as well. At this stage, he only observes the supreme soul within everybody and loves to all without any selfish desires. The Yogī who attains to the perfect knowledge by practising the meditation does not again turns back to this mortal world.

एवं विशोध्य तत्त्वानि योगी निःस्पृहचेतसा। यथा निरिन्धनो वह्निः स्वयमेव प्रशाम्यति॥ १६३॥

Thus the Yogī makes his heart free from all kinds of material fevers like the fire which has no fuel to light. He thus gradually investigates the element of Yoga competent enough to make him free from all kinds of worldly passions.

ग्राह्याभावे मनःप्राणो निश्चयज्ञानसंयुतः। शुद्धसत्त्वे परे लीनो जीवः सैन्धवपिण्डवत्॥ १६४॥

Nothing is left worth acceptance for such a Yogī who has acquired that supreme stage. His mind as also the breathing, both becomes prosperous with knowledge of soul and his living soul merged with the element of ever sacrosanct element of supreme soul like the salt that merges with the water and leaves no separate identity.

मोहजालकसंघातं विश्वं पश्यति स्वप्नवत्। सुषुप्तिवद्यश्चरति स्वभावपरिनिश्चलः॥ १६५॥

निर्वाणपदमाश्रित्य योगी कैवल्यमश्नुत इत्युपनिषत्॥

This world is seen by that Yogī like a dream where all people are fastened in the net of illusion as also the attachments. As he becomes undivided by the soul, he lives in the stage of dormance. Such a supreme Yogī definitely attains to the stage of supreme pleasure by enthroning himself on the supreme position of emancipation. This learning of upaniṣad rejuvenates the power of Yogī to attain the emancipation.

ॐ पूर्णमदः .... इति शान्तिः॥

॥इति त्रिशिखिब्राह्मणोपनिषत्समाप्ता॥

***

44. SĪTĀ- UPANIṢAD

सीतोपनिषद्

This Upaniṣad is related to the tradition of Atharvaveda. This Upaniṣad has been originated in the form of a question as a result of the question and answers taken place between the gods and Prajāpati. The everlasting powerful form of Sītā has been discussed among them. Sītā very first has been called in the form of the root nature. The subject matter then proceeds with the literal meaning of the world Sītā, its perceiving of desire and the form of power, her trio form, the Veda and its branch, the Brahmā form of the sound, the form of apparent power, the will power in the form of power of yoga, will-power in the form of enjoyment power and in the form of gallantry. The knowledge so propounded is most benevolent and a number of confusions hovering in the mind of public may be removed by virtue of acquiring this knowledge.

॥शान्तिपाठः॥

ॐ भद्रं कर्णेभिः .... इति शान्तिः॥

देवा ह वै प्रजापतिमब्रुवन्का सीता किं रूपमिति॥१॥ स होवाच प्रजापतिः सा सीतेति। मूलप्रकृतिरूपत्वात्सा सीता प्रकृतिः स्मृता। प्रणवप्रकृतिरूपत्वात्सा सीता प्रकृतिरुच्यते॥२॥ सीता इति त्रिवर्णात्मा साक्षान्मायामयी भवेत्। विष्णुः प्रपञ्चबीजं च माया ईकार उच्यते॥३॥ सकारः सत्यममृतं प्राप्तिःसोमश्च कीर्त्यते। तकारस्तारलक्ष्म्या च वैराजः प्रस्तरः स्मृतः॥४॥ ईकाररूपिणी सोमाऽमृतावयवदिव्यालंकारस्रङ्मौक्तिकाद्याभरणालंकृता महामायाऽव्यक्तरूपिणी व्यक्ता भवति॥५॥ प्रथमा शब्दब्रह्ममयी स्वाध्यायकाले प्रसन्ना। उद्भावनकरी सात्मिका द्वितीया भूतले हलाग्रे समुत्पन्ना। तृतीया ईकाररूपिणी अव्यक्तरूपा भवतीति सीतेत्युदाहरन्ति शौनकीये॥६॥

The gods once asked a question to Prajāpati– O God! What is the form of Sītā? Who is Sītā? We are most curious to have knowledge of it. Having heard this question, Prajāpati Brahmā replied that Śrī Sītā is an apparent form of power. She is called the fundamental nature (Mūla Prakṛti) being her the root cause for creation. Having in the form of Praṇava, Sītā too is called the nature (prakṛti). Sītā is an apparent form of illusion (Yogamāyā). The same Sītā consisting of three letters is an apparent form of Yogamāyā. Lord Viṣṇu is the seed to the worldly illusion. The Yogamāyā of Lord Viṣṇu is in the form of 'Ī' (Īkāra). The indicative of truth, immortality, attainment and the moon is 'Sa' the letter 'Ta' with its seed has been called in the form of Mahālakṣmī because it extends the light everywhere. Irrespective of having in the intangible form of great illusion, Sītā is the form of 'Ī', is seen duly adorned with the immortal parts of body and divine ornaments. The creator of great illusion, goddess Sītā has three forms. She is pleased with perseverance, with the wisdom and appears in the form of the word Brahma (Śabda Brahma). She was appeared in her second form and by the strike of the plough in this earth and as a daughter to great king Janaka. In her third form *i.e.* in the form of 'Ī' she remains unseen. These three forms of Sītā have been described in the system of Śaunaka.

श्रीरामसान्निध्यवशाज्जगदानन्दकारिणी। उत्पत्तिस्थितिसंहारकारिणी सर्वदेहिनाम्॥७॥ सीता भगवती ज्ञेया मूलप्रकृतिसंज्ञिता। प्रणवत्वात्प्रकृतिरिति वदन्ति ब्रह्मवादिन इति॥८॥ अथातो ब्रह्मजिज्ञासेति च॥९॥

Goddess Sītā with her everlasting and the proximate touch with Lord Śrī Rāma does to the welfare of the world. She is the cause far creation, maintenance and destruction of all living organisms. Goddess Sītā adorned with six kinds of luxuries and is the kind of root nature and is worth knowledge. The persons known to Brahma say her nature, being her in the form of Praṇava. In the aphorism of Brahma (Brahmasūtra) *i.e.* 'Athāto Brahma Jijñāsā', her tangible and intangible both forms has been laid down.

सा सर्ववेदमयी सर्वदेवमयी सर्वलोकमयी सर्वकीर्तिमयी सर्वधर्ममयी सर्वाधारकार्यकारणमयी महालक्ष्मीर्देवेशस्य भिन्नाभिन्नरूपा चेतनाचेतनात्मिका ब्रह्मस्थावरात्मा तद्गुणकर्मविभागभेदाच्छरीररूपा देवर्षिमनुष्यगन्धर्वरूपा असुरराक्षसभूतप्रेतपिशाचभूतादिभूतशरीररूपा भूतेन्द्रियमनःप्राणरूपेति च विज्ञायते॥१०॥

That goddess Sītā is in the form of all Vedas, all gods, present equally in all worlds, in the form of all religions, in the form of all living-organisms and the soul of all matters. Owing to the difference by the reason of the deed and the property (Guṇa) of all living-organisms, she herself is in the form of all physical structures. She is in the form of men, gods, hermits and Gandharva. She is different than the Lord Mahānārāyaṇa in the form of Mahālakṣmi, yet there is no distinction and difference.

सा देवी त्रिविधा भवति शक्त्यासना इच्छाशक्तिः क्रियाशक्तिः साक्षाच्छक्तिरिति॥११॥ इच्छाशक्तिस्त्रिविधा भवति। श्रीभूमिनीलात्मिका भद्ररूपिणी प्रभावरूपिणी सोमसूर्याग्निरूपा भवति॥१२॥ सोमात्मिका ओषधीनां प्रभवति कल्पवृक्षपुष्पफललतागुल्मात्मिका औषधभेषजात्मिका अमृतरूपा देवानां महस्तोमफलप्रदा अमृतेन तृप्तिं जनयन्ती देवानामन्नेन पशूनां तृणेन तत्तज्जीवानाम्॥१३॥

That Sītā in the form of power is in trio-form as also the apparent form of power. The power of action, will power and the power of knowledge are the three species of power. Her form as will-power is of three kinds. She laminates with the light of moon, Sun and fire while in the form of Śri devī, Bhudevī and Nīlādevī, thereby does welfare to all. In order to maintain the medicines, she is the form of moon. She herself has been appeared in the form of Kalpavṛksa, fruits, flowers and the medicines as also the divine medicines in the form of creepers and plants. She endows the gods with the fruit of Mahastoma offering by virtue of her moon form. She satiates the gods, the people and all creatures by providing the nectar, food and the grass respectively.

सूर्यादिसकलभुवनप्रकाशिनी दिवा च रात्रिः कालकलानिमेषमारभ्य घटिकाष्टयामदिवसवाररात्रिभेदेन पक्षमासर्त्वयनसंवत्सरभेदेन मनुष्याणां शतायुःकल्पनया प्रकाशमाना चिरक्षिप्रव्यपदेशेन निमेषमारभ्य परार्धपर्यन्तं कालचक्रं जगच्चक्रमित्यादिप्रकारेण चक्रवत्परिवर्तमानाः सर्वस्यैतस्यैव कालस्य विभागविशेषाः प्रकाशरूपाः कालरूपा भवन्ति॥ १४॥

That Sītā gives light to all Bhuvanas like the sun etc. She is enshrined fulfilling the desire of living for hundred years counted under the system of time as second, hours, eight states of a day, the night, the month, the fortnight, the season, the Ayana (six months division of year), Samvatsara (the period of a year) etc. with the discrimination of sooner and later. The cycle of time from a moment to the period of years is called the cycle of the world. Its all parts and limbs having in the form of Sītā, those have been stated in the form of time and light.

अग्निरूपा अन्नपानादिप्राणिनां क्षुत्तृष्णात्मिका देवानां मुखरूपा वनौषधीनां शीतोष्णरूपा काष्ठेष्वन्तर्बहिश्च नित्यानित्यरूपा भवति॥ १५॥

She is existed in the form of fire within the creatures and in the form of thirst and hunger for sipping and eating the water and food respectively. She is in the form of the mouth for the gods, in the form of winter and summer for the medicines found in the forests and she is existed in and outside all woods.

श्रीदेवी त्रिविधं रूपं कृत्वा भगवत्संकल्पानुगुण्येन लोकरक्षणार्थं रूपं धारयति। श्रीरिति लक्ष्मीरिति लक्ष्यमाणा भवतीति विज्ञायते॥ १६॥

Sītā appears in the form of Mahālakṣmī for protecting all the worlds in compliance with the divine resolutions made in the trio-form of Śrīdevī and she appears in the form of Śrī, Lakṣmī and Lakṣyamāṇā.

भूदेवी ससागराम्भःसप्तद्वीपा वसुन्धरा भूरादिचतुर्दशभुवनानामाधाराधेया प्रणवात्मिका भवति॥

That form of goddess Sītā is called Bhūdevī in which she appears in the form of Praṇava to shelter the earth with seven seas and seven islands and fourteen Bhuvanās etc.

नीला च मुखविद्युन्मालिनी सर्वौषधीनां सर्वप्राणिनां पोषणार्थं सर्वरूपा भवति॥ १८॥

Goddess Sītā appears in multiform for maintenance of all medicines and the creatures who in the form of goddess Nīlā illumines like the illusion of lightening (Vidyunmālinī).

समस्तभुवनस्याधोभागे जलाकारात्मिका मण्डूकमयेति भुवनाधारेति विज्ञायते॥ १९॥

In the form of Ādyā-Śakti, goddess Sītā provides shelter to all Bhuvanās and the lower parts of them by turning into form of the water.

क्रियाशक्तिस्वरूपं हरेर्मुखान्नादः। तन्नादाद्बिन्दुः। बिन्दोरोंकारः। ओंकारात्परतो रामवैखानसपर्वतः। तत्पर्वते कर्मज्ञानमयीभिर्बहुशाखा भवन्ति॥ २०॥

Śrī Sītā in the form of power of action to Supreme Soul has been originated in the form of sound came out from of mouth of Lord Śrī Hari. Bindu (iota) was originated from that sound and the 'Oṁ' was from that iota. Beyond Oṁ there is a mountain namely Vaikhānas in the form of Réma. Countless branches of that mountain in the form of knowledge and action has been stated.

तत्र त्रयीमयं शास्त्रमाद्यं सर्वार्थदर्शनम्। ऋग्यजु:सामरूपत्वात्त्रयीति परिकीर्तिता।। २१।।

हेतुना कार्यसिद्धेन चतुर्धा परिकीर्तिता। ऋचो यजूंषि सामानि अथर्वाङ्गिरसस्तथा।। २२।।

चातुर्होत्रप्रधानत्वाल्लिङ्गादित्रितयं त्रयी। अथर्वाङ्गिरसं रूपं सामऋग्यजुरात्मकम्।। २३।।

At the same mountain, there is existed the primitive scripture (Ādiśāstra) consisting of three Vedas and revealing all meaning. Having in the form of Ṛg (poetry), Yaju (prose) and Sāma (epic poetry), it is called consisting of three Vedas. This very vedatrayī is called with four names for the accomplishment of the work. Their names are Ṛg, Yaju, Sāma and Atharva. Inspite of being vehemently dependent on offering, these are called only three vedas form of Sāma, Yajur and Ṛg.

तथा दिशन्त्याभिचारसामान्येन पृथक्पृथक्। एकविंशतिशाखायामृग्वेद: परिकीर्तित:।। २४।।

शतं च नवशाखासु यजुषामेव जन्मनाम्। साम्न: सहस्रशाखा: स्यु: पञ्चशाखा अथर्वण:।। २५।।

वैखानसमतस्तस्मिन्नादौ प्रत्यक्षदर्शनम्। स्मर्यते मुनिभिर्नित्यं वैखानसमत: परम्।। २६।।

कल्पो व्याकरणं शिक्षा निरुक्तं ज्योतिषं छन्द एतानि षडङ्गानि।। २७।।

उपाङ्गमयनं चैव मीमांसान्यायविस्तर:। धर्मज्ञसेवितार्थं च वेदवेदोऽधिकं तथा।। २८।।

निबन्धा: सर्वशाखा च समयाचारसङ्गति:।

धर्मशास्त्रं महर्षीणामन्त:करणसम्भृतम्। इतिहासपुराणाख्यमुपाङ्गं च प्रकीर्तितम्।। २९।।

वास्तुवेदो धनुर्वेदो गान्धर्वश्च तथा मुने। आयुर्वेदश्च पञ्चैते उपवेदा: प्रकीर्तिता:।। ३०।।

दण्डो नीतिश्च वार्ता च विद्या वायुजय: पर:। एकविंशतिभेदोऽयं स्वप्रकाश: प्रकीर्तित:।। ३१।।

On the basis of the specific procedures, these four are described separately. Twenty-one branches of Ṛgveda, one hundred and nine of Yajurveda, one thousand of Sāmaveda and only five of Atharvaveda have been described. The first Vaikhānas opinion among Vedas has been considered as the apparent philosophy. This is the reason the Saints always recite Vaikhānas (Śrī Rāma). The Saints have stated the Vedas as consisting of six organs *i.e.*, Kalpa, grammar, education, etymology, astrology and the rhyme. The extention of Mīmāṁsā (commentary) Ayana (Vedānta) and the justice consisting of three parts. The person expert in religion consider the study on the parts and the limbs of veda coherent with them, most essential. Under all branches of Vedas, essays have been compassed with a view to make the human conduct according to the scriptures time to time. The saints have enriched the scripture of religion (Smṛtis) with their divine knowledge. The Saints have composed the five Sub-Vedas *i.e.*, history, Purāṇa, Architect Veda (Vāstuveda), Archery Veda (Dhanurveda), Veda of Dance (Gāndharva Veda) and Veda of medicine (Āyurveda). Simultaneously, the twenty-one divisions *i.e.*, business, penal provision, polity, policy, learning accomplishment on yoga and attainment of the supreme element etc. are already published volumes.

वैखानसऋषेः पूर्वं विष्णोर्वाणी समुद्भवेत्। त्रयीरूपेण संकल्प्य इत्थं देही विजृम्भते॥ ३ २॥

संख्यारूपेण संकल्प्य वैखानसऋषेः पुरा। उदितो यादृशः पूर्वं तादृशं शृणु मेऽखिलम्। शश्वद्ब्रह्ममयं रूपं क्रियाशक्तिरुदाहृता॥ ३ ३॥

साक्षाच्छक्तिर्भगवतः स्मरणमात्ररूपाविर्भावप्रादुर्भावात्मिका निग्रहानुग्रहरूपा शान्तितेजोरूपा व्यक्ताव्यक्तकारणचरणसमग्रावयवमुखवर्णभेदाभेदरूपा भगवत्सहचारिणी अनपायिनी अनवरतसहाश्रयिणी उदितानुदिताकारानिमेषोन्मेषसृष्टिस्थितिसंहारतिरोधानानुग्रहादिसर्वशक्तिसामर्थ्यात्साक्षाच्छक्तिरिति गीयते॥ ३ ४॥

In the ancient time, Lord Viṣṇu speech was appeared in the heart of Saint Vaikhānas as in the form of trio-Vedas. By virtue of resolution as the Saint Vaikhānas depicted that speech in the respective columns is worth. Listening and listen to the same from me, that power of action continuously appearing in the form of Brahma is the apparent power of god. Ādyā Śakti goddess Sītā reveals the world in its various forms only when a resolution is made by the gods and she herself appears in all visible forms of the world. That kind-hearted, most disciplined embodiment of peace and splendour, tangible and intangible cause, the foot, all organs, mouth, various kinds of bodies and in exclusive form, Śrī Sītā follows the resolution made by the god and she is integrated to god, she is immortal, she resorts to god, she is in the form of visible feature as also invisible, cause for creation, maintenance and destruction as eye opening and closing, showering with mercy and having cause for holding all powers, is in the apparent form of power.

इच्छाशक्तिस्त्रिविधा प्रलयावस्थायां विश्रमणार्थं भगवतो दक्षिणवक्षःस्थले श्रीवत्साकृतिर्भूत्वा विश्राम्यतीति सा योगशक्तिः॥ ३ ५॥

Śrī Sītā is in the form of trio-will-power. She retires on the right chest of the god in the form of Śrī Vatsa for the purpose of getting rest in course of the devastation caused by her in the form of Yogmāyā.

भोगशक्तिर्भोगरूपा कल्पवृक्षकामधेनुचिन्तामणिशङ्खपद्मनिध्यादिनवनिधिसमाश्रिता भगवदुपासकानां कामनयाऽकामनया वा भक्तियुक्ता नरं नित्यनैमित्तिककर्मभिरग्निहोत्रादिभिर्वा यमनियमासनप्राणायाम-प्रत्याहारधारणाध्यानसमाधिभिर्वालमनण्वपि गोपुरप्राकारादिभिर्विमानादिभिः सह भगवद्विग्रहार्चापूजोपकरणैरर्चनैः स्नानादिभिर्वा पितृपूजादिभिरन्नपानादिभिर्वा भगवत्प्रीत्यर्थमुक्त्वा सर्वं क्रियते॥ ३ ६॥

She is in apparent form of enjoyment with the power of enjoy. Śrī Sītā is in the form of Kalpavṛksa, Kāmadhenu, Cintāmaṇi, couch, Lotus (the great Lotus), crocodile, tortoise etc., nine wealth (Nidhi). The devotees to god who perform the worship of him daily by their deeds in the form of offering and take cares of the parts of yoga *i.e.*, Yama, Niyama, Āgama, Prāṇāyāma, Pratyāhāra, Dhāraṇā, Dhyāna, Samādhi etc. are given a number of good stuffs inspite of having their reluctance. Goddess Sītā performs all activities made for the pleasure of god like the material used in worship, the worship of forefathers (pitṛ-pūjā), pilgrimage and bathing in the holy places as also the food and essence etc.

अथातो वीरशक्तिश्चतुर्भुजाऽभयवरदपद्मधरा किरीटाभरणयुता सर्वदेवैः परिवृता कल्पतरुमूले चतुर्भिर्गजै रत्नघटैरमृतजलैरभिषिच्यमाना सर्वदैवतैर्ब्रह्मादिभिर्वन्द्यमाना अणिमाद्यष्टैश्वर्ययुता संमुखे कामधेनुना स्तूयमाना वेदशास्त्रादिभिः स्तूयमाना जयाद्यप्सरस्स्त्रीभिः परिचर्यमाणा आदित्यसोमाभ्यां दीपाभ्यां प्रकाश्यमाना तुम्बुरुनारदादिभिर्गीयमाना राकासिनीवालीभ्यां छत्रेण ह्लादिनीमायाभ्यां चामरेण स्वाहास्वधाभ्यां व्यजनेन भृगुपुण्यादिभिरभ्यर्च्यमाना देवी दिव्यसिंहासने पद्मासनारूढा सकलकारणकार्यकरी लक्ष्मीर्देवस्य पृथग्भवनकल्पना। अलंचकार स्थिरा प्रसन्नलोचना सर्वदेवतैः पूज्यमाना वीरलक्ष्मीरिति विज्ञायत इत्युपनिषत्॥ ३७॥

In the four arms of Śrī Sītā, Abhaya (fearlessness), Varada (a posture for booning) and Lotus are duly adorned. She is adorned with all ornaments including the crown etc. The holy water is being sprinkled on her at the root of Kalpavṛksa through the gold vessels held by four elephants. She is surrounded by all gods and the Brahmā etc. gods are submitting her pray. The eight accomplishments including Aṇimā etc. always with Śrī Sītā who is being worshipped by Kāmadhenu and served by the divine maids and dancers. The god-like vedas are praying her. The Sun and the Moon in the form of lamp are illuminating that place. The sages like Nārada and Tumburu etc. are reciting the hymns for her pleasure. The goddess Rākā and Sinī are stood with the royal umbrella in their hands. She is fanned air with Svāhā and Svadhā. The power of illusion and exhilaration both are moving to and fro the swing. The great hermit Bhṛgu and Puṇya etc. are worshipping her. The goddess Sītā in the form of Mahālakṣmi who is in herself the cause and action for all; is seated in the divine turone duly erected on the eight petals Lotus. She is adorned with the divine ornaments. That goddess Sītā in the form of gallant Lakṣmī with gaiety glance, worshipped by all gods should be recognized with the essence of knowledge.

ॐ भद्रं कर्णेभिः.... इति शान्तिः॥

॥इति सीतोपनिषत्समाप्ता॥

***

45. YOGACŪḌĀMAṆI- UPANIṢAD

योगचूडामण्युपनिषद्

This Upaniṣad is related to the tradition of Sāmaveda. It contains guidelines entirely regarding the procedure of awakening the soul power through the practise of Yoga. The subject matter of this Upaniṣad proceeds with enunciation of six parts in Yoga i.e. Āsana, Prāṇāyāma, Pratyāhāra, Dhāraṇā, Dhyāna and Samādhi, the knowledge of physical element is necessary for the accomplishment of Yoga. The knowledge of Mūlādhāra, observation of supreme flame in kuṇḍalinī (Yonisthāna), the discus of nerves, the distinct places of nerves, the circulation of oxygen (Prāṇa Vāyu) in nerves and their actions, the motions of living-soul with Prāṇas, research on Ajapā Gāyatrī, penetration of the door for emancipation through kuṇḍalinī, three bondage (Mūlabandha, Jālandhara Bandha and Uḍḍiyāna Bandha, the posture of khecari, Vajrolī etc. and their characteristics, the nature of the great posture (Mahāmudrā), special process for the Japa of Praṇava (Oṁ), uniformity in Praṇava and Brahma, the meaning of the parts of Oṁ (A, U, M), the worship of forerunner Brahma through Turīyoṅkāra, worship of Praṇava and Haṁsa, the Japa of Praṇava as giving knowledge of self-realization and emancipation, the necessity of Prāṇajaya for the devotee reciting Praṇava, accomplishment of Prāṇāyāma through purifying the nerves, Prāṇāyāma in regular routine as also with specific quantum, distinct fruits of each part to the Yoga and their interrelation, revelation of sound through the exercise of Ṣaṇmukhī, exercise on Prāṇāyāma and necessity of giving up the attachment with the sensory issues while exercising on Prāṇāyāma or breath-controlling. The person sitting on penance according to this Upaniṣad, undoubtedly attains to the supreme position (crown position) in the field of Yoga. This Supreme upaniṣad has an important place in Upaniṣad relating to Yoga.

॥शान्तिपाठः॥

ॐ आप्यायन्तु .... इति शान्तिः॥

योगचूडामणिं वक्ष्ये योगिनां हितकाम्यया। कैवल्यसिद्धिदं गूढं सेवितं योगवित्तमैः॥ १॥

I describe this Yogacūḍāmanyupaniṣad for the interest of Yogis. It is most cryptic and provides with emancipation, worth exercising by the persons expert in Yoga.

आसनं प्राणसंरोधः प्रत्याहारश्च धारणा। ध्यानं समाधिरेतानि योगाङ्गानि भवन्ति षट्॥ २॥

एकं सिद्धासनं प्रोक्तं द्वितीयं कमलासनम्। षट्चक्रं षोडशाधारं त्रिलक्ष्यं व्योमपञ्चकम्॥ ३॥

स्वदेहे यो न जानाति तस्य सिद्धिः कथं भवेत्। चतुर्दलं स्यादाधारं स्वाधिष्ठानं च षड्दलम्॥ ४॥

नाभौ दशदलं पद्मं हृदये द्वादशारकम्। षोडशारं विशुद्धाख्यं भ्रूमध्ये द्विदलं तथा॥ ५॥

The Yoga has been stated with six parts. These are Āsana, Prāṇāyāma, Pratyāhāra, Dhāraṇā, Dhyāna and Samādhi. Two kinds of Āsanās are described here out of which one is Siddhāsana and the other is Padmāsana. How the devotee can attain success if he is not able to see within his body the six discus (Ṣaṭcakra), sixteen premises (Ṣoḍaśādhāra), aims (Trilakṣya) and the five ethers? Out of the six discus existing in the body, the basic discus (Mūlādhāra cakra) contains four petals and the Svādhiṣṭhāna cakra contains six petals. A discus containing ten petals is existed in the navel zone, the lotus discus (Padma Cakra) with twelve petals in the heart, the purified discus (Viśuddha Cakra) contains sixteen petals and a discus containing two petals is existed amid the eyebrows. It is also called the discus of obedience (Ājñā Cakra).

सहस्रदलसंख्यातं ब्रह्मरन्ध्रे महापथि। आधारं प्रथमं चक्रं स्वाधिष्ठानं द्वितीयकम्॥ ६॥

योनिस्थानं द्वयोर्मध्ये कामरूपं निगद्यते। कामाख्यं तु गुदस्थाने पङ्कजं तु चतुर्दलम्॥ ७॥

तन्मध्ये प्रोच्यते योनिः कामाख्या सिद्धवन्दिता। तस्य मध्ये महालिङ्गं पश्चिमाभिमुखं स्थितम्॥ ८

A Lotus containing one thousand petals is existed in the great path (Mahāpatha) of Brahmarandhra. The Mūlādhāra is the first discus and the Svādhiṣṭhāna is the second. Kuṇḍalinī is existed in the intervening place of both. Being it a cause for origin, it is called in the form of sex (Kāmarūpa). In the zone of anus, there is existed a lotus containing four petals which has been stated as Kāma (the sex). The Mahāliṅga worshipped by the men of accomplishments amid the same and facing the west is existed.

नाभौ तु मणिवद्बिम्बं यो जानाति स योगवित्। तप्तचामीकराभासं तडिल्लेखेव विस्फुरत्॥ ९॥

त्रिकोणं तत्पुरं वह्नेरधोमेढ्रात्प्रतिष्ठितम्। समाधौ परमं ज्योतिरनन्तं विश्वतोमुखम्॥ १०॥

The person is only Yogi who knows the discus of Maṇipūra in the shape of the gem located at the navel zone. The triangle shaped fire luminating like the lightening and with the lustre of the gold is existed in the spinal chord. The supreme flame luminating everywhere is seen at that very place when the devotee moves through the stage of meditation.

तस्मिन्दृष्टे महायोगे यातायातो न विद्यते। स्वशब्देन भवेत्प्राणः स्वाधिष्ठानं तदाश्रयः॥ ११॥

स्वाधिष्ठानाश्रयादस्मान्मेढ्रमेवाभिधीयते। तन्तुना मणिवत्प्रोतो योऽत्र कन्दः सुषुम्नया॥ १२॥

Having seen the flame of fire at the time of exercise on Yoga, the birth and the death cycle of the world is left forever. The abode of the Prāṇa (breathing) has been stated in Svādhiṣthana Cakra. The breathing too is called Sva. Having its location in the Svādhiṣṭhāna, it is called spine (Meḍhra). As the thread is interwined with the gems, the batch of nerves is interwined with spinal chord.

तन्नाभिमण्डले चक्रं प्रोच्यते मणिपूरकम्। द्वादशारे महाचक्रे पुण्यपापविवर्जिते॥ १३॥

तावज्जीवो भ्रमत्येवं यावत्तत्त्वं न विन्दति। ऊर्ध्वं मेढ्रादधो नाभेः कन्दे योनिः खगाण्डवत्॥ १४॥

तत्र नाड्यः समुत्पन्नाः सहस्राणां द्विसप्ततिः। तेषु नाडीसहस्रेषु द्विसप्ततिरुदाहृता॥ १५॥

प्रधानाः प्राणवाहिन्यो भूयस्तासु दश स्मृताः। इडा च पिङ्गला चैव सुषुम्ना च तृतीयगा॥ १६॥

गान्धारी हस्तिजिह्वा च पूषा चैव यशस्विनी। अलम्बुसा कुहूश्चैव शङ्खिनी दशमी स्मृता॥ १७॥

The Maṇipūra discus is void of the vice and the good well. It is existed in the navel zone and contains twelve petals. The living-soul is compelled to move with the cycle of world until thorough knowledge of it is obtained. The Kuṇḍalinī like an egg of a bird is existed between the spine and the navel. It is the root from where as much as the seventy-two thousand nerves are sprouted and spreaded all over the body. Out of them, seventy-two nerves are called the cardinal nerves. The most pioneer nerves are in ten number. These are Iḍā, Piṅgalā, Suṣumnā, Gāndhārī, Hastijihvā, Pūṣā, Yaśasvinī, Alambuṣā, Kuhū and Śaṅkhinī.

एतन्नाडीमहाचक्रं ज्ञातव्यं योगिभिः सदा। इडा वामे स्थिता भागे दक्षिणे पिङ्गला स्थिता॥ १८॥
सुषुम्ना मध्यदेशे तु गान्धारी वामचक्षुषि। दक्षिणे हस्तिजिह्वा च पूषा कर्णे च दक्षिणे॥ १९॥
यशस्विनी वामकर्णे चानने चाप्यलम्बुसा। कुहूश्च लिङ्गदेशे तु मूलस्थाने तु शङ्खिनी॥ २०॥

The Yogis should be awarded of this great discus of the nerves. The Iḍā nerve is existed at the left side of the nose and the Piṅgalā nerve at the right in the body. The spinal nerve is existed between these two nerves. The Hastijivhā is existed in the right eye and the Gāndhārī in the left eye. The Pūṣā and Yaśasvinī nerves are existed in the right and left ears respectively. The Alambusā nerve is existed in the mouth, the Kuhū nerve in the genital organ and the Śaṅkhinī nerve is existed in the root place (Mūlasthāna).

एवं द्वारं समाश्रित्य तिष्ठन्ते नाडयः क्रमात्। इडापिङ्गलासौषुम्नाः प्राणमार्गे च संस्थिताः॥ २१॥

At each and every door of the entire body, there exists a nerve everywhere and the Iḍā, Piṅgalā as also Suṣumnā nerves are existed on the way of breathing.

सततं प्राणवाहिन्यः सोमसूर्याग्निदेवताः। प्राणापानसमानाख्या व्यानोदानौ च वायवः॥ २२॥
नागः कूर्मोऽथ कृकरो देवदत्तो धनंजयः। हृदि प्राणः स्थितो नित्यमपानो गुदमण्डले॥ २३॥
समानो नाभिदेशे तु उदानः कण्ठमध्यगः। व्यानः सर्वशरीरे तु प्रधानाः पञ्च वायवः॥ २४॥

Lord Sun, Moon and the fire are the conductor of breathings. The breathing air is in the five forms which are called Prāṇa, Apāna, Udāna, Samāna and Vyāna respectively. The sub-breathing are also of five kinds. These are Nāga, Kūrma, Kṛkara, Devadutta and Dhanañjaya.

उद्गारे नाग आख्यातः कूर्म उन्मीलने तथा। कृकरः क्षुत्करो ज्ञेयो देवदत्तो विजृम्भणे॥ २५॥

The main breathing is existed within heart, the Apāna in the anus, the Samāna in the navel region, the Udāna in the entire body. These cardinal breathings are existed in fine places in the body.

न जहाति मृतं वापि सर्वव्यापी धनंजयः। एते नाडीषु सर्वासु भ्रमन्ते जीवजन्तवः॥ २६॥

The sub-breathing namely Nāga is ousted in eructation, the kūrma in winking, the kṛkara in sneezing and the Devadutta is existed in yawning.

आक्षिप्तो भुजदण्डेन यथा चलति कन्दुकः। प्राणापानसमाक्षिप्तस्तथा जीवो न तिष्ठति॥ २७॥

The Dhanañjaya wind is circulated in the body so continuously that it doesn't leave the body even after the death. The living soul circulates in all these nerves.

प्राणापानवशो जीवो ह्यधश्चोर्ध्वं च गच्छति। वामदक्षिणमार्गाभ्यां चञ्चलत्वान्न दृश्यते।। २८।।

This living soul having enslaved of the prāṇa etc. wind perpetually moves up and down as also through right and the left. Since this movement is most rapid, it is impossible to observe and feel.

[As the ball kicked by the players move frequently to and fro, the living-soul too cannot make himself stable owing to the circulation of Prāṇa, Apāna etc. winds viz., he always remains moving or dynamic.]

रज्जुबद्धो यथा श्येनो गतोऽप्याकृष्यते पुनः। गुणबद्धस्तथा जीवः प्राणापानेन कर्षति।। २९।।

As the bird whose wings are ties with a string frequently pulled down, this living soul too is pulled by the Prāṇa and Apāna etc. winds particularly because of bound with the properties (Guṇās).

प्राणापानवशो जीवो ह्यधश्चोर्ध्वं च गच्छति। अपानः कर्षति प्राणं प्राणोऽपानं च कर्षति। ऊर्ध्वाधःसंस्थितावेतौ यो जानाति स योगवित्।। ३०।।

As the Prāṇa pulls the Apāna and similarly the Apāna pulls the Prāṇa, this living soul as a result of this pulling moves frequently up and down. He is truly an expert in yoga who knows such process of moving up and downward of the Prāṇa or the living soul.

हकारेण बहिर्याति सकारेण विशेत्पुनः। हंसहंसेत्यमुं मन्त्रं जीवो जपति सर्वदा।। ३१।।

The Respiration with 'Sa' sound is inhaled and with 'Ha' sound it is exhaled. This living-soul always does the silent recital of the Haṁsa hymns.

षट्शतानि दिवारात्रौ सहस्राण्येकविंशतिः। एतत्संख्यान्वितं मंत्रं जीवो जपति सर्वदा।। ३२।।

So busy frequently in the night and the day with the silent recital (Japa), this living soul thus recites twenty one thousand six hundred hymns in a day.

अजपा नाम गायत्री योगिनां मोक्षदा सदा। अस्याः संकल्पमात्रेण सर्वपापैः प्रमुच्यते।। ३३।।

अनया सदृशी विद्या अनया सदृशो जपः। अनया सदृशं ज्ञानं न भूतं न भविष्यति।। ३४।।

This Ajapa Gāyatrī is only the means of providing emancipation to the Yogis. All vices are left when mere resolution is made for this recital. No any learning, Japa (silent recital) and knowledge, equal to it was existed in past and not expected to be in future.

कुण्डलिन्या समुद्भूता गायत्री प्राणधारिणी। प्राणविद्या महाविद्या यस्तां वेत्ति स वेदवित्।। ३५।।

This Gāyatrī is a learning of Prāṇa and the great learning as it holds the breathing (Prāṇa) which has been originated from Kuṇḍalinī. The person known to this fact is the true knower of the Veda.

कन्दोर्ध्वे कुण्डलीशक्तिरष्टधा कुण्डलाकृतिः। ब्रह्मद्वारमुखं नित्यं मुखेनाच्छाद्य तिष्ठति।। ३६।।

The power of kuṇḍalinī always exists by covering the door of Brahma through its mouth and it is spreaded in the shape of eight ear-rings (kuṇḍals) just at the upper portion of the conjunction (kanda of) the nerves.

येन द्वारेण गन्तव्यं ब्रह्मद्वारं मनोमयम्। मुखेनाच्छाद्य तद्द्वारं प्रसुप्ता परमेश्वरी॥ ३७॥

This power of supreme goddess (Kuṇḍalinī) is slept by covering through its mouth the door of Brahma, (the spinal chord) to which the entrance is made.

प्रबुद्धा वह्नियोगेन मनसा मरुता सह। सूचीवद्गात्रमादाय व्रजत्यूर्ध्वं सुषुम्नया॥ ३८॥

It ascends like a needle within the spinal nerve in the company of the mind and the breathing as light when it is awakened through the Yoga of fire (Agni Yoga).

उद्घाटयेत्कवाटं तु यथा कुञ्चिकया गृहम्। कुण्डलिन्यां तथा योगी मोक्षद्वारं प्रभेदयेत्॥ ३९॥

The Yogis open the door of emancipation through kuṇḍalinī as the door lock is opened by inserting the key.

कृत्वा संपुटितौ करौ दृढतरं बध्वा तु पद्मासनं गाढं वक्षसि संनिधाय चुबुकं ध्यानं च तच्चेष्टितम्।
वारंवारमपानमूर्ध्वमनिलं प्रोच्चारयेत्पूरितं मुञ्चन्प्राणमुपैति बोधमतुलं शक्तिप्रभावान्नरः॥ ४०॥

The desirous of exercising Prāṇayāma should sit firmly on Padmāsana,, put his hands one on the other in the lap, try to touch the chest through the chin by vowing the head down and exhale and inhale the air frequently alongwith the mind concentrated on the Brahma. He should inhale the breathing air and left up the Apāna wind. A man exercising Prāṇāyāma this way obtains unique power in body and mind both.

अङ्गानां मर्दनं कृत्वा श्रमसंजातवारिणा। कट्वम्ललवणत्यागी क्षीरभोजनमाचरेत्॥ ४१॥

The perspiration oozing from the body as a result of exercise on Prāṇāyāma so made, should be smear over the body and abandon the use of saline, sour and bitter taste eatables. He should emphasize on milk and the eatables made from the milk.

ब्रह्मचारी मिताहारी योगी योगपरायणः। अब्दादूर्ध्वं भवेत्सिद्धो नात्र कार्या विचारणा॥ ४२॥

It is undoubtedly true that a great accomplishment in Yoga will be acquired if the practise is made with following the rules of celibacy and the diet both.

सुस्निग्धमधुराहारश्चतुर्थांशविवर्जितः। भुञ्जते शिवसंप्रीत्या मिताहारी स उच्यते॥ ४३॥

The person exercising Yoga should always take the delicious and the fatty food. He should made a provision for his diet in which only half part of belly for food, one fourth for water and one fourth part of belly should be void or blank. The person who takes care of this proportion and offers that food firstly to the god is called Mitāhārī (the balanced diet taker).

कन्दोर्ध्वे कुण्डलीशक्तिरष्टधा कुण्डलाकृतिः। बन्धनाय च मूढानां योगिनां मोक्षदा सदा॥ ४४॥

The power of kuṇḍalinī at the upper portion of the nerve cluster (kanda) with eight whirls gives emancipation to the Yogis while it creates bondage for the persons hovering in the realm of ignorance.

महामुद्रा नभोमुद्रा ओड्याणं च जलन्धरम्। मूलबन्धं च यो वेत्ति स योगी मुक्तिभाजनम्॥४५॥

The person known to Mahāmudrā, Nabhomudrā, Uḍḍiyāṇa Bandha, Jālandhara Bandha and the Mūlabandha, definitely attains to emancipation.

पार्ष्णिघातेन संपीड्य योनिमाकुञ्चयेद्दृढम्। अपानमूर्ध्वमाकृष्य मूलबन्धो विधीयते॥४६॥

The procedure of doing Mūlabandha is to press the place of genital organ through the ankle and thus to shrink it firmly and to pull upward the Apāna wind.

अपानप्राणयोरैक्यं क्षयान्मूत्रपुरीषयोः। युवा भवति वृद्धोऽपि सततं मूलबन्धनात्॥४७॥

Thus a harmony is established between the Prāṇa and Apāna and it reduces the flow of excreta and the urine as well. As a result of thorough practise on Mūlabandha, an old too turns into a young chap.

ओड्याणं कुरुते यस्मादविश्रान्तं महाखगः। ओड्डियाणं तदेव स्यान्मृत्युमातङ्गकेसरी॥४८॥

As the vulture etc. birds fly at the more distance for getting relax in the sky, the exercise on Uḍḍiyāṇa Bandha is like a lion to defeat the elephant in the form of death (the large birds feel extreme rest while on changing the pattern of their flying in the sky. They thus obtain the fresh power).

उदरात्पश्चिमं ताणमधोनाभेर्निगद्यते। ओड्याणमुदरे बन्धस्तत्र बन्धो विधीयते॥४९॥

To stretch the belly below the navel is called paścimottāna. At the same place in the belly, the Uḍḍiyāṇa Bandha too is exercised.

बध्नाति हि शिरोजातमधोगामि नभोजलम्। ततो जालन्धरो बन्धः कष्टदुःखौघनाशनः॥५०॥

The Jālandhara Bandha retains at the upper portion, the water of ether (that oozes by the khecari posture) flown downward in the body. It resists this water and diminishes the sorrows and pains.

जालन्धरे कृते बन्धे कण्ठसंकोचलक्षणे। न पीयूषं पतत्यग्नौ न च वायुः प्रधावति॥५१॥

While exercising the Jālandhara Bandha the head is bent front-side and the chin touches the heart in this posture. By doing this, the nectar neither oozes on the fire nor moves towards wind. It thus becomes stable and stagnant.

कपालकुहरे जिह्वा प्रविष्टा विपरीतगा। भ्रुवोरन्तर्गता दृष्टिर्मुद्रा भवति खेचरी॥५२॥

While exercising the khecari Mudrā, one should fix the sight at the middle of both brows and the tongue should be inserted at the middle of palate by turning it back towards the throat.

न रोगो मरणं तस्य न निद्रा न क्षुधा तृषा। न च मूर्च्छा भवेत्तस्य यो मुद्रां वेत्ति खेचरीम्॥५३॥

The person known and doing exercise continuously on Khecari Mudrā get rid of the ailments, death, feeling of hunger and thirst as also from the swooning.

पीड्यते न च रोगेण लिप्यते न स कर्मभिः। बाध्यते न च केनापि यो मुद्रां वेत्ति खेचरीम्॥५४॥

The knower of Khecari Mudrā neither suffers from any ailment nor he is attached to the worldly activities and no any kinds of hurdle even access to him.

चित्तं चरति खे यस्माज्जिह्वा चरति खे यतः। तेनेयं खेचरी मुद्रा सर्वसिद्धनमस्कृता॥ ५५॥

All Yogis salute to the Khecari Mudrā because acquired expertise on the same, the mind as also the tongue both start moving in the sky.

बिन्दुमूलशरीराणि शिरास्तत्र प्रतिष्ठिताः। भावयन्ती शरीराणि आपादतलमस्तकम्॥ ५६॥

All veins spreaded all over the body from the head to the feet and the nourishment of all parts of the body have their basic nucleus on the Khecari Mudrā.

खेचर्या मुद्रितं येन विवरं लम्बिकोर्ध्वतः। न तस्य क्षीयते बिन्दुः कामिन्यालिङ्गितस्य च॥ ५७॥

As a result of perpetual exercise on Khecari Mudrā, if the tongue covers the entire cavity of the palate; it provides power to control the semen to the extent that it doesn't discharge even if the couplation is enjoyed with a woman.

यावद्बिन्दुः स्थितो देहे तावन्मृत्युभयं कुतः। यावद्बद्धा नभोमुद्रा तावद्बिन्दुर्न गच्छति॥ ५८॥

There is no fear of the death unless the semen is not discharged and existed in the body as a result of the expertise on Khecari Mudrā, the yogi has applied thereto.

ज्वलितोऽपि यथा बिन्दुः संप्राप्तश्च हुताशनम्। व्रजत्यूर्ध्वं गतः शक्त्या निरुद्धो योनिमुद्रया॥ ५९॥

In case, the semen is discharged in the fiercely blazing element of the fire, it too can be retained forcely and made flowing upward as a result of exercising the Yoni Mudrā.

स पुनर्द्विविधो बिन्दुः पाण्डरो लोहितस्तथा। पाण्डरं शुक्लमित्याहुर्लोहिताख्यं महारजः॥ ६०॥

The semen is of two colours i.e. white and the red. The white is called the Venus and the red is called Mahāraja.

सिन्दूरव्रातसंकाशं रविस्थानस्थितं रजः। शशिस्थानस्थितं शुक्लं तयोरैक्यं सुदुर्लभम्॥ ६१॥

The abode of Raja is at the Ravisthāna, luminating like Sindūra and the abode of Venus is in the Candrasthāna. A combination of Venus and Raja is availed with most difficulty.

बिन्दुर्ब्रह्मा रजः शक्तिर्बिन्दुरिन्दू रजो रविः। उभयोः सङ्गमादेव प्राप्यते परमं पदम्॥ ६२॥

The semen is in the form of Brahma and the Raja is in the form of Śakti. Further, this semen is in the form of Moon and the Raja is in the form of Sun. The supreme position is attained when both of them are joined with each other.

वायुना शक्तिचालेन प्रेरितं च यथा रजः। याति बिन्दुः सदैकत्वं भवेद्दिव्यवपुस्तदा॥ ६३॥

When the wind (Prāṇāyāma) establishes the harmony of the dynamic Raja with the semen under the posture of Śakticalinī, the body then becomes divine.

शुक्लं चन्द्रेण संयुक्तं रजः सूर्येण संगतम्। तयोः समरसैकत्वं यो जानाति स योगवित्॥ ६४॥

The devotee expert in Yoga is only said when he is known to the process of combining the Raja in the Sun and the Venus in the moon and integration of both with each other.

शोधनं नाडिजालस्य चालनं चन्द्रसूर्ययोः। रसानां शोषणं चैव महामुद्राभिधीयते॥ ६५॥

Mahāmudrā is a posture by exercising which the cluster of nerves is purified, make the Sun and the Moon moving and the essence is observed.

वक्षोन्यस्तहनुः प्रपीड्य सुचिरं योनिं च वामाङ्घ्रिणा हस्ताभ्यामनुधारयन्प्रसरितं पादं तथा दक्षिणम्। आपूर्य श्वसनेन कुक्षियुगलं बध्वा शनै रेचयेत्सेयं व्याधिविनाशिनी सुमहती मुद्रा नृणां कथ्यते॥ ६६॥

The Mahāmudrā is made when the place of genital organ is pressed by the left foot, the chin touches the heart, the right foot is stretched straightly and gripping the feet with all fingers with both hands and these are kept in both arm pits. Thus, a long and deep respiration is made. The exercise of Mahāmudrā destroys all kinds of ailments.

चन्द्रांशेन समभ्यस्य सूर्यांशेनाभ्यसेत्पुनः या तुल्या तु भवेत्संख्या ततो मुद्रां विसर्जयेत्॥ ६७॥

In course of doing exercise, the air should be inhaled through the left nose (Candra Aṅśa) and Recana should be made. Then, the air should be inhaled through the right nose (Sūrya Aṅśa). The exercise should be stopped when the flow of inhaling from the right and left nose becomes equal.

नहि पथ्यमपथ्यं वा रसाः सर्वेऽपि नीरसाः। अतिभुक्तं विषं घोरं पीयूषमिव जीर्यते॥ ६८॥

The coarse food or the stale food even is digested as a result of exercise on Mahāmudrā. In case, over diet is taken or even poison is gobbled up by mistake, that too is digested like a nectar.

क्षयकुष्ठगुदावर्तगुल्माजीर्णपुरोगमाः। तस्य रोगाः क्षयं यान्ति महामुद्रां तु योऽभ्यसेत्॥ ६९॥

The person exercising Mahāmudrā gets rid of the tuberculosis, leprosy, piles, appendicitis, constipation etc. and all other ailments prognosticated.

कथितेयं महामुद्रा महासिद्धिकरी नृणाम्। गोपनीया प्रयत्नेन न देया यस्य कस्यचित्॥ ७०॥

This Mahāmudrā is endowed with the great accomplishment to the man who practises it. This excellent posture should be kept in a secret and should not be told to the persons not entitled for it.

पद्मासनं समारुह्य समकायशिरोधरः। नासाग्रदृष्टिरेकान्ते जपेदोंकारमव्ययम्॥ ७१॥

The Japa (silent recital) of Oṁ should be made by sitting in a posture of Padmāsana in solitude and by keeping the body erect from the waist to the head and fixing the eyes at the foreportion of the nose.

ॐ नित्यं शुद्धं बुद्धं निर्विकल्पं निरञ्जनं निराख्यातमनादिनिधनमेकं तुरीयं यद्भूतं भवद्भविष्यत् परिवर्तमानं सर्वदाऽनवच्छिन्नं परं ब्रह्म तस्माज्जाता परा शक्तिः स्वयंज्योतिरात्मिका। आत्मन आकाशः संभूतः। आकाशाद्वायुः। वायोरग्निः। अग्नेरापः। अद्भ्यः पृथिवी। एतेषां पञ्चभूतानां पतयः पञ्च सदाशिवेश्वररुद्रविष्णुब्रह्माणश्चेति। तेषां ब्रह्मविष्णुरुद्राश्चोत्पत्तिस्थितिलयकर्तारः। राजसो ब्रह्मा सात्त्विको विष्णुस्तामसो रुद्र इति एते त्रयो गुणयुक्ताः। ब्रह्मा देवानां प्रथमः संबभूव। धाता च सृष्टौ विष्णुश्च स्थितौ रुद्रश्च नाशे भोगाय चेन्द्रः प्रथमजा बभूवुः। एतेषां ब्रह्मणो लोका देवतिर्यङ्नरस्थावराश्च जायन्ते। तेषां

मनुष्यादीनां पञ्चभूतसमवाय: शरीरम्। ज्ञानकर्मेन्द्रियैर्ज्ञानविषयै: प्राणादिपञ्चवायुमनोबुद्धिचित्ताहंकारै: स्थूलकल्पितै: सोऽपि स्थूलप्रकृतिरित्युच्यते। ज्ञानकर्मेन्द्रियैर्ज्ञानविषयै: प्राणादिपञ्चवायुमनोबुद्धिभिश्च सूक्ष्मस्थोऽपि लिङ्गमेवेत्युच्यते। गुणत्रययुक्तं कारणम्। सर्वेषामेवं त्रीणि शरीराणि वर्तन्ते। जाग्रत्स्वप्नसुषुप्तितुरीयाश्चेत्यवस्थाश्चतस्र: तासामवस्थानामधिपतयश्चत्वार: पुरुषा विश्वतैजसप्राज्ञात्मानश्चेति। विश्वो हि स्थूलभुङ् नित्यं तैजस: प्रविविक्तभुक्। आनन्दभुक्तथा प्राज्ञ: सर्वसाक्षीत्यत: पर:॥७२॥

The Oṁ as a luminating Parāśakti appeared itself from the perfect Brahma living in an exclusive mood, nameless, pure, conscienceful, everlasting, untorn, beyond the death, Turīya and of equal entity in the past, future and the present. The ether was originated from the supreme soul, the wind from the ether, the fire from the wind. The water from the fire and the earth from the water was thus originated. The five gods i.e. Sadāśiva, Īśvara, Rudra, Viṣṇu and Brahmā are the five masters of these five great elements (Mahābhūta). Out of these five gods, Lord Brahmā is the creator, Lord Viṣṇu is nourisher and the Lord Rudra is the destroyer. Lord Viṣṇu was the Sattva property, Lord Brahmā has Rajas and Lord Rudra has the Tamas property. Lord Brahmā was very first originated among the gods. Lord Brahmā was originated for the creation of Sṛṣṭi, Lord Viṣṇu for its development, Lord Rudra for its destruction and Lord Indra for the enjoyment. The people, gods, Tiryaka, men and the immovables were originated by Lord Brahmā. The body of men etc. is built with the combination of five elements. The basic cause for the formidable composition of the sensory organs, executive organs, issues of senses, Prāṇa etc. five winds, the mind, the wisdom, the citta and the ego are called the formidable nature (Prakṛti). The sensory organs, executive organs, the issues of senses i.e. word, touch, complexion, essence and the smell, five winds, the mind and the wisdom are called the micro body. The causative body is with three properties. All living-organisms have three bodies i.e. formidable, micro and the cause. These are four states of mind i.e. awakened, dreaming, dormance and Turīya. The splendour, the conscious, the world and the soul are the ruler of all these states. The world consumes the formidable, the splendour consumes the solitude, the conscious consumes the pleasure and the soul is called beyond them all.

प्रणव: सर्वदा तिष्ठेत्सर्वजीवेषु भोगत:। अभिरामस्तु सर्वासु ह्यवस्थासु ह्यधोमुख:॥७३॥

The omnipresent Praṇava (the supreme soul) continuously remains reluctant at the time of the consumption of all pleasant states of the living-soul.

अकार उकारो मकारश्चेति त्रयो वर्णास्त्रयो वेदास्त्रयो लोकास्त्रयो गुणास्त्रीण्यक्षराणि त्रय: स्वरा एवं प्रणव: प्रकाशते। अकारो जाग्रति नेत्रे वर्तते सर्वजन्तुषु। उकार: कण्ठत: स्वप्ने मकारो हृदि सुप्तित:॥७४॥

The three letters embedded with the Praṇava i.e. Oṁ are the A, V, and the M. These are three Vedas, three worlds, three properties (Guṇās) three letters (Akṣara) and the Oṁ is illuminated in these three vowels. The 'A' resides in the eyes of all living-organisms at the state of awakening. At the state of sleeping, the 'U' resides in the throat and the 'M' resides in the heart region at the state of dormance.

विराड्विश्वः स्थूलश्चाकारः। हिरण्यगर्भस्तैजसः सूक्ष्मश्च उकारः। कारणाव्याकृतप्राज्ञश्च मकारः। अकारो राजसो रक्तो ब्रह्मा चेतन उच्यते। उकारः सात्त्विकः शुक्लो विष्णुरित्यभिधीयते॥ ७५॥

मकारस्तामसः कृष्णो रुद्रश्चेति तथोच्यते। प्रणवात्प्रभवो ब्रह्मा प्रणवात्प्रभवो हरिः॥ ७६॥

प्रणवात्प्रभवो रुद्रः प्रणवो हि परो भवेत्। अकारे लीयते ब्रह्मा ह्युकारे लीयते हरिः॥ ७७॥

मकारे लीयते रुद्रः प्रणवो हि प्रकाशते। ज्ञानिनामूर्ध्वगो भूयादज्ञाने स्यादधोमुखः॥ ७८॥

एवं वै प्रणवस्तिष्ठेद्यस्तं वेद स वेदवित्। अनाहतस्वरूपेण ज्ञानिनामूर्ध्वगो भवेत्॥ ७९॥

This formidable and gigantic world is 'A' the micro turaṇyagarbha, full of splendour is called 'U' and the undisclosed cause 'M' is called conscience. The nature of 'A' is Rajas, it is of reddish colour and has been stated as Brahmā, the creator of this universe. The 'U' is of Satva nature, its colour is white and it has been stated as Lord Viṣṇu, the nourisher of the world. The nature of 'M' is 'Tamas', its colour is black and it has been stated as Rudra, the destroyer of this world. Thus, the Praṇava (Oṁ) has been stated as the cause of origin of Lord Brahmā, Viṣṇu and Rudra. The Praṇava too is the unborn cause and the supreme element. The creator Brahmā is embedded in the scope of 'A', Lord Viṣṇu in the scope of 'U' and Lord Rudra in the scope of 'M'. Only this Praṇava remains luminating everywhere. This Praṇava has been stated ascendant for the learned people and descendant for the people hovering in the alley of ignorance. Thus, the Praṇava is enshrined equally everywhere. He is only known to Veda who is aware of this fact among the learned devotees. This Praṇava is of ascendant motion with perpetuity.

तैलधारामिवाच्छिन्नं दीर्घघण्टानिनादवत्।
प्रणवस्य ध्वनिस्तद्वत्तदग्रं ब्रह्म चोच्यते॥ ८०॥

The Anāhata Nāda with the sound of Oṁ like a serious tone of a gong and inseparated like the stream of oil as its route which is called Brahma.

ज्योतिर्मयं तदग्रं स्यादवाच्यं बुद्धिसूक्ष्मतः। ददृशुर्ये महात्मानो यस्तं वेद स वेदवित्॥ ८१॥

The great soul (men) is only known to Veda who is reckoned with the fact that the foreportion (Mūla) of the Praṇava, worth-knowing by application of micro wisdom is ever-luminating and beyond the speech i.e. undescribable in the words.

जाग्रन्नेत्रद्वयोर्मध्ये हंस एव प्रकाशते। सकारः खेचरी प्रोक्तस्त्वंपदं चेति निश्चितम्॥ ८२॥

हकारः परमेशः स्यात्तत्पदं चेति निश्चितम्। सकारो ध्यायते जन्तुर्हकारो हि भवेद्ध्रुवम्॥ ८३॥

The Haṁsa (Swan) luminates continuously amid both eyes when the living-soul is in the awakened state. The 'Sa' has been stated in the form of Khecari and it is definitely in the form of 'Īvaṁ'. The foot 'Ha' is the indicative of supreme soul which is definitely in the form of the foot 'Tat'. The living-soul who meditates on 'Sa' definitely becomes in the form of 'Ha'. The same is the worship of 'So'ham' and 'Tattvamasi'.

[The saint is revealing the uniformity and integrity between two knowledgeable sentences i.e. So'ham' and 'Tatīvam'. When the devotee observes 'Sva' with outlook of element, it reckons with 'So'Hamasmi' and when he observes outward, the 'Tattvamasi' is perceived by him.]

इन्द्रियैर्बध्यते जीव आत्मा चैव न बध्यते। ममत्वेन भवेज्जीवो निर्ममत्वेन केवलः॥८४॥

The sensory organs tie the living organisms in the bondage but these cannot fasten the soul. As long as the affection remains, the living-soul is existed but it gets the form of emancipation as soon as the ties of affection are broken.

भूर्भुवः स्वरिमे लोकाः सोमसूर्याग्निदेवताः। यस्य मात्रासु तिष्ठन्ति तत्परं ज्योतिरोमिति॥८५॥

Oṁ is that supreme form of light in whose mātrā the Sun, the moon, the fire god and the words 'Bhuḥ', 'Bhuvaḥ', 'Svaḥ'.

क्रिया इच्छा तथा ज्ञानं ब्राह्मी रौद्री च वैष्णवी। त्रिधा मात्रास्थितिर्यत्र तत्परं ज्योतिरोमिति॥८६॥

In the three mātrās of Oṁ luminating with supreme light, the action, desire and knowledge as also the powers of Brahmā and Viṣṇu are enshrined.

वचसा तज्जपेन्नित्यं वपुषा तत्समभ्यसेत्। मनसा तज्जपेन्नित्यं तत्परं ज्योतिरोमिति॥८७॥

One should do Japa through his tongue and do activities through the body always for the Praṇava. By reciting silently in the mind one should make him stable in that very Oṁ in the form of supreme light.

शुचिर्वाप्यशुचिर्वापि यो जपेत्प्रणवं सदा। न स लिप्यति पापेन पद्मपत्रमिवाम्भसा॥८८॥

The person doing Japa of Oṁ at any stage either holy or unholy doesn't entrap in the marsh of the evil. He always remains unattached like the lotus leaf which has no affection with the droplets of water.

चले वाते चलो बिन्दुर्निश्चले निश्चलो भवेत्। योगी स्थाणुत्वमाप्नोति ततो वायुं निरुन्धयेत्॥८९

As long as the wind will be blown, the semen (Bindu) will also be dynamic but the Yogi attains to stability when the wind is stopped. Hence, the stability of wind i.e. Prāṇāyāma should be exercised.

यावद्वायुः स्थितो देहे तावज्जीवो न मुञ्चति। मरणं तस्य निष्क्रान्तिस्ततो वायुं निरुन्धयेत्॥९०॥

The living-soul will remain stable in the body as long as the wind is existed in it. The outblowing of the wind from the body is the death, therefore, one should restrain the wind i.e. should do Prāṇāyāma.

यावद्बद्धो मरुत् देहे तावज्जीवो न मुञ्चति। यावद्दृष्टिर्भ्रुवोर्मध्ये तावत्कालभयं कुतः॥९१॥

The living-soul cannot move out from the body till the wind is duly bound within it. The person able to fix his sight between both eyebrows, conquers the time (kāla) and seldom have any fear of it.

अल्पकालभयाद्ब्रह्मा प्राणायामपरो भवेत्। योगिनो मुनयश्चैव ततः प्राणान्निरोधयेत्॥९२॥

Lord Brahmā too does Prāṇāyāma with an intention to get rid of the fear of premature age. The yogis and the hermits therefore do exercise of the Prāṇāyāma for retaining to the breathing.

षड्विंशदङ्गुलिर्हंसः प्रयाणं कुरुते बहिः। वामदक्षिणमार्गेण प्राणायामो विधीयते॥ ९३॥

This breathing comes out twenty six fingers by means of respiration. The Prāṇāyāma should be exercised by using both nostrils, viz., from the left and the right nostril.

शुद्धिमेति यदा सर्वं नाडीचक्रं मलाकुलम्। तदैव जायते योगी प्राणसंग्रहणक्षमः॥ ९४॥

The yogī becomes able to restrain the breathings when the cycle of nerve is fully purified from all kinds of dirt.

बद्धपद्मासनो योगी प्राणं चन्द्रेण पूरयेत्। धारयेद्वा यथाशक्त्या भूयः सूर्येण रेचयेत्॥ ९५॥

In order to exercise Yoga, one should do Baddha Padmāsana and the wind should be inhaled through the moon nerve (Left nostril) viz. do Pūraka. The inhaled air then to be restrained under the process of Kumbhaka and ultimately this air should be exhaled through the sun nerve (right nostril) under the process of Recana.

अमृतोदधिसंकाशं गोक्षीरधवलोपमम्। ध्यात्वा चन्द्रमसं बिम्बं प्राणायामे सुखी भवेत्॥ ९६॥

The person exercising Prāṇāyāma attains all pleasures if he meditates on the moon point (Candra bimba) of white colour like the milk of cow extracted from the ocean of the nectar.

स्फुरत्प्रज्वलसंज्वालापूज्यमादित्यमण्डलम्। ध्यात्वा हृदि स्थितं योगी प्राणायामे सुखी भवेत्॥ ९७॥

Further, the yogi attains pleasure if he does meditation on Lord Sun like a blazing flame in the heart Lotus coincide to Prāṇāyāma.

प्राणं चेदिडया पिबेन्नियमितं भूयोऽन्यथा रेचयेत्पीत्वा पिङ्गलया समीरणमथो बद्ध्वा त्यजेद्वामया। सूर्याचन्द्रमसोरनेन विधिना बिन्दुद्वयं ध्यायतः शुद्धा नाडिगणा भवन्ति यमिनो मासद्वयादूर्ध्वतः॥ ९८॥

One should very first inhale the air from the left nostril under the process of Pūraka and thus make mighty the nerve of Iḍā. He then do contrary to it i.e. Recana through the right nostril and thus make two powerful to the nerve of Piṅgalā. In case, exercise of meditation in the manner aforesaid on the moon and the sun both in course of Prāṇāyāma is done, all nerves are purified merely within two months.

यथेष्टधारणं वायोरनलस्य प्रदीपनम्। नादाभिव्यक्तिरारोग्यं जायते नाडिशोधनात्॥ ९९॥

As a result of having the nerves purified, under exercise of nerve purifying Prāṇāyāma, the man concerned is unable to restrain the air in suffice quantum. It increases his power of digestion inside, strong resistance of the ailments and the divine sound starts to be listened.

प्राणो देहस्थितो यावदपानं तु निरुन्धयेत्। एकश्वासमयी मात्रा ऊर्ध्वाधो गगने गतिः॥ १००॥

The Apāna wind is to be withheld or restrained tili the air inhaled stays in under the process of Kumbhaka in Prāṇāyāma. By doing this the equal quantum of the respiration starts moving up and down.

रेचकः पूरकश्चैव कुम्भकः प्रणवात्मकः। प्राणायामो भवेदेवं मात्राद्वादशसंयुतः॥ १०१॥

One should do Prāṇāyāma containing twelve mātrās considering that the three processes of Prāṇāyāma i.e. Pūraka, Kumbhaka and Recaka are nothing else but one of an apparent forms of Praṇava (Oṁ).

मात्राद्वादशसंयुक्तौ दिवाकरनिशाकरौ। दोषजालमबध्नन्तौ ज्ञातव्यौ योगिभिः सदा॥ १०२॥

This Prāṇāyāma containing twelve mātrās with the meditation on Lord Sun and moon, diminishes all defects of the person doing exercise of Prāṇāyāma.

पूरकं द्वादशं कुर्यात्कुम्भकं षोडशं भवेत्। रेचकं दश चोंकारः प्राणायामः स उच्यते॥ १०३॥

The Prāṇāyāma with twelve mātrās in Pūraka, sixteen mātrās in kumbhaka and ten mātrās in Recaka is called Prāṇāyāma of Oṁ.

अधमे द्वादश मात्रा मध्यमे द्विगुणा मता। उत्तमे त्रिगुणा प्रोक्ता प्राणायामस्य निर्णयः॥ १०४॥

The Prāṇāyāma of twelve mātrās falls in common category, Prāṇāyāma with double mātrās then it falls in the middle category and the Prāṇāyāma with tripple mātrās than it, falls in the best category.

अधमे स्वेदजननं कम्पो भवति मध्यमे। उत्तमे स्थानमाप्नोति ततो वायुं निरुन्धयेत्॥ १०५॥

This means– common Prāṇāyāma brings perspiration to the body, the middle Prāṇāyāma makes the body shivering and the body starts uplifting from the seat in best category of Prāṇāyāma. One should therefore emphasize on the best category of Prāṇāyāma.

बद्धपद्मासनो योगी नमस्कृत्य गुरुं शिवम्। नासाग्रदृष्टिरेकाकी प्राणायामं समभ्यसेत्॥ १०६॥

One should be seated on Baddha Padmāsana in solitude in order to exercise Yoga and after saluting the teacher in the form of Śiva. One should start practising Prāṇāyāma by fixing his sight on the foreportion of the nose.

द्वाराणां नव संनिरुध्य मरुतं बध्वा दृढां धारणां नीत्वा कालमपानवह्निसहितं शक्त्या समं चालितम्।
आत्मध्यानयुतस्त्वनेन विधिना विन्यस्य मूर्ध्नि स्थिरं यावत्तिष्ठति तावदेव महतां सङ्गो न संस्तूयते॥ १०७॥

The men practising Prāṇāyāma should withheld the wind by restraining the incoming and outgoing nine doors of wind and establish the Apāna with meditation on the soul in the mind firmly by taking it in through the route of Kuṇḍalinī and by blending it with the fire and making ascendant by exercising the Śakticalinī Mudrā. He requires no company of great men till the Apāna remains stable in the mind viz. he himself becomes the best great man.

प्राणायामो भवेदेवं पातकेन्धनपावकः। भवोदधिमहासेतुः प्रोच्यते योगिभिः सदा॥ १०८॥

This Prāṇāyāma is analogous to a bridge in order to cross the worldly ocean and as offenly said by yogis, it is like fire that burns into ashes the fuel of evil.

आसनेन रुजं हन्ति प्राणायामेन पातकम्। विकारं मानसं योगी प्रत्याहारेण मुञ्चति॥ १०९॥

By virtue of doing yogāsana, the ailments are removed. The evils are destroyed by exercising the Prāṇāyāma and the ailments relating to mind are destroyed when the man exercises Pratyāhāra.

धारणाभिर्मनोधैर्यं याति चैतन्यमद्भुतम्। समाधौ मोक्षमाप्नोति त्यक्त्वा कर्म शुभाशुभम्॥ ११०॥

The mind of yoga becomes courageous by virtue of the holding power of Yoga. As a result of meditation, all deeds either good or evil are diminished and he attains to the emancipation.

प्राणायामद्विषट्केन प्रत्याहारः प्रकीर्तितः। प्रत्याहारद्विषट्केन जायते धारणा शुभा॥ १११॥

The stage of Pratyāhāra is achieved when twelve time Prāṇāyāma is exercised and the Dhāraṇā providing with the delicious fruits is achieved when Pratyāhāra is exercised upto twelve times. Similarly, the twice time exercise of Dhāraṇā leads to the attention and the twice time attention, as the expert in Yoga have opined; the state of meditation is obtained.

धारणा द्वादश प्रोक्तं ध्यानं योगविशारदैः। ध्यानद्वादशकेनैव समाधिरभिधीयते॥ ११२॥

The person arriving at the state of meditation obtains the equal spirit everywhere and all time. Nothing is left to do and nor the deeds performed fasten the men when this stage is attained. The living-soul thus get rid of the cycle of death and birth.

यत्समाधौ परंज्योतिरनन्तं विश्वतोमुखम्। तस्मिन्दृष्टे क्रियाकर्म यातायातो न विद्यते॥ ११३॥

One should very first sit firmly on the seat by putting the ankles on spine. Then the eyes, ears and nose are to be sucked by using fingers and the air is taken through mouth. In the succeeding step, the Apāna wind should be made ascendant from below and both these winds should be retained in the region of heart. Then making it ascendant and giving stability to the mind one should be engrossed with it. The yogis by doing this exercise obtains the particular sense of equality.

संबद्धासनमेढ्रमङ्घ्रियुगलं कर्णाक्षिनासापुटद्वाराद्यङ्गुलिभिर्नियम्य पवनं वक्त्रेण वा पूरितम्। बध्वा वक्षसि बह्वपानसहितं मूर्ध्नि स्थिरं धारयेदेवं याति विशेषतत्त्वसमतां योगीश्वरास्तन्मनाः॥ ११४॥

When the dynamic wind from up and down both sides become stable in the region of heart, the devotee then starts listening to the great sounds and the sound is heard like the gong etc. musical elements. Thus the Nāda yoga is accomplished.

गगनं पवने प्राप्ते ध्वनिरुत्पद्यते महान्। घण्टादीनां प्रवाद्यानां नादसिद्धिरुदीरिता॥ ११५॥

As a result of exercising Prāṇāyāma following the rules made therefore, all kinds of ailments are driven away. If Prāṇāyāma is not made, the patients by body amounts to a place of origin for the ailments.

प्राणायामेन युक्तेन सर्वरोगक्षयो भवेत्। प्राणायामवियुक्तेभ्यः सर्वरोगसमुद्भवः॥ ११६॥

The uncountable ailments are risen besides cough, asthma, head, ears, hiccup and the eye ache due to arising distortions in the wind.

हिक्का कासस्तथा श्वासःशिरःकर्णाक्षिवेदनाः। भवन्ति विविधा रोगाः पवनव्यत्ययक्रमात्॥

The violent animals like elephant, lion, tiger etc. are enslaved by virtue of the gradual practise or exercise made. The same way, one should enslave the breathing air gradually by virtue of continuous exercise. In case, it cannot be done in a systematic manner, he will definitely be ruined.

यथा सिंहो गजो व्याघ्रो भवेद्वश्यः शनैः शनैः। तथैव सेवितो वायुरन्यथा हन्ति साधकम्॥ ११८॥

The success is achieved when the breathing air is inhaled in an appropriate manner and exhaled as also withheld in an appropriate manner.

युक्तंयुक्तं त्यजेद्वायुं युक्तंयुक्तं प्रपूरयेत्। युक्तंयुक्तं प्रबध्नीयादेवं सिद्धिमवाप्नुयात्॥ ११९॥

To resist the sensory organs like the eyes, ears etc. from their rapid movement towards the worldly issues and engage them for doing endeavour to arrive at the destination (aim) is called Pratyāhāra.

चरतां चक्षुरादीनां विषयेषु यथाक्रमम्। तत्प्रत्याहरणं तेषां प्रत्याहारः स उच्यते॥ १२०॥

यथा तृतीयकाले तु रविः प्रत्याहरेत्प्रभाम्। तृतीयाङ्गस्थितो योगी विकारं मानसं हरेत्॥ इत्युपनिषत्॥ १२१॥

As the evening falls, the Sun gradually shrinks back his light and it is fully shrinked at the fall of evening, the yogi in the similar fashion, if becomes able proceeds by winning three states, three properties and three bodies and thus enshrines in his third part (third part of higher yoga i.e. meditation); all defects of his mind are compounded. This is all what this Upaniṣad explains.

ॐ आप्यायन्तु .... इति शान्तिः॥

॥इति योगचूडामण्युपनिषत्समाप्ता॥

***

46. NIRVĀṆO- UPANIṢAD

निर्वाणोपनिषद्

This Upaniṣad is related to Ṛgveda. A broad description regarding emancipation, the supreme aim of human life to liberate the cycle of birth and death has been made herein.

The cryptic doctrines of Paramahaṁsa recluse has been described in a mysterious way and through the formal system in this Upaniṣad. An introduction of a Paramahaṁsa recluse has been very first given and then the importance of consecration, perceiving to God, thinking in playway, the meeting, an alm, the conduct etc. has been described in perspect to the Paramahaṁsa recluse. Subsequently, the actual position of Maṭha, knowledge, intention, quilt, Āsana, skill, preaching of Tāraka, rule, unbinding, sacrifice, thread braid and emancipation etc. in perspect to the recluse has been described and it is stated that this very is the philosophy which should be assigned with only to a devoted pupil or to ones own son. The common person cannot reap the benefit of any kind from this philosophy.

॥शान्तिपाठः॥

ॐ वाङ्मे मनसि................. इति शान्तिः।

अथ निर्वाणोपनिषदं व्याख्यास्यामः। परमहंसः सोऽहम्। परिव्राजकाः पश्चिमलिङ्गाः। मन्मथक्षेत्रपालाः। गगनसिद्धान्तः। अमृतकल्लोलनदी। अक्षयं निरञ्जनम्। निःसंशयः ऋषिः। निर्वाणो देवता। निष्कुलप्रवृत्तिः। निष्केवलज्ञानम्॥ १-११॥

Now the Nirvāṇopaniṣad is being described. They who are Paramahaṁsa, Parivrājaka are always with Paśeimaliṅga (the symbol at the climax position). They are like a kṣetrapāla or watchman to resist the entrance of god of sex. Their doctrines are compared with the sky, viz., reluctant and widely extended like sky. They are in mood of the soul river with the immortal waves. Their complexion is everlasting, immortal and unattached. Their saint is doubtlessness and emancipation is their god. Their propensity is beyond their clan or Gotra. Their knowledge is liberated from all kinds of the qualifications.

ऊर्ध्वाम्नायः। निरालम्बपीठः। संयोगदीक्षा। वियोगोपदेशः। दीक्षासंतोषपावनं च। द्वादशादित्यावलोकनम्। विवेकरक्षा। करुणैव केलिः। आनन्दमाला। एकान्तगुहायां मुक्तासनसुखगोष्ठी। अकल्पितभिक्षाशी। हंसाचारः। सर्वभूतान्तर्वर्ती हंस इति प्रतिपादनम्॥ १२-२४॥

They does their practice for the higher position. Their seat is without any base, their coherence with the supreme soul is only consecration. Their preaching is to liberate from the world. Their pious duty is to be satisfy sons (the stage of great devastation because twelve sons simultaneously arise only at the time of great devastation). They protect themselves by an appellation of their discretion. To be kind to all living-organisms is their game. Self pleasure is their garland. It is their meeting to be seated in comfortably and freely in a solitary cave. To live on alms and not cooked by themselves is their food. They perform their activities like the haṁsa, viz., they do all justice as the haṁsa separates water from the milk. It is their pronouncement that the soul residing within all living-organisms is the Swan.

धैर्यकन्था। उदासीनकौपीनम्। विचारदण्ड:। ब्रह्मावलोकयोगपट्ट:। श्रियां पादुका। परेच्छाचरणम्। कुण्डलिनीबन्ध:। परापवादमुक्तो जीवन्मुक्त:। शिवयोगनिद्रा च। खेचरीमुद्रा च। परमानन्दी। निर्गुणगुणत्रयम्। विवेकलभ्यम्। मनोवागगोचरम्। अनित्यं जगद्यज्जनितं स्वप्नजगदभ्रगजादितुल्यम्। तथा देहादिसंघातं मोहगुणजालकलितं तद्रज्जुसर्पवत्कल्पितम्। विष्णुविध्यादिशताभिधानलक्ष्यम्। अङ्कुशो मार्ग:। शून्यं न संकेत:। परमेश्वरसत्ता। सत्यसिद्धयोगो मठ:। अमरपदं न तत्स्वरूपम्। आदिब्रह्मस्वसंवित्। अजपा गायत्री। विकारदण्डो ध्येय:॥

Courage is the quilt of those recluse. The propensity of reluctance is their nicker (Laṅgoṭī). Good thoughts are their stick and perceiving Brahma is their monogram of yoga. Wealth is their slipper (they treat the wealth trivial as a slipper). They do all activities and take birth on the will of good. Kuṇḍalinī is their tie. They are liberated soul and make themselves free from the habit of crticizing others. Coherence with all benevolent god is only their sleep. They feel supreme pleasure by holding the posture of sleep and khecari. That Brahma is beyond the three properties, i.e., Satva, Rajas and Tamas. It can be attained only when sole discretion is exercised. It is not attainable through the mind and the speech. This world is mortal and whosoever has been born here is like a dream and an elephant like formation of the cloud in the sky, this body in the similar fashion is full of distortions like affections of snake in a string. The Brahma known with many hundred names like Viṣṇu, Brahmā etc. is the ultimate aim. To control the senses is the only way to attain Brahma. That way to attain Brahma is not a void indication, viz., free from the divine powers like Lord Viṣṇu etc. The entity of god is on all living-organisms. The yoga well tied to truth and accomplished is the Maṭha of that recluse. The heaven is not the complexion of self while that of the primitive Brahma is knowledge. The Japa silently of So'haṁ is Gāyatrī. To establish control on defects is the aim.

मनोनिरोधिनी कन्था। योगेन सदानन्दस्वरूपदर्शनम्। आनन्दभिक्षाशी। महाश्मशानेऽप्यानन्दवने वास:। एकान्तस्थानम्। आनन्दमठम्। उन्मन्यवस्था। शारदा चेष्टा। उन्मनी गति:। निर्मलगात्रम्। निरालम्बपीठम्। अमृतकल्लोलानन्दक्रिया। पाण्डरगगनमहासिद्धान्त:। शमदमादिदिव्यशक्त्याचरणे क्षेत्रपात्रपटुता। परावरसंयोग:। तारकोपदेश:। अद्वैतसदानन्दो देवता॥

The propensity to control ones mind is the quite. The recluse perceive the true pleasure of Para Brahma through yoga. They feed on alms of pleasure. They reside with gaiety as would be in Ānandavana even in the deserted crematorium. Solitude only is their Maṭha, their meditated state is the luminating endeavour. Their motion is without option and restrictions. Their body is all pure and their seat is without base. To enjoy on the waves of the immortal ocean is their prime activity. Cidākāśa is their great principle. It is their skill to aware of the place and the person while applying the divine powers like Śama, Dama etc. Their coherence with Brahma is the preaching of Tāraka. The absolute and single pleasure of truth is their god.

नियमः स्वान्तरिन्द्रियनिग्रहः। भयमोहशोकक्रोधत्यागस्त्यागः। परावरैक्यरसास्वादनम्। अनियामकत्वनिर्मलशक्तिः। स्वप्रकाशब्रह्मतत्त्वे शिवशक्तिसंपुटितप्रपञ्चच्छेदनम्। तथा पत्राक्षाक्षिकमण्डलभावाभावदहनम्। बिभ्रत्याकाशाधारम्। शिवं तुरीयं यज्ञोपवीतम्। तन्मया शिखा। चिन्मयं चोत्सृष्टिरण्डम् संततोक्षिकमण्डलम्। कर्मनिर्मूलनं कथा। मायाममताहंकारदहनम्। श्मशाने अनाहताङ्गी। निस्त्रैगुण्यस्वरूपानुसन्धानं समयं भ्रान्तिहननम्। कामादिवृत्तिदहनम्। काठिन्यदृढकौपीनम्। चिराजिनवासः। अनाहतमन्त्रं अक्रिययैव जुष्टम्। स्वेच्छाचारस्वस्वभावो मोक्षः। परं ब्रह्म प्लववदाचरणम्। ब्रह्मचर्यशान्तिसंग्रहणम्। ब्रह्मचर्याश्रमेऽधीत्य वानप्रस्थाश्रमेऽधीत्य स सर्वसंविन्न्यासं संन्यासम्। अन्ते ब्रह्माखण्डाकारम्। नित्यं सर्वसंदेहनाशनम्॥ ४९-६०॥

To control the senses is the rule of those recluse. It is their sacrifice to abandon the fear, the affection, agony and the anger. They enjoy the coherence with the supreme Brahma. It is their sacrosanct power not to enslave anybody and give respect to all. They split up the illusion by the power of Śiva in the self-luninating Brahma. They burnt down into ashes the possession and non-possession on trio-bodies i.e. causative body, micro body and the formidable body. They hold the base in the garb of ether. Lord Śiva or Brahma as existed in the state of Turiya is their sacrificial thread and the knowledge of Brahma is their braid. Having on the supreme position, this movable as also immovable entire creation is in the form of Brahma under their perceiving. Not to tie with the result of action is their story. They move in the crematorium without taking least care of their body in order to burn into ashes the illusion, affection and the ego as well. They are beyond the trio-prioritise i.e. Satva, Rajas and Tamas. Their all efforts is to kill the confusion. They burn the propensities like a sensuality etc. They put on the laṅgoṭī and observe the rules rigidly. They only put on the hide of deer as clothes upto prolong time. They observe the hymn is garb of Anāhat sound by keeping themselves inactive. Their habit is to act as per the instructions given by their soul and it is the emancipation to which they attain. The recluse behaving like a knowledge boat to achieve the aim i.e. Parabrahma very first observes celibacy to cool down his temperament. On having involved in studies , in course of the period fixed for celibacy, he does the concentration, meditation and the practical application in the āśrama of Vānaprastha also. As a result of the well-knit knowledge which he acquires in course of Vānaprastha, the worldly knowledge is entirely abandoned by him. This very stage is called reclusion. Finally, he arrives at the state of integrated form of everlasting Brahma and all confusions are then decayed.

एतन्निर्वाणदर्शनं शिष्यं पुत्रं विना न देयमित्युपनिषत्॥ ६१॥

This very is the elemental philosophy of the emancipation. It should reproached only either to the devoted pupil or an obedient son or the suitable person to observe the vital elements embedded within it and nobody else. Hence, the common people should not be preached of this Upaniṣad. This very is the mystery of this Upaniṣad.

ॐ वाङ्मे मनसि..................... इति शान्तिः॥

॥इति निर्वाणोपनिषत्समाप्ता॥

***

47. MAṆḌALABRĀHMAṆA- UPANIṢAD

मण्डलब्राह्मणोपनिषद्

॥शान्तिपाठः॥

ॐ पूर्णमदः .... इति शान्तिः॥

॥प्रथमं ब्राह्मणम्॥

॥प्रथमः खण्डः॥

याज्ञवल्क्यो ह वै महामुनिरादित्यलोकं जगाम।
तमादित्यं नत्वा भो भगवन्नादित्यात्मतत्त्वमनुब्रूहीति॥ १॥
स होवाच नारायणः। ज्ञानयुक्तयमाद्यष्टाङ्गयोग उच्यते॥ २॥
शीतोष्णाहारनिद्राविजयः सर्वदा शान्तिर्निश्चलत्वं विषयेन्द्रियनिग्रहश्चैते यमाः॥ ३॥
गुरुभक्तिः सत्यमार्गानुरक्तिः सुखागतवस्त्वनुभवश्च तद्वस्त्वनुभवेन।
तुष्टिर्निःसङ्गता एकान्तवासो मनोनिवृत्तिः फलानभिलाषो वैराग्यभावश्च नियमाः॥ ४॥
सुखासनवृत्तिश्चिरवासश्चैवमासननियमो भवति॥ ५॥
पूरककुम्भकरेचकैः षोडशचतुःषष्टिद्वात्रिंशत्संख्यया यथाक्रमं प्राणायामः॥ ६॥
विषयेभ्य इन्द्रियार्थेभ्यो मनोनिरोधनं प्रत्याहारः॥ ७॥
विषयव्यावर्तनपूर्वकं चैतन्ये चेतःस्थापनं धारणं भवति॥ ८॥
सर्वशरीरेषु चैतन्यैकतानता ध्यानम्॥ ९॥ ध्यानविस्मृतिःसमाधिः॥ १०॥
एवं सूक्ष्माङ्गानि। य एवं वेद स मुक्तिभाग्भवति॥ ११॥

Brāhmaṇa I

Oṁ. The great Muni Yājñavalkya went to Ādityaloka (the sun's world) and saluting him (the Puruṣa of the sun) said: "O reverened sir, describe to me the Ātma-tattva (the tattva or truth of Ātmā)."

(To which), Nārāyaṇa (viz., the Puruṣa of the sun) replied : "I shall describe the eightfold yoga together with Jñāna. The conquering of cold and heat as well as hunger and sleep, the preserving of (sweet) patience and unruffledness ever and the restraining of the organs (from sensual objects)— all these come under (or are) yama. Devotion to one's Guru, love of the true path, enjoyment of objects producing happiness, internal satisfaction, freedom from association, living in a retired place, the controlling of the manas and not longing after the fruits of actions and a state of vairāgya— all these consitute niyama. The sitting in any posture pleasant to one and clothed in tatters (or bark) is prescribed for āsana (posture). Inspiration, restraint of breath and expiration, which have respectively 16, 64 and 32 (mātrās) constitute prāṇāyāma (restraint of breath). The restraining of the mind from the object of senses is pratyāhāra (subjugation of the senses). The contemplation of the oneness of consciousness in all objects is dhyāna. The mind having been drawn away from the objects of the senses, the fixing of the caitanya (consciousness) (on one alone) is dhāraṇā. The forgetting of oneself in dhyāna is samādhi. He who thus knows the eight subtle parts of yoga attains salvation.

॥द्वितीयः खण्डः॥

देहस्य पञ्च दोषा भवन्ति कामक्रोधनिःश्वासभयनिद्राः॥ १॥

तन्निरासस्तु निःसंकल्पक्षमालघ्वाहाराप्रमादतातत्त्वसेवनम्॥ २॥

निद्राभयसरीसृपं हिंसादितरङ्गं तृष्णावर्तं दारपङ्कं संसारवार्धिं तरीतुं सूक्ष्ममार्गमवलम्ब्य सत्त्वादिगुणानतिक्रम्य तारकमवलोकयेत्॥ ३॥

भ्रूमध्ये सच्चिदानन्दतेजःकूटरूपं तारकं ब्रह्म॥ ४॥ तदुपायं लक्ष्यत्रयावलोकनम्॥ ५॥

मूलाधारादारभ्य ब्रह्मरन्ध्रपर्यन्तं सुषुम्ना सूर्याभा। तन्मध्ये तडित्कोटिसमा मृणालतन्तुसूक्ष्मा कुण्डलिनी। तत्र तमोनिवृत्तिः। तद्दर्शनात्सर्वपापनिवृत्तिः॥ ६॥

तर्जन्यग्रोन्मीलितकर्णरन्ध्रद्वये फूत्कारशब्दो जायते।

तत्र स्थिते मनसि चक्षुर्मध्यनीलज्योतिः पश्यति। एवं हृदयेऽपि॥ ७॥

तर्जनी अँगुली के अग्रभाग से दोनों कानों को बन्द करने पर उस (साधक) के कर्णछिद्रों से

बहिर्लक्ष्यं तु नासाग्रे चतुःषडष्टदशद्वादशाङ्गुलीभिः क्रमान्नीलद्युतिश्यामत्वसदृग्रक्त-भङ्गीस्फुरत्पीतवर्णद्वयोपेतं व्योमत्वं पश्यति स तु योगी॥ ८॥

चलनदृष्ट्या व्योमभागवीक्षितुः पुरुषस्य दृष्ट्यग्रे ज्योतिर्मयूखा वर्तन्ते। तद्दृष्टिः स्थिरा भवति॥ ९

शीर्षोपरि द्वादशाङ्गुलिमानं ज्योतिः पश्यति तदाऽमृतत्वमेति॥ १०॥

मध्यलक्ष्यं तु प्रातश्चित्रादिवर्णसूर्यचन्द्रवह्निज्वाला वलीवत्तद्विहीनान्तरिक्षवत्पश्यति॥ ११॥

तदाकाराकारी भवति॥ १२॥

अभ्यासान्निर्विकारं गुणरहिताकाशं भवति। विस्फुरत्तारकाकारगाढतमोपमं पराकाशं भवति। कालानलसमं द्योतमानं महाकाशं भवति। सर्वोत्कृष्टपरमाद्वितीयप्रद्योतमानं तत्त्वाकाशं भवति। कोटिसूर्यप्रकाशसंकाशं सूर्याकाशं भवति॥ १३॥

एवमभ्यासात्तन्मयो भवति य एवं वेद॥ १४॥

"The body has five stains (viz.,) passion, anger, outbreathing, fear, and sleep. The removal of these can be effected respectively by absence of saṅkalpa, forgiveness, moderate food, carefulness, and a spiritual sight of tattvas. In order to cross the ocean of saṁsāra where sleep and fear are the serpents, injury, etc., are the waves, tṛṣṇā (thirst) is whirlpool, and wife is the mire, one should adhere to the subtle path and overstepping tattva and other guṇas should look out for Tāraka. Tāraka is brahman which being in the middle of the two eyebrows, is of the nature of of the spiritual effulgence of Saccidānanda. The (spiritual) seeing through the three lakṣyas (or the three kinds of introvision) is the means to It (Brahman). Suṣumnā which is from the mūlādhāra to brahmarandhra has the radiance of the sun. In the centre of it, is kuṇḍalinī shining like crores of lightning and subtle as the thread in the lotus-stalk. Tamas is destroyed there. Through seeing it, all sins are destroyed. When the two ears are closed by the tips of the forefingers, a phūtkāra (or booming) sound is heard. When the mind is fixed on it, it sees a blue light between the eyes as also in the heart. (This is antarlakṣya or internal introvision). In the bahirlakṣya (or external introvision) one sees in order before his nose at distance of 4, 6, 8, 10, and 12 digits, the space of blue colour, then a colour resembling Śyāma (indigo-black) and then shining as rakta (red) wave and then with the two pīta (yellow and orange red) colours. Then he is a yogin. When one looks at the external space, moving the eyes and sees streaks of light at the corners of his eyes, then his vision can be made steady. When one sees jyotis (spiritual light) above his head 12 digits in length, then he attains the state of nectar. In the madhyalakṣya (or the middle one), one sees the variegated colours of the morning as if the sun, the moon and the fire had joined together in the ākāśa that is without them. Then he comes to have their nature (or light). Through practice, he becomes one with ākāśa devoid of all guṇas and peculiarities. As first ākāśa with its shining starts becomes to him Parākāśa as dark as tamas itself, and he becomes one with Parākāśa shining with stars and sleep as tamas. (Then) he becomes one with Mahā-ākāśa resplendent (as) with the fire of the deluge. Then he becomes one with Tattva-ākāśa, lighted with the brightness which is the highest and the best of all. Then he becomes one with Sūrya-ākāśa (sun-ākāśa) brightened by a crore of suns. By practising thus, he becomes one with them. He who knows them becomes thus.

॥तृतीय: खण्ड:॥

तद्योगं च द्विधा विद्धि पूर्वोत्तरविभागतः। पूर्वं तु तारकं विद्यादमनस्कं तदुत्तरमिति। तारकं द्विविधम् मूर्तितारकममूर्तितारकमिति। यदिन्द्रियान्तं तन्मूर्तितारकम्। यद्भ्रूयुगातीतं तदमूर्तितारकमिति॥ १॥

उभयमपि मनोयुक्तमभ्यसेत्। मनोयुक्तान्तरदृष्टिस्तारकप्रकाशाय भवति॥ २॥

भ्रूयुगमध्यबिले तेजस आविर्भावः। एतत्पूर्वतारकम्॥ ३॥

उत्तरं त्वमनस्कम्। तालुमूलोर्ध्वभागे महज्ज्योतिर्विद्यते। तद्दर्शनादणिमादिसिद्धिः॥ ४॥

लक्ष्येऽन्तर्बाह्यायां दृष्टौ निमेषोन्मेषवर्जितायां चेयं शाम्भवी मुद्रा भवति। सर्वतन्त्रेषु गोप्यमहाविद्या भवति। तज्ज्ञानेन संसारनिवृत्तिः। तत्पूजनं मोक्षफलदम्॥ ५॥

अन्तर्लक्ष्यं जलज्ज्योतिःस्वरूपं भवति। महर्षिवेद्यं अन्तर्बाह्येन्द्रियैरदृश्यम्॥ ६॥

"Know that yoga is twofold through its division into the pūrva (earlier) and the uttara (latter). The earlier is tāraka and the later is amanaska (the mindless). Tāraka is divided into mūrti (with limitation) and amūrti (without limitation). That is mūrti tāraka which goes to the end of the sense (or exists till the sense are conquered). That is amūrti tāraka which goes beyond the two eyebrows (above the senses). Both these should be performed through manas. Antardṛṣṭi (internal vision) associated with manas comes to aid tāraka. Tejas (spiritual light) appears in the hole between the two eyebrows. This tāraka is the earlier one. The later is amanaska. The great jyotis (light) is above the root of the palate. By seeing it, one gets the siddhis, aṇimā. etc. Śāmbhavī-mudrā occurs when the lakṣya (spiritual vision) is internal while the (physical) eyes are seeing externally without winking. This is the great science which is concealed in all the tantras. When this is known, one does not stay in saṁsāra. Its worship (or practice) gives salvation. Antarlakṣya is of the nature of Jalajyotis (or waterjyotis). It is known by the great Ṛṣis and is invisible both to the internal and external sences.

॥चतुर्थः खण्डः॥

सहस्रारे जलज्ज्योतिरन्तर्लक्ष्यम्। बुद्धिगुहायां सर्वाङ्गसुन्दरं पुरुषरूपमन्तर्लक्ष्यमित्यपरे। शीर्षान्तर्गतमण्डलमध्यगं पञ्चवक्त्रमुमासहायं नीलकण्ठं प्रशान्तमन्तर्लक्ष्यमिति केचित्। अङ्गुष्ठमात्रः पुरुषोऽन्तर्लक्ष्यमित्येके॥ १॥

उक्तविकल्पं सर्वमात्मैव। तल्लक्ष्यं शुद्धात्मदृष्ट्या वा यः पश्यति स एव ब्रह्मनिष्ठो भवति॥ २॥

जीवः पञ्चविंशकः स्वकल्पितचतुर्विंशतितत्त्वं परित्यज्य षड्विंशः परमात्माहमिति निश्चयाज्जीवन्मुक्तो भवति॥ ३॥

एवमन्तर्लक्ष्यदर्शनेन जीवन्मुक्तिदशायां स्वयमन्तर्लक्ष्यो भूत्वा परमाकाशाखण्डमण्डलो भवति॥ ४॥

"Sahasrāra (viz., the thousand-petalled lotus of the pineal gland) Jalajyotis is the antarlakṣya. Some say the form of Puruṣa in the cave of buddhi beautiful in all its parts is antarlakṣya. Some again say that the all-quiescent Nīlakaṇṭha accompanied by Umā (his wife) and having five mouths and later in the midst of the sphere in the brain is antarlakṣya. While others say that the Puruṣa of the dimension of a thumb is antarlakṣya. A few again say antarlakṣya is the One Self made supreme through introvision in the state of jīvanmukta. All the different statements above made pertain to Ātmā alone. He alone is a Brahmaniṣṭha who sees that the above lakṣya is the pure Ātmā. The jīva which in the twenty-fifth tattva, having abandoned the twenty-four tattvas, becomes a jīvanmukta through the conviction that the twenty-sixth tattva (viz.,) Paramātmā is 'I' alone. Becoming one with antarlakṣya (brahman) in the emancipated state by means of antarlakṣya (introvision), jīva becomes one with the partless sphere of Paramākāśa.

"Thus ends the first Brāhmaṇa."

॥द्वितीयं ब्राह्मणम्॥

॥प्रथमः खण्डः॥

अथ ह याज्ञवल्क्य आदित्यमण्डलपुरुषं पप्रच्छ। भगवन्नन्तर्लक्ष्यादिकं बहुधोक्तम्। मया तन्न ज्ञातम्। तद्ब्रूहि मह्यम्॥ १॥

तदु होवाच पञ्चभूतकारणं तडित्कूटाभं तद्वच्चतुःपीठम्। तन्मध्ये तत्त्वप्रकाशो भवति। सोऽतिगूढ अव्यक्तश्च॥ २॥

तज्ज्ञानप्लवाधिरूढेन ज्ञेयम्। तद्बाह्याभ्यन्तर्लक्ष्यम्॥ ३॥

तन्मध्ये जगल्लीनम्। तन्नादबिन्दुकलातीतमखण्डमण्डलम्। तत्सगुणनिर्गुणस्वरूपम्। तद्वेत्ता विमुक्तः॥ ४॥

आदावग्निमण्डलम्। तदुपरि सूर्यमण्डलम्। तन्मध्ये सुधाचन्द्रमण्डलम्। तन्मध्येऽखण्डब्रह्मतेजो मण्डलम्। तद्विद्युल्लेखावच्छुक्लभास्वरम्। तदेव शाम्भवीलक्षणम्॥ ५॥

तद्दर्शने तिस्रो दृष्टयः अमा प्रतिपत् पूर्णिमा चेति। निमीलितदर्शनममादृष्टिः। अर्धोन्मीलितं प्रतिपत्। सर्वोन्मीलनं पूर्णिमा भवति। तासु पूर्णिमाभ्यासः कर्तव्यः॥ ६॥

तल्लक्ष्यं नासाग्रम्। यदा तालुमूले गाढतमो दृश्यते। तदभ्यासादखण्डमण्डलाकारज्योतिर्दृश्यते। तदेव सच्चिदानन्दं ब्रह्म भवति॥ ७॥

एवं सहजानन्दे यदा मनो लीयते तदा शाम्भवी भवति। तामेव खेचरीमाहुः॥ ८॥

तदभ्यासान्मनःस्थैर्यम्। ततो बुद्धिस्थैर्यम्॥ ९॥

तच्चिह्नानि आदौ तारकवद्दृश्यते। ततो वज्रदर्पणम्। तत उपरि पूर्णचन्द्रमण्डलम्। ततो नवरत्न प्रभामण्डलम्। ततो मध्याह्नार्कमण्डलम्। ततो वह्निशिखामण्डलं क्रमाद्दृश्यते॥

Brāhmaṇa II

Then Yājñavalkya asked the Puruṣa in the sphere of the sun : "O Lord, antarlakṣya has been described many times, but it has never been understood by me (clearly). Pray describe it to me. "He replied : "It is the source of the five elements, has the lustre of many (streaks of) lightning, and has four seats having (or rising from) 'That' (Brahman). In its midst, there arises the manifestation of tattva. It is very hidden and unmanifested. It can be known (only) by one, who has gone into the boat of jñāna. It is the object of both bahir and antar (external and internal) lakṣyas. In its midst is absorbed the whole world. It is the vast partless universe beyond Nāda, Bindu and Kalā. Above it (viz., the sphere of agni) is the sphere of the sun; in its midst is the sphere of the nectary moon; in its midst is the sphere of the partless Brahma-tejas (or the spiritual effulgence of Brahman). It has the brightness of Śukla (white light) like the ray of lightning. It alone has the characteristic of Śāmbhavī. In seeing this, there are three kinds of ḍṛṣṭi (sight) viz., amā (the new moon), pratipat (the first day of lunar fortnight), and pūrṇimā (the full moon). The sight of amā is the one (seen) with closed eyes. That with half opened eyes is pratipat; while that with fully opened eyes is pūrṇimā. Of these, the practice of pūrṇimā should be resorted to. Its lakṣya (or aim) is the tip of the nose. Then is seen a deep darkness at the root of the palate. By practising thus, a jyoti (light) of the form of an endless sphere is seen. This alone is Brahman, the Saccidānanda. When the mind is absorbed in bliss thus naturally produced, then does Śāmbhavī take place. She (Śāmbhavī) alone is called Khecarī. By practising it (viz., the mudrā), a man obtains firmness of mind. Through it, he obtain firmness of vāyu. The following are the signs : first it is seen like a star; then a reflecting (or dazzling) diamond; then the sphere of full moon; then the sphere of the brightness of nine gems; then the sphere of the midday sun; then the sphere of the flame of agni (fire); all these are seen in order.

॥द्वितीय: खण्ड:॥

तदा पश्चिमाभिमुखप्रकाशः स्फटिकधूम्रबिन्दुनादकलानक्षत्रखद्योतदीपनेत्रसवर्णनवरत्नादिप्रभा दृश्यन्ते। तदेव प्रणवस्वरूपम्॥ १॥

प्राणापानयोरैक्यं कृत्वा धृतकुम्भको नासाग्रदर्शनदृढभावनया द्विकराङ्गुलिभिः षण्मुखीकरणेन प्रणवध्वनिं निशम्य मनस्तत्र लीनं भवति॥ २॥

तस्य न कर्मलेपः। रवेरुदयास्तमययोः किल कर्म कर्तव्यम्। एवंविधश्चिदादित्यस्योदयास्तमयाभावात्सर्वकर्माभावः॥ ३॥

शब्दकाललयेन दिवारात्र्यतीतो भूत्वा सर्वपरिपूर्णज्ञानेनोन्मन्यवस्थावशेन ब्रह्मैक्यं भवति। उन्मन्या अमनस्कं भवति॥ ४॥

तस्य निश्चिन्ता ध्यानम्। सर्वकर्मनिराकरणमावाहनम्। निश्चयज्ञानमासनम्। उन्मनीभावः पाद्यम्। सदाऽमनस्कमर्घ्यम्। सदादीप्तिरपारामृतवृत्तिः स्नानम्। सर्वत्र भावना गन्धः। दृक्स्वरूपावस्थानमक्षताः। चिदाप्तिः पुष्पम्। चिदग्निस्वरूपं धूपः। चिदादित्यस्वरूपं दीपः। परिपूर्णचन्द्रामृतरसस्यैकीकरणं नैवेद्यम्। निश्चलत्वं प्रदक्षिणम्। सोऽहंभावो नमस्कारः। मौनं स्तुतिः। सर्वसंतोषो विसर्जनमिति य एवं वेद॥ ५॥

"(Thus much for the light in pūrva or first stage.) Then there is the light in the western direction (in the uttara or second stage). Then the lustres of crystal, smoke, bindu, nāda, kalā, star, firefly, lamp, eye, gold, and nine gems, etc. are seen. This alone is the form of Praṇava. Having united Prāṇa and Apāna and holding the breath in kumbhaka, one should fix his concentration at the tip of his nose and making ṣaṇmukhi with the fingers of both his hands, one hears the sound of Praṇava (Oṁ) in which manas becomes absorbed. Such a man has not even the touch of karma. The karma of (Sandhyāvandana or the daily prayers) is verily performed at the rising or setting of the sun. As there is no rising or setting (but only the ever shining) of the sun of Cit (the higher consciousness) in the heart of a man who knows thus, he has no karma to perform. Rising above (the conception of) day and night through the annihilation of sound and time, he becomes one with Brahman through the all-full jñāna and the attaining of the state of unmanī (the state above manas). Through the state of unmanī, he becomes amanaska (or without manas).

"Not being troubled by any thoughts (of the world) then constitutes of dhyāna. The abandoning of all karmas constitutes āvāhana (invocation of god). Being firm in the unshaken (spiritual) wisdom constitutes āsana (posture). Being in the state of unmanī constitutes the pādya (offering of water for washing the feet of god). Preserving the state of amanaska (when manas is offered as sacrifice) constitutes the arghya (offering of water as oblation generally). Being in state of eternal brightness and shoreless nectar constitutes snāna (bathing). The contemplation of Ātmā as present in all constitutes (the application to the idol of) sandal. The remaining in the real state of dṛk (spiritual eye) is (the worshipping with) akṣata (non-broken rice). The attaining of Cit (consciousness) is (the worshipping with) flower. The real state of agni (fire) of Cit is the dhūpa (burning of incense). The state of the sun of Cit is the dīpa (light waved before the image). The union of oneself with the nectar of full moon is the naivēdya (offering of food, etc.). The immobility in that state (of the ego being one with all) is pradakṣiṇa (going round the image). The conception of 'I am He' is namaskāra (prostration). The silence then is the stuti (praise). The all-contentment (or serenity then) is the visarjana (giving leave to god or finishing worship). (This is the worship of Ātmā by all Rāja-yogins). He who knows this knows all.

॥तृतीय: खण्ड:॥

एवं त्रिपुट्यां निरस्तायां निस्तरङ्गसमुद्रवन्निवातस्थितदीपवदचलसंपूर्णभावाभावविहीनकैवल्य-ज्योतिर्भवति॥ १॥

जाग्रन्निद्रान्त:परिज्ञानेन ब्रह्मविद्भवति॥ २॥

सुषुप्तिसमाध्योर्मनोलयाविशेषेऽपि महदस्त्युभयोर्भेदस्तमसि लीनत्वान्मुक्तिहेतुत्वाभावाच्च॥ ३॥

समाधौ मृदिततमोविकारस्य तदाकाराकारिताखण्डाकारवृत्त्यात्मकसाक्षिचैतन्ये प्रपञ्चलय: संपद्यते प्रपञ्चस्य मन:कल्पितत्वात्॥ ४॥

ततो भेदाभावात् कदाचिद्बहिर्गतेऽपि मिथ्यात्वभानात्। सकृद्विभातसदानन्दानुभवैकगोचरो ब्रह्मवित्तदेव भवति॥ ५॥

यस्य संकल्पनाश: स्यात्तस्य मुक्ति: करे स्थिता।

तस्माद्भावाभावौ परित्यज्य परमात्मध्यानेन मुक्तो भवति॥ ६॥

पुन:पुन: सर्वावस्थासु ज्ञानज्ञेयौ ध्यानध्येयौ लक्ष्यालक्ष्ये दृश्यादृश्ये चोहापोहादि परित्यज्य जीवन्मुक्तो भवेत्। य एवं वेद॥ ७॥

"When the tripuṭi are thus dispelled, he becomes the kaivalya jyotis without bhāva (existence) or abhāva (non-existence), full and motionless, like the ocean without tides or like the lamp without wind. He becomes a brahmavit (knower of brahman) by cognising the end of the sleeping state, even while in the waking state. Though the (sam) mind is absorbed in suṣupti as also in samādhi, there is much difference between them. (In the former case) as the mind is absorbed in tamas, it does not become the means of salvation, (but) in samādhi as the modifications of tamas in him are rotted away, the mind raises itself to the nature of the Partless. All that is no other than Sākṣī-Caitanya (witness-consciousness or the Higher Self) into which the absorption of the whole universe takes place, inasmuch as the universe is but a delusion (or creation) of the mind and is therefore not different from it. Though the universe appears perhaps as outside of the mind, still it is unreal. He who knows Brahman and who is the sole enjoyer of brāhmic bliss which is eternal and has dawned once (for all in him)— that man becomes one with Brahman. He in whom saṅkalpa perishes has got mukti in his hand. Therefore one becomes an emancipated person through the contemplation of Paramātmā. Having given up both bhāva and abhāva, one becomes jīvanmukta by leaving off again and again in all states jñāna (wisdom) and jñāna (object of wisdom), dhyāna (meditation) and dhyeya (object of meditation), lakṣya (the aim) and alakṣya (non-aim), dṛśya (the visible) and adṛśya (the non-visible and ūha (reasoning) the apoha (negative reasoning). He who knows this knows all.

॥चतुर्थः खण्डः॥

पञ्चावस्थाः जाग्रत्स्वप्नसुषुप्तितुरीयतुरीयातीताः॥ १॥

जाग्रति प्रवृत्तो जीवः प्रवृत्तिमार्गासक्तः। पापफलनरकादि मास्तु शुभकर्मफलस्वर्गमस्त्विति काङ्क्षते॥ २॥

एवं स एव स्वीकृतवैराग्यात्कर्मफलजन्माऽलं। संसारबन्धनमलमिति विमुक्त्यभिमुखो निवृत्तिमार्गप्रवृत्तो भवति॥ ३॥

स एव संसारतारणाय गुरुमाश्रित्य कामादि त्यक्त्वा विहितकर्माचरन्साधनचतुष्टयसंपन्नो हृदयकमलमध्ये भगवत्सत्तामात्रान्तर्लक्ष्यरूपमासाद्य सुषुप्त्यवस्थाया मुक्तब्रह्मानन्दस्मृतिं लब्ध्वा एक एवाहमद्वितीयः कंचित्कालमज्ञानवृत्त्या विस्मृतजाग्रद्वासनानुफलेन तैजसोऽस्मीति तदुभयनिवृत्त्या प्राज्ञ इदानीमस्मीत्यहमेक एव स्थानभेदादवस्थाभेदस्य परंतु नहि मदन्यदिति जातविवेकः शुद्धाद्वैतब्रह्माहमिति भिदागन्धं निरस्य स्वान्तर्विजृम्भितभानुमण्डलध्यानतदाकाराकारितपरंब्रह्माकारितमुक्तिमार्गमारूढः परिपक्वो भवति॥ ४॥

संकल्पादिकं मनो बन्धहेतुः। तद्वियुक्तं मनो मोक्षाय भवति॥ ५॥

तद्वांश्चक्षुरादिबाह्यप्रपञ्चोपरतो विगतप्रपञ्चगन्धः सर्वजगदात्मत्वेन पश्यंस्त्यक्ताहंकारो ब्रह्माहमस्मीति चिन्तयन्निदं सर्वं यदयमात्मेति भावयन्कृतकृत्यो भवति॥ ६॥

"There are five avasthās (states), viz., jāgrat (waking), svapna (dreaming), suṣupti (dreamless sleeping), the turya (fourth) and turyātīta (that beyond the fourth). The jīva (ego) that is engaged in the waking state becomes attached to the pravṛtti (worldly) path and is the participator of naraka (hell) as the fruit of sins. He desires svarga (heaven) as the fruit of his virtuous actions. This very same person becomes (afterwards) indifferent to all these saying, "Enough of the births tending to actions, the fruits of which tend to bondage till the end of this mundane existence." Then he pursues the nivṛtti (return) path with a view to attain emancipation. And this person then takes refuge in a spiritual instructor in order to cross this mundane existence. Giving up passion and others, he does only those he is asked to do. Then having acquired the four sādhanas (means to salvation), he attains, in the middle of the lotus of his heart, the Reality of antarlakṣya that is but the Sat of Lord and begins to recognise (or recollect) the bliss Brahman which he had left (or enjoyed) in the suṣupti state. At last he attains this state of discrimination (thus) : 'I think I am the non dual one only. I was in ajñāna for some time (in the waking state and called therefore Viśva). I became somehow (or involuntarily) a Taijasa (in the dreaming state) through the reflection (in that state) of the affinities of the forgotton waking state; and now I am a Prājña through the disappearance of those two states. Therefore I am one only. I (appear) as more than one through the difference of state and place. And there is nothing of differentiation of class besides me.' Having expelled even the smack of the difference (of conception) between 'I' and 'That' through the thought 'I am the pure and secondless Brahman', and having attained the path of salvation which is of the nature of parabrahman, after having become one with It through the dhyāna of the sun's sphere as shining with himself, he becomes fully ripened forgetting salvation. Saṅkalpa and others are the causes of the bondage of the mind; and the mind devoid of these becomes fit for salvation. Possessing such a mind free from all (saṅkalpa, etc.,) and withdrawing himself out of the odour of the universe, he looks upon all the worlds as Ātmā, abandons the conception of 'I', thinks 'I am Brahman' and considers all these as Ātmā. Through these, he becomes one who had done his duty.

॥पञ्चमः खण्डः॥

सर्वपरिपूर्णतुरीयातीतब्रह्मभूतो योगी भवति। तं ब्रह्मेति स्तुवन्ति॥ १॥

सर्वलोकस्तुतिपात्रः सर्वदेशसंचारशीलः परमात्मगगने बिन्दुं निक्षिप्य शुद्धाद्वैताजाड्य-सहजामनस्कयोगनिद्राखण्डानन्दपदानुवृत्त्या जीवन्मुक्तो भवति॥ २॥

तच्चानन्दसमुद्रमग्ना योगिनो भवन्ति॥ ३॥

तदपेक्षया इन्द्रादयः स्वल्पानन्दाः। एवं प्राप्तानन्दः परमयोगी भवतीत्युपनिषत्॥ ४॥

"The yogin is one that has realised Brahman that is all full beyond turya. They (the people) extol him as Brahman; and becoming the object of the praise of the whole world, he wanders over different countries. Placing the bindu in the ākāśa of Paramātmā and pursuing the path of the partless bliss produced by the pure, secondless, stainless, and innate yoga sleep of amanaska, he becomes an emancipated person. Then the yogin becomes immersed in the ocean of bliss. When compared to it, the bliss of Indra and others is very little. He who gets this bliss is the supreme yogin.

"Thus ends the second Brāhmaṇa."

॥तृतीयं ब्राह्मणम्॥

॥प्रथमः खण्डः॥

याज्ञवल्क्यो महामुनिर्मण्डलपुरुषं पप्रच्छ स्वामिन्नमनस्कलक्षणमुक्तमपि विस्मृतं पुनस्तल्लक्षणं ब्रूहीति॥ १॥

तथेति मण्डलपुरुषोऽब्रवीत्। इदममनस्कमतिरहस्यम्। यज्ज्ञानेन कृतार्थो भवति तन्नित्यं शांभवीमुद्रान्वितम्॥ २॥

परमात्मदृष्ट्या तत्प्रत्ययलक्ष्याणि दृष्ट्वा तदनु सर्वेशमप्रमेयमजं शिवं परमाकाशं निरालम्बमद्वयं ब्रह्मविष्णुरुद्रादीनामेकलक्ष्यं सर्वकारणं परंब्रह्मात्मन्येव पश्यमानो गुहाविहरणमेव निश्चयेन ज्ञात्वा भावाभावादिद्वन्द्वातीतः संविदितमनोन्मन्यनुभवस्तदनन्तरमखिलेन्द्रियक्षयवशादमनस्कसुखब्रह्मानन्दसमुद्रे मनः प्रवाहयोगरूपनिवातस्थितदीपवदचलं परंब्रह्म प्राप्नोति॥ ३॥

ततः शुष्कवृक्षवन्मूर्च्छानिद्रामयनिःश्वासोच्छ्वासाभावान्नष्टद्वन्द्वः सदाऽचञ्चलगात्रः परमशान्तिं स्वीकृत्य मनःप्रचारशून्यं परमात्मनि लीनं भवति॥ ४॥

पयःस्रावानन्तरं धेनुस्तनक्षीरमिव सर्वेन्द्रियवर्गे परिनष्टे मनोनाशो भवति तदेवामनस्कम्॥ ५॥

तदनु नित्यशुद्धः परमात्माहमेवेति तत्त्वमसीत्युपदेशेन त्वमेवाहमहमेव त्वमिति तारकयोगमार्गेणाखण्डानन्दपूर्णः कृतार्थो भवति॥ ६॥

Brāhmaṇa III

The great sage Yājñavalkya then asked the Puruṣa in the sphere (of the sun) : "O Lord, though the nature of amanaska has been defined (by you), yet I forget it (or do not understand it clearly). Therefore please explain it again to me." Accordingly the Puruṣa said: "This amanaska is a great secret. By knowing this, one becomes a person who has done his duty. One should look upon it as Paramātmā, associated with Śāmbhavī-mudrā and should know also all those that can be known through a cognition of them. Then seeing Parabrahman is his own Ātmā as the Lord of all, the immeasurable, the birthless, the auspicious, the supreme ākāśa, the supportless, the secondless, the only goal of Brahmā, Viṣṇu and Rudra and the cause of all and assuring himself that he who plays in the cave (of the heart) is such a one, he should raise himself above the dualities of existence and non-existence; and knowing the experience of the unmanī of his manas, he then attains the state of Parabrahman which is motionless as a lamp in a windless place, having reached the ocean of brāhmic bliss by means of the river of amanaskayoga through the destruction of all his sense. Then he resembles a dry tree. Having lost all (idea of) the universe through the disappearance of growth, sleep, disease, expiration and inspiration, his body being always steady, comes to have a supreme quiescence, being devoid of the movements of his manas and becomes absorbed in Paramātmā. The destruction of manas takes place after the destruction of the collective senses, like cow's udder (that shrivels up) after the milk has been drawn. It is this that is amanaska. By following this, one becomes always pure and becomes one that has done his duty, having been filled with the partless bliss by means of the path of tāraka-yoga through the initiation into the sacred sentences 'I am Paramātmā', 'That are You', 'I am You alone', 'You are I alone', etc.

॥द्वितीयः खण्डः॥

परिपूर्णपराकाशमग्नमनाः प्राप्तोन्मन्यवस्थः संन्यस्तसर्वेन्द्रियवर्गोऽनेकजन्मार्जितपुण्यपुञ्जपक्वकैवल्य-फलोऽखण्डानन्दनिरस्तसर्वक्लेशकश्मलो ब्रह्माहमस्मीति कृतकृत्यो भवति॥ १॥

त्वमेवाहं न भेदोऽस्ति पूर्णत्वात्परमात्मनः। इत्युच्चरन्त्समालिङ्ग्य शिष्यं ज्ञप्तिमनीनयत्॥ २॥

"When his manas is immersed in the ākāśa and he becomes all-full, and when he attains the unmanī state, having abandoned all his collective senses, he conquers all sorrows and impurities through the partless bliss, having attained the fruits of kaivalya, ripened through the collective merits gathered in all his pervious lives and thinking always 'I am Brahman', becomes one that has done his duty. 'I am You alone'. There is no difference between You and me owing to the fullness of Paramātmā. Saying thus, he (the Puruṣa of the sun) embraced his pupil and made him understand it.

"Thus ends the third Brāhmaṇa."

॥चतुर्थं ब्राह्मणम्॥

॥प्रथमः खण्डः॥

अथ ह याज्ञवल्क्यो मण्डलपुरुषं पप्रच्छ व्योमपञ्चकलक्षणं विस्तरेणानुब्रूहीति॥ १॥

स होवाचाकाशं पराकाशं महाकाशं। सूर्याकाशं परमाकाशमिति पञ्च भवन्ति॥ २॥

स बाह्याभ्यन्तरमन्धकारमयमाकाशम्। स बाह्यस्याभ्यन्तरे कालानलसदृशं पराकाशम्। सबाह्याभ्यन्तरेऽपरिमितद्युतिनिभं तत्त्वं महाकाशम्। सबाह्याभ्यन्तरे सूर्यनिभं सूर्याकाशम्। अनिर्वचनीयज्योतिः सर्वव्यापकं निरतिशयानन्दलक्षणं परमाकाशम्॥ ३॥

एवं तत्तल्लक्ष्यदर्शनात्तत्तद्रूपो भवति॥ ४॥

नवचक्रं षडाधारं त्रिलक्ष्यं व्योमपञ्चकम्। सम्यगेतन्न जानाति स योगी नामतो भवेत्॥ ५॥

Brāhmaṇa IV

The Yājñavalkya addressed the Puruṣa in the sphere (of the sun) thus : "Please explain to me in detail the nature of the fivefold division of ākāśa." He replied : "there are five (viz.,) : ākāśa, parākāśa, mahākāśa, sūryākāśa and paramākāśa. That which is of the nature of darkness, both in and out is the first ākāśa. That which has the fire of the deluge, both in and out is truly mahākāśa, That which has the brightness of the sun, both in and out is sūryākāśa. That brightness which is indescribable, all-pervading and of the nature of unrivalled bliss is paramākāśa. By cognising these according to this description, one becomes of their nature. He is yogin only in name, who does not cognise well the nine cakras, the six ādhāras, the three lakṣyas and the five ākāśa. Thus ends the fourth Brāhmaṇa."

॥पञ्चमं ब्राह्मणम्॥

॥प्रथमः खण्डः॥

सविषयं मनो बन्धाय निर्विषयं मुक्तये भवति॥ १॥

अतः सर्वं जगच्चित्तगोचरम्। तदेव चित्तं निराश्रयं मनोन्मन्यवस्थापरिपत्वं लययोग्यं भवति॥

तल्लयं परिपूर्णे मयि समभ्यसेत्। मनोलयकारणमहमेव॥ ३॥

अनाहतस्य शब्दस्य तस्य शब्दस्य यो ध्वनिः। ध्वनेरन्तर्गतं ज्योतिर्ज्योतिरन्तर्गतं मनः॥ ४॥

यन्मनस्त्रिजगत्सृष्टिस्थितिव्यसनकर्मकृत्। तन्मनो विलयं याति तद्विष्णोः परमं पदम्॥ ५॥

तल्लयाच्छुद्धाद्वैतसिद्धिर्भेदाभावात्। एतदेव परमतत्त्वम्॥ ६॥

स तज्ज्ञो बालोन्मत्तपिशाचवज्जडवृत्त्या लोकमाचरेत्॥ ७॥

एवममनस्काभ्यासेनैवनित्यतृप्तिरल्पमूत्रपुरीषमितभोजनदृढाङ्गाजाड्यनिद्रादृग्वायुचलनाभावब्रह्मदर्शनाज्ज्ञात-सुखस्वरूपसिद्धिर्भवति॥ ८॥

Brāhmaṇa V

"The manas influenced by worldly objects is liable to bondage; and that (manas) which is not so influenced by these is fit for salvation. Hence all the world becomes an object of citta; whereas the same citta when it is supportless and well-ripe in the state of unmanī, becomes worthy of laya (absorption in Brahman). This absorption you should learn from me who am the all-full. I alone am the cause of the absorption of manas. The manas is within the jyotis (spiritual light) which again is latent in the spiritual sound which pertains to the anāhata (heart) sound. That manas which is the agent of creation, preservation, and destruction of the three worlds— that same manas becomes absorbed in that which is the highest seat of Viṣṇu; through such an absorption, one gets the pure and secondless state, owing to the absence of difference then. This alone is the highest truth. He who knows this, will wander in the world like a lad or an idiot or a demon or a simpleton. By practising this amanaska, one is ever contented, his urine and faeces become diminished, his food becomes lessened : he becomes strong in body and his limbs are free from disease and sleep. Then his breath and eyes being motionless, he realises Brahman and attains the nature of bliss.

एवं चिरसमाधिजनितब्रह्मामृतपानपरायणोऽसौ संन्यासी परमहंस अवधूतो भवति। तद्दर्शनेन सकलं जगत्पवित्रं भवति। तत्सेवापरोऽज्ञोऽपि मुक्तो भवति। तत्कुलमेकोत्तरशतं तारयति। तन्मातृपितृजायापत्यवर्गं च मुक्तं भवतीत्युपनिषत्॥ ९॥

"That ascetic who is intent on drinking the nectar of Brahman produced by the long practice of this kind of samādhī, becomes a paramahaṁsa (ascetic) or an avadhūta (naked asetic). By seeing him, all the world becomes pure, and even an illiterate person who serves him is freed from bondage. He (the ascetic) enables the member of his family for one hundred and one generations to cross the ocean of saṁsāra; and his mother, father, wife, and childern— all these are similarly freed. Thus ends the fifth Brāhmaṇa."

ॐ पूर्णमदः .... इति शान्तिः॥

॥इति मण्डलब्राह्मणोपनिषत्समाप्ता॥

***

48. DAKṢIṆĀMŪRTI-UPANIṢAD

दक्षिणामूर्त्यूपनिषद्

This upaniṣad is part and parcel to the tradition of Krṣna Yajurveda. The element of Śiva has been highlighted in this upaniṣad. This upaniṣad is propounded in the form of questionnaire, as a result of questions and answers transacted between the Śaunaka etc. hermit and the sage Mārkaṇḍeya. What has been described initially in this upaniṣad is attainment of the long life by virtue of knowledge of the element of Śiva. Some questions have been raised in order to know the element of Śiva and the sage Mārkaṇḍeya in a rejoinder has preached the most mysterious element of lord Śiva. A description of hymn containing twenty-four letters, nine letters, eighteen letters as also twelve letters has been given in continuance. The loyalty to the hymn king Anuṣṭubha has been explained and it has been made ex-facie clear. The element of Śiva can be known only when a sheer reverence to the hymn is retained within heart. In the concluding hymn, the fruits of perceive and perseverance on upaniṣad has been laid down.

॥शान्तिपाठः॥

ॐ सह नाववतु .... इति शान्तिः॥

ब्रह्मावर्ते महाभाण्डीरवटमूले महासत्राय समेता महर्षयः शौनकादयस्ते ह समित्पाणयस्तत्त्वजिज्ञासवो मार्कण्डेयं चिरंजीविनमुपसमेत्य पप्रच्छुः केन त्वं चिरं जीवसि केन वानन्दमनुभवसीति॥ १॥

Once upon a time, the hermits Śaunaka etc. has commenced a long term offering under a Banyan tree namely Mahābhāṇḍīra in the country of Brahmāvarta. In order to acquire the element of knowledge, these hermits stood on their seat most humbly and raised a question before the long-lived hermit Mārkaṇḍeya. (They asked) O hermit! "How had you acquired the long life and tell us that how you feel the infinite pleasure with your life?"

परमरहस्यशिवतत्त्वज्ञानेनेति स होवाच॥ २॥ किं तत्परमरहस्यशिवतत्त्वज्ञानम्। तत्र को देवः। के मन्त्राः। को जपः। का मुद्रा। का निष्ठा। किं तज्ज्ञानसाधनम्। कः परिकरः। को बलिः। कः कालः। किं तत्स्थानमिति॥ ३॥

He replied that it is the knowledge of most cryptic Śiva's element which has bestowed me with the long life. The hermits again asked– "What is the knowledge of Śiva's element? Who is the god of it? What are the hymns worth-summoning it? What is the Japa (silent recital) for it? What is the posture for recital? What are the precautions required for the recital of Śiva's element? What are the means providing with that knowledge? What are the things required for the recital of Śiva's element? What is the offering prescribed therefore? What is most appropriate time for the recital? What is the suitable premise for attaining to Śiva's element?"

स होवाच। येन दक्षिणामुखः शिवोऽपरोक्षीकृतो भवति तत्परमरहस्यशिवतत्त्वज्ञानम्॥४॥

यः सर्वोपरमे काले सर्वानात्मन्युपसंहृत्य स्वात्मानन्दसुखे मोदते प्रकाशते वा स देवः॥५॥

The hermit Mārkaṇḍeya replied– "The knowledge of most mysterious Śiva's element appears with his southern mouth (Dakṣiṇāmukha). The god of this knowledge element is competent to cover this whole universe within him at the time of great devastation (Mahā Pralaya) and he always live self-luminating and self-enjoying in the soul.

Some examples providing with the perception, the purified knowledge through hymns are being given in the successive hymns.

अत्रैते मन्त्ररहस्यश्लोका भवन्ति। मेधा दक्षिणामूर्तिमन्त्रस्य ब्रह्मा ऋषिः। गायत्री छन्दः। देवता दक्षिणास्यः। मन्त्रेणाङ्गन्यासः॥६॥

The hymns revealing the mystery has been now described. Lord Brahmā is the hermit to this hymn of Dakṣiṇāmūrti knowledge, Gāyatrī is the rhyme and god is Dakṣiṇāmukha. One should summon the hymn on the entire organs of the body.

ॐ आदौ नम उच्चार्य ततो भगवते पदम्। दक्षिणेति पदं पश्चान्मूर्तये पदमुद्धरेत्। अस्मच्छब्दं चतुर्थ्यन्तं मेधां प्रज्ञां पदं वदेत्। प्रमुच्चार्य ततो वायुबीजं च्छं च ततः पठेत्। अग्निजायां ततस्त्वेष चतुर्विंशाक्षरो मनुः॥७॥

The syllable 'Oṁ Namaḥ' should be pronounciated and then the word 'Bhagavate' is to be recited. Therefore in a seriatim, the word Dakṣiṇā, then Mūrtaye, then this singular number of the fourth Pada of the word 'Asmad' i.e. 'Mahyaṁ' and finally the Padas i.e. 'Medhāṁ Prajñāṁ' should be recited. Then the letter 'Pra' and the seed of the wind 'Ya' and the pada 'ccha' and finally the wife of fire i.e. 'Svāhā' Pada should be pronounciated. Thus, this is a Manu hymn containing twenty-four letters.

Thus this hymn in its complete form is– "Oṁ Namo Bhagavate Dakṣiṇāmūrtaye Mahyam Medhām Prajñām Prayaccha Svāhā".

ध्यानम्। स्फटिकरजतवर्णं मौक्तिकीमक्षमालाममृतकलशविद्यां ज्ञानमुद्रां कराग्रे। दधतमुरगकक्ष्यं चन्द्रचूडं त्रिनेत्रं विधृतविविधभूषं दक्षिणामूर्तिमीडे॥८॥

Meditation– I pray Dakṣiṇāmurtaye (lord Śiva) of white complexion analogous to the silver and sphaṭika (a species of gem). Under his possession, the posture of knowledge, the learning that provides with immortal element and Akṣamālā made of pearls lies. He has three eyes, the moon resides on his forehead, the snakes have covered his waist region and he appears in multiform. I meditate on him under this presumption of lord Śiva.

मन्त्रेण न्यासः। आदौ वेदादिमुच्चार्य स्वराद्यं सविसर्गकम्।

पञ्चार्णं तत उद्धृत्य अतरं सविसर्गकम्। अन्ते समुद्धरेत्तारं मनुरेष नवाक्षरः॥९॥

Procedure for summoning the hymn on various organs of the body– firstly, the ab-initio letter of Veda i.e. Oṁ should be recited and used with the Visarga. Then the compound of five letters i.e. Dakṣiṇāmūrtiḥ is to be recited. The Pada 'Atara' with a visarga should be pronounciated and finally the Tara i.e. the Oṁ is to be recited. It is the Manu hymn containing nine letters.

मुद्रां भद्रार्थदात्रीं सपरशुहरिणं बाहुभिर्बाहुमेकं जान्वासक्तं दधानो भुजगवरसमाबद्धकक्ष्यो वटाधः।

आसीनश्चन्द्रखण्डप्रतिघटित जटाक्षीरगौरस्त्रिनेत्रो दद्यादाद्यः शुकाद्यैर्मुनिभिरभिवृतो भावशुद्धिं भवो नः॥ १०॥

We meditate on lord Śaṅkara who is enthroned under the Banyan tree in the posture of keeping his one hand on the pubic region, who has held an axe and the posture of hyena in both hands and the posture of rendering fearlessness through the other hand who has wrapped king Cobra on his waist region and the moon of second day of fortnight (Dvitīya) is enshrined within his hair. His body is as white as the milk, he has three eyes and he is always surrounded by the hermits and saints like Śuka etc. May that god clean our heart and provide us with the benevolence.

मन्त्रेण न्यासः ब्रह्मर्षिन्यासः-तारं ब्लूं नम उच्चार्य मायां वाग्भवमेव च। दक्षिणापदमुच्चार्य ततः स्यान्मूर्तये पदम्॥ ११॥

ज्ञानं देहि पदं पश्चाद्वह्निजायां ततो न्यसेत्। मनुरष्टादशार्णोऽयं सर्वमन्त्रेषु गोपितः॥ १२॥

Now the Manu hymn containing eighteen letters is described. While reciting this hymn, one should very first blutter 'Tāraṁ' i.e. 'Oṁ', then 'Blūm Namaḥ', thereafter the seed of illusion i.e. 'Hrīṅ', seed of speech 'En', 'Dakṣiṇā', 'Mūrtaye' and 'Jñānam Dehi' should be recited respectively. Finally, the pada 'Svāhā' should be recited. Thus the complete hymn so recited is– 'Oṁ Blum Namoh Hrīṅ En Dakṣiṇā Mūrtaye Jñānam Dehi Svāhā'. This hymn is most confidential and mysterious among all hymns.

भस्मव्यापाण्डराङ्गः शशिशकलधरो ज्ञानमुद्राक्षमालावीणापुस्तैर्विराजत्करकमलधरो योगपट्टाभिरामः। व्याख्यापीठे निषण्णो मुनिवरनिकरैः सेव्यमानः प्रसन्नः सव्यालः कृत्तिवासाः सततमवतु नो दक्षिणामूर्तिरीशः॥ १३॥

Meditation– May the lord 'Dakṣiṇāmūrti' always protect us whose entire body has become white owing to smearing the ash, who has held the moon on his head, whose hands are equipped with garland of Rudrākṣa, lyre, holy book and who is in the posture of knowledge. Further, whose complexion is fascinating by the decent towel (which is found with the yogis) and who is enthroned on the chair of Vyāsa.

मन्त्रेण न्यासः। (ब्रह्मर्षिन्यासः)। तारं परां रमाबीजं वदेत्साम्बशिवाय च।

तुभ्यं चानलजायां च मनुर्द्वादशवर्णकः॥ १४॥

वीणां करैः पुस्तकमक्षमालां बिभ्राणमभ्राभगलं वराढ्यम्।

फणीन्द्रकक्ष्यं मुनिभिः शुकाद्यैः सेव्यं वटाधः कृतनीडमीडे॥ १५॥

The hymns for summoning them on different parts of body are in a seriatim 'Oṁ',

'Hrīm', 'Śrīm' (Ramā Bīja), Sāmbaśivāya, Tubhyam and the Svāhā. Thus, twelve letters containing Manu hymn is 'Oṁ Hrīm Śrīm Sāmbaśivāya Tubhyam Svāhā'. (For meditation, it should be presumed that) I pray lord Śaṅkara who have held lyre, holy book and Akṣamālā in his hands, whose one hand is in the posture of fearlessness and whose region of throat is fascinating like the thundering cloud of dark colour, who is greatest among the great king, Cobra is wrapped round the region of his waist, who is seated under Banyan tree and surrounded by the saints like Śuka etc.

विष्णु ऋषिरनुष्टुप् छन्दः। देवता दक्षिणास्यः। मन्त्रेण न्यासः। तारं नमो भगवते तुभ्यं वटपदं ततः। मूलेति पदमुच्चार्य वासिने पदमुद्धरेत्॥१६॥ वागीशाय ततः पश्चान्महाज्ञानपदं ततः। दायिने पदमुच्चार्य मायिने नम उद्धरेत्॥१७॥

'Nyāsa' (summoning the hymn on the different organs) should be performed with the knowledge that the saint to this hymn is lord Viṣṇu, rhyme is Anuṣṭubha and the god is Dakṣiṇāmukha. The seriatim to recite this hymn is– firstly, recital of Oṁ, then 'Namo Bhagavate Tubhyam', then Vaṭa Mūla, then Vāsine, Vāgīśāya, Mahājñāna, Dāyine Māyine and lastly Namaḥ word should be recited. Thus the complete form of the hymn is– 'Oṁ Namo Bhagvate Tubhyam Vaṭamūla Vāsine Vāgīśāya Mahājñāna Dāyine Māyine Namaḥ.'

आनुष्टुभो मन्त्रराजः सर्वमन्त्रोत्तमोत्तमः॥१८॥ ध्यानम्। मुद्रापुस्तकवह्निनागविलसद्बाहुं प्रसन्नाननं मुक्ताहारविभूषणं शशिकलाभास्वत्किरीटोज्ज्वलम्। अज्ञानापहमादिमादिमगिरामर्थं भवानीपतिं न्यग्रोधान्तनिवासिनं परगुरुं ध्यायाम्यभीष्टाप्तये॥१९॥ मौनमुद्रा। सोऽहमिति यावदास्थितिः सा निष्ठा भवति॥२०॥

This is the king hymn 'Anuṣṭubha'. It is supreme among all other hymns. (The procedure for meditation is) we meditate on lord Śiva for attaining to the desired destination who are residing under the Banyan tree, who is the first primitive man, who is looking excellent with hands holding the posture of fearlessness, the book and the dreadful snakes poisonous to the extent fire itself, who is always happy, whose chest is fascinating with the garlands of pulse, who have the crown of moon, who destroy the effect of the ignorance and who cannot be known merely by the words. In the silent posture, the loyalty is only existed when the yogi takes care of the realisation to the effect that 'I myself is that supreme soul' standing life-long.

तदभेदेन मन्त्राम्रेडनं ज्ञानसाधनम्॥२१॥ चित्ते तदेकतानता परिकरः॥२२॥ अङ्गचेष्टार्पणं बलिः॥२३॥ त्रीणि धामानि कालः॥२४॥ द्वादशान्तपदं स्थानमिति॥२५॥

The means of knowledge is a continuos Japa of Manu hymns with the presumption that these hymns are inseparable to the perfect knowledge (Parabrahma). To concentrate on that supreme soul too is the entire material or apparatus for acquiring this knowledge. To establish a perpetual check on the temptations of sensory organs and employing them on the benevolent acts is only the offerings. The three abodes (the ego, the ignorance and the position conscious are in the apparent and micro form) too are the Kāla (time). This hymn with twelve letters too is the real premise as the heart or Sahastrāra is the only premise suitable for attaining the supreme soul.

ते ह पुनः श्रद्दधानास्तं प्रत्यूचुः। कथं वाऽस्योदयः। किं स्वरूपम्। को वाऽस्योपासक इति॥ २६॥

स होवाच। वैराग्यतैलसंपूर्णे भक्तिवर्तिसमन्विते। प्रबोधपूर्णपात्रे तु ज्ञप्तिदीपं विलोकयेत्॥ २७॥

मोहान्धकारे निःसारे उदेति स्वयमेव हि। वैराग्यमरणिं कृत्वा ज्ञानं कृत्वा तु चित्रगुम्॥ २८॥

गाढतामिस्त्रसंशान्त्यै गूढमर्थं निवेदयेत्। मोहभानुजसंक्रान्तं विवेकाख्यं मृकण्डुजम्॥ २९॥

तत्त्वाविचारपाशेन बद्धं द्वैतभयातुरम्। उज्जीवयन्निजानन्दे स्वस्वरूपेण संस्थितः॥ ३०॥

Those hermits again raised a question before sage Mārkaṇḍeya that how does it arise? What is nature? And who is its priest? Saint Yājñavalkya replied– "A lamp of knowledge of the oil of detachment and the Vartikā (the cotton strip) of devotion luminates with the inspiration (fire) of knowledge i.e. the equally omnipresence of divine entity is seen in the form of soul. The knowledge devotion and the detachment are the essential ingredients for perceiving the god. The lamp of the soul automatically starts luminating because with the entrance of these ingredients, the darkness of ignorance is removed forever. One should make endeavour to know the cryptic meaning i.e., the inherent supreme element in order to remove the darkness of ignorance by churning in the sea of detachment through a log of knowledge. The perception of that supreme element is only possible when one has engaged himself for obtaining the knowledge and compliance with the rules of detachment. Thinking on the supreme element too is a string that fastens the Saturn of attachment who is frightened and anxious of the duality which Mārkaṇḍeya in the form of discretion revives by thinking on the supreme element even if trapped by the death. It means thinking on the element of soul gradually establishes the concerned devotee within the supreme soul thereby the supreme pleasure is enjoyed.

शेमुषी दक्षिणा प्रोक्ता सा यस्याभीक्षणे मुखम्। दक्षिणाभिमुखः प्रोक्तः शिवोऽसौ ब्रह्मवादिभिः॥ ३१॥

सर्गादिकाले भगवान्विरिञ्चिरुपास्यैनं सर्गसामर्थ्यमाप्य। तुतोष चित्ते वाञ्छितार्थांश्च लब्ध्वा धन्यः सोऽस्योपासको भवति धाता॥ ३२॥

The wit in the form of element knowledge that luminates the Brahma is called Dakṣinā. It is a gateway or the mouth to perceive the Brahma. This is the reason, the persons knowing Brahma has named it Dakṣiṇāmukha Śiva. The Prajāpati lord Brahmā had worshipped just at the beginning of this creation (Sṛṣṭi) to Dakṣiṇāmukha Śiva. He could get the power to create this universe only as a result of this worship and the blessings that came forward. Thus, lord Brahmā realised the supreme pleasure on completion of his resolution. Hence, Prajāpati Brahma is the only priest by Dakṣiṇāmukha Śiva.

य इमां परमरहस्यशिवतत्त्वविद्यामधीते स सर्वपापेभ्यो मुक्तो भवति।

य एवं वेद स कैवल्यमनुभवतीत्युपनिषत्॥ ३ ३॥

The person who recites this most secret learning i.e., Śiva's element get rid of all evils committed in the previous births and the person who establishes deed identity with it by virtue of continuous thinking and digesting, attains to the emancipation. This is pronounced by this upaniṣad.

॥इति दक्षिणामूर्त्युपनिषत्समाप्ता॥

***

49. ŚARABHA-UPANIṢAD

शरभोपनिषद्

This Upaniṣad is related to the tradition of Atharvaveda. The supremacy of lord Śiva has been described in this Upaniṣad. This Upaniṣad has appeared as a result of questions and answers transacted between the great hermit Paippalāda and Lord Brahmā. This Upaniṣad thus commences with the questions raised by the hermit paippalāda as who is the best along Lord Brahmā, Viṣṇu and Rudra? Lord Brahmā among them. Lord Rudra has once killed Nṛsiṁha in disguise of Śarabha (Śiva) On the same premise having it related to Śarabha (Śiva) this Upaniṣad is called Śarabhopniṣad. The gods prayed Lord Rudra and disguise of Śarabha and thus the supremacy of Śarabha has been confirmed by them. This Upaniṣad also contains the grace of Lord Rudra. The fruit of perceiving the real form of Lord Śhia is also described herein. The subject matter of this Upaniṣad then precedes to the extreme magnificence of Lord Rudra, the unity and uniformity between Lord Viṣṇu and Śiva, the supremacy of Lord Śiva and specific roles regarding preaching of this Upaniṣad. Lastly the magnificence of this Upaniṣad and the fruit of listening to as also perseverance of this Upaniṣad has been described and it is thus concluded.

॥शान्तिपाठः॥

ॐ भद्रं कर्णेभिः......... इति शान्तिः॥

अथ हैनं पैप्पलादो ब्रह्माणमुवाच भो भगवन् ब्रह्मविष्णुरुद्राणां मध्ये को वाऽधिकतरो ध्येयः स्यात्तत्त्वमेव नो ब्रूहीति॥ १॥

The great Ṛṣi Paippalāda once asked Prajāpati– 'O Lord! Kindly make me to know who is the best adorable god among Lords, Brahmā, Viṣṇu and Śiva?'

तस्मै स होवाच पितामहश्च हे पैप्पलाद श्रृणु वाक्यमेतत्॥ २॥

Lord Prajāpati replied– O Paippalāda! Listen to attentively what I am going to tell you.

बहूनि पुण्यानि कृतानि येन तेनैव लभ्यः परमेश्वरोऽसौ।
यस्याङ्गजोऽहं हरिरिन्द्रमुख्या मोहान्न जानन्ति सुरेन्द्रमुख्याः॥ ३॥

That supreme god can be realised when a pile of great deeds are performed. The god from which all was originated, is even unknown to the main gods like Viṣṇu, Indra and Surendra owing to the impact of sheer affection.

प्रभुं वरेण्यं पितरं महेशं यो ब्रह्माणं विदधाति तस्मै।
वेदांश्च सर्वान्प्रहिणोति चाग्र्यं तं वै प्रभुं पितरं देवतानाम्॥ ४॥

That god holds very first, the Lord Brahmā, he is only adorable, sole administrator, creator, the greatest god and he is the supreme god who very first inspire to compare the Vedas. He only is the administrator of all and the creator (father) of all gods.

ममापि विष्णोर्जनकं देवमीड्यं योऽन्तकाले सर्वलोकान्संजहार।
स एकः श्रेष्ठश्च सर्वशास्ता स एव वरिष्ठश्च॥५॥

That god is the creator (father) of Lord Viṣṇu and myself. He destroys this entire world in course of the great devastation (Mahāpralaya). That god is saluted. He is alone the regulating authority, the senior most and the best among all.

यो घोरं वेषमास्थाय शरभाख्यं महेश्वरः। नृसिंहं लोकहन्तारं संजघान महाबलः॥६॥

That Maheśvara, full of supreme power had beheaded Nṛsiṁha by holding a gigantic form of Śarabh.

[The above used statement appears, in exagerated form. In the Pūrvatāpinyupaniṣad, the supreme appeared for creation of this universe has been given a qualitative name of Nṛsiṁha.]

हरिं हरन्तं पादाभ्यामनुयान्ति सुरेश्वराः। मा वधीः पुरुषं विष्णुं विक्रमस्व महानसि॥७॥

When Lord Rudra, the god of all had abducted Lord Viṣṇu by catching him at foot; all gods prayed him that he should have mercy on Lord Viṣṇu and should not slaughter him.

कृपया भगवान्विष्णुं विददार नखैः खरैः। चर्माम्बरो महावीरो वीरभद्रो बभूव ह॥८॥

(Hearing to the pray made by gods) Lord Rudra had badly pierced the body of Lord Viṣṇu by stern blows of his acute nails. That most chivalrous Lord Rudra has been addressed as Vīrabhadra at that time he was put on leather apparel at that moment.

स एको रुद्रो ध्येयः सर्वेषां सर्वसिद्धये। यो ब्रह्मणः पञ्चमवक्त्रहन्ता तस्मै रुद्राय नमो अस्तु॥९॥

Thus only Lord Rudra is adorable to all and he only is endoer of all accomplishments, salute is conveyed to, who had stained the fifth mouth of Lord Brahmā.

यो विस्फुलिङ्गेन ललाटजेन सर्वं जगद्भस्मसात्संकरोति। पुनश्च सृष्ट्वा पुनरप्यरक्षदेवं स्वतन्त्रं प्रकटीकरोति। तस्मै रुद्राय नमो अस्तु॥१०॥

Lord Rudra is saluted who burn into ashes this entire world by setting fire of his third eye existed in the forehead and who is competent to do re-origin and protect it.

यो वामपादेन जघान कालं घोरं पपेऽथो हालाहलं दहन्तम्। तस्मै रुद्राय नमो अस्तु॥११॥

The god who had killed the time (kāla) merely with a blow of left foot and sipped the most fatal poison is saluted. He was Lord Rudra.

यो वामपादार्चितविष्णुनेत्रस्तस्मै ददौ चक्रमतीव हृष्टः। तस्मै रुद्राय नमो अस्तु॥१२॥

The Lord Rudra who had provided Lord Viṣṇu with a discus (Cakra) when Lord Viṣṇu had offered his eyes on his left foot; is saluted.

यो दक्षयज्ञे सुरसङ्घान्विजित्य विष्णुं बबन्धोरगपाशेन वीरः। तस्मै रुद्राय नमो अस्तु॥१३॥

Lord Rudra who had defeated all gods present in the offering arranged by Prajāpati Dakṣa and who had tied Lord Viṣṇu with the card of serpents (Nāgapūśa); is saluted. He is all mighty among gods.

यो लीलयैव त्रिपुरं ददाह विष्णुं कविं सोमसूर्याग्निनेत्रः। सर्वे देवाः पशुतामवापुः स्वयं तस्मात्पशुपतिर्बभूव। तस्मै रुद्राय नमो अस्तु॥ १४॥

We salute Lord Rudra who had three eyes i.e., the sun, moon and the fire, who has skilfully beheaded the monster tripura, who had subjugated all gods and they become animal by which he was call Paśupati.

यो मत्स्यकूर्मादिवराहसिंहान्विष्णुं क्रमन्तं वामनमादिविष्णुम्। विविक्लवं पीड्यमानं सुरेशं भस्मीचकार मन्मथं यमं च। तस्मै रुद्राय नमो अस्तु॥ १५॥

We salute Lord Rudra who is the promoter of Lord Viṣṇu's incarnated forms, like Matsya (fish), Kūrma (tortoise), Varāha (pig), Nṛsiṁha, Vāmana (dwarf), etc., who had made Indra badly tired and who had turned into ashes the god of sex (Kāma) and god of death (Yama).

एवंप्रकारेण बहुधा प्रतुष्टा क्षमापयामासुर्नीलकण्ठं महेश्वरम्॥ १६॥

Thus the gods had asked apology from Maheśvara whose throat is of blue colour, by virtue of submitting a number of prays to him.

तापत्रयसमुद्भूतजन्ममृत्युजरादिभिः। नानाविधानि दुःखानि जहार परमेश्वरः॥ १७॥

That supreme god then decayed the three kinds of pains and the hardship of a number of kinds including the birth, death, old age etc.

एवमङ्गीकरोच्छिवः प्रार्थनं सर्वदेवानाम्। शङ्करो भगवानाद्यो ररक्ष सकलाः प्रजाः॥ १८॥

Thus listening to a number of pray from gods, Lord Śaṅkara accepted them, felt exhilaration and protected the subject as a whole.

यत्पादाम्भोरुहद्वन्द्वं मृग्यते विष्णुना सह। स्तुत्वा स्तुत्यं महेशानमवाङ् मनसगोचरम्। भक्त्या नम्रतनोर्विष्णोः प्रसादमकरोद्विभुः॥ १९॥

Lord Maheśvara, adorable with all kinds of pray, beyond the power of speech, worshipped by Lord Viṣṇu became happy when Lord Viṣṇu saluted him with the great obeisance.

यतो वाचो निवर्तन्ते अप्राप्य मनसा सह। आनन्दं ब्रह्मणो विद्वान्न बिभेति कदाचनेति॥ २०॥

The scholar perceiving the Brahma in the form of pleasure doesn't fall in the alley of fear because to perceive Brahma is a herculion task to which a strong combination of mind and speech too fails to access.

अणोरणीयान्महतो महीयानात्मास्य जन्तोर्निहितो गुहायाम्। तमक्रतुं पश्यति वीतशोको धातुः प्रसादान्महिमानमीशम्॥ २१॥

The Sensitivity of supreme sole in enshrined in the most micro than a molecule as also the most greatest form in the heart cavity of this living sole (organism).

वसिष्ठवैयासकिवामदेवविरिञ्चिमुख्यैर्हृदि भाव्यमानः। सनत्सुजातादिसनातनाद्यैरीड्यो महेशो भगवानादिदेवः॥ २२॥

Lord Maheśvara is the primitive god on which the great hermits like Vasiṣṭha, Vāmadeva, Brahma and Śukadeva are concentrated and as number of prays are summited by hermits like Sanatsujāta, Sanātana etc.

सत्यो नित्यः सर्वसाक्षी महेशो नित्यानन्दो निर्विकल्पो निराख्यः। अचिन्त्यशक्तिर्भगवान्गिरीशः स्वाविद्यया कल्पितमानभूमिः॥ २३॥

Nobody is able to know about the extreme power of Lord Girīśa. That Lord is immortal, truth, evident to all, in the form of perpetual pleasure and beyond the options. We do mere imagination regarding his abode etc. Owing to our ignorance because that Lord is unknown to all is reality and word can't describe his actual existence.

अतिमोहकरी माया मम विष्णोश्च सुव्रत। तस्य पादाम्बुजध्यानाद्दुस्तरा सुतरा भवेत्॥ २४॥

"O great resolute! The illusion (māyā) applied by him is unsurpassable because it enchants Lord Viṣṇu and myself too. One can cross this sphere of illusion only when he meditates on the lotus feet of Lord Rudra.

विष्णुर्विश्वजगद्योनिः स्वांशभूतैः स्वकैः सह। ममांशसंभवो भूत्वा पालयत्यखिलं जगत्॥ २५॥

Lord Viṣṇu only is the god who originates this whole universe. In the company of the creatures as part and parcel of him, he is originated by me and provides this whole universe with maintenance.

विनाशं कालतो याति ततोऽन्यत्सकलं मृषा।

ॐ तस्मै महाग्रासाय महादेवाय शूलिने। महेश्वराय मृडाय तस्मै रुद्राय नमो अस्तु॥ २६॥

Everything in this universe is perished under the cruel clutches of the time (Kāla). By this reason whateven is existed here, that all is false. Lord Mahādeva, the holder of trident and making all creatures the morsel and the god of earth Rudra who always showers with grace on the creatures is saluted.

एको विष्णुर्महद्भूतं पृथग्भूतान्यनेकशः। त्रींल्लोकान्व्याप्य भूतात्मा भुङ्क्ते विश्वभुगव्ययः॥ २७॥

It is only Lord Viṣṇu who is absolutely distinct, great and excellent in all kinds of creations. He enjoys the material pleasures by living within all creatures yet he is integrated and beyond the enjoyments.

चतुर्भिश्च चतुर्भिश्च द्वाभ्यां पञ्चभिरेव च। हूयते च पुनर्द्वाभ्यां स मे विष्णुः प्रसीदतु॥ २८॥

May Lord Viṣṇu begraceful to me, who is offered with morsels (āhuti) in a seriatim of two times, four time two and five as also two time again that is 4+4+2+5+2.

ब्रह्मार्पणं ब्रह्म हविर्ब्रह्माग्नौ ब्रह्मणा हुतम्। ब्रह्मैव तेन गन्तव्यं ब्रह्मकर्मसमाधिना॥ २९॥

The above hymn discusses the procedure of offering (Yajña) in which the gods are summoned and offered with morsel. The shore of Lord Viṣṇu between the whole process of offering has been described herein.

शरा जीवास्तदङ्गेषु भाति नित्यं हरिः स्वयम्। ब्रह्मैव शरभः साक्षान्मोक्षदोऽयं महामुने॥ ३०॥

The morsel offered to Brahma too is Brahma. It is offered in the fire of Brahma and this offering is made by the Brahma too. The process of offering too is Brahma. Hence, only Brahma is worth attainable by the Yogi who is duly meditated.

मायावशादेव देवा मोहिता ममतादिभिः। तस्य माहात्म्यलेशांशं वक्तुं केनाप्यशक्यते॥ ३१॥

The living sole in whose parts of body, Lord Hari himself is residing; called 'śara' hence the Brahma endouer of immensipation foots Brahma.

परात्परतरं ब्रह्म यत्परात्परतो हरिः। परात्परतरो हीशस्तस्मात्तुल्योऽधिको न हि॥ ३२॥

Who can able to describe even a slight magnificence of the god by whose illusion and affection; the gods too are enchanted. Hari is beyond the Parātparabrahma and Īśa is beyond Hari. Therefore nobody is either equal or greater than Īśa.

[The creation and its regulating factors have been revealed in the five categories. The system of development gets perfection and the creation gets perfection when five factors are duly assembled there with. The illusion of world (Jagatprapañca) formed by the five elements is called mortal (kṣara). The Īśvara (immortal) is greater than it, the Brahma (most extended) is beyond to it and Hari (who removes for vice, and be) is beyond to it, while the Īśa (administrator of all) has been told beyond to these all. Thus three orderly evolution of the creation (Sṛṣṭi) and its regalating factors has been described herein with the five forms.]

एक एव शिवो नित्यस्ततोऽन्यत्सकलं मृषा। तस्मात्सर्वान्परित्यज्य ध्येयान्विष्ण्वादिकान्सुरान्॥ ३३

शिव एव सदा ध्येयः सर्वसंसारमोचकः। तस्मै महाग्रासाय महेश्वराय नमः॥ ३४॥

Everything else than Lord Śiva is false and Lord Śiva is only immortal. One should therefore concentrate his mind on Lord Śiva by shrinking it is Lord Śiva who provides the living sole with emancipation. Lord Maheśvara is saluted because he liberates the living soles from the worldly ties and he make as his morsel to all of them (he merges all living organisms with him and cut the time of great devastation.

पैप्पलादं महाशास्त्रं न देयं यस्य कस्यचित्। नास्तिकाय कृतघ्नाय दुर्वृत्ताय दुरात्मने॥ ३५॥ दाम्भिकाय नृशंसाय शठायानृतभाषिणे। सुव्रताय सुभक्ताय सुवृत्ताय सुशीलिने॥ ३६॥ गुरुभक्ताय दान्ताय शान्ताय ऋजुचेतसे। शिवभक्ताय दातव्यं ब्रह्मकर्मोक्तधीमते॥ ३७॥ स्वभक्तायैव दातव्यमकृतघ्नाय सुव्रत। न दातव्यं सदा गोप्यं यत्नेनैव द्विजोत्तम॥ ३८॥

This great Upnaiṣad (learning as obtained by the hermit Paippalāda should not be preached to all. The persons not eligible to this preaching are the ungrateful, atheist, wicked, strewed, egoist, liar, rude and cruel. The eligible persons are– a trace devotee, performer of legal activities, modest, abselient to teacher, bonafied; unactual, spiritual devotee to Lord Śiva, interested for learning Brahma, loyal, philan tropist. In case eligible person is not seen it is better to keep mum in order to protect the holyness of this learning.

एतत्पैप्पलादं महाशास्त्रं योऽधीते श्रावयेद्द्विजः। स जन्ममरणेभ्यो मुक्तो भवति। यो जानीते सोऽमृतत्वं च गच्छति। गर्भवासाद्विमुक्तो भवति। सुरापानात्पूतो भवति। स्वर्णस्तेयात्पूतो भवति। ब्रह्महत्यात्पूतो भवति। गुरुतल्पगमनात्पूतो भवति। स सर्वान्वेदानधीतो भवति। स सर्वान्देवान्ध्यातो भवति। स समस्तमहापातकोपपातकात्पूतो भवति। तस्मादविमुक्तमाश्रितो भवति। स सततं शिवप्रियो भवति। स शिवसायुज्यमेति। न स पुनरावर्तते न स पुनरावर्तते। ब्रह्मैव भवति। इत्याह भगवान्ब्रह्मेत्युपनिषत्।। ३९।।

A person who reads himself and makes the Brāhmaṇas to listen this Upaniṣad, definitely cross the worldly sea where ties like birth and death are existed. The person known to it attains immortality and thus enjoys the liberty from frequent birth through the womb. The persons reciting it is ex-honourated from the heinous crimes like hafting of god, sipping liquor, murder of Brāhmaṇa and cohibition with the wife of his teacher etc. and acquires the fruit of learning all Vedas. He becomes innocent after relieving from the henious and the trivial evils. He attains shelter or Lord Śiva enjoys his regular favour and thus merges with Lord Śiva too. He doesn't fall in the pray of re-birth. He attains the form of Brahma. Thus the Upaniṣad as revealed by Lord Brahmā is concluded.

ॐ भद्रं कर्णेभिः .... इति शान्तिः।।

।।इति शरभोपनिषत्समाप्ता।।

***

50. SKANDA-UPANIṢAD

स्कन्दोपनिषद्

॥शान्तिपाठः॥

ॐ सहनाववतु........ इति शान्तिः॥

अच्युतोऽस्मि महादेव तव कारुण्यलेशतः। विज्ञानघन एवास्मि शिवोऽस्मि किमतः परम्॥ १॥
न निजं निजवद्भात्यन्तःकरणजृम्भणात्। अन्तःकरणनाशेन संविन्मात्रस्थितो हरिः॥ २॥
संविन्मात्रस्थितश्चाहमजोऽस्मि किमतः परम्। व्यतिरिक्तं जडं सर्वं स्वप्रवच्च विनश्यति॥ ३॥
चिज्जडानां तु यो द्रष्टा सोऽच्युतो ज्ञानविग्रहः। स एव हि महादेवः स एव हि महाहरिः॥ ४॥
स एव ज्योतिषां ज्योतिः स एव परमेश्वरः। स एव हि परब्रह्म तद्ब्रह्माहं न संशयः॥ ५॥
जीवः शिवः शिवो जीवः स जीवः केवलः शिवः। तुषेण बद्धो व्रीहिः स्यात्तुषाभावेन तण्डुलः॥ ६॥
एवं बद्धस्तथा जीवः कर्मनाशे सदाशिवः। पाशबद्धस्तथा जीवः पाशमुक्तः सदाशिवः॥ ७॥
शिवाय विष्णुरूपाय शिवरूपाय विष्णवे। शिवस्य हृदयं विष्णुर्विष्णोश्च हृदयं शिवः॥ ८॥
यथा शिवमयो विष्णुरेवं विष्णुमयः शिवः। यथान्तरं न पश्यामि तथा मे स्वस्तिरायुषि॥
यथान्तरं न भेदाः स्युः शिवकेशवयोस्तथा॥ ९॥
देहो देवालयः प्रोक्तः स जीवः केवलः शिवः।

Oṁ. O Mahādeva (Lord of Devas), I am indestructible through a small portion of Your grace. I am replete with Vijñāna. I am Śiva (Bliss). What is higher than It? Truth does not shine as such on account of display of the antaḥkaraṇa (internal organs). Through the destruction of the antaḥkaraṇa, Hari abides as Samvit (Consciousness) alone. As I also am of the form of Samvit, I am without birth. What is higher than It? All inert things being other (than Ātmā) perish like dream. That acyuta (the indestructible or Viṣṇu), who is the seer of the conscious and the inert, is of the form of Jñāna. He only is Mahādeva. He only is Mahā-Hari (Mahā-Viṣṇu). He only is the Jyotis of all Jyotis (or Light of all lights). He only is Parameśvara. He only is Parabrahman. That Brahman I am. There is no doubt (about it). Jīva is Śiva. Śiva is Jīva. That Jīva is Śiva alone. Bound by husk, it is paddy; freed from husk, it is rice. In like manner Jīva is bound (by karma). If karma perishes, he (Jīva) is Sadāśiva. So long as he is bound by the bonds of karma, he is Jīva. If freed from its bonds, then he is Sadāśiva. Prostrations on account of Śiva who is of the form of Viṣṇu, and on account of Viṣṇu who is of the form of Śiva. The heart of Viṣṇu is Śiva. The heart of Śiva is Viṣṇu. As I see no difference (between these two), therefore to me are prosperity and life. There is no difference between Śiva and Keśava (Viṣṇu). The body is said to be the divine temple. The Śiva (in the body) is the God Sadāśiva (in the temple).

त्यजेदज्ञाननिर्माल्यं सोऽहंभावेन पूजयेत्॥ १०॥

अभेददर्शनं ज्ञानं ध्यानं निर्विषयं मनः। स्नानं मनोमलत्यागः शौचमिन्द्रियनिग्रहः॥ ११॥

ब्रह्मामृतं पिबेद्भैक्षमाचरेद्देहरक्षणे। वसेदेकान्तिको भूत्वा चैकान्त द्वैतवर्जिते।

इत्येवमाचरेद्धीमान्स एवं मुक्तिमाप्नुयात्॥ १२॥

श्रीपरमधाम्ने स्वस्ति चिरायुष्योन्नम इति। विरिञ्चिनारायणशंकरात्मकं नृसिंह देवेश तव प्रसादतः। अचिन्त्यमव्यक्तमनन्तमव्ययं वेदात्मकं ब्रह्म निजं विजानते॥ १३॥

Having given up the cast-off offerings of ajñāna, one should worship Him with the thought "I am He". To see (oneself) as not different (from Him) is (jñāna) wisdom. To make the mind free from sensual objects is dhyāna (meditation). The giving up of the stains of the mind is Snāna (bathing). The subjugation of the senses is śauca (cleansing). The nectar of Brahman should be drunk. For the upkeep of the body, one should go about for alms and eat. He should dwell alone in a solitary place without a second. He should be with the sole thought of the non-dual One. The wise person who conducts himself thus, attains salvation. Prostrations on account of Sarīmat Param-Jyotis (Supreme Light) abode! May prosperity and long life attend (me). O Narasiṁha! O Lord of Devas! through Your grace, persons cognize the true nature of Brahman that is unthinkable, undifferentiated, endless, and immutable, through the forms of the Gods, Brahmā, Nārāyaṇa and Śaṅkara.

तद्विष्णोः परमं पदं सदा पश्यन्ति सूरयः। दिवीव चक्षुराततम्॥ १४॥

तद्विप्रासो विपन्यवो जागृवांसः समिन्धते। विष्णोर्यत्परमं पदमित्येतन्निर्वाणानुशासनमिति वेदानुशासनमिति वेदानुशासनमित्युपनिषत्॥ १५॥

Like the eye (which sees without any obstacle the things) spread in the ākāśa so the wise always see the supreme abode of Viṣṇu. Brāhmaṇas with divine eyes who are always spiritually awake, praise in diverse ways and illuminate the supreme abode of Viṣṇu. Thus is the teaching of the Vedas for salvation.

॥इति स्कन्दोपनिषत्समाप्ता॥

***

51. ADVAYATĀRAKOPANIṢAD

अद्वयतारकोपनिषद्

"Rāja Yoga" has been described in detail in this Upaniṣad which is related to Śukla Yajurveda. Its consequence has been discussed as the attainment of Brahma. The measure of exercising "Yoga" and its results has been discussed very first while making resolution to explain the "Tārakayoga". Subsequently, the nature of "Tāraka", the method of investigating the trio-aims, internal aim, exterior aim and the middle aim have been described alongwith their characteristics. Apart from it, the nature of two kinds of Tāraka, achievement of the tārakayoga, the nature of tārakayoga, Sambhan Mudrā (posture), the option of internal aim, characteristics of the teacher and finally the fruits of listening to upaniṣad has been described.

Thus, an endeavour (penance) to attain "Tāraka Brahma" has been furnished as an easiest measure for making oneself liberate from all worldly ties.

॥शान्तिपाठः॥

ॐ पूर्णमदः पूर्णमिदं पूर्णात्पूर्णमुदच्यते।

पूर्णस्य पूर्णमादाय पूर्णमेवावशिष्यते॥

ॐ शान्तिः शान्तिः शान्तिः॥

The perfect knowledge (Parabrahma) expressed as "Oṁ" is absolute from all angles and this creation (Sṛṣṭi) is also perfect in itself. This whole (complete) universe has been originated from that perfect element. In case this perfection is extracted out from that perfect element, the resultant or the residual part also remains perfect. May the fevers and fatigues of material, metaphysical and celestial be cooled-down.

अथातोऽद्वयतारकोपनिषदं व्याख्यास्यामो यतये जितेन्द्रियाय शमदमादिषड्गुणपूर्णाय॥ १॥

Now, the explanation on Advayatārakopaniṣad is made for the devotees full of command on sensory organs and of well-balanced temperament (Śama) etc. six merits, the hermits, recluse and for them who have extreme control on their senses.

चित्स्वरूपोऽहमिति सदा भावयन्सम्यङ् निमीलिताक्षः किंचिदुन्मीलिताक्षो वान्तर्दृष्ट्या भ्रूदहरादुपरि सच्चिदानन्दतेजःकूटरूपं परंब्रह्मावलोकयंस्तद्रूपो भवति॥ २॥

He merges with Brahma by keeping his eyes close or half-opened to establish an spirit at the upper place of brows as– "I am in garb of the heart" and by feeling true pleasure and observes Brahma in the light of that pleasure undeviated.

गर्भजन्मजरामरणसंसारमहद्भयात्संतारयति तस्मात्तारकमिति। जीवेश्वरौ मायिकौ विज्ञाय सर्वविशेषं नेति नेतीति विहाय यदवशिष्यते तदद्वयं ब्रह्म॥ ३॥

Tāraka Brahma is considered what is perfect knowledge (Brahma) with excellent splendour and save from womb, birth, old age, death and murder like sins. Assuming the living-organisms and god both covered by the illusion (Māyā) who abandons all others by saying "it is unlimited" (Neti-Neti), can attain the residual i.e. "one or unique Brahma". (The residual after abandoning material ties is the true and purified knowledge).

तत्सिद्ध्यै लक्ष्यत्रयानुसंधानः कर्तव्यः॥ ४॥

In order to avail the shelter of that perfect knowledge (Parabrahma), the research of three aims is only the act possible.

देहमध्ये ब्रह्मनाडी सुषुम्ना सूर्यरूपिणी पूर्णचन्द्राभा वर्तते। सा तु मूलाधारादारभ्य ब्रह्मरन्ध्रगामिनी भवति। तन्मध्ये तडित्कोटिसमानकान्त्या मृणालसूत्रवत्सूक्ष्माङ्गी कुण्डलिनीति प्रसिद्धास्ति। तां दृष्ट्वा मनसैव नरः सर्वपापविनाशद्वारा मुक्तो भवति। फालोर्ध्वगललाटविशेषमण्डले निरन्तरं तेजस्तारकयोगविस्फुरणेन पश्यति चेत्सिद्धो भवति। तर्जन्यग्रान्मीलितकर्णरन्ध्रद्वये तत्र फूत्कारशब्दो जायते। तत्र स्थिते मनसि चक्षुर्मध्यगतनीलज्योतिःस्थलं विलोक्यान्तर्दृष्ट्या निरतिशयसुखं प्राप्नोति। एवं हृदये पश्यति। एवमन्तर्लक्ष्यलक्षणं मुमुक्षुभिरुपास्यम्॥ ५॥

In the middle part of the body of that Yogī, the Brahma nerve "suṣumnā" (spinal nerve) is luminated with the light of moon. It is extended from Mūlādhāra (at the anus and in the middle of genital organs) to the brahmarandhra (where the spinal cord penetrates into brain). In the middle portion of this nerve, the micro shaped Kuṇḍalinī is existed. This "Kuṇḍalinī" is shining like crores of electric currents. The man becomes entitle to avail emancipation by exoneration of all sins committed. The person who sees regularly the splendour existed in the specific region on the brain, becomes a perfect devotee and achieves the desired success. By keeping close the holes of both ears by the tips of the index fingers a hissing sound (like that of a snake) is heard. By focusing the mind and observing the blue flame in the middle of eyes, most pleasure is felt. The same is observed in the heart too. The devotee keeping the desire for emancipation (Mumukṣu) should exercise the "inner aims" (worth feeling in the heart).

[The man gets impetus to commit crime due to attachment for the extraneous pleasures. This tendency to commit an offence arises on the basis of the above attachments. On being observance through to the competency of the Kuṇḍalinī existing in the heart, man becomes confident that the source of pleasure lies in the heart. This is the reason the offensive tendency does not emerge for the extraneous achievements.]

अथ बहिर्लक्ष्यलक्षणं नासिकाग्रे चतुर्भिः षड्भिरष्टभिर्दशभिर्द्वादशभिः क्रमादङ्गुलान्ते नीलद्युतिश्यामत्वसदृग्रक्तभङ्गीस्फुरत्पीतशुक्लवर्णद्वयोपेतव्योम यदि पश्यति स तु योगी भवति। चलदृष्ट्या व्योमभागवीक्षितुः पुरुषस्य दृष्ट्यग्रे ज्योतिर्मयूखा वर्तन्ते। तद्दर्शनेन योगी भवति। तप्तकाञ्चनसंकाशज्योतिर्मयूखा अपाङ्गान्ते भूमौ वा पश्यति तद्दृष्टिः स्थिरा भवति। शीर्षोपरि द्वादशाङ्गुलसमीक्षितुरमृतत्वं भवति। यत्र कुत्र स्थितस्य शिरसि व्योमज्योतिर्दृष्टं चेत्स तु योगी भवति॥ ६॥

Now, the characteristics of extraneous aim" are described. He is called the real Yogī who can regularly see the element of ether, of colour yellowish white, the ether of reddish colour, blue and dark colour from a distance from the point of nose to four, six, eight, ten or twelve fingers respectively. By observing in ether (the void place) by that dynamic sight, the rays of light are seen apparently clear. A Yogī can only see those divine rays. When in the both corners of eyes, the ray of light (Mayūkha) is seen like the hot gold, his sight then is concentrated. The "Yogī" attains immortality who sees that ray at a distance of twelve fingers. The person who sees that ray from ether irrespective of the distance above head, become the perfect Yogī.

अथ मध्यलक्ष्यलक्षणं प्रातश्चित्रादिवर्णाखण्डसूर्यचक्रवद्वह्निज्वालावलीवत्तद्विहीनान्तरिक्षवत्पश्यति। तदाकाराकारितयावतिष्ठति। तद्भूयोदर्शनेन गुणरहिताकाशं भवति। विस्फुरत्तारकाकारसंदीप्यमानागाढतमोपमं परमाकाशं भवति। कालानलसमद्योतमानं महाकाशं भवति। सर्वोत्कृष्टपरमद्युतिप्रद्योतमानं तत्त्वाकाशं भवति। कोटिसूर्यप्रकाशवैभवसंकाशं सूर्याकाशं भवति। एवं बाह्याभ्यन्तरस्थव्योमपञ्चकं तारकलक्ष्यम्। तद्दर्शी विमुक्तफलस्तादृग्व्योमसमानो भवति। तस्मात्तारक एव लक्ष्यममनस्कफलप्रदं भवति॥ ७॥

We now describe the characteristics of the "middle aim". Who sees the integrated sun in the colours, citra etc. and in the circular shape, like the flame of fire and the space without them, becomes analogous to that shape and enshrined the same way. Further, he becomes ether form merely by observing him (sun). He is luminated with the stars and becomes supreme ether like the dark of the dawn. The "Great Ether" (Māhākāśa) is luminated as the fire of the time (Kālāgni). The "element of ether" is of the best light and acute flame. The "ether of sun" (Sūryākāśa) is analogous to the crore suns. The fire ethers thus, enshrined externally and internally are the aims of the "tāraka-brahma". The observer of sky through this procedure, becomes entitle to emancipation by cutting-off all ties like the ether itself. The aim of Tāraka has been said endower with un-imagined fruits.

तत्तारकं द्विविधं पूर्वार्धतारकमुत्तरार्धममनस्कं चेति। तदेष श्लोको भवति। तद्योगं च द्विधा विद्धि पूर्वोत्तरविधानतः। पूर्वं तु तारकं विद्यादमनस्कं तदुत्तरमिति॥ ८॥

Two methods of this "tāraka yoga" has been explained. The first is the half-first and second is second-successive. The hymn referred to it in this context is– "This yoga is of two kinds the first is the first-half and the other is the second-half. The former has been said "Tāraka" and the later Amanaska (void mind)."

अक्ष्यन्तस्तारयोश्चन्द्रसूर्यप्रतिफलनं भवति। तारकाभ्यां सूर्यचन्द्रमण्डलदर्शनं ब्रह्माण्डमिव पिण्डाण्डशिरोमध्यस्थाकाशे रवीन्दुमण्डलद्वितयमस्तीति निश्चित्य तारकाभ्यां तद्दर्शनमात्राण्युभयैक्यदृष्ट्या मनोयुक्तं ध्यायेत्। तद्योगाभावे इन्द्रियप्रवृत्तेरनवकाशात्। तस्मादन्तर्दृष्ट्या तारक एवानुसंधेयः॥ ९॥

We see the sun and moon by our tāraka (cornea). As we see the sun and moon in this universe (Brahmāṇḍa), we should in the similar fashion, always observe the sun and moon under presumption, in the middle of our head in the form of universe and considering them of the same form, ponder upon them with concentration because all sensory organs start engrossing in luxuries if such is not presumed. It is therefore, necessary for a devotee that he should develop a trend to research regularly the Tāraka through his intuition.

तत्तारकं द्विविधं मूर्तितारकममूर्तितारकं चेति। यदिन्द्रियान्तं तन्मूर्तिमत्। यद्भ्रूयुगातीतं तदमूर्तिमत्। सर्वत्रान्त:पदार्थविवेचने मनोयुक्ताभ्यास इष्यते तारकाभ्यां सदूर्ध्वस्थ सत्त्वदर्शनान्मनोयुक्तेनान्तरीक्षणेन सच्चिदानन्दस्वरूपं ब्रह्मैव। तस्माच्छुक्लतेजोमयं ब्रह्मेति सिद्धम्। तद्ब्रह्म मन:सहकारिचक्षुषान्तर्दृष्ट्या वेद्यं भवति। एवममूर्तितारकमपि मनोयुक्तेन चक्षुषैव दहरादिकं वेद्यं भवति रूपग्रहणप्रयोजनस्य मनश्चक्षुरधीनत्वाद्बाह्यवदान्तरेऽप्यात्ममनश्चक्षु:संयोगेनैव रूपग्रहणकार्योदयात्। तस्मान्मनोयुक्तान्तर्दृष्टिस्तारक-प्रकाशा भवति॥ १०॥

Two methods have been told for this "tāraka". The first is tangible and the other is intangible. Whatever in the mind is called tangible Tāraka and the Tāraka existing outside both brows is intangible. While discussing about the inner matters, one should do the exercise through concentration. By analysis regularly in ones heart (full of Satva merit), the luminating perfect Brahma in garb of true pleasure above the both cornea of eyes is seen. It reveals that the Brahma is full of splendour and in white colour. That Brahma should be seen by intuition of the eyes. It makes able to know that the Brahma is full of splendour and white colour. The intangible Tāraka too, is known through the same process of the mind's eyes. The mind is dependent to the eyes in the matter of seeing the complexion. Analogous to the external, the internal cognisance of the complexion is also made by these two. This is the reason, the light of Tāraka becomes by the eyes including the mind.

भ्रूयुगमध्यबिले दृष्टिं तद्द्वारोर्ध्वस्थिततेज आविर्भूतं तारकयोगो भवति। तेन सह मनोयुक्तं तारकं सुसंयोज्य प्रयत्नेन भ्रूयुग्मं सावधानतया किंचिदूर्ध्वमुत्क्षेपयेत्। इति पूर्वभागी तारकयोग:। उत्तरं त्वमूर्तिमदमनस्कमित्युच्यते। तालुमूलोर्ध्वभागे महान् ज्योतिर्मयूखो वर्तते। तद्योगिभिर्ध्येयम्। तस्मादणिमादिसिद्धिर्भवति॥ ११॥

The man who sees the light with splendour a little above the place where both brows are by his intuition, is the Tāraka Yogī. By establishing the fair union of "tāraka" with the mind, both brows should be stayed above a little distance. This is called the first-half of Tāraka. The second-half portion is called intangible. Above the root of palate a great circle of rays is existed. The meditation of the same is the aim of yogis. It is the cause for the axioms like Aṇimā etc.

अन्तर्बाह्यलक्ष्ये दृष्टौ निमेषोन्मेषवर्जितायां सत्यां शांभवी मुद्रा भवति। तन्मुद्रारूढज्ञानिनिवासाद्भूमि: पवित्रा भवति। तद्दृष्ट्या सर्वे लोका: पवित्रा भवन्ति। तादृशपरमयोगिपूजा यस्य लभ्यते सोऽपि मुक्तो भवति॥ १२॥

When the sight (power to observe) competent to see the internal and external aim becomes stable, this stage is called the Śambhavī Mudrā (Posture). The residence of the scholar, having this posture is treated very sacrosanct. and all worlds become sacred only by his single sight. The worshipper of this supreme Yogī, becomes entitle to emancipation.

अन्तर्लक्ष्यजलज्योतिः स्वरूपं भवति। परमगुरूपदेशेन सहस्रारे जलज्योतिर्वा बुद्धिगुहानिहितज्योतिर्वा षोडशान्तस्थतुरीयचैतन्यं वान्तर्लक्ष्यं भवति। तद्दर्शनं सदाचार्यमूलम्॥ १३॥

The internal aim turns into a white flame. The internal aim (Antarlakṣya) is existed within the sixteen arts or the flame existing in the cavity of wit or the luminating flame existed in the lotus of thousand petals and it is known only when the supreme teacher graces with his teaching. This philosophy is the root of etiquette.

आचार्यो वेदसम्पन्नो विष्णुभक्तो विमत्सरः। योगज्ञो योगनिष्ठश्च सदा योगात्मकः शुचिः॥ १४॥

गुरुभक्तिसमायुक्तः पुरुषज्ञो विशेषतः। एवं लक्षणसंपन्नो गुरुरित्यभिधीयते॥ १५॥

The person known to Vedas, enlightened, devotee to lord Viṣṇu, liberated from the defect like manipulation etc. expert in yoga, loyal to yoga, yogātma (devotee to yoga), sacrosanct, obedient to teacher and specially engaged in the attainment of god is called a teacher by virtue of all these characteristics.

गुशब्दस्त्वन्धकारः स्याद्रुशब्दस्तन्निरोधकः। अन्धकारनिरोधित्वाद्गुरुरित्यभिधीयते॥ १६॥

The literal meaning of "gu" letter is darkness and "ru" means competent to resist the darkness. Therefore, the composite meaning of the word "Guru" is a person who drives away the ignorance.

गुरुरेव परं ब्रह्म गुरुरेव परा गतिः। गुरुरेव परा विद्या गुरुरेव परायणम्॥ १७॥

Guru is the supreme soul and supreme Brahma (knowledge). Teacher (Guru) too is the supreme motion, he is Parāvidyā (metaphysics) and he is the best shelter.

गुरुरेव परा काष्ठा गुरुरेव परं धनम्। यस्मात्तदुपदेष्टासौ तस्माद्गुरुतरो गुरुरिति॥ १८॥

Teacher (guru) is the climax and the supreme wealth. It should be presumed that the person who preaches the best is the best teacher or the teacher of the teachers.

यः सकृदुच्चारयति तस्य संसारमोचनं भवति। सर्वजन्मकृतं पापं तत्क्षणादेव नश्यति। सर्वान्कामानवाप्नोति। सर्वपुरुषार्थसिद्धिर्भवति। य एवं वेदेत्युपनिषत्॥ १९॥

The person who once recite this upaniṣad or guru, crosses peacefully this worldly ocean. The sins accumulated since birth are decayed. All desires and ambitions are fulfilled. All industry meet success and achievement. The person known to this is the real scholar of upaniṣad. This is the upaniṣad, a sole cause for all achievements.

ॐ पूर्णमदः .... इति शान्तिः॥

॥इति अद्वयतारकोपनिषत्समाप्ता॥

***

52. RĀMAPŪRVATĀPINYU-UPANIṢAD

रामपूर्वतापिन्यूपनिषद्

This Upaniṣad is related to the tradition of Atharvaveda. It reveals the elemental form of Lord Rāma. There are five divisions made in this Upaniṣad which also are called Upaniṣad themselves. In the first Upaniṣad, the meaning of Lord Rāma has been duly explained. Subsequently, the contents of this Upaniṣad proceeds as an imagination of exclusive devotion necessary for the devotees, the exhilaration of Lord Rāma through Japa of hymns and worship of Yantra. In the second Upaniṣad, the key word (bīja) Rāma has been enumerated as omnipresent and residing in all souls. In the third Upaniṣad, the hymn and Yantrās for the worship of Lord Rāma and goddess Sītā has been described. In the fourth Upaniṣad, the content proceeds as the meaning of Rāma hymns containing six letters, the prays submitted by gods to Lord Rāma, the prosperity while Rāma was enthroned, the method of writing, Rāmayantra, the seriatim of the garland hymn and the worship of Yantra. Lastly in the fifth Upaniṣad, the manner of worshipping the piṭha (Yantrpiṭha) including the purity of soul (Bhūta śuddhi and the provision of the icon worship has been enumerated. Thus, the Upaniṣad is concluded with referring to the desired doctrine for attaining to emancipation by virtue of the grace of Lord Rāma.

॥शान्तिपाठः॥

ॐ भद्रं कर्णेभिः .... इति शान्तिः॥

॥प्रथमोपनिषद्॥

चिन्मयेऽस्मिन्महाविष्णौ जाते दशरथे हरौ। रघोः कुलेऽखिलं राति राजते यो महीस्थितः॥ १॥

स राम इति लोकेषु विद्वद्भिः प्रकटीकृतः। राक्षसा येन मरणं यान्ति स्वोद्रेकतोऽथवा॥ २॥

रामनाम भुवि ख्यातमभिरामेण वा पुनः। राक्षसान्मर्त्यरूपेण राहुर्मनसिजं यथा॥ ३॥

प्रभाहीनांस्तथा कृत्वा राज्यार्हाणां महीभृताम्। धर्ममार्गं चरित्रेण ज्ञानमार्गं च नामतः॥ ४॥

तथा ध्यानेन वैराग्यमैश्वर्यं स्वस्य पूजनात्। तथा रात्यस्य रामाख्या भुवि स्यादथ तत्त्वतः॥ ५॥

रमन्ते योगिनोऽनन्ते नित्यानन्दे चिदात्मनि। इति रामपदेनासौ परं ब्रह्माभिधीयते॥ ६॥

Lord Hari Mahāviṣṇu had appeared in the most renowned clan of Raghu on this earth in Daśaratha's house. Rāma is who was the all-giver (*rā-ti*), who rules (*rā-jate*) over the kingdom of earth (*ma-hī*). The wise ones had given him the name of *Rā-ma* (Rāma) in this world, because the profusion of his power, who kills the monsters approaching to death owing to their evil doings. He became famous as Rāma on this earth because of loveliness (*abhi-rāma*). (He was the cause of pleasure and relief for all hearts). He is Rāma because he had eradicated the clan of monsters in the namely form and the same way as the demon head (Rāhu) gobbles up the shining complexion of moon. He is Rāma, because he leads to the path of religion to the kings and rulership (rā) by the submission of his ideal character and he leads to the way of knowledge to the person reciting his name. He endows with the emancipation when concentration is made and prosperity when his icon is duly worshipped. Perhaps this was the cause for his popularity as Rāma on this earth. It is, indeed, effect that the supreme god Parabrahman is known with this name of Rāma on which the Yogins delight (*ra-mante*) in him, and who is in itself endless, everlasting pleasure and supreme soul in the form of Cid.

चिन्मयस्याद्वितीयस्य निष्कलस्याशरीरिणः। उपासकानां कार्यार्थं ब्रह्मणो रूपकल्पना॥७॥

The supreme soul in the form of Cid is unique, Niṣkala (spotless) and without the physical body but such in tangible and invisible Brahma appears in a physical body in order to fulfil the desires of devotees.

रूपस्थानां देवतानां पुंस्त्र्यङ्गास्त्रादिकल्पना। द्विचत्वारिषडष्टानां दश द्वादश षोडश॥८॥
अष्टादशामी कथिता हस्ताः शङ्खादिभिर्युताः। सहस्रान्तास्तथा तासां वर्णवाहनकल्पना॥९॥
शक्तिसेनाकल्पना च ब्रह्मण्येवं हि पञ्चधा। कल्पितस्य शरीरस्य तस्य सेनादिकल्पना॥१०॥

The gods existing in the form of supreme god too has been imagined in the form of men, women, parts, weapons etc. In the various visible forms of supreme Lord, an imagination of being his two, six, eight, ten, twelve, sixteen and eighteen hands which with a variety of insignia, conches and others are furnished. He has many thousand hands when he holds the gigantic form. One attributes to them also colour, weapons, powers and military forces. In the perfect Brahma (in the form of Lord Viṣṇu, Śiva, Durgā, Sun and Ganeśa etc. five kinds of bodies and their distinct army etc. has been imagined.

ब्रह्मादीनां वाचकोऽयं मन्त्रोऽन्वर्थादिसंज्ञकः। जप्तव्यो मन्त्रिणा नैवं विना देवः प्रसीदति॥११॥
क्रियाकर्मेज्याकर्तॄणामर्थं मन्त्रो वदत्यथ। मननात्त्राणनान्मन्त्रः सर्ववाच्यस्य वाचकः॥१२॥
सोऽभयस्यास्य देवस्य विग्रहो यन्त्रकल्पना। विना यन्त्रेण चेत्पूजा देवता न प्रसीदति॥१३॥

The Rāma hymn is according to its meaning as it tells all about from Brahmā to the entire inert and sensitive world. Lord Rāma is pleased when the devotee makes Japa (silent recital) of this hymn under compliance with the procedure made. The devotees arranging ceremonies for hymn for a particular accomplishment, the objective inherent to the ambition is an ex-phasi in the hymn (viz., every hymn consistent with the ambition reveals the clarity of the purpose). As the hymn is recited and duly protected, it is an orator to all orations.

सोऽभयस्यास्य देवस्य विग्रहो यन्त्रकल्पना। विना यन्त्रेणा चेत्पूजा देवता न प्रसीदति॥१३॥

That hymn is in the form of Yantra (diagram) describing to nature of Parabrahma, is the form of Rāma who drives away all fears. Do not worship without a diagram, if the deity is to be gracious to you.

॥द्वितीयोपनिषद्॥

स्वर्भूर्ज्योतिर्मयोऽनन्तरूपी स्वेनैव भासते। जीवत्वेन समो यस्य सृष्टिस्थितिलयस्य च॥ १॥

कारणत्वेन चिच्छक्त्या रज:सत्त्वतमोगुणै:। यथैव वटबीजस्थ: प्राकृतश्च महान्द्रुम:॥ २॥

तथैव रामबीजस्थं जगदेतच्चराचरम्। रेफारूढा मूर्तय: स्यु: शक्तयस्तिस्र एव चेति॥ ३॥

The formula *'Rāma Rāmāya namaḥ'*

As the perfect Brahma appears automatically, it is called self-born (Svabhū). He is full of light as it is illumined by its own light. Irrespective of being in the physical form, he is endless. He luminates with his own power. He is existed in the form of living soul within all creatures by virtue of its sensitivity and becomes the cause for the creation, maintenance and the merger through the Sattva, Rajas and Tamas properties. As the fig seed already contains the large grown up tree, so the germ of the word *Rāma* contains the whole animate world in it. The three forms of Brahmā, Viṣṇu and Maheśa are stood on the premise of 'R' letter applied with the world Rāma and the three forces too, (*i.e.* power of creation, sustenance and destruction).

॥तृतीयोपनिषद्॥

सीतारामौ तन्मयावत्र पूज्यौ जातान्याभ्यां भुवनानि द्विसप्त।

स्थितानि च प्रहितान्येव तेषु ततो रामो मानवो माययाऽधात्॥ १॥

जगत्प्राणायात्मनेऽस्मै नम: स्यान्नमस्त्वैक्यं प्रवदेत्प्राग्गुणेनेति॥ २॥

Worship Sītā and Rāma as arising out of it and from them proceeds the creation, sustenance and destruction. The fourteen worlds has been originated from them. These Bhuvanas are dependent to both of them and merges with them also. Lord Rāma had made him to appear by virtue of his power of illusion (Māyā). Salutation to him, the Ātman, the world-breath! Praise his oneness with the primordial Guṇas.

॥चतुर्थोपनिषद्॥

जीववाची नमो नाम चात्मा रामेति गीयते। तदात्मिका या चतुर्थी तथा चायेति गीयते॥ १॥

मन्त्रोऽयं वाचको रामो वाच्य: स्याद्योग एतयो:। फलदश्चैव सर्वेषां साधकानां न संशय:॥ २॥

यथा नामी वाचकेन नाम्नो योऽभिमुखो भवेत्। तथा बीजात्मको मन्त्रो मन्त्रिणोऽभिमुखोभवेत्॥

The word *Namaḥ* here means Jīva. The word *Rāma* means the Ātman; but the dative in– *āya* (*caturthī*-Rāmāya) aims at the con-substantiality of the two. Lord Rāma is the subject to the hymn Rāmāya Namaḥ. The concentration of the mind on such form of Lord simultaneous to the silent recital of formula fulfils the desire of devotees and there is no scope left for the doubt of those who use it. Just as a person bearing a name, turns towards the one who calls by that name, so also the formula, budding from the germ, turns towards him who employs it. [Lord Rāma immediately appears before the devotee who summons him through the seed hymn as described above.]

बीजशक्तिं न्यसेद्दक्षवामयोः स्तनयोरपि। कीलो मध्ये विना भाव्यः स्ववाञ्छाविनियोगवान्॥ ४॥

One should wear the Germ and the Force on the right and the left breast; and the Kīlaka 'Yama' on the heart. Simultaneous to it, the devotee should do Viniyoga (to drop the water from palm) for attaining to the desired accomplishment.

सर्वेषामेव मन्त्राणामेष साधारणः क्रमः। अत्र रामोऽनन्तरूपस्तेजसा वह्निना समः॥ ५॥

The same procedure is commonly adopted for the successful application of all formulas in course of concentration and thinking one should firmly stand on the presumption that being eternal, here on earth too Rāma is like fire in lustre.

स त्वनुष्णगुविश्वश्चेदग्नीषोमात्मकं जगत्। उत्पन्नः सीतया भाति चन्द्रश्चन्द्रिकया यथा॥ ६॥

The Agniṣomātmaka (the male and female form) world is perceived when Rāma is in the company of Sītā who is illuminated by the light of modesty. He glows along with Sītā, like the moon with the moon-light.

प्रकृत्या सहितः श्यामः पीतवासा जटाधरः। द्विभुजः कुण्डली रत्नमाली धीरो धनुर्धरः॥ ७॥

प्रसन्नवदनो जेता धृष्ट्यष्टकविभूषितः। प्रकृत्या परमेश्वर्या जगद्योन्याङ्किताङ्कभृत्॥ ८॥

Rāma with his ever exhilarating power Sītā is adorned fascinatingly. His complexion is dark, he puts on a yellow garment, he has matted hairs. Two-armed, with ear-rings and pearl-strings, he sits there, wielding a bow on shoulder. He is always of cheerful countenance and confident of victory. He is adorned with the eight accomplishments of luxuries i.e. Aṇimā etc. Goddess Sītā in the form of causative nature, the origin of this universe is adorned in his left.

हेमाभया द्विभुजया सर्वालंकृतया चिता। श्लिष्टः कमलधारिण्या पुष्टः कोसलजात्मजः॥ ९॥

दक्षिणे लक्ष्मणेनाथ सधनुष्पाणिना पुनः। हेमाभेनानुजेनैव तथा कोणत्रयं भवेत्॥ १०॥

The goddess Sītā has a golden complexion, two arms adorned with all divine ornaments and she has held a lotus flower in her hand. Kauśalyā's son is made happy embraced with both arms by her. To his right stands Lakṣmaṇa, wielding a bow in hand. His younger brother, gold-hued, thus a triangle shaped structure is formed

तथैव तस्य मन्त्रस्य यस्याणुश्च स्वङेन्तया। एवं त्रिकोणरूपं स्यात्तं देवा ये समाययुः॥ ११॥

स्तुतिं चक्रुश्च जगतः पतिं कल्पतरौ स्थितम्। कामरूपाय रामाय नमो मायामयाय च॥ १२॥

नमो वेदादिरूपाय ओङ्काराय नमो नमः। रमाधराय रामाय श्रीरामायात्ममूर्तये॥ १३॥

जानकीदेहभूषाय रक्षोघ्नाय शुभाङ्गिने। भद्राय रघुवीराय दशास्यान्तकरूपिणे॥ १४॥

Similar is the case with the formula : The end, the name and the dative give it too, a triangular form. [The hymn containing six letters is formed i.e. 'Rām Rāmāya Namaḥ' is formed when Sva i.e. Rāma's fourth classification is added with Jīva].

The ruler of this world Rāma enshrined on the throne studded with gems under the Kalpavṛkṣa was prayed by these gods– "We salute Lord Rāma, who is in the form of cupid or taking form at will and him possessed of magical powers! We salute Rāma who is in the form of Oṁ, the initial cause for composition of Vedas. We salute Rāma, as the bearer of loveliness, as the embodiment of the Ātman! To whom who is exclusive ornament of the body of Sītā, who is beheader of monsters, who is having beautiful limbs, who is the gracious hero of the Raghus, and who killed the ten-headed one.

रामभद्र महेष्वास रघुवीर नृपोत्तम। भो दशास्यान्तकास्माकं रक्षां देहि श्रियं च ते॥ १५॥

O All benevolent Lord Rāma! O great archer! O hero of Raghu race! O the best king and O beheader of ten-headed one! Please protect us and endow us the prosperity and the wealth which is related to us.

त्वमैश्वर्यं दापयाथ संप्रत्याश्वरिमारणम्। कुर्विति स्तुत्य देवाद्यास्तेन सार्धं सुखं स्थिता:॥ १६॥

O Rāma! Grant us divine rulership. The gods, praising him thus, passed their days happily until he had killed the monster Khara, the enemy.

स्तुवन्त्येवं हि ऋषयस्तदा रावण आसुर:। रामपत्नीं वनस्थां य: स्वनिवृत्त्यर्थमाददे॥ १७॥

स रावण इति ख्यातो यद्वा रावाच्च रावण:। तद्व्याजेनेक्षितुं सीतां रामो लक्ष्मण एव च॥ १८॥

विचेरतुस्तदा भूमौ देवीं संदृश्य चासुरम्। हत्वा कबन्धं शबरीं गत्वा तस्याज्ञया तया॥ १९॥

पूजितो वायुपुत्रेण भक्तेन च कपीश्वरम्। आहूय शंसतां सर्वमाद्यन्तं रामलक्ष्मणौ॥ २०॥

Ṛṣis praise Rāma– The hermits also remained busy in praying Lord Rāma like the gods too. Subsequent to the death of Khara etc. monsters, Rāvaṇa, descendant by Asura, entered into the forest and abducted Sītā, the wife of Rāma as a cause for his destruction. As he had abducted Sītā residing in the forest, he was called Rāvaṇa (the Ra from the word Rāma and Vaṇa from the word Vana forms Rāvaṇa when both are added). The next approach is that he made all creatures weeping (Rutāna), therefore, he is called Rāvaṇa. The next approach is that he had cried loudly when lord Śaṅkara enhanced the weight of Kailāśa mountain wished to carried away from its original place, hence, noise (Rāva) making had given him the name of Rāvaṇa. Subsequent to the abduction of Sītā, Lord Rāma and Lakṣmaṇa, started moving around the forest in search of her. They beheaded the monster kabandha when he attacked on them and visited at the hermitage of Śabarī according to the suggestion given by while dying. Śabarī entertained them very humbly and with a due respect. They later on met with Hanumān, a devotee son of wind, who had established friendship between Sugrīva, the king of monkeys and Lord Rāma. On having friendship established, both brothers explained the tragedy in detail.

स तु रामे शङ्कित: सन्प्रत्ययार्थं च दुन्दुभे:। विग्रहं दर्शयामास यो रामस्तमचिक्षिपत्॥ २१॥

सप्त सालान्विभिद्याशु मोदते राघवस्तदा। तेन हृष्ट: कपीन्द्रोऽसौ सरामस्तस्य पत्तनम्॥ २२॥

जगामागर्जदनुजो वालिनो वेगतो गृहात्। तदा वाली निर्जगाम तं वालिनमथाहवे॥ २३॥

Sugrīva was doubtful regarding the valour of Rāma and he showed Rāma the dreadful body of demon Dundubhi. Lord Rāma thrown away the carcass of Dundubhi within a second. He immediately penetrated the seven Śāla trees by a single arrow. Thus, the doubts hovering in mind of Sugrīva was effaced like a camphor and he became very happy. Lord Rāma also felt gaiety by assuring his friend Sugrīva. Lord Rāma entered in the city of Sugrīva subsequently where Sugrīva challenged his elder brother Bāli to come out for war. Having heard this challenge Bāli came out like a storm from his home.

निहत्य राघवो राज्ये सुग्रीवं स्थापयेत्ततः। हरीनाहूय सुग्रीवस्त्वाह चाशाविदोऽधुना॥ २४॥

आदाय मैथिलीमद्य ददताश्वाशु गच्छत। ततस्ततार हनुमानब्धि लङ्कां समाययौ॥ २५॥

Śrī Raghuvīra had killed Bāli and enthroned Sugrīva on the state of Kiṣkindhā. Sugrīva, the king of monkeys then called his all warriors and addressed them "O Brave monkeys! You have duly seen all countries. Go immediately and entrust Sītā to Lord Rāma as a result of your successful investigation". Lord Hanumān then reached in Laṅkā by crossing the sea.

सीतां दृष्ट्वाऽसुरान्हत्वा पुरं दग्ध्वा तथा स्वयम्। आगत्य रामेण सह न्यवेदयत तत्त्वतः॥ २६॥

He saw Sītā there, killed a number of monsters and burnt the entire city of Laṅkā into ashes. He then came back to Lord Rāma and explained everything, whatever he perceived also observed there.

तदा रामः क्रोधरूपी तानाहूयाथ वानरान्। तैः सार्धमादायास्त्राणि पुरीं लङ्कां समाययौ॥ २७॥

Lord Rāma then became very furious. Having severely annoyed of the behaviour of Rāvaṇa, the king of Laṅkā, he called upon the entire army of monkeys and invaded on Laṅkā with the arms and weapons.

तां दृष्ट्वा तदधीशेन सार्धं युद्धमकारयत्। घटश्रोत्रसहस्राक्षजिद्भ्यां युक्तं तमाहवे॥ २८॥

हत्वा विभीषणं तत्र स्थाप्याथ जनकात्मजाम्। आदायाङ्कस्थितां कृत्वा स्वपुरं तैर्जगाम सः॥ २९॥

Lord Rāma ensued war with Rāvaṇa, the king of Laṅkā when every pros and cons were duly investigated and scrutinized. He killed Rāvaṇa including his brother Kumbhakarṇa, and his son Meghanāda in this fight for truth. Having conquered the Laṅkā, he enthroned Vibhīṣaṇa as king and seated Jānakī at his left on Puṣpaka Vimāna along with monkeys to leave for Ayodhyā.

ततः सिंहासनस्थः सन् द्विभुजो रघुनन्दनः। धनुर्धरः प्रसन्नात्मा सर्वाभरणभूषितः॥ ३०॥

मुद्रां ज्ञानमयीं याम्ये वामे तेजः प्रकाशिनीम्। धृत्वा व्याख्याननिरतश्चिन्मयः परमेश्वरः॥ ३१॥

Raghunandana, holder of two sturdy arms is adorned on the throne of Ayodhyā kingdom. The great archer Rāma is always smiling and well-decorated with the ornaments. That supreme god, full of truth, meditation and pleasure is seated in the posture of preaching. At his left hand, the posture is of a warrior i.e. Dhanurmayī Mudrā and in the right hand, he is holding the posture of knowledge.

उदग्दक्षिणयोः स्वस्य शत्रुघ्नभरतौ ततः। हनूमन्तं च श्रोतारमग्रतः स्यात्त्रिकोणगम्॥ ३२॥

भरताधस्तु सुग्रीवं शत्रुघ्नाधो विभीषणम्। पश्चिमे लक्ष्मणं तस्य धृतच्छत्रं सचामरम्॥ ३३॥

तदधस्तौ तालवृन्तकरौ त्र्यस्रं पुनर्भवेत्। एवं षट्कोणमादौ स्वदीर्घाङ्गैरेष संयुतः॥ ३४॥

Bharata is seating at right and the Śatrughna is at the left of Rāma. The devotee Hanumān in the form of obedience adorned within the triangle and with clasping hands. Sugrīva is standing below Bharata and Vibhīṣaṇa is below Śatrughna. Lakṣamaṇa is standing with royal umbrella at the back of Rāma. Below Lakṣmaṇa, both brothers i.e. Bharata and Śatrughna are stood and the fan of palm tree leaves are in their hands. Bharata, Śatrughna and Lakṣmaṇa thus form the next position of a triangle. Śrī Raghuvīra is within the circle of the large letters in the form of seed hymn.

द्वितीयं वासुदेवाद्यैराग्नेयादिषु संयुतः। तृतीयं वायुसूनुं च सुग्रीवं भरतं तथा॥ ३५॥

विभीषणं लक्ष्मणं च अङ्गदं चारिमर्दनम्। जाम्बवन्तं च तैर्युक्तस्ततो धृष्टिर्जयन्तकः॥ ३६॥

विजयश्च सुराष्ट्रश्च राष्ट्रवर्धन एव च। अशोको धर्मपालश्च सुमन्त्रश्चैभिरावृतः॥ ३७॥

At the next circle and in the direction like Agnaya etc., there are Vāsudeva etc., (Saṅkarṣaṇa, Śānti, Śrī, Sarasvatī, Aniruddha and Rati). They exist in the second circle added with the first. In the third circle, Bharata, Śatrughna, Hanumān, Vibhīṣaṇa, Sugrīva, Lakṣmaṇa, Aṅgada and Jāmbavanta are counted. Their existence remains in the third circle inspite of they are surrounded by Dhṛṣṭi, Jayanta, Vijaya, Surāṣṭra, Rāṣṭravardhana, Aśoka, Dharmapāla and Sumantra.

ततः सहस्रदृग्वह्निर्धर्मज्ञो वरुणोऽनिलः। इन्द्वीशधात्रनन्ताश्च दशभिश्चैभिरावृतः॥ ३८॥

When Lord Rāma is surrounded by the ten Dikpālas (the master of directions) i.e., Indra fire, Dharmarāja, Varuṇa, Nirṛti, wind, Moon, Brahmā, Īśana and Anant; the fourth circle is then formed.

बहिस्तदायुधैः पूज्यो नीलादिभिरलंकृतः। वसिष्ठवामदेवादिमुनिभिः समुपासितः॥ ३९॥

At the exterior part of these Dikpāla is their weapons. The adorable Rāma is seen fascinating when he is surrounded by these arms and weapons as also with Nala etc. monkeys. Vasiṣṭha, Vāmadeva etc. hermits too are there in their company, keep themselves busy with pray of Lord Rāma.

एवमुद्देशतः प्रोक्तं निर्देशस्तस्य चाधुना। त्रिरेखापुटमालिख्य मध्ये तारद्वयं लिखेत्॥ ४०॥

तन्मध्ये बीजमालिख्य तदधः साध्यमालिखेत्। द्वितीयान्तं च तस्योर्ध्वं षष्ठ्यन्तं साधकं तथा॥ ४१॥

The complete structure of Yantra for worship is being told after the discuss in on the Yantra for worship. One should draw two triangles with the even lines and the dual. Praṇava at the middle of these two triangles should be written separately. In the middle of the dual Praṇava, the basic seed Rāma should be written and the described objective is to be written below it. At the upper portion of the basic seed (Rāma) should be written by dividing it in six parts and the desire should be written after two divisions so made.

कुरु द्वयं च तत्पार्श्वे लिखेद्बीजान्तरे रमाम्। तत्सर्वं प्रणवाभ्यां च वेष्टयेच्छुद्धबुद्धिमान्॥ ४२॥

The foot of 'Kuru' should be written at each colateral part in the left and right. The seed (key) and at the upper portion of the desired object, Śrī Bīja should be written. The scholar person should write all these in such a manner that these may be within the scope of both Praṇava (Oṁ).

दीर्घभाजि षडस्रे तु लिखेद्बीजं हृदादिभिः। कोणपार्श्वे रमामाये तदग्रेऽनङ्गमालिखेत्॥ ४३॥

The basic seed should be written with the long sound vowel on six angles. 'Hṛdya Namaḥ' etc. should be written in a seriatim with each of them. The seed letters (Bījākṣara) i.e., Srīṁ, Hrīṁ and klīṁ should be written in the colateral parts of the angle.

क्रोधं कोणाग्रान्तरेषु लिख्य मन्त्र्यभितो गिरम्। वृत्तत्रयं साष्टपत्रं सरोजे विलिखेत्स्वरान्॥ ४४॥

केसरे चाष्टपत्रे च वर्गाष्टकमथालिखेत्। तेषु मालामनोर्वर्णान्विलिखेदूर्मिसंख्यया॥ ४५॥

अन्ते पञ्चाक्षराण्येवं पुनरष्टदलं लिखेत्। तेषु नारायणाष्टार्णांल्लिख्य तत्केसरे रमाम्॥ ४६॥

तद्वहिर्द्वादशदलं विलिखेद्द्वादशाक्षरम्। अथोंनमो भगवते वासुदेवाय इत्ययम्॥ ४७॥

In the foreportion and inner portions of the angle, the Krodhabīja 'Hum' should be written and the Sarsavatī Bīja 'Aim' should be written on both colateral sides of the same. Three spherical lines should be then drawn. The first will be on Ṣaṭkoṇa, the second in the middle and the third at the forepart of the petals. Simultaneous to these spherical lines, a lotus containing eight petals should also be drawn. At the bottom part of lotus all vowels should be written in a seriatim of two letters together. Above these vowels, the eight square (Aṣṭavarga) of consonants should be written. Above this eight square, fourty-seven letters of the garland hymn are to be written in the couple of six letters each. Thus, at the last petal of lotus the space for five letters will remain. One more lotus containing eight petals should again be drawn. One letter each of the hymn Oṁ Namaḥ Nārāyaṇāya should be written on its petals and the Rāmabīja (Srīṁ) should be written on its bottom. One more thus containing twelve petals should be drawn over it and one letter each of the hymn 'Oṁ Namaḥ Bhagvate Vāsudevāya? i.e. twelve letters hymn should be written on each petal of that lotus.

आदिक्षान्तान्केसरेषु वृत्ताकारेण संलिखेत्। तद्वहिः षोडशदलं लिख्य तत्केसरे ह्रियम्॥ ४८॥

वर्मास्त्रनतिसंयुक्तं दलेषु द्वादशाक्षरम्। तत्सन्धिष्विरजादीनां मन्त्रान्मन्त्री समालिखेत्॥ ४९॥

ह्रं स्रं भ्रं व्रं ल्रं अं श्रं ज्रं च लिखेत्सम्यक्ततो बहिः। द्वात्रिंशारं महापद्मं नादबिन्दुसमायुतम्॥ ५०॥

In the bottom of the lotus containing twelve petals and letters from 'A' to 'Kṣa' (sixteen vowels and thirty-five consonants) should be written in the spherical form. Thus at each bottom there will be four letters and at the last, the seven letters. One more lotus containing sixteen petals exterior to it should be also drawn. A letter on each petal of the twelve letters hymn 'Oṁ Hrīṁ Bhartāgrasa Rāma Klīṁ Svāhā' and 'Huṁ Phaṭ Namaḥ' should be written in orderly manner on the sixteen petals. At the joining spot of the petals, the Bīja hymn of Hanumān and Dhṛṣti etc. Bīja hymns should be written. These hymns are 'Hrṁ Straṁ Bhraṁ Braṁ Lraṁ Aṁ Śraṁ and Jraṁ as also Ghraṁ Jraṁ Vraṁ straṁ Raṁ Aṁ Dhraṁ and straṁ. Further, one more large lotus containing thirty-two petals should also be drawn exterior to it and it should be with the sound and iota both.

विलिखेन्मन्त्रराजार्णांस्तेषु पत्रेषु यत्नतः। ध्यायेदष्टवसूनेकादशरुद्रांश्च तत्र वै॥ ५१॥

द्वादशेनांश्च धातारं वषट्कारं च तद्बहिः। भूगृहं वज्रशूलाढ्यं रेखात्रयसमन्वितम्॥ ५२॥

द्वारोपेतं च राश्यादिभूषितं फणिसंयुतम्। अनन्तो वासुकिश्चैव तक्षः कर्कोटपद्मकः॥ ५३॥

महापद्मश्च शङ्खश्च गुलिकोऽष्टौ प्रकीर्तिताः। एवं मण्डलमालिख्य तस्य दिक्षु विदिक्षु च॥ ५४॥

The thirty-two letters of the king hymn Nārasiṁha are to be written on these petals in the same petal Nyāsa and concentration should be made of Aṭavasu, eleven Rudra, twelve Ādityas and holder of all Vaṣaṭkāra should be made. (The Aṣṭavasu are Dhruva, Dhara, Soma, Aap, Anika, Anala, Pratyūṣa and Prabhāsa respectively). The eleven Rudras are Hara, Bahurūpa, Tryambaka, Aparājita, Śambhu, Vṛṣākapi, Kapardī, Raivata, Mṛgavyādha, Śarva and Kapālī. The twelve Ādityas are Dhātā, Aryamā, Mitra, Varuṇa, Aṁśa, Bhaga, Indra Vivarvāṇa, Pūjā, Parjanya, Tvaṣṭā and Viṣṇu). A Bhūgṛha Yantra should be drawn in the exterior part of that thirty two letter petal lotus. Its three lines are the inspiration of the Satva, Rajas and Tamas properties. A gate should also be formed in it like the doors made in the pavilion. The Bhūgṛha so made should be decorated with Rāśis. It is held by eight Nāgās (serpents) from eight directions and sub-directions. Their names are Anana, Vāsuki, Takṣaka, Karkoṭaka, Padma, Mahāpadma, Śaṅkha and Gulika respectively.

नारसिंहं च वाराहं लिखेन्मन्त्रद्वयं तथा। कूटो रेफानुग्रहेन्दुनादशक्त्यादिभिर्युतः॥ ५५॥

यो नृसिंहः समाख्यातो ग्रहमारणकर्मणि। अन्त्यार्धीशवियद्बिन्दुनादैर्बीजं च सौकरम्॥ ५६॥

Having written the Bhūgṛha Yantra, the seed hymn of Nārasiṁha around and seed hymn of Vārāha in the angles should be written. The seed hymn of Nārasiṁha is 'Kṣraun' formed by 'Ka' 'Ṣ' 'R' compassion (Au), Indu (Anusvāra) the sound and the power (illusion). This hymn endows with the desired accomplishment when applied for destruction of enemy and hurdle created by the stars etc. When the Antya varṇa 'Ha' is added with 'U' and the iota (Anusvāra), sound and the power etc. is added, it forms the Vārāha seed hymn (Hum).

हुंकारं चात्र रामस्य मालामन्त्रोऽधुनेरितः। तारो नतिश्च निद्रायाः स्मृतिर्मेदश्च कामिका॥ ५७॥

रुद्रेण संयुता वह्निर्मेधामरविभूषिता। दीर्घा क्रूरयुता ह्लादिन्यथो दीर्घसमायुता॥ ५८॥

क्षुधा क्रोधिन्यमोघा च विश्वमप्यथ मेधया। युक्ता दीर्घज्वालिनी च सुसूक्ष्मा मृत्युरूपिणी॥ ५९॥

सप्रतिष्ठा ह्लादिनी त्वक्क्ष्वेलप्रीतिश्च सामरा। ज्योतिस्तीक्ष्णाग्निसंयुक्ता श्वेतानुस्वारसंयुता॥ ६०॥

कामिकापञ्चमूलान्तस्तान्तान्तो थान्त इत्यथ। स सानन्तो दीर्घयुतो वायुः सूक्ष्मयुतो विषः॥ ६१॥

कामिका कामका रुद्रयुक्ताथोऽथ स्थिरातपा। तापिनी दीर्घयुक्ता भूरनलोऽनन्तगोऽनिलः॥ ६२॥

नारायणात्मकः कालः प्राणाम्भो विद्यया युतः। पीतारातिस्तथा लान्तो योन्या युक्तस्ततो नतिः॥ ६३॥

The Vārāha seed hymn i.e. Hum should also be written in the angles of this Yantra. Now, the garland hymn relating to Rāma will be described. It is with Praṇava (Oṁ), Namaḥ, Nidrā (Bha), Smṛti (Ga), Meda (Va), Kāmikā (Ta) and Rudra (E). It is with the fire (Ra), wisdom (Gha) immortal (U) added with the prolong time (Na), moon (Anusvāra) after Lhādinī (Dā), the prolong time (Na) is with Mānadākalā (Ā). After it there is kṣudhā (Ya). By adding these letters, the part of hymn 'Oṁ Namaḥ Bhagvate Raghunandanayo' is formed. The Krodhini (Ra) is with Amoghā (kṣ) and the world (O) is adorned with wisdom (Gh). It is a compound form of Dīrghā (Na), Vanhikalā (V) and micro Rudra (I). Thereafter, it is added with the Mṛtya Praṇavakaiā (Ś), is adorned with A in the form of basis for pronunciation. Lasting, the Lhādinī (Dā) and Tvaka (Ya) are existed. This conjoint form constructs the hymn Rakṣoghnāviśadāya. The Kṣvela (Ma) is with Prīti (Dh) and Amara (U). The Jyoti (R) is added with the Tīkṣṇā (P) and fire (Ra) as also with Anusvāra, Śvetā (Sa). Then the fifth letter after 'Ta' (Na), the letter (Va) after (La), one letter lapsed after 'Ta' (Da) is added with Anant (A) leaving aside (Na). Then conjoint wind (Ya) from the large vowel (Ā), the poison (M) formed by small 'I' Kāmikā (Ta) and Kāmikā (Ta) added with Rudra (Ai). Then Sthirā (Ja) is with 'Ai' mara and 'Sa' letter. Thus, the hymn formed is 'Madhura prasanna Vadanāyāmitatejase.' Then, 'Tāpinī' (Ba), the large (La), 'Bhū' i.e., the bīja of large 'Ā' is added and in its company, there is Anita (Ya). Thus, the Valāya is proved. Anantage Anala viz. Rā is with the bīja of the Ā. Then the Kāla (Ma) and Prāṇa (Ya) is existed with the bīja of the Nārāyaṇa shape. Thus, Rāmaya is formed. The Ambhas with learning is 'Va' joined with the mora of 'I'. Then Pītā (Ṣ), Rāti, (Na) and Va after La is formed with Yoni (Ai). Thus Viṣṇave is formed. Lastly, the Saluting 'Nati' (Namaḥ) and Praṇava Oṁ are existed.

सप्तचत्वारिंशद्वर्णगुणान्तः सगुणः स्वयम्। राज्याभिषिक्तस्य तस्य रामस्योक्तक्रमाल्लिखेत्॥ ६४॥

This garland hymn with coronation and fourty-seven letters is related with Rāma. This hymn is Oṁ Namaḥ Bhagavate Raghunandanāya Rakṣoghnaviśadāya Madhuraprasanna Vadanāyāmitatejase Valāya Rāmāya Viṣṇave Namaḥ Oṁ! Inspite of being in apparent form, it liberates the devotees from the ties of 'Triguṇamayi māyā'. This hymn should be written in the manner aforesaid.

इदं सर्वात्मकं यन्त्रं प्रागुक्तमृषिसेवितम्। सेवकानां मोक्षकरमायुरारोग्यवर्धनम्॥ ६५॥

अपुत्राणां पुत्रदं च बहुना किमनेन वै। प्राप्नुवन्ति क्षणात्सम्यगत्र धर्मादिकानपि॥ ६६॥

The aforesaid Yantra is in the form of all. The hermits and Saints have exercised this Yantra and the ancient teachers too have delivered their preachings. The devotee as a result of it obtains the healthy body, promotion of age and also the wish for liberty. The issueless persons are blessed with sons, what is the use for telling more except the fact that its devotee avails all accomplishments immediately. By virtue of the penance so made, the desired purposes like religion, knowledge, detachment etc. are fulfilled.

इदं रहस्यं परममीश्वरेणापि दुर्गमम्। इदं यन्त्रं समाख्यातं न देयं प्राकृते जने॥६७॥

This most cryptic and secret Yantra is inaccessible even for the supreme scholar without learning it through the great teacher. The common persons not entitled to follow it should be seldom pleased.

॥पञ्चमोपनिषद्॥

ॐ भूतादिकं शोधयेद्द्वारपूजां कृत्वा पद्माद्यासनस्थः प्रसन्नः।
अर्चाविधावस्य पीठाधरोर्ध्वपार्श्वार्चनं मध्यपद्मार्चनं च॥ १॥
कृत्वा मृदुलश्लक्ष्णसुतूलिकायां रत्नासने देशिकमर्चयित्वा।
शक्तिं चाधाराख्यकां कूर्मनागौ पृथिव्यब्जे स्वासनाधः प्रकल्प्य॥ २॥

The devotee should purify all elements in a happy mood by sitting in the posture of Padmāsana after worship of the door (Dvārapūjā). Under the provision of worship made for Lord Rāma, the lower portion of the throne, upper portion as also both colateral parts are to be worshipped. Above the throne, the eight petals lotus should also be worshipped in the middle portion. The throne studded with gems should be made smooth by putting the cotton made. Cushions on them and the teachers in the form of supreme soul should be worshipped on that seat. In the lower portion of the Piṭha and below the seat of Lord Rāma, the Ādhāra Śaktī, Kūrma, Nāga (serpent) and earth form two lotus flowers should be presumed and worshipped.

विघ्नेशं दुर्गां क्षेत्रपालं च वाणीं बीजादिकांश्चाग्निदेशादिकांश्च।
पीठस्याङ्घ्रिष्वेव धर्मादिकांश्च नत्वा पूर्वाद्यासु दिक्ष्वर्चयेच्च॥ ३॥
मध्ये क्रमादर्कविध्वग्नितेजांस्युपर्युपर्यादिमैरर्चितानि।
रजः सत्त्वं तम एतानि वृत्तत्रयं बीजाढ्यं क्रमाद्भावयेच्च॥ ४॥

Then Lord Gaṇeśa (who removes the), the master of the territory (Kṣetrapāla), Durgā and Vāṇi (Speech) should be worshipped with the Bīja hymn and these are to be worshipped in Āgneya etc. directions by using Caturthī. Subsequently, in the feet of that Piṭha, the existing Dharma, Artha, Kāma and Mokṣa should be worshipped in the east etc. directions. Then, the sun, moon, and fire as worshipped by the great men in the upper middle portion of the Piṭha should be worshipped. The Bīja hymn existing as a symbol of Satvas, Rajas and Tamas in the Yantra, three circles too should be worshipped properly.

आशाव्याशास्वप्यथात्मानमन्तरात्मानं वा परमात्मानमन्तः।
ज्ञानात्मानं चार्चयेत्तस्य दिक्षु मायाविद्ये ये कलापारतत्त्वे॥ ५॥
संपूजयेद्विमलादींश्च शक्तीरभ्यर्चयेद्देवमावाहयेच्च।
अङ्गव्यूहानिलाजाद्यैश्च पूज्य धृष्ट्यादिकैर्लोकपालैस्तदस्त्रैः॥ ६॥
वसिष्ठाद्यैर्मुनिभिर्नीलमुख्यैराराधयेद्राघवं चन्दनाद्यैः।

मुख्योपहारैर्विविधैश्च पूज्यैस्तस्मै जपादींश्च सम्यक्प्रकल्प्य॥७॥

The eight petals formed in the angles and directions should be then worshipped. The petals existing in the angles should be worshipped by assuming the form of soul, internal soul, supreme soul and the soul of knowledge in a seriatim beginning with the Āgneya angle. The element of illusion, the art (Kalā) and the metaphysics (Parā) should be worshipped in the east etc. directions. The Vimalā etc. powers should be then worshipped in a systematic manner. After the summonation and worship of the cardinal god, the heart, head etc. should be worshipped by sprinkling the water in the company of Dhṛṣṭi (Jayanta, Vijaya, Surāṣṭra etc.,) Lokapāla (Indra, Yama, Nirrti etc). Their arms and weapons like thunderbolt, śakti, Daṇḍa etc., Vasiṣṭha, Vāmadeva, Jāvāla, Gautama etc. Lord Rāma should be worshipped with different manners and a number of best present and smearing of the sandal etc. Simultaneously, the devotee should offer the silent recital with the prescribed manner to him.

एवंभूतं जगदाधारभूतं रामं वन्दे सच्चिदानन्दरूपम्।
गदारिशङ्खाब्जधरं भवारिं स यो ध्यायेन्मोक्षमाप्नोति सर्वः॥८॥

We salute Śrī Raghuvīra who holds Gadā, discus, conch and lotus in his hands, who shatters the ties of the world, who is the supporter of the world, most magnificent and in the form of truth, pleasure and peace (Saccidānanda). All devotees who worship by following the same procedure definitely attains to the salvation.

विश्वव्यापी राघवो यस्तदानीमन्तर्दधे शङ्खचक्रे गदाब्जे।
धृत्वा रमासहितः सानुजश्च सपत्तनः सानुगः सर्वलोकी॥९॥

At the time of closing the phase of his physical activities, Lord Rāma was vanished with his conch, discus, gadā and the Lotus even without leaving the physical body behind. He entered into the supreme abode with Sītā by holding by usual form. He was followed by his family members, relatives, all brothers, all subject and the descendants of the enemy like Vibhīsaṇa etc. to his supreme abode.

तद्भक्ता ये लब्धकामाश्च भुक्त्वा तथा पदं परमं यान्ति ते च।
इमा ऋचः सर्वकामार्थदाश्च ये ते पठन्त्यमला यान्ति मोक्षम्॥१०॥

His devotees obtain the means of enjoyment desired by them. They accept the supreme position after their death. The devotees reciting these Ṛcās are competent enough to fulfill all desires and provide with the wealth; attain to the position of emancipation after duly purifying their minds and conscience.

ॐ भद्रं कर्णेभिः .... इति शान्तिः॥

॥इति रामपूर्वतापिन्युपनिषत्समाप्ता॥

53. MUDGALA-UPANIṢAD

मुद्गलोपनिषद्

This Upaniṣad is a part and parcel of Ṛgveda. There are four parts in this Upaniṣad. In its first part, indications to disclose the mysteries and the meanings of the sixteen hymns used in the Puruṣa Sūkta as contemplated in the Yajurveda. In the second part, the part relating to the two persons (described and undescribed persons) of Puruṣa Sūkta in the preachings given to lord Indra who had come for shelteration to the god are described. In this very part, the advises and the fruit of offering in the fire in the garb of described person by presuming the body as material for offering to lord Brahmā by Aniruddha (the described person). In third part, a description of worshipping that person in his varied forms by the devotees of various species (Yonis) and the fruit of realising that person is given. In the fourth part, the eccentricity of that person and various factors of his appearance have been described. Finally, the discipline to be applied for disclosing this secret knowledge has been explained.

।।शान्तिपाठः।।

वाङ्मे मनसि.......इति शान्तिः।।

।।प्रथमः खण्डः।।

ॐ पुरुषसूक्तार्थनिर्णयं व्याख्यास्यामः। पुरुषसंहितायां पुरुषसूक्तार्थः संग्रहेण प्रोच्यते।
सहस्रशीर्षेत्यत्र सशब्दोऽनन्तवाचकः। अनन्तयोजनं प्राह दशाङ्गुलवचस्तथा।।१।।

The meaning accepted by Puruṣa Sūkta is described (the lord Vāsudeva while describing had said to lord Indra). In Puruṣa Saṁhitā, the meaning of this Sūkta is being summarily spoken. The term 'Sahasra' as applied in Puruṣa Sūkta indicates the endlessness. Similarly, the expression 'Daśāṅgulam' too transpires a distance of endless miles (Yojanas).

[The word 'Saśabdo' as used here is also available is 'Sahasro' which is more appropriate then it.]

तस्य प्रथमया विष्णोर्देशतो व्याप्तिरीरिता। द्वितीयया चास्य विष्णोः कालतो व्याप्तिरुच्यते।।२।।

In this first hymn 'Śāstra Śīrṣa' of Puruṣa Sūkta, a broad description of the omnipresent magnificence of lord Viṣṇu has been given. The second hymn i.e. 'Puruṣa's Evedam..' of Puruṣa Sūkta too is indicative of the ever-lasting presence of the master of the world lord Viṣṇu. He is omnipresent always. He remains existing always.

विष्णोर्मोक्षप्रदत्वं च कथितं तु तृतीयया। एतावानिति मन्त्रेण वैभवं कथितं हरेः।।३।।

The third hymn of Puruṣa Sūkta tells lord Viṣṇu, a god providing with emancipation. In the third hymn i.e. 'Etāvanasya..' an elaborate description of the magnificence as also the power of lord Hari has been given.

एतेनैव य मन्त्रेण चतुर्व्यूहो विभाषितः। त्रिपादित्यनया प्रोक्तमनिरुद्धस्य वैभवम्।।४।।

In this batch of three hymns, the form of lord relating to 'Caturvyūha' has been described. In the fourth hymn i.e. 'Tripāda' an elaboration of the wide prosperity of the Caturvyūha in garb of Aniruddha has been given.

तस्माद्विराडित्यनया पादनारायणाद्धरेः। प्रकृते पुरुषस्यापि समुत्पत्तिः प्रदर्शिता।।५।।

In the fifth hymn i.e. 'Tasmādvirāḍ' of Puruṣa Sūkta, the nature (illusion) and the person (living-organism) sheltered to lord Hari has been revealed as appearing through the lord Nārāyaṇa in garb of magnificence of the foot.

यत्पुरुषेणेत्यनया सृष्टियज्ञः समीरितः। सप्तास्यासन्परिधयः समिधश्च समीरिताः।।६।।

An offering in garb of the universe has been propounded through the hymn 'Yatpuruṣeṇa' of this very Sūkta and the material used in such offering has been described as the 'Saptāsyāsan Paridhayaḥ'.

तं यज्ञमिति मन्त्रेण सृष्टियज्ञः समीरितः। अनेनैव च मन्त्रेण मोक्षश्च समुदीरितः।।७।।

This very offering of universe has been propounded by the successive hymn i.e. 'Tan Yajñam' of this very Sūkta. A description of emancipation coincide has been described by this very hymn.

तस्मादिति च मन्त्रेण जगत्सृष्टिः समीरिता। वेदाहमिति मन्त्राभ्यां वैभवं कथितं हरेः।।८।।

By the seven hymns including 'Tasmād' etc. of Puruṣa Sūkta, the genesis of this whole universe has been described. By two hymns i.e. 'Vedāham' etc. a special description of the magnificence of lord Hari is obtained.

यज्ञेनेत्युपसंहारः सृष्टेर्मोक्षस्य चेरितः। य एवमेतज्ञानाति स हि मुक्तो भवेदिति।।९।।

A conclusive description of the creation and the emancipation has been made by the hymn i.e. 'Yajñena Yajñamaya..'. The person who abreast with the knowledge of Puruṣa Sūkta in the same fashion, definitely attains the emancipation.

।।द्वितीयः खण्डः।।

अथ तथा मुद्गलोपनिषदि पुरुषसूक्तस्य वैभवं विस्तरेण प्रतिपादितम्। वासुदेव इन्द्राय भगवज्ज्ञानमुपदिश्य पुनरपि सूक्ष्मश्रवणाय प्रणतायेन्द्राय परमरहस्यभूतं पुरुषसूक्ताभ्यां खण्डद्वयाभ्यामुपादिशत्।।१।।

Thus the specific magnificence of Puruṣa Sūkta as propounded in the first part of Mudgalopaniṣad, the same knowledge was given by lord Vāsudeva to lord Indra while preaching. With an intention to rehear that minutest knowledge of the element, lord Indra came under shelter of lord Vāsudeva most humbly. The god provided lord Indra that secret knowledge of benevolence in two parts of the Puruṣa Sūkta.

द्वौ खण्डावुच्येते। योऽयमुक्तः स पुरुषो नामरूपज्ञानगोचरं संसारिणामतिदुर्ज्ञेयं विषयं विहाय क्लेशादिभिः संक्लिष्टदेवादिजिहीर्षया सहस्रकलावयवकल्याणं दृष्टमात्रेण मोक्षदं वेषमाददे। तेन वेषेण भूम्यादिलोकं व्याप्यानन्तयोजमत्यतिष्ठत्।।२।।

Two parts of Puruṣa Sūkta has been prescribed the gigantic person as contemplated in this Sūkta is inaccessible to all the living-organisms of this universe specially due to having its existence beyond any name, complexion as also the knowledge. He held the form of unlimited arts with an intention to save the specific living-beings like the gods etc. and for welfare of all living-organisms by abandoning this inaccessible form. This form is as a benevolent that it provides emancipation by mere vision of it. By this very complexion, he covered all the worlds including the earth and thus he extended his coverage upto unlimited miles (Yojanas).

पुरुषो नारायणो भूतं भव्यं भविष्यच्चासीत्। स एष सर्वेषा मोक्षदश्चासीत्। स च सर्वस्मान्महिनो ज्यायान्। तस्मान्न कोऽपि ज्यायान्॥३॥

The perfect man prior to the creation of this universe i.e. lord Śrīnārāyaṇa too was existed in the form of trio-periods i.e. the past, the present and the future. He only is renderer of emancipation to all these living-organisms. He too is specific among the most mighty people. Nothing else is so specific as the gigantic person himself is. He is almighty.

महापुरुष आत्मानं चतुर्धा कृत्वा त्रिपादेन परमे व्योम्नि चासीत्।
इतरेण चतुर्थेनानिरुद्धनारायणेन विश्वान्यासन्॥४॥

That supreme soul (person) has made him to appear in Caturvyūhas by dividing himself into four parts. Out of them, three parts i.e. Vāsudeva, Pradyumna and Saṅkarṣaṇa reside in the supreme abode Vaikuṇṭha. This whole universe was created by lord Śrī Nārāyaṇa renowned with the name of Aniruddha as the fourth part of that supreme soul.

[The three feet of that gigantic man are restricted to the higher worlds only. One foot namely Aniruddha (which was not restricted) has created this universe. The rest of three names are not given in the hymn still the names of god on the basis of Aniruddha have been accepted by the scholars. These feet are Vāsudeva (who provides accommodation to all), Pradyumna (specially luminant) and Saṅkarṣaṇa (creating attraction) still these are undescribed]

स च पादनारायणो जगत्स्रष्टुं प्रकृतिमजनयत्। स समृद्धकायः सन्सृष्टिकर्म न जज्ञिवान्। सोऽनिरुद्धनारायणस्तस्मै सृष्टिमुपादिशत्। ब्रह्मंस्तवेन्द्रियाणि याजकानि ध्यात्वा कोशभूतं दृढं ग्रन्थिकलेवरं हविर्ध्यात्वा मां हविर्भुजं ध्यात्वा वसन्तकालमाज्यं ध्यात्वा ग्रीष्ममिध्मं ध्यात्वा शरदृतुं रसं ध्यात्वैवमग्नौ हुत्वाङ्गस्पर्शात्कलेवरो वज्रं हीष्यते। ततः स्वकार्यान्सर्वप्राणिजीवान्सृष्ट्वा पश्चाद्याः प्रादुर्भविष्यन्ति। ततः स्थावरजङ्गमात्मकं जगद्भविष्यति॥५॥

Lord Nārāyaṇa created the nature for the creation of universe with his four feet. Lord Brahmā (the nature) could not understand the mystery of the creation of the universe even after attaining the body. Nārāyaṇa in his Aniruddha form subsequently preached lord Brahmā the manner for the creation of the universe. He said– "O Brahmā! Consider your speech etc. all senses as the person who perform offering. Assume your body appeared from the pipe of the lotus and mighty as the material for offering, feel the spring season as ghee, summer of fuel and the pleasant season as the essence. Having offering thus made to the fire, your body will be mightiest and the thunderbolt too could be turned down by a mere touch of such body. As a result of such offering, the commune of all living-organisms will appear. Thus, this entire world enriched with the movable and immovable organisms will gets its birth and become apparent.

एतेन जीवात्मनोर्योगे मोक्षप्रकारश्च कथित इत्यनुसंधेयम्।।६।।

Thus the attainment of emancipation by virtue of assimilation of the organism and the soul has been described.

य इमं सृष्टियज्ञं जानाति मोक्षप्रकारं च सर्वमायुरेति।।७।।

The devotee who is well-understood to the method of this offering and the emancipation, becomes capable to avail the full age life.

।।तृतीयः खण्डः।।

एको देवो बहुधा निविष्ट अजायमानो बहुधा विजायते।।१।।

He is an absolute god but inserted in his varied forms. He seldom gets birth yet takes birth in varied ways.

तमेतमग्निरित्यध्वर्यव उपासते। यतुरित्येष हीदं सर्वं युनक्ति। सामेति छन्दोगाः। एतस्मिन्हीदं सर्वे प्रतिष्ठितम्। विषमति सर्पाः। सर्प इति सर्पविदः। ऊर्गिति देवाः। रयिरिति मनुष्याः। मायेत्यसुराः। स्वधेति पितरः। देवजन इति देवजनविदः। रूपमिति गन्धर्वः। गन्धर्व इत्यप्सरसः।।२।।

All Adhvaryus has worshiped that gigantic person as the fire god. The follower of Yajurveda consider that god as Yajuḥ and engages him in all their rituals. The persons following Sāmaveda know him in the form of Sāma. He definitely is present everywhere in the form of this very gigantic person. The serpent (dynamic organism) accept it in the form of poison and the knower to the serpent (yogī) attains him in the form of dynamic breathing (organism). The gods entertain that gigantic person in the form of nectar and the ordinary people consider it as wealth and thus survive their life. The demons know him as illusion, the late fore-fathers consider him as Svadhā (the offering to the late fore-fathers), the worshipper of gods accept him in the form of god, the Gandharvas are identified with him in the form of beauty and complexion and the Damsel know him in the form of Gandharva.

तं यथायथोपासते तथैव भवति। तस्माद् ब्राह्मणः पुरुषरूपं परंब्रह्मैवाहमिति भावयते। तद्रूपो भवति। य एवं वेद।।३।।

The element of supreme soul changes its form according to the recognition of the devotee while worshipping him. Hence, the people known to the Brahman should develop the spirituality as I myself is the perfect man and the supreme Brahman. By virtue of such presumption, the devotee attains the same form of that god, the person who duly understands this mystery himself becomes as that supreme soul is.

।।चतुर्थः खण्डः।।

तद्ब्रह्म तापत्रयातीतं षट्कोशविनिर्मुक्तं षडूर्मिवर्जितं पञ्चकोशातीतं षड्भावविकारशून्यमेवमादि-सर्वविलक्षणं भवति।।१।।

That Brahma (perfect person) is free from trio-fevers, beyond from six treasures, without six brain vagaries, free from five cells and beyond from the six pollution's of the spirit. Thus, that Brahma is excellent than all.

तापत्रयं त्वाध्यात्मिकधिभौतिकाधिदैविकं कर्तृकर्मकार्यज्ञातृज्ञानज्ञेयभोक्तृभोगभोग्यमिति त्रिविधम्।।२।।

These trio-fevers are metaphysical, physical and celestial embedding in them– the doer, deed, action, knower, knowledge, knowable and endurer, enjoyment, enjoyable. Thus, inspite of these being singular, these are of three kinds.

त्वङ्मांसशोणितास्थिस्नायुमज्जाः षट्कोशाः।।३।।

The six treasures (Dhātu) are the skin, the flesh, the bones, the veins, the blood and the marrow respectively.

कामक्रोधलोभमोहमदमात्सर्यमित्यरिषड्वर्गः।।४।।

The sensuality, anger, greed, attachment, ego and manipulation are six enemies.

अन्नमयप्राणमयमनोमयविज्ञानमयानन्दमया इति पञ्चकोशाः।।५।।

The foot, the breathing, the mind, the science (conscious) and the pleasure are the five cells in the body.

प्रियात्मजनवर्धनपरिणामक्षयनाशाः षड्भावाः।।६।।

The six kinds of pollution found in the spirit is to become beloved, to arise, to increase, to change, deterioration or diminishing and the destruction's respectively.

अशनायापिपासाशोकमोहजरामरणानीति षडूर्मयः।।७।।

The six waves are the hunger, passion, gloom, attachment, old age and death respectively.

कुलगोत्रजातिवर्णाश्रमरूपाणि षड्भ्रमाः।।८।।

The clan, gotra, caste, varṇa, āśrama and the complexion are the six illusions.

एतद्योगेन परमपुरुषो जीवो भवति नान्यः।।९।।

The perfect person gets birth by virtue of the combination of these all and nobody other may be competent to get such birth.

य एतदुपनिषदं नित्यमधीते सोऽग्निपूतो भवति। स वायुपूतो भवति। स आदित्यपूतो भवति। अरोगी भवति। श्रीमांश्च भवति। पुत्रपौत्रादिभिः समृद्धो भवति। विद्वांश्च भवति। महापातकात्पूतो भवति। सुरापानात्पूतो भवति। अगम्यागमनात्पूतो भवति। मातृगमनात्पूतो भवति। दुहितृस्नुषाभिगमनात्पूतो भवति। स्वर्णस्तेयात्पूतो भवति। वेदिजन्महानात्पूतो भवति। गुरोरशुश्रूषणात्पूतो भवति। अयाज्ययाजनात् पूतो भवति। अभक्ष्यभक्षणात्

पूतो भवति। उग्रप्रतिग्रहात्पूतो भवति। परादारगमनात्पूतो भवति। कामक्रोधलोभमोहेर्ष्यादिभिरबाधितो भवति। सर्वेभ्यः पापेभ्यो मुक्तो भवति। इह जन्मनि पुरुषो भवति॥१०॥

The person who goes over this Upaniṣad in a routine way becomes so sacrosanct as the fire itself. He is purified like the wind. He becomes as dynamic as the sun itself and becomes free from all ailments. He is blessed with son and daughters as well as all prosperity. He becomes a scholar and also becomes free from all sins. He is exonerated from the default of any misconduct. He becomes exonerated from any misbehave, whatsoever if any did for his mother. He further is exonerated of all defaults, if any entered within him for his daughter and sister. He becomes exonerated from the offence of thefting the gold etc. precious stones. He gets acquittal from the evil as arising due to lapses of the chapters already studied on Vedas. He becomes exonerated from the sins if any committed owing to any polluted material is dropped into the performance of offering. He further exonerated from the evil spirits arising like any lenience or laxity in the service of teacher. He becomes exonerated from evil tendencies like to eat viciated or stable things. He becomes exonerated from the evil some spirit if any has trapped him any time. He never is fastened with the evils which may be committed owing to the passions like sensuality, anger, attachment, greed, ego, manipulation etc. That man becomes purified from all kinds of sins and attains purity by virtue of realisation of a supreme soul in his extant life.

The meaning for this sentence should be taken most precisely. Often the people understand it that the man becomes exonerated from the evils he has committed. Due to compulsion of evil, some tendencies but what the saint wants to convey here is that his intuition becomes free from all kinds of sins. However, the evil deeds once committed by him will certainly punish him because there is no option but to consume the fruit of deeds performed by the man. The scholar having well-enlightened, smells the reality, therefore, he never indulges in the enticement of the evil tendencies.

तस्मादेतत्पुरुषसूक्तर्थमतिरहस्य राजगुह्यं गुह्यदपि गुह्यतरं नादीक्षितायोपदिशेत्। नानूचानाय। नायज्ञशीलाय। नावैष्णवाय। त्रायोगिने न बाहुभाषिणे। नाप्रियवाहिने। नासंवत्सरवेदिति। नातुष्टाय। नानधीतवेदायोपदिशेत्॥११॥

Thus the meaning of this 'Puruṣa Sūkta' is most cryptic. This 'Sūkta' is a secret for the king, the god and more cryptic than the cryptic itself is. One should not preach this Puruṣa Sūkta to a man who is not duly trained by a teacher. Inspite of having intelligent who does not ask with curiosity, who does not perform the offering, does not follow the Vaiṣṇava cult, who is not well-controlled, multi-lingual and speaking harshly, who does not study the Vedas once in a year, who is not content and further who has not gone over the Vedas (either not studied or taught), he is not eligible to have the knowledge of 'Puruṣa Sūkta'. Hence, one should not teach him this 'Puruṣa Sūkta'.

गुरुरप्येवंविच्छुचौ देशे पुण्यनक्षत्रे प्राणानायम्य पुरुषं ध्यायन्नुपसन्नाय शिष्याय दक्षिणकर्णे पुरुषसूक्तार्थमुपदिशेद्विद्वान्। न बहुशो वेदत्। यातयामो भवति। असकृत्कर्णमुपदिशते। एतत्कुर्वाणोऽध्येताध्यापकश्च इह जन्मनि पुरुषो भवतीत्युपनिषत्।।१२।।

The teacher well-known to Vedas as also duly conversant with the meaning of this 'Puruṣa Sūkta' should preach his obedient and devotee disciple to his right ear by taking care of the place, the ceremony, the location of the planets and by doing breathing control (Prāṇāyāma) and reciting the perfect man. He should not talk more otherwise such a preaching or the best knowledge gets polluted owing to no seriousness thus, the meaning of this 'Sūkta' should be preached to many devotee disciples. The teacher as also the student both become the perfect men even in their extant life.

।।शान्तिपाठः।।

ॐ वाङ्मे मनसि..... इति शान्तिः

।।इति मुद्गलोपनिषद् सम्पूर्णा ।।

***

54. ŚĀṆḌILYA-UPANIṢAD

शाण्डिल्योपनिषद्

॥शान्तिपाठः॥

ॐ भद्रं कर्णेभिः..........इति शान्तिः॥

॥प्रथमोऽध्यायः॥

शाण्डिल्यो ह वा अथर्वाणं पप्रच्छ आत्मलाभोपायभूतमष्टाङ्गयोगमनुब्रूहीति। स होवाचाथर्वा यमनियमासनप्राणायामप्रत्याहारधारणाध्यानसमाधयोऽष्टाङ्गानि। तत्र दश यमाः। तथा नियमाः। आसनान्यष्टौ। त्रयः प्राणायामाः। पञ्च प्रत्याहाराः। तथा धारणा। द्विप्रकारं ध्यानम्। समाधिस्त्वेकरूपः। तत्राहिंसासत्यास्तेयब्रह्मचर्यदयार्जवक्षमाधृतिमिताहारशौचानि चेति यमा दश। तत्राहिंसा नाम मनोवाक्कायकर्मभिः सर्वभूतेषु सर्वदाऽक्लेशजननम्। सत्यं नाम मनोवाक्कायकर्मभिर्भूतहितयथार्थाभिभाषणम्। अस्तेयं नाम मनोवाक्कायकर्मभिः परद्रव्येषु निःस्पृहता। ब्रह्मचर्यं नाम सर्वावस्थासु मनोवाक्कायकर्मभिः सर्वत्र मैथुनत्यागः। दया नाम सर्वभूतेषु सर्वत्रानुग्रहः। आर्जवं नाम मनोवाक्कायकर्मणां विहिताविहितेषु जनेषु प्रवृत्तौ निवृत्तौ वा एकरूपत्वम्। क्षमा नाम प्रियाप्रियेषु सर्वेषु ताडनपूजनेषु सहनम्। धृतिर्नामार्थहानौ स्वेष्टबन्धुवियोगे तत्प्राप्तौ सर्वत्र चेतःस्थापनम्। मिताहारो नाम चतुर्थांशावशेषकसुस्निग्धमधुराहारः। शौचं नाम द्विविधं बाह्यमान्तरं चेति। तत्र मृज्जलाभ्यां बाह्यम्। मनःशुद्धिरान्तरम्। तदध्यात्मविद्यया लभ्यम्॥ १॥

Chapter I

Oṁ. Śāṇḍilya questioned Atharvan thus : "Please tell me about the eight aṅgas (parts) of Yoga which is the means of attaining to Ātmā."

Atharvan replied : "The eight aṅgas of yoga are yama, niyama, āsana, prāṇāyāma, pratyāhāra, dhāraṇā, dhyāna and samādhi. Of these, yama is of ten kinds : and so is niyama. There are eight āsanas. Prāṇāyāma, is of three kinds; pratyāhāra is of five kinds : so also is dhāraṇā. Dhyāna is of two kinds and samādhi is of one kind only.

"Under yama (forbearance) are ten: ahiṁsā, satya, asteya, brahmacarya, dayā, ārjava, kṣamā, dhṛti, mitāhāra and śauca. Of these, ahiṁsā is the not causing of any pain to any living being at any time through the actions of one's mind, speech, or body. Satya is the speaking of the truth that conduces to the well-being of creatures, through the actions of one's mind, speech, or body. Asteya is not coveting of another's property through the actions of one's mind, speech, or body. Brahmacarya is the refraining from sexual intercourse in all places and in all states in mind, speech or body. Dayā is kindliness towards all creatures in all places. Ārjava is the preserving of equanimity of mind, speech, or body in the performance or non-performance of the actions ordained or forbidden to be done. Kṣamā is the bearing patiently of all pleasant or unpleasant things, such as praise or blow. Dhṛti is the preserving of firmness of mind during the period of gain or loss of wealth or relatives. Mitāhāra is the taking of oily and sweet food, leaving one-fourth of the stomach empty. Śauca is of two kinds, external and internal. Of these, the external is the cleansing of the body by earth and water; the internal is the cleansing of the mind. This (the latter) is to be obtained by means of the adhyātma-vidyā (science of Self).

॥द्वितीय: खण्ड:॥

तप:सन्तोषास्तिक्यदानेश्वरपूजनसिद्धान्तश्रवणह्रीमतिजपव्रतानि दश नियमा:। तत्र तपो नाम विध्युक्तकृच्छ्रचान्द्रायणादिभि: शरीरशोषणम्। संतोषो नाम यदृच्छालाभसंतुष्टि:। आस्तिक्यं नाम वेदोक्तधर्माधर्मेषु विश्वास:। दानं नाम न्यायार्जितस्य धनधान्यादे: श्रद्धयार्थिभ्य: प्रदानम्। ईश्वरपूजनं नाम प्रसन्नस्वभावेन यथाशक्ति विष्णुरुद्रादिपूजनम्। सिद्धान्तश्रवणं नाम वेदान्तार्थविचार:। ह्रीर्नाम वेदलौकिकमार्गकुत्सितकर्मणि लज्जा। मतिर्नाम वेदविहितकर्ममार्गेषु श्रद्धा। जपो नाम विधि वदुरूपदिष्टवेदाविरुद्धमन्त्राभ्यास:। तद्द्विविधं वाचिकं मानसं चेति। मानसं तु मनसा ध्यानयुक्त म्। वाचिकं द्विविधमुच्चैरुपांशुभेदेन। उच्चैरुच्चारणं यथोक्तफलम्। उपांशु सहस्रगुणम्। मानसं कोटिगुणम्। व्रतं नाम वेदोक्तविधिनिषेधानुष्ठाननैयत्यम्॥ १॥

"Under niyama (religious observances), are ten, viz., tapas, santoṣa, āstikya, dāna, Īśvarapūjana, siddhānta-śravaṇa, hrīḥ, mati, japa and vrata. Of these tapas, is the emancipation of the body through the observances of such penances as kṛcchra, cāndrāyaṇa, etc., according to rules. Santoṣa is being satisfied with whatever comes to us of its own accord. Āstikya is the belief in the merits or demerits of actions as stated in the vedas. Dāna is the giving with faith to deserving persons, money, grains, etc., earned lawfully. Īśvarapūjana is the worshipping of Viṣṇu, Rudra, etc., with pure mind according to one's power. Siddhānta-śravaṇa is the inquiry into the singificance of Vedānta. Hrīḥ is the shame felt in the performance of things contrary to the rules of the Vedas and of society. Mati is the faith in the paths laid down by the Vedas. Japa is the practising of the mantras into which one is duly initiated by his spiritual instructor, and which is not against (the rules of) the Vedas. It is of two kinds— the spoken and the mental. The mental is associated with contemplation by the mind. The spoken is of two kinds— the loud and low. The loud pronunciation gives the reward as stated (in the Vedas) : (while) the low one (gives) a reward thousand times (that). The mental (gives) a reward a crores (of times that). Vrata is the regular observance of or the refraining from the actions enjoined or prohibited by the Vedas.

॥तृतीय: खण्ड:॥

स्वस्तिकगोमुखपद्मवीरसिंहभद्रमुक्तमयूराख्यान्यासनान्यष्टौ। स्वस्तिकं नाम जानूर्वोरन्तरे सम्यक्कृत्वा पादतले उभे। ऋजुकाय: समासीन: स्वस्तिकं तत्प्रचक्षते॥ १॥

सव्ये दक्षिणगुल्फं तु पृष्ठपार्श्वे नियोजयेत्। दक्षिणेऽपि तथा सव्यं गोमुखं गोमुखं यथा॥ २॥

अङ्गुष्ठेन निबध्नीयाद्धस्ताभ्यां व्युत्क्रमेण च। ऊर्वोरुपरि शाण्डिल्य कृत्वा पादतले उभे।

पद्मासनं भवेदेतत्सर्वेषामपि पूजितम्॥ ३॥

एकं पादमथैकस्मिन्विन्यस्योरुणि संस्थितः। इतरस्मिंस्तथा चोरुं वीरासनमुदीरितम्॥ ४॥

दक्षिणं सव्यगुल्फेन दक्षिणेन तथेतरम्। हस्तौ च जान्वोः संस्थाप्य स्वाङ्गुलीश्च प्रसार्य च॥ ५॥

व्यात्तवक्त्रो निरीक्षेत नासाग्रं सुसमाहितः। सिंहासनं भवेदेतत्पूजितं योगिभिः सदा॥ ६॥

योनिं वामेन संपीड्य मेढ्रादुपरि दक्षिणम्। भ्रूमध्ये च मनोलक्ष्यं सिद्धासनमिदं भवेत्॥ ७॥

गुल्फौ तु वृषणस्याधः सीवन्याः पार्श्वयोः क्षिपेत्। पादपार्श्वे तु पाणिभ्यां दृढं बद्ध्वा सुनिश्चलम्। भद्रासनं भवेदेतत्सर्वव्याधिविषापहम्॥ ८॥

संपीड्य सीविनीं सूक्ष्मां गुल्फेनैव तु सव्यतः। सव्यं दक्षिणगुल्फेन मुक्तासनमुदीरितम्॥ ९॥

अवष्टभ्य धरां सम्यक् तलाभ्यां तु करद्वयोः। हस्तयोः कूर्परौ चापि स्थापयेन्नाभिपार्श्वयोः॥ १०॥

समुन्नतशिरः पादो दण्डवद्व्योम्नि संस्थितः। मयूरासनमेतत्तु सर्वपापप्रणाशनम्॥ ११॥

शरीरान्तर्गताः सर्वे रोगा विनश्यन्ति। विषाणि जीर्यन्ते॥ १२॥

येन केनासनेन सुखधारणं भवत्यशक्तस्तत्समाचरेत्॥ १३॥

येनासनं विजितं जगत्त्रयं तेन विजितं भवति॥ १४॥

यमनियमासनाभ्यासयुक्तः पुरुषः प्राणायामं चरेत्। तेन नाड्यः शुद्धा भवन्ति॥ १५॥

"Āsanas (the postures) are chiefly) eight. viz., svastika, gomukha, padma, vīra, siṁha, bhadra, mukta and mayūra–

"Svastika is the sitting at ease with the body erect, placing each foot between the thighs and knees of the other. Gomukha is (the sitting at ease with the body erect) placing the hollow of the left foot under the side of the right posteriors and the hollow of the right foot under the side of the left posteriors, resembling Gomukha (cow's face). Padma is (the sitting at ease with the body erect), placing the back of each foot in the thigh of the other, the right hand grasping the right toe and the left hand the left toe. This, O Śāṇḍilya, is praised by all. Vīra is the sitting at ease (with the body erect), placing one foot on the thigh of the other and the other foot underneath the corresponding (opposite thigh). Siṁha is (the sitting at ease with the body erect), pressing the right side (of the thigh) with the hollow of left heel and vice versa. Rest your hands on the knees, spread out the fingers, open your mouth and carefully fix your gaze on the tip of your nose. This is always praised by the yogins. Siddha is (the siting at ease with the body erect), pressing the perineum with the left heel and placing the heel of the right foot above the genital rogan, concentrating the mind between the two eyebrows. Bhadra is (the sitting at ease with the body erect), pressing the two ankles of the two feet firmly together against the Sīvinī (viz., lower part of the seed) and binding the knees firmly with the hands. This is the bhadra which destroys all diseases and poisons. Mukta is (the sitting at ease with the body erect), pressing with the left heel the right side of the tender part of the Sīvinī, and with the right heel the left side of the tender part of the Sīvinī. Mayūri— (lit., peacock), Rest your body upon the ground with both palms and place your elbows on the sides of the navel, lift up the head and feet and remain like a stick in the air, (like the plant balance in gymnastics). This is the mayūra posture which destroys all sins. By these, all the diseases within the body are destroyed; all the poisons are digested. Let the person who is unable to practise all these postures betake himself to any one (of these) which he may find easy and pleasant. He who conquers (or gets mastery over) the postures— he conquers the three worlds. A person who has the practice of yama and niyama should practise prāṇāyāma; by that the nāḍīs become purified."

॥चतुर्थः खण्डः॥

अथ हैनमथर्वाणं शाण्डिल्यः पप्रच्छ केनोपायेन नाड्यः शुद्धाः स्युः। नाड्यः कतिसंख्याकाः। तासामुत्पत्तिः कीदृशी। तासु कति वायवस्तिष्ठन्ति। तेषां कानि स्थानानि। तत्कर्माणि कानि। देहे यानि यानि विज्ञातव्यानि तत्सर्वं मे ब्रूहीति॥ १॥

स होवाचाथर्वा। अथेदं शरीरं षण्णवत्यङ्गुलात्मकं भवति। शरीरात्प्राणो द्वादशाङ्गुलाधिको भवति॥ २॥ शरीरस्थं प्राणमग्निना सह योगाभ्यासेन समं न्यूनं वा यः करोति स योगिपुङ्गवो भवति॥ ३॥

देहमध्ये शिखिस्थानं त्रिकोणं तप्तजाम्बूनदप्रभं मनुष्याणाम्। चतुष्पदां चतुरश्रम्। विहङ्गानां वृत्ताकारम्। तन्मध्ये शुभा तन्वी पावकी शिखा तिष्ठति॥ ४॥

गुदाद्द्व्यङ्गुलादूर्ध्वं मेढ्राद्द्व्यङ्गुलादधो देहमध्यं मनुष्याणां भवति। चतुष्पदां हृन्मध्यम्। विहगानां तुन्दमध्यम्। देहमध्यं नवाङ्गुलं चतुरङ्गुलमुत्सेधायतमण्डाकृति॥ ५॥

तन्मध्ये नाभिः। तत्र द्वादशारयुतं चक्रम्। तच्चक्रमध्ये पुण्यपापप्रचोदितो जीवोभ्रमति॥ ६ तन्तुपञ्जरमध्यस्थलूतिका यथा भ्रमति तथा चासौ तत्र प्राणश्चरति। देहेऽस्मिञ्जीवः प्राणारूढो भवेत्॥ ७॥

नाभेस्तिर्यगध ऊर्ध्वं कुण्डलिनीस्थानम्। अष्टप्रकृतिरूपाऽष्टधा कुण्डलीकृता कुण्डलिनी शक्तिर्भवति। यथावद्वायुसंचारं जलान्नादीनि परितः स्कन्धपार्श्वेषु निरुध्यैनं मुखेनैव समावेष्ट्य ब्रह्मरन्ध्रं योगकाले चापानेनाग्निना च स्फुरति। हृदयाकाशे महोज्ज्वला ज्ञानरूपा भवति॥ ८॥

मध्यस्थकुण्डलिनीमाश्रित्य मुख्या नाड्यश्चतुर्दश भवन्ति। इडा पिङ्गला सुषुम्ना सरस्वती वारुणी पूषा हस्तिजिह्वा यशस्विनी विश्वोदरी कुहूःशङ्खिनी पयस्विनी अलम्बुसा गान्धारीति नाड्यश्चतुर्दश भवन्ति॥ ९॥

तत्र सुषुम्ना विश्वधारिणी मोक्षमार्गेति चाचक्षते। गुदस्य पृष्ठभागे वीणादण्डाश्रिता मूर्धपर्यन्तं ब्रह्मरन्ध्रे विज्ञेया व्यक्ता सूक्ष्मा वैष्णवी भवति॥ १०॥

सुषुम्नायाः सव्यभागे इडा तिष्ठति। दक्षिणभागे पिङ्गला। इडायां चन्द्रश्चरति। पिङ्गलायां रविः। तमोरूपश्चन्द्रः। रजोरूपो रविः। विषभागो रविः। अमृतभागश्चन्द्रमाः। तावेव सर्वकालं धत्तः। सुषुम्ना कालभोक्त्री भवति। सुषुम्नापृष्ठपार्श्वयोः सरस्वतीकुहू भवतः। यशस्विनीकुहूमध्ये वारुणी प्रतिष्ठिता भवति। पूषासरस्वतीमध्ये पयस्विनी भवति। गान्धारीसरस्वतीमध्ये यशस्विनी भवति। कन्दमध्येऽलम्बुसा भवति। सुषुम्नापूर्वभागे मेढ्रान्तं कुहूर्भवति। कुण्डलिन्या अधश्चोर्ध्वं वारुणी सर्वगामिनी भवति। यशस्विनी सौम्या च

पादाङ्गुष्ठान्तमिष्यते। पिङ्गला चोर्ध्वगा याम्यनासान्तं भवति। पिङ्गलायाः पृष्ठतो याम्यनेत्रान्तं पूषा भवति। याम्यकर्णान्तं यशस्विनी भवति। जिह्वाया ऊर्ध्वान्तं सरस्वती भवति। आसव्यकर्णान्तमूर्ध्वगा शङ्खिनी भवति। इडापृष्ठभागात्सव्यनेत्रान्तगा गान्धारी भवति। पायुमूलादधोर्ध्वगाऽलम्बुसा भवति। एतासु चतुर्दशसु नाडीष्वन्या नाड्यः संभवन्ति। तास्वन्यास्तास्वन्या भवन्तीति विज्ञेयाः। यथाऽश्वत्थादिपत्रं सिराभिर्व्याप्तमेवं शरीरं नाडीभिर्व्याप्तम्॥ ११॥

The Śāṇḍilya questioned Atharvan thus : "By what means are the nāḍīs purified ? How many are they in number? How do they arise? What vāyus (vital airs) are located in them? What are their seats? What are their functions? Whatever is worthy of being known in the body, please tell me." To that Atharvan replied (thus): "This body is ninety-six digits in length. Prāṇa extends twelve digits beyond the body. He who through the practice of yoga reduces his prāṇa within his body to make it equal to or not less than the fire in it becomes the greatest of the yogins. In men, the region of fire which is triangular in form and brilliant as the molten gold is situated in the middle of the body. In four-footed animals, it (fire) is quadrangular. In birds, it is round. In its (the region of fire's) centre, the purifying, beneficial, and subtle flame is situated. Two digits above the anus and two digits below the sexual organ is the centre of the body for men. For four-footed animals, it is the middle of the heart. For birds, it is the middle of the body. Nine digits from (or above) the centre of the body and four digits in length and breadth is situated an oval form. In its midst is the navel. In it, is situated the cakra (viz., wheel) with twelve spokes. In the middle of the cakra, the jīva (Ātmā) wanders, driven by its good and bad deeds. As a spider flies to and fro within a web of fine threads, so prāṇa moves about here. In this body, the jīva rides upon prāṇa. Lying in the middle of the navel and above it, is the seat of kuṇḍalinī. The kuṇḍalinī śakti is of the form of eight prakṛtis (matter) and coils itself eight ways or (times). The movement of vāyus (vital airs) checks duly the food and drink all round by the side of skandha. It closes by its head (the opening of) the brahmarandhra, and during the time of (the practice of) yoga is awakened by the fire (in the apāna): then it shines with great brilliancy in the ākāśa of the heart in the shape of wisdom. Depending upon Kuṇḍalinī which is situated in the centre, there are fourteen principal nāḍīs (viz.,) Iḍā, Piṅgalā, Suṣumnā, Sarasvatī, Vāruṇī, Pūṣā, Hastijihvā, Yaśasvinī, Viśvodharī, Kuhūḥ, Śaṅkhinī, Payasvinī, Alambusā and Gāndhārī. Of them, Suṣumnā is said to be the sustainer of the universe and the path of salvation. Situated at the back of the anus, it is attached to the spinal column and extends to the brahmarandhra of the head and is invisible and subtle and is vaiṣṇavī (or has the śakti force of Viṣṇu). On the left of suṣumnā is situated Iḍā, and on the right is Piṅgalā. The moon moves in Iḍā and the sun in Piṅgalā. The moon is of the nature of tamas and the sun of rajas. The poison share is of the sun and the nectar of the moon. They both direct (or indicate) time and Suṣumnā is the enjoyer (or consumer) of time. To the back and on the side of Suṣumnā are situate Sarasvatī and Kuhūḥ respectively. Between Yaśasvinī and Kuhūḥ stands Vāruṇī. Between Pūṣā and Sarasvatī lies Payasvinī. Between Gāndharī and Sarasvatī is situated Yaśasvinī. In the centre of the navel is Alambusā. In front of Suṣumnā there is Kuhūḥ, which proceeds as far as the genital organ.

Above and below kuṇḍalinī is situated Vāruṇī, which proceeds everywhere. Yaśasvinī which is beautiful (or belonging to the moon), proceeds to the great toes. Piṅgalā goes upwards to the right nostril. Payasvinī goes to right ear. Sarasvatī goes to the upper part or the tongue and Śāṅkhinī to the left ear, (while Gāndhārī goes from the back of Iḍā to the left eye. Alambusā goes upwards and downwards from the root of the anus. From these fourteen nāḍīs, other (minor) nāḍīs spring; from them springing others, and from them springing others; so it should be known. As the leaf of the aśvattha three (ficus religiosa) etc., is covered with minute fibres so also is this body permeated with nāḍīs.

प्राणापानसमानोदानव्याना नागकूर्मकृकरदेवदत्तधनञ्जया एते दश वायवः सर्वासु नाडीषु चरन्ति॥ १२॥

आस्यनासिकाकण्ठनाभिपादाङ्गुष्ठद्वयकुण्डल्यधश्चोर्ध्वभागेषु प्राणः संचरति। श्रोत्राक्षिकटिगुल्फघ्राणगलस्फिग्देशेषु व्यानः संचरति। गुदमेढ्रोरुजानूदरवृषणकटिजङ्घानाभिगुदाग्न्यगारेष्वपानः संचरति। सर्वसंधिस्थ उदानः। पादहस्तयोरपि सर्वगात्रेषु सर्वव्यापी समानः। भुक्तान्नरसादिकं गात्रेऽग्निना सह व्यापयन्द्विसप्ततिसहस्रेषु नाडीमार्गेषु चरन्समानवायुरग्निना सह साङ्गोपाङ्गकलेवरं व्याप्नोति। नागादिवायवः पञ्च त्वगस्थ्यादिसंभवाः। तुन्दस्थं जलमन्नं च रसादिषु समीरितं तुन्दमध्यगतः प्राणस्तानि पृथक्कुर्यात्। अग्नेरुपरि जलं स्थाप्य जलोपर्यन्नादीनि संस्थाप्य स्वयमपानं संप्राप्य तेनैव सह मारुतः प्रयाति देहमध्यगतं ज्वलनम्। वायुना पालितो वह्निरपानेन शनैर्देहमध्ये ज्वलति। ज्वलनो ज्वालाभिः प्राणेन कोष्ठमध्यगतं जलमत्युष्णमकरोत्। जलोपरि समर्पितव्यञ्जनसंयुक्तमन्नं वह्निसंयुक्तवारिणा पक्वमकरोत्। तेन स्वेदमूत्रजलरक्तवीर्यरूपरसपुरीषादिकं प्राणः पृथक्कुर्यात्। समानवायुना सह सर्वासु नाडीषु रसं व्यापयञ्छ्वासरूपेण देहे वायुश्चरति। नवभिर्व्योमरन्ध्रैः शरीरस्य वायवः कुर्वन्ति विण्मूत्रादिविसर्जनम्। निश्वासोच्छ्वासकासश्च प्राणकर्मोच्यते। विण्मूत्रादिविसर्जनमपानवायुकर्म। हानोपादानचेष्टादि व्यानकर्म। देहस्योन्नयनादिकमुदानकर्म। शरीरपोषणादिकं समानकर्म। उद्गारादि नागकर्म। निमीलनादि कूर्मकर्म। क्षुत्करणं कृकरकर्म। तन्द्रा देवदत्तकर्म। श्लेष्मादि धनञ्जयकर्म॥ १३॥

"Prāṇa, Apāna, Samāna, Udāna, Vyāna, Nāga, Kūrma, Kṛkara, Devadatta and Dhanañjaya— these ten vāyus (vital airs) move in all the nāḍīs. Prāṇa moves in the nostrils, the throat, the navel, the two great toes and the lower and the upper parts of kuṇḍalinī. Vyāna moves in the ear, the eye, the loins, the ankles, the nose, the throat and the buttocks. Apāna moves in the anus, the genitals, the thighs, the knees, the stomach, the seeds, the loins, the calves, the navel, and the seat of the anus of fire. Udāna lives in all the joints and also in the hands and legs. Samāna lives, permeating in all parts of the body. Along with the fire in the body, it causes the food and drink taken in, to spread in the body. It moves in the seventy-two thousand nāḍīs and pervades all over the body along with the fire. The five vāyus beginning with Nāga go towards the skin, the bones, etc. The prāṇa which is in the navel separates the food and drink which is there and brings about the rasas (juices) and others. Placing the water above the fire and the food above (or in) the water, it goes to the Apāna and along with it, fans up the fire in the centre of the body. The fire thus fanned up by the Apāna gradually increases in brightness in the middle of the body. Then it causes through its flames the water which is brought in the bowels by the Prāṇa to grow hot. The fire with the water causes the food and condiments, which are placed above, to be boiled to a proper degree. Then Prāṇa separates these into sweat, urine, water, blood, semen, the fæces, and the like. And along with the Samāna, it takes the juice (or essence) to all the nāḍīs and moves in the body in the shape of breath. The vāyus excrete the urine, the fæces, etc., through the nine openings in the body which are connected with the outside air. The functions of Prāṇa are inspiration, expiration, and cough. Those Apāna are excretion of the fæces and the urine. Those of Vyāna are (such actions as) giving and taking. Those of Udāna are keeping the body straight, etc. Those of Samāna are nourishing the body. Those of Nāga are vomiting, etc.; of Kūrma, the movement of the eyelids; the Kṛkara, the causing, of hunger, etc., of Devadatta idleness, etc., and Dhanañjaya, phlegm.

एवं नाडीस्थानं वायुस्थानं तत्कर्म च सम्यग्ज्ञात्वा नाडीसंशोधनं कुर्यात्॥ १४॥

"Having thus acquired a thorough knowledge of the seat of the nāḍīs and of the vāyus with their functions, one should begin with the purification of the nāḍīs.

॥पंचम: खण्ड:॥

यमनियमयुत: पुरुष: सर्वसङ्गविवर्जित: कृतविद्य: सत्यधर्मरतो जितक्रोधो गुरुशुश्रूषानिरत: पितृमातृविधेय: स्वाश्रमोक्तसदाचारविद्वच्छिक्षित: फलमूलोदकान्वितं तपोवनं प्राप्य रम्यदेशे ब्रह्मघोषसमन्विते स्वधर्मनिरतब्रह्मवित्समावृते फलमूलपुष्पवारिभि: सुसंपूर्णे देवायतने नदीतीरे ग्रामे नगरे वापि सुशोभनमठं नात्युच्चनीचायतमल्पद्वारं गोमयादिलिप्तं सर्वरक्षासमन्वितं कृत्वा तत्र वेदान्तश्रवणं कुर्वन्योगं समारभेत्॥ १॥

आदौ विनायकं संपूज्य स्वेष्टदेवतां नत्वा पूर्वोक्तासने स्थित्वा प्राङ्मुख उदङ्मुखो वापि मृद्वासनेषु जितासनगतो विद्वान्समग्रीवशिरोनासाग्रदृग्भ्रूमध्ये शशभृद्बिम्बं पश्यन्नेत्राभ्याममृतं पिबेत्। द्वादशमात्रया इडया वायुमापूर्योदरे स्थितं ज्वालावलीयुतं रेफबिन्दुयुक्तमग्निमण्डलयुतं ध्यायेद्रेचयेत्पिङ्गलया। पुन: पिङ्गलयाऽऽपूर्य कुम्भित्वा रेचयेदिडया॥ २॥

त्रिचतुस्त्रिचतु:सप्तत्रिचतुर्मासपर्यन्तं त्रिसंधिषु तदन्तरालेषु च षट्कृत्व आचरेन्नाडीशुद्धिर्भवति। तत: शरीरे लघुदीप्तिवह्निवृद्धिनादाभिव्यक्तिर्भवति॥ ३-४॥

A person possessed of yama and niyama, avoiding all company, having finished his course of study, delighting in truth and virtue, having conquered (his) anger, being engaged in the service of his spiritual instructor and having been obedient to his parents and well instructed in all the religious practices and the knowledge of his order of life, should go to a sacred grove abounding in fruits, roots, and water. There he should select a pleasant spot always resouding with the chanting of the Vedas, frequented by the knowers of Brahman that persevere in the duties of their orders of life and filled with fruits, roots, flowers, and water. (Else) either in a temple or on the banks of a river or in a village or in a town, he should build a beautiful monastery. It should be neither too long nor too high, should have a small door, should be besmeared well with cow-dung and should have every sort of protection. There listening to exposition of Vedānta, he should begin to practice yoga. In the beginning having worshipped Vināyaka (Gaṇeśa), he should salute his Īṣṭa-Devatā (tutelary deity) and sitting in any of the above-mentioned postures of a soft seat, facing either the east or the north and having conquered them, the learned man keeping his head and neck erect and fixed his gaze on the tip of his nose, should see the sphere of the moon between his eyebrows and drink the nectar (flowing there from through his eyes). Inhaling the air through Iḍā for the space of twelve mātrās, he should contemplate on the sphere of fire situated in the belly as surrounded with flames and having as its seed j (ra); then he should exhale it through Piṅgalā. Again inhaling it through Piṅgalā and retaining it (within), he should exhale it through Iḍā. For the period of twenty-eight months, he should practise six times at every sitting through the three sandhyās (morning, noon, and evening) and during the intervals. By this, the nāḍīs become purified. Then the body becomes light and bright, the (gastric) fire is increased (within) and there is the manifestation of nāda (internal sound).

॥षष्ठ: खण्ड:॥

प्राणापानसमायोग: प्राणायामो भवति। रेचकपूरककुम्भकभेदेन स त्रिविध:। ते वर्णात्मका:। तस्मात्प्रणव एव प्राणायाम:॥ १-२॥

पद्माद्यासनस्थ: पुमान्नासाग्रे शशभृद्बिम्बज्योत्स्नाजालवितानिताकारमूर्ती रक्ताङ्गी हंसवाहिनी दण्डहस्ता बाला गायत्री भवति। उकारमूर्ति: श्वेताङ्गी तार्क्ष्यवाहिनी युवती चक्रहस्ता सावित्री भवति। मकारमूर्ति: कृष्णाङ्गी वृषभवाहिनी वृद्धा त्रिशूलधारिणी सरस्वती भवति॥ ३॥ अकारादित्रयाणां सर्वकारणमेकाक्षरं परंज्योति: प्रणवं भवतीति॥ ४॥

ध्यायेत् इडया बाह्याद्वायुमापूर्य षोडशमात्राभिरकारं चिन्तयन्पूरितं वायुं चतु:षष्टिमात्राभि: कुम्भयित्वोकारं ध्यायन्पूरितं पिङ्गलया द्वात्रिंशन्मात्रया मकारमूर्तिध्यानेनैवं क्रमेण पुन:-पुन: कुर्यात्॥ ५॥

"Prāṇāyāma is said to be union of Prāṇa and Apāna. It is of three kinds— expiration, inspiration, and cessation. They are associated with the letters of (Sanskrit) alphabet (for the right performance of prāṇāyāma). Therefore Praṇava (Oṁ) only is said to be Prāṇāyāma. sitting in the padma posture, the person should meditate that there is at the tip of his nose Gāyatrī, a girl of red complexion surrounded by the numberless rays of the image of the moon and mounted on a haṁsa (Swan) and having a mace in hand. She is the visible symbol of the latter A. The letter U has as its visible symbol Sāvitrī, a young woman of white colour having a disk in her hand and riding on a garuḍa (eagle). The letter M has as its visible symbol Sarasvatī, an aged woman of black colour riding on a bull, having a trident in her hand. He should meditate that the single letter— the supreme light— the praṇava (Oṁ)— is the origin or source of these three letters A, U. and M. Drawing up the air thorugh Iḍā for the space of sixteen mātrās, he should meditate on the letter A during that time; retaining the inspired air for the space of sixty-four mātrās, he should meditate on the letter U during the time; he should then exhale the inspired air for the space of thirty-two mātrās, meditating on the letter M during that time. He should practise this in the above order over and over again.

॥सप्तमः खण्डः॥

अथासनदृढो योगी वशी मितहिताशनः सुषुम्नानाडीस्थमलशोषार्थं योगी बद्धपद्मासनो वायुं चन्द्रेणापूर्य यथाशक्ति कुम्भयित्वा सूर्येण रेचयित्वा पुनः सूर्येणापूर्य कुम्भयित्वा चन्द्रेण विरेच्य यया त्यजेत्तया संपूर्य धारयेत्। तदेते श्लोका भवन्तिप्राणं प्रागिडया पिबेन्नियमितं भूयोऽन्यया रेचयेत्पीत्वा पिङ्गलया समीरणमथो बद्ध्वा त्यजेद्वामया। सूर्याचन्द्रमसोरनेन विधिनाऽभ्यासं सदा तन्वतां शुद्धा नाडिगणा भवन्ति यमिनां मासत्रयादूर्ध्वतः॥ १॥

प्रातर्मध्यन्दिने सायमर्धरात्रे तु कुम्भकान्। शनैरशीतिपर्यन्तं चतुर्वारं समभ्यसेत्॥ २॥

कनीयसि भवेत्स्वेदः कम्पो भवति मध्यमे। उत्तिष्ठत्युत्तमे प्राणरोधे पद्मासनं भवेत्॥ ३॥

जलेन श्रमजातेन गात्रमर्दनमाचरेत्। दृढता लघुता चापि तस्य गात्रस्य जायते॥ ४॥

अभ्यासकाले प्रथमं शस्तं क्षीराज्यभोजनम्। ततोऽभ्यासे स्थिरीभूते न तावन्नियमग्रहः॥ ५॥

यथा सिंहो गजो व्याघ्रो भवेद्वश्यः शनैःशनैः। तथैव सेवितो वायुरन्यथा हन्ति साधकम्॥ ६॥

"Then having become firm in the posture and preserved perfect self-control, the yogin should, in order to clear away the impurities of the Suṣumnā, sit in the padmāsana (padma posture), and having inhaled the air through the left nostril, should retain it as long as he can and should exhale it through the right. Then drawing it again through the right and having retained it, he should exhale it through the left in the order that he should draw it through the same nostril by which he exhaled it before and retained it. In this context, occur (to memory) the following verses : "In the beginning having inhaled the breath (Prāṇa) through the left nostril, according to the rule, he should exhale it through the other; then having inhaled the air through the right nostril, should retain it and exhale it through the other." To those who practise according to these rules through the right and left nostrils, the nāḍīs become purified within three months. He should practise cessation of breath at sunrise, in the midday, at sunset and at midnight slowly till eighty (times a day) for four weeks. In the early stages, perspiration is produced; in the middle stage the tremor of the body, and in the last stage levitation in the air. These (results) ensue out of the repression of the breath, while sitting in the padma posture. When perspiration arises with effort, he should rub his body well. By this, the body becomes firm and light. In the early course of his practice, food with milk and ghee is excellent. One sticking to this rule becomes firm in his practice and gets no tāpa (or burning sensation in the body). As lions, elephants and tigers are gradually tamed, so also the breath, when rightly managed (comes under control); else it kills the practitioner.

युक्तंयुक्तं त्यजेद्वायुं युक्तंयुक्तं च पूरयेत्। युक्तंयुक्तं च बध्नीयादेवं सिद्धिमवाप्नुयात्॥ ७॥

यथेष्टधारणाद्वायोरनलस्य प्रदीपनम्। नादाभिव्यक्तिरारोग्यं जायते नाडिशोधनात्॥ ८॥

विधिवत्प्राणसंयामैर्नाडीचक्रे विशोधिते। सुषुम्नावदनं भित्त्वा सुखाद्विशति मारुतः॥ ९॥

मारुते मध्यसंचारे मनःस्थैर्यं प्रजायते। यो मनः सुस्थिरो भावः सैवावस्था मनोन्मनी॥ १०॥

पूरकान्ते तु कर्तव्यो बन्धो जालन्धराभिधः। कुम्भकान्ते रेचकादौ कर्तव्यस्तूड्डियाणकः॥ ११

अधस्तात्कुञ्चनेनाशु कण्ठसंकोचने कृते। मध्ये पश्चिमतानेन स्यात्प्राणो ब्रह्मनाडिगः॥ १२॥

अपानमूर्ध्वमुत्थाप्य प्राणं कण्ठादधो नयन्। योगी जराविनिर्मुक्तः षोडशो वयसा भवेत्॥ १३॥

"He should (as far as is consistent with his health and safety) properly exhale it, properly inhale it or retain it properly. Thus (only) will he attain success. By thus retaining the breath in an approved manner and by the purification of the nāḍīs, the brightening of the (gastric) fire, the hearing distinctly of (spiritual) sounds and (good) health result. When the nervous centres have become purified through the regular practice of Prāṇāyāma, the air easily forces its way up through the mouth of the Suṣumnā which is in the middle. By the contraction of the muscles of the neck and by the contraction of the one below (viz.,) Apāna the Prāṇa (breath) goes into the Suṣumnā which is in the middle from the west nāḍī Drawing up the Apāna and forcing down the Prāṇa from the throat, the yogin free from ol age becomes a youth of sixteen.

सुखासनस्थो दक्षनाड्या बहिःस्थं पवनं समाकृष्याकेशमानखाग्रं कुम्भयित्वा सव्यनाड्या रेचयेत्। तेन कपालशोधनं वातनाडीगतसर्वरोगसर्वविनाशनं भवति॥ १३-१॥

हृदयादिकण्ठपर्यन्तं सस्वनं नासाभ्यां शनैः पवनमाकृष्य यथाशक्ति कुम्भयित्वा इडया विरेच्य गच्छंस्तिष्ठन्कुर्यात्। तेन श्लेष्महरं जठराग्निवर्धनं भवति॥ १३-२॥

वक्त्रेण सीत्कारपूर्वकं वायुं गृहीत्वा यथाशक्ति कुम्भयित्वा नासाभ्यां रेचयेत्। तेन क्षुत्तृष्णालस्यनिद्रा न जायन्ते॥ १३-३॥

"Seated in pleasant posture and drawing up the air through the right nostril and retaining it inside from the top of the hair to the toe nails, he should exhale it through the same nostril. Through it, the brain becomes purified and the diseases in the air nāḍīs are destroyed. Drawing up the air through the nostrils with noise (so as to fill the space) from the heart to the neck, and having retained it (within) as long as possible, he should exhale it through the nose. Through this, hunger, thirst, idleness and sleep do not arise.

जिह्वया वायुं गृहीत्वा यथाशक्ति कुम्भयित्वा नासाभ्यां रेचयेत्। तेन गुल्मप्लीहज्वरपित्तक्षुधादीनि नश्यन्ति॥ १३-४॥

"Taking in the air through the mouth (wide open) and having retained it as long as possible, he should expel it through the nose. Through this (such diseases as) gulma, pleeha (both being splentic diseases), bile and fever as also hunger, etc., are destroyed.

अथ कुम्भकः। स द्विविधः सहितः केवलश्चेति। रेचकपूरकयुक्तः सहितः। तद्विवर्जितः केवलः। केवलसिद्धिपर्यन्तं सहितमभ्यसेत्। केवलकुम्भके सिद्धे त्रिषु लोकेषु न तस्य दुर्लभं भवति। केवलकुम्भकात्कुण्डलिनीबोधो जायते॥॥ १३-५॥ ततः कृशवपुः प्रसन्नवदनो निर्मललोचनोऽभिव्यक्तनादो निर्मुक्तरोगजालो जितबिन्दुः पटूवग्निर्भवति॥ १३-६॥

"Now we shall proceed to kumbhaka (restraint of breath). It is of two kinds— sahita and kevala. That which is coupled with expiration and inspiration is called sahita. That which is devoid of these is called kevala (alone). Until you become perfect in kevalas, practise sahita. To one who has mastered kevala, there is nothing unattainable in the three worlds. By kevala-restraint of breath, the knowledge of kuṇḍalinī arises. Then he becomes lean in body, serene in face and clear-eyed, hears the (spiritual) sounds distinctly, becomes free from all diseases and conquers his (bindu) seminal fluid, his gastric fire being increased.

अन्तर्लक्ष्यं बहिर्दृष्टिर्निमेषोन्मेषवर्जिता। एषा सा वैष्णवी मुद्रा सर्वतन्त्रेषु गोपिता॥ १४॥

अन्तर्लक्ष्यविलीनचित्तपवनो योगी सदा वर्तते दृष्ट्या निश्चलतारया बहिरधः पश्यन्नपश्यन्नपि। मुद्रेयं खलु खेचरी भवति सा लक्ष्यैकताना शिवा शून्याशून्यविवर्जितं स्फुरति सा तत्त्वं पदं वैष्णवी॥ १५॥

अर्धोन्मीलितलोचनः स्थिरमना नासाग्रदत्तेक्षणश्चन्द्रार्कावपि लीनतामुपनयन्निष्पन्दभावोत्तरम्। ज्योतीरूपमशेषबाह्यरहितं देदीप्यमानं परं तत्त्वं तत्परमस्ति वस्तुविषयं शाण्डिल्य विद्धीह तत्॥ १६॥

तारं ज्योतिषि संयोज्य किंचिदुन्नमयन्भ्रुवौ। पूर्वाभ्यासस्य मार्गोऽयमुन्मनीकारकः क्षणात्॥ १७॥ तस्मात्खेचरीमुद्रामभ्यसेत्। तत उन्मनी भवति। ततो योगनिद्रा भवति। लब्धयोगनिद्रस्य योगिनः कालो नास्ति॥॥ १७.१॥

शक्तिमध्ये मनः कृत्वा शक्तिं मानसमध्यगाम्।
मनसा मन आलोक्य शाण्डिल्य त्वं सुखी भव॥ १८॥

खमध्ये कुरु चात्मानमात्ममध्ये च खं कुरु। सर्वं च खमयं कृत्वा न किंचिदपि चिन्तय॥

बाह्यचिन्ता न कर्तव्या तथैवान्तरचिन्तिका। सर्वचिन्तां परित्यज्य चिन्मात्रपरमो भव॥ २०॥

कर्पूरमनले यद्वत्सैन्धवं सलिले यथा। तथा च लीयमानं सन्मनस्तत्त्वे विलीयते॥ २१॥

ज्ञेयं सर्वप्रतीतं च तज्ज्ञानं मन उच्यते। ज्ञानं ज्ञेयं समं नष्टं नान्यः पन्था द्वितीयकः॥ २२॥

ज्ञेयवस्तुपरित्यागाद्विलयं याति मानसम्। मानसे विलयं याते कैवल्यमवशिष्यते॥ २३॥

Oṁ. Centring one's mind on an inward object while his eyes are looking outside without the shutting and opening of his eyelids, has been called Vaiṣṇavīmudrā. This is kept hidden in all the tāntric works. With his mind and breath absorbed in an internal object, the yogin, though he does not really see the objects outside and under him, still (appears to) see them with eyes in which the pupils are motionless. This is called Khecarīmudrā. It has as its sphere of extension one object and is very beneficial. (Then) the real seat of Viṣṇu, which is void and non-void, dawns on him. With eyes half closed and with a firm mind, fixing his eyes on the tip of his nose and becoming absorbed in the sun and moon, he after remaining thus unshaken (becomes conscious of) the thing which is of the form of light, which is free from all externals, which is resplendent, which is the supreme truth and which is beyond. O Śāṇḍilya, know this to be Tat (That). Merging the sound in the light and elevating the brows a little, this is of the way of (or is part of) the former practice. This brings about the state of Unmanī which causes the destruction of the mind. Therefore he should practise the Khecarīmudrā. Then he attains to the state of Unmanī and falls into the yoga sleep (trance). To one who obtains this yoga sleep, time does not exist. Placing the mind in the midst of śakti and śakti in the midst of the mind and looking on the mind with the mind, O Śāṇḍilya be happy. Place the Ātmā in the midst of ākāśa and ākāśa in the midst of Ātmā, and having reduced everything to ākāśa, do not think anything else. You should not (then) entertain thoughts, either external or internal. Abandoning all thoughts, become abstract. As comphor in fire and salt in water become absorbed, so also the mind becomes absorbed in the Tattva (Truth). What is termed manas (mind) is the knowledge of everything that is known and its clear apprehension. When the knowledge and the object cognised are lost alike, there is no second path (or that is the only path). By its giving up all cognition of objects, it (the mind) it absorbed and when the mind is absorbed, kaivalya (isolation) alone remains.

द्वौ क्रमौ चित्तनाशस्य योगो ज्ञानं मुनीश्वर। योगस्तद्वृत्तिरोधो हि ज्ञानं सम्यगवेक्षणम्॥ २४॥

तस्मिन्निरोधिते नूनमुपशान्तं मनो भवेत्। मनः स्पन्दोपशान्त्यायं संसारः प्रविलीयते॥ २५॥

सूर्यालोकपरिस्पन्दशान्तौ व्यवहृतिर्यथा। शास्त्रसज्जनसंपर्कवैराग्याभ्यासयोगतः॥ २६॥

अनास्थायां कृतास्थायां पूर्वं संसारवृत्तिषु। यथाभिवाञ्छितध्यानाच्चिरमेकतयोहितात्॥ २७॥

"For the destruction of the citta, there are two ways— yoga and jñāna. O prince of sages! yoga is the (forcible) repression of modifications of the mind, and jñāna is the thorough inquiry into them. When the modifications of the mind are repressed, it (the mind) verily obtains peace. Just as the actions of the people cease with the stopping of the fluctuations of the mind sun (viz., with sunset), so when the fluctuations of the mind cease, the cycle of births and deaths comes to an end. (Then) the fluctuations of prāṇa are prevented, when one has no longing for this mundane existence or when he has gratified his desires therein, through the study of religious books, the company of good men, indifference (to enjoyments), practice and yoga or long contemplation with intentness on any desired (higher) object or through practising one truth firmly.

एकतत्त्वदृढाभ्यासात्प्राणस्पन्दो निरुध्यते। पूरकाद्यनिलायामाद्दृढाभ्यासादखेदजात्॥ २८॥

एकान्तध्यानयोगाच्च मनःस्पन्दो निरुध्यते। ओङ्कारोच्चारणप्रान्तशब्दतत्त्वानुभावनात्।

सुषुप्ते संविदा ज्ञाते प्राणस्पन्दो निरुध्यते॥ २९॥

तालुमूलगतां यत्नाज्जिह्वयाक्रम्य घण्टिकाम्। ऊर्ध्वरन्ध्रं गते प्राणे प्राणस्पन्दो निरुध्यते॥ ३०॥

प्राणे गलितसंवित्तौ तालूर्ध्वं द्वादशान्तगे। अभ्यासादूर्ध्वरन्ध्रेण प्राणस्पन्दो निरुध्यते॥ ३१॥

द्वादशाङ्गुलपर्यन्ते नासाग्रे विमलेऽम्बरे। संविद्दृशि प्रशाम्यन्त्यां प्राणस्पन्दो निरुध्यते॥ ३२॥

भ्रूमध्ये तारकालोकशान्तावन्तमुपागते। चेतनैकतने बद्धे प्राणस्पन्दो निरुध्यते॥ ३३॥

ओमित्येव यदुद्भूतं ज्ञानं ज्ञेयात्मकं शिवम्। असंस्पृष्टविकल्पांशं प्राणस्पन्दो निरुध्यते॥ ३४॥

चिरकालं हृदेकान्तव्योमसंवेदनान्मुने। अवासनमनोध्यानात्प्राणस्पन्दो निरुध्यते॥ ३५॥

एभिः क्रमैस्तथान्यैश्च नानासंकल्पकल्पितैः। नानादेशिकवक्त्रस्थैः प्राणस्पन्दो निरुध्यते॥ ३६॥

"By the repression of the breath through inhalation, etc., by continual practice therein which does not cause fatigue, and by meditating in a secluded place, the fluctuations of the mind are arrested. Through the right realisation of the true nature of the sound which is at the extreme end of the pronunciation of the syllable Oṁ (viz., Ardhamātrā), and when suṣupti (dreamless sleeping state) is rightly cognised through consciousness, the fluctuations of prāṇa are repressed. When the passage at the root of the palate which is like the bell, viz., uvula, is closed by the tongue with effort and when the breath goes up through (the upper hole), then the fluctuations of prāṇa are stopped. When the consciousness (samvit) is merged in prāṇa, and when through practice the prāṇa goes through the upper hole into the dvādaśānta (the twelfth centre) above the palate, then the fluctuations of prāṇa are stopped. When the eye of consciousness (viz., the spiritual or third eye) becomes calm and clear so as to be able to distinctly see in the transparent ākāśa at a distance of twelve digits from the tip of his nose, then the fluctuations of prāṇa are stopped. When the thoughts arising in the mind are bound up in the calm contemplation of the world of tāraka (star or eye) between one's eyebrows and are (thus) destroyed, then the fluctuations cease. When the knowledge which is of the form of the knowable, which is beneficent and which is untouched by any modifications arises in one and is known as Oṁ only and no other, then the fluctuations of prāṇa cease. By the contemplation for a long time of the ākāśa which is in the heart, and by the contemplation of the mind free from vāsanās, then the fluctuations of prāṇa cease. By these methods and verious others suggested by (one's) thought and by means of the contact of the many (spiritual) guides, the fluctuations cease.

आकुञ्चनेन कुण्डलिन्याः कवाटमुद्घाट्य मोक्षद्वारं विभेदयेत्॥ ३६-ख॥

येन मार्गेण गन्तव्यं तद्द्वारं मुखेनाच्छाद्य प्रसुप्ता।

कुण्डलिनी कुटिलाकारा सर्पवद्वेष्टिता भवति॥ ३६-ग॥

सा शक्तिर्येन चालिता स्यात्स तु मुक्तो भवति। सा कुण्डलिनी कण्ठोर्ध्वभागे सुप्ता चेद्योगिनां मुक्तये भवति। बन्धनायाधो मूढानाम्॥ ३६-घ॥

इडादिमार्गद्वयं विहाय सुषुम्नामार्गेणागच्छेत्तद्विष्णोः परमं पदम्॥ ३६-ङ॥

मरुदभ्यसनं सर्वं मनोयुक्तं समभ्यसेत्। इतरत्र न कर्तव्या मनोवृत्तिर्मनीषिणा॥ ३७॥

दिवा न पूजयेद्विष्णुं रात्रौ नैव प्रपूजयेत्। सततं पूजयेद्विष्णुं दिवारात्रं न पूजयेत्॥ ३८॥

सुषिरो ज्ञानजनकः पञ्चस्रोतः समन्वितः। तिष्ठते खेचरी मुद्रा त्वं हि शाण्डिल्य तां भज॥ ३९॥

सव्यदक्षिणनाडीस्थो मध्ये चरति मारुतः। तिष्ठते खेचरी मुद्रा तस्मिन्स्थाने न संशयः॥ ४०॥

इडापिङ्गलयोर्मध्ये शून्यं चैवानिलं ग्रसेत्। तिष्ठन्ती खेचरी मुद्रा तत्र सत्यं प्रतिष्ठितम्॥ ४१॥

सोमसूर्यद्वयोर्मध्ये निरालम्बतले पुनः। संस्थिता व्योमचक्रे सा मुद्रा नाम्ना च खेचरी॥ ४२क॥

छेदनचालनदोहैः फलां परां जिह्वां कृत्वा दृष्टिं भ्रूमध्ये स्थाप्य कपालकुहरे जिह्वा विपरीतगा यदा भवति तदा खेचरी मुद्रा जायते। जिह्वा चित्तं च खे चरति तेनोर्ध्वजिह्वः पुमानमृतो भवति॥ ४२-ख॥

वामपादमूलेन योनिं संपीड्य दक्षिणपादं प्रसार्य तं कराभ्यां धृत्वा नासाभ्यां वायुमापूर्य कण्ठबन्धं समारोप्योर्ध्वतो वायुं धारयेत्। तेन सर्वक्लेशहानिः। ततः पीयूषमिव विषं जीर्यते। क्षयगुल्मगुदावर्तजीर्णत्वगादिदोषा नश्यन्ति। एष प्राणजयोपायः सर्वमृत्यूपघातकः॥ ४२ग॥

वामपादपार्ष्णियोनिस्थाने नियोज्य दक्षिणचरणं वामोरूपरि संस्थाप्य वायुमापूर्य हृदये चुबुकं निधाय योनिमाकुञ्च्य मनोमध्ये यथाशक्ति धारयित्वा स्वात्मानं भावयेत्। तेनापरोक्षसिद्धिः॥

"Having by contraction opened the door of kuṇḍalinī one should force open the door of mokṣa. Closing with her mouth the door through which one ought to go, the kuṇḍalinī sleeps spiral in form and coiled up like a serpent. He who causes this kuṇḍalinī to move—he is an emancipated person. If this kuṇḍalinī were to sleep in the upper part of the neck of any yogin, it goes towards his emancipation. (If it were to sleep) in the lower part (of the body), it is for the bondage of the ignorant. Leaving the two nāḍīs, Iḍā and the other (Piṅgalā), it (prāṇa) should move in the Suṣumnā. That is the supreme seat of Viṣṇu. One should practise control of breath with the concentration of the mind. The mind should not be allowed by a clever man to rest on any other thing. One should not worship Viṣṇu during the day alone. One should not worship Viṣṇu during the night alone; but should always worship Him, and should not worship Him merely during day and night. The wisdom-producing opening (near uvula) has five passages. O Śāṇḍilya this is the khecarīmudrā, practise it. With one who sits in the khecarīmudrā, the vāyu which was flowing before through the left and right nāḍīs now flows through the middle one (Suṣumnā). There is no doubt about it. You should swallow the air through the void (Suṣumnā) between Iḍā and Piṅgala. In that place is khecarīmudrā situated, and that is the seat of Truth. Again that is khecarīmudrā which is situated in the end ākāśa-cakra (in the head) in the nirālamba (supportless) seat between the sun and moon (viz., Iḍā and Piṅgalā). When the tongue has been lengthened to the length of a kalā (digit) by the incision and by rubbing and milking it (viz., the tongue), fix the gaze between the two eyebrows and close the hole in the skull with the tongue reversed. This is khecarīmudrā. When the tongue and the citta (mind) both move in the ākāśa (khecarī) then the person with his tongue raised up becomes immortal. Firmly pressing the yoni (perineum) by the left heel, stretching out the right leg, grasping the feet with hands and inhaling the air through the nostrils, practise kaṇṭhabandha, retaining the air upwards. By that, all afflictions are destroyed; then poison is digested as if it were nectar. Asthma, splenetic disease, the turning up of the anus and the problems of the skin are removed. This is the means of conquering prāṇa and destroying death. Pressing the yoni by the left heel, place the other foot over the left thigh : inhale the air, rest the chin on the chest, contract the yoni and contemplate, (as far as possible), your Ātmā as situated within your mind. Thus is the direct perception (of truth) attained.

बाह्यात्प्राणं समाकृष्य पूरयित्वोदरे स्थितम्। नाभिमध्ये च नासाग्रे पादाङ्गुष्ठे च यत्नतः॥४३॥

धारयेन्मनसा प्राणं सन्ध्याकालेषु वा सदा। सर्वरोगविनिर्मुक्तो भवेद्योगी गतक्लमः॥४४क॥

नासाग्रे वायुविजयं भवति। नाभिमध्ये सर्वरोगविनाशः।

पादाङ्गुष्ठधारणाच्छरीरलघुता भवति॥४४-ख॥

रसनाद्वायुमाकृष्य यः पिबेत्सततं नरः। श्रमदाहौ तु न स्यातां नश्यन्ति व्याधयस्तथा॥४५॥

सन्ध्ययोर्ब्राह्मणः काले वायुमाकृष्य यः पिबेत्। त्रिमासात्तस्य कल्याणी जायते वाक् सरस्वती॥४६॥

एवं षणमासाभ्यासात्सर्वरोगनिवृत्तिः। जिह्वया वायुमानीय जिह्वामूले निरोधयेत्। यः पिबेदमृतं विद्वान्सकलं भद्रमश्नुते॥४७॥

आत्मन्यात्मानमिडया धारयित्वा भ्रुवोऽन्तरे। विभेद्य त्रिदशाहारं व्याधिस्थोऽपि विमुच्यते॥

नाडीभ्यां वायुमारोप्य नाभौ तुन्दस्य पार्श्वयोः। घटिकैकां वहेद्यस्तु व्याधिभिः स विमुच्यते॥

मासमेकं त्रिसन्ध्यं तु जिह्वयारोप्य मारुतम्। विभेद्य त्रिदशाहारं धारयेत्तुन्दमध्यमे॥५०॥

ज्वराः सर्वेऽपि नश्यन्ति विषाणि विविधानि च। मुहूर्तमपि यो नित्यं नासाग्रे मनसा सह। सर्वं तरति पाप्मानं तस्य जन्मशतार्जितम्॥५१॥

Inhaling the prāṇa from outside and filling the stomach with it, centre the prāṇa with the mind in the middle of the navel, at the tip of the nose and at the toes during the sandhyās (sunset and sunrise) or at all times. (Thus) the yogin is freed from all diseases and fatigue. By centring his prāṇa at the tip of his nose, he obtains mastery over the elephant of air; by centring it at the middle of his navel, all diseases are destroyed; by centring it at the toes, his body becomes light. He who drinks the air (drawn) through the tongue destroys fatigue, thirst and diseases. He who drinks the air with his mouth during the two sandhyās and the last two hours of the night, within three months the auspicious Sarasvatī (goddess of speech) is present in his vāk (speech) viz., (he becomes eloquent and learned in his speech). In six months, he is free from all diseases. Drawing the air by the tongue, retain the air at the root of the tongue. The wise man thus drinking nectar enjoys all prosperity. Fixing the Ātmā in the Ātmā itself in the middle of the eyebrows, (having inhaled) through Iḍā and breaking through (centre) thirty times, even a sick man is freed from disease. He who draws the air through the nāḍīs and retains it for twenty-four minutes in the navel and in sides of the stomach becomes freed from disease. He who for the space of a month during the three sandhyās (sunset), sunrise, and midnight or noon) draws the air through the tongue, pierces thirty times and retains his breath in the middle of his navel, becomes freed from all fevers and poisons. He who retains the prāṇa together with the mind at the tip of his nose even for space of a muhūrta (forty-eight minutes), destroys all sins that were committed by him during one hundred births.

तारसंयमात्सकलविषयज्ञानं भवति। नासाग्रे चित्तसंयमादिन्द्रलोकज्ञानम्। तदधश्चित्त-संयमादग्निलोकज्ञानम्। चक्षुषि चित्तसंयमात्सर्वलोकज्ञानम्। श्रोत्रे चित्तस्य संयमाद्यमलोकज्ञानम्। तत्पार्श्वे

संयमान्निर्ऋतिलोकज्ञानम्। पृष्ठभागे संयमाद्वरुणलोकज्ञानम्। वामकर्णे संयमाद्वायुलोकज्ञानम्। कण्ठे संयमात्सोमलोकज्ञानम्। वामचक्षुषि संयमाच्छिवलोकज्ञानम्। मूर्ध्नि संयमाद्ब्रह्मलोकज्ञानम्। पादाधोभागे संयमादतललोकज्ञानम्। पादे संयमाद्वितललोकज्ञानम्। पादसन्धौ संयमान्नितललोकज्ञानम्। जङ्घे संयमात्सुतललोकज्ञानम्। जानौ संयमान्महातललोकज्ञानम्। ऊरौ चित्तसंयमाद्रसातललोकज्ञानम्। कटौ चित्तसंयमात्तलातललोकज्ञानम्। नाभौ चित्तसंयमाद्भूलोकज्ञानम्। कुक्षौ संयमाद्भुवर्लोकज्ञानम्। हृदि चित्तस्य संयमात्स्वर्लोकज्ञानम्। हृदयोर्ध्वभागे चित्तसंयमान्महर्लोकज्ञानम्। कण्ठे चित्तसंयमाज्जनोलोकज्ञानम्। भ्रूमध्ये चित्तसंयमात्तपोलोकज्ञानम्। मूर्ध्नि चित्तसंयमात्सत्यलोकज्ञानम्।

"Through the samyama of tāra (Oṁ), he knows all things. By retaining the mind at the tip of his nose, he acquires a knowledge of Indra-world; below that, he acquires a knowledge of Agni-(fire) world, Through the samyama of citta in the eye, he gets a knowledge of all worlds : in the ear, a knowledge of Yama-(the god of death) world : in the sides of the ear, a knowledge of Nrṛti-world: in the back of it (the ear), a knowledge of Varuṇa-world: left ear, a knowledge of Vāyu-world: in the throat, a knowledge of Soma (moon) world : in the left eye, a knowledge of Śiva-world : in the head, a knowledge of brahmā-world: in the soles of the feet, a knowledge of Atala-world : in the feet, a knowledge of Vitala-world : in the ankles, a knowledge of Nitala (rather Sutala) world : the calves, a knowledge of Sutala (rather Talātāla world) : in the knees, a knowledge of Mahātala world : in the thighs, a knowledge of Rasātala world : in the loins, a knowledge of Talātala (rather Pātāla) world : in the navel, a knowledge of Bhūrloka (earth world) : in the stomach, a knowledge of Bhuvar (world) : in the heart, a knowledge of Suvar (world) : in the place above the heart, a knowledge of Mahar world : in the throat, a knowledge of Jana world : in the middle of the brows, a knowledge of Tapa world : in the head, a knowledge of Satya world.

धर्माधर्मसंयमादतीतानागतज्ञानम्। तत्तज्जन्तुध्वनौ चित्तसंयमात्सर्वजन्तुरुतज्ञानम्। संचितकर्मणि चित्तसंयमात्पूर्वजातिज्ञानम्। परचित्ते चित्तसंयमात्परचित्तज्ञानम्। कायरूपे चित्तसंयमादन्यादृश्यरूपम्। बले चित्तसंयमाद्धनुमदादिबलम्। सूर्ये चित्तसंयमाद्भुवनज्ञानम्। चन्द्रे चित्तसंयमात्ताराव्यूहज्ञानम्। ध्रुवे तद्गतिदर्शनम्। स्वार्थसंयमात्पुरुषज्ञानम्। नाभिचक्रे कायव्यूहज्ञानम्। कण्ठकूपे क्षुत्पिपासानिवृत्तिः। कूर्मनाड्यां स्थैर्यम्। तारे सिद्धदर्शनम्। कायाकाशसंयमादाकाशगमनम्। तत्तत्स्थाने संयमात्तत्तत्सिद्धयो भवन्ति॥ ५ २॥

"By conquering dharma and adharma, one knows the past and the future. By centring it on the sound of every creature, a knowledge of the cry (or language) of the animal is produced. By centring it, the sañcita-karma (past karma yet to be enjoyed), a knowledge of one's previous births arises in him. By centring it on the mind of another, a knowledge of the mind (or thoughts) of others is induced. By centring it on the kāya-rūpa (or form of the body), other forms are seen. By fixing it on the bala (strength), the strength of persons like Hanumān is obtained. By fixing it on the sun, a knowledge of the worlds arises. By fixing it on the moon, a knowledge of the constellation is produced. By fixing it on the Dhruva (Polar star) a perception of its motion is induced. By fixing it on his own (Self), one acquires the knowledge of Puruṣa; on the navel, he attains a knowledge of the kāya-vyūha (mystical arrangement of all the particles of the body so as to enable a person to wear out his whole karma in one life): on the well of the throat, freedom from hunger and thirst arises : on the Kūrma nāḍī (which is situated in the well of the throat), a firmness (of concentration) takes place. By fixing it on the tārā (pupil of the eye), he obtains the sight of the siddhas (spiritual personages). By conquering the ākāśa in the body, he is able to soar in the ākāśa : (in short) by centring the mind in any place, he conquers the siddhis appertaining to that place.

॥अष्टमः खण्डः॥

अथ प्रत्याहारः। स पञ्चविधः विषयेषु विचरतामिन्द्रियाणां बलादाहरणं प्रत्याहारः। यद्यत्पश्यति तत्सर्वमात्मेति प्रत्याहारः। नित्यविहितकर्मफलत्यागः प्रत्याहारः। सर्वविषयपराङ्मुखत्वं प्रत्याहारः। अष्टादशसु मर्मस्थानेषु क्रमाद्धारणं प्रत्याहारः॥ १॥

पादाङ्गुष्ठगुल्फजङ्घाजानूरुपायुमेढ्रनाभिहृदयकण्ठकूपतालुनासाक्षिभ्रूमध्यललाटमूर्ध्नि स्थानानि। तेषु क्रमादारोहावरोहक्रमेण प्रत्याहरेत्॥ २॥

"Then comes pratyāhāra, which is of five kinds. It is the drawing away of the organs from attaching themselves to the objects of senses. Contemplating upon everything that one sees as Ātmā is pratyāhāra. Renouncing the fruits of one's daily actions is pratyāhāra. Turning away from all objects of sense is pratyāhāra. Dhāraṇā in the eighteen important places (mentioned below is pratyāhāra, (viz.,) the feet, the toes, the ankles, the calves, the knees, the thighs, the anus, the penis, the navel, the heart, the well of the throat, the palate, the nose, the eyes, the middle of the brows, the forehead, and the head in asending and descending orders.

॥नवमः खण्डः॥

अथ धारणा। सा त्रिविधा आत्मनि मनोधारणं दहराकाशे बाह्याकाशधारणं पृथिव्यप्तेजोवाय्वाकाशेषु पञ्चमूर्तिधारणं चेति॥ १॥

"Then (comes) dhāraṇā. It is of three kinds, (viz.,) fixing the mind in the Ātmā, bringing the external ākāśa into the ākāśa of the heart and contemplating the five mūrtis (forms of devatās) in the five elements— earth, āpas, fire, vāyu, and ākāśa.

॥दशमः खण्डः॥

अथ ध्यानम्। तद्द्विविधं सगुणं निर्गुणं चेति। सगुणं मूर्तिध्यानम्। निर्गुणमात्मयाथात्म्यम्॥ १॥

"Then comes dhyāna. It is of two kinds, saguṇa (with guṇas or quality) and nirguṇa (without quality). Saguṇa is the meditation of a mūrti. Nirguṇa is on the reality of Self.

॥एकादशः खण्डः॥

अथ समाधिः। जीवात्मपरमात्मैक्यावस्था त्रिपुटीरहिता परमानन्दस्वरूपा शुद्धचैतन्यात्मिका भवति॥ १॥

"Samādhi is the union of the Jīvātmā (individual self) and the Paramātmā (higher self) without the threefold state, (viz., the knower, the known, and the knowledge). It is of the nature of extreme bliss and pure consciousness.

"Thus ends the first chapter of Śāṇḍilya Upaniṣad"

॥द्वितीयोऽध्याय:॥

अथ ह शाण्डिल्यो ह वै ब्रह्मऋषिश्चतुर्षु वेदेषु ब्रह्मविद्यामलभमान: किं नामेत्यथर्वाणं भगवन्तमुपसन्न: पप्रच्छाधीहि भगवन् ब्रह्मविद्यां येन श्रेयोऽवाप्स्यामीति॥ १॥

स होवाचाथर्वा शाण्डिल्य सत्यं विज्ञानमनन्तं ब्रह्म॥। २॥

यस्मिन्निदमोतं च प्रोतं च। यस्मिन्निदं सं च विचैति सर्वं यस्मिन्विज्ञाते सर्वमिदं विज्ञातं भवति। तदपाणिपादमचक्षु:श्रोत्रमजिह्वमशरीरमग्राह्यमनिर्देश्यम्॥ ३॥

यतो वाचो निवर्तन्ते अप्राप्य मनसा सह। यत्केवलं ज्ञानगम्यम्। प्रज्ञा च यस्मात्प्रसृता पुराणी। यदेकमद्वितीयम्। आकाशवत्सर्वगतं सुसूक्ष्मं निरञ्जनं निष्क्रियं सन्मात्रं चिदानन्दैकरसं शिवं प्रशान्तममृतं तत्परं च ब्रह्म। तत्त्वमसि तज्ज्ञानेन हि विजानीहि॥ ४॥

य एको देव आत्मशक्तिप्रधान: सर्वज्ञ: सर्वेश्वर: सर्वभूतान्तरात्मा सर्वभूताधिवास: सर्वभूतनिगूढो भूतयोनिर्योगैकगम्य:। यश्च विश्वं सृजति विश्वं बिभर्ति विश्वं भुङ्क्ते स आत्मा। आत्मनि तं तं लोकं विजानीहि॥ ५॥

मा शोचीरात्मविज्ञानी शोकस्यान्तं गमिष्यसि॥ ६॥

Chapter II

Then the Brahmarṣi Śāṇḍilya not obtaining the knowledge of Brahman in the four Vedas, approached the Lord Atharvan and asked him : "What is it? Teach me the science of Brahman by which I shall obtain that which is most excellent."

Atharvan replied : "O Śāṇḍilya, Brahman is satya, vijñāna and ananta in which all the (world) is interwoven, warp-wise and woof-wise, from which all originated and into which all are absorbed, and which being known makes everything else known. It is without hands and feet, without eyes and ears, without tongue or without body, and is unreachable and undefinable. From which, vāk (speech) and mind return, being unable to obtain (or reach) It. It is to be cognised by jñāṇa and yoga. From which, prajñā of old sprang. That which is one and non-dual, that which pervades everything like ākāśa, which is extremely subtle, without a blemish, sat (be-ness) only, the essence of the bliss of consciousness, beneficent, calm and immortal and which is beyond, That is Brahman. You are that. Know That by wisdom. He who is the one, the shining, the giver of the power of Ātmā, the omniscient, the lord of all, and the inner soul of all beings, who lives in all beings, who is hidden in all beings and the sources of all beings, who is reachable only through yoga and who creates, supports and destroys everything— He is Ātmā. Know the several worlds in the Ātmā. Do not grieve, O knower of Ātmā, thou shall reach the end of pains."

॥तृतीयोऽध्याय:॥

॥प्रथम: खण्ड:॥

अथ हैनं शाण्डिल्योऽथर्वाणं पप्रच्छ यदेकमक्षरं निष्क्रियं शिवं सन्मात्रं परंब्रह्म। तस्मात्कथमिदं विश्वं जायते कथं स्थीयते कथमस्मिल्लीयते। तन्मे संशयं छेत्तुमर्हसीति॥ १॥

Then Śāṇḍilya questioned Atharvan thus : "From the Brahman that is Oṁ, imperishable, actionless, beneficial, sat (be-ness) only and supreme, how did this universe arise? How does it exist in It? and how is it absorbed in It? Please solve me this doubt."

स होवाचाथर्वा सत्यं शाण्डिल्य परब्रह्म निष्क्रियमक्षरमिति। अथाप्यस्यारूपस्य ब्रह्मणस्त्रीणि रूपाणि भवन्ति सकलं निष्कलं सकलनिष्कलं चेति॥ २-३॥

यत्सत्यं विज्ञानमानन्दं निष्क्रियं निरञ्जनं सर्वगतं सुसूक्ष्मं सर्वतोमुखमनिर्देश्यममृतमस्ति तदिदं निष्कलं रूपम्॥ ४॥

अथास्य या सहजास्त्यविद्या मूलप्रकृतिर्माया लोहितशुक्लकृष्णा। तया सहायवान् देव: कृष्णपिङ्गलो महेश्वर ईष्टे। तदिदमस्य सकलं रूपम्॥ ५॥

अथैष ज्ञानमयेन तपसा चीयमानोऽकामयत बहुस्यां प्रजायेयेति। अथैतस्मात्तप्यमा-नात्सत्यकामात्त्रीण्यक्षराण्यजायन्त। तिस्रो व्याहृतयस्त्रिपदा गायत्री त्रयो वेदास्त्रयो देवास्त्रयो वर्णास्त्रयोऽग्नयश्च जायन्ते। योऽसौ देवो भगवान्सर्वैश्वर्यसंपन्न: सर्वव्यापी सर्वभूतानां हृदये संनिविष्टो मायावी मायया क्रीडति स ब्रह्मा स विष्णु: स रुद्र: स इन्द्र: स सर्वे देवा: सर्वाणि भूतानि स एव पुरस्तात्स एव पश्चात्स एवोत्तरत: स एव दक्षिणत: स एवाधस्तात्स एवोपरिष्टात्स एव सर्वम्। अथास्य देवस्यात्मशक्तेरात्मक्रीडस्य भक्तानुकम्पिनो दत्तात्रेयरूपा सुरूपा तनूरवासा इन्दीवरदलप्रख्या चतुर्बाहुरघोरापापकाशिनी। तदिदमस्य सकलनिष्कलं रूपम्॥ ६॥

Atharvan replied : The Supreme Brahman, the Truth, is the imperishable and the actionless. Then from the formless Brahman, three forms (or aspects) arose, (viz.,) niṣkalā (partless,) sakalā (with parts), and sakalā-niṣkalā (with and without parts). That which is satya, vijñāna and ānanda, That which is actionless, without any impurity, omnipresent, extermely subtle, having faces in every direction, undefinable and immortal— that is His niṣkalā aspect. Maheśvara (the great Lord) who is black and yellow rules with avidyā, mūlaprakṛti or māyā that is red, white, and black, and that is co-existent with Him. This is his sakalā-niṣkalā aspect. Then the Lord desired (or willed) by his spiritual wisdom (thus) : May I become many"; may I bring forth? Then from this Person who was contemplating and whose desires are fulfilled, three letters sprang up. Three vyāhṛtis, the three-footed Gāyatrī, the three Vedas, the three devas, the three varṇas (colours or castes) and the three fires sprang. That Supreme Lord who is endowed with all kinds of wealth, who is all pervading, who is situated in the hearts of all beings, who is the Lord of māyā and whose from is māyā— he is Brahmā. He is Viṣṇu : He is Rudra : He is Indra : He is all the devas : He is all the bhūtas (elements or beings) : He only is before : He only is behind : He only is on our left : He only is on our right : He only is below : He only is above : He only is the all. That form of him as Dattātreya, who sports with his Śakti, who is kind to his devotees, who is brilliant as fire, resembling the petals or a red lotus and is of four hands, who is mild and shines sinlessly— this is His sakala form."

॥द्वितीयः खण्डः॥

अथ हैनमथर्वाणं शाण्डिल्यः पप्रच्छ भगवन्सन्मात्रं चिदानन्दैकरसं कस्मादुच्यते परं ब्रह्मेति। स होवाचाथर्वा यस्माच्च बृहति बृंहयति च सर्वं तस्मादुच्यते परंब्रह्मेति॥ १-२॥

अथ कस्मादुच्यते आत्मेति। यस्मात्सर्वमाप्नोति सर्वमादत्ते सर्वमत्ति च तस्मादुच्यते आत्मेति॥ ३-४॥

अथ कस्मादुच्यते महेश्वर इति। यस्मान्महत ईशः शब्दध्वन्या चात्मशक्त्या च महत ईशते तस्मादुच्यते महेश्वर इति॥ ५-६॥

अथ कस्मादुच्यते दत्तात्रेय इति। यस्मात्सुदुश्चरं तपस्तप्यमानायात्रये पुत्रकामायातितरां तुष्टेन भगवता ज्योतिर्मयेनात्मैव दत्तो यस्माच्चानसूयायामत्रेस्तनयो ऽभवत्तस्मादुच्यते दत्तात्रेय इति॥

अथ योऽस्य निरुक्तानि वेद स सर्वं वेद। अथ यो ह वै विद्ययैनं परमुपास्ते सोऽहमिति स ब्रह्मविद्भवति॥ ९-१०॥

अत्रैते श्लोका भवन्ति। दत्तात्रेयं शिवं शान्तमिन्द्रनीलनिभं प्रभुम्। आत्ममायारतं देवमवधूतं दिगम्बरम्॥ ११॥ भस्मोद्धूलितसर्वाङ्गं जटाजूटधरं विभुम्। चतुर्बाहुमुदाराङ्गं प्रफुल्लकमलेक्षणम्॥ १२॥ ज्ञानयोगनिधिं विश्वगुरुं योगिजनप्रियम्। भक्तानुकम्पिनं सर्वसाक्षिणं सिद्धसेवितम्॥ १३॥ एवं यः सततं ध्यायेद्देवदेवं सनातनम्। स मुक्तः सर्पपापेभ्यो निःश्रेयसमवाप्नुयात्॥ १४॥ इत्यों सत्यमित्युपनिषद्॥ १५॥

Then Śāṇḍilya questioned Atharvan, "O Lord, that which is Sat only and the essence of the bliss of consciousness— why is He called Parabrahman?"

Atharvan replied : "Because He increases bṛhati and causes to increase everything (bṛhanti) so he is called Prarabrahman. Why is He called Ātmā? Since He obtains (āpnoti) everything, since He takes back everything and since He is everything, so he is called Ātmā. Why is He called Maheśvara (the great Lord)? Since by the sound of the words Mahat-Īśa (the great Lord) and by His own power, the great Lord governs everything. Why is He called Dattātreya? Because the Lord being extremely pleased with Atri (Ṛṣi) who was performing a most difficult penance and who had expressed his desire to see Him who is light itself, offered Himself (datta) as their son, and because the woman Anasūyā was his mother and Atri was his father. Therefore he who knows the (secret) meaning knows everything. He who always contemplates on the supreme that It is himself becomes a knower of Brahman. Here these ślokas (stanzas) occur (to memory). 'He who contemplates always the Lord of Lords and the ancient thus— as Dattātreya, the beneficent, the calm, of the colour of sapphire, one who delights in his own māyā and the Lord who has shaken off everything, as naked and as one whose whole body is besmeared with the holy ashes, who has matted hair, who is the Lord of all, who has four arms, who is bliss in appearance, whose eyes are like full-blown lotus, who is the store of jñāna and yoga, who is the spiritual instructor of all the worlds and who is dear to all the yogins, and one who is merciful towards His devotees, who is the witness of all and who is worshipped by all the siddhas is freed from all sins and will attain (the Spirit).'

"O Satyam (truth)."

ॐ भद्रं कर्णेभिः .... इति शान्तिः॥

॥इति शाण्डिल्योपनिषत्समाप्ता॥

***

55. PAIṄGALOPANIṢAD

पैङ्गलोपनिषद्

॥शान्तिपाठः॥

ॐ पूर्णमदः .... इति शान्तिः॥

Adhyāya I

अथ ह पैङ्गलो याज्ञवल्क्यमुपसमेत्य द्वादशवर्षशुश्रूषापूर्वकं परमरहस्यकैवल्यमनुब्रूहीति पप्रच्छ॥ १॥

Oṁ. Paiṅgala, having served under Yājñavalkya for twelve years, asked him to initiate him into the supreme mysteries of Kaivalya.

स होवाच याज्ञवल्क्यः सदेव सोम्येदमग्र आसीत्।

तन्नित्यमुक्तमविक्रियं सत्यज्ञा नानन्दं परिपूर्णं सनातनमेकमेवाद्वितीयं ब्रह्म॥ २॥

तस्मिन्मरुशुक्तिकास्थाणुस्फटिकादौ जलरौप्यपुरुषरेखादिवल्लोहितशुक्लकृष्णगुणमयी गुणसाम्यानिर्वाच्या मूलप्रकृतिरासीत्। तत्प्रतिबिम्बितं यत्तत्साक्षिचैतन्यमासीत्॥ ३॥

To which Yājñavalkya replied thus : "O gentle one, at first, this (univeıse) was Sat (Bee-ness) only. It (Sat) is spoken of as Brahman which is ever free (from the trammels of matter), which is changeless, which is Truth, Wisdom, and Bliss, and which is full, permanent, and one only without a second. In It, was like a mirage in desert, silver in mother-of-pearl, a person in the pillar, of colour, etc., in the crystals, mūlaprakṛti, having in equal proportions the guṇas, red, white, and black, and being beyond the power of speech. That which is reflected in it is Sākṣi-Caitanya (lit., the witness-consciousness).

सा पुनर्विकृतिं प्राप्य सत्त्वोद्रिक्ताऽव्यक्ताख्यावरणशक्तिरासीत्। तत्प्रतिबिम्बितं यत्तदीश्वरचैतन्यमासीत्। स स्वाधीनमायः सर्वज्ञः सृष्टिस्थितिलयानामादिकर्ता जगदङ्कुररूपो भवति स्वस्मिन्विलीनं सकलं जगदाविर्भावयति। प्राणिकर्मवशादेष पटो यद्वत् प्रसारितः प्राणिकर्मक्षयात् पुनस्तिरोभावयति। तस्मिन्नेवाखिलं विश्वं संकोचितपटवद्वर्तते॥ ४॥

ईशाधिष्ठितावरणशक्तितो रजोद्रिक्ता महदाख्या विक्षेपशक्तिरासीत्।

तत्प्रतिबिम्बितं यत्तद्धिरण्यगर्भचैतन्यमासीत्। स महत्तत्त्वाभिमानी स्पष्टास्पष्टवपुर्भवति॥ ५॥

It (mūlaprakṛti) undergoing again change becomes with the preponderance of Sattva (in it), Āvaraṇa Śakti names avyakta. That which is reflected in it (Avyakta) is Īśvara-Caitanya. He (Īśvara) has Māyā under his control, is omniscient, the original cause of creation, preservation, the dissolution, and the seed of this universe. He causes the universe which was latent in Him. To manifest itself through the bonds of karma of all creatures like a painted canvas unfurled. Again through the extinction of their karmas, he likes it disappear.

In Him alone is latent all the universe, wrapped up like a painted cloth. Then from the supreme (āvaraṇa) Śakti, dependent on (or appertaining) to Īśvara, arose, through the preponderance of Rajas, Vikṣepa Śakti called Mahat. That which is reflected in it is Hiraṇyagarbha-Caitanya.

हिरण्यगर्भाधिष्ठितविक्षेपशक्तितस्तमोद्रिक्ताहंकाराभिधा स्थूलशक्तिरासीत्। तत्प्रतिबिम्बितं यत्तद्विराट्चैतन्यमासीत्। स तदभिमानी स्पष्टवपुः सर्वस्थूलपालको विष्णुः प्रधानपुरुषो भवति। तस्मादात्मन आकाशः संभूतः। आकाशाद्वायुः। वायोरग्निः। अग्नेरापः। अद्भ्यःपृथिवी। तानि पञ्च तन्मात्राणि त्रिगुणानि भवन्ति॥६॥

Presiding (as He does) over Mahat, He (Hiraṇyagarbha) has a body, both manifested and unmanifested. From Vikṣepa Śakti of Hiraṇyagarbha arose, through the preponderance of Tamas, the gross Śakti called ahaṁkāra. That which is reflected in it is Virāṭ-Caitanya. He (Virāṭ) presiding over it (anaṁkara) and possessing a manifested body becomes Viṣṇu, the chief Puruṣa and protector of all gross bodies. From that Ātmā arose ākāśa; from ākāśa arose vāyu, from vāyu agni, from agni apas, and from apas Pṛthivī. The five tanmātrās (rudimentary properties) alone are the guṇas (of the above five).

स्रष्टुकामो जगद्योनिस्तमोगुणमधिष्ठाय सूक्ष्मतन्मात्राणि भूतानि स्थूलीकर्तुं सोऽकामयत। सृष्टेः परिमितानि भूतान्येकमेकं द्विधा विधाय पुनश्चतुर्धा कृत्वा स्वस्वेतरद्वितीयांशैः पञ्च पञ्चधा संयोज्य पञ्चीकृतभूतैरनन्तकोटिब्रह्माण्डानि तत्तदण्डोचितचतुर्दशभुवनानि तत्तद्भुवनोचितगोलकस्थूल-शरीराण्यसृजत्॥७॥

स पञ्चभूतानां रजोंशांश्चतुर्धा कृत्वा भागत्रयात्पञ्चवृत्त्यात्मकं प्राणमसृजत्। स तेषां तुर्यभागेन कर्मेन्द्रियाण्यसृजत्॥८॥

That generating cause of the universe (Īśvara) wishing to create and having assumed tamoguṇa, wanted to convert the elements which were subtle tanmātrās into gross ones. In order to create the universe, he divided into two parts each of those divisible elements; and having divided each moiety into four parts, made a fivefold mixture, each element having moiety of its own original element and one-fourth of a moiety of each of the other elements, and thus evolved out of the fivefold classified gross elements, the many myriads of Brahmāṇḍas (Brahmā's egg or macrocosm), the fourteen worlds pertaining to each sphere, and the spherical gross bodies (microcosm) fit for the (respective) worlds. Having divided the Rajas-essence of the five elements into four parts, He out of three such parts created (the five) prāṇas having fivefold functions. Again out of the (remaining) fourth part, He created Karmendriyas (the organs of action).

स तेषां सत्त्वांशं चतुर्धा कृत्वा भागत्रयसमष्टितः पञ्चक्रियावृत्त्यात्मकमन्तःकरणमसृजत्।
स तेषां सत्त्वतुरीयभागेन ज्ञानेन्द्रियाण्यसृजत्॥९॥

सत्त्वसमष्टित इन्द्रियपालकानसृजत्। तानि सृष्टान्यण्डे प्राचिक्षिपत्। तदाज्ञया समष्ट्यण्डं व्याप्य तान्यतिष्ठन्। तदाज्ञयाऽहंकारसमन्वितो विराट् स्थूलान्यरक्षत्। हिरण्यगर्भस्तदाज्ञया सूक्ष्माण्यपालयत्॥१०॥

Having divided their Sattva-essence into four parts, He out of three such parts created the antaḥkaraṇa (internal organ) having fivefold functions. Out of the (remaining) fourth part of Sattva-essence, He created the jñānendriyas (organs of sense). Out of the collective totality of Sattva-essence, He created the devatās (deities) ruling over the organs of sense and actions. Those (devatās) He created, He located then in the spheres (pertaining to them). They through His orders, began to pervade the macrocosm. Through His orders, Viraṭ associated with ahaṁkāra created all the gross things. Through His orders, Hiraṇyagarbha protected the subtle things.

अण्डस्थानि तानि तेन विना स्पन्दितुं चेष्टितुं वा न शेकुः। तानि चेतनीकर्तुं सोऽकामयत ब्रह्माण्डब्रह्मरन्ध्राणि समस्तव्यष्टिमस्तकान्विदार्य तदेवानुप्राविशत्। तदा जडान्यपि तानि चेतनवत्स्वकर्माणि चक्रिरे॥ ११॥

सर्वज्ञेशो मायालेशसमन्वितो व्यष्टिदेहं प्रविश्य तया मोहितो जीवत्वमगमत्। शरीरत्रयतादात्म्यात्कर्तृत्वभोक्तृत्वतामगमत्। जाग्रत्स्वप्नसुषुप्तिमूर्च्छामरणधर्मयुक्तो घटीयन्त्रवदुद्विग्नो जातो मृत इव कुलालचक्रन्यायेन परिभ्रमतीति॥ १२॥

Without Him, they that were located in their spheres were unable to move or to do anything. Then he wished to infuse Cetanā (life) into them. Having pierced the Brahmāṇḍa (Brahmā's egg or macrocosm) and brahmarandhras (heads-fontanelle) in all the microcosmic heads, he entered within. Though they were (at first) inert, they were then able to perform karmas like beings of intelligence The omniscient Īśvara entered the microcosmic bodies with a particle of Māyā and being deluded by that Māyā, acquired the state of Jīva. Identifying the three bodies with Himself, He acquired the state of the actor and enjoyer. Associated with the attributes of the states of Jāgrat, svapna, suṣupti, trance, and death and being immersed in sorrow, he is (whirled about and) deluded like water-lift of potter's wheel, as if subject to birth and death.

Adhyāya II

अथ पैङ्गलो याज्ञवल्क्यमुवाच सर्वलोकानां सृष्टिस्थित्यन्तकृद्विभुरीशः कथं जीवत्वमगमदिति॥ १॥

Paiṅgala again addressed Yājñavalkya thus : "How did Īśvara, who is the creator, preserver, and destroyer and the Lord of all the worlds, acquire the state of Jīva?"

स होवाच याज्ञवल्क्यः स्थूलसूक्ष्मकारणदेहोद्भवपूर्वकं जीवेश्वरस्वरूपं विविच्य कथयामीति सावधानेनैकाग्रतया श्रूयताम्। ईशः पञ्चीकृतमहाभूतलेशानादाय व्यष्टिसमष्ट्यात्मकस्थूलशरीराणि यथाक्रममकरोत्। कपालचर्मान्त्रास्थिमांसनखानि पृथिव्यंशाः। रक्तमूत्रलालास्वेदादिका अबंशाः। क्षुत्तृष्णोष्णमोहमैथुनाद्या अग्न्यंशाः। प्रचारणोत्तारणाश्वासादिका वाय्वंशाः। कामक्रोधादयो व्योमांशाः। एतत्संघातं कर्मणि संचितं त्वगादियुक्तं बाल्याद्यवस्थाभिमानास्पदं बहुदोषाश्रयं स्थूलशरीरं भवति॥ २॥

To which Yājñavalkya replied : "I shall tell in detail the nature of Jīva and Īśvara, together with a description of the origin of the gross, subtle, and kāraṇa (causal) bodies. Hear attentively with one-pointed mind. "Īśvara having taken a small portion of the quintuplicated mahā-bhūtas (the great elements), made in regular order the gross bodies, both collective and segregate. The skull, the skin, the intestines, bone, flesh, and nails are of the essence of pṛthivī. Blood, urine, saliva, sweat and others are of the essence of āpas. Hunger, thirst, heat, delusion, and copulation are of the essence of agni. Walking, lifting, breathing and others are of the essence of vāyu. Passion, anger, etc., are of the essence of ākāśa. The collection of these having touch and the rest is this gross body that is brought about by karma, that is the seat of egoism in youth and other states and that is the abode of many sins.

अथापञ्चीकृतमहाभूतरजोंशभागत्रयसमष्टितः प्राणमसृजत्। प्राणापानव्यानोदानसमानाः प्राणवृत्तयः। नागकूर्मकृकरदेवदत्तधनंजया उपप्राणाः। हृदासननाभिकण्ठसर्वाङ्गानि स्थानानि। आकाशादिरजोगुणतुरीयभागेन कर्मेन्द्रियमसृजत्। वाक्पाणिपादपायूपस्थास्तद्वृत्तयः। वचनादानगमनविसर्गानन्दास्तद्विषयाः। एवं भूतसत्त्वांशभागत्रयसमष्टितोऽन्तःकरणमसृजत्। अन्तःकरणमनोबुद्धिचित्ताहंकारास्तद्वृत्तयः। संकल्पनिश्चयस्मरणाभिमानानुसंधानास्तद्विषयाः। गलवदननाभिहृदयभ्रूमध्यं स्थानम्। भूतसत्त्वतुरीयभागेन ज्ञानेन्द्रियमसृजत्। श्रोत्रत्वक्चक्षुर्जिह्वाघ्राणास्तद्वृत्तयः। शब्दस्पर्शरूपरसगन्धास्तद्विषयाः। दिग्वातार्कप्रचेतोऽश्विवह्नीन्द्रोपेन्द्रमृत्युकाः। चन्द्रो विष्णुश्चतुर्वक्त्रः शंभुश्च करणाधिपाः॥ ३॥

Then he created prāṇas out of the collective three parts of Rajas-essence of the fivefold divided elements. The modifications of prāṇa are prāṇa, apāna, vyāna, udāna, and samāna; nāga, kūrma, kṛkara, devadatta and dhanañjaya are the auxiliary prāṇas. (Of the first five), the heart, anus, navel, throat and the whole body are respectively the seats. Then He created the karmendriyas out of the fourth part of the Rajas-guṇa. Of ākāśa and the rest the mouth, legs, hands, and the organs of secretion and excretion are the modifications. Talking, walking, lifting, excreting, and enjoying are their functions. Likewise out of the collective three parts of Sattva-essence, He created the antaḥkaraṇa (internal organ). Antaḥkarana, manas, buddhi, citta and ahaṁkāra are the modifications. Saṅkalpa (thought), certitude, memory, egoism, and anusandhāna (inquiry) are their functions. Throat, face, navel, heart, and the middle of the brow are their seats. Out of the (remaining) fourth part of Sattva-essence, He created the Jñānendriyas (organs of sense). Ear, skin, eyes, tongue, and nose are the modifications. Sound, touch, form, taste, and odour are their functions. Dik (the quarters), Vāyu, Arka (the sun), Varuṇa, Aśvini Devas, Indra, Upendra, Mṛtyu (the God of death), Prajāpati, the Moon, Viṣṇu, the four-faced Brahmā and Śambhu (Śiva) are the presiding deities of the organs.

अथान्नमयप्राणमयमनोमयविज्ञानमयानन्दमयाः पञ्च कोशाः। अन्नरसेनैव भूत्वाऽन्नरसेनाभिवृद्धिं प्राप्यान्नरसमयपृथिव्यां यद्विलीयते सोऽन्नमयकोशः। तदेव स्थूलशरीरम्। कर्मेन्द्रियैः सह प्राणादिपञ्चकं प्राणमयकोशः। ज्ञानेन्द्रियैः सह मनो मनोमयकोशः। ज्ञानेन्द्रियैः सह बुद्धिर्विज्ञानमयकोशः। एतत्कोशत्रयं लिङ्गशरीरम्। स्वरूपाज्ञानमानन्दमयकोशः। तत् कारणशरीरम्॥ ४॥

अथ ज्ञानेन्द्रियपञ्चकं कर्मेन्द्रियपञ्चकं प्राणादिपञ्चकं वियदादिपञ्चकमन्तःकरणचतुष्टयं कामकर्मतमांस्यष्टपुरम्॥ ५॥

There are the five kośas (sheaths), viz., annamaya, prāṇamaya, manomaya, vijñānamaya and ānandamaya. Annamaya, sheath is that which is created and developed out of the essence of food, and is absorbed into the earth which is of the form of food. It alone is the gross body. The prāṇas with the karmendriya (organs of action) is the prāṇamaya sheath. Manas with the jñānendriyas (organs of sense) is the manomaya sheath. Buddhi with the jñānendriyas is the vijñānamaya sheath. These three sheaths constitute the liṅgaśarīra (or the subtle body). (That which tends to) the ajñāna (ignorance) of the Reality (of Ātmā) is the ānandamaya sheath. This is the kāraṇa body. Moreover the five organs of sense, the five organs of action, the five prāṇas and others, the five ākāśa and other elements, the four internal organs, avidyā, passion, karma, and tamas— all these constitute this town (of body).

ईशाज्ञया विराजो व्यष्टिदेहं प्रविश्य बुद्धिमधिष्ठाय विश्वत्वमगमत्। विज्ञानात्मा चिदाभासो विश्वो व्यावहारिको जाग्रत्स्थूलदेहाभिमानी कर्मभूरिति च विश्वस्य नाम भवति॥ ६॥

ईशाज्ञया सूत्रात्मा व्यष्टिसूक्ष्मशरीरं प्रविश्य मन अधिष्ठाय तैजसत्वमगमत्।

तैजसः प्रातिभासिकः स्वप्नकल्पित इति तैजसस्य नाम भवति॥ ७॥

ईशाज्ञया मायोपाधिरव्यक्तसमन्वितो व्यष्टिकारणशरीरं प्रविश्य प्राज्ञत्वमगमत्।

प्राज्ञोऽविच्छिन्नः पारमार्थिकः सुषुप्त्यभिमानीति प्राज्ञस्य नाम भवति॥ ८॥

Virāṭ, under the orders of Īśvara having entered this microcosmic body, and having buddhi as his vehicle, reaches the state of Viśva. Then he goes by the several names of Vijñānātmā, Cidābhāsa, Viśva, Vyāvahārika, the one presiding over the waking gross body and the one generated by karma. Sūtrātmā, under the orders of Īśvara, having entered the micro-cosmic subtle body, and having manas as his vehicle, reaches the Taijasa state, Then he goes by the names of taijasa, prātibhāsika and svapnakalpita (the one breed out of dream). Then under the orders of Īśvara, he who is coupled with avyakta, the vehicle of Māyā having entered the microcosmic kāraṇa body, reaches the state of prajñā. He goes then by the names of prājña, avicchinna, and pāramārthika and suṣupti-abhimānī (the presider over suṣupti).

अव्यक्तलेशाज्ञानाच्छादितपारमार्थिकजीवस्य तत्त्वमस्यादिवाक्यानि ब्रह्मणैकतां जगुर्नेतरयोर्व्यावहारिक-प्रातिभासिकयोः॥ ९॥

अन्तःकरणप्रतिबिम्बितचैतन्यं यत्तदेवावस्थात्रयभाग्भवति।

स जाग्रत्स्वप्नसुषुप्त्यवस्थाः प्राप्य घटीयन्त्रवदुद्विग्नो जातो मृत इव स्थितो भवति॥ १०॥

Such sacred sentences, as Tattvamasi (That are You) and others, speak of the identify with the Brahman of the Pāramārthika-Jīva enveloped by ajñāna, which is but a small particle of avyakta; but not vyāvahārika and prātibhāsika (Jīvas). It is only that caitanya which is reflected in antaḥkaraṇa that attains the three states. When it assumes the three states of jāgrat, svapna, and suṣupti, it is like a water-lift as if grieved, born and dead.

अथ जाग्रत्स्वप्नसुषुप्तिमूर्च्छामरणाद्यवस्थाः पञ्च भवन्ति। तत्तद्देवताग्रहान्वितैः श्रोत्रादिज्ञानेन्द्रियैः शब्दाद्यर्थविषयग्रहणज्ञानं जाग्रदवस्था भवति। तत्र भ्रूमध्यं गतो जीव आपादमस्तकं व्याप्य कृषिश्रवणाद्यखिलक्रियाकर्ता भवति। तत्तत्फलभुक् च भवति। लोकान्तरगतः कर्मार्जितफलं स एव भुङ्क्ते। स सार्वभौमवद्व्यवहाराच्छ्रान्त अन्तर्भवनं प्रवेष्टुं मार्गमाश्रित्य तिष्ठति॥

करणोपरमे जाग्रत्संस्कारार्धप्रबोधवद्ग्राह्यग्राहकरूपस्फुरणं स्वप्नावस्था भवति। तत्र विश्व एव जाग्रद्व्यवहारलोपान्नाडीमध्यं चरंस्तैजसत्वमवाप्य वासनारूपकं जगद्वैचित्र्यं स्वभासा भासयन्यथेप्सितं स्वयं भुङ्क्ते॥ १२॥

There are five avasthās— jāgrat, svapna, suṣupti, mūrchā (trace), and death. Jāgrat avasthā is that in which there is the perception of objects, of sound, etc. through the grace of the devatā presiding over each of them. In it, the Jīva, being in the middle of the eyebrows and pervading the body from head to foot, becomes the agent of actions, such as doing, hearing, and others. He becomes also the enjoyer of the fruits thereof; and such a person doing karma for the fruits thereof goes to other worlds and enjoys the same there. Like an emperor tired of worldly acts (in the waking state), he strives to find the path to retire into his abode within. The svapna avasthā is that in which, when the senses are at rest, there is the manifestation of the knower and the known, along with the affinities of (things enjoyed in) the waking state, In this state Viśva alone, its actions in the waking state having ceased, reaches the state of Taijasa (of tejas or effulgence), who moves in the middle of the nāḍīs (nerves), illuminates by his lustre the heterogeneity of this universe which is of the form of affinities, and himself enjoys according to his wish.

चित्तैककरणा सुषुप्त्यवस्था भवति। भ्रमविश्रान्तशकुनिः पक्षौ संहृत्य नीडाभिमुखं यथा गच्छति तथा जीवोऽपि जाग्रत्स्वप्नप्रपञ्चे व्यवहृत्य श्रान्तोऽज्ञानं प्रविश्य स्वानन्दं भुङ्क्ते॥

अकस्मान्मुद्गरदण्डाद्यैस्ताडितवद्भयाज्ञानाभ्यामिन्द्रियसंघातैः कम्पन्निव मृततुल्या मूर्च्छा भवति॥ १४॥

The suṣupti avasthā is that in which the citta is sole organ (at play). Just a bird, tired of roaming, flies to its nest with its stomach filled, so the Jīva being tired of the acts of the world in the waking and dreaming states, enters ajñāna and enjoys bliss. Then trance is attained which resembles death, and in which one with his collection of organs quails, as it were, through fear and ajñāna, like one beaten unexpectedly by a hammer, club or any other weapon.

जाग्रत्स्वप्नसुषुप्तिमूर्च्छावस्थानामन्याब्रह्मादिस्तम्बपर्यन्तं सर्वजीवभयप्रदा स्थूलदेहविसर्जनी मरणावस्था भवति॥ १५॥

कर्मेन्द्रियाणि ज्ञानेन्द्रियाणि तत्तद्विषयान्प्राणान्संहृत्य कामकर्मान्वित अविद्याभूतवेष्टितो जीवो देहान्तरं प्राप्य लोकान्तरं गच्छति। प्राक्कर्मफलपाकेनावर्तान्तरकीटवद्विश्रान्तिं नैव गच्छति॥ १६॥

Then death avasthā is that which is other than the avasthās of jāgrat, svapna, suṣupti, and trance, which produces fear in all Jīvas from Brahmā down to small insects and which dissolves the gross body. The Jīva, that is surrounded by avidyā and the subtle elements, takes with it the organs of sense and action, their objects, and prāṇas along with the kāmic karmas and goes to another world, assuming another body. Through the ripening of the fruits of previous karmas, the Jīva has no rest like an insect in a whirlpool. It is only after many births that the desire of emancipation arises in man through the ripening of good karma.

सत्कर्मपरिपाकतो बहूनां जन्मनामन्ते नृणां मोक्षेच्छा जायते। तदा सद्गुरुमाश्रित्य चिरकालसेवया बन्धं मोक्षं कश्चित्प्रयाति॥ १७॥

अविचारकृतो बन्धो विचारान्मोक्षो भवति। तस्मात्सदा विचारयेत्। अध्यारोपाप वादत: स्वरूपं निश्चयीकर्तुं शक्यते। तस्मात्सदा विचारयेज्जगज्जीवपरमात्मनो जीवभावजगद्भावबाधे प्रत्यगभिन्नं ब्रह्मैवावशिष्यत इति॥ १८॥

Then having restored to a good Guru and served under him for a long time, one out of many attains mokṣa, free form bondage. Bondage is through non-inquiry and mokṣa through inquiry. Therefore there should always be inquiry (into Ātmā). The Reality should be ascertained through adhyāropa (illusory attribution) and apavāda (withdrawl or recession of that idea). Therefore there should be always inquiring into the universe, Jīva and Paramātmā. Were the true nature of Jīva and the universe known, then there remains Brahman which is non-different from Pratyagātmā."

Adhyāya III

अथ हैनं पैङ्गल: पप्रच्छ याज्ञवल्क्यं महावाक्यविवरणमनुब्रूहीति॥ १॥

Then Paiṅgala asked Yājñavalkya to offer an exposition on the mahāvākyas (sacred sentences of the Vedas).

स होवाच याज्ञवल्क्यस्तत्त्वमसि त्वं तदसि त्वं ब्रह्मास्यहं ब्रह्मास्मीत्यनुसंधानं कुर्यात्॥ २

To which Yājñavalkya replied : "One should scrutinise (the sacred sentences), Tattvamasi (That are You), Tvamtadasi (You aet That), Tvambrahmāsmi (You art Brahman) and Ahambrahmāsmi (I am Brahman).

तत्र पारोक्ष्यशबल: सर्वज्ञत्वादिलक्षणो मायोपाधि: सच्चिदानन्दलक्षणो जगद्योनिस्तत्पदवाच्यो भवति। स एवान्त:करणसंभिन्नबोधोऽस्मत्प्रत्ययावलम्बनस्त्वंपदवाच्यो भवति। परजीवोपाधिमायाविद्ये विहाय तत्त्वंपदलक्ष्यं प्रत्यगभिन्नं ब्रह्म॥ ३॥

The word 'Tat' denotes the cause of the universe that is variegated beyond perception, has the characteristics of omniscience, has Māyā as His vehicle and has the attributes of Saccidānanda. It is He that is the basis of the notion 'I' which has the differentiated knowledge produced by antaḥkaraṇa; and it is He that is denoted by the word "Tvam" (You). That is the undifferentiated Brahman which remains as the aim (or meaning) of the words Tat and Tvam after freeing itself from Māyā and Avidyā which are respectively the vehicles of Paramātmā and Jīvātmā.

तत्त्वमसीत्यहं ब्रह्मास्मीति वाक्यार्थविचार: श्रवणं भवति। एकान्तेन श्रवणार्थानुसंधानं मननं भवति। श्रवणमनननिर्विचिकित्स्येऽर्थे वस्तुन्येकतानवत्तया चेत:स्थापनं निदिध्यासनं भवति। ध्यातृध्याने विहाय

निवातस्थितदीपवद्ध्येयैकगोचरं चित्तं समाधिर्भवति॥ ४॥

The inquiry into the real significance of the sentences Tattvamasi and aham brahmāsmi forms (what is called) śravaṇa (hearing— the first state of inquiry). To inquire in solitude into the significance of śravaṇa is manana. The concentration of the mind with one-pointedness upon that which should be sought after by śravaṇa and manana is nididhyāsana. Samādhi is that state in which Citta having given up (the conception of the difference of) the meditator and the meditation, becomes of the form of the meditated like a lamp in place without wind.

तदानीमात्मगोचरा वृत्तय: समुत्थिता अज्ञाता भवन्ति। ता: स्मरणादनुमीयन्ते। इहानादिसंसारे संचिता: कर्मकोटयोऽनेनैव विलयं यान्ति। ततोऽभ्यासपाटवात्सहस्रश: सदाऽमृतधारा वर्षन्ति। ततो योगवित्तमा: समाधिं धर्ममेघं प्राहु:। वासनाजाले नि:शेषममुना प्रविलापिते कर्मसंचये पुण्यपापे समूलोन्मूलिते प्राक्परोक्षमपि करतलामलकवद्वाक्यमप्रतिबद्धापरोक्षसाक्षात्कारं प्रसूयते। तदा जीवन्मुक्तो भवति॥ ५॥

Then arise the modifications pertaining to Ātmā. Such (modifications) cannot be known; but they can only be inferred through memory (of the samādhi state). The myriads of karmas committed in this beginningless cycle of rebirths are annihilated only through them. Through proficiency in practice, the current of nectar always rains down in diverse ways. Therefore those who know Yoga call this Samādhi, dharma-megha (cloud). Through these (modifications of Ātmā), the collection of affinities is absorbed without any remainder whatever. When the accumulated good and bad karmas are wholly destroyed, these sentences (Tattvamasi and Aham brahmāsmi), like the myrobalan in the palm of the hand, bring him face to face with the ultimate Reality, though It was before invisible. Then he becomes a Jīvanmukta.

ईश: पञ्चीकृतभूतानामपञ्चीकरणं कर्तुं सोऽकामयत। ब्रह्माण्डतद्गतलोकान्कार्यरूपांश्च कारणत्वं प्रापयित्वा तत:सूक्ष्माङ्गं कर्मेन्द्रियाणि प्राणांश्च ज्ञानेन्द्रियाण्यन्त:करणचतुष्टयं चैकीकृत्य सर्वाणि भौतिकानि कारणे भूतपञ्चके संयोज्य भूमिं जले जलं वह्नौ वह्निं वायौ वायुमाकाशे चाकाशमहंकारे चाहंकारं महति महदव्यक्तेऽव्यक्तं पुरुषे क्रमेण विलीयते। विराड्‍ढिरण्यगर्भेश्वरा उपाधिविलयात्परमात्मनि लीयन्ते॥ ६॥

Īśvara wished to produce non-quintuplication (or involution) in the fivefold differentiated elements. Having drawn into their cause Brahmā's egg and its effects of worlds, and mixed together the subtle organs of sense and action and the four internal organs and dissolved all things composed of the elements into their cause, the five elements, he then caused Pṛthivī to merge into water, water into agni, agni into vāyu, and vāyu into ākāśa, ākāśa into ahaṁkāra, ahaṁkāra into mahat, mahat into avyakta, and avyakta into puruṣa in regular order. Virāṭ, Hiraṇyagarbha and Īśvara being freed form the vehicle of Māyā, are absorbed into Paramātmā.

पञ्चीकृतमहाभूतसंभवकर्मसंचितस्थूलदेह: कर्मक्षयात्सत्कर्मपरिपाकतोऽपञ्चीकरणं प्राप्य सूक्ष्मेणैकीभूत्वा कारणरूपत्वमासाद्य तत्कारणं कूटस्थे प्रत्यगात्मनि विलीयते। विश्वतैजसप्राज्ञा: स्वस्वोपाधिलयात्प्रत्यगात्मनि लीयन्ते॥ ७॥

This gross body composed of the five differentiated elements and obtained through accumulated karma, is merged into its subtle state of non-quintuplicated elements, through the extinction of (bad) karma and increase of good karma, then attains its kāraṇa (causal) state and (finally) is absorbed into its cause, (viz.,) Kūṭastha-Pratyagātmā. Viśva and Taijasa and Prājña, their upādhi (of avidyā) having become extinct, are absorbed in Pratyagātmā. This sphere (of universe) being burnt up by the fire of Jñāna is absorbed along with its cause into Paramātmā.

अण्डं ज्ञानाग्निना दग्धं कारणैःसह परमात्मनि लीनं भवति। ततो ब्राह्मणः समाहितो भूत्वा तत्त्वंपदैक्यमेव सदा कुर्यात्। ततो मेघापायेंऽशुमानिवात्माऽऽविर्भवति॥ ८॥

Therefore a Brāhmaṇa should be careful and always meditate upon the identity of Tat and Tvam. Then Ātmā shines, like the sun freed from the (obscuration of the) clouds. One should meditate upon Ātmā in the midst (of the body) like a lamp within a jar.

ध्यात्वा मध्यस्थमात्मानं कलशान्तरदीपवत्। अङ्गुष्ठमात्रमात्मानमधूमज्योतिरूपकम्॥ ९॥ प्रकाशयन्तमन्तःस्थं ध्यायेत्कूटस्थमव्ययम्। ध्यायन्नास्ते मुनिश्चैव चासुप्तेरामृतेस्तु यः॥ १०॥ जीवन्मुक्तः स विज्ञेयः स धन्यः कृतकृत्यवान्। जीवन्मुक्तपदं त्यक्त्वा स्वदेहे कालसात्कृते। विशत्यदेहमुक्तत्वं पवनोऽस्पन्दतामिव॥ ११॥

अशब्दमस्पर्शमरूपमव्ययं तथाऽरसं नित्यमगन्धवच्च यत्। अनाद्यनन्तं महतः परं ध्रुवं तदेव शिष्यत्यमलं निरामयम्॥ १२॥

Ātmā, the Kūṭastha, should be meditated upon as being of the size of a thumb, as being of the nature of the jyotis (light) without smoke, as being within, illuminating all and as being indestructible. That Muni (sage) who meditates (upon Ātmā always) until sleep or death comes upon him passes into the state of Jīvanmukta emancipation like the immovable state of the wind. Then there remains the One (Brahman) without sound, touch, free from destruction, without taste or odour, which is eternal, which is without beginning or end, which is beyond the Tattva of Mahat, and which is permanent and without stain or disease."

Adhyāya IV

अथ हैनं पैङ्गलः पप्रच्छ याज्ञवल्क्यं ज्ञानिनः किं कर्म का च स्थितिरिति॥ १॥

Then Paiṅgala addressed Yājñavalkya thus : "To the wise, what is their karma? And what is their state?"

स होवाच याज्ञवल्क्यः। अमानित्वादिसंपन्नो मुमुक्षुरेकविंशतिकुलं तारयति। ब्रह्मविन्मात्रेण कुलमेकोत्तरशतं तारयति॥ २॥

To which Yājñavalkya replied: "A lover of mokṣa, having humility and other possessions (or virtues), enables twenty-one generations to cross (to Ātmā). One through his being a Brahmavit alone enables 101 generations to cross.

आत्मानं रथिनं विद्धि शरीरं रथमेव च। बुद्धिं तु सारथिं विद्धि मनः प्रग्रहमेव च॥ ३॥

इन्द्रियाणि हयानाहुर्विषयांस्तेषु गोचरान्। जङ्गमानि विमानानि हृदयानि मनीषिणः॥४॥

आत्मेन्द्रियमनोयुक्तं भोक्तेत्याहुर्महर्षयः। ततो नारायणः साक्षाद्धृदये सुप्रतिष्ठितः॥५॥

Know Ātmā to be the rider and the body as the chariot. Know also buddhi as the charioteer and manas as the reins. The wise say the organs are the horses, the objects are the roads (through which the horses travel) and the hearts are the moving balloons. Maharṣis say that Ātmā, when associated with the sense organs and means, is the enjoyer. Therefore it is the actual Nārāyaṇa alone that is established in the heart.

प्रारब्धकर्मपर्यन्तमहिनिर्मोकवद्व्यवहरति। चन्द्रवच्चरते देही स मुक्तश्चानिकेतनः॥६॥

तीर्थे श्वपचगृहे वा तनुं विहाय याति कैवल्यम्। प्राणानवकीर्य याति कैवल्यम्॥७॥

तं पश्चाद्दिग्बलिं कुर्यादथवा खननं चरेत्। पुंसः प्रव्रजनं प्रोक्तं नेतराय कदाचन॥८॥

Till his prārabdha karma is worn out, he exists (in his body) as in the (case-off) slough of a serpent (without any desire for the body.) An emancipated person having such a body roves about like a moon-gladdening all with no settled place of abode. He given up his body whether in a sacred place, or in a caṇḍāla's (out-caste's) house (without any distinction whatever), and attains salvation. Such a body (when seen by a person) should be offered as a sacrifice of dik (the quarters) or should be buried (undergrund). It is only to Puruṣa (the wise) that the sannyāsa (renunciation) is ordained and not to others.

नाशौचं नाग्निकार्यं च न पिण्डं नोदकक्रिया। न कुर्यात्पार्वणादीनि ब्रह्मभूताय भिक्षवे॥९॥

दग्धस्य दहनं नास्ति पक्वस्य पचनं यथा। ज्ञानाग्निदग्धदेहस्य न च श्राद्धं न च क्रिया॥१०॥

यावच्चोपाधिपर्यन्तं तावच्छुश्रूषयेद्गुरुम्। गुरुवद्गुरुभार्यायां तत्पुत्रेषु च वर्तनम्॥११॥

In case of the death of an ascetic who is of the form (or has attained the nature) of Brahman, there is no pollution (to be observed); neither the ceremonies of fire (as burning the body, homa etc.,); nor the piṇḍa (balls of rice), nor ceremonies of water, nor the periodical ceremonies (monthly and yearly). Just as a food once cooked is not again cooked, so a body once burnt (by the fire of wisdom) should not be burnt (or exposed to fire) again. To one whose body was burnt by the fire of wisdom there is neither śrāddha (required to be performed), nor (funeral) ceremony. So long as there is the upādhi (of non-wisdom) in one, so long should he serve the Guru. He should conduct himself towards his Guru's wife and children as he does to his Guru.

शुद्धमानसः शुद्धचिद्रूपः सहिष्णुः सोऽहमस्मि सहिष्णुः सोऽहमस्मीति प्राप्ते ज्ञानेन विज्ञाने ज्ञेये परमात्मनि हृदि संस्थिते देहे लब्धशान्तिपदं गते तदा प्रभामनोबुद्धिशून्यं भवति॥१२॥

अमृतेन तृप्तस्य पयसा किं प्रयोजनम्। एवं स्वात्मानं ज्ञात्वा वेदैः प्रयोजनं किं भवति। ज्ञानामृततृप्तयोगिनो न किंचित्कर्तव्यमस्ति। तदस्ति चेन्न स तत्त्वविद्भवति। दूरस्थोऽपि न दूरस्थः पिण्डवर्जितः पिण्डस्थोऽपि प्रत्यगात्मा सर्वव्यापी भवति॥१३॥

हृदयं निर्मलं कृत्वा चिन्तयित्वाप्यनामयम्। अहमेव परं सर्वमिति पश्येत्परं सुखम्॥१४॥

If being of a pure mind, of the nature of immaculate cit and resigned, and having the discrimination arising from the attainment of wisdom "I am He", he should concentrate his heart on Paramātmā and obtain firm peace in his body, then he becomes of the nature of Jyotis, void of manas and buddhi. Of what avail is milk to one content with nectar? Of what avail are the Vedas to him who has known his Ātmā thus? For a Yogin content with the nectar of wisdom, there is nothing more to be done. If he has to do anything, then he is not a knower of Tattva. Pratyagātmā though far (or difficult of attainment), is not far; though in the body, he is devoid of it (since) he is all-pervading. After having purified the heart and contemplated on the One without disease (viz., Brahman), the cognizing of 'I' as the supreme and the all is the highest bliss.

यथा जले जलं क्षिप्तं क्षीरे क्षीरं घृते घृतम्। अविशेषो भवेत्तद्वज्जीवात्मपरमात्मनो:॥ १५॥

देहे ज्ञानेन दीपिते बुद्धिरखण्डाकाररूपा यदा भवति तदा विद्वान्ब्रह्मज्ञानाग्निना कर्मबन्धं निर्दहेत्॥ १६॥

तत: पवित्रं परमेश्वराख्यमद्वैतरूपं विमलाम्बराभम्। यथोदके तोयमनुप्रविष्टं तथात्मरूपो निरुपाधिसंस्थित:॥ १७॥

Like water mixed with water, milk with milk, and ghee with ghee, so Jīvātmā and Paramātmā are without difference. When the body is rendered bright through wisdom and the buddhi becomes of the partless One, then the wise man burns the bondage of karma through the fire of Brahmajñāna. Then be becomes purified, of the nature of the non-dual named Parameśvara and the light like the stainless ākāśa. Like water mixed with water, so Jīva(-Ātmā) becomes upādhi-less (or freed from the bonds of matter). Ātmā is invisible like vāyu. Though he is within and without, he is the immovable Ātmā. Through the torch of wisdom, the internal Ātmā sees (or knows).

स बाह्यमभ्यन्तरनिश्चलात्मा ज्ञानोल्कया पश्यति चान्तरात्मा॥ १८॥

यत्र यत्र मृतो ज्ञानी येन वा केन मृत्युना। यथा सर्वगतं व्योम तत्र तत्र लयं गत:॥ १९॥

घटाकाशमिवात्मानं विलयं वेत्ति तत्त्वत:। स गच्छति निरालम्बं ज्ञानालोकं समन्तत:॥ २०

तपेद्वर्षसहस्राणि एकपादस्थितो नर:। एतस्य ध्यानयोगस्य कलां नार्हति षोडशीम्॥ २१॥

A wise man, in whatever place or manner he dies, is absorbed in that place like the all-pervading ākāśa. It should be known that Ātmā is absorbed as truly as the ākāśa in the pot (when broken). Then he attains the all-pervading wisdom-light that is without support. Though men should perform tapas standing on one leg for a period of 1,000 years, it will not in the least, be equal to one-sixteenth part of dhyānayoga.

इदं ज्ञानमिदं ज्ञेयं तत्सर्वं ज्ञातुमिच्छति। अपि वर्षसहस्रायु: शास्त्रान्तं नाधिगच्छति॥ २२॥

विज्ञेयोऽक्षरतन्मात्रो जीवितं वापि चञ्चलम्। विहाय शास्त्रजालानि यत्सत्यं तदुपास्यताम्॥ २३

One desirous of knowing what jñāna (wisdom) and jñeya (the object to be known) are, will not be able to attain his desired end, even though he may study the Śāstras for 1,000 years. That which is alone should be known as the indestructible. That which exists (in this world) is only impermanent. (Therefore) after having given up (the study of) the many Śāstras, one should worship that which is satya (truth).

अनन्तकर्म शौचं च जपो यज्ञस्तथैव च। तीर्थयात्राभिगमनं यावत्तत्त्वं न विन्दति॥ २४॥

अहं ब्रह्मेति नियतं मोक्षहेतुर्महात्मनाम्। द्वे पदे बन्धमोक्षाय न ममेति ममेति च॥ २५॥

ममेति बध्यते जन्तुर्निर्ममेति विमुच्यते। मनसो ह्युन्मनीभावे द्वैतं नैवोपलभ्यते॥ २६॥

The many karmas, purity (of mind and heart), japa (the muttering of mantras), sacrifice and pilgrimages— all these should be observed till Tattva is known. For Mahātmans (noble souls) to be always in (the conception of) 'I am Brahman' conduces to their salvation. There are two causes (that lead) to bondage and emancipation. They are 'mine' and 'not mine'. Through 'mine' creatures are bound, whereas through 'not mine' they are released from bondage. When the mind attains the state of Unmanīi (above manas, viz., when it is destroyed), then there is never the conception of duality.

यदा यात्युन्मनीभावस्तदा तत्परमं पदम्। यत्र यत्र मनो याति तत्र तत्र परं पदम्॥ २७॥

तत्र तत्र परं ब्रह्म सर्वत्र समवस्थितम्। हन्यान्मुष्टिभिराकाशं क्षुधार्तः खण्डयेत्तुषम्।

नाहंब्रह्मेति जानाति तस्य मुक्तिर्न जायते॥ २८॥

When the Unmanī state occurs, then is the supreme-Seat (attained). (After which) wherever the mind goes, there is the supreme Seat (to it, viz., the mind enjoys salvation wherever it is). That which is equal in all is Brahman alone. One may attain the power to strike the ākāśa with his fist; he may appeases his hunger by eating husks (of grain), but never shall he attain emancipation who has not the self-cognition, 'I am Brahman'.

य एतदुपनिषदं नित्यमधीते सोऽग्निपूतो भवति। स वायुपूतो भवति। स आदित्यपूतो भवति। स ब्रह्मपूतो भवति। स विष्णुपूतो भवति। स रुद्रपूतो भवति। स सर्वेषु तीर्थेषु स्नातो भवति। स सर्वेषु वेदेष्वधीतो भवति। स सर्ववेदव्रतचर्यासु चरितो भवति। तेनेतिहासपुराणानां रुद्राणां शतसहस्राणि जप्तानि फलानि भवन्ति। प्रणवानामयुतं जप्तं भवति। दश पूर्वान्दशोत्तरान्पुनाति। स पङ्क्तिपावनो भवति। स महान्भवति। ब्रह्महत्यासुरापानस्वर्णस्तेयगुरुतल्पगमनतत्संयोगिपातकेभ्यः पूतो भवति॥ २९॥

Whoever recites this Upaniṣad becomes as immaculate as Agni. He becomes as pure as Brahmā. He becomes as pure as Vāyu. He becomes like one who has bathed in all the holy waters. He becomes like one who has studied all the Vedas. He becomes like one that has undergone all vedic observances. He obtains the fruit of the recitation of Itihāsas, Purāṇas and Rudramantras a lakh of times. He becomes like one that has pronounced Praṇava (Oṁ) ten thousand times. He purifies his ancestors ten degrees removed and his descendants ten degree removed. He becomes purified of all those that sit with him for dinner. He becomes a great personage. He becomes purified from the sins of the murder of a Brāhmaṇa, the drinking of alcohol, theft of gold, and sexual cohabitation with Guru's wife, and from the sins of associating with those that commit such sins.

तद्विष्णोः परमं पदं सदा पश्यन्ति सूरयः। दिवीव चक्षुराततम्॥ ३०॥

तद्विप्रासो विपन्यवो जागृवांसः समिन्धते। विष्णोर्यत्परमं पदम्। ॐ सत्यमित्युपनिषद्॥ ३१॥

"Like the eye pervading the Āsās (seeing without effort everything above), a wise man sees (always) the supreme seat of Viṣṇu. The Brāhmaṇas who have always their spiritual eyes wide open praise and illuminate in diverse ways the supreme Seat of Viṣṇu. Oṁ : This Upaniṣad is truth."

ॐ पूर्णमदः................. इति शान्तिः॥

॥इति पैङ्गलोपनिषत्समाप्ता॥

***

56. BHIKṢUKOPANIṢAD

भिक्षुकोपनिषद्

॥शान्तिपाठः॥

ॐ पूर्णमदः.................. इति शान्तिः॥

ॐ अथ भिक्षूणां मोक्षार्थिनां कुटीचकबहूदकहंसपरमहंसाश्चेति चत्वारः॥ १॥

कुटीचका नाम गौतमभरद्वाजयाज्ञवल्क्यवसिष्ठप्रभृतयोऽष्टौ ग्रासांश्चरन्तो योगमार्गे मोक्षमेव प्रार्थयन्ते॥ २॥

Among bhikṣus (religious mendicants) who long for mokṣa (salvation), there are four kinds, viz,. Kuṭīcaka, Bahūdaka, Haṁsa and Paramahaṁsa. Gautama, Bharadvāja, Yājñavalkya, Vasiṣṭha and others belong to the first kind. They take eight mouthfuls (of food daily) and strive after mokṣa alone through the path of yoga.

अथ बहूदका नाम त्रिदण्डकमण्डलुशिखायज्ञोपवीतकाषायवस्त्रधारिणो ब्रह्मर्षिगृहे मधुमांसं वर्जयित्वाऽष्टौ ग्रासान्भैक्षाचरणं कृत्वा योगमार्गे मोक्षमेव प्रार्थयन्ते॥ ३॥

The second kind carry the (bamboo) staves (tied together) and a waterpot, and wear tuft of hair (śikhā), sacred thread (yajñopavīta) and red-colourd cloth. They take eight mouthfuls of food in the house of Brahmarṣis, abstain from flesh and alcohol and strive after emancipation alone through the path of yoga.

अथ हंसा नाम ग्राम एकरात्रं नगरे पञ्चरात्रं क्षेत्रे सप्तरात्रं तदुपरि न वसेयुः। गोमूत्रगोमयाहारिणो नित्यं चान्द्रायणपरायणा योगमार्गे मोक्षमेव प्रार्थयन्ते॥ ४॥

Then the Haṁas should live not more than a night in a village, five nights in a town, and seven nights in a sacred place, partaking daily of cow's urine and cow's dung, observing cāndrāyaṇa and striving after mokṣa alone through the path of yoga.

अथ परमहंसा नाम संवर्तकारुणिश्वेतकेतुजडभरतदत्तात्रेयशुकवामदेवहारीतकप्रभृतयोऽष्टौ ग्रासांश्चरन्तो योगमार्गे मोक्षमेव प्रार्थयन्ते। वृक्षमूले शून्यगृहे श्मशानवासिनो वा साम्बरा वा दिगम्बरा वा। न तेषां धर्माधर्मौ लाभालाभौ शुद्धाशुद्धौ द्वैतवर्जिता समलोष्टाश्मकाञ्चनाः सर्ववर्णेषु भैक्षाचरणं कृत्वा सर्वत्रात्मैवेति पश्यन्ति। अथ जातरूपधरा निर्द्वन्द्वा निष्परिग्रहाः शुक्लध्यानपरायणा आत्मनिष्ठाः प्राणसंधारणार्थं यथोक्तकाले भैक्षमाचरन्तः शून्यागारदेवगृहतृणकूट वल्मीकवृक्षमूलकुलालशालाग्निहोत्रशालानदीपुलिनगिरिकन्दर-कुहरकोटरनिर्झरस्थण्डिले तत्र ब्रह्ममार्गे सम्यक्संपन्नाः शुद्धमानसाः परमहंसाचरणेन संन्यासेन देहत्यागं कुर्वन्ति ते परमहंसा नामेत्युपनिषत्॥ ५॥

Paramahaṁsas like Samvartaka, Āruṇi, Śvetaketu, Jaḍabharata, Dattātreya, Śuka,

Vāmadeva, Hārītaka and others take eight mouthfuls and strive after mokṣa alone through the path of yoga. They live clothed or naked at the foot of trees, in ruined houses, or in burning grounds, With them, there are no dualities as dharma and adharma, gain and loss, and purity and impurity. They look upon gold and stone and clod of earth with the same eye (indifference), live on alms, begging from all without any distinction of caste and look upon everything as Ātmā alone. Being (naked) as nature made them, being free from the sense of duality and from covetousness, being engaged in pure contemplation (śukladhyāna), meditating on Ātmā, and begging at stated times, simply to keep the body and soul together, they reside in ruined houses, temples, straw-huts, ant-hills, the foot of trees, potteries, the places of agnihotra, the sand in the bed of rivers, mountain-caves, cavities, the hollows of trees, waterfalls, and sthaṇḍila (the level square piece of ground prepared for sacrifice). Having advanced far in the path of Brahman, and being pure in mind, they quit this body through the methods prescribed for Paramahaṁsa Sannyāsins. These are the Paramahaṁsas.

ॐ पूर्णमदः .... इति शान्तिः॥

॥इति भिक्षुकोपनिषत्समाप्ता॥

***

57. MAHOPANIṢAD

महोपनिषद्

This upaniṣad is related to the tradition of Sāmaveda. This large in volume upaniṣad has been descended as a result of questions raised and answers given by the great king Janaka, Ṛbhu and Nidāgha respectively. There are six chapters in this Mahopaniṣad.

In the first chapter, the uniqueness and the godly element of Nārāyaṇa has been enumerated. Then the contents to this Mahopaniṣad proceeds as the origin of yajñīya stoma, fourteen Puruṣa and a virgin, the origin of the Puruṣa with twenty five elements, origin of Rudra, four month Brahma, vyāhṛti, rhyme, veda and the gods, the gigantic form of Nārāyaṇa and the achievement of Nārāyaṇa in the heart. The contents in the second chapter are anxiety of Śukadeva even after self acquired knowledge all benevolent and metaphysics, Śukadeva condemning the preaching of Vyāsa, Śukadeva's visit to the king Janaka, Śukadeva's trial by Janaka, colloque striked between Janaka and Śukadeva, the discretion of ties and salvation, stage of soul liberty, the stage when physical sense vanishes (Videha), removal of the doubts raised by Śukadeva and attainment of peace of Śukadava. The issues described in third chapter are– the concept of Nidāgha, the perishable nature of the world, voidness of ego, temptation, etc. condemn to the body and its stage, the misery of the world, condemn to the female, the splitting up of the directions etc. and the curiosity of essence by virtue of detachment etc. The fourth chapter embeds the issues like– four measures for emancipation, the method of self-analyse as contemplated in holy-books (Śāstras), the form of meditation (Samādhi), state of air, liberty, soul satisfaction by śama (conscience), contentment and self-peace (Atma-viśrānti), myth of the apparent or formidable world, the stage of bondage and salvation by attachment and detachment, psychology of the world, samādhi is the perception of sensitivity, the fallacy of worldly living, attainment of Brahma in cool temperament, the magnificence of the easiest knowledge of Brahma, attainment of salvation by remission of the passion, the fundamental resolution of ties and salvation and the method for giving-up the proud of material things (Anātmābhimāna). The fifth chapter contains an introduction of knowledge and ignorance, stability on nature salvation when nature is split-up, seven rules of knowledge and ignorance, the conduct of liberated soul, eligibility criterion for knowledge, Perception to Brahma is the measure to attain Brahma, Perception of sensitivity on merger of mind, measures to cool down the illusory, knowledge of world, detachment or reluctance from the worldly subjects, (issues), giving-up the ego is the sole measure to destroy the temptation, the bondage and liberation from the progress of mind and deteriorations, the mind eligible to learning (vidyā), attainment of Brahma possible only when escaped from illusion, the origin of Brahma under illusion, and the root out or eradication by world is possible when the resolution (ambition) is destroyed. The subject matter of sixth chapter is– attainment of godly element by the practice of Samādhi, the pattern of worship adopted by scholars, the gloomy condoms of stupids, measures to decay the mind, measures of giving-up the passion, magnificence of liberated soul, method of giving-up the temptation, four kinds of determination (resolution), wanting of world for the person loyal to exclusive (one) thought, loyalty to Brahma of the person desirous to salvation and finally, the fruits for perserverance and preaching of this upaniṣad are enumerated.

Thus, we observe that this upaniṣad as it name implies, provides appropriate guidelines with persons practising metaphysics by bringing efficiently countless topics of importance.

॥शान्तिपाठः॥

ॐ आप्यायन्तु ममाङ्गानि वाक् प्राणश्चक्षुः श्रोत्रमथो बलमिन्द्रियाणि च सर्वाणि। सर्वं ब्रह्मौपनिषदं माहं ब्रह्म निराकुर्यां मा मा ब्रह्म निराकरोदनिराकरणमस्त्वनिराकरणं मेऽस्तु तदात्मनि निरते य उपनिषत्सु धर्मास्ते मयि सन्तु ते मयि सन्तु॥ ॐ शान्तिः शान्तिः शान्तिः॥

O supreme god! May my all organs and limbs of body attain proper growth. May the speech, eyes, ears etc. sensory organs and executive organs, all breathings (Prāṇa), the physical and mental power be strong and develop with brilliance and splendour. May I seldom reject the nature of Brahma as propounded in upaniṣad and that Brahma should also not abandon us any time. May that Brahma always make me to feel that he is always near to me. (The mutual nexus) should always be strengthened. May all religions enumerated in upaniṣads exist in me undeviated and luminating always while I engross in that element of supreme soul. O supreme soul! may trio-fevers (pains) be cooled down.

Chapter - I

अथातो महोपनिषदं व्याख्यास्यामः॥१॥ तदाहुरेको ह वै नारायण आसीन्न ब्रह्मा नेशानो नापो नाग्नीषोमौ नेमे द्यावापृथिवी न नक्षत्राणि न सूर्यो न चन्द्रमाः॥२॥ स एकाकी न रमते॥३॥

Now (after pray submitted to lord) the discussion of Mahopaniṣad commences. Lord Nārāyaṇa was alone at the initial time of creation (Sṛṣṭi). Lord Brahmā, Rudra, Apaḥ (water), fire and Soma etc. gods were not in existence besides Nārāyaṇa. This world of sun (Dyuloka) and earth too were absent and the planets, Moon and Sun etc. also were nowhere. In the circumstance, that gigantic person alone was very unhappy because of no company.

तस्य ध्यानान्तःस्थस्य यज्ञस्तोममुच्यते॥४॥ तस्मिन् पुरुषाश्चतुर्दश जायन्ते एका कन्या दशेन्द्रियाणि मन एकादशं तेजो द्वादशोऽहंकारस्त्रयोदशकः प्राणश्चतुर्दश आत्मा पञ्चदशी बुद्धिः भूतानि पञ्च तन्मात्राणि पञ्च महाभूतानि स एकः पञ्चविंशतिः पुरुषः॥५॥ तत्पुरुषं पुरुषो निवेश्य नास्य प्रधानसंवत्सरा जायन्ते। संवत्सरादधिजायन्ते॥६॥

The Dhyāna (concentration) as existed in the conscience of that gigantic-person (Puruṣa) was called yajñastoma i.e. the best offering. A virgin and fourteen Puruṣa were originated from him. The fourteen Puruṣa are ten senses including sensory and executive organs, the eleventh was the mind full of splendour, the twelfth was ego and thirteenth and fourteenth were Prāṇa and soul respectively. The virgin is called the wisdom. Besides these, five tanmātrās in the micro form and five Mahābhūtas were originated. Thus, with the harmony of these twenty five elements, the body of a gigantic Puruṣa was built. The primitive man (Ādipuruṣa) in the form of supreme soul had entered into that gigantic body. The cardinal saṁvatsara etc. are not originated form such puruṣa made as a result of combination of twenty five elements. These are originated by the saṁvatsara in the form of Kāla of primitive-Puruṣa.

अथ पुनरेव नारायणः सोऽन्यत्कामो मनसा ध्यायत। तस्य ध्यानान्तःस्थस्य ललाटात्त्र्यक्षः शूलपाणिः पुरुषो जायते। बिभ्रच्छ्रियं यशः सत्यं ब्रह्मचर्यं तपो वैराग्यं मन ऐश्वर्यं सप्रणवा व्याहृतय ऋग्यजुःसामाथर्वाङ्गिरसः सर्वाणि छन्दांसि तान्यङ्गे समाश्रितानि। तस्मादीशानो महादेवो महादेवः॥७॥

That gigantic Puruṣa lord Nārāyaṇa then sat on meditation and resolute for another desire. Owing to deep meditation, a puruṣa (man) holding a trident in hand and three eyes was appeared out from his forehead. The fame, truth, celibacy, penance, detachment, controlled mind, prosperity, and pleasure and all syllables including 'Oṁ', Ṛg, Yajuḥ, Sāma, Atharva etc. four Vedas and all rhymes were enshrined in the body of that prominent Puruṣa. Owing to these characteristics, he attained popularity as Īśāna and Mahādeva.

अथ पुनरेव नारायणः सोऽन्यत्कामो मनसा ध्यायत। तस्य ध्यानान्तःस्थस्य ललाटात्स्वेदोऽपतत्। ता इमाः प्रतता आपः। ततस्तेजो हिरणमयमण्डम्। तत्र ब्रह्मा चतुर्मुखोऽजायत॥८॥

That lord Nārāyaṇa again sat on meditation with one more resolute desire. In the process, perspiration started oozing from his forehead. That droplets of perspiration converted in Āpaḥ (the fundamental active element of nature) and spreaded all over the ground. This Āpaḥ originated the oval in the form of Hiraṇyagarbha, full of splendour and it gave birth to Lord Brahmā.

सोऽध्यायत्। पूर्वाभिमुखो भूत्वा भूरिति व्याहृतिर्गायत्रं छन्द ऋग्वेदोऽग्निर्देवता। पश्चिमाभिमुखो भूत्वा भुवरिति व्याहृतिस्त्रैष्टुभं छन्दो यजुर्वेदो वायुर्देवता। उत्तराभिमुखो भूत्वा स्वरिति व्याहृतिर्जागतं छन्दः सामवेदः सूर्यो देवता। दक्षिणाभिमुखो भूत्वा मह इति व्याहृतिरानुष्टुभं छन्दोऽथर्ववेदः सोमो देवता॥९॥

That Pitāmaha lord Brahmā had meditated on several gods all around and all directions. While facing the East, he concentrated on Bhuḥ Vyāhṛti, Gāyatrī rhyme, Ṛgveda and lord Agni. Facing the west, he concentrated on Bhuvaḥ Vyāhṛti, Triṣṭupa rhyme, and lord Vāyu including, Yajurveda while facing North, he concentrated on Svaḥ Vyāhṛti, Jagati rhyme, Sāmaveda and the Sun god and facing the south, he concentrated on Mahaḥ Vyāhṛti, Anuṣṭupa rhyme, Atharvaveda and the Soma god.

[The concentration enumerated for gods reveals that these all gods started appearing at the same time i.e. all were so originated.]

सहस्रशीर्षं देवं सहस्राक्षं विश्वशंभुवम्। विश्वतः परमं नित्यं विश्वं नारायणं हरिम्॥१०॥

Lord Brahmā then meditated on lord Nārāyaṇa holding many thousand heads, eyes, all benevolent, omnipresent, everlasting and enshrined in all forms.

विश्वमेवेदं पुरुषस्तद्विश्वमुपजीवति। पतिं विश्वेश्वरं देवं समुद्रे विश्वरूपिणम्॥११॥

This lord Nārāyaṇa is in the form of entire world. The worldly living is entirely dependent on this gigantic puruṣa. Lord Brahmā attained a glimpse of lord Nārāyaṇa, the nourisher of this entire world, universal form, God of universe, and resorting to Yoganidrā in kṣirasāgara while he was in meditation.

पद्मकोशप्रतीकाशं लम्बत्याकोशसंनिभम्। हृदयं चाप्यधोमुखं संतत्यै सीत्कराभिश्च॥ १२॥
तस्य मध्ये महानर्चिर्विश्वार्चिर्विश्वतोमुखम्। तस्य मध्ये वह्निशिखा अणीयोर्ध्वा व्यवस्थिता॥ १३॥
तस्याः शिखाया मध्ये पुरुषः परमात्मा व्यवस्थितः।
स ब्रह्मा स ईशानः सेन्द्रः सोऽक्षरः परमः स्वराट्॥ इति महोपनिषत्॥ १४॥

The lengthy and downward facing heart in the shape of Padmakośa (the shell of lotus flower) duly developed, emanates the hissing sound frequently. There is a great flame ever laying in the middle of that heart. This very flame is giving light to this whole universe by distributing the element of immortal light in ten directions like the flame of a lamp (Dīpaka). In the middle of that flame a very thin flame of fire rising upward is existed. The element of supreme soul (gigantic puruṣa) resides at the middle of that flame. He is Brahmā, Viṣṇu, Īśāna and Indra, the king of gods too. He too is everlasting letter (Akṣara) and supreme Svarāṭ. It is Mahopaniṣad.

[According to Physiology, there is a place at the middle of heart which is known as pacemaker. The vibrations in a rhythmic frequency are arisen from here and it gives motion to the heart. The scientists still could not clarify the basic reason for such heart beating. The saint has perhaps perceived the same spot as of sensitive flame.]

Chapter - II

शुको नाम महातेजाः स्वरूपानन्दतत्परः। जातमात्रेण मुनिराड् यत्सत्यं तदवाप्तवान्॥ १॥ तेनासौ स्वविवेकेन स्वयमेव महामनाः। प्रविचार्य चिरं साधु स्वात्मनिश्चयमाप्तवान्॥ २॥

Lord hermit Śuka used to remain engross in thinking of the issues pertaining to soul and he was full of genius. He had yielded the knowledge of truth and the metaphysics just after his birth. Hence, he resolved for acquiring the nature of soul after prolong thinking and observation by virtue of his self-discretion.

अनाख्यत्वादगम्यत्वान्मनः षष्ठेन्द्रियस्थितेः। चिन्मात्रमेवमात्माणुराकाशादपि सूक्ष्मकः॥ ३॥ चिदणोः परमस्यान्तःकोटिब्रह्माण्डरेणवः। उत्पत्तिस्थितिमभ्येत्य लीयन्ते शक्तिपर्ययात्॥ ४॥ आकाशं बाह्यशून्यत्वादनाकाशं तु चित्त्वतः। न किंचिद्यदनिर्देश्यं वस्तु सत्तेति किंचन॥ ५॥ चेतनोऽसौ प्रकाशत्वाद्वेद्याभावाच्छिलोपमः। स्वात्मनि व्योमनि स्वस्थे जगदुन्मेषचित्रकृत्॥ ६॥

Having beyond the words (Vacanas) inaccessible and enshrined in the sixth sense i.e. mind; this soul is in the shape of molecule, cinmātra and more micro than the ether. The crores of reṇukas in the form of Brahmāṇḍa frequently appear and merge after enshrining as per the power or energy within this molecule in the form of supreme mind. The soul is like ether because of being its void from outside. And having endurable feature it is ether like. It is not objective because it has no complexion or shape still having an entity, it is objective. It is sensitive because of being in the form of light and it is inert like the rock because of being not an issue of heart-touching (pricks). It creates different kinds of universe within the ether of soul existing within the heart.

तद्धामात्रमिदं विश्वमिति न स्यात्ततः पृथक्। जगद्भेदोऽपि तद्भानमिति भेदोऽपि तन्मयः।।७।। सर्वगः सर्वसंबन्धो गत्यभावान्न गच्छति। नास्त्यसावाश्रयाभावात्सद्रूपत्वादथास्ति च।।८।। विज्ञानमानन्दं ब्रह्म रातेर्दातुः परायणम्। सर्वसंकल्पसंन्यासश्चेतसा यत्परिग्रहः।।९।। जाग्रतः प्रत्ययाभावं यस्याहुः प्रत्ययं बुधाः। यत्संकोचविकासाभ्यां जगत्प्रलयसृष्टयः।।१०।। निष्ठा वेदान्तवाक्यानामथ वाचामगोचरः। अहं सच्चित्परानन्दब्रह्मैवास्मि न चेतरः।।११।।

This would being mere light of that very soul is not distinct from that element of soul. The discrimination seen in soul of the world that too is not separate from that soul. Having related to all, the motion of that soul is everywhere however being in the form of truth, it is in garb of entity. It is the supreme position of the generous (donor) person. It is full of pleasure and conscience as also entertain the giving-up of all resolutions from the mind. The scholars tell perceiving of it when the awaking stage is not felt. The world is created and destroyed by its evolvement and shrinking. I am that supreme soul Brahman embedding within the truth, mind and pleasure which is undescribable and loyal to the sentences of vedānta.

स्वयैव सूक्ष्मया बुद्ध्या सर्वं विज्ञातवाञ्छुकः। स्वयं प्राप्ते परे वस्तुन्यविश्रान्तमनाः स्थितः।।१२।। इदं वस्त्विति विश्वासं नासावात्मन्युपाययौ। केवलं विररामास्य चेतो विषयचापलम्। भोगेभ्यो भूरिभङ्गेभ्यो धाराभ्य इव चातकः।।१३।।

Thus, the hermit Śukadeva had acquired all knowledge by virtue of his micro wisdom and he enshrined with continuously engrossed mind on the element of supreme soul. He got firm faith on its being the thing and nothing is distinct from it. As the Cātaka by drinking the torrent of rushing down from the clouds, Śukadeva's mind got stability and he got the stage of emancipation by abstaining it from the caprice generated due to involvement in number of worldly enjoyments.

एकदा सोऽमलप्रज्ञो मेरावेकान्तसंस्थितः। पप्रच्छ पितरं भक्त्या कृष्णद्वैपायनं मुनिम्।।१४।। संसाराडम्बरमिदं कथमभ्युत्थितं मुने। कथं च प्रशमं याति किं यत्कस्य कदा वद।।१५।।

That genius hermit i.e. Śukadeva had once visited at Meru mountain where his father Śrīkṛṣṇa Dvaipāyana were living a life of recluse. He conveyed due respect and asked him– "O great hermit! how had the illusion of this world appeared and by what way is it destroyed? What it is? Of whom and when is it originated? Please, tell us all about it in detail.

एवं पृष्टेन मुनिना व्यासेनाखिलमात्मजे। यथावदखिलं प्रोक्तं वक्तव्यं विदितात्मना।।१६।। अज्ञासिषं पूर्वमेवमहमित्यथ तत्पितुः। स शुकः स्वकया बुद्ध्या न वाक्यं बहु मन्यते।।१७।। व्यासोऽपि भगवान्बुद्ध्वा पुत्राभिप्रायमीदृशम्। प्रत्युवाच पुनः पुत्रं नाहं जानामि तत्त्वतः।।१८।। जनको नाम भूपालो विद्यते मिथिलापुरे। यथावद्वेत्त्यसौ वेद्यं तस्मात्सर्वमवाप्स्यसि।।१९।। पित्रेत्युक्तः शुकः प्रायात्सुमेरोर्वसुधातलम्। विदेहनगरीं प्राप जनकेनाभिपालिताम्।।२०।।

On being asked by Śukadeva, the renowned metaphysician Vyāsa told everything regarding the question but Śukadeva did not give any particular honour to the explanation made by his father considering that the same thing is known to him since prolong past. Having understood this poor exception of Śukadeva, lord Vyāsa told– O Sun! I do not know with essence all the issues asked by you. In case, your curiosity is not duly quenched, go to king Janaka who is ruling on Mithilā country and refer the same to him. He shall satisfy you because he is most genius king. O Son! you can get everything from him. Having heard this from his father, Śukadeva came down from the mountain Sumeru. In the plains and entered into Mithilāpurī duly protected by the great king Janaka.

आवेदितोऽसौ याष्टीकैर्जनकाय महात्मने। द्वारि व्याससुतो राजञ्छुकोऽत्र स्थितवानिति॥ २१॥ जिज्ञासार्थं शुकस्यासावास्तामेवेत्यवज्ञया। उक्त्वा बभूव जनकस्तूष्णीं सप्त दिनान्यथ॥ २२॥ ततः प्रवेशयामास जनकः शुकमङ्गणे। तत्राहानि स सप्तैव तथैवावसदुन्मनाः॥ २३॥ ततः प्रवेशयामास जनकोऽन्तःपुराजिरे। राजा दृश्यते तावदिति सप्त दिनानि तम्॥ २४॥ तत्रोन्मदाभिः कान्ताभिर्भोजनैर्भोगसंचयैः। जनको लालयामास शुकं शशिनिभाननम्॥ २५॥ ते भोगास्तानि भोज्यानि व्यासपुत्रस्य तन्मनः। नाजह्रुर्मन्दपवना बद्धपीठमिवाचलम्॥ २६॥ केवलं सुसमः स्वच्छो मौनी मुदितमानसः। संपूर्ण इव शीतांशुरतिष्ठदमलः शुकः॥ २७॥

The doorkeepers of king Janaka informed him when they saw the hermit Śukadeva, at the gate. They said– "O king! Śrī Śukadeva, the son of Vyāsa has come at the palatial gate and he wants to see you." Lord Janaka with an intention to try his temperament, delivered the message that he should stay at the same place till further message from him is not delivered. The king then kept mum in the matter till the next seven days. He then called in Śukadeva with due respect however did not talk with him for further seven days. He then called him with respect in the compound of his private palace (Antaḥpura), but did not appear before him for another seven days. In the private palace, Śukadeva was provided with the maids, several kinds of tasty food (eatables) but such amenities did not deviate the mind of Śukadeva as the breeze of wind cannot push the mountain from its place. In that Antaḥpura too, Śukadeva remained easy, free from anxiety, innocent and enshrined like a full-moon.

परिज्ञातस्वभावं तं शुकं स जनको नृपः। आनीय मुदितात्मानमवलोक्य ननाम ह॥ २८॥ निःशेषितजगत्कार्यः प्राप्ताखिलमनोरथः। किमीप्सितं तवेत्याह कृतस्वागतमाह तम्॥ २९॥ संसाराडम्बरमिदं कथमभ्युत्थितं गुरो। कथं प्रशममायाति यथावत्कथयाशु मे॥ ३०॥ यथावदखिलं प्रोक्तं जनकेन महात्मना। तदेव यत्पुरा प्रोक्तं तस्य पित्रा महाधिया॥ ३१॥ स्वयमेव मया पूर्वमभिज्ञातं विशेषतः। एतदेव हि पृष्टेन पित्रा मे समुदाहृतम्॥ ३२॥ भवताप्येष एवार्थः कथितो वाग्विदां वर। एष एव हि वाक्यार्थः शास्त्रेषु परिदृश्यते॥ ३३॥ मनोविकल्पसंजातं तद्विकल्पपरिक्षयात्। क्षीयते दग्धसंसारो निःसार इति निश्चितः॥ ३४॥ तत्किमेतन्महाभाग सत्यं ब्रूहि ममाचलम्। त्वत्तो विश्रममाप्नोति चेतसा भ्रमता जगत्॥ ३५॥

Thus, Śrī Śukadeva was called in for direct interview by the king Janaka when his conduct was duly tried. The king saluted him when he saw him happy and told humbly– "O revered Śukadeva! You are fully satisfied. Kindly, tell me that what does you desire now?" Imbibed in curiosity Śukadeva replied– "O great teacher! kindly, tell me that how this worldly illusion has been originated and how is it effaced?" The great scholar Janaka explained with essence all matters which were already told by his father. Śukadeva then reacted– "O best teacher! I myself has acquired sufficient knowledge of it and Vyāsa, my father had also told the same when it was asked to him, you also have repeated the same and the holy books (Śāstras) further confirm it. The illusion is created due to the options adopted by the mind and it is when that option loses its existence. This world is condemnable, it is true, then what this all (life etc.) is? O great scholar king! Kindly explain the factual position. My mind is misdirected about the perception of this world. So, please, explain the reality so that my anxiety may cool-down.

श्रृणु तावदिदानीं त्वं कथ्यमानमिदं मया। श्रीशुक ज्ञानविस्तारं बुद्धिसारान्तरान्तरम्॥३६॥
यद्विज्ञानात्पुमान्सद्यो जीवन्मुक्तत्वमाप्नुयात्॥३७॥ दृश्यं नास्तीति बोधेन मनसो दृश्यमार्जनम्। संपन्नं
चेत्तदुत्पन्ना परा निर्वाणनिर्वृतिः॥३८॥ अशेषेण परित्यागो वासनाया य उत्तमः। मोक्ष इत्युच्यते सद्भिः स
एव विमलक्रमः॥३९॥ ये शुद्धवासना भूयो न जन्मानर्थभागिनः। ज्ञातज्ञेयास्त उच्यन्ते जीवन्मुक्ता
महाधियः॥४०॥ पदार्थभावनादार्ढ्यं बन्ध इत्यभिधीयते। वासनातानवं ब्रह्मन्मोक्ष इत्यभिधीयते॥४१॥

The king Janaka then said–"O Śukadeva! I am now going to tell you in detail regarding this knowledge. Please, listen to attentively. This knowledge is an essence to all 'knowledges and a mystery to all mysteries. Hence, the knower to it attains to emancipation immediately. Janaka (king of Vaideha) told that the mind is purified in toto when this apparent world is severely neglected considering it void altogether. As soon as this sense gets perfection, the devotee attains supreme peace within no time. The person giving-up the passions it tantamounts to the real and the best sacrifice and this absolutely purified stage has been stated an emancipation by the scholars. O great genius Śukadeva! The people engrossed in purified desires, living worthful life and knower of knowable elements only are called liberated from worldly ties. The attachment to worldly things is bondage and decay of passions or attachment too is called the emancipation.

तपःप्रभृतिना यस्मै हेतुनैव विना पुनः। भोगा इह न रोचन्ते स जीवन्मुक्त उच्यते॥४२॥ आपतत्सु
यथाकालं सुखदुःखेष्वनारतः। न हृष्यति ग्लायति यः स जीवन्मुक्त उच्यते॥४३॥
हर्षामर्षभयक्रोधकामकार्पण्यदृष्टिभिः। न परामृश्यते योऽन्तः स जीवन्मुक्त उच्यते॥४४॥ अहंकारमयीं त्यक्त्वा
वासनां लीलयैव यः। तिष्ठति ध्येयसंत्यागी स जीवन्मुक्त उच्यते॥४५॥

Who does not fond of worldly enjoyments habitually in wanting of the penance etc. means, that man is only said as liberated soul. He only is liberated soul who does not attached to the feeling of vicissitudes, who neither becomes happy nor sad. Liberated soul is that man who enjoys freedom from the defects like happiness, misery, fear, sensuality, anger and agony etc. He who gives up the passion blended in ego in easiest way and keeps the spirit of sacrifice while involving the mind is really carved the liberated soul.

ईप्सितानीप्सिते न स्तो यस्यान्तर्वर्तिदृष्टिषु। सुषुप्तिवद्यश्चरति स जीवन्मुक्त उच्यते॥४६॥ अध्यात्मरतिरासीनः पूर्णः पावनमानसः। प्राप्तानुत्तमविश्रान्तिर्न किंचिदिह वाञ्छति। यो जीवति गतस्नेहः स जीवन्मुक्त उच्यते॥४७॥ संवेद्येन हृदाकाशे मनागपि न लिप्यते। यस्यासावजडा संवित्स जीवन्मुक्त उच्यते॥४८॥ रागद्वेषौ सुखं दुःखं धर्माधर्मौ फलाफले। यः करोत्यनपेक्ष्यैव स जीवन्मुक्त उच्यते॥४९॥ मौनवान्निरहंभावो निर्मानो मुक्तमत्सरः। यः करोति गतोद्वेगः स जीवन्मुक्त उच्यते॥५०॥

The man is only carved liberated soul who always is initiative, nor attached at the material desire and who always moves living in equal stage like dormant and without desire. He who is engrossed in the soul, whose mind is perfect and purified, who does not desire anything of this perishing world by virtue of making his habit peace loving and modest is called living a liberated life. The man who moves in this world without any attachment is called living a liberated life. Whose heart does not attach to any of the material and who is full of time knowledge is carved living a liberated life. The man keeping, himself busy, on his works always and living beyond the feeling of attachment envy, vicissitude, respect, insult, good-evil and desire for fruit or ambition is called living a liberated life. The scholars say a man is living liberated life, who does his deeds by leaving the ego, respect, malice, melancholic and the resolutions.

सर्वत्र विगतस्नेहो यः साक्षिवदवस्थितः। निरिच्छो वर्तते कार्ये स जीवन्मुक्त उच्यते॥५१॥ येन धर्ममधर्मं च मनोमननमीहितम्। सर्वमन्तः परित्यक्तं स जीवन्मुक्त उच्यते॥५२॥ यावती दृश्यकलना सकलेयं विलोक्यते। सा येन सुष्ठु संत्यक्ता स जीवन्मुक्त उच्यते॥५३॥ कट्वम्ललवणं तिक्तममृष्टं मृष्टमेव च। सममेव च यो भुङ्क्ते स जीवन्मुक्त उच्यते॥५४॥ जरामरणमापच्च राज्यं दारिद्र्यमेव च। रम्यमित्येव यो भुङ्क्ते स जीवन्मुक्त उच्यते॥५५॥ धर्माधर्मौ सुखं दुःखं तथा मरणजन्मनी। धिया येन सुसंत्यक्तं स जीवन्मुक्त उच्यते॥५६॥

The person actually loves the life fully liberated who deals with all worldly objects without any attachment and keeps himself busy on the work without expecting or awakening for its fruits. The person who has left behind the good and evil, engrossing on worldly issues and all desires is only liberated soul. The scholar who equally takes the sour, pungent, bitter, saline tastes and reluctantly takes the food whatever it is, is the liberated soul. The person always living in contentment irrespective of it being old age, death, adversity, prosperity etc., is the liberated soul. The person who has given-up entirely the feeling of good, evil, pleasure, sorrow and birth as also death etc. from his heart, is really the liberated soul.

उद्वेगानन्दरहितः समया स्वच्छया धिया। न शोचते न चोदेति स जीवन्मुक्त उच्यते॥५७॥ सर्वेच्छाः सकलाः शङ्काः सर्वेहाः सर्वनिश्चयाः। धिया येन परित्यक्ताः स जीवन्मुक्त उच्यते॥५८॥ जन्मस्थितिविनाशेषु सोदयास्तमयेषु च। सममेव मनो यस्य स जीवन्मुक्त उच्यते॥५९॥

न किंचन द्वेष्टि तथा न किंचिदपि काङ्क्षति। भुङ्क्ते यः प्रकृतान्भोगान्स जीवन्मुक्त उच्यते॥६०
शान्तसंसारकलनः कलावानपि निष्कलः। यः सचित्तोऽपि निश्चित्तः स जीवन्मुक्त उच्यते॥६१॥ यः
समस्तार्थजालेषु व्यवहार्यपि निःस्पृहः। परार्थेष्विव पूर्णात्मा स जीवन्मुक्त उच्यते॥६२॥

The person beyond the feeling of anxiety and pleasure and lives equal with his purified wisdom either it is the agony or gaiety, all desires and ambitions, passions and all resolutions thoroughly are given-up from mind, enjoys the pleasure of all liberated soul. The person whose mind remains undeviated at all stages like origin, maintenance and the collapse (destruction) as also at the pace of progress and fall, is really living the liberated life. One who does not have jealous and envy for any person as also seldom expects anything from others, who reluctantly and silently bears the pleasures and pains imposed on him due to past deeds (Prārabdha), is truly the liberated soul. Who has given-up the deserted to have worldly enjoyments, inspite of having mind who has ignored the inspiration given by mind, can only be said living the liberated life. The person irrespective of being enshrined at the centre of the worldly network of wealth, keeps himself detached like a religious man who throws it as the others' wealth, is really great person who perceives the element of supreme soul in his soul and thus, lives fully liberated life.

जीवन्मुक्तपदं त्यक्त्वा स्वदेहे कालसात्कृते। विशत्यदेहमुक्तत्वं पवनोऽस्पन्दतामिव॥६३॥
विदेहमुक्तो नोदेति नास्तमेति न शाम्यति। न सन्नासन्न दूरस्थो न चाहं न च नेतरः॥६४॥

That man of expiry on his material body leaves behind the stage of liberated soul and attains to the stage where the body requires no more like a stagnant wind. At this stage, the living soul neither progress nor fall and it seldom perishes. This stage is beyond the scope of truth and false and he does not live distant or near to anybody.

ततः स्तिमितगम्भीरं न तेजो न तमस्ततम्। अनाख्यमनभिव्यक्तं सत्किंचिदवशिष्यते॥६५॥ न शून्यं नापि
चाकारि न दृश्यं नापि दर्शनम्। न च भूतपदार्थौघसदनन्ततया स्थितम्॥६६॥ किमप्यव्यपदेशात्मा
पूर्णात्पूर्णतराकृतिः। न सन्नासन्न सदसन्न भावो भावनं न च॥६७॥ चिन्मात्रं चैत्यरहितमनन्तमजरं शिवम्।
अनादिमध्यपर्यन्तं यदनादि निरामयम्॥६८॥

The stage wherein body does not require (videha) is a serious and stunned stage. At this stage, neither light is seen everywhere nor the darkness. An element of truth remains therein which can not be given any name and expression. That neither is void or apparent, Neither visible nor vision form. The communes of living bodies and matter too are not found therein. It is such a stunning element, whose nature cannot be even imagined. His shape and nature too becomes perfect. He is not truth, neither false and further nor in their blended form. He is beyond the spirit and sense both. He is merely sensitive but at the same time, it is without mind and infinite. It is beyond the effect of old age, always benevolent (Śiva form) and renders growth to the soul. He is free from defects and it has no beginning (Anādī).

द्रष्टृदर्शनदृश्यानां मध्ये यद्दर्शनं स्मृतम्। नातः परतरं किंचिन्निश्चयोऽस्त्यपरो मुने॥६९॥ स्वयमेव त्वया ज्ञातं गुरुतश्च पुनः श्रुतम्। स्वसंकल्पवशाद्बद्धो निःसंकल्पाद्विमुच्यते॥७०॥ तेन स्वयं त्वया ज्ञातं ज्ञेयं यस्य महात्मनः। भोगेभ्यो ह्यरतिर्जाता दृश्याद्वा सकलादिह॥७१॥ प्राप्तं प्राप्तव्यमखिलं भवता पूर्णचेतसा। स्वरूपे तपसि ब्रह्मन्मुक्तस्त्वं भ्रान्तिमुत्सृज॥७२॥ अतिबाह्यं तथा बाह्यमन्तराभ्यन्तरं धियः। शुक पश्यन्न पश्येस्त्वं साक्षी संपूर्णकेवलः॥७३॥

He has been said in the form of mere observance (Darśana) in the middle of the Tripuṭī (Trio centre) to observer, scene and the (Darśana). O Śukadeva! No other decision can be taken besides it in the same context. You have understood yourselves to this metaphysics (Tattvajñāna) and already heard from your father that the living soul falls to the prey of bondage as a result of his power of resolution and attains to salvation through resolution too. You have yourselves acquired that metaphysics, knowing to which, the gentlemen gradually set aside the attachment for enjoyments and all apparent objects. You have obtained all receivable matters by virtue of attaining to project stage of sensitivity. You are existing in the stage of penance. O Brāhmaṇa! you has accessed to the stage of liberty. Hence, leave the doubts. O Śukadeva! you observe the exterior and most exterior as also the interior and most interior still does not see (viz. remain unaffected even-after observance thereof). You are existed as witness to this all in the stage of perfect emancipation or liberty.

विशश्राम शुकस्तूष्णीं स्वस्थे परमवस्तुनि। वीतशोकभयायासो निरीहश्छिन्नसंशयः॥७४॥ जगाम शिखरं मेरोः समाध्यर्थमखण्डितम्॥७५॥ तत्र वर्षसहस्राणि निर्विकल्पसमाधिना। देशे स्थित्वा शशामासावात्मन्यस्नेहदीपवत्॥७६॥ व्यपगतकलनाकलङ्कशुद्धः स्वयममलात्मनि पावने पदेऽसौ। सलिलकण इवाम्बुधौ महात्मा विगलितवासनमेकतां जगाम॥

Having heard this metaphysics, Śukadeva attained peace as his agony, fear, the stress, doubt and desire all were dispersed and he relaxed in the soul in the form of supreme element. He returned back to the peak of Sumeru mountain for absolute meditation (Samādhi). He there attained supreme peace by exclusive (Nirvikalpa) meditation making him introvert like the lamp without oil many thousand years. As the water drops get the ocean form by merging with the same, Śukadeva merged with his position of soul by attaining liberty from the defective resolutions, the passions and making his mind pure, innocent and the nature, all holy.

Chapter - III

निदाघो नाम मुनिराट् प्राप्तविद्यश्च बालकः। विहृतस्तीर्थयात्रार्थं पित्रानुज्ञातवान्स्वयम्॥१॥ सार्धत्रिकोटितीर्थेषु स्नात्वा गृहमुपागतः। स्वोदन्तं कथयामास ऋभुं नत्वा महायशाः॥२॥ सार्धत्रिकोटितीर्थेषु स्नानपुण्यप्रभावतः। प्रादुर्भूतो मनसि मे विचारः सोऽयमीदृशः॥३॥

The hermit Nidāgha, son of the great hermit Ṛbhu, set-out for pilgrimage alone on permission obtained from his father. He came back to home after taking a bath in three and half crore pilgrim places. That great illustrious hermit had described the complete detail of his pilgrimage before his father Ṛbhu on his return. He said– "O father! the outcome or blessing obtained as a result of having bath in three and half crore pilgrim places is that the best thoughts are originating in my heart.

जायते मृयते लोको म्रियते जननाय च। अस्थिराः सर्व एवेमे सचराचरचेष्टिताः॥४॥ सर्वापदां पदं पापा भावा विभवभूमयः। अयःशलाकासदृशाः परस्परमसङ्गिनः। श्लिष्यन्ते केवला भावा मनःकल्पनयानया॥५॥ भावेष्वरतिरायाता पथिकस्य मरुष्विव। शाम्यतीदं कथं दुःखमिति तप्तोऽस्मि चेतसा॥६॥ चिन्तानिचयचक्राणि नानन्दाय धनानि मे। संप्रसूतकलत्राणि गृहाण्युग्रापदामिव॥७॥ इयमस्मिन् स्थितोदारा संसारे परिपेलवा। श्रीर्मुने परिमोहाय सापि नूनं न शर्मदा॥८॥ आयुः पल्लवकोणाग्रलम्बाम्बुकणभङ्गुरम्। उन्मत्त इव संत्यज्य याम्यकाण्डे शरीरकम्॥९॥

विषयाशीविषासङ्गपरिजर्जरचेतसाम्। अप्रौढात्मविवेकानामायुरायासकारणम्॥१०॥

There are the five kośas (sheaths), viz., annamaya, prāṇamaya, manomaya, vijñānamaya, and ānandamaya. Annamaya, sheath is that which is created and developed out of the essence of food, and is absorbed into the earth which is of the form of food. It alone is the gross body. The prāṇas with the karmendriya (organs of action) is the prāṇamaya sheath. Manas with the jñānendriyas (organs of sense) is the manomaya sheath. Buddhi with the jñānendriyas is the vijñānamaya sheath. These three sheaths constitute the liṅgaśarīra (or the subtle body). (That which tends to) the ajñāna (ignorance) of the Reality (of Ātmā) is the ānandamaya sheath. This is the kāraṇa body. Moreover the five organs of sense, the five organs of action, the five prāṇas and others, the five ākāśa and other elements, the four internal organs, avidyā, passion, karma, and tamas— all these constitute the abode of adversities. The living soul indeed cannot avail pleasure from them. As the hanged droplet of water remains for second at the forepart of a leave, the life of a man similarly is temporary and it brittles with seconds. I would have to depart like an intoxicated man by leaving this mortal body untimely. Whose mind has become rigid and unchanging as a result of prolong company with the shake of attachment and passion and who one deprived of the mature knowledge on element (essence), only suffers throughout their life.

ग्रन्थनं च तरङ्गाणामास्था नायुषियुज्यते॥११॥ प्राप्यं संप्राप्यते येन भूयो येन न शोच्यते। पराया निर्वृतेः स्थानं यत्तज्जीवितमुच्यते॥१२॥ तरवोऽपि हि जीवन्ति जीवन्ति मृगपक्षिणः। स जीवति मनो यस्य मननेनोपजीवति॥१३॥ जातास्त एव जगति जन्तवः साधुजीविताः। ये पुनर्नेह जायन्ते शेषा जरठगर्दभाः॥१४॥ भारो विवेकिनः शास्त्रं भारो ज्ञानं च रागिणः। अशान्तस्य मनो भारो भारोऽनात्मविदो वपुः॥१५॥

It may be possible to warp the wind, split-up the sky in pieces and intertwining of the waves of water, however apparently herculian task even then it is not possible to have faith and obesiance in life. The real life can be said only when the matter worth receiving is obtained and it may seldom be cause for agony as also provide with supreme peace. The trees, deers and birds too live their life, but the man continuously engrossed in thinking on the issue of soul only lives the real life. Only the lores of those creatures born in this world is particular, who are not compelled to fall in the discus of the birth and death. Distinct from this, are like an old ass who is compelled to carry the load inspite of not capable to do the same. The holy-books (Śāstra) is like carrying the load for the learned person. The knowledge is like a burden to the person attached to affection and envy. The mind of an impatient man is burdensome to him. And the persons alien to the soul feel burden of their body too.

अहंकारवशादापदहंकाराद्दुराधय:। अहंकारवशादीहा नाहंकारात्परो रिपु:॥ १६॥ अहंकारवशाद्यद्यन्मया
भुक्तं चराचरम्। तत्तत्सर्वमवस्त्वेव वस्त्वहंकाररिक्तता॥ १७॥ इतश्चेतश्च सुव्यग्रं व्यर्थमेवाभिधावति। मनो दूरतरं
याति ग्रामे कौलेयको यथा॥ १८॥ क्रूरेण जडतां याता तृष्णाभार्यानुगामिना। वश: कौलेयकेनैव
ब्रह्मन्मुक्तोऽस्मि चेतसा॥ १९॥ अप्यब्धिपानान्महत: सुमेरून्मूलनादपि। अपि
वह्न्यशनाद्ब्रह्मन्विषमश्चित्तनिग्रह:॥ २०॥ चित्तं कारणमर्थानां तस्मिन्सति जगत्त्रयम्। तस्मिन्क्षीणे जगत्क्षीणं
तच्चिकित्स्यं प्रयत्नत:॥ २१॥

Ego is the sole motive that calls in all kinds of adversities. It gives rise to the malafides and multiform desires as also ambitions arise therefrom. This is the reason, the ego is the most dreadful enemy to a man. Having caught in the trap of ego, the consumption of movable and immovables made by we, were all false and illusive in their forms. Complete decay of ego is the reality of life. The essence really is being free from ego. This mind runs to and fro impatiently for no cause and redundanity. It wanders to distant fields for no cause. Its habit is like a wandering dog in a village. I too had become inert falling in the trap of cruel mind and wandering behind the bitch of temptation. "O Brahman! I here now become scot-free from that trap. O Brahman! to control the mind is more difficult than drinking the sea entirely, uprooting the mountain of Sumeru and gobbling up the fire. This mind entertains the worldly material within its exterior and interior perceving. On this very basis, the existence of the world in its three stages i.e. awaken, dreaming and dormance depends. This world is destroyed on destructure of the mind. Hence, the proper treatment is to be given to the mind.

यां यामहं मुनिश्रेष्ठ संश्रयामि गुणश्रियम्। तां तां कृन्तति मे तृष्णा तन्त्रीमिव कुमूषिका॥ २२॥ पदं
करोत्यलङ्घ्येऽपि तृप्ता विफलमीहते। चिरं तिष्ठति नैकत्र तृष्णा चपलमर्कटी॥ २३॥ क्षणमायाति पातालं क्षणं
याति नभ:स्थलम्। क्षणं भ्रमति दिक्कुञ्जे तृष्णा हृत्पद्मषट्पदी॥ २४॥ सर्वसंसारदु:खानां तृष्णैका दीर्घदु:खदा।
अन्त:पुरस्थमपि या योजयत्यतिसंकटे॥ २५॥ तृष्णाविषूचिकामन्त्रश्चिन्तात्यागो हि स द्विज। स्तोकेनानन्दमायाति
स्तोकेनायाति खेदताम्॥ २६॥

O great hermit! my temptation cuts the great merits (guṇas) resorted by me in the similar way as the wicked mouse cut the strings of the lyre. This temptation is like a caprice monkey who wants to put his foot at the spot where there is no base and worth jumping. Irrespective to glut, he desires different fruits. He does not stay for long at a place and runs to and fro (from sky to under earth) within seconds. It starts strolling in the groves of directions. It is like a bee that moves round the lotus heart. This temptation is the cause for pouring in prolong pains of this mortal world and throws in great danger even to the king who lives in well protected private palace (Antaḥpura). This temptation is an epidemic like cholera. It can be destroyed only by that best Brāhmaṇa who has abandoned the worry in toto. Excessive pleasure is obtained when the worry is abandoned. Its little particles even throw the mind in immense pain.

नास्ति देहसमः शोच्यो नीचो गुणविवर्जितः॥ २७॥ कलेवरमहंकारगृहस्थस्य महागृहम्। लुठत्वभ्येतु वा स्थैर्यं किमनेन गुरो मम॥ २८॥ पङ्क्तिबद्धेन्द्रियपशुं वल्गत्तृष्णागृहाङ्गणम्। चित्तभृत्यजनाकीर्णं नेष्टं देहगृहं मम॥ २९॥ जिह्वामर्कटिकाक्रान्तवदनद्वारभीषणम्। दृष्टदन्तास्थिशकलं नेष्टं देहगृहं मम॥ ३०॥

Nothing other is trivial, meritless and worth agony than the body. The ego couple resides in this vast house of body. I does not worry at all for having this body existed prolong or destroyed in a short span. It is not any way, desired by me because the animals in garb of senses are standing in queue, the temptation in garb of monkey wanders continuously in the compound and the servants in garb of propensity of mind are appointed in this house of body. This gate in garb of mouth has been so frightened of the coercion exercised by the monkey tongue that even in beginning, the bones in garb of teeth are being seen. (viz. in posture to increase the fear). I do not like such house of the body.

रक्तमांसमयस्यास्य सबाह्याभ्यन्तरे मुने। नाशैकधर्मिणो ब्रूहि कैव कायस्य रम्यता॥ ३१॥ तडित्सु शरदभ्रेषु गन्धर्वनगरेषु च। स्थैर्यं येन विनिर्णीतं स विश्वसितु विग्रहे॥ ३२॥ शैशवे गुरुतो भीतिर्मातृतः पितृतस्तथा। जनतो ज्येष्ठबालाच्च शैशवं भयमन्दिरम्॥ ३३॥ स्वचित्तबिलसंस्थेन नानाविभ्रमकारिणा। बलात्कामपिशाचेन विवशः परिभूयते॥ ३४॥ दासाः पुत्राः स्त्रियश्चैव बान्धवाः सुहृदस्तथा। हसन्त्युन्मत्तकमिव नरं वार्धककम्पितम्॥ ३५॥ दैन्यदोषमयी दीर्घा वर्धते वार्धके स्पृहा। सर्वापदामेकसखी हृदि दाहप्रदायिनी॥ ३६॥

O the great hermit! how this mortal body may be beautiful when it is covered with the blood and flesh etc. from exterior to the interior? Only a man can faith on the longevity of this mortal body who has ascertained it in the lightening of pleasant weather (Śarada Ṛtu) and in the city of Gandharva. The childhood is an abode of fear as the child has fear of his teachers, parents, people, senior boys and other people. On approaching to youth, one is badly defeated due to compulsion of the devil lust that resides in the cave of mind and traps in various kinds of doubts and illusions. In the phase of old age, the servants, sons and daughters, women and relatives too start laughing when they see the trembling man like an intoxicant. The desires and ambitions spurt up excessive while the body becomes unable in old age. This old age is the good-friend to all adversities that burn the heart jointly.

क्वचिद्वा विद्यते यैषा संसारे सुखभावना। आयुः स्तम्बमिवासाद्य कालस्तामपि कृन्तति॥ ३७॥ तृणं पांसुं महेन्द्रं च सुवर्णं मेरुसर्षपम्। आत्मंभरितया सर्वमात्मसात्कर्तुमुद्यतः। कालोऽयं सर्वसंहारी तेनाक्रान्तं जगत्त्रयम्॥ ३८॥

Where is the pleasure expected by the worldly creatures in this mortal world? The time (kāla) is busy in the process of cutting the age like a straw of grass. This time (kāla) is so mighty as it can convert a tiny straw and dust particle into the great mountain Mahendra and the vast mountains like golden Sumeru into a mustard seed. It is competent enough to destroy all and always prepared to gobble up to the hunger. And the three worlds are frightened of the attack of this mighty time (kāla).

मांसपाञ्चालिकायास्तु यन्त्रलोलेऽङ्गपञ्जरे। स्नाय्वस्थिग्रन्थिशालिन्याः स्त्रियः किमिव शोभनम्॥ त्वङ्मांसरक्तबाष्पाम्बु पृथक्कृत्वा विलोचने। समालोकय रम्यं चेत्किं मुधा परिमुह्यसि॥ ४०॥ मेरुशृङ्गतटोल्लासिगङ्गाचलरयोपमा। दृष्टा यस्मिन्मुने मुक्ताहारस्योल्लासशालिता॥ ४१॥ श्मशानेषु दिगन्तेषु स एव ललनास्तनः। श्वभिरास्वाद्यते काले लघुपिण्ड इवान्धसः॥ ४२॥ केशकज्जलधारिण्यो दुःस्पर्शा लोचनप्रियाः। दुष्कृताग्निशिखा नार्यो दहन्ति तृणवन्नरम्॥ ४३॥

What can be said fascinating or attractive in the body of woman made of nerves and joints of bones like a puppet in the cage of dynamic and caprice organs? Observe this body by separating the skin on the eyes the flesh, blood and tears etc. and then see if any thing looks fascinating. What is the use of involving in attachment when nothing here is attractive? O hermit! the woman who is caprice, like the waves of goddess Gaṅgā that exhilaratingly falls down from the peaks of Sumeru mountain, who is seen adorned with the garland of pearls, the nipple, in the body form (Piṇḍa) of that very woman is eaten by the dogs in the cremation ground when she is dead. The women adornes with hair and kājala and which are seen fascinating burn the man like straw by the flames of fire in the form of wrong creation of the creator (Vidhātā).

ज्वलतामतिदूरेऽपि सरसा अपि नीरसाः। स्त्रियो हि नरकाग्नीनामिन्धनं चारु दारुणम्॥ ४४॥ कामनाम्ना किरातेन विकीर्णा मुग्धचेतसः। नार्यो नरविहङ्गानामङ्गबन्धनवागुराः॥ ४५॥ जन्मपल्वलमत्स्यानां चित्तकर्दमचारिणाम्। पुंसां दुर्वासनारज्जुर्नारी बडिशपिण्डिका॥ ४६॥ सर्वेषां दोषरत्नानां सुसमुद्गिकयानया। दुःखशृङ्खलया नित्यमलमस्तु मम स्त्रिया॥ ४७॥ यस्य स्त्री तस्य भोगेच्छा निःस्त्रीकस्य क्व भोगभूः। स्त्रियं त्यक्त्वा जगत्त्यक्तं जगत्त्यक्त्वा सुखी भवेत्॥ ४८॥

These are in the form of fuel that puts in pain like the blaged fire of hell at a distance. These appear full of essence yet void of essence in reality. The hunter (kirāta) in the name of sex has extended the cord in the form of woman for binding (fastening) the deers in the form of men. These men are fishes in the pond of life and move continuously in the mud of the mind. In order to trap these men in the form of fishes, the woman is like the forage duly tied in the cord of the vicious passion or lust. This woman is like the ocean that gives births to all defecting gems. May this chain of sorrow always be away from us. The desire for copulation arises only when the woman is with a man and there is no cause for enjoyment if the woman is absent. The world of a man is left as soon as he abandons his wife and a man can attain pleasure only when he takes leave from this mortal world. He indeed can enjoy the real pleasure.

दिशोऽपि न हि दृश्यन्ते देशोऽप्यन्योपदेशकृत्। शैला अपि विशीर्यन्ते शीर्यन्ते तारका अपि॥४९॥
शुष्यन्त्यपि समुद्राश्च ध्रुवोप्यध्रुवजीवन:। सिद्धा अपि विनश्यन्ति जीर्यन्तो दानवादय:॥५०॥ परमेष्ठ्यपि
निष्ठावान्हीयते हरिरप्यज:। भावोऽप्यभावमायाति जीर्यन्ते वै दिगीश्वरा:॥५१॥ ब्रह्मा विष्णुश्च रुद्रश्च सर्वा वा
भूतजातय:। नाशमेवानुधावन्ति सलिलानीव वाडवम्॥५२॥ आपद: क्षणमायान्ति क्षणमायान्ति संपद:। क्षणं
जन्माथ मरणं सर्वं नश्वरमेव तत्॥५३॥ अशूरेण हता: शूरा एकेनापि शतं हतम्। विषं विषयवैषम्यं न विषं
विषमुच्यते॥५४॥ जन्मान्तरघ्ना विषया एकजन्महरं विषम्। इति मे दोषदावाग्निदग्धे संप्रति चेतसि॥५५॥

(This world is all perishing, when it goes to the stage undescribable) the directions also are vanished, the crunches too become a lesson giving for others viz., these merge with the trench of mighty time (kāla), the mountains are splited up, and the stars too shattered and fall, the life of Dhruva, planets etc. becomes temporary and even changing. The great ascetics and yogis too are destroyed, the demons etc. loss their power and suffer from old age. Pitāmaha Brahmā and lord Viṣṇu who resides prolong and permanent and beyond the birth too are vanished. Every availability turns into scarcity and the ruler of direction also suffer from old age and unwealth. As the water from all oceans rushes towards Vaḍvānala (sea fire), the great gods and all creatures start rushing to waters destruction. If the adversities befall adversities within seconds, the prosperity and luxuries too not take time in gathering around the man, the birth and death both take hardly seconds. All these activities are mortal. The cowards kill the gallants in this world and sometime a single man becomes cause for destruction of many hundred thousands people. The anomaly inserted into mind as a result of enjoying matters is in the form of poison. The apparent poison is not called so fierce as the enjoyment of material objects because it only kills the single life while the later poison kills many lives (births) that one obtained in the cycle of birth and death. My mind burnt of the fire (Dāvānala) of defects appears the same at this point of time.

स्फुरन्ति हि न भोगाशा मृगतृष्णासर:स्वपि। अतो मां बोधयाशु त्वं तत्त्वज्ञानेन वै गुरो॥५६॥
नो चेन्मौनं समास्थाय निर्मानो गतमत्सर:। भावयन्मनसा विष्णुं लिपिकर्मार्पितोपम:॥५७॥

Inspite of standing on the pond of mirage (temptation), the passion for material enjoyments is not within me. O father! O teacher! hence, make me to know the metaphysics immediately. I request you for the same. Please, quench my curiosity otherwise I will sat on Maunvrata (resolute to keep mum) by keeping my mind attentive on lord Viṣṇu like a statue.

Chapter-IV

निदाघ तव नास्त्यन्यज्ज्ञेयं ज्ञानवतां वर। प्रज्ञया त्वं विजानासि ईश्वरानुगृहीतया। चित्तमालिन्यसंजातं
मार्जयामि भ्रमं मुने॥१॥ मोक्षद्वारे द्वारपालाश्चत्वार: परिकीर्तिता:। शमो विचार: संतोषश्चतुर्थ:
साधुसङ्गम:॥२॥ एकं वा सर्वयत्नेन सर्वमुत्सृज्य संश्रयेत्। एकस्मिन्वशगे यान्ति चत्वारोऽपि वशं गता:॥३॥

Having heard all matters disclosed by his son, Nidāgha, the great hermit Ṛbhu said– O lord! you are the best among all scholars. Nothing now has been left for you worth knowing. You have already understood everything as a result of your own confidence (wisdom) under the grace of god. O hermit! I will remove the doubt still arisen in your mind due to some impurity. The Śama (controlling mind), thought, contentment and good company have been stated as four watchman to the gate of salvation. Out of them others automatically are enslaved easily if only one is resorted to.

शास्त्रैः सज्जनसंपर्कपूर्वकैश्च तपोदमैः। आदौ संसारमुक्त्यर्थं प्रज्ञामेवाभिवर्धयेत्॥ ४॥ स्वानुभूतेश्च शास्त्रस्य गुरोश्चैवैकवाक्यता। यस्याभ्यासेन तेनात्मा सततं चावलोक्यते॥ ५॥

In order to attain salvation from this mortal world, extensive to the true knowledge by resorting to control on senses (Dama), perseverance on holy books and company of gentle men is very first required. The self perceiving, the preaching of teachers and the words contemplated in holy books (Śāstra) should continuously bring into practice and propensity of self-thinking should be enhanced.

संकल्पाशानुसंधानवर्जनं चेत्प्रतिक्षणम्। करोषि तदचित्तत्वं प्राप्त एवासि पावनम्॥ ६॥ चेतसो यदकर्तृत्वं तत्समाधानमीरितम्। तदेव केवलीभावं सा शुभा निर्वृतिः परा॥ ७॥ चेतसा संपरित्यज्य सर्वभावात्मभावनाम्। यथा तिष्ठसि तिष्ठ त्वं मूकान्धबधिरोपमः॥ ८॥ सर्वं प्रशान्तमजमेकमनादिमध्यमाभास्वरं स्वदनमात्रमचैत्यचिह्नम्। सर्वं प्रशान्तमिति शब्दमयी च दृष्टिर्बाधार्थमेव हि मुधैव तदोमितीदम्॥ ९॥ सर्वं किंचिदिदं दृश्यं दृश्यते चिज्जगद्गतम्। चिन्निष्पन्दांशमात्रं तन्नान्यदस्तीति भावय॥ १०॥ नित्यप्रबुद्धचित्तस्त्वं कुर्वन्वापि जगत्क्रियाम्। आत्मैकत्वं विदित्वा त्वं तिष्ठाक्षुब्धमहाब्धिवत्॥ ११॥

You would have already arrived at the stage of emancipation if the propensity of resolution and research on the hope have been abandoned by you. The idleness of mind is the restriction (control) of the mental trends viz., meditation. This too is said the stage of salvation and all benevolent supreme peace. It is possible only when you can live like deaf, dumb and blinds in this world by giving the self-spirit up from all worldly things properly. The sight that express the words like everything is lying in peace, single, beyond the birth, only perceivable and beyond the mind, is redundant. It functions as hurdle on the way to self-realisation. Whatever is seen in illusion (the world), that essentially is in the form of "Oṁ" (Praṇava). Whatever is seen at this stage that scenes are also seen in the world of mind and it is a part of the stunned mind. You should therefore, presume that there is nothing existed here except the sensitive mind. Be undeviate in mind with strong faith like the ocean that always remains unaffected by knowing the unity of soul through always sensitive mind and coincide to it, perform the worldly deeds undisturbed. The deeds performed with such spirituality can grow the possibilities of before us.

तत्त्वावबोध एवासौ वासनातृणपावकः। प्रोक्तः समाधिशब्देन न तु तूष्णीमवस्थितिः॥ १२॥ निरिच्छे संस्थिते रत्ने यथा लोकः प्रवर्तते। सत्तामात्रे परे तत्त्वे तथैवायं जगद्गणः॥ १३॥ अतश्चात्मनि कर्तृत्वमकर्तृत्वं च वै मुने। निरिच्छत्वादकर्तासौ कर्ता संनिधिमात्रतः॥ १४॥ ते द्वे ब्रह्मणि विन्देत कर्तृताकर्तृते मुने। यत्रैवैष

चमत्कारस्तमाश्रित्य स्थिरो भव॥ १५॥ तस्मान्नित्यमकर्ताहमिति भावनयेद्धया। परमामृतनाम्नी सा समतैवावशिष्यते॥ १६॥

The self realisation is analoguous to the fire that burns the passion straws. It too is called Samādhi (meditation). It is not meditation that one should sit idly and quietly. As the people not desiring the gem, naturally attract a while when they see it lying at a place, the entire world same way attracts to the element of supreme soul existing merely as an entity. O son! the action and inaction both are existed in this soul. It becomes inactive if there is not desire adhered but it becomes active as soon as any desire is added with it. O hermit! the action and inaction both reside in the immortal supreme soul. At which you could see this phenomenon, it is advised that you should enshrine on the same. Only the entity namely supreme nectar (Parama Amṛta) remains when presumption is made that "I am always inactive (Akarttā)".

निदाघ शृणु सत्त्वस्था जाता भुवि महागुणाः। ते नित्यमेवाभ्युदिता मुदिताः ख इवेन्दवः॥ १७॥ नापदि ग्लानिमायान्ति निशि हेमाम्बुजं यथा। नेहन्ते प्रकृतादन्यद्रमन्ते शिष्टवर्त्मनि॥ १८॥ आकृत्यैव विराजन्ते मैत्र्यादिगुणवृत्तिभिः। समाः समरसाः सौम्य सततं साधुवृत्तयः॥ १९॥ अब्धिवद्धृतमर्यादा भवन्ति विशदाशयाः। नियतिं न विमुञ्चन्ति महान्तो भास्करा इव॥ २०॥

O Nidāgha! hence, the creatures adorned with sattva property in this world are only great virtuous. They only feel gaiety like the moon existed in the sky as they avail accession to always. The people existed in sattva property do not fade like golden lotus in the adversities of the night like. They do not hanker after other matters same as otherwise the enjoyments available to them and always stroll through the route prescribed in the holy books (śāstras). They automatically keep their mind all suitable and the virtues like friendliness, kindness, crazy and detachment etc. always make them popular among the societies. O Modest! they always remain in undeviated form and engage themselves in the benevolent professions. They become generous so vast as the ocean inspite of being beyond the tradition. They like lord sun always proceed on their way predestined.

कोऽहं कथमिदं चेति संसारमलमाततम्। प्रविचार्यं प्रयत्नेन प्राज्ञेन सह साधुना॥ २१॥ नाकर्मसु नियोक्तव्यं नानार्येण सहावसेत्। द्रष्टव्यः सर्वसंहर्ता न मृत्युरवहेलया॥ २२॥ शरीरमस्थि मांसं च त्यक्त्वा रक्ताद्यशोभनम्। भूतमुक्तावलीतन्तुं चिन्मात्रमवलोकयेत्॥ २३॥ उपादेयानुपतनं हेयैकान्तविसर्जनम्। यदेतन्मनसो रूपं तद्बाह्यं विद्धि नेतरत्॥ २४॥ गुरुशास्त्रोक्तमार्गेण स्वानुभूत्या च चिद्घने। ब्रह्मैवाहमिति ज्ञात्वा वीतशोको भवेन्मुनिः॥ २५॥

One should think inner the question "who am I? while sitting in the company of scholars and the gentlemen." (The second question worth consideration is) how the illusive of this gigantic universe had arisen? He should not involve himself in the redundant or useless works and always try to avoid the company of evil doers. He should not neglect the fact that death is ultimate truth and it kills all. The body, bones, flesh and blood etc. should be considered hatred and may be neglected. Focus should be made on the supreme father, the supreme soul intertwined within the creatures as the thread intertwines the garlands of pearls. It is the standing habit of mind that it runs after the useful and abandons useless things forever. It is however exterior and not internal. This fact should not be dispensed with any time. Following the approach suggested by teacher and contemplated in holy-book (śāstra) regarding the element of supreme soul and considering by self-perceiving that "I myself am Brahma", one should make one self scot-free from the agony.

यत्र निशितासिशतपातनमुत्पलताडनवत्सोढव्यमग्निदाहो हिमसेचनमिवाङ्गारावर्तनं चन्दनचर्चेव निरवधिनाराचविकिरपातो निदाघविनोदनधारागृहशीकरवर्षणमिव स्वशिरश्छेदः सुखनिद्रेव मूकीकरणमाननमुद्रेव बाधिर्यं महानुपचय इवेदं नावहेलनया भवितव्यमेवं दृढवैराग्याद्बोधो भवति। गुरुवाक्यसमुद्भूतस्वानुभूत्यादिशुद्धया। यस्याभ्यासेन तेनात्मा सततं चावलोक्यते॥ २६॥

At this stage the fatal injury like dragger, turns in the tender touch of lotus and the affect of burning in fire turns in the repressing impact of bathe in the cold water, viz., the tolerance is increased manifold. Lying on fire balls (Aṅgāra) appears as tender as the body is smeared with the sandal. The injury caused by a number of arrows seems like the droplets pumped from a shower for retiring the pain of scrotching heat. Beheading seems snoring sleep, dumbing (by chilling the tongue) appears silent-penance, and making deaf (by penetrating the ears) seems pleasure going which is fact when any news of progress is heard. This stage however does not avail when neglection is made. Its attainment is only possible when one holds strong resolution and self-realisation free from attachments. Self-realisation can be possible only when a man does regular exercise on the purity of inner soul through the means suggested by teacher and the holy-books as also through the intuition (inner perceiving).

विनष्टदिग्भ्रमस्यापि यथापूर्वं विभाति दिक्। तथा विज्ञानविध्वस्तं जगन्नास्तीति भावय॥ २७॥ न धनान्युपकुर्वन्ति न मित्राणि न बान्धवाः। न कायक्लेशवैधुर्यं न तीर्थायतनाश्रयः। केवलं तन्मनोमात्रमयेनासाद्यते पदम्॥ २८॥

As the directions are known properly as before when the illusion is destroyed, one should make a presumption in the similar fashion that the world does not exists when the ignorance is effaced by the particular knowledge of facts. A man can get the supreme position only when he is merged with cinmātra (knowledge of element) and this position is not obtained as a result of support from wealth, friends, near and dears, healthy body (recovered from ailments) and not by residing in the pilgrim place.

यानि दुःखानि या तृष्णा दुःसहा ये दुराधयः। शान्तचेतःसु तत्सर्वं तमोऽर्केष्विव नश्यति॥ २९॥ मातरीव परं यान्ति विषमाणि मृदूनि च। विश्वासमिह भूतानि सर्वाणि शमशालिनि॥ ३०॥ न रसायनपानेन न लक्ष्म्यालिङ्गितेन च। न तथा सुखमाप्नोति शमेनान्तर्यथा जनः॥ ३१॥ श्रुत्वा स्पृष्ट्वा च भुक्त्वा च दृष्ट्वा ज्ञात्वा शुभाशुभम्। न हृष्यति ग्लायति यः स शान्त इति कथ्यते॥ ३२॥ तुषारकरबिम्बाच्छं मनो यस्य निराकुलम्। मरणोत्सवयुद्धेषु स शान्त इति कथ्यते॥ ३३॥ तपस्विषु बहुज्ञेषु याजकेषु नृपेषु च। वनवत्सु

गुणाढ्येषु शमवानेव राजते॥ ३४॥ संतोषामृतपानेन ये शान्तास्तृप्तिमागताः। आत्मारामा महात्मानस्ते महापदमागताः॥ ३५॥ अप्राप्तं हि परित्यज्य संप्राप्ते समतां गतः। अदृष्टखेदाखेदो यः संतुष्ट इति कथ्यते॥ ३६॥ नाभिनन्दत्यसंप्राप्तं प्राप्तं भुङ्क्ते यथेप्सितम्। यः स सौम्यसमाचारः संतुष्ट इति कथ्यते॥ ३७॥ रमते धीर्यथाप्राप्ते साध्वीवाऽन्तःपुराजिरे। सा जीवन्मुक्ततोदेति स्वरूपानन्ददायिनी॥ ३८॥

The learned persons become satiated and quiet after sipping the nectar of contentment, only attain the position of supreme soul (Mahāpada). One who does not worry about non-receivable thing and not reveal any excess gaiety when receivable thing is received, who does not observe vicissitudes; he really is contended person. One who does not long for scarce thing (or unreceived thing) and consumes that available thing as per need, that modest and active with the best conduct and balanced temperament person is said a contended person. The stage of all liberated and natural pleasure giving is availed only when the wisdom enjoys the things obtained in a common course of action as the chaste wife lives satisfied within the compound of the private palace (Antaḥpura).

यथाक्षणं यथाशास्त्रं यथादेशं यथासुखम्। यथासंभवसत्सङ्गमिमं मोक्षपथक्रमम्। तावद्विचारयेत्प्राज्ञो यावद्विश्रान्तिमात्मनि॥ ३९॥ तुर्यविश्रान्तियुक्तस्य निवृत्तस्य भवार्णवात्। जीवतोऽजीवतश्चैव गृहस्थस्याथवा यतेः॥ ४०॥ नाकृतेन कृतेनार्थो न श्रुतिस्मृतिविभ्रमैः। निर्मन्दर इवाम्भोधिः स तिष्ठति यथास्थितः॥ ४१॥

The scholars should strive regularly— the path of emancipation by formulating their living suitable to the time and the place (location or country) happily and as per the holy-books (śāstra) as also in the company of gentlemen so far it possible unless they avail with soul satisfaction. Either the couple or recluse whatsoever, has if arrived at the stage of Turīya (free from worldly attachments) and no more passions for worldly enjoyment are left in his mind, will attain all pleasures irrespective of being his busy in the worldly life or not and he does any works or sits like an idle man. He needn't falling in the trap of illusion created regarding veda and other holy-books. He obtains everything by virtue of concentration in the soul like a quiet sea without the churning mountain i.e. Madirācala.

सर्वात्मवेदनं शुद्धं यदोदेति तदात्मकम्। भाति प्रसृतिदिक्कालबाह्यं चिद्रूपदेहकम्॥ ४२॥
एवमात्मा यथा यत्र समुल्लासमुपागतः। तिष्ठत्याशु तथा तत्र तद्रूपश्च विराजते॥ ४३॥

The exterior entire world extended in directions and time (kāla) appears in the form of mind when the propensity of unity (oneness) arises from the perceiving of the pure element of soul for all living creatures. Thus, the soul takes place immediately at which form it feels gaiety and enshrines there accordingly.

यदिदं दृश्यते सर्वं जगत्स्थावरजङ्गमम्। तत्सुषुप्ताविव स्वप्नः कल्पान्ते प्रविनश्यति॥ ४४॥ ऋतमात्मा परं ब्रह्म सत्यमित्यादिका बुधैः। कल्पिता व्यवहारार्थं यस्य संज्ञा महात्मनः॥ ४५॥ यथा कटकशब्दार्थः पृथग्भावो न काञ्चनात्। न हेम कटकात्तद्वज्जगच्छब्दार्थता परा॥ ४६॥

As the dream seen in the dormant stage vanishes on awaking, the world as seen with the movable and immovable properties, is destroyed at the advent of the great devastation

(Pralaya). This soul is in causative form ab-initio and it is supreme God and the perfect Brahma (knowledge). These all names are given by the scholars and the great souls (greatman) for practical purposes. As the term bangle (kaṅkaṇa) and its meaning have no distinct existence and the bangle made of gold does keep separate existence than the term bangle; the meaning of the term "world" in the same fashion too is Brahma and nothing except and else it.

तेनेयमिन्द्रजालश्रीर्जगति प्रवितन्यते। द्रष्टुर्दृश्यस्य सत्तान्तर्बन्ध इत्यभिधीयते॥४७॥ द्रष्टा दृश्यवशाद्बद्धो दृश्याभावे विमुच्यते। जगत्त्वमहमित्यादिसर्गात्मा दृश्यमुच्यते॥४८॥ मनसैवेन्द्रजालश्रीर्जगति प्रवितन्यते। यावदेतत्संभवति तावन्मोक्षो न विद्यते॥४९॥

That immortal supreme god (Parabrahma) has extended this dragnet (Indrajāla) in the form of world. The inter relation between the observer and the scene is called the bond (Bandha). The observer falls in the bondage of scene when he is enslaved of the same. He attains salvation in the absence of the scene. This world and the narrow spirit that discriminates the objects by saying "it is your" "that is mine" are called the scene. The illusions for living in this world are knitted only by the mind. Until and unless such imagination of mind are destroyed, no way for emancipation would till then is seen.

ब्रह्मणा तन्यते विश्वं मनसैव स्वयंभुवा। मनोमयमतो विश्वं यन्नाम परिदृश्यते॥५०॥ न बाह्ये नापि हृदये सद्रूपं विद्यते मनः। यदर्थं प्रतिभानं तन्मन इत्यभिधीयते॥५१॥ संकल्पनं मनो विद्धि संकल्पस्तत्र विद्यते। यत्र संकल्पनं तत्र मनोऽस्तीत्यवगम्यताम्॥५२॥ संकल्पमनसी भिन्ने न कदाचन केनचित्। संकल्पजाते गलिते स्वरूपमवशिष्यते॥५३॥

This world should be considered as creation of mind because this world is the mental creation (Sṛṣṭi) of lord Brahmā. This mind nowhere either externally or internally is enshrined in the form of truth. The information or knowledge of the matters and objects is called the mind. As this mind always moves with resolution, the resolution should therefore, considered mind too. Nobody could draw dividing line between the resolution and the mind. The soul only remains when all kinds of resolutions are destroyed.

अहं त्वं जगदित्यादौ प्रशान्ते दृश्यसंभ्रमे। स्यात्तादृशी केवलता दृश्ये सत्तामुपागते॥५४॥ महाप्रलयसंपत्तौ ह्यसत्तां समुपागते। अशेषदृश्ये सर्गादौ शान्तमेवावशिष्यते॥५५॥ अस्त्यनस्तमितो भास्वानजो देवो निरामयः। सर्वदा सर्वकृत्सर्वः परमात्मेत्युदाहृतः॥५६॥ यतो वाचो निवर्तन्ते यो मुक्तैरवगम्यते। यस्य चात्मादिकाः संज्ञाः कल्पिता न स्वभावतः॥५७॥

When the narrow spirit like "it is mine", "that is your" and the world etc. scenes, on cooling down the vagary of the dragnet (indrajāla) obtains the entity viz., the supreme element, the man concerned then attains to the state of salvation. When this entire apparent world losses its existence on the adorent of the great devastation (Mahā Pralaya), the soul only remains for further creation. The sun in the form of soul does not move to set (diminish or vanish), it is all purified god and unborn, it is in all forms and all executor, inaccessible to the power of expression, only known to the liberated scholars and the name given as soul (Ātmā) is mere imagination and not actual (it is called immortal Parabrahma Parameśvara).

चित्ताकाशं चिदाकाशमाकाशं च तृतीयकम्। द्वाभ्यां शून्यतरं विद्धि चिदाकाशं महामुने॥५८॥ देशाद्देशान्तरप्राप्तौ संविदो मध्यमेव यत्। निमेषेण चिदाकाशं तद्विद्धि मुनिपुङ्गव॥५९॥ तस्मिन्निरस्तनिःशेषसंकल्पस्थितिमेषि चेत्। सर्वात्मकं पदं शान्तं तदा प्राप्नोष्यसंशयः॥६०॥ उदितौदार्यसौन्दर्यवैराग्यरसगर्भिणी। आनन्दस्यन्दिनी यैषा समाधिरभिधीयते॥६१॥ दृश्यासंभवबोधेन रागद्वेषादितानवे। रतिर्बलोदिता यासौ समाधिरभिधीयते॥६२॥ दृश्यासंभवबोधो हि ज्ञानं ज्ञेयं चिदात्मकम्। तदेव केवलीभावं ततोऽन्यत्सकलं मृषा॥६३॥

The three ethers are stated namely– the Cittākāśa, Cidākaśa and the physical ether. O hermit! the Cidākāśa has been told as most micro ether. O great hermit! one should understand Cidākāśa the intervening time of eyewinking length in course of moving to other country (subject) form the one and former country. You should definitely attain the peaceful position of all souls if you enshrine in that prominent cidākāśa by leaving aside all resolutions. The stage availed after accessing to the state of cidākāśa is decent, liberated and imbibed with the essence of detachment and full of pleasure and it is called the Sahaja Samādhi. When nonexistence of the apparent objects is known and all defects like attachment, envy etc. are removed, the pleasure in concentration through the prolong and confirmed practice is arisen and it is called the samādhi (meditation). When the conscience is known about the voidness of this apparent world, the reluctant knowledge is then called the perfect knowledge free from all doubts. That too is the worth knowing element of cida, the emancipated form of the soul and everything else it is false.

मत्त ऐरावतो बद्धः सर्षपीकोणकोटरे। मशकेन कृतं युद्धं सिंहौघैरेणुकोटरे॥६४॥ पद्माक्षे स्थापितो मेरुर्निगीर्णो भृङ्गसूनुना। निदाघ विद्धि तादृक्त्वं जगदेतद्भ्रमात्मकम्॥६५॥ चित्तमेव हि संसारो रागादिक्लेशदूषितम्। तदेव तैर्विनिर्मुक्तं भवान्त इति कथ्यते॥६६॥ मनसा भाव्यमानो हि देहतां याति देहकः। देहवासनया मुक्तो देहधर्मैर्न लिप्यते॥६७॥ कल्पं क्षणीकरोत्यन्तः क्षणं नयति कल्पताम्। मनोविलाससंसार इति मे निश्चिता मतिः॥६८ नाविरतो दुश्चरितान्नाशान्तो नासमाहितः। नाशान्तमनसो वापि प्रज्ञानेनैनमाप्नुयात्॥६९॥

As it is impossible to fasten the intoxicated Airāvata elephant with a hole made in the mustard seed, fight of mosquitos against lions in the hole made of the dust particles and as the story as of gobbling the mountain sumeru existed on the petal of lotus up by the bee may not be true, the existence of world in the similar fashion cannot be possible at all. O Nidāgha! you, therefore, should consider its existence mere illusionary.

The mind viciated with the defects, the attachment, envy etc. too is the world. The liberated mind from all defects is called the end of world, viz., attachment of the salvation. The soul becomes relating to the body when the mind stresses perpetually on body. The soul liberated from the physical ties of passions, it only then does not involve with physical activities of mind. It is the mind that turns the kalpa (period many hundred years) in seconds and makes the seconds as the kalpa. Hence, as per my mind, this world is only a game of mind. The person cannot avail self realisation who has not abandoned the vices and evils, who is not of concentrated mind and whose mind is impatient.

तद्ब्रह्मानन्दमद्वन्द्वं निर्गुणं सत्यचिद्घनम्। विदित्वा स्वात्मनो रूपं न बिभेति कदाचन॥७०॥ परात्परं यन्महतो महान्तं स्वरूपतेजोमयशाश्वतं शिवम्। कविं पुराणं पुरुषं सनातनं सर्वेश्वरं सर्वदेवैरुपास्यम्॥७१॥ अहं ब्रह्मेति नियतं मोक्षहेतुर्महात्मनाम्। द्वे पदे बन्धमोक्षाय निर्ममेति ममेति च। ममेति बध्यते जन्तुर्निर्ममेति विमुच्यते॥७२॥

The man becomes free from all fears when he realises within him that perfect Brahma (Parabrahma) full of pleasure, beyond the virtues (guṇas), always true and cidaghana. A determination to the effect that– "I am that immortal Brahma, greatest among the great, the best, full of splendour, immortal, benevolent, omniscient, Purāṇa Puruṣa, Sanātana, Sarveśvara and adorable as also worshipped by all gods becomes the means of salvation for the great souls (men). Then one two causes for ties and salvation. The first out of them is the affection and the other is to abandon the affection. The affection throws the living soul in the ties while attains salvation when the same is abandoned.

जीवेश्वरादिरूपेण चेतनाचेतनात्मकम्। ईक्षणादिप्रवेशान्ता सृष्टिरीशेन कल्पिता। जाग्रदादिविमोक्षान्तः संसारो जीवकल्पितः॥७३॥ त्रिणाचिकादियोगान्ता ईश्वरभ्रान्तिमाश्रिताः। लोकायतादिसांख्यान्ता जीवविभ्रान्तिमाश्रिताः॥७४॥ तस्मान्मुमुक्षुभिर्नैव मतिर्जीवेशवादयोः। कार्या किंतु ब्रह्मतत्त्वं निश्चलेन विचार्यताम्॥७५॥

The imagination of this creation (Sṛṣṭi) embedding all movables and immovables within has been made by the almighty. The scope of this world extends from the living soul and godly form to the Ikṣaṇa viz., beginning from the resolution of Brahma of its merger with the entire world from awaking stage to attachment of salvation is imagined by the living soul. The knowledge under Kaṭhopaniṣad beginning from Triṇā ciketāgni to Śvetāśvatara is dependent to the doubts regarding divinity. The philosophic knowledge beginning from the system of cārvāka to the doctrine of Sāṁkhya to Kapila (the knowledge propounded in the systems like Sāṁkhya etc.) is the basis for the doubt of the living soul. The person desirous of salvation should therefore, follow continuously and firmly the element of Brahma instead of confusing the wisdom on the arguments regarding the living soul and the god.

अविशेषेण सर्वं तु यः पश्यति चिदन्वयात्। स एव साक्षाद्विज्ञानी स शिवः स हरिर्विधिः॥७६॥ दुर्लभो विषयत्यागो दुर्लभं तत्त्वदर्शनम्। दुर्लभा सहजावस्था सद्गुरोः करुणां विना॥७७॥ उत्पन्नशक्तिबोधस्य त्यक्तनिःशेषकर्मणः। योगिनः सहजावस्था स्वयमेवोपजायते॥७८॥ यदा ह्येवैष एतस्मिन्नल्पमप्यन्तरं नरः। विजानाति तदा तस्य भयं स्यान्नात्र संशयः॥७९॥ सर्वगं सच्चिदानन्दं

ज्ञानचक्षुर्निरीक्षते। अज्ञानचक्षुर्नेक्षेत भास्वन्तं भानुमन्धवत्॥ ८०॥ प्रज्ञानमेव तद्‌ब्रह्म सत्यं प्रज्ञानलक्षणम्। एवं ब्रह्मपरिज्ञानादेव मर्त्योऽमृतो भवेत्॥ ८१॥ भिद्यते हृदयग्रन्थिश्छिद्यन्ते सर्वसंशयाः। क्षीयन्ते चास्य कर्माणि तस्मिन्दृष्टे परावरे॥ ८२॥

Scholar is the man who considers the entire apparent world in the form of an ordinary (Nirhśeṣa) mind. That is Śiva and Viṣṇu too. To abandon the passions and attachment is very scarce, to acquire the knowledge of element (Tattva Jñāna) too is difficult but to avail the stage of easiness (Sahajāvasthā) is the most tough. The person who has abandoned the attachment with all deeds and awakened his power of conscious, automatically attains the said state of easiness. There is fear still remains for the person if any slight difference is perceived and it is undoubtedly, true. The supreme god, perfect Brahma and universal form Brahma can be seen by the eyes of conscious. As the blind cannot see the lord sun, the person deprived of such eyes cannot see the immortal Brahma. That Brahma is in the form of conscious. Truth is the characteristic of conserves. The mortal living soul (jīva) attains to immortality only when his conscious realises the Brahma. As soon as the cause and action from Brahma is realised, the knots fastened in the heart are opened, all doubts are effaced and all deeds (Prārabdha etc.) are decayed.

अनात्मतां परित्यज्य निर्विकारो जगत्स्थितौ। एकनिष्ठतयान्तःस्थः संविन्मात्रपरो भव॥ ८३॥

मरुभूमौ जलं सर्वं मरुभूमात्रमेव तत्। जगत्त्रयमिदं सर्वं चिन्मात्रं स्वविचारतः॥८४

लक्ष्यालक्ष्यमतिं त्यक्त्वा यस्तिष्ठेत्केवलात्मना। शिव एव स्वयं साक्षादयं ब्रह्मविदुत्तमः॥८५॥

अधिष्ठानमनौपम्यामवाङ्मनसगोचरम्। नित्य विभुं सर्वगतं सुसूक्ष्मं च तदव्ययम्॥८६॥

सर्वशक्तिर्महेशस्य विलासो हि मनो जगत्। संयमासंयमाभ्यां च संसारः शान्तिमन्वगात्॥८७॥

O son Nidāgha! Engross in the sensitive soul by enshrining with exclusive loyalty in the inner conscious, keeping free from the defects in the worldly position and giving up the spirit that doubts on the existence of soul. As the water seen by mirage of the desert is found the desert instead of water, the entire world with trio stages i.e. awaking, dreaming and dormance should be deemed false until discretion is duly exercised. The person who becomes exclusively loyal to his soul by giving-up the contextual and free wisdom, is only the best scholar of Brahma and in the form of apparent Śiva. The scope of this world is unique and it is beyond the approach of the speech and the mind. It is with everlasting, sovereign, omniscient, most micro and in integrated form. This universe is mere mental play of almighty lord Śiva. All these worldly illusions (Prapañca) are cooled down by the control (assumption, attention and meditation) and decontrol (easy knowledge).

मनोव्याधेश्चिकित्सार्थमु कथयामि ते। यद्यत्स्वाभिमतं वस्तु तत्त्यजन्मोक्षमश्नुते॥ ८८॥

स्वायत्तमेकान्तहितं स्वेप्सिततत्यागवेदनम्। यस्य दुष्करतां यातं धिक्तं पुरुषकीटकम्॥ ८९॥ स्वपौरुषैकसाध्येन स्वेप्सिततत्यागरूपिणा। मनः प्रशममात्रेण विना नास्ति शुभा गतिः॥ ९०॥ असंकल्पनशस्त्रेण छिन्नं चित्तमिदं यदा। सर्वं सर्वगतं शान्तं ब्रह्म संपद्यते तदा॥ ९१॥ भव भावनया मुक्तो मुक्तः परमया धिया। धारयात्मानमव्यग्रो ग्रस्तचित्तं चितः पदम्॥ ९२॥

O hermit Nidāgha! I tell the remedy for the cure of the defects (diseases) arising in your mind. An abandonment of the objects deserved and for when the mind becomes caprice to obtain, is the mean of attaining the salvation. Condemn to the insect in the form of man for whom giving-up the desired worldly matters (things), liking for living in solitude and living under subjugation of soul is difficult. It is the best route for the real peace of mind if a man can give up his desired things and objects by virtue of self endeavour. No other position is else it. When this mind is duly pruned or curtailed, by the blows of the arms in the form of giving up the resolutions, the omni form, omni initiative and the Brahma in the form of peace is than obtained. Hence, be enshrine or cinmātra by controlling the mind and acquiring the supreme conscious after leaving the spirit of illusion (Prapañca).

**परं पौरुषमाश्रित्य नीत्वा चित्तमचित्तताम्। ध्यानतो हृदयाकाशे चिति चिच्चक्रधारया। मनो मारय निःशङ्कं
त्वां प्रबध्नन्ति नारयः॥९३॥ अयं सोऽहमिदं तन्म एतावन्मात्रकं मनः। तदभावनमात्रेण दात्रेणेव
विलीयते॥९४॥ छिन्नाभ्रमण्डलं व्योम्नि यथा शरदि धूयते। वातेन कल्पकेनैव तथान्तर्धूयते मनः॥९५॥
कल्पान्तपवना वान्तु यान्तु चैकत्वमर्णवाः। तपन्तु द्वादशादित्या नास्ति निर्मनसः क्षतिः॥ ।९६॥
असंकल्पनमात्रैकसाध्ये सकलसिद्धिदे। असंकल्पातिसाम्राज्ये तिष्ठावष्टब्धतत्पदः॥९७॥**

Oppress the mind by the acute edge of the sides in garb of citta always enjoyed in the element of sensitiveness by resorting to the exercise in the form of the best industry, the detachment and by thinking in ether from heart carrying the mind at the stage of inert (Acittavasthā) and thus, your all doubts will be eradicated and the enemies in the form of sensuality etc. will not be able to tie you. The spirit discriminating the worldly objects by establishing his direct attachment with them is called the mind. The mind can be decayed when such spirits are abandoned. As the lumps of clouds shattered in the ether of pleasant season (Śarada Ṛtu) are vanished by the strokes of wind, the mind too vanishes by virtue of good thoughts. A man not dwelling in the ebb. Of mind can not be damaged any way even if forty nine winds start blowing together, all oceans assemble and integrated and the twelve suns start showering heat simultaneously. Only a means of resolutionlessness becomes cause for all achievements (Siddhi's). Hence, be enshrine on the ever extended realm of resolutionlessness by resorting to the Tatpada.

**न हि चञ्चलताहीनं मनः क्वचन दृश्यते। चञ्चलत्वं मनोधर्मो वह्नेर्धर्मो यथोष्णता॥९८॥ एषा हि चञ्चला
स्पन्दशक्तिश्चित्तत्वसंस्थिता। तां विद्धि मानसीं शक्तिं जगदाडम्बरात्मिकाम्॥ यत्तु चञ्चलताहीनं
तन्मनोऽमृतमुच्यते। तदेव च तपः शास्त्रसिद्धान्ते मोक्ष उच्यते॥१००॥ तस्य चञ्चलता यैषा त्वविद्या
वासनात्मिका। वासनाऽपरनाम्नीं तां विचारेण विनाशय॥१०१॥**

The stable mind is seen nowhere as capriceness is the usual propensity of the mind. The same way as the fire performs its usual nature i.e. to provide with heat, this very vibrating power of caprice nature is the usual propensity of the mind. The same mental power should be considered the easy nature of the worldly illusion (Prapañca). The mind which is made stable by practice is called the nectar and it is the penance. It is called emancipation in view of the approach of scripture (holy books). The caprice nature of mind is ignorance and the passion is its nature. The passion is evening like and it should be abolished by the good thoughts.

पौरुषेण प्रयत्नेन यस्मिन्नेव पदे मनः। योज्यते तत्पदं प्राप्य निर्विकल्पो भवानघ॥ १०२॥
अतः पौरुषमाश्रित्य चित्तमाक्रम्य चेतसा। विशोकं पदमालम्ब्य निरातङ्कः स्थिरो भव॥ १०३॥
मन एव समर्थं हि मनसो दृढनिग्रहे। अराज्ञा कः समर्थः स्याद्राज्ञो निग्रहकर्मणि॥ १०४॥
तृष्णाग्राहगृहीतानां संसारार्णवपातिनाम्। आवर्तैरूह्यमानानां दूरं स्वमन एव नौः १०५॥
मनसैव मनश्छित्त्वा पाशं परमबन्धनम्। भवादुत्तारयात्मानं नासावन्येन तार्यते॥ १०६॥

O innocent hermit! acquire the exclusive meditation when you could obtain the objective determined and the mind applied thereupon. Obtain peace by living away from the fear and resort to the stage where there is no place for agony and it should be done by enslaving the mind through the mind restified as a result of thorough practice. The mind free from the defects of attachment to worldly issues can only be successful in controlling the mind in toto. A king can be defeated by the other king only and not by other common people. The mind full of detachment and duly purified can only save/protect the persons who are already fall prey of the temptation, a crocodile like and misdirected from their mission during to bitter fall in the worldly ocean and trapped in whirlpool. Such a mind can only turn into a batch to ferry them across the ocean. O hermit! destroy this dragnet by such innocent mind. Then you will automatically cross the sea of this world. Nobody else is competent to cross this vast sea of the world.

या योदेति मनोनाम्नी वासना वासितान्तरा। तां तां परिहरेत्प्राज्ञस्ततोऽविद्याक्षयो भवेत्॥ १०७॥ भोगैकवासनां त्यक्त्वा त्यज त्वं भेदवासनाम्।भावाभावौ ततस्त्यक्त्वा निर्विकल्पः सुखी भव॥ १०८॥ एष एव मनोनाशस्त्वविद्यानाश एव च। यत्तत्संवेद्यते किंचित्तत्रास्थापरिवर्जनम्। अनास्थैव हि निर्वाणं दुःखमास्थापरिग्रहः॥ १०९॥ अविद्या विद्यमानैव नष्टप्रज्ञेषु दृश्यते। नाम्नैवाङ्गीकृताकारा सम्यक्प्रज्ञस्य सा कुतः॥ ११०॥

It is the supreme duty of a learned person that he should curtail the dirt of passion from the mind time to time because it fastly covers the heart (conscious). The ignorance (Avidyā) by virtue of continuous and periodical cleaning, is destroyed. Abandon first the passion for enjoyments (Bhoga), then the passion in the form of discrimination and by giving up these both passions by exclusive (Nirvikalpa) and attain the perfect pleasure. It has been said that in order to remove ignorance, first removal of mind is must. Don't faith on everything whatever is perceived by the mind. Giving up faith is the stage of salvation and living dependable to the faith is the misery. The man void of conscious, becomes storehouse of ignorance (Avidyā). The man of consciousness does not accept the ignorance even a least at all.

तावत्संसारभृगुषु स्वात्मना सह देहिनम्। आन्दोलयति नीरन्ध्रं दुःखकण्टकशालिषु॥ ११११॥ अविद्या यावदस्यास्तु नोत्पन्ना क्षयकारिणी। स्वयमात्मावलोकेच्छा मोहसंक्षयकारिणी॥ ११२॥ अस्याः परं प्रपश्यन्त्याः स्वात्मनाशः प्रजायते। दृष्टे सर्वगते बोधे स्वयं ह्येषा विलीयते॥ ११३॥ इच्छा मात्रमविद्येयं तन्नाशो मोक्ष उच्यते। स चासंकल्पमात्रेण सिद्धो भवति वै मुने॥ ११४॥ मनागपि मनोव्योम्नि वासनारजनीक्षये। कलिका तनुतामेति चिदादित्यप्रकाशनात्॥ ११५॥

Until and unless self desire for self realisation arises, the ignorance (Avidyā) continuously confuses the living soul (Jīva) with her in the illusory world full of physical pains. Only self-realisation tarnishes the curtain of illusion and shows the reality. This ignorance is automatically destroyed when it faces even once the element of supreme soul. The ignorance is vanished when the knowledge of supreme soul is acquired or perceived. The nature of ignorance is mere desire and decay of desire entirely has been called the emancipation. O hermit! this desire ceases only when the resolution is fully diminished, otherwise, the decay of desire is impossible. The darkness in the form of Kali is ruined when the sun of mind grips it within the scope of light.

चैत्यानुपातरहितं सामान्येन च सर्वगम्। यच्चित्तत्वमनाख्येयं स आत्मा परमेश्वरः॥ ११६॥ सर्वं च खल्विदं ब्रह्म नित्यचिद्घनमक्षतम्। कल्पनान्या मनोनाम्नी विद्यते नहि काचन॥ ११७॥ न जायते न म्रियते किंचिदत्र जगत्त्रये। न च भावविकाराणां सत्ता क्वचन विद्यते॥ ११८॥ केवलं केवलाभासं सर्वसामान्यमक्षतम्। चैत्यानुपातरहितं चिन्मात्रमिह विद्यते॥ ११९॥ तस्मिन्नित्ये तते शुद्धे चिन्मात्रे निरुपद्रवे। शान्ते शमसमाभोगे निर्विकारे चिदात्मनि॥ १२०॥ यैषा स्वभावाभिमतं स्वयं संकल्प्य धावति। चिच्चैत्यं स्वयमम्लानं मननान्मन उच्यते॥ १२१॥

The mind becomes able to move everywhere when it abandons the worldly desires and temptations. Such undescribable stage of mind is known as the soul and the supreme soul. This all truly is Brahma. He is immortal and in the form of the cidaghan. It too is integrated (Avyaya). The imagination of the name of mind besides it is made, that has nowhere any existence. That is a mere doubt. Nobody takes birth and dies in these three worlds. The perceived defects of thinking have also no existence. Only Cinmātra, an omnipresent, integrated (Avyaya) judged by mere imagination and not going after the topics of mind, is existed here. The mind itself only moves with resolution in that everlasting, omnipresent, pure, cinmātra, nonviolent, peaceful and cidātmā existed in the form of mental control (śama), moves with resolution according to its nature. That state of resolute mind inspite of being innocent, is called mind because it thinks deep in every issue.

अतः संकल्पसिद्धेयं संकल्पेनैव नश्यति। नाहं ब्रह्मेति संकल्पात्सुदृढाद्बध्यते मनः। सर्वं ब्रह्मेति संकल्पात्सुदृढान्मुच्यते मनः॥ १२२॥ कृशोऽहं दुःखबद्धोऽहं हस्तपादादिमानहम्। इति भावानुरूपेण व्यवहारेण बध्यते॥ १२३॥ नाहं दुःखी न मे देहो बन्धः कोऽस्यात्मनि स्थितः। इति भावानुरूपेण व्यवहारेण मुच्यते॥ १२४॥ नाहं मांसं न चास्थीनि देहादन्यः परोऽस्म्यहम्। इति निश्चितवानन्तः क्षीणाविद्यो विमुच्यते॥ १२५॥

The mind so perfected by resolution, destroys by the resolution too. The mind does not fall in ties when strong resolution as "I am not Brahma" is made and further it attains to emancipation with the strong resolution i.e. "This all is Brahma". The living soul falls in ties when he deals with considering that– "I am thin and lean", "I am suffering from sorrows", "I am hand to mouth", If the mind resolves that "I am in gaiety", "I am not in body but enshrined in the element of soul. So where are the ties that may fasten me", it then avails emancipation. Whose ignorance has been destroyed as a result of resolution to the effect that "I am not the flesh" "I am not the bone", he only can attain to emancipation.

कल्पितेयमविद्येयमनात्मन्यात्मभावनात्। परं पौरुषमाश्रित्य यत्नात्परमया धिया। भोगेच्छां दूरतस्त्यक्त्वा
निर्विकल्पः सुखी भव॥१२६॥ मम पुत्रो मम धनमहं सोऽयमिदं मम। इतीयमिन्द्रजालेन वासनैव
विवल्गति॥१२७॥ मा भवाज्ञो भव ज्ञस्त्वं जहि संसारभावनाम्। अनात्मन्यात्मभावेन किमज्ञ इव
रोदिषि॥१२८॥ कस्तवायं जडो मूको देहो मांसमयोऽशुचिः। यदर्थं सुखदुःखाभ्यामवशः
परिभूयसे॥१२९॥ अहो नु चित्रं यत्सत्यं ब्रह्म तद्विस्मृतं नृणाम्। तिष्ठतस्तव कार्येषु मास्तु
रागानुरञ्जना॥१३०॥ अहो नु चित्रं पद्मोत्थैर्बद्धास्तन्तुभिरद्रयः। अविद्यमाना या विद्या तया विश्वं खिलीकृतम्।
इदं तद्वज्रतां यातं तृणमात्रं जगत्त्रयम्॥१३१॥

It is mere imagination due to ignorance that arises attachment for the things which are void of soul. Pass your life with perfect pleasure by resorting to exercise and detachment, industry with sheer application of wisdom, giving-up the desire for enjoyment and by exclusive devotion (without option). The temptations and attachments like– "This is my son" "my wealth", "I am this" "I am that" etc. are playing different ways by spreading the number of illusions (Prapañca). You don't be fool, be wise and destroy such worldly attachments in toto. Why are you weeping like fools due to attachments with the issues not related to the soul? What relation is of you with this body of flesh, impure, dumb, and inert for which you are disturbed by vicissitudes. How is it surprising that the men have forgotten the everlasting Brahma, the only truth. Be busy always with your duties and deeds but don't left your mind fall in the trap of the ignorance, deeds etc. How is it surprising that the mountains are tied by the fibres of the lotus stemp considering as if these are the strong cords. This multiform world is impressed of the ignorance (Avidyā) which has actually no existence at all. Owing to the influence of that ignorance (Avidyā), the trio worlds, the awaking, dreaming and dormance are seeming strong as the thunderbolt while these are trivial as the straw.

Chapter - V

अथापरं प्रवक्ष्यामि शृणु तात यथायथम्। अज्ञानभूः सप्तपदा ज्ञभूः सप्तपदैव हि॥१॥
पदान्तराण्यसंख्यानि प्रभवन्त्यन्यथैतयोः। स्वरूपावस्थितिर्मुक्तिस्तद्भ्रंशोऽहंत्ववेदनम्॥२॥ शुद्धसन्मात्रसंवित्तेः
स्वरूपान्न चलन्ति ये। रागद्वेषादयो भावास्तेषां नाज्ञत्वसंभवः॥३॥ यः स्वरूपपरिभ्रंशश्चैत्यार्थे चितिमज्जनम्।
एतस्मादपरो मोहो न भूतो न भविष्यति॥४॥ अर्थादर्थान्तरं चित्ते याति मध्ये तु या स्थितिः। सा

ध्वस्तमननाकारा स्वरूपस्थितिरुच्यते॥ ५॥ संशान्तसर्वसंकल्पा या शिलावदवस्थितिः। जाग्रन्निद्राविनिर्मुक्ता सा स्वरूपस्थितिः परा॥ ६॥ अहन्तांशे क्षते शान्ते भेदनिष्पन्दचित्तता। अजडा या प्रचलति तत्स्वरूपमितीरितम्॥ ७॥

The great hermit Ṛbhu again said– O son! Listen to whatever I say. The knowledge and ignorance both has portfolios seven each. A numerous other roles also arise in between them. Basically, the ego is the factor that separates the living soul from its fundamental nature. Emancipation is nothing else than to maintain in the basic nature. The conscious of pure entity is the form of soul and the devotees undeviating from that state of conscious, seldom fall under influence of the nervous attachment, envy etc. defects arising due to ignorance. The sinking of mind from the soul-nature to the nature of temptation is the state of drawing in affection. No other state may be and shall be when the living souls suffers from attachments. The state of mind just at the intervening moments when the conscious shifts from a state to another is considered the "isolation of thinking". However the state of inaction availed when the resolutions are cooled down like a stone boulder is called the "Parā" state wherein the state of awaking and dreaming both also are inactivated. The state when the mind becomes peaceful, sensitive (awakened) and beyond the sense of discrimination as a result of complete of ego, is called the state of the soul in natural form (Svarupāvasthā).

बीजजाग्रत्तथा जाग्रन्महाजाग्रत्तथैव च। जाग्रत्स्वप्नस्तथा स्वप्नः स्वप्नजाग्रत्सुषुप्तिकम्॥ ८॥ इति सप्तविधो मोहः पुनरेष परस्परम्। श्लिष्टो भवत्यनेकाग्र्यं शृणु लक्षणमस्य तु॥ ९॥

Seven kinds of attachment has been stated– 1. awakening of cause, 2. state of awakening, 3. Most awakening state, 4. Awakening-dreaming state, 5. Dreaming state, 6. dreaming-awakening state, 7. state of dormance respectively. These further hold uncounted forms as a result of blending with each other. Now, listen to the characteristics of these separately.

प्रथमं चेतनं यत्स्यादनाख्यं निर्मलं चितः। भविष्यच्चित्तजीवादिनामशब्दार्थभाजनम्॥ १०॥ बीजरूपस्थितं जाग्रद्बीजजाग्रत्तदुच्यते। एषा ज्ञप्तेर्नवावस्था त्वं जाग्रत्संस्थितिं शृणु॥ ११॥

The first state i.e. awakening of cause is the state that defines the nature, citta, jīva etc. words which are nameless and it is the state of the pure sensitivity. This state is popularly known as the sprouting of seed state and it is the first step towards the affection. This is the innovative state of the knower. Now, listen to the real position of the awakened state.

नवप्रसूतस्य परादयं चाहमिदं मम। इति यः प्रत्ययः स्वस्थस्तज्जाग्रत्प्रागभावनात्॥ १२॥ अयं सोऽहमिदं तन्म इति जन्मान्तरोदितः। पीवरः प्रत्ययः प्रोक्तो महाजाग्रदिति स्फुटम्॥ १३॥ अरूढमथवा रूढं सर्वथा तन्मयात्मकम्। यज्जाग्रतो मनोराज्यं यज्जाग्रत्स्वप्न उच्यते॥ १४॥ द्विचन्द्रशुक्तिकारूप्यमृगतृष्णादिभेदतः। अभ्यासं प्राप्य जाग्रत्तत्स्वप्नो नानाविधो भवेत्॥ १५॥

The incoming of the spirit like– "This is I am", "This is mine" i.e. "I" and "my" spirit in the heart of new born living soul (Jīva) is the second state of affection because such spirit are not earlier it. The most awakened state is the state in which the spirits like– "This is that man", "This is I", "That thing is mine" etc. are revealed by the concerned living soul including the nature acquainted in previous births.

The imaginative composition of mind as revealed at the time of his engrossing on any thought, or using some prevalent or non-prevalent words in the state of awakening is called the state of awakening-dreaming (i.e. day dreaming) seeming two moons in place of one, silver in oyster and water in the desert etc. are the several kinds of awakening-dreaming (day dreaming).

अल्पकालं मया दृष्टमेतन्नोदेति यत्र हि। परामर्शः प्रबुद्धस्य स स्वप्न इति कथ्यते॥१६॥ चिरं संदर्शनाभावादप्रफुल्लं बृहद्वचः। चिरकालानुवृत्तिस्तु स्वप्नो जाग्रदिवोदितः॥१७॥ स्वप्नजाग्रदिति प्रोक्तं जाग्रत्यपि परिस्फुरत्। षडवस्थापरित्यागे जडा जीवस्य या स्थितिः॥१८॥ भविष्यद्दुःखबोधाढ्य सौषुप्तिः सोच्यते गतिः। जगत्तस्यामवस्थायामन्तस्तमसि लीयते॥१९॥

The state of dreaming is the state in which the scene seem sometime before not seen again and only memory of the scene is left with the living soul. Then there comes the state of dreaming-awakening state. In this state, the dream stays till long hours with a number of activities still remain inchoate and the dream that arise like awakening or it is seen when the man is in the state of awakening. When the living soul avails in the inert state after crossing these six states, this state is called the dormance. The man recollects in mind the pains pertaining to the past. This world merges with internal darkness at this state.

सप्तावस्था इमाः प्रोक्ता मया ज्ञानस्य वै द्विज। एकैका शतसंख्यात्र नानाविभवरूपिणी॥२०॥ इमां सप्तपदां ज्ञानभूमिमाकर्णयानघ। नानया ज्ञातया भूयो मोहपङ्के निमज्जति॥२१॥

O Brāhmaṇa! I told the seven roles of the attachment due to ignorance to you. Every role out of it, is full of different kinds of luxuries and holds multiforms in different states. O innocent son! I am now going to tell you the seven roles of knowledge. The man does not fall in the marsh of attachment if he is well known to the same.

वदन्ति बहुभेदेन वादिनो योगभूमिकाः। मम त्वभिमता नूनमिमा एव शुभप्रदाः॥२२॥ अवबोधं विदुर्ज्ञानं तदिदं साप्तभूमिकम्। मुक्तिस्तु ज्ञेयमित्युक्ता भूमिकासप्तकात्परम्॥२३॥

The scholar have told a number of kinds of the Yoga but I consider only these seven roles specially advantageous. The conscious so arisen by these seven roles too is called the knowledge. The emancipation availed under these seven roles is called "knowable".

ज्ञानभूमिः शुभेच्छाख्या प्रथमा समुदाहृता। विचारणा द्वितीया तु तृतीया तनुमानसी॥२४॥ सत्त्वापत्तिश्चतुर्थी स्यात्ततोऽसंसक्तिनामिका। पदार्थभावना षष्ठी सप्तमी तुर्यगा स्मृता॥२५॥ आसामन्तःस्थिता मुक्तिर्यस्यां भूयो न शोचति। एतासां भूमिकानां त्वमिदं निर्वचनं शृणु॥२६॥

Śubhecchā (good wishes) name has been given to the first role of knowledge. Similarly, the second is vicāraṇā, the third is "tanumānasī", the fourth is sattvāpatti, fifth is "Asaṅsakti", sixth is "Padārtha Bhāvanā" and the seventh is "Turyagā". The emancipation giving cautions for not again falling in melancholic is inherent in these roles. Now, listen to these roles in detail.

स्थित: किं मूढ एवास्मि प्रेक्षेऽहं शास्त्रसज्जनैः। वैराग्यपूर्वमिच्छेति शुभेच्छेत्युच्यते बुधैः॥२७॥ शास्त्रसज्जनसंपर्कवैराग्याभ्यासपूर्वकम्। सदाचारप्रवृत्तिर्या प्रोच्यते सा विचारणा॥२८॥

I will discuss with the great men and persue the Śāstra on the issue that– "Why am I in confused mind?" The curiosity so arising in mind prior to adopting the detachment is given the name as "Śubhecchā" by the scholars. The propensities of etiquette appear then as a result of consult and discuss with the scholars, persual of Śāstra thereby with exercise and detachment, this role of knowledge is called vicāraṇā.

विचारणाशुभेच्छाभ्यामिन्द्रियार्थेषु रक्तता। यत्र सा तनुतामेति प्रोच्यते तनुमानसी॥२९॥ भूमिकात्रितयाभ्यासाच्चित्ते तु विरतेर्वशात्। सत्त्वात्मनि स्थिते शुद्धे सत्त्वापत्तिरुदाहृता॥३०॥

The state when as a result of Śubhecchā and Vicāraṇā, the attachment for the issues pertaining to sensory organs is dimished– it is called "Tanumānasī" when the mind due to exercises on these three roles attains to the spirit of detachment and when it enshrines in the sattva form, this state is called the "Sattvāpatti".

दशाचतुष्टयाभ्यासादसंसर्गकला तु या। रूढसत्त्वचमत्कारा प्रोक्ताऽसंसक्तिनामिका॥३१॥ भूमिकापञ्चकाभ्यासात्स्वात्मारामतया दृढम्। आभ्यन्तराणां बाह्यानां पदार्थानामभावनात्॥३२॥ परप्रयुक्तेन चिरं प्रयत्नेनावबोधनम्। पदार्थभावना नाम षष्ठी भवति भूमिका॥३३॥ **दशाचतुष्टयाभ्यासादसंसर्गकला तु या। रूढसत्त्वचमत्कारा प्रोक्ताऽसंसक्तिनामिका॥३१॥ भूमिकापञ्चकाभ्यासात्स्वात्मारामतया दृढम्। आभ्यन्तराणां बाह्यानां पदार्थानामभावनात्॥३२॥ परप्रयुक्तेन चिरं प्रयत्नेनावबोधनम्। पदार्थभावना नाम षष्ठी भवति भूमिका॥३३॥**

The kalā (art) without contact (Saṁsarga) is called "Asaṅsakti". The ever brilliant kalā is attained when all these roles are well practiced. Subsequent to the sufficient exercise of these five roles when the man engrosses with his sensitivity and the attachment for the worldly objects is destroyed from externally and internally, the sixty role namely, "Padārtha Bhāvanā" is then availed.

भूमिषट्कचिराभ्यासाद्भेदस्यानुपलम्भनात्। यत्स्वभावैकनिष्ठत्वं सा ज्ञेया तुर्यगा गतिः॥३४॥ एषा हि जीवन्मुक्तेषु तुर्यावस्थेति विद्यते। विदेहमुक्तिविषयं तुर्यातीतमतः परम्॥३५॥

The discriminatory wit is diminished on maturity of these six roles and devotee attains firm loyalty on the soul. This state is called the "Turyagā" state. Only the persons of liberated soul can avail this "Turyāvasthā". The next to this state, there comes the state beyond "Turyāvasthā" i.e. "Turyātīta Avasthā" which is the subject of "Videha Mukti" i.e. Emancipation from the senses of the body.

ये निदाघ महाभागाः सप्तमीं भूमिमाश्रिताः। आत्मारामा महात्मानस्ते महत्पदमागताः॥३६॥ जीवन्मुक्ता न मज्जन्ति सुखदुःखरसस्थिते। प्रकृतेनाथ कार्येण किंचित्कुर्वन्ति वा न वा॥३७॥

O innocent! The lucky persons who have attained the saptaṁ Turyagāvasthā definitely entertain the great soul Mahatpada (Parama Pada) engrossed in the soul. Such liberated soul remain uninvolved to the feeling of the pleasure and grief. They do not attach even to the duties and deeds on which they always and thoroughly keep themselves busy.

पार्श्वस्थबोधिता: सन्त: पूर्वाचारक्रमागतम्। आचारमाचरन्त्येव सुप्तबुद्धवदुत्थिता:॥३८॥ भूमिकासप्तकं चैतद्धीमतामेव गोचरम्। प्राप्य ज्ञानदशामेतां पशुम्लेच्छादयोऽपि ये॥३९॥ सदेहा वाप्यदेहा वा ते मुक्ता नात्र संशय:। ज्ञप्तिर्हि ग्रन्थिविच्छेदस्तस्मिन्सति विमुक्तता॥४०॥

As the man suddenly awakes when he is awakened by the family members, the scholars perform the tradition of good conduct by keeping themselves busy on executing great deeds. If the animals and the Mleccha (evil doer and born in lower of society) are known any way to these seven roles, they too attain emancipation either in existing life or after death. There is no scope for any doubt. The knowledge is nothing else but an opening of all knot tied in heart and emancipation is certain on attainment of the knowledge.

मृगतृष्णाम्बुबुद्ध्यादिशान्तिमात्रात्मकस्त्वसौ। ये तु मोहार्णवात्तीर्णास्तै: प्राप्तं परमं पदम्॥४१॥ ते स्थिता भूमिकास्वासु स्वात्मलाभपरायणा:। मन: प्रशमनोपायो योग इत्यभिधीयते॥४२॥

When one is confused of water at a state of mirage, the same of confusion to mind is called ignorance (Avidyā). The decay of ignorance is the emancipation. The persons who have crossed the ocean of attachment are really entitled to the supreme position (Parama Pada). The man busy in efforts for self-realisation are only enshrined on these roles. The means giving perfect peace to mind is called yoga.

सप्तभूमि: स विज्ञेय: कथितास्ताश्च भूमिका:। एतासां भूमिकानां तु गम्यं ब्रह्माभिधं पदम्॥४३॥ त्वत्ताऽहन्तात्मता यत्र परता नास्ति काचन। न क्वचिद्भावकलना न भावाभावगोचरा॥४४॥ सर्वं शान्तं निरालम्बं व्योमस्थं शाश्वतं शिवम्। अनामयमनाभासमनामकमकारणम्॥४५॥ न सन्नासन्न मध्यं तं न सर्वं सर्वमेव च। मनोवचोभिरग्राह्यं पूर्णात्पूर्णं सुखात्सुखम्॥४६॥ असंवेदनमाशान्तमात्मवेदनमाततम्। सत्ता सर्वपदार्थानां नान्या संवेदनादृते॥४७॥

These seven roles of yoga have been already told above under Jñānabhūmi. The aim of these roles is to attain the position of Brahma. As the entity of worldly objects is mere soul-sensitivity and nothing apart from it; the wisdom relating to attachment becomes zero and discrimination of attachment and detachment diminishes when, the narrow pace of thinking such as "It is mine", "that is your" and discriminations between self and others is completely effaced. The structure (nature) of Brahma is peaceful, non-dependence, ether form, everlasting, Śiva, pure, non-perceiving, undescribable, non-causative, non-truth, non-myth, non-middle, incomplete and complete too, un-entertainable to mind and speech, perfect than perfection, more pleasurous than pleasure, beyond the approach of sensitivity, in the form of soul conceiving tenderised and extended. This sensitive (caitanya) Brahma is not different than the entity of all matters and the sole basis of its attainment is the due feeling.

संबन्धे द्रष्टृदृश्यानां मध्ये दृष्टिर्हि यद्वपुः। द्रष्टृदर्शनदृश्यादिवर्जितं तदिदं पदम्॥ ४८॥ देशाद्देशं गते चित्ते मध्ये यच्चेतसो वपुः। अजाड्यसंविन्मननं तन्मयो भव सर्वदा॥ ४९॥ अजाग्रत्स्वप्ननिद्रस्य यत्ते रूपं सनातनम्। अचेतनं चाजडं च तन्मयो भव सर्वदा॥ ५०॥ जडतां वर्जयित्वैकां शिलाया हृदयं हि तत्। अमनस्कस्वरूपं यत्तन्मयो भव सर्वदा। चित्तं दूरे परित्यज्य योऽसि सोऽसि स्थिरो भव॥ ५१॥ पूर्वं मनः समुदितं परमात्मतत्त्वात्तेनाततं जगदिदं सविकल्पजालम्। शून्येन शून्यमपि विप्र यथाम्बरेण नीलत्वमुल्लसति चारुतराभिधानम्॥ ५२॥

The form of sight in between the observer and the scene as perceived is the position of realisation distinct than the observer, scene and the observation. One should engross himself continuously in ever sensitive form at the stage that falls between the movement of mind from one issue (country) to another. Always stand stable in the everlasting form which is beyond the awakening, dreaming and dormance and the inert as also the sensitive. Always engross in the state of non-mental (Amanaska) which is attained after giving up the store like position of heart i.e. the ignorance. Remain stable in the state where you are by giving-up the mind from a distance. The mind was very first originated from the element of the supreme soul and subsequently, this world in the form of dignity of options (vikalpajāla) has been originated. O Brāhmaṇa! The zero is the cause for creation of zero. For an instance, the ether is zero but the fascinating blue scene gets birth from the same.

संकल्पसंक्षयवशाद्गलिते तु चित्ते संसारमोहमिहिका गलिता भवन्ति।
स्वच्छं विभाति शरदीव खमागतायां चिन्मात्रमेकमजमाद्यमनन्तमन्तः॥ ५३॥

The propensities of mind are melted when the resolution is destroyed and the fog spreaded inner the world in the form of attachment is shattered. Then that exclusive Brahma in the form of cinmātra, unborn, Ādya, Ananta, is ultimately adorned like moon in the clear sky of the pleasant season (Śarada Ṛtu).

अकर्तृकमरङ्गं च गगने चित्रमुत्थितम्। अद्रष्टृकं स्वानुभवमनिद्रस्वप्नदर्शनम्॥ ५४॥
साक्षिभूते समे स्वच्छे निर्विकल्पे चिदात्मनि। निरिच्छं प्रतिबिम्बन्ति जगन्ति मुकुरे यथा॥ ५५॥

The sky appears printed without the artist and the colour. The sleepless dream is seen self felt without the observer (looker). This cidātmā is like an evident, unbiased, clear and exclusive mirror. All the three worlds are being seen in it without any ambitions or desires.

एकं ब्रह्म चिदाकाशं सर्वात्मकमखण्डितम्। इति भावय यत्नेन चेतश्चाञ्चल्यशान्तये॥ ५६॥ रेखोपरेखावलिता यथैका पीवरी शिला। तथा त्रैलोक्यवलितं ब्रह्मैकमिह दृश्यताम्॥ ५७॥

In order to cool-down the caprice nature of mind, one should forcily presume that the Brahma is one in all forms, in the form of Cidākāśa and integrated. As the lines and sub-lines are drawn on a thick boulder of stone the same way, the Brahma with three worlds should be seen.

द्वितीयकारणाभावादनुत्पन्नमिदं जगत्। ज्ञातं ज्ञातव्यमधुना दृष्टं द्रष्टव्यमद्भुतम्॥ ५८॥ विश्रान्तोऽस्मि चिरं श्रान्तश्चिन्मात्रान्नास्ति किंचन। पश्य विश्रान्तसंदेहं विगताशेषकौतुकम्॥ ५९॥

To say that in the absence of any other cause different than Brahma was not responsible for creating this universe is absolutely unbelieving the same as to say horns on the head of a rabbit. I (the solitoque of Ṛbhu) have thus, known to knowable the specialities expected are seen and I am now badly tored. (O Nidāgha) observe the cinmātra by enjoying liberty from the entire worldly illusion and doubts. Understand that nothing is here except cinmātra.

निरस्तकल्पनाजालमचित्तत्वं परं पदम्। त एव भूमतां प्राप्ताः संशान्ताशेषकिल्बिषाः॥६०॥ महाधियः शान्तधियो ये याता विमनस्कताम्। जन्तोः कृतविचारस्य विगलद्वृत्तिचेतसः॥६१॥ मननं त्यजतो नित्यं किंचित्परिणतं मनः। दृश्यं संत्यजतो हेयमुपादेयमुपेयुषः॥६२॥ द्रष्टारं पश्यतो नित्यमद्रष्टारमपश्यतः। विज्ञातव्ये परे तत्त्वे जागरूकस्य जीवतः॥६३॥ सुप्तस्य घनसंमोहमये संसारवर्त्मनि। अत्यन्तपक्ववैराग्यादरसेषु रसेष्वपि॥६४॥ संसारवासनाजाले खगजाल इवाधुना। त्रोटिते हृदयग्रन्थौ श्लथे वैराग्यरंहसा॥६५॥ कातकं फलमासाद्य यथा वारि प्रसीदति। तथा विज्ञानवशतः स्वभावः संप्रसीदति॥६६॥

The innocent devotees only attain to the Brahma who have cut the tie of resolution and who have attached to great position where no disturbance of the element of mind remains. The persons who have become vimanaska by enslaving the mind, the peacefulness in mind is the indicative of their acute wisdom. The thoroughful people on Vedānta, whose mental aptitudes has been diminished and where minds have become stable due to regular exercise for giving up the mental resolutions, the dissolves of salvation who are giving up the hatred and useful both kinds of scenes, who is always initiative (observer) viz., busy on doing self-realisation and non-observer viz., who do not see the illusion (prapañca), who pass that life by keeping themselves specially aware of the knowable supreme element, who has been slept on the stable spirit of detachment for the things either full of essence or essenceless, whose cords of worldly affection and temptation has been cut by vehemetic spirit of detachment like the ties of a bird cut by the the mouse and the knots tied in heart has been loosened; their nature becomes so rectified and pure as the water is purified by the fruit of Nirmali.

नीरागं निरुपासङ्गं निर्द्वन्द्वं निरुपाश्रयम्। विनिर्याति मनो मोहाद्विहङ्गः पञ्जरादिव॥६७॥ शान्तसंदेहदौरात्म्यं गतकौतुकविभ्रमम्। परिपूर्णान्तरं चेतः पूर्णेन्दुरिव राजते॥६८॥

The mind is liberated from the lies of affection like a bird liberated from the cage on being its free from the affection, unattached, puzzles and the basis (Ādhāra). The persons whose malafides have cooled-down, who are free from the illusion (Prapañca), their mind (citta) attains particular image like the full moon.

नाहं न चान्यदस्तीह ब्रह्मैवास्मि निरामयम्। इत्थं सदसतोर्मध्याद्यः पश्यति स पश्यति॥६९॥ अयत्नोपनतेष्वक्षिदृग्दृश्येषु यथा मनः। नीरागमेव पतति तद्वत्कार्येषु धीरधीः॥७०॥ परिज्ञायोपभुक्तो हि भोगो भवति तुष्टये। विज्ञाय सेवितश्चोरो मैत्रीमेति न चोरताम्॥७१॥

I am mere Brahma free from all defects and neither I myself nor anything here is, which vigil is so at the middle of truth and false is really the Brahma worth realisation. As the mind is attracted towards the scenes worth observance usually and without attachment, the men of stable mind are engaged in performance of the duties and the works. The enjoyment taken deliberated becomes the cause for satisfaction the same way as the thief deliberately engaged in service performs friendship by learning the theft.

अशङ्कितापि संप्राप्ता ग्रामयात्रा यथाऽध्वगैः। प्रेक्ष्यते तद्वदेव ज्ञैर्भोगश्रीरवलोक्यते॥७२॥ मनसो निगृहीतस्य लीलाभोगोऽल्पकोऽपि यः। तमेवालब्धविस्तारं क्लिष्टत्वाद्बहु मन्यते॥७३॥ बद्धमुक्तो महीपालो ग्रासमात्रेण तुष्यति। परैरबद्धो नाक्रान्तो न राष्ट्रं बहु मन्यते॥७४॥

The scholar observes the enjoyments and luxuries with the same surprise as it is felt by the traveller who suddenly has come in a village whose he never thought to visit. The devotee of controlled mind gives up even a little quantum of unearned or recovered free of cost (labour) considering it enough to bring pains and puzzles. The king who satisfies with a morsel of food but after freedom from the captivity of enemy, he only considers the prosperity in abundance as trivial if the same has been returned by the enemy under pity.

हस्तं हस्तेन संपीड्य दन्तैर्दन्तान्विचूर्ण्य च। अङ्गान्यङ्गैरिवाक्रम्य जयेदादौ स्वकं मनः॥७५॥ मनसो विजयान्नान्या गतिरस्ति भवार्णवे। महानरकसाम्राज्ये मत्तदुष्कृतवारणाः। आशाशरशलाकाढ्या दुर्जया हीन्द्रियारयः॥७६॥

One should try to win his mind by friction of two hands, grind teeth of both jaws against each other and by pushing his body parts one against another viz., exercise all valour and courage to win the mind. There is no other measure to cross this ocean of world than to win one's own mind. The intoxicated elephants are marching in the form of evils in this dreadful realm of hell. It is most different to win the enemies in the form of senses who are well equipped with the arrows and draggers of hope.

प्रक्षीणचित्तदर्पस्य निगृहीतेन्द्रियद्विषः। पद्मिन्य इव हेमन्ते क्षीयन्ते भोगवासनाः॥७७॥ तावन्निशीव वेताला वसन्ति हृदि वासनाः। एकतत्त्वदृढाभ्यासाद्यावन्न विजितं मनः॥७८॥ भृत्योऽभिमतकर्तृत्वान्मन्त्री सर्वार्थकारणात्। सामन्तश्चेन्द्रियाक्रान्तेर्मनो मन्ये विवेकिनः॥७९॥

The passions for worldly enjoyments are diminished the same way as the lotus plant is dried-up in the snowfall season when the enemies in the form of senses are enslaved and the ego is entirely destroyed. The passion stands undeviated in the mind until the mind is not controlled by virtue of a firm practice on integrity. I opine that the men of discreet turn their mind into servant for getting the desired thing to be done, secretary for the fulfilment of all objectives and feudal for imposing control on his senses.

लालनात्स्निग्धललना पालनात्पालकः पिता। सुहृदुत्तमविन्यासान्मनो मन्ये मनीषिणः॥८०॥ स्वालोकतः शास्त्रदृशा स्वबुद्ध्या स्वानुभावतः। प्रयच्छति परां सिद्धिं त्यक्त्वात्मानं मनःपिता॥ सुहृष्टः

सुदृढः स्वच्छः सुक्रान्तः सुप्रबोधितः। स्वगुणेनोर्जितो भाति हृदि हृद्यो मनोमणिः॥८२॥ एनं मनोमणिं ब्रह्मन्बहुपङ्ककलङ्कितम्। विवेकवारिणा सिद्ध्यै प्रक्षाल्यालोकवान्भव॥८३॥

According to my opinion, the mind of scholar is like a maid full of affection as a result of loving care and like a father as a result of providing with maintenance. The mind in the form of father extends the way of supreme accomplishment by the gentle behave prescribed by the scriptures (holy-books), by the light of knowledge gathered through experience and discreet wisdom. The beautiful mind in the form of gem, very sturdy, firm, innocent, self-enslaved, duty sensitive and with acute splendour of true-soul merit is adorned in the heart. O Brāhmaṇa! make this mind in the form of a gem dazzling with light (polish) in order to accomplishment of means by cleaning it with water of discretions because it is badly imbued with the mud of passion and temptations.

विवेकं परमाश्रित्य बुद्ध्या सत्यमवेक्ष्य च। इन्द्रियारीनलं छित्त्वा तीर्णो भव भवार्णवात्॥८४॥

You will be able to scatter the rivals in the form of sensory organs by resorting to the time discretion, and investigating the truth by application of wisdom. Only then you can cross the worldly sea.

आस्थामात्रमनन्तानां दुःखानामाकरं विदुः। अनास्थामात्रमभितः सुखानामालयं विदुः॥८५॥ वासनातन्तुबद्धोऽयं लोको विपरिवर्तते। सा प्रसिद्धातिदुःखाय सुखायोच्छेदमागता॥८६॥ धीरोऽप्यतिबहुज्ञोऽपि कुलजोऽपि महानपि। तृष्णया बध्यते जन्तुः सिंहः शृङ्खलया यथा॥८७॥ परमं पौरुषं यत्नमास्थायादाय सूद्यमम्। यथाशास्त्रमनुद्वेगमाचरन्को न सिद्धिभाक्॥८८॥

The faith (hope) only is the cause for origin of a number of pains and the life reluctant (non-hoping) is to be considered the abode of pleasure. This world tied with the thread of temptations moves frequently in the cycle of birth and death. That renowned temptation enters for shattering all pleasures and puts the living soul on blazing fire of hardships. The courageous, aristocrat, most renewed and the greatmen too are tied with the fascinating cord of the affection. Who does not acquire accomplishments by performing the activities compared by the scriptures (holy-books), resorting the supreme industry and engaging himself in the best enterprise or arocation?

अहं सर्वमिदं विश्वं परमात्माहमच्युतः। नान्यदस्तीति संवित्त्या परमा सा ह्यहंकृतिः॥८९॥ सर्वस्माद्व्यतिरिक्तोऽहं वालाग्रादप्यहं तनुः। इति या संविदो ब्रह्मन्द्वितीयाहंकृतिः शुभा॥९०॥ मोक्षायैषा न बन्धाय जीवन्मुक्तस्य विद्यते॥९१॥

The ego based on self-realisations. On the facts– "I am in the form of world", "I am in the form of exclusive supreme soul", "nothing is left besides me" has been considered the best conscious ego. The second ego that inspires thinking– "I am more micro than the foreportion of a hair" provides with the emancipation. It does not traps in ties. Only liberated souls hold such ego with them.

पाणिपादादिमात्रोऽयमहमित्येष निश्चयः। अहंकारस्तृतीयोऽसौ लौकिकस्तुच्छ एव सः॥९२॥ जीव एव दुरात्मासौ कन्दः संसारदुस्तरोः। अनेनाभिहतो जन्तुरधोऽधः परिधावति॥९३॥ अनया दुरहंकृत्या भावात्संत्यक्तयाचिरम्। शिष्टाहंकारवाञ्जन्तुः शमवान्याति मुक्तताम्॥९४॥

The assumption to the effect that– "I am merely a man of formidable body" exists in third kind of worldly ego and it has been stated meanest ego. The creature of such vicious ego is the root cause for the tree of this world full of pains. The creature suffered from it continuously proceeds to the destruction. The creatures giving-up such meanest and trouble enhancing ego and holding the best ego since long avail emancipation.

प्रथमौ द्वावहंकारावङ्गीकृत्य त्वलौकिकौ। तृतीयाहंकृतिस्त्याज्या लौकिकी दुःखदायिनी॥९५॥ अथ ते अपि संत्यज्य सर्वाहंकृतिवर्जितः। स तिष्ठति तथात्युच्चैः परमेवाधिरोहति॥९६॥

One should accept the initial two celestial egos and leave the third kind of worldly e[illegible] that becomes cause for dismal. All these egos' should be abandoned and be innocent wh[illegible] the means of power are increased because the superior position is only then possible.

भोगेच्छामात्रको बन्धस्तत्त्यागो मोक्ष उच्यते। मनसोऽभ्युदयो नाशो मनोनाशो महोदयः। ज्ञमनो नाशमभ्येति मनोऽज्ञस्य हि शृङ्खला॥९७॥ नानन्दं न निरानन्दं न चलं नाचलं स्थिरम्। न सन्नासन्न चैतेषां मध्यं ज्ञानिमनो विदुः॥९८॥ यथा सौक्ष्म्याच्चिदाभास्य आकाशो नोपलक्ष्यते। तथा निरंशश्चिद्भावः सर्वगोऽपि न लक्ष्यते॥९९॥

The desire for enjoyment has been said the bondage and emancipation is attained when it is abandoned. The cause for progress of mind is its destruction. Destruction of mind is the identity of the lucky persons. The mind of scholars is destroyed. The mind for the persons trapped in ignorance is the cause of binding. The mind neither is pleasure given nor cause for sadness to the scholars. It is not movable, immovable, stable, truth and false and the state of it too is unknown. The ingrained sensitive entity is not perceived through eyes inspite of being it omnipresent as the ether illumined in the mind (Citta) is not seen due to being in micro form.

सर्वसंकल्परहिता सर्वसंज्ञाविवर्जिता। सैषा चिदविनाशात्मा स्वात्मेत्यादिकृताभिधा॥१००॥

आकाशशतभागाच्छा ज्ञेषु निष्कलरूपिणी। सकलामलसंसारस्वरूपैकात्मदर्शिनी॥१०१॥

नास्तमेति न चोदेति नोत्तिष्ठति न तिष्ठति। न च याति न चायाति न च नेह न चेह चित्॥१०२॥

This cidātmā (supreme soul) is known as everlasting and self-soul and it is beyond the names and the resolutions. It reveals itself only in the form of the entire world of innocence. It is hundred times clean than the ether, innocent and unfabricated (Niṣkala) in the eyes of scholars. That sensitive entity neither arises nor sets. It is beyond the cycle of birth and death, neither stands nor seated permanently. It is neither here and nor there.

सैषा चिदमलाकारा निर्विकल्पा निरास्पदा॥१०३॥

आदौ शमदमप्रायैर्गुणैः शिष्यं विशोधयेत्। पश्चात्सर्वमिदं ब्रह्म शुद्धस्त्वमिति बोधयेत्॥ १०४॥
अज्ञस्यार्धप्रबुद्धस्य सर्वं ब्रह्मेति यो वदेत्। महानरकजालेषु स तेन विनियोजितः॥ १०५॥

That cidātmā is without shelter, beyond option and in the form of purity. It is necessary for a teacher to rectify the heart of his pupil by imbibing the properties (Guṇās) like Śama (control), Dama (to oppress) etc. He must then give this knowledge of Brahma by proper monitoring. He should say that he (pupil) is the pure Brahma form and everything here is in the form of Brahma. To say everything in the form of Brahman before the person of immature mind and the fool is like pushing him into the gross hell.

[The saint says here that initially non-discriminate (exclusive) knowledge should not be given to the pupil, the devotee. It is necessary first that his mind should be made pure through śama, dama, etc. parts of yoga by explaining. He can not give up the undesirable until his mind is purified and thus, the non-discriminative preaching is proved futile.]

प्रबुद्धबुद्धेः प्रक्षीणभोगेच्छस्य निराशिषः। नास्त्यविद्यामलमिति प्राज्ञस्तूपदिशेद्गुरुः॥ १०६॥
सति दीप इवालोकः सत्यर्क इव वासरः। सति पुष्प इवामोदश्चिति सत्यं जगत्तथा॥ १०७॥

Whose passions for enjoyment have been decayed, ambitions have been diminished and the wisdom is awakening, the same devotee should be preached the vedānta by the teacher. There is no existence of the defects in the form of ignorance (Avidyā). As the day when the sun rises and light from the lamp (dīpaka) as also the perfume from the flower is definite, the wind is existed on the sensitivity (caitanya).

प्रतिभासत एवेदं न जगत्परमार्थतः। ज्ञानदृष्टौ प्रसन्नायां प्रबोधविततोदये॥ १०८॥
यथावज्ज्ञास्यसि स्वस्थो मद्वाग्वृष्टिजलाबलम्। अविद्ययैवोत्तमया स्वार्थनाशोद्यमार्थया॥ १०९॥
विद्या संप्राप्यते ब्रह्मन्सर्वदोषापहारिणी। शाम्यति ह्यस्त्रमस्त्रेण मलेन क्षाल्यते मलम्॥ ११०॥
शमं विषं विषेणैति रिपुणा हन्यते रिपुः। ईदृशी भूतमायेयं या स्वनाशेन हर्षदा॥ १११॥

This world actually is void and it merely perceives to the eyes. When your sight of knowledge will become wide of all covers (fully disclosed) and imbued with the knowledge of light, you will in that circumstance be stable in your own form. You will then be duly understood the reality of my preaching. O Brahman! The attainment of learning, removing all defects caused by the ignorance can be possible only by prolong exercise of ignorance (Avidyā). A weapon is made void of effect only by the next weapon and the impurity is washed by application of impurity. The poison kills poison and the enemy kills enemy. This illusion of creatures (Bhūtamāyā) too is exhilarated on its decay.

न लक्ष्यते स्वभावोऽस्या वीक्ष्यमाणैव नश्यति। नास्त्येषा परमार्थेनेत्येवं भावनयेद्धया॥ ११२॥
सर्वं ब्रह्मेति यस्यान्तर्भावना सा हि मुक्तिदा। भेददृष्टिरविद्येयं सर्वथा तां विसर्जयेत्॥ ११३॥

Its form is not perceived easily but it is destroyed as and when it is seen. It is ignorance (Avidyā) that has discriminant view and giving it up altogether is for all good. It is theme assure for attainment of salvation when firmly understood and remain undeviated on the inner spirit that the illusion has actually no existence and everything is in the form of Brahma.

मुने नासाद्यते तद्धि पदमक्षयमुच्यते। कुतो जातेयमिति ते द्विज मास्तु विचारणा॥ ११४॥

इमां कथमहं हन्मीत्येषा तेऽस्तु विचारणा। अस्तं गतायां क्षीणायामस्यां ज्ञास्यसि तत्पदम्॥ ११५॥

यत एषा यथा चैषा यथा नष्टेत्यखण्डितम्। तदस्या रोगशालाया यत्नं कुरु चिकित्सने॥ ११६॥

O the best hermit! Akṣyapada is called which is not found by resorting to the illusion. O Brahman! You should not imagine about the creator of this illusion or the source from which it is originated but emphasize on how it may be shattered. You will attain everlasting position only when this illusion is reduced and destroyed in toto. One should make endevour to eradicate the basic reason of this disease when the characteristics of its appearance, its nature and the able measures for destroying it are duly understood.

यथैषा जन्मदु:खेषु न भूयस्त्वां नियोक्ष्यति। स्वात्मनि स्वपरिस्पन्दैः स्फुरत्यच्छैश्चिदर्णवः॥ ११७॥

एकात्मकमखण्डं तदित्यन्तर्भाव्यतां दृढम्। किंचित्क्षुभितरूपा सा चिच्छक्तिश्चिन्मयार्णवे॥ ११८॥

तन्मयैव स्फुरत्यच्छा तत्रैवोर्मिरिवार्णवे। आत्मन्येवात्मना व्योम्नि यथा सरसि मारुतः॥ ११९॥

तथैवात्मात्मशक्त्यैव स्वात्मन्येवैति लोलताम्। क्षणं स्फुरति सा दैवी सर्वशक्तितया तथा॥ १२०॥

The cidātmā is in undivided form. It should be the firm determination so that (this illusion) may not rotate you frequently around the cycle of birth and death. The mind in the form of an ocean may raise its wanes (the liberation of pure and innocent thoughts) all time. This cidātmā in some way is slightly feeling distress in the cinmaya sea. The pure cinmaya waves are raising upward like the sea waves. As the wind automatically blows on waves in the pond of ether, the soul is vibrated in waves by virtue of power of soul in ones own soul.

देशकालक्रियाशक्तिर्न यस्याः संप्रकर्षणे। स्वस्वभावं विदित्वोच्चैरप्यनन्तपदे स्थिता॥ १२१॥

The awakened power (cetanā śakti) cannot be driven by the time, place and power of action however, when it is known to its usual position, it enshrines on the unending high position.

रूपं परिमितेनासौ भावयत्यविभाविता। यदैवं भावितं रूपं तया परमकान्तया॥ १२२॥

तदैवैनामनुगता नामसंख्यादिका दृशः। विकल्पकलिताकारं देशकालक्रियास्पदम्॥ १२३॥

This power in sensitivity is confined to the complexion feelings in the state of ignorance. The name and quantum etc. qualifications are added with it when the complexion conscious is inserted in that supreme entity of pecularity.

चितो रूपमिदं ब्रह्मन्क्षेत्रज्ञ इति कथ्यते। वासनाः कल्पयन्सोऽपि यात्यहंकारतां पुनः॥ १२४॥

अहंकारो विनिर्णेता कलङ्की बुद्धिरुच्यते। बुद्धिः संकल्पिताकारा प्रयाति मननास्पदम्॥ १२५॥

O Brahman! the form of awakened power that entertains the options and gives shelter to the place, time and action; is carved Kṣetrajña (knower of the area) and this same is again said ego when it is engrossed in passions. When the ego is defected and determined, it is caused wisdom. When the wisdom turns into the resolution, it holds the form of a discreet mind.

मनो घनविकल्पं तु गच्छतीन्द्रियतां शनैः। पाणिपादमयं देहमिन्द्रियाणि विदुर्बुधाः॥ १२६॥

The glance of the sensory form is gradually seen when the mind sinks in the deep ocean. The scholars consider the sensory to this formidable body with hands and feet added.

एवं जीवो हि संकल्पवासनारज्जुवेष्टितः। दुःखजालपरीतात्मा क्रमादायाति नीचताम्॥ १२७॥

इति शक्तिमयं चेतो घनाहंकारतां गतम्। कोशकारक्रिमिरिव स्वेच्छया याति बन्धनम्॥ १२८॥

The living soul fastened with the cord of resolution and passions, proceeds forward to dismay frequently and he is badly trapped in the dragnet of sorrows. The mighty mind binds himself after having arrived at the state of dense ego like the silk-worm.

स्वयं कल्पिततन्मात्राजालाभ्यन्तरवर्ति च। परां विवशतामेति शृङ्खलाबद्धसिंहवत्॥ १२९॥

The power of mind is enslaved like a lion tied with the chain in the form of Tanmātrā resolved by itself.

क्वचिन्मनः क्वचिद्बुद्धिः क्वचिज्ज्ञानं क्वचित्क्रिया। क्वचिदेतदहंकारः क्वचिच्चित्तमिति स्मृतम्॥ क्वचित्प्रकृतिरित्युक्तं क्वचिन्मायेति कल्पितम्। क्वचिन्मलमिति प्रोक्तं क्वचित्कर्मेति संस्मृतम्॥ क्वचिद्बन्ध इति ख्यातं क्वचित्पुर्यष्टकं स्मृतम्। प्रोक्तं क्वचिदविद्येति क्वचिदिच्छेति संमतम्॥

This very soul is known somewhere as mind, somewhere as knowledge (Jñāna), the action, ego and somewhere as mind. It is called somewhere nature (Prakṛti) and as illusion (Māyā). It is called somewhere ties and somewhere, the micro body. Further, somewhere it is called ignorance (Avidyā) and somewhere the desire.

इमं संसारमखिलमाशापाशविधायकम्। दधदन्तःफलैर्हीनं वटधाना वटं यथा॥ १३३॥

The weaver of the hope dragnet holds the entire world the same way as the seed of fruitless banyan holds the banyan tree.

चिन्तानलशिखादग्धं कोपाजगरचर्वितम्। कामाब्धिकल्लोलरतं विस्मृतात्मपितामहम्॥ १३४॥

This mind was signed by the flame of fire in the form of worry, bitten by the anger python and trapped in the waves of the lust ocean. It has forgotten its grandfather, the soul.

समुद्धर मनो ब्रह्मन्मातङ्गमिव कर्दमात्। एवं जीवाश्रिता भावा भवभावनयाहिताः॥ १३५॥ ब्रह्मणा कल्पिताकारा लक्षशोऽप्यथ कोटिशः। संख्यातीताः पुरा जाता जायन्तेऽद्यापि चाभितः॥ उत्पतस्यन्तेऽपि चैवान्ये कणौघा इव निर्झरात्। केचित्प्रथमजन्मानः केचिज्जन्मशताधिकाः॥ १३७॥ केचिच्चासंख्यजन्मानः केचिद्द्वित्रिभवान्तराः। केचित्किन्नरगन्धर्वविद्याधरमहोरगाः॥ १३८॥

O Brahman! Do upliftment of this mind alike the elephant trapped in the marshes. The dependent spirit of loving soul have already brought in many millions, crores and uncountable forms under the imagination of Brahma. There too are originated continuously and will also be originated like the droplets from a fountain in future. Some have originated first time, some more than hundred time, some numerous time and some have brought in two or three times. Some are originated in the form of Kinnara, Gandharva, Vidyādhara and Nāga (serpents).

केचिदर्केन्दुवरुणास्त्र्यक्षाधोक्षजपद्मजाः। केचिद्ब्राह्मणभूपालवैश्यशूद्रगणाः स्थिताः॥ १३९॥

केचित्तृणौषधीवृक्षफलमूलपतङ्गकाः। केचित्कदम्बजम्बीरसालतालतमालकाः॥ १४०॥

केचिन्महेन्द्रमलयसह्यमन्दरमेरवः। केचित्क्षारोदधिक्षीरघृतेक्षुजलराशयः॥ १४१॥

Some have held the form of Sun, Moon, Varuṇa, Hari, Śiva and Brahma. Some are in the form of Brahman, Kṣatriya, Vaiśya, Śūdra etc. Similarly, some are in the form of medicine, straw, tree, fruit, root and the leaves while some are in the form of lemon, kadamba, mango, palm and tamāla tree. Some are in the form of the mountains namely, Mahendra, Malaya, Sahya, Mandara, Meru etc. Some others are in the form of saline sea, some are milk, ghee, cane juice and the water form.

केचिद्विशालाः ककुभः केचिन्नद्यो महारयाः। विहरन्त्युच्चकैः केचिन्निपतन्त्युत्पतन्ति च॥ १४२॥

कन्दुका इव हस्तेन मृत्युनाऽविरतं हताः। भुक्त्वा जन्मसहस्राणि भूयः संसारसंकटे॥ १४३॥

पतन्ति केचिदबुधाः संप्राप्यापि विवेकताम्। दिक्कालाद्यनवच्छिन्नमात्मतत्त्वं स्वशक्तितः॥ १४४॥

लीलयैव यदादत्ते दिक्कालकलितं वपुः। तदेव जीवपर्यायवासनावेशतः परम्॥ १४५॥

मनः संपद्यते लोलं कलनाकलनोन्मुखम्। कलयन्ती मनःशक्तिरादौ भावयति क्षणात्॥ १४६॥

आकाशभावनामच्छां शब्दबीजरसोन्मुखीम्। ततस्तद्घनतां यातं घनस्पन्दक्रमान्मनः॥ १४७॥

भावयत्यनिलस्पन्दं स्पर्शबीजरसोन्मुखम्। ताभ्यामाकाशवाताभ्यां दृढाभ्यासवशात्ततः॥ १४८॥

Some are flown in the form of rivers flowing with torrents, some are in the form of extended directions, some lift up, some fall and some again move upward. Like the ball throwing up and down in the hands, some rise up and fall by the strokes of death. There are numerous other persons too who are scholars and always perform the great deeds (benevolent to all) still they move frequently under the cycle of birth and death inspite of already born and died thousand times. When the element of soul un-intercepted by the time and directions holds the body by its own power, this living soul then holds the form of caprice mind and having enslaved to the passions starts making resolutions. That mind-power with resolution imagines the clear sky within seconds and the seeds of words start sprouting within it. Subsequently, that very mind is engrossed in the imagination of deep vibration and then light vibration having turned in excessive density.

शब्दस्पर्शस्वरूपाभ्यां संघर्षाज्जन्यतेऽनलः। रूपतन्मात्रसहितं त्रिभिस्तैः सह संमितम्॥ १४९॥

मनस्तादृग्गुणगतं रसतन्मात्रवेदनम्। क्षणाच्चेतत्यपां शैत्यं जलसंवित्ततो भवेत्॥ १५०॥

The seed in the form of touch are germinated from that mind. Subsequently, the fire is originated as a result of friction between the ether in the form of word and touch form and the air which is caused by virtue of firm exercise. The mind soaked with the three properties (Sattva, Rajas and Tamas) imagines the cold water within a second while perceiving the essence Tanmātra and thus, he feels the touch of water.

[The fire is originated in the form of electrical charge owing to friction caused by the force of air in the sky. The factors of air (i.e. Hydrogen and oxygen) and turned into water with the combination of fire with them. The science can understand this action in the formidable form of matter while the seers perceive it even in the form of micro Tanmātras too.]

ततस्तादृग्गुणगतं मनो भावयति क्षणात्। गन्धतन्मात्रमेतस्माद्भूमिसंवित्ततो भवेत्॥ १५१॥
अथेत्थंभूततन्मात्रवेष्टितं तनुतां जहत्। वपुर्वह्निकणाकारं स्फुरितं व्योम्नि पश्यति॥ १५२॥

The mind then within next second imagines the small Tanmātra by virtue of its four properties (guṇas). Similarly as a compound of five properties, that mind sees the body shining in the shape of fire balls (flames) after giving up its micro form.

[The saint herein is revealing the cycle of development from the micro to the formidable form. The system of evolution of the breathing cells (Prāṇamaya-kośa) has been told in the form of formidable fire flames than the micro mental cell (kośa). This breathing from mind too takes the form of formidable body when it is duly matured. The saint is telling herein this process analogues to melting the pieces of gold and casting them in a specific shape.]

अहंकारकलायुक्तं बुद्धिबीजसमन्वितम्। तत्पुर्यष्टकमित्युक्तं भूतहृत्पद्मषट्पदम्॥ १५३॥
तस्मिंस्तु तीव्रसंवेगाद्भावयद्भासुरं वपुः। स्थूलतामेति पाकेन मनो बिल्वफलं यथा॥ १५४॥

That body with the elocution (kalā) of ego and the seed of wisdom is called Puryaṣṭaka. It is like the bee murmuring in the lotus hearts of creatures. The mind gets formidable shape when on the state of maturity (Pāka). It imagines a body full of splendour of acute sentiments like the fruit of the Bilva (A tree whose leaves are offered to lord Śiva).

मूषास्थद्रुतहेमाभं स्फुरितं विमलाम्बरे। संनिवेशमथादत्ते तत्तेजः स्वस्वभावतः॥ १५५॥
ऊर्ध्वं शिरः पिण्डमयमधः पादमयं तथा। पार्श्वयोर्हस्तसंस्थानं मध्ये चोदरधर्मिणम्॥ १५६॥
कालेन स्फुटतामेत्य भवत्यमलविग्रहम्। बुद्धिसत्त्वबलोत्साहविज्ञानैश्वर्यसंस्थितः॥ १५७॥

That splendour starts crystalling accuracy to this nature in the clear ether by getting shining like the melted gold in Mūṣā (used for melting the gold). It gradually end within a certain time frame, gets full development and turns into the shape of a human-body. At the upper side, it gets the shape of head, shape of feet in lower, arms shape collaterally and belly shape in the middle portion. It than gets the wisdom, semen, strength, courage, conscience and the luxuries.

स एव भगवान्ब्रह्मा सर्वलोकपितामहः। अवलोक्य वपुर्ब्रह्मा कान्तमात्मीयमुत्तमम्॥ १५८॥
चिन्तामभ्येत्य भगवांस्त्रिकालामलदर्शनः। एतस्मिन्परमाकाशे चिन्मात्रैकात्मरूपिणि॥ १५९॥
अदृष्टपारपर्यन्ते प्रथमं किं भवेदिति। इति चिन्तितवान्ब्रह्मा सद्योजातामलात्मदृक्॥ १६०॥

That body becomes the grand father (Pitāmaha) lord Brahmā of all worlds. Lord Brahmā, knower of the Past, Future and Present prima-facie thought the moment while observing his attractive and the best complexion that neither beginning nor end to this supreme ether in the form of cinmātra soul, is seen. He got the holy conscious of soul (Dṛṣti) immediately when he thought of the first creation. (What should be done at first?)

अपश्यत्सर्गवृन्दानि समतीतान्यनेकशः। स्मरत्यथो स सकलान्सर्वधर्मगुणक्रमात्॥ १६१॥

लीलया कल्पयामास चित्राः संकल्पतः प्रजाः। नानाचारसमारम्भा गन्धर्वनगरं यथा॥ १६२॥

तासां स्वर्गापवर्गार्थं धर्मकामार्थसिद्धये। अनन्तानि विचित्राणि शास्त्राणि समकल्पयत्॥ १६३॥

He saw numerous sarga (scenes) of the creation (Sṛṣti) made in the past. As a result of this vision, the system of all religious properties (guṇa) were emerged in his memory. He originated the subject of numerous colour and complexion bearing subject in the space like gandharvaloka full of resolution. For accomplishment of their four industries i.e. Dharma, Artha, Kāma and Mokṣa, he made the imagination (composition) of different śāstras preaching numerous excellent issues and the heavens and hells as well.

विरञ्चिरूपान्मनसः कल्पितत्वाज्जगत्स्थितेः। तावत्स्थितिरियं प्रोक्ता तन्नाशे नाशमाप्नुयात्॥ १६४॥

न जायते न म्रियते क्वचित्किंचित्कदाचन। परमार्थेन विप्रेन्द्र मिथ्या सर्वं तु दृश्यते॥ १६५॥

कोशमाशाभुजङ्गानां संसाराडम्बरं त्यज। असदेतदिति ज्ञात्वा मातृभावं निवेशय॥ १६६॥

The existence of world being the imagination of the Brahma from mind, its life is correlated to the life of Brahma. O best Brāhmaṇa! Nobody neither gets life nor is dead anywhere. It is all false apparently seen. The world full of illusions (Prapañca) is a cage of serpents in the form of hope. It is all good to stable in Mātṛbhāva (spirit) by considering it a fallacy.

गन्धर्वनगरस्यार्थे भूषितेऽभूषिते तथा। अविद्यांशे सुतादौ वा कः क्रमः सुखदुःखयोः॥ १६७॥

धनदारेषु वृद्धेषु दुःखयुक्तं न तुष्टता। वृद्धायां मोहमायायां कः समाश्वासवानिह॥ १६८॥

यैरेव जायते रागो मूर्खस्याधिकतां गतैः। तैरेव भागैः प्राज्ञस्य विराग उपजायते॥ १६९॥

The city of Gandharva whether adorned or not, it still is trivial. Similarly, these sons of Avidyā (ignorance) etc. are also illusion. It is cause of pain to attach with them. It is redundant to worry for the increase of wealth and wife etc. There is no scope for satisfaction at all in it. Who has become able to attain peace and pleasure as a result of their growth in this world? The scholars remain unattached to the things by whose growth the foolish people feel pleasure.

अतो निदाघ तत्त्वज्ञ व्यवहारेषु संसृतेः। नष्टं नष्टमुपेक्षस्व प्राप्तं प्राप्तमुपाहर॥ १७०॥

अनागतानां भोगानामवाञ्छनमकृत्रिमम्। आगतानां च संभोग इति पण्डितलक्षणम्॥ १७१॥

शुद्धं सदसतोर्मध्यं पदं बुद्ध्वावलम्ब्य च। सबाह्याभ्यन्तरं दृश्यं मा गृहाण विमुञ्च मा॥ १७२॥

O metaphysician Nidāgha! One should accept at ease the things available in this world and give up the desire for the things which are not available. It is prudency that one should not hanker for the things that reccived and utilise the things easily available. By due analysation between the true and false and resorting to that what is true and not, either entertaining of giving up the exterior as also interior scenes is the prudency.

यस्य चेच्छा तथाऽनिच्छा ज्ञस्य कर्मणि तिष्ठतः। न तस्य लिप्यते प्रज्ञा पद्मपत्रमिवाम्बुभिः॥ १७३॥

यदि ते नेन्द्रियार्थश्रीः स्पन्दते हृदि वै द्विज। तदा विज्ञातविज्ञेयः समुत्तीर्णो भवार्णवात्॥ १७४॥

उच्चैःपदाय परया प्रज्ञया वासनागणात्। पुष्पाद्गन्धमपोह्यारं चेतोवृत्तिं पृथक्कुरु॥ १७५॥

As the lotus petal does not get the tint of mud even having immersed there, the scholars treating the willing and un-willing as equal, do not attached to then while performing the deeds. O Brāhmaṇa! You have definitely crossed the worldly sea by acquiring the knowledge of the knowable thing if the sensory issues are not stirring in your heart. The great position can be attained if the propensity of mind is immediately removed from the odour of the passion flowers by developing the special knowledge.

संसाराम्बुनिधावस्मिन्वासनाम्बुपरिप्लुते। ये प्रज्ञानावमारूढास्ते तीर्णाः पण्डिताः परे॥ १७६॥

न त्यजन्ति न वाञ्छन्ति व्यवहारं जगद्गतम्। सर्वमेवानुवर्तन्ते पारावारविदो जनाः॥ १७७॥

अनन्तस्यात्मतत्त्वस्य सत्तासामान्यरूपिणः। चितश्चेत्योन्मुखत्वं यत्तत्संकल्पाङ्कुरं विदुः॥ १७८॥

लेशतः प्राप्तसत्ताकः स एव घनतां शनैः। याति चित्तत्वमापूर्य दृढं जाड्याय मेघवत्॥ १७९॥

The learned have crossed this ocean of world waving with the endless water of passions who are sailing on the boat of true knowledge. The knower of the worldly illusions neither give up the worldly dealing nor desire for the same. They instead, remain reluctant to the same. The scholars have considered the sprouting of resolution as the attachment of the sensitivity in the form of element of soul with the worldly issues. That resolutions gradually turn into thick layer when they get even a little space. They later on become firm as the clouds and create the inert position when they fully grip (cover) the ether of mind.

भावयन्ति चितिश्चैत्यं व्यतिरिक्तमिवात्मनः। संकल्पतामिवायाति बीजमङ्कुरतामिव॥ १८०॥

संकल्पनं हि संकल्पः स्वयमेव प्रजायते। वर्धते स्वयमेवाशु दुःखाय न सुखाय यत्॥ १८१॥

मा संकल्पय संकल्पं मा भावं भावय स्थितौ। संकल्पनाशने यत्तो न भूयोऽननुगच्छति॥ १८२॥

He gets the state of resolution by treating the sensitive issues separate from him like the sprouting state of a seed. Its action by resolution automatically is revealed and it gets rapid growth. However it causes sorrow and not any way the cause for pleasure. Resist the action of resolution that originates in the mind. He should not imagine the material affection for them. The persons who already have determined for destroying the resolution, should not again follow the same.

भावनाऽभावमात्रेण संकल्पः क्षीयते स्वयम्। संकल्पेनैव संकल्पं मनसैव मनो मुने॥ १८३॥

छित्त्वा स्वात्मनि तिष्ठ त्वं किमेतावति दुष्करम्। यथैवेदं नभः शून्यं जगच्छून्यं तथैव हि॥ १८४॥

तण्डुलस्य यथा चर्म यथा ताम्रस्य कालिमा। नश्यति क्रियया विप्र पुरुषस्य तथा मलम्।। १८५।।

जीवस्य तण्डुलस्येव मलं सहजमप्यलम्। नश्यत्येव न संदेहस्तस्मादुद्योगवान्भवेत्।। १८६।।

The resolution automatically is destroyed when the affection is abandoned. O great hermit! The resolution through resolution and the mind through mind should be destroyed. This world too is void like the ether. O Brāhmaṇa! As the dark tint of copper and the husk of paddy is destroyed by adopting the special procedure, the defects of a man can be removed through the prolong exercise. The defects within the living soul are natural like the hust of the paddy however there can not be doubted on possibility of their distinction if due endeavour is made. Hence, attempt to be industrious person by setting upon the nature of soul and nothing like impossible is here. The defects covering the sensitivity are compared with the husk of paddy. As the rice becomes eatable when decorticated while it is necessary to be for reproduction, the scholar entertains it by removing the defects and the possibility of falling in rebirth cycle is also held-out.

Chapter - VI

अन्तरास्थां परित्यज्य भावश्रीं भावनामयीम्। योऽसि सोऽसि जगत्यस्मिल्लीलया विहरानघ।। १।।

सर्वत्राहमकर्तेति दृढभावनयानया। परमामृतनाम्नी सा समतैवावशिष्यते।। २।।

O innocent one! move with gaiety and in your real nature in this world by giving up the inner believe and the spirit of affection. Treat yourselves Akartta everywhere and thus, the uniformity of supreme immortal name is not left as a result of such detached spirit for action.

खेदोल्लासविलासेषु स्वात्मकर्तृतयैकया। स्वसंकल्पे क्षयं याते समतैवावशिष्यते।। ३।।

समता सर्वभावेषु यासौ सत्यपरा स्थितिः। तस्यामवस्थितं चित्तं न भूयो जन्मभाग्भवेत्।। ४।।

The sorrows and exhilaration as also gaiety are self-creation of the man. The spirit of equity only remains when the resolution is decayed. The cycle of birth and death is ceased when the actual position of equity among all matters is held with loyalty within the mind.

अथवा सर्वकर्तृत्वमकर्तृत्वं च वै मुने। सर्वं त्यक्त्वा मनः पीत्वा योऽसि सोऽसि स्थिरो भव।। ५।।

शेषस्थिरसमाधानो येन त्यजसि तत्त्यज। चिन्मनःकलनाकारं प्रकाशतिमिरादिकम्।। ६।।

वासनां वासितारं च प्राणस्पन्दनपूर्वकम्। समूलमखिलं त्यक्त्वा व्योमसाम्यः प्रशान्तधीः।। ७।।

O hermit! be stable firmly in your natural nature by controlling the mind and giving up all duties and non-duties (kartṛy and Akartavya). Give up then the spirit that enables you developing detachment and do meditation. The sensitivity too has held the shape of resolution and it too is in the form of light and darkness. You therefore, should become innocent and peaceful mind like the ether by giving up entirely the passions, coincide the beating of breathing (vibration due to respiration).

हृदयात्संपरित्यज्य सर्ववासनपङ्क्तयः। यस्तिष्ठति गतव्यग्रः स मुक्तः परमेश्वरः।। ८।।

दृष्टं द्रष्टव्यमखिलं भ्रान्तं भ्रान्त्या दिशो दश। युक्त्या वै चरतो ज्ञस्य संसारो गोष्पदाकृतिः॥ ९॥

सबाह्याभ्यन्तरे देहे ह्यध ऊर्ध्वं च दिक्षु च। इत आत्मा ततोऽप्यात्मा नास्त्यनात्ममयं जगत्॥ १०॥

The man is only in peace and liberty who gives up all affections from the heart. He is only the supreme god. He is competent observing the worth seeing matters due to confusion while strolling in the ten directions. The world becomes worth crossing easily like the cow hoof for the scholars who bring substantial reforms in their practical attitude and attempts. This world does not become without soul for him because the soul is existed in and out of body, up and down as also in all directions.

न तदस्ति न यत्राहं न तदस्ति न तन्मयम्। किमन्यदभिवाञ्छामि सर्वं सच्चिन्मयं ततम्॥ ११॥

समस्तं खल्विदं ब्रह्म सर्वमात्मेदमाततम्। अहमन्य इदं चान्यदिति भ्रान्तिं त्यजानघ॥ १२॥

तते ब्रह्मघने नित्ये संभवन्ति न कल्पिताः। न शोकोऽस्ति न मोहोऽस्ति न जरास्ति न जन्म वा॥

O innocent! Give up the confused thinking that accepts "It is other" "I am different" (i.e. discriminative spirit). There is no place left where my existence is nil. If existence is void it is only of the matter. When the truth and cinmaya element is existed everywhere, what is the thing that should be desired by me? This all is in the form of Brahma and the soul is extended within all. There is no possibility of imagination in the Brahma who is omnipresent and always full of truth mind and pleasure (Saccidānanda). This element is beyond the agony, affection, old age and birth.

यदस्तीह तदेवास्ति विज्वरो भव सर्वदा। यथाप्राप्तानुभवतः सर्वत्रानभिवाञ्छनात्॥ १४॥

त्यागादानपरित्यागी विज्वरो भव सर्वदा। यस्येदं जन्म पाश्चात्त्यं तमाश्वेव महामते॥ १५॥

विशन्ति विद्या विमला मुक्ता वेणुमिवोत्तमम्। विरक्तमनसां सम्यक्स्वप्रसङ्गादुदाहृतम्॥ १६॥

द्रष्टृदृश्यसमायोगात्प्रत्ययानन्दनिश्चयः। यस्तं स्वमात्मतत्त्वोत्थं निष्पन्दं समुपास्महे॥ १७॥

द्रष्टृदर्शनदृश्यानि त्यक्त्वा वासनया सह। दर्शनप्रत्ययाभासमात्मानं समुपास्महे॥ १८॥

Whatever is existed in the element of soul, that is only everything. One should therefore, live happily always and everywhere without tempting for any material thing and accepting reluctantly whatever is available under the easy process. Thus, one should live free from agony under the spirit that neither gives up nor accepts. O great genius! The pure learning is inserted in the mind of a person, analoguous to the pearl of the best quality who is in his last birth (viz. who will not hence forth get rebirth). The scholars full of the spirit of detachment have revealed by virtue of their conscious acquired by experience that the feeling of gaiety to the observer as a result of the scene observed; is the vibration arisen from the element of soul to which we worship with the best way.

द्वयोर्मध्यगतं नित्यमस्तिनास्तीति पक्षयोः। प्रकाशनं प्रकाशानामात्मानं समुपास्महे॥ १९॥

We are worshipper (devotee) of the ever luminating soul by giving up the trio i.e. observer, scene and the observation (looking at the scene) alongwith the thinking for the passions. We worship the everlasting soul that gives light to the light existing amid the Āsti (it is existing) and Nāsti (It has no existence).

संत्यज्य हृद्गुहेशानं देवमन्यं प्रयान्ति ये। ते रत्नमभिवाञ्छन्ति त्यक्तहस्तस्थकौस्तुभाः॥ २०॥

उत्थितानुत्थितानेतानिन्द्रियारीन्पुनः पुनः। हन्याद्विवेकदण्डेन वज्रेणेव हरिर्गिरीन्॥ २१॥

That element of soul is existing within our hearts in the form of Maheśvara. The people doing endeavour for attainment of other thing otherwise than this soul, desire for other gem leaving behind the Kaustubha maṇi (the best gem) already in their possession. Like spliting up the mountains by Indra though He blows of thunderbolt, the enemies either mighty or weak, are to be hurt of using the stick of discretion.

संसाररात्रिदुःस्वप्ने शून्ये देहमये भ्रमे। सर्वमेवापवित्रं तद्दृष्टं संसृतिविभ्रमम्॥ २२॥

अज्ञानोपहतो बाल्ये यौवने वनिताहतः। शेषे कलत्रचिन्तार्तः किं करोति नराधमः॥ २३॥

सतोऽसत्ता स्थिता मूर्ध्नि रम्याणां मूर्ध्न्यरम्यता। सुखानां मूर्ध्नि दुःखानि किमेकं संश्रयाम्यहम्॥ २४

Whatever the extension of the illusion is seen in the mirage of this inert and nightmare form body in the night of world, all that is beyond the purity, the living organism gripped of ignorance in childhood, hurt by wife in youth and worried of wife and sons etc. at the last stage cannot do anything good for him. The fallacy is ruling on the head of the truth, the ugly on the beauty and the sorrow on the pleasures. To whom should I resort in the circumstance?

येषां निमेषणोन्मेषौ जगतः प्रलयोदयौ। तादृशाः पुरुषा यान्ति मादृशां गणनैव का॥ २५॥

संसार एव दुःखानां सीमान्त इति कथ्यते। तन्मध्ये पतिते देहे सुखमासाद्यते कथम्॥ २६॥

What to say of the common persons like me when the greatest person (Puruṣa) whose eye opening and closing does the creation and destruction of this world too meet to the cruel death? This mortal world too has been considered the climax of sorrows. How their pleasure can be felt by the body born in such world?

प्रबुद्धोऽस्मि प्रबुद्धोऽस्मि दुष्टश्चोरोऽयमात्मनः। मनो नाम निहन्म्येनं मनसास्मि चिरं हृतः॥ २७॥

मा खेदं भज हेयेषु नोपादेयपरो भव। हेयादेयदृशौ त्यक्त्वा शेषस्थः सुस्थिरो भव॥ २८॥

I have become known, I am awakened. The wicked thief which has stolen my soul is nobody else but my defective mind only. It has enslaved me by stealing from myself since long past which cannot be ascertained. I am now awaken. Hence, I will destroy it. Don't be sad for hatred matters and don't tempt for the useful matters as well. Be stable on the residual (Śeṣa) by giving up the spirit calculating hatred and useful.

निराशता निर्भयता नित्यता समता ज्ञता। निरीहता निष्क्रियता सौम्यता निर्विकल्पता॥ २९॥

धृतिर्मैत्री मनस्तुष्टिर्मृदुता मृदुभाषिता। हेयोपादेयनिर्मुक्ते ज्ञे तिष्ठन्त्यपवासनम्॥ ३०॥

गृहीततृष्णाशबरीवासनाजालमाततम्। संसारवारिप्रसृतं चिन्तातन्तुभिराततम्॥ ३१॥

अनया तीक्ष्णया तात छिन्धि बुद्धिशलाकया। वात्ययेवाम्बुदं जालं छित्त्वा तिष्ठ तते पदे॥ ३२॥

The despair, fearlessness, stability, smartness, equity, detachment, inactivity, modesty, courage, absoluteness, amity, contentment, politeness, and humble speech etc. properties (guṇa) reside in the conscious person who is beyond the accessibility of hatred and useful considerations. You have been gripped in the network of passion made by the Bhīlanī (rude woman) of temptation and this world as mirage has been spreaded all around by the rays of worry. O son Nidāgha! As the network of clouds is scattered by the storm, enshrine in your extended (fully developed) nature by shattering that network by the blows of this sharp edge spear made of knowledge.

मनसैव मनश्छित्त्वा कुठारेणेव पादपम्। पदं पावनमासाद्य सद्य एव स्थिरो भव॥ ३३॥

तिष्ठन्गच्छन्स्वपञ्जाग्रन्निवसन्नुत्पतन्पतन्। असदेवेदमित्यन्तं निश्चित्यास्थां परित्यज॥ ३४॥

दृश्यमाश्रयसीदं चेत्तत्सच्चित्तोऽसि बन्धवान्। दृश्यं संत्यजसीदं चेत्तदाऽचित्तोऽसि मोक्षवान्॥

As an axe cuts down the tree when it is fixed on a handle made of tree, be stable by attaining the immortal position immediately by cutting the mind through the mind. Always faith firmly on overall fallacy of this world when you stand, walk, awake, sleep, reside, sit, rise and fall. Give up the faith on the visible matters. Abandon the faith of the apparent or visible matters because it will bind you if resorted to these visible matters and you become able for emancipation if the visible matters are abandoned in toto and the mind is made void.

नाहं नेदमिति ध्यायंस्तिष्ठ त्वमचलाचलः। आत्मनो जगतश्चान्तर्द्रष्टृदृश्यदशान्तरे॥ ३६॥

दर्शनाख्यं स्वमात्मानं सर्वदा भावयन्भव। स्वाद्यस्वादकसंत्यक्तं स्वाद्यस्वादकमध्यगम्॥ ३७॥

स्वदनं केवलं ध्यायन्परमात्ममयो भव। अवलम्ब्य निरालम्बं मध्येमध्ये स्थिरो भव॥ ३८॥

Reside undeviated like a mountain by thinking that neither I myself nor this world is consider yourself as an observing soul between the soul and the world and in the situation of observer and the observed (scene). Be enshrine in the form of supreme soul by mere feeling the taste amid the tasty matter and the person (karttā) enjoying taste and not considering yourself the man who enjoys the taste. Stable on a place by resorting to independent position in between the process.

रज्जुबद्धा विमुच्यन्ते तृष्णाबद्धा न केनचित्। तस्मान्निदाघ तृष्णां त्वं त्यज संकल्पवर्जनात्॥ ३९॥

एतामहंभावमयीमपुण्यां छित्त्वाऽनहंभावशलाकयैव। स्वभावजां भव्यभवान्तभूमौ भव प्रशान्ताखिलभूतभीतिः॥ ४०॥

अहमेषां पदार्थानामेते च मम जीवितम्। नाहमेभिर्विना किंचिन्न मयैते विना किल॥ ४१॥

इत्यन्तर्निश्चयं त्यक्त्वा विचार्य मनसा सह। नाहं पदार्थस्य न मे पदार्थ इति भाविते॥ ४२॥

अन्तःशीतलया बुद्ध्या कुर्वतो लीलया क्रियाम्। यो नूनं वासनात्यागो ध्येयो ब्रह्मन्प्रकीर्तितः॥ ४३॥

The persons tied by cord may be freed but the creatures tied with temptation can not be freed any ways. O son Nidāgha! Do attempts to leave temptation by giving up the resolution. Walk in the beautiful world of supreme mission in a fearless state by penetrating this temptation full of ego and sins arisen by nature through the spear beyond the ego. I am made of all these matters and these are my life, I am nothing without them and these too are nothing without me, are the resolutions worth giving up from your inner mind. Make a firm spirit and imagine in mind that I am not made of these matters and these are not mine. O Brahman! The forgo of passion by thinking patiently and with stable mind and performing the duties (deeds) in general manner, is really stated as the real objective (intention).

सर्वं समतया बुद्ध्या यः कृत्वा वासनाक्षयम्। जहाति निर्ममो देहं नेयोऽसौ वासनाक्षयः॥ ४४॥

अहंकारमयीं त्यक्त्वा वासनां लीलयैव यः। तिष्ठति ध्येयसंत्यागी स जीवन्मुक्त उच्यते॥ ४५॥

The person who becomes free from the sense of affection by giving up the passion for ever and establishing the sense of equity, only he can abandon the physical ties. The giving up of passion is hence, the supreme duty. The man is only liberated soul who gives up the passion full of ego and enshrines after duly giving up the desired thing.

निर्मूलं कलनां त्यक्त्वा वासनां यः शमं गतः। ज्ञेयं त्यागमिमं विद्धि मुक्तं तं ब्राह्मणोत्तमम्॥ ४६॥

The person attaining to the supreme power by leaving entirely the passion in the form of resolution is worth admiration for such sacrifice. Consider only him the actually liberated and excellent among the persons known to Brahma.

द्वावेतौ ब्रह्मतां यातौ द्वावेतौ विगतज्वरौ। आपतत्सु यथाकालं सुखदुःखेष्वनारतौ॥ ४७॥

संन्यासियोगिनौ दान्तौ विद्धि शान्तौ मुनीश्वर। ईप्सितानीप्सिते न स्तो यस्यान्तर्वर्तिदृष्टिषु॥ ४८॥

सुषुप्तवद्यश्चरति स जीवन्मुक्त उच्यते। हर्षामर्षभयक्रोधकामकार्पण्यदृष्टिभिः॥ ४९॥

न हृष्यति ग्लायति यः परामर्शविवर्जितः। बाह्यार्थवासनोद्भूता तृष्णा बद्धेति कथ्यते॥ ५०॥

Both of these attain to the element of Brahma and these only are free from the worldly fevers (pains). O hermit! The recluse exercising Sāma and dama and the yogis do not suffer from vicissitude bestowed any time. Who has given up the state where desires are felt or hate is expressed, who lives in the state of dormance, who is without passions, is called the liberated soul. He neither becomes happy nor sad in the event of pleasure, sorrow, fear, anger, lust and miseriness. The temptation arising from the exterior issues has been stated fastening.

सर्वार्थवासनोन्मुक्ता तृष्णा मुक्तेति भण्यते। इदमस्तु ममेत्यन्तमिच्छां प्रार्थनयान्विताम्॥ ५१॥

तां तीक्ष्णशृङ्खलां विद्धि दुःखजन्मभयप्रदाम्। तामेतां सर्वभावेषु सत्स्वसत्सु च सर्वदा॥ ५२॥

संत्यज्य परमोदारं पदमेति महामनाः। बन्धास्थामथ मोक्षास्थां सुखदुःखदशामपि॥ ५३॥

त्यक्त्वा सदसदास्थां त्वं तिष्ठाक्षुब्धमहाब्धिवत्। जायते निश्चयः साधो पुरुषस्य चतुर्विधः॥ ५४॥

आपादमस्तकमहं मातापितृविनिर्मितः। इत्येको निश्चयो ब्रह्मन्बन्धायासविलोकनात्॥ ५५॥

अतीतः सर्वभावेभ्यो वालाग्रादप्यहं तनुः। इति द्वितीयो मोक्षाय निश्चयो जायते सताम्॥ ५६॥

जगज्जालपदार्थात्मा सर्व एवाहमक्षयः। तृतीयो निश्चयश्चोक्तो मोक्षायैव द्विजोत्तम॥ ५७॥

The temptation without the passion for all kinds of issues, ensures emancipation. The idea with desire for any thing only becomes cause for sorrow, fear and birth as well. Treat it as gross binding nature. The people of great soul, attain the position of supreme liberty by giving-up the desire/ambition entirely for the matters in the form of truth and untrue. Enshrine like the pacific ocean by abandoning forever the faith on the entity of binding, emancipation, and the faith/belief on the true and false in the form of pleasure and grief. O great soul! There are four kinds of determination made by a man. The first out of them is that I have been originated as result of parents harmony from the head to feet. O Brahman! now listen to the second determination which is made while watching at the sorrows in binding– "I am the soul in more micro form than the foreportion of a hair and is beyond all worldly illusions and defects." This determination gives emancipation to the scholars. O Brahman! the third determination is that– "I am the soul of all inert and living matter of this world." I am in universal form and un-decaying. This third determination too becomes the cause for emancipation of the man definitely.

अहं जगद्वा सकलं शून्यं व्योम समं सदा। एवमेष चतुर्थोऽपि निश्चयो मोक्षसिद्धिदः॥५८॥
एतेषां प्रथमः प्रोक्तस्तृष्णया बन्धयोग्यया। शुद्धतृष्णास्त्रयः स्वच्छा जीवन्मुक्ता विलासिनः॥५९
सर्वं चाप्यहमेवेति निश्चयो यो महामते। तमादाय विषादाय न भूयो जायते मतिः॥६०॥

Now listen to the fourth determination. The fourth determination i.e. "I or this world and everything is void like the ether" provides the man with emancipation. Out of these four determinations, the first is of fastening nature and with the binding of temptation. The other three determinations are with the clean and pure temptation (free from binding) and the man with three determinations enjoys the liberty and the element of souls. O the best genius hermit! "I myself is everything" is the determination that enables the wisdom to give-up the misery.

शून्यं तत्प्रकृतिर्माया ब्रह्मविज्ञानमित्यपि। शिवः पुरुष ईशानो नित्यमात्मेति कथ्यते॥६१॥
द्वैताद्वैतसमुद्भूतैर्जगन्निर्माणलीलया। परमात्ममयी शक्तिरद्वैतैव विजृम्भते॥६२॥
सर्वातीतपदालम्बी परिपूर्णैकचिन्मयः। नोद्वेगी न च तुष्टात्मा संसारे नावसीदति॥६३॥

The void (zero) known as soul too is called nature (Prakṛti) illusion, knowledge of Brahma, Puruṣa, Īśāna, Śiva, everlasting and knowledge of Brahma. The exclusive power (Dvaita) in the form of supreme soul is developing with the art of creation of the things originated from dvaita and advaita in this world. The people neither do any enterprise (work) nor satisfy by resorting to the position of soul beyond all kinds of illusion and love in the state of Cinmaya, do not fall prey of the worldly agony.

प्राप्तकर्मकरो नित्यं शत्रुमित्रसमानदृक्। ईहितानीहितैर्मुक्तो न शोचति न काङ्क्षति॥६४॥
सर्वस्याभिमतं वक्ता चोदितः पेशलोक्तिमान्। आशयज्ञश्च भूतानां संसारे नावसीदति॥६५॥

O son! the man who performs the works received in routine, looks equally the enemy and friend, freed from desire and hate, neither laments nor desire for any of the things, softspoken, responding humbly to the questions raised and competent to know the spirits of all creatures, does not fall to prey of the worldly sorrows.

पूर्वां दृष्टिमवष्टभ्य ध्येयत्यागविलासिनीम्। जीवन्मुक्ततया स्वस्थो लोके विहर विज्वरः॥६६॥

अन्तःसंत्यक्तसर्वाशो वीतरागो विवासनः। बहिःसर्वसमाचारो लोके विहर विज्वरः॥६७॥

Walk in this world like a liberated soul with inner-eyes, keeping free from luxury, without falling prey of worldly pains and by enshrining on the inner soul. Always be active while moving in this world happily, vomiting out the hopes of all kinds from heart, free from affection and passion and complying with all worldly customs and traditions by exterior mind.

बहिःकृत्रिमसंरम्भो हृदि संरम्भवर्जितः। कर्ता बहिरकर्तान्तर्लोके विहर शुद्धधीः॥६८॥

त्यक्ताहंकृतिराश्वस्तमतिराकाशशोभनः। अगृहीतकलङ्काङ्को लोके विहर शुद्धधीः॥६९॥

Move in this world everywhere by making the heart free from anger but its revelation artificially outward, and be subject (Karttā) of deed outward while Akarttā (the state that diminishes ego) inward. Don't loose the place of mind and by giving-up the ego, be free from the darkness of enigmity for ever. Walk in the world by attaining the pure and rectified life as sky and the pure and true wisdom.

उदारः पेशलाचारः सर्वाचारानुवृत्तिमान्। अन्तःसङ्गपरित्यागी बहिःसंभारवानिव॥७०॥

अन्तर्वैराग्यमादाय बहिराशोन्मुखेहितः। अयं बन्धुरयं नेति गणना लघुचेतसाम्॥७१॥

उदारचरितानां तु वसुधैव कुटुम्बकम्। भावाभावविनिर्मुक्तं जरामरणवर्जितम्॥७२॥

प्रशान्तकलनारम्यं नीरागं पदमाश्रय। एषा ब्राह्मी स्थितिः स्वच्छा निष्कामा विगतामया॥७३॥

The man liberal and of best conduct should do efforts outwardly by following the rules of etiquette and prudency inspite of detachment from all activities inward. Holding detachment entirely in the heart one should do best behave (industry) as an optimist extraneously. It is mine (friend) and that is not, are the meanest thoughts of cunning people. This whole earth is like family to the great men. Resort to such a position free from affection and heart touching in which the man gets liberty from the discriminant thinking, beyond the death and birth and where all resolutions duly attain peace. This position is holy, innocent and free from attachments. It is called as Brāhmī position.

आदाय विहरन्नेवं संकटेषु न मुह्यति। वैराग्येणाथ शास्त्रेण महत्त्वादिगुणैरपि॥७४॥ यत्संकल्पहरार्थं तत्स्वयमेवोन्नयन्मनः। वैराग्यात्पूर्णतामेति मनो नाशवशानुगम्॥७५॥ आशया रक्ततामेति शरदीव सरोऽमलम्। तमेव भुक्तिविरसं व्यापारौघं पुनःपुनः॥७६॥ दिवसे-दिवसे कुर्वन्प्राज्ञः कस्मान्न लज्जते। चिच्चैत्यकलितो बन्धस्तन्मुक्तौ मुक्तिरुच्यते॥७७॥

The man moving in the world under such conscious does not even fall in the trap of affection in the adversity. The resolution is destroyed by the knowledge of śāstra or detachment and great bonafide virtues. Thus, the mind so processed, starts promoting automatically. The mind attaining the perfection by the detachment, that very mind becomes full of affection like a clean pond in the pleasant season (Śarada Ṛtu) when it is lured of hope. However, why the learned people once detached of the enjoyments do not feel hesitation while engaging such mind in the dealing of attachment etc. frequently and again and again? The combination of mind and worldly issues is called binding to exonerate from that combination (yoga) is called emancipation.

चिदचैत्या किलात्मेति सर्वसिद्धान्तसंग्रहः। एतन्निश्चयमादाय विलोकय धियेद्धया॥७८॥
स्वयमेवात्मनात्मानमानन्दं पदमाप्स्यसि। चिदहं चिदिमे लोकाश्चिदाशाश्चिदिमाः प्रजाः॥७९॥
दृश्यदर्शननिर्मुक्तः केवलामलरूपवान्। नित्योदितो निराभासो द्रष्टा साक्षी चिदात्मकः॥८०॥

The mind void of worldly issues as a result of firm determination is called the soul. This very is the essence of the doctrine of all vedānta. See yourself by the awakened heart under presumption of this doctrine as absolute truth in itself. Endless position of pleasure will be acquired as a result of such analysis. I am in the form of mind. All these worlds are mind and the direction as also all these communes of creatures are in the form of mind. The Cidātmā (mental soul) in the form of evidence, un-perceivable and in the rectified form is being observer to the day to day activities after relieving from the lies of the observed (the scene) and observance.

चैत्यनिर्मुक्तचिद्रूपं पूर्णज्योतिःस्वरूपकम्। संशान्तसर्वसंवेद्यं संविन्मात्रमहं महत्॥८१॥
संशान्तसर्वसंकल्पः प्रशान्तसकलैषणः। निर्विकल्पपदं गत्वा स्वस्थो भव मुनीश्वर॥८२॥

I am in the form of mind and great knowledge (Saṁvit) after having freed from the passions for worldly issues, and the sentiments and when I have become a flame of light. O hermit! enshrine in the soul by cooling down absolutely all resolutions, giving up all temptations and entering into the exclusive (Nirvikalpa) position.

य इमां महोपनिषदं ब्राह्मणो नित्यमधीते। अश्रोत्रियः श्रोत्रियो भवति। अनुपनीत उपनीतो भवति। सोऽग्निपूतो भवति। स वायुपूतो भवति। स सूर्यपूतो भवति। स सोमपूतो भवति। स सत्यपूतो भवति। स सर्वपूतो भवति। स सर्वैर्देवैर्ज्ञातो भवति। स सर्वेषु तीर्थेषु स्नातो भवति। स सर्वैर्देवैरनुध्यातो भवति। स सर्वक्रतुभिरिष्टवान्भवति। गायत्र्याः षष्टिसहस्राणि जप्तानि फलानि भवन्ति। इतिहासपुराणानां रुद्राणां शतसहस्राणि जप्तानि फलानि भवन्ति। प्रणवानामयुतं जप्तं भवति। आचक्षुषः पङ्क्तिं पुनाति। आसप्तमान्पुरुषयुगान्पुनाति। इत्याह भगवान्हिरण्यगर्भः। जप्येनामृतत्वं च गच्छतीत्युपनिषत्॥८३॥

The best Brāhmaṇa reciting this Mahopaniṣad daily becomes śrotriya if he is not śrotriya and upanīta if he is not upanīta. He becomes holy as the fire, pure like air and becomes somapūta and satyapūta. He becomes perfectly pure. He achieves popularity among all gods. He receives the fruit of bathing in all pilgrim-places. He becomes able to resolve for arranging all offerings. He receives the fruit of reciting (Japa) many thousand times of the great hymn of Gāyatrī merely by going-over this upaniṣad. He further receives the fruit of reciting many thousand times the History-Purāṇa and Rudra. He receives the fruit of Japa (Silent recital) of Praṇava (Oṁ) ten thousand times. He makes holy the line

(Paṅkti) upto which he has observed. Lord Hiraṇyagarbha Brahmā has said that immortality is attained merely by recital (Japa) of this upaniṣad. This very is the mystery of this upaniṣad.

ॐ आप्यायन्तु ....इति शान्तिः॥

॥इति महोपनिषत्समाप्ता॥

***

58. ŚĀRĪRAKOPANIṢAD

शारीरकोपनिषद्

॥शान्तिपाठः॥

ॐ सह नाववतु .... इति शान्तिः॥

ॐ अथातः पृथिव्यादिमहाभूतानां समवायं शरीरम्। यत्कठिनं सा पृथिवी यद्द्रवं तदापो यदुष्णं तत्तेजो यत्संचरति स वायुर्यत्सुषिरं तदाकाशम्॥ १॥

श्रोत्रादीनि ज्ञानेन्द्रियाणि। श्रोत्रमाकाशे वायौ त्वगग्नौ चक्षुरप्सु जिह्वा पृथिव्यां घ्राणमिति। एवमिन्द्रियाणां यथाक्रमेण शब्दस्पर्शरूपरसगन्धाश्चेति विषयाः पृथिव्यादिमहाभूतेषु क्रमेणोत्पन्नाः॥ २॥

वाक्पाणिपादपायूपस्थाख्यानि कर्मेन्द्रियाणि। तेषां क्रमेण वचनादानगमनविसर्गानन्दाश्चैते विषयाः पृथिव्यादिमहाभूतेषु क्रमेणोत्पन्नाः॥ ३॥

Oṁ. The body is a compound of pṛthivī (earth) and other mahābhūtas (primordial elements, as āpas or water, agni or fire, vāyu or air, and ākāśa (in the body), that which is hard is (of the essence of) earth; that which is liquid is (of the essence of) water; that which is hot is (of the essence of) fire; that which moves about is (of the essence of) vāyu; that which is perforated is (of the essence of) ākāśa. The ear and others are the jñānendriyas (organs of sense). The ear is of the essence of ākāśa, the skin of the essence of vāyu, the eye of the essence of fire, the tongue of the essence of water, and the nose of the essence of earth; sound, touch, form, taste, and odour being respectively the objects of perception for these organs. There arose respectively out of the primordial elements, beginning with earth.

मनोबुद्धिरहंकारश्चित्तमित्यन्तःकरणचतुष्टयम्। तेषां क्रमेण संकल्पविकल्पाध्यवसायाभिमानावधारणास्वरूपाश्चैते विषयाः। मनःस्थानं गलान्तं बुद्धेर्वदनमहंकारस्य हृदयं चित्तस्य नाभिरिति॥ ४॥

अस्थिचर्मनाडीरोममांसाश्चेति पृथिव्यंशाः। मूत्रश्लेष्मरक्तशुक्रस्वेदा अबंशाः। क्षुत्तृष्णा-लस्यमोहमैथुनान्यग्नेः। प्रचारणविलेखनस्थूलाक्ष्युन्मेषनिमेषादि वायोः। कामक्रोधलोभमोह-भयान्याकाशस्य॥ ५॥

शब्दस्पर्शरूपरसगन्धाः पृथिवीगुणाः। शब्दस्पर्शरूपरसाश्चापां गुणाः। शब्दस्पर्शरूपाण्यग्निगुणाः। शब्दस्पर्शाविति वायुगुणौ। शब्द एक आकाशस्य॥ ६॥

The mouth, the hands, the legs, the organs of excretion and the organs of generation are the karmendriyas (or organs of action). Their functions are respectively talking, lifting, walking, excretion, and enjoyment. Antaḥkaraṇa (or the internal organ) is of four kinds—manas, buddhi, ahaṁkāra, and citta. Their functions are respectively saṅkalpa-vikalpa, (or will thought and about), determination, egoism, and memory. The seat of manas is the end of the throat, that of buddhi the face, that of ahaṁkāra the heart, and that of citta, the navel. The bone, skin, nāḍīs, nerves, hair, and flesh are of the essence of earth. Urine, phlegm, blood, śukla (or sperm), and sweat are of the essence of water. Hunger, thirst, sloth, delusion, and (desire of) copulation are of the essence of fire. Walking, scratching, opening and closing the gross eyes, etc., are of the essence of vāyu. Desire, anger, avarice, delusion, and fear are of the essence of ākāśa.

सात्त्विकराजसतामसलक्षणानित्रयो गुणाः॥७॥

अहिंसा सत्यमस्तेयब्रह्मचर्यापरिग्रहाः। अक्रोधो गुरुशुश्रूषा शौचं संतोष आर्जवम्॥८॥

अमानित्वमदम्भित्वमास्तिकत्वमहिंस्रता। एते सर्वे गुणाः ज्ञेयाः सात्त्विकस्य विशेषतः॥९॥

अहं कर्ताऽस्म्यहं भोक्ताऽस्म्यहं वक्ताऽभिमानवान्। एते गुणा राजसस्य प्रोच्यन्ते ब्रह्मवित्तमैः॥

निद्रालस्ये मोहरागौ मैथुनं चौर्यमेव च। एते गुणास्तामसस्य प्रोच्यन्ते ब्रह्मवादिभिः॥११॥

Sound, touch, form, taste, and odour are the properties of earth : sound, touch, form, and taste are the properties of water : sound, touch, and form, are the properties of fire : sound and touch are the properties of vāyu : sound alone is property of ākāśa. There are three guṇas (or qualities), sāttvika, rājasa, and tāmasa. Non-killing veracity, nor stealing, continence, non-covetousness, refraining from anger, serving the Guru, purity (in mind and body), contentment, right conduct, abstinence from self-praise, freedom from pompousness, firm conviction in the existence of God, and not causing any injury to others— all these are to be known as sāttvika-guṇas chiefly. I am the actor, I am the enjoyer, I am the speaker, and I am the egoistic— such are said by knowers of Brahman to be rājasa-guṇas. Sleep, sloth, delusion, desire, copulation, and theft are said by expounders of the Vedas to be tāmasa-guṇas.

ऊर्ध्वे सात्त्विको मध्ये राजसोऽधस्तामस इति॥१२॥

सत्यज्ञानं सात्त्विकम्। धर्मज्ञानं राजसम्। तिमिरान्धं तामसमिति॥१३॥

Those having sattva-guṇa (go) up (viz., higher spheres)— those having rājasa-guṇa (stay) in the middle (viz., the sphere of earth)— those having tāmasa-guṇa (go) down (viz., to hell, etc.,). Perfect (or divine) knowledge is of sāttvika-guṇa; knowledge of dharma is of rājasa-guṇa, the mental darkness is of tāmasa.

जाग्रत्स्वप्नसुषुप्तितुरीयमिति चतुर्विधा अवस्थाः। ज्ञानेन्द्रियकर्मेन्द्रियान्तःकरणचतुष्टयं चतुर्दशकरणयुक्तं जाग्रत्। अन्तःकरणचतुष्टयैरेव संयुक्तः स्वप्नः। चित्तैककरणा सुषुप्तिः। केवलजीवयुक्तमेव तुरीयमिति॥१४॥

उन्मीलितनिमीलितमध्यस्थजीवपरमात्मनोर्मध्ये जीवात्मा क्षेत्रज्ञ इति विज्ञायते॥१५॥

बुद्धिकर्मेन्द्रियप्राणपञ्चकैर्मनसा धिया। शरीरं सप्तदशभिः सुसूक्ष्मं लिङ्गमुच्यते॥१६॥

Jāgrata (waking state), svapna (dreaming state), suṣupti (dreamless sleeping state), and turya (the fourth state beyond these three) are the four states. Jāgrata is (the state) having (the play of) the fourteen organs, the organs of sense (five), the organs of action (five), and the four internal organs. Svapna is (the state) associated with the four internal organs. Suṣupti is (the state) where the citta is the only organ. Turya is that state having jīva alone.

Regarding jīvātmā and Paramātmā (enjoying the three states) of a person with opened eyes, the closed eyes, and with eyes in an intermediate state with neither, jīva is said to be the kṣetrajña (the lord of the body). The organs of sense (five), the organs of action (five), prāṇas, (five), manas, and buddhi— all these seventeen are said to constitute the sūkṣma or liṅga (viz., subtle) body.

मनो बुद्धिरहंकार खानिलाग्निजलानि भूः। एताः प्रकृतयस्त्वष्टौ विकाराः षोडशापरे॥ १७॥ श्रोत्रं त्वक्चक्षुषी जिह्वा घ्राणं चैव तु पंचमम्। पायूपस्थौ करौ पादौ वाक्चैव दशमी मता॥ शब्दः स्पर्शश्च रूपं च रसो गन्धस्तथैव च। त्रयोविंशतिरेतानि तत्त्वानि प्रकृतानि तु॥ १९॥ चतुर्विंशतिरव्यक्तं प्रधानं पुरुषः परः इत्युपनिषत्॥ २०॥

Manas, buddhi, ahaṁkāra, ākāśa, vāyu, fire, water, and earth— these are the eight prakṛtis (on matter) : ear, skin, eye, tongue, nose the fifth, the organs of excretion, the organs of secretion, hands, legs, speech the tenth, sound, from, touch, taste, and odour are the fifteen modifications (of the above eight prakṛtis). Therefore the tattvas are twenty-three. The twenty-fourth is avyakta (the undifferentiated matter) or pradhāna. Puruṣa is other than (or superior to) this.

ॐ सह नाववतु .... इति शान्तिः॥

॥इति शारीरकोपनिषत्समाप्ता॥

***

59. TURĪYĀTĪTA-UPANIṢAD

तुरीयातीतोपनिषद्

This Upaniṣad is related to the tradition of Śukla Yajurveda. It is also called as Turīyātītādhūtopaniṣad. The question and answers are transacted between Lord Brahmā and Ādinārāyaṇa in this Upaniṣad in which Lord Brahmā has asked his father Ādinārāyaṇa, the route of recluse who is Turīyātīta. Ādinārāyaṇa, has described this route a scarce one and described the modus operandi of a recluse along with his conduct, behave, mode of concentration and meditation. He has told that the recluse ultimately obtains the Supreme aim of his life. Finally, this Upaniṣad is concluded with explaining its importance.

॥शान्तिपाठः॥

ॐ पूर्णमदः .... इति शान्तिः॥

अथ तुरीयातीतावधूतानां कोऽयं मार्गस्तेषां का स्थितिरिति सर्वलोक पितामहो भगवन्तं पितरमादिनारायणं परिसमेत्योवाच। तमाह भगवान्नारायणो योऽयमवधूतमार्गस्थो लोके दुर्लभतरो नतु बाहुल्यो यद्येको भवति स एव नित्यपूतः स एव वैराग्यमूर्तिः स एव ज्ञानाकारः स एव वेदपुरुष इति ज्ञानिनो मन्यन्ते। महापुरुषो यस्तच्चित्तं मय्येवावतिष्ठते। अहं च तस्मिन्नेवावस्थितः। सोऽयमादौ तावत्क्रमेण कुटीचको बहूदकत्वं प्राप्य बहूदको हंसत्वमवलम्ब्य हंसः परमहंसो भूत्वा स्वरूपानुसंधानेन सर्वप्रपञ्चं विदित्वा दण्डकमण्डलुकटिसूत्रकौपीनाच्छादनं स्वविध्युक्तक्रियादिकं सर्वमप्सु संन्यस्य दिगम्बरो भूत्वा विवर्णजीर्णवल्कलाजिनपरिग्रहमपि संत्यज्य तदूर्ध्वममन्त्रवदाचरन्क्षौराभ्यङ्गस्नानोर्ध्वपुण्ड्रादिकं विहाय लौकिकवैदिकमप्युपसंहृत्य सर्वत्र पुण्यापुण्यवर्जितो ज्ञानाज्ञानमपि विहाय शीतोष्णसुखदुःखमानावमानं निर्जित्य वासनात्रयपूर्वकं निन्दाऽनिन्दागर्वमत्सरदम्भदर्पेच्छाद्वेषकामक्रोधलोभमोहहर्षामर्षासूयात्मसंरक्षणादिकं दग्ध्वा स्ववपुः कुणपाकारमिव पश्यन्नयत्नेनानियमेन लाभालाभौ समौ कृत्वा गोवृत्त्या प्राणसंधारणं कुर्वन्यत्प्राप्तं तेनैव निर्लोलुपः सर्वविद्यापाण्डित्यप्रपञ्चं भस्मीकृत्य स्वरूपं गोपयित्वा ज्येष्ठाऽज्येष्ठत्वानपलापकः सर्वोत्कृष्टत्वसर्वात्मकत्वाद्वैतं कल्पयित्वा मत्तो व्यतिरिक्तः कश्चिन्नान्योऽस्तीति देवगुह्यादिधनमात्मन्युपसंहृत्य दुःखेन नोद्विग्नः सुखेन नानुमोदको रागे निःस्पृहः सर्वत्र शुभाशुभयोरनभिस्नेहः सर्वेन्द्रियोपरमः स्वपूर्वापन्नाश्रमाचारविद्याधर्मप्राभवमननुस्मरन्त्यक्तवर्णाश्रमाचारः सर्वदा दिवानक्तसमत्वेनास्वप्नः सर्वत्र सर्वदा संचारशीलो देहमात्रावशिष्टो जलस्थलकमण्डलुः सर्वदानुन्मत्तो बालोन्मत्तपिशाचवदेकाकी संचरन्नसंभाषणपरः स्वरूपध्यानेन निरालम्बमवलम्ब्य स्वात्मनिष्ठानुकूलेन सर्वं विस्मृत्य तुरीयातीतावधूतवेषेणाद्वैतनिष्ठापरः प्रणवात्मकत्वेन देहत्यागं करोति यः सोऽवधूतः स कृतकृत्यो भवतीत्युपनिषत्॥

Once Lord Brahmā went to his father Ādinārāyaṇa and asked– "O Lord! Kindly tell me the route of a recluse who is beyond the state of route Turīya including the strata of his feeling? Lord Nārāyaṇa replied– 'persons moving on the routes of an Avadhūta are rare. They are in least number. However, the scholars say that if there is one such Avadhūta, he is seen an embodiment by detachment, knowledge, purity and a man learnt veda. Such a great man always enshrining his mind in me and I my self enshrine within him. Initially, one becomes kuṭīcaka. Then Bahūdaka and ultimately resorts to the elements of Haṁsa. On having availed this state, he then turns into this supreme Paramahaṁsa. He does research with his own soul and having known to the mystery of all illusions, He immerses his stick, Kamaṇḍala, Laṅgota, Kaupīna, garments and all regular actions in the water. Thus he becomes fully naked or uncovered body, the hide of deer, all kinds of hymns, shaving, bathing, putting Tripuṇḍra on forehead, giving up all worldly and vedic activities and even abandons the good and bad feelings as also the ignorance. He equally endures the pains of weather i.e. heat and cold, vicissitudes, honour and insult etc. He burns into ashes the trio-passion of his body, the feeling of criticism, praise, ego, vanity, boost, malice, desire, envy, anger, greed, affection, gay, sorrow, impurity and self-protection etc. He observes his body as a corpse. He treats the loss and profit equally keeping himself inactive all through. He lives on contentment and satisfies with whatever is met for food like a cow. He keeps himself free from greed, the learning and pedantry and hides his innermost expressions as a stupid. No scope for big and small is left in his heart. He keeps the notion of the single god and observes it on every universal thing. He consider that there is nothing else than me. He keep the divine mysteries duly accumulated within his heart and neither aggrieved in sorrow nor leaves on gaiety. Affection has no place in his heart and good or bad happenings do not put any impact on him. All his senses are cooled down. He becomes reluctant to all preceding Āśrama, learning, religion and influence and abandons the etiquettes prescribed by Varṇāśrama. Having inspired with the thought that the day and night are equal he never sleeps and remains dynamic always and at every place. His body merely is as residual and servant to the Brahma because he applies his body only to acquire the Brahma (knowledge). He treats as Kamaṇḍala to the well and the ponds. He is always reluctant. However, outwardly he moves alone like a child, intoxicated man and demon etc. He doesn't talk with any person and always engrosses in concentration of his genuine form. He reforest to where there is no shelter and having deep loyalty to his soul. He forgets all. The person who thus converts himself in an Avadhūta going beyond the state of Turīya and engrosses himself in Praṇava with sanctity and devotion, definitely attains to emancipation after his physical death. This very fact has been pronounced by this Upaniṣad.

॥ॐ पूर्णमदः .... इति शान्तिः॥

॥इति तुरीयातीतोपनिषत्समाप्ता॥

***

60. SAṄNYĀSA-UPANIṢAD

संन्यासोपनिषद्

This Upaniṣad is related to the tradition of Sāmaveda. There are two chapters in it. The contents in the first chapter are an introduction of reclusion procedure for obtaining, and behaviour as also pragmatic activities required for it. The second chapter is with prolix details. Its opening has been made with the four means i.e. discretion, reluctance, six properties and desire for emancipation. A detailed description on the criterion for reclusion has been given. While describing the kinds of recluse the classification in– (i) reluctant recluse, (ii) knowledge recluse (iii) the recluse enriched with the knowledge and detachment and the recluse who observes it in his activities have been explained. Later on six types of reclusion i.e. Kuṭīcaka, Bahūdaka, Haṁsa, Paramahaṁsa, Turīyātīta and Avadhūta has been described in orderly manner. The position of knowledge on soul or self-realization as also its nature has been described. The holiness in behave and a provision to satiate with the lesser food obtained on alms has been described. An instruction for keeping away from wife, enjoyments etc. physical pleasures has been given. Thus, it is suggested that one should engross himself on the soul daily and by putting a strict control on activities as also on diet. One should do the Japa of Oṁkāra because it originates the light of Brahma in his bosom and he thus becomes entitled to emancipation.

॥शान्तिपाठः॥

ॐ आप्यायन्तु ....इति शान्तिः॥

Chapter first

अथातः संन्यासोपनिषदं व्याख्यास्यामो योऽनुक्रमेण संन्यस्यति स संन्यस्तो भवति। कोऽयं संन्यास उच्यते। कथं संन्यस्तो भवति। य आत्मानं क्रियाभिर्गुप्तं करोति मातरं पितरं भार्यां पुत्रान्बन्धूननुमोदयित्वा ये चास्यर्त्विजस्तान्सर्वांश्च पूर्ववद्वृणीत्वा वैश्वानरेष्टिं निर्वपेत्सर्वस्वं दद्याद्यजमानस्य गा ऋत्विजः सर्वैः पात्रैः समारोप्य यदाहवनीये गार्हपत्ये वान्वाहार्यपचने सभ्यावसथ्ययोश्च प्राणापानव्यानोदानसमानान्सर्वान्सर्वेषु समारोपयेत्। सशिखान्केशान्विसृज्य यज्ञोपवीतं छित्त्वा पुत्रं दृष्ट्वा त्वं यज्ञस्त्वं सर्वमित्यनुमन्त्रयेत्। यद्यपुत्रो भवत्यात्मानमेवेमं ध्यात्वाऽनवेक्षमाणः प्राचीमुदीचीं वा दिशं प्रव्रजेच्च। चतुर्षु वर्णेषु भिक्षाचर्यं चरेत्। पाणिपात्रेणाशनं कुर्यात् औषधवदशनमाचरेत्। औषधवदशनं प्राश्नीयात्। यथालाभमश्नीयात्प्राणसंधारणार्थं यथा मेदोवृद्धिर्न जायते। कृशो भूत्वा ग्राम एकरात्रं नगरे पञ्चरात्रं चतुरो मासान्वार्षिकान्ग्रामे वा नगरे वापि वसेत्। पक्षा वै मासो इति द्वौ मासौ वा वसेत्। विशीर्णवस्त्रं वल्कलं वा प्रतिगृह्णीयान्नान्यत्प्रतिगृह्णीयाद्यद्यशक्तो भवति क्लेशतस्तप्यते तप इति। यो वा एवं क्रमेण संन्यस्यति यो वा एवं पश्यति किमस्य यज्ञोपवीतं कास्य शिखा कथं वास्योपस्पर्शनमिति। तं होवाचेदमेवास्य तद्यज्ञोपवीतं यदात्मध्यानं विद्या शिखा नीरैः सर्वत्रावस्थितैः कार्यं निर्वर्तयन्नुदरपात्रेण जलतीरे निकेतनम्। ब्रह्मवादिनो वदन्त्यस्तमित आदित्ये कथं वास्योपस्पर्शनमिति।

तान्होवाच यथाहनि तथा रात्रौ नास्य नक्तं न दिवा तदप्येतदृषिणोक्तम्। सकृद्दिवा हैवास्मै भवति य एवं विद्वानेतेनात्मानं संधत्ते॥ १॥

Saṅnyāsopaniṣad is now the subject-matter of our description. The person giving up this mortal world through his orderly manners is only the recluse. A question thus arises that to which can be said the reclusion? What is the nature of a recluse? Its answer is a person who for the upliftment of his soul abandons all the activities approved by the parents, wife, the sons, brothers, etc., who performs the offering of vaiśvānara subsequent to a salute to be conveyed to the Ṛtvijas. It is advisable that the client at this auspicious occasion should donate everything and the Ṛtvij should be offered the material with the bodies in which it is kept. A recluse should impose in the five airs– i.e. Prāṇa, Apāna, Vyāna, Udāna and Samāna.. The fire at the time of memory (Āvasaṭhya) and in Āhavanīya, Gārhapatya and Dakṣiṇāgni fires, with the Vedic age fire. He should cut clear his all hair. He should further abandon the sacrificial thread and while observing his son he should say you are in the offering and you are in the universal form. He should depart then towards the East or the North direction by addressing his own soul the same when he has no son. He should accept alm from all the four Varṇas i.e. Brāhmaṇas, Kṣatriyas, Vaiśyas, and Śūdras. He should take food after getting food in the bowl. The food should be taken under presumption as if it is a medicine. In other words, it can be said that a man should take food only to the extent that he could do something great or only to the extent that it may preserve the breathing. This food should also be entertained like a medicine free from fat and all impurities that develops excitement. Thus, he should stay at night in a village and five nights in a city. During raing season, the recluse should stay either in a village or city up to the period of two months counting by the fortnights. He should live on rags or the clothes and of barks of the trees. No others kind of garments should be a entertaining. Thus throwing oneself into penance to show severe extent is the best ground on which a man reaming active. The person who accepts reclusion in this orderly manner has answers to all questions like what is the sacrificial thread, the braid and the Ācamana. Answer to these all questions is then naturally obtained. Concentration is only the sacrificial like a braid. His belly acts like a bowl to sip the water and his resort is at the bank of the pool. Similar are the characteristics of the person who know Brahma very well. What kind of Ācamana is for them at the time when Lord Sun departs to the west. Answer to this question is that the night and the day both are equal to a recluse. He neither has a meaning for the night nor for day. He keeps himself indulged in the investigation of his soul and as per scholars, all night and days are like a day for such a recluse.

चत्वारिंशत्संस्कारसंपन्नः सर्वतो विरक्तश्चित्तशुद्धिमेत्याशासूयेर्ष्याहंकारं दग्ध्वा साधनचतुष्टयसंपन्न एव संन्यस्तुमर्हति॥ १॥

The criterion to be a recluse is that he should have performed in the past the forty kinds of ceremony, reluctant to all, keeping the mind always refined, burning the hopes, expectations, envy, jealousy, ego and enriched with the four means, i.e., discretion, renunciation, six virtues, element of emancipation. The discretion refers to the day to day knowledge of the objective world, no desires for the material and metaphysical world, the six property pertains to the virtues like control, purify, reluctance, obeisance, detachment and the conclusion and a strong will for emancipation.

संन्यासे निश्चयं कृत्वा पुनर्न च करोति यः। स कुर्यात्कृच्छ्रमात्रं तु पुनः संन्यस्तुमर्हति॥ २॥

The ascetic determined to reclusion if doesn't implement the same, he may do a severe penance and can re-entertain the life of a recluse.

संन्यासं पातयेद्यस्तु पतितं न्यासयेत्तु यः। संन्यासविघ्नकर्त्ता च त्रीनेतान्पतितान्विदुः॥ ३॥

The person befallen from the reclusion, who consecrate reclusion to the trapped persons or who put hurdles in entertaining the reclusion are called severely befallen and trodden person.

अथ षण्डः पतितोऽङ्गविकलः स्त्रैणो बधिरोऽर्भको मूकः पाषण्डश्चक्री लिङ्गी कुष्ठी वैखानसहरद्विजौ भृतकाध्यापकः शिपिविष्टोऽनग्निको नास्तिको वैराग्यवन्तोऽप्येते न संन्यासार्हाः। संन्यस्ता यद्यपि महावाक्योपदेशे नाधिकारिणः॥ ४॥

The person enriched with detachment aren't eligible to consecrate with reclusion if those are eunuch, degraded, handicapped, effeminate, deaf, child, talkative, boost, conspirator, leaper, the soothsayers and the man befallen from the position of Brāhmaṇa. Salaried teacher, unbalanced temperament, non-performer of offering, the atheist etc., these are not eligible to the consecration of reclusion inspite of their keen detachment to the worldly affairs. They do not become the authoritative while preaching the great sentence even if they accept reclusion.

आरूढपतितापत्यं कुनखी श्यावदन्तकः। क्षयीतथाङ्गविकलो नैव संन्यस्तुमर्हति॥ ५॥

The children of an uncultured man whose nails are worst type, teeth are dirty and full of foul smell, entrapped in T.B., handicapped etc. is to entitle to accept the consecration of reclusion.

संप्रत्यवसितानां च महापातकिनां तथा। व्रात्यानामभिशस्तानां संन्यासं नैव कारयेत्॥ ६॥

The consecration of reclusion shouldn't be given to the person who have become detached from the worldly affairs suddenly, who are criminal, uncultured and criticized by the society.

व्रतयज्ञतपोदानहोमस्वाध्यायवर्जितम्। सत्यशौचपरिभ्रष्टं संन्यासं नैव कारयेत्। एते नार्हन्ति संन्यासमातुरेण विना क्रमम्॥ ७॥

The person devoid of resolution, offering, penance, generosity, worship and perseverance are vacate of the truth and purity. These are not entitled to the consecration of reculsion. A few among them may be the prompt recluse but these do not fulfill the procedural requirement.

ॐ भूः स्वाहेति शिखामुत्पाट्य यज्ञोपवीतं बहिर्न निवसेत्। यशो बलं ज्ञानं वैराग्यं मेधां प्रयच्छेति यज्ञोपवीतं छित्त्वा ॐ भूः स्वाहेत्यप्सु वस्त्रं कटिसूत्रं च विसृज्य संन्यस्तं मयेति त्रिवारमभिमन्त्रयेत्॥ ८॥

One should cut clean his braid by reciting Oṁ Bhūḥ Svāhā but the sacrificial thread shouldn't be abandoned. It is the second step when by reciting. "O offering! Endow us with power, knowledge, renunciation and intelligence. The sacrificial thread is cut into pieces. Thrice time recital should be made of Saṁnyastaṁ Maye (I have accepted reclusion) the waist thread should be immersed into a pond with recital of Oṁ Bhūḥ Svāhā."

संन्यासिनं द्विजं दृष्ट्वा स्थानाच्चलति भास्करः। एष मे मण्डलं भित्त्वा परं ब्रह्माधिगच्छति॥ ९॥

Lord Sun starts moving to and fro when it looks at the recluse and the Brāhmaṇa, having afraid to their emerge in the perfect Brahma by penetrating the orbit of Sun.

षष्टिं कुलान्यतीतानि षष्टिमागामिकानि च। कुलान्युद्धरते प्राज्ञः संन्यस्तमिति यो वदेत्॥ १०॥

The person who say in affirmation "I have become a recluse" crosses his sixty preceding generation and sixty forth coming generations from the worldly sea.

ये च संतानजा दोषा ये दोषा देहसंभवाः। प्रैषाग्निर्निर्दहेत्सर्वांस्तुषाग्निरिव काञ्चनम्॥ ११॥

The defects fallen through the heredity and the defects of his own body are burnt down by him. The same way as the fire of Tuṣā burnts down the impurity of the gold.

सखा मा गोपायेति दण्डं परिग्रहेत्॥ १२॥

O friend! Protect us, should be recited while accepting a stick.

दण्डं तु वैणवं सौम्यं सत्वचं समपर्वकम्। पुण्यस्थलसमुत्पन्नं नानाकल्मषशोधितम्॥ १३॥

अदग्धमहतं कीटैः पर्वग्रन्थिविराजितम्। नासादघ्नं शिरस्तुल्यं भ्रुवोर्वा बिभृयाद्यतिः॥ १४॥

The stick should be straight, bamboo specie with bark, it should have the even number of knots. Its place of origin should be pure, there should be no spot on such stick, it should neither be affected by fire nor hold in by the pesticides etc. There should be knots and it should be upto the height of nose, braid or the brows in the measurement.

दण्डात्मनोस्तु संयोगः सर्वथा तु विधीयते। न दण्डेन विना गच्छेदिषुक्षेपत्रयं बुधः॥ १५॥

The combination of stick and the soul is always good. If a stick is not with a recluse, he should only move within the periphery crossed by an arrow thrice time.

जगज्जीवनं जीवनाधारभूतं मा ते मा मन्त्रयस्व सर्वदा सर्वसौम्येति कमण्डलुं परिगृह्य योगपट्टाभिषिक्तो भूत्वा यथासुखं विहरेत्॥ १६॥

O modest! You hold the basic element of life, water, live in contact with me by declaring it. A recluse should hold a Kamaṇḍala in hand, a monogram of yoga with him and should move with all pleasure everywhere.

त्यज धर्ममधर्मं च उभे सत्यानृते त्यज। उभे सत्यानृते त्यक्त्वा येन त्यजसि तत्त्यज॥ १७॥

A recluse should abandon all kinds of good and bad as also the false and the truth. The false and the truth as it laterward should also be left abandoned ultimately.

वैराग्यसंन्यासी ज्ञानसंन्यासी ज्ञानवैराग्यसंन्यासी। कर्मसंन्यासीति चातुर्विध्यमुपागत:।। १८।।

There are four kinds of recluse the first reluctant recluse, second conscious recluse, the third a recluse full of a mixture of knowledge and reluctance both and the fourth a recluse by activities.

तद्यथेति। दृष्टानुश्रविकविषयवैतृष्ण्यमेत्य। प्राक्पुण्यकर्मविशेषात्संन्यस्त: स वैराग्यसंन्यासी।। १९।।

The person who has accepted reclusion after developing the spirit of detachment from the audio-video affairs of this world and as a result of the fruits for the deeds previously performed is called Vairāgya Sannyāsi.

[According to Sāṅkhya yoga, the visible matters are perceived in the form of complexion, essence, odour etc., and the wealth and property, the wife, the royal luxuries etc. The Audio objects are the matters as heard from the Veda and holy books. These are also of two kinds (A) the pleasures of divine abode, the heaven senselessness for the physique and engross with the nature. (B) The divine odour, essence etc., the accomplishment like Aṇimā, Garimā etc. The reluctant recluse remains unattached with the above two kinds of affairs.]

शास्त्रज्ञानात्पापपुण्यलोकानुभवश्रवणात्प्रपञ्चोपरतो देहवासनां शास्त्रवासनां लोकवासनां त्यक्त्वा वमनान्नमिव प्रवृत्तिं हेयं मत्वा साधनचतुष्टयसंपन्नो य: संन्यस्यति स एव ज्ञानसंन्यासी।।२०।।

The person who as a result of knowledge with the holy books, the study of good and bad as also the worldly experiences, keeping always awake, who abandons the physical luxuries (passion for a son, wealth, prestige), passion for the holy book but, only a sheer devotion and faith on holy books, who considers as vomitted by means of four i.e. discretion, reluctance, six property and the element of emancipation is called a conscious recluse.

क्रमेण सर्वमभ्यस्य सर्वमनुभूय ज्ञानवैराग्याभ्यां स्वरूपानुसंधानेन देहमात्रावशिष्ट: संन्यस्य जातरूपधरो भवति स ज्ञानवैराग्यसंन्यासी।। २१।।

A recluse enriched with the knowledge and reluctance accepts the reclusion through a prolong practise in orderly manner by observing all experiences, under the knowledge to know properly the element of detachment and who treats the body as a residual.

ब्रह्मचर्यं समाप्य गृही भूत्वा वानप्रस्थाश्रममेत्य वैराग्याभावेऽप्याश्रमक्रमानुसारेण य: संन्यस्यति स कर्मसंन्यासी।। २२।।

The characteristics as to accept reclusion by observing the rules made therefore after systematic entrance and glut with the Āśramas of celibacy, couple Vānaprastha, are called held by a recluse of activity (karma Saṁnyāsī).

स संन्यास: षड्विधो भवति कुटीचकबहूदकहंस। परमहंसतुरीयातीतावधूताश्चेति।। २३।।

There are six kinds of reclusion. These are Kuṭīcaka, Buhūdaka, Haṁsa, Paramahaṁsa, Turīyātīta and Avadhūta.

कुटीचक: शिखायज्ञोपवीती दण्डकमण्डलुधर: कौपीनशाटीकन्थाधर: पितृमातृगुर्वाराधनपर: पिठरखनित्रशिक्यादिमात्रसाधनपर एकत्रान्नादनपर: श्वेतोर्ध्वपुण्ड्रधारी त्रिदण्ड:।। २४।।

The recluse of Kuṭīcaka holds the braid and sacrificial thread on his body. He beside these, accepts a stick, Kamaṇḍala, Kaupīna, (nicker), bed sheet, a bag also. He is obedient to his parents and the teacher. He holds a kettle, a spade and cinka with him. He takes food at the uniform place. He smears a white Tripuṇḍra on his forehead and he holds a trident also.

बहूदकः शिखादिकन्थाधरस्त्रिपुण्ड्रधारी। कुटीचकवत्सर्वसमो इ मधुकरवृत्त्याष्टकवलाशी॥ २५॥

The recluse Bahūdaka holds the braid etc. a bag and smears up Tripuṇḍra. He alike Kuṭīcaka lives on alms and only takes eight morsels of food at a time.

हंसो जटाधारी त्रिपुण्ड्रोर्ध्वपुण्ड्रधारी। असंक्लृप्तमाधुकरान्नाशी कौपीनखण्डतुण्डधारी॥ २६॥

A recluse namely Haṁsa holds large matted hair, Tripuṇḍra and Vrdhvapuṇḍra, asks for food from alien places and puts on a Kaupīna (nicker) on his body.

परमहंसः शिखायज्ञोपवीतरहितः पञ्चगृहेषु करपात्री एककौपीनधारी।
शाटीमेकामेकं वैणवं दण्डमेकशाटीधरो वा भस्मोद्धूलनपरः सर्वत्यागी।॥ २७॥

A Paramahaṁsa recluse abandons the braid and sacrificial thread, survives on alm, accepted in hand from five houses, holds a nicker, a bedsheet and a bamboo stick with him or he abandons everything except a bedsheet and the ash to smear on Gods.

तुरीयातीतो गोमुखवृत्त्या फलाहारी अन्नाहारी।
चेद्गृहत्रये देहमात्रावशिष्टो दिगम्बरः कुणपवच्छरीरवृत्तिकः॥ २८॥

The recluse Turīyātīta abandons everything, lives on cow, profession, accepts alm of fruits or cereal from three houses, keeps his body naked and thus he survives considering his body as a corpse.

अवधूतस्त्वनियमः पतिताभिशस्तवर्जनपूर्वकं सर्ववर्णेष्वजगरवृत्त्याहारपरः स्वरूपानुसंधानपरः॥ २९॥
जगत्तावदिदं नाहं सवृक्षतृणपर्वतम्। यद्बाह्यं जडमत्यन्तं तत्स्यां कथमहं विभुः। कालेनाल्पेन विलयी देहो नाहमचेतनः॥ ३०॥

The recluse namely Avadhūta does not observe any kind of the rule. He obtains his food under the python profession from all castes barring the evil doers and spotted persons. He always keeps himself busy in the investigation of his own genuine form. He discriminates the entire universe consisting of the tree, grass and vegetation as also the mountains. He considers the happenings of extraneous world as most inert. He considers that he is gigantic and can't live with the exterior world. He considers himself a resolution of the time and living enduring life.

जडया कर्णशष्कुल्या कल्प्यमानक्षणस्थया। शून्याकृतिः शून्यभवः शब्दो नाहमचेतनः॥ ३१॥

He thinks I am not an inert world because it stays for a moment. I am not in the form of dormance which has no feature.

त्वचा क्षणविनाशिन्या प्राप्योऽप्राप्योऽयमन्यथा। चित्प्रसादोपलब्धात्मा स्पर्शो नाहमचेतनः॥ ३२॥

This skin varying its size and perishable in seconds is distinct from me. I am not that inert touch who obtains the self-perceiving by virtue of the sensitivity.

त्वचा क्षणविनाशिन्या प्राप्योऽप्राप्योऽयमन्यथा। चित्प्रसादोपलब्धात्मा स्पर्शो नाहमचेतनः॥ ३२॥

I am not a caprice mind and not a power of vibration that arise trivially through a matter from the tongue.

लब्धात्मा जिह्वया तुच्छो लोलया लोलसत्तया। स्वल्पस्पन्दो द्रव्यनिष्ठो रसो नाहमचेतनः॥ ३३॥

I am merely a witness and I am not a perception of inert and sensitive that destroys when the scene and the observer are merged with.

दृश्यदर्शनयोर्लीनं क्षयि क्षणविनाशिनोः। केवले द्रष्टरि क्षीणं रूपं नाहमचेतनः॥ ३४॥

I am not a trivial inert odour because it comes out from the inert material and judged by the nose.

नासया गन्धजडया क्षयिण्या परिकल्पितः। पेलवोऽनियताकारो गन्धो नाहमचेतनः॥ ३५॥

I am a recluse not trapped in the illusion of five sensory organs, without perseverance, peaceful and all pure sensitivity.

निर्ममोऽमननः शान्तो तपपञ्चेन्द्रियभ्रमः। शुद्धचेतन एवाहं कलाकलनवर्जितः॥३६॥

चैत्यवर्जितचिन्मात्रमहमेषोऽवभासकः। सबाह्याभ्यन्तरव्यापी निष्कलोऽहं निरञ्जनः। निर्विकल्पचिदाभास एक आत्मास्मि सर्वगः॥ ३७॥

I am luminating with Cinmātra light which is beyond the sensitivity. I am an element of the soul that is present in and out, Cid and omnipresent.

मयैव चेतनेनेमे सर्वे घटपटादयः। सूर्यान्ता अवभास्यन्ते दीपेनेवात्मतेजसा॥ ३८॥

I am sensitivity that constitutes the radiance like a lamp from the pitcher, cloth etc. to the sun.

मयैवैताः स्फुरन्तीह विचित्रेन्द्रियवृत्तयः। तेजसान्तः प्रकाशेन यथाग्निकणपङ्क्तयः॥ ३९॥

These all senses arise from the light within my bosom and all varied professions also eminates from it. These eminate the same way as the sparks from the fire.

अनन्तानन्दसंभोगा परोपशमशालिनी। शुद्धेयं चिन्मयी दृष्टिर्जयत्यखिलदृष्टिषु॥ ४०॥

This holy and divine view provides with everlasting, endless, extreme peace enabling to enjoy the pleasure. It conquers all other kinds of outlooks.

सर्वभावान्तरस्थाय चैत्यमुक्तचिदात्मने। प्रत्यक्चैतन्यरूपाय मह्यमेव नमो नमः॥ ४१॥

This liberated soul resides permanently among all kinds of spirits. It is the Cid that should liberated from the sensitive stage. This soul all sensitive is saluted.

विचित्राः शक्तयः स्वच्छाः समा या निर्विकारया। चिता क्रियन्ते समया कलाकलनमुक्तया॥ कालत्रयमुपेक्षित्र्या हीनायाश्चैत्यबन्धनैः। चितश्चैत्यमुपेक्षित्र्याः समतैवावशिष्यते॥ ४३॥

These excellent, clean and equity powers have been originated from the power of mind without imagination and the heart. This power of mind is sovereign and fully liberated from the bindings of this apparent world in trio-time (Kāla).

सा हि वाचामगम्यत्वादसत्तामिव शाश्वतीम्। नैरात्मसिद्धात्मदशामुपयातैव शिष्यते॥४४॥ ईहानीहामयैरन्तर्या चिदावलिता मलैः। सा चिन्नोत्पादितुं शक्ता पाशबद्धेव पक्षिणी॥४५॥ इच्छाद्वेषसमुत्थेन द्वन्द्वमोहेन जन्तवः। धराविवरमग्नानां कीटानां समतां गताः॥४६॥

It is indescribable, an everlasting, an entity not in existence and it remains as rest analogous to the reluctant soul. The power of kind as existed in the state of desire and hate is covered of impurities and enable to fly like a bird caught in a case. Owing to a sense of duality, born as a result of desire and envy, these are like the insects and bacterias, fall in the trench of earth.

आत्मनेऽस्तु नमो मह्यमविच्छिन्नचिदात्मने। परामृष्टोऽस्मि बुद्धोऽस्मि प्रोदितोऽस्म्यचिरादहम्॥४७

A salute is conveyed to this inseparated soul in the form of cid. I am developed and duly perceived of apparent knowledge.

उद्धतोऽस्मि विकल्पेभ्यो योऽस्मि सोऽस्मि नमोऽस्तु ते। तुभ्यं मह्यमनन्ताय मह्यं तुभ्यं चिदात्मने॥

I am stubborn, beyond the operations, I am, what am I, Salute to me. You and I both are endless. I and you both are the cidātma. Convey salute to both.

नमस्तुभ्यं परेशाय नमो मह्यं शिवाय च। तिष्ठन्नपि हि नासीनो गच्छन्नपि न गच्छति। शान्तोऽपि व्यवहारस्थः कुर्वन्नपि न लिप्यते॥४९॥

Salute is conveyed to the supreme Īśvara and Śiva who is within me. This soul doesn't enshrine while sitting, doesn't move while in dynamic action, indulges and behave insipte of always in peace. It does the function but never attached with the fruit of action.

सुलभश्चायमत्यन्तं सुज्ञेयश्चाप्तबन्धुवत्। शरीरपद्मकुहरे सर्वेषामेव षट्पदः॥५०॥

This soul is easy to find, it is like a friend in need and it is like a bee in the Lotus flower of body.

न मे भोगस्थितौ वाञ्छा न मे भोगविसर्जने। यदायाति तदायातु यत्प्रयाति प्रयातु तत्॥५१॥

I am not hungry for the worldly enjoyment and on other side I am not tempt to abandon the enjoyments. Let come whatever it is and let go whatever is gone.

मनसा मनसि च्छिन्ने निरहंकारतां गते। भावेन गलिते भावे स्वस्थस्तिष्ठामि केवलः॥५२॥

Only the soul remains healthy and hearty on destruction of spirit, crush of ego and separation of mind from mind.

मनसा मनसि च्छिन्ने निरहंकारतां गते। भावेन गलिते भावे स्वस्थस्तिष्ठामि केवलः॥५२॥

I am void of spirit, ego, the vacation of mind, in action, loss of vibration and only a soul in purity. Where my enemy may be?

निर्भावं निरहंकारं निर्मनस्कमनीहितम्। केवलास्पन्दशुद्धात्मन्येव तिष्ठति मे रिपुः॥५३॥

The world free from ego living the cage of my body has departed to alien peace after cutting the string of passion.

तृष्णारज्जुगणं छित्त्वा मच्छरीरकपञ्जरात्। न जाने क्व गतोड्डीय निरहंकारपक्षिणी॥५४॥

Only a man lives true life who is not affiliated with the activities handled by him, whose mind is free from attachment and who observes all creatures with equal eye.

यस्य नाहंकृतो भावो बुद्धिर्यस्य न लिप्यते। यः समः सर्वभूतेषु जीवितं तस्य शोभते॥५५॥

The best recluse whose bosom is all cool, whose wisdom is liberated from the feelings of affection, envy etc. and who observes this world as if he is witness to it, lives the real life.

योऽन्तःशीतलया बुद्ध्या रागद्वेषविमुक्तया। साक्षिवत्पश्यतीदं हि जीवितं तस्य शोभते॥५६॥

The recluse enjoys the pleasure of true life, who has acquired perfection in knowledge, who has abandoned pondering on the aspect of good and bad and who has enjoined the mind in the mind.

ग्राह्यग्राहकसंबन्धे क्षीणे शान्तिरुदेत्यलम्। स्थितिमभ्यागता शान्तिर्मोक्षनामाभिधीयते॥५८॥

An extreme pleasure starts rising when the relation of commodity and consumer is destroyed. The peace is called the emancipation.

भ्रष्टबीजोपमा भूयो जन्माङ्कुरविवर्जिता। हृदि जीवद्विमुक्तानां शुद्धा भवति वासना॥५९॥

As the fried seed doesn't spout, the slight passion in the heart of person who actually has obtained the liberty from life.

पावनी परमोदारा शुद्धसत्त्वानुपातिनी। आत्मध्यानमयी नित्या सुषुप्तिस्थेव तिष्ठति॥६०॥

They always perform actions of philanthropy, always generous, abide by the truth, concentrate on soul and remain in their actual form.

चेतनं चित्तरिक्तं हि प्रत्यक्चेतनमुच्यते। निर्मनस्कस्वभावत्वान्न तत्र कलनामलम्॥६१॥

This soul is called an element of sensitivity only when the element of sensitivity is liberated from the mind. When the habit is without the mind no faults are appeared therefrom.

सा सत्यता सा शिवता सावस्था पारमात्मिकी। सर्वज्ञता सा संतृप्तिर्नतु यत्र मनः क्षतम्॥६२॥

It is Śiva, it is truth and the supreme soul locates here. It is omniscience, a perfect glut and not at the stage, where the mind is deviated between the feeling of 'it is! mine and that is yours!'

प्रलपन्विसृजन्गृह्णन्नुन्मिषन्निमिषन्नपि। निरस्तमननानन्दःद संविन्मात्रपरोऽस्म्यहम्॥६३॥

I abandon, accept, do conversation, open and close the eyes still I am soul in concentration, pleasure and in the form of knowledge.

मलं संवेद्यमुत्सृज्य मनो निर्मूलयन्परम्। आशापाशानलं छित्त्वा संविन्मात्रपरोऽस्म्यहम्॥ ६४॥

I am only in the form of knowledge after removing the mind in sensitivity and making it without desire as also after cutting down the knot of hope.

अशुभाशुभसंकल्पः संशान्तोऽस्मि निरामयः। नष्टेष्टानिष्टकलनः संविन्मात्रपरोऽस्म्यहम्॥ ६५॥

I am located in a healthy state after obtaining a due peace and liberty from the good and bad resolutions. I could be in knowledge form after giving up the sense of good and evil.

आत्मतापरते त्यक्त्वा निर्विभागो जगत्स्थितौ। वज्रस्तम्भवदात्मानमवलम्ब्य स्थिरोऽस्म्यहम्।
निर्मलायां निराशायां स्वसंवित्तौ स्थितोऽस्म्यहम्॥ ६६॥

I am enshrined perfectly in shelter with the equity of soul after giving up the affection and envy, the discrimination, the hunger for fame in this mortal world. I an enshrined in the position of soul where there is no place for imagination and hope and only an innocent knowledge.

ईहितानीहितैर्मुक्तो हेयोपादेयवर्जितः। कदान्तस्तोषमेष्यामि स्वप्रकाशपदे स्थितः॥ ६७॥

I have attained to the emancipation with a spirit of inert and active as also hatred and useful. When will I obtain the contentment of Soul? When I will be enshrined on the position of automatic light.

कदोपशान्तमननो धरणीधरकन्दरे। समेष्यामि शिलासाम्यं निर्विकल्पसमाधिना॥ ६८॥

When will I do concentration and meditation peacefully getting a seat in the cave of a rock. When will I become inactive or inert like a boulder by virtue of the exclusive meditation.

निरंशध्यानविश्रान्तिमूकस्य मम मस्तके। कदा तार्णं करिष्यन्ति कुलायं वनपत्रिणः॥ ६९॥

Upto when will I be able to concetrate on everlasting Brahma so undeviated that the cuckoo bird construct a nest on our head.

संकल्पपादपं तृष्णालतं छित्त्वा मनोवनम्। विततां भुवमासाद्य विहरामि यथासुखम्॥ ७०॥

I move with pleasure in the ever-extended field after crossing a vast forest of mind by cutting the resolution trees and the creepers of temptation.

पदं तदनुयातोऽस्मि केवलोऽस्मि जयाम्यहम्। निर्वाणोऽस्मि निरीहोऽस्मि निरंशोऽस्मि निरीप्सितः॥ ७१॥ स्वच्छतोर्जितता सत्ता हृद्यता सत्यता ज्ञता। आनन्दितोपशमता सदा प्रमुदितोदिता। पूर्णतोदारता सत्या कान्तिसत्ता सदैकता॥ ७२॥ इत्येवं चिन्तयन्भिक्षुः स्वरूपस्थितिमञ्जसा। निर्विकल्पस्वरूपज्ञो निर्विकल्पो बभूव ह॥ ७३॥

I am the form of that everlasting position. I am exclusive. I am in the form of victory and I had become liberated soul, a simple man, reluctant to desires, clean, full of splendour, a ruler and in the form of truth and knowledge. A recluse should enshrine within his own soul by making himself free from the feeling of pleasure, happiness, perfection, generosity, truth, non-duality etc. One should be exclusive in his practical deeds too when he had realized the one and the exclusive form.

आतुरो जीवति चेत्क्रमसंन्यासः कर्तव्यः। न शूद्रस्त्रीपतितोदक्या संभाषणम्। न यतेर्देवपूजनोत्सवदर्शनम्। तस्मान्न संन्यासिन एष लोकः। आतुरकुटीचकयोर्भूर्लोकभुवर्लोकौ। बहूदकस्य स्वर्गलोकः। हंसस्य तपोलोकः। परमहंसस्य सत्यलोकः। तुरीयातीतावधूतयोः स्वात्मन्येव कैवल्यं स्वरूपानुसंधानेन भ्रमरकीटन्यायवत्॥७४॥

If the prompt recluse is living with a desire for reclusion, he should do endeavour to obtain it in orderly manner. He should not converse with the Śūdra, the women, the shrewd, the man of enigma and the female in course of menstruation. A recluse shouldn't go to see the functions organised for any good. These worldly affairs, aren't for a recluse. The Bhūḥ and Bhuvaḥ world is for the prompt and Kuṭīcaka recluse, the heaven for Bahūdaka, the world of penance, for Haṁsa and the world of truth for Paramahaṁsa. The people under category of Avadhūta and Turīyātīta are enshrined in the element of their soul by investigating their genuine form analogous to a bee.

स्वरूपानुसंधानव्यतिरिक्तान्यशास्त्राभ्यास उष्ट्रकुङ्कुमभारवद्व्यर्थः। न योगशास्त्र प्रवृत्तिः। न सांख्यशास्त्राभ्यासः। न मन्त्रतन्त्रव्यापारः। नेतरशास्त्रप्रवृत्तिर्यतेरस्ति। अस्ति चेच्छवालंकारवत्कर्माचारविद्यादूरः। न परिव्राण्णामसंकीर्तनपरो यद्यत्कर्म करोति तत्तत्फलमनुभवति। एरण्डतैलफेनवत्सर्वं परित्यजेत्। न देवताप्रसादग्रहणम्। न बाह्यदेवाभ्यर्चनं कुर्यात्॥७५॥

A perseverance on number of holy books in orderly manner is redundant for a recluse and he only does investigation with his own form. Such move is useless as loading saffron on the back of a camel. A recluse is prohibited to follow the trend of yoga to do business with the hymns of Sāṁkhya Śāstra and to observe the trend of any holy book. In case, any recluse engages himself, it is like ornament on a dead body and it is prejudicial to the function and learning of a recluse. A recluse shouldn't participate in the functions organized for summoning the gods and deities. He should think that he is compelled to born with the fruit whatever action is made. He therefore should abandon these all activities as the froth is disappeared from the caster oil. The recluse neither should accept any Prasāda offered to any god and goddesses nor worship any exterior god.

स्वव्यतिरिक्तं सर्वं त्यक्त्वा मधुकरवृत्त्याहारमाहरन्कृशीभूत्वा मेदोवृद्धिमकुर्वन्विहरेत्। माधुकरेण करपात्रेणास्यपात्रेण वा कालं नयेत्। आत्मसंमितमाहारमाहरेदात्मवान्यतिः॥७६॥

The recluse should abandon everything except his soul and should live on alm confined to the hand. It will reduce the formation of fat in his body. He should move regularly and pass his life on alms in hand or the bowl in the form of mouth. A recluse should take food to the extent two parts by dividing the capacity of a belly into four parts. One part should contain water and the part should be left vacate for the circulation of wind.

भैक्षेण वर्तयेन्नित्यं नैकान्नाशी भवेत्क्वचित्। निरीक्षन्ते त्वनुद्विग्नास्तद्गृहं यत्नतो व्रजेत्॥७८॥

A recluse should always live dependent on alms. He shouldn't accept the food only from a home. The persons who watch at their path patiently and do request should only be visited for lunch or dinner.

पञ्चसप्तगृहाणां तु भिक्षामिच्छेत्क्रियावताम्। गोदोहमात्रमाकाङ्क्षेन्निष्क्रान्तो न पुनर्व्रजेत्॥७९॥

A recluse should go for alm only at five or seven houses who are cultured. He should only wait there to the extent a cow takes time in milking. He shouldn't re-visit at the same place from where he once has obtained the alm.

नक्ताद्वरश्चोपवास उपवासादयाचित:। अयाचिताद्वरं भैक्षं तस्मात्भैक्षेण वर्तयेत्॥८०॥

The fast is better than the dinner and the thing uncalled for is more better than the fast, Begging is more better than the thing obtained without begging. One should therefore resort to alm to extent it is possible.

नैव सव्यापसव्येन भिक्षाकाले विशेद्गृहान्। नातिक्रामेद्गृहं मोहाद्यत्र दोषो न विद्यते॥८१॥

One shouldn't enter into a house from the left and right directions while going for alm. The house absorbed from defects shouldn't be left either by mistake or by affection viz., the cultured house is the best place for an alm in purity.

श्रोत्रियान्नं न भिक्षेत श्रद्धाभक्तिबहिष्कृतम्। व्रात्यस्यापि गृहे भिक्षेच्छ्रद्धाभक्तिपुरस्कृते॥८२

If a person known to Veda is void of obeisance and devotion, no alm from his house should be accepted while a house full of obedience and devotion is suitable for alm even if it is not cultured.

माधूकरमसंक्लृप्तं प्राक्प्रणीतमयाचितम्। तात्कालिकं चोपपन्नं भैक्षं पञ्चविधं स्मृतम्॥८३॥

The alm for recluse is of five kinds. These are unresolved Mādhūkara, words used for begging, unexpected, immediate and casual.

मन: संकल्परहितांस्त्रीन्गृहान्पञ्च सप्त वा। मधुमक्षिकवत्कृत्वा माधूकरमिति स्मृतम्॥८४॥

The unresolved Mādhūkara is the kind of alm which is accepted in small quantum like a bee from any three, five or seven houses without having any resolution in the mind.

प्रात:काले च पूर्वेद्युर्यद्भक्तै: प्रार्थितं मुहु:। तद्भैक्षं प्राक्प्रणीतं स्यात्स्थितिं कुर्यात्तथापि वा॥८५॥

The alm accepted under promise or for which words are used is a process to accept it under compliance with the request made by the concerned person in the morning or on the previous day.

भिक्षाटनसमुद्योगाद्येन केन निमन्त्रितम्। अयाचितं तु तद्भैक्षं भोक्तव्यं च मुमुक्षुभि:॥८६॥

In case, any person invites the recluse while he is on move for alm, the recluse should accept alm at his house.

उपस्थानेन यत्प्रोक्तं भिक्षार्थं ब्राह्मणेन तत्। तात्कालिकमिति ख्यातं भोक्तव्यं यतिभि: सदा॥

सिद्धमन्नं यदा नीतं ब्राह्मणेन मठं प्रति। उपपन्नमिति प्राहुर्मुनयो मोक्षकाङ्क्षिण:॥८८॥

If any Brāhmaṇa request a recluse to accept food in his home at a time when the recluse is on move for alm, it is called as an immediate alm and it is worth to accept always. In case, any Brāhmaṇa brings food for a recluse in the hermitage of that recluse, it is called the derivative alm.

चरेन्माधुकरं भैक्षं यतिर्म्लेच्छकुलादपि। एकान्नं नतु भुञ्जीत बृहस्पतिसमादपि। याचितायाचिताभ्यां च भिक्षाभ्यां कल्पयेत्स्थितम्॥८९॥

A recluse shouldn't hesitate to ask for alm even from a Mleccha (an-uncultured and lower rung of society) when a dire need is felt: however, he shouldn't accept the food continuously from a single house. That house may be so cultured as that of Bṛhaspati but it is prohibited for a recluse to visit daily there. A recluse should live either on the alm for which words are used or a casual alm.

न वायुः स्पर्शदोषेण नाग्निर्दहनकर्मणा। नापो मूत्रपुरीषाभ्यां नान्नदोषेण मस्करी॥९०॥

It is a common tendency of the wind that it touches all, the fire burns all, the water wets all. Hence, even after a lump of urine and dust is thrown upon them, these do to accept such pollutions. Similarly, a recluse is not polluted as a reason of the defect get mixed in him.

विधूमे सन्नमुसले व्यङ्गारे भुक्तवज्जने। कालेऽपराह्णे भूयिष्ठे भिक्षाचरणमाचरेत्॥९१॥

A yogī should accept alm afternoon when the fire is not blazing with smoke and doing any sound, it is fully extinct and all other people present there could have taken their food.

अभिशस्तं च पतितं पाषण्डं देवपूजकम्। वर्जयित्वा चरेद्भैक्षं सर्ववर्णेषु चापदि॥९२॥

In course of any mishappening or adversity, a recluse can accept his alm from all Varṇas and castes except the infamous families, the shrewd, egoist and once fallen from their position.

घृतं श्वमूत्रसदृशं मधु स्यात्सुरया समम्। तैलं सूकरमूत्रं स्यात्सूपं लशुनसंमितम्॥

माषापूपादि गोमांसं क्षीरं मूत्रसमं भवेत्। तस्मात्सर्वप्रयत्नेन घृतादीन्वर्जयेद्यतिः॥९३-९४॥

The ghee is like a dog urine for recluse. The honey is like liquor, the oil is like the pork's urine, the commodities mixed with garlic, the pulse of Urad. The sweeten flower etc. are like the beef and the milk is like urine. Hence, the recluse should accept an alm without ghee etc. fatty things.

घृतसूपादिसंयुक्तमन्नं नाद्यात्कदाचन। पात्रमस्य भवेत्पाणिस्तेन नित्यं स्थितिं नयेत्। पाणिपात्रश्चरन्योगी नासकृद्भैक्षमाचरेत्॥९५॥ आस्येन तु यदाहारं गोवन्मृगयते मुनिः। तदा समः स्यात्सर्वेषु सोऽमृतत्वाय कल्पते॥९६॥

A recluse should never accept the spicy and firy food blended with ghee and Juice. Only hand is the vessel to accept the food for a recluse. One should always accept alm from that vessel only. A single time food in a day should be maintained and food in two times should be strictly avoided. The recluse who accepts the food only to the extent of his mouth capacity like a cow, viz., who doesn't stock it , attains to immortality by virtue of his spirit of equity.

आज्यं रुधिरमिव त्यजेदेकत्रान्नं पललमिव गन्धलेपनमशुद्धलेपनमिव क्षारमन्त्यजमिव वस्त्रमुच्छिष्टपात्रमिवाभ्यङ्गं स्त्रीसङ्गमिव मित्राह्लादकं मूत्रमिव स्पृहां गोमांसमिव ज्ञातचरदेशं चण्डालवाटिकामिव स्त्रियमहिमिव सुवर्णं कालकूटमिव सभास्थलं श्मशानस्थलमिव राजधानीं कुम्भीपाकमिव शवपिण्डवदेकत्रान्नं न देवतार्चनम्। प्रपञ्चवृत्तिं परित्यज्य जीवन्मुक्तो भवेत्॥ ९७॥

One should abandon the ghee etc. and the food accumulated treating it like blood and the flesh respectively. The recluse should abandon the odour and a cosmetics treating it rubbish, the salt considering it a snatcher, the garments as the state vessels, the massage like copulation, jokes and irony of friends like urine, the proud like beef, the alm from the house of friends and familiar like Cāṇḍāla, the women like snakes, the gold, like poison the assemblies like cremation ground, the capital like Kumbhīpāka hell, the food from a single home like corpse. He should seldom do the worship and recital for gods. He should try to be a free soul after giving up all worldly illusions.

आसनं पात्रलोपश्च संचयः शिष्यसंचयः। दिवास्वापो वृथालापो यतेर्बन्धकराणि षट्॥ ९८॥

The Āsana, the vessel, passion for accumulation of money, to make disciple, sleeping in the day and keeping the mind busy in trivial matters are the six things that throw a recluse in the ties.

वर्षाभ्योऽन्यत्र यत्स्थानमासनं तदुदाहृतम्। उक्तालाब्वादिपात्राणामेकस्यापीह संग्रहः॥ ९९॥

यतेः संव्यवहाराय पात्रलोपः स उच्यते। गृहीतस्य तु दण्डादेर्द्वितीयस्य परिग्रहः॥ १००॥

A place unwet of water is called Āsana. Only a pātra (vessel) should be kept with recluse. It is remission of vessel when a recluse adopts other vessels. To accept the stick of other on occasion of losing one is called Parigraha.

कालान्तरोपभोगार्थं संचयः परिकीर्तितः। शुश्रूषालाभपूजार्थं यशोऽर्थं वा परिग्रहः॥ १०१॥

It is called accumulation to collect the worldly luxuries with an intention to enjoy in further to accept service from any person, to do worship and perform any activities for the fame is also Parigraha.

शिष्याणां नतु कारुण्याच्छिष्यसंग्रह ईरितः। विद्या दिवा प्रकाशत्वादविद्या रात्रिरुच्यते॥ १०२॥

One should only make disciple to a person who is clean heart and most curious for sheltering with a view to welfare. Accumulation of disciples is a trend when unwanted disciples are made. The learning is known as day and the ignorance is as night for reclusion.

विद्याभ्यासे प्रमादो यः स दिवास्वाप उच्यते। आध्यात्मिकीं कथां मुक्त्वा भिक्षावार्तां विना तथा। अनुग्रहं परिप्रश्नं वृथाजल्पोऽन्य उच्यते॥ १०३॥

Any laxity towards the practise in learning is called sleeping in the day. It is considered trivial involvement when discussions are made on other wise matters than a story leading to metaphysics and common queries and replies.

एकान्नं मदमात्सर्यं गन्धपुष्पविभूषणम्। ताम्बूलाभ्यञ्जने क्रीडा भोगाकाङ्क्षा रसायनम्॥ १०४॥ कत्थनं कुत्सनं स्वस्ति ज्योतिश्च क्रयविक्रयम्। क्रिया कर्मविवादश्च गुरुवाक्यविलङ्घनम्॥ १०५॥ संधिश्च विग्रहो यानं मञ्चकं शुक्लवस्त्रकम्। शुक्रोत्सर्गो दिवास्वापो भिक्षाधारस्तु तैजसम्॥ १०६॥ विषं चैवायुधं बीजं हिंसां तैक्ष्ण्यं च मैथुनम्। त्यक्तं संन्यासयोगेन गृहधर्मादिकं व्रतम्॥ १०७॥ गोत्रादिचरणं सर्वं पितृमातृकुलं धनम्। प्रतिषिद्धानि चैतानि सेवमानो व्रजेदधः॥ १०८॥

A recluse should immediately abandon a single cereal (food staff), proud and vanity, odour, flower, ornaments, eating bettle, do massage, involve in playing games, ambition for enjoyment, do chemicalisation, do flattery, do criticize, do discussions on bargaining of any commodity, deliberation of the routine affairs, debate and dispute, violation to the principle laid down by teacher, the matters pertaining to dispute and harmony, the cot, white garments, discharge of semen, sleeping in the day, the begging bowl, gold, the poison, the weapon, the living soul, violence, the anger and couplation. The things prohibited are in brief the activities prescribed by Gotra etc., the inherent properties of parents. Enjoying these things pulls down the recluse to trap into worldly affairs.

सुजीर्णोऽपि सुजीर्णासु विद्वांस्त्रीषु न विश्वसेत्। सुजीर्णास्वपि कन्थासु सज्जते जीर्णमम्बरम्॥ १०९॥

स्थावरं जङ्गमं बीजं तैजसं विषमायुधम्। षडेतानि न गृह्णीयाद्यतिर्मूत्रपुरीषवत्॥ ११०॥

A learned recluse approaching to the old age shouldn't even faith on an old woman because an old cloth is stuck with the old quilt. The recluse shouldn't accept the immovable and movable things, the seeds, the gold, the poison, the weapon etc. considering these six things like the urine and night soil.

नैवाददीत पाथेयं यतिः किंचिदनापदि। पक्वमापत्सु गृह्णीयाद्यावदन्नं न लभ्यते॥ १११॥

A recluse shouldn't keep anything with him except the expenses necessary for transit and that too in course of adversity. In case the cereal is not available, the recluse may take the cooked food.

नीरुजश्च युवा चैव भिक्षुर्नावसथे वसेत्। परार्थं न प्रतिग्राह्यं न दद्याच्च कथंचन॥ ११२॥

A recluse, healthy and youth, shouldn't stay at any house. He neither should accept anything from others nor should give his own things to them.

दैन्यभावात्तु भूतानां सौभगाय यतिश्चरेत्। पक्वं वा यदि वाऽपक्वं याचमानो व्रजेदधः॥ ११३॥

A recluse should always be kind to all living organisms for their well-beings. The recluse who accepts the alm of cooked and uncooked food certainly attains to the worst position.

अन्नपानपरो भिक्षुर्वस्त्रादीनां प्रतिग्रही। आविकं वानाविकं वा तथा पट्टपटानपि॥ ११४॥

प्रतिगृह्य यतिश्चैतान्पतत्येव न संशयः। अद्वैतं नावमाश्रित्य जीवन्मुक्तत्वमाप्नुयात्॥ ११५॥

A recluse who takes special care for his taste, puts on woollen or cotton clothes and sometimes accept the silk clothes certainly befalls to a hellish position. He should instead of it ride on the sip of non-duality and gems the stage of all liberty.

वाग्दण्डे मौनमातिष्ठेत्कायदण्डे त्वभोजनम्। मानसे तु कृते दण्डे प्राणायामो विधीयते॥ ११६॥

A recluse should keep silence if he wishes to punish the speech. To punish the body, he should stop eating and hold the fast for long. He should do Prāṇāyāma if he wants to punish the mind.

[All living-organisms are tied with their activities and attain liberty by application of their self-knowledge. This is the season, the scholar recluse, always, keeps them away from all activities.]

रथ्यायां बहुवस्त्राणि भिक्षा सर्वत्र लभ्यते। भूमिः शय्यास्ति विस्तीर्णा यतयः केन दुःखिताः॥

The old and used cloth in lump can be easily found in the streets and colonies and the alm too is available everywhere. This earth is sufficely extended for sleeping. Hence, a recluse shouldn't fall in the trap of sorrow.

प्रपञ्चमखिलं यस्तु ज्ञानाग्नौ जुहुयाद्यतिः। आत्मन्यग्नीन्समारोप्य सोऽग्निहोत्री महायतिः॥ ११९॥

A recluse should burn into ashes in the fire of knowledge all kinds of worldly illusions. A recluse who can embed the knowledge fire in his innermost soul, is only said a great scholar and Agnihotri.

प्रवृत्तिर्द्विविधा प्रोक्ता मार्जारी चैव वानरी। ज्ञानाभ्यासवतामोतुर्वानरीभाक्तमेव च॥ १२०॥

There are two kinds of propensities among the recluse. The first is Mārjarī and the second is Vānarī. The recluse doing exercise on knowledge have the Mārjarī propensities and the otherwise category is of Vānarī.

नापृष्टः कस्यचिद्ब्रूयान्न चान्यायेन पृच्छतः। जानन्नपि हि मेधावी जडवल्लोक आचरेत्॥ १२१॥

A recluse shouldn't speak with any person not desirous of talking. He should also keep silence if someone raises any unjusticiable querry. Inspite of scholar, a recluse should remain innocent as a stupid.

सर्वेषामेव पापानां सङ्घाते समुपस्थिते। तारं द्वादशसाहस्रमभ्यसेच्छेदनं हि तत्॥ १२२॥

In case, if any evil is committed or atmosphere is seated, the recluse should do a Japa of Tāraka hymns upto twelve thousand in number and thus try to nip the evil at the bud.

यस्तु द्वादशसाहस्रं प्रणवं जपतेऽन्वहम्। तस्य द्वादशभिर्मासैः परं ब्रह्म प्रकाशते इत्युपनिषद्॥ १२३॥

A recluse is duly introduced with the everlasting perfect Brahma within his heart in a period of twelve months when he recites Oṁ in order of twelve thousand times per day. This Upaniṣad pertaining to reclusion is thus fall of mystery.

ॐ आप्यायन्तु .... इति शान्तिः॥

॥इति संन्यासोपनिषत्समाप्ता॥

61. AKṢAMĀLIKA-UPANIṢAD

अक्षमालिकोपनिषद्

This upaniṣad is related to Ṛgveda. In a questionnaire pattern, it has been framed as a result of discussion between Prajāpati Brahmā and Kumāra Kārttikeya (Guha). The topic of discussion is the enshrine of Akāra, Ukāra etc. in the basil-bead garland (aksamālā).

The curiosity very first has been raised regarding Akṣamālā (basil-garland). The questions raised are– what are the characteristics of Akṣamālā? How many kinds of it? How many aphorisms are in it? How is it intertwined? How many letters (varṇa) are enshrined in it? and who are the gods represented by it? Subsequently, the characteristics of Akṣamālā, concept of Brahma residing in it, the rectificatory (amending) approach, establishing recognition of a god particular with every bead of the garland, the prescribed Japas (silent recital) for attaining intimacy with the god, hymn, learning and the element, an exclusive devotion to Akṣamālā with presumption that everything is covered by it, psalm to Akṣamālā and finally the fruits of listening to this upaniṣad have been discussed.

॥शान्तिपाठ:॥

ॐ वाङ्मे मनसि प्रतिष्ठिता मनो मे वाचि प्रतिष्ठितमाविरावीर्म एधि। वेदस्य म आणीस्थ: श्रुतं मे मा प्रहासीरनेनाधीतेनाहोरात्रान्संदधाम्यृतं वदिष्यामि सत्यं वदिष्यामि। तन्मामवतु तद्वक्तारमवतु अवतु मामवतु वक्तारमवतु वक्तारम्॥ ॐ शान्ति: शान्ति: शान्ति:॥

O the supreme soul! Let me attain a position in which my speech within mind and mind within speech merged. Please, enable me to perceive your apparent feature. Enable me to know Vedas in essence. Let me endow with a viable memory not losing to whatever has been gained. May I be able to establish unbreaking relation between the day and night by virtue of this studious attitude (i.e. my study remains continue). I shall speak the fact (Ṛta) and truth always. May lord Brahmā guard me and the orator (the teacher). Should three fevers be cooled-down.

अथ प्रजापतिर्गुहं पप्रच्छ भो ब्रह्मन्नक्षमालाभेदविधिं ब्रूहीति। सा किं लक्षणा कति भेदा अस्या: कति सूत्राणि कथं घटनाप्रकार: के वर्णा: का प्रतिष्ठा कैवास्याधिदेवता किं फलं चेति॥ १॥

Once upon a time Prajāpati asked the lord Guha (Kārtikeya)– "O lord! Kindly tell the distinct method of Akṣamālā (basil-garland). What is the characteristics of that garland? How many kinds of it? Further, how many aphorism of it? The cause of action or event (kinds of intertwining) are of what nature? What are the letters (Akṣara)? What is the concept regarding it? Who is the god representing/regulating it? and What is the outcome of if?"

तं गुहः प्रत्युवाच प्रवालमौक्तिकस्फटिकशङ्खरजताष्टापदचन्दनपुत्रजीविकाब्जे रुद्राक्षा इति। आदिक्षान्तमूर्तिः सावधानभावा। सौवर्णं राजतं ताम्रं चेति सूत्रत्रयम्। तद्विवरे सौवर्णं तद्दक्षपार्श्वे राजतं तद्वामे ताम्रं तन्मुखे मुखं तत्पुच्छे पुच्छं तदन्तरावर्तनक्रमेण योजयेत्॥ २॥

Lord Guha replied– "O Brahman! This Akṣamālā is of ten kinds– made of corel, pearl, sphaṭika (precious stone), conch, silver, gold, sandal, Putrajīvikā, lotus and rudrākṣa. These are worn with a procedure and the beads represent the letters from "a" to "kṣa". There are three kinds of threads for intertwining these beads i.e. made of gold, silver and copper. The gold thread should be in the hold of beads, silver at the right, the copper in left side of the beads of this Akṣamālā. These should be intertwined in a manner that mouth of every bead in juxtaposition and the tail juxtapose to the tail of another bead.

यदस्यान्तरं सूत्रं तद्ब्रह्म। यद्दक्षपार्श्वे तच्छैवम्। यद्वामे तद्वैष्णवम्। यन्मुखं सा सरस्वती। यत्पुच्छं सा गायत्री। यत्सुषिरं सा विद्या। या ग्रन्थिः सा प्रकृतिः। ये स्वरास्ते धवलाः। ये स्पर्शास्ते पीताः। ये परास्ते रक्ताः॥ ३॥

The innermost thread is Brahmā. The right is Śiva and the left is Viṣṇu. The mouth is Sarasvatī (goddess of wit) and tail is Gāyatrī. The hold in every bead is learning (vidyā) and the knot is nature. The vowel (svara) being detached (satva) are in white colour. The consonants (touch) being blended form of Satva and Tamas are yellow and beyond to these properties (excluding Satva and Tamas) are of red colour because of Rajas property.

अथ तां पञ्चभिर्गव्यैरमृतैः पञ्चभिर्गव्यैस्तनुभिः शोधयित्वा पञ्चभिर्गव्यैर्गन्धोदकेन संस्नाप्य तस्मात्सोङ्कारेण पत्रकूर्चेन स्नपयित्वाष्टभिर्गन्धैरालिप्य सुमनःस्थले निवेश्याक्षतपुष्पैराराध्य प्रत्यक्षमादिक्षान्तैर्वर्णैर्भावयेत्॥ ४॥

Subsequently (after intertwining the garland) it should be made sanctitive by immersing in the milk of Nandā etc. five species of cows and by rubbing duly with Pañcagavya (cow urine, cow-dung, milk, curd and ghee) and further by cleaning with Pañcagavya (curd of Nandā etc. five species of cows). Then, the garland should be soaked into the perfumed water and "Oṁ" should be recited. The leaves then should fold and made a funnel like and water should be sprinkled on it. The eight kind of scented items (Aṣṭagandha) i.e. Takkola, Usīra, camphor etc. should be smeared on it and then enshrined on the metal "Maṇiśilā". It should be worshipped with Akṣata (rice) and flowers. Every bead of the garland should be spelled systematically from the letter "a" to "kṣa".

ओमंकार मृत्युंजय सर्वव्यापक प्रथमेऽक्षे प्रतितिष्ठ। ओमाङ्काराकर्षणात्मक सर्वगत द्वितीयेऽक्षे प्रतितिष्ठ। ओमिङ्कार पुष्टिदाक्षोभकर तृतीयेऽक्षे प्रतितिष्ठ। ओमीङ्कार वाक्प्रसादकर निर्मल चतुर्थेऽक्षे प्रतितिष्ठ। ओमुङ्कार सर्वबलप्रद सारतर पञ्चमेऽक्षे प्रतितिष्ठ। ओमूङ्कारोच्चाटनकर दुःसह षष्ठेऽक्षे प्रतितिष्ठ। ओमृङ्कार संक्षोभकर चञ्चल सप्तमेऽक्षे प्रतितिष्ठ। ओमॄङ्कार संमोहनकरोज्ज्वलाष्टमेऽक्षे प्रतितिष्ठ। ओम्लृङ्कार विद्वेषणकर मोहक नवमेऽक्षे प्रतितिष्ठ। ओम्लॄंकार मोहकर दशमेऽक्षे प्रतितिष्ठ। ओमेङ्कार सर्ववश्यकर शुद्धसत्त्वैकादशेऽक्षे प्रतितिष्ठ। ओमैङ्कार शुद्धसात्त्विक पुरुषवश्यकर द्वादशेऽक्षे प्रतितिष्ठ। ओमोङ्काराखिलवाङ्मय नित्यशुद्ध

त्रयोदशेऽक्षे प्रतितिष्ठ। ओमौङ्कार सर्ववाङ्मय वश्यकर शान्त चतुर्दशेऽक्षे प्रतितिष्ठ। ओमङ्कार गजादिवश्यकर मोहन पञ्चदशेऽक्षे प्रतितिष्ठ। ओम:कार मृत्यनाशनकर रौद्र षोडशेऽक्षे प्रतितिष्ठ। ॐ कंकार सर्वविषहर कल्याणप्रद सप्तदशेऽक्षे प्रतितिष्ठ। ॐ खंकार सर्वक्षोभकर व्यापकाष्टादशेऽक्षे प्रतितिष्ठ। ॐ गंकार सर्वविघ्नशमन महत्तरैकोनविंशेऽक्षे प्रतितिष्ठ ॐ घंकार सौभाग्यप्रद स्तम्भनकर विंशेऽक्षे प्रतितिष्ठ। ॐ ङंकार सर्वविषनाशकरोग्रैकविंशेऽक्षे प्रतितिष्ठ। ॐ चङ्काराभिचारघ्न क्रूर द्वाविंशेऽक्षे प्रतितिष्ठ। ॐ छंकार भूतनाशकर भीषण त्रयोविंशेऽक्षे प्रतितिष्ठ। ॐ जङ्कार कृत्यादिनाशकर दुर्धर्ष चतुर्विंशेऽक्षे प्रतितिष्ठ। ॐ झंकार भूतनाशकर पञ्चविंशेऽक्षे प्रतितिष्ठ। ॐ ञंकार मृत्युप्रमथन षड्विंशेऽक्षे प्रतितिष्ठ। ॐ टंकार सर्वव्याधिहर सुभग सप्तविंशेऽक्षे प्रतितिष्ठ। ॐ ठंकार चन्द्ररूपाष्टाविंशेऽक्षे प्रतितिष्ठ। ॐ डङ्कार गरुडात्मक विषघ्न शोभनैकोनत्रिंशेऽक्षे प्रतितिष्ठ। ॐ ढंकार सर्वसंपत्प्रद सुभग त्रिंशेऽक्षे प्रतितिष्ठ। ॐ णंकार सर्वसिद्धिप्रद मोहकरैकत्रिंशेऽक्षे प्रतितिष्ठ। ॐ तंकार धनधान्यादिसंपत्प्रद प्रसन्न द्वात्रिंशेऽक्षे प्रतितिष्ठ। ॐ थङ्कार धर्मप्राप्तिकर निर्मल त्रयस्त्रिंशेऽक्षे प्रतितिष्ठ। ॐ दङ्कार पुष्टिवृद्धिकर प्रियदर्शन चतुस्त्रिंशेऽक्षे प्रतितिष्ठ। ॐ धङ्कार विषज्वरनिघ्न विपुल पञ्चत्रिंशेऽक्षे प्रतितिष्ठ। ॐ नङ्कार भुक्तिमुक्तिप्रद शान्त षट्त्रिंशेऽक्षे प्रतितिष्ठ।ॐ पङ्कार विषविघ्ननाशन भव्य सप्तत्रिंशेऽक्षे प्रतितिष्ठ। ॐ फङ्काराणिमादिसिद्धिप्रद ज्योतीरूपाष्टत्रिंशेऽक्षे प्रतितिष्ठ। ॐ बंकार सर्वदोषहर शोभनैकोनचत्वारिंशेऽक्षे प्रतितिष्ठ। ॐ भंकार भूतप्रशान्तिकर भयानक चत्वारिंशेऽक्षे प्रतितिष्ठ। ॐ मंकार विद्वेषिमोहनकरैकचत्वारिंशेऽक्षे प्रतितिष्ठ। ॐ यङ्कार सर्वव्यापक पावन द्विचत्वारिंशेऽक्षे प्रतितिष्ठ। ॐ रंकार दाहकर विकृत त्रिचत्वारिंशेऽक्षे प्रतितिष्ठ। ॐ लंकार विश्वंभर भासुर चतुश्चत्वारिंशेऽक्षे प्रतितिष्ठ। ॐ वंकार सर्वाप्यायनकर निर्मल पञ्चचत्वारिंशेऽक्षे प्रतितिष्ठ। ॐ शंकार सर्वफलप्रद पवित्र षट्चत्वारिंशेऽक्षे प्रतितिष्ठ। ॐ षंकार धर्मार्थकामद धवल सप्तचत्वारिंशेऽक्षे प्रतितिष्ठ। ॐ संकार सर्वकारण सार्ववर्णिकाष्टचत्वारिंशेऽक्षे प्रतितिष्ठ। ॐ हंकार सर्ववाङ्मय निर्मलैकोनपञ्चाशदक्षे प्रतितिष्ठ। ॐ ळङ्कार सर्वशक्तिप्रद प्रधान पञ्चाशदक्षे प्रतितिष्ठ। ॐ क्षंकार परापरतत्त्वज्ञापक परंज्योतीरूप शिखामणौ प्रतितिष्ठ॥ ५॥

O Akāra! You are winner of death, therefore, by seated on this first bead. O Ākāra! You are omnipresent by virtue of your magnetic power of attraction. Please, be seated on this second bead. O Ikāra! You are endower of power and peace. Please, be seated on this third bead. O Īkāra! You are endower of elegance to the speech and always sacrosanct. Hence, enshrine on this fourth bead. O Ukāra! You are endower of all strength. Please, be seated on this fifth bead. O Ūkāra! You are innocent and almighty. Please, be seated on this sixth bead. O Ṛkāra! You make caprice to the mind, so, please shrine on this seventh bead. O Ṛṛkāra! you are spell bounder and ever luminating. So, please enshrine on this eighth bead. O lṛkāra! you are exhibitor of inimity and most cryptic as also know everything. So, please be seated on this ninth bead. O lṛṛkara! you are creator of attachment. So, please enshrine on this tenth bead. O Ekāra! you enslave to all and truth in yourselves, so enshrine on this eleventh bead. O Aikāra! you are always pure enrich with the satva property. You enslave the persons. So, please enshrine on this twelfth bead. O Okāra! you are the literature (all commune of words) and always pure, so enshrine on this thirteenth bead. O

Aukāra! you also are group of words, enslaver to all and always in peace. So, please enshrine on this fourteenth bead. O Ankāra! you enslave the elephant etc. and enchanter. So, please, enshrine on this fifteenth bead. O Aḥkāra! you destroy the death and dreadful. So, please enshrine on this sixteenth bead. O Kakāra! you are destroyer of all poisons and renderer of welfare. So, please enshrine on this seventeenth bead. O Khakāra! you are omnipresent and aggrieve all. Please, enshrine on this eighteenth bead. O Gakāra! you compound all hurdles and senior most. Please, enshrine on this nineteenth bead. O Ghakāra! you endow fortune and resist the power of enchanting. Please, enshrine on the twentieth bead. O Ṅkāra! you are destroyer of all beings and stubborn. Please, enshrine on this twenty first bead. O Cakāra! you make motionless and most cruel. Please, enshrine on this twenty second bead. O Chakāra! you destroy the living organism and fierce. Please, enshrine on this twenty third bead. O Jakāra! you destroy Kṛtya (wit of anger) and gallant. So, enshrine on this twenty fourth bead. O Jhakāra! you kill the living organisms. So, enshrine on this twenty fifth bead. O Ñkāra! you churn the death. So, enshrine on this twenty sixth bead. O Ṭakāra! you are destroyer of all ailments. Please, enshrine on this twenty seventh bead. O Ṭhakāra! you are in the form of moon. Please, enshrine on this twenty eighth bead. O Ḍakāra! you are destroyer of poison like eagle and beautiful. Enshrine please, on this twenty ninth bead. O Ḍhakāra! you endow with the properties and modest. Please, enshrine on this thirtieth bead. O Ṇakāra! you endow with all axioms and create affection. Enshrine on this thirty first bead. O Takāra! you endow with wealth and cereal etc. properties and always happy. So, please, enshrine on this thirty second bead. O Thakāra! you suggest means for performing great deeds (Brahma) and always in peace. Please, enshrine on this thirty third bead. O Dakāra! you endow with growth and glut and perceive always beautiful. Please, enshrine on this thirty fourth bead. O Dhakāra! you are killer of fever and poison. Please, enshrine on this thirty fifth bead. O Nakāra! you endow with enjoyment, emancipation and peace. Please, enshrine on this thirty sixth bead. O Pakāra! you are killer of poison and hurdles. You endow with benevolence. Please, enshrine on this thirty seventh bead. O Phakāra! you are enriched with Aṇimā, Garimā etc. eight axioms (achievements of a devotee) and always luminating. Please, enshrine on this thirty eighth bead. O Bakāra! you efface all distorts and beautiful. Enshrine on this thirty ninth bead. O Bhakāra! you kill the hurdle created by ghosts and dangerous. Enshrine on this fortieth bead. O Makāra! you enchant the enemy or raising inimity and creator of affection. Please, enshrine on this forty first bead. O Yakāra! you are omnipresent and sacred. Please enshrine on this forty second bead. O Rakāra! you create burns, jealousy and fever. You are defaced. Enshrine on this forty third bead. O Lakāra! you nourish the world and full of splendour. Enshrine on this forty fourth bead. O Vakāra! you satiate all and sacred. Enshrine on forty fifth bead. O Śakāra! you endow with all fruits and sacred. Enshrine on this forty sixth bead. O Ṣakāra! you endow with the great deeds (Dharma), wealth (Artha) and sensuality (Kāma) and your complexion is white. Please, enshrine on this forty seventh bead. O Sakāra! you are cause for all articles and related to all varṇas (four varṇas).

Enshrine on this forty eighth bead. O hakāra! you are all literature (all letters or literature) and sacred. Please enshrine on this forty ninth bead. O lhakāra! you endow with all powers and prominent. Please, enshrine on this fiftieth bead. O Kṣakāra! you are teller of the essence existing in this as also that worlds. Please enshrine on Śikhāmaṇi (the cardinal bead).

अथोवाच ये देवाः पृथिवीषदस्तेभ्यो नमो भगवन्तोऽनुमदन्तु शोभायै पितरोऽनुमदन्तु शोभायै ज्ञानमयीमक्षमालिकाम्॥ ६॥

He told thereafter– "we salute the gods existed in this earth." O god! give your kind consent for accepting this garland by me. The forefathers are requested for the image this garland would bear. Let the Pitṛ (Agnisvatta etc.) approve wearing this Akṣamālikā.

अथोवाच ये देवा अन्तरिक्षसदस्तेभ्य ॐ नमो भगवन्तोऽनुमदन्तु शोभायै पितरोऽनुमदन्तु शोभायै ज्ञानमयीमक्षमालिकाम्॥ ७॥

He then said– "Salute is conveyed to the gods residing in the space. May these gods enshrine on the garland of knowledge including Pitṛs (late forefathers_and bless for its image."

अथोवाच ये देवा दिविषदस्तेभ्यो नमो भगवन्तोऽनुमदन्तु शोभायै पितरोऽनुमदन्तु शोभायै ज्ञानमयीमक्षमालिकाम्॥ ८॥

He again said– "May the gods residing in heaven enshrine on this garland of knowledge and approve its image including pitṛs with blessing hands."

अथोवाच ये मन्त्रा या विद्यास्तेभ्यो नमस्ताभ्यश्चोन्नमस्तच्छक्तिरस्याः प्रतिष्ठापयति॥ ९॥

He further added– "Salute is conveyed to the hymns existed in this world (about 7 crore) as also to the learning (vidyās) including sixty arts. May their powers enshrine on it."

अथोवाच ये ब्रह्मविष्णुरुद्रास्तेभ्यः सगुणेभ्य ॐ नमस्तद्वीर्यमस्याः प्रतिष्ठापयति॥ १०॥

He continued– "Salute is conveyed repeatedly to lord Brahmā, Viṣṇu and Rudra alongwith their chivalry. May! their chivalry enshrine on it."

अथोवाच ये सांख्यादितत्त्वभेदास्तेभ्यो नमो वर्तध्वं विरोधेनिवर्तध्वम्॥ ११॥

He added– "Salute is conveyed to the ninety six sāṁkhya etc. philosophies. May these bless for progress and keep at a distance, the position of conflict and inimity."

अथोवाच ये शैवा वैष्णवाः शाक्ताः शतसहस्रशस्तेभ्यो नमो नमो भगवन्तोऽनुमदन्त्वनुगृह्णन्तु॥ १२॥

He again said– "Salute is conveyed to the thousands of devotees and followers to the sect of Śiva, Viṣṇu and Śakti. May these all grace with approval."

अथोवाच याश्च मृत्योः प्राणवत्यस्ताभ्यो नमो नमस्तेनैतां मृडयत मृडयत॥ १३॥

Lastly, we told– "Salute is conveyed to the subordinate or dependent powers of the death. Please, be graceful on us with this psalm and endow with pleasure to their devotees through this akṣamālikā.

पुनरेतस्यां सर्वात्मकत्वं भावयित्वा भावेन पूर्वमालिकामुत्पाद्यारभ्य तन्मयीं महोपहारैरुपहृत्य आदिक्षान्तैरक्षरैरक्षमालामष्टोत्तरशतं स्पृशेत्॥ १४॥

Again this half garland of fifty beads should be completed by adding fifty more beads with the same spirit and summon of the letters (Akṣara) thereafter, eight more beads should be spelled with the letters– a, ka, ca, ta, ṭa, pa, ya, sa as previously done. Now, one hundred eight beads will be intertwined with the garland (the śikhāmaṇi will enshrine by "kṣa" as before and the garland should be made by adopting this process).

अथ पुनरुत्थाप्य प्रदक्षिणीकृत्यों नमस्ते भगवति मन्त्रमातृकेऽक्षमाले सर्ववशंकर्यों नमस्ते भगवति मन्त्रमातृकेऽक्षमालिके शेषस्तम्भिन्यों नमस्ते भगवति मन्त्रमातृकेऽक्षमाले उच्चाटन्यों नमस्ते भगवति मन्त्रमातृकेऽक्षमाले विश्वामृत्यों मृत्युंजयस्वरूपिणि सकलोद्दीपिनि सकललोकरक्षाधिके सकललोकोज्जीविके सकललोकोत्पादिके दिवाप्रवर्तिके रात्रिप्रवर्तिके नद्यन्तरं यासि देशान्तरं यासि द्वीपान्तरं यासि लोकान्तरं यासि सर्वदा स्फुरसि सर्वहृदि वासयसि। नमस्ते परारूपे नमस्ते पश्यन्तीरूपे नमस्ते मध्यमारूपे नमस्ते वैखरीरूपे सर्वतत्त्वात्मिके सर्वविद्यात्मिके सर्वशक्त्यात्मिके सर्वदेवात्मिके वसिष्ठेन मुनिनाराधिते विश्वामित्रेण मुनिनोपजीव्यमाने नमस्ते नमस्ते॥ १५॥

After psalm offered to Akṣamālikā, it should be picked up and on moving round (Parikramā) one should again pray– "O goddess Mantramātṛke! O Akṣamāle! you resist the motion of all, you create melancholia and turn all in lunacy. Please, accept obeisance. You are in form of death to all and you also are conqueror of death. You excite all. You are saviour of all worlds, endow life to all, create everything, administrator of day and night and powerful to move from a river to another, from a coming to all other countries, islands, and throughout the world. You are present at all places. You regularly appear and luminate the heart by perpetual inspirations (vibrations). You dwell in all hearts. You are in the form of speeches known as Parā, Paśyantī, Madhyamā and Vaikharī etc. You hold all elements, all learning, you are the supreme power and worshipped by all gods. You are prayed by Vasiṣtha and worshipped by the saint Viśvāmitra. You are repeatedly saluted.

प्रातरधीयानो रात्रिकृतं पापं नाशयति। सायमधीयानो दिवसकृतं पापं नाशयति। तत्सायंप्रात: प्रयुञ्जान: पापोऽपापो भवति। एवमक्षमालिकया जप्तो मन्त्र: सद्य: सिद्धिकरो भवतीत्याह भगवान्गुह: प्रजापतिमित्युपनिषत्॥ १६॥

The person reciting this upaniṣad in morning absolves from the evils committed in the night. Recital in evening effaces all evils committed in the day. The person who recites in morning as also in evening, absolves from evils irrespective of their size. Lord Guha finally said that the hymn recited silently (Japa) on such garland duly spelled calling the presence of gods on all its beads; fructifies immediately.

ॐ वाङ्मे मनसि .... इति शान्ति:॥

॥ इति अक्षमालिकोपनिषत्समाप्ता॥

62. EKĀKṢARA-UPANIṢAD

एकाक्षरोपनिषद्

The saint feel a single letter (unperishing) supreme soul as the vital element of the life circulated throughout the world and as breathing taking a flow in the spinal nerve and as Soma in the space. A single letter has thus considered as almighty in this Upaniṣad allied to the Kṛṣṇa Yajurveda. The saint observes it activating as the god of removing hindrances namely 'Ariṣṭanemi' and Kumāra Kārtikeya. In this Upaniṣad, the saint has advised to worship that immortal letter and remove all illusions due to ignorance thereby integrate with the flame which is free from all worldly ties. The same element of supreme soul has been told that it bears all the characteristics of god Indra, Rudra and the Sun as also it is extended to all the four Vedas and the dynamic as also inert world. As a succinct note, it can be said that a single letter is almighty and one should pray it for a proper lead in life from birth to the emancipation i.e. physical death but metaphysical revival.

।।शान्तिपाठः।।

ॐ सह नाववतु....... इति शान्तिः।।

Pray for Peace

एकाक्षरं त्वक्षरेऽत्रास्ति सोमे सुषुम्नायां चेह दृढी स एकः।
त्वं विश्वभूर्भूतपतिः पुराणः पर्जन्य एको भुवनस्य गोप्ता।।१।।

O Lord! You are 'Akṣara' (i.e. immortal), you are Soma, Para Brahma (perfect knowledge) and you exist within a single letter (an immortal element) with your entity by moving through the route of spinal nerve to the Sahastrāra. You too are the cause of world, the master of all living-organisms, the person described in Purāṇa and in all forms. You only protect all the worlds by pouring with the rain.

विश्वे निमग्नेपदवीः कवीनां त्वं जातवेदो भुवनस्य नाथः।
अजातमग्रे स हिरण्यरेता यज्ञस्त्वमेवैकविभुः पुराणः।।२।।

O Almighty! You too are existed as the life force throughout the world and within every drain of the earth. You are only shelter to the intuitive saints and the poets. You only are protector of all the worlds. You too are in garb of fire and in garb of offering. You only are a gigantic and perfect man.

When the resolution of creation (Sṛṣṭi) is baked in the splendour of Brahma (knowledge), it is then said 'Hiraṇyagarbha' and when the perfect knowledge shows the feed of resolution, it is called 'Hiraṇyaretā'.

प्राणः प्रसूतिर्भुवनस्य योनिर्व्याप्तं त्वया एकपदेन विश्वम्।
त्वं विश्वभूर्योनिपारः स्वगर्भे कुमार एको विशिखः सुधन्वा।।३।।

As the thread is essential to every bead of a garment, you are in the same fashion exist as the main thread in garb of breathing throughout the world as also a cause of its origin. You only have measured the whole universe by a single pace therefore you only are the origin place of this whole creation of the universe. You too are protector of this universe in garb of breathing and as omnipresent as the Lord Viṣṇu himself and you hold the supreme bow like 'Kumāra Kārtikeya'.

वितत्य बाणं तरुणार्कवर्णं व्योमान्तरे भासि हिरण्यगर्भः।
भासा त्वया व्योम्नि कृतः सुताक्ष्यस्त्वं वै कुमारस्त्वमरिष्टनेमिः॥४॥

O Supreme soul!! You only attract the arrow towards yourself like the splendour of the Sun as it shines in the noon. You are in the form of luminated 'Hiraṇyagarbha' in the ether-like heart of all these living-beings created by the illusion. It is your divine light by which lord Sun lights in the ether. You are existed in the form of Kārtikeya, who are the army-general of the gods and you regulates all hurdles like an eagle.

त्वं वज्रभृद्भूतपतिस्त्वमेव कामः प्रजानां निहितोऽसि सोमे।
स्वाहा स्वधा यच्च वषट् करोति रुद्रः पशूनां गुहया निमग्नः॥५॥

O Supreme soul! You are thunder-holding Indra and the Rudra who removes all worldly ailments and thus you are the king of all subjects. You too are existed in the world of moon in the form of late fore-fathers who provide with the desired results and you also are the offering and obeisance performed for the satiation of the gods and late fore-fathers i.e. you are in the form of 'Svāhā, Svadhā' and 'Vaṣaṭkara'. You only are existing in the heart of all living-organisms.

धाता विधाता पवनः सुपर्णो विष्णुर्वराहो रजनी रहश्च।
भूतं भविष्यत्प्रभवः क्रियाश्च कालः क्रमस्त्वं परमाक्षरं॥६॥

O Lord! You too are Brahmā in garb of breathing and the creator of this whole universe. You also are the wind, the eagle, the Viṣṇu, Varāha, night and the day. You too are the past, the future as also the present. All activities, the movement of time and the supreme letter i.e. the non-perishing element Oṁ, are nothing else but you yourself.

ऋचो यजूंषि प्रसवन्ति वक्त्रात्सामानि सम्राड्वसुरन्तरिक्षम्।
त्वं यज्ञनेता हुतभुग्विभुश्च रुद्रास्तथा दैत्यगणा वसुश्च॥७॥

You too are originator of Ṛgveda, Yajurveda and Sāmaveda through your mouth. You are king Vasu, the space, the performer of the procedure of offering, entertainer of the share of offering and almighty. You too are eleven Rudras, demons and omnipresent Vasu also.

स एष देवोऽम्बरगश्च चक्रे अन्येऽभ्यधिष्ठेत तमो निरुन्ध्यः।
हिरणमयं यस्य विभाति सर्वं व्योमान्तरे रश्मिमिमंसुनाभिः॥८॥

O Supreme soul! You are existed in the orbit of Sun and everywhere as also in the heart of living-organisms for removing their darkness of ignorance with your various forms. You also are the Brahmāṇḍagarbhinī (holding this universe in its womb), Sunābhi (the best navel centre or illusion) existing in the ether of gigantic heart. The ever-luminated rays as existing in the planets like Sun etc. are also your rays.

स सर्ववेत्ता भुवनस्य गोप्ता नाभि प्रजानां निहिता जनानाम्।
प्रोता त्वमोता विचितिः क्रमाणां प्रजापतिश्छन्दमयो विगर्भः॥९॥

That (gigantic Brahma) is omniscient, protector of all worlds as also the navel of all the living communes. You too are all intuitive. You also are the relief's of a varied kinds of emotions. You too are existed in the form of Prajāpati within the womb of lord Viṣṇu and you too are Veda (rhyme).

सामैश्चिदन्तो विरजश्च बाहुं हिरण्मयं वेदविदां वरिष्ठम्।
यमध्वरे ब्रह्मविदः स्तुवन्ति सामैर्यजुर्भिः क्रतुभिस्त्वमेव॥१०॥

The learned persons were known to Veda, get rid of the property of Raja (Rajoguṇa), cannot able to know the gigantic person by golden complexion through the study of Sāma etc. Vedas. The person well-known to Brahma worship you through the hymns of Yajurveda in the offerings and the person following Sāmaveda also worship you through the Sāma hymns.

त्वं स्त्री पुमांस्त्वं च कुमार एकस्त्वं वै कुमारी ह्यथ भूस्त्वमेव।
त्वमेव धाता वरुणश्च राजा त्वं वत्सरोऽग्न्यर्यम एव सर्वम्॥११॥

O Supreme soul! You alone are the woman, man, bachelor as also the spinster. You too are the earth. You are Brahma, Varuṇa, the king, Saṁvatsara (period of a year), fire and the sun. You are everything.

मित्रः सुपर्णश्चन्द्र इन्द्रो वरुणो रुद्रस्त्वष्टा विष्णुः सविता गोपतिस्त्वम्।
त्वं विष्णुर्भूतानि तु त्रासि दैत्यांस्त्वयावृतं जगदुद्भवगर्भः॥१२॥

O Supreme man! You also are the sun, the eagle (Garuḍa), the moon, Varuṇa, Rudra, Prajāpati, Viṣṇu, the Sun and the master of sensory organs like the mouth etc. Gopati. You too are lord Viṣṇu and only saviour from the atrocities of the demons to the mankind as a whole. You too are the father of this world in the form of 'Bhūgarbha'. The whole universe is covered by you.

त्वं भूर्भुवः स्वस्त्वं हि स्वयंभूरथ विश्वतोमुखः।
य एवं नित्यं वेदयते गुहाशयं प्रभुं पुराणं सर्वभूतं हिरण्मयम्।
हिरण्मयं बुद्धिमतां परां गतिं स बुद्धिमान्बुद्धिमतीत्य तिष्ठतीत्युपनिषत्॥१३॥

You are competent to take auto birth (Svayaṁbhū) and with the mouth everywhere (Viśvatomukha). You too are residing in the worlds like Bhūḥ, Bhuvaḥ, Svaḥ etc. worlds. The man who know the primitive person (almighty) existing in the region of the heart cavity as the breathing and the light itself, obtains the supreme position of the scholars and his ignorance is effaced in toto. This only is Upaniṣad (mysterious knowledge).

॥शान्तिपाठः॥

ॐ सह नाववतु....... इति शान्तिः॥

॥इति एकाक्षरोपनिषत्समाप्ता॥

63. SŪRYOPANIṢAD

सूर्योपनिषद्

This Upaniṣad is related to the tradition of Atharvaveda. The uniformity between the Sun and the Brahma has been described in this smallest Upaniṣad. The Saint, god, rhyme etc. to this Upaniṣad has been very first enumerated. The inseparability of the Sun and the soul has been then propounded. The subject-matter then proceeds with the origin of world by the (splendour of Sun), the worship of god Sun, the universal Brahma form of Sun god, pray to god sun, the eight letters containing hymn of the Sun and the lastly, the fruit of the recital. The fact worth taking in notice is that the time when the Sun exist in the Hasta planet (the month of October or Aśvina) has been considered the best time for reciting this Upaniṣad. The man conquers the death by virtue of following this rule. This Upaniṣad has been then concluded with this great magnificence.

॥शान्तिपाठः॥

ॐ भद्रं कर्णेभिः........ इति शान्तिः॥

अथ सूर्याथर्वाङ्गिरसं व्याख्यास्यामः। ब्रह्मा ऋषिः। गायत्री छन्दः। आदित्यो देवता। हंसः सोऽहमग्निनारायणयुक्तं बीजम्। हल्लेखा शक्तिः। वियदादिसर्गसंयुक्तं कीलकम्। चतुर्विधपुरुषार्थसिद्ध्यर्थे विनियोगः। षट्स्वरारूढेन बीजेन षडङ्गं रक्ताम्बुजसंस्थितम्। सप्ताश्वरथिनं हिरण्यवर्णं चतुर्भुजं पद्मद्वयाभयवरदहस्तं कालचक्रप्रणेतारं श्रीसूर्यनारायणं य एवं वेद स वै ब्राह्मणः॥१॥

Now the Atharvāṅgirasa hymns pertaining to god Sun are described. The Saint to this hymn is Brahmā, the rhyme is Gāyatrī and the god is Āditya. 'Haṁsaḥ' 'So'ham' is the seed with fire god and the power is curiosity (Hṛllekhā). The Kīlaka is allied to the ether etc. creation. This hymn is applied for the purpose of accomplishment to four industries (Puruṣārtha). The person only is Brahman (knower of Brahma) who knows Lord Sun as enshrined with the seed on six sounds, consisting of six limbs, seated on red, lotus, rode on the chariot consisting of seven horses, gold complexion, holder of four hands, lotus in two hands and the posture of booning and posture of fearlessness in two hands and who inspires the cycle of time.

ॐ भूर्भूवः सुवः। ॐ तत्सवितुर्वरेण्यं भर्गो देवस्य धीमहि। धियो यो नः प्रचोदयात्॥२॥

The Brāhmaṇa doing concentration under the presumption that Lord Sun is present everywhere in the trio-world consisting of Bhūḥ, Bhuvaḥ and Svaḥ in the form of the supreme soul (Praṇava) attains to the emancipation. (He should say) I concentrate on the best splendour of Lord Savitā who originates this whole world. May that Savitā lead my wisdom to the right path.

सूर्य आत्मा जगतस्तस्थुषश्च। सूर्याद्वै खल्विमानि भूतानि जायन्ते। सूर्याद्यज्ञः पर्जन्योऽन्नमात्मा॥३॥

Lord Sun is the soul of the entire inert and sensitive world. All creatures are originated by the Sun. The offering, cloud, cereals and the soul (sensitivity) etc. all arise from the Sun-god.

नमस्त आदित्य। त्वमेव प्रत्यक्षं कर्मकर्तासि। त्वमेव प्रत्यक्षं ब्रह्मासि। त्वमेव प्रत्यक्षं विष्णुरसि। त्वमेव प्रत्यक्षं रुद्रोऽसि। त्वमेव प्रत्यक्षमृगसि। त्वमेव प्रत्यक्षं यजुरसि। त्वमेव प्रत्यक्षं सामासि। त्वमेव प्रत्यक्षमथर्वासि। त्वमेव सर्वं छन्दोऽसि॥४॥

O Lord Āditya! We salute you. You are the performer of all direct deeds. You apparently are lord Brahmā, Visṇu and Rudra. You too are Ṛk, Yajus, Sāma and Atharvaveda. You are the apparent form of all rhymes.

आदित्याद्वायुर्जायते। आदित्याद्भूमिर्जायते। आदित्यादापो जायन्ते। आदित्याज्जोतिर्जायते। आदित्याद्व्योम दिशो जायन्ते। आदित्याद्देवा जायन्ते। आदित्याद्वेदा जायन्ते। आदित्यो वा एष एतन्मण्डलं तपति। असावादित्यो ब्रह्म। आदित्योऽन्तःकरणमनोबुद्धिचित्ताहंकाराः। आदित्यो वै व्यानः समानोदानोऽपानः प्राणः। आदित्यो वै श्रोत्रत्वक्चक्षूरसनघ्राणाः। आदित्यो वै वाक्पाणिपादपायूपस्थाः। आदित्यो वै शब्दस्पर्शरूपरसगन्धाः। आदित्यो वै वचनादानागमनविसर्गानन्दाः। आनन्दमयो ज्ञानमयो विज्ञानमय आदित्यः॥५॥

The wind, earth, water and flame too are originated from the sun. He is the cause for origin of ether and the directions. The gods and the Vedas too are originated from him. Lord Sun only gives heat and light to this universe. This Sun too is Brahma. He is in the form of heart, mind, wisdom, and ego. Lord Sun is enshrined in the form of five breathing i.e., Rudra, Apāna, Samāna, Udāna and Vyāna also. He is performing the functions of the five sensory organs i.e. ears, skin, eyes, tongue and nose. He too is in the form of five executive organs i.e. speech, hand, feet, anus and genital. Lord Āditya is in the form of Tanmātrā to five sensory organs i.e. the world, touch, complexion, essence and smell as also five executive organs i.e. statement (words), giving, moving, excretion and pleasure. He is full of pleasure, knowledge and in the conscience form.

नमो मित्राय भानवे मृत्योर्मा पाहि। भ्राजिष्णवे विश्वहेतवे नमः। सूर्याद्भवन्ति भूतानि सूर्येण पालितानि तु। सूर्ये लयं प्राप्नुवन्ति यः सूर्यः सोऽहमेव च। चक्षुर्नो देवः सविता चक्षुर्न उत पर्वतः। चक्षुर्धाता दधातु नः। आदित्याय विद्महे सहस्रकिरणाय धीमहि। तन्नः सूर्यः प्रचोदयात्। सविता पश्चात्तात्सविता पुरस्तात्सवितोत्तरात्तात्सविताधरात्तात्। सविता नः सुवतु सर्वतातिं सविता नो रासतां दीर्घमायुः॥६॥

Salutation is conveyed to Lord Sun and Mitra, O Lord! Please protect us from the clutches of death. Salute is conveyed to Lord Sun who is ever-luminating and the cause for the creation of world. The creation, maintenance and destruction of all inert and sensitive creatures is caused from the Sun. I myself is what Lord Sun is. Lord Savitā is our eyes. Lord Sun renowned with the name of Parvara (who is able to fill with the light and energy both) is in the form of eyes. May Lord Āditya provide our eyes the power to observe everything. We are known to Āditya. We concentrate our mind on Lord Sun adorned with the thousand rays and may that Lord Sun provide us with great inspirations. Lord Savitā is in the front, at the rear, at North (left) and at the South (right). May Lord Savitā generate all desired matters for us. May that Lord provide us with longevity.

ॐ इत्येकाक्षरं ब्रह्म। घृणिरिति द्वे अक्षरे। सूर्य इत्यक्षरद्वयम्। आदित्य इति त्रीण्यक्षराणि एतस्यैव सूर्यस्याष्टाक्षरो मनुः॥७॥

The Praṇava Oṁ is one letter Brahma. 'Ghṛṇiḥ' and 'Sūryaḥ' are the hymns containing two letters each and 'Ādityaḥ' contains three letters. The great hymn is formed with these eight letters when all these are combined.

यः सदाऽहरहर्जपति स वै ब्राह्मणो भवति स वै ब्राह्मणो भवति। सूयोभिमुखो जप्त्वा महाव्याधिभयात्प्रमुच्यते। अलक्ष्मीर्नश्यति। अभक्ष्यभक्षणात्पूतो भवति। अगम्यागमनात्पूतो भवति। पतितसंभाषणात्पूतो भवति। असत्संभाषणात्पूतो भवति। मध्याह्ने सूर्याभिमुखः पठेत्। सद्योत्पन्नपञ्चमहापातकात्प्रमुच्यते। सैषां सावित्री विद्यां न किंचिदपि न कस्मैचित्प्रशंसयेत्। य एतां महाभागः प्रातः पठति स भाग्यवाञ्जायते। पशून्विन्दति। वेदार्थं लभते। त्रिकालमेतज्जप्त्वा क्रतुशतफलमवाप्नोति। यो हस्तादित्ये जपति स महामृत्युं तरति स महामृत्युं तरति य एवं वेद इत्युपनिषत्॥८॥

The person reciting this hymn daily is only Brāhmaṇa. An apprehension of prolong ailments is effaced by virtue of reciting this hymn while facing Lord Sun. The pauperity of the devotee is vanished forever and he gets rid of the defects caused by eating the forbidden or course things. He further gets rid of the defect arising on moving through inaccessible way (or wrong path), trifle and jeering, gossips, false statement etc. This upaniṣad should be recited by facing Sun in the noon time. The person doing this exonerates from the five kinds of heinous evils. It has been said Sāvitrī Vidyā (learning). One should not make any statement or appreciation to any of the person. The person reciting it in the morning becomes lucky and attains the livestock, life, cows etc. and the vital learning of Vedas. A fruit of many hundred offerings is obtained as a result of reciting this Upaniṣad thrice times a day. The person who recites this Upaniṣad when Lord Sun enshrines on Hasta planet i.e. in the month of October or Aśvina; conquers on the death too. The person who is known to this fact too crosses the death easily. This is the matter disclosed by this Upaniṣad (a mysterious learning).

॥ ॐ भद्रं कर्णेभिः......... इति शान्तिः॥

॥इति सूर्योपनिषत्समाप्ता॥

64. AKṢYUPANIṢAD

अक्ष्युपनिषद्

This Upaniṣad is related to the white (Śukla) Yajurveda. The Cākṣuṣmati Vidyā and Yogavidyā has been highlighted in a questionnaire pattern between the hermit Sāṅkṛti and Āditya wherein one has raised questions and the other has replied/answered them. This Upaniṣad has been divided in two parts. In its first part, Cākṣuṣmati Vidyā has been described. In the second part the nature of Brahma Vidyā has been elaborated and then several portfolios of Yoga for acquiring Brahmavidyā has been described. There are seven portfolios of Yoga described in this upaniṣad. The devotee gradually attains accession to in the field of Yoga vidyā by adopting Yoga. He arrives at the apparent vision of the Brahma when he practices the seventh position. At the end, a description regarding Brahma in the form of Oṁ has been made which is viable enough to achieve the position of Brahma by systematic knowledge and practical application of the same. He then perceives himself as Brahma particularly when he finds himself in the stage of supreme perception of the extreme and exclusive pleasure. This is the main topic laid-down by this upaniṣad.

॥शान्तिपाठः॥

ॐ सह नाववतु। सह नौ भुनक्तु। सह वीर्यं करवावहै। तेजस्विनावधीतमस्तु मा विद्विषावहै॥

ॐ शान्तिः शान्तिः शान्तिः॥

Recital for Peace

The supreme soul! Wish you please protect both of us (the teacher and disciple) simultaneously. Nourish us simultaneously. May both of us be powerful simultaneously. The learning acquired by us be full of splendour and intelligence should there be no place for inimity and rivalry between us. O mighty! may the trio fevers (material, metaphysical and celestial) be cooled down and undepleting peace attained.

॥प्रथमः खण्डः॥

अथ ह सांकृतिर्भगवानादित्यलोकं जगाम। तमादित्यं नत्वा चाक्षुष्मतीविद्यया तमस्तुवत्॥ ॐ नमो भगवते श्रीसूर्यायाक्षितेजसे नमः। ॐ खेचराय नमः। ॐ महासेनाय नमः। ॐ तमसे नमः। ॐ रजसे नमः। ॐ सत्त्वाय नमः। ॐ असतो मा सद्गमय। तमसो मा ज्योतिर्गमय। मृत्योर्माऽमृतं गमय। हंसो भगवाञ्छुचिरूपः प्रतिरूपः। विश्वरूपं घृणिनं जातवेदसं हिरणमयं ज्योतीरूपं तपन्तम्। सहस्त्ररश्मिः शतधा वर्तमानः पुरुषः प्रजानामुदयत्येष सूर्यः। ॐ नमो भगवते श्रीसूर्यायादित्यायाक्षितेजसेऽहोऽवाहिनि वाहिनि स्वाहेति। एवं चाक्षुष्मतीविद्यया स्तुतः श्रीसूर्यनारायणः सुप्रीतोऽब्रवीच्चाक्षुष्मतीविद्यां ब्राह्मणो यो नित्यमधीते न तस्याक्षिरोगो भवति। न तस्य कुलेऽन्धो भवति। अष्टौ ब्राह्मणान्ग्राहयित्वाथ विद्यासिद्धिर्भवति। य एवं वेद स महान्भवति॥ १॥

Part - I

Once upon a time, lord Sāṅkṛti visited in the world of sun (Ādityaloka). Having arrived there, they saluted lord Sun and worshipped him by Cākṣuṣmati vidyā. Salute is conveyed to lord Sun who gives light to the eyes. The mover in the sky, lord sun is saluted. Salute is conveyed to the commander who holds a huge army of thousands rays. Salute to lord Sun who is in the form of Tamas. Salute to sun in Rajas form and Satva form. O god sun! lead us from false to the truth. Lead us from darkness to light. Lead us from death to immortality. Lord Sun is sacred and creator of shadow (reflection). We bring in our memory, the holder of varied universal forms, luminated by the beams of light, omniscient (Jātveda), illustrated like gold, in the form of light-flames, and full of heat. He is appearing before all living organisms with thousand beams and in many hundred forms. In the form of light to our eyes, the son of Aditi is saluted. We are dedicated for the conductor and holder of this universe, the sun god. As a result of worship through this Cākṣuṣmati vidyā, lord sun was pleased enough and began to say– the Brāhmaṇa worshipping me daily with recital of this Cākṣuṣmati vidyā, does not suffer from eye-ailments and his clan also attains healthy eye-sight. This vidyā becomes fruitful when eight Brāhmaṇas are taught this vidyā. The person known to this vidyā attains greatness.

[The sun-god has been considered 'Pratirūpa' and 'Viśvarūpa'. According to science, whatever we see, it is because of reflection made by him. This is the reason, sun is considered Pratirūpa (counter form). Whatever we see in the light of the day, those all are the several forms of sun light and merely variation is seen due to their kinds. This is the reason for which the sun has been said universal (Viśvarūpa)].

॥द्वितीयः खण्डः॥

अथ ह सांकृतिरादित्यं पप्रच्छ भगवन्ब्रह्मविद्यां मे ब्रूहीति। तमादित्यो होवाच। सांकृते शृणु वक्ष्यामि तत्त्वज्ञानं सुदुर्लभम्। येन विज्ञातमात्रेण जीवन्मुक्तो भविष्यसि॥ १॥

Sāṅkṛti then said to lord sun– "O lord! Please, teach me the "Brahmavidyā". Lord sun replied– "O Saṅkṛti! listen to the most rare knowledge of element to which I am going to tell you. You will attain emancipation on acquiring this knowledge.

सर्वमेकमजं शान्तमनन्तं ध्रुवमव्ययम्। पश्यन्भूतार्थचिद्रूपं शान्त आस्व यथासुखम्॥ २॥

अवेदनं विदुर्योगं चित्तक्षयमकृत्रिमम्। योगस्थः कुरु कर्माणि नीरसो वाथ मा कुरु॥ ३॥

Live in peace and please by observing all living organisms one, seldom born (Ajanmā), silent, infinite, Pole-state (stable), integrated and sensitive (living) because of the knowledge of element. There should be no place for other in mind except the soul and supreme soul. This state of mind is Yoga and this is the real control of passion. Therefore, perform duties and actions by establishing mind in Yoga and there should be no time when dullness and reluctance may peep into the conscious of working.

विरागमुपयात्यन्तर्वासनास्वनुवासरम्। क्रियासूदाररूपासु क्रमते मोदतेऽन्वहम्॥ ४॥

ग्राम्यासु जडचेष्टासु सततं विचिकित्सते। नोदाहरति मर्माणि पुण्यकर्माणि सेवते॥ ५॥

(The first procedure of Avedana Yoga is as herein described). The heart and mind both gradually start moving away from the stage of thinking on the objects of worldly pleasures. The devotee feels pleasure in performing the benevolent activities daily and in routine manner. He always hates the abrupt mode and manners of the ignorant people and removes out such attitudes, if any, he finds in his personality. He does not disclose the private secrets of any person before others. He always keeps his mind and hands busy on executing the great deeds.

अनन्योद्वेगकारीणि मृदुकर्माणि सेवते। पापाद्बिभेति सततं न च भोगमपेक्षते॥ ६॥

स्नेहप्रणयगर्भाणि पेशलान्युचितानि च। देशकालोपपन्नानि वचनान्यभिभाषते॥ ७॥

He does the acts that keep others in peace and seldom knock down in the trench of excitement. His deeds thus, are performed benevolent and philanthropic. He fears of committing crime and does not tempted to the means of consumption (luxuries). He used the words revealing love and affection as also suitable to the time, place and person with courtesy.

मनसा कर्मणा वाचा सज्जनानुपसेवते। यतःकुतश्चिदानीय नित्यं शास्त्राण्यवेक्षते॥ ८॥

He makes all endeavour to sit in the company of great persons and involves himself in their service by engaging mind, speech and the deeds. He reads holy literature daily and shows no miserity in procuring them.

तदासौ प्रथमामेकां प्राप्तो भवति भूमिकाम्। एवं विचारवान्यः स्यात्संसारोत्तारणं प्रति॥ ९॥

स भूमिकावानित्युक्तः शेषस्त्वार्य इति स्मृतः। विचारनाम्नीमितरामागतो योगभूमिकाम्॥ १०॥

He is called executing his first portfolio at this stage. The man who is fond of crossing the deep worldly ocean, only gives priority to such thought. He is called Bhūmikāvān (promoter) while the rest of people are said Arya (Best in comparison to others). The follower of the second approach of Yoga have the following characteristics.

श्रुतिस्मृतिसदाचारधारणाध्यानकर्मणः। मुख्यया व्याख्यया ख्याताञ्छ्रयति श्रेष्ठपण्डितान्॥ ११॥

He attains shelter to such renowned scholars who are famous for the best explanation of Veda, Smṛti, etiquette, conception and the meditation.

पदार्थप्रविभागज्ञः कार्याकार्यविनिर्णयम्। जानात्यधिगतश्चान्यो गृहं गृहपतिर्यथा॥ १२॥

मदाभिमानमात्सर्यलोभमोहातिशायिताम्। बहिरप्यास्थितामीषत्त्यजत्यहिरिव त्वचम्॥ १३॥

इत्थंभूतमतिः शास्त्रगुरुसज्जनसेवया। सरहस्यमशेषेण यथावदधिगच्छति॥ १४॥

He knows the division and position of the matters properly and become expert in deciding the nature of act whether good or wrong when he acquires mastery in the holy-books worth listening to the excessity of ego, vanity, manipulation, greed and attachments etc. does not make him puzzle. Extraneous dealing if any, remain attached to him, that also is abandoned by him as the snake casts off his slough. The devotee full of such holy knowledge acquires even most cryptic knowledge as a result of his hard industry and with co-operation and assistance that he receives from the scriptures, teacher and the great-men.

असंसर्गाभिधामन्यां तृतीयां योगभूमिकाम्। ततः पतत्यसौ कान्तः पुष्पशय्यामिवामलाम्॥ १५

यथावच्छास्त्रवाक्यार्थे मतिमाधाय निश्चलाम्। तापसाश्रमविश्रान्तैरध्यात्मकथनक्र मैः॥ १६॥

शिलाशय्याऽऽसनासीनो जरयत्यायुराततम्। वनावनिविहारेण चित्तोपशमशोभिना॥ १७॥

असङ्गसुखसौख्येन कालं नयति नीतिमान्। अभ्यासात्साधुशास्त्राणां करणात्पुण्यकर्मणाम्॥ १८

जन्तोर्यथावदेवेयं वस्तुदृष्टिः प्रसीदति। तृतीयां भूमिकां प्राप्य बुद्धोऽनुभवति स्वयम्॥ १९॥

He enters in the third stage of Yoga named as Asaṅsarga hereafter and the same as any person lays on the neat and clean bed well decorated. As the holy-books say, he enjoins his stable mind on them, resides in the āśrama of ascetics and engaged him discussing on the metaphysics and spends his whole life bearing troubles of resting on the bed made of stones. That man of polity puts his relations out from the material luxuries, lives in the tropical forests suitable to provide with peace to mind and passes his life by consuming the easily available means of pleasure. The perseverance on the holy books and by reason of performing great deeds, the power of observation is rectified. The devotee perceives this stage as a result of self-recognition.

द्विप्रकारमसंसर्गं तस्य भेदमिमं शृणु। द्विविधोऽयमसंसर्गः सामान्यः श्रेष्ठ एव च॥ २०॥

नाहं कर्त्ता न भोक्ता च न बाध्यो न च बाधकः। इत्यसंजनमर्थेषु सामान्यासङ्गनामकम्॥ २१॥

प्राक्कर्मनिर्मितं सर्वमीश्वराधीनमेव वा। सुखं वा यदि वा दुःखं कैवात्र मम कर्तृता॥ २२॥

भोगाभोगा महारोगाः संपदः परमापदः। वियोगायैव संयोगा आधयो व्याधयोऽधियाम्॥ २३॥

कालश्च कलनोद्युक्तः सर्वभावाननारतम्। अनास्थयेति भावानां यदभावनमान्तरम्।

वाक्यार्थलब्धमनसः सामान्योऽसावसङ्गमः॥ २४॥

Asaṅsarga is of two kinds from an angle of common and particular classification. (Now these kinds are to be described.) The attitude for making oneself detached from the worldly luxuries considering him not a Kartā, enjoyer and interceptor is called Asaṅsarga. To conceive that everything is the consideration for the deeds performed in previous life or everything is under the supreme soul and what is the existence or influence of the deeds performed by me in the position of grief or happiness? Excess collection of means of luxuries is in the form of incurable disease and all luxuries are the cause of calamities. The last consequence of all combinations is the betterment. The mental worries are ailments for the persons looming large in ignorance. All transitory matters are perishing and the mighty time (Kāla) is busy in making them his morsel. The common Asaṅsarga is, that generates pains for the lack of the world objects and this only takes place when holy scriptures are not read or listened to heartily.

अनेन क्रमयोगेन संयोगेन महात्मनाम्। नाहं कर्तेश्वरः कर्ता कर्म वा प्राक्तनं मम॥ २५॥

कृत्वा दूरतरे नूनमिति शब्दार्थभावनम्। यन्मौनमासनं शान्तं तच्छ्रेष्ठासङ्ग उच्यते॥ २६॥

As a result of perpetual touch with the great men, one who says that he is not Kartā (the performer of actual), god is the performer or the deeds performed by me in previous life are the performer. All worries and the meaning and proportion to words are thus, surrendered to almighty or the previous deeds. What remains thereafter is the silence (control on mind and senses), the Āsana (internal stage) and a spirit in peace (losing the extraneous spirit) and it is called the best Asaṅsarga.

संतोषामोदमधुरा प्रथमोदेति भूमिका। भूमिप्रोदितमात्रोऽन्तरमृताङ्कुरिकेव सा॥ २७॥

एषा हि परिमृष्टान्तरन्यासां प्रसवैकभूः। द्वितीयां च तृतीयां च भूमिकां प्राप्नुयात्ततः॥ २८॥

श्रेष्ठा सर्वगता ह्येषा तृतीया भूमिकात्र हि। भवति प्रोज्झिताशेषसंकल्पकलनः पुमान्॥ २९॥

भूमिकात्रितयाभ्यासादज्ञाने क्षयमागते। समं सर्वत्र पश्यन्ति चतुर्थीं भूमिकां गताः॥ ३०॥

अद्वैते स्थैर्यमायाते द्वैते च प्रशमं गते। पश्यन्ति स्वप्नवल्लोकं चतुर्थीं भूमिकां गताः॥ ३१॥

In the land of heart, the first stage or trend arises as pleasing and satisfactory as the sprouting of the small shoot of nectar. It appears melodious to the large extent. The land for sprouting of other and the rest of trends becomes ready in the heart. The second and third trend originating subsequently is also accessed to and acquired mastery by the devotee easily. As the devotee gives up all tendencies based on resolutions, the third stage therefore is counted in the supreme category. Owing to strong conception of the integrated view, the duality automatically ceases. The devotee accepts this world as a dream when the fourth stage is arrived at.

भूमिकात्रितयं जाग्रच्चतुर्थी स्वप्न उच्यते। चित्तं तु शरदभ्रांशविलयं प्रविलीयते॥ ३२॥

सत्त्वावशेष एवास्ते पञ्चमीं भूमिकां गतः। जगद्विकल्पो नोदेति चित्तस्यात्र विलापनात्॥ ३३॥

पञ्चमीं भूमिकामेत्य सुषुप्तपदनामिकाम्। शान्ताशेषविशेषांशस्तिष्ठत्यद्वैतमात्रकः॥ ३४॥

गलितद्वैतनिर्भासो मुदितोऽन्तःप्रबोधवान्। सुषुप्तघन एवास्ते पञ्चमीं भूमिकां गताः॥ ३५॥

अन्तर्मुखतया तिष्ठन्बहिर्वृत्तिपरोऽपि सन्। परिश्रान्ततया नित्यं निद्रालुरिव लक्ष्यते॥ ३६॥

कुर्वन्नभ्यासमेतस्यां भूमिकायां विवासनः। षष्ठीं तुर्याभिधामन्यां क्रमात्पतति भूमिकाम्॥ ३७॥

यत्र नासन्नसद्रूपो नाहं नाप्यनहंकृतिः। केवलं क्षीणमननमास्तेऽद्वैतेऽतिनिर्भयः॥ ३८॥

निर्ग्रन्थिः शान्तसंदेहो जीवन्मुक्तो विभावनः। अनिर्वाणोऽपि निर्वाणश्चित्रदीप इव स्थितः॥ ३९॥

षष्ठ्यां भूमावसौ स्थित्वा सप्तमीं भूमिमाप्नुयात्। विदेहमुक्तताऽत्रोक्ता सप्तमी योगभूमिका॥ ४०॥

First three stages are the awaken form and the fourth stage is called the dream. On arriving at the fifth stage, the world by feelings for luxuries is merged like the clouds of the pleasant season. Only Satva remains thereafter. Owing to merging of the heart, the worldly options do not arise. The fifth stage known as Suṣupta Pada locates the devotee in absolute stage when all sense of discrimination is cooled down. On removal of duality, the devotee attains self-realisation, feels pleasure and attains Suṣuptāghan (the pleasing stage). He always remains introvert inspite of extrovert dealing and always appears sleepy and dull like a tired man. Achieving expertise in this stage and on being devoid of attachments, the devotee, enters gradually in the sixth stage which is called "Turya". This is a stage where the truth and false lose their recognition, ego and humbleness is absent and having devoid of thinking tendency in the pure absolute stage, he obtains fearlessness. The doubts effaces on having disclosure of all the glands existing in the heart. Devoidness of the spirit takes place when the devotee attains emancipation. His position becomes as that of the devotee obtained the emancipation even when he actually has not availed of the same. He in that stage lives undeviated like an inert lamp. Having achieved the sixth, he attains the seventh stage. The seventh stage is considered when the devotee is living but forgets all care of body and becomes liberate from the attachments and worldly ties.

अगम्या वचसां शान्ता सा सीमा सर्वभूमिषु। लोकानुवर्तनं त्यक्त्वा त्यक्त्वा देहानुवर्तनम्॥ ४१॥

शास्त्रानुवर्तनं त्यक्त्वा स्वाध्यासापनयं कुरु। ओंकारमात्रमखिलं विश्वप्राज्ञादिलक्षणम्॥ ४२॥

वाच्यवाचकताभेदात् भेदेनानुपलब्धितः। अकारमात्रं विश्वः स्यादुकारस्तैजसः स्मृतः॥ ४३॥

प्राज्ञो मकार इत्येवं परिपश्येत्क्रमेण तु। समाधिकालात्प्रागेव विचिन्त्यातिप्रयत्नतः॥ ४४॥

स्थूलसूक्ष्मक्रमात्सर्वं चिदात्मनि विलापयेत्। चिदात्मानं नित्यशुद्धबुद्धमुक्तसदद्वयः॥ ४५॥

परमानन्दसंदोहो वासुदेवोऽहमोमिति। आदिमध्यावसानेषु दुःखं सर्वमिदं यतः॥ ४६॥

तस्मात्सर्वं परित्यज्य तत्त्वनिष्ठो भवानघ। अविद्यातिमिरातीतं सर्वाभासविवर्जितम्॥ ४७॥

आनन्दममलं शुद्धं मनोवाचामगोचरम्। प्रज्ञानघनमानन्दं ब्रह्मास्मीति विभावयेत्। इत्युपनिषत्॥ ४८॥

This stage is of supreme peace and it is undescribable any way by using the speech. It is like border line to all stages and all stages of Yoga end with it. (All stages get their terminal herein). The confined shackles of worldly etiquette, physical activities and following the track of the holy-book as suggested therein is left behind and affiliations with them are cut-off at this stage. This whole universe in the form of universe, perception and splendour is nothing else but the syllable Oṁ. Here establishes unity in the addressed and who addresses and achievement of this stage is not possible until discrimination ceases. These should be known as– the first move or 'Oṁ' i.e. 'a' is the world, 'u' is splendour and 'm' is the perception. Before the time of meditation (Samādhi), one should merge in the supreme soul by systematic exercise of thinking and making analysis, all that is material, tangible and in the minutest form residing in mind. Accepting his own complexion as that of the supreme soul, one should develop conformed faith on– I am immortal, sacred, wise, liberated, entity, unique, explorer of supreme pleasure and Vāsudeva 'Oṁ'. As this attachment is the main cause for trouble in beginning, in the middle and at the end, therefore, O innocent! abandon this all and be loyal to the element. One should develop a mentality that he himself is liberated from the darkness of ignorance, free from all kinds of illusions, sacred, pleasure, invisible from the mind and speech, full of perception, Brahma in garb of pleasure. This is upaniṣad (the secret learning).

॥ ॐ सह नाववतु .... इति शान्तिः॥

॥ इति अक्ष्युपनिषत्समाप्ता॥

65. ADHYĀTMOPANIṢAD

अध्यात्मोपनिषद्

॥शान्तिपाठः॥

ॐ पूर्णमदः पूर्णमिदं पूर्णात्पूर्णमुदच्यते।

पूर्णस्य पूर्णमादाय पूर्णमेवावशिष्यते॥

ॐ शान्तिः शान्तिः शान्तिः॥

अन्तःशरीरे निहितो गुहायामज एको नित्यमस्य पृथिवी शरीरं यः पृथिवीमन्तरे संचरन् यं पृथिवी न वेद। यस्यापः शरीरं योऽपोऽन्तरे संचरन् यमापो न विदुः। यस्य तेजः शरीरं यस्तेजोऽन्तरे संचरन् यं तेजो न वेद। यस्य वायुः शरीरं यो वायुमन्तरे संचरन् यं वायुर्न वेद। यस्याकाशः शरीरं य आकाशमन्तरे संचरन् यमाकाशो न वेद। यस्य मनः शरीरं यो मनोऽन्तरे संचरन् यं मनो न वेद। यस्य बुद्धिः शरीरं यो बुद्धिमन्तरे संचरन् यं बुद्धिर्न वेद। यस्याहंकारः शरीरं योऽहंकारमन्तरे संचरन् यमहंकारो न वेद। यस्य चित्तं शरीरं यश्चित्तमन्तरे संचरन् यं चित्तं न वेद। यस्याव्यक्तं शरीरं योऽव्यक्तमन्तरे संचरन् यमव्यक्तं न वेद। यस्याक्षरं शरीरं योऽक्षरमन्तरे संचरन् यमक्षरं न वेद। यस्य मृत्युः शरीरं यो मृत्युमन्तरे संचरन् यं मृत्युर्न वेद। स एष सर्वभूतान्तरात्माऽपहतपाप्मा दिव्यो देव एको नारायणः। अहं ममेति यो भावो देहाक्षादावनात्मनि। अध्यासोऽयं निरस्तव्यो विदुषा ब्रह्मनिष्ठया॥ १॥

The One *Aja* (unborn) is ever located in the cave (of the heart) within the body. (*Pṛthivī*) the earth is His Body; though he pervades the earth, it does not know Him. The waters are His body; though He pervades the waters, they do not know Him. *Agni* is His body; though He pervades *agni*, it does not know Him. *Vāyu* is His body: though he pervades *vāyu*, it does not know Him. *Ākāśa* is His body; though He pervades *ākāśa*, it does not know Him. *Manas* is His body; though He pervades *manas*, it does not know Him. *Buddhi* is His body; though he pervades *buddhi*, it does not know him. *Ahaṁkāra* is His Body; though He pervades *ahaṁkāra*, it does not know Him. *Citta* is His body; though He pervades *Citta*, it does not know Him. *Avyakta* is His body; though He pervades *avyakta*, It does not know Him. *Akṣara* is His body; though He pervades *akṣara*, it does not know Him. *Mṛtyu* is His body; though He pervades *Mṛtyu*, it does not know Him. He who is the inner soul of all creatures and the purifier of sins, is the one divine Lord Nārāyaṇa.

ज्ञात्वा स्वं प्रत्यगात्मानं बुद्धितद्वृत्तिसाक्षिणम्। सोऽहमित्येव तद्वृत्त्या स्वान्यत्रात्ममतिं त्यजेत्॥ २॥

लोकानुवर्तनं त्यक्त्वा त्यक्त्वा देहानुवर्तनम्। शास्त्रानुवर्तनं त्यक्त्वा स्वाध्यासापनयं कुरु॥ ३॥

स्वात्मन्येव सदा स्थित्या मनो नश्यति योगिनः। युक्त्या श्रुत्या स्वानुभूत्या ज्ञात्वा सार्वात्म्यमात्मनः॥ ४॥

निद्राया लोकवार्तायाः शब्दादेरात्मविस्मृतेः। क्वचिन्नावसरं दत्त्वा चिन्तयात्मानमात्मनि॥ ५॥

मातापित्रोर्मलोद्भूतं मलमांसमयं वपुः। त्यक्त्वा चण्डालवद्दूरं ब्रह्मीभूय कृती भव॥ ६॥

घटाकाशं महाकाश इवात्मानं परात्मनि। विलाप्याखण्डभावेन तूष्णीं भव सदा मुने॥ ७॥

स्वप्रकाशमधिष्ठानं स्वयंभूय सदात्मना। ब्रह्माण्डमपि पिण्डाण्डं त्यज्यतां मलभाण्डवत्॥ ८॥

चिदात्मनि सदानन्दे देहरूढामहंधियम्। निवेश्य लिङ्गमुत्सृज्य केवलो भव सर्वदा॥ ९॥

यत्रैष जगदाभासो दर्पणान्तः पुरं यथा। तद्ब्रह्माहमिति ज्ञात्वा कृतकृत्यो भवानघ॥ १०॥

अहंकारग्रहान्मुक्तः स्वरूपमुपपद्यते। चन्द्रवद्विमलः पूर्णः सदानन्दः स्वयंप्रभः॥ ११॥

The wise should through the practice of deep meditation of *Brahman* leave off the (recurrent) conception of 'I' and 'mine' in the body and the senses which are other than *Ātmā*. Having known himself as *Pratyagātmā*, the witness of *buddhi* and its actions, one should ever think "So'ham" ("I am That") and leave off the idea of *Ātmā* in all others. Shunning the pursuits of the world, the body and the *Śāstras*, set about removing the false attribution of self. In the case of a *Yogin* staying always in his own *Ātmā*, his mind perishes, having known his *Ātmā* as the *Ātmā* of all, through inference, Vedas and self-experience. Never giving slightest scope to sleep, worldly talk, sounds, etc., think of *Ātmā*, (in yourself) to be the (supreme) *Ātmā*. Shun at a distance like a *caṇḍāla* (the thought of) the body, which is generated out of the impurities of parents and is composed of excreta and flesh. Then you will be become *Brahman* and be (in a) blessed (state). O Sage, having dissolved (*Jīva-*) *Ātmā* into *paramātmā* with the thought of its being partless, like the ether of a jar in the universal ether, be ever in a state of taciturnity. Having become that which is the seat of all *Ātmās* and the self-resplendent, give up the macrocosm and microcosm like an impure vessel. Having merged into *Cidātmā*, which is ever blissful, the conception of "I" which is rooted in the body, and having removed the (conception of) *Liṅga* (here the sign of separateness), become ever the *Kevala* (alone). Having known "I am that *Brahman*" in which alone the universe appears like a town in a mirror, become one that has performed (all) his duty, O sinless one. The ever-blissful and the self-effulgent One being freed from the grip of *ahaṁkāra* attains its own state, like the spotless moon becoming full (after eclipse).

क्रियानाशाद्भवेच्चिन्तानाशोऽस्माद्वासनाक्षयः। वासनाप्रक्षयो मोक्षः सा जीवन्मुक्तिरिष्यते॥ सर्वत्र सर्वतः सर्वब्रह्ममात्रावलोकनम्। सद्भावभावनादार्ढ्याद्वासनालयमश्नुते॥ १३॥ प्रमादो ब्रह्मनिष्ठायां न कर्तव्यः कदाचन। प्रमादो मृत्युरित्याहुर्विद्यायां ब्रह्मवादिनः॥ १४॥

यथाऽपकृष्टं शैवालं क्षणमात्रं न तिष्ठति। आवृणोति तथा माया प्राज्ञं वापि पराङ् मुखम्॥ १५॥

जीवतो यस्य कैवल्यं विदेहोऽपि स केवलः। समाधिनिष्ठतामेत्य निर्विकल्पो भवानघ॥ १६॥

With the extinction of actions, there arises the extinction of *cintā*. From it arises the decay of *vāsanās*; and from the latter, arises *mokṣa*; and this is called *Jīvanmukti*. Looking upon everything in all places and times as *Brahman* brings about the destruction of *Vāsanās* through the force of *vāsanās* of *sāttvika* nature. Carelessness in *Brahmaniṣṭhā* by (or meditation of *Brahman*) should not in the least be allowed (to creep in). Knowers of *Brahman* style (this) carelessness, in Brāhmic science, is death (itself). Just as the moss (momentarily) displaced (in a tank) again resumes its original position, in a moment, so *Māyā* envelops even the wise, should they be careless (even for a moment). He who attains the *Kaivalya* state during life becomes a *Kevala* even after death of his body. Ever devoted to *samādhi*, become a *nirvikalpa* (or the changeless one), O sinless one. the *granthi* (or knot) of the heart, full of *ajñāna*, is broken completely only when one sees his *Ātmā* as secondless through *nirvikalpa samādhi*.

अज्ञानहृदयग्रन्थेर्निःशेषविलयस्तदा। समाधिनाऽविकल्पेन यदाऽद्वैतात्मदर्शनम्।। १७।।

अत्रात्मत्वं दृढीकुर्वन्नहमादिषु संत्यजन्। उदासीनतया तेषु तिष्ठेद्घटपटादिवत्।। १८।।

ब्रह्मादिस्तम्बपर्यन्तं मृषामात्रा उपाधयः। ततः पूर्णं स्वमात्मानं पश्येदेकात्मना स्थितम्।। १९।।

स्वयं ब्रह्मा स्वयं विष्णुःस्वयमिन्द्रः स्वयं शिवः। स्वयं विश्वमिदं सर्वं स्वस्मादन्यन्न किंचन।। २०

स्वात्मन्यारोपिताशेषाभासवस्तुनिरासतः। स्वयमेव परंब्रह्म पूर्णमद्वयमक्रियम्।। २१।।

असत्कल्पो विकल्पोऽयं विश्वमित्येकवस्तुनि। निर्विकारे निराकारे निर्विशेषे भिदा कुतः।। २२

द्रष्टृदर्शनदृश्यादिभावशून्ये निरामये। कल्पार्णव इवात्यन्तं परिपूर्णे चिदात्मनि।। २३।।

तेजसीव तमो यत्र विलीनं भ्रान्तिकारणम्। अद्वितीये परे तत्त्वे निर्विशेषे भिदा कुतः।। २४।।

एकात्मके परे तत्त्वे भेदकर्त्ता कथं वसेत्। सुषुप्तौ सुखमात्रायां भेदः केनावलोकितः।। २५।।

चित्तमूलो विकल्पोऽयं चित्ताभावे न कश्चन। अतश्चित्तं समाधेहि प्रत्यग्रूपे परात्मनि।। २६।।

अखण्डानन्दमात्मानं विज्ञाय स्वस्वरूपतः। बहिरन्तः सदानन्दरसास्वादनमात्मनि।। २७।।

Now, having strengthened the conception of *Ātmā* and well given up that of "I" in the body, one should be indifferent as he would be towards jars, cloth, etc. From Brahmā down to a pillar, all the *upādhis* are only unreal, hence one should see (or cognize) his *Ātmā* as all-full and existing by itself (alone). Brahmā is *Svayam* (*Ātmā*); Viṣṇu is *Ātmā*; Rudra is *Ātmā*; Indra is *Ātmā*; all this universe is *Ātmā* and there is nothing but *Ātmā*. By expelling (from the mind) without any remainder all objects which are superimposed on one's *Ātmā*, one becomes himself *Parabrahman* the full, the secondless and the actionless. How can there be the heterogeneity of the universe of *saṅkalpa* and *vikalpa* in that One Principle which is immutable, formless and homogeneous? When there is no difference between the seer, the seen, and sight, there being the decayless and *Cidātmā*, full like the ocean at the end of a *Kalpa* and effulgent, all darkness, the cause of false perception, merges in it. How can there be heterogeneity in that one supreme Principle which is alike? How can there be heterogeneity in the highest *Tattva* which is One? Who has observed any heterogeneity in *suṣupti* (the dreamless sleep), where there is happiness only? This *vikalpa* has its root in *Citta* only. When *Citta* is not, there is nothing. Therefore unite the *Citta* with *Paramātman* in its *Pratyāgātmika* state. If one knows *Ātmā* as unbroken bliss in itself, then he drinks always the juice (or essence) of bliss in his *Ātmā*, whether internally or externally.

वैराग्यस्य फलं बोधो बोधस्योपरतिः फलम्। स्वानन्दानुभवाच्छान्तिरेषैवोपरतेः फलम्॥ २८॥

यद्युत्तरोत्तराभावे पूर्वपूर्वं तु निष्फलम्। निवृत्तिः परमा तृप्तिरानन्दोऽनुपमः स्वतः॥ २९॥

मायोपाधिर्जगद्योनिः सर्वज्ञत्वादिलक्षणः। पारोक्ष्यशबलःसत्याद्यात्मकस्तत्पदाभिधः॥ ३०॥

आलम्बनतया भाति योऽस्मत्प्रत्ययशब्दयोः। अन्तःकरणसंभिन्नबोधः स त्वंपदाभिधः॥ ३१॥

मायाविद्ये विहायैव उपाधी परजीवयोः। अखण्डं सच्चिदानन्दं परं ब्रह्म विलक्ष्यते॥ ३२॥

इत्थं वाक्यैस्तदर्थानुसंधानं श्रवणं भवेत्। युक्त्या संभावितत्वानुसंधानं मननं तु तत्॥ ३३॥

ताभ्यां निर्विचिकित्सेऽर्थे चेतसः स्थापितस्य यत्। एकतानत्वमेतद्धि निदिध्यासनमुच्यते॥ ३४

ध्यातृध्याने परित्यज्य क्रमाद्ध्येयैकगोचरम्। निवातदीपवच्चित्तं समाधिरभिधीयते॥ ३५॥

वृत्तयस्तु तदानीमप्यज्ञाता आत्मगोचराः। स्मरणादनुमीयन्ते व्युत्थितस्य समुत्थिताः॥ ३६॥

अनादाविह संसारे संचिताः कर्मकोटयः। अनेन विलयं यान्ति शुद्धो धर्मो विवर्धते॥ ३७॥

धर्ममेघमिमं प्राहुः समाधिं योगवित्तमाः। वर्षत्येष यथा धर्मामृतधाराः सहस्रशः॥ ३८॥

अमुना वासनाजाले निःशेषं प्रविलापिते। समूलोन्मूलिते पुण्यपापाख्ये कर्मसंचये॥ ३९॥

वाक्यमप्रतिबद्धं सत्प्राक्परोक्षावभासते। करामलकवद्बोधमपरोक्षं प्रसूयते॥ ४०॥

वासनानुदयो भोग्ये वैराग्यस्य तदावधिः। अहंभावोदयाभावो बोधस्य परमावधिः॥ ४१॥

लीनवृत्तेरनुत्पत्तिर्मर्यादोपरतेस्तु सा। स्थितप्रज्ञो यतिरयं यः सदानन्दमश्नुते॥ ४२॥

ब्रह्मण्येव विलीनात्मा निर्विकारो विनिष्क्रियः। ब्रह्मात्मनोः शोधितयोरेक भावावगाहिनि॥ ४३॥

निर्विकल्पा च चिन्मात्रा वृत्तिः प्रज्ञेति कथ्यते। सा सर्वदा भवेद्यस्य स जीवन्मुक्त इष्यते॥ ४४॥

देहेन्द्रियेष्वहंभाव इदंभावस्तदन्यके। यस्य नो भवतः क्वापि स जीवन्मुक्त इष्यते॥ ४५॥

न प्रत्यग्ब्रह्मणोर्भेदं कदापि ब्रह्मसर्गयोः। प्रज्ञया यो विजानाति स जीवन्मुक्त इष्यते॥ ४६॥

साधुभिः पूज्यमानेऽस्मिन्पीड्यमानेऽपि दुर्जनैः। समभावो भवेद्यस्य स जीवन्मुक्त इष्यते॥ ४७॥

विज्ञातब्रह्मतत्त्वस्य यथापूर्वं न संसृतिः। अस्ति चेन्न स विज्ञातब्रह्मभावो बहिर्मुखः॥ ४८॥

सुखाद्यनुभवो यावत्तावत्प्रारब्धमिष्यते। फलोदयः क्रियापूर्वो निष्क्रियो नहि कुत्रचित्॥ ४९॥

अहं ब्रह्मेति विज्ञानात् कल्पकोटिशतार्जितम्। संचितं विलयं याति प्रबोधात्स्वप्नकर्मवत्॥ ५०

The fruit of *vairāgya* is bodha (spiritual wisdom); the fruit of *bodha* is *uparati* (renunciation); *śānti* (sweet patience) is attained out of the enjoyment of the bliss of one's *Ātmā*, and this *śānti* is the fruit of *uparati*. If the latter in each of these is absent, the former is useless. *Nivṛtti* (or the return path) leads to the highest contentment and (spiritual) bliss is said to be beyond all analogy. That which has *Māyā* as its *upādhi* is the womb of the world; that true one which has the attribute of omniscience, etc. and has the variegated mystery is denoted by the word "*Tat*" (that). That is called *Apara* (the other or inferior) which shines through meditation upon the idea and the world *asmat* and the consciousness of which is developed by *antaḥkaraṇa*. By separating the *upādhis, Māyā* and *avidyā* from *Parā* and

Jīva (cosmic and human *Ātmās* respectively) one realises *Parabrahman* which is partless and *saccidānanda*. Making the mind dwell upon such sentences (or ideas) as the above constitutes *śravaṇa* (hearing). It becomes *manana* (contemplation) when such ideas are quited (in one) through logical reasoning. When (their) meaning is confirmed through these (two processes) the concentration of the mind on it alone constitutes *nididhyāsana*. That is called *samādhi* in which the *citta*, rising above the conception of the contemplator and contemplation, merges gradually into the contemplated, like a light undisturbed by the wind. Even the mental states are not known (at the time when one is within the scope of *Ātmā*). But they are only inferred from the recollection which takes place after *samādhi*. Through this *samādhi* are destroyed crores of *karmas* which have accumulated during cycles of births without beginning and pure *dharma* is developed. Knowers of *Yoga* call this *samādhi*, *dharma-megha* (cloud), in as much as it showers nectarine drops of *karma* in great quantities, when all the hosts of *vāsanās* are destroyed entirely through this, and when the accumulated *karmas*, virtuous and sinful, are rooted out. Then that in which speech was hidden till now, appears no longer so, and shines as *Sat*; and direct cognition reveals itself, like the myrobalan in the palm of the hand. *Vairāgya* starts from where the *vāsanās* cease to arise towards objects of enjoyment. The cessation of the rising of the idea of "I" is the highest limit of *buddhi*; *uparati* beings from where the mental states once destroyed do not again arise. That ascetic is said to possess *Sthitaprajñā* who enjoys bliss always and whose mind is absorbed in *Brahman* that is formless and actionless. That state of mind is termed *prajñā* that realises the oneness of *Brahman* and *Ātmā* after deep inquiry, and that has the *vṛtti* of *nirvikapla* and *cinmātra*. He who possessess this always is *Jīvanmukta*. He is a *Jīvanamukta* who has neither the conception of "I" in the body and the senses of the conception of another (different from himself) in everything else. He is a *Jīvanamukta* who sees through his *prājña* no difference between his own *Ātmā* and *Brahman* as well as between *Brahman* and the universe, He is a *Jīvanamukta* who preserves equanimity of mind, either when revered by the good or reviled by the vicious. One who has cognized the true nature of *Brahman* is not subject to rebirth as before. But were he so subjected, then he is not a true knower, the knowing of *Brahman* being external only. A man is subject to *prārabdha* so long as he is affected by pleasure, etc. The attainment of a result is always preceded by action; and nowhere is it without *karma*. Through the cognition, "I am *Brahman*" are destroyed the *karmas* accumulated during hundreds of crores of previous births, like the actions in the dreaming state (that are destroyed) during the waking state.

An ascetic having known himself as associateless and indifferent like ether, is not at all affected by any of his *karmas* at any time. Just as the ether is not affected by the alcoholic smell through its contact with a pot, so *Ātmā* is not affected by the *guṇas* produced by its *upādhi*. The *Prārabdha karma* that has begun to act before the dawn of *jñāna* is not checked by it; and one should reap its fruit, as in the case of an arrow discharged at a target. An arrow that is discharged towards an object with the idea that it is tiger, does not stop when it (the tiger) is found to be a cow; but it (even) pierces the mark through its speed, without stopping. When one realises his *Ātmā* as free from old age and death, then how will *prārabdha* affect him? *Prārabdha* accomplishes (its work) only when one considers his body as *Ātmā*. This conception of *Ātmā* as body is not at all a desirable one; so it should be given up along with *prārabdha*, since it is simply a delusion to attribute *prārabdha* to this body. How can there be reality to that which is super-imposed upon another? How can there be birth to that which is not real? How can there be death to that which is not born? How can there be *prārabdha* to that which is unreal? The Veda speaks of *prārabdha* in an external sense only, to satisfy those foolish persons that doubt, saying : "If *jñāna* can destroy all the results of *ajñāna* (such as body, etc.), then whence is the existence of this body to such a one?" But not to inculcate to the wise the existence of the body.

स्वमसङ्गमुदासीनं परिज्ञाय नभो यथा। न श्लिष्यते यतिः किंचित्कदाचिद्भाविकर्मभिः॥५१॥

न नभो घटयोगेन सुरागन्धेन लिप्यते। तथाऽऽत्मोपाधियोगेन तद्धर्मैर्नैव लिप्यते॥५२॥

ज्ञानोदयात्पुराऽऽरब्धं कर्म ज्ञानान्न नश्यति। अदत्त्वा स्वफलं लक्ष्यमुद्दिश्योत्सृष्टबाणवत्॥५३॥

व्याघ्रबुद्ध्या विनिर्मुक्तो बाणः पश्चात्तु गोमतौ। न तिष्ठति भिनत्त्येव लक्ष्यं वेगेन निर्भरम्॥५४

अजरोऽस्म्यमरोऽस्मीति य आत्मानं प्रपद्यते। तदात्मना तिष्ठतोऽस्य कुतः प्रारब्धकल्पना॥५५॥

प्रारब्धं सिद्ध्यति तदा यदा देहात्मना स्थितिः। देहात्मभावो नैवेष्टः प्रारब्धं त्यज्यतामतः॥५६॥

प्रारब्धकल्पनाप्यस्य देहस्य भ्रान्तिरेव हि॥५७॥ अध्यस्तस्य कुतस्तत्त्वमसत्यस्य कुतो जनिः। अजातस्य कुतो नाशः प्रारब्धमसतः कुतः॥५८॥

ज्ञानेनाज्ञानकार्यस्य समूलस्य लयो यदि। तिष्ठत्ययं कथं देह इति शङ्कावतो जडान्॥५९॥

समाधातुं बाह्यदृष्ट्या प्रारब्धं वदति श्रुतिः। न तु देहादिसत्यत्वबोधनाय विपश्चिताम्॥६०॥

परिपूर्णमनाद्यन्तमप्रमेयमविक्रियम्। सद्घनं चिद्घनं नित्यमानन्दघनमव्ययम्॥६१॥

प्रत्यगेकरसं पूर्णमनन्तं सर्वतोमुखम्। अहेयमनुपादेयमनाधेयमनाश्रयम्॥६२॥

निर्गुणं निष्क्रियं सूक्ष्मं निर्विकल्पं निरञ्जनम्। अनिरूप्यस्वरूपं यन्मनोवाचामगोचरम्॥६३॥ सत्समृद्धं स्वतःसिद्धं शुद्धं बुद्धमनीदृशम्। एकमेवाद्वयं ब्रह्म नेह नानास्ति किंचन॥६४॥

स्वानुभूत्या स्वयं ज्ञात्वा स्वमात्मानमखण्डितम्। ससिद्धः ससुखं तिष्ठन् निर्विकल्पात्मनात्मनि॥

क्व गतं केन वा नीतं कुत्र लीनमिदं जगत्। अधुनैव मया दृष्टं नास्ति किं महदद्भुतम्॥६६॥

किं हेयं किमुपादेयं किमन्यत्किं विलक्षणम्। अखण्डानन्दपीयूषपूर्णे ब्रह्ममहार्णवे॥६७॥

न किंचिदत्र पश्यामि न शृणोमि न वेद्म्यहम्। स्वात्मनैव सदानन्दरूपेणास्मि स्वलक्षणः॥६८

असङ्गोऽहमनङ्गोऽहमलिङ्गोऽहमहं हरिः। प्रशान्तोऽहमनन्तोऽहं परिपूर्णश्चिरन्तनः॥६९॥

अकर्ताऽहमभोक्ताऽहमविकारोऽहमव्ययः। शुद्धो बोधस्वरूपोऽहं केवलोऽहं सदाशिवः॥७०॥

Ātmā is all-full, beginningless, immeasurable, unchangeable, replete with *Sat*, *Cit*, and *Ānanda*, decayless, the one essence, the eternal, the differentiated, the plenum, the endless, having its face everywhere, the one that can neither be given up nor taken up, the one that can neither be supported nor be made to support, the *guṇa*-less, the actionless, the subtle, the changeless, the stainless, the indescribable, the true nature one's *Ātmā*, above the reach of speech and mind, the one full *Sat*, the self-existent, the immaculate, the enlightened, and incomparable; such is *Brahman*, one only without a second. There are not in the least many. He who knows his *Ātmā* himself through his own cognition, as the one who is not restricted by any, is a *Siddha* (one that has accomplished his object), who has identified his *Ātmā* with the one changeless *Ātmā*. Whither is this world gone, then? How did it appear? Where is it absorbed? It was seen by me just now, but now it is gone. What a great miracle! What is fit to be taken in? And what to be rejected? What is other (than *Ātmā*)? And what is different (from It)? In this mighty ocean of *Brahman* full of the nectar of undivided bliss, I do not see, hear, or know anything. I remain in my *Ātmā* only and in my own nature of *Sat*, *Ānandarūpa*. I am an *asaṅga* (or the associateless). I am without any attributes. I am *Hari* (the Lord taking away sin). I am the quiescent, the endless, the all-full and the ancient. I am neither the agent nor the enjoyer. I am the changeless and the decayless. I am of the nature of pure enlightenment. I am the one and the perpetual bliss.

एतां विद्यामपान्तरतमाय ददौ। अपान्तरतमो ब्रह्मणे ददौ। ब्रह्मा घोराङ्गिरसे ददौ। घोराङ्गिरा रैक्वाय ददौ। रैक्वो रामाय ददौ। रामः सर्वेभ्यो भूतेभ्यो ददावित्येतन्निर्वाणानुशासनं वेदानुशासनं वेदानुशासनमित्युपनिषत्॥ ७१॥

This science was imparted to *Apāntaratama* who gave it to Brahmā. Brahmā gave it to *Ghora-Aṅgiras*. *Ghora-Aṅgiras* gave it to *Raikva*, who gave it to Rāma. And Rāma gave it to all beings. This is the teaching of *Nirvāṇa*; and this is the teaching of the Vedas; yea, this is the teaching of the Vedas.

ॐ पूर्णमदः .... इति शान्तिः॥

॥इत्यध्यात्मोपनिषत्समाप्ता॥

66. KUṆḌIKOPANIṢAD

कुण्डिकोपनिषद्

This Upaniṣad is related to Sāmaveda. From hymn 1 to 13 the entrance of a couple in reclusion when the liabilities of couple life are duly discharge as also the routine has been highlighted. The introvert penance of the recluse has been then enumerated. It has been said that one should know the process of descending the Brahma sensitivity by means of the silent recital and concentration and he should feel it everywhere in the form of soul sensitivity. Thereafter, the penance of the upliftment of the living sensitivity by means of the Anāhata Nāda under due control to Tanmātrās, this specific order of penance has been enumerated most clearly here.

॥शान्तिपाठः॥

आप्यायन्तु .... इति शान्तिः॥

ब्रह्मचर्याश्रमे क्षीणे गुरुशुश्रूषणे रतः। वेदानधीत्यानुज्ञात उच्यते गुरुणाश्रमी॥ १॥

When the stage of celibacy is over, study on Vedas is completed and the teacher has aloud the persons to return his home by taking a leave from his service such a man is called Āśramaī.

दारमाहृत्य सदृशमग्निमाधाय शक्तितः। ब्राह्मीमिष्टिं यजेत्तासामहोरात्रेण निर्वपेत्॥ २॥

A prudent man should accept the wife matching with him and by entertaining the fire according to his power, he should earn his livelihood keeping him adhered to the offering of Brahma.

संविभज्य सुतानर्थे ग्राम्यकामान्विसृज्य च। संचरन्वनमार्गेण शुचौ देशे परिभ्रमन्॥ ३॥

The wealth earned till then should be divided among the sons, all affairs relating to the home and house (domestic) should be assigned to the sons and should depart for the forest by moving through the holy places.

वायुभक्षोऽम्बुभक्षो वा विहितैः कन्दमूलकैः। स्वशरीरे समाप्याथ पृथिव्यां नाश्रु पातयेत्॥ ४॥

The recluse should protect his body by inhaling the air and drinking water or the roots and the fruits as prescribed by the holy books. He should not wail considering the world of all confined to his body viz., he should not lament for his near and dears.

सह तेनैव पुरुषः कथं संन्यस्त उच्यते। सनामधेयो यस्मिस्तु कथं संन्यस्त उच्यते॥ ५॥

Nobody can be recluse by attending to or executing all these ordinary affairs. It is merely an observance of the ordinary rules and the rules made for recluse are more typical and best than it. In Order to observe these rites, one should enter into past couple life

(Vānaprastha Āśrama) by duly giving up the fire and the provision of varṇāśrama as a result of attaining to the emancipation through the life of a recluse.

तस्मात्फलविशुद्धाङ्गी संन्यासं संहितात्मनाम्। अग्निवर्णं विनिष्क्रम्य वानप्रस्थं प्रपद्यते॥ ६॥

One should enter into past couple stage not desiring for fruit of action, giving up the fire and abandoning the system to varṇāśrama thereby attain to emancipation through process of renouncement.

लोकवद्धार्ययाऽऽसक्तो वनं गच्छति संयतः। संत्यक्त्वा संसृतिसुखमनुतिष्ठति किं मुधा॥ ७॥

किंवा दुःखमनुस्मृत्य भोगांस्त्यजति चोच्छ्रितान्। गर्भवासभयाद्भीतः शीतोष्णाभ्यां तथैव च॥ ८॥

What is the benefit for performing the ceremonies in the forest by resorting to it and giving up the worldly pleasures and like ordinary people? Further why the man threatened of the vicissitudes of life, feeling of cold and the heat as also apprehension of sprouting within the womb abandon the worldly enjoyments?

गुह्यं प्रवेष्टुमिच्छामि परं पदमनामयमिति। संन्यस्याग्निमपुनरावर्तनं यन्मृत्युर्जायमावहमिति। अथाध्यात्ममन्त्राञ्जपेत्। दीक्षामुपेयात्काषायवासाः। कक्षोपस्थलोमानि वर्जयेत्। ऊर्ध्वबाहुर्विमुक्तमार्गो भवति। अनिकेतश्चरेद्भिक्षाशी। निदिध्यासनं दध्यात्। पवित्रं धारयेज्जन्तुसंरक्षणार्थम्। तदपि श्लोका भवन्ति। कुण्डिकां चमसं शिक्यं त्रिविष्टपमुपानहौ। शीतोपघातिनीं कन्थां कौपीनाच्छादनं तथा॥ ९॥ पवित्रं स्नानशाटीं च उत्तरासङ्गमेव च। अतोऽतिरिक्तं यत्किंचित्सर्वं तद्वर्जयेद्यतिः॥ १०॥

The reason behind performing these activities is that the recluse desires to enter into that supreme and mighty position. He always and continuously remembers the Mahākāla that conquers the death. He recites the metaphysical hymns always and entertains consecration after putting up the saffron cloths. He cuts clean all hair. He wanders voluntarily by uplifting his both arms towards the sky. He lives on alms and thus survives having no home of his own. He should do Nididhyāsna continuously. He should hold (a stick) for protection from the animals. He should keep with him a Kamaṇḍala, Camasa (spoon), Śikya, Triviṣṭapa, a quilt for defence from the water, a Laṅgotī (nicker), a dhotī for bathing and a towel, All other things except these, should be abandoned by recluse.

नदीपुलिनशायी स्याद्देवागारेषु बाह्यतः। नात्यर्थं सुखदुःखाभ्यां शरीरमुपतापयेत्॥ ११॥

He should sleep at the bank of a river voluntarily if he may does. The body should not be in pain without any specific reason therefore.

स्नानं पानं तथा शौचमद्भिः पूताभिराचरेत्। स्तूयमानो न तुष्येत निन्दितो न शपेत्परान्॥ १२॥

He should use the pure water for bathing, drinking and cleaning purposes. He should neither be happy if praise is made nor curse any person if he condemns him.

भिक्षादिवैदलं पात्रं स्नानद्रव्यमवारितम्। एवं वृत्तिमुपासीनो यतेन्द्रियो जपेत्सदा॥ १३॥

A vessel for alm and water for bathing should be acquired by application of all efforts (because these are mandatory) to do physical cleaning. Thus, the saint should always keep oneself engrossed on silent reciting and do all whatever is ideal.

विश्वाय मनुसंयोगं मनसा भावयेत्सुधीः। आकाशाद्वायुर्वायोर्ज्योतिर्ज्योतिष आपोऽद्भ्यः पृथिवी। एतेषां भूतानां ब्रह्म प्रपद्ये। अजरममरमक्षरमव्ययं प्रपद्ये। मय्यखण्डसुखाम्भोधौ बहुधा विश्ववीचयः। उत्पद्यन्ते विलीयन्ते मायामारुतविभ्रमात्॥ १४॥

The scholars should develop propensity of mind that the Brahma in garb of universe and the latter Brahma i.e. Praṇava or Manu both are the same and there is no distinction between them.

I have attained the state of the Brahma, an omnipresent and everlasting among the elements in an orderly manner— the sky, the wind, the fire, the water, and the earth. I have acquired the state of immortality, everlasting, integrate and free from the impact of old age.

[A picturesque or concentration on or at the systematic origin of the Brahmi sensitivity from micro to formidable form has been described here in. In the successive hymns, the process of moving sensitivity from formidable to the micro form has been highlighted.]

न मे देहेन संबन्धो मेघेनेव विहायसः। अतः कुतो मे तद्धर्मा जाग्रत्स्वप्नसुषुप्तिषु॥ १५॥

As the cloud has no nexus with sky, I have in the similar fashion no nexus with the body, what relation I could have then with the dormance, dreaming, and awakening stage of this body?

आकाशवत्कल्पविदूरगोऽहमादित्यवद्भास्यविलक्षणोऽहम्।
अहार्यवन्नित्यविनिश्चलोऽहमम्भोधिवत्पारविवर्जितोऽहम्॥ १६॥

I (the living soul) is beyond the imagination like the sky and distinct from the attractive matters shining gold like the sun. I remain stable like the mountain and inaccessible like the sea.

नारायणोऽहं नरकान्तकोऽहं पुरान्तकोऽहं पुरुषोऽहमीशः।
अखण्डबोधोऽहमशेषसाक्षी निरीश्वरोऽहं निरहं च निर्ममः॥ १७॥

I myself is Nārāyaṇa. I am Narkāntaka (one who stained the monster Naraka), Purāntaka (killer or Tripurāsura), the man and the god too. I am known to unrebuttable knowledge, witness to all creatures without Īśvara (nobody is my administrator), without ego and affection.

तदभ्यासेन प्राणापानौ संयम्य तत्र श्लोका भवन्ति। वृषणापानयोर्मध्ये पाणी आस्थाय संश्रयेत्। संदश्य शनकैर्जिह्वां यवमात्रे विनिर्गताम्॥ १८॥

Now, we describe about the exercise of Prāṇa and Apāna. He should put his both hands at the middle place of testis and anus. He should gradually push his tongue by the teeth and take it out equal to the length of a barley seed.

माषमात्रां तथा दृष्टिं श्रोत्रे स्थाप्य तथा भुवि। श्रवणे नासिके गन्धा यतः स्वं न च संश्रयेत्॥ १९॥

He should make stable his sight on the airs and earth by investigating the aim equal to the length of a Urad seed.

[The successive hymns i.e., 20, 21, 22 explains the manner of penance in which all Tanmātrās are restricted, the sound generated as a result of the exercise made in the heart and adding by this procedure the self sensitivity to the sensitivity of Brahma. The sage has given the hints for the process of self-perceiving by establishing control on all Tanmātrās existing in the body in the hymn 18 and 19. A combination of the formidable and micro processes is existed in it. The inner perceiving can be obtained only with the five Tanmātrās i.e. the word, the touch complexion, essence and smell. That iota may be at the somewhere place in the mind and at the adjunction of the nose root and the ear root. Where the sensing cells for the smell are existed, concentration through inner eyes cannot get any place due to presence of smell into nostrils and words in the air. Thus, a strong perceiving of the sensitivity of Brahma viz. the inner most position can only be possible when all Tanmātrās of exterior world are set aside.]

अथ शैवपदं यत्र तद्ब्रह्म ब्रह्म तत्परम्। तदभ्यासेन लभ्येत पूर्वजन्मार्जितात्मनाम्॥ २०॥

The person engrossed with Brahma attains the complexion of Brahma himself and he is Śiva. A continuous practise and the great deeds performed in the previous birth are the only means for availing that everlasting Brahma.

संभूतैर्वायुसंश्रावैर्हृदयं तप उच्यते। ऊर्ध्वं प्रपद्यते देहाद्भित्त्वा मूर्धानमव्ययम्॥ २१॥

The origin of sound through wind is called the penance of heart. It accesses to the mind by uplifting and penetrating the body.

[Smell arises as a result of the conduction of the earth element in common life. The taste gets excitement as a result of activated water and the essence through the perceiving of smell. As a result of excitement through essence, the power of digestion (Jaṭharāgni) increases. The circulation of wind and the breathing increases due to acuteness of fire. The power of enjoying various worldly pleasures increases due to dynamicity of the breathing. At the state of meditation of yoga, a restriction is imposed on Tanmātrās and these are proceeded to the innermost pleasure by reducing their acuteness towards perceiving the physical pleasures. Having the breathing and the wind existed in the body, dynamic, the perceiving of immortal Anāhata Nāda generates. This sound activates the Sahasrāra and Brahmarandhra existing in the mind and thus opens the way of supreme position.]

स्वदेहस्य तु मूर्धानं ये प्राप्य परमां गतिम्। भूयस्ते न निवर्तन्ते परावरविदो जनाः॥ २२॥

To obtain mental power in this body is called the supreme position. The person who successfully attains this position, is liberated from the cycle of the birth and death.

न साक्षिणं साक्ष्यधर्माः संस्पृशन्ति विलक्षणम्। अविकारमुदासीनं गृहधर्माः प्रदीपवत्॥ २३॥

As nobody can influence the lamp lighted in the home, the defects of witness or evidence doesn't even touch the witness who is unbiased and without any defect.

[The persons residing in a home perform all their activities in the light of the lamp but the lamp has nothing to bear with their activities. The same way the sensitivity of a yogin originates the situation of performing various activities through the body yet it remains uninfluenced itself.]

जले वापि स्थले वापि लुठत्वेष जडात्मकः। नाहं विलिप्ये तद्धर्मैर्घटधर्मैर्नभो यथा॥ २४॥

I (the living Soul) am sensitive therefore, not under affection of this inert body either it lays on water or on the land.

निष्क्रियोऽस्म्यविकारोऽस्मि निष्कलोऽस्मि निराकृतिः। निर्विकल्पोऽस्मि नित्योऽस्मि निरालम्बोऽस्मि निर्द्वयः॥ २५॥

सर्वात्मकोऽहं सर्वोऽहं सर्वातीतोऽहमद्वयः। केवलाखण्डबोधोऽहं स्वानन्दोऽहं निरन्तरः॥ २६॥

I am inactive, without defects, artless, without any particular shape, exclusive, immortal, sovereign, unique, soul of all organisms, beyond the ties of time and only one. I am in the form of integrated knowledge and I myself is always in pleasure.

स्वमेव सर्वतः पश्यन्मन्यमानः स्वमद्वयम्। स्वानन्दमनुभुञ्जानो निर्विकल्पो भवाम्यहम्॥

I only see myself at all moments, realize myself single, enjoy the pleasure and I am exclusive (strong resolute).

गच्छंस्तिष्ठन्नुपविशञ्छयानो वाऽन्यथापि वा। यथेच्छया वसेद्विद्वानात्मारामः सदा मुनिरित्युपनिषत्॥ २८॥

This Upnaniṣad pronounces that such a scholar always live in contentment, with sources of survival voluntarily chosen and everywhere and everytime he feels satisfaction irrespective of his posture and activity.

ॐ आप्यायन्तु..................इति शान्तिः॥

॥इति कुण्डिकोपनिषत्समाप्ता॥

67. SĀVITRYUPANIṢAD

सावित्र्युपनिषद्

This Upaniṣad is related to the tradition of Sāmaveda. In this smallest Upaniṣad, an integrity has been propounded under a presumption of multiform Savitā and Sāvitrī. The couplet of Savitā Sāvitrī and their cause and action has been enumerated in the beginning. The three feet of Sāvitrī, the fruit of acquiring the knowledge of Sāvitrī (learning), conquer on death by virtue of having it, the formation of Balā and Atibalā hymns and lastly this Upaniṣad has been concluded with a dialogue on magnificence of learning.

॥शान्तिपाठः॥

ॐ आप्यायन्तु .... इति शान्तिः॥

कः सविता का सावित्री अग्निरेव सविता पृथिवी सावित्री स यत्राग्निस्तत्पृथिवी यत्र वै पृथिवी तत्राग्निस्ते द्वे योनिः तदेकं मिथुनम्॥१॥ कः सविता का सावित्री वरुण एव सविताऽऽपः सावित्री स यत्र वरुणस्तदापो यत्र वा आपस्तद्वरुणस्ते द्वे योनिः तदेकं मिथुनम्॥२॥ कः सविता का सावित्री वायुरेव सविताकाशः सावित्री स यत्र वायुस्तदाकाशो यत्र वा आकाशस्तद्वायुस्ते द्वे योनिस्तदेकं मिथुनम्॥३॥ कः सविता का सावित्री यज्ञ एव सविता छन्दांसि सावित्री स यत्र यज्ञस्तत्र छन्दांसि यत्र वा छन्दांसि स यज्ञस्ते द्वे योनिस्तदेकं मिथुनम्॥४॥ कः सविता का सावित्री स्तनयित्नुरेव सविता विद्युत्सावित्री स यत्र स्तनयित्नुस्तद्विद्युत् यत्र वा विद्युत्तत्र स्तनयित्नुस्ते द्वे योनिस्तदेकं मिथुनम्॥५॥ कः सविता का सावित्री आदित्य एव सविता द्यौः सावित्री स यत्रादित्यस्तद्द्यौर्यत्र वा द्यौस्तदादित्यस्ते द्वे योनिस्तदेकं मिथुनम्॥६॥ कः सविता का सावित्री चन्द्र एव सविता नक्षत्राणि सावित्री स यत्र चन्द्रस्तन्नक्षत्राणि यत्र वा नक्षत्राणि स चन्द्रमास्ते द्वे योनिस्तदेकं मिथुनम्॥७॥ कः सविता का सावित्री मन एव सविता वाक् सावित्री स यत्र वा मनस्तद्वाक् यत्र वा वाक् तन्मनस्ते द्वे योनिस्तदेकं मिथुनम्॥८॥ कः सविता का सावित्री पुरुष एव सविता स्त्री सावित्री स यत्र पुरुषस्तत्स्त्री यत्र वा स्त्री स पुरुषस्ते द्वे योनिस्तदेकं मिथुनम्॥९॥

Who is Savitā and who is Sāvitrī? The fire is Savitā and the earth is Sāvitrī. The earth too is enshrined where there is fire and where there is earth there is fire. Both of them are the conjoint cause for creation of this universe (yoni). Both of them has a couplet. Who is Savitā and who is Sāvitrī? God Varuṇa is Savitā and the water (Āpaḥ) is Sāvitrī. Āpaḥ is also existed where there is God Varuṇa and where Āpaḥ is, god Varuṇa too is existed there. Both of them are a singly couple. Who is Savitā and who is Sāvitrī? The god wind is Savitā and the ether is Sāvitrī. Where there is wind, there is the ether is Sāvitrī. Where there is wind, there is the ether and where is ether, the wind is also existed there. Both of them are the cause for creation (yoni) and there is a singly couple of them. Who is Savitā and who is Sāvitrī? The god of offering is Savitā and the rhyme is Sāvitrī. Where there is god of offering, the rhyme is also existed there and the rhyme is where the god of offering is existed. Both of them are jointly the cause of creation and there is a single couple of them. To whom Savitā is called and who is Sāvitrī? The thundering clouds are Savitā and the lightening is Sāvitrī. Where there is thundering cloud, there is lightening and there thundering clouds are where there is lightening. Both of them are jointly the cause of creation and hence a singly couple. What is Savitā and what is Sāvitrī? The Āditya is Savitā and the world of Sun (Dyuoka) is Sāvitrī. Where there is Āditya, the world of Sun is existed and where there is world of Sun, the Āditya is existed. Both of them are jointly the cause for creation and have a single couple. Who is Savitā and who is Sāvitrī? The moon is Savitā and the planets are Sāvitrī. The planets are where is the moon and the moon is existed where the planets are and have a singly couple. Who is Savitā and who is Sāvitrī? The mind is Savitā and the speech organ is Sāvitrī. Where there is mind, there is the power of speech and where is the power of speech, there is existed the mind. Both of them are jointly the cause for creation and have a singly couple. Who is Savitā and who is Sāvitrī? The man is called Savitā and the woman is Sāvitrī. Where there is man, woman is existed and where there is women, the man is existed. Both of them are jointly the cause of creation and have a singly couple.

तस्या एव प्रथमः पादो भूस्तत्सवितुर्वरेण्यमित्यग्निर्वै वरेण्यमापो वरेण्यं चन्द्रमा वरेण्यम्॥ १०॥ तस्या एव द्वितीयः पादो भर्गमयोऽपो भुवो भर्गो देवस्य धीमहीत्यग्निर्वै भर्ग आदित्यो वै भर्गश्चन्द्रमा वै भर्गः॥ ११॥ तस्या एष तृतीयः पादः स्वर्धियो यो नः प्रचोदयादिति। स्त्री चैव पुरुषश्च प्रजनयतः॥ १२॥ यो वा एतां सावित्रीमेवं वेद स पुनर्मृत्युं जयति॥ १३॥

The first foot of that great power Sāvitrī is 'Bhūḥ Tatsaviturvareṇyam'. The fire is adorable and the water is adorable. The moon too is adorable. The second foot of that great power Sāvitrī is the laminating water 'Bhavaḥ' Bhargodevasyadhimahī. The fire is that splendour (Bharga) and Āditya is that Bharga in the form of light. This third foot of that great power Sāvitrī is 'Svaḥ' Dhiyo Yo Naḥ Pracodayāt'. The men and women which complying with the rules of their couple life attempt to know this goddess Sāvitrī, they become able to enslave the death and thus access to the element of immortality.

बलातिबलयोर्विराट् पुरुष ऋषिः। गायत्री छन्दः। गायत्री देवता। अकारोकारमकारा बीजाद्याः। क्षुधादिनिरसने विनियोगः। क्लीमित्यादिषडङ्गन्यासः। ध्यानम्। अमृतकरतलार्द्रौ सर्वसंजीवनाढ्यावघहरणसुदक्षौ वेदसारे मयूखे। प्रणवमयविकारौ भास्कराकारदेहौ सततमनुभवेऽहं तौ बलातिबलान्तौ। ॐ ह्रीं बले महादेवि ह्रीं महाबले क्लीं चतुर्विधपुरुषार्थसिद्धिप्रदे तत्सवितुर्वरदात्मिके ह्रीं वरेण्यं भर्गो देवस्य वरदात्मिके अतिबले सर्वदयामूर्ते बले सर्वक्षुद्भ्रमोपनाशिनि धीमहि धियो यो नो जाते प्रचुर्यः या प्रचोदयादात्मिके प्रणवशिरस्कात्मिके हुं फट् स्वाहा॥ १४॥ एवं विद्वान् कृतकृत्यो भवति सावित्र्या एव सलोकतां जयतीत्युपनिषत्॥ १५॥

The sages to both learning are, Balā and Atibalā who are gigantic person (Virāt Puruṣa), the rhyme is Gāyatrī. And the god too is Gāyatrī. Its seed is 'A', power is 'U' and the kīlaka is 'M'. It is applied in order to remain away from the hunger. One should do six kinds Nyāya of them with reciting the seed hymn 'Klīṁ', (The process of six kinds Nyāya is Oṁ Klīṁ Hṛdayāya Namaḥ, Oṁ Klīṁ Śrase Svāhā, Oṁ Klīṁ Śikhāya Vaṣaṭ and Oṁ Klīṁ Astrāya Phaṭ). The concentration process is now described– 'Whose hands are wet of the nectar, who is soaked with all kinds of reviving powers, who is fully competent to decay the evils and who is the essence of Veda, full of the light rays, in the form of Oṁ, free from all kinds of defects and whose body is luminating like Lord Sun. I always perceive the gods who are the master of Balā and Atibalā learnings (the hymn for the master of Balā and Atibalā learning is given in Sanskrit above whose indication is Oṁ Hṛīṁ Bale Mahādevi.. .. .. .. Huṁ Phaṭ Svāhā. The person reckoning with this great learning of Sāvitrī attains to all accomplishments in his life. He attains to the abode of goddess Sāvitrī. This Upaniṣad thus leads the people towards developing their knowledge on this great learning.

ॐ आप्यायन्तु .... इति शान्तिः॥

॥इति सावित्र्युपनिषत्समाप्ता॥

68. ĀTMOPANIṢAD

आत्मोपनिषद्

This Upaniṣad is related to the tradition of Atharvaveda. The different positions of Soul, internal Soul and the Supreme Soul to the element of Soul has been made clear in this Upaniṣad as per name given to it. The active sense in body and the sensory organs etc. has been stated as Soul. The Soul residing in various factors, the five elements of the nature has been stated as internal Soul and the flow of sensitivity beyond all these factors has been stated as the Supreme Soul (Brahma). As the Sun is seen gripped by the demon head (Rāhu) but actually it seldom grips the Sun, in the similar fashion it seems gripped by ignorance. However, actually it does not happen. The Saint has thus revealed the facts of life coincide to the facts of solar eclipse. The worldly confusions and the easy liberated stage of the Soul has been explained with the examples of confusing snake on a chord and the process of get rid of the snake from the slough. The Brahma has been proved by resorting to the basis of names, word meaning and the comparative materials.

॥शान्तिपाठः॥

ॐ भद्रं कर्णेभिः ....इति शान्तिः॥

अथाङ्गिरास्त्रिविधः पुरुषोऽजायतात्माऽन्तरात्मा परमात्मा चेति॥ १-क॥

The Supreme Soul (Puruṣa) known as Āṅgira under an outlook of the organ, organ holder and expert to know the organs appeared in trio-form i.e. Soul, internal Soul and the Supreme Soul.

त्वक् चर्ममांसरोमाङ्गुष्ठाङ्गुल्यः पृष्ठवंशनखगुल्फोदरनाभिमेढकट्यूरुकपोलश्रोत्र भ्रूललाटबाहुपार्श्वशिरोधमनिकाऽक्षीणि भवन्ति जायते म्रियत इत्येष बाह्यात्मा॥ १-ख॥

(The nature of Soul, internal Soul and Supreme Soul is being described.) It is the soul that rotates with the cycle of birth and death by means of the skin (Tvak), flesh (Māṅsa), hide (Carma), hair, thumb, fingers, back, nails thighs, belly, navel, genital, waist, pubic, forehead, eyebrow, skill arms, collateral parts, head, and eyes etc. (formidable body).

अथान्तरात्मा नाम पृथिव्यापस्तेजोवायुराकाशेच्छाद्वेषसुखदुःखकाममोह विकल्पनादिभिः स्मृतिलिङ्ग उदात्तानुदात्तह्रस्वदीर्घप्लुतस्खलितगर्जितस्फुटितमुदितनृत्तगीतवादित्रप्रलय विजृम्भितादिभिः श्रोता घ्राता रसयिता मन्ता बोद्धा कर्त्ता विज्ञानात्मा पुरुषः पुराणन्यायमीमांसाधर्मशास्त्राणीति श्रवणघ्राणाकर्षणकर्मविशेषणं करोत्येषोऽन्तरात्मा॥ १-ग॥

The internal Soul (viz., the intuitive sensitivity existing invasively in the apparent matters is that listens to, smells, drink, concentrates, knows, executes, by the earth, water, vicissitudes, attachment, lust, plea and option etc., memory, gender, Udātta, (sharp tone).

Anudātta (neither high or low), short vowel, long vowel, long drawn etc. (kind of vowels), discharged, thunder, sprout, wink, dance, song, playing musical instruments, devastation (Pralaya), development etc. and who is known to the holy books like Purāṇa, Nyāya, Mimāṁsā etc. and completes the peculiar work as also the hearing, smelling, enchanting etc.

अथ परमात्मा नाम यथाक्षर उपासनीयः। स च प्राणायामप्रत्याहारधारणाध्यानसमाधियोगानुमानाध्यात्मचिन्तकं वटकणिका वा श्यामाकतण्डुलो वा वालाग्रशतसहस्रविकल्पनाभिः स लभ्यते नोपलभ्यते न जायते न म्रियते न शुष्यति न क्लिद्यते न दह्यति न कम्पते न भिद्यते न च्छिद्यते निर्गुणः साक्षीभूतः। शुद्धो निरवयवात्मा केवलः सूक्ष्मो निष्कलो निरञ्जनो निर्विकारः शब्दस्पर्शरूपरसगन्धवर्जितो निर्विकल्पो निराकाङ्क्षः सर्वव्यापी सोऽचिन्त्यो निर्वर्ण्यश्च पुनात्यशुद्धान्यपूतानि। निष्क्रियस्तस्य संसारो नास्ति॥ १-घ॥

The letter as addressed in the name of supreme Soul (the syllable Oṁ) is adorable. It can be perceived and even not perceived when concentration is made by resorting to Prāṇāyāma, Pratyāhāra, Dhāraṇā, concentration, meditation, yoga, conjecture, self-thinning, who is most micro as many thousand parts of the foreportion of their hair, the micro seed of Banyan tree and the tiny rice of Śyāmāka species. It seldom appeases and seldom dies. It is neither dry nor wet. It is neither dynamic nor vibrates. It neither cracks nor reinforced. It is beyond the properties (Guṇa), with all proofs, holy, a Soul without organs, micro, clear, unattached, free from defects, without the word, touch, complexion, essence and the smell, beyond the knowledge, imagination, ambition, omnipresent, beyond concentration and a supreme Soul which cannot be known accurately cleans the impure and makes it pure. He is without action and that supreme Soul is without world as it has no world.

The meaning of the word 'world' is dynamic or changeable. The Supreme Soul always remains in uniform feature therefore it is not changeable. Hence he has been stated without world within this outlook. In the successive hymns, it has been stated that, in case the element of Soul is perceived, it is been everywhere.

आत्मसंज्ञः शिवः एक एवाद्वयः सदा। ब्रह्मरूपतधा ब्रह्म केवलं प्रतिभासते॥ १-ङ॥

That supreme purity, benevolent, exclusive, unique form of Brahma known as the Soul perceives as only the Brahma.

जगद्रूपतयाप्येतद्ब्रह्मैव प्रतिभासते। विद्याऽविद्यादिभेदेन भावाऽभावादिभेदतः॥ २॥

The Brahma is seen in the form of this world. Whatever is been by the discrimination of Vidyā (learning), Avidyā (ignorance), Bhāva (spirit), Abhāva (morbidity) etc. is the form of that everlasting Brahma.

गुरुशिष्यादिभेदेन ब्रह्मैव प्रतिभासते। ब्रह्मैव केवलं शुद्धं विद्यते तत्त्वदर्शने॥ ३॥

The Brahma is seen even when the discrimination of teacher and disciple etc. is taken for consideration. Indeed, the Brahma in the form of light of purity is existed everywhere.

न च विद्या न चाविद्या न जगच्च न चापरम्। सत्यत्वेन जगद्भानं संसारस्य प्रवर्तकम्॥४॥

असत्यत्वेन भानं तु संसारस्य निवर्तकम्। घटोऽयमिति विज्ञातुं नियमः को न्वपेक्षते॥५॥

There is neither learning nor ignorance, neither the world nor any other thing is true but the feeling of world as truth is the basic cause for this creation or the promoter motive of this universe. As no other proofs are expected for the pitcher kept at the apparent place, the realisation of the world being untrue is as the force that provides with emancipation.

विना प्रमाणसुष्ठुत्वं यस्मिन्सति पदार्थधीः। अयमात्मा नित्यसिद्धः प्रमाणे सति भासते॥६॥

As the knowledge of the matter put in front of the eyes need no proof to have knowledge, this Soul always proved appears in its apparent form viz., there is no need of proof for Brahma because everything of this Brahma is in the form of Brahma.

न देशं नापि कालं वा न शुद्धिं वाप्यपेक्षते। देवदत्तोऽहमित्येतद्विज्ञानं निरपेक्षकम्॥७॥

As the person known to the name of Devadutta etc. becomes confident with, that element of Soul does not expect any place, time or the purity.

तद्वद्ब्रह्मविदोऽप्यस्य ब्रह्माहमिति वेदनम्। भानुनेव जगत्सर्वं भास्यते यस्य तेजसा॥८॥

A presumption of 'I myself' and Brahma made by the knower of the Brahma is the direct perception of the Brahma as this whole world is lighted by the Sun, the entire Brahmāṇḍa is luminated by the splendour of that Brahma.

अनात्मकमसत्तुच्छं किं नु तस्यावभासकम्। वेदशास्त्रपुराणानि भूतानि सकलान्यपि। येनार्थवन्ति तं किं नु विज्ञातारं प्रकाशयेत्॥९॥

As a direct proof to the existence of Brahma, there is nothing and any proof if given will be untrue and trifle. Who will educate this preposition? (viz. None will) Brahma is self-luminating and the Vedas, Scriptures, Puraṇas and all living-organisms are meaningful only through the light of Brahma.

क्षुधां देहव्यथां त्यक्त्वा बालः क्रीडति वस्तुनि॥१०॥

तथैव विद्वान् रमते निर्ममो निरहं सुखी। कामान्निष्कामरूपी संचरत्येकचरो मुनिः॥११॥

As a child is engrossed in playing with the attractive things (dolls) so attentively of sometimes he forgets the hunger and any kinds of pains in the body, the scholars engross with Brahma by keeping themselves free from the attachments, ego etc. and always live in a happy mood. That knower of Soul gives up all desires and starts moving hither and thither aloofly in the form of a recluse (Muni).

स्वात्मनैव सदा तुष्टः स्वयं सर्वात्मना स्थितः। निर्धनोऽपि सदा तुष्टोऽप्यसहायो महाबलः॥१२॥

The person poor in worldly view always feels contentment when he presumes his Soul present everywhere and who satisfies with his soul and the helpless person too thinks himself most mighty.

नित्यतृप्तोऽप्यभुञ्जानोऽप्यसमः समदर्शनः। कुर्वन्नपि न कुर्वाणश्चाभोक्ता फलभोग्यपि॥१३॥

He always remains satiated inspite of taking nothing as food. His behaviour is seemed abnormal but be looks all creatures as equal, irrespective by busy on work, he seems inactive and irrespective of enjoying the fruit of action, he is considered of without enjoyment.

[The Sage makes is clear in the hymn no. 15 to 16 that the Sun is perceived dark owing the eclipse or the dense clouds however it actually is not gripped by them. Nobody should develop the presumption making the scriptures unscientific on the basis of the cases or examples referred by the Sages particularly with an intention to make the common people duly understand the contents.]

शरीर्यप्यशरीर्येष परिच्छिन्नोऽपि सर्वगः। अशरीरं सदा सन्तमिदं ब्रह्मविदं क्वचित्॥ १४॥

प्रियाप्रिये न स्पृशतस्तथैव च शुभाशुभे। तमसा ग्रस्तवद्भानादग्रस्तोऽपि रविर्जनैः॥ १५॥

ग्रस्त इत्युच्यते भ्रान्त्या ह्यज्ञात्वा वस्तुलक्षणम्। तद्वद्देहादिबन्धेभ्यो विमुक्तं ब्रह्मवित्तमम्॥ १६॥

पश्यन्ति देहिवन्मूढाः शरीराभासदर्शनात्। अहिनिर्ल्वयनीवायं मुक्तदेहस्तु तिष्ठति॥ १७॥

That Soul resides in body still it is without body. It is bound with the body still most dynamic. This is the reason the scholar of Brahma being without body remains unattached to the favourite and unfavourite knowledge (viz., It does not consider anything favourable and unfavourable). The good and bad cannot touch such Soul. All creatures are equal in the eye of such scholars. As the people assume the Sun gripped by the demon head, however, actually it has not happened, the fools consider the scholar of Brahma as the common Soul tied with the body etc., but the actual position of the scholar (the Soul) is that he always remains liberated with the body analogous to slough of the snake.

इतस्ततश्चाल्यमानो यत्किंचित्प्राणवायुना। स्रोतसा नीयते दारु यथानिम्नोन्नतस्थलम्॥ १८॥

This body is moved hither and thither by the power of the breathing wind as the woods are brought up and down by the waves of fountains and rivers etc.

दैवेन नीयते देहो तथा कालोपभुक्तिषु। लक्ष्यालक्ष्यगतिं त्यक्त्वा यस्तिष्ठेत्केवलात्मना॥ १९॥ शिव एव स्वयं साक्षादयं ब्रह्मविदुत्तमः। जीवन्नेव सदा मुक्तः कृतार्थो ब्रह्मवित्तमः॥ २०॥

Lord Śiva is the apparent god among the scholars known to Brahma and the ascetics who becomes stable and does not observe the direct and indirect motions of this material world by duly resorted to his Soul is truly, like Śiva. He takes the events and the happenings the same way as our destiny tends to our body to feel vicissitudes. Such scholars duly known to Brahma and alike to Lord Śiva attains to emancipation even in this material life.

उपाधिनाशाद्ब्रह्मैव सद्ब्रह्माप्येति निर्द्वयम्। शैलूषो वेषसद्भावाभावयोश्च यथा पुमान्॥ २१॥

This Soul merges with Brahma when all material feelings are destroyed as a person able to disguise his body in varied is deemed an acrobatic. He too is deemed the natural man when he leaves the camouflaged complexions.

तथैव ब्रह्मविच्छ्रेष्ठः सदा ब्रह्मैव नापरः। घटे नष्टे यथा व्योम व्योमैव भवति स्वयम्॥ २२॥

Similarly, the person known to Brahma becomes Brahma himself. He looks different than Brahma nearly by his physical structure but his masterpiece of mind always acts as per the sheer guidance of Brahma. Thus, he himself is Brahma and there is nothing else than it. As the ether, turns into the universal ether when the pitcher is broken viz., the ether or sky is been only to the extent of the mouth of the pitcher but the usual or eternal sky embeds such notional sky within itself when the pitcher is broken.

तथैवोपाधिविलये ब्रह्मैव ब्रह्मवित्स्वयम्। क्षीरं क्षीरे यथा क्षिप्तं तैलं तैले जलं जले॥ २३॥
संयुक्तमेकतां याति तथाऽऽत्मन्यात्मविन्मुनिः। एवं विदेहकैवल्यं सन्मात्रत्वमखण्डितम्॥ २४॥ ब्रह्मभावं प्रपद्यैष यतिर्नावर्तते पुनः। सदात्मकत्वविज्ञानदग्धाविद्यादिवर्ष्मणः॥ २५॥

In the same way, the Scholar known to Brahma himself becomes Brahma when this body and its properties are destroyed. As the milk, oil and water get their uniform shape when these are mixed with the milk, oil and water respectively. The situation of the hermit, expert in metaphysics and the Soul is integrated and there is no distinction at all. Thus as a result of attaining to the position of emancipation, where there is no feeling for the material things, the devotee attainss to Brahma and thus crosses the cycles of death and birth because the conscience on metaphysics, burns into ashes is ignorance.

अमुष्य ब्रह्मभूतत्वाद्ब्रह्मणः कुत उद्भवः। मायाक्लृप्तौ बन्धमोक्षौ न स्तः स्वात्मनि वस्तुतः॥ २६॥

How can it be possible that such an ascetic would take rebirth when once he had attained to the Brahma. The ties created by illusion and the emancipation has no place in that Brahma.

यथा रज्जौ निष्क्रियायां सर्पाभासविनिर्गमौ। आवृतेः सदसत्त्वाभ्यां वक्तव्ये बन्धमोक्षणे॥ २७॥

As the likeliness of snake even in the dead chord is effaced when the person applies his mind and takes the real cognisance of the chord. He then treat it of a chord and not as a snake. The truth and false spirits are nothing else but the ties and emancipation respectively.

नावृतिर्ब्रह्मणःकाचिदन्याभावादनावृतम्। अस्तीति प्रत्ययो यश्च यश्च नास्तीति वस्तुनि॥ २८॥
बुद्धेरेव गुणावेतौ न तु नित्यस्य वस्तुनः। अतस्तौ मायया क्लृप्तौ बन्धमोक्षौ न चात्मनि॥ २९॥

The Brahma is without cover or it is in fully disclosed form. Why it is so, it is because there are no options in Brahma. It is an adept of wisdom that creates faith on the existence of anything or non-existence but it is not an issue with the everlasting Brahma. This is the reason, the ties and emancipation has no place within the Soul because these are the only generation of illusions (Māyā).

[The Saint wants to make it clear that the ties or emancipation are not for Soul and these are only for wisdom. This wisdom revolves round the conscience of the narrow. Thinking as this is mine and that is yours, while the Soul is existed fully liberated.]

निष्कले निष्क्रिये शान्ते निरवद्ये निरञ्जने। अद्वितीये परे तत्त्वे व्योमवत्कल्पना कुतः॥ ३०॥

How the imagination of the ether in a pitcher and the ether gigantic can be made in the Supreme element of Soul, beyond the art, inactive tender, free from evils and invisible.

न निरोधो न चोत्पत्तिर्न बद्धो न च साधकः। न मुमुक्षुर्न वै मुक्त इत्येषा परमार्थता।।३१।।

The truth prevails that the perfect Brahma neither takes birth and nor it is beyond the birth. It is neither an ascetic nor desirous of the emancipation and he neither is fastened with worldly ties nor absolutely free from worldly ties.

[That Brahma is not beyond the birth because it appears with the body that takes birth. On thing to bring in notice is that the birth is taken by the body and nor by the sensitivity as a number of vessels usually are made and broken time to time but the water kept on them is free to cycle of birth and decay. Hence, it is unborn with the same spirit, we can't say that Brahma has emancipated and not desirous of emancipation or free from the ties.]

ॐ भद्रं कर्णेभिः ....इति शान्तिः।।

।।इत्यात्मोपनिषत्समाप्ता।।

69. PĀŚUPATABRAHMOPANIṢAD

पाशुपतब्रह्मोपनिषद्

This Upaniṣad is related to the tradition of Atharvaveda. It is a collection of questions and their answers i.e. questionnaire where is question were raised by Bālakilya saint and answers were given by Svayambhū Brahma. This Upaniṣad is divided into two chapters i.e. Pūrva Kāṇḍa and Uttarakāṇḍa.

In the first cantos i.e, Pūrva Kāṇḍa, There have been raised seven questions about the regular (Administrator) of this world. Answers to these questions has been given in an ordering manner. Subsequently, the contents described are Karūa's role in Sṛṣṭi Yajña, offering relating to research on sound, Hamsa form of the supreme soul, consistency in yajña sūtra and Brahmasūtra, offering propensity of Praṇava Hamsa, the functional mental offering of Brahma Sandhyā, Research on unformity of Hamsa and Praṇava, emancipation as a result of observance to Hamsātma vidyā containing ninety six sūtras, more importance of internal offering than the exterior offering; horse sacrifice (Aśvamedha) in the form of and Tāraka Hamsa Jyoti.

In the second or successive uttarkāṇḍa, the subject matter for description is the evolvement first, property of Brahma (Brahma Sampatti) and then world in the supreme soul, the method of Hamsārka praṇava meditation, mind and sensory organs inspired by Lord Śiva, others perception in the soul due to the impact of illusion, self realisation and its nexus with the knowledge of Brahma, the manner to acquire the best learning like truth etc., emancipation of the metaphysician (Atma-Jñānī) from the cycle of birth and death, no use of having discretion of consumption (Bhakṣyābhakṣya) and finally the stage of perception when the scholar sees all within him. Thus, very cryptic principles relating to Brahma has been widely described in this Upaniṣad.

॥शान्तिपाठः॥

ॐ भद्रं कर्णेभिः .... इति शान्तिः॥

॥पूर्वकाण्डः॥

अथ ह वै स्वयंभूर्ब्रह्मा प्रजाः सृजानीति कामकामो जायते कामेश्वरो वैश्रवणः॥ १॥

Once Lord Brahmā resolved for creating the subject. In order to that creation, Kāmeśvara (Rudra) and Vaiśravaṇa were originated.

वैश्रवणो ब्रह्मपुत्रो वालखिल्यः स्वयंभुवं परिपृच्छति जगतां का विद्या का देवता जाग्रत्तुरीययोरस्य को देवो यानि कस्य वशानि कालाः कियत्प्रमाणाः कस्याज्ञया रविचन्द्रग्रहादयो भासन्ते कस्य महिमा गगनस्वरूप एतदहं श्रोतुमिच्छामि नान्यो जानाति त्वं ब्रूहि ब्रह्मन्॥ २॥

Vaiśrvaṇa Vālakhilya, a saint, son of Brahma then asked– O Lord, what is this material (Jagata) learning? Who are the gods of awaking and stage of meditation (turīyāvasthā)? To whom the world is enslaved? What is the proof (Pramāṇa) of Kāla? By whose order the sun and moon etc. planets are luminated? Whose magnificence is wide like the sky? We want to listen the answers to all these questions? Nobody otherwise you is known the answers to these questions. O Brahman! please therefore, provide us with solution to these questions.

स्वयंभूरुवाच कृत्स्नजगतां मातृका विद्या॥ ३॥

Lord Brahmā told the Matṛkā Vidyā (learning of letters) is the learning that originates this whole world.

द्वित्रिवर्णसहिता द्विवर्णमाता त्रिवर्णसहिता। चतुर्मात्रात्मकोङ्कारो मम प्राणात्मिका देवता॥ ४॥

It consists two letters (Haṁsa) and three letters (Praṇava). The learning of two letters also comprises three letters (Praṇava). The syllable "Oṁ" is my god of breathing.

अहमेव जगत्त्रयस्यैकः पतिः॥ ५॥

I am above is the master of trio-lokas (i.e, I provide maintenance to all).

मम वशानि सर्वाणि युगान्यपि॥ ६॥

All ears live under my guidance and control.

अहोरात्रादयो मत्संवर्धिताः कालाः॥ ७॥

The Ahorātra viz. the day and nights have been originated by me too.

मम रूपा रवेस्तेजश्चन्द्रनक्षत्रग्रहतेजांसि च॥ ८॥

The splendour existing in the Sun, Moon and in all planets as also stars etc. too is my own form.

गगनो मम त्रिशक्तिमायास्वरूपो नान्यो मदस्ति॥ ९॥

This ether with trio power i.e. Satva, Rajas and Tamas is also my illusory form. Nothing except me is existing anywhere.

तमोमायात्मको रुद्रः सात्त्विकमायात्मको विष्णू राजसमायात्मको ब्रह्मा। इन्द्रादयस्तामसराजसात्मिका न सात्त्विकः कोऽपि। अघोरः सर्वसाधारणस्वरूपः॥ १०॥

Lord Rudra is in the illusory form of the Tamas property, Viṣṇu is of the Satva property and lord Brahmā is of Rajas property. Indra etc. gods bear the fine blend of Rajas and Tamas property. No god out of them bears satva property. Only Aghora (Śiva) is in the common and an ordinary form.

समस्तयागानां रुद्रः पशुपतिः कर्ता।

रुद्रो यागदेवो विष्णुरध्वर्युर्होतेन्द्रो देवता यज्ञभुग् मानसं ब्रह्म महेश्वरं ब्रह्म॥ ११॥

The Karttā (performer) of all offerings are Paśupati Lord Rudra, Lord Viṣṇu is Adhvaryu of offering and lord Indra is Hotā (who recites hymn). The mental form Brahma of Maheśvara-Brahma is the enjoyed of such offering.

मानसो हंसः सोऽहं हंस इति। तन्मययज्ञो नादानुसंधानम्। तन्मयविकारो जीवः॥ १२॥

The form of that mental (Mānasa) Brahma too is "Hansaḥ so'haṁ. The offering performed for attaining to this engrossment is a research of sound (Nāda-Anusandhāna). The living soul is the defect of Tanmaya (that sensitivity). Haṁsa Sādhanā and so'haṁ Sādhanā have been accepted as one. The sound "Haṁsaḥ" appears as so'haṁ from the other side. In the spiritual outlook both presumptions– "I myself is that" (Haṁsaḥ) and that too is (so'haṁ) are indicator of the integrity established between the living soul (jīva) and Brahma.

परमात्मस्वरूपो हंसः। अन्तर्बहिश्चरति हंसः। अन्तर्गतोऽनवकाशान्तर्गतसुपर्णस्वरूपो हंसः॥ १३॥

(That) "Haṁsa" is the form of supreme soul. (That) Haṁsa frequently moves internally and externally. At the premise of external regular frequency, this Haṁsa exists in the form of suparṇa (god-perfect Brahma).

षण्णवतितत्त्वतन्तुवद्व्यक्तं चित्सूत्रत्रयचिन्मयलक्षणं नवतत्त्वत्रिरावृतं ब्रह्मविष्णुमहेश्वरात्मकमग्नित्रयकलोपेतं चिद्ग्रन्थिबन्धनम् अद्वैतग्रन्थिः॥ १४॥ यज्ञसाधारणाङ्गं बहिरन्तर्ज्वलनं यज्ञाङ्गलक्षणब्रह्मस्वरूपो हंसः॥ १५॥

The sacrificial thread (Yajñopavīta) in the form of Haṁsa with all characteristics of Brahma is revealed in ninety six fibres, contains nine elements owing to have three properties, made of three threads i.e. truth, mind and pleasures, added with three fires in the form of Brahmā, Viṣṇu and Maheśa, tied with the mental knot, contains the Advaita knot (the Brahma knot) and exhibitor of the exterior and conscience in the form of the general part of the offering.

The sacrificial thread (Yajñopavīta) has been described herein as the Brahmasūtra. The saint is describing herein the sensitive elements on the basis of which the apparent sacrificial thread is made. The three fibres of the raw thread are rolled (wrapped) ninety six times on the article measuring four fingers. It is spanned by making three fold. Thus, nine fibres are assembled as side. This sacrificial thread of three folds is then joined with a knot. The Brahma knot is fixed after the initial knots. The saint has made analysis of them. Only sixteen elements have not been described while other matters are clear in the connotation of the hymn. It has been explained in the appendix to Chāndogya of Sāmaveda this way "Tithivarañca nakṣatraṁ tattvaveda guṇānvitam. Kālatrayaṁ ca Māsāśca, Brahmasūtraṁ, hi ṣaṇṇavam" viz. 25 elements, 3 properties, 15 tithis, 7 days, 27 stars, 4 Vedas, 3 Kālas and 12 months. Thus the Brahmasūtra is of 96 elements.

उपवीतलक्षणसूत्रब्रह्मगा यज्ञाः। ब्रह्माङ्गलक्षणयुक्तो यज्ञसूत्रम्। तद्ब्रह्मसूत्रम्। यज्ञसूत्रसंबन्धी ब्रह्मयज्ञः तत्स्वरूपः॥ १६॥

Thus, the thread with the characteristics of sacrificial thread is in the form of offering. It is the symbol of Brahma. This, Yajñasūtra (sacrificial thread) is of Brahma characteristics and it is Brahmasūtra. Hence the sacrificial thread and Brahma Brahmyajña both are the form of each other.

अङ्गानि मात्राणि। मनोयज्ञस्य हंसो यज्ञसूत्रम्। प्रणवं ब्रह्मसूत्रं ब्रह्मयज्ञमयम्। प्रणवान्तर्वर्ती हंसो ब्रह्मसूत्रम्। तदेव ब्रह्मयज्ञमयं मोक्षक्रमम्॥ १७॥

Its Aṅgas (parts) are mātrās. This Brahma sūtra too is the Haṁsa of this mental yajña. This Praṇava with Brahma yajña too is Brahmasūtra, the internal Haṁsa of Praṇava too is Brahmasūtra. This Brahmayajña is the means of salvation.

The real objective of holding extraneous Brahmasūtra is to awake and make viable to the internal Brahmasūtra. With the adoption of recession (Sannyāsa) the extraneous thread is abandoned because the ascetic is reached at the fully matured stage of internal Brahmasūtra.

ब्रह्मसंध्याक्रिया मनोयाग:। संध्याक्रिया मनोयागस्य लक्षणम्॥ १८॥

Brahmasandhyā is an action of mental yajña while the sandhyā kriyā is the characteristic of mental offering. The people considering completion of their liability my merely repeating Brahma Sandhyā as the formidable ritual and do not awake/ develop the same as the mental yajña, can not get the fruit of Sandhyā Vandana to the extent, the same has been stated in the scriptures.

यज्ञसूत्रप्रणवब्रह्मयज्ञक्रियायुक्तो ब्राह्मण:। ब्रह्मचर्येण चरन्ति देवा:। हंससूत्रचर्या यज्ञा:। हंसप्रणवयोरभेद:॥ १९॥

Brāhmaṇas are the people who observe the procedure of sacrificial thread, Praṇava and the Brahma yajña. The gods move in the state of celibacy. The Haṁsa and Praṇava in the form of thread (Sūtra) are equal. There is no discrimination between them.

हंसस्य प्रार्थनास्त्रिकाला:। त्रिकालास्त्रिवर्णा:। त्रेताग्न्यनुसंधानो याग:। त्रेताग्न्यात्माकृतिवर्णोङ्कारहंसानुसंधानोऽन्तर्याग:॥ २०॥

The pray of Haṁsa is made thrice time (trikāla). Three Kālas are three varṇa (A, U, and M). This yajña is performed by the research of three fires. The formation of soul in forms of three fires and a research of Haṁsa in the form of 'Oṁ' too is the internal yajña.

चित्स्वरूपवत्तन्मयं तुरीयस्वरूपम्। अन्तरादित्ये ज्योति:स्वरूपो हंस:॥ २१॥

It is nature of the state of meditation (Turīyāvasthā). The Haṁsa in the internal Āditya (Sun) too is located in the form of Jyoti.

यज्ञाङ्गं ब्रह्मसंपत्ति:। ब्रह्मप्रवृत्तौ तत्प्रणवहंससूत्रेणैव ध्यानमाचरन्ति॥ २२॥

The part of Yajña (yajñāṅga) is the property of Brahma. One should therefore, move by the meditation (Dhyāna) in the worship of Haṁsa in the form of praṇa for attaining to Brahma.

प्रोवाच पुन: स्वयंभुवं प्रतिजानीते ब्रह्मपुत्रो ऋषिर्वालखिल्य:। हंससूत्राणि कतिसंख्यानि कियद्वा प्रमाणम्॥ २३॥

Brahmaputra Vālakhilya again askes Lord Brahmā (Svayaṁbhū) O Lord! "How may one Haṁsa sūtra and how may proofs one of that existed. You are competent to know everything.” Please, have grace for telling the same.

हृद्यादित्यमरीचीनां पदं षण्णवतिः। चित्सूत्रघ्राणयोः स्वर्निर्गता प्रणवाधारा षडङ्गुलदशाशीतिः॥ २४॥

Lord Brahmā then replied— there one ninety six rays of the heart Sun. The stream coming out from the thread of mind i.e. nose (Ghrāṇa) with the vowels too is of ninety six finger measurement.

वामबाहुदक्षिणकट्योरन्तश्चरति हंसः परमात्मा ब्रह्मगुह्यप्रकारो नान्यत्र विदितः॥ २५॥

The supreme soul Haṁsa resides in the middle of dakṣiṇa kaṭyata (at the back of waist of right side) and the left shoulder (viz in the region of heart) but nobody knows or can gather information of that secret issue.

जानन्ति तेऽमृतफलकाः। सर्वकालं हंसं प्रकाशकम्। प्रणवहंसान्तर्ध्यानप्रकृतिं विना न मुक्तिः॥

The persons know that all time (Sarvakāla) luminating Haṁsa who have attained to the immortality, emancipation cannot be awarded conducting meditation inward made on the Haṁsa in the form of Praṇava.

नवसूत्रान्परिचर्चितान्। तेऽपि यद्ब्रह्म चरन्ति। अन्तरादित्यं न ज्ञातं मनुष्याणाम्॥ २७॥

The people holding (wearing) this sacrificial thread of nine threads, do worship to it by assuming it as Brahma but these people do no introduce with or realise the Brahma in garb of sun existed in the heart.

जगदादित्यो रोचत इति ज्ञात्वा ते मर्त्या विबुधास्तपनप्रार्थनायुक्ता आचरन्ति॥ २८॥

Considering that this sun luminates the universe, those wise people worship him for holiness and knowledge.

वाजपेयः पशुहर्ता अध्वर्युरिन्द्रो देवता अहिंसा धर्मयागः परमहंसोऽध्वर्युः परमात्मा देवता पशुपतिः॥ २९॥

Vājapeya Yajña (specific offering of knowledge) is depressor of animal spirit (remover of the ignorance). The Adhvaryu to this Yajña and god is Indra (supreme God). It is a religious offering aranged/performed under the of non-voilence. Its adhraryu is Paramhaṁsa and the god is Paśupati, the supreme soul.

ब्रह्मोपनिषदो ब्रह्म। स्वाध्याययुक्ता ब्राह्मणाश्चरन्ति॥ ३०॥

The Brahma as performed in Veda and Upaniṣad is the element of supreme soul and worshipped by the scholars of Brahma who have devoted themselves in perseverance.

अश्वमेधो महायज्ञकथा। तद्राज्ञा ब्रह्मचर्यमाचरन्ति। सर्वेषां पूर्वोक्तब्रह्मयज्ञक्रमं मुक्तिक्रममिति॥ ३१॥

The knowledge to this Mahāyajña is Aśvamedha Yajña (offering performed by horse sacrifice). The scholars resorting to it do activities prescribed or allowed by the knowledge of Brahma. All Brahma Yajña (deeds) described earlier too are competent in providing with emancipation.

ब्रह्मपुत्रः प्रोवाच। उदितो हंस ऋषिः। स्वयंभूस्तिरोदधे। रुद्रो ब्रह्मोपनिषदो हंसज्योतिः पशुपतिः प्रणवस्तारकः

स एवं वेद॥३२॥

Brahmaputra again said– "The knowledge relating to Brahma has been appeared." Lord Savaymbhū (Brahmā) vanished after hearing this. The Haṁsa Jyoti as described in this Upaniṣad is Rudra and the supporter for crossing the ocean of world be Praṇava (Oṁ) too is Paśupati (Brahma). One should know him this way.

॥उत्तरकाण्डः॥

हंसात्ममालिकावर्णब्रह्मकालप्रचोदिता। परमात्मा पुमानिति ब्रह्मसंपत्तिकारिणी॥१॥

Japa of Haṁsa too is the letter Brahma. It inspires for attending to Brahma. This Brahma too is supreme soul and supreme person. This Brahma is enriched with the property of Brahma.

अध्यात्मब्रह्मकल्पस्याकृतिः कीदृशी कथा। ब्रह्मज्ञानप्रभासन्ध्या कालो गच्छति धीमताम्। हंसाख्यो देवमात्माख्यमात्मतत्त्वप्रजः कथम्॥२॥

The person who has become Brahma like by virtue of his self-knowledge, nothing is left for saying anything about him. The scholars used to spend their full time in discussing Brahma and worship him. Where else the subject may be when integrity is established between Haṁsa and the soul.

अन्तः प्रणवनादाख्यो हंसः प्रत्ययबोधकः। अन्तर्गतप्रमागूढं ज्ञाननालं विराजितम्॥३॥

The Haṁsa known through the sound of 'Oṁ' as emanated from the heart gives understanding to the entire knowledge. The extensor knowledge of the world is obtained by virtue of the cryptic knowledge directly perceived.

शिवशक्त्यात्मकं रूपं चिन्मयानन्दवेदितम्। नादबिन्दुकला त्रीणि नेत्रविश्वविचेष्टितम्॥४॥

The conjoint form of Śiva and Śakti is worth knowing in a state of pleasure. This world is activated with three eyes (awakening) i.e. sound, point (Bindu) and Kalā.

त्रियंगानि शिखा त्रीणि द्वित्रीणि संख्यमाकृतिः। अन्तर्गूढप्रमा हंसः प्रमाणान्निर्गतं बहिः॥५॥

His number (the shape) is known in three Aṅgas (parts), three braids and two or three moons. When he is thus, vanished, the knowledge of this cryptic soul then appears as proof in the exterior.

ब्रह्मसूत्रपदं ज्ञेयं ब्राह्म्यं विध्युक्तलक्षणम्। हंसार्कप्रणवध्यानमित्युक्तो ज्ञानसागरे॥६॥

Having obtained the knowledge of Brahma as the thread (key) to the world one should himself be adorned with the characteristics of Brahma and the Sun in the form of Haṁsa should be kept in mind in a regular manner. It is the preaching of the scholars.

एतद्विज्ञानमात्रेण ज्ञानसागरपारगः। स्वतः शिवः पशुपतिः साक्षी सर्वस्य सर्वदा॥७॥

Thus, one can cross the oceans of knowledge only after having such particular perceiving. Lord Paśupati Brahma in the form of Lord Śiva is always its evidence (witness).

As the entrapping of the persons doing more worship to learning (vidyā) has been stated in the hymn "Andhaṁ tamaḥ praviśanti.. .. etc. of Iśopaniṣads, the extremity of knowledge of both kinds i.e. inert and sensitive in the form of Metaphysics has not been considered appropriate. It appears that the statement knowledge as drawing sea and crossing it has been given only by taking the above fact in mind.

सर्वेषां तु मनस्तेन प्रेरितं नियमेन तु। विषये गच्छति प्राणश्चेष्टते वाग्वदत्यपि॥ ८॥

This very Lord Śiva inspire, regulate and strike a balance in the mind of all people because the mind indulges to the subject (viṣaya) by the impact of it. The breathing activates and by the speech reveals the activities proposed and performed.

चक्षुः पश्यति रूपाणि श्रोत्रं सर्वं शृणोत्यपि। अन्यानि खानि सर्वाणि तेनैव प्रेरितानि तु॥ ९॥
स्वं स्वं विषयमुद्दिश्य प्रवर्तन्ते निरन्तरम्। प्रवर्तकत्वं चाप्यस्य मायया न स्वभावतः॥ १०॥

Because of the inspiration from almighty, the eyes observe the complexions and the scenes, the ears listen, and all sensory organs are motivated. These are continuously activated to the respective motives (subject) performing to them. This propensity, the engross in motives (subject) is the illusion (Māyā). It does not take place habitually but due to illusion.

श्रोत्रमात्मनि चाध्यस्तं स्वयं पशुपतिः पुमान्। अनुप्रविश्य श्रोत्रस्य ददाति श्रोत्रतां शिवः॥ ११॥

The ears are dependent to the soul and Paśupati Brahma himself enters into the ears and give power of hearing to that Śiva.

मनः स्वात्मनि चाध्यस्तं प्रविश्य परमेश्वरः। मनस्त्वं तस्य सत्त्वस्थो ददाति नियमेन तु॥ १२॥

The mind too is habitual (engrossed) within the self-conscience (Antarātmā) and it is the supreme god (perfect knowledge) that enters into it, regulate by placing it in sattva and provides with the brilliance of mind (Manastva).

स एव विदितादन्यस्तथैवाविदितादपि। अन्येषामिन्द्रियाणां तु कल्पितानामपीश्वरः॥ १३॥ तत्तद्रूपमनुप्राप्य ददाति नियमेन तु। ततश्चक्षुश्च वाक्चैव मनश्चान्यानि खानि च॥ १४॥ न गच्छन्ति स्वयंज्योतिः स्वभावे परमात्मनि। अकर्तृविषयप्रत्यक्प्रकाशं स्वात्मनैव तु॥ १५॥ विना तर्कप्रमाणाभ्यां ब्रह्म यो वेद वेद सः। प्रत्यगात्मा परंज्योतिर्माया सा तु महत्तमः॥ १६॥

Such supreme god activates all sensory organs but that Maheśvara is different altogether than the people approach and imagination of that Brahma. Only the perfect Brahma (supreme god) gives suitable form to these all sensory organs and regularise them too. These eyes, mind and the speech etc. all sensory organs therefore, and by this very reason, can not avail the self-luminating element (form) of the supreme soul, viz., can not able to know to the fact that the supreme soul is distinct (separate) from the inner subject, should without resorting to the logic and proofs do effort to know him through his self conscience. He thus, arrive at the true knowledge of the element of supreme soul. This soul is in the form of supreme light while that illusion is in the form of sheer darkness.

तथा सति कथं मायासंभवः प्रत्यगात्मनि। तस्मात्तर्कप्रमाणाभ्यां स्वानुभूत्या च चिद्घने॥१७॥
स्वप्रकाशैकसंसिद्धे नास्ति माया परात्मनि। व्यावहारिकदृष्ट्येयं विद्याविद्या न चान्यथा॥१८॥

Therefore the integrity of Pratyapātmā and the soul is no way possible. It are in knowledge through his logic, proofs, and experience that there is no illusion in the supreme soul, self-luminating and sensitive. The subjects of Vidyā (learning) and Avidyā (ignorance) are pragmatic and those have no nexus with the supreme soul.

तत्त्वदृष्ट्या तु नास्त्येव तत्त्वमेवास्ति केवलम्। व्यावहारिकदृष्टिस्तु प्रकाशाव्यभिचारतः॥१९॥
प्रकाश एव सततं तस्मादद्वैत एव हि। अद्वैतमिति चोक्तिश्च प्रकाशाव्यभिचारतः॥२०॥

In all way true outlook, all this is false. Only the element is the real truth. It appears the same and in pragmatic view, it is seen. The light is only existed everlasting. Thus, it is Advaita because Advaita only is said inseparable from the light.

प्रकाश एव सततं तस्मान्मौनं हि युज्यते। अयमर्थो महान्यस्य स्वयमेव प्रकाशितः॥२१॥ न स जीवो न च ब्रह्म न चान्यदपि किंचन। न तस्य वर्णा विद्यन्ते नाश्रमाश्च तथैव च॥२२॥ न तस्य धर्मोऽधर्मश्च न निषेधो विधिर्न च। यदा ब्रह्मात्मकं सर्वं विभाति तत एव तु॥२३॥ तदा दुःखादिभेदोऽयमाभासोऽपि न भासते। जगज्जीवादिरूपेण पश्यन्नपि परात्मवित्॥२४॥ न तत्पश्यति चिद्रूपं ब्रह्मवस्त्वेव पश्यति। धर्मधर्मित्ववार्ता च भेदे सति हि भिद्यते॥२५॥

A light everywhere and continuously is so existed. Silence approach is better than to by something more about it. The man automatically known to it is not a living soul (Jīva), not Brahma and not any thing otherwise. It has no Varṇa nor it is an Āśrama. He is neither involved in religion, evils, nor prohibition and the law. When Brahma is all apparent to him, he does to feel at all the distinction between these worldly palms and sorrows. The person known to the supreme soul as the perfect knowledge (Parabrahma) sees this world of different creatures but the distinction cannot be seen by him. He observes continuously the only Brahma in the form of mind (cit). The subjects pertaining to the religion and the religious themselves having some distinction; these are appeared different to each other.

भेदाभेदस्तथा भेदाभेदः साक्षात्परात्मनः। नास्ति स्वात्मातिरेकेण स्वयमेवास्ति सर्वदा॥२६॥

It is only the sensitivity of supreme soul that exists always in its present form and the other all distinction etc. and all similarity and differences are embedded within that supreme soul.

ब्रह्मैव विद्यते साक्षाद्वस्तुतोऽवस्तुतोऽपि च। तथैव ब्रह्मविज्ञानी किं गृह्णाति जहाति किम्॥२७॥

The thing or non-thing (Avastu) whatever is existing that all is the apparent perfect Brahma (Prabrahma). How the person knows to Brahma can accept one and neglect, reject other in such circumstance?

अधिष्ठानमनौपम्यमवाङ्मनसगोचरम्। यत्तदद्रेश्यमग्राह्यमगोत्रं रूपवर्जितम्॥ २८॥ अचक्षुःश्रोत्रमत्यर्थं तदपाणिपदं तथा। नित्यं विभुं सर्वगतं सुसूक्ष्मं च तदव्ययम्॥ २९॥ ब्रह्मैवेदममृतं तत्पुरस्ताद्ब्रह्मानन्दं परमं चैव पश्चात्। ब्रह्मानन्दं परमं दक्षिणे च ब्रह्मानन्दं परमं चोत्तरे च॥ ३०॥

The perfect knowledge (Parabrahma) is beyond the comparison, inaccessible to the speech and mind, beyond seeing through eyes, unentertainable, without clan (Gotra) without any form (complexion), without eyes, ears, hands, and feet etc. everlasting, almightly omniscient, most minuscule, absolute, and beyond the clutter of death. He is creator and supporter to all, and existed as the pleasure of Brahma (Brahmānanda) at front, rear, north, south, i.e. at all directions and the best nectar of veda. That perfect knowledge (Parabrahma) is existed at the left and right both sides.

स्वात्मन्येव स्वयं सर्वं सदा पश्यति निर्भयः। तदा मुक्तो न मुक्तश्च बद्धस्यैव विमुक्तता॥ ३१॥

Thus that best devotee every moment sees fearlessly to all in his conscience (Antarātmā). The devotee of such nature, irrespective of his being scholar or innocent (Ajñānī); he avails emancipation.

एवंरूपा परा विद्या सत्येन तपसापि च। ब्रह्मचर्यादिभिर्धर्मैर्लभ्या वेदान्तवर्त्मना॥ ३२॥

Thus, the Para-vidyā (metaphysics), truth penance and celibacy etc. religions too are obtained through the route of Vedānta.

स्वशरीरे स्वयंज्योतिःस्वरूपं पारमार्थिकम्। क्षीणदोषाः प्रपश्यन्ति नेतरे माययाऽऽवृताः॥ ३३॥

The great yogī devotees can see the self luminating supreme soul (Parabrahma) whose heart is pure absolutely, and the defects are decayed, the people engrossed in illusion (Māyā) can not see that supreme Lord.

एवं स्वरूपविज्ञानं यस्य कस्यास्ति योगिनः। कुत्रचिद्गमनं नास्ति तस्य संपूर्णरूपिणः॥ ३४॥

The yogin devotee, understood to his nature attains to the perfection and seldom falls prey to the cycle of birth and death (Āvāgamana).

आकाशमेकं संपूर्णं कुत्रचिन्न हि गच्छति। तद्वद्ब्रह्मात्मविच्छ्रेष्ठः कुत्रचिन्नैव गच्छति॥ ३५॥

As only sky is existed everywhere without come and go anywhere, the yogī known to him as Brahma, can not move anywhere.

अभक्ष्यस्य निवृत्त्या तु विशुद्धं हृदयं भवेत्। आहारशुद्धौ चित्तस्य विशुद्धिर्भवति स्वतः॥ ३६॥

The mind is fully purified when control on diet in only made i.e. checks on forbidden diet. The mind automatically purifies when purity in diet is established.

चित्तशुद्धौ क्रमाज्ज्ञानं त्रुट्यन्ति ग्रन्थयः स्फुटम्। अभक्ष्यं ब्रह्मविज्ञानविहीनस्यैव देहिनः॥ ३७॥

The knowledge starts increasing systematically when the mind is purified in toto. The knots of ignorances then are destroyed. However, control on diet is necessary for the person who still has not attained to the knowledge of Brahma.

न सम्यग्ज्ञानिनस्तद्वत्स्वरूपं सकलं खलु। अहमन्नं सदान्नाद इति हि ब्रह्मवेदनम्॥ ३८॥

Its reason is that the nature of scholar is not found so discriminative as it found in the stupid. The scholar thinks that I, the conjumer (Bhoktā) is Brahma and the food eaten too is I myself.

ब्रह्मविद्ग्रसति ज्ञानात्सर्वं ब्रह्मात्मनैव तु। ब्रह्मक्षत्रादिकं सर्वं यस्य स्यादोदनं सदा॥ ३९॥

The devotee who is yogī known to Brahma, always sees all living organisms in the form of Brahma. By this very reason, the concept of Brāhmaṇa, Kṣatriya etc. too is entertainable for him.

यस्योपसेचनं मृत्युस्तं ज्ञानी तादृशः खलु। ब्रह्मस्वरूपविज्ञानाज्जगद्भोज्यं भवेत्खलु॥ ४०॥

The devotee, whose food (eatable) is the death, attains the same form and this whole world too becomes entertainable to him.

जगदात्मतया भाति यदा भोज्यं भवेत्तदा। ब्रह्मस्वात्मतया नित्यं भक्षितं सकलं तदा॥ ४१॥

The world becomes in the form of eatable when it is perceived as the sons and the immortal Brahma in the form of soul eats (consumes) it regularly.

यदाभानेन रूपेण जगद्भोज्यं भवेत्तु तत्। मानतः स्वात्मना भातं भक्षितं भवति ध्रुवम्॥ ४२॥

The nature of soul that turns the world in the form of eatable matters when it is perceived and definitely it is consumed by the Brahma.

स्वस्वरूपं स्वयं भुङ्क्ते नास्ति भोज्यं पृथक् स्वतः। अस्ति चेदस्तितारूपं ब्रह्मैवास्तित्वलक्षणम्॥ ४३॥

Thus, the Brahma eats its nature himself. Its reason is that the eatable matter is not distinct and separate from the Brahma. The nature of entity that too is the characteristic of existence.

अस्तितालक्षणा सत्ता सत्ता ब्रह्म न चापरा। नास्ति सत्तातिरेकेण नास्ति माया च वस्तुतः॥ ४४॥

The characteristics of entity too is known as existence and it does not differ from the Brahma. There is no other entity then Brahma and the illusion (Māyā) too is not real matter.

योगिनामात्मनिष्ठानां माया स्वात्मनि कल्पिता। साक्षिरूपतया भाति ब्रह्मज्ञानेन बाधिता॥ ४५॥

The yogis, the devotees, imagine illusion through his heart. It appears as an evidence to restricted by virtue of the knowledge of Brahma to the devotees (Ascetics).

ब्रह्मविज्ञानसंपन्नः प्रतीतमखिलं जगत्। पश्यन्नपि सदा नैव पश्यति स्वात्मनः पृथक्॥ ४६॥ इत्युपनिषत्॥

Thus, duly perceived of the Brahma as perfect knowledge and science, the learned devotees does not treat it distinct and separate him irrespective of his observance directly of the world. This Upaniṣad (secret knowledge) contains this all very specifically.

ॐ भद्रं कर्णेभिः .... इति शान्तिः॥

॥इति पाशुपतब्रह्मोपनिषत्समाप्ता॥

70. PARABRAHMOPANIṢAD

परब्रह्मोपनिषद्

This Upaniṣad is related to the tradition of Atharvaveda. There are twenty hymns wherein the reclusion has been described as the best measure to attain the Parabrahma. This Upaniṣad commences with a question raised by Mahāśāla Śaunaka in which he has asked the hermit Pippalāda about the pre-destination of the worldly objects prior to the creation. The next question is that how Lord Hiraṇyagarbha originated. Those things and what are they? The sage Pippalāda has explained this very question in prolix and it has been suggested that one should resort to Aṣṭākapāla and Aṣṭāṅga yoga in order to know the primitive cause for the creation, the supreme entity. A most influensive description for the life of a recluse has been described thereafter. It has been suggested that the recluse should definitely put an inner most sacrificial thread and the braid instead of exterior sacrificial thread and the braid. It has been also added that the man is only entitled to emancipation and can be said a true ascetic only when he has put on a braid of fire and knowledge of also the sacrificial thread. At the conclusion, it has been suggested that the exterior braid and the sacrificial thread should be abandoned and the braid in the form of Oṁ and sacrificial thread only can provide with the emancipation.

॥शान्तिपाठः॥

ॐ भद्रं कर्णेभिः ....इति शान्तिः॥

अथ हैनं महाशालः शौनकोऽङ्गिरसं भगवन्तं पिप्पलादं विधिवदुपसन्नः पप्रच्छ दिव्ये ब्रह्मपुरे संप्रतिष्ठिता भवन्ति खलु। कथं सृज्यन्ते। नित्यात्मन एष महिमा। विभज्य एष महिमा विभुः। क एषः। तस्मै स होवाच। एतत्सत्यं यत्प्रब्रवीमि ब्रह्मविद्यां वरिष्ठां देवेभ्यः प्राणेभ्यः। परब्रह्मपुरे विरजं निष्कलं शुभ्रमक्षरं विरजं विभाति। स नियच्छति मधुकरराश्या निर्मकः। अकर्मस्वपुरस्थितः। कर्मतरः कर्षकवत्फलमनुभवति। कर्ममर्मज्ञाता कर्म करोति। कर्ममर्म ज्ञात्वा कर्म कुर्यात्। को जालं विक्षिपेदेको नैनमपकर्षत्यपकर्षति॥ १॥

Once the learned Śaunaka asked Lord Pippalāda (born in the Gotra of Aṅgirasa) Whether all things proposed for the creation with the universe wherein divine abode of Brahma prior to their origin in this universe viz., Whether those were enshrined in the heart ether of Lord Hirṇyagarbha? How the magnificent Lord create them by dividing into suitable classes out froṃ within? What is the magnificence of this very sovereign Lord? viz., What these actually are?" The hermit Pippalāda replied– "The learning of Brahma to what I will tell you is true. It provides the ten breathing i.e. Prāṇa, Apāna etc. senses, and the truth to entertain their respective subjects. It is viraja what for the trio-properties including Rajas etc. and Niṣkala (the sixteen arts including Prāṇa etc.) in the abode of Parabrahma. This is the reason for its being pure and everlasting. It is called Nirmaka because it builds the ties and liberty for the living-organisms and adorns beyond the Guṇas. This builder of supreme soul effaces the ignorance of the persons desirous of emancipation and enables them to perceive that all sensitive supreme soul has nothing left to do for that Parabrahma, it remains all inactive. The man of worldly eye performs a number of activities in order to enjoy the fruit from this and that world. He thus enjoys the fruits of action like a former. The scholar well-known to the mystery of action always performs it as worship to god in order to purify his mind. The scholar who considers himself as the Brahma and desires liberty from the illusion and further who knows that it is the action that determines the inferior and superior position of a man, always does the action according to his āśrama and without hankering for the fruits. Who is such a scholar dashing himself down as a result of entrapped in the net of various actions instead of engrossing his mind in the Brahma? Its answer is that there is none viz. the person who performs his duties as worship to Lord and remains unattached to the fruit of action seldom is trapped in the worldly objects.

प्राणदेवताश्चत्वारः। ताः सर्वा नाड्यः सुषुप्तश्येनाकाशवत्। यथा श्येनः खमाश्रित्य याति स्वमालयं कुलायम्। एवं सुषुप्तं ब्रूत। अयं च परं च स सर्वत्र हिरणमये परे कोशे। अमृता ह्येषा नाडीत्रयं संचरति। तस्य त्रिपादं ब्रह्म। एषात्रेष्य ततोऽनुतिष्ठति। अन्यत्र ब्रूत। अयं च परं च सर्वत्र हिरणमये परे कोशे। यथैष देवदत्तो यष्ट्या च ताड्यमानो नैवैति। एवमिष्टापूर्तकर्मा शुभाशुभैर्न लिप्यते। यथा कुमारको निष्काम आनन्दमभियाति। तथैष देवः स्वप्न आनन्दमभिधावति। वेद एव परं ज्योतिः। ज्योतिषा मा ज्योतिरानन्दयत्येवमेव। तत्परं यच्चित्तं परमात्मानमानन्दयति। शुभ्रवर्णमाजायतेश्वरात्। भूयस्तेनैव मार्गेण स्वप्नस्थानं नियच्छति। जलूकाभाववद्व्यर्थाकाममाजायतेश्वरात्। तावतात्मानमानन्दयति। परसंधि यदपरसन्धीति। तत्परं नापरं त्यजति। तदैवं कपालाष्टकं संधाय य एष स्तन इवावलम्बते सेन्द्रयोनिः स वेदयोनिरिति। अत्र जाग्रति शुभाशुभातिरिक्तः शुभाशुभैरपि कर्मभिर्न लिप्यते। य एष देवोऽन्यदेवस्य संप्रसादोऽन्तर्याम्यसङ्गचिद्रूपः पुरुषः। प्रणवहंसः परं ब्रह्म। न प्राणहंसः। प्रणवो जीवः। आद्या देवता निवेदयति। य एवं वेद। तत्कथं निवेदयते। जीवस्य ब्रह्मत्वमापादयति॥ २॥

A person who is made known by his teacher that he himself is the supreme flame and pleasure as also a ray of sun etc. luminating stars, the light and he is in the form of pleasure always lives in gaiety. Similarly, whose heart is duly devoted to Parabrahma, attains the supreme soul and enjoys with every moment or always enjoys the pleasure within his soul. The white colour is originated from the Lord and it keeps a man in pleasure. Thus, an exclusive meditation establishing the breathing in the middle of the both eyes, the devotee rests in dreaming, viz., he attains as a result of such exercise. The stage of dreaming and perceives 'Tattvamasi' 'Ahaṁ Brahmāsmi' thereby relax the soul. As a leech moves easily from a straw to another, the scholar too easily moves from awaking to the dreaming stage. Again, he can abandon the stage of awaking by entering into the stage of dreaming. By the grace of Lord, he enjoys the pleasure of moving in the three stages (awaking, dreaming and dormance) immediately and voluntarily. Thus, the living soul enjoys its soul by resorting to the Savikalpa and Nirvikalpa meditation. This element of soul then abandons the ignorance creating hurdle in joining the living soul with the supreme soul. Thus, the element of soul illumining with the knowledge always remains automatically.

In case, the common knowledge of Brahma is not attained through mere listening about it, one should resort to kapālāṭaka. Kapālāṭaka has eight parts. These are Yama, Niyama, Āsana, Prāṇāyāma, Pratyāhāra, Dhāraṇā, Dhyāna and Samādhi. The knowledge of Brahma by purifying the heart through these exercises should be acquired. This Kapālāṭaka hangs like the beast (the banana flower existing in the region of the heart) by the eight kinds of yoga. It uplifts and develops while exercising the Indrayoni (a route to attain the supreme soul) known as Vedayoni always awakes there in. The person who concentrates on Īśvara in his heart Lotus, goes beyond the good and bad, thereby no involvement with them. The characteristics of that god is now explained. It endows pleasure to other gods, intuitive, sensitive, Puruṣa, exclusive, Oṁ, and the supreme Brahma. It is not the Prāṇahaṁsa. Prāṇahaṇsa has been referred here as cardinal breathing because this issue is of Parabrahma and not of breathing). Praṇava is the living soul because it is worth to know by the size of the component to Oṁ that Oṁ is the form of living soul, called the primitive god. The person duly known to it does not locate discrimination between the living soul and the Brahma. He always lays down the unity between them and seldom thinks and discrimination therein.

[The Saint has said the eight parts of yoga as kapālāṭaka herein. By virtue of his spiritual perception he observe him as a Lotus flower. As the hung and closed Lotus rises up and blossoms in the presence of Sunlight, the propensities of yoga in dormance awake and upraise when the sensitivity of Brahma is added there with.]

सत्त्वमथास्य पुरुषान्तःशिखोपवीतत्वम्। ब्राह्मणस्य मुमुक्षोरन्तःशिखोपवीतधारणम्। बहिर्लक्ष्यमाणशिखायज्ञोपवीतधारणं कर्मिणो गृहस्थस्य। अन्तरुपवीतलक्षणं तु बहिस्तन्तु-वदव्यक्तमन्तस्तत्त्वमेलनम्।। ३।।

The essence of this Puruṣa Brahma is the internal braid and sacrificial thread. The Brāhmaṇa desirous of emancipation should hold them. It is for couple to put on the extraneous braid and the sacrificial thread. The internal braid and the sacrificial thread is not so apparent as the extraneous is. These are invisible and they joins with the element of Brahma.

न सन्नासन्न सदसद्भिन्नाभिन्नं न चोभयम्। न सभागं न निर्भागं न चाप्युभयरूपकम्। ब्रह्मात्मैकत्वविज्ञानं हेयं मिथ्यात्वकारणादिति।। ४।।

The nature of ignorance is neither truth, nor false. It is neither distinct nor integrated and it is not the mixed form of them. Similarly, it has no division, it is not free from division to the mixed form of the both. Until and unless, the knowledge, accepting that every one is Brahma is acquired, the ignorance remains. Being it all false, it is worth giving up and hatred when the true knowledge of Brahma is acquired.

पञ्चपाद्ब्रह्मणो न किंचन। चतुष्पादन्तर्वर्तिनोऽन्तर्जीवब्रह्मणश्चत्वारि स्थानानि। नाभिहृदयकण्ठमूर्धसु जाग्रत्स्वप्नसुषुप्तितुरीयावस्थाः। आहवनीयगार्हपत्यदक्षिणसभ्याग्निषु। जागरिते ब्रह्मा स्वप्ने विष्णुः सुषुप्तौ रुद्रस्तुरीयमक्षरं चिन्मयम्। तस्माच्चतुरवस्था। चतुरङ्गुलवेष्टनमिव षण्णवतितत्त्वानि तन्तुवद्विभज्य तदाहितं

त्रिगुणीकृत्य द्वात्रिंशत्तत्त्वनिष्कर्षमापाद्य ज्ञानपूतं त्रिगुणस्वरूपं त्रिमूर्तित्वं पृथग्विज्ञाय नवब्रह्माख्यनवगुणोपेतं ज्ञात्वा नवमानमितं त्रि:पुनस्त्रि गुणीकृत्य सूर्येन्द्वग्निकलास्वरूपत्वेनैकीकृत्याद्यन्तरेकत्वमपि मध्ये त्रिरावृत्य ब्रह्म विष्णुमहेश्वरत्वमनुसंधायाद्यन्तमेकीकृत्य चिद्ग्रन्थावद्वैतग्रन्थिं कृत्वा नाभ्यादिब्रह्म बिलप्रमाणं पृथक् पृथक् सप्तविंशतितत्त्वसंबन्धं त्रिगुणोपेतं त्रिमूर्तिलक्षणलक्षित मप्येकत्वमापाद्य वामांसादिदक्षिणाकट्यन्तं विभाव्याद्यन्तग्रहसंमेलनमेवं ज्ञात्वा मूलमेकं सत्यं मृणमयं विज्ञातं स्याद्वाचारम्भणं विकारो नामधेयं मृत्तिकेत्येव सत्यम्। हंसेति वर्णद्वयेनान्त:शिखोपवीतित्वं निश्चित्य ब्राह्मणत्वं ब्रह्मध्यानार्हत्वं यतित्वमलक्षितान्त: शिखोपवीतित्वमेवं बहिर्लक्षितकर्मशिखाज्ञानोपवीतं गृहस्थस्याभासब्राह्मणत्वस्य केशसमूहशिखाप्रत्यक्षकार्पासतन्तुकृतोपवीतत्वम्। चतु: चतुर्गुणीकृत्य चतुर्विंशतितत्त्वापादनतन्तुकृत्त्वं नवतत्त्वमेकमेव परंब्रह्म तत्प्रतिसरयोग्यत्वाद्बहुमार्गप्रवृत्तिं कल्पयन्ति। सर्वेषां ब्रह्मादीनां देवर्षीणां मनुष्याणां मुक्तिरेका। ब्रह्मैकमेव। ब्राह्मणत्वमेकमेव। वर्णाश्रमाचारविशेषा: पृथक्पृथक् शिखा वर्णाश्रमिणामेककैव। अपवर्गस्य यते: शिखायज्ञोपवीतमूलं प्रणवमेकमेव वदन्ति। हंस: शिखा। प्रणव उपवीतम्। नाद: संधानम्। एष धर्मो नेतरो धर्म:। तत्कथमिति। प्रणवहंसो नादस्त्रिवृत्सूत्रं स्वहृदि चैतन्ये तिष्ठति त्रिविधं ब्रह्म। तद्विद्धि प्रापञ्चिकशिखोपवीतं त्यजेत्॥५॥

The confusion to the effect whether the Brahma is in the form of ignorance or not is nothing because the Pañcapāda Brahma (awaking, dreaming, Turīya and beyond Turīya) embeds everything within it. There are four places of the Brahma in garb of living soul as existed under Catuṣpāda in macro and micro form. These are navel, heart, throat and the head. The Brahma is attained in four stages. These are awaking, dreaming, dormance and Turīya. One should consider as soul to the extent possible in the fires i.e. Āhavanīya, Gārhapatya, Dakṣiṇā and Sabhya. The Lord Brahmā awaking Lord Viṣṇu in dreaming, Lord Rudra in dormance and the latter Brahma in Turīya stage is worth concentration.

Now, the Brahma is described in the form of sacrificial thread because a recluse puts on this sacrificial thread in the form of Brahma. The four stages as described above are the measurement of four fingers (the sacrificial thread is made by rolling it in four fingers). It is rolled six times. Ninety six elements are rolled up in it. Dividing it into three parts, every part should contain the thirty-two elements and by multiplying it by three, the resultant ninety-six conclusions are arrived. Its form of knowledge, trio-properties (Satva, Rajas and Tamas) are the three threads intertwined with it and the three gods complexion creating distinct nine threads should be treated as nine Brahma. The arts of Sun, moon and the fire i.e. three should multiply with this nine and then it should be intertwined. Further, the three frequencies i.e. the primitive, middle and the last and by doing research on Brahmā, Viṣṇu and Maheśa; these frequencies by taking one after another from beginning to the end, a single knot should be made and put on from navel zone to the Brahmarandhra. The sacrificial thread with three intertwined rolls rebel the trio-properties related to the twenty-seven elements distinctly and joining the three threads in one presuming its length from left shoulder to the right portion of the waist, it can purify the heart. One should deem regarding this sacrificial thread that the basic element is the one irrespective of joining different elements from the beginning to the end of it. As a number of vessels are made by using the clay but the basic elements is the clay, everything in the similar fashion is made by Brahma but no entity is distinct than it. Hence, presuming himself the Brahma is the innermost braid and the element of sacrificial thread. This presumption enables to obtain the element of Brāhmaṇa i.e. the ability to concentrate on Brahma and element of reclusion. The persons who have attained the element of Brahman and the recluse keep and put on the internal braid the invisible sacrificial thread. The visible or the apparent braid in garb of activity and the sacrificial thread in garb of knowledge are for the couples. The visible cluster of hair i.e. braid and the sacrificial thread made of the cotton thread are only indication of the element of Brāhmaṇa and his ability to perform the Vedic ceremonies. The maxim of sacrificial thread are in combination of twenty-four elements multiplied by four i.e. ninety-six elements lay down the Brahma in the form of element. The nine elements (thread) of the sacrificial thread also lay down the Brahma. Brahma is one but a number of people suggests numerous measures as (Sāṁkhya yoga etc.) for attainment of it. For all Brāhmaṇa, hermit and the hymn beings, the emancipation, the Brahma and the element of Brahmāṇa are the same. The ceremonies and varṇāśramas are separate and in many numbers. The nature of braid is the one for all varṇas. The persons entitled to emancipation state that the root of braid and the sacrificial thread is Oṁ. The knowledge of Brahma is braid and the Oṁ is the sacrificial thread for the ascetics and the sound of Oṁ is the thing that joins them.

Their (recluse) is this single religion and nothing apart from it. What kind of this religion is? A question which has been answered as—This Oṁ is the Brahma and the sound is the three intertwining threads. It is existed with its own magnificence. It enshines in the heart in the form of sensitivity. This Brahma is of two kinds. The first is 'Parā' and the second is 'Aparā'. The person desirous of emancipation should abandon the visible braid and the sacrificial thread if he has arrived at the stage in which he observes nothing other than his own soul.

सशिखं वपनं कृत्वा बहि:सूत्रं त्यजेद्बुध:। यदक्षरं परंब्रह्म तत्सूत्रमिति धारयेत्॥ ६॥

The persons who have arrived at the stage described above should cut their hair including the braid and the visible sacrificial thread should be immersed into water and they should only put on the letter Brahma as the sacrificial thread.

पुनर्जन्मनिवृत्त्यर्थं मोक्षस्याहर्निशं स्मरेत्। सूचनात्सूत्रमित्युक्तं सूत्रं नाम परं पदम्॥ ७॥

The ascetic should always remember the emancipation for liberating himself from the trap of rebirth. The thread in the form of Brahma is called the maxim providing with the supreme position being it an informant.

तत्सूत्रं विदितं येन स मुमुक्षु: स भिक्षुक:। स वेदवित्सदाचार: स विप्र: पंक्तिपावन:॥ ८॥

Only the man is true desirous of emancipation, consecrator, known to Veda enlightened and the Brāhmaṇa who is known to the maxim of Brahma. He makes all the people pure in heart to whom he get in touch with.

येन सर्वमिदं प्रोतं सूत्रे मणिगणा इव। तत्सूत्रं धारयेद्योगी योगविद्ब्राह्मणो यति:॥ ९॥

The maxim or the thread pertaining to the Parabrahma who has entertained in a single thread this entire Brahmāṇḍa like the beats of gem actually entitles the man putting it on a yogī, a Brāhmaṇa known to yoga and an ascetic.

बहि:सूत्रं त्यजेद्विप्रो योगविज्ञानतत्पर:। ब्रह्मभावमिदं सूत्रं धारयेद्य: स मुक्तिभाक्। नाशुचित्वं न चोच्छिष्टं तस्य सूत्रस्य धारणात्॥ १०॥

The person engrossed acquiring knowledge, known to yoga and the Brahma should give up the extraneous thread because the man is only entitled to emancipation who holds the sacrificial thread with the spiritual Brahma. Having that thread duly put on, no apprehension of impurity, stateness, remains any more.

सूत्रमन्तर्गतं येषां ज्ञानयज्ञोपवीतिनाम्। ते तु सूत्रविदो लोके ते च यज्ञोपवीतिन:॥ ११॥

The worldly people putting on the sacrificial thread are the true person if the knowledge in depth is embedded with it.

ज्ञानशिखिनो ज्ञाननिष्ठा ज्ञानयज्ञोपवीतिन:। ज्ञानमेव परं तेषां पवित्रं ज्ञानमीरितम्॥ १२॥

The person holding braid of knowledge, loyalty to knowledge and sacrificial thread of knowledge know that the knowledge is only supreme because it is knowledge which is stated as the supreme sacrosanct.

अग्नेरिव शिखा नान्या यस्य ज्ञानमयी शिखा। स शिखीत्युच्यते विद्वान्नेतरे केशधारिण:॥ १३॥

The person who have no exterior braid see as otherwise the braid of knowledge brilliant as the fire itself; have really the braid and the rest of people have only hair. As the scholars say.

कर्मण्यधिकृता ये तु वैदिके लौकिकेऽपि वा। ब्राह्मणाभासमात्रेण जीवन्ते कुक्षिपूरका:। व्रजन्ते निरयं ते तु पुनर्जन्मनि जन्मनि॥ १४॥

The Brāhmaṇas whose activities are confined only to perform ceremonies either Vedic or the worldly are mere Brāhmaṇas because they only live for their stomach. They definitely fall in the hell at the end of every birth they receive (they suffer from a number of pains in the hell that embeds the cycle of birth and death in this universe.

वामांसदक्षकट्यन्तं ब्रह्मसूत्रं तु सव्यत:। अन्तर्बहिरिवात्यर्थं तत्त्वतन्तुसमन्वितम्। नाभ्यादिब्रह्मरन्ध्रान्तप्रमाणं धारयेत्सुधी:॥ १५॥

It is all good for the scholars that they should put on a sacrificial thread as lengthy as to touch the right side of the waist from the left shoulder. This suggestion is for putting on the extraneous sacrificial thread. So far as the innermost sacrificial thread is concerned, it is made of the fibre in garb of the supreme element and it should be put on from the navel zone to the Brahmarandhra.

तेभिर्धार्यमिदं सूत्रं क्रियाङ्गं तन्तुनिर्मितम्। शिखा ज्ञानमयी यस्य उपवीतं च तन्मयम्। ब्राह्मण्यं सकलं तस्य नेतरेषां तु किंचन॥ १६॥

Thus, the sacrificial thread made of this fibre in garb of supreme element and in the form of various aspects of the numerous activities should be put on. Everything is in the form of Brahma for the persons who put on the braid and sacrificial thread of knowledge and there is nothing except Brahma for them.

इदं यज्ञोपवीतं तु परमं यत्परायणम्। विद्वान्यज्ञोपवीती संधारयेद्यः स मुक्तिभाक्।। १७।।

The scholar putting on the sacrificial thread of Brahma and the supreme element is really entitled to put it on and emancipation.

बहिरन्तश्चोपवीती विप्रः संन्यस्तुमर्हति। एकयज्ञोपवीती तु नैव संन्यस्तुमर्हति।। १८।।

The Brāhmaṇa putting on the exterior and interior both sacrificial threads is only entitled to the reclusion viz., he performs the worldly and vedic ceremonies and observing the rules prescribed therefore and it is possible only when the exterior sacrificial thread is out on while the internal sacrificial thread leads to know. The element of Brahma thereby creates the propensity of detachment and enables to the reclusion. Hence, the Brāhmaṇa putting on a single sacrificial thread is not entitled to the reclusion.

तस्मात्सर्वप्रयत्नेन मोक्षापेक्षी भवेद्यतिः। बहिःसूत्रं परित्यज्य स्वान्तःसूत्रं तु धारयेत्।। १९।।

The ascetic therefore should do all efforts to be desirous of emancipation and put on the internal sacrificial thread by giving up the exterior thread.

बहिःप्रपञ्चशिखोपवीतित्वमनादृत्य प्रणवहंसशिखोपवीतित्वमवलम्ब्य मोक्षसाधनं कुर्यादित्याह भगवाञ्छौनक इत्युपनिषत्।। २०।।

(Finally) Lord Śaunaka said that one should do all efforts for emancipation be giving up the exterior braid and sacrificial thread and by resorting to the braid of Praṇavahaṁsa (Oṁ) and the sacrificial thread of knowledge. This very is the cryptic learning.

ॐ भद्रं कर्णेभिः ....इतिः शान्तिः।।

।।इति परब्रह्मोपनिषत्समाप्ता।।

71. AVADHŪTOPANIṢAD

अवधूतोपनिषद्

This Upaniṣad is related to Kṛṣṇa Yajurveda. Lord Dattātreya describes the form and importance of Avadhūta state when the question was raised by Sāṁkṛti in this upaniṣad. It has also been described that how the concerned man receive higher accomplishments as a result of the best elements inserted in the state of Avadhūta.

॥शान्तिपाठः॥

ॐ सह नाववतु। सह नौ भुनक्तु। सह वीर्यं करवावहै। तेजस्विनावधीतमस्तु मा विद्विषावहै॥

ॐ शान्तिः शान्तिः शान्तिः॥

O supreme soul! I protect us (the teacher and the disciple) both concomitantly. Please provide us maintenance. May both of us obtain the power simultaneously. May the learning duly digested be sharp. May both of us do not envy and attach with each other. O the powerful soul! compound our trio-pains i.e supernatural, metaphysical and celestial. May the undeputing stock of peace is enjoyed.

अथ ह सांकृतिर्भगवन्तमवधूतं दत्तात्रेयं परिसमेत्य पप्रच्छ। भगवन्कोऽवधूतस्तस्य का स्थितिः किं लक्ष्म किं संसरणमिति। तं होवाच भगवो दत्तात्रेयः परमकारुणिकः॥१॥ अक्षरत्वाद्वरेण्यत्वाद्धूतसंसारबन्धनात्। तत्त्वमस्यादिलक्ष्यत्वादवधूत इतीर्यते॥२॥

Sāṁkṛti went to Lord Dattātreya and asked– "O Lord! Who is Avadhūta! What kind of his state is ? What is the characteristics of Avadhūta and what kind of physical treatment he does?" Listening to these questions– "The generous Lord Dattāreya replied– "Avadhūta is the living organism with resolute, mind adorable, free from the worldly ties and known to the connotation of Tattvamasi etc. sentences. In other words, the letter 'A' is immortal, the letter 'Va' is vareṇya, the letter Dhū is free from worldly ties and the letter 'Ta' is the aim of Tattvamasi etc. sentences. When these letters are gathered or added the word Avadhūta is constructed.

यो विलङ्घ्याश्रमान्वर्णानात्मन्येव स्थितः सदा। अतिवर्णाश्रमी योगी अवधूतः स कथ्यते॥३॥

The Yogī always engrossed in the Soul, uplifted from the provision of Āśrama and Varṇa is called Avadhūta viz., a yogi devoid to holding Varṇāśrama.

तस्य प्रियं शिरः कृत्वा मोदो दक्षिणपक्षकः। प्रमोद उत्तरः पक्ष आनन्दो गोष्पदायते॥४॥

The favourite to Yogī is Brahma, the gaiety is his right hand and luxuries is the left while the pleasure is his nucleus soul. The position of his Soul becomes analogous to the hoof of a cow.

[This same context has appeared in Tattirīyopaniṣad also]

गोवालसदृशं शीर्षे नापि मध्ये न चाप्यथः। ब्रह्म पुच्छं प्रतिष्ठेति पुच्छाकारेण कारयेत्। एवं चतुष्पदं कृत्वा ते यान्ति परमां गतिम्॥५॥

One should not engross in that head (gaiety) the lower organs (pleasures and luxuries) as the middle (pleasure) by assuming them as Soul. If it is not so then that what is to be presumed as Soul? Its answer is that the Brahma should be known in the shape of a tale because the Brahma is recognised as a tail of a cow. The Yogī attain the supreme position by virtue of their appropriate knowledge of the Brahma.

न कर्मणा न प्रजया धनेन त्यागेनैके अमृतत्वमानशुः॥६॥

Immortality can be availed by virtue of sacrifice and it cannot be availed even if a number of activities are performed. It can be availed by the subject and through the wealth.

स्वैरं स्वैरविहरणं तत्संसरणम्। साम्बरा वा दिगम्बरा वा। न तेषां धर्माधर्मौ न मेध्यामेध्यौ।

सदा सांग्रहण्येष्ट्याश्वमेधमन्तर्यागं यजते। स महामखो महायोगः॥७॥

To behave according to the desires is the world of these Yogīs. Out of them a number of people put on garments while a number of people live naked. There is nothing like religion nor the evil, the holy and nuisance etc. for these Yogīs in their extreme aim i.e. to control the sensory organs, that Yogīs always do in their heart the offering of horses (Aśvamedha) by concentrating in the heart. It is their great offering and the great yoga.

कृत्स्नमेतच्चित्रं कर्म। स्वैरं न विगायेत्तन्महाव्रतम्। न स मूढवल्लिप्यते॥८॥

The state of internal Aśvamedha has been stated as the state in which the streams of extrovert powers duly surrendered to the sensitivity of supreme Soul or giving the extrovert mind up. This accomplishment is called the great offering or the great yoga. The entire conduct of these yogins, excellent deeds performed by them should not be condemned. They do not involve in the good and the evil etc. like persons living in the alley of ignorance. They perpetually and voluntarily move everywhere without any sense of attachment.

यथा रविः सर्वरसान्प्रभुङ्क्ते हुताशनश्चापि हि सर्वभक्षः।

तथैव योगी विषयान्प्रभुङ्क्ते न लिप्यते पुण्यपापैश्च शुद्धः॥९॥

As Lord Sun entertains all kinds of essences and the fire entertains everything; the Yogī inspite of enjoying the worldly pleasures, does not made responsible for the good or evil etc. particularly because of his heart duly made pure.

आपूर्यमाणमचलप्रतिष्ठं समुद्रमापः प्रविशन्ति यद्वत्।

तद्वत्कामा यं प्रविशन्ति सर्वे स शान्तिमाप्नोति न कामकामी॥१०॥

As the water inserts in the ocean which has attained the undeviated prestige (position), the Yogī remains undeviated inspite of existence of the passion for worldly issues and attains peace. The person tempted or curious for the enjoyments of worldly issues cannot attain the peace as it is obtained by the Yogī.

न निरोधो न चोत्पत्तिर्न बद्धो न च साधकः। न मुमुक्षुर्न वै मुक्त इत्येषा परमार्थता॥ ११॥

The real position is that neither origin nor cessation is in existence and further nobody is devotee and no one is fastened. Similarly, nobody is desirous of emancipation and none is liberated.

ऐहिकामुष्मिकव्रातसिद्ध्यै मुक्तेश्च सिद्धये। बहुकृत्यं पुरा स्यान्मे तत्सर्वमधुना कृतम्॥ १२॥ तद्देव कृतकृत्यत्वं प्रतियोगिपुरःसरम्। दुःखिनोऽज्ञाः संसरन्तु कामं पुत्राद्यपेक्षया॥ १३॥ परमानन्दपूर्णोऽहं संसरामि किमिच्छया। अनुतिष्ठन्तु कर्माणि परलोकयियासवः॥ १४॥ सर्वलोकात्मकः कस्मादनुतिष्ठामि किं कथम्। व्याचक्षतां ते शास्त्राणि वेदानध्यापयन्तु वा॥ १५ येऽत्राधिकारिणो मे तु नाधिकारोऽक्रियत्वतः। निद्राभिक्षे स्नानशौचे नेच्छामि न करोमि च॥ १६ द्रष्टारश्चेत्कल्पयन्तु किं मे स्यादन्यकल्पनात्। गुञ्जापुञ्जादि दह्येत नान्यारोपितवह्निना। नान्यारोपितसंसार धर्मानेवमहं भजे॥ १७॥

It was necessary for me to do very first for the accomplishment of deeds in this and that world and for the accomplishment of the emancipation but now all this has been performed. Thus, the Avadhūta doing investigations deeply within each yoga always feels glut by adopting this presumption. He then says in the state of concentration that the fools were entangled with the cycle of birth and death full of dismay only due to their passion for sun etc. but I am fulfilled with the supreme pleasure and there is no desire that could entangle me with this world. Why should I perform and of the deeds when I am the Soul of all worlds and all the-worlds are within me. Let the persons do activities with an intention to attain emancipation. As I am idle (inactive) and have not right to preach and teach, let the persons righteous do preaching and teaching of the Vedas. I have not even slight worry about this sleep, alm, bathing and to excrete. Let the people of intuitive label imagine otherwise; there is no advantage to me for such imagination. The people may confuse of fire while seeing the red Guñja but such imagination may not burn the Guñja into ashes. The worldly religions are not imposed on me therefore I do not pray for any.

शृण्वन्त्वज्ञाततत्त्वास्ते जानन्कस्माच्छृणोम्यहम्। मन्यन्तां संशयापन्ना न मन्येऽहमसंशयः॥ १८॥

Let the people listen to whatever they want because of no realisation with the element that I (Avadhūta) is competent to know the element. Hence, no cause for my listening. Let the person confused be do concentration. As there is no confusion in my mind (Avadhūta) needn't concentrate on any matter issue.

विपर्यस्तो निदिध्यासे किं ध्यानमविपर्यये। देहात्मत्वविपर्यासं न कदाचिद्भजाम्यहम्॥ १९॥

Nididhyāsana is for the people falling in the contradictory knowledge, the concentration is not required where there is no contradiction. I (Avadhūta) do not fall in the contradiction that considers the body as Soul. The Nididhyāsana is therefore not required.

अहं मनुष्य इत्यादिव्यवहारो विनाप्यमुम्। विपर्यासं चिराभ्यस्तवासनातोऽवकल्पते॥ २०॥

The behaviour of a man is due to the contradictory knowledge and such contradiction takes place only due to the passion exercised till long.

आरब्धकर्मणि क्षीणे व्यवहारो निवर्तते। कर्मक्षये त्वसौ नैव शाम्येद्ध्यानसहस्रत:॥ २१॥

Such dealing or behaviour is ceased only when accumulated deeds are destroyed. But this behaviour is not cooled down even if concentration is made thousand times until the destruction of accumulated deeds is made.

विरलत्वं व्यवहृतेरिष्टं चेद्ध्यानमस्तु ते। बाधिकर्मव्यवहृतिं पश्यन्ध्यायाम्यहं कुत:॥ २२॥

You should concentrate voluntarily if any desire for practical deed remains. But no such behaviour or deed is worthful in my mind, why should I then concentrate on it.

विक्षेपो नास्ति यस्मान्मे न समाधिस्ततो मम। विक्षेपो वा समाधिर्वा मनस: स्याद्विकारिण:॥ २३॥

I needn't go in the state of meditation because my mind is undeviated all time. The mind becomes caprice only when it entertains the defects and to remove these defects, the meditation is then required. I am always in the form of perceiving hence the meditation cannot give any new or different to my perceiving.

नित्यानुभवरूपस्य को मेऽत्रानुभव: पृथक्। कृतं कृत्यं प्रापणीयं प्राप्तमित्येव नित्यश:॥ २४॥
व्यवहारो लौकिको वा शास्त्रीयो वाऽन्यथापि वा। ममाकर्तुरलेपस्य यथारब्धं प्रवर्तताम्॥ २५॥

Whatever I wished to do, it was done and always obtained whatever was worth obtaining. Why should I then do any otherwise behaviour or the behaviour prescribed by worldly rites and holy books? This is the reason I do nothing. I am not involved into attachment for anything. Whatever happens naturally, I accept and perform the same.

अथवा कृतकृत्योऽपि लोकानुग्रहकाम्यया। शास्त्रीयेणैव मार्गेण वर्तेऽहं मम का क्षति:॥ २६॥

What harm is caused to me if I follow the holy book and the prescribed rules in orders to do some good for common people inspite of fully satisfied viz., fully detached.

देवार्चनस्नानशौचभिक्षादौ वर्ततां वपु:। तारं जपतु वाक्तद्वत्पठत्वाम्नायमस्तकम्॥ २७॥
विष्णुं ध्यायतु धीर्यद्वा ब्रह्मानन्दे विलीयताम्। साक्ष्यहं किंचिदप्यत्र न कुर्वे नापि कारये॥ २८॥

I merely like a witness at the time when the physical attitude does pray to gods, take bath, discharge of night soil and urine, education etc., the speech busy in reciting Praṇava, recital of Upaniṣad takes place, the wit always concentrate in Lord Viṣṇu or engrossed in Brahma. I (Avadhūta) neither any of the activity out of these nor I make anyone to perform them.

कृतकृत्यतया तृप्त: प्राप्तप्राप्यतया पुन:। तृप्यन्नेवं स्वमनसा मन्यतेऽसौ निरन्तरम्॥ २९॥

I (Avadhūta) is fully satiated because of perfection and I have received all that I wished. I regularly presume in my mind the same way satiation.

धन्योऽहं धन्योऽहं नित्यं स्वात्मानमञ्जसा वेद्मि। धन्योऽहं धन्योऽहं ब्रह्मानन्दो विभाति मे स्पष्टम्॥ ३०॥

I am granted because I know the everlasting, immortal element of Soul easily. I am granted because the pleasure of Brahma provides me with the clear light.

धन्योऽहं धन्योऽहं दु:खं सांसारिकं न वीक्षेऽद्य। धन्योऽहं धन्योऽहं स्वस्याज्ञानं पलायितं क्वापि।। ३१।।

धन्योऽहं धन्योऽहं कर्तव्यं मे न विद्यते किंचित्। धन्योऽहं धन्योऽहं प्राप्तव्यं सर्वमत्र संपन्नम्।। ३२।।

धन्योऽहं धन्योऽहं तृप्तेर्मे कोपमा भवेल्लोके। धन्योऽहं धन्योऽहं धन्यो धन्य: पुन: पुनर्धन्य:।। ३३।।

अहो पुण्यमहो पुण्यं फलितं फलितं दृढम्। अस्य पुण्यस्य संपत्तेरहो वयमहो वयम्।। ३४।।

अहो ज्ञानमहो ज्ञानमहो सुखमहो सुखम्। अहो शास्त्रमहो शास्त्रमहो गुरुरहो गुरु:।। ३५।।

I am granted because I seldom perceive the misery of this perishing world. I am granted because my ignorance has been destroyed very early. I am granted because nothing remains worth doing for me. I am granted because I have received whatever was desired by me. I am granted because my satiation is unique. I am always granted. The fruits of this great deed have been firmly obtained by me. All of us are thankful to this great deed. The knowledge, the pleasure, the holy books and the teachers all are worth thanks.

इति य इदमधीते सोऽपि कृतकृत्यो भवति। सुरापानात्पूतो भवति। स्वर्णस्तेयात्पूतो भवति। ब्रह्महत्यात्पूतो भवति। कृत्याकृत्यात्पूतो भवति। एवं विदित्वा स्वेच्छाचारपरो भूयादोंसत्यमित्युपनिषत्।। ३६।।

The person doing perseverance of this Upaniṣad gets perfection in his life. As a phenomenal impact of this Upaniṣad, the intoxicants, the thieves, murderer of Brāhmaṇa and committing prohibited deeds also converts in a man of great virtues. Its mere recital purifies the heart of a man. Having acquired this knowledge the man engages himself in executing great deeds. The Oṁ (Brahma) is only truth and it is clear by this Upaniṣad.

ॐ सह नाववतु..........इति शान्ति:।।

।।इति अवधूतोपनिषत् समाप्ता।।

72. DEVYUPANIṢAD

देव्युपनिषद्

This upaniṣad falls under the tradition of Atharvaveda. This upaniṣad is described in a questionnaire form containing the questions and answers which had taken place between the gods and the goddess (Mahādevī). The universal form of the power of mind has been described very first and it has been explained that it is the mind that has multiform and it resides with all living-organisms. The subject matter of this upaniṣad then comprises the psalm of goddess performed by the gods, the upliftment of the primitive learning, the magnificence of primitive learning, explanation on Bhuvaneśi, single letter hymn; the nine-letter learning of Mahācaṇḍī and lastly the fruits of acquiring this learning. This upaniṣad is in its tiny exterior form but it is most important in the outlook of the penance for goddess by means of Tantra.

॥शान्तिपाठः॥

ॐ भद्रं कर्णेभिः .... इति शान्तिः॥

सर्वे वै देवा देवीमुपतस्थुः। कासि त्वं महादेवि॥ १॥ साब्रवीदहं ब्रह्मस्वरूपिणी। मत्तः प्रकृतिपुरुषात्मकं जगच्छून्यं चाशून्यं च अहमानन्दानानन्दाः विज्ञानाविज्ञानेऽहम्। ब्रह्मा ब्रह्मणी वेदितव्ये। इत्याहाथर्वणी श्रुतिः॥ २॥

All gods appeared before the goddess and submitted– "O great goddess! Who are you? Kindly make us to know your identity." The goddess replied– "O gods! I am in the form of Brahma. This world, a compound of nature and the person has been originated by me. It is void from me (for the fools) and with me (for the scholars). I am with and without pleasure. I am the conscience and without conscience. It is definite that I am Brahma worth knowing and I too am beyond the Brahma. The Atharvaveda contains this very hymn.

अहं पञ्च भूतान्यपञ्चभूतानि। अहमखिलं जगत् वेदोऽहमवेदोऽहम्। विद्याहमविद्याहम्। अजाहमनजाहम्। अधश्चोर्ध्वं च तिर्यक्चाहम्॥ ३॥ अहं रुद्रेभिर्वसुभिश्चराम्यहमादित्यैरुत विश्वदेवैः। अहं मित्रावरुणावुभौ बिभर्म्यहमिन्द्राग्नी अहमश्विनावुभौ॥ ४॥ अहं सोमं त्वष्टारं पूषणं भगं दधाम्यहम्। विष्णुमुरुक्रमं ब्रह्माणमुत प्रजापतिं दधामि॥ ५॥ अहं दधामि द्रविणं हविष्मते सुप्राव्ये२यजमानाय सुन्वते। अहं राष्ट्री सङ्गमनी वसूनामहं सुवे पितरमस्य मूर्धन्॥ ६॥

I am the compound form of five elements and I myself is the great element which is free from all these elements. I myself is this whole universe which is visible, I myself is Veda (knowledge) as also Aveda (ignorance) too. I am the learning and I myself is the illusion. I myself is the nature as also beyond the nature. I am up and down as also the sides (right and left) or everything. I am omnipresent and move everywhere in the form of Rudras and Vasus. I move everywhere in the form of the sun and Viśvadeva. I provide maintenance and care to the Mitra and Varuṇa, Indra and the fire as also both Aśvini kumāras. I am bearer of Soma, Tvaṣṭa and Bhaga. I hold lord Viṣṇu, Brahmā and Prajāpati for the purpose of achieving regulatory power on three worlds with ever-extended legs. I also hold the wealth enriched of the material for offering on behalf of the client who performs offerings with obeisance and offers Soma with utmost care. I am the administrator and ruler of this whole universe. I provide the devotee wealth, I am the knowledge itself and I am the pioneer god among the gods who please with offerings. I originate the supreme soul who administers this whole universe.

मम योनिरप्स्वन्तः समुद्रे। य एवं वेद स देवीपदमाप्नोति॥७॥

ते देवा अब्रुवन्। नमो देव्यै महादेव्यै शिवायै सततं नमः।

नमः प्रकृत्यै भद्रायै नियताः प्रणताः स्म ताम्॥८॥

My residence is inherent in the element of 'Ap' (the fundamental factors of creation, five elements etc.) and in the heart lotus of all living-organisms. The person known to this fact attains to the magnificence and powers of goddess. The gods again submitted– "O Goddess! We bow our heads most reverently. You are the benevolent goddess who makes the great persons to perform their great deeds undivided. We salute you. You are in the form of nature and you are the only source of welfare. We again salute such great goddess in a routine manner.

तामग्निवर्णां तपसा ज्वलन्तीं वैरोचनीं कर्मफलेषु जुष्टाम्।

दुर्गां देवीं शरणमहं प्रपद्ये सुतरां नाशयते तमः॥९॥

देवीं वाचमजनयन्त देवास्तां विश्वरूपाः पशवो वदन्ति।

सा नो मन्द्रेषमूर्जं दुहाना धेनुर्वागस्मानुपसुष्टुतैतु॥१०॥

We resort to the mother goddess Durgā for the yield of the fruit of action whose complexion is analogous to the fire, who is shining by virtue of the penance and who is full of the light. Please decay the darkness of ignorance which has trapped us. The breathing gods had originated the speech ever-illuminating namely Vaikharī which is used by all the living-organisms in its pleasing form. May the mother goddess in the form of speech who bestows with all pleasures with food as also with divine powers like the cow (Kāmadhenu), be appear before us as a result of our great psalms and perfect devotion.

कालरात्रिं ब्रह्मस्तुतां वैष्णवीं स्कन्दमातरम्। सरस्वतीमदितिं दक्षदुहितरं नमामः पावनां शिवाम्॥११॥

महालक्ष्मीश्च विद्महे सर्वसिद्धिश्च धीमहि। तन्नो देवी प्रचोदयात्॥१२॥

We salute to the goddess who bestows with the welfare and removes all the evils committed in her multiform i.e. Vaiṣṇavī, Skandamātā, Sarasvatī, Aditi (mother of all gods) and the daughter of Dakṣa, duly worshipped by Veda and who is analogous to Kālarātri. We enshrine within our heart and summon regularly the goddess bestowing with all axioms which is known as Mahālakṣmī. May that goddess leave us to acquire the true knowledge and great perceptions.

अदितिर्ह्यजनिष्ट दक्ष या दुहिता तव। तां देवा अन्वजायन्त भद्रा अमृतबन्धवः॥ १३॥
कामो योनिः कामकला वज्रपाणिर्गुहा हसा मातरिश्वाभ्रमिन्द्रः।
पुनर्गुहा सकला मायया च पुरूच्येषा विश्वमाताऽऽदिविद्योम्॥ १४॥

O Dakṣa! Your daughter Aditi is adorable after giving birth to the gods and she has originated all immortal gods. (The fundamental and primitive learning is, thus, contemplated). This fundamental learning has been evolved by sex, vagina, vajrapāṇī, art of copulation (Kāmakalā), cavity, the letters (Ha and Sa), the wind, the ether, Indra, the re-cavity, the letter (Sa, Ka, La) and by the specific form of illusion etc. (giver of multi-pleasures or dynamic everywhere or in the form of luxury) and in the form of Brahma.

[The above hymns are indicative of the fundamental hymns pertaining to Ādi Vidyā. In the scriptures pertaining to the Tantra (systems) an indication of the letters relating to specific word has been given. According to it, 'Ka' is for sex, E for vagina, I for the art of copulation, La for Vajrapāṇī, Hṛni for cavity, Ha-Sa for Hasa, Ka for Mātariśva, Ha for ether, La for Indra, Hrīṅ for re-cavity, Sa-Ka-La for Sakala, Hrīṅ for illusion.]

एषात्मशक्तिः। एषा विश्वमोहिनी पाशाङ्कुशधनुर्बाणधरा। एषा श्रीमहाविद्या॥ १५॥
य एवं वेद स शोकं तरति॥ १६॥ नमस्ते अस्तु भगवति भवती मातरस्मान्पातु सर्वतः॥ १७॥

This mother of universe is the supreme power of soul who fascinates this whole world. She bears a string, goad, arrow and the bow and she too is known with the name of Śrī Mahāvidyā (great learning). The person known to this fact is exonerated from the agony and grief. O goddess! We salute you. Please protect us by providing with all safety.

सैषाऽष्टौ वसवः। सैषैकादश रुद्राः। सैषा द्वादशादित्याः। सैषा विश्वेदेवाः सोमपा असोमपाश्च। सैषा यातुधाना असुरा रक्षांसि पिशाचा यक्षाः सिद्धाः। सैषा सत्त्वरजस्तमांसि। सैषाब्रह्मविष्णुरुद्ररूपिणी। सैषा प्रजापतीन्द्रमनवः। सैषा ग्रहा नक्षत्रज्योतींषि कलाकाष्ठादिकालरूपिणी। तामहं प्रणौमि नित्यम्॥ १८॥
तापापहारिणीं देवीं भुक्तिमुक्तिप्रदायिनीम्। अनन्तां विजयां शुद्धां शरण्यां शिवदां शिवाम्॥ १९॥

The saint now states the nature of goddess. That mother of this universe is in the form of eight Vasus, eleven Rudras and twelve suns. The all Viśvadevas including Soma sipping and non-sipping are existed in the womb of universal mother. This mother too is in the form of devil, demon, monster, asura, yakṣa and siddha etc. She is the three properties i.e. Satva, Rajas, Tamas. She is in the form of lord Brahmā, Viṣṇu and Rudra. She also is Prajāpati, Indra and Manu. She is the stars, planets and all sub-planets. As also she is in the form of Kāla (time) equipped with the art (kalā) and Kāṣṭhā etc. We always salute the goddess who removes all fatigues and tensions, who endows with the enjoyments and emancipation, who is full of infinite merits and who commands on the victory, who is free from defaults, who is worth-resorting, who endows with welfare as also who always renders pleasing results to her devotees.

वियदीकारसंयुक्तं वीतिहोत्रसमन्वितम्। अर्धेन्दुलसितं देव्या बीजं सर्वार्थसाधकम्॥ २०॥
एवमेकाक्षरं मंत्रं यतयः शुद्धचेतसः। ध्यायन्ति परमानन्दमया ज्ञानाम्बुराशयः॥ २१॥

The Bīja (seed) word Hrīṅ is a compound of Viyad (ether), I, Vītihotra (with fire) and the half-moon (mora). It is competent enough to fulfill all desires and ambitions of the devotees. The saints following the rules of celibacy, whose heart is free from the passions, who are well-realised to the supreme pleasure and further who has acquired the immense knowledge, concentrate their mind continuously on this one letter Brahma.

वाङ्माया ब्रह्मभूस्तस्मात्षष्ठं वक्त्रसमन्वितम्। सूर्योऽ वामश्रोत्रबिन्दु:संयुक्ताष्टात्तृतीयक:॥ २२॥

नारायणेन संयुक्तो वायुश्चाधरसंयुत:। विच्चे नवार्णकोऽर्ण: स्यान्महदानन्ददायक:॥ २३॥

The nine letter hymn, i.e. Oṁ Eam Hrīṅ Klīm Cāmuṇḍāyae Vicce endows with the supreme pleasure and the position analogous to the Brahma itself. The various letters used as a component to this hymn represent as– Eam represents the power of speech, the Hrīṅ represents the illusion, Klīm represents Brahma (a represents Vakāra i.e. sixth consonant, 'M' represent the sun, 'A' represents the left ear, 'U' represents the right ear, 'Mun' represents Bindu (point), 'da' represents the third letter from the Ta, Ya represents the air, the 'e' represents the lips and the last word is Vicce. It also represents the lips.

[The meaning of above hymn is that O great Sarasvatī in the form of mind, O Mahālakṣmī in the form of truth, O Mahākālī in the form of pleasure, we always concentrate on you in order to acquire the learning of Brahma. We salute you. Please make us able to attain emancipation and please untie the chord of ignorance.]

हृत्पुण्डरीकमध्यस्थां प्रात:सूर्यसमप्रभाम्। पाशाङ्कुशधरां सौम्यां वरदाभयहस्तकाम्।

त्रिनेत्रां रक्तवसनां भक्तकामदुघां भजे॥ २४॥

नमामि त्वामहं देवीं महाभयविनाशिनीम्। महादुर्गप्रशमनीं महाकारुण्यरूपिणीम्॥ २५॥

The goddess enshrining in the middle of the lotus heart, illuminating like the sun in the dawn, holding the string and the goad, modest, whose hands are in the posture of bestowing with fearlessness and the boons, who has three eyes, red garments and who fulfills the desires of all her devotees. O goddess! I worship you because you remove all fears, you are competent to remove the turbulence and you are full of generosity.

यस्या: स्वरूपं ब्रह्मादयो न जानन्ति तस्मादुच्यतेऽज्ञेया। यस्या अन्तो न विद्यते तस्मादुच्यतेऽनन्ता। यस्या ग्रहणं नोपलभ्यते तस्मादुच्यतेऽलक्ष्या। यस्या जननं नोपलभ्यते तस्मादुच्यतेऽजा। एकैव सर्वत्र वर्तते तस्मादुच्यत एका। एकैव विश्वरूपिणी तस्मादुच्यते नैका। अत एवोच्यतेऽज्ञेयाऽनन्ताऽलक्ष्याऽजैका नैकेति॥ २६॥

The gods do not know the form of goddess and she has been therefore addressed as Ajñeya (unknown). She is everlasting, therefore, her name is Ananta beyond the end. She is called Alakṣya because of non-apparent. Nothing is known regarding her birth therefore she is addressed as Ajā. She is omnipresent alone therefore she is called Eka. She is existed alone in her universal form, hence, she is called Naika. By the reason above said her names are Ajñeya, Ananta, Ajā, Eka and Naika respectively.

मन्त्राणां मातृका देवी शब्दानां ज्ञानरूपिणी। ज्ञानानां चिन्मयातीता शून्यानां शून्यसाक्षिणी॥ २७॥ यस्याः परतरं नास्ति सैषा दुर्गा प्रकीर्तिता। तां दुर्गां दुर्गमां देवीं दुराचारविघातिनीम्। नमामि भवभीतोऽहं संसारार्णवतारिणीम्॥ २८॥

That goddess is existed in Matṛkā which is the root letter in all hymns and she is existed in the form of knowledge with all worlds. She dwells within knowledge in the form of Cinmayātītā and Śūnyasākṣiṇī with the zero. Having unique and the best, she is renowned with the name of Durgā. I, who was badly frightened with the worldly ties salute Durgā because she only can save me from misbehaves and can row my boat safely on the worldly ocean because her arts are supreme and she is rare to access.

इदमथर्वशीर्षं योऽधीते स पञ्चाथर्वशीर्षजपफलमवाप्नोति। इदमथर्वशीर्षं ज्ञात्वा योऽर्चां स्थापयति॥ २९॥ शतलक्षं प्रजप्त्वापि नार्चासिद्धिं च विन्दति। शतमष्टोत्तरं चास्याः पुरश्चर्याविधिः स्मृतः॥ ३०॥ दशवारं पठेद्यस्तु सद्यः पापैः प्रमुच्यते। महादुर्गाणि तरति महादेव्याः प्रसादतः॥

The person reciting these hymns of this Atharvaśīrṣa, easily attains the fruits of performing Japa (silent recital) on all the five Atharvaśīrṣas. The person who establishes the idol without proper knowledge of this Atharvaśīrṣa does not acquires the axiom even if he would perform many thousands and lakhs Japas. The method of confessing such omissions is very easy and the devotee would have performed Japa only for one hundred and eight time. The person who recites it as little as ten times, attains easy pass with all safety even in course of suffering from a number of turbulence with the kind grace of great goddess and the evils committed by him are removed within moments.

प्रातरधीयानो रात्रिकृतं पापं नाशयति। सायमधीयानो दिवसकृतं पापं नाशयति। तत्सायंप्रातः प्रयुञ्जानः पापोऽपापो भवति। निशीथे तुरीयसंध्यायां जप्त्वा वाक्सिद्धिर्भवति। नूतनप्रतिमायां जप्त्वा देवतासान्निध्यं भवति। प्राणप्रतिष्ठायां जप्त्वा प्राणानां प्रतिष्ठा भवति। भौमाश्विन्यां महादेवीसंनिधौ जप्त्वा महामृत्युं तरति। य एवं वेदेत्युपनिषत्॥ ३२॥

By virtue of recital in the morning, the devotee is exonerated from the evils committed in the night and by virtue of recital of this upaniṣad on evening, all evil deeds committed in the day are exonerated. The miscreants involved in the evil deeds are also exonerated if recital is made two times a day. Recital of this upaniṣad before newly established idol opportune the devotee to have abundant grace of the god. The devotee crosses the gross death if he performs Japa before the idol of great goddess on Amṛta siddhi Yoga i.e. on Tuesday when the Aśvinī planet is apparent to the Earth. What this Devyupaniṣad pronounces is that the person having proper identity to this upaniṣad, crosses the gross death without one or other puzzles.

ॐ भद्रं कर्णेभिः .... इति शान्तिः॥

॥इति देव्युपनिषत्समाप्ता॥

73. TRIPUROPANIṢAD

त्रिपुरोपनिषद्

This upaniṣad falls under the tradition of Ṛgveda. The nature of the power that is held by the heart (cit) has been described in the opening lines and this power is then prayed. The complexion of Kāmeśvara, cover (Avarṇa) god, the fruits of Śiva Kāma Sundarī Vidyā, the nature of Ādimūla Vidyā, the fruits for knowledge of Ādi Vidyā to recluse, meditation for the average person, performance of ceremony for the material devotees and its fruits as also attainment of the element of knowledge by the devotee free from attachment has been described in it. This upaniṣad is related to Āgama Vidyā (i.e. Tantra Vidyā). This is the reason a majority of words are in the form of symbols (code). And only measure to attain knowledge (Brahma) has been explained by virtue of worship with recital of the root hymns (Bīja Mantra) in this upaniṣad. Thus this upaniṣad is among a few upaniṣads which are difficult to understand for the common people.

॥शान्तिपाठः॥

ॐ वाङ्मे मनसि .... इति शान्तिः॥

तिस्रः पुरस्त्रिपथा विश्वचर्षणा अत्राकथा अक्षराः संनिविष्टाः।
अधिष्ठायैना अजरा पुराणी महत्तरा महिमा देवतानाम्॥ १॥

This power observing all with the same eye, immortal as also standing sensitive is more greater than its magnificence. It enshrines with three bodies (Puras), three routes and the letter 'Akatha' etc. inserted in Śrī Cakra.

[The expression three Puras is meant for the material, micro and causative body. The expression three route is meant by the knowledge, deed and worship (knowledge, conscience and perception). Further, the expression Akatha etc. letter is meant by the letters from 'A to Kṣa'.]

नवयोनीर्नवचक्राणि दधिरे नवैव योगा नव योगिन्यश्च।
नवानां चक्रा अधिनाथा स्योना नव भद्रा नव मुद्रा महीनाम्॥ २॥

That sensitive power is illuminating in the form of nine yonis, nine cycles, nine yogas, nine yoginis, the foundation powers of nine cycles, nine bhadras and magnificent nine postures.

[The specific words used in this hymn are explained as– Nava yoni is meant by nine yonis (the great powers like Mahā-tripura Sundarī etc.) drawn in Śrī Cakra Yantra, Nava Cakra is meant by endower with all pleasures and axioms, all protector, remover of all ailments, winner of all wealth, endower with all fortunes, creator of all melancholia, suppliant to all curses and pleasure giver to the three worlds. The foundation power of nine Cakras are Mahā Tripura Sundarī, Tripuramba, Tripura Siddha, Tripura Mālinī, Tripuraśrī, Tripura Vāsinī, Tripura Sundarī, Tripureśī and Tripura. Nine yogas are Yama, Niyana, Āsana, Prāṇāyāma, Pratyāhāra, Dhāraṇā, Dhyāna, Samādhi and Sahaja yoga. Nava yognis are nine powers residing in nine cakras. Nine postures are Yoni, Bīja, Khecharī, Mahāṅkuśa, Mahāmodinī, Sarvavasankarī, Sarvakarṣiṇī, Sarvavidravinī and Sarva Saṅkṣovhiṇī. Nine Bhadras are the nine powers like Kāmeśvaris etc.]

एका स आसीत्प्रथमा सा नवासीदा सोनविंशादा सोनत्रिंशात्।
चत्वारिंशादथ तिस्रः समिधा उशतीरिव मातरो माऽऽविशन्तु॥ ३॥

Nine Bhadras in their initial form, nine elements conjointly, forty powers and three Samidhas should insert within my heart (wherein a wish to attain Brahma resides) like a mother who desires all welfare for her sons i.e. should enter into my heart.

[Nineteen elements are five sensory organs + five executive organs + five breathings and four powers of perception (antaḥkaraṇa). Twenty-nine elements are nineteen elements + five subjects (word, touch, complexion, essence, smell) + five sub-breathings. Forty powers are fourteen external and internal senses and their ruler + three deeds (exemplary, thoughtful, undiscreet) + four properties (Vikṣepa, Āvaraṇa, Mudita, Karuṇā) + world with discrimination of world etc., Turīya, Prājña etc. Three Samidhās are– action, knowledge, temptation, knowledge conscience and due knowledge.]

ऊर्ध्वज्वलज्ज्वलनं ज्योतिरग्रे तमो वै तिरश्चीनमजरं तद्रजोऽभूत्।
आनन्दनं मोदनं ज्योतिरिन्दोरेता उ वै मण्डला मण्डयन्ति॥ ४॥

The flame rising upward and luminating is perceived very first. Contrary to it, the slanting flame has originated the properties of Rajas. This flame provides with pleasure and gaiety as also gives the modesty etc. tranquil merits.

यास्तिस्रो रेखाः सदनानि भूस्त्रीस्त्रिविष्टपास्त्रिगुणास्त्रिप्रकाराः।
एतत्त्रयं पूरकं पूरकाणां मन्त्री प्रथते मदनो मदन्या॥ ५॥

The three lines, four abodes, three premises, three Viṣṭapa, three merits and three kinds of each are the means of providing with trio-perfection. In the hymn (Śrī Cakra), the Madana (the god of passion) should attain victory by virtue of the power that satiated the passion.

[Three lines are the action, knowledge and ambition. Four abodes are awakening, dreaming, dormance and Turīya or the eyes, throat, heart and the Sahastrāra Cakra. Three Bhūḥ are Bhūḥ, Bhuvaḥ and Svaḥ. Three Viṣṭapa and three merits are Tamas, Rajas and Satva. Three kinds of each are (i) Tamas– Satva Dhan + Tamas, Rajas + Tamas, Tamas + Tamas, (ii) Rajas– Satva + Rajas, Rajas + Rajas, Tamas + Rajas, (iii) Satva– Satva + Satva, Satva + Rajas, Satva + Tamas.]

मदन्तिका मानिनी मंगला च सुभगा च सा सुन्दरी सिद्धिमत्ता।
लज्जा मतिस्तुष्टिरिष्टा च पुष्टा लक्ष्मीरुमा ललिता लालपन्ती॥ ६॥

The number of cover god to their family is fifteen. These are Madantikā, Māninī, Maṅgalā, Subhagā, Sundarī, Siddhimattā, Lajjā, Mati, Tuṣṭi, Iṣta, Puṣṭa, Lakṣmī, Umā, Lalitā and Lālapantī.

इमां विज्ञाय सुधया मदन्ती परिसृता तर्पयन्तः स्वपीठम्।
नाकस्य पृष्ठे महतो वसन्ति परं धाम त्रैपुरं चाविशन्ति॥ ७॥

The devotee by virtue of identity with these immortal properties perceive pleasures, satiate the Svapiṭha (Śrī Cakra Piṭha) with milk etc., reside in the great heaven and avails absolute satisfaction on accessing to the supreme abode of Traipura.

कामो योनिः कामकला वज्रपाणिर्गुहा हसा मातरिश्वाभ्रमिन्द्रः।

पुनर्गुहा सकला मायया च पुरूच्येषा विश्वमाताऽऽदिविद्या॥ ८॥

The nature of Ādimāla learning is– This specific learning has been evolved with Kāma, Yoni, Kāma Kalā, Vajrapāṇi, Guha, Hasā, Mātariśvā, Abhra, Indra, Punarguhā, Sakalā and illusion etc.

[In the above hymn, the codes for Ādividyā have been applied. These are Kāma - Ka, Yoni - E, Kāma Kalā - I, Vajrapāṇi - La, Guha - Hrīṅ, Hasā - Ha, Sa, Mātariśvā - Ka, Abhra - Ha, Indra - La, Sakalā - Sa, Ka, La, Māyā - Hriṅ. These all varṇas are symbol to the learning of Prāṇavivātmika etc.]

षष्ठं सप्तममथ वह्निसारथिमस्या मूलत्रिकमादेशयन्तः।

कथ्यं कविं कल्पकं काममीशं तुष्टुवांसो अमृतत्वं भजन्ते॥ ९॥

The six letter (Ha - Śiva Bīja), seventh letter (Sa - Śakti Bīja) and Vahnisārathi (Ka - Kāmeśa-Bīja) of Ādi Vidyā, its Mūlatrika (Ha, Sa, Ka) is recited to the extent it can be expressed and by virtue of offering psalms to Kāmamīśa analogous to the poet (intuitive who knows the past, future and the present who knows the three tenses) avail immortality.

पुरं हन्त्रीमुखं विश्वमातू रवे रेखा स्वरमध्यं तदेषा।

बृहत्तिथिर्दश पञ्चा च नित्या सषोडशिकं पुरमध्यं बिभर्ति॥ १०॥

(That goddess) Pura, Hantrimukha, (Ha-Sa-Ka), the form of universal, mother, line of sun (the form of the cycle of sun), Svara Madhya (I, O form) etc. forms, the Bṛhattithi (from Nimeśa to the end of Kalpa) and fifteen etc. (fifteen days, the name of days and planets etc., Nitya (availed of divine spirits), Saṣoḍaśika (sixteenth day including the full moon day), Puramadhya (based on once ignorance or attachment). (All these are the forms in which that goddess enshrines and appears before her devotees.)

यद्वा मण्डलाद्वा स्तनबिम्बमेकं मुखं चाधस्त्रीणि गुहासदनानि।

कामीकलां कामरूपां चिकित्वा नरो जायते कामरूपश्च कामः॥ ११॥

The person born in the superior clan (Aristocrat) should not worship for satiating the passion because it involves the concerned devotee in the cycle of birth and death. However, for others meditation on the art of supreme lord, Kāma Kalā which is situated in the cavity of trio-body (the apparent, micro and causative body) of an excellent beautiful lady (Sundarī) whose complexion is illuminated with the light of sun and moon, whose mouth and one breast downward is always fruitful because they satiate their passions voluntarily thereby attain the fruit of satisfaction.

परिसृतं झषमाजं पलं च भक्तानि योनीः सुपरिष्कृताश्च।

निवेदयन्देवतायै महत्यै स्वात्मीकृते सुकृते सिद्धिमेति॥ १२॥

Similarly, keeping aside the consideration of soul, such persons offer as Prasāda to the great goddess which are their eatables (the meat and liquor etc.) duly cooked by them and then eat the same. By doing so they can achieve success if great deeds are performed by them irrespective of the Tamas diet they have consumed.

सृण्येव सितया विश्वचर्षणि: पाशेनैव प्रतिबध्नात्यभीकान्।

इषुभि: पञ्चभिर्धनुषा च विध्यत्यादिशक्तिररुणा विश्वजन्या॥ १३॥

The persons involved in such route of passion, goddess Sarasvatī, Lakṣmī, Gaurī etc. throw them in the dreadful whirlpool of this world after fastening them properly and penetrate their hearts by shooting five arrows (the five sensory organs) which these goddess do not provide them with the opportunity of emancipation.

भग: शक्तिर्भगवान्काम ईश उभा दाताराविह सौभगांनाम्।

समप्रधानौ समसत्त्वौ समोजौ तयो: शक्तिरजरा विश्वयोनि:॥ १४॥

Lord Kāma and god (Kāmeśvara) both make their devotee to attain the position of Brahma who is free from attachment and whose heart is full of six luxuries (all kinds of luxuries, great deeds, fame, wealth, knowledge and reclusion), who is generous, full of Satva merit and who has acquired a splendour by virtue of celibacy. This universal mother (Śrī Satī) is enshrined in the middle of Śiva Śakti or Kāma god. This goddess is known as Ajara and she is distinct then the three bodies i.e. the apparent, micro and causative.

परिसृता हविषा भावितेन प्रसंकोचे गलिते वैमनस्क:।

शर्व: सर्वस्य जगतो विधाता धर्ता हर्ता विश्वरूपत्वमेति॥ १५॥

(This goddess) becomes satiated by the offering of knowledge, conscience and due perception made by the devotee who is free from attachments and it destroys the ignorance and the illusions which are standing in his benevolent route. Thus the devotee becomes reluctant to the worldly feelings and attains to the universal from with the powers of creation, nutrition and destruction (Lord Brahmā, Viṣṇu and Maheśa) to this whole universe.

इयं महोपनिषत्त्रैपुर्या यामक्षरं परमो गीर्भिरीट्टे। एषर्ग्यजु: परमेतज्ज सामायमथर्वेयमन्या चविद्या॥

This great upaniṣad with its name Traipura is praised with the hymns in the form of speech duly enlightened and full of undepleting knowledge which is stored in four Vedas, i.e. Ṛg, Yaju, Sāma and Atharva as also other fourteen learning's (Purāṇa, Nyāya and Mimaṁsā etc.).

ॐ ह्रीं ॐ ह्रीमित्युपनिषत्॥ १७॥

Oṁ Hriṅ is the element of the heart (cit) and the power. This only is an element of most sensitive power.

॥इति त्रिपुरोपनिषत्समाप्ता॥

74. KAṬHARUDROPANIṢAD

कठरुद्रोपनिषद्

This Upaniṣad is a part and parcel to the branch of Kṛṣṇa Yajurveda. It is also called as Kaṇṭharudropaniṣad. Lord Prajāpati has discussed on the element of soul including the method of entering into the stage of a recluse when the gods has realised the questions regarding Brahmavidyā. The method of getting admission into the stage of reclusion is in first three Kaṇḍikās. From the fourth to eleventh kaṇḍikā, various disciplines worth observing after adopting the life of a recluse have been described. The Brahma and the illusions including Tanmātrās and the structurisation of Brahmāṇḍa has been then enumerated. The god, living soul, Pramātā, proof, Prameya and the fruit etc. is substantiated as the supreme element of soul while explaining the mystery of the Pañca Ātmā and Pañca Kośa. Finally, this complete dialogue has been said as the essence of Vedānta.

॥शान्तिपाठः॥

ॐ सह नाववतु ....इति शान्तिः॥

देवा ह वै भगवन्तमब्रुवन्नधीहि भगवन्ब्रह्मविद्याम्। स प्रजापतिरब्रवीत्॥ १॥

All gods once visited to Lord Brahmā and requested O Lord! Kindly preach us the learning of Brahma. Prajāpati Brahmā then replied–

सशिखान्केशान्निष्कृष्य विसृज्य यज्ञोपवीतं निष्कृष्य ततः पुत्रं दृष्ट्वा त्वं ब्रह्मा त्वं यज्ञस्त्वं वषट्कारस्त्वमोंकारस्त्वं स्वाहा त्वं स्वधा त्वं धाता त्वं विधाता। अथ पुत्रो वदत्यहं ब्रह्माहं यज्ञोऽहं वषट्कारोऽहमोंकारोऽहं स्वाहाहं स्वधाहं धाताहं विधाताहं त्वष्टाहं प्रतिष्ठास्मीति। तान्येतान्यनुव्रजन्नाश्रुमापातयेत्। यदश्रुमापातयेत्प्रजां विच्छिन्द्यात्। प्रदक्षिणमावृत्त्यैतच्चैतच्चानवेक्षमाणाः प्रत्यायन्ति। स स्वर्ग्यो भवति॥ २॥

One should say to his son— you are Brahmā, the offering, the Vaṣaṭkāra, the syllable Oṁ, the Svāhā, the Svadhā, Dhātā and you are Vidhātā after cleaning all the hairs from the head and giving up the sacrificial thread. Hearing to this son should say—I am Brahmā, the offering, Vaṣaṭkāra, the Oṁkāra, the Svāhā and Svadhā, the Dhātā, Vidhātā, Tvaṣṭā and Pratiṣṭhā. Thus, the recluse when followed by his son and wife at the moment when he is going out from the house of a reclusion, should not weep or express any kind of pain. In case, he weeps at that time, the children will certainly do the same. In case, the family members turn back to their houses after merely conveying their salute, the recluse of so detached definitely attains to the abode of the gods.

[The sentences as the father make his son to repeat have most important intention. The person in the couple stage should make his son fully independent and feeling dignity to take over the responsibility of his father so that he should not suffer from the inferiority complex when his father departs to the forest. It reveals through the words of son that he is ready to perform ideally the responsibilities assigned by father and his self-confidence has been awaken. If the relatives do not face any agony while leaving their father, it definitely reveals that those have no attachment with the father and have full confidence to tackle with the responsibilities.]

ब्रह्मचारी वेदमधीत्य वेदोक्ताचरितब्रह्मचर्यो दारानाहृत्य पुत्रानुत्पाद्य ताननुरूपो पाधिभिर्वितत्येष्ट्वा च शक्तितो यज्ञैस्तस्य संन्यासो गुरुभिरनुज्ञातस्य बान्धवैश्च। सोऽरण्यं परेत्य द्वादशरात्रं पयसाग्निहोत्रं जुहुयात्। द्वादशरात्रं पयोभक्षः स्यात्। द्वादशरात्रस्यान्तेऽग्नये वैश्वानराय प्रजापतये च प्राजापत्यं चरुं वैष्णवं त्रिकपालमग्निम्। संस्थितानि पूर्वाणि दारुपात्राण्यग्नौ जुहुयात्। मृण्मयान्यप्सु जुहुयात्। तैजसानि गुरवे दद्यात्। मा त्वं मामपहाय परागाः। नाहं त्वामपहाय परागामिति। गार्हपत्यदक्षिणाग्न्याहवनीयेष्वरणिदेशाद्भस्ममुष्टिं पिबेदित्येके। सशिखान्केशान्निष्कृष्य विसृज्य यज्ञोपवीतं भूः स्वाहेत्यप्सु जुहुयात्। अत ऊर्ध्वमनशनमपां प्रवेशमग्निप्रवेशनं वीराध्वानं महाप्रस्थानं वृद्धाश्रमं वा गच्छेत्। पयसा यं प्राश्नीयात्सोऽस्य सायंहोमः। यत्प्रातः सोऽयं प्रातः। यद्दर्शे तद्दर्शम्। यत्पौर्णमास्ये तत्पौर्णमास्यम्। यद्वसन्ते केशश्मश्रुलोमनखानि वापयेत्सोऽस्याग्निष्टोमः॥ ३॥

An entrance into the life of a recluse may be taken when a person has made study on Vedas and the holy books during the period of celibaces, enjoyed the couple life after marriage, reproduced children, educated them, perform the ceremonies according to his capacity, hosted the offerings etc. and then duly allowed by the friends and teachers. The person so entering into the reclusion should do agnihotra by milk offering upto twelve nights in the forest. He should live on the milk till twelve days. After the successful end of twelve nights should look after for the Vaiśvānara fire and Prajāpati, the morsel looked on three clay pots for Lord Viṣṇu and Rudra. The wooden vessels used in course of Agnihotra should also be offered to fire in the form of morsel (Āhuti). The earthen pots should be left in the pond and the objects made of gold etc., should be given to his teacher. While offering the gold articles, he should say "You should not go away leaving me and I would not go away leaving you." According to some holy books, the person should thereafter take a fistfull as existing as residual of three kinds of fire i.e., Gārhapatya, Dakṣiṇāgni and Āhavanīya. The hairs including the braid should be cut and the sacrificial thread with reciting Oṁ Bhūḥ Svāhā should be dropped in the pond after taking it out from the body. He should then do Mahāprasthāna by observing the penance like giving up food, remaining stable in the water, entering into fire and following the way of gallants or he should move to stay in the hermitage of any old recluse. Whatever food he takes including milk and water is his offering performed in the evening and it is his morning offering, whatever he takes in the morning, the food taken by him on the day of first fortnight (Amāvasyā) is Darśayajña. The food taken on the full moon day is Paurṇamāsya Yajña. Agniṣṭoma is the offering when he makes clean his hair, beard, moustache, the hairs grown on the body and nails in the spring season.

[The spirit to join every common activity of the life of offering and it too by giving up the Agnihotra as prescribed under ritual is very clearly expressed here. The perfection of the propensity of reclusion is not possible by giving up the rituals without adopting the high labelled penance of the life.]

संन्यस्याग्निं न पुनरावर्तयेन्मृत्युर्जयमावहमित्यध्यात्ममन्त्राञ्जपेत्। स्वस्ति सर्वजीवेभ्य इत्युक्त्वाऽऽत्मानमनन्यं ध्यायन् तदूर्ध्वबाहुर्विमुक्तमार्गो भवेत्। अनिकेतश्चरेत्। भिक्षाशी यत्किंचिन्नाद्यात्। लवैकं न धावयेज्जन्तुसंरक्षणार्थं वर्षवर्जमिति। तदपि श्लोका भवन्ति॥ ४॥

The fire should not be blazed or summoned after when the reclusion is adopted. He should only do the silent recital of the celestial hymns like mṛtyuñjayamāha mantra. He should wish for the welfare of all living organisms, concentrate on the element of soul, by lifting hands upward should move on the way devoid of illusion by living a homeless ascetic. He should not take anything else to what he received on alms. He should not stay even for a single moment anywhere and frequently move everywhere. He may stay at a single place for four months during rainy season in order to avoid from any kind of violence. There are some hymns revealing the discipline of a recluse.

कुण्डिकां चमसं शिक्यं त्रिविष्टपमुपानहौ। शीतोपघातिनीं कन्थां कौपीनाच्छादनं तथा॥ ५॥ पवित्रं स्नानशाटीं च उत्तरासङ्गमेव च। यज्ञोपवीतं वेदांश्च सर्वं तद्वर्जयेद्यतिः॥ ६॥ स्नानं पानं तथा शौचमद्भिः पूताभिराचरेत्। नदीपुलिनशायी स्याद्देवागारेषु वा स्वपेत्॥ ७॥ नात्यर्थं सुखदुःखाभ्यां शरीरमुपतापयेत्। स्तूयमानो न तुष्येत निन्दितो न शपेत्परान्॥ ८॥

The person desirous of reclusion should abandon the Kuṇḍikā, the vessel used for offering, the bag made, the shelves, shoes, the clothes covering the upper body except part covered by Laṅgoti. He should abandon the Kathari, the cloth covering the body upside the Laṅgoti, the Pavitri made of Kuśā grass, the garments to be put on offer taking the garment covering the upper part of the body. The garment put on the upper part of the body, the sacrificial thread and a propensity to go over the veda should be there. He should perform his bathing, drinking and exerting etc. activities by using the pure water. He should either sleep at the bank of the river or in the temple of god. He should either do not enjoy, rest for much time, put his body in pains due to severe physical labour. He should neither feel any happiness by listening to his pray. He should be so tolerant that seldom abuse or curse at the time where either topic is flattery to him or the flay by others.

ब्रह्मचर्येण संतिष्ठेदप्रमादेन मस्करी। दर्शनं स्पर्शनं केलिः कीर्तनं गुह्यभाषणम्॥ ९॥ संकल्पोऽध्यवसायश्च क्रियानिर्वृत्तिरेव च। एतन्मैथुनमष्टाङ्गं प्रवदन्ति मनीषिणः॥ १०॥ विपरीतं ब्रह्मचर्यमनुष्ठेयं मुमुक्षुभिः। यज्जगद्भासकं भानं नित्यं भाति स्वतः स्फुरत्॥ ११॥

The recluse should pass his life by holding the resolution for celibacy free from laxity and laziness. The learned person have described the eight kinds of copulation (Maithuna), which are watching the ladies, touching, playing, discussing, conversing on the issues govern with the sensuality, resolution for the sex, attempts for copulation and doing the intercourse.

स एष जगतः साक्षी सर्वात्मा विमलाकृतिः। प्रतिष्ठा सर्वभूतानां प्रज्ञानघनलक्षणः॥ १२॥

न कर्मणा न प्रजया न चान्येनापि केनचित्। ब्रह्मवेदनमात्रेण ब्रह्माप्नोत्येव मानवः॥ १३॥

The thing that gives light to the world, self-luminated with light is the witness of this entire world and it is the soul of the fair complexion. It is in the form of self-conscience. All living-communes are enshrined in that Brahma. A person cannot realize that supreme soul by his deeds through the children and through any other means because it is only realised by the perceiving of Brahma through soul.

तद्विद्याविषयं ब्रह्म सत्यज्ञानसुखाद्वयम्। संसारे च गुहावाच्ये मायाज्ञानादिसंज्ञिके॥ १४॥ निहितं ब्रह्म यो वेद परमे व्योम्नि संज्ञिते। सोऽश्नुते सकलान्कामान्क्रमेणैव द्विजोत्तमः॥ १५॥ प्रत्यगात्मानमज्ञानमायाशक्तेश्च साक्षिणम्। एकं ब्रह्माहमस्मीति ब्रह्मैव भवति स्वयम्॥ १६॥

That unique Brahma in the form of truth, knowledge and pleasure is existed in this world which is known as the illusion, ignorance, cavity (Guhā). This Brahma can be only realised by virtue of the true knowledge. The person known to this everlasting Brahma as existed in the immortal abode of the ether, he definitely attains to all his desires in a seriatim. His all desires are fulfilled. The person who knows the Pratyagātmā as "I am in the form of Brahma, definitely becomes Brahma himself because that Pratyagātmā is the witness to the ignorance and the power of illusion.

[The ascetic duly realized with Brahma becomes able to understand the mysterious facts that how the visible world is originated by the invisible element of the soul. This system of creation has been made all clear in the successive hymns.]

ब्रह्मभूतात्मनस्तस्मादेतस्माच्छक्तिमिश्रितात्। अपञ्चीकृत आकाशः संभूतो रज्जुसर्पवत्॥ १७॥ आकाश०ाद्वायुसंज्ञस्तु स्पर्शोऽपञ्चीकृतः पुनः। वायोरग्निस्तथा चाग्नेराप अद्भ्यो वसुन्धरा॥ १८॥ तानि सर्वाणि सूक्ष्माणि पञ्चीकृत्येश्वरस्तदा। तेभ्य एव विसृष्टं तद्ब्रह्माण्डादि शिवेन ह॥ १९॥ ब्रह्माण्डस्योदरे देवा दानवा यक्षकिन्नराः। मनुष्याः पशुपक्ष्याद्यास्तत्तत्कर्मानुसारतः॥ २०॥

As the snake is perceived in the chord, the word etc. Tanmātrās have been originated by the mighty soul in the form of Brahma. Subsequently, the non-illusory Tanmātrās (touch) known as wind has been originated. The Īśvara in the form of Śiva classified them into five micro elements, thereby created the Brahmāṇḍa etc. In the abdomen of Brahmāṇḍa, the yonis of gods, monster, Yakṣa, Kinnara, men, animals, birds etc. according to the account of their previous deeds has been created.

[The chord seems as snake only till it is not duly seen by the observer. The first unit of the matter is atom. The atom of all matters have been formed as a result of varied combination with the electron, protron and neutron etc. The existence of all matters is ceased for the persons able to see the element of soul which is the basic element to all.]

अस्थिस्नाय्वादिरूपोऽयं शरीरं भाति देहिनाम्। योऽयमन्नमयो ह्यात्मा भाति सर्वशरीरिणः॥ २१॥ ततः प्राणमयो ह्यात्मा विभिन्नश्चान्तरस्थितः। ततो मनोमयो ह्यात्मा विभिन्नश्चान्तरस्थितः॥ २२॥ ततो विज्ञान आत्मा तु ततोऽन्यश्चान्तरः स्वतः। आनन्दमय आत्मा तु ततोऽन्यश्चान्तरस्थितः॥ २३॥ योऽयमन्नमयः सोऽयं पूर्णः प्राणमयेन तु। मनोमयेन प्राणोऽपि तथा पूर्णः स्वभावतः॥ २४॥ तथा मनोमयो ह्यात्मा पूर्णो ज्ञानमयेन तु। आनन्देन सदा पूर्णः सदा ज्ञानमयः सुखम्॥ २५॥ तथानन्दमयश्चापि ब्रह्मणोऽन्येन साक्षिणा। सर्वान्तरेण पूर्णश्च ब्रह्म नान्येन केनचित्॥ २६॥

The bodies of all living-organisms built of bone, nerves etc. is illustrated according to their deeds. The soul taking food as exhibited by the means of the formidable body is different than the breathing soul which is residing within this formidable soul surviving on food. A distinct and more micro soul than it is the mental soul living within the breathing soul. The more micro soul than it is the mental soul living within the breathing soul. The more micro soul than it is soul of the conscience. It resides within the mental soul. One more micro soul in the pleasure giving soul, tt resides with in the conscience soul. The soul surviving on food is perfect with the breathing soul and the breathing soul is supplement to the mental soul. The mental soul is with the conscience soul and it further is perfect with the soul giving pleasure. The soul giving pleasure is the supplement to the intuitive, omnipresent and all witness Brahma. This Brahma is perfect itself and it requires no combination with the other.

[The mystery of Pañcākāśa and Pañca Ātmā has been made apparent here. Every body receives structure by the soul surviving on food. The energy from the breathing soul, the desires from mental soul, the natural talents and outstanding etc. from the conscience soul and feelings of pleasure from the soul of pleasure. When it is appeared by the formidable means, it is called soul and having it most micro, it is called Kośa (treasure).]

यदिदं ब्रह्मपुच्छाख्यं सत्यज्ञानाद्वयात्मकम्। सारमेव रसं लब्ध्वा साक्षाद्देही सनातनम्॥२७॥ सुखी भवति सर्वत्र अन्यथा सुखिता कुतः। असत्यस्मिन्परानन्दे स्वात्मभूतेऽखिलात्मनाम्॥२८ को जीवति नरो जातु को वा नित्यं विचेष्टते। तस्मात्सर्वात्मना चित्ते भासमानो ह्यसौ नरः॥२९ आनन्दयति दुःखाढ्यं जीवात्मानं सदा जनः। यदा ह्येवैष एतस्मिन्नदृश्यत्वादिलक्षणे॥३०॥ निर्भेदं परमाद्वैतं विन्दते च महायतिः। तदेवाभयमित्यन्तं कल्याणं परमामृतम्॥३१ सद्रूपं परमं ब्रह्म त्रिपरिच्छेदवर्जितम्। यदा ह्येवैष एतस्मिन्नल्पमप्यन्तरं नरः॥३२॥ विजानाति तदा तस्य भयं स्यान्नात्र संशयः। अस्यैवानन्दकोशेन स्ताम्बान्ता विष्णुपूर्वकाः॥३३ भवन्ति सुखिनो नित्यं तारतम्यक्रमेण तु। तत्तत्पदविरक्तस्य श्रोत्रियस्य प्रसादिनः॥३४॥ स्वरूपभूत आनन्दः स्वयं भाति परे यथा। निमित्तं किंचिदाश्रित्य खलु शब्दः प्रवर्तते॥३५॥ यतो वाचो निवर्तन्ते निमित्तानामभावतः। निर्विशेष परानन्दे कथं शब्दः प्रवर्तते॥३६॥ तस्मादेतन्मनः सूक्ष्मं व्यावृत्तं सर्वगोचरम्। यस्माच्छ्रोत्रत्वगक्ष्यादिखादिकर्मेन्द्रियाणि च॥३७॥

The unique perfect knowledge in the form of knowledge and truth is the resort of all. It is an essence and in the form of essence to all. This living soul enjoys the pleasure everywhere as a result of obtaining this everlasting element. Where besides it is the feeling of pleasure? In the absence of this supreme pleasure in garb of soul nobody can live and do any activity in his life. The perfect knowledge and then everlasting supreme soul as perceived in the heart of all, always renders pleasure to the living soul who is entrapped in the network of sorrows. The person who attains the unique Brahma enriched with the symptoms of non-visibility is the real recluse. The perfect knowledge in the grab of the truth uncovered by the time, place and the person is benevolent, equal to supreme immortality and the position of fearlessness. There is no doubt, the man is afraid of the birth and the death until any hurdle is perceived by the man, from the tiny and trivial straw to the Lord Viṣṇu, all enjoy the pleasure always in a good proportion to their deeds from the treasure of pleasure. The persons who are unattached with the enjoyment of this and that world, automatically perceive this pleasure. This perceiving is undescribable in the words because it is felt according to the position of supreme soul. It is a well-known fact that the words need something as a base for an expression while having devoid of the base in the supreme element the speech comes back empty from them. The element that provides with the supreme pleasure is devoid of all qualifying designations therefore how can the words may be formed to describe the same? This mind moves to and fro by virtue of most micro and confined power because the sensory organs like eyes, skin, ears etc., their issues and the executive organs i.e.., speech, the hands and the feet etc. have limited power.

व्यावृत्तानि परं प्राप्तुं न समर्थानि तानि तु। तद्ब्रह्मानन्दमद्वन्द्वं निर्गुणं सत्यचिद्घनम्॥३८॥ विदित्वा स्वात्मरूपेण न बिभेति कुतश्चन। एवं यस्तु विजानाति स्वगुरोरुपदेशत:॥३९॥ स साध्वसाधुकर्मभ्यां सदा न तपति प्रभु:। तप्यतापकरूपेण विभातमखिलं जगत्॥४०॥

These all sensory organs therefore are not able to obtain the element of supreme soul. The person who realizes as his own form the exclusive, beyond merits, the truth and the pleasure of conscience Brahma, doesn't feel a slight fear anywhere. Thus, the celibate man who enjoys the pleasure of Brahma by the means of self-realization through teacher's preaching doesn't suffer from agony caused by the truth and false. The material enjoyment are the soul cause for the pains and the heart is its feeler. This entire world is activated as the heart and the issues related to it.

[The material science has invented the sensors to perceive the vibration of the matter but the sensor to feel the vibration of the spirit is the heart. The combination of the competence as established by the vibrations created as a result of the worldly enjoyments and felt by the heart is the root cause for this illusory world and nothing else than it. This is in the same manner as the matter reflects the light rays and the eyes having competency to feel give a particular structure to the matter.]

प्रत्यगात्मतया भाति ज्ञानाद्वेदान्तवाक्यजात्। शुद्धमीश्वरचैतन्यं जीवचैतन्यमेव च॥४१॥ प्रमाता च प्रमाणं च प्रमेयं च फलं तथा। इति सप्तविधं प्रोक्तं भिद्यते व्यवहारत:॥४२॥ मायोपाधिविनिर्मुक्तं शुद्धमित्यभिधीयते। मायासंबन्धश्चेशो जीवोऽविद्यावशस्तथा॥४३॥ अन्त:करणसंबन्धात्प्रमातेत्यभिधीयते। तथा तद्वृत्तिसंबन्धात्प्रमाणमिति कथ्यते॥ अज्ञातमपि चैतन्यं प्रमेयमिति कथ्यते। तथा ज्ञातं च चैतन्यं फलमित्यभिधीयते॥४५॥

It has been described in the Vedas and the holy books that the Brahma is in the form of every soul. The seven elements i.e. Brahma, Īśvara, living soul, Pramātā, proof, Prameya and the fruit are distinct and separate under the practical observation. The supreme soul is in the form of pure sensitivity and it always remains free from the names, qualification and designations framed by the illusion. It is Īśvara in the form of illusion and living soul because of enslaved to the ignorance. This very Brahma is called Pramātā (knower) when it establishes the relation with the heart. The combination of perceiving and the heart, it attains to a proven name. The sensitive Brahma is Prameya until the search goes on and the fruit attains the name when the research is succeeded or the Brahma is realized.

[The learned person therefore concentrate his brain continuously on the stage of emancipation under the presumption that "I am free from all qualifications."]

सर्वोपाधिविनिर्मुक्तं स्वात्मानं भावयेत्सुधीः। एवं यो वेद तत्त्वेन ब्रह्मभूयाय कल्पते॥४६॥
सर्ववेदान्तसिद्धान्तसारं वच्मि यथार्थतः। स्वयं मृत्वा स्वयं भूत्वा स्वयमेवावशिष्यते॥४७॥

The person thus known to the essence always becomes able to attain the element of Brahma. I have told in the original form the essence of all doctrines to the vedānta. The living soul gets birth himself, attain to death and remains as residual in proportion to his deeds. This all is an art of soul and there is no other element same as otherwise the soul.This very is the mystery of this Upaniṣad.

ॐ सह नाववतु ....इति शान्तिः॥

॥इति कठरुद्रोपनिषत्समाप्ता॥

75. BHĀVANOPANIṢAD

भावनोपनिषद्

This upaniṣad relates to the tradition of Atharvaveda. The descriptions of the appearance of most mighty form by having seated on Śrīcakra by Parāmbā Tripurasundarī has been made herein. It has been said very first white descending the god-element of Lord Śiva that he is called Śiva as a result of cooperating and support received from "Śakti". Subsequently, the spirit of Śrīcakra in three bodies i.e. formidable, micro and causative has been enumerated. Thus, the orderly elements are– summering of divine (godly) powers, the process of Āsana, Pādya etc. and the fruits of such spirit made. It has been finally told that the devotee thus, living loyal of spirit till the three ceremonies (Muhūrta), becomes free from all worldly ties. He becomes solely the form of Brahma. That devotee is called "Śivayogī". Thus, this upaniṣad is concluded.

॥शान्तिपाठः॥

ॐ भद्रं कर्णेभिः .... इति शान्तिः॥

श्रीगुरुः सर्वकारणभूता शक्तिः॥ १॥

The most revered Śrī Sadguru alone is the supreme causative power and above all. The literal meaning of the term "guru" is "one who destroys the darkness of ignorance. This peculiarity lies with the supreme Śiva. Only He is competent to create, maintain and destroy. He therefore, has been said as supreme causative power.

[For what motive the Śrīcakra is proved (acquired) in the body? This body is with nine holes and this Śrīcakra is fertilise with nine powers (from Vimala to Iśāna). The mother of this body is Kurukullā Bali Devī and Vārāhī is in the form of father. The Dharma etc. four industries (Puruṣārtha) are in the form of its four oceans supported by the body.]

केन नवरन्ध्ररूपो देहः। नवशक्तिरूपं श्रीचक्रम्। वाराही पितृरूपा। कुरुकुल्ला बलिदेवता माता। पुरुषार्थाः सागराः। देहो नवरत्नद्वीपः। आधारनवकमुद्राः शक्तयः। त्वगादिसप्तधातुभिरनेकैः संयुक्ताः संकल्पाः कल्पतरवः। तेजः कल्पकोद्यानम्। रसनया भाव्यमाना मधुराम्लतिक्तकटुकषायलवणभेदाः षड्रसाः षडृतवः। क्रियाशक्तिः पीठम्। कुण्डलिनी ज्ञानशक्तिर्गृहम्। इच्छाशक्तिर्महात्रिपुरसुन्दरी। ज्ञाता होता ज्ञानमग्निः ज्ञेयं हविः। ज्ञातृज्ञानज्ञेयानामभेदभावनं श्रीचक्रपूजनम्। नियतिसहिताः शृङ्गारादयो नव रसा अणिमादयः। कामक्रोधलोभमोहमदमात्सर्यपुण्यपापमया ब्राह्म्याद्यष्टशक्तयः। पृथिव्यप्तेजोवाय्वाकाशश्रोत्रत्वक्चक्षुर्जिह्वा-घ्राणवाक्पाणिपादपायूपस्थमनोविकाराः षोडश शक्तयः। वचनादानगमनविसर्गानन्दहानोपेक्षा-बुद्ध्योऽनङ्गकुसुमादिशक्तयोऽष्टौ। अलम्बुसा कुहूर्विश्वोदरी वरुणा हस्तिजिह्वा यशस्वत्यश्विनी गान्धारी पूषा शङ्खिनी सरस्वतीडा पिङ्गला सुषुम्ना चेति चतुर्दश नाड्यः। सर्वसंक्षोभिण्यादिचतुर्दशारगा देवताः। प्राणापानव्यानोदानसमाननागकूर्मकृकरदेवदत्तधनंजया इति दश वायवः। सर्वसिद्धिप्रदा देव्यो बहिर्दशारगा

देवता:। एतद्वायुदशकसंसर्गोपाधिभेदेन रेचकपूरकशोषकदाहकप्लावका अमृतमिति प्राणमुख्यत्वेन पञ्चविधोऽस्ति। क्षारको दारक: क्षोभको मोहको जृम्भक इत्यपालनमुख्यत्वेन पञ्चविधोऽस्ति। तेन मनुष्याणां मोहको दाहको भक्ष्यभोज्यलेह्यचोष्यपेयात्मकं चतुर्विधमन्नं पाचयति। एता दश वह्निकला: सर्वात्वाद्यन्तर्दशारगा देवता:। शीतोष्णसुखदु:खेच्छासत्त्वरजस्तमोगुणा वशिन्यादिशक्तयोऽष्टौ। शब्दस्पर्शरूपरसगन्धा: पञ्चतन्मात्रा: पञ्च पुष्पबाणा मन इक्षुधनु:। वश्यो बाणो राग: पाश:। द्वेषोऽङ्कुश:। अव्यक्तमहत्तत्त्वमहदहंकार इति कामेश्वरीवज्रेश्वरीभगमालिन्योऽन्तस्त्रिकोणाग्रगा देवता:। पञ्चदशतिथिरूपेण कालस्य परिणामावलोकनस्थिति: पञ्चदश नित्या श्रद्धानुरूपाधिदेवता। तयो: कामेश्वरी सदानन्दघना परिपूर्णस्वात्मैक्यरूपा देवता॥ २॥

The fundamental powers of this is Mahātripurasundarī etc. (from yoni mudrā to Sarva Śanikṣobhiṇī), are in nine numbers. The varied form of resolution and compromise (saṅkalpa and nikalpa) with skin etc. seven dhātus and numerous exterior and interior defects are kalpa vrkṣa. The living soul (Jīva) in the form of splendour (different that that supreme soul and enjoying in varied ways) is the garden. The taste felt by the tongue i.e. sweet, sour, pungen, bitter, sahine and astringent are the six seasons. The power known as action is the Pīṭha. The power of discretion in the form of Kuṇḍalinī is gṛha. The will power too is adorable Bhagvatī (goddess) known as Mahātripurasundarī. The knower is Hotā, knowledge is Arghya and know how (the known element) is in the form of morsel (Hari). It is the real worship of Śrīcakra when no discrimination is left among knower, knowledge and know how. The nexus of the Aṇimā etc. axioms (i.e. Aṇimā, Laghimā, Mahimā, Īśitva, Vaśitva, Prākāmya, Bhakti, desire (icchā), yield (Prāpti) and liberation from all desires) is with nine essences i.e. Śṛgāra, Vīra, Karuṇa etc. including the assessment of nature (Niyati). There are eight powers viz. sensuality, anger, greed, attachment, ego, malice, Brāhmī with good and evil etc. The earth, water, splendour, air, ether, ear, skin, eyes, tongue, nose, speech, hands, feet, arms, penis and the mond etc. defects (originated from the original nature) are the sixteen powers. Speech (to speak), to lake (Entertain), to move, to excrete, pleasure, removable (Tyājya), negative with and the vagary of sex (Anaṅga Kusuma) etc. are eight powers. Alambusā, Kuhū, Viśvodarī, Varuṇā, Hastijihvā, Yaśasvinī, Gāndhāri, Pūṣā, Śaṅkhinī, Sarasvatī, Iḍā, Piṅgalā, Suṣumnā etc. fourteen nerves including sarvasaṅkṣobhiṇī etc. are the fourteen gods (caturdaśāra). Prāṇa, Apāna, Udāna, Samāna, Vyāna, Nāga, Kūrma, Kṛkara, Devadatta, Dhanañjaya, these ten Praṇās, sarvasiddhipradā etc. goddesses are exterior Daśāra gods by of contract and discriminator with the category of these ten airs. There are mainly four kinds of Prāṇās in nectar (immortal) form. These are Recaka, Pūraka, Śoṣaka, Dāhaka and Plāvaka. Those digest the four kinds of food i.e. which are cheered, licked, sucked and drunk and full of taste as also in warm state. This air, in the form of Kalā (art) too is sarvajñātva etc. The Vaśiṁ etc. eight powers are : Winter, summer, pleasure, sorrow, desire, sattva, Rajas, Tamas. The five Tanmātrās are word, touch, complexion, essence (rose) and perfume (smell) etc. These are five arrows of flower and the mind is a bow made of sugar-cane i.e. these complexion etc. five arrows are thrown out by the mind. The arrow is intrapped, attachment (affective) is the cord and envy is the god. The gods enshrined on the forepoint of internal triangle are Avyakta, Mahatattava, Ahaṁkāra, Kāmeśvarī, Vajreśvarī and Bhagamālinī etc. There are fifteen Ādidevatas (super gods) who observe the quantum of time in the form of fifteen tithis. The Ādyāpradhara Kāmeśvarī among Vajreśvarī and Bhagamālinī is in the form of truth, mind and pleasure as also the god integrated form of Brahma and the soul.

[Herein the procedure for śrī yantra lekhana is enumerated. The point (Bindu), Trikaṇa, Aṣṭāra, Antardaśāra, Bahirdaśāra, Caturdaśāra, Aṣṭadala Padma, (Ṣodaśadalapadma and Caturāṣṭra etc. are its defining words used for writing the Śrīyantra.]

सलिलमिति सौहित्यकारणं सत्त्वं। कर्तव्यमकर्तव्यमिति भावनायुक्त उपचारः। अस्ति नास्तीति कर्तव्यता उपचारः। बाह्याभ्यन्तःकरणानां रूपग्रहणयोग्यताऽस्त्वित्यावाहनम्। तस्य बाह्याभ्यन्तःकरणानामेकरूपविषयग्रहणमासनम्। रक्तशुक्लपदैकीकरणं पाद्यम्। उज्ज्वलदा-मोदानन्दासनदानमर्घ्यम्। स्वच्छं स्वतःसिद्धमित्याचमनीयम्। चिच्चन्द्रमयीति सर्वाङ्गस्रवणं स्नानम्। चिदग्निस्वरूपपरमानन्दशक्तिस्फुरणं वस्त्रम्। प्रत्येकं सप्तविंशतिधा भिन्नत्वेनेच्छाज्ञान-क्रियात्मकब्रह्मग्रन्थिमद्रसतन्तुब्रह्मनाडी ब्रह्मसूत्रम्। स्वव्यतिरिक्तवस्तुसङ्गरहितस्मरणं विभूषणम्। स्वच्छस्वपरिपूर्णतास्मरणं गन्धः। समस्तविषयाणां मनसः स्थैर्येणानुसंधानं कुसुमम्। तेषामेव सर्वदा स्वीकरणं धूपः। पवनावच्छिन्नोर्ध्वज्वलनसच्चिदुल्काकाशदेहो दीपः। समस्तयातायातवर्ज्यं नैवेद्यम्। अवस्थात्रयाणामेकीकरणं ताम्बूलम्। मूलाधारादाब्रह्मरन्ध्रपर्यन्तं ब्रह्मरन्ध्रादामूलाधारपर्यन्तं गतागतरूपेण प्रादक्षिण्यम्। तुर्यावस्था नमस्कारः। देहशून्यप्रमातृतानिमज्जनं बलिहरणम्। सत्यमस्ति कर्तव्यमकर्तव्यमौदासीन्यनित्यात्मविलापनं होमः। स्वयं तत्पादुकानिमज्जनं परिपूर्णध्यानम्॥ ३॥

The element of truth in the form of integrated hymn gods (guru Mantra) too is the action (karttavya) and not following the integrated form is undoing (Akarttavya). The Bhāvanā yoga (combination of spirit) is its worship. The action (continuous research) of Asti (Brahma is in existence) and Nāsti (Brahma is not in existence) is the remedy (processing). The summoning is the ability to entertain the form of exterior and interior causes. To entertain subjects by integrated form of exterior and interior sensory organs is the Āsana (seat). The Red and white Pada (the Sattva and Tamas properties) in integrated form is Pādya. To maintain always in the pleasure form Brahma (Ānandamaya Brahma) ever luminating and its liberal contribution (to educate the eligible disciple) is Arghya. To keeps ones' clean and self purified is Ācamana. Sweating from all organs of body as a result of industry made through the mental power in the form of mind is bathe. Awaking the power of supreme soul in the form of mental energy (fire) is the apparel. The spinal nerve located in the middle of the Brahma knot (granthi) (Viṣṇu and Rudra) is Brahmasūtra (the sacrificial thread) because this is symbol to the Brahma itself. The Brahma-granthi is in the form of desire, knowledge and action etc. having its presence with three properties (i.e. Sattva, Rajas and Tamas) and alongwith twenty seven kinds of each of them. Not recollecting regarding the thing not one's own is the ornament. To assume Brahma in white complexion and everything is merged with it is the "smell". To research in all subjects by keeping the mind stable (under) is the flower and to accept it is the "Dhūpa" (odour giving stick). The body in the form of luminating ether with truth, mind ulkā (light) in the spinal cord (nerve) integrated with Prāṇa and Apāna at the time of Prāṇāyāma (yoga based on wind) is the lamp (Dīpa). To restrict the motion of mind and concentrating it on single subject at the material time is Naivedya (the sweet thing offered to god). To establish unity among three stages (i.e. awakening, dreaming, and dormance) is the betel (Tāmbūla). The frequent movement from Mūlādhāra to Brahmarandhra vice versa is Pradakṣinā. To maintain at the fourth stage i.e. Tūrīyāvasthā is Namaskāra. Sinking into intertia of the body viz. treating soul as sensitive and body as inert thereby standing undeviated is "Bali" (sacrifice). To do continuous self-analysis on the issues like doing, undoing, reluctance on the basis of everlasting soul and under determination that element of one's soul is the truth– is yajña. To sink or imbibe on the feet of that perfect Brahma (the gigantic person– supreme soul) is the perfect meditation (Dhyāna). (It may be said that the convention of aptitudes and conscience in the manner abovesaid enables the devotee to perceive directly the supreme soul. There is then left no requirement of material things in order to submit the pray to almighty).

एवं मुहूर्तत्रयं भावनापरो जीवन्मुक्तो भवति। तस्य देवतात्मैक्यसिद्धिः। चिन्तितकार्याण्ययत्नेन सिद्ध्यन्ति। स एव शिवयोगीति कथ्यते॥४॥

The person (Ascetic or devotee) developing, ability to maintain the abovesaid spiritual perception upto three ceremonies (Muhūrta), definitely attains to emancipation. He then becomes Brahma himself and his desired deeds are completed without employing any special endeavour attempts. Such devotee is only said "Śivayogī".

॥ इति भावनोपनिषत्समाप्ता॥

76. RUDRAHṚDAYOPANIṢAD

रुद्रहृदयोपनिषद्

This Upaniṣad is related to the Kṛṣṇa Yajurveda. Lord Śiva and Viṣṇu has been told inseparable and integrate in it. This Upaniṣad begins in the form of questions and answers which had taken place between the Śukadeva and Vedavyāsa. Śrī Śukadeva very first has asked Śrī Vyāsa that who is the greatest god among all gods? Its answers has been given that it is Lord Rudra who is the greatest among all gods. Thereafter the content of this Upaniṣads proceeds as the unity of Lord Śiva and Viṣṇu, trio aspects of the soul i.e. soul, supreme soul and internal soul, trio embodiment of Lord Rudra i.e. Brahmā, Viṣṇu and Maheśa, removal of all vices by the worship of Lord Rudra, the nature of Parā and Aparā Vidya (learning), the supreme truth (Akṣara knowledge) and the destruction of world, worship of Praṇava for desirous people of salvation, the discrimination between the living-soul and the god is imaginative and the removal of agony and affection when exclusive (Advaita). This Upaniṣad is most useful for removing the discriminant wisdom and enabling to know the exclusive wisdom (non-discriminant). The misdirected society as easily being seen may avail a proper lead by virtue of learning this Upaniṣad. It will certainly show them the path duly illumined by the non-discriminant rays of knowledge.

॥शान्तिपाठः॥

ॐ सह नाववतु .... इति शान्तिः॥

हृदयं कुण्डली भस्मरु द्राक्षगणदर्शनम्। तारसारं महावाक्यं पञ्चब्रह्माग्निहोत्रकम्। प्रणम्य शिरसा पादौ शुको व्यासमुवाच ह। को देवः सर्ववेदेषु कस्मिन्देवाश्च सर्वशः॥ १॥

The five Upaniṣads i.e. Rudrahṛdaya, Yogakuṇḍalī, Bhasma Jāvāla, Rudrakṣa Jāvāla and Gaṇapati enumerate the basic element of Praṇava (Oṁ). These are called the five great hymn for the offering related to the knowledge of Brahma and these too have been called the great sentences of the Vedas. Śrī Śukadeva saluted his father duly by vowing his head on his feet and asked him– "O Lord! Who is the exclusive god described by Vedas and who is the god in which all gods reside?"

कस्य शुश्रूषणान्नित्यं प्रीता देवा भवन्ति मे। तस्य तद्वचनं श्रुत्वा प्रत्युवाच पिता शुकम्॥ २॥

Kindly again tell me the name of god by whose worship all other gods will be graceful to me. Lord Vyāsa replied on hearing this question from him–

सर्वदेवात्मको रुद्रः सर्वे देवाः शिवात्मकाः। रुद्रस्य दक्षिणे पार्श्वे रविर्ब्रह्मा त्रयोऽग्नयः॥ ३॥

"O Śukadeva! God Rudra is the god in which all gods resides and these all gods are in the form of Rudra. The Sun, Brahmā and three kinds of fire (Gārhapatya, Dakṣiṇāgni and Āhavanīya) are existed at the right collateral part of the Rudra."

वामपार्श्वे उमा देवी विष्णुः सोमोऽपि ते त्रयः। या उमा सा स्वयं विष्णुर्यो विष्णुः स हि चन्द्रमाः॥४॥

The goddess Umā, Lord Viṣṇu and Soma i.e. three divine powers are existed at his left collateral parts. Lord Viṣṇu is the same Umā and the moon is the Lord Viṣṇu.

ये नमस्यन्ति गोविन्दं ते नमस्यन्ति शंकरम्। येऽर्चयन्ति हरिं भक्त्या तेऽर्चयन्ति वृषभध्वजम्॥५॥

To vow before Govinda will be deemed as salute convey to Lord Śaṅkara. The persons worshipping Lord Viṣṇu with sheer devotion, they too worship Vṛṣabhadhvaja i.e. the Lord Rudra.

ये द्विषन्ति विरूपाक्षं ते द्विषन्ति जनार्दनम्। ये रुद्रं नाभिजानन्ति ते न जानन्ति केशवम्॥६॥

The persons keeping envy of Virūpākṣa (Lord Śaṅkara), seldom attain the grace of Lord Janārdana. The persons unknown to the form of Rudra too are unknown altogether of Keśava.

रुद्रात्प्रवर्तते बीजं बीजयोनिर्जनार्दनः। यो रुद्रः स स्वयं ब्रह्मा यो ब्रह्मा स हुताशनः॥७॥

Lord Rudra too is the seed form to the origin of the living-organism and Lord Viṣṇu is in vagina form (viz. the field) of that seed. Lord Rudra too is Brahmā himself and whosoever is Brahma. He too is the fire Lord.

ब्रह्मविष्णुमयो रुद्र अग्नीषोमात्मकं जगत्। पुँल्लिङ्गं सर्वमीशानं स्त्रीलिङ्गं भगवत्युमा॥८॥

Lord Rudra too is Brahmā and Viṣṇu as also this world with fire and Soma also is in the form of Rudra. All creatures in masculine gender are in the form of Rudra and the feminine gender are in the form of goddess Umā in this world.

उमारुद्रात्मिकाः सर्वाः प्रजाः स्थावरजङ्गमाः। व्यक्तं सर्वमुमारूपमव्यक्तं तु महेश्वरम्॥९॥

The creation (Sṛṣṭi) of all inert and sensitive is in the form of Rudra and Umā. The tangible world is in the form of Umā and the intangible form of this world is in the form of Maheśvara.

उमाशंकरयोगो यः स योगो विष्णुरुच्यते। यस्तु तस्मै नमस्कारं कुर्याद्भक्तिसमन्वितः॥१०॥

आत्मानं परमात्मानमन्तरात्मानमेव च। ज्ञात्वा त्रिविधमात्मानं परमात्मानमाश्रयेत्॥११॥

The harmony of Umā and Śiva too is called Viṣṇu. The persons saluting Lord Viṣṇu with sheer devotion, attains to the supreme soul after thoroughly known to the trio souls i.e., the soul, supreme soul and the inner soul (conscience).

अन्तरात्मा भवेद् ब्रह्मा परमात्मा महेश्वरः। सर्वेषामेव भूतानां विष्णुरात्मा सनातनः॥१२॥

The inner soul (conscience) is Brahmā, the supreme soul is Maheśvara and the everlasting soul of all living-organisms is Lord Viṣṇu.

अस्य त्रैलोक्यवृक्षस्य भूमौ विटपशाखिनः। अग्रं मध्यं तथा मूलं विष्णुब्रह्ममहेश्वराः॥१३॥

The branches and stamps of this tree in the form of three worlds are spreaded on the earth. Lord Viṣṇu is at its foreportion, Lord Brahmā is the trunk and Lord Maheśvara is the root of this tree.

कार्यं विष्णुः क्रिया ब्रह्मा कारणं तु महेश्वरः। प्रयोजनार्थं रुद्रेण मूर्तिरेका त्रिधा कृता॥ १४॥

Lord Viṣṇu is in the form of work, Lord Brahmā in the form of action and Lord Maheśvara is in the form of cause. Thus, Lord Rudra too has held in the three forms to his single icon (power) according to the purpose.

धर्मो रुद्रो जगद्विष्णुः सर्वज्ञानं पितामहः॥ १५॥

श्रीरुद्र रुद्र रुद्रेति यस्तं ब्रूयाद्विचक्षणः। कीर्तनात्सर्वदेवस्य सर्वपापैः प्रमुच्यते॥ १६॥

The religion is in the form of Rudra, the world is in the form of Viṣṇu and the entire knowledge is in the form of Brahmā. The scholar reciting the name of Rudra frequently, attains the fruit of worship to all gods and he becomes innocent and abandons all evil doings.

रुद्रो नर उमा नारी तस्मै तस्यै नमो नमः॥ १७॥ रुद्रो ब्रह्मा उमा वाणी तस्मै तस्यै नमो नमः। रुद्रो विष्णुरुमा लक्ष्मीस्तस्मै तस्यै नमो नमः॥ १८॥ रुद्रः सूर्य उमा छाया तस्मै तस्यै नमो नमः। रुद्रः सोम उमा तारा तस्मै तस्यै नमो नमः॥ १९॥ रुद्रो दिवा उमा रात्रिस्तस्मै तस्यै नमो नमः। रुद्रो यज्ञ उमा वेदिस्तस्मै तस्यै नमो नमः॥ २०॥ रुद्रो वह्निरुमा स्वाहा तस्मै तस्यै नमो नमः। रुद्रो वेद उमा शास्त्रं तस्मै तस्यै नमो नमः॥ २१॥ रुद्रो वृक्ष उमा वल्ली तस्मै तस्यै नमो नमः। रुद्रो गन्ध उमा पुष्पं तस्मै तस्यै नमो नमः॥ २२॥ रुद्रोऽर्थ अक्षरः सोमा तस्मै तस्यै नमो नमः। रुद्रो लिङ्गमुमा पीठं तस्मै तस्यै नमो नमः॥ २३॥ सर्वदेवात्मकं रुद्रं नमस्कुर्यात्पृथक्पृथक्। एभिर्मंत्रपदैरेव नमस्यामीशपार्वतीम्॥ २४॥ यत्र यत्र भवेत्सार्धमिमं मन्त्रमुदीरयेत्। ब्रह्महा जलमध्ये तु सर्वपापैः प्रमुच्यते॥ २५॥

Lord Rudra and the goddess Umā is saluted in the form of men and women respectively. Rudra is Brahmā and the Umā is the speech. These both forms of Rudra and Umā are saluted. Similarly, salute is conveyed to Rudra as Viṣṇu and Umā of goddess Lakṣmī. Lord Sun in the form of Rudra and shadow in the form of Umā is saluted. Lord Rudra and Umā both are saluted in their respective forms of moon and the stars. Two forms of Rudra and Umā are saluted in which Rudra is the day and the Umā is the night further, Rudra as offering and the Umā as ultra are saluted. Again Lord Rudra as fire and Umā as Svāhā (sacrifice) are saluted. Lord Rudra in the form of Veda and Umā in the form of Śāstra (holy books) are saluted. Lord Śaṅkara in the form of tree and Umā in the form of creeper are saluted. Lord Śaṅkara and Umā are further saluted assuming them in the form of smell and flower effectively. Lord Śaṅkara in the form of meaning and the goddess Umā is in the form of letter and both are thus saluted. Lord Śaṅkara and Umā are saluted in form of Liṅga and Piṭha. Thus, in the form of all gods, the Rudra should be saluted separately. I salute Lord Śiva and goddess Pārvatī by reciting these feet of hymns. Irrespective of living anywhere, a man should always do silent reciting of this hymn. Even if, the men has committed the murder of a Brāhmaṇa, he too is exonerated from the evil so committed if this hymn is recited by entering in the water of the river.

सर्वाधिष्ठानमद्वन्द्वं परं ब्रह्म सनातनम्। सच्चिदानन्दरूपं तदवाङ्मनसगोचरम्॥ २६॥

तस्मिन्सुविदिते सर्वं विज्ञातं स्यादिदं शुक। तदात्मकत्वात्सर्वस्य तस्माद्भिन्नं नहि क्वचित्॥ २७॥

O Śuka! All these mysteries are properly known when the sheltering place of all, beyond the puzzles of the mind, in the form of the truth, the pleasure and the penance, beyond perceiving through the mind and the speech, the everlasting supreme Brahma is duly known because nothing here is distinct than the Brahma and everything is in its form.

द्वे विद्ये वेदितव्ये हि परा चैवापरा च ते। तत्रापरा तु विद्यैषा ऋग्वेदो यजुरेव च॥ २८॥

सामवेदस्तथाथर्ववेदः शिक्षा मुनीश्वर। कल्पो व्याकरणं चैव निरुक्तं छन्द एव च॥ २९॥

ज्योतिषं च यथा नात्मविषया अपि बुद्धयः। अथैषा परमा विद्या ययात्मा परमाक्षरम्॥ ३०॥

The knowable two learnings i.e. the Parā and Aparā are important for the devotee. In the scope of the Aparā learning, the Ṛk, Yajus, Sāma, Atharva, education, kalpa, grammar, etymology, rhyme and the astrology are existed. O the best hermit! Besides the topic of soul, this learning contains all kinds of knowledge pertaining to the wisdom the Parā learning has been called, resorting to which the self-realization is obtained. That element of soul is everlasting.

यत्तदद्रेश्यमग्राह्यमगोत्रं रूपवर्जितम्। अचक्षुः श्रोत्रमत्यर्थं तदपाणिपदं तथा॥ ३१॥

नित्यं विभुं सर्वगतं सुसूक्ष्मं च तदव्ययम्। तद्भूतयोनिं पश्यन्ति धीरा आत्मानमात्मनि॥ ३२॥

That element of soul neither is seen nor entertainable. He is beyond the name, the complexion and the clan. He is beyond the eyes, perception of eyes, ears and the hands as also the feet. He is omnipresent, everlasting, omniscient, most micro and free from all kinds of defects. He is the origin place of all creatures. The learned persons always watch that element of supreme soul in their own conscience (inner soul).

यः सर्वज्ञः सर्वविद्यो यस्य ज्ञानमयं तपः। तस्मादत्रान्नरूपेण जायते जगदावलिः॥ ३३॥

That Brahma too is the resorting place to all learnings (Vidyā) and it is omniscient (who knows all about the past, future and the present). This inert and sensitive world has been originated by the penance of knowledge in the form of the cereals (food) and the enjoyer (Bhoktā).

सत्यवद्भाति तत्सर्वं रज्जुसर्पवदास्थितम्। तदेतदक्षरं सत्यं तद्विज्ञाय विमुच्यते॥ ३४॥

As the snake is perceived or likely in cord, this world as it perceived is similarly existed in the Brahma. The men duly known that the immortal Brahma is the truth, attains to the position of emancipation.

ज्ञानेनैव हि संसारविनाशो नैव कर्मणा। श्रोत्रियं ब्रह्मनिष्ठं स्वगुरुं गच्छेद्यथाविधि॥ ३५॥

The worldly cord can be cut out only by application of the knowledge and it cannot be sheltered by the activity. Hence, the devotee should visit regularly for acquiring the knowledge before his teacher and who is loyal to Brahma and well known to the same.

गुरुस्तस्मै परां विद्यां दद्याद्ब्रह्मात्मबोधिनीम्। गुहायां निहितं साक्षादक्षरं वेद चेन्नरः॥ ३६॥

छित्त्वाऽविद्यामहाग्रन्थिं शिवं गच्छेत्सनातनम्। तदेतदमृतं सत्यं तद्बोद्धव्यं मुमुक्षुभिः॥ ३७॥

The teacher should preach the Parā learning making to understand the absolute form of soul and the Brahma to such devotee. The devotee introduced or realised to that letter Brahma (Akṣara Brahma) existed in the cavity of the heart attains to the everlasting Śiva after setting aside the hard blend (knot) of the ignorance. The devotees desirous of emancipation assume it as the supreme element of soul worth-knowing.

धनुस्तारं शरो ह्यात्मा ब्रह्म तल्लक्ष्यमुच्यते। अप्रमत्तेन वेद्धव्यं शरवत्तन्मयो भवेत्॥ ३८॥

The Praṇava is said a bow and the soul is said an arrow. One should setting aside the giving up of the laxity and luxury hit at the aim of the Brahma. Alike the arrow penetrating the target (aim), the devotee should also engross himself in the entity of Brahms.

लक्ष्यं सर्वगतं चैव शरः सर्वगतो मुखः। वेद्धा सर्वगतश्चैव शिवलक्ष्यं न संशयः॥ ३९॥

The target of Brahma is omniscient, the arrow in the form of soul mouths from all sides and in case the archer i.e. devotee too is omniscient, he definitely hit at the target in the form of Śivā.

न तत्र चन्द्रार्कवपुः प्रकाशते न वान्ति वाताः सकला देवताश्च।
स एष देवः कृतभावभूतः स्वयं विशुद्धो विरजः प्रकाशते॥ ४०॥

The supreme soul at whose ever holy abode, the sun and moon seldom are illumined, where the wind god and all other gods cannot access, that supreme soul illumines in the form of pure and intangible one when due attention is made by the devotees.

द्वौ सुपर्णौ शरीरेऽस्मिञ्जीवेशाख्यौ सह स्थितौ। तयोर्जीवः फलं भुंक्ते कर्मणो न महेश्वरः॥ ४१॥

The two birds i.e. the living soul and the god, reside in this tree of the body. The bird in the form of living soul enjoys the fruit of action but the god is only observer and seldom enjoys the fruits of action.

केवलं साक्षिरूपेण विना भोगं महेश्वरः। प्रकाशते स्वयं भेदः कल्पितो मायया तयोः॥ ४२॥

The god is illuminated only as an evidence and it seldom enjoys the fruit of action. The discrimination between the living soul and god has been made on the basis of illusion (Māyā).

घटाकाशमठाकाशौ यथाकाशप्रभेदतः। कल्पितौ परमौ जीवशिवरूपेण कल्पितौ॥ ४३॥

As the Ghatākāśa and Maṭhākāśa two are national kinds of the ether, the kinds of supreme soul of living soul and gods too are based on imagination.

तत्त्वतश्च शिवः साक्षाच्चिज्जीवश्च स्वतः सदा। चिच्चिदाकारतो भिन्ना न भिन्ना चित्त्वहानितः॥

The living soul in the form of Cid actually is the apparent Śiva. The difference between the living-soul and the god is perceived only due to discrimination of the size and the level of cinmaya but there is no difference between the nature of them. In case, any discrimination between the nature would be, their form of mind then certainly destroyed.

चितश्छिन्न चिदाकाराद्भिद्यते जडरूपत:। भिद्यते चेज्जडो भेदश्चिदेका सर्वदा खलु॥४५॥

The difference as found mind to mind is not in the form of the size of Cid but it is national due to inert calibre (name given to it). The discriminant view in itself is full of inert because the mind holds the equal nature at all places.

तर्कतश्च प्रमाणाच्च चिदेकत्वव्यवस्थिते:। चिदेकत्वपरिज्ञाने न शोचति न मुह्यति॥४६॥

अद्वैतं परमानन्दं शिवं याति तु केवलम्॥४७॥

The unity of the mind is confirmed by the device and the proof both. Hence, the person duly known to the unity of mind neither falls to the pray of agony nor he is fastened with the ties of affection (he is fully exonerated from such ties). He after arriving at this state, attains to the element of Śiva in the form of giving exclusive pleasure.

अधिष्ठानं समस्तस्य जगत: सत्यचिद्घनम्। अहमस्मीति निश्चित्य वीतशोको भवेन्मुनि:॥४८॥

The god in the form of truth and cidghana is sheltering place to this entire universe. The learned persons determines as– "that too is I myself" (I myself is that supreme soul) and thus make them free from the agony.

स्वशरीरे स्वयं ज्योति:स्वरूपं सर्वसाक्षिणम्। क्षीणदोषा: प्रपश्यन्ति नेतरे माययावृता:॥४९॥

Those persons only can see in their conscience that self-luminated and all evident god as a result of long penance whose vices and evils are fully destroyed but the persons engrossed in the illusion of this world, always remain denial of perceiving that supreme flame.

एवं रूपपरिज्ञानं यस्यास्ति परयोगिन:। कुत्रचिद्गमनं नास्ति तस्य पूर्णस्वरूपिण:॥५०॥

The great men full of knowledge to their soul, do not rotate around the cycle of birth and death because at that stage those become yogis of higher accomplishments.

आकाशमेकं संपूर्णं कुत्रचिन्नैव गच्छति। तद्वत्स्वात्मपरिज्ञानी कुत्रचिन्नैव गच्छति॥५१॥

As this entire ether always remains stable and seldom moves, the learned person duly attain to self-realization does not move anywhere.

स यो ह वै तत्परमं ब्रह्म यो वेद वै मुनि:। ब्रह्मैव भवति स्वस्थ: सच्चिदानन्दमातृक:॥५२॥

The scholar definitely known to perfect Brahma (Para Brahma) makes himself stable in the form acquired by him as a result of sheer penance and he himself is called the Brahma in the form of Saccidānanda (The state of supreme pleasure and truth).

ॐ सह नाववतु .... इति शान्ति:॥

॥इति रुद्रहृदयोपनिषत्समाप्ता॥

77. YOGAKUṆḌALYUPANIṢAD

योगकुण्डल्युपनिषद्

॥शान्तिपाठः॥

ॐ सह नाववतु .... इति शान्तिः॥

Chapter I

हेतुद्वयं हि चित्तस्य वासना च समीरणः। तयोर्विनष्ट एकस्मिंस्तद्द्वावपि विनश्यतः॥ १॥
तयोरादौ समीरस्य जयं कुर्यान्नरः सदा। मिताहारश्चासनं च शक्तिचालस्तृतीयकः॥ २॥
एतेषां लक्षणं वक्ष्ये श‍ृणु गौतम सादरम्। सुस्निग्धमधुराहारश्चतुर्थांशविवर्जितः॥ ३॥
भुज्यते शिवसंप्रीत्यै मिताहारः स उच्यते। आसनं द्विविधं प्रोक्तं पद्मं वज्रासनं तथा॥ ४॥
ऊर्वोरुपरि चेद्धत्ते उभे पादतले यथा। पद्मासनं भवेदेतत्सर्वपापप्रणाशनम्॥ ५॥
वामाङ्घ्रिमूलकन्दाधो ह्यन्यं तदुपरि क्षिपेत्। समग्रीवशिरःकायो वज्रासनमितीरितम्॥ ६॥
कुण्डल्येव भवेच्छक्तिस्तां तु संचालयेद्बुधः। स्वस्थानादाभ्रुवोर्मध्यं शक्तिचालनमुच्यते॥ ७
तत्साधने द्वयं मुख्यं सरस्वत्यास्तु चालनम्। प्राणरोधमथाभ्यासादृज्वी कुण्डलिनी भवेत्॥ ८॥
तयोरादौ सरस्वत्याश्चालनं कथयामि ते। अरुन्धत्येव कथिता पुराविद्भिः सरस्वती॥ ९॥
यस्याः संचालनेनैव स्वयं चलति कुण्डली। इडायां वहति प्राणे बद्ध्वा पद्मासनं दृढम्॥ १०॥
द्वादशाङ्गुलदैर्घ्यं च अम्बरं चतुरङ्गुलम्। विस्तीर्य तेन तन्नाडीं वेष्टयित्वा ततः सुधीः॥ ११॥
अङ्गुष्ठतर्जनीभ्यां तु हस्ताभ्यां धारयेद्दृढम्। स्वशक्त्या चालयेद्वामे दक्षिणेन पुनःपुनः॥ १२॥
मुहूर्तद्वयपर्यन्तं निर्भयाच्चालयेत्सुधीः। ऊर्ध्वमाकर्षयेत्किंचित्सुषुम्नां कुण्डलीगताम्॥ १३॥
तेन कुण्डलिनी तस्याः सुषुम्नाया मुखं व्रजेत्। जहाति तस्मात्प्राणोऽयं सुषुम्नां व्रजति स्वतः॥ १४॥
तुन्दे तु ताणं कुर्याच्च कण्ठसंकोचने कृते। सरस्वत्याश्चालनेन वक्षसश्चोर्ध्वगो मरुत्॥ १५॥
सूर्येण रेचयेद्वायुं सरस्वत्यास्तु चालने। कण्ठसंकोचनं कृत्वा वक्षसश्चोर्ध्वगो मरुत्॥ १६॥
तस्मात्संचालयेन्नित्यं शब्दगर्भां सरस्वतीम्। यस्याः संचालनेनैव योगी रोगैः प्रमुच्यते॥ १७॥
गुल्मं जलोदरः प्लीहा ये चान्ये तुन्दमध्यगाः। सर्वे तु शक्तिचालेन रोगा नश्यन्ति निश्चयम्॥ १८॥

Citta has two causes, vāsanās and (prāṇa) vāyu. If one of them is controlled, then both are controlled. Of these two, a person should control (prāṇa) vāyu always through moderate food, postures and thirdly śakti-cāla. I shall explain the nature of these. Listen to it, O Gautama. One should take a sweet and nutritious food, leaving a fourth (of his stomach) unfilled in order to please Śiva (the patron of yogin). This is called moderate food. Posture herein required is of two kinds, padma and vajra. Placing the two heels over the two opposite thighs (respectively) is the padma (posture) which is the destroyer of all sins. Placing one heel below the mūlakanda and the other over it and sitting with the neck, body had head erect is the vajra posture. The śakti (mentioned above) is only kuṇḍalinī. A wise man should take it up from its place (viz., the navel, upwards) to the middle of the eyebrows. This is called śakti-cāla. In practising it, two things are necessary, Sarasvatīcāla and the restraint of prāṇa (breath). Then through practice, kuṇḍalinī (which is spiral) becomes straightened. Of these two, I shall explain to you first Sarasvatī-cāla. It is said by the wise of old that Sarasvatī is no other than Arundhatī. It is only by rousing her up that kuṇḍalinī is roused. When prāṇa (breath) is passing through (one's) Iḍā (left nostril), he should assume firmly padma-posture and should lengthen (inwards) 4 digits the ākāśa of 12 digits. Then the wise man should bind the (sarasvatī) nādi by means of this lengthened (breath) and holding firmly together (both his ribs near the navel) by means of the forefingers and thumbs of both hands, (one hand on each side) should stir up kuṇḍalinī with all his might from right to left often and often; for a period of two muhūrtas (48 minutes), he should be stirring it up fearlessly. Then he should draw up a little when kuṇḍalinī enters suṣumnā. By this means, kuṇḍalinī enters the mouth of suṣumnā. Prāṇa (also) having left (that place) enters of itself the suṣumnā (along with kuṇḍalinī). By compressing the neck, one should also expand the navel. Then by shaking sarasvatī, prāṇa goes above (to) the chest. Through the contraction of the neck, prāṇa goes above from the chest. Sarasvatī who has sound in her womb should be shaken (or thrown into vibration) each day. Therefore by merely shaking it, one is cured of diseases. Gulma (a splenetic disease), jalodara (dropsy), plīha (a splenetic disease) and all other diseases arising within the belly, are undoubtedly destroyed by shaking this Śakti.

प्राणरोधमथेदानीं प्रवक्ष्यामि समासतः। प्राणश्च देहगो वायुरायामः कुम्भकः स्मृतः॥ १९॥

स एव द्विविधः प्रोक्तः सहितः केवलस्तथा। यावत्केवलसिद्धिः स्यात्तावत्सहितमभ्यसेत्॥ २०॥

सूर्योज्जायी शीतली च भस्त्री चैव चतुर्थिका। भेदैरेव समं कुम्भो यः स्यात्सहितकुम्भकः॥ २१॥

I shall now briefly describe to you prāṇāyāma. Prāṇa is the vāyu that move in the body and its restraint within is known as kumbhaka. It is of two kinds, sahita and kevala. One should practise sahita till he gets kevala. There are four bhedas (lit., piercings or divisions) viz., sūrya, ujjāyī, śītalī and bhastrī. The kumbhaka associated with these four is called sahita-kumbhaka.

पवित्रे निर्जने देशे शर्करादिविवर्जिते। धनुः प्रमाणपर्यन्ते शीताग्निजलवर्जिते॥ २२॥

पवित्रे नात्युच्चनीचे ह्यासने सुखदे सुखे। बद्धपद्मासनं कृत्वा सरस्वत्यास्तु चालनम्॥ २३॥

दक्षनाड्या समाकृष्य बहिष्ठं पवनं शनैः। यथेष्टं पूरयेद्वायुं रेचयेदिडया ततः॥ २४॥

कपालशोधने वापि रेचयेत्पवनं शनैः। चतुष्कं वातदोषं तु कृमिदोषं निहन्ति च॥ २५॥

Being seated in the padma posture upon a pure and pleasant seat which gives ease end is neither too high nor too low, and in a place which is pure, lovely and free from pebbles, etc., and which for the length of a bow is free from cold, fire, and water, one should shake (or throw into vibration) Sarasvatī; slowly inhaling the breath from outside, as long as he desires, through the right nostril, he should exhale it through the left nostril. He should exhale it after purifying his skull (by forcing the breath up). This destroys the four kinds of evils caused by vāyu as also by intestinal worms.

पुनः पुनरिदं कार्यं सूर्यभेदमुदाहृतम्। मुखं संयम्य नाडीभ्यामाकृष्य पवनं शनैः॥ २६॥
यथा लगति कण्ठात्तु हृदयावधि सस्वनम्। पूर्ववत्कुम्भयेत्प्राणं रेचयेदिडया ततः॥ २७॥
शीर्षोदितानलहरं गलश्लेष्महरं परम्। सर्वरोगहरं पुण्यं देहानलविवर्धनम्॥ २८॥
नाडीजलोदरं धातुगतदोषविनाशनम्। गच्छतस्तिष्ठतः कार्यमुज्जाय्याख्यं तु कुम्भकम्॥ २९॥

This should be done often and it is this which is spoken of as sūryabheda. Closing the mouth and drawing up slowly the breath as before with the nose through both the nāḍīs (or nostrils) and retaining it in the space between the heart and the neck, one should exhale it through the left nostril. This destroys the heat caused in the head as well as the phlegm in the throat. It removes all diseases, purifies his body and increases the (gastric) fire within. It removes also the evils arising in the nāḍīs, jalodara (water-belly or dropsy) and dhātus. This kumbhaka is called ujjāyī and may be practised (even) when walking or standing.

जिह्वया वायुमाकृष्य पूर्ववत्कुम्भकादनु। शनैस्तु घ्राणरन्ध्राभ्यां रेचयेदनिलं सुधीः॥ ३०॥
गुल्मप्लीहादिकान्दोषाक्षयं पित्तं ज्वरं तृषाम्। विषाणि शीतली नाम कुम्भकोऽयं निहन्ति च॥

Drawing up the breath as before through the tongue with (the hissing sound of) I and retaining it as before, the wise man should slowly exhale it through (both) the nostrils. This is called śītalī kumbhaka and destroys diseases, such as gulma, plīha, consumption, bile, fever, thirst and poison.

ततः पद्मासनं बद्ध्वा समग्रीवोदरः सुधीः। मुखं संयम्य यत्नेन प्राणं घ्राणेन रेचयेत्॥ ३२॥
यथा लगति कण्ठात्तु कपाले सस्वनं ततः। वेगेन पूरयेत् किंचिद्धृत्पद्मावधि मारुतम्॥ ३३॥
पुनर्विरेचयेत्तद्वत्पूरयेच्च पुनः पुनः। यथैव लोहकाराणां भस्त्रा वेगेन चाल्यते॥ ३४॥
तथैव स्वशरीरस्थं चालयेत्पवनं शनैः। यथा श्रमो भवेद्देहे तथा सूर्येण पूरयेत्॥ ३५॥
यथोदरं भवेत्पूर्णं पवनेन तथा लघु। धारयन्नासिकामध्यं तर्जनीभ्यां विना दृढम्॥ ३६॥
कुम्भकं पूर्ववत्कृत्वा रेचयेदिडयानिलम्। कण्ठोत्थितानलहरं शरीराग्निविवर्धनम्॥ ३७॥
कुण्डलीबोधकं पुण्यं पापघ्नं शुभदं सुखम्। ब्रह्मनाडीमुखान्तस्थकफाद्यर्गलनाशनम्॥ ३८॥
गुणत्रयसमुद्भूतग्रन्थित्रयविभेदकम्। विशेषेणैव कर्तव्यं भस्त्राख्यं कुम्भकं त्विदम्॥ ३९॥

Seated in the padma posture with belly and neck erect, the wise man should close the mouth and exhale with care through the nostrils. Then he should inhale a little with speed up to the heart, so that the breath may fill the space with noise between the neck and skull. Then he should exhale in the same way and inhale often and often. Just as the bellows of a smith are moved (viz., stuffed with air within and then the air is let out), so he should move the air within his body. If the body gets tired, then he should inhale through the right nostril. If his belly is full of vāyu, then he should press well his nostrils with all his fingers except his forefinger, and performing kumbhaka as before, should exhale through the left nostril. This frees one from diseases of fire in (or inflammation of) the throat, increases the gastric fire within, enables one to know the kuṇḍalinī, produces purity removing sins, gives happiness and pleasure and destroys phlegm which the bolt (or obstacle) to the door at the mouth of brahmanāḍī (viz., suṣumnā). It pierces also the three granthis (or knots) differentiated through the three guṇas. This kumbhaka is known as bhastrī and should especially be performed.

चतुर्णामपि भेदानां कुम्भके समुपस्थिते। बन्धत्रयमिदं कार्यं योगिभिर्वीतकल्मषैः॥४०॥

प्रथमो मूलबन्धस्तु द्वितीयोड्डीयणाभिधः। जालन्धरस्तृतीयस्तु तेषां लक्षणमुच्यते॥४१॥

अधोगतिमपानं वै ऊर्ध्वगं कुरुते बलात्। आकुञ्चनेन तं प्राहुर्मूलबन्धोऽयमुच्यते॥४२॥

अपाने चोर्ध्वगे याते संप्राप्ते वह्निमण्डले। ततोऽनलशिखा दीर्घा वर्धते वायुना हता॥४३॥

ततो यातौ वह्न्यपानौ प्राणमुष्णस्वरूपकम्। तेनात्यन्तप्रदीप्तेन ज्वलनो देहजस्तथा॥४४॥

तेन कुण्डलिनी सुप्ता संतप्ता संप्रबुध्यते। दण्डाहतभुजङ्गीव निःश्वस्य ऋजुतां व्रजेत्॥४५॥

बिलप्रवेशतो यत्र ब्रह्मनाड्यन्तरं व्रजेत्। तस्मान्नित्यं मूलबन्धः कर्तव्यो योगिभिः सदा॥४६॥

कुम्भकान्ते रेचकादौ कर्तव्यस्तूड्डियाणकः। बन्धो येन सुषुम्नायां प्राणस्तूड्डीयते यतः॥४७॥

तस्मादुड्डीयणाख्योऽयं योगिभिः समुदाहृतः। सति वज्रासने पादौ कराभ्यां धारयेद्दृढम्॥४८॥

गुल्फदेशसमीपे च कन्दं तत्र प्रपीडयेत्। पश्चिमं ताणमुदरे धारयेद्धृदये गले॥४९॥

शनैः शनैर्यदा प्राणस्तुन्दसन्धिं निगच्छति। तुन्ददोषं विनिर्धूय कर्तव्यं सततं शनैः॥५०॥

पूरकान्ते तु कर्तव्यो बन्धो जालन्धराभिधः। कण्ठसंकोचरूपोऽसौ वायुमार्गनिरोधकः॥५१॥

अधस्तात्कुञ्चनेनाशु कण्ठसंकोचने कृते। मध्ये पश्चिमताणेन स्यात्प्राणो ब्रह्मनाडिगः॥५२॥

पूर्वोक्तेन क्रमेणैव सम्यगासनमास्थितः। चालनं तु सरस्वत्याः कृत्वा प्राणं निरोधयेत्॥५३॥

प्रथमे दिवसे कार्यं कुम्भकानां चतुष्टयम्। प्रत्येकं दशसंख्याकं द्वितीये पञ्चभिस्तथा॥५४॥

विंशत्यलं तृतीयेऽह्नि पञ्चवृद्ध्या दिनेदिने। कर्तव्यः कुम्भको नित्यं बन्धत्रयसमन्वितः॥५५॥

Through these four ways when kumbhaka is near (or is about to be performed), the sinless yogin should practise the three bandhas. The first is called mūlabandha. The second is called uḍḍiyāna, and the third is jālandhara. Their nature will be thus described. Apāna (breath) which has a downward tendency is forced up by one bending down. This process is called mūlabandha. When apāna is raised up and reaches the sphere of agni (fire), then the flame of agni grows long, being blown about by vāyu. Then agni and apāna come to (or commingle with) prāṇa in a heated state. Through this agni which is very fiery, there airses in the body the flamming (or the fire) which rouses the sleeping kuṇḍalinī through its heat. Then this kuṇḍalinī makes a hissing noise, becomes erect like a serpent beaten with stick and enters the hole of brahmanāḍī (suṣumnā). Therefore yogin should daily practise mūlabandha often. Uḍḍiyāna should be performed at the end of kumbhaka and at the beginning of expiration. Because prāṇa uḍḍīyatē (viz., goes up) the suṣumnā in this bandha, therefore it called uḍḍiyāna by the yogins. Being seated in the vajra posture and holding firmly the two toes by the two hands, he should press at the kanda and at the place near the two ankles. Then he should gradually upbear the tāna (thread or nāḍī) which is on the western side first to udara (the upper part of the abdomen above the navel), then to the heart and then to the neck. When prāṇa reaches the sandhi (junction) of navel, slowly it removes the impurities (or diseases) in the navel. Therefore this should be frequently practised. The bandha called jālandhara should be practised at the end of kumbhaka. This jālandhara is of the form of contraction of the neck and is an impediment to the passage of vāyu (upwards). When the neck is contracted at once by bending downwards (so that the chin may touch the breast), prāṇa goes through brahmanāḍī on the western tāna in the middle. Assuming the seat as mentioned before, one should stir up sarasvatī and control prāṇa. On the first day, kumbhaka should be done four times; on the second day it should be done ten times, and then five times separately; on the third day, twenty times will do, and afterwards kumbhaka should be performed with three bandhas and with an increase of five times each day.

दिवा सुप्तिर्निशायां तु जागरादतिमैथुनात्। बहुसंक्रमणं नित्यं रोधान्मूत्रपुरीषयोः॥५६॥
विषमासनदोषाच्च प्रयासप्राणचिन्तनात्। शीघ्रमुत्पद्यते रोगः स्तम्भयेद्यदि संयमी॥५७॥
योगाभ्यासेन मे रोग उत्पन्न इति कथ्यते। ततोऽभ्यासं त्यजेदेवं प्रथमं विघ्नमुच्यते॥५८॥
द्वितीयं संशयाख्यं च तृतीयं च प्रमत्तता। आलस्याख्यं चतुर्थं च निद्रारूपं तु पञ्चमम्॥५९॥
षष्ठं तु विरतिर्भ्रान्तिः सप्तमं परिकीर्तितम्। विषयं चाष्टमं चैव अनाख्यं नवमं स्मृतम्॥६०॥
अलब्धियोगतत्त्वस्य दशमं प्रोच्यते बुधैः। इत्येतद्विघ्नदशकं विचारेण त्यजेद्बुधः॥६१॥
प्राणाभ्यासस्ततः कार्यो नित्यं सत्त्वस्थया धिया। सुषुम्ना लीयते चित्तं तथा वायुः प्रधावति॥६२॥
शुष्के मले तु योगी च स्याद्गतिश्चलिता ततः। अधोगतिमपानं वै ऊर्ध्वगं कुरुते बलात्॥६३॥
आकुञ्चनेन तं प्राहुर्मूलबन्धोऽयमुच्यते। अपानश्चोर्ध्वगो भूत्वा वह्निना सह गच्छति॥६४॥
प्राणस्थानं ततो वह्निः प्राणापानौ च सत्वरम्। मिलित्वा कुण्डलीं याति प्रसुप्ता कुण्डलाकृतिः॥
तेनाग्निना च संतप्ता पवनेनैव चालिता। प्रसार्य स्वशरीरं तु सुषुम्ना वदनान्तरे॥६६॥
ब्रह्मग्रन्थिं ततो भित्त्वा रजोगुणसमुद्भवम्। सुषुम्नावदने शीघ्रं विद्युल्लेखेव संस्फुरेत्॥६७॥
विष्णुग्रन्थिं प्रयात्युच्चैः सत्वरं हृदि संस्थिता। ऊर्ध्वं गच्छति यच्चान्ते रुद्रग्रन्थिं तदुद्भवम्॥६८॥
भ्रुवोर्मध्यं तु संभिद्य याति शीतांशुमण्डलम्। अनाहताख्यं यच्चक्रं दलैः षोडशभिर्युतम्॥६९॥
तत्र शीतांशुसंजातं द्रवं शोषयति स्वयम्। चलिते प्राणवेगेन रक्तं पित्तं रवेर्ग्रहात्॥७०॥
यातेन्दुचक्रं यत्रास्ते शुद्धश्लेष्मद्रवात्मकम्। तत्र सिक्तं ग्रसत्युष्णं कथं शीतस्वभावकम्॥७१॥
तथैव रभसा शुक्लं चन्द्ररूपं हि तप्यते। ऊर्ध्वं प्रवहति क्षुब्धा तदैवं भ्रमतेतराम्॥७२॥
तस्यास्वादवशाच्चित्तं बहिष्ठं विषयेषु यत्। तदेव परमं भुक्त्वा स्वस्थः स्वात्मरतो युवा॥७३॥

प्रकृत्यष्टकरूपं च स्थानं गच्छति कुण्डली। क्रोडीकृत्य शिवं याति क्रोडीकृत्य विलीयते॥७४॥
इत्यधोर्ध्वरजः शुक्लं शिवे तदनु मारुतः। प्राणापानौ समौ याति सदा जातौ तथैव च॥७५॥
भूतेऽल्पे चाप्यनल्पे वा वाचके त्वतिवर्धते। धावयत्यखिला वाता अग्निमूषाहिरण्यवत्॥७६॥
आधिभौतिकदेहं तु आधिदैविकविग्रहे। देहोऽतिविमलं याति चातिवाहिकतामियात्॥७७॥
जाड्यभावविनिर्मुक्तममलं चिन्मयात्मकम्। तस्यातिवाहिकं मुख्यं सर्वेषां तु मदात्मकम्॥७८॥
जायाभवविनिर्मुक्तिः कालरूपस्य विभ्रमः। इति तं स्वरूपा हि मती रज्जुभुजङ्गवत्॥७९॥
मृषैवोदेति सकलं मृषैव प्रविलीयते। रौप्यबुद्धिः शुक्तिकायां स्त्रीपुंसोर्भ्रमतो यथा॥८०॥
पिण्डब्रह्माण्डयोरैक्यं लिङ्गसूत्रात्मनोरपि। स्वापाव्याकृतयोरैक्यं स्वप्रकाशचिदात्मनोः॥८१॥

Diseases are generated in one's body through the following causes, viz., sleeping in daytime, late vigils over night, excess of sexual intercourse, moving in crowd, the checking of the discharge of urine and faeces, the evil of unwholesome food and laborious mental operation with prāṇa. If yogin is afraid of such diseases (when attacked by them), he says, "My disease hae arisen from my practice of yoga." Then he will discontinue this practice. This is said to be the first obstacle to yoga. The second (obstacle) is doubt; the third is carelessness; the fourth, laziness; the fifth, sleep; the sixth, the not leaving of objects (of sense); the seventh, erroneous perception; the eighth, sensual object; the ninth, want of faith; and the tenth, the failure to attain the truth of yoga. A wise man should abandon these ten obstacles after great deliberation. The practice of prāṇāyāma should be performed daily with the mind firmly fixed on Truth. Then citta is absorbed in suṣumnā, and prāṇa (therefore) never moves. When the impurities (of citta) are thus removed and prāṇa is absorbed in suṣumnā, he becomes a (true) yogin. Apāna, which has a downward tendency should be raised up with effort by the contraction (of the anus), and this is spoken of as mūlabandha. Apāna thus raised up mixes with agni and then they go up quickly to the seat of prāṇa. Then prāṇa and apāna uniting with one another go to kuṇḍalinī, which is coiled up and sleep. Kuṇḍalinī being heated by agni and stirred up by vāyu, extends her body in the mouth of suṣumnā, pierces the brahmagranthi formed of rajas, and flashes at once like lightning at the mouth of suṣumnā. Then it goes up at once through viṣṇugranthi to the heart. Then it goes up through rudragranthi and above it to the middle of the eyebrows; having pierced this place, it goes up to the maṇḍala (sphere) of the moon. It dries up the moisture produced by the moon in the anāhatacakra having sixteen petals. When the blood is agitated through the speed of prāṇa, it becomes bile from its contact with the sun, after which it goes to the sphere of the moon where it becomes of the nature of the flow of pure phlegm. How does it (blood) which is very cold become hot when it flows there? (Since) at the same time the intense white form of moon is speedily heated. Then being agitated, it goes up. Through taking in this, citta which was moving amidst sensual objects externally, it restrained there. The novice enjoying this high state attains peace and becomes devoted to Ātmā. Kuṇḍalinī assumes the eight forms of prakṛti (matter) and attain Śiva by encircling him and dissolves itself in Śiva. Thus rajas-śukla (seminal fluid) which rises up goes to Śiva alone with marut (vāyu): prāṇas and apāna which are always produced become equal. Prāṇas flow in all things, great and small, describable or indescribable, as fire in gold. Then this body which is ādhibhautika (composed of elements) becomes ādhidaivata (relating to a tutelar deity) and is thus purified. Then it attains the stage of ativāhika. Then the body being freed from the inert state becomes stainless and of the nature of Cit. In it, the ativāhika become the chief of all, being of the nature of That. Like the conception of the snake in a rope, so the idea of the release from wife and saṁsāra is the delusion of time. Whatever appears is unreal. Whatever is absorbed is unreal. Like the illusory conception of silver in the mother-of-pearl, so is the idea of man and woman. The microcosm and the microcosm are one and the same; so also the liṅga and sūtrātma, svabhāva (substance) and form and the self-resplendent light and Cidātmā.

शक्तिः कुण्डलिनी नाम बिसतन्तुनिभा शुभा। मूलकन्दं फणाग्रेण दृष्ट्वा कमलकन्दवत्॥८२॥

मुखेन पुच्छं संगृह्य ब्रह्मरन्ध्रसमन्विता। पद्मासनगतः स्वस्थो गुदमाकुञ्च्य साधकः॥८३॥

वायुमूर्ध्वगतं कुर्वन्कुम्भकाविष्टमानसः। वाय्वाघातवशादग्निः स्वाधिष्ठानगतो ज्वलन्॥८४॥

ज्वलनाघातपवनाघातैरुन्निद्रितोऽहिराट्। ब्रह्मग्रन्थिं ततो भित्त्वा विष्णुग्रन्थिं भिनत्त्यतः॥८५॥

रुद्रग्रन्थिं च भित्त्वैव कमलानि भिनत्ति षट्। सहस्रकमले शक्तिः शिवेन सह मोदते॥८६॥

सैवावस्था परा ज्ञेया सैव निर्वृतिकारिणी॥८७॥ इति॥

The Śakti named kuṇḍalinī, which is like a thread in the the lotus and is resplendent, is biting with the upper end of its hood (namely, mouth) at the root of the lotus the mūlakanda. Taking hold of its tail with its mouth, it is in contact with the hole of brahmarandhra (or suṣumnā). If a person seated in the padma posture and having accustomed himself of the contraction of his anus makes his vāyu go upward with the mind intent on kumbhaka, then agni comes to svādhiṣṭhāna flamming, owing to the blowing of vāyu. From the blowing of vāyu and agni, the chief (kuṇḍalinī) pierces open the brahmagranthi and then viṣṇugranthi. Then it pierces rudragranthi, after that, (all) the six lotuses (or plexuses). Then Śakti is happy with Śiva in sahasrāra kamala (1,000 lotuses seat or pineal gland). This should be known as the highest avasthā (state) and it alone is the giver of final beatitude. Thus ends the first chapther.

Chapter II

अथाहं संप्रवक्ष्यामि विद्यां खेचरिसंज्ञिकाम्। यथा विज्ञानवानस्या लोकेऽस्मिन्नजरोऽमरः॥१॥

मृत्युव्याधिजराग्रस्तो दृष्ट्वा विद्यामिमां मुने। बुद्धिं दृढतरां कृत्वा खेचरीं तु समभ्यसेत्॥२॥

जरामृत्युगदघ्नो यः खेचरीं वेत्ति भूतले। ग्रन्थतश्चार्थतश्चैव तदभ्यासप्रयोगतः॥३॥

तं मुने सर्वभावेन गुरुं मत्वा समाश्रयेत्। दुर्लभा खेचरी विद्या तदभ्यासोऽपि दुर्लभः॥४॥

अभ्यासं मेलनं चैव युगपन्नैव सिध्यति। अभ्यासमात्रनिरता न विन्दन्ते ह मेलनम्॥५॥

अभ्यासं लभते ब्रह्मञ्जन्मजन्मान्तरे क्वचित्। मेलनं तत्तु जन्मनां शतान्तेऽपि न लभ्यते॥ ६॥
अभ्यासं बहुजन्मान्ते कृत्वा तद्भावसाधितम्। मेलनं लभते कश्चिद्योगी जन्मान्तरे क्वचित्॥ ७॥
यदा तु मेलनं योगी लभते गुरुवक्त्रतः। तदा तत्सिद्धिमाप्नोति यदुक्ता शास्त्रसंततौ॥ ८॥
ग्रन्थतश्चार्थतश्चैव मेलनं लभते यदा। तदा शिवत्वमाप्नोति निर्मुक्तः सर्वसंसृतेः॥ ९॥
शास्त्रं विनापि संबोद्धुं गुरवोऽपि न शक्नुयुः। तस्मात्सुदुर्लभतरं लभ्यं शास्त्रमिदं मुने॥ १०॥
यावन्न लभ्यते शास्त्रं तावद्गां पर्यटेद्यतिः। यदा संलभ्यते शास्त्रं तदा सिद्धिः करे स्थिता॥ ११॥
न शास्त्रेण विना सिद्धिर्दृष्टा चैव जगत्त्रये। तस्मान्मेलनदातारं शास्त्रदातारमच्युतम्॥ १२॥
तदभ्यासप्रदातारं शिवं मत्वा समाश्रयेत्। लब्ध्वा शास्त्रमिदं मह्यमन्येषां न प्रकाशयेत्॥ १३॥
तस्मात्सर्वप्रयत्नेन गोपनीयं विजानता। यत्रास्ते च गुरुर्ब्रह्मन्दिव्ययोगप्रदायकः॥ १४॥
तत्र गत्वा च तेनोक्तविद्यां संगृह्य खेचरीम्। तेनोक्तः सम्यगभ्यासं कुर्यादादावतन्द्रितः॥ १५॥
अनया विद्यया योगी खेचरीसिद्धिभाग्भवेत्। खेचर्या खेचरीं युञ्जन्खेचरीबीजपूरया॥ १६॥
खेचराधिपतिर्भूत्वा खेचरेषु सदा वसेत्। खेचरावसथं वह्निमम्बुमण्डलभूषितम्॥ १७॥
आख्यातं खेचरीबीजं तेन योगः प्रसिध्यति। सोमांशनवकं वर्णं प्रतिलोमेन चोद्धरेत्॥ १८॥
तस्मात् त्र्यंशकमाख्यातमक्षरं चन्द्ररूपकम्। तस्मादप्यष्टमं वर्णं विलोमेन परं मुने॥ १९॥
तथा तत्परमं विद्धि तदादिरपि पञ्चमी। इन्दोश्च बहुभिन्ने च कूटोऽयं परिकीर्तितः॥ २०॥
गुरूपदेशलभ्यं च सर्वयोगप्रसिद्धिदम्। यत्तस्य देहजा माया निरुद्धकरणाश्रया॥ २१॥
स्वप्नेऽपि न लभेत्तस्य नित्यं द्वादशजप्यतः। य इमां पञ्च लक्षाणि जपेदपि सुयन्त्रितः॥ २२॥
तस्य श्रीखेचरीसिद्धिः स्वयमेव प्रवर्तते। नश्यन्ति सर्वविघ्नानि प्रसीदन्ति च देवताः॥ २३॥
वलीपलितनाशश्च भविष्यति न संशयः। एवं लब्ध्वा महाविद्यामभ्यासं कारयेत्ततः॥ २४॥
अन्यथा क्लिश्यते ब्रह्मन्न सिद्धिः खेचरीपथे। यदभ्यासविधौ विद्यां न लभेद्यः सुधामयीम्॥ २५॥
ततः संमेलकादौ च लब्ध्वा विद्यां सदा जपेत्। नान्यथा रहितो ब्रह्मन्न किंचित्सिद्धिभाग्भवेत्॥
यदिदं लभ्यते शास्त्रं यदा विद्यां समाश्रयेत्। ततस्तदोदितां सिद्धिमाशु तां लभते मुनिः॥ २७॥
तालुमूलं समुत्कृष्य सप्तवासरमात्मवित्। स्वगुरूक्तप्रकारेण मलं सर्वं विशोधयेत्॥ २८॥
स्नुहिपत्रनिभं शस्त्रं सुतीक्ष्णं स्निग्धनिर्मलम्। समादाय ततस्तेन रोममात्रं समुच्छिनेत्॥ २९॥
हित्वा सैन्धवपथ्याभ्यां चूर्णिताभ्यां प्रकर्षयेत्। पुनः सप्तदिने प्राप्ते रोममात्रं समुच्छिनेत्॥ ३०॥
एवं क्रमेण षाण्मासं नित्योद्युक्तः समाचरेत्। षाण्मासाद्रसनामूलं सिराबन्धं प्रणश्यति॥ ३१॥
अथ वागीश्वरीधाम शिरो वस्त्रेण वेष्टयेत्। शनैरुत्कर्षयेद्योगी कालवेलाविधानवित्॥ ३२॥
पुनः षाण्मासमात्रेण नित्यं संघर्षणान्मुने। भ्रूमध्यावधि चाप्येति तिर्यक्कर्णबिलावधि॥ ३३॥
अधश्च चुबुकं मूलं प्रयाति क्रमचारिता। पुनः संवत्सराणां तु तृतीयादेव लीलया॥ ३४॥
केशान्तमूर्ध्वं क्रमति तिर्यक्शाखावधिर्मुने। अधस्तात्कण्ठकूपान्तं पुनर्वर्षत्रयेण तु॥ ३५॥

ब्रह्मरन्ध्रं समावृत्य तिष्ठेदेव न संशयः। तिर्यक् चूलितलं याति अधः कण्ठबिलावधिः॥ ३६॥
शनैः शनैर्मस्तकाच्च महावज्रकपाटभित्। पूर्वं बीजयुता विद्या ह्याख्याता याऽतिदुर्लभा॥ ३७॥
तस्याः षडङ्गं कुर्वीत तया षट्स्वरभिन्नया। कुर्यादेवं करन्यासं सर्वसिद्ध्यादिहेतवे॥ ३८॥
शनैरेवं प्रकर्तव्यमभ्यासं युगपन्न हि। युगपद्वर्तते यस्य शरीरं विलयं व्रजेत्॥ ३९॥
तस्माच्छनैः शनैः कार्यमभ्यासं मुनिपुङ्गव। यदा च बाह्यमार्गेण जिह्वा ब्रह्मबिलं व्रजेत्॥ ४०॥
तदा ब्रह्मार्गलं ब्रह्मन्दुर्भेद्यं त्रिदशैरपि। अङ्गुल्यग्रेण संघृष्य जिह्वामात्रंनिवेशयेत्॥ ४१॥
एवं वर्षत्रयं कृत्वा ब्रह्मद्वारं प्रविश्यति। ब्रह्मद्वारे प्रविष्टे तु सम्यङ् मथनमाचरेत्॥ ४२॥
मथनेन विना केचित्साधयन्ति विपश्चितः। खेचरीमन्त्रसिद्धस्य सिध्यते मथनं विना॥ ४३॥
जपं च मथनं चैव कृत्वा शीघ्रं फलं लभेत्। स्वर्णजां रौप्यजां वापि लोहजां वा शलाकिकाम्॥ ४४॥
नियोज्य नासिकारन्ध्रं दुग्धसिक्तेन तन्तुना। प्राणान्निरुध्य हृदये सुखमासनमात्मनः॥ ४५॥
शनैः सुमथनं कुर्याद्भ्रूमध्ये न्यस्तचक्षुषी। षाण्मासं मथनावस्था भावेनैव प्रजायते॥ ४६॥
यथा सुषुप्तिर्बालानां यथा भावस्तथा भवेत्। न सदा मथनं शस्तं मासे मासे समाचरेत्॥ ४७॥
सदा रसनया योगी मार्गं न परिसंक्रमेत्। एवं द्वादशवर्षान्ते संसिद्धिर्भवति ध्रुवा॥ ४८॥
शरीरे सकलं विश्वं पश्यत्यात्मविभेदतः। ब्रह्माण्डोऽयं महामार्गो राजदन्तोर्ध्वकुण्डली॥ ४९॥

I shall hereafter describe the science called khecarī which is such that one who knows it is freed from old age and death in this world. One who is subject to the pains of death, disease and old age should, O sage, on knowing this science make his mind firm and practise khecarī. One should regard that person as his Guru on earth who knows khecarī, the destroyer of old age and death, both from knowing the meaning of books and practice, and should perform it with all his heart. The science of khecarī is not easily attainable, as also its practice. Its practice and melana are not accomplished simultaneously. Those that are bent upon practice alone do not get melana. Only some get the practice, O Brahman, after several births, but melana is not obtained even after a hundred births. Having undergone the practice after several births, some (solitary) yogin gets the melana in some future bitrth as the result of his practice. When a yogin gets this melana from the mouth of his Guru, then he obtains the siddhis mentioned in the several books. When a man gets this melana through books and the significance, then he attains the state of Śiva freed from all rebirth. Even Guru may not be able to know this without books. Therefore this science is very difficult to master. An ascetic should wander over the earth so long as he fails to get this science, and when this science is obtained, then he has got the siddhi in his hand (viz., mastered the psychical powers). Therefore one should regard as Acyuta (Viṣṇu) the person who imparts the melana, as also him who gives out the science. He should regard as Śiva him who teaches the practice. Having got this science from me, you should not reveal it to others. Therefore one who knows this should protect it with all his efforts (viz., should never give it out except to persons who deserve it). O Brahman, one should go to the place where lives the Guru, who is able to teach the divine yoga and there learn from him the science khecarī, and being then teach the divine yoga and there learn from him the science khecarī, and being then thought well by him, should at first practise it carefully. By means of this science, a person will attain the siddhi of khecarī. Joining with khecarī śakti (viz., kuṇḍalinī śakti) by means of the (science) of khecarī which contains the bīja (seed of letter) of khecarī, one becomes the lord of the khecaras (Devas) and lives always amongst them. Kheharī bījā (seed-letter) is spoken of as agni encircles with water and as the abode of khecaras (Devas). Through this yoga, siddhi is mastered. The ninth (bīja) letter of somāṁśa (soma or moon part) should also be pronounced in the reverse order. Then a letter composed of three aṁśas of the form of moon has been described; and after that, the eighth letter should be pronounced in the reverse order; then consider it as the supreme and its beginning as the fifth, and this is said to the kūṭa (horns) of the several bhinnas (or parts) of the moon. This which tends to the accomplishment of all yogas, should be learnt through the initiation of a Guru. He who recites this twelve times every day, will not get even in sleep that māyā (illusion) which is born in his body and which is the source of all vicious deeds. He who recites this five lakhs of times with every great care— to him the science of khecarī will reveal itself. All obstacles vanish and the devas are pleased. The destruction of valīpalita (viz., wrinkle and grayness of hair) will take place without doubt. Having acquired this great science, one should practise it afterwards. If not, O Brahman, he will suffer without getting any siddhi in the path of khecarī. If one does not get this nectarlike science in his practice, he should get it in the beginning of melana and recite it always; (else) one who is without never gets siddhi. As soon as he gets this science, he should practise it; and then the sage will soon get the siddhi. Having drawn out the tongue from the root of palate, a knower of Ātmā should clear the impurity (of the tongue) for seven days according to the advice of his Guru. He should take a sharp knife which is oiled and cleaned and which resembles the leaf of the plant snuhī ("Euphorbia antiquorum") and should cut for the space of a hair (the fraenum Lingui). Having powdered saindhava (rock-salt) and pathya (sea-salt), he should apply it to the place. On the seventh day, he should again cut for the space of a hair. Thus for the space of six months, he should continue it always gradually with great care. In six months, Śiro-bandha (bandha at the head) which is at the root of the tongue is destroyed. Then the yogin who knows timely action should encircle with Śīro-vastra (lit., the cloth of the head) the Vāk-Īśvarī (the deity presiding over speech) and should draw (it) up. Again by daily drawing it up for six months, it comes, O sage, as far as the middle of the eyebrows and obliquely up to the opening of the ears; having gradually practised, it goes to the root of the chin. Then in three years, it goes up easily to the end of the hair (of the head). It goes up obliquely to Śākha and downwards to the well of the throat. In another three years, it occupies brahmarandhra and stops there without doubt. Crosswise it goes up to the top of the head and downwards to the well of the throat. Gradually it opens the great adamantine door in the head. The rare science (of khecarī) bīja has been explained before. One should perform the six aṅgas (parts) of this mantra by pronouncing it in six different intonations. One should do this in order to attain all the siddhis; and this karanyāsam should be done gradually and not all at a time, since the body of one who does it all at once will soon decay. Therefore it should be practised, O best of sages, little by little. When the tongue goes to the brahmarandhra through the outer path, then one should place the tongue after moving the bolt of Brahmā which cannot be mastered by the devas. On doing this for three years with the point of the finger, he should make the tongue enter within : then it enters brahmadvāra (or hole). On entering the brahmadvāra, one should practise mathana (churning) well. Some intelligent men attain siddhi even without mathana. One who is versed in khecarī Mantra accomplishes it without mathana. By doing the japa and mathana, one reaps the fruits soon. By connecting a wire made of gold, silver or iron with the nostrils by means of a thread soaked in milk, one should restrain his breath in his heart and seated a convenient posture with his eyes concentrated between his eyebrows, he should perform mathana slowly. In six months, the state of mathana becomes natural like sleep in children. And it is not advisable to do mathana always. It should be done (once) only in every month. A yogin should not reolve his tongue in the path. After doing this for twelve years, siddhis are surely obtained. Then he sees the whole universe in his body as not being different from Ātmā. This path of the ūrdhvakuṇḍalinī (higher kuṇḍalinī), O chief of kings conquers the macrocosm. Thus ends the second chapter.

Chapter III

मेलनमन्त्र: ह्रीं भं सं मं पं सं क्षम्। पद्मज उवाच। अमावास्या च प्रतिपत्पौर्णमासी च शंकर।
अस्या: का वर्ण्यते संज्ञा एतदाख्याहि तत्त्वत:।। १।।
प्रतिपद्दिनतोऽकाले अमावास्या तथैव च। पौर्णमास्यां स्थिरीकुर्यात्स च पन्था हि नान्यथा।। २।।
कामेन विषयाकाङ्क्षी विषयात्काममोहित:। द्वावेव संत्यजेन्नित्यं निरञ्जनमुपाश्रयेत्।। ३।।
अपरं संत्यजेत्सर्वं यदीच्छेदात्मनो हितम्। शक्तिमध्ये मन: कृत्वा मन: शक्तेश्च मध्यगम्।। ४।।
मनसा मन आलोक्य तत्त्यजेत्परमं पदम्। मन एव हि बिन्दुश्च उत्पत्तिस्थितिकारणम्।। ५।।
मनसोत्पद्यते बिन्दुर्यथा क्षीरं घृतात्मकम्। न च बन्धनमध्यस्थं तद्वै कारणमानसम्।। ६।।
चन्द्रार्कमध्यमा शक्तिर्यत्रस्था तत्र बन्धनम्। ज्ञात्वा सुषुम्नां तद्भेदं कृत्वा वायुं च मध्यगम्।। ७।।
स्थित्वासौ बैन्दवस्थाने घ्राणरन्ध्रे निरोधयेत्। वायुं बिन्दुं समाख्यातं सत्त्वं प्रकृतिमेव च।। ८।।
षट् चक्राणि परिज्ञात्वा प्रविशेत्सुखमण्डलम्। मूलाधारं स्वाधिष्ठानं मणिपूरं तृतीयकम्।। ९।।
अनाहतं विशुद्धिं च आज्ञाचक्रं च षष्ठकम्। आधारं गुदमित्युक्तं स्वाधिष्ठानं तु लैङ्गिकम्।। १०।।
मणिपूरं नाभिदेशं हृदयस्थमनाहतम्। विशुद्धि: कण्ठमूले च आज्ञाचक्रं च मस्तकम्।। ११।।
षट् चक्राणि परिज्ञात्वा प्रविशेत्सुखमण्डले। प्रविशेद्वायुमाकृष्य तथैवोर्ध्वं नियोजयेत्।। १२।।
एवं समभ्यसेद्वायुं स ब्रह्माण्डमयो भवेत्। वायुं बिन्दुं तथा चक्रं चित्तं चैव समभ्यसेत्।। १३।।

Melanamantra— ह्रीं (Hrīm), भं (bham), सं (sam), फं (pham), सं (sam), and क्षं (kṣam).

The lotus-born (Brahmā) said : O Śaṅkara, (among) new moon (the first day of the lunar fortnight) and full moon, which is spoken of as its mantra's) sign? In the first day of lunar fortnight and during new moon and full moon (days), It should be made firm and there is no other way (or time). A man longs for an object through passion and is infatuated with passion for objects. One should always leave these two and seek the Nirañjana (stainless). He should abandon everything else which he thinks is favourable to himself. Keeping the manas in the midst of śakti, and śakti in the midst of manas, one should look into manas by means of manas. Then he leaves even the highest stage. Manas alone is the bindu, the cause of creation and preservation. It is only through manas that bindu is produced, like the curd from milk. The organs of manas is not that which is situated in the middle of bandhana. Bandhana is there where Śakti is between the sun and moon. Having known suṣumnā and its bheda (piercing) and making the vāyu go in the middle, one should stand in the seat of bindu, and close the nostrils, Having known vāyu, the above-mentioned bindu and the sattva-prakṛti as well as the six cakras, one should enter the sukha-maṇḍala (viz., the sahasrāra or pineal gland, the sphere of happinss). There are six cakras. Mūlādhāra is in the anus; svādhiṣṭhana is near the genital organ; maṇipūraka is in the navel; anāhata is in the heart; viśuddhi is at the root of the neck and ajñā is in the head (between the two eyebrows). Having known these six maṇḍalas (spheres), one should enter the sukhamaṇḍala (pineal gland), drawing up the vāyu and should sent it (vāyu) upwards. He who practises thus (the control of) vāyu becomes one with brahmāṇḍa (the macrocosm). He should practise (or master) vāyu, bindu, citta, and cakra.

समाधिमेकेन सममममृतं यान्ति योगिनः। यथाग्निर्दारुमध्यस्थो नोत्तिष्ठेन्मथनं विना॥ १४॥
विना चाभ्यासयोगेन ज्ञानदीपस्तथा न हि। घटमध्यगतो दीपो बाह्ये नैव प्रकाशते॥ १५॥
भिन्ने तस्मिन्घटे चैव दीपज्वाला च भासते। स्वकायं घटमित्युक्तं यथा दीपो हि तत्पदम्॥ १६॥
गुरुवाक्यसमाभिन्ने ब्रह्मज्ञानं स्फुटीभवेत्। कर्णधारं गुरुं प्राप्य कृत्वा सूक्ष्मं तरन्ति च॥ १७॥
अभ्यासवासनाशक्त्या तरन्ति भवसागरम्। परायामङ्कुरीभूय पश्यन्त्यां द्विदलीकृता॥ १८॥
मध्यमायां मुकुलिता वैखर्यां विकसीकृता। पूर्वं यथोदिता या वाग्विलोमेनास्तगा भवेत्॥ १९॥
तस्या वाचः परो देवः कूटस्थो वाक्प्रबोधकः। सोऽहमस्मीति निश्चित्य यः सदा वर्तते पुमान्॥ २०
शब्दैरुच्चावचैर्नीचैर्भाषितोऽपि न लिप्यते। विश्वश्च तैजसश्चैव प्राज्ञश्चेति च ते त्रयः॥ २१॥
विराड्ढिरण्यगर्भश्च ईश्वरश्चेति ते त्रयः। ब्रह्माण्डं चैव पिण्डाण्डं लोका भूरादयः क्रमात्॥ २२॥
स्वस्वोपाधिलयादेव लीयन्ते प्रत्यगात्मनि। अण्डं ज्ञानाग्निना तप्तं लीयते कारणैः सह॥ २३॥
परमात्मनि लीनं तत्परं ब्रह्मैव जायते। ततः स्तिमितगम्भीरं न तेजो न तमस्ततम्॥ २४॥
अनाख्यमनभिव्यक्तं सत्किंचिदवशिष्यते। ध्यात्वा मध्यस्थमात्मानं कलशान्तरदीपवत्॥ २५॥
अङ्गुष्ठमात्रमात्मानमधूमज्योतिरूपकम्। प्रकाशयन्तमन्तःस्थं ध्यायेत्कूटस्थमव्ययम्॥ २६॥
विज्ञानात्मा तथा देहे जाग्रत्स्वप्नसुषुप्तितः। मायया मोहितः पश्चाद्बहुजन्मान्तरे पुनः॥ २७॥

सत्कर्मपरिपाकात्तु स्वविकारं चिकीर्षति। कोऽहं कथमयं दोषः संसाराख्य उपागतः॥२८॥

Yogins attain the nectar of equality through samādhi alone. Just as the fire latent in (sacrificial) wood does not appear without churning, so the lamp of wisdom does not arise without the abhyāsa yoga (or practice of yoga). The fire placed in a vessel does not give light outside. When the vessel is broken, its light appears without. One's body is spoken of as the vessel, and the seat of 'That' is the fire (or light) within; and when (the body) is broken through the words of a Guru, the light of brahmajñāna becomes resplendent. With the Guru as the helmsman, one crosses the subtle body and the ocean of saṁsāra through the affinities of practice. That vāk (power of speech) which sprouts in parā, gives fourth two leaves in paśyantī, buds forth in madhyamā and blossoms in vaikharī— that vāk which has before been described, reaches the state of the absorption of sound, reversing the above order (viz., beginning with vaikharī, etc). Whoever thinks that He who is great lord of that vāk, who is the undifferentiated and who is the illuminator of that vāk is Self; whoever thinks over thus, is never affected by words, high or low (or good or bad). The three (aspects of consciousness), viśva, taijasa and prāṇa (in man), the three Virāṭ, Hiraṇyagarbha, and Īśvara in the universe, the egg of the universe, the egg of man and the seven worlds— all these in turn are absorbed in Pratyagātma through the absorption of their respective upādhis (vehicles). The egg being heated by the fire of jñāna is absorbed with its kāraṇa (cause) into Paramātmā (Universal Self). Then it becomes one with Parabrahman. It is then neither steadiness nor depth, neither light nor darkness, neither describable nor distinguishable. Sat (Be-ness) alone remains. One should think of Ātmā as being within the body like a light in a vessel. Ātmā is of the dimensions of a thumb, is a light without smoke and without form, is shining within (the body) and is undifferentiated and immutable.

जाग्रत्स्वप्ने व्यवहरन्त्सुषुप्तौ क्व गतिर्मम। इति चिन्तापरो भूत्वा स्वभासा च विशेषतः॥२९॥

अज्ञानात्तु चिदाभासो बहिस्तापेन तापितः। दग्धं भवत्येव तदा तूलपिण्डमिवाग्निना॥३०॥

दहरस्थः प्रत्यगात्मा नष्टे ज्ञाने ततः परम्। विततो व्याप्य विज्ञानं दहत्येव क्षणेन तु॥३१॥

मनोमयज्ञानमयान्त्सम्यग्दग्ध्वा क्रमेण तु। घटस्थदीपवच्छश्वदन्तरेव प्रकाशते॥३२॥

The Vijñāna Ātmā that dwells in this body is deluded by māyā during the states of waking, dreaming, and dreamless sleep; but after many births, owing to the effect of good karma, it wishes to attain its own state. Who am I? How has this stain of mundane existence accrued to me? What becomes in the dreamless sleep of me who am engaged in business in waking and dreaming states? Just as a bale of cotton is burnt by fire, so the Cidābhāsa which is the result of non-wisdom, is burnt by the (wise) thoughts like the above and by its own supreme illuminations. The outer burning (of body as done in world) is no burning at all. When the worldly wisdom is destroyed, Pratyagātma that is in the dahara (ākāśa or ether of the heart) obtains vijñāna, diffusing itself everywhere and burns in an instant jñānamaya and manomaya (sheaths). After this, He himself shines always within, like a light within a vessel.

ध्यायन्नास्ते मुनिश्चैवमासुप्तेरामृतेस्तु यः। जीवन्मुक्तः स विज्ञेयः स धन्यः कृतकृत्यवान्॥ ३ ३॥
जीवन्मुक्तपदं त्यक्त्वा स्वदेहे कालसात्कृते। विशत्यदेहमुक्तत्वं पवनोऽस्पन्दतामिव॥ ३ ४॥
अशब्दमस्पर्शमरूपमव्ययं तथाऽरसं नित्यमगन्धवच्च यत्।
अनाद्यनन्तं महतः परं ध्रुवं तदेव शिष्यत्यमलं निरामयम्॥ इत्युपनिषत्॥ ३ ५॥

That muni who contemplates thus till sleep and till death is to be known as a jīvanmukta. Having done what ought to be done, he is a fortunate person. And having given up (even) the state of a jīvanmukta, he attains videhamukti (emancipation in a disembodied state), after his body wears off. He attains the state, as if of moving in the air. Then That alone remains which is soundless, touchless, formless and deathless, which is the rasa (essence), eternal and odourless, which had neither beginning nor end, which is greater than the great, and which is permanent, stainless and decayless.

॥ॐ सह नाववतु ...... इति शान्तिः॥

॥इति योगकुण्डल्युपनिषत्समाप्ता॥

78. RUDRĀKṢAJĀBĀLOPANIṢAD

रुद्राक्षजाबालोपनिषद्

This Upaniṣad is related to the tradition of Sāmaveda. It is the cardinal objective of Upaniṣad to reveal the excessive importance of Rudrākṣa. Initially, there is discussion between Bhusuṇḍa and Kālāgnirudra. Bhusuṇḍa has asked about the origin of Rudrākṣa and the first of its holding. Kālāgnirudra, the lord has given its answer in detail. He has described in a sensation the origin of Rudrākṣa, the fruit of holding and japa (silent recital) of rudrākṣa, the best medium and mean kinds of rudrākṣa, its kinds– Brāhmaṇa, Kṣatriya, Vaiśya, and Śūdra, acceptable, non-acceptable rudrākṣa, the provision of holding rudrākṣa in braid etc. places, holding hymns, distinction of rudrākṣa according their mouth (from one mouth to fourteen mouths), the rules prohibiting flesh diet etc. for the persons holding rudrākṣa and last by the fruit of knowing rudrākṣa learning has been described. Thus, everything about rudrākṣa has been explained in detail.

॥शान्तिपाठः॥

ॐ आप्यायन्तु......... इति शान्तिः॥

अथ हैनं कालाग्निरुद्रं भुसुण्डः पप्रच्छ कथं रुद्राक्षोत्पत्तिः। तद्धारणात्किं फलमिति॥१॥

Bhusuṇḍa once asked Kālāgnirudra– 'O god! How the rudrākṣa was originated and what is the benefit availed by holding it?'

तं होवाच भगवान्कालाग्निरुद्रः त्रिपुरवधार्थमहं निमीलिताक्षोऽभवम्। तेभ्यो जलबिन्दवो भूमौ पतितास्ते रुद्राक्षा जाताः। सर्वानुग्रहार्थाय तेषां नामोच्चारमात्रेण दशगोप्रदानफलं दर्शनस्पर्शनाभ्यां द्विगुणं फलमत ऊर्ध्वं उक्तं न शक्नोमि॥२॥

Lord Kālāgnirudra then replied– "The drops of water were fell on the ground from the eyes and they turned into Rudrākṣa when I closed eyes for meditation in order to kill the monster Tripura. I am saying for the benevolence of all that even the name recited as rudrākṣa endows with the fruit of giving ten cows in donation and two tones more fruit is obtained when rudrākṣa is seen and touched. What more can be said in the master.

तत्रैते श्लोका भवन्ति– कस्मिंस्थितं तु किं नाम कथं वा धार्यते नरैः। कतिभेदमुखान्यत्र कैर्मंत्रैर्धार्यते कथम॥३॥

These hymns have been contemplated about it (the question is) where it is existed? What is its name? How the man should hold ? How many kinds of it are? What hymns are to be recited while holding it?

दिव्यवर्षसहस्राणि चक्षुरुन्मीलितं मया। भूमावक्षिपुटाभ्यां तु पतिता जबबिन्दवः॥४॥

(Answer is) at the state of meditation when I opened the eyes after the flux of one thousand divine years, water drops came out from eyes and fell on the earth.

तत्राश्रुबिन्दवो जाता महारुद्राक्षवृक्षकाः। स्थावरत्वमनुप्राप्य भक्तानुग्रहकारणात्॥५॥

That drops on the same spot of earth were turned into the shape of Mahārudrākṣa tree and became stable for doing grace on the devotees.

भक्तानां धारणात्पापं दिवारात्रिकृतं हरते। लक्षं तु दर्शनात्पुण्यं कोटिस्तद्धारणाद्भवेत्॥६॥

तस्य कोटिशतं पुण्यं लभते धारणान्नरः। लक्षकोटिसहस्राणि लक्षकोटिशतानि च॥७॥

तज्जपाल्लभते पुण्यं नरो रुद्राक्षधारणात्। धात्रीफलप्रमाणं यच्छ्रेष्ठमेतदुदाहृतम्॥८॥

It removes the sins committed by the devotee in the day and night who holds it. Mere seeing it endows with lakh times and crore times fruits when it is held. The devotee holding it obtains a billion time more fruit than its Japa (silent recital). It becomes hundred time to lakh and thousand time than one lakh crore of the same if it is held with sheer obedience. The man obtains the fruit of rudra-japa when it is held by him. The rudrākṣa equal to the size of a myrobalan is considered as the best rudrākṣa.

[The fruitfulness of seeing and holding the rudrākṣa has been decribed herein. Generally, its exceptional power is untraced but the devotees and the people holding rudrākṣa opine that simultaneous to the excessive property of metaphysics, the rudrākṣa is powerful remedy for the heart ailments. It appears that its magnificence has been described exaggeratly here.]

बदरीफलमात्रं तु मध्यमं प्रोच्यते बुधैः। अधमं चणमात्रं स्यात्प्रक्रियैषा मयोच्यते॥९॥

The rudrākṣa in the size of jujube plum (badarī fruit) is stated as medium and the rudrākṣa of gram seeds size is mean (Adhama). Now, the procedure (for holding) is described.

ब्राह्मणः क्षत्रिया वैश्याः शूद्राश्चेति शिवाज्ञया। वृक्षा जाताः पृथिव्यां तु तज्जातीयाः शुभाक्षकाः॥१०॥

That all benevolent rudrākṣa was originated as directed by Lord Śiva in the form of the Brāhmaṇa, Kṣatriya, Vaiśya and Śūdra for the welfare of the respective castes.

श्वेतास्तु ब्राह्मणा ज्ञेयाः क्षत्रिया रक्तवर्णकाः। पीतास्तु वैश्या विज्ञेयाः कृष्णाः शूद्रा उदाहृताः॥११॥

The white colour rudrākṣa is stated Brāhmaṇa, the red colour, Kṣatriya, yellow, the Vaiśya and the black colour rudrākṣa is stated as Śūdra.

ब्राह्मणो बिभृयाच्छ्वेतान्रक्तान्राजा तु धारयेत्। पीतान्वैश्यस्तु बिभृयात्कृष्णाञ्छूद्रस्तु धारयेत्॥१२॥

The Brāhmaṇa should hold white, the kṣatriya red, the Vaiśya yellow and the Śūdra should hold the black rudrākṣa.

समाः स्निग्धा दृढाः स्थूलाः कण्टकैः संयुताः शुभाः। कृमिदष्टं छिन्नभिन्नं कण्टकैर्हीनमेव च॥१३॥

व्रणयुक्तमयुक्तं च षड्रुद्राक्षाणि वर्जयेत्। स्वयमेव कृतद्वारं रुद्राक्षं स्यादिहोत्तमम्॥१४॥

The sturdy, smooth, spherical uniformly, and with their horn's, rudrākṣa is considered best and the six kinds of rudrākṣa i.e. eaten by insect, splited without horn, holed by insects and ugly are forbidden. However, the natural hole beaning rudrākṣa is stated as the best rudrākṣa.

यत्तु पौरुषयत्नेन कृतं तन्मध्यमं भवेत्। समान्स्त्रिग्धान् दृढान् स्थूलान् क्षौमसूत्रेण धारयेत्।।१५।।

The rudrākṣa in which hole is made (for intertwining with the garland) is stated as medium. In order to hold, the uniform in size and shape, smooth, solid, and thick rudrākṣa should be intertwined in the silk thread.

सर्वगात्रेण सौम्येन सामान्यानि विचक्षणः। निकषे हेमरेखाभा यस्य रेखा प्रदृश्यते।।१६।।

तदक्षमुत्तमं विद्यात्तद्धार्यं शिवपूजकैः। शिखायामेकरुद्राक्षं त्रिंशतं शिरसा वहेत्।।१७।।

The size of all rudrākṣa should be common, tender and uniform. The devotees to lord Śiva should hold the rudrākṣa on which the golden lines are seen. One rudrākṣa on braid and thirty rudrākṣa should be hold on herd duly inter-thrived with a garland.

षट्त्रिंशतं गले दध्याद्बाहो षोडशषोडश। मणिबन्धे द्वादशैव स्कन्धे पञ्चदशं वहेत्।।१८।।

Thirty six rudrākṣa round the throat, sixteen each on arms, twelve rudrākṣa on the wrist and fifteen on shoulder should be held.

अष्टोत्तरशतैर्मालामुपवीतं प्रकल्पयेत्। द्विसरं त्रिसरं वापि सराणां पञ्चकं तथा।।१९।।

सराणां सप्तकं वापि बिभृयात्कण्छदेशतः। मुकुटे कुण्डले चैव कर्णिकाहारकेऽपि वा।।२०।।

A garland containing one hundred eight rudrākṣa should be held like the sacrificial thread (upavīta). A garland (compact of three garlands in one) should be held on the neck. The rudrākṣas should be held as ear-rings, Kuṇḍala and as the crown too.

केयूरकटके सूत्रं कुक्षिबन्धे विशेषतः। सुप्ते पीते सदाकालं रुद्राक्षं धारयेन्नरः।।२१।।

A garland intertwined with specific thread should be held in awaking and sleeping i.e., all time as wristlace and Kukṣibanda (round the armpit).

त्रिषतह त्वधमं पञ्चशतं मध्यममुच्यते। सहस्रमुत्तमं प्रोक्तमेवं भेदेन धारयेत्।।२२।।

The rudrākṣas should be held when the distinction is known properly that holding one thousand rudrākṣa is the best, five hundred, the medium and three hundred rudrākṣa as mean (Adhama).

शिरसीशानमंत्रेण कण्ठे तत्पुरुषेण तु। अघोरेण गले धार्यं तेनैव हृदयेऽपि च।।२३।।

While holding on head, the hymn "Īśānaḥ sarva hidyānāṁ," the hymn "Tatpuruṣā vidmahe mahāderāya, while holding round the throat and "Aghorebhyo" should be recited while holding rudrākṣa in the neck and chest.

अघोरबीजमन्त्रेण करयोर्धारयेत्सुधीः। पञ्चादशदक्षग्रथितान्व्योव्याप्यपि चोदरे।।२४।।

पञ्च ब्रह्मभिरङ्गैश्च त्रिमाला पञ्च सप्त च। ग्रथित्वा मूलमन्त्रेण सर्वाण्यक्षाणि धारयेत्।।२५।।

The scholars should hold rudrākṣa by reciting Aghora Bīja hymn. While inserting the thread in the hole made in middle portion, the fifty letters falling from A to Kṣa should be recited with sheer obeisance. The rudrākṣa should then be spelled with the hymn of five Brahma or the hymn containing five letters i.e. "Oṁ Namaḥ śivāye". Then he should hold like seven, five or three garlands after intertwining with recital of the basic hymn according to Akṣamālikopaṇisad.

अथ हैनं भगवन्तं कालाग्निरुद्रं भुसुण्डः पप्रच्छ रुद्राक्षाणां भेदेन यदक्षं यत्स्वरूपं यत्फलमिति। तत्स्वरूपं मुखयुक्तमरिष्टनिरसनं कामाभीष्टफलं ब्रूहीति होवाच॥२६॥

Then Bhusuṇḍa raised a query before lord Kālāgnirudra regarding the kinds of rudrākṣa, their nature and the fruit of holding them. He requester further to tell about effacing the adversity and attainment of desired front from the distinct mouths of rudrākṣa.

तत्रैते श्लोका भवन्ति–

एकवक्त्रं तु रुद्राक्षं परतत्त्वस्वरूपकम्। तद्धारणात्परे तत्त्वे लीयते विजितेन्द्रियः॥२७॥

These are the hymns about it. The rudrākṣa of one mouth is the apparent form of supreme element. The person who holds sensory organs of (controlling), they engrosses in the supreme element (Parātpara tattva) Śiva.

द्विवक्त्रं तु मुनिश्रेष्ठ चार्धनारीश्वरात्मकम्। धारणादर्धनारीशः प्रीयते तस्य नित्यशः॥२८॥

O great hermit! The rudrākṣa of two mouths has been stated in Ardhanārīśvara form. Lord Śiva always grace the person holding such rudrākṣa.

त्रिमुखं चैव रुद्राक्षमग्नित्रयस्वरूपकम्। तद्धारणाच्च हुतभुक्तस्य तुष्यति नित्यदा॥२९॥

The rudrākṣa of three mouths is stated in the form of trio fire (Agnitraya) lord fire always be graceful for that devotee.

चतुर्मुखं तु रुद्राक्षं चतुर्वक्त्रस्वरूपकम्। तद्धारणाच्चतुर्वक्त्रः प्रीयते तस्य नित्यदा॥३०॥

The four mouth rudrākṣa is stated in the form of caturmukha Lord (Brahmā). Lord Brahmā always be grateful to him.

पञ्चवक्त्रं तु रुद्राक्षं पञ्चब्रह्मस्वरूकम्। पञ्चवक्त्रः स्वयं ब्रह्म पुंहत्यां च व्यपोहति॥३१॥

The rudrākṣa of five mouths is stated Pañcabrahma i.e., lord Śiva of some mouths. Lord Śiva in the form of Brahmā effaces the deject of homicide himself.

षड्वक्त्रमपि रुद्राक्षं कार्तिकेयाधिदैवतम्। तद्धारणान्महाश्रीः स्यान्महदारोग्यमुत्तमम्॥३२॥

The six mouths rudrākṣa is stated in the form of Kārtikeya. Goddess Mahālakṣmī graces on such person and provides good health.

मतिविज्ञानसंपत्तिशुद्धये धारयेत्सुधीः। विनायकाधिदैवं च प्रवदन्ति मनीषिणः॥३३॥

Scholars consider it in the form of Lord Gaṇeśa. Hence they opine that the wise people should hold it for the increase of learning, wisdom and wealth.

सप्तवक्त्रं तु रुद्राक्षं सप्तमात्रधिदैवतम्। तद्धारणान्महाश्रीः स्यान्महदारोग्यमुत्तमम्॥३४॥

The rudrākṣa of seven mouth is in the form of seven worlds, seven Mātṛśakti (Brahmā, Vaiṣṇavī etc.). Great health and best health in ensured by holding it.

महती ज्ञानसंपत्तिः शुचिर्धारणतः सदा। अष्टवक्त्रं तु रुद्राक्षमष्टमात्रधिदैवतम्॥३५॥

वस्वष्टकप्रियं चैव गङ्गाप्रीतिकरं तथा। तद्धारणादिमे प्रीता भवेयुः सत्यवादिनः।।३६।।

Excellent knowledge and wealth is received as a result of holding it with purity always. The rudrākṣa of eight mouth is said in the form of eight mothers. It is also called favourite to Aṣṭavasu. It is favourite to Gaṅgā also. The truthful man gets grace of these three by holding it.

नववक्त्रं तु रुद्राक्षं नवशक्त्याधिदैवतम्। तस्य धारणमात्रेण प्रीयन्ते नव शक्तयः।।३७।।

The nine mouth rudrākṣa is called the god holding nine powers. The holder of it attains the grace and pleasure of nine powers.

दशवक्त्रं तु रुद्राक्षं यमदैवत्यमीरितम्। दर्शनाच्छान्तिजनकं धारणान्नात्र संशयः।।३८।।

The rudrākṣa of ten mouth is called in the form of god Yama (god of death). There is not even an iota of doubt that its mere seeing gives peace and holding gives supreme peace.

एकादशमुख त्वक्षं रुद्रैकादशदैवतम्। तदिदं दैवतं प्राहुः सदा सौभाग्यवर्धनम्।।३९।।

The rudrākṣa of eleven mouths is called in the form of eleven rudra. The eleven rudra always enhance the luck.

रुद्राक्षं द्वादशमुखं महाविष्णुस्वरूपकम्। द्वादशादित्यरूपं च बिभर्त्येव हि तत्परः।।४०।।

The twelve mouth rudrākṣa is considered in the form of Mahāviṣṇu. It is also considered in the form of twelve suns too. The person holding it become Tatpara viz., in the form of lord Mahāviṣṇu and twelve suns.

त्रयोदशमुखं त्वक्षं कामदं सिद्धिदं शुभम्। तस्य धारणमात्रेण कामदेवः प्रसीदति।।४१।।

The rudrākṣa of thirteen mouth has been considered endower of desires and accomplishment. Its more holding ensures the grace of Kāmadeva (the god of love). It has been stated all way benevolent.

चतुर्दशमुखं चाक्षं रुद्रनेत्रसमुद्भवम्। सर्वव्याधिहरं चैव सर्वदारोग्यमाप्नुयात्।।४२।।

The origin of fourteen mouth rudrākṣa has been taken place from the eyes of apparent lord Rudra. It endows with robust wealth and acts like panacea.

मद्यं मांसं च लशुनं पलाण्डुं शिग्रुमेव च। श्लेष्मातकं विड्वराहमभक्ष्यं वर्जयेन्नरः।।४३।।

The devotee holding rudrākṣa should abandon eating garlic, onion, Śigru (mushroom like thing), viḍvarāha (a vegetable), liquor and the flesh etc. for hidden things.

ग्रहणे विषुवे चैवमयने संक्रमेऽपि च। दर्शेषु पूर्णमासे च पूर्णेषु दिवसेषु च।
रुद्राक्षधारणात्सद्यः सर्वपापैः प्रमुच्यते।।४४।।

The man immediately gets rid of the evils if the rudrākṣa is held on Amāvasyā (the fifteenth day of dark fortnight), full-moon day at the adjunct of Āyaṇa (Uttārāyaṇa-Dakṣiṇāyana), at the time of transition (Saṁkrānti) of Libra, Aries etc., the day when the tone of day and night is equal at the tone of sun set, and at the time of eclipse (Sun and moon).

रुद्राक्षमूलं तद्ब्रह्म तन्नालं विष्णुरेव च। तन्मुखं रुद्र इत्याहुस्तद्बिन्दुः सर्वदेवताः॥४५॥

Brahma resides in the base, lord Viṣṇu at the spot of hold, Śiva on the lines drawn on rudrākṣa i.e. mouth and all gods reside in the horn form spots of rudrākṣa.

अथ कालाग्निरुद्रं भगवन्तं सनत्कुमारः पप्रच्छाधीहि भगवन्रुद्राक्षधारणविधिम्। तस्मिन्समये निदाघजडभरतदत्तात्रेयकात्यायनभरद्वाजकपिलवसिष्ठपिप्पलादयश्च कालाग्निरुद्रं परिसमेत्योचुः। अथ कालाग्निरुद्रः किमर्थं भवतामागमनमिति होवाच। रुद्राक्षधारणविधिं वै सर्वे श्रोतुमिच्छामह इति॥४६॥

The king hermit Sanatkumara then asked lord Kālāgnirudra– "O lord! Please tell me the manner of holding rudrākṣa." Nidāgha, Jaḍabharata, Dattātreya, Kātyāyana, Bharadvāja, Kapila, Vasiṣṭha, Pippalāda etc. hermits in the meantime seated on Āsanas around lord Kālāgnirudra. Lord Kālāgnirudra then asked them– "why all of you have come here?" The hermits replied that they also are curious to know the manner of holding rudrākṣa.

अथ कालाग्निरुद्रः प्रोवाच। रुद्रस्य नयनादुत्पन्ना रुद्राक्षा इति लोके ख्यायन्ते। अथ सदाशिवः संहारकाले संहारं कृत्वा संहाराक्षं मुकुलीकरोति। तन्नयनाज्जाता रुद्राक्षा इति होवाच। तस्माद्रुद्राक्षत्वमिति कालाग्निरुद्रः प्रोवाच॥४७॥

Lord Kālāgnirudra then told– "It is called rudrākṣa as it has originated form the eyes of lord Rudra. When Lord Śiva at the time of great devastation (pralaya) closed his destructive eyes after destruction made by him, rudrākṣa was originated. This is the reason for its recognition as rudrākṣa. Thus lord Kālāgnirudra told the facts related to the origin of rudrākṣa.

तद्रुद्राक्षे वाग्विषये कृते दशगोप्रदानेन यत्फलमवाप्नोति तत्फलमश्नुते। स एष भस्मज्योती रुद्राक्ष इति। तद्रुद्राक्षं करेण स्पृष्ट्वा धारणमात्रेण त्रिसहस्त्रगोप्रदानफलं भवति। तद्रुद्राक्षे कर्णयोर्धार्यमाणे एकादशसहस्त्रगोप्रदानफलं भवति। एकादशरुद्रत्वं च गच्छति। तद्रुद्राक्षे शिरसि धार्यमाणे कोटिगोप्रदानफलं भवति। एतेषां स्थानानां कर्णयोः फलं वक्तुं न शक्यमिति होवाच॥४८॥

The fruit obtained as a result of giving ten cows as gift is same as reciting the name of rudrākṣa. It is also called as Bhasmajyoti rudrākṣa, Holding rudrākṣa after touching it with hands ensures the fruit as world have obtained after giving two thousand cows in gift. On holding rudrākṣa, one acheives the fruit of donation made of eleven thousand cows. The person holding it attains eleven rudras. The fruit as world here obtained after giving one crore cows in gift merely ensured when rudrākṣa is held on the head. The fruit of holding it on ear etc. place (organs) is even indescribable.

य इमां रुद्राक्षजाबालोपनिषदं नित्यमधीते बालो वा युवा वा वेद स महान्भवति। स गुरुः सर्वेषां मन्त्राणामुपदेष्टा भवति। एतैरेव होमं कुर्यात्। एतैरवार्चनम्। तथा रक्षोघ्नं मृत्युतारकं गुरुणा लब्धं कण्ठे बाहौ शिखायां वा बध्नीत्। सप्तद्वीपवति भूमिर्दक्षिणार्थं नावकल्पते। तस्माच्छ्रद्धया यां कांचिद्गां दद्यात्सा दक्षिणा भवति। य इमामुपनिषदं ब्राह्मणः प्रातरधीयानो रात्रिकृतं पापं नाशयति। सायमधीयानो दिवसकृतं पापं नाशयति। मध्याह्नेऽधीयानः षड्जन्मकृतं पापं नाशयति। सायं प्रातः प्रयुञ्जानोऽनेकजन्मकृतं पापं नाशयति।

षट्सहस्रलक्षगायत्रीजफलमवाप्नोति। ब्रह्महत्यासुरापानस्वर्णस्तेयगुरुदारगमनतसंयोगपातकेभ्य: पूतो भवति। सर्वतीर्थफलमश्नुते। पतितसंभाषणात्पूतो भवति। पङ्क्तिशतसहस्रपावनो भवति। शिवसायुज्यमवाप्नोति। न च पुनरावर्तते न च पुनरावर्तत इत्यों सत्यमित्युपनिषत्॥४९॥

The youth, child whatsoever the devotee is, attains supreme knowledge if he recites this Rudrākṣajābālopaniṣad daily. He becomes teacher and preacher (who teaches hymns). Worship and offering should be made with reciting this Upaniṣad hymn. For suppression of monsters and the death, the rudrākṣa should be tied around the neck, or the braid by obtaining it from the learned teacher. The gift to the extent this entire earth containing seven islands too is less for such a teacher. Hence, whatever is given with respect and honour, that should be considered as Dakṣiṇā (gift to teacher). The evils committed in the night are decayed by the impact of reciting this Upaniṣad in morning and the evils committed in the day, are effaced when it is recited in the evening daily. The devotee doing recital in the noon, effaces his evils committed in the previous six births. He attains liberty from the evils committed during many births by virtue of reciting this Upaniṣad in morning and evening daily and thus, gets the fruit of six thousand lakh japa of Gāyatrī hymn. He even is exonerated from the evils like gold thefting, sipping liquor, murder of Brāhmaṇa and debauch with the wife of teacher etc. and thus attains holiness. He further attains the fruit of visiting pilgrimage. The evil attaching and good diminishing by the reason of contact with the evil doers is resisted and he becomes innocent and is dated from the vicious impacts. Such devotee makes holy, many hundred thousands people by removing their ignorance. Thus, he gets the form of Lord Śiva himself and seldown rotates with the cycle of birth and death. "Oṁ" only is truth and this is all this Upaniṣad says.

ॐ आप्यायन्तु......... इति शान्ति:॥

॥इति रुद्राक्षजाबालोपनिषत्समाप्ता॥

79. GAṆAPATYUPANIṢAD

गणपत्युपनिषद्

This upaniṣad falls under the tradition of Atharvaveda. Lord Gaṇeśa has been worshipped very first and then the Gaṇapati existed in the form of soul within all living-organisms has been prayed. Subsequently, Gaṇapati Manu viz., the ceretum of the world Gaṇapati, meditation thereupon, the hymn relating to Gaṇapati garland, the fruits of this knowledge, the rules framed for transacting this learning, application of hymns for fulfilling the desires and finally the fruits of listening to this upaniṣad have been described. It appears clearly that all upaniṣad of ancient time give an impetus to worship gods in their physical form. The same impetus can be seen in this upaniṣad also. Gaṇapati has been enshrined in the form of Brahma but his personified form has been widely described.

॥शान्तिपाठः॥

ॐ भद्रं कर्णेभिः .... इति शान्तिः॥

नमस्ते गणपतये॥१॥ त्वमेव प्रत्यक्षं तत्त्वमसि। त्वमेव केवलं कर्तासि। त्वमेव केवलं धर्तासि। त्वमेव केवलं हर्तासि। त्वमेव सर्वं खल्विदं ब्रह्मासि। त्वं साक्षादात्मासि॥२॥ नित्यं ऋतं वच्मि। सत्यं वच्मि॥३॥

Salutation to lord Gaṇapati. You are an apparent and direct element. You are the only cause, only nourisher and only destroyer. You only are existed in all these forms. You are an apparent form of the soul. You always speak the matter beyond the truth and always propound whatever is true.

अव त्वं माम्। अव वक्तारम्। अव श्रोतारम्। अव दातारम्। अव धातारम्। अवानूचानमव शिष्यम्। अव पश्चात्तात्। अव पुरस्तात्। अव चोत्तरात्तात्। अव दक्षिणात्तात्। अव चोर्ध्वात्तात्। अवाधरात्तात्। सर्वतो मां पाहि पाहि समन्तात्॥४॥

Protect me and my teacher. Protect all the audience. Protect to who gives knowledge, protect the holder of knowledge. Protect to who converts knowledge into practical actions and protect the disciple (myself). Protect me from front side, back side, from north, south, up and down. Protect me from all around. Provide me guardianship all around.

त्वं वाङ्मयस्त्वं चिन्मयः। त्वमानन्दमयस्त्वं ब्रह्ममयः। त्वं सच्चिदानन्दाद्वितीयोऽसि। त्वं प्रत्यक्षं ब्रह्मासि। त्वं ज्ञानमयो विज्ञानमयोऽसि॥५॥

You are the literature (in the form of letters). You are in the form of pleasure, Brahma and immortality. You are unique and holder of the truth, the mind and the pleasure (Saccidānanda). You are apparent Brahma and you are in the form of knowledge and science also.

सर्वं जगदिदं त्वत्तो जायते। सर्वं जगदिदं त्वत्तस्तिष्ठति। सर्वं जगदिदं त्वयि लयमेष्यति। सर्वं जगदिदं त्वयि प्रत्येति। त्वं भूमिरापोऽनलोऽनिलो नभः। त्वं चत्वारि वाक्पदानि। त्वं गुणत्रयातीतः। त्वं कालत्रयातीतः। त्वं देहत्रयातीतः। त्वं मूलाधारस्थितोऽसि नित्यम्। त्वं शक्तित्रयात्मकः। त्वां योगिनो ध्यायन्ति नित्यम्। त्वं ब्रह्मा त्वं विष्णुस्त्वं रुद्रस्त्वमिन्द्रस्त्वमग्निस्त्वं वायुस्त्वं सूर्यस्त्वं चन्द्रमास्त्वं ब्रह्म भूर्भुवः सुवरोम्॥ ६॥

This whole world has been originated by you. It is enshrined within you. It merges within you. This whole world is appearing within you. You are in the form of the earth, water, fire, wind and the ether. You also are the four divisions of speech i.e. Para, Paśyanti, Madhyama and Vaikhāri etc. You are beyond the three properties i.e. Satva, Rajas and Tamas. You are beyond the three times (Kāla) i.e. the past, present and the future. You are beyond three bodies i.e. physical, micro and the causative. You always enshrined in the cycle of Mūlādhāra. You only are the three powers i.e. will power, power of action and power of discretion. The yogis always recall you. You only are Brahmā, Viṣṇu, Rudra, Indra, fire, wind, sun, moon and the Brahma. You are the three worlds i.e. Bhūḥ, Bhuvah, Svah as also the perfect knowledge (Para Brahma) known as the syllable Oṁ.

गणादिं पूर्वमुच्चार्य वर्णादिं तदनन्तरम्। अनुस्वारः परतरः। अर्धेन्दुलसितम्। तारेण रुद्धम्। एतत्तव मनुस्वरूपम्॥ ७॥

Recite the initial letter 'G' very first. Then the initial letter of varṇas 'A' should be recited. Thereafter Anusvāra is recited. Thus, the 'Gaṇ' enshrined with the half-mora (Ardha Candra) having restricted by the syllable Oṁ is the form of your root hymn.

गकारः पूर्वरूपम्। अकारो मध्यमरूपम्। अनुस्वारश्चान्त्यरूपम्। बिन्दुरुत्तररूपम्। नादः संधानम्। संहिता संधिः। सैषा गणेशविद्या॥ ८॥

Its first form 'Ga' is (G), the middle form is 'A', Anusvāra is the terminal form and point is its answer form. Sound is its application (Sandhāna) and Saṁhitā is called its joints (Sandhi). The learning of Gaṇeśa (Gaṇeśa Vidyā) is in this form.

गणक ऋषिः। निचृद्गायत्री छन्दः। श्रीमहागणपतिर्देवता। ॐ गम्। (गणपतये नमः)॥ ९॥

The saint of this hymn is Gaṇaka. The rhyme is 'Nicṛdgāyatrī' and the god is 'Śrī Mahā Gaṇapati'. 'Oṁ Gam Gaṇapataye Namaḥ' is considered as the great hymn.

एकदन्ताय विद्महे वक्रतुण्डाय धीमहि। तन्नो दन्ती प्रचोदयात्॥ १०॥

We know lord Gaṇeśa as 'Ekadanta'. We meditate on Vakratuṇḍa. May that tooth-bearer (Danti) motivate us towards the benevolent route (This hymn is called Gaṇeśa-Gāyatrī Mantra).

एकदन्तं चतुर्हस्तं पाशमङ्कुशधारिणम्। अभयं वरदं हस्तैर्बिभ्राणं मूषकध्वजम्॥ ११॥

रक्तं लम्बोदरं शूर्पकर्णकं रक्तवाससम्। रक्तगन्धानुलिप्ताङ्गं रक्तपुष्पैः सुपूजितम्॥ १२॥

भक्तानुकम्पिनं देवं जगत्कारणमच्युतम्। आविर्भूतं च सृष्ट्यादौ प्रकृतेः पुरुषात्परम्॥ १३॥

एवं ध्यायति यो नित्यं स योगी योगिनां वरः॥ १४॥

The devotee who worships daily the 'Ekadanta', four-armed, holding the posture of elephant, 'Abhaya' (fearlessness) and holding a string (Pāśa) and goad (Aṅkuśa) in his four hands, bearing a flag mouse-marked, red-coloured, a huge stomach, huge ears like the Śūrpa, covered by the red-colour garments, body duly smeared by red sandal, worshipped properly with the red-flowers, always graceful to the devotees, cause of creation of the universe, undivided, born prior to the creation of this universe and beyond the nature and the person is the best and excellent among all the Yogīs.

नमो व्रातपतये नमो गणपतये नमः प्रमथपतये नमस्तेऽस्तु लम्बोदरायैकदन्ताय विघ्नविनाशिने शिवसुताय श्रीवरदमूर्तये नमो नमः॥ १५॥

The commander of commune of all gods is saluted, salute is conveyed to Gaṇapati, 'Pramathapati' i.e. the soldier of lord Śiva, 'Lambodara', 'Ekadant', killer of the hurdles, son of lord Śiva and 'Śrī Varadamūrti'.

एतदथर्वशिरो योऽधीते स ब्रह्मभूयाय कल्पते। स सर्वविघ्नैर्न बाध्यते। स सर्वतः सुखमेधते। स पञ्चमहापातकोपपातकात्प्रमुच्यते। सायमधीयानो दिवसकृतं पापं नाशयति। प्रातरधीयानो रात्रिकृतं पापं नाशयति। सायंप्रातः प्रयुंजानोऽपापो भवति। धर्मार्थकाममोक्षं च विन्दति॥ १६॥

This is the upaniṣad of Atharvaveda. The person who does study on this upaniṣad becomes entitled to the position of Brahma. The hurdles irrespective of their nature, do not resist his way. He avails pleasure and peace everywhere. That person is liberated from the five kinds of evils and the other minor evils. The recital made in the light destroys the sins committed in the day and the recital in the morning compounds the evils committed in the night. The person who recites this upaniṣad in morning and evening both times, he becomes innocent. He becomes able to avail four industries i.e. the Dharma, benevolent concept, the Artha (wealth), the Kāma (the splendour and sensuality) and the Mokṣa (emancipation).

इदमथर्वशीर्षमशिष्याय न देयम्। यो यदि मोहाद्दास्यति स पापीयान्भवति॥ १७॥

Only a disciple should be preached of this 'Atharva Śirṣa' upaniṣad and it should not be preached to any other. The learned person who, by the reason of any attachment, does this, becomes sinister.

सहस्रावर्तनाद्यं यं काममधीते तं तमनेन साधयेत्। अनेन गणपतिमभिषिञ्चति स वाग्मी भवति। चतुर्थ्यामनश्नञ्जपति स विद्यावान्भवति। इत्यथर्वणवाक्यम्। ब्रह्माद्याचरणं विद्यात्। न बिभेति कदाचनेति। यो दूर्वाङ्कुरैर्यजति स वैश्रवणोपमो भवति। यो लाजैर्यजति स यशोवान्भवति। स मेधावान्भवति। यो मोदकसहस्रेण यजति स वाञ्छितफलमवाप्नोति। यः साज्यसमिद्भिर्यजति स सर्वं लभते स सर्वं लभते। अष्टौ ब्राह्मणान्सम्यग्ग्राहयित्वा सूर्यवर्चस्वी भवति। सूर्यग्रहणे महानद्यां प्रतिमासंनिधौ वा जप्त्वा सिद्धमन्त्रो भवति। महाविघ्नात्प्रमुच्यते। महापापात्प्रमुच्यते। महादोषात्प्रमुच्यते॥ १८॥

The person who recites this upaniṣad for one hundred times, avails everything whatever he desires. The person who adores lord Gaṇeśa as per the procedure quoted in this universe becomes an expert orator. The person who recites this on the fourth day of the fortnight, holding the fast, definitely becomes a scholar. This is a sentence of 'Atharvana'. The person who knows the provision of sitting on penance with the hymns of this upaniṣad, does not becomes frightened. The person who worships lord Gaṇapati with the shoots of Dhruva definitely becomes rich like the Kubera (wealth-god). The person who offers the 'Laja' (the Khila of the paddy) becomes illustrious and intelligent. The person who performs offering with 'Modakas' (a sweet), avails the desired fruits. The person who performs offering with ghee and the fuel obtains everything. His all ambitions are fulfilled. The person who contributes this learning of upaniṣad to eight Brāhmaṇas and make them well understood, becomes enriched with splendour analogous to the sun. At the time of solar eclipse, this learning of upaniṣad having recited expressly and silently before an idol or the great river, it becomes fruitful to him. He is liberated from all hurdles and the sins as well. He is liberated from all defects irrespective of their size.

स सर्वविद्भवति स सर्वविद्भवति। य एवं वेदेत्युपनिषत्॥ १९॥

The person who thus develops well understanding with this upaniṣad, becomes omniscient and nothing remains unknown to him. This is the magnificence of this upaniṣad under Atharvaveda.

॥ॐ भद्रं कर्णेभिः .... इति शान्तिः॥

॥इति गणपत्युपनिषद् समाप्त॥

80. TĀRASĀRO-UPANIṢAD

तारसारोपनिषद्

॥शान्तिपाठः॥

ॐ यन्नारायणतारार्थसत्यज्ञानसुखाकृति। त्रिपान्नारायणाकारं तद्ब्रह्मैवास्मि केवलम्॥

ॐ पूर्णमद इति शान्तिः॥

हरिः ॐ॥ बृहस्पतिरुवाच याज्ञवल्क्यं यदनु कुरुक्षेत्रं देवानां देवयजनं सर्वेषां भूतानां ब्रह्मसदनं तस्माद्यत्र क्वचन गच्छेत्तदेव मन्येतेति। इदं वै कुरुक्षेत्रं देवानां देवयजनं सर्वेषां भूतानां ब्रह्मसदनमविमुक्तं वै कुरुक्षेत्रं देवानां देवयजनं सर्वेषां भूतानां ब्रह्मसदनम्। अत्र हि जन्तोः प्राणेषूत्क्रममाषेणु रुद्रस्तारकं ब्रह्म व्याचष्टे येनासावमृतीभूत्वा मोक्षी भवति। तस्मादविमुक्तमेव निषेवेत। अविमुक्तं न विमुञ्चेत्। एवमेवैष भगवन्निति वै याज्ञवल्क्यः॥१॥

Oṁ. Bṛhaspti asked Yājñavalkya : "That which is called Kurukṣetra is place of the sacrifice of the Devas and the spiritual seat of all beings. Therefore where should one go in order that he may cognize Kurukṣetra, the place of the sacrifice of the Devas and the spiritual seat of all beings?" (To which Yājñavalkya replied :) "Avimukta is Kurukṣetra, the place of the sacrifice of the Devas and of the study of Brahman, because it is there that Rudra initiates one into the Tāraka brahman when prāṇa (life) goes out. Through this, one becomes immortal and the enjoyer of mokṣa. Therefore one should always be in the midst of that place avimukta, and should never leave, O revered sir, avimukta." Thus said Yājñavalkya.

अथ हैनं भारद्वाजः पप्रच्छ याज्ञखल्क्यं किं तारकम्। किं तारयतीति। स होवाच याज्ञवल्क्यः। ॐ नमो नारायणायेति तारकं चिदात्मकमित्युषासितव्यम्। ओमित्येकाक्षरमात्मस्वरूपम्। नम इति द्व्यक्षरं प्रकृतिस्वरूपम्। नारायणायेति पञ्चाक्षरं परंब्रह्मस्वरूपम्। इति य एवं वेद। सोऽमृतो भवति। ओमिति ब्रह्मा भवति। नकारो विष्णुर्भवति। मकारो रुद्रो भवति। नकार ईश्वो भवति। रकारोऽण्डं विराड्‌ भवति। यकारः पुरुषो भवति। णकारो भगवान्भवति। यकारः परमात्मा भवति। एतद्वै नारायणस्याष्टाक्षरं वेद परमपुरुषो भवति। अयमृग्वेदः प्रथमः पादः॥१॥

Then Bhāradvāja asked Yājñavalkya : "What is tāraka? What is that which causes one to cross (this mundane existence)." Two which Yājñavalkya replied : "Oṁ-Namo-Nārāyaṇāye is the tāraka. It should be worshipped as Cidātma. Oṁ is a single syllable and of the nature of Ātmā. Namaḥ is of two syllables and is of the nature of prakṛti (matter). Nārāyaṇāye is of five syllables and is of the nature of parabrahman. He who knows this becomes immortal. Through Oṁ, is Brahma produced; through Na is Viṣṇu produced;

through Ma is Rudra produced; through Nā is Īśvara produced; through Rā is the Aṇḍa-Virāṭ (or Virāṭ of the universe) produced; through ya is Puruṣa produced; through Nā is Bhagavān (Lord) produced; and through Ya is Paramātmā produced. This Aṣṭākṣara (eight syllables) of Nārāyaṇa is the supreme and the highest Puruṣa. Thus is the Ṛgveda with the first foot (or half).

ॐ मित्येतदक्षरं परं ब्रह्म। तदेवोपासितव्यम्। एतदेव सूक्ष्माष्टाक्षरं भवति। तदेतदष्टात्मकोऽष्टधा भवति। अकार: प्रथमोक्षरो भवति। उकारो द्वितीयाक्षरो भवति। मकारास्तृतीयाक्षरो भवति। बिन्दूस्तुतरीयाक्षरो भवति। नाद: पञ्चमाक्षरो भवति। कला षष्ठाक्षरो भवति। कलातीता सप्तमाक्षरो भवति। तत्परश्चाष्टमाक्षरो भवति। तारकत्वात्तारको भवति। तदेव तारकं ब्रह्म त्वं विद्धि। तदेवोपासितव्यम्। अत्रैते श्लोका भवन्ति।।

अकारादाभवद्ब्रह्मा जाम्बवानितिसंज्ञक:। उराकाक्षकसंभूत उपेन्द्रो हरिनायक:।।१।।

मकाराक्षकसंभूत: शिवस्तु हनुमान्समृत:। बिन्दुरीश्वरसंज्ञस्तु शत्रुघ्नश्चक्रराट् खयम्।।२।।

नादो महाप्रभुर्ज्ञेयो भरत: शङ्खनामक:। कलाया: पुरुष: साक्षाल्लक्ष्मणो धरणीधर:।।३।।

कलातीता भगवती स्वय सीतेति संज्ञिता। तत्पर: परमात्मा च श्रीराम: पुरषोत्तम:।।४।।

ओमित्येतदक्षरमिदं सर्वम्। तस्योपव्याख्यानं भूतं भव्यं भविष्यद्यच्चान्यत्तत्त्वमन्त्रवर्णदेवताछन्दो-ऋक्कलाशक्तिसृष्ट्यात्मकमिति। य वं वेद। यजुर्वेदो द्वितीय: पाद:।।२।।

That which is Oṁ is the indestructible, the supreme, and Brahman. That alone should be worshipped. It is this that is of the eight subtle syllables. And this becomes eight, being of eight forms. A is the first letter; U is the second; M is the third; Bindu is the fourth; Nāda is the fifth; Kalā is the sixth; Kalātīta (the beyond kalā) is the seventh; and that which is beyond these is the eighth. It is called Tāraka, because it enables one to cross this mundane existence. Know that Tāraka alone is Brahman and it alone should be worshipped. The (following) verses may be quoted here : "From the letter A came Brahmā named Jāmbavān (the bear). From the letter U came Upendra, named Hari. From the letter M came Śiva, known as Hanumān. Bindu is named Īśvara and is Śatrughna, the Lord of the discus itself. Nāda should be known as the great Lord named Bharata and the sound of the conch itself. From Kalā came the Puruṣa himself as Lakṣmaṇa and the bearer of the earth. Kalātīta is known as the goddess Sītā Herself. That which is beyond is the Paramātmā named Śrī-Rāma and is the highest Puruṣa. All this is the explanation of the letter Oṁ, which is the past, the present, and future, and which is other than these (viz.,). tattva, mantra, varṇa (colour), devatā (deity), chandas (metre), ṛk, kāla, śakti, and sṛṣṭi (creation). He who knows this becomes immortal. (Thus is) Yajurveda with the second foot."

अथ हैनं भारद्वाजो याज्ञवल्क्यमुवाच कैर्मन्त्रै: परमात्मा प्रीतो भवति स्वात्मानं दर्शयति तन्नो ब्रूहि भगव इति। स होवाच यात्रवल्क्य:।

Then Bhāradvāja asked Yājñavalkya : "Through what mantra is Paramātmā pleased and shows his own Ātmā (to persons) ? Please tell this." Yājñavalkya replied–

ॐ या ह वै श्रीपरमात्मा नारायण: स भगवानकारवाच्यो जाम्बवान्भूर्भूव: सुवस्तस्मै वै नमोनम:।।१।।

"(1st Mantra) : Oṁ. He who is Śrī-Paramātmā, Nārāyaṇa and the Lord described by (the letter) A and is Jāmbavān (the bear) and Bhūḥ, Bhuvaḥ, Svaḥ : Salutation to Him."

ॐ यो ह वै श्रीपरमात्मा नारायणः स भगवानुकारवाच्य उपेन्द्रस्वरूपो हरिनायको भुर्भुवः सुवस्तसै् वै नमोनमः॥२॥

"(2nd Mantra :) He who is Paramātmā, Nārāyaṇa, and the Lord described by (the letter) U and is Upendra (or) Hari and Bhūḥ, Bhuvaḥ,and Svaḥ : Salutation to Him."

ॐ यो ह वै परमात्मा नारायणः स भगवान्मकारवाच्यः शिवस्वरूपो हनूमामन्भूर्भुवः सुवस्तस्मै वै नमोनमः॥३॥

"(3rd Mantra :) Oṁ. He who is Śrī-Paramātmā, Nārāyaṇa, and the Lord described by (the letter) M and is of the form of Śiva (or) Hanumān and Bhūḥ, Bhuvaḥ, and Svaḥ : Salutation to Him."

ॐ यो ह वै परमात्मा नारायणः स भगवान्बिन्दुस्वरूपः शत्रुघ्नो भूर्भवः सुवस्तस्मै वै नमोनमः॥४॥

"(4th Mantra :) Oṁ. He who is Śrī-Paramātmā, Nārāyaṇa, the Lord of Śatrughna of the form of Bindu and the Bhuḥ, Bhuvaḥ and Svaḥ : Salutation to Him."

ॐ यो ह वै परमात्मा नारायणः स भगवान्नादस्वरूपो भरतो भूर्भुवः सुवस्तस्मै वै नमोनमः॥५॥

"(5th Mantra :) Oṁ. He who is Śrī-Paramātmā, Nārāyaṇa, and the Lord, and is Bharata of the form of Nāda and the Bhuḥ, Bhuvaḥ and Svaḥ. : Salutation to Him."

ॐ यो ह वै परमात्मा नारायणः स भगवान्कलास्वरूपो लक्ष्मणो भूर्भुवः सुवस्तस्मै वै नमोनमः॥६॥

"(6th Mantra :) Oṁ. He who is Śrī-Paramātmā, Nārāyaṇa, and the Lord, and is Lakṣmaṇa of the form of Kalā and the Bhūḥ, Bhuvaḥ, Svaḥ : Salutation to Him."

ॐ यो ह वै परमात्मा नारायणः स भगवान्कलातीता भगवती सीता चित्स्वरूपा भूर्भुवः सुवस्तस्मै वै नमोनमः॥७॥

"(7th Mantra :) Oṁ. He who is Śrī-Paramātmā, Nārāyaṇa, and the Lord, and is Kalātīta, the Goddess Sītā, of the form of Cit and the Bhuḥ, Bhuvaḥ, and Svaḥ : Salutation to Him."

यथा प्रथमन्त्रोक्तावाद्यन्तौ तथा सर्वमन्त्रेषु द्रष्टव्यम्। उकारवाच्य उपेन्द्रस्वरूपो हरिनायकः २ मकरावाच्यः शिवस्वरूपो हनुमान् ३ बिन्दुस्वरूपः शत्रुघ्नः ४ नादस्वरूपो भरतः ५ कलास्वरूपो लक्ष्मणः ६ कलातीता भगवती सीता चित्स्वरूपा ७ ॐ यो ह वै श्रीपरमात्मा नारायणः स भगवांस्तत्परः परमपुरुषः पुराणपुरुषोत्तमो नित्यशुद्धबुद्धमुक्तसत्यपरमानन्ताद्वयपरिपूर्णः परमात्मा ब्रह्मैवाहं रामोऽस्मि भूर्भुवः सुवस्तमै नमोनमः॥८॥

"(8th Mantra :) Oṁ. He who is "Śrī-Paramātmā, Nārāyaṇa, and the Lord what is beyond that (Kalātīta), is the supreme Puruṣa, and is the ancient Puruṣottama, the eternal, the immaculate, the enlightened, the emancipated, the true, the highest bliss, the endless, the secondless, and the all-full— that Brahman is myself. I am Rāma and the Bhuḥ, Bhuvaḥ, and Svaḥ : Salutation to Him."

एतदष्टविधमन्त्रं योऽधीते सोऽग्निपूतो भवति। स वायुपूतो भवति। स आदित्यपूतो भवति। स स्थाणुपूतो भवति। स सर्वैर्देवैर्ज्ञातो भवति। तेनेतिहासपुराणनां रुद्राणां शतसहस्राणि जप्तानि फलानि भवन्ति। श्रीमन्नारायणाष्टाक्षरानुस्मरणेन गायत्र्याः शतसहस्रं जप्तं भवति। प्रणवानामयुतं जप्तं भवति। दशपूर्वान्दशोत्तरान्पुनाति। नारायणपदमवाप्नोति य एवं वेद। तद्विष्णोः परमं पदं सदा पश्यन्ति सूरयः दिवीव चक्षुराततम्। तद्विप्रासो विपन्यवो जागृवांसः समिन्धते। विष्णोर्यत्परमं पदम्।। इत्युपनिषद्।। सामवेदस्तृतीयः पादः।।३।।

He who has mastered this eightfold mantra is purified by Agni; he is purified by Vāyu; he is purified by the sun; he is purified by Śiva; he is known by all the Devas. He attains the fruit of reciting Itihāsas, Purāṇas, Rudra (Mantras), a hundred thousand times. He who repeatedly remembers (or recites) the Aṣṭākṣara (the eight-syllabled mantra) of the Nārāyaṇa gains the fruit of the recitation of Gāyatrī hundred thousand times or of Praṇava (Oṁ) a myriad of times. He purifies (his ancestors) ten (degrees) above and (his descendants) ten (degrees) below. He attains the state of Nārāyaṇa. He who knows this attains the state of Nārāyaṇa. He who knows this (attains the state of Nārāyaṇa).

Like the eye (which sees without any obstacle) the things spread (in the sky), the wise even sees this supreme seat of Viṣṇu. Brāhmaṇas who are spiritually awaken praise in diverse ways and illuminate the supreme abode of Viṣṇu. (Thus is) the Sāmaveda with the third foot.

ॐ पूर्णमद......इति शान्तिः। हरिः ॐ तत्सत्।।

।।इति तारसारोपनिषत्समाप्ता।।

81. MAHĀVĀKYOPANIṢAD

महावाक्योपनिषद्

This Upaniṣad is related to Atharvaveda. There are twelve hymns in it. The most cryptic knowledge or mystery has been disclosed before the gods under the speeches of Lord Brahmā. These should be expressed only before the desirous persons whose practical activities are also consisting of the Satva properties, the introvert as also the service to the teachers.

The cardinal proposition of this Upaniṣad is the element of soul, it is covered by the darkness of ignorance. The genuine form of the element of soul appears analogous to the colour of sun and he is duly introduced with the sun, the supreme flame, the supreme Śiva, the supreme luxuries and the supreme Brahma. It endows with the perceiving and attainment of immortality for the supreme pleasure. This cryptic knowledge has been concluded along with explaining the magnificence of Upaniṣad.

॥शान्तिपाठः॥

ॐभद्रं कर्णेभिः..........इति शान्तिः॥

अथ होवाच भगवान्ब्रह्मापरोक्षानुभवपरोपनिषदं व्याख्यास्यामः॥ १॥

गुह्याद्गुह्यतर मेषा न प्राकृतायोपदेष्टव्या। सात्त्विकायान्तर्मुखाय परिशुश्रूषवे॥ २॥

Lord Brahmā once (in the presence of gods) said– "O Gods! The feelings beyond the senses are given by Upaniṣad to which is described here. This Upaniṣad shouldn't be revealed before people of an ordinary propensities because it is most cryptic. However, preaching on this Upaniṣad should be made before the persons instilled with the Sattva, properties, introvert and devotee to the service of teachers.

अथ संसृतिबन्धमोक्षयोर्विद्याविद्ये चक्षुषी उपसंहृत्य विज्ञायाविद्यालोकाण्डस्तमोदृक्॥ ३॥

As a result of going over this Upaniṣad, the ascetic presuming Ahambrahmāsmi closes his eyes of learning and ignorance, the main causative to bondage and emancipation of the world and thus resorting to the due perception, he becomes, liberate of having an eye of ignorance or darkness towards the world of illusion.

तमो हि शारीरप्रपञ्चमाब्रह्मस्थावरान्तमनन्ताखिलाजाण्डभूतम्।
निखिलनिगमोदितसकामकर्मव्यवहारो लोकः॥ ४॥

This is a darkness in the form of ignorance that covers the elements of soul. It is Avidyā i.e., ignorance and this very thing is the cause for the integrated scope from this body to the Brahma of this inert including active world. It is due to the ignorance that makes a difference from the Brahma and a separate entity is felt to have existence. The directions on what to do and not to doing Vedas is because the ignorance in the form of darkness as compelled it to appear.

नैषोऽन्धकारोऽयमात्मा। विद्या हि काण्डान्तरादित्यो ज्योतिर्मण्डलं ग्राह्यं नापरम्॥५॥

A man should do perseverance ceaselessly on learning the true knowledge until and unless the ever luminating feature of ones soul is known and it is self-luminating due to its origin from Brahma. It is learning severely distinct, self-luminating in garb of sun. It province is luminated with the supreme flame. That only is entertainable because that is dependent mainly on Brahma and except Brahma there is nothing otherwise.

असावादित्यो ब्रह्मेत्यजपयोपहितं हंसः सोऽहम्। प्राणापानाभ्यां प्रतिलोमानुलोमाभ्यां समुपलभ्यैवं सा चिरं लब्ध्वा त्रिवृदात्मनि ब्रह्मण्यभिध्यायमाने सच्चिदानन्दः परमात्माविर्भवति॥६॥

This Brahma in the form of Sun is a supreme Soul known as the Haṁsa residing in the body with the Ajapa Japa of inhale and exhale. Presuming as the part and parcel of supreme soul know as Haṁsa and by obtaining the knowledge of Prāṇa, Apāna, the inhale and exhale of the wind and by virtue of sitting on prolong penance; the macro, individual and the unitary soul attains Brahma through this learning. The perfect Brahma in the form of truth, mind and pleasure is originated.

सहस्रभानुमच्छुरिता पूरितत्वादलीया पारावारपूर इव। नैषा समाधिः। नैषा योगसिद्धिः। नैषा मनोलयः। ब्रह्मैक्यं तत्॥७॥ आदित्यवर्णं तमसस्तु पारे। सर्वाणि रूपाणि विचित्य धीरः। नामानि कृत्वाऽभिवदन्यदास्ते॥८॥

That trend of the best element of knowledge is luminated with the light of many thousand Suns. This trend is without wave and alike the immense water of sea filled with the essence of Brahma and without the rhyme. Such a state of mind is not perceived in meditation, immersion of mind and accomplishment of yoga but it is only the unity of living Soul and Brahma. That element of Soul, i.e. Brahma is beyond ignorance and luminates with the light of a Sun. The scholars convert themselves in the form of Brahma to which Parātpara Brahma, they ponder after duly understood about the mortality of this name and the complexion.

धाता पुरस्ताद्यमुदाजहार। शक्रः प्रविद्वान्प्रदिशश्चतस्रः तमेवं विद्वानमृत इह भवति। नान्यः पन्था अयनाय विद्यते॥९॥

Lord Brahmā very first spoke this situation and the same has been stated by the divine king Indra who is a barrier and excellent among all gods. The scholar knowing that everlasting Brahma, this way, attains to the immortality. No other way leads to the emancipation otherwise than it.

यज्ञेन यज्ञमयजन्त देवाः। तानि धर्माणि प्रथमान्यासन्। ते ह नाकं महिमानः सचन्ते। यत्र पूर्वे साध्याः सन्ति देवाः॥१०॥

The gods Indra etc. observing the great essence of religion summoned the gigantic offering through the material of their knowledge i.e. Jñāna Yajña. They are luminating in the divine abode which is full of magnificence and the abode of the great men and great souls.

सोऽहमर्कः परं ज्योतिरर्कज्योतिरहं शिवः।

आत्मज्योतिरहं शुक्रः सर्वज्योतिरसावदोम्॥ ११॥

I am that Sun, I am that supreme flame of Sun and I am Śiva (the element that does welfare). I am that flame of the great soul. I am the Śukra (Venus) that endows light with all and I never live separate than that supreme entity.

य एतदथर्वशिरोऽधीते। प्रातरधीयानो रात्रिकृतं पापं नाशयति। सायमधीयानो दिवसकृतं पापं नाशयति। तत्सायं प्रातः प्रयुञ्जानः पापोऽपापो भवति। मध्यन्दिनमादित्याभिमुखोऽधीयानः पञ्चमहापातकोपपातकात्प्रमुच्यते। सर्ववेदपारायणपुण्यं लभते। श्रीमहाविष्णुसायुज्यमवाप्नोतीत्युपनिषत्॥ १२॥

By reciting this Upaniṣad in morning liberated a person from all evils and the person reciting it in the evening becomes free from the evils committed in the day. Heinous crimes and offences even are absorbed if a person recites this Upaniṣad in every morning and evening. The person reciting this Upaniṣad becomes liberated from all other kinds of heinous offences too. He obtains the consequence of world that he achieves after study on four Vedas and thus attains to the form of Lord Viṣṇu.

ॐ भद्रं कर्णेभिः ...... इति शान्तिः॥

॥इति महावाक्योपनिषत्समाप्ता॥

82. PAÑCABRAHMOPANIṢAD

पञ्चब्रह्मोपनिषद्

॥शान्तिपाठः॥

ॐ सह नाववतु..............इति शान्तिः॥

This Upaniṣad is related to the tradition of Kṛṣṇa Yajurveda. There are fourty one hymns in it. This Upaniṣad commences with a question regarding the first thing originated with the creation which was asked by hermit Śākala to Paippalāda. The hermit Paippalāda very first told about the origin of Sadyojāta, Aghora, Vāmadeva, Tatapuruṣa and Īśāna and their nature was described thereafter. These five are called as Pañcabrahma. It has been stated that the devotee who acquires the knowledge by perception through a presumption that he himself is Pañcabrahma within his soul, definitely attains to emancipation and enjoys the pleasure of sipping the nectar Brahma. Finally, this Upaniṣad has been concluded with description of magnificence of the learning to Pañcabrahma and with instructions to do research with the element of Sadāśiva as existed in the heart Lotus.

अथ पैप्पलादो भगवान्भो किमादौ किं जातमिति। सद्यो जातमिति किं भगव इति। अघोर इति। किं भगव इति। वामदेव इति। किं वा पुनरिमे भगव इति। तत्पुरुष इति। किं वा पुनरिमे भगव इति। सर्वेषां दिव्यानां प्रेरयिता ईशान इति। ईशानो भूतभव्यस्य सर्वेषां देवयोनिनाम्॥ १॥

Once a hermit asked Paippalāda— "what was originated very first with the creation? Paippalāda replied— "The Brahma namely Sadyojāta was very first originated." Śākala asked– "Whether any more of discrimination besides it is also therein? Paippalāda replied "Yes! It is Aghora" Śākala again asked– "Whether this is the only discrimination?" Paippalāda replied– "No one more discrimination also exists and it is Tatapuruṣa." Śākala asked again– "Very well! Whether these four are only discrimination?" Paippalāda relied "No! One more discrimination that inspires the god is Īśāna. It is a ruler of the past and future as also all species of gods."

कति वर्णाः। कति भेदाः। कति शक्तयः। यत्सर्वं तद्गुह्यम्॥ २॥

"How many varṇa (colours) are of it? Further, how many kinds of and how many powers are in existence. These all matters are most confidential. Therefore, these should be hidden from the person who are not entitled to it.

तस्मै नमो महादेवाय महारुद्राय॥ ३॥ प्रोवाच तस्मै भगवान्महेशः॥ ४॥

The Lord Mahārudra in garb of Mahādeva is saluted. It was Lord Maheśa who preached all these matters to the hermit Paippalāda.

गोप्याद्गोप्यतरं लोके यद्यस्ति शृणु शाकल। सद्योजातं मही पूषा रमा ब्रह्मा त्रिवृत्स्वरः॥ ५॥

ऋग्वेदो गार्हपत्यं च मन्त्राः सप्त स्वरास्तथा। वर्णं पीतं क्रिया शक्तिः सर्वाभीष्टफलप्रदम्॥ ६॥

O Śākala! Listen to what is most cryptic among the cryptic matters of this world. It is the Brahma namely Sadyojāta. The Mahī, Pūṣā, Ramā, trio-properties (Satva, Rajas and Tamas), the vowels including 'A' etc. Ṛgveda, Garhapatya (fire), a number of hymns (Namaḥ Śivāya etc), seven musical notations (Sā, Re, Ga, Ma, Pa, Dha, Ni), yellow colour and the power namely action etc. are the various forms of this Brahma who endow with the desired accomplishments.

अघोरं सलिलं चन्द्रं गौरी वेदद्वितीयकम्। नीरदाभं स्वरं सान्द्रं दक्षिणाग्निरुदाहृतम्॥ ७॥

पञ्चाशद्वर्णसंयुक्तं स्थितिरिच्छाक्रियान्वितम्। शक्तिरक्षणसंयुक्तं सर्वाघौघविनाशनम्॥ ८॥

सर्वदुष्टप्रशमनं सर्वैश्वर्यफलप्रदम्॥ ९॥

The water, moon, Gaurī, Yajurveda, Nīrdābha (radiance as of clouds), vowels, smooth, Dakṣiṇāgni, etc. are the form of Aghora. Apart from these, the letters in fifty numbers (from A to Kṣa), the position including them, with the will-power and the power of action as also power to conserve the energy are the other forms of Aghora. This form of Brahma eliminates all evils, beheads all shrewds, and it provides with the fruits of all luxuries.

वामदेवं महाबोधदायकं पावकात्मकम्। विद्यालोकसमायुक्तं भानुकोटिसमप्रभम्॥ १०॥

प्रसन्नं सामवेदाख्यं गानाष्टकसमन्वितम्। धीरस्वरमधीनं चाहवनीयमनुत्तमम्॥ ११॥

ज्ञानसंहारसंयुक्तं शक्तिद्वयसमन्वितम्। वर्णं शुक्लं तमोमिश्रं पूर्णबोधकरं स्वयम्॥ १२॥

धामत्रयनियन्तारं धामत्रयसमन्वितम्। सर्वसौभाग्यदं नृणां सर्वकर्मफलप्रदम्॥ १३॥

अष्टाक्षरसमायुक्तमष्टपत्रान्तरस्थितम्॥ १४॥

Vāmadeva, another form of Brahma provides with great knowledge, it is in the form of blazing fire, it luminates with the light of learning, its splendour is alike crore suns and it is always in the form of pleasure. Its one more form is comprised of Aṣṭagāna (seven songs as stated in Sāmaveda and one more as per Bharata Śāstra), the slow vowel (Ā, Ā, Ā, M) and the best Āhavanīya knowledge and the power of distraction. Its complexion is white, property is Tamas, perfect in knowledge, regulator of trio-abodes (awaking etc.), trio-abodes (the universe, the splendour, the conscience), endower of fortune, the fruit of action and it resides on a lotus of eight petals i.e., heart-lotus and it possesses eight letters (A, Ka, Cha, Ta, Ta, Pa, Ya, Śa) or with eight letters in Om Namaḥ Mahā Devāya.

यत्तत्तत्पुरुषं प्रोक्तं वायुमण्डलसंवृतम्। पञ्चाग्निना समायुक्तं मन्त्रशक्तिनियामकम्॥ १५॥

पञ्चाशत्स्वरवर्णाख्यमथर्ववेदस्वरूपकम्। कोटिकोटिगणाध्यक्षं ब्रह्माण्डाखण्डविग्रहम्॥ १६

वर्णं रक्तं कामदं च सर्वाधिव्याधिभेषजम्। सृष्टिस्थितिलयादीनां कारणं सर्वशक्तिधृक्॥ १७॥

अवस्थात्रितयातीतं तुरीयं ब्रह्मसंज्ञितम्। ब्रह्मविष्णवादिभिः सेव्यं सर्वेषां जनकं परम्॥ १८॥

Another Brahma Tatapuruṣa regulates the power of hymn of joining with the five fires blazed by the atmosphere. This Brahma is renowned with the fifty number of the vowel and consonants, it is in the form of Atharvaveda, the head of many crores Gaṇas viz., its body is the entire Brahmāṇḍa. He is of red complexion, he fulfils all desires and an excellent remedy to all kinds of mental and physical ailments. He is the sole cause for the origin, nutrition and destruction of this world. He is beyond the three states and live in the state of Turīya (the fourth state and known as Brahma). He originates all and worshipped by Lord Brahmā and Viṣṇu always.

ईशानं परमं विद्यात्प्रेरकं बुद्धिसाक्षिणम्। आकाशात्मकमव्यक्तमोंकारस्वरभूषितम्॥ १९॥

सर्वदेवमयं शान्तं शान्त्यतीतं स्वराद्बहिः। अकारादिस्वराध्यक्षमाकाशमयविग्रहम्॥ २०॥

पञ्चकृत्यनियन्तारं पञ्चब्रह्मात्मकं बृहत्॥ २१॥ पञ्चब्रह्मोपसंहारं कृत्वा स्वात्मनि संस्थितः।

स्वमायावैभवान्सर्वान्संहृत्य स्वात्मनि स्थितः॥ २२॥ पञ्चब्रह्मात्म कातीतो भासते स्वस्वतेजसा।

आदावन्ते च मध्ये च भासते नान्यहेतुना॥ २३॥

Another Brahma Īśāna should be known as an inspirer in the form of the supreme element of soul. He is a witness to the wisdom, omnipresent, inexpressive and adorned with the vowel of Oṁ. He is in the form of all gods, always in peace, beyond the peace viz., always in peace, beyond the vowels (viz., the vowels cannot describe him), he is the god of 'A' etc. vowels and he is of gigantic body. He is the controller of the five functions i.e., creation, maintenance, destruction, provision and grace as also a gigantic Pañcabrahma. He concludes Pañcabrahma, enshrines in his soul, destroys all by virtue of his magnificent illusion and always enshrines in his soul. He is self-luninating and beyond the Pañcabrahma and doesn't perceive by any cause in the beginning, middle and the end. He is self-luminating and svayambhū. (self-born).

मायया मोहिताः शंभोर्महादेवं जगद्गुरुम्। न जानन्ति सुराः सर्वे सर्वकारणकारणम्। न संदृशे तिष्ठति रूपमस्य परात्परं पुरुषं विश्वधाम॥ २४॥ येन प्रकाशते विश्वं यत्रैव प्रविलीयते। तद्ब्रह्म परमं शान्तं तद्ब्रह्मास्मि परं पदम्॥ २५॥

The gods, the teachers to this entire universe and the cause for all causes do not know the god of the gods (Mahādeva) due to the illusion created by Lord Śambhu. A common eye cannot perceive that gigantic person who provides with light to this entire universe. That supreme everlasting Brahma by which this world is luminated and gets merged with always lives in peace. That unique supreme position is of nothing else but I myself is the same.

पञ्चब्रह्ममिदं विद्यात्सद्योजातादिपूर्वकम्। दृश्यते श्रूयते यच्च पञ्चब्रह्मात्मकं स्वयम्॥ २६॥

पञ्चधा वर्तमानं तं ब्रह्मकार्यमिति स्मृतम्। ब्रह्मकार्यमिति ज्ञात्वा ईशानं प्रतिपद्यते॥ २७॥

पञ्चब्रह्मात्मकं सर्वं स्वात्मनि प्रविलाप्य च। सोऽहमस्मीति जानीयाद्विद्वान्ब्रह्मामृतो भवेत्॥ २८॥

इत्येतद्ब्रह्म जानीयाद्यः स मुक्तो न संशयः॥ २९॥

Sadyojāta etc. are the Pañcabrahma. Everything whatever is being perceived in this movable and immovable world or whatever is being heard; that all is in the form of

Pañcabrahma. That Sadyojāta has been stated as Brahmakārya enshrined in the five forms. By virtue of knowledge to this Brahmakārya Īśāna is attained. The learned person competent to merge that Pañcabrahma in his soul viz., if he develops the notion that "I myself is Pañcabrahma and in the form of Pañcabrahma, definitely enjoys the pleasure of Brahma nectar. There is no doubt at all for the emancipation of the man who realises the form of Brahma by this way.

पञ्चाक्षरमयं शम्भुं परब्रह्मस्वरूपिणम्। नकारादियकारान्तं ज्ञात्वा पञ्चाक्षरं जपेत्॥ ३०॥

सर्वं पञ्चात्मकं विद्यात्पञ्चब्रह्मात्मतत्त्वत:॥ ३१॥ पञ्चब्रह्मात्मिकीं विद्यां योऽधीते भक्तिभावित:।

स पञ्चात्मकतामेत्य भासते पञ्चधा स्वयम्॥ ३२॥

The five letter hymn i.e., Namaḥ Śivāya should be recited. It starts with the letter 'Na' and ends with the letter 'Ya' and this five letter hymn describes Lord Śambhu as Parabrahma. One should perceive all objects as Pañcabrahma and this element of Pañcabrahma should be observed everywhere. The person who reads the learning of Pañcabrahma with full devotion, definitely becomes Pañcabrahma himself and attains a close touch with it.

एवमुक्त्वा महादेवो गालवस्य महात्मन:। कृपां चकार तत्रैव स्वान्तर्धिमगमत्स्वयम्॥ ३३॥

Lord Mahādeva explained this knowledge to the hermit Gālava and then merged with the soul.

यस्य श्रवणमात्रेणाश्रुतमेव श्रुतं भवेत्। अमतं च मतं ज्ञातमविज्ञातं च शाकल॥ ३४॥

एकेनैव तु पिण्डेन मृत्तिकायाश्च गौतम। विज्ञातं मृण्मयं सर्वं मृदभिन्नं हि कार्यकम्॥ ३५॥

O Śākala! Its mere listening makes a man to listen everything even if it is beyond listening. All awareness either experienced or not arise and all alien doctrines automatically join with the knowledge of the man. O Gautama! As the lump of clay endows the perfect knowledge of the thing analogous to it due to inseparability of the cause and action, all kinds of material knowledge is obtained as and when Pañcabrahma is known.

एकेन लोहमणिना सर्वं लोहमयं यथा। विज्ञातं स्यादथैकेन नखानां कृन्तनेन च॥ ३६॥

सर्वं कार्ष्णायसं ज्ञातं तदभिन्नं स्वभावत:। कारणाभिन्नरूपेण कार्यकारणमेव हि॥ ३७॥

As all elements of iron are known by a Lohamaṇi, the nail-cutter gives suffice knowledge of the arms made of iron. It is natural that all things analogous to it will certainly be the same because the action not distinct to the cause always becomes in the form of the cause.

तद्रूपेण सदा सत्यं भेदेनोक्तिर्मृषा खलु। तच्च कारणमेकं हि न भिन्नं नोभयात्मकम्॥ ३८॥

भेद: सर्वत्र मिथ्यैव धर्मादेरनिरूपणात्। अतश्च कारणं नित्यमेकमेवाद्वयं खलु। अत्र कारणमद्वैतं शुद्धचैतन्यमेव हि॥ ३९॥

In case, any action is deemed as its cause, it is always true. If it is said otherwise, the statement will be false because the cause for all actions is the same. It is neither distinct nor of otherwise nature. The distinction whatever is felt at all places, its reason only depicts the absence of locating the nature of that thing. Hence, the cause really is one and it cannot be otherwise. This is the reason the cause for this inert and active world is only the pure sensitivity.

अस्मिन्ब्रह्मपुरे वेश्म दहरं यदिदं मुने। पुण्डरीकं तु तन्मध्ये आकाशो दहरोऽस्ति तत्। स शिवः सच्चिदानन्दः सोऽन्वेष्टव्यो मुमुक्षुभिः॥४०॥ अयं हृदि स्थितः साक्षी सर्वेषामविशेषतः। तेनायं हृदयं प्रोक्तः शिवः संसारमोचकः। इत्युपनिषत्॥४१॥

O hermit! Daharākāśa is existed in Dahara (within heart) and is the only resort of Brahma i.e. body which is also called Puṇḍarika (Lotus). The persons desirous to emancipation should trace Lord Śiva in the form of truth, mind and the pleasure in Daharākāśa. This Śiva always enshrines in the lotus heart and it is witness to all by virtue of its common eye. This is the reason that the heart is addressed as Śiva and emancipation is attributed only to the effort of this best.

ॐ स ह नाववतु ....इति शान्तिः॥

॥इति पञ्चब्रह्मोपनिषत्समाप्ता॥

83. PRĀṆĀGNIHOTROPANIṢAD

प्राणाग्निहोत्रोपनिषद्

The Upaniṣad is related to the tradition of Kṛṣṇayajurveda. The cardinal objective of this Upaniṣad is the purification of the heart because it enables easy access to the knowledge of Brahma. The pronouncing of explanation regarding the "Śārīra Yajña and its outcome has been very first described. Subsequently, the exterior Prāṇāgnihotra, with procedure has been made ex-facie. The other contents included in this Upaniṣad are Apara Brahma vidyā known as Śārīrāgni Darśana, Śārīra Yajña by śārīrāgni vidyā and lastly the importance of perseverance on this Prāṇāgnihotra vidyā has been described. It has been stated that the devotee going over attentively on this Upaniṣad attains to purity in heart thereby emancipation in the phase of very life. This Upaniṣad has been concluded with the above contents.

॥शान्तिपाठः॥

ॐ सह नाववतु..... इति शान्तिः॥

अथातः सर्वोपनिषत्सारं संसारज्ञानातनीतमन्नसूक्तं शारीरयज्ञं व्याख्यास्यामः। यस्मिन्नेव पुरुषः शरीरे विनाप्यग्निहोत्रेण विनापि सांख्ययोगेन संसारविमुक्तिर्भवति॥१॥

Now the explanation on the Annasūkta and Śārīra-yajña (sacrifice offered in one's own body) starts under this Upaniṣad which is beyond the worldly knowledge and an essence of all Upaniṣads. The liberation is easily attained from this world in this present human body without the Agnihotra and the knowledge of Sāṁkhya and Yoga.

स्वेन विधिनान्नं भूमौ निक्षिप्य या ओषधीः सोमराज्ञीरिति तिसृभिरन्नपत इति द्वाभ्यामनुमन्त्रयते॥

Placing the cereals on the earth (viz. on the alter) with pursuance of due procedure, it should be processed with "Yo auṣadhaḥ.. (i.e, three hymns) and two Ṛcās i.e., Anna Pate.. and Yadannamagni...

Now the meaning to the aforesaid three hymns and two Ṛcās is orderly mentioned herein-

यो ओषधः सोमराज्ञीर्बह्वीः शतविचक्षणाः। बृहस्पतिप्रसूतास्ता नो मुञ्चन्त्वंहसः॥३॥

The god soma, the owner (creator) of medicines, is prime god. He is competent in removing many hundred diseases that infest in their multifarious species. These medicines of specific qualities have been prepared by lord Bṛhaspati (the teacher of all gods). May these medicines remove all kinds of wees and ailments and make us healthy.

याः फलिनीर्या अफला अपुष्पा याश्च पुष्पिणीः। बृहस्पतिप्रसूतास्ता नो मुञ्चन्त्वंहसः॥४॥

May the medicines bearing fruits, barren or foundless, flowering and non-flowering etc.

all make us free from the prospective wees and ailments. These all (medicines) are duly prepared by Lord Bṛhaspati (by an expert Vaidya).

जीवला नघारिषां मा ते बध्नाम्योषिधम्। यातयायुरुपाहरादप रक्षांसि चातयात्।।५।।

The evergreen medicine is being tied (viz. entertained) by me. May it ensure for protection from the elements decaying the age.

अन्नपतेऽन्नस्य नो धेह्यनमीवस्य शुष्मिणः। प्रप्रदातारं तारिष ऊर्जं नो धेहि द्विपदे चतुष्पदे।।६।।

O the owner of food (cereal) Lord fire! Please arrange the hygienic food (cereal) for us all. Please provide the generous people with due maintenance. Please, provide own sons, grand-sons and the pet animals too with food (cereals).

यदन्नमग्निर्बहुधा विराद्धि रुद्रैः प्रजग्धं यवि वा पिशाचैः।
सर्वं तदीशानो अभयं कृणोतु शिवमीशानाय स्वाहा।।७।।

Lord Īśāna make the benevolent food free from all defects which is kept by fire for the subject by protecting the same from Rudras and demons (Piśācās). This morsel (āhuti) is offered to that Lord Śiva (Īśānadeva).

[The cereals should be touched by reciting the hymns from serial 4 to 7 respectively. This cereal should be then processed with the droprets of water (Prakṣaṇa) by reciting two hymns mentioned in hymn nos. 8 and 9.]

अन्तश्चरसि भूतेषु गुहायां विश्वतोमुखः। त्वं यज्ञस्त्वं ब्रह्मा त्वं रुद्रस्त्वं विष्णुस्त्वं वषट्कार आपो ज्योती रसोऽमृतं ब्रह्म भूर्भुवः सुवरों नमः।।८।।

You are Yajña (offering), Brahmā, Viṣṇu, Vaṣaṭkāra, Apaḥ (water) flame, essence Rasa) Nectar (Amṛt), Brahma, Bhūḥ, Bhuvaḥ and Svaḥ who reside within the heart of living organisms by virtue of omnipresence and move ceaselessly. You are saluted.

आपः पुनन्तु पृथिवीं पृथिवी पूता पुनातु माम्। पुनन्तु ब्रह्मणस्पतिर्ब्रह्मपूता पुनातु माम्।
यदुच्छिष्टमभोज्यं यद्वा दुश्चरितं मम। सर्वं पुनन्तु मामापोऽसतां च प्रतिग्रहं स्वाहा।।९।।

O Āpaḥ (water)! Purify the earth and so purified earth should make me pure. May this Brahmapūta earth! make us holy. May Lord water! Remove the staleness, unhygienic and disorders inserted within me and thus make us holy. This morsel is being offered for the same.

अमृतमस्यमृतोपस्तरणमस्यमृतं प्राणे जुहोम्यमाशिष्यान्तोऽसि। ॐ प्राणाय स्वाहा। ॐ अपानाय स्वाहा। ॐ व्यानाय स्वाहा। ॐ उदानाय स्वाहा। ॐ समानाय स्वाहा। ॐ ब्रह्मणे स्वाहा। ॐ ब्रह्मणि म आत्माऽमृतत्वायेति।।१०।।

(Thus, two times the water should be sprinkled with hymn reciting and then water in right palm with left hand touching the alter) one should recite 'Amṛtamasyamṛtopastaraṇamasi (viz O water! You are in nectar form and provide immortal coverage). Then, making research with (realisation) soul, the morsel (the water taken in palm as Āhuti) should be offered to breathing (Prāṇa) by reciting coincide "Amṛtaṁ prāṇe.."(the material equal to nectar has been taken) the morsel (Āhuti) is this offered for Apāna, Vyāna, Udāna and Samāna as also for Brahma. May my soul enjoy the essence of nector (immortality) in Brahma.

कनिष्ठिकाङ्गुल्याङ्गुष्ठेन च प्राणे जुहोति अनामिकयापाने मध्यमया व्याने सर्वाभिरुदाने प्रदेशिन्या समाने।।११।।

The morsel (Āhuti) should be offered to breathing (Prāṇa) by little finger and thumb, by ring finger to Apāna, by middle finger to vyāna and by all fingers to Samāna.

[A hint of having five breathing (praṇas) link with different figures of hand has been given. It is a matter of research that how the five breathings are satiated by using different fingers while offering the morsel (Āhuti).]

तूष्णीमेकामेकऋचा जुहोति द्वे आहवनीये एकां दक्षिणाग्नौ एकां गार्हपत्ये एकां सर्वप्रायश्चित्तीये।।१२।।

One morsel (Āhuti) should be offered by silent recital (Japa) of the hymn 'Prāṇāya Svāhā, two morsels on Āhavanīya by reciting (Japa) of "Apānāya Svāhā, one in Dakṣiṇāgni, one in gārhapatya and one in sarvaprāyaścittīya fire.

अथापिधानमस्यमृतत्वायोपस्पृश्य पुनरादाय पुनरुपस्पृशेत्।।१३।।

Thus after offering five morsels, and following the hymn 'Atha purastāt coparitācca abdhiḥ pandadhāti" i.e. eating the food; the disclosed form should be touched for immortality, then it should be taken and again touched.

सव्ये प्राणावाऽऽपो गृहीत्वा हृदयमन्वालभ्य जपेत्। प्राणोऽग्निः परमात्मा पञ्चवायुभिरावृतः। अभयं सर्वभूतेभ्यो न मे भीतिः कदाचन।।१४।।

Japa should be made by keeping the hand nearer to the heart (hṛdyālambhana) and taking water in the left hand. The cardinal breathing (Mukhya Prāṇa) is the supreme soul surrounded by five kinds of air (i.e. Prāṇa, Apāna, Vyāna, Udāna and Samāna). May it make me free from all kinds of fear prognosticated of all living organisms (creatures) and should I not fear of them.

विश्वोऽसि वैश्वानरो विश्वरूपं त्वया धार्यते जायमानम्। विश्वं त्वाहुतयः सर्वा यत्र ब्रह्माऽमृतोऽपि।।१५।।

O united Prāṇa! you are in universal form. You too hold this entire world in garb of gigantic Vaiśvānara, that Vaiśvānara is existed in the body of all living organism. You are in the form of immortal Brahma (Brahmamṛta). This universe created by you merges in the form of morsels (Āhutis) in Turīyāgni.

महानवोऽयं पुरुषो योऽङ्गुष्ठाग्रे प्रतिष्ठितः। तमद्भिः परिषिञ्चामि सोऽस्यान्ते अमृताय च।।१६।।

You exist in the form of innovative person every moment at the five part of both thumbs in feet as prāṇa. At the end of food, I satiate you for obtaining the immortality.

अनावित्येष बाह्यात्मा ध्यायेताग्निहोत्रं जुहोमीति। सर्वेषामेव सूनुर्भवति। अस्य यज्ञपरिवृता आहुतीर्होमयति।।१७।।

That (person in the form of breathing) is enriched of specific efforts. The exterior soul therefore should do meditation on them. This person does offering (Agnihotra) daily in the form of breathing. (As the supreme soul provides you with maintenance as the fathers do) you therefore are son like to all. Making this presumption you offer morsel while arranging the āhuti.

स्वशरीरे यज्ञं परिवर्तयामीति। चत्वारोऽग्नयस्ते किं नारमर्धया:॥१८॥

(I) convert the offering in my body. Four kinds of fire are considered in this body. It is in most micro form. These all are merely of half-moras (Ardhamātrika).

तत्र सूर्योऽग्निर्नाम सूर्यमण्डलाकृति: सहस्त्ररश्मिपरिवृत एकऋषिर्भूत्वा मूर्धनि तिष्ठति। यस्मादुक्तो दर्शनाग्निर्नाम चतुराकृतिराहवनीयो भूत्वा मुखे तिष्ठति। शारीरोऽग्निर्नाम जराप्रणुदा हविरवस्कन्दति। अर्धचन्द्राकृतिर्दक्षिणाग्निर्भूत्वा हृदये तिष्ठति। तत्र कोष्ठाग्निरितिकोष्ठाग्निर्नामाशितपीतलीढस्वादितं सम्यग् व्यष्ट्यं विषयित्वा गार्हपत्यो भूत्वा नाभ्यां तिष्ठति॥१९

The five namely 'Sūryāgni', out of these four fires is like the orbital shape of the sun. These five reside in the mind (Mūrdhā) with countless rays and ever extended form (As it is popular that Turīyani Mūrdhni (Saṁsthitam). Since this living soul is seen everywhere in the form of God, it has been soul, Darśanāgni. It resided in the mouth with virad etc. four forms and worth summoning (Āhavanīya). The Śārīra Agni (Hiraṇyagarbha) that ignites the formidable body, weakened by the old age etc., is dependent on it. It gobbles up the formidable morsel (Hari) in the form of Prapañca (artificial processes) which is existed in the heart of all living organisms as Dakṣiṇāgni in the form of half moon (Ardhacandra). It digests the eaten, drunk, licked and gobbled up items by duly cooking them and resides in navel zone in the form of Gārhapatya-agni.

प्रायश्चित्तयस्त्वधस्तात्तिर्यक् तिस्रो हिमांशुप्रभाभि: प्रजननकर्मा॥२०॥

Thus, the propensities of mind are existed in the lower parts of the body. The curvy propensities (Tiryak) and himāṅśu (the moon in the form of mind) illuminating the three stages i.e., awaking, dreaming and dormant are competant to do every thing. He illumines everything.

अस्य शारीरयज्ञस्य यूपरशनाशोभितस्य को यजमान: का पत्नी के ऋत्विज: के सदस्या: कानि यज्ञपात्राणि कानि हवींषि का वेदि: काऽन्तर्वेदि: को द्रोणकलश: को रथ: क: पशु: कोऽध्वर्यु: को होता को ब्राह्मणाच्छंसी क: प्रतिप्रस्थाता क: प्रस्तोता को मैत्रावरुण: क उद्गाता का धारा क: पोता के दर्भा: क: स्त्रुव: काज्यस्थाली कावाघारौ कावाज्यभागौ केऽत्र याजा: के अनुयाजा: केडा क: सूक्तवाक: क: शंयोर्वाक: काऽहिंसा के पत्नीसंयाजा: को यूप: का रशना का इष्टय: का दक्षिणा किमवभृथमिति॥२१॥

Who is the client (Yajamāna) of this Śārīra Yajña deprived of the pillar (Yūpa) and Cord (Raśanā), who are wife, Ṛtvij and members? Who are vessels for offering (Yajña), morsel (Hari), alter (Vedī), internal alter (Antarvedikā), Kalaśa, chariot, animal (for offering), Adhvaryu, Hotā, Brāhmaṇācchaṁsī, Pratiprasthātā, Prastotā, Maitrāvaruṇa, udgātā, dhārā (winnower), Potā, Darbha (Kuśā grass), Śruvā (spoon like apparatus), Ājyasthālī (ghee vessel), Āghāra,, Ājyabhāgam, Yāja, Anuyāja, Iḍa, Sūktavāk, Śaṁyorvāk, Ahiṁsā, Patnī, Saṁyāja, Yūpa (pillar) Raśana (Lord), Iṣṭa, Dakṣiṇā and (Avabhṛtha) made at the time of completism of the offerings? (viz., all above said things, material etc, are required while performing the offering. Śārīra Yajña also requires these all but what and where these are all?).

अस्य शारीरयज्ञस्य यूपरशनाशोभितस्य को यजमानः बुद्धिः पत्नी वेदा महर्त्विजः अहंकारोऽध्वर्युः चित्तं होता प्राणो ब्राह्मणाच्छंसी अपना प्रतिप्रस्थाता व्यानः प्रस्तोता उदान उद्गाता समानो मैत्रावरुणः शरीरं वेदिः नासिकाऽन्तर्वेदिः मूर्धा द्रोणकलशः पादो रथः दक्षिणहस्तः स्रुवः सव्यहस्त आज्यस्थाली श्रोत्रे आघारौ चक्षुषी आज्यभागौ ग्रीवा धारा पोता तन्मात्राणि सदस्याः महाभूतानि प्रयाजाः भूतानि गुणा अनुयाजाः जिह्वेडा दन्तोष्ठौ सूक्तवाकः तालुः शंयोर्वाकः स्मृतिर्दया क्षान्तिरहिंसा पत्नीसंयाजाः ओंकारो यूपः आशा रशना मनो रथः कामः पशुः केशा दर्भा बुद्धीन्द्रियाणि यज्ञपात्राणि कर्मेन्द्रयाणि हवींषि अहिंसा इष्टयः त्यागो दक्षिणा अवभूथं मरणात् सर्वा ह्यस्मिन्देवताः शरीरेऽधिसमाहिताः॥२२॥

The Śārīra Yajña which has no pillar and cord holds the soul as Yajamāna (client), wisdom is wife, Vedas are the great Ṛtvij, ego is Adhvaryu, mind is Hotā, Prāṇa (breathing) is Brāhmaṇācahhaṁsī, Apāna is Pratiprasthātā, Vyāna is Prastotā, Udāna is udgātā, Samāna is Maitrā Varuṇa, body is alter, Nāsikā (nose) is inner-alter, head is kalāśa, feet one chariot, right hand is Śruvā, left is ghee vessel, ears are Āghāra, eyes are part of Ājya, neck is Dhārā and Potā, tanmātrās are members, the Pañca Mahābhūta is Prayāja, the living orgamisms are property (Gaṇa) and Anuyāja, tongue is Iḍā, teeth and lips are Sūktavāk, palatal is Śaṁyorvāk, the memory, kindness and peace are non-violence (Ahiṁsā) and Patnīsaṁyāja, Oṁ is pillar, hope is cord, mind is chariot, lust is animal, hair are Kuśa grass, sensory organs are vessels for offering, executive organs are morsel (Hari), Ahiṁsā (Non-violence) is Iṣṭas,, sacrifice is Dakṣiṇā (donation) and the death is Avabhṛtha bath. The offering performed under such presumption, deferentially endows the fruits in toto, and all gods then enter in this body.

वाराणस्यां मृतो वापि इदं वा ब्राह्मणः पठेत्। एकेन जन्मना जन्तुर्मोक्षं च प्राप्नुयादिति मोक्षं च प्राप्नुयादित्युपिषत्॥२३॥

This Upaniṣad produces that either the death of a person in Kāśī or persued of this Upaniṣad, he definitely shall attain the mind purifying knowledge and the emancipation (mokṣa) too.

॥इति प्राणाग्निहोत्रोपनिषत् समाप्ता॥

84. GOPĀLAPŪRVATĀPINYUPANIṢAD

गोपालपूर्वतापिन्युपनिषद्

This upaniṣad falls under the tradition of Atharvaveda. Lord Kṛṣṇa as a particular Brahma has been laid down in it and at a conclusion he has been referred to as a Brahma who is invisible as also intangible. This upaniṣad has been commenced in the form of a questionnaire as a result of questions and answers transacted between the saints and lord Brahmā himself.

In the opening lines, a psalm to lord Kṛṣṇa with keen devotion has been made in the form of Maṅgalācaraṇa. The supreme element of divinity in the personality of lord Kṛṣṇa then has been described. This upaniṣad then advances to describe the nature of lord Kṛṣṇa, a particular meditation, on a specific form of him, the recital of hymn pertaining to lord Kṛṣṇa, the psalm to lord Kṛṣṇa, a provision for the worship, description of the hymn (Aṣṭadarśana) as a mean of the creation, source of attaining self-knowledge, description of the creation of universe from the five feet used in the hymn, psalm to lord Govinda in five feet, meditation on Gopāla Kṛṣṇa as also the manner of Japa (silent recital) and the psalm has been elaborated in detail. At the concluding part, the importance of this upaniṣad has been explained.

॥शान्तिपाठः॥

ॐ भद्रं कर्णेभिः .... इति शान्तिः॥

कृषिर्भूवाचकः शब्दो नश्च निर्वृतिवाचकः। तयोरैक्यं परं ब्रह्म कृष्ण इत्यभिधीयते॥
सच्चिदानन्दरूपाय कृष्णायाक्लिष्टकर्मणे। नमो वेदान्तवेद्याय गुरवे बुद्धिसाक्षिणे॥ १॥

The 'Kṛṣ' word is indicative of entity and the 'Ṇa' is indicative of the pleasure. The combination of both these words i.e. 'Kṛs' plus 'Ṇa' laid down the name of lord Kṛṣṇa. Salutation is conveyed to lord Kṛṣna, who is competent to do everything, whose complexion is comprising trio-elements i.e. the truth, the spirit and the pleasure (Saccidānanda), who is worth-knowing through Vedas and witness to our wit as also a teacher to this whole universe.

मुनयो ह वै ब्राह्मणमूचुः। कः परमो देवः। कुतो मृत्युर्बिभेति। कस्य विज्ञानेनाखिलं विज्ञातं भवति। केनेदं विश्वं संसरतीति॥ २॥

Once upon a time the saints raised a question before lord Brahmā– "O lord! Kindly tell us who is the supreme god? By whom the death is frightened? Who is the entity, if the element is known, nothing is left to known then? Who is that supreme power under whose instructions, this cycle of birth and death is tackled?"

तदु होवाच ब्राह्मणः। कृष्णो वै परमं दैवतम्। गोविन्दान्मृत्युर्बिभेति। गोपीजनवल्लभज्ञानेनैतद्विज्ञातं भवति। स्वाहेदं विश्वं संसरतीति॥ ३॥

While forwarding a solution to all these questions, lord Brahmā said to the saints– "O dear saints! Lord Kṛṣṇa is only the supreme god. The death even frightens if the name as Govinda is recited. If any person is known entirely to the essence of lord Kṛṣṇa, he becomes master to all knowledge. This world, under the motivation of the power of illusion (Māyā) in the form of Svāhā, always remains engaged in the cycle of birth and the death."

तदु होचुः। कः कृष्णः। गोविन्दश्च कोऽसाविति। गोपीजनवल्लभश्च कः। का स्वाहेति॥४॥

Those saints again raised a query– "O Lord! who is lord Śrī Kṛṣṇa and Govinda? Who is the beloved to Gopīs (the maids engaged in the buying and selling of milk and milk products) and kindly tell us who is Svāhā?"

तानुवाच ब्राह्मणः। पापकर्षणो गोभूमिवेदविदितो गोपीजनविद्याकलापीप्रेरकः। तन्माया चेति सकलं परं ब्रह्मैव तत्। यो ध्यायति रसति भजति सोऽमृतो भवतीति॥५॥ ते होचुः किं तद्रूपं किं रसनं किमाहो तद्भजनं तत्सर्वं विविदिषतामाख्याहीति॥६॥

Reacting on the request made by the saints, lord Brahmā explained these words and satisfying them– "O dear saints! It is the power of lord Kṛṣṇa that only can convert the brain of people to apply it in executing holy deeds instead of evils. He only is in the form of omniscient Hari namely Govinda who has mastery on nourishing the cow, the land and the speech of Vedas. That beloved to Gopīs is the only inspiration of learning and the art to all Gopīs and Svāhā is the power of illusion (Māyā Śakti) handled by lord Kṛṣṇa. This power is the phenomenon of Brahma (knowledge). Thus, the person who meditates on the perfect Brahma (knowledge) renowned with the name of lord Kṛṣṇa and recites daily his holy names as also engages him in psalms and pray in commune, attains immortality. Those saints again asked– "O revered god! What form of lord Kṛṣṇa would be fit for the meditation? Please describe what kind of perceptions are availed as a result of reciting his name and what is the manner in which lord Kṛṣṇa should be worshipped? Kindly satisfy us by describing the solution to these queries in detail."

तदु होवाच हैरण्यो गोपवेषमभ्राभं तरुणं कल्पद्रुमाश्रितम्॥७॥

On submission of the saints, the Hiraṇyagarbha Brahmā told– "O dear saints! Listen to more clearly the description for the complexion of lord Kṛṣṇa worth meditation. His appearance is like the boys who rear the cows, his complexion is as dark as the clouds bearing the fresh water. He is in his teens and he is enshrined under the divine Kalpavṛkṣa.

तदिह श्लोका भवन्ति–सत्पुण्डरीकनयनं मेघाभं वैद्युताम्बरम्। द्विभुजं ज्ञानमुद्राढ्यं वनमालिनमीश्वरम्॥८॥
गोपगोपाङ्गनावीतं सुरद्रुमतलाश्रितम्। दिव्यालंकरणोपेतं रत्नपङ्कजमध्यगम्॥९॥
कालिन्दीजलकल्लोलसङ्गिमारुतसेवितम्। चिन्तयंश्चेतसा कृष्णं मुक्तो भवति संसृतेः॥१०॥

These hymns has been contemplated in this context. The eyes of lord Kṛṣṇa are analogous to the white blossomed lotus. He is in the posture of meditation with both arms. A long garland made of the wild flowers is embellishing his neck. He is the great god and covered all around by the Gopas (cow-rearing boys) and the maids. He is seated under the

Kalpavṛkṣa. His body is embellished with divine garments and ornaments as well. He is seated just at the middle portion of the lotus made of the gems on the throne studded with gems. The cold breeze blowing by kissing the all caprice waves of Yamunā is engaged in the service of lord Kṛṣṇa. The devotee who can focus his mind in such fascinating complexion of lord Kṛṣṇa attains emancipation from all these worldly ties.

तस्य पुना रसनमिति जलभूमीन्दुसंपातः कामादिकृष्णायेत्येकं पदम्। गोविन्दायेति द्वितीयम्। गोपीजनेति तृतीयम्। वल्लभायेति तुरीयम्। स्वाहेति पञ्चममिति॥ ११॥ पञ्चपदं जपन्पञ्चाङ्गं द्यावाभूमिसूर्याचन्द्रमसौ साग्नी तद्रूपतया ब्रह्म संपद्यते ब्रह्म संपद्यत इति॥ १२॥

Now in the ceretum the pleasure of recital to the name of lord Kṛṣṇa and the hymn pertaining to him are described. The word 'Klīṁ' a group of (Ka) water, (La) land, 'Ī', E, Induḥ (Anusvāra) too is the seed of Kāma (sex or inspiration). The foot 'Kṛṣṇāya' should be pronunciated by placing this root hymn in the beginning. Thus the first foot to the whole hymn is– 'Klīṁ Kṛṣṇāya'. The second foot is 'Govindāya', the third foot is 'Gopījana', the fourth foot is Vallabhāya and Svāhā is the fifth foot. Thus with the five feet, this hymn is 'Klīm Kṛṣṇāya Govindāya Gopījana Vallabhāya Svāhā'. This hymn is known as 'Pañcapadi' (hymn with five feet). Having illustrative to the earth, the ether, the sun, the moon and the fire, this phenomenal hymn is the conjoint form of the five limbs. The devotee who performs the psalm and Japa by this hymn, attains to lord Śrī Kṛṣṇa who himself is the perfect Brahma (knowledge).

तदेष श्लोकः– क्लीमित्येतदादावादाय कृष्णाय गोविन्दाय गोपीजनवल्लभायेति बृहन्मानव्या सकृदुच्चरेद्योऽसौ गतिस्तस्यास्ति मङ्क्षु नान्या गतिः स्यादिति॥ १३॥

This hymn is contemplated in this context. The devotee who will pronunciate the feet– 'Kṛṣṇāya, Govindāya, Gopījana Vallabhāya' by placing the root of sex (Kāmabīja), 'Klīṁ' in the beginning alongwith the pronunciation of Svāhā, definitely and at the earliest attains to the highest position. There is no other option regarding the position for that devotee.

भक्तिरस्य भजनम्। तदिहामुत्रोपाधिनैराश्येनामुष्मिन्मनः कल्पनम्। एतदेव च नैष्कर्म्यम्॥ १४॥

The inseparable devotion of lord Kṛṣṇa is only the psalm. The nature of real psalm is to abandon the attachments like passion, to enjoy the luxuries of this and that world and to devote the mind alongwith all sensory organs on the holy name of lord Kṛṣṇa. It is only the real recursion.

कृष्णं तं विप्रा बहुधा यजन्ति गोविन्दं सन्तं बहुधाऽऽराधयन्ति।
गोपीजनवल्लभो भुवनानि दध्रे स्वाहाश्रितो जगदैजत्सुरेताः॥ १५॥

The scholars duly known to Vedas perform worship to lord Kṛṣṇa in varied ways. They offer their pray with varied manners to lord Śrī Kṛṣṇa renowned with the name of Govinda. That Gopījana Vallabha too nourishes all the worlds and that lord with his supreme power of resolution and has created this universe by resorting to the power of illusion which is known as Svāhā.

वायुर्यथैको भुवनं प्रविष्टो जन्येजन्ये पञ्चरूपो बभूव।
कृष्णस्तथैकोऽपि जगद्धितार्थं शब्देनासौ पञ्चपदो विभातीति॥ १६॥

As the element of air is spreaded in the expanse of this whole world and it is called breathing (Prāṇa) within the body of every living-organisms in its five forms; lord Śrī Kṛṣṇa also in the same fashion is one and alone but known with the five feet of separate name in this hymn as described above.

ते होचुरुपासनमेतस्य परमात्मनो गोविन्दस्याखिलाधारिणो ब्रूहीति॥ १७॥

All those saints again asked– "O lord! How the supreme Brahma Govinda, a great shelter to the whole world; is worshipped? Kindly educate us in detail."

तानुवाच यत्तस्य पीठं हैरण्याष्टपलाशमम्बुजं तदन्तरालिकानलास्त्रयुगं तदन्तरालाद्यर्णाखिलबीजं कृष्णाय नम इति बीजाढ्यं स ब्रह्माणमादायानङ्गगायत्रीं यथावद्व्यालिख्य भूमण्डलं शूलवेष्टितं कृत्वाङ्गवासुदेवादिरुक्मिण्यादिस्वशक्तीन्द्रादिवसुदेवादिपार्थादिनिध्यावीतं यजेत्संध्यासु प्रतिपत्तिभिरुपचारैः। तेनास्याखिलं भवत्यखिलं भवतीति॥ १८॥

Lord Brahmā with the description of the back of lord Kṛṣṇa (Gopala Yantra) told those saints– "O dear saints! One should draw a lotus containing eight petals with gold on the back. In the middle of this lotus, two reverse triangles should be drawn. Thus there will be six angles made. In the middle of these angles, 'Klīṁ' (Kāmabīja) as the initial letter should be written on the hypotenuse. This hymn is pre-dominant mean for attaining success in all the activities. Now each letter of the hymn 'Kṛṣṇāya Namaḥ' with the seed hymn 'Klīṁ' should be written in every angle so made. A space should be then created duly covered by eight thunderbolts with quoting therein the hymn of Brahma (the learning of Gopala that comprises eighteen letters) and the 'Kāma Gāyatrī' (Kāmadevāya with Vidmahe Puṣpavaṇāya Dhimahi', Tannonaṅgah Pracodayāt). Then the 'Pīṭha Yantra' duly protected by eight covers including Indra, Vasudeva, Pārtha and Nidhi as also Svaśakti including Aṅga, Vasudeva etc. and Rukmiṇī should be worshipped with this hymn. Lord Kṛṣṇa should be worshipped complying with sixteen modes of worship after meditation, three times a day. The devotee who becomes able to perform this complete procedure can avail easily everything i.e. Dharma (great conception), Artha (the wealth), Kāma (the sex or inspiration) and the Mokṣa (the emancipation).

तदिह श्लोका भवन्ति–एको वशी सर्वगः कृष्ण ईड्य एकोऽपि सन्बहुधा यो विभाति।
तं पीठगं येऽनुभजन्ति धीरास्तेषां सिद्धिः शाश्वती नेतरेषाम्॥ १९॥

These hymns are in this context. lord Kṛṣṇa only is adorable because he regulates all persons and omnipresent. Inspite of being one, he is seen in multiform. The person who worships lord Kṛṣṇa by duly enshrining him on the above Pīṭha, attains the everlasting pleasure and no body others.

नित्यो नित्यानां चेतनश्चेतनानामेको बहूनां यो विदधाति कामान्।

तं पीठगं येऽनुभजन्ति धीरास्तेषां सुखं शाश्वतं नेतरेषाम्॥ २०॥

Lord Kṛṣṇa who is immortal in immortals, most sensitive among sensitive, scholar and who fulfills the desires of all, the devotee worshipping him by enshrining on the above said Pīṭha, is only blessed with the eternal pleasure and no body others.

एतद्विष्णोः परमं पदं ये नित्योद्युक्तास्तं यजन्ति न कामात्।
तेषामसौ गोपरूपः प्रयत्नात्प्रकाशयेदात्मपदं तदेव॥ २१॥

The person who worship lord Viṣṇu (lord Kṛṣṇa) with this hymn complying with the procedure and who do not anticipate anything besides lord Kṛṣṇa, that Śyāma Sundara in garb of Gopala make him to realize his nature and the most everlasting abode without delay.

यो ब्रह्माणं विदधाति पूर्वं यो विद्यां तस्मै गोपायति स्म कृष्णः।
तं ह देवमात्मबुद्धिप्रकाशं मुमुक्षुः शरणं व्रजेत्॥ २२॥

Lord Śrī Kṛṣṇa who make appear lord Brahmā in the initial stage of the creation and who preaches lord Brahmā, the learning of Veda and make him to recite these Vedas, such is lord Kṛṣṇa and the person fond of attaining emancipation should definitely resort to him.

ओङ्कारेणान्तरितं ये जपन्ति गोविन्दस्य पञ्चपदं मनुम्।
तेषामसौ दर्शयेदात्मरूपं तस्मान्मुमुक्षुरभ्यसेन्नित्यशान्त्यै॥ २३॥

The great devotees who recite the renowned hymn containing eighteen letters and five feet with the syllable Oṁ, definitely see the complexion of Śrī Govinda. The man desirous of emancipation from all worldly ties should recite the above described hymn in order to attain everlasting peace.

एतस्मा एव पञ्चपदादभूवन्गोविन्दस्य मनवो मानवानाम्।
दशार्णाद्यास्तेऽपि संक्रन्दनाद्यैरभ्यस्यन्ते भूतिकामैर्यथावत्॥ २४॥

All hymns arisen from the above hymn of five feet that contain ten letters; also are benevolent to the humanity. The gods Indra etc. desirous of luxuries do 'Japa' of the hymns containing ten letters etc. with meditation and Nyāsa (to summon god for all organs of the body).

ते पप्रच्छुस्तदु होवाच ब्रह्मसदनं चरतो मे ध्यातः स्तुतः परमेश्वरः परार्धान्ते सोऽबुध्यत। गोपवेषो मे पुरुषः पुरस्तादाविर्बभूव। ततः प्रणतो मयानुकूलेन हृदा मह्यमष्टादशार्णस्वरूपं सृष्टये दत्त्वान्तर्हितः। पुनस्ते सिसृक्षतो मे प्रादुरभूत्तेष्वक्षरेषु विभज्य भविष्यज्जगद्रूपं प्रकाशयन्। तदिह कादापो लात्पृथिवीतोऽग्निर्बिन्दोरिन्दुस्तत्संपातात्तदर्क इति क्लींकारादसृजं कृष्णादाकाशं खाद्वायुरुत्तरात्सुरभिविद्याः प्रादुरकार्षमकार्षमिति। तदुत्तरात्स्त्रीपुंसादिभेदं सकलमिदं सकलमिदमिति॥ २५॥

Lord Brahmā told on enquiry made by the saints– "O saints! I survive upto two 'Parardha'. One 'Parardha' has been already passed in meditation and hymns to god ceaselessly. Only then the lord was attracted towards me. Śyāma Sundara in garb of a

'Gopa' appeared before me as the supreme person. I bowed unto his feet with the keen devotion. The lord was pleased and with a grace preached me the hymn containing eighteen letters for creation of the universe and then vanished. Later on, at the juncture when I became passionate to create the universe, he again appeared before me and provided me with a glimpse of the prospective world in all the letters of that hymn. So inspired by lord Kṛṣṇa, I originated the water by the letter 'Ka', the earth by 'La', the fire by 'Ī', the moon by Anusvāra (half circle) and the god son by the commune of all these. Similarly, I made appear the element of ether and the wind by the ether by virtue of the second foot of hymn 'Kṛṣṇāya'. I originated 'Kāmadhenu' (divine cow) and the learning of Vedas etc. from the third foot 'Govindāya'. Then from the fourth foot 'Gopījana Vallabhāya', the women and men etc. were originated and lastly the movable and immovable, inert and sensitive world was originated from the fifth foot 'Svāhā'.

[The hymn described above contains eighteen letters which are 'Klīṁ' Kṛṣṇāya Govindāya Gopījana Vallabhāya Svāhā'.]

एतस्यैव यजनेन चन्द्रध्वजो गतमोहमात्मानं वेदयति। ओंकारालिकं मनुमावर्तयेत्। सङ्गरहितोऽभ्यानत्॥ २६॥

In the ancient times, the king Candradhvaja made himself get rid of attachment by virtue of worship to lord Kṛṣṇa and by 'Japa' and meditation on the hymn containing eighteen letters alongwith Oṁ. Thus as a blessing, he got self-knowledge thereby attained the emancipation.

तद्विष्णोः परमं पदं सदा पश्यन्ति सूरयः। दिवीव चक्षुराततम्॥ २७॥

The scholars and the devotees ceaselessly adore the ever-lasting supreme abode of lord Viṣṇu (Śrī Kṛṣṇa). He analogous to the sun-god is ether present everywhere and every direction in garb of the light.

तस्मादेनं नित्यमावर्तयेन्नित्यमावर्तयेदिति॥ २८॥

The hymn containing eighteen letters is the only mean for attainment of the everlasting abode of that god. Therefore this divine hymn should be recited daily.

तदाहुरेके यस्य प्रथमपदाद्भूमिर्द्वितीयपदाज्जलं तृतीयपदात्तेजश्चतुर्थपदाद्वायुश्चरमपदाद्व्योमेति। वैष्णवं पञ्चव्याहृतिमयं मन्त्रं कृष्णावभासकं कैवल्यस्य सृत्यै सततमावर्तयेत्सततमावर्तयेदिति॥ २९॥

Some saints say that the hymn containing eighteen letters provides with the splendour to the complexion of lord Kṛṣṇa with its five feet. These five feet are– the first is 'Klīṁ' i.e. element of the earth, the second 'Kṛṣṇāya' is the element of water, the third 'Govindāya' is splendour (element of fire), the fourth foot 'Gopījana Vallabhāya' is the element of wind and the last and fifth feet is the element of ether. This hymn should always be recited and a meditation should be made upon for the sake of attainment of the emancipation.

तदत्र गाथाः– यस्य चाद्यपदाद्भूमिर्द्वितीयात्सलिलोद्भवः। तृतीयात्तेज उद्भूतं चतुर्थाद्गन्धवाहनः॥ ३०॥

पञ्चमादम्बरोत्पत्तिस्तमेवैकं समभ्यसेत्। चन्द्रध्वजोऽगमद्विष्णोः परमं पदमव्ययम्॥ ३१॥

It is a well-settled dictum in this context that the hymn containing eighteen letters should always be recited and the meditation should be made upon who has originated the earth by its first foot, the water by second foot, the splendour (fire) by the third foot, the air by the fourth foot and the ether by the fifth foot. It is the magnificence of this hymn that made the king Candradhvaja able to attain the everlasting abode of lord Kṛṣṇa.

ततो विशुद्धं विमलं विशोकमशेषलोभादिनिरस्तसङ्गम्।
यत्तत्पदं पञ्चपदं तदेव स वासुदेवो न यतोऽन्यदस्ति॥ ३२॥

That abode (Goloka) is most sacrosanct, holy, free from agony, greed etc. as also free from all kinds of attachment. That abode is not distinct than the hymn containing five feet as described above. That hymn in itself is the apparent Vāsudeva and nothing distinct than him.

तमेकं गोविन्दं सच्चिदानन्दविग्रहं पञ्चपदं वृन्दावनसुरभूरुहतलासीनं सततं समरुद्गणोऽहं परमया स्तुत्या तोषयामि॥ ३३॥

That lord Govinda is in the form of five feet hymn. His appearance is enriched of the truth, the meditation and the pleasures. He always is enthroned under a divine tree (Kalpa Vṛkṣa) on the throne studded with gems in Vṛndāvana. I (Brahmā) with Marudgaṇas (the wind) please that lord Śrī Kṛṣṇa with recital of excellent psalms.

ॐ नमो विश्वस्वरूपाय विश्वस्थित्यन्तहेतवे। विश्वेश्वराय विश्वाय गोविन्दाय नमो नमः॥ ३४॥

Lord Govinda is saluted ceaselessly who himself is in garb of this entire world, the sole cause of nourishing and destroying as also the universal and the only regulator of this whole world.

नमो विज्ञानरूपाय परमानन्दरूपिणे। कृष्णाय गोपीनाथाय गोविन्दाय नमो नमः॥ ३५॥

The beloved of the maids (Gopīs) lord Govinda is ceaselessly saluted as he is the treasure of knowledge and the supreme pleasure. He is competent absolutely to fascinate all the living organisms.

नमः कमलनेत्राय नमः कमलमालिने। नमः कमलनाभाय कमलापतये नमः॥ ३६॥

Salute is conveyed to lord Kamalapati (Kṛṣṇa) from whose navel, the lotus has been arisen, who wears the garland of lotus flowers on his neck and holds the fascinating beauty of the lotus flower in his both eyes.

बर्हापीडाभिरामाय रामायाकुण्ठमेधसे। रमामानसहंसाय गोविन्दाय नमो नमः॥ ३७॥

Lord Govinda looking beautiful with the wing of peacock on forehead, whose mind and the power of memory never frustrated, who is worshipped by all and who is a flamingo to the mind of Rāma, Gopīs and Śrī Rādhā.

कंसवंशविनाशाय केशिचाणूरघातिने। वृषभध्वजवन्द्याय पार्थसारथये नमः॥ ३८॥

Lord Śrī Kṛṣṇa is saluted frequently as he was the charioteer to Arjuna, killer of

Kaṁsa's clan and who had slaughtered Keśi and Caṇūra as also who is worshipped by Vṛṣabhadhvaja (lord Śiva).

वेणुवादनशीलाय गोपालायाहिमर्दिने। कालिन्दीकूललोलाय लोलकुण्डलधारिणे॥ ३९॥

वल्लवीवदनाम्भोजमालिने नृत्तशालिने। नमः प्रणतपालाय श्रीकृष्णाय नमो नमः॥ ४०॥

Whose common interest is playing the flute, who is nourisher of all cows and who is competent to split up the ego of a cobra named Kāli, who is busy on dancing at the hoods in Kāliyāhrada on the bank of Kālindī with most dynamic speed, whose ear rings are sparkling due to dynamic dance, whose body organs are fascinating like the fresh garland of fresh lotus and who is entirely seeming excellent, such lord Kṛṣṇa, most generous to the devotees is frequently saluted.

नमः पापप्रणाशाय गोवर्धनधराय च। पूतनाजीवितान्ताय तृणावर्तासुहारिणे॥ ४१॥

Lord Kṛṣṇa is saluted who destroys the evils and the evil-doers, who holds the mountain Govardhana on his little finger in order to protect the life of citizens, who had killed she devil Pūtanā and the devil Tṛṇavarta.

निष्कलाय विमोहाय शुद्धायाशुद्धवैरिणे। अद्वितीयाय महते श्रीकृष्णाय नमो नमः॥ ४२॥

Lord Śrī Kṛṣṇa is frequently saluted as he is beyond the odds, absolutely free from attachment, most holy and supreme, enemy to obnoxious and brusque demons and nobody is distinct and separate from him.

प्रसीद परमानन्द प्रसीद परमेश्वर। आधिव्याधिभुजङ्गेन दष्टं मामुद्धर प्रभो॥ ४३॥

O supreme lord! You are full of pleasure therefore, pray on me and accept me under your grace. O god! the snakes in garb of mental and physical pains have bitten me. Hence, protect me from all these pains.

श्रीकृष्ण रुक्मिणीकान्त गोपीजनमनोहर। संसारसागरे मग्नं मामुद्धर जगद्गुरो॥ ४४॥

O lord Kṛṣṇa! O darling to Rukmiṇī! O Śyāma Sundara! You fascinate the heart of Gopīs, I am drowning in this worldly ocean. O the teacher of world! Please protect me.

केशव क्लेशहरण नारायण जनार्दन। गोविन्द परमानन्द मां समुद्धर माधव॥ ४५॥

O Keśava! O ever-competent Nārāyaṇa to relieving from pains! O the master of this world! O Govinda! You are the source of supreme pleasure. O Mādhava! have mercy on me and please protect me.

अथैवं स्तुतिभिराराधयामि तथा यूयं पञ्चपदं जपन्तः श्रीकृष्णं ध्यायन्तः संसृतिं तरिष्यथेति होवाच हैरण्यगर्भः॥ ४६॥

O great saints! As I (Brahmā) worship lord Kṛṣṇa with recital of these psalms, all of you in the same fashion should keep yourself busy on worship to lord Kṛṣṇa with meditation and a hymn containing eighteen letters and five feet as I have previously described. You will definitely cross this ocean of world. Thus lord Brahmā preached to those saints and hermits.

अमुं पञ्चपदं मन्त्रमावर्तयेद्यः स यात्यनायासतः केवलं तत्पदं तत्॥४७॥ अनेजदेकं मनसो जवीयो नैनद्देवा आप्नुवन्पूर्वमर्षदिति॥४८॥ तस्मात्कृष्ण एव परमो देवस्तं ध्यायेत् तं रसयेत् तं भजेत् तं भजेदित्यों तत्सदित्युपनिषत्॥४९॥

The man worshipping lord Kṛṣṇa regularly with the recital and meditation of above said eighteen letters and five feet hymns, definitely attains to the supreme everlasting position of that god. That supreme position is not dynamic but stabble and standing. It is rather different matter that it is more dynamic than that of the mind. Having a stable place for god in such a mind, it is unique. Any god or the speech etc. sensory organs seldom are competent to access there. He already has approached to the extent the position of sensory organs. Hence, lord Kṛṣṇa is only the supreme immortal god worth-reciting frequently. One should enjoy the pleasure of reciting his name in garb of the nectar with recital of the hymn and only that god should be worshipped daily. One should always engage himself in recital of this psalm. Oṁ (the supreme soul) is the only truth. Thus this upaniṣad is concluded.

ॐ भद्रं कर्णेभिः .... इति शान्तिः॥

॥इति गोपालपूर्वतापिन्युपनिषत्समाप्ता॥

85. KṚṢṆOPANIṢAD

कृष्णोपनिषद्

This upaniṣad is related to the tradition of Atharvaveda. It has been commenced as a questionnaire between the saints and the god. Accordingly, the several acts of lord have been appeared in the garb of several characters. It has been said in a concluding note that lord Śrī Kṛṣṇa has made the Vaikuntha Dhāma and all residents of heaven to appear on the earth. Lord Rāma has undertaken to again appear in the form of lord Kṛṣṇa. The person whosoever, knows that lord this way, attains the fruit of all pilgrimage and enjoys emancipation for ever from the physical bondage. This upaniṣad approaches to conclusion with elaboration of blessings to which the devotee avails.

॥शान्तिपाठः॥

ॐ भद्रं कर्णेभिः शृणुयाम देवा भद्रं पश्येमाक्षभिर्यजत्राः।
स्थिरैरङ्गैस्तुष्टुवाꣳ सस्तनूभिर्व्यशेम देवहितं यदायुः॥
स्वस्ति न ऽ इन्द्रो वृद्धश्रवाः स्वस्ति नः पूषा विश्ववेदाः।
स्वस्ति नस्तार्क्ष्यो अरिष्टनेमिः स्वस्ति नो बृहस्पतिर्दधातु॥
ॐ शान्तिः शान्तिः शान्तिः॥

Recital for peace.

O lord! should we listen to benevolent matters, see benevolent scenes and pass the complete age conferred to by almighty with sturdy and healthy organs of the body in the welfare deeds. May lord Indra, enriched with great fame bestow with our welfare. May the omniscient god Pūṣā do our welfare. May Ariṣṭanemi (motion of which cannot be resisted), the eagle (garuḍa) and Jupiter do our welfare. May the trio fevers be cooled down.

श्रीमहाविष्णुं सच्चिदानन्दलक्षणं रामचन्द्रं दृष्ट्वा सर्वाङ्गसुन्दरं मुनयो वनवासिनो विस्मिता बभूवुः। तं होचुर्नोऽवद्यमवतारान्वै गण्यन्ते आलिङ्गामो भवन्तमिति। भवान्तरे कृष्णावतारे यूयं गोपिका भूत्वा मामालिङ्गथ अन्ये येऽवतारास्ते हि गोपा नः स्त्रीश्च नो कुरु।

अन्योन्यविग्रहं धार्यं तवाङ्गस्पर्शनादिह। शश्वत्स्पर्शयितास्माकं गृह्णीमोऽवतारान्वयम्॥ १॥
रुद्रादीनां वचः श्रुत्वा प्रोवाच भगवान्स्वयम्। अङ्गसङ्गं करिष्यामि भवद्वाक्यं करोम्यहम्॥ २॥

The reclused saints were overwhelmed with surprise on seeing lord Rāmacandra (incarnate to lord Viṣṇu) who had beautiful limbs of the body and ever-shining complexion with the tree pleasure. (On having order to appear on earth issued by lord Brahmā) the saints said to him (lord Rāma) we do not consider it well to appear on the earth. We are keenly interested to have proximate relation with you. (Lord Rāma said) you will get my proximate relation (love and affection) during my next incarnation as Kṛṣṇa. When all of you will appear as Gopīka (milk-maid). (The saints again said) we want to be Gopa (cowherd) and Gopīka (milk-maid) in our rebirth. In the circumstance of having your proximity, we accept the body of Gopīka etc. because, we will be able to achieve the pleasure of carnal relations. Having heard this affectionate submission of Rudra etc. all gods, lord Rāma himself said– O Gods! I definitely provide you with an opportunity to touch the organs and all limbs of my body. I will certainly lead to fulfilment of your desire.

मोदितास्ते सुराः सर्वे कृतकृत्याधुना वयम्। यो नन्दः परमानन्दो यशोदा मुक्तिगेहिनी॥ ३॥

माया सा त्रिविधा प्रोक्ता सत्त्वराजसतामसी। प्रोक्ता च सात्त्विकी रुद्रे भक्ते ब्रह्मणि राजसी॥ ४॥

तामसी दैत्यपक्षेषु माया त्रेधा ह्युदाहृता। अजेया वैष्णवी माया जप्येन च सुता पुरा॥ ५॥

देवकी ब्रह्मपुत्रा सा या वेदैरुपगीयते। निगमो वसुदे०वो यो वेदार्थः कृष्णरामयोः॥ ६॥

स्तुवते सततं यस्तु सोऽवतीर्णो महीतले। वने वृन्दावने क्रीडन्गोपगोपीसुरैः सह॥ ७॥

गोप्यो गाव ऋचस्तस्य यष्टिका कमलासनः। वंशस्तु भगवान् रुद्रः शृङ्गमिन्द्रः सगोसुरः॥ ८॥

गोकुलं वनवैकुण्ठं तापसास्तत्र ते द्रुमाः। लोभक्रोधादयो दैत्याः कलिकालस्तिरस्कृतः॥ ९॥

Having obtained this assurance from supreme person, the lord Rāma, all gods became glad enough and said– "We have now arrived to the climax of our penance." All gods then appeared for the purpose of serving the lord. The form of supreme pleasure, thus, had born in garb of Nanda and the goddess of emancipation in herself, in garb of Yaśodā herself. The renowned illusion (Māyā) has been described in the three forms. Out of them first is Satva, second the Rajas and the third is Tamas. The devotee to god Rudra is the representative of Satva, Brahmā, the Rajas and the demons are representative of Tamas. Besides these, Vaiṣṇavī illusion (Māyā) cannot be conquered by all persons. Lord Brahmā himself was also failed to enslave this illusion (Māyā) in the long ancient. The Vaiṣṇava illusion enriched with Brahma vidyā (learning) and further, which is worshipped by the Gods, has been appeared in the garb of Devakī. The Nigamas viz., Veda are Vasudeva, who regularly worship my gigantic form (the perfect person, Nārāyaṇa). The Brahma purported form of Veda had appeared in the form of Śrī Balarāma and Śrī Kṛṣṇa on this earth. That proposed essence to ideal Veda, plays with Gopa (cowherds) and Gopīs (milk-maid) in Vṛndāvana, the Ṛcās of Vedas and the cows of lord Śrī Kṛṣṇa and Gopīs. Brahmā has attained the complexion of the stick and lord Rudra has become Rudra-vaṁśa (flute). Sagosura Indra (viz. god Indra holding the thunderbolt) has held the form Śṛnga (A musical instrument made of horns). The forest renowned as Gokula (where Vaikuṇṭha is enshrined itself). The great souls (Mahātmā) are engrossed in penance in garb of the druma (trees). The six defects i.e. greed, attachment etc. has obtained the form of demons and devils. These all demons are destroyed merely by reciting the name of lord Kṛṣṇa in Kali era.

गोपरूपो हरिः साक्षान्मायाविग्रहधारणः। दुर्बोधं कुहकं तस्य मायया मोहितं जगत्॥ १०॥

दुर्जया सा सुरैः सर्वैर्धृष्टिरूपो भवेद्द्विजः। रुद्रो येन कृतो वंशस्तस्य माया जगत्कथम्॥ ११॥

बलं ज्ञानं सुराणां वै तेषां ज्ञानं हृतं क्षणात्। शेषनागोभवेद्रामः कृष्णो ब्रह्मैव शाश्वतम्॥ १२॥

अष्टावष्टसहस्रे द्वे शताधिक्यः स्त्रियस्तथा। ऋचोपनिषदस्ता वै ब्रह्मरूपा ऋचः स्त्रियः॥ १३॥

द्वेषश्चाणूरमल्लोऽयं मत्सरो मुष्टिको जयः। दर्पः कुवलयापीडो गर्वो रक्षः खगो बकः॥ १४॥

दया सा रोहिणी माता सत्यभामा धरेति वै। अघासुरो महाव्याधिः कलिः कंसः स भूपतिः॥ १५॥

शमो मित्रः सुदामा च सत्याक्रूरोद्धवो दमः। यः शङ्खः स स्वयं विष्णुर्लक्ष्मीरूपो व्यवस्थितः॥ १६॥

दुग्धसिन्धौ समुत्पन्नो मेघघोषस्तु संस्मृतः। दुग्धोदधिः कृतस्तेन भग्नभाण्डो दधिग्रहे॥ १७॥

क्रीडते बालको भूत्वा पूर्ववत्सुमहोदधौ। संहारार्थं च शत्रूणां रक्षणाय च संस्थितः॥ १८॥

कृपार्थे सर्वभूतानां गोप्तारं धर्ममात्मजम्। यत्स्रष्टुमीश्वरेणासीत्तच्चक्रं ब्रह्मरूपधृक्॥ १९॥

Lord Śrī Hari himself has retained the character of a Gopa for playing his chief portfolio. This material world is trapped by the illusion (Māyā). By this reason, the mystery of lord Kṛṣṇa's illusion is difficult task to realise. This illusion as spreaded by lord Kṛṣṇa is inaccessible even for the Gods also. How can this common world may know the illusion of lord by which lord Brahmā has been formed a stock and which has compelled lord Śiva to become a flute? Undoubtedly, the lord's illusion has abducted or seized the power of discretion lying with the gods within moments. Śrī Śeṣanāga was born in garb of Balarāma and the Sanātana Brahma was appeared in garb of lord Śrī Kṛṣṇa. Rukmiṇī etc. sixteen thousand one hundred eight queens of lord Śrī Kṛṣṇa are the Ṛcās and upaniṣad. Besides the Ṛcās in garb of Brahma, had appeared in garb of Gopikas in the land of Braja, inimity is in garb of Cāṇūra Malla. Manipulation (Matsara) is in the form of Muṣṭika, a demon most difficult to win, and the vanity is in the form of the elephant namely, Kuvalayāpīḍa. The ego appeared in garb of Bakāsura, a demon moving in the sky. The kindness appeared in garb of Rohiṇī, the mother and the earth appeared in garb of Satyabhāmā. "Mahāvyādhi" in garb of Aghāsura and "Kali" himself appeared in the form of "Kaṁsa". Sudāmā, the friend of Kṛṣṇa is Śama, Akrūra in the form of the truth and Uddhava in form of Dama appeared. Conch itself is in form of lord Viṣṇu and having brother of Lakṣmī, it also is in the form of Lakṣmī too. It has appeared as a result of churning Kṣīrasāgara. Its deep sound is analogous to thundering clouds. The lord had broken the pitchers, full of milk and curd and it was flown. It represents the Kṣīrasāgara. The lord Kṛṣṇa played in the curd and milk so flown during his childhood. He is always prepared for killing the enemies and providing the saints with protection. Lord Kṛṣṇa had appeared on this earth in order to bless all living organisms beyond cause and for accession to his son like religion (the benevolent concepts). One should presume accordingly while worshipping. God Mahākāla (Śiva) had produced a discuss for assigning it to lord Hari. The discuss in hands of lord Kṛṣṇa too is in garb of Brahma (knowledge).

जयन्तीसंभवो वायुश्चमरो धर्मसंज्ञितः। यस्यासौ ज्वलनाभासः खड्गरूपो महेश्वरः॥ २०॥

कश्यपोलूखलः ख्यातो रज्जुर्माताऽदितिस्तथा। चक्रं शङ्खं च संसिद्धिं बिन्दुं च सर्वमूर्धनि॥ २१॥

यावन्ति देवरूपाणि वदन्ति विबुधा जनाः। नमन्ति देवरूपेभ्य एवमादि न संशयः॥ २२॥
गदा च कालिका साक्षात्सर्वशत्रुनिबर्हिणी। धनुः शार्ङ्गं स्वमाया च शरत्कालः सुभोजनः॥ २३॥
अब्जकाण्डं जगद्बीजं धृतं पाणौ स्वलीलया। गरुडो वटभाण्डीरः सुदामा नारदो मुनिः॥ २४॥
वृन्दा भक्तिः क्रिया बुद्धिः सर्वजन्तुप्रकाशिनी। तस्मान्न भिन्नं नाभिन्नमाभिर्भिन्नो न वै विभुः॥ २५॥
भूमावुत्तारितं सर्वं वैकुण्ठं स्वर्गवासिनाम्॥ २६॥
सर्वतीर्थफलं लभते य एवं वेद। देहबन्धाद्विमुच्यते इत्युपनिषत्॥

The religion (benevolent conception) has hold the appearance of cradle. The wind god appeared in garb of Vaijayantī Mālā (specific garland) and Maheśvara has accepted to be a dragger that shines like fire. Saint Kaśyapa is enshrined in the form of mortar (Ūkhala) and goddess mother Aditi has appeared in garb of the string. As Anusvārs enshrines on the letters (Akṣara), the ether enshrining above all, should be considered as an umbrella of lord Śrī Kṛṣṇa. The learned great men like Vyāsa, Vālmikī etc. worships to which forms of gods and at which the people, bow their heads considering as god, they all receive only resort of lord Kṛṣṇa. The Gadā (a weapon for hitting purposes) as enshrined in the hand of lord Kṛṣṇa is in garb of goddess Kali who kills all enemies. Vaiṣṇavī illusion is in the form of Śārṅgadhanuṣa and the Kāla (god of death) is an arrow of god. The lord has caught the seed like lotus of this world in his hand. The Garuḍa (divine eagle) has retained the form of Banyan tree and the divine saint Nārada has appeared in the form of Sudāmā, his close friend. Bhakti (devotion) has retained the form of Vṛndā. The wit providing with light to all living organism is the power of action of lord. This is the reason, these Gopa and Gopīkas etc. are inseparable to lord Śrī Kṛṣṇa and he himself is not separate from them. That lord Śrī Kṛṣṇa has made all residents of heaven and the Vaikuṇṭha-Dhāma (an abode of lord Viṣṇu) on the earth. The person, who considers or realises that lord with this pious presumption, obtains the fruit of all pilgrimage and enjoys liberty from all physical ties. This upaniṣad conveys the same concept.

॥ॐ भद्रं कर्णेभिः .... इति शान्तिः॥

॥इति कृष्णोपनिषत्समाप्ता॥

86. VARĀHOPANIṢAD

वराहोपनिषद्

श्रीमद्वाराहोपनिषद्वेद्याखण्डसुखाकृति।

त्रिपान्नारायणाख्यं तद्रामचन्द्रपदं भजे।।१।।

ॐ सह नाववत्विति शान्तिः।।

।।प्रथमोऽध्यायः।।

हरिः ॐ। अथ ऋभुर्वै महामुनिर्देवमानेन द्वादशवत्सरं तपश्चचार। तदवसाने वराहरूपी भगवान्प्रादुरभूत्। स होवाचोत्तिष्ठोत्तिष्ठ वरं वृणीष्वेति। सोदतिष्ठत्। तस्मै नमस्कृत्योवाच भगवन्कामिभिर्यद्यत्कामितं तत्तत्त्वत्सकाशात्स्वप्नेऽपि न याचे। समस्तवेदशास्त्रेतिहासपुराणानि समस्तविद्याजालानि ब्रह्मादयः सुराः सर्वे त्वद्रूपज्ञानन्मुक्तिमाहुः। अतस्त्वद्रूपप्रतिपादिकां ब्रह्मविद्यां ब्रूहीति होवाच। तथेति स होवाच वराहरूपी भगवान्। चतुर्विंशतितत्त्वानि केचिदिच्छन्ति वादिनः। केचित्षट्त्रिंशत्तत्त्वानि केचित्षण्णवतीनि च।।१।।

Chapter I

The great sage Ṛbhu performed penance for twelve deva (divine) years. At the end of the time, the Lord appeared before him in the form of a boar. He said : "Rise, rise and choose your boon." The sage got up and having prostrated himself before him said : "O Lord, I will not, in my dream, wish of Your those things that are desired by the worldy. All the Vedas, Śāstras, Itihāsa and all the hosts of the other sciences, as well as Brahmā and all the other Devas, speak of emancipation as resulting from a knowledge of Your nature. So Impart to me that science of Brahman which treats of Your nature."

Then the boar-shaped Bhagavān Lord) said : "Some disputants hold that there are twenty-four tattvas (principles) and some thirty-six, while other maintain that there are ninety-six.

तेषां क्रमं प्रवक्ष्यामि सावदानमनाः शृणु। ज्ञानेन्द्रियाणि पञ्चैव श्रोत्रत्वग्लोचनादयः।।२।।

कर्मेन्द्रियाणि पञ्चैव वाक्पाण्यङ्घ्र्यादयः क्रमात्। प्राणादयस्तु पञ्चैव पञ्च शब्दादयस्तथा।।३।।

मनोबुद्धिरहंकारश्चित्तं चेति चतुष्टयम्। चतुर्विंशतितत्त्वानि तानि ब्रह्मविदो विदुः।।४।।

एतैस्तत्त्वैः समं पञ्चीकृतभूतानि पञ्च च। पृथिव्यापस्तथा तेजो वायुराकाशमेव च।।५।।

देहत्रयं स्थूलसूक्ष्मकारणानि विदुर्बुधाः। अवस्था त्रितयं चैव जाग्रत्स्वप्न सुषुप्तयः।।६।।

आहत्य तत्त्वजातानां षट्त्रिंशन्मुनयो विदुः। पूर्वोक्तैस्तत्त्वजातैस्तु समं तत्त्वानि योजयेत्।।७।।

I shall relate them in their order. Listen with an attentive mind. The organs of sense are five, viz., ear, skin, eye and others. The organs of action are five, viz., mouth, hand, leg and others, Prāṇas (vital airs) are five; Sound and other (viz., rudimentary principles) are five. Manas, buddhi, citta and ahaṁkāra are four; thus those that know Brahman know these to be the twenty-four tattvas. Besides these, the wise hold the quintuplicated elements to be five, viz. : earth, water, fire, vāyu and ākāśa; the bodies to be three, viz., : the gross, the subtle and the kāraṇa or causal; the states of consciousness to be three viz., : the waking, the dreaming and the dreamless sleeping. The munis know the total collection of tattvas to be thirty-six (coupled with jīva).

षड्भावविकृतिश्चास्ति जायते वर्धतेऽपि च। परिणामं क्षयं नाशं षड्भावविकृतिं विदुः॥८॥

अशना च पिपासा च शोकमोहौ जरा मृतिः। एते षडूर्मयः प्रोक्ताः षट्कोशानथ वच्मि ते॥९॥

त्वक्र रक्तं मांसमेदोमज्जास्थानी निबोधत। कामग्रोधौ लोभमोहौ मदो मात्सर्यमेव च॥१०॥

एतेऽरिषड्वा विश्वश्च तैजसः प्राज्ञ एव च। जीवत्रयं सत्त्वरजस्तमांसि च गुणत्रयम्॥११॥

प्रारब्धागाम्यर्जितानि कर्मत्रयमितीरितम्। वचनादामगमनविसर्गानन्दपञ्चकम्॥१२॥

संकल्पोऽध्यवसायश्च अभिमानोऽवधारणा। मुदिता करुणा मैत्री उपेक्षा च चतुष्टयम्॥१३॥

दिग्वातार्कप्रचेतोऽश्विवह्नीन्द्रोपेन्द्रमृत्युकाः। तथा चन्द्रश्चतुर्वक्त्रो रुद्रः क्षेत्रज्ञ ईश्वरः॥१४॥

आहत्य तत्त्वजातानां षण्णवत्यस्तु कीर्तिताः। पूर्वोक्ततत्त्वजातानां वैलक्षण्यमनामयम्॥१५॥

वराहरूपिणं मां ये भजन्ति मयि भक्तितः। विमुक्ताज्ञानतत्कार्या जीवन्मुक्ता भवन्ति ते॥१६॥

ये षण्णवतितत्त्वज्ञा यत्र कुत्राश्रमे रताः। जटी मुण्डी शिखी वापि मुच्यते नात्र संशयः॥१७॥

"With these tattvas, there are six changes, viz. : existence, birth, growth, transformation, decay and destruction. Hunger, thirst, grief, delusion, old age and death are said to be the six infirmities. Skin, blood, flesh, fat, marrow and bones are said to be the six sheaths. Passion, anger, avarice, delusion, pride and malice are the six kinds of foes. Viśva, Taijasa and prājña are the three aspects of the jīva. Sattva, rajas and tamas are the three guṇas (qualities). Prārabdha, sañcita and āgāmin are the three karmas. Talking, lifting, walking, excerting and enjoying the five actions (of the organs of action); and there are also thought, certainty, egoism, compassion, memory (funtions of manas, etc.,), complacency, sympathy and indifference : dik (the quarters), Vāyu, Sun, Varuṇa, Aśvini devas, Agni, Indra, Upendra, and Mṛtyu (death) : and then the moon, the fourfaced Brahmā, Rudra, Kṣetrajña, and Īśvara. Thus these are the ninety-six tattvas. Those that worship, with devotion, me of the form of boar, who am other than the aggregate of these tattvas and am without decay are released from ajñāna and its effects and becoms jīvanmuktas. Those that know these ninety-six tattvas will attain salvation in whatever order of life they may be, whether they have matted hair or are of shaven head or have (only) their tuft of hair on. There is no doubt of this. Thus ends the first chapter."

॥द्वितीयोऽध्यायः॥

ऋभुर्नाम महायोगी क्रोडरूप रमापतिम्। वरिष्ठां ब्रह्मविद्यां त्वमधीहि भगवन्मम।
एवं स पृष्टो भगवान्प्राह भक्तार्तिभञ्जनः॥१॥
स्ववर्णाश्रमधर्मेण तपसा गुरुतोषणात्। साधनं प्रभवेत्पुंसा वैराग्यदिचतुष्टयम्॥२॥
नित्यानित्यविवेकश्च इहामुत्र विरागता। शमादिषङ्कसंपत्तिर्मुमुक्षा तां समभ्यसेत्॥३॥
एवं जितेन्द्रियो भूत्वा सर्वत्र ममतामतिम्। विहाय साक्षिचैतन्ये मयि कुर्यादहंमतिम्॥४॥
दुर्लभं प्राप्य मानुष्यं तत्रापि नरविग्रहम्। ब्राह्मण्यं च महाविष्णोर्वेदान्तश्रवणादिना॥५॥
अतिवर्णाश्रमं रूपं सच्चिदानन्दलक्षणम्। यो न जानाति सोऽविद्वान्कदा मुक्तो भविष्यति॥६॥
अहमेव सुखं नान्यदन्यच्चेन्नैव तत्सुखम्। अमदर्थं न हि प्रेयो मदर्थं न स्वतः प्रियम्॥७॥
परप्रेमास्पदतया मा न भूवमहं सदा। भूयासमिति यो द्रष्टा सोऽहं विष्णुर्मुनीश्वर॥८॥
न प्रकाशोऽहमित्युक्तिर्यत्प्रकाशैकबन्धना। स्वप्रकाशं तमात्मानमप्रकाशः कथं स्पृशेत्॥९
स्वयं भातं निराधारं ये जानन्ति सुनिश्चितम्। ते हि विज्ञानसंपन्ना इति मे निश्चिता मतिः॥१०॥

Chapter II

The great Ṛbhu (again) addressed the Lord of Lakṣmī of the from of boar thus : "O Lord, place initiate me into the supreme Brahmavidyā (or science)." Then the Lord who removes the miseries of his devotees being thus questioned, answered thus : "Through (the right observance of) the duties of one's own caste and orders of life, through religious austerities and through the pleasing of the Guru (by serving him rightly), arise to persons the four, vairāgya, etc. They are the discrimination of the eternal from the non-eternal; indifference to the enjoyments of this and the other worlds; acquisition of the six virtues, sama, etc., and the longing after liberation. These should be practised. Having subdued the sensual organs and having given up the conception of 'mine' in all objects, you should place your consciousness of 'I' in (or identify yourself with) me, who am the witness caitanya (consciousness). To be born as a human being is difficult— more difficult it is to be born as a male being— and more so is it to be born as a Brāhmaṇa. Even then, if the fool does not cognise through the hearing, etc., of vedānta, the true nature of the Saccidānanda (of Brahman) that is all-prevading, and that is beyond all caste and orders of life, when will he obtain mokṣa? I alone am happiness. There is none other. If there is said to be another, then it is not happiness. There is no such things as love, except on my account. The love that is on account of me is not natural to me. As I am the seat of supreme love, that 'I am not' is not. He who is sought after by all, saying "I should become such", is myself, the all-pervading. How can non-light affect Ātmā, the self-shining which is no other than the light when originates the words 'I am not light'. My firm conviction is, whoever knows for certain that (Ātmā) which is self-shining and has itself no basis (to rest upon), is one of vijñāna.

स्वपूर्णात्मातिरेकेण जगज्जीवेश्वरादयः। न सन्ति नास्ति माया च तेभ्यश्चाहं विलक्षणः॥११॥

अज्ञानान्धतमोरूप कर्मधर्मादिलक्षणम्। स्वयंप्रकाशात्मानं नैव मां स्प्रष्टुमर्हति॥१२॥

सर्वसाक्षिणमात्मानं वर्णाश्रमविवर्जितम्। ब्रह्मरूपतया पश्यन्ब्रह्मैव भवति स्वयम्॥१३॥

भासमानमिदं सर्वं मानरूपं परं पदम्। पश्यन्वेदान्तमानेन सद्य एव विमुच्यते॥१४॥

देहात्मज्ञानवज्ज्ञानं देहात्मज्ञानबाधकम्। आत्मन्येव भवेद्यस्य स नेच्छन्नपि मुच्यते॥१५॥

सत्यज्ञानानन्दपूर्णलक्षणं तमसः परम्। ब्रह्मानन्दं सदा पश्यन्कथं बध्येत कर्मणा॥१६॥

त्रिधामसाक्षिणं सत्यज्ञानान्ददिलक्षणम्। तवमहंशब्दलक्ष्यार्थमसक्तं सर्वदोषतः॥१७॥

सर्वगं सच्चिदात्मानं ज्ञानचक्षुर्निरीक्षते अज्ञानचक्षुर्नेक्षेत भास्वन्तं भानुमन्धवत्॥१८॥

प्रज्ञानमेव तद्ब्रह्म सत्यप्रज्ञानलक्षणम्। एवं ब्रह्मपरिज्ञानादेव मर्त्योऽमृतो भवेत्॥१९॥

तद्ब्रह्मानन्दमद्वन्द्वं निर्गुणं सत्यचिद्घनम्। विदित्वा स्वात्मनो रूपं न बिभेति कुश्चन॥२०॥

चिन्मात्रं सर्वगं नित्यं संपूर्णं सुखमद्वयम्। साक्षाद्ब्रह्मैव नान्योऽस्तीत्येवं ब्रह्मविदां स्थितिः॥२१॥

अज्ञस्य दुःखौघमयं ज्ञस्यानन्दमयं जगत्। अन्धं भुवनमन्धस्य प्रकाशं तु सुचक्षुषाम्॥२२॥

अनन्ते सच्चिदानन्दे मयि वाराहरूपिणि। स्थितेऽद्वितीयभावः स्यात्को बन्धः कश्च मुच्यते॥२३॥

स्वरूपं तु चिन्मात्रं सर्वदा सर्वदेहिनाम्। नैव देहादिसंघातो घटवद्दृशिगोचरः॥२४॥

स्वात्मनोऽन्यदिवाभातं चराचरमिदं जगत्। स्वात्ममात्रतया बुद्ध्वा तदस्मीति विभावय॥२५॥

स्वस्वरूपं स्वयं भुङ्क्ते नास्ति भोज्यं पृथक् स्वतः। अस्ति चेदस्तितारूपं ब्रह्मैवास्तित्वलक्षणम्२६॥

ब्रह्मविज्ञानसंपन्नः प्रतीतमखिलं जगत्। पश्यन्नपि सदा नैव पश्यति स्वात्मनः पृथक्॥२७॥

मत्स्वपरूरिज्ञानात्कर्मभिर्न स बध्यते॥२८॥

यः शरीरेन्द्रियादिभ्यो विहीनं सर्वसाक्षिणम्। परमार्थैकविज्ञानं सुखात्मानं स्वयंप्रभम्॥२९॥

स्वस्वरूपतया सर्वं वेद स्वानुभयेन यः। स धीरः स तु विज्ञेयः सोऽहं तत्त्वं ऋभो भव॥३०॥

अतः प्रपञ्चानुभवः सदा न हि स्वरूपबोधानुभवः सदा खलु।

इति प्रपश्यन्तपरिपूर्णवेदनो न बन्धमुक्तो न च बद्ध एव तु॥३१॥

स्वस्वरूपानुसंधानान्नृत्यन्तं सर्वसाक्षिणम्। मुहूर्तं चिन्तयेन्मां यः सर्वबन्धैः प्रमुच्यते॥३२॥

सर्वभूतान्तरस्थाय नित्यमुक्तचिदात्मने। प्रत्यक्चैतन्यरूपाय मह्यमेव नमोनमः॥३३॥

त्वं वाहमस्मि भगवो देवतेऽहं वै त्वमसि। तुभ्यं मह्यमनन्ताय मह्यं तुभ्यं चिदात्मने॥३४॥

नमो मह्यं परेशाय नमस्तुभ्यं शिवाय च। किं करोमि क्व गच्छामि किं गृह्णामि त्यजामि किम्॥३५॥

यन्मया पूरितं विश्वं महाकल्पाम्बुना यथा। अन्तःसङ्गं बहिःसङ्गमात्मसङ्गं च यस्त्यजेत्।

सर्वसङ्गनिवृत्तात्मा स मामेति न संशयः॥३६॥

अहिरिव जनयोगं सर्वदा वर्जयेद्यः कुणपमिव सुनारीं त्यक्तुकामो विरागी।

विषमिव विषयादीन्मन्यमानो दुरन्ताञ्जगति परमहंसो वासुदेवोऽहमेव॥३७॥

इदं सत्यमिदं सत्यं सत्यमेतदिहोच्यते। अहं सत्यं परं ब्रह्म मत्तः किंचिन्न विद्यते॥३८॥

"The universe, jīva, Īśvara, māyā and others do not really exist, except, my full Ātmā. I have not their characteristics. Karma which has dhāraṇā and other attributes and is of the form of darkness and ajñāna is not fit to touch (or effect) me, who am Ātmā, the self-resplendent. That man who sees (his) Ātmā which is all-witness and is beyond all caste and orders of life as of the nature of Brahman, becomes himself Brahman. Whoever sees, through the evidence of Vedānta, this visible universe as the Supreme Seat which is of the form of light, attains mokṣa at once. When that knowledge which dispels the idea that this body (alone) is Ātmā, arises firmly in one's mind as was before the knowledge that this body (alone) is Ātmā, then that person, even though he does not desire mokṣa, gets it. Therefore how will a person be bound by karma, who always enjoys the bliss of Brahman which has the characteristics of Saccidānanda, and which is other than ajñāna? Persons with spiritual eyes see Brahman, that is the witness of the three states that has the characteristics of be-ness, wisdom and bliss, that is the underlying meaning of the words 'Thou' (Tvam) and 'I' (Aham), and that is untouched by all the stains. As a blind man does not see the sun that is shining, so an ignorant person does not see (brahman). Prajñāna alone is Brahman. It has truth and prajñāna as its characteristics. By thus cognising Brahman well, a person becomes immortal. One who knows his own Ātmā as Brahman, that is bliss, and without duality and guṇas (qualities), and that is truth and absolute consciousness is not afraid of anything. That which is consciousness alone, which is all-pervading, which is eternal, which is all-full, which is of the form of bliss, and which is indestructible, is the only true Brahman. It is the settled determination of Brahmajñanīs that there is naught else but that. As the world appears dark to the blind and bright to those having good eyes, so this world full of manifold miseries to the ignorant is full of happiness of the wise. In me, of the form of boar, who am infinite and the Bliss of absolute Consciousness, if there is the conception of non-dualism, where then is bondage? And who is the one to be emancipated? The real nature of all embodied objects is ever the absolute Consciousness. Like the pot seen by the eyes, the body and its aggregates are not (viz., do not really exist). Knowing, as Ātmā, all the locomotive and fixed worlds that appear as other than Ātmā, meditate upon them as 'It I am'. Such a person then enjoy his real nature. There is no other to be enjoyed than one-Self. If there is anything that is then Brahman alone has that attribute. One who is perfect in Brahmajñāna, though he always sees this established universe, does not see it other than his Ātmā. By cognising clearly my form, one is not trammelled by karma. He is an undaunted person who by his own experience cognises as his own real nature all (the universe and Brahman) that is without the body and the organs of sense— that is the all-witness— that is the one vijñāna, that is the blissful Ātmā (as contrasted with jīvātmā or the lower self) and that is self-resplendent. He is one that should be known as . . . (myself). O Ṛbhu, may you become He. After this, there will be never any experience of world. Thereafter there will always be the experience of wisdom of one's own true nature. One who has thus known fully Ātmā has neither emancipation nor bondage. Whoever meditates, even for the muhūrta (48 minutes) through the cognition of one's own real form, upon Him who is dancing as the all-witness, is released from all bondage. Prostrations— prostrations to me who am in all the elements, who am the Cidātmā (viz., Ātmā of the nature of wisdom) that is eternal and free and who am the Pratyagātmā. O Devatā, you are I. I am you. Prostrations on account of myself and yourself who are infinite and who are Cidātmā, myself being the supreme Īśa (Lord) and yourself being Śiva (of a generous nature). What should I do? Where should I go? What should I reject? (Nothing, because) the universe is filled by me as with the waters of the universal deluge. Whoever gives up (fond) love of the external, love of the internal and love of the body and thus gives up all associations, is merged in me. There is no doubt about it. That Paramahaṁsa (ascetic) who, though living in the world, keeps aloof from human congregation as from serpent, who regards a beautiful woman as a (living) corpse and the endless sensual objects as position, and who has abandoned all passion and is indifferent towards all objects is no other than Vāsudeva, (viz.,) myself. This is satya (truth). This is nothing but truth. It is turth alone that is now said. I am Brahman, the turth. There is naught else but I.

उप समीपे यो वासो जीवात्मपरमात्मनोः। उपवासः स विज्ञेयो न तु कायस्य शोषणम्॥३९॥
कायशोषणमात्रेण का तत्र ह्यविवेकिनाम्। वल्मीकताडनादेव मृतः किं नु महोरगः॥४०॥
अस्ति ब्रह्मेति चेद्वेद परोक्षज्ञानमेव तत्। अहं ब्रह्मेति चेद्वेद सात्रात्कारः स उच्यते॥४१॥
यस्मिन्काले स्वमात्मानं योगी जानाति केवलम्। तस्मात्कालात्समारभ्य जीवन्मुक्तो भयेदसौ॥४२॥
अहं ब्रह्मेति नियतं मोक्षहेतुर्महात्मनाम्। द्वे पदे बन्धमोक्षाय निर्ममेति ममेति च॥४३॥
ममेति बध्यते जन्तुर्निर्ममेति विमुच्यते। बाह्यचिन्ता न कर्तव्या तथैवान्तरचिन्तिका।
सर्वचिन्ता समुत्सृज्य स्वस्थो भव सदा ऋभो॥४४॥

"(The word) 'Upavāsa' (lit., dwelling near) signifies the dwelling near (or union) of jīvātmā and Paramātmā and not (the religious observance as accepted by the world) emanciating the body through fasts. To the ignorant, what is the use of the mere drying up of the body? By beating about the hole of a snake, can we be said to have killed the big snake within. A man is said to attain parokṣa (indirect) wisdom when he knows (theoreticaly) that there is Brhaman; but he is said to attain sākṣātkāra (direct cognition) when he knows (or realises) that he is himself Brahman. When a yogin knows his Ātmā to be the absoulte, then he becomes a jīvanmukta. To mahātmās, to be always in the state 'I am Brahman' conduces to their salvation. There are two words for bondage and mokṣa. They are 'mine' and 'not mine'. Man is bound by 'mine', but he is released by 'not mine'. He should abandon all the thoughts relating to externals and so also with reference to internals. O Ṛbhu haivng given up all thoughts, you should rest content (in your Ātmā) ever.

संकल्पमात्रकलनेन जगत्समग्रं संकल्पमात्रकलने हि जगद्विलासः।
संकल्पमात्रमिदमुत्सृज निर्विकल्पमाश्रित्य मामकपदं हृदि भावयस्व॥४५॥

मच्चिन्तनं मत्कथनमन्योन्यं मत्प्रभाषणम्। मदेकपरमो भूत्वा कालं नय महामते॥४६॥
चिदिहास्तीति चिन्मात्रमिदं चिन्मयमेव च। चित्त्वं चिदहमेते च लोकाश्चिदिति भावय॥४७॥
रागं नीरागतां नीत्वा निर्लेपो भव सर्वदा। अज्ञानजन्यकर्त्रादिकारकोत्पन्नकर्मणा॥४८॥
श्रुत्युत्पन्नात्मविज्ञानप्रतीपो बाध्यते कथम्। अनात्मतां परित्यज्य निर्विकारो जगत्स्थितौ॥४९।
एकनिष्ठतयान्तस्थसंदविन्मात्रपरो भव। घटाकाशमठाकाशौ महाकाशे प्रतिष्ठितौ॥५०॥
एवं मयि चिदाकशे जीवेशौ परिकल्पितौ। या च प्रागात्मनो माया तथान्ते च तिरस्कृता॥५१॥
ब्रह्मवादिभिरुद्गीता सा मायेति विवेकत:। मायातत्कार्यविलये नेश्वरत्वं न जीवता॥५२॥
तत: शुद्धश्चिदेवाहं व्योमवन्निरुपाधिक:। जीवेश्वरादिरूपेण चेतनाचेतनात्मकम्॥५३॥
ईक्षणादिप्रवेशान्ता सृष्टिरीशेन कल्पिता। जाग्रदादिविमोक्षान्त: संसारो जीवकल्पित:॥५४॥
त्रिणाचिकादियोगान्ता ईश्वरभ्रान्तिमाश्रिता:। लोकायतदिसांख्यान्ता जीवविश्रान्तिमाश्रिता:॥५५॥
तस्मान्मुमुक्षुभिनैव मतिर्जीवेशवादयो:। कार्या किंतु ब्रह्मतत्त्वं निश्चलेन विचार्यताम्॥५६॥
अद्वितीयब्रह्मतत्त्वं न जानन्ति यथा तथा। भ्रान्ता एवाखिलास्तेषां क्व मुक्ति: क्वेह वा सुखम्॥५७॥
उत्तमाधमभावश्चेत्तेषां स्यादस्ति तेन किम्। स्वप्नस्थराज्यभिक्षाभ्यां प्रबुद्ध: स्पृशते खलु॥५८॥
अज्ञाने बुद्धिविलये निद्रा सा भण्यते बुधै:। विलीनाज्ञानतत्कार्ये मयि निद्रा कथं भवेत्॥५९॥
बुद्धे: पूर्णविकासोऽयं जागर: परिकीर्त्यते। विकारादिविहीनत्वाज्जागरो मे न विद्यते॥६०॥
सूक्ष्मनाडिषु संचारो बुद्धे: स्वप्न: प्रजायते। संचारधर्मरहिते मयि स्वप्नो न विद्यते॥६१॥
सुषुप्तिकाले सकले विलीने तमसावृते। स्वरूपं महदानन्दं भुङ्क्ते विश्वविवर्जित:॥६२॥
अविशेषेण सर्वं तु य: पश्यति चिदन्वयात्। स एव साक्षाद्विज्ञानीं स शिव: स हरिर्विधि:॥६३॥
दीर्घस्वप्नमिदं यत्तद्दीर्घं वा चित्तविभ्रमम्। दीर्घं वापि मनोराज्यं संसारं दु:खमागरम्।
सुप्तेरुत्थाय सुप्त्यन्तं ब्रह्मैकं प्रविचिन्त्यताम्॥६४॥
आरोपितस्य जगत: प्रविलापनेन चित्तं मदात्मकतया परिकल्पितं न:।
शत्रून्निहस्य। गुरुषट्कगणान्निपाताद्गन्धद्विपो भवति केवलमद्वितीय:॥६५॥
अद्यास्तमेतु वपुराशक्षितारमास्तां कस्तावत्तापि मम चिद्वपुषो विशेष:।
कुम्भे विनश्यति चिरं समवस्थिते वा कुम्भाम्बरस्य नहि कोऽपि विशेषलेश:॥६६॥
अहिनिर्ल्वयनी सर्पनिर्मोको जीववर्जित:। वल्मीके पतितस्तिष्ठेत्तं सर्पो नाभिमन्यते॥६७॥
एवं स्थूल च सूक्ष्मं च शरीरं नाभिमन्यते। प्रत्यग्ज्ञानशिखिध्वसो मिथ्याज्ञाने सहेतुके।
नेति नेतीति रूपत्वादशरीरो भवत्ययम्॥६८॥
शास्त्रेण न स्यात्परमार्थदृष्टि: कार्यक्षमं पश्यति चापरोक्षम्।
प्रारब्धनाशत्प्रतिभाननाश एवं त्रिधा नश्यति चात्ममाया॥६९॥
ब्रह्मत्वे योजिते स्वामिञ्जीवभावो न गच्छति। अद्वैते बोधिते तत्त्वे वासना विनिवर्तते॥७०॥

प्रारब्धान्ते देहहानिर्मायेति क्षीयतेऽखिला। अस्तीत्युक्ते जगत्सर्वं सद्रसं ब्रह्म तद्भवेत्॥७१॥

"The creation, sentient as well as non-sentient from īkṣaṇā (thinking) to praveśa (entry) (as stated in Chāndogya-Upaniṣad, Prapāthaka VI, Khaṇḍas II and III) of those having the forms of jīvas and Īśvara is due to the creation (or illusion) of Īśvara; while the saṁsāra (worldly existence) from the waking state to salvation is due to the creation of jīva. So the karmas ordained in the sacrifice (called) Triṇācaka (so called after Naciketas of Kaṭhopaniṣad) to yoga are dependent upon the illusion of Īśvara; while (the systems form) Lokāyata (atheistical system) to sāṁkhya rest on the illusion of jīva. Therefore aspirants after salvation should never make their heads enter into the field of controversy regarding jīva and Īśvara. But with an undisturbed mind, the tattvas of Brahman should be investigated. Those who do not cognise the tattva of the secondless Brahman are all deluded person only. When (then) is salvation of them? When then is happiness (to them) in this universe? What if they have the thoughts of superiority and inferiority (of Īśvara and jīva)? Will sovereignity and mendicancy (experienced by a person) in the dreaming state affect him in his waking state? When buddhi is absorbed in ajñāna, then it is termed, by the wise, sleep. When then is sleep to me who have not ajñāna and its effects? When buddhi is in full bloom, then it is said to be the jāgrat (waking state). As I have no changes, etc., there is no waking state to me. The moving about of buddhi in the subtle nāḍīs constitutes the dreaming state. In me without the act of moving about, there is no dreaming. Then at the time of suṣupti when all things are absorbed, enveloped by tamas, he then enjoys the highest bliss of his own nature in an invisible state. If he sees everything as Cit without any difference, he alone is an actual vijñānī. He alone is Śiva. He alone is Hari. He alone is Brahmā. This mundane existence which is an ocean of sorrow, is nothing but a long-lived dream, or an illusion of the mind or a long-lived reign of the mind. From the rising from sleep till going to bed, the one Brahman alone should be contemplated upon. By causing to be absorbed this universe which is but a super-imposition, the citta partakes of my nature. Having annihilated all the six powerful enemies, through their destruction become the non-dual, one like the scent-elephant. Whether the body perishes now or lasts the age of moon and stars, what matters it to me having Cit alone as my body? What matters it to the ākāśa in the pot, whether it (the pot) is destroyed now or exists for a long time. While the slough of a serpent lies cast off lifeless in its hole, it (the serpent) does not evince any affection towards it. Likewise the wise do not identify themselves with their gross and subtle bodies. If the delusive knowledge (that the universe is real) with its cause should be destroyed by the fire of ātmajñāna, the wise man becomes bodiless, through the idea 'It (Brahman) is not this; It is not this.' Through the study of Śāstras, the knowledge of reality (of the universe) perishes. Through direct perception of truth, one's fitness for action (in this universe) ceases. With the cessation of prārabdha (the portion of the past karma which is being enjoyed in this life), the destruction of the manifestation (of the universe) takes place. Māyā is thus destroyed in a threefold manner. If within himself no identification (of jīva) with Brahman takes place, the state (of the separateness) of jīva does not perish. If the non-dual one is truly discerned, then all affinities (for objects) ceases. With the cessation of prārabdha (arising from the cessation of affinities), there is that of the body. Therefore it is certain that māyā perishes thus entirely.

भातीत्युक्ते जगत्सर्वं भानं ब्रह्मैव केवलम्। मरुभूमो जलं सर्वं मरुभूमात्रमेव तत्।
जगत्त्रयमिदं सर्वं चिन्मात्रं स्वविचारतः।।७२।।
अज्ञानमेव न कुतो जगतः प्रसङ्गो जीवेशदेशिकविकल्पकथातिदूरे।
एकान्तकेवलचिदेकरसस्वभावे ब्रह्मैव केवलमहं परिपूर्णमस्मिं।।७३।।
बोधचन्द्रमसि पूर्णविग्रहे मोहराहुमुषितात्मतेजसि। स्नानदानयजनादिकाः क्रिया मोचनावधि वृथैव तिष्ठते।।७४।।
सलिले सैन्धवं यद्वत्साम्यं भवति योगतः। तथात्ममनसोरैक्यं समाधिरिति कथ्यते।।७५।।
दुर्लभो विषयत्यागो दुर्लभं तत्त्वदर्शनम्। दुर्लभा सहजावस्था सद्गुरोः करुणां विना।।७६।।
उत्पन्नशक्तिबोधस्य त्यक्तिःशेषकर्मणः। योगिनः सहजावस्था स्वयमेव प्रकाशते।।७७।।
रसस्य मनसश्चैव चञ्चलत्वं स्वभावतः। रसो बद्धो मनो बद्धं किं न सिद्धयति भूतले।।७८।।
मूर्च्छितो हरति व्याधिं मृतो जीवयति स्वयम्। बद्धः खेचरतां धत्त ब्रह्मत्वं रसचेतसि।।७९।।
इन्द्रियाणां मनो नाथो मनोनाथस्तु मारुतः। मारुतस्य लयो नाथस्तन्नाथं लयमाश्रय।।८०।।
निश्चेष्टो निर्विकारश्च लयो जीवति योगिनाम्। उच्छिन्नसर्वसंकल्पो निःशेषाशेषचेष्टितः।
स्वावगम्यो लयः कोऽपि मनसां वागगोचरः।।८१।।
पुङ्खानुपुङ्खविषयेक्षणतत्परोऽपि ब्रह्मावलोकनधियं न जहाति योगी।
सङ्गीततालयावाद्यवशं गतापि मौलिस्थकुम्भपरिरक्षणधीर्नटीव।।८२।।
सर्वचिन्तां परित्यज्य सावधानेन चेतसा। नाद एवानुसंधेयो योगसाम्राज्यमिच्छता।।८३।।

"If it is said that all the universe is, that Brahman alone is that is of the nature of Sat. If it is said that the universe shines, then it is Brahman alone that shines. (The mirage of) all the water in an oasis is really no other than the oasis itself.

Through inquiry of one's Self, the three worlds (above, below and middle) are only of the nature of Cit. In Brahman, which is one and alone, the essence of whose nature is absolute Consciousness and which is remote from the differences of Jīva, Īśvara and Guru, there is no ajñāna. Such being the case, where then is the occasion for the universe there? I am that Brahman which is all full. While the full moon of wisdom is robbed of its lustre by the rāhu (one of the two nodes of the moon) of delusion, all actions such as the rites of bathing, alms-giving and sacrifice performed during the time of eclipse are all fruitless. As salt dissolved in water becomes one, so if Ātmā and manas become unidentified, it is termed samādhi. Without the grace of a good (perfect) Guru, the abandonment of sensual objects is very difficult of attainment; so also the perception of (divine) truth and the attainment of one's true state. Then the state of being in one's own self shines of its own accord in a yogin in whom jñanaśakti has dawned and who has abandoned all karmas. The (property of) fluctuation is natural to mercury and mind. If either mercury is bound (or consolidated) or mind is bound (or controlled), what then on this earth cannot be accomplished? He who obtains mūrcchā cures all diseases. The dead are brought to life again. He who has bound (his mind or mercury) is able to move in the air. Therefore mercury and mind confer upon one the state of Brahman. The master of indriyas (the organs) is manas (mind). The master of manas is prāṇa. The master of prāṇa is laya (absorption yoga). Therefore laya-yoga should be practised. To the yogins, laya (-yoga) is said to be without actions and changes. This laya (absorption) of mind which is above speech and in which one has to abandon all saṅkalpas and to give up completely all actions, should be known through one's own (experience). As an actress, though subject (or dancing in harmony) to music, cymbals and other musical instruments of time, has her mind intent upon the protection of the pot on her head, so the yogin, though intent for the time being upon the hosts of objects, never leaves off the mind contemplating on Brahman. The person who desires all the wealth of yoga should, after having given up all thoughts, practise with a subdued mind concentration on nāda (spiritual sound) alone."

॥तृतीयोऽध्यायः॥

नहि नानास्वरूपं स्यादेकं वस्तु कदाचन। तस्मादखण्ड एवास्मि यन्मदन्यन्न किंचन॥१॥
दृश्यते श्रूयते यद्यद्ब्रह्मणोऽन्यत्र तद्भवेत्। नित्यशुद्धविमुक्तैकमखण्डानन्दमद्वयम्।
सत्यं ज्ञानमनन्तं यत्परं ब्रह्माहमेव तत्॥२॥
आनन्दरूपोऽहमखण्डबोधः परात्परोऽहं घनचित्प्रकाशः।
मेघा यथा व्योम न च स्पृशन्ति संसारदुःखानि न मां स्पृशन्ति॥३॥
सर्वं सुखं विद्धि सुदुःखनाशात्सर्वं सद्रूपमसत्यनाशात्।
चिद्रूपमेव प्रतिभानयुक्तं तस्मादखण्डं मम रूपमेतत्॥४॥
न हि जनिर्मरणं गमनागमौ न च मलं विमलं न च वेदनम्।
चिन्मयं हि सकलं विराजते स्फुटतरं परमस्य तु योगिनः॥५॥
सत्यचिद्घनमखण्डमद्वयं सर्वदृश्यरहितं निरामयम्।
यत्पदं विमलमद्वयं शिवं तत्सदाहमिति मौनमाश्रय॥६॥

Chapter III

The One Principle cannot at any time become of manifold forms. As I am the partless, there is none else but myself. Whatever is seen and whatever is heard is no other than Brahman. I am that Parabrahman, which is the eternal, the immaculate, the free, the one, the undivided bliss, the non-dual, the truth, the wisdom, and the endless. I am of the nature of bliss; I am of undivided wisdom; I am the supreme of the supreme; I am the resplendent absolute Consciousness. As the clouds do not touch the ākāśa, so the miseries attendant of mundane existence do not affect me. Know all to be happiness through the annihilation of sorrow and all to be of the nature of sat (be-ness) through the annihilation of asat (not be-ness). It is only the nature of Cit (Consciousness) that is associated with this visible universe. Therefore my form is partless. To an exalted yogin, there is neither birth nor death, nor going (to other spheres), nor returning (to earth); there is no stain or purity or knowledge but (the universe) shines to him as absolute Consciousness. Practise always silence 'I am (viz., that you yourself are) Parabrahman' which is truth and absolute Consciousness, which is undivided and non-dual, which is invisible, which is stainless, which is pure, which is secondless, and which is beneficent.

जन्ममृत्युसुखदु:खवर्जितं जातिनीकुलगोत्रदूरगम्। चिद्विवर्तजगतोऽस्य कारणं तत्सदाहमिति मौनमाश्रय।।७।।

पूर्णमद्वयखण्डचेतनं विश्वभेदकलनादिवर्जितम्। अद्वितीयपरसंविदंशकं तत्सदाहमिति मौनमाश्रय।।८।।

It (Brahman) is not subject to birth and death, happiness and misery. It is not subject to caste, law, family and gotra (clan). Practice silence— I am Cit which is the vivarta-upādāna (viz., the illusory cause) of the universe. Always practice silence— I am (viz., you are) the Brahman, that is the full, the secondless, the undivided consciousness which has neither the relationship nor the differences existing in the universe and which partakes of the essence of the non-dual and the supreme Sat and Cit.

केनाप्यबाधिततत्वेन त्रिकालेऽप्येकरूपत:। विद्यमानत्वमस्त्येतत्सद्रूपत्वं सदा मम।।९।।

निरुपाधिकनित्यं यत्सुप्तौ सर्वसुखात्परम्। सुखरूपत्वमस्त्येतदानन्दत्वं सदा मम।।१०।।

दिनकरकिरणैर्हि शार्वरं तमो न निबिडतरं झटिति प्राणशमेति घनतरभवकारणं तमो यद्धरिदिनकृत्प्रभया न चान्तरेण।।११।।

मम चरणस्मरणेन पूजया च स्वकतमस: परिमुच्यते हि जन्तु:।

न हि मरणप्रभवप्रणाशहेतुर्मम चरणस्मरणादृतेऽस्ति किंचित्।।१२।।

आदरेण यथा स्तौति धनवन्तं धनेच्छया। तथा चेद्विश्वकर्तारं को न मुच्येत बन्धनात्।।१३।।

That which always is and that which preserves the same nature during the three periods of time, unaffected by anything, is my eternal form Sat. Even the state of happiness which is eternal without upādhis (vehicles) and which is superior to all the happiness derivable from suṣupti is of my bliss only. As by the rays of the sun, thick gloom is soon destroyed, so darkness, the cause of rebirth is destroyed by Hari (Viṣṇu) viz., the sun's lustre. Through the contemplation and worship of my (Hari's) feet, every person is delivered from his ignorance. The manas of destroying deaths and births is only through the contemplation of my feet. As a lover of wealth praises a wealthy man, so if with earnestness a person praises the Cause of the universe, who will not be delivered from bondage?

आदित्यसंनिधौ लोकश्चेष्टते स्वयमेव तु। तथा मत्संनिधावेव समस्तं चेष्टते जगत।।१४।।

शुक्तिकाया यथा तारं कल्पितं मायया तथा। महदादि जगन्मायामयं मय्येव केवलम्।।१५।।

चण्डालदेहे पश्वादिस्थावरे ब्रह्मविग्रहे। अन्येषु तारतम्येन स्थितेषु न तथा ह्यहम्॥१६॥

विनष्टदिग्भ्रमस्यापि यथापूर्वं विभाति दिक्। तथा विज्ञानविध्वस्तं जगन्मे भाति तन्न हि॥१७॥

न देहो नेन्द्रियप्राणो न मनोबुद्ध्यहंकृति। न चित्तं नैव माया च न च व्योमादिकं जगत्॥१८॥

न कर्ता नैव भोक्ता च न च भोजयिता तथा। केवलं चित्सदानन्दब्रह्मैवाहं जनार्दनः॥१९॥

As in presence of the sun the world of its own accord begins to perform its actions, so in my presence all the worlds are animated to action. As to the mother-of-pearl, the illusory conception of silver is falsely attributed, so to me is falsely attributed through māyā this universe which is composed of mahat, etc. I am not with those differences that are (observable) in the body of low caste men, the body of cow, etc., the fixed ones, bodies of brāhmaṇas and others. As to a person, even after being relieved from the misconception of the directions, the (same misconception of) direction continues (as before) just so is to me the universe though destroyed by vijñāna. Therefore the universe is not. I am neither the body nor the organs of sense and action, nor prāṇas, nor manas, nor buddhi, nor ahaṁkāra, nor citta, nor māyā, nor the universe including ākāśa and others. Neither am I the actor, the enjoyer, nor he who causes the enjoyment. I am Brahman that is Cit, Sat and Ānanada alone and that is Janārdana (Viṣṇu).

जलस्य चलनादेव चञ्चलत्वं यथा रवेः। तथाहंकारसंबन्धादेव संसार आत्मनः॥२०॥

चित्तमूलं हिं संसारस्तत्प्रयत्नेन शोधयेत्। हन्त चित्तमहत्तायां कैषा विश्वासता तव॥२१॥

क्व धनानि महीपानां ब्राह्मणः क्व जगन्ति वा। प्राक्तनानि प्रयातानि गताः सर्गपरम्पराः। कोटयो ब्रह्मणां याता भूपा नष्टाः परागवत्॥२२॥

स चाध्यात्माभिमानोऽपि विदुषोऽयासुरत्वतः। विदूषोऽप्यासुरश्चेत्स्यान्निष्फलं तत्त्वदर्शनम्॥२३॥

उत्पाद्यमाना रागाद्या विवेकज्ञानवह्निना। यदा तदैव दह्यन्ते कुतस्तेषां प्ररोहणम्॥२४॥

यथा सुनिपुणः सम्यक् परदोषेक्षणे रतः। तथा चेन्निपुणः स्वेषु को न मुच्यते बन्धनात्॥२५॥

अनात्मविदमुक्तोऽपि सिद्धिजालानि वाञ्छति। द्रव्यमन्त्रक्रियाकालयुक्त्याप्नोति मुनीश्वरः॥२६॥

नात्यमज्ञस्यैष विषय आत्मज्ञो ह्यात्ममात्रदृक्। आत्मनात्मनि संतृप्तो नाविद्यामनुधावति॥२७॥

ये केचन जगद्भावस्तानविद्यामयान्विदु। कथं तेषु किलात्मज्ञस्त्यक्तविद्यो निमज्जति॥२८॥

द्रव्यमन्त्रक्रियाकालयुक्तयः साधुसिद्धिदाः। परमात्मपदप्राप्तौ नोपकुर्वन्ति काञ्चन॥२९॥

सर्वेच्छाकलनाशान्तवात्मलाभोदयाभिधः। स पुनः सिद्धिवाञ्छायां कथमर्हत्यचित्ततः॥३०॥

As, through the fluctuation of water, the sun (reflected therein) is moved, so Ātmā arises in this mundane existence through its mere connection with ahaṁkāra. This mundane existence has citta as its root. This (citta) should be cleansed by repeated effort. How is it you have your confidence in the greatness of citta? Alas, where is all the wealth of the kings ! Where are the Brahmās? Where are all the worlds ? All old ones are gone. Many fresh evolutions have occurred. Many crores of Brahmās have passed away. Many kings have fitted away like particles of dust. Even to a jñānī, the love of the body may arise through the asure (demoniacal) nature. If the asura nature should arise in a wise man, his knowledge of truth becomes fruitless. Should rajas and other generated in us be burnt by the fire of discriminative (divine) wisdom, how can they germinate again? Just as a very intelligent person delights in the shortcomings of another, so if one finds out his own faults (and corrects them) who will not be relieved from bondage? O Lord of munis, only he who has not ātmajñāna and who is not an emancipated person, longs after siddhis. He attains such siddhis through medicine, (or wealth), mantras, religious works, time and skill. In the eyes of an ātmajñānī, these siddhis are of no importance. One who has become an ātmajñānī, one who has his sight solely on ātmā, and one who is content with Ātmā (the higher self) through (his) ātmā (or the lower self), never follows (the dictates of) avidyā. Whatever eixsts in this world, he knows to be of the nature of avidyā. How then will an ātmajñānī who has relinquished avidyā be immersed in (or affected by) it. Through medicines, mantras, religious work, time and skill (or mystical expressions) lead to the development of siddhis, yet they cannot in any way help one to attain the seat of Paramātmā. How then can who is ātmajñānī and who is without his mind be said to long after siddhis, while all the actions of his desires are controlled?

।।चतुर्थोऽध्याय:।।

अथ ह ऋभुं भगवन्तं निघाघ: पप्रच्छ जीवन्मुक्तिलक्षणमनुब्रूहीति। तथेति स होवाच। सप्तभूमिषु जीवन्मुक्ताश्चत्वार:। शुभेच्छा प्रथमा भूमिका भवति। विचारणा द्वितीया। तनुमानसी तृतीया। सत्त्वापत्तिस्तुरीया। असंसक्ति: पञ्चमी। पदार्थभावना षष्ठी। तुरीयगा सप्तमी। प्रणवात्मिका भूमिका अकारोकारमकारार्धमात्रात्मिका। स्थूलसूक्ष्मबीजसाक्षिभेदेनाकारादयश्चतुर्विधा:।

Chapter IV

On another occasion Nidāgha asked Lord Ṛbhu to enlighten him as to the characteristics of jīvanmukti. To which Ṛbhu replied in the affirmative and said the following :

In the seven bhūmikās (states of development of wisdom) there are four kinds of jīvanmuktas. Of these the first stage is śubhecchā (good) desire; the second is vicāraṇā (inquiry); the third is tanumānasī (or attainment of śattva); the fifth is asamsakti (non-attachment); the sixth is the padārthabhāvanā (analysis of objects) and the seventh is the turīya (fourth or final stage). The bhūmikā which is of the form of praṇava (Oṁ) is formed of (or is divided into) akāra— A, ukāra— U, makāra— M, and ardhamātrā. Akāra and other are of four kinds on account of the differnce of sthūla (gross), sūkṣma (subtle,) bīja (seed or causal), and sākṣī (witness.). Their avasthās are four– waking, dreaming, dreamless sleeping and turīya (fourth). He who is in (or the entity that identifies itself with) the waking state in the gross aṁśa (essence or part) of akāra is named Viśva; in the subtle essence, he is termed Taijasa; in the bīja essence, he is termed Prājña; and in the Sākṣī essence, he is termed Turīya.

तदवस्था जाग्रत्स्वप्नसुषुप्तितुरीयाः। अकारस्थूलांशे जाग्रद्विश्वः। सूक्ष्मांशे तत्तैजसः। बीजांशे तत्प्राज्ञः। साक्ष्यंसे तत्तुरीयः। उकारस्थूलांशे स्वप्नविश्वः। सूक्ष्मांशे तत्तैजसः। बीजांशे तत्प्राज्ञः। साक्ष्यंसे तत्तुरीयः। मकारस्थूलांशे सुषुप्तविश्वः। सूक्ष्मांशे तत्तैजसः। बीजांशे तत्प्राज्ञः। साक्ष्यंसे तत्तुरीयः। अर्धमात्रास्थूलांशे तुरीयविश्वः। सूक्ष्मांशे तत्तैजसः। बीजांशे तत्प्राज्ञः। साक्ष्यंसे तुरीयतुरीयः।

He who is in the dreaming state (or the entity which identifies itself with the dreaming state) in the gross essence of ukāra is Viśva; in the subtle essence, he is termed Taijasa; in the bīja essence, he is termed Prājñā; and in the sākṣī essence, he is termed Turīya.

He who is in the suṣupti state in the gross essence of makāra is termed Viśva; in the subtle essence, Taijasa; in the bīja essence, he is termed Prājña; and to the sākṣī essence, he is termed Turīya.

He who is in turīya state in the gross essence of ardhamātrā is termed Turīya-viśva. In the subtle, he is termed Taijasa; in the bīja essence, he is termed Prājña; and in the sākṣī essence, he is termed Turīya-turīya.

अकारतुरीयांशाः प्रथमद्वितीयतृतीयभूमिकाः। उकारतुरीयांशा चतुर्थी भूमिका। मकारतुरीयांशा पञ्चमी। अर्धमात्रातुरीयांशा षष्ठी। तदतीता सप्तमी। भूमित्रयेषु विहरन्मुमुक्षुर्भवति। तुरीयभूम्यां विहरन्ब्रह्मविद्भवति। पञ्चमभूम्यां विहरन्ब्रह्मविद्वरिष्ठो भवति। षष्ठभूम्यां विहरन्ब्रह्मविद्वरीयान्भवति। सप्तमभूम्यां विरहन्ब्रह्मविद्वरिष्ठो भवति। तत्रैते श्लोका भवन्ति। ज्ञानभूमिः शुभेच्छा स्यात्प्रथमा समुदीरिता। विचारणा द्वितीया तु तृतीया तनुमानसा।।१।।

सत्त्वापत्तिश्चतुर्थी स्यात्ततोऽसंसक्तिनामिका। पदार्थभावना षष्ठी सप्तमी तुर्यगा स्मृता।।२।।

The turīya essence of akāra is (or embraces) the first, second and third (bhūmikās or stages of the seven). The turīya essence of ukāra embraces the fourth bhūmikā. The turīya essence of makāra embraces the fifth bhūmikā. The turīya essence of ardhamātrā is the sixth stage. Beyond this, is the seventh stage.

One who functions in the (first) three bhūmikā is called mumukṣu; one who functions in the fourth bhūmikā is called brahmavit; one who functions in the sixth bhūmikā is called a brahmavidvara; one who functions in the sixth bhūmikā is called a brahmavidvarīya; and one in the seventh bhūmikā is called a brahmavidvariṣṭha. With reference to this, there are ślokas. They are :

'Śubhecchā is said to be the first jñanabhūmi (or stage of wisdom); vichāraṇā, the second; tanumānasī, the third; sattvāpatti, the fourth; then come asamsakti as the fifth, padārthabhāvanā as the sixth and turīya as the seventh.'

स्थितः किं मूढ एवास्मि प्रेक्ष्योऽहं शास्त्रसज्जनैः। वैराग्यपूर्वमिच्छेति शुभेच्छेत्युच्यते बुधैः।।३।।

शास्त्रसज्जनसंपर्कवैराग्याभ्यासपूर्वकम्। सदाचार प्रवृत्तिर्या प्रोच्यते सा विचारणा।।४।।

विचारणाशुभेच्छामिन्द्रियार्थेषुरक्तता। यत्र सा तनुतामेति प्रोच्यते तनुमानसी।।५।।

The desire that arises in one through sheer vairāgya (after resolving) 'Shall I be ignorant? I will be seen by the Śāstras and the wise (or I will study the books and be with the wise)' is termed by the wise as Śubhecchā. The association with the wise and Śāstras and the following of the right path preceding the practice of indifference is termed vicāraṇā. That stage wherein the hankering after sensual objects is thinned through the first and second stages is said to be tanumānasī.

भूमिकात्रितयाभ्यासाच्चित्तेऽर्थविरतेर्वशात्। सत्वात्मनि स्थिते शुद्धे सत्त्वापत्तिरूदाहता।।६।।

दशाचतुष्टयाभ्यासादसंसर्गफला तु या। रूढसत्वचमत्कारा प्रोक्ता संसक्तिनामिका।।७।।

भूमिकापञ्चकाभ्यासात्स्वात्मारामतया भृशम्। आभ्यन्तराणां बाह्यानां पदार्थानामभावनात्।।८।।

परप्रयुक्तेन चिरं प्रत्ययेनावबोधनम्। पदार्थभावना नाम षष्ठी भवति भूमिका।।९।।

That stage wherein having become indifferent to all sensual objects through the exercise in the (above) three stages, the purified citta rests on Ātmā which is of the nature of sat is called sattvāpatti. The light (or manifestation) of sattvaguṇa that is firmly rooted (in one) without any desire for the fruits of actions through the practice in the above four stages is termed asamsakti. That stage wherein through the practice in the (above) five stages one, having found delight in Ātmā, has no conception of the internals or externals (through before him) and engages in actions only when impelled to do so by others is termed padārthabhāvanā, the sixth state.

षड्भूमिकाचिराभ्यासाद्भेदस्यानुपलम्भनात्। यत्स्वभावैकनिष्ठत्वं सा ज्ञेया तुर्यगा गतिः।।१०।।

शुभेच्छादित्रयं भूमिभेदाभेदयुतं स्मृतम्। यथावद्वेद बुद्ध्येदं जगज्जाग्रति दृश्यते।।११।।

अद्वैते स्थैर्यमायाते द्वैते च प्रशमं गते। पश्यन्ति स्वप्नवल्लोकं तुर्यभूमिसुयोगतः।।१२।।

विच्छिन्नशरदभ्रांशविलयं प्रविलीयते।

The states wherein after exceedinlgy long practice in the (above) stages one is (immovably) fixed in the contemplation of Ātmā alone without the difference (of the universe) is the seventh stage called turīya. The three stages beginning with Śubhecchā are said to be attained with (or amidst) differences and non-differences. (Because) the universe one sees in the waking state he thinks to be really existent, when the mind is firmly fixed on the non-dual. One and the conception of duality is put down, then he sees this universe as a dream through his union with the fourth stage. As the autumnal cloud being dispersed vanishes, so this universe perishes.

सत्वावशेष एवास्ते हे निगाघ दृढीकुरु।।१३।।

पञ्चभूमिं समारुह्य सुषुप्तिपदनामिकाम्। शान्ताशेषविशेषांशस्तिष्ठत्यद्वैतमात्रके।।१४।।

अन्तर्मुखतया नित्यं बहिर्वृत्तिपरोऽपि सन्। परिश्रान्ततया नित्यं निद्रालुरिव लक्ष्यते।।१५।।

कुर्वन्नभ्यासमेतस्यां भूम्यां सम्यग्विवासनः। सप्तमी गुढसुप्त्याख्या क्रमप्राप्ता पुरातनी।।१६।।

O Nidāgha, be convinced that such a person has only sattva remaining. Then having ascended the fifth stage called suṣuptipada (dreamless sleeping state), he remains simply in the non-dual state, being freed from all the various differences. Having always introvision though ever participating in external actions, those that are engaged in the practice of this (sixth stage) are seen like one sleeping when fatigued (viz., being freed from all affinities). (Lastly) the seventh stage which is the ancient and which is called guḍhasupti is generally attained.

यत्र नासन्न सद्रूपो नाहं नाप्यनहंकृतिः। केवलं क्षीणमनन आस्तेऽद्वैतेऽतिनिर्भयः॥१७॥

अन्तशून्यो बहिःशून्यः शून्यकुम्भ इवाम्बरे। अन्तःपूर्णो बहिःपूर्णः पूर्णकुम्भ इवार्णवे॥१८॥

मा भव ग्राह्यभावात्मा ग्राहकात्मा च मा भव। भावनामखिलां त्यक्त्वा यच्छिष्टं तन्मयो भव॥१९॥

द्रष्टृदर्शनदृश्यानि त्यक्त्वा वासनया सह। दर्शनप्रथमाभासमात्मानं केवलं भज॥२०॥

Then one remains in that secondless state without fear and with his consciousness almost annihilated where there is neither sat nor asat, neither self nor not-self. Like an empty pot in the ākāśa, there is void both within and, without; like a filled vessel in the midst of an ocean, he is full both within and without. Do not become either the knower or the known. May you become the Reality which remains after all thoughts are given up. Having discarded (all the distinctions of) the seer, the sight and the seen with their affinities, meditate solely upon Ātmā which shines as the supreme Light.

यथास्थितमिदं यस्य व्यवहारवतोऽपिच। अस्तंगतं स्थितं व्योम स जीवन्मुक्त उच्यते॥२१॥

नोदेति नास्तमायाति सुखे दुःखे मनःप्रभा। यथाप्राप्तस्थितिर्यस्य स जीवन्मुक्त उच्यते॥२२॥

यो जागर्ति सुषुप्तिस्थो यस्य जाग्रन्न विद्यते। यस्य निर्वासनो बोधः स जीवन्मुक्त उच्यते॥२३॥

रागद्वेषभयादीनामनुरूपं चरन्नपि। योऽन्तर्व्योमवदच्छन्नः स जीवन्मुक्त उच्यते॥२४॥

He is said to be a jīvanmukta (emancipated person) in whom, thought participating in the material concerns of the world, the universe is not seen to exist like the invisible ākāśa. He is said to be a jīvanmukta, the light of whose mind never sets or rises in misery or happiness, and who does not seek to change what happens to him (viz., either to diminish his misery or increase his happiness). He is said to be a jīvanmukta who thought in his suṣupti is awake and to whom the waking state is unknown and whose wisdom is free from the affinities (of objects).

यस्य नाहंकृतो भावो बुद्धिर्यस्य न लिप्यते। कुर्वतोऽकुर्वतो वापि स जीवन्मुक्त उच्यते॥२५॥

यस्मान्नोद्विजते लोको लोकान्नोद्विजते च यः। हर्षामर्षभयोन्मुक्तः स जीवन्मुक्त उच्यते॥२६॥

यः समस्तार्थजालेषु व्यवहार्यपि शीतलः। परार्थेष्विव पूर्णात्मा स जीवन्मुक्त उच्यते॥२७॥

प्रजहाति यदा कामान्सर्वांश्चित्तगतान्मुने। मयि सर्वात्मके तुष्टः स जीवन्मुक्त उच्यते॥२८॥

चैत्यवर्जितचिन्मात्रे पदे परमपावने। अक्षुब्धचित्तो विश्रान्तः स जीवन्मुक्त उच्यते॥२९॥

इदं जगदहं सोऽयं दृशयजातमवास्तवम्। यस्य चित्ते न स्फुरति स जीवन्मुक्त उच्यते॥३०॥

He is said to be a jīvanmukta whose heart is pure like ākāśa, though acting (as if) in consonance to love, hatred, fear and others. He is said to be a jīvanmukta, who has not the conception of his being the actor and whose buddhi is not attached to material objects, whether he performs actions or not. He is said to be a jīvanmukta, of whom people are not afraid, who is not afraid of people and who has given up joy, anger and fear. He is said to be a jīvanmukta who, though participating in all the illusory objects, is cool amidst them and is a full Ātmā, (being) as if they belonged to other. O muni, he is called a jīvanmukta who, having eradicated all the desires of his citta, is (fully) content with me who am the Ātmā of all. He is said to be a jīvanmukta who rests with an unshaken mind in that all pure abode which is Cinmātrā and free from all the modifications of citta. He is said to be a jīvanmukta in whose citta do not dawn (the distinctions of) the universe, I, he, You and others that are visible and unreal.

सद्ब्रह्मणि स्थिरे स्फारे पूर्णे विषयवर्जिते। आचार्यशास्त्रमार्गेण प्रविश्यायु स्थिरो भव।।३१।।
शिवो गुरुः शिवो वेदः शिव देवः शिव प्रभुः। शिवोऽस्म्यहं शिवः सर्वं शिवादन्यत्र किंचन।।३२।।
तमेव धीरो विज्ञाय प्रज्ञां कुर्वीत ब्राह्मणः। नानुध्यायाद्बहूञ्छब्दान्वाचो विग्लापनं हि तत्।।३३।।
शुको मुक्तो वामदेवोऽपि मुक्तस्ताभ्यां विना मुक्तिभाजो न सन्तिः।
शुकमार्गं येऽनुसरन्ति धीराः सद्यो मुक्तास्ते भवन्तीह लोके।।३४।।
वामदेवं येऽनुसरन्ति नित्यं मृत्वा जनित्वा च पुनःपुनस्तत्।
ते वै लोके क्रममुक्ता भवन्ति योगैः सांख्यैः कर्मभिः सत्त्वयुक्तैः।।३५।।

Through the path of the Guru and Śāstras, enter soon Sat— the Brahman that is immutable, great, full and without objects— and be firmly seated there. Śiva alone is Guru; Śiva alone is Vedas; Śiva alone is Lord; Śiva alone is I; Śiva alone is all. There is none other than Śiva. The undaunted Brāhmaṇa having known Him (Śiva) should attain wisdom. One need not utter many words as they but injure the organs of speech. (The Ṛṣi) Śuka is mukta (emancipated person). (The Ṛṣi) Vāmadeva is a mukta. There are no others (who have attained emancipation) than through these (viz., the two paths of these two Ṛṣis), those brave men who follow the path of Śuka in this world become sadyomuktas (viz., emancipated) immediately after (the body were away); while those who always follow the path of vedānta in this world are subject again and again to rebirths and attain krama (gradual) emancipation, through yoga, sāṁkhya and karmas associated with Sattva (guṇa).

शुकश्च वामदेवश्च द्वे सृती देवनिर्मिते। शुको विहङ्गमः प्रोक्तो वामदेवः पिपीलिका।।३६।।
अतद्व्यावृत्तिरूपेण साक्षाद्विधिमुखेन वा। महावाक्यविचारेण सांख्ययोगसमाधिना।।३७।।
विदित्वा स्वात्मनो रूपं संप्रज्ञातसमाधितः। शुकमार्गेण विरजाः प्रयान्ति परमं पदम्।।३८।।
यमाद्यासनजायासहठाभ्यासात्पुनःपुनः। विघ्नबाहुल्यसंजात अणिमादिवशादिह।।३९।।
अलब्ध्वापि फलं सम्यक्पुनर्भूत्वा महाकुले। पुनर्वासनयैवायं योगाभ्यासं पुनश्चरन्।।४०।।
अनेकजन्माभ्यासेन वामदेवेन वे पथा। सोऽपि मुक्तिं समाप्नोति तद्विष्णो परमं पदम्।।४१।।
द्वाविमावपि पन्थानौ ब्रह्मप्राप्तिकरौ शिवौ। सद्योमुक्तिप्रदश्चैक क्रममुक्तिप्रदः परः।

Thus there are two paths laid down by the Lord of Devas (viz.,) the Śuka and Vāmadeva paths. The Śuka path is called the bird's path : while the Vāmadeva path is called the ant's path. Those persons that have cognised the true nature of their Ātmā through the mandatory and prohibitory injunctions (of the Vedas), the inquiry into (the true meaning of) mahāvākyas (The sacred sentences of the Vedas), the samādhi of sāṁkhya yoga or asamprajñāta samādhi and that have thereby purified themselves, attain the supreme seat through the Śuka path. Having, through haṭhayoga practice with the pain caused by yama, postures, etc., become liable to the ever recurring obstacles caused by aṇimā and other (siddhis) and having not obtained good results, one is born again in a great family and practises yoga through his previous (kārmic) affinities. Then through the practice of yoga during many lives, he attains salvation (viz.,) the supreme seat of Viṣṇu through the Vāmadeva path. Thus there are two paths that lead to the attainment of Brahman and that are beneficent. The one confers instantaneous salvation and the other confers gradual salvation.

अत्र को मोहः कः शोक एकत्वमनुपश्यतः॥४२॥

यस्यानुभवपर्यन्ता बुद्धिस्तत्त्वे प्रवर्तते। तद्दृष्टिगोचराः सर्वे मुच्यन्ते सर्वपातकैः॥४३॥

खेचरा भूचराः सर्वे ब्रह्मविद्दृष्टिगोचराः। सद्य एव विमुच्यन्ते कोटिजन्मार्जितैरघैः॥४४॥इति चतुर्थोऽध्यायः॥४॥

"To one that sees (all) as the one (Brahma), where is delusion? Where is sorrow? Those that are under the eyes of those whose buddhi is solely occupied with the truth (of Brahman) that is the end of all experience are released from all heinous sins. All beings inhabiting heaven and earth that fall under the vision of Brahmavits are at once emancipated from the sins committed during many crores of births."

॥पञ्चमोऽध्यायः॥

अथ हैनं ऋभुं भगवन्तं निदाघः पप्रच्छ योगाभ्यासविधिमनुब्रूहिति। तथेति स होवाच। पञ्चभूतात्मको देहः पञ्चमण्डलपूरितः। काठिन्यं पृथिवीमेका पानीयं तद्द्रवाकृति॥१॥

दीपनं च भवेत्तेजः प्रचारो वायुलक्षणम्। आकाशः सत्त्वतः सर्वं ज्ञातव्यं योगमिच्छता॥२॥

षट्शतान्यधिकान्यत्र सहस्राण्येकविंशतिः। अहोरात्रवहैः श्वासैर्वायुमण्डलघाततः॥३॥

तत्पृथ्वीमण्डले क्षीणे वलिरायाति देहिनाम्। तद्वदापो गणापाये केशाः स्युः पाण्डुराः क्रमात्॥४॥

तेजःक्षये क्षुधा कान्तिर्नश्यते मारुतक्षये। वेपथुः संभवेन्नित्यं नाम्भसेनैव जीवति॥५॥

इत्थंभूतं क्षयान्नित्यं जीवितं भूतधारणम्। उड्याणं कुरुते यस्मादविश्रान्तं महाखगः॥६॥

उड्डियाणं तदेव स्यात्तत्र बन्दोऽमिधीयते। उड्डियाणे ह्यसौ बन्धो मृत्युमातङ्गकेशरी॥७॥

तस्य मुक्तिस्तनोः कायात्तस्य बन्धो हि दुष्करः। अग्नौ तु चालिते कुक्षौ वेदना जायते भृशम्॥८॥

न कार्या क्षुधि तेनापि नापि विण्मूत्रवेगिना। हितं मितं च भोक्तव्यं स्तोकं स्तोकमनेकधा॥९॥

मृदुमध्यममन्त्रेषु क्रमान्मन्त्रं लयं हठम्। लयमन्त्रहठा योगा योगो ह्यष्टाङ्गसंयुतः॥१०॥

Chapter V

Then Nidāgha asked Lord Ṛbhu to enlighten him as to the rules (to be observed) in the practice of Yoga. Accordingly He (the Lord) said thus:

"The body is composed of the five elements. It is filled with five maṇḍalas (spheres). That which is hard is Pṛthivī (earth), one of them; that which is liquid is Āpas; that which is bright is Tejas (fire); motion is the property of vāyu; that which pervades everywhere is Ākāśa. All these should be known by an aspirant after Yoga. Through the blowing of Vāyumaṇḍala in this body, (there are caused) 21,600 breaths every day and night. If there is a diminution in the Pṛthivīmaṇḍala, there arise folds in the body; if there is diminution in the essence of Āpas, there arises gradually greyness of hair; if there is diminution in the essence of Tejas, there is loss of hunger and lustre; if there is diminution in the essence of Vāyu, there is incessant tremor; if there is diminution in the essence of Ākāśa, one dies. The jīvita (viz., Prāṇa) which possesses these elements havings no place to rest (in the body) owing to the diminution of the elements, rises up like birds flying up in the air. It is for this reason that it is called Uḍyāṇa (lit., flying up). With reference to this, there is said to be a bandha (binding, also meaning a posture called Uḍḍiyāṇabandha, by which this flight can be arrested). This Uḍḍiyāṇabandha is to (or does away with) death, as a lion to an elephant. Its experience is in the body, as also the bandha. Its binding (in the body) is hurtful. If there is agitation of Agni (fire) within the belly, then there will be caused much of pain. Therefore this (Uḍḍiyāṇabandha) should not be practised by one who is hungry or who has urgency to make water or void excrement. He should take many times in small quantities proper and moderate food. He should practise Mantrayoga, Layayoga and Haṭhayoga, through mild, middling and transcendental methods (or periods) respectively. Laya, Mantra and Haṭhayogas have each (the same) eight subservients.

यमश्च नियमश्चैव तथा चासनमेव च। प्राणायामस्तथा पश्चात्प्रत्याहारस्तथा परम्॥११॥
धारणा च तथा ध्यानं समाधिश्चाष्टमो भवेत्। अहिंसा सत्यमस्तेयं ब्रह्मचर्यं दयार्जवम्॥१२॥
क्षमा धृतिर्मिताहारः शौचं चेति समा दश। तपः सन्तोषमास्तिक्यं दानमीश्वरपूजनम्॥१३॥
सिद्धान्तश्रवणं चैव ह्रीर्मतिश्च जपो व्रतम्। एते हि नियमाः प्रोक्ता दशधैव महामते॥१४॥
एकादशासनानि स्युश्चक्रादि मुनिसत्तम। चक्रं पद्मासनं कूर्मं मयूरं कुक्कुटं तथा॥१५॥
वीरासनं स्वास्तिकं च भद्रं सिंहासनं तथा। मुक्तासनं गोमुखं च कीर्तितं योगवित्तमैः॥१६॥
सव्योरु दक्षिणे गुल्फे दक्षिणं दक्षिणेतरे। निदध्यादृजुकायस्तु चक्रासनमिदं मतम्॥१७॥
पूरकः कुम्भकस्तद्वद्रेचकः पूरकः पुनः। प्राणायामः स्वनाडीभिस्तस्मान्नाडीः प्रचक्षते॥१८॥

They are yama, niyama, āsana, prāṇāyāma, pratyāhāra, dhāraṇā, dhyāna and samādhi. (Of these), yama is of ten kinds. They are non-injury, truth, non-coveting continence, compassion, straight forwardness, patience, courage, moderate eating and purity (bodily and mental). Niyama is of ten kinds. They are tapas (religious austerities), contentment, belief in the existence of God or Vedas, charity, worship of Īśvara (or God), listening to the exposition of religious doctrines, modesty, a (good) intellect, japa (muttering or Prayers), and vrata (religious observances). There are eleven postures beginning with cakra. Cakra, padma, kūrma, mayūra, kukkuṭa, vīra, svastika, bhadra, siṁha, mukta and gomukha, are the postures enumerated by the knowers of yoga. Placing the left ankle on the right thigh and the right ankle is the posture "Cakra". Prāṇāyāma should be practised again and again in the following order, viz., inspiration, restraint of breath and expiration. The prāṇāyāma is done through the nāḍīs (nerves). Hence it is called the nāḍīs themselves.

शरीरं सर्वजन्तूनां षण्णवत्यङ्गुलात्मकम्। तन्मध्ये पायुदेशात्तु द्व्यङ्गुलात्परतः परम्॥१९॥
मेढ्रदेशादधस्तात्तु द्व्यङ्गुलान्मध्यमुच्यते। मेढ्रान्नताङ्गुलादूर्ध्वं नाडीनां कन्दमुच्यते॥२०॥
चतुरङ्गुलमुत्सेधं चतुरङ्गुलमायतम्। अण्डाकारं परिवृतं मेदोमज्जास्थिशोणितैः॥२१॥
तत्रैव नाडीचक्रं तु द्वादशारं प्रतिष्ठितम्। शरीर ध्रियते येन वर्तते तत्र कुण्डली॥२२॥
ब्रह्मरन्ध्रं सुषुम्णा या वदनेन पिधाय सा। अलम्बुसा सुषुम्णायाः कुहूर्नाडी वसत्यसौ॥२३॥
अनन्तरायुग्यमे तु वारुणा च यशस्विनी। दक्षिणारे सुषुम्णायाः पिङ्गला वर्तते क्रमात्॥२४॥
तदन्तरारयोः पूषा वर्तते च पयस्विनी। सुषूम्ना पश्चिमे चारे स्थिता नाडी सरस्वती॥२५॥

"The body of every sentient being is ninety-six digits long. In the middle of the body, two digits above the anus and two digits below the sexual organ, is the centre of the body (called Mūlādhāra). Nine digits above the genitals, there is kanda of nāḍīs which revolves, oval-shaped, four digits high and four digits broad. It is surrounded by fat, flesh, bone, and blood. In it, is situated a nāḍī-cakra (wheel of nerves) having twelve spokes. Kuṇḍalī by which this body is supported is there. It is covering by its face the Brahmarandhra (viz., Brahmā's hole) of Suṣumnā. (By the side) of Suṣumnā dwell the nāḍīs Alambusā and Kuhūḥ. In the next two (spokes) are Vāruṇā and Yaśasvinī. On the spoke south of Suṣumnā is, in regular course piṅgalā. On the next two spokes, are Pūṣā and Payasvinī. On the spoken west of Suṣumnā is the nāḍī called Payasvinī. On the spoke west of Suṣumnā is the nāḍī called Sarasvatī.

शङ्खिनी चैव गान्धारी तदनन्तरयोः स्थिते। उत्तरे तु सुषुम्नाया इडाख्या निवसत्यसौ॥२६॥
अनन्तरं हस्तिजिह्वा ततो विश्वोदरी स्थिता। प्रदक्षिणक्रमेणैव चक्रस्यारेषु नाड्यः॥२७॥
वर्तन्ते द्वादश होता द्वादशानिलवाहकाः। पटवत्संस्थिता नाड्यो नानावर्णाः समीरिताः॥२८॥
पटमध्यं तु यत्स्थानं नाभिचक्रं चदुच्यते। नादाधारा समाख्याता ज्वलन्ती नादरूपिणी॥२९॥
पररन्ध्रा सुषुम्ना च चत्वारो रत्नपूरिताः। कुण्डल्या पिहितं शश्वद्ब्रह्मरन्ध्रस्य मध्यमम्॥३०॥
एवमेतासु नाडीषु धरन्ति दश वायवः। एवं नाडीगतिं वायुगतिं ज्ञात्वा विचक्षणः॥३१॥
समग्रीवशिरःकायः संवृतास्य सुनिश्चलः। नासाग्रे चैव हृन्मध्ये बिन्दुमध्ये तुरीयकम्॥३२॥
स्रवन्तममृतं पश्येन्नेत्राभ्यां सुसमाहितः। अपानं मुकुलीकृत्य पायुमाकृष्य चौन्मुखम्॥३३॥

प्रणवेन समुत्थाप्य श्रीबीजेन निवर्तयेत्। स्वात्मानं च श्रियं ध्यायेदमृतप्लावनं ततः॥३४॥

कालवञ्चनमेतद्धि सर्वमुख्यं प्रचक्षते। मनसा चिन्तितं कार्यं मनसा येन सिध्यति॥३५॥

जलेऽग्निज्वलनाच्छाखापल्लवानि भवन्ति हि। नाधन्यं जागतं वाक्यं विपरीता भवेत्क्रिया॥३६॥

On the next two spokes are Śaṅkhinī and Gāndhārī. To the north of Suṣumnā dwells Iḍā; in the next is Hastijihvā; in the next is Viśvodarā. In these spokes of the wheel, the twelve nāḍīs carry the twelve vāyus from left to right (to the different parts of the body). The nāḍīs are like (i.e., woven like the warp and woof of) cloth. They are said to have different colours. The central portion of the cloth (here the collection of the nāḍīs) is called the nābhicakra (navel plexus). Jvalantī, Nādarūpinī, Pararandhrā and Suṣumnā are called the (basic) supports of nāda (spiritual sound). These four nāḍīs are of ruby colour. The central portion of Brahmarandhra is again and again covered by Kuṇḍalī. Thus ten vāyus move in these nāḍīs. A wise man who has understood the course of nāḍīs and vāyus should, after keeping his neck and body erect with his mouth closed, contemplate immovably upon turyaka (Ātmā) at the tip of his nose, in the centre of his heart and in the middle of bindu and should see, with a tranquil mind through the (mental) eyes, the nectar flowing from there. Having closed the anus and drawn up the vāyu and caused it to rise through (the repetition of) praṇava (Oṁ), he should complete with Śrī bīja. He should contemplate upon his Ātmā as Śrī (or Parāśakti) and as being bathed by nectar. This is Kālavañcana (lit., time illusion). It is said to be the most important of all. Whatever is thought of by the mind is accomplished by the mind itself. (Then) agni (fire) will flame in jala (water) and in the flame (of agni) will arise the branches and blossoms. Then the words uttered and the actions done regarding the universe are not in vain.

मार्गे बिन्दुं समाबध्य वह्निं प्रज्वाल्य जीवने। शोषयित्वा तु सलिलं तेन कायं दृढं भवेत्॥३७॥

गुदयोनिसमायुक्त आकुञ्चत्येककालतः। अपानमूर्ध्वगं कृत्वा समानोऽन्ने नियोजयेत्॥३८॥

स्वात्मानं च श्रियं ध्यायेदमृतप्लावनं ततः। बलं समारभेद्योगं मध्यमद्वारमागतः॥३९॥

भावयेदूर्ध्वगत्यर्थं प्राणापानसुयोगतः। एष योगो वरो देहे सिद्धिमार्गप्रकाशकः॥४०॥

यथैवापाङ्गतः सेतुः प्रवाहस्य निरोधकः। तथा शरीरगा च्छाया ज्ञातव्या योगिभिः सदा॥४१॥

सर्वासामेव नाडीनामेष बन्धः प्रकीर्तितः। बन्धस्यास्य प्रसादेन स्फुटीभवति देवता॥४२॥

एवं चतुष्पथो बन्धो मार्गत्रयनिरोधकः। एवं विकासयन्मार्गं येन सिद्धाः सुसङ्गताः॥४३॥

उदानमूर्ध्वगं कृत्वा प्राणेन सह वेगतः। बन्धोऽयं सर्वनाडीनामूर्ध्वं याति निरोधकः॥४४॥

अयं च संपुटो योगो मूलबन्धोऽप्ययं मतः। बन्धत्रयमनेनैव सिद्ध्यत्यभ्यासयोगतः॥४५॥

दिवारात्रमविच्छिन्नं यामेयामे यदा यदा। अनेनाभ्यासयोगेन वायुरभ्यसितो भवेत्॥४६॥

वायावभ्यसिते वह्निः प्रत्यहं वर्धते तनौ। वह्नौ विवर्धमाने तु सुखमन्नादि जीर्यते॥४७॥

अन्नस्य परिपाकेन रसवृद्धिः प्रजायते। रसे वृद्धिं गते नित्यं वर्धन्ते धातवस्तथा॥४८॥

धातूनां वर्धनेनैव प्रबोधो वर्धते तनौ। दह्यन्ते सर्वपापानि जन्मकोट्यर्जितानि च॥४९॥

By checking the bindu in the path, by making the fire flame up in the water and by causing the water to dry up, the body is made firm. Having contracted simultaneously the anus and yoni (the womb) united together, he should draw up Apāna and unite with it Samāna. He should contemplate upon his Ātmā as Śiva and then as being bathed on nectar. In the central part of each spoke, the yogin should commence to concentrate bala (will or strength). He should try to go up by the union of Prāṇa and Apāna. This most important yoga brightens up in the body the path of siddhis. As a dam across the water serves as an obstacle to the floods, so it should ever be known by the yogins that the chāyā of the body is (to jīva). This bandha is said of all nāḍīs. Through the grace of this bandha, Devatā (goddess) become visible. This bandha of four feet serves as a check to the three paths. This brightens up the path through which the siddhas obtained (their siddhis). If with Prāṇa is made to rise up soon Udāna, this bandha checking all nāḍīs goes up. This is called Sampuṭayoga or Mūlabandha. Through the practising of this yoga, the three bandhas are mastered. By practising day and night intermittingly or at any convenient time, the vāyu will come under his control. With the control of vāyu, agni (the gastric fire) in the body will increase daily. With the increase of agni, food, etc., will be easily digested. Should food be properly digested, there is increase of rasa (essence of food). With the daily increase of rasa, there is the increase of dhātus (spiritual substances). With the increase of dhātus, there is the increase of wisdom in the body. Thus all the sings collected together during many crores of births are burnt up.

गुदमेढ्रान्तरालस्थं मूलाधारं त्रिकोणकम्। शिवस्य बिन्दुरूपस्य स्थानं तद्धि प्रकाशकम्॥५०॥

यत्र कुण्डलिनि नाम परा शक्तिः प्रतिष्ठिता। यस्मादुत्पद्यते वायुर्यस्माद्वह्निः प्रवर्धते॥५१॥

यस्मादुत्पद्यते बिन्दुर्यस्मान्नादः प्रवर्धते। यस्मादुत्पद्यते हंसो यस्मादुत्पद्यते मनः॥५२॥

मूलधारादिषटचक्रं शक्तिस्थानमुदीरितम्। कण्ठदुपरि मूर्बान्तं शांभवं स्थानमुच्यते॥५३॥

नाडीनामाश्रयः पिण्डो नाट्यः प्राणस्य चाश्रयः। जीवस्य निलयः प्राणो जीवो हंसस्य चाश्रयः॥५४॥

हंसः शक्तेरधिष्ठानं चराचरमिदं जगत्।

In the centre of the anus and the genitals, there is the triangular Mūlādhāra. It illumines the seat of Śiva of the from of bindu. There is located the Parāśakti named kuṇḍalinī. From the seat, vāyu arises. From the seat, agni becomes increased. From that seat, bindu originates and nāda becomes increased. From that seat, Haṁsa is born. From that seat, manas is born. The six cakras beginning with Mūlādhāra are said to be the seat of Śakti (Goddess). From the neck to the top of the head is said to be the seat of Śambhu (Śiva). To the nāḍīs, the body is the support (or vehicle); to Prāṇa, the nāḍīs are the support; to jīva, Prāṇa, is the dwelling place; to Haṁsa, jīva is the support; to Śakti, Haṁsa is the seat and the locomotive and fixed universe.

निर्विकल्पः प्रसन्नात्मा प्राणायामं समभ्यसेत्॥५५॥

सम्यग्बन्धत्रयस्थोऽपि लक्ष्यलक्षणकारणम्। वेद्यं समुद्धरेन्नित्यं सत्यसंधानमानसः॥५६॥

रेचकं पूरकं कुम्भमध्ये निरोधयेत्। दृश्यमाने परे लक्ष्ये ब्रह्मणि स्वयमाश्रितः॥५७॥

बाह्यस्थविषयं सर्वं रेचकः समुदाहृतः। पूरकं शास्त्रविज्ञान कुम्भकं स्वगतं स्मृतम्॥५८॥

एवमभ्यासचित्तश्चेत्स मुक्तो नात्र संशयः। कुम्भकेन समारोप्य कुम्भकेनैव पूरयेत्॥५९॥

कुम्भेन कुम्भयेत्कुम्भं तदन्तस्थः परं शिवम्। पुनरास्फालयेदद्य सुस्थिरं कण्ठमुद्रया॥६०॥

वायूनां गतमावृत्य धृत्वा पूरककुम्भकौ। समहस्तयुगं भूमौ समं पादयुगं तथा॥६१॥

वेधकक्रमयोगेन चतुष्पीठं तु वायुना। आस्फालयेन्महामेरुं वायुवक्रे प्रकोटिभिः॥६२॥

पुटद्वयं समाकृष्य वायुः स्फुरति सत्वरम्। सोमसूर्याग्निसंबन्धाज्जानीयादमृताय वै॥६३॥

मेरुमध्यगता देवाश्चलन्ते मेरुचालनात्। आदौ संजायत क्षिप्र वेधोऽस्य ब्रह्मग्रन्थितः॥६४॥

ब्रह्मग्रन्थिं ततो भित्त्वा विष्णुग्रन्थिं भिनत्त्यसौ। विष्णुग्रन्थि ततो भित्त्वा रुद्रग्रन्थिं भिनत्त्यसौ॥६५॥

रुद्रग्रन्थिं ततो भित्त्वा छित्त्वा मोहमलं तथा। अनेकजन्मसंस्कारगुरुदेवप्रसादतः॥६६॥

Being without distraction and of a calm mind, one should practise prāṇāyāma. Even a person who is well-skilled in the practice of the three bandhas should try always to cognise with a true heart that Principle which should be known and is the cause of all objects and their attributes. Both expiration and inspiration should (be stopped and made to) rest in restraint of breath (alone). He should depend solely on Brahman which is the highest aim of all visibles. (The giving out of) all external objects is said to be recaka (expiration). The (taking in of the) spiritual knowledge of the Śāstras is said to be pūraka (Inspiration) and (the keeping to oneself of) such knowledge is said to be kumbhaka (or restraint of breath). He is an emancipated person who practises thus such a citta. There is no doubt about it. Through kumbhaka, it (the mind) should be always taken up, and through kumbhaka alone it should be filled up within. It is only through kumbhaka that kumbhaka should be firmly mastered. Within it is Paramaśiva. That (vāyu) which is non-motionless should be shaken again through kaṇṭha-mudrā (throat-posture). Having checked the course of vāyu, having become perfect in the practice of expiration and restraint of breath and having planted evenly on the ground the two hands and the two feet, one should pierce the four seats through vāyu through the three yogas. He should shake Mahāmeru with the (aid of) prakoṭis (forces) at the mouth of vāyu. The two puṭas (cavities) being drawn, vāyu throbs quickly. The union of moon, sun and agni should be known on account of nectar. Through the motion of Meru, the devatās who stay in the centre of Meru move. At first in his Brahmagranthi, there is produced soon a hole (or passage). Then having pierced Brahmagranthi, he pierces Viṣṇu-granthi : then he pierces Rudra-granthi.

योगाभ्यासात्तो वेधो जायते तस्य योगिनः। इडापिङ्गलयोर्मध्ये सुषुम्नानाडिमण्डले॥६७॥

मुद्राबन्धविशेषेण वायुमूर्ध्वं च कारयेत्। ह्रस्वो दहति पापानि दीर्घो मोक्षदायकः॥६८॥

आप्यायनः प्लुतो वापि त्रिविधोच्चारणेन तु। तैलधारामिवाच्छिन्नं दीर्घघण्टानिनादवत्॥६९॥

अवाच्यं प्रणवस्याग्रं यस्तं वेद स वेदवित्। ह्रस्वं बिन्दुगतं दैर्घ्यं ब्रह्मरन्ध्रगतं प्लुतम्।

द्वादशान्तगतं मन्त्रं प्रसादं मन्त्रसिद्धये॥७०॥

सर्वविघ्नहरश्चायं प्रणवः सर्वदोषहा। आरम्भश्च घटश्चैव पुनः परिचयस्तथा।।७१।।
निषपत्तिश्चेति कथिताश्चतस्रस्तस्य भूमिकाः। कारणत्रयसंभूतं बाह्य कर्म परित्यजन्।।७२।।
आन्तरं कर्म कुरुते यत्रारम्भः स उच्यते। वायुः पश्चिमतो वेधं कुर्वन्नापुर्य सुस्थिरम्।।७३।।
यत्र तिष्ठति सा प्रोक्ता घटाख्या भूमिका बुधैः। न सजीवो न निर्जीवः काये तिष्ठति निश्चलम्।
यत्र वायुः स्थिरः खे स्यात्सेयंः प्रथमभूमिका।।७४।।
यत्रात्मना सृष्टिलयौ जीवन्मुक्तिदशागतः। सहजः कुरुते योगं सेयं निष्पत्तिभूमिका।।७५।।

Then to the yogin comes vedha (piercing) through his liberation from the impurities of delusion, through the religious ceremonies (performed) in various births, through the grace of Gurus and devatās and through the practice of yoga. In the maṇḍala (sphere or region) of Suṣumnā (situated between Iḍā and Piṅgalā) vāyu should be made to rise up through the feature known as Mudrā-bandha. The short pronunciation (of Praṇava) frees (one) from sins, its long pronunciation confers (on one) mokṣa. So also its pronunciation in āpyāyana or pluta svara (tone). He is a knower of Veda, who through the above-mentioned three ways or pronunciation knows the end of Praṇava which is beyond the power of speech, like the never-ceasing flow of oil or the long-drawn bell-sound. The short svara goes to bindu. The long svara goes to brahmarandhra : the pluta to dvādaśānta (twelfth centre). The mantras should be uttered on account of getting mantra siddhis. This Praṇava (Oṁ) will remove all obstacles. It will remove all sins. Of this, are four bhūmikās (states) predicated, viz., ārambha, ghaṭa, paricaya and niṣpatti. Ārambha is that state in which one having abandoned external karmas performed by the three organs (mind, speech and body), is always engaged in mental karma only. It is said by the wise that the ghaṭa state is that in which vāyu having forced an opening on the western side and being full, is firmly fixed there. Paricaya state is that in which vāyu is firmly fixed to ākāśa, neither associated with jīva nor not, while the body is immovable. It is said that niṣpatti state is that in which there take place creation and dissolution through Ātmā or that state in which a yogin having become a jīvanmukta performs yoga without effort.

एतदुपनिषदं योऽधीते सोऽग्निपूतो भवति। स वायुपूतो भवति। सुरापानात्पूतो भवति। स्वर्णस्तेयात्पूतो भवति। स जीविन्मुक्तो भवति। तदेतदृचाभ्युक्तम्। तद्विष्णोः परमं पदं सदा पश्यन्ति सूरयः। दिवीव चक्षुराततम्। तद्विप्रासो विपन्यवो जागृवांसः समिन्धते। विष्णोर्यत्परमं पदमित्यपनिषत्।

"Whoever recites this Upaniṣad becomes immaculate like agni. Like vāyu, be becomes pure. He becomes freed from the sin of drinking alcohol. He becomes freed from the sins of the theft of gold. He becomes a Jīvanmukta. This is what is said by the Ṛgveda. Like the eye pervading the ākāśa (seeing without effort everything above), a wise man sees (always) the supreme seat of Viṣṇu. The brāhmaṇas who have always their spiritual eyes wide open praise and illuminate in diverse ways the spiritiual seat of Viṣṇu.

ॐ सह नाववत्विति शान्तिः।। हरि ॐ तत्सत्।

।।इति वराहोपनिषत्समाप्ता।।

87. GARUḌOPANIṢAD

गरुडोपनिषद्

This upaniṣad falls under the tradition of Atharvaveda. The learning of Garuḍa has been described coincide mentioning the tradition of teacher and the student from lord Brahmā to saint Bharadvāja in this upaniṣad. Garuḍa vidyā is purported to the learning of effacing the poison (Viṣa Nivāraṇa). This upaniṣad contains the process of killing the effect of poison which is inserted in the body of mankind as a result of bite by the poisonous insects including the serpents.

This upaniṣad very first describes the tradition of student and the teacher followed in this learning by the commune of Garuḍa vidyā. At the last, this upaniṣad has been concluded with propounding in detail the hymn used for Garuḍa Mala.

॥शान्तिपाठः॥

ॐ भद्रं कर्णेभिः .... इति शान्तिः॥

गारुडब्रह्मविद्यां प्रवक्ष्यामि यां ब्रह्मविद्यां नारदाय प्रोवाच नारदो बृहत्सेनाय बृहत्सेन इन्द्राय इन्द्रो भरद्वाजाय भरद्वाजो जीवत्कामेभ्यः शिष्येभ्यः प्रायच्छत्॥ १॥

Om̐! I will preach now the Gāruḍa-Brahma-Vidyā. Brāhmaṇa taught the Brahman-science to Nārada, Nārada to Bṛhatsena, Bṛhatsena to Indra, Indra to Bharadvāja, Bharadvāja to his pupils who were curious to preserve their life.

अस्याः श्रीमहागरुडब्रह्मविद्याया ब्रह्मा ऋषिः। गायत्री छन्दः। श्रीभगवान्महागरुडो देवता। श्रीमहागरुडप्रीत्यर्थे मम सकलविषविनाशनार्थे जपे विनियोगः॥ २॥

The seer (Ṛṣi) to 'Śrī Garuḍa Brahma Vidyā' is lord Brahmā, Chanda is Gāyatrī and lord Mahā Garuḍa is the god. Its 'Viniyoga' (application) is made for appreciation of lord Maha Garuḍa and for killing and effect of all sort of poisons inserted in me.

[Now the process of Nāganyāsa (summoning gods in various organs of body) with recital of following hymns.]

ॐ नमो भगवते अङ्गुष्ठाभ्यां नमः। श्रीमहागरुडाय तर्जनीभ्यां स्वाहा। पक्षीन्द्राय मध्यमाभ्यां वषट्। श्रीविष्णुवल्लभाय अनामिकाभ्यां हुम्। त्रैलोक्यपरिपूजिताय कनिष्ठिकाभ्यां वौषट्। उग्रभयंकरकालानलरूपाय करतलकरपृष्ठाभ्यां फट्। एवं हृदयादिन्यासः॥ ३॥

'Om̐ Namo Aṅguṣṭhābhyam̐ Namaḥ– (touch both thumbs by the index finger of both hands), Śrī Mahā Garuḍāya Tarjanībhyām Svāhā (touch both index fingers by the thumbs). 'Pakṣīndrāya Madhyamābhyām̐ Vaṣaṭ' (touch the middle finger by the thumbs). 'Śrī Viṣṇu Vallabhāya Anāmikābhyām̐ Hum' (touch the ring finger by the thumbs). 'Trailokyaparipūjitāya Kaniṣṭhakābhyām̐ Vauṣaṭ' (touch the little fingers by the thumbs).

'Ugra Bhayankara.....Karatalakarapṛṣṭhābhyāṁ Phaṭ' (touch the upper and lower palm of both hands). Similarly, the heart etc. (head, braid, chest, eyes etc.) should also be touched by the five fingers of the right hand.

भूर्भुवः सुवरोमिति दिग्बन्धः॥४॥

The process of defence from all directions should be made with the recital of Bhūḥ, Bhuvaḥ, Svaḥ and Oṁ.

[Now the meditation is described for which one should meditate on Mahā Garuḍa while reading the following hymns with reverence.]

ध्यानम्। स्वस्तिको दक्षिणं पादं वामपादं तु कुञ्चितम्। प्राञ्जलीकृतदोर्युग्मं गरुडं हरिवल्लभम्। अनन्तो वामकटको यज्ञसूत्रं तु वासुकिः। तक्षकः कटिसूत्रं तु हारः कर्कोट उच्यते। पद्मो दक्षिणकर्णे तु महापद्मस्तु वामके। शङ्खः शिरःप्रदेशे तु गुलिकस्तु भुजान्तरे। पौण्ड्रकालिकनागाभ्यां चामराभ्यां सुवीजितम्। एलापुत्रकनागाद्यैः सेव्यमानं मुदान्वितम्। कपिलाक्षं गरुत्मन्तं सुवर्णसदृशप्रभम्। दीर्घबाहुं बृहत्स्कन्धं नागाभरणभूषितम्। आजानुतः सुवर्णाभमाकट्योस्तुहिनप्रभम्। कुङ्कुमारुणमाकण्ठं शतचन्द्रनिभाननम्। नीलाग्रनासिकावक्त्रं सुमहच्चारुकुण्डलम्। दंष्ट्राकरालवदनं किरीटमुकुटोज्ज्वलम्। कुङ्कुमारुणसर्वाङ्गं कुन्देन्दु-धवलाननम्। विष्णुवाह नमस्तुभ्यं क्षेमं कुरु सदा मम। एवं ध्यायेत्त्रिसंध्यासु गरुडं नागभूषणम्। विषं नाशयते शीघ्रं तूलराशिमिवानलः॥५॥

Meditation– Whose right foot is in the shape of Svastika, the left foot is bent on knees, both hands are clasped in the posture of salutation, dearest to lord Viṣṇu, holder of the Cobra named Anant as a bangle to his left hand, holder of the Cobra Vāsuki as the sacrificial thread (Yajñopavīta), holder of Takṣaka (poisonous serpent) as scarf and Karkoṭa as garland round the neck, holder of the Cobra Padma like ear-ring and Mahā Padma in the left ear, the Śaṅkha serpent on head, Gulikā (Cobra) in the middle of arms, the Cobras Pauṇḍra and Kālika as fans, worshipped with devotion by the serpents Elā and Putrakā, yellowish eyes luminating like gold, prolongated arms, broad shoulders, well decorated with the ornaments of Cobras, golden complexion, long legs, white lustre like snow in the waist region, red body like Kuṁkuma, illustrious mouth like hundred moons, the front portion of nose and the mouth bluish, ears trimmed with the huge rings, huge mouth with fires jaws, holder of radiating crown, red organs like Kuṁkuma, white mouth like moon and the kunda flower and the vehicle of lord Viṣṇu known as god Garuḍa is saluted. Do our welfare always. Lord Garuḍa trimmed with the Cobras should be meditated in the three intervening time of the day. Lord Garuḍa will definitely be pleased and kill the effect of poison as the fire burns into ashes the pile of cotton.

ओमीमों नमो भगवते श्रीमहागरुडाय पक्षीन्द्राय विष्णुवल्लभाय त्रैलोक्यपरिपूजिताय उग्रभयंकरकालानलरूपाय वज्रनखाय वज्रतुण्डाय वज्रदन्ताय वज्रदंष्ट्राय वज्रपुच्छाय वजपक्षालक्षितशरीराय ओमीमेह्येहि श्री महागरुडाप्रतिशासनास्मिन्नाविशाविश दुष्टानां विषं दूषय दूषय स्पृष्टानां विषं नाशय नाशय दन्दशूकानां विषं दारय दारय प्रलीनं विषं प्रणाशय प्रणाशय सर्वविषं नाशय नाशय हन हन दह दह पच पच भस्मीकुरु भस्मीकुरु हुं फट् स्वाहा॥६॥

Salutation is conveyed to lord Mahā Garuḍa who is the king of birds, dearest to lord Viṣṇu, worshipped by the three worlds, fires and dreadful like Kālāgni, holder of rigid nails and beak, acute teeth, hard jaws, stiff tail and the stiff wings. O Mahā Garuḍa! Please come and enshrine this suitable sheet. Please appear here. Kill the effect of poison created by the wicked persons. Destroy the poison that inserts merely by a contact. Please kill the effect of poison inserted by the crawling poisonous snakes. Please delete the poison inserted clandestinely. Kill the effects of all kinds of poisons. Kill it and burn it as also digest it. Please burn all poisons, burn them immediately. The offering should be made for the pleasure of lord Garuḍa with the recital of hymn 'Huṁ Phaṭ'.

चन्द्रमण्डलसंकाश सूर्यमण्डलमुष्टिक। पृथ्वीमण्डलमुद्राङ्ग श्रीमहागरुड विषं हर हर हुं फट् स्वाहा॥७॥

You are analogous to the circle of moon. The circle of sun is within your fist. You hold the postures like the circle of this earth. O lord Mahā Garuḍa! Please, kill the effect of all poisons and destroys them. This offering is for the pleasure of lord Garuḍa with the root hymn 'Huṁ Phaṭ'.

ॐ क्षिप स्वाहा॥८॥

O lord Garuḍa! Accept this offering for setting aside the serpents and the poison to which they create.

ओमीं सचरति सचरति तत्कारी मत्कारी विषाणां च विषरूपिणी विषदूषिणी विषशोषणी विषनाशिनी विषहारिणी हतं विषं नष्टं विषमन्तःप्रलीनं विषं प्रनष्टं विषं हतं ते ब्रह्मणा विषं हतमिन्द्रस्य वज्रेण स्वाहा॥९॥

The ever-increasing poison that kills the living-organism has been destroyed by the learning of Brahma. That kills the effect of poison, itself is poisonous making the poison vicious, observe, destroy and abducting is itself in the form of Brahma. The violent poison, the hidden poison etc. has been destroyed by that learning of Brahma. The thunderbolt of Indra supported while killing the effect of this poison. This offering is being made for the same.

ॐ नमो भगवते महागरुडाय विष्णुवाहनाय त्रैलोक्यपरिपूजिताय वज्रनखवज्रतुण्डाय वज्रपक्षालंकृतशरीराय एह्येहि महागरुड विषं छिन्धि छिन्धि आवेशयावेशय हुं फट् स्वाहा॥१०॥

This offering with recital of 'Huṁ Phaṭ' is for the purpose of salutation to lord Mahā Garuḍa, vehicle of lord Viṣṇu, worshipped in three worlds, holder of the nails and beak as stiff as the thunderbolt and holder of the stiff wings. We summon you lord Garuḍa. Please come and with your kind arrival, please destroy the effect of this poison.

सुपर्णोऽसि गरुत्मान्त्रिवृत्ते शिरो गायत्रं चक्षुः स्तोम आत्मा साम ते तनूर्वामदेव्यं बृहद्रथन्तरे पक्षौ यज्ञायज्ञियं पुच्छं छन्दांस्यङ्गानि धिष्णिया शफा यजूंषि नाम। सुपर्णोऽसि गरुत्मान्दिवं गच्छ सुवः पत॥११॥

O sky-fleeing lord Mahā Garuḍa! You are dynamic as lord Fire and you have the nice wings. Your head is 'Trivṛtta', your eyes are Gāyatra (Sāma), the Bṛhada and Rathantara

Sāma are in the form of your two wings. The offerings are your inner soul, all rhymes are your body organs and Yajuḥ is your name. The Sāma named Vāmadeva is your body, Yajña Yajñiya Sāma is your tail and the fire existing in 'Dhiṣṇiya' is your nails. O lord Garuḍa! Please move towards the divine world and attain the heaven.

ओमीं ब्रह्मविद्यामममावास्यायां पौर्णमास्यायां पुरोवाच सचरति सचरति तत्कारी मत्कारी विषनाशिनी विषदूषिणी विषहारिणी हतं विषं नष्टं विषं प्रनष्टं विषं हतमिन्द्रस्य वज्रेण विषं हतं ते ब्रह्मणा विषमिन्द्रस्य वज्रेण स्वाहा॥ १२॥

This learning of Brahma was told on the day of full moon and on the last day of the month (Amāvasyā) in the ancient times. The learning of Brahma (Brahma Vidyā) is the poison of poisons i.e. the poison-killer. It kills the effect of ever-increasing and violent poison. It abducts and viciates the poison. The learning in the form of Brahma had destroyed the violent poison and the clandestine poison as also the murderous poison through the thunderbolt the effect of poison through this thunderbolt. This offering is made for the same purpose.

तत्स्त्र्यम्। यद्यनन्तकदूतोऽसि यदि वानन्तकः स्वयं सचरति सचरति तत्कारी मत्कारी विषनाशिनी विषदूषिणी हतं विषं नष्टं विषं हतमिन्द्रस्य वज्रेण विषं हतं ते ब्रह्मणा विषमिन्द्रस्य वज्रेण स्वाहा॥ १३॥

May you be Anantaka's messenger, or be Anantaka himself, the 'Tatstryaṁ' (a root hymn that kills effect of all kinds of poison) will destroy you. The poison that kills us and them has been destroyed by a stroke of Indra's thunderbolt under the motivation of Brahma Vidyā, who is poison to all poisons and holds the power to extinct them. The thunderbolt of Indra also have supported to extinct this poison. This offering is made for the same.

यदि वासुकिदूतोऽसि यदि वा वासुकिः स्वयं सचरति सचरति तत्कारी मत्कारी विषनाशिनी विषदूषिणी हतं विषं नष्टं विषं हतमिन्द्रस्य वज्रेण विषं हतं ते ब्रह्मणा विषमिन्द्रस्य वज्रेण स्वाहा॥ १४॥

Irrespective of yours being a messenger from Vāsuki (a poisonous serpent) or you yourself are Vāsuki, the Brahma Vidyā will kill you. The poison as increasing for the purpose of killing either us or them has been extincted by a stroke of Indra's thunderbolt under the motivation of the learning of Brahma who is a poison to the poisons and competent enough the viciate, to kill, to destroy and to seize all poisons. This learning is the knowledge in itself. This offering is made for the same purpose.

यदि तक्षकदूतोऽसि यदि वा तक्षकः स्वयं सचरति सचरति तत्कारी मत्कारी विषनाशिनी विषदूषिणी हतं विषं नष्टं विषं हतमिन्द्रस्य वज्रेण विषं हतं ब्रह्मणा विषमिन्द्रस्य वज्रेण स्वाहा॥ १५॥

Irrespective of yours being a messenger from Takṣaka or you yourself being a Takṣaka, will be killed by the learning of Brahma. The violent poison created for killing them or us has been viciated, destroyed and extincted by the Brahma Vidyā that in itself is the poison of poisons. It has destroyed that violent poison by a mere stroke of Indra's thunderbolt because of being it in the garb of Brahma. While destroying this poison, lord Indra's thunderbolt has also supported. This offering is made for the same purpose.

यदि कर्कोटकदूतोऽसि यदि वा कर्कोटकः स्वयं सचरति सचरति तत्कारी मत्कारी विषनाशिनी विषदूषिणी हतं विषं नष्टं विषं हतमिन्द्रस्य वज्रेण विषं हतं ते ब्रह्मणा विषमिन्द्रस्य वज्रेण स्वाहा॥ १६॥

Irrespective of yours being a messenger from Karkoṭaka or you yourself are a Karkoṭaka, you will be killed by the Brahma Vidyā. The ever-increasing and circulating violent poison has been destroyed, viciated and extincted by the learning of Brahma because it is the poison of poisons. The learning of Brahma has destroyed it by a violent stroke made by the thunderbolt of lord Indra. The thunderbolt of lord Indra has also supported while extincting this poison. This offering is made for the same purpose.

यदि पद्मकदूतोऽसि यदि वा पद्मकः स्वयं सचरति सचरति तत्कारी मत्कारी विषनाशिनी विषदूषिणी हतं विषं नष्टं विषं हतमिन्द्रस्य वज्रेण विषं हतं ते ब्रह्मणा विषमिन्द्रस्य वज्रेण स्वाहा॥ १७॥

Irrespective of yours being a messenger of Padmaka or you yourself are Padmaka, you will be killed by the learning of Brahma. The ever-increasing violent poison which has been created either them or us has been destroyed by the learning of Brahma because it is the poison of poisons. This learning in garb of Brahma and so competent has destroyed such a violent poison by the stroke of lord Indra's thunderbolt. Lord Indra's thunderbolt has also supported for the destruction of such poison. This offering is being made on the behalf of same.

यदि महापद्मकदूतोऽसि यदि वा महापद्मकः स्वयं सचरति सचरति तत्कारी मत्कारी विषनाशिनी विषदूषिणी हतं विषं नष्टं विषं हतमिन्द्रस्य वज्रेण विषं हतं ते ब्रह्मणा विषमिन्द्रस्य वज्रेण स्वाहा॥ १८॥

Irrespective of yours being a messenger from Mahā Padmaka or you yourself will be Maha Padmaka, you will be killed by the learning of Brahma. The learning of Brahma is poison of poisons and it is competent enough to kill themselves or ourselves. The learning of Brahma is competent enough for viciating, killing, destroying and seizing the poison. It has destroyed such violent poison by using the Indra's thunderbolt which has co-operated entirely. This offering is made on the behalf of the same.

यदि शङ्खकदूतोऽसि यदि वा शङ्खकः स्वयं सचरति सचरति तत्कारी मत्कारी विषनाशिनी विषदूषिणी विषहारिणी हतं विषं नष्टं विषं हतमिन्द्रस्य वज्रेण विषं हतं ते ब्रह्मणा विषमिन्द्रस्य वज्रेण स्वाहा॥ १९॥

Irrespective of yours being a messenger from Śaṅkhaka or you yourself are Śaṅkhaka, you will be destroyed by the learning of Brahma. The ever-increasing poison of killing effect either them or ourselves has been destroyed by the learning of Brahma who itself is the poison of poisons. It is competent enough to viciate, to kill, to destroy and to seize all poisons. It has destroyed that violent poison by the stroke of Indra's thunderbolt. While destroying it, Indra's thunderbolt has also supported. This offering is made for the same purpose.

यदि गुलिकदूतोऽसि यदि वा गुलिकः स्वयं सचरति सचरति तत्कारी मत्कारी विषनाशिनी विषदूषिणी विषहारिणी हतं विषं नष्टं विषं हतमिन्द्रस्य वज्रेण विषं हतं ते ब्रह्मणा विषमिन्द्रस्य वज्रेण स्वाहा॥ २०॥

Irrespective of yours being a messenger from Gulika or you yourself are Gulika, you will be killed by the learning of Brahma. The ever-increasing poison with killing effect either to them or ourselves has been destroyed by the learning of Brahma because it is the poison of poisons and competent enough to viciate, to kill, to destroy and to seize the poison. Such learning in the garb of Brahma has destroyed that violent poison by the stroke of lord Indra's thunderbolt. While destroying this poison, lord Indra's thunderbolt has also supported. This offering is being made for the same purpose.

यदि पौण्ड्रकालिकदूतोऽसि यदि वा पौण्ड्रकालिक: स्वयं सचरति सचरति तत्कारी मत्कारी विषनाशिनी विषदूषिणी विषहारिणी हतं विषं नष्टं विषं हतमिन्द्रस्य वज्रेण विषं हतं ते ब्रह्मणा विषमिन्द्रस्य वज्रेण स्वाहा।। २१।।

Irrespective of your being a messenger from Pauṇḍra Kālika or you yourself are Pauṇḍra Kālika, you will be killed by the learning of Brahma. The poison of poisons i.e. the learning of Brahma is competent enough to viciate, to kill, to destroy and to seize the violent poison with killing effect either to them or to ourselves. It has destroyed that violent poison by the help of a stroke of lord Indra's thunderbolt. Lord Indra's thunderbolt also have supported while killing this poison. This offering is being made for the same purpose.

यदि नागकदूतोऽसि यदि वा नागक: स्वयं सचरति सचरति तत्कारी मत्कारी विषनाशिनी विषदूषिणी विषहारिणी हतं विषं नष्टं विषं हतमिन्द्रस्य वज्रेण विषं हतं ते ब्रह्मणा विषमिन्द्रस्य वज्रेण स्वाहा।। २२।।

Irrespective of yours beings a messenger from Nāgaka or you yourself are Nāgaka, you will be destroyed by the learning of Brahma. The learning of Brahma having the poison of poisons is competent enough to viciate, to kill, to destroy and to seize the violent poison with effect of killing either ourselves or them. The learning in garb of Brahma has destroyed that violent poison by the stroke of Indra's thunderbolt. Lord Indra's thunderbolt has also supported while destroying this poison. This offering is being made for the same purpose.

यदि लूतानां प्रलूतानां यदि वृश्चिकानां यदि घोटकानां यदि स्थावरजङ्गमानां सचरति सचरति तत्कारी मत्कारी विषनाशिनी विषदूषिणी विषहारिणी हतं विषं नष्टं विषं हतमिन्द्रस्य वज्रेण विषं हतं ते ब्रह्मणा विषमिन्द्रस्य वज्रेण स्वाहा।। २३।।

Either you are spider, the largest spider, the scorpion, the horse, serpent or the inert or dynamic poisonous insect. The violent poison increasing and circulating for killing us or them has been killed by the learning of Brahma, most competent to viciate, to kill, to destroy and to seize such violent poisons because it is the poison of the poisons. By assistance of lord Indra's thunderbolt, this learning of Brahma has destroyed such violent poison. This offering is being made on the behalf of the same.

अनन्तवासुकितक्षककर्कोटकपद्मकमहापद्मकशङ्खकगुलिकपौण्ड्रकालिकनागक इत्येषां दिव्यानां महानागानां महानागादिरूपाणां विषतुण्डानां विषदन्तानां विषदंष्ट्राणां विषाङ्गानां विषपुच्छानां विश्वचाराणां वृश्चिकानां लूतानां प्रलूतानां मूषिकाणां गृहगौलिकानां गृहगोधिकानां घ्रणासानां

गृहगिरिगह्वरकालानलवल्मीकोद्भूतानां तार्णानां पार्णानां काष्ठदारुवृक्षकोटरस्थानां मूलत्वग्दारुनिर्यास-पत्रपुष्पफलोद्भूतानां दुष्टकीटकपिश्वानमार्जारजम्बुकव्याघ्रवराहाणां जरायुजाण्डजोद्भिज्जस्वेदजानां शस्त्रबाणक्षतस्फोटव्रणमहाव्रणकृतानां कृत्रिमाणामन्येषां भूतवेतालकूष्माण्डपिशाचप्रेतराक्षसयक्षभय प्रदानां विषतुण्डदंष्ट्राणां विषाङ्गानां विषपुच्छानां विषाणां विषरूपिणी विषदूषिणी विषशोषिणी विषनाशिनी विषहारिणी हतं विषं नष्टं विषमन्त:प्रलीनं विषं प्रनष्टं विषं हतं ते ब्रह्मणा विषमिन्द्रस्य वज्रेण स्वाहा।।२४।

The learning of Brahma is the poison of poisons i.e., it viciates, absorbs, destroys and removes the effect of poisons either it is of 'Anantaka Vāsuki, Takṣaka, Karakoṭaka, Padmaka, Mahā Padmaka, Śaṅkhaka, Gulika, Pauṇḍra, Kālika' etc. Cobras and other all divine great Cobras and in the form of great Cobras, living-beings of poisonous beak, poisonous teeth, poisonous jaws, poisonous organs, poisonous tales, moving everywhere like poisonous scorpion, spider, large spider, mouse, grand-shrew, lizard, despicable poisonous insects, poisonous insect that move on floor, walls and small holes in the houses, ants, termite etc., the insects residing in grass, leaves, wood, tree, holes in the trees etc. the insects generating from the bark, leaves, flowers and fruits etc. of the trees as also in its root and trunks, the poisonous wild animals, like monkey, dogs, cats, jackals, tiger, pig, the other animals and the men etc., the germs arising from the eggs, plants and trees from sweating glands, the weapons, the arrows etc., the toxic arising in the injured parts of the body, wounds, large wounds, the supernatural powers frightening i.e. the ghost, Vetāla, Kuṣmaṇḍa, Preta, Piśāca, demon, Yakṣa etc., the birds of poisonous beaks, poisonous jaws, poisonous organs. May that learning of Brahma destroys all these poisons and spoil their effect. That Brahma Vidyā has destroyed these fatal poisons, clandestine poisons and the poisons of killing effect. The thunderbolt of lord Indra has also assisted while destroying these poisons. This offering is being made for the same purpose.

य इमां ब्रह्मविद्याममावास्यायां पठेच्छृणुयाद्वा यावज्जीवं न हिंसन्ति सर्पा:। अष्टौ ब्राह्मणान्ग्राहयित्वा तृणेन मोचयेत्। शतं ब्राह्मणान् ग्राहयित्वा चक्षुषा मोचयेत्। सहस्रं ब्राह्मणान् ग्राहयित्वा मनसा मोचयेत्। सर्पाञ्जलेन मुञ्चन्ति। तृणेन मुञ्चन्ति। काष्ठेन मुञ्चन्तीत्याह भगवान्ब्रह्मेत्युपनिषत्।। २५।।

The devotee who recites or hears to this Brahma vidyā on the last day of the month, remains unbitten by the snake– like poisonous insects throughout his life. He who teaches it to eight Brāhmaṇas, he releases (from the effects of snake-bite) by merely touching with grass. One who teaches it to a hundred Brāhmaṇas he releases by a mere glance. One who teaches it to a thousand Brāhmaṇas, he releases by the mere thought. Thus he releases with grass, with a piece of wood, with ashes. Lord Brahmā has pronounced the same before all seers in this Upaniṣad. This is the essence inherited to this upaniṣad.

।।शान्तिपाठ:।।

ॐ भद्रं कर्णेभि: .... इति शान्ति:।।

।।इति गरुडोपनिषत्समाप्ता।।

88. KALISANTARAṆOPANIṢAD

कलिसंतरणोपनिषद्

॥शान्तिपाठ:॥

ॐ सह नाववतु .... इति शान्ति:॥

द्वापरान्ते नारदो ब्रह्माणं जगाम कथं भगवन् गां पर्यटन्कलिं संतरेयमिति। स होवाच ब्रह्मा साधु पृष्टोऽस्मि सर्वश्रुतिरहस्यं गोप्यं तच्छृणु येन कलिसंसारं तरिष्यसि। भगवत आदिपुरुषस्य नारायणस्य नामोच्चारणमात्रेण निर्धूतकलिर्भवति॥ १॥

At the end of Dvāpara yuga, Nārada went the Brahmā and addressed him thus : "O Lord, how shall I, roaming over the earth, be able to cross Kali?" To which Brahmā thus replied : "Well asked. Hearken to that which all Śrutis (the Vedas) keep secret and hidden, through which one may cross the saṁsāra (mundane existence) of Kali. He shakes off (the evil effects of) Kali through the mere uttering of the name of the Lord Nārāyaṇa, who is the primeval Puruṣa." Again Nārada asked Brahmā : "What is the name?" To which Hiraṇyagarbha (Brahmā) replied thus : (the words are :)" 1. Harē; 2. Rāma, 3. Harē, 4. Rāma 5. Rāma, 6. Rāma 7. Harē, 8. Harē; 9. Harē, 10. Kṛṣṇa 11. Harē, 12. Kṛṣṇa, 13. Kṛṣṇa, 14. Kṛṣṇa 15. Harē, 16. Harē. These sixteen names (words) are destructive of the evil effects of Kali. No better means than this is to be seen in all the Vedas. These (sixteen names) destory of āvaraṇa (or the centripetal force which produces the sense of individuality) of jīva surrounded by the sixteen kalās (rays). Then like the sphere of the sun which shines fully after the clouds (screening it) disperse, Parabrahman (alone) shines."

नारद: पुन: पप्रच्छ तन्नाम किमिति। स होवाच हिरण्यगर्भ:। हरे राम हरे राम राम राम हरे हरे। हरे कृष्ण हरे कृष्ण कृष्ण कृष्ण हरे हरे। इति षोडशकं नाम्नां कलिकल्मषनाशनम्। नात: परतरोपाय: सर्ववेदेषु दृश्यते। इति षोडशकलावृतस्य जीवस्यावरणविनाशनम्। तत: प्रकाशते परं ब्रह्म मेघापाये रविरश्मिमण्डलीवेति॥ २॥

Nārada asked : "O Lord, what are the rules to be observed with reference to it. To which Brahmā replied that there were no rules for it. Whoever in a pure or an impure state, utters these always, attains the same world of, or proximity with, or the same form of, or absorption into Brahmā.

पुनर्नारद: पप्रच्छ भगवन्कोऽस्य विधिरिति। तं होवाच नास्य विधिरिति। सर्वदा शुचिरशुचिर्वा पठन्ब्राह्मण: सलोकतां समीपतां सरूपतां सायुज्यतामेति। यदास्य षोडशीकस्य सार्धत्रिकोटीर्जपति तदा ब्रह्महत्यां तरति। तरति वीरहत्याम्। स्वर्णस्तेयात्पूतो भवति। पितृदेवमनुष्याणामपकारात्पूतो भवति। सर्वधर्मपरित्यागपापात्सद्य: शुचितामाप्नुयात् सद्यो मुच्यते सद्यो मुच्यत इत्युपनिषत्॥ ३॥

Whoever utters three and a half koṭis (or thirty-five millions) times this *mantra* composed of sixteen names (or words) crosses the sin of the murder of a *Brāhmaṇa*. He becomes purified from the sin of the theft of gold. He becomes purified from the sin of cohabitation with a woman of low caste. he is purified from the sin of wrong done to pitṛs, devas, and men. Having given up all dharmas, he becomes freed at once from all sins. He is at once released from all bondage. That he is at once released from bondage is the *Upaniṣad*.

ॐ सह नाववतु .... इति शान्तिः॥

॥इति कलिसंतरणोपनिषत्समाप्ता॥

89. JĀBĀLYUPANIṢAD

जाबाल्युपनिषद्

This Upaniṣad is a part and parcel to Sāmaveda. There are only twenty three hymns in it. A questionnaire type formation of three hymns has been made regarding the supreme element in which is Paippalādi, the son of Pippalāda and Lord Jābāli have been discussed. The first question has been asked regarding the introduction of the element, living soul, animal and Īśa and the measure for the attainment of the emancipation. The hermit Jābāli has replied for all these questions. Finally the magnificence of the knowledge laid down by this upaniṣad has been described and the contents is this set a rest.

॥शान्तिपाठः॥

ॐ आप्यायन्तु ....इति शान्तिः॥

अथ हैनं भगवन्तं जाबालिं पैप्पलादिः पप्रच्छ भगवन्मे ब्रूहि परमतत्त्वरहस्यम्॥ १॥

किं तत्त्वं को जीवः कः पशुः क ईशः को मोक्षोपाय इति॥ २॥

स तं होवाच साधु पृष्टं सर्वं निवेदयामि यथाज्ञातमिति॥ ३॥

पुनः स तमुवाच कुतस्त्वया ज्ञातमिति॥ ४॥ पुनः स तमुवाच षडाननादिति॥ ५॥

पुनः स तमुवाच तेनाथ कुतो ज्ञातमिति॥ ६॥ पुनः स तमुवाच तेनेशानादिति॥ ७॥

पुनः स तमुवाच कथं तस्मात्तेन ज्ञातमिति॥ ८॥ पुनः स तमुवाच तदुपासनादिति॥ ९॥

पुनः स तमुवाच भगवन्कृपया मे सरहस्यं सर्वं निवेदयेति॥ १०॥

The hermit Paippalādi (the son of Paippalāda) asked Lord Jābāli– "O Lord kindly explain the mystery of the supreme element for me? What is element? Who is living soul? Who is animal? Who is Īśa and what is the way to attain emancipation?" The hermit Jābāli said– "You indeed has asked a question of vital importance. I describe all whatever is known to me regarding this topic. Paippalādi asked– "Kindly tell me that from where have you acquired this knowledge?" Jābāli replied– "It is from Ṣaḍānana". Paippalādi asked again– "where from Ṣaḍānana was known to it?" Jābāli replied– "he acquired this knowledge from Īśana." Paippalādi asked again "From where he acquired it?" Jābāli replied– "he acquired this knowledge by virtue of worship." Hearing this, Paippalādi asked– " O Lord! Kindly disclose this mystery in detail to me."

स तेन पृष्टः सर्वं निवेदयामास तत्त्वम्। पशुपतिरहंकाराविष्टःसंसारी जीवः स एव पशुः। सर्वज्ञः पञ्चकृत्यसंपन्नः सर्वेश्वर ईशः पशुपतिः॥ ११॥ के पशव इति पुनः स तमुवाच॥ १२॥ जीवाः पशव उक्ताः। तत्पतित्वात्पशुपतिः॥ १३॥ स पुनस्तं होवाच कथं जीवाः पशव इति। कथं तत्पतिरिति॥ १४॥ स तमुवाच

यथा तृणाशिनो विवेकहीनाः परप्रेष्याः कृष्यादिकर्मसु नियुक्ताः सकलदुःखसहाः स्वस्वामिबध्यमाना गवादयः पशवः। यथा तत्स्वामिन इव सर्वज्ञ ईशः पशुपतिः॥ १५॥ तज्ज्ञानं केनोपायेन जायते॥ १६॥ पुनः स तमुवाच विभूतिधारणादेव॥ १७॥ तत्प्रकारः कथमिति। कुत्र कुत्र धार्यम्॥ १८॥

Jābāli replied– "I explain the entire element. Lord Paśupati himself turns into the worldly living organisms when it falls in the trap of ego. Such a living soul is the animal. Paśupati is omnipresent and lord to all who perform the five kinds of activities. Paippalādi asked again– "Who is animals?" Jābāli replied– "It is living organism which has been called an animal owing to the master of living organism, he is called Paśupati." He further asked– "what form of that animal is? And how Paśupati is the master to him? The Saint Jābāli replied– "As the grass eater, stupid, slave to any other, employed in agriculture etc. activities born with a number of pains and tied by their master i.e. the cow etc. animals, these living organisms too are fastened by the god. As the people are master to the animals, the master to all living organisms is the omniscient Paśupati." Paippalādi asked again– "How can that knowledge be acquired?" Jābāli replied– "By holding as that knowledge can be acquired." Paippalādi asked– "What is the method of holding it? At what places it should be held?"

पुनः स तमुवाच सद्योजातादिपञ्चब्रह्ममन्त्रैर्भस्म संगृह्याग्निरिति भस्मेत्यनेनाभिमन्त्र्य मानस्तोक इति समुद्धृत्य जलेन संसृज्य त्र्यायुषमिति शिरोललाटवक्षःस्कन्धेष्विति तिसृभिस्त्र्यायुषैस्त्र्यम्बकैस्तिस्रो रेखाः प्रकुर्वीत। व्रतमेतच्छाम्भवं सर्वेषु वेदेषु वेदवादिभिरुक्तं भवति। तत्समाचरेन्मुमुक्षुर्न पुनर्भवाय॥ १९॥

Then Jābāli replied– "That knowledge should be collected by reciting Sadyojāta etc. five hymns pertaining to Brahma. It should then be spelled by reciting Agniriti hymn. It should be picked up by reciting Mānastoka and it should be held on head, forehead, chest and shoulders by reciting Tryāyuṣam (Yaju 3.62) and belting it by adding water. Three lines should be then drawn by reciting three Trayāṣa and three Tryambaka (Yaju 3.60) hymns. The reader of Veda has been told as Sāmbhava Vrata in Veda. The person observing this process doesn't fall in the trap of birth and death. The hymns abbreviated above are hymns from Yajurveda has been referred there to. The hymns are five hymns of Sadyojāta etc.– "Oṁ Sadyojātaṁ Prapadāmi Sadhojatāya Vai Namo Namaḥ Bhava Bhave Nāti Bhave Bhavasya Maṁ Bhavodbhavāya Namaḥ' (1) 'Vamadevāya Namoh Jyesthāya Namaḥ. Śreṭyāya Namo Rudrāya Namaḥ Kālāya Namaḥ Kal Vikarṇāya Namo Valavikarṇāya Namaḥ (2) Valāya Nomo Vala Pramatranāya Namaḥ. Sarvabhutadamanāya Namo Namaḥ (3) Aghorebhyotha Ghorebhyo Ghoraghoratatebhyaḥ Sarvebhyaḥ Sarvasarvebhyoḥ Namaste'astu Rudrarūpebhyaḥ (4) Tatpuruṣāya Vidamahe Mahādevā dhimahi Tanno Rudraḥ Pracodayāta (5) (Rudrādhyāyī) Agniriti Om Agniriti bhaṣma! Vayuritibhaṣma Jalamiti Bhaṣma Sthalamiti bhaṣmsaVyometibhaṣma Sarva Ha Va Idam Bhaṣma Man Etāni Caksūṁṣi Bhaṣmani Iti."

अथ सनत्कुमारः प्रमाणं पृच्छति। त्रिपुण्ड्रधारणस्य
त्रिधा रेखा आललाटादाचक्षुषोराभ्रुवोर्मध्यतश्च॥ २०॥

On being asked about the testimony, Sanatkumara told that the three horizontal lines in the middle of the entire forehead should be drawn upto the brows and eyes.

याऽस्य प्रथमा रेखा सा गार्हपत्यश्चाकारो रजो भूर्लोकः स्वात्मा क्रियाशक्तिः ऋग्वेदः प्रातःसवनं प्रजापतिर्देवो देवतेति। याऽस्य द्वितीया रेखा सा दक्षिणाग्निरुकारः सत्त्वमन्तरिक्षमन्तरात्मा चेच्छाशक्तिर्यजुर्वेदो माध्यन्दिनसवनं विष्णुर्देवो देवतेति। याऽस्य तृतीया रेखा साऽऽहवनीयो मकारस्तमो द्यौर्लोकः परमात्मा ज्ञानशक्तिः सामवेदस्तृतीयसवनं महादेवो देवतेति॥ २१॥

Its first line is in the form of the Gārhapatya fire, Rajas property, 'A' letter, the abode of earth, the action of ones own soul, synonym to power, Ṛgveda form and Prātaḥ Savana. Its god is Prajāpati himself. The second line is in the form of Dakṣiṇāgni, Satva property, 'U' letter, the space, the will-power of ones inner soul, Yajurveda and in the form of Mādhyandina Savana. Its god is Lord Viṣṇu. The third line is in the form of Āhavanīya fire, 'M' letter, Tamas property, abode of Sun, the power of knowledge to the supreme soul, Sāmaveda and in form of third Savana. Its god is Mahādeva himself.

त्रिपुण्ड्रं भस्मना करोति यो विद्वान्ब्रह्मचारी गृही वानप्रस्थो यतिर्वा स महापातकोपपातकेभ्यः पूतो भवति। स सर्वान् वेदानधीतो भवति। स सर्वान्देवान्ध्यातो भवति। स सर्वेषु तीर्थेषु स्नातो भवति। स सकलरुद्रमन्त्रजापी भवति। न स पुनरावर्तते न स पुनरावर्तते॥ इति॥ २२॥ ॐ सत्यमित्युपनिषत्॥ २३॥

The person who holds the Tripuṇḍra from ash attains to the mystery of the tripuṇḍra as revealed in the preceding hymn. He may be a celibate, couple, vānaprasthi or recluse. He is liberated from all kinds of evils either greater or smaller. He observes all Vedas, concentrates on all gods acquires the fruits as of all pilgrim places and automatically enjoys the fruits which would be of Japa on Rudra hymns. The person so observing the rules of holding Tripuṇḍra seldom falls prey to the cycle of birth and death. This Upaniṣad is thus included with the disclosure of this fact.

ॐ आप्यायन्तु ....इति शान्तिः॥

॥इति श्रीजाबाल्युपनिषत्समाप्ता॥

90. SAUBHĀGYALAKṢMYUPANIṢAD

सौभाग्यलक्ष्म्युपनिषद्

This Upaniṣad is related to the tradition of Ṛgveda. The magnificent letters of Śrī aphorism has been made basis for description of the hymn, discus etc. of the goddess. It has been presented in the form of a questionaire where in questions and answers were transacted between the gods on one side and Śrī Nārāyaṇa on the other side. This Upaniṣad is divided in three parts. The first part has been started with the curiosity of Saubhāgyalakṣmī Vidyā. The subject-matter then is concentration on Saubhāgyalakṣmī, the Saints etc. of Śrī Sūkta, the discus of Saubhāgyalakṣmī, the Saint to one letter containing hymn etc., the one letter containing discus and the special hymn of Lakṣmī. In the second part, the Jñāna yoga for the eligible persons, the yoga or Prāṇāyāma with Ṣaṇmukhī posture, description of three knots from which the sound arises, propensity of integrated Brahma, exclusive spirit and the characteristics of meditation has been described. In the third part, the nine discuses (Nava Cakra) i.e. Mulādhāra, Svādhiṣṭhāna, navel, heart, throat, palate, brow, Brahmarandhra and Ākāśa have been enumerated and lastly the fruit of the study of Upaniṣad has been explained.

ॐ वाङ्मे मनसि .... इति शान्तिः।

॥प्रथमः खण्डः॥

अथ भगवन्तं देवा ऊचुर्हे भगवन्नः कथय सौभाग्यलक्ष्मीविद्याम्॥ १॥

All gods once appeared before Lord Nārāyaṇa and requested– "O Lord ! kindly preach us the learning of Saubhāgyalakṣmī."

तथेत्यवोचद्भगवानादिनारायणः सर्वे देवा यूयं सावधानमनसो भूत्वा श‍ृणुत। तुरीयरूपां तुरीयातीतां सर्वोत्कटां सर्वमन्त्रासनगतां पीठोपपीठदेवतापरिवृतां चतुर्भुजां श्रियं हिरण्यवर्णामिति पञ्चदशर्ग्भिर्ध्यायेत्॥ २॥

Lord Nārāyaṇa replied– "O Gods ! It is all good now, listen to attentively what I say. One should concentrate his mind on the goddess Śrī Lakṣmī with reciting 'Hiraṇyavarṇam' .. .. etc. fifteen Ṛcās of Śrī Sūkta. She is beyond the three stages i.e., formidable, micro and cause, who is beyond the stage of Turīya concommitantly being in form of Turīya, she is scarce to perceive and she is enshrined on the seat of all hymns. She is surrounded by the gods seated on Pīṭhas and sub-Pīṭhas and she has four arms.

अथ पञ्चदश ऋगात्मकस्य श्रीसूक्तस्यानन्दकर्दमचिक्लीतेन्दिरासुता ऋषयः। श्रीरित्याद्या ऋचः चतुर्दशानामृचामानन्दाद्यृषयः। हिरण्यवर्णाद्याद्यत्रयस्यानुष्टुप् छन्दः। कांसोस्मीत्यस्य बृहती छन्दः। तदन्ययोर्द्वयोस्त्रिष्टुप्। पुनरष्टकस्यानुष्टुप्। शेषस्य प्रस्तारपङ्क्तिः। श्र्यग्निर्देवता। हिरण्यवर्णामिति बीजम्। कांसोऽस्मीति शक्तिः। हिरणमया चन्द्रा रजतस्रजा हिरण्यस्रजा हिरण्याहिरण्यवर्णेति प्रणवादिनमोन्तैश्चतुर्थ्यन्तैरङ्गन्यासः। अथ वक्त्रत्रयैरङ्गन्यासः। मस्तकलोचनश्रुतिघ्राणवदन-कण्ठबाहुद्वयहृदयनाभिगुह्यपायूरुजानुजङ्घेषु श्रीसूक्तैरेव क्रमशो न्यसेत्॥ ३॥

The intuitive saint to the fifteen Ṛcās of above Śrī Sūkta are Ānanda (the Son of Indirā), Ciklīta and Kardama. The intuitive hermit to the first hymn is Śrī viz. Indirā and Ānanda, Kardama and Ciklīta etc., hermits are the saints to fourteen hymns. The rhyme to first three Ṛcās is Anustup, rhyme to fourth, Ṛcā is Triṣṭupa. The rhyme to the Ṛcās from seven to fourteen i.e., eight Ṛcās is anuṣṭup and the rhyme to the fifteenth Ṛcā is Prastāra Paṅkti. The gods to these hymns are the Śrī and the fire 'Hiraṇyavarṇaṁ' is the seed to all hymns falling within this aphorism and its power (Śakti) is 'Kānsomi' One should do Aṅganyāsa with reciting at the beginning Oṁ and in the end Namaḥ to the words Hiraṇya, Hiraṇyavarṇa in the fourth classification (Vibhakti). Then·Aṅganyāsa should be made with reciting Vaktratraya (hymn). The process of Nyāsa in a systematic manner and with reciting the Ṛcās of Śrī Sūkta on the head, eyes, ears, nose, mouth, throat, arms, heart, navel, genital, anus, pubic, leg, thigh etc. parts of the body. (Then the following hymn should be recited in the state of concentration).

अरुणकमलसंस्था तद्रजःपुञ्जवर्णा करकमलधृतेष्टाऽभीतियुग्माम्बुजा च।
मणिकटकविचित्रालंकृताकल्पजालैः सकलभुवनमाता संततं श्रीः श्रियै नः॥४॥

May the mother goddess of entire worlds Śrī Mahālakṣmī shower prosperity on us. She is in reddish complexion seated on a pious petal of lotus, yellowish as the lotus honey, two lotus flowers in two hands each, as also the boning posture and the posture of fearlessness in other two hands, adorned with excellent influence of the bangles studded with gems and adorned with all kinds of ornaments.

तत्पीठकर्णिकायां ससाध्यं श्रीबीजम्। वस्वादित्यकलापद्मेषु श्रीसूक्तगतार्धार्धर्चा तद्बहिर्यः शुचिरिति मातृकया च श्रियं यन्त्राङ्गदशकं च विलिख्य श्रियमावाहयेत्॥५॥

Inside the seed to be (Pīṭha Karṇikā) the Śrī seed (Śrīṁ) should be written with special attempt. The half hymn of Śrī Sūkta in the middle of the ground circle and on the lotus containing eight petals, twelve petals and sixteen petals each should be then written. Outside that seed to be, the Mātṛka letters i.e., 'Yaḥ Śuciḥ Prayato Bhūtvā etc. should be written viz., after writing the hymn containing sixteen petals and above from 'A' to 'Kṣa' should be written. Thus, the Śrī Cakra consisting of the parts i.e. Praṇava, Ṣaṭkoṇa, Bhūvṛtta, Aṣṭadala, Bhūvṛtta, Dvādaśadala, Bhūvṛtta. Ṣoḍaśadala, Bhūvṛtta and Nirbhūvṛtta should be made and Śrī is to be summoned.

अङ्गैः प्रथमावृतिः। पद्मादिभिर्द्वितीया। लोकेशैस्तृतीया। तदायुधैस्तुरीया वृतिर्भवति। श्रीसूक्तैरावाहनादि। षोडशसहस्रजपः॥६॥

The worship to the first layer is performed through the hymns of Aṅganyāsa. The worship to second layer is made through the Nidhis like Padma etc., the third layer worship is made through the Lokapālās (Indra etc.) and the worship to fourth layer is made through their arms and weapons like thunderbolt etc. The deeds pertaining to summon the gods are performed with reciting the hymns of Śrī Sūkta. As a next effort, the Puraścaraṇa with reciting sixteen thousand hymns has been provided.

सौभाग्यरमैकाक्षर्या भृगुनिचृद्गायत्री। श्रिय ऋष्यादय:। शमिति बीजशक्ति:। श्रामित्यादि षडङ्गम्।।७।।

(The sage of worship to Saubhāgyalakṣmī hymn is Bhṛgu, the rhyme is Nicṛd Gāyatrī and the god is Śrī. 'Śaṁ' is the seed. The process of Aṅganyāsa is to be performed with reciting Śram etc. Then, concentration should be made according to the meaning of the successive hymns as mentioned below.

भूयाद्भूयो द्विपद्माभयवरदकरा तप्तकार्तस्वराभा शुभ्राभ्राभेभयुग्मद्वयकरधृतकुम्भाद्भिरासिच्यमाना। रक्तौघाबद्धमौलिर्विमलतरदुकूलार्तवालेपनाढ्या पद्माक्षी पद्मनाभोरसि कृतवसति: पद्मगा श्री: श्रियै न:।।८।।

May the goddess Śrī Lakṣmī grace on us with the best luxuries by enshrining on the lotus seat who has held louts flowers in her both hands and whose two other hands are in the posture of boning and fearlessness respectively. Whose complexion of body is like the melted gold. The goddess who is bathing with the water pouring from vessels held by two elephants in their trunks, who are in the complexion of white clouds. A reddish colour and gem-studded crown is adorned on her head. Her apparels are excessively clean, whose eyes are like that of lotus, whose parts and organs of body are smeared with the sandal etc. scented matters consistent with the existing season and who resides in the heart zone of Lord Viṣṇu.

तत्पीठम्। अष्टपत्रं वृत्तत्रयं द्वादशराशिखण्डं चतुरस्रं रमापीठं भवति। कर्णिकायां ससाध्यं श्रीबीजम्। विभूतिरुन्नति: कान्ति: सृष्टि: कीर्ति: सन्नतिर्व्युष्टि: सत्कृष्टिर्ऋद्धिरिति प्रणवादिनमोन्तैश्चतुर्थ्यन्तैर्नवशक्तिं यजेत्।।९।।

After the concentration so made, the Pīṭha Yantra is described in this Pīṭha Yantra, there is a Ramā Pīṭha analogous to the shape of quadrangle, three circles, the lotus containing eight petals. The Śrī seed 'Śrīṁ' should be mentioned with special attempt on that seed. For eg. Śrīṁ Śrī Ramā Devi Jusstām should be recited and then call of the Nature, Pīṭhanyāsa and Nyāsa with the saints etc. should be made. Subsequently, the worship should be performed to the nine powers i.e. Vibhūti, Kānti, Unnati, Kīrti, Sṛṣṭi, Sannati, Vyuṣṭi, Riddhi and Satkṛṣṭi should be performed by using each name in fourth classification (Vibhakti) and by adding Oṁ in the beginning and Namaḥ in the end of each name.

अङ्गै: प्रथमावृति:। वासुदेवादिभिर्द्वितीया। बालक्यादिभिस्तृतीया। इन्द्रादिभिश्चतुर्थी भवति। द्वादशलक्षजप:।।१०।।

Thereafter the first layer should be worshipped through Aṅganyāsa. The worship of second layer is to be performed by praying to Vāsudeva etc. (Vāsudeva, Saṅkarṣaṇa, Pradyumna and Aniruddha). Now by the third layer worship to Bālāki etc. (Bālāki, Vimalā, Kamalā, Vibhiśikā, Vanamālikā, Malikā and Vasumālikā) should be performed. Then, in the worship of fourth layer, Indra etc. all gods and with their weapons including thunderbolt should be worshipped. For Purascarṇa, twelve Lakh hymns should be recited in a regular framework.

श्रीलक्ष्मीर्वरदा विष्णुपत्नी वसुप्रदा हिरण्यरूपा स्वर्णमालिनी रजतस्रजा स्वर्णप्रभा स्वर्णप्राकारा पद्मवासिनी पद्महस्ता पद्मप्रिया मुक्तालंकारा चन्द्रसूर्या बिल्वप्रिया ईश्वरी भुक्तिर्मुक्तिर्विभूतिर्ऋद्धिः समृद्धिः कृष्टिः पुष्टिर्धनदा धनेश्वरी श्रद्धा भोगिनी भोगदा सावित्री धात्री विधात्रीत्यादिप्रणवादिनमोन्ताश्चतुर्थ्यन्ता मन्त्राः। एकाक्षरवदङ्गादिपीठम्। लक्षजपः। दशांशं तर्पणम्। दशांशं हवनम्। द्विजतृप्तिः॥ ११॥

Now the system of Śrīṁ, Hrīṁ, Śrīṁ learning which contains three letters is being described. Its system of worship is analogous to the worship of one letter hymn. Only a slight difference is existed in the third layer worship. In the beginning of this learning, Oṁ and in the end word Namaḥ is to be added and every name should be used in its fourth classification (Vibhakti). These names are Śrī, Lakṣmī, Vardā, Viṣṇupatni, Vasupradā, Hiraṇyarupā, Svarṇamālinī, Rajatastrajā, Svarṇapriyā, Svarṇaprākārā, Padmavāsinī, Padmapriyā, Candrasūryā, Muktālaṅkārā, Bilvapriyā, Īśvarī, Bhukti, Mukti, Vibhūti, Riddhi, Samṛddhi, Kṛṣṭi, Puṣṭi, Dhanadā, Dhaneśvarī, Śraddhā, Bhoginī, Bhogadā, Sāvitrī, Dhātrī and Vidhātrī etc. and thus worship is to be made. The worship of Pīṭha is to be made with Aṅganyāsa like the one letter hymn. One lakh hymns are to be recited for Purascarṇa. The one tenth part of the Japa is Tarpaṇa, one tenth part of Tarpaṇa is Havana and one-tenth part of Havana is feeding of Brāhmaṇas. (This is the rule formed for Purascarṇa)

निष्कामानामेव श्रीविद्यासिद्धिः। न कदापि सकामानामिति॥ १२॥

This learning of Śrī Lakṣmī can be acquired only by the devotees who are free from all kinds of attachments. They attain accomplishment to this learning.

॥द्वितीयः खण्डः॥

अथ हैनं देवा ऊचुस्तुरीयया मायया निर्दिष्टं तत्त्वं ब्रूहीति। तथेति स होवाच-योगेन योगो ज्ञातव्यो योगो योगात्प्रवर्धते। योऽप्रमत्तस्तु योगेन स योगी रमते चिरम्॥ १॥ समापय्य निद्रां सुजीर्णेऽल्पभोजी श्रमत्याज्यबाधे विविक्ते प्रदेशे। सदा शीतनिस्तृष्ण एष प्रयत्नोऽथ वा प्राणरोधो निजाभ्यासमार्गात्॥ २॥ वक्त्रेणापूर्य वायुं हुतवहनिलयेऽपानमाकृष्य धृत्वा स्वाङ्गुष्ठाद्यङ्गुलीभिर्वरकरतलयोः षड्भिरेवं निरुध्य। श्रोत्रे नेत्रे च नासापुटयुगलमथोऽनेन मार्गेण सम्यक्पश्यन्ति प्रत्ययांशं प्रणवबहुविधध्यानसंलीनचित्ताः॥ ३॥

All gods then raised the next question to Lord Nārāyaṇa– "O God! Please tell us all in context to the specified elements of the Turīya illusion (Māyā)". Lord Nārāyaṇa started describing the matter by saying 'very well' in reply (he said O Gods!) attempts to know the yoga through yoga itself is to be made because yoga is promoted only by resorting to yoga. The yogi who remains attentive to his yoga by leaving aside the laxity, only can enjoy the pleasure for unlimited period. The devotee who uses the material only to the extent necessary for performance of the deeds viz. Mitabhogi, gives up the attachment, every and the dormance, defects and malafides in the form of attachment and performs the concentration in solitude because of Brahma. He in a continuous manner does practise for establishment of the soul into the element of supreme soul. He always tends to the penance of Rājayoga in order to set aside the feelings of heat and cold etc. pain. The yogis under exercise of Prāṇāyāma inhale the wind from mouth and set it in their belly. Thus, they push the Apāna wind from the navel region to the cell of digestion (Jaṭharāgni). They put their all fingers including the thumb and both palms on both ears, eyes and nostrils and do the continuous exercise of Prāṇāyāma. Thus, they do concentration on Oṁ in various ways and by merging themselves with it realize the element of ever-sensitive soul.

श्रवणमुखनयननासानिरोधनेनैव कर्तव्यम्। शुद्धसुषुम्नासरणौ स्फुटममलं श्रूयते नादः॥४॥

विचित्रघोषसंयुक्तानाहते श्रूयते ध्वनिः। दिव्यदेहश्च तेजस्वी दिव्यगन्धोऽप्यरोगवान्॥५॥

संपूर्णहृदयः शून्ये त्वारम्भे योगवान्भवेत्। द्वितीयां विघटीकृत्य वायुर्भवति मध्यगः॥६॥

One more method for the practise of Prāṇāyāma has been stated in which the eyes, ears, mouths and nostrils are closed. By following that process, the spinal nerve is purified and the strong sound of Oṁ can be heard with clarity. On hearing to the sound in undisturbed cycle (Anāhata cakra) excellent and of varied nature, words are heard. By virtue of such exercise, the devotee becomes full of splendour and a divine smell starts emanating out from his body. He attains the divine body and fully developed heart in the healthy state. By virtue of the continuous listening to this sound coming out from the spinal nerve, the man practising becomes well-supported by yoga just in the Mūlādhāra Cakra from where the spinal nerve starts ascending. This nerve then penetrates the Svādhiṣṭhāna cakra and going out from the whole in its nucleus, the oxygen enters into the spinal nerve.

दृढासनो भवेद्योगी पद्माद्यासनसंस्थितः। विष्णुग्रन्थेस्ततो भेदात्परमानन्दसंभवः॥७॥

अतिशून्यो विमर्दश्च भेरीशब्दस्ततो भवेत्। तृतीयां यत्नतो भित्त्वा निनादो मर्दलध्वनिः॥८॥

Having duly seated on Padmāsana etc. postures and by entering into the third Maṇipūraka cakra, the supreme pleasure is obtained without any extra efforts when the illusion (Viṣṇugranthi) is penetrated (This illusion is the sole cause for the growth of excessive desires and ambitions). When the oxygen (Prāṇa Vāyu) overleaps the void (Māyā) while ascending and when it does friction with the nerve, a sound like trumpet is heard therefrom. At the time, when the oxgyen penetrates the Maṇipura cakra, a sound like Mṛdaṅga (drum like sounding instrument) is heard.

महाशून्यं ततो याति सर्वसिद्धिसमाश्रयम्। चित्तानन्दं ततो भित्त्वा सर्वपीठगतानिलः॥९॥

The oxygen thereafter penetrates other Cakras and accesses to great void (Ākāśa Cakra). All kinds of accomplishment are easily attained. From there the oxygen thereafter penetrates the feeling of pleasure and becomes dynamic in all cakrās.

निष्पत्तौ वैणवः शब्दः क्वणतीति क्वणो भवेत्। एकीभूतं तदा चित्तं सनकादिमुनीडितम्॥१०॥

अन्तेऽनन्तं समारोप्य खण्डेऽखण्डं समर्पयन्। भूमानं प्रकृतिं ध्यात्वा कृतकृत्योऽमृतो भवेत्॥११॥

On the completion of this exercise, a sound like flute comes out and it automatically arises in the form of Praṇava (Oṁ). According to Sanaka etc. sages, the entire aptitude is engrossed while listening to the sound of Oṁ. The devotee then, finally becomes able in imposing the living soul on the element of supreme soul from this Ākāśa Cakra. He attains immortality by surrounding the soul engrossed in illusions to the supreme soul and by doing concentration on the omnipresent scope of soul.

योगेन योगं संरोध्य भावं भावेन चाञ्जसा। निर्विकल्पं परं तत्त्वं सदा भूत्वा परं भवेत्॥ १२॥

अहंभावं परित्यज्य जगद्भावमनीदृशम्। निर्विकल्पे स्थितो विद्वान्भूयो नाप्यनुशोचति॥ १३॥

By virtue of the yoga beyond the knowledge, one should enslave the peculiar Jñāna yoga and put checks on the spiritual meditation by the exclusive meditation. The yogin duly succeed in exclusive meditation, attains to the state of emancipation which directly adheres to the element of supreme soul. The egotism of such yogi is set aside by virtue of exclusive meditation and the world in the form of illusion as residing in the element of soul is also vanished. Thus the scholars go beyond the worries like 'This is I' and 'This is mine' etc. worries that arise frequently in the mind of the common people.

सलिले सैन्धवं यद्वत्साम्यं भवति योगतः। तथात्ममनसोरैक्यं समाधिरभिधीयते॥ १४॥

यदा संक्षीयते प्राणो मानसं च प्रलीयते। तदा समरसत्वं यत्समाधिरभिधीयते॥ १५॥

यत्समत्वं तयोरत्र जीवात्मपरमात्मनोः। समस्तनष्टसंकल्पः समाधिरभिधीयते॥ १६॥

प्रभाशून्यं मनःशून्यं बुद्धिशून्यं निरामयम्। सर्वशून्यं निराभासं समाधिरभिधीयते॥ १७॥

स्वयमुच्चलिते देहे देही नित्यसमाधिना। निश्चलं तं विजानीयात्समाधिरभिधीयते॥ १८॥

यत्रयत्र मनो याति तत्रतत्र परं पदम्। तत्रतत्र परं ब्रह्म सर्वत्र समवस्थितम्॥ १९॥

As the water and the salt get mixed and no identity of the salt remains separately, the oxygen when exists in the process of kumbhaka under the exercise of Prāṇāyāma and the mental propensities are weakened, the integrated state of the mind with soul like the stream of oil is called meditation. When all resolution are decayed as a result of unity established between the living soul and the supreme soul, the stage so formed is called meditation. When the mind and the wisdom are entirely merged being senseless to the world, when nothing is felt and everything seems like zero or essenceless, such a stage is called meditation. When the living soul exists underrated, stable and in the form of light inspite of the to and fro movement of body, this stage is called meditation. Wheresoever the mind of such a yogī is moved, a supreme position is attained thereto. The perfect knowledge (Para Brahma) is equally felt to that yogi at all places.

॥तृतीयः खण्डः॥

अथ हैनं देवा ऊचुर्नवचक्रविवेकमनुब्रूहीति। तथेति स होवाच–आधारे ब्रह्मचक्रं त्रिरावृतं भगमण्डलाकारम्। तत्र मूलकन्दे शक्तिः पावकाकारं ध्यायेत्। तत्रैव कामरूपपीठं सर्वकामप्रदं भवति। इत्याधारचक्रम्॥ १॥

All gods again requested Lord Nārāyaṇa– "O Lord! please tell us about the discretion of nine Cakrās for the welfare of us all". Lord Nārāyaṇa started explaining the same by reciprocating very well to the gods. (He told) The Brahma Cakra is existed in Mūlādhāra. It is in three circles in the form of yoni. The great power kuṇḍalinī is existed in the shape of a serpent in sleeping posture just at the root of the seed to be. Concentration should be made on that power in the form of the blazing fire until it is awakened i.e. the place of Devitripurā is existed. As a result of worship to that goddess, all kinds of enjoyments are obtained. The same description has been given regarding the first cakra namely the Mūlādhāra cakra.

द्वितीयं स्वाधिष्ठानचक्रं षड्दलम्। तन्मध्ये पश्चिमाभिमुखं लिङ्गं प्रवालाङ्कुरसदृशं ध्यायेत्। तत्रैवोड्याणपीठं जगदाकर्षणसिद्धिदं भवति॥ २॥

The second Cakra is with six petals and called Svādhiṣṭhāna Cakra. A Śivaliṅga in red colour like the shoot of coral should be bring in concentration by facing the west direction at the back of the seed to be to that six petal lotus. Uḍyāṇa Pīṭha is existed there. An accomplishment of fascinating the entire world is obtained by virtue of its worship.

तृतीयं नाभिचक्रं पञ्चावर्तं सर्पकुटिलाकारम्। तन्मध्ये कुण्डलिनीं बालार्ककोटिप्रभां तडित्प्रभां (तनुमध्यां) ध्यायेत्। सामर्थ्यशक्तिः सर्वसिद्धिप्रदा भवति। मणिपूरकचक्रम्॥ ३॥

The third Cakra is encircled by five times and it is curvy like the serpent. It is called the navel cakra. Concentration on great power of kuṇḍalinī luminating with the splendour of many crores rising suns and whose organs are so tender as the lightening. A great power is attained when this power is awakened and it renders with all kinds of accomplishment, it is the Maṇipūraka Cakra.

हृदयचक्रमष्टदलमधोमुखम्। तन्मध्ये ज्योतिर्मयलिङ्गाकारं ध्यायेत्। सैव हंसकला सर्वप्रिया सर्वलोकवश्यकरी भवति॥ ४॥

The fourth discus is called Anāhata Cakra. It is also known as Hṛdaya Cakra. It is in the form of eight petal lotus and its mouth is downward. One should concentrate on the ever-luminating liṅga within this discus. This luminating Liṅga is popularly known as Haṁsa Kalā. It is favourite to all and a power dominating the three worlds is attained on its awakening.

कण्ठचक्रं चतुरङ्गुलम्। तत्र वामे इडा चन्द्रनाडी दक्षिणे पिङ्गला सूर्यनाडी तन्मध्ये सुषुम्नां श्वेतवर्णां ध्यायेत्। य एवं वेदानाहतसिद्धिदा भवति॥ ५॥

The fifth discus has acquired popularity as Viśuddhākhya Cakra and its location is on the throat. It is of four fingers measurement. The Iḍā (nerve of Candra) and Piṅgalā (the nerve of Sun) are enshrined at the left and right respectively to this discus. One should concentrate on the spinal nerve of white consistency amid these two nerves. The men known to it attains mastery on Anāhata, the sound.

तालुचक्रम्। तत्रामृतधाराप्रवाहः। घण्टिकालिङ्गमूलचक्ररन्ध्रे राजदन्तावलम्बिनीविवरं दशद्वादशारम्। तत्र शून्यं ध्यायेत्। चित्तलयो भवति॥ ६॥

At the upper portion of this discus, another discus Tālu Cakra is enshrined. A stream of nectar perpetually flows from there. There are ten or twelve petals in tālu cakra. The hole like a discus at the root of the glottis and extended upto the root of teeth contains this tālu cakra. The mind enters into void (zero) when concentration on void is made within this discus.

सप्तमं भ्रूचक्रमङ्गुष्ठमात्रम्। तत्र ज्ञाननेत्रं दीपशिखाकारं ध्यायेत्। तदेव कपालकन्दवाक्सिद्धिदं भवत्याज्ञाचक्रम्॥७॥

The seventh Bhrū Cakra is analogues to the shape of a thumb. An eye of knowledge is worth concentration in the shape of flame within that two petal lotus. A knowledge of Kapāla Kanda (the causative functions invisible and the power of speech to explain it) is accomplished entirely when this Bhrū Cakra is awakened. The discuss so framed is called Ajñāna Cakra.

ब्रह्मरन्ध्रं निर्वाणचक्रम्। तत्र सूचिकागृहेतरं धूम्रशिखाकारं ध्यायेत्। तत्र जालन्धरपीठं मोक्षप्रदं भवतीति परब्रह्मचक्रम्॥८॥

The eighth discus is called Nirvāṇa Cakra. It is also known as Brahmarandhra. It is analogous to the shape of the needle pointed. The shape of Dhūmraśikhā perpetually dynamic should be concentrated therein. Here is existed the Jālandhara Pīṭha. Emancipation is availed as a result of perpetual concentration on that discus. Hence, the yogis called it Parabrahma Cakra too.

नवममाकाशचक्रम्। तत्र षोडशदलपद्ममूर्ध्वमुखं तन्मध्यकर्णिकात्रिकूटाकारम्। तन्मध्ये ऊर्ध्वशक्तिः। तां पश्यन्ध्यायेत्। तत्रैव पूर्णगिरिपीठं सर्वेच्छासिद्धिसाधनं भवति॥९॥

The nineth discus is called Ākāśa Cakra. Within this discus, a sixteen petal lotus with mouth upward; is existed. The hypotenuse of its middle place, having generator of three virtues, it has three ridges analogous to a mountain. In the middle of that discus, the power duly bowed is found at the upper portion. One should concentrate on that power. The Purṇagiri Pīṭha is too existed at that place. Concentration on this Pīṭha enables the devotee to accomplish all desires intertwined.

सौभाग्यलक्ष्म्युपनिषदं नित्यमधीते सोऽग्निपूतो भवति। स वायुपूतो भवति। स सकलधनधान्यसत्पुत्रकलत्रहयभूगजपशुमहिषीदासीदासयोगज्ञानवान्भवति। न स पुनरावर्तते न स पुनरावर्तत इत्युपनिषत्॥१०॥

The person reciting this Saubhāgyalakṣmī Upaniṣad regularly is as holy as the fire and air both. Thus, he becomes prosperous with the easy access to wealth, food, wife, children, elephant, horses, buffaloes, cows, servants and the maids and becomes scholar. On the completion of the destined period (life), he easily attains to the everlasting position of supreme soul. As per the awakening secured by this Upaniṣad, he doesn't return back or fall from that position ever.

ॐ वाङ्मे मनसि ...... इति शान्तिः॥

॥इति सौभाग्यलक्ष्म्युपनिषत्समाप्ता॥

91. SARASVATĪ-RAHASYOPANIṢAD

सरस्वतीरहस्योपनिषद्

This Upaniṣad is related to the tradition of Kṛṣṇa Yajurveda. This Upaniṣad has got its form in a questionnaire in which questions and answers session has taken place between the hermits and the great hermit Āśvalāyana. The form of Mahā Sarasvatī has been described with the essence herein. In the beginning, Sarasvatī vidyā containing ten hymns and the sole mean for the knowledge of essence (tattva). The subject matter then proceeds as the saint to this learning, the rhyme, the saints in separate for ten hymns and the god as also the rhyme, pray to mother Sarasvatī, the element of Brahma in goddess Sarasvatī, the element of nature and the element of man (puruṣatva), the illusion (māyā), the tenability of illusion and its impact, the tenet of two powers, the form of living organism, the destruction of discriminant mentality after decay of the tensility of illusion, the descriptions of the part of Brahma and nature in this visible world, the procedure of meditation in the substance of Brahma, six kinds of meditations and the position of exclusive realization. It has been made undoubtedly clear that the devotee attains to emmancipation by virtue of the knowledge acquired through this Upaniṣad.

॥शान्तिपाठः॥

ॐ वाङ्मे मनसि .... इति शान्तिः॥

ऋषयो ह वै भगवन्तमाश्वलायनं संपूज्य पप्रच्छुः-केनोपायेन तज्ज्ञानं तत्पदार्थावभासकम्। यदुपासनया तत्त्वं जानासि भगवन्वद॥१॥ सरस्वतीदशश्लोक्या सऋचा बीजमिश्रया। स्तुत्वा जप्त्वा परां सिद्धिमलभं मुनिपुङ्गवाः॥२॥

All hermits visited at the hermitage of Lord Āśvalāyana and honoured him with all respect and due compliance with the procedure wait for. They stood then and raised a question with closing hands– "O Lord! how can the knowledge be acquired which enables to realize the element of supreme sole as the meaning of the foot 'tat'? kindly tell us the element of knowledge acquired as a result of penance made by you for the divine power." Lord Āśvalāyana replied with clarity and in order to satisfy the hermits– "O hermits! I have obtained the immortal accomplishment (parāsiddhi) by virtue of the incessant pray and Japa (silent recital) of the hymns pertaining to mother Sarasvatī with the ten ṛcās of Ṛgveda as the seed hymn (Bījamantra).

ऋषय ऊचुः-कथं सारस्वतप्राप्तिः केन ध्यानेन सुव्रत। महासरस्वती येन तुष्टा भगवती वद॥३॥

The hermits then asked the second question– "O the king hermit! You are performer of great deeds with your best resolutions. How and by what kind of concentration you were enabled to obtain the Śārasvata hymn and thus mother Mahā Sarasvatī was pleased? Kindly tell us the process you had adopted for that purpose."

स होवाचाश्वलायनः- अस्य श्रीसरस्वती दशश्लोकीमहामन्त्रस्य अहमाश्वलायन ऋषिः। अनुष्टुप् छन्दः। श्रीवागीश्वरी देवता। यद्वागिति बीजम्। देवीं वाचमिति शक्तिः। प्रणो देवीति कीलकम्। विनियोगस्तत्प्रीत्यर्थे। श्रद्धा मेधा प्रज्ञा धारणा वाग्देवता महासरस्वतीत्येतैरङ्गन्यासः॥४॥

The renowned hermit Āśvalāyana replied– "O saints! (Āśvalāyana) myself is the saint to this great hymn of Śrī Sarasvatī which consists of ten hymns. Its rhyme is anuṣṭup and the god is Śrī Vāgīśvarī. Its seed hymn is yadvāga and 'devīṁvācaṁ' is its power, its Kīlaka is 'praṇodevī' and it has been applied (viniyoga) with the pleasure of the god Śri Vāgīsvarī. The Aṅganyāsa (summoning gods on the different part of body) is made by reciting the hymns namely, Śraddhā (obeisance), Prajñā (conscience), dhāraṇā (presumption), Vāgdevatā (god of speech) and Mahā Sarasvatī etc.

नीहारहारघनसारसुधाकराभां कल्याणदां कनकचम्पकदामभूषाम्। उत्तुङ्गपीनकुचकुम्भमनोहराङ्गीं वाणीं नमामि मनसा वचसा विभूत्यै॥५॥

(After Aṅganyāsa) the process of concentration is described. One should concentrate his mind as 'I' bow and pray by using my mind and power of speech with a motive of accomplishment of outstanding, the Vāṇī (Goddess Sarasvatī) who is with the white brilliance like the beauty of snow, garland of pearl, camphor and the moon, who is all benevolent, duly adorned with garlands of yellow jasmine and whose parts of body are most fascinating with the breast duly developed.

ॐ प्रणो देवीत्यस्य मन्त्रस्य भरद्वाज ऋषिः। गायत्री छन्दः। श्रीसरस्वती देवता। प्रणवेन बीजशक्तिः कीलकम्। इष्टार्थे विनियोगः। मन्त्रेण न्यासः॥६॥

The hymn namely Oṁ Praṇodevī is with its saint Bharadvāja, the rhyme is Gāyatrī and the god is Śrī Sarasavtī. The Prāṇava (Oṁ namaḥ) is the seed (bīja), power (śakti) and kīlaka. It has been applied for the accomplishment of desired objectives. The Aṅganyāsa too is made by reciting this hymn.

या वेदान्तार्थतत्त्वैकस्वरूपा परमार्थतः। नामरूपात्मना व्यक्ता सा मां पातु सरस्वती॥७॥

May mother Sarasvatī provide me with perfect protection whose nature is the sole element of Brahma, the substantial meaning of the vedānta and who is known with various names and several complexions

ॐ प्रणो देवी सरस्वती वाजेभिर्वाजिनीवती। धीनामवित्र्यवतु॥८॥

May mother Sarasvatī, the goddess provides us with the food etc. in abundance because She is the greatest donor, her stock of food is undepleted and she provides her devotees and the persons arrange offerings for her pleasure with sheer protection.

आ नो दिव इति मन्त्रस्य अत्रिर्ऋषिः। त्रिष्टुप् छन्दः। सरस्वती देवता। ह्रीमिति बीजशक्तिः कीलकम्। इष्टार्थे विनियोगः। मन्त्रेण न्यासः॥९॥

The saint to the hymn "Ā no divaḥ-----" is Atri, the rhyme is Triṣṭup and the god is Sarasvatī. 'Hṛṅ' is the seed, power and kīlaka of this hymn. This hymn is applied for the fulfilment of desired objectives. The process of Nyāsa is too performed by this very hymn.

या साङ्गोपाङ्गवेदेषु चतुर्ष्वेकैव गीयते। अद्वैता ब्रह्मणः शक्तिः सा मां पातु सरस्वती॥ १०॥

May mother goddess Sarasvatī, provide us with protection because she is the exclusive power of the supreme. Īśvara is the form of perfect knowledge (Parabrahma) and the four vedas as also their parts and the limbs (aṅga/upaṅga) pray to her exclusively.

ह्रीं आ नो दिवो बृहतः पर्वतादा सरस्वती यजतागंतु यज्ञम्। हवं देवी जुजुषाणा घृताची शग्मां नो वाचमुशती शृणोतु॥ ११॥

May the mother goddess Sarasvatī come at our place of offering descending from the world of sun (in the form of light) and by crossing the clouds analogous to the shape of vast mountains. She is adorable to us all. May that goddess Sarasvatī voluntarily listen to over pleasing hymns recited by us and feel all pleasure.

पावका न इति मन्त्रस्य मधुच्छन्द ऋषिः। गायत्री छन्दः। सरस्वती देवता। श्रीमिति बीजशक्तिः कीलकम्। इष्टार्थे विनियोगः। मन्त्रेण न्यासः॥ १२॥

The saint to the hymn "Pāvakā naḥ----" is Madhucchanda, the rhyme is Gāyatrī and the god is Sarasvatī, the seed, power and kīlaka to this hymn is 'Śriṁ'. This hymn is applied for the accomplishment of desire. Aṅganyāsa too is performed by this very hymn.

या वर्णपदवाक्यार्थस्वरूपेणैव वर्तते। अनादिनिधनानन्ता सा मां पातु सरस्वती॥ १३॥

May mother goddess Sarasvatī provide us with protection who is existed every where in letter, word (pada) and sentence etc. in the form of meaning, who is beyond the beginning and the end and who is in uncountable complexions, properties (guṇa) etc.

श्रीं पावका नः सरस्वती वाजेभिर्वाजिनीवती। यज्ञं वष्टु धिया वसुः॥ १४॥

May mother goddess Sarasvatī be present in our offering and provide all co-operation until it is completed who makes all devotees holy and well to do, who has undepleted stock of food etc. and who is cause for the yield of wealth after due performance of the deeds etc. requisite for it.

चोदयित्रीति मन्त्रस्य मधुच्छन्द ऋषिः। गायत्री छन्दः। सरस्वती देवता। ब्लूमिति बीजशक्तिः कीलकम्। मन्त्रेण न्यासः॥ १५॥

The saint to the hymn "Codayitrī----" is Madhucchanda, the rhyme is Gāyatrī and the god is Sarasvatī. 'Blūṁ' is the seed, power and kīlaka of this hymn. It is applied for obtaining the desired wealth. The Aṅganyāsa is too made through reciting this hymn.

अध्यात्ममधिदैवं च देवानां सम्यगीश्वरी। प्रत्यगास्ते वदन्ती या सा मां पातु सरस्वती॥ १६॥

May mother goddess Sarasvatī provide all of us protection who is the administrator of all gods viz. inspiring power, who is in the form of metaphysics and the supreme divine and who is existed in the form of Madyamā speech.

ब्लूं चोदयित्री सूनृतानां चेतन्ती सुमतीनाम्। यज्ञं दधे सरस्वती॥ १७॥

The goddess who inspires for using the humble and true words, who every moment monitors the intelligent industrious people by making ex-facie their supreme duty; such mother goddess Sarasvatī has hold this offering made by us (devotees).

महो अर्णं इति मन्त्रस्य मधुच्छन्द ऋषिः। गायत्री छन्दः। सरस्वती देवता। सौरिति बीजशक्तिः कीलकम्। मन्त्रेण न्यासः॥ १८॥

The saint of "Mahoarṇaḥ-----" is Madhucchanda, the rhyme is Gāyatrī and the god is Sarasvatī. The 'Sauḥ' is the seed, the power and the kīlaka of this hymn. The power of Nyāsa too is performed by reciting this hymn.

अन्तर्याम्यात्मना विश्वं त्रैलोक्यं या नियच्छति। रुद्रादित्यादिरूपस्था यस्यामावेश्य तां पुनः। ध्यायन्ति सर्वरूपैका सा मां पातु सरस्वती॥ १९॥

May mother goddess Sarasvatī provide us protection who controls the three worlds by virtue of her intuitive power and who is enshrined in the form of Rudra and Āditya etc. god.

सौः महो अर्णः सरस्वती प्रचेतयति केतुना। धियो विश्वा विराजति॥ २०॥

The mother goddess Sarasavtī originated in the form of a river identifying with the unending stock of water and embedded within her by virtue of her work in a flow. She awakes the duty concious of all kinds through her divine form.

चत्वारि वागिति मन्त्रस्य उचथ्यपुत्र ऋषिः। त्रिष्टुप् छन्दः। सरस्वती देवता। ऐमिति बीजशक्तिः कीलकम्। मन्त्रेण न्यासः॥ २१॥

The hermit to the hymn "Catvārivāk----" is 'Dīghratamā,' the son of 'ucathya' the rhyme is triṣṭup and the god is Sarasavtī. 'Aiṅ' is the seed, the power and the kīlaka of this hymn. This hymn is applied with the motive of accomplishment to the desired objectives. The process of Nyāsa too is performed by this hymn.

या प्रत्यग्दृष्टिभिर्जीवैर्व्यज्यमानानुभूयते। व्यापिनी ज्ञप्तिरूपैका सा मां पातु सरस्वती॥ २२॥

May mother goddess Sarasvatī provide as with protection who is being perceived in a number of forms for all living organisms who have the power of initiation and who is enshrined at all places in the form worth knowing.

ऐं चत्वारि वाक् परिमिता पदानि तानि विदुर्ब्राह्मणा ये मनीषिणः। गुहा त्रीणि निहिता नेङ्गयन्ति तुरीयं वाचो मनुष्या वदन्ति॥ २३॥

The speech entirely has been divided into four parts. These are called Parā, Paśyantī, Madhyamā and Vaikhārī respectively. These speeches are known to the learned Brāhmaṇa and scholars. The three speeches i.e. Parā, Paśyantī and Madhyamā are enshrined in the cavity of heart. These therefore are not revealed outside but the fourth speech i.c. vaikhārī is only used by the human beings in their conversation made with others.

यद्वाग्वदन्तीति मन्त्रस्य भार्गव ऋषिः। त्रिष्टुप् छन्दः। सरस्वती देवता। क्लीमिति बीजशक्तिः कीलकम्। मन्त्रेण न्यासः॥ २४॥

The Saint to hymn "Yadvāgvadantī----" is Bhārgava, the rhyme is Triṣṭup and the god is Sarasvatī. Klīṁ is the seed, power and Kīlaka of this hymn. The process of Nyāsa too is performed by reciting this hymn.

नामजात्यादिभिर्भेदैरष्टधा या विकल्पिता। निर्विकल्पात्मना व्यक्ता सा मां पातु सरस्वती॥ २५॥

May mother goddess Sarasvatī provide us all protection who is in the eight forms as a result of classification under name, caste etc. and concommitently is being seen in the single form.

क्लीं यद्वाग्वदन्त्यविचेतनानि राष्ट्री देवानां निषसाद मन्द्रा। चतस्र ऊर्जं दुदुहे पयांसि क्व स्विदस्याः परमं जगाम॥ २६॥

When the power of speech attains the offering by educating the fools, who please all gods and originates the divine spirits (Rāṣṭri), mother Sarasvatī in the same time exploits the food and water for the four directions (caturdik) where these the essence embeded in Madhyamā speech go?

देवीं वाचमिति मन्त्रस्य भार्गव ऋषिः। त्रिष्टुप् छन्दः। सरस्वती देवता। सौरिति बीजशक्तिः कीलकम्। मन्त्रेण न्यासः॥ २७॥

The intuitive saint to the hymn "Devīṁ Vācaṁ----" is Bhārgava. The rhymn is Triṣṭup and the god is Sarasvatī. The 'sauḥ' is the seed power, (Śakti) and the Kīlaka. The process of Nyāsa should be performed by evicting this hymn.

व्यक्ताव्यक्तगिरः सर्वे वेदाद्या व्याहरन्ति याम्। सर्वकामदुघा धेनुः सा मां पातु सरस्वती॥ २८॥

May mother goddess Sarasvatī provide us her kind protection whose expressive and in-expressive speech is used by all living organisms including gods etc. and who is in the form of speech, who is competent to provide with all desired things like milk from Kāmadhenu.

सौः देवीं वाचमजनयन्त देवास्तां विश्वरूपाः पशवो वदन्ति। सा नो मन्द्रेषमूर्जं दुहाना धेनुर्वागस्मानुपसुष्टुतैतु॥ २९॥

May mother goddess Sarasvatī in the form of speech be present before all of us (devotees) duly pleased by the best hymns. That luminating vaikhārī speech has been originated by the breathing gods, which is used by all creatures and who is pleasure giver like Kāmadhenu as also provides with food (cereals and power both).

उत त्व इति मन्त्रस्य बृहस्पतिर्ऋषिः। त्रिष्टुप् छन्दः। सरस्वती देवता। समिति बीजशक्तिः कीलकम्। मन्त्रेण न्यासः॥ ३०॥

The initative saint to the hymn "Utatvaḥ------" is Bṛhaspati. The rhyme is Triṣṭup and the god is Sarasvatī. 'Sam' is the seed, power (Śakti) and Kīlaka. The Nyāsa should be performed with this very hymn.

यां विदित्वाखिलं बन्धं निर्मथ्याखिलवर्त्मना। योगी याति परं स्थानं सा मां पातु सरस्वती॥ ३१॥

May mother goddess Sarasvatī provide us all with protection to whom realized by

Yogīs as Brahma Vidyā and then they are liberated from all worldly ties and the supreme immortal position is secured when the rout of this learning is followed.

सं उत त्वः पश्यन्न ददर्श वाचमुत त्वः शृण्वन्न शृणोत्येनाम्।
उतो त्वस्मै तन्वं विसस्रे जायेव पत्य उशती सुवासाः॥ ३२॥

There are a few people who can't perceive the apparent power of speech even if they face and see it frequently in their life. Again, there are some more people who listens yet they can't listen for the real purposes. However, there are rare people for whom the goddess of speech makes herself so disclosed as the wife adorned with descent apparels and ornaments offers herself fully disclosed before her husband.

अम्बितम इति मन्त्रस्य गृत्समद ऋषिः। अनुष्टुप् छन्दः।
सरस्वती देवता। ऐमिति बीजशक्तिः कीलकम्। मन्त्रेण न्यासः॥ ३३॥

The initative Saint to the hymn "Ambitama ----" is Gṛtsamada. The rhyme is Anuṣṭup and the god is Sarasvatī. The 'Aiṁ' is the seed, power and kīlaka. The process of Nyāsa too is performed by reciting this very hymn.

नामरूपात्मकं सर्वं यस्यामावेश्य तां पुनः। ध्यायन्ति ब्रह्मरूपैका सा मां पातु सरस्वती॥ ३४॥

May mother goddess Sarasvatī provide us all with protection in the form of Brahma. She is worshipped by all scholars of Brahma while living in this illusory world which is recognised with the name and the complexion. They thus surrender this illusory network at the feet of goddess Sarasvatī.

ऐं अम्बितमे नदीतमे देवितमे सरस्वति। अप्रशस्ता इव स्मसि प्रशस्तिमम्ब नस्कृधि॥ ३५॥

O mother goddess Sarasvatī! You are the greatest among all motherly powers, rivers and goddesses. We are suffering from the lack of wealth and this world is beating us like a pauper. O mother! Kindly provide us with all kinds of upliftments which make us prosperous from all angles.

चतुर्मुखमुखाम्भोजवनहंसवधूर्मम। मानसे रमतां नित्यं सर्वशुक्ला सरस्वती॥ ३६॥
नमस्ते शारदे देवि काश्मीरपुरवासिनि। त्वामहं प्रार्थये नित्यं विद्यादानं च देहि मे॥ ३७॥
अक्षसूत्राङ्कुशधरा पाशपुस्तकधारिणी। मुक्ताहारसमायुक्ता वाचि तिष्ठतु मे सदा॥ ३८॥
कम्बुकण्ठी सुताम्रोष्ठी सर्वाभरणभूषिता। महासरस्वती देवी जिह्वाग्रे संनिविश्यताम्॥ ३९॥
या श्रद्धा धारणा मेधा वाग्देवी विधिवल्लभा। भक्तजिह्वाग्रसदना शमादिगुणदायिनी॥ ४०॥
नमामि यामिनीनाथलेखालंकृतकुन्तलाम्। भवानीं भवसंतापनिर्वापणसुधानदीम्॥ ४१॥
यः कवित्वं निरातङ्कं भुक्तिमुक्ती च वाञ्छति। सोऽभ्यर्च्यैनां दशश्लोक्या नित्यं स्तौति सरस्वतीम्॥ ४२॥

May goddess Sarasvatī enshrines daily in Mānasarovara of mind who moves like flaming in the lotus forest of Prajāpati Brahmā's mouth and who lights all directions with her white brilliance. O goddess Sarasvatī! You reside in the province of Kāśmīra. We salute you. I pray you daily. Kindly grace me with the true learning. You are the imparter of

Vidyā (learning). A garland made of pearls is always adorned in your breast region. O goddess Sarasvatī! please always be enshrined on my tongue. May goddess Mahā Sarasvatī whose throat is conch like, whose lips are copper like and who is adorned with all ornaments; be enshrined at the forepart of my tongue at ease. May mother goddess Sarasvatī reside on our tongue always and provide us (devotees) the six kinds of properties, individual śama, dama etc. She is in forms of obeisance, faith, wisdom and mistress of the law (Vidhivallabhā). I pray mother Bhavānī Sarasvatī who has hair duly adorned by candra-kalā, who is like a nectar flowing river and decaying the pains of the world. The person desirous of poetic power, enjoyment, fearlessness and immunisation, should worship with keen devotion daily mother Sarasvati with reciting these 10 hymns.

तस्यैवं स्तुवतो नित्यं समभ्यर्च्य सरस्वतीम्। भक्तिश्रद्धाभियुक्तस्य षण्मासात्प्रत्ययो भवेत्॥४३॥

ततः प्रवर्तते वाणी स्वेच्छया ललिताक्षरा। गद्यपद्यात्मकैः शब्दैरप्रमेयैर्विवक्षितैः॥४४॥

अश्रुतो बुध्यते ग्रन्थः प्रायः सारस्वतः कविः॥४५॥

इत्येवं निश्चयं विप्राः सा होवाच सरस्वती। आत्मविद्या मया लब्धा ब्रह्मणैव सनातनी।

ब्रह्मत्वं मे सदा नित्यं सच्चिदानन्दरूपतः॥४६॥

प्रकृतित्वं ततः सृष्टं सत्त्वादिगुणसाम्यतः। सत्यमाभाति चिच्छाया दर्पणे प्रतिबिम्बवत्॥४७॥

तेन चित्प्रतिबिम्बेन त्रिविधा भाति सा पुनः। प्रकृत्यवच्छिन्नतया पुरुषत्वं पुनश्च ते॥४८॥

The person who performs worship of goddess Sarasvatī complying with the procedure and does pray to her daily with keen devotion and obeisance, he definitely attains her grace within the short span of six months. As a result of this accomplishment, the speech full of elegant letters in the form of words, prose and poetry starts emanating automatically with unique elocution from the mouth of such devotee. The poet graced by goddess Sarasvatī enables to know even the connotation orient sriptures even without hearing to from others. O Brāhmaṇas! Mother goddess Sarasvatī herself had pronounced this fact with confirmation. We obtained the learning of soul, true and immortal from Prajāpati Brahmā and I have now acquired the element of Brahma, immortal and full of everlasting pleasure subsequently, this nature we created by taking in equal proportions the free properties i.e., the Sattva, Rājas and Tāmas as the reflection is seen in the mirror, the element of sensitivity appears true in the nature. It is the reflection of that sensitive element which enables perceiving the nature in three forms. You have got this living body as a result of the combination made in the nature.

शुद्धसत्त्वप्रधानायां मायायां बिम्बितो ह्यजः। सत्त्वप्रधाना प्रकृतिर्मायेति प्रतिपाद्यते॥४९॥

सा माया स्ववशोपाधिः सर्वज्ञस्येश्वरस्य हि। वश्यमायत्वमेकत्वं सर्वज्ञत्वं च तस्य तु॥५०॥

सात्त्विकत्वात्समष्टित्वात्साक्षित्वाज्जगतामपि। जगत्कर्तुमकर्तुं वा चान्यथा कर्तुमीशते।

यः स ईश्वर इत्युक्तः सर्वज्ञत्वादिभिर्गुणैः॥५१॥

The pre-dominance of Sattva property in the nature is called illusion. The element of sensitivity as reflected within that illusion consisting of Sattva property is called Brahma. That illusion is the designation (name) dependent to the Brahma. The main characteristics of that gigantic Brahma is that it controls the illusion and it is unique as also omniscient. That Brahma as a reason of being witness to all worlds, over extended and full of sattva property, it is competent to create, not create and do some different deed from as that of creation. This is the reason that element of sensitivity is called Īśvara particularly because it is enriched with the element of omniscience etc. properties.

शक्तिद्वयं हि मायाया विक्षेपावृतिरूपकम्। विक्षेपशक्तिर्लिङ्गादि ब्रह्माण्डान्तं जगत्सृजेत्॥५२॥
अन्तर्दृग्दृश्ययोर्भेदं बहिश्च ब्रह्मसर्गयोः। आवृणोत्यपरा शक्तिः सा संसारस्य कारणम्॥५३॥

There are two powers wilth illusion (Māyā). These are known as Vikṣepa and Āvaraṇa. The former power i.e. vikṣepa creates everything from the body liṅga to the entire world including Brahmāṇḍa. The later power i.e. Āvaraṇa is the power of Aparā. It is corporate, the discriminant cause existed in Brahma and the creation (Sṛṣṭi) in the innermost world. This power is only main cause for the worldly ties.

साक्षिणः पुरतो भातं लिङ्गदेहेन संयुतम्। चितिच्छायासमावेशाज्जीवः स्याद्व्यावहारिकः॥५४॥

The evident (Sākṣī) seems it in the formation of liṅga and the body. The living organism performing activities in this visible world is originated when the virtual image of the sensitive element is added with the causative nature.

अस्य जीवत्वमारोपात्साक्षिण्यप्यवभासते। आवृतौ तु विनष्टायां भेदे भातेऽपयाति तत्॥५५॥ तथा सर्गब्रह्मणोश्च भेदमावृत्य तिष्ठति। या शक्तिस्तद्वशादब्रह्म विकृतत्वेन भासते॥५६॥ अत्राप्यावृतिनाशेन विभाति ब्रह्मसर्गयोः। भेदस्तयोर्विकारः स्यात्सर्गे न ब्रह्मणि क्वचित्॥५७॥ अस्ति भाति प्रियं रूपं नाम चेत्यंशपञ्चकम्। आद्यत्रयं ब्रह्मरूपं जगद्रूपं ततो द्वयम्॥५८॥ अपेक्ष्य नामरूपे द्वे सच्चिदानन्दतत्परः। समाधिं सर्वदा कुर्याद्धृदये वाथ वा बहिः॥५९॥

The worldly discrimination starts being clear as and when the power of Āvaraṇa is decayed, viz., this power keeps a distance between the element of sensitivity and the state of unconsciousness. At that state, the position of living element is discharged and the power enshrined by extending the discrimination of Brahma is duly reckoned with. Thus the Brahma enslaved by that power starts appearing defective. The discrimination of Brahma and creation (Sṛṣṭi) starts clear as soon as the Āvaraṇa is furnished. The Brahma being free from defects, the creation only falls in the defective position. The five parts (Aṁśa) has been stated as– Asti (is existed), Bhāti (appears or seems), priya (in the form of pleasure) Rūpa (complexion) and Nāma (designation) and complexion have been told as the form of the world. It is the coherence of designation and complexion by virtue of which the supreme element of sole (truth, mind and pleasure) enshrines in the form of world. The devotee should therefore, always engross in the meditation from in and out both.

सविकल्पो निर्विकल्पः समाधिर्द्विविधो हृदि। दृश्यशब्दानुभेदेन स विकल्पः पुनर्द्विधा॥६०॥ कामाद्याश्चित्तगा दृश्यास्तत्साक्षित्वेन चेतनम्। ध्यायेद्दृश्यानुविद्धोऽयं समाधिः सविकल्पकः॥६१॥ असङ्गः

सच्चिदानन्दः स्वप्रभो द्वैतवर्जितः। अस्मीतिशब्दविद्धोऽयं समाधिः सविकल्पकः॥६२॥ स्वानुभूतिरसावेशाद्दृश्यशब्दाद्यपेक्षितुः। निर्विकल्पः समाधिः स्यान्निवातस्थितदीपवत्॥६३॥ हृदीव बाह्यदेशेऽपि यस्मिन्कस्मिंश्च वस्तुनि। समाधिराद्यसन्मात्रान्नामरूपपृथक्कृतिः॥ स्तब्धीभावो रसास्वादात्तृतीयः पूर्ववन्मतः। एतैः समाधिभिः षड्भिर्नयेत्कालं निरन्तरम्॥६५॥

There are two kinds of meditation out of which one is called compromising (Savikalpa) and the other is exclusive (Nirvikalpa). The first meditation is also in two forms. The one is known as perception through the observation (Dṛśyānuviḍdha) and the other is perception through the second (Śabdānuviddha). One should consider that the defects like sensuality etc., usually arising in the mind are visible and sensitive sole is their witness. The first kind of meditation i.e. Savikalpa Samādhi is called perception through the sound. A devotee who neglects the scenes and the sounds and is engroved with perception of sole attains the state of exclusive meditation. At that state he stands undedicated like the flame of a lamp when the wind is not blowing. This Nirvikalpa and Savikalpa meditation is enshrined in the heart. Similarly when the mind is attracted towards a thing in particular, the meditation is obtained. The first kind of meditation is obtained when the discretion of the observer and the scene is applied. The second kind of meditation depicts the concentration of the sensitive element residing under the discriminative cognisance of each thing as per its name and complexion. The third kind of meditation has been stated as analogous to the earlier one. In the state of this meditation, the omnipresent essence of sensitivity is perceived and the change so generated makes the devotee fully stunned. Everyman should pass his life practicing continuously these six kinds of meditations.

देहाभिमाने गलिते विज्ञाते परमात्मनि। यत्र यत्र मनो याति तत्र तत्र परामृतम्॥६६॥ भिद्यते हृदयग्रन्थिश्छिद्यन्ते सर्वसंशयाः। क्षीयन्ते चास्य कर्माणि तस्मिन्दृष्टे परावरे॥६७॥ मयि जीवत्वमीशत्वं कल्पितं वस्तुतो न हि। इति यस्तु विजानाति स मुक्तो नात्र संशयः॥ इत्युपनिषत्॥६८॥

The knowledge of supreme soul rises only when the physical ego is entirely decayed. As a result of this best knowledge originated, the mind attains the pleasure of immortality everywhere and at every place where even it goes. All kinds of confusions are seized at that state and the knots made in the heart are automatically untied. All kinds of deeds performed or committed by the man meet to non-est when the art full and the artless Brahma is realized. The discriminations between living element and element of god are removed. The person known to this fact really is the liberated soul and there is no scope for any doubts. This very thing is pronounced by this knowledge of Upaniṣad.

ॐ वाङ्मे मनसि .... इति शान्तिः॥

॥इति सरस्वतीरहस्योपनिषत्समाप्ता॥

92. BAHVṚCOPANIṢAD

बह्वृचोपनिषद्

This Upaniṣad is related to Ṛgveda. Ṛṣi describes the feature of Ādiśakti who is the cardinal cause for creation of this world. The form "power of mind" has been very first clarified herein. All creations even from Brahmā to the inerts (immovables) have been originated from that very "Power of mind". The words, meanings and complexion (nature) etc. originated from the "Power of mind" are unique. The sensitive power existed in exterior and interior is equal and the same. That very power is existing in the form of "Ambā" etc. names. She is in the form of Parabrahma. The persons duly known to this very "Power of mind" in the form of Brahma, enshrine to that supreme ether for ever. This Upaniṣad is concluded with these contents.

॥शान्तिपाठः॥

ॐ वाङ्मे मनसि....... इति शान्तिः॥

देवी ह्येकाग्र आसीत्। सैव जगदण्डमसृजत्। कामकलेति विज्ञायते। शृङ्गारकलेति विज्ञायते॥१॥

Only Goddess was present prior to the creation of Sṛṣṭi (universe). The structurisation of Sṛṣṭi was performed by her. That goddess is removed with the name of Kāmakalā (sexual art) and Śṛṅgārakalā (art of trimming).

तस्या एव ब्रह्मा अजीजनत्। विष्णुरजीजनत्। रुद्रोऽजीजनत्। सर्वे मरुद्गणा अजीजनन्। गन्धर्वाप्सरसः किंनरा वादित्रवादिनः समन्तादजीजनन्। भोग्यमजीजनत्। सर्वमजीजनत्। सर्वं शाक्तमजीजनत्। अण्डजं स्वेदजमुद्भिज्जं जरायुजं यत्किंचैतत्प्राणिस्थावरजङ्गमं मनुष्यमजीजनत्॥२॥

Lord Brahmā, Viṣṇu and Rudra were originated by that goddess. All Marutas, the singer Gandharvas, the dancing fairies and blower of musical instruments i.e Kinnaras were originated from her. All kinds of consumable material was originated from her. That goddess as mother of the world, has created all beings getting birth from oval, sweat, water and womb etc., including all movable, immovable as also the people.

सैषाऽपरा शक्तिः। सैषा शांभवी विद्या कादिविद्येति वा हादिविद्येति वा सादिविद्येति वा रहस्यम्। ओमों वाचि प्रतिष्ठा॥३॥

That (goddess) too is called the Aparā Śakti. She too is called Śāmbhavī, Kādi, Hādi, and Sādi vidyās (learnings). She is full of secret. She too is "Oṁ (Praṇava). That goddess is situated on tongue (Vāgīndriya) of all living organisms because she is full of truth, mind, and pleasure i.e., "Oṁ".

[Several experiments made when Śāstra Tantra, give the hint of being integrity between the element of soul and supreme soul. It too has been called learning here. For example Śāmbhavī Vidyā enables a man to realise the supreme benevolent god, Kādividyā is meant by "Ka" etc (Ka, e, ī, l Hriṅ) see (key) hymns continuing Vidyā, Hādi vidyā is the learning that contains seed (key) hymns 'Ha' etc (Ha, sa, Ka, Ha, la, Hrīṅ) and Sādi Hiyā is the learning that contains seed (key) hymns Sa etc. (Sa, Ka, La, Hrīṅ).]

सैव पुरत्रयं शरीरत्रयं व्याप्य बहिरन्तरवभासयन्ती देशकालवस्त्वन्तरसङ्गान्महात्रिपुरसुन्दरी वै प्रत्यक् चितिः॥४॥

That (goddess) is spreading light externally and internally both by extending three stages (awaking, dreaming and dormant) and three bodies (formidable, micro and causative). That great tripura sundarī dwells within country, time and the subject beyond attachment and in garb of Pratyak (perceiving) sensitivity.

सैवात्मा ततोऽन्दसत्यमनात्मा। अत एषा ब्रह्मसंवित्तिर्भावाभावकलाविनिर्मुक्ता चिद्विद्याद्वितीयब्रह्मसंवित्तिः सच्चिदान्दलहरी महात्रिपुरसुन्दरी बहिरन्तरनुप्रविश्य स्वयमेकैव विभाति। यदस्ति सन्मात्रम्। यद्विभाति चिन्मात्रम्। यत्प्रियमानन्दं तदेतत्सर्वाकारा महात्रिपुरसुन्दरी। त्वं चाहं च सर्वं विश्वं सर्वदेवता। इतरत्सर्वं महात्रिपुरसुन्दरी। सत्यमेकं ललिताख्यं वस्तु तदद्वितीयमखण्डार्थं परं ब्रह्म॥५॥

That (goddess) is in the form of soul. Everything except her is false and beyond the soul. She is in the form of Brahmavidyā, power of vidyā free from the spirit and spiritless and she too is worth introducing the unique Brahma. That Mahā Tripurasundarī alone is adorned herself by entering external and internally. Out of the three forms of that goddess i.e. Asti, Bhāti and Priya, the Asti is a monitor of the sanmātra, the Bhāti is of cinmātra and the Priya (intimate) is full of pleasure. Thus Śrīmahā tripura Sundarī is existed in all forms. You and I, this whole world, all gods and everything other is Śrīmahātripurasundarī. The sole thing (Power) is lalitā and it is the everlasting truth. This is unique, integrated, immortal supreme element of the soul.

पञ्चरूपपरित्यागादस्वरूपप्रहाणतः। अधिष्ठानं परं तत्त्वमेकं सच्छिष्यते महत् इति॥६॥

By abandonment of the five forms i.e. Asti, Bhāti, Priya, name and complexion and not giving up her self form, the residual entity stable is the supreme element of immortality.

प्रज्ञानं ब्रह्मेति वा अहं ब्रह्मास्मीति वा भाष्यते। तत्त्वमसीत्येव संभाष्यते। अयमात्मा ब्रह्मेति वा अहं ब्रह्मास्मीति वा ब्रह्मैवाहमस्मीति वा॥७॥

That supreme element of soul is expressed through Prajñāna Brahma, or is a Brahma, "This soul is Brahma" or "I myself is Brahma" or "I am that Brahma is " etc. sentences.

योऽहमस्मीति वा सोऽहमस्तीति वा योऽसौ सोऽहमस्मीति वा या भाष्यते सैषा षोडशी श्रीविद्या पञ्चदशाक्षरी श्रीमहात्रिपुरसुन्दरी बालाम्बिकेति बगलेति वा मातङ्गीति स्वयंवरकल्याणीति भुवनेश्वरीति चामुण्डेति चण्डेति वाराहीति तिरस्तकरिणीति राजमातङ्गीति वा शुकश्यामलेति वा लघुश्यमालेति वा अश्वारूढेति वा प्रत्यङ्गिरा धूमावती सावित्री सरस्वती गायत्री ब्रह्मानन्दकलेति॥८॥

Ṣoḍaśī Śrīvidyā is which is addressed in Vedas by the overments (vacana) like "That I am", "I am that" "what that is" "That am too" etc. That Śrīmahātripurasundarī with hymn containing fifteen letters in known as Bālā, Ambikā, Bagalā, Mātaṅgī, Svayaṁvara-kalyāṇī, Bhuvaneśvarī, Cāmuṇḍā, Caṇḍī, Vārāhī, Tirastakariṇī, Rājamātaṅgī, Śukaśyāmalā, Laghuśyāmalā, Aśvāruḍhā, Pratyaṅgirā, Dhūmāvatī, Sāvitrī, Sarasavtī, Gāyatrī, Brahmānandakalā etc.

ऋचो अक्षरे परमे व्योमन्। यस्मिन्देवा अधि विश्वे निषेदुः। यस्तन्न वेद किमृचा करिष्यति। य इत्तद्विदुस्त इमे समासते॥९॥

Ṛcās, letter (Akṣara) exist in the immortal supreme ether. All gods duly reside within ether. The person who did not make endeavour for acquiring that best and everlasting knowledge, what can be obtained by mere perseverance of Oṁ Ṛcās? The person who acquire knowledge of that supreme ether by virtue of their strong determination, only they enshrine in the supreme ether for ever, Thus this Upaniṣad has been concluded.

॥इति बह्वृचोपनिषत्समाप्ता॥

93. MUKTIKOPANIṢAD

मुक्तिकोपनिषद्

ईशाद्यष्टोत्तरशतवेदान्तपटलाशयम्।
मुक्तिकोपनिषद्वेद्यं रामचन्द्रपदं भजे॥१॥
हरिः ॐ पूर्णमिद इति शान्तिः॥

॥प्रथमोऽध्यायः॥

ॐ अयोध्यानगरे रम्ये रत्नमण्डपमध्यमे। सीताभरतसौमित्रिशत्रुघ्नाद्यैः समन्वितम्॥१॥
सनकाद्यैर्मुनिगणैर्वसिष्ठाद्यैः शुकादिभिः। अन्यैर्भागवतैश्चापि स्तूयमानमहर्निशम्॥२॥
धीविक्रियासहस्राणां साक्षिणं निर्विकारिणम्। स्वरूपध्याननिरतं समाधिविरमे हरिम्॥३॥
भक्त्या शुश्रूषया रामं स्तुवन्पप्रच्छ मारुतिः। राम त्वं परमात्मासि सच्चिदानन्दविग्रहः॥४॥
इदानीं त्वां रघुश्रेष्ठं प्रणमामि मुहुर्मुहुः। त्वद्रूपं ज्ञातुमिच्छामि तत्त्वतो राम मुक्तये॥५॥
अनायासेन येनाहं मुच्येयं भवबन्धनात्। कृपया वद मे राम येन मुक्तो भवाम्यहम्॥६॥

Addressing with devotion and obedience Śrī-Rāma— the Lord Hari, at the end of his Samādhi, who being Himself changeless is the witness of the thousands of changes of Buddhi, and who ever rests in Svarūpa-Dhyāna (the meditation on Reality) while seated under the bejwelled dome of the palace in the lovely city of Ayodhyā, in the midst of Sītā, Bharata and Saumitri (Lakṣmaṇa), Śatrughna and others, eulogised day and night by Sanaka and other hosts of Munis, as well as by Vasiṣṭha, Śukra, and other devotees of Viṣṇu— Hanumān, after praising them, asked : "O Rāma, You are Paramātmā of the nature of Saccidānanda. O foremost of the family of Raghu, I make prostrations to You again and again. O Rāma, I wish to know for the sake of emancipation, Your nature as it really is. O Rāma, be You gracious enough to tell me that by which I shall be easily released from the bondage of mundane existence and by which I shall attain salvation."

साधु पृष्टं महाबाहो वदामि शृणु तत्त्वतः। वेदान्ते सुप्रतिष्ठोऽहं वेदान्तं समुपाश्रय॥७॥
वेदान्ताः के रघुश्रेष्ठ वर्तन्ते कुत्र ते वद। हनूमञ्छृणु वक्ष्यामि वेदान्तस्थितिमञ्जसा॥८॥
निश्वासभूता मे विष्णोर्वेदा जाताः सुविस्तराः। तिलेषु तैलवद्वेदे वेदान्तः सुप्रतिष्ठितः॥९॥
राम वेदाः कतिविधास्तेषां शाखाश्च राघव। तासूपनिषदः काः स्युः कृपया वद तत्त्वतः॥१०॥

(Śrī Rāma replied :) "O mighty-armed one, well as led: hearken then to the truth uttered by Me. I am well established in Vedānta (or the end of Vedas or knowledge). Have You recourse to Vedānta well."

(Hanumān again asked :) "O foremost of Raghus, what are Vedāntas? Where do they abide? Pray enlighten me". (Śrī-Rāma replied :) "O Hanumān, listen to me. I shall truly describe to you the nature of Vedānta. Through the expiratory breath of Myself— Viṣṇu, the Vedas were generated as many. Like the oil in the sesamum seeds, Vedānta is well established (or latent in the Vedas)".

(Hanumān asked again :) "O Rāma, how many are the Vedas and their branches? O Rāghava, what are the Upaniṣads? Please, through Your grace, tell me truly."

श्रीराम उवाच

ऋग्वेदादिविभागेन वेदाश्चत्वार ईरिताः। तेषां शाखा ह्यनेकाः स्युस्तासूपनिषदस्तथा॥११॥
ऋग्वेदस्य तु शाखाः स्युरेकविंशतिसंख्यकाः। नवाधिकशतं शाखा यजुषो मारुतात्मज॥१२॥
सहस्रसंख्यया जाताः शाखाः साम्नः परन्तप। अथर्वणस्य शाखाः स्युः पञ्चाशद्भेदतो हरे॥१३॥
एकैकस्यास्तु शाखाया एकैकोपनिषन्मता। तासामेकामृचं यश्च पठते भक्तितो मयि॥१४॥
स मत्सायुज्यपदवीं प्राप्नोति मुनिदुर्लभाम्। राम केचिन्मुनिश्रेष्ठा मुक्तिरेकेति चक्षिरे॥१५॥
केचित्त्वन्नामभजनात्काश्यां तारोपदेशतः। अन्येतु सांख्ययोगेन भक्तियोगेन चापरे॥१६॥
अन्ये वेदान्तवाक्यार्थविचारात्परमर्षयः। सालोक्यादिविभागेन चतुर्धा मुक्तिरीरिता॥१७॥

(Śrī-Rāma said :) "Through the divisions of Ṛgveda and others, the Vedas are said to be four in number. Their branches are many. So also the Upaniṣads. In Ṛgveda, there are branches, 21 in number. O son of Vāyu, there are 109 branches in Yajurveda. O conqueror of enemies, there are 1,000 branches in Sāmaveda, O best of Monkeys, there are 50 branches in Atharvaveda. In each branch, there is one Upaniṣad. Whoever with devotion to Me studies even one of the Ṛks (hymns) in these, attains the state of absorption, rare for the Munis to attain."

(Hanumān asked :) "O Rāma, some excellent Munis have said there is one kind of salvation only, while other [stated that salvation is attained] through the uttering of Your name or the initiation into Tāraka (Oṁ) at Kāśī (Vārāṇasī); others through Sāṁkhya-Yoga, others through the Yoga of Devotion; other Maharṣis through the meditation upon the meaning of Mahāvākyas (the sacred sentences of the Vedas). Salvation is stated to be of four kinds through the divisions of Śālokya and others."

सहोवाच श्रीरामः

कैवल्यमुक्तिरेकैव पारमार्थिकरूपिणी। दुराचाररतो वापि मन्नामभजनात्कपे॥१८॥
सालोक्यमुक्तिमाप्नोति न तु लोकान्तरादिकम्।
काश्यां तु ब्रह्मनालेऽस्मिन्मृतो मत्तारमाप्नुयात्॥१९॥
पुनरावृत्तिरहितां मुक्तिं प्राप्नोति मानवः। यत्र कुत्रापि वा काश्यां मरणे च महेश्वरः॥२०॥
जन्तोर्दक्षिणकर्णे तु मत्तारं समुपादिशेत्। निर्धूताशेषपापौघो मत्सारूप्यं भजत्ययम्॥२१॥

(Śrī-Rāma replied :) "There is only one true emancipation. O Kapi (Monkey), even a person addicted to evil practices attains the salvation of Sālokya (My world) through the uttering of My name, but not of other worlds. Should one die in Brahma-nāla (the lotus-stalk— also street) in Kāśī, he attains My Tāraka (Mantra). Such a person attains salvation without any rebirth; wherever he may die in Kāśī, Maheśvara initiates him by whispering My Tāraka (Mantra) into his right ear. Such person, freed from all sins, attains my Svarūpa (Form). It is this that is termed Sālokya-Sārūpya salvation. The twice-born who is of virtuous conduct and who without diverting his intelligence on any other, meditates upon Me, the All-Ātmā, attains Sāmīpya (nearness) to Me.

सैव सालोक्यसारूप्यमुक्तिरित्यभिधीयते। सदाचाररतो भूत्वा द्विजो नित्यमनन्यधीः॥२२॥

मयि सर्वात्मके भावो मत्सामीप्यं भजत्ययम्। सैव सालोक्यसारूप्यसामीप्या मुक्तिरिष्यते॥२३॥

गुरूपदिष्टमार्गेण ध्यायन्मद्‌गुणमव्ययम्। मत्सायुज्यं द्विजः सम्यग्भजेद्भ्रमरकीटवत्॥२४॥

सैव सायुज्यमुक्तिः स्याद्ब्रह्मानन्दकरी शिवा। चतुर्विधा तु या मुक्तिर्मदुपासनया भवेत्॥२५॥

इयं कैवल्यमुक्तिस्तु केनोपायेन सिध्यति। माण्डूक्यमेकमेवालं मुमुक्षूणां विमुक्तये॥२६॥

तथाप्यसिद्धं चेज्ज्ञानं दसोपनिषदं पठ। ज्ञानं लब्ध्वाचिरादेव मामकं धाम यास्यसि॥२७॥

तथापि दृढता नो चेद्विज्ञानस्याञ्जनासुत। द्वात्रिंशाख्योपनिषदं समभ्यस्य निवर्तय॥२८॥

विदेहमुक्ताविच्छा चेदष्टोत्तरशतं पठ। तासां क्रमं सशान्ति च शृणु वक्ष्यामि तत्त्वतः॥२९॥

ईशकेनकठप्रश्नमुण्डमाण्डूक्यतित्तिरिः। ऐतरेयं च छान्दोग्यं बृहदारण्यकं तथा॥३०॥

ब्रह्मकैवल्यजाबालश्वेताश्वो हंस आरुणिः। गर्भो नारायणो हंसो बिन्दुर्नादशिरः शिखा॥३१॥

मैत्रायणी कौषीतकी बृहज्जाबालतापनी। कालाग्निरुद्रमैत्रेयी सुबालक्षुरिमन्त्रिका॥३२॥

सर्वसारं निरालम्बं रहस्यं वज्रसूचिकम्। तेजोनादध्यानविद्यायोगतत्त्वात्मबोधकम्॥३३॥

परिव्राट् त्रिशिखी सीता चूडा निर्वाणमण्डलम्।दक्षिणा शरभं स्कन्दं महानारायणाह्वयम्॥३४॥

रहस्यं रामतपनं वासुदेवं च मुद्गलम्। शाण्डिल्यं पैङ्गलं भिक्षुमहच्छारीरकं शिखा॥३५॥

तुरीयातीतसंन्यासपरिव्राजाक्षमालिका। अव्यक्तैकाक्षरं पूर्णा सूर्याक्ष्यध्यात्मकुण्डिका॥३६॥

सावित्र्यात्मा पाशुपतं परं ब्रह्मावधूतकम्। त्रिपुरातपनं देवीत्रिपुरा कठभावना।

हृदयं कुण्डली भस्म रुद्राक्षगणदर्शनम्॥३७॥

तारसारमहावाक्यपञ्चब्रह्माग्निहोत्रकम्। गोपालपतनं कृष्णं याज्ञवल्क्यं वराहकम्॥३८॥

शाट्यायनी हयग्रीवं दत्तात्रेयं च गारुडम्। कलिजाबालिसौभाग्यरहस्यऋचमुक्तिका॥३९॥

एवमष्टोत्तरशतं भावनात्रयनाशनम्। ज्ञानवैराग्यदं पुंसां वासनात्रयनाशनम्॥४०॥

It is this that is termed Sālokya-Sārūpya-Sāmīpya salvation. The twice-born who according to the path opened by the teacher, meditates upon My immutable Reality attains Sāyujya (absorption) into Me, like the caterpillar into the wasp. This is the Sāyujya salvation which is productive of Brahmic bliss and auspicious. Thus these kinds of salvation arise through the Upāsanā (worship) of Me.

The only means by which the final emancipation is attained is through Māṇḍūkya-Upaniṣad alone, which is enough for the salvation of all aspirants. If Jñāna is not attained thereby, study the 10 Upaniṣads; you shall soon attain Jñāna, and then My Seat. O son of Añjanā, if your Jñāna is not made firm, practise (study) well the 32 Upaniṣads. You shall get release. If you strives after Videhamukti (or disembodied salvation), study the 108 Upaniṣads. I will truly state in order the (names of the) Upaniṣads with their Śānti (purification Mantras). Hearken to them. (They are :) Īśa, Kena, Kaṭha, Praśna, Muṇḍa, Māṇḍūkya, Tittiri, Aitareya, Chāndogya, Bṛhadāraṇyaka, Brahma, Kaivalya, Jābāla, Śvetāśvatara, Haṁsa, Āruṇi, Garbha, Nārāyaṇa, Parama Haṁsa, (Amṛta)-Bindu, (Amṛta)-Nāda, (Atharva)-Śira, (Atharva)-Śikhā, Maitrāyaṇī, Kauṣītaki, (Bṛhat)-Jābāla, (Nārasiṁha)-Tāpanī, Kālāgnirudra, Maitreyī, Subāla, Kṣurikā, Mantrikā, Sarvasāra, Nirālamba, (Śuka)-Rahasya, Vajrasūcikā, Tejo-(Bindu), Nāda-(Bindu), Dhyāna-(Bindu), (Brahma)-Vidyā, Yoga-Tattva, Ātmabodhaka, Parivrāṭ (Nārada-Parivrājaka), (Tri)-Śikhī, Sītā, (Yoga)-Cūḍā-(Maṇi), Nirvāṇa, Maṇḍala-(Brāhmaṇa), Dakṣiṇā-(Mūrti), Śarabh-Skanda, (Tripādvibhūtī)-Mahā-Nārāyaṇa, Advaya-(Tāraka), (Rāma)-Rahasya, (Rāma)-Tāpanī, Vāsudeva, Mudgala, Śāṇḍilya, Paiṅgala, Bhikṣu, Mahat-Śāriraka, (Yoga)-Śikhā, Triyatīta, Saṁnyāsa, (Paramahaṁsa)-Parivrājaka, Akṣamālikā, Avyakta, Ekākṣara, (Anna)-Pūrṇa, Sūrya, Akṣi, Adhyātma, Kuṇḍikā, Sāvitrī, Ātmā, Pāśupata, Parabrahma, Avadhūta, Tripuratapaṇī, Devī, Tripura, Kaṭha, Bhāvanā, (Rudra)-Hṛdaya, (Yoga)-Kuṇḍalinī, Bhasma-(Jābāla), Rudrākṣa, Gaṇapati, Darśana, Tārasāra, Mahāvākya, Pañcabrahma, (Prāṇa)-Agnihotra, Gopāla-Tāpanī, Kṛṣṇa, Yājñavalkya, Varāha, Śātyāyanī, Hayagrīva, Dattātreya, Garuḍa, Kali-(Santāraṇa), Jābāla, Saubhāgya, Sarasvatī-rahasya, Bahvṛca and Muktikā. These 108 (Upaniṣads) are able to do away with the three Bhāvanās [of doubt, vain thought and false thought], conferring Jñāna and Vairāgya and destroying the three Vāsanās [of book-lore, world and body].

पूर्वोत्तरेषु विहिततत्तच्छान्तिपुरःसरम्। वेदविद्याव्रतस्नातदेशिकस्य मुखात्स्वयम्॥४१॥

गृहीत्वाष्टोत्तरशतं ये पठन्ति द्विजोत्तमाः। प्रारब्धक्षयपर्यन्तं जीवन्मुक्ता भवन्ति ते॥४२॥

ततः कालवशादेव प्रारब्धे तु क्षयं गते। वैदेहीं मामकीं मुक्तिं यान्ति नास्त्यत्र संशयः॥४३॥

सर्वोपनिषदां मध्ये सारमष्टोत्तरं शतम्। सकृच्छ्रवणमात्रेण सर्वाघौघनिकृन्तनम्॥४४॥

मयोपदिष्टं शिष्याय तुभ्यं पवननन्दन। इदं शास्त्रं मयादिष्टं गुह्यमष्टोत्तरं शतम्॥४५॥

ज्ञानतोऽज्ञानतो वापि पठतां बन्धमोचकम्। राज्यं देयं धनं देयं याचतः कामपूरणम्॥४६॥

इदमष्टोत्तरशतं न देयं यस्य कस्यचित्। नास्तिकाय कृतघ्नाय दुराचाररताय वै॥४७॥

मद्भक्तिविमुखायापि शास्त्रगर्तेषु मुह्यते। गुरुभक्तिविहीनाय दातव्यं न कदाचन॥४८॥

सेवापराय शिष्याय हितपुत्राय मारुते। मद्भक्ताय सुशीलाय कुलीनाय सुमेधसे॥४९॥

सम्यक् परीक्ष्य दातव्यमेवमष्टोत्तरं शतम्। यः पठेच्छृणुयाद्वापि स मामेति न संशयः। तदेतदृचाभ्युक्तम्। विद्या ह वै ब्राह्मणमाजगाम गोपाय मा शेवधिष्टेऽहमस्मि। असूयकायानृजवे शठाय मा मा ब्रूया वीर्यवती तथा स्याम्।

यमेव विद्याश्रुतमप्रमत्तं मेधाविनं ब्रह्मचर्योपपन्नम्। तस्मा इमामुपसन्नाय सम्यक् परीक्ष्य दद्याद्वैष्णवीमात्मनिष्ठाम्।।१।। इति।।

"The twice-born— after learning the 108 Upaniṣads, together with the Śānti as prescribed both before and after from the mouth of a Guru well-versed in the observances of Vedic knowledge and study— become Jīvanmuktas till the destruction of their Prārabdha; in course of time as Prārabdha is destroyed, they attain My disembodied salvation. There is no doubt of it. O son of Vāyu, these 108 Upaniṣads, which are the essence of all the Upaniṣads, and are capable of destroying all sins through their mere study, have been imparted by Me to you as a disciple. This science of the 108 Upaniṣads taught by Me, is occult one, and will free persons from bondage, whether they read them with or without knowledge. To gratify the desire of a supplicant, a kingdom may be given or wealth, but never shall the 108 Upaniṣads be imparted to an atheist, an ungrateful person, one intent on vicious actions, one having no devotion towards Me, or one who loses his path in the cave of books. On no account shall they be given to one devoid of devotion.

O Māruti, it is only after a thorough examination that they should be imparted to a disciple doing service (to a Guru), to a well-disposed son, or to one devoted to Me, following good observances, belonging to a good family, and being of good intelligence. Whoever studies or hears the 108 Upaniṣads attains Me. There is no doubt of this. This is stated in the Ṛk (verse) thus— Vidyā (Sarasvatī) went to a Brāhmaṇa (and addressed him) thus : 'Protect me. I shall be Your treasure. Do not confide me to the envious, to one not treading the right path, or to the rogue. Then I shall be potent'. Impart this Ātmaniṣṭha-Vidyā relating to Viṣṇu to one after well examining him who had studied much, is alert, intelligent, observant of the vow of celibacy, and serving [the Guru]."

अथ हैनं श्रीरामचन्द्रं मारुतिः पप्रच्छ ऋग्वेदादिविभागेन पृथक् शान्तिमनुब्रूहीति। स होवाच श्रीरामः। ऐतरेयकौषीतकीनादबिन्द्वात्मप्रबोधनिर्वाणमुद्गलाक्षमालिकात्रिपुरासौभाग्यबह्वृचानामृग्वेदगतानां दशसंख्याका - नामुपनिषदां वाङ्मे मनसीति शान्तिः।।१।।

ईशावास्यबृहदारण्यजाबालहंसपरमहंससुबालमन्त्रिकानिरालम्बत्रिशिखीब्राह्मणमण्डलब्राह्मणाद्वयतारक-पैङ्गलभिक्षुतुरीयातीताध्यात्मतारसारयाज्ञवल्क्यशाट्यायनीमुक्तिकानां शुक्लयजुर्वेदगतानामेकोनविंशति-संख्याकानामुपनिषदां पूर्णमदं इति शान्तिः।।२।।

Then Hanumān asked Śrī-Rāmacandra to relate the Śānti of each Upaniṣad according to the divisions of Ṛgveda and others to which they belong. To which Śrī-Rāma replied: "Aitareya, Kauṣītakī, Nāda-(Bindu), Ātma-Bodha, Nirvāṇa, Mudgala, Akṣamālikā, Tripurā, Saubhāgya and Bahvṛca— these 10 Upaniṣads are of Ṛgveda and have the Śānti beginning with 'Vāṅme-Manasi, etc.'. Īśā, Bṛhadāraṇyaka, Jābāla, Haṁsa, (Parama)-Haṁsa, Subāla, Mantrikā, Nirālamba, Triśikhī Brāhmaṇa, Maṇḍala-Brāhmaṇa, Advaya-Tāraka, Paiṅgala, Bhikṣu, Turīyātīta, Adhyātma, Tārasāra, Yājñavalkya, Śāṭyāyanī, and Muktika— these 19 Upaniṣads are of Śukla Yajurveda and have the Śānti beginning with 'Pūrṇamada, etc."

कठवल्लीतैत्तिरीयकब्रह्मकैवल्यश्वेताश्वतरगर्भनारायणामृतबिन्दुमृतनादकालाग्निरुद्रक्षुरिकासर्वसार-शुकरहस्यतेजोबिन्दुध्यानबिन्दुब्रह्मविद्यायोगतत्त्वदक्षिणामूर्तिस्कन्दशारीरकयोगशिखैकाक्षराक्ष्यवधूतकठरुद्रहृदय-योगकुण्डलिनीपञ्चब्रह्मप्राणाग्निहोत्रवराहकलिसंतरणसरस्वतीरहस्यानां कृष्णयजुर्वेदगतानां द्वात्रिंशत्संख्याकानामुपनिषदां सह नाववत्विति शान्तिः॥३॥

"Kaṭha, Taittirīya, Brahma, Kaivalya, Śvetāśvatara, Garbha, Nārāyaṇa, (Amṛta)-Bindu, (Amṛta)-Nāda, Kālāgnirudra, Kṣurikā, Sarvasāra, Śukarahasya, Tejo-(Bindu), Dhyāna-(Bindu), (Brahma)-Vidyā, Yoga-Tattva, Dakṣiṇā-(Mūrti), Skanda-Śārīraka, (Yoga)-Śikhā, Ekākṣara, Akṣi, Avadhūta, Kara, (Rudra)-Hṛdaya, (Yoga)-Kuṇḍalinī, Pañcabrahma, (Prāṇa)-Agnihotra, Varāha, Kali-(Santaraṇa), and Sarasvatīrahasya,— these 32 Upaniṣads are of Kṛṣṇa Yajurveda and have the Śānti beginning with 'Sahanāvavatu, etc."

केनच्छान्दोग्यारुणिमैत्रायणिमैत्रेयीवज्रसूचिकायोगचूडामणिवासुदेवमहत्संन्यासाव्यक्तकुण्डिकासावित्री-रुद्राक्षजाबालदर्शनजाबालीनां सामवेदगतानां षोडशसंख्याकानामुपनिपदामाप्यायन्त्विति शान्तिः॥४॥

"Kena, Chāndogya, Āruṇi, Maitrāyaṇī, Maitreyī, Vajrasūcikā, (Yoga)-Cūḍā-(Maṇi), Vāsudeva, Mahat-Sannyāsa, Avyakta, Kuṇḍikā, Sāvitrī, Rudrākṣa, Jābāla, Darśana, and Jābālī— these 16 Upaniṣads are of Sāmaveda and have the Śānti beginning with 'Āpyāyantu, etc.'

प्रश्नमुण्डकमाण्डूक्याथार्वशिरोऽथर्वशिखाबृहज्जाबालनृसिंहतापनीनारदपरिव्राजक सीताशरभ-महानारायणरामरहस्यरामातपनीशाण्डिल्यपरमहंसपरिव्राजकान्नपूर्णासूर्यात्मपाशुपतपरब्रह्मत्रिपुरातपनीदेवी-भावनाब्रह्मजाबालगणपतिमहावाक्यगोपालपनकृष्णहयग्रीवदत्तात्रेयगारुडानामथर्ववेदगतानामेक-त्रिंशत्संख्याकानामुपनिषदां भद्रं कर्णेभिरिति शान्तिः॥५॥

"Praśna, Muṇḍaka, Māṇḍūkya, (Atharva)-Śira, (Atharva) Śikhā, (Bṛhat)-Jābāla, (Nṛsiṁha)-Tāpanī, (Nérada)-Parivrājaka, Sītā, Śarabha, Mahā-Nārāyaṇa, (Rāma)-Rahasya, (Rāma)-Tāpanī, Śāṇḍilya, (Paramahaṁsa)-Parivrājaka, (Anna)-Pūrṇā, Sūrya Ātmā, Pāśupata, Parabrahma, Tripuratāpanī, Devī, Bhāvanā, Bhasma-(Jābāla), Gaṇapati, Mahāvākya, Gopāla-Tāpanī, Kṛṣna, Hayagrīva, Dattātreya, and Garuḍa,— These 31 Upaniṣads on Atharvaveda have the Śānti commencing with 'Bhadram-Karṇebhiḥ, etc'.

मुमुक्षवः पुरुषाः साधनचतुष्टयसंपन्नाः श्रद्धावन्तः सुकुलभवं श्रोत्रियं शास्त्रवात्सल्यगुणवन्तमकुटिलं सर्वभूतहिते रतं दयासमुद्रं सद्गुरुं विधिवदुपसंगम्योपहारपाण्योऽष्टोत्तरशतोपनिषदं विधिवदधीत्य श्रवणमन्ननिदिध्यासनानि नैरन्तर्येण कृत्वा प्रारब्धक्षयाद्देहत्रयभङ्गं प्राप्योपाधिविनिर्मुक्तघटाकाशवत्परिपूर्णता विदेहमुक्तिः।

सैव कैवल्यमुक्तिरिति। अतएव ब्रह्मलोकस्था अपि ब्रह्ममुखाद्वेदान्तश्रवणादि कृत्वा तेन सह कैवल्यं लभन्ते। अतः सर्वेषां कैवल्यमुक्तिर्ज्ञानमात्रेणोक्ता। न कर्मसांख्ययोगोपासनादिभिरित्युपनिषद्। इति प्रथमोऽध्यायः॥१॥

"Persons desirous of emancipation and having developed the four means of salvation should, with presents in then hands, approach a Guru full of faith, of good family, proficient in Vedas, scripture-loving, of good qualities, straightforward, intent upon the welfare of all beings, and an ocean of compassion; and after studying under him, according to the rules, the 108 Upaniṣads, he should ever be going through the process of studying, thinking and reflecting upon them. With the cessation of the three bodies through the destruction of Prārabdha, they attain the state of Plenum without any Upādhis like the ether in the pot (after the pot is broken). This is the embodied salvation, this is the final emancipation. Therefore even those in Brahmaloka through the studying of Vedānta from the mouth of Brahmā attain with Him the final emancipation. Hence to all these is stated the final emancipation through the Jñāna path, and not through Karma, Sāṁkhya-Yoga, and other Upāsanās. Thus is the Upaniṣad."

॥द्वितीयोऽध्यायः॥

तथा हैनं श्रीरामन्द्रं मारुतिः पप्रच्छ। केयं वा तत्सिद्धिः सिद्ध्या वा किं प्रयोजनमिति। सहोवाच श्रीरामः। पुरुषस्य कर्तृत्वभोक्तृत्वसुखदुःखादिलक्षणश्चित्तधर्मः क्लेशरूपत्वाद्बन्धो भवति। तन्निरोधनं जीवन्मुक्तिः। उपाधिविनिमुक्तघटाकाशवत्प्रारब्धक्षयाद्विदेहमुक्तिः।

जीवन्मुक्तिविदेहमुक्त्योरष्टोत्तरशतोपनिषदः प्रमाणम्। कर्तृत्वादिदुःखनवृत्तिद्वारा नित्यानन्दावाप्तिः प्रयोजनं भवति। तत्पुरुषप्रयत्नसाध्यं भवति। यथा पुत्रकामेष्टिना पुत्रं वाणिज्यादिना वित्तं ज्योतिष्टोमेन स्वर्गं तथा पुरुषप्रयत्नसाध्यवेदान्तश्रवणादिजनितसमाधिना जीवन्मुक्त्यादिलाभो भवति।

सर्ववासनाक्षयात्तल्लाभः। अत्र श्लोका भवन्ति। उच्छास्त्रं शास्त्रितं चेति पौरुषं द्विविधं मतम्। तत्रोच्छास्त्रमनर्थाय परमार्थाय शास्त्रितम्॥१॥

लोकवासनाय जन्तोः शास्त्रवासनयापि च। देहवासनया ज्ञानं यथावन्नैव जायते॥२॥

द्विविधो वासनाव्यूहः शुभश्चैवाशुभश्च तौ। वासनौघेन शुद्धेन तत्र चेदनुनीयसे॥३॥

तत्क्रमेणाशु तेनैव मामकं पदमाप्नुहि। अथ चेदशुभो भावस्त्वां योजयति संकटे॥४॥

प्राक्तनस्तदसौ यत्नाज्जेतव्यो भवता कपे। शुभाशुभाभ्यां मार्गाभ्यां वहन्ती वासनासरित्॥५॥

पौरुषेण प्रयत्नेन योजनीया शुभे पथि। अशुभेषु समाविष्टं शुभेष्वेवावतारयेत्॥६॥

अशुभाच्चालितं याति शुभं तस्मादपीतरत्। पौरुषेण प्रयत्नेन लालयेच्चित्तबालकम्॥७॥

द्रागभ्यासवशाद्याति यदा ते वासनोदयम्। तदाभ्यासस्य साफल्यं विद्धि त्वममरिमर्दन॥८॥

Adhyāya II

Again Māruti (Hanumān) addressed Śrī-Rāmacandra thus : "What is Jīvanmukti? what is Videhamukti? What is the authority therein? What about its perfection? What is the object of such a perfection?"

(Śrī-Rāma replied :) "The Dharma of a man's Citta that has the characteristics of agency and enjoyment is fraught with pains and hence tends towards bondage. The control of it (the Citta) is Jīvanmukti. Videhamukti follows when through the extinction of Prārabdha, the removal of the vehicles [of the bodies] takes place like the ether in the pot [after the pot is broken]. The authority on the points of Jīvanmukti and Videhamukti is the 108 Upaniṣads. Its object [of perfection] is the attaining of eternal bliss through the removal of the pains of agency, etc. This has to be achieved through human efforts. Like progeny obtained through the Putrakāmeṣṭi sacrifice, wealth in trade, or heaven through the Jyotiṣṭoma sacrifice, so Jīvanmukti is gained through Samādhi arising through Vedāntic study, and accomplished through human efforts. It has to be won through the extinction of all Vāsanās. Regarding it, there are verses thus : "The efforts of man are stated to be of two kinds, those that transcend scriptures and those that are according to scriptures. Those that transcend scriptures tend to harn while those that are according to scriptures tend to Reality." To men, true Jñāna does not arise through the Vāsanās of the world, scripture and body. Vāsanā is divided into two, the pure and the impure. If you are led by the pure Vāsanās, you shall thereby soon reach by degrees My Seat. But should the old impure Vāsanās land you in danger, they should be overcome through efforts. This river of Vāsanās towards objects, which flows in the pure and impure paths, should be diverted to the pure path through human efforts. The impure ones have to be transmuted into the pure. That which is diverted from the impure turns towards the pure. So also the reverse. This child, Citta has to be fondled through human efforts. O killer of enemies, it is only when through means of practice both Vāsanās quite abandon you, that you will be able to realise the effects of [such] practice. Even in the case of doubt, the pure Vāsanās alone should be practised.

संदिग्धायामपि भृशं शुभामेव समाचर। शुभायां वासनावृद्धौ न दोषाय मरुत्सुत।।९।।
वासनाक्षयविज्ञानमनोनाशा महामते। समकालं चिराभ्यास्ता भवन्ति फलदा मताः।।१०।।
त्रय एवं समं यावन्नाभ्यस्ताश्च पुनः पुनः। तावन्न पदसंप्राप्तिर्भवत्यपि समाशतैः।।११।।
एकैकशो निषेव्यन्ते यद्येते चिरमप्यलम्। तन्न सिद्धिं प्रयच्छन्ति मन्त्राः संकीर्तिता इव।।१२।।
त्रिभिरेतैश्चिराभ्यस्तैर्हृदयग्रन्थयो दृढाः। निःशङ्कमेव त्रुठ्यन्ति बिसच्छेदाद्गुण इव।।१३।।
जन्मान्तरशताभ्यस्ता मिथ्या संसारवासना। सा चिराभ्यासयोगेन विना न क्षीयते क्वचित्।।१४।।
तस्मात्सौम्य प्रयत्नेन पौरुषेण विवेकिना। भोगेच्छां दूरतस्त्यक्त्वा त्रयमेव समाश्रय।।१५।।
तस्माद्वासनया युक्तं मनो बद्धं विदुर्बुधाः। सम्यग्वासनया त्यक्तं मुक्तिमित्यभिधीयते।

"O son of Vāyu, there is nothing wrong in the increase of the pure Vāsanās. The extinction of Vāsanās, Vijñāna and the destruction of Manas [as these three] when practised together for a long time are regarded, O great and intelligent one, as fruitful. So long as these are not equally practised again and again, so long the [Supreme] Seat is not attained, even after the lapse of hundreds of years. Even should one of these [three] be practised for a long time, it will not yield its fruit like a Mantra imperfectly done. Through the practice of these for a long time, the firm knots of the heart are cut, without doubt, like the breaking of the threads in a lotus-stalk rent in twain. The illusory Sāṁsārika Vāsanā that has arisen through the practice of [many] hundreds of lives never perishes except through the practice of Yoga for a long time. Therefore, O Somya [disciple], after having put away to a distance the desire of enjoyment through discriminative human effort, resort to these three alone. The wise know that a mind associated with Vāsanā tends to bondage, while a mind well freed from Vāsanā is said to be an emancipated one.

मनोनिर्वासनीभावमाचराशु महाकपे॥१६॥

सम्यगालोचनात्सत्याद्वासना प्रविलीयते। वासनाविलये चेतः शममायाति दीपवत्॥१७॥

वासनां संपरित्यज्य मयि चिन्मात्रविग्रहे। यस्तिष्ठति गतव्यग्रः सोऽहं सच्चित्सुखात्मकः॥१८॥

समाधिमथ कार्याणि मा करोतु करोतु वा। हृदयोनात्तसर्वेहो मुक्त एवोत्तमाशयः॥१९॥

नैष्कर्म्येण न तस्यार्थस्तस्यार्थोऽस्ति न कर्मभिः।

न ससाधानजाप्याभ्यां यस्य निर्वासनं मनः॥२०॥

संत्यक्तवासनान्मौनादृते नास्त्युत्तमं पदम्॥२१॥

वासनाहीनमप्येतचक्षुरादीन्द्रियं स्वतः। प्रवर्तते बहिः स्वाऽर्थे वासनामात्रकारणम्॥२२॥

अयत्नोपनतेष्वक्षि दृग्द्रव्येषु यथा पुनः। नीरागमेव पतति तद्वत्कार्येषु धीरधीः॥२३॥

भावसंवित्प्रकटितामनुरूपा च मारुते। चित्तस्योत्पत्त्युपरमा वासनां मुनयो विदुः॥२४॥

दृढाभ्यस्तपदार्थैकभावनादतिचञ्चलम्। चित्तं संजायते जन्मजरामरणकारणम्॥२५॥

वासनावशतः प्राणस्पन्दस्तेन च वासना। क्रियते चित्तबीजस्य तेन बीजाङ्कुरक्रमः॥२६॥

O Mahā-kapi (great Monkey) practise the state of a mind devoid of Vāsanā. Vāsanā perishes through well-conducted deliberation and truth. Through the absorption of Vāsanās, Manas attains quiescence like a lamp [without oil]. He whose mind, devoid of destruction, is [centred] on Me as of the nature of Cinmātra [consciousness alone], abandoning the Vāsanās, is no other than Myself of the nature of Saccidānanda. Whether Samādhi and Karma are performed or not, one who has a supreme Citta with a heart devoid of all desires is an emancipated person. He whose mind is freed from Vāsanās is not subject to the fruits arising from the performance or non-performance of actions, or Samādhi of Jñāna. Except through the entire giving up of Vāsanās and through Mouna (the observance of silence towards objects), the Supreme Seat is not attained. Though devoid of Vāsanās, the eye and other organs are involuntarily prompted to their (respective) external objects through habit. Just as the eye without any desire sees without any effort the objects that fall on it, so also the undaunted man of intelligence enters into the affairs (of the world) without any desire. O Māruti, the Munis know that Vāsanā which is manifested through the consciousness of objects, which is of the nature of the object itself, and which is the cause of the origination and absorption of Citta. This excessively fluctuating Citta is the cause of birth, dotage and death, due to the identification of itself with objects practised firmly [for a long time]. Like the analogy of the seed and the tree, the variation of Prāṇa arises through Vāsanā and (vice versa) the Vāsanā through the former— these forming the need of Citta.

द्वे बीजे चित्तवृक्षस्य प्राणस्पन्दनवासने। एकस्मिंश्च तयोः क्षीणे क्षिप्रं द्वे अपि नश्यतः॥२७॥
असङ्गव्यवहारत्वाद्भवभावनवर्जनात्।
शरीरनाशदर्शित्वाद्वासनां न प्रवर्तते। वासनासंपरित्यागाच्चित्तं गच्छत्यचित्तताम्॥२८॥
अवासनत्वात्सततं यदा न मनुते मनः। अमनस्ता तदोदेति परमोपशमप्रदा॥२९॥
अव्युत्पन्नमना यावद्भवानज्ञाततत्पदः। गुरुशास्त्रप्रमाणैस्तु निर्णितं तावदाचार॥३०॥
ततः पक्वकषायेण नूनं विज्ञानं वस्तुना। शुभोऽप्यसौ त्वया त्याज्यो वासनौघो निराधिना॥३१॥

To the tree of Citta, there are two seeds: the vibration of Prāṇa and Vāsanā. Should either of them perish, both perish soon. Through the actions of the world being done without attachment, through the abandoning of the [thought of the) reality of the universe and the conviction of the distractibility of the body, Vāsanā does not arise. Through the complete giving up of Vāsanā, Citta becomes not-Citta. When the mind does not think at all, being completely devoid of Vāsanā, then dawns the state of mindlessness which confers the great peace. So long as you are without a mind of (true) discrimination and are not a knower of the Supreme Seat, so long should you follow whatever has been decided by the teacher and the authorities of the sacred books. When your sins are burnt up and you are a knower of the Reality without any anxiety then all the Vāsanās even should be given up.

द्विविधश्चित्तनाशोऽस्ति सरूपोऽरूप एव च। जीवन्मुक्तः सरूपः स्यादरूपो देहमुक्तिगः॥३२॥
अस्य नाशमिदानीं त्वं पावने शृणु सादरम्॥३३॥
चित्तनाशाभिधानं हि यदा ते विद्यते पुनः। मैत्र्यादिभिर्गुणैर्युक्तं शान्तिमेति न संशयः।
भूयोजन्मविनिर्मुक्तं जीवन्मुक्तस्य तन्मनः॥३४॥
सरूपोऽसौ मनोनाशो जीविन्मुक्तस्य विद्यते। अरूपस्तु मनोनासो वैदेहीमुक्तिगो भवेत्॥३५॥
सहस्राङ्कुरशाखात्मफलपल्लवशालिनः॥३६॥

The destruction of Citta is of two kinds, that with form and that without form. (The destruction of) that with form is of the Jīvanmukta; (the destruction of), that without form being of the Videhamukta. O son of Vāyu, hearken to (the means of) the destruction of Citta. That is said to be destruction of Citta when it, associated with all the attributes of Maitrī (friendship) and others, becomes quiescent (without any resurrection). There is no doubt of it. Then the Manas of a Jīvanmukta is free from fresh rebirth; to him, there is the destruction of Manas with form. But to the Videhamukta, there is the destruction of Manas without form.

अस्य संसारवृक्षस्य मनोमूलमिदं स्थितम्। संकल्प एव तन्मन्ये संकल्पोपशमेन तत्॥३७॥
शोषयाशु यथा शोषमेति संसारपादपः। उपाय एक एवास्ति मनसः स्वस्य निग्रहे॥३८॥
मनसोऽभ्युदयो नाशो मनोनाशो महोदयः। ज्ञमनो नाशमभ्येति मनो ज्ञस्य हि शृङ्खला॥३९॥
तावन्निशीव वेताला वल्गन्ति हृदि वासनाः। एकतत्त्वदृढाभ्यासाद्यावन्न विजितं मनः॥४०॥

प्रक्षीणचित्तदर्पस्य निगृहीतेन्द्रियद्विषः। पद्मिन्य इव हेमन्ते क्षीयन्ते भोगवासनाः॥४१॥

हस्तं हस्तेन संपीड्य दन्तैर्दन्तान्विचूर्ण्य च। अङ्गान्यङ्गैः समाक्रम्य जयेदादौ स्वकं मनः॥४२॥

It is Manas that is the root of the tree of Saṁsāra with its thousands of shoots, branches, tender, leaves and fruits. I think it to be Saṅkalpa alone. In order that the trees of Saṁsāra may wither soon, dry up its root through the quiescence of Saṅkalpa. There is only one means to control one's mind. That is to destroy the mind as soon as it rises. That is the (great) dawn. In the case of the wise, the mind is destroyed : but in the case of ignorant, it is indeed a fetter. So long as the mind is not destroyed through the firm practice of the One Reality, so long as Vāsanās are prancing about in the heart like Betāla (goblin) in the night-time, the Vāsanās of enjoyment of one who has destroyed the egoism of Citta and controlled organs, the enemies, decay like lotuses in mid-winter, pressing one hand against the other, setting teeth against teeth, and forcing one limb against the order, he should first conquer his mind.

उपाविश्योपविश्यैकां चिन्तकेन मुहुर्मुहुः। न शक्यते मनो जेतुं विना युक्तिमनिन्दिताम्॥४३॥

अङ्कुशेन विना मत्तो यथा दुष्टमतङ्गजः। अध्यात्मविद्याधिगमः साधुसंगतिरेव च॥४४॥

वासनासंपरित्यागः प्राणस्पन्दनिरोधनम्। एतास्ता युक्तयः पुष्टाः सन्ति चित्तजयेकिल॥४५॥

सतीषु युक्तिष्वेतासु हठान्नियमयन्ति ये। चेतसो दीपमुत्सृज्य विचिन्वन्ति तमोऽञ्जनैः॥४६॥

विमूढाः कर्तुमुद्युक्ता ये हठाच्चेतसो जयम्। ते निवध्नन्ति नागेन्द्रमुन्मत्तं बिसतन्तुभिः॥४७॥

It is not possible on the part of the one-thoughted to control the mind by sitting up again and again except through the approved means. As a vicious rutting elephant is not subject to control except through the goad, so in the matter of the control of the mind, the effective means are the attainment of spiritual knowledge, association with the wise, the entire abdication of all Vāsanās and the control of prāṇas. While such are the (prescribed) means, should persons try to control the mind through violence, they are like those that search in darkness, having thrown aside the light (in their hands). Those who endeavour to control the mind through force are but trying to bind a mad elephant with the filaments of a lotus-stalk.

द्वे बीजे चित्तवृक्षस्य वृत्तिव्रततिधारिणः। एकं प्राणपरिस्पन्दो द्वितीयं दृढभावना॥४८॥

सा हि सर्वगता संवित्प्राणास्पन्देन चाल्यते। चित्तैकाग्र्याद्यतो ज्ञानमुक्तं समुपजायते॥४९॥

तत्साधनमथो ध्यानं यथावदुपदिश्यते। विनाप्यविकृतिं कृत्स्नां संभवव्यत्ययक्रमात्।

यशोऽरिष्टं च चिन्मात्रं चिदानन्दं विचिन्तय॥५०॥

अपानेऽस्तंगते प्राणो यावन्नाभ्युदितो हृदि। तावत्सा कुम्भकावस्था योगिभिर्यानुभूयते॥५१॥

बहिरस्तंगतें प्राणे यावन्नापान उद्गतः। तावत्पूर्णां समावस्थां बहिष्ठं कुम्भकं विदुः॥५२॥

ब्रह्माकारमनोवृत्तिप्रवाहोऽहंकृतिं विना। संप्रज्ञातसमाधिः स्याद्ध्यानाभ्यासप्रकर्षतः॥५३॥

प्रशान्तवृत्तिकं चित्तं परमानन्ददायकम्। असंप्रज्ञातनामायं समाधिर्योगिना प्रियः॥५४॥

प्रभाशून्यं मनःशून्यं बुद्धिशून्यं चिदात्मकम्। अतद्व्यावृत्तिरूपोऽसौ समाधिर्मुनिभावितः॥५५॥
ऊर्ध्वपूर्णमधःपूर्णं मध्यपूर्णं शिवात्मकम्। साक्षाद्विधिमुखो ह्येष समाधिः पारमार्थिकः॥५६॥

To the tree of the mind having the ever-growing branches of modifications, there are two seeds. One is the fluctuation of Prāṇa, and the other is the firmness of Vāsanā. The (One) All-pervading Consciousness is agitated by the fluctuation of Prāṇas. The means of Dhyāna by which (the one) Jñāna is attained through the one-pointedness of the mind is now imparted to you after duly resolving back the things originated (in the universe) with all their changes, meditate upon that which remains— (viz.), Cinmātra (the consciousness alone), which is also Cidānanda (conscious-bliss). The wise say that the interval experienced by Yogins after the inspiration and before the (next) expiration is (the internal) Kumbhaka (cessation of breath); while the interval of complete equilibrium after expiration and before the next inspiration is the external Kumbhaka. Through the force of the practice of Dhyāna, the current of the modification of Manas devoid of Self that is of Brāhmic nature is said to be Samprajñāta Samādhi, while the mind with the utter quiescence of modifications that confers upon the supreme bliss is said to be Asamprajñāta-Samādhi that is dear to Yogins. This (state) that is devoid of light, Manas and Buddhi, and that is of the nature of Cit. (consciousness merely) is styled by the Munis Atadvyāvṛtti Samādhi (a Samādhi that does not care or require the aid of another). It is Plenum above, below and in the middle, and is of the nature of Śiva (auspiciousness). This noumenal (of occult) Samādhi is itself Vidhi-Mukha (sanctioned by books of Brahmā).

दृढभावनया त्यक्तपूर्वापरविचारणम्। यदादानं पदार्थस्य वासना सा प्रकीर्तिता॥५७॥
भावितं तीव्रसंवेगादात्मना यत्तदेव सुः। भवत्याशु कपिश्रेष्ठ विगतेतरवासनः॥५८॥
तादृग्रूपो हि पुरुषो वासनाविवशीकृतः। संपश्यति यदैवैतत्सद्वस्त्विति विमुह्यति॥५९॥
वासनावेगवैचित्र्यात्स्वरूपं न जहाति तत्। भ्रान्तं पश्यति दुर्दृष्टिः सर्वं मदवशादिव॥६०॥
वासना द्विविधा प्रोक्ता शुद्धा च मलिना तथा। मलिना जन्महेतुः स्याच्छुद्धा जन्मविनाशिनी॥६१॥
अज्ञानसुधनाकारा घनाहंकारशालिनी। पुनर्जन्मकरी प्रोक्ता मलिना वासना बुधैः।
पुनर्जन्माङ्कुरं त्यक्त्वा स्थितिः संभृष्टबीजवत्॥६२॥
बहुशास्त्रकथाकन्थारोमन्थेन वृथैव किम्। अन्वेष्टव्यं प्रयत्नेन मारुते ज्योतिरान्तरम्॥६३॥
दर्शनादर्शने हित्वा स्वयं केवलरूपतः। य आस्ते कपिशार्दूल ब्रह्म स ब्रह्मवित्स्वयम्॥६४॥

The clinging to objects without previous or subsequent deliberation through intense longing is stated to be Vāsanā. O chief of Monkeys, whatever is meditated upon by a person with ardent impetuosity without any other Vāsanā— that he soon becomes. A person that is entirely subject to Vāsanā becomes of the nature of that, when he regards this (universe) as Sat (the Reality), then he is subject to delusion. Because of the many strong Vāsanā, he does not abandon the nature of the universe. This person of wrong vision sees everything under infatuation like one deluded. Vāsanās are of two kinds— the pure and the impure. The impure ones are the cause of rebirth, while the pure are the destroyers of it. The impure are said by the wise to be of the nature of intense Ajñāna, associated with the great Ahaṁkāra and generative of rebirth. Of what avail is the chewing again and again of the many Śāstric stories to one that has abandoned the seed of re-birth, having turned it into a burnt one? O Māruti, you should with effort, seek the effulgence within. O tiger of Monkeys, whoever, after having abandoned the visible and the invisible, is as the One alone is not a mere knower of Brahman but is Brahman itself.

अधीत्य चतुरो वेदान्सर्वशास्त्राण्यनेकश:। ब्रह्मतत्त्वं न जानाति दर्वी पाकरसं यथा।।६५।।

स्वदेहाशुचिगन्धेन न विरज्येत य: पुमान्। विरागकारणं तस्य किमन्यदुपदिश्यते।।६६।।

अत्यन्तमलिनो देहो देही चात्यन्तनिर्मल:। उभयोरन्तरं ज्ञात्वा कस्य शौचं विधीयते।।६७।।

बद्धो हि वासनाबद्धो मोक्ष: स्याद्वासनाक्षय:। वासनां संपरित्यज्य मोक्षार्थित्वमपि त्यज।।६८।।

मानसीर्वासना: पूर्वं त्यक्त्वा विषयवासना:। मैत्र्यादिवासनानाम्नीर्गृहाणामलवासना:।।६९।।

ता अप्यत: परित्यज्य ताभिर्व्यवहन्नपि। अन्त:शान्त: समस्नेहो भव चिन्मात्रवासन:।।७०।।

तामप्यथ परित्यज्य मनोबुद्धिसमन्विताम्। शेषस्थिरसमाधानो मयि त्वं भव मारुते।।७१।।

अशब्दमस्पर्शमरूपमव्ययं तथाऽरसं नित्यमगन्धवच्च यत्।

अनामगोत्रं मम रूपमीदृशं भजस्वं नित्यं पवनात्मजार्तिहन्।।७२।।

दृशिस्वरूपं गगनोपमं परं सकृद्विभातं त्वजमेकमक्षरम्।

अलेपकं सर्वगतं यद्द्वयं तदेव चाहं सकलं विमुक्तॐ।।७३।।

दृशिस्तु शुद्धोऽहमविक्रियात्मको न मेऽस्ति कश्चिद्विषय: स्वभावत:।

पुरस्तिरश्चोर्ध्वमधश्च सर्वत: सूपूर्णभूमाहमितीह भावय।।७४।।

अजोऽमरश्चैव तथाजरोऽमृत: स्वयंप्रभ: सर्वगतोऽहमव्यय:।

न कारणं कार्यमतीत्य निर्मल: सदैव तृप्तोऽहमितीह भावय।।७५।।

जीवन्मुक्तपदं त्यक्त्वा स्वदेहे कालसात्कृते। विशत्यदेहमुक्तत्वं पवनोऽस्पन्दतामिव।।७६।।

One who having studied the four Vedas and the various books does not cognize the reality of Brahman is like the ladle ignorant of the taste of the dainty. Therefore what other advice of indifference can be imparted to a person that has not attained the indifference to the impure Vāsanā of delusion (or body)? This body is very impure while the one (Ātmā) that dwells in it is very pure. When the differences between the two are (thus) known, what then may be ordained as the purification? The bondage of Vāsanā is the (real) bondage, while the destruction of Vāsanā is salvation. After wholly abandoning the Vāsanās, give up even the desire for salvation. After first giving up the Vāsanā of objects dependent upon the Vāsanā of the mind, attract unto the pure Vāsanās associated with Maitrī (friendship) and others. Though engaged in the world with these pure Vāsanās, give up them too and retire within the quiescent desires and become of the form of the longing after Cit alone. Then, O

Māruti ! giving up that also associated as it is with Manas and Buddhi, may you now left alone become firm in Me in Samādhi. O son of Vāyu! always worship My Reality that is destructive of pains, without sound, touch, form, decay, taste, destruction or smell, and without name and Gotra [clan]. I am that non-dual One (Brahman) that is of the nature of the visible (Jñāna), like unto the Ākāśa, supreme, always shining, without birth, non-dual, without destruction, without attachment and pervading all. I am the All, and of the nature of salvation. One should ever meditate upon Me thus : 'I am of the form the visible [Jñāna] the pure, of changeless nature and have really no objects in Me. I am the ever-full Brahman, transverse and across, up and down. Also meditate upon Me thus : 'I am birthless, deathless, ageless, immortal, self-shining, all-pervading, destructionless, causeless, pure beyond the effect (of the universe) and ever content.' When one's becomes a prey to time, he gives up the state of Jīvanmukti, as the wind attains the motionless state.

तदेतदृचाभ्युक्तम्। तद्विष्णोः परमं पदं सदा पश्यन्ति सूरयः। दिवीव चक्षुराततम्।

तद्विप्रासो विपन्यवो जागृवांसः समिन्धते। विष्णोर्यत्परमं पदम्। ॐ सत्यमितयुपनिषद्। ॐ पूर्णमदः पूर्णमिदं पूर्णात्पूर्णमुदच्यते। पूर्णस्य पूर्णमादाय पूर्णमेवावशिष्यते।। ॐ शान्तिः शान्तिः शान्तिः।। हरिः ॐ तत्सत्।।

"The following is said in the Ṛg [-Veda] also : Like the eye which is spread in the Ākāśa (seeing all things without any obstacle), so the wise ever see the Supreme Seat of Viṣṇu. The Brāhmaṇas that have ever the Divine vision praise in diverse ways and illumine the Supreme Seat of Viṣṇu."

ॐ सह नाववतु .... इति शान्तिः।।

।।इति मुक्तिकोपनिषत्समाप्ता।।

94. AMṚTABINDU-UPANIṢAD

अमृतबिन्दूपनिषद्

अमृतबिन्दूपनिषद्वेद्यं यत्परमाक्षरम्।
तदेव हि त्रिपाद्रामचन्द्राख्यं नः परा गतिः।।

ॐ सह नाववत्विति शान्तिः।।

ॐ मनो हि द्विविधं प्रोक्तं शुद्धं चाशुद्धमेव च। अशुद्धं कामसंकल्पं शुद्धं कामविवर्जितम्।।१।।
मन एव मनुष्याणां कारणं वन्धमोक्षयोः। बन्धाय विषयासक्तं मुक्त्यै निर्विषयं स्मृतम्।।२।।
यतो निर्विषयस्यास्य मनसो मुक्तिरिष्यते। तस्मान्निर्विषयं नित्यं मनः कार्यं मुमुक्षुणा।।३।।
निरस्तविषयासङ्गं संनिरुद्धं मनो हृदि। यदा यात्युन्मनीभावं तदा तत्परमं पदम्।।४।।
तावदेव निरोद्धव्यं यावद्धृदि गतं क्षयम्। एतज्ज्ञानं च मोक्षं च अतोऽन्यो ग्रन्थविस्तरः।।५।।
नैव चिन्त्यं न चाचिन्त्यमचिन्त्यं चिन्त्यमेव च। पक्षपातविनिर्मुक्तं ब्रह्म संपद्यते तदा।।६।।
स्वरेण संधयेद्योगमस्वरं भावयेत्परम्। अस्वरेण हि भावेन भावो नाभाव इष्यते।।७।।
तदेव निष्कलं ब्रह्म निर्विकल्पं निरञ्जनम्। तद्ब्रह्माहमिति ज्ञात्वा ब्रह्म संपद्यते ध्रुवम्।।८।।
निर्विकल्पमनन्तं च हेतुदृष्टान्तवर्जितम्। अप्रमेयमनाद्यं च ज्ञात्वा च परमं शिवम्।।९।।
न निरोधो न चोत्पत्तिर्न वन्धो न च शासनम्। न मुमुक्षा न मुक्तिश्च इत्येषां परमार्थता।।१०।।
एव एवात्मा मन्तव्यो जाग्रत्स्वप्नसुषुप्तिषु। स्थानत्रयाद्यतीतस्य पुनर्जन्म न विद्यते।।११।।
एक एव हि भूतात्मा भूते भूते व्यवस्थितः। एकधा बहुधा चैव दृश्यते जलचन्द्रवत्।।१२।।
घटसंभृतमाकाशं लीयमाने घटे यथा। घटो लीयेत नाकाशं तद्वज्जीवो घटोपमः।।१३।।
घटवद्विविधाकारं भिद्यमानं पुनः पुनः। तद्भग्नं न च जानाति स जानाति च नित्यशः।।१४।।
शब्दमायावृतो यावत्तावत्तिष्ठति पुष्करे। भिन्ने तमसि चैकत्वमेकमेवानुपस्यति।।१५।।
शब्दाक्षरं परं ब्रह्म यस्मिन्क्षीणे यदक्षरम्। तद्विद्वानक्षरं ध्यायेद्यदीच्छेच्छान्तिमात्मनः।।१६।।

Oṁ. Manas (mind) is said to be of two kinds, the pure and the impure. That which is associated with the thought of desire is the impure, while that which is without desire is the pure. To men, their mind alone is the cause of bondage or emancipation. That mind which is attracted by objects of sense tends to bondage, while that which is not so attracted tends to emancipation. Now inasmuch as to a mind without a desire for sensual objects there is stated to be salvation, therefore an aspirant after emancipation should render his mind ever free from all longing after material objects. When a mind freed from the desires for objects and controlled in the heart attains the reality of Ātmā, then is it in the Supreme Seat. Till that which arises in the heart perishes, till then it (Manas) should be controlled. This only is (true) wisdom. This only is true Dhyāna (meditation). Other ways are but long or tedious. It (Brahman) is not at all one that can be contemplated upon. It is not one that cannot be contemplated upon. It is not capable of contemplation, (and yet) it should be contemplated upon. Then one attains Brahman that is devoid of partiality. Yoga should be associated with Svara (sound, accent). (Brahman) should be meditated upon without Svara. By meditating without Svara upon Brahman, that which is cannot become non-existent. Such a Brahman is partless, devoid of fancy and quiescent (or free from the action of mind). Whoever cognizes "I" to be that Brahman attains certainly Brahman. A wise man having known that Brahman, that is without fancy, without and without cause, or example, beyond inference and without beginning, is emancipated. There is (for him then) no destruction, no creation, no person in bondage, no devotee, no aspirant for salvation, no emancipated person. This is the truth. Ātmā that should be contemplated upon is One in (the three states), the waking, the dreaming, and the dreamless sleep. There is no rebirth to him who goes beyond the three states. The one Bhūtātmā of all beings is in all beings. Like the moon (reflected) in water, he appears as one and as many. While a pot is being carried (from one place to another), the Ākāśa (ether) that is within it is not carried (along with it). As the pot alone is carried, Jīva (within the body) may be likened to the Ākāśa. Like the pot, the body has various kinds of forms. The body which perishes again and again is not conscious of its own destruction. But he (the Jīva) knows (it) always. He who is enveloped by the Māyā of sound, is never able to come to (or see) the sun (of Parabrahman) from the darkness (of ignorance). Should such darkness be cleared, then he alone sees the non-dual state. Parabrahman is Śabdākṣara. What remains after the cessation of Śabda-Vedas, that is Akṣara (indestructible), should be meditated upon by a learned man who wishes to secure quiescence to his Ātmā.

द्वे विद्ये वेदितव्ये तु शब्दब्रह्म परं च यत्। शब्दब्रह्मणि निष्णातः परं ब्रह्माधिगच्छति॥१७॥

ग्रन्थमभ्यस्य मेधावी ज्ञानविज्ञानतत्त्वतः। पलालमिव धान्यार्थी त्यजेद्ग्रन्थमशेषतः॥१८॥

गवामनेकवर्णानां क्षीरस्याप्येकवर्णता। क्षीरवत्पश्यते ज्ञानं लिङ्गिनस्तु गवां यथा॥१९॥

घृतमिव पयसि निगूढं भूते भूते च वसति विज्ञानम्। सततं मन्थयितव्यं मनसा मन्थानभूतेन॥२०॥

ज्ञाननेत्रं समादाय चरेद्वह्निमतः परम्। निष्कलं शान्तं तद्ब्रह्माहमिति स्मृतम्॥२१॥

सर्वभूताधिवासं य यद्भूतेषु वसत्यधि। सर्वानुग्राहकत्वेन तदस्म्यहं वासुदेवः तदस्म्यहं वासुदेव इति॥२२॥

सहेति शान्तिः॥

Two Vidyās (sciences) are fit to be known, viz., Śabdabrahman and Parabrahman. One who has completely mastered Śabdabrahman attains Parabrahman. Having studied well the books, the learned man should perseverance studiously in Jñāna (the acquisition of knowledge) and Vijñāna (Self-realisation according to such knowledge). Then he should discard the whole of the books, as a person in quest of grain gives up the straw. Though there are cows of different colours, yet their milk is of the same colour. Like milk is seen Jñāna, and like cows are seen the different kinds of forms (in the universe). As ghee is latent in milk, so is Vijñāna (Self-realisation) latent in every being. Through churning always, the Manas with the churning-stick of Manas and the string of Jñāna, Parabrahman that is partless, calm and quiescent should be brought out like fire from the wood. I am the Brahman. That Vāsudeva who is support of all beings, who lives in all and who protects all creatures is Myself. That Vāsudeva is Myself. Such is the Upaniṣad.

।।इति अमृतबिन्दूपनिषत्समाप्ता।।

95. SVASAMVEDYO-UPANIṢAD

स्वसंवेद्योपनिषद्

The main objective of this Upaniṣad is to realize the element of soul within ones heart and to manage the sensitivity. A single hymn in it is divided in four smaller parts. In the first part, the living-organisms are compared with water bubble. It has been stated that the commune of living-organisms is merged with the perfect Brahma in form of nectar-ocean as the water bubble is merged with the water and integrated to the extent of no separate recognition, the commune of living-organisms merges with the perfect Brahma but this state is possible only when the knowledge is duly acquired. The living-organisms generally are covered with ignorance. It has been stated in the second part that all times are with the activity and the nature. In reality, there is no good or evil neither right nor wrong and it is the reality of the element of soul. No meaning of hell and heaven is for a person who is beyond the feeling of it. In the third subpart, the knowledge of element has been inserted into the cavity and it has been stated that the common people has no interest to go through this route. The persons only worshipping the icon like things of physical presence, only wander to and fro in ignorance. The metaphysician doesn't discriminate under the blessed eye of sensitivity among the Lord Brahmā, Viṣṇu, Rudra, dog, donkey and even in a cat. In the last subpart i.e. the fourth part, a secret to serve all by considering them with the element of soul has been explained. Finally, the importance of a teacher has been explained. It has been made ex-phasi that everything can be known with the grace of the teacher. The person who considers teacher, the supreme among all, definitely attains to the liberated soul.

ॐ सर्वेषां प्राणिबुद्‌बुदानां निरंजनाव्यक्तामृतनिधौ विलयविलासः स्थितिर्विजृम्भते। तेषामेव पुनर्भवनं नो इहास्ति। स यथा मृत्पिण्डे घटानां तन्तौ पटानां तथैवेति भवति। वस्तुतो नोपादानमत एव नोपादेयमत एव न निमित्तमत एव न विद्या न पुराणं नो वेदा नेतिहासा इति न जगदिति न ब्रह्मा नो विष्णुः नाथ रुद्रो नेश्वरो न बिन्दुः नो कलेति अग्रे मध्येऽवसाने सर्वं यथावस्थितं यथावस्थितज्ञानं तेषां नो भवत्यागमपुराणेतिहासधर्मशास्त्रेषु धृताभिमानास्ते। यत्तानि तु मुग्धतरमुनिशब्दवाच्यैः जीवबुद्‌बुदैः रचितानीति भवन्ति। तत्र प्रामाण्यं तादृशानामेव। ते त्वज्ञानेनावृताः सयत्नेन गर्भास्तदप्येष श्लोको भवति। तदत्र श्लोको भवति॥ १-क॥

It is all apparent and truth to arise from and merge with the nectar ocean of the water-bubbles (the creatures). It always happens. The persons engrossed in Brahma do revolve round the cycle of birth and death. Their position is like a pitcher in the lump of clay and the position of cloth in its thread. He is neither a comparable object nor on its behalf and not of use in reality. It is not learning, Purāṇa, the Veda and the history. It is neither a world nor Brahmā, Viṣṇu, Rudra, Īśvara and it is not an iota and any art. The living-organisms remain untouched to the knowledge in the sequence of beginning, middle and because they become egoistic on their study in Purāṇa, history and the holy books. This happens because those living-organisms are formed of the bubbles in garb of great preaching made by the hermit living-organisms. At that reference, it is the acceptable proof. Those are covered with ignorance. They acquire knowledge only when special efforts are made. Still this dictum is well-settled that all living-organisms are full of ignorance and affection.

इह तेनाप्यज्ञानेन नो किञ्चित्। अथ यथावस्थितज्ञानेन किंचित् नेति यदस्ति तदस्ति यन्नास्ति नास्ति तत्। कालकर्मात्मकमिदं स्वभावात्मकं चेति। न सुकृतं नो दुष्कृतम्। अत एव सुमेरुदातारो गोदातारो वा गोघ्नैः ब्राह्मणघ्नैः सुरापानैः पश्यतोहरैः परोक्षहरैर्वा गुरुपापनिष्ठैः सर्वपापनिष्ठैः समानास्त एते। तैश्च न गौः न ब्राह्मणः न सुरा न पश्यतोहरः न परोक्षहरः न गुरुपापानि न लघुपापानि मत एव तन्निष्ठाः मत एव न निर्वाणं नो निरय इति तदप्येष श्लोको भवति॥ १-ख॥

Here is nothing to take with the ignorance and affection location of knowledge. It is the existence to what it is. It is not which as no existence. All these times are of functional and natural tendency. There is nothing right and wrong. Hence, the gold donor, cow donor or cow-killer, Brāhmaṇa killar, intoxicant, thief teacher, (evil-doer) and the persons always involved in offence are equal for them. It is not cow, not Brāhmaṇa, not intoxicant, no any deceit, not a thief and neither heinous offences nor the petty offences. For them, the objective is the supreme because it is the only topic of their loyalty. He has nothing to bear with hell and heaven. This very is the real meaning of this hymn.

तत्त्वज्ञानं गुहायां निविष्टमज्ञानिकृतमार्गं सुष्ठु वदन्ति। ते तत्र साभिमाना वर्तन्ते। पुष्पितवचनेन मोहितास्ते भवन्ति। स यथातुरा भिषग्ग्रहणकाले बाला अपथ्याहितगुडादिना जनन्या वञ्चिता इति नानादेवता गुरुकर्मतीर्थनिष्ठाश्च ते भवन्ति। केचिद्वयं वैदिका इति वदन्ति। नान्येऽस्मभ्यम्। केचिद्वयं सर्वशास्त्रज्ञा इति। केचिद्वयं देवानुग्रहवन्तः। केचिद्वयं स्वप्ने उपास्यदेवताभाषिणः। केचिद्वयं देवा इति। केचिद्वयं श्रीमद्रमारमणनलिनभृङ्गा इति। केचित्तु नृत्यन्तु। केचित्तु मूर्खा वयं परमभक्ता इति वदन्तो रुदन्ति पतन्ति च। ये केचनैते ते सर्वेऽप्यज्ञानिनः। ये तु ज्ञानिनो भवन्ति ये तत्त्वज्ञानिनश्च तैस्तेषां को विशेषः। मत एव केषाञ्चित्कैश्चिद्भेदः। मत एव यत्र विरिञ्चिविष्णुरुद्रा ईश्वरश्च गच्छन्ति तत्रैव श्वानो गर्दभाः मार्जाराः कृमयश्च मत एव न श्वानगर्दभौ न मार्जारः न कृमिः नोत्तमाः न मध्यमाः न जघन्याः। तदप्येष श्लोको भवति॥ १-ग॥

It has been stated that the knowledge of element is inserted into cavity. The route followed by ignorant people has been stated the best route because they move in the same with pride. They frequently enchant to the sweet words. As the mothers due to pure affection give medicine to their children by blending the Jaggery with it while Jaggery is strictly prohibited, the gods are cheated by the people performing the worship of a number of gods, teacher, visit at number of pilgrim places and the person performing great deeds viz., they always wish for their supreme position behind performing these all activites. Some people declare themselves as expert in Veda while a few other seldom express it. A few people consider themselves a knower to all holy books and some consider them as blessed by deity. According to some people, they are instructed by their deity in dreaming and thus they predict about the thefting and recovery of goods. A group of people consider themselves as gods. Some says that they are Vaiṣṇava i.e. a bee murmuring on the Lotus Viṣṇu. Some people are proud of their being devoted while a few stupid weeps and fall into hell even after they declare themselves the best devotee. There is also a commune of people who is in the depth of ignorance. The scholars and the metaphysicians has specific characteristics. Only a difference in opinion is seen among them. It is the universe opinion that the dog, donkey, cat and the insect also go where Lord Brahmā, Viṣṇu, Rudra, Śiva and the Īśvara are. It is also a universal fact that the dogs, donkeys, cats and the insects are neither best nor better and even not good. (All has their appropriate place in this universe). This hymn discloses the same meaning.

न तच्छब्दः न किंशब्दः न सर्वे शब्दाः न माता नो पिता न बन्धुः न भार्या न पुत्रो न मित्रं नो सर्वे तथापि साधकैरात्मस्वरूपं वेदितुमिच्छद्भिर्जीवन्मुमुक्षुभिः सन्तः सेव्याः। भार्या पुत्रो गृहं धनं सर्वं तेभ्यो देयम्। कर्माद्वैतं न कार्यं भावाद्वैतं तु कार्यं। निश्चयेन सर्वाद्वैतं कर्तव्यम्। गुरौ द्वैतमवश्यं कार्यम्। यतो न तस्मादन्यत्। येन सर्वमिदं प्रकाशितम्। कोऽन्यः तस्मात्परः। स जीवन्मुक्तो भवति स जीवन्मुक्तो भवति। य एवं वेद। य एवं वेद॥ १-घ॥

Hence, there is neither Tat nor a word kiṁ in existence, viz., the question and answer is nothing and there are also no otherwise words. When there is no mother, father, brother, wife, son, friends and all others are not present, the ascetics do service to the saints with a view to know about the soul and to attain emancipation. One should surrender all worldly things which he had to his wife and son viz., he should abandon affection about them. He shouldn't think duality while performing the activities. He should be exclusive and a concentration should be in full and on a single work at a time. This sense of duality can be imposed on teachers because nobody is greater than him. This whole universe gets light from him viz., everything can be known with the mercy of a teacher. Nobody else is greater than him. The person duly known to this fact duly enjoys the pleasure of duality.

॥इति स्वसंवेद्योपनिषत् समाप्ता॥

96. ŚIVASAṄKALPA-UPANIṢAD

शिवसङ्कल्पोपनिषद्

This Upaniṣad too is a part and parcel of Śukla Yajurveda (chapter 34, hymns 1-6) like the Īśopaniṣad. There are only six hymns in which the excellent powers of mind have been described and it is prayed that the mind of so excellent powers should be made with the welfare resolutions. The mind of a man is most powerful and it is most difficult to divide it from the resolutions made by it. This is the reason the saints pray for making it a mind that can make the resolution for the well-being of all living-organisms. The hymns are constituted so spiritual and including the essence that it is given a recognition of being an independent Upaniṣad.

यज्जाग्रतो दूरमुदैति दैवं तदु सुप्तस्य तथैवैति।
दूरङ्गमं ज्योतिषां ज्योतिरेकं तन्मे मनः शिवसङ्कल्पमस्तु॥१॥

O God! The mind is equipped with so excellent powers that in awakening and even indormant stage; it moves to distant places. This mind too is the monitor of all sensory organs and it is definitely a sole means of the living-organisms. May our mind of such excellent powers be resolved with benevolent thoughts.

येन कर्माण्यपसो मनीषिणो यज्ञे कृण्वन्ति विदथेषु धीराः।
यदपूर्वं यक्षमन्तः प्रजानां तन्मे मनः शिवसङ्कल्पमस्तु॥२॥

O God! May our mind resorting to which the scholars perform the offering etc., great deeds, existing in the body of all living-organisms and enshrined with the reverend spirits while performing the higher deeds including the offerings; be enable to fabricate the all benevolent resolutions.

यत्प्रज्ञानमुत चेतो धृतिश्च यज्ज्योतिरन्तरमृतं प्रजासु।
यस्मान्न ऋते किञ्चन कर्म क्रियते तन्मे मनः शिवसङ्कल्पमस्तु॥३॥

O God! This mind is enriched with acute knowledge, sensitive and full of courage. It is residing in the heart of all living-beings in the form of ever-lasting light and in garb of the flame. Nothing can be done in the absence of mind. Therefore, please make our mind enable to resolve for all benevolent deeds.

येनेदं भूतं भुवनं भविष्यत् परिगृहीतममृतेन सर्वम्।
येन यज्ञस्तायते सप्तहोता तन्मे मनः शिवसङ्कल्पमस्तु॥४॥

By virtue of the powers inherent to this ever-lasting mind, all matters hidden under the coverage of the past, future and the present can be disclosed. The extension of offering (great deeds) is made by the seven kinds of great men (offerer). May such mighty mind be resolved for all-benevolent deeds.

यस्मिन्नृचः साम यजूंषि यस्मिन् प्रतिष्ठिता रथनाभाविवाराः।
यस्मिंश्चित्तं सर्वमोतं प्रजानां तन्मे मनः शिवसङ्कल्पमस्तु॥५॥

The Ṛcās of all Vedas are existing in the mind. The hymns of Sāma and Yajurveda are set-up in it as the sticks are fixed in the wheel of a chariot and all knowledge regarding the living-beings is embedded in this mind. May such mighty mind be resolved with all-benevolent deeds.

सुषारथिरश्वानिव यन्मनुष्यान्नेनीयतेऽभीशुभिर्वाजिन इव।
हृत्प्रतिष्ठं यदजिरं जविष्ठं तन्मे मनः शिवसङ्कल्पमस्तु॥६॥

As the expert charioteer drives the horses in a proper way to the destination by controlling them through the rein, the mind in the same fashion, leads the people to their aims. This most dynamic and free from the ties of old age is existed in our heart. May such mighty mind be resolved with performing all-benevolent deeds.

॥इति शिवसंकल्पोपनिषत्समाप्ता॥

97. CĀKṢUṢOPANIṢAD

चाक्षुषोपनिषद्

This upaniṣad falls under the tradition of Kṛṣṇa Yajurveda. As its name implies, this upaniṣad contains the hymns competent enough to remove the diseases caused to human eyes. Initially and just in the opening lines, the significance of this upaniṣad has been elaborated. The saint, the god, the rhyme and the application (Viniyoga) to this upaniṣad have been then described. Lord sun who is the sole master to the eyes is requested for removal of the diseases infested to the eyes. It is prayed to him that the darkness of ignorance is to be removed and this world of living-organisms entirely to be made free from the ties of illusions and ignorance of virtue by providing with the divine splendour. This upaniṣad has been then concluded.

॥शान्तिपाठः॥

ॐ सह नाववतु .... इति शान्तिः॥

ॐ अथातश्चाक्षुषीं पठितसिद्धविद्यां चक्षूरोगहरां व्याख्यास्यामः। यच्चक्षूरोगाः सर्वतो नश्यंति। चाक्षुषी दीप्तिर्भविष्यतीति। तस्याश्चाक्षुषीविद्याया अहिर्बुध्न्य ऋषिः। गायत्री छन्दः। सूर्यो देवता। चक्षूरोगनिवृत्तये जपे विनियोगः। ॐ चक्षुः चक्षुः चक्षुः तेजः स्थिरो भव। मां पाहि पाहि। त्वरितं चक्षूरोगान् शमय शमय। मम जातरूपं तेजो दर्शय दर्शय। यथाऽहं अन्धो न स्यां तथा कल्पय कल्पय। कल्याणं कुरु कुरु। यानि मम पूर्वजन्मोपार्जितानि चक्षुः प्रतिरोधकदुष्कृतानि सर्वाणि निर्मूलय निर्मूलय। ॐ नमः चक्षुस्तेजोदात्रे दिव्याय भास्कराय। ॐ नमः करुणाकरायामृताय। ॐ नमः सूर्याय। ॐ नमो भगवते सूर्याक्षितेजसे नमः। खेचराय नमः। महते नमः। रजसे नमः। तमसे नमः। असतो मा सद्गमय। तमसो मा ज्योतिर्गमय। मृत्योर्मा अमृतं गमय। उष्णो भगवाञ्छुचिरूपः। हंसो भगवान् शुचिरप्रतिरूपः। य इमां चक्षुष्मतीविद्यां ब्राह्मणो नित्यमधीते न तस्याक्षिरोगो भवति। न तस्य कुले अन्धो भवति। अष्टौ ब्राह्मणान् ग्राहयित्वा विद्यासिद्धिर्भवति॥ १॥

The Cakṣuṣī Vidyā (learning related to the eyes) worth-pleasing merely by slight reading is now described. This learning is competent to remove all sorts of the diseases pertaining to the eyes from the root. The eyes get splendour by virtue of recital to this upaniṣad. The intuition to the hymn relating to this learning is the sage 'Ahirbudhnya'. Its rhyme is Gāyatrī and the god is lord sun. In order to remove the eye-ailments it is applied. O the sole god sun to the eyes! Be enshrined in the splendour form of eyes. Please protect me and remove the eye-ailments immediately. Please me able to see the divine splendour analogous to the gold. Kindly suggest me a measure sufficient enough to protect my eyes from the blindness. Kindly shower with grace for welfare to all. The evils committed by me in the previous births resulting to destroy my eye-sight should be uprooted for which I solicit to you. Lord sun shining with the divine flame and endower to the eyes, a divine splendour is saluted. Salute is conveyed to merciful and immortal lord in garb of Oṁ. Lord sun is saluted. Lord sun who are the splendour to eyes is saluted. Lord sun who moves all through in the ether is saluted. The noble and the best form sun is saluted. Creator of activity by virtue of Rajas, lord sun is saluted. The resort to Tamas (merging the darkness within himself), lord sun is saluted. O lord! Please, lead us all from fallacy to the truth. Lead us all from the darkness of ignorance to the light of knowledge and from mortality to immortality. All heating lord sun is in the garb of purity. Lord sun is the embodiment of purity and excellent in the garb of this Svaḥ. Nothing else is worth-comparing with the splendour form of lord sun. The scholar who recites it daily, does not suffer from any kind of eye-ailments. No body in his clan suffers from the blindness. This learning becomes favourable and work same if it is duly made to understand to as much as eight Brāhmaṇas.

ॐ विश्वरूपं घृणिनं जातवेदसं। हिरणमयं पुरुषं ज्योतिरूपं तपन्तम्।
विश्वस्य योनिं प्रतपन्तमुग्रं पुरः प्रजानामुदयत्येष सूर्यः॥ २॥

Lord sun is in the form of the trio i.e. the truth, meditation and the pleasure. This whole world is his own form. He is shining with rays and he knows all regarding the three tenses (Kāla) i.e. past, present and the future providing with heat to this universe in the form of golden person (Hiraṇyamaya Puruṣa). He creates this whole universe and all of us salute to the lord sun luminating with the acute light. Lord sun in this apparent form is arising before all living-organisms.

ॐ नमो भगवते आदित्याय अहोवाहिन्यहोवाहिनी स्वाहा। ॐ वयः सुपर्णा उपसेदुरिन्द्रं प्रियमेधा ऋषयो नाधमानाः। अपध्वान्तमूर्णूहि पूर्द्धि चक्षुर्मुमुग्ध्यस्मान्निधयेव बद्धान्। पुण्डरीकाक्षाय नमः। पुष्करेक्षणाय नमः। अमलेक्षणाय नमः। कमलेक्षणाय नमः। विश्वरूपाय नमः। महाविष्णवे नमः॥ ३॥

Salute to lord Sun. The light coming from the sun survives the day. We offer the great sacrifice for lord sun. All saints like Priyamedhā etc. appeared in the form of birds with fascinating wings before lord sun and started praying– O lord! Remove this darkness of ignorance from us all. Please make our eyes glowing and please have a grace to make free all the living-organisms from the ties of darkness i.e. ignorance. Salute is given to lord Puṇḍarīkākṣa. Salute is conveyed to Puṣkarekṣaṇa. Similarly, salute and request both is conveyed to Amalekṣaṇa, Kamalekṣaṇa, the world form and great lord Viṣṇu.

ॐ सह नाववतु ....इति शान्तिः॥

॥इति चाक्षुषोपनिषत् समाप्ता॥

98. MANTRIKOPANIṢAD

मन्त्रिकोपनिषद्

ॐ पूर्णमदः पूर्णमिदं पूर्णात्पूर्णमुदच्यते।

पूर्णस्य पूर्णमादाय पूर्णमेवावशिष्यते।।

ॐ शान्तिः शान्तिः शान्तिः।।

This Upaniṣad is related to the Śukla Yajurveda. According to its composer, this living soul perceives itself a part and parcel of the supreme soul yet it cannot observe the supreme soul in its easy form. It is only possible when attachment to body and the darkness of ego both are shattered. Commonly, the people are curious and have senses only for the ever-lasting and undivided false illusion (Māyā). It is however necessary to perceive the supreme soul residing within the inner most cell in the garb of a swan. This supreme soul has been described as– expressive, inexpressive, dual, integrated, micro and in gigantic forms. The sole secret of all hymns is the Brahma. The saint has said it celibate, undivided like a pillar, fructified in the form of world and puller of this world cart.

ॐ अष्टपादं शुचिं हंसिं त्रिसूत्रमणुमव्ययम्। त्रिवर्त्मानं तेजसोऽहं सर्वतः पश्यन्न पश्यति।।१।।

We perceive that sensitivity of supreme soul through the trio-ways (devotion, knowledge and action) but unable to see him. It has eight feet, sacred complexion, haṁsa form, trio-aphorism, nature (micro, macro, both blended), minutest, absolute and ever-luminating.

भूतसंमोहने काले भिन्न तमसि वैखरे। अन्तः पश्यन्ति सत्त्वस्था निर्गुणं गुणगह्वरे।।२।।

That supreme sensitivity of the soul is beyond the properties (Guṇas), yet it is included in the cavity of property (guṇa). The common people are engrossed in the darkness created by the most alluring attachments etc. but the people of 'Satva' properties always see him in their heart.

अशक्यः सोऽन्यथा द्रष्टुं ध्यायमानः कुमारकैः। विकारजननीमज्ञामष्टरूपामजां ध्रुवाम्।।३।।

The people looming in ignorance cannot see that sensitivity of supreme soul even if they otherwise concentrate their thoughts thereupon because the illusions (Māyā) that create all distortions is ignorance and it has eight forms (the five elements, mind, wit and ego). This illusion in the form of nature has its undivided effect on the pupil.

ध्यायतेऽध्यासिता तेन तन्यते प्रेर्यते पुनः। सूयते पुरुषार्थं च तेनैवाधिष्ठितं जगत्।।४।।

It is only the meditation that enables a man to know the illusion. This illusion ensures the extension or the progress of the metaphysical living-organisms and they are inspired to make them free from the worldly bondages. This world is only existed by virtue of the industry made by that metaphysical person.

गौरनाद्यन्तवती सा जनित्री भूतभाविनी। सितासिता च रक्ता च सर्वकामदुघा विभोः॥५॥

This illusion in the form of a cow has two powers, i.e., the power of genesis and power of destruction. It is helpful to all and it nourishes all living-beings. It has white, dark and red colours (Sat, Raja and Tama) and it fulfills all desires.

पिबन्त्येनामविषयामविज्ञातां कुमारकाः। एकस्तु पिबते देवः स्वच्छन्दोऽत्र वशानुगः॥६॥

All living-organisms are busy in milking this illusion in the form of a cow but that supreme man is alien and different from the objects of this illusion. He regulates all the living-organisms alone and by keeping himself independent, he sips the milk extracted from the illusion cow.

ध्यानक्रियाभ्यां भगवान्भुङ्क्तेऽसौ प्रसहद्विभुः। सर्वसाधारणीं दोग्ध्रीं पीयमानां तु यज्वभिः॥७॥

That god (the celestial person) enjoys the illusion cow through meditation and great deeds which is milked by the common people and offered by the person engaged in offering. He thus extends the scope of this illusion.

पश्यन्त्यस्यां महात्मानः सुवर्णं पिप्पलाशनम्। उदासीनं ध्रुवं हंसं स्नातकाध्वर्यवो जगुः॥८॥

The great persons eat the fruit of this pippala world looking so nice and even in the illusion of this world, they observe that supreme man of detachment and the supreme soul. All devotees and learned people worship that soul.

शंसन्तमनुशंसन्ति बहवृचाः शास्त्रकोविदाः। रथन्तरं बृहत्साम सप्तवैधैस्तु गीयते॥९॥

The person well-learnt to the scriptures and the worshipper by the means of their hymns and psalms respectively worship that supreme person and recite seven ways the 'Bṛhatsāma' and 'Rathantara' for him.

मन्त्रोपनिषदं ब्रह्म पदक्रमसमन्वितम्। पठन्ति भार्गवा ह्येते ह्यथर्वाणो भृगूत्तमाः॥१०॥

The secret of hymns too is Brahma. These are recited in the serial and the foot of Atharvaveda by the descendants of Bhṛgu known as 'Bhārgava'.

सब्रह्मचारिवृत्तिश्च स्तम्भोऽथ फलितस्तथा। अनड्वान्रोहितोच्छिष्टः पश्यन्तो बहुविस्तरम्॥११॥

This supreme person is celibate, undivided like a pillar, full of worldly fruits, puller of the world cart, void of the Rajas property, enriched with the Satva property and seen in his universal form.

कालः प्राणश्च भगवान्मृत्युः शर्वो महेश्वरः। उग्रो भवश्च रुद्रश्च ससुरः सासुरस्तथा॥१२॥

This supreme person (enriched with the six kinds of luxuries) is in the form of the time (Kāla), breathing (Prāṇa), death, Śarva, Maheśvara, universe, Rudra, Ugra (violent), God and demon too.

प्रजापतिर्विराट् चैव पुरुषः सलिलमेव च। स्तूयते मन्त्रसंस्तुत्यैरथर्वविदितैर्विभुः॥१३॥

That supreme god is adorable for all in the form of Prajāpati, gigantic man and the water etc. gods. His vast form is perceived by Atharvaveda.

तं षड्विंशक इत्येते सप्तविंश तथापरे। पुरुषं निर्गुणं सांख्यमथर्वशिरसो विदुः।।१४।।

Some says him the twenty-sixth element while some other say the twenty-seventh element. The person well-learnt to Upaniṣad say him as 'Nirguṇa Sāṁkhya Puruṣa' (having no particular form still within all).

चतुर्विंशतिसंख्यातं व्यक्तमव्यक्तमेव च। अद्वैतं द्वैतमित्याहुस्त्रिधा तं पञ्चधा तथा।।१५।।

Some consider him a compound of twenty-four elements (Sāṁkhya Darśana). Some of them, apparent (world) and some intangible (nature), some consider him dual (the living-organisms and Brahma) and some consider absolute (Brahma). Similarly, some consider him as holding three forms (Brahmā, Viṣṇu, Maheśa) and some consider him as holding five forms (Brahmā, Viṣṇu, Maheśa, Gaurī and Gaṇeśa).

ब्रह्माद्यं स्थावरान्तं च पश्यन्ति ज्ञानचक्षुषः। तमेकमेव पश्यन्ति परिशुभ्रं विभुं द्विजाः।।१६।।

A number of intuitive persons perceive him as extended to in an absolute entity and most sacred from Brahma (greatest and most sensitive form) to the inert and dead matters.

यस्मिन्सर्वमिदं प्रोतं ब्रह्म स्थावरजंगमम्। तस्मिन्नेव लयं यान्ति स्रवन्त्यः सागरे यथा।।१७।।

This whole world (inert and sensitive both) has been incorporated within that Brahma. As the rivers in the end merge with the ocean, this whole universe too merges within the Brahma.

यस्मिन्भावाः प्रलीयन्ते लीनाश्चाव्यक्ततां ययुः। पश्यन्ति व्यक्ततां भूयो जायन्ते बुद्बुदा इव।।१८।।

As the bubble arises and merges in the water, the scholars consider the Brahma in which all organisms are originated and become invisible when merging with it.

क्षेत्रज्ञाधिष्ठितं चैव कारणैर्विद्यते पुनः। एवं स भगवान्देवं पश्यन्त्यन्ये पुनः पुनः।।१९।।

He is inserted within all living-organisms in the form Kṣetrajña (one who knows everything regarding the respective region) and he knows all the causes behind the effect. The learned devotee see him repeatedly who are well-known to these facts.

ब्रह्म ब्रह्मेत्यथायान्ति ये विदुर्ब्राह्मणास्तथा। अत्रैव ते लयं यान्ति लीनाश्चाव्यक्तशालिनः।।
लीनाश्चाव्यक्तशालिन इत्युपनिषत्।।२०।।

The persons well-known to Brahma definitely are merged in the Brahma and they obtain all pleasure in their invisible forms. This is the secret of this Upaniṣad.

।।शान्तिपाठः।।

।।ॐ पूर्णमदः पूर्णमिदं.... इति शान्तिः।।

।।इति मंत्रिकोपनिषत्समाप्ता।।

99. GĀYATRYUPANIṢAD

गायत्र्युपनिषद्

This Upaniṣad is in the form of a compilation of eight Kaṇḍikās falling from thirty-one to thirty-eight of Gopath Brāhmaṇa allied to the Atharvaveda. By means of colloquy striked between the saints like Maudgalya and Maitreyī, the great learning of Gāyatrī have been described here. In the first and second Kaṇḍikā, the introductory part is given including the definition of the terms 'Savithu', 'Vareṇyam', 'Bhargoḥ', 'Devasya', 'Dhiyoḥ', 'Pracodayāt' etc. of the Gāyatrī hymn. In the third Kaṇḍikā, the inseparability of lord Sun and Sāvitrī and their varied forms have been described. In the fourth, fifth and sixth Kaṇḍikās, an explanation and the scope of three feet of the great hymn of Gāyatrī are enunciated respectively. In the seventh and the eight Kaṇḍikā, an exposition of the equal sound of the Brahma, the offering and the Brāhmaṇa has been given.

।।प्रथमा कण्डिका।।

एतद्ध स्मैतद्विद्वांसमेकादशाक्षम्मौद्गल्यं ग्लावो मैत्रेयोऽभ्याजगाम स तस्मिन् ब्रह्मचर्यं वसतो विज्ञायोवाच किं स्विन्मर्या अयं तं मौद्गल्योऽध्येति यदस्मिन् ब्रह्मचर्ये वसतीति।।१।।

First Kaṇḍikā

'Glāva Maitreya' (the disciple of Maitreyī clan) came to the scholar Maudgalya (Mudgal clan) who was enriched with eleven eyes (the knowledge or the sense organs) having seen the resident celibates in the hermitage of Maudgalya, he sarcastically asked– "What does this Maudgalya teach to his pupils?"

Eleven aspects used in this hymn indicates his being extra-ordinarily intelligent. It also used as an authoritative word. It is meant by the ten sensory organs or the breathings i.e. five breathings plus five sub-breathings and the eleventh is the ever-awaken element of the soul. This is the reason, he was said as possessing eleven aspects.

तद्धि मौद्गल्यस्यान्तेवासी शुश्राव सः आचार्यायावृज्याचचष्टे दुरधीयानं वा अयं भवन्तमवोचद्योऽयमद्यातिथिर्भवति किं सौम्य विद्वानिति त्रीन् वेदान् ब्रूते भो३इति।।२।।

The pupil of Maudgalya went to his teacher and informed him saying that this guest is declaring you a stupid. Maudgalya asked– "Whether he is scholar?" The pupil replied– "Yes sir, he is professor of three Vedas."

तस्य सौम्य यो विस्पष्टो विजिगीषोऽन्तेवासी तन्मे ह्वयेति।।३।।

"O dear! Then bring in the student of our guest who is most intelligent, scholar, intuitive and competent to me"– Maudgalya said to his pupil.

तमाजुहाव तमभ्युवाचासाविति भो३इति किं सौम्य त आचार्योऽध्येतीति, त्रीन् वेदान् ब्रूते भो३इति।।४।।

He brought that student and said to his teacher– "Honourable teacher! This one is the student possessing all properties as suggested by you." He asked to him– "Dear student! What does your teacher do?" The student said– "Sir! He is Professor of three Vedas."

यन्नु खलु सौम्यास्माभिः सर्वे वेदा मुखतो गृहीताः कथन्त एवमाचार्यो भाषते कथं नु शिष्टाः शिष्टेभ्य एवं भाषेरन् यं ह्येनमहं प्रश्नं प्रच्छामि न तं विवक्ष्यति न ह्येनमध्येतीति॥५॥

O dear student! Why your teacher say that I am stupid when all Vedas are well-learned to me. Does he even ignorant to the manner of talking with the civilised persons? I, therefore, ask a question and in case, a proper reply to it is not given, it will be purported that he does not teach Veda.

तां भवान् प्रब्रवीत्विति स चेत्सौम्य दुरधीयानो भविष्यत्याचार्योवाच ब्रह्मचारी ब्रह्मचारिणे सावित्रीं प्राहेति वक्ष्यति तत्त्वं ब्रूयात् दुरधीयानन्तं वै भवान् मौद्गल्यमवोचत् स त्वा यं प्रश्नमप्राक्षीन्न तं व्यवोचः पुरा संवत्सरादर्त्तिमाकृष्यसीति॥६॥

O dear student! in case, he is ignorant, it will be said by him that the subject taught by the teacher to his celibate pupil is Sāvitrī. You should say that he had condemned Maudgalya as being a stupid and say him that Maudgalya will ask you a question and in case the same is not duly answered, you would have to suffer severe pains till the period of a year.

॥द्वितीया कण्डिका॥

स ह मौद्गल्यः स्वमन्तेवासिनमुवाच, परेहि सौम्य ग्लावं मैत्रेयमुपसीदाधीहि भोः सावित्रीं गायत्रीञ्चतुर्विंशतियोनिं द्वादशमिथुनां यस्या भृग्वङ्गिरसश्चक्षुर्यस्यां सर्वमिदं श्रितम्॥१॥

Second Kaṇḍikā

The saint Maudgalya then said to his pupil– "O dear student! Go to Glāva Maitreya and say– O teacher! Tell us about the Sāvitrī and Gāyatrī with its twelve couplets and twenty-four minutest nucleus. All and every is sheltered to it, therefore, please teach us about that Gāyatrī."

स तत्राजगाम यत्रेतरो बभूव, तं ह पप्रच्छ स ह न प्रतिपेदे, तं होवाच दुरधीयानं तं वै भवान् मौद्गल्यमवोचत् स त्वा यं प्रश्नमप्राक्षीत्रं तं व्यवोचः पुरासंवत्सरादार्त्तिमाकृष्यसीति॥२॥

Under the instruction of his teacher, the Maudgalya's pupil visited at the hermitage of Maitreya. He asked a question but the Maitreya could not reply. He then said to him– "O lord! You had told Maudgalya a stupid one. He has asked this question and in case, you are failed to answer, you would suffer from the severe pains for the period of a year."

स ह मैत्रेयः स्वानन्तेवासन उवाच यथार्थं भवन्तो यथागृहं यथामनो विप्रसृज्यन्तां दुरधीयानं वा अहं मौद्गल्यमवोचं स मा यं प्रश्नमप्राक्षीन्न तं व्यवोचं तमुपैष्यामि शान्तिं करिष्यामीति॥३॥

The saint Maitreya expressed the reality before his pupils and said– "Please return back voluntarily to your home. I had told the saint Maudgalya as unworthy but I could not answer to the question he has asked to me. I would now go to him and satisfy him by the possible means."

स ह मैत्रेयः प्रातः समित्पाणिर्मौद्गल्यमुपससादासावाग्रहं भो मैत्रेयः किमर्थमिति दुरधीयानं वा अहं भवन्तमवोचं त्वं मा यम्प्रश्नमप्राक्षीर्न्न तं व्यवोचं त्वामुपेव्यामि शान्ति करिष्यामीति॥४॥

He reached to Maudgalya with most enlightened manner by taking the fuel in his hands in the morning. On accessing to there he said– "O revered teacher! I am Maitreya." Maudgalya asked– "How have you come here?" Maitreya replied– "Sir! I could not reply to the question asked by you. I would now satisfy you by my personal services. Hence, I have come here."

स होवाचात्र वा उपेतञ्च सर्वञ्च कृतं पापकेन त्वा यानेन चरन्तमाहूरथोऽयं मम कल्याणस्तंते ददामि तेन याहीति॥५॥

The saint Maudgalya said– "You have come here and without observing your pure or impure thoughts, I provide you with the chariot of all benevolent thoughts. Please let us come riding on it."

[The chariot means a carrier that brings a man to his destination. Every person attains the motion of his life according to the thoughts which he possesses within heart. The people who expect welfare always resort to the welfare thoughts.]

स होवाचैतदेवात्रात्विषञ्चानृशंस्यञ्च यथा भवानाहोपायामित्येवं भवन्तमिति तं होपेयाय तं होपेत्य पप्रच्छ किंस्विदाहुर्भोः सवितुर्वरण्यं भर्गो देवस्य कवयः किमाहुर्धियो विचक्ष्व यदि ताः प्रवेक्ष्य प्रचोदयात्सविता याभिरेतीति॥६॥

Sage Maitreya said– "Your statement is true and immersed in the thoughts that provide with fearnessless to all. I am before you to perform everything in pursuance with your instruction." He appeared with a manner before the saint Maudgalya and began to ask– "O teacher! What is the adorable element of the Sun? What is the 'bharga' of that god? What answer to this question is provided by the intuitive? What explanation they give to the element of wisdom by resorting to which that god moves after getting an entrance into the world of Sun?"

तस्मा एतत् प्रोवाच वेदाश्छन्दांसि सवितुर्वरेण्य भर्गो देवस्य कवयोऽन्नमाहुः। कर्माणि धियस्तदु ते ब्रवीमि प्रचोदयात्सविता याभिरेतीति॥७॥

The saint Maudgalya said to Maitreya– "The Vedic rhymes are the elements adorable to the sun-god. The wise people consider the food as the 'Bharga' of that god. The deed is only that element of wisdom motivating to which that god takes movements.

[The sun-god is motivator of all. The motivating element as referred to in the rhymes too are adorable and the undescribed ether flow is not worth-adoration because these are beyond to the power of entertainment as vested with the mankind. The savvy (Dhi) is called wisdom. It seems that the saint want to convey the movement of sun-god with the power of motivating the wisdom towards the deeds.]

तमुपसंगृह्य पप्रच्छाधीहि भोः कः सविता का सावित्री॥८॥

Hearing this, the saint Maitreya asked humbly to Maudgalya– "O revered teacher! Kindly tell me that what is the Sun and what is Sāvitrī?"

॥तृतीय खण्डिका॥

मन एव सविता, वाक् सावित्री, यत्र ह्येव मनस्तद् वाक्, यत्र वै वाक् तन्मन इत्येते द्वे योनी एकं मिथुनम्॥१॥

Third Kaṇḍikā

The saint Maudgalya said– "The mind too is the Sun (the motivating element) and the speech is Sāvitrī (the motivated element). Where there is mind, there is speech and where there is speech there resides the mind. Both of them are couple and in the form of Yoni (the centre of genesis).

अग्निरेव सविता, पृथिवी सावित्री यत्र ह्येवाग्निस्तत्पृथिवी यज्ञ वे पृथिवी तदग्निरित्येते द्वे योनी एकं मिथुनम्॥२॥

The fire too is the Sun and the earth is Sāvitrī. Where there is fire, the earth is also there and where the earth is, the fire also exists there. Thus, the fire and the earth both are couples as the centre of genesis (Yoni).

वायुरेवा सविताऽन्तरिक्षं सावित्री यत्र ह्येव वायुस्तदन्तरिक्षं, यत्र वा अन्तरिक्षं तद्वायुरित्येते द्वे योनी एकं मिथुनम्॥३॥

The wind is the Sun and the space is Sāvitrī. The wind is where the space is and where the space is existed the wind is also there. Both of them i.e. the wind and the space are the couples and the centre of genesis.

आदित्य एव सविता द्यौः सावित्री यत्र ह्येवादित्यस्तद्द्यौर्यत्र वै द्यौस्तदादित्य इत्येते द्वे योनी एकं मिथुनम्॥४॥

The Sun is the Savitā and the world of Sun is Sāvitrī, where there is the Sun, there is 'Dyau' and where there is Dyau there is Sun, both of them are a couplet and nucleus of genesis.

चन्द्रमा एव सविता, नक्षत्राणि सावित्री, यत्र ह्येव चन्द्रमास्तन्नक्षत्राणि यत्र वै नक्षत्राणि तच्चन्द्रमा, इत्येते द्वे योनी एकं मिथुनम्॥५॥

The moon is Savitā and the planet is Sāvitrī. Where there is moon, there is planet and where there is planet there is the moon. Both of them are a couplet and a nucleus of genesis.

अहरेव सविता, रात्रिः सावित्री, यत्र ह्येवाहस्तद्रात्रिर्यत्र वै रात्रिस्तदहरित्येते द्वे योनी एकं मिथुनम्॥६॥

The day is Savitā and the night is Sāvitrī, where there is the day, there is night. And where there is night, there is day. Both of them are nucleus of genesis and a couplet.

उष्णमेव सविता, शीतं सावित्री, यत्र ह्येवोष्णं, तच्छीतं, यत्र वै शीतं तदुष्णमित्येते द्वे योनी एकं मिथुनम्।।७।।

The heat is Savitā and cold is Sāvitrī, where there is heat, there is cold and where there is cold, there is heat. Both of them are couplet and the nucleus of genesis.

अब्भ्रमेव सविता वर्षं सावित्री यत्र ह्येवाब्भ्रन्तद्वर्षं यत्र वै वर्षं तदब्भ्रमित्येते द्वे योनी एकं मिथुनम्।।८।।

The cloud is Savitā and the raining is Sāvitrī. Where there is cloud, there is rain and where there is rain, there is cloud. Both of them are a couplet and a nucleus of genesis.

विद्युदेव सविता स्तनयित्नुः सावित्री यत्र ह्येव विद्युत् तत् स्तनयित्नुः यत्र वै स्तनयित्नुस्तद्विद्युदित्येते द्वे योनी एकं मिथुनम्।।९।।

The lightening is Savitā and its thundering is Sāvitrī. Where there is lightening, there is thundering and where there is thundering, there also exist lightening. Both of them are a couplet and a nucleus of genesis.

प्राण एव सविता अन्नं सावित्री, यत्र ह्येव प्राणस्तदन्नं यत्र वा अन्नं तत् प्राण इत्येते द्वे योनी एकं मिथुनम्।।१०।।

The breathing is Savitā and the food is Sāvitrī. Where there is breathing, there is food and where there is food, there is breathing. Both of them are a couplet and a nucleus of genesis.

वेदा एव सविता छन्दांसि सावित्री, यत्र ह्येव वेदान्तच्छन्दांसि यत्र वै च्छन्दांसि तद् वेदा इत्येते द्वे योनी एकं मिथुनम्।।११।।

The Vedas are Savitā and the rhymes are Sāvitrī. Where there are Veda there are rhymes and where there are rhymes, there are Veda. Both of them are a couplet and a nucleus of genesis.

यज्ञ एव सविता दक्षिणा सावित्री, यत्र ह्येव यज्ञस्तत् दक्षिणा यत्र वै दक्षिणास्तद्यज्ञ इत्येते द्वे योनी एकं मिथुनम्।।१२।।

The offering is Savitā and the donation is Sāvitrī. Where there is donation, there is offering and where there is offering, there is donation. Both of them are a couplet and a nucleus of genesis.

एतद्ध स्मैतद्विद्वांसमोपाकारिमासस्तुर्ब्रह्मचारी ते संस्थित इत्यथैत आसस्तुराचित इव चितो बभूवाथोत्थाय प्रावाजीदित्येतद्वाऽहं वेद नैतासु योनिष्वित एतेभ्यो वा मिथुनेभ्यः सम्भूतो ब्रह्मचारी मम पुरायुषः प्रेयादिति।।१३।।

Thereafter Glāva Maitreya said to Maudgalya– "O learned teacher! I am obliged to you. This celibate is present for your service. This celibate has become fulfilled of knowledge on arrival here." With these words, Maitreya stood and spoke while strolling– "I am now well-known that my celibate affiliated to these couples and nucleus of genesis will not attain premature death."

।।चतुर्थीकण्डिका।।

ब्रह्म हेदं श्रियं प्रतिष्ठामायतनमैक्षत तत्तपस्व यदि तद् व्रते ध्रियेत तत्सत्ये प्रत्यतिष्ठत्।।१।।

Fourth Kaṇḍikā

Maudgalya said to Maitreya– "This Brahma too is in the form of wealth, prestige and shelter. Hence, you should do penance. In case, a resolution for penance is made, one will attain the truth."

स सविता सावित्र्या ब्राह्मणं सृष्ट्वा तत् सावित्रीं पर्य्यदधात् तत् सवितुर्वरेण्यमिति सावित्र्याः प्रथमः पादः।।२।।

That lord Savitā reproduced Brāhmaṇa (enriched of the knowledge of Brahma) with the co-operation of Sāvitrī and made him to know the hymn of Sāvitrī. Tatsaviturvareṇyam is the first foot of the Sāvitrī hymn."

पृथिव्यर्चं समदधादृचाऽग्निमग्निनां श्रियं श्रिया स्त्रियं स्त्रिया मिथुनं मिथुनेनं प्रजां प्रजया कर्म कर्मणा तपस्तपसा सत्यं सत्येन ब्रह्म ब्रह्मणा ब्राह्मणं ब्राह्मणेन व्रतं व्रतेन वै ब्राह्मणः संशितोभवत्यशून्यो भवत्यविच्छिन्नः।।३।।

The lord Sun added Ṛk with the earth. Similarly, the fire was added with Ṛk, the wealth with the fire, the woman with the wealth, the couple with the woman, the subject with the couple, the deed with the subject, the penance with the deed, the truth with the penance, the Brahma with the truth, the Brāhmaṇa with the Brahma and the resolution with the Brāhmaṇa. By virtue of that resolution, the Brāhmaṇa gets splendour, perfection and integration.

भवत्यविच्छिन्नोऽस्य तन्तुरविच्छिन्नं जीवनं भवनं भवति य एव वेदं यश्चैवं विद्वानेवमेतं सावित्र्याः प्रथमं पादं व्याचष्टे।४।।

The scholar who assumes this first foot of Sāvitrī hymn in the similar fashion and explains it everywhere, his clan as also his life becomes integrated.

।।पञ्चमी कण्डिका।।

भर्गो देवस्य धीमहीति सावित्र्या द्वितीयः पादोऽन्तरिक्षेण यजुः समदधात् यजुषा वायुं, वायुनाऽभ्रमभ्रेण वर्ष, वर्षेणौषधिवनस्पतीनोषधि वनस्पतिभिः पशून् पशुभिः कर्म कर्मणा तपस्तपसा सत्यं, सत्येन ब्रह्म, ब्रह्मणा, ब्राह्मणं, ब्राह्मणेन व्रतं व्रतेन वै ब्राह्मणः संशितो भवत्यशून्यो भवत्यविच्छिन्नः।।१।।

Fifth Kaṇḍikā

The second foot of Sāvitrī hymn is 'Bhargo Devasya Dhīmahī'. You lord Sun added 'Yajus' with the space, the wind was added with the Yajus, the cloud with the wind, the rain with the cloud, the medicines and vegetation's with the rain, the animals with the medicine and the vegetation's, the deeds with the animals, the penance with the deeds, the deeds with the truth, the Brahma with the truth, the Brāhmaṇa with the Brahma and the resolution with the Brāhmaṇa. It is only his resolution that provides the Brāhmaṇa with splendour, perfection and the integrity.

भवत्यविच्छिन्नोऽस्य तन्तुरविच्छिन्नं जीवनं भवति य एव वेदं यश्चैवं विद्वानेवमेतं सावित्र्याः द्वितीयं पादं व्याचष्टे।।२।।

The learned person who is known to the second foot (the element of Bharga) of Sāvitrī and explains this way, his clan as also his life both avail integrity.

।।षष्ठी कण्डिका।।

धियो यो नः प्रचोदयादिति सावित्र्यास्तृतीयः पादो दिवा साम समदधात्साम्नाऽऽदित्यमादित्येनरश्मीन्रश्मिभिर्वर्षं, वर्षेणौषधिवनस्पतीनोषधिवनस्पतिभिः पशून् पशुभिः कर्म कर्मणा तपस्तपसा सत्यं, सत्येन ब्रह्म, ब्रह्मणा, ब्राह्मणेन व्रतं व्रतेन वै ब्राह्मणः संशितो भवत्यशून्याभवत्यविच्छिन्नः।।१।।

Sixth Kaṇḍikā

The third foot of Sāvitrī is 'Dhiyo Yo Naḥ Pracodayāt'. That lord Sun added Sāma with the world of Sun. Similarly, Āditya was added with the Sāma, the rays were added with the Āditya, the rain was added with the rays, the medicine and the vegetation is added with rain, the animals is added with the medicines and vegetation, the deed was added with the animals, the penance is added with the deed, the truth was added with the penance, the Brahma is added with the truth, the Brahma was added with truth, and the resolution is added with the Brāhmaṇa. It is the resolution that provides the Brāhmaṇa with splendour, perfection and integrity.

भवत्यविच्छिन्नोऽस्य तन्तुरविच्छिन्नं जीवनं भवति य एव वेदं यश्चैवं विद्वानेवमेतं सावित्र्यास्तृतीयं पादं व्याचष्टे।४।।

The person known to this third foot of Sāvitrī and explains it in the same way, his clan as also life both avail integrity.

।।सप्तमी कण्डिका।।

तेन ह वा एवं विदुषा ब्राह्मणेन ब्रह्माभिपन्नं ग्रसितं परामृष्टम्।।१।।

Seventh Kaṇḍikā

The Brāhmaṇa well-known to the three feet of Sāvitrī emanates the power of Brahman duly obtained, hold and applied with the allied experiences.

ब्रह्मणाऽऽकाशमभिपन्नं ग्रसितं परामृष्टमाकाशेन वायुरभिपन्नो ग्रसितः परामृष्टो वायुना ज्योतिरभिपन्नं ग्रसितं परामृष्टं ज्योतिषाऽपोभिपन्ना ग्रसिताः परामृष्टा अद्भिर्भूमिरभिपन्ना ग्रसिता परामृष्टा भूम्याऽन्नमभिपन्नं ग्रसितं परामृष्टमन्नेन प्राणोऽभिपन्नो ग्रसितः परामृष्टः प्राणेन मनोऽभिपन्नं ग्रसितं परामृष्टं मनसा वागभिपन्ना ग्रसिता परामृष्टा वाचा वेदा अभिपन्ना ग्रसिताः परामृष्टा वेदैर्यज्ञोऽभिपन्नो ग्रसितः परामृष्टस्तानि ह वा एतानि द्वादशमहाभूतान्येव विधिप्रतिष्ठितानि तेषां यत्र एव पराद्ध्र्यः।।२।।

The ether along with the Brahma is acquired, held and applied with the allied experiences. The wind with the ether is also acquired, held and applied with allied experiences. Similarly, the flame is acquired, held and applied with allied experiences with the water. The water with the flame, the earth with the water, the food with the earth, the breathing with the food, the mind with the breathing, the speech with the mind, the Veda with the speech and the offerings with the Veda are acquired, held and applied with allied experiences. The twelve vital elements (Mahā Bhūta) out of such learned persons are enshrined. The offerings is the best among them.

।।अष्टमी कण्डिका।।

तं ह स्मैतमेवं विद्वांसो मन्यन्ते विद्मनमिति याथातथ्यमविद्वांसो यज्ञो वेदेषु प्रतिष्ठितो वेदो वाचि प्रतिष्ठिता वाङ् मनसि प्रतिष्ठिता मनः प्राणे प्रतिष्ठितं प्राणोऽन्ने प्रतिष्ठितो ऽन्नं भूमौ प्रतिष्ठितं भूमिरप्सु प्रतिष्ठिता आपो ज्योतिषि प्रतिष्ठिता ज्योतिर्वायौ प्रतिष्ठितं वायुराकाशे प्रतिष्ठित आकाशं ब्रह्मणि प्रतिष्ठितं ब्रह्म ब्राह्मणे ब्रह्मविदि प्रतिष्ठितं यो ह वा एवं वित् स ब्रह्मवित् पुण्यां च कीर्तिं लभते सुरभींश्च गन्धान् सोऽपहतपाप्मानन्तांश्रियमश्नुते य एवं वेद, यश्चैव विद्वानेवमेतां मातरं सावित्रीसम्पदमुपनिषदमुपास्त इति ब्राह्मणम्।।१।।

Eighth Kaṇḍikā

The scholars who believe of their knowledge to the offering really are ignorant. This offering is enshrined in Vedas, the Vedas are enshrined in the speech, the speech is enshrined in the mind, the mind in the breathing, the breathing in food, the food in the earth, the earth in water, the water in the splendour (fire), the splendour in the wind, the wind in the ether, the ether in the Brahma and the Brahma in the person who is well-known to the Brahma. The person who knows the motion of these twelve vital elements attains fame and pleasure and enjoys a life full of higher deeds (perfume). He attains gigantic luxuries after duly exonerated from the evils.

।।गायत्र्युपनिषत्समाप्ता।।

100. TULASYUPANIṢAD

तुलस्युपनिषद्

Among the most ancient upaniṣads, one of the upaniṣad Tulasī is also existed. Tulasī (basil) is a well-known plant acceptable to both person either he is atheist or have faith on god. The persons devotee to god, sow the seed of basil with great reverence. They obtain blessing with the worship to the basil plant systematically after bath and application of the flower, scented stick and the lamp presuming it as the god itself. Irrespective of non-observance to the recital and worship, the atheist also accept the utility of basil particularly owing to medicinal qualities to which it possesses.

The celestial properties of basil has been enumerated in this upaniṣad. At the beginning, the saint, the god, the rhyme etc. to this upaniṣad has been described and the magnificence of it has been laid down thereafter. The five parts (the root, the stem, the leaves, the flowers and the seed) of basil plant are most useful for removal of the ailments and evolution of the celestial properties. Its leaves should not be plucked in night as also on any auspicious day. It has been deemed as immortal and effacing the evils. This plant is most darling to lord Viṣṇu. Lastly, the significance of this upaniṣad even on mere hearing has been described and thus it has been concluded.

अथ तुलस्युपनिषदं व्याख्यास्यामः। नारद ऋषिः। अथर्वाङ्गिरश्छन्दः। अमृता तुलसी देवता। सुधा बीजम्। वसुधा शक्तिः। नारायणः कीलकम्। श्यामां श्यामवपुर्धरां ऋक्स्वरूपां यजुर्मनां ब्रह्माथर्वप्राणां कल्पहस्तां पुराणपठितां अमृतोद्भवां अमृतरसमञ्जरीं अनन्तां अनन्तरसभोगदां वैष्णवीं विष्णुवल्लभां मृत्युजन्मनिबर्हणीं दर्शनात्पापनाशिनीं स्पर्शनात्पावनीं अभिवन्दनाद्रोगनाशिनीं सेवनान्मृत्युनाशिनीं वैकुण्ठार्चनाद्विपद्धन्त्रीं भक्षणात् वयुनप्रदां प्रादक्षिण्याद्दारिद्र्यनाशिनीं मूलमृल्लेपनान्महापापभञ्जिनीं घ्राणतर्पणादन्तर्मलनाशिनीं य एवं वेद स वैष्णवो भवति। वृथा न छिन्द्यात्। दृष्ट्वा प्रदक्षिणं कुर्यात्। रात्र्यां न स्पृशेत्। पर्वणि न विचिन्वेत्। यदि विचिन्वति स विष्णुहा भवति। श्रीतुलस्यै स्वाहा। विष्णुप्रियायै स्वाहा। अमृतायै स्वाहा। श्रीतुलस्यै विद्महे विष्णुप्रियायै धीमहि। तन्नो अमृता प्रचोदयात्॥ १॥

अमृतेऽमृतरूपासि अमृतत्वप्रदायिनि। त्वं मामुद्धर संसारात् क्षीरसागरकन्यके॥ २॥

श्रीसखि त्वं सदानन्दे मुकुन्दस्य सदा प्रिये। वरदाभयहस्ताभ्यां मां विलोकय दुर्लभे॥ ३॥

Now description of Tulasyupaniṣad is made. Saint to this upaniṣad is Nārada, rhyme is Atharvāṅgirasa, god is the immortal Tulsī, seed is the nectar, power is the earth and Nārāyaṇa is the 'Kīlaka'. It has dark complexion and dark colour. It is in the form of Ṛgveda, its mind is Yajurveda, breathing is 'Brahmārthavaveda'. Renowned in Vedas and Purāṇas its magnificence is recognised when one does the study of Vedas and Purāṇas, arisen by the nectar, its buds are filled with the nectar, beyond the death, endows with various sorts of essence and enjoyments, destroyer of the evils merely by the appearance, in the form of supreme Viṣṇu, darling to lord Viṣṇu, destroyer to the cycle of birth and death, making pious merely by touch, remover of all ailments by mere salute, endows with immortality by mere use, destroyer of the crisis on submission to lord Viṣṇu while worship, endows with the power of breathing if eaten, killer of poverty by mere Pradakṣiṇā i.e., one circle round the basil plant and destroyer of the ever big evils merely by smearing the clay existing in its roots. It kills the internal impurity by mere smelling. The person is real devotee to lord Viṣṇu who is known to this fact. The plant of basil should not be plucked in the vagary of mind. One should take a circle round the basil wherever this plant is seen. It should not be touched in the nights. The basil plant should not be plucked on any auspicious day or any festival because the person not complying with this rule does enmity to lord Viṣṇu. The darling to lord Viṣṇu and the immortal basil is saluted. We know the basil plants as per the holy books and the advises given by our teacher. We sit on meditation to the basil plant which is beloved to lord Viṣṇu. May that immortal plant motivate our power of discretion to work for an immortality. O the daughter of milk ocean! You are immortal and having immortal you render the immortality. Therefore let me pass from this worldly ocean with utmost liberty. O a friend to Lakṣmī! You are the pleasure in yourself and darling to lord Viṣṇu always. Therefore, O rarest goddess! Please put me under your eye and care in the posture of fearlessness and always blessing.

अवृक्षवृक्षरूपासि वृक्षत्वं मे विनाशय। तुलस्यतुलरूपासि तुलाकोटिनिभेऽजरे॥ ४॥

अतुले त्वतुलायां हि हरिरेकोऽस्ति नान्यथा। त्वमेव जगतां धात्री त्वमेव विष्णुवल्लभा॥ ५॥

O Tulasī! You are seen in the form of a tree (inert), however you are plant (most sensitive). Hence, destroy the inertia dwelling with me. O goddess of excellent stature! You are unique and unborn. The crores of measures applied for comparison are blunt to compare you with any of the other. O unique! It is lord Viṣṇu analogous to you and no body else. You are beloved of lord Viṣṇu and nourish this whole world.

त्वमेव सुरसंसेव्या त्वमेव मोक्षदायिनी। त्वच्छायायां वसेल्लक्ष्मीस्त्वन्मूले विष्णुरव्ययः॥ ६॥

All the gods are under your service and you provide with emancipation. Lord Viṣṇu resides in your root and lord Lakṣmī resides under your shadow.

समन्ताद्देवताः सर्वाः सिद्धचारणपन्नगाः। यन्मूले सर्वतीर्थानि यन्मध्ये ब्रह्मदेवताः॥ ७॥

यदग्रे वेदशास्त्राणि तुलसीं तां नमाम्यहम्। तुलसि श्रीसखि शुभे पापहारिणि पुण्यदे॥ ८॥

नमस्ते नारदनुते नारायणमनः प्रिये। ब्रह्मानन्दाश्रुसंजाते वृन्दावननिवासिनि॥ ९॥

I salute Tulasī in whose root all gods, saints, poets, serpents and pilgrimage are situated all around, lord Brahmā resides in the middle and the holy scriptures of Vedas resides on the top. O Tulasī! You are friend to Lakṣmī, ever-benevolent, destroyer of all sins and inspirer to great deeds. Arising from the tears flown in the mood of pleasure of Brahmā, you (Tulasī) reside in Vṛndāvana. Salute is conveyed to which is worshipped by Nārada and beloved to lord Nārāyaṇa.

सर्वावयवसंपूर्णे अमृतोपनिषद्रसे। त्वं मामुद्धर कल्याणि महापापाब्धिदुस्तरात्॥ १०॥

सर्वेषामपि पापानां प्रायश्चित्तं त्वमेव हि। देवानां च ऋषीणां च पितॄणां त्वं सदा प्रिये॥ ११॥

विना श्रीतुलसीं विप्रा येऽपि श्राद्धं प्रकुर्वते। वृथा भवति तच्छ्राद्धं पितॄणां नोपगच्छति॥ १२

तुलसीपत्रमुत्सृज्य यदि पूजां करोति वै। आसुरी सा भवेत् पूजा विष्णुप्रीतिकरी न च॥ १३॥

यज्ञं दानं जपं तीर्थं श्राद्धं वै देवतार्चनम्। तर्पणं मार्जनं चान्यन्न कुर्यात्तुलसीं विना॥ १४॥

तुलसीदारुमणिभिः जपः सर्वार्थसाधकः। एवं न वेद यः कश्चित् स विप्रः श्वपचाधमः॥ १५

O the form of perfection! You are the essence and complexion to the immortal upaniṣad. O benevolent gods! Make us able to cross the ocean of evils. O Tulasī! You are in the form of regret to all evils and by the same reason you are beloved to all gods, saints and pitṛs (fore-fathers). In case, basil leaves are not used by the Brāhmaṇas in Śrāddha (reverence to late fore-fathers), that complete performance meet to failure. If someone worships the god without the basil leaves, it is considered worship to demon instead of god and same is not accepted by the lord Viṣṇu. The offerings, the donations, the Japa, pilgrimage, Śrāddha, Tarpaṇa, Mārjana and worship etc. should not be performed without the basil leaves. The garland made of the basil beads fulfills all desires. The Brāhmaṇa unknown to this fact is as mean as a Caṇḍāla (evil-doer).

इत्याह भगवान् ब्रह्माणं नारायणः, ब्रह्मा नारदसनकादिभ्यः सनकादयो वेदव्यासाय, वेदव्यासः शुकाय, शुको वामदेवाय, वामदेवो मुनिभ्यः, मुनयो मनुभ्यः प्रोचुः। य एवं वेद स स्त्रीहत्यायाः प्रमुच्यते। स वीरहत्यायाः प्रमुच्यते। स ब्रह्महत्यायाः प्रमुच्यते। स महाभयात् प्रमुच्यते। स महादुःखात् प्रमुच्यते। देहान्ते वैकुण्ठमवाप्नोति वैकुण्ठमवाप्नोति। इत्युपनिषत्॥ १६॥

Thus, this fact was explained by lord Nārāyaṇa to lord Brahmā, lord Brahmā to Nārada and the saints like Sanaka etc., Sanaka etc. to Vedavyāsa, Vedavyāsa to Śukadeva, Śukadeva to Vāmadeva, Vāmadeva to the saints and the saints had explained it to the human beings. The person known to this fact is exonerated from the evil of killing his wife, brother, Brāhmaṇa and becomes fearless from all kinds of apprehensions. He is liberated from the trap of the miseries. He attains to Vaikuṇṭha Loka (region of lord Viṣṇu) after his death. Thus, this upaniṣad is concluded.

॥ इति तुलस्युपनिषत् समाप्ता॥

101. CATURVEDOPANIṢAD

चतुर्वेदोपनिषद्

This is a small upaniṣad. A brief detail of the appearance of four Vedas have been given here. Very first, the commencement of the creation has been described. In continuation, appearance of the hymns, rhymes and Veda has been described from the four mouths of Lord Brahmā in posture of meditation which were located in the four directions. The most wide feature of the gigantic person has been elaborated thereafter. At last, the fruits of listening to this upaniṣad has been explained.

ॐ अथातो महोपनिषदमेव तदाहुः। एको ह वै नारायण आसीत्। न ब्रह्मा न ईशानो नापो नाग्निः न वायुः नेमे द्यावापृथिवी न नक्षत्राणि न सूर्यः। स एकाकी नर एव। तस्य ध्यानान्तस्स्थस्य ललाटात् स्वेदोऽपतत्। ता इमा आपः। ता एते नो हिरण्यमयमन्नम्। तत्र ब्रह्मा चतुर्मुखोऽजायत। स ध्यातपूर्वामुखो भूत्वा भूरिति व्याहृतिः गायत्रं छन्द ऋग्वेदः। पश्चिमामुखो भूत्वा भूरिति व्याहृतिस्त्रैष्टुभं छन्दः यजुर्वेदः। उत्तरामुखो भूत्वा भुवरिति व्याहृतिर्जागतं छन्दः सामवेदः। दक्षिणामुखो भूत्वा जनदिति व्याहृतिरानुष्टुभं छन्दोऽथर्ववेदः॥ १॥

Now this great upaniṣad is highlighted. Prior to creation of this universe, only Nārāyaṇa was existed. Neither Brahmā nor Śiva was existed at that time. Besides it nobody like the earth, wind, ether, planet and even sun etc. was present at that time. Only a man (gigantic person) was existed. The gigantic person was sat on penance and his forehead was perspirated while in meditation. This sweating was nothing else but the water. This water is in garb of Hiraṇyamaya food and lord Brahmā holding four mouths was appeared from it. That Brahma sat on meditation facing the east and originated Bhūḥ, Gāyatrī rhyme, Ṛgveda. Similarly, by facing the west, he originated the hymn Bhūḥ, Triṣṭup rhyme and Yajurveda; by facing north, the hymn Bhuvaḥ, Jagati rhyme and Sāmaveda and finally by facing the south he originated 'Janat' hymn (Sambhavatah Janah), Anuṣṭup rhyme and the Atharvaveda.

[The four hymns from the mouth of lord Brahmā has been described here. However, due to some discrimination in the recital, the hymn 'Bhūḥ' has been described twice but Svaḥ is omitted.]

सहस्रशीर्षं देवं सहस्राक्षं विश्वसंभवम्। विश्वतः परमं नित्यं विश्वं नारायणं हरिम्॥ २॥

विश्वमेवेदं पुरुषं तं विश्वमुपजीवति। ऋषिं विश्वेश्वरं देवं समुद्रे तं विश्वरूपिणम्॥ ३॥

पद्मकोशप्रतीकाशं लम्बत्याकोशसन्निभम्। हृदये चाप्यधोमुखं सतस्यत्यैशीत्कराभिश्च॥ ४॥

तस्य मध्ये महानग्निर्विश्वार्चिर्विश्वतोमुखः। तस्य मध्ये वह्निशिखा अणीयोर्ध्वा व्यवस्थिता॥ ५

तस्याः शिखाया मध्ये परमात्मा व्यवस्थितः। स ब्रह्मा स ईशानः सोऽक्षरः परमः स्वराट्॥ ६॥

That immortal god (gigantic person) has thousand heads and one thousand eyes. That supreme god is always omnipresent because this whole universe is originated by him. That god also is renowned with the words like Nārāyaṇa and Hari. This whole universe is living and awakened by virtue of resort to the supreme gigantic person who is residing in the ocean and in universal form. He alone is the master of this world in the form of a holy man. This gigantic person is 'hung' like a cell to the ovary of lotus flower who performs everything by application of his powers. The supreme fire is existed in the middle of him whose flames are blazing all around. In the middle, there is also 'Vahniśikhā'. It is situated over the 'Aṇīya'. That gigantic person or Para Brahma is situated in the middle of that supreme flame. He too is Brahmā, Śiva, Akṣara (Brahma) and self-luminating sovereign god.

य इमां महोपनिषदं ब्राह्मणोऽधीते अश्रोत्रियः श्रोत्रियो भवति। अनुपनीतः उपनीतो भवति। सोऽग्निपूतो भवति। स वायुपूतो भवति। स सूर्यपूतो भवति। स सोमपूतो भवति। स सत्यपूतो भवति। स सर्वैर्देवैर्ज्ञातो भवति। स सर्वेषु तीर्थेषु स्नातो भवति। तेन सर्वैः क्रतुभिरिष्टं भवति। गायत्र्याः षष्टिसहस्त्राणि जप्तानि भवन्ति। इतिहासपुराणानां सहस्त्राणि जप्तानि भवन्ति। प्रणवानामयुतं जप्तं भवति। आचक्षुषः पङ् क्तिं पुनाति। आसप्तमात् पुरुषं पुनाति। जाप्येन अमृतत्वं च गच्छति अमृतत्वं च गच्छति इत्याह भगवान् हिरण्यगर्भः॥७॥

The Brāhmaṇa (devotee) who read this great Upaniṣad becomes 'Śotriya' if he is not. In case, 'Mundane' ceremony is not celebrated, he still becomes entitle to hold the sacrificial thread (Yajñopavīta). He is as holy as the fire, wind, sun, soma and the truth. All gods start realizing him. It should be deemed as if he has visited on all pilgrimages and performed all kinds of offerings as also 'Japa' of Gāyatrī hymn for sixty thousand times and further one thousand times study performed in the history as also in Purāṇas. It will also be deemed that he has already performed 'Japa' of Oṁ for ten thousand times. Such a person becomes so competent as to make sacred to the human communities even by a mere glance. He makes the seven successive generations so enlightened that they perform great deeds. According to lord Hiraṇyagarbha the person doing perseverance of this Upaniṣad definitely attains to the immortality.

देवा ह वै स्वर्गं लोकमायंस्ते देवा रुद्रमपृच्छंस्ते देवा ऊर्ध्वबाहवो रुद्रं स्तुवन्ति। भूस्त्वादिर्मध्यं भुवस्ते स्वस्ते शीर्षं विश्वरूपोऽसि ब्रह्मैकस्त्वं द्विधा त्रिधा शान्तिस्त्वं हुतमहुतं दत्तमदत्तं सर्वमसर्वं विश्वमविश्वं कृतमकृतं परमपरं परायणं च त्वम्। अपाम सोमममृता अभूमागन्म ज्योतिरविदाम देवा नमस्याम धूर्तेरमृतं मृतं मर्त्यं च सोमसूर्यपूर्वजगदधीतं वा यदक्षरं प्राजापत्यं सौम्यं सूक्ष्मं ग्राहं ग्राहेण भावं भावेन सौम्यं सौम्येन सूक्ष्मं सूक्ष्मेण ग्रसति तस्मै महाग्रासाय नमः॥८॥

Once all gods get together in the heaven, started offering psalms to lord Rudra by uplifting hands and asked– "O Lord! Yours origin is Bhūḥ, the middle is Bhuvaḥ and the end is Svaḥ. You are universal. You are only in garb of Brahma, dual in garb of the living soul and Brahma, trio in garb of the living-soul, the Brahma and the illusion as also the supreme soul. You also are the thing already offered (Huta), not offered 'Ahuta', the things given or not given, everything 'Sarva', nothing 'Asarva', the world-non world, performed, unperformed, under control, beyond control and the end. May all of us sip the nectar in garb of Soma. May we obtain the divine flame. O Lord! We salute you and are devotee to you. The immortality, mortality, the earth, soma, sun, the non-world, Akṣara (Adhita), Prājāpatya, modesty and the micro is obtained in seriatim to the spirit, physical intake, cordial and the intuitional intake. Such mightiest god Rudra is saluted.

॥इति चतुर्वेदोपनिषत्समाप्ता॥

102. GĀYATRĪ-RAHASYOPANIṢAD

गायत्रीरहस्योपनिषद्

The great learning of Gāyatrī has been appreciated everywhere in four Vedas, Brāhmaṇas, Upaniṣads, Purāṇas, Smṛtis etc. and its magnificence is taken under the cognisance of great power of Gāyatrī. In this Upaniṣad too, that great hymn and the great power has been disclosed. The commencement of this Upaniṣad has been made in a questionnaire form that contains the questions and answers transacted between saint Yājñavalkya and self-born Brahmā. The ceretum of the appearance of Gāyatrī has been very first given. Gāyatrī and its hymns has been clarified or duly explained in a questionnaire form thereafter. It is the wisest form. For example, the gotra of Gāyatrī, the letter, the foot, the arm-pit, the head, the saint, the rhyme, the power, the limbs, twenty-four powers of twenty-four letters, twenty-four saints for twenty-four letters, twenty-four flowers for twenty-four letters, fatal form of twenty-four sorts of sins, the divine, the abode of divine powers in limbs and organs of the Gāyatrī etc. Finally the Upaniṣad has been concluded by enunciating the special power of destroying the evils.

ॐ स्वस्ति सिद्धम्। ॐ नमो ब्रह्मणे। ॐ नमस्कृत्य याज्ञवल्क्य ऋषिः स्वयंभुवं परिपृच्छति। हे ब्रह्मन् गायत्र्या उत्पत्तिं श्रोतुमिच्छामि। अथातो वसिष्ठः स्वयंभुवं परिपृच्छति। यो ब्रह्मा स ब्रह्मोवाच। ब्रह्मज्ञानोत्पत्तेः प्रकृतिं व्याख्यास्यामः। को नाम स्वयंभूः पुरुष इति। तेनाङ्गुलीमथ्यमानात् सलिलमभवत्। सलिलात् फेनमभवत्। फेनाद्बुद्बुदमभवत्। बुद्बुदादण्डमभवत्। अण्डाद्ब्रह्माभवत्। ब्रह्मणो वायुरभवत्। वायोरग्निरभवत्। अग्नेरोङ्कारोऽभवत्। ओंकाराद्व्याहृतिरभवत्। व्याहृत्याः गायत्र्यभवत्। गायत्र्याः सावित्र्यभवत्। सावित्र्याः सरस्वत्यभवत्। सरस्वत्याः सर्वे वेदा अभवन्। सर्वेभ्यो वेदेभ्यः सर्वे लोका अभवन्। सर्वेभ्यो लोकेभ्यः सर्वे प्राणिनोऽभवन्॥ १॥

May all achieve welfare. Salutation is conveyed to lord Brahmā (knowledge). The saint Yājñavalkya asked lord Brahmā after the salutation so conveyed– "O Brahman! We want to know how Gāyatrī has been originated?" Saint Vasiṣtha also have asked the same from lord Brahmā. Lord Brahmā who is born from the Brahma (knowledge) replied– "The causative nature for the origin of knowledge of Brahma is now explained. Who is the man known as Svayaṁbhuva? He is the same Purāṇa Puruṣa. He has made appear the water by churning through the finger. Thus the froth was arisen from the water, bubble from the froth, egg from the bubble, Brahma from the egg, ear from Brahma, fire from ear, Oṁ from fire, hymn from Oṁ, Gāyatrī from hymn, Sāvitrī from Gāyatrī, Sarasvatī from Sāvitrī, four Vedas from Sarasvatī, all worlds from four Vedas and finally all living-organisms from the worlds.

अथातो गायत्री व्याहृतयश्च प्रवर्तन्ते। का च गायत्री काश्च व्याहृतयः। किं भूः किं भुवः किं सुवः किं महः किं जनः किं तपः किं सत्यं किं तत् किं सवितुः किं वरेण्यं किं भर्गः किं देवस्य किं धीमहि किं धियः किं यः किं नः किं प्रचोदयात्। ॐ भूरिति भुवो लोकः। भुव इत्यन्तरिक्षलोकः। स्वरिति स्वर्गलोकः।

मह इति महर्लोकः। जन इति जनोलोकः। तप इति तपोलोकः। सत्यमिति सत्यलोकः। तदिति तदसौ तेजोमयं तेजोऽ ग्निर्देवता। सवितुरिति सविता सावित्रमादित्यो वै। वरेण्यमित्यत्र प्रजापतिः। भर्ग इत्यापो वै भर्गः। देवस्य इतीन्द्रो देवो द्योतत इति स इन्द्रस्तस्मात् सर्वपुरुषो नाम रुद्रः। धीमहीत्यन्तरात्मा। धिय इत्यन्तरात्मा परः। य इति सदाशिवपुरुषः। नो इत्यस्माकं स्वधर्मे प्रचोदयादिति प्रचोदितकाम इमान् लोकान् प्रत्याश्रयते यः परो धर्म इत्येषा गायत्री॥२॥

A description of Gāyatrī and the hymns is now commences from here. The question arises that who is Gāyatrī and what are the hymn? What is Bhūḥ? What is Bhuvaḥ? What is Svaḥ? What is Mahaḥ? What is Janaḥ? What is Tapaḥ? What is truth? What is Tat? What is Savituḥ? What is Vareṇyam? What is Bhargaḥ? What is Devasya? What is Dhīmahi? What is Dhiyaḥ? What is Yaḥ? What is Naḥ? And what is Pracodayāt? The answer to these questions are that 'Oṁ Bhūḥ' is the world on this earth, Bhvaḥ is the space, Svaḥ is the heaven, Mahaḥ is the world of Mahar, Janaḥ is the world of people. Tapaḥ is the world of ascetics. Satyam is the world of truth. Tat is the fire full of spledour, Savituḥ is the sun, Devasya is lord Indra, who is promulgated by Rudra namely, Sarva Puruṣa symbol of luxuries. Dhīmahi is indicative of internal soul, Dhiyaḥ is indicative of the next eternal soul (the Brahma), Yaḥ is the indicative of Lord Sadāśiva, Naḥ is indicative of its own form i.e. an indicative of this meaning. Thus, all these make cognisance of the perpetual form in the ceretum as already has been described. Pracodayāt is an indicative of the motive and the concept (religion) that provides shelter to all these worlds is Gāyatrī.

सा च किं गोत्रा कत्यक्षरा कति पादा। कति कुक्षयः! कानि शीर्षाणि। सांख्यायनगोत्रा सा चतुर्विंशत्यक्षरा गायत्री त्रिपादा चतुष्पादा। पुनस्तस्याश्चत्वारः पादाः षट् कुक्षिकाः पञ्च शीर्षाणि भवन्ति। के च पादाः काश्च कुक्षयः कानि शीर्षाणि। ऋग्वेदोऽस्याः प्रथमः पादो भवति। यजुर्वेदो द्वितीयः पादः। सामवेदस्तृतीयः पादः। अथर्ववेदश्चतुर्थः पादः। पूर्वा दिक् प्रथमा कुक्षिर्भवति। दक्षिणा द्वितीया कुक्षिर्भवति। पश्चिमा तृतीया कुक्षिर्भवति। उत्तरा चतुर्थी कुक्षिर्भवति। ऊर्ध्वा वै पञ्चमी कुक्षिर्भवति। अधः षष्ठी कुक्षिर्भवति। व्याकरणोऽस्याः प्रथमः शीर्षो भवति। शिक्षा द्वितीयः। कल्पस्तृतीयः। निरुक्तश्चतुर्थः। ज्योतिषामयनमिति पञ्चमः। का दिक् को वर्णः किमायतनं कः स्वरः किं लक्षणं कान्यक्षरदैवतानि क ऋषयः कानि छन्दांसि काः शक्तयः कानि तत्त्वानि के चावयवाः। पूर्वायां भवतु गायत्री। मध्यमायां भवतु सावित्री। पश्चिमायां भवतु सरस्वती। रक्ता गायत्री। श्वेता सावित्री। कृष्णा सरस्वती। पृथिव्यन्तरिक्षं द्यौरायतनानि॥३॥

Further the questions arise– what is the gotra of that Gāyatrī? How many letters it bear? How many feet it has, how many arm-pits and the places of her head and the mind etc. are? An answer to these questions are– Her gotra is 'Sāṁkhyāyan'. It has twenty-four letters, it has three and four feet. Then she has four feet, six arm-pits and five heads. The next questions are– Who are her feet, the arm-pits and the heads? Its answer is that Ṛgveda is its first foot, Yajurveda is the second foot, Sāmaveda is the third foot and Atharvaveda is fourth foot. Her east is the first arm-pit, south is the second arm-pit, west is the third arm-pit and the north is the fourth arm-pit. Similarly, the upward direction is the fifth arm-pit and the downward direction is sixth arm-pit. The grammar is her first head, the education is her second head, the kalpa is her third head, the etymology is her fourth head, the astrology is her fifth head. Again the questions are– Which colour of goddesses are enshrined on the particular direction? What is their scope, what are the sound and characteristics? What are the letters of which those goddesses are mistress? Who are the saints of them? Who are rhymes? Who are powers, elements and their organs? Answers to these questions are– "Gāyatrī is existed in the east direction and she is of red colour. The white colour Sāvitrī is existed in the south, dark colour Sarasvatī in the west and this colour recognition at the time of meditation proves appropriate; the earth, the ether and the heaven are the abodes and the premises of extended form for these trio-powers."

अकारोकारमकाररूपोदात्तादिस्वरात्मिका। पूर्वा सन्ध्या हंसवाहिनी ब्राह्मी। मध्यमा वृषभवाहिनी माहेश्वरी। पश्चिमा गरुडवाहिनी वैष्णवी। पूर्वाह्णकालिका सन्ध्या गायत्री कुमारी रक्ता रक्ताङ्गी रक्तवासिनी रक्तगन्धमाल्यानुलेपनी पाशाङ्कुशाक्षमालाकमण्डलुवरहस्ता हंसारूढा ब्रह्मदैवत्या ऋग्वेदसहिता आदित्यपथगामिनी भूमण्डलवासिनी। मध्याह्नकालिका सन्ध्या सावित्री युवती श्वेताङ्गी श्वेतवासिनी श्वेतगन्धमाल्यानुलेपनी त्रिशूलडमरुहस्ता वृषभारूढा रुद्रदैवत्या यजुर्वेदसहिता आदित्यपथगामिनी भुवोलोके व्यवस्थिता। सायं सन्ध्या सरस्वती वृद्धा कृष्णाङ्गी कृष्णवासिनी कृष्णगन्धमाल्यानुलेपना शङ्खचक्रगदाभयहस्ता गरुडारूढा विष्णुदैवत्या सामवेदसहिता आदित्यपथगामिनी स्वर्गलोकव्यवस्थिता॥ ४॥

That Gāyatrī contains the vowel 'A, U and M' as also 'Svarita' (composite vowel). At the time of thrice recital, she has the form of Brāhmī, rode on Swan in the morning, Maheśvarī, rode on the bull in the noon and Vaiṣṇavī, rode on the eagle (Garuḍa) in the evening. At the time of morning recital, Gāyatrī has reddish complexion, a virgin, reddish organs, wearing red garments, red sandal and garlands, holder of goad, a string (Pāśa), holder of basil garland (Akṣamālā) water-pot (particularly used by ascetics) in her hands as also a hand in the posture of bestowing boons (Varada), rode on the Swan, Brāhmī with divine powers, holder of Ṛgveda, dynamic in the ether as also residing on the earth. At the time of recital in the noon, she is Sāvitrī, a spinster holder of white-organs, white complexion, wearing white garments, smearing white sandals and holding garlands, rode on the bull with the trident and Ḍamaru (a musical instrument particular with lord Śiva), the super god Rudra and holder of Yajurveda. She is dynamic in the ether and particularly resides in the world of sun (Bhuvaḥ). The evening recital is in the form of goddess Sarasvatī. She is old, dark-complexioned, wearing dark garments, smearing an odouring garland in black colour, holding the Śaṅkha, discuss, the Gadā (a heavy weapon), rode on eagle whose super-god is lord Viṣṇu. She holds Sāmaveda, moves through the route of lord sun and resides in the heaven.

अग्निवायुसूर्यरूपाऽऽहवनीयगार्हपत्यदक्षिणाग्निरूपा ऋग्यजुःसामरूपा भूर्भुवः स्वरिति व्याहृतिरूपा प्रातर्मध्याह्नतृतीयसवनात्मिका सत्त्वरजस्तमोगुणात्मिका जाग्रत्स्वप्नसुषुप्तरूपा वसुरुद्रादित्यरूपा गायत्रीत्रिष्टुब्जगतीरूपा ब्रह्मशङ्करविष्णुरूपेच्छाज्ञानक्रियाशक्तिरूपा स्वराड्विराड्वषड्ब्रह्मरूपेति। प्रथममाग्नेयं

द्वितीयं प्राजापत्यं तृतीयं सौम्यं चतुर्थमीशानं पञ्चममादित्यं षष्ठं गार्हपत्यं सप्तमं मैत्रमष्टमं भगदैवतं नवममार्यमणं दशमं सावित्रमेकादशं त्वाष्ट्रं द्वादशं पौष्णं त्रयोदशमैन्द्राग्नं चतुर्दशं वायव्यं पञ्चदशं वामदेवं षोडशं मैत्रावरुणं सप्तदशं भ्रातृव्यमष्टादशं वैष्णवमेकोनविंशं वामनं विंशं वैश्वदेवमेकविंशं रौद्रं द्वाविंशं कौबेरं त्रयोविंशमाश्विनं चतुर्विंशं ब्राह्ममिति प्रत्यक्षरदैवतानि। प्रथमं वासिष्ठं द्वितीयं भारद्वाजं तृतीयं गार्ग्यं चतुर्थमौपमन्यवं पञ्चमं भार्गवं षष्ठं शाण्डिल्यं सप्तमं लौहितमष्टमं वैष्णवं नवमं शातातपं दशमं सनत्कुमार-मेकादशं वेदव्यासं द्वादशं शुकं त्रयोदशं पाराशर्यं चतुर्दशं पौण्ड्रकं पञ्चदशं क्रतुं षोडशं दाक्षं सप्तदशं काश्यपमष्टादशमात्रेयमेकोनविंशमगस्त्यं विंशमौद्दालकमेकविंशमाङ्गिरसं द्वाविंशं नामिकेतुं त्रयोविंशं मौद्गल्यं चतुर्विंशमाङ्गिरसं वैश्वामित्रमिति प्रत्यक्षराणा०मृषयो भवन्ति॥ ५॥

This Gāyatrī is in the form of fire, wind and the sun. She is the trio-fire i.e. Āhavanīya, Gārhapatya and DakṣIṇā. She is in the form of Ṛk, Yajuī and Sāmaveda, the hymns i.e. Bhūḥ, Bhuvaḥ and Svaḥ, the trio-recital i.e. in morning, in noon and in evening. She is of three properties i.e. Satva, Rajas and Tamas, dormant, dreaming, awakened, Vasu, Rudra and the Sun. She is in the form of trio-rhymes i.e. Gāyatrī, Triṣṭup and Jagati etc. She is in the form of lord Brahmā, Śiva and lord Viṣṇu. She is in the form of the ambition, knowledge and power of action as also in the form of trio-Brahma i.e. Svarāṭ, Virāṭ and Vaṣaṭ. The god of the first letter, to this Gāyatrī hymn is the fire, Prajāpati is of the second, the moon is of the third, Īṣana is of fourth, the Sun is of fifth, the fire Gārhapatya is of sixth, Maitra of the seventh, the Bhaga of the eighth, Aryama is of ninth, Savitā is of tenth, Tvaṣṭra is of eleventh, Paųṣa is of twelfth, Indrāgni is of the thirteenth, the wind is of fourteenth, the god Vāma is of fifteenth, Maitra Varuṇa is of sixteenth, Bhrātṛavya of the seventeenth, lord Viṣṇu is of eighteenth, lord Vāmana is of the nineteenth, the god Vaiśva is of the twentieth, god Rudra is of twenty-first, lord Kubera (wealth-god) is of twenty-second, Aśvinikumara is of the twenty-third and lord Brahmā is of the twenty-fourth letter. (Now twenty-four saints to these twenty-four letters are described. The saint to its first letter is Vasiṣtha, of second Bharadvāja, of third Gārgya, of fourth Upamanyu, of fifth Bhṛgu, of sixth Śāṇḍilya, of seventh Lohita, of eighth lord Viṣṇu, of ninth Śatātapa, of tenth Sanatkumāra, of eleventh Vedavyāsa, of twelfth Śukadeva, of thirteenth Pārāśara, of fourteenth Pauṇḍraka, of fifteenth Kratu, of sixteenth Dakṣa, of seventeenth Kaśyapa, of eighteenth Atri, of nineteenth Agastya, of twentieth Uddālaka, of twenty-first Āṅgirasa, of twenty-second Nāmiketu, of twenty-third Mudgala and of twenty-fourth Viśvāmitra who was born in the clan of Āṅgira. Thus these are the twenty-four saints separately to each and every letter.

गायत्रीत्रिष्टुब्जगत्यनुष्टुप्पङ्क्तिबृहत्युष्णिगदितिरिति त्रिरावृत्तेन छन्दांसि प्रतिपाद्यन्ते। प्रह्लादिनी प्रज्ञा विश्वभद्रा विलासिनी प्रभा शान्ता मा कान्तिः स्पर्शा दुर्गा सरस्वती विरूपा विशालाक्षी शालिनी व्यापिनी विमला तमोऽपहारिणी सूक्ष्मावयवा पद्मालया विरजा विश्वरूपा भद्रा कृपा सर्वतोमुखीति चतुर्विंशतिशक्तयो निगद्यन्ते। पृथिव्यप्तेजोवाय्वाकाशगन्धरसरूपस्पर्शशब्दवाक्यानि पादपायूपस्थत्वक्चक्षुःश्रोत्रजिह्वाघ्राण-मनोबुद्ध्यहङ्कारचित्तज्ञानानीति प्रत्यक्षराणां तत्त्वानि प्रतीयन्ते। चम्पकातसीकुङ्कुमपिङ्गलेन्द्रनीलाग्नि-

प्रभोद्यत्सूर्यविद्युत्तारकसरोजगौरमरकतशुक्लकुन्देन्दुशङ्खपाण्डुनेत्रनीलोत्पलचन्दनागुरुकस्तूरीगोरोचन (मल्लिका केतकी) घनसाररान्निभं प्रत्यक्षरमनुस्मृत्य समस्तपातकोपपातकमहापातकागम्यागमनगोहत्या-ब्रह्महत्याभ्रूणहत्यावीरहत्यापुरुषहत्याऽऽजन्मकृतहत्या स्त्रीहत्यागुरुहत्यापितृहत्याप्राण हत्याचराचरहत्याऽभक्ष्य-भक्षणप्रतिग्रहस्वकर्मविच्छेदनस्वाम्यार्तिहीनकर्मकरणपरधनापहरणशूद्रान्नभोजनशत्रुमारणचण्डालीगमनादिसमस्त पापहरणार्थं संस्मरेत्॥ ६॥

The hymns with their three frequencies have been laid down as Triṣṭup, Jagati, Anuṣṭup, Paṅkti, Bṛhati, Uṣṇik. The description of twenty-four powers with Gāyatrī is– Prahlādinī, Prajñā, Viśvabhadrā (that does welfare to the whole universe), Vilāsinī (enjoyer of luxury), Prabhā (light), Śāntā (peace-giver), Mā, Kānti (radiance), Sparśā, Durgā, Sarasvatī, Virūpā, Viśālākṣī, Śālinī, Vyāpinī, Vimalā, Tamopahāriṇī (that removes the ignorance/darkness), Sūkṣmāvayavā (slim), Padmālayā, Virajā, Viśvarūpā, Bhadrā, Kṛpā and Sarvatomukhī. The twenty-four elements for every letter separately in Gāyatrī are the earth, the water, the splendour, the wind, the ether, the smell, the essence, complexion, touch, word, speech, feet, anus and penis etc. Further the skin, the eyes, the ears, the tongue, the nose, the mind, the wit, the heart, the ego and the knowledge. (The flowers for every letter out of twenty-four letters in Gāyatrī separately are)– Campaka, Atasī (a blue colour flower), Kuṁkuma, Piṅgala, Indranīla, Agniprabhā, Udyatsūrya (sunflower), Vidyuttāraka, Lotus, Gaura, Markata, Śukla, Kunda, Indu, Śaṅkh, Pāṇḍunetra, Nīlakamala, Sandal, Aguru, Musk-flower, Gorocana, Mallikā, Ketakī and Karpūra. (Now the twenty-four kinds of evils are–) The evils, petty evils, heinous evils, Agamyāgamana (vagina relation made to which that should not be), cow-slaughtering, murder of Brāhmaṇa, abortion, murder of brother, murder of person, murders committed since many previous years, murder of wife, murder of teacher, murder of father, suicide, murder of the living-organisms either movable or immovable etc. The evil of murder arising due to eating which are prohibited, evil due to accepting donation, abandonment of ones duty, the evils committed in the form of not comply with the duties assigned by the owner (employer), evil committed by thefting other's wealth, the evil attached due to entertaining food cooked by the obnoxious person (Śūdra), sin due to attack on enemy and the sin committed by enjoying cohesion with the wife of Cāṇḍāla etc. For exonerating from all these sins one should always keep in mind his activities.

मूर्धा ब्रह्मा शिखान्तो विष्णुर्ललाटं रुद्रश्चक्षुषी चन्द्रादित्यौ कर्णौ शुक्रबृहस्पती नासापुटे अश्विनौ दन्तोष्ठावुभे सन्ध्ये मुखं मरुतः स्तनौ वस्वादयो हृदयं पर्जन्य उरमाकाशो नाभिरग्निः कटिरिन्द्राग्नी जघनं प्राजापत्यमूरू कैलासमूलं जानुनी विश्वेदेवौ जङ्घे शिशिरः गुल्फानि पृथिवीवनस्पत्यादीनि नखानि महती अस्थीनि नवग्रहा असृक्केतुर्मांसमृतुसन्धयः कालद्वयास्फालनं संवत्सरो निमेषोऽहोरात्रमिति वाग्देवीं गायत्रीं शरणमहं प्रपद्ये॥ ७॥

I attain to shelter of Gāyatrī who is enriched with the power of speech, whose head is Brahmā (abode of knowledge), the braid is lord Viṣṇu, forehead is lord Rudra, eyes are the sun and moon, ears are the Venus and the Jupiter (nostrils are Aśvini kumāra), the lips are both conjoining point of the day (Sandhyā), mouth is the wind, breast is Vasu, chest is the cloud, stomach is the ether, the navel is the fire, the waist is Indrāgni, the leg is Prājāpatya, the thighs are the basic places of Kailāsa, both knees are the god of universe, the calves are ŚIśira, ankles are the vegetation of earth, the nails are the supreme element, the bones are nine planets, the intestines are Ketu (demon tail), flesh is the joint of seasons, the ear indicative of the movement of both times (Kāla) is Samvatsara and wink is the day and night.

य इदं गायत्रीरहस्यमधीते तेन क्रतुसहस्रमिष्टं भवति। य इदं गायत्री रहस्यमधीते दिवसकृतं पापं नाशयति। प्रातर्मध्याह्नयोः षण्मासकृतानि पापानि नाशयति। सायं प्रातरधीयानो जन्मकृतं पापं नाशयति। य इदं गायत्रीरहस्यं ब्राह्मणः पठेत् तेन गायत्र्याः षष्टिसहस्रलक्षाणि जप्तानि भवन्ति। सर्वान् वेदानधीतो भवति। सर्वेषु तीर्थेषु स्नातो भवति। अपेयपानात् पूतो भवति। अभक्ष्यभक्षणात् पूतो भवति। वृषलीगमनात् पूतो भवति। अब्रह्मचारी ब्रह्मचारी भवति। पंक्तिषु सहस्रपानात् पूतो भवति। अष्टौ ब्राह्मणान् ग्राहयित्वा ब्रह्मलोकं स गच्छति। इत्याह भगवान् ब्रह्मा॥८॥

The man who recites this mystery of Gāyatrī should deem that he has performed many thousands offerings. By virtue of the recital of this mystery, all sins committed in the day due to inadvertence are decayed. The person who recites this mystery in the morning and the noon is exonerated from all sins committed in the period of six months viz., be becomes innocent. The evils committed in course of the cycle of pre-births are absolutely destroyed who recites this daily in morning as also in the evening. The recital of this mystery of Gāyatrī by any of the Brāhmaṇa should be treated that he has made Japas (silent recital) of Gāyatrī hymn to the extent sixty thousand lakhs. Again it should be deemed that he has duly persued all four Vedas and made pilgrimage to all the holy places. He is exonerated from the evil which is attached with his personality due to intoxication. Further he is exonerated from the evil of taking prohibited diet, enjoying intercourse with the women of inferior caste (Śūdra) and inspite of non-celibate his personality shines with the splendour of a celibate person. Irrespective of his being intake of prohibited things in the queue or commune not less than one thousand times, he still becomes sacred by virtue of recital of this mystery. Lord Brahmā had told saint Yājñavalkya that such a devotee to Gāyatrī hymns attains to and arise at the abode of Brahmā as a grace for making eight Brāhmaṇas well-explained to this mystery of Gāyatrī.

॥इति गायत्रीरहस्योपनिषत् समाप्ता॥

103. PRAṆAVA-UPANIṢAD

प्रणवोपनिषद्

The syllable of Praṇava i.e. Oṁ has been described in this Upaniṣad as its name already symbolises. The syllable Oṁ has been called the expression of the perfect knowledge in letters form. The consistency of three gods, three times, three fires and three Vedas has been made with the three moras of this syllable i.e. a, u, m. It has been said that the syllable Oṁ is circulated in seventy-two thousand nerves including the nerves of Iḍā, Piṅgalā and Suṣumnā. Finally it has been said that the devotee attains the immortality who establish their perfect identity with the Brahma by means of the syllable Oṁ.

पुरस्ताद्ब्रह्मणस्तस्य विष्णोरद्भुतकर्मणः। रहस्यं ब्रह्मविद्याया धृताग्निं संप्रचक्षते।।१।।

Now the mystery of the Brahma learning (Brahma Vidyā) that holds the fire capable enough in burning the accumulated account of the deeds and equipped with all excellent deeds of lord Viṣṇu in the form of Brahma is now described.

ओमित्येकाक्षरं ब्रह्म यदुक्तं ब्रह्मवादिभिः। शरीरं तस्य वक्ष्यामि स्थानकालत्रयं तथा।।२।।

The persons learned to Brahma has said the syllable Oṁ an unique and immortal Brahma. His body, the place and the trio-time i.e. the past, the present and the future is now described.

तत्र देवास्त्रयः प्रोक्ता लोका वेदास्त्रयोऽग्नयः। तिस्रो मात्रार्धमात्रा च प्रत्यक्षस्य शिवस्य तत्।।३।।

In the syllable Oṁ in the garb of Brahma, the three gods (Brahmā, Viṣṇu and Maheśa), three worlds (Bhūḥ, Bhuvaḥ, Svaḥ), three Vedas (Ṛk, Yajus, Sāma), three fires (Gārhapatya, Dakṣiṇāgni, Āhavanīya), three complete moras and one half mora (a, u, m and Anusvāra) are embedded. It is his apparent form of welfare (Śiva).

ऋग्वेदो गार्हपत्यं च पृथिवी ब्रह्म एव च। अकारस्य शरीरं तु व्याख्यातं ब्रह्मवादिभिः।।४।।

The persons learned to Brahma have told the Ṛgveda, the earth, the Gārhapatya fire and lord Brahmā as in the body form of 'Akāra' in three letters of the syllable Oṁ.

यजुर्वेदोऽन्तरिक्षं च दक्षिणाग्निस्तथैव च। विष्णुश्च भगवान् देव उकारः परिकीर्तितः।।५।।

The Yajurveda, the space, the southern fire and lord Viṣṇu are the elements that are described in the garb of 'Ukāra' in the three letters of the syllable Oṁ.

सामवेदस्तथा द्यौश्चाहवनीयस्तथैव च। ईश्वरः परमो देवो मकारः परिकीर्तितः।।६।।

The Sāmaveda, the world of Sun, the fire, Āhavanīya and the supreme god 'Śiva' are described in garb of 'Makāra' in the three letters of Oṁ.

सूर्यमण्डलमाभाति ह्यकारश्चन्द्रमध्यगः। उकारश्चन्द्रसंकाशस्तस्य मध्ये व्यवस्थितः।।७।।

The form of the orbit of Sun is the form of 'Akāra' in the letters of Oṁ. The form of the orbit of moon is described as 'Ukāra' and it is located in the middle of Oṁ.

मकारश्चाग्निसंकाशो विधूमो विद्युतोपमः। तिस्रो मात्रास्तथा ज्ञेयाः सोमसूर्याग्नितेजसः॥८॥

The last letter 'Makāra' of Oṁ is in the form of that fire which is without smoke and analogous to the lightening. The three moras of the syllable Oṁ should be considered as the splendour of the moon, the sun and the fire.

शिखा च दीपसंकाशा यस्मिन्नु परिवर्तते। अर्धमात्रा तथा ज्ञेया प्रणवस्योपरि स्थिता॥९॥

The ascendant flame of the lamp is like the half-moon on the syllable Oṁ i.e. the half mora.

पद्मसूत्रनिभा सूक्ष्मा शिखाभा दृश्यते परा। नासादिसूर्यसंकाशा सूर्यं हित्वा तथापरम्॥१०॥

The light of the minutest upper end of the flame analogous to the tube of a lotus is seen in the region of mind. This second flame is located by holding the splendour analogous to the Sun from the nostril by penetrating the orbit of the sun.

द्विसप्ततिसहस्राणि नाडिभिसत्वा तु मूर्धनि। वरदं सर्वभूतानां सर्वं व्याप्यैव तिष्ठति॥११॥

That upper flame (the half mora of the syllable Oṁ) in garb of the fire provides all living-organisms the life through the seventy-two thousand nerves and it is located by covering all these nerves.

कांस्यघण्टानिनादः स्याद्यदा लिप्यति शान्तये। ओङ्कारस्तु तथा योज्यः श्रुतये सर्वमिच्छति॥१२॥

That devotee attains peace proxy to the emancipation and he listens to the sound analogous to the gong made of bronze at that time. This is the form of the syllable Oṁ. All devotees wish to listen this form with the sound.

यस्मिन् स लीयते शब्दस्तत्परं ब्रह्म गीयते। सोऽमृतत्वाय कल्पते सोऽमृतत्वाय कल्पते इति॥१३॥

The devotee who is engrossed in the vibration of the Oṁ syllable, becomes in the form of Brahma himself. It is definite that he attains the immortality at this stage.

॥इति प्रणवोपनिषत्समाप्ता॥

104. NĪLARUDRA-UPANIṢAD

नीलरुद्रोपनिषद्

॥शान्तिपाठः॥

ॐ भद्रं कर्णेभिः .... इति शान्तिः॥

This upaniṣad is related to the tradition of Atharvaveda. There are three parts in this upaniṣad. The Rudra form of Nīlakaṇṭha Rudra has been described in this upaniṣad.

In the first part of this upaniṣad, the Rudra form (i.e. the weeping posture) of lord Rudra has been described. He has been prayed for cooling down such dreadful form and to appear in the welfare form. In the second part, the Gopāla (Kṛṣṇa) form of lord Rudra has been depicted and he has been addressed as the lord who holds the crown of peacock wing. He has been told as Indra also in somewhere other places. The most mighty weapons of lord Rudra has been also made a subject of elucidation. In the third part, the form of Nīlakaṇṭha has been duly explained. Lord Rudra has been prayed addressing as Kedāreśvara, Virupākṣa (Trinetra) etc. names given to him according to the specific characteristics of lord Rudra and he has been prayed as the lord who had once drunk the dreadful poison with an intention to protect all the living-organisms of this universe. Thus, with these contents, this upaniṣad has been concluded.

॥प्रथमःखण्डः॥

अपश्यं त्वावरोहन्तं दिवितः पृथिवीमवः। अपश्यं रुद्रमस्यन्तं नीलग्रीवं शिखण्डिनम्॥ १॥

दिव उग्रोऽवारुक्षत् प्रत्यस्थाद्भूम्यामधि। जनासः पश्यतेमं नीलग्रीवं विलोहितम्॥ २॥

एष एत्यवीरहा रुद्रो जलासभेषजीः। वित्तेऽक्षेममनीनशद्वातीकारोऽप्येतु ते॥ ३॥

I saw you, coming down from divine abode (heaven) upon the earth here, I saw the shooting Rudra, the dark-necked, curly-haired. From heaven he descended on dreadful, and planted his feet on the earth; O people! Have a sight at him bright-red and the dark-necked. Lord Rudra destroys the evils in garb of disease by insertion within the medicines existed in the water. He is the basis of life for all living-organisms. May lord Rudra come to you for destroying the mishappenings and supplying with the means which are not yet available.

नमस्ते भवभामाय नमस्ते भवमन्यवे। नमस्ते अस्तु बाहुभ्यामुतो त इषवे नमः॥ ४॥

यामिषुं गिरिशन्त हस्ते बिभर्ष्यस्तवे। शिवां गिरित्र तां कुरु मा हिꣳसीः पुरुषं जगत्॥ ५॥

O lord Rudra! salutation to your furious complexion. O Nīlakaṇṭha Rudra! Salutation to your arms, and salutation to your arrows too. O rejoincer-in-hills! The arrow, which, you hold in your hand to shoot, make it gracious to us, hill-guardian, Please don't destroy our near and dears by blowing that arrow (do not strike my people).

शिवेन वचसा त्वा गिरिशाच्छा वदामसि। यथा नः सर्वमिज्जगदयक्ष्मं सुमना असत्॥६॥

या त इषुः शिवतमा शिवं बभूव ते धनुः। शिवा शरव्या या तव तया नो मृड जीवसे॥७॥

O Dweller on the Mountain, we salute you with auspicious hymn, by the virtue of that the whole world will become favourable to us and we will be free from all kinds of pain. Your kindest arrow and your gracious bow, also your gracious bow-shot, mercy on us, so that we may live.

या ते रुद्र शिवा तनूरघोराऽपापकाशिनी। तया नस्तन्वा शंतमया गिरिशन्ताभिचाकशत्॥८॥ असौ यस्ताम्रो अरुण उत बभ्रुर्विलोहितः। ये चेमे रुद्रा अभितो दिक्षु श्रिताः सहस्रशोऽवैषां हेड ईमहे॥९॥

With your gracious appearance, not terrible, not harmful, with your most wholesome appearance, O mountain-dweller, show yourself to us. The one who shines, dark and red, and brownish and in blazing red, the thousands of Rudras darting to all sides around, I beg their fury away from us.

॥द्वितीयः खण्डः॥

अपश्यं त्वावरोहन्तं नीलग्रीवं विलोहितम्। उत त्वा गोपा अदृशन्नुत त्वोदहार्यः॥१॥

उत त्वा विश्वा भूतानि तस्मै दृष्टाय ते नमः। नमो अस्तु नीलशिखण्डाय सहस्राक्षाय वाजिने॥२॥

They saw you descending with a dark neck, in blazing red. They saw you, the cowherds, and the women fetching water, Yea, everybody saw you. Salutation to you, whom they saw. Salutation to him, the dark-haired one, who is the thousand-eyed, comes as a hero, and to all his legions too. Let me pay a tribute of salutation.

अथो ये अस्य सत्वानस्तेभ्योऽहमकरं नमः। नमांसि त आयुधायानातताय धृष्णवे॥३॥

उभाभ्यामकरं नमो बाहुभ्यां तव धन्वने। प्रमुञ्च धन्वनस्त्वमुभयोरार्त्नियोर्ज्याम्॥४॥

O lord Rudra! We salute all your weapons many times which are most powerful however of no use this time. We convey our salute with clasping hands to your grand bow. Please take out the string of your bow for the rival king as also for whom you favour viz., remove even the possibility of the war by cooling down the temperament.

याश्च ते हस्त इषवः परा ता भगवो वप। अवतत्य धनुस्त्वꣳ सहस्राक्ष शतेषुधे॥५॥

निशीर्य शल्यानां मुखा शिवो नः शंभुराभर। विज्यं धनुः शिखण्डिनो विशल्यो बाणवाꣳउत॥६॥

Please turn back in rest to the arrow which has been taken out by you for its application in the war. O thousand eyed one! Your bow in hundred quivers break off your arrows and bring us help. His bow is now stringless, His quiver without an arrow, His missiles have disappeared, Bliss-bringer is his sheath of sword.

अनेशन्नस्येषव आभुरस्य निषङ्गथिः। परि ते धन्वनो हेतिरस्मान्वृणक्तु विश्वतः॥७॥

अथो य इषुधिस्तवारे अस्मिन्निधेहि तम्। या ते हेतिर्मीढुष्टम हस्ते बभूव ते धनुः॥८॥

May the missile shooting from your bow pass by us in all directions. Indeed, loosen your quiver itself and keep it far away from us.

Or rather take up as weapon your bow, O prosperous god, with it as defender from diseases to protect us from all sides.

तया त्वं विश्वतो अस्मानयक्ष्मया परिब्भुज। नमो अस्तु सर्पेभ्यो ये के च पृथिवीमनु॥ ९॥

ये अन्तरिक्षे ये दिवि तेभ्यः सर्पेभ्यो नमः। ये वाभिरोचने दिवि ये च सूर्यस्य रश्मिषु॥ १०॥

येषामप्सु सदस्कृतं तेभ्यः सर्पेभ्यो नमः। या इषवो यातुधानानां ये वा वनस्पतीनाम्।

ये वाऽवटेषु शेरते तेभ्यः सर्पेभ्यो नमः॥ ११॥

Salutation to the snakes also, to such as are on the earth, and also to the snakes in atmosphere, also salutation to those in heaven.

Those in the radiant regions of heaven, those too, that are in the sun's rays, and those that live in the watery abyss, salutation to those snakes too.

Salutation to theoe snakes too, who are as arrows of the imps shoot down from trees above, and those who nest in earth-holes.

॥तृतीयः खण्डः॥

यः स्वजनान्नीलग्रीवो यः स्वजनान्हरिः। कल्माषपुच्छमोषधे जम्भयोताश्वरुन्धति॥ १॥

He who is the Blue-necked god (*Śiva*) to his people, He who is quite Hari (*Viṣṇu*) to his own, Him with a many-coloured tail, O healing her, Quick grind to pieces, Arundhati.

बभ्रुश्च बभ्रुकर्णश्च नीलग्रीवश्च यः शिवः। शर्वेण नीलकण्ठेन भवेन मरुतां पिता॥ २॥

The [goblin] is brown and brown-eared. But with a circle of black neck is Śiva, through him, Śarva, the black-haired, through Bhava, who the father (read *pitrā*) of the winds is.

विरूपाक्षेण बभ्रुणा वाचं वदिष्यतो हतः। शर्व नीलशिखण्ड वीर कर्मणि कर्मणि॥ ३॥

Through him with eyes enormous, strike [read : *hata*] by the brown, him who only speaks a word, through him wholly dark-haired at work, a hero's work.

इमामस्य प्राशं जहि येनेदं विभजामहे। नमो भवाय। नमश्शर्वाय। नमः कुमाराय शत्रवे। नमः सभाप्रपादिने। यस्याश्वतरौ द्विसरौ गर्दभावभितस्सरौ। तस्मै नीलशिखण्डाय नमः। नीलशिखण्डाय नमः॥ ४॥

Check the demand that he makes, so that we could share it here. Salutation to Śiva, salutation to Śarva. Salutation to him, the ever-young fighter! Salutation to him, the black-haired, when he comes to the assembly and lets his fawn-coloured mules, and asses graze around. Salutation to him, the black-haired, when he comes to the assembly, when he comes to the assembly.

ॐ भद्रं कर्णेभिः .... इति शान्तिः॥

॥इति नीलरुद्रोपनिषत्समाप्ता॥

105. ĀŚRAMOPANIṢAD

आश्रमोपनिषद्

This Upaniṣad is most important when we analyse it with the weightage of content. It is related to Athravaveda. The provision of Āśramas i.e. celibate, couple, past-couple, and reclusion have been explained consisting its all aspects and the disciplines in a brief manner. The four hymns tell about four Āśramas.

॥शान्तिपाठः॥

ॐ भद्रं कर्णेभिः ....इति शान्तिः॥

अथातश्चत्वार आश्रमाः षोडशभेदा भवन्ति। तत्र ब्रह्मचारिणश्चतुर्विधा भवन्ति गायत्रो ब्राह्मणः प्रजापत्यो बृहन्निति। य उपनयनादूर्ध्वं त्रिरात्रमक्षारलवणाशी गायत्रीमन्त्रे स गायत्रः। योऽष्टाचत्वारिंशद्वर्षाणि वेदब्रह्मचर्यं चरेत्प्रतिवेदं द्वादश वा यावद्ग्रहणान्तं वा वेदस्य स ब्राह्मणः। स्वदारनिरत ऋतुकालाभिगामी सदा परदारवर्जी प्राजापत्यः। अथवा चतुर्विंशतिवर्षाणि गुरुकुलवासी ब्राह्मणोऽष्टाचत्वारिंशद्वर्षवासी च प्राजापत्यः। आ प्रायणाद्गुरोरपरित्यागी नैष्ठिको बृहन्निति॥ १॥

There are four Āśramas (modes of life) with their sixteen subclasses. There are four kinds of Brahmacāriṇas– Gāyatra, Brāhmaṇa, Prājāpatya and Bṛhan. Who remains occupied with Gāyatrī-mantra after the sacrificial thread ceremony unto three nights and without taking salt in the food; is called Gāyatra. One who keeps himself busy on the study of Vedas upto fourty-eight years of his life in celibacy and allocates twelve years period for the study of a Vedas and who observes celibacy until the due knowledge on Veda acquired; is called Brāhmaṇa. One who copulates with wife only in Ṛtukāla (the time of a woman's menstrual discharge) and doesn't establish sexual relation with the females else his wife is called Prājāpatya. Or also– Who resides in the house of his teacher upto twenty-four years is called Brāhmaṇa and who resides for fourty-eight years is called Prājāpatya. The celibate who is quite perfect and doesn't leave his teacher throughout life is called Bṛhan.

गृहस्था अपि चतुर्विधा भवन्ति वार्त्ताकवृत्तयः शालीनवृत्तयो यायावरा घोरसंन्यासिकाश्चेति। तत्र वार्त्ताकवृत्तयः कृषिगोरक्षवाणिज्यमगर्हितमुपयुञ्जानाः शतसंवत्सराभिः क्रियाभिर्यजन्त आत्मानं प्रार्थयन्ते। शालीनवृत्तयो यजन्तो न याजयन्तोऽधीयाना नाध्यापयन्तो ददतो न प्रतिगृह्णन्तः शतसंवत्सराभिः क्रियाभिर्यजन्त आत्मानं प्रार्थयन्ते। यायावरा यजन्तो याजयन्तोऽधीयाना अध्यापयन्तो ददतः प्रतिगृह्णन्तः शतसंवत्सराभिः क्रियाभिर्यजन्त आत्मानं प्रार्थयन्ते। घोरसंन्यासिका उद्धृतपरिपूताभिरद्भिः कार्यं कुर्वन्तः प्रतिदिवसमाहृतोञ्छवृत्तिमुपयुञ्जानाः शतसंवत्सराभिः क्रियाभिर्यजन्त आत्मानं प्रार्थयन्ते॥ २॥

Also the Gṛhasthas (householders) are of four kinds. These are Vārttāka-vṛtti, Śālīna-vṛtti (modesty), Yāyāvaras and the Ghora-saṁnyāsikas. Those are Vārttāka-vṛttis (living on agriculture) who engaged in agriculture, animal husbandry and the business permitted under the prevalent law of the country and do the worship of Soul by organising the offerings upto hundred years of their life. Śālīna-vṛttis (living a modest life) are they, who arrange offering the messiness but they do not offer on behalf of others. They study but doesn't teach others. They provide others with gift but doesn't receive any. Thus they worship the soul engaging themselves in offering upto hundred years. Yāyāvaras (having no fixed abode) are the couple who do offering and make others to do the same. They read and make others to read. They get and give the gifts. Thus they worship the soul by performing sacrificial acts upto hundred years. The Ghora-saṁnyāsins are they who perform their acts taking the pure water only, survive on the grains fallen on the ground picked up every day. Thus, they worship the soul by performing the offerings upto hundred years.

वानप्रस्था अपि चतुर्विधा भवन्ति वैखानसा उदुम्बरा बालखिल्याः फेनपाश्चेति। तत्र वैखानसा अकृष्ट पच्यौषधिवनस्पतिभिर्ग्रामबहिष्कृताभिरग्निपरिचरणं कृत्वा पञ्चमहायज्ञ क्रियां निर्वर्तयन्त आत्मानं प्रार्थयन्ते। उदुम्बराः प्रातरुत्थाय यां दिशमभिप्रेक्षन्ते तदाहृतोदुम्बरबदरनीवारश्यामाकैरग्निपरिचरणं कृत्वा पञ्चमहायज्ञक्रियां निर्वर्तयन्त आत्मानं प्रार्थयन्ते। बालखिल्या जटाधराश्चीरचर्मवल्कलपरिवृताः कार्तिक्यां पौर्णमास्यां पुष्पफलमुत्सृजन्तः शेषानष्टौ मासान् वृत्त्युपार्जनं कृत्वाऽग्निपरिचरणं कृत्वा पञ्चमहायज्ञक्रियां निर्वर्तयन्त आत्मानं प्रार्थयन्ते। फेनपा उन्मत्तकाः शीर्णपर्णफलभोजिनो यत्र यत्र वसन्तोऽग्निपरिचरणं कृत्वा पञ्चमहायज्ञक्रियां निर्वर्तयन्त आत्मानं प्रार्थयन्ते॥ ३॥

The past-couple āśrama (Vānaprastha) is also of four kinds. These are Vaikhānas, Udumbara, Bālakhilya and Phenapa. The Vaikhānas person survive on the cereals self-grown and the medicines and vegetation's duly matured by expelled or refused by the villagers. They do Pañca Mahāyajña and thus worship the Soul. Udumbara are the persons who get up early in the morning and perform the Pañca Mahāyajña by offering the Udumbara, Badara, Nīvāra etc. as the material. The Bālakhilyas are the persons who had matted hair, put on the hide of animals and the bark of trees as cloths, take as food the flowers and the fruits upto four months, abandon the accumulated flowers and fruits on the full moon day in Kārtika month. The rest of eight months they earn for their living and perform the Pañca Mahāyajña. The Phenap are the persons who do the worship of soul by using the torn leaves and fruits like a man suffering from insane. They live wherever they get the space and thus do the worship of soul by performing the Pañca Mahāyajña.

परिव्राजका अपि चतुर्विधा भवन्ति कुटीचका बहूदका हंसाः परमहंसाश्चेति। तत्र कुटीचराः स्वपुत्रगृहेषु भिक्षाचर्यं चरन्त आत्मानं प्रार्थयन्ते। बहूदकास्त्रिदण्डकमण्डलुशिक्यपक्षजलपवित्रपात्रपादुकासन-शिखायज्ञोपवीतकौपीनकाषायवेषधारिणः साधुवृत्तेषु ब्राह्मणकुलेषु भैक्षाचर्यं चरन्त आत्मानं प्रार्थयन्ते। हंसा एकदण्डधराः शिखावर्जिता यज्ञोपवीतधारिणः शिक्यकमण्डलुहस्ता ग्रामैकरात्रवासिनो नगरे तीर्थेषु पञ्चरात्रं वसन्त एकरात्रद्विरात्रकृच्छ्रचान्द्रायणादि चरन्त आत्मानं प्रार्थयन्ते। परमहंसा नदण्डधरा मुण्डाः कन्थाकौपीनवाससोऽव्यक्तलिङ्गा अव्यक्ताचारा अनुन्मत्ता उन्मत्तवदाचरन्तस्त्रिदण्डकमण्डलु शिक्यपक्षजल-

पवित्रपात्रपादुकासनशिखायज्ञोपवीतानां त्यागिनः शून्यागारदेवगृहवासिनो न तेषां धर्मो नाधर्मो न चानृतं सर्वंसहा:सर्वसमा: समलोष्टाश्मकाञ्चना यथोपपन्नचातुर्वर्ण्यभैक्षाचर्यं चरन्त आत्मानं मोक्षयन्त आत्मानं मोक्षयन्त इति॥४॥

The recluses are also of four kinds. The first are called Kuṭīcaka, the second Bahūdaka, the third Haṁsa and the fourth Paramahaṁsa. Kuṭīcaka are the recluse who do meditation on Soul by surviving on alms from the houses of their sons etc. Bahūdaka are the recluse who meditate on the element of soul by putting the brown apparels, the nicker (Laṅgoti), sacrificial thread, braid, a seat, the slippers, a vessel for water, a bag, Kamaṇḍala and a trident and surviving on alms from the houses of good Brāhmaṇas. The Haṁsa are the recluse who hold a stick, a carry bag, the sacrificial thread and Kamaṇḍala. They do not grow the braid on their head and hold only a stick. They live for a night in a village and for five nights in city and pilgrim place. They do meditation on the element of soul by observing one or two nights in the fast namely Kṛcchra-Cāndrāyaṇa etc. Parama Haṁsa are the recluse who doesn't hold the stick, clean their hair from the head and hold Kantha and Kaupīna. Their penis (liṅga) is unseen and they always remain silent and stable. They behave like the intoxicants while they never use the intoxications. They abandon the trident, Kamaṇḍala, a carry bag for collecting alms, the holy pot of water, slipper, seat, braid and the sacrificial thread etc. They live in a barren house or the abode of god (Devālaya). The good or bad and the truth or false has no meaning for them. They bear with everything, they see equally to all the deem, do distinction between a stone, a lump of clay and the gold. They live on alms given by all four Varṇas and always live in contentment. They make free the soul from the tie and do all measure to liberate the soul.

ॐ भद्रं कर्णेभि ....इति शान्तिः॥

॥इति आश्रमोपनिषत्समाप्ता॥

106. NṚSIṀHAṢAṬCAKRA-UPANIṢAD

नृसिंहषट्चक्रोपनिषद्

This is smallest upaniṣad when we analyse its contents. This upaniṣad has been come into existence as a result of the questions and answers taken place between the Gods and the Prajāpati. Thus, it is in the form of a questionnaire. The gods one raised their curiosity regarding the 'Narasiṁha Cakra' before Prajāpati. Lord Prajāpati has provided with proper answers to the question raised by the gods. During the session of questions, Prajāpati explained that the above Cakra is existed in six numbers. Assuming it as base, this upaniṣad is called 'Nṛsiṁhaṣaṭcakropaniṣad'. Lord Prajāpati while explaining the name of six discuss (Cakra) told that the first discuss is called Ācakra, the second is Sucakra, the third is Mahācakra, fourth is Sakalalokarakṣaṇacakra. The fifth is Dyūtacakra and the sixth is Asurāntakacarka. Subsequently, the gods had asked the distinctions and the manners for holding these Cakras to which Prajāpati had answered with more clarity. The gods again asked in respect of the place at which these cakras are to be held. Lord Prajāpati duly explained the places and the benefits arising as a result of holding these cakras. Finally, this upaniṣad has been concluded with explaining the fruits of perservence on this upaniṣad.

ॐ देवा ह वै सत्यं लोकमायंस्तं प्रजापतिमपृच्छन्नारसिंहचक्रन्नो ब्रूहीति। तान्प्रजापतिर्नारसिंहचक्रमवोचत्। षड्वै नारसिंहानि चक्राणि भवन्ति। यत्प्रथमं तच्चतुररं यद्द्वितीयं तच्चतुररं यत्तृतीयं तदष्टारं यच्चतुर्थं तत्पञ्चारं यत्पञ्चमं तत्पञ्चारं यत्षष्ठं तदष्टारं तदेतानि षडेव नारसिंहानि चक्राणि भवन्ति॥ १॥

Once upon a time the gods reached at the abode of truth and asked Prajāpati (Lord Brahmā)– O lord! Please preach us regarding the identity of Nārasiṁha cakra. Hearing to the request so made by the gods, lord Brahmā started preaching them the identity of Nārasiṁha cakra. He told that this cakra is in six numbers. There are four blades with the first and the second cakra, eight blades with the third, five blades with the fourth, five blades with the fifth and eight blades with the sixth cakra. Thus the six cakras are called Nārasiṁha cakra.

अथ कानि नामानि भवन्ति। यत्प्रथमं तदाचक्रं यद्द्वितीयं तत्सुचक्रं यत्तृतीयं तन्महाचक्रं यच्चतुर्थं तत्सकललोकरक्षणचक्रं यत्पञ्चमं तद्द्यूतचक्रं यद्वै षष्ठं तदसुरान्तकचक्रं तदेतानि षडेव नारसिंहचक्रनामानि भवन्ति॥ २॥

Further the gods asked the names given to the above cakras. Lord Brahmā told that their names are– Ācakra, Sucakra, Mahācakra, Sakalalokarakṣaṇa cakra, Dyūcakra and Asurāntaka cakra respectively. These are the six names for these six cakras.

अथ कानि त्रीणि वलयानि भवन्ति। यत्प्रथमं तदान्तरवलयं भवति। यद्द्वितीयं तन्मध्यमं वलयं भवति। यत्तृतीयं तद्बाह्यं वलयं भवति। तदेतानि त्रीण्येव वलयानि भवन्ति। यदा तद्बैतद्बीजं यन्मध्यमं तां नारसिंहगायत्रीं यद्बाह्यं तन्मन्त्रः॥ ३॥

The gods later on asked about the three rings (valaya) of these cakras. Thus they were curious to know the names of these rings (valaya). Lord Brahmā explained that the first is Āntara, the second is Madhyama and the third is Bāhya. These are called the three rings of these cakras. The Madhyama bīja (key) out of these is called Nārasiṁha Gāyatrī and the Bāhya or the exterior is the mantra (hymn).

अथ किमान्तरं वलयम्। षड्वान्तराणि वलयानि भवन्ति। यन्नारसिंहं तत्प्रथमस्य यन्माहालक्ष्म्यं तद्द्वितीयस्य यत्सारस्वतं तत्तृतीयस्य यस्य यत्कामं देवं तच्चतुर्थस्य यत्प्रणवं तत्पञ्चमस्य यत्क्रोधदैवतं तत्षष्ठस्य। तदेतानि षण्णां नारसिंहचक्राणां षडान्तराणि वलयानि भवन्ति॥४॥

How many kinds of Āntaravalaya? Having asked this question, lord Brahmā while answering told that those are in six numbers. Nārasiṁhaṁ is of first, Mahālakṣmyaṁ is of second, Sarāsvata is of third, the Iṣṭadeva if any is of fourth, the Oṁ is of fifth and Krodhadaivata is of the sixth. Thus there are six Āntaravalaya (internal rings) in the six Nārasiṁha cakras.

अथ किं मध्यमं वलयम्। षड्वै मध्यमानि वलयानि भवन्ति। यन्नारसिंहाय तत्प्रथमस्य यद्विद्महे तद्द्वितीयस्य यद्वज्रनखाय तत्तृतीयस्य यद्धीमहि तच्चतुर्थस्य यत्तन्नस्तत्पञ्चमस्य यत्सिंहः प्रचोदयादिति तत्षष्ठस्य। तदेतानि षण्णां नारसिंहचक्राणां षण्मध्यमानि वलयानि भवन्ति॥५॥

When the gods asked the strength of the Madhyama valayas, lord Brahmā told that these are also of six kinds. Narasiṁhāya is of first, Vidmahe is of second, Vajranakhāya is of third, Dhīmayi is of fourth, Tannaḥ is of fifth and Siṁhaḥ pracodayāt is the name of the sixth valaya. Thus these six Nārasiṁha cakras have Madhyama valayas of six kind.

अथ किं बाह्यं वलयम्। षड्वै बाह्यानि वलयानि भवन्ति। यदाचक्रं यदात्मा तत्प्रथमस्य यत्सुचक्रं यत्प्रियात्मा तद्द्वितीयस्य यन्महाचक्रं यज्ज्योतिरात्मा तत्तृयीयस्य यत्सकललोकरक्षणचक्रं यन्मायात्मा तच्चतुर्थस्य यदाचक्रं यद्योगात्मा तत्पञ्चमस्य यदसुरान्तकचक्रं यत्सत्यात्मा तत्षष्ठस्य। तदेतानि षण्णां नारसिंहचक्राणां षट् बाह्यानि वलयानि भवन्ति॥६॥

The gods again asked about the quantum and the names of the Bāhya valayas. Lord Brahmā while answering this question told that Bāhya valayas are also of six kinds. The first is the Ācakra and the soul. The seconds of Sucakra and Priyātmā. The third is of Mahācakra and Jyotirātmā, the protective cakra and the soul of illusion (Māyātmā) is the fourth, the Ācakra and Yogātmā is the fifth and the Asurāntaka cakra and Satyātmā is of the sixth. Thus these six Nārasiṁha cakras have Bāhya valayas of six kind.

[The whole hymn describes about the Ācakra in the first exterior ring but the fifth ring again has been extracted while the Dyūtacakra has been accepted as the fifth ring before it. Hence, this change is worth consideration. It is to be seen and judged that why such differentiation has been made.]

क्वैतानि न्यस्यानि। यत्प्रथमं तद्धृदये यद्द्वितीयं तच्छिरसि यत्तृतीयं तच्छिखायां यच्चतुर्थं तत्सर्वेष्वङ्गेषु यत्पञ्चमं तत्सर्वेषु (?) यत्षष्ठं तत्सर्वेषु देशेषु। य एतानि नारसिंहानि चक्राण्येतेष्वङ्गेषु बिभृयात् तस्यानुष्टुप् सिध्यति। तं भगवान् नृसिंहः प्रसीदति। तस्य कैवल्यं सिद्धयति। तस्य सर्वे लोकाः सिध्यन्ति। तस्य सर्वे

जनाः सिद्ध्यन्ति। तस्मादेतानि षण्णां नारसिंहचक्राण्यङ्गेषु न्यस्यानि भवन्ति। पवित्रं च एतत्तस्य न्यसनम्। न्यसनान्नृसिंहानन्दी भवति। कर्मण्यो भवति। ब्रह्मण्यो भवति। अन्यसनान्न नृसिंहानन्दी भवति। न कर्मण्यो भवति। तस्मादेतत्पवित्रं तस्य न्यसनम्॥७॥

Where the Nyāsa (a procedure for summoning the gods to enshrine on the different parts of the body) for these hymns should be made? Viz. at what place these should be held? Lord Brahmā while answering this very query raised by the gods told that the first should be held in the heart, the second on the head, the third on the braid, the fourth in all organs, the fifth on every part and organs of the body as also. The sixth and the last should be held on the entire body. The person holding these cakras in all the parts of his body, attains to success on Anuṣṭup. Lord Nṛsiṁha is pleased on him and with the grace of lord Nṛsiṁha, he attains to the ēmancipation. He thus accustoms with all worlds and acquires them as also all people (all near and dear) follows him heartily. These are the places for doing Nyāsa in the parts of six Nārsiṁha cakras. The Nyāsa so made is most holy. As a result of making this Nyāsa the man pleases lord Nṛsiṁha. He becomes aware of what to do and don't i.e. his power of discretion is developed and he becomes well known to the Brahma (knowledge). The person who doesn't know the procedure of Nyāsa, lord Nṛsiṁha seldom pleases on him and he can't obtain the power of discretion. This Nyāsa therefore is most sacrosanct and the procedure of Nyāsa makes the devotee holy in heart and mind both and thus he automatically attains to the peace and pleasure.

[In the above hymn and specially in the matter of Nyāsa all parts of body in the fourth Nyāsa and all places in the sixth Nyāsa has been described but why the place is not prescribed with the word 'All' has been not described in the fifth Nyāsa is worth consideration?]

यो वा एतं नारसिंहं चक्रमधीते स सर्वेषु वेदेष्वधीतो भवति। स सर्वेषु यज्ञेषु याजको भवति। स सर्वेषु तीर्थेषु स्नातो भवति। स सर्वेषु मन्त्रेषु सिद्धो भवति। स सर्वत्र शुद्धो भवति। स सर्वरक्षो भवति। भूतपिशाचशाकिनीप्रेतवंताकनाशको भवति। स निर्भयो भवति। तदेतन्नाश्रद्दधानाय प्रब्रूयात्तदेतन्नाश्रद्दधानाय प्रब्रूयादिति॥८॥

The person doing perseverance on this Nārasiṁhacakra upaniṣad becomes able to study all Vedas too. He is considered as Karttā (performer) of all offerings viz. it is deemed that he has performed all kinds of offerings (Yajña). Further, it is considered that he also has completed his pilgrimage too. He attains to success on all hymns and he becomes holy personality in his material life. He becomes able to protect all. He attains to the powers more than suffice to destroy the ghost, demons, the magician, the evil spirit and the malice created by evil doers as also all other species (Yonis) that become a cause of terror for the gentle man. He becomes fearless. This Nārasiṁha cakra should not be pleased or discussed to or among the persons void of obeisance at any of the circumstances.

॥इति नृसिंहषट्चक्रोपनिषत् समाप्ता॥

107. RĀDHOPANIṢAD

राधोपनिषद्

This Upaniṣad is related to the tradition of Ṛgveda. It has been presented in the form of questionnaire taken place between the Sanaka etc. hermit and Hirṇyagarbha Brahmā. The Sanaka etc. hermits asked very first to Lord Brahmā that who is the supreme god and the supreme power (goddess). Replying to this question, Lord Brahmā have said that Lord Śrī Kṛṣṇa is the supreme god and Śrī Rādhā is his internal power and the best goddess. Since Rādhā was worshipped by Lord Kṛṣṇa, she has been given the name of Rādhikā. Subsequently, the magnificent powers of Rādhā have been enumerated. Then, the twenty-eight names of Rādhā have been stated and it has been told that the person can avail salvation by reciting and doing perseverance on these names. Finally, the pioneer role of Rādhā in the process of incarnation has been accepted by saying the power of Rādhā as the power of Līlā.

॥शान्तिपाठः॥

ॐ वाङ्मे ....इति शान्तिः॥

ओमथोर्ध्वं मन्थिन ऋषयः सनकाद्या भगवन्तं हिरण्यगर्भमुपासित्वोचुः देवः कः परमो देवताः का वा तच्छक्तयः तासु च का वरीयसी भवतीति सृष्टिभूता च केति। स होवाच हे पुत्रकाः शृणुतेदं ह वाव गुह्याद् गुह्यतरमप्रकाश्यं यस्मै कस्मै न देयम्। स्निग्धाय ब्रह्मवादिने गुरुभक्ताय, देयमन्यथा दातुर्महदवम्भीत। कृष्णो ह वै हरिः परमो देवः षड्विधैश्वर्य्यैः परिपूर्णो भगवान् गोपीगोपसेव्यो वृन्दाऽऽराधितो वृन्दावनादिनाथः स एकः सर्वेश्वरः। तस्य ह वै द्वैततनु नारायणोऽखिल ब्रह्माण्डाधिपतिरेकः प्रकृतेः प्राचीनो नित्यः। एवं हि तस्य शक्तयस्त्वनेकधा। आह्लादिनीसन्धिनीज्ञानेच्छाक्रियाद्याबहुविधः शक्तयः। तास्वाह्लादिनी वरीयसी परमान्तरङ्गभूता राधा कृष्णेन आराध्यत इति राधा कृष्णं समाराधयति सदेति राधिका गान्धर्वेति व्यपदेश्यत इति। येयं राधा यश्च कृष्णो रसाब्धिर्देहेनैकः क्रीडनार्थं द्विधाभूत्॥ १॥

Once the hermit Sanaka etc. Urdhvaretā have realised a question with humble request to Lord Brahmā– "O Lord! Who is the supreme god? What are the powers of him? What power among all powers is the most grand and initial reason of the creation (Sṛṣṭi)?" Lord Brahmā replied– "O sons! I am going to tell you the most secret mystery, you should attentively listen to it. The person who is not obedient to his teacher, not follows the rules of celibacy, void of the application, is not any way entitle to know this mystery because to preach such people even brings the evil-some consequences. Lord Kṛṣṇa only is the most pioneer god. The Gopa and Gopīs always serve that Lord Śrī kṛṣṇa who is full of six luxuries. The king of Vṛndāvana, worshipped by Vṛndā is only the god of all. His one form is of Śrī Nārāyaṇa who is the ruler of this whole universe. He is beyond the nature and everlasting. The god of all, Lord Kṛṣṇa has numerous power like Āhlādinī, Sandhinī, Jñāna, Icchā, Kriyā etc. Out of them Āhlādinī is the most pioneer power. This power too is called the most imbibed power of Lord Kṛṣṇa and addressed of Śrī Rādhā. She is called Rādhikā because Lord Kṛṣṇa worship her. Lord Kṛṣṇa is the adorable god for Rādhā. She is addressed as Gāndharvā too. All Gopīs, all pioneer queens of Lord Kṛṣṇa and Śrī Lakṣmī are the part and parcel of Śrī Rādhikā. Lord Kṛṣṇa in the form of a sea full of essence, has divided himself into two forms for playing with gaiety.

[In the above hymn, the context of Lord Kṛṣṇa worshipped by Vṛndā and the names like Gāndharvā, Sanātanī vidyā, goddess of breathing etc. given to Rādhā have a particular meaning. Vṛndā is purported to the commune or the batch and the divine sensitivity. (Kṛṣṇa) is influenced to a greater extent only through the group pray. The imbibed power of that sensitivity is Rādhā who endows with accomplishments to the efforts of devotees. The Gāndharvā is the holding power of the earth, the ray and the senses. Hence, she has been addressed as Sanātanī vidyā and the goddess of breathing etc. The numerous names and the qualities of Rādhā should be seen in the same prospect in order to have the actual meaning.]

एषा वै हरेः सर्वेश्वरी सर्वविद्या सनातनी कृष्णप्राणाधिदेवी चेति, विविक्ते वेदाः स्तुवन्ति, यस्या गतिं, वक्तुं न चोत्सहे सर्वं यस्य प्रसीदति तस्य करतलावकलितम्परमधामेति। एतामवज्ञाय यः कृष्णमाराधयितुमिच्छति, स मूढतमो मूढतमश्चेति॥ २॥

Goddess Rādhikā is the soul power of supreme god Lord Śrī Kṛṣṇa and she is the everlasting Vidyā in a learning acquired by him as also the goddess of breathing to Lord Kṛṣṇa for Vedas in a state of meditation always prays her. The Saints well-known to Brahma too cannot know her excellent arts (Gati). O Sons! I cannot access to the magnificence of goddess Rādhikā even if I recite the same throughout my life. The person graced by goddess Rādhikā accesses to the supreme abode easily. He is the greatest foolish among fools who worship Lord Kṛṣṇa without identity with Śrī Rādhā.

अथ हैतानि नामानि गायन्ति श्रुतयः। राधा रासेश्वरी रम्या कृष्णमन्त्राधिदेवता। सर्वाद्या सर्ववन्द्या च वृन्दावनविहारिणी। वृन्दाराध्या रमाऽशेषगोपीमण्डलपूजिता। सत्या सत्यपरा सत्यभामा श्रीकृष्णवल्लभा। वृषभानुसुता गोपी मूलप्रकृतीश्वरी। गान्धर्वा राधिका रम्या रुक्मिणी परमेश्वरी। परात्परतरा पूर्णा पूर्णचन्द्रनिभानना। भुक्तिमुक्तिप्रदा नित्यं भवव्याधिविनाशिनी इत्येतानि नामानि यः पठेत् स जीवन्मुक्तो भवति। इत्याह हिरण्यगर्भो भगवानिति॥ ३॥

The Vedas recite the names of Śrī Rādhā. These are (i) Rādhā, (ii) Rāseśvarī, (iii) Ramyā, (iv) Kṛṣṇa mantrādhi devatā (v) Sarvādyā, (vi) Sarvavandyā, (vii) Vṛndāvana Vihāriṇī, (viii) Vṛndā rādhyā, (ix) Ramā, (x) Aśeṣa Gopīmaṇḍalapūjitā, (xi) Satyā, (xii) Satyaparā, (xiii) Satyabhāmā, (xiv) Śrī Kṛṣṇa Vallabhā, (xv) Vṛṣabhānusutā, (xvi) Gopī, (xvii) Mūlaprakṛtī, (xviii) Īśvarī, (xix) Gāndharvā, (xx) Rādhikā, (xxi) Ramya (xxii) Rukmiṇī, (xxiii) Parameśvarī, (xxiv) Parātparatarā, (xxv) Pūrṇā, (xxvi) Pūrṇacandrā, Nibhānanā, (xxvii) Bhuktimuktipradā and (xxviii) Bhavavādhivināśinī. Lord Brahmā says that person reciting these names attains to fully enjoyable life.

सन्धिनी तु धामभूषणशय्यासनादि मित्रभृत्यातिरूपेण परिणत मृत्युलोकावतरणकाले मातृपितृरूपेण चाऽऽसीदित्यनेकावतारकारणज्ञानशक्तिस्तु क्षेत्रज्ञशक्तिरिति इच्छाभूता मायासत्त्वरजस्तमोमयी बहिरङ्गा

जगत्कारणभूता सैवाविद्यारूपेण जीवबन्धनभूता क्रियाशक्तिस्तु लीलाशक्तिरिति। य इमामुपनिषदमधीते सोऽव्रती व्रती भवति, स वायुपूतो भवति, स सर्वपूतो भवति, राधाकृष्णप्रियो भवति स यावच्चक्षुःपातं पंक्तिं पुनाति॥४॥

The Sandhinī Śaktī (power of combination) is converted in the form of abode, ornament, bed cushions, friends and servants etc. as also in the form of a in this earth (Mṛtyuloka). This power is only considered the cause for incarnation of Lord. The power of knowledge is only the power of expert knowledge regarding territory and the power of illusion is embedded in the will power. This power is stated as inert power owing to its extraneous form as Satva, Rajas and Tamas; the basic cause for the creation of this universe. It has been stated illusion (Māyā) as it fastens the living soul in the form of ignorance. This is the reason for stating this power of action as the god's art (Līlā Śaktī). The persons reciting this Upaniṣad become resolute to beyond resolution. They are purified like the wind and become able to spread everywhere the purity. Such persons get the supreme blessing of Lord Śrī Kṛṣṇa and Śrī Rādhā. Every area at which they visit or even observe automatically turns into all purified form.

॥इति राधोपनिषत्समाप्ता॥

108. RUDROPANIṢAD

रुद्रोपनिषद्

It is a smallest Upaniṣad containing only three hymns. The characteristics of a best Brāhmaṇa have been very first discussed in it and explanation has been given that the best Brāhmaṇa engages himself in the worship of Lord Śiva (viz., for the welfare of all creatures). The Brāhmaṇa not devotee to Lord Śiva falls in the category of the Cāṇḍāla (meanest person). The Cāṇḍāla (person born in lower caste) but Śiva's devotee has been appreciated saying that the ash in the hands of Cāṇḍāla is better than the ash obtained after offering made in the fire, air, land, water and ether etc. All has been considered in the form of ash worth putting on head. Lord Śiva has been stated as Prāṇa liṅgī (which is recognised by the effects of breathing). The Cāṇḍāla, devotee to Śiva has also been considered as the best Prāṇaliṅgī. Then Lord Śiva and teacher has been told equal to worship and honour. The person who worships Lord Śiva and teacher considering them equal, definitely becomes eligible to receive favour of Śiva after exonerating from the sins committed during a number of previous births. Thus, this Upaniṣad has been concluded with suggestion to shelter Lord Śiva and the teacher.

विश्वमयो ब्राह्मणः शिवं व्रजति। ब्राह्मणः पञ्चाक्षरमनुभवति। ब्राह्मणः शिवपूजारतः। शिवभक्तिविहीनश्चेत् स चण्डाल उपचण्डालः। चतुर्वेदज्ञोऽपि शिवभक्त्यान्तर्भवतीति स एव ब्राह्मणः। अधमश्चाण्डालोऽपि शिवभक्तोऽपि ब्राह्मणाच्छ्रेष्ठतरः। ब्राह्मणस्त्रिपुण्ड्रधृतः। अत एव ब्राह्मणः। शिवभक्तेरेव ब्राह्मणः। शिवलिङ्गार्चनयुतश्चाण्डालोऽपि स एव ब्राह्मणाधिको भवति। अग्निहोत्रभसिताच्छिवभक्तचाण्डालहस्तविभूतिः शुद्धा। कपिशा वा श्वेतजापि धूम्रवर्णा वा। विरक्तानां तपस्विनां शुद्धा। गृहस्थानां निर्मलविभूतिः। तपस्विभिः सर्वभस्म धार्यम्। यद्वा शिवभक्तिसंपुष्टं सदापि तद्भसितं देवताधार्यम्॥ १॥

The Brāhmaṇa in the form of universe (i.e. full of spirit of universal brotherhood) accesses to Śiva (the welfare). That Brāhmaṇa perceives the Pañcākṣara (Namaḥ Śivāya). The Brāhmaṇa always busy with the worship of Lord Śiva is the best Brāhmaṇa. He will be considered as Cāṇḍāla or sub-Cāṇḍāla if he is not a devotee to Śiva inspite of learned in four vedas. The person who is peculiarly introvert to the devotion of Lord Śiva is only Brāhmaṇa. The mean (Cāṇḍāla) too is considered better than Brāhmaṇa if he is soaked with devotion of Lord Śiva. The Brāhmaṇa holding (smearing) Tripuṇḍra on his forehead is the best Brāhmaṇa. The element or essence of his being Brāhmaṇa is depicted by it. With the keen devotion to Śiva, he will be called Brāhmaṇa. The Cāṇḍāla too is Brāhmaṇa if he worships the liṅga of Śiva. The ash in the hands of Śiva devotee Cāṇḍāla is better and more fruitful than the ash obtained from the offering. This ash is of three kinds– (1) copper colour (2) white and (3) Brown as the smoke. The pure ash for the detached ascetics and clean ash for the family (Gṛhastha) is considered the best ash. The ascetics should smear all kinds of ash. The ash soaked with Śiva's devotion, viz., the devotion of Śiva in the form of knowledge is worth entertaining of all gods and it should be smeared (held).

ॐ अग्निरिति भस्म। वायुरिति भस्म। स्थलमिति भस्म। जलमिति भस्म। व्योमेति भस्म इत्याद्युपनिषत्कारणात् तत् कार्यम्। अन्यत्र 'विश्वतश्चक्षुरुत विश्वतोमुखो विश्वतोहस्त उत विश्वतस्पात्। सं बाहुभ्यां नमति सं पतत्रैर्द्यावापृथिवी जनयन् देव एकः।'इ तस्मात्प्राणलिङ्गी शिवः। शिव एव प्राणलिङ्गी। जटाभस्मधारोऽपि प्राणलिङ्गी हि श्रेष्ठः। प्राणलिङ्गी शिवरूपः। शिवरूपः प्राणलिङ्गी। जङ्गमरूपः शिवः। शिव एव जङ्गमरूपः। प्राणलिङ्गिनां शुद्धसिद्धिर्न भवति। प्राणलिङ्गिनां जङ्गमपूज्यानां पूज्यतपस्विनामधिकश्चण्डालोऽपि प्राणलिङ्गी। तस्मात्प्राणलिङ्गी विशेष इत्याह। य एवं वेद स शिवः। शिव एव रुद्रः प्राणलिङ्गी नान्यो भवति॥ २॥

It should be held with presumption that the all elements like fire, air, land, water and ether etc. are in the form of ash, It has been started elsewhere– "That god sees all, talks with all and he has hand as also feet. That sole god originates with his own hands, the earth and the sky. He is worth saluting by all. Hence Prāṇaliṅgī (where is recognised by breathing) is Śiva. Śiva is Prāṇaliṅgī. The god holding matted hair and ash only is the best Prāṇaliṅgī. The Prāṇaliṅgī is Śiva form and the form of Śiva is Prāṇaliṅgī. Śiva is in dynamic form (Jaṅgam) and the dynamic form is Śiva. Prāṇaliṅgī do not attain the pure accomplishment (siddhi). The dynamic (Jaṅgama) are revered among Prāṇaliṅgīs and Cāṇḍāla devoted to Lord Śiva too is the best Prāṇaliṅgī. Prāṇaliṅgī, therefore, is called the best Brāhmaṇa. The person known to this fact becomes Śiva himself. Rudra is Prāṇaliṅgī and nobody else can be Prāṇaliṅgī.

ॐ आत्मा परशिवद्वयो गुरुः शिवः। गुरूणां सर्वविश्वमिदं विश्वमन्त्रेण धार्यम्। दैवाधीनं जगदिदम्। तद्दैवं तन्मन्त्रात् तनुते। तन्मे दैवं गुरुरिति। गुरूणां सर्वज्ञानिनां गुरुणा दत्तमेतदन्नं परब्रह्म। ब्रह्म स्वानुभूतिः। गुरुः शिवो देवः। गुरुः शिव एव लिङ्गम्। उभयोर्मिश्रप्रकाशत्वात्। प्राणवत्त्वात् महेश्वरत्वाच्च शिवस्तदैव गुरुः। यत्र गुरुस्तत्र शिवः। शिवगुरुस्वरूपो महेश्वरः। भ्रमरकीटकार्येण दीक्षिताः शिवयोगिनः शिवपूजापथे गुरुपूजाविधौ च महेश्वरपूजनान्मुक्ताः। लिङ्गाभिषेकं निर्माल्यं गुरोरभिषेकतीर्थं महेश्वरपादोदकं जन्ममालिन्यं क्षालयन्ति। तेषां प्रीतिः शिवप्रीतिः। तेषां तृप्तिः शिवतृप्तिः। तैश्च पावनो वासः। तेषां निरसनं शिवनिरसनम्। आनन्दपारायणः। तस्माच्छिवं व्रजन्तु। गुरुं व्रजन्तु। इत्येव पावनम्॥ ३॥

This soul is Brahma and in the form of Śiva. It is in the form of teacher and Śiva. The teachers should hold this whole world with the universal spirit (hymn) viz., they should strike a balance in the world by doing proper publicity and circulation of Vedic hymns. This world is under gods and that gods provide strength as a result of reciting these hymns. That god is teacher of us all. This food (cereal) endowed by all teachers and the teacher to omniscients is in the form of perfect knowledge (Parabrahma). Brahma is understood by self-realisation. Lord Śiva is teacher and the teacher (Guru) Śiva is in the form of liṅga. The invisible (Nirākāra) Brahma has been depicted in vedas. As a reason of coming out both in light and having in the form of Prāṇa (breathing) and Maheśvara, Śiva is the supreme teacher. Where there is teacher, there is Śiva. That Maheśvara is in the form of Śiva as also in the form of a teacher. Complying with the bee insect doctrine (A dictum has gained populating that the insect Bhṛngī catches other insects in his hole and then starts murmuring around him. The insects captive gradually get in hesion and converted wholly as the Bhṛngī is) the exclusive devotee to lord Śiva and teacher equally achieve the state of sheer mediation and thus attains to emancipation. Coronation of Śiva liṅga (viz. duly sprinkling water, smearing tripuṇḍra water, reciting hymns in a prescribed manner therefore) effaces the evils of devotee forever. The evils accumulated since many births in past are decayed when the devotee does coronation of Śiva-liṅga and the teacher both with all loyalty and devotion. Devotion to Śiva-liṅga and the teacher is revelation of lore for lord Śiva. Śiva satiates when these two are satiated. To live in close touch of them is the supreme holy deed. Their remission is deemed the remission of Śiva's grace. The person known to this fact always feel pleasure within him. To obtain shelter of lord Śiva, the pious shelter of a teacher is also necessary. Doing this always is the pure and the best deed.

॥इति रुद्रोपनिषत्समाप्ता॥

109. ĀTMAPŪJĀ-UPANIṢAD

आत्मपूजोपनिषद्

The element of soul existed in the body and the method of worship to god of soul has been explained in this Upaniṣad. How the different activities of life can be skilfully converted in the form of pray and worship, has been explained in this Upaniṣad and this has been stated that the path to welfare too extends in garb of emancipation by virtue of such walks of life.

ॐ तस्य निश्चिन्तनं ध्यानम्। सर्वकर्मनिराकरणमावाहनम्। निश्चलज्ञानमासनम्। समुन्मनीभावः पाद्यम्। सदामनस्कमर्घ्यम्। सदादीप्तिराचमनीयम्। वराकृतप्राप्तिः स्नानम्। सर्वात्मकत्वं दृश्यविलयो गन्धः। दृगविशिष्टात्मानः अक्षताः। चिदादीप्तिः पुष्पम्। सूर्यात्मकत्वं दीपः। परिपूर्णचन्द्रामृतरसैकीकरणं नैवेद्यम्। निश्चलत्वं प्रदक्षिणम्। सोऽहंभावो नमस्कारः। परमेश्वरस्तुतिर्मौनम्। सदासन्तोषो विसर्जनम्। एवं परिपूर्णराजयोगिनः सर्वात्मकपूजोपचारः स्यात्। सर्वात्मकत्वं आत्माधारो भवति। सर्वनिरामयपरिपूर्णोऽहमस्मीति मुमुक्षूणां मोक्षैकसिद्धिर्भवति।। इत्युपनिषत्।।

Concentration incessantly on that element of soul is the concentration for him. The removal or remission of all deeds is the summoning of that god. The undeviated knowledge is his seat. The vessels (pādya) is the spirit that always concentrates on the element of soul. A perpetual concentration on the same is Arghya. The ceaseless lustre of soul is Ācamana. The yield of superiority is the bath of that supreme element. The merger of all perceiving of soul (the meditation of zero) is the perfume. The inner eyes are the Akṣata. The flame of mind (sensitivity) is the flower and the sun form of that element of soul is the lamp (Dīpaka). The full moon and its integrated nectar essence is Naivedya. The well-planned movement of that soul is Pradakṣiṇā. I myself is that Brahma, is the spirit that salutes him. To maintain introvert nature (silent) is the worship of that soul. To live always in contentment is the visarjana. Thus, the universal worship and pray of the perfect Rājayogi, is the basis of that element of soul. The desire for emancipation is fulfilled only when the devotee presumes that I am the perfect Brahma and gets rid of all ailments and adversities. This is to what this Upaniṣad (the knowledge of element) says.

।।इति आत्मपूजोपनिषत् समाप्ता।।

110. YOGARĀJA-UPANIṢAD

योगराजोपनिषद्

This is an Upaniṣad composed on Yoga. As its name implies, it is the best Upaniṣad among all other Upaniṣads composed on Yoga. This name indeed has been given for the same and taking in view the peculiarities to which it contains. There are twenty one hymns in aggregate in which the doctrines of yoga has been explained in easy words. In the beginning, the four Yogas i.e. Mantra yoga, Laya yoga, Haṭha yoga and Rāja yoga have been enumerated. The contents then followed is the four pioneer parts of yoga, i.e., Āsana, Prāṇāyāma, Dhyāna and Samādhi, nine discus i.e., Brahmacakra, Svādhiṣṭhāna Cakra, Nābhi Cakra, Hṛdaya Cakra, Kaṇṭha Cakra, Tālukā Cakra, Bhrū Cakra, Brahmarandhra Cakra and Vyoma Cakra with the procedure of meditation and finally this Upaniṣad has been concluded after describing the fruit of perseverance and meditation of discuss (Cakras).

योगराजं प्रवक्ष्यामि योगिनां योगसिद्धये। मन्त्रयोगो लयश्चैव राजयोगो हठस्तथा॥ १॥

Now this yogarāja upaniṣad containing the four kinds of yogas i.e. Mantra yoga, Laya yoga, Haṭha yoga and Rāja yoga in order to special achievements for the yogis is to be described.

योगश्चतुर्विधः प्रोक्तो योगिभिस्तत्त्वदर्शिभिः। आसनं प्राणसंरोधो ध्यानं चैव समाधिकः॥ २॥

The experts in yoga has told four kinds of yoga, i.e., Āsana, Prāṇāyāma, Dhyāna and meditation.

एतच्चतुष्टयं विद्धि सर्वयोगेषु सम्मतम्। ब्रह्मविष्णुशिवादीनां मन्त्रं जाप्यं विशारदैः॥ ३॥

These four have been described as confirmed with all yogas. The scholars should do Japa and the hymns pertaining to Viṣṇu and Lord Śiva.

साध्यते मन्त्रयोगस्तु वत्सराजादिभिर्यथा। कृष्णद्वैपायनाद्यैस्तु साधितो लयसंज्ञितः॥ ४॥

The Mantra yoga was confirmed by Vatsa Rājā etc. and the Laya yoga, was confirmed by Kṛṣṇadvaipāyana etc. hermits.

नवस्वेव हि चक्रेषु लयं कृत्वा महात्मभिः। प्रथमं ब्रह्मचक्रं स्यात् त्रिरावृत्तं भगाकृति॥ ५॥

The great men make the higher accomplishment on yoga by merging in it nine kinds of discus. The three time surrounded Bhaga (triangle form) is the first discus which has been said the Brahma Cakra.

अपाने मूलकन्दाख्यं कामरूपं च तज्जगुः। तदेव वह्निकुण्डं स्यात् तत्त्वकुण्डलिनी तथा॥ ६॥

The Mūlakanda (cluster of nerves) in the form of sex is existed at the place of Apāna. It too has been called Agni kuṇḍa and Tattva Kuṇḍalinī.

तां जीवरूपिणीं ध्यायेज्ज्योतिष्ठं मुक्तिहेतवे। स्वाधिष्ठानं द्वितीयं स्याच्चक्रं तन्मध्यगं विदुः॥ ७॥

One should concentrate on that Jīva form flame with a desire of emancipation. The Scholars have stated a second discus namely the Svādhiṣṭhāna Cakra at the middle of the same.

पश्चिमाभिमुखं लिङ्गं प्रवालाङ् कुरसन्निभम्। तत्रोद्रीयाणपीठेषु तं ध्यात्वाकर्षयेज्जगत्॥ ८॥

A Liṅga is existed facing the west ever-luminating like Pravālāṅkura (sprout of red colour). One should attract the world by concentrating mind on that luminating sprout under the Udrīyāṇa Pīṭha, a (Svādhiṣṭhāna Cakra).

तृतीयं नाभिचक्रं स्यात्तन्मध्ये तु जगत् स्थितम्। पञ्चावर्तां मध्यशक्तिं चिन्तयेद्विद्युदाकृति॥ ९॥

The third discus is the Nābhi Cakra and the existence of world has been stated within it. The power analogous to the lightening should be bring into attention which is of five frequencies between that discus.

तां ध्यात्वा सर्वसिद्धीनां भाजनं जायते बुधः। चतुर्थे हृदये चक्रं विज्ञेयं तदधोमुखम्॥ १०॥

The scholar as a result of concentrating his brain on that discus attains to all accomplishments. It is to be deemed that the fourth discus is existed in the heart and its mouth is downward.

ज्योतीरूपं च तन्मध्ये हंसं ध्यायेत् प्रयत्नतः। तं ध्यायतो जगत् सर्वं वश्यं स्यान्नात्र संशयः॥ ११॥

In the middle of that discus, one should make endeavour to concentrate on the haṁsa in the form of light. The entire world is enslaved as a result of concentration made thereupon and one should not anyway doubt on it.

पञ्चमं कण्ठचक्रं स्यात् तत्र वामे इडा भवेत्। दक्षिणे पिङ्गला ज्ञेया सुषुम्ना मध्यतः स्थिता॥ १२॥

The fifth discus has been stated as Kaṇṭha Cakra. It has been told that Iḍā is existed at its left, Piṅgalā at right and the Suṣumnā in the middle.

तत्र ध्यात्वा शुचि ज्योतिः सिद्धीनां भाजनं भवेत्। षष्ठं च तालुकाचक्रं घण्टिकास्थान मुच्यते॥

All kinds of accomplishments are availed by virtue of making concentration on the holy light in the Kaṇṭha Cakra. The sixth has been stated as Talukā Cakra and this very discus is called Gaṇṭikā place too.

दशमद्वारमार्गं तद्राजदन्तं च तज्जगुः। तत्र शून्ये लयं कृत्वा मुक्तो भवति निश्चितम्॥ १४॥

The route to the tenth door is also stated as Rājadanta. The man definitely attains to the emancipation by merging the mind in the void (zero) existing there.

भ्रूचक्रं सप्तमं विद्याद्बिन्दुस्थानं च तद्विदुः। भ्रुवोर्मध्ये वर्तुलं च ध्यात्वा ज्योतिः प्रमुच्यते॥ १५॥

The Seventh is the Bhrū Cakra. It is also called the place of Vidyā and Bindu. The yogis attain to emancipation by virtue of concentration made on the spherical flame existing in the middle of brows.

अष्टमं ब्रह्मरन्ध्रं स्यात् परं निर्वाणसूचकम्। तं ध्यात्वा सूतिकाग्रामं धूमाकारं विमुच्यते॥ १६॥

The indicative of supreme salvation, the eighth discus is called Brahmarandhra. The yogi attains to the emancipation by virtue of making concentration on that origin place (Sūtikā grāma) shining with the brown colour.

तच्च जालन्धरं ज्ञेयं मोक्षदं नीलचेतसम्। नवमं व्योमचक्रं स्यादश्रैः षोडशभिर्युतम्॥ १७॥

That endower of emancipation and the bluish spot should be considered the Jālandhara Pīṭha. The ninth discus has been stated that it contains sixteen petals.

संविद्ब्रूयाच्च तन्मध्ये शक्तिरुद्धा स्थिता परा। तत्र पूर्णां गिरौ पीठे शक्तिं ध्यात्वा विमुच्यते॥ १८॥

The Parāśaktī existed in the middle of that discus containing sixteen emancipation is a result of concentration to be made on Purnāgirī Pīṭha for perfect power at the middle of that discuss.

एतेषां नवचक्राणामेकैकं ध्यायतो मुनेः। सिद्धयो मुक्तिसहिताः करस्थाः स्युर्दिने दिने॥ १९॥

The yogi who does concentration gradually one after another on the above said nineth discus definitely attains to emancipation including all accomplishment day-today.

एको दण्डद्वयं मध्ये पश्यति ज्ञानचक्षुषा। कदम्बगोलकाकारं ब्रह्मलोकं व्रजन्ति ते॥ २०॥

The yogis who observe two sticks (Daṇḍa) in the middle of the spherical discus analogous to the cluster of Kadamba by virtue of their learned eye, attain to the above Brahma.

ऊर्ध्वशक्तिनिपातेन अधःशक्तेर्निकुञ्चनात्। मध्यशक्तिप्रबोधेन जायते परमं सुखं जायते परमं सुखम्। इति॥ २१॥

Supreme pleasure is attained when the upper power is dropped and lower power is shrinked as also the middle power is awakened. It is definite as this Upaniṣad states.

॥इति योगराजोपनिषत् समाप्ता॥

111. ŚĀṬYĀYANĪYA-UPANIṢAD

शाट्यायनीयोपनिषद्

This Upaniṣad is related to the tradition of Yajurveda. There are fourty hymns in it in which the life of a recluse particularly the reclusion of Viṣṇuliṅga has been described. The mind very first has been explained as the cause for binding and emancipation. Then, the four means i.e., discretion renounce, control etc. properties and the element of desire for emancipation, the form of kuṭīcaka and the four forms of the religion, yoga and the offering etc., for the recluse, their duties, the rules pertaining to their residence, the position of the ascetic known to the knowledge of soul, and in flirting of evil if the rules are violated, have been described. Finally, the outcome of penance for the recluse of Viṣṇuliṅga has been explained. It has been pronounced that the precedent and successive as much as thirty generation of a Viṣṇuliṅga recluse clan enjoy the pleasure of emancipation. That recluse himself becomes entitle to the position of Brahma.

॥शान्तिपाठः॥

ॐ पूर्णमद .... इति शान्तिः॥

मन एव मनुष्याणां कारणं बन्धमोक्षयोः। बन्धाय विषयासक्तं मुक्त्यै निर्विषयं स्मृतम्॥१॥

The mind is only cause for binding and emancipation of the human beings. The mind lured in the worldly issues etc. is the cause for binding and the mind detached and reluctant to the worldly passions is the cause for emancipation.

समासक्तं सदा चित्तं जन्तोर्विषयगोचरे। यद्येवं ब्रह्मणि स्यात्तत्को न मुच्येत बन्धनात्॥२॥

In case, the mind is attached to Brahma in the same proportion as it is attached to worldly affairs; there are no worldly ties from which one cannot be liberated viz. all bindings are cut down.

चित्तमेव हि संसारस्तत्प्रयत्नेन शोधयेत्। यच्चित्तस्तन्मयो भाति गुह्यमेतत्सनातनम्॥३॥

This mind is the world and every person should purify his mind through exercise. The person becomes Brahma who stakes his mind on Brahma. It is fact universally settled and most cryptic.

नावेदविन्मनुते तं बृहन्तं नाब्रह्मवित्परमं प्रैति धाम। विष्णुक्रान्तं वासुदेवं विजानन्विप्रो विप्रत्वं गच्छते तत्त्वदर्शी॥४॥

The gigantic form has no existence for the person not known to the element of Veda. He doesn't accept the existence of it. The man vacate of Brahma knowledge can't access to the self-luminating abode. It is only the prudent and metaphysician Brahma that can feel the touch of Ahaṁbrahmāsmi in his soul. Who is omnipresent, eminent and intuitive can attain to the element of Brahma and the element of liberated soul.

अथ ह यत्परं ब्रह्म सनातनं ये श्रोत्रिया अकामहता अधीयुः। शान्तो दान्त उपरतस्तितिक्षुर्योऽनूचानो ह्यभिजज्ञौ समानःत्यक्तेषणो ह्यनृणस्तं विदित्वा मौनी वसेदाश्रमे यत्र कुत्र॥५॥

The person who like Sanaka etc. hermits abandon their worldly passions and desire, acquire mastery in Veda can only understand the real nature of that supreme Brahma. They thus become in the form of Brahma. Such a man establishes a strong control on his sensory organs, he is glut of worldly enjoyments. He is reluctant, full of tolerance, known to Veda and understand that Brahma like the best desirous of emancipation. Such a man is away from the desires, liberated from the debts of father and the teacher. He resides at a solitary place and in a hermitage under a keen concentration.

अथाश्रमं चरमं संप्रविश्य यथोपपत्तिं पञ्चमात्रां दधानः॥६॥

One should enter into the stage of ultimate reclusion and attain to emancipation by accepting the five mātrās including the force, trident etc.

त्रिदण्डमुपवीतं च वासः कौपीनवेष्टनम्। शिक्यं पवित्रमित्येतद्बिभृयाद्यावदायुषम्॥७॥

He should hold trident, sacrificial thread, a cloth for covering shoulders, kaupīna (nicker), the Śikya and the water purifying Kuśa.

पञ्चैतास्तु यतेर्मात्रास्ता मात्रा ब्रह्मणे श्रुताः। न त्यजेद्यावदुत्क्रान्तिरन्तेऽपि निखनेत्सह॥८॥

These five mātrās of a yogi are embedded in Brahma (Oṁ). One shouldn't abandon them. All these should be buried in ground with the body after death.

विष्णुलिङ्गं द्विधा प्रोक्तं व्यक्तमव्यक्तमेव च। तयोरेकमपि त्यक्त्वा पतत्येव न संशयः॥९॥

The two kinds of marks have been stated of Viṣṇuliṅga reclusion out of which one is expressive and another is inexpressive. The recluse is misdirected if he abandons anyone out of them. There is nothing to doubt on it.

त्रिदण्डं वैष्णवं लिङ्गं वि प्राणां मुक्तिसाधनम्। निर्वाणं सर्वधर्माणामिति वेदानुशासनम्॥१०॥

The trident is known as a special mark of Viṣṇuliṅga recluse. This mark ensures emancipation for the Brāhmaṇas. This marks is in the form of Vedic discipline and renunciation of all religions.

अथ खलु सौम्य कुटीचको बहूदको हंसः परमहंस इत्येते परिव्राजकाश्चतुर्विधा भवन्ति। सर्व एते विष्णुलिङ्गिनः शिखिन उपवीतिनः शुद्धचित्ता आत्मानमात्मना ब्रह्म भावयन्तः शुद्धचिद्रूपोपासनरता जपयमवन्तो नियमवन्तः सुशीलिनः पुण्यश्लोका भवन्ति। तदेतदृचाभ्युक्तम्। कुटीचको बहूदकश्चापि हंसः परमहंस इव वृत्त्या च भिन्नाः। सर्व एते विष्णुलिङ्गं दधाना वृत्त्या व्यक्तं बहिरन्तश्च नित्यम्॥११॥

O modest! There are four kinds of recluse known as– Kuṭīcaka, Bahūdaka, Haṁsa and Paramahaṁsa. All these four put on sacrificial thread, raise a braid, a sacrosanct mind, worshipper of Brahma under presumption of it, these, abiding by Japa and Yama, Niyama etc. and of sober habits. A hymn on it is– "The Kuṭīcaka Bahūdaka, Haṁsa and Paramahaṁsa have their distinct propensities. These hold the marks of reclusion inward and outward as also these are expressive and inexpressive both."

पञ्चयज्ञा वेदशिः प्रविष्टाः क्रियावन्तोऽमि संगता ब्रह्मविद्याम्। त्यक्त्वा वृक्षं वृक्षमूलं श्रितासः संन्यस्तपुष्पा रसमेवाश्नुवानाः। विष्णुक्रीडा विष्णुरतयो विमुक्ता विष्ण्वात्मका विष्णुमेवापियन्ति॥ १२॥

These perform the five kinds of offering i.e. Japa of Gāyatrī hymn, yoga, penance, perseverance and knowledge as also listen to the meaning of Upaniṣads. These observe the prescribed rules for them and resort to Brahmavidyā. These resort to the root of world tree instead of its stem and branches and enjoy the essence of Brahma by giving up all apparent ceremonies. These recluse play with Lord Viṣṇu by giving up the exterior playfulness and concentrate on the soul as Viṣṇu.

त्रिसंध्यं शक्तितः स्नानं तर्पणं मार्जनं तथा। उपस्थानं पञ्चयज्ञान्कुर्यादामरणान्तिकम्॥ १३॥

All person should perform throughout their life Sandhyā in morning, at noon and in the evening as also the bath, Tarpaṇa, Mārjana, Upasthāna and Pañcayajña (offering for gods, forefathers, humanity or the gust, for creatures and for Brahma) essentially.

दशभिः प्रणवैः सप्तव्याहृतिभिश्चतुष्पदा। गायत्रीजप यज्ञश्च त्रिसंध्यं शिरसा सह॥ १४॥

One should do Japa and ten Praṇava including seven derivatives (Bhūḥ, Bhuvaḥ, Svaḥ, Mahaḥ, Javaḥ, Tapaḥ and Satyam) and fourfeet, Gāyatrī, Japa with Āpojyotī etc. and the offering with three times Sandhyā.

योगयज्ञः सदैकाग्र्यभक्त्या सेवा हरेर्गुरोः। अहिंसा तु तपोयज्ञो वाङ्मनःकायकर्मभिः॥ १५॥

One should continuously engage himself in the offering in the form of non-violent penance through the mind, speech, action, service to teacher and yoga with keen devotion and concentration as also service to Lord Viṣṇu.

नानोपनिषदभ्यासः स्वाध्यायो यज्ञ ईरितः। ओमित्यात्मानमव्यग्रो ब्रह्मण्यग्नौ जुहोति यत्॥ १६॥

A study on all Upaniṣads has been stated as an offering of perseverance. The morsel is given to the fire of Brahma in the form of soul by reciting Oṁ, viz., the soul is engrossed in the Brahma.

ज्ञानयज्ञः स विज्ञेयः सर्वयज्ञोत्तमोत्तमः। ज्ञानदण्डा ज्ञानशिखा ज्ञानयज्ञोपवीतिनः॥ १७॥

That Oṁ has been stated the best offering of knowledge among all other offerings. The knowledge is the fundamental base to all these offerings, the knowledge is the braid and it is sacrificial thread also.

शिखा ज्ञानमयी यस्य उपवीतं च तन्मयम्। ब्राह्मण्यं सकलं तस्य इति वेदानुशासनम्॥ १८

According to the discipline of Veda, all things belonging to a man are in the form of Brahma whose braid and sacrificial thread are the knowledge.

अथ खलु सोम्यैते परिव्राजका यथा प्रादुर्भवन्ति तथा भवन्ति। कामक्रोधलोभमोहदम्भदर्पासूयाममत्वाहंकारादींस्तितीर्य मानावमानौ निन्दास्तुती च वर्जयित्वा वृक्ष इव तिष्ठासेत्। छिद्यमानो न ब्रूयात्। तदेवं विद्वांस इहैवामृता भवन्ति। तदेतदृचाभ्युक्तम्। बन्धुपुत्रमनुमोदयित्वानवेक्ष्यमाणो द्वन्द्वसहः प्रशान्तः। प्राचीमुदीचीं वा निर्वर्तयंश्चरेत॥ १९॥

O dear modest! It has been explained that how these recluse are originated. These recluse cross the stages when the people are trapped in sensuality, greed, affection, boosting, proud, nature of criticising others, attachment, ego etc. They remain undeviated and stable like a tree before the strokes of respect, insult, condemn and appreciation. They say nothing while cut down or trouped in pains. The scholars thus enjoy the pleasure of immortal and liberated soul in this very world. A hymn referring it is he should seldom look for the brother, childern etc. often providing them maintenance upto a long period. He should move to and fro with an intention to research on his own actual form and boldly face all the strokes of pain and sorrow.

पात्री दण्डी युगमात्रावलोकी शिखी मुण्डी चोपवीती कुटुम्बी। यात्रामात्रं प्रतिगृह्णन्मनुष्यात् अयाचितं याचितं वोत भैक्षं॥ २०॥

The recluse who observe the living soul and the supreme soul in its integrated form who hold a bow and stick, who grow matted hairs on their head, whose only family is the sacrificial thread should live on alm either asking for it or without and thus sustain his body to ensure the frequent movements and observations of this universe.

मृद्दार्वलाबूफलंतन्तुपर्णपात्रं तत्तथा यथा तु लब्धम्। क्षाणं क्षामं तृणं कन्थाजिने च पर्णमाच्छादनं स्यादहतं वा विमुक्तः॥ २१॥

He should accept a pātra either made of clay or gourd, the coir, intertwined by the fibres or made of the leaf. He should accept the āsana made of mat, from the bark of a tree or from hay, from the hide of a black deer and from the leaves not hold by the insects.

ऋतुसन्धौ मुण्डयेन्मुण्डमात्रं नाधो नाक्षं जातु शिखां न वापयेत्। चतुरो मासान्ध्रुवशीलतः स्यात्स यावत्सुप्तोऽन्तरात्मा पुरुषो विश्वरूपः॥ २२॥

The recluse should clean his hair at the time of the adjunct of the coming season but the recluse of kuṭīcaka category should not cut his matted hair. He should remain at a place fully stable upto four mouth because Lord Nārāyaṇa in their gigantic form sleeps upto that time.

अन्यानथाष्टौ पुनरुत्थितेऽस्मिन्स्व कर्मलिप्सुर्विहरेद्वा वसेद्वा। देवाग्न्यगारे तरुमूले गुहायां वसेदसङ्गोऽलक्षितशीलवृत्तः। अनिन्धनो ज्योतिरिवोपशान्तो न चोद्विजेदुद्विजेद्यत्र कुत्र॥ २३॥

Thus, the recluse desirous of obtaining the stages like hearing, concentration and meditation etc. should reside at a place and perform his deeds continuously. He can resort elsewhere for it. He should make his residence in a temple close to the root of a tree or in a cave. Thus, living in solitude, and refrain from the public contact he should live with cool temperament like the fire without fuel. He shouldn't be attracted to any body and treat all creatures equal.

आत्मानं चेद्विजानीयादयमस्मीति पूरुषः। किमिच्छन्कस्य कामाय शरीरमनुसंज्वरेत्॥ २४॥

The desire to provide maintenance to this body automatically is effaced when one's soul is realised as Brahma, viz., one shouldn't care for his physique when such a state of mind is achieved.

तमेव धीरो विज्ञाय प्रज्ञां कुर्वीत ब्राह्मणः। नानुध्यायाद्बहूञ्छब्दान्वाचो विग्लापनं हि तत्॥ २५॥

A patient Brāhmaṇa should establish his wisdom on Brahma after an actual cognisance with the perfect Brahma. He shouldn't fall in the trap of harangues because it is mere abuse to the speech.

बाल्येनैव हि तिष्ठासेन्निर्विद्य ब्रह्मवेदनम्। ब्रह्मविद्यां च बाल्यं च निर्विद्य मुनिरात्मवान्॥ २६॥

He should desire to be stable with reluctance. He should develop a firm determination that there is nothing except Brahma. Thus, having a due recognition made with Brahma one should observe the soul everywhere.

यदा सर्वे प्रमुच्यन्ते कामा येऽस्य हृदि श्रिताः। अथ मर्त्योऽमृतो भवत्यत्र ब्रह्म समश्नुते॥

This mortal man becomes immortal and sips the pleasure of Brahma when all desires residing in the heart are cooled down.

अथ खलु सोम्येदं परिव्राज्यं नैष्ठिकमात्मधर्मं यो विजहाति स वीरहा भवति। स ब्रह्महा भवति। स भ्रूणहा भवति। स महापातकी भवति। य इमां वैष्णवीं निष्ठां परित्यजति। स स्तेनो भवति। गुरुतल्पगो भवति। समित्रध्रुग्भवति। स कृतघ्नो भवति। स सर्वस्मा ल्लोकात्प्रच्युतो भवति। तदेतदृचाभ्युक्तम्। स्तेनः सुरापो गुरुतल्पगामी मित्रध्रुगेते निष्कृतेर्यान्ति शुद्धिम। व्यक्तमव्यक्तं वा विधृतं विष्णुलिङ्गं त्यजन्न शुध्येदखिलैरात्मभासा॥ २८॥

O dear modest! The person who violates the rules prescribed for a recluse becomes analogous to the murderer of Brāhmaṇa, killer of industry, killer of womb and a heinous criminal. The recluse who gives up his loyalty to Viṣṇu becomes a thief. He becomes a debaucher even with the wife of his teacher, rival to his friend and all ungrateful. He thus falls in the trap of misery after such serious misdirections. These hymns refer it– "The thief, the intoxicant, debaucher to the wife of teacher, rival to friend, may regain purity by virtue of lamenting for the same but the recluse can't regain purity if he has infringed either expressively or impliedly framed for the Viṣṇuliṅga recluse.

त्यक्त्वा विष्णोर्लिङ्गमन्तर्बहिर्वा यः स्वाश्रमं सेवतेऽनाश्रमं वा। प्रत्यापत्तिं भजते वातिमूढो नैषां गतिः कल्पकोट्यापि दृष्टा॥ २९॥

The recluse who stays in his hermitage by giving up the in and out Viṣṇuliṅga or gives up the traditions, is surrounded with adversities all time and he can't see or acquire a true position even in the indefinite period of time.

त्यक्त्वा सर्वाश्रमान्धीरो वसेन्मोक्षाश्रमे चिरम्। मोक्षाश्रमात्परिभ्रष्टो न गतिस्तस्य विद्यते॥ ३०॥

A patient man should reside prolong the hermitage of emancipation after giving up all Āśramas. He has no place to stay if he is befallen from the Āśrama of emancipation.

पारिव्राज्यं गृहीत्वा तु यः स्वधर्मे न तिष्ठति। तमारूढच्युतं विद्यादिति वेदानुशासनम्॥ ३१॥

The person who can't maintain himself in the duty for which he is engaged after accepting the Āśrama of a recluse, is nothing else but an offender because he has cheated to the Āśrama concerned. It is the discipline of Veda.

अथ खलु सोम्येमं सनातनमात्मधर्मं वैष्णवीं निष्ठां लब्ध्वा यस्तामदूषयन्वर्तते स वशी भवति। स पुण्यश्लोको भवति। स लोकज्ञो भवति। स वेदान्तज्ञो भवति। स ब्रह्मज्ञो भवति। स सर्वज्ञो भवति। स स्वराड् भवति। स परं ब्रह्म भगवन्तमाप्नोति। स पितॄन्संबन्धिनो बान्धवान्सुहृदो मित्राणि च भवादुत्तारयति॥ ३२॥

O dear modest! The person who doesn't vitiate the loyalty obtained for Lord Viṣṇu and in his everlasting soul, is only a man who has controlled his senses. He is knower to a wide fame and the element of world. He is known to Brahma, he is omniscient and he attains to the perfect Brahma by turning himself in the form of light. He crosses his forefathers, nears and dears, relatives and all persons in contact from this worldly ocean.

तदेतदृचाभ्युक्तम्। शतं कुलानां प्रथमं बभूव तथा पराणां त्रिशतं समग्रम्। एते भवन्ति सुकृतस्य लोके येषां कुले संन्यसतीह विद्वान्॥ ३३॥

The person who accepts reclusion uplifts his hundred preceding generations and three hundred succeeding generations of his clan. Such genius recluse most scarcely appear in this world and thus bless it with their great deeds.

त्रिंशत्परांस्त्रिंशदपरांस्त्रिशच्च परतः परान्। उत्तारयति धर्मिष्ठः परिव्राडिति वै श्रुतिः॥ ३४॥

According to the Veda, the genius recluse crosses his thirty successive and thirty preceding as also thirty generations prior to it from the worldly oceans.

संन्यस्तमिति यो ब्रूयात्कण्ठस्थप्राणवानपि। तारिताः पितरस्तेन इति वेदानुशासनम्॥ ३५॥

According to the discipline of Veda, the person who declares that he has accepted reclusion even at the time of his last breathe; it is deemed that he has crossed his forefathers from the worldly sea.

अथ खलु सोम्येमं सनातनमात्मधर्मं वैष्णवीं निष्ठां नासमाप्य प्रब्रूयात्। नानूचानाय नानात्मविदे नावीतरागाय नाविशुद्धाय नानुपसन्नाय नाप्रयतमानसायेति ह स्माहुः। तदेतदृचाभ्युक्त म्। विद्या ह वै ब्राह्मणमाजगाम गोपाय मां शेवधिष्टेऽहमस्मि। असूयकायानृजवे शठाय मा मा ब्रूया वीर्यवती तथा स्याम्॥ ३६॥

O dear modest! A scholar should not preach this learning of immortal soul without adopting it practically and this Viṣṇu related religion without royalty. The person who is unknown to Veda, to self-conscious, full of affections, impure heart, stubborn and atheist shouldn't be preached, this Upaniṣad. The hymns confirming this fact are– "The Brahmavidyā came to Brāhmaṇa and said– "O Brāhmaṇa! protect me I am your treasure. Don't preach about me to the person who are shrewd, stupid, artful and who criticize others. In case, if it is done, my influence will he entirely effaced.

यमेवैष विद्याच्छुचिमप्रमत्तं मेधाविनं ब्रह्मचर्योपपन्नम्। अस्मा इमामुपसन्नाय सम्यक् परीक्ष्य दद्याद्वैष्णवीमात्मनिष्ठाम्॥ ३७॥

The person entitled to educate is a man of purity in heart, egoless, cautious, celibate and well-tried. He only can do the best use of this learning pertaining to Lord Viṣṇu.

अध्यापिता ये गुरुं नाद्रियन्ते विप्रा वाचा मनसा कर्मणा वा। यथैव तेन न गुरुर्भोजनीयस्तथैव चान्नं न भुनक्ति श्रुतं तत्॥ ३८॥

The person who doesn't have any respect for their teacher and who don't reveal it through their mind, speech and actions, their education is only an illusion and worth nothing. The person of philanthropic ideology doesn't entertain the food offered by them and the teachers too do not accept the food. According to Veda, a recluse also refrain from taking food at the home of such ungrateful.

गुरुरेव परो धर्मो गुरुरेव परा गतिः। एकाक्षरप्रदातारं यो गुरुं नाभिनन्दति। तस्य श्रुतं तपो ज्ञानं स्रवत्यामघटाम्बुवत्॥ ३९॥

The teacher is the supreme religion and also the supreme position. As the water kept in a coarse pitcher gradually percolates living it empty, the persons education, penance and knowledge is decayed gradually who has no respect for the teacher who always provides with the knowledge.

यस्य देवे परा भक्तिर्यथा देवे तथा गुरौ। स ब्रह्मवित्परं प्रेयादिति वेदानुशासनम् इत्युपनिषत्॥

The person who has a strong faith on gods and the same faith on teacher; is the supreme devotee. Such a person of knowledge attains to the supreme position. It is the discipline contemplated in Veda and it is the directions. Thus, this Upaniṣad has been concluded.

ॐ पूर्णमदः .... इति शान्तिः॥

॥इति शाट्यायनीयोपनिषत्समाप्ता॥

112. LĀṄGŪLOPANIṢAD

लाङ्गूलोपनिषद्

This Upaniṣad appears to be of later stage. It describes about the tāntric form of 'Hanumat Sādhanā'. Under this special Sādhanā, there is found a reference of Ṛṣi, Devatā, Chanda, Bīja, Śakti and Kīlaka. The Upaniṣad starts with the recital of Ṛṣi, Devatā etc. related to Hanumat Sādhanā. After that there is a description of Nyāsa (related to heart), Dhyāna, Mantra, Japa and Āhuti. This Upaniṣad is primarily related to Sādhanā. The verses used in this Upaniṣad are used only during the Japa and Dhyāna procedure and not in gaining any tattva-jñāna. Therefore only a direction for employing the ślokas of this Upaniṣad has been mentioned here. In the end there is a mention of the ritual followed related to this sādhanā. Lord Śiva told this mantra to Vīrabhadra (one of his chief gaṇa) and through Vīrabhadra, it has been imparted to the entire world. All wishes are fufilled by reciting this Upaniṣad during morning, noon and evening.

ॐ अस्य श्रीअनन्तघोरप्रलयज्वालाग्निरौद्रस्य वीरहनुमत्साध्यसाधनाघोरमूलमन्त्रस्य ईश्वर ऋषिः। अनुष्टुप् छन्दः। श्रीरामलक्ष्मणौ देवता। सौ बीजम्। अञ्जनासूनुरिति शक्तिः। वायुपुत्र इति कीलकम्। श्रीहनुमत्प्रसादसिद्ध्यर्थं भूर्भुवस्स्वर्लोकसमासीनतत्त्वंपदशोधनार्थं जपे विनियोगः॥ १॥

The Ṛṣi to this extremely terrible, jvālāgni Rudra, courageous, fierce mūla-mantra of Hanumat Sādhanā is Īśvara, rhyme is Anuṣṭup and devatas are Śrī Rāma-Lakṣmaṇa, Bīja are hundred, Śakti is Añjanāsuta and Kīlaka is Vāyuputra. This mantra of Hanumat Sādhanā is recited for gratifying the universal 'Tattva' (This is You).

[This way after reciting the mantra 'Oṁ Asya Śrī..........Jape Viniyogaḥ', the water should be left on the earth. After that, the Aṅganyāsa (touching of various body parts) should be done by reciting the following hymns.]

ॐ भूः नमो भगवते दावानलकालाग्निहनुमते अङ्गुष्ठाभ्यां नमः। हृदयाय नमः। ॐ भुवः नमो भगवते चण्डप्रतापहनुमते तर्जनीभ्यां नमः। शिरसे स्वाहा। ॐ स्वः नमो भगवते चिन्तामणिहनुमते मध्यमाभ्यां नमः। शिखायै वषट्। ॐ महः नमो भगवते पातालगरूडहनुमते अनामिकाभ्यां नमः। कवचाय हुम्। ॐ जनः नमो भगवते कालाग्निरुद्रहनुमते कनिष्ठिकाभ्यां नमः। नेत्रत्रयाय वौषट्। ॐ तपः सत्यं नमो भगवते भद्रजातिविकटरुद्रवीरहनुमते करतलकरपृष्ठाभ्यां नमः। अस्त्राय फट्। पाशुपतेन दिग्बन्धः॥ २॥

Oṁ Bhūḥ Namo...............Aṅguṣṭhābhyām Namaḥ. Hrdayāya Namaḥ.

Oṁ Bhuvaḥ Namo...............Tarjanībhyām Namaḥ. Śirase Svāhā.

Oṁ Svaḥ Namo...............Madhyamābhyām Namaḥ. Śikhāyai Vaṣaṭ.

Oṁ Mahaḥ Namo...............Anāmikābhyām Namaḥ. Kavacāya Hum.

Oṁ Janaḥ Namo...............Kaniṣṭhikābhyām Namaḥ. Netratrayāya Vauṣaṭ.

Oṁ Tapaḥ Satyam Namo...............Karatalakarapṛṣṭhābhyām Namaḥ. Astraāya Phaṭ.

अथ ध्यानम्-

वज्राङ्गं पिङ्गनेत्रं कनकमयलसत्कुण्डलाक्रान्तगण्डं
दम्भोलिस्तम्भसारप्रहरणविवशीभूतरक्षोऽधिनाथम्।
उद्यल्लाङ्गूलघर्षप्रचलजलनिधिं भीमरूपं कपीन्द्रं
ध्यायन्तं रामचन्द्रं प्लवगपरिवृढं सत्त्वसारं प्रसन्नम्॥ ३॥

The meditation should be done on lord Hanumān who is, ever happy, Vajra like, beautifully built body, eyes like Piṅgala, ear-rings made of gold, making helpless the Rākṣasa king (Rāvaṇa) with the strong blow, frightening the ocean by fire on tail, having terrible form, lord of monkeys, extremely courageous, best among the monkeys and always in the contemplation of lord Rāma.

[Doing dhyāna this way, the worship of lord Hanumān should be done without any materials and again Japa and sacrificial offerings should be done with the following mantras.]

इति मानसोपचारैः संपूज्य,ॐ नमो भगवते दावानलकालाग्निहनुमते (जयश्रियो जयजीविताय) धवलीकृतजगत्त्रय वज्रदेह वज्रपुच्छ वज्रकाय वज्रतुण्ड वज्रमुख वज्रनख वज्रबाहो वज्ररोम वज्रनेत्र वज्रदन्त वज्रशरीर सकलात्मकाय भीमकर पिङ्गलाक्ष उग्र प्रलयकाल-रौद्र वीरभद्रावतार शरभसालुवभैरवदोर्दण्ड लङ्कापुरीदाहन उदधिलङ्घन दशग्रीवकृतान्त सीताविश्वास ईश्वरपुत्र अञ्जनागर्भसंभूत उदयभास्करबिम्बानलग्रासक देवदानवऋषिमुनिवन्द्य पाशुपतास्त्रब्रह्मास्त्रबैलवास्त्र-नारायणास्त्रकालशक्तिकास्त्रदण्डकास्त्रपाशाघोरास्त्रनिवारण पाशुपतास्त्रब्रह्मास्त्रबैलवास्त्रनारायणास्त्रमृड सर्वशक्तिग्रसन ममात्मरक्षाकर परविद्यानिवारण आत्मविद्यासंरक्षक अग्निदीप्त अथर्वणवेदसिद्धस्थिरकालाग्निनिराहारक वायुवेग मनोवेग श्रीरामतारकपरब्रह्मविश्वरूपदर्शन लक्ष्मणप्राणप्रतिष्ठानन्दकर स्थलजलाग्निमर्मभेदिन् सर्वशत्रून् छिन्धि छिन्धि मम वैरिणः खादय खादय मम संजीवनपर्वतोत्पाटन डाकिनीविध्वंसन सुग्रीवसख्यकरण निष्कलङ्क कुमारब्रह्मचारिन् दिगम्बर सर्वपाप सर्वग्रह कुमारग्रह सर्वं छेदय छेदय भेदय भेदय भिन्धि भिन्धि खादय खादय टङ्क टङ्क ताडय ताडय मारय मारय शोषय शोषय ज्वालय ज्वालय हारय हारय देवदत्तं नाशय नाशय अतिशोषय अतिशोषय मम सर्वं च हनुमन् रक्ष रक्ष ॐ ह्रां ह्रीं ह्रूं हुं फट् घे घे स्वाहा॥ ४॥

Oṁ Namo Bhagavate Dāvānala Kālāgni Hanumate..........Hanuman Rakṣa Rakṣa Oṁ Hrāṁ Hrīṁ Hrūṁ Huṁ Phaṭ Ghe Ghe Svāhā.

ॐ नमो भगवते चण्डप्रतापहनुमते महावीराय सर्वदुःखविनाशनाय ग्रहमण्डलभूत-मण्डलप्रेतपिशाचमण्डलसर्वोच्चाटनाय अतिभयङ्करज्वर माहेश्वरज्वर-विष्णुज्वर-ब्रह्मज्वर-वेताल ब्रह्मराक्षस ज्वर-पित्तज्वर-श्लेष्मसान्निपातिकज्वर-विषमज्वर-शीतज्वर-एकाहिकज्वर-द्व्याहिकज्वर-त्र्यैहिकज्वर-चातुर्थिकज्वर-अर्धमासिकज्वर-मासिकज्वर- षाण्मासिकज्वर-सांवत्सरिकज्वर-अस्थ्यन्तर्गतज्वर-महापस्मार-श्रमिकापस्मारांश्च भेदय भेदय खादय खादय ॐ ह्रां ह्रीं ह्रूं हुं फट् घे घे स्वाहा॥ ५॥

Oṁ Namo Bhagavate Caṇḍapratāpa Hanumate..........Khādaya Khādaya Oṁ Hrāṁ Hrīṁ Hrūṁ Huṁ Phaṭ Ghe Ghe Svāhā.

ॐ नमो भगवते चिन्तामणिहनुमते अङ्गशूल-अक्षिशूल-शिरश्शूलगुल्मशूल-उदरशूल-कर्णशूल-नेत्रशूल गुदशूल-कटिशूल-जानुशूल-जङ्घाशूल-हस्तशूल-पादशूल-गुल्फशूल-वातशूल-पित्तशूल-पायुशूल-स्तनशूल-परिणामशूल-परिधामशूल-परिबाणशूल-दन्तशूल-कुक्षिशूल सुमनश्शूल-सर्वशूलानि निर्मूलय निर्मूलय दैत्यदानवकामिनीवेतालब्रह्मराक्षस-कोलाहलनागपाशानन्तवासुकितक्षककार्कोटकलिङ्गपद्मक-कुमुदज्वलरोगपाशमहामारीन् कालपाशविषं निर्विषं कुरु कुरु ॐ ह्रां ह्रीं ह्रूं हुं फट् घे घे स्वाहा॥६॥

Oṁ Namo Bhagavate Cintāmaṇi Hanumate..........Nirviṣam Kuru Kuru Oṁ Hrāṁ Hrīṁ Hrūṁ Huṁ Phaṭ Ghe Ghe Svāhā.

ॐ ह्रीं श्रीं क्लीं ग्लां ग्लीं ग्लूं ॐ नमो भगवते पातालगरुडहनुमते भैरववनगतगज-सिंहेन्द्राक्षीपाशबन्धं छेदय छेदय प्रलयमारुत कालाग्निहनुमन् शृङ्खलाबन्धं विमोक्षय विमोक्षय सर्वग्रहं छेदय छेदय मम सर्वकार्याणि साधय साधय मम प्रसादं कुरु कुरु मम प्रसन्न श्रीरामसेवकसिंह भैरवस्वरूप मां रक्ष रक्ष ॐ ह्रां ह्रीं ह्रूं ह्रां ह्रीं क्ष्मौं भ्रैं श्रां श्रीं क्लां क्लीं क्रां क्रीं ह्रां ह्रीं ह्रूं ह्रैं ह्रौं ह्रः ह्रां ह्रीं हुं ख ख जय जय मारण मोहन घूर्ण घूर्ण दम दम मारय मारय वारय वारय खे खे ह्रां ह्रीं ह्रूं हुं फट् घे घे स्वाहा॥७॥

Oṁ Hrīṁ Śrīṁ Klīṁ Glāṁ Glīṁ Glūṁ Oṁ Namo Bhagavate Pātālagaruḍahanumate..........Vāraya Vāraya..........Ghe Ghe Svāhā.

ॐ नमो भगवते कालाग्निरौद्रहनुमते भ्रामय भ्रामय लव लव कुरु कुरु जय जय हस हस मादय मादय प्रज्वलय प्रज्वलय मृडय मृडय त्रासय त्रासय साहय साहय वशय वशय शामय शामय अस्त्रत्रिशूलडमरुखड्गकालमृत्युकपालखट्वाङ्गधर अभयशाश्वत हुं हुं अवतारय अवतारय हुं हुं अनन्तभूषण परमन्त्र-परयन्त्र-परतंत्र-शतसहस्त्र-कोटितेजःपुञ्जं भेदय भेदय अग्निं बन्धय बन्धय वायुं बन्धय बन्धय सर्वग्रहं बन्धय बन्धय अनन्तादिदुष्टनागानां द्वादशकुलवृश्चिकानामेकादशलूतानां विषं हन हन सर्वविषं बन्धय बन्धय वज्रतुण्ड उच्चाटय उच्चाटय मारणमोहनवशीकरणस्तम्भनजृम्भणाकर्षणोच्चाटनमिलनविद्वेषणयुद्धतर्कमर्माणि बन्धय बन्धय ॐ कुमारीपदत्रिहारबाणोग्रमूर्तये ग्रामवासिने अतिपूर्वशक्ताय सर्वायुधधराय स्वाहा अक्षयाय घे घे घे घे ॐ लं लं लं घ्रां घ्रौं स्वाहा ॐ ह्लां ह्लीं ह्लूं हुं फट् घे घे स्वाहा॥८॥

Oṁ Namo Bhagavate Kālāgniraudra Hanumate.......... Ghe Ghe Svāhā.

ॐ श्रां श्रीं श्रूं श्रैं श्रौं श्रः ॐ नमो भगवते भद्रजानिकटरुद्रवीरहनुमते टं टं टं लं लं लं लं देवदत्तदिगम्बराष्टमहाशक्त्यष्टाङ्गधर अष्टमहाभैरवनवब्रह्मस्वरूप दशविष्णुरूप एकादशरुद्रावतार द्वादशार्कतेजः त्रयोदशसोममुख वीरहनुमन् स्तंभिनीमोहिनीवशीक-रिणीतन्त्रैकसावयव नगरराजमुखबन्धन बलमुखमकरमुखसिंहमुखजिह्वामुखानि बन्धय बन्धय स्तम्भय स्तम्भय व्याघ्रमुखसर्ववृश्चिकाग्निज्वालाविषं निर्गमय निर्गमय सर्वजनवैरिमुखं बन्धय बन्धय पापहर वीर हनुमन् ईश्वरावतार वायुनन्दन अञ्जनासुत बन्धय बन्धय श्रीरामचन्द्रसेवक ॐ ह्रां ह्रां ह्रां आसय आसय ह्रीं ह्लां घ्रीं क्रीं यं भैं म्रं म्रः हट् हट् खट् खट् सर्वजन-विश्वजन-शत्रुजन-वश्यजन-सर्वजनस्य दृशं लं लां श्रीं ह्रां ह्रीं मनः स्तम्भय स्तम्भय भञ्जय भञ्जय अद्रि ह्रीं वं ही ही मे सर्व ही ही सागर ही ही वं वं सर्वमन्त्रार्थाथर्वणवेदसिद्धिं कुरु कुरु स्वाहा॥९॥

Oṁ Śrāṁ Śrīṁ Śrūṁ Śraiṁ Śrauṁ Śraḥ Oṁ Namo Bhagavate Bhadrajānikaṭarudravīra Hanumate.......... Sarvamantrārthātharvaṇavedasiddhiṁ Kuru Kuru Svāhā.

श्रीरामचन्द्र उवाच। श्रीमहादेव उवाच। श्रीवीरभद्रस्तौ उवाच। त्रिसन्ध्यं यः पठेन्नरः॥

This mantra was conveyed to Vīrabhadra by lord Śrī Rāmacandra and Śiva and thus, obtained the entire mode of reciting this mantra. Whosoever do sandhyā of this very Upaniṣad during morning, noon and evening, he surely attains all his wishes.

॥इति लाङ्गूलोपनिषत्समाप्ता॥

Thus finishes the volume 2 of the present edition of 112 Upaniṣads (Sanskrit text and English Translation)

ABBREVIATIONS

(संकेतसूची)

अक्ष०	अक्षमालिकोपनिषद्
अक्षि०	अक्ष्युपनिषद्
अथर्वशि०	अथर्वशिर उपनिषद्
अद्व०ता०	अद्वयतारकोपनिषद्
अध्या०	अध्यात्मोपनिषद्
अ०ना०	अमृतनादोपनिषद्
अमृ०बि०	अमृतबिन्दुपनिषद्
अव०	अवधूतोपनिषद्
आ०पू०	आत्मपूजोपनिषद्
आ०बो०	आत्मबोधोपनिषद्
आत्मो०	आत्मोपनिषद्
आरु०	आरुण्युपनिषद्
आश्र०	आश्रमोपनिषद्
ईश०	ईशावास्योपनिषद्
एका०	एकाक्षरोपनिषद्
ऐत०	ऐतरेयोपनिषद्
क०रु०	कठरुद्रोपनिषद्
कलिसं०	कलिसंतरणोपनिषद्
कठ०	कठोपनिषद्
का०रु०	कालाग्निरुद्रोपनिषद्
कुण्डि०	कुण्डिकोपनिषद्
कृष्ण०	कृष्णोपनिषद्
केन०	केनोपनिषद्
कैव०	कैवल्योपनिषद्
कौ०ब्रा०	कौषीतकि ब्राह्मणोपनिषद्
क्षुरि०	क्षुरिकोपनिषद्
गण०	गणपत्युपनिषद्
गरुड०	गरुडोपनिषद्
गर्भो०	गर्भोपनिषद्
गा०रह०	गायत्रीरहस्योपनिषद्
गाय०	गायत्र्युपनिषद्
गो०पूर्व०	गोपालपूर्वतापिन्युपनिषद्
च०वे०	चतुर्वेदोपनिषद्
चा०	चाक्षुषोपनिषद्
छान्दो०	छान्दोग्योपनिषद्
जा०द०	जाबालदर्शनोपनिषद्
जाबा०	जाबालोपनिषद्
जाबालि०	जाबाल्युपनिषद्
तार०	तारसारोपनिषद्
तुलसी०	तुलस्युपनिषद्
तुरी०	तुरीयातीतोपनिषद्
ते०बि०	तेजबिन्दूपनिषद्
तैत्ति०	तैत्तिरीयोपनिषद्
त्रिपुरा०	त्रिपुरोपनिषद्
त्रि०ब्रा०	त्रिशिखिब्राह्मणोपनिषद्
द०मू०	दक्षिणामूर्त्युपनिषद्
देवी०	देव्युपनिषद्
द्वयो०	द्वयोपनिषद्
ध्या०बि०	ध्यानबिन्दूपनिषद्
ना०परि०	नारदपरिव्राजकोपनिषद्
ना०बि०	नादबिन्दूपनिषद्
नारा०	नारायणोपनिषद्
निरा०	निरालम्बोपनिषद्
निर्वा०	निर्वाणोपनिषद्
नी०द्र०	नीलरुद्रोपनिषद्
नृ०पूर्व०	नृसिंहपूर्वतापिन्युपनिषद्
नृ०षट्०	नृसिंहषट्चक्रोपनिषद्
पं०ब्र०	पंचब्रह्मोपनिषद्
प०ब्र०	परब्रह्मोपनिषद्
प०हं०	परमहंसोपनिषद्

पा०ब्र०	पाशुपतब्रह्मोपनिषद्
पैङ्ग०	पैङ्गलोपनिषद्
प्रण०	प्रणवोपनिषद्
प्रश्न०	प्रश्नोपनिषद्
प्रा०हो०	प्राणाग्निहोत्रोपनिषद्
बह्वृ०	बह्वृचोपनिषद्
बृह०	बृहदारण्यकोपनिषद्
ब्र०बि०	ब्रह्मबिन्दूपनिषद्
ब्र०वि०	ब्रह्मविद्योपनिषद्
ब्रह्म०	ब्रह्मोपनिषद्
भाव०	भावनोपनिषद्
भिक्षु०	भिक्षुकोपनिषद्
मं०ब्रा०	मण्डलब्राह्मणोपनिषद्
म०वा०	महावाक्योपनिषद्
मन्त्रि०	मन्त्रिकोपनिषद्
महो०	महोपनिषद्
माण्डू०	माण्डूक्योपनिषद्
मुक्ति०	मुक्तिकोपनिषद्
मुण्डक०	मुण्डकोपनिषद्
मुद्ग०	मुद्गलोपनिषद्
मैत्रे०	मैत्रेय्युपनिषद्
याज्ञ०	याज्ञवल्क्योपनिषद्
यो०कु०	योगकुण्डल्युपनिषद्
यो०चू०	योगचूडामण्युपनिषद्
यो०त०	योगतत्त्वोपनषिद्
यो०रा०	योगराजोपनिषद्
राधा०	राधोपनिषद्
रामपूर्व०	रामपूर्वतापिन्युपनिषद्
रुद्र०	रुद्रोपनिषद्
रुद्र०जा०	रुद्राक्षजाबालोपनिषद्
रुद्रह०	रुद्रहृदयोपनिषद्
लाङ्गूल०	लाङ्गूलोपनिषद्
व०सू०	वज्रसूचिकोपनिषद्
वरा०	वराहपनिषद्
शरभ०	शरभोपनिषद्
शाट्या०	शाट्यायनीयोपनिषद्
शाण्डि०	शाण्डिल्योपनिषद्
शारी०	शारीरकोपनिषद्
शि०सं०	शिवसंकल्पोनिषद्
शु०र०	शुकरहस्योपनिषद्
श्वेता०	श्वेताश्वतरोपनिषद्
संन्या०	संन्यासोपनिषद्
स०र०	सरस्वतीरहस्योपनिषद्
स०सा०	सर्वसारोपनिषद्
सावि०	सावित्र्युपनिषद्
सीता०	सीतोपनिषद्
सुबा०	सुबालोपनिषद्
सूर्य०	सूर्योपनिषद्
सौ०ल०	सौभाग्यलक्ष्म्युपनिषद्
स्कं०	स्कंदोपनिषद्
स्व०	स्वसंवेद्योपनिषद्
हंस०	हंसोपनिषद्

मन्त्रानुक्रमणिका

INDEX OF VERSES

।।इति मन्त्रानुक्रमणिका समाप्ता।।